LIBRARY OF CONGRESS

Subject Headings

Volume I

A–Jury

Eighth Edition

Subject Cataloging Division—PROCESSING DEPARTMENT

LIBRARY OF CONGRESS   WASHINGTON   1975

Burnett
#2

Sales Information

These publications are sold by the Cataloging Distribution Service Division, Library of Congress, Building 159, Navy Yard Annex, Washington, D.C. 20541. Their purchase may be charged against card accounts of subscribers to the card service; others must pay in advance by check or money order made payable to the *Chief, Cataloging Distribution Service Division, Library of Congress.* Payment from foreign countries for these publications may be made with Unesco book coupons. Prices include postage.

Library of Congress Subject Headings, 8th ed., 1975, 98-frame prepublication microfiche and 2 vol., price to be announced.

Library of Congress Subject Headings, 8th ed., 1975, 2 vol., $35.

Supplement to LC Subject Headings. Subscription includes three quarterly issues and an annual cumulation.
  1974 cumulation, $35
  1975 subscription, $35

An Introduction to Library of Congress Subject Headings, 1975, reprinted from the *Library of Congress Subject Headings,* 8th ed., $4

Subject Headings for Children's Literature, 2nd ed., 1975, reprinted from the *Library of Congress Subject Headings,* 8th ed., $2

Library of Congress Cataloging in Publication Data

United States. Library of Congress. Subject Cataloging Division.
  Library of Congress subject headings.

  Previous editions have title: Subject headings used in the dictionary catalogs of the Library of Congress.
  Incorporates material through 1973; kept up to date by quarterly cumulative supplements.
  1. Subject headings. I. Title.
Z695.U4749   1975   025.3'3   73–14630
ISBN 0-8444-0101-3
ISBN 0-8444-0100-5 (Suppl.)

Preface

When the seventh edition (1966) of the present work, then entitled *Subject Headings Used in the Dictionary Catalogs of the Library of Congress,* was printed by photocomposition from computer-produced tape, it was hoped that a base had been developed into which subsequent supplements could be merged and a new edition published in a relatively short time when needed. Technical shortcomings quickly made it evident that this hope was an oversimplification. Finally it was decided that the only approach to a new edition was that of reformatting the seventh edition and each supplement through 1972 with a consequent merge of all pieces into one list. This large task was assigned to the MARC Development Office of the Library of Congress and the Editorial Section of the Subject Cataloging Division. Through their combined efforts this eighth edition was realized.

The headings and their references are the results of the day-to-day efforts of the subject catalogers in identifying new concepts and new terminology and incorporating them into a rapidly growing base. Eugene Frosio, the principal subject cataloger of the Library, is responsible for the expansion of the introduction, which makes it much more a guide to subject heading application than it has been in previous editions.

We are particularly indebted to the members of the MARC Development Office who provided not only the technical assistance needed in implementation but also tolerant guidance through the misty no-man's-land between the wonders and the limitations of computer technology. They and our own editorial staff are likewise to be commended for their participation in a last-minute decision to include in the eighth edition all new and modified subject headings adopted through 1973 instead of 1972 as originally planned and announced.

WILLIAM J. WELSH
Director, Processing Department

EDWARD J. BLUME
Chief, Subject Cataloging Division

Contents

Symbols

sa (see also)   indicates a reference to a related or subordinate topic

x (see from)   indicates a reference from an expression not itself used as a heading

xx (see also from)   indicates a related heading from which a *sa* reference is made

Introduction

The eighth edition of the Library of Congress list of subject headings contains the headings established and applied by the Library through December 1973, with some exceptions noted below. Subsequent additions to and changes in these headings will be found in the supplements, starting with 1974, to be issued quarterly as cumulations, followed by annual volumes which will in turn be cumulated each year.

FORMAT

This edition follows the format of the seventh edition with certain exceptions:

Filing Arrangement

Because of the need for efficient arrangement of bibliographic entries by computer, a new set of filing rules has been followed. Although not yet applied to the Library of Congress card catalogs, the rules are being used in the computer-generated bibliographic products of the LC Processing Department.

Although the new rules retain features of systematic arrangement found in manually produced LC catalogs, they differ significantly in that a basic principle is to file a heading strictly as expressed in its written form, word by word. A word is defined as consisting of one or more letters or numerals set off by spaces or marks of significant punctuation, such as the hyphen.

Another change is that numbers which are expressed in digits, both arabic and roman, precede alphabetic characters and are arranged according to increase in numeric value. Thus it may be necessary to look under more than one possible form to find a heading, i.e., under numeric or alphabetic version.

Those rules having the greatest effect on the filing arrangement in the subject heading list are explained in the sections following.

ABBREVIATIONS

Abbreviations, acronyms, and initials without interior punctuation (e.g., Dr., ALGOL, IBM) are filed as words.

Initials separated by punctuation are filed as separate words at the beginning of their alphabetic group.

Note the change in filing in the following example:

Old format	New format
C-coefficient	C-coefficient
CCPM test	C.F. & I. clause
C.F. & I. clause	**C.O.D. shipments**
C.O.D. shipments	Ca Gaba Indians
CTC system (Railroads)	**Cazcan Indians**
Ca Gaba Indians	CCPM test
Cazcan Indians	**Crystals**
Crystals	CTC system (Railroads)

"Gt.Brit." and "U.S." are now spelled out as "Great Britain" and "United States" in most subject headings and in class numbers. The abbreviations will continue to be used in parenthetical geographical qualifiers added at the end of a corporate heading, e.g., **Independent Labour Party (Gt.Brit.).**

HEADINGS WITH QUALIFIERS

Inverted headings now file ahead of headings with parenthetical qualification, e.g.:

Old format	New format
Children	**Children**
Children (International law)	**Children, Adopted**
Children (Roman law)	**Children, Vagrant**
Children, Adopted	**Children (International law)**
Children, Vagrant	**Children (Roman law)**

HEADINGS WITH PERIOD SUBDIVISIONS

Some subdivisions representing historical periods under place or topical headings which were previously filed in a chronological sequence could not easily be handled by the computer because the periods were not in numeric form. All of these headings have been changed in the eighth edition by substituting or adding explicit dates, e.g., **"Rome**—History—Aboriginal and early period" becomes **"Rome**—History—To 510 B.C."; **"U.S.**—History—Civil War" becomes **"United States**—History—Civil War, 1861–1865."** Likewise all variations of phrase subdivisions with a terminal date have been reduced to a simple form, e.g., **"France**—History—Carlovingian and early period to 987" becomes simply **"France**—History—To 987."

Period subdivisions beginning with the same date and ending with various dates were previously filed with the broadest period first. Since the new filing system follows a numeric progression, the shortest period is now filed first, e.g.:

Great Britain—History—To 55 B.C.
Great Britain—History—To 449
Great Britain—History—To 1066
Great Britain—History—To 1485

In any subject heading, subordinate elements that follow a dash are grouped in the following order: (a) period subdivisions, (b) form and topical subdivisions, and (c) geographical subdivisions. The first group is arranged chronologically, the other two groups alphabetically. These distinctions are maintained at every level of subject subdivision.

Music Headings

Although a large number of existing music headings have been printed in the current edition, in the future LC will not be printing all examples of headings with qualifiers specifying instruments or vocal parts when the main heading has a general scope note, with or without a general *see also* reference (for an example of such a heading, see **Trios** in the main list). Those headings which will not be printed in future editions for specific combinations of instruments include **Brass trios,** etc.; **Wind trios,** etc.; **Woodwind trios,** etc.; **Trios,** etc.; **String trios,** etc.; **Songs** and **Choruses.** New music subject headings for concertos and duets are always printed because specific cross references are needed.

The decision not to print all combinations of instruments under certain forms is based on the fact that the order of instruments listed in qualifiers has now been firmly established and an appropriate heading can be formulated as needed by following the sequence of instruments given: (1) keyboard instruments, (2) wind instruments, (3) plectral instruments, (4) percussion instruments, (5) bowed string instruments, (6) unspecified instruments, and (7) continuo. The instruments in each category are given in alphabetical order with the exception of bowed string instruments, which are given in score order, e.g., **Octets (Piano, clarinet, flute, oboe, percussion, violin, viola, violoncello); Octets (Piano, clarinet, flute, guitar, mandolin, accordion, percussion, double bass); Quartets (Flute, violin, viola, continuo).** An exception to the order of instruments occurs in duets where the solo instrument is accompanied by a chordal instrument, which is given last, e.g., **Bassoon and piano music; Violin and guitar music; Sonatas (Violin and piano); Duets (Unspecified instrument and piano).**

When two or more of an instrument are needed for performance, the arabic number is now placed after the name of the instrument and enclosed by curves, e.g., **Sonatas (Pianos (2), 8 hands); Violins (2) with string orchestra; Trios (Piano, unspecified instruments (2)).** This rearrangement of the number of instruments to a position following the name of the instrument is a format change to facilitate computer filing.

It should also be noted that some headings in the current list contain abbreviations for the words "instrument" and "part" in qualifiers. These words should now be spelled in full since such abbreviations are no longer used on LC printed cards.

HEADINGS OMITTED

The present edition, like its predecessors, omits as a matter of policy certain categories of headings (so-called "nonprint" headings), for the greater part proper names, used on LC printed cards. Individual examples of these omitted categories, however, are intentionally included in the main list in some instances to show the standard subdivisions which may be used in connection with them. For a listing of these individual examples (by subject), see "Headings Serving as Patterns for Sets of Subdivisions," in this introduction. The principal categories of omitted headings are:

1. Individual persons. However, Thomas Aquinas, Shakespeare, Wagner, Lincoln, Washington, and Napoleon have been included to show by example the subdivisions appropriate for use under names of individual philosophers, literary authors, musicians, and statesmen.

2. Family names.

3. Gods and goddesses; legendary characters.

4. Most corporate bodies, including governments and their agencies, religious bodies, societies, institutions, or firms.

5. Places and regions, except when they form an integral part of other headings; when subdivisions under them must be shown, as in the case of historical periods; or when the scope of the heading is indicated in a scope note.

6. Archaeological sites.

7. Natural features such as bays, capes, deserts, lakes, mountains, rivers, and volcanoes.

8. Structures such as aqueducts, bridges, canals, dams, reservoirs, buildings, castles, historic houses, and forts.

9. Metropolitan areas; parkways, roads, squares, streets; city quarters.

10. Parks, forests and forest preserves, and wildlife refuges.

11. Most sacred books, anonymous religious classics, or special prayers.

12. Works of art, motion pictures, and television programs.

13. Systematic names of families, genera, and species in botany and zoology; references from scientific to popular names. However, when the English names of biological taxa present no ambiguity, they are preferred for use and are consequently printed in the list.

14. Chemical compounds.

FORMATION OF HEADINGS

The choice and form of the headings and references in the list have been guided for many years by the principles and practices set forth by David Judson Haykin, chief of the Subject Cataloging Division from 1940 to 1952, in his *Subject Headings: a Practical Guide* (Washington, Government Printing Office, 1951).

A typical entry consists of the main heading in boldface

type, e.g., **Alphabet, Life on other planets, Nuclear physics,** followed, in lightface roman, by reference tracings, subdivisions, and other indications affecting its use in the system.

Class Numbers

Many of the headings are followed by Library of Congress class numbers which generally represent the most common aspect of a subject. If several aspects of a subject are covered by different class numbers, the latter are qualified by a term indicating the specific discipline to show the distinction, e.g.:

Diesel motor (*TJ795*)
Norwegian language (*PD2571–2699*)
Shellfish (*Cookery, TX753; Public health, RA602.S2;*
  Shellfish as food, TX387; Zoology, QL401–445)

Class numbers are added only when there is a close correspondence between the subject heading and the provisions of the Library of Congress classification schedules. Since these, as well as the subject heading list, are subject to continuous revision, the class numbers in the list should not be used without verification in the latest editions of the schedules and their supplements.

Scope Notes

Scope notes are provided when needed to ensure consistency of subject usage by specifying the range of subject matter to which a heading is applied in the Library's catalogs, by drawing necessary distinctions between related headings, or by stating which of several meanings of a term is the one to which its use in the Library's catalogs is limited. These notes appear in the list immediately following the headings with which they are used. A typical example may be found under the heading **Civil service.**

References

After the class number and scope note, if any exist for a particular heading, is listed the record of the cross references associated with the heading; *sa* (*see also*) is the abbreviation preceding the references to be made to headings for related and subordinate topics; *x* (*see* from) designates references that are to be made to the heading from expressions not used as headings, that are in general synonymous with, or alternative forms of, the heading; *xx* (*see also* from) is a record of the headings from which *sa* references are to be made to the heading. Each of the tracings in the reference block appears also in the list in its alphabetical position, the *sa*'s and *xx*'s as headings, the *x*'s in the following form: Labor-unions *See* **Trade-unions;** Physics, Nuclear *See* **Nuclear physics.**

The basic list of subject headings provides a complete picture of reference for those included. For the convenience of other libraries wishing to follow LC principles in developing references, we are including here some examples of references for typical nonprint headings, i.e., headings from normally omitted categories.

STANDARD REFERENCE PATTERNS FOR NONPRINT HEADINGS

ARCHAEOLOGICAL SITES
  Standard references:
    [site name] site, [country]
      xx [country] [1]—Antiquities
      Excavations (Archaeology)—[country] [1]
      [ethnic group, culture, period, etc., often with
        subdivision "Antiquities"]

  Examples (including particular categories of sites):
    Aguacatal site, Mexico
      xx Excavations (Archaeology)—Mexico
      Mayas—Antiquities
      Mexico—Antiquities

    Tuilerie Cave, France
      x Grotte de la tuilerie, France
      xx Bronze age—France
      Caves—France
      Excavations (Archaeology)—France
      France—Antiquities
      Neolithic period—France

    Mozia, San Pantaleo
      x Motya, San Pantaleo
      Motye, San Pantaleo
      xx Cities and towns, Ruined, extinct, etc.—Italy
      Excavations (Archaeology)—Italy
      Italy—Antiquites, Phenician
      Phenicians in San Pantaleo
      San Pantaleo—Antiquities, Phenician

ART COLLECTIONS (private)
  Standard references:
    [name of owner]—Art collections
      x [alternative name of the collection]
      xx Art—Private collections

  Examples (including a collection now in a museum):
    Heinemann, Lore—Art collections
      x Collection of Lore and Rudolf Heinemann
      Heinemann Collection
      xx Art—Private collections

    Howard, Loretta Hines—Art collections
      x Loretta Hines Howard Collection
      New York (City).   Metropolitan Museum of
        Art.   Loretta Hines Howard Collection
      xx Art—Private collections

ART WORKS (movable art)
  Standard references:
    [artist.   name of work]
      x [name of work] ([art form])
      xx [subject of the work, if applicable]
      [institution where located, except paintings]
      [art form or medium—country, except paintings]

---

[1] The name of the pertinent country is indicated here and in the patterns below because it is the entity most commonly applied. However, the name of a geographic area larger than country is also permissible, if warranted by the individual case in question. Also, for Canada, Great Britain, and the United States, the name of the pertinent province, constituent country, or state may be applied if appropriate.

Examples:

Leonardo da Vinci, 1452–1519.   Penitent Magdalen
 x Penitent Magdalen (Painting)
 xx Mary Magdalene, Saint—Art

Riemenschneider, Tilmann, d. 1531.   Windsheim altar of the Twelve Apostles
 x Altar of the Twelve Apostles (Sculpture)
  Windsheim altar of the Twelve Apostles (Sculpture)
 xx Altarpieces, Gothic—Germany
  Apostles in art
  Heidelberg.   Kurpfälzisches Museum

ART WORKS (permanently located art)
Standard references:
[city, or building of which the art is a part.   name of work]
 x [name of work, city]
 xx [artist, if known]
  [subject of the work, if applicable]
  [art form or medium—country]
  [city—art form, if topical subdivision exists]

Examples:

Paris.   Statue équestre de Louis XV
 x Statue équestre de Louis XV, Paris
 xx Bouchardon, Edmé, 1698–1762
  Louis XV, King of France, 1710–1774—Monuments, etc.
  Paris—Statues
  Sculpture—France

Hallstatt, Austria.   Pfarrkirche.   Marienaltar
 x Marienaltar, Hallstatt, Austria
 xx Altars—Austria
  Mary, Virgin—Art

BRIDGES (in cities)
Standard references:
[city]—Bridges—[name of bridge]
 x [name of bridge, city]
  [alternate name of bridge, city]
  [city.   name of bridge]
 xx [type of bridge]
  [river or water body]—Bridges
  Bridges—[country]

Example:
New York (City)—Bridges—Brooklyn Bridge
 x Brooklyn Bridge, New York
  New York (City).   Brooklyn Bridge
  New York and Brooklyn Bridge, New York
 xx Bridges—New York (State)
  Bridges, Suspension
  East River—Bridges

BRIDGES (outside of cities)
Standard references:
[name of bridge, country]
 x [alternate name of bridge, if any, country]
 xx [type of bridge]
  [river or water body]—Bridges
  Bridges—[country]

Example:
Forth Bridge, Scot.
 xx Bridges—Scotland
  Bridges, Cantilever
  Forth, Firth of—Bridges

BUILDINGS, HOUSES, ETC. (in cities)
Standard references:
[city.   name of structure]
 x [name of structure, city]
  [alternate name of structure, city]
 xx [kind of structure—country]
  [name of famous owner, if appropriate]—Homes (and haunts)
  Architecture, Domestic—[country] (add for houses, if appropriate)
  [city—topical subdivision, if appropriate subdivision exists]

Examples:
Lienz, Austria.   Schloss Bruck
 x Bruck Castle, Lienz, Austria
  Schloss Bruck, Lienz, Austria
 xx Castles—Austria
  Lienz, Austria—Castles

Lienz, Austria.   Schloss Bruck.   Dreifaltigkeitskapelle
 x Dreifaltigkeitskapelle, Lienz, Austria
 xx Chapels—Austria
  Lienz, Austria—Churches

Bordeaux.   Palais Rohan
 x Palais Rohan, Bordeaux
  Rohan Palace, Bordeaux
 xx Bordeaux—Palaces
  Palaces—France

Washington, D.C.   Cedar Hill
 x Cedar Hill, Washington, D.C.
 xx Douglass, Frederick, 1817?–1895—Homes
  Historic buildings—Washington, D.C.
  Washington, D.C.—Dwellings

Philadelphia.   316 Market Street
 x Philadelphia.   Market Street No. 316
 xx Duane, William, 1760–1835—Homes
  Historic buildings—Pennsylvania
  Philadelphia—Dwellings

BUILDINGS, HOUSES, ETC. (outside of cities)
Standard references:
[name of structure, country]
 x [alternate name of structure, country]
 xx [kind of structure—country]
  [name of famous owner, if appropriate]—Homes (and haunts)
  Architecture, Domestic—[country] (add for houses, if appropriate)

Examples:
Eringerfeld, Ger.
 xx Castles—Germany

Garthright House, Va.
  xx Architecture, Domestic—Virginia
      Historic buildings—Virginia
      Richmond National Battlefield Park, Va.

Fort Foote, Md.
  x Foote, Fort, Md.
  xx Fortification—Maryland

Huntercombe Manor, Eng.
  xx Historic buildings—England
      Manors—England

Lyndon B. Johnson National Historic Site, Tex.
  x Johnson National Historic Site, Tex.
  xx Historic buildings—Texas
      Historic sites—Texas
      Johnson, Lyndon Baines, Pres. U.S.,
          1908–1973—Homes
      National parks and reserves—United States

CITY SECTIONS
  Standard references:
  [name of section, city]
    x [city.   name of section]

  Example:
  Pláka, Athens
    x Athens.   Pláka

DAMS
  Standard references:
  [name] Dam, [country]
    xx Dams—[river]
        Dams—[country]

  Example:
  Mattmark Dam, Switzerland
    xx Dams—Saaservisp River, Switzerland
        Dams—Switzerland

DEITIES
  Standard references:
  [name of deity, with qualifier often added to designate
          religion]
    xx Gods, [qualifier to designate religion]

  Example:
  Kamakshi (Hindu deity)
    xx Gods, Hindu

GARDENS (in cities)
  Standard references:
  [city.   name of garden]
    x [alternate name of garden, city]
       [name of garden, city]
    xx Gardens—[country]
        [special location, if appropriate]

  Example:
  Paris.   Jardin du Luxembourg
    x Jardin du Luxembourg, Paris
       Luxembourg Garden, Paris
       Paris.   Luxembourg Garden
    xx Gardens—France
        Paris.   Palais du Luxembourg

GARDENS (outside of cities)
  Standard references:
  [name of garden, country]
    xx Gardens—[country]

  Example:
  Compton Acres, Eng.
    xx Gardens—England

GEOGRAPHIC FEATURES
  Standard references:
  [name of feature, country]
    xx [type of feature—country]

  Examples:
  Clarence River, Australia
    xx Rivers—Australia

  Niedere Tauern, Austria
    x Tauern, Niedere, Austria
    xx Alps, Eastern
        Mountains—Austria

  Erna Plains, Italy
    x Piani d'Erna, Italy
    xx Plains—Italy

HURRICANES
  Standard references:
  [area under discussion]—Hurricane, [year]
    x [name of hurricane] (Hurricane, [year])
    xx Hurricanes
        [area hit by hurricane]—Hurricane, [year]

  Example:
  Pennsylvania—Hurricane, 1972
    x Agnes (Hurricane, 1972)
    xx Atlantic States—Hurricane, 1972
        Hurricanes

METROPOLITAN AREAS
  Standard references:
  [city] metropolitan area, [country]
    sa [city]—Suburbs and environs
    xx [city]
        [city]—Suburbs and environs
        Metropolitan areas—[country, without
            exception]

  Example:
  Pensacola metropolitan area, Fla.
    sa Pensacola, Fla.—Suburbs and environs
    xx Metropolitan areas—United States
        Pensacola, Fla.
        Pensacola, Fla.—Suburbs and environs

NATIONAL PARKS
  Standard references:
  [name of park, country]
    xx National parks and reserves—[country,
            without exception]
        Parks—[country]
        [name of larger system, if applicable]

Example:
Nationalpark Bayerischer Wald, Ger.
  x Bayerischer Wald, Nationalpark, Ger.
  xx Bavarian Forest
    National parks and reserves—Germany
    Parks—Germany

RAILROAD LINES
Standard references:
  [name of railroad as subject]
    x [alternate name of railroad, if any]
    [name of railroad as corporate body]
      (For subject entry see reference)
    xx Railroads—[country, without exception]
    [type of railroad, if appropriate]

Example:
Manitou and Pike's Peak Railway
  x Pike's Peak Railway
    Manitou and Pike's Peak Railway Company
      (For subject entry see reference)
    xx Rack-railroads
    Railroads—United States

TRIALS HAVING NAMES
Standard references:
  [name of trial, city, dates]
    x [alternate name of trial, city, dates]
    [city name of trial, dates]
    xx Trials ([type of crime])—[country]
    [group to which defendant(s) belong, if any]

Example:
Black Panthers Trial, New York, 1970–1971
  x Bomb Conspiracy Trial, New York,
    1970–1971
    New York City Bomb Conspiracy Trial,
    1970–1971
    xx Black Panther Party
    Trials (Conspiracy)—New York (State)

SUBDIVISION PRACTICE

Main headings may be subdivided by several kinds of subdivisions, which are discussed separately below.

Topical Subdivisions

Topical subdivisions are used under main headings (or other topical subdivisions) to limit the concept expressed by the heading to a special subtopic, e.g., **Invalids**—Recreation; **Locomotives**—Dynamics. Those topical subdivisions which have been found appropriate for a main heading have been listed under that heading following the cross references. Many of these subdivisions occur with great frequency and are also included in the special list of commonly occurring subdivisions which follows in this introduction.

Form Subdivisions

Form subdivisions are used to specify the special form in which the material on a particular subject is organized (e.g., congresses, dictionaries, periodicals, etc.) and as

such are added as the last element to any heading, after main heading or subdivision. In general, a heading without special form subdivision should be interpreted as designating general discussions or treatises on the subject. Those form subdivisions which are of general application under all topics are normally not included in the listing of subdivisions considered appropriate under specific main headings. For a complete list of form subdivisions used in the LC system, including guidelines for their use, see the special list of commonly occurring subdivisions in this introduction.

Period Subdivisions

Period subdivisions are used to denote chronological sequence under countries or topical headings. Those for countries are given in the main list under the subdivision "History," except when they are coextensive with the reign of an individual ruler. They are omitted from the list under the subdivisions "Foreign relations" and "Politics and government" because they largely correspond to those for "History." Period subdivisions under other subdivisions, e.g., "Description and travel" and "Economic conditions," have not been incorporated in the list because of space limitations.

Period subdivisions are also used to mark significant dates in the evolution of the literature on a subject, e.g., **"Philosophy, French**—18th century," or to divide arbitrarily a large file by date of publication, e.g., **Aeronautics**—Early works to 1900; **Mathematics**—1961–

Local Subdivisions

Many subject headings (and certain subdivisions) may be subdivided by the name of a country or other political entity, region, or geographic feature. These headings are followed in the basic list by one of two designations, (*Direct*) or (*Indirect*). The former indicates that the local subdivision follows directly after the subject heading, e.g.:

Banks and banking—United States
Banks and banking—Ohio
Banks and banking—Cleveland

The designation (*Indirect*) indicates in general that the name of the relevant country is to be interposed between the subject heading and the name of any subordinate political, administrative, or geographical division within the country, e.g.:

Agriculture—Chile—Patuende Valley
Music—Switzerland—Zürich

To this normal pattern for indirect subdivision there are, however, several exceptions: the names of certain cities, states, provinces, divisions, etc., and of certain categories of political and geographic entities are always used directly after the subject heading. A list of these exceptions follows:

1. The states, provinces, constituent countries, or territories of the United States, Canada, and Great Britain, e.g., **Postal service**—California, not **Postal service**—United States—California. These entities are further subdivided, if required, by names of counties, cities, or other subordinate units, e.g.:

Music—Illinois—Chicago
Education—California—San Diego County
Sports—England—London

2. The states, provinces, or major divisions of the following countries:

> Australia
> Austria
> France (old provinces only)
> Germany
> Germany, West
> Italy (regions only)
> Netherlands
> USSR

If, however, a subordinate locality such as a county or city in any of these countries is to be named, the name of the country is interposed between the subject heading and the place name, as in the normal pattern for indirect subdivision, e.g.:

> **Agriculture**—Ukraine
> BUT **Agriculture**—Russia—Kiev (Province)
> **Education**—Siberia
> BUT **Education**—Russia—Irkutsk (City)
> **Music**—Bavaria
> BUT **Music**—Germany—Munich

3. Historic kingdoms and principalities, mediatized states, e.g.:

> Naples (Kingdom)
> Fürstenberg (Principality)
> Wertheim (Grafschaft)

4. Ecclesiastical jurisdictions (provinces, archdioceses, dioceses, etc.) which do not fall wholly within a single political jurisdiction.

5. Physiographic regions which do not fall wholly within or are not identified with one political jurisdiction, such as certain bodies of water, mountain ranges, watersheds, or islands, e.g.:

> **Geology**—Rocky Mountains
> **Geology**—Alps

However, names of regions and geographic features lying wholly within a single jurisdiction are treated in the same manner as in categories 1 and 2 above:

> **Geology**—California—San Bernardino Mountains
> **Geology**—Russia—Volga Valley
> **Geology**—Australia—Gippsland
> BUT **Geology**—Italy, Southern
> **Geology**—Brazil, Northeast

A clear exception to regular indirect subdivision is the use of "Siberia" directly after the subject heading, even though it is wholly contained in the USSR and does not incorporate the country name as part of its own designation.

6. The cities of Washington, D.C., and New York (City) as well as the jurisdiction of the District of Columbia.

Some headings designated "indirect" may not be subdivided by names of cities. These headings are instead used as subject subdivisions under names of cities; that is, the name of the city is subdivided by the subject, e.g.:

> **Libraries**—Illinois—LaSalle County
> BUT **Chicago**—Libraries (not **Libraries**—Illinois—Chicago)
> **Fire prevention**—California
> BUT **Los Angeles**—Fires and fire prevention

For each subject heading that is to be used in this manner, the following reference is given: "also subdivision . . .

under names of cities, e.g. . . ." Due to certain changes in practice which have evolved since the compilation of the main list, however, it is essential to verify the use of such headings as subdivisions by referring to the list of subdivisions used under cities which is included in this introduction.

ORDER OF PRECEDENCE OF LOCAL SUBDIVISION. If both local subdivision and topical or form subdivision are to be applied in cataloging a work, the order of subdivisions is as follows: (1) When the words (*Direct*) or (*Indirect*) follow the main heading, the geographic name is interposed between the main heading and the subdivision, e.g.:

> **Construction industry** (*Direct*)
> —Finance
> **Construction industry**—Poland—Finance

(2) When the words (*Direct*) or (*Indirect*) follow the subject subdivision, the local subdivision is placed at the end, e.g.:

> **Construction industry** (*Direct*)
> —Law and legislation (*Direct*)
> **Construction industry**—Law and legislation—Poland

When a main heading is first divided by place and then by subject, a general *see also* reference is made in the Library of Congress catalogs in the following form:

> **Construction industry**—Finance
> *See also*
> **Construction industry**—[local subdivision]—Finance

Headings Serving as Patterns for Sets of Subdivisions

In this section certain headings are identified as representative of different categories of headings in relation to subdivision practice. In the headings list these representative headings will serve as examples of the patterns of subdivisions appropriate to their particular categories. Many of the representative headings are from categories that would normally be excluded from the main subject heading list (such as names of individuals, sacred books, universities, etc.) but have been retained because they have distinctive sets of subdivisions. Other headings are designated representative because they possess greater detail in their subdivision development than others of the same category, although all headings of the category are included in the main subject heading list. Occasionally, several headings are used to represent one category since no single heading was found to possess all of the requisite subdivisions. The intention in all instances is to use these representative headings to illustrate the total range of possibilities in applying subdivisions in each category. To conserve space, in the future LC will concentrate subdivision development solely on these representative headings and exclude entirely from the subject heading list those subdivisions under other headings belonging to the same category. Following is the list of representative headings established through the fall of 1973. They are arranged first by major discipline and then by special category.

Subject Field	Category	Representative Heading
Philosophy and Religion	Philosophers	Thomas Aquinas, Saint
	Founders of religion	Jesus Christ
	Monastic and religious orders	Jesuits
	Religions	Christianity
	Christian denominations	Catholic Church
		Baptists
	Sacred works	Bible
	Special theological topics	Salvation
The Arts	Literary authors	Shakespeare
	Languages	English language
	Literatures	English literature
	Musicians	Wagner
History and Geography	Rulers, statesmen, etc.	Lincoln
		Washington
		Napoleon
	Legislative bodies	United States. Congress
	Armies and navies	United States. Army
		United States. Navy
	Wars	World War, 1939–1945
		United States—History—Civil War, 1861–1865
	Jurisdictions	United States
		New York (City)
	Ethnic groups, minorities, etc.	Negroes
		Jews
		Indians of North America
Education	Types of institutions	Schools
		Universities and colleges
	Universities	Harvard University
Social Sciences	Industries	Retail trade
		Construction industry
	Classes of persons	Children
		Students
		Women
Science and Technology	Transportation systems	Railroads
	Vehicles	Automobiles
	Buildings	Dwellings
		Factories
	Materials	Concrete
		Metals
	Mechanical equipment	Machinery
		Construction equipment
	Chemicals	Copper
	Organs and regions of the body	Heart
		Brain
	Diseases	Cancer
		Tuberculosis
	Plants	Fungi
	Animals	Fishes
	Crops	Fruit
	Livestock	Cattle

Subdivisions Under Place Names

Since no geographical heading in the printed headings list shows all possible subdivisions appropriate to that category, we are listing all subdivisions which can be applied to names of (1) regions, countries, provinces, etc., and (2) cities.

I

UNDER REGIONS, COUNTRIES, STATES, ETC.
Abstracting and indexing
Abstracts
Addresses, essays, lectures
Administrative and political divisions
Aerial exploration
Aerial photographs
Air defenses
Air defenses, Civil
Air defenses, Military
Altitudes
Anecdotes, facetiae, satire, etc.
Annexation to [name of country]
Anniversaries, etc.
Antiquities
Appropriations and expenditures
Armed Forces
Bibliography
Bio-bibliography
Biography
Biography—Anecdotes, facetiae, satire, etc.
Biography—Portraits
Blizzard, [year]
Book reviews
Boundaries
Census, [year]
Centennial celebrations, etc.
Charters
Charters, grants, privileges
Church history
Civil defense
Civilization
Climate
Clubs
Coast defenses
Collected works
Colonies
Colonization
Commerce
Commercial policy
Congresses
Constitutional history
Constitutional law
Courts and courtiers
Cyclone, [year]
Defenses
Description and travel
Description and travel—Aerial
Description and travel—Guide-books
Description and travel—Tours
Description and travel—Views
Dictionaries and encyclopedias
Diplomatic and consular service
Diplomatic and consular service—Privileges and immunities
Directories
Directories—Telephone
Discovery and exploration
Distances, etc.
Drama
Economic conditions
Economic integration
Economic policy
Emigration and immigration
Executive departments
Exiles
Exploring expeditions
Fairs
Famines
Fiction
Foreign economic relations
Foreign opinion
Foreign population
Foreign relations
Foreign relations administration
Forest policy
Frontier troubles
Gazetteers
Genealogy
Gentry
Gold discoveries
Government property
Government publications
Government vessels
Governors
Historical geography
Historical geography—Maps
Historiography
History
History—Anecdotes, facetiae, satire, etc.
History—Prophecies
History—Sources
History, Comic, satirical, etc.
History, Local
History, Military
History, Naval
Hurricane, [year]
Hurricanes
Imprints
Industries
Intellectual life
International status
Juvenile drama
Juvenile fiction
Juvenile films
Juvenile literature
Juvenile phonorecords
Juvenile poetry
Kings and rulers
Languages
Learned institutions and societies
Literary collections
Literatures
Manufactures
Maps

Maps—Bibliography
Maps, Outline and base
Maps, Physical
Maps, Pictorial
Maps, Topographic
Massacre, [date]
Military policy
Militia
Miscellanea
Moral conditions
Name
National security
Native races
Naval militia
Navigation
Neutrality
Nobility
Officials and employees
Officials and employees—Appointment, qualifications,
    tenure, etc.
Officials and employees—Pensions
Officials and employees—Salaries, allowances, etc.
Periodicals
Photo maps
Poetry
Politics and government
Popular culture
Population
Presidents
Princes and princesses
Proclamations
Provinces
Public buildings
Public lands
Public works
Race question
Registers
Relations (general) with . . .
Relations (military) with . . .
Relief models
Religion
Religious and ecclesiastical institutions
Religious life and customs
Road maps
Royal household
Rural conditions
Scientific bureaus
Seal
Social conditions
Social life and customs
Social policy
Social registers
Songs and music
States
Statistical services
Statistics
Statistics, Medical
Statistics, Vital
Surveys
Territorial expansion
Territories and possessions
Tidal wave, [year]
Tornado, [year]

Typhoon, [year]
Voting registers
Yearbooks
Zoning maps

II
UNDER CITIES
Abstracting and indexing
Abstracts
Addresses, essays, lectures
Aerial photographs
Air defenses
Air defenses, Civil
Air defenses, Military
Almshouses
Ambulance service
Amusements
Anecdotes, facetiae, satire, etc.
Anniversaries, etc.
Antiquities
Armories
Auditoriums, convention facilities, etc.
Avalanche, [year]
Bars, saloons, etc.
Bathing beaches
Bibliography
Bio-bibliography
Biography
Biography—Anecdotes, facetiae, satire, etc.
Biography—Portraits
Blizzard, [year]
Bombardment, [year]
Book reviews
Boundaries
Bridges
Buildings
Canals
Capture, [year]
Carnival
Castles
Cemeteries
Census, [year]
Centennial celebrations, etc.
Charities
Charters
Charters, grants, privileges
Church history
Churches
Civic improvement
Civil defense
Civilization
Climate
Clubs
Collected works
Commerce
Congresses
Conservatories of music
Convents
Correctional institutions
Courtyards
Cyclone, [year]
Demonstration, [date]
Description

Slaughter-houses
Social conditions
Social life and customs
Social policy
Social registers
Songs and music
Sports facilities
Stables
Statistical services
Statistics
Statistics, Medical
Statistics, Vital
Statues
Stock-yards
Stores, shopping centers, etc.
Storm, [year]
Street-cleaning
Streets
Suburbs and environs
Surveys
Synagogues
Temples
Theater disaster, [year]
Theaters
Tidal wave, [year]
Tombs
Topes
Tornado, [year]
Towers
Transit systems
Typhoon, [year]
Underground areas
Voting registers
Walls
Wards
Water-supply
Yearbooks
Zoning maps

Most Commonly Used Subdivisions

A "key to the subject subdivisions used on the printed catalogue cards" was last issued by the Library of Congress in 1924, in the sixth edition of *Subject Subdivisions* (Washington, U.S. Govt. Printing Office, 1924), and represented a complete transcript of the LC subdivision file as it existed at that time. Today this same card file has grown to fill a considerable number of trays, has become increasingly complex, and contains much obsolete information. Therefore, although there is an acute need for a practical guide to subdivision practice which would complement the basic list of subject headings, no useful purpose would be served today by reproducing this entire file.

For this edition of the subject heading list a new approach to providing a usage guide has been attempted. Instead of including a complete register of LC subdivisions, only the most important and most commonly used form and topical subdivisions have been recorded (approximately one-third of all the subdivisions in the LC file). In addition to limiting the number of entries, other important changes in the presentation have been introduced. For each subdivision in the 1924 list there

was a note of all the headings under which it had been previously established. In the present guide, however, only a general statement is made as to the types of headings under which the subdivisions are applicable. In the previous publication almost no instructions were given for use; in the present list each subdivision which could offer difficulties in application is provided with a scope note explaining to the cataloger the points to observe in assigning the subdivision, the nature of the publication to which it should be assigned, how it may overlap in meaning with other subdivisions, and what other related or similar subdivisions should be considered at the same time. In some cases directions for assigning duplicate subject entries are also indicated if required by the subdivision under consideration.

In summarizing LC practice for any given subdivision, no attempt has been made to express the total range of possibilities; only the range of actual recorded usage as reflected in the LC subdivision file has been indicated.

The guidelines provided here should help to achieve uniformity in subdivision practice in American libraries, precisely because this information is included with the basic list of subject headings and is thus available to all at the crucial point in the cataloging process. Many of the subdivisions listed have had different meanings over the years because precise definitions were not always readily available. Now LC catalogers as well as those in other institutions will be able to assign each subdivision in all fields with approximately the same meaning. The reading public should also benefit from the definitions of particular subdivisions observed in the subject card catalog.

Since this list of subdivisions is intentionally incomplete, the user must understand what kinds of subdivisions are recorded here. The criteria for selection are as follows:

1. Subdivisions applicable to more than one major subject area were generally included, whereas those pertaining to a single field were omitted.

2. Most subdivisions given under pattern headings in the subject heading list itself, including standard subdivisions for wars, armies, individual persons, universities, churches, sacred works, etc., were omitted (see exceptions noted in paragraph 5 below as well as the section in the introduction pertaining to pattern subject headings, p. xiii).

3. Subdivisions used only rarely were generally excluded.

4. All standard subdivisions used under place names were automatically included regardless of frequency of use.

5. A pattern subdivision or a subdivision pertinent to a single subject field was sometimes included to distinguish it from related or similar subdivisions.

The information presented here should not be regarded as permanent. To maintain currency it must be altered, refined, expanded, or corrected on a continuing basis as errors or lacunae are discovered or as new problems arise. All changes in practice will be announced in a subsequent supplement to this edition. It should also be noted that the guidelines presented in this section represent practice in effect at the beginning of 1974. Since numerous changes in practice in the Subject Cataloging Division were set into motion only shortly before this date, some aspects of subdivision practice observed in the main list of subject headings may not coincide with these guidelines. As these discrepancies are discovered they will be corrected.

Users of this section are cautioned that the *see* and *see also* references provided under each subdivision refer only to other subdivisions in this section and are not to be taken as references to subject headings in the main list.

SYMBOLS used in designating references
   sa(*see also*) indicates a related or subordinate topic to be consulted
   x(*see from*) indicates a reference made from an expression not itself used as a heading

ABBEYS *see* CONVENTS; MONASTERIES

ABBREVIATIONS
Use as a form subdivision under topical headings for lists of abbreviations of words or phrases, e.g., **Engineering —Abbreviations**. If the work in hand is not in English, make a second entry under the subject heading **Abbreviations** qualified by the name of the language, e.g., **Abbreviations, German.**
   sa   Acronyms
         Notation

ABILITY TESTING
Use under topical headings for discussion of tests for native aptitude or acquired proficiency in particular fields, e.g., **Economics—Ability testing**. Do not use the subdivision under subjects for which phrase headings designating the special ability have been provided, e.g., **Mathematical ability; Creative ability.** In these cases and also under psychological subjects use the subdivision "Testing."

ABSTRACTING AND INDEXING
Use under topical or geographic headings for discussions of methods used in abstracting or indexing works published on those topics.
   sa   Indexes
   x   Indexing

ABSTRACTS
Use as a form subdivision under topical or geographic headings for works listing publications on those topics together with short summaries. As a rule these summaries should include substantive information (as distinct from annotated bibliographies where only descriptive comments are normally offered). For abstracts of works by or about one person or one organization use the subdivision "Abstracts" under the name of the person or organization.
   sa   Bibliography
         Book reviews
         Digests
   x   Summaries of publications

ACCIDENTS
Use under topical headings, particularly under types of industries or trades, structures or equipment, technical processes, etc. Under particular sports or games use the subdivision "Accidents and injuries."
   sa   Ambulance service
         Explosion
         Fires and fire prevention
         Safety measures

Theater disaster
   x   Injuries

ACCIDENTS AND INJURIES
Use under types of sports or games.
   x   Injuries

ACCOUNTING
Use under topical headings, particularly under special trades, professions, business activities, and types of institutions, as well as under names of particular institutions.
   sa   Auditing and inspection
         Inventories

ACRONYMS
Use as a form subdivision under topical headings or names of languages (except English) for lists of words formed from the initial letter or letters of each of the successive parts of a compound term, e.g., **Engineering—**Acronyms; **Russian language**—Acronyms. Therefore, each non-English work may require two subject headings, one to designate the topic and one to designate the language.
   sa   Abbreviations

ADDRESSES, ESSAYS, LECTURES
Use as a form subdivision under topical or geographic headings for collected miscellaneous papers or essays, including anthologies or readings, by one or more authors in one volume or set of volumes; or for one paper or essay dealing with a topic as a whole in general terms. Do not use the subdivision for works consisting of essays brought together according to a preconceived plan to form a unified whole, such as in the case of comprehensive treatises where each chapter is by a different author (i.e., composite works); in such cases use no subdivision. For anthologies which are made up of works so comprehensive in scope (e.g., collected treatises) that they cannot be designated compilations of papers, essays, studies, etc., use the subdivision "Collected works." For collected papers delivered at congresses use the subdivision "Congresses." For literary anthologies use the subdivision "Literary collections."
   sa   History—Sources
         Interviews
         Sermons
         Sources
         Speeches in Congress
   x   Anthologies
         Collected papers
         Essays
         Festschriften
         Lectures
         Papers
         Readings

ADMINISTRATION
Use under types of institutions or names of particular institutions, including especially libraries, schools, medical services, etc., for works on directing or conducting the affairs of those establishments, e.g., **Research libraries—**Administration; **Community schools**—Administration; **Health facilities**—Administration; **Columbia University—**Administration. For the management of types of industries or businesses, industrial plants or processes, special activities, as well as particular government agencies, use the subdivision "Management." For the administration of

particular jurisdictions use the subdivision "Politics and government." Do not use the subdivision under subjects for which phrase headings have been provided, e.g., **Police administration.**

> *sa* Foreign relations administration
> Officials and employees
> State supervision

ADMINISTRATIVE AND POLITICAL DIVISIONS
Use under names of regions or jurisdictions.

> *sa* Boundaries
> Departments
> Provinces
> States
> Wards
> *x* Political divisions

AERIAL DESCRIPTION *see* **DESCRIPTION—AERIAL;**
DESCRIPTION AND TRAVEL—AERIAL

AERIAL EXPLORATION
Use under names of geographic areas for the discovery and exploration of those areas when accomplished from the air.

> *x* Exploration, Aerial

AERIAL PHOTOGRAPHS
Use as a form subdivision under geographic headings for collections of photographs taken from conventional aircraft.

> *sa* Maps
> Photo maps
> Photographs from space
> *x* Photographs, Aerial

AGENCIES, GOVERNMENT *see* **EXECUTIVE DEPARTMENTS**

AIR CONDITIONING
Use under types of buildings, factories, vehicles, or other constructions.

> *x* Conditioning, Air
> Purification of air

AIR DEFENSES
Use under names of regions or countries for works on preventing or minimizing the effects of air attacks.

> *x* Air raids, Protective measures against
> Protective measures against air raids

AIR DEFENSES, CIVIL
> *x* Civil air defenses

AIR DEFENSES, MILITARY
> *x* Military air defenses

AIR RAIDS, PROTECTIVE MEASURES AGAINST *see* **AIR DEFENSES**

ALMSHOUSES
Use under names of cities.
> *x* Poorhouses

ALTITUDES
Use under names of regions, countries, states, etc.
> *x* Elevations

ALUMNI
Use under types of schools or other institutions, or under names of individual schools or other institutions.

AMATEURS' MANUALS
Use as a form subdivision under technical headings for works of instruction for nonprofessionals on how to acquire a skill or perform an operation, e.g., **Brewing—Amateurs' manuals.**

AMBULANCE SERVICE
Use under names of cities.

AMUSEMENTS
Use under names of cities.

> *sa* Auditoriums, convention facilities, etc.
> Discotheques
> Nightclubs, dance halls, etc.
> Popular culture
> Recreational activities
> Theaters
> *x* Entertainments

ANALOGIES, ELECTROMECHANICAL
see **ELECTROMECHANICAL ANALOGIES**

ANALYSIS
Use under kinds of substances or chemicals (a) for works on methods of analyzing these items, or for works presenting the results of analysis in the case of substances not produced naturally; or (b) for works on methods of analyzing a sample to determine the presence of these items, or to determine the quantities of these items present. For the results of the analysis of natural substances of unfixed composition use the subdivision "Composition." For the physical or mechanical testing of substances use the subdivision "Testing."

> *x* Chemical analysis

ANECDOTES
Use as a form subdivision under names of prominent persons, including literary authors, or under names of wars, for collections of brief, usually biographical, narratives of true, interesting, often humorous incidents involving those persons or occurring during those wars. For anecdotal writings on subjects other than particular persons or wars use the subdivision "Anecdotes, facetiae, satire, etc."

ANECDOTES, FACETIAE, SATIRE, ETC.
Use as a form subdivision (a) under topical headings or names of organizations for anecdotal or humorous writings about those subjects; or (b) under names of regions, countries, cities, etc., for humorous writings about those places. Assign the subdivision as required regardless of whether the work in hand consists of true narratives or pieces issued solely as products of the imagination. For works which consist of collections of true anecdotes rather than complete biographies about particular persons of particular places use the subdivision "Biography—Anecdotes, facetiae, satire, etc." under the name of the place. For collections of miscellaneous humorous or anecdotal writings concerning the history of particular places use the subdivision "History—Anecdotes, facetiae, satire, etc." under the name of the place. For comprehensive humorous histories of particular places use the subdivision "History, Comic, satirical, etc." under the name of the place. For anecdotes about individual persons or wars use the subdivision "Anecdotes" under the name

of the individual person or war. For other humorous works about individual persons (with the exception of literary authors) or individual wars use the subdivision "Cartoons, satire, etc." under the name of the person, or the subdivision "Humor, caricatures, etc." under the name of the war. With the exception of anecdotes, assign to humorous writings about literary authors the following phrase heading [**name of author**] **in fiction, drama, poetry, etc.;** in order to bring out the humorous aspect assign a second subject heading of the type **American [German, Swiss, etc.] wit and humor** as appropriate for the work in hand.

    sa Caricatures and cartoons
        Parodies, travesties, etc.
    x Facetiae
        Humor
        Jokes
        Satire

ANIMAL BEHAVIOR *see* BEHAVIOR

ANNEXATION TO [name of country]
    Use under names of regions, countries, states, etc.
    sa Territorial expansion

ANNIVERSARIES, ETC.
    Use under names of individual persons, societies or institutions, historic events, or places.
    sa Centennial celebrations
        Festivals, etc.
    x Celebrations, anniversaries, etc.

ANNUALS (YEARBOOKS) *see* YEARBOOKS

ANSWERS TO QUESTIONS *see* MISCELLANEA

ANTHOLOGIES *see* ADDRESSES, ESSAYS, LECTURES; COLLECTED WORKS

ANTHOLOGIES, LITERARY *see* LITERARY COLLECTIONS

ANTIQUITIES
    Use under names of regions, countries, cities, etc., or ethnic groups, for works which reconstruct the past of these places or peoples by a study of ruins, ancient monuments, excavated artifacts, and other material remains. Use the subdivision under names of ethnic groups only if the group in question has been extant in modern times, e.g., **Pueblo Indians**—Antiquities. When used under place names, qualify the subdivision "Antiquities" by the name of the group to which the antiquities in question belong, but only if the distribution of the group was spread over what is today a vast and diversified area, e.g., "Antiquities, Celtic"; "Antiquities, Roman"; LC uses only the following qualifiers: Buddhist, Byzantine, Celtic, Germanic, Hindu, Phenician, Roman, Slavic, and Turkish. In the case of all other groups the subdivision "Antiquities" is used unqualified. In the case of archaeological reports which discuss more than one site of a particular locality, assign, if possible, at least two headings, one to designate the antiquities of the place and one to designate the group in question (or the culture, period, empire, etc.). Examples: 1. **Egypt**—Antiquities. 2. **Neolithic period**—Egypt. Or, 1. **Slovakia**—Antiquities, Celtic. 2. **Celts in Slovakia.** If the name of the place in question corresponds precisely to the name of the group (e.g., Gaul vs. Gauls; Rome vs.

Romans), omit the heading designating the group (e.g., if "**Gaul**—Antiquities" is assigned to a work, the heading **Gauls** is omitted). In the case of individual archaeological sites, assign only the name of the site, e.g., **El Khiam site, Jordan.** (For the required references to individual site names see the section on pattern references in the introduction to this volume.)

APARTMENT BUILDINGS *see* DWELLINGS

APPARATUS AND SUPPLIES *see* EQUIPMENT AND SUPPLIES

APPLIANCES, SAFETY *see* SAFETY APPLIANCES

APPLIANCES AND SUPPLIES *see* EQUIPMENT AND SUPPLIES

APPLICATIONS, INDUSTRIAL *see* INDUSTRIAL APPLICATIONS

APPLICATIONS, SCIENTIFIC *see* SCIENTIFIC APPLICATIONS

APPLICATIONS, THERAPEUTIC *see* THERAPEUTIC USE

APPOINTMENT, QUALIFICATIONS, TENURE, ETC.
    Use under classes of public employees for discussions on the conditions of appointment of these persons to office, e.g., **Judges**—Appointment, qualifications, tenure, etc. For the appointment to office of public employees in particular jurisdictions use the subdivision "Officials and employees—Appointment, qualifications, tenure, etc." For the appointment to office of employees in individual government agencies use the subdivision "Appointments, promotions, salaries, etc." under the name of the agency. For the selection and appointment of teachers or other classes of professionals who are not necessarily government employees use the subdivision "Selection and appointment"; for their tenure use the subdivision "Tenure."
    x Qualifications
        Tenure

APPOINTMENTS, PROMOTIONS, SALARIES, ETC.
    Use under names of individual government agencies (except military organizations) for discussions on the conditions of employment in those individual agencies. For specific aspects of employment in the same agencies use the appropriate subdivision under the name of the agency subdivided by the subdivision "Officials and employees," e.g., **United States. Federal Bureau of Investigation**—Officials and employees—Pensions. For the conditions of employment of public employees in general there exists no single subdivision, only subdivisions denoting various aspects of the topic. Therefore, for works discussing special aspects of this topic in connection with the public employees in a particular jurisdiction, use the appropriate subdivision for the aspect in question under the name of the jurisdiction subdivided by the subdivision "Officials and employees," e.g., **United States**—Officials and employees—Salaries, allowances, etc. For the subdivisions used under the subdivision "Officials and employees" see the examples listed under "**United States**—Officials and employees" in the main list of subject headings. For conditions of employment of particular categories of public employees use the appropriate subdivision for the special aspect in question under the category, e.g., **Police**—Salaries, pensions, etc.; **Judges**—Appointment, qualifications, tenure, etc.
    sa Appointment, qualifications, tenure, etc.
        Pensions

Salaries, pensions, etc.

   x Conditions of employment in government agencies

APPROPRIATIONS AND EXPENDITURES

Use under names of jurisdictions, government agencies, institutions, etc., for works which discuss public monies that have been allotted or spent for specified purposes. In order to designate appropriations made by the national or central government for local use assign the subject heading appropriate for the work in hand, e.g., **Grants-in-aid; Intergovernmental fiscal relations; Federal aid to education,** and subdivide by the name of the jurisdiction receiving the funds.

   x Expenditures, Public

ARCHAEOLOGY *see* **ANTIQUITIES**

ARCHITECTURAL DRAWINGS *see* **DESIGNS AND PLANS**

ARCHITECTURE *see* **BUILDINGS; DESIGN AND CONSTRUCTION**

ARCHIVES

Use as a form subdivision under names of individual persons, families, or corporate bodies for collections of documents or historical records, including notes, correspondence, minutes, photographs, legal papers, etc., which have been accumulated generally as a result of their public or private activities.

   sa Autographs
         Charters
         Charters, grants, privileges
         Manuscripts
         Records and correspondence
         Sources

ARENAS, SPORTS *see* **SPORTS FACILITIES**

ARMED FORCES

Use under names of regions or countries. For secondary subdivisions to be used under this subdivision, see the list provided under the heading **"United States—Armed Forces"** in the main list of subject headings.

   sa Fortifications, military installations, etc.
         Militia
   x Forces, Armed
         Military Forces

ARMORIAL INSIGNIA *see* **HERALDRY**

ARMORIES

Use under names of cities for works discussing collectively the government-owned buildings or sites which are used for storing arms, training reserves, or in some instances manufacturing arms.

   x Arsenals

ARSENALS *see* **ARMORIES**

ART

Use as a form or topical subdivision under names of individual persons who lived before 1400, as well as under names of deities or legendary figures, for works consisting of reproductions of works of art in which these persons are depicted, or for works discussing these persons as themes in art. For real persons living after 1400 use the subdivision "Portraits, etc." or "Portraits, caricatures, etc." For

works consisting of reproductions of works of art focusing on other subjects, as well as discussions on the representation of other subjects in art, assign the phrase heading **[subject] in art,** e.g., **Hand in art; Horses in art.** Assign also phrase headings of this type for reproductions of works of art about particular places, as well as discussions on the depiction of particular places in art, e.g., **Russia in art.** For works consisting of reproductions which are not offered primarily for the sake of their artistic value use the subdivisions "Description—Views," "Description and travel—Views," "Pictorial works." Also use the subdivision "Art" under names of Indian tribes for works on their art. For the art of other ethnic groups assign the heading **Art** with the appropriate adjectival qualifier for the name of the group, e.g., **Art, Berber.**

   sa Iconography
         Illustrations
         Monuments
         Monuments, etc.
         Portraits

ART COLLECTIONS

Use under the name of the original owner of a private art collection, the owner being an individual person, a family, or a corporate body. Also use the heading "[name of original owner]—Art collections" for a private collection donated or sold to a public institution if the collection is still known by its original name; make a reference, however, from the name of the public institution with the official name of the collection as a subhead to the heading "[name of original owner]—Art collections," e.g., New York (City). Metropolitan Museum of Art. Loretta Hines Howard Collection *see* **Howard, Loretta Hines**—Art collections. For a work that describes a particular named collection assign a heading not only for the name of the collection, but also a heading to designate the particular nature of the collection, e.g., 1. **Engravings**—Catalogs. 2. [name of original owner]—Art collections.

   x Collections, Art

ATLASES

Use as a form subdivision under scientific or technical headings for comprehensive, often systematically arranged collections of illustrative plates, charts, etc., usually with each representative item provided with caption. For miscellaneous diagrams illustrating scientific or technical subjects use the subdivision "Charts, diagrams, etc." Under place names use the subdivision "Maps."

   sa Drawings

ATLASES, HISTORICAL *see* **HISTORICAL GEOGRAPHY—MAPS**

AUDIO-VISUAL AIDS

Use under topical headings, for discussions on the use of audio-visual aids as tools to advance the field in question toward its goals but not to fulfill an educational function, e.g., **Art**—Audio-visual aids. For the use of audio-visual aids as aids in the learning and teaching of a subject, use the subdivision "Audio-visual aids" under educational headings, e.g., "**Adult education**—Audio-visual aids"; or use the subdivision "Study and teaching—Audio-visual aids" under topical headings. For the use of particular aids in particular fields assign the appropriate phrase heading, e.g., **Television in agriculture.**

>   *sa*   Films for [name of language] speakers
>   Juvenile films
>   Juvenile phonorecords
>   Phonorecords for [name of language] speakers
>   Pictorial works
>   *x*   Visual aids, Audio

AUDIO-VISUAL AIDS—CATALOGS

Use as a form subdivision under topical headings for works which list audio-visual materials on a particular topic in more than one form. For works which list one form only use the subdivision appropriate for that form directly under the subject, e.g., **German literature**—Discography; **Medicine**—Film catalogs.

>   *sa*   Discography
>   Film catalogs
>   Phonotape catalogs

AUDITING AND INSPECTION

Use under types of industries, trades, etc., in socialist countries, or under government controlled enterprises in non-socialist countries.

>   *sa*   Accounting
>   *x*   Inspection and auditing

AUDITORIUMS, CONVENTION FACILITIES, ETC.

Use under names of cities for works dealing collectively with the public buildings used for theatrical productions, concerts, lectures, congresses, etc.

>   *sa*   Theaters
>   *x*   Concert halls
>   Convention facilities
>   Halls, Music
>   Music hall

AUTHORSHIP

Use under names of disciplines or under particular literary forms for the techniques of writing or marketing works on those subjects or in those forms. Do not use under disciplines for which special phrase headings have been provided, e.g., **Technical writing.** Also use the subdivision under names of individual authors for discussions of the validity of attributing certain works to them.

>   *sa*   Historiography
>   Language
>   Technique
>   *x*   Writing

AUTOGRAPHS

Use as a form or topical subdivision under classes of persons or names of individual persons for collections or discussions about the autographs (including holographs or signatures) of these persons. Note: The subdivision should be used only for works in which the interest is in the handwriting of the individuals in question, rather than in the subject of the manuscripts on which the handwriting is found.

>   *sa*   Manuscripts
>   *x*   Holographs
>   Signatures (Writing)

AUTOMATED TEACHING *see* PROGRAMMED INSTRUCTION

AUTOMATIC CONTROL

Use under types of machinery or technical devices, e.g.,

Power presses—Automatic control; **Kilns**—Automatic control.

>   *x*   Control, Automatic

AUTOMATION

Use under types of factories, industries, processes, systems, or institutions, e.g., **Machine-shops**—Automation; **Electronic industries**—Automation; **Electroplating**—Automation; **Railroads**—Automation; **Libraries**—Automation.

AVALANCHE, [year]

Use under names of villages, mountains, etc.

AWARDS

Use under topical headings, e.g., **Journalism**—Awards.

>   *sa*   Competitions
>   *x*   Prizes (Rewards)
>   Rewards (Prizes, etc.)

BARROOMS *see* BARS, SALOONS, ETC.

BARS, SALOONS, ETC.

Use under names of cities.

>   *sa*   Nightclubs, dance halls, etc.
>   *x*   Barrooms
>   Beer halls
>   Drinking establishments
>   Halls, Beer
>   Saloons
>   Taprooms
>   Taverns (Bars)

BASE MAPS *see* MAPS, OUTLINE AND BASE

BATHING BEACHES

Use under names of cities.

>   *x*   Beaches, Bathing

BEACHES, BATHING *see* BATHING BEACHES

BEER HALLS *see* BARS, SALOONS, ETC.

BEHAVIOR

Use under types of animals, or groups of animals. For human behavior or special kinds of human behavior use the relevant phrase heading, e.g., **Human behavior; Food habits.**

>   *sa*   Psychology
>   *x*   Animal behavior
>   Habits, Animal

BEHAVIOR, ETHICAL *see* CONDUCT OF LIFE

BIBLICAL TEACHING

Use under religious or secular subjects for works which discuss what the Bible teaches on those subjects.

>   *x*   Teaching of the Bible

BIBLIOGRAPHY

Use as a form subdivision under subjects for lists of printed books, or printed books and serials, which pertain to those subjects. For lists of serials or periodicals alone use the subdivision "Periodicals—Bibliography" under the subject. For lists of works by or about one person or organization use the subdivision "Bibliography" under the name of the person or organization. For works which contain lists of the works of authors active in particular fields, as well as biographical information about those authors, use the subdivision "Bio-bibliography" under the name of the field. For bibliographies of bibliographies in a particular field assign headings constructed as follows: **Bibliography**—Bibliography—[topic]. Do not use the subdivision "Bibliography" in connection with nonbook materials or manuscripts (except maps). Since bibliographies are often indexed it may be difficult to distinguish between indexes, which stress the subject approach to publications, and bibliographies, which merely list publications. For any bibliography which is indexed in sufficient detail as to be usable also as an index to the subject use the subdivision "Indexes" instead of the subdivision "Bibliography." To distinguish between an annotated bibliography and an abstract see instructions provided under the subdivision "Abstracts."

> *sa* Book reviews
> Imprints
> Manuscripts
> Maps—Bibliography
> Translations from [name of language]—
>   Bibliography
> Translations into [name of language]—
>   Bibliography
> *x* Book lists
> Lists of books

BIBLIOGRAPHY—CATALOGS

Use as a form subdivision under subjects for lists of books or books and serials which are held by one organization or library, assembled as a private collection, or issued by an individual publisher. If such catalogs are limited to lists of serials or periodicals use the subdivision "Periodicals—Bibliography—Catalogs" under the subject. For the catalog of a named book collection use the name of the collection without the subdivision "Catalogs," e.g., **Jefferson, Thomas, Pres. U.S., 1743-1826**—Library.

> *sa* Periodicals—Bibliography—Catalogs

BIBLIOGRAPHY—FIRST EDITIONS

Use as a form or topical subdivision under particular kinds of literature, including their special forms, or under names of authors, for lists or discussions about first editions of literary works, e.g., **English literature**—Bibliography—First editions; **English poetry**—Bibliography—First editions; **Wodehouse, Pelham Grenville, 1881-**—Bibliography—First editions.

> *x* First editions
> Editions, First

BIBLIOGRAPHY—METHODOLOGY *see* BIBLIOGRAPHY—THEORY, METHODS, ETC.

BIBLIOGRAPHY—THEORY, METHODS, ETC.

Use under subjects for the methodology of preparing bibliographies on those subjects.

> *x* Bibliography—Methodology

BIBLIOGRAPHY—UNION LISTS

Use as a form subdivision under subjects for the records of the holdings of two or more libraries of books, or books and serials, on those subjects, e.g., **Science**—Bibliography—Union lists. For the records of holdings of periodicals or serials alone use the subdivision "Periodicals—Bibliography—Union lists." For union lists of particular kinds of

imprints, or publications provided for in the main list of subject headings under the subject heading **Bibliography,** use the subdivision "Union lists" directly under the pertinent heading. Also use the subdivision "Union lists" directly in the case of records of the holdings of nonbook materials. For union lists of books in the libraries of a particular geographic area assign the heading **Catalogs, Union**—[place]. For a union list of books in a particular place on a particular subject assign two headings, one for the place and one for the subject, e.g., 1. **Korea**—Bibliography—Union lists. 2. **Catalogs, Union**—Japan.

BIO-BIBLIOGRAPHY

Use as a form subdivision under subjects, including names of places, literatures, religious orders or sects, or topical headings generally, for works which contain lists of works of authors active in particular fields as well as biographical information about those authors, e.g., **United States**—Bio-biography; **English drama**—Bio-biography; **Jesuits**—Bio-bibliography; **Biology**—Bio-bibliography; **Jews**—Bio-bibliography. Do not use under classes of persons unless the heading for the corresponding subject area does not exist. For example, do not use the subdivision under **Musicians,** but do use it under the subject heading **Music** instead. Do not use the subdivision under names of individual persons.

BIOGRAPHY

Use as a form subdivision under names of regions, countries, cities, etc., classes of persons, ethnic groups, names of organizations, or particular historical events, periods, etc., for collected biography, e.g., **New York (City)**—Biography; **Entertainers**—Biography; **Japanese in Brazil**—Biography; **Harvard University**—Biography; **European War, 1914-1918**—Biography. If a work of collected biography is limited in scope to biographies of persons who lived during a particular historic period of a particular region, country, city, etc., assign two subject headings if possible, one to designate the place and one to designate the period, e.g., 1. **United States**—Biography. 2. **United States**—History—Colonial period, ca, 1600-1775—Biography. If the term representing the special class of persons required by the work in hand does not exist, use the subdivision "Biography" under the name of the relevant discipline, e.g., **Art**—Biography (that is, there is no one available term encompassing every class of person found in the field of art, including artists, dealers, collectors, museum personnel, etc.). Do not use the subdivision "Biography" under names of individual persons except literary authors. In the latter case assign the subdivision "Biography" only when the work in hand is a true biography of an individual literary author. However, if the work contains not only biographical information but also criticism of the author's literary efforts, assign only his name without subdivision. Critical works without biographical information should receive the subdivision "Criticism and interpretation" or other more specific subdivision designating criticism. (For a list of possible subdivisions under names of literary authors see the pattern subdivisions listed under Shakespeare in the main list of subject headings).

For autobiographical accounts of events or impressions experienced by a member of a special profession use the subdivision "Correspondence, reminiscences, etc." under special classes of professional persons. For autobiographical but nonprofessional accounts of experiences of individual persons in connection with a particular activity, event, war, or disease, use the subdivision "Personal narratives."

    sa Anecdotes
         Bio-bibliography
         Chronology
         Directories
         Genealogy
         Homes
         Homes and haunts
         Interviews
         Portraits
    x   Life histories

BIOGRAPHY—ANECDOTES, FACETIAE, SATIRE, ETC.
    Use as a form subdivision under names of regions, countries, cities, etc., for works which consist of collections of anecdotes rather than complete biographies about particular persons in those places. For collections of anecdotes about persons associated with particular topics use the subdivision "Anecdotes, facetiae, satire, etc."

BIOGRAPHY—PORTRAITS
    Use as a form subdivision under names of regions, countries, cities, etc., for collections of portraits of persons who are associated with those places.

BLANK FORMS *see* FORMS

BLIZZARD, [year]
    Use under names of regions or cities.

BOMBARDMENT, [year]
    Use under names of cities.

BOOK COLLECTIONS *see* LIBRARY

BOOK ILLUSTRATIONS *see* ILLUSTRATIONS

BOOK LISTS *see* BIBLIOGRAPHY

BOOK PUBLISHING *see* PUBLISHING

BOOK REVIEWS
    Use as a form subdivision under subjects for collections of descriptive and evaluative accounts of works on those subjects, e.g., **Medicine**—Book reviews; **French literature**—Book reviews; **French imprints**—Book reviews.

    sa Abstracts
         Bibliography
    x   Literary reviews

BOOKS FOR CHILDREN *see* JUVENILE LITERATURE

BORDERS *see* BOUNDARIES

BOUNDARIES *(Direct)*
    Use under names of regions, countries, cities, etc. If used under names of countries, further subdivide, if appropriate, the subdivision to designate the common border with another country, e.g., **United States**—Boundaries—Mexico. Make a second subject entry under a heading with the two place names reversed, e.g., **Mexico**—Boundaries—United States.

    sa Administrative and political divisions
         Frontier troubles
         Historical geography
         Territorial expansion
    x   Borders
         Frontiers (Boundaries)
         Geographic boundaries
         Political boundaries
         Territorial boundaries

BRIDGES
    Use under names of cities, rivers, etc. For individual bridges located in a particular city, further subdivide the subdivision "Bridges" by the name of the bridge, e.g., **New York (City)**—Bridges—Brooklyn Bridge. For individual bridges not located in cities assign as the heading the name of the bridge, e.g., **Glen Canyon Bridge.**

    x   Engineering

BUILDINGS
    Use under names of cities, exhibitions, corporate bodies, or under particular types of institutions or installations, e.g., **Calgary, Alta.**—Buildings; **Olympic Games, Munich, 1972–** —Buildings; **United Nations**—Buildings; **Engineering schools**—Buildings; **Postal service**—Buildings. For individual buildings assign the name of the building, e.g., **Washington, D.C.** White House.

    sa Convents
         Courtyards
         Dwellings
         Laboratories
         Monasteries
         Public buildings
         Stables
         Towers
    x   Architecture
         Historic houses, etc.
         Engineering

BY-PRODUCTS
    Use under types of technical processes or, if not appropriate, under types of industries for secondary products produced during the manufacture of the principal product, e.g., **Lumbering**—By-products; **Cement industries**—By-products.

    sa Waste disposal
    x   Products, Secondary
         Waste products

CABARETS *see* NIGHTCLUBS, DANCE HALLS, ETC.

CAFETERIAS *see* RESTAURANTS

CANALS
    Use under names of cities for works which discuss collectively the canals located in a particular city.

    x   Engineering

CAPTURE, [year]
    Use under names of cities.

CARE AND HYGIENE
    Use under parts of the body, or under age groups who are generally dependent upon the assistance of others, e.g., **Foot**—Care and hygiene; **Infants**—Care and hygiene.

    sa Health and hygiene
    x   Hygiene and care

CARE AND TREATMENT *(Direct)*

Use under classes of physically or mentally handicapped persons for nonmedical care received, e.g., **Mentally ill**—Care and treatment; **Epileptics**—Care and treatment. For the medical care and treatment of diseased persons, i.e., the therapy for particular diseases, assign the name of the disease without subdivision.

sa Almshouses
Health and hygiene
Medical care
Rehabilitation
x Treatment and care

CARICATURES AND CARTOONS

Use as a form subdivision under topical headings, including classes of persons, as well as under names of corporate bodies or individual events except wars, for collections of pictorial humor (cartoons, caricatures, etc.), e.g., **Plumbing**—Caricatures and cartoons; **Sweden**—Social conditions—Caricatures and cartoons; **Mothers**—Caricatures and cartoons; **France. Marine**—Caricatures and cartoons; **Paris**—Riot, 1968—Caricatures and cartoons. For pictorial humor about individual persons use the subdivision "Cartoons, satire, etc." under the name of the person, except in the case of individual literary authors, where the subdivision "Portraits, etc." must be used. For pictorial humor about individual wars use the subdivision "Humor, caricatures, etc." under the name of the war.

x Cartoons
Humor, Pictorial
Pictorial humor

CARNIVAL

Use under names of cities.

CARTOONS *see* CARICATURES AND CARTOONS

CARTOONS, SATIRE, ETC.

Use as a form subdivision under names of individual persons (except literary authors) or under names of anonymous classics for pictorial humor or humorous writings (excluding anecdotes) about those persons or works, e.g., **Dürer, Albrecht, 1471–1528**—Cartoons, satire, etc.; **Bible**—Cartoons, satire, etc. For pictorial humor about individual literary authors use the subdivision "Portraits, etc." under the name of the author. For anecdotes about individual persons, including literary authors, use the subdivision "Anecdotes" under the name of the person. For other humorous writings about individual literary authors assign the following phrase heading: **[name of author] in fiction, drama, poetry, etc.;** to bring out the humorous aspect, assign a second subject heading of the type **American [German, Swiss, etc.] wit and humor** as appropriate for the work in hand.

sa Portraits, caricatures, etc.

CASE STUDIES

Use as a form subdivision under topical headings for single as well as collections of recorded instances illustrating the conditions of a particular field from which general principles may be drawn, e.g., **Juvenile delinquency**—Case studies. For cases in the field of law use the subdivision "Cases"; in the field of medicine use "Cases, clinical reports, statistics."

CASES

Use as a form subdivision under legal headings for compilations of court decisions on particular topics, including such publications as reporters or casebooks for students, e.g., **Estates (Law)**—Cases; **Torts**—Cases.

CASES—DIGESTS *see* DIGESTS

CASES, CLINICAL REPORTS, STATISTICS

Use as a form subdivision under medical headings, including names of diseases, for works consisting of professional description or analysis of one or more case histories on the topic in question, e.g., **Childbirth**—Cases, clinical reports, statistics; **Tuberculosis**—Cases, clinical reports, statistics. Do not use the subdivision for works which consist only of compilations of statistics on particular medical topics; use instead the subdivision "Statistics" under the topic in question, e.g., **Childbirth**—Statistics; **Tuberculosis**—Statistics.

sa Statistics, Medical
x Clinical reports, cases, statistics

CASTLES

Use under names of cities.
sa Palaces
x Châteaux forts (Fortresses)
Feudal castles

CATALOGS

Use as a form subdivision under types of objects, including types of merchandise, art objects, manufactures, publications, collectors' items, technical equipment, etc., for listings of those objects which are available or are located at particular places or occur on a particular market, often systematically arranged with descriptive details, prices, etc., accompanying each entry. For catalogs of books use the subdivision "Bibliography—Catalogs." For catalogs of audio-visual materials (all forms treated collectively) use the subdivision "Audio-visual aids—Catalogs." For catalogs which list only one form of audio-visual materials, e.g., films, the subdivision appropriate for that form should be used, e.g., "Discography," "Film catalogs," "Phonotape catalogs." For catalogs of natural objects or musical instruments use the subdivision "Catalogs and collections." For catalogs of exhibitions use the subdivision "Exhibitions" without further subdivision. For catalogs of objects located permanently in a particular institution assign in addition to the heading of the type "[object]—Catalogs" a heading for the name of the institution. For catalogs of individually named collections, assign in addition to the heading of the type "[object]—Catalogs" a heading for the name of the collection, e.g., [name of original owner]—Art collections.

sa Inventories
Manuscripts—Catalogs
Periodicals—Bibliography—Catalogs
Private collections
Thematic catalogs
x Lists of objects

CATALOGS AND COLLECTIONS

Use as a form or topical subdivision under topical headings for works on collections of natural objects or musical instruments and associated equipment, including catalogs of them, e.g., **Beetles**—Catalogs and collections; **Piano**—Catalogs and collections.

    sa Collection and preservation
    x Collections and catalogs

CATHEDRALS *see* CHURCHES

CELEBRATIONS, CENTENNIAL *see* CENTENNIAL CELEBRATIONS, ETC.

CELEBRATIONS, ANNIVERSARIES, ETC. *see* ANNIVERSARIES, ETC.

CEMETERIES

Use under names of cities.

    sa Sepulchral monuments
        Tombs
    x Graveyards

CENSORSHIP

Use under topical headings, particularly headings denoting forms of communication, including the mass media, as well as under names of wars, e.g., **Art**—Censorship; **Foreign news**—Censorship; **Radio**—Censorship; **World War, 1939–1945**—Censorship.

CENSUS

Use under names of regions, countries, cities, etc., or under names of ethnic groups, for official counts of the population of a place or group, generally including vital statistics and other classified information relating to social and economic conditions. For works which present the results of a specific census add the date of the census to the subdivision, e.g., **Great Britain**—Census, 1966.

    sa Population

CENTENNIAL CELEBRATIONS, ETC.

Use names of regions, countries, cities, etc., or under names of corporate bodies or historic events. For centennial celebrations in connection with persons use the subdivision "Anniversaries, etc."

    x Celebrations, Centennial

CENTERS, MUNICIPAL *see* PUBLIC BUILDINGS

CENTERS, RECREATION *see* RECREATIONAL FACILITIES

CENTERS, SHOPPING *see* STORES, SHOPPING CENTERS, ETC.

CEREMONIES *see* RITES AND CEREMONIES

CERTIFICATION *(Direct)*

Use under types of products, classes of professionals, employees, or tradesmen, or types of industries, for official confirmation that required standards have been met, e.g., **Seeds**—Certification; **Teachers**—Certification; **Air lines**—Certification.

    sa Licenses
        Medcial examinations

CHAIN STORES *see* STORES, SHOPPING CENTERS, ETC.

CHAPELS *see* CHURCHES

CHARITIES

Use under names of cities, ethnic groups, and churches or other corporate bodies.

    sa Almshouses

CHARTERS

Use under names of American colonies, states, cities, etc. e.g., **Virginia**—Charters.

CHARTERS, GRANTS, PRIVILEGES

Use under names of individual countries, cities, etc., except in the case of the colonies, states, cities, etc., of the United States, where the subdivision "Charters" is used.

CHARTS, DIAGRAMS, ETC.

Use as a form subdivision under scientific or technical subjects for miscellaneous diagrams illustrating those subjects, e.g., **Geology**—Charts, diagrams, etc.; **Mine timbering**—Charts, diagrams, etc. For comprehensive collections of plates, charts, etc., illustrating scientific or technical subjects use the subdivision "Atlases." Under geographic names use the subdivision "Maps."

    sa Drawings
        Graphic methods
    x Diagrams
        Outline drawings

CHÂTEAUX FORTS (FORTRESSES) *see* CASTLES

CHEMICAL ANALYSIS *see* ANALYSIS

CHEMICAL COMPOSITION *see* COMPOSITION

CHILDREN'S BOOKS *see* JUVENILE LITERATURE

CHRESTOMATHIES *see* READERS

CHRISTIAN CHURCH HISTORY *see* CHURCH HISTORY

CHRONOLOGY

Use under topical or historical headings or under names of persons for listings of events in order of occurrence, e.g., **Photogrammetry**—Chronology; **History, Ancient**—Chronology; **Wagner, Richard, 1813–1883**—Chronology.

    x Lists of events

CHURCH HISTORY

Use under names of regions, countries, cities, etc., or under names of ethnic groups, for the history of the Christian church in particular places or among particular peoples. If appropriate for the work in hand, further subdivide the subdivision by period subdivisions, e.g., **United States**—Church history—20th century.

    sa Convents
        Monasteries
    x Christian church history

CHURCH TOWERS *see* TOWERS

CHURCHES

Use under names of cities for works discussing collectively the Christian places of worship. If appropriate for the work in hand, further subdivide the subdivision by names of individual denominations or sects, e.g., **Baltimore**—Churches—Protestant Episcopal. For works on individual churches assign the name of the church, e.g., **Baltimore. Christ Church (Protestant Episcopal).**

    sa Mosques
        Synagogues
        Temples
        Topes
    x Cathedrals
        Chapels

CITY IMPROVEMENT *see* CIVIC IMPROVEMENT

CITY SQUARES *see* PLAZAS

CITY STREETS *see* STREETS

CITY ENVIRONS *see* SUBURBS AND ENVIRONS

CITY UNDERGROUND AREAS *see* UNDERGROUND AREAS

CITY WALLS *see* WALLS

CITY ZONING MAPS *see* ZONING MAPS

CIVIC IMPROVEMENT
Use under names of cities.
- *x* City improvement
  Improvement of cities

CIVIL AIR DEFENSES *see* AIR DEFENSES, CIVIL

CIVIL DEFENSE
Use under names of regions, countries, cities, etc.
- *sa* Air defenses, Civil

CIVIL RIGHTS   *(Direct)*
Use under classes of persons or names of ethnic groups for discussions on the rights of persons belonging to these classes or groups to have equal opportunities for employment, schooling, voting, etc., as any other citizen.
- *sa* Censorship
- *x* Human rights
  Rights, Civil

CIVILIZATION
Use under names of regions, countries, cities, etc., for works describing the culture of complex societies. For the civilization of a people not confined to one country assign the appropriate qualified subject heading, e.g., **Civilization, Greek; Civilization, Islamic.** For the culture of a primitive group use the name of the group without subdivision. If appropriate for the work in hand, further subdivide the subdivision "Civilization" to express influences on the civilization under discussion by other civilizations, peoples, etc., e.g., **United States**—Civilization—English [French, German, etc.] influences.
- *sa* Foreign influences
  Intellectual life
  Popular culture
  Social life and customs
- *x* Culture (Civilization)

CLASSIFICATION
Use under names of particular disciplines for works which discuss the systematic breakdown of those topics into subtopics or categories. The subdivision is understood to comprise both method (taxonomy) and underlying theory (systematics). For the classification of books and other library materials on a particular subject use the subject heading constructed as follows: **Classification—Books—[subject]**.
- *sa* Identification
  Nomenclature
- *x* Systematics
  Taxonomy

CLEANING
Use under types of objects or products. Do not use under subjects for which special headings have been provided, e.g., **Street cleaning.**
- *sa* Purification
  Street cleaning
- *x* Washing

CLIMATE
Use under names of regions, countries, cities, etc., for works which discuss the meteorological phenomena of a particular locality averaged statistically over a specific interval of time.
- *x* Weather (Climate)

CLINICAL REPORTS, CASES, STATISTICS
see CASES, CLINICAL REPORTS, STATISTICS

CLUBS
Use under names of regions, countries, cities, etc., for works which discuss collectively the clubs of particular places. Under age or sex groups of man use the subdivision "Societies and clubs."

CLUBS (NIGHTCLUBS) *see* NIGHTCLUBS, DANCE HALLS, ETC.

COAST DEFENSES
Use under names of countries.

CODE NUMBERS
Use as a form subdivision under topical headings for works consisting of lists of code numbers, e.g., **Book industries and trade**—Code numbers. For works listing numbers of this type to be used in information retrieval systems in particular fields assign the heading constructed as follows: **Information storage and retrieval systems**—[subject]—Code numbers.
- *x* Numbers, Code

CODE WORDS
The instructions given under the subdivision "Code numbers" are also applicable here.
- *x* Words, Code

COIN COLLECTIONS
Use under the name of the original owner of a private coin collection, the owner being an individual person, a family, or a corporate body. Also assign the heading "[name of original owner]—Coin collections" for a private collection donated or sold to a public institution if the collection is still known by its original name. For a work which describes a particular named collection assign a heading not only for the name of the collection but also a heading to designate the particular nature of the collection, e.g., 1. **Coins, Greek.** 2. [name of original owner]—Coin collections.
- *x* Collections, Coin

COLD WEATHER CONDITIONS
Use under types of installations, construction activities, or technical processes for procedures to be followed during cold weather conditions.
- *x* Engineering

COLD WEATHER OPERATION
Use under types of machinery or vehicles for operating

procedures during cold weather.

   x   Operation, Cold weather

COLISEUMS *see* **SPORTS FACILITIES**

COLLECTED PAPERS *see* **ADDRESSES, ESSAYS, LECTURES**

COLLECTED WORKS

Use as a form subdivision under topical or geographic headings for (a) the complete or selected works of one author on a topic collected in one volume or a set of volumes; (b) anthologies of major treatises by different authors on a particular topic assembled in one volume or set of volumes (usually, for anthologies on a topic the subdivision "Addresses, essays, lectures" is used. However, in the event that the publication of this type is made up of works so comprehensive in scope that they cannot be regarded as papers, essays, studies, or similar works, use the subdivision "Collected works"); or (c) serial publications on a topic irregularly issued, including monographic series, as well as irregular serials each issue of which consists of papers written by various authors. The use of the subdivision "Collections" in the past for publications of this type was discontinued by LC in 1973.

   sa   Congresses
          Literary collections
          Papal documents
          Periodicals
          Quotations, maxims, etc.
          Sources
          Texts
   x   Anthologies

COLLECTED WORKS—TRANSLATIONS FROM
  [name of language]

Use as a form subdivision under topical headings for works which represent compilations of translated works originally published in a particular language (the language specified in the subdivision), e.g., **Astronautics**—Collected works—Translations from Russian. Do not use the subdivision unless the work in hand represents a publication in which the constituent items were newly assembled and translated at the time of its publication and had not previously appeared in the same arrangement in any language. For compilations of translated works of belles lettres originally published in a particular language use the subdivision "Translation from . . ." directly under the literary form heading.

COLLECTED WORKS—TRANSLATIONS INTO
  [name of language]

Use as a form subdivision under topical headings for works which represent compilations of works originally published in various languages and translated into one language (the language specified in the subdivision), e.g., **Antibiotics**—Collected works—Translations into Russian. Do not use the subdivision unless the work in hand was newly assembled and translated at the time of its publication and the individual works making up the volume had not previously appeared in that arrangement in any language. For compilations of works of belles lettres originally published in various languages and translated into one language use the subdivision "Translations into . . ." directly under the literary form heading.

COLLECTING OF OBJECTS *see* **COLLECTORS AND COLLECTING**

COLLECTION AND PRESERVATION

Use under kinds of natural objects, including particular types of plants or animals, or under antiquities of particular places, for methods of collecting and preserving these objects or specimens, e.g., **Spiders**—Collection and preservation; **Anatomical specimens**—Colleciton and preservation; **Bolivia**—Antiquities—Collection and preservation.

   sa   Catalogs and collections

[COLLECTIONS]

This form subdivision was formerly used by LC under headings in the humanities or social sciences with the same meaning as the existing subdivision "Collected works." It was discontinued in 1973.

COLLECTIONS, ART *see* **ART COLLECTIONS**

COLLECTIONS, BOOK *see* **LIBRARY**

COLLECTIONS, COIN *see* **COIN COLLECTIONS**

COLLECTIONS, ETHNOLOGICAL
  see **ETHNOLOGICAL COLLECTIONS**

COLLECTIONS, PHOTOGRAPH
  see **PHOTOGRAPH COLLECTIONS**

COLLECTIONS, PRIVATE *see* **PRIVATE COLLECTIONS**

COLLECTIONS AND CATALOGS
  see **CATALOGS AND COLLECTIONS**

COLLECTORS AND COLLECTING   *(Direct)*

Use under types of objects for information on how to become a collector of such objects, i.e., methods of assembling and maintaining collections, as well as information on individual collectors in the field. For methods of collecting and preserving natural history and archaeological specimens use the subdivision "Collection and preservation."

   sa   Conservation and restoration
   x   Collecting of objects

COLLEGE EDUCATION *see* **STUDY AND TEACHING** (Higher)

COLONIES

Use under names of countries for works discussing collectively the colonial possessions of these countries. Also use where appropriate the subdivision "[name of country]—Colonies" under topical headings, e.g., **Education**—Great Britain—Colonies. The subdivision "Colonies" may be further subdivided by form or topical subdivisions, as required by the work in hand, e.g., **Great Britain**—Colonies—Administration; **Missions**—Portugal—Colonies—Pictorial works. Additional examples of subdivisions used in such instances are "Economic conditions," "Finance," "History," "Social conditions."

COLONIZATION   *(Direct)*

Use under names of regions or countries which are being colonized, or under classes of persons or names of ethnic groups who are being transplanted to establish colonies in new lands. If used under classes of persons or names of ethnic groups, further subdivide the subdivision by the name of the place where the colony is being established, e.g., **Jews**—Colonization—Argentine Republic.

COMIC HISTORIES *see* HISTORY, COMIC, SATIRICAL, ETC.

COMMERCE *(Direct)*

Use under names of regions, countries, cities, etc., as well as under names of ethnic groups, for discussions of the business activity, including particularly the exchange of commodities on a wide scale, conducted by or within those places or groups. The subdivision under a place name may be further subdivided to designate foreign trade between two specified places, e.g., **United States**—Commerce—Hongkong. For every heading so constructed assign a second heading with the designated places in reversed positions, e.g., **Hongkong**—Commerce—United States. Note: Do not assign headings of this type to bring out trade relations between regions or jurisdiction within a single country.

> *sa* Accounting
> Commercial policy
> Fairs
> Harbor
> Marketing
> Markets
> Stores, shopping centers, etc.
> Trade-marks
> Transportation
> *x* Foreign trade
> Trade

COMMERCIAL POLICY

Use under names of countries.

COMMUNICATION SYSTEMS

Use under types of industries, institutions, or installations, or names of disciplines or individual corporate bodies.

COMPARATIVE METHOD

Use under names of disciplines for works which discuss methods for making comparisons between data relevant to the field in question, e.g., **Social sciences**—Comparative method. Do not use the subdivision for works which present the results of comparative investigations; in the latter case assign the heading appropriate for the particular discipline in question, e.g., **Comparative government; Religions.**

> *sa* Comparative studies

COMPARATIVE STUDIES

Use as a form subdivision under religious headings for works in which particular systems pertaining to the topic under consideration are compared, e.g., **Messiah**—Comparative studies.

COMPETITIONS

Use under names of disciplines or types of activities, e.g., **Architecture**—Competitions; **Baking**—Competitions.

> *sa* Awards
> *x* Contests

COMPOSITION

Use under natural substances of unfixed composition, including soils, plants, animals, farm products, etc., for the results of the chemical analyses of these substances, e.g., **Sea-water**—Composition; **Peat soils**—Composition; **Fishes**—Composition; **Milk**—Composition. For methods of chemical analyses, as well as results of analyses of substances not produced naturally, use the subdivision "Analysis."

> *x* Chemical composition

COMPUTER PROGRAMS

Use as a form subdivision under names of disciplines for works which contain solely lists of machine instructions necessary to solve problems in those fields. For works which are broader in scope and contain in addition to programs discussions about the problems to be solved by use of the computer, programming methods, etc., assign the subject heading **Electronic data processing**—[subject].

> *x* Programs, Computer

CONCERT HALLS *see* AUDITORIUMS, CONVENTION FACILITIES, ETC.

CONCORDANCES

Use as a form subdivision under names of individual authors or under individual works (i.e., author-title or title entries), or under particular literary forms (e.g., **German poetry**), for indexes to the principal words found within the writings of one author, one named work, or one group of specific literary works, especially those indexes which indicate the places in the text or texts where the words occur, often with their immediate context.

> *x* Word indexes

CONDITIONING, AIR *see* AIR CONDITIONING

CONDITIONS OF EMPLOYMENT IN GOVERNMENT AGENCIES *see* APPOINTMENTS, PROMOTIONS, SALARIES, ETC.

CONDUCT OF LIFE

Use under classes of persons (i.e., classes of persons identified on the basis of age, sex, status, nonprofessional activities, etc.) for standards of ethical behavior, or for moral guidance and advice to the individual, e.g., **Wives**—Conduct of life; **Students**—Conduct of life. Enter works limited to etiquette or professionl ethics under such phrase headings as **Etiquette for women; Librarians, Professional ethics for; Nursing ethics.**

> *sa* Discipline
> *x* Behavior, Ethical
> Deportment
> Ethical behavior

CONFERENCES *see* CONGRESSES

CONGRESS, SPEECHES IN *see* SPEECHES IN CONGRESS

CONGRESSES

Use as a form subdivision under topical headings including names of persons, places, or wars, to designate (a) the collected papers delivered at, or published on the occasion of, named or unnamed individual congresses; (b) reports of the proceedings and discussions, program statements, lists of delegates, etc., of such congresses; or (c) combinations of both. Use the subdivision also for proceedings of a society or institution as long as the proceedings are not limited in subject coverage to the internal affairs of the organization; in the latter case the name of the organization is sufficient. Use the subdivision "Addresses essays, lectures" for one or several lectures originally delivered on the occasion of an individual congress but later published under separate cover and no longer strictly identifiable with the original congress.

   sa Auditoriums, convention facilities, etc.
   x Conferences
      Meetings
      Proceedings of congresses
      Symposia

CONSERVATION AND RESTORATION

Use under particular art objects, museum specimens, library materials, types of architecture, etc., for techniques of preserving and restoring these items. For the collection and preservation of natural history or archaeological specimens use the subdivision "Collection and preservation." For the preservation of perishable products, including particular foods, drugs, textiles, etc., use the subdivision "Preservation." For the maintenance and repair of machinery, instruments, vehicles, structures, etc., use the subdivision "Maintenance and repair." Do not use the subdivision "Conservation and restoration" where other usage patterns have been provided, e.g., **Furniture**—Repairing.

   x Restoration and conservation

CONSTITUTIONAL HISTORY

Use under names of countries, states, etc.

CONSTITUTIONAL LAW

Use under names of countries, states, etc., (a) as a form subdivision for texts of the constitutions of those jurisdictions, or (b) as a topical subdivision for legal discussions about the establishment, interpretation, construction, validity, etc., of the constitutions of those jurisdictions. For the history of the formation and development of constitutions of particular countries, states, etc., use the subdivision "Constitutional history."

   sa Charters

CONSULAR AND DIPLOMATIC SERVICE *see* DIPLOMATIC AND CONSULAR SERVICE

CONTESTS *see* COMPETITIONS

CONTINUING EDUCATION *see* STUDYING AND TEACHING (CONTINUING EDUCATION)

CONTRACTS AND SPECIFICATIONS   *(Direct)*

Use as a form or topical subdivision under headings for particular kinds of construction or engineering, e.g., **Pavements**—Contracts and specifications; **Nuclear engineering**—Contracts and specifications. For specifications pertaining to products or merchandise use the subdivision "Specifications."

CONTROL   *(Indirect)*

Use under kinds of pests for their control or extermination. Do not use under subjects for which phrase headings have been provided, e.g., **Mosquito control.** Since October 1972, however, it has not been LC policy to establish phrase headings of this type, and all new headings in this category will use the subdivision "Control."

   x Extermination
      Pest control

CONTROL, AUTOMATIC *see* AUTOMATIC CONTROL

CONTROL, DUST *see* DUST CONTROL

CONTROL, FUME *see* FUME CONTROL

CONTROL, NOISE *see* NOISE CONTROL

CONTROL, PRODUCTION *see* PRODUCTION CONTROL

CONTROL, QUALITY *see* QUALITY CONTROL

CONVENTION FACILITIES *see* AUDITORIUMS, CONVENTION FACILITIES, ETC.

CONVENTS

Use under names of cities.
   sa Monasteries
   x Abbeys
      Cloisters
      Nunneries

COOLING

Use under kinds of equipment or machinery, or perishable products, e.g., **Rocket engines**—Cooling; **Semiconductors**—Cooling; **Milk**—Cooling.
   sa Air conditioning

COOPERATION, INTERNATIONAL *see* INTERNATIONAL COOPERATION

COPIES (FACSIMIILES) *see* FACSIMILES

CORRECTIONAL INSTITUTIONS

Use under names of cities for works discussing collectively those institutions whose function it is to rehabilitate or neutralize the deviant behavior of adult criminals or juvenile delinquents.
   sa Exiles
   x Detention homes
      Halfway houses
      Jails
      Penal institutions
      Penitentiaries
      Prisons
      Reformatories
      Workhouses

CORRESPONDENCE (OFFICE RECORDS) *see* RECORDS AND CORRESPONDENCE

CORRESPONDENCE, REMINISCENCES, ETC.

Use as a form subdivision under classes of professional persons for the collected correspondence of one or more members of a particular profession, or for an individual's autobiographical account of participation in his profession. Do not use under names of individuals. For an autobiographical account of nonprofessional experiences in connection with a particular activity, movement, disease, or war use the subdivision "Personal narratives."
   x Letters (Correspondence)
      Reminiscences, correspondence, etc.

CORROSION

Use under kinds of materials or equipment, e.g., **Steel**—Corrosion; **Water heaters**—Corrosion; **Floors**—Corrosion.

COST OF OPERATION

Use under particular types of machinery or equipment for operating costs. For costs incurred in the operation of an industry, industrial plant, or service use the subdivision "Costs."

   x   Operating costs

COSTS

Use under types of industries, processes, services, or institutions, or under names of disciplines, for the actual outlay of money, time, labor, etc., while carrying out normal activities, e.g., **Grocery trade**—Costs; **Electroplating**—Costs; **Abstracting and indexing services**—Costs; **Nursing homes**—Costs; **Education**—Costs. Do not use the subdivision under types of products unless there is no available heading corresponding to the industry, process, etc., which produces the product (i.e., do not use **Cotton**—Costs; use instead **Cotton growing**—Costs; **Cotton trade**—Costs; etc.). For estimates of costs use the subdivision "Estimates." For operating costs of machinery use the subdivision "Cost of operation." For actual amounts demanded for merchandise, products, etc., at the time of sale on the market use the subdivision "Prices."

COSTUME

Use under classes of persons.

COUNTRY CONDITIONS *see* RURAL CONDITIONS

COURSES OF STUDY *see* CURRICULA

COURTS AND COURTIERS

Use under names of countries.

COURTYARDS

Use under names of cities.

CRITICISM AND HISTORY *see* HISTORY AND CRITICISM

CRITICISM, TEXTUAL

Use under names of sacred works or anonymous classics, individual authors, or special literary forms, for works which attempt to establish original texts, including explanations of obscure passages.

   x   Textual criticism

CRITICISM AND INTERPRETATION

Use under names of authors for evaluations of their works. For criticism and interpretation of special bodies of literature use the subdivision "History and criticism" under the relevant literary form.

   x   Interpretation and criticism

CRITICISM, INTERPRETATION, ETC.

Use under names of sacred works or their parts, or under anonymous classics.

   sa   Criticism, Textual

CULT

Use under names of divine persons or saints for the system of beliefs and rituals connected with them.

   sa   Shrines
   x   Cultus

CULTURAL INFLUENCES *see* FOREIGN INFLUENCES

CULTURE (CIVILIZATION) *see* CIVILIZATION

CULTUS *see* CULT

CURIOSA AND MISCELLANY *see* MISCELLANEA

CURRICULA

Use under types of education, schools, or names of individual schools, for listings of courses offered, or discussions about them, e.g., **Health education**—Curricula; **Junior colleges**—Curricula; **Chicago. University**—Curricula. Except in those cases where education in a particular field has been established as a phrase heading, use the subdivision "Study and teaching" for courses of study in a particular subject field.

   x   Courses of study

CUSTOMS, RELIGIOUS *see* RELIGIOUS LIFE AND CUSTOMS

CUSTOMS, SOCIAL *see* SOCIAL LIFE AND CUSTOMS

CYCLONE, [year]

Use under names of regions or cities.

DAMPNESS *see* MOISTURE

DANCE HALLS *see* NIGHTCLUBS, DANCE HALLS, ETC.

DATA, STATISTICAL *see* STATISTICS

DEAD, MONUMENTS TO THE *see* SEPULCHRAL MONUMENTS

DEAD, REGISTERS OF *see* REGISTERS OF DEAD

DEATH RATE *see* MORTALITY

DEFECTS

Use under types of materials, structures, products, etc., in which defects may exist.

   sa   Corrosion
         Deterioration

DEFENSE MEASURES

Use under types of industries, utilities, installations, etc., for measures undertaken for their protection during times of conflict.

   sa   Military aspects
         Security measures

DEFENSES

Use under names of regions or countries.

   sa   Air defenses
         Armed Forces
         Armories
         Civil defense
         Coast defenses
         Defense measures
         Fortifications, military installations, etc.
         History, Military
         History, Naval
         Military policy
   x   Military defenses

DEMOGRAPHY *see* POPULATION

DEMONSTRATION, [date]

Use under names of cities.

   sa   Riot

DENTAL CARE *(Direct)*
Use under classes of persons.

DEPARTMENT STORES *see* STORES, SHOPPING CENTERS, ETC.

DEPARTMENTS
Use under names of countries whose major administrative divisions are called departments (e.g., Colombia) and only when the name of the country itself is used as a subdivision under a topical heading, e.g., **Budget**—Colombia—Departments. Use for works which discuss collectively the departments of the country in relation to the topic in question.

DEPARTMENTS, EXECUTIVE *see* EXECUTIVE DEPARTMENTS

DEPORTMENT *see* CONDUCT OF LIFE

DESCRIPTION
Use under names of cities, as well as under names of parks, universities, mountain peaks, or other geographic areas of limited size for descriptions of existing conditions or features, including personal impressions of them.
   x Geography
      Travel and description

DESCRIPTION—AERIAL
Use under names of cities or other local areas for descriptions as seen from the air.
   x Aerial description

DESCRIPTION—GAZETTEERS *see* GAZETTEERS

DESCRIPTION—GUIDE-BOOKS
Use as a form subdivision under names of cities, colleges or universities, or other local areas for travelers' handbooks containing information about routes, accommodations, items of cultural interest, etc., e.g., **New York (City)**—Description—Guide-books; **Harvard University**—Description—Guide-books. For guide-books to individual parks, forest reserves, highways, battlefields, or other named lands except college or universities, use the subdivision "Guide-books" directly under the name in question.

DESCRIPTION—MAPS *see* MAPS

DESCRIPTION—TOURS
Use as a form subdivision under names of cities, etc., for guide-books providing planned itineraries for visitors to those cities, usually including descriptions and historical information about items to be seen.
   x Tours

DESCRIPTION—VIEWS
Use under names of cities, parks, universities, mountain peaks, or other local areas for works which consist exclusively or predominantly of views of those places.
   x Views

DESCRIPTION AND TRAVEL
Use under names of regions or jurisdictions larger than cities for geographies or works describing existing conditions or features of those places. Use also for individual accounts of travel in those places. For descriptions of cities, etc., use the subdivision "Description."
   sa Climate
      Discovery and exploration

   x Geography
      Travel and description

DESCRIPTION AND TRAVEL—AERIAL
Use under names of regions or jurisdictions larger than cities for descriptions based on aerial travel and observation.
   x Aerial description

DESCRIPTION AND TRAVEL—GAZETTEERS *see* GAZETTEERS

DESCRIPTION AND TRAVEL—GUIDE-BOOKS
Use as a form subdivision under names of regions or jurisdictions larger than cities for travelers' handbooks containing information about routes, accommodations, items of cultural interest, etc.

DESCRIPTION AND TRAVEL—MAPS *see* MAPS

DESCRIPTION AND TRAVEL—TOURS
Use as a form subdivision under names of regions or jurisdictions larger than cities for guide-books providing planned itineraries for travelers to those places, usually including descriptions and historical information about items to be seen.
   x Tours

DESCRIPTION AND TRAVEL—VIEWS
Use as a form subdivision under names of regions or jurisdictions larger than cities for works which consist exclusively or predominantly of views of those places.
   x Views

DESIGN AND CONSTRUCTION
Use under types of structures, machines, equipment, etc., for works discussing the engineering of those items.
   sa Drawings
      Maintenance and repair
      Materials
      Planning
   x Architecture
      Engineering

DESIGNS AND PLANS
Use as a form subdivision under architectural headings, including types of buildings or rooms, for architectural drawings, e.g., **Architecture, Domestic**—Designs and plans; **Beauty shops**—Designs and plans.
   sa Drawings
   x Architectural drawings
      Plans, Architectural

DETENTION HOMES *see* CORRECTIONAL INSTITUTIONS

DETERIORATION
Use under kinds of substances, materials, products, etc.
   sa Corrosion
      Defects

DEVOTIONS *see* PRAYER-BOOKS AND DEVOTIONS

DIAGRAMS *see* CHARTS, DIAGRAMS, ETC.

DICTIONARIES
Use as a form subdivision under (a) names of languages for comprehensive, alphabetical lists of words in those languages with definitions; (b) topical headings for works consisting of comprehensive, alphabetical lists of

terms pertaining to those topics; or (c) topical headings for encyclopedic works on those topics. For juvenile dictionaries use the subdivision "Dictionaries, Juvenile." Under geographic names or names of ethnic groups use the subdivision "Dictionaries and encyclopedias." Under names of individuals use the subdivision "Dictionaries, indexes, etc." For a listing of the words used by a particular author use the subdivision "Language—Glossaries, etc." under the name of the author. For incomplete lists of the words of a language which may or may not be alphabetically arranged, with or without definitions, use the subdivision "Glossaries, vocabularies, etc." under the name of the language. For lists of expressions, phrases, idioms, etc., found in a particular language use the subdivision "Terms and phrases" under the name of the language. For incomplete lists of the terms associated with a particular topic, or for comprehensive lists of such terms which are not arranged alphabetically, use the subdivision "Terminology" under the topic.

Language dictionaries in one language: Assign the following subject heading: [name of language]—Dictionaries, e.g., **English language**—Dictionaries.

Language dictionaries in two languages: If a dictionary gives the terms of one language in terms of another, assign to it the heading" [name of first language]—Dictionaries" subdivided by the name of the second language (without the word "language"), e.g., **French language**—Dictionaries—German. If the second language is also given in terms of the first, make a second subject entry with the languages reversed, e.g., **German language**—Dictionaries—French.

Polyglot dictionaries: If a polyglot dictionary provides for one language the equivalent terms in several other languages, assign to it the heading "[name of first language]—Dictionaries" subdivided by the subdivision "Polyglot," e.g., **German language**—Dictionaries—Polyglot. If the equivalent of each language is given in terms of the others, assign only the one heading **Dictionaries, Polyglot** without subdivision.

Subject dictionaries in one language: For English language dictionaries within a particular subject area assign the heading "[subject]—Dictionaries." If the dictionary is in a language other than English, assign the heading "[subject]—Dictionaries—[name of language]" (omitting the word "language"), e.g., **Science**—Dictionaries—French.

Subject dictionaries in two languages: If a subject dictionary gives the terms of one language in terms of another assign to it two headings as follows: 1. [subject]—Dictionaries—[first language]. 2. [first language]—Dictionaries—[second language]. If the second language is also given in terms of the first language assign the two additional headings: 3. [subject]—Dictionaries—[second language]. 4. [second language]—Dictionaries—[first language]. Example: 1. **Chemistry**—Dictionaries. 2. **English language**—Dictionaries—German. 3. **Chemistry**—Dictionaries—German. 4. **German language**—Dictionaries—English.

Polyglot subject dictionaries: For a polyglot subject dictionary giving for one language the equivalent terms in several other languages, assign to it the following headings: 1. [subject]—Dictionaries—Polyglot. 2. [first language]—Dictionaries—Polyglot. If the equivalent of each language is given in terms of the others, assign: 1. [subject]

—Dictionaries—Polyglot. 2. **Dictionaries, Polyglot.**
  sa Abbreviations
      Acronyms
      Concordances
      Gazetteers
  x Encyclopedias
      Word lists

DICTIONARIES, JUVENILE
Use as a form subdivision under names of languages or topical headings for dictionaries or encyclopedias for juveniles.
  x Juvenile dictionaries

DICTIONARIES AND ENCYCLOPEDIAS
Use as a form subdivision under names of regions, countries, cities, etc., or under names of ethnic groups.
  sa Gazetteers
  x Encyclopedias

DICTIONARIES, INDEXES, ETC.
Use as a form subdivision under names of individual authors or other persons. Do not use under names of individual works.
  sa Language—Glossaries, etc.

DIGESTS
Use as a form subdivision under legal headings for works consisting of systematically arranged compilations of brief summaries of individual statutes or decisions on particular topics, e.g., **Electioneering**—Law and legislation—Digests; **Land tenure**—Digests.
  x Cases—Digests

DINING ESTABLISHMENTS *see* RESTAURANTS

DIPLOMATIC AND CONSULAR SERVICE *(Direct)*
Use under names of countries for the service of particular countries. Further subdivide the subdivision geographically for the service of a particular country in a particular place. For the service of all countries located in a particular country assign the subject heading **Diplomatic and consular service in [name of country]**.
  x Consular and diplomatic service

DIPLOMATIC AND CONSULAR SERVICE—
PRIVILEGES AND IMMUNITIES
Use under names of countries.

DIPLOMATIC RELATIONS *see* FOREIGN RELATIONS

DIRECTORIES
Use as a form subdivision under (a) names of regions, countries, cities, etc., for alphabetical or classified lists containing the names and addresses of the inhabitants or organizations of a place; (b) topical headings, classes of persons, types of corporate bodies or names of particular corporate bodies for the names, addresses and other identifying data of persons or organizations connected with the entities named; or (c) headings for particular kinds of newspapers or periodicals for alphabetical or classified lists of the pertinent newspapers or periodicals, including names, addresses, and other identifying data, e.g., **American newspapers**—Directories.

For works which list names of persons without addresses or other identifying data use the subdivision "Registers" under the name of the corporate body, class of persons, etc. Reserve use of the subdivision "Directories" under names of subject fields for works which list all of the various types of persons associated with the field, including nonprofessionals, suppliers, etc., as well as perhaps the member organizations. But for works which list merely the professionals within the field use the subdivision under the relevant class of persons, e.g., **Engineers**—Directories. For directories listing only the organizations belonging to a particular field use the subdivision "Directories" under the heading for the societies, etc., of the field, e.g., **Social sciences**—Societies, etc.—Directories. Do not use the subdivision "Directories" under names of objects or products, if a subject heading exists for the specific industry or activity which produces those objects (e.g., use **Rubber industry and trade**—Directories, not **Rubber**—Directories). If the subdivision "Directories" is used under the name of a corporate body, e.g., **"United States. Dept of Agriculture**—Directories," also make a second subject entry, if possible, for the field in which the body specializes, e.g., **Agriculture**—United States—Directories.

DIRECTORIES—TELEPHONE
Use under names of regions, countries, cities, etc., or under names of corporate bodies.
  x   Telephone directories

DISCIPLINE
Use under names of corporate bodies, types of corporate bodies, or classes of persons for the enforcement of rules affecting conduct or action, e.g., **Church of England**—Discipline; **Medical personnel**—Discipline. Do not use under subjects for which phrase headings have been provided, e.g., **School discipline.**

DISCOGRAPHY
Use as a form subdivision under topical headings or under names of authors, composers, or performers, for lists or catalogs of sound recordings on phonodiscs or phonodiscs and phonotapes, e.g., **American literature**—Discography; **Shakespeare, William, 1564–1616**—Discography. For catalogs of sound recordings on phonotapes alone use the subdivision "Phonotape catalogs."
  x   Phonorecord catalogs

DISCOTHEQUES
Use under name of cities.
  sa   Nightclubs, dance halls, etc.

DISCOVERIES OF GOLD see GOLD DISCOVERIES

DISCOVERY AND EXPLORATION
Use under names of regions or countries for the discovery and exploration of unknown territories. If appropriate for the work in hand, further subdivide the subdivision by the nationality of the exploring parties, e.g., **America**—Discovery and exploration—Spanish.
  sa   Exploring expeditions
  x   Exploration and discovery

DISEASES   (Direct)
Use under names of animals, age groups of man, names of ethnic groups, or organs or regions of the body. For diseases of plants use "Diseases and pests."
  sa   Diseases and hygiene

Diseases and pests
Mortality
Therapeutic use

DISEASES AND HYGIENE
Use under names of occupational groups, e.g., **Miners**—Diseases and hygiene.
  x   Hygiene and diseases
Occupational diseases

DISEASES AND PESTS   (Direct)
Use under names of plants or types of plants.
  sa   Control
  x   Pests and diseases
Plant diseases

DISPENSARIES see HOSPITALS

DISPOSAL OF WASTES see WASTE DISPOSAL

DISTANCES, ETC.
Use under names of regions, countries, cities, etc.

DISTRIBUTION OF COMMODITIES see MARKETING

DOCKS, WHARVES, ETC.
Use under names of cities.
  x   Engineering
Piers
Quays
Wharves

DOCUMENTATION   (Direct)
Use under names of disciplines for works which discuss the sum total of all processes by which documents, i.e., objects on which knowledge is recorded, are made available to the seeker of knowledge; such processes should include the following: abstracting, archives, bibliographies, cataloging, classification, indexing, information centers, information storage and retrieval systems, libraries, copying processes, translating services, etc. For works on any one process use the subdivision appropriate for that process.
  sa   Abstracting and indexing
Archives
Bibliography
Code numbers
Code words
Government publications
Information services
Libraries
Translating services

DOCUMENTS, PAPAL see PAPAL DOCUMENTS

DOCUMENTS, PUBLIC see GOVERNMENT PUBLICATIONS

DOCUMENTS (HISTORICAL SOURCES)
  see HISTORY—SOURCES; SOURCES

DRAMA
Use as a form subdivision under subjects for collections of dramas, for collections of dramas by one author, or for individual dramas on any identifiable topic. Exception: In the case of drama about individual literary authors, instead of using the subdivision "Drama" under the name of the author, assign the phrase heading **[author's name]**

in fiction, drama, poetry, etc. For discussions about particular themes in drama assign the phrase heading **[subject] in literature,** except in the case of discussions about particular individuals (all classes of persons) as themes in drama in which case the phrase heading **[name of person] in fiction, drama, poetry, etc.** is assigned.

    sa   Juvenile drama

DRAWING *see* DRAWINGS

DRAWINGS

Use as a form subdivision under technical subjects for collections of drawings, plans, etc., e.g., **Forging machinery**—Drawings. Use also as a topical subdivision for discussions of the technique for making such drawings, unless headings for the technique have been especially provided. That is, since **Automotive drafting** exists, **"Automobiles**—Drawings" is used only as a form heading.

    x   Drawing

DRINKING ESTABLISHMENTS *see* BARS, SALOONS, ETC.

DRYING

Use under names of products or objects dried, e.g., **Peat**—Drying.

DUST CONTROL

Use under types of industries, plants, or processes.

    x   Control, Dust

DUTIES (TAXATION) *see* TAXATION

DWELLINGS

Use (a) under names of cities for works dealing collectively with the residential buildings of those places; or (b) under names of particular ethnic groups or classes of persons for discussions of their dwellings from the standpoint of architecture, construction, ethnology, etc., e.g., **Ainu**—Dwellings; **Aged**—Dwellings. For social or economic aspects of a minority group's housing problems use the subdivision "Housing" under the name of the group. For homes of individual persons or classes of persons use the subdivision "Homes" or "Homes and haunts."

    sa   Castles
           Hotels, motels, etc.
           Palaces
           Royal household
    x   Apartment buildings
           Historic houses, etc.
           Homes (Buildings)
           Houses
           Residential buildings

EARLY WORKS TO 1800

Use as form subdivision under topical headings for works published on those topics before 1800, e.g., **Astronomy**—Early works to 1800. Other dates may be arbitrarily selected if they provide a satisfactory division of the literature in the field in question, e.g., **Psychiatry**—Early works to 1900.

EARTHQUAKE, [year]

Use under names of cities.

ECCLESIASTICAL INSTITUTIONS *see* RELIGIOUS AND ECCLESIASTICAL INSTITUTIONS

ECONOMIC ASPECTS   *(Direct)*

Use under topical headings for works which discuss the economic aspects of a particular topic, e.g., Roads—Economic aspects. Under place names or names of ethnic groups use the subdivision "Economic conditions."

    sa   Commerce
           Economic policy
           Finance

ECONOMIC CONDITIONS

Use under names of regions, countries, cities, etc., or names of ethnic groups.

    sa   Commerce
           Famines
           Industries
    x   Economic geography
           Geography, Economic
           History, Economic

ECONOMIC GEOGRAPHY *see* ECONOMIC CONDITIONS

ECONOMIC INTEGRATAION

Use under names of continents or regions for works discussing the partial integration of the economies of a group of countries.

    x   Economic union
           Integration of economies
           International economic integration

ECONOMIC POLICY

Use under names of countries, cities, etc.

    sa   Commercial policy
           Foreign economic relations
           Forest policy
           Government ownership
           Taxation

ECONOMIC RELATIONS, FOREIGN *see* FOREIGN ECONOMIC RELATIONS

ECONOMIC UNION *see* ECONOMIC INTEGRATION

EDITIONS, FIRST *see* BIBLIOGRAPHY—FIRST EDITIONS

EDUCATION   *(Direct)*

Use under names of ethnic groups, classes of persons, or particular orders or sects for works discussing the education of the entities named. If appropriate for the work in hand, qualify the subdivision to designate the specific age level (all qualifiers which may be added to the subdivision "Study and teaching" to designate age level may be also added to the subdivision "Education"). Example: **Minorities**—Education (Elementary). Or, for works which discuss the education of these groups or persons in specific subject fields, further subdivide the subdivision "Education" by the field of study, e.g., **Blind**—Education—Physics. For the education of particular individuals use the subdivision "Knowledge and learning" under their individual names.

    sa   In-service training
           Instruction and study
           Study and teaching

ELECTROMECHANICAL ANALOGIES

Use under scientific or technical subjects for the solving

of dynamical problems of systems by means of equivalent electrical circuits.

    x   Analogies, Electromechanical

ELEMENTARY EDUCATION *see* STUDY AND TEACHING (ELEMENTARY)

ELEVATIONS *see* ALTITUDES

EMIGRATION AND IMMIGRATION
Use under names of countries for the movement of persons out of or into those countries with the intention of establishing new residences.

    sa Colonization
          Exiles
          Foreign population
    x   Immigration and emigration

EMPLOYEES
Use under types of private industries, services, establishments, or institutions, as well as under names of individual nongovernment institutions for discussions about the employees found within these organizations, including professional and nonprofessional personnel. For public employees use the subdivision "Officials and employees" under the name of the pertinent jurisdiction, government or international agency, or kind of government-administered institution. Do not use the subdivision "Employees" under subjects for which phrase headings have been provided, e.g., **School employees.**

    sa General strike
          Job descriptions
          Medical examinations
          Pensions
          Personnel management
          Recruiting
          Retirement
    x   Personnel
          Staff

EMPLOYMENT *(Direct)*
Use under classes of persons or names of ethnic groups.

    sa Appointments, promotions, salaries, etc.
          Occupations
          Officials and employees—Appointment, qualifications, tenure, etc.
          Vocational guidance

ENCYCLOPEDIAS *see* DICTIONARIES; DICTIONARIES AND ENCYCLOPEDIAS

ENGINEERING *see* BRIDGES; BUILDINGS; CANALS; COLD WEATHER CONDITIONS; DESIGN AND CONSTRUCTION; DOCKS, WHARVES, ETC.; HARBOR; MAINTENANCE AND REPAIR; MATERIALS; PIPELINES; PUBLIC WORKS; RELIABILITY; TOWERS; WATER-SUPPLY

ENTERTAINMENTS *see* AMUSEMENTS

ENVIRONMENTAL ASPECTS *(Direct)*
Use under types of industries, processes, machines, constructions, or chemicals for environmental problems associated with their operation, creation, or use, e.g., **Atomic power-plants**—Environmental aspects; **Automobiles**—Environmental aspects; **Pesticides**—Environmental aspects.

    sa Dust control
          Fume control

          Noise
          Noise control
          Sanitation
          Waste disposal

ENVIRONS OF CITIES *see* SUBURBS AND ENVIRONS

EQUIPMENT AND SUPPLIES
Use under names of disciplines, type of processes, industries, services, laboratories, or institutions, as well as under name of individual corporate bodies. Do not use under subjects for which phrase headings have been provided, e.g., **Electric apparatus and appliances; Chemical apparatus.**

    sa Instruments
          Safety appliances
    x   Apparatus and supplies
          Appliances and supplies
          Supplies and equipment

ESSAYS *see* ADDRESSES, ESSAYS, LECTURES

ESTIMATES *(Direct)*
Use under types of engineering, technical processes, industries, etc., for estimates of the cost of construction, installation, or the carrying out of a task to completion.

    sa Contracts and specifications

ETHICAL ASPECTS *see* MORAL AND RELIGIOUS ASPECTS

ETHICAL BEHAVIOR *see* CONDUCT OF LIFE

ETHICS AND RELIGION *see* RELIGION AND ETHICS

ETHNOLOGICAL COLLECTIONS
Use under the name of the original owner of a private ethnological collection, the owner being an individual person, a family, or a corporate body. Also use the heading "[name of original owner]—Ethnological collections" for a private collection donated or sold to a public institution if the collection is still known by its original name.

    x   Collections, Ethnological

EVALUATION
Use under types of products, institutions, or services for discussions of the ability of equipment to perform as required or on the value of programs or tasks carried out, e.g., **Electronic digital computers**—Evaluation; **Moving-pictures**—Evaluation; **Hygiene, Public**—Evaluation; **Libraries**—Evaluation. For critical analyses of literature, music, or films as art forms use the subdivision "History and criticism." Do not use the subdivision "Evaluation" under classes of persons.

    sa Grading
          Judging
          Quality control
          Reviews
          Testing
          Valuation

EXAMINATIONS
Use under names of disciplines, types of institutions, or names of individual institutions or government agencies for discussions about examinations given on particular subjects or in particular organizations. Do not use under classes of persons unless a heading for the corresponding

subject field does not exist. Further subdivide the subdivision "Examinations" by particular disciplines when used under types of institutions, or names of particular institutions, e.g., **Harvard University**—Examinations—Mathematics. For compilations of examination questions in particular disciplines use the subdivision "Examinations, questions, etc."

    x Tests (Examinations)

EXAMINATIONS, MEDICAL *see* MEDICAL EXAMINATIONS

EXAMINATIONS, QUESTIONS, ETC.

    Use as a form subdivision under topical or geographic headings for compilations of examination questions pertaining to those fields.

    sa Miscellanea
           Problems, exercises, etc.
    x Questions, examinations, etc.

EXAMPLES *see* SPECIMENS

EXECUTIVE DEPARTMENTS

    Use under names of countries, cities, etc., for works discussing collectively those specialized agencies or departments making up the major portion of the executive branch of particular governments.

    sa Scientific bureaus
    x Agencies, Government
           Departments, Executive
           Government agencies

EXERCISES, PROBLEMS, ETC. *see* PROBLEMS, EXERCISES, ETC.

EXHIBITIONS

    Use under (a) names of cities for discussions of exhibitions in those places, e.g., **New York (City)**—Exhibitions; (b) types of objects (or if headings for the objects are lacking, under the relevant subject fields) for descriptions or catalogs or public displays of those objects or items representative of a subject, e.g., **Medals**—Exhibitons; **Geology**—Exhibitions; or (c) names of authors or their individual works, e.g., **Goethe, Johann Wolfgang von, 1749–1832**—Exhibitions. Note: In the field of art the subdivision "Exhibitions" is not used under the name of the artist whose works were exhibited; his name is assigned without subdivision. However, in such cases, additional headings are assigned to bring out art form, theme, etc.

EXILES

    Use under names of regions, countries, islands, etc., to designate places to which persons have been banished.

EXPANSION, TERRITORIAL *see* TERRITORIAL EXPANSION

EXPEDITIONS, EXPLORING *see* EXPLORING EXPEDITIONS

EXPENDITURES, PUBLIC *see* APPROPRIATIONS AND EXPENDITURES

EXPERIMENT STATIONS *see* LABORATORIES

EXPERIMENTS

    Use under scientific or technical headings for discussions about experiments and instructions for carrying them out.

    sa Laboratory manuals

EXPLORATION, AERIAL *see* AERIAL EXPLORATION

EXPLORATION AND DISCOVERY *see* DISCOVERY AND EXPLORATION

EXPLORING EXPEDITIONS

    Use under names of regions or countries.
    x Expeditions, Exploring

EXPLOSION, [year]

    Use under names of cities.

EXPOSITIONS *see* EXHIBITIONS

EXTERMINATION *see* CONTROL

FACETIAE *see* ANECDOTES, FACETIAE, SATIRE, ETC.

FACSIMILES

    Use as a form subdivision under types of manuscripts, printed materials, etc., for exact copies of collections of items originally made or published at an earlier date, e.g., **Manuscripts, Mexican**—Facsimiles; **Maps, Early**—Facsimiles; **Autographs**—Facsimiles; **Bookbinding**—Facsimiles.

    x Copies (Facsimiles)

FAIRS

    Use under names of countries, cities, etc., for descriptions of gatherings of buyers and sellers at a stated time and place for trade.

    sa Exhibitions
    x Trade fairs

FAMINES

    Use under names of regions or countries.

FEES

    Use under classes of professional persons, or types of services, institutions, etc., for charges for services rendered, e.g., **Architects**—Fees; **Social services**—Fees. Do not use under subjects for which phrase headings have been provided, e.g., **Dental fees.**

    sa Salaries, pensions, etc.

FELLOWSHIPS, SCHOLARSHIPS, ETC. *see* SCHOLARSHIPS, FELLOWSHIPS, ETC.

FERRIES

    Use under names of cities.

FESTIVALS, ETC.

    Use under names of schools or cities.
    sa Anniversaries, etc.

FESTSCHRIFTEN *see* ADDRESSES, ESSAYS, LECTURES

FEUDAL CASTLES *see* CASTLES

FICTION

    Use as a form subdivision under subjects for collections of novels or stories on identifiable topics, including collections by one author, e.g., **Slavery in the United States**—Fiction. In the case of individual works of fiction use the subdivision "Fiction" only under names of individual persons for fictionalized biographical works or under historical headings for historical novels based on actual historical events; otherwise, do not assign subject headings to single novels or stories. Exception: In the case of biographical fiction about individual literary authors, instead of using the subdivision "Fiction" under the name of the author, assign the phrase heading **[author's name] in fiction, drama, poetry, etc.,** e.g., **Shakespeare, William, 1564–1616, in fiction, drama, poetry, etc.** For discussions about particular themes in fiction assign the phrase heading **[subject] in literature** except in the case of discussions about particular individuals (all classes of persons) as themes in fiction; where the phrase heading **[name of person] in fiction, drama, poetry, etc.** is assigned. In the case of collections of stories do not use the subdivision under topics for which phrase headings have been provided, e.g., **Sea stories.**

> *sa* Juvenile fiction
> Legends
> Legends and stories
> *x* Novels
> Short stories
> Stories

FIELD GUIDES *see* GUIDE-BOOKS

FIELD WORK
Use under names of disciplines for discussions of the techniques of carrying out work in the field to gain practical experience through firsthand observation.

FIELDS, PLAYING *see* SPORTS FACILITIES

FILM CATALOGS
Use as a form subdivision under topical headings for catalogs of pictorial media intended for projection, i.e., motion pictures, filmstrips, slides, video tapes, etc., on particular topics.

> *x* Filmstrip catalogs
> Moving-picture catalogs

FILMS, JUVENILE *see* JUVENILE FILMS

FILMS FOR [NAME OF LANGUAGE] SPEAKERS
Use as a form subdivision under names of languages for language instruction films to be shown to native speakers of particular languages, e.g., **English language**—Films for Spanish speakers; **Romance languages**—Films for English speakers.

FILMSTRIP CATALOGS *see* FILM CATALOGS

FINANCE
Use under types of industries, services, technical operations, or corporate bodies, as well as under names of individual corporate bodies, for the raising and expenditure of funds. In the case of individual corporate bodies also use the subdivision for works which discuss the budgets of those bodies, e.g., **United Nations**—Finance; insert in the catalog the reference "**United Nations**—Budget *see* **United Nations**—Finance." For the financial affairs of government agencies involving appropriated funds use the subdivision "Appropriations and expenditures."

> *sa* Accounting
> Taxation

FIRE, [year]
Use under names of cities, institutions, structures, etc. for accounts of particular fires.

FIRES AND FIRE PREVENTION
Use under (a) names of cities; (b) types of structures, buildings or institutions; or (c) types of industries; if the relevant headings are avaliable, (b) is preferred to (c). For accounts of particular fires use the subdivision "Fire" under the name of the city, institution, etc.

> *sa* Fire

FIRST EDITIONS *see* BIBLIOGRAPHY—FIRST EDITIONS

FLOOD, [year]
Use under names of cities, rivers, etc., for accounts of particular floods.

FLOODS
Use under names of particular cities, rivers, etc. For accounts of particular floods use the subdivision "Flood."

> *sa* Flood

FOLKTALES *see* LEGENDS

FOOD SERVICE
Use under types of institutions, organized activities, etc., for provisions for meals and food in those enterprises.

FORCES, ARMED *see* ARMED FORCES

FOREIGN ECONOMIC RELATIONS *(Direct)*
Use under names of regions or countries. Further subdivide the subdivision by region or country if required by the work in hand. If so subdivided, make a second subject entry with the two pertinent regions or countries in reversed positions, e.g., 1. **United States**—Foreign economic relations—France. 2. **France**—Foreign economic relations—United States.

> *sa* Commerce
> Economic integration
> *x* Economic relations, Foreign
> International economic relations

FOREIGN INFLUENCES
Use under headings which denote civilizations of particular places, or under particular aspects of those civilizations, including art forms, literary forms, philosophies, intellectual life, etc., for discussions on outside cultural influences on them, e.g., **Great Britain**—Civilization—Foreign influences; **Art, Japanese**—Foreign influences. For works discussing the cultural influence of a specific civilization on another, or on particular aspects of the latter, use the subdivision appropriate for that influence under the heading designating the specific civilization or cultural phenomena being influenced, e.g., **United States**—Civilization—Greek influences; **Civilization, Occidental**—Islamic influences; **Japan**—Intellectual life—American influences; **Painting, Russian**—Occidental influences; **Tales, French**—German influences. Whenever headings of this type are established, make a *see also* reference to it from the heading for the influencing civilization, e.g., **Bavaria**—Civilization *see also* **Art, Hungarian**—Bavarian influences. For the influence of particular persons, religions, art forms, philosophies, events, etc., on other persons or things use the subdivision "Influence."

> *sa* Civilization
> Relations (general) with . . .
> *x* Cultural influences

FOREIGN LANGUAGE TEXT-BOOKS
see TEXT-BOOKS FOR FOREIGNERS

FOREIGN OPINION
Use under names of regions or countries for foreign opinion about those regions or countries. Qualify the subdivision if appropriate to denote the public opinion held by any one region or country, e.g., **United States**—Foreign opinion, British; this means British public opinion about the United States. In each instance in which the qualified subdivision is used, assign as a second subject the heading **Public opinion**—[location of the opinion held], e.g., **Public opinion**—Great Britain.
   sa Foreign public opinion
      Public opinion
   x Opinion, Foreign

FOREIGN POPULATION
Use under names of countries, cities, etc., for works discussing persons born in, belonging to, or characteristic of some country other than the one under consideration. For discussions about specific foreign elements in the population use the phrase heading **[name of group] in [name of place]**, e.g., **Italians in Chicago; Jews, American, in Israel.**
   sa Emigration and immigration

FOREIGN PUBLIC OPINION
Use under names of wars for world opinion (excluding the opinion of the belligerent countries) about a particular war. Qualify the subdivision if appropriate, to denote the public opinion held by any one non-belligerent region or country, e.g., **United States**—History—Civil War, 1861–1865—Foreign public opinion, Austrian. In each instance in which the qualified subdivision is used assign as a second subject the heading **Public opinion**—[location of the opinion held], e.g., **Public opinion**—Austria.
   sa Foreign opinion
      Public opinion

FOREIGN RELATIONS *(Direct)*
Use under names of particular countries (or regions made up of two or more countries) for works which discuss the diplomatic relations between these countries and other sovereign states. If required by the work in hand to designate relations with a specific region or country, further subdivide the subdivision by region or country. If so divided, make a second subject entry with the two names in reversed positions, e.g., 1. **United States**—Foreign relations—Canada. 2. **Canada**—Foreign relations—United States.
   sa Annexation to . . .
      Defenses
      Diplomatic and consular service
      Foreign economic relations
      Frontier troubles
      International status
      Neutrality
      Relations (general) with . . .
      Territorial expansion
   x Diplomatic relations
      International relations

FOREIGN RELATIONS ADMINISTRATION
Use under names of countries.

FOREIGN TRADE *see* COMMERCE

FOREST POLICY
Use under names of countries.

FORMS
Use as a form subdivision under topical headings for works consisting of or containing substantial numbers of blank forms, e.g., **Export sales**—Forms.

FORTIFICATIONS, MILITARY INSTALLATIONS, ETC.
Use under names of cities.
   sa Castles
      Gates
      Walls
   x Forts
      Military installations
      Posts, Military
      Stations, Military

FORTS *see* FORTIFICATIONS, MILITARY INSTALLATIONS, ETC.

FOUNTAINS
Use under names of cities.

FRONTIER TROUBLES
Use under names of countries, provinces, etc.

FRONTIERS (BOUNDARIES) *see* BOUNDARIES

FUME CONTROL
Use under types of industries, plants, or processes.
   x Control, Fume

GALLERIES *see* MUSEUMS

GATES
Use under names of cities.
   sa Walls

GAZETTEERS
Use as a form subdivision under names of regions, countries, cities, etc., for dictionaries of geographic names of those places with descriptions, e.g., **United States**—Gazetteers.
   x Description—Gazetteers
      Description and travel—Gazetteers
      Place name dictionaries

GENEALOGY
Use under names of regions, countries, cities, etc., as well as under names of ethnic groups, classes of persons, etc., for family histories, e.g., **St. Louis**—Genealogy; **French-Canadians**—Genealogy; **Kings and rulers**—Genealogy. For the genealogy of one family use the name of the family as the subject, e.g., **Reynolds family.**
   sa Heraldry
      Nobility

GENERAL STRIKE, [year]
Use under names of cities.
   x Strike, General

GENTRY
Use under names of regions, countries, etc.
   sa Nobility
      Social registers

GEOGRAPHIC ATLASES *see* MAPS

GEOGRAPHIC BOUNDARIES *see* BOUNDARIES

GEOGRAPHY *see* DESCRIPTION; DESCRIPTION AND TRAVEL

GEOGRAPHY, ECONOMIC *see* ECONOMIC CONDITIONS

GEOGRAPHY, HISTORICAL *see* HISTORICAL GEOGRAPHY

GILDS
Use under names of cities.

GLOSSARIES, ETC. *see* LANGUAGE—GLOSSARIES, ETC.

GLOSSARIES, VOCABULARIES, ETC.
Use as a form subdivision under names of languages for incomplete lists of the words of a language which may or may not be alphabetically arranged, with or without definitions. For related subdivisions see the instructions given under the subdivision "Dictionaries."
   x Vocabularies, glossaries, etc.

GOLD DISCOVERIES
Use under names of regions, countries, states, etc.
   x Discoveries of gold

GOVERNMENT *see* POLITICS AND GOVERNMENT

GOVERNMENT AGENCIES *see* EXECUTIVE DEPARTMENTS

GOVERNMENT BUILDINGS *see* PUBLIC BUILDINGS

GOVERNMENT EMPLOYEES
see OFFICIALS AND EMPLOYEES

GOVERNMENT LANDS *see* PUBLIC LANDS

GOVERNMENT OWNERSHIP (*Direct*)
Use under names of industries.
   sa Auditing and inspection
   x Ownership, Government
       Public ownership

GOVERNMENT PROPERTY
Use under names of countries, cities, etc.
   sa Public lands
   x Property, Government
       Public property

GOVERNMENT PUBLICATIONS
Use under names of countries, cities, etc. Qualify the subdivision if the work in hand deals collectively with the publications of particular kinds of jurisdictions within a particular country, e.g., **Canada**—Government publications (Provincial governments).
   x Documents, Public
       Public documents
       Publications, Government

GOVERNMENT SCIENTIFIC AGENCIES
see SCIENTIFIC BUREAUS

GOVERNMENT VESSELS
Use under names of countries.
   x Ships, Government

GOVERNORS
Use under names of countries, provinces, states, etc., except in the case of works dealing collectively with the governors of the United States, for which the heading "**Governors**—United States" is assigned.

GRADING
Use under kinds of industrial or agricultural products for works discussing the assignment of categories of quality to facilitate marketing, e.g., **Tobacco**—Grading.
   sa Labeling

GRANTS, RESEARCH *see* RESEARCH GRANTS

GRAPHIC METHODS
Use under names of disciplines, types of technical processes, scientific phenomena, etc., for the technique of solving problems by means of graphs, e.g., **Linguistics**—Graphic methods; **Shielding (Radiation)**—Graphic methods; **Solar radiation**—Graphic methods.

GRAVESTONES *see* SEPULCHRAL MONUMENTS

GRAVEYARDS *see* CEMETERIES

GUIDANCE, VOCATIONAL *see* VOCATIONAL GUIDANCE

GUIDE-BOOKS
Use as a form subdivision under names of individual parks, forest reserves, highways, battlefields, or other named lands except colleges and universities, for handbooks for travelers containing information about routes, accommodations, items of cultural interest, etc.; e.g., **Sierra National Forest**—Guide-books. Also use the subdivision under types of geographic features for field guides to particular geomorphologic phenomena of an area, e.g., **Caves**—[local subdivision]—Guide-books. Use the subdivision under types of buildings for guides to the architecture of an area, e.g., **Churches**—[local subdivision]—Guide-books. For travel guides to individual cities, universities, mountain peaks, or other geographic areas of limited size use the subdivision "Description—Guide-books." For travel guides to individual regions or jurisdictions larger than cities use the subdivision "Description and travel—Guide-books."
   sa Description—Tours
       Description and travel—Tours
   x Field guides

HABITS, ANIMAL *see* BEHAVIOR

HALFWAY HOUSES *see* CORRECTIONAL INSTITUTIONS

HALLS, BEER *see* BARS, SALOONS, ETC.

HALLS, DANCE *see* NIGHTCLUBS, DANCE HALLS, ETC.

HALLS, MUSIC *see* AUDITORIUMS, CONVENTION
   FACILITIES, ETC.; THEATERS

HANDBOOKS, MANUALS, ETC.
Use as a form subdivision under topical headings for concise reference works in which facts and information pertaining to a certain subject field are arranged for ready reference and consultation rather than for continuous reading and study.
   sa Amateurs' manuals
       Field work
       Guide-books
       Identification
       Laboratory manuals
       Observers' manuals
       Tables

x Manuals
    Vade mecums

HARBOR
    Use under names of cities.
  sa Docks, wharves, etc.
  x Engineering

HEALTH AND HYGIENE (*Direct*)
    Use under particular classes of persons or ethnic groups, e.g., **Boys**—Health and hygiene; **Students**—Health and hygiene; **Mexican Americans**—Health and hygiene. For age groups of man generally dependent by nature on the assistance of others use the subdivision "Care and hygiene." For the health and hygiene of occupational groups use the subdivision "Diseases and hygiene." For particular hygienic customs practiced by religious groups assign inverted headings of the type **Hygiene, Islamic.**
  sa Care and treatment
       Diseases
       Food service
       Hygienic aspects
       Medical care
  x Hygiene

HEALTH CARE *see* MEDICAL CARE

HEATING AND VENTILATION
    Use under types of buildings, factories, vehicles, or other constructions.
  sa Air conditioning
  x Ventilation

HERALDRY
    Use under topical headings, types of industries, or names of individual societies or institutions, for the devising, granting, or use of armorial insignia, e.g., **Medicine**—Heraldry; **Book industries and trade**—Heraldry; **Freemasons**—Heraldry.
  sa Genealogy
       Seal
  x Armorial insignia

HIGHER EDUCATION *see* STUDY AND TEACHING (HIGHER)

HISTORIC HOUSES, ETC. *see* BUILDINGS; DWELLINGS

HISTORICAL ATLASES *see* HISTORICAL GEOGRAPHY—MAPS

HISTORICAL GEOGRAPHY
    Use under names of regions or countries for histories of an area in terms of the changes occurring in its territorial limits.
  sa Boundaries
  x Geography, Historical

HISTORICAL GEOGRAPHY—MAPS
    Use as a form subdivision under names of regions or countries for works consisting of maps of an area at various stages of its history, e.g., **United States**—Historical geography—Maps.
  x Atlases, Historical
       Historical atlases
       History—Maps

HISTORIOGRAPHY
    Use under subjects, including geographic headings, for the theory and technique of writing history; or for the history and criticism of histories previously published in the field in question. Examples: **Education**—Historiography; **United States**—Historiography; **United States**—History—Civil War, 1861–1865—Historiography.
  sa Sources
  x History—Criticism
       History—Historiography

HISTORY
    Use under subjects, including names of regions, countries, cities, etc., for descriptions and explanations of past events within a particular field of knowledge, or in a particular place, e.g., **Aeronautics**—History; **Art**—History; **Catholic Church**—History; **Indians**—History; **Washington, D.C.**—History. Under certain headings especially names of places, the subdivision "History" is further subdivided by period subdivisions, e.g., **United States**—History—Civil War, 1861–1865; **Japan**—History—Heian period, 794–1185; **New York (City)**—History—1865–1898; **Catholic Church**—History—Middle Ages, 600–1500; **Art**—History—17th–18th centuries; **Preaching**—History—20th century; **Theater**—History—To 500. Certain headings which in themselves have a historical connotation are subdivided by period subdivisions without interposing the subdivision "History," e.g., **Christian life**—Early church, ca. 30–600; **Biography**—Middle Ages, 500–1500; **Great Britain**—Economic conditions––1918–1945; **United States**—Social conditions—1960–   . Do not use the subdivision "History" under subjects for which phrase headings have been provided, e.g., **Church history; World history.** Under literary, music, or film form headings use the subdivision "History and criticism."
  sa Anniversaries, etc.
       Antiquities
       Biography
       Chronology
       Church history
       Civilization
       Constitutional history
       Genealogy
       Gold discoveries
       Historical geography
       Kings and rulers
       Massacre
       Origin
       Politics and government
       Relations (general) with . . .

HISTORY—ANECDOTES, FACETIAE, SATIRE, ETC.
    Use as a form subdivision under names of regions, countries, cities, etc., for collections of miscellaneous humorous writings, including anecdotes, concerning the history of those places. For comprehensive humorous histories of particular places use the subdivision "History, Comic, satirical, etc."

HISTORY—CRITICISM *see* HISTORIOGRAPHY

HISTORY—HISTORIOGRAPHY *see* HISTORIOGRAPHY

HISTORY—MAPS *see* HISTORICAL GEOGRAPHY—MAPS

HISTORY—PROPHECIES
    Use under names of regions, countries, cities, etc.

HISTORY—SOURCES

Use as a form or topical subdivision under topical or geographical headings for historical source materials, i.e., collections of, or discussions about, contemporary documents used by subsequent historians in their research, e.g., **Medicine—History—Sources**; **Franciscans in Ireland—History—Sources**; **San Francisco—History—Sources.** Under historical headings, including certain headings of the type [place]—[topic], or under systems of law use the subdivision "Sources" directly, e.g., **Reformation**—Sources; **Pakistan**—Politics and government—Sources; **Roman law**—Sources.

   sa Sources
   x Documents (Historical sources)

HISTORY, COMIC, SATIRICAL, ETC.

Use as a form subdivision under names of regions, countries, cities, etc., for comprehensive humorous histories of those places, e.g., **Great Britain**—History, Comic, satirical, etc. For collections of miscellaneous humorous writings concerning the history of particular places use the subdivision "History—Anecdotes, facetiae, satire, etc."

   x Comic histories
      Humorous histories
      Satirical histories

HISTORY, ECONOMIC *see* ECONOMIC CONDITIONS

HISTORY, LOCAL

Use as a form subdivision under names of regions, countries, states, etc., for the collective histories of several local units. For the history of a single locality use the subdivision "History" under the name of the locality.

   x Local history

HISTORY, MILITARY

Use under names of regions, countries, cities, etc.

   sa Bombardment
      Capture
      Neutrality
      Relations (military) with . . .
      Siege
      Sieges
   x Military history
      Wars

HISTORY, NAVAL

Use under names of regions or countries.

   x Naval history
      Wars

HISTORY, SOCIAL *see* SOCIAL CONDITIONS

HISTORY AND CRITICISM

Use under literary, film, or music form headings, e.g., **English poetry**—History and criticism; **Arthurian romances**—History and criticism; **Erotic films**—History and criticism. Under names of individual authors use the subdivision "Criticism and interpretation."

   sa Book reviews
      Criticism, Textual
      Evaluation
      Historiography
      Reviews
   x Criticism and history

HOLOGRAPHS *see* AUTOGRAPHS

HOMES (*Direct*)

Use under names of statesmen, political figures, etc., for discussions about the dwellings they lived in or their associations with particular places. For works on an individual dwelling use the name of the dwelling, e.g., **Washington, D.C. Cedar Hill.**

HOMES (BUILDINGS) *see* DWELLINGS

HOMES AND HAUNTS (*Direct*)

Use under particular classes of persons or names of individual persons (except statesmen, political figures, etc.) for discussions about the dwellings they lived in or their associations with particular places, e.g., **Architects**—Homes and haunts; **Shakespeare, William, 1564–1616**—Homes and haunts. For works discussing the homes of individual statesmen, etc., use the subdivision "Homes." For works on an individual dwelling use the name of the dwelling, e.g., **Mount Vernon.**

HOSPITALS

Use under name of cities, as well as under names of diseases, types of diseases, or particular ethnic groups.

   x Dispensaries

HOTELS, MOTELS, ETC.

Use under names of cities.

   sa Restaurants
   x Inns
      Motels
      Tourist homes

HOUSEHOLD, ROYAL *see* ROYAL HOUSEHOLD

HOUSES *see* DWELLINGS

HOUSING (*Direct*)

Use (a) under names of minority groups for the social or economic aspects of their housing problems; or (b) under types of domestic animals, e.g., **Laboratory animals**—Housing. For housing for government employees use the subdivision "Officials and employees—Housing" under the name of the jurisdiction in question.

HUMAN RIGHTS *see* CIVIL RIGHTS

HUMOR *see* ANECDOTES, FACETIAE, SATIRE, ETC.

HUMOR, PICTORIAL *see* CARICATURES AND CARTOONS

HUMOR, CARICATURES, ETC.

Use as a form subdivision under names of individual wars for humorous writings or pictorial humor about those wars. For anecdotes pertaining to individual wars use the subdivision "Anecdotes" under the name of the war.

HUMOROUS HISTORIES *see* HISTORY, COMIC, SATIRICAL, ETC.

HURRICANE, [year]

Use under names of regions, countries, cities, etc., for discussions about individual hurricanes.

HURRICANES

Use under names of regions, countries, cities, etc. For accounts of particular hurricanes use the subdivision "Hurricane."

HYGIENE *see* HEALTH AND HYGIENE

HYGIENE AND CARE *see* CARE AND HYGIENE

HYGIENE AND DISEASES *see* DISEASES AND HYGIENE

HYGIENIC ASPECTS *(Direct)*

Use under types of industries, plants, or processes, as well as under types of everyday objects, for works on the inherent nature of those activities or objects as it pertains to the health of persons associated with them, e.g., **Packing-houses**—Hygienic aspects; **Machine-shops**—Hygienic aspects; **Paper money**—Hygienic aspects. For works on the control of environmental conditions of industries, buildings, activity areas, etc., so that they will not be injurious to health use the subdivision "Sanitation." For works on the health of occupational groups use "Diseases and hygiene."

    sa   Diseases
           Physiological aspects
           Physiological effect
           Sanitary affairs

ICONOGRAPHY

Use as a form subdivision under names of individuals, including literary authors, or under particular classes of persons, for works consisting of pictures which relate in some way to those persons, including their portraits, as well as portraits of family and associates, views of birthplaces, residences, results of their creative activity, etc., e.g., **Kafka, Franz, 1883–1924**—Iconography; **Authors, Czech**—Iconography. For works consisting solely of portraits of individuals use the subdivisions "Art," "Portraits," "Portraits, caricatures, etc.," or "Portraits, etc." under the name of the individual.

    sa   Cartoons, satire, etc.
           Medals

IDENTIFICATION

Use as a form subdivision under types of objects, including plants or animals, for manuals or keys which present the salient characters for the purpose of determining the names and relationships of unidentified members of the particular group, e.g., **Firearms**—Identification; **Meat cuts**—Identification; **Soils**—Identification; **Birds**—Identification.

ILLUMINATION *see* LIGHTING

ILLUSTRATIONS

Use as a form or topical subdivision under particular literary forms, names of individual authors, or names of individual works (i.e., author-title or uniform title entries) for the illustrations found in particular bodies of literature, or in single publications, e.g., **Japanese fiction**—Illustrations; **Nursery rhymes**—Illustrations; **Milton, John, 1608–1674**—Illustrations; **Sforza manuscript**—Illustrations. Do not use the subdivision as a form subdivision for the illustrations of an individual illustrated work except in those cases where the illustrations have been reissued separately without text.

    x   Book illustrations

IMMIGRATION AND EMIGRATION
   see EMIGRATION AND IMMIGRATION

IMMUNITIES *see* PRIVILEGES AND IMMUNITIES

IMPRINTS

Use as a form subdivision under particular regions, countries, cities, etc., for lists of works published in those places without consideration as to the language in which they were published. For lists of works published in a particular language without consideration as to the place in which they were published, assign phrase headings of the type **Hebrew imprints.**

    x   National bibliography

IMPROVEMENT OF CITIES *see* CIVIC IMPROVEMENT

IN-SERVICE TRAINING *(Direct)*

Use under particular kinds of professional or paraprofessional personnel for works which discuss their continuing professional education during service to increase their effectiveness on the assignment, e.g., **High school teachers**—In-service training; **Social workers**—In-service training. Do not use the subdivision for on-the-job training of employees, in which case the subject heading **Employees, Training of** is assigned.

    x   Training, In-service

INDEXES

Use as a form subdivision under topical headings for works which provide a comprehensive subject approach to the printed materials, including books, or books and serials, published in a special field of knowledge; the individual subtopics listed in such works may be arranged either alphabetically or systematically. (Since bibliographies are often indexed, it may be difficult to distinguish between indexes, which stress the subject approach to publications, and bibliographies, which merely list publications.) For any bibliography which is indexed in sufficient detail as to be usable also as a comprehensive index to the subject, use the subdivision "Indexes" instead of the subdivision "Bibliography." For indexes to serials or periodicals alone use the subdivision "Periodicals—Indexes." For indexes to collections of manuscripts on particular subjects use the subdivision "Manuscripts—Indexes." For indexes to specific bodies of literature use the subdivision "Indexes" under the appropriate literary form heading, e.g., **English literature**—Indexes. For first-line indexes to poetry or hymns use the subdivision "Indexes" under the appropriate form heading, e.g., **English poetry**—Indexes. For indexes to the published works of an individual author treated collectively use the subdivision "Dictionaries, indexes, etc." under the name of the author. For indexes to individual monographic works (except individual works of belles lettres, if entered under the name of an author) or to individual serial publications (no restrictions as to subject area), use the subdivision "Indexes" under the author-title entry (or under the uniform title for publications entered under title) of the individual publication; in addition to this subject heading assign also the same subject headings that were assigned to the work being indexed subdivided by the subdivision "Indexes." For indexes to individual works of belles lettres, if entered under an individual author, do not use the subdivision "Indexes" under the name of the work; instead, assign two subject headings, one being the name of the author subdivided by "Dictionaries, indexes, etc.," the other being the author-title entry for the individual work without subdivision. For indexes to individual anonymous classics or other works entered under uniform title, use the subdivision "Indexes" under the particular uniform title. For indexes to the principal words found within the writings of one author, one named work, or a group of literary works use the subdivision "Concordances." For indexes to collections of objects use the subdivision "Catalogs" under the name of the object. For works on how to prepare indexes within a particular discipline use the subdivision "Abstracting and indexing" under the name of the discipline.

INDEXING *see* ABSTRACTING AND INDEXING

INDUSTRIAL APPLICATIONS
Use under particular scientific phenomena or substances, e.g., **Ultrasonic waves**—Industrial applications; **Enzymes**—Industrial applications.
   sa Scientific applications
   x Applications, Industrial
      Use, Industrial

INDUSTRIAL EXHIBITIONS *see* EXHIBITIONS

INDUSTRIAL SCHOOLS *see* SCHOOLS

INDUSTRIAL WASTE DISPOSAL *see* WASTE DISPOSAL

INDUSTRIES
Use under names of regions, countries, cities, etc., for discussions of the industries of those places. Use also under names of primitive groups for the crafts and technologies of those groups, e.g., **Australian aborigines**—Industries.
   sa Automation
      Gilds
      Inventories
      Management
      Manufactures

INFLUENCE
Use under names of prominent persons or authors, sects or religions, sacred works, particular art forms, movements, types of organizations, etc., for discussions of their influence, e.g., **Euripides**—Influence; **Baptists**—Influence; **Bible**—Influence; **Sculpture, Greek**—Influence; **Crusades**—Influence; **Monasticism and religious orders**—Influence. On whom or on what this influence was brought to bear remains unspecified (as far as the one subject heading under question is concerned) except in the case of the influence of a literary author on another individual or on the development of a particular discipline (outside of his own field). Formulate headings involving the latter situation in the following manner: [author who influences]—Influence—[person or discipline influenced] e.g., **Shakespeare, William, 1564–1616**—Influence—Emerson; **Shakespeare, William, 1564–1616**—Influence—Music. When headings of this type are assigned, make a second subject entry under the name of the person influenced (without subdivision) or under the heading designating the history of the relevant discipline. For discussions of the influence of particular wars use the subdivision "Influence and results." For discussions on outside cultural influences made on civilizations or particular aspects of them use the subdivision "Foreign influences" or subdivisions of the type "American influences" designating specific influences.

INFORMATION CENTERS *see* INFORMATION SERVICES

INFORMATION SERVICES *(Direct)*
Use under topical headings for information centers and the services which they provide in those subject fields, with stress on the retrieval, analysis, synthesis and dissemination of information to meet the specific requirements of the clientele served by the centers.
   sa Libraries
   x Information centers

INHABITANTS *see* POPULATION

INJURIES *see* ACCIDENTS; ACCIDENTS AND INJURIES

INNOVATIONS, TECHNOLOGICAL
   see TECHNOLOGICAL INNOVATIONS

INNS *see* HOTELS, MOTELS, ETC.

INSIGNIA
Use under names of corporate bodies, including armies and navies, as well as under types of organizations, for discussions of their distinguishing signs of authority, office, or honor.
   sa Heraldry
      Seal

INSPECTION *(Direct)*
Use under (a) particular items of merchandise for methods of examining them to determine their fitness for marketing; (b) types of machines or engineering structures for methods of determining compliance with regulations with respect to fire and other hazards; or (c) names of particular military services for official examinations to determine and report on their state of readiness. Examples: **Lumber**—Inspection; **Locomotives**—Inspection; **United States. Army**—Inspection. Do not use under subjects for which phrase headings have been provided, e.g., **Meat inspection; Mine inspection.**
   sa Grading
      Judging

INSPECTION AND AUDITING *see* AUDITING AND INSPECTION

INSTITUTIONS, SOCIETIES, ETC. *see* SOCIETIES, ETC.

INSTRUCTION AND STUDY *(Direct)*
Use under music subject headings or under names of musical instruments as an equivalent of the subdivision "Study and teaching."

INSTRUMENTS
Use under names of scientific or technical disciplines for discussions of the instruments employed in those fields, e.g., **Nuclear physics**—Instruments; **Internal friction**—Instruments. Do not use under subjects for which phrase headings have been provided, e.g., **Aeronautical instruments.**
   sa Measurement

INTEGRATION OF ECONOMIES *see* ECONOMIC INTEGRATION

INTELLECTUAL LIFE
Use under names of regions, countries, cities, etc., as well as under particular ethnic or religious groups for discussions about the intellectual activities of a people, especially in the arts and letters.

INTERNATIONAL COOPERATION

Use under topical headings for international cooperative activities with or without the active participation of governments, e.g., **Postal service**—International cooperation; **Nature conservation**—International cooperation. Do not use under subjects for which phrase headings have been provided, e.g., **International agricultural cooperation.**

   sa Economic integration
   x Cooperation, International

INTERNATIONAL ECONOMIC INTEGRATION
see ECONOMIC INTEGRATION

INTERNATIONAL ECONOMIC RELATIONS
see FOREIGN ECONOMIC RELATIONS

INTERNATIONAL RELATIONS *see* FOREIGN RELATIONS

INTERNATIONAL STATUS

Use under names of regions, countries, cities, etc.

INTERPRETATION *see* CRITICISM AND INTERPRETATION

INTERVIEWS

Use as a form subdivision under classes of persons for transcripts of what was said during the course of interviews with three or more persons on one or more occasions, e.g., **Statesmen**—Interviews. Also use the subdivision under names of particular literary authors for the transcripts of interviews with those individuals. Do not use the subdivision under topical headings; assign secondary headings (without subdivision) to bring out the topic of the interviews, if appropriate for the work in hand.

INVENTORIES

Use as a form or topical subdivisions under types of industries or institutions for lists of raw materials, supplies, work in process, finished goods, etc., on hand at a particular time, e.g., **Drug stores**—Inventories.

JAIL *see* CORRECTIONAL INSTITUTIONS

JOB DESCRIPTIONS

Use under particular types of employees or professional personnel for summaries of the essential activities involved in the performance of their jobs, e.g., **Librarians**—Job descriptions. If the subject heading for the type of employees is not available, use instead the subdivision under the type of industry or service which is pertinent, e.g., **Flax industry**—Job descriptions; **Hospitals**—Job descriptions. Use the subdivision also under names of corporate bodies, e.g., **United States. Navy**—Job descriptions.

JOBS *see* OCCUPATIONS

JOKES *see* ANECDOTES, FACETIAE, SATIRE, ETC.

JOURNALS *see* PERIODICALS

JUDGING

Use under (a) kinds of farm products, animals, etc., for discussion of methods for evaluating quality, breed, conformation, etc., at a show or exhibit; or (b) kinds of games or sports for discussions of methods for officiating at a contest or athletic event. Examples: **Cattle**—Judging; **Potatoes**—Judging; **Bicycle racing**—Judging.

   x Refereeing
      Umpiring

JUVENILE DICTIONARIES *see* DICTIONARIES, JUVENILE

JUVENILE DRAMA

Use as a form subdivision. Cf. instructions under the subdivision "Drama."

JUVENILE FICTION

Use as a form subdivision. Cf. instructions under the subdivision "Fiction."

JUVENILE FILMS

Use as a form subdivision under subject headings assigned to juvenile pictorial media intended for projection, i.e., juvenile motion pictures, filmstrips, video tapes, etc.

   x Films, Juvenile

JUVENILE LITERATURE

Use as a form subdivision under topical or geographical headings, as well as under names of persons or corporate bodies, for topical publications for children up through the age of 15 (or through the 9th grade). Do not use the subdivision in connection with juvenile belles lettres. For juvenile works of belles lettres on particular topics use the subdivisions "Juvenile fiction," "Juvenile drama," or "Juvenile poetry" under the pertinent heading for the topic. However, if the juvenile work of belles lettres in hand requires a literary form heading, assign either an adult heading without subdivision, e.g., **Ghost stories;** or assign a specific juvenile heading pertinent for the form in question, e.g., **Children's stories; Nursery rhymes.**

   sa Dictionaries, Juvenile
   x Books for children
      Children's books
      Literature, Juvenile

JUVENILE PHONORECORDS

Use as a form subdivision under subject headings assigned to any medium for juveniles on which sound has been recorded for subsequent reproduction, including phonodiscs, phonotapes, etc., e.g. **Astronomy**—Juvenile phonorecords.

   x Phonorecords, Juvenile

JUVENILE POETRY

Use as a form subdivision. Cf. instructions under the subdivision "Poetry."

KINGS AND RULERS

Use under names of regions, countries, empires, ethnic groups, etc.

   sa Courts and courtiers
      Palaces
      Presidents
      Princes and princesses
      Queens
      Royal household
      Sultans
   x Rulers

KNOWLEDGE

Use under names of prominent individuals (including philosophers or theologians) but only if the subdivision is further subdivided by special topics, denoting the knowledge these individuals may have had on incidental topics not central to their careers, e.g., **Homerus**—Knowledge—

Medicine; **Luther, Martin, 1483–1546**—Knowledge—Hebrew language. For their learning and scholarship in general use the subdivision "Knowledge and learning." For philosophers or theologians who have made major contributions in particular fields subdivide their names directly by the field in question, e.g., **Plato**—Ethics; **Plato**—Mathematics.

KNOWLEDGE AND LEARNING
Use under names of prominent individuals (including philosophers or theologians) for their learning and scholarship in general. For their knowledge on incidental topics use the subdivision "Knowledge—[subject]."
   x Learning and knowledge

LABELING (*Direct*)
Use under kinds of products or merchandise, e.g., **Chemicals**—Labeling.

LABOR PRODUCTIVITY
Use under particular industrial processes for works discussing the rate of ouptut of workmen per unit time, usually compared to an established standard, e.g., **Pipefitting**—Labor productivity. When headings for the processes are lacking use the subdivision under types of plants or industries, e.g., **Gas industry**—Labor productivity.
   sa Production standards
   x Productivity, Labor

LABORATORIES
Use under names of cities.
   x Experiment stations
       Research buildings
       Stations, Experiment

LABORATORY MANUALS
Use as a form subdivision under science or technology headings for workbooks containing concise background information and directions for performing work, including experiments, in the laboratory.
   sa Experiments

LAND SURVEYS *see* SURVEYS

LANDS, PUBLIC *see* PUBLIC LANDS

LANDSLIDE, [year]
Use under names of cities.
   sa Avalanche

LANGUAGE
Use under names of individual authors, classes of persons, or fields of knowledge for discussions about the special vocabularies, use of language, phraseology, etc., belonging to those persons or found in those fields, e.g., **Milton, John, 1608–1674**—Language; **Children**—Language; **Medicine**—Language.
   sa Authorship
       Name
       Names
       Terminology

LANGUAGE—GLOSSARIES, ETC.
Use as a form subdivision under names of authors for listing of the words used by those authors.
   x Glossaries, etc.
       Vocabularies, glossaries, etc.

LANGUAGE (NEW WORDS, SLANG, ETC.)
Use under classes of persons, names of schools, or individual wars. For slang occurring in particular disciplines, as well as slang of particular languages, use the subdivision "Slang" under the name of the discipline or language. For new words of particular languages assign the subject heading **Words, New** subdivided by the name of the language, e.g., **Words, New**—English.
   x New words
       Words, New

LANGUAGE TEXT-BOOKS FOR FOREIGNERS
   see TEXT-BOOKS FOR FOREIGNERS

LANGUAGES
Use under names of regions or countries, or under particular ethnic groups which do not speak a common language, for discussions of the languages spoken, e.g., **Europe**—Languages; **Jews**—Languages.
   sa Language
       Language (New words, slang, etc.)
       Literatures
       Readers
       Translating
       Translations

LAUNDRIES, PUBLIC *see* PUBLIC LAUNDRIES

LAW AND LEGISLATION (*Direct*)
Use as a form or topical subdivision under topical headings. Do not use under subjects for which phrase headings have been provided, e.g., **Marriage law.**
   sa Charters
       Charters, grants, privileges
       Constitutional law
       Legal status, laws, etc.
       Privileges and immunities
       Safety regulations
   x Legislation

LEARNED INSTITUTIONS AND SOCIETIES
Use as a topical subdivision under names of regions, countries, cities, etc., for works discussing collectively the various learned institutions or societies of a particular place. For societies devoted to special fields of knowledge use the subdivision "Societies, etc.," under the heading for the field.

LEARNING AND KNOWLEDGE
   see KNOWLEDGE AND LEARNING

LECTURES *see* ADDRESSES, ESSAYS, LECTURES

LEGAL STATUS, LAWS, ETC. (*Direct*)
Use under classes of persons, types of occupational groups, or names of ethnic groups.
   sa Civil rights

LEGENDS
Use this subdivision in connection with stories coming down from the past popularly taken as historical though not verifiable. Use (a) as a form subdivision under names of historical persons or legendary figures, objects, etc., for the texts of European pre-1500 legends, e.g., **Alexius, Saint**—Legends; **Grail**—Legends (further subdivide the subdivision "Legends" by "History and criticism" for dis-

cussions about legends of this type, e.g., **Grail**—Legends —History and criticism); (b) as a form or topical subdivision under certain religious subjects, e.g., **Angels**—Legends; **Crosses**—Legends; **Martyrs**—Legends; or (c) as a form subdivision under names of Indian tribes. For texts of pre-1500 European romances use the subdivision "Romances." For the legends of particular ethnic groups (except Indians) assign as appropriate either the subject heading **Legends** or **Tales** qualified by the name of the group, e.g. **Legends, Jewish; Tales, Xosa.** For legends involving particular subjects (except those indicated above), assign the phrase heading **[subject] (in religion, folk-lore, etc.),** e.g., **Dolls (in religion, folk-lore, etc.).** However, for the texts of legends about particular kinds of animals use the subdivision "Legends and stories" under the appropriate heading for the animal.

> *x* Folktales
> Stories, Folk
> Tales, Folk

LEGENDS AND STORIES

Use as a form subdivision under names of animals for one or more legends or stories on those particular animals.

> *x* Stories

LEGISLATION *see* LAW AND LEGISLATION

LETTERS (CORRESPONDENCE)

> *see* CORRESPONDENCE, REMINISCENCES, ETC.

LIBRARIES

Use under names of cities. Also use under names of corporate bodies having library systems of more than one library for which no corporate heading exists, e.g., **Santa Catarina, Brazil. Universidade Federal**—Libraries.

> *x* Public libraries

LIBRARY

Use under the name of the owner or collector for works which discuss an individual privately owned book collection. Also use the heading "[name of owner]—Library" for a private library donated or sold to a public institution, if the library is still known by its original name; make a reference, however, from the name of the public institution with the official name of the library as subhead to the heading "[name of owner]—Library," e.g., Newberry Library, Chicago. Greenlee Collection *see* **Greenlee, William Brooks**—Library. If the donated library has no official name of its own, make a *see also* reference from the name of the public institution to the same type of heading for the library in question.

> *x* Book collections
> Collections, Book

LICENSES (*Direct*)

Use under types of professions, employees, occupational groups, etc., or under particular types of industries or businesses for discussions of the permission granted in accordance with law by competent authority to engage in business or perform work, e.g., **Flight engineers**—Licenses; **Milk trade**—Licenses.

> *x* Permits

LIFE HISTORIES *see* BIOGRAPHY

LIGHTING

Use under names of cities for the provision of lighting, including street lighting, in individual cities. Also use under types of vehicles, structures, buildings, rooms, installations, etc., e.g., **Ships**—Lighting; **Bridges**—Lighting; **Theaters**—Lighting; **Physical education facilities**—Lighting.

> *x* Illumination
> Street lighting

LISTS OF BOOKS *see* BIBLIOGRAPHY

LISTS OF EVENTS *see* CHRONOLOGY

LISTS OF OBJECTS *see* CATALOGS

LITERARY COLLECTIONS

Use as a form subdivision under topical or geographic headings, as well as under names of individual persons (except literary authors) or corporate bodies, for literary anthologies involving two or more literary forms, e.g., **Fishing**—Literary collections; **Canada**—Literary collections. For literary anthologies about individual literary authors assign the phrase heading **[name of author] in fiction, drama, poetry, etc.**

> *x* Anthologies, Literary

LITERARY REVIEWS *see* BOOK REVIEWS

LITERATURE, JUVENILE *see* JUVENILE LITERATURE

LITERATURES

Use as a form subdivision under names of regions or certain countries, where two or more languages are spoken but with one predominating, for collections of literary works in those several languages, e.g., **United States**—Literatures; **Russia**—Literatures. Do not use the subdivision under names of places for which phrase headings have been provided; in general, it has been LC policy to use phrase headings for countries or regions where no single language predominates, e.g., **African literature; Indic literature; Belgian literature; Swiss literature. America**—Literatures, by exception, is used for the collective literatures of the Western hemisphere by contrast with **American literature** which usage has equated with the English-language literature of the United States. Both the subdivision "Literatures" and the phrase headings are further subdivided by "History and criticism" for discussions of the literatures.

LOCAL HISTORY *see* HISTORY, LOCAL

LOCATION

Use under types of installations, businesses, structures, etc., e.g., **Atomic power plants**—Location; **Banks and banking**—Location; **Roads**—Location.

> *x* Spatial economics

MAGAZINES *see* PERIODICALS

MAINTENANCE AND REPAIR

Use under kinds of objects, including machinery, equipment, instruments, vehicles, structures, etc., which are maintained and repaired. For objects for which no maintenance aspect is involved use the subdivision "Repairing." For preserving and restoring particular art objects, museum specimens, historic buildings, etc., use the subdivision "Conservation and restoration."

sa Collection and preservation
x Engineering
Mending

MANAGEMENT

Use under types of industries or businesses, industrial plants or processes, special activities, names of disciplines, as well as under names of particular government agencies, for works which discuss the function of planning, organizing, directing and controlling an enterprise, activity, or affairs within a particular discipline, e.g., **Clothing trade —Management; Beauty shops**—Management; **Rolling-mills**—Management; **Strip mining**—Management; **Camps** —Management; **Festivals**—Management; **Engineering**—Management; **United States. Veterans Administration**—Management. For the management of particular institutions or types of institutions use the subdivision "Administration." Do not use the subdivision "Management" under subjects for which phrase headings have been provided, e.g., **Office management.**

sa Labor productivity
Location
Planning
Practice
Production control
Production standards
Quality control
Records and correspondence

MANNERS AND CUSTOMS *see* SOCIAL LIFE AND CUSTOMS

MANUALS *see* HANDBOOKS, MANUALS, ETC.

MANUFACTURES

Use under names of regions, countries, cities, etc., for discussions about articles manufactured in those places.

sa By-products
Commerce
Marketing
Materials
Patents
Reliability
Specifications
Technological innovations
x Products

MANUSCRIPTS

Use as a topical subdivision for works which discuss writings made by hand, including those made by typewriter, under (a) names of authors or sacred works; (b) names of particular religions; (c) particular classes of authors or types of literature, e.g., **Authors, Polish**—Manuscripts; **Christian literature, Early**—Manuscripts; or (d) topical headings, e.g., **Physics**—Manuscripts. Do not use as a form subdivision for individual works in manuscript form.

sa Archives
Autographs

MANUSCRIPTS—CATALOGS

Use as a form subdivision for lists of works in manuscript form.

MANUSCRIPTS—INDEXES

Use as a form subdivision under the same kinds of headings appropriate for the subdivision "Manuscripts"

for indexes to the particular group of manuscripts under discussion.

MAPS

Use as a form subdivision under names of regions, countries, cities, etc., or under topical headings, including particular languages, wars, or disciplines, for individual maps or for collections of maps (including geographic atlases), e.g., **Russia**—Maps; **Catalan language**—Maps; **European War, 1914–1918—Maps; Market surveys**—Maps; **United States—History—1865–1898**—Maps; **Postal service**—United States—Maps.

sa Aerial photographs
Historical geography—Maps
Photo maps
Relief models
Road maps
Zoning maps
x Geographic atlases

MAPS—BIBLIOGRAPHY

Use as a form subdivision for lists of maps.

MAPS, OUTLINE AND BASE

Use as a form subdivision under names of regions, countries, etc.

x Base maps
Outline maps

MAPS, PHYSICAL

Use under names of regions, countries, etc.

x Physical maps

MAPS, PICTORIAL

Use as a form subdivision under names of regions, countries, cities, etc.

x Pictorial maps

MAPS, TOPOGRAPHIC

Use under names of regions, countries, etc.

x Topographic maps

MARKETING

Use under types of commodities or products for works which discuss the process of moving goods from the producer through the trade channels to the consumer, e.g., **Hardware**—Marketing; **Graphic arts**—Marketing; **Farm produce**—Marketing. Do not use the subdivision "Marketing" under commodities or products for which the corresponding heading for the industry has been provided, e.g., **Automobile industry and trade,** not **Automobiles**—Marketing. Exception: In the case of farm produce use the subdivision "Marketing" for works which discuss the marketing of those products from the point of view of the farmer; for works which discuss the marketing of those same products from the point of view of the commodity dealer use the appropriate heading for the industry. Examples: "**Farm produce**—Marketing" and **"Produce trade"** are both valid headings, as are "**Cotton**—Marketing" and **"Cotton trade."**

x Stores, shopping centers, etc.

MARKETS

Use under names of cities.

MASS CULTURE *see* POPULAR CULTURE

MASSACRE, [date]
Use under names of regions, countries, cities, etc., for specific massacres. Do not use under names of places in cases where names of specific massacres have been established as phrase headings, e.g., **Katyn Forest Massacre, 1940; St. Bartholomew's Day, Massacre of, 1572.**

MATERIALS
Use under names of scientific or technical disciplines for discussions on the basic substances (e.g., particular alloys, chemicals, etc.) used in the construction of the devices, apparatus or structures normally associated with the discipline, e.g., **Electronics**—Materials; **Nuclear engineering**—Materials. Also use the subdivision under particular types of equipment or constructions for discussions about the materials out of which they are made, e.g., **Space vehicles**—Materials; **Boots and shoes**—Materials. Do not use the subdivision under subjects for which phrase headings have been provided, e.g., **Molding materials.**
   x   Engineering

MATHEMATICAL MODELS
Use under topical headings for works which represent the operation of a specific process or system in mathematical terms. The sum total of the mathematical expressions may represent the process or system exactly or only approximately. Examples: **Air**—Pollution—Mathematical models; **Asia**—Economic conditions—Mathematical models; **Kidneys**—Mathematical models.
   sa   Computer programs

MATHEMATICS
Use under topical subjects for the mathematics employed in those fields, e.g., **Astronomy**—Mathematics; **Carpentry**—Mathematics. Do not use the subdivision under subjects for which phrase headings have been provided, e.g., **Business mathematics.**
   sa   Mathematical models

MAXIMS *see* QUOTATIONS; QUOTATIONS, MAXIMS, ETC.

MEASUREMENT
Use under scientific or technical subjects for the technique of making measurements, e.g., **Glaciers**—Measurement; **Magnetic fields**—Measurement; **Mechanical wear**—Measurement; **Soil moisture**—Measurement. Do not use under subjects for which special headings have been provided, e.g., **Colorimetry; Length measurement.**
   sa   Observers' manuals
          Weight
          Weights and measures

MECHANICAL TESTING *see* TESTING

MEDALS
Use under topical headings, as well as under names of individual persons, for discussions about a medal or medals issued to commemorate an action, event, person, or group of persons, e.g., **Sports**—Medals; **Cook, James, 1728–1779**—Medals; **Popes**—Medals.

MEDICAL CARE (*Direct*)
Use under classes of persons, particular occupational groups, or ethnic groups for professional medical care received, e.g., **Aged**—Medical care; **Merchant seamen**—Medical care; **Negroes**—Medical care.

   sa   Care and hygiene
          Dental care
          Diseases and hygiene
          Hospitals
          Rehabilitation
   x   Health care

MEDICAL EXAMINATIONS
Use under classes of persons, types of employees or insurance, or particular military services, e.g., **Athletes**—Medicial examinations; **Air pilots**—Medical examinations; **Insurance, Life**—Medical examinations; **United States. Army**—Medical examinations.
   x   Examinations, Medical
          Physical examinations

MEDICAL STATISTICS *see* STATISTICS, MEDICAL

MEDITATIONS
Use as a form subdivision under religious headings (including names of persons) for works containing descriptions of thoughts or reflections on the spiritual significance of these topics, e.g., **Future life**—Meditations; **Lord's prayer**—Meditations; **Christmas**—Meditations; **Mary, Virgin**—Meditations.
   sa   Prayer-books and devotions

MEETINGS *see* CONGRESSES

MEMBERSHIP
Use under names of religions or denominations, international agencies, political parties, or types of organizations for works which discuss conditions of membership in those bodies, e.g., **United Nations**—Membership.

MENDING *see* MAINTENANCE AND REPAIR; REPAIRING

METHODOLOGY
Use under names of disciplines for the principles of procedure as they pertain to the field in question, as well as a listing of the directions to be followed in order to proceed, e.g., **Ethnology**—Methodology. For works presenting methods alone, without theory, use the subdivision "Technique."
   sa   Bibliography—Theory, methods, etc.
          Comparative method
          Research

MILITARY AIR DEFENSES *see* AIR DEFENSES, MILITARY

MILITARY ASPECTS
Use under types of industries.
   sa   Defense measures

MILITARY DEFENSES *see* DEFENSES

MILITARY FORCES *see* ARMED FORCES

MILITARY HISTORY *see* HISTORY, MILITARY

MILITARY INSTALLATIONS
see FORTIFICATIONS, MILITARY INSTALLATIONS, ETC.

MILITARY POLICY
Use under names of countries.

MILITARY RELATIONS *see* RELATIONS (MILITARY) WITH . . .

MILITIA
Use under name of regions, countries, states, etc.
   sa   Naval militia

MISCELLANEA

Use as a form subdivision under topical headings, names of places, or literary authors (a) for works consisting of compilations of curious or miscellaneous facts about the topic in question without continuous text; or (b) for certain monographic works which because of their special nature should not be entered under general works (i.e., the unsubdivided subject heading), and yet there is no other appropriate subdivision under which to enter them. Include in this latter group works in which the text is written in question and answer form. LC previously assigned headings of the type "**Questions and answers**—[topic]" to works in question and answer form. However, beginning in September 1973, the use of topical subdivisions under the heading **Questions and answers** was dropped and the subdivision "Miscellanea" used in its place. The subdivisions "Curiosa" and "Curiosa and miscellany" were dropped earlier in favor of "Miscellanea." Examples: **Medicine**—Miscellanea; **Bible**—Miscellanea; **Ferrara**—Miscellanea; **India**—History—Miscellanea; **Shakespeare, William, 1564–1616**—Miscellanea. For works which consist of single papers with continuous text and which present a noncomprehensive treatment of the topic use the subdivision "Addresses, essays, lectures."

   sa Anecdotes
   x Answers to questions
       Curiosa and miscellany
       Questions and answers
       Wonders

MODELING METHODS *see* SIMULATION METHODS

MODELS

Use under types of objects, e.g., **Furniture**—Models; **Towers**—Models; **Magnetic amplifiers**—Models. Do not use under subjects for which phrase headings have been provided, e.g., **Ship models.**

   sa Electromechanical analogies
       Facsimiles
       Mathematical models
       Relief models
       Simulation methods
       Standards

MOISTURE

Use under types of farm produce, inanimate objects, or technical equipment for discussions on the moisture contained therein, e.g., **Grain**—Moisture; **Rocks**—Moisture; **Electric insulators and insulation**—Moisture.

   x Dampness

MONASTERIES

Use under names of cities.
   sa Convents
   x Abbeys

MONUMENTS

Use under names of cities or classes of persons for discussions about the monuments located in a particular city or those made to commemorate a particular category of persons, e.g., popes, presidents, etc. For monuments erected in honor of particular persons use the subdivision "Monuments, etc." under the name of the person.

   sa Sepulchral monuments
       Statues

MONUMENTS, ETC.

Use under names of individual persons or families.

MORAL AND RELIGIOUS ASPECTS

Use under topical headings, e.g., **Automobiles**—Moral and religious aspects; **Boxing**—Moral and religious aspects. For the morality of peoples of particular places use the subdivision "Moral conditions" under the name of the place. For the significance of particular objects or concepts in religious beliefs or practices assign headings of the type **[topic] (in religion, folk-lore, etc.)**, e.g., **Fire (in religion, folk-lore, etc.).**

   sa Biblical teaching
       Conduct of life
   x Ethical aspects
       Religious aspects

MORAL CONDITIONS

Use under names of regions, countries, cities, etc.

MORGUES

Use under names of cities.

MORTALITY

Use as a form or topical subdivision under names of diseases or classes of persons for works which list or discuss the number of deaths during a given time due to a particular disease or occurring in a particular group.

   sa Registers of dead
   x Death rate

MOSQUES

Use under names of cities.

MOTELS *see* HOTELS, MOTELS, ETC.

MOTIVES, THEMES *see* THEMES, MOTIVES

MOUNTAIN PASSES *see* PASSES

MOVING-PICTURE CATALOGS *see* FILM CATALOGS

MUNICIPAL BUILDINGS *see* PUBLIC BUILDINGS

MUNICIPAL CENTERS *see* PUBLIC BUILDINGS

MUSEUMS

Use (a) under topical headings, as well as under names of individual wars, for works discussing collectively the museums devoted to special fields of interest, e.g., **Photography**—Museums; **Stalingrad, Battle of, 1942–1943**—Museums; or (b) under names of cities for works discussing collectively the museums located in those places. For museums devoted to particular persons use the subdivision "Museums, relics, etc." under the name of the person.

   sa Art collections
       Catalogs and collections
       Coin collections
       Ethnological collections
       Photograph collections
       Private collections
   x Galleries

MUSEUMS, RELICS, ETC.

Use under names of particular persons or families.
   x Relics

MUSIC AND SONGS *see* SONGS AND MUSIC

MUSIC HALLS *see* AUDITORIUMS, CONVENTION FACILITIES, ETC.; THEATERS

MUSICAL SETTINGS
Use as a form subdivision under names of authors for musical scores in which the texts or a text of the author in question has been set to music. For works which discuss the settings, further subdivide the subdivision by the subdivision "History and criticism," e.g., **Shakespeare, William, 1564–1616**—Musical settings—History and criticism.
   x Settings, Musical

NAME
Use under individual proper names, including names of persons, deities, places, corporate bodies, or ethnic groups, for discussions of the name's origin, history, validity, etc.

NAMES
Use under types of objects (e.g., vehicles, stars, real estate), animals (e.g., pets, horses), events (e.g., wars), or organizations (e.g., schools, sects) for rules, customs, etc., in the naming of the individual item in question. Also use the subdivision under names of Indian tribes for the names belonging to the tribe in question. In the case of other ethnic groups assign the subject heading **Names** qualified by the name of the group, or the name of the language spoken by the group, e.g., **Names, Jewish; Names, Semitic.** Also use the subdivision "Names" under names of sacred works for discussions of the names found in those works, e.g., **Bible**—Names. For lists of names use the subdivision "Registers." For works on the origin of names of a particular language assign the subdivision "Etymology—Names" under the name of the language, with a second subject entry denoting the special category of names under consideration and the locality in which they occur, e.g., 1. **English language**—Etymology—Names. 2. **Names, Geographical**—England.
   sa Directories
          Gazetteers
          Genealogy
          Nomenclature
          Trade-marks

NARRATIVES, PERSONAL *see* PERSONAL NARRATIVES

NATIONAL BIBLIOGRAPHY *see* IMPRINTS

NATIVE RACES
Use under names of regions or countries settled in modern times for works dealing with the political relations between the present government of the area in question and all of its aboriginal inhabitants discussed collectively, e.g., **Australia**—Native races. (Exception: Under names of Indian tribes use the subdivision "Government relations.")

NAVAL HISTORY *see* HISTORY, NAVAL

NAVAL MILITIA
Use under names of regions, countries, states, etc.

NAVIGATION
Use under names of oceans, lakes, rivers, etc.
   sa Canals
          Harbor

NEUTRALITY
Use under names of countries or neutralized areas.

NEW WORDS *see* LANGUAGE (NEW WORDS, SLANG, ETC.)

NIGHTCLUBS, DANCE HALLS, ETC.
Use under names of cities.
   sa Bars, saloons, etc.
          Discotheques
          Theaters
   x Cabarets
          Clubs, Night
          Dance halls
          Halls, Dance

NOBILITY
Use under names of countries.
   sa Gentry
          Heraldry

NOISE
Use under types of vehicles, machinery, or equipment for discussions of the noise generated (and its control, if appropriate). For works on the abatement of noise occurring in particular institutions or industries use the subdivision "Noise control." Do not use the subdivision "Noise" under subjects for which phrase headings have been provided, e.g., **Traffic noise.**

NOISE CONTROL
Use under particular types of institutions or industries for the abatement of noise in these establishments, e.g., **Hospitals**—Noise control; **Mineral industries**—Noise control.
   x Control, Noise

NOMENCLATORS *see* NOMENCLATURE

NOMENCLATURE
Use as a form or topical subdivision under names of scientific or technical disciplines, or particular types of substances, plants, or animals for systematically derived lists of names or designations which have been formally adopted or sanctioned by usage; or for discussions of the prinicples involved in the creation and application of such names.
   sa Classification
   x Nomenclators

NOTATION
Use as a form subdivision under scientific or technical headings for works containing the symbols, formulae, or signs used in the practice or exposition of a subject.
   sa Abbreviations
   x Symbols (Science and technology)

NOVELS *see* FICTION

NUMBERS, CODE *see* CODE NUMBERS

NUNNERIES *see* CONVENTS

OBSERVATIONS
Use as a form or topical subdivision under scientific headings for works consisting of numerical data obtained by the observation of natural phenomena or for discussions on the processing and use of these data. For manuals

on how to make observations use the subdivision "Observers' manuals."

sa Observers' manuals

OBSERVERS' MANUALS

Use as a form subdivision under scientific headings for instruction books on making observations of natural phenomena.

OCCUPATIONAL DISEASES *see* DISEASES AND HYGIENE

OCCUPATIONS

Use under names of regions, countries, or cities for works discussing or describing the jobs or career possibilities occurring in particular places.

sa Employment
Job descriptions
Vocational guidance
x Jobs

OFFICE BUILDINGS

Use under names of cities.

OFFICE RECORDS *see* RECORDS AND CORRESPONDENCE

OFFICIALS AND EMPLOYEES

Use under names of countries, cities, etc., under names of individual government or international agencies, or under kinds of government-administered institutions for the public employees of those jurisdictions, agencies, or institutions, e.g., **United States**—Officials and employees; **United States. Dept. of Defense**—Officials and employees; **United Nations**—Officials and employees; **Prisons**—Officials and employees. The term "public employees" refers here to all employees of a government, including civil service employees, appointees, elected officials, temporary help, etc. For works dealing solely with the civil service employees of a particular place assign the heading **Civil service** subdivided by the name of the place. For works on the employees of private industries, services, firms, or institutions use the subdivision "Employees." For further subdivision of the subdivision "Officials and employees" see the examples listed under **"United States**—Officials and employees" in the main list of subject headings. A few of the possible subdivisions are provided below.

sa Governors
Kings and rulers
Presidents
x Government employees
Public employees

OFFICIALS AND EMPLOYEES—
APPOINTMENT, QUALIFICATIONS, TENURE, ETC.

Use under names of countries, cities, etc., for works discussing the conditions of appointment to office in the case of public employees of particular jurisdictions. For the appointment to office of particular categories of public employees use the subdivision "Appointment, qualifications, tenure, etc." under the particular category. For the appointment to office of employees in individual government agencies use the subdivision "Appointments, promotions, salaries, etc." under the name of the agency.

sa Salaries, allowances, etc.

OFFICIALS AND EMPLOYEES—PENSIONS

Use under names of countries, cities, etc., or under names of individual government agencies (except military services). For the pensions of particular categories of public employees use the subdivision "Salaries, pensions, etc." (or the subdivision "Pensions" in the case of headings involving the phrase "officials and employees," e.g., **Municipal officials and employees**—Pensions).

sa Pensions

OFFICIALS AND EMPLOYEES—
SALARIES, ALLOWANCES, ETC.

Use under names of countries, cities, etc., or under names of individual government agencies (except military organizations).

OPERATION, COLD WEATHER
see COLD WEATHER OPERATION

OPERATING COSTS *see* COST OF OPERATION

OPINION, FOREIGN *see* FOREIGN OPINION

OPINION, PUBLIC *see* PUBLIC OPINION

ORIGIN

Use under names of ethnic groups, races, religions, or certain topics such as life, man, etc.

OUTLINE DRAWINGS *see* CHARTS, DIAGRAMS, ETC.

OUTLINE MAPS *see* MAPS, OUTLINE AND BASE

OUTLINES, SYLLABI, ETC.

Use as a form subdivision under topical headings for brief statements of the principal elements of a subject to be studied, usually arranged by headings and subheadings.

x Syllabi

OUTPUT STANDARDS *see* PRODUCTION STANDARDS

OWNERSHIP, GOVERNMENT *see* GOVERNMENT OWNERSHIP

PACKAGING

Use under types of products or merchandise for the techniques of wrapping, sealing and labeling such items for marketing.

sa Labeling

PACKING

Use under types of products or commodities for the techniques of preparing these items for safe storage or shipment.

PALACES

Use under names of cities.

sa Castles
Court and courtiers

PAPAL DOCUMENTS

Use as a form subdivision under topical headings for individual or collections of papal documents or other papal pronouncements since 1500 on particular topics, e.g., **Family**—Papal documents. For documents issued before 1500 assign the subject heading **Bulls, Papal** without topical subdivision; assign additional subject headings to designate bulls on special topics.

x Documents, Papal

PAPERS *see* ADDRESSES, ESSAYS, LECTURES

PARKS

Use under names of cities. For individual parks located in particular cities further subdivide the subdivision "Parks" by the name of the park, e.g., **New York (City)—Parks—Central Park**. For individual parks not located in cities assign as the heading the name of the park directly, e.g., **Patapsco State Park, Md.**

sa Plazas

PARODIES, TRAVESTIES, ETC.

Use as a form subdivision under names of literary authors or under titles of anonymous classics for works which imitate closely for comic effect the language and style of the author in question or which represent debased and distorted imitations of individual works. For imitations of individual works, when said works are not anonymous, make a second subject entry under the name of the work (i.e., an author-title entry) without subdivision.

x Travesties

PASSES

Use under (a) names of mountains for descriptions of the mountain passes of particular mountainous regions, e.g., **Alps—Passes**; or (b) under types of transportation systems for discussions of those tickets which allow free transportation, e.g., **Motor bus lines—Passes**.

x Mountain passes

PATENTS

Use as a form or topical subdivision under kinds of products, processes, or names of disciplines, e.g., **Saws—Patents**.

sa Trade-marks

PENAL INSTITUTIONS *see* CORRECTIONAL INSTITUTIONS

PENITENTIARIES *see* CORRECTIONAL INSTITUTIONS

PENSIONS

Use under classes of nonprofessional employees, workers, tradesmen, etc.; also under certain classes of persons. Examples: **Fishermen—Pensions**; **Blind—Pensions**. For pensions of professional employees or categories of public employees use the subdivision "Salaries, pensions, etc." (Exception: For those headings involving the phrase "officials and employees" use the subdivision "Pensions," e.g., **Municipal officials and employees—Pensions**.) For pensions of other public employees use the subdivision "Officials and employees—Pensions" under the name of the pertinent agency or jurisdiction, or assign the heading **Civil service pensions** subdivided by the name of the jurisdiction.

PERIODICALS

Use as a form subdivision under topical or geographic headings for serials issued indefinitely at regular intervals, generally more frequently than annually, each issue of which normally contains separate articles or other writings.

sa Societies, periodicals, etc.

Yearbooks

PERIODICALS—BIBLIOGRAPHY

Use as a form subdivision under topical headings for lists of serials or periodicals on a particular topic.

PERIODICALS—BIBLIGRAPHY—CATALOGS

Use as a form subdivision under topical headings for lists of serials or periodicals which are held by one organization or library, assembled as a private collection, or issued by an individual publisher.

PERIODICALS—BIBLIOGRAPHY—UNION LISTS

Use as a form subdivision under subjects for the records of the holdings of two or more libraries of periodicals or serials on those subjects, e.g., **Science—Periodicals—Bibliography—Union lists**.

PERIODICALS—INDEXES

Use as a form subdivision under topical headings for indexes to serials or periodicals on a particular topic, including indexes to single serials or periodicals. When the subdivision is used for single serials or periodicals, use also the subdivision "Indexes" under the author-title entry (or the uniform title for works entered under title) of the work being indexed (see instructions under the subdivision "Indexes").

PERIODICALS, SOCIETIES, ETC.

see SOCIETIES, PERIODICALS, ETC.

PERMITS *see* LICENSES

PERSONAL NARRATIVES

Use as a form subdivision under classes of persons, types of activities, names of diseases, or wars for autobiographical accounts of nonprofessional experiences in connection with these particular pursuits, misfortunes, or events, e.g., **Conscientious objectors—Personal narratives**; **Church work with youth—Personal narratives**; **Rheumatism—Personal narratives**; **Armenian massacres, 1915–1923—Personal narratives**. For an individual's autobiographical account of participation in his profession use the subdivision "Correspondence, reminiscences, etc." under classes of professional persons.

x Narratives, Personal

PERSONNEL *see* EMPLOYEES

PERSONNEL MANAGEMENT

Use under types of organizations or establishments, or under names of individual government agencies, including the military services.

sa Discipline

Recruiting

PEST CONTROL *see* CONTROL

PESTS AND DISEASES *see* DISEASES AND PESTS

PHILOSOPHY

Use under (a) names of literary authors for the personal philosophy of those authors; or (b) special fields of knowledge for the basic theory of those fields. For the general philosophy of individual philosophers assign as the subject heading the name of the philosopher without subdivision. For the philosophy of particular ethnic or religious groups, or particular countries, assign the heading **Philosophy** with the appropriate adjectival qualifier, e.g., **Philosophy, Hindu** (except in the case of American Indian groups for which the subdivision "Philosophy" is used, e.g., **Hopi Indians—Philosophy**).

sa Knowledge and learning

Methodology

x Theory

PHONORECORD CATALOGS
  see DISCOGRAPHY; PHONOTAPE CATALOGS

PHONORECORDS, JUVENILE see JUVENILE PHONORECORDS

PHONORECORDS FOR [NAME OF LANGUAGE] SPEAKERS
  Use as a form subdivision under names of languages
for language instruction phonorecords to be used by native
speakers of particular languages, e.g., **Spanish language**—
Phonorecords for English speakers.

PHONOTAPE CATALOGS
  Use as a form subdivision under topical headings, or
under names of authors, composers, or performers, for
lists or catalogs of sound recordings on phonotapes.
  x   Phonorecord catalogs

PHOTO MAPS
  Use as a form subdivision under names of regions,
countries, cities, etc., for aerial photographs of a particular
place upon which grids and other data pertinent to maps
have been added.

PHOTOGRAPH COLLECTIONS
  Use under the name of the original owner of a private
photograph collection, the owner being an individual person, a family, or a corporate body. Also use the heading
"[name of original owner]—Photograph collections" for
a private collection donated or sold to a public institution
if the collection is still known by its original name. Also
use the subdivision "Photograph collections" under names
of individual public institutions for works discussing
unnamed photograph collections owned by them.
  x   Collections, Photograph

PHOTOGRAPHS, AERIAL see AERIAL PHOTOGRAPHS

PHOTOGRAPHS FROM SPACE
  Use as a form subdivision under topical headings for
collections of photographs taken from outer space, e.g.,
Clouds—Photographs from space; **Moon**—Photographs
from space.
  sa Aerial photographs
  x   Space photographs

PHRASES AND TERMS see TERMS AND PHRASES

PHYSICAL EXAMINATIONS see MEDICAL EXAMINATIONS

PHYSICAL MAPS see MAPS, PHYSICAL

PHYSIOLOGICAL ASPECTS
  Use under topical headings for works which discuss the
interrelationships between an individual's activity, pursuit,
mental state, etc., and his physiology, e.g., **Automobile
driving**—Physiological aspects; **Music**—Physiological aspects; **Depression, Mental**—Physiological aspects.

PHYSIOLOGICAL EFFECT
  Use under names of chemicals, drugs, poisons, etc., or
under particular phenomena or environmental conditions,
for discussions on the effect that these items have on the
functions and activities of living matter, e.g., **Adrenalin**—
Physiological effect; **Beta rays**—Physiological effect; **Cold**
—Physiological effect; **Pollution**—Physiological effect.
  sa Toxicology

PICTORIAL HUMOR see CARICATURES AND CARTOONS

PICTORIAL MAPS see MAPS, PICTORIAL

PICTORIAL WORKS
  Use as a form subdivision under topical headings for
works which consist exclusively or predominantly of pictures accompanied either with captions or with scarcely
any text. For works which do contain some text in addition
to accompanying illustrations do not use this subdivision.
For pictorial works consisting of views of particular regions or jurisdictions larger than cities use the subdivision
"Description and travel—Views." For pictorial works consisting of views of particular cities use the subdivision
"Description—Views." For reproductions of works of art
embracing particular themes assign the phrase heading
[subject] in art, e.g., **Hand in art;** these themes may also
represent particular places, e.g., **Russia in art.** Also use the
subdivision "Pictorial works" under classes of persons, unless the pictures in question place stress on the visual
identity of individuals in which case the subdivision
"Portraits" is used. Do not use the subdivision "Pictorial
works" under names of persons; for pictorial works about
an individual person use one of the following subdivisions:
Art; Iconography; Portraits, caricatures, etc.; Portraits, etc.
  sa Aerial photographs
      Atlases
      Caricatures and cartoons
      Drawings
      Illustrations
      Photographs from space
      Posters
  x   Pictures

PICTURES see PICTORIAL WORKS

PIERS see DOCKS, WHARVES, ETC.

PIPE LINES
  Use under names of substances or materials transported
by means of pipe lines, or under types of machinery or
industrial plants which employ piping in their construction,
e.g., **Coal**—Pipe lines; **Refrigeration and refrigerating
machinery**—Pipe lines; **Chemical plants**—Pipe lines.

PLANNING
  Use under kinds of services, facilities, institutions,
etc., e.g., **Heliports**—Planning; **Winter sports facilities**—
Planning; **Municipal junior colleges**—Planning. Do not
use under subjects for which phrase headings have been
provided, e.g., **Library planning.**
  sa Commercial policy
      Economic policy
      Forest policy
      Social policy

PLACE NAME DICTIONARIES see GAZETTEERS

PLANS, ARCHITECTURAL see DESIGNS AND PLANS

PLANT DISEASES see DISEASES AND PESTS

PLAYGROUNDS
  Use under names of cities.

PLAYING FIELDS see SPORTS FACILITIES

PLAZAS
  Use under names of cities. For individual plazas located

in particular cities further subdivide the subdivision "Plazas" by the name of the plaza, e.g., **New York (City)—Plazas—Washington Square.**

sa Parks
x City squares
Squares, City

POETRY

Use as a form subdivision under subjects for collections of poems, collections of poems by one author, or individual poems on any identifiable topic. Exception: In the case of poems about individual literary authors, instead of using the subdivision "Poetry" under the name of the author, assign the phrase heading **[author's name] in fiction, drama, poetry, etc.** For discussions about particular themes in poetry assign the phrase heading **[subject] in literature,** except in the case of discussions about particular individuals (all classes of persons) as themes in poetry, in which case the phrase heading **[name of person] in fiction, drama, poetry, etc.** is assigned.

sa Juvenile poetry

POISONOUS PROPERTIES *see* TOXICOLOGY

POLICE

Use under names of cities.

POLITICAL ACTIVITY

Use under classes·of persons or occupational groups, kinds of organizations or particular organizations, particular armed forces or military agencies, e.g., **Young adults—Political activity; High school teachers—Political activity; Trade-unions—Political activity; Mexico—Armed Forces —Political activity; Nigeria. Army—Political activity.**

POLITICAL ASPECTS

Use under topical subjects, e.g., **Dancing—Political aspects.**

POLITICAL BOUNDARIES *see* BOUNDARIES

POLITICAL DIVISIONS *see* ADMINISTRATIVE AND POLITICAL DIVISIONS

[POLITICS]

This subdivision, formerly used under names of geographic regions larger than countries, was dropped as a valid subdivision by LC in October 1972 and replaced by the subdivision "Politics and government."

POLITICS AND GOVERNMENT

Use under names of regions, countries, cities, etc., as well as under names of ethnic groups, for works on political or governmental matters relating to the jurisdictions or peoples in question. Exception: In the case of Indian tribes use the subdivision "Tribal government" under the name of the tribe or group of tribes. For the political activity of particular classes of persons (e.g., farmers, young adults) use the subdivision "Political activity."

sa Administration
Administrative and political divisions
Appropriations and expenditures
Civil rights
Constitutional history
Constitutional law

Executive departments
Exiles
Foreign relations
Governors
Legal status, laws, etc.
Law and legislation
Native races
Officials and employees
Police
Political aspects
Voting registers
x Government

POOR

Use under names of cities.
sa Almshouses
Charities

POORHOUSES *see* ALMSHOUSES

POPULAR CULTURE

Use under names of regions, countries, cities, etc., for discussions of the literature, art, music, etc., produced for the people, i.e., for mass consumption.
x Mass culture

POPULAR WORKS

Use as a form subdivision under names of disciplines, or under legal headings, for works written for the layman, e.g., **Oceanography—Popular works; Emigration and immigration law—Popular works.**

POPULATION

Use under names of regions, countries, cities, etc., for statistical studies of the characteristics of human populations of particular places, especially with reference to the size and density, growth, distribution, migration, and vital statistics, and the effect of all these on social and economic conditions.
sa Census
Foreign population
Statistics, Vital
x Demography
Inhabitants

PORTRAITS

Use as a form subdivision under classes of persons, names of ethnic groups, or wars, as well as under headings denoting local biography, for works consisting of reproductions of paintings, photographs, etc. (usually with faces emphasized) of individuals associated with these categories, groups, events, or places, e.g., **Children—Portraits; Maoris—Portraits; European War, 1914–1918—Portraits; Japan—Biography—Portraits.** For pictures of persons of a special class in which the class rather than the individuals of the class are emphasized, and which are not issued for their artistic value or biographical information, use the subdivision "Pictorial works" ("**Children—Pictorial works**" is a possible heading for a pictorial study of children in which the interest is sociological). For collections of paintings, drawings, etc., which have as a theme a particular class of persons, and for which the subdivision "Portraits" does not apply, assign the phrase heading **[class of persons] in art,** e.g., **Horsemen in art.** Also use the latter phrase heading for discussions about the representation of classes of persons in works of art. For collections of portraits of individual persons use the subdivision "Art," "Portraits, caricatures, etc.," or "Portraits, etc."

> sa Biography—Portraits
> Caricatures and cartoons

PORTRAITS, CARICATURES, ETC.

Use as a form subdivision under names of individual persons (or families) likely to be caricatured, including statesmen, politicians, rulers, etc., (but excluding persons who lived before 1400) for portraits or portraits and caricatures of those persons. For pictorial humor alone about those persons use the subdivision "Cartoons, satire, etc." For portraits of persons who lived before 1400 use the subdivision "Art."

PORTRAITS, ETC.

Use as a form subdivision under names of individuals (or families), except statesmen, etc., or persons who lived before 1400, for portraits or portraits and caricatures of those persons. For pictorial humor about those persons alone use the subdivision "Cartoons, satire, etc.," except in the case of individual literary authors when the subdivision "Portraits, etc." is also used. For portraits of individual statesmen, politicians, rulers, etc., use the subdivision "Portraits, caricatures, etc." For portraits of individual persons who lived before 1400, as well as of individual legendary figures or deities, use the subdivision "Art."

POSTERS

Use as a form subdivision under topical headings, including particularly names of historical events or individual historical periods. Do not use under subjects for which phrase headings have been established, e.g., **Theatrical posters.**

POSTS, MILITARY see FORTIFICATIONS,
  MILITARY INSTALLATIONS, ETC.

PRACTICE

Use under types of professions for the techniques of running a professional service, e.g., **Medicine**—Practice; **Interior decoration**—Practice. Do not use under subjects for which phrase headings have been provided, e.g., **Practice of law.**

> x Professional practice

PRAYER-BOOKS AND DEVOTIONS

Use as a form subdivision under (a) classes of persons or names of particular churches or denominations for individual books of prayers or devotions intended for use by those persons or bodies; (b) names of individual saints or divine persons for books of devotions which are to be directed to those persons whose help or prayers are requested; or (c) names of religious days, special events, or activities for books of prayers or devotions to be said on those occasions. Examples: **Catholic Church**—Prayer-books and devotions; **Husbands**—Prayer-books and devotions; **Holy Spirit**—Prayer-books and devotions; **Lent**—Prayer-books and devotions; **Camping**—Prayer-books and devotions. For any work in hand it may be necessary to use the subdivision under several categories of subjects in order to bring out all aspects. Further subdivide the subdivision by the language of the text, e.g., **Prisoners of war**—Prayer-books and devotions—French; or by the sub-

division "History and criticism" for discussions of the texts, e.g., **Lutheran Church**—Prayer-books and devotions—History and criticism. Do not use the subdivision "Prayer-books and devotions" under subjects for which phrase headings have been provided, e.g., **Jewish prayers.**

> sa Meditations
> x Devotions

PRESCHOOL EDUCATION see STUDY AND TEACHING
  (PRESCHOOL)

PRESERVATION

Use under kinds of perishable products, including particular foods, drugs, textiles, etc. For the preservation of particular art objects, museum specimens, library materials, historic structures, etc., use the subdivision "Conservation and restoration." For the maintenance and repair of objects requiring such service, including machinery, instruments, vehicles, structures, etc., use the subdivision "Maintenance and repair." For the preservation of natural history or archaeological specimens use the subdivision "Collection and preservation."

> sa Cooling
> Corrosion
> Deterioration
> Drying
> Protection
> Storage

PRESIDENTS

Use under names of countries, universities, etc. Exception: For presidents of the United States assign the heading **Presidents**—United States.

PREVENTION

Use under kinds of diseases, physical disabilities, or particular situations to be avoided, e.g., **Cancer**—Prevention; **Blindness**—Prevention; **Conception**—Prevention. Do not use the subdivision in connection with particular kinds of accidents; use instead the subdivision "Safety measures" or a special phrase heading concerned with safety (e.g., use **Railroads**—Safety measures, not **Railroads**—Accidents—Prevention; use **Traffic safety,** not **Traffic accidents**—Prevention).

> sa Control
> Dust control
> Fume control
> Fires and fire prevention
> Noise control

PRICES (*Direct*)

Use under kinds of merchandise, products, art objects, etc., for amounts demanded for them at the time of sale on the market. Use also under types of industries where one general subject heading for the products of that industry is lacking, e.g., **Construction industry**—Prices. For prices of professional services use the subdivision "Fees." For prices charged for products or services if adjusted to a specific standard or scale use the subdivision "Rates." For price catalogs use the subdivision "Catalogs."

> sa Costs
> Valuation

PRIMARY EDUCATION see STUDY AND TEACHING (PRIMARY)

PRINCES AND PRINCESSES
Use under names of countries.

PRISONS *see* CORRECTIONAL INSTITUTIONS

PRIVATE COLLECTIONS (*Direct*)
Use under kinds of objects collected for discussions of various privately owned collections, e.g., **Porcelain**—Private collections. For discussions of individual private collections use the subdivision "Art collections" or similar subdivisions under the name of the original owner.
   sa   Catalogs and collections
        Coin collections
        Ethnological collections
        Library
        Photograph collections
   x   Collections, Private

PRIVILEGES AND IMMUNITIES
Use under names of international organizations, particular legislative bodies or universities, as well as under types of organizations.
   sa   Charters, grants, privileges
        Diplomatic and consular services—Privileges and immunities
   x   Immunities

PRIZES (REWARDS) *see* AWARDS

PROBLEMS, EXERCISES, ETC.
Use as a form subdivision under topical headings for compilations of practice problems or exercises, often with answers, pertinent to the study of a particular subject.
   sa   Examinations, questions, etc.
   x   Exercises, problems, etc.

PROCEEDINGS OF CONGRESSES *see* CONGRESSES

PROCLAMATIONS
Use under names of countries.
   sa   Posters

PRODUCTION CONTROL
Use under types of industrial processes or plants for the procedures of planning, routing, scheduling, dispatching, and expediting the flow of materials, parts, and assemblies within the plant, e.g., **Oil well drilling**—Production control; **Steel-works**—Production control. Use the subdivision under types of industries when headings for the processes or plants are unavailable, e.g., **Coke industries**—Production control.
   x   Control, production

PRODUCTION STANDARDS
Use under types of industrial processes for the unit time value for the accomplishment of a work task as determined by work measurement techniques, e.g., **Electric welding**—Production standards. When headings for the processes are unavailable use the subdivision under types of industrial plants or, those failing, under types of industries.
   sa   Labor productivity
   x   Output standards
        Time standards

PRODUCTIVITY, LABOR *see* LABOR PRODUCTIVITY

PRODUCTS *see* MANUFACTURES

PRODUCTS, SECONDARY *see* BY-PRODUCTS

PROFESSIONAL PRACTICE *see* PRACTICE

PROGRAMMED INSTRUCTION
Use under topical headings (a) for discussions on prepared, presequenced instruction in which the individual learner is able to govern the sequence and pacing of the instruction process usually through the use of a teaching machine; or (b) as a form subdivision for programmed texts, i.e., sequenced self-correction instruction texts. Examples: **Physiology**—Programmed instruction; **Business education**—Programmed instruction.
   x   Automated teaching
        Programmed texts

PROGRAMMED TEXTS *see* PROGRAMMED INSTRUCTION

PROGRAMS, COMPUTER *see* COMPUTER PROGRAMS

PROPERTY, GOVERNMENT *see* GOVERNMENT PROPERTY

PROPERTY VALUATION *see* VALUATION

PROPHECIES
Use under individual sacred works, names of persons or deities, wars, or classes of persons.
   sa   History—Prophecies

PROTECTION
Use under kinds of equipment, structures, industries or plants, parts of the body, or classes of persons for discussions on preserving these items from physical damage or harm. Do not use under subjects for which phrase headings have been provided, e.g., **Birds, Protection of.**
   sa   Safety measures
        Security measures
        Storage

PROTECTIVE MEASURE AGAINST AIR RAIDS *see* AIR DEFENSES

PROVINCES
Use under names of countries whose major administrative divisions are called provinces (e.g., Canada) for discussion of the provinces collectively in relation to a special topic. Use the subdivision only when the name of the country is used as a subdivision under a topical heading, e.g., **Civil service**—Canada—Provinces.

PSYCHOLOGICAL ASPECTS
Use under topical headings for works which discuss the influence of particular situations, conditions, activities, environments, or objects on the mental condition or personality of the individual, e.g., **Air warfare**—Psychological aspects; **Cancer**—Psychological aspects; **Smoking**—Psychological aspects; **Atomic bomb shelters**—Psychological aspects; **Dolls**—Psychological aspects. Under classes of persons, names of ethnic groups, types of animals, or religious subjects use the subdivision "Psychology."

PSYCHOLOGY
Use under classes of persons, names of ethnic groups, or kinds of animals for discussions about their mental processes or characteristics. Also use the subdivision under religious subjects for the psychological aspects of those subjects, e.g., **Faith**—Psychology. For the influence of

particular situations, environments, activities, or objects on the mentality of the individual use the subdivision "Psychological aspects." Do not use the subdivision "Psychology" under classes of afflicted persons, if the heading for the affliction or disease is available (e.g., use **Deafness**—Psychological aspects, not **Deaf**—Psychology). Also use the subdivision "Psychology" under names of individual philosophers for their contributions in the field of psychology. Use the subdivision "Knowledge—Psychology" under names of literary authors for their incidental knowledge of the subject of psychology.

- *sa* Ability testing
- Behavior

PUBLIC BUILDINGS

Use under names of regions, countries, cities, etc., for works discussing collectively (a) the buildings used by the public which are located in those places, or (b) the government buildings owned by a particular jurisdiction (i.e., the jurisdictional name under which the subdivision is used refers to building ownership, not location). When a country or state is named in accordance with (b) above, if appropriate, further subdivide by place, normally a city name, to designate location. In those cases where the physical location of the buildings and the responsible jurisdiction are not identical, assign two headings to bring out both aspects. For example, a work discussing the federal government buildings of New York City would require: 1. **New York (City)**—Public buildings. 2. **United States**—Public buildings—New York (City). Do not assign headings to bring out the jurisdictional aspect for jurisdictions below the state or provincial level.

- *sa* Almshouses
- Armories
- Auditoriums, convention facilities, etc.
- Bars, saloons, etc.
- Churches
- Correctional institutions
- Hospitals
- Hotels, motels, etc.
- Libraries
- Morgues
- Museums
- Nightclubs, dance halls, etc.
- Office buildings
- Public comfort stations
- Restaurants
- Stores, shopping centers, etc.
- Theaters
- *x* Centers, Municipal
- Government buildings
- Municipal buildings
- Municipal centers

PUBLIC COMFORT STATIONS

Use under names of cities.

PUBLIC DOCUMENTS *see* GOVERNMENT PUBLICATIONS

PUBLIC EMPLOYEES *see* OFFICIALS AND EMPLOYEES

PUBLIC LANDS

Use under names of regions, countries, states, etc.

- *sa* Territories and possessions

- *x* Government lands
- Lands, Public

PUBLIC LAUNDRIES

Use under names of cities.

- *x* Laundries, Public

PUBLIC LIBRARIES *see* LIBRARIES

PUBLIC OPINION

Use under topical headings for discussions or results of surveys on the predominant attitudes of a community on a topic, e.g., **Express highways**—Public opinion. In order to bring out the location of the persons having the opinion make a second subject entry under a heading of the following type: **Public opinion**—[place]. Example: for Japanese opinion about American telephones assign: 1. **Telephone**—United States—Public opinion. 2. **Public opinion**—Japan. Use the subdivision "Public opinion" under names of individual wars unless it is necessary to limit the opinion held to that of nonparticipants, in which case the subdivision "Foreign public opinion" is used. For the public opinion held by one region or country about another use the subdivision "Foreign opinion."

- *x* Opinion, Public

PUBLIC OWNERSHIP *see* GOVERNMENT OWNERSHIP

PUBLIC PROPERTY *see* GOVERNMENT PROPERTY

PUBLIC RELATIONS

Use under names of corporate bodies for discussions on the policies and methods which promote their standing in the community.

- *sa* Public opinion
- *x* Relations, Public

PUBLIC SCHOOLS *see* SCHOOLS

PUBLIC WORKS

Use under names of regions, countries, cities, etc., for discussions of construction financed by public funds for public use in those places.

- *x* Engineering

PUBLICATIONS, GOVERNMENT *see* GOVERNMENT PUBLICATIONS

PUBLISHING

Use under types of literature, imprints, or names of corporate bodies, e.g., **Children's literature**—Publishing; **French imprints**—Publishing; **Methodist Church**—Publishing. For publishing of works on particular subjects assign the appropriate phrase heading, e.g., **Technical publishing.**

- *x* Book publishing

PURIFICATION

Use under types of things to be purified, e.g., **Chemicals**—Purification; **Sewage**—Purification.

- *sa* Cleaning

PURIFICATION OF AIR *see* AIR CONDITIONING

QUALIFICATIONS *see* APPOINTMENT, QUALIFICATIONS, TENURE, ETC.

QUALITY CONTROL

Use under types of processes or plants for discussions on the procedures to be used in establishing and maintaining acceptable limits of variation for products and services, e.g., **Forging**—Quality control; **Packing-houses**—Quality control. Use the subdivision under types of industries when headings for processes or plants are unavailable, e.g., **Food industry and trade**—Quality control. Do not use the subdivision under types of products.

    sa Defects
    x Control, Quality

QUAYS *see* DOCKS, WHARVES, ETC.

QUEENS

Use under names of countries.

QUESTIONS AND ANSWERS *see* MISCELLANEA

QUESTIONS, EXAMINATIONS, ETC.
    see EXAMINATIONS, QUESTIONS, ETC.

QUOTATIONS

Use as a form subdivision under names of persons or classes of persons for compilations of quotations taken from the writings of individuals or groups of individuals, e.g., **Chaucer, Geoffrey, d. 1400**—Quotations; **Presidents**—United States—Wives—Quotations. For compilations of quotations on particular subjects use the subdivision "Quotations, maxims, etc."

    x Maxims
       Sayings

QUOTATIONS, MAXIMS, ETC.

Use as a form subdivision under topical headings for compilations of quotations on particular subjects taken from the writings of one or more authors, e.g., **Joy**—Quotations, maxims, etc.

RACE QUESTION

Use under names of regions, countries, cities, etc., for discussions about race relations and their attendant problems in particular places.

RATES

Use as a form or topical subdivision under types of services, utilities, transportation systems, etc., for prices charged for services provided or items sold according to a specific ratio, scale or standard. Exception: for types of insurance, investments, or taxes use the subdivision "Rates and tables," e.g., **Sales tax**—Rates and tables.

READERS

Use as a form subdivision under names of individual languages (except English) for reading texts to be used in learning those languages, e.g., **German language**—Readers. Further subdivide the subdivision by topic or form when the reader in hand is limited to particular subject fields or literary forms, e.g., **German language**—Readers—Medicine; **German language**—Readers—Science fiction. For English language readers assign the subject heading **Readers.** For English readers on particular subjects subdivide the heading **Readers** by the subject, e.g., **Readers**—Agriculture.

    x Chrestomathies

READINGS *see* ADDRESSES, ESSAYS, LECTURES

RECORDS AND CORRESPONDENCE

Use under types of industries, businesses, or agencies, or under names of individual corporate bodies, including government agencies for works on preparing, using, filing, indexing, storing, etc., of office records and correspondence.

    sa Archives
       Forms
    x Correspondence (Office records)
       Office records

RECREATION

Use under classes of persons or names of ethnic groups.

RECREATION CENTERS *see* RECREATIONAL FACILITIES

RECREATIONAL ACTIVITIES

Use under names of cities.

    sa Amusements
       Recreation

RECREATIONAL FACILITIES

Use under names of cities.

    sa Parks
       Playgrounds
       Recreational use
       Sports facilities
    x Centers, Recreation
       Recreation centers

RECREATIONAL USE

Use under kinds of land or geographic features, including bodies of water, as well as under particular named land areas or bodies of water, e.g., **Farms**—Recreational use; **Reservoirs**—Recreational use; **Atchafalaya River**—Recreational use.

RECRUITING

Use under types of professional employees, e.g., **Art teachers**—Recruiting; **United States**—Officials and employees—Recruiting. For the recruitment of employees of particular government agencies (except military organizations) use the subdivision "Appointments, promotions, salaries, etc." under the name of the agency. For the recruitment of personnel for particular military organizations use the subdivision "Recruiting, enlistment, etc." under the name of the organization, e.g., **United States. Air Force**—Recruiting, enlistment, etc.

REFEREEING *see* JUDGING

REFORMATORIES *see* CORRECTIONAL INSTITUTIONS

REGISTERS

Use as a form subdivision under names of regions, countries, cities, etc., particular ethnic groups, corporate bodies, including government agencies, wars, or under classes of persons, for lists of names without addresses and other identifying data. Also use the subdivision under types of named objects for lists of their names, e.g., **Ocean liners**—Registers; **Reservoirs**—Registers.

    sa Alumni
       Directories
       Social registers
       Voting registers

REGISTERS OF DEAD
Use as a form subdivision under names of wars or military organizations.
   x   Dead, Registers of

REHABILITATION (*Direct*)
Use under classes of persons suffering from a particular handicap, disease, undesirable condition, etc., for discussions of professional services administered or required for purposes of restoring to normal health or activity, e.g., **Crippled children**—Rehabilitation; **Epileptics**—Rehabilitation; **Narcotic addicts**—Rehabilitation.

RELATIONS (GENERAL) WITH [NAME OF REGION OR JURISDICTION]
Use under names of regions, countries, or cities, etc., for general relations between one region or jurisdiction and another, e.g., **Hongkong**—Relations (general) with Europe; **Europe**—Relations (general) with Russia; **Latin America**—Relations (general) with the United States. For each relationship designated by means of this subdivision assign a second subject heading using the same subdivision with the two regions or jurisdictions in reversed positions, e.g., **Europe**—Relations (general) with Hongkong. Note: the subdivision should not be used to bring out relations between regions or jurisdictions in one country. For general relations of a region or jurisdiction with three or more regions or jurisdictions use the general subdivision "Relations (general) with foreign countries," e.g., **United States**—Relations (general) with foreign countries. For commercial relations use the subdivision "Commerce." For diplomatic relations use the subdivision "Foreign relations." For military relations use the subdivision "Relations (military) with . . . ." For cultural influences on the civilization of particular regions or countries use the subdivision "Foreign influences" or headings of the type **Great Britain**—Civilization—American influences.
   sa   Foreign economic relations
        International cooperation

RELATIONS (MILITARY) WITH [NAME OF REGION OR JURISDICTION]
Use under names of regions, countries, or cities, etc., for military relations between one region or jurisdiction and another. For each relationship indicated by means of this subdivision assign a second subject heading using the same subdivision with the two regions or jurisdictions in reversed positions. For the relations of a region or jurisdiction with three or more regions or jurisdictions use the general subdivision "Relations (military) with foreign countries."
   x   Military relations

RELATIONS, PUBLIC *see* PUBLIC RELATIONS

RELIABILITY
Use under types of equipment, machines, technical systems, or industrial plants.
   x   Engineering

RELICS *see* MUSEUMS, RELICS, ETC.

RELIEF MODELS
Use under names of regions, countries, cities, etc.

RELIGION
Use under names of regions or countries, ethnic groups, schools or other institutions, kinds of institutions, or under names of individual persons (except literary authors) for discussions of the various religions practiced in a particular place, or for the religion of particular peoples, institutions, individuals, etc. For works limited to the discussion of one religion in a particular place assign the appropriate heading for that religion, e.g., **Christianity**—France. For works discussing the religious customs of particular places use the subdivision "Religious life and customs." Under names of literary authors use the subdivision "Religion and ethics." Under names of Indian tribes use the subdivision "Religion and mythology."
   sa   Biblical teaching
        Church history
        Churches
        Cult
        Moral and religious aspects
        Sermons
        Shrines

RELIGION—SOCIETIES, ETC. *see* RELIGIOUS AND ECCLESIASTICAL INSTITUTIONS

RELIGION AND ETHICS
Use under names of individual literary authors for discussions of the role of religion and ethics in their lives and their influence on their works. Under names of prominent, nonliterary persons use the subdivision "Religion."
   x   Ethics and religion

RELIGIOUS AND ECCLESIASTICAL INSTITUTIONS
Use under names of regions, countries, cities, etc.

RELIGIOUS ASPECTS *see* MORAL AND RELIGIOUS ASPECTS

RELIGIOUS LIFE
Use under classes of persons for works descriptive of their general religious and devotional life, or for works seeking to foster such religious life, e.g., **Widows**—Religious life.
   sa   Conduct of life
        Meditations
        Prayer-books and devotions

RELIGIOUS LIFE AND CUSTOMS
Use under names of regions, countries, cities, etc., for descriptions of the religious practices and customs of those places.
   sa   Rites and ceremonies
   x   Customs, Religious

REMINISCENCES, CORRESPONDENCE, ETC.
   see CORRESPONDENCE, REMINISCENCES, ETC.

REPAIRING
Use only under types of objects which normally require no maintenance, e.g., **Glassware**—Repairing. For all other types of objects, including machines, instruments, structures, etc., use the subdivision "Maintenance and repair."
   sa   Conservation and restoration
   x   Mending

RESEARCH (*Direct*)
Use under topical headings for descriptions of proposed

research in particular subject fields, including such details as management, finance, personnel, special projects, methodology, goals, etc. Do not use the subdivision for works which discuss results of research. Do not use the subdivision under subjects for which phrase headings have been provided, e.g., **Feed research.** Although many phrase headings now exist in the list of subject headings, since July 1973 LC has established all new research headings using the subdivision "Research."

RESEARCH BUILDINGS *see* LABORATORIES

RESEARCH GRANTS (*Direct*)
Use under topical headings, e.g., **Environmental engineering**—Research grants. For those subjects for which phrase research headings have been provided, use the subdivision under the research headings, e.g., **Medical research**—Research grants.
   x   Grants, Research

RESIDENTIAL BUILDINGS *see* DWELLINGS

RESTAURANTS
Use under names of cities.
   sa Bars, saloons, etc.
       Nightclubs, dance halls, etc.
   x   Cafeterias
       Dining establishments

RESTORATION AND CONSERVATION
see CONSERVATION AND RESTORATION

RETAIL STORES *see* STORES, SHOPPING CENTERS, ETC.

RETIREMENT
Use under classes of persons, including particular classes of employees.

REVIEWS
Use as a form subdivision under types of artistic production or nonbook materials for descriptive and critical works, e.g., **Performing arts**—Reviews; **Phonotapes**—Reviews. For reviews of books in a topical area, use the subdivision "Book reviews" under the topic; for book reviews not limited to a specific topic the heading **"Books —Reviews"** is used.

REWARDS (PRIZES, ETC.) *see* AWARDS

RIGHTS, CIVIL *see* CIVIL RIGHTS

RIOT, [date]
Use under names of cities or schools.
   sa Demonstration

RIOTS, [date]
Use under names of cities or schools.

RITES AND CEREMONIES
Use under names of ethnic groups.
   x   Ceremonies

ROAD MAPS
Use under names of regions, countries, cities, etc.
   x   Street maps

ROMANCES
Use as a form subdivision under names of historical persons or legendary figures for tales in verse written in medieval times based chiefly on legends, chivalric love, and adventure, e.g., **Tristan**—Romances. Do not use under subjects for which phrase headings have been provided, e.g., **Arthurian romances.** Further subdivide the subdivision "Romances" by "History and criticism" for discussions about individual romances, e.g., **Tristan**—Romances History and criticism.

ROYAL HOUSEHOLD
Use under names of countries.
   sa Court and courtiers
       Palaces
   x   Household, Royal

RULERS *see* KINGS AND RULERS

RURAL CONDITIONS
Use under names of regions, countries, states, etc., for works which describe living conditions in the rural regions. For popular or literary works on living in the country assign the subject heading **Country life**—[place].
   x   Country conditions

SAFETY APPLIANCES
Use under types of machines, vehicles, industrial plants, occupations, etc.
   x   Appliances, Safety

SAFETY MEASURES
Use under types of objects, chemicals, materials, machines, installations, industries, or activities, or names of disciplines, for discussions of measures to be taken to prevent accidents or injury. Do not use under subjects for which phrase headings have been provided, e.g., **Traffic safety.**
   sa Accidents
       Accidents and injuries
       Safety appliances
       Safety regulations

SAFETY REGULATIONS
Use under the same headings under which the subdivision "Safety measures" is used, for safety rules or orders which have the force of law.

SALARIES, ALLOWANCES, ETC.
Use only under the subdivision "Officials and employees" or under headings involving the phrase "officials and employees," e.g., **United States**—Officials and employees —Salaries, allowances, etc.; **County officials and employees**—Salaries, allowances, etc. For all other classes of professional employees or public employees use the subdivision "Salaries, pensions, etc." For works dealing solely with pensions of public employees use the subdivision "Officials and employees—Pensions," the subdivision "Pensions," or the heading **Civil service pensions,** depending upon the particular category of public employees in question.
   sa Officials and employees—Salaries, allowances, etc.

SALARIES, PENSIONS, ETC.
Use under particular legislative bodies, classes of professional persons, or kinds of administrative or public employees for discussions of fixed compensations received by the employees or legislative members in question, e.g., **United States. Congress**—Salaries, pensions, etc.; **Artists**

—Sweden—Salaries, pensions, etc.; **Judges**—Salaries, pensions, etc.; **School employees**—Salaries, pensions, etc.; **Psychiatric hospitals**—Employees—Salaries, pensions, etc. For the salaries of the public employees in particular jurisdictions or government agencies use the subdivision "Officials and employees—Salaries, allowances, etc." For the wages of workers, tradesmen, etc., assign the heading **Wages** subdivided by the class of workmen in question. Do not use the subdivision "Salaries, pensions, etc." under kinds of military personnel.

> *sa* Fees
> Officials and employees—Pensions

SALOONS *see* BARS, SALOONS, ETC.

SANITARY AFFAIRS
Use under names of individual institutions, especially names of schools or universities, government agencies, military agencies, etc.

SANITATION
Use under types of buildings, industrial plants, public vehicles, recreational areas, etc., for works on the control of environmental conditions to promote good health, e.g., **Dairy plants**—Sanitation; **Railroads**—Sanitation; **Trailer camps**—Sanitation. If the appropriate heading designating the type of plant in question is lacking, use the corresponding heading for the industry and trade. Under names of individual corporate bodies use the subdivision "Sanitary affairs."

> *sa* Dust control
> Environmental aspects
> Fume control
> Heating and ventilation
> Lighting
> Noise
> Noise control
> Public comfort stations
> Public laundries
> Street-cleaning
> Sewerage
> Waste disposal
> Water-supply

SATIRE *see* ANECDOTES, FACETIAE, SATIRE, ETC.

SATIRICAL HISTORIES
see HISTORY, COMIC, SATIRICAL, ETC.

SAYINGS *see* QUOTATIONS; QUOTATIONS, MAXIMS, ETC.

SCHOLARSHIPS, FELLOWSHIPS, ETC. (*Direct*)
Use under (a) topical headings for works discussing scholarships, etc., offered in particular fields of study; or (b) names of ethnic groups or particular categories of students for works discussing educational assistance programs for particular ethnic groups or students. Examples: **Biology**—Scholarships, fellowships, etc.; **African studies**—Scholarships, fellowships, etc.; **Negroes**—Scholarships, fellowships, etc.; **College students, Negro**—Scholarships, fellowships, etc. For scholarships offered by particular schools use the subdivision "Funds and scholarships" under the name of the school.

> *sa* Research grants
> *x* Fellowships, scholarships, etc.

SCHOOLS
Use under names of cities.

> *x* Industrial schools
> Public schools
> Trade schools
> Vacation schools

SCIENTIFIC APPLICATIONS
Use under particular technical devices or processes which are used to further the advancement of science, e.g., **Artifical satellites**—Scientific applications; **Photography**—Scientific applications.

> *sa* Industrial applications
> *x* Applications, Scientific
> Use, Scientific

SCIENTIFIC BUREAUS
Use under names of countries, cities, etc., for discussions on government scientific agencies in those places.

> *x* Government scientific agencies

SEAL
Use under names of jurisdictions or other corporate bodies or under names of prominent individuals for discussions of the devices (such as emblems, symbols, or words) used for the signatures of these jurisdictions, organizations, or individuals to authenticate written matter purportedly issued by them.

SECONDARY EDUCATION *see* STUDY AND TEACHING (SECONDARY)

SECURITY MEASURES
Use under types of buildings, establishments, installations, industries, or names of corporate bodies, including particularly government agencies, for discussions of measures to be taken, including the use of security personnel, to prevent espionage, sabotage, observation, theft, etc.

> *sa* Defense measures
> Protection

SELECTION AND APPOINTMENT
Use under categories of teachers or other professionals who are not necessarily public employees, e.g., **College teachers**—Selection and appointment; **Psychiatrists**—Selection and appointment. For the appointment to office of public employees use the subdivision "Appointment, qualifications, tenure, etc."

SEPULCHRAL MONUMENTS
Use under names of cities.

> *sa* Cemeteries
> Tombs
> *x* Dead, Monuments to the
> Gravestones

SERMONS
Use as a form subdivision under (a) topical headings, particularly theological headings, or under names of individual saints or divine persons, for single sermons or collections of sermons on those topics or persons; or (b) names of individual religious bodies for sermons intended for use by those bodies. For any work in hand it may be necessary to use the subdivision under several categories of headings in order to bring out all aspects. For collections of sermons delivered on the occasion of special

religious events or ceremonies, assign the appropriate phrase heading, e.g., **Funeral sermons; Christmas sermons; Children's sermons.**

SETTINGS, MUSICAL *see* MUSICAL SETTINGS

SEWERAGE
　Use under names of cities for works discussing their sewage disposal systems.
　　x　Sewers

SEWERS *see* SEWERAGE

SHIPMENT *see* TRANSPORTATION

SHIPS, GOVERNMENT *see* GOVERNMENT VESSELS

SHOPPING CENTERS *see* STORES, SHOPPING CENTERS, ETC.

SHOPS *see* STORES, SHOPPING CENTERS, ETC.

SHORT STORIES *see* FICTION

SHRINES
　Use under names of cities.

SIEGE, [year]
　Use under names of cities, castles, forts, etc.

SIEGES, [years]
　Use under names of cities, castles, forts, etc.

SIGNATURES (WRITING) *see* AUTOGRAPHS

SIMULATION METHODS
　Use under topical headings for works which discuss comprehensively the development or use of several types of models for studying particular systems, processes, or concepts. For works which discuss the simulation of a particular system, process, or concept using only one model type (e.g., mathematical models, physical models, simulators, gaming models), assign only the heading appropriate for the model type, e.g., **Shipping**—Mathematical models; **Hydraulic models; Space simulators; Management games.**
　　sa　Electromechanical analogies
　　　　Mathematical models
　　　　Models
　　x　Modeling methods

SLANG
　Use under names of languages or special fields of knowledge for the slang occurring in those languages or disciplines, e.g., **English language**—Slang; **Medicine**—Slang. For the slang used by particular classes of persons, found in particular schools, or generated on the occasion of particular wars, use the subdivision "Language (New Words, slang, etc.)."

SLAUGHTER-HOUSES
　Use under names of cities.

SOCIAL ASPECTS (*Direct*)
　Use under topical headings for works which discuss the impact of the item, activity, principle, or discipline in question on modern society and vice versa, e.g., **Automobiles**—Social aspects; **Blood**—Transfusion—Social aspects; **Baptism**—Social aspects; **Journalism**—Social aspects. Do

not use under topics for which phrase headings have been provided, e.g., **War and society.**

SOCIAL CONDITIONS
　Use under names of regions, countries, cities, etc., or ethnic groups for discussions of the sociology of those places or groups, including particularly such subtopics of sociology as social problems, stability, change, interaction, adjustment, structure, institutions, etc.
　　sa　Almshouses
　　　　Charities
　　　　Emigration and immigration
　　　　Housing
　　　　Moral conditions
　　　　Poor
　　　　Race question
　　　　Riot
　　　　Riots
　　　　Rural conditions
　　　　Social policy
　　　　Sociological aspects
　　x　History, Social
　　　　Social history
　　　　Sociology

SOCIAL HISTORY *see* SOCIAL CONDITIONS

SOCIAL LIFE AND CUSTOMS
　Use under names of regions, countries, cities, etc., or ethnic groups for works discussing the folkways, manners, customs, ceremonies, popular traditions, etc., of those places or groups.
　　sa　Amusements
　　　　Costume
　　　　Court and courtiers
　　　　Fairs
　　　　Festivals, etc.
　　　　Intellectual life
　　　　Languages
　　　　Popular culture
　　　　Religious life and customs
　　　　Social aspects
　　　　Social conditions
　　x　Customs, Social
　　　　Manners and customs

SOCIAL POLICY
　Use under names of regions, countries, cities, etc., for works discussing governmental programs or plans.
　　sa　Correctional institutions

SOCIAL REGISTERS
　Use as a form subdivision under names of regions, countries, cities, etc., for lists of names of the socially prominent of those places.

SOCIETIES AND CLUBS
　Use as a topical subdivision under particular age or sex groups for works on associations devoted to these groups. Such works may discuss methods of establishing and conducting these associations, or treat specific associations collectively. Examples: **Aged**—Societies and clubs; **Boys**—Societies and clubs. For the clubs of particular places use the subdivision "Clubs."

SOCIETIES, ETC.

Use as a topical subdivision under topical headings for works discussing two or more societies or institutions active in a particular subject field, e.g., **Veterinary medicine**—Societies, etc. Do not use the subdivision under those topics for which phrase headings have been provided, e.g. **Medical societies.** LC formerly also used the subdivision as a form subdivision for individual serial society publications if they contained information both on the topic in which the issuing society specialized and information about the business matters of the society. This practice was discontinued in 1971. The assignment of headings to an individual serial society publication containing substantive information as well as information about the issuing society is now as follows: 1. Topic subdivided by the appropriate form subdivision: "Periodicals"; "Collected works"; "Yearbooks." 2. Name of the society (without form subdivision). If the publication contains only business information about the society, omit Tracing 1. If it contains only substantive information, omit Tracing 2. In order to provide topical access in the subject catalog to those works receiving only the name of a society, make a *see also* reference from the topic to the name of the society, as shown by the following example: **Psychology**—Societies, etc. *see also* **Canadian Psychological Association.** For works discussing collectively the various learned institutions or societies of a particular place use the subdivision "Learned institutions and societies." For works about societies specializing in the career and accomplishments of individual persons use the subdivision "Societies, periodicals, etc.," under the name of the person.

- *sa* Clubs
  - Congresses
  - Executive departments
  - Gilds
  - Insignia
  - Membership
  - Religious and ecclesiastical institutions
  - Scientific bureaus
  - Societies and clubs
- *x* Institutions, societies, etc.

SOCIETIES, PERIODICALS, ETC.

Use as a form subdivision under names of individual persons for periodicals, yearbooks, or serial society publications devoted to the individual in question. Also use the subdivision as a topical subdivision for works discussing journals or societies specializing in the career and accomplishments of the person in question.

- *x* Periodicals, societies, etc.

SOCIOLOGICAL ASPECTS

Use under kinds of institutions for works discussing the impact of the inherent nature of the institution in question on group interaction within the institution, and vice versa, e.g., **Hospitals**—Sociological aspects.

SOCIOLOGY *see* SOCIAL CONDITIONS

SONGS AND MUSIC

Use as a form subdivision under topical headings, as well as under names of corporate bodies, persons (except religious persons), or places (except names of countries) for collections or single works of vocal or instrumental music about the topic or entity named. For works which discuss songs or music encompassing particular subjects, further subdivide the subdivision by "History and criticism." For songs or music about particular religious persons or deities assign the phrase heading **[person] in music**, e.g., **Jean d' Arc, Saint, 1412–1431, in music.**

- *sa* Musical settings
  - Thematic catalogs
- *x* Music and songs

SOURCES

Use as a form subdivision under historical headings, including certain headings of the type [place]—[topic], or under systems of law, for historical source materials, i.e., compilations of contemporary writings to be used by subsequent historians in their research, e.g., **Reformation**—Sources; **United States**—History—Civil War, 1861–1865—Sources; **Pakistan**—Politics and government—Sources; **Roman law**—Sources. Also use the subdivision as a topical subdivision for discussions of such writings. Under particular nonhistorical topics use the subdivision "History—Sources," e.g., **Technology**—History—Sources. Note: The subdivision "History" is uniformly used, if appropriate, under certain headings of the type [place]—[topic], e.g., **United States**—Commerce—History; instead of using the subdivision "Sources" directly in the case of such headings, use the subdivision "History—Sources," e.g., **United States**—Commerce—History—Sources. Also use the subdivision "Sources" under names of individual literary authors, author-title headings for individual works, or particular literary forms for sources and inspiration for literary works, e.g., **Defoe, Daniel, 1661?–1731. Robinson Crusoe**—Sources; **English drama**—Sources.

- *sa* Archives
- *x* Documents (Historical sources)

SPACE PHOTOGRAPHS *see* PHOTOGRAPHS FROM SPACE

SPATIAL ECONOMICS *see* LOCATION

SPECIFICATIONS *(Direct)*

Use as a form or topical subdivision under kinds of products or merchandise for detailed written descriptions of an item to be manufactured or supplied, such as are normally found in the terms of a contract, e.g., **Knit goods**—Specifications. For specifications pertaining to construction use the subdivision "Contracts and specifications."

SPECIMENS

Use as a form subdivision under kinds of publications or printed matter, or under kinds of objects which may appear as illustrative samples accompanying books, e.g., **Expurgated books**—Specimens; **Advertising**—Specimens; **Bookbinding**—Specimens; **Photoengraving**—Specimens; **Seals (Numismatics)**—Specimens. For works which discuss natural history specimens use the subdivisions "Catalogs and collections," or "Collection and preservation."

- *sa* Facsimiles
- *x* Examples

SPEECHES IN CONGRESS

Use as a form subdivision under topical headings for single speeches or compilations of speeches on those topics, e.g., **Silver question**—Speeches in Congress; **Trusts, Industrial**—Speeches in Congress.

x Congress, Speeches in
United States Congress, Speeches in

SPORTS ARENAS *see* SPORTS FACILITIES

SPORTS FACILITIES
Use under names of cities.
x Arenas, Sports
Coliseums
Fields, Playing
Playing fields
Sports arenas
Stadia

SQUARES, CITY *see* PLAZAS

STABLES
Use under names of cities.

STADIA *see* SPORTS FACILITIES

STAFFS *see* EMPLOYEES

STANDARDS   *(Direct)*
Use under topical headings, particularly under kinds of materials or equipment, names of disciplines, or kinds of establishments, for descriptions of the example or model set up and established by authority which all others should follow, e.g., **Lumber**—Standards; **Electric engineering**—Standards; **Libraries**—Standards.
sa Certification
Contracts and specifications
Inspection
Production standards
Specifications
Weights and measures

STATE SUPERVISION
Use under topical headings, e.g., **Banks and banking**—State supervision; **Local government**—State supervision.
x Supervision, State

STATES
Use under names of countries whose major administrative divisions are called states (e.g., United States) for discussions of the states collectively in relation to a specific topic. Use the subdivision only when the name of the country is used as a subdivision under a topical heading, e.g., **Civil service**—India—States.

STATIONS, EXPERIMENT *see* LABORATORIES

STATIONS, MILITARY
see FORTIFICATIONS, MILITARY INSTALLATIONS, ETC.

STATISTICAL METHODS
Use under topical headings for discussions of the methods of solving problems in those fields through the use of statistics, e.g., **Engineering**—Statistical methods. In certain fields phrase headings have been provided to designate statistical methods (for example, see the scope note under **Library statistics** in the main list of subject headings.)

STATISTICAL SERVICES
Use under names of regions, countries, cities, etc., or under topical headings.

STATISTICS
Use as a form subdivision under names of regions, countries, cities, etc., as well as under topical headings, including medical headings, for compilations of numerical data on a particular place or topic, e.g., **Italy**—Statistics; **Education**—Statistics; **Children**—Statistics; **Tuberculosis**—Statistics. For compilations of medical statistics data pertaining to particular places use the subdivision "Statistics, Medical." For compilations of the vital statistics of particular places use the subdivision "Statistics, Vital." Do not use the subdivision under subjects for which phrase headings have been provided, e.g., **Industrial statistics.**
sa Cases, clinical reports, statistics
Census
Observations
Population
Statistical methods
Statistical services
Tables
x Data, Statistical

STATISTICAL, MEDICAL
Use as a form subdivision under names of regions, countries, cities, etc., for compilations of medical statistical data on those places. For statistics on medical topics use the subdivision "Statistics." For collections of cases on a particular topic in which information is presented in the form of analyses of each of the individual cases, use the subdivision "Cases, clinical reports, statistics."
x Medical statistics

STATISTICAL, VITAL
Use as a form subdivision under names of regions, countries, cities, etc., as well as under names of ethnic groups, for compilations of birth, marriage, and death statistics.
sa Mortality
Population
Statistics, Medical
x Vital statistics

STATUES
Use under names of cities.

STOCK-YARDS
Use under names of cities.
sa Slaughter-houses

STORAGE
Use under kinds of commodities, foods, materials, industrial products, etc., for their safekeeping in a warehouse or other depository.
sa Packing

STORES, SHOPPING CENTERS, ETC.
Use under names of cities.
x Centers, Shopping
Chain stores
Department stores
Retail stores
Shopping centers
Shops

STORIES *see* FICTION; LEGENDS AND STORIES

STORIES, FOLK *see* LEGENDS

STORM, [year]
Use under names of localities or cities.
- *sa* Blizzard
  Cyclone
  Hurricanes
  Tornado
  Typhoon

STREET-CLEANING
Use under names of cities.

STREET LIGHTING *see* LIGHTING

STREET MAPS *see* ROAD MAPS

STREETS
Use under names of cities. For individual streets located in particular cities further subdivide the subdivision "Streets" by the name of the street, e.g., **Washington, D.C. —Streets—Pennsylvania Avenue.**
- *sa* Street-cleaning
- *x* City streets

STRIKE, GENERAL *see* GENERAL STRIKE

STUDENTS
Use under names of schools, universities, etc.
- *sa* Alumni

STUDY AND TEACHING (*Direct*)
Use under topical headings for works which discuss both methods of studying and teaching in the field in question, as well as educational facilities and activities in that field, including institutions, courses, programs, students, funds, etc. In the place of headings of the type "[topic]— Study and teaching," certain very broad disciplines have been provided with phrase headings which have the identical meaning, e.g., **Agricultural education.** In such disciplines, the heading "[topic]—Study and teaching" is restricted in meaning to methods of studying and teaching. Under music headings use the subdivision "Instruction and study." For education intended for individual religious bodies, classes of persons or ethnic groups use the subdivision "Education." For the learning and scholarship in general of individual persons use the subdivision "Knowledge and learning."
- *sa* Alumni
  Curricula
  Examinations
  In-service training
  Programmed instruction
  Research
  Research grants
  Schools
  Scholarships, fellowships, etc.
  Students
  Teacher training
  Text-books
  Vocational guidance
- *x* Teaching and study

STUDY AND TEACHING—AUDIO-VISUAL AIDS
Use under topical headings for general discussions on aids to the learning and teaching of a subject which make use of hearing and sight, e.g., **Art**—Study and teaching— Audio-visual aids. Under particular kinds of education use the subdivision "Audio-visual aids." For audio-visual aids which do not fill an educational function use the subdivision "Audio-visual aids" under the particular field.
- *sa* Films for [name of language] speakers
  Phonorecords for [name of language] speakers
- *x* Teaching aids, Audio-visual

STUDY AND TEACHING (CONTINUING EDUCATION) (*Direct*)
- *x* Continuing education

STUDY AND TEACHING (ELEMENTARY) (*Direct*)
- *x* Elementary education

STUDY AND TEACHING (HIGHER) (*Direct*)
- *x* College education
  Education

STUDY AND TEACHING (PRESCHOOL) (*Direct*)
- *x* Preschool education

STUDY AND TEACHING (PRIMARY) (*Direct*)
- *x* Primary education

STUDY AND TEACHING (SECONDARY) (*Direct*)
- *x* Secondary education

SUBJECTS IN ART *see* THEMES, MOTIVES

SUBURBS AND ENVIRONS
Use under names of cities for the lands or regions associated with a particular city, including the neighboring residential areas lying outside of the city as well as smaller satellite jurisdictions, but not including the city itself. For the metropolitan area associated with a particular city assign the appropriate phrase heading, e.g., **Pensacola metropolitan area, Fla.** For indefinite regions of individual cities, including the city itself and its surrounding territory, the exact size of which is vague and varies according to each author discussing it, assign the appropriate phrase heading, e.g., **Barcelona region, Venezuela.**
- *x* City environs
  Environs of cities

SULTANS
Use under names of countries.

SUMMARIES OF PUBLICATIONS *see* ABSTRACTS

SUPERVISION, STATE *see* STATE SUPERVISION

SUPPLIES AND EQUIPMENT *see* EQUIPMENT AND SUPPLIES

SUPPLY OF WATER *see* WATER-SUPPLY

SURVEYS
Use under names of regions, countries, cities, etc., for works presenting the results of land surveys. For other kinds of surveys use the appropriate phrase heading, e.g., **Snow surveys; Social surveys.**
- *sa* Altitudes
  Distances, etc.
  Maps
- *x* Land surveys

SYLLABI *see* OUTLINES, SYLLABI, ETC.

SYMBOLS (SCIENCE AND TECHNOLOGY) *see* NOTATION

SYMPOSIA *see* CONGRESSES

SYNAGOGUES
Use under names of cities.

SYSTEMATICS *see* CLASSIFICATION

TABLES
Use as a form subdivision under topical headings for works in tabular form which present systematic listings of results already computed, worked out, or processed, and which are to be used as reference tools to reduce the labor of investigators in future computations, e.g., **Alcohol**—Tables; **Gas lasers**—Tables; **Irrigation canals and flumes**—Tables; **Ellipsometry**—Tables. Use of the subdivisions "Tables and ready-reckoners," "Tables, calculations, etc.," and "Tables, etc." was discontinued by LC in October 1972.
> *sa* Chronology
> Statistics

TALES, FOLK *see* LEGENDS

TAPROOMS *see* BARS, SALOONS, ETC.

TAVERNS (BARS) *see* BARS, SALOONS, ETC.

TAXATION *(Direct)*
Use under topical headings for discussions of the taxes (a) which are levied on income-producing activities (e.g., business establishments, industries, services, etc.); or (b) which are levied on articles of value (luxury articles, property, commodities, etc.); or (c) which apply to particular classes of persons, especially employed persons. Examples: **Animal industry**—Taxation; **Hospitals**—Taxation; **Fur**—Taxation; **Drugs** — Taxation; **Investments** — Taxation; **Accountants**—Taxation; **Husband and wife**—Taxation. Do not use under subjects for which phrase headings have been provided, e.g., **Property tax; Taxation of bonds, securities, etc.**
> *x* Duties (Taxation)

TAXONOMY *see* CLASSIFICATION

TEACHER TRAINING
Use under topical headings or types of education for works discussing the methods and programs to train teachers in particular fields of study or special educational subjects, e.g., **Art**—Teacher training; **Health education**—Teacher training; **Activity programs in education**—Teacher training.
> *x* Training of teachers

TEACHING AIDS, AUDIO-VISUAL *see* STUDY AND TEACHING—AUDIO-VISUAL AIDS

TEACHING AND STUDY *see* STUDY AND TEACHING

TEACHING OF THE BIBLE *see* BIBLICAL TEACHING

TECHNIQUE
Use under (a) names of disciplines, particularly disciplines involving laboratory routines, for nontheoretical works describing the actual steps or methods to be followed in performing the tasks required in a particular field of study or endeavor, e.g., **Art**—Technique; **Bacteriology**—Technique; or (b) under literary form headings for works on the art of writing in particular forms, e.g., **Farce**—Technique; **Western stories**—Technique. Do not use the subdivision under headings for particular literary forms in those cases where special subject headings have been provided, e.g., **Essay; Poetics.** Also use the subdivision "Technique" under names of literary authors for discussions of their individual techniques of writing.
> *x* Writing

TECHNOLOGICAL INNOVATIONS
Use under technical subjects for discussions of the processes by which new products or techniques in those fields are developed and introduced into the economic system, e.g., **Instrument manufacture**—Technological innovations.
> *x* Innovations, Technological

TELEPHONE DIRECTORIES *see* DIRECTORIES—TELEPHONE

TEMPLES
Use under names of cities.

TENURE *see* APPOINTMENT, QUALIFICATIONS, TENURE, ETC.

TERMINOLOGY
Use under topical headings (a) as a form subdivision for lists of the special terms or expressions used in those fields, not alphabetically arranged or not comprehensive if alphabetical; or (b) as a topical subdivision for discussions about the terminology of a particular subject field. For comprehensive, alphabetical lists of terms use the subdivision "Dictionaries." Under legal headings use the subdivision "Terms and phrases." Also use the subdivision "Terms and phrases" under names of languages for lists of expressions, phrases, idioms, etc., found in a particular language. For incomplete lists of the words of a language with or without definitions use the subdivision "Glossaries, vocabularies, etc." under the name of the language.
> *sa* Name
> Names
> Nomenclature
> Slang

TERMS AND PHRASES
Use as a form or topical subdivision under (a) legal headings for works which list or discuss the special legal terms or expressions used in those fields; or (b) names of languages for works which list or discuss expressions, phrases, idioms, etc., found in those languages.
> *sa* Terminology
> *x* Phrases and terms

TERRITORIAL BOUNDARIES *see* BOUNDARIES

TERRITORIAL EXPANSION
Use under names of countries.
> *sa* Annexation to . . .
> *x* Expansion, Territorial

TERRITORIES AND POSSESSIONS
Use under names of countries for works discussing collectively the territories and possessions of those countries. Also use the subdivision where appropriate when the name of the country in question is used as a subdivision under a topical heading, e.g., **Taxation**—United States—Territories and possessions.
> *sa* Colonies

TESTING
Use under (a) types of engineering materials or forms for works describing methods of testing these items for their mechanical or physical properties; (b) types of instruments, equipment, products, or structures for tests on the quality of their performance or function; (c) drugs or other substances for tests on the efficiency of their action; or (d) psychological headings for methods of making psychological tests in those fields. In cases (a) through (c) above use the subdivision also for works providing results of individual tests. Examples: **Brass**—Testing; **Diesel motor**—Testing; **Fungicides**—Testing; **Aggressiveness (Psychology)**—Testing.
- sa   Ability testing
  Analysis
  Evaluation
  Grading
  Inspection
  Quality control
  Specifications
- x   Mechanical testing

TESTS (EXAMINATIONS) *see* EXAMINATIONS

TEXT-BOOKS
Use as a topical subdivision under topical headings for works which discuss the books presenting a particular subject in an organized and simplified manner for purposes of learning, e.g., **Social sciences**—Text-books. Do not use the subdivision as a form subdivision for individual text-books (the several examples in the subject heading list which violate this principle, e.g., **Geography**—Text-books, represent an earlier practice no longer followed).
- sa   Programmed instruction
  Readers
  Text-books for foreigners

TEXT-BOOKS FOR FOREIGNERS
Use as a form subdivision under names of languages for textbooks to be used in learning the particular language in question as a foreign language. If the textbook in hand is written for native speakers of a specific language, further subdivide the subdivision by the name of that language, e.g., **English language**—Text-books for foreigners—German.
- sa   Films for [name of language] speakers
  Phonorecords for [name of language] speakers
- x   Foreign language text-books
  Language text-books for foreigners

TEXTS
Use as a form subdivision under names of rare or exotic languages for collections of texts in those languages on all possible subjects. Also use the subdivision as a form subdivision under headings designating songs or special kinds of songs for works consisting of the words alone to one or more songs with the music omitted, e.g., **Negro spirituals**—Texts; **Songs, American**—Texts; **Music, Popular (Songs, etc.)**—Texts. For collections of texts in the field of belles lettres assign the appropriate literary headings, e.g., **American poetry.**

TEXTUAL CRITICISM *see* CRITICISM, TEXTUAL

THEATER DISASTER, [date]
Use under names of cities.

THEATERS
Use under names of cities.
- sa   Nightclubs, dance halls, etc.
- x   Hall music
  Music halls

THEMATIC CATALOGS
Use as a form subdivision under particular musical forms or names of composers for listings of the themes of musical compositions.

THEMES, MOTIVES
Use under particular literary or art forms for general discussions of the themes, etc., occurring or possible in the form in question, e.g., **Folk literature, Polynesian**—Themes, motives; **Painting**—Themes, motives; **Illustration of books**—Themes, motives.
- x   Motives, themes
  Subjects in art

THEORY *see* PHILOSOPHY

THERAPEUTIC USE
Use under types of substances, plants, foods, physical phenomena, activities, etc., for discussions of their use in curing disease.
- x   Applications, Therapeutic
  Use, Therapeutic

TIDAL WAVE, [year]
Use under names of regions, countries, cities, etc.
- x   Wave, Tidal

TIME STANDARDS *see* PRODUCTION STANDARDS

TOMB
Use under names of persons.

TOMBS
Use under names of cities, royal families, categories of rulers, etc., e.g., **Alexandria, Egypt**—Tombs; **Japan**—Royal families—Tombs; **Popes**—Tombs. For tombs of individual persons use the subdivision "Tomb" under the name of the person.

TOPES
Use under names of cities (mainly in India).

TOPOGRAPHIC MAPS *see* MAPS, TOPOGRAPHIC

TORNADO, [year]
Use under names of regions, countries, cities, etc.

TOURIST HOMES *see* HOTELS, MOTELS, ETC.

TOURS *see* DESCRIPTION—TOURS; DESCRIPTION AND TRAVEL—TOURS

TOWERS
Use under names of cities.
- x   Church towers
  Engineering

TOXICOLOGY
Use under topical headings, especially kinds of chemicals or substances, for discussions on their poisonous effect on man or animals. Do not use under subjects for which phrase headings have been provided, e.g., **Lead-**

poisoning. For the effect of chemical substances on plants assign phrase headings of the type **Plants, Effect of [substance] on,** e.g., **Plants, Effect of arsenic on.**

    x   Poisonous properties

TRADE *see* COMMERCE

TRADE FAIRS *see* FAIRS

TRADE-MARKS

Use as a form or topical subdivision under kinds of merchandise for works listing or discussing the words, letters, or symbols adopted and used by the manufacturers or dealers of these items to distinguish them from the goods of others, e.g., **Glassware**—Trade-marks; **Cosmetics**—Trade-marks. If the work in hand is concerned with the trade-marks of an industry rather than a specific product use the subdivision under the heading for the pertinent industry, e.g., **Plastic industry and trade**—Trade-marks.

TRADE SCHOOLS *see* SCHOOLS

TRAINING, IN-SERVICE *see* IN-SERVICE TRAINING

TRAINING OF TEACHERS *see* TEACHER TRAINING

TRANSIT SYSTEMS

Use under names of cities or metropolitan areas for general discussions on the public transportation systems of those places. For works discussing particular systems of particular places assign the heading appropriate for that system, e.g., **Subways**—[name of city].

TRANSLATING

Use under (a) names of languages for general works on the techniques of translating works originally published in those languages; or (b) individual sacred works, particular literary forms, or names of disciplines for discussions of the techniques of translating those specific works, or works in those forms or subject fields. Examples: **English language**—Translating; **Koran**—Translating; **Poetry**—Translating; **Mathematics**—Translating. If the work in hand discusses how to translate from one language into another specific language modify the subdivision as follows: "Translating into [name of language]," e.g., **German language**—Translating into English. If the work in hand discusses how to translate one language into another, as well as the reverse direction, assign two headings as appropriate, e.g., 1. **German language**—Translating into English. 2. **English language**—Translating into German.

    sa   Translating services

TRANSLATING SERVICES

Use under names of disciplines.

TRANSLATIONS

Use as a topical subdivision under names of individual authors for discussions about translations of their works, including discussions about single works which have been translated. If appropriate, further qualify the subdivision by the name of the language into which the work or works have been translated, e.g., **Shakespeare, William, 1564–1616**—Translations, German.

TRANSLATIONS FROM [NAME OF LANGUAGE]

Use as a form subdivision under particular literary forms for works which represent compilations of translated works of belles lettres originally published in a particular language (the language specified in the subdivision), e.g., **English drama**—Translations from Danish. Do not use the subdivision unless the work in hand represents a publication in which the constituent items were newly assembled and translated at the time of its publication and did not previously appear in the same arrangement in any language. If the work in hand represents a compilation of works translated from many languages use the subdivision "Translations from foreign literature." If only two languages are involved (the original language and the language of the translation) make a second subject entry in order to bring out the language into which the translations were made, e.g., 1. **English poetry**—Translations from French. 2. **French poetry**—Translations into English. For compilations of translated works on a topic originally published in a particular language use the subdivision "Collected works—Translations from . . . " under the topic.

TRANSLATIONS FROM [NAME OF LANGUAGE]—
    BIBLIOGRAPHY

Use as a form subdivision under topical headings for lists of works on a particular topic which have been translated from a particular language, e.g., **Geophysics**—Translations from Russian—Bibliography. If the work in hand lists translations from many languages use the subdivision "Translations from foreign literature—Bibliography."

TRANSLATIONS INTO [NAME OF LANGUAGE]

Use as a form subdivision under particular literary forms for works of belles lettres which represent compilations of works originally published in various languages and translated into one language (the language specified in the subdivision), e.g., **Belgian poetry**—Translations into English. Do not use the subdivision unless the work in hand was newly assembled and translated at the time of its publication, and the individual works making up the volume did not previously appear in that arrangement in any language. If the work in hand represents a compilation of works translated into many languages use the subdivision "Translations into foreign languages." If only two languages are involved (the original language and the language of the translation), make a second subject entry in order to bring out the name of the original language, e.g., 1. **French poetry**—Translations into English. 2. **English poetry**—Translations from French. For compilations of works on a topic translated into one language use the subdivision "Collected works—Translations into . . . " under the particular topic.

TRANSLATIONS INTO [NAME OF LANGUAGE]—
    BIBLIOGRAPHY

Use as a form subdivision under topical headings for lists of works on a particular topic which have been translated into a particular language, e.g., **Geophysics**—Translations into English—Bibliography. If the work in hand lists translations into many languages use the subdivision "Translations into foreign languages—Bibliography."

TRANSPORTATION

Use under types of objects, merchandise, persons, etc., transported. Also use the subdivision under names of agencies or wars for the transportation carried out by or during them, e.g., **United States. Army**—Transportation; **World War, 1939–1945**—Transportation. When used under classes of persons further subdivide the subdivision "Transportation" by locality if appropriate for the work in hand, e.g., **School children**—Transportation—Ohio.

    sa Commerce
        Ferries
        Government vessels
        Navigation
        Packing
        Pipe lines
        Stables
        Storage
        Transit systems
    x Shipment

TRAVEL AND DESCRIPTION
    see DESCRIPTION; DESCRIPTION AND TRAVEL

TRAVESTIES *see* PARODIES, TRAVESTIES, ETC.

TREATMENT AND CARE *see* CARE AND TREATMENT

TYPHOON, [year]
    Use under names of regions, countries, cities, etc.

UMPIRING *see* JUDGING

UNDERGROUND AREAS
    Use under names of cities.
    x City underground areas

UNION LISTS
    Use as a form subdivision under (a) particular kinds of nonbook materials, or (b) in the case of printed materials, under particular kinds of imprints, or (c) particular kinds of publications provided for in the main list of subject headings under the subject heading **Bibliography,** for catalogs of these materials held by two or more libraries, e.g., **Microcards**—Union lists; **Italian imprints**—Union lists; **Bibliography**—Early printed books—Union lists. For union lists of publications on special subjects use the subdivision "Bibliography—Union lists."

UNITED STATES CONGRESS, SPEECHES IN
    see SPEECHES IN CONGRESS

USE, INDUSTRIAL *see* INDUSTRIAL APPLICATIONS

USE, SCIENTIFIC *see* SCIENTIFIC APPLICATIONS

USE, THERAPEUTIC *see* THERAPEUTIC USE

VACATION SCHOOLS *see* SCHOOLS

VADE MECUMS *see* HANDBOOKS, MANUALS, ETC.

VALUATION *(Direct)*
    Use under particular types of property, businesses, structures, etc., for discussions of the value set upon them as their estimated or determined market value, e.g., **Farms**—Valuation; **Public utilities**—Valuation; **Bridges**—Valuation.
    x Property valuation

VENTILATION *see* HEATING AND VENTILATION

VIEWS *see* DESCRIPTION—VIEWS; DESCRIPTION AND TRAVEL—VIEWS

VISUAL AIDS, AUDIO *see* AUDIO-VISUAL AIDS

VITAL STATISTICS *see* STATISTICS, VITAL

VOCABULARIES, GLOSSARIES, ETC. *see* GLOSSARIES, VOCABULARIES, ETC.; LANGUAGE—GLOSSARIES, ETC.

VOCATIONAL GUIDANCE
    Use under types of industries, trades, establishments, or under particular subject fields, for works intended to assist persons to choose a career in these fields, advising them how to prepare for, enter, and progress in them, and what specific working conditions to expect, e.g., **Ceramic industries**—Vocational guidance; **Baking**—Vocational guidance; **Camps**—Vocational guidance; **Technology**—Vocational guidance. Also use the subdivision under names of individual organizations or under types of organization, e.g., **United States. Navy**—Vocational guidance; **Police**—Vocational guidance. Do not use the subdivision under classes of employees if a heading exists for the activity or field, e.g., **Jewelry trade**—Vocational guidance, not **Jewelers**—Vocational guidance. Only if no heading exists for the activity or field, may the subdivision be used under classes of employees, e.g., **Dental hygienists**—Vocational guidance. Whenever the subdivision is used under a type of activity or field, make a *see also* reference from the class of employees to the heading, e.g., **Automobile mechanics** *see also* **Automobiles**—Maintenance and repair—Vocational guidance. For vocational guidance in professional fields assign the phrase heading **[name of discipline] as a profession,** e.g., **Engineering as a profession.**
    sa Employment
        Occupations
    x Guidance, Vocational

VOTING REGISTERS
    Use as a form subdivision under names of countries, cities, or other electoral districts.

WALLS
    Use under names of cities.
    sa Gates
    x City walls

WARDS
    Use under names of cities.

WARS *see* HISTORY, MILITARY; HISTORY, NAVAL

WASHING *see* CLEANING

WASTE DISPOSAL
    Use under types of industries, plants, or industrial processes.
    sa By-products
    x Disposal of wastes
        Industrial waste disposal
        Waste products

WASTE PRODUCTS *see* BY-PRODUCTS; WASTE DISPOSAL

WATER-SUPPLY
    Use under names of cities, as well as under types of installations, plants, industries, processes, etc.
    sa Fountains
    x Engineering
        Supply of water

WAVE, TIDAL *see* TIDAL WAVE

WEATHER (CLIMATE) *see* CLIMATE

WEIGHT

Use under kinds of objects or substances for discussions of the techniques of making weight measurements, or for the results of measurements made on individual examples of the item in question, e.g., **Air**—Weight; **Aeroplanes**—Weight. Under types of farm produce use the subdivision "Weight and measurement," e.g., **Poultry**—Weight and measurement.

WEIGHTS AND MEASURES

Use under types of commodities or merchandise for the special systems of weights and measures established for the particular item in question, e.g., **Aggregates (Building materials)**—Weights and measures.

WHARVES *see* DOCKS, WHARVES, ETC.

WONDERS *see* MISCELLANEA

WORD INDEXES *see* CONCORDANCES

WORD LISTS *see* DICTIONARIES

WORDS, CODE *see* CODE WORDS

WORDS, NEW *see* LANGUAGE (NEW WORDS, SLANG, ETC.)

WORKHOUSES *see* CORRECTIONAL INSTITUTIONS

WRITING *see* AUTHORSHIP; TECHNIQUE

YEARBOOKS

Use as a form subdivision under topical headings, as well as under names of places, for publications appearing annually, each volume of which summarizes those accomplishments or events of the year occurring in those subject fields, e.g., **Medicine**—Yearbooks. Do not use the subdivision for annuals which do not summarize; instead use the subdivision "Periodicals" for publications of this type. Do not use the subdivision "Yearbooks" for annuals which summarize the events of a year in an individual organization active in a particular field (such as company reports or annual reports of institutions); in such instances, if no substantive information is provided in the publication in hand, assign as the subject heading only the name of the company or institution. However, a *see also* reference should be provided in the subject catalog under the topic in question subdivided by "Societies, etc." to the name of the company or institution. For publications which summarize in the style of yearbooks but appear biennially or semiannually also use "Yearbooks."
sa Societies, periodicals, etc.
x Annuals (Yearbooks)

ZONING MAPS

Use under names of regions, countries, cities, etc.
x City zoning maps

☆U.S. GOVERNMENT PRINTING OFFICE: 1975 O—552—623

Subject Headings For Children's Literature

ANNOTATED CARD PROGRAM

In the fall of 1965 the Library of Congress initiated the Annotated Card Program. The purpose of this program was to provide a more appropriate and in-depth subject treatment of juvenile titles and thus offer easier subject access to these materials. This was accomplished chiefly through a more liberal application of the Library of Congress subject headings—the standard or master list contained in these two volumes. In some cases this necessitated a reinterpretation in application as well as the simplification of certain headings and, in a few instances, required the creation of new headings to provide access to materials for which no headings had previously existed. Through these three steps catalogers have arrived at a list of approximately 309 headings and subdivisions to date which vary in application and form from standard LC subject headings. The Annotated Card Program (AC) list is in effect a list of exceptions to the master LC list and should therefore be consulted in conjunction with the latter. (AC headings appear in brackets on the LC cards coded AC.)

While the AC list entails certain departures from the standard LC list its original intent was not to exist primarily as a third list. The AC list was to provide a liberal extension of the standard LC list and any departure from LC was to be guided by the *Sears List of Subject Headings,* the Committee on Cataloging of Children's Materials of the American Library Association, and the needs of children's libraries as articulated by authorities in the field. Nonetheless, it was recognized that users of LC annotated catalog cards for children's literature needed an explicit statement regarding the authority lists used for the subject headings assigned and a statement of the policies followed in assigning them.

In 1969, *Subject Headings for Children's Literature* was published. It explained guiding principles of the AC program and listed those headings that varied from LC standard headings in application or form. Since that date the list has grown by over 100 headings. New policies have been initiated and old ones changed or terminated as feedback was received from the ALA Committee on Cataloging of Children's Materials and from the field.

This updated introduction explains the ways in which AC headings depart from standard LC headings in form and policy. It includes sources consulted in establishing headings, terms not used, and subdivisions that are an exception to LC standard policies or patterns. The list of AC headings is printed complete with scope notes and cross references, and since it is a list of exceptions to the LC, it is to be used in conjunction with the standard list. Additions to this list will be found in the issues of *Supplement to LC Subject Headings.*

A representative from the Children's Literature Cataloging Section, which administers the Annotated Card Program, has worked closely with the ALA Committee on Cataloging of Children's Materials. The committee has provided a forum for those concerned with the cataloging of children's materials, forwarding the comments and suggestions from interested persons in the field to the Library of Congress as well as making specific recommendations of its own.

The committee has considered the problems of cataloging for children's collections, particularly the lack of uniformity prevalent in cataloging children's materials among various sources. As a step toward urging standardization, the committee recommended at the 1969 ALA Midwinter Conference "the adoption of Library of Congress cataloging of children's materials as the national standard."

Application of Subject Headings

With a few exceptions the bracketed headings used on AC cards are standard LC subject headings. Some of the chief differences between the AC and LC headings are in application rather than terminology. For example:

(1) Elimination of subdivisions such as "Juvenile fiction" and "Juvenile literature" which would be useless in a children's literature catalog.

(2) The application of subject headings to fiction when such headings can provide a helpful approach to the literature. For example, if a story adds to the reader's information about a country, a social problem, or a profession, such headings are used as: **Switzerland**—Social life and customs—Fiction; **Drug abuse**—Fiction; **Teachers**—Fiction. Abstract concepts such as **Friendship**—Fiction are also recognized.

(3) The use of both specific and general subject headings. In a catalog for a children's collection a young reader can locate a biographical work through (a) the specific name of the individual, (b) the broader heading of the individual's career or particular contribution, or (c) the period of history in which the individual flourished and was influential if it is pertinent to the work being cataloged. For example: 1. **Bickerdyke, Mary Ann (Ball) 1817–1901.** 2. **Nurses and nursing.** 3. **United States**—History—Civil War, 1861–1865.

(4) The use of both popular and scientific terms. For material intended for very young children, the popular term is used, as in the headings **Weather** and **Fossils.** When the book is intended for older children, both the popular and scientific terms are frequently traced. Thus a single card may carry such tracings as: 1. **Weather** 2. **Meteorology.** Or 1. **Fossils** 2. **Paleontology.** When books are intended for young adults, ordinarily only the scientific terminology is provided; for example, **Meteorology** or **Paleontology.**

(5) Use of headings denoting form or kind. Such headings, created to make certain types of material more accessible to the reader, include **Joke books, Counting games, Stories without words.**

Categories of AC Headings

The headings used on annotated cards represent four categories: standard LC, modified LC, standard Sears, and new headings established for exclusive use on annotated cards.

By far the most numerous are the standard LC headings assigned in the usual way. Included are topical headings, most proper names, geographic names, and subdivisions. The following tracings selected at random illustrate this usage: **Chemistry, Analytic**—Laboratory manuals; **Conductors (Music); Isotopes; Negro athletes; Socially handicapped; Utah**—History; **Vietnamese Conflict, 1961–** ; **Warren, Earl, 1891.**

The modified LC headings, many of which conform to usage in the Sears list, consist of the following types of adjustments: (1) Spelling and hyphenation are modernized in such headings as **Airplanes; Bullfights; Caddis flies; Folklore, Gypsy; Trotsky, Leon;** and **Columbus, Christopher.** (2) Subdivision is often used rather than inversion or qualification, for example: **Animals**—Infancy; **American poetry**—Collections; **Cookery**—Meat; **Speech**—Disorders. (3) Subdivided headings are in some instances made adjectival headings, such as **Christmas poetry.** (4) Superfluous words and phrases are deleted in such headings as **Picture books** [for children] and **Lumbermen**—Language [(New words, slang, etc.)].

Sears headings and subdivisions which appear to be more appropriate than those in the LC list are adopted for use. The following Sears headings and subdivisions are typical: **Alphabet books; Parades; Pigs; Robbers and outlaws; "Collections".**

Certain headings are established specifically for use on LC annotated cards when neither Sears nor the LC lists provide suitable terminology, form, or scope. Into this group fall such headings as **Clay modeling; Parties;** and **Stories without words.**

In establishing a heading that varies from the LC, catalogers consult a considerable number of sources in arriving at the term thought to be the most effective for AC purposes. Literature in the subject area is consulted; spelling is accepted from *Webster's Third New International Dictionary,* with the exception of hyphenated terms; indexing sources widely used by the public, such as *The Reader's Guide to Periodical Literature* and *The New York Times Index,* are checked for their indexing terms. Sears is consulted, as are leading children's encyclopedias and a number of other reference sources usually found in public and school libraries.

Subdivisions

AC PRACTICE

While many of the most commonly used subdivisions of general application listed in the introductory material of *Library of Congress Subject Headings* can be used in a card catalog devoted exclusively to children's literature, some needed modifications in form or application. The following subdivisions are exceptions to the LC list and should be used by the librarian in conjunction with the LC standard subdivision list.

BIOGRAPHY

Used for both collected and individual biographies but only under names of ethnic groups and under subject fields where no specific term designates the profession or contribution of the biographee. For example, **Indians of North America**—Biography, and **Football**—Biography, but **Engineers,** without subdivision, for biographies of persons belonging to this occupational group.

COLLECTIONS

Used for publications containing works by more than one author and in such headings as **American poetry**—Collections.

FICTION

Used under all subjects.

GEOGRAPHY

Used under the names of states, regions or countries.

HABITS AND BEHAVIOR

Used under any kind of animal, bird, reptile, or fish.

PICTORIAL WORKS

Used under all pictorial matter.

STORIES

See Fiction.

VOCATIONAL GUIDANCE

Used under vocations for which a college degree is not required.

SUBDIVISIONS AND QUALIFIERS NOT USED

The subdivision "United States" and the qualifying term "American" are not often used since most of the materials purchased by children's libraries in the United States reflect an American orientation rather than an international one. Thus **Bridges**—United States becomes simply **Bridges,** a heading which can be used both for works about United States bridges and for works about bridges in several different countries. However, other geographical subdivisions are retained and are used for books limited in scope to a particular country or a particular state, as in the heading **Bridges**—Great Britain.

An exception is made for subject headings for topics whose treatment is predominantly international in scope, such as **Art, Folklore,** and **Music.** Where the presentation is limited to the United States, qualification or subdivision is used, for example: **Art, American; Folklore**—United States; **Music, American.**

The qualifying term "Children's" is usually deleted so that a heading such as **Children's parties** becomes simply **Parties.** Similarly, **Children's songs** becomes **Songs. Children in [Poland]** is an exception to this and is always used with the second heading [**Poland**]—Social life and customs.

Names

Names of persons are anglicized to concur with popular English usage such as **Christopher Columbus** (rather than Cristoforo Colombo) and **William Tell** (rather than Wilhelm Tell). These proper names appear in the AC list and those used that do not agree with LC usage will appear in the supplements to the subject heading list.

Geographic and place names, as established by LC, are based on the form determined by the United States Board on Geographical Names.

Exceptions to LC usage of the names of plants and animals are listed. For those not appearing consult the LC standard list.

The list and introduction were prepared in the Subject Cataloging Division by the Children's Literature Cataloging Section. Special acknowledgement and thanks to Priscilla Moulton (Director, Brookline Public School Libraries, Brookline, Mass.), who served as chairman of the ALA *ad hoc* Committee on Cataloging of Children's Materials (1967–72); Winifred Duncan (Chicago Public Schools), who became chairman of the permanent committee (1972–); and to those librarians who served as members of the committee. Their suggestions, recommendations, and cooperation have been of immense value.

The following list includes all Annotated Card headings which vary in application or form from the standard LC subject headings. The AC list is to be used in conjunction with the list of LC subject headings and its cross-reference structure is to be observed with the list of exceptions noted below. Some of the headings which first appeared in *Subject Headings for Children's Literature* (1969) have since been incorporated into the 10th edition of the Sears list. The symbols of these headings have been adjusted to indicate they are now Sears headings.

ANNOTATED CARD
SUBJECT HEADINGS LIST

† LC heading included for use of subdivision
    or reference structure
$ New application of LC heading
* Modified LC heading
** Sears heading
Unmarked New heading
  sa see also
   x Refer from (*see*)
  xx Refer from (*see also*)

---

* **Acrobats and acrobatics**

* **Airplane racing**

* **Airplanes**

* **Airplanes, Military**

  Airplanes, Vertically rising
    See Vertically rising airplanes

* **Airships**

† **Alphabet**
    Here are entered works on the his-
    torical development of letters of
    the alphabet. ABC books that
    teach letters are entered under
    Alphabet books. Works on sample
    alphabets, lettering, calligraphy,
    etc. are entered under Alphabets.

** **Alphabet books**
    Note under Alphabet

  **Alphabet books, French, [German, Spanish,
    etc.]**

† **Alphabets**
    Note under Alphabet

* **Alpine animals**
    x Alpine fauna

  Alpine fauna
    See Alpine animals

* **Amateur motion pictures**
    x Amateur moving-pictures

  Amateur moving-pictures
    See Amateur motion pictures

$ **American [Danish, English, etc.] poetry**
    Here are entered collections of
    poetry by individual American
    [Danish, English, etc.] authors.
    Collections of poetry by several
    authors of the same nationality
    are entered under American [Dan-
    ish, English, etc.] poetry—Col-
    lections.

*   —**Collections**
    Note under American [Danish,
    English, etc.] poetry

  Animal distribution
    x Geographical distribution of animals
      and plants
      Zoogeography

† **Animals**
    —**Age**
*   —**Air transportation**
** —**Courtship**
*   —**Food habits**
*   —**Habitations**
*   —**Infancy**

*   —**Migration**
*   —**Training**
*   —**Treatment**

  Animals, Prehistoric
    See Prehistoric animals

* **Animals in numismatics**

  Anteaters

* **Arachnids**

* **Art metalwork**

* **Atomic power plants**

† **Australian aborigines**
*   —**Legends**
    x Legends
      Legends, Australian (Aboriginal)

$ **Automata**
    Here are entered works on robots
    which do not take human form.
    sa Robots
    xx Robots

† **Baseball**
*   —**Anecdotes**

* **Basset hounds**

† **Beetles**
** —**Collection and preservation**

** **Behavior**
    sa Conduct of life
      Etiquette
    xx Conduct of life
      Etiquette

* **Bell founders**

† **Bible**
*   —**Selections**

† **Bible. O.T.**
*   —**Selections**

** **Bicycles and bicycling**
    x Tricycles

* **Bird song**

* **Birdhouses**

  Birds, Extinct
    See Extinct birds

* **Birthstones**

  Boots and shoes
    See Shoes and boots

  Brigands and robbers
    See Robbers and outlaws

* **Bullfights**

* **Burglar alarms**

** **Buried treasure**
    x Sunken treasure
      Treasure trove

* **Bus drivers**
    x Motor bus drivers

* **Buses**
    x Motor buses

* **Cabinetwork**

  Cable cars
    xx Railroads, Cable

* **Caddis flies**

* **Calculating machines**

$ **Camping**
    Here are entered works on both
    organized camps and techniques
    of outdoor camping.
    sa Music camps
    x Camps

  Camps
    See Camping

† **Card tricks**
    sa Magic tricks
    xx Magic tricks

* **Cardinal (Bird)**

  Cardiovascular system
    See Circulatory system

* **Casserole recipes**

  Cattails

* **Cave animals**
    x Cave fauna

* **Cave drawings**

* **Cave dwellers**

* **Cave dwellings**

  Cave fauna
    See Cave animals

  Chickens
    sa Roosters
    xx Poultry
      Roosters

† **Chivalry**
    Here are entered nonfiction works
    only. Works of fiction are entered
    under Knights and knighthood—
    Fiction.
    —**Fiction**
    See Knights and knighthood—Fic-
    tion

† **Christian life**
    Here are entered works on the effect
    of Christian religions on everyday
    life.
    sa Religious life
    xx Religious life

* **Christmas poetry**

Circulatory system
   x Cardiovascular system
Circus stories
Clay modeling
   xx Modeling
* Cliff dwellers
* Cliff dwellings
* Clipper ships
* Cockfighting
† Collective settlements
      Here are entered works on large communal settlements. For works dealing with small communal settlements and those associated with the communal movement of the 1960's and 1970's use Communes.
  —China
   x Communes (China)
Colombo, Cristoforo
  See Columbus, Christopher
* Color variation (Biology)
* Columbus, Christopher
   x Colombo, Cristoforo
Communes
  Note under Collective settlements
Communes (China)
  See Collective settlements—China
† Conduct of life
      Here are entered works on moral and ethical values in everyday life.
   sa Behavior
   xx Behavior
* Conifers
Conjuring
  See Magic tricks
† Cookery
*   —Fruit
*   —Herbs
*   —Meat
*   —Vegetables
** Corn
   x Maize
* Coronado, Francisco Vásquez de, 1510–1554
   x Vásquez de Coronado, Francisco, 1510–1554
     Vázquez de Coronado, Francisco, 1510–1554
Corpulence
  See Weight control
** Counting books
Counting games
   xx Mathematical recreations
     Number games
Courtesy
  See Etiquette
Creative activities and seat work
  See Handicraft
    Indoor games
    Mathematical recreations
    Puzzles
* Decision making
* Desert animals
   x Desert fauna
Desert fauna
  See Desert animals

Desert flora
  See Desert plants
* Desert plants
   x Desert flora
* De Soto, Hernando, 1500 (ca.)–1542
   x Soto, Hernando de, 1500 (ca.)–1542
Detective and mystery stories
  See Mystery and detective stories
† Diet
   sa Weight control
   xx Weight control
Digestive system
* Dinosaurs
   xx Fossils
* Dollhouses
† Drama
  —Collections
    See Plays—Collections
† Drug abuse
   x Drugs and youth
† Drugs
   x Drugs and youth
Drugs and youth
  See Drug abuse
    Drugs
Eating customs
Education of women
  See Women—Education
Egg-laying mammals
  See Monotremes
† Electromagnetism
**   —Experiments
* Emotional problems
† English language
  —Orthography and spelling
    See English language—Spelling
*   —Spelling
   x English language—Orthography and spelling
*   —Textbooks for foreigners
$ Entertaining
   sa Parties
   xx Parties
* Ericson, Leif, d. ca. 1020
   x Leif Ericson, d. ca. 1020
    Leiv Eiriksson, d. ca. 1020
† Eskimos
  —Legends
   x Legends
† Espionage
      Here are entered works on the art and techniques of espionage.
   sa Intelligence service
     Spies
   xx Intelligence service
     Spies
  —Fiction
    See Spy stories
Essayists, American, [French, German, etc.]
$ Etiquette
      Here are entered works on prescribed patterns and conventions of social behavior.
   sa Behavior
   x Courtesy
   xx Behavior

Excretion
  See Excretory system
† Excretory organs
   sa Excretory system
Excretory system
   x Excretion
   xx Excretory organs
* Extinct birds
   x Birds, Extinct
† Family
  —Prayer-books and devotions
    See Prayer books and devotions
Family life
Family problems
* Fire departments
* Fire engines
* First aid
* Fish culture
* Fly casting
* Folk songs
* Folklore
   x Legends
    Tales
  —[country subdivision]
      Here are entered collections of folklore originating in a particular country. Collections of folklore of ethnic groups not limited by country are entered under the heading Folklore, American [Czech, Jewish, etc.]
* Folklore, American, [Czech, Jewish, etc.]
  Note under Folklore—[country subdivision]
* Folklore, French Canadian
* Folklore, Gypsy
* Forest animals
   x Forest fauna
Forest fauna
  See Forest animals
Forest flora
  See Forest plants
* Forest plants
   x Forest flora
** Fossils
   sa Dinosaurs
     Prehistoric animals
  —Collectors and collecting
* Fox hunting
* French Canadians
* Freshwater animals
   x Freshwater fauna
* Freshwater biology
* Freshwater ecology
Freshwater fauna
  See Freshwater animals
* Fruit culture
* Gallflies
* Game and game birds
† Games
  —Fiction
    See Play—Fiction
Gas and oil engines
  See Internal combustion engines
Generative organs, Female
  See Reproductive system, Female

Generative organs, Male
 See Reproductive system, Male
Geographical distribution of animals and
    plants
 See Animal distribution
    Plant distribution

* Germans in Pennsylvania
    x Pennsylvania Germans
Gilds
 See Guilds
Gipsies
 See Gypsies
* Gliding
Gravitation
 See Gravity
† Gravity
    x Gravitation
* Grooming
    x Grooming for men
Grooming for men
 See Grooming

Groundhog
 See Woodchuck

Groundhog Day
* Guilds
    x Gilds
* Guinea pigs
* Gypsies
    x Gipsies
† Handicraft
    x Creative activities and seat work

* Hermit crabs
* Hindenburg (Airship)
History and condition of women
 See Women—History

† Honesty
    x Truthfulness and falsehood
* Horror stories
    x Horror tales
Horror tales
 See Horror stories
Horse breeding
 See Horses—Breeding

* Horse racing
* Horse shows
Horse-training
 See Horses—Training

† Horses
*   —Breeding
      x Horse breeding
*   —Training
      x Horse-training

Horseshoe crabs
* Hummingbirds

Humorous stories
Ice skating
    x Skating
Improvisation (Acting)
 See Plays—Improvisation

† Indians
*   —Treatment
      x Indians, Treatment of
Indians, Treatment of
 See Indians—Treatment

† Indians of North America, [South America,
    etc.]
† —Legends
    x Legends
† Indoor games
    x Creative activities and seat work
† Intelligence service
    Here are entered works on the organ-
    ization, function, and activities of
    particular intelligence services.
  sa Espionage
    Spies
  xx Expionage
    Spies
  —Fiction
    Here are entered fictional works
    on the activities of agents of an
    intelligence service.
  sa Spy stories
  xx Spy stories

Internal combustion engines
    x Gas and oil engines
* Jackrabbits
Jellyfishes
Joke books
    xx Wit and humor
* Jungle animals
    x Jungle fauna

Jungle fauna
 See Jungle animals
Jungle stories
Kinkajou
† Knights and knighthood
  —Fiction
    x Chivalry—Fiction
    Note under Chivalry

** Labor unions
    x Trade-unions

* Ladybugs
Learning
    This heading is used only with sub-
    divisions.
* —Psychology

Left and right
    Here are entered works on left and
    right as indications of location or
    direction. Works on political
    beliefs are entered under Right
    and left (Political science).
    Works on the physical charac-
    teristic of favoring one hand or
    the other are entered under Left-
    and right-handedness.
    x Right and left

† Left- and right-handedness
    Note under Left and right
Legends
 See Australian aborigines—Legends
    Eskimos—Legends
    Folklore
    Indians of North America, [South
    America, etc.]—Legends
    subdivision Fiction under special
    subjects

Legends, Australian (Aboriginal)
 See Australian aborigines—Legends

Leif Ericson, d. ca. 1020
 See Ericson, Leif, d. ca. 1020

Leiv Eiriksson, d. ca. 1020
 See Ericson, Leif, d. ca. 1020
* Letter writing
* Lifesaving
Lights
* Lightships
** Lumber and lumbering
  —Terminology
    Here are entered works dealing
    with technical terms of the
    industry.
  sa Lumbermen—Language
  xx Lumbermen—Language
† Lumbermen
* —Language
    Here are entered works dealing
    with slang used by men in
    lumber camps, etc.
  sa Lumber and lumbering—Ter-
    minology
  xx Lumber and lumbering—Ter-
    minology
Lunar petrology
 See Moon rocks
* Machine tools
Magalhães, Fernão de, d. 1521
 See Magellan, Ferdinand, d. 1521

* Magellan, Ferdinand, d. 1521
    x Magalhães, Fernão de, d. 1521

† Magic
  sa Magic tricks
  xx Magic tricks

Magic tricks
    Here are entered books of simple
    tricks.
  sa Card tricks
    Magic
    x Conjuring
  xx Card tricks
    Magic

Maize
 See Corn
* Makeup, Theatrical
* Marine animals
    x Marine fauna
Marine fauna
 See Marine animals
Marine flora
 See Marine plants
* Marine plants
    x Marine flora

† Marmots
    Here are entered works on several
    species of marmots.
  sa Woodchuck
Marsh flora
 See Marsh plants

* Marsh plants
    x Marsh flora

* Marsupials

† Mathematical recreations
  sa Counting games
    Number games
    x Creative activities and seat work
* Mayflies

Measuring
    x Mensuration

Mensuration
  See Measuring
† **Mental illness**
  Here are entered works on specific kinds of mental illness and on the special problems encountered by those dealing with mentally ill persons.
  sa Mentally ill
  xx Mentally ill

† **Mentally ill**
  Here are entered works on mentally ill persons and their relationship to their environment.
  sa Mental illness
  xx Mental illness

* **Metalwork**
† **Modeling**
  sa Clay modeling
* **Mole crickets**
* **Monorails**
  Monotremata
  See Monotremes
* **Monotremes**
  x Egg-laying mammals
  Monotremata
* **Moon (in religion, folklore, etc.)**
  Moon rocks
  x Lunar petrology
† **Moths**
** —Collection and preservation
* **Motion picture actors and actresses**
  x Moving-picture actors and actresses
* **Motion picture cartoons**
  x Moving-picture cartoons
* **Motion pictures**
  x Moving-pictures
* **Motion pictures as a profession**
  x Moving-pictures as a profession
  Motor bus drivers
  See Bus drivers
  Motor buses
  See Buses
  Motor trucks
  See Trucks
* **Motorboat racing**
* **Motorboats**
* **Mound builders**
* **Mouth organ**

  Moving-picture actors and actresses
  See Motion picture actors and actresses
  Moving-picture cartoons
  See Motion picture cartoons
  Moving-pictures
  See Motion pictures
  Moving-pictures as a profession
  See Motion pictures as a profession
† **Muscles**
  sa Muscular system
* **Muscular system**
  x Musculoskeletal system
  xx Muscles
  Musculoskeletal system
  See Muscular system
* **Music, Popular**
  Music camps
  xx Camping

* **Mysteries and miracle plays**
* **Mystery and detective stories**
  x Detective and mystery stories
* **Nature printing and nature prints**
* **Negro cowboys**
  x Negroes as cowboys
* **Negro social workers**
  x Negroes as social workers
* **Negro soldiers**
  x Negroes as soldiers
  Negroes as cowboys
  See Negro cowboys
  Negroes as social workers
  See Negro social workers
  Negroes as soldiers
  See Negro soldiers
* **Nonsense verses**
** **Number games**
  sa Counting games
  xx Mathematical recreations
  Number systems
  x Numeration
  Numeration
  See Number systems
† **Odonata**
** —Collection and preservation
* **Orphans**
  Here are entered works on orphans and orphan homes.
* **Outboard motorboats**
  Outlaws
  See Robbers and outlaws
** **Parades**
  Parakeets
** **Parties**
  sa Entertaining
  xx Entertaining
  Pearl diving
  Here are entered works on old methods of diving with rocks, baskets, etc.
  sa Pearl industry and trade
  xx Pearl industry and trade
† **Pearl industry and trade**
  Here are entered works on the modern industry and modern diving methods.
  sa Pearl diving
  xx Pearl diving
  Pennsylvania Germans
  See Germans in Pennsylvania
  Physically handicapped, Teachers of the
  See Teachers of the physically handicapped
† **Photography**
* —Collections
  Here are entered collections of photographs by one or more photographers intended as examples of the art of photography.
  Phytogeography
  See Plant distribution
* **Picture books**
  sa Stories without words
** **Pigs**
  x Swine
* **Pipelines**
* **Plant breeding**

  Plant distribution
  x Geographical distribution of animals and plants
  Phytogeography
* **Planetariums**
† **Play**
  —Fiction
  x Games—Fiction
  Plays
  Here are entered single or collected works by one author or joint authors. Collections of plays by several authors are entered under Plays—Collections.
  —Collections
  x Drama—Collections
  Note under Plays
  —Improvisation
  x Improvisation (Acting)
  —Production and direction
* **Poison ivy**
  Pond flora
  See Pond plants
* **Pond plants**
  x Pond flora
* **Popcorn**
* **Portrait painters**
* **Postage stamps**
† **Poultry**
  sa Chickens
* **Prairie dogs**
* **Prayer books and devotions**
  x Family—Prayer-books and devotions

  Prehistoric animals
  x Animals, Prehistoric
  xx Fossils

* **Prejudices**
$ **Primers**
  This heading is not subdivided by date or subject.
* **Prisoners and prisons**
  Private secretaries
  See Secretaries
† **Puzzles**
  x Creative activities and seat work
† **Race problems**
  sa subdivision Race relations *under place names*
* **Rack railroads**
* **Radio, Shortwave**
† **Railroads, Cable**
  sa Cable cars
$ **Readers**
  This heading is not subdivided by date or subject.
* **Recycling (Waste)**
* **Religious life**
  Here are entered works on the religious and monastic life of monks, priests, saints, nuns, etc.
  sa Christian life
  xx Christian life
  Reproductive system, Female
  x Generative organs, Female
  Reproductive system, Male
  x Generative organs, Male
  Respiratory system

sa Witches
xx Witches

** Witches
Here are entered works on Halloween witches and other witches of fantasy.
sa Witchcraft
xx Witchcraft

Woman
See Women

* Women
x Woman
* —Education
x Education of women
* —History
x History and condition of women
—Rights of women
See Women's rights
Women as teachers
See Women teachers
* Women teachers
x Women as teachers

* Women's rights
x Women—Rights of women

* Wood carving

Woodchuck
x Groundhog
xx Marmots

* X rays
Zoogeography
See Animal distribution

Symbols

sa *(see also)*   indicates a reference to a related or subordinate topic

x *(see from)*   indicates a reference from an expression not itself used as a heading

xx *(see also from)*   indicates a related heading from which a *sa* reference is made

Library of Congress Subject Headings

4-H clubs *(Indirect)* *(S533)*
  sa International farm youth exchange
    project
  xx Agricultural education
    Boys—Societies and clubs
    Girls—Societies and clubs
 — Accounting
 — Juvenile literature
 — Public relations
    x Public relations—4-H clubs
97 Sen (Fighter planes)
  x Nakajima Ki. 27 (Fighter planes)
  xx Fighter planes
A-5 rocket
  xx Rockets (Ordnance)
    V-1 bomb
    V-2 rocket
A-20 bomber
  x Boston bomber
    Havoc bomber
  xx Bombers
A-36 (Fighter-bomber planes)
  See Mustang (Fighter planes)
A-C carrier control systems
  See Carrier control systems
A.D.C.
  See Child welfare
A Distinctly Empirical Prover of Theorems
  See ADEPT (Computer program)
A.J.S. motorcycle
A priori
  x Apriori
  xx Knowledge, Theory of
    Logic
    Reasoning
A3D bomber
  See Skywarrior bomber
A3J Vigilante (Bomber)
  See Vigilante bomber
A4D bomber
  See Skyhawk bomber
Aachen
 — Siege, 1944
    xx World War, 1939-1945—Campaigns
      —Germany
Aardvark *(QL737.E2)*
  x Ant bear
  xx Tubulidentata
Aarhus, Denmark
 — Great Lockout, 1899

Aaronic Priesthood (Mormonism)
    (BX8643.A2)
  x Mormons and Mormonism—Aaronic
    Priesthood
  xx Priesthood, Universal
Aba-Mbos
  See Fingos
Ababua language *(PL8035)*
  xx Bantu languages
Ababuas
  x Babuas
    Mangbuas
  xx Ethnology—Zaire
Abaca
  See Manila hemp
Abacus *(QA75)*
  sa Quipu
  x Soroban
  xx Mathematical instruments
    Quipu
  Note under Digital counters
 — Pictorial works
Abalones *(QL430.5.H3)*
  x Ear-shells
    Ormers
    Sea-ears
  xx Gasteropoda
    Shellfish fisheries
 — Behavior
Abalones, Fossil *(QE809.A)*
Abaluyia (Bantu tribe)
  See Baluyia (Bantu tribe)
Abambos
  See Fingos
Abandon-ship food packets
  See Survival and emergency rations
Abandoned children *(Direct)* *(HV873-887)*
  sa Foundlings
    Orphans and orphan-asylums
  x Children, Abandoned
  xx Child welfare
    Children
    Orphans and orphan-asylums
 — Law and legislation *(Direct)*
    xx Children—Law
Abandoned vehicles
  See Abandonment of automobiles
Abandonment (Marine insurance)
  See Insurance, Marine
Abandonment (Maritime law) *(Direct)*
  xx Debtor and creditor
    Liability (Law)

    Limited liability
    Maritime law
Abandonment of automobiles *(Direct)*
  x Abandoned vehicles
    Automobiles—Abandonment
  xx Abandonment of property
    Automobiles—Environmental aspects
    Automobiles—Laws and regulations
Abandonment of family
  See Desertion and non-support
Abandonment of property *(Direct)*
  sa Abandonment of automobiles
    Refugee property
  x Dereliction (Civil law)
  xx Bona vacantia
    Possession (Law)
    Property
    Renunciation (Law)
Abandonment of property (Roman law)
Abarambo language
  See Barambu language
Abatement of taxes
  See Tax remission
Abattoirs
  See Slaughtering and slaughter-houses
    subdivision Slaughter-houses *under*
    names of cities
Abazin language *(PK9201.A2)*
  xx Caucasian languages
 — Tapanta dialect
    See Tapanta dialect
Abbadides
  xx Spain—History—Arab period, 711-1492
Abbasids *(DS234-8)*
  xx Arabs
    Caliphs
    Islamic Empire
    Mesopotamia—History—634-1534
Abbé language
  See Abe language
Abbey language
  See Abe language
Abbeys *(Indirect)* *(Architecture,*
    NA4800-6113; Church history,
    BX2501-2749; Local history, D-F)
  sa Cathedrals
    Convents and nunneries
    Monasteries
    Priories
  xx Architecture
    Church architecture
    Church history

Abbeys *(Indirect) (Architecture,*
NA4800-6113; Church history,
BX2501-2749; Local history, D-F)
(Continued)
    Convents and nunneries
    Monasteries
  — Pictorial works
Abbots *(Indirect)*
   xx Christian biography
    Superiors, Religious
  — Appointment, call, and election
Abbots (Canon law) *(BX1939.A)*
   xx Bishops (Canon law)
    Monasticism and religious orders
     (Canon law)
Abbots nullius (Canon law)
   xx Bishops (Canon law)
Abbreviations
   sa Acronyms
    Ciphers
    Code names
    Periodicals—Abbreviations of titles
    Shorthand
    Signs and symbols
    Technical reports—Abbreviations of
     titles
    subdivision Abbreviations *under*
     subjects, e.g. Associations,
     institutions, etc.—Abbreviations;
     Law—Abbreviations
   x Brachygraphy
    Chemical symbols
    Contractions
   xx Ciphers
    Paleography
    Shorthand
    Signs and symbols
    Writing
Abbreviations, English, ₍French, Hebrew, etc.₎
   x English ₍French, Hebrew, etc.₎ language
    —Abbreviations
Abbreviations, Legal
  See Law—Abbreviations
Abderhalden reaction
   xx Blood—Analysis and chemistry
    Chemical reactions
    Chemical tests and reagents
    Enzymes
Abdomen *(Regional anatomy, QM543)*
   sa Abdominal compression reaction
    Groin
    Intestines
    Kidneys
    Liver
    Peritoneum
    Stomach
    Viscera
   xx Viscera
  — Abscess
  — Blood-vessels
  — — Radiography
  — Cancer *(RC280.A2; RD668)*
  — Diseases *(RC944)*
    sa Abdomen—Radiography
    Abdominal angina
    Abdominal pain
    Acute abdomen
  — — Atlases
  — Examination
   x Celioscopy
  — Paracentesis
  — Radiography
   xx Abdomen—Diseases
  — Surgery *(RD540-547)*
    sa Appendicitis
    Intestines—Surgery
   x Laparotomy
    Surgery, Abdominal
    Example under Surgery

— — Atlases
— Tumors *(RC280.A2; RD668)*
— Wounds and injuries *(RD131)*
Abdominal aneurysm
   xx Aortic aneurysms
Abdominal angina
   x Angina abdominis
   xx Abdomen—Diseases
Abdominal aorta
   xx Aorta
  — Radiography
  — Surgery
Abdominal compression reaction
   xx Abdomen
    Muscles
    Reflexes
    Respiration
Abdominal decompression
   x Decompression, Abdominal
   xx Atmospheric pressure—Physiological
    effect
    Therapeutics, Physiological
Abdominal pain
   sa Acute abdomen
   xx Abdomen—Diseases
    Diagnosis
Abduction *(Direct) (HV6571-4)*
   sa Kidnapping
   xx Criminal law
    Impediments to marriage
    Kidnapping
    Offenses against the person
Abduction (Canon law)
Abduction (Logic)
   xx Logic
    Reasoning
    Syllogism
Abduction (Roman law)
Abe language
   x Abbé language
    Abbey language
   xx Kwa languages
Abelam (New Guinea tribe)
   xx Ethnology—New Guinea
Abelian categories
   x Categories, Abelian
   xx Categories (Mathematics)
Abelian equations
  See Equations, Abelian
Abelian functions
  See Functions, Abelian
Abelian groups *(QA171)*
   sa Homology theory
   x Commutative groups
   xx Groups, Theory of
Abelian varieties
   x Varieties, Abelian
   xx Geometry, Algebraic
Abercrombie's Ticonderoga Campaign, 1758
   sa Ticonderoga, Battle of, 1758
Aberdeen-Angus cattle *(SF193.A14;*
    SF199.A14)
   x Angus cattle
    Polled Aberdeen cattle
    Polled Angus cattle
   xx Beef cattle
   Example under Cattle breeds
Aberfan, Wales
  — Landslides
Aberratio ictus *(Direct)*
   xx Criminal attempt
    Criminal intent
Aberration *(Astronomy, QB163; Physics,*
    QC671)
   xx Astronomy, Spherical and practical
    Optics
Aberration, Chromatic and spherical
  See Achromatism

    Lenses
    Mirrors
    Optical instruments
Abert squirrel *(QL737.R68)*
   xx Squirrels
Abettors
  See Accomplices
Abherents
   x Parting agents
    Release agents
    Slip agents
   xx Adhesion
    Surface chemistry
  — Patents
Abhidharma
   sa Matter (Buddhism)
   xx Buddha and Buddhism
    Philosophy, Buddhist
Abhiras
  See Abhirs
Abietic acid *(QD341.A2)*
   x Sylvic acid
Abigar language
  See Nuer language
Ability
   sa Athletic ability
    Creative ability
    Educational acceleration
    Executive ability
    Inefficiency, Intellectual
    Leadership
    Learning ability
    Mathematical ability
    Mechanical ability
    Mental tests
    Motor ability
    Musical ability
    Spelling ability
   xx Executive ability
    Psychology
    Success
  — Testing *(BF431)*
    sa Clergy, Rating of
    Clerical ability and aptitude tests
    Comprehension—Testing
    Creative ability—Testing
    Employees, Rating of
    Executives, Rating of
    General aptitude test battery
    Lincoln-Oseretsky motor
     development scale
    Mathematical ability—Testing
    Maze tests
    Mechanical ability—Testing
    Mental tests
    Motor ability—Testing
    Moving-pictures in ability testing
    Musical ability—Testing
    Occupational aptitude tests
    Physical fitness—Testing
    Prediction of scholastic success
    Scholastic aptitude test
    School superintendents and
     principals, Rating of
    Selective service college qualification
     test
    Self-evaluation
    Spelling ability—Testing
    Supervisors, Rating of
    Teachers, Rating of
    United States. Army—Officer
     efficiency reports
    subdivision Ability testing *under*
     subjects, e.g. Salesmen and
     salesmanship—Ability testing
   x Ability tests
    Aptitude tests
   xx Educational tests and measurements

Employees, Rating of
Prediction (Psychology)
Teachers, Rating of
Ability, Distribution of
Ability, Executive
See Executive ability
Ability, Influence of age on
   sa Age and employment
   xx Adult education
      Age and employment
      Mental discipline
      Mind and body
      Old age
Ability, Mechanical
   See Mechanical ability
Ability, Musical
   See Musical ability
Ability grouping in education *(LB3061)*
   sa Educational acceleration
      Nongraded schools
   x Classification of school children
      Graded schools
      Grouping by ability
      Grouping, Homogeneous
      Homogeneous grouping
      Streaming (Education)
   xx Education
      Educational psychology
      Grading and marking (Students)
      Mental tests
      School management and organization
Ability tests
   See Ability—Testing
Abiogenesis
   See Life—Origin
      Spontaneous generation
Abiosis
   See Cryptobiosis
Abipone Indians *(F2230.2)*
   xx Guaycuru Indians
      Indians of South America
Abipone language *(PM5301)*
   sa Guaycuruan languages
   xx Guaycuruan languages
      Indians of South America—Languages
Abiri language
   See Birri language
Abitibi Indians *(E99.A12)*
   x Abittibi Indians
   xx Algonquian Indians
      Indians of North America
Abittibi Indians
   See Abitibi Indians
Abkhasians
   See Abkhazians
Abkhazian drama *(Direct)*
Abkhazian language *(PK9201.A3)*
   xx Caucasian languages
Abkhazian philology *(PK9201.A2)*
Abkhazian poetry *(Direct)* *(Collections,*
      PK9201.A37; History, PK9201.A35)
Abkhazians *(DK34.A)*
   x Abkhasians
   xx Ethnology—Caucasus
ABL automatic rifles
   See Fabrique nationale automatic rifles
Ablation (Aerothermodynamics)
   x Ablation phenomena
      Atmospheric entry problems
   xx Aerothermodynamics
      Heat—Transmission
      Mass transfer
      Melting points
      Vaporization, Heats of
Ablation phenomena
   See Ablation (Aerothermodynamics)
ABM (Antiballistic missiles)
   See Antimissile missiles

Abnaki calendar
   See Calendar, Abnaki
Abnaki Indians *(E99.A13)*
   sa Arosaguntacook Indians
      Malecite Indians
      Passamaquoddy Indians
      Penobscot Indians
      Wawenock Indians
   x Kennebec Indians
      Tarratine Indians
      Wabanaki Indians
   xx Algonquian Indians
      Indians of North America
   — Calendar
      See Calendar, Abnaki
   — Legends
   — — Juvenile literature
   — Missions
   — Treaties *(E99.A13)*
Abnaki language *(PM551)*
   xx Algonquian languages
      Penobscot language
Abnormal children
   See Exceptional children
      Handicapped children
Abnormal E (Ionosphere)
   See Sporadic E (Ionosphere)
Abnormal psychology
   See Psychology, Pathological
Abnormal reflexes
   See Reflexes, Abnormal
Abnormalities
   See Deformities
      Monsters
Abnormalities (Animals) *(QL991)*
      Works on abnormalities in a particular
      animal are entered here and also under
      name of animal, *e.g.* 1. Abnormalities
      (Animals) 2. Cats. Works on physical
      abnormalities in man are entered un-
      der the heading Deformities.
   sa subdivision Abnormities and
      deformities *under names of organs,*
      regions and systems of the body, e.g.
      Eye—Abnormities and deformities;
      Head—Abnormities and deformities;
      Nervous system—Abnormities and
      deformities
   x Animals, Abnormalities of
      Teratology
   xx Monsters
      Morphology (Animals)
Abnormalities (Plants) *(QK664)*
      Works on abnormalities in a particular
      plant are entered here and also under
      name of plant, *e.g.* 1. Abnormalities
      (Plants) 2. Podophyllum.
   sa Peloria
      Prolification
   x Botany—Teratology
      Fasciations
      Plants—Deformities
      Teratology
   xx Botany—Anatomy
      Botany—Morphology
      Plants
Abolition of slavery
   See Abolitionists
      Slavery
Abolitionists
   x Abolition of slavery
   xx Slavery in the United States
   — Juvenile literature
Aborigines
   See Ethnology
      Native races
      names of aboriginal races, e.g. Indians

Aborigines, Australian
   See Australian aborigines
Abors *(DS485.A86)*
   sa Gallongs
      Shimongs
   x Adis
   xx Ethnology—Assam
   — Anthropometry
   — Religion
Abortifacients
   xx Abortion
Abortion *(Direct)* *(HQ767; Medical*
      jurisprudence, RA1067; Obstetrical
      operations, RG734; Obstetrics,
      RG648)
   sa Abortifacients
   x Feticide
      Miscarriage
   xx Birth control
      Criminal law
      Fetus, Death of the
      Infanticide
      Obstetrics
      Offenses against the person
      Sex and law
   — Complications and sequelae
   — Personal narratives
   — Psychological aspects
   — Public opinion
   — Religious aspects
Abortion, Septic
   x Septic abortion
Abortion, Therapeutic
   x Therapeutic abortion
Abortion (Canon law)
Abortion (Jewish law) *(Direct)*
Abortion in animals *(SF871)*
   sa Brucellosis in cattle
   xx Cattle—Diseases
      Horses—Diseases
      Veterinary medicine
Aboukir, Battle of, 1798
   See Nile, Battle of the, 1798
Aboukir, Battle of, 1801
   See Alexandria, Battle of, 1801
Abrahamites (Bohemia)
   x Bohemian Deists
      Deists, Bohemian
      Israelites (Bohemia)
Abrasive industry
   See Abrasives industry
Abrasive wheels
   See Grinding wheels
Abrasives *(Mechanical engineering, TJ1296;*
      Mineral resources, TN936)
   sa Abrasives industry
      Grinding wheels
      Shot (Pellets)
   xx Ceramics
   — Standards *(Direct)*
   — Testing *(TA455.A3)*
Abrasives industry *(Direct)*
   x Abrasive industry
   xx Abrasives
   — Accounting *(HF5686.A15)*
   — Automation *(TJ1296)*
   — Collective labor agreements
      See Collective labor agreements—
          Abrasives industry
   — Costs
Abri dialect (Sudan)
   See Nirere dialect
Abridged books
   See Books, Condensed
Abrogation of legislation
   See Repeal of legislation
Abron (African people)
   x Brong (African people)

Abron (African people) *(Continued)*
  xx Ethnology—Africa, Central
        Ethnology—Africa, West
Absahrokee Indians
  See Crow Indians
Absaroka Indians
  See Crow Indians
Abscess *(RD641)*
  sa Subphrenic abscess
        Suppuration
        subdivision Abscess *under names of*
          organs and regions of the body, e.g.
          Liver—Abscess; Pelvis—Abscess
  xx Suppuration
        Ulcers
Abscission (Botany) *(QK763)*
  sa Defoliation
  x Plants—Shedding
        Shedding (Botany)
  xx Defoliation
Absence, Leave of
  See Leave of absence
Absence and presumption of death *(Direct)*
  sa Civil death
        Death—Proof and certification
  x Absentees (Law)
        Death, Declaration of
        Death, Presumption of
        Declaration of death
        Presumption of death
  xx Civil death
        Death—Proof and certification
        Missing persons
  — Conflict of laws
        See Conflict of laws—Absence and
          presumption of death
**Absence and presumption of death (Canon
  law)** *(BX1939)*
**Absence and presumption of death (Islamic
  law)**
**Absence and presumption of death (Jewish
  law)**
  sa Agunah
Absence from school
  See School attendance
Absence without leave *(Direct)*
  x Absent without leave
        AWOL
  xx Military offenses
Absent treatment
  See Mental healing
Absent voting
  See Voting, Absent
Absent without leave
  See Absence without leave
Absentee voting
  See Voting, Absent
Absenteeism
  xx Agriculture—Economic aspects
        Land tenure
        Taxation
Absenteeism (Labor) *(Direct)* *(HD5115)*
  sa Sick leave
  x Employee absenteeism
        Labor absenteeism
  xx Labor and laboring classes
        Labor supply
        Personnel management
Absentees (Law)
  See Absence and presumption of death
Absinthe
  Example under Liqueurs
Absite
  See Brannerite
Absolute, The *(BD416)*
  sa Brahman
        One (The One in philosophy)
  xx Metaphysics

One (The One in philosophy)
        Ontology
Absolute differential calculus
  See Calculus of tensors
Absolute liability
  See Strict liability
Absolute rights
  See Natural law
Absolution
  sa Confession
        Forgiveness of sin
        Indulgences
        Penance
        Power of the keys
  xx Church discipline
        Confession
        Forgiveness of sin
        Indulgences
        Penance
Absolution (Canon law) *(BX1939.A)*
  x Reserved cases (Canon law)
  xx Faculties (Canon law)
        Penance (Canon law)
Absolutism
  See Despotism
Absorbent paper
  xx Paper
Absorptiometer
  xx Absorption of light
        Spectrophotometer
        Spectrum analysis—Instruments
Absorption
  sa Gases—Absorption and adsorption
        Photoabsorption
        Sorbents
  x Sorption
  xx Chemistry, Physical and theoretical
        Packed towers
Absorption, Atmospheric
  See Solar radiation
Absorption (Heat)
  See Heat—Radiation and absorption
Absorption (Physiology) *(QP88)*
  sa Chyle
        Digestion
        Fat
        Ingestion
        Intestinal absorption
        Lymphatics
        Osmosis
        Pinocytosis
        Plants—Absorption of water
        Skin
  xx Biological physics
        Nutrition
        Osmosis
        Physiological chemistry
        Physiology
Absorption in soils
  See Soil absorption
Absorption of gases
  See Gases—Absorption and adsorption
Absorption of light *(QC437)*
  sa Absorptiometer
        Interstellar reddening
  x Selective absorption
  xx Light
        Optics
Absorption of sound *(QC233)*
  sa Anechoic chambers
        Architectural acoustics
        Soundproofing
  x Sound absorption
        Sound—Absorption
  xx Architectural acoustics
        Sound
  — Charts, diagrams, etc.
  — Measurement

  — Tables, etc.
Absorption spectra *(QC437)*
  sa Astronomical spectroscopy
        Atomic absorption spectroscopy
        Fraunhofer lines
        Heat—Radiation and absorption
        Internal reflection spectroscopy
        Molecular spectra
        Spectrum analysis
        subdivision Spectra *under subjects, e.g.*
        Drugs—Spectra
  x Selective absorption
  xx Exciton theory
        Spectrum analysis
  — Punched card systems
        See Punched card systems—
          Absorption spectra
  — Tables, etc.
Abstinence
  See Fasting
        Temperance
Abstract algebra
  See Algebra, Abstract
Abstract and title companies
  See Title companies
Abstract art
  See Art, Abstract
Abstract automata
  See Machine theory
Abstract cinematography
  See Cinematography, Abstract
Abstract companies
  See Title companies
Abstract expressionism *(Direct)*
  sa Color-field painting
  xx Art, Abstract
        Expressionism (Art)
Abstract impressionism
  xx Art, Abstract
        Impressionism (Art)
Abstract machines
  See Machine theory
Abstract metrics
  See Distance geometry
Abstract paintings
  See Art, Abstract
Abstract photography
  See Photography, Abstract
Abstract writing
  See Abstracting
Abstracters (Land titles)
  See Title companies
Abstracting *(English, PE1477)*
  sa Indexing
        subdivision Abstracting and indexing
          under specific subjects, e.g.
          Chemistry—Abstracting and
          indexing
  x Abstract writing
        Précis writing
  xx Content analysis (Communication)
        Documentation
        Rhetoric
  — Chronology
Abstracting and indexing services *(Indirect)*
  sa Information storage and retrieval
          systems
  x Indexing and abstracting services
  xx Bibliography
        Documentation
        Indexes
  — Costs
Abstraction
  sa Categorization (Psychology)
        Concepts
  xx Attention
        Educational psychology
        Logic

4

Psychology
Abstraction in photography
    See Photography, Abstract
Abstracts
    sa Dissertations, Academic—Abstracts
        subdivision Abstracts *under specific*
            subjects, e.g. Science—Abstracts
Abstracts of title   *(Direct)*
    sa Conveyancing
        Deeds
        Land titles
        Title companies
        Title examinations
    xx Conveyancing
        Deeds
        Real property
        Vendors and purchasers
Abua language
    x Abuan language
    xx Abua-Ogbia languages
Abua-Ogbia languages   *(PL8037)*
    sa Abua language
    x Kugbo dialect
        Odual dialect
        Ogbia dialect
Abuan language
    See Abua language
Abukir, Battle of, 1801
    See Alexandria, Battle of, 1801
Abulas language
Abuse
    See Invective
Abuse of administrative power   *(Direct)*
    sa Amparo (Writ)
        Ombudsman
    x Administrative power, Abuse of
        Excess of power (Administrative law)
    xx Administrative discretion
        Administrative law
        Judicial review of administrative acts
Abuse of administrative power (Roman law)
Abuse of power
    See Despotism
Abuse of process
    See False imprisonment
        Process
Abusive treatment (Divorce)
    See Legal cruelty
Abyss
Abyss in literature
Abyssal zone
    sa Ocean bottom
    x Deep-sea zone
    xx Ocean bottom
        Oceanography
Abyssinian cat   *(SF449.A)*
Abyssinian Church
    See Ethiopic Church
Abyssinian Expedition, 1867-1868   *(DT386.3;*
        Natural history, QH195.A2)
Abyssinian manuscripts
    See Manuscripts, Ethiopic
Abyssinian music
    See Music, Ethiopic
Abyssino-Italian War, 1895-1896
    See Italo-Ethiopian War, 1895-1896
Acacia
    sa Locust (Tree)
        Wattle (Tree)
    xx Leguminosae
    — Diseases and pests   *(Indirect)*
            (SB608.A)
Acacia (Gum)
    See Gum arabic
Acacian Schism
    See Schism, Acacian, 484-519
Academic achievement
    sa Motivation in education

Prediction of scholastic success
    x Achievement, Academic
        Scholastic success
    xx Success
Academic achievement and personality
    See Personality and academic achievement
Academic adjustment
    See Student adjustment
Academic costume   *(LB2389)*
    x Academic dress
        Caps and gowns
        College gowns
        Gowns, College
        Hoods
    xx Costume
Academic decorations of honor
    See Decorations of honor, Academic
Academic degrees
    See Degrees, Academic
Academic dishonesty
    See Cheating (Education)
Academic dissertations
    See Dissertations, Academic
Academic dress
    See Academic costume
Academic etiquette
    x Academic protocol
        Protocol, Academic
    xx Etiquette
Academic freedom
    See Teaching, Freedom of
        University autonomy
Academic librarians
    See College librarians
Academic motivation
    See Motivation in education
Academic probation
    See College attendance
Academic protocol
    See Academic etiquette
Academic terms
    See Universities and colleges—Terminology
Academies, Catholic
    See Catholic academies
Academies, Evangelical
    See Evangelical academies
Academies, Talmudic
    See Talmudic academies
Academies (Learned societies)
    See Learned institutions and societies
        Societies
Academy awards (Moving-pictures)
    x Moving-picture academy awards
        Moving-pictures—Academy awards
        Oscars (Moving-pictures)
    xx Moving-pictures—Awards
Acadian chickadee
    See Brown-headed chickadee
Acadian flycatcher
Acadians
    xx French-Canadians
Acadians in Louisiana, [Maine, the United
        States, etc.]
    — Juvenile literature
    — Registers
    — Songs and music
Acagchemin Indians
    See Juaneño Indians
Acalculia   *(RJ496.A25)*
    xx Brain—Diseases
        Mathematical ability
Acanthocephala   *(QL391.A2)*
    xx Nemathelminthes
        Worms, Intestinal and parasitic
Acanthodii
    xx Fishes, Fossil
Acantholysis bullosa
    See Epidermolysis bullosa

Acari
    See Mites
Acaricides
    See Miticides
Acarida
    See Mites
Acaridea
    See Mites
Acarina
    See Mites
        Ticks
Acarology   *(QL458.A2)*
    sa Mites
        Ticks
    xx Mites
        Ticks
        Zoology
Acaxee Indians   *(F1219)*
    xx Indians of Mexico
Accadians (Sumerians)
    See Sumerians
Accawai Indians
    sa Patamona Indians
    x Akavais Indians
    xx Carib Indians
        Indians of South America
Accawai language   *(PM5308)*
    sa Cariban languages
    xx Cariban languages
        Indians of South America—Languages
Accelerated conduction
    See Wolff-Parkinson-White syndrome
Accelerated erosion
    See Soil erosion
Accelerated reading
    See Developmental reading
        Rapid reading
Acceleration, Negative
    See Acceleration (Mechanics)
Acceleration (Mechanics)
    sa Inertia (Mechanics)
    x Acceleration, Negative
        Deceleration
    xx Mechanics
        Motion
        Speed
Acceleration (Physiology)
    sa Human centrifuge
    xx Space medicine
        Stress (Physiology)
    — Electromechanical analogies
Acceleration in education
    See Educational acceleration
Acceleration principle (Economics)
    x Accelerator (Economics)
    xx Capital investments—Mathematical
        models
Accelerator, Van de Graaff
    See Van de Graaff generator
Accelerator (Economics)
    See Acceleration principle (Economics)
Accelerators, Electron
    See Particle accelerators
Accelerators, Linear
    See Linear accelerators
Accelerators, Plasma
    See Plasma accelerators
Accelerators, Vulcanization
    See Vulcanization accelerators
Accelerometers   *(TL589.2.A3)*
    sa Speedometers
    xx Aeronautical instruments
        Speed-indicators
        Vibration—Measurement
    — Testing
Accents and accentuation
    sa subdivision Accents and accentuation
        under names of languages

5

Accents and accentuation *(Continued)*
    x Grammar, Comparative and general—
        Accents and accentuation
        Language and languages—Accents and
          accentuation
        Language and languages—Stress
        Stress (Linguistics)
    xx Versification
Accentuation (Music)
    See Musical accentuation
Acceptance, Social
    See Social acceptance
Acceptance (Contracts)
    See Offer and acceptance
Acceptance sampling *(TS156.4)*
    xx Quality control
        Sampling (Statistics)
    — Tables
Acceptance trials of ships
    See Ship trials
Acceptances
    Here are entered works on trade or bank
    acceptances as credit instruments.
    Works on the legal aspects of accept-
    ances are entered under the heading
    Bills of exchange.
    sa Bills of exchange
        Discount
    xx Banks and banking
        Bills of exchange
        Credit
        Discount
        Drafts
        Negotiable instruments
    — Taxation
        See Bills of exchange—Taxation
Acceptilation
    See Extinguishment of debts (Roman law)
Access roads to airports
    See Airports—Access roads
Access roads to ferries
    See Ferries—Access roads
Access to airports *(Direct) (TL725.3.A2)*
    sa Airports—Access roads
    x Airport access
        Transportation to airports
    xx Airports
        Urban transportation
Access to books in libraries
    See Open and closed shelves
Access to documents in archives
    See Restricted collections in archives
Access to the sea (International law)
    xx Maritime law
        Transit by land (International law)
Accession (Law) *(Direct)*
    sa Accretion (Law)
        Confusion of goods
        Specification (Civil law)
    xx Accretion (Law)
        Acquisition of property
        Alluvion
        Confusion of goods
        Specification (Civil law)
Accession to treaties
    See Treaties—Accession
Accessions, Cooperative (Libraries)
    See Acquisitions, Cooperative (Libraries)
Accessories, Road
    See Roads—Accessories
Accessories (Civil law)
    See Appurtenances
Accessories (Criminal law)
    See Accomplices
Accessories (Dress)
    See Dress accessories
Accessory contracts
    See Accessory obligations

Accessory obligations *(Direct)*
    sa Mortgages
        Pledges (Law)
        Suretyship and quaranty
    x Accessory contracts
    xx Contracts
        Obligations (Law)
Accident (Casus fortuitus) *(Direct)*
    sa Vis major (Civil law)
    x Casus fortuitus
    xx Contracts
        Impossibility of performance
        Liability (Law)
        Vis major (Civil law)
Accident insurance
    See Insurance, Accident
Accident law *(Direct)*
    sa Assistance in emergencies
        Damages
        Employers' liability
        Fireworks—Laws and regulations
        Industrial safety—Law and legislation
        Liability for aircraft accidents
        Liability for building accidents
        Liability for marine accidents
        Liability for mine accidents
        Liability for nuclear damages
        Liability for railroad accidents
        Liability for school accidents
        Liability for skiing accidents
        Liability for space vehicle accidents
        Liability for sports accidents
        Liability for traffic accidents
        Negligence
        Negligence, Contributory
        Personal injuries
        Torts
        Traffic violations
        Workmen's compensation
    x Accidents—Laws and legislation
        Injuries (Law)
        Law, Accident
    xx Negligence
        Occupations, Dangerous
        Personal injuries
        Torts
    — Cases
Accident neuroses
    See Traumatic neuroses
Accident prevention
    See Accidents—Prevention
Accident proneness
    See Accidents—Psychological aspects
Accidental nuclear excursions
    See Nuclear reactors—Accidents—1961
Accidents *(Direct)*
    sa Ambulance service
        Ambulances
        Asphyxia
        Assistance in emergencies
        Burns and scalds
        Children's accidents
        Crash injuries
        Disasters
        Drowning
        Dust explosion
        Electricity, Injuries from
        Employers' liability
        Explosions
        Falls (Accidents)
        Fires
        First aid in illness and injury
        Foreign bodies (Surgery)
        Home accidents
        Ice accidents
        Industrial accidents
        Life-saving
        Lightning

        Marine accidents
        Medical emergencies
        Mine accidents
        Motor-boats—Accidents and injuries
        Nursing home accidents
        Occupations, Dangerous
        Office accidents
        Physically handicapped
        Poisons
        School accidents
        Shipwrecks
        Shock
        Steam-boiler explosions
        Steamboat disasters
        Traffic accidents
        Traumatism
        subdivision Accidents *under subjects,*
          e.g. Coal mines and mining—
          Accidents; Theaters—Accidents; *also*
          subdivision Accidents and injuries
          under sports and games, e.g. Sports
          —Accidents and injuries; Football—
          Accidents and injuries; *also*
          subdivision Wounds and injuries
          under names of regions and organs
          of the body; and subdivision
          Ambulance service *under names of*
          cities, e.g. London—Ambulance
          service
    x Emergencies
        Emergencies, Medical
        Injuries
    xx Disasters
        Diseases—Causes and theories of
          causation
        First aid in illness and injury
        Medical emergencies
        Violent deaths
    — Adjustment of claims
    — Laws and legislation
        See Accident law
    — Prevention *(HV675-7)*
        sa Eye—Protection
          Industrial safety
          Safety education
          Safety education, Industrial
          Safety regulations
          Safety signs
          subdivisions Safety appliances *and*
          Safety measures *under subjects,*
          e.g. Railroads—Safety appliances;
          Automobiles—Safety measures
        x Accident prevention
          Prevention of accidents
        xx Occupations, Dangerous—Safety
          appliances
          Safety appliances
    — — Film catalogs
    — — Juvenile literature
    — — Study and teaching
        See Safety education
    — Psychological aspects
        x Accident proneness
Accidents, Aircraft
    See Aeronautics—Accidents
Accidents, Home
    See Home accidents
Accidents, Industrial
    See Industrial accidents
Accidents, Marine
    See Marine accidents
Accidents, Occupational
    See Industrial accidents
Accidents, School
    See School accidents
Accidents, Spacecraft
    See Astronautics—Accidents

Accidents, Traffic
   See Traffic accidents
Acclamations (Liturgy)
   x Liturgical acclamations
   xx Liturgies
      Rites and ceremonies
Acclimatization *(Indirect)* *(Animal culture, SF87; Zoology, QH543)*
   sa Altitude, Influence of
      Animal introduction
      Man—Influence of climate
      Stock and stock-breeding
      Tropics—Diseases and hygiene
   x Environment
   xx Adaptation (Biology)
      Bioclimatology
      Biology
      Man—Influence of climate
      Man—Influence of environment
      Stock and stock-breeding
      Tropics—Diseases and hygiene
      Zoology—Ecology
Acclimatization (Plants) *(Indirect)* *(Botany, QK913; Plant culture, SB109)*
   sa Botany—Ecology
      Plant introduction
   xx Agriculture
      Botany
      Botany—Ecology
      Gardening
      Horticulture
      Phytogeography
      Plant introduction
      Plants
Accommodation (Psychology)
   See Adjustment (Psychology)
Accommodation coefficient
   xx Gases—Absorption and adsorption
Accommodation indorsements *(Direct)*
   x Aval
      Indorsements, Accommodation
   xx Bills of exchange
      Indorsements
      Suretyship and guaranty
Accompaniment, Musical
   See Musical accompaniment
Accomplices *(Direct)*
   sa Principals (Criminal law)
      Receiving stolen goods
      Respondeat superior
   x Abettors
      Accessories (Criminal law)
      Principal and accessory
   xx Criminal law
      Principals (Criminal law)
Accomplices (Canon law) *(BX1939.A25)*
   xx Criminal law (Canon law)
Accord and satisfaction *(Direct)*
   sa Composition (Law)
      Compromise (Law)
      Novation
   x Dation in payment
   xx Discharge of contracts
      Payment
      Performance (Law)
Accord and satisfaction (Roman law)
   x Datio in solutum
Accordeon
   See Accordion
Accordion *(History and construction, ML990.A4)*
   sa Bandonion
      Concertina
   x Accordeon
      Piano accordion
   xx Bandonion
      Concertina
   Example under Musical instruments

— Construction *(ML990.A4)*
— Instruction and study *(MT680)*
   sa Accordion music—Teaching pieces
— Methods
— — Juvenile *(MT801.A3)*
— — Self-instruction *(MT680)*
   x Accordion—Self-instruction
— Self-instruction
   See Accordion—Methods—
      Self-instruction
Accordion and guitar music *(M298)*
   x Guitar and accordion music
Accordion and piano music *(M284.A3; M285.A3)*
   sa Concertos (Accordion)—Solo with piano
   x Piano and accordion music
Accordion and piano music (Jazz) *(M284.A3; M285.A3)*
Accordion and vibraphone music
   See Vibraphone and accordion music
Accordion and zither music
   See Zither and accordion music
Accordion band
   See Accordion ensembles
Accordion ensembles
      Here are entered compositions for two or more accordions.
   sa Canons, fugues, etc. (Accordion ensemble)
      Country-dances (Accordion ensemble)
      Gavottes (Accordion ensemble)
      Minuets (Accordion ensemble)
      Polonaises (Accordion ensemble)
      Waltzes (Accordion ensemble)
   x Accordion band
   xx Accordion music
      Instrumental music
Accordion music *(M175.A4)*
   sa Accordion ensembles
      Accordion with chamber orchestra
      Accordion with orchestra
      Accordion with plectral ensemble
      Accordion with string orchestra
      Canons, fugues, etc. (Accordion)
      Concertos (Accordion)
      Concertos (Accordion with chamber orchestra)
      Concertos (Accordion with plectral ensemble)
      Concertos (Accordion with string orchestra)
      Ländler (Accordion)
      Marches (Accordion)
      Overtures arranged for accordion
      Polkas (Accordion)
      Rondos (Accordion)
      Sonatas (Accordion)
      Suites (Accordion)
      Tangos (Accordion)
      Waltzes (Accordion)
      Quartets, [Trios, etc.] *followed by specifications which include the accordion*
— Teaching pieces *(MT680)*
   xx Accordion—Instruction and study
Accordion music (Jazz) *(M175.A4)*
Accordion with chamber orchestra *(M1039.4.A3)*
   sa Concertos (Accordion with chamber orchestra)
   xx Accordion music
      Chamber-orchestra music
      Concertos (Accordion with chamber orchestra)
Accordion with orchestra *(M1039.4.A3)*
   sa Concertos (Accordion)
      Suites (Accordion with orchestra)

   xx Accordion music
      Concertos (Accordion)
      Orchestral music
Accordion with plectral ensemble *(M1360)*
   sa Concertos (Accordion with plectral ensemble)
   xx Accordion music
      Concertos (Accordion with plectral ensemble)
      Plectral ensembles
Accordion with string orchestra *(M1105-6)*
   sa Concertos (Accordion with string orchestra)
   xx Accordion music
      Concertos (Accordion with string orchestra)
      String-orchestra music
Accordionists *(ML399; ML419)*
Account current
   See Accounts current
Accountability
   See Criminal liability
      Liability (Law)
Accountability in education
   See Educational accountability
Accountants *(Direct)*
   sa Accounting as a profession
      Auditors
      Tax consultants
      Women as accountants
   x Bookkeepers
      Certified public accountants
      Public accountants
— Correspondence, reminiscences, etc.
— Fees
— Legal status, laws, etc. *(Direct)*
   sa Accounting—Law
   xx Accounting—Law
— Taxation *(Direct)*
Accountants, Professional ethics for
   xx Professional ethics
Accounting *(HF5601-5689)*
   sa Accounting and price fluctuations
      Accounts current
      Accounts receivable
      Amortization
      Auditing
      Average of accounts
      Bookkeeping
      Business losses
      Business mathematics
      Card system in business
      Cost accounting
      Depreciation
      Disclosure in accounting
      Financial statements
      Fiscal year
      Foreign exchange—Accounting
      Income accounting
      Inflation (Finance) and accounting
      Inventories
      Liabilities (Accounting)
      Liquidation
      Machine accounting
      Municipal finance—Accounting
      Productivity accounting
      Realization (Accounting)
      Reserves (Accounting)
      Sales accounting
      Surplus (Accounting)
      Tax accounting

Accounting *(HF5601-5689) (Continued)*
    subdivision Accounting *under names of*
    industries, professions, trades, etc.,
    e.g. Dairying—Accounting;
    Corporations—Accounting; *and*
    subdivision Accounting *under*
    Finance, Public—⌐local subdivision⌐,
    e.g. Finance, Public—Great Britain—
    Accounting
    x Small business—Accounting
    xx Arithmetic
        Auditing
        Bookkeeping
        Business
        Business education
        Controllership
— Anecdotes, facetiae, satire, etc.
— Classification
— Examinations
    Note under Examinations
— Examinations, questions, etc.
    Here are entered collections of ques-
    tions actually set in examinations.
    Problems for classroom use or pri-
    vate study are entered under Ac-
    counting—Problems, exercises, etc.
— Forms, blanks, etc.
    See Business—Forms, blanks, etc.
— History *(Direct)*
— Juvenile literature
— Law *(Direct)*
    sa Accountants—Legal status, laws, etc.
        Auditors—Legal status, laws, etc.
        Tax accounting
    x Accounting law
        Auditing—Law
    xx Accountants—Legal status, laws, etc.
        Commercial law
— — Digests
— Machine methods
    See Machine accounting
— Problems, exercises, etc.
— Programmed instruction
— Research
— Social aspects *(Direct)*
— Study and teaching *(Direct)*
    x Bookkeeping—Study and teaching
Accounting and inflation (Finance)
    See Inflation (Finance) and accounting
Accounting and price fluctuations
    x Price fluctuations and accounting
    xx Accounting
        Prices
Accounting as a profession *(HF5629)*
    xx Accountants
Accounting law
    See Accounting—Law
Accounting machines *(Machines, HF5688;*
    Manufacture, TK4100-4101; Use,
    HF5629)
    sa Bookkeeping machines
    x Electric accounting machines
    xx Calculating-machines
        Machine accounting
        Office equipment and supplies
        Punched card systems
        Tabulating machines
Accounts, Collecting of
    See Collecting of accounts
Accounts, Running
    See Accounts current
Accounts current *(Direct)*
    sa Collecting of accounts
        Settlements (Law)
    x Account current
        Accounts, Running
        Running accounts
    xx Accounting

Commercial law
    Credit
    Debtor and creditor
    Set-off and counterclaim
Accounts receivable *(HF5681.A3)*
    sa Collecting of accounts
        Commercial finance companies
    x Factoring (Finance)
    xx Accounting
        Credit
        Financial statements
Accounts receivable finance companies
    See Commercial finance companies
        Instalment plan
Accra language
    See Gã language
Accreditation (Education)
    sa subdivision Accreditation *under types*
    of schools, e.g. High schools—
    Accreditation; Theological
    seminaries—Accreditation; *and*
    subdivision Study and teaching
    under specific subjects, e.g. Industrial
    arts—Study and teaching ⌐for the
    accreditation of programs of study in
    particular subjects⌐
Accreditation of hospitals
    See Hospitals—Accreditation
Accreditation of nursing schools
    See Nursing schools—Accreditation
Accreditation of schools of public health
    See Schools of public health—Accreditation
Accreditation of theological seminaries
    See Theological seminaries—Accreditation
Accrediting of hospitals
    See Hospitals—Accreditation
Accretion (Law) *(Direct)*
    sa Accession (Law)
        Alluvion
    xx Accession (Law)
        Acquisition of property
        Co-heirs
Accretion (Roman law)
Acculturation
    sa Assimilation (Sociology)
        Detribalization
        Diffusion of innovations
        East and West
        Intercultural education
        North and south
        Socialization
    x Culture contact
        Development education
    xx Anthropology
        Assimilation (Sociology)
        Civilization
        Culture
        Ethnology
        Race problems
— Juvenile literature
Accumulated earnings tax
    See Undistributed profits tax
Accumulations (Law)
    See Perpetuities
Accumulators, Electric
    See Storage batteries
Accumulators, Hydraulic
    See Hydraulic accumulators
Accusation
    See Charges and specifications
        (Courts-martial)
        Indictments
        Informations
        Police charges
ACE
    See Automatic checkout equipment
Acephala
    See Lamellibranchiata

Acetabulum (Anatomy)
    xx Pelvis
— Surgery
Acetal resins
    x Polyformaldehyde resins
    xx Gums and resins, Synthetic
        Plastics
        Polymers and polymerization
Acetate film
    See Safety film
Acetate silk
    See Rayon
Acetic acid *(Chemical technology,*
    TP248.A18; Chemistry, QD305.A2)
    sa Chloroacetic acids
        Glycine
        Indoleacetic acid
        Vinegar
Acetolysis
Acetone *(QD305.K2)*
    xx Urine
Acetonemia *(RB145; Diseases of children,*
    RJ416.A)
    sa Ketogenic diet
    x Ketonemia
        Ketosis
    xx Acidosis
        Diabetes
        Urine—Analysis and pathology
— Cases, clinical reports, statistics
Acetophenetidin
    x Phenacetin
    Example under Analgesics
Acetylene *(Chemical technology, TP765-770;*
    Chemistry, QD305.H8)
    sa PVP
    x Biacetylene
        Butadiine
        Butadiyne
        Diacetylene
    xx Gas
        Gas lighting
        Lighting
    Example under Gases
Acetylene as fuel
    xx Gas as fuel
        Motor fuels
Acetylene black
    See Carbon-black
Acetylene compounds *(QD305.H8)*
— Spectra
Acetylene crystals
Acetylene generators *(TP769)*
    xx Gas-producers
— Safety measures
Acetylene lamps
    xx Lamps
Achaean League *(DF236-7)*
    x Achaian League
Achaeans *(DF135)*
Achaemenian inscriptions
    sa Cuneiform inscriptions
        Cuneiform writing
    x Behistun inscriptions
        Inscriptions, Achaemenian
        Inscriptions, Behistun
    xx Cuneiform inscriptions
        Cuneiform writing
        Elamite language
        Old Persian inscriptions
Achagua Indians
    xx Indians of South America
Achagua language
    xx Arawakan languages
        Indians of South America—Languages
Achaian League
    See Achaean League

Achalasia of the cardia
  See Cardiospasm
Achaotinne Indians
  See Slave Indians
Aché Indians
  See Guayaqui Indians
Acheotenne Indians
  See Slave Indians
Achetoetinne Indians
  See Slave Indians
Acheulian culture *(Indirect)*
  xx Paleolithic period
Achievement, Academic
  See Academic achievement
Achievement motivation *(LB1065)*
  sa Level of aspiration
  xx Educational psychology
    Motivation (Psychology)
Achievement tests
  See Examinations
Achievements (Heraldry) *(CR41.A)*
  sa Hatchments
  xx Hatchments
    Heraldry
Achilles, Tendon of
  See Tendon of Achilles
Achilles reflex
  x Ankle reflex
  xx Reflexes
    Tendon of Achilles
Achinese language *(PL5191-4)*
  xx Malayan languages
Achinese literature
Acholi (African people)
  See Acoli (African people)
Acholi language
  See Acoli language
Achomawi Indians *(E99.A15)*
  sa Madehsi Indians
  x Pit River Indians
  xx Indians of North America
    Palaihnihan Indians
    Shastan Indians
Achomawi language *(PM561)*
  x Achumawi language
  xx Palaihnihan languages
    Shastan languages
Achondroplasia
  See Rickets, Fetal
Achromatism *(QC385)*
  x Aberration, Chromatic and spherical
    Chromatic aberration (Optics)
  xx Dispersion
    Lenses
    Optical instruments
    Optics
Achumawi language
  See Achomawi language
ACI test
  See Adult-child interaction test
Acid-base equilibrium
  sa Buffer solutions
  xx Biological chemistry
  — Programmed instruction
Acid mine drainage *(Indirect)* *(TD899.M5)*
  x Mine acid drainage
  xx Mine drainage
Acid phosphate
  See Superphosphates
Acid proteinase
  See Pepsin
Acidity function
  xx Acids
    Dissociation
Acidity of soils
  See Soil acidity
Acidization of oil wells
  See Oil wells—Acidization

Acidosis *(RB147)*
  sa Acetonemia
Acids *(Technology, TP213)*
  sa Acidity function
    names of acids, e.g. Sulphuric acid
  xx Chemistry
  Example under Chemicals
  — Basicity
    x Basicity of acids
    xx Chemistry, Physical and theoretical
  — Effect on plants
    See Plants, Effect of acids on
  — Handling and transportation *(TP213)*
    xx Chemical engineering
      Corrosion and anti-corrosives
      Transportation
  — Physiological effect *(QP905-917)*
  — Programmed instruction
  — Tariff
    See Tariff on acids
  — Toxicology
Acids, Fatty *(QD305.A2)*
  sa Essential fatty acids
    Fatty acid metabolism
    Fatty acid synthesis
    Quercetin
  x Fatty acids
  — Analysis
  — Patents
Acids, Inorganic *(Chemistry, QD167;*
    Technology, TP213-217)
  Individual acids are entered under their
    specific names, but the prefixes ortho-,
    meta-, para-, pyro-, per-, hypo- are
    usually omitted.
  Example under Chemistry, Inorganic
  — Safety measures
  — Tables, etc.
Acids, Organic *(Chemistry, QD305.A2,*
    QD341.A2; Technology, TP247.2)
  Individual acids are entered under their
    specific names, but the prefixes α-, β-,
    γ-, di-, tri-, tetra-, iso-, ortho-, para-,
    meta- are usually omitted.
  sa Perkin reaction
  Example under Chemistry, Organic
Ackia, Battle of, 1736 *(F347.A25)*
  xx Indians of North America—Wars—
    1600-1750
Acknowledgment of children *(Direct)*
  xx Illegitimacy
    Parent and child (Law)
    Paternity
Acknowledgments *(Direct)*
  sa Conveyancing
    Deeds
    Forms (Law)
    Justices of the peace
    Notaries
  xx Conveyancing
    Deeds
    Notaries
    Real property
Acne *(RL131)*
  xx Sebaceous glands—Diseases
Acne rosacea
  See Rosacea
Acolhua Indians
  See Tezcucan Indians
Acoli (African people)
  x Acholi (African people)
  xx Ethnology—Uganda
Acoli language *(PL8041)*
  x Acholi language
    Acooli language
    Gang language
    Lwo language
    Shuli language

  xx Nilotic languages
Acolytes
  See Altar boys
Acoma dialect *(PM1511)*
  xx Keres language
Acoma Indians *(E99.A16)*
  xx Indians of North America
    Pueblo Indians
Aconite *(Pharmacy, RS165.A; Therapeutics,*
    RM666.A)
  xx Myocardial depressants
Acooli language
  See Acoli language
Acorns
  xx Oak
Acorns as food
  xx Food
Acoustic adaptation
  See Auditory adaptation
Acoustic coagulation
  See Sonic coagulation
Acoustic emission *(TA418.84)*
  x Emission, Acoustic
  xx Acoustical engineering
    Materials—Testing
    Stress waves
Acoustic engineering
  See Acoustical engineering
Acoustic filters
  x Filters, Acoustic
    Sound filters
  xx Architectural acoustics
    Music—Acoustics and physics
    Sound—Apparatus
    Sound-waves
Acoustic holography *(QC244.5)*
  x Acoustic imaging (Holography)
    Acoustical holography
    Sonoholography
    Sonoptography
    Sound holography
  xx Holography
    Interference (Sound)
Acoustic imaging (Holography)
  See Acoustic holography
Acoustic impedance *(QC233)*
  x Impedance, Acoustic
  xx Sound-waves
  — Instruments *(QC227)*
    x Instruments, Acoustic impedance
Acoustic load
  See Sound pressure
Acoustic logging (Oil wells)
  See Oil well logging, Acoustic
Acoustic models
  x Models, Acoustic
  xx Acoustical engineering
    Engineering models
Acoustic nerve
  x Auditory nerve
  xx Auditory pathways
    Nerves, Cranial
  — Tumors
    x Acoustic tumors
Acoustic phenomena in nature
  sa Barisal guns
    Echo
    Thunderstorms
  x Detonations
    Mist-poeffers
    Mistpouffers
    Nature, Acoustic phenomena in
  xx Sound
Acoustic pressure
  See Sound pressure
Acoustic radiation pressure *(QC243)*
  sa Sound pressure
  x Radiation pressure, Acoustic

Acoustic radiation pressure *(QC243)*
 (Continued)
  xx Atmospheric pressure
    Sound pressure
    Sound-waves
Acoustic shock
  See Sound pressure
Acoustic streaming *(QC243.3.A25)*
  x Sound streaming
    Streaming, Acoustic
    Streaming, Sound
  xx Fluid dynamics
    Sound-waves
    Vortex-motion
Acoustic trauma
  xx Hearing disorders
    Noise—Physiological effect
Acoustic tumors
  See Acoustic nerve—Tumors
Acoustic vases
  See Vases, Acoustic
Acoustic velocity meters
  x Sonic velocity flow meters
  xx Flow meters
Acoustic well logging
  See Oil well logging, Acoustic
Acoustical engineering *(TA365)*
  sa Acoustic emission
    Acoustic models
    Anechoic chambers
    Architectural acoustics
    Auditoriums—Electronic sound control
    Electro-acoustics
    Music—Acoustics and physics
    Noise
    Noise control
    Oil well logging, Acoustic
    Sonic coagulation
    Sound laboratories
    Sound pressure
    Sound studios
    Soundproofing
    Telecommunication
    Theaters—Electronic sound control
    Ultrasonic waves—Industrial
      applications
    Underwater acoustics
  x Acoustic engineering
    Sonic engineering
    Sonics
    Sound engineering
    Sound-waves—Industrial applications
  xx Sound
Acoustical holography
  See Acoustic holography
Acoustical materials
  x Soundproofing materials
  — Tables, calculations, etc.
  — Testing
Acoustics
  See Architectural acoustics
    Hearing
    Molecular acoustics
    Music—Acoustics and physics
    Sound
    Underwater acoustics
Acoustics laboratories
  See Sound laboratories
Acousto-optical devices
  See Acoustooptical devices
Acoustooptical devices
  x Acousto-optical devices
    Opto-acoustic devices
    Optoacoustic devices
  xx Optical data processing
    Sound-waves
Acquiescence (Law) *(Direct)*
  xx Civil procedure
    Consent (Law)

    Silence (Law)
Acquiescence (Psychology)
  x Agreement (Psychology)
  xx Adjustment (Psychology)
Acquired characters, Heredity of
  See Inheritance of acquired characters
Acquired characters, Inheritance of
  See Inheritance of acquired characters
Acquisition of Near East publications,
  [scientific publications, serial
  publications, etc.]
  x Near East publications [Scientific
    publications, Serial publications,
    etc.], Acquisition of
  xx Acquisitions (Libraries)
Acquisition of property *(Direct)*
  sa Accession (Law)
    Accretion (Law)
    Alluvion
    Confusion of goods
    Constitutum possessorium
    Occupancy (Law)
    Prescription (Law)
    Singular succession
    Specification (Civil law)
    Transfer (Law)
    Trover and conversion
    Universal succession
  x Property, Acquisition of
  xx Property
    Transfer (Law)
Acquisition of property (Islamic law)
Acquisition of property (Jewish law)
Acquisition of property (Roman law)
Acquisition of territory *(JX4088)*
  sa Annexation (International law)
    Occupancy (International law)
  x Territory, Acquisition of
  xx Territory, National
  — Cases
    sa Minquiers and Ecrehos case
Acquisitions, Cooperative (Libraries)
  sa Farmington plan
    Latin American Cooperative
      Acquisitions Program
    National Program for Acquisitions and
      Cataloging
  x Accessions, Cooperative (Libraries)
    Centralized acquisitions (Libraries)
    Centralized purchasing (Libraries)
  xx Centralized processing (Libraries)
    Library cooperation
Acquisitions (Libraries)
  sa Acquisition of Near East publications,
    [scientific publications, serial
    publications, etc.]
    Books—Prices
    Books—Want lists
    Exchanges, Literary and scientific
    Farmington plan
    Latin American Cooperative
      Acquisitions Program
    Libraries—Gifts, legacies
    National Program for Acquisitions and
      Cataloging
    Searching, Bibliographical
  x Book buying (Libraries)
    Libraries—Accession department
    Libraries—Order department
    Library acquisitions
  xx Processing (Libraries)
  — Automation
Acquittals *(Direct)*
  x Acquittals (Criminal procedure)
  xx Criminal procedure
    Judgments, Criminal
Acquittals (Criminal procedure)
  See Acquittals

Acra language
  See Gã language
Acrania
  See Protochordates
Acrasiales *(QK635)*
  x Acrasieae
    Acrasina
    Cellular slime molds
    Slime molds, Cellular
  xx Myxomycetes
Acrasieae
  See Acrasiales
Acrasina
  See Acrasiales
Acre, Israel
  — Siege, 1799 *(DC226.A)*
Acre
Acreage allotments *(Direct)*
  xx Agricultural administration
    Agriculture and state
Acrilan
  See Acrylic fibers
Acrobatics
  See Acrobats and acrobatism
Acrobats and acrobatism *(GV551-3)*
  sa Gymnastics
    Ski acrobatics
    Stunt men
    Tumbling
  x Acrobatics
    Balancing (Gymnastics)
    Contortion
  xx Circus
    Gymnastics
  — Terminology
Acrobats and acrobatism in art *(N8217.A3)*
  xx Art
Acrodermatitis
  xx Skin—Inflammation
Acrodynia
  x Erythroedema
    Pink disease
Acrodystrophic neuropathy
  xx Bones—Diseases
    Perception, Disorders of
    Ulcers
Acrogens
  See Cryptogams
    Ferns
    Mosses
Acromegaly
  xx Hypertrophy
    Myxedema
    Pituitary body
Acronyms
    Here are entered general works and
    works on English acronyms. Works
    dealing with the acronyms of other
    languages are entered under names of
    specific languages, with subdivision
    Acronyms, *e.g.* Russian language—
    Acronyms.
  sa *subdivision* Acronyms *under subjects*
  x English language—Acronyms
    Initialisms
  xx Abbreviations
    Code names
Acrostics *(PN6369-6377)*
  sa Double-crostics
Acrothoracica *(QL444.C5)*
  x Boring barnacles
    Burrowing barnacles
  xx Cirripedia
Acrylic fibers
  x Acrilan
  xx Textile fibers, Synthetic
  — Patents
  — Testing

Acrylic fibers, Orlon
   See Orlon
Acrylic painting
   See Polymer painting
Acrylic resins
   xx Dental materials
      Gums and resins, Synthetic
Act (Philosophy)
   sa Agent (Philosophy)
   xx Agent (Philosophy)
      Philosophy
Act of God
   See Vis major (Civil law)
Act of state
   sa Government liability
      Political questions and judicial power
   x Matter of state
      State, Act of
      State, Matter of
   xx Constitutional law
      Government liability
      International law
      Political questions and judicial power
      Prerogative, Royal
      Rule of law
      Sovereignty
   — Cases
      sa Sabbatino case
Act psychology
   See Intentionalism
Act-tune
   See Entr'acte music
ACTH
   x Adrenocorticotropic hormones
      Corticotrophic hormones
      Corticotropin
   xx Cortisone
      Pituitary hormones
   — Analysis
Actinaria
   See Sea-anemones
Acting
   sa Acting for television
      Actors
      Actresses
      Amateur theatricals
      College and school drama
      Commedia dell' arte
      Drama
      Drama in education
      Expression
      Gesture
      Impersonators, Female
      Impersonators, Male
      Improvisation (Acting)
      Mime
      Movement (Acting)
      Moving-picture acting
      Pageants
      Pantomime
      Stage fencing
      Stage fighting
      Stage fright
      Stanislavsky method
      Theater
   x Histrionics
      Stage
   xx Actors
      Actresses
      Amateur theatricals
      Drama
      Drama in education
      Elocution
      Expression
      Theater
   — Auditions
      Example under reference from Auditions
   — Costume

      See Costume
   — Juvenile literature
   — Make-up
      See Make-up, Theatrical
   — Quotations, maxims, etc.
   — Study and teaching   *(Direct)*
      x Dramatic education
Acting as a profession
   sa Actors—Psychology
   xx Moving-pictures as a profession
      Theater as a profession
   — Juvenile literature
Acting for moving-pictures
   See Moving-picture acting
Acting for television
   x Television acting
   xx Acting
Acting out (Psychology)
   sa Transference (Psychology)
   xx Psychoanalysis
      Psychology
Actiniaria
   See Sea-anemones
Actinide element metabolism
   xx Metabolism
Actinide elements   *(QD172.A3)*
   sa names of specific elements, e.g.
      Plutonium, Uranium
   x Actinide series
      Actinides
   xx Chemical elements
      Radioactive substances
   — Spectra
Actinide series
   See Actinide elements
Actinides
   See Actinide elements
Actinium
   sa Becquerel rays
      Radioactivity
   xx Radioactive substances
   — Isotopes
      x Actinium isotopes
         Isotopic actinium
Actinium isotopes
   See Actinium—Isotopes
Actinometer   *(QC912)*
   sa Solar radiation
   xx Meteorological instruments
Actinomycin
   xx Antibiotics
Actinomycin C
   xx Antibiotics
Actinomycosis   *(Practice of medicine, RC120;*
      Veterinary medicine, SF784)
   x Lumpy jaw
Actinotherapy
   See Phototherapy
      Ultra-violet rays—Therapeutic use
Actinozoa
   See Anthozoa
Actio de in rem verso
   See Agency (Roman law)
Actio de peculio
   See Agency (Roman law)
Actio exercitoria
   See Agency (Roman law)
Actio in fraudem legis
   See Evasion (Law)
Actio in rem
   See Actions in rem
Actio institoria
   See Agency (Roman law)
Actio pauliana
   See Fraudulent conveyances
Actio popularis
   See Popular actions

Actio realis
   See Actions in rem
Actio rei persequendae causa
   See Actions in rem
      Torts (Roman law)
Actio tributoria
   See Agency (Roman law)
Action, Catholic
   See Catholic action
Action in art   *(NC785)*
   sa Futurism (Art)
   xx Animal locomotion
      Animals in art
      Art
      Futurism (Art)
      Human figure in art
      Human locomotion
Action research   *(Direct)*
   xx Social action
      Social science research
Action songs
   See Games with music
Actions and defenses   *(Direct)*
   sa Actions on the case
      Bills of particulars
      Choses in action
      Citizen suits (Civil procedure)
      Civil procedure
      Class actions (Civil procedure)
      Complaints (Civil procedure)
      Complaints (Criminal procedure)
      Costs (Law)
      Defense (Civil procedure)
      Defense (Criminal procedure)
      Ejectment
      Equity
      Estoppel
      Evidence (Law)
      Extraordinary remedies
      Forcible entry and detainer
      Forms (Law)
      Injunctions
      Joinder of actions
      Limitation of actions
      Lis pendens
      Matrimonial actions
      Nisi prius
      Parties to actions
      Pleading
      Popular actions
      Possessory actions
      Private prosecutors
      Remedies (Law)
      Replevin
      Self-defense (Law)
      Separate actions
      Torts
      Trespass
      Trover and conversion
   x Defense (Law)
      Interpleader
      Personal actions
      Real actions
      Suits (Law)
   xx Civil procedure
      Pleading
      Procedure (Law)
      Remedies (Law)
      Trial practice
   — Cases
   —— Digests
      See Actions and defenses—Digests
   — Digests
      x Actions and defenses—Cases—
         Digests

        GEOGRAPHIC SUBDIVISIONS

   — Rome

Actions and defenses (Direct)

GEOGRAPHIC SUBDIVISIONS

— Rome (Continued)
    See Actions and defenses (Roman
      law)
Actions and defenses (Administrative law)
    (Direct)
    xx Administrative law
    Judicial review of administrative acts
Actions and defenses (Canon law)
Actions and defenses (Greek law)
Actions and defenses (Islamic law)
    x Da'wā (Islamic law)
Actions and defenses (Roman law)
    x Actions and defenses—Rome
Actions in rem (Direct)
    sa Petitory actions
    x Actio in rem
    Actio realis
    Actio rei persequendae causa
    In rem actions
    Proceedings in rem
    Real actions
    Rei vindicatio
    Vindicatio rei
    xx Admiralty
    Property
Actions in rem (Germanic law)
Actions in rem (Roman law)
Actions on the case (Direct)
    x Case (Action)
    Trespass on the case
    xx Actions and defenses
Actium, Battle of, 31 B.C. (DG269)
    xx Rome—History—Civil War, 43-31 B.C.
Activated carbon
    See Carbon, Activated
Activated charcoal
    See Carbon, Activated
Activated nitrogen
    See Active nitrogen
Activated sludge process (Sewage purification)
    See Sewage—Purification—Activated sludge
      process
Activation analysis
    See Radioactivation analysis
Active nitrogen
    x Activated nitrogen
    xx Ionization of gases
    Nitrogen
Active site (Biochemistry)
    See Binding sites (Biochemistry)
Active transport
    See Biological transport
Activities, Student
    See Student activities
Activity coefficients (Chemistry, QD501;
    Electrochemistry, QD561; Solution,
    QD541-3)
    x Activity theory
    xx Chemical reaction, Conditions and laws
      of
    Chemical reaction, Rate of
    Chemical reactions
    Electrolytes
    Electromotive force
    Ions—Migration and velocity
    Solution (Chemistry)
Activity programs in education (Direct)
    (LB1027)
    sa Creative activities and seat work
    Project method in teaching
    x Activity schools
    xx Creative activities and seat work
    Education—Experimental methods
    Project method in teaching
— Teacher training (Direct)

Activity schools
    See Activity programs in education
Activity theory
    See Activity coefficients
Actors (Direct) (PN2205-2217)
    Here are entered works on actors includ-
      ing both men and women. Works
      about women actors alone or women
      as actors are entered under the head-
      ing Actresses.
    sa Acting
    Actresses
    Blacklisting of entertainers
    Children as actors
    Comedians
    Impersonators, Male
    Make-up, Theatrical
    Moving-picture actors and actresses
    Theater
    Trade-unions—Actors
    x Stage
    xx Acting
    Actresses
    Artists
    Entertainers
    Theater
    Theater and society
    Theaters—Employees
— Biography
    Example under Autobiographies; Biogra-
      phy
— Caricatures and cartoons
— Correspondence, reminiscences, etc.
    xx Theater—Anecdotes, facetiae, satire,
      etc.
— Language (New words, slang, etc.)
— Legal status, laws, etc. (Direct)
    (PN2042-5)
    xx Theater—Laws and regulations
    Example under Labor laws and legislation
— Portraits
    x Art and theater
    xx Theater in art
— Psychology
    xx Acting as a profession
— Religious life
— Salaries, pensions, etc. (Direct)
— Social status
    See Theater and society
Actors, Negro
    See Negro actors
Actors, Professional ethics for (PN2056)
    x Actors' ethics
    xx Ethics
    Professional ethics
Actors' ethics
    See Actors, Professional ethics for
Actors in art
    xx Art
Actors in literature
    xx Occupations in literature
Actresses (Direct) (PN2205-2217)
    sa Acting
    Actors
    Impersonators, Female
    Moving-picture actors and actresses
    Theater
    x Stage
    Women as actors
    xx Acting
    Actors
    Theater
    Theaters—Employees
    Woman—Biography
Note under Actors
— Biography
— Correspondence, reminiscences, etc.
— Juvenile literature

— Portraits
    x Art and theater
    xx Theater in art
Actresses in literature
Acts, Administrative
    See Administrative acts
Acts, Human
    See Human acts
Acts, Juristic
    See Juristic acts
Acts of trade and navigation, 1649-1696
    See Navigation acts, 1649-1696
Actual cash value insurance
    See Insurance, Replacement cost
Actuarial science
    See Insurance, Life
    Insurance, Life—Mathematics
    Insurance—Mathematics
Actuarial statistics
    See Insurance—Rates and tables
    Insurance—Statistical methods
    Insurance—Statistics
Actuaries
    xx Insurance—Mathematics
    Mathematicians
— Legal status, laws, etc. (Direct)
Actus legitime ecclesiastici
    See Legitimate ecclesiastical acts
Acua-Shavante Indians
    See Akwē-Shavante Indians
Acuen-Xavante Indians
    See Akwē-Shavante Indians
Acuerdo de Cartagena countries
Aculeata
    See Ants
    Bees
    Wasps
Acupuncture (RN184)
    sa Baunscheidtism
    Reflexotherapy
    xx Counter-irritants
— Atlases
Acupuncture anesthesia (RD85.A25)
    xx Anesthesia
Acute abdomen
    x Surgical abdomen
    xx Abdomen—Diseases
    Abdominal pain
Acute catarrhal jaundice
    See Hepatitis, Infectious
Acute epidermal necrolysis
    See Toxic epidermal necrolysis
Acylation
Acyloin reaction
    xx Chemical reactions
Ad Dominum (Music)
    See Psalms (Music)—120th Psalm
Ad te, Domine, clamabo (Music)
    See Psalms (Music)—28th Psalm
Ad valorem tariff
    See Tariff
Adages
    See Maxims
    Proverbs
Adaiel language
    See Afar language
ADAM (Computer program)
Adam kadmon
    xx Cabala
Adamawa dialect
    See Fulah language
Adamites
    sa Brethren of the Free Spirit
    xx Heresies and heretics—Early church,
      ca. 30-600
    Hussites
    Sects, Medieval

Adams spectral sequences
   xx Algebraic topology
      Sequences (Mathematics)
      Spectral theory (Mathematics)
Adams-Stokes syndrome
   x Morgagni-Adams-Stokes syndrome
      Stokes-Adams syndrome
   xx Heart block
Adan language
   See Adangme language
Adana, Turkey (City)
   — Massacre, 1909   *(DS51.A2)*
Adangme language
   x Adan language
      Dangme language
   xx Kwa languages
Adapazari, Turkey
   — Earthquake, 1943
Adaptability (Psychology)   *(BF335)*
   sa Adaptation level (Psychology)
      Adjustment (Psychology)
      Dissonance (Psychology)
      Purdue non-language adaptability test
      Rigidity (Psychology)
   xx Adjustment (Psychology)
      Experience
      Psychology
Adaptation (Biology)   *(QH546; Plants,*
      QK915-924)
   sa Acclimatization
      Bergmann's rule
      Cold adaptation
      Genetics
      Man—Influence of environment
      Origin of species
      Stress (Physiology)
   x Environment
   xx Biology
      Evolution
      Genetics
      Self-organizing systems
      Transmutation of animals
      Variation (Biology)
      Zoology—Ecology
   — Juvenile literature
   — Mathematics
Adaptation (Music)
   See Arrangement (Music)
Adaptation (Physiology)   *(QP84)*
   sa Auditory adaptation
      Eye—Adaptation
   x Compensation (Physiology)
   xx Physiology
Adaptation (Psychology)
   See Adjustment (Psychology)
Adaptation level (Psychology)
   xx Adaptability (Psychology)
      Adjustment (Psychology)
Adaptation to cold
   See Cold adaptation
Adaptations, Film
   See Film adaptations
Adaptations, Radio
   See Radio adaptations
Adaptations, Stage
   See Stage adaptations
Adaptations, Television
   See Television adaptations
Adaptations (Copyright)
   See Copyright—Adaptations
Adaptive control systems
   sa Feedback control systems
   x Self-adaptive control systems
   xx Artificial intelligence
      Feedback control systems
      Self-organizing systems
   — Mathematical models

Adari language
   See Harari language
Adat law   *(Direct)*
      Here are entered works on the native cus-
      tomary law of Indonesia. Works on
      adat law of specific areas are entered
      under this heading with local subdivi-
      sion, *e.g.* Adat law—Banca (Island)
   sa special legal headings with Adat law
      added in parentheses, e.g. Civil
      procedure (Adat law); Domestic
      relations (Adat law)
   x Civil law (Adat law)
   — Research

GEOGRAPHIC SUBDIVISIONS

   — Banca (Island)
      Example under Adat law
Adayev horse   *(SF293.A3)*
Added-value tax
   See Value-added tax
Addicere (The word)
   xx Civil procedure (Roman law)
      Roman law—Language
Adding-machines
   See Calculating-machines
Addison's disease   *(RC659)*
   sa Hemochromatosis
   x Bronzed skin
   xx Adrenal glands—Diseases
      Hemochromatosis
   — Psychosomatic aspects   *(RC659)*
Addition   *(QA115)*
   xx Arithmetic
      Ready-reckoners
   — Problems, exercises, etc.
   — Programmed instruction
Addition polymerization   *(Chemical*
      technology, TP156.P6; Chemistry,
      QD281.P6)
   x Emulsion polymerization
      Free-radical polymerization
      Ionic polymerization
   xx Polymers and polymerization
Addition reactions
   xx Chemical reactions
   — Tables
Additive compounds
   See Food additives
      subdivisions Additives, Antistatic
      additives, *etc. under subjects, e.g.*
      Storage batteries—Additives;
      Petroleum products—Antistatic
      additives
Additive functions
   xx Functions
Additive process (Probability theory)
   See Random walks (Mathematics)
Additives, Food
   See Food additives
Address, Forms of
   See Forms of address
Address, Titles of
   See Forms of address
      Titles of honor and nobility
Addresses
   See Baccalaureate addresses
      Lectures and lecturing
      Orations
      Speeches, addresses, etc.
Addressing machines, Electronic
   See Electronic addressing machines
Addressing of envelopes
   See Envelopes, Addressing of
Addressing services
   See Letter services
Adelaide, Bahamas, in art

Adélie penguin
   xx Penguins
   — Behavior
   — Juvenile literature
Adelphians
   See Messalians
Aden
   — Riot, 1947
Adenitis
   See Lymphadenitis
Adenocarcinoma
   xx Cancer
Adenohypophysis
   x Anterior pituitary gland
   xx Pituitary body
   — Aging
Adenoids
   xx Nose—Diseases
      Pharynx—Diseases
   — Surgery
Adenolymphoma
   xx Lymphoma
Adenoma
   xx Tumors
Adenomatosis, Pulmonary
   See Pulmonary adenomatosis
Adenomyosis
   See Endometriosis
Adenosinetriphosphate synthesis
   xx Biosynthesis
Adenovirus diseases
   xx Virus diseases
Adenoviruses
   xx Viruses
ADEPT (Computer program)   *(QA171)*
   x A Distinctly Empirical Prover of
      Theorems
   xx Automatic theorem proving
Adhesion   *(QC183)*
   sa Abherents
      Cohesion
   xx Adsorption
      Cohesion
Adhesions   *(RD647.A3)*
   xx Diseases—Complications and sequelae
      Surgery—Complications and sequelae
Adhesive joints
   x Glued joints
   xx Joints (Engineering)
   — Testing   *(TA492.A3)*
Adhesive plaster
   x Adhesive tape
      Plaster, Adhesive
   xx Bandages and bandaging
Adhesive tape
   See Adhesive plaster
Adhesives   *(TP967-970)*
   sa Cement
      Cements, Adhesive
      Glue
      Gum arabic
      Metal bonding
      Mortar
      Mucilage
      Paste
      headings beginning with the word
      Adhesive
   x Agglutinants
   xx Cement
      Cements, Adhesive
      Glue
      Mucilage
   — Laboratory manuals
   — Patents
   — Radiation effects
      See Adhesives, Effect of radiation on
   — Tables, calculations, etc.
   — Testing

Adhesives, Effect of radiation on
  x Adhesives, Irradiated
    Adhesives—Radiation effects
    Radiation—Effect on adhesives
  xx Radiation
Adhesives, Irradiated
  See Adhesives, Effect of radiation on
Adhesives in surgery
  xx Surgical instruments and apparatus
Adhesives industry *(Direct)*
    (HD9999.A4-44)
Adiabatic demagnetization *(QC278)*
  x Demagnetization, Adiabatic
    Magnetic cooling
  xx Cooling
    Low temperatures
Adiaphora *(BT32)*
  x Middle things
  xx Casuistry
    Christian ethics
    Rites and ceremonies
    Theology, Doctrinal
Adiaspiromycosis
  x Haplomycosis
  xx Fungi, Pathogenic
    Lungs—Diseases
Adibasis
  See Adivasis
Adighe
  See Adyghe
Adighe language
  See Adyghe language
Adipocere
  xx Fat
Adipose tissues *(QM565)*
  x Fat tissue
    Fatty tissue
  xx Connective tissues
    Tissues
  — Transplantation
  — Tumors
Adis
  See Abors
Adivasis
  x Adibasis
  xx Ethnology—India
Adiyah language
  See Bube language
Adja dialect
  See Aja dialect
Adjaua language
  See Yao language
Adjective
  See Grammar, Comparative and general—
    Adjective
    subdivision Adjective *under names of*
      languages and groups of languages
Adjective administrative law
  See Administrative procedure
Adjective law
  See Procedure (Law)
Adjoining landowners *(Direct)*
  sa Boundaries (Estates)
    Dilapidations
    Light and air (Easement)
    Nuisances
    Party walls
    Right of way
    Servitudes
  x Landowners, Adjoining
    Neighbor's rights
  xx Boundaries (Estates)
    Real property
    Right of way
    Servitudes
Adjoining landowners (Roman law)
Adjudication, Administrative
  See Administrative procedure

Adjustment, Social
  See Social adjustment
Adjustment (Psychology)
  sa Acquiescence (Psychology)
    Adaptability (Psychology)
    Adaptation level (Psychology)
    Conflict (Psychology)
    Defense mechanisms (Psychology)
    Passivity (Psychology)
    Student adjustment
  x Accommodation (Psychology)
    Adaptation (Psychology)
    Maladjustment (Psychology)
  xx Adaptability (Psychology)
    Psychology
Adjustment (Students)
  See Student adjustment
Adjustment letters
  sa Complaints (Retail trade)
  xx Commercial correspondence
Adjustment of claims
  See Insurance, Accident [Fire, etc.]—
    Adjustment of claims
    Insurance—Adjustment of claims
Adjustments (Retail trade)
  See Complaints (Retail trade)
Adjutants
Adjuvants, Immunological
  x Immunological adjuvants
  xx Antigens and antibodies
Administration
  See Administration of estates
    Administrative and political divisions
    Administrative law
    Civil service
    Management
    Political science
    State, The
    subdivision Politics and government
      under names of countries, states,
      cities, etc.
Administration, Agricultural
  See Agricultural administration
Administration, Nursing service
  See Nursing service administration
Administration, Public
  See Public administration
Administration of criminal justice
  See Criminal justice, Administration of
Administration of estates *(Indirect)*
    Here are entered only works on the man-
    agement of estates, *e.g.* of landholders
    or native princes in British India.
    Works on the administration of estates
    of deceased persons are entered under
    Executors and administrators or Pro-
    bate law and practice.
  x Administration
    Estates, Administration of
  xx Land tenure
    Real property
Administration of justice
  See Justice, Administration of
Administrative ability
  See Executive ability
Administrative acts *(Direct)*
  sa Judicial review of administrative acts
  x Acts, Administrative
  xx Administrative law
    Administrative procedure
    Juristic acts
Administrative adjudication
  See Administrative procedure
Administrative advisory bodies
  See Executive advisory bodies
Administrative agencies *(Direct)*
  sa Executive advisory bodies
    Independent regulatory commissions

    subdivision Executive departments
      under names of countries, cities, etc.
  x Executive agencies
    Executive departments
    Government agencies
    Government departments
  xx Administrative law
    Public administration
  — Management
  — Rules and practice *(Direct)*
    sa subdivision Rules and practice *under*
      names of particular agencies, e.g.
      United States. Atomic Energy
      Commission—Rules and practice
    xx Administrative procedure
Administrative and political divisions
  sa Economic zoning
    Election districts
    Gerrymander
    Judicial districts
    Local government
    subdivision Administrative and political
      divisions *under names of countries,*
      cities, etc.; also subdivision Wards
      under names of cities
  x Administration
    Political divisions
  xx Administrative law
    Decentralization in government
    Local government
    Proportional representation
    Representative government and
      representation
Administrative appeals
  See Administrative remedies
Administrative arbitration
  See Arbitration (Administrative law)
Administrative communication
  See Communication in management
Administrative courts *(Direct)*
    Here are entered works on the organiza-
    tion of official bodies concerned with
    administrative adjudication, including
    administrative courts of the continen-
    tal European type as well as, in Eng-
    lish-speaking countries, those quasi-
    judicial agencies (within departments
    or independent, such as boards, com-
    missions, etc.) which perform adminis-
    trative judicial functions.
  sa Administrative remedies
    Customs courts
    Examiners (Administrative procedure)
    Exhaustion of administrative remedies
    International administrative courts
    Judicial review of administrative acts
    Social insurance courts
    Tax courts
    names of individual administrative
      courts, e.g. France. Conseil d'État;
      Prussia. Oberverwaltungsgericht;
      and names of administrative courts
      with special jurisdiction, e.g. Great
      Britain. Railway Rates Tribunal;
      United States. Court of Claims;
      United States. Federal Trade
      Commission
  x Administrative tribunals
    Courts, Administrative
    Tribunals, Administrative
  xx Administrative law
    Administrative procedure
    Courts
Administrative courts, International
  See International administrative courts
Administrative discretion *(Direct)*
  sa Abuse of administrative power
    Bias (Law)

14

Judicial discretion
Political questions and judicial power
x Discretion, Administrative
Discretion (Law)
xx Administrative law
Dispensations (Law)
Judicial discretion
Rule of law
Administrative economic councils *(Direct)*
Here are entered works dealing with administrative councils. Works dealing with planning or advisory councils are entered under Economic councils.
x Economic councils, Administrative
xx Economic councils
Note under Economic councils
Administrative fees
See Fees, Administrative
Administrative international courts
See International administrative courts
Administrative law *(Direct) (JF1571; By country, JK-JQ)*
sa Abuse of administrative power
Actions and defenses (Administrative law)
Administrative acts
Administrative agencies
Administrative and political divisions
Administrative courts
Administrative discretion
Administrative procedure
Administrative remedies
Administrative responsibility
Arbitration (Administrative law)
Civil service
Colonies—Administration
Concessions
Constitutional law
De facto doctrine
Delegation of powers
Executions (Administrative law)
Executive advisory bodies
Fees, Administrative
Government liability
Independent regulatory commissions
Initiative, Right of
Judicial review of administrative acts
Limitation of actions (Administrative law)
Local government
Mandamus
Municipal corporations
Police power
Police regulations
Public administration
Public contracts
Public domain
Public institutions—Law and legislation
Public officers
Rule of law
Sanctions, Administrative
x Administration
Law, Administrative
xx Civil service
Constitutional law
Political science
Public administration
Public law
— Codification
— Digests
— Interpretation and construction
— Popular works
— Research
— Study and teaching *(Direct)*
Administrative law (Canon law)
Administrative libraries
See Libraries, Governmental, administrative, etc.

Administrative penalties
See Sanctions, Administrative
Administrative power, Abuse of
See Abuse of administrative power
Administrative procedure *(Direct)*
sa Administrative acts
Administrative agencies—Rules and practice
Administrative courts
Administrative remedies
Examiners (Administrative procedure)
Judicial review of administrative acts
Licenses
Representation in administrative proceedings
Sanctions, Administrative
Social insurance courts
Tax courts
subdivision Executive departments *under names of countries, states, cities, etc.*
x Adjective administrative law
Adjudication, Administrative
Administrative adjudication
Administrative rule making
Rule making, Administrative
xx Administrative law
Competent authority
Procedure (Law)
— Costs
— Digests
— Examinations, questions, etc.
Administrative reconsideration
See Administrative remedies
Administrative regulations
See Delegated legislation
Administrative rehearing
See Administrative remedies
Administrative remedies *(Direct)*
sa Exhaustion of administrative remedies
Ombudsman
Tax protests and appeals
x Administrative appeals
Administrative reconsideration
Administrative rehearing
Appeals, Administrative
Reconsideration, Administrative
Rehearing, Administrative
Remedies, Administrative
xx Administrative courts
Administrative law
Administrative procedure
Appellate procedure
Judicial review of administrative acts
— Digests
Administrative responsibility *(Direct)* *(JF1621)*
Here are entered works on the personal liability of government officials to the state or to individuals for torts committed in office. Works on the criminal law pertaining to such acts are entered under the heading Misconduct in office. Discussions of the liability of the state for wrongful acts of officials are entered under the heading Government liability.
sa Denial of justice
Government liability
Impeachments
Misconduct in office
x Responsibility, Administrative
xx Administrative law
Liability (Law)
Torts
Administrative rule making
See Administrative procedure

Administrative rules
See Delegated legislation
Administrative sanctions
See Sanctions, Administrative
Administrative tribunals
See Administrative courts
Administrator-student relationships
See Student-administrator relationships
Administrator-teacher relationships
See Teacher-administrator relationships
Administrators, Arts
See Arts administrators
Administrators and executors
See Executors and administrators
Administrators apostolic *(BX1939.A3)*
Here are entered works dealing with persons appointed by the Pope to administer a diocese when its bishop is prohibited or prevented from exercising his office, or when a diocese is vacant and there is no chapter to elect a vicar capitular.
The term is also used for administrators appointed by the Pope to govern ecclesiastical institutions under similar circumstances.
Since 1918 the term has been used for appointees to an administrature apostolic, a provisional form of diocese.
sa Vicars capitular
x Apostolic administrators
xx Bishops (Canon law)
Canon law
Dioceses (Canon law)
Vicars capitular
Admirals *(Indirect)*
xx Naval biography
— Correspondence, reminiscences, etc.
— Portraits
sa United States. Navy—Biography—Portraits
xx United States. Navy—Biography—Portraits
Admiralty *(Direct)*
sa Actions in rem
Arrest of ships
Liability for marine accidents
xx Commercial law
Courts
Maritime law
Admission for practice before administrative agencies
See Representation in administrative proceedings
Admission of nonimmigrants *(Direct)*
x Nonimmigrants, Admission of
Tourists, Admission of
xx Aliens
Emigration and immigration law
International travel regulations
Passports
Admission officers, College
See College admission officers
Admission to college
See Universities and colleges—Admission
Admission to the bar *(Direct)*
sa Bar examinations
xx Lawyers
Practice of law
Admissions, Taxation of
See Amusements—Taxation
Admissions (Law) *(Direct)*
xx Civil procedure
Confession (Law)
Evidence (Law)
Admonition
Adobe construction
See Building, Adobe

Adobe houses
  x Adobes
    Houses, Adobe
  xx Architecture, Domestic
    Brick houses
    Building, Adobe
    Dwellings
Adobes
  See Adobe houses
Adolescence *(HQ35; Child study, LB1135;*
    Diseases, RJ550; Somatology,
    GN63)
  sa High school personality questionnaire
    Newspapers and children
    Puberty
    Social case work with youth
    Youth
    headings beginning with the word
      Adolescent
  x Teen-age
  xx Child study
    Parent and child
    Puberty
    Youth
  — Caricatures and cartoons
    See Youth—Caricatures and cartoons
  — Health and hygiene
    See Youth—Health and hygiene
  — Juvenile literature
  — Photography
    See Photography of youth
  — Psychology
    See Adolescent psychology
  — Research
    See Youth—Research
  — Stories
Adolescence in literature
  sa Youth in literature
  xx Youth in literature
Adolescent boys
  sa Religious education of adolescent boys
  x Teen-age boys
  xx Boys
    Puberty
    Youth
Adolescent girls *(HQ798)*
  sa Pregnant schoolgirls
  x Teen-age girls
  xx Girls
    Puberty
    Youth
  — Juvenile literature
Adolescent psychiatry *(Indirect) (RJ503)*
  xx Child psychiatry
    Psychiatry
  — Cases, clinical reports, statistics
Adolescent psychology *(Indirect) (BF724)*
  x Adolescence—Psychology
    Youth—Psychology
  xx Child study
    Psychology
  — Cases, clinical reports, statistics
  — Research *(Direct) (BF724)*
    xx Psychological research
      Youth—Research
Adolescent suicide
  See Youth—Suicidal behavior
Adonhiramite masonry
  See Freemasons, Adonhiramite
Adopted children
  See Children, Adopted
Adoptianism
  See Adoptionism
Adoption *(Direct) (HV875)*
  sa Children, Adopted
    Foster home care
    Interracial adoption
  x Child placing

  xx Children—Law
    Foster home care
    Foundlings
    Guardian and ward
    Impediments to marriage
    Parent and child (Law)
  — Domicile
    See Domicile in domestic relations
  — Juvenile literature
  — Personal narratives
  — Research *(Direct)*
Adoption (Canon law)
Adoption (Hindu law)
  Example under Hindu law
Adoption (Jewish law)
Adoption (Roman law)
Adoption (Theology)
  xx God—Fatherhood
    Mystical union
Adoptionism *(BT1320)*
  x Adoptianism
Adouma language
  See Aduma language
Adowa, Battle of, 1896
  xx Italo-Ethiopian War, 1895-1896
Adrenal cortex
  sa Adrenocortical hormones
    Zona reticularis
  xx Adrenal glands
  — Aging
  — Diseases
    sa Cushing's syndrome
      Hyperadrenocorticism
  — Transplantation
  — Tumors
Adrenal cortex hormones
  See Adrenocortical hormones
Adrenal glands
  sa Adrenal cortex
    Adrenal medulla
    Adrenalin
    Chromaffin cells
  x Adrenals
    Suprarenal bodies
    Suprarenal capsules
  xx Kidneys
  — Blood-vessels
  — Diseases
    sa Addison's disease
      Adrenogenital syndrome
    xx Kidneys—Diseases
  — Excision
    x Adrenalectomy
  — Innervation
  — Radiography
  — Tumors
Adrenal medulla
  xx Adrenal glands
Adrenal-pituitary function tests
  See Pituitary-adrenal function tests
Adrenal steroids
  See Adrenocortical hormones
Adrenalectomy
  See Adrenal glands—Excision
Adrenalin *(Physiological effect, QP951;*
    Therapeutics, RM292)
  x Epinephrin
  xx Adrenal glands
    Bronchodilator agents
  Example under Animal extracts
  — Physiological effect
Adrenalin metabolism
  xx Metabolism
Adrenals
  See Adrenal glands
Adrenergic agents
  See Sympathomimetic agents

Adrenergic blocking agents
  See Sympatholytic agents
Adrenergic mechanisms
  xx Sympathin
Adrenocortical hormones
  sa Aldosterone
    Corticosterone
    Cortisone
    Glucocorticoids
    Hydrocortisone
  x Adrenal cortex hormones
    Adrenal steroids
    Corticoids
    Corticosteroids
  xx Adrenal cortex
    Steroid hormones
  — Therapeutic use
    xx Hormone therapy
Adrenocortical hyperplasia
  See Hyperadrenocorticism
Adrenocorticotropic hormones
  See ACTH
Adrenogenital syndrome
  xx Adrenal glands—Diseases
    Sexual disorders
Adrenolytic agents
  See Sympatholytic agents
Adrianople, Battle of, 378 *(DF559)*
  xx Rome—History—Empire, 284-476
    Visigoths
Adriatic question
  xx European War, 1914-1918—Territorial
    questions
    World War, 1939-1945—Territorial
    questions
Adriatic race
  See Dinaric race
Adsorption
  sa Adhesion
    Carbon, Activated
    Chemisorption
    Heat of adsorption
    Ion exchange
    Permeability
    Porosity
    Saline water conversion—Adsorption
      process
    Sorbents
    Wetting agents
  x Sorption
  xx Chemistry, Physical and theoretical
    Packed towers
    Separation (Technology)
    Surface chemistry
  — Juvenile literature
Adsorption of gases
  See Gases—Absorption and adsorption
Adsuki bean
  See Azuki bean
Adularia
  sa Moonstones
  xx Feldspar
Adulation
  See Toadyism
Adult-child interaction test
  x ACI test
  xx Mental tests
Adult dropouts
  See Adult education dropouts
Adult education *(Direct) (LC5201-6660)*
  sa Ability, Influence of age on
    Adult education and state
    Bachelor of liberal studies
    Catholic Church—Adult education
    Continuing education centers
    Education of the aged
    Elementary education of adults
    Folk high schools

Lutheran Church—Adult education
Personnel service in adult education
Radio in adult education
Reading (Adult education)
Religious education of adults
Television in adult education
  x Adults, Education of
    Education of adults
    Life-long education
  xx Education
— Audio-visual aids
— Curricula
— Evaluation
  xx Educational surveys
— Federal aid
    See Federal aid to adult education
— Finance
  sa Adult education fees
    Federal aid to adult education
— Law and legislation (Direct)
  sa Federal aid to adult education
  xx Educational law and legislation
— Motivation
    See Motivation in adult education
— Personnel service
    See Personnel service in adult
      education
— Research (Direct)
    x Adult education research
— Teacher training
Adult education and libraries
    See Libraries and adult education
Adult education and state (Direct)
    x State and adult education
  xx Adult education
    Education and state
Adult education dropouts
    x Adult dropouts
  xx Dropouts
Adult education fees (Direct)
    x Fees, Adult education
  xx Adult education—Finance
Adult education of women (Direct)
  xx Education of women
Adult education research
    See Adult education—Research
Adult education teachers (Direct)
  xx Teachers
Adult elementary education
    See Elementary education of adults
Adulterated coins
  xx Coinage
    Coins
    Numismatics
Adulterations
  sa Drugs—Adulteration and analysis
    Food adulteration and inspection
    Liquors
    Seed adulteration and inspection
  xx Chemistry, Technical
    Sanitary chemistry
Adultery (Direct) (HQ806-8)
  sa Commandments, Ten—Adultery
    Cuckolds
    Trials (Adultery)
  xx Criminal law
    Impediments to marriage
    Marriage law
    Sex crimes
— Stories
Adultery (Aztec law)
  xx Law, Aztec
Adultery (Canon law)
  xx Marriage (Canon law)
Adultery (Canon law, Orthodox Eastern)
  xx Criminal law (Canon law, Orthodox
    Eastern)

Marriage (Canon law, Orthodox
    Eastern)
Adultery (Inca law)
  xx Law, Inca
Adultery (Jewish law)
Adultery (Roman law)
Adulthood (BF724.5)
  sa Aged
    Old age
  xx Age (Psychology)
    Genetic psychology
    Growth
    Maturation (Psychology)
— Caricatures and cartoons
Adults, Education of
    See Adult education
Aduma language (PL8045)
    x Adouma language
    Douma language
    Duma language
  xx Bantu languages
Advaita (B132.A3)
  sa Nagesh sect
    Shaktivisitadvaitavedanta
    Viśistādvaita
  xx Hinduism
    Pantheism
    Philosophy, Hindu
    Vedanta
Advance guards
    See Guard duty
Advance wages
    See Wages—Advances
Advanced placement programs (Education)
  xx Educational acceleration
    School credits
Advanced radar traffic control systems
    (Aeronautics)
    See Radar air traffic control systems
Advent
  sa Second Advent
— Comparative studies (BL325.A)
— Prayer-books and devotions
— Songs and music
    See Advent music
Advent hymns
  xx Hymns
Advent music
    x Advent—Songs and music
  xx Church music
    Music
    Sacred vocal music
Advent sermons (BV40)
  xx Sermons
Adventists (BX6101-6193)
  sa Seventh-Day Adventists
    x Second Adventists
Adventure and adventurers (G525-530)
  sa Discoveries (in geography)
    Escapes
    Explorers
    Frontier and pioneer life
    Heroes
    Sea stories
    Seafaring life
    Shipwrecks
    Soldiers of fortune
    Underwater exploration
    Voyages and travels
    Women and the sea
    x Adventurers
    Mystery stories
  xx Voyages and travels
— Personal narratives
— Philosophy
— — Juvenile literature
— Stories
    See Adventure stories

Adventure and adventurers in literature
Adventure and Beagle Expedition, 1826-1830
    (F2936)
Adventure stories (Collections, PN6071.A38;
    History, PN3448.A3)
  sa Detective and mystery stories
    Science fiction
    Sea stories
    Western stories
    x Adventure and adventurers—Stories
  xx Fiction
Adventurers
    See Adventure and adventurers
Adventures, Joint
    See Joint adventures
Adversaria
    See Commonplace-books
    Marginalia
Adversary in the Bible
    See Enemy in the Bible
Adverse enjoyment
    See Adverse possession
Adverse interest (Agency)
    See Conflict of interests (Agency)
Adverse possession (Direct)
  sa Ejectment
    Prescription (Law)
    x Adverse enjoyment
    Possession, Adverse
  xx Ejectment
    Land titles
    Limitation of actions
    Possession (Law)
    Prescription (Law)
    Real property
Adverse possession (Canon law)
Adverse possession (Roman law)
Advertisement writing
    See Advertising copy
Advertising (Direct) (HF5801-6191)
    Also subdivided by topic, e.g. Advertising
      —Agriculture, Advertising—Banks
      and banking.
    Works on advertising by nationals of one
      country in foreign countries are en-
      tered under Advertising, American,
      [French, etc.]
  sa Advertising cards
    Advertising specialties
    Better-business bureaus
    Bill-posting
    Catalogs, Commercial
    Color in advertising
    Commercial art
    Cooperative advertising
    Display of merchandise
    Help-wanted advertising
    Humor in advertising
    Letter services
    Mailing lists
    Market surveys
    Marketing
    Packaging
    Premiums (Retail trade)
    Prize contests in advertising
    Propaganda
    Public relations
    Publicity
    Radio advertising
    Sales promotion
    Salesmen and salesmanship
    Samples (Commerce)
    Sex in advertising
    Showrooms
    Slogans
    Television advertising
    Testimonials in advertising
    Trading-stamps

Advertising *(Direct) (HF5801-6191)*
(Continued)
  x Advertising, Consumer
    Advertising, Retail
    Advertising—Retail trade
    Consumer advertising
    Retail advertising
  xx Business
    Industrial publicity
    Propaganda
    Public relations
    Publicity
    Retail trade
    Sales promotion
    Salesmen and salesmanship
 — Agents
   See Advertising agencies
 — Agriculture
   Note under Advertising
 — Anecdotes, facetiae, satire, etc.
 — Banks and banking
   xx Bank marketing
   Note under Advertising
 —— Law and legislation *(Direct)*
    xx Advertising laws
     Banking law
 — Bicycle industry
   sa Bicycles and tricycles—Posters
   x Bicycle industry—Advertising
 — Biography
 — Churches *(BV653)*
   sa Church announcements
    Church bulletins
    Journalism, Religious
    Public relations—Churches
   xx Church management
    Church publicity
    Mass media in religion
    Public relations—Churches
 — Cigarettes
   xx Advertising—Tobacco trade
 —— Law and legislation *(Direct)*
    xx Advertising laws
 — Clothing and dress
   sa Fashion shows
 — Cost control
 — Costs
 — Directories
   x Advertising, Magazine—Directories
    Advertising, Newspaper—Directories
 — Examinations, questions, etc.
 — Farm produce
   x Advertising—Produce trade
    Farm produce—Advertising
    Produce trade—Advertising
 — Food
   x Food industry and trade—
     Advertising
    Produce trade—Advertising
 —— Law and legislation *(Direct)*
    xx Advertising laws
     Food law and legislation
 — Government
   See Government advertising
 — Juvenile literature
 — Law
   See Advertising laws
    Advertising—Lawyers
 — Lawyers
   x Advertising—Law
   xx Legal ethics
 —— Law and legislation *(Direct)*
    xx Advertising laws
 — Libraries
   sa Libraries and radio
    Library exhibits
    Public relations—Libraries
   x Libraries—Advertising
    Library advertising

   xx Library extension
    Public relations—Libraries
 — Marriage
   See Matrimonial advertisements
 — Mathematical models
 — Periodicals
   sa House organs
 — Photographic apparatus
   x Photography—Apparatus and
     supplies—Advertising
 — Problems, exercises, etc.
 — Produce trade
   See Advertising—Farm produce
 — Psychological aspects
   sa Motivation research (Marketing)
 — Quotations, maxims, etc.
 — Retail trade
   See Advertising
 — Schools
   sa School publicity
   xx School publicity
 — Shopping centers
   x Shopping centers—Advertising
 — Specimens
 — Taxation
   See Taxation of advertising
 — Terminology
 — Tobacco trade
   sa Advertising—Cigarettes
 — Underdeveloped areas
   See Underdeveloped areas—
     Advertising
Advertising, American, ₍French, etc.₎
Note under Advertising
Advertising, Art in
  See Art and industry
    Commercial art
Advertising, Classified
  sa Help-wanted advertising
  x Classified advertising
    Want ads
  xx Advertising, Newspaper
Advertising, Color in
  See Color in advertising
Advertising, Consumer
  See Advertising
Advertising, Cooperative
  See Cooperative advertising
Advertising, Direct-mail
  sa Catalogs, Commercial
    Circular letters
    Mail-order business
    Sales letters
  x Advertising, Mail
    Direct advertising
    Direct-mail advertising
    Junk mail
  xx Catalogs, Commercial
    Commercial correspondence
    Mail-order business
Advertising, Government
  See Government advertising
Advertising, Humor in
  See Humor in advertising
Advertising, Industrial
  x Industrial advertising
Advertising, Legal
  See Legal advertising
Advertising, Magazine *(Direct)*
  x Magazine advertising
    Periodical advertising
  xx Periodicals
 — Directories
   See Advertising—Directories
Advertising, Mail
  See Advertising, Direct-mail
Advertising, Moving-pictures in
  See Moving-pictures in advertising

Advertising, Newspaper *(Direct)*
  sa Advertising, Classified
    Advertising fliers
  x Newspaper advertising
  xx Newspapers
 — Directories
   See Advertising—Directories
 — Vocational guidance
Advertising, Outdoor *(Direct)*
  sa Advertising cards
    Bill-posting
    Billboards
    Posters
    Show-windows
    Sign painting
    Signs and sign-boards
    Skywriting
  x Outdoor advertising
 — Law and legislation *(Direct)*
   xx Advertising laws
Advertising, Photography in
  See Photography, Advertising
Advertising, Pictorial
  See Commercial art
    Posters
Advertising, Point-of-sale
  sa Display of merchandise
    Show-windows
    Showrooms
    Signs and sign-boards
  x Point-of-purchase advertising
    Point-of-sale advertising
Advertising, Political
  sa Press and politics
    Radio in politics
    Telephone in politics
    Television in politics
  x Advertising in politics
    Political advertising
  xx Electioneering
    Press and politics
Advertising, Prize contests in
  See Prize contests in advertising
Advertising, Public interest
  See Advertising, Public service
Advertising, Public service
  x Advertising, Public interest
    Public interest advertising
    Public service advertising
  xx Public relations
Advertising, Radio
  See Radio advertising
Advertising, Retail
  See Advertising
Advertising, Subliminal
  See Subliminal projection
Advertising, Television
  See Television advertising
Advertising, Transportation
  See Advertising cards
Advertising agencies *(Direct)*
  x Advertising—Agents
    Advertising business
 — Accounting
 — Law and legislation *(Direct)*
   xx Advertising laws
Advertising art
  See Commercial art
Advertising as a profession
 — Juvenile literature
Advertising business
  See Advertising agencies
Advertising campaigns
  sa Market surveys
  x Campaigns, Advertising
  xx Market surveys

Advertising cards *(HF5851; Card and sign writing, TT360)*
- sa Cigarette cards
  Sailing cards
- x Advertising, Transportation
  Business cards
  Cards, Advertising
  Show cards
  Tradesmen's cards
- xx Advertising
  Advertising, Outdoor
  Industrial design coordination
— Collectors and collecting

Advertising copy
- sa Copy writers
- x Advertisement writing
  Copy, Advertising
  Copy writing
- xx Authorship

Advertising fliers
- x Circulars, Advertising
  Fliers, Advertising
  Flyers, Advertising
  Handbills, Advertising
- xx Advertising, Newspaper

Advertising in politics
  See Advertising, Political

Advertising laws *(Direct)* *(HF5817-5819)*
  Here are entered works on the legal aspects of advertising. Works on the law of public notice are entered under the heading Legal advertising.
- sa Advertising agencies—Law and legislation
  Advertising—Banks and banking—Law and legislation
  Advertising—Cigarettes—Law and legislation
  Advertising—Food—Law and legislation
  Advertising—Lawyers—Law and legislation
  Advertising, Outdoor—Law and legislation
  Bill-posting—Laws and regulations
  Billboards—Law and legislation
  Competition, Unfair
  Radio advertising—Law and legislation
  Slogans—Law and legislation
  Television advertising—Law and legislation
- x Advertising—Law
  Law, Advertising
- xx Competition, Unfair
  Press law
  Public relations and law
  Trade regulation

Advertising layout and typography
- x Advertising typography
  Layout and typography, Advertising
  Typography, Advertising
- xx Newspaper layout and typography
  Printing
  Printing, Practical—Make-up
  Type and type-founding

Advertising management
- xx Management
Advertising novelties
  See Advertising specialties
Advertising photography
  See Photography, Advertising

Advertising research
- sa Market surveys
- xx Market surveys
  Research

Advertising specialties
- x Advertising novelties
- xx Advertising

Premiums (Retail trade)
Advertising typography
  See Advertising layout and typography
Advisory bodies, Executive
  See Executive advisory bodies
Advisory committees in education
  See Citizens' advisory committees in education
Advisory committees in education, Parents'
  See Parents' advisory committees in education
Advisory committees in science
  See Citizens' advisory committees in science
Advisory committees in technology
  See Citizens' advisory committees in technology
Advisory opinions *(Direct)*
- sa Attorneys general's opinions
  City attorneys' opinions
- xx Judicial opinions
  Law reports, digests, etc.
Advisory opinions (Islamic law) *(Direct)*
- sa Fatwās
Advocates
  See Lawyers
Adya dialect
  See Aja dialect
Adyghe
- x Adighe
- xx Circassians
  Ethnology—Russia
— Economic conditions
Adyghe language *(PK9201.A4)*
- sa Circassian language
  Kabardian language
- x Adighe language
- xx Caucasian languages
  Circassian language
  Kabardian language
Adyghe philology *(Direct)*
Adyghe prose literature *(Direct)*
Adzes *(Anthropology, GN447.A3; Carpenter's tools, TS5618)*
- xx Axes
Adzes (in religion, folk-lore, etc.) *(BV168.A)*
- x Folk-lore of adzes
- xx Religion, Primitive
Adzhar dialect *(Direct)* *(PK9201.A54)*
- xx Georgian language
Adzuki bean
  See Azuki bean
Aediles
- x Ediles
- xx Rome—Officials and employees
  Tribunus plebis
Aegean civilization
  See Civilization, Aegean
Aekyom language
AEMOVE (Computer program)
- xx IBM 360 (Computer)—Programming
Aeolian harp *(ML1005-6)*
- x Eolian harp
- xx Harp
Aeolian pipe-organ
  See Player-organ
Aeolian-vocalion *(ML1055.A3)*
- x Vocalion, Aeolian
- xx Musical instruments (Mechanical)
  Phonograph
Aequiprobabilism
  See Probabilism
Aequitas
  See Equity (Roman law)
Aerated concrete
  See Lightweight concrete
Aerated water flow
  See Water—Air entrainment

Aeration of grain
  See Grain aeration
Aeration of reservoirs
  See Reservoirs—Aeration
Aeration of rivers
  See Rivers—Aeration
Aeration of sewage
  See Sewage—Purification—Aeration
Aeration of soil
  See Soil aeration
Aeration of water
  See Water—Aeration
Aeration of yeast
  See Yeast—Aeration
Aerial attacks on cities
  See subdivision Bombardment *under names of cities, e.g.* London—Bombardment, 1940
Aerial bombing
  See Bombing, Aerial
Aerial bombs
  See Bombs
  Projectiles, Aerial
Aerial dusting in agriculture
  See Aerial spraying and dusting in agriculture
Aerial fertilizing *(Indirect)*
- x Aerial topdressing
- xx Aeronautics in agriculture
  Fertilizers and manures
Aerial geography
  See Geography, Aerial
Aerial gunnery
- sa Fire control (Aerial gunnery)
- x Air gunnery
  Flexible gunnery
- xx Aeronautics, Military
  Air warfare
  Gunnery
Aerial law
  See Aeronautics—Laws and regulations
Aerial navigation
  See Navigation (Aeronautics)
Aerial observation
  See Aeronautics, Military—Observations
Aerial photogrammetry *(TA593)*
- sa Aerial photography in archaeology
  Aerial photography in road surveying
  Aerial triangulation
  Airborne profile recorder
  Photography, Aerial
  Stereoplanigraph
- x Aerial photographic surveying
- xx Aerial photography in geography
  Aeronautics in geodesy
  Photogrammetry
  Photographic surveying
  Photography, Aerial
— Apparatus and supplies
— Laboratory manuals
— Specifications *(Direct)*
Aerial photograph reading
  See Photographic interpretation
  Photographic interpretation (Military science)
Aerial photographic equipment
  See Photography, Aerial—Apparatus and supplies
Aerial photographic surveying
  See Aerial photogrammetry

Aerial photographs

Here are entered works on the handling, maintenance, and indexing of aerial photographs in unbound collections. Works on the taking of aerial photographs, and their applications in special fields, are entered under Photography, Aerial. Works on their interpretation are entered under Photographic interpretation.

  sa subdivision Aerial photographs *under names of countries, cities, etc., e.g.* California—Aerial photographs
  x Air photos
    Airphotos
  xx Photographs
    Photography, Aerial

Aerial photography
  See Photography, Aerial

Aerial photography in agriculture
  sa Aerial photography in botany
    Aerial photography in forestry
    Aerial photography in soil surveys
  xx Aeronautics in agriculture
    Photography, Aerial

Aerial photography in archaeology
  xx Aerial photogrammetry
    Archaeology
    Photography, Aerial

Aerial photography in botany
  sa Aerial photography in forestry
  xx Aerial photography in agriculture
    Botany
    Photography, Aerial
    Vegetation surveys

Aerial photography in cryopedology
  xx Cryopedology
    Photography, Aerial

Aerial photography in forestry
  xx Aerial photography in agriculture
    Aerial photography in botany
    Aeronautics in forestry
    Photography, Aerial

Aerial photography in geography
  sa Aerial photogrammetry
  xx Photography, Aerial
    Photography in geography
    Physical geography

Aerial photography in geology
  sa Aerial photography in submarine geology
  x Photogeology
  xx Geology
    Photography, Aerial
    Photography in geology

Aerial photography in geomorphology
  xx Geomorphology
    Photography, Aerial

Aerial photography in glaciology
  xx Glaciology
    Photography, Aerial

Aerial photography in hydrogeology
  xx Hydrogeology
    Photography, Aerial

Aerial photography in hydrology
  xx Hydrology
    Photography, Aerial

Aerial photography in road surveying
  xx Aerial photogrammetry
    Photography, Aerial
    Roads—Surveying

Aerial photography in soil surveys
  xx Aerial photography in agriculture
    Photography, Aerial
    Soil-surveys

Aerial photography in submarine geology
  xx Aerial photography in geology
    Photography, Aerial
    Submarine geology

Aerial photography in traffic engineering
  xx Photography, Aerial
    Traffic engineering

Aerial projectiles
  See Projectiles, Aerial

Aerial propellers
  See Propellers, Aerial

Aerial railroads
  See Railroads, Atmospheric

Aerial reconnaissance
  See Aeronautics, Military—Observations

Aerial reconnaissance in geodesy
  See Aeronautics in geodesy

Aerial rockets
  See Projectiles, Aerial
    Rockets (Aeronautics)
    Rockets (Ordnance)

Aerial servitudes
  See Avigation easements

Aerial spraying and dusting in agriculture *(Indirect)*
  x Aerial dusting in agriculture
  xx Aeronautics in agriculture
    Spraying and dusting in agriculture
  — Economic aspects *(Indirect)*
  — Safety measures

Aerial spraying in mosquito control
  See Aeronautics in mosquito control

Aerial strategy
  See Air warfare

Aerial tactics
  See Air warfare

Aerial topdressing
  See Aerial fertilizing

Aerial triangulation
  x Aerotriangulation
    Phototriangulation
    Stereotriangulation
  xx Aerial photogrammetry
    Triangulation

Aerial views
  See subdivision Description and travel—Aerial *under names of countries, regions, etc.; and subdivision* Description—Aerial *under names of cities and of universities and colleges, etc.*

Aerial warfare
  See Air warfare

Aerobatic flying
  See Stunt flying

Aerobatics
  See Stunt flying

Aerobee rocket
  sa WAC Corporal rocket
  xx Rockets, Sounding
    WAC Corporal rocket
  Example under Rockets (Aeronautics)

Aerobic bacteria
  See Bacteria, Aerobic

Aerodromes
  See Airports

Aerodynamic control of aeroplanes
  See Aeroplanes—Control surfaces

Aerodynamic forces
  See Aerodynamic load
    Drag (Aerodynamics)
    Lift (Aerodynamics)

Aerodynamic heating
  sa Artificial satellites—Atmospheric entry
    Ballistic missiles—Atmospheric entry
    Space vehicles—Atmospheric entry
  x Heat barrier
    Heating, Aerodynamic
    Thermal barrier
  xx Aerodynamics
    Aerothermodynamics
    Friction
    Heat
    Thermodynamics

Aerodynamic load *(TL574.P7)*
  sa Blast effect
    Drag (Aerodynamics)
    Gust loads
    Lift (Aerodynamics)
    Sound pressure
  x Aerodynamic forces
    Pressure distribution (Aircraft)
  xx Aerodynamics
    Aeroplanes—Design and construction
    Strains and stresses

Aerodynamic measurements *(TL573)*
  sa Gust loads—Measurement
    Rocket engines—Thrust—Measurement
  x Measurements, Aerodynamic
  xx Physical measurements

Aerodynamic noise *(TL574.N6)*
  sa Aeroplanes—Noise
    Boundary layer noise
    Jet planes—Noise
    Rocket engines—Noise
    Sonic boom
  xx Noise
    Turbulence

Aerodynamical laboratories
  See Aeronautical laboratories

Aerodynamics *(QA930; TL570-574)*
  sa Aerodynamic heating
    Aerodynamic load
    Aerodynamics, Supersonic
    Aerodynamics, Transonic
    Aeroelasticity
    Aeronautics
    Aerostatics
    Artificial satellites—Atmospheric entry
    Automobiles—Aerodynamics
    Ballistic missiles—Atmospheric entry
    Ballistic ranges
    Blades
    Body of revolution
    Boundary layer
    Buffeting (Aerodynamics)
    Cascades (Fluid dynamics)
    Downwash (Aerodynamics)
    Drag (Aerodynamics)
    Flutter (Aerodynamics)
    Gas flow
    Ground-cushion phenomenon
    Hinge moments (Aerodynamics)
    Interference (Aerodynamics)
    Lift (Aerodynamics)
    Mach number
    Magnus effect
    Pitching (Aerodynamics)
    Reynolds number
    Rolling (Aerodynamics)
    Space vehicles—Atmospheric entry
    Spin (Aerodynamics)
    Stability of aeroplanes
    Stability of helicopters
    Stability of rockets
    Stalling (Aerodynamics)
    Turbulence
    Vertically rising aeroplanes—Aerodynamics
    Vortex-motion
    Wakes (Aerodynamics)
    Whirling arms (Aerodynamics)
    Wind tunnels
    Yawing (Aerodynamics)
    subdivision Aerodynamics *under subjects, e.g.* Compressors—Aerodynamics
  x Aerodynamics, Subsonic
    Streamlining

Subsonic aerodynamics
  xx Aeronautics
    Air
    Dynamics
    Fluid dynamics
    Gas dynamics
    Pneumatics
    Wind tunnels
— Electromechanical analogies
— Juvenile literature
— Laboratory manuals
— Notation
— Tables, etc.

Aerodynamics, Hypersonic *(TL571.5)*
  sa Hypersonic planes
    Hypersonic wind tunnels
    Plasma sheaths
  x Aerodynamics of hypersonic flight
    Hypersonic aerodynamics
    Hypersonic speeds
    Hypersonics
  xx Aerodynamics, Supersonic
    Mach number
    Sound pressure
— Tables, etc.

Aerodynamics, Subsonic
  See Aerodynamics

Aerodynamics, Supersonic
  sa Aerodynamics, Hypersonic
    Aerothermodynamics
    Shock waves
    Sonic boom
    Supersonic compressors
    Supersonic diffusers
    Supersonic nozzles
    Supersonic planes
    Supersonic speeds
    Supersonic wind tunnels
    Supersonics
  x Aerodynamics of supersonic flight
    High-speed aerodynamics
    Supersonic aerodynamics
  xx Aerodynamics
    High-speed aeronautics
    Sound pressure
— Computer programs
— Tables, etc.

Aerodynamics, Transonic
  sa Aerothermodynamics
    Transonic planes
    Transonic wind tunnels
  x Aerodynamics of transonic flight
    Trans-sonic aerodynamics
    Transonic aerodynamics
    Transonic speeds
  xx Aerodynamics
    High-speed aeronautics
    Sound pressure

Aerodynamics of hypersonic flight
  See Aerodynamics, Hypersonic
Aerodynamics of supersonic flight
  See Aerodynamics, Supersonic
Aerodynamics of transonic flight
  See Aerodynamics, Transonic

Aeroelasticity *(TL570)*
  xx Aerodynamics
    Aeroplanes—Design and construction
    Elastic waves
    Elasticity
    Statics
— Electromechanical analogies

Aerofoils *(TL574.A4)*
  sa Aeroplanes—Control surfaces
    Aspect ratio (Aerofoils)
    Blades
    Boundary layer control
    Camber (Aerofoils)
    Downwash (Aerodynamics)

    Elevators (Aeroplanes)
    Flaps (Aeroplanes)
    Oscillating wings (Aerodynamics)
    Rotors (Helicopters)
    Tabs (Aeroplanes)
  x Airfoils
— Rolling
    See Rolling (Aerodynamics)
— Stalling
    See Stalling (Aeroplanes)
Aerofoils in cascade
  See Cascades (Fluid dynamics)
Aerogastres
  See Myxomycetes
Aerograph
  See Meteorograph
Aerographers, Naval
  See United States. Navy—Aerographers
Aerographer's mates
  See United States. Navy—Aerographers
Aerolites
  See Meteorites
Aerologation
  See Pressure pattern flying
Aerology
  See Meteorology
Aeromagnetic maps
  See Magnetism, Terrestrial—Maps
Aeronautical accidents
  See Aeronautics—Accidents

Aeronautical charts *(Indirect)*
    Here are entered maps giving information
      intended for use in air navigation, such
      as compass rose, isogonic lines, loca-
      tion of landing fields, beacons, hazards
      to air navigation, etc.
  sa Instrument landing systems—Charts,
      diagrams, etc.
    Loran charts
    Plotting charts
  x Aeronautics—Charts, diagrams, etc.
    Charts, Aeronautical
  xx Aids to air navigation
    Airways—Maps
    Maps
    Navigation (Aeronautics)
Aeronautical competitions
  See Aeronautics—Competitions

Aeronautical engineers *(Direct)*
  xx Engineers

Aeronautical instruments *(TL589)*
  sa Accelerometers
    Aeroplanes—Electric equipment
    Air-speed indicators
    Altimeter
    Aneroid barometer
    Artificial horizons (Aeronautical
      instruments)
    Automatic pilot (Aeroplanes)
    Automatic pilot (Helicopters)
    Course-line computers
    Density altitude computers
    Distance measuring equipment (Aircraft
      to ground station)
    Flight engineering
    Flight recorders
    Guidance systems (Flight)
    Gyro compass
    Gyroscope
    Gyroscopic instruments
    Inclinometer
    Inertial navigation (Aeronautics)
    Instrument flying
    Kymograph
    Navigation computer (Aeronautical
      instrument)
    Omnirange system
    Radio beacons

    Radioisotopes in aeronautics
    Rate gyroscopes
    Rockets (Aeronautics)—Aspect
      recording systems
    Stall warning indicators (Aeronautics)
    Tacan
  x Aeroplanes—Instruments
    Aircraft instruments
    Instruments, Aeronautical
  xx Aeroplanes—Electric equipment
— Display systems
    sa Pictorial course computer
    x Airborne display systems
      Pictorial display systems, Airborne
      Pictorial navigation displays
    xx Electronics in aeronautics
      Information display systems
— Maintenance and repair
— Programmed instruction
— Testing
— Trade and manufacture *(Direct)*
Aeronautical journalism
  See Journalism, Aeronautical

Aeronautical laboratories *(TL566-8)*
  x Aerodynamical laboratories
    Laboratories, Aerodynamical
    Laboratories, Aeronautical
  xx Aeronautical research
— Safety measures

Aeronautical libraries *(Z675.A5)*
  sa Information storage and retrieval
      systems—Aeronautics
  x Libraries, Aeronautical
Aeronautical literature searching
  See Information storage and retrieval
      systems—Aeronautics

Aeronautical museums *(Indirect)* *(TL506)*
  xx Museums
  Example under Transportation museums
Aeronautical navigation
  See Navigation (Aeronautics)
Aeronautical patents
  See Aeronautics—Patents

Aeronautical radio stations *(Direct)*
    (TL695)
  sa Consol navigation
    Loran
    Radio beacons
    Radio direction finders
  x Aircraft radio stations
    Airport radio stations
  xx Mobile communication systems
    Radio in aeronautics
    Radio stations
  Example under Mobile radio stations

Aeronautical research *(Indirect)*
  sa Aeronautical laboratories
    Aeronautics, Military—Research
    Aeronautics—Study and teaching
    Astronautical research
    Navigation—Research
    X-15 (Rocket aircraft)
  x Aeronautics—Research
    Research, Aeronautical
  xx Aeronautics—Study and teaching
    Research
    Research, Industrial

Aeronautical societies *(TL500-504)*
  sa Aeronautics—Societies, etc. ₍for
      publications of aeronautical and
      other societies in relation to
      aeronautics₎
  xx Societies

Aeronautical sports *(GV750-770)*
  sa Aeroplane racing
    Aeroplanes—Models
    Balloon racing
    Gliding and soaring

Aeronautical sports *(GV750-770)*
  (Continued)
      Parachuting
      Private flying
      Skydiving
    xx Aeronautics
      Sports
  — Juvenile literature
Aeronautical telecommunication services
  See Aeronautics—Communication systems
Aeronautics *(Indirect) (International law,
      JX5771; Technology, TL500-830;
      Transportation and communication,
      HE9911-9925)*
    sa Aerodynamics
      Aeronautical sports
      Aeroplane racing
      Aeroplanes
      Aerostatics
      Air lines
      Air pilots
      Air-ships
      Air speed
      Airdrop
      Airports
      Airports, Floating
      Airways
      Astronautics
      Balloon ascensions
      Balloons
      Catapults (Aeronautics)
      Classification—Books—Aeronautics
      Condensation trails
      Electricity in aeronautics
      Electronics in aeronautics
      Flight
      Flying-machines
      Flying saucers
      Gliding and soaring
      Helicopters
      High-speed aeronautics
      Interplanetary voyages
      Kites
      Landing aids (Aeronautics)
      Meteorology in aeronautics
      Moving-pictures in aeronautics
      Navigation (Aeronautics)
      Negroes in aeronautics
      Polar regions—Aerial exploration
      Private flying
      Propellers, Aerial
      Radar in aeronautics
      Radio in aeronautics
      Radioisotopes in aeronautics
      Rocketry
      Rockets (Aeronautics)
      Seaplanes
      Stability of aeroplanes
      Vibration (Aeronautics)
      Women in aeronautics
    x Aerostation
      Air navigation
      Aviation
    xx Aerodynamics
      Aeroplanes
      Air-ships
      Balloons
      Communication and traffic
      Flight
      Flying-machines
  — Abbreviations *(TL509)*
  — Abstracting and indexing
  — Accident investigation
      Here are entered works on the meth-
        ods of investigating accidents. Re-
        ports of the investigation of particu-
        lar accidents are entered under
        Aeronautics—Accidents.
    x Aircraft accident investigation

    xx Aeronautics—Accidents
  — Accidents *(TL553.5)*
      Subdivided by date, *e.g.* Aeronautics—
        Accidents—1958.
    sa Aeronautics—Accident investigation
      Aeronautics—Safety measures
      Airports—Bird control
      Drinking and airplane accidents
      Liability for aircraft accidents
      Salvage (Aeroplanes)
      Survival (after aeroplane accidents,
        shipwrecks, etc.)
    x Accidents, Aircraft
      Aeronautical accidents
      Aeroplane accidents
      Aeroplanes—Accidents
      Aeroplanes—Collisions with birds
      Aircraft accidents
      Aviation accidents
      Birds—Collisions with aeroplanes
      Collisions, Aircraft
    xx Aeronautics—Safety measures
      Note under Aeronautics—Accident
        investigation
  — — 1958
      Note under Aeronautics—Accidents

      GENERAL SUBDIVISIONS

  — — Pictorial works
  — Anecdotes, facetiae, satire, etc.
  — Awards *(TL537)*
    xx Rewards (Prizes, etc.)
  — Biography *(TL539-540)*
    sa Air pilots
      Women in aeronautics
  — — Juvenile literature
  — Caricatures and cartoons
  — Charts, diagrams, etc.
      See Aeronautical charts
  — Chronology
  — Communication systems *(TL692)*
    sa Aerospace telemetry
      Airports—Communication systems
      Teletype in aeronautics
    x Aeronautical telecommunication
        services
      Aviation communications
    xx Electronics in aeronautics
      Telecommunication
  — — Maintenance and repair
  — Competitions
    sa Aeroplane racing
      Balloon racing
    x Aeronautical competitions
      Air meets
  — Computer programs
  — Dictionaries, Juvenile
  — Drama
  — Early works to 1900
  — Examinations, questions, etc.
    sa United States. Army Air Forces—
        Examinations
  — Flights *(TL721)*
    sa Daily Mail Transatlantic Air Race,
        1969
      Flights around the world
      Space flight
      Transatlantic flights
      Transpacific flights

      subdivision Aerial exploration *under*
        Antarctic regions, Arctic regions
        *and similar geographic headings
        where subdivisions* Description
        and travel *or* Discovery and
        exploration *are not used; also
        subdivision* Description and travel
        —Aerial *under countries, regions,
        etc. or* Description—Aerial *under
        cities*
    x Aeronautics—Voyages
    xx Voyages and travels
  — Handbooks, manuals, etc. *(TL551)*
  — History *(TL515-532)*
  — — Juvenile literature
  — Hygienic aspects
      See Aeronautics—Sanitary aspects
  — Information services
  — Insurance
      See Insurance, Aviation
  — Juvenile literature *(TL547)*
    x Aeronautics, Commercial—Juvenile
        literature
  — Laws and regulations *(International law,
        JX5771; Transportation and
        communication, HE9915-9925)*
    sa Aeronautics, Commercial—Law and
        legislation
      Aeroplanes—Nationality
      Air charter contracts
      Air pilots—Legal status, laws, etc.
      Air traffic rules
      Aircraft mortgages
      Airport zoning
      Airspace (International law)
      Avigation easements
      Crimes aboard aircraft
      Helicopters—Law and legislation
      Jurisdiction over aircraft
      Liability for aircraft accidents
      Salvage (Aeroplanes)
      Space law
    x Aerial law
      Aerospace law
      Air law
      Aviation law
    xx Aeronautics and state
      Space law
  — — Conflict of laws
      See Conflict of laws—Aeronautics
  — — Criminal provisions
  — Literary collections
  — Medical aspects
      See Aviation medicine
  — Medical service
      See Aeronautics in medicine
        Aeronautics—Relief service
  — Miscellanea
      Example under Curiosities and wonders
  — Music
      See Aeronautics—Songs and music
  — Navigation
      See Navigation (Aeronautics)
  — Patents *(TL513)*
    sa Aeroplanes—Patents
    x Aeronautical patents
  — Periodicals
  — — Juvenile literature
  — Personal narratives
  — Pictorial works *(TL549)*
    sa Aeronautics in art
    xx Aeronautics in art
  — Piloting
      See subdivision Piloting *under specific
        types of aircraft, e.g.*
        Aeroplanes—Piloting; Air-ships
        —Piloting; Fighter planes—
        Piloting; Helicopters—Piloting

— Poetry
  x Aeroplanes—Poetry
    Air-ships—Poetry
    Autogiros—Poetry
    Balloon ascensions—Poetry
    Balloons—Poetry
    Flying-machines—Poetry
    Gliders (Aeronautics)—Poetry
    Helicopters—Poetry
    Seaplanes—Poetry
— Popular works
— Problems, exercises, etc. *(TL560)*
— Psychology
  sa Aeronautics, Military—Psychology
    Fear of flying
  x Aviation psychology
    Flight—Psychological aspects
  xx Air pilots
    Aviation medicine
    Psychology, Applied
  Example under Psychology
— Relief service *(Direct)* *(TL722.8)*
  sa Aeronautics in medicine
    Aeroplane ambulances
    Search and rescue operations
  x Aeronautics—Medical service
  xx Aeroplane ambulances
    Life-saving
— Research
  See Aeronautical research
— Safety measures *(TL553.5; TL697.S3)*
  sa Aeronautics—Accidents
    Aeroplanes—Dispatching
    Aeroplanes—Ditching
    Aeroplanes—Ice prevention
    Aeroplanes—Oxygen equipment
    Air traffic control
    Aircraft survival equipment
    Airport zoning
    Airports—Bird control
    Drinking on aircraft
    Pilot ejection seats
    Pressure suits
    Radar in aeronautics
    Safety harness (Aeronautics)
    United States. Army—Aviation—
      Safety measures
    United States. Navy—Aviation—
      Safety measures
  x Aeroplanes—Safety measures
    Aircraft safety measures
  xx Aeronautics—Accidents
    Propellant actuated devices
— Sanitary aspects *(RA615.2)*
  x Aeronautics—Hygienic aspects
    Aviation hygiene
— Societies, etc.
  xx Aeronautical societies
— Songs and music *(M1977.A; M1978.A;*
    History and criticism, ML3780)
  x Aeronautics in music
    Aeronautics—Music
  Example under Music; Songs
— Statistics *(TL521-530)*
— Study and teaching *(Direct)*
  sa Aeronautical research
    Aeronautics, Military—Study and
      teaching
    Flight training
    Moving-pictures in aeronautics
    Synthetic training devices
  xx Aeronautical research
— Study and teaching (Elementary)
    (LB1594.5)
— Subject headings
  See Subject headings—Aeronautics
— Systems engineering
— Tables *(TL551)*

— Terminology *(TL509)*
— Vocational guidance
  See Aeronautics as a profession
— Voyages
  See Aeronautics—Flights

GEOGRAPHIC SUBDIVISIONS

— Acronyms
— Flights
— — Juvenile literature
Aeronautics, Commercial *(Indirect)*
    (TL515-532; TL552)
  sa Air line police
    Air lines
    Air lines, Local service
    Airports—Landing fees
    Airways
    Helicopter transportation
    Heliports
    Metropolitan helicopter services
    Transport planes
  x Air transport
    Civil aeronautics
    Civil aviation
    Commercial aeronautics
    Commercial aviation
  xx Geography, Aerial
    Transportation
  Example under Traffic engineering
— Accounting
  See Air lines—Accounting
— Chartering *(Direct)*
  sa Air charter contracts
  x Aeroplanes—Chartering
    Air charter
    Charter flight
    Chartering of aeroplanes
— Claims
— Collective bargaining
  See Collective bargaining—
    Aeronautics
— Collective labor agreements
  See Collective labor agreements—
    Aeronautics
— Fares
  See Air lines—Rates
— Finance
  sa Air lines—Cost of operation
    Air lines—Rates
— Freight *(TL720.7)*
  sa Air mail service
    Animals, Air transportation of
  x Aeroplanes—Cargo
    Aeroplanes—Freight
    Air cargo
    Air freight
  xx Express service
    Freight and freightage
— — Juvenile literature
— Juvenile literature
  See Aeronautics—Juvenile literature
— Law and legislation *(Direct)*
  sa Air charter contracts
    Liability for aircraft accidents
  x Air lines—Law and legislation
  xx Aeronautics—Laws and regulations
    Carriers
— Management
— Passenger traffic *(TL720.3)*
  sa Air travel
  x Passenger traffic
  xx Air travel
— — Reservations
    See Air lines—Reservations
— Public opinion
— Rates
  See Air lines—Rates
— Statistics *(TL552)*

— Taxation *(Direct)* *(TL553)*
— Time-tables
  See Air lines—Time-tables
— Vocational guidance
— — Juvenile literature
Aeronautics, Electronics in
  See Electronics in aeronautics
Aeronautics, High-speed
  See High-speed aeronautics
Aeronautics, Military *(Indirect)*
    (UG630-670; International law,
    JX5124)
  sa Aerial gunnery
    Aeroplanes—IFF equipment
    Aeroplanes, Military
    Air bases
    Air defenses, Military
    Air power
    Air raid shelters
    Air warfare
    Aircraft carriers
    Anti-submarine warfare
    Kites (Military and naval
      reconnaissance)
    Parachute troops
    Projectiles, Aerial
    Radar confusion reflectors
    United States—Air National Guard
    United States. Navy—Aviation
    subdivision Aerial operations *under*
      names of wars, e.g. World War,
      1939-1945—Aerial operations; *and*
      subdivision Signaling *under armies,*
      e.g. United States. Army—
      Signaling
  x Aeronautics, Naval
    Military aeronautics
    Military aviation
    Naval aeronautics
    Naval aviation
  xx Armaments
    Military art and science
— Juvenile literature
— Law and legislation *(Direct)*
  sa Air warfare (International law)
— Mathematical models
— Observations *(UG630-670)*
  x Aerial observation
    Aerial reconnaissance
    Reconnaissance, Aerial
— Psychology
  xx Aeronautics—Psychology
    Psychology, Applied
    Psychology, Military
— Research *(Direct)*
  xx Aeronautical research
    Military research
— Sounds
  See Air warfare sounds
— Study and teaching *(Direct)*
  sa Flight simulators
  x Air Force schools
  xx Aeronautics—Study and teaching
    Air warfare
    Military education
Aeronautics, Naval
  See Aeronautics, Military
Aeronautics, Radar in
  See Radar in aeronautics
Aeronautics, Radio in
  See Radio in aeronautics
Aeronautics and civilization
  sa Astronautics and civilization
  x Air-age education
    Civilization and aeronautics
Aeronautics and state *(Indirect)*
    (HE9915-9925)
  sa Aeronautics—Laws and regulations

Aeronautics and state *(Indirect)*
    (HE9915-9925) *(Continued)*
    x State and aeronautics
Aeronautics as a profession *(TL561)*
    sa Air lines—Hostesses
        Air pilots
        Women in aeronautics
    x Aeronautics—Vocational guidance
    — Juvenile literature
Aeronautics in agriculture *(Indirect)*
    (TL722.1)
    sa Aerial fertilizing
        Aerial photography in agriculture
        Aerial spraying and dusting in
          agriculture
    x Aeroplanes in agriculture
    xx Agriculture
Aeronautics in art *(N8217.A4)*
    xx Aeronautics—Pictorial works
        Art
        Flight in art
Aeronautics in astronomy
    sa Balloons in astronomy
    x Aeroplanes in astronomy
    xx Astronomy
Aeronautics in cryopedology
    x Aeroplanes in cryopedology
    xx Cryopedology
Aeronautics in earth sciences
    x Aeroplanes in earth sciences
    xx Earth sciences
Aeronautics in education
    x Aeroplanes in education
        Field trips by air
        Flying classes
    xx Field work (Educational method)
Aeronautics in fisheries
    See Aeronautics in fishing
Aeronautics in fishing
    x Aeronautics in fisheries
        Aeroplanes in fishing
    xx Fishing
Aeronautics in forest fire control
    x Aeroplanes in forest fire control
    xx Aeronautics in forestry
        Forest fires—Prevention and control
    — Juvenile literature
Aeronautics in forestry *(TL722.3)*
    sa Aerial photography in forestry
        Aeronautics in forest fire control
    x Aeroplanes in forestry
    xx Forests and forestry
Aeronautics in geodesy
    sa Aerial photogrammetry
    x Aerial reconnaissance in geodesy
        Aeroplanes in geodesy
    xx Geodesy
Aeronautics in geology
    xx Geology
Aeronautics in hunting
    x Aeroplanes in hunting
    xx Hunting
Aeronautics in hydrometeorology *(Indirect)*
    x Aeroplanes in hydrometeorology
    xx Aeronautics in meteorology
        Hydrometeorology
Aeronautics in literature *(TL554)*
Aeronautics in medicine *(Indirect)*
    sa Aeroplane ambulances
    x Aeronautics—Medical service
        Aeroplanes in medicine
    xx Aeronautics—Relief service
Aeronautics in meteorology *(QC879)*
    Here are entered works on the application
        of aeronautics to meteorological pur-
        poses.
    sa Aeronautics in hydrometeorology

        Atmosphere, Upper—Rocket
          observations
        Balloons, Pilot
        Balloons, Sounding
        Meteorology in aeronautics
        Rockets, Sounding
    xx Meteorology
        Meteorology in aeronautics
Aeronautics in missionary work
    x Aeroplanes in missionary work
    xx Missions
Aeronautics in mosquito control *(RA640)*
    x Aerial spraying in mosquito control
        Aeroplanes in mosquito control
    xx Mosquito control
        Spraying
Aeronautics in music
    See Aeronautics—Songs and music
Aeronautics in oceanography
    x Aeroplanes in oceanography
    xx Oceanography
Aeronautics in police work *(HV8080.A3)*
    x Aeroplanes in police work
    xx Police
        Police patrol
        Traffic police
    — Juvenile literature
Aeronautics in riots
    x Aeroplanes in riots
    xx Police
        Riots
Aeronomy
    See Atmosphere, Upper
Aerophagia
    See Aerophagy
Aerophagy *(RC840)*
    x Aerophagia
    xx Hysteria
        Stomach—Diseases
Aeroplane accidents
    See Aeronautics—Accidents
Aeroplane accidents and drinking
    See Drinking and airplane accidents
Aeroplane ambulances *(TL722.8)*
    sa Aeronautics—Relief service
    x Aeroplanes, Ambulance
    xx Aeronautics in medicine
        Aeronautics—Relief service
        Ambulances
        Aviation medicine
Aeroplane bombs
    See Bombs
Aeroplane brakes
    See Aeroplanes—Brakes
Aeroplane carriers
    See Aircraft carriers
Aeroplane control surfaces
    See Aeroplanes—Control surfaces
Aeroplane cylinders
    See Aeroplanes—Motors—Cylinders
Aeroplane engines
    See Aeroplanes—Motors
Aeroplane exhaust emissions
    See Aircraft exhaust emissions
Aeroplane fabrics
    See Aeroplanes—Fabrics
Aeroplane factories
    x Aircraft factories
        Airplane factories
    xx Aeroplane industry and trade
        Factories
    — Design and construction
    — Fires and fire prevention
Aeroplane fuel
    See Aeroplanes—Fuel
Aeroplane industry and trade *(Direct)*
    (Technology, TL724)
    sa Aeroplane factories

        Aeroplane industry workers
        Strikes and lockouts—Aeroplane
          industry
        Used aircraft
    x Aircraft production
        Aviation industry
    xx Aerospace industries
    — Automation
    — Capital productivity
        xx Capital productivity
    — Collective bargaining
        See Collective bargaining—Aeroplane
          industry
    — Collective labor agreements
        See Collective labor agreements—
          Aeroplane industry
    — Costs
        x Aeroplanes—Cost of construction
    — Equipment and supplies
    — Finance *(TL724.1.F5)*
        x Aircraft financing
    — Job descriptions
    — Labor productivity
    — Management
    — Military aspects
    — Quality control
    — Records and correspondence
    — Subcontracting *(Direct)* *(TL724.1.S78)*
        Example under Subcontracting
Aeroplane industry workers *(Direct)*
    sa Collective bargaining—Aeroplane
        industry
        Collective labor agreements—Aeroplane
        industry
        Wages—Aeroplane industry workers
    x Aeroplane workers
    xx Aeroplane industry and trade
Aeroplane landing mats
    See Landing mats
Aeroplane parts
    See Aeroplanes—Parts
Aeroplane pressurization
    See Aeroplanes—Pressurization
Aeroplane racing *(Direct)* *(GV759)*
    sa Daily Mail Transatlantic Air Race,
        1969
        Model airplane racing
    x Aeroplanes—Racing
    xx Aeronautical sports
        Aeronautics
        Aeronautics—Competitions
        Racing
    — History
    — — Juvenile literature
Aeroplane recognition
    See Aeroplanes—Recognition
Aeroplane seats
    See Aeroplanes—Seats
Aeroplane sounds
    sa Aeroplanes—Noise
        Fighter plane sounds
        Jet plane sounds
    xx Aeroplanes—Noise
        Sounds
    — Juvenile literature
Aeroplane speed records
    See Aeroplanes—Speed records
Aeroplane tires
    See Aeroplanes—Tires
Aeroplane workers
    See Aeroplane industry workers
Aeroplanes *(TL670-688)*
    sa Aeronautics
        Aeroplanes, Private
        Aircraft cabins
        Amphibian planes
        Autogiros
        Convertiplanes

Drag (Aerodynamics)
Drone aircraft
Fan-in-wing aircraft
Flying-machines
Gliders (Aeronautics)
Lift (Aerodynamics)
Lockheed airplanes
Propellers, Aerial
Seaplanes
Stearman airplanes
Supersonic planes
Vertically rising aeroplanes
specific types of aeroplanes, e.g.
Bombers, Fighter planes
  x Airplanes
 xx Aeronautics
Flying-machines
— Accidents
See Aeronautics—Accidents
— Ailerons
See Ailerons
— Air conditioning
 xx Aeroplanes—Climatic factors
— Airworthiness *(TL671.1)*
sa Airworthiness certificates
  x Airworthiness requirements
 xx Aeroplanes—Standards
— Apparatus and supplies *(TL688)*
sa Aeroplanes—Fuel tanks
Aeroplanes—Hydraulic equipment
Aeroplanes—Oxygen equipment
— Assisted take-off
  x Aeroplanes—Jet-assisted take-off
Assisted take-off of aircraft
JATO
Jet-assisted take-off (Aircraft)
RATO
Rocket-assisted take-off (Aircraft)
 xx Aeroplanes—Take-off
— — Juvenile literature
— Atomic power
See Aeroplanes—Nuclear power
plants
— Batteries
 xx Aeroplanes—Electric equipment
— Bearings *(TL697.B4)*
 xx Bearings (Machinery)
— Brakes *(TL683.B7)*
  x Aeroplane brakes
 xx Aeroplanes—Landing gear
Example under Brakes
— Buffeting
See Buffeting (Aerodynamics)
— Cargo
See Aeronautics, Commercial—
Freight
— Catalogs *(TL686)*
— Cavities
See Cavities (Aeroplanes)
— Chartering
See Aeronautics, Commercial—
Chartering
— Climatic factors
sa Aeroplanes—Air conditioning
Aeroplanes—Cold weather operation
Aeroplanes—Ice prevention
Aeroplanes—Rain erosion
 xx Engineering meteorology
Meteorology in aeronautics
— Cockpits *(TL681.C6)*
sa Aeroplanes—Field of view
 xx Aircraft cabins
— Cold weather operation
 xx Aeroplanes—Climatic factors
Polar regions—Aerial exploration
Example under Cold
— Collectors and collecting *(TL506.5)*
— Collisions with birds

See Aeronautics—Accidents
— Compressed-air equipment
See Aeroplanes—Pneumatic
equipment
— Condensation trails
See Condensation trails
— Control surfaces *(Technology, TL676;
Theory, TL574.C6)*
sa Ailerons
Boundary layer control
Elevators (Aeroplanes)
Flaps (Aeroplanes)
Hinge moments (Aerodynamics)
Spoilers (Aeroplanes)
  x Aerodynamic control of aeroplanes
Aeroplane control surfaces
 xx Aerofoils
Aeroplanes—Control systems
Boundary layer control
— Control systems *(TL678)*
sa Aeroplanes—Control surfaces
Aeroplanes—Handling characteristics
Automatic pilot (Aeroplanes)
Servomechanisms
  x Control systems of aeroplanes
 xx Flight control
— Corrosion
— Cost of construction
See Aeroplane industry and trade—
Costs
— Cost of operation
  x Aeroplanes—Operating costs
— Cowlings
See Aeroplanes—Motors—Cowlings
— Crews
See Flight crews
— Design and construction *(TL671.2)*
sa Aerodynamic load
Aeroelasticity
Aeroplanes—Motors—Design and
construction
Aeroplanes—Nacelles
Aeroplanes—Sheet-metal work
Aeroplanes—Weight
Aeroplanes—Welding
Aircraft drafting
Airframes
Monocoque construction
 xx Lightweight construction
Example under Engineering design; *and
under reference from* Aircraft con-
struction
— — Amateurs' manuals
— — Juvenile literature
— Diesel motors
See Aeroplanes—Motors (Diesel)
— Disinfection *(TL555)*
 xx Aviation medicine
Disinfection and disinfectants
— Dispatching *(TL725.3.D4)*
 xx Aeronautics—Safety measures
Air traffic control
— Distance measuring equipment
See Distance measuring equipment
(Aircraft to ground station)
— Ditching
  x Ditching of aircraft
Emergency landings (over water)
Forced landings (over water)
 xx Aeronautics—Safety measures
Aeroplanes—Landing
Survival (after aeroplane accidents,
shipwrecks, etc.)
— Dopes and doping
See Aeroplanes—Fabrics
— Drafting
See Aircraft drafting
— Drawing

See Aeroplanes—Drawings
— Drawings
  x Aeroplanes—Drawing
 xx Aircraft drafting
— Ejection seats
See Pilot ejection seats
— Electric equipment *(TL690-691)*
sa Aeronautical instruments
Aeroplanes—Batteries
Aeroplanes—Electric wiring
Aeroplanes—Lighting
 xx Aeronautical instruments
Electricity in aeronautics
Landing aids (Aeronautics)
— — Cooling
 xx Heat—Transmission
— — Testing
— Electric wiring *(TL691.W5)*
 xx Aeroplanes—Electric equipment
Electric wiring
— Electronic equipment *(TL693)*
sa Aeroplanes—Radio equipment
  x Airborne electronic equipment
 xx Electronic apparatus and appliances
Electronics in aeronautics
Landing aids (Aeronautics)
— — Cooling *(TL693)*
 xx Heat—Transmission
Example under Cooling
— — Testing
— Engines
See Aeroplanes—Motors
— Escape devices
See Pilot ejection seats
— Examinations, questions, etc.
— Exhaust emissions
See Aircraft exhaust emissions
— Fabrics *(TL699.F2)*
  x Aeroplane fabrics
Aeroplanes—Dopes and doping
 xx Aeroplanes—Materials
— Field of view *(TL681.C6)*
  x Aeroplanes—Range of vision
Field of view from aeroplanes
Range of vision from aeroplanes
 xx Aeroplanes—Cockpits
— Fires and fire prevention *(TL697.F5)*
— Flaps
See Flaps (Aeroplanes)
— Flight recorders
See Flight recorders
— Flight testing
  x Flight testing of aeroplanes
 xx Aeroplanes—Testing
— — Juvenile literature
— Flying, Private
See Private flying
— Flying qualities
See Aeroplanes—Handling
characteristics
— Freight
See Aeronautics, Commerical—
Freight
— Fuel *(TL704.7)*
sa Gasoline—Anti-knock and
anti-knock mixtures
Jet planes—Fuel
  x Aeroplane fuel
Aviation gasoline
 xx Gasoline—Anti-knock and
anti-knock mixtures
Motor fuels
— — Pipe lines
— Fuel systems
sa Aeroplanes—Fuel tanks
— — Vapor lock
  x Vapor lock in aeroplanes
 xx Gasoline

— Operating costs
    See Aeroplanes—Cost of operation
— Operation
    See Aeroplanes—Piloting
— Oxygen equipment *(TL697.O8)*
    x Oxygen equipment in aeroplanes
    xx Aeronautics—Safety measures
       Aeroplanes—Apparatus and supplies
       Respirators
— Painting
— Parawings
    x Parawings
    xx Aeroplanes—Wings
— Parts
    x Aeroplane parts
    xx Machine parts
— Patents *(TL513)*
    xx Aeronautics—Patents
— Performance *(TL671.4)*
— Piloting *(TL710)*
    sa Aeroplanes—Taxiing
       Flight navigators
       Flight simulators
       Flight training
       Instrument flying
       Link trainers
       Stunt flying
       subdivision Piloting *under specific*
         types of aircraft, e.g. Fighter
         planes—Piloting; Helicopters—
         Piloting
    x Aeroplanes—Operation
    xx Air pilots
       Flight training
       Navigation (Aeronautics)
    Example under reference from Aeronau-
       tics—Piloting; Air pilotage; Piloting
       (Aeronautics)
— — Juvenile literature
— — Mathematical models
    x Air pilots—Mathematical models
       Pilot dynamic capability models
    xx Human engineering
       Man-machine systems
— — Programmed instruction
— Pilots
    See Air pilots
— Pitching
    See Pitching (Aerodynamics)
— Pneumatic equipment
    sa Aeroplanes—Pressurization
    x Aeroplanes—Compressed-air
       equipment
— Poetry
    See Aeronautics—Poetry
— Pressurization
    x Aeroplane pressurization
       Aircraft cabins, Pressurized
       Cockpits, Pressurized
       Pressurized cabins (Aircraft)
       Pressurized cockpits (Aircraft)
    xx Aeroplanes—Pneumatic equipment
       Atmospheric pressure
— Private flying
    See Private flying
— Propeller-turbine engines
    See Aeroplanes—Turbine-propeller
       engines
— Propellers
    See Propellers, Aerial
— Racing
    See Aeroplane racing
— Radar equipment *(TL696.2)*
    sa Airborne profile recorder
    xx Radar in aeronautics
    Example under reference from Airborne
       radar
— Radiators *(TL702.R3)*

    xx Radiators
— Radio antennas *(TL694.A6)*
    x Aircraft antennas
    xx Aeroplanes—Radio equipment
       Radio—Antennas
— Radio control
    xx Radio in aeronautics
— Radio equipment
    sa Aeroplanes—Radio antennas
    x Airborne radio equipment
       Radio equipment, Airborne
    xx Aeroplanes—Electronic equipment
       Mobile communication systems
       Radio in aeronautics
— — Reliability
— Radio operators
    See Flight radio operators
— Rain erosion
    x Rain erosion (Aeronautics)
    xx Aeroplanes—Climatic factors
       Erosion
       Erosion of metals
       Rain and rainfall
— Ramjet engines
    x Jet planes—Motors
       Ramjet engines, Aircraft
       Ramjet plane engines
    xx Aeroplanes—Jet propulsion
— — Air intakes *(TL709.5.I5)*
    x Air inlets (Jet planes)
       Air intakes (Jet planes)
       Supersonic inlets (Jet planes)
— — Combustion
— — Control systems
— — Diffusers
    xx Diffusers
— — Testing
— Range of vision
    See Aeroplanes—Field of view
— Recognition
    sa Aeroplanes—Identification marks
       Aeroplanes—IFF equipment
       Radar in aeronautics
    x Aeroplane recognition
       Aeroplanes, Military—Recognition
       Aircraft identification
       Aircraft recognition
    xx Aeroplanes—Identification marks
       Aircraft spotting
— Refueling *(TL711.R4)*
    x Refueling of aeroplanes
    xx Motor fuels
— Registers *(Direct)* *(TL512)*
    sa Aeroplanes—Registration and
       transfer
    Example under reference from Registers
— Registration and transfer *(Direct)*
    sa Aeroplanes—Nationality
    x Registration of aeroplanes
    xx Aeroplanes—Registers
       Non-contentious jurisdiction
       Recording and registration
— Rigging *(TL671.5)*
    Example under reference from Rigging
— Rivets and riveting
    See Rivets and riveting, Aircraft
— Rocket engines
    x Aeroplanes—Rocket propulsion
       Rocket planes—Motors
       Rocket propulsion (Aeroplanes)
    xx Aeroplanes—Jet propulsion
       Rocket planes
       Rocketry
       Rockets (Aeronautics)
    Example under Rocket engines
— Rocket propulsion
    See Aeroplanes—Rocket engines
— Rolling

    See Rolling (Aerodynamics)
— Safety measures
    See Aeronautics—Safety measures
— Seats *(TL685.5.S4)*
    x Aeroplane seats
       Aircraft seats
       Seats, Aeroplane
    xx Chairs
— — Specifications *(Direct)*
— Sheet-metal work
    x Aircraft sheet-metal work
    xx Aeroplanes—Design and
       construction
       Sheet-metal work
— Skis *(TL683.S6)*
    xx Aeroplanes—Landing gear
— Soundproofing
    Example under Soundproofing
— Specifications *(TL671.1)*
— Speed
    sa Aeroplanes—Speed records
— Speed records
    x Aeroplane speed records
    xx Aeroplanes—Speed
    Example under Speed records
— Spin
    See Spin (Aerodynamics)
— Stability
    See Stability of aeroplanes
— Stalling
    See Stalling (Aeroplanes)
— Standards *(TL671.1)*
    sa Aeroplanes—Airworthiness
       Gliders (Aeronautics)—Standards
— Steel
    See Aircraft steel
— Stresses
    See Airframes
— Structures
    See Airframes
— Sweepback
    See Aeroplanes—Wings, Swept-back
— Tail surfaces *(TL677.T3)*
    sa Elevators (Aeroplanes)
— Take-off *(TL711.T3)*
    sa Aeroplanes—Assisted take-off
       Aircraft carriers—Flight decks
    Example under references from Aircraft
       take-off; Take-off of aircraft
— Tariff
    See Duty-free importation of aircraft
— Taxation *(Direct)*
    xx Taxation of personal property
— Taxiing
    x Taxiing (of aircraft)
    xx Aeroplanes—Piloting
— Terminology
— Testing *(TL671.7)*
    sa Aeroplanes—Flight testing
— Tires
    x Aeroplane tires
— Turbine-propeller engines *(TL709.3.T8)*
    x Aeroplanes—Propeller-turbine
       engines
       Aeroplanes—Turboprop engines
       Propjet engines (Aeroplanes)
       Turboprop engines (Aeroplanes)
       Turbopropeller jet engines
         (Aeroplanes)
    xx Aeroplanes—Jet propulsion
       Aircraft gas-turbines
       Gas-turbines
       Propellers, Aerial
— Turbojet engines
    x Jet planes—Motors
       Turbojet plane engines
    xx Aeroplanes—Jet propulsion
       Aircraft gas-turbines

Aeroplanes *(TL670-688)*
— Turbojet engines *(Continued)*
Gas-turbines
— — Air intakes *(TL709.5.I5)*
   x Air inlets (Jet planes)
   Air intakes (Jet planes)
   Supersonic inlets (Jet planes)
— — Bearings
— — Blades *(TL709)*
   Example under Blades
— — Combustion
— — Control systems
— — Cooling *(TL709.5.C6)*
— — Diffusers
   xx Diffusers
— — Ignition
— — Lubrication
— — Testing
— Turboprop engines
   See Aeroplanes—Turbine-propeller
     engines
— Valves
   See Aeroplanes—Motors—Valves
— Vibration
   See Vibration (Aeronautics)
— Weight
   xx Aeroplanes—Design and
     construction
   Aeroplanes—Materials
— Welding *(TL671.5)*
   x Aircraft welding
   xx Aeroplanes—Design and
     construction
   Example under Welding
— Wheels
   See Aeroplanes—Landing gear
— Windshields
— Wings *(TL672-3; TL675)*
   sa Aeroplanes—Nacelles
   Aeroplanes—Parawings
   Ailerons
   Camber (Aerofoils)
   Fan-in-wing aircraft
   Oscillating wings (Aerodynamics)
   Transonic planes—Wings
   x Wings (Aeroplanes)
   xx Ailerons
   Airframes
   Oscillating wings (Aerodynamics)
   Wings
— — Testing
— Wings, Canard
   x Canard wings (Aeroplanes)
— Wings, Cruciform *(TL673.C7)*
   x Cruciform wings (Aeroplanes)
— Wings, Delta
   See Aeroplanes—Wings, Triangular
— Wings, Oblique
   See Aeroplanes—Wings, Swept-back
— Wings, Ogee
   x Ogee wings (Aeroplanes)
— Wings, Rectangular *(TL673.R4)*
   x Rectangular wings (Aeroplanes)
— Wings, Swept-back *(TL673.S9)*
   x Aeroplanes—Sweepback
   Aeroplanes—Wings, Oblique
— Wings, Trapezoidal
   x Trapezoidal wings (Aeroplanes)
— Wings, Triangular *(TL673.T7)*
   x Aeroplanes—Wings, Delta
   Delta wings (Aeroplanes)
   Triangular wings (Aeroplanes)
— Yawing
   See Yawing (Aerodynamics)
Aeroplanes, Ambulance
See Aeroplane ambulances
Aeroplanes, Company
   x Company aeroplanes

Aeroplanes, Diesel
   See Aeroplanes—Motors (Diesel)
Aeroplanes, Drone
   See Drone aircraft
Aeroplanes, Government
   See Aeroplanes, Military
   Government aircraft
Aeroplanes, Hypersonic
   See Hypersonic planes
Aeroplanes, Jet propelled
   See Aeroplanes—Jet propulsion
   Jet planes
Aeroplanes, Magnetism of
   See Magnetism of aircraft
Aeroplanes, Military *(TL685.3)*
   sa Albatross (Amphibian planes)
   Bombers
   Fighter planes
   Hercules (Turboprop transports)
   Jet planes, Military
   JN-4D (Training planes)
   North American airplanes (Military
     aircraft)
   Training planes
   subdivision Aviation supplies and stores
     under armies, navies, etc., e.g.
     United States. Navy—Aviation
     supplies and stores
   x Aeroplanes, Government
   Aircraft, Government
   Government aeroplanes
   Government-owned aircraft
   Military aeroplanes
   xx Aeronautics, Military
   Air warfare
   Government aircraft
   United States. Air Force—Weapons
     systems
— Armament
   sa Aeroplanes, Military—Rocket
     launchers
   Air-to-air rockets
   Fire control (Aerial gunnery)—
     Equipment
   x Aircraft armament
   xx Arms and armor
— Design and construction
— Flight testing
   x Flight testing of aeroplanes
   xx Aeroplanes, Military—Testing
— Maintenance and repair
— Pictorial works
— Recognition
   See Aeroplanes—Recognition
— Rocket launchers
   x Aircraft rocket launchers
   xx Aeroplanes, Military—Armament
   Example under Rocket launchers (Ord-
     nance)
— Testing
   sa Aeroplanes, Military—Flight testing
— Turrets *(General and Army,*
     UG630-635; Navy, VG90-95)
   x Aircraft turrets
   Gun turrets
   Revolving turrets
Aeroplanes, Personal
   See Aeroplanes, Private
Aeroplanes, Pilotless
   See Guided missiles
Aeroplanes, Private
   sa Beechcraft 17 (Aeroplanes)
   Beechcraft (Aeroplanes)
   Cessna 150 (Private planes)
   Cessna 180 (Private planes)
   Cessna (Aeroplanes)
   Private flying
   x Aeroplanes, Personal

   Personal aeroplanes
   Personal aircraft
   Private aeroplanes
   xx Aeroplanes
   Private flying
Aeroplanes, Rocket propelled
   See Rocket planes
Aeroplanes, Supersonic
   See Supersonic planes
Aeroplanes, Tailless
   x All-wing aeroplanes
   Flying wing (Aeroplanes)
   Tailless aeroplanes
Aeroplanes, Transonic
   See Transonic planes
Aeroplanes, Used
   See Used aircraft
Aeroplanes, Vertically rising
   See Vertically rising aeroplanes
Aeroplanes in agriculture
   See Aeronautics in agriculture
Aeroplanes in art
   xx Art
Aeroplanes in astronomy
   See Aeronautics in astronomy
Aeroplanes in cryopedology
   See Aeronautics in cryopedology
Aeroplanes in earth sciences
   See Aeronautics in earth sciences
Aeroplanes in education
   See Aeronautics in education
Aeroplanes in fishing
   See Aeronautics in fishing
Aeroplanes in forest fire control
   See Aeronautics in forest fire control
Aeroplanes in forestry
   See Aeronautics in forestry
Aeroplanes in geodesy
   See Aeronautics in geodesy
Aeroplanes in hunting
   See Aeronautics in hunting
Aeroplanes in hydrometeorology
   See Aeronautics in hydrometeorology
Aeroplanes in medicine
   See Aeronautics in medicine
Aeroplanes in missionary work
   See Aeronautics in missionary work
Aeroplanes in mosquito control
   See Aeronautics in mosquito control
Aeroplanes in oceanography
   See Aeronautics in oceanography
Aeroplanes in police work
   See Aeronautics in police work
Aeroplanes in riots
   See Aeronautics in riots
Aerosleighs
   See Motor sledges
Aerosol filling
   See Pressure packaging
Aerosol packaging
   See Pressure packaging
Aerosol sniffing
   x Sniffing, Aerosol
   xx Drug abuse
   Gases, Asphyxiating and poisonous
Aerosol therapy
   xx Aerosols
   Inhalation therapy
Aerosols
   sa Aerosol therapy
   Contamination (Technology)
   Fume control
   Pressure packaging
   Sonic coagulation
   xx Air—Pollution
   Atomization
— Mathematical models

Aerospace industries *(Direct)*
 sa Aeroplane industry and trade
  Guided missile industries
 x Aircraft production
 Example under reference from Industries
 — Accidents
 — Costs
  See Aerospace industries—Estimates
   and costs
 — Employees
 — Estimates and costs *(Direct)* *(TL872)*
  x Aerospace industries—Costs
 — Vocational guidance
Aerospace law
 See Aeronautics—Laws and regulations
  Space law
Aerospace medicine
 See Aviation medicine
  Space medicine
Aerospace telemeter
 See Aerospace telemetry
Aerospace telemetry *(TL694.T35)*
 sa Telemeter (Physiological apparatus)
 x Aerospace telemeter
 xx Aeronautics—Communication systems
  Astronautics—Communication systems
  Astronautics—Optical communication
   systems
  Electronic measurements
  Electronics in aeronautics
  Telemeter
Aerospace weapons systems
 See United States. Air Force—Weapons
  systems
  United States. Navy—Weapons
  systems
Aerostatics *(QC168; TL578)*
 xx Aerodynamics
  Aeronautics
Aerostation
 See Aeronautics
Aerotherapeutics
 See Aerotherapy
Aerotherapy *(RM824-9)*
 sa Inhalation therapy
 x Aerotherapeutics
  Air, Rarefied—Therapeutics
 xx Inhalation therapy
Aerothermodynamics
 sa Ablation (Aerothermodynamics)
  Aerodynamic heating
  Artificial satellites—Atmospheric entry
  Ballistic missiles—Atmospheric entry
  Plasma sheaths
 x Thermoaerodynamics
 xx Aerodynamics, Supersonic
  Aerodynamics, Transonic
  Astronautics
  High-speed aeronautics
  Thermodynamics
Aerotriangulation
 See Aerial triangulation
Aesthetic form
 See Form (Aesthetics)
Aesthetics *(Art, N61-79; Philosophy, BH)*
 sa Art
  Art and literature
  Art and morals
  Art—Philosophy
  Classicism
  Color
  Criticism
  Cubism
  Dadaism
  Dancing—Philosophy
  Dilettantism
  Expressionism (Art)
  Fantastic, The (Aesthetics)

  Form (Aesthetics)
  Futurism (Art)
  Harmony (Aesthetics)
  Idealism in art
  Idealism in literature
  Impressionism (Art)
  Indians of North America—Aesthetics
  Information theory in aesthetics
  Kitsch
  Lettrism
  Literature—Aesthetics
  Literature—Psychology
  Movement, Aesthetics of
  Moving-pictures—Aesthetics
  Music and architecture
  Music—Philosophy and aesthetics
  Naturalism in art
  Naturalism in literature
  Nature (Aesthetics)
  Painting
  Particularity (Aesthetics)
  Poetry
  Post-impressionism (Art)
  Proportion
  Realism in art
  Realism in literature
  Rhythm
  Romanticism
  Sculpture
  Spatialism (Art)
  Sublime, The
  Surrealism
  Symmetry
  Ugliness
  Ut pictura poesis (Aesthetics)
  Worth
  subdivision Aesthetics *under names of*
   persons
 x Art—Analysis, interpretation,
   appreciation
  Beautiful, The
  Beauty
  Esthetics
  Taste (Aesthetics)
 xx Art
  Criticism
  Literature—Psychology
  Philosophy
  Proportion
  Symmetry
 — Early works to 1800 *(N62-65;*
   BH91-188)
 — Juvenile literature *(BH220)*
 — Physiological aspects
 — Quotations, maxims, etc.
 — Terminology
Aesthetics, American, ⌈Greek, Indic, etc.⌉
 x American ⌈Greek, Indic, etc.⌉ aesthetics
Aesthetics, Ancient *(Art, N61; Philosophy,*
 BH91-116)
Aesthetics, Communist
 See Communist aesthetics
Aesthetics, Medieval *(Art, N61; Philosophy,*
 BH131-6)
Aesthetics, Modern *(Art, N61; Philosophy,*
 BH151-208)
 x Modern aesthetics
 — 16th century *(Art, N61; Philosophy,*
   BH161-8)
 — 17th century *(Art, N61; Philosophy,*
   BH171-8)
 — 18th century *(Art, N61; Philosophy,*
   BH181-8)
 — 19th century *(Art, N61; Philosophy,*
   BH191-8)
 — 20th century *(Art, N61; Philosophy,*
   BH201-8)

Aesthetics, Oriental *(BH101-2)*
 x Oriental aesthetics
Aestimatum *(Direct)*
 x Contractus aestimatorius
 xx Bailments
  Commission merchants
  Contracts
Aetas (Philippine Negritos)
 xx Negritos
Aether
 See Ether
Aethiopic . . .
 See Ethiopic . . .
Aetiology
 See Diseases—Causes and theories of
  causation
Aetolian League *(DF236-7)*
Afade dialect *(PL8046.A2)*
 x Áffadéh dialect
 xx Chadic languages
  Kotoko dialects
Afar language *(PJ2421)*
 sa Saho language
 x Adaiel language
  Danakil language
  Dankali language
 xx Cushitic languages
  Saho language
Afara
 See Limba
Afara (African tribe)
 xx Arabs in Africa
Áffadéh dialect
 See Afade dialect
Affect (Psychology)
 sa Emotions
  Temperament
 xx Emotions
  Psychology
Affection
 See Friendship
  Kindness
  Love
Affections, Alienation of
 See Alienation of affections
Affidavits *(Direct)*
 sa Depositions
 xx Evidence, Documentary
  Evidence (Law)
  Oaths
  Witnesses
Affiliation (Psychology)
 xx Attitude (Psychology)
  Social psychology
Affine geometry
 See Geometry, Affine
Affinity, Chemical
 See Chemical affinity
Affinity (Canon law)
Affinity (Canon law, Orthodox Eastern)
Affinity (Greek law)
Affinity (Law) *(Direct)*
 sa Marriage with deceased wife's sister
 xx Domestic relations
  Impediments to marriage
Affinity (Roman law)
Affixes
 See Grammar, Comparative and general—
   Affixes
  subdivision Affixes *under names of*
   languages and groups of languages
Affliction
 See Suffering
Afforestation *(Indirect) (SD409)*
 sa Forests and forestry
  Reforestation
  Tree planting
 x Forest planting

Afforestation *(Indirect)* *(SD409)*
  (Continued)
    Forestation
    Planting
  xx Forests and forestry
    Hurricane protection
    Natural resources
    Reforestation
    Tree planting
Affray *(Direct)*
  x Fray
  xx Assault and battery
    Breach of the peace
    Criminal law
    Riots
Affreightment
  See Bills of lading
    Charter-parties
    Freight and freightage
Afghan hounds *(SF429.A4)*
Afghan language
  See Pushto language
Afghan Wars
  x India—History—Afghan Wars,
    1838-1919
  xx Eastern question (Central Asia)
  — Postal service
Afghans
  See Pushtuns
Aflatoxins
  xx Mycotoxins
Afrasiyabids
Africa
  — Climate
    Example under Tropics—Climate
  — — Maps
      Example under Maps
  — Colonization
    Example under Colonization
  — Commerce
  — — United States
      Note under United States—Com-
      merce—Africa, ⌈Belgium, China,
      etc.⌉
  — History
  — — To 1884
  — — — Juvenile literature
  — — 19th century
  — — 1884-1960
  — — 1960-
  — Kings and rulers
  — — Juvenile literature
  — Maps
    Example under Maps
  — Native races
    Example under Native races; Race prob-
      lems
Africa, Central
  Example under Scientific expeditions
Africa, North
  x Barbary States
  — Economic conditions
  — — Maps
      Example under Maps
  — History *(DT160-177)*
  — — To 647
  — — 647-1517
    sa Aghlabids
  — — 1517-1882
    sa Hafsides
      United States—History—
        Tripolitan War, 1801-1805
      United States—History—War
        with Algeria, 1815
  — — 1882-
Africa, South
  — History *(DT730-995)*
  — — To 1836 *(DT773)*
    sa Slachters Nek Rebellion, 1815

  — — Kafir Wars, 1811-1878
    x Kafir Wars
  — — Great Trek, 1836-1840 *(DT773)*
    x Great Trek
    xx Boers
      Cape of Good Hope—History
  — — — Juvenile literature
  — — South African War, 1899-1902
      See South African War, 1899-1902
  — — Rebellion, 1914-1915
  — Native races
    Example under Native races
  — Race question
    x Apartheid
  — — Juvenile literature
Africa, North, in literature
Africa, Southern, studies
  See Southern African studies
Africa in literature
  sa Angola in literature
Africa in moving-pictures
  xx Moving-pictures
African-Americans
  See Negroes
African art
  See Art, African
African-Asian politics
  See Afro-Asian politics
African cooperation
  sa Pan-Africanism
  xx International cooperation
    Pan-Africanism
African daisy
  See Gerbera
African drama *(Direct)*
African drama (English)
  See English drama—African authors
African elephant
  xx Elephants
  — Behavior
  — Control *(Indirect)*
  — Juvenile literature
  — Legends and stories
African fiction *(Direct)*
African horse sickness
  xx Horses—Diseases
African languages
  sa names of languages, e.g. Bantu
    languages, Fulah language, Timne
    language; *also subdivision* Languages
    under names of African countries,
    regions, etc., e.g. Nigeria—
    Languages
African literature *(PL8010-8013)*
  x Negro literature (African)
African literature (English)
  See English literature—African authors
African literature (French)
  See French literature—African authors
African literature (Portuguese)
  See Portuguese literature—African authors
African lymphoma
  See Burkitt's lymphoma
African masks
  See Masks, African
African music
  See Music, African
African oil-palm
  See Oil-palm
African philology
African poetry *(Direct)*
African poetry (English)
  See English poetry—African authors
African poetry (Portuguese)
  See Portuguese poetry—African authors
African prose literature *(Direct)*

African prose literature (English)
  See English prose literature—African
    authors
African relations
  See Pan-Africanism
African sculpture
  See Sculpture, African
African students in the United States, ⌈etc.⌉
African studies *(Direct)*
  sa Afro-Asian studies
    Near East studies
  — Fellowships
    See African studies—Scholarships,
      fellowships, etc.
  — Scholarships, fellowships, etc. *(Direct)*
    x African studies—Fellowships
African sugar-cane
  See Sorgo
African swine fever
  x East African swine fever
    Swine fever, African
    Wart-hog disease
African swine fever virus
  xx Viruses
African tales
  See Tales, African
African trypanosomiasis
  xx Trypanosomiasis
African violets *(Botany, QK495.G4; Culture,*
    SB413.A4)
  x Usambara violets
  — Varieties
African wild ass *(QL737.U62)*
  x Asses
    Wild ass, African
Africander cattle *(SF199.A3)*
  x Afrikander cattle
Africanders
  See Boers
Africanization *(Direct)*
  Here are entered works dealing with the
  practice by African nations of replac-
  ing non-African civil servants, busi-
  nessmen, etc., with local people.
Africans
  — Psychology
Africans in Austria, ⌈etc.⌉
Africans in foreign countries
Africans in literature
Afridis
  xx Pushtuns
Afrikaanders
  See Boers
Afrikaans-Arabic dialect
  See Arabic-Afrikaans dialect
Afrikaans ballads
  See Ballads, Afrikaans
Afrikaans children's stories
  See Children's stories, Afrikaans
Afrikaans drama *(Collections, PT6565;*
    History, PT6520)
Afrikaans essays
  x South African essays (Afrikaans)
Afrikaans fiction *(Collections, PT6570;*
    History, PT6525)
  sa Children's stories, Afrikaans
Afrikaans folk-songs
  See Folk-songs, Afrikaans
Afrikaans hymns
  See Hymns, Afrikaans

Afrikaans language *(PF861-884)*
 The language spoken and written by the descendants of the Dutch colonists in South Africa, gradually evolved and differentiated from the Dutch South African dialects of the earlier periods. The name, first used about 1861, was gradually adopted by the press, and later recognized as an official language by legislative enactment.
 For material concerning any Dutch South African dialect not conforming to the Dutch as spoken or written in the Netherlands, use the heading Afrikaans language, or Dutch language—Dialects—Africa, South, as the case may be. If necessary use both headings.
 x Afrikander language
  Cape Dutch
  Taal
— Dialects
— — Arabic
  See Arabic-Afrikaans dialect
Afrikaans literature *(PT6500-6590)*
 x South African literature (Afrikaans)
— 20th century

GENERAL SUBDIVISIONS

— Pictorial works
Afrikaans newspapers
 Note under Newspapers
Afrikaans periodicals
Afrikaans poetry *(Collections, PT6560; Folk literature, PT6545; History, PT6515)*
 x South African poetry (Afrikaans)
Afrikaans prose literature *(Collections, PT6570; History, PT6525)*
 x South African prose literature (Afrikaans)
Afrikaans wit and humor *(PN6222.A)*
Afrikander cattle
 See Africander cattle
Afrikander language
 See Afrikaans language
Afrikanders
 See Boers
Afro-American studies *(Direct)* *(E184.7)*
 sa Afro-Latin American studies
  Negroes—History—Study and teaching
 x Black studies
 xx Negroes—Education
  Negroes—History—Study and teaching
  Negroes—Race identity
— Audio-visual aids
— Public opinion
Afro-Americans
 See Negroes
Afro-Asian politics *(DS33.3)*
 x African-Asian politics
  Asian-African politics
 xx World politics
— Sources
Afro-Asian studies *(Direct)*
 Here are entered works on the study of Africa and Asia combined, including their history, geography, language, general culture, etc.
 xx African studies
  Area studies
  Oriental studies
Afro-Latin American studies *(Direct)*
 xx Afro-American studies
Afroasiatic languages *(PJ990)*
 sa Chadic languages
  Coptic language
  Egyptian language
  Hamito-Semitic languages

Afşar (Turkish tribe)
 See Afshar (Turkish tribe)
Afshar (Turkish tribe) *(GN630.A18)*
 x Afşar (Turkish tribe)
  Avşar (Turkish tribe)
 xx Turks
Aftasides
After-dinner speeches
 sa Introduction of speakers
  Speeches, addresses, etc.
  Toasts
 xx Orations
  Speeches, addresses, etc.
  Toasts
After-images
 sa Eidetic imagery
  Phosphenes
 x Spectrum, Ocular
 xx After-sensations
  Fatigue, Mental
  Imagery (Psychology)
  Phosphenes
  Senses and sensation
  Vision
After-sensations
 sa After-images
 xx Senses and sensation
  Touch
Aftereffects, Figural
 See Figural aftereffects
Afterglow (Physics) *(QC711.8.A34)*
 sa Luminescence
  Phosphorescence
 xx Electric discharges through gases
Afternoon teas
Aftosa fever
 See Foot-and-mouth disease
Agadir, Morocco
— Earthquake, 1960
Agammaglobulinemia
 x Gamma globulin deficiency
  Hypogammaglobulinemia
 xx Immunopathology
Agape
 sa Love feasts
 xx Fasts and feasts
  Lord's Supper
  Love feasts
  Love (Theology)
  Rites and ceremonies
  Sacred meals
Agar
 xx Algae
Agarabe language
 x Agarabi language
 xx Papuan languages
Agarabi language
 See Agarabe language
Agarias *(DS432.A)*
 x Agariyas
 xx Ethnology—India
Agariyas
 See Agarias
Agarwals *(DS422.C3)*
 x Agrawāls
 xx Caste—India
Agate ware
 xx Enameled ware
  Kitchen utensils
Agates *(Indirect)*
 xx Quartz
Agathyrsi
Agau language *(PJ2425)*
 sa Bilin language
  Kemant language
  Quara language
 x Agaw language
 xx Bilin language

  Cushitic languages
  Hamitic languages
  Quara language
Agave *(SB317.A2)*
 sa Mescal
  Pulque
  Sisal hemp
  Tequila
 x Maguey
— Therapeutic use
Agaw language
 See Agau language
Agazzi method of teaching *(LB775.A4125)*
 xx Education, Preschool
Age
 sa Age groups
  Longevity
  Middle age
  Old age
  Youth
  subdivision Age *under subjects, e.g.* Domestic animals—Age; Earth—Age; Meteorites—Age
— Juvenile literature
— Physiological effect
  See Aging
Age (Law) *(Direct)*
 sa Age of consent
  Capacity and disability
 xx Capacity and disability
  Impediments to marriage
  Marriage law
— Conflict of laws
  See Conflict of laws—Age
Age (Psychology)
 sa Adulthood
  Age and intelligence
  Childishness
  Maturation (Psychology)
 xx Developmental psychology
  Genetic psychology
  Psychology, Physiological
Age (Roman law)
Age and crime
 See Crime and age
Age and employment *(Direct)*
 sa Ability, Influence of age on
  Children—Employment
  Life span, Productive
  Retired military personnel—Employment
  Youth—Employment
 x Aged—Employment
  Employment and age
  Middle age and employment
  Middle aged workers
  Old age and employment
  Older workers
 xx Ability, Influence of age on
  Discrimination in employment
— United States
  sa United States—Officials and employees, Retired—Employment
Age and intelligence
 x Age and mental ability
  Intellect and age
  Intelligence and age
  Mental ability and age
 xx Age (Psychology)
  Intellect
Age and mental ability
 See Age and intelligence
Age determination (Zoology)
 sa subdivision Age determination *under names of individual animals and groups of animals, e.g.* Horses—Age determination; Domestic animals—Age determination

Age determination (Zoology) *(Continued)*
  x Zoology—Age determination
Age factors in disease
  sa Aging
    Geriatrics
    Pediatrics
    subdivision Age factors *under medical*
      topics, e.g. Cancer—Age factors
  xx Aging
Age groups
  sa Conflict of generations
  x Groups, Age
  xx Age
    Anthropology
    Social groups
    Sociology
Age groups in art
Age groups in literature
Age hardening
  See Precipitation hardening
Age of consent *(Direct)*
  xx Age (Law)
    Consent (Law)
    Marriage law
Age of meteorites
  See Meteorites—Age
Age of rocks
  See Geological time
    Geology, Stratigraphic
Aged *(Direct)* *(HV1451-1493)*
  sa Aged, Killing of the
    Aging
    Church work with the aged
    Cruelty to the aged
    Gerontocracy
    Life span, Productive
    Old age assistance
    Police services for the aged
    Retirement income
    Social case work with the aged
    Social work with the aged
  x Gerontology
    Senior citizens
  xx Adulthood
    Old age
  — Biography
  — Books and reading
    See Books and reading for the aged
  — Care and hygiene
    sa Geriatric nursing
      Geriatrics
      Nursing homes
      Physical education for the aged
    xx Geriatrics
  — Conduct of life *(BJ1691)*
  — Correspondence, reminiscences, etc.
  — Dental care *(Direct)*
    Example under Dental care
  — Dwellings *(NA7195.A4)*
    x Housing for the aged
    xx Architecture and the aged
      Housing
  — — Fires and fire prevention
  — — Public opinion
  — Education
    See Education of the aged
  — Employment
    See Age and employment
  — Hospital care *(Indirect)* *(RC954.3-6)*
    xx Hospital care
  — Legal status, laws, etc. *(Direct)*
  — Library service
    See Libraries and the aged
  — Medical care *(Direct)*
    x Medical assistance programs
      Medical care for the aged
    xx Charities, Medical
      Old age assistance

— — Public opinion
— Nutrition
— Personality
    See Aged—Psychology
— Portraits *(TR680)*
— Prayer-books and devotions *(BV4580)*
    Subdivided by language.
    x Aged—Prayer-books and devotions
      —English
— — English
    See Aged—Prayer-books and
      devotions
— Programmed instruction
— Psychiatric care
    See Geriatric psychiatry
— Psychology
    x Aged—Personality
      Aging—Psychological aspects
      Old age—Psychological aspects
— Public opinion
— Recreation *(GV184)*
    x Invalids—Recreation
— Rehabilitation
— Religious life *(BV4580)*
    sa Church work with the aged
— Research
    See Old age—Research
— Sermons *(BV4316.A4)*
— Sexual behavior
— — Caricatures and cartoons
— Societies and clubs
— Surgery
    xx Surgery
— Transportation *(Direct)*
— Wounds and injuries
Aged, Killing of the
  x Killing of the aged
  xx Aged
    Cruelty to the aged
    Euthanasia
    Manners and customs
    Murder
    Old age
Aged and architecture
  See Architecture and the aged
Aged as consumers *(Direct)*
  xx Consumers
Agencies, Employment
  See Employment agencies
Agencies, Recreation
  See Recreation agencies
Agencies, Theatrical
  See Theatrical agencies
Agency (Jewish law)
Agency (Law) *(Direct)*
  sa Bailments
    Brokers
    Commercial agents
    Commercial travelers
    Commission merchants
    Conflict of interests (Agency)
    Franchises (Retail trade)
    Independent contractors
    Mandate (Contract)
    Master and servant
    Power of attorney
    Proxy
    Real estate business—Law and
      legislation
    Respondeat superior
    Ship brokers
  x Attorneys
    Principal and agent
  xx Brokers
    Commercial agents
    Commercial law
    Contracts
    Independent contractors

    Mandate (Contract)
    Master and servant
    Partnership
  — Conflict of laws
    See Conflict of laws—Agency
Agency (Philosophy)
  See Agent (Philosophy)
Agency (Roman law)
  x Actio de in rem verso
    Actio de peculio
    Actio exercitoria
    Actio institoria
    Actio tributoria
Agent (Philosophy)
  sa Act (Philosophy)
  x Agency (Philosophy)
    Agents
    Person (Philosophy)
  xx Act (Philosophy)
    Philosophy
Agent-nouns *(Aryans, P632; English,*
      PE1205; German, PF3201)
Agents
  See Agent (Philosophy)
Agents, Colonial
  See Colonial agents
Agents, Commercial
  See Commercial agents
Agents, Manufacturers'
  See Manufacturers' agents
Agents, Stabilizing
  See Stabilizing agents
Agents of foreign principals in the United
    States
  See Foreign propagandists in the United
    States
Agents provocateurs *(Direct)*
  xx Police
    Spies
Agfa camera
Aggada
  — Commentaries
  — Greek influences
Agglomeration
  sa Coagulation
  x Clustering of particles
  xx Briquets
    Bulk solids
    Clay
    Coagulation
    Compacting
    Particles
  — Patents
Agglomeration, Sonic
  See Sonic coagulation
Agglutinants
  See Adhesives
Agglutination *(QR185)*
  sa Agglutinins
    Blood—Agglutination
    Hemagglutinin
    Typhoid fever—Diagnosis—
      Agglutination reaction
  xx Bacteria
    Immunity
    Serum diagnosis
Agglutinins *(QR185)*
  sa Cold agglutinin syndrome
    Hemagglutinin
    Leucoagglutinins
    Rh factor
  xx Agglutination
Aggravating circumstances *(Direct)*
  sa Extenuating circumstances
  x Aggravation (Law)
  xx Criminal law
    Criminal liability
    Extenuating circumstances

Aggravation (Law)
   See Aggravating circumstances
Aggregates
   See Set theory
Aggregates (Building materials)
   sa Alkali-aggregate reactions
      Gravel
      Sand
      Slag
      Stone, Crushed
   x Mineral aggregates
   xx Building materials
  — Electric properties
  — Hygienic aspects
  — Standards
  — Storage
  — Testing
  — Transportation
  — Weights and measures
Aggregation, Cell
   See Cell aggregation
Aggression (International law)
   xx Arbitration, International
      Crimes against peace
      International law
      International offenses
      Mediation, International
      War (International law)
Aggressive behavior in animals
   sa Animal fighting
   x Animal aggression
   xx Aggressiveness (Psychology)
      Agonistic behavior in animals
      Animals, Habits and behavior of
      Social hierarchy in animals
Aggressiveness (Child psychology)
   xx Child study
Aggressiveness (Psychology) *(Child study,*
   LB1117)
   sa Aggressive behavior in animals
      Defensiveness (Psychology)
      Fighting (Psychology)
      Hostility (Psychology)
      Violence
   xx Defensiveness (Psychology)
      Fighting (Psychology)
      Psychology
  — Testing
Aghlabids *(DT199)*
   x Aghlabites
   xx Africa, North—History—647-1517
Aghlabites
   See Aghlabids
Agibba (African people)
   See Murle (African people)
Agility
   See Motor ability
Agincourt, Battle of, 1415 *(DC101.5.A2)*
   xx Hundred Years' War, 1339-1453
  — Juvenile literature
  — Sources
Aging
   sa Age factors in disease
      subdivision Aging *under subjects, e.g.*
        Nervous system—Aging
   x Age—Physiological effect
      Senescence
   xx Age factors in disease
      Aged
      Developmental biology
      Longevity
      Middle age
      Old age
  — Psychological aspects
     See Aged—Psychology
        Genetic psychology
  — Research

Agiryama (Bantu tribe)
   See Giryama (Bantu tribe)
Agistment
   See Pasture, Right of
Agitators (Machinery)
   See Mixing machinery
Agitophasia
   See Cluttering (Speech pathology)
Aglemiut dialect *(PM21)*
   x Aglemute dialect
   xx Eskimo language
      Hyperborean languages
Aglemute dialect
   See Aglemiut dialect
Agnatha
   sa Hagfish
      Lampreys
Agnatha (Insects)
   See May-flies
Agnes (Hurricane, 1972)
   See Pennsylvania—Hurricane, 1972
Agni (African tribe) *(GN655.A; Ivory Coast,*
   DT545)
  — Psychology
Agnosia *(RC382)*
Agnosticism *(Philosophic agnosticism, B808;*
   Religion, BL2700-2790; Skepticism,
   B837; Skepticism in France, B1917;
   Theory of knowledge, BD150-232)
   sa Atheism
      Belief and doubt
      Positivism
      Rationalism
      Skepticism
   xx Atheism
      Belief and doubt
      Christianity—Controversial literature
      Faith
      Free thought
      God
      Irreligion
      Positivism
      Rationalism
      Religion
      Secularism
      Skepticism
      Truth
  — Controversial literature
Agnosticism in literature
   xx Literature
Agnus Dei (Sacramental) *(BX2310.A)*
Agona (African people)
   xx Ethnology—Ghana
Agoneaseah Indians
   See Iroquois Indians
Agonistic behavior in animals
   sa Aggressive behavior in animals
      Animal defenses
      Animal fighting
   xx Animals, Habits and behavior of
Agonists
   See Circumcellions
Agoraphobia
   xx Fear
Agranulocytosis *(RC640)*
   x Leucopenia, Malignant
      Malignant leucopenia
   xx Blood—Diseases
      Granulocytopenia
Agraphia
   x Dysgraphia
   xx Brain—Diseases
      Writing
Agrarian laws of Rome
Agrarian question
   See Agriculture and state
      Agriculture—Economic aspects
      Land tenure

Agrarian reform
   See Land reform
Agrawāls
   See Agarwals
Agreement (Psychology)
   See Acquiescence (Psychology)
Agreements
   See Contracts
Agreements, Interstate
   See Interstate agreements
Agribusiness
   See Agricultural industries
      Agriculture—Economic aspects
Agricultural accidents
   See Agriculture—Accidents
Agricultural accounting
   See Agriculture—Accounting
Agricultural administration *(Indirect)*
   (S484)
   sa Acreage allotments
      Agricultural extension work
      Farm production quotas
   x Administration, Agricultural
      Agricultural programs
   xx Agriculture and state
Agricultural assistance
    Here are entered works on international
     aid to agriculture given to under-
     developed areas in the form of techni-
     cal assistance.
   x Foreign aid to agriculture
   xx International agricultural cooperation
      Technical assistance
Agricultural assistance, American, ₍Danish,
   etc.₎ *(Indirect)*
   x American ₍Danish, etc.₎ agricultural
      assistance
Agricultural associations
   See Agricultural societies
Agricultural attachés
   x Attachés
   xx Diplomatic and consular service
Agricultural bacteriology
   See Bacteriology, Agricultural
Agricultural banks
   See Agricultural credit
      Banks and banking
      Mortgage banks
Agricultural botany
   See Botany, Economic
Agricultural census
   See Agriculture—Statistics
Agricultural chemicals
   sa Algicides
      Fertilizers and manures
      Fungicides
      Growth inhibiting substances
      Growth promoting substances
      Herbicides
      Hormones (Plants)
      Insecticides
      Pesticides
      Seeds—Disinfection
      Trace elements
   xx Agricultural chemistry
  — Environmental aspects
     sa Pesticides—Environmental aspects
     xx Agricultural ecology
     Example under reference from Environ-
       ment
  — Law and legislation *(Direct)*
     xx Agricultural laws and legislation
  — Safety measures
  — Spectra
  — Standards
  — Toxicology
Agricultural chemistry *(S583-8)*
   sa Agricultural chemicals

Agricultural chemistry *(S583-8)*
(Continued)
      Chemurgy
      Dairy products—Analysis and
         examination
      Feeds—Analysis
      Fertilizers and manures
      Insect chemosterilization
      Insect sterilization
      Nitrification
      Plants—Chemical analysis
      Soil chemistry
      Soils
      Soils—Composition
      Wood—Chemistry
   x Chemistry, Agricultural
   xx Chemistry
      Fertilizers and manures
      Soils
 — Experiments
 — Laboratory manuals
 — Tables, etc.
 — Technique *(S587)*
 — Terminology
Agricultural climatology
  See Crops and climate
Agricultural clubs
  See Agricultural societies
Agricultural colleges *(Indirect) (S537-9)*
      Here are entered works which deal with
      the history, description, and statistics
      of agricultural colleges. *Cf.* Agricul-
      tural education, which covers general
      and comprehensive works on educa-
      tion in agriculture, and Agriculture—
      Study and teaching, covering works on
      methods of instruction.
  sa Agricultural education
      Agricultural extension work
   x Agricultural schools
   xx Agricultural education
      Agriculture—Study and teaching
      Schools
      Universities and colleges
  Note under Agriculture—Study and teaching
 — Alumni
 — Faculty
   xx College teachers
Agricultural colonies *(Indirect) (HD1516)*
      Here are entered works on settlement of
      the land by organized groups. General
      works on occupation of the land are
      entered under the heading Land settle-
      ment. The heading Colonization is
      used for works on colonial settlement.
  sa Allotment of land
      Jews—Colonization
      Mennonites—Colonization
      Migration, Internal
      Negroes—Colonization
      Penal colonies
      Rehabilitation, Rural
   x Labor colonies
   xx Cities and towns—Growth
      Colonies
      Colonization
      Emigration and immigration
      Land
      Land settlement
      Land tenure
      Poor
      Public lands
      Rehabilitation, Rural
Agricultural commodities
  See Farm produce
Agricultural communication
  See Communication in agriculture
Agricultural conservation program
  See Rural environment assistance program

Agricultural contracts
  See Contracts, Agricultural
Agricultural cooperation
  See Agriculture, Cooperative
Agricultural cooperation, International
  See International agricultural cooperation
Agricultural cooperative credit associations
      (Indirect) (HG2041-2051)
  sa Banks and banking, Cooperative
   x Cooperative credit associations,
      Agricultural
      Farmers' cooperatives
   xx Agricultural credit
      Agricultural societies
      Banks and banking, Cooperative
      Cooperative societies
Agricultural corporations
  See Farm corporations
Agricultural courts and procedure *(Direct)*
   x Agricultural procedure (Law)
   xx Agricultural laws and legislation
      Civil procedure
      Courts
      Non-contentious jurisdiction
      Procedure (Law)
Agricultural credit *(Indirect) (Banking,*
      HG2041-2051; Theory,
      HD1439-1440)
  sa Agricultural cooperative credit
      associations
      Agricultural price supports
      Forest credit
      Mortgage banks
      Mortgage loans
   x Agricultural banks
      Agricultural warrants
      Credit, Agricultural
      Crédit foncier
      Land credit
      Rural credit
      Warrants, Agricultural
   xx Agriculture—Economic aspects
      Banks and banking
      Credit
      Government lending
      Hurricane protection
      Mortgage banks
      Mortgages
 — Problems, exercises, etc.
Agricultural ecology *(Indirect) (S601)*
  sa Agricultural chemicals—Environmental
      aspects
      Crops and climate
      Pesticides—Environmental aspects
   x Agriculture—Ecology
   xx Ecology
 — Terminology
Agricultural economics
  See Agriculture—Economic aspects
Agricultural economics as a profession
   xx Agriculture as a profession
Agricultural education *(Indirect) (S531-9)*
      Here are entered comprehensive treatises
      on education in agriculture. *Cf.*
      Agricultural colleges, under which
      heading are entered works about the
      colleges, descriptive, historical, statis-
      tical, etc., and Agriculture—Study and
      teaching, which covers works dealing
      with methods of instruction.
  sa 4-H clubs
      Agricultural colleges
      Agricultural extension work
      Agricultural laborers—Education
      County agricultural agents
      Dairy schools
      Farmers' institutes
      Forestry schools and education

      Missions—Agricultural work
   x Education, Agricultural
   xx Agricultural colleges
      Agricultural extension work
      Education
      Technical education
      Vocational education
  Note under Agriculture—Study and teaching
 — Audio-visual aids *(S531.5)*
  sa Moving-pictures in agriculture
      Radio in agriculture
   x Agricultural extension work—
      Audio-visual aids
 — Curricula
 — Finance
 — Law and legislation *(Direct)*
 — Research *(Direct)*
   xx Educational research
 — Teacher training
   x Agriculture—Teacher training
   xx Agriculture—Study and teaching
      Agriculture teachers
Agricultural engineering *(S671-760)*
  sa Agricultural engineers
      Agricultural processing
      Drainage
      Electricity in agriculture
      Farm buildings
      Farm equipment
      Farm roads
      Fertilizers and manures—Preservation
        and storage
      Forestry engineering
      Irrigation engineering
   x Agricultural mechanics
      Engineering, Agricultural
      Farm mechanics
   xx Agricultural machinery
      Bioengineering
      Electricity in agriculture
      Engineering
      Farm buildings
      Farm engines
      Farm equipment
 — Laboratory manuals
 — Problems, exercises, etc.
 — Tables, calculations, etc.
   xx Agriculture—Tables and
      ready-reckoners
 — Vocational guidance
  See Agricultural engineering as a
      profession
Agricultural engineering as a profession
  sa Agricultural machinery operators—
      Vocational guidance
   x Agricultural engineering—Vocational
      guidance
   xx Agricultural engineers
      Agriculture as a profession
Agricultural engineers *(Direct)*
  sa Agricultural engineering as a profession
   xx Agricultural engineering
      Agriculturists
Agricultural estimating and reporting
      (Indirect)
  sa Agriculture—Authorship
      Agriculture—Statistics
      Crop yields
   x Crop estimating
      Crop reporting
   xx Agriculture—Authorship
      Agriculture—Statistics
      Crop yields
Agricultural exhibitions *(Indirect) (S551-9)*
  sa Horticultural exhibitions
      Livestock exhibitions
      particular exhibitions, e.g. Toronto.
        Canadian National Exhibition

x Agricultural fairs
   Agriculture—Exhibitions
   Exhibitions, Agricultural
xx Exhibitions
   Fairs
— Finance
— Juvenile literature
Agricultural experiment stations *(Indirect)*
   (S541-3)
sa Agricultural extension work
x Agricultural experimentation
   Experimental farms
   Farms, Experimental
   Stations, Agricultural experiment
xx Agricultural research
   Agriculture and state
   Agriculture—Experimentation
   Agriculture—Study and teaching
Agricultural experimentation
   See Agricultural experiment stations
   Agriculture—Experimentation
Agricultural extension research
   See Agricultural extension work—Research
Agricultural extension work *(Direct)* *(S544)*
sa Agricultural education
   Community development
   County agricultural agents
   Farmers' institutes
   Home demonstration work
   Television in agriculture
x Extension work, Agricultural
xx Agricultural administration
   Agricultural colleges
   Agricultural education
   Agricultural experiment stations
   Agriculture and state
   Agriculture—Information services
   Community development
— Audio-visual aids
   See Agricultural education—
      Audio-visual aids
— Research
   x Agricultural extension research
      Extension research, Agricultural
— Underdeveloped areas
   See Underdeveloped areas—
      Agricultural extension work
Agricultural fairs
   See Agricultural exhibitions
Agricultural geography *(Indirect)*
sa Crop zones
   Geography, Economic
   Soil geography
x Geography, Agricultural
xx Geography, Economic
   Physical geography
— Methodology
Agricultural implements *(Indirect)* *(S676)*
sa Garden tools
   Gardening—Equipment and supplies
   Rice—Implements and machinery
   Spraying equipment
   Viticulture—Equipment and supplies
   names of particular implements, e.g.
      Plows, Scythes
x Agricultural tools
   Farm implements
   Farm tools
   Tools, Agricultural
xx Agricultural machinery
   Farm equipment
   Implements, utensils, etc.
   Tools
— Catalogs
— Juvenile literature
— Prices *(Direct)* *(S676)*
— Repairing
— Testing

— Trade and manufacture *(Direct)*
Agricultural industries *(Direct)*
sa Agricultural processing industries
   Farm supply industries
x Agribusiness
xx Agriculture—Economic aspects
— Employees
   sa Agricultural industries—Vocational
      guidance
— Management
— Study and teaching (Higher) *(Direct)*
   (S530-539)
— Vocational guidance
   xx Agricultural industries—Employees
Agricultural innovations *(Indirect)*
x Innovations, Agricultural
   Technological change in agriculture
Agricultural instruments *(S676.5)*
x Instruments, Agricultural
xx Agricultural machinery
   Farm equipment
   Scientific apparatus and instruments
Agricultural insurance
   See Insurance, Agricultural
Agricultural journalism
   See Journalism, Agricultural
Agricultural laboratories *(Indirect)*
x Agriculture—Laboratories
   Laboratories, Agricultural
Agricultural laborers *(Indirect)*
   (HD1521-1539)
sa Agricultural machinery operators
   Agricultural wages
   Allotment of land
   Collective labor agreements—
      Agriculture
   Disguised unemployment
   Livestock workers
   Migrant labor
   Migration, Internal
   Peasantry
   Peonage
   Rural-urban migration
   Strikes and lockouts—Agricultural
      laborers
   Trade-unions—Agricultural laborers
   Vineyard laborers
x Agricultural workers
   Farm laborers
   Farm workers
xx Farmers
   Peasantry
   Unemployment, Seasonal
Example under Labor and laboring classes; *and*
     under reference from Laborers
Note under Manpower
— Caricatures and cartoons
— Diseases and hygiene *(HD7269.A29)*
— Education
   xx Agricultural education
— History
— — Juvenile literature
— Housing
   See Housing, Rural
— Juvenile literature
— Medical care *(Direct)*
— Nutrition
— Pensions *(Direct)*
   xx Collective farms—Pensions
— — Examinations, questions, etc.
— Pictorial works
— Political activity
   xx Politics, Practical
— Research
Agricultural laborers, Costa Rican, [**Mexican,**
   etc.] *(Direct)*
xx Agricultural laborers, Foreign

Agricultural laborers, Foreign *(Direct)*
sa Agricultural laborers, Costa Rican,
   [Mexican, etc.]
x Foreign agricultural laborers
xx Alien labor
Agricultural laborers in literature
Agricultural laws and legislation *(Direct)*
   (General, HD109; United States,
   HD185-6; Other countries,
   HD301-1130)
sa Agricultural chemicals—Law and
      legislation
   Agricultural courts and procedure
   Agriculture, Cooperative—Law and
      legislation
   Animal industry—Law and legislation
   Collective farms—Law and legislation
   Collective settlements—Law and
      legislation
   Consolidation of land holdings
   Contracts, Agricultural
   Cooperative marketing of farm produce
      —Law and legislation
   Farm corporations
   Farm law
   Farm mechanization, Cooperative—Law
      and legislation
   Farm production quotas
   Land tenure—Law
   Machine-tractor stations—Law and
      legislation
   Nurseries (Horticulture)—Laws and
      legislation
   Plant quarantine
   Produce trade—Law and legislation
   Rural electrification—Law and
      legislation
   Soil conservation—Laws and legislation
   State farms—Law and legislation
   Viticulture—Law and legislation
x Agriculture—Laws and legislation
   Law, Agricultural
xx Agriculture and state
— Colonies
   See Agricultural laws and legislation,
      Colonial
— Criminal provisions
— Study and teaching *(Direct)*
   GEOGRAPHIC SUBDIVISIONS

— [country]
— — Colonies
   Note under Agricultural laws and
      legislation, Colonial
Agricultural laws and legislation, Colonial
   Here are entered general and comparative works only. Works on agricultural
   laws and legislation of the colonies of
   an individual country are entered under the heading Agricultural laws and
   legislation with subdivision [country]
   —Colonies. Works dealing with a spe-
   cific colony are entered under the
   same heading, subdivided by the name
   of the colony.
x Agricultural laws and legislation—
      Colonies
   Colonial agricultural laws
   Colonies—Agricultural laws and
      legislation
Agricultural laws and legislation (Islamic law)
Agricultural laws and legislation (Jewish law)
sa Jubilee (Judaism)
   Sabbatical year (Judaism)
   Terumah
   Tithes—Jews
Agricultural laws and legislation (Roman law)

Agricultural libraries *(Direct)* *(Z675.A8)*
  sa Information storage and retrieval
        systems—Agriculture
  x Libraries, Agricultural
  xx Agriculture—Documentation
        Communication in agriculture
  — Underdeveloped areas
        See Underdeveloped areas—
              Agricultural libraries
Agricultural literature
  sa Agriculture—Bibliography
  x Agriculture—Literature
  xx Agriculture—Bibliography
        Agriculture—History
Agricultural literature searching
  See Information storage and retrieval
        systems—Agriculture
Agricultural machinery *(Indirect)*
        (S671-760)
  sa Agricultural engineering
        Agricultural implements
        Agricultural instruments
        Corn machinery
        Corn planters (Machines)
        Cotton planters (Machines)
        Cultivators
        Drill (Agricultural implement)
        Electricity in agriculture
        Fanning-mills
        Farm engines
        Farm equipment
        Farm mechanization
        Farm trailers
        Feed-grinders
        Fertilizer spreaders
        Fruit grading machinery
        Gardening—Equipment and supplies
        Harrows
        Harvesting machinery
        Horticultural machinery
        Machine-tractor stations
        Milking machines
        Mowing-machines
        Planters (Agricultural machinery)
        Plows
        Potato machinery
        Potato planters (Machines)
        Rice—Implements and machinery
        Rice processing machines
        Scythes
        Separators (Machines)
        Silage machinery
        Spraying equipment
        Tea machinery
        Threshing machines
        Tillage
        Traction-engines
        Transplanting machines
        Viticulture—Equipment and supplies
  x Farm machinery
  xx Farm equipment
        Farm supply industries
        Implements, utensils, etc.
        Machine-tractor stations
        Tools
  Example under Machinery
  — Automatic control *(TJ1480)*
  — Cost of operation
        x Agricultural machinery—Operating
              costs
  — Design and construction
  — Dynamics
  — Economic aspects *(Direct)*
  — Electric equipment
        xx Electricity in agriculture
  — Hydraulic drive *(TJ1480)*
  — Hydraulic equipment
  — Juvenile literature

  — Lubrication
  — Maintenance and repair
        sa Agricultural machinery—
              Replacement
        x Agricultural machinery—Repairing
        xx Agricultural machinery—
              Replacement
        Farm shops
  — — Costs
  — — Laboratory manuals
  — — Production standards
  — — Safety measures
  — Models
  — Noise
  — Operating costs
        See Agricultural machinery—Cost of
              operation
  — Parts
  — Patents
  — Pictorial works
  — Prices *(Direct)*
  — Production standards
  — Reliability
  — Repairing
        See Agricultural machinery—
              Maintenance and repair
  — Replacement
        sa Agricultural machinery—
              Maintenance and repair
        x Replacement of agricultural
              machinery
        xx Agricultural machinery—
              Maintenance and repair
  — Safety measures
  — Seats
  — Standards
  — Study and teaching (Higher) *(Direct)*
        (S678.5)
  — Testing *(TJ1480)*
  — Tires
  — — Repairing
  — Trade and manufacture *(Direct)*
        (HD9486)
        Example under Farm supply industries
  — — Accounting
  — — Automation
  — — Collective labor agreements
        See Collective labor agreements—
              Agricultural machine
              industry
  — — Finance
  — — Technological innovations
  — — Underdeveloped areas
        See Underdeveloped areas—
              Agricultural machinery
              industry
  — Transmission devices
  — Transportation
Agricultural machinery operators *(Indirect)*
  x Farm equipment operators
  xx Agricultural laborers
  — Vocational guidance
        xx Agricultural engineering as a
              profession
  — — Juvenile literature
Agricultural mapping *(Indirect)* *(S494.5.C3)*
  xx Agriculture—Maps
        Cartography
Agricultural maps
  See Agriculture—[local subdivision]—Maps
        Agriculture—Maps
Agricultural marketing
  See Farm produce—Marketing
        Produce trade
Agricultural mathematics *(S566)*
  x Agriculture—Mathematics
        Business mathematics—Agriculture
  — Problems, exercises, etc.

Agricultural mechanics
  See Agricultural engineering
Agricultural mechanization
  See Farm mechanization
Agricultural meteorology
  See Meteorology, Agricultural
Agricultural microbiology *(QR51)*
  sa Bacteriology, Agricultural
        Fungi in agriculture
        Micro-organisms, Nitrogen-fixing
        Soil micro-organisms
        Veterinary microbiology
  x Microbiology, Agricultural
  xx Microbiology
        Plant diseases
  — Laboratory manuals
Agricultural museums *(Indirect)* *(S549)*
  x Agriculture—Museums
  xx Museums
Agricultural pests *(Indirect)* *(SB599-999)*
  sa Farm produce—Storage—Diseases and
              injuries
        Farm produce—Transportation—
              Diseases and injuries
        Fungi in agriculture
        Garden pests
        Host plants
        Insects, Injurious and beneficial
        Nematode diseases of plants
        Pest control
        Plant diseases
        Plant quarantine
        Repellents
        Spraying and dusting in agriculture
        Weeds
        subdivision Diseases and pests *under*
              names of crops, etc., e.g. Cotton—
              Diseases and pests; Fruit—Diseases
              and pests; Trees—Diseases and pests
  xx Horticulture
        Insects, Injurious and beneficial
        Parasites
        Pests
        Plant quarantine
        Zoology, Economic
  — Biological control
        See Pest control—Biological control
  — Identification
  — Juvenile literature
Agricultural photography
  See Photography, Agricultural
Agricultural physics *(S589-600)*
  sa Crops and climate
        Soil physics
  xx Physics
        Soils
  — Laboratory manuals
  — Mathematical models *(S589)*
Agricultural policy
  See Agriculture and state
Agricultural population
  See Rural population
Agricultural price policy
  See Agricultural price supports
        Agricultural prices
Agricultural price supports *(Direct)*
  x Agricultural price policy
        Agricultural subsidies
  xx Agricultural credit
        Agricultural prices
        Agriculture and state
        Price regulation
        Produce trade
Agricultural prices *(Direct)*
  sa Agricultural price supports
        Farm income
        Farm produce—Marketing
        Food prices

Produce trade
   x Agricultural price policy
   Agriculture—Prices
   xx Agriculture—Economic aspects
   Farm income
   Prices
Agricultural procedure (Law)
   See Agricultural courts and procedure
Agricultural processing *(S698)*
   Here are entered general works on the processing of agricultural products. Works restricted to the processing of food are entered under the heading Food industry and trade. Material dealing with special aspects and methods of processing are entered under specific headings such as Farm produce—Grading; Grain—Drying; Poultry, Dressing of.
   sa Feed processing
   Food industry and trade
   Fruit processing
   Poultry processing
   Vegetable processing
   x Farm produce—Processing
   Processing, Agricultural
   xx Agricultural engineering
   — Patents
Agricultural processing industries *(Direct)*
   sa specific agricultural processing industries, e.g. Canning and preserving—Industry and trade; Meat industry and trade
   xx Agricultural industries
Agricultural processing industry workers *(Direct)*
   sa Wages—Agricultural processing industry workers
Agricultural production functions
   See Agriculture—Economic aspects—Mathematical models
   Farm management—Mathematical models
Agricultural production quotas
   See Farm production quotas
Agricultural products
   See Farm produce
   Produce trade
Agricultural programs
   See Agricultural administration
Agricultural proverbs
   See Agriculture—Quotations, maxims, etc.
Agricultural research *(Indirect)*
   sa Agricultural experiment stations
   Agriculture, Cooperative—Research
   Agriculture—Experimentation
   Arid regions—Research
   Cacao research
   Citrus fruits—Research
   Coffee research
   Dairy research
   Drainage research
   Farm management research
   Fertilizers and manures—Research
   Field experiments
   Forestry research
   Fruit-culture—Research
   Grain research
   Horticultural research
   Insecticides—Research
   Irrigation research
   Oilseed plants—Research
   Pasture research
   Plant-breeding—Research
   Plant diseases—Research
   Plants—Disease and pest resistance—Research
   Plants, Protection of—Research

Poultry research
Range research
Soil conservation—Research
Soil research
Stock and stock-breeding—Research
Tea research
Tillage—Research
Tobacco research
Viticulture—Research
Water conservation—Research
   x Agriculture—Research
   xx Research
   — Finance
Agricultural safety
   See Agriculture—Safety measures
Agricultural schools
   See Agricultural colleges
Agricultural societies *(Indirect)* *(S1-20)*
   sa Agricultural cooperative credit associations
   Agriculture—Societies, etc. *[for publications of agricultural and other societies in relation to agriculture]*
   Cow testing associations
   Farmers' institutes
   Patrons of Husbandry
   x Agricultural associations
   Agricultural clubs
   Farm life clubs
   Farmers' organizations
   xx Agriculture, Cooperative
   Boys—Societies and clubs
   Country life
   Societies
   — Abbreviations
Agricultural statistics
   See Agriculture—Statistical methods
   Agriculture—Statistics
Agricultural subsidies
   See Agricultural price supports
   Soil bank program
Agricultural supplies
   See Farm equipment
Agricultural surpluses
   See Surplus agricultural commodities
Agricultural taxes
   See Agriculture—Taxation
Agricultural teachers
   See Agriculture teachers
Agricultural tools
   See Agricultural implements
Agricultural wages *(Direct)*
   x Wages—Agricultural laborers
   xx Agricultural laborers
   Agriculture—Economic aspects
Agricultural warrants
   See Agricultural credit
   Chattel mortgages
Agricultural wastes *(Indirect)*
   sa Animal waste
   Compost
   Dairy waste
   Farm manure
   x Wastes, Agricultural
   xx Factory and trade waste
   Note under Recycling (Waste, etc.)
Agricultural water-supply
   See Water-supply, Agricultural
Agricultural work of missions
   See Missions—Agricultural work
Agricultural workers
   See Agricultural laborers
Agricultural writing
   See Agriculture—Authorship
Agriculture *(Indirect)* *(S; HD1405-2206)*
   sa Acclimatization (Plants)
   Aeronautics in agriculture
   Animal industry

Antibiotics in agriculture
Aquaculture
Arid regions agriculture
Botany, Economic
Burning of land
Cattle
Chemurgy
Clearing of land
Communication in agriculture
Crop yields
Crops and climate
Dairying
Domestic animals
Drainage
Dry farming
Electricity in agriculture
Electronics in agriculture
Ensilage
Explosives in agriculture
Family farms
Farm buildings
Farm life
Farm management
Farm produce
Farm risks
Farmers
Farmers' institutes
Farms
Farms, Location of
Fertilizers and manures
Field crops
Floriculture
Food industry and trade
Forage plants
Forests and forestry
Fruit
Fruit-culture
Gardening
Gleaning
Grain
Grasses
Hill farming
Horticulture
Insects, Injurious and beneficial
International agricultural cooperation
Irrigation
Irrigation farming
Land
Land tenure
Meadows
Métayer system
Negroes as farmers
Oilseed plants
Organic farming
Part-time farming
Pastures
Plant-breeding
Plant spacing
Plastics in agriculture
Radio in agriculture
Radioactive tracers in agriculture
Radioisotopes in agriculture
Reclamation of land
Rotation of crops
Rural population
Seeds
Shifting cultivation
Soil science
Soil-surveys
Soils
Sowing
State farms
Stock and stock-breeding
Threshing
Tillage
Trees
Vegetable gardening
Vegetables

Agriculture *(Indirect)* *(S; HD1405-2206)*
(Continued)
    Viticulture
    Waste lands
    Water in agriculture
    Water-supply, Agricultural
    Women in agriculture
    headings beginning with the word
      Agricultural, *and names of*
      agricultural products, e.g.
      Buckwheat, Oats, Rye
  x Agronomy
    Crops
    Farming
    Husbandry
    Planting
  xx Industrial arts
    Land
    Life sciences
— Abbreviations
— Abstracting and indexing
— Accidents *(Indirect)* *(HD7269.A52)*
  sa Agriculture—Safety measures
  x Agricultural accidents
— Accounting *(S567-9)*
  sa Agriculture—Costs
    Collective farms—Accounting
    Communes (China)—Accounting
  x Agricultural accounting
    Farm accounting
    Farms—Accounting
  xx Farm management
— — Problems, exercises, etc.
— Anecdotes, facetiae, satire, etc.
— Atlases
— Auditing and inspection
— Authorship
  sa Agricultural estimating and reporting
  x Agricultural writing
  xx Agricultural estimating and reporting
— Awards
  xx Rewards (Prizes, etc.)
— Bibliography
  sa Agricultural literature
  xx Agricultural literature
— Capital productivity
  xx Capital productivity
— Charts, diagrams, etc.
— Collective labor agreements
  See Collective labor agreements—
    Agriculture
— Competitions
— Costs *(S567)*
  sa Collective farms—Costs
  xx Agriculture—Accounting
    Agriculture—Economic aspects
— Defense measures
  x Agriculture and defense
— Documentation *(Indirect)*
  sa Agricultural libraries
    Agriculture—Information services
    Information storage and retrieval
      systems—Agriculture
    Punched card systems—Agriculture
  Example under Documentation
— — Economic aspects *(Direct)*
— Early works to 1800
— Ecology
  See Agricultural ecology
— Economic aspects *(Indirect)*
  sa Absenteeism
    Agricultural credit
    Agricultural industries
    Agricultural prices
    Agricultural wages
    Agriculture—Costs
    Agriculture—Taxation
    Diminishing returns
    Farm income

    Farm management
    Farm produce—Marketing
    Farm rents
    Farm tenancy—Economic aspects
    Farms—Recreational use
    Farms, Size of
    Forests and forestry—Economic
      aspects
    Geography, Economic
    Land tenure
    Métayer system
    Produce trade
    Rehabilitation, Rural
    Rent
  x Agrarian question
    Agribusiness
    Agricultural economics
  xx Land
  Example under Economics
— — 1945-

GENERAL SUBDIVISIONS

— — Mathematical models
  x Agricultural production functions
    Production functions, Agricultural
  xx Economics—Mathematical models

GENERAL SUBDIVISIONS

— — Papal documents
— — Pictorial works
— — Public opinion
— — Research *(Direct)*
— Exhibitions
  See Agricultural exhibitions
— Experimentation
  sa Agricultural experiment stations
    Field experiments
  x Agricultural experimentation
  xx Agricultural research
— — Statistical methods
— — Tables, calculations, etc.
— Fellowships
  See Agriculture—Scholarships,
    fellowships, etc.
— Germanic tribes
  x Germanic tribes—Agriculture
— History
  sa Agricultural literature
— Hygienic aspects
— Information services
  sa Agricultural extension work
  xx Agriculture—Documentation
    Communication in agriculture
— Job descriptions
— Juvenile literature
— Labor productivity
  x Collective farms—Labor productivity
  Example under Labor productivity
— Laboratories
  See Agricultural laboratories
— Laboratory manuals
— Laws and legislation
  See Agricultural laws and legislation
— Literature
  See Agricultural literature
— Maps
  sa Agricultural mapping
    Soils—Maps
  x Agricultural maps
    Maps, Agricultural
— Mathematical models *(S494.5.M3)*
— Mathematics
  See Agricultural mathematics
— Moral and religious aspects
— Museums
  See Agricultural museums
— Pictorial works
— Poetry

— Political aspects
  See Agriculture and politics
— Prices
  See Agricultural prices
— Production standards
— Public relations
  See Public relations—Agriculture
— Punched card systems
  See Punched card systems—
    Agriculture
— Quotations, maxims, etc.
  x Agricultural proverbs
    Proverbs, Agricultural
— Readers
  See Readers—Agriculture
— Research
  See Agricultural research
— Safety measures *(S565)*
  x Agricultural safety
  xx Agriculture—Accidents
    Farm management
— Safety regulations *(Direct)*
— Scholarships, fellowships, etc.
  x Agriculture—Fellowships
  xx Agriculture—Study and teaching
— Social aspects *(Direct)*
  xx Social change
    Sociology, Rural
— Societies, etc.
  xx Agricultural societies
— Standards
— Statistical methods
  x Agricultural statistics
— Statistics
  sa Agricultural estimating and reporting
    Crop yields
  x Agricultural census
    Agricultural statistics
    Crop reports
    Crop statistics
  xx Agricultural estimating and reporting
    Crop yields
    Food supply
    Prices
  Example under Statistics
— Study and teaching *(S531-9)*
  Here are entered works which deal
  purely with methods of instruction.
  Cf. Agricultural colleges, under
  which heading are entered works
  about the colleges, descriptive, historical, statistical, etc., and Agricultural education, which covers general and comprehensive works on
  education in agriculture.
  sa Agricultural colleges
    Agricultural education—Teacher
      training
    Agricultural experiment stations
    Agriculture—Scholarships,
      fellowships, etc.
    Agriculture teachers
    Forestry schools and education
— Subject headings
  See Subject headings—Agriculture
— Tables and ready-reckoners *(S413)*
  sa Agricultural engineering—Tables,
    calculations, etc.
    Forests and forestry—Tables and
    ready-reckoners
— Taxation *(Direct)*
  sa Farm produce—Taxation
  subdivision Taxation *under names of*
    agricultural products, e.g. Peanuts
    —Taxation, Tea—Taxation; *and*
    kinds of taxes affecting
    agriculture, e.g. Income tax
  x Agricultural taxes

Taxation of agriculture
    xx Agriculture—Economic aspects
— Teacher training
    See Agricultural education—Teacher
        training
— Tropics
    sa Tropical crops
    x Tropical agriculture
    xx Tropics
    Example under Tropics
— Underdeveloped areas
    See Underdeveloped areas—
        Agriculture
— Vocational guidance
    See Agriculture as a profession

GEOGRAPHIC SUBDIVISIONS

— ⌜local subdivision⌝
— — Maps
    x Agricultural maps
    Maps, Agricultural
Agriculture, Cooperative *(Indirect)*
    (HD1483-6; HD1491)
    Here are entered works which deal with
    cooperation in the production as well
    as in the disposal of agricultural pro-
    ducts.
    sa Agricultural societies
        Bees (Cooperative gatherings)
        Collective farms
        Cooperative cold-storage lockers
        Cooperative marketing of farm produce
        Cooperative marketing of livestock
        Farm mechanization, Cooperative
        Grain elevators, Cooperative
        Patrons of Husbandry
    x Agricultural cooperation
        Cooperation, Agricultural
        Cooperative agriculture
        Cooperative societies, Agricultural
        Farmers' cooperatives
    xx Contracts, Agricultural
        Cooperation
        International cooperation
— Accounting
— Biography
— Employees
    See Agriculture, Cooperative—
        Officials and employees
— Finance
— Law and legislation *(Direct)*
    xx Agricultural laws and legislation
— — Digests
— Management
— Officials and employees
    x Agriculture, Cooperative—
        Employees
— Public opinion
— Research *(Direct)*
    xx Agricultural research
— Taxation *(Direct)*
— Underdeveloped areas
    See Underdeveloped areas—
        Agriculture, Cooperative
Agriculture, Electronics in
    See Electronics in agriculture
Agriculture, Folk-lore of
    See Folk-lore of agriculture
Agriculture, Primitive *(Indirect)* *(GN424-6)*
    sa Indians of Central America—
        Agriculture
        Indians of North America—Agriculture
        Indians of South America—Agriculture
    x Primitive agriculture
    xx Industries, Primitive
        Society, Primitive
Agriculture, Soilless
    See Hydroponics

Agriculture and Christianity
    See Christianity and agriculture
Agriculture and defense
    See Agriculture—Defense measures
Agriculture and politics *(Direct)*
    x Agriculture—Political aspects
        Politics and agriculture
    xx Politics, Practical
Agriculture and state *(Indirect)*
    sa Acreage allotments
        Agricultural administration
        Agricultural experiment stations
        Agricultural extension work
        Agricultural laws and legislation
        Agricultural price supports
        Allotment of land
        Farm production quotas
        Land reform
        Rehabilitation, Rural
        Surplus agricultural commodities
    x Agrarian question
        Agricultural policy
        State and agriculture
    xx Economic policy
        Industry and state
        Land reform
— Mathematical models

GEOGRAPHIC SUBDIVISIONS

— United States
    sa Cropland conversion program
        Feed grain program
        Rural environmental assistance
            program
        Soil bank program
Agriculture and water
    See Water-supply, Agricultural
Agriculture as a profession
    sa Agricultural economics as a profession
        Agricultural engineering as a profession
        Farm management as a profession
        Forestry as a profession
        Horticulture as a profession
        Soil conservation as a profession
    x Agriculture—Vocational guidance
    xx Agriculturists
        Occupations
        Professions
        Vocational guidance
— Juvenile literature
Agriculture teachers *(Direct)* *(S531-9)*
    sa Agricultural education—Teacher
        training
    x Agricultural teachers
    xx Agriculture—Study and teaching
        Teachers
— Salaries, pensions, etc. *(Direct)*
Agriculturists *(Direct)*
    sa Agricultural engineers
        Agriculture as a profession
        Farmers
        Horticulturists
        Plant pathologists
    x Agronomists
— Biography
— Books and reading
— Correspondence, reminiscences, etc.
— Fees
— Legal status, laws, etc. *(Direct)*
Agronomists
    See Agriculturists
Agronomy
    See Agriculture
Agrostology
    See Grasses
Agta language *(PL5550)*
    xx Negrito languages (Philippine)

Aguaruna dialect *(PM5337.A5)*
    sa Jivaran languages
    xx Indians of South America—Languages
        Jivaran languages
Ague
    See Malarial fever
Agul language *(PK9201.A6)*
    xx Caucasian languages
Agunah
    sa Divorce (Jewish law)
    xx Absence and presumption of death
        (Jewish law)
        Desertion and non-support (Jewish law)
        Divorce (Jewish law)
        Marriage (Jewish law)
        Woman—Legal status, laws, etc.
        (Jewish law)
Ahansala
    x Ihansalen
    xx Berbers
        Ethnology—Morocco
Aharaibu Indians
    See Guaharibo Indians
Ahiṃsā
    x Non-harming (Ethics)
        Non-injury (Ethics)
    xx Buddhist ethics
        Hindu ethics
        Jaina ethics
        Nonviolence
        Passive resistance
Ahirs *(DS432.A)*
    x Abhiras
    xx Ethnology—India
Ahl-i Hadīth *(BP195.A3-32)*
    xx Islamic sects
Ahmadiyya
    x Aḥmedīya
        Qadiani
        Qadiyani
    xx Islamic sects
— Missions
Ahmadiyya (Sufism)
    See Badawiyah
Ahmadnagar (Kingdom)
    xx India—History—1500-1765
Ahmedabad
— Riots, 1964
Aḥmedīya
    x Ahmadiyya
Ahom language *(PL4251.A4)*
    xx Indochinese languages
        Tai languages
Aht Indians
    See Nootka Indians
Aht language
    See Nootka language
Ahtena Indians *(E99.A28)*
    x Ahtinné Indians
        Atnah Indians
        Atnatana Indians
        Yellow Knives (Indians)
    xx Athapascan Indians
        Indians of North America
Ahtinné Indians
    See Ahtena Indians
Aichi Hino automobile
    See Hino automobile
AID (Computer program)
    x Automatic Interaction Detector
        Program
Aid to dependent children
    See Child welfare
Aid to developing countries
    See Economic assistance
        Technical assistance
Aid to underdeveloped areas
    See Economic assistance

Aid to undeveloped areas
  See Technical assistance
Aids to air navigation *(Direct)*
  sa Aeronautical charts
    Airways
    Electronics in aeronautics
    Meteorology in aeronautics
    Radar in aeronautics
    Radio in aeronautics
    names of specific equipment and
      systems, e.g. Runway localizing
      beacons; Instrument landing systems
  x Air navigation aids
    Navigational aids (Aeronautics)
  xx Aids to navigation
    Airways
    Electronics in aeronautics
    Meteorology in aeronautics
    Navigation (Aeronautics)
  — Costs
  — Defense measures
    xx War damage, Industrial
  — Inspection
  — Maintenance and repair
  — Research *(Direct)*
Aids to navigation *(Direct)* *(Signaling,*
    VK381-397; Lighthouse service,
    VK1000-1249)
  sa Aids to air navigation
    Astronautics in navigation
    Beacons
    Buoys
    Electronics in navigation
    Fog-bells
    Fog-signals
    Ice breaking operations
    Lighthouses
    Nautical charts
    Radar in navigation
    Radio in navigation
    Transit (Navigation satellite)
  x Marine aids
    Marine signals
  xx Marine service
    Navigation
    Signals and signaling
  — Lists *(VK1150-1246)*
    x Light lists
      Lists of lights
Aikido *(GV1111)*
  xx Hand-to-hand fighting, Oriental
    Self-defense
Ailanthus moth *(Sericulture, SF459; Zoology,*
    QL561.S2)
  x Ailanthus silkworm
    Cynthia silk moth
    Eria silk moth
    Eria silkworm
  xx Moths
    Sericulture
    Silkworms
Ailanthus silkworm
  See Ailanthus moth
Ailerons *(TL677.A5)*
  sa Aeroplanes—Wings
    Flaps (Aeroplanes)
    Spoilers (Aeroplanes)
  x Aeroplanes—Ailerons
  xx Aeroplanes—Control surfaces
    Aeroplanes—Wings
    Spoilers (Aeroplanes)
Ailette, Battle of the, 1917
  See Aisne, Battle of the, 1917
Aimara language
  See Aymara language
Aimores
  See Botocudo Indians

Aino language
  See Ainu language
Ainos
  See Ainu
Ainu
  x Ainos
  xx Ethnology—Japan
  — Anthropometry
  — Caricatures and cartoons
  — Dwellings
  — Implements
  — Juvenile literature
  — Origin
  — Religion *(BL2370.A5)*
  — Rites and ceremonies
  — Social conditions
Ainu ballads and songs
Ainu in art
Ainu language *(PL495)*
  x Aino language
  xx Hyperborean languages
Air
  sa Aerodynamics
    Atmosphere, *and headings beginning*
      with the word Atmospheric
    Bubbles
    Sea air
    Ventilation
  xx Atmosphere
    Hygiene
    Meteorology
  — Analysis *(QD121)*
    sa Air—Pollution—Measurement
      Air sampling apparatus
      Argon
      Xenon
  — Bacteriology
    See Air—Microbiology
  — Experiments
  — Juvenile literature
  — Microbiology
    sa Communicable diseases
    x Air—Bacteriology
    xx Germ theory of disease
      Sanitary microbiology
  — Optical properties
    sa Meteorological optics
    xx Meteorological optics
  — Pollution *(Direct)*
    sa Aerosols
      Air pollution control industries
      Air quality
      Aircraft exhaust emissions
      Automobile exhaust gas
      Dust
      Dust control
      Fume control
      Motor vehicles—Pollution control
        devices
      Odor control
      Odors
      Radioactive pollution of the
        atmosphere
      Smog
      Smoke
    x Air pollution
      Air pollution control
      Atmosphere—Pollution
    xx Air quality
      Environmental health
      Pollution
  — — Caricatures and cartoons
  — — Classification
  — — Economic aspects *(Direct)*
  — — Experiments
  — — Juvenile literature
  — — Juvenile literature
  — — Law and legislation *(Direct)*

    sa Air—Pollution—Standards
    x Air pollution law
    xx Environmental law
  — — Mathematical models
  — — Measurement
    sa Air quality monitoring stations
      Smokemeters
    xx Air—Analysis
  — — Physiological effect
    sa Plants, Effect of air pollution on
  — — Pictorial works
  — — Psychological aspects
  — — Research *(Direct)*
    x Air pollution research
  — — Research grants *(Direct)*
  — — Standards *(Direct)*
    x Air pollution standards
    xx Air—Pollution—Law and
      legislation
  — — Study and teaching *(Direct)*
  — — Tables, calculations, etc.
  — Purification
    sa Air conditioning
      Air filters
      Germicidal lamps
    xx Air quality management
      Disinfection and disinfectants
      Gases—Purification
  — — Equipment and supplies
    xx Pollution control equipment
  — — Patents
  — Quality
    See Air quality
  — Radioactive pollution
    See Radioactive pollution of the
      atmosphere
  — Separation
    See Gases—Separation
  — Tables, calculations, etc.
  — Thermal properties *(QC880)*
  — Weight
Air, Compressed
  See Compressed air
Air, Ionized
  sa Ionosphere
  x Ionized air
  xx Gases, Ionized
    Ionization of gases
  — Industrial applications
  — Physiological effect
  — Therapeutic use
Air, Liquid
  See Liquid air
Air, Moisture of
  See Humidity
Air, Rarefied
  sa Mirages
  x Rarefied air
  — Therapeutic use
    See Aerotherapy
Air (Easement)
  See Light and air (Easement)
Air-age education
  See Aeronautics and civilization
Air-age geography
  See Geography, Aerial
Air attachés
  See Military attachés
Air base names
  See Air bases—Names
Air bases *(Indirect)*
  sa Intercontinental ballistic missile bases
  x Air bases, Military
    Air bases, Naval
    Air stations, Military
    Air stations, Naval
    Military air bases
    Military air stations

Naval air bases
Naval air stations
xx Aeronautics, Military
Airports
Intercontinental ballistic missile bases
Military bases
— Economic aspects *(Direct)*
— Electronic equipment
— — Maintenance and repair
— Fires and fire prevention
— Names
x Air base names
— Runways
sa Landing mats
x Airstrips
Landing strips
Runways (Aeronautics)
xx Pavements
— Safety measures
— Water-supply
Air bases, American, [**British, Russian, etc.**]
(Indirect)
Air bases, Military
See Air bases
Air bases, Naval
See Air bases
Air-bearing lift
See Ground-cushion phenomenon
Air-bearing vehicles
See Ground-effect machines
Air-bladder (in fishes) *(QL855)*
sa Weberian apparatus
x Gas bladder
Swim bladder
Swimbladder
Swimming-bladder
xx Fishes—Anatomy
Weberian apparatus
Air-borne infection
See Airborne infection
Air-borne troops
See Airborne troops
Air-brakes *(TF420-430)*
sa Brakes
New York air-brake
Railroads—Safety appliances
Westinghouse air-brake
x Railroads—Air-brakes
xx Brakes
Pneumatic machinery
— Maintenance and repair *(TF420)*
Air brush art
See Airbrush art
Air buildings
See Air-supported structures
Air cargo
See Aeronautics, Commercial—Freight
Air cargo dropping
See Airdrop
Air carrier operating certificates
See Air lines—Certification
Air charter
See Aeronautics, Commercial—Chartering
Air charter contracts *(Direct)*
x Charter contracts, Air
xx Aeronautics, Commercial—Chartering
Aeronautics, Commercial—Law and
legislation
Aeronautics—Laws and regulations
Charter-parties
Contracts
Air-compressors *(TJ990-992)*
sa Compressed air
Diesel locomotives—Compressors
x Compressors, Air
xx Compressors
— Automatic control *(TJ990)*
— Inspection

— Safety measures
Air conditioning *(TH7687)*
sa Dampness in buildings
Refrigeration and refrigerating
machinery
Ventilation
subdivision Air conditioning *under
specific subjects, e.g.* Factories—Air
conditioning
xx Air—Purification
Dampness in buildings
Environmental engineering (Buildings)
Refrigeration and refrigerating
machinery
Ventilation
— Climatic factors *(TH7687)*
x Air conditioning and climate
Air conditioning and weather
xx Atmospheric temperature
Humidity
Winds
Example under Climatology; *and under
reference from* Climatic factors
— Control
xx Air conditioning—Equipment and
supplies
Thermostat
Example under Automatic control
— Ducts
See Air ducts
— Equipment and supplies
sa Air conditioning—Control
— — Appraisal
See Air conditioning—Equipment
and supplies—Valuation
— — Design and construction
— — Maintenance and repair
— — Noise
— — Tariff
See Tariff on air conditioning
equipment and supplies
— — Valuation
x Air conditioning—Equipment and
supplies—Appraisal
— Estimates
— Handbooks, manuals, etc.
— Hygienic aspects
— Problems, exercises, etc.
— Safety regulations *(Direct)*
xx Gases, Asphyxiating and poisonous
—Laws and legislation
— Tables, calculations, etc.
— Vocational guidance
Air conditioning and climate
See Air conditioning—Climatic factors
Air conditioning and weather
See Air conditioning—Climatic factors
Air conditioning from central stations
x District air conditioning
xx Refrigeration and refrigerating
machinery
Air conditioning industry *(Direct)*
xx Heating and ventilation industry
Air controlmen, Naval
See United States. Navy—Air controlmen
Air crews
See Flight crews
Air curtains
x Air doors
Curtains, Air
xx Doors
Heating
Ventilation
Air-cushion vehicles
See Ground-effect machines
Air-cushions

Air defenses
Here are entered general works on pre-
venting and minimizing the military
and civil effects of air attacks. Works
limited to the military aspects are en-
tered under Air defenses, Military.
Works limited to the protection of
civilians from air attacks are entered
under Air defenses, Civil. Works dealing with civil defense in general are
entered under Civil defense.
sa Air raid shelters
Aircraft spotting
Blackouts in war
Building, Bombproof
Chemical warfare
Civil defense
Gas masks
Gases, Asphyxiating and poisonous—
War use
Telegraph—Defense measures
Telephone—Defense measures
subdivision Air defenses *under names
of countries, cities, etc.*
x Air raid defensive measures
Air defenses, Civil
sa Air raid wardens
subdivision Air defenses, Civil *under
names of countries, cities, etc.*
xx Civil defense
Note under Air defenses
— Equipment and supplies
Air defenses, Military *(Anti-aircraft guns,
UF625; Military aeronautics,
UG630-635)*
sa Anti-aircraft artillery
Anti-aircraft guns
Antimissile missiles
Ballistic missile early warning system
Distant early warning system
Radar defense networks
Surface-to-air missiles
subdivision Air defenses, Military *under
names of countries, cities, etc.*
xx Aeronautics, Military
Air warfare
Attack and defense (Military science)
Note under Air defenses
Air doors
See Air curtains
Air ducts *(TH7683.D8)*
x Air conditioning—Ducts
Air pipes
Ducts, Air
Hot-air heating—Ducts
Pipes, Air
Ventilation—Ducts
xx Exhaust systems
Pipe
Air easements
See Avigation easements
Air-engines
sa Compressed air
Stirling engines
x Hot-air engines
xx Compressed air
Engines
Air-entrained concrete
See Lightweight concrete
Air-entraining cements *(TA434)*
sa Lightweight concrete
xx Cement
Lightweight concrete
Air filters *(TH7683.A3)*
sa Motor vehicles—Motors—Air filters
Tractors—Motors—Air filters
xx Air—Purification
Dust—Prevention

Air filters *(TH7683.A3)* *(Continued)*
    Filters and filtration
    Water—Purification
Air flow *(TJ1025)*
    sa Air jets
        Gas flow
        Permeability
    xx Gas flow
Air Force chaplains
    See Chaplains, Military
Air Force facilities
    See United States. Air Force—Facilities
Air Force law *(Direct)*
    xx Military law
        United States. Air Force
        United States. Army Air Forces
Air Force schools
    See Aeronautics, Military—Study and
        teaching
Air Force translator
    See United States. Air Force translator
Air Force wives
    x Dependents of military personnel
        Families of military personnel
        Military dependents
        Military families
    xx Etiquette
        Wives
Air forces
    sa individual air forces under names of
        countries, e.g. United States. Air
        Force
    x Military power
    xx Air power
        Armed Forces
Air frames
    See Airframes
Air freight
    See Aeronautics, Commercial—Freight
Air gunnery
    See Aerial gunnery
Air guns
    x Air pistols
        Air rifles
    xx Firearms
Air heaters
    sa Steam-boilers—Air preheating
    x Air preheaters
        Heaters, Air
    xx Heat exchangers
Air hoar
    See Ice fog
Air hostesses
    See Air lines—Hostesses
Air inlets (Jet planes)
    See Aeroplanes—Jet propulsion—Air
        intakes
        Aeroplanes—Ramjet engines—Air
        intakes
        Aeroplanes—Turbojet engines—Air
        intakes
        Cavities (Aeroplanes)
Air intakes (Jet planes)
    See Aeroplanes—Jet propulsion—Air
        intakes
        Aeroplanes—Ramjet engines—Air
        intakes
        Aeroplanes—Turbojet engines—Air
        intakes
        Cavities (Aeroplanes)
Air jets *(TJ1030)*
    sa Ground-cushion phenomenon
        Jet flaps (Aeroplanes)
        Lift fans
    xx Air flow
        Jets
Air law
    See Aeronautics—Laws and regulations

Air layering *(SB125)*
    x Chinese layerage
        Layering of plants
        Plant layering
    xx Plant propagation
Air lift pumps *(TJ925)*
    sa Oil wells—Gas lift
    xx Compressed air
        Pumping machinery
Air-line hostesses
    See Air lines—Hostesses
Air line police *(Direct)*
    sa Airport police
    x Air lines—Police
        Police, Air line
    xx Aeronautics, Commercial
        Air lines—Employees
        Airport police
        Police, Private
    — United States
        x Air police (United States)
Air-line reservation systems
    See Air lines—Reservations
Air lines *(Indirect)* *(TL552; TL720)*
    Here are entered works dealing with es-
    tablished systems of aerial transporta-
    tion, and companies owning or operat-
    ing them. Material on individual sys-
    tems or companies is entered under
    specific heading.
    sa Air lines, Local service
        Airways
    x Airlines
        Aviation industry
    xx Aeronautics
        Aeronautics, Commercial
        Air travel
        Airways
    — Accounting *(TL720.2)*
        x Aeronautics, Commercial—
          Accounting
    — Baggage
    — — Mathematical models
    — Certification
        x Air carrier operating certificates
        Air lines—Licenses
        Airline certificates
        Certification of air lines
    — Collective bargaining
        See Collective bargaining—
          Aeronautics
    — Collective labor agreements
        See Collective labor agreements—
          Aeronautics
    — Cost of operation *(TL720.2)*
        xx Aeronautics, Commercial—Finance
    — Employees *(Direct)*
        sa Air line police
          Air lines—Hostesses
          Air pilots
          Collective bargaining—Aeronautics
          Collective labor agreements—
            Aeronautics
          Flight crews
          Flight engineers
          Flight navigators
          Strikes and lockouts—Air lines
    — — Medical examinations
        x Physical examination of air line
          employees
        xx Aviation medicine
        Example under reference from Medi-
        cal examinations
    — — Salaries, pensions, etc. *(Direct)*
        x Wages—Air line employees
    — Equipment and supplies
    — Fares
        See Air lines—Rates

    — Finance *(TL720)*
    — Food service
        Example under Food service
    — Hijacking
        See Hijacking of aircraft
    — Hostesses *(HD6073)*
        x Air hostesses
        Air-line hostesses
        Air stewardesses
        Stewardesses (Air lines)
        xx Aeronautics as a profession
        Air lines—Employees
        Flight crews
        Women in aeronautics
    — — Correspondence, reminiscences, etc.
        (TL539-540)
    — — Juvenile literature
    — Labor productivity
    — Law and legislation
        See Aeronautics, Commercial—Law
          and legislation
    — Licenses
        See Air lines—Certification
    — Management
        x Air transport management
    — — Mathematical models
    — Police
        See Air line police
    — Rates *(TL720.2)*
        x Aeronautics, Commercial—Fares
        Aeronautics, Commercial—Rates
        Air lines—Fares
        xx Aeronautics, Commercial—Finance
    — Reservations
        x Aeronautics, Commercial—Passenger
          traffic—Reservations
        Air-line reservation systems
    — — Electronic data processing
        See Electronic data processing—Air
          lines—Reservations
    — Time-tables
        x Aeronautics, Commercial—
          Time-tables
Air lines, Local service *(Direct)* *(TL726)*
    x Feeder air lines
        Local service air lines
    xx Aeronautics, Commercial
        Air lines
    — Finance
Air mail service *(Indirect)* *(General,*
    HE6238; United States, HE6496)
    sa Air mail stamps
        Air mail subsidies
        Pigeon post
        Rocket mail
    xx Aeronautics, Commercial—Freight
        Postal service
    — United States
        x Postal service—United States—Air
          mail
Air mail stamps *(Direct)*
    xx Air mail service
        Postage-stamps
Air mail subsidies *(Direct)*
    xx Air mail service
        Subsidies
Air masses *(Indirect)* *(QC880)*
    sa Fronts (Meteorology)
    xx Atmospheric circulation
        Fronts (Meteorology)
Air meets
    See Aeronautics—Competitions
Air myelography
    See Pneumomyelography
Air National Guard (United States)
    See United States—Air National Guard
Air navigation
    See Aeronautics

Navigation (Aeronautics)
Air navigation aids
   See Aids to air navigation
Air navigators
   See Flight navigators
Air-passages
   See Respiratory organs
Air photos
   See Aerial photographs
Air-pilot guides *(Direct) (TL726)*
   sa Pilot guides
   xx Pilot guides
Air pilotage
   See subdivision Piloting under specific types
      of aircraft, e.g. Aeroplanes—Piloting;
      Air-ships—Piloting; Fighter planes—
      Piloting; Helicopters—Piloting
Air pilots *(Direct) (Training, TL712)*
   sa Aeronautics—Psychology
      Aeroplanes—Piloting
      Astronauts
      Negroes in aeronautics
      Trade-unions—Air pilots
      Women in aeronautics
   x Aeroplanes—Pilots
      Aviators
      Pilots (Aeronautics)
   xx Aeronautics
      Aeronautics as a profession
      Aeronautics—Biography
      Air lines—Employees
      Flight crews
— Biography *(TL539)*
— Correspondence, reminiscences, etc.
— Diseases and hygiene
      xx Aviation medicine
— Juvenile literature
— Legal status, laws, etc. *(Direct)*
      xx Aeronautics—Laws and regulations
— Licenses *(Direct)*
— Mathematical models
      See Aeroplanes—Piloting—
         Mathematical models
— Medical examinations
      x Physical examination of air pilots
— Prayer-books and devotions
         Subdivided by language.
— Religious life
— Salaries, pensions, etc.
      x Wages—Air pilots
Air pipes
   See Air ducts
Air piracy
   See Hijacking of aircraft
Air pistols
   See Air guns
Air plants
   See Epiphytes
Air police (United States)
   See Air line police—United States
      United States. Air Force—Air police
Air pollution
   See Air—Pollution
Air pollution control
   See Air—Pollution
      Air quality management
Air pollution control industries *(Direct)*
   xx Air—Pollution
Air pollution law
   See Air—Pollution—Law and legislation
Air pollution research
   See Air—Pollution—Research
Air pollution standards
   See Air—Pollution—Standards
Air ports
   See Airports
Air power
   sa Air forces

Air warfare
   x Military power
   xx Aeronautics, Military
      Air warfare
Air preheaters
   See Air heaters
Air pressure support
   See Air-supported structures
Air propellers
   See Propellers, Aerial
Air-pump *(Physics, QC166; Pneumatic
      machinery, TJ955)*
   x Pneumatic pump
   xx Pneumatic machinery
      Pumping machinery
Air quality *(Direct) (TD883)*
   sa Air—Pollution
   x Air—Quality
      Quality of air
   xx Air—Pollution
— Management
      See Air quality management
— Standards *(Direct)*
— Statistical methods

GEOGRAPHIC SUBDIVISIONS

— United States
— — States
Air quality management *(Indirect)*
   sa Air—Purification
   x Air pollution control
      Air quality—Management
   xx Environmental protection
Air quality monitoring stations *(Indirect)*
   xx Air—Pollution—Measurement
Air raid alerts
   See Air raid warning systems
Air raid defensive measures
   See Air defenses
Air raid shelters *(Indirect)*
   sa Atomic bomb shelters
      Building, Bombproof
   x Bomb shelters
      Shelters, Air raid
   xx Aeronautics, Military
      Air defenses
      Building, Bombproof
      Civil defense
      Underground construction
Air raid sirens
   See Air raid warning systems
Air raid wardens *(Direct)*
   x Wardens (Civilian defense)
   xx Air defenses, Civil
      Civil defense
Air raid warning systems
   sa Conelrad
      Radar defense networks
   x Air raid alerts
      Air raid sirens
      Aircraft warning systems
      Attack warning systems
   xx Civil defense
      Signals and signaling
Air rescue service
   See Search and rescue operations
Air resistance
   sa Drag (Aerodynamics)
      Skin friction (Aerodynamics)
   xx Wind-pressure
Air resupply
   See Airdrop
Air rifles
   See Air guns
Air rights
   See Airspace (Law)
Air rule of the road
   See Air traffic rules

Air-sacs (of birds) *(QL855)*
   xx Birds—Anatomy
      Respiratory organs
Air sampling apparatus
   xx Air—Analysis
      Atmosphere
      Meteorological instruments
Air-sea interaction
   See Ocean-atmosphere interaction
Air-sea rescue
   See Search and rescue operations
Air-ship gases
   See Balloon gases
Air-ships *(TL650-668)*
   sa Aeronautics
      Balloons
      Propellers, Aerial
   x Airships
      Balloons, Dirigible
      Blimps
      Dirigible balloons
   xx Aeronautics
      Balloons
— Design and construction *(TL660)*
— Insurance
      See Insurance, Aviation
— Motors *(TL701-4)*
      sa Aeroplanes—Motors
      xx Aeroplanes—Motors
         Gas and oil engines
      Example under Motors
— Piloting *(TL663)*
      Example under reference from Aeronau-
         tics—Piloting; Air pilotage; Piloting
         (Aeronautics)
— Poetry
      See Aeronautics—Poetry
Air space (International law)
   See Airspace (International law)
Air space (Law)
   See Airspace (Law)
Air speed
   x Airspeed
   xx Aeronautics
Air-speed indicators *(TL589.2.A5)*
   xx Aeronautical instruments
Air stations, Military
   See Air bases
Air stations, Naval
   See Air bases
Air stewardesses
   See Air lines—Hostesses
Air strategy
   See Air warfare
Air supply
   See Airdrop
Air-supported structures
   sa Buildings, Plastic
      Expandable space structures
   x Air buildings
      Air pressure support
      Expandable structures
      Inflatable structures
      Pneumatic buildings
      Structures, Air-supported
   xx Lightweight construction
      Structural engineering
Air tactics
   See Air warfare
Air-to-air missiles
   See Falcon (Missile)
Air-to-air rockets
   x Aircraft rockets
   xx Aeroplanes, Military—Armament
      Rockets (Ordnance)
Air traffic control *(Indirect) (TL725.3.T)*
   sa Aeroplanes—Dispatching
      Airports—Traffic control

Air traffic control *(Indirect)* *(TL725.3.T)*
  (Continued)
    Distance measuring equipment (Aircraft
      to ground station)
    Electronics in aeronautics
    Omnirange system
    Radar air traffic control systems
    Tacan
  xx Aeronautics—Safety measures
    Airports—Communication systems
  — Computer programs
  — Electronic equipment
  — Equipment and supplies *(TL725.3.T7)*
    xx Electronics in aeronautics
      Signals and signaling
      Telecommunication
  — Examinations, questions, etc.
  — Law and legislation
    See Air traffic rules
  — Mathematical models
  — Research *(Direct)*
  — Vocational guidance
Air traffic control simulators
  xx Synthetic training devices
Air traffic rules *(Direct)*
  x Air rule of the road
    Air traffic control—Law and legislation
    Rules of the air
  xx Aeronautics—Laws and regulations
  — Criminal provisions
Air traffic rules, International
  x Air traffic rules (International law)
    International air traffic rules
  xx International law
Air traffic rules (International law)
  See Air traffic rules, International
Air transport
  See Aeronautics, Commercial
Air transport management
  See Air lines—Management
Air transportation of animals
  See Animals, Air transportation of
Air travel
  sa Aeronautics, Commercial—Passenger
    traffic
    Air lines
  x Routes of travel
  xx Aeronautics, Commercial—Passenger
    traffic
    Communication and traffic
    Transportation
    Travel
    Voyages and travels
  — Anecdotes, facetiae, satire, etc.
    (TL554.5)
Air-turbines
  sa Rotors
    Wind power
  xx Pneumatic machinery
    Turbines
    Wind power
    Windmills
Air warfare *(UG630)*
  sa Aerial gunnery
    Aeronautics, Military—Study and
      teaching
    Aeroplanes, Military
    Air defenses, Military
    Air power
    Aircraft spotting
    Anti-aircraft guns
    Atomic warfare
    Bombing, Aerial
    Chemical warfare
    Projectiles, Aerial
    subdivision Aerial operations *under*
      names of wars, e.g. World War,
      1939-1945—Aerial operations
  x Aerial strategy

    Aerial tactics
    Aerial warfare
    Air strategy
    Air tactics
  xx Aeronautics, Military
    Air power
    Atomic warfare
    Military art and science
    Strategy
    Tactics
    War
  — Juvenile literature
  — Mathematical models
  — Psychological aspects
Air warfare (International law)
  xx Aeronautics, Military—Law and
    legislation
    War (International law)
Air warfare sounds
  x Aeronautics, Military—Sounds
  xx Sounds
Airborne computers
  xx Computers
    Electronics in aeronautics
Airborne display systems
  See Aeronautical instruments—Display
    systems
Airborne electronic equipment
  See Aeroplanes—Electronic equipment
    Rockets (Aeronautics)—Electronic
      equipment
Airborne fire control systems
  See Fire control (Aerial gunnery)—
    Equipment
Airborne forces
  See Airborne troops
Airborne infection
  x Air-borne infection
    Infection, Airborne
  xx Communicable diseases
    Infection
Airborne profile recorder *(TR696)*
  x Profile recorder, Airborne
    Radar profile recorder
  xx Aerial photogrammetry
    Aeroplanes—Radar equipment
    Altimeter
Airborne radar
  See subdivision Radar equipment *under*
    types of aircraft, e.g. Aeroplanes—
    Radar equipment; Guided missiles—
    Radar equipment
Airborne radio equipment
  See Aeroplanes—Radio equipment
Airborne troops
  sa Parachute troops
    subdivision Airborne troops *under*
      armies, e.g. Germany. Heer—
      Airborne troops; United States.
      Army—Airborne troops
  x Air-borne troops
    Airborne forces
    Glider troops
    Sky-troops
  — Sounds
    xx Sounds
Airbrush art *(Direct)* *(NC915.A35)*
  x Air brush art
  xx Drawing—Instruction
    Painting—Technique
  Note under Spray painting
Aircraft, Atomic
  See Atomic aircraft
Aircraft, Government
  See Aeroplanes, Military
    Government aircraft
Aircraft accident investigation
  See Aeronautics—Accident investigation

Aircraft accidents
  See Aeronautics—Accidents
Aircraft accidents, Liability for
  See Liability for aircraft accidents
Aircraft antennas
  See Aeroplanes—Radio antennas
Aircraft armament
  See Aeroplanes, Military—Armament
Aircraft cabins
  sa Aeroplanes—Cockpits
  x Cabins, Aircraft
  xx Aeroplanes
  — Insulation
    xx Insulation (Heat)
Aircraft cabins, Pressurized
  See Aeroplanes—Pressurization
Aircraft carburetors
  See Aeroplanes—Motors—Carburetors
Aircraft carrier flight decks
  See Aircraft carriers—Flight decks
Aircraft carriers *(V874-5)*
  sa Atomic aircraft carriers
  x Aeroplane carriers
    Airplane carriers
    Carriers, Aircraft
    Carriers (Warships)
  xx Aeronautics, Military
    Warships
  — Flight decks
    x Aircraft carrier flight decks
      Carrier flight decks
      Flight decks, Aircraft carrier
    xx Aeroplanes—Landing
      Aeroplanes—Take-off
  — Juvenile literature
  — Pictorial works
Aircraft carriers, Atomic
  See Atomic aircraft carriers
Aircraft construction
  See subdivision Design and construction
    under types of aircraft, e.g.
      Aeroplanes—Design and
      construction; Seaplanes—Design and
      construction
Aircraft crews
  See Flight crews
Aircraft drafting *(TL671.25)*
  sa Aeroplanes—Drawings
  x Aeroplanes—Drafting
    Aircraft drawing
    Drafting, Aircraft
    Drawing, Aircraft
  xx Aeroplanes—Design and construction
    Mechanical drawing
Aircraft drawing
  See Aircraft drafting
Aircraft engine industry *(Direct)*
  — Management
Aircraft engines
  See Aeroplanes—Motors
Aircraft exhaust emissions *(TD886.7)*
  x Aeroplane exhaust emissions
    Aeroplanes—Exhaust emissions
    Exhaust emissions (Aircraft)
  xx Air—Pollution
Aircraft factories
  See Aeroplane factories
Aircraft financing
  See Aeroplane industry and trade—Finance
Aircraft gas-turbines
  sa Aeroplanes—Turbine-propeller engines
    Aeroplanes—Turbojet engines
  x Gas-turbines, Aircraft
  xx Gas-turbines
  — Automatic control
  — Combustion
  — Fuel systems
  — Lubrication

— Reliability
— Vibration
Aircraft handling group
   See United States. Navy—Aviation
      boatswain's mates
Aircraft heating
   See Aeroplanes—Heating and ventilation
Aircraft hydraulic equipment
   See Aeroplanes—Hydraulic equipment
Aircraft identification
   See Aeroplanes—Recognition
      Gliders (Aeronautics)—Recognition
      Helicopters—Recognition
Aircraft IFF equipment
   See Aeroplanes—IFF equipment
Aircraft instruments
   See Aeronautical instruments
Aircraft landing
   See subdivision Landing *under particular*
      types of aircraft, e.g. Aeroplanes—
      Landing; Seaplanes—Landing
Aircraft landing aids
   See Landing aids (Aeronautics)
Aircraft markings
   See Aeroplanes—Identification marks
Aircraft mechanics (Persons)
   See Aviation mechanics (Persons)
Aircraft mortgage guaranty
   See Insurance, Aircraft mortgage
Aircraft mortgages *(Direct)*
   sa Insurance, Aircraft mortgage
   x Aeroplanes—Mortgages
      Mortgages, Aircraft
   xx Aeronautics—Laws and regulations
      Chattel mortgages
Aircraft noise
   See Aeroplanes—Noise
      Jet planes—Noise
Aircraft production
   See Aeroplane industry and trade
      Aerospace industries
Aircraft radio stations
   See Aeronautical radio stations
Aircraft recognition
   See Aeroplanes—Recognition
      Gliders (Aeronautics)—Recognition
      Helicopters—Recognition
Aircraft riveting
   See Rivets and riveting, Aircraft
Aircraft rocket launchers
   See Aeroplanes, Military—Rocket launchers
Aircraft rockets
   See Air-to-air rockets
Aircraft safety measures
   See Aeronautics—Safety measures
Aircraft seats
   See Aeroplanes—Seats
Aircraft sheet-metal work
   See Aeroplanes—Sheet-metal work
Aircraft spotting
   sa Aeroplanes—Recognition
   x Spotting, Aircraft
   xx Air defenses
      Air warfare
      Civil defense
Aircraft steel *(TL699.S8)*
   x Aeroplanes—Steel
      Steel, Aircraft
   xx Aeroplanes—Materials
      Steel alloys
      Steel, Structural
  — Testing
Aircraft stress analysis
   See Airframes
Aircraft structures
   See Airframes
Aircraft survival equipment
   sa Clothing, Protective

Life-preservers
    Parachutes
    Pilot ejection seats
    Survival and emergency rations
   x Sea rescue equipment
    Survival and emergency equipment
      (Airborne)
    Survival kits
   xx Aeronautics—Safety measures
    Life-saving apparatus
    Survival (after aeroplane accidents,
      shipwrecks, etc.)
    Survival and emergency equipment
Aircraft take-off
   See subdivision Take-off *under particular*
      types of aircraft, e.g. Aeroplanes—
      Take-off; Seaplanes—Take-off
Aircraft turrets
   See Aeroplanes, Military—Turrets
Aircraft warning systems
   See Air raid warning systems
Aircraft welding
   See Aeroplanes—Welding
Aircrews
   See Flying crews
Airdromes
   See Airports
Airdrop *(TL711.D7; Military, UC330-335)*
   x Air cargo dropping
    Air resupply
    Air supply
    Cargo dropping (Aeroplane)
   xx Aeronautics
    Delivery of goods
    Parachutes
    Transportation, Military
Airedale terriers *(SF429.A6)*
   xx Terriers
Aires (Dance)
   x Relaciones (Dance)
Aires camera
Airfield landing mats
   See Landing mats
Airfoils
   See Aerofoils
Airframes *(TL671.6)*
   sa Aeroplanes—Fuselage
    Aeroplanes—Landing gear
    Aeroplanes—Nacelles
    Aeroplanes—Wings
   x Aeroplanes—Stresses
    Aeroplanes—Structures
    Air frames
    Aircraft stress analysis
    Aircraft structures
   xx Aeroplanes—Design and construction
    Structural frames
  — Fatigue
    x Fatigue of airframes
    xx Materials—Fatigue
Airglow
   sa Auroras
   x Day airglow
    Night airglow
    Twilight airglow
   xx Atmosphere, Upper
    Auroras
    Luminescence
    Meteorological optics
  — Charts, diagrams, etc.
  — Observations
Airline certificates
   See Air lines—Certification
Airliners
   See Transport planes
Airlines
   See Air lines

Airphotos
   See Aerial photographs
Airplane accidents, Liability for
   See Liability for aircraft accidents
Airplane carriers
   See Aircraft carriers
Airplane factories
   See Aeroplane factories
Airplanes
   See Aeroplanes
Airport access
   See Access to airports
Airport bird control
   See Airports—Bird control
Airport buildings
   See Airports—Buildings
Airport control towers
   See Airports—Control towers
Airport drainage *(TL725.3.D7)*
   x Airports—Drainage
   xx Airports
    Drainage
Airport landing fees
   See Airports—Landing fees
Airport management
   See Airports—Management
Airport noise *(Direct) (TL725.3.N6)*
   x Airports—Noise
   xx Aeroplanes—Noise
    City noise
    Noise
    Transportation noise
Airport planning
   See Airports—Planning
Airport police *(Direct)*
   sa Air line police
   x Airports—Police
    Police, Airport
   xx Air line police
Airport radio stations
   See Aeronautical radio stations
Airport towers
   See Airports—Control towers
Airport zoning *(Direct)*
   sa Avigation easements
   x Airports—Aerial approach protection
    Airports—Approach zones
    Airports—Zoning
   xx Aeronautics—Laws and regulations
    Aeronautics—Safety measures
    Airports
    Airports—Laws and regulations
    Zoning
    Zoning law
Airports *(Indirect) (TL725-6)*
   sa Access to airports
    Air bases
    Airport drainage
    Airport zoning
    Heliports
    International airports
    Intra-airport transportation
    Landing aids (Aeronautics)
    Runway localizing beacons
    Seaplane bases
   x Aerodromes
    Air ports
    Airdromes
   xx Aeronautics
    Terminals (Transportation)
  — Abstracts
  — Access roads *(Direct)*
    x Access roads to airports
    xx Access to airports
    Roads
  — Aerial approach protection
    See Airport zoning
  — Approach zones

Airports *(Indirect)* *(TL725-6)*
— Approach zones *(Continued)*
   See Airport zoning
— Bird control *(TL725.3.B5)*
   x Airport bird control
     Airports—Runways—Bird control
     Bird control, Airport
     Birds—Control at airports
   xx Aeronautics—Accidents
     Aeronautics—Safety measures
     Bird control
     Birds, Injurious and beneficial
— Buildings
   sa Airports—Control towers
     Hangars
   x Airport buildings
— — Soundproofing
— Cold weather conditions
   sa Slush on pavements, runways, etc.
   Example under Cold
— Communication systems *(TL725.3.C63)*
   sa Air traffic control
   xx Aeronautics—Communication
     systems
     Telecommunication
— Contracts and specifications *(TL725.2)*
   x Airports—Specifications
   xx Building—Contracts and
     specifications
— Control towers *(TL725.3.C64)*
   x Airport control towers
     Airport towers
     Control towers (Airports)
     Traffic control towers (Airports)
   xx Airports—Buildings
     Airports—Traffic control
     Towers
— Defense measures
   xx War damage, Industrial
— Design and construction
— Drainage
   See Airport drainage
— Economic aspects *(Direct)*
— Employees *(Direct)*
   sa Wages—Airport employees
— — Medical examinations
   x Physical examination of airport
     employees
— Equipment and supplies *(TL725.3.E6)*
   sa Airports—Radar equipment
— Fees
   sa Airports—Landing fees
   xx Airways—Finance
— Finance *(TL725.3.F5)*
   sa Airports—Price policy
— Fires and fire prevention *(TL730.1)*
— Juvenile literature
— Landing aids
   See Landing aids (Aeronautics)
— Landing fees *(TL725.3.L3)*
   sa International airports—Landing fees
   x Airport landing fees
     Landing fees (Airports)
   xx Aeronautics, Commercial
     Airports—Fees
— Landscape architecture
   xx Landscape architecture
— Laws and regulations
   sa Airport zoning
     Avigation easements
— Lighting *(TL725.3.L5)*
   xx Landing aids (Aeronautics)
— — Terminology
— Location *(TL725.3.L6)*
   x Location of airports
   xx Airports—Planning
— Maintenance and repair
— — Costs

— Management *(TL725.3.M2)*
   x Airport management
— Noise
   See Airport noise
— Planning *(TL725.3.P5)*
   sa Airports—Location
   x Airport planning
— — Mathematical models *(TL725.3.P5)*
— Police
   See Airport police
— Price policy
   xx Airports—Finance
     Price policy
— Radar equipment
   xx Airports—Equipment and supplies
     Airports—Traffic control
— Runways *(TL725.3.R8)*
   sa Slush on pavements, runways, etc.
   x Airstrips
     Landing strips
     Runways (Aeronautics)
   xx Pavements
— — Bird control
   See Airports—Bird control
— — Maintenance and repair
— — Mathematical models *(TL725.3.R8)*
— Safety measures
— Specifications
   See Airports—Contracts and
     specifications
— Terminology
— Traffic control
   sa Airports—Control towers
     Airports—Radar equipment
   xx Air traffic control
— — Display systems
   x Control tower display systems
   xx Electronics in aeronautics
     Information display systems
— — Mathematical models
— Visibility *(TL557.V5)*
   x Visibility conditions at airports
     Visual range at airports
   xx Atmospheric transparency
     Meteorological optics
     Meteorology in aeronautics
— Water-supply
— Zoning
   See Airport zoning
Airports, Floating *(TL725.7)*
   x Seadromes
   xx Aeronautics
Airports of entry
   See International airports
Airships
   See Air-ships
Airsickness
   See Motion sickness
Airspace (International law) *(JX5771)*
   sa Jurisdiction over aircraft
   x Air space (International law)
     Freedom of the air
   xx Aeronautics—Laws and regulations
     International law
     Sovereignty
     Space law
Airspace (Law) *(Direct)*
   sa Avigation easements
   x Air rights
     Air space (Law)
   xx Property
     Real property
Airspace (Roman law)
Airspace easements
   See Avigation easements
Airspace over highways
   See Express highways—Airspace utilization

Airspeed
   See Air speed
Airspeed airplanes
Airstrips
   See Air bases—Runways
     Airports—Runways
Airway (Medicine)
   xx Respiration
Airways *(Indirect)* *(TL725-733)*
   Here are entered works dealing with air
     routes along which are maintained aids
     to air navigation, such as landing
     fields, beacon lights, etc.
   sa Aids to air navigation
     Air lines
     Radio beacons
   xx Aeronautics
     Aeronautics, Commercial
     Aids to air navigation
     Air lines
     Geography, Aerial
— Finance *(TL725.3)*
   sa Airports—Fees
— Guide-books
— Lighting *(TL725.3.L5)*
— — Terminology
— Maps
   sa Aeronautical charts
Airworthiness certificates *(Direct)*
   x Certificates of airworthiness
   xx Aeroplanes—Airworthiness
     Aeroplanes—Inspection
     Helicopters—Airworthiness
Airworthiness requirements
   See Aeroplanes—Airworthiness
     Helicopters—Airworthiness
Airy differential equation
   See Airy functions
Airy functions
   x Airy differential equation
     Airy integral
     Functions, Airy
   xx Differential equations, Linear
Airy integral
   See Airy functions
Aisne, Battle of the, 1914 *(DA545.A5)*
   xx European War, 1914-1918—Campaigns
     —France
Aisne, Battle of the, 1917 *(D545.A5)*
   x Ailette, Battle of the, 1917
   xx European War, 1914-1918—Campaigns
     —France
Aisne, Battle of the, 1918 *(DA545.A5)*
   xx European War, 1914-1918—Campaigns
     —France
Aisors
   See Assyrians
Aït Atta (Berber tribe)
   xx Berbers
     Ethnology—Morocco
     Ethnology—Sahara
Aix, Battle of, 102 B.C.
   See Aquae Sextiae, Battle of, 102 B.C.
Aix-la-Chapelle, Peace of, 1668 *(D276.A3)*
Aix-la-Chapelle, Peace of, 1748 *(D294)*
   xx Austrian Succession, War of, 1740-1748
     United States—History—King George's
     War, 1744-1748
Aja dialect
   x Adja dialect
     Adya dialect
   xx Ewe language
Ajawa language
   See Yao language
Ajibba (African people)
   See Murle (African people)
Ajivikas *(BL2020.A4)*
   xx Buddha and Buddhism

Free will and determinism
Jainism
Universalism
AK 8 moving-picture camera
Akā language
　See Akan language
Akan language *(PL8046.A6)*
　sa Baoule language
　　Fanti language
　　Tshi language
　x Akā language
　xx Kwa languages
　　Tshi language
Akans (African people) *(DT510.42)*
　sa Ashantis
　　Fantis
　　Missions to Akans (African people)
　xx Ashantis
　　Ethnology—Ghana
　　Fantis
　— Music
　　xx Music, African
　— Religion *(BL2480.A)*
　— Tribal government
Akarimojong language
　See Karamojong language
Akas *(DS432.A44)*
　xx Ethnology—India—North East Frontier
　　　Agency
Akatziroi
　See Khazars
Akavais Indians
　See Accawai Indians
Akermanite *(Indirect)*
　xx Melilite
Akha language
　See Kaw language
Akha people
　See Kaw people
Akhwakh language *(PK9201.A7)*
　x Alwal language
　xx Caucasian languages
AKI (Computer program language)
Akimbu (Bantu people)
　See Kimbu (Bantu people)
Akinski dialect
　See Akkinski dialect
Akita dogs *(SF429.A65)*
Akkadian (East Semitic) language
　See Assyro-Babylonian language
Akkadians
　　Not to be confused with the Sumerians, a
　　non-Semitic race called "Akkadians"
　　in the earlier works of Assyriology.
　— Religion
Akkadians (Sumerians)
　See Sumerians
Akkinski dialect *(PK9201.A73)*
　x Akinski dialect
　xx Caucasian languages
Akō gishi
　See Forty-seven Rōnin
Akō Vendetta, 1702
　See Japan—History—Akō Vendetta,1702
Akomu
　See Ilomba
Akoniken language
　See Tzoneca language
Akra language
　See Gā language
Aku language
　See Yoruba language
Akutagawa shō
Akvavit
　See Aquavit
Akwa'ala Indians *(F1221.A4)*
　xx Indians of Mexico
　　Yuman Indians

Akwē-Shavante Indians *(F2520.1.A4)*
　x Acua-Shavante Indians
　　Acuen-Xavante Indians
　　Chavante-Akwē Indians
　　Crisca Indians
　　Crixá Indians
　　Puxití Indians
　　Shavante-Akwē Indians
　　Tapacuá Indians
　　Xavante-Acuen Indians
　xx Indians of South America
　　Tapuya Indians
Alabados *(ML3086)*
　xx Folk-songs, Spanish—Southwest, New
　　Hymns, Spanish
Alabama
　— History *(F321-355)*
　— — To 1819
　— — 1819-1950
　— — Creek War, 1836
　　　See Creek War, 1836
　— — Civil War, 1861-1865 *(E495;*
　　　　　Confederate, E551)
　— — 1951-
Alabama claims *(JX238.A4-7)*
　sa Washington, Treaty of, 1871
　x Geneva award
　xx Claims
　　United States—Claims against Great
　　　Britain
　　United States—History—Civil War,
　　　1861-1865—Claims
　Example under Neutrality
Alabama Coal Strike, 1894
Alabama Indians
　See Alibamu Indians
Alabamine *(QD181.A15)*
Alabaster *(TN989.A3)*
Alabaster sculpture *(Direct)*
　xx Sculpture
Alabaster sculpture, English, [etc.] *(Direct)*
　x English [etc.] alabaster sculpture
Alabiformes
　See Synbranchiformes
Alacaluf Indians *(F2823.A4)*
　x Alakaluf Indians
　　Alikaluf Indians
　　Alikuluf Indians
　　Alookooloop Indians
　　Alukoeluf Indians
　xx Fuegians
　　Indians of South America
Alacaluf language *(PM5378)*
　xx Indians of South America—Languages
Aladdin oven
　xx Cookery
　　Stoves
Aladian (African people)
　See Alagya (African people)
Aladian language
　x Aladyā language
　　Alagya language
　　Alladian language
　xx Kwa languages
Aladyā language
　See Aladian language
Alagya (African people)
　x Aladian (African people)
　　Alladian (African people)
　　Aragya (African people)
　　Jack-Jack (African people)
　xx Ethnology—Ivory Coast
Alagya language
　See Aladian language
Alahmares
　See Nasrides
Alakaluf Indians
　See Alacaluf Indians

Alakhagira
　See Alakhiyas
Alakhgirs
　See Alakhiyas
Alakhiyas *(BL1245.A5)*
　x Alakhagira
　　Alakhgirs
　　Alakhnamis
　xx Hindu sects
Alakhnamis
　See Alakhiyas
Alam El Halfa, Battle of, 1942
　See Alam Halfa, Battle of, 1942
Alam Halfa, Battle of, 1942 *(D766.9)*
　x Alam El Halfa, Battle of, 1942
　xx World War, 1939-1945—Campaigns—
　　Africa, North
Alamance, Battle of, 1771
Alamanni
　See Alemanni
al 'Alamayn, Battle of, 1942 *(D766.9)*
　x Alamein, Battle of, 1942
　　El Alamein, Battle of, 1942
　　World War, 1939-1945—Campaigns—
　　　Egypt
　xx World War, 1939-1945—Campaigns—
　　Africa, North
　— Juvenile literature
Alamein, Battle of, 1942
　See al 'Alamayn, Battle of, 1942
Alamo
　— Juvenile literature
　— Siege, 1836
　— — Juvenile literature
Alan (Hound)
　x Alant
Åland question *(DK465.A4)*
Alani
　sa Jazyge
　　Roxolani
　x Alans
　xx Ossetes
　　Sarmatians
　　Scythians
Alanine metabolism
　xx Amino acid metabolism
Alans
　See Alani
Alant
　See Alan (Hound)
Alarm reaction
　xx Animals, Habits and behavior of
Alarodian language
　See Vannic language
Alaska
　— History
　— — To 1867
　— — 1867-1959
　— — 1959-

　— — Pictorial works
　— Tidal wave, 1958
　— Tidal wave, 1964
Alaska cod
　See Pacific cod
Alaska in literature
Alaska Railroad
　— Employees
　　Example under Railroads—Employees
Alastrim
　x Amaas
　xx Smallpox
Alaudidae
　See Larks
Alawa language
　x Galawa language
　xx Australian languages

Alawites
    See Nosairians
'Alawīyīn
    See Nosairians
Albacore
    x Albicore
    xx Tuna
Albania
    — History
    ——— Turkish Wars, 15th century
    ——— 1944-
    ———— Pictorial works
Albanian language *(PG9501-9599)*
Albanian literature *(PG9601-9678)*
    xx Balkan Peninsula—Literatures
Albanian philology
Albanian poetry *(Direct)*
Albanian studies *(Direct)*
Albanians *(DR701.S49-85; Greece,*
       DF747.A3)
    sa Ghegs
Albany
    — Charities
        Example under reference from Homes
          (Institutions)
Albarrada, Battle of, 1631
Albas
    xx Lyric poetry
       Poetry
Albatross (Amphibian planes)
    x Grumman Albatross
       HU-16 (Amphibian planes)
    xx Aeroplanes, Military
       Amphibian planes
Albatrosses *(QL696.P6)*
    sa Buller's albatross
       Laysan albatross
       Royal albatross
       Short-tailed albatross
       Wandering albatross
    x Diomedeidae
    xx Sea birds
       Tubinares
Albedo *(QC912.5)*
    xx Earth—Surface
       Extraterrestrial radiation
       Solar radiation
Albedo, Infra-red
    See Infra-red albedo
Albers-Schoenberg disease
    See Osteopetrosis
Albert Schweitzer prijs
    x Schweitzer prijs
Albicore
    See Albacore
Albigenses *(BX4873-4893; Wars, DC83.2-3)*
    sa Bogomiles
       Muret, Battle of, 1213
       Waldenses
    x Cathari
       Catharists
    xx Church history—Middle Ages,
       600-1500
    Example under Persecution
Albigensian art
    See Art, Albigensian
Albinism
    See Albinos and albinism
Albinos and albinism *(Anthropology, GN199;*
       Zoology, QL767)
    sa Color of man
    x Albinism
       Leucoderma
       Leucopathy
    xx Color of man
       Pigmentation disorders
    — Juvenile literature

Albite
    xx Feldspar
Ålborg Vaerft Strike, 1971-1972
Albright's hereditary osteodystrophy
    See Pseudo-pseudohypoparathyroidism
Albuera, Battle of, 1811 *(DC233.A5)*
    xx Peninsular War, 1807-1814
Albumin *(QP551)*
    sa Serum albumin
    x Toxalbumins
Albumin metabolism
    xx Metabolism
Albuminuria *(RC905; Diseases of children,*
       RJ476.A3; Diseases of pregnancy,
       RG575)
    sa Bright's disease
       Urine—Analysis and pathology
    xx Bright's disease
       Kidneys—Diseases
       Proteinuria
Albumose *(QP551)*
Albumosuria *(RC905)*
Albums
Albums, Autograph
    See Autograph albums
Albums, Postage-stamp
    See Postage-stamps—Albums
Alcaldes
    See Mayors
Alcaloids
    See Alkaloids
Alcatraz Island, Calif.
    — History
    ——— Indian occupation, 1969-1971
        x Indian occupation of Alcatraz
          Island, Calif., 1969-1971
        xx Indians of North America—
          Government relations—1934-
Alcedinidae
    See Kingfishers
Alcestis in literature
Alchemists *(QD24)*
    xx Chemists
       Philosophers
    — Biography *(QD24)*
    ——— Juvenile literature
Alchemy *(QD24-26.5; History, QD13)*
    sa Elixir of life
       Magic
       Medicine, Magic, mystic, and spagiric
    x Hermetic art and philosophy
       Hermetic medicines
       Metals, Transmutation of
       Philosophers' egg
       Philosophers' stone
       Stone, Philosophers'
       Transmutation of metals
    xx Chemistry
       Chemistry—History
       Elixir of life
       Gold
       Magic
       Occult sciences
       Superstition
    — Juvenile literature
Alcock comet *(QB727)*
Alcohol *(Chemistry, QD305.A4; Technology,*
       TP593; Trade, HD9391)
    sa Alcoholic beverages
       Alcoholism
       Avertin
       Distillation
       Distilling industries
       Liquor problem
       Liquor traffic
       Liquors
       Oxo process
       Temperance

       names of alcoholic liquors, e.g. Brandy,
       Rum, Whiskey
    x Ethanol
       Ethyl alcohol
       Intoxicants
    xx Alcohols
       Citrus fruits—By-products
       Distillation
    Example under Stimulants
    — Analysis *(TP511)*
    — Costs
    — Law and legislation *(Direct)*
       sa Distilleries—Law and legislation
         Liquor laws
       x Alcoholic beverage control
    — Patents
    — Physiological effect *(Physiology,*
       QP915.A3; Temperance,
       HV5060-5065)
       sa Alcohol—Toxicology
         Drinking and airplane accidents
         Drinking and traffic accidents
         Hangover cures
         Plants, Effect of alcohol on
         Wine—Physiological effect
       xx Temperance
    ——— Juvenile literature
    — Prices *(Direct)*
    — Punched card systems
       See Punched card systems—Alcohol
    — Quotations, maxims, etc.
    — Standards *(Direct)*
    — Tables *(TP609)*
    — Tariff
       See Tariff on alcohol
    — Taxation *(Direct) (HD9350.8;*
       Licensing, HV5084-7)
       sa Distilleries—Law and legislation
         Liquor traffic—Taxation
       x Alcohol tax
       xx Liquor traffic—Taxation
    — Therapeutic use *(RM666.A3)*
    — Toxicology
       xx Alcohol—Physiological effect
Alcohol, Denatured *(Technology, TP593;*
       Trade, HD9399)
    x Alcohol, Industrial
       Denatured alcohol
       Industrial alcohol
       Methylated spirit
Alcohol, Industrial
    See Alcohol, Denatured
Alcohol and children *(Direct)*
    x Children and alcohol
    xx Alcoholism
       Liquor problem
       Temperance
Alcohol and Jews
    x Drinking and Jews
       Jews and alcohol
    xx Alcoholism
       Liquor problem
       Temperance
Alcohol and military personnel *(Direct)*
    x Military personnel and alcohol
    xx Liquor problem
Alcohol and Negroes
    x Drinking and Negroes
       Negroes and alcohol
    xx Alcoholism
       Liquor problem
       Temperance
Alcohol and women *(Direct) (HV5137)*
    x Drinking and women
       Female alcoholism
       Female drinking
       Women and alcohol
    xx Alcoholism

Liquor problem
Temperance
Alcohol and youth (Direct)
  x Drinking and youth
    Juvenile drinking
    Youth and alcohol
  xx Alcoholism
    Drugs and youth
    Liquor problem
    Temperance
  — Juvenile literature
Alcohol as fuel (TP358)
  xx Liquid fuels
    Motor fuels
Alcohol education
  See Temperance—Study and teaching
Alcohol in blood
  See Blood alcohol
Alcohol in the body (QP801.A3)
  sa Blood alcohol
  x Alcohol intoxication
    Blood alcohol level
    Drunkenness testing
  xx Physiological chemistry
Alcohol intoxication
  See Alcohol in the body
    Alcoholism
Alcohol motors (TJ800)
  x Internal combustion engines
  xx Motors
Alcohol tax
  See Alcohol—Taxation
Alcoholates (QD341.A4)
Alcoholic beverage control
  See Alcohol—Law and legislation
    Liquor laws
Alcoholic beverage industry
  See Brewing industry
    Distilling industries
    Wine and wine making
Alcoholic beverages
  sa Beer
    Cocktails
    Liquors
    Temperance
    Wine and wine making
  x Intoxicants
  xx Alcohol
    Beverages
  — Analysis (TP511)
  — Patents
  — Standards (Direct)
Alcoholic psychoses
  sa Delirium tremens
    Korsakoff's syndrome
  xx Psychoses
Alcoholics (Direct)
  sa Church work with alcoholics
    Social work with alcoholics
  x Drunkards
    Inebriates
  xx Alcoholism
    Liquor problem
    Temperance
  — Hospitals and asylums (Direct)
    xx Alcoholism—Treatment
    Asylums
    Hospitals
  — Law and legislation (Direct)
    xx Mental health laws
  — Personal narratives
  — Personality
    See Alcoholics—Psychology
  — Psychology
    x Alcoholics—Personality
    Alcoholism—Psychological aspects
  — Rehabilitation (Direct)
    sa Social case work with alcoholics

— — Evaluation
Alcoholism (Direct) (Disease, RC565; Temperance, HV5001-5720)
  Used chiefly for medical works; includes works on drunkenness, dipsomania, etc.
  The general heading for works on the temperance question is Temperance, under which are entered books on the temperance movement, popular and controversial works, and fiction. Under Liquor problem are entered works of an administrative or local character. Liquor traffic is used for the liquor industry, Liquor laws for the legal side of the question, and Liquors for the technical side. Special topics, e.g. Local option, Gothenburg system, Prohibition, License system, take special headings.
  sa Alcohol and children
    Alcohol and Jews
    Alcohol and Negroes
    Alcohol and women
    Alcohol and youth
    Alcoholics
    Children of alcoholic parents
    Korsakoff's syndrome
  x Alcohol intoxication
    Dipsomania
    Drunkenness
    Inebriety
    Intemperance
    Intoxication
  xx Alcohol
    Drug abuse
    Liquor problem
    Temperance
  Notes under Liquor laws; Liquor problem; Liquor traffic; Liquors; Prohibition; Temperance
  — Anecdotes, facetiae, satire, etc.
  — Cases, clinical reports, statistics
  — Complications and sequelae
  — Early works to 1800
  — Juvenile literature
  — Mortality
  — Psychological aspects
    See Alcoholics—Psychology
  — Punched card systems
    See Punched card systems—Alcohol
  — Research (Direct)
  — Study and teaching
    See Temperance—Study and teaching
  — Treatment (Direct)
    sa Alcoholics—Hospitals and asylums
    x Gold-cure
    Keeley cure
  — — Costs
Alcoholism and airplane accidents
  See Drinking and airplane accidents
Alcoholism and crime (HV5053-5)
  Here are entered works on the relation between alcoholism and criminal behavior or the incidence of crime. Works on alcoholic intoxication as a criminal offense or as a factor of criminal liability are entered under the heading Drunkenness (Criminal law)
  sa Drunkenness (Criminal law)
  x Crime and alcoholism
  xx Crime and criminals
    Drunkenness (Criminal law)
  Note under Drunkenness (Criminal law)
Alcoholism and employment
  x Employment and alcoholism
  xx Personnel management
Alcoholism and religion
  x Religion and alcoholism

  xx Liquor problem
    Temperance
Alcoholism and traffic accidents
  See Drinking and traffic accidents
Alcoholism education
  See Temperance—Study and teaching
Alcoholometer (TP517)
  sa Liquors—Gaging and testing
  x Alcohometer
    Spirit-meter
  xx Distillation
    Liquors—Gaging and testing
Alcoholometry
  See Liquors—Gaging and testing
Alcohols (Chemistry, QD305.A4, QD341.A4; Manufacture, TP248.A5)
  sa Alcohol
    Cyclitols
    Rutin
    Sorbitol
  Example under Chemistry, Organic
  — Analysis
  — Programmed instruction
  — Tables
Alcoholysis (QD305.A4)
  sa Solvolysis
Alcohometer
  See Alcoholometer
ALCOM (Computer program language)
  x Algebraic compiler
    Symbolic language
Alcoran
  See Koran
Alcyonaria (QL377.C6)
  sa Gorgonacea
    Sea-pens
  x Octocorallia
  xx Anthozoa
    Coelenterata
Aldehydes (QD305.A6; QD341.A6)
  sa Cannizzaro reaction
    Oxo process
    Perkin reaction
    Phenolic resins
    Schiff reaction
  xx Oxo compounds
  Example under Chemistry, Organic
  — Reactivity
    Example under Reactivity (Chemistry)
Alder
  sa European green alder
    Red alder
  — Diseases and pests
    sa Alder blight
Alder blight
  xx Alder—Diseases and pests
Alder flea-beetle
  xx Flea-beetles
Alder flycatcher
Alder woodwasp
  xx Wasps
Aldermen
  See City councilmen
Aldine type
  See Type and type-founding—Italic type
Aldol condensation
  xx Condensation products (Chemistry)
Aldosterone
  xx Adrenocortical hormones
Aldosterone antagonists
  xx Antimetabolites
Aldosterone synthesis
  xx Biosynthesis
Aldosteronism
  See Hyperaldosteronism
Ale (TP578)
  sa Beer
    Malt

Ale (TP578) (Continued)
    Porter
    xx Beer
        Brewing
        Brewing industry
        Malt liquors
Ale-houses
    See Hotels, taverns, etc.
Ale-pump (TP517)
    xx Pumping machinery
Aleatory contracts
    See Contracts, Aleatory
Aleatory music
    See Chance composition
        Chance compositions
Alekon-Gerard process
    See Front-screen projection
Alemanni (DD78.A5)
    x Alamanni
    xx Germanic tribes
Alembertian operator
    See D'Alembertian operator
Aleppo oak
    xx Oak
Alesia, Battle of, 52 B.C. (DC62)
    x Alise-Sainte-Reine, France—Siege, 52
        B.C.
    xx Gaul—History—58 B.C.-511 A.D.
Aleut language (PM31-34)
    x Aleutian language
        Eleuth language
    xx Hyperborean languages
Aleutian disease of minks
    See Mink Aleutian disease
Aleutian Indians
    See Aleuts
Aleutian language
    See Aleut language
Aleuts (E99.A34)
    x Aleutian Indians
    xx Eskimos
        Indians of North America
Alewife
Alexandria, Egypt
    — Riots, 1921 (DT107.8)
    — Siege, 48-47 B.C.
        See Alexandrine War, 48-47 B.C.
    — Siege, 1882 (DT107.4)
    — Tombs
        Example under Tombs
Alexandria, Va.
    — Capture by the British, 1814
Alexandria, Battle of, 1801 (DC226.A3)
    x Aboukir, Battle of, 1801
        Abukir, Battle of, 1801
        Canopus, Battle of, 1801
Alexandrian school (Ethics, BJ221-4;
        Philosophy, B630-708)
    sa Neoplatonism
    xx Neoplatonism
Alexandrian school, Christian (B631)
    sa Antiochian school
    x Christian Alexandrian school
    xx Antiochian school
        Apologetics—Early church, ca. 30-600
        Church history—Primitive and early
            church, ca. 30-600
        Theology, Doctrinal—History—Early
            church, ca. 30-600
Alexandrine verse
Alexandrine War, 48-47 B.C. (DT92.7)
    x Alexandria, Egypt—Siege, 48-47 B.C.
    xx Egypt—History—332-30 B.C.
Alexia
    sa Dyslexia
        Reading disability
    x Word-blindness
    xx Aphasia

Brain—Diseases
    Dyslexia
    Reading disability
Alexins
    See Complements (Immunity)
Alfa Romeo automobile
Alfalfa (Indirect) (SB205.A4)
    x Brazilian clover
        Chilean clover
        French clover
        Lucerne (Plant)
        Purple medic
        Spanish trefoil
    xx Forage plants
        Hay
    — Breeding
        See Alfalfa breeding
    — Disease and pest resistance
    — Diseases and pests (SB608.A5)
        sa names of pests, e.g. Alfalfa
            caterpillar
    — Drying
    — Fertilizers and manures
    — Genetics
    — Irrigation
        x Alfalfa irrigation
    — Marketing
    — Seed
    — Silage
        See Alfalfa silage
    — Varieties
    — Water requirements
        Example under Plants—Water require-
            ments
    — Weed control
        Example under Weed control
Alfalfa as feed
    sa Alfalfa silage
Alfalfa breeding
    x Alfalfa—Breeding
    xx Plant-breeding
Alfalfa caterpillar
    Example under Alfalfa—Diseases and pests;
        Caterpillars
Alfalfa irrigation
    See Alfalfa—Irrigation
Alfalfa leafcutter-bee (QL568.M4)
    x Leafcutter-bee, Alfalfa
        Leafcutting-bee, Alfalfa
Alfalfa looper
Alfalfa silage
    x Alfalfa—Silage
    xx Alfalfa as feed
    Example under Ensilage
Alfalfa weevil
    xx Beetles
    — Biological control (Indirect)
        xx Alfalfa weevil—Control
    — Control (Indirect)
        sa Alfalfa weevil—Biological control
Alfred P. Sloan national scholarships
    x Sloan national scholarships
    xx Scholarships—United States
Alfures (GN663)
    x Alfuros
    xx Malay race
        Papuans
Alfuros
    See Alfures
Algae (Indirect) (QK564-580)
    sa Agar
        Algology
        Chlorophyceae
        Chrysophyceae
        Coenobic plants
        Coralline algae
        Cyanophyta
        Diatoms

Freshwater algae
        Kelp
        Marine algae
        Nitrogen-fixing algae
        Pyrrhophyta
        Water bloom
    x Hydrophytes
    xx Algology
        Aquatic resources
        Cryptogams
        Marine flora
        Phytoplankton
    Example under Botany
    — Classification
    — Control
        See Algae control
    — Cultures and culture media
    — Economic aspects
        sa Algae as food
        xx Marine resources
    — Growth
        xx Growth (Plants)
    — — Measurement
    — Juvenile literature
        x Algology—Juvenile literature
Algae, Fossil (QE955)
    sa Stromatolites
Algae, Nitrogen-fixing
    See Nitrogen-fixing algae
Algae as food
    sa Nori
    x Algal food
    xx Algae—Economic aspects
        Food
Algae control (Indirect)
    x Algae—Control
    xx Aquatic weed control
        Water bloom
Algal bloom
    See Water bloom
Algal food
    See Algae as food
ALGAMS (Computer program language)
        (QA76.73)
Algarrobilla
Algebra (QA152-263)
    sa Algorithms
        Binomial theorem
        Combinations
        Combinatorial analysis
        Congruences and residues
        Determinants
        Diophantine analysis
        Elimination
        Equations
        Factors (Algebra)
        Forms (Mathematics)
        Groups, Theory of
        Interpolation
        Logarithms
        Mathematical analysis
        Modules (Algebra)
        Numbers, Theory of
        Partitions (Mathematics)
        Permutations
        Probabilities
        Products, Infinite
        Sequences (Mathematics)
        Series
        Spinor analysis
    xx Mathematical analysis
        Mathematics
    — Early works to 1800 (QA35)
    — Examinations, questions, etc.
    — Graphic methods
        sa Equations—Numerical solutions
            Geometry, Analytic
        x Graphic algebra

xx Equations—Numerical solutions
 Geometry, Analytic
— Juvenile literature
— Problems, exercises, etc. *(QA157)*
— Programmed instruction
— Terminology

Algebra, Abstract *(QA266)*
 sa Algebra, Boolean
  Algebra, Homological
  Algebra, Universal
  Fields, Algebraic
  Genetic algebras
  Groups, Theory of
  Jordan algebras
  Lattice theory
  Lie algebras
  Logic, Symbolic and mathematical
  Matrices
  Nonassociative algebras
 x Abstract algebra
 xx Algebra, Universal
  Logic, Symbolic and mathematical
  Set theory
— Problems, exercises, etc.

Algebra, Boolean *(QA266)*
 sa Caratheodory measure
  Lattice theory
 x Boolean algebra
  Boole's algebra
 xx Algebra, Abstract
  Groups, Theory of
  Logic, Symbolic and mathematical
  Set theory
— Problems, exercises, etc.
— Programmed instruction

Algebra, Commutative
 See Commutative algebra

Algebra, Difference *(QA247.4)*
 x Difference algebra
  Difference fields
 xx Algebra, Differential
  Difference equations

Algebra, Differential *(QA247.4)*
 sa Algebra, Difference
 x Differential algebra
  Differential fields
 xx Differential equations
  Fields, Algebraic

Algebra, Homological *(QA169)*
 sa Categories (Mathematics)
  Functor theory
 x Homological algebra
 xx Algebra, Abstract
  Homology theory

Algebra, Matrix
 See Matrices
Algebra, Multiple
 See Algebra, Universal
Algebra, Steenrod
 See Steenrod algebra

Algebra, Universal *(QA251-263)*
 sa Algebra, Abstract
  Algebras, Linear
  Ausdehnungslehre
  Calculus of operations
  Categories (Mathematics)
  Matrices
  Numbers, Complex
  Quaternions
  Vector analysis
 x Algebra, Multiple
  N-way algebra
 xx Algebra, Abstract
  Numbers, Complex

Algebra of currents
 x Current algebra
 xx Quantum field theory

Algebra of logic
 See Logic, Symbolic and mathematical
Algebraic compiler
 See ALCOM (Computer program language)
Algebraic configurations in hyperspace
 See Hyperspace
Algebraic curves
 See Curves, Algebraic
Algebraic fields
 See Fields, Algebraic
Algebraic functions
 See Functions, Algebraic
Algebraic geometry
 See Geometry, Algebraic
Algebraic groups, Linear
 See Linear algebraic groups
Algebraic ideals
 See Ideals (Algebra)

Algebraic number theory
 sa Class field theory
  Valuation theory
 xx Fields, Algebraic
  Numbers, Theory of
Algebraic numbers
 See Fields, Algebraic
Algebraic rings
 See Rings (Algebra)

Algebraic spaces
 x Spaces, Algebraic
 xx Geometry, Algebraic
Algebraic surfaces
 See Surfaces, Algebraic

Algebraic topology *(QA611)*
 sa Adams spectral sequences
  CW complexes
  Eilenberg-Moore spectral sequences
  Fiber spaces (Mathematics)
  Homology theory
  Hopf algebras
  K-theory
  Measure theory
  Sheaves, Theory of
  Steenrod algebra
 xx Topology

Algebraic varieties
 sa Linear algebraic groups
 x Varieties, Algebraic
 xx Geometry, Algebraic
  Linear algebraic groups
Algebras, Associative
 See Associative algebras
Algebras, Banach
 See Banach algebras
Algebras, Clifford
 See Clifford algebras
Algebras, Cylindric
 See Cylindric algebras
Algebras, Function
 See Function algebras
Algebras, Genetic
 See Genetic algebras
Algebras, Hilbert
 See Hilbert algebras
Algebras, Hopf
 See Hopf algebras
Algebras, Jordan
 See Jordan algebras
Algebras, L1
 See L1 algebras
Algebras, Lie
 See Lie algebras

Algebras, Linear *(QA251)*
 sa Calculus of operations
  Clifford algebras
  Complexes
  Jordan algebras
  Lie algebras
  Line geometry

  Nonassociative algebras
  Substitutions, Linear
  Tensor products
  Topology
  Vector spaces
 x Linear algebras
 xx Algebra, Universal
  Calculus of operations
  Line geometry
  Mathematical analysis
  Spaces, Generalized
  Topology
— Problems, exercises, etc.
— Programmed instruction
Algebras, Measure
 See Measure algebras
Algebras, Nonassociative
 See Nonassociative algebras
Algebras, Operator
 See Operator algebras
Algebras, Polyadic
 See Polyadic algebras
Algebras, Topological
 See Topological algebras
Algebras, Von Neumann
 See Von Neumann algebras
Algebras, W
 See C*-algebras
  Von Neumann algebras

ALGEC (Computer program language)
 x Algorithmic economics language
ALGEM (Computer program language)
Algeria
— History *(DT271-299)*
— — To 647
— — 647-1516
— — 1516-1830
— — English Expedition, 1620-1621
— — Spanish Expedition, 1775
— — English Expedition, 1816
— — French Expedition, 1830
— — 1830-1962
— — 1945-1962
— — — Refugees
   xx Refugees, Algerian
— — — 1962-
— War with the United States, 1815
  See United States—History—War
   with Algeria, 1815

Algerian febrifuge
Algerian literature (French)
 See French literature—Algerian authors
Algerian poetry (French)
 See French poetry—Algerian authors
Algerians
Algerians in foreign countries
Algic languages
 See Algonquian languages
Algicides *(SB951)*
 xx Agricultural chemicals
  Pesticides
Algiers, Battle of, 1816 *(DT291)*
ALGOL (Computer program language)
 sa BALGOL (Computer program
  language)
  KALDAS (Computer program
  language)
  MALGOL (Computer program
  language)
  NELIAC (Computer program language)
  SIMULA (Computer program language)
 x Algorithmic language
  Symbolic language
 xx SIMULA (Computer program language)
— Problems, exercises, etc.
— Programmed instruction
Algol (Variable star)
 See Stars, Variable

Algology *(QK564-580)*
　sa Algae
　x Phycology
　xx Algae
　　Microbiology
　— Juvenile literature
　　　See Algae—Juvenile literature
　— Technique *(QK565.2)*
Algonkian Indians
　See Algonquian Indians
Algonkian period
　See Geology, Stratigraphic—Algonkian
Algonkin Indians *(E99.A349)*
　xx Algonquian Indians
　　Indians of North America
　— Juvenile literature
　— Legends
Algonkin language *(PM599)*
　xx Algonquian languages
Algonquian Indians *(E99.A35)*
　sa Abitibi Indians
　　Abnaki Indians
　　Algonkin Indians
　　Arapaho Indians
　　Arosaguntacook Indians
　　Bocootawwonauke Indians
　　Brotherton Indians
　　Cheyenne Indians
　　Chippewa Indians
　　Conoy Indians
　　Cree Indians
　　Delaware Indians
　　Esopus Indians
　　Fox Indians
　　Gay Head Indians
　　Illinois Indians
　　Kickapoo Indians
　　Lumbee Indians
　　Mahican Indians
　　Malecite Indians
　　Manahoac Indians
　　Mascouten Indians
　　Mashpee Indians
　　Massachuset Indians
　　Menominee Indians
　　Miami Indians
　　Micmac Indians
　　Minisink Indians
　　Missisauga Indians
　　Mistassin Indians
　　Mohegan Indians
　　Montagnais Indians
　　Montauk Indians
　　Moravian Indians
　　Munsee Indians
　　Narraganset Indians
　　Nascapee Indians
　　Nauset Indians
　　Nipissing Indians
　　Nipmuc Indians
　　Norridgewock Indians
　　Oka Indians
　　Ottawa Indians
　　Pamunkey Indians
　　Passamaquoddy Indians
　　Pennacook Indians
　　Penobscot Indians
　　Pequawket Indians
　　Pequot Indians
　　Piankashaw Indians
　　Piegan Indians
　　Pocasset Indians
　　Potawatomi Indians
　　Potomac Indians
　　Powhatan Indians
　　Quinnipiac Indians
　　Rappahannock Indians
　　Sauk Indians

　　Scaticook Indians (Conn.)
　　Scaticook Indians (N.Y.)
　　Shawnee Indians
　　Shinnecock Indians
　　Siksika Indians
　　Sokoki Indians
　　Stockbridge Indians
　　Têtes de Boule Indians
　　Timiskaming Indians
　　Wachuset Indians
　　Wamesit Indians
　　Wampanoag Indians
　　Wappinger Indians
　　Wea Indians
　x Algonkian Indians
　xx Indians of North America
　— Legends
　— Names
　— Religion and mythology
　— Social life and customs
　— — Juvenile literature
Algonquian languages *(PM600-609)*
　sa Abnaki language
　　Algonkin language
　　Amikwa language
　　Arapaho language
　　Atsina language
　　Cheyenne language
　　Chippewa language
　　Cree language
　　Delaware language
　　Fox language
　　Illinois language
　　Kickapoo language
　　Malecite language
　　Massachuset language
　　Menominee language
　　Miami language
　　Micmac language
　　Missisauga language
　　Mohegan language
　　Montagnais language
　　Munsee language
　　Narraganset language
　　Nascapee language
　　Nipissing language
　　Ottawa language
　　Passamaquoddy language
　　Penobscot language
　　Potawatomi language
　　Quinnipiac language
　　Quioucohanock language
　　Shawnee language
　　Siksika language
　x Algic languages
　xx Chippewa language
　　Cree language
　　Delaware language
　　Illinois language
　　Malecite language
　　Massachuset language
　　Micmac language
　　Missisauga language
　　Mohegan language
　　Montagnais language
　　Munsee language
　　Narraganset language
　　Nipissing language
　　Quinnipiac language
　　Quioucohanock language
　　Siksika language
　Example under Indians of North America—
　　Languages
Algorism
　See Algorithms
Algorithmic economics language
　See ALGEC (Computer program language)

Algorithmic language
　See ALGOL (Computer program language)
　　BALGOL (Computer program
　　language)
　　MAD (Computer program language)
Algorithms
　sa Branch and bound algorithms
　　Machine theory
　　Machine translating
　　Numerical analysis
　　Programming (Electronic computers)
　　Programming languages (Electronic
　　computers)
　　Programming (Mathematics)
　　Recursive functions
　　Transformations (Mathematics)
　x Algorism
　　Euclid's algorithm
　xx Algebra
　　Arithmetic—Foundations
Algraphy
　x Aluminum plate-printing
　xx Lithography
Alhamarides
　See Nasrides
Alhambra
　Example under Architecture, Islamic
　— Juvenile literature
Alhenna
　See Henna
Alibamu Indians *(E99.A4)*
　x Alabama Indians
　xx Indians of North America
　　Muskhogean Indians
Alibi *(Direct)*
　xx Defense (Criminal procedure)
Alicyclic compounds
　x Aliphatic-cyclic compounds
　　Cyclo-aliphatic compounds
　Example under Chemistry, Organic
Alides
　See Alids
Alids
　sa Shiites
　x Alides
　xx Shiites
Alien and Sedition laws, 1798 *(E327-8)*
　sa Kentucky and Virginia resolutions of
　　1798
　x Sedition law, 1798
　xx Kentucky and Virginia resolutions of
　　1798
Alien animals
　See Animal introduction
Alien labor *(Direct)*
　sa Agricultural laborers, Foreign
　　Children of alien laborers
　　Frontier workers
　x Alien workers
　　Foreign labor
　　Foreign workers
　　Immigrant labor
　xx Aliens
　　Emigration and immigration
　　Labor and laboring classes
　　Labor laws and legislation
　　Labor laws and legislation, International
　— Education *(Direct)*
Alien labor, Canadian, [French, etc.] *(Direct)*
　xx Canadians [French, etc.] in foreign
　　countries
　— Juvenile literature
Alien plants
　See Plant introduction
Alien property *(Direct)* *(JX4263.P6)*
　sa Eminent domain (International law)
　　Enemy property
　　Refugee property

American [British, Swiss, etc.] property in foreign countries
    x Foreign property
    Property, Alien
    xx Aliens
    Enemy property
    International law
— Appraisal
    See Alien property—Valuation
— Valuation *(Direct)*
    x Alien property—Appraisal
    xx Indemnity

    GEOGRAPHIC SUBDIVISIONS

— France
    sa Droit d'aubaine

    GEOGRAPHIC SUBDIVISIONS

— Italy, [Sweden, Switzerland, etc.]
    sa German property in Italy, [Sweden, Switzerland, etc.]

    GEOGRAPHIC SUBDIVISIONS

— Korea, [Manchuria, etc.]
    sa Japanese property in Korea, [Manchuria, etc.]

Alien radio stations
    See Foreign radio stations
Alien workers
    See Alien labor
Alienation, Restraints on
    See Restraints on alienation
Alienation, Social
    See Alienation (Social psychology)
Alienation (Law)
    See Transfer (Law)
Alienation (Philosophy) *(B808.2)*
    sa Isolation (Philosophy)
    x Estrangement (Philosophy)
    xx Philosophy
Alienation (Rhetoric)
    xx Rhetoric
Alienation (Social psychology)
    sa Social isolation
    x Alienation, Social
    Estrangement (Social psychology)
    Rebels (Social psychology)
    Social alienation
    xx Social isolation
    Social psychology
Alienation (Social psychology) in literature
Alienation (Social psychology) in moving-pictures
    xx Moving-pictures
Alienation (Theology) *(BT731)*
    xx Theology, Doctrinal
Alienation of affections *(Direct)*
    x Affections, Alienation of
    xx Betrothal—Law
    Breach of promise
    Divorce
    Marriage law
    Torts
Alienists
    See Psychiatrists
Aliens *(Indirect) (Emigration and immigration, JV6001-9500; European War: United States, D570.8.A6, Other countries, D636.A3-Z; World War: United States, D769.8.A6, Other countries, D801; Nationality and alienage, JX4203-4270)*
    sa Admission of nonimmigrants
    Alien labor
    Alien property
    Allegiance
    Business enterprises, Foreign
    Calvo doctrine and clause

    Citizenship
    Corporations, Foreign
    Deportation
    Diplomatic protection
    Drago doctrine
    Droit d'aubaine
    Expatriation
    Frontier workers
    International travel regulations
    Naturalization
    Pilgrims and pilgrimages—Law and legislation
    Refugees, Political—Legal status, laws, etc.
    Repatriation
    Security for costs
    Self-determination, National
    Taxation of aliens
    Japanese in San Francisco; *and similar headings*
    x Enemy aliens
    Foreigners
    xx Allegiance
    Citizenship
    Conflict of laws
    Deportation
    Emigration and immigration
    International law
    International travel regulations
    Naturalization
    Refugees, Political—Legal status, laws, etc.
    Example under Status (Law)
— Anecdotes, facetiae, satire, etc.
    See Ethnic wit and humor
— Political activity
    xx Politics, Practical
— Taxation
    See Taxation of aliens

    GEOGRAPHIC SUBDIVISIONS

— United States
    x United States—Aliens
Aliens, Taxation of
    See Taxation of aliens
Aliens (Greek law)
Aliens (Islamic law) *(Direct)*
    sa Dhimmis
    Example under Islamic law
Aliens (Jewish law)
    sa Gentiles in the Old Testament
    Example under Jewish law
Aliens (Roman law)
    sa Jus gentium (Roman law)
    Example under Roman law
Aliens in literature
Aligarh movement
Alignment, Optical
    See Optical tooling
Alignment charts
    See Nomography (Mathematics)
Alignment of automobile bodies
    See Automobiles—Bodies—Alignment
Alignment of automobile wheels
    See Automobiles—Wheels—Alignment
Alikaluf Indians
    See Alacaluf Indians
Alikuluf Indians
    See Alacaluf Indians
Alimentary canal *(Comparative anatomy, QL856-863; Human anatomy, QM301-345)*
    sa Digestive organs
    Gastrointestinal gas
    x Alimentary tract
    Gastrointestinal tract
— Blood-vessels
    See Digestive organs—Blood-vessels

— Cancer
— — Diagnosis
— Diseases
    See Digestive organs—Diseases
— Exploration
— Foreign bodies
— Hemorrhage
    See Gastrointestinal hemorrhage
— Inflammation
    xx Digestive organs—Diseases
— Innervation
    See Digestive organs—Innervation
— Obstructions
    xx Digestive organs—Diseases
— Radiography
— Surgery
— — Complications and sequelae
— Tumors
Alimentary pastes
    See Macaroni products
Alimentary tract
    See Alimentary canal
Alimentation
    See Nutrition
Alimony *(Direct)*
    sa Separate maintenance
    xx Divorce
    Matrimonial actions
    Support (Domestic relations)
— Taxation *(Direct)*
Alimony (Jewish law)
    sa Ketuba
Aliphatic-cyclic compounds
    See Alicyclic compounds
Alise-Sainte-Reine, France
— Siege, 52 B.C.
    See Alesia, Battle of, 52 B.C.
Alison, Sweet
    See Sweet alyssum
Alizarin *(TP918.A4)*
    xx Coal-tar colors
    Madder
Alizarin black
    See Naphthazarin
Aljamía
    x Portuguese language—Arabic alphabet
    Spanish language—Arabic alphabet
Alkali-aggregate reactions
    sa Concrete—Defects
    xx Aggregates (Building materials)
    Chemical reactions
    Concrete—Chemistry
    Concrete—Defects
Alkali disease
    See Selenosis
Alkali industry and trade *(Technology, TP201-223)*
    sa Barilla
    Potash industry and trade
    Soda industry
    xx Soda industry
    Example under Chemistry, Technical
Alkali lands *(S595)*
    sa Solonetz soils
    x Alkali soils
    xx Irrigation
    Reclamation of land
    Soils
    Soils, Salts in
Alkali metal electrodes
    See Electrodes, Alkali metal
Alkali metal halide crystals
Alkali metals *(QD172.A4)*
    sa Francium
    xx Light metals
— Analysis
— Safety measures
— Spectra

Alkali metals *(QD172.A4)* *(Continued)*
— Thermal properties
Alkali proteinase
See Trypsin
Alkali rocks
See Alkalic igneous rocks
Alkali soils
See Alkali lands
Alkalic igneous rocks *(QE462.A4)*
x Alkali rocks
Alkaline igneous rocks
Igneous rocks, Alkaline
xx Rocks, Igneous
Alkalies *(Chemistry, QD172.A4; Technology, TP201-223)*
sa Ammonia
Lye
Potassium
Sodium
Example under Chemicals; Chemistry, Inorganic
— Handling and transportation
— Physiological effect
— Prices *(Direct)*
Alkaline earth metals *(QD172.A42)*
sa Alkaline earths
xx Light metals
— Analysis
Alkaline earths
xx Alkaline earth metals
Alkaline igneous rocks
See Alkalic igneous rocks
Alkaline phosphatase
Alkaloids *(Botany, QK898.A4; Chemistry, QD421; Pharmacology, QP921)*
sa names of alkaloids, e.g. Atropine, Belladonna, Strychnine
x Alcaloids
xx Nitrogen compounds
Example under Chemistry, Organic
— Physiological effect *(QP921)*
sa Medicine, Dosimetric
Plants, Effect of alkaloids on
xx Medicine, Dosimetric
— Spectra
— Tables, etc.
— Therapeutic use *(RM666.A4; Pharmacology, QP921)*
Example under Therapeutics
Alkalosis *(RB145)*
Alkanes
See Paraffins
Alkoran
See Koran
Alkyd resins
xx Gums and resins, Synthetic
Alkylation *(QD281.A5)*
sa Methylation
xx Chemical reactions
Hydrocarbons
Petroleum—Refining
All (Philosophy) *(BD397)*
x Allness
xx Ontology
Whole and parts (Philosophy)
All Fools' Day
See April Fools' Day
All Hallows' Eve
See Halloween
All Saints' Day *(BV67)*
xx Church year
Fasts and feasts
Saints
All Saints' Day sermons
xx Sermons
All Souls' Day
xx Fasts and feasts
Purgatory

All Souls' Day sermons
xx Sermons
All-Star Baseball Game
xx Baseball
— Juvenile literature
All-Star Football Game
xx Football
All terrain vehicle racing *(Direct)*
xx All terrain vehicles
Automobile racing
All terrain vehicles
sa All terrain vehicle racing
Dune buggies
Snowmobiles
Tracklaying vehicles
x Terrain vehicles
xx Motor vehicles
— Environmental aspects *(Direct)*
— Juvenile literature
All-wing aeroplanes
See Aeroplanes, Tailless
Alladian (African people)
See Alagya (African people)
Alladian language
See Aladian language
Allah
See God (Islam)
Allanite *(Indirect)* *(TN948.A5)*
x Orthite
xx Epidote
Allantoin metabolism
xx Metabolism
Allegiance *(Direct)* *(JC328; Nationality, JX4203-4270)*
sa Aliens
Citizenship
Dual nationality
Naturalization
Self-determination, National
x Loyalty, Political
xx Aliens
Citizenship
Government, Resistance to
International law
Naturalization
Political science
Self-determination, National
Note under Loyalty
Allegiance, Oath of, 1606
See Oath of allegiance, 1606
Allegorical costume
xx Costume
Allegories
Here are entered collections of allegories. Works on allegory as a literary form are entered under the heading Allegory.
sa Apocalyptic art
Fables
Parables
x Allegory (Art)
xx Exempla
Fables
Fiction
Homiletical illustrations
Parables
Tales
Allegory *(PN56.A5)*
sa Apocalyptic literature
Personification in literature
xx Personification in literature
Note under Allegories
Allegory (Art)
See Allegories
Symbolism in art
Allegory (Literature)
See Symbolism in literature

Allegory in literature
See Symbolism in literature
Allelism
See Allelomorphism
Allelomorphism
sa Complementation (Genetics)
x Allelism
xx Chromosomes
Genetics
Allelopathy
xx Botany—Ecology
Plant physiology
Alleluia (Music)
x Alleluja (Music)
xx Chants (Plain, Gregorian, etc.)— History and criticism
Alleluja (Music)
See Alleluia (Music)
Allemande
x Allmayne
Almain
Almand
Allemandes
Here are entered collections of allemande music for various mediums. Individual allemandes and collections of allemandes for a specific medium are entered under the heading followed by specification of medium.
Allemandes (Orchestra) *(M1048; M1060)*
xx Orchestral music
Allemandes (String quartet) *(M450-454)*
xx String quartets
Allemandes (Viols (3)) *(M990)*
xx String trios (Viols (3))
Allen and Wheelock firearms
xx Firearms
Allen organ *(ML597)*
xx Electronic organ
Allen radiation belts
See Van Allen radiation belts
Allene crystals
Allentiac language *(PM5386)*
x Guarpe language
xx Indians of South America—Languages
Allergic encephalomyelitis
x Disseminated vasculomyelinopathy
Hyperergic encephalomyelitis
xx Autoimmune diseases
Encephalomyelitis
Allergy *(RC583-598)*
sa Anaphylaxis
Antihistamines
Cellular immunity
Contact dermatitis
Cookery for allergics
Drug allergy
Favism
Food allergy
Immune complexes
Pediatric allergy
Respiratory allergy
Skin tests
x Hypersensitivity (Immunology)
xx Anaphylaxis
Immunity
Immunopathology
Serumtherapy
— Cases, clinical reports, statistics
— Diagnosis
— Personal narratives
— Psychosomatic aspects
— Research grants *(Direct)*
Allethrin
Alleys
See Streets
Alliance, Dual, 1879
See Dual Alliance, 1879

Alliance, Holy
See Holy Alliance
Alliance, Triple . . .
See Triple Alliance . . .
Alliance for progress
sa Social progress trust fund
xx Economic assistance in Latin America
Technical assistance in Latin America
Alliance of the Three Emperors, 1872
See Three Emperors' League, 1872
Alliance of the Three Emperors, 1881
See Three Emperors' League, 1881
Alliances *(JX4005)*
x Treaties of alliance
xx International relations
Treaties
Allied health education
See Paramedical education
Allied health personnel *(Indirect)*
sa Dental assistants
Dental hygienists
Dental technicians
Medical record librarians
Medical secretaries
Nurses' aides
Operating room technicians
Pharmacy technicians
Physicians' assistants
x Paramedical personnel
Paramedics
Allied rat
xx Rats
Alligator hunting *(SK305.A)*
xx Alligators
Alligator-pear
See Avocado
Alligators *(QL666.C9)*
sa Alligator hunting
— Juvenile literature
Alligators, Fossil *(QE862.C8)*
Alliteration
xx Rime
Versification
Allmayne
See Allemande
Allness
See All (Philosophy)
Allocation of time
See Time allocation
Allocations, Industrial
See Priorities, Industrial
Allodial tenure
See Allodium
Allodium *(Direct)*
x Allodial tenure
xx Feudal law
Land tenure—Law
Udal system
Allogeneic homografts
See Homografts
Allografts
See Homografts
Allometry
xx Growth
Allophanates *(QD305.A2)*
Allophanite
Allorhythmia
See Arrhythmia
Allotment of land *(Direct)* *(HD1519)*
Here are entered works on the assign-
ment of small plots of land to laborers
for cultivation as a subsidiary source of
income.
sa Part-time farming
Working-men's gardens
x Land, Allotment of
xx Agricultural colonies
Agricultural laborers

Agriculture and state
Charities
Labor and laboring classes
Land tenure
Part-time farming
Rehabilitation, Rural
Allotriognathi
See Lampridiformes
Allotropy *(QD470)*
xx Chemical elements
Chemistry, Physical and theoretical
— Problems, exercises, etc.
Allowances, Children's
See Children's allowances
Allowances, Family
See Family allowances
Alloxan
xx Diabetes
Uric acid
Alloxuric substances *(Physiological
chemistry, QP801; Practice of
medicine, RC903; Secretions,
QP211)*
sa Urine—Analysis and pathology
Xanthine
xx Metabolism
Nitrogen excretion
Physiological chemistry
Purines
Urine—Analysis and pathology
Alloy plating *(TS693)*
x Electrodeposition of alloys
xx Alloys
Electroplating
Alloys *(Magnetic induction, QC761;
Materials of engineering, TA490;
Metallography, TN690; Technology,
TS650)*
sa Alloy plating
Alnicos
Amalgamation
Amalgams
Brass
Bronze
Heat resistant alloys
Magnetic alloys
Metallurgy
Nonferrous alloys
Pewter
Aluminum alloys; Copper alloys; Nickel
alloys; Steel alloys; Tin alloys; *and
similar headings*
x Metallic alloys
xx Amalgamation
Brass
Chemistry, Technical
Metallic composites
Metallurgical analysis
Metallurgy
Metals
Phase rule and equilibrium
Solder and soldering
— Analysis
Example under Metallurgical analysis
— Catalogs
— Corrosion
— Defects
— Fatigue
— Juvenile literature
— Patents
— Specifications *(TA490)*
— Testing *(TA490)*
— — Laboratory manuals
— Thermal properties
— — Charts, diagrams, etc.
Alloys, Heat resistant
See Heat resistant alloys

Alloys, Nonferrous
See Nonferrous alloys
Allport-Vernon study of values test
(BF698.8.A4)
x Study of values test, Allport-Vernon
xx Personality tests
Worth
Allspice
x Jamaica pepper
Pimento (Allspice)
Allusions *(PN43)*
sa Terms and phrases
subdivision Allusions *under names of
prominent authors, etc.*
xx Terms and phrases
Allusive arms (Heraldry)
See Canting arms (Heraldry)
Alluvial fans *(Indirect)* *(GB591-8)*
xx Alluvial plains
Alluvium
Sedimentation and deposition
Alluvial plains *(GB591-8)*
sa Alluvial fans
Alluvium
Deltas
subdivision Alluvial plain *under names
of rivers, e.g.* Mississippi River—
Alluvial plain
x Bottom lands
xx Deltas
Alluvion
sa Accession (Law)
xx Accretion (Law)
Acquisition of property
Riparian rights
Alluvium *(QE699)*
sa Alluvial fans
Silt
xx Alluvial plains
Geology
Rivers
Soils
Allyl halides
xx Halides
Alma, Battle of the, 1854 *(DK215.1)*
xx Crimean War, 1853-1856
Almain
See Allemande
Almanac publishing *(Direct)*
xx Publishers and publishing
Almanacs *(AY; Nautical, QB8; Weather,
QC999)*
sa Calendars
Chronology
Literary calendars
Music—Almanacs, yearbooks, etc.
Nautical almanacs
Yearbooks
x Annuals
xx Astronomy
Calendars
Chronology
Street literature
Yearbooks
Almanacs, American, ₍Belgian, Dutch, etc.₎
(Direct)
x American ₍Belgian, Dutch, etc.₎
almanacs
Almanacs, Children's *(AY81.J8)*
x Children's almanacs
Almanacs, Jewish
x Jewish almanacs
Almand
See Allemande
Almaricians
See Amalricians
Almeida, Portugal
— Siege, 1762

Almohades
  x Muwāḥḥadis
  xx Islamic Empire
Almond *(SB401)*
  — Tariff
    See Tariff on almonds
Almond moth
  See Fig-moth
Almoravides
  xx Spain—History—Arab period, 711-1492
Almost complex manifolds *(QA649)*
  x Manifolds, Almost complex
  xx Complex manifolds
    Geometry, Differential
Almost periodic functions
  x Functions, Almost periodic
  xx Fourier series
Alms and almsgiving
  See Charities
    Charity
Alms and almsgiving (Islam)
  See Islam—Charities
Almsgiving, Buddhist
  See Buddhist giving
Almshouses *(Indirect)* *(HV61, HV85-527)*
  sa Old age homes
    Poor
    subdivision Almshouses *under names of*
      cities
  x Benevolent institutions
    Charitable institutions
    Homes (Institutions)
    Poor farms
    Poorhouses
    Workhouses (Poorhouses)
  xx Asylums
    Charities
    Children—Institutional care
    Hospitals
    Institutional care
    Old age homes
    Poor
    Public institutions
    Public welfare
  — Law and legislation *(Direct)*
    xx Charity laws and legislation
      Poor laws
      Public welfare—Law
Almucantar *(QB103)*
  xx Astronomical instruments
Alnicos
  xx Alloys
    Magnetic materials
Alogi *(BT1323)*
  x Alogians
  xx Church history—Primitive and early
    church, ca. 30-600
    Logos
Alogians
  See Alogi
Aloin *(QP925.A4)*
Alombrados
  See Alumbrados
Alomwe (Bantu people)
  See Lomwe (Bantu people)
Alookooloop Indians
  See Alacaluf Indians
Alopecia
  See Baldness
Alouette (Artificial satellite)
  xx Artificial satellites
Alp (The word)
Alpaca *(QL737.U54; SF401.A4)*
Alpaca (Textile)
Alpenhorn *(History and construction,*
  ML980)
  sa Lur
  x Alpine horn

  xx Horn (Musical instrument)
    Lur
ALPHA (Electronic computer system)
Alpha decay
  x Decay, Alpha
  xx Alpha rays
    Radioisotopes—Decay
Alpha globulin
  sa Ceruloplasmin
  xx Globulin
Alpha particles
  See Alpha rays
Alpha ray spectrometry
  x Spectrometry, Alpha ray
  xx Spectrometer
    Spectrum analysis
Alpha rays *(QC721)*
  sa Alpha decay
    Delta rays
  x Alpha particles
  xx Delta rays
    Ionizing radiation
    Neutrons
    Protons
    Radiation
    Radioactivity
  — Scattering
Alphabet
  Here are entered general and comparative works dealing with the Semitic alphabet and its ancient and modern
  derivatives, or with similar series of
  characters, employed to represent the
  sounds of a language. *Cf.* note under
  Writing.
  sa Alphabets
    Arabic alphabet
    Brahmi alphabet
    Celtiberian alphabet
    Cuneiform writing
    Cypriote syllabary
    Cyrillic alphabet
    Devanagari alphabet
    Extinct languages
    Glagolitic alphabet
    Indians—Writing
    Inscriptions, Linear A
    Jawi alphabet
    Kharosthi alphabet
    Paleography
    Pasigraphy
    hPhags-pa-alphabet
    Phonetic alphabet
    Runes
    Siyāqat alphabet
    Writing
    subdivision Alphabet *or* Writing *under*
      groups of languages or under
      particular languages, e.g. Greek
      language—Alphabet; Slavic languages
      —Writing
  x Letters of the alphabet
    Roman alphabet
  xx Extinct languages
    Hieroglyphics
    Paleography
    Transliteration
    Writing
  Note under Writing
  — Juvenile literature
  — Transliteration
    See Transliteration
Alphabet, Initial teaching
  See Initial teaching alphabet
Alphabet, Phonetic
  See Phonetic alphabet
Alphabet, Unifon
  See Unifon alphabet

Alphabet (in religion, folk-lore, etc.)
  sa Alphabet rhymes
    Bijas
    Devanagari alphabet (in religion,
      folk-lore, etc.)
    English language—Alphabet (in
      religion, folk-lore, etc.)
    Hebrew language—Alphabet (in
      religion, folk-lore, etc.)
    Writing (in religion, folk-lore, etc.)
  x Folk-lore of the alphabet
    Symbolism of letters
  xx Cryptography
    Religion, Primitive
    Writing (in religion, folk-lore, etc.)
Alphabet rhymes *(GR486)*
  x Rhyming alphabets
  xx Alphabet (in religion, folk-lore, etc.)
    Folk-lore
    Nursery rhymes
Alphabeting *(Z695.95)*
  sa Files and filing (Documents)
    Shelf-listing (Library science)
  x Book numbers
    Notation (for books in libraries)
    Numeration of books in libraries
  xx Files and filing (Documents)
  — Programmed instruction
Alphabets *(Art, NK3600-3620; Calligraphy,*
  Z43; Comparative grammar,
  P211-213; Fancy work, TT773;
  Mechanical drawing, T371)
  sa Illumination of books and manuscripts
    Initials
    Lettering
    Monograms
    Telegraph—Alphabets
  x Ornamental alphabets
  xx Alphabet
    Decoration and ornament
    Illumination of books and manuscripts
    Initials
    Lettering
    Monograms
    Penmanship
    Sign painting
Alpine agriculture
  See Hill farming
Alpine clubs
  See Mountaineering—Societies, etc.
Alpine farming
  See Hill farming
Alpine fauna *(Indirect)*
  xx Zoology
  — Juvenile literature
Alpine flora *(Indirect)* *(Botany, QK331,*
  QK937; Culture, SB421)
  sa Alpine gardens
    Edelweiss
  x Flora
    Mountain flora
  xx Botany
    Mountain ecology
    Plants
Alpine gardens *(SB421; SB459)*
  xx Alpine flora
    Rock gardens
Alpine horn
  See Alpenhorn
Alpine ibex
  See Bouquetin
Alpine mountain goat
  See Bouquetin
Alpine race *(GN549.A)*
  sa Celts
  x Alpines
  xx Celts

Alpine regions
    xx Crop zones
        Mountains
    — Climate
Alpine wild goat
    See Bouquetin
Alpines
    See Alpine race
Alport's syndrome
    x Oto-oculorenal syndrome
    xx Deafness—Genetic aspects
        Ear—Diseases
        Eye—Diseases and defects
        Kidneys—Diseases
Alps
    — Passes
        Example under Mountain passes; Valleys
Alps in literature
Alsace in literature
Alsace-Lorraine question *(DD801.A31-57)*
    xx Franco-German War, 1870-1871
Alsatian poetry (French)
    See French poetry—Alsatian authors
Alsatian wolf dogs
    See German shepherd dogs
Alsatians in Germany, ⌐Italy, etc.⌐
Alsea Indians *(E99.A5)*
    xx Indians of North America
Alsea language *(PM610.A3)*
Alsike clover
    xx Clover
Alsnö, Ordinance of, 1280
    x Alsnöstadgan
        Ordinance of Alsnö, 1280
    xx Sweden—History—To 1397
Alsnöstadgan
    See Alsnö, Ordinance of, 1280
Altai language
    See Oirot language
Altaians
    See Ural-Altaic tribes
Altaic languages *(PL1-9)*
    sa Chuvashian language
        Finno-Ugrian languages
        Manchu language
        Mongolian languages
        Soyot language
        Tungusic languages
        Turko-Tataric languages
        Uigur language
        Ural-Altaic languages
        Yakut language
    x Scythian languages
    xx Turko-Tataric languages
        Ural-Altaic languages
Altar boys *(Catholic Church, BX1972)*
    sa Seises
    x Acolytes
        Servers
    xx Clergy—Minor orders
        Mass
Altar-cloths *(BV167)*
    xx Church vestments
        Liturgical objects
Altar gilds
    x Altar guilds
        Gilds, Altar
    xx Church societies
Altar guilds
    See Altar gilds
Altar prayers *(BX2048)*
    xx Catholic Church. Liturgy and ritual
Altar screens
    See Screens (Church decoration)
Altarpieces *(Direct)*
    x Predellas
        Reredos
        Retables

    xx Christian art and symbolism
        Church decoration and ornament
        Church furniture
        Screens (Church decoration)
Altarpieces, Baroque *(Direct)*
    x Baroque altarpieces
Altarpieces, Flemish, ⌐German, etc.⌐ *(Direct)*
    x Flemish ⌐German, etc.⌐ altarpieces
Altarpieces, Gothic *(Direct)*
    x Gothic altarpieces
Altarpieces, Renaissance *(Direct)*
    x Renaissance altarpieces
Altarpieces, Romanesque *(Direct)*
    x Romanesque altarpieces
Altars *(Direct)* *(Architecture, NA5060;*
        Christian, BV195)
    sa Sacrament houses
    xx Church decoration and ornament
        Church furniture
Altars, Baroque *(Direct)*
    x Baroque altars
Altars, Gothic *(Direct)*
    x Gothic altars
Altars, Hindu
    x Hindu altars
Altars, Renaissance *(Direct)*
    x Renaissance altars
Altars (Canon law) *(BX1939.A5)*
    xx Sacred places (Canon law)
Altars with pulpits
    xx Pulpits
Alterants
    See Alteratives
Alteration, Chromatic
    See Chromatic alteration (Music)
Alteratives
    x Alterants
    xx Materia medica
        Therapeutics
Alternating current dynamos
    See Dynamos—Alternating current
Alternating current generators
    See Dynamos—Alternating current
Alternating current machinery
    See Electric machinery—Alternating
        current
Alternating currents
    See Electric currents, Alternating
Alternating generations
    See Generations, Alternating
Alternative convictions *(Direct)*
    x Convictions, Alternative
    xx Criminal procedure
        Judgments
Alternative schools
    See Free schools
Alternators, Electric
    See Dynamos—Alternating current
Altimeter
    sa Airborne profile recorder
        Altitudes—Measurement
        Radio altimeters
    xx Aeronautical instruments
        Altitudes—Measurement
        Meteorological instruments
Altitude, Influence of *(QP82)*
    sa Anoxemia
        Erythremia
        Man—Influence of environment
        Mountain sickness
        Plants, Effect of altitude on
    xx Acclimatization
        Atmospheric pressure—Physiological
          effect
        Climatology, Medical
        Man—Influence of environment

Altitude gyro
    See Artificial horizons (Aeronautical
        instruments)
Altitudes *(GB491-8)*
    sa Contours (Cartography)
        subdivision Altitudes *under names of*
        countries, states, etc., e.g. United
        States—Altitudes; New York (State)
        —Altitudes
    x Elevations
        Heights
    xx Physical geography
    — Measurement *(Meteorology, QC895;*
        Surveying, TA606-9)
        sa Altimeter
            Barometric hypsometry
            Leveling
            Refraction, Terrestrial
            Saint Hilaire method
        x Hypsometry
            Tables of heights
        xx Altimeter
            Barometric hypsometry
            Refraction, Terrestrial
            Topographical surveying
        Example under Mensuration
Altix camera
Altmark, Truce of, 1629
    x Marienburg, Truce of, 1629
        Stuhmsdorf, Treaty of, 1629
    xx Swedish-Polish War, 1617-1629
Alto cornet
    See Alto horn
Alto horn *(ML975-6)*
    x Alto cornet
        Alto saxhorn
        Mellophone
    xx Fluegelhorn
        Horn (Musical instrument)
Alto horn and piano music *(M270-271)*
    sa Sonatas (Alto horn and piano)
    x Piano and alto horn music
Alto horn music *(M110)*
    sa Quartets, ⌐Trios, etc.⌐, Wind quartets,
        ⌐trios, etc.⌐ *followed by specifications*
        which include the alto horn
Alto saxhorn
    See Alto horn
Altranstädt, Peace of, 1707 *(DL743.A5)*
Altruism *(BJ1474)*
    sa Egoism
        Helping behavior
        Self-denial
        Self-interest
        Self-sacrifice
    xx Charity
        Conduct of life
        Egoism
        Ethics
        Hedonism
        Self-interest
        Social ethics
Altuzzo, Battle of, 1944
    x Monte Altuzzo, Battle of, 1944
    xx World War, 1939-1945—Campaigns—
        Italy
Aluconidae
    See Owls
Alukoeluf Indians
    See Alacaluf Indians
Alulu language
    See Alur language
Alum *(RM666.A42; Water purification,*
    TD468)
    — Therapeutic use
Alum-stone
    See Alunite

Alumbrados *(Spanish Inquisition, BX1735)*
   x Alombrados
   xx Illuminati
      Mysticism
Alumina-silica catalysts
   See Silica-alumina catalysts
Aluminosilicates
   See Aluminum silicates
Aluminothermy *(TS227)*
   xx Metallurgy
      Thermit
      Welding
Aluminum *(Chemistry, QD181.A4;*
      Production, TN775)
   sa Aluminum foil
      Aluminum silicates
      Classification—Books—Aluminum
      Creep of aluminum
      Soils—Aluminum content
   xx Aluminum silicates
      Light metals
   — Analysis *(QD137.A6)*
   — Anodic oxidation *(TS694.2)*
      xx Aluminum coatings
      Example under Metals—Anodic oxida-
        tion
   — Brazing
      Example under Brazing
   — Corrosion
      sa Aluminum coatings
      Example under Corrosion and anti-corro-
        sives
   — Creep
      See Creep of aluminum
   — Electrometallurgy *(TN775)*
   — Fatigue
      xx Aluminum—Testing
   — Finishing
      x Aluminum finishing
      Example under Metals—Finishing
   — Isotopes
   — — Decay
   — — Spectra
   — Juvenile literature
   — Metallography *(TN693.A5)*
   — Metallurgy *(TN775)*
   — Protective coatings
      See Aluminum coatings
   — Spectra
   — Tables, calculations, etc.
   — Tariff
      See Tariff on aluminum
   — Testing
      sa Aluminum—Fatigue
   — Toxicology
   — Welding
Aluminum, Powdered
   See Aluminum powder
Aluminum, Structural *(TA480.A6)*
   sa Aluminum construction
      Plates, Aluminum
   x Structural aluminum
   xx Aluminum construction
   — Corrosion
   — Specifications
   — Testing
   — Vibration
Aluminum alloy forgings
   See Aluminum forgings
Aluminum alloy plates
   See Plates, Aluminum
Aluminum alloys *(Manufacture, TS555;*
      Metallurgy, TN775)
   sa Aluminum bronze
      Aluminum-chromium alloys
      Aluminum-copper alloys
      Aluminum-copper-magnesium alloys
      Aluminum founding

      Aluminum-magnesium alloys
      Aluminum-magnesium-silicon alloys
      Aluminum-magnesium-zinc alloys
      Aluminum-manganese alloys
      Aluminum-silver alloys
      Aluminum-uranium alloys
      Aluminum-yttrium alloys
      Aluminum-zinc alloys
      Aluminum-zirconium alloys
      Nickel-aluminum alloys
      Nickel-chromium-aluminum alloys
      Steel-aluminum alloys
      Titanium-aluminum-vanadium alloys
   xx Alloys
      Light metals
   — Analysis
   — Anodic oxidation *(TS694.2)*
   — Corrosion
   — Fatigue
   — Fracture
   — Heat treatment
      x Heat treatment of aluminum alloys
   — Hydrogen content *(TN693.A5)*
      x Hydrogen in aluminum alloys
      xx Gases in metals
   — Metallurgy
   — Patents
   — Spectra
   — Testing
   — Welding
Aluminum boats
   x Boats, Aluminum
   xx Boats and boating
Aluminum brass tubes
   See Tubes, Aluminum brass
Aluminum bridges
   See Bridges, Aluminum
Aluminum bronze *(TS650)*
   xx Aluminum alloys
      Bronze
   — Welding
Aluminum building
   See Aluminum construction
Aluminum castings
   xx Aluminum founding
      Metal castings
   — Radiography
Aluminum cell *(TK2798)*
   xx Electric current rectifiers
      Electric transformers
Aluminum-chromium alloys
   x Chromium-aluminum alloys
   xx Aluminum alloys
      Chromium alloys
   — Magnetic properties
Aluminum coating
   Here are entered works on aluminum ap-
      plied as a coating to surfaces of other
      materials. Works on coatings applied
      to the surfaces of aluminum objects are
      entered under Aluminum coatings.
   sa Calorizing
   xx Corrosion and anti-corrosives
      Electroplating
      Metal coating
      Metal spraying
      Plating
   Note under Aluminum coatings
Aluminum coatings
   Here are entered works on coatings ap-
      plied to the surfaces of aluminum ob-
      jects. Works on aluminum applied as a
      coating to surfaces of other materials
      are entered under Aluminum coating.
   sa Aluminum—Anodic oxidation
   x Aluminum—Protective coatings
   xx Aluminum—Corrosion
      Protective coatings

   Note under Aluminum coating
   — Optical properties
Aluminum compounds
Aluminum construction *(TA690)*
   sa Aluminum, Structural
      Aluminum windows
      Bridges, Aluminum
      Ships, Aluminum
   x Aluminum building
      Aluminum structures
      Building, Aluminum
      Structures, Aluminum
   xx Aluminum, Structural
      Building
      Lightweight construction
   — Patents
   — Standards *(Direct)*
   — Tables, calculations, etc.
Aluminum-copper alloys
   sa Duralumin
   x Copper-aluminum alloys
   xx Aluminum alloys
      Copper alloys
   — Radiation effects
      See Aluminum-copper alloys, Effect of
        radiation on
Aluminum-copper alloys, Effect of radiation on
   x Aluminum-copper alloys, Irradiated
      Aluminum-copper alloys—Radiation
        effects
      Radiation—Effect on aluminum-copper
        alloys
   xx Radiation
Aluminum-copper alloys, Irradiated
   See Aluminum-copper alloys, Effect of
      radiation on
Aluminum-copper-magnesium alloys
   xx Aluminum alloys
      Copper alloys
      Magnesium alloys
   — Testing
Aluminum crystals
Aluminum films
   xx Metallic films
   — Radiation effects
      See Aluminum films, Effect of
        radiation on
Aluminum films, Effect of radiation on
   x Aluminum films—Radiation effects
   xx Radiation
Aluminum finishing
   See Aluminum—Finishing
Aluminum foil
   xx Aluminum
      Aluminum in packaging
      Metal foils
Aluminum forgings *(TS555)*
   x Aluminum alloy forgings
      Forged aluminum
   xx Forging
Aluminum forming
   x Aluminum working
      Forming of aluminum
      Working of aluminum
   xx Metal-work
Aluminum founding *(TS555)*
   sa Aluminum castings
   x Aluminum foundry practice
   xx Aluminum alloys
      Founding
   — Safety measures
Aluminum foundry practice
   See Aluminum founding
Aluminum in packaging
   sa Aluminum foil
   x Aluminum packaging
   xx Packaging

Aluminum in soils
    See Soils—Aluminum content
Aluminum in the body *(QP535.A4)*
Aluminum industry and trade *(Direct)*
        (HD9539.A6)
    sa Light metals industry
        Strikes and lockouts—Aluminum
            industry
        Wages—Aluminum industry
    — Accounting
    — Automation
    — Collective labor agreements
            See Collective labor agreements—
                Aluminum industry
    — Defense measures *(UA929.95.A5)*
    — Employees
    — Government ownership *(Direct)*
    — Labor productivity
    — Safety measures
    — Safety regulations *(Direct)*
Aluminum ingots
    x Ingots, Aluminum
Aluminum-iron alloys
    See Iron-aluminum alloys
Aluminum-magnesium alloys
    x Magnesium-aluminum alloys
    xx Aluminum alloys
        Light metals
        Magnesium alloys
    — Magnetic properties
Aluminum-magnesium-silicon alloys
    xx Aluminum alloys
        Magnesium alloys
        Silicon alloys
Aluminum-magnesium-zinc alloys
    xx Aluminum alloys
        Magnesium alloys
        Zinc alloys
    — Corrosion
Aluminum-manganese alloys
    x Manganese-aluminum alloys
    xx Aluminum alloys
        Manganese alloys
    — Spectra
Aluminum mines and mining *(Indirect)*
Aluminum-nickel alloys
    See Nickel-aluminum alloys
Aluminum ores *(Indirect)*
    sa Bauxite
Aluminum organic compounds
    See Organoaluminum compounds
Aluminum packaging
    See Aluminum in packaging
Aluminum pipe
    See Pipe, Aluminum
Aluminum plate-printing
    See Algraphy
Aluminum plates (Structural)
    See Plates, Aluminum
Aluminum powder
    x Aluminum, Powdered
        Powdered aluminum
    xx Metal powders
Aluminum roofing
    See Roofing, Aluminum
Aluminum ships
    See Ships, Aluminum
Aluminum silicates *(QD181.S6)*
    sa Aluminum
        Andalusite
        Beryl
        Clay
        Kaolin
        Mullite
        Pyrophyllite
        Sillimanite
        Vesuvianite
    x Aluminosilicates

Silicoaluminates
    xx Aluminum
        Silicates
    — Spectra
Aluminum-silver alloys
    x Silver-aluminum alloys
    xx Aluminum alloys
        Silver alloys
Aluminum-steel alloys
    See Steel-aluminum alloys
Aluminum structures
    See Aluminum construction
Aluminum-uranium alloys
    x Uranium-aluminum alloys
    xx Aluminum alloys
        Uranium alloys
Aluminum windows
    xx Aluminum construction
        Metal windows
Aluminum wire *(TK3305)*
    xx Wire
    — Tables, calculations, etc.
Aluminum working
    See Aluminum forming
Aluminum-yttrium alloys
    x Yttrium-aluminum alloys
    xx Aluminum alloys
        Yttrium alloys
Aluminum-zinc alloys
    x Zinc-aluminum alloys
    xx Aluminum alloys
        Zinc alloys
    — Testing
Aluminum-zirconium alloys
    x Zirconium-aluminum alloys
    xx Aluminum alloys
        Zirconium alloys
Alumni
    See subdivisions Alumni and Registers
        under Universities and colleges; and
        similar headings
Alumnol
Alunite *(Indirect)*
    x Alum-stone
Alur (African tribe)
    xx Ethnology—Uganda
        Ethnology—Zaire
        Nilo-Hamitic tribes
Alur language
    x Alulu language
        Aluru language
        Dho Alur
        Lur language
    xx Nilotic languages
Aluru language
    See Alur language
Alvars *(BL1171)*
    xx Saints, Hindu
        Vaishnavism
Alveolar nerve
    x Dental nerve
    — Surgery
Alvis automobile
Alwal language
    See Akhwakh language
Alyssum, Sweet
    See Sweet alyssum
Alzheimer's disease
    See Presenile dementia
Amaas
    See Alastrim
Amabaca
    See Bhaca (African tribe)
Amadi language
    See Ma language
Amafengos
    See Fingos

Amafingos
    See Fingos
Amaguaco Indians
    See Amahuaca Indians
Amahlubi tribe
Amahuaca Indians
    x Amaguaco Indians
        Amajuaca Indians
        Amawaka Indians
        Ameuhaque Indians
        Ipitinere Indians
        Sayaco Indians
    xx Indians of South America
Amahuaca language
    x Amawaca language
    xx Indians of South America—Languages
        Panoan languages
Amajuaca Indians
    See Amahuaca Indians
Amalgam electrodes
    See Electrodes, Amalgam
Amalgamation *(TN763)*
        Here are entered works relating to the
        separation of precious metals, espe-
        cially gold, from any accompanying
        mineral matter by means of mercury.
        Works relating to the combination of
        mercury with other metals, and the re-
        sulting amalgams, are entered under
        the heading Amalgams.
    sa Alloys
        Mercury
    xx Alloys
        Metals
Amalgamation of corporations
    See Consolidation and merger of
        corporations
Amalgamation of land
    See Consolidation of land holdings
Amalgams *(Chemistry, QD181.H65;
        Technology, TS650)*
    sa Dental amalgams
    xx Alloys
        Mercury
        Metals
    Note under Amalgamation
Amalgams (Linguistics) *(P245)*
    xx Grammar, Comparative and general—
        Word formation
        Phonemics
Amalricians *(BT1325)*
    sa Brethren of the Free Spirit
    x Almaricians
        Amauriani
    xx Brethren of the Free Spirit
        Pantheism
        Sects, Medieval
Amana furniture
    See Furniture, Amana
Amanaya language
    See Nzima language
Amanori
    See Nori
Amaqaba (Bantu tribe)
    See Qaba (Bantu tribe)
Amaqwathi (Bantu tribe)
    See Qaba (Bantu tribe)
Amarascogin Indians
    See Arosaguntacook Indians
Amardic language
    See Elamite language
Amarigna language
    See Amharic language
Amateur art
    See Art, Amateur
Amateur circus *(GV1838)*
    x Play circus
    xx Amateur theatricals

Amateur circus *(GV1838)* *(Continued)*
    Circus
Amateur journalism *(PN4825-4830)*
    sa College and school journalism
    xx Journalism
        Press
Amateur moving-pictures
    x Moving-pictures, Amateur
        Personal films
    xx Amateur theatricals
        Cinematography
    — Juvenile literature
Amateur radio stations *(Direct)* *(TK9956)*
    x Radio stations, Amateur
    xx Radio—Amateurs' manuals
        Radio stations, Short wave
    — Law and legislation *(Direct)*
        xx Radio—Laws and regulations
Amateur theatricals *(Direct)*
    (PN3151-3191)
        Works limited to plays for children are
        entered under Children's plays.
    sa Acting
        Amateur circus
        Amateur moving-pictures
        Bible plays
        Charades
        Children's plays
        College and school drama
        College theater
        Drama festivals
        Improvisation (Acting)
        Make-up, Theatrical
        Pantomime
        Shadow pantomimes and plays
        Tableaux
        Women in amateur theatricals
    x Private theatricals
        Theatricals, Amateur
    xx Acting
        Amusements
        Drama
        Theater
    Note under Children's plays
    — Plots, themes, etc.
        x Amateur theatricals—Stories, plots,
            etc.
            Amateur theatricals—Themes,
               motives
        xx Plots (Drama, novel, etc.)
    — Production and direction
        xx Theater—Production and direction
    — Stories, plots, etc.
        See Amateur theatricals—Plots,
            themes, etc.
    — Themes, motives
        See Amateur theatricals—Plots,
            themes, etc.
Amateurism in sports
    See Professionalism in sports
Amatsuyashiro Yamakage Shinto
    See Yamakage (Sect)
Amauriani
    See Amalricians
Amaurosis
    See Blindness
Amaurotic family idiocy
    x Tay-Sachs' disease
    xx Brain—Diseases
        Idiocy
        Lipid metabolism disorders
Amawaca language
    See Amahuaca language
Amawaka Indians
    See Amahuaca Indians
Amazon Valley in literature

Amazons *(HQ1139; Classical mythology,*
    BL820.A6)
    xx Women as soldiers
Amba
    See Baamba (African tribe)
Ambalakaran
    See Muthurajas
Ambari hemp
    See Ambary hemp
Ambary hemp *(Botany, QK495.M27; Culture,*
    SB261.A; Fiber, TS1544.A)
    x Ambari hemp
        Bimlipatum jute
        Brown Indian hemp
        Deccan hemp
        Gambo hemp
        Kenaf
    xx Fibers
        Hemp
        Hibiscus
Ambassadors *(JX1621-1894)*
    sa Diplomatic privileges and immunities
        Fetiales
        Legates, Papal
        Nuncios, Papal
    x Embassies
        Ministers (Diplomatic agents)
    xx Diplomatic and consular service
        Diplomats
        International relations
Amber *(Indirect)* *(Carving, NK6000;*
    Mineralogy, QE391.A5)
    xx Marine resources
Amber art objects *(Direct)* *(NK6000)*
Ambergris
    xx Perfumes
Ambete (African people)
    See Mbete (African people)
Ambiguity
    xx Semantics
Ambili language
    See Birri language
Ambition *(BJ1533.A4)*
Ambivalence
    xx Emotions
        Psychology
Amblyopia
    sa Pleoptics
    xx Blindness
        Eye—Diseases and defects
Amblypoda
    xx Mammals, Fossil
Ambo (African tribe)
    sa Kuanyama (African tribe)
    x Kambonsenga (African tribe)
        Ndonga (African tribe)
        Ovambo (African tribe)
        Ovampo (African tribe)
    xx Bantus
        Ethnology—Zambia
Amboina Massacre, 1623
Amboinese languages *(PL5206-9)*
    xx Malayan languages
Ambries
    See Aumbries
Ambrim language
    See Ambrym language
Ambrine
Ambrones
    xx Celts
Ambrosia beetles
    x Timber beetles
    xx Beetles
Ambrosian chant
    See Catholic Church. Liturgy and ritual.
        Ambrosian rite
Ambrotype *(TR370)*
    xx Photography

Ambry
    See Aumbries
Ambrym language
    sa Lonwolwol dialect
    x Ambrim language
    xx Melanesian languages
Ambu dialect
    See Annobon dialect
Ambulance drill
    See First aid in illness and injury
Ambulance service *(Indirect)*
    sa subdivision Ambulance service *under*
        names of cities, e.g. London—
        Ambulance service; *and subdivision*
        Transport of sick and wounded
        under armies, e.g. United States.
        Army—Transport of sick and
        wounded
    xx Accidents
        First aid in illness and injury
        Rescue work
    — Juvenile literature
Ambulances *(RA995-6)*
    sa Aeroplane ambulances
        subdivision Ambulances *under armies,*
        e.g. United States. Army—
        Ambulances
    xx Accidents
        Carriages and carts
        First aid in illness and injury
        Health facilities
        Hospitals—Emergency service
        Rescue work
        Surgery, Military
        Vehicles
        Vehicles, Military
Ambulatory care
    See Hospitals—Outpatient services
Ambushes and surprises *(U167)*
    xx Tactics
Ambuun (Bantu tribe)
    See Babunda (Bantu tribe)
Ameba
    See Amoeba
Amebiasis
    sa Liver abscess, Amebic
    x Amebic dysentery
        Amoebiasis
        Amoebic dysentery
    xx Dysentery
        Medical protozoology
Amebic dysentery
    See Amebiasis
Amebic liver abscess
    See Liver abscess, Amebic
Ameboid movement
    See Amoeboid movement
Amen (Liturgy)
    xx Amens (Music)
        Jews. Liturgy and ritual
        Liturgies
Amended and supplemental pleading *(Direct)*
    x Amended pleading
        Amendments (Pleading)
        Pleading, Amended
        Pleading, Supplemental
        Supplemental pleading
    xx Pleading
Amended pleading
    See Amended and supplemental pleading
Amendments, Constitutional
    See Constitutional amendments
Amendments (Parliamentary practice)
    xx Parliamentary practice
Amendments (Pleading)
    See Amended and supplemental pleading
Amenorrhea *(RG171)*
    xx Menstruation disorders

Amens (Music)
  sa Amen (Liturgy)
  xx Sacred vocal music
Amerescoggin Indians
  See Arosaguntacook Indians
America
  x American Republics
  — Antiquities
    sa Indians—Antiquities
      Paleo-Indians
  — Bibliography *(Z1201-1939)*
    x Americana
  —— Catalogs *(Z1207)*
  —— Early *(Z1202-3)*
  — Biography
  —— Dictionaries
  —— Juvenile literature
  — Civilization
    x Civilization, American
  —— Pictorial works
  — Climate
  — Commerce
  — Congresses
  — Description and travel
  —— 1951-

GENERAL SUBDIVISIONS

  —— Gazetteers
  —— Juvenile literature
  —— Maps
      See America—Maps

GENERAL SUBDIVISIONS

  —— Views
  — Discovery and exploration
    sa United States—Exploring expeditions
    x Latin America—Discovery and
        exploration
      North America—Discovery and
        exploration
      United States—Discovery and
        exploration
    Example under Discoveries (in geography)
  —— Drama
  —— Dutch, ₁English, French, etc.₁
  ——— Juvenile literature
  ——— Pictorial works
  —— Fiction
  —— Historiography
  —— Juvenile literature
  —— Maps
      xx America—Maps
  —— Norse
      x Northmen in America
  ——— Juvenile literature
  —— Pictorial works
  —— Poetry
  —— Pre-Columbian
      sa Indians—Transpacific influences
  ——— Juvenile literature
  —— Sources
  —— Spanish
      x Conquistadors
  ——— Juvenile literature
  — Early accounts to 1600
  — Economic conditions
  — Emigration and immigration
  — Foreign relations
      Here are entered works on relations,
      concerted or otherwise, between
      the Americas and single countries,
      or groups of countries, outside the
      western hemisphere, *e.g.* America
      —Foreign relations—Russia,
      ₁Europe, etc.₁
    x American Republics
  —— Treaties

      See Pan-American treaties and
          conventions

GEOGRAPHIC SUBDIVISIONS

  —— Russia, ₁Europe, etc.₁
      Example under America—Foreign relations
  — History *(E18)*
  —— To 1810
  ——— 1810-
  ——— 20th century

GENERAL SUBDIVISIONS

  —— Chronology
  —— Juvenile literature
      x America—History, Juvenile

GENERAL SUBDIVISIONS

  —— Philosophy
  —— Poetry
  —— Sources
  ——— Juvenile literature
  — History, Juvenile
      See America—History—Juvenile
          literature
  — Intellectual life
  — Learned institutions and societies
  — Literatures
    sa Spanish American literature
      *national literatures of individual
        countries of America, e.g.
        Brazilian literature, Canadian
        literature*
    x American literatures
      Literatures of America
    xx American literature
      Literature
      Spanish American literature
  — Maps
    sa America—Discovery and exploration
        —Maps
    x America—Description and travel—
        Maps
  — Name
      Example under Names
  — Politics
      Here are entered comprehensive
      works on politics and government
      in the western hemisphere or in
      three or more countries of the two
      Americas.
    sa Latin America—Politics
      Pan-Americanism
    x American Republics
  — Presidents
  —— Registers
  — Social conditions
  — Statistics
America in art
  xx Art
America in literature
American (Artificial language) *(PM8077)*
  xx Languages, Artificial
American aborigines
  See Indians
      Indians of North America
      Indians of South America
      similar headings
American aesthetics
  See Aesthetics, American
American agricultural assistance
  See Agricultural assistance, American
American almanacs
  See Almanacs, American
American anatomists
  See Anatomists, American
American architecture
  See Architecture, American

American artificial satellites
  See Artificial satellites, American
American artists
  See Artists, American
American arts
  See Arts, American
American authors
  See Authors, American
American automobiles
  See Automobiles, American
American ballads and songs *(Direct)*
      *(Collections, PS583-619; History,
      PS309-324)*
  sa Ballads, American
      Campaign songs
      Folk-songs, American
      National songs, American
      Political ballads and songs, American
      Songs, American
      War-songs, American
  Note under Songs, American, ₁English,
      French, etc.₁
American banks and banking
  See Banks and banking, American
American Bantam automobile *(TL215.A)*
  x Bantam automobile
American bison
  See Bison, American
American black dialect
  See Negro-English dialects
American book-plates
  See Book-plates, American
American books abroad *(Z479)*
  x Books abroad, American
  xx American literature—History and
      criticism
American bottles
  See Bottles, American
American bullterriers
  See Staffordshire terriers
American buttons
  See Buttons, American
American Cancer Society
  Example under Voluntary health agencies
American cartoonists
  See Cartoonists, American
American checkered giant rabbits *(SF455)*
  x Checkered giant rabbits
  Example under Rabbit breeds
American children's writings
  See Children's writings, American
American Christian drama
  See Christian drama, American
American Christian poetry
  See Christian poetry, American
American civil engineers
  See Civil engineers, American
American Civil War
  See United States—History—Civil War,
      1861-1865
American clocks and watches
  See Clocks and watches, American
American coffee bean
  See Kentucky coffeetree
American collages
  See Collages, American
American coverlets
  See Coverlets, American
American crime stories
  See Crime stories, American
American cut glass
  See Cut glass, American
American detective plays
  See Detective and mystery plays, American
American diaries *(Collections, PS669;
      History, PS409)*
  xx Diaries

American didactic drama
    See Didactic drama, American
American dissertations
    See Dissertations, Academic—United States
American dog tick *(QL458.A2)*
    xx Rocky Mountain spotted fever
       Tularemia
American dogwood
    See Flowering dogwood
American dollar
    See Dollar, American
American dollar (Coin)
    See Dollar, American (Coin)
American drama *(Direct)* *(Collections,*
    PS623-635; History, PS330-351)
    sa Christian drama, American
       Detective and mystery plays, American
       Didactic drama, American
       One-act plays, American
— To 1775
— Revolutionary period, 1775-1783

GENERAL SUBDIVISIONS

— Biography
    See Dramatists, American

GENERAL SUBDIVISIONS

— Negro authors
    x Negro drama (American)
       Negro drama—United States

GENERAL SUBDIVISIONS

— Stories, plots, etc.
American drama (Comedy) *(History,*
    PS336.C7)
American drama (Tragedy) *(History,*
    PS336.T7)
American drawings
    See Drawings, American
American dry-points
    See Dry-points, American
American eagle
    See Bald eagle
American Education Week *(LB3562)*
    x Education Week
    Example under reference from Weeks (Special
       observances)
American elk
    See Elk
American elm *(Botany, QK495.U4)*
    x White elm
    xx Elm
— Diseases and pests
    See Elm—Diseases and pests
American English
    See English language in the United States
American engravers
    See Engravers, American
American engraving
    See Engraving, American
American essays *(Direct)* *(Collections,*
    PS680-688; History, PS420-428)
    Here are entered collections of essays by
       several authors.
American fantastic fiction
    See Fantastic fiction, American
American fiction *(Direct)* *(Collections, PZ1;*
    History, PS371-9)
    sa Crime stories, American
       Dime novels
       Fantastic fiction, American
       Historical fiction, American
       Horror tales, American
       Short stories, American
       Western stories
    xx Fiction
— 18th century
— 19th century

— 20th century

GENERAL SUBDIVISIONS

— Book reviews
— Jewish authors
    x Jewish fiction (American)

GENERAL SUBDIVISIONS

— Negro authors
    x Negro fiction (American)
       Negro fiction—United States

GENERAL SUBDIVISIONS

— Stories, plots, etc.
American firearms
    See Firearms, American
American folk-songs
    See Folk-songs, American
American foul brood
    See Foul brood, American
American foxhounds *(SF429.A7)*
    xx Foxhounds
American gems
    See Gems, American
American genre paintings
    See Genre paintings, American
American glassware
    See Glassware, American
American gunsmiths
    See Gunsmiths, American
American Heart Association
    Example under Voluntary health agencies
American horror tales
    See Horror tales, American
American hymns
    See Hymns, English
American Indians
    See Indians
       Indians of North America
       Indians of South America
       similar headings
American insurance companies
    See Insurance companies, American
American ivories
    See Ivories, American
American language
    See English language in the United States
American leishmaniasis
    See Leishmaniasis, Mucocutaneous
American letters *(Collections, PS670-678;*
    History, PS410-418)
American librarians
    See Librarians, American
American literature *(Direct)* *(Collections,*
    PS504-688; History, PS1-478)
    sa America—Literatures
       Christian literature, American
       College readers
       German-American literature; Spanish
          American literature;
          Swedish-American literature; *and*
          similar headings
    x United States—Literature (English)
    xx United States—Literatures
    Example under Bibliography
    Notes under College readers; Readers
— Colonial period, ca. 1600-1775
    (PS185-191)
— Revolutionary period, 1775-1783
    (PS193)
— 1783-1850 *(PS208)*
— 19th century *(PS201-214)*
— 20th century *(PS221-8)*
— Anecdotes, facetiae, satire, etc.
— Armenian authors
    x Armenian literature (English)
— Bibliography *(Z1225-1231)*
    sa Catalogs, Publishers'—United States

— — First editions *(Z1231.F5)*
    x Authors, American—First editions
    Example under Bibliography—First
       editions
— Biography
    See Authors, American—Biography
— Catholic authors *(Collections, PS508.C3;*
    Collections of poetry, PS591.C3)
    x American poetry—Catholic authors
    Example under Catholic authors
— Competitions
— Finnish authors
    x Finnish literature (American)
— History and criticism
    sa American books abroad
    Example under reference from Bibliogra-
       phy, Critical
— Indian authors
    x Indian literature (English)
— Jewish authors
    x Jewish literature (American)
— Latin American authors
    sa American literature—Mexican
       American authors
    x Latin American literature (English)
— Mexican American authors
    x Chicano literature
       Mexican American literature
    xx American literature—Latin American
       authors
— Negro authors *(Collections, PS508.N3)*
    x Negro literature (American)
       Negro literature—United States
— Oriental authors
    x Oriental literature (English)
American literature (Czech)
    See Czech-American literature
American literature (Danish)
    See Danish-American literature
American literature (French) *(PQ3920-3939)*
    Duplicate entry is made under French lit-
       erature—American authors.
    sa French-Canadian literature
    Note under French literature—American au-
       thors
American literature (Irish) *(Collected poems,*
    PS595.I; Collections, PS508.I;
    History, PS153.I)
    Duplicate entry is made under Irish liter-
       ature—American authors.
    Note under Irish literature—American authors
American literature (Lithuanian)
    See Lithuanian-American literature
American literature (Polish)
    See Polish-American literature
American literature (Russian)
    See Russian-American literature
American literatures
    See America—Literatures
American lithographers
    See Lithographers, American
American lithographs
    See Lithographs, American
American lobster
    xx Lobsters
— Behavior
American long rifle
    See Kentucky rifle
American love poetry
    See Love poetry, American
American loyalists *(E277)*
    sa Church of England in America—
       Clergy, Loyalist
       Hickey Plot, 1776
       United Empire loyalists
       United States—History—Revolution,
          1775-1783—Regimental histories—
          American loyalist

x Loyalists, American
   Tories, American
   United States—History—Revolution,
     1775-1783—Loyalists
xx United Empire loyalists
   United States—History—Revolution,
     1775-1783—Biography
— Juvenile literature

— Canada, [Connecticut, Massachusetts, etc.]
American marine painting
  See Marine painting, American
American medical assistance
  See Medical assistance, American
American merganser
  xx Mergansers
American messianism
  See Messianism, American
American military music
  See Military music, American
American miniature cases
  See Miniature cases, American
American missions
  See Missions, American
American mistletoe
  See Dwarf mistletoe
American moving-picture cartoons
  See Moving-picture cartoons, American
American mural painting and decoration
  See Mural painting and decoration,
    American
American mystery plays
  See Detective and mystery plays, American
American narrative poetry
  See Narrative poetry, American
American newspapers *(Direct) (History,*
  etc., PN4840-4899)
  sa Negro newspapers (American)
    German-American newspapers;
     Italian-American newspapers;
     Spanish American newspapers; *and*
     similar headings
  xx Newspapers
  Note under Newspapers
— Circulation
    sa Readership surveys
    xx Newspaper circulation
— Facsimilies
— Foreign language press *(PN4884-5;*
    Directories, Z6953.5)
— Juvenile literature
— Language
— Sections, columns, etc.
    xx Newspapers—Sections, columns, etc.
— Taxation
    xx Newspapers—Taxation
American orations *(Direct) (Collections,*
  PS660-668; History, PS400-408)
  Here are entered collections of orations
    by several authors.
  sa College orations
  xx Orations
— Colonial period, ca. 1600-1775
— 20th century
American orators
  See Orators, American
American oyster
  x Atlantic oyster
    Eastern oyster
    Virginia oyster
  xx Oysters
American paintings
  See Paintings, American
American paperweights
  See Paperweights, American

American Party *(JK2341)*
  Subdivided by locality, *e.g.* American
    Party. Rhode Island.
  x Know-Nothing Party
    Native American Party
  xx Nativism
American Party. Rhode Island
  Note under American Party
American patriotic poetry
  See Patriotic poetry, American
American periodicals *(Direct) (History, etc.,*
  PN4840-4900)
  sa Negro periodicals (American)
    Italian-American periodicals;
     Norwegian-American periodicals;
     Spanish American periodicals; *and*
     similar headings
  Notes under Content analysis (Communica-
    tion); Periodicals
— Anecdotes, facetiae, satire, etc.
— Caricatures and cartoons
— Circulation
    sa Readership surveys
    xx Periodicals—Circulation
— Collectors and collecting *(Direct)*
— Information services
American pewter
  See Pewter, American
American philosophy
  See Philosophy, American
American pilgrims and pilgrimages
  See Pilgrims and pilgrimages, American
American pistols
  See Pistols, American
American poetry *(Direct) (PS)*
  sa Christian poetry, American
    Haiku, American
    Narrative poetry, American
    Patriotic poetry, American
    Political poetry, American
    Protest poetry, American
    Russian poetry—American authors
    Sonnets, American
    German-American poetry; Spanish
     American poetry; *and similar*
     headings
— Colonial period, ca. 1600-1775 *(PS312)*
— Revolutionary period, 1775-1783
    (PS314)
— 1783-1850 *(PS319)*
— 19th century *(PS316-321)*
— 20th century *(PS324)*
— — Readings with music
    Example under reference from Read-
     ings with music

— Catholic authors
    See American literature—Catholic
     authors

— Eskimo authors
    x Eskimo poetry (American)

— Explication
— Indian authors
    Note under Indians—Poetry

— Negro authors
    x Negro poetry (American)
    Negro poetry—United States

— Stories, plots, etc.

American poetry (French) *(PQ3910;*
  PQ3914)
  Duplicate entry is made under French
    poetry—American authors.
  sa French-Canadian poetry
  Note under French poetry—American authors
American poetry (Russian)
  See Russian-American poetry
American poetry (Swedish)
  See Swedish-American poetry
American poetry (Ukrainian)
  See Ukrainian-American poetry
American political satire
  See Political satire, American
American portrait painting
  See Portrait painting, American
American portraits
  See Portraits, American
American posters
  See Posters, American
American printmakers
  See Printmakers, American
American prints
  See Prints, American
American prisoners' writings
  See Prisoners' writings, American
American propaganda
  See Propaganda, American
American property in Canada, [Iceland, the
  Czechoslovak Republic, etc.]
American property in foreign countries
  xx Alien property
American prose literature *(Direct)*
  (Collections, PS643-659; History,
  PS362-379)
— Colonial period, ca. 1600-1775 *(PS651)*
— Revolutionary period, 1775-1783

— Negro authors
    x Negro prose literature (American)
American protest poetry
  See Protest poetry, American
American Railway Union Strike, 1894
  See Chicago Strike, 1894
American Republics
  See America
    America—Foreign relations
    America—Politics
    Pan-Americanism
American Revolution
  See United States—History—Revolution,
    1775-1783
American revolvers
  See Revolvers, American
American saddle horse *(SF293.A)*
  x Saddle horse, American
American satire
  See Satire, American
American school reading readiness tests
  xx Mental tests
    Reading readiness
American schools
  See Schools, American [for works on
    American schools in foreign
    countries]
    Schools—United States [for works on
    schools in the United States]
American shad *(QL638.C64)*
  x White shad
  xx Shad
American silversmithing
  See Silversmithing, American
American silverware
  See Silverware, American
American singing games
  See Singing games, American

American smelt (QL638.O45)
xx Smelts
American songs
See Songs, American
American sonnets
See Sonnets, American
American Spanish War, 1898
See United States—History—War of 1898
American spoons
See Spoons, American
American stemware
See Stemware, American
American still-life painting
See Still-life painting, American
American stilt
See Black-necked stilt
American students in Europe, ⌜France, Norway, etc.⌝
— Information services
American studies (Direct)
sa Americanists
American synagogue art
See Synagogue art, American
American tales
See Tales, American
American teachers in foreign countries
x Teachers abroad, American
xx Americans in foreign countries
Teachers in foreign countries
— Employment
x Foreign teaching positions
International teaching positions
Overseas teaching positions
Teaching positions abroad
American teachers in the Argentine Republic, ⌜Turkey, etc.⌝
x Teachers in the Argentine Republic, ⌜Turkey, etc.⌝, American
American theatrical posters
See Theatrical posters, American
American thoroughbred horse
See Thoroughbred horse
American tinsmiths
See Tinsmiths, American
American tinware
See Tinware, American
American trypanosomiasis
See Chagas' disease
American veterans' writings
See Veterans' writings, American
American war-songs
See War-songs, American
American water-colors
See Water-colors, American
American wit and humor (Direct)
(Collections, PN6157-6162; History, PS430-438)
Here are entered collections from several authors and individual authors who have not written in other literary forms.
sa Negro wit and humor
German-American wit and humor; Irish-American wit and humor; and similar headings
xx Wit and humor
American wit and humor, Pictorial (NC1420-1429)
sa Caricatures and cartoons—United States
xx Wit and humor, Pictorial
— Moral and religious aspects
American wood-engraving
See Wood-engraving, American
American wood-engravings
See Wood-engravings, American
American woodcock
See Woodcock

American wormseed-oil
See Chenopodium oil
Americana
See subdivision Bibliography under America and under names of parts of the continent, regions, countries, cities, etc.
Americanism (Catholic controversy) (BX1407.A5)
sa Modernism—Catholic Church
xx Catholic Church in France
Catholic Church in the United States
Modernism—Catholic Church
Americanisms (PE2801-3101)
Here are entered works dealing with the usage of words and idiomatic expressions peculiar to the United States. Works on the English language in the United States as a whole, its history, structure, orthography, pronunciation, etc., are entered under English language in the United States with appropriate subdivisions as used under English language. Works dealing with local deviations from conventional English in the United States are entered under English language in the United States—Dialects—⌜local subdivision⌝
x English language—Americanisms
xx English language—Dialects
English language in the United States
Note under English language in the United States
Americanists (Direct)
xx American studies
Americanization (Citizenship, JK1758; Education, LC3731-3)
sa Libraries and foreign population
xx Assimilation (Sociology)
Civics
Americans in Borneo, ⌜China, Cuba, etc.⌝
— Anecdotes, facetiae, satire, etc.
— Caricatures and cartoons
— Legal status, laws, etc.
— Public opinion
Americans in Cuba
sa Venceremos Brigade
Americans in foreign countries
sa American teachers in foreign countries
United States—Officials and employees in foreign countries
— Employment
x Employment in foreign countries
Overseas employees
Americans in literature
America's Cup races
xx Yacht racing
Americium (QD181.A5)
xx Radioactive substances
Amerindian . . .
See Indian . . .
Amerinds
See Indians
Amethysts (Mineralogy, QD394.A6)
Ametropia
See Eye—Accommodation and refraction
Ameuhaque Indians
See Amahuaca Indians
Amharas
xx Ethiopians
Ethnology—Ethiopia
Amharic essays (Direct)
Amharic language (PJ9201-9250)
x Amarigna language
xx Ethiopian languages
Amharic poetry (PJ9262; PJ9266)

Amharic wit and humor (Direct)
(Collections, PN6222.E; History, PJ9264)
Amherst's Expedition against Ticonderoga and Crown Point, 1759
Ami (Formosan people)
x Amis (Formosan people)
xx Ethnology—Formosa
Ami 6 automobile (TL215.A45)
xx Citroën automobile
Ami 8 automobile (TL215.A)
xx Citroën automobile
Amic acids (QD305.A7; QD341.A7)
xx Nitrogen compounds
Amides (QD305.A7; QD341.A7)
sa Polyamides
Amidines (QD341.A7)
Amido-benzene
See Aniline
Amiens, Battle of, 1870 (DC309.A5)
x Villers-Bretonneux, Battle of, 1870
xx Franco-German War, 1870-1871
Amiens, Battle of, 1918 (D545.A56)
xx European War, 1914-1918—Campaigns —France
Amiens, Battle of, 1940 (D756.5.A)
xx World War, 1939-1945—Campaigns— France
Amiens, Treaty of, 1802 (DC222.5)
Amikwa language (PM610.A6)
xx Algonquian languages
Amillennialism
See Millennialism
Amination (QD281.A6)
sa Voigt reaction
xx Amines
Amine metabolism
xx Metabolism
Amines (QD305.A8; QD341.A8)
sa Amination
Deamination
Dibenamine
Histamine
Naphthylamines
xx Deamination
Example under Chemistry, Organic
— Analysis
— Physiological effect
— Programmed instruction
Amines in the body
Amino acid metabolism (QP801.A5)
sa Alanine metabolism
Aspartic acid metabolism
Glycine metabolism
Phenylalanine metabolism
Tryptophan metabolism
xx Amino acids
Metabolism
Amino acid metabolism, Inborn errors of
x Aminoacidopathies
xx Metabolism, Inborn errors of
Amino acid synthesis
xx Biosynthesis
Amino acids (QD305.A7; QD341.A7; Physiology, QP801.A5)
sa Amino acid metabolism
Glycine
Leucine
Polyamides
Tyrosine
— Analysis
— Programmed instruction
— Tables, etc.
— Therapeutic use
Amino acids in animal nutrition (SF98.A4)
sa Lysine in animal nutrition
x Feeds—Amino acid content
xx Feeding

Proteins in animal nutrition
Amino-formaldehyde resins
  See Aminoplastics
Amino groups
  xx Radicals (Chemistry)
Amino resins
  See Aminoplastics
Aminoacetic acid
  See Glycine
Aminoacidopathies
  See Amino acid metabolism, Inborn errors
    of
Aminoplastics *(TP986.A)*
  x Amino-formaldehyde resins
    Amino resins
    Aminoplasts
  xx Plastics
    Urea derivatives
Aminoplasts
  See Aminoplastics
Amirids
  xx Spain—History—Arab period, 711-1492
Amis (Formosan people)
  See Ami (Formosan people)
Amiscogging Indians
  See Pequawket Indians
Amish *(BX8129.A5-6; E184.M45; F160.M45)*
  x Old Order Amish
  xx Mennonites
  — Doctrinal and controversial works
  — Hymns
  — Social life and customs
  — — Pictorial works
Amish cookery
  See Cookery, Mennonite
Amish in Pennsylvania, [etc.]
Amishgo language *(PM3516)*
  x Amuzgo language
  xx Mixtec language
Amitosis *(QH605)*
  x Direct cell division
  xx Cell division
Ammeter *(QC544.A5)*
  xx Electric meters
Ammocoetes
  xx Lampreys
Ammocoetes populations
  xx Animal populations
Ammonia *(Chemistry, QD181.N15;*
    Manufacture, TP223; Therapeutics,
    RM666.A5)
  sa Liquid ammonia
  x Anhydrous ammonia
  xx Alkalies
  Example under Refrigerants; Stimulants
  — Analysis
  — Law and legislation *(Direct)*
  — Physiological effect *(QP913.N15)*
    sa Plants, Effect of ammonia on
  — Spectra
  — Storage
  — Toxicology
Ammonia as fertilizer
  xx Fertilizers and manures
Ammonia in animal nutrition
  x Feeds—Ammonia content
  xx Feeding
    Proteins in animal nutrition
Ammonia intoxication
  x Intoxication, Ammonia
  xx Metabolism, Disorders of
Ammonites
  See Ammonoidea
Ammonium cobalt bases
  See Cobalt-ammonium compounds
Ammonium compounds
  sa Chromium-ammonium compounds

Ammonium compounds as disinfectants
  xx Disinfection and disinfectants
Ammonium ions
  xx Ions
Ammonium reineckate
  See Reinecke salt
Ammonium salts
  sa Reinecke salt
  xx Salts
Ammonoidea *(QE807.A5)*
  sa Clymeniida
  x Ammonites
  xx Cephalopoda, Fossil
    Mollusks, Fossil
  — Pictorial works
Ammon's horn
  See Hippocampus (Brain)
Ammunition *(UF700-780)*
  sa Bombs
    Cartridges
    Gunpowder
    Handloading of ammunition
  xx Armaments
    Explosives
    Gunnery
    Gunpowder
    Projectiles
    Shooting, Military
  — Containers
  — Law and legislation
    See Firearms—Laws and regulations
  — Transportation
Amnesia *(RC394.A5)*
  sa Aphasia
  xx Aphasia
    Brain—Diseases
    Memory
    Memory, Disorders of
Amnestic confabulatory syndrome
  See Korsakoff's syndrome
Amnesty *(Direct)*
  sa Pardon
  xx Criminal justice, Administration of
    Pardon
    Punishment
  — United States
    xx Reconstruction
Amniocentesis *(RG628)*
  xx Amniotic liquid
    Fetus—Diseases—Diagnosis
Amnion *(Embryology, QL975; Human*
    embryology, QM611)
  xx Fetal membranes
Amniotic fluid embolism
  x Amniotic liquid embolism
  xx Embolism
    Pregnancy, Complications of
Amniotic liquid *(Embryology, QL975;*
    Human embryology, QM611)
  sa Amniocentesis
  x Liquor amnii
  xx Body fluids
    Embryology
    Pregnancy
  — Analysis and chemistry
    xx Biological chemistry
    Medicine, Clinical
Amniotic liquid embolism
  See Amniotic fluid embolism
Amoeba *(QL368.A5)*
  x Ameba
  xx Unicellular organisms
Amoebaea
  See Amoebida
Amoebiasis
  See Amebiasis
Amoebic dysentery
  See Amebiasis

Amoebic liver abscess
  See Liver abscess, Amebic
Amoebida *(QL368.A5)*
  sa Amoeboid movement
  x Amoebaea
    Amoebina
  xx Sarcodina
Amoebina
  See Amoebida
Amoeboid movement
  x Ameboid movement
  xx Amoebida
    Animal locomotion
Amoor cork tree
  See Amur cork tree
Amoraim
  sa Tannaim
  xx Rabbis
    Talmud
    Tannaim
Amorites *(DS72.5)*
Amorphous substances
  sa Colloids
    Glass
  — Magnetic properties
Amortization *(Direct)*
  sa Corporation reserves
    Reserves (Accounting)
    Sinking-funds
  xx Accounting
    Corporation reserves
    Finance
    Loans
    Reserves (Accounting)
  — Tables, etc.
    See Interest and usury—Tables, etc.
Amortization deductions *(Direct)*
  x Emergency facilities, Amortization of
  xx Depreciation allowances
    Tax deductions
Amortization tables
  See Annuities—Tables
    Interest and usury—Tables, etc.
AMOS (Computer program)
  x Associative memory organizing system
  xx Compiling (Electronic computers)
Ampale language
  sa Wojokeso dialect
Amparo (Writ) *(Direct)*
  xx Abuse of administrative power
    Civil procedure
    Constitutional law
    Criminal procedure
    Extraordinary remedies
    Habeas corpus
    Judicial review
    Writs
Ampelidae
  See Waxwings
Amperes *(QC536)*
  sa Current balance (Electric meter)
Amperometric analysis
  See Conductometric analysis
Ampfing, Battle of, 1322
  See Mühldorf, Battle of, 1322
Amphibian planes
  sa Albatross (Amphibian planes)
    Loening (Amphibian plane)
  xx Aeroplanes
    Seaplanes
  — Piloting
Amphibians *(Indirect)* *(QL641-669)*
  sa Anura
    Urodela
  x Batrachia
  xx Herpetology
    Vertebrates
  — Anatomy *(QL669)*

Amphibians *(Indirect)* *(QL641-669)*
— Anatomy *(QL669)* *(Continued)*
  sa subdivision Amphibians *under*
    Digestive organs, Nervous system,
    Sense-organs
— Behavior
  sa subdivision Behavior *under names of*
    particular amphibians, e.g. Toads
    —Behavior
— — Juvenile literature
— Catalogs and collections *(QL645)*
— Classification
— Collection and preservation
— Digestive organs
  See Digestive organs—Amphibians
— Diseases
— Evolution
  xx Vertebrates—Evolution
— Generative organs
  See Generative organs—Amphibians
— Geographical distribution
— Identification
  Example under Identification
— Juvenile literature
— Larvae
  See Larvae—Amphibians
— Metamorphosis
  xx Metamorphosis
— Nervous system
  See Nervous system—Amphibians
— Physiology *(QL669.2)*
— Pictorial works
— Sense-organs
  See Sense-organs—Amphibians
Amphibians, Fossil
  sa Anura, Fossil
    Salamanders, Fossil
    Stegocephali
Amphibians as pets *(SF459.A45)*
  sa Frogs as pets
— Juvenile literature
Amphibious motor vehicles
  See Motor vehicles, Amphibious
Amphibious warfare
    Here are entered works on the joint com-
    bat operations of air, land, and sea
    forces.
  sa Landing craft
    Landing operations
    Underwater demolition teams
    subdivision Amphibious operations
      under names of wars, e.g. World
      War, 1939-1945—Amphibious
      operations
  x Combined operations (Military science)
    Joint operations (Military science)
    Troops, Landing of
  xx Landing operations
    Unified operations (Military science)
  Note under Landing operations
Amphiboles *(Indirect)*
  sa Amphibolite
    Hornblende
  xx Silicates
Amphibolite *(Indirect)* *(QE399)*
  xx Amphiboles
Amphictyonic league *(DF85)*
Amphimixis
  See Fertilization (Biology)
    Reproduction
Amphineura *(QL430.1)*
  sa Chitons
    Solenogastres
  xx Gasteropoda
    Mollusks
Amphineura, Fossil
  xx Mollusks, Fossil

Amphipoda *(Indirect)* *(QL444.A5)*
  xx Arthrostraca
    Crustacea
    Malacostraca
— Classification
Amphitheaters *(Direct)*
  xx Architecture
Amphoras *(Direct)* *(NK4650.A6)*
  xx Vases, Greek
— Classification
Amplifiers, Dielectric
  See Dielectric amplifiers
Amplifiers, Direct current
  See Direct current amplifiers
Amplifiers, Fluid
  See Fluid amplifiers
Amplifiers, Light
  See Light amplifiers
Amplifiers, Magnetic
  See Magnetic amplifiers
Amplifiers, Parametric
  See Parametric amplifiers
Amplifiers, Rotating
  See Rotating amplifiers
Amplifiers, Transistor
  See Transistor amplifiers
Amplifiers, Vacuum-tube *(QC544.V3)*
  sa Distributed amplifiers
    Feedback (Electronics)
    Traveling-wave tubes
  x Vacuum-tube amplifiers
  xx Radio—Apparatus and supplies
    Vacuum-tubes
  Example under Amplifiers (Electronics)
Amplifiers (Electronics) *(TK7872.A5)*
  sa Automatic gain control
    Video amplifiers
    names of specific types of amplifiers,
      e.g. Amplifiers, Vacuum-tube;
      Masers; Transistor amplifiers
  x Electronic amplifiers
    Radio amplifiers
  xx Electronics
— Patents
— Problems, exercises, etc.
— Reliability
Ampulla of Vater
  x Ampulla Vateri
  xx Bile-ducts
Ampulla Vateri
  See Ampulla of Vater
Ampullas, Coronation *(CR4480)*
  x Coronation ampullas
    Eagle (Ampulla)
  xx Christian antiquities
    Church plate
    Coronations
    Crown jewels
Ampuls *(RS201.A5)*
  xx Injections
    Pharmacy
Amputation *(RD553)*
  sa Amputees
    Causalgia
  xx Surgery
    Surgery, Military
    Surgery, Operative
Amputation stumps
— Blood-vessels
— — Radiography
  xx Angiography
Amputations of arm *(RD557)*
  xx Arm—Surgery
Amputations of foot
  xx Foot—Surgery
Amputations of leg *(RD560)*
  x Gritti's amputation
    Knee—Amputation

Leg—Amputation
Amputees
  xx Amputation
    Physically handicapped
— Personal narratives
— Psychology
  x Phantom limbs
  xx Psychology, Applied
    Psychology, Physiological
    Senses and sensation
— Rehabilitation
  sa Artificial limbs
  Note under Rehabilitation
Amritsar, India
— Massacre, 1919 *(DS480.5)*
Amsterdam
— Riots, 1966
AMTRAN (Electronic computer system)
Amueixa language
  See Lorenzan language
Amuesa language
  See Lorenzan language
Amulets *(GR600)*
  sa Charms
    Medicine, Magic, mystic, and spagiric
    Scarabs
    Talismans
  xx Archaeology
    Charms
    Demonology
    Folk-lore
    Magic
    Superstition
    Talismans
    Witchcraft
Amulets, Egyptian *(Direct)*
  x Egyptian amulets
Amulets, Tunisian, [etc.] *(Direct)*
  x Tunisian [etc.] amulets
Amulets (Hinduism)
  sa Yantras
  xx Magic, Hindu
Amulets (Islam) *(BP190.5.A5)*
  xx Magic, Islamic
Amulets (Judaism) *(BM729.A4)*
  xx Magic, Jewish
Amur cork tree
  x Amoor cork tree
  xx Cork-tree
Amur Valley in literature
Amusement parks *(GV1835; GV1851-5)*
  sa Merry-go-round
    Picnic grounds
    Railroads, Miniature
  x Carnivals (Circus)
    Side shows
    Sideshows
  xx Circus
    Parks
— Safety regulations *(Direct)*
Amusements *(Indirect)*
  sa Amateur theatricals
    Aquatic sports
    Balls (Parties)
    Burlesque (Theater)
    Campfire programs
    Cards
    Charades
    Children's parties
    Church entertainments
    Circus
    College sports
    Concerts
    Conjuring
    Creative activities and seat work
    Dancing
    Entertaining
    Family recreation

Fortune-telling
Games
Hobbies
Indoor games
Literary recreations
Mathematical recreations
Moving-pictures
Musical recreations
Performing arts
Play
Psychological recreations
Puzzles
Recreation
Riddles
School sports
Scientific recreations
Soldiers—Recreation
Sports
Tableaux
Theater
Toys
Vaudeville
Ventriloquism
Wild west shows
Winter sports
    subdivision Amusements *under names*
      of cities, e.g. Boston—Amusements
  x Children—Recreation
Entertainments
Pastimes
Recreations
  xx Entertaining
Games
Indoor games
Play
Recreation
Sports
Note under Social surveys
— Early works to 1800
— Juvenile literature
— Laws and regulations
— Moral and religious aspects *(BV4597)*
    Example under Christian ethics; Ethics;
      Religious ethics
— Taxation *(Direct)* *(HJ5797)*
  sa Moving-picture industry—Taxation
  x Admissions, Taxation of
Gate receipts, Taxation of
Taxation of admissions
Tickets of admission, Taxation of
  xx Moving-picture industry—Taxation
    Example under Internal revenue

Amusia
  xx Aphasia
Memory, Disorders of
Music—Physiological aspects
Music—Psychology
Psychology, Pathological
Amuzgo language
  See Amishgo language
AMX automobile
Amygdala (Brain)
  See Amygdaloid body
Amygdaloid body *(QL933;QP376)*
  x Amygdala (Brain)
Amygdaloid nucleus
  xx Basal ganglia
Amygdaloid nucleus
  See Amygdaloid body
Amylase
  See Diastase
Amyloid degeneration
  See Amyloidosis
Amyloidosis
  x Amyloid degeneration
  xx Metabolism, Disorders of
Protein metabolism disorders

Amylolysis
  xx Starch
Sugar
Amyotonia congenita
  See Myotonia congenita
Amyotrophic lateral sclerosis
  x Sclerosis, Amyotrophic lateral
  xx Atrophy, Muscular
Neuromuscular diseases
Amyotrophy
  See Atrophy, Muscular
Amyrin *(QD419)*
Ana
  See Anecdotes
Aphorisms and apothegms
Epigrams
Maxims
Proverbs
Quotations
Table-talk
Anabaptists *(Direct)* *(BX4929-4946)*
  sa Baptists
Church of the Brethren
Mennonites
Peasants' War, 1524-1525
  x Catabaptists
Habans
  xx Baptists
Peasants' War, 1524-1525
Reformation
Anabiosis
  See Cryptobiosis
Anabolic steroids
  xx Steroids
Anabolism
  See Metabolism
Anachronisms, Literary
  See Errors and blunders, Literary
Anacreontic poetry *(Direct)*
  xx Poetry
Anacreontic poetry, German, [etc.] *(Direct)*
  x German [etc.] anacreontic poetry
  xx German poetry
Anadis
  See Yanadis
Anadromous fishes
  See Fishes, Anadromous
Anadromous rainbow trout
  See Steelhead (Fish)
Anaemia
  See Anemia
Anaerobic bacteria
  See Bacteria, Anaerobic
Anaesthesia
  See Anesthesia
Anaesthetics
  See Anesthetics
Anagrams *(Collections, PN6366-6377;*
    Games, GV1507.A5; Poetry,
    PN1525)
  sa Chronograms
  xx Anonyms and pseudonyms
Chronograms
Monograms
Puzzles
— Glossaries, vocabularies, etc.
    (GV1507.A5)
    xx English language—Glossaries,
      vocabularies, etc.
Anaiteum language
  See Aneityum language
Anal character
  See Anus (Psychology)
Anal eroticism
  See Anus (Psychology)
Anal reflex
  See Anus (Psychology)

Analcime *(Indirect)* *(QE391.A55)*
  x Analcite
Analzim
  xx Zeolites
Analcite
  See Analcime
Analgesia
  sa Analgesics
Preanesthetic medication
  xx Anesthesia
Analgesics
  sa names of individual analgesics, e.g.
    Acetophenetidin
  x Pain-killing drugs
  xx Analgesia
Anesthetics
— Testing
Analog calculating-machines
  See Analog computers
Electronic analog computers
Analog computer circuits
  See Electronic analog computers—Circuits
Analog computers
  sa Electronic analog computers
Integrators
Planimeter
Slide-rule
  x Analog calculating-machines
Analog machines
Analyzing machines
  xx Calculating-machines
Mathematical instruments
— Terminology
Analog-digital converters
  See Analog-to-digital converters
Analog machines
  See Analog computers
Analog multipliers *(TK7872.M8)*
  x Multipliers (Electronic
    calculating-machines)
  xx Vacuum-tube circuits
Analog-to-digital converters *(TK7887.6)*
  x Analog-digital converters
  xx Computer input-output equipment
Digital electronics
Electronic data processing
— Reliability
Analogies, Electromechanical
  See Electromechanical analogies
Analogies test, Miller
  See Miller analogies test
Analogy *(BD190)*
  xx Knowledge, Theory of
Reasoning
Analogy (Islamic law)
  See Islamic law—Interpretation and
    construction
Analogy (Law)
  See Law—Interpretation and construction
Analogy (Linguistics)
  x Grammar, Comparative and general—
    Analogy
Language and languages—Analogy
Linguistic analogy
  xx Linguistics
Analogy (Religion) *(Apologetics,*
  BT1100-1101; Natural theology,
  BL210)
  sa Anthropomorphism
Correspondences, Doctrine of
  xx Apologetics
Natural theology
Analysis, Chromatographic
  See Chromatographic analysis
Analysis, Conformational
  See Conformational analysis
Analysis, Discriminant
  See Discriminant analysis

Analysis, Electrochemical
   See Electrochemical analysis
Analysis, Electrolytic
   See Electrochemical analysis
Analysis, Factorial
   See Factor analysis
Analysis, Fourier
   See Fourier analysis
Analysis, Global (Mathematics)
   See Global analysis (Mathematics)
Analysis, Interaction (Education)
   See Interaction analysis in education
Analysis, Job
   See Job analysis
Analysis, Linguistic (Linguistics)
   See Linguistic analysis (Linguistics)
Analysis, Linguistic (Philosophy)
   See Analysis (Philosophy)
Analysis, Logical
   See Analysis (Philosophy)
Analysis, Metallurgical
   See Metallurgical analysis
Analysis, Microscopic
   See Metallography
      Microscope and microscopy
Analysis, Philosophical
   See Analysis (Philosophy)
Analysis, Spectrum
   See Spectrum analysis
Analysis, Stochastic
   See Stochastic analysis
Analysis, Volumetric
   See Volumetric analysis
Analysis (Chemistry)
   See Chemistry, Analytic
Analysis (Mathematics)
   See Calculus
      Functions
      Harmonic analysis
      Mathematical analysis
Analysis (Philosophy) *(B808.5)*
  sa Linguistic analysis (Linguistics)
     Logical positivism
     Semantics (Philosophy)
   x Analysis, Linguistic (Philosophy)
     Analysis, Logical
     Analysis, Philosophical
     Analytical philosophy
     Linguistic analysis (Philosophy)
     Logical analysis
     Philosophical analysis
     Philosophy, Analytical
  xx Languages—Philosophy
     Logical positivism
     Methodology
     Philosophy
     Semantics (Philosophy)
Analysis of blood
   See Blood—Analysis and chemistry
Analysis of colors
   See Colors—Analysis
Analysis of content (Communication)
   See Content analysis (Communication)
Analysis of cottonseed
   See Cottonseed—Analysis
Analysis of cottonseed oil
   See Cottonseed oil—Analysis
Analysis of food
   See Food adulteration and inspection
      Food—Analysis
Analysis of oil
   See Oil analysis
Analysis of sea-water
   See Sea-water—Analysis
Analysis of soils
   See Soils—Analysis
Analysis of time series
   See Time-series analysis

Analysis of variance *(QA276)*
  sa Experimental design
     Multivariate analysis
     Response surfaces (Statistics)
     Sampling (Statistics)
   x Variance analysis
  xx Experimental design
     Mathematical statistics
     Sampling (Statistics)
     Statistics
 — Programmed instruction
Analysis situs
   See Topology
Analysor, Neural
   See Neural analyzers
Analytic continuation
   x Continuation, Analytic
  xx Functions of several complex variables
Analytic functions *(QA331)*
  sa Analytic spaces
     Function algebras
     Hyperfunctions
     Siegel domains
   x Functions, Analytic
     Functions, Holomorphic
     Functions, Monogenic
     Functions, Regular
     Holomorphic functions
     Monogenic functions
     Regular functions
  xx Functions of complex variables
     Series, Taylor's
 — Problems, exercises, etc.
Analytic mappings
   x Mappings, Analytic
  xx Functions of several complex variables
Analytic spaces
  sa Complex manifolds
   x Spaces, Analytic
  xx Analytic functions
     Functions of several complex variables
Analytical chemistry
   See Chemistry, Analytic
Analytical geometry
   See Geometry, Analytic
Analytical mechanics
   See Mechanics, Analytic
Analytical philosophy
   See Analysis (Philosophy)
Analytico-synthetic classification
   See Classification, Faceted
Analyzers, Magnetic (Nuclear physics)
   See Magnetic analyzers (Nuclear physics)
Analyzers, Neural
   See Neural analyzers
Analyzing machines
   See Analog computers
Analzim
   See Analcime
Anang (African tribe)
  xx Ethnology—Nigeria
     Ibibios
Ānāpānasmṛti
   x Mindfulness of breathing
  xx Breath and breathing (in religion,
     folk-lore, etc.)
     Meditation (Buddhism)
Anaphora (Liturgy)
   See Lord's Supper (Liturgy)
Anaphylaxis *(QR185)*
  sa Allergy
     Antihistamines
     Serum sickness
   x Hypersusceptibility
  xx Allergy
     Immunity
     Serumtherapy
     Toxins and antitoxins

Anaplasmosis *(SF967.A)*
   x Gall sickness
     South African gall sickness
  xx Cattle—Diseases
Anarchism and anarchists *(Indirect)*
        (HX821-970)
  sa Anomy
     Direct action
     Liberty
     Socialism
     Syndicalism
     Terrorism
   x Anarchy
  xx Crime and criminals
     Liberty
     Nihilism
     Political crimes and offenses
     Political science
     Socialism
     Syndicalism
 — Chronology
 — Correspondence, reminiscences, etc.
 — Jews
 — Quotations, maxims, etc.
Anarchy
   See Anarchism and anarchists
Anasagunticook Indians
   See Arosaguntacook Indians
Anasazi culture
   See Pueblo Indians
Anastenaria
Anastomosis, Portacaval
   See Portacaval anastomosis
Anathema
   See Excommunication
Anatidae
   Notes under Water-birds; Waterfowl
Anātman
  sa Ātman
     No-mind (Buddhism)
   x Anattā
     Nirātman
     Non-self
  xx Ātman
     Philosophy, Buddhist
     Philosophy, Hindu
     Self (Philosophy)
     Soul
Anatomical laboratories *(QM41)*
   x Anatomy—Laboratories
     Laboratories, Anatomical
Anatomical models, Human
   See Anatomy, Human—Models
Anatomical museums *(QL814; QM51)*
  xx Medical museums
     Museums
Anatomical specimens *(QL814)*
   x Specimens, Anatomical
  xx Injections, Anatomical
 — Collection and preservation
Anatomists *(QM16)*
  xx Scientists
Anatomists, American, ₍French, etc.₎
   x American ₍French, etc.₎ anatomists
Anatomy
  sa Body composition
     Dissection
     Histology
     Nervous system
     Organs (Anatomy)
     Physiology
     Veterinary anatomy
     subdivision Anatomy *under subjects,*
      e.g. Cattle—Anatomy; Ear—
      Anatomy; Ferns—Anatomy; Wood—
      Anatomy
  xx Biology
     Medicine

Physiology
— Abstracts
— Early works to 1800
— Laboratories
    See Anatomical laboratories
— Terminology
Anatomy, Artistic *(NC760)*
  sa Human figure in art
    Medicine and art
    Proportion (Anthropometry)
    Proportion (Art)
  x Artistic anatomy
  xx Art
    Drawing
    Human figure in art
    Medicine and art
    Nude in art
    Proportion (Art)
Anatomy, Comparative *(QL801-950)*
  sa Homology (Biology)
    Man—Origin
    Morphology
    names of organs and regions of the body, e.g. Eye, Brain, Pelvis
  x Comparative anatomy
    Comparative morphology
    Zoology—Morphology
    Zootomy
  xx Evolution
    Man—Origin
    Zoology
  Note under Morphology (Animals)
— Atlases
— Catalogs and collections
— Examinations, questions, etc.
— Juvenile literature
— Laboratory manuals *(QL812)*
  sa Dissection
    Veterinary anatomy—Laboratory manuals
  xx Dissection
    Zoology—Laboratory manuals
Anatomy, Dental
  See Teeth
Anatomy, Human *(QM)*
  sa Body, Human
    Extremities (Anatomy)
    Woman—Anatomy and physiology
    names of organs and regions of the body, e.g. Heart, Pelvis, Skull
  x Human anatomy
  xx Body, Human
    Human biology
    Somatology
— Atlases *(QM25)*
  Example under Atlases
— Charts, diagrams, etc. *(QM33)*
  x Manikins
— Early works to 1800 *(QM21)*
— Examinations, questions, etc. *(QM32)*
— Juvenile literature
— Laboratory manuals *(QM34-39)*
  sa Human dissection
  xx Dissection
    Human dissection
— Models
  x Anatomical models, Human
— Programmed instruction
— Terminology *(QM81)*
Anatomy, Microscopic
  See Histology
Anatomy, Morbid
  See Anatomy, Pathological
Anatomy, Pathological *(RB24-57)*
  sa Autopsy
    Pathology
  x Anatomy, Morbid
    Morbid anatomy

    Pathological anatomy
  xx Pathology
— Atlases
Anatomy, Practical
  See Human dissection
Anatomy, Regional
  See Anatomy, Surgical and topographical
Anatomy, Surgical and topographical *(QM531-549)*
  sa names of organs and regions of the body
  x Anatomy, Regional
    Regional anatomy
    Surgical anatomy
    Topographical anatomy
  xx Surgery
Anatomy, Vegetable
  See Botany—Anatomy
Anatomy, Veterinary
  See Veterinary anatomy
Anatomy of plants
  See Botany—Anatomy
Anattā
  See Anātman
Ancestor cult
  See Ancestor worship
Ancestor worship *(Direct)* *(BL467)*
  sa Apotheosis
    Tutelaries (Shinto)
  x Ancestor cult
    Dead, Worship of the
  xx Dead (in religion, folk-lore, etc.)
    Funeral rites and ceremonies
    Religion, Primitive
    Worship
Ancestor worship (Hinduism) *(BL1215.A55)*
  sa Śrāddha (Hindu rite)
  xx Hinduism
Ancestral debts
  See Claims against decedents' estates
Ancestry
  See Genealogy
    Heredity
Anchor davits
  See Davits
Anchor ring
  See Torus (Geometry)
Anchor stations (Oceanography)
  See Oceanographic research stations
Anchor stones
Anchorage
  sa Deep-sea moorings
    Harbors of refuge
    Marinas
    subdivision Harbor—Anchorage *under names of cities, e.g.* New York (City)—Harbor—Anchorage
  x Mooring of ships
    Ships—Anchorage
  xx Marinas
Anchorage (Structural engineering)
  sa Guy anchors
    Rock bolts
    Shoring and underpinning
  xx Foundations
    Shoring and underpinning
    Soil mechanics
Anchorites
  See Hermits
Anchors *(VM791)*
  sa Capstan
    Windlasses
Anchors, Deadman
  See Guy anchors
Anchors, Ground
  See Guy anchors
Anchors, Guy
  See Guy anchors

Anchors, Rock
  See Rock bolts
Anchovies
  sa Cookery (Anchovies)
    Northern anchovy
    Peruvian anchovy
  xx Clupeiformes
Ancient art, ⌐geography, history, etc.⌐
  See Art ⌐Geography, History, etc.⌐, Ancient
Ancient biography
  See Biography—To 500
Ancient Chinese language
  See Chinese language—Archaic Chinese
Ancient lights
  See Light and air (Easement)
Ancon, Treaty of, 1883 *(F3097.3)*
  xx War of the Pacific, 1879-1884
Ancona
— Earthquake, 1972
Anconas (Poultry) *(SF489.A6)*
Ancones
  xx Architecture—Details
Andaki Indians
  See Andaqui Indians
Andalusia in literature
Andalusians (Poultry) *(SF489.A65)*
Andalusite *(Indirect)*
  xx Aluminum silicates
    Silicates
Andaman languages
Andaqui Indians *(F2270.2.A)*
  x Andaki Indians
  xx Ethnology—Colombia
    Indians of South America
Ande (Artificial language)
  xx Languages, Artificial
Ande Indians
  See Campa Indians
Ande language
  See Campa language
Andean programme
  xx United Nations—Technical assistance
Andematunnum
  See Lingones
Anders Jahre prize
  See Jahre prize
Andhra language
  See Telugu language
Andorite
Andorobo
  See Dorobo (African people)
Andorra in literature
Andreas-Gryphius-Preis
  x Ostdeutscher Literaturpreis
Andrews' Raid, 1862
  See Chattanooga Railroad Expedition, 1862
Andrews' Railroad Raid
  See Chattanooga Railroad Expedition, 1862
Androgenic zone
  See Zona reticularis
Androgens
  xx Androstane
  Example under Hormones, Sex
Androids
  x Robots
  xx Automata
Andromeda (Nebula)
  xx Nebulae
Andropogon sorghum
  See Sorghum
Androscoggin Indians
  See Arosaguntacook Indians
Androsovo, Treaty of, 1667
  See Andrusovo, Treaty of, 1667
Androstane
  sa Androgens
    Hormones, Sex
  xx Steroids

Andrusovo, Treaty of, 1667
    x Androsovo, Treaty of, 1667
Anecdotes *(Direct) (Collections,*
        PN6259-6268; Historical, D10)
    sa Children—Anecdotes and sayings
        Exempla
        Homiletical illustrations
        Last words
        Table-talk
        subdivision Anecdotes *under names of*
        wars and prominent persons, e.g.
        United States—History—Revolution,
        1775-1783—Anecdotes; Lincoln,
        Abraham, Pres. U.S., 1809-1865—
        Anecdotes; *and subdivision*
        Anecdotes, facetiae, satires, etc.
        under particular subjects, e.g. Art—
        Anecdotes, facetiae, satire, etc.;
        Literature—Anecdotes, facetiae,
        satire, etc.
    x Ana
    xx Biography
        Wit and humor
Anecdotes, Legal
    See Law—Anecdotes, facetiae, satire, etc.
Anecdotes, Medical
    See Medicine—Anecdotes, facetiae, satire,
        etc.
Anecdotes, Musical
    See Music—Anecdotes, facetiae, satire, etc.
        Musicians—Correspondence,
        reminiscences, etc.
Anechoic chambers
    xx Absorption of sound
        Acoustical engineering
        Noise
Aneityum language *(PL6217)*
    x Anaiteum language
    xx Melanesian languages
Anelasticity
    See Internal friction
Anemia *(RC641)*
    sa Aplastic anemia
        Blood
        Brain—Anemia
        Hemoglobinopathy
        Hemolytic anemia
        Hemorrhage
        Hookworm disease
        Hypochromic anemia
        Infectious anemia
        Iron deficiency anemia
        Leukemia
        Liver extract
        Megaloblastic anemia
        Pernicious anemia
        Sickle cell anemia
        Thalassemia
    x Anaemia
    — Dietary aspects
        See Anemia—Nutritional aspects
    — Nutritional aspects
        x Anemia—Dietary aspects
        Diet and anemia
        Nutrition and anemia
Anemia, Drepanocytic
    See Sickle cell anemia
Anemia, Infectious
    See Infectious anemia
Anemia, Microcytic hypochromic
    See Hypochromic anemia
Anemia in pregnancy *(RG580.A5)*
    xx Pregnancy, Complications of
Anemometer *(QC932)*
    sa Hot-wire anemometer
    xx Meteorological instruments
        Wind-pressure

Anemometer, Laser
    See Laser Doppler velocimeter
Anencephalus *(Indirect)*
    xx Brain—Abnormities and deformities
        Dysraphia
Anerbengerichte (Germany)
Aneroid barometer *(QC896)*
    sa Barometric hypsometry
    x Barometer, Aneroid
    xx Aeronautical instruments
        Barometric hypsometry
        Meteorological instruments
    Example under Physical instruments
Anesthesia *(RD79-87)*
    sa Acupuncture anesthesia
        Analgesia
        Anesthesia in dentistry
        Anesthesia in obstetrics
        Anesthesia in ophthalmology
        Anesthesia in veterinary surgery
        Anesthesiology
        Anesthetics
        Anesthetists
        Brain—Puncture
        Conduction anesthesia
        Geriatric anesthesia
        Hypnotism in surgery
        Inhalation anesthesia
        Muscle relaxants
        Paravertebral anesthesia
        Pediatric anesthesia
        Peridural anesthesia
        Preanesthetic medication
        Refrigeration anesthesia
    x Anaesthesia
    xx Anesthesiology
        Anesthetics
    — Complications and sequelae
        Example under Diseases—Complications
        and sequelae
    — Instruments
        See Anesthesiology—Apparatus and
        instruments
    — Jurisprudence *(Direct)*
    — Measurement
Anesthesia, Conduction
    See Conduction anesthesia
Anesthesia, Electric
    See Electric anesthesia
Anesthesia, Endotracheal
    See Intratracheal anesthesia
Anesthesia, Epidural
    See Peridural anesthesia
Anesthesia, Extradural
    See Peridural anesthesia
Anesthesia, Inhalation
    See Inhalation anesthesia
Anesthesia, Intratracheal
    See Intratracheal anesthesia
Anesthesia, Intravenous
    See Intravenous anesthesia
Anesthesia, Local
    See Local anesthesia
Anesthesia, Neurolept
    See Neuroleptanesthesia
Anesthesia, Paravertebral
    See Paravertebral anesthesia
Anesthesia, Peridural
    See Peridural anesthesia
Anesthesia, Spinal
    See Spinal anesthesia
Anesthesia adjuvants
    xx Anesthesiology
        Pharmacology
Anesthesia in childhood
    See Pediatric anesthesia
Anesthesia in dentistry *(RK510)*
    sa Hypnotism in dentistry

    x Anesthetics in dentistry
        Dental anesthesia
    xx Anesthesia
        Dentistry, Operative
Anesthesia in obstetrics *(RG732)*
    sa Hypnotism in obstetrics
    x Anesthetics in obstetrics
        Obstetric anesthesia
        Obstetrics, Anesthetics in
    xx Anesthesia
        Labor, Complicated
        Obstetrics
Anesthesia in oncology
    xx Oncology
Anesthesia in ophthalmology *(RE82)*
    x Anesthetics in ophthalmology
        Ophthalmology, Anesthetics in
    xx Anesthesia
Anesthesia in otolaryngology
    x Anesthetics in otolaryngology
        Otolaryngology, Anesthetics in
Anesthesia in urology
    x Urologic anesthesia
    xx Urology
Anesthesia in veterinary surgery
    x Anesthetics in veterinary surgery
    xx Anesthesia
        Animal immobilization
        Veterinary surgery
Anesthesiologists
    See Anesthetists
Anesthesiology
    sa Anesthesia
        Anesthesia adjuvants
        Anesthetics
    xx Anesthesia
    — Apparatus and instruments
        x Anesthesia—Instruments
    — — Standards
    — Examinations, questions, etc.
    — Research
        See Anesthesiology research
    — Study and teaching *(Direct)*
    — — Mathematical models
    — Vocational guidance
        See Anesthesiology as a profession
Anesthesiology as a profession
    x Anesthesiology—Vocational guidance
Anesthesiology research *(Direct)*
    x Anesthesiology—Research
    xx Medical research
        Research
Anesthetics *(RD79-87)*
    sa Analgesics
        Anesthesia
        Avertin
        Chloroform
        Curare
        Ether (Anesthetic)
        Falicaine
        Halothane
        Nupercaine
        Penthrane
        Sedatives
        Trichloroethylene
    x Anaesthetics
    xx Anesthesia
        Anesthesiology
        Materia medica
        Pain
        Sedatives
        Surgery
    — Administration
    — Safety measures
    — Toxicology
Anesthetics, Local
    See Local anesthesia

Anesthetics in dentistry
   See Anesthesia in dentistry
Anesthetics in obstetrics
   See Anesthesia in obstetrics
Anesthetics in ophthalmology
   See Anesthesia in ophthalmology
Anesthetics in otolaryngology
   See Anesthesia in otolaryngology
Anesthetics in veterinary surgery
   See Anesthesia in veterinary surgery
Anesthetists *(Indirect)*
   x Anesthesiologists
   xx Anesthesia
  — Fees
Aneuploidy
   xx Chromosome numbers
Aneurisms
   See Aneurysms
Aneurysms *(RC693)*
   sa Aortic aneurysms
      Intracranial aneurysms
      Renal artery aneurysms
      Ventricular aneurysms
   x Aneurisms
   xx Blood-vessels—Diseases
Aneurysms, Aortic
   See Aortic aneurysms
Aneurysms, Arteriovenous
   See Fistula, Arteriovenous
Anga (Papuan people)
   See Kukukuku (Papuan people)
Angaco, Battle of, 1841 *(F2846)*
Angal Heneng language
Angami language *(PL4001.A65)*
   xx Naga languages
Angami Nagas
   See Nagas
Angary, Right of
   sa Eminent domain
      Requisitions, Military
   x Requisitions (of neutral vessels and
      cargoes)
      Right of angary
      Ships, Requisition of
   xx Eminent domain
      International law
      Maritime law
      Requisitions, Military
      Seizure of vessels and cargoes
      War, Maritime (International law)
Angas language *(PL8047)*
   sa Hausa language
      Ron language
   x Angass language
      Karaṅ language
   xx Chadic languages
      Hausa language
      Ron language
Angass language
   See Angas language
Angel fish *(SF458.A5)*
   Example under Tropical fish
Angelica *(RS165.A5)*
Angelology
   See Angels
Angels *(Comparative religion, BL477;*
      Theology, BT965-8)
   sa Ark of the Covenant
      Divine messengers in literature
      Guardian angels
   x Angelology
      Cherubim
      Seraphim
   xx Heaven
      Spirits
      Theology, Doctrinal
  — Art *(N8090)*
  — Cultus

   xx Worship
  — Early works to 1800
  — History of doctrines
  — Juvenile literature
  — Legends
  — Prayer-books and devotions
      Subdivided by language.
Angels (Buddhism)
   xx Gods, Buddhist
Angels (Islam) *(BP166.89)*
   x Islamic angelology
      Muslim angelology
   xx Spirits (Islam)
   Example under Islam
  — Koranic teaching
Angels (Judaism) *(BM645.A6)*
Anger *(Ethics, BJ1535.A6; Psychology,*
      BF575.A5)
   sa Wrath
   x Indignation
   xx Conduct of life
      Deadly sins
      Emotions
      Ethics
      Wrath
   Example under Vices
  — Juvenile literature
Anger of God
   See God—Wrath
Angico gum
   x Brazilian gum
      Para gum
Angina abdominis
   See Abdominal angina
Angina Ludovici
   See Neck—Abscess
Angina maligna
   x Cynanche maligna
Angina pectoris *(RC685.A6)*
   x Stenocardia
   xx Heart—Diseases
Angiocardiography
   xx Blood-vessels—Diseases—Diagnosis
      Diagnosis, Radioscopic
      Heart—Diseases—Diagnosis
Angiography
   sa Amputation stumps—Blood-vessels—
      Radiography
      Arteries—Radiography
      Brain—Blood-vessels—Radiography
      Cineangiography
      Coronary arteries—Radiography
      Eye—Blood-vessels—Radiography
      Liver—Blood-vessels—Radiography
      Lungs—Blood-vessels—Radiography
      Pancreas—Blood-vessels—Radiography
      Retina—Blood-vessels—Radiography
      Spinal cord—Blood-vessels—
      Radiography
      Spleen—Blood-vessels—Radiography
      Veins—Radiography
   x Blood-vessels—Radiography
   xx Diagnosis, Radioscopic
      Radiography
  — Atlases
  — Complications and sequelae
Angioid streaks
   xx Retina—Diseases
Angioma
Angiomatosis
   xx Blood-vessels—Diseases
Angioneurotic edema
   x Quincke's disease
   xx Edema
Angioscotometry
   See Scotoma
Angiospasm
   xx Blood-vessels

Angiosperms *(QK495.A)*
   sa Diapensiales
      Dicotyledons
      Magnoliales
      Monocotyledons
      Scitamineae
      Urticales
   x Flowering plants
   xx Phanerogams
  — Classification
Angiosperms, Fossil *(QE980)*
   x Magnoliophyta, Fossil
Angiostrongylosis
   xx Medical parasitology
Angle *(QA482)*
   sa Euler angles
      Goniometry
      Rectangle
   xx Geometry
  — Juvenile literature
Angle trisection
   See Trisection of angle
Angler-fishes *(QL638.L75)*
   x Goosefish
Anglia automobile
   xx Ford automobile
Anglican chant
   See Chants (Anglican)
Anglican Church
   See Church of England
Anglican churches
   See Churches, Anglican
Anglican Communion *(BX5003-9)*
  — Clergy
  — Confirmation
      See Confirmation—Anglican
         Communion
  — Continuity
      See Continuity of the church—
         Anglican Communion
  — Government
  — Liturgical movement
      See Liturgical movement—Anglican
         Communion
  — Parish missions
      See Parish missions—Anglican
         Communion
  — Relations
      sa Lambeth Quadrilateral
  — Sermons *(BX5008)*
Anglican converts
   See Converts, Anglican
Anglican monasticism and religious orders
   See Monasticism and religious orders,
      Anglican
      Monasticism and religious orders for
      women, Anglican
Anglican orders *(BX5178)*
      Here are entered works dealing with the
      question at issue between the Anglican
      Communion and the Catholic Church
      as to whether the episcopate of the An-
      glican Communion is in the true line of
      apostolic succession.
   x Orders, Anglican
   xx Apostolic succession
      Church of England—Clergy
      Continuity of the church—Anglican
         Communion
      Episcopacy
Anglican theology
   See Theology, Anglican
Angling
   See Fishing
Anglo-American law
   See Common law
      Law—Great Britain
      Law—United States

Anglo-American Polar Expedition, 1906-1908
Anglo-Burmese War, 1824-1826
   See Burmese War, 1824-1826
Anglo-Catholicism *(BX5121)*
   sa Catholicity
   x Catholic movement (Anglican
      Communion)
   xx Catholic Church
      Church of England
      Church of England—Parties and
       movements
      Oxford movement
      Protestant Episcopal Church in the
       U.S.A.
Anglo-Dutch War . . .
   x British-Dutch War
      Dutch-English War
Anglo-Dutch War, 1652-1654 *(DJ193)*
Anglo-Dutch War, 1664-1667 *(DJ180-182)*
   — Sources
Anglo-Dutch War, 1672-1674
   See Dutch War, 1672-1674
Anglo-Dutch War, 1780-1784 *(DJ205-6)*
Anglo-French Intervention in Egypt, 1956
   See Egypt—History—Intervention, 1956
Anglo-French War . . .
   x British-French War
      Franco-English War
      French-English War
Anglo-French War, 1294-1298
Anglo-French War, 1512-1513 *(DA337;*
     DC108)
   x Spurs, Battle of the, 1513
   xx Holy League against France, 1511-1513
Anglo-French War, 1666-1667 *(D274.5-6;*
     English history, DA448; French
     history, DC127.3-8)
Anglo-French War, 1689-1697
   See United States—History—King William's
      War, 1689-1697
Anglo-French War, 1755-1763 *(DA500-510;*
     DC133; DD409-412)
   sa Port Mahon—Siege, 1756
      United States—History—French and
       Indian War, 1755-1763
   xx Seven Years' War, 1756-1763
Anglo-French War, 1778-1783 *(DA510;*
     DC136)
   sa Ouessant, Battle of, 1778
Anglo-French War, 1793-1802 *(DA520;*
     DC220-222)
Anglo-German naval agreement, 1935
   x German-British naval agreement, 1935
Anglo-Indian dialect
   See Hobson-jobson
Anglo-Indian fiction *(History, PR9735-9)*
Anglo-Indian literature *(PR9700-9799)*
   For literature by English residents of
     India.
   sa English literature—Indic authors
   Note under English literature—Indian authors
Anglo-Indian poetry *(Collections,*
     PR9755-9769; History,
     PR9726-9732)
   For poetry by English residents of India.
   sa English poetry—Indic authors
   Note under English poetry—Indic authors
Anglo-Indians *(DS432.A)*
   xx Eurasians
      Miscegenation
Anglo-Iranian oil dispute
Anglo-Israelism *(DS131)*
   sa Lost tribes of Israel
   xx Jews
      Lost tribes of Israel
Anglo-Norman dialect *(PC2941-8)*
Anglo-Norman horse

Anglo-Norman letters *(Collections, PR1344;*
     History, PR913)
   xx French letters
Anglo-Norman literature *(Collections,*
     PR1119-1120; History, PR251-369)
Anglo-Norman poetry *(Collections, PR1203;*
     History, PR311-369)
Anglo-Russian treaty, 1942 *(D749.5.A)*
   x Anglo-Soviet treaty, 1942
      British-Soviet treaty, 1942
      Russo-British treaty, 1942
      Russo-English treaty, 1942
   xx World War, 1939-1945—Diplomatic
      history
      World War, 1939-1945—Treaties
Anglo-Saxon art industries and trade
   See Art industries and trade, Anglo-Saxon
Anglo-Saxon calendar
   See Calendar, Anglo-Saxon
Anglo-Saxon civilization
   See Civilization, Anglo-Saxon
Anglo-Saxon decoration and ornament
   See Decoration and ornament, Anglo-Saxon
Anglo-Saxon inscriptions
   See Inscriptions, Anglo-Saxon
Anglo-Saxon language *(PE101-299)*
   x English language—To 1100
      Old English language
   xx Germanic languages
      Old Saxon language
Anglo-Saxon law
   See Law, Anglo-Saxon
Anglo-Saxon literature *(Collections,*
     PR1490-1508; History, PR171-236)
   x English literature—To 1100
      Old English literature
Anglo-Saxon magic
   See Magic, Anglo-Saxon
Anglo-Saxon manuscripts
   See Manuscripts, Anglo-Saxon
Anglo-Saxon names
   See Names, Anglo-Saxon
Anglo-Saxon philology
Anglo-Saxon poetry *(Collections,*
     PR1490-1508; History, PR201-217)
   x English poetry—To 1100
Anglo-Saxon race *(CB216-220)*
   Here are entered works on the nations of
     Anglo-Saxon descent. Works on the
     early Anglo-Saxons are entered under
     the heading Anglo-Saxons.
   xx Lost tribes of Israel
      Teutonic race
   Note under Anglo-Saxons
Anglo-Saxon riddles
   See Riddles, Anglo-Saxon
Anglo-Saxons *(DA150-162)*
   Here are entered works on the Anglo-
     Saxons until the time of the conquest
     (approximately) Material dealing with
     the nations of Anglo-Saxon descent is
     entered under the heading Anglo-
     Saxon race.
   sa Jutes
   xx Saxons
   Note under Anglo-Saxon race
   — Kings and rulers
     xx Great Britain—Kings and rulers
Anglo-Soviet treaty, 1942
   See Anglo-Russian treaty, 1942
Anglo-Spanish War . . .
   x British-Spanish War
      Spanish-English War
Anglo-Spanish War, 1718-1720 *(DA498-9;*
     DP194)
   xx Quadruple Alliance, 1718
Anglo-Spanish War, 1739-1748
   sa Austrian Succession, War of, 1740-1748

      Porto Bello, Panama—Siege, 1739
   x Jenkins' Ear, War of
   xx Austrian Succession, War of, 1740-1748
Anglo-Spanish War, 1762-1763 *(DA505-512;*
     DP199)
   xx Seven Years' War, 1756-1763
Anglo-Spanish War, 1779-1783 *(DA505-512;*
     DP199)
Angola
   — Massacre, 1961
   — Native races
     Example under Native races
Angola in literature
   xx Africa in literature
Angola language
   See Kimbundu language
Angoni
   sa Missions to Angoni
Angoni
   sa Bhaca (African tribe)
   x Ngoni
   xx Ethnology—Malawi
Angoni law
   See Law, Angoni
Angora cat *(SF449)*
   sa Persian cat
   x Long hair cat
      Longhair cat
   xx Persian cat
   Example under Cat breeds
Angora goat *(SF385)*
   sa Mohair
   xx Goats
Angora rabbits *(SF455)*
Angostura bark *(RS165.A6)*
   x Angustura bark
Angular correlations (Nuclear physics)
   sa Beta ray spectrometry
      Gamma ray spectrometry
   xx Nuclear reactions
   — Charts, diagrams, etc.
   — Tables, etc.
Angular momentum
   sa Angular momentum (Nuclear physics)
      Moments of inertia
      Torque
   x Moment of momentum
      Momentum, Angular
   xx Moments of inertia
      Momentum (Mechanics)
      Rotational motion (Rigid dynamics)
      Torque
Angular momentum (Nuclear physics)
   sa Clebsch-Gordan coefficients
      Nuclear orientation
      Nuclear spin
      Racah coefficients
      Regge trajectories
   xx Angular momentum
      Nuclear moments
      Nuclear physics
      Particles (Nuclear physics)
      Quantum theory
Angus cattle
   See Aberdeen-Angus cattle
Angustura bark
   See Angostura bark
Anhalonium
   See Peyote
Anhidrosis
   xx Sweat glands—Diseases
Anhydrides *(QD305.A2; QD341.A2)*
Anhydrite *(Indirect)*
   xx Evaporites
Anhydrobiosis *(QH524)*
   xx Cryptobiosis
Anhydrous ammonia
   See Ammonia

Anicca (Buddhism)
  See Impermanence (Buddhism)
Aniline *(QD341.A8; TP914)*
  x Amido-benzene
    Benzene, Amido-
  Example under Chemistry, Organic
Aniline black *(TP918.A5)*
  xx Coal-tar colors
Aniline colors
  See Coal-tar colors
Aniline printing
  See Flexography
Animal aggression
  See Aggressive behavior in animals
Animal babies
  See Animals, Infancy of
Animal baiting
  See Bull-fights
    Cock-fighting
    Dog-fighting
Animal behavior
  See Animals, Habits and behavior of
Animal black
  See Animal charcoal
Animal blood groups
  See Blood groups in animals
Animal bodies, Disposal of
  See Dead animals, Removal and disposal of
Animal camouflage
  See Camouflage (Biology)
Animal cemeteries
  See Pet cemeteries
Animal charcoal *(Sugar manufacture, TP378)*
  sa Bone products
  x Animal black
    Bone black
    Charcoal, Animal
  xx Bone products
Animal collecting
  See Wild animal collecting
Animal collectors
  See Wild animal collectors
Animal colonies *(Indirect) (QL364.5)*
  Here are entered works on groupings of physically interconnected animals having a common ancestry through asexual reproduction. Works on groups of animals which are characterized by specific social patterns due to their proximity, interrelationships, and/or similarities are entered under the heading Animal societies.
  sa Coelenterata
    Hemichordata
    Polyzoa
    Sponges
  x Colonial animals
    Coloniality (Zoology)
    Zooids
  xx Colonies (Biology)
    Invertebrates
    Reproduction, Asexual
  Note under Animal societies
Animal coloration
  See Color of animals
Animal communication
  sa Animal sounds
    Sound production by animals
  x Animal language
    Communication among animals
  — Juvenile literature
Animal courtship
  See Courtship of animals
Animal culture *(Indirect) (SF)*
  sa Domestic animals
    Fish-culture
    Fur farming
    Game bird culture

    Laboratory animals
    Pets
    Poultry
    Small animal culture
    Stock and stock-breeding
  x Animal husbandry
  xx Animals
    Zoology, Economic
  — Early works to 1800
Animal dealers
  sa Pet industry
    Pet shops
    Wild animal trade
  xx Wild animal trade
Animal defenses
  sa Animal weapons
    Camouflage (Biology)
    Glands, Odoriferous
    Mimicry (Biology)
  x Defense mechanisms of animals
    Defense mechanisms (Zoology)
    Self-defense in animals
    Self-protection in animals
  xx Agonistic behavior in animals
    Animal weapons
    Animals, Habits and behavior of
  — Juvenile literature
Animal diseases
  See Veterinary medicine
Animal drawing
  See Animal painting and illustration
Animal electricity
  See Electrophysiology
Animal extracts *(Pharmacology, QP951; Therapeutics, RM283-298)*
  sa Organotherapy
    names of particular extracts, e.g. Adrenalin, Pancreatin
  x Opotherapy
  xx Organotherapy
    Zoology, Medical
Animal fibers *(TS1545)*
  sa specific fibers, e.g. Silk, Wool
  x Textile fibers, Animal
  xx Textile fibers
  — Testing
Animal fighting
  sa Bull-fights
    Cock-fighting
    Dog-fighting
  x Fighting
  xx Aggressive behavior in animals
    Agonistic behavior in animals
Animal fighting in art
  xx Animals in art
Animal films
  Here are entered individual fiction films in which animals are the principal characters. Animated cartoons featuring animals, are entered under Moving-picture cartoons.
  xx Animals, Legends and stories of
    Feature films
    Moving-pictures
Animal fluids and humors
  See Body fluids
Animal folklore
  See Animal lore
Animal food *(TX371-389)*
  sa Vegetarianism
    names of particular animal foods and food products, e.g. Dairy products, Eggs, Meat, Pork
  x Animal-origin food
    Animals as food
    Animals, Edible
    Food animals
  xx Diet

    Food
  — Toxicology *(RA1259)*
    xx Food poisoning
Animal forms in design
  See Design, Decorative—Animal forms
Animal genetics
  sa Animal mutation breeding
    Fish genetics
    Insect genetics
  xx Genetics
  — Statistical methods
Animal gut industries *(Direct)*
  sa Catgut
    Sausage casings
    Sutures
  x Gut industries
  xx Animal products
    Meat industry and trade
  — Standards *(Direct)*
Animal heat *(QP135)*
  sa Body temperature
    Thermometers and thermometry, Medical
  x Calor animalis
  xx Body temperature
    Calorimeters and calorimetry
    Heat
    Physiological chemistry
    Physiology
  — Juvenile literature
Animal homes
  See Animals, Habitations of
Animal hospitals
  See Veterinary hospitals
Animal housing *(Indirect)*
  sa Cattle houses and equipment
    Kennels
    Laboratory animals—Housing
    Poultry houses and equipment
    Sheep houses and equipment
    Stables
    Swine houses and equipment
  x Domestic animals—Housing
    Housing, Animal
    Livestock buildings
Animal husbandry
  See Animal culture
    Domestic animals
    Stock and stock-breeding
Animal immobilization
  sa Anesthesia in veterinary surgery
  x Animal restraint
    Immobilization of animals
    Restraint of animals
  xx Veterinary medicine
Animal industry *(Indirect) (Economics, HD9410-9429)*
  sa Cattle trade
    Dairying
    Domestic animals
    Fur farming
    Marketing of livestock
    Pet industry
    Poultry industry
    Stock and stock-breeding
    Wages—Animal industry
  xx Agriculture
    Stock and stock-breeding
  — Accounting
    x Stock and stock-breeding— Accounting
  — Exhibitions
  — Law and legislation *(Direct)*
    sa Domestic animals—Law
      Pasture, Right of
      Veterinary hygiene—Law and legislation
    x Cattle trade—Law and legislation

Animal industry *(Indirect) (Economics, HD9410-9429)*
— Law and legislation *(Direct)*
(Continued)
    Livestock laws
    Stock and stock-breeding—Law and legislation
   xx Agricultural laws and legislation
    Domestic animals—Law
    Veterinary hygiene—Law and legislation
— Prices *(Direct)*
— Taxation *(Direct)*
   x Cattle trade—Taxation
— Vocational guidance
Animal instinct
  See Instinct
Animal intelligence *(QL785)*
  sa Animals, Habits and behavior of
    Instinct
    Learning, Psychology of
    Maze tests
    Psychology, Comparative
   subdivision Psychology *under names of specific animals, e.g.* Horses—Psychology
  x Intelligence of animals
  xx Animals, Habits and behavior of
    Instinct
    Psychology, Comparative
— Juvenile literature
Animal introduction *(Indirect)*
  sa Domestic animals
    Game and game-birds
  x Alien animals
  xx Acclimatization
    Fish-culture
    Game and game-birds
    Zoogeography
    Zoology, Economic
— Juvenile literature
Animal kingdom
  See Zoology
Animal language
  See Animal communication
    Animal sounds
    Sound production by animals
Animal light
  See Phosphorescence
Animal locomotion *(QP301)*
  sa Action in art
    Amoeboid movement
    Brachiation
    Crawling and creeping
    Flight
    Horses—Paces, gaits, etc.
    Running
    Swimming
    Walking
  x Animals, Movements of
    Movements of animals
  xx Animal mechanics
    Locomotion
    Muscles
— Juvenile literature
Animal lore *(GR820-830; QL89)*
  sa Animal worship
    Animals, Legends and stories of
    Animals, Mythical
    Animals, Prosecution and punishment of
    Bestiaries
    Bugonia
    Dragons
    Ethnozoology
    Folk-lore
    Leopard men
    Natural history
    Parapsychology and animals

    Salamanders
    Unicorns
    Vampires
    Werwolves
  x Animal folklore
    Animal symbolism
    Animals in folk-lore
    Animals (in religion, folk-lore, etc.)
    Folk-lore of animals
    Imaginary animals
    Symbolism of animals
    Zoological mythology
  xx Animals in literature
    Animals, Legends and stories of
    Animals, Mythical
    Bestiaries
    Dragons
    Folk-lore
    Natural history
    Nature (in religion, folk-lore, etc.)
    Superstition
— Juvenile literature
Animal luminescence
  See Bioluminescence
Animal magnetism *(Psychical research, BF1111-1156; Therapeutics, RZ430)*
  sa Clairvoyance
    Hypnotism
    Magnetic healing
    Mesmerism
  x Human magnetism
    Magnetism, Animal
    Magnetism, Human
    Mind-cure
  xx Hypnotism
    Magnetic healing
    Magnetism
    Mental suggestion
    Mesmerism
    Therapeutics, Suggestive
Animal marking *(Indirect)*
  sa Bird-banding
    Fish tagging
  x Animal tagging
    Marking of animals
    Tagging of animals
  xx Wildlife management
    Zoological research
Animal mechanics *(QP303)*
  sa Animal locomotion
    Flight
    Human mechanics
    Standing position
  x Animals, Movements of
    Movements of animals
  xx Biomechanics
    Mechanics
    Physiology
Animal migration *(QL754)*
  sa Animal navigation
    Animal orientation
    Birds—Migration
  x Animals, Migration of
    Migration of animals
  xx Animal navigation
    Animals, Habits and behavior of
    Zoogeography
— Juvenile literature
Animal mutation
  sa Animal mutation breeding
  x Mutation of animals
  xx Mutation (Biology)
Animal mutation breeding
  xx Animal genetics
    Animal mutation
    Mutation breeding
    Stock and stock-breeding

Animal names, Popular
  See Zoology—Nomenclature (Popular)
Animal navigation
  sa Animal migration
    Animal orientation
    Bird navigation
  xx Animal migration
    Animal orientation
    Animals, Habits and behavior of
    Navigation
Animal nursing
  See Veterinary nursing
Animal nutrition
  See Feeding
    Nutrition
Animal oils
  See Oils and fats
Animal orientation
  sa Animal navigation
    Echolocation (Physiology)
    Phototaxis
  xx Animal migration
    Animal navigation
    Animals, Habits and behavior of
    Orientation
Animal-origin food
  See Animal food
Animal painters
  x Animaliers
Animal painters, Belgian, ₍French, etc.₎ *(Direct)*
  x Belgian ₍French, etc.₎ animal painters
Animal painting and illustration *(Drawing, NC780; Painting, ND1380)*
  Here are entered works on the art of animal painting and illustration. Popular works containing chiefly pictures and photographs of animals are entered under the heading Animal pictures. Scientific works of which the plates form the more important feature are entered under the heading Zoology—Pictorial works.
  sa Animals in art
    Bees in art
    Birds in art
    Design, Decorative—Animal forms
   subdivision Pictures, illustrations, etc. *under names of animals, e.g.* Cats—Pictures, illustrations, etc.
  x Animal drawing
  xx Animals in art
    Art
    Painting
  Notes under Animal pictures; Zoology—Pictorial works
— Juvenile literature
Animal parasites
  See Parasites
Animal photography
  See Photography of animals
Animal pictures *(Animal culture, SF76; Art, N7660)*
  Here are entered collections of illustrations which are mainly popular in character. Scientific works are entered under the heading Zoology—Pictorial works. *Cf.* Animal painting and illustration.
  sa Domestic animals—Pictorial works
    Natural history—Pictorial works
   subdivisions Pictorial works *and* Pictures, illustrations, etc. *under names of animals*
  x Animals—Pictorial works
  xx Animals in art
    Natural history—Pictorial works
    Pictures

Notes under Animal painting and illustration;
    Zoology—Pictorial works
  — Juvenile literature
Animal pigments
  sa Bile pigments
    Blood—Pigments
    Chromatophores
    Color of animals
    Melanin
    Visual pigments
  x Pigments in animals
  xx Chromatophores
    Color of animals
    Pigments (Biology)
Animal poetry
  See Animals—Poetry
Animal poisons
  See Venom
Animal populations *(Indirect)*
  sa Ammocoetes populations
    Arthropod populations
    Bird populations
    Fish populations
    Home range
    Mammal populations
    Population genetics
    Reptile populations
    Rodent populations
  x Population biology
    Populations, Animal
  xx Colonies (Biology)
    Ecology
    Population
    Wildlife management
    Zoology—Ecology
  — Juvenile literature
  — Mathematical models
Animal products
  sa Animal gut industries
    Bone products
    Dairy products
    Meat
    Raw materials
    Slaughtering and slaughter-houses—
      By-products
    names of particular products, e.g. Hides
      and skins, Ivory, Wool
  x Products, Animal
  xx Chemistry, Technical
    Commercial products
  — Analysis
  — — Laboratory manuals
  — Marketing
  — Quality control *(TS1955)*
Animal psychology
  See Psychology, Comparative
Animal quarantine
  See Quarantine, Veterinary
Animal remains (Archaeology) *(Indirect)*
  (CC76.5.A5)
  sa Kitchen-middens
  x Zooarchaeology
    Zoology in archaeology
  xx Archaeology—Methodology
    Bones
    Paleoecology
    Paleontology
Animal restraint
  See Animal immobilization
Animal sculptors *(Direct)*
  x Animaliers
  xx Sculptors
Animal sculpture *(Direct)*
  xx Animals in art
    Sculpture
Animal signs
  See Animal tracks

Animal societies
  Here are entered works on groups of animals which are characterized by specific social patterns due to their proximity, interrelationships, and/or
  similarities. Works on groupings of
  physically interconnected animals
  having a common ancestor through
  asexual reproduction are entered under the heading Animal colonies.
  sa Insect societies
    Social behavior in animals
  xx Biotic communities
    Zoology—Ecology
  Note under Animal colonies
  — Juvenile literature
Animal sounds
  sa Bird-song
    Fish sounds
    Game calling (Hunting)
    Insect sounds
    Vocal sac
  x Animal language
  xx Animal communication
    Bioacoustics
    Nature sounds
    Sound production by animals
  — Juvenile literature
Animal stories
  See Animals, Legends and stories of
Animal symbolism
  See Animal lore
Animal tagging
  See Animal marking
Animal taxonomy
  See Zoology—Classification
Animal technicians
  See Laboratory animal technicians
Animal tracks *(QL768)*
  sa Tracking and trailing
  x Animal signs
    Tracks of animals
  xx Tracking and trailing
  — Juvenile literature
  — Pictorial works
Animal training
  See Animals, Training of
Animal traps *(Indirect) (SK283.2)*
  x Traps, Animal
  xx Trapping—Equipment and supplies
  — Collectors and collecting *(Direct)*
Animal trials and punishment
  See Animals, Prosecution and punishment
  of
Animal waste *(Indirect)*
  sa Farm manure
    Slaughtering and slaughter-houses—
      By-products
  x Farm waste
    Livestock waste
    Packing-house waste
    Slaughtering and slaughter-houses—
      Waste
  xx Agricultural wastes
    Factory and trade waste
Animal weapons *(QL940-943)*
  sa Animal defenses
    specific animal weapons, e.g. Antlers,
      Horns
  x Defense mechanisms of animals
    Defense mechanisms (Zoology)
    Self-defense in animals
    Self-protection in animals
  xx Animal defenses
    Morphology (Animals)
  — Juvenile literature
Animal worship *(Direct) (BL439-443)*
  sa Serpent worship

  x Animals (in religion, folk-lore, etc.)
    Zoolatry
  xx Animal lore
    Nature worship
Animalcules *(QL365)*
  sa Infusoria
    Microscope and microscopy
  xx Micro-organisms
    Zoology
Animaliers
  See Animal painters
    Animal sculptors
Animals
  sa Animal culture
    Animals and civilization
    Aquatic animals
    Circus animals
    Zoo animals
  xx Zoology
  — Air transportation
    See Animals, Air transportation of
  — Caricatures and cartoons
  — Food
    See Animals, Food habits of
  — Identification
    x Zoology—Identification
    xx Zoology—Classification
  — Juvenile literature
  — Legends and stories
    See Animals, Legends and stories of
  — Pictorial works
    See Animal pictures
  — Poetry
    x Animal poetry
      Animals, Treatment of—Poetry
  — Quotations, maxims, etc.
  — Songs and music *(M1977.A5;*
    M1978.A5)
  — Tariff
    See Duty-free importation of animals
  — Transportation
    sa Animals, Air transportation of
      Railroads—Livestock transportation
      subdivision Transportation *under*
      specific animals and groups of
      animals, e.g. Sheep—
      Transportation; Domestic animals
      —Transportation
    x Animals, Transportation of
      Stock and stock-breeding—
      Transportation by rail
      Transportation of animals
  — Transportation, Air
    See Animals, Air transportation of
Animals, Abnormalities of
  See Abnormalities (Animals)
Animals, Air transportation of
  x Air transportation of animals
    Animals—Air transportation
    Animals—Transportation, Air
    Transportation of animals by air
  xx Aeronautics, Commercial—Freight
    Animals—Transportation
  — Juvenile literature
Animals, Aquatic
  See Aquatic animals
Animals, Bloodsucking
  See Bloodsucking animals
Animals, Color of
  See Color of animals
Animals, Cruelty to
  See Animals, Treatment of
Animals, Diseases of
  See Veterinary medicine
Animals, Domestic
  See Domestic animals
Animals, Domestication of
  See Domestication

Animals, Edible
   See Animal food
Animals, Experimental
   See Laboratory animals
Animals, Extinct
   See Extinct animals
Animals, Feral
   See Feral livestock
Animals, Fictitious
   See Animals, Mythical
Animals, Food habits of *(QL756)*
   sa Food chains (Ecology)
     Game and game-birds—Feeding and
      feeds
      subdivisions Feeding and feeds *and*
      Food *under kinds of animals, e.g.*
      Cattle—Feeding and feeds; Deer—
      Food
   x Animals—Food
     Feeding behavior
     Food habits of animals
     Food of animals
   xx Animals, Habits and behavior of
     Food
   — Juvenile literature
Animals, Fossil
   See Paleontology
Animals, Geographical distribution of
   See Zoogeography
Animals, Habitations of *(QL756)*
   sa Habitat selection
     Nest building
   x Animal homes
   — Identification
   — Juvenile literature
Animals, Habits and behavior of
      (QL750-785)
   sa Aggressive behavior in animals
     Agonistic behavior in animals
     Alarm reaction
     Animal defenses
     Animal intelligence
     Animal migration
     Animal navigation
     Animal orientation
     Animals as artists
     Animals, Food habits of
     Animals, Infancy of
     Animals, Legends and stories of
     Behavior genetics
     Burrowing animals
     Courtship of animals
     Crustacea—Behavior
     Displacement activity (Animal
      behavior)
     Eliminative behavior
     Herding behavior in animals
     Hibernation
     Insect societies
     Instinct
     Irritability
     Mimicry (Biology)
     Nature study
     Nest building
     Nocturnal animals
     Parental behavior in animals
     Ritualization
     Sexual behavior in animals
     Social behavior in animals
     Solunar theory
     Territoriality (Zoology)
     Tracking and trailing
   x Animal behavior
     Behavior (Psychology)
     Ethology
     Habits of animals
   xx Animal intelligence
     Animals, Legends and stories of

Hibernation
   Nature study
   Zoology
   — Juvenile literature
   — Laboratory manuals
   — Mathematical models
   — Terminology
Animals, Imaginary
   See Animals, Mythical
Animals, Infancy of
   sa Parental behavior in animals
   x Animal babies
     Baby animals
     Infancy of animals
   xx Animals, Habits and behavior of
     Parental behavior in animals
   — Juvenile literature
   — Pictorial works
   — — Juvenile literature
Animals, Injurious and beneficial
   See Zoology, Economic
Animals, Irritability of
   See Irritability
Animals, Legends and stories of *(QL791-5;*
     PZ)
   sa Animal films
     Animal lore
     Animals, Habits and behavior of
     Animals in literature
     Buffaloes (in religion, folk-lore, etc.)
     Cats (in religion, folk-lore, etc.)
     Cows (in religion, folk-lore, etc.)
     Fables
     Nature study
     Swan (in religion, folk-lore, etc.)
     Dogs—Legends and stories; Elephants
      —Legends and stories; *and similar*
      headings
   x Animal stories
     Animals—Legends and stories
     Legends and stories of animals
     Zoological mythology
   xx Animal lore
     Animals, Habits and behavior of
     Animals in literature
     Fables
     Folk-lore
     Nature stories
     Nature study
Animals, Migration of
   See Animal migration
Animals, Movements of
   See Animal locomotion
     Animal mechanics
     Irritability
Animals, Mythical *(GR820-830)*
   sa Animal lore
     Dragons
     Griffins
     Mermaids
     Sea monsters
     Unicorns
     Vampires
     Werwolves
     Zoology—Pre-Linnean works
   x Animals, Fictitious
     Animals, Imaginary
     Fictitious animals
     Imaginary animals
     Mythical animals
     Zoological mythology
   xx Animal lore
     Dragons
     Mythology
   — Juvenile literature
Animals, Mythical, in art *(N7745.A5)*
   xx Art
     Symbolism in art

— Juvenile literature
Animals, Nocturnal
   See Nocturnal animals
Animals, Parthenogenesis in
   See Parthenogenesis (Animals)
Animals, Photography of
   See Photography of animals
Animals, Poisonous
   See Poisonous animals
Animals, Predatory
   See Predatory animals
Animals, Prosecution and punishment of
      (GT6715)
   x Animal trials and punishment
     Trials of animals
   xx Animal lore
     Superstition
Animals, Protection of
   See Animals, Treatment of
     Wildlife conservation
Animals, Rare
   See Rare animals
Animals, Respiration of
   See Respiration
Animals, Sea
   See Marine fauna
Animals, Sound production by
   See Sound production by animals
Animals, Training of *(GV1829-1831)*
   sa Cats—Training
     Dogs—Training
     Domestication
     Horse-training
   x Animal training
     Training of animals
   xx Circus
     Domestication
     Menageries
Animals, Transmutation of
   See Transmutation of animals
Animals, Transportation of
   See Animals—Transportation
Animals, Treatment of *(Direct)*
      (HV4701-4959)
   sa Check-rein
     Curb-bit
     Hunting—Moral and religious aspects
     Vivisection
   x Animals, Cruelty to
     Animals, Protection of
     Humane treatment of animals
     Kindness to animals
     Prevention of cruelty to animals
     Protection of animals
   xx Cruelty
     Domestic animals
     Ethics
   — Juvenile literature
   — Law and legislation *(Direct)*
   — Moral and religious aspects
   — Poetry
     See Animals—Poetry
   — Societies, etc.
     x Humane societies
   — Study and teaching
     See Humane education
Animals, Treatment of (Jewish law)
Animals, Useful and harmful
   See Zoology, Economic
Animals, War use of *(UH87-100)*
   sa Dogs, War use of
Animals (in numismatics)
Animals (in religion, folk-lore, etc.)
   See Animal lore
     Animal worship
Animals and children
   See Children and animals

Animals and civilization *(QL85)*
  sa Zoology, Economic
  xx Animals
     Civilization
  — Juvenile literature
Animals and parapsychology
  See Parapsychology and animals
Animals as artists *(QL785)*
  x Apes as artists
    Art production by animals
  xx Animals, Habits and behavior of
Animals as carriers of disease
  sa Dogs as carriers of disease
    Gasteropoda as carriers of disease
    Insects as carriers of disease
    Rodents as carriers of disease
  xx Communicable diseases
    Diseases—Transmission
    Virus-vector relationships
    Zoology, Medical
  — Juvenile literature
Animals as food
  See Animal food
Animals as parents
  See Parental behavior in animals
Animals as represented on the stage
  x Animals in the theater
    Theater—Animals
  xx Animals in literature
    Theater
Animals in art
  sa Action in art
    Animal fighting in art
    Animal painting and illustration
    Animal pictures
    Animal sculpture
    Bulls ₍Horses, etc.₎ in art
    Design, Decorative—Animal forms
  xx Animal painting and illustration
    Art
Animals in folk-lore
  See Animal lore
Animals in literature
  sa Animal lore
    Animals as represented on the stage
    Animals, Legends and stories of
    Birds in literature; Horses in literature;
      and similar headings
  x Animals in poetry
  xx Animals, Legends and stories of
Animals in moving-pictures
  xx Moving-pictures
Animals in poetry
  See Animals in literature
Animals in police work
  sa Police dogs
  x Police animals
  — Juvenile literature
Animals in research
  See Laboratory animals
Animals in the Bible
  See Bible—Natural history
Animals in the theater
  See Animals as represented on the stage
Animated cartoons
  See Moving-picture cartoons
Animated cartoons by computer
  See Computer animation
Animation, Computer
  See Computer animation
Animation (Cinematography) *(TR897.5)*
  sa Computer animation
    Moving-picture cartoons
  xx Moving-picture cartoons
Animism *(GN471)*
  sa Bon (Tibetan religion)
    Fetishism
    Hylozoism

    Idealism
    Idols and images
    Materialism
    Panpsychism
    Soul
    Soul worship
    Spiritualism
    Transmigration
  xx Fetishism
    Folk-lore
    Hylozoism
    Mana
    Soul
Anions *(QD553)*
  — Spectra
Anisomyaria, Fossil
  xx Lamellibranchiata, Fossil
Anisotropic crystals
  See Anisotropy
Anisotropy
  x Anisotropic crystals
  xx Crystallography
    Matter—Properties
Anitya (Buddhism)
  See Impermanence (Buddhism)
Ankle *(QM131)*
  sa Anklebone
  — Ankylosis
  — Diseases
    sa Ankle—Radiography
  — Excision
    See Excision of ankle
  — Fracture
  — Innervation
  — Radiography
    xx Ankle—Diseases
  — Surgery
  — Wounds and injuries
Ankle-bone
  See Anklebone
Ankle reflex
  See Achilles reflex
Anklebone
  x Ankle-bone
    Astragalus (Anklebone)
  xx Ankle
Ankylosing spondylitis *(RD771.A5)*
  x Bechterew's disease
    Marie-Struempell disease
    Spondylarthritis ankylopoietica
    Spondylitis ankylopoietica
  xx Spine—Diseases
Ankylosis
  sa Arthrodesis
    subdivision Ankylosis *under names of*
     specific joints, e.g. Shoulder joint—
     Ankylosis
Ankylostoma
  See Hookworms
Ankylostomiasis
  See Hookworm disease
ANNA project
  See Project ANNA
Annals
  See Chronology, Historical
    History
Annamese
  See Vietnamese
Annapolis
  — Riot, 1847
Annates *(BX1950)*
  sa Church finance
    Tithes
  x First fruits
  xx Church finance
    Fees, Ecclesiastical
    Tithes

Annealing of crystals
  xx Crystals
Annealing of glass *(TP858)*
  xx Glass manufacture
Annealing of metals
  sa Tempering
  xx Metals—Heat treatment
    Recrystallization (Metallurgy)
    Steel—Heat treatment
Annelida *(Indirect)* *(QL391.A6)*
  sa Archiannelida
    Chaetopoda
    Earthworms
    Gephyrea
    Leeches
    Myzostomaria
    Oligochaeta
    Polychaeta
    Tube worms
  — Identification
  — Juvenile literature
Annexation (County government) *(Direct)*
  x County annexation
  xx Cities and towns—Growth
    County government
    Local government
Annexation (International law)
  sa subdivision Annexation *under names of*
    territories annexed, e.g. Baltic States
    —Annexation to Russia; Texas—
    Annexation to the United States
  x Cession of territory
  xx Acquisition of territory
    International law
    Territory, National
Annexation (Municipal government) *(Direct)*
    (United States, JS344.A5)
  x Municipal annexation
  xx Cities and towns—Growth
    Local government
    Metropolitan areas
    Metropolitan government
    Municipal corporations
    Municipal government
    Municipal incorporation
  — Public opinion
Annihilation
  See Annihilationism
Annihilation, Positron
  See Positron annihilation
Annihilation, Proton and antiproton
  See Proton and antiproton annihilation
Annihilation (Nuclear reactions)
  See Annihilation reactions
Annihilation reactions *(QC794)*
  sa Positron annihilation
    Proton and antiproton annihilation
  x Annihilation (Nuclear reactions)
  xx Nuclear reactions
    Particles (Nuclear physics)
    Photons
Annihilationism *(BT930)*
  Here are entered works dealing with the
    theory that at death the body and soul
    of man are annihilated.
  sa Future punishment
  x Annihilation
    Conditionalism
    Conditioned immortality
    Immortality, Conditional
    Mortalism
  xx Death
    Eschatology
    Future punishment
    Immortality
    Nirvana
    Universalism

Anniversaries *(AS7)*
  sa Church anniversaries
    Days
    Festivals
    Holidays
    Wedding anniversaries
    subdivision Anniversaries, etc. *under*
      Biography, *names of individuals,*
      historic events, institutions, and
      places, e.g. Lincoln, Abraham, Pres.
      U.S., 1809-1865—Anniversaries, etc.;
      Harvard University—Anniversaries,
      etc.; *also subdivision* Centennial
      celebrations, etc. *under names of*
      places and historic events, e.g.
      Colorado—Centennial celebrations,
      etc.
  x Commemorations
  xx Days
    Festivals
    Holidays
    Memorials
Anniversary editions of newspapers
  See Newspapers—Anniversary editions
Anniversary rites and ceremonies
  See Memorial rites and ceremonies
Anniversary volumes
  See Festschriften
Anno santo
  See Holy Year
Annobon dialect
  x Ambu dialect
Annotations and citations (Law) *(Direct)*
  sa Citation of legal authorities
    Law reports, digests, etc.
  x Citations (Law)
    Legal citations
  xx Law reports, digests, etc.
  Note under Citation of legal authorities
Announcements, Business
  See Business announcements
Announcing for radio
  See Radio announcing
Announcing for television
  See Television announcing
Annual assessment work on mining claims
  See Mining claims
Annual improvement factor
  See Wages and labor productivity
Annual income guarantee
  See Guaranteed annual income
Annual parallax
  See Parallax—Stars
Annual reports, Corporate
  See Corporation reports
Annual wage plans
  See Wages—Annual wage
Annual wild rice
  See Wild rice
Annuals
  See Almanacs
    Calendars
    Gift-books (Annuals, etc.)
    Yearbooks
Annuals (Plants)
  x Therophytes
  xx Floriculture
    Flowers
    Plants, Cultivated
  — Pictorial works
Annuities *(Direct)* *(Life insurance,*
  HG8790-8793; Taxation, HJ4631)
  sa Pensions
    Survivors' benefits
    Variable annuities

    subdivisions Pensions *and* Salaries,
    pensions, etc. *under subjects, e.g.*
    Lawyers—Pensions; United States.
    Congress—Salaries, pensions, etc.
  xx Contracts, Aleatory
    Insurance, Life
    Investments
    Pensions
  — Tables *(HG8793)*
    sa Interest and usury—Tables, etc.
    x Amortization tables
    xx Interest and usury—Tables, etc.
  — Taxation *(Direct)*
Annuities, Variable
  See Variable annuities
Annulment of marriage
  See Marriage—Annulment
Annunciation of the Virgin Mary
  See Mary, Virgin—Annunciation
Anodic oxidation of metals
  See Metals—Anodic oxidation
Anodizing
  See Metals—Anodic oxidation
Anointings
  See Unction
Anomaeans
  See Eunomianism
Anomalies, Gravity
  See Gravity anomalies
Anomalous water
  See Polywater
Anomie
  See Anomy
Anomy
  x Anomie
  xx Anarchism and anarchists
    Government, Resistance to
    Social psychology
    Sociology
    State, The
Anonymous architecture
  See Architecture, Anonymous
Anonymous classics (Cataloging)
  See Cataloging of anonymous classics
Anonymous letters *(HV6632)*
  x Poison pen letters
  xx Anonyms and pseudonyms
    Criminal psychology
    Letters
Anonymous painters *(Direct)*
  x Masters, Unnamed
    Unnamed masters
  xx Painters
Anonymous paintings *(Direct)*
  x Paintings without authors
  xx Paintings
Anonyms and pseudonyms *(Z1041-1115)*
  sa Anagrams
    Anonymous letters
    Homonymous authors
    Imaginary books and libraries
    Imprints (in books), Fictitious
  x Fictitious names
    Names, Fictitious
    Noms de plume
    Pseudonyms
  xx Authors
    Bibliography
    Names, Personal
  — Law and legislation *(Direct)*
    xx Names, Personal—Law
Anonyms and pseudonyms, American,
  [English, French, etc.]
  x Authors, American [English, French,
    etc.]—Pseudonyms
Anoplura *(Indirect)* *(QL503.A6)*
  sa Bird-lice
    Lice

  x Phthiraptera
  xx Bird-lice
    Insects
Anorexia
  sa Appetite
  xx Appetite
Anorexia nervosa
Anorexigenic agents
  See Weight reducing preparations
Anorthosite *(QE461)*
  xx Feldspar
    Rocks, Igneous
Anostraca
  xx Branchiopoda
ANOVA 45 (Computer program)
Anoxaemia
  See Anoxemia
Anoxemia
  sa Oxygen in the body
  x Anoxaemia
    Anoxhemia
    Anoxia
    Hypoxemia
    Hypoxia
    Oxygen deficiency in the blood
  xx Altitude, Influence of
    Asphyxia
    Aviation medicine
    Blood—Analysis and chemistry
    Hemoglobin
    Oxygen in the body
    Oxygen—Physiological effect
    Respiration
Anoxhemia
  See Anoxemia
Anoxia
  See Anoxemia
Ansar *(BP75.5)*
  x Helpers of Muḥammad, the prophet
  xx Companions of Muḥammad, the
    prophet
Ansarii
  See Nosairians
Anschluss movement, 1918-1938
  xx Austria—History—1918-1938
    Germany—History—1918-1933
    Germany—History—1933-1945
Anserma Indians
  x Ansermas
  xx Indians of South America
Ansermas
  See Anserma Indians
Answers to questions
  See Questions and answers
Ant
  See Ants
Ant bear
  See Aardvark
Ant control *(Indirect)*
  sa Imported fire ant—Control
  x Ants—Control
Ant lions *(QL513.M)*
  xx Neuroptera
Antagonism (Bacteria)
  See Antibiosis
Antagonists, Enzyme
  See Enzyme inhibitors
Antaisaka
  x Antisaka
Antaisaka dialect *(PL5379)*
  x Antesaka dialect
  xx Malagasy language—Dialects
Antalcidas, Peace of, 387 B.C. *(DF231.55)*
  xx Greece—History—Corinthian War,
    395-386 B.C.
Antandroy dialect
  xx Malagasy language

Antarctic expeditions
  See Antarctic regions
    names of expeditions, e.g. United States
      Exploring Expedition, 1838-1842;
      and names of ships
Antarctic flora
  See Botany—Antarctic regions
Antarctic regions   *(G850-890; Botany,*
    QK474; Meteorology, QC994.9;
    Natural history, QH84.2; Terrestrial
    magnetism, QC825.9; Zoology,
    QL106)
  sa Physical geography—Antarctic regions
    Scientific expeditions
    South Pole
    names of exploring expeditions and
      names of explorers
  x Antarctic expeditions
    Antarctic regions—Description and
      travel
    Antarctic regions—Discovery and
      exploration
    Expeditions, Antarctic
    Polar expeditions
  xx Discoveries (in geography)
    Earth
    Polar regions
    South Pole
  Example under Scientific expeditions; Voyages
    and travels
  — Aerial exploration
    xx Aeronautics—Flights
  —— Juvenile literature
  — Description and travel
    See Antarctic regions
  — Discovery and exploration
    See Antarctic regions
  — International status
    Example under International law
  — Juvenile literature
Ante-nuptial contracts
  See Antenuptial contracts
Antediluvian animals
  See Paleontology
Antélangue (Artificial language)   *(PM8079.7)*
  xx Languages, Artificial
Antelope ground squirrel
  See White-tailed antelope squirrel
Antelopes   *(Indirect) (QL737.U5)*
  sa Blue antelope
    Elands
    Gnus
    Oryx
    Pronghorn antelope
    Sable antelope
    Saiga
    Uganda Kob
    White-eared kob
  xx Deer
    Ruminantia
  Example under Zoology
  — Legends and stories
Antelopes, Fossil   *(QE882.U3)*
Antemoro (Madagascan people)
  xx Ethnology—Madagascar
Antenna arrays
  sa Phased array antennas
  xx Antennas (Electronics)
Antenna feeds   *(TK7871.6)*
  x Feeds, Antenna
  xx Antennas (Electronics)
    Radio lines
Antennas, Phased array
  See Phased array antennas
Antennas, Radar
  See Radar—Antennas
Antennas, Radio
  See Radio—Antennas

Antennas (Electronics)   *(TK7872.A6)*
  sa Antenna arrays
    Antenna feeds
    Microwave lenses
    Microwave pillboxes
    Phased array antennas
    Radar—Antennas
    Radar confusion reflectors
    Radio—Antennas
    Radio, Short wave—Antennas
    Radio telescope
    Television—Antennas
  xx Electronic apparatus and appliances
  — Computer programs
  — Tables, calculations, etc.
Antenuptial contracts   *(Direct)*
  sa Settlements (Law)
  x Ante-nuptial contracts
    Marriage articles
    Marriage contracts
    Prenuptial contracts
  xx Husband and wife
    Settlements (Law)
Antenuptial contracts (Canon law)
Anterior commissure
  x Commissure, Anterior
  xx Brain—Anatomy
Anterior pituitary gland
  See Adenohypophysis
Anterior spinal paralysis
  See Poliomyelitis
Antesaka dialect
  See Antaisaka dialect
Anthelmintics   *(RM635)*
  sa Nematocides
    Pumpkin seed
    Santonin
  x Vermifuges
  xx Anti-infective agents
    Gastrointestinal agents
    Medical helminthology
    Veterinary helminthology
Anthem
  xx Church music
    Musical form
Anthems
    Here are entered collections of anthems
    and separately published anthems. The
    heading is used only as a second head-
    ing, *e.g.* 1. Choruses, Sacred (Mixed
    voices, 5 parts) with orchestra—To
    1800. 2. Anthems.
  sa Choruses, Sacred
Anthems, National
  See National songs
Anthocerotales   *(QK557)*
  xx Liverworts
Anthocyanidins
  xx Anthocyanin
    Color of flowers
    Plant pigments
Anthocyanin   *(QK898.A6)*
  sa Anthocyanidins
  xx Color of flowers
    Glucosides
    Plant pigments
Anthologies   *(PN6010-6054)*
    Here are entered collections of general
    interest, too broad to use more specific
    headings such as Literature—Collec-
    tions; Quotations; Sports stories, etc.
  sa Gift-books (Annuals, etc.)
    Literature—Collections
    Readers
    names of literatures
  x Chrestomathies
Anthomedusae   *(QL377.H9)*
  xx Hydrozoa

Anthophora
  See Mason-bees
Anthozoa   *(QL377.C5-7)*
  sa Alcyonaria
    Corals
    Madreporaria
    Sea-anemones
    Sea-pens
    Zoantharia
  x Actinozoa
  xx Coelenterata
    Marine fauna
Anthracene   *(QD393)*
  sa Phenanthrene
Anthracene crystals
  — Radiation effects
    See Anthracene crystals, Effect of
      radiation on
Anthracene crystals, Effect of radiation on
  x Anthracene crystals—Radiation effects
  xx Radiation
Anthracite coal   *(Indirect) (HD9450-9559;*
    TN820-823)
  xx Coal
    Fuel
Anthracite Coal Strike, 1887-1888
    (HD5325.M63 1887)
  Note under Strikes and lockouts
Anthracite Coal Strike, 1902   *(HD5325.M63*
    1902)
Anthracite Coal Strike, 1922   *(HD5325.M63*
    1922)
Anthracite Coal Strike, 1925-1926
    (HD5325.M63 1925)
Anthracnose   *(SB741.A55)*
  sa Coffee anthracnose
  xx Fungi in agriculture
Anthracosauria   *(QE868.A48)*
  x Batrachosauria
Anthracosis
  See Lungs—Dust diseases
Anthranil   *(QD401)*
Anthraquinones   *(QD305.K2)*
  — Spectra
Anthrax   *(RC121.A6; Bacteriology,*
    QR201.A6)
  sa Pustule, Malignant
  x Cumberland disease
  xx Occupational diseases
  Example under Bacterial diseases
  — Preventive inoculation   *(RM755)*
    Example under Inoculation; *and under*
      reference from Preventive inocula-
      tion
Anthrax, Symptomatic   *(Veterinary medicine,*
    SF787)
  x Black quarter
    Blackleg
    Symptomatic anthrax
  xx Cattle—Diseases
Anthropo-geography   *(Indirect) (GF)*
  sa Communication in anthropogeography
    Geography, Political
    Geopolitics
    Human ecology
    Man—Influence of climate
    Man—Influence of environment
    Man—Migrations
    Regionalism
  x Environment
    Geographical distribution of man
    Geography, Social
    Human geography
  xx Anthropology
    Emigration and immigration
    Ethnology
    Geography
    Geopolitics

Anthropo-geography *(Indirect)* *(GF)*
(Continued)
    History
    Human ecology
    Man—Influence of environment
   Note under Geography, Historical
— Juvenile literature   *(GF37)*
— Methodology
Anthropological institutes
   See Anthropological societies
Anthropological museums and collections
    (Indirect) *(GN35-41)*
   sa Archaeological museums and
      collections
    Ethnological museums and collections
   xx Museums
Anthropological research   *(Direct)*
   x Anthropology—Research
   xx Research
Anthropological societies   *(Indirect)*
   x Anthropological institutes
Anthropologists   *(Indirect)* *(GN20-21)*
   sa Anthropology as a profession
   xx Anthropology as a profession
    Scientists
— Juvenile literature
Anthropologists, Women
Anthropology   *(GN)*
   sa Acculturation
    Age groups
    Anthropo-geography
    Anthropometry
    Applied anthropology
    Archaeology
    Assimilation (Sociology)
    Civilization
    Color of man
    Componential analysis in anthropology
    Craniology
    Educational anthropology
    Ethnology
    Ethnopsychology
    Historical sociology
    Language and languages
    Man
    Mathematical anthropology
    Medical anthropology
    National characteristics
    Nomads
    Social change
    Somatology
    Technical assistance—Anthropological
      aspects
    Woman
   names of races, tribes, etc., e.g.
    Caucasian race; Guayaqui Indians;
    and subdivision Race question *under*
    names of countries, e.g. United
    States—Race question
   xx Civilization
    Man
— Abstracts
— Anecdotes, facetiae, satire, etc.
— Classification   *(GN34)*
— Early works to 1870
— Field work
   x Field work (Anthropology)
   xx Anthropology—Methodology
— Juvenile literature   *(GN31.5)*
— Methodology
   sa Anthropology—Field work
    Mathematical anthropology
— Publishing
   See Anthropology publishing
— Research
   See Anthropological research
— Vocational guidance
   See Anthropology as a profession

Anthropology, Biblical
   See Man (Theology)
Anthropology, Criminal
   See Criminal anthropology
Anthropology, Doctrinal
   See Man (Theology)
Anthropology, Philosophical
   See Philosophical anthropology
Anthropology, Physical
   See Somatology
Anthropology, Prehistoric
    Here are entered works on the science, its
    history, methods, scope, etc. Works
    treating of prehistoric man are entered
    under the heading Man, Prehistoric,
    and under names of countries, cities,
    etc., with subdivision Antiquities.
   sa Archaeology
   x Prehistoric anthropology
   xx Man, Prehistoric
Anthropology, Structural
   See Structural anthropology
Anthropology, Theological
   See Man (Theology)
Anthropology as a profession
   sa Anthropologists
   x Anthropology—Vocational guidance
   xx Anthropologists
Anthropology publishing   *(Z286.A5)*
   x Anthropology—Publishing
   xx Publishers and publishing
Anthropometry   *(Indirect)* *(GN51-59;*
    GV435)
   sa Bertillon system
    Body size
    Body weight
    Craniology
    Craniometry
    Criminal anthropology
    Fingerprints
    Indians of North America—
      Anthropometry
    Palmprints
    Physical fitness—Testing
    Proportion (Anthropometry)
   x Criminal anthropometry
    Skeletal remains
   xx Anthropology
    Bioengineering
    Body size
    Craniometry
    Ethnology
    Man
    Somatology
   Notes under Bones; Skeleton
— Eskimos
   See Eskimos—Anthropometry
— Instruments   *(GN53)*
— Jews
   See Jews—Anthropometry
— Lapps
   See Lapps—Anthropometry
— Polynesians
   See Polynesians—Anthropometry
— Statistical methods
— Tables, etc.
Anthropomorphism   *(BL215)*
   xx Analogy (Religion)
    Ejection (Psychology)
    God
    Symbolism
Anthropophagy
   See Cannibalism
Anthroposophy   *(BP595)*
   sa Karma
    Reincarnation
    Theosophy
   x Human science

   xx Karma
    Reincarnation
    Theosophy
— Controversial literature
Anti-acceleration suits
   See Pressure suits
Anti-aircraft artillery
   sa Anti-aircraft guns
    Artillery, Coast
   x Artillery, Anti-aircraft
   xx Air defenses, Military
    Artillery
    Artillery, Coast
Anti-aircraft guns   *(UF625)*
   sa Artillery
    Machine-guns
   xx Air defenses, Military
    Air warfare
    Anti-aircraft artillery
    Artillery
    Machine-guns
Anti-aircraft missiles
   See Falcon (Missile)
    Nike rocket
Anti-American propaganda
   See Propaganda, Anti-American
Anti-antibodies
   xx Antigens and antibodies
Anti-blackout suits
   See Pressure suits
Anti-Catholicism   *(Direct)* *(BX1766)*
   sa Catholic Church—Doctrinal and
      controversial works
   x Antipapism
   xx Catholic Church—Doctrinal and
      controversial works
    Prejudices and antipathies
— United States
   sa Nativism
Anti-clericalism   *(Direct)*
   xx Catholic Church—Doctrinal and
      controversial works—Protestant
      authors
    Church and state
    Freemasons and Catholic Church
    Secularism
— Anecdotes, facetiae, satire, etc.
Anti-clericalism in literature
Anti-colonialism
   See Colonies
Anti-comintern pact   *(D749.5.A)*
   x Anti-communist pact
   xx World War, 1939-1945—Diplomatic
    history
    World War, 1939-1945—Treaties
Anti-communist movements   *(Direct)*
   sa Propaganda, Anti-communist
   x Anti-communist resistance
    Underground, Anti-communist
   xx Communism
— Juvenile literature
— Personal narratives
Anti-communist pact
   See Anti-comintern pact
Anti-communist propaganda
   See Propaganda, Anti-communist
Anti-communist resistance
   See Anti-communist movements
Anti-corrosive paint
   See Corrosion and anti-corrosives
Anti-discrimination laws
   See Race discrimination
Anti-freeze solutions
   xx Automobiles—Apparatus and supplies
    Chemical inhibitors
    Freezing points
Anti-German propaganda
   See Propaganda, Anti-German

Anti Indians
See Campa Indians
Anti-infective agents
 sa Anthelmintics
  Antibiotics
  Antimalarials
  Antitubercular agents
  Antiviral agents
  Bacteriocins
  Chemotherapy
  Phytoncides
 x Antibacterial agents
  Antimicrobial agents
  Bacteriocidal agents
  Bacteriostatic agents
 xx Chemotherapy
Anti-inflammatory agents
See Antiphlogistics
Anti-injunction law
See Injunctions
Anti-Japanese movements, Korean
See Korean resistance movements,
 1905-1945
Anti-Japanese propaganda
See Propaganda, Anti-Japanese
Anti-knock compounds
See Gasoline—Anti-knock and anti-knock
 mixtures
 Motor fuels—Anti-knock and
 anti-knock mixtures
Anti language
See Campa language
Anti-Nazi movement *(DD256.3)*
 sa Munich. Universität—Riot, Feb. 18,
  1943
 x German resistance movement
  Resistance movements (World War,
   1939-1945)
  Underground movements (World War,
   1939-1945)
  World War, 1939-1945—Resistance
   movements
  World War, 1939-1945—Underground
   movements—Germany
 xx Germany—History—1933-1945
  National socialism
 — Personal narratives
 — Pictorial works
Anti-obesity drugs
See Weight reducing preparations
Anti-Polish propaganda
See Propaganda, Anti-Polish
Anti-poverty legislation (United States)
See Economic assistance, Domestic—Law
 and legislation—United States
Anti-poverty program (United States)
See Economic assistance, Domestic—
 United States
Anti-poverty programs
See Economic assistance, Domestic
Anti-Reformation
See Counter-Reformation
Anti-rent troubles, New York, 1839-1846
 (HD199)
Anti-Russian propaganda
See Propaganda, Anti-Russian
Anti-submarine warfare
 sa Depth charges
  Destroyer escorts
  Destroyers (Warships)
  Mines, Submarine
  Sonar
  Submarine chasers
 x ASW
 xx Aeronautics, Military
  Destroyers (Warships)
  Submarine warfare

Antiarin
 xx Upas
Antiarrhythmia agents
See Myocardial depressants
Antibabele (Artificial language) *(PM8080)*
 xx Languages, Artificial
Antibacterial agents
See Anti-infective agents
Antiballistic missiles
See Antimissile missiles
Antibiosis
 sa Antibiotics
  Interferons
 x Antagonism (Bacteria)
  Bacterial antagonism
 xx Antibiotics
Antibiotic residues
 — Analysis
Antibiotics *(Pharmacy, RS161; Therapeutics,*
  RM265-7)
 sa Actinomycin
  Actinomycin C
  Antibiosis
  Aureomycin
  Bacitracin
  Chloromycetin
  Circulin
  Erythromycin
  Heptamycin
  Mycostatin
  Neomycin
  Nisin
  Penicillin
  Phytoncides
  Plants, Effect of antibiotics on
  Rifomycin
  Streptomycin
  Subtilin
  Terramycin
  Vancomycin
 xx Anti-infective agents
  Antibiosis
  Chemotherapy
  Microbial metabolites
  Phytoncides
 — Side effects
  x Side effects of antibiotics
 — Standards
 — Study and teaching
 — — Audio-visual aids
 — Testing *(RS190.A5)*
  sa Micro-organisms, Effect of
   antibiotics on
Antibiotics in agriculture
 sa Antibiotics in animal nutrition
  Antibiotics in veterinary medicine
  Plants, Effect of antibiotics on
 xx Agriculture
Antibiotics in animal nutrition
 xx Antibiotics in agriculture
  Antibiotics in nutrition
  Feeding
  Medicated feeds
Antibiotics in food preservation
 xx Food—Preservation
Antibiotics in nutrition
 sa Antibiotics in animal nutrition
 xx Nutrition
Antibiotics in veterinary medicine
 xx Antibiotics in agriculture
  Veterinary medicine
Antibiotics resistance in micro-organisms
See Drug resistance in micro-organisms
Antibodies
See Antigens and antibodies
Antibody-antigen complexes
See Immune complexes

Anticancer agents
See Antineoplastic agents
Anticholesteremic agents
 x Cholesterol inhibitors
  Hypocholesteremic agents
 xx Chemotherapy
Anticholinergic agents
See Parasympatholytic agents
Anticholinesterase agents
See Cholinesterase inhibitors
Antichresis *(Direct)*
 xx Mortgages
  Pledges (Law)
Antichrist *(BT985)*
 xx End of the world
  Eschatology
  Jesus Christ
 — History of doctrines
Anticoagulants (Medicine)
 sa Coumarins
 xx Blood—Coagulation
  Rodenticides
Anticollision lights, Aircraft
See Aeroplanes—Lighting
Anticonvulsants
 x Antiepileptics
 xx Convulsions
  Muscle relaxants
Anticyclones *(Indirect)*
 x High (Meteorology)
  High-pressure system (Meteorology)
 xx Atmospheric pressure
  Dynamic meteorology
  Winds
Antidepressants
 x Psychic energizers
 xx Depression, Mental
  Psychopharmacology
Antidiabetics *(RC661.A1)*
 sa Insulin
 xx Diabetes
Antidiuretic hormone
See Vasopressin
Antidotes
 sa Toxins and antitoxins
 x Antipoisonous agents
 xx Poisons
  Toxins and antitoxins
Antidumping duties *(Direct)*
 x Countervailing duties
 xx Dumping (Commercial policy)
  Tariff
Antiemetics
 xx Neuropharmacology
  Vomiting
Antiepileptics
See Anticonvulsants
Antietam, Battle of, 1862 *(E474.65)*
Antietam Campaign
See Maryland Campaign, 1862
Antiferromagnetism
 xx Ferromagnetism
Antifibrillatory agents
See Myocardial depressants
Antifibrinolytic agents
 sa Trasylol
 x Fibrinolysis inhibitors
 xx Enzyme inhibitors
  Fibrinolysin
Antifoaming agents *(TP159.A47)*
 x Defoaming agents
  Foam inhibitors
  Foam regulators
 xx Chemicals
  Foam
 — Patents
Antigen-antibody complexes
See Immune complexes

Antigens and antibodies
   sa Adjuvants, Immunological
      Anti-antibodies
      Autoantibodies
      Carcinoembronic antigens
      Cardiolipin
      Fluorescent antibody technique
      Gamma globulin
      Haptens
      Hepatitis associated antigen
      Hormone antagonists
      Immunofluorescence
      Immunoglobulins
      Isoantigens
      Precipitin reaction
      Rh factor
   x Antibodies
   xx Immunity
      Immunoglobulins
      Immunology
      Serology
      Serumtherapy
      Toxins and antitoxins
  — Analysis
     sa Immunoassay
  — Catalogs and collections
Antigorite
   xx Serpentine
Antihistamines
   xx Allergy
      Anaphylaxis
      Histamine
Antihormones
   See Hormone antagonists
Antihypertensive agents
   See Hypotensive agents
Antilleans
Antilleans in France, [etc.]
Antilymphocytic serum
   xx Immunological tolerance
      Serum
  — Computer programs
Antimalarials
   xx Anti-infective agents
      Malarial fever
Antimasonic Party *(E381-390; F123;*
     HS525-7)
   xx Freemasons
Antimatter
   xx Matter—Properties
Antimetabolites *(QP801.A)*
   sa Aldosterone antagonists
      Antivitamins
      Folic acid antagonists
   x Competitive antagonists (Metabolism)
      Metabolic antagonists
   xx Antimitotic agents
      Antineoplastic agents
      Enzyme inhibitors
      Metabolism
Antimicrobial agents
   See Anti-infective agents
Antimilitarism
   See Militarism
Antimissile missiles
   x ABM (Antiballistic missiles)
      Antiballistic missiles
   xx Air defenses, Military
      Guided missiles
  — Juvenile literature
Antimitotic agents
   sa Antimetabolites
   xx Mitosis
      Mutagenesis
Antimony *(Chemistry, QD181.S3;*
     Metallurgy, TN799.A6; Mining,
     TN490.A6)
   x Stibium

Example under Chemicals
— Isotopes
   x Antimony isotopes
      Isotopic antimony
— — Decay
— Prices *(Direct)*
— Therapeutic use *(RM666.A55)*
     sa Tartar emetic
— Toxicology
Antimony alloys
   sa Antimony-tin alloys
      Bismuth-antimony alloys
      Lead-antimony alloys
Antimony-bismuth alloys
   See Bismuth-antimony alloys
Antimony compounds *(QD181.S3)*
   sa Organoantimony compounds
Antimony isotopes
   See Antimony—Isotopes
Antimony-lead alloys
   See Lead-antimony alloys
Antimony ores *(Indirect)* *(TN490.A6)*
Antimony organic compounds
   See Organoantimony compounds
Antimony-tin alloys
   x Tin-antimony alloys
   xx Antimony alloys
      Tin alloys
Antineoplastic agents
   sa Antimetabolites
      Beet juice—Therapeutic use
      Krebiozen
      Nitrogen mustards
   x Anticancer agents
      Cytotoxic drugs
      Drugs, Antineoplastic
      Drugs, Cytotoxic
   xx Cancer
      Cancer—Chemotherapy
      Tumors
Antineutrinos *(QC721)*
   xx Neutrinos
Antinomianism
   sa Brethren of the Free Spirit
      Law and gospel
      Libertines (Spirituals)
      Neonomianism
      Ranters
   xx Assurance (Theology)
      Calvinism
      Congregationalism
      Good works (Theology)
      Law (Theology)
      Theology, Doctrinal
Antinomy *(Kant, B2799.A6)*
Antinomy of the liar
   See Liar paradox
Antinuclear factors
   xx Autoantibodies
Antioch, School of
   See Antiochian school
Antiochene school
   See Antiochian school
Antiochian school
      Here are entered works dealing with the theories of a group of early Christian theologians at Antioch. Common to all of them was a grammatico-historical method of interpreting the Bible in opposition to the allegorical method of the Alexandrian school and a dogmatic theory which tended to separate the divine and human in the person of Christ.
   sa Alexandrian school, Christian
   x Antioch, School of
      Antiochene school
   xx Alexandrian school, Christian

Bible—Criticism, interpretation, etc.—
     History
     Church history—Primitive and early
      church, ca. 30-600
     Jesus Christ—History of doctrines
     Theology, Doctrinal—History—Early
      church, ca. 30-600
Antioxidants
   xx Chemical inhibitors
Antipapism
   See Anti-Catholicism
Antipatharia
   See Antipathidea
Antipathidea
   x Antipatharia
Antipathies
   See Prejudices and antipathies
Antiphlogistics *(RM321)*
   x Anti-inflammatory agents
   xx Antipyretics
      Inflammation
Antiphonaries (Music)
   sa Antiphons (Music)
   xx Catholic Church. Liturgy and ritual.
      Antiphonary
      Sacred vocal music
Antiphons (Music)
   xx Antiphonaries (Music)
      Sacred vocal music
Antipoisonous agents
   See Antidotes
Antipopes *(BX957)*
   x Pseudo-popes
   xx Papacy—History
      Popes
Antiproton and proton annihilation
   See Proton and antiproton annihilation
Antipyretics *(Therapeutics, RM321)*
   sa Antiphlogistics
     names of individual antipyretics, e.g.
      Antipyrin, Phesin
   xx Body temperature
      Fever
      Materia medica
      Therapeutics
Antipyrin *(Therapeutics, RM666.A56)*
   Example under Antipyretics
Antiquarian book trade
   See Antiquarian booksellers
Antiquarian booksellers *(Direct)*
     (Z286.A55; Z287-550; Z998-1000.5)
   sa Bibliography—Rare books
      Book collecting
      Books—Want lists
      Out-of-print books
   x Antiquarian book trade
      Secondhand booksellers
   xx Bibliography—Rare books
      Book collecting
      Books—Want lists
      Booksellers and bookselling
      Out-of-print books
— Correspondence, reminiscences, etc.
Antique dealers *(Direct)*
   sa Mail-order antique business
   xx Art dealers
Antique mail-order business
   See Mail-order antique business
Antiques
   See Collectors and collecting
     subdivision Collectors and collecting
      under subjects, e.g. Furniture—
      Collectors and collecting
Antiques in interior decoration
   xx Art objects—Collectors and collecting
      Interior decoration
Antiquities
   sa Archaeology

Aryan antiquities
Buddhist antiquities
Byzantine antiquities
Christian antiquities
Classical antiquities
Forgery of antiquities
Germanic antiquities
Gold articles, Prehistoric
Hindu antiquities
Illyrian antiquities
Islamic antiquities
Oriental antiquities
Phenician antiquities
Punic antiquities
Shinto antiquities
Slavic antiquities
Turkish antiquities
   subdivision Antiquities *under names of*
    countries, cities, etc.
  x Archaeological specimens
 xx Archaeology
— Collection and preservation
   sa Archaeological museums and
    collections
   xx Archaeological museums and
    collections
Antiquities, Aryan
  See Aryan antiquities
Antiquities, Biblical
  See Bible—Antiquities
Antiquities, Buddhist
  See Buddhist antiquities
Antiquities, Byzantine
  See Byzantine antiquities
Antiquities, Christian
  See Christian antiquities
Antiquities, Classical
  See Classical antiquities
Antiquities, Ecclesiastical
  See Christian antiquities
Antiquities, Forgery of
  See Forgery of antiquities
Antiquities, Germanic
  See Germanic antiquities
Antiquities, Grecian
  See Classical antiquities
    Greece—Antiquities
Antiquities, Hindu
  See Hindu antiquities
Antiquities, Illyrian
  See Illyrian antiquities
Antiquities, Industrial
  See Industrial archaeology
Antiquities, Islamic
  See Islamic antiquities
Antiquities, Legal
  See Law—Antiquities
Antiquities, Muslim
  See Islamic antiquities
Antiquities, Oriental
  See Oriental antiquities
    subdivision Antiquities *under names of*
     countries, cities, etc.
Antiquities, Phenician
  See Phenician antiquities
Antiquities, Prehistoric
  See Archaeology
    Man, Prehistoric
    subdivision Antiquities *under names of*
     countries, cities, etc.
Antiquities, Punic
  See Punic antiquities
Antiquities, Roman
  See Classical antiquities
    Rome—Antiquities
    Rome (City)—Antiquities
    subdivision Antiquities, Roman *under*
     names of countries, cities, etc.

Antiquities, Shinto
  See Shinto antiquities
Antiquities, Slavic
  See Slavic antiquities
Antiquities, Turkish
  See Turkish antiquities
Antiquity of man
  See Man—Origin
Antisaka
  See Antaisaka
Antisemitism *(Direct) (DS145)*
  sa Jews—Persecutions
    Jews—Segregation
  xx Jewish question
    Prejudices and antipathies
    Race problems
Antisemitism and Christianity
  See Christianity and antisemitism
Antisemitism in motion pictures
    (PN1995.9.A55)
  xx Moving-pictures
Antiseptic medication *(RM647-8)*
  x Medication, Antiseptic
  xx Therapeutics
Antiseptic surgery
  See Surgery, Aseptic and antiseptic
Antiseptics *(Surgery, RD91; Therapeutics,*
    RM400)
  sa Asepsis and antisepsis
    Biogan
    Clavicin
    Cytisine
    Disinfection and disinfectants
    Glycozone
    Hydrozone
    Metals as antiseptics
    Phenols
    Surgery, Aseptic and antiseptic
    Vioform
  xx Asepsis and antisepsis
    Bacteriology
    Disinfection and disinfectants
    Putrefaction
    Surgery
    Surgery, Aseptic and antiseptic
Antiseptics in obstetrics *(RG730)*
  x Obstetrics, Antiseptics in
Antisera
  See Immune serums
Antislavery
  See Slavery
Antispasmodics
  sa Barbiturates
    Muscle relaxants
Antistatic agents (Textiles)
  x Textile industry and fabrics—Antistatic
    agents
  xx Electrostatics
    Textile chemistry
— Patents
Antistatic compounds
  See Petroleum products—Antistatic
    additives
Antitank guns *(UF628)*
  xx Artillery, Field and mountain
    Gunnery
    Ordnance
    Tank warfare
    Tanks (Military science)
Antitank warfare
  See Tank warfare
Antitheses (in religion, folk-lore, etc.)
  See Polarity (in religion, folk-lore, etc.)
Antithrombotic agents
  See Fibrinolytic agents
Antithyroid drugs
  See Thyroid antagonists

Antitoxins
  See Toxins and antitoxins
Antitrinitarianism *(Direct)*
  sa Arianism
    Socinianism
    Trinity—Controversial literature
    Unitarianism
  xx Theology, Doctrinal—History
    Trinity
Antitrust laws
  See Trusts, Industrial—Law
Antitubercular agents
  x Drugs, Antitubercular
    Tuberculosis—Chemotherapy
  xx Anti-infective agents
    Chemotherapy
    Tuberculosis
Antitussive agents
  x Drugs, Antitussive
  xx Chemotherapy
    Cough
Antiviral agents
  x Drugs, Antiviral
    Virus diseases—Chemotherapy
  xx Anti-infective agents
    Chemotherapy
    Virus diseases
Antiviruses
  See Virus inhibitors
Antivitamins *(QP801.A)*
  xx Antimetabolites
    Vitamins
Antivivisection
  See Vivisection
Antlers *(QL942)*
  xx Horns
  Example under Animal weapons
— Therapeutic use *(RM666.A57)*
Antlers (in religion, folk-lore, etc.)
  x Folk-lore of antlers
  xx Religion, Primitive
Antliata
  See Diptera
Antoinism *(BX9998.A6)*
  xx Spiritualism
Antoninianus (Coin)
Antonyms
  See subdivision Synonyms and antonyms
    under names of languages, e.g.
    English language—Synonyms and
    antonyms
Antrum of Highmore
  See Maxillary sinus
Antrustions
  x Trustis
  xx Merovingians
    Salic law
Ants *(Indirect) (QL568.F7)*
  sa Army ants
    Carpenter ants
    Fungus ants
    Honey-ants
    Imported fire ant
    Myrmecophilous plants
  x Aculeata
    Ant
    Formicidae
  xx Hymenoptera
    Insect societies
    Insects
— Anatomy
— Behavior
    sa Parasitic ants
    Example under Insects—Behavior
— Control
    See Ant control
— Juvenile literature

Ants *(Indirect)* *(QL568.F7)*
(Continued)
— Legends and stories *(Juvenile, PZ10.3;*
   Zoology, QL795.A65)
— Parasites
  See Parasites—Ants
Ants, Fossil *(QE832.H9)*
Ants, Parasitic
  See Parasitic ants
Ants (in religion, folk-lore, etc.)
  x Folk-lore of ants
  xx Religion, Primitive
Antwerp
— Festivals, etc.
  Example under Festivals
— Longshoremen's Strike, 1907
— Siege, 1584-1585
— Siege, 1832 *(DH652)*
— Siege, 1914 *(D542.A6)*
  xx European War, 1914-1918—
    Campaigns—Belgium
Anuak language
  x Yambo language
  xx Nilotic languages
Anuaks
  x Anwaks
    Anyuaas
    Jambos
    Niuaks
  xx Luo (Nilotic tribe)
Anuclear cells
  See Anucleate cells
Anucleate cells
  x Anuclear cells
  xx Cell nuclei
    Cells
    Unicellular organisms
Anudha language
  See Florida language
Anufo dialect
  x Chakosi dialect
  xx Anyi language
Anura *(Indirect)* *(QL668.E2)*
  sa Toads
  x Ecaudata
    Salientia
  xx Amphibians
— Physiology
Anura, Fossil *(QE868.A5)*
  xx Amphibians, Fossil
Anuria
  x Urination, Absence of
    Urine—Suppression
Anus
— Abnormities and deformities
— Cancer
— Diseases *(RC864-6)*
  xx Proctology
— Surgery *(RD544; RD672)*
  xx Surgery, Orificial
Anus (Psychology)
  sa Scatology
  x Anal character
    Anal eroticism
    Anal reflex
  xx Psychoanalysis
    Psychology, Physiological
    Sex (Psychology)
Anwaks
  See Anuaks
Anxiety
  sa Avoidance (Psychology)
    Defensiveness (Psychology)
    Escape (Psychology)
    Fear
    Obsessive-compulsive neuroses
    Peace of mind
    Shame
    Test anxiety

    Worry
  x Tension
  xx Emotions
    Fear
    Worry
  Example under Neuroses
— Juvenile literature
— Pictorial works
Anxiety (Child psychology)
  sa Kinder-Angst-Test
    Separation anxiety (Child psychology)
  xx Child study
Anxiety in literature
  sa Hypochondria in literature
  xx Emotions in literature
Anyi language
  sa Anufo dialect
  xx Kwa languages
Anyuaas
  See Anuaks
Anzanic language
  See Elamite language
Anzio Beachhead, 1944
  xx World War, 1939-1945—Campaigns—
    Italy
Ao language *(PL4001.A7)*
  x Chungli dialect
    Hatigorria language
    Mongsen dialect
    Mungsen dialect
    Zungi dialect
    Zwingi dialect
  xx Naga languages
Aodad
  See Barbary sheep
Aonas
  See Ona Indians
Aonik language
  See Ona language
Aorta *(QL835; QM191)*
  sa Abdominal aorta
    Aortic aneurysms
    Ductus arteriosus
  xx Arteries
    Blood—Circulation
    Blood-vessels
    Chest
— Abnormities and deformities
  sa Aortic coarctation
— Diseases *(RC691)*
  sa Aorta—Radiography
    Aortic valve stenosis
    Fistula, Branchial cleft
— — Diagnosis
— Innervation
— Radiography
  xx Aorta—Diseases
— Surgery
— Wounds and injuries
Aortic aneurysms *(RC693)*
  sa Abdominal aneurysm
  x Aneurysms, Aortic
  xx Aneurysms
    Aorta—Diseases
Aortic bodies
  See Aortic paraganglia
Aortic coarctation
  x Coarctation of the aorta
  xx Aorta—Abnormities and deformities
Aortic glands
  See Aortic paraganglia
Aortic paraganglia *(QP188.A6)*
  x Aortic bodies
    Aortic glands
    Organs of Zuckerkandl
    Preaortal paraganglia
    Zuckerkandl-organs
    Zuckerkandl's bodies

  xx Chromaffin cells
Aortic regurgitation
  See Heart—Valves—Diseases
Aortic stenosis
  See Aortic valve stenosis
Aortic valve
— Diseases
— Surgery
Aortic valve stenosis
  x Aortic stenosis
  xx Aorta—Diseases
    Heart—Valves—Diseases
Aoudad
  See Barbary sheep
Aowin language
  See Brissa language
Apa Tanis
  xx Ethnology—Assam
Apabhraṃśa language *(PK1421-9)*
  xx Prakrit languages
Apabhraṃśa literature *(PK1428)*
Apabhraṃśa philology
  xx Prakrit philology
Apabhraṃśa poetry
Apache Indians *(E99.A6)*
  sa Jicarilla Indians
    Lipan Indians
    Mescalero Indians
    Mimbreño Indians
    Mogollon Indians
    Warm Spring Apache Indians
  x Chiricahua Indians
  xx Athapascan Indians
    Indians of North America
— Wars
— Wars, 1872-1873
— Wars, 1883-1886 *(E83.88)*
  xx Indians of North America—Wars—
    1866-1895
Apache language *(PM631)*
  xx Athapascan languages
Apache Mohave Indians
  See Yavapai Indians
Apalachee Indians
  x Appalachian Indians
  xx Indians of North America
    Muskhogean Indians
Apalachee language *(PM633)*
  x Appalachian language
  xx Muskhogean languages
Apalachicola Indians *(E99.A63)*
  x Appalachicola Indians
    Blount Indians
    Blunt Indians
  xx Indians of North America
Apalai Indians *(F2520.1.A62)*
  x Aparai Indians
  xx Carib Indians
    Indians of South America
Apalakiri Indians *(F2520.1.A)*
  x Kalapalo Indians
  xx Indians of South America
Aparai Indians
  See Apalai Indians
APAREL (Computer program language)
  xx PL I (Computer program language)
Apartheid
  See Africa, South—Race question
    Negroes in South Africa—Segregation
    Segregation
Apartment houses *(Direct)* *(Architecture,*
    NA7860; Service, TX957-8)
  sa Church work with apartment dwellers
    Garden apartments
    High-rise apartment buildings
    Housing management
    Landlord and tenant
    Real estate management

```
            x Flats                            Children—Language              Apocatastasis
            Houses, Apartment                  Handicapped children              See Restorationism
          xx Architecture, Domestic          — Education                       Apocryphal books (New Testament)
            Dwellings                         — Personal narratives                This heading is used only with subdivi-
            Landlord and tenant            Aphid control                             sions.
        — Accounting  (HF5686.A)               See Plant-lice—Control          — Criticism, interpretation, etc.
        — Cost of operation                 Aphididae                          Apocryphal books (Old Testament)
            x Apartment houses—Operating costs   See Plant-lice                   This heading is used only with subdivi-
        — Electric equipment                Aphids                                  sions.
        — Fires and fire prevention            See Plant-lice                  — Criticism, interpretation, etc.
        — Heating and ventilation          Aphorisms and apothegms  (PN6269-6278)  — Theology
        — Landscape architecture             sa Epigrams                       Apocynum  (Therapeutics, RM666.A6)
          xx Landscape architecture            Maxims                          Apodal fishes
        — Lighting                             Medicine—Aphorisms                 See Eels
        — Maintenance and repair               Proverbs                        Apodes
        — — Estimates  (Direct)                Quotations                         See Eels
        — Operating costs                      Table-talk                      Apodiformes
            See Apartment houses—Cost of       Wellerisms                        sa Humming-birds
                operation                      subdivision Quotations, maxims, etc.   Swifts
        — Security measures                      under certain subjects, e.g. Music—   x Cypseliformes
        — Social aspects  (Direct)               Quotations, maxims, etc.            Macrochires
        — Soundproofing                      x Ana                                  Micropodiformes
      Apartment houses, Cooperative  (Direct)    Apothegms                      Apodization
          sa Condominium (Housing)             Gnomes (Maxims)                   xx Diffraction
           x Cooperative apartment houses      Sayings                         Apogamy  (QK826)
          xx Condominium (Housing)          xx Epigrams                          sa Parthenogenesis (Plants)
            Cooperative societies              Maxims                            xx Apomixis
            Housing, Cooperative               Proverbs                            Parthenogenesis (Plants)
            Joint tenancy                      Quotations                          Plants—Reproduction
      Apartment houses, Prefabricated       Aphrodisiacs  (Sex relations, HQ12)    Reproduction, Asexual
          See Prefabricated apartment houses   xx Drugs and sex                Apollo lyre
      Apatite  (Indirect)  (Mineral resources,   Materia medica                   See Lyre-guitar
            TN948.A7; Mineralogy, QE391.A6)      Medicine, Magic, mystic, and spagiric  Apollo project
          sa Urtite                              Sexual instinct                   See Project Apollo
           x Phosphorite                     Aphthae                           Apologetics  (BT1095-1255)
          xx Phosphate rock                    See Thrush (Mouth disease)        sa Analogy (Religion)
        — Analysis                          Aphthae tropicae                       Bible—Evidences, authority, etc.
      Apayao                                   See Sprue                           Catholic Church—Apologetic works
          See Isneg                         Aphthous fever                         Faith and reason
      Apayao language                          See Foot-and-mouth disease          Judaism—Controversial literature
          See Isneg language               Apiacá Indians                         Natural theology
      Apertometer                            xx Indians of South America           Religion and science
          xx Microscope and microscopy         Tupi Indians                       Theodicy
      Aperture card systems                 Apiculture                             Witness bearing (Christianity)
          See Microfilm aperture card systems  See Bee culture                    subdivision Doctrinal and controversial
      Apes  (QL737.P9)                      Apinagé Indians  (F2520.1.A65)            works under names of particular
          sa Chimpanzees                      x Apinayé Indians                       denominations; and also subdivision
            Gibbons                          xx Indians of South America             Apologetic works under religions
            Gorillas                            Tapuya Indians                        and denominations, e.g. Catholic
            Orang-utans                     Apinayé Indians                           Church—Apologetic works;
          xx Primates                          See Apinagé Indians                    Mormons and Mormonism—
        — Behavior                          APL (Computer program language)          Apologetic works
        — Juvenile literature              Aplacophora                          x Christian evidences
      Apes (in religion, folk-lore, etc.)  (GR730.A6)   See Solenogastres          Christianity—Apologetic works
           x Folk-lore of apes            Aplastic anemia                          Christianity—Evidences
          xx Religion, Primitive             xx Anemia                             Evidences, Christian
      Apes as artists                      Aplite                                  Evidences of Christianity
          See Animals as artists             xx Dikes (Geology)                    Fundamental theology
      Apes as pets  (SF459.A)                  Rocks, Igneous                      Polemics (Theology)
        — Juvenile literature              Apnoea                                  Theology, Fundamental
      Aphakia                                 xx Respiration                     xx Theology, Doctrinal
          xx Crystalline lens              Apocalyptic art  (NX650.A6)          — Early church, ca. 30-600  (BT1115-1116)
            Eye—Abnormalities and deformities   sa Apocalyptic literature          sa Alexandrian school, Christian
      Aphasia  (RC425)                        x Art, Apocalyptic                   xx Christian literature, Early
          sa Alexia                           xx Allegories                          Church history—Primitive and early
            Amnesia                             Apocalyptic literature               church, ca. 30-600
            Amusia                              Symbolism in art                     Theology, Doctrinal—History—Early
            Aphasic children               Apocalyptic literature  (BS646; BS1705)    church, ca. 30-600
            Dyslalia                           sa Apocalyptic art               — Middle Ages, 600-1500  (BT1100)
          xx Amnesia                            x Literature, Apocalyptic          xx Church history—Middle Ages,
            Brain—Diseases                     xx Allegory                            600-1500
            Memory, Disorders of                 Apocalyptic art                     Theology, Doctrinal—History—
            Psychology, Pathological            Bible—Prophecies                     Middle Ages, 600-1500
            Speech, Disorders of                Eschatology                    — 17th century  (BT1100)
        — Personal narratives                   Hebrew literature              — 18th century  (BT1100)
      Aphasic children                          Jewish literature              — 19th century  (BT1101-5)
           x Children, Aphasic                  Prophecies                     — 20th century  (BT1101-5)
          xx Aphasia                            Revelation                     — History
```

Apologetics (BT1095-1255)
— History (Continued)
— — 16th century
— — 18th century
— — 19th century
— — 20th century
— Methodology
Apologetics, Islamic
See Islam—Apologetic works
Apologetics, Jewish
See Judaism—Apologetic works
Apologetics, Missionary (BV2063)
Here are entered works on methods of
presenting Christianity in the foreign
mission fields, as well as works on
Christianity which are prepared for the
foreign mission fields.
x Missionary apologetics
Apologetics, Muslim
See Islam—Apologetic works
Apologetics, Sikh
See Sikhism—Apologetic works
Apomixis
sa Apogamy
xx Plants—Reproduction
Reproduction, Asexual
Apomorphine
xx Emetics
Morphine
Apono language
See Shira language
Apoplexy (RC394.A7)
sa Stroke patients
x Cerebral hemorrhage
Hemorrhage, Cerebral
xx Brain—Diseases
Brain—Hemorrhage
Paralysis
— Cases, clinical reports, statistics
— Personal narratives
See Stroke patients—Personal
narratives
Aporidea (QL391.P7)
sa Gastrotaenia
xx Cestoda
Apostasy
sa Dogma
Heresy
Schism
Sects
Turncoats
xx Dogma
Faith
Heresy
Offenses against religion
Sects
Apostasy (Islam)
Apostasy (Judaism) (BM720.H5)
Apostles (BS2440)
sa Evangelists (Bible)
Jesus Christ—Brethren
Jesus Christ—Sending of the twelve
x Disciples, Twelve
xx Bible—Biography
Christian biography
Church history—Primitive and early
church, ca. 30-600
Saints
— Biblical teaching (Pauline theology,
BS2655.A6)
— Juvenile literature
— Legends
Apostles' Creed (BT992-3)
sa Communion of saints
xx Creeds
— Early works to 1800
— Meditations
— Pictures, illustrations, etc.

Apostles in art
Apostleship
See Apostolate (Theology)
Apostolate, Lay
See Catholic action
Apostolate, Liturgical
See Liturgical movement—Catholic Church
Apostolate (Theology) (BV601.2)
x Apostleship
xx Mission of the church
Theology, Doctrinal
— History of doctrines
Apostolic administrators
See Administrators apostolic
Apostolic Church
See Church history—Primitive and early
church, ca. 30-600
Apostolic Fathers (Collective biography,
BR1705; Patrology, BR60-67)
x Fathers, Apostolic
xx Christian biography
Christian literature, Early
Church history—Primitive and early
church, ca. 30-600
Fathers of the church
— Concordances
See Christian literature, Early—
Concordances
Apostolic prefects
See Vicars apostolic
Apostolic succession (BV665)
sa Anglican orders
Bishops
Catholic Church—Clergy
Church of England—Clergy
Episcopacy
Popes
x Succession, Apostolic
xx Bishops
Catholic Church—Clergy
Church of England—Clergy
Episcopacy
Papacy
— History of doctrines
Apostolic vicars
See Vicars apostolic
Apostolicity
See Church—Apostolicity
Apostrophe
xx Punctuation
Apothecaries
See Pharmacists
Apothecary jars
x Jars, Apothecary
Example under Pharmacy paraphernalia
Apothecium
Apothegms
See Aphorisms and apothegms
Apotheosis (BL465)
Here are entered works dealing with the
deification of rulers, heroes, and others
either at death or during life.
sa Emperor worship
Emperors
Heroes
Kings and rulers (in religion, folk-lore,
etc.)
Roman emperors
Superman
x Deification
xx Ancestor worship
Emperors
Heroes
Religion, Primitive
Apotheosis in literature
Apoyao
See Isneg

Appalachian dulcimer
See Dulcimer
Appalachian Indians
See Apalachee Indians
Appalachian language
See Apalachee language
Appalachicola Indians
See Apalachicola Indians
Appaloosa horse
xx Indian ponies
Appanage
sa Civil list
xx Civil list
Apparatus, Chemical
See Chemical apparatus
Apparatus, Electric
See Electric apparatus and appliances
Apparatus, Electrochemical
See Electrochemical apparatus
Apparatus, Medical
See Medical instruments and apparatus
Apparatus, Ophthalmological
See Eye, Instruments and apparatus for
Apparatus, Orthopedic
See Orthopedic apparatus
Apparatus, Physiological
See Physiological apparatus
Apparatus, Scientific
See Scientific apparatus and instruments
Apparatus, Surgical
See Surgical instruments and apparatus
Apparatus, Volumetric
See Volumetric apparatus
Apparatus for the blind
See Blind, Apparatus for the
Apparent position calculators, Artificial
satellite
See Artificial satellites—Apparent position
calculators
Apparitions (BF1445-1486)
sa Demonology
Ghosts
Hallucinations and illusions
Jesus Christ—Apparitions and miracles
(Modern)
Mary, Virgin—Apparitions and miracles
(Modern)
Materialization
Mediums
Miracles
Poltergeists
Spiritualism
Theophanies
Visions
x Phantoms
Specters
xx Demonology
Ghosts
Hallucinations and illusions
Psychical research
Spirits
Spiritualism
Superstition
Theophanies
Visions
Appeal
See Appellate procedure
Appeal as from an abuse
xx Appellate procedure
Church and state
Ecclesiastical courts
Jurisdiction
Jurisdiction (Canon law)
Appeals, Administrative
See Administrative remedies
Appeals in forma pauperis (Direct)
xx Appellate procedure
In forma pauperis

Appellate courts *(Direct)*
   sa Appellate procedure
      Courts of last resort
   xx Appellate procedure
      Courts
      Courts of last resort
   — United States
         Works on individual appellate courts
           are entered under the official head-
           ing for the court, *e.g.* United States.
           Circuit Court of Appeals (1st Cir-
           cuit); United States. Court of Ap-
           peals for the district of Columbia
           Circuit.
Appellate procedure *(Direct)*
   sa Administrative remedies
      Appeal as from an abuse
      Appeals in forma pauperis
      Appellate courts
      Briefs
      Certiorari
      Civil procedure
      Courts of last resort
      Criminal procedure
      Exceptions (Law)
      Judicial review of administrative acts
      Law and fact
      New matter (Civil procedure)
      New trials
      Pleading
      Prospective overruling
      Reformatio in pejus
      Tax protests and appeals
      Trial practice
      Waiver of appeal
      Writ of error
   x Appeal
   xx Appellate courts
      Civil procedure
      Courts
      Criminal procedure
      Procedure (Law)
      Trial practice
   — Forms
Appellate procedure (Canon law)
      (BX1939.A6)
Appellate procedure (Roman law)
Appendectomy
   xx Appendicitis
Appendicitis *(RD542)*
   sa Appendectomy
      Appendix (Anatomy)
   x Perityphlitis
   xx Abdomen—Surgery
      Intestines—Diseases
      Intestines—Surgery
   — Cases, clinical reports, statistics
Appendix (Anatomy) *(Comparative anatomy,*
      QL863; Human anatomy, QM345)
   x Appendix vermiformis
      Vermiform appendix
   xx Appendicitis
      Cecum
      Intestines
   Example under Vestigial organs
Appendix vermiformis
   See Appendix (Anatomy)
Apperception *(BF321; Educational*
      psychology, LB1067)
   sa Attention
      Comprehension
      Consciousness
      Knowledge, Theory of
      Number concept
      Perception
   xx Comprehension
      Educational psychology
      Knowledge, Theory of

      Perception
      Psychology
   — Testing *(BF433.A6)*
      sa Children's apperception test
         School apperception method
         Thematic apperception test
         Three-dimensional personality test
      xx Projective techniques
Appetency
   See Desire
Appetite
   sa Anorexia
      Children—Nutrition—Psychological
         aspects
      Diet
      Hunger
   xx Anorexia
      Hunger
Appetite depressants
   See Weight reducing preparations
Appetizers
   See Cookery (Appetizers)
Applause, demonstrations, etc.
   sa Theater—Applause, demonstrations,
         etc.
Applause in theaters
   See Theater—Applause, demonstrations,
         etc.
Apple *(Indirect) (SB363)*
   sa Cookery (Apples)
      Crabapple
   Example under Fruit; Fruit trees
   — Breeding
      See Apple breeding
   — Cooperative marketing
      xx Apple—Marketing
      Example under Cooperative marketing of
         farm produce
   — Diseases and pests *(SB608.A6)*
      sa Apple—Storage—Diseases and
         injuries
         names of diseases and pests, e.g.
         Apple blotch, Apple-maggot,
         Crown-gall disease
   — Genetics
   — Grading
   — Handling
      See Apple handling
   — Harvesting *(SB363.35)*
   — Juvenile literature
   — Marketing
      sa Apple—Cooperative marketing
      Example under Fruit—Marketing
   — Packaging
      Example under Food containers
   — Packing
      Example under Packing for shipment
   — Prices *(Direct)*
   — Standards *(Direct) (SB363.5)*
   — Storage
      Example under Fruit—Storage
   — — Diseases and injuries *(Indirect)*
         (SB608.A6)
      xx Apple—Diseases and pests
   — Transportation
      Example under Fruit—Transportation
   — Varieties
Apple, Frozen
   x Frozen apple
   xx Food, Frozen
Apple-aphis
Apple blotch
   Example under Apple—Diseases and pests
Apple blue mold *(SB608.A6)*
   x Blue mold disease of apples
Apple breeding *(Indirect)*
   x Apple—Breeding
   xx Plant-breeding

Apple fruit-borer
Apple handling
   x Apple—Handling
   xx Fruit handling
Apple juice
   sa Cider
   xx Cider
      Fruit juices
Apple juice, Frozen concentrated
   x Frozen concentrated apple juice
   xx Fruit juices, Concentrated
      Fruit juices, Frozen
Apple leaf-sewer
Apple-maggot
   Example under Apple—Diseases and pests
Apple powdery mildew
Apple products
   xx Canning and preserving
Apple root-borer
Apple sawfly *(QL568.T3; Agricultural pests,*
      SB945.A)
   — Control *(Indirect)*
Apple scab
Apple-scald
Apple sucker
   x European apple sucker
      Psylla mali
Apple-tree borers
   Example under Borers (Insects)
Apple-tree tent caterpillar
   See Eastern tent caterpillar
Apple-tree weevil
   xx Beetles
Apple worm
Appliances, Electric
   See Electric apparatus and appliances
Applications for office
   x Office, Applications for
   xx Civil service
Applications for positions *(HF5383)*
   sa Employment interviewing
      Employment references
      Interviewing
      Résumés (Employment)
   xx Business
      Personnel management
      Success
Applied anthropology *(GN27)*
   xx Anthropology
Applied art
   See Art industries and trade
Applied linguistics
   sa Language data processing
      Machine translating
      Mathematical linguistics
   xx Linguistics
Applied mechanics
   See Mechanics, Applied
Applied photography
   See Photography, Applied
Applied psychology
   See Psychology, Applied
Applied science
   See Technology
Appliqué *(NK9100-9199)*
   xx Fancy work
      Needlework
   — Juvenile literature

Appointment to office
    See subdivision Officials and employees—
        Appointment, qualifications, tenure,
        etc. *under names of countries, cities,*
        etc.; and subdivision Appointments,
        promotions, salaries, etc. *under*
        names of departments or institutions;
        and subdivision Appointments and
        retirements *under armies, navies,*
        etc., e.g. United States—Officials and
        employees—Appointment,
        qualifications, tenure, etc.; United
        States. Dept. of Agriculture—
        Appointments, promotions, salaries,
        etc.; United States. Army—
        Appointments and retirements
Appointments and schedules (Medicine)
    See Medical appointments and schedules
Appomattox Campaign, 1865 *(E477.67)*
  — Juvenile literature
Apportionment
Apportionment (Election law) *(Direct)*
    sa Election districts
    x Reapportionment (Election law)
    xx Election districts
        Representative government and
        representation
Apposition (Grammar)
    See Grammar, Comparative and general—
        Apposition
    subdivision Apposition *under names of*
        languages and groups of languages
Appraisal
    See Assessment
        Valuation
Appraisal (Customs administration)
    See Customs appraisal
Appraisal of books
    See Bibliography—Best books
        Books and reading
        Criticism
        Literature—History and criticism
Appreciation of art
    See Art appreciation
Appreciation of moving-pictures
    See Moving-pictures—Appreciation
Appreciation of music
    See Music—Analysis, appreciation
Apprehension
    See Perception
Apprentices *(Direct) (HD4881-5; Printers'*
      apprentices, Z122.5)
    sa Compagnonnages
        Education, Cooperative
        Employees, Training of
        Interns (Business)
        Interns (Civil service)
        Learners, Industrial
        Wages—Apprentices
    x Work experience
    xx Artisans
        Children—Employment
        Employees, Training of
        Labor and laboring classes
        Learners, Industrial
        Master and servant
        Servants
        Technical education
  — Health and hygiene
Apprentices (Greek law)
Approaches, Bridge
    See Bridge approaches
Approbations (Hebrew literature)
    x Haskamah
        Hasskama
    xx Censorship (Judaism)
        Hebrew literature
        Liberty of the press

Appropriated funds, Executive impoundment of
    See Executive impoundment of
        appropriated funds
Appropriation (Theology)
    xx God
        Theology, Doctrinal
        Trinity
Appropriation and impropriation
    See Secularization
Appropriations, Indian
    See Indians of North America—
        Appropriations
Appropriations and expenditures
    See Expenditures, Public
        subdivision Appropriations and
        expenditures *under names of*
        countries, states, etc. and under
        names of departments, institutions,
        etc., e.g. United States—
        Appropriations and expenditures;
        United States. War Dept.—
        Appropriations and expenditures
Approval, Social
    See Social acceptance
        Social desirability
Approximant, Padé
    See Padé approximant
Approximate computation
    See Numerical analysis
Approximation computation
    See Numerical analysis
Approximation theory *(QA221)*
    sa Born approximation
        Chebyshev approximation
        Chebyshev systems
        Form factor (Nuclear physics)
        Hartree-Fock approximation
        Hypercircle method
        Interpolation
        Numerical analysis
        Padé approximant
        Perturbation (Mathematics)
        Spline theory
        WKB approximation
    x Theory of approximation
    xx Chebyshev systems
        Functional analysis
        Functions
        Interpolation
        Polynomials
Appurtenances *(Direct)*
    sa Fixtures (Law)
    x Accessories (Civil law)
    xx Fixtures (Law)
        Personal property
        Real property
        Things (Law)
Appurtenances (Roman law)
Apraxia
    xx Psychomotor disorders
Apricot *(Indirect) (SB379.A7)*
    sa Cookery (Apricots)
    Example under Stone fruit
  — Packing
April Fools' Day *(GT4995.A6)*
    x All Fools' Day
  — Juvenile literature
Apriori
    See A priori
Aprons
    xx Clothing and dress
Apsarases
Apses (Architecture) *(NA2880)*
    xx Architecture—Details
APT (Computer program language)
    x Automatically programmed tools
        (Computer program language)

Aptal
    See Ephthalites
Aptera
    See Thysanura
Aptitude tests
    See Ability—Testing
Apytere Indians
    See Mbya Indians
Aquaculture *(Indirect)*
    sa Fish-culture
        Mariculture
    x Aquiculture
    xx Agriculture
  — Juvenile literature
Aquaculture, Marine
    See Mariculture
Aquae Sextiae, Battle of, 102 B.C.
      (DG255.5)
    x Aix, Battle of, 102 B.C.
Aquafers
    See Aquifers
Aqualung
    x Scuba
    xx Respirators
        Skin diving—Equipment and supplies
Aquarium fish breeding *(SF458.2)*
    sa Tropical fish breeding
    x Aquarium fishes—Breeding
Aquarium fishes
    sa Goldfish
        Marine aquarium fishes
        Tropical fish
    xx Fishes
  — Breeding
      See Aquarium fish breeding
  — Diseases and pests *(Indirect) (SF458.5)*
  — Juvenile literature
Aquarium plants
    xx Fresh-water flora
Aquarium reactors
    See Swimming pool reactors
Aquarium water
    xx Water—Composition
Aquariums *(Indirect) (QH68; QL78-79)*
    sa Fish-culture
        Marine aquariums
        Water gardens
    xx Fish-culture
        Fishes
        Fresh-water biology
        Fresh-water fauna
        Natural history—Technique
        Vivariums
  — Anecdotes, facetiae, satire, etc.
  — Juvenile literature
Aquariums, Marine
    See Marine aquariums
Aquariums, Public *(Indirect) (QL78-79)*
    x Public aquariums
Aquariums, Saltwater
    See Marine aquariums
Aquatic animals *(Indirect) (QL120)*
    sa Aquatic invertebrates
        Aquatic mammals
        Fishes
        Fresh-water fauna
        Insects, Aquatic
        Marine fauna
    x Animals, Aquatic
        Aquatic fauna
        Water animals
    xx Animals
        Aquatic biology
        Zoology
  — Juvenile literature
  — Physiology
Aquatic biology *(Indirect) (QH90)*
    sa Aquatic animals

Aquatic ecology
Aquatic microbiology
Aquatic plants
Benthos
Estuarine biology
Fresh-water biology
Marine biology
Neuston
Plankton
Vertical distribution (Aquatic biology)
  x Hydrobiology
    Water biology
  xx Biology
Aquatic birds
  See Water-birds
Aquatic chemistry
  See Water chemistry
Aquatic ecology *(Indirect) (QH541.5.W3)*
  sa Fresh-water ecology
    Marine ecology
  xx Aquatic biology
    Ecology
  — Experiments
  — Laboratory manuals
Aquatic fauna
  See Aquatic animals
Aquatic flora
  See Aquatic plants
Aquatic insects
  See Insects, Aquatic
Aquatic invertebrates *(Indirect)*
  sa Freshwater invertebrates
    Insects, Aquatic
    Marine invertebrates
  xx Aquatic animals
    Invertebrates
Aquatic mammals *(Indirect)*
  sa Marine mammals
  xx Aquatic animals
    Mammals
  — Juvenile literature
Aquatic microbiology *(Indirect) (QR105)*
  sa Freshwater microbiology
    Marine microbiology
  xx Aquatic biology
    Microbiology
  — Technique
Aquatic nuisances
  See Aquatic pests
Aquatic pests
  sa Aquatic weeds
    Marine borers
  x Aquatic nuisances
  xx Fresh-water biology
    Marine biology
    Pests
Aquatic plants *(Indirect) (Botany, QK916;*
    Culture, SB423)
  sa Water gardens
    Water-lilies
  x Aquatic flora
    Hydrobotany
    Water plants
  xx Aquatic biology
    Botany
    Fresh-water flora
    Gardening
    Marine flora
    Plants
    Water gardens
  Example under Floriculture
  — Economic aspects
  — Identification
  — Laboratory manuals
  — Pictorial works
Aquatic resources *(Indirect)*
  sa Algae
    Fisheries

Fishery products
Fishery resources
Marine resources
Wetlands
  x Resources, Aquatic
  xx Natural resources
Aquatic sports *(Direct) (GV771-840)*
  sa Boat jousting
    Boats and boating
    Canoes and canoeing
    Coasts—Recreational use
    Fishing
    Logrolling (Aquatic sports)
    Rafting (Sports)
    Regattas
    Rowing
    Sailing
    Surfing
    Swimming
    Water skiing
    Yachts and yachting
  x Camps—Water programs
    Water sports
  xx Amusements
    Boats and boating
    Coasts—Recreational use
    Sports
  — Accidents and injuries
    x Aquatic sports—Injuries
      Water safety
    xx Aquatic sports—Safety measures
  — Injuries
    See Aquatic sports—Accidents and
      injuries
  — Juvenile literature
  — Safety measures
    sa Aquatic sports—Accidents and
      injuries
    x Water safety
Aquatic sports facilities *(Direct)*
Aquatic weed control *(Indirect)*
  sa Algae control
  x Aquatic weed eradication
    Aquatic weeds—Control
    Aquatic weeds—Eradication
  xx Weed control
Aquatic weed eradication
  See Aquatic weed control
Aquatic weeds *(Indirect)*
  xx Aquatic pests
    Weeds
  — Control
    See Aquatic weed control
  — Eradication
    See Aquatic weed control
  — Identification
Aquatint *(NE1820)*
  xx Engraving
    Etching
Aquatints *(Direct)*
Aquatints, Belgian, [etc.] *(Direct)*
  x Belgian [etc.] aquatints
Aquavit
  x Akvavit
Aqueducts *(TD398)*
  sa Canal aqueducts
  names of aqueducts, e.g. Croton
    Aqueduct
  x Conduits
  xx Channels (Hydraulic engineering)
    Civil engineering
    Engineering
    Hydraulic structures
    Water—Distribution
    Water-supply
Aqueous humor *(Animals, QL949; Man,*
    QM511)
  xx Eye

Lacrimal organs
Aquiculture
  See Aquaculture
Aquiculture, Marine
  See Mariculture
Aquifers *(Indirect)*
    Here are entered works on the geology of
    water-bearing strata. Works on water
    contained in aquifers are entered un-
    der Water, Underground.
  x Aquafers
    Water-bearing formations
  xx Hydrogeology
    Water, Underground
  — Electromechanical analogies *(GB665)*
  — Mathematical models *(GB665)*
Arab architecture
  See Architecture, Islamic
Arab art
  See Art, Islamic
Arab civilization
  See Civilization, Arab
Arab coins
  See Coins, Arab
Arab costume
  See Costume, Arab
Arab countries
  x Arabic speaking states
  xx Islamic countries
    Near East
Arab Empire
  See Islamic Empire
Arab-Israel Border Conflicts, 1949-
  See Israel-Arab Border Conflicts, 1949-
Arab-Israel War, 1948-1949
  See Israel-Arab War, 1948-1949
Arab-Israel War, 1967-
  See Israel-Arab War, 1967-
Arab-Jewish relations
  See Jewish-Arab relations
Arab logicians
  See Logicians, Arab
Arab philosophy
  See Philosophy, Arab
Arab refugees
  See Refugees, Arab
Arab riots, 1920
  See Palestine—History—Arab riots, 1920
Arab riots, 1929
  See Palestine—History—Arab riots, 1929
Arab riots, 1936
  See Palestine—History—Arab riots, 1936
Arab studies
  See Arabic studies
Arabesques *(NK1575)*
  sa Decoration and ornament
    Grotesque
  xx Decoration and ornament
Arabian horse *(SF293.A8)*
  sa Barbary horse
  Example under Horse breeds
Arabian oryx
  x Beatrix oryx
  xx Oryx
Arabic-Afrikaans dialect
  x Afrikaans-Arabic dialect
    Afrikaans language—Dialects—Arabic
    Arabic language—Dialects—Africa,
      South
  xx Languages, Mixed
Arabic alphabet *(PJ6123)*
  sa Jawi alphabet
  x Arabic language—Alphabet
  xx Alphabet
Arabic astrology
  See Astrology, Arabic
Arabic astronomy
  See Astronomy, Arabic

Arabic ballads and songs *(Direct)*
Arabic drama
Arabic drama (Comedy) *(Direct)*
Arabic gazels
   See Gazels, Arabic
Arabic imprints *(Direct)*
Arabic inscriptions
   See Inscriptions, Arabic
Arabic Islamic prayers
   See Islamic prayers, Arabic
Arabic language *(PJ6001-7134)*
   sa Mahri language
      Sokotri language
   Example under Semitic languages
  — Alphabet
     See Arabic alphabet
  — Business Arabic
  — Dialects
  — — Judeo-Arabic
     xx Jews—Languages
       GEOGRAPHIC SUBDIVISIONS
  — — Africa, South
     See Arabic-Afrikaans dialect
  — Translating
    sa Dragomen
  — Writing
     See Writing, Arabic
Arabic language in Lebanon, [etc.]
Arabic libraries *(Z675.A82)*
   x Libraries, Arabic
Arabic literature *(PJ7501-8518)*
   sa Ismaili literature
      Koran as literature
      Shiite literature
  — To 622
  — 622-750
  — 750-1258
  — 1258-1800
  — 1801-
  — 20th century
       GENERAL SUBDIVISIONS
  — Cataloging
     See Cataloging of Arabic literature
       GENERAL SUBDIVISIONS
  — Christian authors
  — Coptic authors
     x Coptic literature (Arabic)
       GENERAL SUBDIVISIONS
  — Jewish authors
     Duplicate entry is made under Jewish
       literature (Arabic)
     Note under Jewish literature (Arabic)
       GENERAL SUBDIVISIONS
  — Themes, motives
  — Egypt
     xx Egyptian literature
  — Lebanon
     x Lebanese literature (Arabic)
  — Malta
     x Maltese literature
Arabic manuscripts
   See Manuscripts, Arabic
Arabic mathematics
   See Mathematics, Arabic
Arabic medicine
   See Medicine, Arabic
Arabic names
   See Names, Arabic
Arabic newspapers
Arabic numismatics
   See Numismatics, Arabic
Arabic orations
Arabic periodicals *(PN5449.A)*

Arabic philology *(PJ6001-6071)*
Arabic philosophy
   See Philosophy, Arab
     Philosophy, Islamic
     Physicians, Arabic
Arabic physicians
   See Physicians, Arabic
Arabic poetry *(Direct) (Collections,*
     PJ7631-7661; History, PJ7541-7561)
   sa Gazels, Arabic
      Qasidas, Arabic
      Zajal
  — To 622
  — 622-750
  — 750-1258
  — 1258-1800
  — 1801-
  — 20th century
       GENERAL SUBDIVISIONS
  — Christian authors
  — Jewish authors
     x Jewish poetry (Arabic)
Arabic prose literature
   sa Maqamah
Arabic proverbs
   See Proverbs, Arabic
Arabic-Spanish poetry
   See Mozarabic poetry
Arabic speaking states
   See Arab countries
Arabic students in the United States, [etc.]
Arabic studies *(Direct)*
   x Arab studies
   xx Near East studies
Arabic wit and humor *(Direct) (PN6222.A)*
Arabism *(DS38)*
   sa Panarabism
     Panislamism
   x al-'Urūbah
Arabs *(DS218-219)*
   sa Abbasids
     Bedouins
     Buwayhids
     Hammudites
     Hashimites
     Hudhayl tribe
     Juhaynah (Arab tribe)
     North Africans
     Omayyads
     Ouled Naïl
     Quraysh (Arab tribe)
     Tamim
   xx North Africans
     Saracens
   Example under Semites
  — Religion
Arabs in Africa
   sa Afara (African tribe)
Arabs in Italy, [Mesopotamia, Sicily, etc.]
  — Economic conditions
  — Legal status, laws, etc.
  — Political and social conditions
Arabs in literature
Arabs in Palestine
   sa Jewish-Arab relations
     Palestine—History—Arab riots, 1920
     Palestine—History—Arab riots, 1929
     Palestine—History—Arab riots, 1936
   xx Jewish-Arab relations
Arabs in Spain *(DP98-123)*
   Here are entered general treatises on
    Arabic culture and political history.
    Works on Arabs under Christian gov-
    ernment are entered under the heading
    Moriscos.
   sa Moriscos
     Mudéjares

     Omayyads in Spain
Arachides
   See Peanuts
Arachis oil
   See Peanut oil
Arachnida *(Indirect) (QL451-9)*
   sa Arthrogastra
     Eurypterida
     Mites
     Pentastomida
     Spiders
     Tardigrada
     Whip scorpions
     Xiphosura
   xx Arthropoda
     Invertebrates
  — Anatomy
  — Behavior
     sa subdivision Behavior *under names of*
       particular arachnids, e.g.
       Scorpions—Behavior
  — Juvenile literature
  — Physiology
  — Pictorial works
Arachnida, Fossil
   sa Spiders, Fossil
Arachnitis
   See Arachnoiditis
Arachnoiditis
   x Arachnitis
   xx Meninges—Diseases
Arad, Romania (Judet)
  — Flood, 1970
Aragats computer
   xx Electronic digital computers
  — Programming
Aragon
  — History
  — — Interregnum, 1410-1412
Aragon in literature
Aragonite
   xx Calcium carbonite
Aragya (African people)
   See Alagya (African people)
Arahuna language
   See Araona language
Arains *(DS432.A67)*
   xx Ethnology—India—Punjab
Arakanese
Arakanese in East Pakistan
   x Mags
     Marma
   xx Ethnology—Bangladesh
Aramaic incantations
   See Incantations, Aramaic
Aramaic inscriptions
   See Inscriptions, Aramaic
Aramaic language *(PJ5201-5329)*
   Here are entered works treating of the
    Aramaic language and its eastern and
    western branches and dialects in gen-
    eral, as well as works on Biblical
    Aramaic (in former times erroneously
    called Chaldee or Chaldean) *i.e.* the
    language in which portions of the Old
    Testament and the translations known
    as "Targums" were written.
   sa Inscriptions, Nabataean
     Mandaean language
     Palmyrene language
     Samaritan Aramaic language
     Samaritan language
     Syriac language
     Syriac language, Modern
     Syriac language, Palestinian
   x Aramean language
     Biblical Aramaic language
     Chaldaic language

Chaldean language
  Chaldee language
  xx Bible—Language, style
    Languages—Religious aspects
    Syriac language
    Talmud—Language, style
Aramean language
  See Aramaic language
Arameans *(DS59.A7)*
Aranda language *(PL7101.A6)*
  x Aranta language
    Arunta language
  xx Australian languages
Aranda tribe *(DU122.A; Anthropology,*
    GN666)
  x Aranta tribe
    Arunndta tribe
    Arunta tribe
  xx Australian aborigines
Araneida
  See Spiders
Aranjuez, Treaty of, 1777 *(F1929.B7)*
Aranta language
  See Aranda language
Aranta tribe
  See Aranda tribe
Araona language *(PM5453)*
  x Arahuna language
    Arauna language
  xx Indians of South America—Languages
    Tacanan languages
Arapaho Indians *(E99.A7)*
  xx Algonquian Indians
    Indians of North America
Arapaho language *(PM635)*
  sa Atsina language
  xx Algonquian languages
Arapaima
  x Paiche
    Piraruca
Arapesh language *(PL6621.A7)*
  xx Papuan languages
Arapesh tribe *(New Guinea, GN671.N5)*
Arara Indians
  xx Indians of South America
Ararge language
  See Harari language
Arasa language
  x Arasairi language
  xx Indians of South America—Languages
Arasairi language
  See Arasa language
Araucana *(SF489.A68)*
Araucanian Indians *(F3126)*
  sa Huilliche Indians
    Pampean Indians
    Pehuenche Indians
  x Araucanos
    Auca Indians
    Mapuche Indians
  xx Indians of South America
    Pampean Indians
  — Legal status, laws, etc.
  — Religion and mythology
  — Rites and ceremonies
  — Wars
Araucanian language *(PM5461-9)*
  sa Moluche language
    Pehuenche language
  x Mapuche language
  xx Indians of South America—Languages
Araucanian literature *(PM5468)*
Araucanian poetry *(Direct)*
Araucanos
  See Araucanian Indians
Arauna language
  See Araona language

Arawak Indians
  sa Moxo Indians
    Taino Indians
  x Arrague Indians
  xx Indians of South America
    Indians of the West Indies
Arawak language *(PM5476)*
  xx Arawakan languages
    Indians of South America—Languages
Arawakan Indians *(F2230.2.A)*
  xx Indians of South America
Arawakan languages *(PM5476)*
  sa Achagua language
    Arawak language
    Bauré language
    Campa language
    Campa languages
    Chuntaquiro language
    Culina language
    Goajiro language
    Guahibo language
    Ipurina language
    Lorenzan language
    Matsigenka language
    Taino language
  xx Indians of South America—Languages
Arbedo, Battle of, 1422 *(DQ98)*
  x Bellinzone, Battle of, 1422
    San Paolo, Battle of, 1422
  xx Switzerland—History—1032-1499
Arbela, Battle of, 331 B.C.
  See Gaugamela, Battle of, 331 B.C.
Arbitrage
  xx Commodity exchanges
    Securities
    Speculation
    Stock-exchange
Arbitration, Administrative
  See Arbitration (Administrative law)
Arbitration, Industrial *(Direct)*
    (HD5481-5630)
  sa Collective bargaining
    Grievance procedures
    Labor courts
    Mediation and conciliation, Industrial
    Strikes and lockouts
  x Industrial arbitration
  xx Collective bargaining
    Industrial relations
    Labor and laboring classes
    Labor courts
    Labor disputes
    Mediation and conciliation, Industrial
    Negotiation
    Strikes and lockouts
    Trade-unions
Example under Industrial relations
  — Anecdotes, facetiae, satire, etc.
  — Cases
Arbitration, International *(JX1901-1991)*
  sa Aggression (International law)
    Commissions of inquiry, International
    Diplomatic negotiations in international
      disputes
    Disarmament
    Geneva protocol, 1924
    Hague. Permanent Court of
      Arbitration
    International courts
    Jurisdiction (International law)
    Mediation, International
    Renunciation of war treaty, Paris, Aug.
      27, 1928
  x International arbitration
  xx Disarmament
    International cooperation
    International law
    International relations

Jurisdiction (International law)
    Mediation, International
    Negotiation
    Pacific settlement of international
      disputes
    Peace
    Peaceful change (International
      relations)
    Treaties
    War (International law)
  — Digests
Arbitration (Administrative law) *(Direct)*
  x Administrative arbitration
    Arbitration, Administrative
  xx Administrative law
Arbitration agreements, Commercial *(Direct)*
  x Arbitration clauses, Commercial
    Commercial arbitration agreements
    Compromise (Arbitration agreement)
    Submission (Arbitration agreement)
  xx Arbitration and award
Arbitration and award *(Direct)*
  sa Arbitration agreements, Commercial
    Compromise (Law)
  x Awards
    Commercial arbitration
  xx Civil procedure
    Commercial law
    Compromise (Law)
    Courts
    Discharge of contracts
    Remedies (Law)
  — Costs
  — Forms
Arbitration and award, International
  x Commercial arbitration, International
    International arbitration and award
  xx Commercial courts
    Commercial law
    International courts
Arbitration and award (Canon law)
Arbitration and award (Roman law)
Arbitration clauses, Commercial
  See Arbitration agreements, Commercial
Arboledas, Colombia
  — Earthquake, 1950
Arbor Day *(SD363)*
  sa Tree planting
  xx Holidays
    Tree planting
  Example under Schools—Exercises and recre-
      ations
  — Juvenile literature
Arboretums *(Indirect)* *(QK479)*
  sa Botanical gardens
    individual arboretums, e.g. Harvard
      University. Arnold Arboretum
  xx Botanical gardens
Arboriculture *(Indirect)*
  sa Forests and forestry
    Fruit-culture
    Nurseries (Horticulture)
    Stocks (Horticulture)
    Tree breeding
    Trees
  xx Forests and forestry
    Fruit-culture
    Horticulture
    Nurseries (Horticulture)
    Ornamental horticulture
    Shrubs
    Trees
  — Costs
Arbors and mandrels
  x Mandrels
  — Standards
Arboviruses
  See Arthropod-borne viruses

Arc, Electric
   See Electric arc
Arc, Mercury
   See Mercury arc
Arc image furnaces
   See Image furnaces
Arc-jet engines
   See Arc-jet rocket engines
Arc-jet rocket engines
   x Arc-jet engines
     Arc-jet thrusters
     Electrothermal rocket engines
   xx Electric rocket engines
   — Fuel systems
     xx Fuel pumps
Arc-jet thrusters
   See Arc-jet rocket engines
Arc lamps
   See Electric lamps, Arc
Arc light
   See Electric lighting, Arc
Arc measures *(QB291)*
     Here are entered accounts of measure-
       ments of an arc of the earth's surface,
       whether meridian, parallel or oblique.
   sa Geodesy
   xx Earth—Figure
     Geodesy
Arc spectra *(QC454.A7)*
   x Spectra, Arc
     Spectrum, Arc
   xx Electric arc
     Flame spectroscopy
     Spectrum analysis
Arc welding
   See Electric welding
Arcades *(Direct)*
   sa Shopping malls
   xx Shopping centers
     Shopping malls
Arcadia in literature
   xx Utopias in literature
Arch
   See Arches
Arch dams *(TC547)*
   x Dams, Arch
   xx Concrete dams
   — Foundations *(TC547)*
Archaean period
   See Geology, Stratigraphic—Archaean
Archaeogastropoda
   x Archeogastropoda
     Aspidobranchia
     Diotocardia
   xx Gasteropoda
     Prosobranchiata
Archaeological chemistry
   x Chemistry, Archaeological
   xx Archaeology—Methodology
     Chemistry, Analytic
Archaeological collections
   See Archaeological museums and
     collections
Archaeological expeditions *(CC100; CC105)*
   sa subdivision Antiquities *under names of*
     countries, regions, etc.; also names of
     expeditions
   x Expeditions, Archaeological
   xx Excavations (Archaeology)
Archaeological forgeries
   See Forgery of antiquities
Archaeological illustration
   xx Drawing—Scientific applications
     Illustration of books
Archaeological museums and collections
     (Indirect)
   sa Antiquities—Collection and
     preservation

Classical antiquities
   Indians of Mexico—Museums
   Indians of North America—Museums
   x Archaeological collections
   xx Anthropological museums and
     collections
     Antiquities—Collection and
     preservation
     Museums
   — Catalogs
Archaeological radiography
   See Radiography in archaeology
Archaeological societies *(Indirect)*
   sa Archaeology—Societies, etc. *[for*
     publications of archaeological and
     other societies in relation to
     archaeology]
   xx Societies
Archaeological specimens
   See Antiquities
Archaeological surveying *(CC73-75)*
   xx Archaeology—Methodology
     Excavations (Archaeology)
     Surveying
Archaeologists *(Direct)*
   sa Archaeology as a profession
   xx Historians
   — Correspondence, reminiscences, etc.
Archaeology *(CC; Art, N; Indian and other*
     American antiquities, E-F; National
     antiquities other than American,
     DA-DU; Prehistoric antiquities, GN;
     Social antiquities, manners and
     customs: general, GT)
   sa Aerial photography in archaeology
     Amulets
     Antiquities
     Architecture, Ancient
     Architecture, Primitive
     Arms and armor, Primitive
     Arrowheads
     Art, Prehistoric
     Art, Primitive
     Bone implements
     Christian art and symbolism
     Cliff-dwellings
     Copper age
     Cromlechs
     Earthworks (Archaeology)
     Epitaphs
     Ethnology
     Excavations (Archaeology)
     Fibula (Archaeology)
     Fishing, Primitive
     Fortification, Primitive
     Funeral rites and ceremonies
     Gems
     Heraldry
     Hill figures
     Historic sites
     Indians—Antiquities
     Industrial archaeology
     Industries, Primitive
     Inscriptions
     Insect forms in art and archaeology
     Iron age
     Kitchen-middens
     Magnetometry in archaeology
     Man, Prehistoric
     Medals, Ancient
     Monuments—Preservation
     Mounds
     Mummies
     Mythology
     Navigation, Primitive
     Numismatics
     Obelisks
     Picture-writing

     Pottery
     Projectile points
     Protohistory
     Pyramids
     Rock paintings
     Round towers
     Sculpture, Primitive
     Seven Wonders of the World
     Spindle-whorls
     Stele (Archaeology)
     Stone age
     Stone implements
     Temples
     Terremare
     Tombs
     Underwater archaeology
     subdivision Antiquities *under names of*
     regions, countries, etc.
   x Antiquities, Prehistoric
     Archeology
     Paleoethnography
     Prehistoric antiquities
     Prehistory
     Ruins
   xx Anthropology
     Anthropology, Prehistoric
     Antiquities
     Art
     Auxiliary sciences of history
     Civilization
     Classical antiquities
     Copper age
     Ethnology
     Excavation (Archaeology)
     History
     History, Ancient
     Iron age
     Philology
     Stone age
   — Audio-visual aids
   — Classification
   — Law and legislation *(Direct) (CC130)*
     sa Treasure-trove
     xx Archaeology and state
       Treasure-trove
   — Methodology *(CC73-75)*
     sa Animal remains (Archaeology)
       Archaeological chemistry
       Archaeological surveying
       Dendrochronology
       Magnetometry in archaeology
       Photography in archaeology
       Plant remains (Archaeology)
       Radiocarbon dating
       Radiography in archaeology
       Soil science in archaeology
       Underwater archaeology
   — Societies, etc.
     xx Archaeological societies
   — State aid
     See Archaeology and state
Archaeology, Biblical
   See Bible—Antiquities
Archaeology, Christian
   See Christian antiquities
Archaeology, Classical
   See Classical antiquities
Archaeology, Medieval
   sa Art, Medieval
   x Medieval archaeology
   xx Middle Ages
Archaeology, Submarine
   See Underwater archaeology
Archaeology and state *(Indirect)*
   sa Archaeology—Law and legislation
   x Archaeology—State aid
     Public archaeology
     State aid to archaeology

State and archaeology
Archaeology as a profession
　xx Archaeologists
Archaeozoic period
　See Geology, Stratigraphic—Archaean
Archaic Chinese language
　See Chinese language—Archaic Chinese
Archbishoprics
　See Dioceses
Archbishops
　See Bishops
　　Metropolitans
Archdeacons *(Direct) (Catholic Church,*
　BX1911; Church of England,
　BX5179)
　sa Chorepiscopi
　　Rural chapters
　　Rural deans
　x Archpriests
　xx Dioceses
　　Rural deans
Archean period
　See Geology, Stratigraphic—Archaean
Archebiosis
　See Spontaneous generation
Archegenesis
　See Spontaneous generation
Archeogastropoda
　See Archaeogastropoda
Archeology
　See Archaeology
Archeozoic period
　See Geology, Stratigraphic—Archaean
Archer-fishes
Archers
　x Bowmen
Archery *(Direct) (GV1185-9)*
　sa Bow and arrow
　xx Bow and arrow
　　Shooting
　Example under Sports
　— Early works to 1800
　— Juvenile literature
Archery in art
　xx Art
　　Sports in art
Arches *(TG327-340)*
　sa Bridges, Arched
　　Centering of arches
　　Culverts
　　Roofs, Shell
　x Arch
　xx Architecture
　　Bridges
　　Building
　　Civil engineering
　　Engineering
　　Masonry
Arches, Concrete
　x Concrete arches
　xx Concrete construction
Arches, Metal *(TG410)*
Arches, Oblique *(TG329)*
　x Oblique arches
Arches, Triumphal *(Direct) (NA9360-9380)*
　x Triumphal arches
　xx Architecture, Ancient
　　Architecture, Roman
　　Monuments
Archi *(DK34.A7)*
　x Archintsy
　　Arshishtuw
　　Arshishuw
　xx Ethnology—Caucasus
Archiannelida
　xx Annelida
　　Chaetopoda

Archibald prize
　x Sulman prize
　　Wynne prize
　xx Art—Competitions
Archicembalo *(ML653-5)*
　xx Piano
Archil
　See Orchil
Archimedean screw *(TJ901)*
　x Spiral pump
　　Water screw
　xx Hydraulic machinery
Archintsy
　See Archi
Architects *(Direct) (NA)*
　sa Architectural technicians
　　Architecture as a profession
　　Building designers
　　City planners
　　Landscape architects
　　Women as architects
　xx Artists
　— Biography
　— Certification *(Direct)*
　　x Certification of architects
　　xx Architects—Legal status, laws, etc.
　— Correspondence, reminiscences, etc.
　— Fees *(NA2570)*
　　xx Architectural practice—Costs
　　Example under Fees, Professional
　— Interviews
　— Legal status, laws, etc. *(Direct)*
　　sa Architects—Certification
　　　Building laws
　　　Engineering law
　　x Architectural law and legislation
　　　Architecture—Law and legislation
　　xx Building laws
　　Example under Status (Law)
Architects, Islamic
　See Architects, Muslim
Architects, Muslim
　x Architects, Islamic
　　Islamic architects
　　Muslim architects
　xx Islam—Biography
Architects, Women
　See Women as architects
Architects and community
　x Community and architects
Architectural acoustics *(NA2800)*
　sa Absorption of sound
　　Acoustic filters
　　Electro-acoustics
　　Reverberation time
　　School buildings—Acoustics
　　Sound—Measurement
　　Sound studios
　　Sound—Transmission
　　Soundproofing
　x Acoustics
　　Buildings—Acoustics
　xx Absorption of sound
　　Acoustical engineering
　　Environmental engineering (Buildings)
　　Sound
　　Theaters—Construction
Architectural casts
　sa Architectural models
　xx Architectural models
　　Plaster casts
　Note under Casts
Architectural decoration and ornament
　See Decoration and ornament, Architectural
Architectural design
　sa Architectural drawing
　　Architecture—Composition, proportion,
　　etc.

　　Architecture—Details
　　Decoration and ornament, Architectural
　　Structural design
　x Design, Architectural
　xx Design
　　Structural design
Architectural designs
　See Architecture—Designs and plans
Architectural details
　See Architecture—Details
Architectural drawing *(NA2700-2780)*
　sa Architectural rendering
　　Architecture—Designs and plans
　　Architecture—Details
　x Drawing, Architectural
　　Plans
　xx Architectural design
　　Drawing
　　Mechanical drawing
Architectural engineering
　See Building
　　Building, Iron and steel
　　Strains and stresses
　　Strength of materials
　　Structures, Theory of
Architectural inscriptions *(Direct)*
　(NA4050.I5)
　x Architectural lettering
　　Building inscriptions
　　House inscriptions
　　Inscriptions, Architectural
　xx Inscriptions
　　Lettering
Architectural ironwork *(Direct) (NA3950;*
　TH1651-5)
　sa Architectural metal-work
　　Building fittings
　xx Architectural metal-work
　　Building fittings
　　Ironwork
　　Wrought-iron
Architectural ironwork, English, ₍French,
　German, etc.₎
Architectural law and legislation
　See Architects—Legal status, laws, etc.
　　Building laws
　　Engineering law
Architectural lettering
　See Architectural inscriptions
Architectural libraries *(Z675.A83)*
　x Libraries, Architectural
　xx Art libraries
Architectural lighting
　See Lighting, Architectural and decorative
Architectural metal-work *(TA685;*
　TH1651-5)
　sa Architectural ironwork
　　Art metal-work
　　Building fittings
　　Finials
　x Metal-work, Architectural
　xx Architectural ironwork
　　Art metal-work
　　Building fittings
　　Metal-work
Architectural models *(NA2790)*
　sa Architectural casts
　　Miniature rooms
　　Structural frames—Models
　x Buildings—Models
　　Models, Architectural
　xx Architectural casts
　　Artists' preparatory studies
　　Miniature objects
　　Models and modelmaking
Architectural orders
　See Architecture—Orders

Architectural perspective
  See Perspective
Architectural photography
  See Photography, Architectural
Architectural polychromy
  See Color in architecture
Architectural practice *(Direct)*
  sa Architecture as a profession
     Decision-making in architecture
     Group work in architecture
  x Architectural services
     Architecture—Practice
  xx Architecture as a profession
  — Costs
     sa Architects—Fees
  — Marketing
       See Architectural services marketing
Architectural rendering
  sa Architecture—Sketch-books
  x Architectural renderings
  xx Architectural drawing
     Architecture—Sketch-books
     Perspective
     Shades and shadows
Architectural renderings
  See Architectural rendering
Architectural schools
  See Schools of architecture
Architectural services
  See Architectural practice
Architectural services marketing *(Direct)*
  x Architectural practice—Marketing
  xx Sales promotion
Architectural societies *(Indirect)*
  xx Societies
Architectural symbolism
  See Symbolism in architecture
Architectural technicians *(Direct)*
  xx Architects
Architectural writing
  x Architecture—Authorship
  xx Authorship
Architecture *(Direct) (NA)*
  sa Abbeys
     Amphitheaters
     Arches
     Architecture, Tropical
     Archive buildings
     Bank buildings
     Basilicas
     Bosses (Architecture)
     Building
     Building materials
     Buildings
     Castles
     Cathedrals
     Cave architecture
     Church architecture
     Club-houses
     Color in architecture
     Columns
     Concrete construction
     Decision-making in architecture
     Decoration and ornament, Architectural
     Entrance halls
     Environmental engineering (Buildings)
     Exhibition buildings
     Factories
     Farm buildings
     Follies (Architecture)
     Fountains
     Glass construction
     Group work in architecture
     Half-columns
     Hospitals—Construction
     Indians—Architecture
     Light in architecture
     Lighting, Architectural and decorative

Mannerism (Architecture)
     Mercantile buildings
     Military architecture
     Modular coordination (Architecture)
     Monuments
     Mosques
     Moving-picture theaters
     Municipal buildings
     Naval architecture
     Obelisks
     Office buildings
     Orientation (Architecture)
     Palaces
     Pediments
     Public buildings
     School buildings
     Sepulchral monuments
     Skyscrapers
     Space frame structures
     Spherical buildings
     Spires
     Strains and stresses
     Strength of materials
     Structural engineering
     Symbolism in architecture
     Tall buildings
     Temples
     Tenement-houses
     Theaters—Construction
     Tombs
     Towers
     Tympana (Architecture)
     Vaults (Architecture)
     headings beginning with the word
       Architectural
  x Building design
     Construction
  xx Art
     Building
     Buildings
     Engineering
Note under Buildings
  — Authorship
     See Architectural writing
  — Caricatures and cartoons
  — Climatic factors
     See Architecture and climate
  — Competitions *(NA2335-2360)*
     sa Kenchikugyō Kyōkai shō
        Pairotto hausu gijutsu kōan kyōgi
     Example under Rewards (Prizes, etc.);
        and under references from Compe-
        titions; Prize competitions
  — Composition, proportion, etc. *(NA2760)*
     sa Space (Architecture)
     x Architecture—Proportion
        Proportion (Architecture)
     xx Architectural design
        Composition (Art)
  — Congresses
  — Conservation and restoration
     sa Buildings—Repair and reconstruction
     x Architecture—Restoration
        Buildings, Restoration of
        Conservation of buildings
        Restoration of buildings
     xx Buildings—Repair and reconstruction
  — — Finance
  — Decoration and ornament
     See Decoration and ornament,
        Architectural
  — Designs and plans *(NA2600-2635)*
     sa Hospitals—Construction
        Theaters—Construction
     x Architectural designs
        Architecture—Plans
        Designs, Architectural
     xx Architectural drawing

Architecture—Sketch-books
  — Details *(NA2835-3060)*
     sa Ancones
        Apses (Architecture)
        Balconies
        Bases (Architecture)
        Capitals (Architecture)
        Caryatids
        Ceilings
        Chimneys
        Church architecture—Details
        Corbels
        Cornices
        Domes
        Doorways
        Façades
        Fireplaces
        Floors
        Foundations
        Friezes
        Gables
        Grilles
        Moldings
        Plinths
        Porches
        Roofs
        Screens
        Staircases
        Vanes
        Windows
        Woodwork
     x Architectural details
        Buildings—Details
        Details, Architectural
     xx Architectural design
        Architectural drawing
  — Early works to 1800 *(NA2515-2517)*
  — Examinations
  — Exhibitions *(NA2430-2460)*
  — Guide-books
  — Handbooks, manuals, etc.
  — Historiography
  — Influence of climate
     See Architecture and climate
  — Juvenile literature *(NA2555)*
  — Law and legislation
     See Architects—Legal status, laws,
        etc.
        Building laws
        Engineering law
  — Manuscripts
  — Mathematical models
  — Modular design
     See Modular coordination
        (Architecture)
  — Orders *(NA2810-2817)*
     x Architectural orders
        Orders, Architectural
  — Pictorial works
  — Plans
     See Architecture—Designs and plans
  — Practice
     See Architectural practice
  — Proportion
     See Architecture—Composition,
        proportion, etc.
  — Psychological aspects
  — Restoration
     See Architecture—Conservation and
        restoration
  — Sketch-books
     sa Architectural rendering
        Architecture—Designs and plans
     xx Architectural rendering
  — Study and teaching *(Direct)*
     sa Schools of architecture
     xx Schools of architecture
  — Terminology

— Views

— Egypt, ₍Italy, Japan, etc.₎
    sa Architecture, Egyptian, ₍Italian,
        Japanese, etc.₎
    xx Architecture, Egyptian, ₍Italian,
        Japanese, etc.₎

— — Juvenile literature

Architecture, American, ₍French, etc.₎
    (Direct)
    x American ₍French, etc.₎ architecture

Architecture, Ancient *(NA210-340)*
    sa Arches, Triumphal
        Basilicas
        Capitols
        Pyramids
        Seven Wonders of the World
        Temples
        Architecture, Egyptian; Architecture,
          Greek; *and similar headings*
    xx Archaeology
  — Juvenile literature

Architecture, Anonymous *(NA203)*
    Here are entered works dealing with ar-
    chitecture and architectural styles of
    "folk" character developed from in-
    digenous sources or borrowed from
    traditional sources by untrained and
    unidentified practitioners.
    x Anonymous architecture
        Non-professional architecture

Architecture, Arab
  See Architecture, Islamic

Architecture, Assyro-Babylonian
    (NA220-221)
    sa Ziggurats
    x Assyro-Babylonian architecture

Architecture, Aztec
  See Indians of Mexico—Architecture

Architecture, Baroque *(Direct) (NA590)*
    x Baroque architecture

Architecture, Buddhist
    sa Architecture, Zen
        Stūpas
        Temples, Buddhist
    x Buddhist architecture

Architecture, Byzantine *(NA370-373)*
    x Byzantine architecture

Architecture, Carlovingian *(Direct)*
    x Carlovingian architecture
        Carolingian architecture
    xx Architecture, Medieval

Architecture, Carthusian *(Direct)*
    x Carthusian architecture
    xx Architecture, Medieval

Architecture, Cave
  See Cave architecture

Architecture, Celtic
    x Celtic architecture

Architecture, Church
  See Church architecture

Architecture, Cistercian *(Direct) (NA4820)*
    x Cistercian architecture
    xx Architecture, Gothic
        Church architecture

Architecture, Cluniac
    x Cluniac architecture

Architecture, Colonial *(Direct) (NA707)*
    sa subdivision Historic houses, etc. *under*
      names of countries, cities, etc.
    x Colonial architecture
  — Juvenile literature

Architecture, Domestic *(Direct)*
    (NA7100-7786)
    sa Adobe houses

Apartment houses
Bathrooms
Bedrooms
Brick houses
Bungalows
Children's rooms
Concrete houses
Cottages
Country homes
Decks (Architecture, Domestic)
Dining rooms
Earth houses
Farm buildings
Farmhouses
Fishing lodges
Grass huts
Half-timbered houses
House construction
Hunting lodges
Labor and laboring classes—Dwellings
Living rooms
Patios
Pergolas
Prefabricated houses
Recreation rooms
Row houses
Single story houses
Sod houses
Solar houses
Stone houses
Suburban homes
Summer homes
Terrace houses
Wooden-frame houses
Youth—Dwellings
  x Architecture, Rural
    Domestic architecture
    Garden architecture
    Houses
    Residences
    Rural architecture
    Villas
  xx Cottages
    Dwellings
    Farm buildings
    Suburban homes
— Conservation and restoration
    x Architecture, Domestic—Restoration
— Designs and plans *(NA7127-7135)*
    x House plans
— Juvenile literature
— Location
    See Homesites
— Public opinion
— Restoration
    See Architecture, Domestic—
        Conservation and restoration

Architecture, Domestic, in art
    xx Art

Architecture, Domestic, in literature

Architecture, Early Christian
    x Early Christian architecture

Architecture, Ecclesiastical
  See Church architecture

Architecture, Egyptian *(NA1581-5; Ancient,*
    NA215-216)
    sa Architecture—Egypt
    x Egyptian architecture
    xx Architecture, Ancient
        Architecture—Egypt

Architecture, Gallo-Roman *(Direct)*
    x Gallo-Roman architecture
    xx Architecture, Roman

Architecture, Georgian *(NA640; NA707;*
    NA966)
    x Georgian architecture

Architecture, Germanic *(NA1061-1088)*
    x Germanic architecture

Architecture, Gothic *(Direct) (NA440-489)*
    sa Architecture, Cistercian
        Cathedrals
        Church architecture
        Decoration and ornament, Gothic
        Gothic revival (Architecture)
    x Gothic architecture
    xx Cathedrals
        Christian antiquities
        Church architecture

Architecture, Greek *(NA270-285)*
    sa Capitals (Architecture), Corinthian
        Columns, Corinthian
        Columns, Doric
        Columns, Ionic
        Greek revival (Architecture)
        Palaces
        Temples
        Architecture—Greece, *and particular*
          buildings, e.g. Athens. Parthenon
    x Greek architecture
    xx Architecture, Ancient
        Architecture—Greece

Architecture, Grotto
  See Cave architecture

Architecture, Hindu *(Direct)*
    x Hindu architecture

Architecture, Iberian
    sa Architecture, Portuguese
        Architecture, Spanish
    x Iberian architecture

Architecture, Industrial *(Direct) (NA6400)*
    sa Industrial buildings
    x Industrial architecture
  — Designs and plans

Architecture, Islamic *(Direct) (NA380-388)*
    sa Minarets
        Mosques
        particular buildings, e.g. Alhambra
    x Arab architecture
        Architecture, Arab
        Architecture, Moorish
        Architecture, Muslim
        Architecture, Saracenic
        Islamic architecture
        Moorish architecture
        Muslim architecture
        Saracenic architecture

Architecture, Italian
    sa Architecture—Italy
    x Italian architecture
    xx Architecture—Italy

Architecture, Jacobean
    x Jacobean architecture
    xx Architecture, Renaissance

Architecture, Jaina
    x Jaina architecture
    xx Jainism

Architecture, Japanese
    sa Architecture—Japan
        Architecture, Shoin
        Architecture, Sukiya
    x Japanese architecture
    xx Architecture—Japan
  — Heian period, 794-1185 *(NA1553.3)*
  — Occidental influences
    xx Civilization, Occidental

Architecture, Jesuit *(NA4820)*
    x Jesuit architecture
    xx Architecture, Renaissance
        Church architecture

Architecture, Jewish
    sa Synagogue architecture
        Synagogues
        Tabernacle
        Temples
        particular temples, etc., e.g. Jerusalem.
          Temple

Architecture, Jewish (Continued)
  x Jewish architecture
Architecture, Library
  See Library architecture
Architecture, Lombard
  x Lombard architecture
  xx Architecture, Medieval
Architecture, Manueline *(NA1325)*
  x Manueline architecture
Architecture, Maori
  x Maori architecture
  xx Architecture, Primitive
Architecture, Medieval *(Direct)*
    (NA350-497)
  sa Architecture, Carlovingian
    Architecture, Carthusian
    Architecture, Lombard
    Architecture, Norman
    Architecture, Romanesque
    Castles
    Cathedrals
  x Medieval architecture
  xx Middle Ages
Architecture, Military
  See Military architecture
Architecture, Minoan *(Direct)*
  x Minoan architecture
Architecture, Modern *(Direct)*
    (NA500-680)
  sa Neoclassicism (Architecture)
  x Modern architecture
  — 17th-18th centuries *(Direct)*
  — 19th century *(Direct)*
    sa Architecture, Victorian
      Romanesque revival (Architecture)
  — 20th century *(Direct)*
    sa Brutalism (Architecture)
      Constructivism (Architecture)
      Functionalism (Architecture)
      Romanesque revival (Architecture)
Architecture, Moorish
  See Architecture, Islamic
Architecture, Moravian *(Direct)*
  x Moravian architecture
Architecture, Mozarabic
  x Mozarabic architecture
Architecture, Muslim
  See Architecture, Islamic
Architecture, Mycenaean *(Direct)*
  x Mycenaean architecture
Architecture, Naval
  See Naval architecture
    Ship-building
Architecture, Norman *(NA423-9)*
  x Norman architecture
  xx Architecture, Medieval
Architecture, Norse
  x Norse architecture
Architecture, Oriental *(NA1460-1579)*
  sa Mosques
    Temples
    particular mosques, temples, etc., e.g.
      Jerusalem. Temple; Taj Mahal
  x Oriental architecture
Architecture, Portuguese *(Direct)*
  x Portuguese architecture
  xx Architecture, Iberian
Architecture, Primitive *(NA205-7;*
    Anthropology, GN414)
  sa Architecture, Maori
  xx Archaeology
Architecture, Prison
  See Prisons—Construction
Architecture, Renaissance *(Direct)*
    (NA510-575)
  sa Architecture, Jacobean
    Architecture, Jesuit
    Mannerism (Architecture)

  x Renaissance architecture
Architecture, Rococo *(Direct)* *(NA590)*
  x Rococo architecture
Architecture, Roman *(Direct)* *(NA310-340)*
  sa Arches, Triumphal
    Architecture, Gallo-Roman
    Architecture—Rome
    Palaces
    Temples
  x Roman architecture
  xx Architecture—Rome
Architecture, Romanesque *(Direct)*
    (NA390-419)
  sa Romanesque revival (Architecture)
  x Romanesque architecture
  xx Architecture, Medieval
Architecture, Rural
  See Architecture, Domestic
    Bungalows
    Cottages
    Country homes
    Farm buildings
Architecture, Saracenic
  See Architecture, Islamic
Architecture, Sassanid *(Direct)*
  x Sassanid architecture
Architecture, Shaker
  x Shaker architecture
Architecture, Shoin *(Direct)*
  x Shoin architecture
    Shoinzukuri
  xx Architecture, Japanese
Architecture, Spanish *(NA1301-1313)*
  sa Architecture—Spain
  x Spanish architecture
  xx Architecture, Iberian
    Architecture—Spain
Architecture, Sukiya *(Direct)*
  sa Chashitsu (Japanese tearooms)
  x Sukiya architecture
  xx Architecture, Japanese
Architecture, Tropical
  xx Architecture
    Architecture and climate
Architecture, Victorian *(Direct)*
  sa Gothic revival (Architecture)
  x Victorian architecture
  xx Architecture, Modern—19th century
    Gothic revival (Architecture)
Architecture, Zen
  x Zen architecture
  xx Architecture, Buddhist
Architecture (in numismatics)
  xx Numismatics
Architecture and climate *(Indirect)*
  sa Architecture, Tropical
    Heliodon
  x Architecture—Climatic factors
    Architecture—Influence of climate
    Climate and architecture
    Climate, Influence of
  xx Climatology
Architecture and communism
  See Communism and architecture
Architecture and liturgy
  See Liturgy and architecture
Architecture and mentally handicapped
    children *(Direct)*
  x Mentally handicapped children and
    architecture
  xx Architecture and the mentally
    handicapped
    Mental retardation facilities
Architecture and music
  See Music and architecture
Architecture and religion
  sa Church architecture
    Liturgy and architecture

    Orientation (Architecture)
  x Religion and architecture
  xx Church architecture
Architecture and society *(Direct)*
    (NA2543.S6)
  x Architecture and sociology
    Society and architecture
    Sociology and architecture
Architecture and sociology
  See Architecture and society
Architecture and solar radiation
    (NA2542.S6)
  x Sun protection in architecture
  xx Solar radiation
Architecture and space
  See Space (Architecture)
Architecture and the aged *(Direct)*
    (NA2545.A3)
  sa Aged—Dwellings
  x Aged and architecture
  xx Architecture and the handicapped
Architecture and the handicapped *(Direct)*
    (NA2545)
  sa Architecture and the aged
    Architecture and the mentally
      handicapped
    Architecture and the physically
      handicapped
  x Handicapped and architecture
Architecture and the mentally handicapped
    (Direct)
  sa Architecture and mentally handicapped
    children
  x Mentally handicapped and architecture
  xx Architecture and the handicapped
    Mental retardation facilities
Architecture and the physically handicapped
    (Direct) *(NA2545.P5)*
  sa Housing for physically handicapped
  x Physically handicapped and
    architecture
  xx Architecture and the handicapped
    Physically handicapped
Architecture and youth *(Direct)*
  sa Day nurseries
    Kindergartens
    Playgrounds
    Recreation centers
    School buildings
    Youth—Dwellings
    Youth hostels
  x Youth and architecture
Architecture as a profession *(NA1995)*
  sa Architectural practice
  xx Architects
    Architectural practice
Architecture in art
  xx Art
Architecture in literature *(PN56.A; English*
    literature, PR149.A)
  Example under Literature, Comparative—
    Themes, motives
Archival material on microfilm
  See Documents on microfilm
Archival resources on Bohemia, ⌈the United
    States, etc.⌉ *(Direct)*
Archive buildings *(CD981)*
  x Buildings, Archive
  xx Architecture
  Example under Buildings
Archives *(Indirect)* *(CD931-4279;*
    Directories, CD941; Handbooks,
    CD950-965)
  sa Business records
    Cartularies
    Charters
    Church records and registers
    Court records

Diplomatics
Historical libraries
Manuscripts
Public land records
Public records
Restricted collections in archives
Temple records and registers
subdivision Archives *under subjects,*
   e.g. Universities and colleges—
   Archives
  x Documents
Historical record preservation
Manuscript depositories
Manuscript repositories
Manuscripts—Depositories
Manuscripts—Repositories
Preservation of historical records
Public records—Preservation
  xx Auxiliary sciences of history
Bibliography
Cartularies
Charters
Diplomatics
Documentation
History—Sources
Information services
Public records
Records
— Calendars
   See Archives—Inventories, calendars,
     etc.
— Cataloging
   See Cataloging of archival material
— Catalogs
   See Archives—Inventories, calendars,
     etc.
— Classification
   See Classification—Archives
— Handbooks, manuals, etc.
— History
— — To 500   *(CD996)*
— — 500-1500
— Inventories, calendars, etc.
   x Archives—Calendars
Archives—Catalogs
Calendars, Archival
Inventories of archives
— Law and legislation   *(Direct)*

GEOGRAPHIC SUBDIVISIONS

— United States
   sa Presidents—United States—Archives
   x United States—Archives
Archives, Diocesan
  x Diocesan archives
  xx Church records and registers
Archives, Family
  See Family archives
Archives (Canon law)
Archives and photography
  See Photography—Archive applications
Archivists   *(Direct)*
Archons   *(DF83; Athens, DF277-285)*
  sa Cosmetes
Archostemata
  xx Beetles
Archostemata, Fossil
Archpriests
  See Archdeacons
Arctic blue-grass
Arctic char fishing   *(SH691.A7)*
  xx Fishing
Arctic clothing
  See Clothing, Cold weather

Arctic conditions
  See subdivision Cold weather conditions
   under specific subjects, e.g.
   Transportation, Military—Cold
   weather conditions
Arctic expeditions
  See Arctic regions
   names of expeditions, e.g. Grinnell
   Expedition, 1st, 1850-1851; *and*
   names of ships
Arctic flora
  See Botany—Arctic regions
Arctic fox
  xx Foxes
  Example under Fur-bearing animals
Arctic fox, Fossil
Arctic grayling
  x Grayling, Arctic
Grayling, Michigan
Grayling, Montana
Michigan grayling
Montana grayling
Arctic medicine
  x Cold weather medicine
Medicine, Arctic
  xx Cold—Physiological effect
Medicine
Arctic Ocean
  Example under Ocean
Arctic races   *(GN673)*
  sa Eskimos
Indians of North America—Alaska
Lapps
  x Ethnology—Arctic regions
Hyperboreans
Paleoasiatics
Paleosiberians
Arctic raspberry
  xx Raspberries
Arctic regions   *(G600-830; Botany, QK474;*
   Meteorology, QC994.8; Natural
   history, QH84.1; Terrestrial
   magnetism, QC825.8; Zoology,
   QL105)
  sa North Pole
Northeast Passage
Northwest Passage
Sanitary engineering, Low temperature
Scientific expeditions
Transportation, Military—Cold weather
  conditions
  names of exploring expeditions, e.g.
  Yenisei Expedition, 1876
  x Arctic expeditions
Arctic regions—Description and travel
Arctic regions—Discovery and
  exploration
Expeditions, Arctic
Polar expeditions
  xx Discoveries (in geography)
Earth
North Pole
Polar regions
Example under Scientific expeditions
— Aerial exploration
  xx Aeronautics—Flights
— American [Canadian, Russian, etc.]
  exploration   *(G630)*
— Description and travel
  See Arctic regions
— Discovery and exploration
  See Arctic regions
— Juvenile literature
— Research
  See Arctic research
Arctic research   *(Direct)*
  x Arctic regions—Research
  xx Research

Arctic sanitary engineering
  See Sanitary engineering, Low temperature
Arctic tern
  xx Terns
Arctic transportation
  See Transportation, Military—Cold weather
   conditions
Arcturus   *(QB805.A7)*
Ardeatine Massacre, 1944
  x Rasella Massacre, 1944
  xx World War, 1939-1945—Atrocities
Ardeidae
  See Herodiones
Herons
Ardennes, Battle of the, 1944-1945
   (D756.5.A7)
  x Bastogne, Battle of, 1944-1945
Bulge, Battle of the
  xx World War, 1939-1945—Campaigns—
   France (1944-1945)
Ardennes in art
Ardennes in literature
Ardhamagadhi language
  x Paiya language
Are are language
  See Areare language
Area bibliographers
  See Area specialist bibliographers
Area linguistics
  See Areal linguistics
Area measurement   *(Mathematical geography,*
   GA23)
  sa Cartometry
Length measurement
Planimeter
  subdivision Area *under names of*
   regions
  x Measurement of area
  xx Earth—Figure
Geodesy
Geography, Mathematical
Geometry, Plane
Length measurement
Mensuration
Surveying
— Tables, etc.
Area research
  See Area studies
Area septalis
  See Septum (Brain)
Area specialist bibliographers   *(Direct)*
  x Area bibliographers
  xx Area studies
Bibliographers
Area studies   *(D16.25)*
  sa Afro-Asian studies
Area specialist bibliographers
Geography—Study and teaching
Japanese studies; Occidental studies;
  Southeast Asian studies; *and similar*
  headings
  x Area research
Foreign area studies
  xx Education
Geography—Study and teaching
Area technical-vocational centers
  See Area vocational-technical centers
Area vocational-technical centers   *(Direct)*
  x Area technical-vocational centers
  xx Industrial arts—Study and teaching
Technical education
Vocational education
Areal linguistics
  sa Languages in contact
  x Area linguistics
  xx Linguistics
Areare language   *(PL6311.Z9A)*
  x Are are language

Areare language   (PL6311.Z9A)
(Continued)
   xx Melanesian languages
Areas, Law of (Mechanics)
   See Law of areas (Mechanics)
Areas (Building)
   See Areaways
Areaways   (TH3000)
   x Areas (Building)
   xx Building
Areca nut
   See Betel nut
Arecuna Indians   (F2380.1.A7)
   x Arekuna Indians
     Jarecoune Indians
     Jaricuna Indians
     Pemon Indians
     Taulipang Indians
     Taurepan Indians
   xx Indians of South America
— Legends
Arecuna language
   sa Pemón dialects
   x Arekuna language
   xx Cariban languages
     Indians of South America—Languages
Arekuna Indians
   See Arecuna Indians
Arekuna language
   See Arecuna language
Arena theater
   x Central staging
     Circus theater
     Penthouse theater
     Round stage
     Theater-in-the-round
   xx Theater
Areolar tissue
   See Connective tissues
Areometer
   See Hydrometer
Arere
   See Obeche
Aretine pottery
   See Pottery, Arretine
Aretine vases
   See Vases, Arretine
Argali
   xx Mountain sheep
Argand burner
   xx Gas-burners
     Oil burners
Argelès-sur-Mer (Concentration camp)
   Example under Concentration camps
Argentaffinoma
   See Carcinoid
Argentine ant
   Example under Insects, Injurious and benefi-
   cial
Argentine ballads and songs   (Collections,
     PQ7760-7761; History, PQ7680)
   sa Folk-songs, Argentine
     National songs, Argentine
     Songs, Argentine
   xx Spanish American ballads and songs
Argentine-Brazilian War, 1825-1828   (F2726)
   sa Ituzaingó, Battle of, 1827
     Sarandi, Battle of, 1825
   x Brazilian-Argentine War, 1825-1828
Argentine carols
   See Carols, Argentine
Argentine drama   (Collections, PQ7764-7770;
     History, PQ7683-7695)
Argentine essays
Argentine farces
Argentine fiction   (Direct)
Argentine Friesian cattle
   See Holando-Argentino cattle
Argentine imprints   (Direct)

Argentine literature   (PQ7600-7799)
   xx Spanish American literature
Argentine newspapers   (History, etc.,
     PN5001-5010)
Argentine periodicals   (History, etc.,
     PN5001-5010)
Argentine philology
Argentine poetry   (Direct)   (Collections,
     PQ7749-7763; History,
     PQ7661-7681)
— 19th century
— 20th century
Argentine prose literature   (Direct)
Argentine Republic
— History   (F2801-3021)
       Includes early works on the La Plata
       region before the formation of the
       viceroyalty of La Plata in 1776.
— — To 1810
— — — Juvenile literature
— — 1515-1535
— — 1535-1617
— — 1617-1776
— — Guarani War, 1754-1756
       See Seven Reductions, War of the,
       1754-1756
— — 1776-1810
— — English invasions, 1806-1807
— — 1810-
— — War of Independence, 1810-1817
       sa Martín García, Battle of, 1814
          Suipacha, Battle of, 1810
— — — Religious aspects
— — 1817-1860
       sa Cañada de la Cruz, Argentine
          Republic, Battle of, 1820
          Pago Largo, Battle of, 1839
          San Gregorio, Battle of, 1853
— — 1860-1910
       sa Pozo de Vargas, Battle of, 1867
— — Revolution, 1890
— — 1910-
— — 1910-1943
— — Revolution, 1930
— — 1943-   (F2849)
— — Revolution, 1955
— — Coup d'état, 1966
       x Argentine Republic—History—
          Revolution, 1966
— — Revolution, 1966
       See Argentine Republic—History—
       Coup d'état, 1966
Argentine rummy
   See Canasta (Game)
Argentine students in Bolivia, ₍etc.₎
Argentine teachers in Cuba, ₍etc.₎
   x Teachers in Cuba, ₍etc.₎, Argentine
Argentine wit and humor   (Collections,
     PQ7785; History, PQ7715)
Argentines
   x Argentinians
Argentines in Cuba, ₍the United States, etc.₎
Argentines in foreign countries
Argentinians
   See Argentines
Argillite   (Indirect)
   x Mudrock
   xx Clay
     Shale
     Slate
Argobba language
Argon   (QD181.A6)
   sa Krypton
     Metargon
     Neon
   xx Air—Analysis
     Gases, Rare
     Krypton

Neon
   Example under Gases
— Isotopes
   sa Potassium-argon dating
   x Radioargon
— — Spectra
— Spectra
Argon-potassium dating
   See Potassium-argon dating
Argonauts
   x Golden Fleece
   xx Mythology
     Mythology, Classical
— Art
— Juvenile literature
Argonne, Battle of the, 1915   (D545.A6)
   xx European War, 1914-1918—Campaigns
     —France
Argonne, Battle of the, 1918   (D545.A63)
   xx European War, 1914-1918—Campaigns
     —France
Argot
   See Cant
     Slang
Argot des marchands d'images
   See Ochweśnicki jargon
Argumentation
   See Debates and debating
     Logic
     Oratory
     Reasoning
     Syllogism
Arguments, Legal
   See Forensic orations
Argus camera
Argus project
   See Project Argus
Argyllshire Gathering
Argyria   (RA1231.S5)
   x Argyriasis
     Argyrism
   xx Pigmentation disorders
     Silver—Physiological effect
Argyriasis
   See Argyria
Argyrism
   See Argyria
Argyroneta aquatica
   See Water-spiders
Arhar
   See Pigeon-pea
Arhats
   x Lohans
   xx Saints, Buddhist
Arhouaques-Kaggaba
   See Kagaba Indians
Arhuaco Indians   (F2270.2.A67)
   x Aruaco Indians
   xx Indians of South America
Arhythmia
   See Arrhythmia
Arianism   (BT1350)
   sa Eunomianism
     Jesus Christ—Divinity
     Socinianism
     Unitarianism
   x Humanitarianism (Religion)
   xx Antitrinitarianism
     Church history—Primitive and early
       church, ca. 30-600
     Jesus Christ—Divinity
     Socinianism
     Trinity
     Unitarianism
Arias
   See Songs
Ariboflavinosis   (RC299.A)
   x Pellagra sine pellagra

xx Deficiency diseases
    Pellagra
    Riboflavin
Arica, Battle of, 1880
    xx War of the Pacific, 1879-1884
Arickara Indians
    See Arikara Indians
Arickaree Indians
    See Arikara Indians
Arid regions *(Indirect)*
    sa Deserts
    x Arid zones
      Semiarid regions
    xx Crop zones
      Irrigation
      Water-supply
  — Research *(Direct)*
    x Arid zone research
    xx Agricultural research
Arid regions agriculture *(Indirect)* *(SB110)*
    sa Dry farming
      Irrigation farming
    x Dryland farming
    xx Agriculture
Arid zone research
    See Arid regions—Research
Arid zones
    See Arid regions
Ariel (Artificial satellite)
    xx Artificial satellites
      Astronautics—International cooperation
      Ionospheric research
Arikara hymns
    See Hymns, Arikara
Arikara Indians *(E99.A8)*
    x Arickara Indians
      Arickaree Indians
      Ree Indians
    xx Caddoan Indians
      Indians of North America
Arikara language *(PM636.A7)*
    xx Caddoan languages
Arisah
    See Bulgur
Aristocracy *(Political science, JC411-417; Social classes, HT647)*
    sa Democracy
      Nobility
      Upper classes
      subdivision Nobility under names of countries, e.g. Germany—Nobility
    xx Democracy
      Equality
      Nobility
      Political science
      Sociology
      Upper classes
  — Anecdotes, facetiae, satire, etc.
Aristocracy in literature
Aristocratic education
    See Upper classes—Education
Aristotype *(TR395)*
    xx Photography—Printing processes— Silver
Arita porcelain *(NK4399.A7)*
    sa Imari porcelain
      Kakiemon porcelain
    x Porcelain, Arita
Arithmetic *(QA101-145; Primitive, GN476.1)*
    sa Accounting
      Addition
      Average
      Cube root
      Decimal system
      Division
      Duodecimal system
      Fractions
      Metric system

      Multiplication
      Number line
      Numbers, Real
      Numeration
      Octal system
      Percentage
      Quinary system
      Ratio and proportion
      Square root
      Subtraction
      Time-rate-distance tables
    xx Mathematics
      Numbers, Real
      Set theory
  Example under Text-books
  — To 1846
  — 1846-1880
  — 1881-1900
  — 1901-1960 *(QA106)*
  — 1961- *(QA107)*
  — Caricatures and cartoons
  — Examinations
  — Examinations, questions, etc. *(QA139)*
  — Foundations *(QA248)*
    sa Algorithms
      Gödel's theorem
      Recursive functions
    x Foundations of arithmetic
    xx Mathematics—Philosophy
  — Juvenile literature
  — Problems, exercises, etc.
  — Programmed instruction
  — Remedial teaching *(QA135)*
    x Remedial arithmetic
    xx Remedial teaching
  — Study and teaching (Elementary)
  — Study and teaching (Preschool) *(Direct)* *(QA135.5)*
  — Study and teaching (Primary) *(Direct)*
    sa Arithmetic readiness
    x Number games
      Number study
Arithmetic, Commercial
    See Business mathematics
Arithmetic, Floating-point
    See Floating-point arithmetic
Arithmetic, Mechanical
    See Calculating-machines
Arithmetic, Mental
    x Mental arithmetic
Arithmetic, Pharmaceutical
    See Pharmaceutical arithmetic
Arithmetic and logic units, Computer
    See Computer arithmetic and logic units
Arithmetic functions
    x Functions, Arithmetic
    xx Functions of complex variables
      Numbers, Theory of
Arithmetic readiness
    xx Arithmetic—Study and teaching (Primary)
Arithmetic series
    See Series, Arithmetic
Arithmetical ability
    See Mathematical ability
Arithmomancy
    See Fortune-telling by numbers
ARITMA computer *(QA76.8.A)*
    xx Electronic digital computers
Arizona
  — History *(F806-820)*
  — — To 1950
  — — Civil War, 1861-1865
  — — 1951-
Ark, Holy
    See Ark of the law
Ark, Noah's
    See Noah's Ark

Ark of the Covenant
    x Mercy seat
    xx Angels
      Cultus, Jewish
      Jews—Antiquities
      Tabernacle
      Yom Kippur
Ark of the law *(BM657.A85)*
    x Ark, Holy
      Aron ha-kodesh
      Holy ark
    xx Cultus, Jewish
      Synagogues
Arkansas
  — History *(F406-420)*
  — — Civil War, 1861-1865 *(E496; Confederate, E553)*
Arlis II (Drifting ice station)
    xx Drifting ice stations
      Ice islands
Arm *(Comparative anatomy: general, QL950.7; muscles, QL831; skeleton, QL821; Human anatomy: muscles, QM165; skeleton, QM117; Surgical and topographical anatomy, QM548)*
    sa Axilla
      Humerus
      Radius
    xx Extremities (Anatomy)
  — Blood-vessels
    x Blood-vessels, Brachial
  — — Diseases
  — Fracture
  — Innervation
    x Nerves, Brachial
  — Muscles
    xx Muscles
  — Prosthesis
    See Artificial arms
  — Surgery *(RD551-7)*
    sa Amputations of arm
Arm pain
    See Brachialgia
Armada, 1588 *(DA360)*
    x Spanish Armada
  — Juvenile literature
Armadillos *(QL737.E2)*
    x Chlamydophoridae
      Dasypodidae
    xx Edentata
  — Juvenile literature
Armadillos, Fossil
    xx Edentata, Fossil
Armaments
    Here are entered general works on military strength, including military personnel, munitions, natural resources and industrial war potential. Works on the implements of war and the industries producing them are entered under the heading Munitions.
    Works on the armament of a particular country are entered under the name of the country with subdivision Defenses, *e.g.* United States—Defenses.
    sa Aeronautics, Military
      Ammunition
      Armed Forces
      Armies
      Disarmament
      Firearms industry and trade
      Industrial mobilization
      Munitions
      Navies
      Ordnance

Armaments *(Continued)*
 armies, navies, etc. of individual
  countries, e.g. Germany. Heer;
  Spain. Armada; United States.
  Army
 xx Military art and science
 Note under Munitions
Armans
 See Arumanians
Armatoli
 See Martoloses
Armatures *(TK2477)*
 sa Electric motors—Windings
 x Electric armatures
 xx Dynamos
  Electric apparatus and appliances
  Electric motors
Armed Forces
 sa Air forces
  Armies
  Combatants and noncombatants
   (International law)
  Navies
  Sociology, Military
  Soldiers
  specific branches of the Armed Forces
   under names of countries, e.g.
   United States. Army; *and*
   subdivision Armed Forces *under*
   names of countries, regions,
   international organizations, etc., e.g.
   United States—Armed Forces;
   United Nations—Armed Forces
 x Armed Services
 xx Armaments
  Military art and science
— Abbreviations
— Anecdotes, facetiae, satire, etc.
— Appropriations and expenditures
— Civic action
  Here are entered works on the non-
  military use of armed forces for so-
  cial and economic development.
  sa subdivision Civic action *under names*
   of armies, navies, etc., e.g. United
   States—Armed Forces—Civic
   action
 x Civic action of Armed Forces
  Military civic action
— Discharge
  See Military discharge
— Equipment
— Insignia
  xx Insignia
— Journalism
  See Journalism, Military
— Mascots *(U750)*
  Example under Pets; *and under refer-*
   ences from Mascots, Military; Mili-
   tary mascots
— Officers, Retired
  See Retired military personnel
— Personnel management
— Political activity
  xx Sociology, Military
— Prayer-books and devotions
  Subdivided by language.
  x Soldiers—Prayer-books and
   devotions
— Registers
— Retired military personnel
  See Retired military personnel
— Supplies and stores
— Vocational guidance
Armed Forces Day *(U43.U)*
 x Army Day
  Navy Day
 xx United States—Armed Forces

Armed Forces in foreign countries
 sa Military occupation
  subdivision Armed Forces—Foreign
   countries *under names of countries,*
   e.g. United States—Armed Forces—
   Foreign countries
Armed Forces newspapers
 See Journalism, Military
Armed merchant ships
 sa European War, 1914-1918—Naval
  operations
  World War, 1939-1945—Naval
  operations
 x Merchant ships, Armed
 xx Armored vessels
  Maritime law
  Merchant marine
  Merchant ships
  Submarine warfare
  War, Maritime (International law)
Armed Neutrality, 1780 and 1800
 See Neutrality, Armed
Armed Services
 See Armed Forces
Armenia
— History
—— To 428
—— Artaxiad (Artashesian) dynasty, 189
   B.C.-1 A.D.
—— Arsacid (Arshakuni) dynasty, 66-428
—— 428-1522
—— Persian and Greek rule, 429-640
   sa Awarayr, Battle of, 451
—— Arab period, 640-885
—— Bagratuni dynasty, 885-1045
—— Turkic-Mongol domination, 1045-1522
   sa Cilicia—History—Armenian
    Kingdom, 1080-1375
—— 1522-1800
—— 1801-1900
   sa Armenian massacres, 1894-1896
    Armenian question
—— 1901-
   sa Armenian massacres, 1915-1923
    Armenian question
—— 1917-1921
   Includes the Armenian Republic,
   1918-1920.
—— 1921-
Armenia in art
Armenia in literature
Armenia in the Bible
Armenian Church in Palestine, [etc.]
Armenian Church monasteries
 See Monasteries, Armenian
Armenian drama *(Direct)* *(Collections,*
  PK8537-8; History, PK8521)
Armenian fiction *(Direct)*
Armenian genocide, 1915-1923
 See Armenian massacres, 1915-1923
Armenian imprints *(Direct)*
— Publishing
Armenian language *(PK8001-8454)*
 xx Aryan languages
— Writing
  See Writing, Armenian
Armenian language, Classical *(PK8001-8099)*
 x Old Armenian language
Armenian language, Middle
Armenian language, Modern
— East Armenian *(PK8451-8499)*
 x East Armenian language
— West Armenian *(PK8351-8449)*
 x West Armenian language
Armenian literature *(PK8500-8958)*
— 20th century

— Cataloging
  See Cataloging of Armenian literature
Armenian literature (English)
 See American literature—Armenian authors
Armenian manuscripts
 See Manuscripts, Armenian
Armenian massacres, 1894-1896 *(Direct)*
 xx Armenia—History—1801-1900
  Armenian question
Armenian massacres, 1909 *(Direct)*
 xx Armenian question
Armenian massacres, 1915-1923 *(Direct)*
  (DS195.5)
 x Armenian genocide, 1915-1923
 xx Armenia—History—1901-
  Armenian question
  European War, 1914-1918—Atrocities
— Personal narratives
Armenian mythology
 See Mythology, Armenian
Armenian periodicals
Armenian poetry
Armenian prose literature *(Direct)*
Armenian question *(DS194-5)*
 sa Armenian massacres, 1894-1896
  Armenian massacres, 1909
  Armenian massacres, 1915-1923
 xx Armenia—History—1801-1900
  Armenia—History—1901-
Armenian studies *(Direct)*
Armenian type
 See Type and type-founding—Armenian
  type
Armenian wit and humor, Pictorial *(Direct)*
Armenians *(DS161-199)*
Armenians in foreign countries
— Caricatures and cartoons
Armenians in Russia, [Turkey, etc.]
— Legal status, laws, etc.
Armies
 sa Disarmament
  Mercenary troops
  Militarism
  Military art and science, *and references*
   under that heading
  Military service, Compulsory
  Navies
  Recruiting and enlistment
  Sociology, Military
  Soldiers
  Standing army
  War, Cost of
  World War, 1939-1945—Manpower
  France. Armée; Italy. Esercito;
   United States. Army; *and similar*
   headings
 x Army
  Military power
 xx Armaments
  Armed Forces
  Military art and science
  Military statistics
  Navies
  Soldiers
  Strategy
  War
— Accounting
— Commissariat *(UC700-780)*
  sa Cookery, Military
  Forage
  Operational rations (Military
   supplies)

subdivisions Commissariat *and*
Supplies and stores *under armies,*
e.g. France. Armée—
Commissariat; France. Armée—
Supplies and stores
  x Armies—Supplies
Army supplies
Commissariat
Mess
Military equipment, supplies, etc.
Rations
  xx Military supplies
— Discipline
  See Military discipline
— Equipment *(UC460-465)*
  x Military equipment, supplies, etc.
— Insignia *(UC530-535)*
  xx Insignia
— Maneuvers
  See Military maneuvers
— Medical and sanitary affairs
  sa Medicine, Military
  subdivision Sanitary affairs *under*
    armies, e.g. United States. Army
    —Sanitary affairs; *and subdivision*
    Medical and sanitary affairs *under*
    wars, e.g. World War, 1939-1945
    —Medical and sanitary affairs
  xx War—Medical aspects
— Motorization
  See Motorization, Military
— Music
  See Military music
    Music in the army
    War-songs
— Non-commissioned officers
  sa subdivision Non-commissioned
    officers *under armies, e.g.* United
    States. Army—
    Non-commissioned officers
  xx Armies—Officers
— Officers *(UB410-415)*
  sa Armies—Non-commissioned officers
  subdivision Officers *under armies,*
    e.g. United States. Army—
    Officers
  x Army officers
— Organization
  sa Armies—Staffs
  x Army organization
  xx Armies—Staffs
    Military law
— Remount service
  See Remount service
— Staffs *(UB220-225)*
  sa Armies—Organization
    Marshals
    Orders, Preparation of (Military
    science)
  under names of countries, the
    designation of the general staff,
    e.g. France. Armée. État-major;
    United States. War Dept.
    General Staff
  x General staffs
    Military staffs
    Staffs, Military
  xx Armies—Organization
— Supplies
  See Armies—Commissariat
    Military supplies
  subdivision Supplies and stores
    under armies, e.g. France.
    Armée—Supplies and stores
Armies, Colonial
  sa subdivision Colonial forces *under*
    armies, e.g. Great Britain. Army—
    Colonial forces

  x Colonial armies
    Colonies—Armies
Armies, Cost of *(UA17)*
  sa War, Cost of
  x Cost of armies
  xx Disarmament
    Peace
    War, Cost of
Arminianism *(BX6195-7)*
  sa Arminians
    Calvinism
    Methodism
    Neonomianism
  xx Calvinism
Arminians *(BX6195-7)*
  sa Remonstrants
  xx Arminianism
    Reformed Church
    Remonstrants
Armiñon, Battle of, 1837 *(DP219.2)*
  x Carga de Armiñon
    Combate de Armiñon
    Zambrana, Battle of, 1837
  xx Portugal—History—1826-1853
    Spain—History—Carlist War,
    1833-1840
Armistice Day
  See Veterans Day
Armistices *(JX5173)*
  sa Flags of truce
  x Truces
  xx Peace
    War (International law)
Armor
  See Arms and armor
Armor-plate *(V900-925)*
  xx Armored vessels
    Naval art and science
    Warships
Armored cars (Tanks)
  See Tanks (Military science)
Armored military vehicles
  See Armored vehicles, Military
Armored trains *(UG345)*
  x Trains, Armored
  xx Military art and science
    Railroads—Trains
Armored vehicles, Military
  sa Tanks (Military science)
  x Armored military vehicles
    Combat vehicles
    Vehicles, Armored (Military science)
  xx Tanks (Military science)
    Vehicles, Military
— Maintenance and repair
Armored vessels *(V799-800)*
  sa Armed merchant ships
    Armor-plate
    Turret ships
    Turrets
    Warships
  x Iron-clad vessels
    Ironclads
    Vessels, Armored
  xx Naval architecture
    Naval art and science
    Navies
    Ship-building
    Ships
    Warships
— Juvenile literature
Armorers *(Direct)*
Armorers' marks
  x Arms and armor—Marks
    Marks, Armorers'
Armorial book-plates
  See Book-plates, Heraldic

Armorial bookbindings
  See Bookbinding—Armorial bindings
Armoric language
  See Breton language
Armoric literature
  See Breton literature
Armories *(Indirect)* *(UA)*
  sa Arsenals
    Military museums
  xx Arsenals
    Military architecture
    Military museums
Armour Research Reactor
  x ARR (Nuclear reactor)
  xx Atomic energy research
    Nuclear reactors
Armpit
  See Axilla
Arms, Artificial
  See Artificial arms
Arms, Coats of
  See Devices
    Heraldry
Arms, Profession of
  See Military service as a profession
Arms and armor *(U800-825; Art,*
        NK6600-6699; Industry, HD9743)
  sa Aeroplanes, Military—Armaments
    Bayonets
    Daggers
    Damascening
    Firearms
    Miniature arms
    Ordnance
    Pistols
    Rifles
    Sabers
    Shields
    Spears
    Swords
    Tournaments
  x Armor
    Weapons
  xx Art industries and trade
    Costume
    Military art and science
    Military paraphernalia
— Collectors and collecting
— Conservation and restoration
— Corrosion
— Exhibitions
    Here are entered works dealing with
    antiquarian collections, exhibits of
    ancient and medieval weapons, his-
    toric battle relics, etc.
  sa Military museums
  xx Military museums
— Juvenile literature
— Marks
  See Armorers' marks
— Private collections *(Direct)*
— Terminology
Arms and armor, Ancient *(Direct)*
Arms and armor, English, ⌜**Spanish, etc.**⌝
        (Direct)
  x English ⌜Spanish, etc.⌝ arms and armor
— Juvenile literature
Arms and armor, Islamic
  x Arms and armor, Muslim
    Islamic arms and armor
    Muslim arms and armor
Arms and armor, Muslim
  See Arms and armor, Islamic
Arms and armor, Primitive *(GN498)*
  sa Boomerangs
    Bow and arrow
    Indians—Arms and armor

Arms and armor, Primitive *(GN498)*
   (Continued)
          Indians of North America—Arms and
            armor
          Indians of South America—Arms and
            armor
          Patu
          Projectile points
          Throwing-sticks
   xx Archaeology
      Ethnology
      Industries, Primitive
Arms control
   See Disarmament
Armstrong gun
   xx Ordnance
Army
   See Armies
      Military art and science
      Standing army
      France. Armée; Italy. Esercito;
         United States. Army; *and similar*
         headings
Army ants *(QL568.F7)*
   xx Ants
Army appropriation bills
   See subdivision Appropriations and
        expenditures *under armies, e.g.*
        United States. Army—
        Appropriations and expenditures
Army aviation (United States Army)
   See United States. Army—Aviation
Army Day
   See Armed Forces Day
Army life
   See subdivision Military life *under armies,*
      e.g. France. Armée—Military life;
      United States. Army—Military life
Army-McCarthy controversy, 1954
   See McCarthy-Army controversy, 1954
Army motorization
   See Motorization, Military
Army newspapers
   See Journalism, Military
Army officers
   See Armies—Officers
Army organization
   See Armies—Organization
      subdivision Organization *under armies,*
      e.g. France. Armée—Organization;
      United States. Army—Organization
Army package power reactors
   xx Atomic power-plants
      Nuclear reactors
Army posts
   See Military posts
Army reactors (PM)
   x PM reactors
   xx Pressurized water reactors
Army schools
   See Military education
      Military post schools
Army supplies
   See Armies—Commissariat
      Military supplies
      subdivision Supplies and stores *under*
      armies, e.g. United States. Army—
      Supplies and stores
Army wagons
   See Vehicles, Military
Army wives *(U750-773)*
   x Dependents of military personnel
      Families of military personnel
      Military dependents
      Military families
   xx Etiquette
      Wives
Army-worms *(SB945.A8)*
   sa Cotton-worm

      Fall army-worms
   xx Caterpillars
Arnaville, Battle of, 1944
   x Moselle River, Battle of the, 1944
   xx World War, 1939-1945—Campaigns—
      Alsace
Arnel
   See Triacetate
Arnhem, Battle of, 1944 *(D763.N4)*
   xx World War, 1939-1945—Campaigns—
      Netherlands
Arnica (Drug)
   xx Materia medica, Vegetable
Arnica oil
Arolla pine
   See Swiss pine
Aroma of food
   See Food—Odor
Aromani
   See Arumanians
Aromatic compounds
   — Physiological effect
   — Problems, exercises, etc.
   — Reactivity
   — Spectra
   — Tables
Aromatic plant products
   See Essences and essential oils
Aromatic plants *(Indirect)*
   sa Essences and essential oils
      Lavender (Plant)
      Lemon-grass oil
      Sweet goldenrod
      Vetiver
   xx Botany
      Essences and essential oils
      Plants, Cultivated
Aromatic plants (in religion, folk-lore, etc.)
   x Folk-lore of aromatic plants
   xx Plant-lore
      Religion, Primitive
Aromunes
   See Arumanians
Aron ha-kodesh
   See Ark of the law
Aroostook War, 1839 *(E398)*
   xx Northeast boundary of the United
      States
Arorai language
   See Gilbertese language
Arosaguntacook Indians
   x Amarascogin Indians
      Amerescoggin Indians
      Anasagunticook Indians
      Androscoggin Indians
      Bescommonconty Indians
   xx Abnaki Indians
      Algonquian Indians
      Indians of North America
Arosi language *(PL6311.Z9A)*
   xx Melanesian languages
Arousal (Physiology)
   xx Physiology
      Psychology, Physiological
ARR (Nuclear reactor)
   See Armour Research Reactor
Arrah
   — Siege, 1857
      xx India—History—Sepoy Rebellion,
      1857-1858
Arraignment *(Direct)*
   xx Preliminary examinations (Criminal
      procedure)
Arrangement (Music)
   sa Instrumentation and orchestration
   x Adaptation (Music)
      Transcription (Music)
   xx Instrumentation and orchestration

      Music
   — Copyright
      See Copyright—Adaptations
Arras, Battle of, 1917 *(D545.A7)*
   sa Vimy Ridge, Battle of, 1917
   xx European War, 1914-1918—Campaigns
      —France
Arras, Battle of, 1940 *(D756.5.A78)*
   xx World War, 1939-1945—Campaigns—
      France
Arras, Treaty of, 1485 *(DC102.535)*
Array, Commissions of
   See Commissions of array
Arrest *(Direct)*
   sa Bail
      Fugitives from justice
      Juvenile detention homes
      Preventive detention
      Speedy trial
   x Pretrial detention
   xx Criminal justice, Administration of
      Detention of persons
      Imprisonment
      Process
      Provisional remedies
   Note under Preventive detention
   — France
      sa Lettres de cachet
Arrest (Police methods)
   sa Police pursuit driving
   x Arresting
   xx Police
Arrest of judgment *(Direct)*
   xx Judgments
      Motions (Law)
Arrest of ships *(Direct)*
   x Ships—Arrest
      Ships, Arrest of
   xx Admiralty
      Attachment and garnishment
      Maritime law
      Security (Law)
Arrest records
   See Criminal registers
Arresting
   See Arrest (Police methods)
Arrest's comet *(QB723.A7)*
Arretine pottery
   See Pottery, Arretine
Arretine vases
   See Vases, Arretine
Arrha
   See Earnest
Arrhythmia *(RC685.A65)*
   sa Auricular fibrillation
      Heart block
      Heart—Palpitation
      Paroxysmal tachycardia
      Tachycardia
      Ventricular fibrillation
      Wolff-Parkinson-White syndrome
   x Allorhythmia
      Arhythmia
   xx Heart beat
      Heart—Diseases
      Heart—Palpitation
   — Atlases
   — Diagnosis
Arrow (Fighter planes)
   See Pfeil (Fighter planes)
Arrow-heads *(GN498.B78)*
   xx Archaeology
      Bow and arrow
      Indians of North America—Antiquities
      Projectile points
Arrowroot
Arrows
   See Bow and arrow

Arroyo Hondo, Battle of, 1821
  xx Mexico—History—Wars of
      Independence, 1810-1821
Arruague Indians
  See Arawak Indians
Arsenal Football Club
  Example under Soccer clubs
Arsenals *(Indirect) (UF540-545)*
  sa Armories
      Military museums
      subdivision Arsenals *under names of
        cities*
  xx Armories
      Military architecture
      Military museums
Arsenate of lead
  See Lead arsenate
Arsenates
Arseniasis
  See Arsenic poisoning
Arsenic *(Chemistry, QD181.A7;
    Pharmacology, QP913.A7)*
  sa Copper-arsenic alloys
      Paris green
      Sandell-Kolthoff reaction
      Soils—Arsenic content
  — Analysis
  — Isotopes
  — — Decay
  — Physiological effect *(QP913.A7)*
  — Spectra
  — Therapeutic use *(RM666.A7)*
  — Toxicology
      See Arsenic poisoning
Arsenic compounds
  sa Organoarsenic compounds
Arsenic-copper alloys
  See Copper-arsenic alloys
Arsenic in soils
  See Soils—Arsenic content
Arsenic in the body
Arsenic organic compounds
  See Organoarsenic compounds
Arsenic poisoning *(RA1231.A7)*
  x Arseniasis
      Arsenic—Toxicology
      Arsenicism
  xx Occupational diseases
      Occupations, Dangerous
  Note under Poisons
Arsenic poisoning (Plants)
  See Plants, Effect of arsenic on
Arsenicism
  See Arsenic poisoning
Arshishtuw
  See Archi
Arshishuw
  See Archi
Arson *(Direct) (HV6638)*
  sa Arson investigation
      Liability for fire damages
      Pyromania
      Trials (Arson)
  x Incendiarism
  xx Criminal law
      Offenses against property
Arson investigation
  xx Arson
      Criminal investigation
      Fire investigation
Arsphenamine *(RM666.A77)*
Art *(Direct) (N)*
      Here are entered general works on the
        visual arts (architecture, painting,
        sculpture, etc.) Works on the arts in
        general, are entered under Arts.
  sa Acrobats and acrobatism in art
      Action in art

Actors in art
Aeronautics in art
Aeroplanes in art
Aesthetics
Anatomy, Artistic
Animal painting and illustration
Animals in art
Animals, Mythical, in art
Archaeology
Archery in art
Architecture
Architecture, Domestic, in art
Architecture in art
Art nouveau
Art objects
Artisans in art
Artists
Artists and models in art
Artists' preparatory studies
Arts and crafts movement
Astrology in art
Automobiles in art
Ballet in art
Balloons in art
Bamboo in art
Battles in art
Biology in art
Blue in art
Books in art
Boots and shoes in art
Bread in art
Breast in art
Bridges in art
Bronzes
Buildings in art
Bulls in art
Butterflies in art
Cadaver in art
Camellia in art
Camels in art
Caricature
Carnations in art
Carriages and carts in art
Carving (Art industries)
Catfishes in art
Cats in art
Caves in art
Children in art
Christian art and symbolism
Chrysanthemums in art
Church in art
Churches in art
Circus in art
Cities and towns in art
Classical antiquities in art
Classicism in art
Clocks and watches in art
Clouds in art
Clowns in art
Collage
Collectors and collecting
Color in art
Commercial art
Community art projects
Composition (Art)
Corals in art
Corpulence in art
Costume
Costume in art
Councils and synods in art
Country life in art
Courage in art
Courts and courtiers in art
Cowboys in art
Creation (Literary, artistic, etc.)
Cricket in art
Crying in art
Cube in art

Cubism
Dancing in art
Deadly sins in art
Decoration and ornament
Deer in art
Deluge in art
Dentistry in art
Design, Decorative
Dinners and dining in art
Dogs in art
Dots (Art)
Dragons in art
Drapery in art
Drawing
Drinking in art
Dwarfs in art
Eagle in art
Education in art
Eggs in art
Elephants in art
Emotions in art
Engraving
Erotic art
Etching
Exoticism in art
Expressionism (Art)
Eye in art
Eyeglasses in art
Face in art
Fairs in art
Family in art
Fans in art
Farm life in art
Fencing in art
Fig tree in art
Fire in art
Fishermen in art
Fishes in art
Five (The number) in art
Flight in art
Flower arrangement in art
Flowering plum in art
Folk art
Folly in art
Fools and jesters in art
Forests in art
Forgery of works of art
Foxes in art
Friendship in art
Fruit in art
Fur garments in art
Futurism (Art)
Games in art
Gardens in art
Geese in art
Gems
Genre (Art)
Gesture in art
Glass painting and staining
Glyptics
Gold in art
Grapes in art
Graphic arts
Grief in art
Grotesque in art
Group work in art
Hair in art
Hand in art
Harbors in art
Head in art
Hermits in art
Heroes in art
History in art
Horsemanship in art
Horsemen in art
Horses in art
Human figure in art
Humanism in art

Art *(Direct)* *(N)* *(Continued)*

Hunger in art
Hunting in art
Idealism in art
Illumination of books and manuscripts
Illustration of books
Imitation (in art)
Interior decoration
Interior decoration in art
Jewelry
Kabuki in art
Kings and rulers in art
Labor and laboring classes in art
Landscape in art
Lasers in art
Laughter in art
Laundresses in art
Laundry in art
Letters in art
Lettrism
Light in art
Lightning in art
Line (Art)
Lions in art
Lithography
Liturgical dramas in art
Lotus in art
Love in art
Magic in art
Man, Prehistoric, in art
Mannerism (Art)
Marriage in art
Mate (Tea) in art
Medicine and art
Men in art
Mines and mineral resources in art
Miniature painting
Minnesingers in art
Mirrors in art
Mobiles (Sculpture)
Monastic and religious life in art
Money in art
Mongols in art
Monkeys in art
Monks in art
Monsters in art
Months in art
Moon in art
Mosaics
Mothers in art
Mountains in art
Mural painting and decoration
Muses in art
Music in art
Mythology, Classical, in art
Nationalism and art
Naturalism in art
Negroes in art
Night in art
Nimbus (Art)
Notaries in art
Nude in art
Occupations in art
Old age in art
Olympic games in art
Outer space in art
Owls in art
Painting
Papacy in art
Paper stretching (Art)
Paradise in art
Parks in art
Pastel drawing
Peace in art
Peafowl in art
Peasants in art
Peddlers and peddling in art
Performing arts

Photography, Artistic
Photography of art
Pictures
Pine tree in art
Pitchers in art
Plants in art
Politics in art
Pomegranate in art
Poor in art
Portraits
Posters
Potatoes in art
Pottery
Prayer in art
Preraphaelitism
Primitivism in art
Processions in art
Project Apollo in art
Proportion (Art)
Psychiatry in art
Pure Land Buddhism in art
Railroads in art
Realism in art
Reptiles in art
Roads in art
Rope in art
Rosary in art
Ruins in art
Salutations in art
Santos (Art)
Scales (Weighing instruments) in art
Scatology in art
Sculpture
Sea gods in art
Sea in art
Seasons in art
Self-realization in art
Serpent worship in art
Serpents in art
Shells in art
Shoemakers in art
Sick in art
Silhouettes
Skating in art
Slavery in art
Sleep in art
Smoking in art
Soccer in art
Soldiers in art
Soul in art
Space (Art)
Spirals in art
Sports in art
Square in art
Still-life in art
Stone pictures
String in art
Students in art
Suffering in art
Sumo in art
Sun in art
Sunlight in art
Sutjeska River, Battle of the, 1943, in art
Swine in art
Symbolism in art
Tanning in art
Technology in art
Textile industry and fabrics in art
Theater in art
Thinker in art
Time in art
Titles of works of art
Tobacco in art
Tree worship in art
Triumph in art
Tropics in art
Turtles in art

Twelve tribes of Israel in art
Unfinished works of art
Vices in art
Violence in art
Virtues in art
Votive offerings in art
War in art
Water waves in art
Weepers (Mourners) in art
Whaling in art
White in art
Windmills in art
Wine in art
Witchcraft in art
Women in art
Words in art
Wrestling in art
Writing in art
Youth in art
America in art; Greece in art;
Nuremberg in art; Ruhr Valley in
art; *and similar headings; also
subdivision* Art *under special
headings, e.g.* Saints—Art
x Arts, Fine
Fine arts
Iconography
Visual arts
xx Aesthetics
Civilization
Note under Arts
— Ability testing
— Analysis, interpretation, appreciation
See Aesthetics; Art—Philosophy; Art
—Study and teaching; Art
criticism; Painting; Pictures;
and similar headings
— Anecdotes, facetiae, satire, etc.
(N7460-7470)
Example under Anecdotes; Wit and hu-
mor
— Audio-visual aids
— — Catalogs
— Biography
— Caricatures and cartoons
— Cataloging
See Cataloging of art
— Catalogs
Here are entered dealers' and general
sales catalogs. For catalogs of exhi-
bitions use Art—Exhibitions; for
catalogs of private collections use
Art—Private collections. Catalogs
of the art galleries of a city are en-
tered under Art—[city]—Catalogs,
e.g. Art—London—Catalogs.
xx Art—Prices
Drawings—Prices
— Censorship *(N8740)*
x Art censorship
— — Chronology
— Certification
— Collectors and collecting *(Direct)*
sa Art as an investment
x Art collectors
— Competitions
sa Archibald prize
Certamen Nacional de
Investigaciones Visuales
Deutscher Kunstpreis der Jugend
Example under Rewards (Prizes, etc.);
and under reference from Prize
competitions
— Composition
See Composition (Art)
— Congresses
— Conservation and restoration

See Art objects—Conservation and
  restoration
— Copyright
  See Copyright—Art
— Criticism
  See Art criticism
— Early works to 1800
— Education
  See Art—Study and teaching
— Examinations, questions, etc.
— Exhibitions
  xx Paintings—Exhibitions
  Note under Art—Catalogs
— Exhibitions, Traveling
  x Art exhibitions, Traveling
    Traveling art exhibitions
  xx Educational exhibits, Traveling
— Expertising
  sa Expertising, X-ray
    Paintings—Expertising
  Example under reference from Expertis-
    ing
— Federal aid
  See Federal aid to the arts
— Fellowships
  See Art—Scholarships, fellowships,
    etc.
— Film catalogs
— Finance
  sa Federal aid to the arts
— Forgeries
  See Forgery of works of art
— Galleries and museums *(N400-490)*
  This heading is used for the general
    subject only, not for particular gall-
    eries nor for the galleries of a par-
    ticular country or city. For the lat-
    ter use Art—[country or city]—
    Galleries and museums. References
    are made from Art—[city]—Galler-
    ies and museums to individual gall-
    eries, *e.g.* Art—Washington, D.C.
    —Galleries and museums *see also*
    Corcoran Gallery of Art, Washing-
    ton, D.C.; Art—Boston—Galleries
    and museums *see also* Boston. Mu-
    seum of Fine Arts.
  x Art galleries
    Art museums
    Art—Museums
    Galleries (Art)
    Picture-galleries
  xx Museums
    Paintings—Exhibitions
— — Juvenile literature
— Graduate work
  x Graduate study in art
    Graduate work in art
  xx Art—Study and teaching
— Historiography *(N8370)*
  Example under Historiography
— History *(N5300-7415)*
  sa Art criticism
— — 17th-18th centuries
  See Art, Modern—17th-18th
    centuries—History
— — 19th century
  See Art, Modern—19th century—
    History
— — 20th century
  See Art, Modern—20th century—
    History
— — 17-18th centuries

GENERAL SUBDIVISIONS

— — Juvenile literature
— — Pictorial works
— Juvenile literature *(N7440)*

— Lighting *(N460)*
— Marketing
  sa Art dealers
— Museums
  See Art—Galleries and museums
— Negroes
  See Negro art
— Philosophy
  x Art—Analysis, interpretation,
    appreciation
    Beautiful, The
    Beauty
  xx Aesthetics
  Example under Philosophy
— Poetry
— Prices *(Direct)*
  sa Art as an investment
    Art—Catalogs
    Engravings—Prices; Paintings—
    Prices; *and similar headings*
  xx Drawings—Prices
— Private collections *(Direct)*
    (N5210-5297)
  sa Royal houses—Art collections
    subdivision Private collections *under*
    Engravings, Paintings, Sculpture;
    and similar headings
  Note under Art—Catalogs
— Psychology *(N70)*
  sa Art and mental illness
— Quotations, maxims, etc. *(PN6084.A8)*
— Readers
  See Readers—Art
— Rhythm
  See Proportion (Art)
— Scholarships, fellowships, etc. *(N347)*
  x Art fellowships
    Art—Fellowships
    Art scholarships
  xx Art schools
    Art—Study and teaching
— Societies, etc.
  x Clubs, Art
— Study and teaching *(Direct)*
  sa Art—Graduate work
    Art in universities and colleges
    Art—Scholarships, fellowships, etc.
    Art schools
    Pictures—Copying
  x Art—Analysis, interpretation,
    appreciation
    Art education
    Art—Education
    Education, Art
  xx Art schools
  Example under Study, Method of
— Study and teaching (Elementary)
    (Direct)
— Study and teaching (Preschool) *(Direct)*
— Study and teaching (Primary) *(Direct)*
— Study and teaching (Secondary) *(Direct)*
— Subjects
  See Art—Themes, motives
— Tariff
  See Tariff on works of art
— Teacher training *(Direct)*
— Technique *(N7430-7433)*
  sa Chiaroscuro
    Texture (Art)
    subdivision Technique *under*
    Painting, Sculpture; *and similar*
    headings
— — Juvenile literature
— Terminology *(N33)*
— Thefts
  See Art thefts
— Themes, motives
  x Art—Subjects

— Therapeutic use
  See Art therapy
— Trade
  See Art industries and trade

  GEOGRAPHIC SUBDIVISIONS

— Africa, [Italy, Spain, etc.]
  sa Art, African, [Italian, Spanish, etc.]
  xx Art, African, [Italian, Spanish, etc.]

  GEOGRAPHIC SUBDIVISIONS

— Boston
— — Galleries and museums
  Note under Art—Galleries and mu-
    seums

  GEOGRAPHIC SUBDIVISIONS

— England
  xx Art—Great Britain

  GEOGRAPHIC SUBDIVISIONS

— Great Britain
  sa Art—England

  GEOGRAPHIC SUBDIVISIONS

— London
— — Catalogs
  Note under Art—Catalogs

  GEOGRAPHIC SUBDIVISIONS

— Washington, D.C.
— — Galleries and museums
  Note under Art—Galleries and mu-
    seums

Art, Abstract *(Direct) (N6490)*
  sa Abstract expressionism
    Abstract impressionism
    Concrete art
    Kinetic sculpture
    Minimal art
    Modernism (Art)
    Vorticism
  x Abstract art
    Abstract paintings
    Art, Non-objective
    Non-objective art
    Non-objective paintings
    Paintings, Abstract
    Paintings, Non-objective
  xx Art, Modern—20th century
    Modernism (Art)
— Caricatures and cartoons
Art, African, [Italian, Spanish, etc.] *(Direct)*
  The references indicated here are general
    in application. Exceptions to this pat-
    tern and examples of additional refer-
    ences required in specific cases are
    shown under the headings below.
  sa Art—Africa, [Italy, Spain, etc.]
  x African [Italian, Spanish, etc.] art
  xx Art—Africa, [Italy, Spain, etc.]
    Decoration and ornament
— Chinese [Roman, etc.] influences
— History
— — Juvenile literature
— Influence
— Juvenile literature
Art, Albigensian *(N6246)*
  x Albigensian art
  xx Art, Medieval
Art, Amateur *(Direct)*
  x Amateur art
Art, Ancient *(N5315-5899)*
  sa Art, Greco-Bactrian
    Art, Greco-Roman
    Art, Primitive
    Classical antiquities
    Seven Wonders of the World

Art, Ancient (N5315-5899) (Continued)
  Terra-cottas
  Art, Greek; Art, Roman; and similar
    headings
  x Ancient art
— Juvenile literature
Art, Apocalyptic
  See Apocalyptic art
Art, Applied
  See Art industries and trade
Art, Arab
  See Art, Islamic
Art, Asian (Direct)
  sa Art, Oriental
  x Art, Asiatic
    Asiatic art
  xx Art, Oriental
Art, Asiatic
  See Art, Asian
Art, Australian (Aboriginal) (Direct)
  x Australian aborigines—Art
  xx Art, Primitive
Art, Aztec
  See Aztecs—Art
Art, Bactrian
  sa Art, Greco-Bactrian
Art, Baroque (Direct)
  sa Painting, Baroque
  x Baroque art
— Influence
— Jesuit [etc.] influences
Art, British
  sa Art, English
Art, Buddhist (Direct)
  sa Art, Zen
    Buddhism and art
    Buddhist art and symbolism
    Hell (Buddhism)—Art
    Pretas (Buddhism)—Art
    Pure Land Buddhism in art
  x Buddhist art
  xx Art, Greco-Bactrian
Art, Byzantine (Direct)
  x Byzantine art
  xx Art, Medieval
— Influence
Art, Carlovingian
  x Carlovingian art
    Carolingian art
  xx Art, Medieval
Art, Celtic
  xx Art, Irish
Art, Chinese
  sa Art, Taoist
Art, Christian
  See Christian art and symbolism
Art, Cistercian
  x Cistercian art
  xx Art, Medieval
Art, Cluniac
  x Cluniac art
Art, Colonial (Direct)
  x Colonial art
Art, Commercial
  See Commercial art
Art, Conceptual
  See Conceptual art
Art, Concrete
  See Concrete art
Art, Decorative (NK)
  sa Bronzes
    Decoration and ornament
    Design, Decorative
    Embroidery
    Enamel and enameling
    Fore-edge painting
    Furniture
    Graffito decoration

Illustration of books
Mosaics
Mural painting and decoration
Needlework
Pottery
Screens
Tapestry
Textile design
Tole painting
Vase-painting
  x Arts, Decorative
    Decorative art
    Decorative arts
    Painting, Decorative
  xx Art industries and trade
    Decoration and ornament
    Design, Decorative
— Psychological aspects
Art, Early Christian (Direct) (N7832)
  x Early Christian art
  xx Christian art and symbolism
Art, Early Gothic
  See Art, Gothic—Early Gothic
Art, Early Renaissance
  See Art, Renaissance—Early Renaissance
Art, Ecclesiastical
  See Christian art and symbolism
Art, Effect of
  See Art therapy
Art, English
  xx Art, British
Art, Erotic
  See Erotic art
Art, Exotic
  See Exoticism in art
Art, Folk
  See Folk art
Art, Georgian (Direct)
  x Georgian art
Art, Germanic
  x Art, Teutonic
    Teutonic art
Art, Gothic
  x Gothic art
  xx Art, Medieval
— Early Gothic (Direct)
  x Art, Early Gothic
    Early Gothic art
— High Gothic (Direct)
  x Art, High Gothic
    High Gothic art
— Late Gothic (Direct)
  x Art, Late Gothic
    Late Gothic art
Art, Graphic
  See Graphic arts
Art, Greco-Bactrian
  sa Art, Buddhist
    Art, Greek
    Art, Oriental
  xx Art, Ancient
    Art, Bactrian
    Art, Greek
    Art, Oriental
Art, Greco-Roman
  This heading is used for works dealing
    specifically with Roman art exhibiting
    strong Greek influence and produced
    almost exclusively by Greek artists,
    particularly in Italy until about 100
    A.D.
  x Greco-Roman art
  xx Art, Ancient
    Art, Greek
    Art, Roman
Art, Greek
  sa Art, Greco-Bactrian
    Art, Greco-Roman

Art, Hellenistic
  xx Art, Ancient
    Art, Greco-Bactrian
    Classical antiquities
— Juvenile literature
Art, Hellenistic (Direct)
  x Hellenistic art
  xx Art, Greek
Art, High Gothic
  See Art, Gothic—High Gothic
Art, High Renaissance
  See Art, Renaissance—High Renaissance
Art, Hindu (Direct)
  sa Art, Vaishnava
  x Hindu art
Art, Ibo (Direct)
  x Art, Igbo
    Ibo art
    Igbo art
Art, Igbo
  See Art, Ibo
Art, Immoral
  See Erotic art
— Law and legislation
  See Obscenity (Law)
Art, Incomplete
  See Unfinished works of art
Art, Indian
  See Indians—Art
    Indians of Central America [Mexico,
      North America, etc.]—Art
    subdivision Art under Indian tribes
Art, Iranian
  x Art, Persian
Art, Irish
  sa Art, Celtic
Art, Islamic (N6260-6271)
  sa Islam and art
  x Arab art
    Art, Arab
    Art, Moorish
    Art, Muslim
    Art, Saracenic
    Islamic art
    Moorish art
    Muslim art
    Saracenic art
— Juvenile literature
Art, Jaina (Direct)
  x Jaina art
Art, Japanese
  sa Art, Shinto
    Namban art
— To 794 (N7353.2)
— Heian period, 794-1185 (N7353.3)
— 1185-1600 (N7353.4)
— Edo period, 1600-1868 (N7353.5)
— Meiji period, 1868-1912 (N7354.5)
Art, Jesuit
  x Jesuit art
Art, Jewish (Direct)
  sa Hanukkah lamp
    Jewish art and symbolism
    Judaism and art
    Menorah
    Synagogue art
  x Hebrew art
  xx Judaism and art
Art, Kinetic
  See Kinetic art
Art, Korean
— Yi dynasty, 1392-1910 (N7363.4)
Art, Late Gothic
  See Art, Gothic—Late Gothic
Art, Maya
  See Mayas—Art
Art, Medieval (Direct) (N5940-6311)
  sa Art, Albigensian

Art, Byzantine
Art, Carlovingian
Art, Cistercian
Art, Gothic
Art, Merovingian
Art, Norman
Art, Ottonian
Art, Romanesque
Illumination of books and manuscripts
x Medieval art
xx Archaeology, Medieval
Civilization, Medieval
Middle Ages
— Byzantine [etc.] influences
— Subjects
  See Art, Medieval—Themes, motives
— Themes, motives
  x Art, Medieval—Subjects
Art, Merovingian (N6243)
  x Merovingian art
  xx Art, Medieval
Art, Minimal
  See Minimal art
Art, Minoan (Direct)
  x Minoan art
Art, Modern (Direct)
  sa Gothic revival (Art)
  Neoclassicism (Art)
  x Modern art
  xx Arts, Modern
— 17th-18th centuries (Direct)
— — French [etc.] influences
— — History
  x Art—History—17th-18th
  centuries
— 19th century (Direct)
  sa Art, Victorian
  Biedermeier (Art)
  Impressionism (Art)
  Neo-impressionism (Art)
  Post-impressionism (Art)
  Tonalism
— — History
  x Art—History—19th century
— — Juvenile literature
— — Subjects
  See Art, Modern—19th century—
  Themes, motives
— — Themes, motives
  x Art, Modern—19th century—
  Subjects
— 20th century (Direct)
  sa Art, Abstract
  Art deco
  Assemblage (Art)
  Conceptual art
  Concrete art
  Constructivism (Art)
  Cubism
  Dadaism
  Environment (Art)
  Expressionism (Art)
  Fauvism
  Found objects (Art)
  Futurism (Art)
  Happening (Art)
  Kinetic art
  Letter-pictures
  Minimal art
  Modernism (Art)
  Multiple art
  New objectivity (Art)
  Optical art
  Orphism (Art)
  Pop art
  Post-impressionism (Art)
  Purism (Art)
  Spatialism (Art)

Surrealism
Vorticism
  x Contemporary art
  xx Modernism (Art)
— — Anecdotes, facetiae, satire, etc.
— — Caricatures and cartoons
— — History
  x Art—History—20th century
— — Primitive [etc.] influences
— — Subjects
  See Art, Modern—20th century—
  Themes, motives
— — Themes, motives
  x Art, Modern—20th century—
  Subjects
Art, Modernist
  See Modernism (Art)
Art, Moorish
  See Art, Islamic
Art, Multiple
  See Multiple art
Art, Municipal (Direct) (Aesthetics of
  cities, NA9000-9425; Public art,
  N8700-8850)
  Works treating of municipal art in a par-
  ticular city are usually entered here
  and also under city, subdivision Public
  works, e.g. 1. Art, Municipal—Boston.
  2. Boston—Public works.
  sa Art commissions
  Cities and towns—Planning
  Municipal buildings
  x Civic art
  Municipal art
  Municipal improvements
  xx Cities and towns
  Cities and towns—Planning
  Urban beautification
— Boston
  Note under Art, Municipal
Art, Muslim
  See Art, Islamic
Art, Namban
  See Namban art
Art, Nanban
  See Namban art
Art, Negro
  See Negro art
Art, Non-objective
  See Art, Abstract
Art, Norman
  x Norman art
  xx Art, Medieval
Art, Optical
  See Optical art
Art, Oriental (Direct) (N7260)
  sa Art, Asian
  Art, Greco-Bactrian
  Occidentals in Oriental art
  x Oriental art
  xx Art, Asian
  Art, Greco-Bactrian
— Greek [etc.] influences
Art, Ottonian (Direct)
  x Ottonian art
  xx Art, Medieval
Art, Parsic
  x Parsees—Art
  Parsic art
Art, Persian
  See Art, Iranian
Art, Polynesian
  xx Art, Primitive
Art, Pop
  See Pop art
Art, Popular
  See Art industries and trade
  Folk art

Art, Prehistoric (Direct) (Fine arts, N5310;
  Prehistoric archaeology, GN799.A)
  sa Rock paintings
  subdivision Antiquities under names of
  countries, cities, etc.
  x Prehistoric art
  xx Archaeology
  Art, Primitive
  Man, Prehistoric
— Juvenile literature
Art, Primitive (Direct) (N5310)
  sa Art, Australian (Aboriginal)
  Art, Polynesian
  Art, Prehistoric
  Eskimos—Art
  Folk art
  Idols and images
  Indians—Art
  Indians of North America—Art
  Paintings, Australian (Aboriginal)
  Sculpture, Primitive
  x Primitive art
  xx Archaeology
  Art, Ancient
  Ethnology
  Folk art
  Society, Primitive
— Juvenile literature
— Private collections
Art, Regional (Direct) (N7428)
Art, Renaissance
  sa Little masters (Artists)
  x Renaissance art
— Early Renaissance (Direct)
  x Art, Early Renaissance
  Early Renaissance art
— High Renaissance (Direct)
  x Art, High Renaissance
  High Renaissance art
— Islamic [etc.] influences
Art, Rococo (Direct) (N6410)
  sa Sculpture, Rococo
  x Rococo art
Art, Roman
  sa Art, Greco-Roman
  xx Art, Ancient
  Classical antiquities
Art, Romanesque (Direct) (N6280)
  x Romanesque art
  xx Art, Medieval
— Byzantine [etc.] influences
Art, Saracenic
  See Art, Islamic
Art, Shinto (Direct) (N7350-7359)
  x Shinto art
  xx Art, Japanese
Art, Synagogue
  See Synagogue art
Art, Tantric
  x Tantric art
  xx Tantrism
Art, Tantric-Buddhist (Direct)
  x Tantric-Buddhist art
  xx Tantric Buddhism
Art, Taoist
  x Taoist art
  xx Art, Chinese
Art, Teutonic
  See Art, Germanic
Art, Tudor (Direct)
  x Tudor art
Art, Unfinished
  See Unfinished works of art
Art, Vaishnava (Direct)
  x Vaishnava art
  xx Art, Hindu
Art, Victorian (Direct)
  x Victorian art

Art, Victorian *(Direct) (Continued)*
    xx Art, Modern—19th century
Art, Visigothic *(N6242)*
    x Visigothic art
Art, Zen *(Direct)*
    sa Bodhidharma dolls
    x Zen art
    xx Art, Buddhist
Art and Buddhism
    See Buddhism and art
Art and communism
    See Communism and art
Art and fashion
    See Fashion and art
Art and history
    Here are entered works on the relation
    between art and history. Works deal-
    ing with the representation of histori-
    cal events and characters are entered
    under History in art.
    sa Art and war
    History in art
    subdivisions Art and the war; Humor,
    caricatures, etc.; *and* Iconography
    under particular wars, e.g. Spain—
    History—Civil War, 1936-1939—Art
    and the war
    x History and art
    xx History in art
Art and homosexuality
    See Homosexuality and art
Art and industry
    sa Art patronage
    Commercial art
    Industry in art
    x Advertising, Art in
    Industry and art
    xx Commercial art
Art and insanity
    See Art and mental illness
Art and Islam
    See Islam and art
Art and Judaism
    See Judaism and art
Art and law
    See Law and art
Art and literature *(Art, N72; English*
    literature, PR149.A; German
    literature, PT112; Literature, PN53)
    sa Ut pictura poesis (Aesthetics)
    x Literature and art
    Literature and painting
    Literature and sculpture
    Painting and literature
    Sculpture and literature
    xx Aesthetics
    Literature
Art and medicine
    See Medicine and art
Art and mental illness *(Art, N71.5;*
    Medicine, RC455)
    x Art and insanity
    Artists, Insane
    Insanity and art
    Mental illness and art
    Psychiatry and art
    Psychotic art
    xx Art—Psychology
Art and morals *(N70-72)*
    sa Erotic art
    Music and morals
    Nude in art
    Theater—Moral and religious aspects
    x Morals and art
    xx Aesthetics
    Erotic art
    Ethics
    Nude in art

Art and moving-pictures *(N72.M6)*
    sa Art in moving-pictures
    x Moving-pictures and art
Art and music
    sa Music in art
    x Music and art
    xx Music in art
Art and mythology *(N7760)*
    sa Gods (in numismatics)
    Mythology, Classical, in art
    Sea gods in art
    Serpent worship in art
    Tree worship in art
    x Mythology in art
    xx Art and religion
    Mythology
Art and nationalism
    See Nationalism and art
Art and nature
    See Nature (Aesthetics)
Art and photography *(N72.P5)*
    x Photography and art
Art and psychoanalysis
    See Psychoanalysis and art
Art and race
    x Race and art
    xx Ethnopsychology
Art and religion
    sa Art and mythology
    Buddhism and art
    Catholic Church and art
    Christian art and symbolism
    Gods in art
    Idols and images
    Islam and art
    Judaism and art
    Orthodox Eastern Church and art
    Sea gods in art
    x Religion and art
    xx Art and society
    Christian art and symbolism
Art and revolutions *(Direct)*
    sa Socialist realism in art
    x Revolutions and art
    xx Arts and revolutions
    Politics in art
Art and science
    sa Medicine and art
    Scientific illustration
    x Science and art
    xx Science and the humanities
Art and socialism
    See Socialism and art
Art and society *(N72)*
    sa Art and religion
    Art and state
    Art industries and trade
    Folk art
    x Art and sociology
    Society and art
    Sociology and art
Art and sociology
    See Art and society
Art and state *(Indirect) (N8700-8850)*
    sa Art and war
    Art commissions
    Federal aid to the arts
    State encouragement of science,
    literature, and art
    Theater and state
    x State and art
    xx Art and society
    Education and state
    State encouragement of science,
    literature, and art
    Note under Art patronage
Art and technology *(N72.T4)*
    x Technology and art

Art and the Catholic Church
    See Catholic Church and art
Art and the Orthodox Eastern Church
    See Orthodox Eastern Church and art
Art and theater
    See Actors—Portraits
    Actresses—Portraits
    Theater in art
    Theaters—Decoration
    Theaters—Stage-setting and scenery
Art and vision disorders *(N71.8)*
    x Vision disorders and art
Art and war
    Here are entered works on the relation
    between art and war, including the
    functions of art in wartime and the
    mobilization and specialized services
    of artists in the war effort.
    sa Art treasures in war
    War memorials
    subdivisions Art and the war; Humor,
    caricatures, etc.; Iconography *under*
    names of wars
    x War and art
    xx Art and history
    Art and state
Art appreciation
    x Appreciation of art
    xx Art criticism
    — Testing
      sa McAdory art test
Art as a profession
    xx Artists
    — Juvenile literature
Art as an investment *(N8680)*
    sa special types of art as an investment,
    e.g. Porcelain as an investment;
    Prints as an investment
    xx Art—Collectors and collecting
    Art—Prices
    Capital investments
Art auctions *(Direct)*
    xx Auctions
Art calendars
    xx Calendars
Art censorship
    See Art—Censorship
Art centers
    Here are entered works on community art
    centers in general. Works on an in-
    dividual art center are entered under
    its name.
    x Community art centers
    xx Community centers
Art collectors
    See Art—Collectors and collecting
    Art objects—Collectors and collecting
Art commissions *(Direct)*
    x Commissions, Art
    xx Art and state
    Art, Municipal
    Education and state
    State encouragement of science,
    literature, and art
Art criticism *(Direct) (N7435-6; Art critics,*
    N8370-8375)
    sa Art appreciation
    Newspapers—Sections, columns, etc.—
    Reviews
    x Art—Analysis, interpretation,
    appreciation
    Art—Criticism
    Arts—Criticism
    xx Art—History
    Arts—History
    Criticism
    Note under Criticism
    — Terminology

Art dealers *(Direct)* *(N8610-8660)*
  sa Antique dealers
  xx Art—Marketing
  — Caricatures and cartoons
  — Correspondence, reminiscences, etc.
Art deco *(Direct)* *(N6494.A7)*
  x Decoration and ornament—Art deco
  xx Art, Modern—20th century
    Art nouveau
Art education
  See Art—Study and teaching
Art exhibitions, Traveling
  See Art—Exhibitions, Traveling
Art fellowships
  See Art—Scholarships, fellowships, etc.
Art festivals *(Direct)*
  sa Dance festivals
    Drama festivals
    Moving-picture festivals
    Music festivals
    Performing arts festivals
  xx Festivals
Art forgeries
  See Forgery of works of art
Art galleries
  See Art—Galleries and museums
Art glass lampshades
  See Lampshades, Glass
Art in advertising
  See Commercial art
Art in literature *(PN56.A; Medieval*
  literature, PN682.A7)
Art in motion
  See Kinetic art
Art in moving-pictures
  Here are entered works dealing with
  moving-pictures on art subjects, both
  instructional and documentary.
  x Films on art
    Moving-pictures about art
  xx Art and moving-pictures
    Moving-pictures
Art in Negro universities and colleges
  xx Art in universities and colleges
    Negro universities and colleges
Art in universities and colleges
  sa Art in Negro universities and colleges
    College teachers as artists
    Print rental service
  xx Art—Study and teaching
    Universities and colleges
Art industries and trade *(Direct)* *(NK)*
  sa Arms and armor
    Art, Decorative
    Arts and crafts movement
    Damascening
    Folk art
    Fretwork
    Jewelry
    Marquetry
    particular industries, trades, etc., e.g.
      Glass painting and staining; Leather
      work; Mosaics
  x Applied art
    Art, Applied
    Art, Popular
    Art—Trade
    Arts, Decorative
    Decorative arts
    Peasant art
  xx Art and society
    Folk art
    Industrial arts
  Note under Folk art
  — Exhibitions
  — Museums
    See Industrial museums
  — Study and teaching *(Direct)*

Art industries and trade, Anglo-Saxon,
  ⌈**Germanic, etc.**⌉ *(Direct)*
  x Anglo-Saxon ⌈Germanic, etc.⌉ art
    industries and trade
  — Terminology
Art industries and trade, Colonial American
  See Art industries and trade, Early
    American
Art industries and trade, Early American
  (Direct)
  x Art industries and trade, Colonial
    American
    Colonial American art industries and
    trade
    Early American art industries and trade
Art industries and trade, Gothic *(Direct)*
  x Gothic art industries and trade
Art industries and trade, Islamic
  (NK720-725)
  x Art industries and trade, Muslim
    Islamic art industries and trade
    Muslim art industries and trade
Art industries and trade, Medieval
  — Juvenile literature
Art industries and trade, Muslim
  See Art industries and trade, Islamic
Art industries and trade, Renaissance
  — Juvenile literature
Art industries and trade, Shaker *(Direct)*
  sa Furniture, Shaker
  x Shaker art industries and trade
Art industries and trade, Victorian *(Direct)*
  x Victorian art industries and trade
Art insurance
  See Insurance, Art
Art libraries *(Direct)* *(Z675.A85)*
  sa Architectural libraries
  x Libraries, Art
  Example under Libraries; Libraries, Special
Art metal-work *(Direct)* *(NK6400-8450;*
  TS; TT)
  sa Architectural metal-work
    Bronze doors
    Bronzes
    Cloisonné
    Coppersmithing
    Damascening
    Engraving (Metal-work)
    Filigree
    Goldsmithing
    Goldweights
    Indians—Metal-work
    Indians of Central America—
      Metal-work
    Indians of Mexico—Metal-work
    Indians of North America—Metal-work
    Indians of South America—Metal-work
    Ironwork
    Jewelry
    Lead-work
    Medals
    Niello
    Pewter
    Pewtercraft
    Plaques, plaquettes
    Porringers
    Repoussé work
    Silversmithing
    Tinsmithing
  x Decorative metal-work
    Metal-work, Art
  xx Architectural metal-work
    Metal-work
  — Collectors and collecting
  — Juvenile literature
Art metal-work, Ancient *(Direct)* *(NK6407)*
Art metal-work, Early Christian *(Direct)*
  x Early Christian art metal-work

Art metal-work, Egyptian, ⌈**Greek, etc.**⌉
  (Direct)
  x Egyptian ⌈Greek, etc.⌉ art metal-work
Art metal-work, Islamic *(NK6473)*
  x Art metal-work, Muslim
    Islamic art metal-work
    Muslim art metal-work
Art metal-work, Muslim
  See Art metal-work, Islamic
Art metal-work, Oriental *(NK6472)*
  x Oriental art metal-work
Art metal-work, Primitive *(Direct)*
Art metal-workers *(Direct)*
  sa Goldsmiths
    Jewelers
    Silversmiths
    Swordsmiths
    Tinsmiths
  xx Artists
    Metal-workers
Art museums
  See Art—Galleries and museums
Art nouveau *(Direct)*
  sa Art deco
    Decoration and ornament—Art
    nouveau
  x Jugendstil
    Stile liberty
  xx Art
  — Collectors and collecting *(Direct)*
Art objects *(Direct)* *(NK)*
  sa Miniature objects
    Relics and reliquaries
    Reproduction of art objects
    classes of art objects and names of
      particular objects, e.g. Bronzes,
      Glassware, Jewelry, Metal-work,
      Plate, Pottery, Rings
  x Bric-a-brac
  xx Art
    Decoration and ornament
  — Catalogs
    Here are entered dealers' and general
    sales catalogs. For catalogs of exhi-
    bitions use Art objects—Exhibi-
    tions; for catalogs of private collec-
    tions use Art objects—Private col-
    lections.
  — Collectors and collecting *(Direct)*
    (NK1125-1130)
    sa Antiques in interior decoration
      Art objects as an investment
    x Art collectors
  — — Juvenile literature
  — Conservation and restoration *(N8560)*
    x Art—Conservation and restoration
      Conservation of art objects
      Preservation of art objects
      Restoration of art objects
    Example under Cultural property, Pro-
      tection of
  — Exhibitions *(NK510-520)*
    Note under Art objects—Catalogs
  — Fires and fire prevention *(N8750)*
  — Packing *(N8585)*
  — Prices *(Direct)*
    sa Art objects as an investment
  — Private collections *(NK530-570)*
    Note under Art objects—Catalogs
Art objects, Ancient *(Direct)*
Art objects, Buddhist *(Direct)*
  x Buddhist art objects
Art objects, Byzantine *(Direct)*
  x Byzantine art objects
Art objects, Classical *(NK665-680)*
  xx Classical antiquities
Art objects, Early Christian *(Direct)*
  x Early Christian art objects

Art objects, Edwardian *(Direct)*
    x Edwardian art objects
Art objects, Egyptian, ⌐German, Italian, etc.¬
    (Direct)
    x Egyptian ⌐German, Italian, etc.¬ art
       objects
  — Oriental ⌐etc.¬ influences
  — Pictorial works
Art objects, Forgery of
    See Forgery of works of art
Art objects, Hindu *(Direct)*
    x Hindu art objects
Art objects, Islamic *(Direct)*
    x Art objects, Muslim
      Islamic art objects
      Muslim art objects
Art objects, Jade
    See Jade art objects
Art objects, Maori
    x Maori art objects
Art objects, Medieval *(Direct)*
Art objects, Muslim
    See Art objects, Islamic
Art objects, Oriental *(NK1037)*
    sa Inksticks
    x Oriental art objects
Art objects, Renaissance *(Direct)*
    x Renaissance art objects
Art objects, Rococo *(Direct)*
    x Rococo art objects
Art objects, Romanesque *(Direct)*
    x Romanesque art objects
Art objects, Shinto *(Direct)*
    x Shinto art objects
Art objects, Victorian *(Direct)*
    x Victorian art objects
Art objects as an investment
    xx Art objects—Collectors and collecting
      Art objects—Prices
      Investments
Art patronage *(Direct)* *(N8410)*
    Here are entered works dealing with the
    patronage of art by individuals and
    corporations. Works on government
    sponsorship of art are entered under
    Art and state; State encouragement of
    science, literature, and art.
    sa Art patrons
      Arts—Endowments
      subdivision Art patronage *under names*
      of individuals, families, firms, etc.,
      e.g. Napoléon I, Emperor of the
      French, 1769-1821—Art patronage
    x Business patronage of the arts
      Patronage of art
    xx Art and industry
Art patrons *(Direct)*
    sa subdivision Art patronage *under names*
      of individuals, families, firms, etc.,
      e.g. Napoléon I, Emperor of the
      French, 1769-1821—Art patronage
    xx Art patronage
  — Portraits
Art photography
    See Photography of art
Art povera
    See Conceptual art
Art production by animals
    See Animals as artists
Art projects, Community
    See Community art projects
Art robberies
    See Art thefts
Art scholarships
    See Art—Scholarships, fellowships, etc.
Art schools *(Direct)*
    sa Art—Scholarships, fellowships, etc.
      Art—Study and teaching

    xx Art—Study and teaching
      Drawing—Instruction
      Painting—Study and teaching
      Schools
  — Entrance requirements
Art societies *(Indirect)*
    Here are entered works about art socie-
    ties. For society publications dealing
    with art use subdivision Societies, etc.
    under the headings Art, Painting,
    Sculpture, and similar headings.
    xx Societies
Art stealing
    See Art thefts
Art teachers *(Direct)*
    sa Artists as teachers
    xx Teachers
  — Recruiting *(Direct)*
Art thefts *(Direct)*
    x Art robberies
      Art stealing
      Art—Thefts
      Thefts, Art
    xx Larceny
      Thieves
Art therapy *(RC489.A)*
    sa Modeling—Therapeutic use
    x Art, Effect of
      Art—Therapeutic use
      Psychiatry and art
    xx Occupational therapy
      Psychotherapy
  — Cases, clinical reports, statistics
Art treasures, Protection of
    See Cultural property, Protection of
Art treasures in war *(N8750; European War,*
    N6491)
    sa European War, 1914-1918—Art and
      the war
      Spain—History—Civil War, 1936-1939
        —Art and the war
      World War, 1939-1945—Art and the
        war
    xx Art and war
      Cultural property, Protection of
      (International law)
Art typing *(Z50.2)*
    x Designs for typing
    xx Typewriting
Arte povera
    See Conceptual art
Arterial catheterization *(RC78.7.A7)*
    xx Arteries
      Catheters
      Injections, Intra-arterial
Arterial grafts
    xx Transplantation of organs, tissues, etc.
      Vascular grafts
  — Atlases
  — Preservation
    xx Preservation of organs, tissues, etc.
Arterial obstructions
    See Arterial occlusions
Arterial occlusions
    sa Embolism
    x Arterial obstructions
Arteries *(QL835; QM191)*
    sa Aorta
      Arterial catheterization
      Blood—Circulation
      Blood-vessels
      Carotid artery
      Celiac artery
      Coronary arteries
      Femoral artery
      Iliac artery
      Meningeal artery
      Mesenteric artery

      Pulmonary artery
      Renal artery
      Subclavian artery
      Thoracic arteries
      Veins
      Vertebral artery
    xx Blood—Circulation
      Blood-vessels
      Veins
  — Abnormities and deformities
  — Calcification
    Example under Calcification
  — Diseases *(RC691)*
    sa Arteries—Radiography
    names of diseases, e.g. Fistula,
      Arteriovenous
  — Inflammation
  — Ligature *(RD598)*
    sa Carotid artery—Ligature
      Iliac artery—Ligature
      Veins—Ligature
  — Radiography
    x Arteriography
    xx Angiography
      Arteries—Diseases
  — Surgery
  — Wounds and injuries
    sa Hemorrhage
    xx Hemorrhage
Arteriography
    See Arteries—Radiography
Arteriosclerosis *(RC691)*
    sa Cerebral arteriosclerosis
    x Atherosclerosis
  — Dietary aspects
    See Arteriosclerosis—Nutritional
      aspects
  — Nutritional aspects
    x Arteriosclerosis—Dietary aspects
      Diet and arteriosclerosis
      Nutrition and arteriosclerosis
Arteriosclerosis obliterans
    x Obliterative arteriosclerosis
Arteriovenous anastomosis
    sa Portacaval anastomosis
    xx Fistula, Arteriovenous
Arteriovenous aneurysms
    See Fistula, Arteriovenous
Arteriovenous fistula
    See Fistula, Arteriovenous
Artesian basins *(Indirect)*
    sa Artesian wells
    xx Hydrogeology
Artesian wells *(Direct)* *(TD410)*
    sa Boring
    xx Artesian basins
      Boring
      Hydraulic structures
      Water-supply
      Wells
Arthritics
    xx Arthritis
      Physically handicapped
  — Rehabilitation
Arthritis
    sa Arthritics
      Cookery for arthritics
      Periarthritis
    xx Joints—Diseases
  — Cases, clinical reports, statistics
  — Dietary aspects
    See Arthritis—Nutritional aspects
  — Nutritional aspects
    x Arthritis—Dietary aspects
      Diet and arthritis
      Nutrition and arthritis
  — Personal narratives

x Arthritis deformans—Personal
narratives
Arthritis, Infectious
See Infectious arthritis
Arthritis deformans *(RC933)*
sa Joints—Diseases
Sjogren's syndrome
x Arthrosis deformans
Osteoarthritis
Rheumatic gout
Rheumatoid arthritis
xx Collagen diseases
Gout
Joints—Diseases
Rheumatism
— Diagnosis
— Immunological aspects
— Personal narratives
See Arthritis—Personal narratives
— Psychosomatic aspects
Arthritis deformans in children *(RJ520.R5)*
x Juvenile arthritis deformans
Juvenile rheumatoid arthritis
Still's disease
xx Collagen diseases
Arthrocentesis
x Arthrotomy
Joints—Paracentesis
Joints—Puncture
xx Paracentesis
Arthrodesis *(RD686)*
xx Ankylosis
Joints—Surgery
Arthrogastra *(Indirect)*
xx Arachnida
Arthrogryposis
x Arthromyodysplasia, Congenital
Congenital arthromyodysplasia
Guérin-Stern syndrome
Myodystrophia fetalis deformans
xx Joints—Diseases
Arthromyodysplasia, Congenital
See Arthrogryposis
Arthropathy
See Joints—Diseases
Arthroplasty *(RD686)*
xx Joints—Surgery
Surgery, Plastic
Arthropod-borne viruses
sa Semliki Forest virus
Tick-borne encephalitis viruses
x Arboviruses
xx Virus diseases
Viruses
Arthropod populations *(Indirect)*
sa Insect populations
xx Animal populations
Arthropoda *(Indirect)* *(QL434-599)*
sa Arachnida
Crustacea
Insects
Myriapoda
Pentastomida
Symphyla
Tardigrada
xx Invertebrates
— Anatomy
— Catalogs and collections
— Collection and preservation
— Identification *(QL438)*
— Physiology
sa Ecdysis
Arthropoda, Fossil *(QE815-832)*
sa Trilobites
Xiphosura
Arthroscopy
xx Endoscope and endoscopy
Joints—Examination

Arthrosis deformans
See Arthritis deformans
Arthrostraca *(QL444.A7)*
sa Amphipoda
Isopoda
xx Crustacea
Malacostraca
Arthrotomy
See Arthrocentesis
Artichokes *(SB351.A8)*
sa Cookery (Artichokes)
Jerusalem artichoke
— Marketing
— Prices *(Direct)*
— Storage
Article
See Grammar, Comparative and general—
Article
subdivision Article *under names of*
languages and groups of languages
Articles, Thirty-nine
See Church of England. Articles of
religion
Articles of association
See Articles of incorporation
Articles of faith, Thirteen (Judaism)
See Thirteen articles of faith (Judaism)
Articles of incorporation *(Direct)*
sa By-laws
Certificates of incorporation
x Articles of association
xx Charters
Corporation law
Incorporation
Articles of partnership *(Direct)*
xx Partnership
Articles of war
See Military law
Articulata
xx Brachiopoda
Articulata, Fossil
sa Strophomenida
Terebratulida, Fossil
xx Brachiopoda, Fossil
Articulated locomotives
See Locomotives, Articulated
Articulation (Education) *(LB2350)*
sa Eight-Year Study
x Integration in education
xx Education—Curricula
School management and organization
Articulations
See Joints
Artificial arms *(RD756)*
x Arm—Prosthesis
Arms, Artificial
xx Artificial limbs
Artificial atmospheres (Space environment)
x Atmospheres, Artificial (Space
environment)
Controlled atmospheres (Space
environment)
Gaseous environment (Space
environment)
Habitable atmospheres (Space
environment)
xx Closed respiratory systems (Space
environment)
Gases
Space medicine
Artificial blood circulation
See Blood—Circulation, Artificial
Artificial clouds *(QC921.5)*
xx Clouds
Weather control
Artificial consciousness
See Conscious automata

Artificial deformities
See Deformities, Artificial
Artificial delay lines
See Delay lines
Artificial diamonds
See Diamonds, Artificial
Artificial eyes
See Eyes, Artificial
Artificial feeding *(RM223-4)*
sa Tube feeding
x Feeding, Artificial
xx Nutrition
Artificial fever
See Fever therapy
Artificial fibers
See Textile fibers, Synthetic
Artificial flies
See Flies, Artificial
Artificial flower industry *(Direct)*
sa Wages—Artificial flower industry
— Collective labor agreements
See Collective labor agreements—
Artificial flower industry
Artificial flowers *(TT890-894)*
sa Feather flowers
Wax flowers
x Flowers, Artificial
xx Fancy work
Millinery
— Juvenile literature
Artificial food
See Food, Artificial
Artificial fruit
x Fruit, Artificial
Artificial fur
x Fur, Artificial
xx Fur
— Cleaning
Artificial ground-water recharge
See Water, Underground—Artificial
recharge
Artificial heart
See Blood—Circulation, Artificial
Perfusion pump (Heart)
Artificial hibernation
xx Hibernation
Hypothermia
Artificial horizons
See Horizons, Artificial
Artificial horizons (Aeronautical instruments)
x Altitude gyro
Climb and bank indicators
Gyro horizon
Gyro vertical (Instruments)
xx Aeronautical instruments
Gyroscope
Artificial impregnation
See Artificial insemination
Artificial insemination *(SF105.5)*
Here are entered general works and
works on artificial insemination of
livestock. Works on artificial insemi-
nation in humans are entered under
the heading Artificial insemination,
Human.
x Artificial impregnation
Impregnation, Artificial
Insemination, Artificial
xx Stock and stock-breeding
— Law and legislation *(Direct)*
Artificial insemination, Human *(Catholic*
moral theology, BX1759.5.A7;
Obstetrics, RG134)
Note under Artificial insemination
— Law and legislation *(Direct)*
xx Sex and law
Artificial insemination, Human (Canon law)

Artificial intelligence
    sa Adaptive control systems
        Automatic theorem proving
        Error-correcting codes (Information
           theory)
        GPS (Computer program)
        Machine translating
        Perceptrons
        Question-answering systems
    x Artificial thinking
        Electronic brains
        Intellectronics
        Intelligence, Artificial
        Intelligent machines
        Machine intelligence
        Thinking, Artificial
    xx Bionics
        Digital computer simulation
        Electronic data processing
        Logic machines
        Machine theory
        Self-organizing systems
        Simulation methods
Artificial islands
    sa Satellite launching ships
    x Drilling platforms
        Islands, Artificial
        Offshore structures
        Radar islands
        Texas towers
    xx Oil well drilling, Submarine
        Radar defense networks
  — Safety measures
Artificial joints
    xx Prosthesis
Artificial kidney *(RC901.7.A7)*
    x Kidney, Artificial
    xx Artificial organs
        Hemodialysis
        Hospitals—Nephrological services
        Uremia
Artificial languages
    See Languages, Artificial
Artificial leather
    See Leather, Artificial
Artificial leaves
    x Foliage, Artificial
        Leaves, Artificial
Artificial legs
    x Leg—Prosthesis
    xx Artificial limbs
Artificial light gardening
    xx Gardening
        Greenhouse management
        House plants
        Plants, Effect of light on
  — Costs
Artificial limb fitters *(Direct)*
    sa Wages—Artificial limb fitters
Artificial limbs *(RD756)*
    sa Artificial arms
        Artificial legs
    x Limbs, Artificial
    xx Amputees—Rehabilitation
        Orthopedic apparatus
        Prosthesis
  — Research *(RD756)*
Artificial membranes
    See Membranes (Technology)
Artificial mineral waters
    See Mineral waters, Artificial
Artificial minerals
    sa Precious stones, Artificial
    x Minerals, Artificial
        Minerals, Synthetic
    xx Mineralogy
        Synthetic products

Artificial modification of clouds
    See Rain-making
Artificial organs
    sa Artificial kidney
        Pacemaker, Artificial (Bladder)
        Pacemaker, Artificial (Heart)
        Perfusion pump (Heart)
        Prosthesis
    x Organs, Artificial
    xx Prosthesis
        Surgery
Artificial pacemaker (Bladder)
    See Pacemaker, Artificial (Bladder)
Artificial pacemaker (Heart)
    See Pacemaker, Artificial (Heart)
Artificial palate
    x Palate, Artificial
Artificial persons
    See Juristic persons
Artificial pneumoperitoneum
    See Pneumoperitoneum, Artificial
Artificial radioactivity
    See Induced radioactivity
Artificial recharge of ground water
    See Water, Underground—Artificial
        recharge
Artificial reefs
    xx Fisheries
        Fishing
        Reefs
Artificial resins
    See Gums and resins, Synthetic
Artificial respiration *(RC87)*
    sa Asphyxia
        Drowning, Restoration from
        Iron lung
        Respirators
    x Respiration, Artificial
    xx Asphyxia
        Drowning, Restoration from
        First aid in illness and injury
        Resuscitation
  — Complications and sequelae
Artificial sampling
    See Monte Carlo method
Artificial satellite launching
    See Artificial satellites—Launching
Artificial satellite re-entry
    See Artificial satellites—Atmospheric entry
Artificial satellite sounds
    xx Sounds
Artificial satellites *(TL796)*
        Here are entered works on artificial satel-
           lites in general and on the satellites or-
           biting around the earth. Works on ar-
           tificial satellites of other celestial bo-
           dies are entered under Artificial satel-
           lites subdivided by the name of the
           body, *e.g.* Artificial satellites—Sun.
    sa Alouette (Artificial satellite)
        Ariel (Artificial satellite)
        Astronautics in meteorology
        Astronautics in navigation
        Discoverer (Artificial satellite)
        Expandable space structures
        Explorer (Artificial satellite)
        Geodetic satellites
        Meteorological satellites
        Project Vanguard
        Scientific satellites
        Space stations
        Transit (Navigation satellite)
        Vanguard (Artificial satellite)
        Voskhod (Manned satellite)
        Vostok (Manned satellite)
    x Earth satellites
        Orbiting vehicles
        Satellite vehicles

        Satellites, Artificial
    xx Astronautics
        Astronautics in meteorology
        Satellites
        Space vehicles
  — Apparent position calculators
    x Apparent position calculators,
        Artificial satellite
        Calculators, Satellite apparent
        position
        Satellite apparent position calculators
    xx Artificial satellites—Tracking
    Example under Astronautical instru-
        ments
  — Atmospheric entry
    x Artificial satellite re-entry
        Atmospheric re-entry (from space)
        Re-entry aerodynamics
        Re-entry problems (Astronautics)
        Re-entry trajectories
    xx Aerodynamic heating
        Aerodynamics
        Aerothermodynamics
        Artificial satellites—Orbits
        Astronautics
        Space trajectories
  — Attitude control systems
    sa Gravity gradient booms
    x Attitude control systems
        (Astronautics)
        Satellite attitude control
    xx Artificial satellites—Control systems
        Astronautical instruments
  — Control systems
    sa Artificial satellites—Attitude control
        systems
    x Control systems of artificial satellites
    xx Flight control
  — Dynamics
  — Equatorial orbits
    x Equatorial orbits (Artificial satellites)
        Equatorial satellites
    xx Artificial satellites—Orbits
  — Juvenile literature
  — Launching
    sa Launch vehicles (Astronautics)
        Satellite launching ships
    x Artificial satellite launching
        Launching of artificial satellites
    xx Rockets (Aeronautics)—Launching
  — — Safety measures
  — Law and legislation
    See Space law
  — Lunar launching
    x Lift-off from the moon
        Lunar launching of artificial satellites
    xx Rocketry
  — Materials
  — Models
  — — Juvenile literature
  — Moon
    sa Lunar probes
        Project Apollo
    x Lunar satellites
    xx Lunar probes
  — — Orbits
    x Lunar satellite orbits
    xx Orbits
        Space trajectories
  — Observers' manuals *(TL796.8)*
  — Optical observations
    sa Baker-Nunn camera
  — Orbits
    sa Artificial satellites—Atmospheric
        entry
        Artificial satellites—Equatorial orbits

subdivision Orbits *under names of*
individual satellites, e.g. Explorer
(Artificial satellite)—Orbits
  xx Astrodynamics
    Orbits
    Space trajectories
—— Graphic methods
—— Tables, etc.
— Public opinion   *(Direct)*
  Example under Public opinion
— Radio observations
— Rotation
— Scientific applications
  sa Orbiting astronomical observatories
    Orbiting geophysical observatories
    Orbiting solar observatories
— Sun   *(TL796.6.S)*
  sa Pioneer (Space probes)
  x Solar artificial satellites
    Sun—Artificial satellites
  Note under Artificial satellites
— Testing
— Tracking
  sa Artificial satellites—Apparent
    position calculators
    Satellite triangulation
    Syncom (Communications satellite)
    —Tracking
  x Flight tracking
    Satellite tracking
    Tracking
  xx Space trajectories
    Tracking radar

    GEOGRAPHIC SUBDIVISIONS

— Jupiter
—— Orbits
— Moon
  sa Lunar Orbiter (Artificial satellite)
Artificial satellites, American, [etc.]
  x American [etc.] artificial satellites
Artificial satellites, Russian *(TL796.5.R)*
  x Russian artificial satellites
    Soviet artificial satellites
    Sputniks
— Optical observations
— Radio observations
Artificial satellites in fingerprint transmission
  xx Fingerprints
Artificial satellites in geographical research
  xx Astronautics in earth sciences
    Geographical research
Artificial satellites in navigation
  xx Astronautics in navigation
    Electronics in navigation
Artificial satellites in telecommunication
  sa Earth stations (Satellite
    telecommunication)
    Project Echo
    Project Relay
    Project Telstar
    Radiotelephone
    Skynet Project
    Syncom (Communications satellite)
    Telegraph, Wireless
    Television
  x Communication satellites
    Communications-relay satellites
    Global satellite communications
    systems
  xx Radio relay systems
    Telecommunication
— Earth stations
  See Earth stations (Satellite
    telecommunication)
— Ground stations
  See Earth stations (Satellite
    telecommunication)

— Law and legislation   *(Direct)*
  xx Space law
    Telecommunication—Law and
    legislation
Artificial silk
  See Rayon
Artificial stone
  See Stone, Artificial
Artificial sunlight therapy
  See Ultra-violet rays—Therapeutic use
Artificial sweeteners
  See Nonnutritive sweeteners
Artificial teeth
  See Prosthodontics
Artificial thinking
  See Artificial intelligence
Artificial vision
  x Visual prosthesis
  xx Blindness
    Prosthesis
    Vision
Artificial weather control
  See Weather control
Artificial wool
  See Wool, Artificial
Artillery *(Indirect) (UF)*
  sa Anti-aircraft artillery
    Anti-aircraft guns
    Fire control (Gunnery)—Optical
    equipment
    Floating batteries
    Ordnance
    Railway artillery
    Range-finding
    France. Armée. Artillerie; United
    States. Army. Artillery; *and*
    similar headings under other
    countries
  x Naval artillery
  xx Anti-aircraft guns
    Batteries
    Gunnery
    Ordnance
    Shooting, Military
— Early works to 1800
— History
—— Pictorial works
— Museums
    See Military museums
— Problems, exercises, etc.
Artillery, Anti-aircraft
  See Anti-aircraft artillery
Artillery, Coast *(Indirect) (UF450-455)*
  sa Anti-aircraft artillery
    Ordnance, Coast
    United States. Army. Coast
    Artillery; *and similar headings under*
    other countries
  x Coast artillery
    Seacoast artillery
  xx Anti-aircraft artillery
    Coast defenses
Artillery, Field and mountain *(Indirect)*
    (UF400-445)
  sa Antitank guns
    Mountain guns
    Switzerland. Armée.
    Gebirgsartillerie; United States.
    Army. Field Artillery; *and similar*
    headings under other countries
  x Field artillery
    Mountain artillery
Artillery, Railway
  See Railway artillery

Artillery drill and tactics *(UF157-302)*
  Here are entered general works only.
  Works on the army of any particular
  country are entered under the name of
  the country with subheading Army.
  Artillery—Drill and tactics.
  sa Gunnery
    Target-practice
  xx Drill and minor tactics
    Military art and science
    Tactics
Artillery ranges
  See Bombing and gunnery ranges
Artiodactyla
  sa Ruminantia
— Anatomy
Artisans *(Direct)*
  sa Apprentices
    Cottage industries
    Home labor
    Journeymen
    Service industries
    particular classes of artisans, e.g.
     Barbers; Cabinet-workers; Weavers
  x Artizans
  xx Cottage industries
    Handicraft
    Industrial arts
    Labor and laboring classes
— Accounting
— Information services
— Language (New words, slang, etc.)
— Pensions
— Pictorial works
— Taxation   *(Direct)*
  xx Business tax
Artisans in art *(N8218)*
  xx Art
Artist and art dealer contracts
  See Artists' contracts
Artistic anatomy
  See Anatomy, Artistic
Artistic photography
  See Photography, Artistic
Artists *(Direct) (N40)*
  sa Actors
    Architects
    Art as a profession
    Art metal-workers
    Authors
    Authors as artists
    Book-plate designers
    Cartoonists
    College teachers as artists
    Commercial artists
    Dancers
    Engravers
    Entertainers
    Etchers
    Illustrators
    Little masters (Artists)
    Musicians
    Painters
    Potters
    Printmakers
    Prisoners as artists
    Prisoners of war as artists
    Sculptors
    Women artists
    Youth as artists
  xx Art
    Arts
    Painters
— Anecdotes, facetiae, satire, etc.
— Autographs
—— Facsimiles
    Example under Autographs—Fac-
    similes

Artists *(Direct)* *(N40)* *(Continued)*
— Biography
— Caricatures and cartoons
— Correspondence, reminiscences, etc.
— Interviews
— Juvenile literature
— Portraits
    x Painters—Portraits
    Example under Portraits
— Psychology
— Salaries, pensions, etc.
Artists, Blind
    sa Sculptors, Blind
    xx Artists, Physically handicapped
        Blind
Artists, Handicapped
    See Artists, Physically handicapped
Artists, Hebrew
    See Artists, Jewish
Artists, Insane
    See Art and mental illness
Artists, Jewish *(Direct)*
    x Artists, Hebrew
        Hebrew artists
        Jewish artists
    xx Jews—Biography
Artists, Medieval *(Direct)*
Artists, Negro
    See Negro artists
Artists, Physically handicapped *(N71.3)*
    sa Artists, Blind
    x Artists, Handicapped
        Handicapped artists
        Physically handicapped artists
    xx Physically handicapped
Artists, Women
    See Women artists
Artists and models in art
    x Artists in art
        Models and artists in art
        Models in art
    xx Art
Artists as teachers
    xx Art teachers
        Teachers
Artists' book-plates
    See Book-plates, Artists'
Artists' brushes
    x Brushes, Artists'
    xx Artists' materials
Artists' contracts *(Direct)*
    x Artist and art dealer contracts
        Contracts, Artists'
    xx Contracts
        Law and art
Artists in art
    See Artists and models in art
Artists in literature
Artists' marks *(N45)*
    sa Calligraphers' marks
        Engravers' marks
        Swordsmiths' marks
    x Marks, Artists'
        Painters' marks
    xx Engravers' marks
        Initials
        Monograms
Artists' materials
    sa Artists' brushes
        Concrete as art material
        Easels
        Painting knives
        Palette knives
        Palettes
        Plastics as art material
    x Painters' materials
    xx Drawing materials—Catalogs
— Formulae, tables, etc.

    x Formulas for artists
— — Juvenile literature
Artists' models
    See Models, Artists'
Artists' preparatory studies *(Direct)*
        (N7433.5)
    Here are entered works dealing with stud-
    ies or sketches by artists preparatory to
    executing works of art in any form.
    sa Architectural models
    x Preliminary sketches (Art)
        Preparatory studies (Art)
        Presentation drawings (Art)
        Sketches, Preparatory (Art)
        Working drawings (Art)
    xx Art
Artizans
    See Artisans
Artom system of wireless telegraphy
    See Telegraph, Wireless—Artom system
Arts *(Direct)*
    Here are entered works on the arts in gen-
    eral, including the visual arts, litera-
    ture and the performing arts. Works
    limited to the visual arts (architecture,
    painting, sculpture, etc.) are entered
    under Art.
    sa Artists
    x Arts,Fine
        Fine arts
    Note under Art
— Administration
    See Arts—Management
— Anecdotes, facetiae, satire, etc.
— Book reviews
— Caricatures and cartoons
— Competitions
    sa Nihon Geijutsuin shō
        Premio Spoleto
— Criticism
    See Art criticism
— Early works to 1800
— Endowments
    xx Art patronage
— Federal aid
    See Federal aid to the arts
— Fellowships
    See Arts—Scholarships, fellowships,
        etc.
— History
    sa Art criticism
— Juvenile literature
— Management *(NX760-770)*
    sa Arts administrators
    x Arts administration
        Arts—Administration
        Arts management
— Marketing
— Mathematics
— Psychology
— Public opinion
— Scholarships, fellowships, etc. *(Direct)*
    x Arts fellowships
        Arts—Fellowships
        Arts scholarships
— Social aspects
    See Arts and society
— Study and teaching *(Direct)*
Arts, American, ₍French, etc.₎ *(Direct)*
    x American ₍French, etc.₎ arts
— Iranian ₍etc.₎ influences
— Juvenile literature
Arts, Associate in
    See Associate in arts degree
Arts, Bachelor of
    See Bachelor of arts degree
Arts, Baroque

Arts, Baroque *(Direct)*
    x Baroque arts
— Historiography
Arts, Buddhist *(Direct)*
    sa Buddhist art and symbolism
    x Buddhist arts
Arts, Classical *(Direct)*
    x Classical arts
Arts, Decorative
    See Art, Decorative
        Art industries and trade
        Arts and crafts movement
        Decoration and ornament
        Design, Decorative
        Interior decoration
        the subjects referred to under these
        headings
Arts, Fine
    See Art
        Arts
Arts, Gothic *(Direct)*
    x Gothic arts
    xx Arts, Medieval
Arts, Graphic
    See Graphic arts
Arts, Islamic *(Direct)*
    x Arts, Muslim
        Islamic arts
        Muslim arts
Arts, Master of
    See Master of arts degree
Arts, Medieval *(Direct)*
    sa Arts, Gothic
Arts, Modern *(Direct)*
    sa Art, Modern
        Gothic revival (Art)
        Literature, Modern
    x Modern arts
— 20th century *(Direct)*
Arts, Mormon *(Direct)*
    x Mormon arts
Arts, Muslim
    See Arts, Islamic
Arts, Negro
    See Negro arts
Arts, Occidental
    This heading is used only with subdivi-
    sions.
— Japanese ₍etc.₎ influences
Arts, Renaissance *(Direct)*
    x Renaissance arts
Arts, Useful
    See Industrial arts
        Technology
Arts, Victorian *(Direct)*
    x Victorian arts
— Italian ₍etc.₎ influences
ARTS (Air traffic control)
    See Radar air traffic control systems
Arts administration
    See Arts—Management
Arts administrators *(Direct)*
    x Administrators, Arts
    xx Arts—Management
        Executives
Arts and crafts movement *(NK1135-1149)*
    sa Basket making
        Beadwork
        Bookbinding
        Carving (Art industries)
        China painting
        Decoration and ornament
        Design, Decorative
        Embroidery
        Enamel and enameling
        Folk art
        Furniture
        Glass painting and staining

Goldsmithing
Graffito decoration
Hand spinning
Hand weaving
Handicraft
Illumination of books and manuscripts
Ironwork
Jewelry
Lace and lace making
Lacquer and lacquering
Leather work
Manual training
Metal-work
Modeling
Mosaics
Mural painting and decoration
Needlework
Pottery
Repoussé work
Rugs
Silversmithing
Stencil work
Tapestry
Weaving
Wood-carving
  x Arts, Decorative
    Decorative arts
  xx Art
    Art industries and trade
    Folk art
    Handicraft
    Industrial arts
    Manual training
    Technical education
Arts and ethics
  See Arts and morals
Arts and mass media
  See Mass media and the arts
Arts and morals *(NX180.E8)*
  sa Literature and morals
    Music and morals
    Theater—Moral and religious aspects
  x Arts and ethics
    Ethics and the arts
    Morals and the arts
Arts and religion *(NX180.R4)*
  x Religion and the arts
Arts and revolutions
  sa Art and revolutions
    Politics in art
  x Revolutions and the arts
  xx Politics in art
Arts and science
  See Science and the arts
Arts and socialism
  See Socialism and the arts
Arts and society *(Direct)*
  x Arts and sociology
    Arts—Social aspects
    Society and the arts
    Sociology and the arts
Arts and sociology
  See Arts and society
Arts and technology
  See Technology and the arts
Arts and trade-unions
  See Trade-unions and the arts
Arts fellowships
  See Arts—Scholarships, fellowships, etc.
Arts in literature
Arts management
  See Arts—Management
Arts scholarships
  See Arts—Scholarships, fellowships, etc.
Aruaco Indians
  See Arhuaco Indians
Arui
  See Barbary sheep

Arulo (Artificial language) *(PM8085)*
  xx Languages, Artificial
Arumani
  See Arumanians
Arumanian dialect *(Direct)* *(PC797)*
  xx Romanian language
Arumanian marriage customs and rites
  See Marriage customs and rites, Arumanian
Arumanians
  x Armans
    Aromani
    Aromunes
    Arumani
    Cincari
    Kutso-Vlachs
    Macedo-Romanians
    Makedo-Romanians
    Pindus Romanians
    Tsintsars
    Vlachs
    Wallachs
  xx Ethnology—Balkan Peninsula
    Romanians
Arumanians in Greece, [etc.]
Arunndta tribe
  See Aranda tribe
Arunta language
  See Aranda language
Arunta tribe
  See Aranda tribe
Arusha (African tribe)
  xx Ethnology—Tanganyika
    Masai
Arusha law
  See Law, Arusha
Arvernes
  See Arverni
Arverni
  x Arvernes
  xx Ethnology—France
    Gauls
Arvin, Calif.
  — Earthquake, 1952
Arya-samaj
  xx Hinduism
  — Biography
Aryan antiquities *(GN539)*
  x Antiquities, Aryan
  xx Antiquities
Aryan civilization
  See Civilization, Aryan
Aryan folk-lore
  See Folk-lore, Aryan
Aryan languages *(P501-769)*
  sa Armenian language
    Baltic languages
    Indo-Aryan languages
    Indo-Iranian languages
    Iranian languages
    Khayasa language
    Phrygian language
    Proto-Aryan language
    Tokharian language
    Venetic language
  x Indo-European languages
    Indo-Germanic languages
    Languages, Aryan
  xx Indo-Aryan languages
    Indo-Iranian languages
    Iranian languages
  Note under Philology, Comparative
  — Etymology
    Example under reference from Etymology
  — Indeclinable words
    Example under reference from Indeclinable words
  — Numerals

  — Reduplication
    Example under reference from Reduplication (in language)
Aryan philology *(P501-769)*
  sa Indo-Aryan philology
    Indo-Iranian philology
    Iranian philology
    Oriental philology
  x Indo-European philology
    Languages, Aryan
    Philology, Aryan
  xx Indo-Aryan philology
    Indo-Iranian philology
    Iranian philology
  Example under Philology
  Note under Philology, Comparative
Aryans *(DS15; GN539)*
  sa Celts
    Germanic tribes
    Greeks
    Hindus
    Latin peoples
    Luwians
    Slavs
    Tokhari
  x Indo-Europeans
    Indo-Germanic peoples
  xx Caucasian race
    Civilization, Aryan
  Example under Ethnology; History, Ancient
  — Religion *(BL660)*
Arylation
Arytenoid ligaments
  See Vocal cords
As (Coin) *(CJ937)*
Asango language
  See Shira language
Asaro language
  sa Lunambe dialect
  xx Papuan languages
Asbestos *(Indirect)* *(TN930)*
  sa Asbestos cement
    Serpentine
    Strikes and lockouts—Asbestos mining
  xx Building materials
    Serpentine
  Example under Geology, Economic
  — Standards
  — Toxicology
Asbestos cement
  sa Pipe, Asbestos-cement
  xx Asbestos
    Cement
  — Quality control
  — Standards *(Direct)*
Asbestos-cement pipe
  See Pipe, Asbestos-cement
Asbestos cement roofing
  See Roofing, Asbestos cement
Asbestos fibers
  x Textile fibers, Asbestos
  xx Inorganic fibers
Asbestos industry *(Direct)*
  — Dust control
  — Hygienic aspects *(RC965.A7)*
Asbestosis
  xx Lungs—Dust diseases
Ascariasis *(RC119.7)*
  x Ascaridiasis
  xx Medical parasitology
Ascarida
  See Ascaridida
Ascaridiasis
  See Ascariasis
Ascaridida
  x Ascarida
  xx Nematoda

Ascension, Feast of the
   See Ascension Day
Ascension (in religion, folk-lore, etc.)
   sa Mi'rāj
      Revelation
   x Folk-lore of ascension
   xx Religion, Primitive
      Revelation
Ascension Day   *(BV57)*
   x Ascension, Feast of the
   xx Church year
      Fasts and feasts
      Jesus Christ—Ascension
Ascension Day music
   xx Church music
      Music
      Sacred vocal music
Ascension of Christ
   See Jesus Christ—Ascension
Ascetical theology
   See Asceticism
      Asceticism—Catholic Church
Asceticism   *(BL625; Christian, BV5021-5068;*
      Ethics, BJ1491)
   sa Christian life
      Fakirs
      Fasting
      Flagellants and flagellation
      Hedonism
      Martyrdom
      Meditation
      Monastic and religious life
      Monastic and religious life of women
      Monasticism and religious orders
      Monasticism and religious orders—
         Dietary rules
      Mysticism
      Perfection
      Prayer
      Retreats
      Spiritual direction
      Spiritual life
      Vows
      Wilderness (Theology)
   x Ascetical theology
      Contempt of the world
      Theology, Ascetical
   xx Christian life
      Church discipline
      Ethics
      Fanaticism
      Monastic and religious life
      Monastic and religious life of women
      Theology, Doctrinal
      Wilderness (Theology)
   — Middle Ages, 600-1500
      xx Church history—Middle Ages,
         600-1500

      GENERAL SUBDIVISIONS

   — Biblical teaching
   — Catholic Church
      x Ascetical theology
         Catholic Church—Asceticism
         Theology, Ascetical
      Example under Catholic Church

      GENERAL SUBDIVISIONS

   — Comparative studies   *(BL625)*
   — Early church, ca. 30-600
      xx Church history—Primitive and early
         church, ca. 30-600
   — Hinduism
      sa Fasting (Hinduism)
         Sannyasi
      x Hindu asceticism
         Hinduism—Asceticism
   — Judaism

      sa Fasting (Judaism)
      x Jewish asceticism
         Judaism—Asceticism
   — Orthodox Eastern Church
      x Orthodox Eastern Church—
         Asceticism
   — Psychology
      xx Psychology, Religious
   — Sermons
Aschaffenburg
   — Siege, 1945
      xx World War, 1939-1945—Campaigns
         —Germany
Asci
   sa Ascospores
   xx Ascomycetes
      Ascospores
Ascidia (Botany)   *(QK649)*
Ascidiacea   *(Indirect)*   *(QL613)*
   x Ascidians
      Sea-squirts
Ascidians
   See Ascidiacea
Ascites
   x Dropsy, Abdominal
      Hydroperitoneum
Asclepiads
Ascomycetes   *(QK623)*
   sa Asci
      Ascospores
      Discomycetes
      Dothideales
      Pezizales
   xx Fungi
ASCOP (Electronic computer system)
Ascorbic acid
   x Vitamin C
   — Physiological effect
   — Therapeutic use
      xx Vitamin therapy
Ascorbic acid deficiency
   sa Scurvy
      Scurvy, Infantile
   xx Avitaminosis
Ascorbic acid in animal nutrition
   xx Feeding
Ascorbic acid metabolism
   xx Vitamin metabolism
Ascospores
   sa Asci
   xx Asci
      Ascomycetes
      Spores (Botany)
Asculum, Battle of
   See Ausculum, Battle of, 279 B.C.
Asdic
   See Sonar
Asepsis and antisepsis
   sa Antiseptics
      Culture contamination (Biology)
      Irrigation (Medicine)
      Surgery, Aseptic and antiseptic
   xx Antiseptics
   — Programmed instruction
Aseptic femoral necrosis
   See Idiopathic femoral necrosis
Aseptic surgery
   See Surgery, Aseptic and antiseptic
Aseptolin   *(RM666.A8)*
Asexual reproduction
   See Reproduction, Asexual
Ash, Pulverized fuel
   See Fly ash
Ash (Tree)
   sa White ash
Ash disposal   *(Conveying machinery, TJ1410)*
   x Ashes, Removal of
   xx Refuse and refuse disposal

Ashango language
   See Shira language
Ashanti goldweights
   See Goldweights, Ashanti
Ashanti language
   See Tshi language
Ashanti law
   See Law, Ashanti
Ashanti War, 1822-1831   *(DT507)*
Ashanti War, 1873-1874   *(DT507)*
Ashanti War, 1900   *(DT507)*
Ashantis   *(DT507)*
   sa Akans (African people)
      Fantis
   xx Akans (African people)
   — Juvenile literature
Ashcan School   *(N6512.5.E4)*
   x Eight (Group of artists)
Asher (Tribe of Israel)
   xx Twelve tribes of Israel
Ashes, Removal of
   See Ash disposal
Ashes (Fertilizer)
   xx Fertilizers and manures
      Fly ash
Ashikaga Shogunate
   xx Japan—History—1333-1600
Ashio-machi, Japan, in art
Ashira language
   See Shira language
Ashkenazic Jews
   See Ashkenazim
Ashkenazim
   x Ashkenazic Jews
   xx Jews
Ashluslay Indians   *(F2230.2.A)*
   xx Indians of South America
Ashluslay language
   See Chulupí language
Āsī language
   See Ossetic language
Asia
   — Defenses
      sa Military assistance
   — Description and travel
      Example under Discoveries (in geogra-
         phy)
   — Languages
      sa Oriental languages
   — Literatures
      See Oriental literature
Asia co-prosperity sphere
   See Greater East Asia co-prosperity sphere
Asian-African politics
   See Afro-Asian politics
Asian cooperation
   xx International cooperation
Asian flu   *(RC150)*
   x Asiatic flu
   xx Influenza
Asian literature
   See Oriental literature
Asian newspapers
Asian periodicals
   sa Southeast Asian periodicals
Asian students in the United States, ₍etc.₎
Asian studies
   See Oriental studies
Asiani
   See Tokhari
Asians
   sa names of individual races, e.g.
      Chinese, East Indians, Mongols
   x Orientals
   xx Ethnology—Asia
Asians in Australia, ₍etc.₎
Asiatic art
   See Art, Asian

Asiatic beetle (SB945.A)
  xx Beetles
    Grasses—Diseases and pests
Asiatic buffalo
  See Water buffalo
Asiatic cholera
  See Cholera, Asiatic
Asiatic Eskimo language
  See Yuit language
Asiatic flu
  See Asian flu
Asiatic proverbs
  See Proverbs, Oriental
Asiatic rice borer
  x Rice borer, Asiatic
  xx Rice—Diseases and pests
Asiento treaty, 1713
  x Assiento treaty, 1713
  xx Utrecht, Treaty of, 1713
Asira language
  See Shira language
Asmat
  xx Ethnology—New Guinea
Asmat language
  xx Papuan languages
Asmoneans
  See Maccabees
Asociación Latinoamericana de Libre
    Comercio countries
  xx Latin America
Asparagin (QP921.A7)
Asparagus (SB325)
  sa Cookery (Asparagus)
  — Disease and pest resistance
  — Diseases and pests (SB608.A8)
    sa Asparagus-beetle
      Asparagus miner
      Asparagus-rust
      Asparagus—Storage—Diseases and
        injuries
      Bacterial soft rot of asparagus
      Example under Vegetables—Diseases
        and pests
  — Fertilizers and manures
  — Genetics
  — Preservation
  — Storage
  — — Diseases and injuries *(Indirect)*
      xx Asparagus—Diseases and pests
  — Transportation
Asparagus-beetle
  xx Asparagus—Diseases and pests
    Beetles
Asparagus miner
  xx Asparagus—Diseases and pests
Asparagus-rust
  xx Asparagus—Diseases and pests
Aspartic acid metabolism
  xx Amino acid metabolism
Aspect (Linguistics)
  See Grammar, Comparative and general—
    Aspect
Aspect ratio (Aerofoils)
  xx Aerofoils
Aspect recording systems of rockets
  See Rockets (Aeronautics)—Aspect
    recording systems
Aspen *(Indirect)* (SD397.A7)
  — Diseases and pests
Aspergillosis, Pulmonary
  See Pulmonary aspergillosis
Aspern, Battle of, 1809 (DC234.6)
  x Essling, Battle of, 1809
    Esslingen, Battle of, 1809
    Marchfeld, Battle of, May 21-22, 1809
  xx Napoléon I, Emperor of the French,
      1769-1821—German and Austrian
      Campaign, 1809

Asphalt *(TN853)*
  sa Asphalt as fuel
    Asphalt concrete
    Asphalt rock
    Pavements, Asphalt
  xx Bitumen
    Bituminous materials
    Concrete
  — Abstracts
  — Electric properties
  — Patents
  — Radiography
  — Testing
Asphalt as fuel
  xx Asphalt
    Fuel
    Liquid fuels
Asphalt cement
  x Asphaltic cement
    Paving asphalt
  xx Bituminous materials
    Cement
    Road materials
  — Grading
  — Specifications
  — Testing
Asphalt concrete
  x Asphaltic concrete
    Concrete, Asphalt
  xx Asphalt
    Concrete
  — Moisture
  — — Measurement
  — Safety measures
  — Testing
  — — Laboratory manuals
Asphalt concrete pavements
  See Pavements, Asphalt concrete
Asphalt flooring
  See Flooring, Asphalt
Asphalt rock
  x Asphalt stone
    Rock asphalt
  xx Asphalt
    Road materials
Asphalt roofing
  See Roofing, Bituminous
Asphalt stone
  See Asphalt rock
Asphaltic cement
  See Asphalt cement
Asphaltic concrete
  See Asphalt concrete
Asphodel (QK495.L72)
Asphyxia *(Diseases of newly born, RJ256;
    First aid, RC87-88; Legal medicine,
    RA1071)*
  sa Anoxemia
    Artificial respiration
    Drowning
    Gases, Asphyxiating and poisonous
  x Asphyxiating gases
    Suffocation
  xx Accidents
    Artificial respiration
    Death—Causes
    First aid in illness and injury
    Gases, Asphyxiating and poisonous
    Gases—Physiological effect
    Respiration
    Violent deaths
Asphyxia neonatorum
  Example under Infants (Newborn)—Diseases
Asphyxiating gases
  See Asphyxia
    Gases, Asphyxiating and poisonous
Aspidobranchia
  See Archaeogastropoda

Aspidospermin (QP921.A75)
Aspiration and aspirators
  sa Chest—Paracentesis
  xx Surgery
Aspiration level
  See Level of aspiration
Aspiration pneumonia (RC772.A8)
  x Aspiration pneumonitis
  xx Pneumonia
Aspiration pneumonitis
  See Aspiration pneumonia
Aspirations, Occupational
  See Vocational interests
Aspirations, Student
  See Student aspirations
Aspirations, Vocational
  See Vocational interests
Aspirin *(Therapeutics, RM666.A82; Trade,
    HD9675.A73)*
Ass, Domestic
  See Donkeys
Assamese language (PK1550-1599)
  xx Indo-Aryan languages, Modern
Assamese literature (PK1560-1588)
Assamese philology (PK1550)
Assamese poetry
Assamese wit and humor
  xx Indic wit and humor
Assaorta-Saho language
  See Saho language
Assassination *(Direct)* (HV6499-6535;
    Political, HV6278)
  sa Assassins
    Murder
    Offenses against heads of state
    Regicides
    Terrorism
  x Manslaughter
    Political murder
  xx Crime and criminals
    Homicide
    Murder
    Offenses against heads of state
    Offenses against the person
    Political crimes and offenses
    Violent deaths
Assassins *(Direct)*
  xx Assassination
    Crime and criminals
  — Biography
  — — Juvenile literature
Assassins (Ismailites) (BP195.A8)
  sa Ismailites
    Nosairians
  xx Batinites
    Islamic sects
    Ismailites
    Regicides
Assateague Indians (E99.A83)
  x Asseteague Indians
  xx Indians of North America
Assault, Criminal
  See Rape
Assault and battery *(Direct)*
  sa Affray
    Assaulting a foreign official
    Indecent assault
    Poisoning
    Trials (Assault and battery)
  x Battery (Law)
  xx Criminal law
    Offenses against the person
    Torts
    Violence (Law)
Assault on foreign officials
  See Assaulting a foreign official
Assaulting a foreign official *(Direct)*
  x Assault on foreign officials

Assaulting a foreign official *(Direct)* *(Continued)*
>> Assaulting public minister
> *xx* Assault and battery
>> International offenses
>> Political crimes and offenses

Assaulting public minister
> *See* Assaulting a foreign official

Assayers *(Assaying, TN550; Biography, TN139-140)*

Assaying *(TN550-580; Mints, HG325-9)*
> *sa* Blowpipe
>> Ores—Sampling and estimation
>> *subdivision* Assaying *under classes of metals and names of specific metals, e.g.* Precious metals—Assaying; Gold —Assaying
> *x* Ores—Analysis
> *xx* Blowpipe
>> Chemistry
>> Metallurgical analysis
>> Metals
>> Mineralogy, Determinative
>> Ores—Sampling and estimation
>> Prospecting
> — Tables, calculations, etc.

Assaying apparatus *(TN575)*
> *xx* Chemical apparatus

Assemblage (Art) *(Direct)*
> *sa* Collage
>> Environment (Art)
> *xx* Art, Modern—20th century
>> Dadaism
>> Found objects (Art)

Assembler language (Computer program language)
> *sa* IBAL (Computer program language)
> *x* Assembly language (Computer program language)
> — Problems, exercises, etc.

Assemblies, Religious
> *See* Religious gatherings

Assembling (Electronic computers)
> *sa* Compiling (Electronic computers)
> *xx* Compiling (Electronic computers)
>> Electronic data processing
>> Electronic digital computers— Programming

Assembling machines
> *x* Assembly machines
> *xx* Assembly-line methods
> — Automatic control *(TJ1317)*
> — Design and construction

Assembly, Right of *(Direct)* *(JC607)*
> *sa* Conventicle act, 1670
>> Freedom of association
>> Liberty of speech
>> Public meetings
>> Riots
> *x* Freedom of assembly
>> Right of assembly
> *xx* Civil rights
>> Freedom of association
>> Liberty
>> Public meetings

Assembly, School
> *See* Schools—Exercises and recreations

Assembly language (Computer program language)
> *See* Assembler language (Computer program language)

Assembly-line balancing
> *x* Balancing of assembly-lines
>> Line balancing (Assembly-lines)

Assembly-line methods
> *sa* Assembling machines
>> Automation
> *x* Production-line methods
> *xx* Automation

>> Factory management
>> Industrial management
>> Manufacturing processes
>> Plant layout
>> Production engineering

Assembly machines
> *See* Assembling machines

Assembly of gods (Greek mythology) in art

Asses
> *See* African wild ass
>> Donkeys

Assessment *(Direct)* *(HJ3241)*
> Here are entered works on tax assessment. Works on the technique of property valuation for other than taxation purposes are entered under specific headings with subdivision Valuation, *e.g.* Real property—Valuation. Works on assessment in a particular field of taxation are entered under the heading covering taxation in that field, *e.g.* Real property tax.
> *sa* Real property—Valuation
>> Taxation, Double
>> Taxation, Exemption from
>> Valuation
> *x* Appraisal
>> Tax assessment
> *xx* Property tax
>> Tax administration and procedure
>> Taxation
> *Note under* Valuation
> — Digests

Assessment insurance
> *See* Insurance, Assessment

Assessment of personality
> *See* Personality assessment

Assessment of technology
> *See* Technology assessment

Assessment work on mining claims
> *See* Mining claims

Assessments, Political
> *See* Campaign funds

Asseteague Indians
> *See* Assateague Indians

Assets, Frozen
> *See* Liquidity (Economics)

Assets, Liquid
> *See* Liquidity (Economics)

Assiento treaty, 1713
> *See* Asiento treaty, 1713

Assietta, Battle of, 1747 *(D293.5.A8)*
> *xx* Austrian Succession, War of, 1740-1748

Assignats *(HG978.2)*
> *xx* Inflation (Finance)—France

Assignment specifications
> *See* Job descriptions

Assignments *(Direct)*
> *sa* Assignments for benefit of creditors
>> Patent assignments
> *x* Cessio bonorum
> *xx* Choses in action
>> Commercial law
>> Debtor and creditor
>> Security (Law)
>> Singular succession
>> Transfer (Law)

Assignments (Roman law)

Assignments for benefit of creditors *(Direct)*
> *sa* Fraudulent conveyances
> *x* Cessio bonorum
> *xx* Assignments
>> Bankruptcy
>> Composition (Law)
>> Debtor and creditor
>> Fraudulent conveyances
>> Trusts and trustees

Assignments for benefit of creditors (Roman law)
> *x* Cessio bonorum

Assimilation (Phonetics)
> *sa subdivision* Assimilation *under names of languages and groups of languages*
> *xx* Phonetics

Assimilation (Sociology)
> *sa* Acculturation
>> Americanization
>> Discrimination
>> Emigration and immigration
>> Emigration and immigration— Psychological aspects
>> Germanization
>> Intercultural education
>> Minorities
>> Race problems
>> *subdivision* Foreign population *under names of countries, cities, etc.*
> *x* Cultural assimilation
> *xx* Acculturation
>> Anthropology
>> Emigration and immigration
>> Minorities
>> Socialization

Assiniboin Indians *(E99.A84)*
> *xx* Indians of North America
>> Siouan Indians

Assiniboin language *(PM638)*
> *xx* Siouan languages

Assistance in emergencies *(Direct)*
> *sa* Disaster relief
>> First aid in illness and injury
>> Necessity (Law)
> *x* Emergencies, Assistance in
>> Emergency assistance
>> Failure to assist in emergencies
>> Good Samaritan laws
> *xx* Accident law
>> Accidents
> — Psychological aspects

Assistance to underdeveloped areas
> *See* Economic assistance

Assistance to undeveloped areas
> *See* Technical assistance

Assistant medical officers
> *See* Physicians' assistants

Assistant student counselors
> *See* Student counselors' assistants

Assistant teachers
> *See* Teachers' assistants

Assisted take-off of aircraft
> *See* Aeroplanes—Assisted take-off

Associate in arts degree
> *x* Arts, Associate in

Associate Presbyterian Church
> Here are entered works on the religious bodies stemming from the Associate Presbytery of Pennsylvania as reconstituted in 1782, after the presbytery of the same name, founded in 1754, was merged into the Associate Reformed Synod.
> *sa* Associate Reformed Presbyterian Church
> *xx* Presbyterian Church in the United States (General)

Associate Reformed Church of North America *(BX8999.A7)*

Associate Reformed Presbyterian Church
> Here are entered works on the religious bodies stemming from the Associated Reformed Synod, founded in 1782 by merger of the Associate Presbytery of Pennsylvania and of the Reformed Presbytery of America.
> *xx* Associate Presbyterian Church

Presbyterian Church in the United
States (General)
Reformed Presbyterian Church
Association
See Social groups
Association, Freedom of
See Freedom of association
Association, Right of
See Freedom of association
Association football
See Soccer
Association of ideas *(BF365-7)*
sa Association tests
Cloze procedure
Conditioned response
Paired-association learning
Perseveration (Psychology)
Reproduction (Psychology)
Trait intercorrelations
Visualization
x Ideas, Association of
Mental association
xx Memory
Perseveration (Psychology)
Psychology
Reproduction (Psychology)
Thought and thinking
Transfer of training
— Juvenile literature
Association tests
sa Remote associates test
xx Association of ideas
Meaning (Psychology)
Memory
Mental tests
Associations, Baptist
See Baptist associations
Associations, International
See International agencies
International cooperation—Societies,
etc.
*particular international agencies,
congresses, societies, etc.*
Associations (Law)
See Corporations, Nonprofit
Unincorporated societies
Associations, institutions, etc. *(Direct)*
sa By-laws
Clubs
Committees
Community life
Cooperation
Cooptation
Freedom of association
Meetings
Membership campaigns
Social group work
Societies
*names of specific types of associations,
institutions, etc., e.g.* Corporations;
Public institutions; Trade and
professional associations; *also
subdivision* Societies, etc. *under
appropriate subjects*
x Institutions, associations, etc.
Organizations
Voluntary associations
Voluntary organizations
xx Societies
— Abbreviations
Example under Abbreviations
— Information services
— Law and legislation *(Direct)*
— Membership, Negro
x Negro membership in associations,
institutions, etc.
xx Negroes
— Taxation *(Direct)*

**Associations, institutions, etc., British,
[Japanese, etc.]** *(Direct)*
x British [Japanese, etc.] associations,
institutions, etc.
Associations, institutions, etc., Foreign
(Direct)
x Foreign associations, institutions, etc.
Foreign institutions, associations, etc.
Institutions, associations, etc., Foreign
— Taxation *(Direct)*
xx Taxation of aliens
Associative algebras
x Algebras, Associative
Associative law (Mathematics)
xx Mathematics
Associative learning
See Paired-association learning
Associative memory organizing system
See AMOS (Computer program)
Associative rings
sa Radical theory
xx Rings (Algebra)
Associative storage *(TK7895.M4)*
x Content-addressed storage
xx Computer storage devices
Assumption
See Hypothesis
Assumption of the Blessed Virgin Mary
See Mary, Virgin—Assumption
**Assumption of the Blessed Virgin Mary, Feast
of the** *(BV50.A7)*
x Feast of the Assumption of the Blessed
Virgin Mary
xx Church year
Fasts and feasts
Mary, Virgin—Assumption
Assurance (Insurance)
See Insurance
Assurance (Theology) *(BT785)*
sa Antinomianism
Inner Light
Perseverance (Theology)
xx Justification
Perseverance (Theology)
Salvation
Theology, Doctrinal
— History of doctrines
Assyria
— Antiquities
x Assyro-Babylonian studies
Assyrian . . .
See Assyro-Babylonian . . .
Assyrians
Here are entered works dealing with
modern adherents of the Nestorian
Church as an element in the popula-
tion of Iraq.
sa Nestorians
x Aisors
East Syrians
xx Nestorians
Assyrians in Canada, [the United States, etc.]
Assyriology
Here are entered works on the science of
Assyrian and Babylonian studies, its
history, scope, etc.
x Assyro-Babylonian studies
xx Oriental studies
Assyro-Babylonian . . .
x Assyrian . . .
Assyro-Babylonian architecture
See Architecture, Assyro-Babylonian
Assyro-Babylonian astrology
See Astrology, Assyro-Babylonian
Assyro-Babylonian astronomy
See Astronomy, Assyro-Babylonian
Assyro-Babylonian calendar
See Calendar, Assyro-Babylonian

Assyro-Babylonian chronology
See Chronology, Assyro-Babylonian
Assyro-Babylonian civilization
See Civilization, Assyro-Babylonian
Assyro-Babylonian cultus
See Cultus, Assyro-Babylonian
Assyro-Babylonian eschatology
See Eschatology, Assyro-Babylonian
Assyro-Babylonian gods
See Gods, Assyro-Babylonian
Assyro-Babylonian inscriptions
See Cuneiform inscriptions
Assyro-Babylonian language *(PJ3101-3595)*
sa Sumerian language
x Akkadian (East Semitic) language
Babylonian language
— Texts
xx Cuneiform inscriptions
Note under Cuneiform inscriptions
Assyro-Babylonian language, Modern
See Syriac language, Modern
Assyro-Babylonian law
See Law—Assyria
Law—Babylonia
Assyro-Babylonian letters
x Babylonian letters
Assyro-Babylonian literature *(PJ3601-3959)*
sa Cuneiform inscriptions
x Babylonian literature
xx Cuneiform inscriptions
— Catalogs
Assyro-Babylonian magic
See Magic, Assyro-Babylonian
Assyro-Babylonian medicine
See Medicine, Assyro-Babylonian
Assyro-Babylonian music
See Music, Assyro-Babylonian
Assyro-Babylonian mythology
See Mythology, Assyro-Babylonian
Assyro-Babylonian philology
Assyro-Babylonian poetry *(Direct)*
Assyro-Babylonian prayers *(PJ3785)*
x Prayers, Assyro-Babylonian
xx Assyro-Babylonian religion
Assyro-Babylonian religion *(BL1620-1625)*
sa Assyro-Babylonian prayers
Gods, Assyro-Babylonian
Sin (Assyro-Babylonian religion)
x Religion, Assyro-Babylonian
Assyro-Babylonian studies
See Assyria—Antiquities
Assyriology
Astasia and astasia-abasia
xx Hysteria
Neurasthenia
Astatine *(QD181.A8)*
xx Halogens
Radioactive substances
Aster yellows
sa Six-spotted leaf-hopper
Asterism (Crystallography) *(QD941)*
xx Crystallography
Mineralogy
Reflection (Optics)
Asteroidea
See Starfishes
Asteroids
See Planets, Minor
Asters *(Botany, QK495.A84; Culture,
SB413.A7)*
Asthenia
Asthenopia
Asthma *(RC591)*
xx Respiratory allergy
— Psychosomatic aspects
Astigmatism *(RE932)*
xx Eye—Abnormities and deformities
Eye—Diseases and defects

Astomida *(Indirect)* *(QL368.C5)*
  xx Ciliata
Aston Martin automobile
Astonishment
  See Surprise
Astor Place Riot, New York, 1849
Astragalus (Anklebone)
  See Anklebone
Astral projection *(BF1389.A7)*
  x Out-of-the-body experiences
  xx Psychical research
Astringents *(RM392)*
  sa Kino
Astrionics
  sa Astronautical instruments
    Astronautics—Communication systems
    Ground support systems (Astronautics)
    Space vehicles—Electronic equipment
    Space vehicles—Radio equipment
  x Astronautics, Electronics in
    Electronics in astronautics
    Space electronics
  xx Astronautical instruments
    Electricity in astronautics
    Electronics
    Electronics in aeronautics
Astrobiology
  See Life on other planets
    Space biology
Astrocytes
  xx Cells
Astrodiagnosis
  See Medical astrology
Astrodynamics *(TL1050)*
  sa Artificial satellites—Orbits
    Astronautical charts
    Astronautics
    Inertial navigation (Astronautics)
    Navigation (Astronautics)
    Relativistic rocket dynamics
    Space flight
    Space trajectories
  xx Astronautics
    Dynamics
    Mechanics, Celestial
    Space flight
  — Computer programs
  — Problems, exercises, etc.
Astrogation
  See Navigation (Astronautics)
Astrographic catalog and chart *(QB6)*
  x Astronomical charts
    Astronomy—Atlases
    Atlases, Astronomical
    Charts, Astronomical
  xx Astronomical photography
    Astronomy—Charts, diagrams, etc.
    Stars—Atlases
    Stars—Catalogs
Astroinertial guidance systems
  See Stellar inertial navigation systems
Astrolabe Expedition, 1826-1829
Astrolabe Expedition, 1837-1840
Astrolabes *(QB85)*
  sa Prismatic astrolabe
  xx Astronomical instruments
  — Early works to 1800 *(QB85)*
Astrology *(BF1651-1729; QB25-26)*
  sa Horoscopes
    Iatrophysical school
    Medical astrology
    Moon—Influence on man
    Occult sciences
    Saturn (Planet)—Influence on man
    Zodiac
  x Hermetic art and philosophy
    Horoscopy
  xx Astronomy

    Divination
    Fortune-telling
    Occult sciences
    Prophecies
    Stars
    Superstition
— Anecdotes, facetiae, satire, etc.
— Caricatures and cartoons
— Controversial literature *(BF1713)*
— Early works to 1800
— History
— — 20th century *(BF1679)*
— Poetry
— Tables *(BF1715)*
Astrology, Arabic, [Assyro-Babylonian, Aztec, Hindu, etc.]
  x Arabic [Assyro-Babylonian, Aztec, Hindu, etc.] astrology
Astrology and birth control
  x Birth control and astrology
Astrology and sex *(BF1729.S4)*
  x Sex and astrology
Astrology in art
  xx Art
Astrology in literature
Astrometry *(QB807)*
    Here are entered works on the art of measuring the position, distance, motion, etc., of the stars. Works on the determination of stellar magnitude by measuring the amount of light are entered under the heading Photometry, Astronomical.
  xx Astronomy
Astronautical accidents
  See Astronautics—Accidents
Astronautical charts *(TL1070)*
    Here are entered maps and charts, including works on them, giving information for use in navigation in space to determine course and location for the astronaut.
  x Astronautics—Charts, diagrams, etc.
    Charts, Astronautical
    Navigation (Astronautics)—Charts, diagrams, etc.
  xx Astrodynamics
    Astronomy—Charts, diagrams, etc.
Astronautical communication systems
  See Astronautics—Communication systems
Astronautical display systems
  See Astronautical instruments—Display systems
Astronautical instruments
  sa Artificial satellites—Attitude control systems
    Astrionics
    Astronautics—Communication systems
    Radioisotopes in astronautics
    Star trackers
    Sun trackers
    headings for special space vehicles with subdivisions for instruments or instrument systems, e.g. Artificial satellites—Apparent position calculators; Ballistic missiles—Guidance systems
  x Instruments, Astronautical
    Space vehicles—Instruments
  xx Astrionics
    Astronautics—Communication systems
    Electronic instruments
    Gyroscopic instruments
    Navigation (Astronautics)
    Space vehicles—Guidance systems
— Display systems
  x Astronautical display systems

    Pictorial display systems, Astronautical
  xx Information display systems
Astronautical museums *(Indirect)*
  x Astronautics—Museums
  xx Museums
Astronautical pilotage
  See Space vehicles—Piloting
Astronautical research *(Direct)*
    (TL858-862)
  sa Rocket research
  x Astronautics—Research
    Research, Astronautical
    Space research
  xx Aeronautical research
    Research
Astronautics *(Indirect)* *(TL787-799)*
    Here are entered general works on the art and science of flying in outer space. Works on the physics of flight beyond earth's atmosphere are entered under Space flight.
  sa Aerothermodynamics
    Artificial satellites
    Artificial satellites—Atmospheric entry
    Astrodynamics
    Astronauts
    Ballistic missiles—Atmospheric entry
    Explosives in astronautics
    Ground support systems (Astronautics)
    Interplanetary voyages
    Launch complexes (Astronautics)
    Manned space flight
    Navigation (Astronautics)
    Outer space
    Outer space—Exploration
    Project Gemini
    Project Mercury
    Project Neptune
    Pyrotechnics in astronautics
    Radioisotopes in astronautics
    Relativistic rocket mechanics
    Rocketry
    Space flight
    Space flight to Mars
    Space flight to the moon
    Space sciences
    Space ships
    Space simulators
    Space stations
    Space vehicles
    Space vehicles—Atmospheric entry
    Women as astronauts
    Women in astronautics
    X-15 (Rocket aircraft)
  xx Aeronautics
    Astrodynamics
    Space flight
    Space sciences
    Space vehicles
  Note under Space sciences
— Abbreviations
— Accidents
    Subdivided by date, *e.g.* Astronautics—Accidents—1967.
  x Accidents, Spacecraft
    Astronautical accidents
    Space vehicles—Accidents
    Spacecraft accidents
— — 1967
    Note under Astronautics—Accidents
— Acronyms
— Anecdotes, facetiae, satire, etc.
— Biography
— — Juvenile literature
— Caricatures and cartoons
— Charts, diagrams, etc.
    See Astronautical charts

120

— Chronology
— Communication systems
    sa Aerospace telemetry
        Astronautical instruments
        Astronautics—Optical
           communication systems
        Television in astronautics
    x Astronautical communication
        systems
        Space communication
        Space communication systems
        Space telecommunication
        Space telecommunication systems
    xx Astrionics
        Astronautical instruments
        Interstellar communication
        Telecommunication
— Contracts and specifications *(Direct)*
    (TL869)
    x Astronautics—Specifications
— Dictionaries
— — Juvenile literature
— Dictionaries, Juvenile
— Economic aspects *(Direct)*
— Experiments *(TL794.3)*
— — Juvenile literature *(TL794.3)*
— Graphic methods
— International cooperation
    sa Ariel (Artificial satellite)
    x International space cooperation
    xx Outer space—Exploration
— Juvenile literature *(TL793)*
— Law and legislation
    See Space law
— Mathematical models
— Museums
    See Astronautical museums
— Nomenclature
— Optical communication systems
    sa Aerospace telemetry
        Lasers
        Television
    x Light communication systems
        Optical space communication
        systems
        Space optical communication
        systems
    xx Astronautics—Communication
        systems
        Laser communication systems
        Lasers
        Optical data processing
        Television
— Patents
    xx Patents
— Pictorial works *(TL793.3)*
— — Juvenile literature
— Piloting
    See Space vehicles—Piloting
— Poetry
— Popular works
— Problems, exercises, etc. *(TL849)*
— Psychology
    See Space flight—Psychological
        aspects
— Research
    See Astronautical research
— Safety measures *(TL867)*
— Specifications
    See Astronautics—Contracts and
        specifications
— Systems engineering
— Terminology *(TL788)*
— Vocational guidance
    See Astronautics as a profession
Astronautics, Electricity in
  See Electricity in astronautics

Astronautics, Electronics in
  See Astrionics
Astronautics, Military *(Indirect)*
    sa Intercontinental ballistic missile bases
    x Astronautics, Naval
        Military astronautics
        Naval astronautics
Astronautics, Naval
  See Astronautics, Military
Astronautics, Photography in
  See Space photography
Astronautics and civilization
    sa Religion and astronautics
        Space law
    x Civilization and astronautics
        Outer space and civilization
        Space age
        Space power
    xx Aeronautics and civilization
        Civilization
— Juvenile literature
Astronautics and ethics *(BJ60)*
    x Ethics and astronautics
Astronautics and Islam
  See Islam and astronautics
Astronautics and religion
  See Religion and astronautics
Astronautics and state *(Indirect)*
    x Space policy
        State and astronautics
    xx Science and state
        Technology and state
Astronautics as a profession *(TL850)*
    sa Women in astronautics
    x Astronautics—Vocational guidance
— Juvenile literature
Astronautics in astronomy
    sa Orbiting astronomical observatories
    xx Astronomy
Astronautics in earth sciences
    sa Artificial satellites in geographical
        research
        Astronautics in geodesy
        Astronautics in geology
        Astronautics in geophysics
        Astronautics in hydrology
        Astronautics in meteorology
        Astronautics in oceanography
    xx Earth sciences
Astronautics in geodesy
    sa Geodetic satellites
        Project ANNA
        Satellite triangulation
    xx Astronautics in earth sciences
        Geodesy
Astronautics in geographical research
    xx Geographical research
Astronautics in geology *(QE33)*
    xx Astronautics in earth sciences
        Geology
Astronautics in geomorphology
    xx Geomorphology
Astronautics in geophysics
    xx Astronautics in earth sciences
        Geophysics
Astronautics in hydrology *(GB665)*
    xx Astronautics in earth sciences
        Hydrology
Astronautics in literature
Astronautics in meteorology *(QC879.5)*
    sa Artificial satellites
        Atmosphere, Upper—Rocket
        observations
        Meteorological satellites
        Photography of clouds
    xx Artificial satellites
        Astronautics in earth sciences
        Meteorology

        Photography of clouds
        Weather forecasting
    Note under Space sciences
— Juvenile literature
Astronautics in navigation *(VK)*
    sa Artificial satellites in navigation
        Transit (Navigation satellite)
    x Terrestrial navigation, Astronautics in
    xx Aids to navigation
        Artificial satellites
        Geographical positions
        Navigation
Astronautics in oceanography *(GC61)*
    xx Astronautics in earth sciences
        Oceanography
Astronautics ships
  See Satellite launching ships
Astronauts *(Direct)*
    sa Space flight training
        Space vehicles—Piloting
        Women as astronauts
    x Cosmonauts
        Space ships—Pilots
    xx Air pilots
        Astronautics
        Manned space flight
— Anecdotes, facetiae, satire, etc.
— Juvenile literature
— Mathematical models
    See Space vehicles—Piloting—
        Mathematical models
— Medical examinations *(TL856)*
    x Physical examination of astronauts
— Nutrition
    x Nutrition in space flight
        Nutrition of astronauts
        Space nutrition
    Example under Nutrition
Astronavigation
  See Navigation (Astronautics)
Astronomers *(Direct)* *(QB35-36)*
    sa Astronomy as a profession
    xx Scientists
— Biography
— Correspondence, reminiscences, etc.
— Juvenile literature
Astronomical charts
  See Astrographic catalog and chart
        Astronomy—Charts, diagrams, etc.
Astronomical clocks *(QB107)*
    sa Calendar watches
        Chronograph
        Chronometer
    x Clocks, Astronomical
    xx Astronomical instruments
        Clocks and watches
Astronomical constants
    sa Astronomical unit
    x Constants, Astronomical
— Tables, etc.
Astronomical geography *(QB631-8)*
    sa Geography, Mathematical
        Latitude
        Longitude
        Meridian lines
        Seasons
    x Geography, Astronomical
    xx Earth
        Geography
        Geography, Mathematical
— Tables, etc.
Astronomical instruments *(QB85-137)*
    sa Almucantar
        Astrolabes
        Astronomical clocks
        Astronomical models
        Astronomical photography
        Chronograph

Astronomy, Hebrew
  See Astronomy, Jewish
Astronomy, Infra-red
  See Infra-red astronomy
Astronomy, Jewish *(QB34)*
  x Astronomy, Hebrew
    Hebrew astronomy
    Jewish astronomy
Astronomy, Khmer *(QB23)*
  x Astronomy, Cambodian
    Cambodian astronomy
    Khmer astronomy
Astronomy, Maya
  See Indians of Central America—
      Astronomy
    Indians of Mexico—Astronomy
Astronomy, Medieval
Astronomy, Mexican Indian
  See Indians of Mexico—Astronomy
Astronomy, Nautical
  See Nautical astronomy
Astronomy, Prehistoric *(GN799.A8)*
  x Prehistoric astronomy
Astronomy, South American Indian
  See Indians of South America—Astronomy
Astronomy, Spherical and practical
      (QB145-237)
  sa Aberration
    Azimuth
    Eclipses
    Ecliptic
    Latitude
    Longitude
    Meridian lines
    Nautical astronomy
    Navigation
    Nutation
    Occultations
    Parallax
    Precession
    Refraction, Astronomical
    Time
    Vernal equinox
  x Spherical astronomy
  xx Geodesy
  — Early works to 1800 *(QB144)*
Astronomy, Statistical
  See Statistical astronomy
Astronomy and state *(Direct)*
  x State and astronomy
Astronomy as a profession *(QB51.5)*
  xx Astronomers
Astronomy in literature
Astrophysics *(QB461)*
      Serial publications of astrophysical obser-
      vatories are entered under 1. As-
      tronomy—Observations. 2. Astrophy-
      sics.
  sa Astronomical spectroscopy
    Cosmic electrodynamics
    Interstellar matter
    Magnetic fields (Cosmic physics)
    Mass loss (Astrophysics)
    Nuclear astrophysics
    Radiative transfer
    Radio astrophysics
    Spectrum analysis
    Stars—Atmospheres
    Stars—Density
    Stars—Evolution
  x Astronomical physics
    Physics, Astronomical
  xx Astronomy
    Cosmic physics
    Physics
    Stars
  — Automation
  — Tables, etc.

Asturians
  xx Ethnology—Spain—Oviedo (Province)
Asturians in Cuba, ⌈Mexico, etc.⌉
Asu (Bantu tribe)
  See Pare (Bantu tribe)
Asu language
  x Athu language
    Chasu language
    Pare language
  xx Bantu languages
Asurs *(DS432)*
  xx Ethnology—India—Bihar (State)
    India—Scheduled tribes
    Mundas
ASW
  See Anti-submarine warfare
Asylum, Right of *(JX4275-4399; HV8652-4)*
  sa Extradition
    Holy Year
    Refugees, Political
    Refugees, Political—Legal status, laws,
      etc.
  x Right of asylum
    Sanctuary (Law)
  xx Church and state
    Deportation
    Ecclesiastical law
    Extradition
    International law
    Neutrality
    Refugees, Political—Legal status, laws,
      etc.
  — Biblical teaching
    x Cities of refuge
  — Cases
    sa Colombian-Peruvian asylum case
Asylum, Right of (in religion, folk-lore, etc.)
  x Folk-lore of the right of asylum
  xx Religion, Primitive
Asylums *(Indirect)*
  sa Alcoholics—Hospitals and asylums
    Almshouses
    Blind—Institutional care
    Deaf—Institutional care
    Incurables—Hospitals and asylums
    Old age homes
    Orphans and orphan-asylums
    Poor
    Psychiatric hospitals
    Woman—Institutional care
    subdivision Benevolent and moral
      institutions and societies *under
      names of cities, e.g.* London—
      Benevolent and moral institutions
      and societies; *and subdivision*
      Charities *under churches, fraternal
      orders, etc.*
  x Benevolent institutions
    Charitable institutions
    Homes (Institutions)
  xx Charities
    Children—Institutional care
    Poor
    Public institutions
    Public welfare
  — Fires and fire prevention
  — Law and legislation *(Direct)*
    xx Charity laws and legislation
      Poor laws
      Public welfare—Law
  — Religious life
Asymptotes *(QA559; QA565)*
  sa Asymptotic expansions
  xx Curves, Plane
Asymptotic developments
  See Asymptotic expansions
Asymptotic expansions
  x Asymptotic developments

  xx Asymptotes
    Convergence
    Difference equations
    Functions
    Numerical analysis
    Series, Divergent
Asynchronous electric motors
  See Electric motors, Induction
AT-6 (Training planes)
  See T-6 (Training planes)
Atabrine
  x Chinacrin
    Quinacrine
  xx Malarial fever
Atacamas
  See Atacameño Indians
Atacamenian language *(PM5521)*
  x Cunza language
Atacameño Indians *(F3070.1.A7)*
  x Atacamas
  xx Indians of South America
Ataiyal
  See Atayal
Ataractic drugs
  See Tranquilizing drugs
Ataraxia *(B187.A8)*
  xx Knowledge, Theory of
    Peace of mind
    Philosophy, Ancient
    Quietude
Atavism
  sa Heredity
  xx Eugenics
    Heredity
Ataxia
  sa Locomotor ataxia
Ataxia, Hereditary
  See Friedreich's disease
Atayal
  sa Tayal language
  x Ataiyal
    Taiyars
  xx Ethnology—Formosa
ATE 80 (Computer)
  xx Electronic digital computers
  — Programming
Atelectasis
  x Collapse of the lungs
    Lungs—Collapse
  xx Lungs—Diseases
Atellanae
  xx Latin drama (Comedy)
Ateso language
  See Teso language
Ath, Belgium
  — Siege, 1697 *(D280.A8)*
**Athabasca and Peace River Treaty Expedition,
      1889** *(F1060.9)*
Athabascan Indians
  See Athapascan Indians
Athabascan languages
  See Athapascan languages
Athanasian Creed *(BT995)*
  xx Creeds
Athanasianism *(BT995)*
  xx Trinity
Athapascan Indians
  sa Ahtena Indians
    Apache Indians
    Chasta Indians
    Chetco Indians
    Chilula Indians
    Chipewyan Indians
    Hupa Indians
    Ingalik Indians
    Jicarilla Indians
    Kaska Indians
    Kato Indians

Athapascan Indians *(Continued)*
    Kawchottine Indians
    Kuitsh Indians
    Kutchin Indians
    Lipan Indians
    Nahane Indians
    Navaho Indians
    Sarsi Indians
    Sinkyone Indians
    Slave Indians
    Tahltan Indians
    Takulli Indians
    Tanai Indians
    Thlingchadinne Indians
    Tinne Indians
    Tolowa Indians
    Tsilkotin Indians
    Wailaki Indians
  x Athabascan Indians
  xx Indians of North America
    Tinne Indians
— Legal status, laws, etc. *(Direct)*
— Legends
Athapascan languages *(PM641)*
  sa Apache language
    Chastacosta language
    Chilula language
    Chipewyan language
    Hupa language
    Ingalik language
    Jicarilla language
    Kato language
    Koyukon language
    Kuitsh language
    Kutchakutchin language
    Navaho language
    Sarsi language
    Slave language
    Takulli language
    Tinne languages
    Tukkuthkutchin language
  x Athabascan languages
  xx Chipewyan language
    Kato language
    Kutchakutchin language
    Kutchin languages
    Navaho language
    Tinne languages
    Tukkuthkutchin language
Atheism *(Direct)* *(BL2700-2790)*
  sa Agnosticism
    Deism
    Lokāyata
    Rationalism
    Skepticism
    Theism
  xx Agnosticism
    Christianity—Controversial literature
    Deism
    Faith
    God
    Irreligion
    Rationalism
    Religion
    Theism
    Theology
— Controversial literature
— Early works to 1800 *(BT1209)*
— Exhibitions and museums
— History
— — Modern period, 1500- *(BL2757-9)*
— Quotations, maxims, etc.
Atheism, Christian
  See Death of God theology
Atheism and Christianity
  See Christianity and atheism
Atheism and the Bible
  See Bible and atheism

Atheism and the Catholic Church
  See Catholic Church and atheism
Atheism in literature
  xx Religion in literature
Athena
  Example under Gods
Athens
— History
    sa Thirty tyrants
Athens. Parthenon
  Example under Architecture, Greek
— Juvenile literature
Athens, Treaty of, 1934
  sa Balkan Entente, 1934-
  x Treaty of Athens, 1934
  xx Balkan Entente, 1934-
Athens in art
Atheriniformes *(QL615)*
Atherosclerosis
  See Arteriosclerosis
Athetosis
  xx Chorea
    Movement disorders
Athletes *(Direct)* *(GV697)*
  sa Deaf as athletes
— Ability testing
    See Athletic ability
— Biography
— — Juvenile literature
— Hygiene *(RA781)*
  xx Hygiene
    Sports medicine
— Juvenile literature
— Legal status, laws, etc. *(Direct)*
— Medical examinations *(RC1225)*
  xx Sports medicine
— Nutrition *(TX361.A8)*
  x Nutrition of athletes
  xx Sports medicine
— Religious life *(BV4596.A8)*
— Retirement
Athletes, Negro
  See Negro athletes
Athletes, Women *(Direct)*
— Biography
Athletes in art
Athletic ability *(GV436)*
  x Athletes—Ability testing
  xx Ability
Athletic accident insurance
  See Insurance, Athletic accident
Athletic clubs *(Direct)* *(GV563)*
  sa Varsity lettermen's clubs
  x Athletics—Societies, etc.
    Sports clubs
  xx Clubs
    Sports
— Taxation *(Direct)*
Athletic equipment
  See Athletics—Apparatus and equipment
Athletic fields *(GV411-413)*
  sa Playgrounds
    Synthetic sporting surfaces
  x Playing fields
  xx Physical education facilities
    Playgrounds
Athletic goods
  See Athletics—Apparatus and equipment
Athletic goods industry
  See Sporting goods industry
Athletic shoes
  sa Sneakers
  x Sport shoes
  xx Athletics—Apparatus and equipment
    Boots and shoes
Athletics *(Indirect)* *(GV561-751)*
  sa Bag punching
    Boxing

    Coaching (Athletics)
    College sports
    Fencing
    Gymnastics
    Insurance, Athletic accident
    Jiu-jitsu
    Jumping
    Olympic games
    Physical education and training
    Professionalism in sports
    Rowing
    Skating
    Sports
    Swimming
    Track-athletics
    Walking
    Weight lifting
    Wrestling
    subdivision Athletics *under names of schools, colleges, etc.*
  x College athletics
  xx Physical education and training
    Sports
— Apparatus and equipment
  sa Athletic shoes
    Mouth protectors
    Sporting goods
    Sporting goods industry
  x Athletic equipment
    Athletic goods
  xx Physical education facilities
    Sporting goods
— Early works to 1800
    See Physical education and training—
      Early works to 1800
— Medical aspects
    See Sports medicine
— Philosophy *(GV342)*
— Public relations
    See Public relations—Sports
— Societies, etc.
    See Athletic clubs
Athu language
  See Asu language
Atimbuka
  See Tumbuka (African tribe)
Atimuca language
  See Timucua language
Atisa language
  x Atissa language
    Epie language
  xx Kwa languages
Atissa language
  See Atisa language
Atlanta Campaign, 1864 *(E476.7)*
Atlantic, Battle of the, 1939-1945
  See World War, 1939-1945—Atlantic
    Ocean
Atlantic bottlenosed dolphin *(QL737.C432)*
  xx Bottlenosed dolphins
Atlantic cable
  See Cables, Submarine—Atlantic
Atlantic cod *(QL638.G2)*
  xx Codfish
Atlantic croaker *(QL638.S34)*
  x Croaker, Atlantic
Atlantic hagfish
  xx Hagfish
Atlantic halibut *(QL638.P7)*
  sa Halibut fisheries
  xx Halibut
Atlantic menhaden
  xx Menhaden
Atlantic midshipman *(QL638.B3)*
  xx Toadfishes
Atlantic Ocean
  Example under Ocean
— Aerial crossings

See Transatlantic flights
Atlantic oyster
   See American oyster
Atlantic pact, 1949
   See North Atlantic treaty, 1949
Atlantic salmon
   sa Ouananiche
   xx Salmon
Atlantic salmon fishing *(Indirect) (SH685)*
   xx Salmon-fishing
Atlantic States
   — Blizzard, 1947
   — History
   — — Civil War, 1861-1865
   — Hurricane, 1955
   — Hurricane, 1964
   — Hurricane, 1972
      sa Pennsylvania—Hurricane, 1972
      x Agnes (Hurricane, 1972)
Atlanto-Mediterranean race
   See Mediterranean race
ATLAS (Computer) *(QA76.8.A)*
   xx Electronic digital computers
Atlas (Missile)
   Example under Intercontinental ballistic missiles
Atlas (Vertebra)
   x Vertebra, First cervical
   xx Vertebrae, Cervical
   — Wounds and injuries
Atlases
      Here are entered geographical atlases of world coverage published in the United States for general use. Atlases of world coverage published in other countries or in a particular language are entered under Atlases, Austrian, ₍British, Cuban, Polish, etc.₎ Works about atlases are entered under Atlases —History.
   sa Bible—Geography
      subdivision Atlases *under subjects, e.g.* Anatomy, Human—Atlases; Obstetrics—Atlases; Worms, Intestinal and parasitic—Atlases; *and subdivision* Maps *under names of countries, cities, etc., e.g.* Germany —Maps; New York (City)—Maps
   x Atlases, American
      Geographical atlases
      Geography—Atlases
   xx Geography
      Maps
   — Early works to 1800
   — History
      Note under Atlases
   — Juvenile literature
Atlases, American
   See Atlases
Atlases, Astronomical
   See Astrographic catalog and chart
      Astronomy—Charts, diagrams, etc.
      Stars—Atlases
Atlases, Austrian, ₍British, Cuban, Polish, etc.₎
   Note under Atlases
Atlases, Historical
   See Classical geography—Maps
      Geography, Ancient—Maps
      Geography, Historical—Maps
      Geography, Medieval—Maps
      subdivision Historical geography—Maps *under names of countries*
Atlases, Optical
   See Optics—Atlases
Atlatl
   See Throwing-sticks

Ātman
   sa Anātman
   x Attan
   xx Anātman
      Philosophy, Buddhist
      Philosophy, Hindu
      Self (Philosophy)
      Soul
Atmometer
Atmosphere *(QC851-999; Circulation, QC931; Mechanics and thermodynamics, QC880)*
   sa Air
      Air sampling apparatus
      Biosphere
      Counterglow
      Ionosphere
      Mesosphere
      Meteorology
      Standard atmosphere
      Tropopause
      Troposphere
      headings beginning with the word Atmospheric
   xx Air
      Earth
      Earth sciences
      Meteorology
   — Juvenile literature
   — Laser observations *(QC975.9)*
      x Atmospheric observations (Laser)
      xx Atmospheric research
      Lasers
   — Pollution
      See Air—Pollution
   — Research
      See Atmospheric research
Atmosphere, Solar
   See Solar atmosphere
Atmosphere, Upper *(Indirect) (QC879)*
   sa Airglow
      Atmospheric ozone
      Atmospheric thermodynamics
      Balloons, Pilot
      Chemosphere
      Clear air turbulence
      Jet stream
      Magnetosphere
      Noctilucent clouds
      Project Argus
      Radiosondes
      Stratosphere
      Thermosphere
      Winds aloft
   x Aeronomy
   xx Kites (Meteorology)
      Radiosondes
   — Charts, diagrams, etc.
   — Radiosonde observations *(QC879)*
      x Upper air observations (Radiosondes)
      xx Ionospheric research
      Radiosondes
   — Rawinsonde observations
      xx Rawinsondes
   — Rocket observations *(QC879)*
      sa Black Brant rocket
      Ionospheric research
      Radiosondes
      Rockets, Sounding
      x High altitude rocket research
      xx Aeronautics in meteorology
      Astronautics in meteorology
      Meteorology
      Rockets (Aeronautics)
      Example under Rocketry
      Note under Rocket research

Atmosphere-ocean interaction
   See Ocean-atmosphere interaction
Atmospheres, Artificial (Space environment)
   See Artificial atmospheres (Space environment)
Atmospheres in space cabins
   See Space cabin atmospheres
Atmospheric absorption of solar radiation
   See Solar radiation
Atmospheric boundary layer
   See Planetary boundary layer
Atmospheric circulation *(Indirect) (QC880)*
   sa Air masses
      Atmospheric turbulence
      Convection (Meteorology)
      Jet stream
      Rossby waves
      Trade-winds
   x Atmospheric motion
      Wind circulation
   xx Climatology
      Meteorology
      Winds
   — Charts, diagrams, etc.
   — Mathematical models
Atmospheric corrosion
   See Corrosion and anti-corrosives
Atmospheric density *(QC880)*
   sa Densitometer (Meteorological instrument)
   x Density, Atmospheric
   xx Specific gravity
Atmospheric electricity *(QC961-972)*
   sa Auroras
      Cloud electrification
      Equatorial electrojet
      Ionization of gases
      Lightning
      Sporadic E (Ionosphere)
      St. Elmo's fire
      Whistlers (Radio meteorology)
   x Electricity, Atmospheric
   xx Auroras
      Electricity
      Geophysics
      Lightning
      Meteorology
      Weather
   — Tables, etc.
Atmospheric entry problems
   See Ablation (Aerothermodynamics)
      Space vehicles—Atmospheric entry
Atmospheric humidity
   See Humidity
Atmospheric motion
   See Atmospheric circulation
Atmospheric nucleation *(QC918)*
   sa Condensation
      Ionization of gases
   x Nucleation, Atmospheric
   xx Cloud physics
      Meteorology
Atmospheric observations (Laser)
   See Atmosphere—Laser observations
Atmospheric optics
   See Meteorological optics
Atmospheric oscillations
   See Atmospheric tides
Atmospheric ozone *(Indirect)*
   xx Atmosphere, Upper
      Ozone
   — Observations
Atmospheric pressure *(QC885-896)*
   sa Acoustic radiation pressure
      Aeroplanes—Pressurization
      Anticyclones
      Density altitude computers
      Magdeburg experiments

Atmospheric pressure *(QC885-896)*
  (Continued)
    Siphons
    Southern oscillation
    x Isobars
    Pressure, Atmospheric
    xx Barometer
    Climatology
    Meteorology
    Pressure
    Weather
  — Charts, diagrams, etc.
  — Observations
  — Physiological effect *(QP82)*
    sa Abdominal decompression
    Altitude, Influence of
    Caisson-disease
    Decompression (Physiology)
    xx Caisson-disease
  — Tables, etc.
Atmospheric radiation *(QC912.3)*
    Here are entered works on the infra-red
    radiation emitted by or propagated
    through the atmosphere. Works on the
    total infra-red radiation emitted from
    the earth's surface are entered under
    Terrestrial radiation.
    sa Energy budget (Geophysics)
    Solar radiation
    Terrestrial radiation
    x Diffuse sky radiation
    Radiation, Atmospheric
    Sky radiation
    xx Energy budget (Geophysics)
    Infra-red rays
    Solar radiation
    Terrestrial radiation
  Note under Terrestrial radiation
Atmospheric radio refractivity *(QC973)*
    x Radio refractivity, Atmospheric
    Radio refractivity of earth's atmosphere
    Refractivity, Atmospheric radio
    xx Radio astronomy
    Radio meteorology
    Refractive index
  — Charts, diagrams, etc.
Atmospheric radioactivity *(Indirect)*
    (QC913)
    sa Atomic energy and meteorology
    xx Atomic energy and meteorology
    Radioactivity
  — Charts, diagrams, etc.
  — Observations
  — Tables, etc.
Atmospheric railroads
  See Railroads, Atmospheric
Atmospheric re-entry (from space)
  See Artificial satellites—Atmospheric entry
  Ballistic missiles—Atmospheric entry
Atmospheric research *(Direct)*
    sa Atmosphere—Laser observations
    x Atmosphere—Research
    xx Meteorological research
    Research
Atmospheric temperature *(Direct)*
    (QC901-6)
    sa Air conditioning—Climatic factors
    Cooling towers—Climatic factors
    Degree days
    Density altitude computers
    Global temperature changes
    Heat budget (Geophysics)
    Temperature inversions
    Urban temperature
    x Isotherms
    xx Climatology
    Heat
    Heat budget (Geophysics)
    Meteorology

    Temperature
    Weather
  — Charts, diagrams, etc. *(QC901)*
  — Measurement
  — Observations
Atmospheric thermodynamics *(QC880.4.T5)*
    x Thermodynamics of the atmosphere
    xx Atmosphere, Upper
    Dynamic meteorology
    Heat budget (Geophysics)
    Thermodynamics
Atmospheric tides
    x Atmospheric oscillations
    xx Tides
Atmospheric transparency *(QC976.T7)*
    sa Airports—Visibility
    xx Atmospheric turbidity
    Meteorological optics
  — Charts, diagrams, etc.
Atmospheric turbidity *(Indirect)*
    (QC976.T7)
    sa Atmospheric transparency
    x Turbidity, Atmospheric
    xx Meteorological optics
    Solar radiation
Atmospheric turbulence
    sa Clear air turbulence
    Gust loads
    Mountain wave
    Turbulent diffusion (Meteorology)
    xx Atmospheric circulation
    Turbulence
Atnah Indians
  See Ahtena Indians
Atnatana Indians
  See Ahtena Indians
Atolls
  See Coral reefs and islands
Atom bomb
  See Atomic bomb
Atomic absorption spectroscopy *(QC454;*
    QD95)
    x Spectroscopy, Atomic absorption
    xx Absorption spectra
    Atomic spectra
    Spectrophotometry
    Spectrum analysis
  — Instruments
    x Instruments, Atomic absorption
    spectroscopy
Atomic aircraft
    sa Aeroplanes—Nuclear power plants
    x Aircraft, Atomic
    Atomic planes
    xx Atomic power
    Transportation, Atomic-powered
  Example under Nuclear propulsion
Atomic aircraft carriers
    x Aircraft carriers, Atomic
    Nuclear-powered aircraft carriers
    xx Aircraft carriers
    Atomic ships
Atomic batteries
    x Nuclear batteries
    Radioactive batteries
    Storage batteries, Atomic energy
    xx Atomic power
    Electric batteries
    Radioisotopes
  — Safety measures
Atomic beams
    x Beams, Atomic
    xx Particle beams
    Proton beams
Atomic blasting
  See Nuclear excavation
Atomic bomb
    sa Atomic energy

    Atomic power
    Hydrogen bomb
    Radioactive fallout
    x Atom bomb
    xx Atomic energy
    Atomic power
    Atomic warfare
    Atomic weapons
    Bombs
    Hydrogen bomb
  Note under Bombs
  — Blast effect
    Example under Blast effect
  — Moral and religious aspects
    See Atomic warfare—Moral and
    religious aspects
  — Physiological effect
    sa Radioactivity—Physiological effect
    xx Radioactivity—Physiological effect
  — — Personal narratives
  — — Pictorial works
  — Safety measures
    sa Atomic bomb shelters
    xx Civil defense
    Radioactivity—Safety measures
    War damage, Industrial
  — — Film catalogs
  — Testing
Atomic bomb (International law)
  See Atomic weapons (International law)
Atomic bomb and disarmament
  See Atomic weapons and disarmament
Atomic bomb shelters *(Indirect)*
    x Atomic shelters
    Bomb shelters
    Fallout shelters
    Shelters, Atomic bomb
    xx Air raid shelters
    Atomic bomb—Safety measures
    Building, Bombproof
    Civil defense
    Radioactive fallout
    Radioactivity—Safety measures
  — Heating and ventilation
    x Atomic bomb shelters—Ventilation
  — Law and legislation *(Direct)*
  — Psychological aspects
    xx Interpersonal relations
    Social psychology
    War—Psychological aspects
  — Ventilation
    See Atomic bomb shelters—Heating
    and ventilation
Atomic clocks
    x Clocks, Atomic
    xx Atomic frequency standards
    Clocks and watches
    Frequency standards
Atomic damages, Liability for
  See Liability for nuclear damages
Atomic energy
    sa Atomic bomb
    Atomic power
    Classification—Books—Atomic energy
    Masers
    Nuclear engineering
    Nuclear fission
    Nuclear fusion
    Nuclear reactors
    Project Plowshare
    x Nuclear energy
    xx Atomic bomb
    Atomic power
    Nuclear physics
  — Abstracts
  — Economic aspects *(Direct)*
    sa Atomic energy industries
    Atomic power industry

Insurance, Atomic hazards
Strikes and lockouts—Atomic energy
industries
—— Public relations
See Public relations—Atomic
energy industries
— Industrial applications
— Information services *(Direct)*
— International control
See Atomic power—International
control
— Juvenile literature
— Law and legislation
See Atomic power—Law and
legislation
— Microcard catalogs *(Z5160)*
Example under Microcards
— Moral and religious aspects
(BR115.A83)
sa Atomic warfare—Moral and religious
aspects
— Physiological effect
sa Atomic medicine
— Popular works
— Research
See Atomic energy research
— Social aspects *(Direct)*
— Tables, etc.
— Underdeveloped areas
See Underdeveloped areas—Atomic
energy
Atomic energy and meteorology
sa Atmospheric radioactivity
Radioactive fallout
Radioactive pollution of the atmosphere
x Meteorology and atomic energy
xx Atmospheric radioactivity
Engineering meteorology
Meteorology
Radioactive pollution
Radioactivity
— Tables, etc.
Atomic energy industries *(Direct)*
(Economics, HD; Technology,
TK9001-9401)
sa Nuclear engineering
individual industries and products, e.g.
Atomic power industry; Reactor fuel
reprocessing; Radioisotopes
x Atomic industries
Nuclear industries
Nuclear reactor supply industry
xx Atomic energy—Economic aspects
Nuclear engineering
— Accidents
— Employees
See Atomic workers
— Finance
— Fires and fire prevention
— Government ownership *(Direct)*
— Instruments
— Job descriptions
— Management
— Public relations
See Public relations—Atomic energy
industries
— Safety regulations
See Atomic power—Law and
legislation
— Security measures
— Vocational guidance
Atomic energy laboratories
See Atomic energy research—Laboratories
Atomic energy research *(Direct)*
sa Armour Research Reactor
x Atomic energy—Research
Atomic research
xx Research

— International cooperation
sa Atomic weapons information
x International cooperation in atomic
energy research
— Laboratories
sa Hot laboratories (Radioactive
substances)
x Atomic research laboratories
Laboratories, Atomic energy
research
xx Chemical laboratories
Physical laboratories
—— Construction
See Atomic energy research—
Laboratories—Design and
construction
—— Design and construction
x Atomic energy research—
Laboratories—Construction
Atomic explosions
See Nuclear explosions
Atomic freighters
x Nuclear-powered cargo vessels
xx Atomic merchant ships
Freighters
Atomic frequency standards *(QC454)*
sa Atomic clocks
xx Frequency standards
Atomic fuel
See Nuclear fuels
Atomic icebreakers *(VM451)*
sa names of individual atomic icebreakers
x Icebreakers, Atomic
Nuclear-powered icebreaking vessels
xx Atomic ships
Ice-breaking vessels
Atomic industries
See Atomic energy industries
Atomic insurance
See Insurance, Atomic hazards
Atomic locomotives *(TJ623)*
xx Atomic power
Locomotives
Transportation, Atomic-powered
Example under Nuclear propulsion
Atomic mass *(Chemistry, QD466; Physics,*
QC173)
sa Mass transfer
subdivision Mass *under names of*
elements or groups of elements, e.g.
Isotopes—Mass
x Mass (Chemistry)
Mass (Nuclear physics)
Nuclear masses
xx Chemistry, Physical and theoretical
Mass (Physics)
Matter—Properties
Nuclear physics
— Measurement
— Tables, etc.
Atomic medicine *(RC91)*
sa Radioactive tracers
x Medicine, Atomic
Nuclear medicine
xx Atomic energy—Physiological effect
Radiation—Physiological effect
Radiobiology
— Apparatus and instruments
Example under Medical instruments and
apparatus
— Laboratory manuals
Atomic merchant ships
sa Atomic freighters
x Nuclear-powered merchant ships
xx Atomic ships
Merchant ships
— Safety measures *(VM776)*
xx Radiation—Safety measures

Atomic models
See Atoms—Models
Atomic nuclei
See Nuclear physics
Atomic orbitals
x Orbitals, Atomic
xx Electrons
Quantum chemistry
Valence (Theoretical chemistry)
Wave mechanics
Atomic piles
See Nuclear reactors
Atomic planes
See Atomic aircraft
Atomic power
sa Atomic aircraft
Atomic batteries
Atomic bomb
Atomic energy
Atomic locomotives
Atomic power-plants
Atomic ships
Atomic workers
Controlled fusion
Fusion reactors
Nuclear excavation
Nuclear propulsion
Nuclear rockets
Nuclear saline water conversion plants
Transportation, Atomic-powered
x Nuclear power
xx Atomic bomb
Atomic energy
Nuclear engineering
— International control
x Atomic energy—International
control
xx World politics—1945-
— Juvenile literature
— Law and legislation *(Direct)*
sa Liability for nuclear damages
Radioactive substances—Safety
regulations
x Atomic energy industries—Safety
regulations
Atomic energy—Law and legislation
Atomic power industry—Safety
regulations
Atomic power—Safety regulations
xx Safety regulations
—— Criminal provisions
—— Digests
— Psychological aspects *(TK9153)*
— Safety regulations
See Atomic power—Law and
legislation
— Security measures
Atomic power engineering
See Nuclear engineering
Atomic power industry *(Direct)*
(Economics, HD9698; Technology,
TK9001-9401)
xx Atomic energy—Economic aspects
Example under Atomic energy industries
— Costs
— Management
— Public relations
See Public relations—Atomic energy
industries
— Safety regulations
See Atomic power—Law and
legislation
Atomic power-plants *(Direct)*
sa Army package power reactors
Boiling water reactors
Gas cooled reactors
Isotopic power generators
Magnetohydrodynamic generators

Atomic power-plants (Direct)
  (Continued)
      Marine nuclear reactor plants
      Submerged atomic power-plants
    x Power-plants, Atomic
    xx Atomic power
      Electric power-plants
  — Accidents
  — Automation
  — Construction
      See Atomic power-plants—Design and
        construction
  — Design and construction
      x Atomic power-plants—Construction
  — Environmental aspects (Direct)
      Example under reference from Environ-
        ment
  — Equipment and supplies
  — Heating and ventilation
      x Atomic power-plants—Ventilation
  — Hygienic aspects
  — Location
  — Management
  — Mathematical models
  — Safety measures
      xx Radioactivity—Safety measures
  — Thermodynamics
  — Ventilation
      See Atomic power-plants—Heating
        and ventilation
  — Waste disposal (TD899.A8)
  — Water-supply
Atomic power-plants, Earthquake-proof
  See Earthquakes and atomic power-plants
Atomic power-plants (Aircraft)
  See Aeroplanes—Nuclear power plants
Atomic power-plants (Saline water conversion)
  See Nuclear saline water conversion plants
Atomic power-plants (Space vehicles)
  See Space vehicles—Nuclear power plants
Atomic-powered automatic weather stations
  See Automatic meteorological stations—
      Isotopic power generators
Atomic-powered transportation
  See Transportation, Atomic-powered
Atomic-powered vehicles
  See Nuclear propulsion
Atomic research
  See Atomic energy research
Atomic saline water conversion plants
  See Nuclear saline water conversion plants
Atomic shelters
  See Atomic bomb shelters
Atomic ship propulsion
  See Marine nuclear reactor plants
Atomic ships (VM317)
    sa Atomic aircraft carriers
      Atomic icebreakers
      Atomic merchant ships
      Atomic warships
      Marine nuclear reactor plants
    x Nuclear-powered ships
      Nuclear ships
    xx Atomic power
      Ships
      Transportation, Atomic-powered
  — Safety measures
      See Marine nuclear reactor plants—
        Safety measures
Atomic ships (International law)
    xx International law
      Maritime law
Atomic spectra
    sa Atomic absorption spectroscopy
      Hyperfine structure
      Isotope shift
      Triplet state
    x Atomic spectroscopy
      Atoms—Spectra

Spectrum, Atomic
    xx Nuclear spectroscopy
      Spectrum analysis
      Triplet state
  — Tables, etc.
Atomic spectroscopy
  See Atomic spectra
Atomic stopping power
  See Stopping power (Nuclear physics)
Atomic structure
  See Atomic theory
Atomic submarines
    sa Fleet ballistic missile weapons systems
    xx Atomic warships
      Fleet ballistic missile weapons systems
      Submarine boats
  — Juvenile literature
Atomic theory (QD461)
    sa Atomism
      Quantum theory
    x Atomic structure
    xx Chemistry, Physical and theoretical
      Quantum theory
Atomic transition probabilities
    x Transition probabilities, Atomic
    xx Nuclear physics
  — Tables, etc.
Atomic transportation
  See Transportation, Atomic-powered
Atomic underground explosions
  See Underground nuclear explosions
Atomic volume
    xx Chemistry, Physical and theoretical
Atomic warfare
    sa Air warfare
      Atomic bomb
      Atomic weapons
      Hydrogen bomb
    x CBR warfare
      Nuclear warfare
    xx Air warfare
      Bombardment
      Military art and science
      Strategy
      Tactics
      War
  — Moral and religious aspects
        (BR115.A85)
      x Atomic bomb—Moral and religious
        aspects
      xx Atomic energy—Moral and religious
        aspects
  — Psychological aspects
      sa Psychological warfare
      xx Morale
        War—Psychological aspects
  — Safety measures
  — Social aspects
      See Atomic warfare and society
Atomic warfare (International law)
  See Atomic weapons (International law)
Atomic warfare and society
    x Atomic warfare—Social aspects
      Society and atomic warfare
    xx Sociology
      War and society
Atomic warships
    sa Atomic submarines
    x Nuclear-powered warships
      Nuclear warships
    xx Atomic ships
      Warships
Atomic weapons
    sa Atomic bomb
      Atomic weapons and disarmament
      Ballistic missiles
      Hydrogen bomb
      Intercontinental ballistic missiles

    x Nuclear weapons
      Weapons, Atomic
    xx Atomic warfare
      Ordnance
  — Public opinion
  — Safety measures
  — Testing (UF767)
      sa Cannikin Project
        Project Argus
        Underground nuclear explosions
      xx Underground nuclear explosions
  — — Detection
        x Detection of atomic weapons tests
Atomic weapons (International law)
    x Atomic bomb (International law)
      Atomic warfare (International law)
    xx International law
      War (International law)
Atomic weapons and disarmament
        (JX1974.7)
    sa Atomic weapons information
      Rapacki plan
    x Atomic bomb and disarmament
      Disarmament and atomic weapons
    xx Atomic weapons
      Disarmament
Atomic weapons information (Direct)
    x Exchange of atomic weapons
        information
    xx Atomic energy research—International
        cooperation
      Atomic weapons and disarmament
      Defense information, Classified
      Military assistance
Atomic weapons information, American,
      ₍British, etc.₎ (Direct)
Atomic weather stations
  See Automatic meteorological stations—
      Isotopic power generators
Atomic weights (QD463-4)
    sa Molecular weights
      Packing fractions
    xx Chemical elements
      Chemistry, Physical and theoretical
      Molecular weights
Atomic workers (Direct)
    sa Strikes and lockouts—Atomic energy
        industries
      Wages—Atomic workers
    x Atomic energy industries—Employees
    xx Atomic power
Atomism (Cosmology, BD646; Greek
        philosophy, B193)
    xx Atomic theory
      Philosophy
      Philosophy, Ancient
      Pluralism
Atomism (Logic)
  See Logical atomism
Atomization (TC173)
    sa Aerosols
      Electrostatic atomization
      Jets
      Spraying
    xx Drops
      Hydraulics
      Jets
      Particles
      Size reduction of materials
      Spraying
Atoms (QC173; Disintegration, QC721)
    sa Binding energy
      Cyclotron
      Deuterons
      Electronegativity
      Electrons
      Hartree-Fock approximation
      Magnetic resonance

Matter
Neutrons
Nuclear models
Nuclear physics
Nuclear shell theory
Nuclides
Optical pumping
Particle accelerators
Protons
Transmutation (Chemistry)
Van der Waals forces
headings beginning with the word
Atomic
xx Chemistry, Physical and theoretical
Matter—Constitution
Neutrons
Protons
Stereochemistry
— Juvenile literature
— Models
x Atomic models
xx Chemical models
— Programmed instruction
— Space arrangement
See Stereochemistry
— Spectra
See Atomic spectra
— Tables, etc. *(QC173)*
Atoms, Nuclei of
See Nuclear physics
Atonality
See Tonality
Atonement *(BT264-5)*
sa Jesus Christ—Priesthood
Precious Blood, Devotion to
Precious Blood, Relics of the
Redemption
Servant of Jehovah
x Jesus Christ—Atonement
xx Guilt
Jesus Christ
Redemption
Sacrifice
Salvation
Sin
Theology, Doctrinal
— Biblical teaching
— History of doctrines *(BT263)*
Atonement, Day of
See Yom Kippur
Atonement (Brahmanism)
xx Brahmanism
Atonement (Hinduism)
xx Hinduism
Atonement (Judaism)
Note under Judaism—History of doctrines
Atoni
xx Ethnology—Timor
Atrial fibrillation
See Auricular fibrillation
Atrial septal defects
xx Heart—Abnormalities and deformities
Atrocities *(Direct)*
sa Massacres
Persecution
xx Crime and criminals
Cruelty
Atrocities, Military
See subdivision Atrocities *under names of
wars, e.g.* World War, 1939-1945—
Atrocities
Atrocities, Political
See Political atrocities
Atrophy, Muscular *(Physiology, QP321;
Surgery, RD688)*
sa Amyotrophic lateral sclerosis
Poliomyelitis
x Amyotrophy

Muscular atrophy
xx Muscles—Diseases
Atropine *(Ophthalmology, RE991;
Pharmacology, QP921.A8;
Therapeutics, RM666.A85)*
sa Belladonna
Homatropin
x Genatropin
xx Belladonna
Mydriatics
Example under Alkaloids
— Physiological effect
— Therapeutic use
— Toxicology *(RA1238.A8)*
Atschoua
See Batwa
Atsera language
x Atzera language
xx Melanesian languages
Atsina Indians *(E99.A87)*
x Gros Ventres of Montana
Gros Ventres of the Prairie
Grosventres of the Prairie
xx Indians of North America
Atsina language *(PM653)*
x Grosventre language
xx Algonquian languages
Arapaho language
Atsugewi Indians *(E99.A875)*
x Pit River Indians
xx Indians of North America
Palaihnihan Indians
Shastan Indians
Atsugewi language *(PM655)*
sa Palaihnihan languages
Shastan languages
xx Palaihnihan languages
Shastan languages
Attacapa Indians *(E99.A88)*
Attacapa language *(PM661)*
Attaché cases
See Briefcases
Attachés
See Agricultural attachés
Commercial attachés
Labor attachés
Military attachés
Attachment and garnishment *(Direct)*
sa Arrest of ships
Seals (Law)
Wages—Exemption
x Garnishment
Sequestration
Trustee process
xx Civil procedure
Commercial law
Debtor and creditor
Executions (Law)
Provisional remedies
Attack and defense (Military science)
(UG443-9)
Here are entered technical military works
on siege warfare. Historical works on
sieges are entered under the heading
Sieges.
sa Air defenses, Military
Bombardment
Civil defense
Coast defenses
Deterrence (Strategy)
Mines, Military
Roadblocks (Military science)
Sapping
Sieges
Smoke screens
x Defense (Military science)
Fortifications, Attack and defense of
Fortress warfare

xx Fortification
Intrenchments
Military art and science
Military engineering
Sieges
Tactics
— Juvenile literature
Attack warning systems
See Air raid warning systems
Attainder
sa Civil death
Forfeiture
xx Civil death
Forfeiture
Attan
See Ātman
Attapulgite
See Fuller's earth
Attapulgus clay
See Fuller's earth
Attar of roses
x Oil of rose
Oleum rosae
Otto of roses
Rose oil
xx Roses
Example under Essences and essential oils
Attempt, Criminal
See Criminal attempt
Attendance, Church
See Church attendance
Attendance, Football
See Football attendance
Attendance, Museum
See Museum attendance
Attendance, School
See School attendance
Attendance officers *(Direct)*
x Attendance teachers
Truant officers
xx School attendance
— Correspondence, reminiscences, etc.
Attendance teachers
See Attendance officers
Attendite, popule (Music)
See Psalms (Music)—78th Psalm
Attention *(Psychology, BF321; Psychology,
Educational, LB1065)*
sa Abstraction
Boredom
Comparison (Psychology)
Fatigue, Mental
Interest (Psychology)
Listening
Set (Psychology)
Vigilance (Psychology)
x Concentration
xx Apperception
Educational psychology
Interest (Psychology)
Memory
Psychology
Thought and thinking
Attention-seeking
xx Inferiority complex
Interest (Psychology)
Psychology
Social interaction
Attenuation equalizers
See Equalizers (Electronics)
Attenuators, Radio
See Radio attenuators
Atticmospicayes Indians
See Thlingchadinne Indians
Attics *(TH3000)*
sa Crawl spaces
x Garrets
xx Dwellings

129

Attitude (Psychology) *(Child study, LB1117; Psychoanalysis, BF175; Sociology, HM251-291)*
  sa Affiliation (Psychology)
    Attitude change
    College students—Attitudes
    Conformity
    Dogmatism
    Empathy
    Ethnic attitudes
    First year teachers—Attitudes
    Frustration
    Health attitudes
    High school students—Attitudes
    High school teachers—Attitudes
    Job satisfaction
    Negro students—Attitudes
    Public opinion
    Role expectation
    Scale analysis (Psychology)
    Socially handicapped children—Attitudes
    Stereotype (Psychology)
    Students—Attitudes
    Teachers—Attitudes
    Teachers college students—Attitudes
  xx Emotions
    Psychology
    Public opinion
    Set (Psychology)
    Social psychology
 — Testing
    Example under Mental tests
Attitude and posture of man
  See Man—Attitude and movement
Attitude change
  x Change of attitude
  xx Attitude (Psychology)
    Judgment
Attitude control systems (Astronautics)
  See Artificial satellites—Attitude control systems
    Space stations—Attitude control systems
    Space vehicles—Attitude control systems
Attiwendaronk Indians
  See Neutral Nation Indians
Attorney and client *(Direct)*
  sa Confidential communications—Lawyers
  xx Lawyers
    Legal ethics
    Practice of law
Attorney-client privilege
  See Confidential communications—Lawyers
Attorneys
  See Agency (Law)
    Lawyers
Attorneys, County
  See County attorneys
Attorneys, Government
  See Government attorneys
Attorneys, Municipal
  See City attorneys
Attorneys-general *(Direct)*
  sa Government litigation
    Public prosecutors
  xx Government attorneys
    Public prosecutors
 — Portraits
 —— Catalogs
Attorneys general's opinions *(Direct)*
  xx Advisory opinions
    Law reports, digests, etc.
Attracting birds
  See Birds, Attracting of
Attracting fish by light
  See Light fishing

Attracting of birds
  See Birds, Attracting of
Attraction, Interpersonal
  See Interpersonal attraction
Attractions *(QA825-7)*
Attractions of ellipsoids *(QA827)*
  sa Rotating masses of fluid
  x Ellipsoids, Attractions of
  xx Earth—Figure
    Potential, Theory of
    Rotating masses of fluid
Attractive nuisance *(Direct)*
  x Nuisance, Attractive
  xx Liability for condition and use of land
    Negligence
    Torts
Attribute (Grammar)
  See Grammar, Comparative and general—Attribute; *and subdivision* Attribute *under names of languages and groups of languages*
Attributes of God
  See God—Attributes
Attribution of paintings
  See Paintings—Attribution
Attrition
  See Penance
    Repentance
Atypical children
  See Exceptional children
Atzera language
  See Atsera language
Aubrac cattle *(SF199.A85; Herd-books, SF193.A)*
Auca Indians
  See Araucanian Indians
Auchenorrhyncha
  xx Homoptera
Auction bridge *(GV1282)*
  sa Contract bridge
    Duplicate auction bridge
    Pirate bridge
  xx Bridge whist
    Whist
Auction-penuchle
  xx Penuchle (Game)
Auction piquet *(GV1295.A8)*
  x Piquet, Auction
Auctioneers *(Direct)*
    Works on the legal status of auctioneers and the law relating to their activities are entered under the heading Auctions.
 — Licenses *(Direct)*
Auctions *(Direct)* *(HF5476)*
  sa Art auctions
    Sales
  x Vendues
  xx Bailments
    Commercial law
    Sales
  Note under Auctioneers
 — Digests
Auctions (Greek law)
Auctions (Roman law)
Auctoritas (The word)
  xx Roman law—Language
Audad
  See Barbary sheep
Audi automobile *(TL215.A8)*
Audible numbers
  See NUMAUDO (Computer program language)
Audiences
  See Moving-picture audiences
    Radio audiences
    similar headings

Audiences, Radio
  See Radio audiences
Audiences, Television
  See Television audiences
Audiences, Theater
  See Theater audiences
Auding
  See Listening
Audio amplifiers, Transistor
  See Transistor audio amplifiers
Audio-lingual approach (Language teaching)
  See Audio-lingual method (Language teaching)
Audio-lingual method (Language teaching)
  sa subdivision Audio-visual instruction *under names of languages for phonorecords, films, and moving-pictures used in language instruction*
  x Audio-lingual approach (Language teaching)
    Aural-oral method (Language teaching)
  xx Language and languages—Study and teaching
    Languages, Modern—Study and teaching
Audio-visual aids
  See Audio-visual materials
Audio-visual education *(Direct)* *(LB1043-1044.9)*
  sa Audio-visual materials
    Instructional materials personnel
    Phonograph in education
    Phonotapes in education
    Photography in education
    Radio in education
    Simulated environment (Teaching method)
    Television in education
    Video tapes in education
    Visual education
    subdivision Audio-visual aids *under subjects, e.g.* Geography—Study and teaching—Audio-visual aids; Music —Analysis, appreciation—Audio-visual aids; *also subdivision* Audio-visual instruction *under names of languages for instruction by means of phonorecords and films, e.g.* English language—Audio-visual instruction
  xx Educational technology
    Instructional materials personnel
    Teaching
    Visual education
Audio-visual education and copyright
  See Copyright and audio-visual education
Audio-visual equipment *(TS2301.A7)*
    Here are entered general works on projectors, screens, sound equipment, pointers, tables, exhibit boards, etc.
  sa names of particular equipment, *e.g.* Moving-picture projectors; Record changers
 — Catalogs *(TS2301.A7)*
 — Standards *(Direct)*
Audio-visual library service *(Z717)*
  sa Instructional materials centers
    Libraries and moving-pictures
    Libraries and pictures
    Libraries and radio
    Libraries and television
    Vertical files (Libraries)
  xx Instructional materials centers
    Libraries
    Library science
Audio-visual materials
  sa Filmstrips

Moving-pictures
Phonorecords
Slides (Photography)
Transparencies
subdivision Audio-visual aids *under*
subjects, e.g. Music—Analysis,
appreciation—Audio-visual aids
  x Audio-visual aids
  xx Audio-visual education
Audio-visual materials, Cataloging of
  See Cataloging of non-book materials
Audio-visual materials centers
  See Instructional materials centers
Audio-visual materials personnel
  See Instructional materials personnel
Audio-visual specialists
  See Instructional materials personnel
Audiology *(Direct)*
  sa Deafness
  xx Hearing
Audiology, Forensic
  See Forensic audiology
Audiometer
  See Audiometry
Audiometry
  x Audiometer
  Hearing—Testing
  xx Hearing
— Programmed instruction
Auditing *(HF5667)*
  sa Accounting
  Disclosure in accounting
  Financial statements
  Legislative auditing
  Tax auditing
  subdivision Accounting *under names of*
  industries, trades, etc., e.g. Dairying
  —Accounting, *unless special*
  provision is made for the use of the
  subdivision Auditing, *e.g.*
  Corporations—Auditing; *also*
  subdivision Auditing and inspection
  under names of industries, trades,
  etc. in socialist countries or
  governmentally controlled
  enterprises in non-socialist countries,
  e.g. Collective farms—Auditing and
  inspection
  xx Accounting
  Bookkeeping
  Controllership
— Law
    See Accounting—Law
— Problems, exercises, etc.
— Statistical methods
Auditing, Legislative
  See Legislative auditing
Auditing, Tax
  See Tax auditing
Auditions
  See subdivision Auditions *under names of*
  activities, e.g. Acting—Auditions;
  Radio broadcasting—Auditions
Auditoriums *(Direct)* *(NA6815)*
  sa Music-halls
  Public buildings
  Theaters
  x Lecture halls
  Lecture theaters
  xx Centers for the performing arts
  Halls
  Public buildings
— Electronic sound control *(TK7882.T5)*
  xx Acoustical engineering
  Electronic apparatus and appliances
  Sound
Auditors *(Direct)*
  xx Accountants

— Legal status, laws, etc. *(Direct)*
  xx Accounting—Law
Auditors (Civil procedure) *(Direct)*
  xx Courts—Officials and employees
Auditory adaptation
  x Acoustic adaptation
  xx Adaptation (Physiology)
  Hearing
Auditory disorders
  See Hearing disorders
Auditory nerve
  See Acoustic nerve
Auditory pathways
  sa Acoustic nerve
  Cerebral cortex
  Cochlear nucleus
  Ear
  Hearing
  x Auditory system
  xx Hearing
Auditory perception
  xx Hearing
  Perception
Auditory system
  See Auditory pathways
Audubon societies *(QL671)*
  xx Birds, Protection of
Audumbaras *(DS432.A9)*
  x Odumbaras
  Udumbaras
  xx Ethnology—India
Auerbach's plexus
  See Myenteric plexus
Auger bits
  See Augers
Auger conveyors
  See Screw conveyors
Auger effect *(QC721)*
  x Auto-ionization
  Autoionization
  xx Electrons
  Internal conversion (Nuclear physics)
  Ionization
  Nuclear physics
  X-rays
— Tables, etc.
Augers
  x Auger bits
  xx Bits (Drilling and boring)
  Carpentry—Tools
Aughrim, Battle of, 1691
Augsburg, Diet of, 1518
  x Diet of Augsburg, 1518
Augsburg, Diet of, 1530
  x Diet of Augsburg, 1530
Augsburg, Diet of, 1548
  x Diet of Augsburg, 1548
Augsburg Confession *(BX8069)*
  xx Reformation
Augury
  See Divination
Augusta, Ga.
— Riot, May 11, 1970
Augustales *(DG83.A7)*
  xx Cultus, Roman
Augustinian Canonesses *(BX4265-8)*
Augustinian Canons *(BX2830)*
Augustinians *(BX2901-2955; Women,*
  BX4265-8)
  sa Birgittines
  x Austin Friars
  Eremites
  St. Augustine, Order of
  xx Friars
  Hermits
  Monasticism and religious orders
— Missions

Augustinians in Austria, ₍France, Germany,
  etc.₎
  Cf. reference from Catholic Church in
  Boston, ₍Canada, Chile, etc.₎
Augustinus, Aurelius, Saint, Bp. of Hippo
— Ethics
    Example under Christian ethics
Aujeszky's disease
  See Pseudorabies
Auks
  sa Razor-billed auk
  xx Sea birds
Aumbries
  x Ambries
  Ambry
  Aumbry
  xx Church decoration and ornament
  Church furniture
  Lord's Supper
Aumbry
  See Aumbries
AUNTIE (Computer system) *(HF5548.4.A9)*
  x Automatic Unit for National Taxation
  and Insurance
  xx Electronic data processing—Finance,
  Public
Aunts
  sa Maiden aunts
  xx Family
  Woman
Aura *(Physiology, QP77; Spiritism,*
  BF1389.A8; Theosophy, BP573.A8)
Aural hospitals
  See Hospitals, Ophthalmic and aural
Aural-oral method (Language teaching)
  See Audio-lingual method (Language
  teaching)
Aureate terms
  sa Euphuism
  xx Baroque literature
  English language—Foreign words and
  phrases
  English language—Style
  English language—Terms and phrases
  Euphuism
Aureola (Art)
  See Nimbus (Art)
Aureomycin *(Pharmacy, RS165.A;*
  Therapeutics, RM666.A)
  xx Antibiotics
Auricula
Auricular confession
  See Confession
Auricular fibrillation
  x Atrial fibrillation
  xx Arrhythmia
Aurignacian culture *(GN775)*
  sa Cro-Magnon man
  xx Cro-Magnon man
  Man, Prehistoric
  Paleolithic period
Aurochs
  See Bison, European
Aurora australis
  See Auroras
Aurora borealis
  See Auroras
Auroral hiss
  See Hiss (Radio meteorology)
Auroral photography
  x Photography, Auroral
  Photography of auroras
  xx Auroras
  Photography
  Photography—Scientific applications
Auroral substorms
  sa Magnetic storms
  x Substorms, Auroral

Auroral substorms *(Continued)*
   xx Auroras
     Magnetic storms
Auroras *(QC971-2)*
   sa Airglow
     Atmospheric electricity
     Auroral photography
     Auroral substorms
     Krypton
     Magnetic storms
     Magnetism, Terrestrial
     Solar activity
   x Aurora australis
     Aurora borealis
     Northern lights
     Polar lights
   xx Airglow
     Atmospheric electricity
     Cosmic physics
     Geophysics
     Magnetism, Terrestrial
     Meteorological optics
     Solar activity
  — Atlases
  — Charts, diagrams, etc.
  — Spectra
Aurunci *(DG225.A)*
   x Ausones
   xx Italy—History—To 476
     Rome—History—To 510 B.C.
Auschwitz Trial, Frankfurt am Main, 1963-1965
Auscultation *(RC76.3)*
   sa Chest—Diseases—Diagnosis
     Phonendoscope
   x Stethoscopy
   xx Chest—Diseases—Diagnosis
     Diagnosis
     Heart—Diseases—Diagnosis
     Lungs—Diseases—Diagnosis
  — Juvenile literature
Auscultation of the heart
  See Heart—Sounds
Ausculum, Battle of, 279 B.C.
   x Asculum, Battle of
     Osculum, Battle of
Ausdehnungslehre *(QA259)*
   x Grassmann's theory of extension
   xx Algebra, Universal
     Mathematics
     Numbers, Complex
     Quaternions
     Spherical harmonics
     Vector analysis
Aushi (African tribe)
  See Ushi (African tribe)
Ausones
  See Aurunci
Austenite *(TN731)*
   sa Steel, Heat resistant
Austerlitz, Battle of, 1805 *(DC227.5.A8)*
   xx Napoléon I, Emperor of the French, 1769-1821—German and Austrian Campaign, 1805
Austin, Tex.
  — Tornado, 1922
Austin automobile *(TL215.A9)*
   sa Morris Mini Minor automobile
   xx BLMC automobiles
Austin Friars
  See Augustinians
Austin-Healey automobile
   sa Sprite automobile
   x Healey automobile
   xx BLMC automobiles
  Example under Automobiles, Racing
Austin Mini automobile
  See Morris Mini Minor automobile

Austin Seven automobile
  See Morris Mini Minor automobile
Australia
  — History
  — — 20th century
  — Native races
     x Australian aborigines—Government relations
  — Politics and government
     Example under Federal government
  — Public lands
     Example under Public lands
Australia. Constitution
  Example under Federal government
Australia antigen
  See Hepatitis associated antigen
Australia in art
Australia in literature
   xx Literature
Australian aboriginal poetry *(Direct)*
   x Australian poetry (Aboriginal)
Australian aborigines *(Direct)*
   sa Aranda tribe
     Bindubi (Australian people)
     Buandik (Australian people)
     Burbung
     Euahlayi tribe
     Gunwinggu (Australian tribe)
     Gurindji (Australian people)
     Kabi tribe
     Kogai tribes
     Kurnai tribe
     Mewite tribe
     Mungarai (Australian tribe)
     Munkan tribe
     Murngin (Australian tribe)
     Murrumbidgee tribes
     Nagarnooks
     Piniridjara (Australian people)
     Pintubi (Australian tribe)
     Pitjandjara (Australian tribe)
     Tiwi (Melville Island people)
     Wakka tribe
     Walbiri tribe
     Worora tribe
     Wunambal (Australian tribe)
   x Aborigines, Australian
     Australians (Native people)
   xx Ethnology—Australia
  — Anthropometry
     sa Australian aborigines—Craniology
  — Antiquities *(GN871-5)*
  — Art
     See Art, Australian (Aboriginal)
  — Civil rights
  — Craniology
     xx Australian aborigines— Anthropometry
  — Economic conditions
     sa Australian aborigines—Employment
  — Education *(Direct)*
  — Employment *(Direct)*
     xx Australian aborigines—Economic conditions
  — Food
  — Government relations
     See Australia—Native races
  — Health and hygiene *(Direct)*
  — Implements
     xx Australian aborigines—Industries
  — Industries
     sa Australian aborigines—Implements
     xx Industries, Primitive
  — Juvenile literature
  — Languages
     See Australian languages
  — Mixed bloods
     x Mixed bloods (Australian aborigines)

   xx Miscegenation
  — Mythology
     See Mythology, Australian (Aboriginal)
  — Psychology
  — Race identity
     x Racial identity of Australian aborigines
     xx Ethnopsychology
     Race awareness
  — Religion
  — Reservations
     x Reservations, Australian aborigine
  — Rites and ceremonies
Australian badgers
  See Wombats
Australian ballads and songs *(Collections, PR9560; History, PR9480)*
   sa Ballads, Australian
     Folk-songs, Australian
     National songs, Australian
     Songs, Australian
     War-songs, Australian
Australian ballot *(JF111; United States, JK2215)*
   x Ballot, Australian
   xx Ballot
     Elections
Australian cattle dog
   x Cattle dog, Australian
   xx Working dogs
Australian English
  See English language in Australia
Australian essays *(Collections, PR9583; History, PR9513)*
  Here are entered collections of essays by several authors.
Australian fiction *(History, PR9497-9507)*
  — 20th century
Australian football *(GV947)*
   xx Football
     Soccer
Australian languages *(PL7001-7101)*
  This term is limited to the aboriginal languages of Australia, and to those languages of adjacent islands which agree with the continental languages in vocabulary and grammatical structure.
  Works including Papuan languages spoken in Australia require an additional entry under the heading Papuan languages.
   sa Alawa language
     Aranda language
     Bandjalang language
     Dargari language
     Djirbal language
     Gugada dialect
     Gumbáingar language
     Gundjun dialects
     Gunwinggu language
     Gupapuyngu language
     Jindjibandji language
     Kalkatungu language
     Kattang language
     Mabuiag language
     Maramungku language
     Maung language
     Murundi language
     Narrinyeri language
     Ngarinjin language
     Ngarluma language
     Nggerikudi language
     Nunggubuyu language
     Nyangumata language
     Pitjandjara language
     Tasmanian languages
     Thangatti language

Walbiri language
Western desert language
Worora language
  x Australian aborigines—Languages
Australian literature *(PR9400-9597)*
  x English literature—Australia
Australian lovebird
  See Budgerigars
Australian mythology
  See Mythology, Australian (Aboriginal)
Australian newspapers *(Direct) (History, etc., PN5510-5590)*
Australian orations *(Direct)*
Australian periodicals *(Direct) (History, etc., PN5510-5590)*
Australian poetry *(Collections, PR9531-9563; History, PR9461-9481)*
Australian poetry (Aboriginal)
  See Australian aboriginal poetry
Australian prose literature *(Direct)*
  — 20th century
Australian shepherd dog *(SF429.A79)*
  xx Sheep dogs
Australian silky terriers
  See Silky terriers
Australian songs
  See Songs, Australian
      Songs, Australian (Aboriginal)
Australian terriers *(SF429.A8)*
  xx Terriers
Australian tomato weevil
  See Vegetable weevil
Australian wit and humor
Australian wit and humor, Pictorial
  (NC1760)
Australians
Australians (Native people)
  See Australian aborigines
Australians in California, ₍etc.₎
  — Anecdotes, facetiae, satire, etc.
Austria
  — Description and travel
  — — Views
      Example under Views
  — History *(DB)*
  — — To 1273
  — — 1273-1519
      sa Dürnkrut, Battle of, 1278
        Mühldorf, Battle of, 1322
  — — 1519-1740
  — — War with Turkey, 1661-1664
      See Austro-Turkish War, 1661-1664
  — — 1740-1789
      sa Silesian wars
  — — 1789-1815
      sa Elchingen, Battle of, 1805
        Lunéville, Treaty of, 1801
        Napoléon I, Emperor of the French, 1769-1821—German and Austrian Campaign, 1805
        Raszyn, Battle of, 1809
        Tyrol—History—Uprising of 1809
        Ulm—Capitulation, 1805
  — — 1789-1900
  — — 1815-1848
  — — Revolution, 1848-1849
      sa Austro-Sardinian War, 1848-1849
        Bohemia—History—Revolution, 1848
        Hungary—History—Uprising of 1848-1849
        Italy—History—Revolution of 1848
        Slovakia—History—Uprising of 1848-1849
        Vienna—Siege, 1848
  — — 1848-1867

  sa Schleswig-Holstein question
      Schleswig-Holstein War, 1864
  — — Italian Campaign, 1859
      See Italy—History—War of 1859
  — — Austro-Prussian War, 1866
      See Austro-Prussian War, 1866
  — — 1867-1918
      sa Dual Alliance, 1879
  — — 20th century
  — — 1918-1938
      sa Anschluss movement, 1918-1938
        Austria—History—Socialist Uprising, February 1934
  — — Socialist Uprising, February 1934
      xx Austria—History—1918-1938
  — — 1938-1945
  — — Allied occupation, 1945-1955
      (D802.A9)
  — — 1955-
Austria, Lower, in literature
  xx Austria in literature
Austria in literature
  sa Austria, Lower, in literature
Austrian artists
  See Artists, Austrian
Austrian ballads and songs
  See Folk-songs, Austrian
      Folk-songs, German
      Folk-songs, Hungarian
      German ballads and songs
      Political ballads and songs, Austrian
Austrian ballads and songs (German)
  See German ballads and songs—Austrian authors
Austrian book-plates
  See Book-plates, Austrian
Austrian coins
  See Coins, Austrian
Austrian drama (German)
  See German drama—Austrian authors
Austrian economists
  See Austrian school of economists
      Economists, Austrian
Austrian fiction (German)
  See German fiction—Austrian authors
Austrian-German Monetary Union of 1857
  x Deutsch-Österreichischer Munz-Verein von 1857
      German-Austrian Monetary Union of 1857
  xx Bimetallism
Austrian glass painting and staining
  See Glass painting and staining, Austrian
Austrian literature
  xx German literature
Austrian literature (German)
  See German literature—Austrian authors
Austrian musicians
  See Musicians, Austrian
Austrian newspapers *(Direct) (History, etc., PN5161-9)*
  xx German newspapers
  — Taxation
Austrian periodicals *(Direct) (History, etc., PN5161-5170)*
  xx German periodicals
Austrian periodicals in foreign countries
Austrian pine
  x Corsican pine
  — Diseases and pests
Austrian poetry (German)
      Duplicate entry is made under German poetry—Austrian authors.
  sa German ballads and songs—Austrian authors
  Notes under German ballads and songs—Austrian authors; German poetry—Austrian authors

Austrian property in Great Britain
Austrian school of economists *(HB98)*
  sa Marginal utility
  x Austrian economists
      Marginalist school of economics
  xx Economics
      Economists
      Value
Austrian students in the United States, ₍etc.₎
Austrian Succession, War of, 1740-1748
    (D291-4; Austria, DB72)
  sa Aix-la-Chapelle, Peace of, 1748
      Anglo-Spanish War, 1739-1748
      Assietta, Battle of, 1747
      English West Indian Expedition, 1739-1742
      Fontenoy, Battle of, 1745
      Füssen, Treaty of, 1745
      Silesian War, 1st, 1740-1742
      Silesian War, 2d, 1744-1745
      St. Augustine Expedition, 1740
      Toulon, Battle of, 1744
      United States—History—King George's War, 1744-1748
      Velletri, Battle of, 1744
  x War of the Austrian Succession, 1740-1748
  xx Anglo-Spanish War, 1739-1748
Austrian wit and humor *(Direct)*
  sa Tyrolese wit and humor
Austrians
  sa Styrians
Austrians in Germany, ₍the United States, etc.₎
  — Legal status, laws, etc.
Austric languages
  See Austroasiatic languages
Austro-German War, 1866
  See Austro-Prussian War, 1866
Austro-Hungarian Compromise, 1867
  x Hungarian-Austrian Compromise, 1867
Austro-Italian War, 1848-1849
  See Austro-Sardinian War, 1848-1849
Austro-Italian War, 1866 *(DG558)*
  sa Custozza, Battle of, 1866
      Lissa, Battle of, 1866
  x Italy—History—Austro-Italian War, 1866
Austro-Prussian War, 1866 *(DD436-440)*
  sa Custozza, Battle of, 1866
      Königgrätz, Battle of, 1866
      Prague, Peace of, 1866
      Trautenau, Battle of, 1866
  x Austria—History—Austro-Prussian War, 1866
      Austro-German War, 1866
      Prussia—History—Austro-Prussian War, 1866
      Seven Weeks' War
  xx Germany—History—1866-1871
  — Medical and sanitary affairs
Austro-Sardinian War, 1848-1849 *(DG553)*
  sa Custozza, Battle of, 1848
      Novara, Battle of, 1849
  x Austro-Italian War, 1848-1849
  xx Austria—History—Revolution, 1848-1849
Austro-Turkish War . . .
  x Turco-Austrian War . . .
Austro-Turkish War, 1661-1664
  sa St. Gotthard, Hungary, Battle of, 1664
      Vasvár, Treaty of, 1664
  x Austria—History—War with Turkey, 1661-1664
      Turkey—History—War with Austria, 1661-1664
Austro-Turkish War, 1716-1718 *(DR545)*
  sa Pozharevats, Peace of, 1718

Austro-Turkish War, 1737-1739   (DR548)
    sa Belgrad, Peace of, 1739
        Russo-Turkish War, 1736-1739
    xx Russo-Turkish War, 1736-1739
Austro-Turkish War, 1788-1790
Austroasiatic languages   (PL4281-4587)
    sa Cham language
        Indochinese languages
        Khasi language
        Mon-Khmer languages
        Munda languages
        Nicobarese language
        Palaung language
        Sakai dialects
        Semang dialects
        Vietnamese language
        Wa language
    x Austric languages
    xx Indochinese languages
Austronesian languages
    See Malay-Polynesian languages
Autarchy   (HD82-85)
    Here are entered works on economic self-sufficiency.
    sa subdivisions Commercial policy *and* Economic policy *under names of countries*
    x Economic self-sufficiency
        Self-sufficiency, Economic
    xx Commercial policy
        Economic policy
Authentication   (Direct)
    sa Legal documents
        Legalization
        Seals (Law)
    xx Contracts
        Legal documents
        Legalization
        Non-contentious jurisdiction
Authentication (Greek law)
Authenticity (Philosophy)
    xx Philosophy
Author and publisher
    See Authors and publishers
Author notation
    See Shelf-listing (Library science)
Authoritarianism
    sa Authority
        Despotism
        Fascism
        National socialism
        Totalitarianism
    xx Authority
        Conservatism
        Political science
Authoritarianism (Psychology)
    See Dogmatism
Authorities, Legal
    See Legal authorities
Authorities, Public
    See Corporations, Government
        Special districts
Authority   (Epistemology, BD209; Political theory, JC571; Social psychology, HM271)
    sa Authoritarianism
        Consensus (Social sciences)
        Despotism
        Divine right of kings
        Example
        Power (Philosophy)
    xx Authoritarianism
        Consensus (Social sciences)
        Despotism
        Political science
Authority, Delegation of
    See Delegation of authority

Authority (Islam)   (BP165.7)
    sa Taqlīd
    xx Islamic theology
Authority (Psychology)
    See Dogmatism
Authority (Religion)   (BT88-92)
    sa Bible—Evidences, authority, etc.
        Catholic Church—Infallibility
        Catholic Church—Teaching office
        Church—Authority
        Church—Credibility
        Church—Teaching office
        Conciliar theory
        Experience (Religion)
        Inner Light
        Liberty of speech in the church
        Popes—Infallibility
        Tradition (Theology)
    xx Power (Theology)
        Theology, Doctrinal
Authority in law
    See Legal authorities
Authorized ecclesiastical acts
    See Legitimate ecclesiastical acts
Authors   (General, PN)
    sa Anonyms and pseudonyms
        Bio-bibliography, *and subdivision* Bio-bibliography *under special subjects and under names of countries, cities, etc.*
        Children as authors
        College teachers as authors
        Lawyers as authors
        Literary quarrels
        Litterateurs
        Nuns as authors
        Physicians as authors
        Prisoners as authors
        Recluses as authors
        Soldiers as authors
        Teachers as authors
        Women authors
        Young men as authors
        names of literatures, e.g. English literature, French literature; *and particular classes of writers, e.g.* Dramatists, Historians, Humorists, Novelists, Poets
    x Literature as a profession
        Literature—Biography
        Writers
    xx Artists
        Authorship
        Bio-bibliography
        Literature—History and criticism
        Litterateurs
    — Anecdotes, facetiae, satire, etc.
    — Autographs   (Z41-42)
    — Biography
    — Caricatures and cartoons
    — Correspondence, reminiscences, etc.
    — Homes and haunts
        See Literary landmarks
    — Interviews
        Example under Interviews
    — Juvenile literature
    — Pensions
        See Authors—Salaries, pensions, etc.
    — Portraits
    — Psychology
        Example under Psychoanalysis
    — Relationship with women
    — Salaries, pensions, etc.   (Direct)
        x Authors—Pensions
Authors, American
    — 19th century
    — — Biography
    — 20th century

    — — Interviews
    — — Portraits
Authors, American, [English, French, etc.]   (Direct)
    Here are entered works in which the personal and strictly biographical element is emphasized rather than the literary. Works in which both elements are combined are entered under the name of the literature treated, with subdivision Bio-bibliography or History and criticism, *e.g.* English literature—Bio-bibliography.
    x American [English, French, etc.] authors
    Notes under Dramatists, English, [French, German, etc.]; Poets, American, [English, French, etc.]
    — Anecdotes, facetiae, satire, etc.
    — Autographs
    — Biography
        x American [English, French, etc.] literature—Biography
    — Caricatures and cartoons
    — Children
    — Correspondence, reminiscences, etc.
    — Fees
    — First editions
        See American literature—Bibliography—First editions; English literature—Bibliography—First editions; French literature—Bibliography—First editions; and similar headings
    — Homes and haunts
    — Interviews
    — Juvenile literature
    — Lists
    — Manuscripts
    — Political activity
    — Political and social views
    — Portraits
    — Pseudonyms
        See Anonyms and pseudonyms, American, [English, French, etc.]
    — Relationship with women
    — Wives
        xx Wives
Authors, Blind
    x Blind authors
    xx Blind
Authors, Catholic
    See Catholic authors
Authors, College
    See College teachers as authors
Authors, Czech
    x Bohemian authors
        Czech authors
Authors, English
    x English authors
        English fiction—Biography
    — 18th century
    — 19th century
    — — Biography
    — 20th century
    — — Portraits
Authors, French
    x French authors
    — 18th century
    — 20th century
Authors, Homonymous
    See Homonymous authors
Authors, Indic
    x East Indian authors
        Indic authors
Authors, Insane
    See Literature and mental illness

Authors, Islamic
  See Muslim authors
Authors, Japanese
  — 20th century
Authors, Laboring class
  Here are entered works on the contribu-
  tions to literature by authors belonging
  to or coming from the laboring classes.
  sa Labor and laboring classes in literature
  x Authors, Proletarian
  Labor and laboring classes—Authors
  Laboring class authors
  Proletarian authors
  Working-class authors
  xx Labor and laboring classes in literature
Authors, Medieval *(PN661-694)*
Authors, Muslim
  See Muslim authors
Authors, Negro
  See Negro authors
Authors, Proletarian
  See Authors, Laboring class
Authors, Russian
  — 20th century
  — — Correspondence, reminiscences, etc.
Authors, Shiite
  See Shiite authors
Authors, University
  See College teachers as authors
Authors, Women
  See Women authors
Authors (Game) *(GV1483)*
Authors and patrons
  sa Literature and state
  x Patronage of literature
  xx Literature and state
  State encouragement of science,
  literature, and art
Authors and printers
  See Authorship—Handbooks, manuals, etc.
  Printing, Practical—Style manuals
Authors and publishers *(Direct)*
  Here are entered works on the relations
  between author and publisher.
  sa Copyright
  Literary agents
  x Author and publisher
  Publishers and authors
  xx Contracts
  Copyright
  Literary agents
  — Antiquity
Authors and readers
  sa Books and reading
  xx Authorship
  Books and reading
  Books—Psychology
Authors and the theater
  sa Playwriting
  xx Playwriting
  Theater
Authors as artists *(Direct)*
  xx Artists
  — Biography
Authors in literature
Authorship *(PN101-249)*
Authorship
  Here are entered guides to authorship in
  general. Guides in individual fields are
  entered under appropriate terms if in
  common usage, *e.g.* Playwriting, Technical writing, Television authorship;
  otherwise under the name of the genre
  or subject with subdivision Authorship, *e.g.* Poetry—Authorship, Sociology—Authorship.

The subdivision Authorship is also used
  under names of individual authors or
  works in cases of dubious or disputed
  authorship, *e.g.* Shakespeare, William,
  1564-1616—Authorship; The Federal-
  ist—Authorship.
  sa Advertising copy
  Architectural writing
  Authors
  Authors and readers
  Autobiography
  Biography (as a literary form)
  Children as authors
  Children's literature—Technique
  Children's stories—Technique
  Copyright
  Creative writing
  Dedications (in books)
  Drama—Technique
  Editing
  Fashion writing
  Fiction—Authorship
  Fiction—Technique
  Historiography
  Imitation (in literature)
  Journalism
  Journalism—Authorship
  Literary forgeries and mystifications
  Literature
  Moving-picture authorship
  New literates, Writing for
  One-act plays—Technique
  Originality (in literature)
  Plagiarism
  Playwriting
  Plots (Drama, novel, etc.)
  Poetry—Authorship
  Proposal writing in the social sciences
  Radio authorship
  Radio plays—Technique
  Report writing
  Short story
  Soldiers as authors
  Television authorship
  Versification
  Women authors
  x Literature as a profession
  Writing as a profession
  Writing (Authorship)
  xx Literature
  — Anecdotes, facetiae, satire, etc. *(PN165)*
  sa Literature—Anecdotes, facetiae,
  satire, etc.
  — Collaboration
  sa Copyright (Joint tenancy)
  x Collaboration in literature
  Joint authors
  Literary collaboration
  xx Copyright
  Intellectual cooperation
  — Economic aspects
  — Handbooks, manuals, etc. *(PN147)*
  sa Medical writing
  Printing, Practical—Style manuals
  Technical writing
  x Authors and printers
  xx Editing
  Printing, Practical—Style manuals
  Proof-reading
  Technical writing
Authorship, Disputed
Autism
  sa Fantasy
  Hallucinations and illusions
  xx Introversion
  Personality, Disorders of
  Self-love (Psychology)
  — Cases, clinical reports, statistics

  — Personal narratives
Auto courts
  See Motels
Auto-da-fe sermons
  xx Catholic Church—Sermons
  Inquisition
Auto demolition derbies
  x Automobile demolition derbies
  Automobile wrecking derbies
  Automobiles—Demolition derbies
  Automobiles—Wrecking derbies
  Demolition derbies, Automobile
  Wrecking derbies, Automobile
Auto-feedback devices in education
  See Teaching machines
Auto-instructional machines
  See Teaching machines
Auto-intoxication *(RB152)*
  x Autotoxaemia
  xx Bacteriology
  Constipation
  Digestion
  Diseases—Causes and theories of
  causation
Auto-ionization
  See Auger effect
Auto mechanics
  See Automobile mechanics
Auto rallies
  See Automobile rallies
Auto-sexing of poultry
  See Poultry sexing
Auto tape players
  See Magnetic recorders and recording—
  Installation in automobiles
Auto thefts
  See Automobile thieves
  Theft from motor vehicles
Auto thieves
  See Automobile thieves
Auto washes
  See Car washes
Auto workers
  See Automobile industry workers
Autoantibodies
  sa Antinuclear factors
  xx Antigens and antibodies
  — Analysis
  xx Medicine, Clinical—Laboratory
  manuals
Autobiographic fiction
  See Fiction, Autobiographic
Autobiographies *(Collections in English,
  CT101)*
  sa Diaries
  subdivision Biography *under particular
  subjects and under names of
  countries, cities, etc., e.g.* Actors—
  Biography; Children in Africa—
  Biography; United States—Biography
  xx Biography
  Diaries
  — Juvenile literature
Autobiography *(CT25)*
  sa Biography (as a literary form)
  Fiction, Autobiographic
  x Autobiography—History and criticism
  Autobiography—Technique
  Memoirs
  xx Authorship
  Biography (as a literary form)
  Literature
  — History and criticism
  See Autobiography
  — Technique
  See Autobiography

Autoclaves *(TP159.A8)*
  sa Chemical engineering—Apparatus and
      supplies
    Pressure vessels
  x Digesters (Chemical engineering)
  xx Boilers
    Chemical engineering—Apparatus and
      supplies
    Pressure vessels
    Steam-boilers
Autocoder (Computer program language)
  — Programmed instruction
Autocodes
  See Programming languages (Electronic
    computers)
Autocorrelation (Statistics)
  sa Time-series analysis
  xx Correlation (Statistics)
    Stochastic processes
    Time-series analysis
Autodigestion
  See Autolysis
Autogenic training
  x Self-hypnosis
  xx Mental suggestion
    Psychotherapy
Autogenous welding
  See Oxyacetylene welding and cutting
Autogiros *(TL715)*
  x Gyroplanes
  xx Aeroplanes
    Flying-machines
  — Poetry
    See Aeronautics—Poetry
Autograph albums
  x Albums, Autograph
  — Juvenile literature
Autograph letters
  See Autographs
Autographic processes
  See Copying processes
Autographs *(Indirect) (Z41-42)*
  sa Books—Owners' marks
    Manuscripts
    Marginalia
    Signatures (Writing)
    subdivision Autographs *under names of*
      prominent authors and under classes
      of persons, e.g. Shakespeare,
      William, 1564-1616—Autographs;
      Musicians—Autographs
  x Autograph letters
    Handwriting
    Letters in manuscript
  xx Biography
    Manuscripts
    Marginalia
    Signatures (Writing)
    Writing
  — Catalogs
    See Autographs—Collections
  — Collections *(Z42)*
    x Autographs—Catalogs
  — Collectors and collecting
  — — Juvenile literature
  — Exhibitions
    xx Bibliographical exhibitions
  — Facsimiles
    sa Signature writing machines
      subdivision Autographs—Facsimiles
      under classes of persons, e.g.
      Artists—Autographs—Facsimiles
    Example under Facsimiles
  — Prices
    Example under Prices
Autoharp *(ML1015)*
  xx Zither
Autoharp music *(M175.A8)*

Autoimmune diseases
  sa Allergic encephalomyelitis
  x Autoimmunologic diseases
  xx Immunopathology
Autoimmunologic diseases
  See Autoimmune diseases
Autoionization
  See Auger effect
Autokinesis *(QP495)*
  x Autokinetic effect
    Charpentier's illusion
  xx Eye—Movements
    Optical illusions
Autokinetic effect
  See Autokinesis
Autolysis
  x Autodigestion
  xx Bacteria
    Cells
    Enzymes
    Physiological chemistry
    Tissues
Automata *(ML1055.A8; TJ215)*
  sa Androids
    Conscious automata
    Machine theory
  x Flute-players, Mechanical
    Robots
  xx Machine theory
    Mechanical movements
    Musical instruments (Mechanical)
    Perpetual motion
    Turing machines
  — Juvenile literature
  — Reliability
Automata in literature
Automated cell identification
  See Diagnosis, Cytologic—Automation
Automated data system analysis technique
  See AUTOSATE
Automated information networks
  See Information networks
Automated instruction
  See Teaching machines
Automated maintenance
  See Automatic checkout equipment
Automated typesetting
  See Computerized typesetting
AUTOMATH (Formal language) *(QA267.3)*
  xx Formal languages
    Mathematical notation
Automatic checkout equipment
  sa Error-correcting codes (Information
    theory)
  x ACE
    Automated maintenance
    Built-in test equipment
    Project ACE
  xx Automation
    Electronic instruments
    Maintenance
    Non-destructive testing
    Repairing
  — Display systems
    xx Information display systems
Automatic computers
  See Computers
Automatic control *(TA165)*
  sa Automatic frequency control
    Automatic gain control
    Automatic pilot (Aeroplanes)
    Automatic pilot (Helicopters)
    Automatic timers
    Automation
    Carrier control systems
    Control boards (Electrical engineering)
    Cybernetics
    Delay lines

    Electric controllers
    Error-correcting codes (Information
      theory)
    Feedback control systems
    Flight control
    Governors (Machinery)
    Guidance systems (Flight)
    Hydraulic control
    Hydraulic presses—Numerical control
    Interconnected electric utility systems
      —Automation
    Lathes—Numerical control
    Machine-tools—Numerical control
    Milling-machines—Numerical control
    Pneumatic control
    Process control
    Rate gyroscopes
    Servomechanisms
    Switching theory
    Temperature control
    Transfer functions
    Woodworking machinery—Numerical
      control
    subdivision Control *under specific types*
      of technical processes and
      equipment, e.g. Air conditioning—
      Control; Nuclear reactors—Control
  x Control engineering
    Control equipment
  xx Automation
    Control theory
    Engineering instruments
    Information theory
  — Drawings
    xx Electric drafting
  — Electromechanical analogies
  — Examinations, questions, etc. *(TJ213.8)*
  — Laboratory manuals
  — Mathematical models
  — Notation
  — Patents
  — Protection *(TJ213)*
  — Reliability
  — Research *(Direct)*
  — Statistical methods
  — Tables, calculations, etc.
  — Terminology
Automatic counting devices
  See Digital counters
Automatic data collection systems
  x Data collection systems, Automatic
    Factory data acquisition systems,
      Automatic
    Factory monitoring systems, Automatic
    In-plant data collection systems,
      Automatic
  xx Automation
    Communication in management
    Data transmission systems
Automatic data processing
  See Electronic data processing
Automatic data processors
  See Computers
Automatic data storage
  See Information storage and retrieval
    systems
Automatic digital computers
  See Electronic digital computers
Automatic doors
  See Mechanically-operated doors
Automatic drafting
  See Computer graphics
Automatic elevators
  See Elevators, Automatic
Automatic factories
  See Automation
Automatic frequency control
  xx Automatic control

Radio frequency

Automatic gain control
  x Automatic volume control
  xx Amplifiers (Electronics)
    Automatic control
    Radio—Receivers and reception

Automatic indexing
  sa Exclusion lists in automatic indexing
    Permutation indexes
  x Indexing, Automatic
    Subject cataloging, Automatic
  xx Catalogs, Subject
    Indexing
    Information storage and retrieval
      systems
    Language data processing
    Subject headings

Automatic information retrieval
  See Information storage and retrieval
    systems

Automatic Interaction Detector Program
  See AID (Computer program)

Automatic load dispatching (Electric power)
  See Interconnected electric utility systems
    —Automation

Automatic machinery
  See Machinery, Automatic

Automatic meteorological observing systems
  See Automatic meteorological stations

Automatic meteorological stations *(Indirect)*
  x Automatic meteorological observing
    systems
    Automatic weather stations
  xx Meteorological stations
  — Isotopic power generators
    x Atomic-powered automatic weather
      stations
      Atomic weather stations
      Radioisotope-powered meteorological
      stations
    Example under Isotopic power genera-
      tors

Automatic pens
  See Signature writing machines

Automatic picture transmission
  xx Data transmission systems

Automatic pilot (Aeroplanes) *(TL589.5)*
  sa Gyro compass
  x Autopilot
    Gyro pilot
    Gyropilot
    Pilot, Automatic
    Robot pilot
  xx Aeronautical instruments
    Aeroplanes—Control systems
    Automatic control
    Flight control
    Gyro compass
    Gyroscope
    Example under Gyroscopic instruments

Automatic pilot (Helicopters)
  x Automatic stabilization equipment
    (Helicopters)
    Helicopter auto-pilot
    Pilot, Automatic
  xx Aeronautical instruments
    Automatic control
    Flight control
    Helicopters
    Radar in aeronautics
    Stability of helicopters

Automatic pilot (Ships)
  sa Gyro compass
  x Automatic steerer
    Gyro pilot
    Gyropilot
    Iron quartermaster
    Pilot, Automatic

— Reliability

Automatic production
  See Automation

Automatic programming languages
  See Programming languages (Electronic
    computers)

Automatic record changers
  See Record changers

Automatic refrigeration
  See Refrigeration and refrigerating
    machinery—Automatic control

Automatic screw machines
  See Screw machines, Automatic

Automatic signature writers
  See Signature writing machines

Automatic speech recognition
  x Mechanical speech recognizer
  xx Computer input-output equipment
    Perceptrons
    Speech, Intelligibility of
    Speech perception
    Speech processing systems
    Voice

Automatic sprinklers
  See Fire sprinklers

Automatic stabilization equipment
  (Helicopters)
  See Automatic pilot (Helicopters)

Automatic steerer
  See Automatic pilot (Ships)

Automatic teaching
  See Teaching machines

Automatic telephone
  See Telephone, Automatic

Automatic theorem proving
  sa ADEPT (Computer program)
  x Theorem proving, Automatic
  xx Artificial intelligence
    Proof theory

Automatic timers *(TJ214.T5)*
  sa Delay lines
  x Timers, Automatic
    Timing devices
  xx Automatic control
    Engineering instruments
    Time measurements

Automatic tracking
  x Tracking, Automatic
  xx Servomechanisms
    Tracking radar

Automatic train control
  See Railroads—Automatic train control

Automatic translating
  See Machine translating

Automatic transmissions, Automobile
  See Automobiles—Transmission devices,
    Automatic

Automatic transmissions, Motor bus
  See Motor buses—Transmission devices,
    Automatic

Automatic typewriters
  xx Typewriters

Automatic Unit for National Taxation and
  Insurance
  See AUNTIE (Computer system)

Automatic volume control
  See Automatic gain control

Automatic weather stations
  See Automatic meteorological stations

Automatic welding
  See Electric welding—Automation
    Welding—Automation

Automatically programmed tools (Computer
  program language)
  See APT (Computer program language)

Automation *(Direct)*
  sa Assembly-line methods
    Automatic checkout equipment

    Automatic control
    Automatic data collection systems
    Feedback control systems
    Machinery, Automatic
    Man-machine systems
    Servomechanisms
    Systems engineering
    subdivision Automation *under specific*
      subjects, e.g. Electronic industries—
      Automation
  x Automatic factories
    Automatic production
    Computer control
    Engineering cybernetics
    Robots
  xx Assembly-line methods
    Automatic control
    Industrial engineering
    Industrial productivity
    Machinery, Automatic
    Machinery in industry
    Mechanization
  — Economic aspects *(Direct)*
    xx Economic history
  — Juvenile literature
  — Social aspects *(Direct)*
  — — Juvenile literature

Automation in documentation
  See Information storage and retrieval
    systems

Automation of instruction
  See Teaching machines

Automatism
  sa Planchette
  xx Consciousness
    Psychomotor disorders
    Subconsciousness

Automobile accessories
  See Automobiles—Apparatus and supplies

Automobile accidents
  See Traffic accidents

Automobile batteries
  See Automobiles—Batteries

Automobile bearings
  See Automobiles—Bearings

Automobile bodies
  See Automobiles—Bodies

Automobile brakes
  See Automobiles—Brakes

Automobile buying
  See Automobile purchasing

Automobile carburetors
  See Automobiles—Motors—Carburetors

Automobile clubs
  See Automobiles—Societies, etc.

Automobile clutches
  See Automobiles—Clutches

Automobile construction workers
  See Automobile industry workers

Automobile cooling systems (Motors)
  See Automobiles—Motors—Cooling

Automobile corrosion
  See Automobiles—Corrosion

Automobile cylinders
  See Automobiles—Motors—Cylinders

Automobile demolition derbies
  See Auto demolition derbies

Automobile doors
  See Automobiles—Doors

Automobile driver education *(Direct)*
    (TL152.6)
  sa Automobile driving simulators
    Traffic safety—Study and teaching
  x Automobile driving—Study and
    teaching
    Driver education
  xx Traffic safety—Study and teaching
  — Curricula

Automobile driver education *(Direct)*
    (TL152.6) *(Continued)*
— Psychological aspects
    xx Educational psychology
Automobile driver education (Elementary)
    (TL152.65)
Automobile driver education (Secondary)
    (TL152.65)
— Finance
Automobile drivers *(Direct)* *(TL152.3)*
    sa Automobile drivers' tests
        Automobile driving
        Automobiles
        Automobiles—Laws and regulations
        Drinking and traffic accidents
        Hit-and-run drivers
        Juvenile automobile drivers
        Police pursuit driving
        Women as automobile drivers
    x Drivers, Automobile
        Motor vehicle drivers
        Motor vehicle operators
    xx Traffic safety
— Juvenile literature *(TL152)*
— Medical examinations
    xx Automobile driving—Physiological
        aspects
        Automotive medicine
— Psychology
    xx Automotive medicine
— Testing
    See Automobile drivers' tests
Automobile drivers, Handicapped
    See Automobile drivers, Physically
        handicapped
Automobile drivers, Physically handicapped
    x Automobile drivers, Handicapped
        Handicapped automobile drivers
        Physically handicapped automobile
        drivers
    xx Physically handicapped
Automobile drivers and drug abuse
    See Drug abuse and automobile drivers
Automobile drivers' licenses *(Direct)*
    sa Automobile drivers' tests
    x Automobiles—Drivers' licenses
        Automobiles—Licenses
        Drivers' licenses, Automobile
        Operators' permits, Automobile
    xx Automobiles—Laws and regulations
— Registers
Automobile drivers' tests
    sa Columbia driver judgment test
        Cyclists' tests
    x Automobile drivers—Testing
        Drivers' tests, Automobile
        Driving tests, Automobile
    xx Automobile drivers
        Automobile drivers' licenses
        Automotive medicine
        Traffic regulations
Automobile driving *(Direct)* *(TL152.5)*
    sa Automobile driving at night
        Automobile driving in bad weather
        Automobile driving in cities
        Automobile driving on highways
        Automobiles—Cold weather operation
        Motor-truck driving
        Stunt driving
    x Automobile operation
        Automobiles—Driving
        Driving, Automobile
    xx Automobile drivers
        Motor vehicle driving
— Backing
    See Automobile driving—Steering
— Braking
    x Automobile driving—Stopping

    xx Automobiles—Brakes
— Juvenile literature
— Parking
    See Automobile driving—Steering
— Passing
    xx Automobile driving—Steering
        Traffic safety
— Physiological aspects
    sa Automobile drivers—Medical
        examinations
    x Physiological aspects of automobile
        driving
    xx Automotive medicine
— Programmed instruction
— Safety measures
    See Traffic safety
— Shifting gear
    xx Automobiles—Transmission devices
— Starting
— Steering
    sa Automobile driving—Passing
    x Automobile driving—Backing
        Automobile driving—Parking
        Automobile driving—Turning
        maneuvers
        Automobile driving—Turns
    xx Automobiles—Steering-gear
        Space-perception
— Stopping
    See Automobile driving—Braking
— Study and teaching
    See Automobile driver education
— Turning maneuvers
    See Automobile driving—Steering
— Turns
    See Automobile driving—Steering
Automobile driving, Medical aspects of
    See Automotive medicine
Automobile driving and drug abuse
    See Drug abuse and automobile drivers
Automobile driving at night
    sa Headlight glare
    x Night driving
    xx Automobile driving
        Night vision
Automobile driving in bad weather
    sa Automobile driving in winter
    xx Automobile driving
        Fog
        Rain and rainfall
        Storms
Automobile driving in cities
    x Automobile driving in suburbs
        Automobile driving in towns
        City driving
    xx Automobile driving
Automobile driving in suburbs
    See Automobile driving in cities
Automobile driving in towns
    See Automobile driving in cities
Automobile driving in winter
    x Winter driving
    xx Automobile driving in bad weather
        Automobiles—Cold weather operation
        Winter
Automobile driving on highways
    x Freeway driving
        Highway driving
    xx Automobile driving
        Express highways
Automobile driving on mountain roads
    x Mountain driving
Automobile driving simulators
    xx Automobile driver education
        Synthetic training devices
Automobile engineering
— Problems, exercises, etc.

Automobile engineering research *(TL158)*
    x Automobile research
        Automobiles—Research
        Automotive engineering research
    xx Research, Industrial
Automobile engineers *(Direct)*
    xx Engineers
— Biography
Automobile engines
    See Automobiles—Motors
Automobile exhaust gas
    sa Diesel motor exhaust gas
        Motor vehicles—Pollution control
        devices
    x Automobiles—Exhaust gas
        Automobiles—Motors—Exhaust
        Exhaust gas (Automobile)
    xx Air—Pollution
        Automobiles—Fuel consumption
        Combustion gases
        Gases
— Analysis *(QD121)*
    x Exhaust gas analysis
— Mathematical models
Automobile fenders
    See Automobiles—Fenders
Automobile filling stations
    See Automobiles—Service stations
Automobile fuel systems
    See Automobiles—Fuel systems
Automobile gasoline consumption
    See Automobiles—Fuel consumption
Automobile graveyards
Automobile guides
    See Automobiles—Road guides
Automobile headlight glare
    See Headlight glare
Automobile identification
    See Automobiles—Identification
Automobile industry and trade *(Direct)*
    sa Automobile industry workers
        Automobile wrecking and used parts
        industry
        Automobiles—Parts—Prices
        Automobiles—Prices
        Automobiles—Service stations
        Automobiles—Showrooms
        Salesmen and salesmanship—
        Automobiles
        Strikes and lockouts—Automobile
        industry
        Tractor industry
    xx Automobiles—Social aspects
    Note under Automobiles—Social aspects
— Automation *(TL240)*
— Collective bargaining
    See Collective bargaining—
        Automobile industry
— Collective labor agreements
    See Collective labor agreements—
        Automobile industry
— Costs
— Electric equipment
— Finance
    x Automobiles—Finance
— Labor productivity
— Law and legislation *(Direct)*
    sa Products liability—Motor vehicles
    xx Automobiles—Laws and regulations
— Management
— Mathematical models
— Public relations
    See Public relations—Automobile
        trade
— Quality control
— Safety measures
— Subcontracting
— Taxation *(Direct)*

— Underdeveloped areas
   See Underdeveloped areas—
      Automobile industry and trade
— Used cars
   See Used car trade
— Vocational guidance
— — Juvenile literature
Automobile industry workers *(Direct)*
   sa Automobile mechanics
     Collective bargaining—Automobile
       industry
     Collective labor agreements—
       Automobile industry
     Strikes and lockouts—Automobile
       industry
     Trade-unions—Automobile industry
       workers
     Wages—Automobile industry workers
   x Auto workers
     Automobile construction workers
     Automobile workers
   xx Automobile industry and trade
— Retirement
Automobile inspection
   See Automobiles—Inspection
Automobile insurance
   See Insurance, Automobile
Automobile law
   See Automobiles—Laws and regulations
Automobile license plates *(Direct)*
   x Automobiles—Licenses
   xx Automobiles—Registration
Automobile maintenance
   See Automobiles—Maintenance and repair
Automobile mechanics *(Direct)*
   sa Automobiles—Maintenance and repair
      —Vocational guidance
     Trade-unions—Automobile mechanics
     Wages—Automobile mechanics
   x Auto mechanics
     Automobile workers
   xx Automobile industry workers
     Mechanics (Persons)
— Juvenile literature
Automobile operation
   See Automobile driving
Automobile ownership
   sa Automobile purchasing
   x Automobiles—Ownership
   xx Automobile purchasing
— Juvenile literature
Automobile parking *(Direct)* *(TL154)*
   sa Campus parking
     Churches—Parking facilities
     Hotels, taverns, etc.—Parking facilities
     Motels—Parking facilities
     Motor-truck parking
     Parking garages
     Recreation areas—Parking facilities
     Trailer parking
   x Automobiles—Parking
     Parking, Automobile
   xx Garages
     Transportation, Automotive
— Anecdotes, facetiae, satire, etc.
— Law and legislation *(Direct)*
   xx Traffic regulations
— Taxation *(Direct)*
Automobile-parking meters
   See Parking meters
Automobile parts
   See Automobiles—Parts
Automobile photography
   See Photography of automobiles
Automobile prices
   See Automobiles—Prices
Automobile purchasing
   sa Automobile ownership

   x Automobile buying
     Automobiles—Purchasing
     Buying, Automobile
     Car buying
     Purchasing, Automobile
   xx Automobile ownership
     Shopping
Automobile racing *(Direct)* *(GV1029)*
   sa All terrain vehicle racing
     Automobile rallies
     Automobiles, Racing
     British Grand Prix Race
     Canadian-American Challenge Cup
     Daily Mirror World Cup Rally, 1970
     Drag racing
     Dune buggy racing
     East African Safari Rally
     German Grand Prix Race
     Grand Prix racing
     Karting
     London-Sydney Marathon
     Model car racing
     Monaco Grand Prix Race
     Racetracks (Automobile racing)
     Sebring Grand Prix Race
     Sports car events
     Tourist Trophy Road Race
     Watkins Glen Grand Prix Race
   xx Racing
     Sports car events
— Biography
— — Juvenile literature
— Caricatures and cartoons
— Juvenile literature
— Pictorial works
— Safety measures
— Terminology
Automobile racing on ice *(GV1029.9.I25)*
   xx Winter sports
— Juvenile literature
Automobile radios
   See Radio—Installation in automobiles
Automobile rallies *(Direct)* *(GV1029.2)*
   sa Daily Mirror World Cup Rally, 1970
     East African Safari Rally
     London-Sydney Marathon
   x Auto rallies
     Rallies, Automobile
     Rallying, Automobile
   xx Automobile racing
     Sports car events
Automobile repair
   See Automobiles—Maintenance and repair
Automobile research
   See Automobile engineering research
Automobile safety belts
   See Automobile seat belts
Automobile scales
   See Motor vehicle scales
Automobile seat belts *(TL159)*
   x Automobile safety belts
     Automobiles—Seat belts
     Lap belts, Automobile
     Safety belts, Automobile
     Seat belts, Automobile
   xx Automobiles—Safety appliances
— Safety regulations *(Direct)*
   xx Automobiles—Laws and regulations
Automobile selling
   See Salesmen and salesmanship—
     Automobiles
Automobile service stations
   See Automobiles—Service stations
Automobile showrooms
   See Automobiles—Showrooms
Automobile sounds
   sa Sports car sounds
   xx Sounds

Automobile spare parts
   See Automobiles—Parts
Automobile speed records
   See Automobiles, Racing—Speed records
Automobile stealing
   See Automobile thieves
Automobile steel
   See Steel, Automobile
Automobile theft investigation *(Direct)*
   xx Automobile thieves
     Criminal investigation
Automobile thefts
   See Automobile thieves
     Theft from motor vehicles
Automobile thieves *(Direct)*
   sa Automobile theft investigation
     Theft from motor vehicles
   x Auto thefts
     Auto thieves
     Automobile stealing
     Automobile thefts
   xx Crime and criminals
     Larceny
     Thieves
Automobile tires
   See Automobiles—Tires
Automobile trailers
   See Automobiles—Trailers
Automobile trains *(TL235)*
   x Trains, Automobile
Automobile transmission
   See Automobiles—Transmission devices
Automobile trucks
   See Motor-trucks
Automobile used parts industry
   See Automobile wrecking and used parts
     industry
Automobile welding
   See Automobiles—Welding
Automobile windows
   See Automobiles—Windows and
     windshields
Automobile windshields
   See Automobiles—Windows and
     windshields
Automobile wiring
   See Automobiles—Electric wiring
Automobile workers
   See Automobile industry workers
     Automobile mechanics
Automobile wrecking and used parts industry
     (Direct)
   x Automobile used parts industry
     Automobiles—Used parts
     Automobiles—Wrecking
     Wrecking, Automobile
   xx Automobile industry and trade
     Wrecking
Automobile wrecking derbies
   See Auto demolition derbies
Automobiles *(Industry and statistics,*
     HD9710; Periodicals, technology,
     history, TL1-445; Sports and
     amusements, GV1021-1030;
     Transportation, HE5601-5720)
   sa Car washes
     Commercial vehicles
     Cycle-cars
     Motor buses
     Motor-trucks
     Motorcycles
     Railroad motor-cars
     Sports cars
     Wreckers (Vehicles)
     headings beginning with the word
      Automobile; and names of
      automobiles, e.g. Chevrolet
      automobile, Ford automobile

Automobiles *(Industry and statistics, HD9710; Periodicals, technology, history, TL1-445; Sports and amusements, GV1021-1030; Transportation, HE5601-5720) (Continued)*
  x Automobiles, Gasoline
    Automobiling
    Cars (Automobiles)
    Gasoline automobiles
    Motor-cars
  xx Automobile drivers
    Locomotion
    Motor vehicles
    Transportation
    Transportation, Automotive
    Vehicles
  Example under Traffic engineering
— Abandonment
    See Abandonment of automobiles
— Accessories
    See Automobiles—Apparatus and
      supplies
— Accidents
    See Traffic accidents
— Aerodynamics *(TL245)*
    xx Aerodynamics
      Automobiles—Design and
        construction
    Example under reference from Streamlining
— Air conditioning
— Alignment of bodies
    See Automobiles—Bodies—Alignment
— Alignment of wheels
    See Automobiles—Wheels—
      Alignment
— Anecdotes, facetiae, satire, etc.
— Apparatus and supplies
    sa Anti-freeze solutions
      Automobiles—Safety appliances
      Automobiles—Service stations
      Motor vehicles—Pollution control
        devices
    x Automobile accessories
      Automobiles—Accessories
— — Prices *(Direct)*
— — Tariff
      See Tariff on automobile parts
— Axles
    xx Axles
— Batteries *(TL272)*
    x Automobile batteries
    Example under Storage batteries
— — Testing
— Bearings
    sa Automobiles—Motors—Bearings
    x Automobile bearings
    xx Bearings (Machinery)
— Bodies *(TL255)*
    sa Automobiles—Doors
    x Automobile bodies
    xx Automobiles—Design and
        construction
— — Alignment
      x Alignment of automobile bodies
        Automobiles—Alignment of
          bodies
— — Maintenance and repair
— — Tariff
      See Tariff on automobile bodies
— Bottled-gas motors
    See Automobiles—Motors
      (Compressed-gas)
— Brakes *(TL275)*
    sa Automobile driving—Braking
    x Automobile brakes
— — Maintenance and repair
— — Testing

— Carburetors
    See Automobiles—Motors—
      Carburetors
— Caricatures and cartoons
— Catalogs
— Chassis
    xx Automobiles—Design and
      construction
— Clutches
    x Automobile clutches
    Example under Clutches (Machinery)
— Cold weather operation
    sa Automobile driving in winter
    xx Automobile driving
      Motor vehicles—Cold weather
        operation
— Collectors and collecting
— — Juvenile literature
— Cooling systems (Motors)
    See Automobiles—Motors—Cooling
— Corrosion
    x Automobile corrosion
    xx Automobiles—Maintenance and
      repair
— Cost of operation
    x Automobiles—Operating costs
— Cylinders
    See Automobiles—Motors—Cylinders
— Demolition derbies
    See Auto demolition derbies
— Design and construction *(TL240)*
    sa Automobiles—Aerodynamics
      Automobiles—Bodies
      Automobiles—Chassis
      Automotive drafting
— — Juvenile literature
— — Mathematical models
— Diesel motors
    See Automobiles—Motors (Diesel)
— Directories *(Direct)*
    x Automobiles—Registers
— Doors
    x Automobile doors
      Doors, Automobile
    xx Automobiles—Bodies
— Drafting
    See Automotive drafting
— Drawing
    See Automobiles—Drawings
— Drawings *(TL240)*
    x Automobiles—Drawing
    xx Automotive drafting
— Drivers' licenses
    See Automobile drivers' licenses
— Driving
    See Automobile driving
— Dynamics
    sa Automobiles—Skidding
— — Mathematical models
— — Programmed instruction
— Electric equipment *(TL272)*
    sa Automobiles—Electric wiring
    x Electric equipment of automobiles
    xx Electricity in transportation
— — Maintenance and repair
— — — Programmed instruction *(TL272)*
— Electric generators
    x Automobiles—Generators, Electric
    xx Dynamos
— Electric wiring *(TL272)*
    x Automobile wiring
    xx Automobiles—Electric equipment
      Electric wiring
— Electronic equipment *(TL272.5)*
    x Automotive electronics
    xx Electronic apparatus and appliances
— Environmental aspects *(Direct)*
    sa Abandonment of automobiles

— Examinations, questions, etc.
— Exhaust gas
    See Automobile exhaust gas
— Fenders *(TL275)*
    x Automobile fenders
      Fenders, Automobile
      Fenders for automobiles
— Finance
    See Automobile industry and trade—
      Finance
— Front-end alignment
    See Automobiles—Wheels—
      Alignment
— Front-wheel drive
    x Front-wheel drive (Automobiles)
    xx Automobiles—Transmission devices
— Fuel consumption *(TL154)*
    sa Automobile exhaust gas
    x Automobile gasoline consumption
      Gasoline consumption of
        automobiles
    xx Gasoline
      Motor fuels
— — Tables, calculations, etc.
— Fuel systems
    sa Automobiles—Motors—Carburetors
      Carburetors
    x Automobile fuel systems
      Automotive fuel systems
    xx Fuel pumps
    Example under reference from Fuel systems
— — Vapor lock
      x Vapor lock in automobiles
      xx Gasoline
        Vapors
— Gas engines
    See Automobiles—Motors
      (Compressed-gas)
— Gas-producers *(TL229.G3)*
    x Automobiles, Gas-generator
    xx Gas as fuel
      Gas-producers
— Gearing
    See Automobiles—Steering-gear
— Generators, Electric
    See Automobiles—Electric generators
— Guides
    See Automobiles—Road guides
— Handling characteristics
    xx Stability of automobiles
— Headlights
    See Automobiles—Lighting
— History
— — Juvenile literature
— Horns *(TL275)*
— — Testing
— Identification
    sa Automobiles—Trade-marks
    x Automobile identification
      Identification of automobiles
— Ignition
    sa Magneto
      Spark-plugs
    x Ignition devices
— — Maintenance and repair
— — Testing
— Inspection *(Direct) (TL285)*
    x Automobile inspection
    xx Automobiles—Laws and regulations
      Automobiles—Testing
      Traffic safety
— Insurance
    See Insurance, Automobile
— Juvenile literature
— Laboratory manuals
— Laws and regulations *(Direct)*
    (HE5619-5720)

sa Abandonment of automobiles
   Automobile drivers' licenses
   Automobile industry and trade—Law
      and legislation
   Automobile seat belts—Safety
      regulations
   Automobiles—Inspection
   Automobiles—Tires—Safety
      regulations
   Liability for traffic accidents
   Products liability—Automobiles
   Traffic courts
   Traffic violations
x Automobile law
   Law, Automobile
   Traffic safety—Law and legislation
xx Automobile drivers
   Highway law
   Traffic safety
— — Cases
— Leasing
   See Automobiles, Rental
— Licenses
   See Automobile drivers' licenses
      Automobile license plates
      Automobiles—Registration
      Automobiles—Taxation
— Lighting (Electric equipment, TL272)
   sa Headlight glare
   x Automobiles—Headlights
      Headlights
— Lubrication (TL153.5)
   xx Motor vehicles—Lubrication
   Example under Lubrication and lubri-
      cants
— Maintenance and repair
   sa Automobiles—Corrosion
      Automobiles—Motors—Maintenance
         and repair
   x Automobile maintenance
      Automobile repair
      Automobiles—Repairing
      Automobiles—Servicing
   Example under Repairing
— — Examinations, questions, etc.
— — Juvenile literature
— — Production standards
— — Rates
— — Safety measures
— — Vocational guidance
   xx Automobile mechanics
— Materials (TL154)
   sa Plastics in automobiles
— Mirrors, Rearview
   See Automobiles—Rearview mirrors
— Models (TL237)
   sa Automobiles, Racing—Models
      Model car racing
   x Model cars
      Toy automobiles
   Example under Models and modelmak-
      ing
— — Juvenile literature
— — Radio control (TL237)
— Moral and religious aspects
— Motors (TL210)
   sa Automobiles, Racing—Motors
      Automotive gas turbines
      Fuel pumps
   x Automobile engines
   Example under Motors
— — Bearings
   xx Automobiles—Bearings
— — Carburetors (TL212)
   x Automobile carburetors
      Automobiles—Carburetors
   xx Automobiles—Fuel systems
   Example under Carburetors

— — Cooling
   x Automobile cooling systems
      (Motors)
      Automobiles—Cooling systems
         (Motors)
      Cooling of automobile engines
   xx Automobiles—Radiators
      Gas and oil engines—Cooling
— — Cylinders
   x Automobile cylinders
      Automobiles—Cylinders
— — Exhaust
   See Automobile exhaust gas
— — Maintenance and repair
   xx Automobiles—Maintenance and
      repair
— — Oil filters (TL214.O5)
   x Automobiles—Oil filters
   xx Filters and filtration
      Oil filters
— — Soundproofing
— — Superchargers
   x Automobiles—Superchargers
— — Testing
— — Valves
   x Automobiles—Valves
   xx Gas and oil engines—Valves
— Motors (Compressed-gas) (TL229.G3)
   x Automobiles—Bottled-gas motors
      Automobiles, Compressed-gas
      Automobiles—Gas engines
      Compressed-gas automobiles
      Gas engines, Automotive
   xx Gas and oil engines
      Gas as fuel
      Gases, Compressed
— Motors (Diesel) (TL229.D5)
   x Automobiles, Diesel
      Automobiles—Diesel motors
— Motors (Two-stroke cycle) (TL210.5)
   x Automobiles, Two-stroke cycle
      Automobiles—Two-stroke cycle
         motors
      Two-stroke cycle automobile motors
— Museums
— Noise
— Oil filters
   See Automobiles—Motors—Oil filters
— Operating costs
   See Automobiles—Cost of operation
— Ownership
   See Automobile ownership
— Painting (TL154)
   xx Carriage and wagon painting
   Example under Painting, Industrial
— Parking
   See Automobile parking
— Parts
   x Automobile parts
      Automobile spare parts
      Automobiles—Spare parts
   xx Machine parts
   Note under Machine parts
— — Prices (Direct)
   xx Automobile industry and trade
— Patents (TL280)
   Example under Patents
— Photography
   See Photography of automobiles
— Pictorial works
— Pneumatic equipment
— Popular works
— Prices (Direct)
   x Automobile prices
   xx Automobile industry and trade
— Products liability
   See Products liability—Automobiles
— Purchasing

   See Automobile purchasing
— Quotations, maxims, etc.
— Radiators (TL275)
   sa Automobiles—Motors—Cooling
   xx Radiators
— — Maintenance and repair
— Radio
   See Radio—Installation in automobiles
— Rearview mirrors
   x Automobiles—Mirrors, Rearview
      Rearview mirrors, Automobile
   xx Mirrors
— Registers
   See Automobiles—Directories
— Registration (Direct) (HE5621-5720)
   sa Automobile license plates
   x Automobiles—Licenses
— Renting
   See Automobiles, Rental
— Repairing
   See Automobiles—Maintenance and
      repair
— Research
   See Automobile engineering research
— Road guides (Direct) (GV1024-5)
   When subdivided by place, make a see
      also reference from the place, with
      subdivision Description and travel
      —Guide-books.
   sa Road maps
   x Automobile guides
      Automobiles—Guides
      Road guides, Automobile
— Safety appliances
   sa Automobile seat belts
      Reflectors (Safety devices)
   xx Automobiles—Apparatus and
      supplies
— Safety measures
   xx Automotive medicine
   Example under Accidents—Prevention
— Seat belts
   See Automobile seat belts
— Selling
   See Salesmen and salesmanship—
      Automobiles
— Service stations (Direct) (TL153)
— Servicing
   See Automobiles—Maintenance and
      repair
— Shock absorbers
   x Shock absorbers, Automobile
   xx Shock (Mechanics)
   Example under Damping (Mechanics)
— Showrooms
   x Automobile showrooms
   xx Automobile industry and trade
      Mercantile buildings
— Signals
   See Signals and signaling, Automobile
— Skidding
   x Skid accidents
      Skidding (Motor vehicles)
   xx Automobiles—Dynamics
      Automobiles—Tires
      Roads
      Traffic accidents
— Social aspects (Direct)
   Here are entered works on the au-
      tomobile as a factor in the social life
      of the community. Commercial au-
      tomobile transportation is entered
      under Transportation, Automotive
      and the economic aspects under
      Automobile industry and trade.
   sa Automobile industry and trade
      Transportation, Automotive
   xx Social history

141

Automobiles *(Industry and statistics, HD9710; Periodicals, technology, history, TL1-445; Sports and amusements, GV1021-1030; Transportation, HE5601-5720)*
— Social aspects *(Direct) (Continued)*

  Transportation, Automotive
— Societies, etc.
  x Automobile clubs
— Spare parts
  See Automobiles—Parts
— Speed
  sa Automobiles, Racing—Speed records
    Speed limits
— Speedometers
  See Speedometers
— Springs and suspension
  x Automobiles—Suspension
  Example under Springs (Mechanism)
— Stability
  See Stability of automobiles
— Starting devices *(TL272)*
— Statistics *(Direct)*
— Steering-gear *(TL259)*
  sa Automobile driving—Steering
  x Automobiles—Gearing
  xx Gearing
    Steering-gear
— Superchargers
  See Automobiles—Motors—Superchargers
— Suspension
  See Automobiles—Springs and suspension
— Tables, calculations, etc.
— Tariff
  See Tariff on automobiles
— Taxation *(Direct) (HD9710)*
    Here are entered works on the taxation of automobiles, commercial and non-commercial. Works on the taxation of automotive carriers are entered under specific headings, *e.g.* Transportation, Automotive—Taxation; Motor bus lines—Taxation.
  x Automobiles—Licenses
    Motor-trucks—Taxation
  xx Roads—Finance
    Taxation of personal property
  Example under reference from Excise
— Terminology
— Testing *(TL285-295)*
  sa Automobiles—Inspection
  Example under Testing
— Tires *(TL270)*
  sa Automobiles—Skidding
    Studded tires
  x Automobile tires
  xx Motor vehicles—Tires
  Example under Tires, Rubber
— — Labeling *(Direct)*
— — Marketing
    See Tire industry
— — Repairing
  x Tire repairing
— — Safety regulations *(Direct)*
  xx Automobiles—Laws and regulations
— — Testing
  x Tire testing
— Touring *(GV1021-5)*
  sa Games for travelers
  xx Travel
— Trade-marks
  x Car badges
  xx Automobiles—Identification
— Trailers *(TL297)*

  sa Boat trailers
    Mobile homes
    Motor bus trailers
    Recreational vehicles
    Trailer camps
    Truck trailers
  x Automobile trailers
    Caravans (Automobile trailers)
  xx Trailers
— — Anecdotes, facetiae, satire, etc.
— — Law and legislation *(Direct)*
— — Maintenance and repair *(TL297)*
— — Parking
    See Trailer parking
— Transmission devices *(TL262)*
  sa Automobile driving—Shifting gear
    Automobiles—Front-wheel drive
  x Automobile transmission
    Automobiles—Gearing
    Transmissions, Automobile
  xx Gearing
  Example under reference from Transmission devices
— Transmission devices, Automatic *(TL263)*
  x Automatic transmissions, Automobile
  xx Hydraulic torque converters
— Transportation
— Two-stroke cycle motors
    See Automobiles—Motors (Two-stroke cycle)
— Upholstery
  xx Upholstery
— Used cars
    See Used cars
— Used parts
    See Automobile wrecking and used parts industry
— Valves
    See Automobiles—Motors—Valves
— Vibration
— Welding
  x Automobile welding
— Wheels *(TL270)*
  Example under Wheels
— — Alignment
  x Alignment of automobile wheels
    Automobiles—Alignment of wheels
    Automobiles—Front-end alignment
    Front-end alignment (Automobile wheels)
    Wheel alignment (Automobiles)
— Windows and windshields *(TL275)*
  sa Automobiles—Windshield wipers
  x Automobile windows
    Automobile windshields
    Windshields (Automobile)
— Windshield wipers
  x Windshield wipers (Automobile)
  xx Automobiles—Windows and windshields
— Wrecking
    See Automobile wrecking and used parts industry
— Wrecking derbies
    See Auto demolition derbies
Automobiles, American, [British, German, etc.]
  x American [British, German, etc.] automobiles
— Juvenile literature
Automobiles, Compact
  sa Corvair automobile
  x Compact automobiles
    Compact cars

Automobiles, Company
  x Company automobiles
    Company cars
  xx Commercial travelers
    Transportation, Automotive
Automobiles, Compressed-gas
  See Automobiles—Motors (Compressed-gas)
Automobiles, Diesel
  See Automobiles—Motors (Diesel)
Automobiles, Electric *(TL220)*
  x Electric automobiles
  xx Electric motors
    Electric vehicles
Automobiles, Foreign
  x Foreign automobiles
    Foreign cars
— Maintenance and repair
Automobiles, Gas-generator
  See Automobiles—Gas-producers
Automobiles, Gas-turbine
  x Automobiles, Turbine-powered
    Gas-turbine automobiles
    Gas-turbine cars
    Turbine cars
— Motors
    See Automotive gas turbines
— Pictorial works
Automobiles, Gasoline
  See Automobiles
Automobiles, Government *(Direct)*
  sa Police vehicles
    subdivision Officials and employees—Travel regulations *under names of countries, states, cities and individual government agencies*
  x Government cars
    Government-owned automobiles
Automobiles, Midget
  See Karts (Midget cars)
Automobiles, Military *(UG680-685)*
  sa Jeep automobile
    Tanks (Military science)
  x Military automobiles
    Motor vehicles in war
  xx Motorization, Military
    Transportation, Military
    Vehicles, Military
— Cold weather operation *(UC340-345)*
— Gearing
    See Automobiles, Military—Transmission devices
— Heating and ventilation *(UC340-345)*
— Maintenance and repair
— Transmission devices
  x Automobiles, Military—Gearing
  xx Gearing
Automobiles, Plastic
  x Plastic automobiles
Automobiles, Racing *(TL236)*
  sa Karts (Midget cars)
    Sports cars
    names of specific racing automobiles, e.g. Austin-Healey automobile
  x Racing automobiles
    Racing cars
  xx Automobile racing
— Aerodynamics
— Chassis
— Fuel systems
— Juvenile literature
— Models
  xx Automobiles—Models
    Model car racing
— — Radio control
— Motors *(TL210)*
  x "Hopped-up" motors
    "Hot" motors

"Souped-up" motors
   xx Automobiles—Motors
— — Carburetors
— Pictorial works
— Speed records
   x Automobile speed records
   xx Automobiles—Speed
Automobiles, Rental *(Direct)*
   x Automobiles—Leasing
     Automobiles—Renting
     Rental automobiles
   xx Lease and rental services
Automobiles, Steam *(TL200)*
   x Steam automobiles
   xx Steam-carriages
— Juvenile literature
Automobiles, Theft from
   See Theft from motor vehicles
Automobiles, Three wheel
   x Three wheel automobiles
     Three-wheelers
Automobiles, Turbine-powered
   See Automobiles, Gas-turbine
Automobiles, Two-stroke cycle
   See Automobiles—Motors (Two-stroke cycle)
Automobiles for the physically handicapped
   xx Physically handicapped
Automobiles in art
   xx Art
Automobiles in moving-pictures
   xx Moving-pictures
Automobiling
   See Automobiles
Automorphic forms *(QA331)*
   x Forms, Automorphic
   xx Forms (Mathematics)
     Functions of several complex variables
Automorphic functions
   See Functions, Automorphic
Automorphisms
   xx Groups, Theory of
Automotive drafting *(TL253)*
   sa Automobiles—Drawings
   x Automobiles—Drafting
     Automotive drawing
     Drafting, Automotive
     Drawing, Automotive
   xx Automobiles—Design and construction
     Mechanical drawing
Automotive drawing
   See Automotive drafting
Automotive electronics
   See Automobiles—Electronic equipment
     Motor vehicles—Electronic equipment
Automotive engineering research
   See Automobile engineering research
Automotive fleets
   See Motor vehicle fleets
Automotive fuel systems
   See Automobiles—Fuel systems
Automotive fuels
   See Motor fuels
Automotive gas turbines
   x Automobiles, Gas-turbine—Motors
   xx Automobiles—Motors
     Gas-turbines
Automotive medicine
   sa Automobile drivers—Medical examinations
     Automobile drivers—Psychology
     Automobile drivers' tests
     Automobile driving—Physiological aspects
     Automobiles—Safety measures
     Crash injuries
     Traffic accidents
   x Automobile driving, Medical aspects of

   xx Medicine
     Transportation medicine
Automotive transport workers
   See Highway transport workers
Automotive transportation
   See Transportation, Automotive
Automotive vehicles
   See Motor vehicles
Automutilation
   See Self-mutilation
Autonomic drugs
   sa Ganglionic blocking agents
     Ganglionic stimulating agents
     Neuroleptanesthesia
     Neuromuscular depolarizing agents
     Parasympatholytic agents
     Parasympathomimetic agents
     Sympatholytic agents
     Sympathomimetic agents
   xx Neuropharmacology
Autonomic ganglia
   See Ganglia, Autonomic
Autonomic nervous system
   See Nervous system, Autonomic
Autonomy
   sa Self-determination, National
   x Independence
     Self-government
   xx International law
     Political science
     Self-determination, National
     Sovereignty
Autonomy, University
   See University autonomy
Autophagic vacuoles *(QH603.L9)*
   x Autophagocytosis
Autophagocytosis
   See Autophagic vacuoles
Autopilot
   See Automatic pilot (Aeroplanes)
Autopsy *(Medical jurisprudence, RA1058; Pathology, RB57)*
   sa Death—Causes
     Exhumation
     Medical examiners (Law)
     Veterinary autopsy
   x Necropsy
     Necroscopy
     Post-mortem examinations
   xx Anatomy, Pathological
     Dead bodies (Law)
     Death—Causes
     Medical jurisprudence
Autoradiography
   x Radioautography
   xx Radioactivity
     Radiography
— Films
— Technique
AUTOSATE
   x Automated data system analysis technique
   xx Electronic data processing
     FORTRAN (Computer program language)
Autosuggestion
   See Hypnotism
     Mental suggestion
     related subjects referred to under these headings
Autosyn
   See Synchros
Autotherapy
   xx Serumtherapy
Autotomy
   sa Regeneration (Biology)
   xx Regeneration (Biology)

Autotoxaemia
   See Auto-intoxication
Autotrophic bacteria
   See Bacteria, Autotrophic
Autoxidation
   See Oxidation
Autumn
   x Fall
— Juvenile literature
Autumnal catarrh
   See Hay-fever
Auvergne in art
Auvergne in literature
Auxiliary military police
   See United States. Army. Corps of Military Police—Foreign auxiliaries
Auxiliary police *(Indirect)*
   sa subdivision Auxiliary police *under names of cities*
   x Police, Auxiliary
   xx Civil defense
     Police
Auxiliary saints
   See Fourteen holy helpers
Auxiliary sciences of history *(C)*
   sa Archaeology
     Archives
     Biography
     Chronology
     Civilization
     Diplomatics
     Genealogy
     Heraldry
     History
     Inscriptions
     Numismatics
     Paleography
   xx History
Auxin metabolism
   xx Metabolism
Auxochromes
   xx Dyes and dyeing
Auyana language
   sa Kosena dialect
   xx Papuan languages
Ava-mbiha Indians
   See Mbya Indians
Aval
   See Accommodation indorsements
Avalanche diodes
   See Zener diodes
Avalanches *(Indirect)* *(QC929.A8)*
   sa Landslides
     Railroads—Snow protection and removal
     subdivision Avalanche *under names of mountains, villages, etc., e.g.* White Mountains—Avalanche, 1826
   xx Natural disasters
     Snow
— Terminology
Avant-garde churches
   See Non-institutional churches
Avant-garde films
   See Experimental films
Avant-garde theater
   See Experimental theater
Avar language
   See Avaric language
Avarair, Battle of, 451
   See Awarayr, Battle of, 451
Avarayr, Battle of, 451
   See Awarayr, Battle of, 451
Avaric drama *(Direct)*
Avaric language *(PK9201.A9)*
   sa Karata language
   x Avar language
   xx Caucasian languages

Avaric literature *(Direct) (Collections, PK9201.A96-9; History, PK9201.A95)*
Avaric poetry *(Direct)*
Avarice *(BJ1535.A8)*
   sa Commandments, Ten—Covetousness
      Egoism
      Misers
   x Covetousness
      Greed
   xx Conduct of life
      Deadly sins
      Egoism
      Ethics
      Wealth, Ethics of
   Example under Vices
Avars
Avascular femoral necrosis
   See Idiopathic femoral necrosis
Avatars
   sa Incarnation
   xx Theosophy
Avausi (African tribe)
   See Ushi (African tribe)
Avenger automobile
   See Cricket automobile
Average
   sa Mean (Philosophy)
   xx Arithmetic
      Probabilities
      Statistics
Average (Maritime law) *(HE970)*
   sa Jettison
   x General average
   xx Contracts, Maritime
      Insurance, Marine
      Jettison
      Maritime law
   — Conflict of laws
      See Conflict of laws—Average
Average ionization potential
   See Stopping power (Nuclear physics)
Average of accounts *(HF5696)*
   x Equation of payments
   xx Accounting
      Bookkeeping
Averaging method (Differential equaltions)
   x Method of averaging (Differential equations)
   xx Differential equations, Nonlinear—Numerical solutions
Aversive stimuli *(BF319.5.A8)*
   xx Avoidance (Psychology)
      Conditioned response
Avertin *(Anesthetics, RD86.A9; Experimental pharmacy, QP915.A8)*
   x Tribromoethanol
   xx Alcohol
      Anesthetics
Avesta *(Texts, translations, criticism, etc., PK6111-6119; Zoroastrianism, BL1515)*
   sa Pahlavi literature
      Parsees
      Zoroastrianism
   x Persian literature—Avestan
      Zend-Avesta
   xx Pahlavi literature
      Parsees
      Zoroastrianism
   Example under Sacred books
Avesta language *(PK6101-9)*
   sa Old Persian language
      Pahlavi language
   x Bactrian language (Old Bactrian)
      Old Bactrian language
      Persian language—Old Persian (Avesta)
      Zend language

   xx Iranian languages
      Old Persian language
Avesta manuscripts
   See Manuscripts, Avesta
Avian encephalomyelitis *(Indirect) (SF995.6.E5)*
   x Encephalomyelitis, Avian
      Epidemic tremor
      Infectious avian encephalomyelitis
   xx Encephalomyelitis
      Poultry—Diseases
   — Diagnosis
Avian leukosis
   sa Avian lymphomatosis
   x Avian lymphoid leukosis
      Leukemia in poultry
      Leukosis, Avian
   xx Leukemia in animals
      Poultry—Diseases
Avian lymphoid leukosis
   See Avian leukosis
Avian lymphomatosis
   x Fowl paralysis
      Lymphomatosis, Avian
      Marek's disease
   xx Avian leukosis
Avian malaria
   See Malarial fever in birds
Avian pneumoencephalitis
   See Newcastle disease
Avian salmonellosis
   See Salmonellosis in poultry
Avian tuberculosis
   See Tuberculosis in poultry
Aviaries *(Indirect) (QL677.8)*
   xx Birds
      Cage-birds
Aviation
   See Aeronautics
Aviation accidents
   See Aeronautics—Accidents
Aviation and geography
   See Geography, Aerial
Aviation boatswain's mates
   See United States. Navy—Aviation boatswain's mates
Aviation communications
   See Aeronautics—Communication systems
Aviation electricians, Naval
   See United States. Navy—Aviation electricians
Aviation gasoline
   See Aeroplanes—Fuel
Aviation guided missilemen, Naval
   See United States. Navy—Aviation guided missilemen
Aviation hygiene
   See Aeronautics—Sanitary aspects
Aviation industry
   See Aeroplane industry and trade
      Air lines
Aviation insurance
   See Insurance, Aviation
Aviation law
   See Aeronautics—Laws and regulations
Aviation machinists, Naval
   See United States. Navy—Aviation machinists
Aviation mechanics (Persons) *(Direct)*
   x Aircraft mechanics (Persons)
      Aviation technicians
   xx Mechanics (Persons)
   — Certification *(Direct)*
Aviation medical examiners
   x Medical examiners, Aviation
   xx Aviation medicine
Aviation medicine *(Indirect) (RC1050-1099)*
   sa Aeronautics—Psychology

      Aeroplane ambulances
      Aeroplanes—Disinfection
      Air lines—Employees—Medical examinations
      Air pilots—Diseases and hygiene
      Anoxemia
      Aviation medical examiners
      Aviation toxicology
      Flight—Physiological aspects
      Space medicine
      Weightlessness simulators
   x Aeronautics—Medical aspects
      Aerospace medicine
      Flight crews—Diseases and hygiene
      Flight—Medical aspects
   xx Medicine
      Space medicine
      Transportation medicine
   — Research *(RC1058)*
      xx Medical research
Aviation physiology
   See Flight—Physiological aspects
Aviation psychology
   See Aeronautics—Psychology
Aviation structural mechanics, Naval
   See United States. Navy—Aviation structural mechanics
Aviation technicians
   See Aviation mechanics (Persons)
Aviation toxicology
   sa Flight—Physiological aspects
   xx Aviation medicine
Aviators
   See Air pilots
Avidyā *(B132.A9)*
   xx Philosophy, Indic
Avigation
   See Navigation (Aeronautics)
Avigation easements *(Direct)*
   x Aerial servitudes
      Air easements
      Airspace easements
      Easements, Avigation
      Flight easements
      Servitudes, Aerial
   xx Aeronautics—Laws and regulations
      Airport zoning
      Airports—Laws and regulations
      Airspace (Law)
      Servitudes
Avignon, Popes at
   See Papacy—History—1309-1378
Avignon in literature
Avionics
   See Electronics in aeronautics
Avitaminosis
   sa Ascorbic acid deficiency
      Tocopherol deficiency
      Vitamin A deficiency
      Vitamin B deficiency
      Vitamin D deficiency
   x Hypovitaminosis
      Vitamin deficiency
   xx Deficiency diseases
Avocado *(SB379.A9)*
   sa Cookery (Avocado)
   x Alligator-pear
   — Diseases and pests
   — Transportation
   — Varieties
Avocations
   See Hobbies
Avocets
   x Avosets
   xx Charadriiformes
Avoidance (Psychology)
   sa Aversive stimuli
      Escape (Psychology)

xx Anxiety
Emotions
Escape (Psychology)
Psychology, Physiological
Avosets
See Avocets
Avro 707 (Jet planes)
xx Jet planes
Avşar (Turkish tribe)
See Afshar (Turkish tribe)
Awa language
xx Papuan languages
Awadhi dialect *(PK2001-7)*
xx Hindi language
Awakening, Great
See Great Awakening
Awakening (Buddhism)
See Enlightenment (Buddhism)
Awakening (Religion)
Here are entered works on the concept of
awakening in various religions. Works
limited to Christian theology are en-
tered under Awakening (Theology)
sa Awakening (Theology)
xx Religion
Salvation
Awakening (Theology)
xx Awakening (Religion)
Pietism
Theology, Doctrinal
Note under Awakening (Religion)
Awarayr, Battle of, 451
x Avarair, Battle of, 451
Avarayr, Battle of, 451
Vardanants', Battle of, 451
xx Armenia—History—Persian and Greek
rule, 429-640
Awards
See Arbitration and award
Rewards (Prizes, etc.)
Awards, Performance
See Performance awards
Awareness
sa Race awareness
xx Cognition
Perception
— Juvenile literature
Awe *(BF575.A)*
xx Emotions
Wonder
Aweikoma Indians
See Shokleng Indians
Awnings
Example under Canvas
AWOL
See Absence without leave
Axes
sa Adzes
Tomahawks
Example under Stone implements
— Classification
Axial flow compressors
See Compressors
Axilla
x Armpit
Fossa axillaris
xx Arm
— Blood-vessels
Axinite *(Indirect)*
Axiological proof of God
See God—Proof, Moral
Axiology
See Worth
Axiom of choice *(QA248)*
x Choice, Axiom of
xx Axiomatic set theory
Axiomatic set theory
sa Axiom of choice

xx Axioms
Logic, Symbolic and mathematical
Set theory
Axioms *(Geometry, QA481; QA681)*
sa Axiomatic set theory
Geometry, Projective—Foundations
Mathematical analysis—Foundations
xx Geometry—Foundations
Mathematics
Parallels (Geometry)
Philosophy
Axis (Vertebra)
x Epistropeus
Vertebra, Second cervical
xx Vertebrae, Cervical
— Wounds and injuries
Axles
sa Automobiles—Axles
Bearings (Machinery)
Car axles
xx Carriage and wagon making
Wheels
— Design and construction
— Standards *(Direct)*
Axolotls *(QL668.C2)*
Axonometric projection
sa Isometric projection
x Axonometry
Projection, Axonometric
xx Geometry, Descriptive
Projection
Axonometry
See Axonometric projection
Axons
x Nerve axons
xx Neurons
Axseed
x Crown vetch
Crownvetch
Ay-bo-le (Dance)
Ayacucho, Battle of, 1824
Ayahuasca *(Botany, QK495.M26)*
x Caapi
xx Botany, Medical
Hallucinogenic drugs
— Therapeutic use
Ayan language
See Bassari language
Ayana language
See Oyana language
Aye-aye
xx Primates
Ayllus
Aymara Indians *(F2230.2.A9)*
sa Callahuaya Indians
Colla Indians
xx Indians of South America
— Land tenure
Example under Indians of South America
—Land tenure
— Missions
Aymara language *(PM5571-9)*
sa Callahuaya language
Cauqui dialect
x Aimara language
xx Indians of South America—Languages
Ayook language
See Mixe language
Ayoré Indians
See Zamucoan Indians
Ayous
See Obeche
Ayrshire cattle *(SF199.A9)*
xx Cows
Ayu
Ayu fishing *(Direct)* *(SH691.A9)*
xx Fishing

Ayubites
See Ayyubids
Ayurvedic medicine
See Medicine, Hindu
Ayyubids
x Ayubites
xx Egypt—History—640-1250
Azalea
— Diseases and pests
— Varieties
Azande *(DT132)*
sa Zande language
x Niam-Niam
Nyam-Nyam
Sandeh
xx Zande language
Azeotropes
xx Boiling-points
Colloids
Distillation
Mixtures
— Tables, etc.
Azerbaijan in art
Azerbaijan in literature
Azerbaijani drama
Azerbaijani fiction *(Direct)*
Azerbaijani language *(PL311-314)*
x Azeri language
xx Turkish language—Dialects
Turko-Tataric languages
Azerbaijani periodicals *(Direct)*
Azerbaijani philology *(Direct)*
Azerbaijani poetry
Azeri language
See Azerbaijani language
Azharot
xx Commandments, Six hundred and
thirteen
Hebrew poetry
Religious poetry, Hebrew
Azimuth *(QB207; Navigation, VK563;*
Surveying, TA597)
sa Meridian lines
xx Astronomy, Spherical and practical
Geodesy
Navigation
Azimuthal projection (Cartography)
x Zenithal projection (Cartography)
xx Map-projection
Azo compounds *(QD305.A9)*
sa Azo dyes
Azo dyes *(TP918)*
sa Congo red
xx Azo compounds
Dyes and dyeing
Azole
See Pyrrol
Azon bombs
xx Bombs
Azotemia
sa Uremia
xx Nitrogen in the body
Renal insufficiency
Uremia
Aztec architecture
See Indians of Mexico—Architecture
Aztec art
See Aztecs—Art
Aztec astrology
See Astrology, Aztec
Aztec calendar
See Calendar, Mexican
Aztec chronology
See Chronology, Mexican
Aztec drama *(Direct)*
Aztec hieroglyphics
See Aztecs—Writing

Aztec inscriptions
   See Aztecs—Writing
Aztec language *(PM4061-9)*
   sa Nahuatl-Spanish dialect
      Pipil language
   x Mexican language
      Nahuatl language
   xx Indians of Mexico—Languages
      Uto-Aztecan languages
Aztec law
   See Law, Aztec
Aztec literature *(PM4068)*
   x Nahuatl literature
   xx Literature
   Notes under Indian literature; Mexican literature
Aztec music
   See Aztecs—Music
Aztec mythology
   See Aztecs—Religion and mythology
Aztec poetry
Azteco-Tanoan Indians *(E77)*
   sa Uto-Aztecan Indians
   xx Aztecs
      Indians of Mexico
      Indians of North America
      Tanoan Indians
      Uto-Aztecan Indians
Aztecs *(F1219)*
   sa Azteco-Tanoan Indians
      Nahuas
      Teco Indians
      Toltecs
   xx Indians of Mexico
      Toltecs
   — Art *(F1219.3.A7)*
      x Art, Aztec
         Aztec art
   — Historiography
   — Juvenile literature
   — Kings and rulers
      Example under Kings and rulers
   — Law
      See Law, Aztec
   — Legends
      x Legends, Aztec
   — Music *(ML3575)*
      x Aztec music
         Music, Aztec
   — Religion and mythology
      x Aztec mythology
         Mythology, Aztec
      xx Indians of Mexico—Religion and
         mythology
   — Rites and ceremonies
   — Wars
   — Writing
      sa Manuscripts, Mexican
      x Aztec hieroglyphics
         Aztec inscriptions
         Hieroglyphics, Aztec
         Inscriptions, Aztec
         Picture-writing, Aztec
      xx Indians of Mexico—Writing
Azuki bean *(QK495.L52; Culture, SB327)*
   x Adsuki bean
      Adzuki bean
   xx Beans
Azygos vein
B-17 (Bombers)
   See B-17 bomber
B-17 bomber
   x B-17 (Bombers)
      Boeing B-17
      Flying Fortress (Bombers)
   xx Boeing bombers
      Bombers

B-24 bomber
   x Liberator (Bombers)
      PB4Y bomber
   xx Bombers
B-25 bomber
   See Mitchell bomber
B-29 (Bombers)
   See B-29 bomber
B-29 bomber
   x B-29 (Bombers)
      Boeing B-29
      Superfortress (Bombers)
   xx Boeing bombers
      Bombers
B-32 bomber
   x Dominator (Bomber)
   xx Bombers
B-36 (Bombers)
   See B-36 bomber
B-36 bomber
   x B-36 (Bombers)
   xx Bombers
B-58 (Bombers)
   See B-58 bomber
B-58 bomber
   x B-58 (Bombers)
      B-58 Hustler (Bombers)
      General Dynamics B-58
      Hustler (Bombers)
   xx Jet planes, Military
      Supersonic bombers
B-58 Hustler (Bombers)
   See B-58 bomber
B cells *(QR185.8.L9)*
   x B lymphocytes
      Bone marrow derived cells
      Bursa equivalent cells
   xx Immunity
      Lymphocytes
B lymphocytes
   See B cells
B.O.D.
   See Biochemical oxygen demand
B.S.A. motorcycle *(TL448.B2)*
   sa Bantam motorcycle
B stars
   xx Stars
Ba (Egyptian religion) *(BL2450.B2)*
Ba-ila
   See Ila (Bantu tribe)
Ba-katlha
   See Kgatla (African tribe)
Ba-Kuba (Bantu tribe)
   See Kuba (Bantu tribe)
Ba-Nyoro
   See Banyoro
Ba-thlapin
   See Thlaping (African tribe)
Ba-Ushi (African tribe)
   See Ushi (African tribe)
Ba-xlapin
   See Thlaping (African tribe)
Baakpe
   See Bakwiri (African people)
Baal (Deity) *(BL1671)*
   x Bel
   Example under Gods
Baamarani dialect *(PJ2395.B2)*
   xx Berber languages
Baamba (African tribe)
   x Amba
   xx Ethnology—Uganda
Babassú palm *(SB299.P3)*
   xx Palms
Babassuê (Cultus)
   See Batuque (Cultus)
Babatana language
   See Bambatana language

Babbitt metal
   xx Lead alloys
      Tin alloys
   — Analysis
Babesiasis
   See Piroplasmosis
Babies
   See Infants
Babili (African people)
   See Wasongola (African people)
Babindja (African people)
   See Wasongola (African people)
Babingas *(DT570)*
   xx Ethnology—East Cameroon
      Pygmies
Babingtonite *(QE391.B2)*
Babira (Bantu tribe)
   See Bira (Bantu tribe)
Babirussa *(QL737.U5)*
   xx Swine
Babism *(BP340)*
   sa Bahaism
   xx Bahaism
      Religions
      Shiites
Babiy Yar Massacre, 1941
   xx Russia—History—German occupation,
      1941-1944
      World War, 1939-1945—Atrocities
      World War, 1939-1945—Jews
Babm
   xx Languages, Artificial
Baboma (Bantu people)
   x Giribuma (Bantu people)
      Ouabuma (Bantu people)
      Uabuma (Bantu people)
      Wabuma (Bantu people)
   xx Bantus
      Ethnology—Zaire
Baboons *(QL737.P9)*
   sa Gelada baboon
      Hamadryas baboon
      Olive baboon
   xx Monkeys
   — Anatomy
   — — Atlases
   — Behavior
   — Juvenile literature
Baboons as laboratory animals
Babouende (Bantu tribe)
   See Babwende (Bantu tribe)
Babuas
   See Ababuas
Babuende (Bantu tribe)
   See Babwende (Bantu tribe)
Babunda (Bantu tribe)
   x Ambuun (Bantu tribe)
      Bambunda (Bantu tribe)
   xx Bantus
      Ethnology—Zaire
Babwende (Bantu tribe) *(DT650)*
   x Babouende (Bantu tribe)
      Babuende (Bantu tribe)
   xx Ethnology—Zaire
Baby animals
   See Animals, Infancy of
Baby books *(HQ779)*
   x Books, Baby
Baby foods
   See Infants—Nutrition
Baby sitters
   x Babysitters
   xx Children—Care and hygiene
      Children—Management
      Infants—Care and hygiene
   — Anecdotes, facetiae, satire, etc.
   — Juvenile literature

Babylonian astronomy
   See Astronomy, Assyro-Babylonian
Babylonian boundary stones
   See Boundary stones, Babylonian
Babylonian calendar
   See Calendar, Assyro-Babylonian
Babylonian captivity, Jewish
   See Jews—History—Babylonian captivity,
     598-515 B.C.
Babylonian captivity, Papal
   See Papacy—History—1309-1378
Babylonian civilization
   See Civilization, Assyro-Babylonian
Babylonian cosmogony
   See Cosmogony, Babylonian
Babylonian exile, Jewish
   See Jews—History—Babylonian captivity,
     598-515 B.C.
Babylonian inscriptions
   See Cuneiform inscriptions
Babylonian language
   See Assyro-Babylonian language
Babylonian letters
   See Assyro-Babylonian letters
Babylonian literature
   See Assyro-Babylonian literature
Babylonian music
   See Music, Assyro-Babylonian
Babylonian mythology
   See Mythology, Assyro-Babylonian
Babylonian sibyl
   x Egyptian sibyl
     Judean sibyl
     Sabbe
     Sambete
   xx Sibyls
Babysitters
   See Baby sitters
BAC Lightning (Fighter plane) *(TL686.B74)*
   x English Electric (BAC) Lightning
     Lightning (BAC fighter plane)
   xx Fighter planes
     Jet planes
BAC TSR 2 (Turbojet fighter planes)
   x TSR 2 (Turbojet fighter planes)
   xx Fighter planes
     Jet planes
Bacalod, Battle of, 1903 *(DS682.B2)*
Bacama (African people)
   See Bachama (African people)
Baccalaureate, International
   See International baccalaureate
Baccalaureate addresses *(BV4255)*
   x Addresses
     Commencement addresses
     Graduation sermons
   xx Sermons
     Speeches, addresses, etc.
     Universities and colleges—Sermons
   — Dartmouth, ₍Mills College, Princeton,
     etc.₎
Baccarat *(GV1295.B3)*
Bacchanalia
   xx Cultus, Roman
Bacchantes
   xx Cultus, Greek
     Dionysia
Bachama (African people)
   x Bacama (African people)
     Bashama (African people)
     Gboare (African people)
   xx Ethnology—Nigeria
   — Religion
Bachelor of arts degree *(LB2383)*
   x Arts, Bachelor of
   Example under Degrees, Academic
Bachelor of liberal studies *(LB2383)*
   x BLS

Liberal studies, Bachelor of
   xx Adult education
     University extension
Bachelors *(HQ800)*
   xx Single people
   — Anecdotes, facetiae, satire, etc.
   — Taxation *(Direct) (HJ5580-5582)*
Bachilele (African tribe)
   See Lele (Bantu tribe)
Bachokwe (Bantu tribe)
   See Chokwe (Bantu tribe)
Bachopi (African tribe)
   See Chopi (African tribe)
Bachua
   See Batwa
Bacillariophyceae
   See Diatoms
Bacillariophyta
   See Diatoms
Bacillary dysentery
   See Shigellosis
Bacille Calmette-Guérin
   See BCG
Bacillus anthracis
   Example under Bacteria, Pathogenic
Bacillus Calmette-Guérin
   See BCG
Bacitracin *(RM666.B2)*
   xx Antibiotics
Back packing
   See Backpacking
Back siphonage (Plumbing)
   See Backsiphonage (Plumbing)
Backache
   x Lumbago
Backbone
   See Spine
Backfield play (Football) *(GV951.3)*
   xx Football
   — Juvenile literature
Backflow connections
   See Cross-connections (Plumbing)
Backgammon *(GV1469.B2)*
   x Trick-track
   Example under Games
Backpacking *(G504.5)*
   x Back packing
     Packing (Transportation)
   xx Camping
     Hiking
     Pack transportation
Backsiphonage (Plumbing)
   sa Cross-connections (Plumbing)
   x Back siphonage (Plumbing)
   xx Cross-connections (Plumbing)
Backward areas
   See Underdeveloped areas
Backward children
   See Mentally handicapped children
     Slow learning children
Backwardation
   See Contango and backwardation
Bacon
   sa Cookery (Bacon)
     Dunmow flitch
   xx Meat
     Pork
   — Packaging
Bacon-Shakespeare controversy
   See Shakespeare, William, 1564-1616—
     Authorship—Baconian theory
Bacon's Rebellion, 1676 *(F229)*
   x Ingram's Rebellion (Virginia)
   xx Virginia—History—Colonial period, ca.
     1600-1775
Bacouba (Bantu tribe)
   See Kuba (Bantu tribe)

Bacteremia
   x Bacteriaemia
     Bacteriemia
   xx Bacterial diseases
     Bacteriology
     Blood
Bacteremic shock
   See Septic shock
Bacteria *(QR75-84)*
   Here are entered works on biological
   studies of bacteria. Works on the
   science are entered under the heading
   Bacteriology.
   sa Agglutination
     Autolysis
     Bacterial cell walls
     Endotoxin
     Fermentation
     Iron bacteria
     L-form bacteria
     Sulphur bacteria
     Viruses
   x Germs
     Microbes
   xx Bacteriology
     Micro-organisms
   Notes under Bacteriology; Fermentation
   — Genetics
     See Bacterial genetics
   — Juvenile literature
     x Bacteriology—Juvenile literature
   — Morphology
     xx Morphology
   — Motility
     sa Flagella (Microbiology)
     x Motility of bacteria
   — Nomenclature
   — Physiology
     sa Bacteria, Effect of radiation on
     Bacterial growth
     x Bacterial physiology
Bacteria, Aerobic
   x Aerobic bacteria
Bacteria, Anaerobic *(QR84)*
   x Anaerobic bacteria
Bacteria, Autotrophic
   x Autotrophic bacteria
Bacteria, Chromogenic *(QR84)*
Bacteria, Denitrifying *(QR105; QR111)*
   sa Micro-organisms, Nitrogen-fixing
     Nitrification
   xx Bacteriology, Agricultural
     Micro-organisms, Nitrogen-fixing
     Nitrification
     Soils—Analysis
Bacteria, Effect of drugs on
   See Micro-organisms, Effect of drugs on
Bacteria, Effect of radiation on
   xx Bacteria—Physiology
     Radiation—Physiological effect
     Radioisotopes in microbiology
Bacteria, Heterotrophic
   x Heterotrophic bacteria
Bacteria, Luminous
   x Luminous bacteria
   xx Bioluminescence
Bacteria, Nitrifying *(QR105; QR111)*
   sa Micro-organisms, Nitrogen-fixing
     Nitrification
     Soils—Bacteriology
   x Nitrobacteria
   xx Bacteriology, Agricultural
     Micro-organisms, Nitrogen-fixing
     Nitrification
     Soils—Analysis
Bacteria, Pathogenic *(QR175-241)*
   sa Bacteria, Phytopathogenic
     Bacterial diseases

Bacteria, Pathogenic (QR175-241)
(Continued)
    Bacteriology, Medical
    Necrosis—Bacteriology
    Pneumococcus
    Rickettsia
    Sarcina
    Soil pollution
    Spirillosis
    Streptococcus
    Streptothrix
    Veterinary bacteriology
    Vibrio comma
    subdivision Bacteriology *under organs*
      and regions of the body, e.g. Eye—
      Bacteriology; Intestines—
      Bacteriology; *and headings beginning*
      with the word Bacillus, *e.g.* Bacillus
      anthracis
  x Disease germs
    Pathogenic bacteria
  xx Bacterial diseases
    Bacteriology, Medical
    Communicable diseases
    Diseases—Causes and theories of
      causation
    Germ theory of disease
    Micro-organisms, Pathogenic
    Soil pollution
    Veterinary bacteriology
— War use
  See Biological warfare
Bacteria, Photosynthetic
  x Photosynthetic bacteria
  xx Photosynthesis
Bacteria, Phytopathogenic *(Indirect)*
    (QR351)
  sa Bacterial diseases of plants
    Plant diseases
  x Phytopathogenic bacteria
  xx Bacteria, Pathogenic
    Bacterial diseases of plants
    Bacteriology, Agricultural
    Micro-organisms, Phytopathogenic
    Plant parasites
    Plants—Bacteriology
— Host plants
Bacteria, Psychrophilic
  x Bacteria, Psychrophite
    Psychrophilic bacteria
    Psychrophite bacteria
Bacteria, Psychrophite
  See Bacteria, Psychrophilic
Bacteria, Sporeforming
  sa Spores (Bacteria)
  x Sporebearing bacteria
    Sporeforming bacteria
Bacteria, Thermophilic *(QR84)*
  x Thermophilic bacteria
  xx Thermophilic fungi
Bacteriaemia
  See Bacteremia
Bacterial antagonism
  See Antibiosis
Bacterial blight of peas *(SB608.P25)*
  xx Peas—Diseases and pests
  Example under Bacterial diseases of plants
Bacterial brown rot of potato
  See Bacterial wilt of potato
Bacterial cell walls
  sa L-form bacteria
  x Cell walls (Bacteria)
  xx Bacteria
Bacterial cultures
  See Bacteriology—Cultures and culture
    media
Bacterial diseases *(Indirect)* *(RC115)*
  sa Bacteremia
    Bacteria, Pathogenic

    Clostridium diseases
    Hemophilus diseases
    names of specific bacterial diseases, e.g.
      Anthrax, Botulism
  xx Bacteria, Pathogenic
    Communicable diseases
Bacterial diseases in animals
  See Veterinary bacteriology
Bacterial diseases of plants *(Indirect)*
    (SB734)
  sa Bacteria, Phytopathogenic
    names of specific diseases, e.g. Bacterial
      blight of peas; Potato ring rot
  xx Bacteria, Phytopathogenic
    Plant diseases
Bacterial genetics
  sa Episomes
    R factors
  x Bacteria—Genetics
  xx Bacteriology
    Microbial genetics
Bacterial gill disease
  x Gill disease, Bacterial
  xx Fishes—Diseases and pests
Bacterial growth
  sa Bacteriology—Cultures and culture
    media
  x Growth (Bacteria)
  xx Bacteria—Physiology
    Growth (Plants)
Bacterial physiology
  See Bacteria—Physiology
Bacterial pigments
  xx Pigments (Biology)
Bacterial resistance to antibiotics
  See Drug resistance in micro-organisms
Bacterial ring rot of potato
  See Potato ring rot
Bacterial shock
  See Septic shock
Bacterial soft rot of asparagus *(SB608.A8)*
  x Soft rot of asparagus, Bacterial
  xx Asparagus—Diseases and pests
Bacterial soft rot of red pepper
  x Soft rot of red pepper
  xx Peppers—Diseases and pests
Bacterial spores
  See Spores (Bacteria)
Bacterial synthesis
  See Microbiological synthesis
Bacterial transformation
  x Transformation, Bacterial
    Transformation (Genetics)
  xx Cell transformation
    Genetic recombination
    Genetic transformation
    Microbial genetics
Bacterial warfare
  See Biological warfare
Bacterial white diarrhea
  See Pullorum disease
Bacterial wilt of potato
  x Bacterial brown rot of potato
    Brown rot of potato
    Potato brown rot
Bacteriemia
  See Bacteremia
Bacteriocidal agents
  See Anti-infective agents
Bacteriocins *(QR92.B3)*
  xx Anti-infective agents
Bacteriological laboratories *(QR63-71)*
  sa Public health laboratories
  x Laboratories, Bacteriological
  xx Microbiological laboratories
    Public health laboratories
— Safety measures

Bacteriological warfare
  See Biological warfare
Bacteriologists
  xx Bacteriology as a profession
    Microbiologists
— Correspondence, reminiscences, etc.
Bacteriology *(QR)*
  Cf. note under Bacteria.
  sa Antiseptics
    Auto-intoxication
    Bacteremia
    Bacteria
    Bacterial genetics
    Bacteriolysis
    Biological products
    Disinfection and disinfectants
    Fermentation
    Germ theory of disease
    Immunity
    Medicine, Preventive
    Putrefaction
    Sewage—Purification
    Sewage—Purification—Biological
      treatment
    Staphylococcus
    Surgery, Aseptic and antiseptic
    Veterinary bacteriology
    subdivision Bacteriology *under*
      particular subjects, e.g. Water—
      Bacteriology
  x Germs
    Microbes
  xx Communicable diseases
    Fermentation
    Fungi
    Germ theory of disease
    Medicine
    Medicine, Preventive
    Microbiology
    Pathology
    Putrefaction
    Science
— Anecdotes, facetiae, satire, etc.
— Apparatus and supplies *(QR71)*
  sa Chemostat
— Atlases
— Catalogs and collections
— Classification *(QR81)*
— Cultures and culture media
  x Bacterial cultures
  xx Bacterial growth
  Example under Cultures (Biology)
— — Catalogs and collections
— Juvenile literature
  See Bacteria—Juvenile literature
— Laboratory manuals *(QR63)*
  sa Food—Bacteriology—Laboratory
    manuals
— Technique *(QR65-69)*
  sa Fermentation tube
    Micrurgy
    Sterilization
— Vocational guidance
  See Bacteriology as a profession
Bacteriology, Agricultural *(QR51; Bacteria in*
    soil, QR111; Bacteria of plant
    diseases, QR351)
  sa Bacteria, Denitrifying
    Bacteria, Nitrifying
    Bacteria, Phytopathogenic
    Cheese—Bacteriology
    Dairy bacteriology
    Dairying
    Milk—Bacteriology
    Nitrification
    Nitrogen—Fixation
    Soil inoculation
    Soils—Bacteriology

subdivision Diseases and pests *under names of crops, etc., e.g.* Fruit—Diseases and pests; Grain—Diseases and pests
  x Agricultural bacteriology
  xx Agricultural microbiology
    Dairy bacteriology
    Soils—Analysis
    Soils—Bacteriology
    Veterinary bacteriology
  — Technique
Bacteriology, Dental
  See Mouth—Bacteriology
Bacteriology, Medical *(QR46)*
  sa Bacteria, Pathogenic
    Diarrhea—Bacteriology
    Escherichia coli infections
  x Medical bacteriology
  xx Bacteria, Pathogenic
    Medical microbiology
  — Technique
Bacteriology, Oral
  See Mouth—Bacteriology
Bacteriology, Sanitary
  See Sanitary microbiology
Bacteriology, Veterinary
  See Veterinary bacteriology
Bacteriology as a profession
  sa Bacteriologists
  x Bacteriology—Vocational guidance
Bacteriolysis *(QR185)*
  sa Bacteriophage
  xx Bacteriology
    Bacteriophage
    Blood
    Serumtherapy
Bacteriophage
  sa Bacteriolysis
    Transduction
  x Bacteriophagy
  xx Bacteriolysis
    Viruses
  — Atlases
  — Experiments
  — Mathematical models
  — Spectra
Bacteriophage lambda *(QR185.B4)*
  xx Episomes
Bacteriophagy
  See Bacteriophage
Bacteriostatic agents
  See Anti-infective agents
Bactrian language (Old Bactrian)
  See Avesta language
Bacwa
  See Batwa
Bad faith (Jewish law)
Bad faith (Law) *(Direct)*
  sa Good faith (Law)
  x Mala fides
  xx Dolus (Civil law)
    Fraud
    Good faith (Law)
Badaga dialect *(PL4641-9)*
  sa Dravidian languages
  xx Dravidian languages
Badakhshani dialect
Badawiyah *(BP189.7.B3-32)*
  x Ahmadiyya (Sufism)
  xx Islamic sects
    Sufism
Badchanim
  See Badḥanim
Baden
  — History
  — — Revolution, 1848-1849
Baden, Treaty of, 1714 *(D283.5)*

Baden language
  See Kunama language
Badger-dogs, German
  See Dachshund
Badgers *(QL737.C2; Legends and stories, QL795.B2)*
  — Legends and stories
Badges *(Heraldry, CR67-69; Manufacture, TS761)*
  xx Heraldry
    Insignia
Badges of honor
  See Decorations of honor
    Insignia
    Medals
    subdivision Medals, badges, decorations, etc. *under armies, navies, etc., e.g.* United States. Navy—Medals, badges, decorations, etc.
Badḥanim *(GT2695.J4)*
  x Badchanim
  xx Fools and jesters
    Jewish poetry
    Marriage customs and rites, Jewish
Badiaranke language
  See Badyaranke language
Badminton (Game) *(GV1007)*
Badoej (Indonesian tribe)
  See Badui (Indonesian tribe)
Badoewi (Indonesian tribe)
  See Badui (Indonesian tribe)
Badr, Battle of, 624
Badschu dialect
  See Badzhuv dialect
Badui (Indonesian tribe)
  x Badoej (Indonesian tribe)
    Badoewi (Indonesian tribe)
    Badujs (Indonesian tribe)
    Baduwi (Indonesian tribe)
  xx Ethnology—Java
Badujs (Indonesian tribe)
  See Badui (Indonesian tribe)
Baduwi (Indonesian tribe)
  See Badui (Indonesian tribe)
Badyara language
  See Badyaranke language
Badyaranké (African people)
  xx Ethnology—Guinea
    Ethnology—Guinea, Portuguese
    Ethnology—Senegal
Badyaranke language
  x Badiaranke language
    Badyara language
    Pajade language
    Pajadinca language
Badzhuv dialect *(PK6996.B)*
  x Badschu dialect
    Badžŭ dialect
    Bajui dialect
  xx Pamir languages
Badžŭ dialect
  See Badzhuv dialect
Baegu (Melanesian people)
  xx Ethnology—Solomon Islands
    Melanesians
Bael (Tree)
  x Bel (Tree)
    Bengal quince
    Bilva
Bafia (African tribe) *(DT570)*
  xx Bantus
Bafia language *(PL8047.5.B4)*
  x Kpa language
  xx Bantu languages
Bag punching *(GV1139)*
  xx Athletics
    Boxing

Bagaduce Expedition, 1779
  See Penobscot Expedition, 1779
Baganda
  x Ganda
    Waganda
  xx Bantus
Bagasse
  sa Newsprint
  xx Paper making and trade
    Sugar-cane
    Sugar—Manufacture and refining—By-products
Bagatelle *(GV1469.B)*
Bagdad pact, 1955
Bagelli tribe
  sa Negrillos
  xx Negrillos
    Pygmies
Bagesu
  See Gisu (Bantu tribe)
Baggage
  See Luggage
Baggage, Railroad
  See Railroads—Baggage
Baggara (African tribe) *(DT132)*
  xx Ethnology—Sudan
Bagging
  x Bags
    Cotton bagging
  xx Containers
    Cotton trade
    Jute
Bagirmi language
  x Barma language
  xx Bongo-Bagirmi languages
Bagishu
  See Gisu (Bantu tribe)
Baĝlama
  xx Lute
    Mandolin
Bagobo language *(PL5551-4)*
  xx Philippine languages
Bagobo tribe
Bagpipe *(ML980)*
  sa Duda
    Gaita
  x Cornemuse
    Musette
  xx Music—Scotland
Bagpipe and drum music *(M298)*
  x Drum and bagpipe music
  xx Bagpipe music
    Percussion music
Bagpipe music *(M145)*
  sa Bagpipe and drum music
    Pipe music
    Trios (Harpsichord, bagpipe, hurdy-gurdy)
    Trios (Harpsichord, bagpipes (2))
    Variations (Bagpipe)
  xx Pipe music
Bagpipe music (Bagpipes (2)) *(M288-9)*
  sa Suites (Bagpipes (2))
Bags
  See Bagging
    Paper bags
Baguhas
  See Baholoholo
Baha'i Faith
  See Bahaism
Bahai youth
  See Youth, Bahai
Bahaism *(Indirect)* *(BP300-395)*
  sa Babism
  x Baha'i Faith
  xx Babism
    Religions
    Shiites

Bahaism *(Indirect)* *(BP300-395)*
  (Continued)
  — Doctrinal and controversial works
  — Government
    Note under Polity (Religion)
  — Juvenile literature
  — Relations
  — — Buddhism, ₍Christianity, Islam, etc.₎
Bahama grass
  See Bermuda grass
Bahamas
  — Hurricane, 1866
Bahamians in Virginia, ₍etc.₎
Bahanga
  See Wanga (Bantu tribe)
Bahasa Indonesia
  See Indonesian language
Bahaya
  See Haya (African tribe)
Bahemba (Bantu people)
    x Baluba-Hemba (Bantu people)
    Hemba (Bantu people)
    Muhemba (Bantu people)
    Muluba-Hemba (Bantu people)
    xx Bantus
    Ethnology—Zaire
Bahera
  See Belleric myrobalan
Bahia, Brazil (City)
  — Capture by the Spaniards, 1625
Bahima (African people)
    sa Banyankole
    Banyoro
    x Bahuma
    Hima
    Huma
    Wahima
Bahinemo language
    xx Papuan languages
Bahing dialect *(PL3801.B2)*
    xx Tibeto-Burman languages
Bahnar language *(PL4311-4314)*
    sa Mon-Khmer languages
    x Banar language
    xx Mon-Khmer languages
Bahnar law
  See Law, Bahnar
Baholoholo
    x Baguhas
    xx Ethnology—Zaire
Bahuma
  See Bahima (African people)
Bahusi (African tribe)
  See Ushi (African tribe)
Bahutu
    x Hutu
    xx Ethnology—Ruanda-Urundi
Baia (African tribe)
  See Baya (African tribe)
Baigas *(DS432)*
    x Bhumia Baigas
    Bygas
    xx Bhuiyas
    Mundas
Bail *(Direct)*
    x Bail jumping
    Bonding (Bail)
    Jumping bail
    xx Arrest
    Criminal justice, Administration of
    Criminal procedure
    Security (Law)
    Suretyship and guaranty
Bail (Roman law)
Bail jumping
  See Bail
Bailecito (Dance) *(GV1796.B25)*
Bailén, Battle of, 1808 *(DC233.B3)*
    x Baylen, Battle of, 1808

  xx Peninsular War, 1807-1814
Bailey bridges
  See Bridges, Prefabricated
Bailiffs *(Direct)* *(HV7983)*
    xx Courts—Officials and employees
  — Fees
    xx Costs (Law)
Bailiffs (Baillis)
  See Baillis
Baillis *(Direct)*
    x Bailiffs (Baillis)
Bailments *(Direct)* *(United States, HF1249)*
    sa Aestimatum
    Auctions
    Carriers
    Deposits (Law)
    Freight forwarders
    Hire
    Hotels, taverns, etc.—Law
    Liens
    Loans for use
    Mandate (Contract)
    Pawnbroking
    Pledges (Law)
    Possession (Law)
    Precarium
    Safe-deposit companies
    xx Agency (Law)
    Carriers
    Commercial law
    Contracts
    Deposits (Law)
    Pawnbroking
    Personal property
    Pledges (Law)
    Possession (Law)
Bailments (Hindu law)
Bailments (Jewish law)
Bailments (Roman law)
Bairam
  See 'Īd al-Fiṭr
Bairo (African people)
    sa Banyankole
    Banyoro
Bait *(SH448)*
    sa Fishing lures
    xx Fishing
Bait-casting *(SH459)*
    x Plug casting
    xx Casting (Fishing)
Baja (African tribe)
  See Baya (African tribe)
Bajau (Malay people)
    xx Ethnology—Malay Archipelago
Bajri tribe
  See Baseri tribe
Bajui dialect
  See Badzhuv dialect
Bajun (African people)
    xx Ethnology—Kenya
  — Juvenile literature
Bakairi Indians *(F2520.1.B)*
    xx Carib Indians
    Indians of South America
Bakairi language *(PM5581)*
    sa Cariban languages
    xx Cariban languages
    Indians of South America—Languages
Bakalahadi
  See Kgalagadi (African people)
Bakas (African tribe)
    xx Pygmies
Bakatla
  See Kgatla (African tribe)
Baked products
    sa Hot dog rolls
    specific baked products, e.g. Bread,
      Cake, Cookies

    x Bakery products
    xx Bakers and bakeries
    Baking
  — Packaging
  — Patents
  — Preservation
  — Quality control
  — Standards *(Direct)*
  — Transportation
Baked products, Frozen
    x Frozen baked products
    xx Food, Frozen
Bakele language
  See Kele language
Bakelite
  Example under Plastics
Baker-Nunn camera
    xx Artificial satellites—Optical
      observations
Bakers and bakeries *(Direct)* *(TX761-778;*
      Bakers, HD8039.B2; Industry,
      HD9057)
    sa Baked products
    Bakery employees
    xx Food processing plants
  — Automation
  — Costs
  — Employees
    See Bakery employees
  — Equipment and supplies
  — — Patents
  — Hygienic aspects
  — Juvenile literature
  — Labor productivity
  — Law and legislation   *(Direct)*
  — Safety measures
  — Vocational guidance
    See Baking—Vocational guidance
Bakery employees *(Direct)*
    sa Trade-unions—Bakery employees
    Wages—Bakery employees
    x Bakers and bakeries—Employees
    Bakery workers
    xx Bakers and bakeries
Bakery products
  See Baked products
Bakery workers
  See Bakery employees
Bakgalagadi
  See Kgalagadi (African people)
Bakgatla
  See Kgatla (African tribe)
Bakhatla
  See Kgatla (African tribe)
Bakhtiari *(DS269.B3)*
Bakhtiari dialect
Baking *(TX761-778)*
    sa Baked products
    Bread
    Cake
    Dough
    Muffins
    Pastry
    Pizza
    Soufflés
    xx Bread
    Cookery
  — Competitions
  — Juvenile literature
  — Tables, calculations, etc.
  — Vocational guidance
    x Bakers and bakeries—Vocational
      guidance
Baking-powder *(TX409; HD9330)*
Bakitara
  See Banyoro
Bakiue
  See Batwa

BAKO (Computer program)
Bakoko (African tribe) *(DT570)*
  xx Bantus
Bakongo (African tribe)
  x Fjort (African tribe)
  xx Bantus
    Ethnology—Zaire
Bakossi (Bantu people)
  x Kossi (Bantu people)
    Nkosi (Bantu people)
  xx Bantus
    Ethnology—Cameroon
Bakota
  See Kota (African tribe)
Bakuba (Bantu tribe)
  See Kuba (Bantu tribe)
Bakuba language
  See Bushongo language
Bakundu language
  x Kundu language
    Lokundu language
  xx Bantu languages
Bakwa
  See Batwa
Bakwedi
  See Bakwiri (African people)
Bakweri
  See Bakwiri (African people)
Bakwileh
  See Bakwiri (African people)
Bakwili
  See Bakwiri (African people)
Bakwiri (African people)
  x Baakpe
    Bakwedi
    Bakweri
    Bakwileh
    Bakwili
    Kpe
    Kweli
    Kwili
    Kwiri
    Mokpe
  xx Bantus
    Ethnology—Cameroons
Balaenoptera
  See Whales
Balahis *(DS485.C6)*
  xx Caste—India
    Ethnology—India—Madhya Pradesh
Balaic language
  See Palaic language
Balaklava, Battle of, 1854 *(DK215.3)*
  x Charge of the Light Brigade
    Light Brigade, Charge of the
  xx Crimean War, 1853-1856
Balala
  See Kgalagadi (African people)
Balalaika *(M1015-1018)*
  sa Domra
    Tambura
  xx Guitar
Balalaika and piano music *(M282-3)*
  sa Sonatas (Balalaika and piano)
    Suites (Balalaika and piano)
    Waltzes (Balalaika and piano)
  x Piano and balalaika music
Balalaika music *(M142.B2)*
  sa Balalaika with chamber orchestra
    Concertos (Balalaika with chamber
      orchestra)
    Domra music
    Trios (Balalaika, guitar, mandolin)
Balalaika with chamber orchestra
    (M1037.4.B3)
  sa Concertos (Balalaika with chamber
    orchestra)
  xx Balalaika music

Chamber-orchestra music
  Concertos (Balalaika with chamber
    orchestra)
Balalaika with chamber orchestra, Arranged
    (M1037.4.B3)
Balali language
  See Teke language
Balamba
  See Lambas
Balambu language
  See Barambu language
Balance *(Weights and measures, QC107)*
  sa Current balance (Electric meter)
    Magnetic balance
    Microbalance
    Thermobalance
    Wind tunnel balances
  xx Mechanics
    Weighing-machines
    Weights and measures
  — Juvenile literature
Balance, Water (Hydrology)
  See Water balance (Hydrology)
Balance (Art)
  See Proportion (Art)
Balance (in religion, folk-lore, etc.)
  x Folk-lore of the balance
    Symbolism of the balance
  xx Religion, Primitive
Balance (Physiology)
  See Equilibrium (Physiology)
Balance beam
  x Beam, Balance
  xx Gymnastics
Balance bridges
  See Balance cocks
Balance cocks *(Art, NK7502)*
  x Balance bridges
  xx Clocks and watches
Balance of nature
  See Ecology
Balance of payments *(Direct)*
  sa Balance of trade
    International clearing
    International liquidity
  x International payments, Balance of
  xx Balance of trade
    Foreign exchange
    International economic relations
    International finance
    International liquidity
  — Graphic methods
  — Mathematical models
  — Underdeveloped areas
    See Underdeveloped areas—Balance
      of payments
Balance of power *(D217; International law,*
    JX1318)
  sa Baltic Entente, 1934-
    Great powers
    Little Entente, 1920-1939
  x Power, Balance of
    Power politics
  xx International relations
Balance of trade *(Direct)* *(HF1014)*
  sa Balance of payments
    Mercantile system
    Payment
  x Trade, Balance of
  xx Balance of payments
    Commerce
    Economics
    Exchange
    Free trade and protection
    Mercantile system
    Payment
    Tariff

Balance sheets
  See Financial statements
Balancing (Gymnastics)
  See Acrobats and acrobatism
Balancing-machines
  See Balancing of machinery
Balancing of assembly-lines
  See Assembly-line balancing
Balancing of machinery *(TJ153)*
  x Balancing-machines
    Machinery—Balancing
    Machines, Balancing of
  xx Machinery
Balangao language
  xx Philippine languages
Balante language
  x Balāt language
    Bulanda language
    Fca language
Balantidium coli *(RC122.B3)*
Balāt language
  See Balante language
Balata
  xx Rubber
    Rubber plants
Balbis *(QA482)*
  xx Geometry, Plane
Balconies *(NA3070)*
  xx Architecture—Details
Balcony gardening *(SB419.5)*
  sa Roof gardening
    Window-gardening
  xx Gardening
    Roof gardening
Bald eagle
  x American eagle
  xx Eagles
  — Juvenile literature
  — Legends and stories
Bald Mountains, N.C. and Tenn., in art
Baldness *(RL91)*
  sa Scalp—Aging
  x Alopecia
  xx Hair—Diseases
    Scalp—Aging
    Scalp—Diseases
Baldwin locomotives *(TJ625.B2-45)*
  xx Locomotives
Baldwin organ *(ML579)*
  x Orga-sonic organ
  xx Electronic organ
Baleen
  See Whalebone
Balega language
  See Kilega language
Baleggas
  See Waregas
Balese (African tribe) *(DT650)*
  x Balissi (African tribe)
    Walese (African tribe)
  xx Ethnology—Zaire
    Mamvu (African tribe)
Balese language *(PL8048)*
  x Lese language
Balfour declaration
  xx Zionism
BALGOL (Computer program language)
  x Algorithmic language
    Burroughs 220 dialect of ALGOL
    Symbolic language
  xx ALGOL (Computer program language)
Balinese ballads and songs *(Direct)*
Balinese drama *(PL5221)*
Balinese language *(PL5221-4)*
  sa Malayan languages
  xx Javanese language
    Malayan languages
Balinese literature *(PL5224)*

Balinese philology
Balinese poetry *(Direct)*
Baling
  sa Cotton baling
    Wool baling
  xx Packing for shipment
Baling hoops
  x Hoops, Baling
  xx Packing for shipment
  — Safety measures
Baling of cotton
  See Cotton baling
Baling of wool
  See Wool baling
Balissi (African tribe)
  See Balese (African tribe)
Balkan Entente, 1934-
  sa Athens, Treaty of, 1934
  xx Athens, Treaty of, 1934
    Eastern question (Balkan)
Balkan League
Balkan literatures
  See Balkan Peninsula—Literatures
Balkan Peninsula
  — History
  —— 20th century
  —— War of 1912-1913 *(DR46)*
    sa Bitola, Battle of, 1912
      Bregalnica, Battle of, 1913
      Bucharest, Treaty of, 1913
      Edirne, Turkey (City)—Siege,
        1912-1913
      Ioánnina, Greece—Siege,
        1912-1913
      Scutari, Albania—Siege,
        1912-1913
    x Turco-Balkan War, 1912-1913
    xx Eastern question (Balkan)
      Serbia—History—1804-1918
  ——— Aerial operations
  ——— Atrocities
  ——— Medical and sanitary affairs
  ——— Regimental histories *(Indirect)*
      Further subdivision by division,
        regiment, etc.
  ——— Territorial questions *(Direct)*
  ——— Women's work
  — Literatures
    sa Albanian literature
      Bulgarian literature
      Greek literature
      Romanian literature
      Turkish literature
      Yugoslav literature
    x Balkan literatures
Balkan pine *(SD397.P565)*
Balkan question
  See Eastern question (Balkan)
Balkan studies *(Direct)*
Balkar language *(PL65.B2)*
  xx Caucasian languages
    Turko-Tataric languages
Balkar literature *(Direct)*
Balkar poetry *(Direct)*
Balkarians *(DK34.B)*
  xx Ethnology—Caucasus
Ball-bearing screws *(TJ1338)*
  xx Screws
Ball-bearings *(TJ1071-3)*
  sa Roller bearings
  xx Bearings (Machinery)
    Roller bearings
  — Standards
  — Testing
Ball games *(Direct)* *(GV861)*
  sa Bowling games
    names of individual games, e.g. Baseball
  xx Games

    Sports
  — Juvenile literature
Ball lightning
  xx Lightning
Ball mills
  xx Milling machinery
  — Automation
Ball-point pens
  xx Pens
Ball room dancing
  See Ballroom dancing
Ball valves
  xx Valves
Ballad opera *(History, ML1950)*
  sa Singspiel
  x Dramatic music
    Music, Dramatic
    Music, Theatrical
    Theatrical music
  xx Ballads, English
    English ballads and songs
    English drama
    English drama (Comedy)
    Musical form
    Opera, English
    Singspiel
Ballad operas *(M1500-1503.5)*
  Subdivided in the same manner as the
    heading Operas.
  xx Operas
Ballad-sheets
  See Broadsides
Ballade *(History and criticism, PN1471)*
Note under Ballades
Ballades *(English literature, PR1194)*
  Here are entered collections of ballades.
    Works on the literary form are entered
    under the heading Ballade.
  xx Poetry
Ballads *(Indirect)* *(History and criticism,*
  PN1376; Music, M1627; Music
  literature, ML3545)
  Includes general works on ballads, com-
    prehensive collections, etc.
  The following distinction is made in the
    entry of works limited to a particular
    country or nationality: 1. For general
    works or for works dealing only with
    the literary aspect of the subject and
    for collections of ballads which contain
    the words but not the music, the head-
    ings English ballads and songs, French
    ballads and songs, etc., are used. 2.
    Works treating chiefly of the musical
    side and collections including both
    words and music take the headings
    Ballads, English; Ballads, French; etc.
  sa Folk-songs
    Political ballads and songs
  xx Folk-songs
    Poetry
    Songs
    Vocal music
  — [country subdivision]
    Here are entered collections of ballads
    of various national and ethnic ori-
    gins which are sung in a particular
    country. References are made to
    and from Ballads with national
    qualification, *e.g.* Ballads—United
    States *see also* Ballads, American;
    Ballads, American *see also* Ballads
    —United States. Additional spe-
    cific references as shown under the
    following headings are made when
    needed.
  — Adirondack Mountains

    See Ballads, American—Adirondack
      Mountains
  — Newfoundland
    sa Ballads, Canadian—Newfoundland
  — United States
    Note under Ballads—[country subdivi-
      sion]
Ballads, American
Note under Ballads—[country subdivision]
  — Adirondack Mountains
    x Ballads—Adirondack Mountains
Ballads, American, [English, French, etc.]
  Subdivided by locality. The references in-
    dicated here are general in application.
    Exceptions to this pattern and exam-
    ples of additional references required
    in specific cases are shown under the
    headings below.
  sa Folk-songs, American, [English,
    French, etc.]
    Political ballads and songs, American,
    [English, French, etc.]
  xx American [English, French, etc.]
    ballads and songs
    Folk-songs, American, [English,
    French, etc.]
    Songs, American, [English, French,
    etc.]
Ballads, American, [English, French, etc.]
  (Instrumental settings)
Ballads, Canadian
  — Newfoundland
    xx Ballads—Newfoundland
Ballads, English
  sa Ballad opera
  Notes under Ballads; English ballads and songs
Ballads, French
Note under Ballads
Ballast (Railroads)
  xx Railroads—Track
Ballast (Ships) *(VK237)*
  sa Ships—Cargo
  xx Navigation
    Ships—Cargo
Ballasts (Electricity)
  xx Electric controllers
    Electric resistors
Balle au tamis (Game)
  x Tamis (Ball game)
Ballet *(Dancing, GV1787; Music, ML3460)*
  Here are entered works on the ballet. Bal-
    let scores are entered under the head-
    ing Ballets.
  sa Choreography
    Pantomime
  xx Choreography
    Dancing
    Drama
    Opera
    Pantomime
  Example under Performing arts
  — Anecdotes, facetiae, satire, etc.
    (GV1795)
  — Costume *(GT1740-1745)*
  — Juvenile films
  — Juvenile literature *(GV1787.5)*
  — Pictorial works
  — Production and direction
    See Dance production
  — Stage-setting and scenery
    x Scenery (Stage)
    Stage scenery
    Stage-setting
  — Study and teaching
    sa Ballet dancing
  — Terminology
Ballet, Water
  See Synchronized swimming

Ballet dance music
    Here are entered works intended for use with ballet dance instruction. Ballet scores are entered under Ballets.
    xx Ballets
        Dance music
Ballet dancers
    See Dancers
Ballet dancing *(GV1788)*
    x Dancing, Ballet
        Toe dancing
    xx Ballet—Study and teaching
    — Accidents and injuries
        x Ballet dancing—Injuries
    — Examinations
    — Injuries
        See Ballet dancing—Accidents and injuries
    — Juvenile literature
Ballet festivals
    See Dance festivals
Ballet in art
    xx Art
        Dancing in art
Ballet in moving-pictures, television, etc. *(GV1779)*
    x Ballet in television
    xx Dancing in moving-pictures, television, etc.
        Moving-pictures
        Television
Ballet in television
    See Ballet in moving-pictures, television, etc.
Ballet production
    See Dance production
Ballets *(Instrumental, M33, M208; Vocal, M1520-1526)*
    Cf. notes under Ballet; Operas.
    sa Ballet dance music
        Pantomimes with music
    xx Pantomimes with music
    Note under Ballet dance music
    — Excerpts
        sa Overtures
        — — Scores *(M1524-5)*
            x Ballets—Scores—Excerpts
        — — Scores (reduced) and parts *(M1524)*
            x Ballets—Scores (reduced) and parts—Excerpts
    — Piano scores *(M1523)*
    — Scores *(M1520)*
    — — Excerpts
        See Ballets—Excerpts—Scores
    — Scores (reduced) and parts *(M1520)*
    — — Excerpts
        See Ballets—Excerpts—Scores (reduced) and parts
    — Stories, plots, etc. *(MT95-100)*
        xx Plots (Drama, novel, etc.)
    — — Juvenile literature
Ballets arranged for flute and piano *(M243-4)*
    xx Flute and piano music, Arranged
Ballets arranged for piano (4 hands) *(M208)*
    xx Piano music (4 hands), Arranged
Ballets arranged for piano (Pianos (2)) *(M1523)*
    xx Piano music (Pianos (2)), Arranged
Ballista *(U875)*
    xx Catapult
Ballistic instruments *(UF830-857)*
    x Instruments, Ballistic
Ballistic missile early warning system *(Direct)*
    x BMEWS
        Early warning systems
    xx Air defenses, Military

Ballistic missiles
    Radar defense networks
Ballistic missile guidance systems
    See Ballistic missiles—Guidance systems
Ballistic missile re-entry
    See Ballistic missiles—Atmospheric entry
Ballistic missiles
    Here are entered works on high-altitude, high-speed atomic missiles which are self-propelled and guided in the first stage of flight only, after which the trajectory becomes natural and uncontrolled. Works on conventional missiles are entered under Projectiles. Works on powered and guided missiles are entered under Rockets (Ordnance) and Guided missiles.
    sa Ballistic missile early warning system
        Fleet ballistic missile weapons systems
        Intercontinental ballistic missiles
        Intermediate-range ballistic missiles
        names of specific missiles, e.g. Corporal (Missile)
    xx Atomic weapons
        Guided missiles
        Rocketry
        Rockets (Aeronautics)
        United States. Air Force—Weapons systems
    — Atmospheric entry
        x Atmospheric re-entry (from space)
            Ballistic missile re-entry
            Re-entry aerodynamics
            Re-entry problems (Astronautics)
            Re-entry trajectories
        xx Aerodynamic heating
            Aerodynamics
            Aerothermodynamics
            Astronautics
            Space trajectories
    — Design and construction
    — Guidance systems
        x Ballistic missile guidance systems
        Example under Astronautical instruments
    — — Testing
    — Juvenile literature
Ballistic photography
    See Photography, Ballistic
Ballistic ranges *(TL567.B33)*
    sa Hypervelocity guns
        Shock tubes
    x Ranges, Ballistic
    xx Aerodynamics
        Wind tunnels
Ballistic tables
    See Ballistics—Tables, calculations, etc.
Ballistics *(UF820-840)*
    sa Gunnery
        Meteorology in rocketry
        Ordnance
        Projectiles
        Shooting, Military
        headings beginning with the word Ballistic
    xx Gunnery
        Naval gunnery
        Ordnance
        Projectiles
        Shooting, Military
    — Early works to 1800
    — Tables, calculations, etc. *(UF820; VF550)*
        x Ballistic tables
Ballistics, Exterior
    x Exterior ballistics
Ballistics, Forensic
    See Forensic ballistics

Ballistics, Interior
    x Interior ballistics
Ballistocardiography
    xx Heart—Diseases—Diagnosis
Balloon ascensions *(TL620)*
    xx Aeronautics
        Balloons
    — Juvenile literature
    — Law and legislation *(Direct)*
    — Poetry
        See Aeronautics—Poetry
Balloon fabrics
    See Balloons—Materials
Balloon gases *(TL666)*
    x Air-ship gases
    xx Gases
Balloon photography
    See Photography, Aerial
Balloon races
    See Balloon racing
Balloon racing *(GV763)*
    x Balloon races
    xx Aeronautical sports
        Aeronautics—Competitions
Balloon tracking
    See Balloons—Tracking
Balloons *(TL609-639)*
    sa Aeronautics
        Air-ships
        Balloon ascensions
        Expandable space structures
    x Military balloons
    xx Aeronautics
        Air-ships
        Expandable space structures
    — History
    — — Juvenile literature
    — Juvenile literature
    — Materials *(TL665; TL699)*
        x Balloon fabrics
    — Pictorial works
    — Poetry
        See Aeronautics—Poetry
    — Scientific applications
    — Tracking
        x Balloon tracking
            Flight tracking
            Tracking
Balloons, Captive *(TL634-7)*
    sa Balloons, Kite
    x Captive balloons
Balloons, Dirigible
    See Air-ships
Balloons, Kite *(TL635)*
    x Kite balloons
    xx Balloons, Captive
        Kites
Balloons, Pilot
    x Pilot balloons
    xx Aeronautics in meteorology
        Atmosphere, Upper
Balloons, Sounding *(TL631)*
    sa Radiosondes
    x Sounding balloons
    xx Aeronautics in meteorology
Balloons in art
    xx Art
Balloons in astronomy *(QB137)*
    xx Aeronautics in astronomy
Ballot *(JF1091-1177; United States, JK2215-2217)*
    sa Australian ballot
        Coupon ballot
        Voting-machines
    x Short ballot
    xx Elections
        Plebiscite
        Politics, Practical

Ballot *(JF1091-1177; United States, JK2215-2217) (Continued)*
    Representative government and representation
    Secrecy (Law)
    Suffrage
    Voting
Ballot, Australian
  See Australian ballot
Ballot, Coupon
  See Coupon ballot
Ballot, Preferential
  See Preferential ballot
Ballot-box *(United States, JK2217)*
  xx Elections
    Voting-machines
Ballots Project *(Z699.4.B17)*
  x Bibliographic Automation of Large Library Operations Using a Time-sharing System
    Project Ballots
  xx Information storage and retrieval systems
    Libraries—Automation
Ballroom dancing *(GV1751)*
  x Ball room dancing
    Social dancing
  xx Dancing
Balls, Decorative
  See Decorative balls
Balls (Parties) *(GV1746-1750; GV1757)*
  Here are entered works dealing with formal dances. Works concerned with less formal dances are entered under Dance parties.
  sa Dance parties
    Dancing
  x Dances
  xx Amusements
    Dance parties
    Dancing
    Entertaining
  Note under Dance parties
Balls (Sporting goods)
  sa Baseballs
    Footballs
    Golf balls
    Tennis balls
  xx Sporting goods
  — Juvenile literature
Ball's Bluff, Battle of, 1861 *(E472.63)*
Balneology *(RM819-822)*
  x Balneotherapy
  xx Mineral waters
    Physical therapy
Balneotherapy
  See Balneology
Balobedu
  See Lobedu
Baloch
  See Baluchis
Balochi language
  See Baluchi language
Balolo (Bantu tribe)
  See Mongo (Bantu tribe)
Balovale
  See Luvale (Bantu tribe)
Balsa craft
  See Balsa wood craft
Balsa wood
  x Balza wood
    Corkwood
  — Testing
Balsa wood craft *(Direct) (TT189)*
  x Balsa craft
  xx Handicraft
    Woodwork
  — Juvenile literature

Balsam fir
  xx Fir
  — Diseases and pests
Balsams
Baltic Entente, 1934- *(DK511.B3)*
  x Entente, Baltic, 1934-
    Little Baltic Union
    Little Union of the Baltic States
  xx Balance of power
Baltic hemp
  See Flax
Baltic languages
  sa Balto-Slavic linguistic unity
    Latvian language
    Lithuanian language
    Prussian language
  x Balto-Slavic languages
  xx Aryan languages
Baltic literature *(Direct)*
Baltic philology
  sa Balto-Slavic linguistic unity
  x Balto-Slavic philology
Baltic question
  See Baltic States
Baltic Sea
  — Sea level
    See Sea level—Baltic Sea
Baltic Sea region in literature
Baltic States
  x Baltic question
  — Annexation to Russia
    Example under Annexation (International law)
  — History
  — — German occupation, 1941-1944
    xx World War, 1939-1945—Baltic States
Baltic studies *(Direct)*
Baltimore
  — Directories
  — — Telephone
    Note under Telephone—Directories
  — Fire, 1904
  — Historic houses, etc.
    Example under Historic houses, etc.
  — Poor
    Example under Charities
Baltimore, Battle of, 1814 *(E356.B2)*
  sa North Point, Battle of, 1814
  x Fort McHenry, Md., Bombardment of
Baltimore oriole
  xx Orioles
Balto-Finnish languages
  See Finnish languages
Balto-Slavic languages
  See Baltic languages
    Balto-Slavic linguistic unity
    Slavic languages
Balto-Slavic linguistic unity
  x Balto-Slavic languages
  xx Baltic languages
    Baltic philology
    Slavic languages
    Slavic philology
Balto-Slavic philology
  See Baltic philology
    Slavic philology
Baluba-Hemba (Bantu people)
  See Bahemba (Bantu people)
Baluchi fiction *(Direct)*
Baluchi language *(PK6851-9)*
  sa Iranian languages
  x Balochi language
    Beloutchi language
    Biluchi language
  xx Iranian languages
Baluchi literature *(Direct) (PK6858)*
  xx Pakistan literature

Baluchi philology
Baluchi poetry *(Collections, PK6858.6; History, PK6858.2)*
Baluchis
  x Baloch
Baluyia (Bantu tribe)
  x Abaluyia (Bantu tribe)
  xx Bantus
    Ethnology—Kenya
    Ethnology—Uganda
Balza wood
  See Balsa wood
BAM P14 (Electronic computer system)
Bamana language
  See Bambara language
Bamangwato
  sa Missions to Bamangwato
  xx Bantus
Bamba (African people)
  See Mbete (African people)
Bamba language
  See Mbete language
Bambara language *(PL8049.B3)*
  sa Mandingo language
  x Bamana language
  xx Mande languages
    Mandingo language
Bambara tribe
Bambatana language
  x Babatana language
    Bumbatana language
  xx Melanesian languages
Bambatha Rebellion, 1906
  See Zulu Rebellion, 1906
Bambete (African people)
  See Mbete (African people)
Bamboo *(Indirect) (SB317.B2)*
  — Varieties
Bamboo in art
  xx Art
Bamboo pipe
  See Pipe (Musical instrument)
Bamboo-pulp industry *(Direct)*
  xx Wood-pulp industry
Bamboo work *(Direct)*
  xx Woodwork
Bambunda (Bantu tribe)
  See Babunda (Bantu tribe)
Bambute
  sa Negrillos
  x Ituri forest pygmies
    Mambuti
    Mbuti
    Wambouti
  xx Ethnology—Zaire
    Negrillos
    Pygmies
  — Juvenile literature
Bamileke (African people)
  sa Bangwa (African people)
  xx Bangwa (African people)
    Ethnology—East Cameroon
Bamongo
  See Mongo language
Bamoun (African tribe)
  See Bamun (African tribe)
Bamu River language
  xx Kiwai languages
Bamum (African tribe)
  See Bamun (African tribe)
Bamun (African tribe) *(DT570)*
  x Bamoun (African tribe)
    Bamum (African tribe)
  xx Ethnology—Cameroons
Bamun language *(PL8050)*
Banabans (Oceanian people)
  xx Ethnology—Ocean Island
    Ethnology—Rambi Island, Fiji Islands

Banach algebras *(QA326)*
  sa C*-algebras
      Function algebras
      Harmonic analysis
      Von Neumann algebras
  x Algebras, Banach
      Banach rings
      Metric rings
      Normed rings
  xx Banach spaces
      Topological algebras
Banach rings
  See Banach algebras
Banach spaces
  sa Banach algebras
      Hilbert space
      Normed linear spaces
  xx Functions of complex variables
      Spaces, Generalized
      Topology
Banality (Law) *(Direct)*
  x Droit de banalité
  xx Feudal law
      Licenses
      Monopolies
Banality (Philosophy)
  xx Naturalism
      Philosophy
      Realism
Banana *(Indirect) (Botany, QK495.M98; Culture, SB379.B2)*
  sa Cookery (Bananas)
      Plantain banana
  Example under Tropical fruit
  — Diseases and pests *(SB608.B16)*
      sa Banana black-end disease
          Banana root borer
          Banana wilt
  — Juvenile literature
  — Packaging
  — Research
      See Banana research
  — Storage
  — Terminology
  — Varieties
Banana black-end disease *(SB608.B16)*
  xx Banana—Diseases and pests
Banana fish
  See Bonefish
Banana flour
  xx Flour
Banana research
  x Banana—Research
  xx Horticultural research
      Research
Banana root borer
  x Banana weevil borer
  xx Banana—Diseases and pests
Banana trade *(Direct)*
  — Law and legislation *(Direct)*
Banana weevil borer
  See Banana root borer
Banana wilt
  x Panama disease
  xx Banana—Diseases and pests
Banar language
  See Bahnar language
Banaro tribe
Banat
  — History
  — — Revolution, 1848-1849
Band music *(M1200-1268)*
  Cf. note under Orchestral music.
  sa Bassoon, clarinet, flute, horn, oboe with
          band
      Bassoon with band
      Boleros (Band)
      Canons, fugues, etc. (Band)

Chorale preludes (Band)
Clarinet with band
Concertos (Band)
Concertos (Bassoon, clarinet, flute,
    horn, oboe with band)
Concertos (Bassoon with band)
Concertos (Clarinet with band)
Concertos (Cornet with band)
Concertos (Cornets (4) with band)
Concertos (Double bass with band)
Concertos (Flute with band)
Concertos (Flutes (3) with band)
Concertos (Flutes (4) with band)
Concertos (Horn with band)
Concertos (Horns (3) with band)
Concertos (Horns (4) with band)
Concertos (Oboe with band)
Concertos (Organ with band)
Concertos (Percussion with band)
Concertos (Piano with band)
Concertos (Saxophone with band)
Concertos (String quartet with band)
Concertos (Trombone and trumpet with
    band)
Concertos (Trombone with band)
Concertos (Trombones (3) with band)
Concertos (Trombones (4) with band)
Concertos (Trumpet with band)
Concertos (Trumpets (3) with band)
Concertos (Tuba with band)
Concertos (Viola and piano with band)
Concertos (Violin with band)
Concertos (Violoncello with band)
Cornet with band
Cornets (4) with band
Country-dances (Band)
Czardas (Band)
Dance-orchestra music
Double bass with band
Fanfares
Flute with band
Flutes (3) with band
Flutes (4) with band
Fox trots (Band)
Galops (Band)
Gavottes (Band)
Horn with band
Marches (Band)
Merengues (Band)
Military music
Minuets (Band)
Monologues with music (Band)
Oboe with band
Orchestral music
Organ with band
Overtures (Band)
Pasodobles (Band)
Passacaglias (Band)
Pavans (Band)
Percussion with band
Piano with band
Polkas (Band)
Polonaises (Band)
Potpourris (Band)
Rondos (Band)
Rumbas (Band)
Sambas (Band)
Sarabands (Band)
Saxophone with band
String quartet with band
Suites (Band)
Symphonic poems (Band)
Symphonies (Band)
Tangos (Band)
Trombone and trumpet with band
Trombone with band
Trombones (3) with band
Trombones (4) with band

Trumpet and drum with band
Trumpet with band
Trumpets (3) with band
Tuba with band
Variations (Band)
Viola and piano with band
Viola with band
Violin with band
Violoncello with band
Waltzes (Band)
Wind ensembles
Wind quartets (Horns (4)) with band
Wind trios (Horns (3)) with band
  x Brass band music
  xx Instrumental music
      Military music
      Orchestral music
  — Analysis, appreciation *(MT125; MT130)*
Band music, Arranged
  sa Concerti grossi arranged for band
Band music, Juvenile *(M1420)*
  x School-orchestra music
Band saws
  xx Saws
  — Welding
Band-tailed pigeon
  xx Game and game-birds
      Pigeons
Band theory of solids
  See Energy-band theory of solids
Banda (African people)
  sa Langbas (African people)
  x Bandas
      Dar Banda
Banda languages
  sa Gólo language
Bandages and bandaging *(RD113)*
  sa Adhesive plaster
      Plaster casts, Surgical
      Splints (Surgery)
  x Dressings (Surgery)
      Surgical dressings
  xx First aid in illness and injury
      Plaster casts, Surgical
      Surgery, Minor
      Wounds—Treatment
Bandas
  See Banda (African people)
Bandboxes
  sa Hatboxes
  xx Boxes
      Hatboxes
Banded anteater
  See Numbat
Banded mongoose *(QL737.C28)*
  xx Mongooses
Bandeiras *(F2528)*
  xx Brazil—History—1549-1762
      Brazil—History—To 1821
Bandi language
  See Gbandi language
Banding of bats
  See Bat-banding
Banding of birds
  See Bird-banding
Bandits
  See Brigands and robbers
Banditti
  See Brigands and robbers
Bandjalang language
  sa Gidabal dialect
      Jugumbir dialect
  x Bandjelang language
      Minyung language
  xx Australian languages
Bandjelang language
  See Bandjalang language

Bandmasters
　　See Bandsmen
　　　　Conductors (Music)
　　　　United States. Army—Bandmasters;
　　　　　and similar headings
Bandmen
　　See Bandsmen
Bandoneon
　　See Bandonion
Bandonion *(ML990)*
　　sa Accordion
　　　　Concertina
　　x Bandoneon
　　xx Accordion
　　　　Concertina
Bandonion music *(M175.B2)*
Bands (Music) *(Direct)* *(ML1300-1354;*
　　　　MT733)
　　sa Conducting
　　　　Dance orchestra
　　　　Drum majors
　　　　Instrumentation and orchestration
　　　　　(Band)
　　　　Orchestra
　　　　Rhythm bands and orchestras
　　　　United States. Army—Bandmasters
　　　　Wind instruments
　　x Brass bands
　　xx Conducting
　　　　Instrumental music—History and
　　　　　criticism
　　　　Military music—History and criticism
　　　　Orchestra
　　　　Wind instruments
　　— Instruction and study
　　— Juvenile literature
Bands of hope *(HV5287.B2-25)*
Bandsmen *(ML399; ML419)*
　　x Bandmasters
　　　　Bandmen
　　xx Musicians
Bandurria *(ML1015-1018)*
　　xx Guitar
　　　　Lute
Bandurria music *(Ml42.B3)*
Bandwith compression, Television
　　See Television bandwidth compression
Banen (African tribe)
　　sa Ndiki (African tribe)
　　xx Ethnology—East Cameroon
Banen language
　　x Banend language
　　　　Tunen language
　　xx Bantu languages
Banend language
　　See Banen language
Bang
　　See Bhang (Drug)
Bangala language *(PL8055)*
　　x Gala language
　　　　Kasandsi language
　　　　Lingala language
　　　　Ngala language
　　xx Bantu languages
Bangalas
　　x Wangalas
　　xx Ethnology—Zaire
Bangangte *(DT584.B3)*
　　xx Bantus
　　　　Ethnology—Cameroon
Bangaru dialect *(PK1940)*
　　x Hariani dialect
　　　　Jatu dialect
　　xx Hindi language
Bangladesh
　　— Cyclone, 1970
　　— History
　　— — Revolution, 1971

　　x Pakistan—History—Civil War,
　　　　1971
　　xx India-Pakistan Conflict, 1971-
　　— — — Atrocities
　　— — — — Foreign public opinion
　　— — — Medical and sanitary affairs
　　— — — Personnal narratives
Bangle (Sikhism)
　　xx Bracelets
　　　　Sikhism
　　　　Symbolism
Bang's disease
　　See Brucellosis in cattle
Bangwa (African people)
　　sa Bamileke (African people)
　　xx Bamileke (African people)
　　　　Ethnology—Cameroons
Baniabungu (African people)
　　See Bashi (African people)
Banja Luka, Yugoslavia
　　— Earthquake, 1969
Banjang (Bantu tribe)
　　See Banyang (Bantu tribe)
Banjaras *(DS432.B35)*
　　xx Ethnology—India
　　— Rites and ceremonies
Banjo *(ML1015-1018)*
　　— Methods *(MT562)*
　　— — Self-instruction *(MT568)*
　　　　x Banjo—Self-instruction
　　— Self-instruction
　　　　See Banjo—Methods—Self-instruction
Banjo and percussion music *(M298)*
　　x Percussion and banjo music
Banjo band
　　See Plectral ensembles
Banjo music *(M120-122)*
　　sa Plectral ensembles
Bank accounting
　　See Banks and banking—Accounting
Bank auditing
　　See Bank examination
Bank buildings *(NA6240-6243)*
　　xx Architecture
Bank clerks
　　See Bank employees
Bank correspondence
　　See Banks and banking—Records and
　　　　correspondence
Bank deposit insurance
　　See Insurance, Deposit
Bank deposits *(Direct)*
　　sa Banks and banking—Government
　　　　guaranty of deposits
　　　　Banks and banking—Night and curb
　　　　　depositories
　　　　Certificates of deposit
　　　　Insurance, Deposit
　　　　Public depositories
　　x Deposits, Bank
　　xx Banks and banking
　　　　Deposit banking
　　　　Money
　　— Accounting
　　　　xx Banks and banking—Accounting
Bank directors *(Direct)*
　　xx Banking law
　　　　Banks and banking
　　　　Directors of corporations
Bank discount
　　See Discount
Bank drafts
　　See Drafts
Bank employees *(Direct)*
　　sa Bank tellers
　　　　Collective bargaining—Banks and
　　　　banking

　　　　Collective labor agreements—Banks and
　　　　　banking
　　　　Savings-banks—Officials and employees
　　　　Strikes and lockouts—Bank employees
　　　　Trade-unions—Bank employees
　　　　Wages—Bank employees
　　x Bank clerks
　　　　Banks and banking—Employees
　　xx Clerks
　　— Examinations
　　— Pensions *(Direct)*
　　　　x Banks and banking—Pensions
　　— Recruiting
Bank examination *(Direct)*
　　sa Banks and banking—Accounting
　　x Bank auditing
　　　　Banks and banking—Auditing
　　　　Banks and banking—Examinations
　　xx Banks and banking
　　　　Banks and banking—State supervision
Bank fees
　　See Banks and banking—Service charges
Bank float *(Direct)*
　　x Banks and banking—Float
　　　　Float (Banking)
　　xx Checks
Bank for International Settlements
　　　　(HG1997.16)
　　x Banque des règlements
　　　　International Settlements, Bank for
　　xx Banks and banking
　　　　European War, 1914-1918—
　　　　　Reparations
Bank holding companies *(Direct)*
　　x Banks and banking, Group
　　　　Banks and banking—Holding
　　　　　companies
　　xx Banks and banking
　　　　Holding companies
Bank investments *(Direct)*
　　x Banks and banking—Investments
　　　　Investments, Bank
　　xx Banks and banking
　　　　Investments
　　— Mathematical models
Bank loans *(Direct)* *(HG1641)*
　　sa Brokers' loans
　　xx Banks and banking
　　　　Loans
　　— Mathematical models　　*(Indirect)*
Bank management
　　x Banks and banking—Management
　　xx Management
Bank marketing
　　sa Advertising—Banks and banking
　　　　Public relations—Banks and banking
　　xx Marketing
Bank mergers *(Direct)*
　　x Merger of banks
　　xx Banks and banking
　　　　Consolidation and merger of
　　　　　corporations
Bank-notes *(Direct)* *(Paper money,*
　　　　HG348-353; United States
　　　　bank-notes, HG607-610; United
　　　　States local, HG621-7; Other
　　　　countries, HG651-l490)
　　sa Banks of issue
　　　　Legal tender
　　　　National bank notes
　　xx Banks and banking
　　　　Banks of issue
　　　　Engraving
　　　　Legal tender
　　　　Money
　　　　National bank notes
　　　　Paper money
　　— Forgeries

xx Counterfeits and counterfeiting
Bank of England *(HG2994-6)*
Example under Banks and banking, Central
Bank of Japan, ⌐**Maryland, North America,**
etc.⌐
— Caricatures and cartoons
Bank protection *(Direct)*
x Banks and banking—Protection
— Law and legislation *(Direct)*
Bank records
See Banks and banking—Records and
correspondence
Bank records on microfilm
xx Microfilms
Bank reserves *(Direct)*
x Reserves, Bank
Security reserve requirements
xx Banks and banking
Bank robberies *(Direct)*
xx Brigands and robbers
Robbery
Thieves
Bank service corporations *(Direct)*
xx Banks and banking
Corporation law
Corporations
Electronic data processing—Banks and
banking
Bank statements
See Banks and banking—Accounting
Bank stocks *(Direct)*
xx Banks and banking
Stocks
Bank tellers
xx Bank employees
— Juvenile literature
— Programmed instruction
Banked blood
See Blood banks
Banker-marks
x Marks, Banker
Marks, Masons'
Masons' marks
Stone-cutters' marks
xx Masonry
Stone-cutting
Bankers *(Direct)*
xx Banks and banking
— Biography
— Correspondence, reminiscences, etc.
Bankers, Jewish
See Banks and banking—Jews
Banking
See Banks and banking
Banking as a profession
x Banks and banking—Vocational
guidance
xx Banks and banking
— Juvenile literature
Banking law *(Direct)*
sa Advertising—Banks and banking—Law
and legislation
Bank directors
Banks and banking, Central—Law and
legislation
Banks and banking, Cooperative—Law
and legislation
Discount
Negotiable instruments
topics in the field of banking, e.g.
Custodianship accounts; Trust
companies
x Banks and banking—Laws and
legislation
Law, Banking
xx Commercial law
Money—Law
Banking law (Roman law)

Banking research
See Banks and banking—Research
Bankruptcy *(Direct) (HG3760-3773)*
sa Assignments for benefit of creditors
Composition (Law)
Corporate reorganizations
Creditors' bills
Fraudulent conveyances
Liquidation
Municipal bankruptcy
Poor debtor's oath
Priorities of claims and liens
Receivers
x Business failures
Cessio bonorum
Failure (in business)
Insolvency
Privileged debts
xx Business mortality
Commercial law
Corporate reorganizations
Debt
Debtor and creditor
Finance
Priorities of claims and liens
— Conflict of laws
See Conflict of laws—Bankruptcy
— Criminal provisions
— Digests
— Popular works
Bankruptcy, Fraudulent
See Fraudulent conveyances
Bankruptcy, Municipal
See Municipal bankruptcy
Bankruptcy, National
See State bankruptcy
Bankruptcy (Canon law) *(BX1939.B3)*
Bankruptcy (Roman-Dutch law)
Example under Roman-Dutch law
Bankruptcy (Roman law)
Banks, Central
See Banks and banking, Central
Banks, Coin
See Coin banks
Banks and banking *(Direct)*
(HG1501-3540)
sa Acceptances
Agricultural credit
Bank deposits
Bank directors
Bank examination
Bank for International Settlements
Bank holding companies
Bank investments
Bank loans
Bank mergers
Bank-notes
Bank reserves
Bank service corporations
Bank stocks
Bankers
Banking as a profession
Banks and banking, Central
Banks of issue
Bills of exchange
Chain banks
Charge account bank plans
Checks
Clearinghouse
Confidential communications—Banking
Consumer credit
Credit
Custodianship accounts
Deposit banking
Development banks
Development credit corporations
Discount
Drive-in banking

Federal home loan banks
Foreign exchange
Forest credit
Free banking
Industrial loan associations
Interest and usury
Investment banking
Land banks
Liquidity (Economics)
Lock box banking
Lombard loans
Money
Mortgage banks
Negotiable instruments
Postal savings-banks
Safe-deposit companies
Savings-banks
School savings-banks
Strikes and lockouts—Bank employees
Syndicates (Finance)
Trust companies
x Agricultural banks
Banking
xx Capital
Credit
Economics
Finance
Financial institutions
Money
— Accounting *(HG1706-8)*
sa Bank deposits—Accounting
x Bank accounting
Bank statements
xx Bank examination
— Anecdotes, facetiae, satire, etc.
— Auditing
See Bank examination
— Branch banks
x Branch banks
xx Branches (Business enterprises)
— Calendars
— Chain banks
See Chain banks
— Collective bargaining
See Collective bargaining—Banks and
banking
— Collective labor agreements
See Collective labor agreements—
Banks and banking
— Confidential communications
See Confidential communications—
Banking
— Correspondent banks
x Correspondent banks
— Costs
— Electronic data processing
See Electronic data processing—Banks
and banking
— Employees
See Bank employees
— Equipment and supplies
sa Electronic data processing—Banks
and banking
— Examinations
See Bank examination
— Examinations, questions, etc.
— Float
See Bank float
— Forms, blanks, etc.
— Government guaranty of deposits
(HG1781-2)
sa Building and loan associations—
Government guaranty of deposits
x Banks and banking—United States—
Government guaranty of deposits
Guaranty of bank deposits
xx Bank deposits
Consumer protection

Banks and banking *(Direct)*
  (HG1501-3540)
  — Government guaranty of deposits
    (HG1781-2) *(Continued)*
    Insurance, Deposit
    Example under Insurance, Government
    Note under Insurance, Deposit
  — Government ownership *(Direct)*
    sa Banks and banking, Central
  — Holding companies
    See Bank holding companies
  — Investments
    See Bank investments
  — Jews
    x Bankers, Jewish
      Jewish bankers
  — Job descriptions
  — Juvenile literature
  — Laws and legislation
    See Banking law
  — Location
  — Management
    See Bank management
  — Mathematical models
  — Night and curb depositories
    x Depositories, Night (Banking)
      Night depositories (Banking)
    xx Bank deposits
  — Nonpar banking
    See Nonpar banking
  — Pensions
    See Bank employees—Pensions
  — Personnel management
  — Programmed instruction
  — Protection
    See Bank protection
  — Public opinion
  — Public relations
    See Public relations—Banks and
      banking
  — Records and correspondence
    x Bank correspondence
      Bank records
  — Research
    x Banking research
  — Seasonal variations
    Example under Seasonal variations (Eco-
      nomics)
  — Security measures
  — Service charges
    sa Nonpar banking
    x Bank fees
      Fees, Bank
  — State supervision
    sa Bank examination
      Banks and banking, Central
  — Statistics
  — Tables, etc.
    xx Interest and usury—Tables, etc.
  — Taxation *(Direct)* *(HG1766-8)*
  — Terminology
  — Trust departments
    See Trust companies
  — Vocational guidance
    See Banking as a profession

      GEOGRAPHIC SUBDIVISIONS

  — United States
    sa National banks (United States)

      GEOGRAPHIC SUBDIVISIONS

  — — Government guaranty of deposits
    See Banks and banking—
      Government guaranty of
      deposits

Banks and banking, American, [British, etc.]
  (Direct)
    x American [British, etc.] banks and
      banking
Banks and banking, Central *(Direct)*
    sa Lombard loans
      Monetary policy
      Open market operations
      *names of individual central banks and
      central banking systems, e.g.* Bank of
      England, Federal Reserve banks
    x Banks, Central
      Central banking
      Central banks
    xx Banks and banking
      Banks and banking—Government
        ownership
      Banks and banking—State supervision
      Banks of issue
      Currency question
      Money
  — Law and legislation *(Direct)*
    xx Banking law
Banks and banking, Colonial
    x Colonial banks and banking
Banks and banking, Cooperative *(Direct)*
  (HG2035-2051)
    sa Agricultural cooperative credit
      associations
      Banks and banking, Trade-union
      Building and loan associations
    x Cooperative banks
      Credit cooperatives
      Credit unions
      People's banks
    xx Agricultural cooperative credit
      associations
      Banks and banking, Trade-union
      Cooperation
      Cooperative societies
      Loans, Personal
  — Law and legislation *(Direct)*
    xx Banking law
Banks and banking, Deposit
    See Deposit banking
Banks and banking, Foreign *(Direct)*
    x Foreign banks and banking
Banks and banking, Group
    See Bank holding companies
Banks and banking, Industrial
    See Industrial loan associations
      Loans, Personal
Banks and banking, International
    sa Euro-dollar market
    x International banking
    xx Financial institutions, International
      International finance
Banks and banking, Investment
    See Investment banking
Banks and banking, Trade-union
    sa Banks and banking, Cooperative
    x Labor bank movement
      Labor banks
      Trade-union banks
      Workers' banks
    xx Banks and banking, Cooperative
Banks of issue *(Direct)*
    sa Bank-notes
      Banks and banking, Central
    xx Bank-notes
      Banks and banking
  — United States
    sa Federal Reserve banks
      National banks (United States)
Banners
    See Flags
Bannock Indians *(E99.B33)*
    xx Indians of North America

Numic Indians
Shoshonean Indians
  — Wars, 1878
    xx Indians of North America—Wars—
      1866-1895
Bannockburn, Battle of, 1314 *(DA783.41)*
Banns
    x Bans
    xx Impediments to marriage
Banque des règlements internationaux
    See Bank for International Settlements
Banquets
    See Dinners and dining
Bans
    See Banns
Bansaw (African people)
    See Nso (African people)
Banso (African people)
    See Nso (African people)
Bantam automobile
    See American Bantam automobile
Bantam motorcycle *(TL448.B3)*
    xx B.S.A. motorcycle
Bantams *(SF489.B2)*
    sa Cochin bantams
      Sebright bantam
Bantoe . . .
    See Bantu . . .
Bantry Bay Expedition, 1796-1797
    See French Expedition to Ireland,
      1796-1797
Bantu . . .
    x Bantoe . . .
Bantu consumers
    See Bantus as consumers
Bantu folk-lore
    See Folk-lore, Bantu
Bantu languages *(PL8025)*
    sa Ababua language
      Aduma language
      Asu language
      Bafia language
      Bakundu language
      Banen language
      Bangala language
      Basa language
      Bati language
      Bemba language
      Bembe language (Lake Tanganyika)
      Benga language
      Benge language
      Bisa language
      Bisio language
      Bobangi language
      Bondei language
      Bube language
      Bukusu language
      Bulu language
      Bushongo language
      Chaga language
      Chewa dialect
      Chindau language
      Chokwe language
      Chopi language
      Congo language
      Digo language
      Diriku language
      Duala language
      Ekoi languages
      Embu language
      Ewondo language
      Fan language
      Ganda language
      Ganguela language
      Giryama language
      Gisu language
      Gogo language
      Gusii language

Holoholo language
Jita language
Kamba language
Kaonde language
Kele language
Kiga language
Kikuyu language
Kilega language
Kimbundu language
Kingwana language
Kioko language
Kitabwa language
Kombe language
Kuanyama languages
Kuria language
Kwangali language
Lamba language
Lenje language
Lilima language
Logooli language
Lonkengo language
Lozi language
Lumbu language (Gabon)
Lunda language
Luvale language
Luyana language
Luyia language
Makonde language
Makua language
Mambwe language
Mbete language
Mbinsa language
Mbunda language (Zambia)
Meru language
Mongo language
Mwamba language
Mwera language
Nande language
Ndonga language
Ndumu language
Ngombe language
Ngonde language
Nika language
Nilamba language
Nkundu language
Ntomba language
Nyamwezi language
Nyaneka language
Nyanja language
Nyankole language
Nyankore-Kiga language
Nyore language
Nyoro language
Nyoro-Tooro language
Ombo language
Orungu language
Pogoro language
Punu language
Ragoli language
Ruanda language
Rundi language
Sagara language
Sakata language
Sena language
Senga language
Shambala language
Sheetswa language
Shira language
Shona language
Soga language
Songe language
Sotho language
Sotho-Tswana languages
Suku language
Swahili language
Swazi language
Taita language
Taveta language

Tebele language
Teke language
Tete language
Tetela language
Thonga language
Tonga language (Inhambane)
Tonga language (Nyasa)
Tonga language (Zambesi)
Tooro language
Umbundu language
Venda language
Vili language
Wanga language
Xosa language
Yao language
Yombe language
Ziba language
Zigula language
   xx Benue-Congo languages
Example under African languages
— Classification
    Example under Language and languages
      —Classification
Bantu law
  See Law, Bantu
Bantu literature
  sa Xosa literature
    names of literatures belonging to the
      Bantu group, e.g. Swahili literature
Bantu marriage customs and rites
  See Marriage customs and rites, Bantu
Bantu philology
  sa Soga philology
Bantus   (DT16.B2; Ethnology, GN657.B2;
      South Africa, DT764.B2)
  sa Ambo (African tribe)
    Baboma (Bantu people)
    Babunda (Bantu tribe)
    Bafia (African tribe)
    Baganda
    Bahemba (Bantu people)
    Bakoko (African tribe)
    Bakongo (African tribe)
    Bakossi (Bantu people)
    Bakwiri (African people)
    Baluyia (Bantu tribe)
    Bamangwato
    Bangangte
    Banyang (Bantu tribe)
    Banyankole
    Banyoro
    Bapedi tribe
    Barundi
    Basuto (African people)
    Batetela (African tribe)
    Baya (African tribe)
    Bemba (African tribe)
    Beti (Bantu tribe)
    Bisio (Bantu tribe)
    Bomvana (African tribe)
    Bube (African tribe)
    Bukusu (Bantu tribe)
    Chokwe (Bantu tribe)
    Chopi (African tribe)
    Embu (Bantu people)
    Evuzok (Bantu people)
    Fingos
    Ghoya (Bantu tribe)
    Giryama (Bantu tribe)
    Gisu (Bantu tribe)
    Gusii (Bantu tribe)
    Hanya (Bantu tribe)
    Haya (African tribe)
    Ila (Bantu tribe)
    Kavirondo (African people)
    Kimbu (Bantu people)
    Kuanyama (African tribe)
    Lambas

    Lele (Bantu tribe)
    Lobedu
    Luenas (Bantu tribe)
    Luguru (Bantu tribe)
    Luvale (Bantu tribe)
    Makonde (Bantu tribe)
    Mamabolo (Bantu people)
    Mashona
    Mbundu (Bantu tribe)
    Meru (African tribe)
    Missions to Bantus
    Mongo (Bantu tribe)
    Mpongwe (Bantu tribe)
    Mwila (Bantu people)
    Ngombe (Bantu tribe)
    Ngonde (African tribe)
    Nguni
    Nyakyusa (African tribe)
    Nyamwezi
    Ovimbundu
    Pare (Bantu tribe)
    Phalaborwa (Bantu tribe)
    Pondos
    Qaba (Bantu tribe)
    Safwa (Bantu tribe)
    Sambyu (Bantu tribe)
    Shambala (Bantu tribe)
    Soga (Bantu tribe)
    Sonjo (Bantu tribe)
    Suku (African tribe)
    Swazi (African tribe)
    Tiriki (Bantu tribe)
    Tooro (Bantu people)
    Topoke (Bantu tribe)
    Tswana (Bantu tribe)
    Valenge (African tribe)
    Venda (Bantu tribe)
    Wabena
    Wachaga
    Wahehe
    Wanga (Bantu tribe)
    Wanyaturu (Bantu tribe)
    Wapangwa (Bantu people)
    Warundi
    Yao (African tribe)
    Zigula (Bantu people)
— Economic conditions
— Education
— — Art, [etc.]
— Migrations
    x Mfecane
    xx Migrations of nations
— Music
— Pictorial works
— Religion
    sa Prayer (Bantu religion)
    Example under Religion, Primitive
— Social conditions
Bantus as consumers
    x Bantu consumers
    xx Consumers
Bantus in Tanzania, [etc.]
— Rites and ceremonies
Banū Hāshīm
  See Hashimites
Banū Hudhayl
  See Hudhayl tribe
Banū Tamim
  See Tamim
Banū 'Umajjo
  See Omayyads
Banu Wattas
  See Wattasids
Banyabongo (African people)
  See Bashi (African people)
Banyang (Bantu tribe)
    x Banjang (Bantu tribe)
    xx Bantus

Banyang (Bantu tribe) *(Continued)*
    Ethnology—Cameroon
Banyankole
    x Nyankole
    xx Bahima (African people)
        Bairo (African people)
        Bantus
Banyoro
    x Ba-Nyoro
        Bakitara
        Bunyoro
        Kitara
        Nyoro (Bantu people)
    xx Bahima (African people)
        Bairo (African people)
        Bantus
Baoa'n language
    See Pao-an language
Baoulé (African people)
    x Baule (African people)
    xx Ethnology—Ivory Coast
Baoulé language
    x Baule language
        Poni language
    xx Akan language
        Kwa languages
Baousi (African tribe)
    See Ushi (African tribe)
Baoussi (African tribe)
    See Ushi (African tribe)
Bapedi tribe
    xx Bantus
Baptism *(BV806-814)*
    sa Baptism and church membership
        Baptismal certificates
        Baptisteries
        Fonts
        Infant baptism
        Innocence (Theology)
        Regeneration (Theology)
        Sponsors
    x Christening
        Immersion, Baptismal
    xx Church membership
        Initiations (in religion, folk-lore, etc.)
        Rites and ceremonies
        Sacraments
        Theology, Doctrinal
        Theology, Practical
    — Anglican Communion, [Catholic Church, etc.]
    — — Juvenile literature
    — Early works to 1800
    — History
    — — Early church, ca. 30-600
        xx Church history—Primitive and
            early church, ca. 30-600
    — — — Sources
        xx Christian literature, Early
    — Juvenile literature
    — Sermons
    — Social aspects
        xx Sociology, Christian
    — Terminology
Baptism, Sailors'
    See Shellbacks
Baptism, Second
    See Martyrdom
Baptism (Canon law) *(BX1939.B3)*
    xx Sacraments (Canon law)
Baptism (Hinduism)
    xx Hinduism
        Tantrism
Baptism (Liturgy)
    xx Catholic Church. Liturgy and ritual
        Liturgics
        Sacraments (Liturgy)

Baptism and Christian union
    x Christian union and baptism
    xx Sacraments and Christian union
Baptism and church membership *(BV820)*
    x Church membership and baptism
    xx Baptism
        Church membership
        Church polity
Baptism for the dead *(BV814)*
    x Dead, Baptism for the
Baptism in blood
    See Martyrdom
Baptism in the Holy Spirit *(BT123)*
    sa Glossolalia
    xx Gifts, Spiritual
        Glossolalia
        Holy Spirit
        Pentecostalism
    — Biblical teaching
Baptismal certificates
    xx Baptism
        Church records and registers
Baptismal fonts
    See Fonts
Baptismal water *(Catholic Church, BX2307.3)*
    Here are entered works dealing with the
        water consecrated on Holy Saturday
        or the eve of Pentecost.
    x Water, Baptismal
    xx Holy water
        Sacramentals
        Water (in religion, folk-lore, etc.)
Baptist associations
    Here are entered works dealing collec-
        tively with the various "associations"
        comprising the Baptist churches of a
        given locality.
    x Associations, Baptist
        Baptists—Associations
    xx Baptists—Government
        Baptists—Societies, etc.
Baptist churches
    See Churches, Baptist
Baptist converts
    See Converts, Baptist
Baptist journalism
    See Press, Baptist
Baptist press
    See Press, Baptist
Baptist theological seminaries
    See Theological seminaries, Baptist
Baptist women
    See Women, Baptist
Baptisteries *(Direct) (General, NA4910; Local, NA5201-6113)*
    sa Fonts
    xx Baptism
        Churches
        Fonts
Baptists *(Direct) (BX6201-6495)*
    sa Anabaptists
        Church of the Brethren
        Mennonites
        Primitive Baptists
        Separate Baptists
        Seventh-Day Baptists
        United American Freewill Baptists
        World War, 1939-1945—Baptists
    xx Anabaptists
    — Associations
        See Baptist associations
    — Biography
    — Catechisms and creeds
    — Clergy *(BX3645)*
        sa Theological seminaries, Baptist
    — — Caricatures and cartoons
    — — Correspondence, reminiscences, etc.

    — Converts
        See Converts, Baptist
    — Doctrinal and controversial works
        Example under Theology, Doctrinal
    — Education
        sa Theological seminaries, Baptist
    — Finance
    — Government
        sa Baptist associations
    — Historiography
    — Hymns
        Note under Hymns
    — Influence
    — Membership
    — Missions
    — Publishing
    — Relations *(BX6329.A1)*
    — — Catholic Church, [etc.]
    — Sermons
    — Societies, etc.
        sa Baptist associations
Baptists, Colored
    See Baptists, Negro
Baptists, Danish, [German, etc.] *(United States, BX6247.A-Z)*
    Here are entered works on Baptists living
        outside their native country who use
        their native language in church ser-
        vices.
    x Danish [German, etc.] Baptists
Baptists, Negro *(BX6440-6460)*
    x Baptists, Colored
        Colored Baptists
        Negro Baptists
    xx Negroes—Religion
Baptitoxine
    See Cytisine
Bar
    See Lawyers
Bar, Horizontal
    See Horizontal bar
Bar associations *(Direct)*
    sa Integrated bar
        Student bar associations
    xx Lawyers
Bar-bells *(GV485)*
Bar examinations *(Direct)*
    x Law—Examinations
    xx Admission to the bar
        Law examinations
Bar Harbor, Me.
    — Fire, 1947
Bar-headed goose
    xx Geese
Bar integration
    See Integrated bar
Bar mitzvah
    sa Confirmation (Jewish rite)
        Youth, Jewish—Religious life
    xx Confirmation (Jewish rite)
        Jews—Rites and ceremonies
Bar mitzvah etiquette *(BJ2078.B3)*
    xx Etiquette
Bar mitzvah sermons
    xx Sermons, Jewish
Bara (Madagascan tribe)
    xx Ethnology—Madagascar
Bara dialect (Madagascar) *(PL5379)*
    xx Malagasy language
Bara language *(PL4001.B3)*
    x Cachari language
        Kachari language
        Mech language
        Plains Kachari language
    xx Bodo languages
al-Barā'ah, Laylat
    See Laylat al-Barā'ah

Barabaig (African people)
    xx Ethnology—Tanzania
       Nilo-Hamitic tribes
Baraka
    See Barakah
Barakah *(BP190.5.B3)*
    x Baraka
      Barkah
    xx Blessing and cursing
      Mana
      Mysticism—Islam
Barambo language
    See Barambu language
Barambu language *(PL8058)*
    x Abarambo language
      Balambu language
      Barambo language
    xx Zande languages
Barasana Indians
    xx Indians of South America
Barb
    See Barbary horse
Barba (African tribe)
    See Bariba (African tribe)
Barbados
    — Hurricane, 1831
Barbarian invasions of Rome *(DG500-514)*
    sa Goths in Italy
      Huns
      Italy—History—476-1492
      Lombards
      Migrations of nations
      Vandals
    x Invasions of Rome, Barbarian
    xx Germanic tribes in the Balkan
       Peninsula
      Goths in Italy
      Lombards
      Migrations of nations
      Vandals
Barbary corsairs
    See Pirates
Barbary horse *(SF293.B3)*
    x Barb
    xx Arabian horse
Barbary Pirates
    See United States—History—Tripolitan
       War, 1801-1805
Barbary sheep
    x Aodad
      Aoudad
      Arui
      Audad
      Maned sheep
      Udad
    xx Mountain sheep
Barbary States
    See Africa, North
    — History *(DT160-329)*
Barbastro city prize
    See Premio Ciudad de Barbastro
Barbecue cookery *(TX840.B3)*
    x Cookery, Barbecue
    xx Cookery (Fish)
      Cookery (Meat)
      Outdoor cookery
Barbed wire *(TS271)*
    xx Wire
    — Collectors and collecting
    — Patents
Barbed wire, Tariff on
    See Tariff on wire
Barbed-wire entanglements
    See Wire obstacles
Barbel (Fish) *(Fishing, SH691.B; Zoology,*
      QL638.C94)
    sa Mahseer

Barberries *(SB386.B2)*
    x Berberis
Barbers *(Direct)* *(Hygienic aspects, RA617;*
      Mechanic trades, TT950-979)
    sa Haircutting
      Shaving
      Trade-unions—Barbers
      Wages—Barbers
    xx Shaving
    Example under Artisans; Service industries
    — Anecdotes, facetiae, satire, etc.
    — Legal status, laws, etc. *(Direct)*
Barbers' chairs, Tariff on
    See Tariff on barbers' chairs
Barbers' supplies *(TT979)*
Barberton daisy
    See Gerbera
Barbiero fever
    See Chagas' disease
Barbiturates *(RM325)*
    xx Antispasmodics
      Hypnotics
      Sedatives
    — Toxicology
Barbizon school *(ND547)*
    xx Landscape painters
Barbus mosal
    See Mahseer
Barcelona
    — History
    —— Revolution, 1909
    — Siege, 1713-1714 *(D283.B3)*
      xx Spanish Succession, War of,
        1701-1714
Barcelona (Province)
    — Flood, 1962
      x Tragic Week in Barcelona, 1909
Barcelona in literature
Barcelona prizes
    See Ciudad de Barcelona prizes
Barcenite *(QE391.B3)*
Bardet-Biedl syndrome
    See Laurence-Moon-Biedl syndrome
Bards and bardism *(ML287-9; ML3653-6)*
    sa Meistersinger
      Minnesingers
      Minstrels
      Scalds and scaldic poetry
      Troubadours
      Trouvères
    xx Druids and Druidism
      Minstrels
      Poetry
      Poets
      Scalds and scaldic poetry
Barea language
    See Baria language
Bareë dialect *(PL5231-4)*
    sa Malayan languages
    xx Malayan languages
Barettini
    See Humiliati
Bargaining
    See Collective bargaining
      Negotiation
Bargello
    See Canvas embroidery
Barges
    sa Sailing barges
      Whalebacks
    xx Canal-boats
      River boats
      Work boats
    — Safety appliances
Bari Indians
    See Motilon Indians
Bari language *(PL8061)*
    sa Kakwa dialect

      Mandara language
    x Dzilio language
    xx Nilo-Hamitic languages
Baria language *(PL8062)*
    x Barea language
      Kolkotta language
      Mogoreb language
      Morda language
      Nere language
    xx Nilo-Hamitic languages
Barias
Bariba (African tribe) *(DT541.42)*
    x Barba (African tribe)
    xx Ethnology—Dahomey
      Ethnology—Nigeria
Barilla *(TP245.S7)*
    xx Alkali industry and trade
      Soda industry
Baris (Insect)
Barisal guns
    xx Acoustic phenomena in nature
Barite *(Indirect)* *(QE391.B35)*
    x Barytes
Baritone (Musical instrument) *(History and*
      construction, ML975-8)
    sa Euphonium
      Trombone
    xx Euphonium
      Trombone
    — Orchestra studies *(MT496)*
      xx Baritone (Musical instrument)—
        Studies and exercises
    — Studies and exercises *(MT496)*
      sa Baritone (Musical instrument)—
        Orchestra studies
Baritone and cornet music *(M288-9)*
    sa Suites (Baritone and cornet)
    x Cornet and baritone music
Baritone and piano music *(M262-3)*
    sa Rondos (Baritone and piano)
      Sonatas (Baritone and piano)
    x Piano and baritone music
Baritone and piano music, Arranged
    (M262-3)
Baritone music
    sa Baritone with string orchestra
      Concertos (Baritone with string
       orchestra)
      Quartets, ₍Trios, etc.₎, Wind quartets,
       ₍trios, etc.₎ *followed by specifications*
       which include the baritone
Baritone with string orchestra *(M1134.B37;*
      M1135.B37)
    sa Concertos (Baritone with string
       orchestra)
    xx Baritone music
      Concertos (Baritone with string
       orchestra)
Barium *(Chemistry, QD181.B2; Mineral*
      industries, TN948.B18)
    sa Soils—Barium content
    Example under Chemicals
    — Analysis
    — Spectra
Barium compounds *(QD181.B2)*
Barium enema
    x Contrast enema
    xx Enema
Barium in soils
    See Soils—Barium content
Barium salts
    xx Salts
Bark
    sa Bark peeling
      Bast
      Cinnamon
      Lenticels
      Pine bark

Bark *(Continued)*
    Quinine
    Wood
    xx Botany—Anatomy
        Lenticels
        Trees
        Wood
  — Photography
    See Photography of bark
  — Tables
Bark as fuel *(TP324)*
    xx Fuel
Bark-beetles *(Indirect)* *(SB945.B3)*
    sa Douglas fir beetle
        Red turpentine beetle
        Spruce bark-beetles
        Tan-bark beetle
        Western pine beetle
    x Engraver beetles
    xx Beetles
        Forest insects
  — Host plants
Bark cloth
    See Tapa
Bark inscriptions
    x Birch bark inscriptions
        Inscriptions on bark
        Novgorod birch bark inscriptions
    xx Paleography
        Writing—Materials and instruments
Bark painting *(Direct)*
    xx Painting, Primitive
Bark peeling
    sa Barkers (Woodworking machinery)
    x Debarking
    xx Bark
        Trees
Bark photography
    See Photography of bark
Bark-weevil *(SB761)*
    xx Beetles
Barkah
    See Barakah
Barkers (Woodworking machinery)
    x Barking machines
        Debarkers (Woodworking machinery)
    xx Bark peeling
Barkhausen effect
    xx Ferromagnetism
Barking machines
    See Barkers (Woodworking machinery)
Barletta
  — Riot, 1931
  — Siege, 1503
      xx Italy—History—1492-1559
Barley *(Indirect)* *(Botany, QK495.H75;*
    Culture, SB191.B2; Trade,
    HD9049.B3-4)
    xx Flour
  Example under Crop yields
  — Disease and pest resistance
  — Diseases and pests *(SB608.B2)*
    sa Barley stripe mosaic virus
  — Genetics
  — Grading
  — Milling
    x Barley milling
        Milling, Barley
  — Varieties
    xx Barley breeding
Barley as feed
Barley breeding
    sa Barley—Varieties
    xx Grain breeding
Barley false stripe
    See Barley stripe mosaic virus
Barley milling
    See Barley—Milling

Barley stripe mosaic virus
    x Barley false stripe
    xx Barley—Diseases and pests
Barley yellow dwarf virus *(SB608.G6)*
    x Cereal yellow dwarf virus
Barlow's disease
    See Scurvy, Infantile
Barma language
    See Bagirmi language
Barmaids
    See Bartenders
Barn owl
    xx Owls
Barn swallow *(QL696.P2)*
    xx Swallows
Barn symbols
    xx Barns
        Hex signs
        House marks
        Signs and symbols
Barnabites *(BX2960.B6)*
    x Paulines
    xx Monasticism and religious orders
Barnacle goose
    xx Geese
Barnacles
    See Cirripedia
Barns *(Indirect)* *(NA8230)*
    sa Barn symbols
        Dairy barns
        Stables
    xx Farm buildings
        Stables
  — Heating and ventilation
  — Water-supply
Barnyard manure
    See Farm manure
Baroa
    See Batwa
Baroclinic field
    See Baroclinicity
Baroclinic instability
    See Baroclinicity
Baroclinicity
    x Baroclinic field
        Baroclinic instability
    xx Meterology
Barometer *(QC886)*
    sa Atmospheric pressure
    xx Meteorological instruments
        Pressure
  — Juvenile literature
Barometer, Aneroid
    See Aneroid barometer
Barometric hypsometry *(QC895)*
    sa Altitudes—Measurement
        Aneroid barometer
        Leveling
    x Hypsometry, Barometric
    xx Altitudes—Measurement
        Aneroid barometer
        Mensuration
        Meteorology
  — Tables
Baron language
    See Ron language
Baronage
    See Peerage
Barons' War, 1263-1267 *(DA227.5)*
    sa Lewes, Eng., Battle of, 1264
  — Sources
Baroque altarpieces
    See Altarpieces, Baroque
Baroque altars
    See Altars, Baroque
Baroque architecture
    See Architecture, Baroque

Baroque art
    See Art, Baroque
Baroque arts
    See Arts, Baroque
Baroque bronzes
    See Bronzes, Baroque
Baroque civilization
    See Civilization, Baroque
Baroque decoration and ornament
    See Decoration and ornament, Baroque
Baroque drawing
    See Drawing, Baroque
Baroque ecclesiastical embroidery
    See Ecclesiastical embroidery, Baroque
Baroque engravings
    See Engravings, Baroque
Baroque furniture
    See Furniture, Baroque
Baroque glass painting and staining
    See Glass painting and staining, Baroque
Baroque glassware
    See Glassware, Baroque
Baroque ivories
    See Ivories, Baroque
Baroque literature
    Duplicate entry is made under the litera-
    ture or literary form concerned, *e.g.* 1.
    Baroque literature. 2. German litera-
    ture—Early modern (to 1700)—His-
    tory and criticism; or, 2. German poe-
    try—Early modern (to 1700)
    sa Aureate terms
        Euphuism
        Gongorism
        Marinism
        Rococo literature
    x Literature, Baroque
    xx Literature, Modern—History and
        criticism
Baroque medals
    See Medals, Baroque
Baroque mural painting and decoration
    See Mural painting and decoration, Baroque
Baroque music
    See Music, Baroque
Baroque painting
    See Painting, Baroque
Baroque paintings
    See Paintings, Baroque
Baroque portraits
    See Portraits, Baroque
Baroque sculpture
    See Sculpture, Baroque
Baroque silversmithing
    See Silversmithing, Baroque
Baroque wood-carving
    See Wood-carving, Baroque
Barotse
    See Lozi (African tribe)
Barotsi
    See Lozi (African tribe)
Barr bodies
    See Sex chromatin
Barracks *(UC400-405)*
    sa subdivision Barracks and quarters *under*
        armies, navies, etc., *e.g.* under
        armies, navies, etc., e.g. *United*
        States. Army—Barracks and
        quarters; United States. Navy—
        Barracks and quarters
    x Military housing
    xx Military architecture
Barracuda automobile *(TL215.B)*
    xx Plymouth automobile
Barracudas
    sa Great barracuda
Barrages *(TC540-555)*
    sa Dams

Rivers—Regulation
subdivision Barrage *under names of rivers, e.g.* Nile River—Barrage
xx Dams

Barratry (Maritime law) *(Direct)*
xx Maritime law
Shipmasters

Barre, Vt.
— Flood, 1927 *(F59.B15)*

Barred dove
xx Pigeons

Barred warbler
x Warbler, Barred

Barrel finishing
See Tumbling (Metal finishing)

Barrel jumping
xx Jumping
Skating

Barrel organ
x Hand-organ
xx Musical instruments (Mechanical)
Organ

Barrel organ, Hydraulic
xx Hydraulic organ

Barrel-organ music
Barrel-shell roofs
See Roofs, Shell

Barrels *(TS890)*
sa Coopers and cooperage
Staves and stave trade
xx Containers
Coopers and cooperage
— Standards
— Tables, calculations, etc.

Barren fig tree (Parable) *(BT378.B2)*
x Fig tree, Barren
xx Fig (in religion, folk-lore, etc.)

Barren grounds caribou *(QL737.U55)*
xx Caribou

Barrier agents (Dermatology)
See Barrier creams

Barrier creams
x Barrier agents (Dermatology)
Protective agents (Dermatology)
xx Ointments

Barrier Forts, Battle of, 1856
x Canton Forts, Battle of, 1856
xx China—History—19th century
United States—History, Naval

Barrier islands *(GB471-8)*
x Offshore bar
xx Islands

Barrier pillars
xx Coal mines and mining

Barrier treaty, 1709 *(D282; DA490)*
Barrier treaty, 1715 *(D282; DA499)*
Barriers, Saline water
See Saline water barriers
Barriers (Military science)
See Obstacles (Military science)
Barristers
See Lawyers
Barrows
See Mounds
Bars, Parallel
See Parallel bars
Bars, Plastic
See Plastic bars
Bars, Reinforcing
See Reinforcing bars
Bars, Steel
See Steel bars

Bars (Engineering)
Here are entered theoretical and technical works on rods and bars as members of engineering structures. Works on the mathematical theories of elasticity in rods are entered under Elastic rods and wires.
sa Girders
Reinforcing bars
Springs (Mechanism)
Steel bars
Struts (Engineering)
x Rods
xx Elastic rods and wires
Structural frames
Note under Elastic rods and wires
— Electromechanical analogies
— Testing *(TA660.B3)*
— Vibration

Bars (Furniture)
xx Furniture
Hotels, taverns, etc.—Furniture, equipment, etc.

Bars (Geomorphology) *(Indirect)*
sa Sand-bars
Bars (Sand)
See Sand-bars

Bartang dialect
xx Pamir languages

Bartenders *(TX950-951; Trade-unions, HD6350.H8)*
sa Wages—Bartenders
x Barmaids
— Anecdotes, facetiae, satire, etc.
— Correspondence, reminiscences, etc.

Barter *(Direct)*
x Exchange (Barter)
xx Commerce
Economics
Money
— Taxation *(Direct)*

Barter (Islamic law)
Barter (Jewish law)
Barter (Roman law)
Barthianism
See Dialectical theology

Bartholin's gland
x Gland of Bartholin
Bartholomew, St., Massacre of
See St. Bartholomew's Day, Massacre of, 1572
Baru language
See Loma language

Barundi *(DT443)*
sa Batutsi
x Warundi
xx Bantus
Ethnology—Burundi
Ethnology—Rwanda
Hamites

Barwe (African people)
sa Tangwena (African people)
x Wabarwe (African people)
xx Ethnology—Mozambique
Ethnology—Rhodesia, Southern

Barylite *(Indirect)*
xx Silicates

Baryons
sa Hyperons
Neutrons
Protons
xx Hadrons
— Spectra
Barytes
See Barite

Baryton *(ML760)*
x Viola di bordone
Viola paredon
xx Viol
Viola da gamba

Baryton music *(M59)*
sa String trios (Baryton, viola, violoncello)
String trios (Baryton, violin, violoncello)

Bas-relief *(NB1280-1291)*
sa Sarcophagi
Sculpture
Wood-carving
xx Decoration and ornament
Relief (Sculpture)
Sculpture

Basa language *(PL8065)*
x Bassa language (Cameroons)
xx Bantu languages
Basa language (Liberia)
See Bassa language (Liberia)

Basakata (African people) *(DT650)*
x Sakata (African people)
xx Ethnology—Zaire
— Religion

Basal ganglia
sa Amygdaloid body
Corpus striatum
Globus pallidus
x Ganglia, Basal
xx Brain
— Diseases

Basal metabolism
sa Thyroid gland function tests
x BMR
xx Energy metabolism
Metabolism

Basalt *(Indirect)*
— Analysis
Basaltes pottery
See Black basaltes
Basare (African people)
See Bassari (African people)
Basari language
See Bassari language
Basco language
See Batan language
Base apparatus
See Base measuring
Base-ball
See Baseball
Base courses (Roads)
See Roads—Base courses
Base-exchange
See Ion exchange
Base flow
See Groundwater flow

Base measuring *(QB303)*
x Base apparatus
xx Geodesy
Base-plates
See Plates, Iron and Steel

Base running (Baseball)
x Running (Baseball)
xx Baseball
— Juvenile literature

Baseball *(GV862-881)*
sa All-Star Baseball Game
Base running (Baseball)
Baseballs
Batting (Baseball)
Catchers (Baseball)
Catching (Baseball)
Fielding (Baseball)
Indoor baseball
No-hitter (Baseball)
Pitchers (Baseball)
Pitching (Baseball)
Softball
World series (Baseball)
x Base-ball

Baseball *(GV862-881)* *(Continued)*
  xx College sports
     Softball
  Example under Ball games; Games; School
     sports; Sports
  — Anecdotes, facetiae, satire, etc. *(GV873)*
     sa Baseball stories
     xx Baseball stories
  — Caricatures and cartoons
  — Economic aspects *(GV880)*
  — History *(Direct)*
  — — Juvenile literature
  — Juvenile literature
  — Pictorial works
  — Records *(GV877)*
  — Rules
  — Societies, etc.
     See Baseball clubs
  — Songs and music *(M1977.S713;
        M1978.S713)*
     xx Sports—Songs and music
  — Statistical methods
  — Umpiring *(GV876)*
     x Umpires (Baseball)
     xx Sports officiating
Baseball and radio
  See Radio and baseball
Baseball and television
  See Television and baseball
Baseball bats
  x Bats, Baseball
  xx Sporting goods
Baseball buttons
  See Baseball insignia
Baseball cards
  xx Cards
Baseball clubs *(GV875.A1)*
  sa names of individual clubs, e.g. New
     York. Baseball club (American
     League)
  x Baseball clubs, Professional
     Baseball—Societies, etc.
     Professional baseball clubs
Baseball clubs, Professional
  See Baseball clubs
Baseball coaching
  xx Coaching (Athletics)
Baseball gloves
  x Gloves, Baseball
  xx Sporting goods
Baseball insignia
  x Baseball buttons
     Baseball pins
  xx Insignia
Baseball managing
  xx Coaching (Athletics)
     Management
Baseball no-hitter
  See No-hitter (Baseball)
Baseball pins
  See Baseball insignia
Baseball stories
  sa Baseball—Anecdotes, facetiae, satire,
     etc.
  x Stories
  xx Baseball—Anecdotes, facetiae, satire,
     etc.
     Fiction
     Sports stories
Baseballs
  xx Balls (Sporting goods)
     Baseball
Basedow's disease
  See Graves' disease
Basel, Council of, 1431-1449 *(BX830 1431)*
Basel, Treaty of, 1795 *(DC222.B3)*
Basement soil
  See Roads—Subgrades

Basements
  sa Crawl spaces
  x Cellars
  xx Foundations
Basenjis
Baseri tribe
  x Bajri tribe
     Basiri tribe
     Basseri tribe
  xx Ethnology—Iran
Bases, Military
  See Military bases
Bases (Architecture) *(NA2873)*
  xx Architecture—Details
     Columns
Bases (Chemistry)
  sa Organic bases
  xx Chemistry
  — Programmed instruction
  — Tables, etc.
Bashama (African people)
  See Bachama (African people)
Bashfulness
  sa Timidity
  x Shyness
  xx Emotions
     Fear
     Timidity
Bashgali language *(PK7055.B3)*
  xx Pisacha languages
Bashi (African people)
  x Baniabungu (African people)
     Banyabongo (African people)
     Wanyambungi (African people)
  xx Ethnology—Zaire
Bashi-Bazouks
Bashi-Lele (African tribe)
  See Lele (Bantu tribe)
Bashilele (African tribe)
  See Lele (Bantu tribe)
Bashkir language *(PL65.B3)*
  xx Turko-Tataric languages
Bashkir literature
Bashkir philology *(PL65.B3)*
Bashkir poetry *(Direct)*
Bashkirs
Basic (Computer program language)
  x Beginner's all-purpose symbolic
     instruction code
  — Problems, exercises, etc.
  — Programmed instruction
Basic English *(PE1073.5)*
  x Thousand-word English
  xx English language
Basicity of acids
  See Acids—Basicity
Basidiomycetes *(QK626-9)*
  sa Gasteromycetes
     Hymenomycetes
     Mushrooms
     Puffballs
     Rusts (Fungi)
     Smuts
     Tremellales
  xx Fungi
Basilar impression
  See Platybasia
Basilar membrane
  xx Ear
     Membranes (Biology)
Basilians
Basilians in Albania, [**Italy, the Sinaitic
     Peninsula, etc.**]
Basilicas *(NA4150)*
  xx Architecture
     Architecture, Ancient
     Church architecture

Basing-point system
  sa F.O.B. clause
  xx Competition, Unfair—United States
     Delivered pricing
     Price discrimination—United States
     Trusts, Industrial—United States
Basiri tribe
  See Baseri tribe
BASIS-E (Information retrieval system)
     (Z699.4.B2)
  x Bibliothekarisch-analytisches System
     zur
  xx Information storage and retrieval
     systems
     Libraries—Automation
Basket-ball
  See Basketball
Basket-Maker Indians *(E99.B37)*
  xx Indians of Mexico
     Indians of North America
     Pueblo Indians—Antiquities
Basket making *(Elementary education,
     LB1543; Ethnology, GN431;
     Manufacture, TS910)*
  Works dealing with collections of basket-
     work are entered under the heading
     Basketwork.
  sa Indians—Basket making
     Indians of North America—Basket
        making
     Indians of South America—Basket
        making
     Palmetto weaving
     Raffia work
     Rush-work
  xx Arts and crafts movement
     Manual training
     Osiers
     Raffia work
     Weaving
  Note under Basketwork
  — Juvenile literature
Basket rummy
  See Canasta (Game)
Basket willows
  See Osiers
Basketball *(Direct)* *(GV885)*
  sa Netball
     subdivision Basketball *under names of
        universities, colleges, schools, etc.,
        e.g.* Harvard University—Basketball
  x Basket-ball
  — Biography
  — — Juvenile literature
  — Caricatures and cartoons
  — Defense
     x Defensive basketball
  — — Juvenile literature
  — History
  — — Juvenile literature
  — Juvenile literature
  — Offense
     x Offensive basketball
  — Pictorial works
  — Refereeing
     See Basketball officiating
  — Rules
  — Training
Basketball coaching
  xx Coaching (Athletics)
Basketball for women *(GV886)*
  x Girls' basketball
  xx Sports for women
  — Pictorial works
Basketball officiating
  x Basketball—Refereeing
  xx Sports officiating

Basketball stories
　　xx Sports stories
Baskets
　　xx Basketwork
　　　　Containers
　　— Catalogs
　　— Prices
Basketwork　*(Direct)*
　　　　Here are entered works dealing with collections of basketwork. Works on the art are entered under the heading Basket making.
　　sa Baskets
　　x Indian baskets
　　Note under Basket making
　　— Collectors and collecting
Basking shark
　　x Bone shark
　　xx Sharks
Basmalah　*(BP183.7.B3)*
　　x Bismillah
　　　　Tasmiyah
　　xx God—Name
　　　　Islamic theology
　　　　Koran
Basongola (African people)
　　See Wasongola (African people)
Basque ballads and songs
Basque drama　*(Direct)*
Basque funeral rites and ceremonies
　　See Funeral rites and ceremonies, Basque
Basque imprints　*(Direct)*　*(Z7009.B3)*
Basque language　*(PH5001-5259)*
　　x Euskara language
Basque literature　*(PH5280-5490)*
Basque literature (Spanish)
　　See Spanish literature—Basque authors
Basque philology
Basque poetry　*(Direct)*
Basques　*(Ethnology, GN549.B3; French history, DC611.B31-322; Spanish history, DP302.B46)*
　　sa Celtiberi
　　　　Ligurians
　　x Biscayans
　　　　Vasques
　　　　Vizcayans
　　xx Celtiberi
　　　　Iberians
Basques in America, ⌜**Canada, Venezuela, etc.**⌝
Basques in foreign countries
Basques in literature
Bass　*(QL638.C3; Fish-culture, SH351.B)*
　　sa Black bass
　　　　Kelp bass
　　　　Rock bass
　　　　Sea bass
　　　　Striped bass
　　　　White bass
　　　　Yellow bass
Bass, Otsego
　　See Whitefishes
Bass drum
　　See Drum
Bass fishing　*(SH681)*
　　sa Black bass fishing
　　　　Striped bass fishing
　　xx Fishing
Bass horn
　　See Tuba
Bass viol
　　See Double bass
　　　　Viola da gamba
Bassa language (Cameroons)
　　See Basa language
Bassa language (Liberia)
　　x Basa language (Liberia)
　　　　Gbasa language

Bassari (African people)
　　x Basare (African people)
　　　　Cemba (African people)
　　　　Tobote (African people)
　　xx Ethnology—Africa, West
Bassari language
　　x Ayan language
　　　　Basari language
　　　　Biyan language
　　　　Wo language
Basse danse　*(ML3465)*
Basseri tribe
　　See Baseri tribe
Basset horn　*(ML990.B35)*
　　xx Clarinet
Basset-horn and piano music　*(M270.B4; M271.B4)*
　　sa Sonatas (Basset horn and piano)
　　x Piano and basset-horn music
　　xx Basset-horn music
　　　　Piano music
Basset-horn music　*(M110.B35)*
　　sa Basset-horn and piano music
　　　　Quintets (Basset horn, clarinets (3), vibraphone)
Basset-hounds　*(SF429.B2)*
　　Example under Hounds
　　— Legends and stories
Basso continuo
　　See Thorough bass
Basso ostinato
　　See Ground bass
Bassoa
　　See Batwa
Bassoon　*(History, ML953)*
　　sa Pommer
　　　　Sarrusophone
　　x Curtall
　　— Construction　*(ML951)*
　　— Orchestra studies　*(MT406)*
　　　　xx Bassoon—Studies and exercises
　　— Repairing　*(ML951)*
　　— Studies and exercises　*(MT405)*
　　　　sa Bassoon—Orchestra studies
Bassoon and clarinet music
　　sa Bassoon and clarinet with orchestra
　　　　Bassoon and clarinet with string orchestra
　　　　Concertos (Bassoon and clarinet)
　　　　Concertos (Bassoon and clarinet with string orchestra)
　　　　Sonatas (Bassoon and clarinet)
　　x Clarinet and bassoon music
Bassoon and clarinet with orchestra　*(M1040-1041)*
　　sa Concertos (Bassoon and clarinet)
　　xx Bassoon and clarinet music
　　　　Concertos (Bassoon and clarinet)
　　　　Orchestral music
Bassoon and clarinet with string orchestra　*(M1105-6)*
　　sa Concertos (Bassoon and clarinet with string orchestra)
　　xx Bassoon and clarinet music
　　　　Concertos (Bassoon and clarinet with string orchestra)
　　　　String-orchestra music
　　— Solos with piano　*(M1106)*
　　　　xx Trios (Piano, bassoon, clarinet), Arranged
Bassoon and continuo music
　　x Continuo and bassoon music
Bassoon and double-bass music　*(M290-291)*
　　x Double-bass and bassoon music
Bassoon and English-horn music　*(M288-9)*
　　sa Suites (Bassoon and English horn)
　　x English-horn and bassoon music
　　xx Bassoon music

English-horn music
Bassoon and flute music　*(M288-9)*
　　sa Bassoon and flute with string orchestra
　　　　Concertos (Bassoon and flute with string orchestra)
　　　　Sonatas (Bassoon and flute)
　　　　Suites (Bassoon and flute)
　　x Flute and bassoon music
Bassoon and flute with string orchestra　*(M1140-1141)*
　　sa Concertos (Bassoon and flute with string orchestra)
　　xx Bassoon and flute music
　　　　Concertos (Bassoon and flute with string orchestra)
Bassoon and harpsichord music　*(M253-4)*
　　sa Sonatas (Bassoon and harpsichord)
　　x Harpsichord and bassoon music
Bassoon and horn music　*(M288-9)*
　　x Horn and bassoon music
Bassoon and oboe music　*(M288-9)*
　　sa Bassoon and oboe with orchestra
　　　　Bassoon and oboe with string orchestra
　　　　Canons, fugues, etc. (Bassoon and oboe)
　　　　Concertos (Bassoon and oboe)
　　　　Concertos (Bassoon and oboe with string orchestra)
　　　　Sonatas (Bassoon and oboe)
　　　　Suites (Bassoon and oboe)
　　x Oboe and bassoon music
Bassoon and oboe with orchestra　*(M1040-1041)*
　　sa Concertos (Bassoon and oboe)
　　xx Bassoon and oboe music
　　　　Concertos (Bassoon and oboe)
　　　　Orchestral music
Bassoon and oboe with string orchestra　*(M1105-6)*
　　sa Concertos (Bassoon and oboe with string orchestra)
　　xx Bassoon and oboe music
　　　　Concertos (Bassoon and oboe with string orchestra)
　　　　String-orchestra music
Bassoon and piano music　*(M253-4)*
　　sa Passacaglias (Bassoon and piano)
　　　　Sonatas (Bassoon and piano)
　　　　Suites (Bassoon and piano)
　　x Duets
　　　　Piano and bassoon music
Bassoon and piano music, Arranged　*(M253-4)*
　　sa Bassoon with chamber orchestra—Solo with piano
　　　　Bassoon with orchestra, Arranged—Solo with piano
　　　　Bassoon with orchestra—Solo with piano
　　　　Bassoon with string orchestra—Solo with piano
　　　　Concertos (Bassoon)—Solo with piano
　　　　Concertos (Bassoon with string orchestra), Arranged—Solo with piano
　　　　Concertos (Bassoon with string orchestra)—Solo with piano
　　　　Suites (Bassoon with orchestra)—Solo with piano
　　　　Suites (Bassoon with string orchestra)—Solo with piano
Bassoon and piccolo music　*(M288-9)*
　　sa Bassoon and piccolo with string orchestra
　　　　Concertos (Bassoon and piccolo with string orchestra)
　　x Piccolo and bassoon music

Bassoon and piccolo with string orchestra
(M1105-6)
  sa Concertos (Bassoon and piccolo with
    string orchestra)
  xx Bassoon and piccolo music
    Concertos (Bassoon and piccolo with
      string orchestra)
    String-orchestra music
Bassoon and recorder music (M288-9)
  sa Bassoon and recorder with string
    orchestra
    Concertos (Bassoon and recorder with
      string orchestra)
  x Recorder and bassoon music
Bassoon and recorder with string orchestra
(M1105-6)
  sa Concertos (Bassoon and recorder with
    string orchestra)
  xx Bassoon and recorder music
    Concertos (Bassoon and recorder with
      string orchestra)
    String-orchestra music
Bassoon and trumpet music (M288-9)
  sa Bassoon and trumpet with string
    orchestra
    Concertos (Bassoon and trumpet with
      string orchestra)
  x Trumpet and bassoon music
Bassoon and trumpet with string orchestra
(M1105-6)
  sa Concertos (Bassoon and trumpet with
    string orchestra)
  xx Bassoon and trumpet music
    Concertos (Bassoon and trumpet with
      string orchestra)
    String-orchestra music
Bassoon and violin music (M290-291)
  sa Bassoon and violin with string orchestra
    Concertos (Bassoon and violin with
      string orchestra)
    Suites (Bassoon and violin)
  x Violin and bassoon music
Bassoon and violin with string orchestra
(M1105-6)
  sa Concertos (Bassoon and violin with
    string orchestra)
  xx Bassoon and violin music
    Concertos (Bassoon and violin with
      string orchestra)
    String-orchestra music
Bassoon and violoncello music (M290-291)
  sa Sonatas (Bassoon and violoncello)
    Suites (Bassoon and violoncello)
  x Violoncello and bassoon music
**Bassoon, clarinet, English horn, flute with
orchestra** (M1040-1041)
  sa Concertos (Bassoon, clarinet, English
    horn, flute)
  xx Concertos (Bassoon, clarinet, English
    horn, flute)
    Orchestral music
    Wind quartets (Bassoon, clarinet,
      English horn, flute)
Bassoon, clarinet, flute, horn, oboe with band
(M1205-6)
  sa Concertos (Bassoon, clarinet, flute,
    horn, oboe with band)
  xx Band music
    Concertos (Bassoon, clarinet, flute,
      horn, oboe with band)
    Wind quintets (Bassoon, clarinet, flute,
      horn, oboe)
**Bassoon, clarinet, flute, horn, oboe with
chamber orchestra** (M1040-1041)
  sa Concertos (Bassoon, clarinet, flute,
    horn, oboe with chamber orchestra)
  xx Chamber-orchestra music

Concertos (Bassoon, clarinet, flute,
  horn, oboe with chamber orchestra)
Wind quintets (Bassoon, clarinet, flute,
  horn, oboe)
— Scores (M1040)
**Bassoon, clarinet, flute, horn, oboe with
orchestra** (M1040-1041)
  sa Concertos (Bassoon, clarinet, flute,
    horn, oboe)
  xx Concertos (Bassoon, clarinet, flute,
    horn, oboe)
    Orchestral music
    Wind quintets (Bassoon, clarinet, flute,
      horn, oboe)
**Bassoon, clarinet, flute, horn, oboe with string
orchestra** (M1105-6)
  sa Concertos (Bassoon, clarinet, flute,
    horn, oboe with string orchestra)
    Suites (Bassoon, clarinet, flute, horn,
      oboe with string orchestra)
  xx Concertos (Bassoon, clarinet, flute,
    horn, oboe with string orchestra)
    String-orchestra music
    Wind quintets (Bassoon, clarinet, flute,
      horn, oboe)
— Scores (M1105)
**Bassoon, clarinet, flute, horn, violoncello with
string orchestra** (M1105-6)
  sa Concertos (Bassoon, clarinet, flute,
    horn, violoncello with string
    orchestra)
  xx Concertos (Bassoon, clarinet, flute,
    horn, violoncello with string
    orchestra)
    Quintets (Bassoon, clarinet, flute, horn,
      violoncello)
    String-orchestra music
**Bassoon, clarinet, flute, oboe, harp with
orchestra** (M1040-1041)
  sa Concertos (Bassoon, clarinet, flute,
    oboe, harp)
  xx Concertos (Bassoon, clarinet, flute,
    oboe, harp)
    Orchestral music
    Quintets (Bassoon, clarinet, flute, oboe,
      harp)
**Bassoon, clarinet, flute, oboe, violins (2),
viola, violoncello with string
orchestra** (M1105-6)
  sa Concertos (Bassoon, clarinet, flute,
    oboe, violins (2), viola, violoncello
    with string orchestra)
  xx Concertos (Bassoon, clarinet, flute,
    oboe, 2 violins, viola, violoncello
    with string orchestra)
    Octets (Bassoon, clarinet, flute, oboe,
      violins (2), viola, violoncello)
    String-orchestra music
— Scores (M1105)
**Bassoon, clarinet, flute, oboe with chamber
orchestra** (M1040-1041)
  sa Concertos (Bassoon, clarinet, flute,
    oboe with chamber orchestra)
    Variations (Bassoon, clarinet, flute,
      oboe with chamber orchestra)
  xx Chamber-orchestra music
    Concertos (Bassoon, clarinet, flute,
      oboe with chamber orchestra)
    Wind quartets (Bassoon, clarinet, flute,
      oboe)
**Bassoon, clarinet, flute, oboe with string
orchestra** (M1105-6)
  sa Concertos (Bassoon, clarinet, flute,
    oboe with string orchestra)
  xx Concertos (Bassoon, clarinet, flute,
    oboe with string orchestra)
    String-orchestra music

Wind quartets (Bassoon, clarinet, flute,
  oboe)
**Bassoon, clarinet, flute, trumpet with string
orchestra** (M1105-6)
  sa Concertos (Bassoon, clarinet, flute,
    trumpet with string orchestra)
  xx Concertos (Bassoon, clarinet, flute,
    trumpet with string orchestra)
    String-orchestra music
    Wind quartets (Bassoon, clarinet, flute,
      trumpet)
— Scores (M1105)
Bassoon, clarinet, flute with string orchestra
(M1105-6)
  sa Concertos (Bassoon, clarinet, flute with
    string orchestra)
  xx Concertos (Bassoon, clarinet, flute with
    string orchestra)
    String-orchestra music
    Wind trios (Bassoon, clarinet, flute)
Bassoon, clarinet, horn, oboe with orchestra
(M1040-1041)
  sa Concertos (Bassoon, clarinet, horn,
    oboe)
  xx Concertos (Bassoon, clarinet, horn,
    oboe)
    Orchestral music
    Wind quartets (Bassoon, clarinet, horn,
      oboe)
**Bassoon, clarinet, horn, oboe with string
orchestra** (M1105-6)
  sa Concertos (Bassoon, clarinet, horn,
    oboe with string orchestra)
  xx Concertos (Bassoon, clarinet, horn,
    oboe with string orchestra)
    String-orchestra music
    Wind quartets (Bassoon, clarinet, horn,
      oboe)
Bassoon, clarinet, oboe with string orchestra
(M1105-6)
  sa Concertos (Bassoon, clarinet, oboe with
    string orchestra)
    Suites (Bassoon, clarinet, oboe with
      string orchestra)
  xx Concertos (Bassoon, clarinet, oboe with
    string orchestra)
    String-orchestra music
    Wind trios (Bassoon, clarinet, oboe)
Bassoon, clarinet, trumpet with orchestra
(M1040-1041)
  sa Concertos (Bassoon, clarinet, trumpet)
  xx Concertos (Bassoon, clarinet, trumpet)
    Orchestral music
    Wind trios (Bassoon, clarinet, trumpet)
**Bassoon, flute, horn, oboe, trumpet with string
orchestra** (M1140-1141)
  sa Concertos (Bassoon, flute, horn, oboe,
    trumpet with string orchestra)
    Suites (Bassoon, flute, horn, oboe,
      trumpet with string orchestra)
  xx Concertos (Bassoon, flute, horn, oboe,
    trumpet with string orchestra)
    String-orchestra music
    Wind quintets (Bassoon, flute, horn,
      oboe, trumpet)
**Bassoon, flute, horn, oboe with chamber
orchestra** (M1040-1041)
  sa Concertos (Bassoon, flute, horn, oboe
    with chamber orchestra)
  xx Chamber-orchestra music
    Concertos (Bassoon, flute, horn, oboe
      with chamber orchestra)
    Wind quartets (Bassoon, flute, horn,
      oboe)
Bassoon, flute, horn, oboe with orchestra
(M1040-1041)
  sa Concertos (Bassoon, flute, horn, oboe)
  xx Concertos (Bassoon, flute, horn, oboe)

Orchestral music
Wind quartets (Bassoon, flute, horn, oboe)

Bassoon, flute, horn, oboe with string orchestra *(M1105-6)*
  sa Concertos (Bassoon, flute, horn, oboe with string orchestra)
  xx Concertos (Bassoon, flute, horn, oboe with string orchestra)
    String-orchestra music
    Wind quartets (Bassoon, flute, horn, oboe)
  — Scores *(M1105)*

Bassoon, horn, trumpet, double bass with orchestra *(M1040-1041)*
  sa Concertos (Bassoon, horn, trumpet, double bass)
  xx Concertos (Bassoon, horn, trumpet, double bass)
    Orchestral music
    Quartets (Bassoon, horn, trumpet, double bass)
  — Scores *(M1040)*

Bassoon music *(M75-77)*
  sa Bassoon and English-horn music
    Bassoon with band
    Bassoon with chamber orchestra
    Bassoon with instr. ensemble
    Bassoon with orchestra
    Bassoon with string orchestra
    Concertos (Bassoon)
    Concertos (Bassoon with band)
    Concertos (Bassoon with chamber orchestra)
    Concertos (Bassoon with string orchestra)
    Recorded accompaniments (Bassoon)
    Sonatas (Bassoon)
    Suites (Bassoon)
    Quartets, ⌈Trios, etc.⌉, Wind quartets, ⌈trios, etc.⌉ *followed by specifications which include the bassoon*

Bassoon music (Bassoons (2)) *(M288-9)*
  sa Sonatas (Bassoons (2))

Bassoon music (Bassoons (2)), Arranged *(M288-9)*

Bassoon music (Bassoons (4))
  See Wind quartets (Bassoons (4))

Bassoon, oboe, trumpet with string orchestra *(M1105-6)*
  sa Concertos (Bassoon, oboe, trumpet with string orchestra)
  xx Concertos (Bassoon, oboe, trumpet with string orchestra)
    String-orchestra music
    Wind trios (Bassoon, oboe, trumpet)

Bassoon, oboe, violin, violoncello with chamber orchestra *(M1040-1041)*
  sa Concertos (Bassoon, oboe, violin, violoncello with chamber orchestra)
  xx Chamber-orchestra music
    Concertos (Bassoon, oboe, violin, violoncello with chamber orchestra)
    Quartets (Bassoon, oboe, violin, violoncello)
  — Scores *(M1040)*

Bassoon, oboe, violin, violoncello with orchestra *(M1040-1041)*
  sa Concertos (Bassoon, oboe, violin, violoncello)
  xx Concertos (Bassoon, oboe, violin, violoncello)
    Orchestral music
    Quartets (Bassoon, oboe, violin, violoncello)
  — To 1800
    — Solos with piano *(M1041)*

  xx Quintets (Piano, bassoon, oboe, violin, violoncello), Arranged

Bassoon players
  See Bassoonists

Bassoon with band *(M1205-6)*
  sa Concertos (Bassoon with band)
  xx Band music
    Bassoon music
    Concertos (Bassoon with band)

Bassoon with band, Arranged *(M1257)*
  — Scores and parts *(M1257)*

Bassoon with chamber orchestra *(M1026-7)*
  sa Concertos (Bassoon with chamber orchestra)
  xx Bassoon music
    Chamber-orchestra music
    Concertos (Bassoon with chamber orchestra)
  — Solo with piano *(M1027)*
    xx Bassoon and piano music, Arranged

Bassoon with instr. ensemble
  xx Bassoon music
    Instrumental ensembles

Bassoon with orchestra *(M1026-7)*
  sa Concertos (Bassoon)
    Suites (Bassoon with orchestra)
  xx Bassoon music
    Concertos (Bassoon)
    Orchestral music
  — Solo with piano *(M1027)*
    xx Bassoon and piano music, Arranged

Bassoon with orchestra, Arranged *(M1026-7)*
  — Solo with piano *(M1027)*
    xx Bassoon and piano music, Arranged

Bassoon with string orchestra *(M1105-6)*
  sa Concertos (Bassoon with string orchestra)
    Suites (Bassoon with string orchestra)
  xx Bassoon music
    Concertos (Bassoon with string orchestra)
    String-orchestra music
  — Solo with piano *(M1106)*
    xx Bassoon and piano music, Arranged

Bassoonists *(ML399)*
  x Bassoon players

Basswood
  See Linden

Basswood oil
  See Linden oil

Bast
  xx Bark
    Fibers

Bast spinning *(TS1727)*
  xx Spinning

Bast work *(TT875)*
  xx Handicraft

Bastaards
  See Griquas

Bastardy
  See Illegitimacy

Bastarnae
  xx Germanic tribes

Bastnaesite
  sa Cerium
    Didymium
    Lanthanum
  x Bastnasite
    Hamartite
  xx Carbonates
    Cerium group

Bastnasite
  See Bastnaesite

Bastogne, Battle of, 1944-1945
  See Ardennes, Battle of the, 1944-1945

Basuku (African people)
  xx Bayaka (African people)
    Ethnology—Zaire

Basuto (African people)
  sa Khwakhwa (African people)
    Pedi (Basuto tribe)
    Tswana (Bantu tribe)
  x Sotho (African people)
  xx Bantus
  — Legal status, laws, etc.

Basuto law
  See Law, Basuto

Basuto pony *(SF315.2.B3)*
  xx Ponies

Bat
  See Bats

Bat-banding
  x Banding of bats
    Marking of bats

Bat falcon *(QL696.A2)*
  xx Falcons

Batak
  sa Karo-Batak
    Missions to Batak
    Pakpak (Indonesian people)
    Simelungun (Indonesian people)
  x Batak (Sumatra)
    Bataks
    Battas (Sumatra)
  xx Ethnology—Sumatra

Batak (Palawan)

Batak (Sumatra)
  See Batak

Batak language *(PL5241-4)*
  sa Karo-Batak dialect
    Simelungun dialect
    Toba-Batak dialect
  x Batta language (Sumatra)
  xx Malayan languages

Bataks
  See Batak

Batalla de Boquerón
  See Boquerón, Battle of, 1932

Batalla de Gondra, 1933
  See Gondra, Battle of, 1933

Batalla de Niquitao, 1813
  See Niquitao, Battle of, 1813

Batalla de Pantano de Vargas, 1819
  See Pantano de Vargas, Battle of, 1819

Batalla de Picuiba-Yrendagué, 1934
  See Picuiba-Yrendagué, Battle of, 1934

Batalla de Santa Rosa, 1856
  See Santa Rosa, Battle of, 1856

Batalla de Toledo, 1933
  See Toledo, Battle of, 1933

Batalla de Vargas, 1819
  See Pantano de Vargas, Battle of, 1819

Batalla del Sauce
  See Sauce, Battle of the, 1870

Batan language *(PL5571)*
  sa Yami language
  x Basco language
    Batanese language
    Ibatan language
    Isamurang language
    Itbayat language
    Ivatan language
    Saptang language
  xx Philippine languages
    Yami language

Batanese language
  See Batan language

Batavians
  xx Germanic tribes

Batch size determination
  See Economic lot size

Bateke (Bantu people)
  x Teke (Bantu people)
    Tio (Bantu people)
  xx Ethnology—Congo (Brazzaville)

Bates laboratory aspirator
   See Separators (Machines)
Bateso
   See Teso tribe
Batetela (African tribe)
   xx Bantus
Bathetic poetry *(PN1059.B; English*
      collections, PR1175)
   sa Bathos
   xx Bathos
      Poetry
Bathing beaches
   sa Bathing customs
      subdivision Bathing beaches *under*
        names of cities, e.g. Chicago—
        Bathing beaches
   xx Beaches
Bathing costume
   See Bathing suits
Bathing customs *(GT2845)*
   xx Bathing beaches
      Baths
   — Caricatures and cartoons
Bathing suits
   x Bathing costume
      Swimsuits
Batholiths *(Indirect)* *(QE461)*
   xx Intrusions (Geology)
Bathometer
   xx Deep-sea sounding
Bathos *(PN203)*
   sa Bathetic poetry
   xx Bathetic poetry
Bathrooms *(Building, TH6485-6496; Interior*
      decoration, NK2117)
   xx Architecture, Domestic
      Dwellings
   — Cleaning
      xx Buildings—Cleaning
      House cleaning
Baths *(Direct)* *(RM801-822; School*
      hygiene, LB3461)
   sa Bathing customs
      Hydrotherapy
      Mikveh
      Nauheim bath
      Shower-baths
      Swimming pools
   x Cleanliness
   xx Hydrotherapy
      Hygiene
      Physical therapy
      Therapeutics, Physiological
      Toilet
Baths, Cold *(RM822.C6)*
Baths, Electric *(RM885)*
   x Electric baths
   xx Electrotherapeutics
Baths, Finnish
   See Sauna
Baths, Hot-air *(RM865-7)*
   sa Baths, Turkish
   x Hot-air baths
   xx Thermotherapy
Baths, Medicated *(RM822.V2)*
   x Medicated baths
Baths, Medieval
Baths, Moor and mud *(RM822.M9)*
   x Baths, Mud
      Mud baths
   xx Earths, Medical and surgical uses of
      Hydrotherapy
Baths, Mud
   See Baths, Moor and mud
Baths, Partial *(RM822.P3)*
   xx Hydrotherapy
Baths, Plating
   See Plating baths

Baths, Public *(Direct)* *(Building, TH4761;*
      Public hygiene, RA605)
   x Public baths
      School baths
   — Employees
      See Public bath employees
   — Public opinion
   — Safety regulations *(Direct)*
Baths, Russian *(RM820)*
   x Russian baths
   xx Baths, Vapor
Baths, Sea *(RM819)*
   x Sea baths
Baths, Turkish *(RM821)*
   x Turkish baths
   xx Baths, Hot-air
Baths, Vapor *(RM822.V2)*
   sa Baths, Russian
      Sauna
   x Vapor-baths
Baths, Warm *(RM822.W2)*
Baths in moving-pictures *(PN1995.9.B3)*
   xx Moving-pictures
Bathymetric maps
   sa subdivision Bathymetric maps *under*
      names of countries, regions, bodies
      of water, etc.
   xx Maps
Bathyscaphe
   xx Diving, Submarine
      Midget submarines
      Oceanographic research
      Oceanographic submersibles
Bathythermograph
   xx Ocean temperature
      Sounding and soundings
      Thermometers and thermometry
Bati
   See Beti (Bantu tribe)
Bati language *(PL8066)*
   x Beti language
   xx Bantu languages
Bati oil
   x Batiputa oil
Baticola Indians
   See Mbya Indians
Batik *(NK9503)*
   xx Dyes and dyeing
   — Juvenile literature
Batinites
   sa Assassins (Ismailites)
   xx Islamic sects
      Ismailites
Batiputa oil
   See Bati oil
Batjva
   See Batwa
Batoa
   See Batwa
Baton Rouge, La.
   — Riot, 1866
Baton Rouge, La., Battle of, 1862
Baton twirling *(MT733.6)*
   sa Drum majoring
   xx Drill and minor tactics
      Drum majoring
Batoro (Bantu tribe)
   See Wanyaturu (Bantu tribe)
Batrachia
   See Amphibians
   — Anatomy *(QL669)*
Batrachosauria
   See Anthracosauria
Bats *(Indirect)* *(QL737.C5)*
   sa Flying foxes
      Pallid bats
      Vampire bats
      headings beginning with the word Bat

   x Bat
      Cheiroptera
      Chiroptera
      Rhinolophus
      Vespertilio
   xx Mammals
   — Juvenile literature
   — Legends and stories
   — Parasites
      See Parasites—Bats
Bats, Baseball
   See Baseball bats
Bats, Fossil
Bats language
   See Tsova-Tush language
Batshwa
   See Batwa
Batswa
   See Batwa
Batta language (Sumatra)
   See Batak language
Battas (African tribe)
Battas (Sumatra)
   See Batak
Battenberg lace *(TT800-805)*
   xx Lace and lace making
Battered child syndrome
   See Cruelty to children
Batteries
   sa Artillery
      Floating batteries
Batteries, Electric
   See Electric batteries
      Storage batteries
Battery (Law)
   See Assault and battery
Battery additives
   See Storage batteries—Additives
Battery chargers *(TK2943)*
   x Chargers, Battery
   xx Storage batteries
Battery radios
   See Portable radios
Battice, Battle of, 1940 *(D756.5.B)*
   xx World War, 1939-1945—Campaigns—
      Belgium
Batting (Baseball) *(GV869)*
   xx Baseball
   — Juvenile literature
Battle, Wager of
   See Wager of battle
Battle-ax cultures
   See Corded Ware culture
Battle-Axes (Sect) *(BX6510.B3)*
Battle-ball *(GV1017.B33)*
Battle-cries *(Heraldry, CR79)*
   sa Slogans
   x War-cries
   xx Cries
      Heraldry
Battle damage repair (Warships)
   See Damage control (Warships)
Battle Island, Battle of, 1756
Battle of Britain
   See Britain, Battle of, 1940
Battle of the Atlantic, 1939-1945
   See World War, 1939-1945—Atlantic
      Ocean
Battle of the Spurs
   See Courtrai, Battle of, 1302
Battle-songs
   See War-songs
Battle sounds
   xx Sounds
Battledeck floor bridges
   See Bridges, Steel plate deck
Battlefield photographers
   See War photographers

Battles *(Indirect)* *(D25)*
　　sa Imaginary wars and battles
　　　Naval battles
　　　names of battles, e.g. Harlem Heights,
　　　　Battle of, 1776; *and subdivision*
　　　　Campaigns *or* Campaigns and battles
　　　　under names of wars, e.g. European
　　　　War, 1914-1918—Campaigns; United
　　　　States—History—Civil War,
　　　　1861-1865—Campaigns and battles
　　x Fighting
　　xx Combat
　　　History
　　　Military art and science
　　　Military history
　　　Naval battles
　　　Sieges
　　　War
　　— Pictorial works
Battles, Naval
　　See Naval battles
Battles in art *(N8260)*
　　xx Art
Battles in literature
　　xx War in literature
Battleships
　　x Dreadnoughts
　　　Pocket battleships
　　xx Warships
　　— Pictorial works
Batua
　　See Batwa
Batuco language
　　See Eudeve language
Batumbuka
　　See Tumbuka (African tribe)
Batumi (City)
　　— General Strike, 1902
Batuque (Cultus) *(BL2592.B3)*
　　x Babassuê (Cultus)
　　xx Religion, Primitive
Batushi (African tribe)
　　See Ushi (African tribe)
Batussi
　　See Batutsi
Batutsi *(DT443)*
　　x Batussi
　　　Tutsi
　　　Watussi
　　xx Barundi
　　　Ethnology—Burundi
　　　Ethnology—Rwanda
Batwa
　　x Atschoua
　　　Bachua
　　　Bacwa
　　　Bakiue
　　　Bakwa
　　　Baroa
　　　Bassoa
　　　Batjva
　　　Batoa
　　　Batshwa
　　　Batswa
　　　Batua
　　　Bekoe
　　　Watshua
　　　Wattua
　　　Wotsschua
　　xx Ethnology—Burundi
　　　Ethnology—Rwanda
　　　Pygmies
Baule (African people)
　　See Baoulé (African people)
Baule language
　　See Baoulé language
Bauls
　　xx Hindu sects

— Hymns
Baungshè dialect
　　See Lai language
Baunscheidtism *(RZ410)*
　　xx Acupuncture
　　　Counter-irritants
　　　Therapeutics
Bauré language *(PM5606)*
　　xx Arawakan languages
　　　Indians of South America—Languages
Bauris *(DS432.B37)*
　　xx Caste—India
　　　Ethnology—India
Baushi (African tribe)
　　See Ushi (African tribe)
Bausi (African tribe)
　　See Ushi (African tribe)
Bautzen, Battle of, 1813 *(DC236.7.B3)*
　　xx Napoléon I, Emperor of the French,
　　　　1769-1821—Campaigns of
　　　　1813-1814
　　　Saxony—History—1423-1815
Bautzen, Ger., Battle of, 1945
　　xx World War, 1939-1945—Campaigns—
　　　　Germany
Bauxite *(Indirect)* *(Mineral industries,*
　　　　TN490.A5; Mineralogy, QE391.B4)
　　xx Aluminum ores
　　— Analysis
Bavaria
　　— History *(DD801.B31-55)*
　　— — To 1180
　　— — 1180-1777
　　　　sa Hiltersried, Battle of, 1433
　　— — 1777-1918
　　— — 1918-1945
Bavaria, Lower, in art
Bavaria in art
Bavaria in literature
Bavarian literature
　　See German literature—Bavaria
Bavarian Succession, War of, 1778-1779
　　　　(DD801.B376)
　　x War of the Bavarian Succession,
　　　　1778-1779
Bavarian wit and humor *(Direct)*
　　xx German wit and humor
Bavarians *(DD801.B34-348)*
　　xx Germanic tribes
Bavarians in foreign countries
Bavenda
　　See Venda (Bantu tribe)
Bavili tribe *(GN654)*
Bawdy songs *(M1977.B38; M1978.B38)*
　　x Dirty songs
　　　Ribald songs
　　xx Humorous songs
　　　Songs
Bawenda
　　See Venda (Bantu tribe)
Baxter Springs, Kan., Battle of, 1863
　　　　(E474.9)
Bay (Tree)
Bay of Pigs invasion
　　See Cuba—History—Invasion, 1961
Bay oil
　　x Myrcia oil
Bay scallop *(QL430.7.P3; SH372)*
　　x Scallop, Common
　　xx Scallops
Baya (African tribe) *(DT584.B35)*
　　x Baia (African tribe)
　　　Baja (African tribe)
　　xx Bantus
　　　Ethnology—Sudan (Region)
Bayaka (African people)
　　sa Basuku (African people)
　　x Jaca (African people)

　　　Mayaka (African people)
　　　Yaka (African people)
　　xx Ethnology—Zaire
Bayaka language
　　See Teke language
Bayes' solution
　　See Bayesian statistical decision theory
Bayesian statistical decision theory
　　　　(QA279.5)
　　x Bayes' solution
　　xx Statistical decision
Bayeux tapestry *(NK3049.B3)*
　　xx Tapestry
　　— Juvenile literature
Baylen, Battle of, 1808
　　See Bailén, Battle of, 1808
Bayonets *(UD400)*
　　xx Arms and armor
Bays *(Indirect)*
　　sa Estuaries
　　　names of bays
　　x Gulfs
　　xx Coasts
　　　Estuaries
Bāza language
　　See Kunama language
Bazaars, Charitable *(HV544)*
　　sa Thrift shops and rummage sales
　　x Bazars, Charitable
　　　Church fairs
　　xx Charities
　　　Fairs
Bazaars, Oriental
　　sa subdivision Bazaars *under names of*
　　　cities, etc.
　　x Bazars, Oriental
　　xx Fairs
　　　Markets
　　　Retail trade
Bazars, Charitable
　　See Bazaars, Charitable
Bazars, Oriental
　　See Bazaars, Oriental
Bāzen language
　　See Kunama language
Bazimbas
　　See Vazimbas
BBK classification
　　See Classification, BBK
BCG
　　sa BCG vaccination
　　x Bacille Calmette-Guérin
　　　Bacillus Calmette-Guérin
　　xx Tuberculosis—Preventive inoculation
BCG vaccination *(Direct)*
　　x Mass BCG vaccination
　　xx BCG
　　　Tuberculosis—Preventive inoculation
　　　Vaccination
Be bop music
　　See Jazz music
Bê language
　　See Li language
Beach birds
　　See Shore birds
Beach erosion *(Direct)*
　　　Works on the prevention of erosion are
　　　　entered under the heading Shore pro-
　　　　tection. Works on coast changes re-
　　　　sulting from erosion or other causes
　　　　are entered under the heading Coast
　　　　changes.
　　sa Coast changes
　　　Shore protection
　　x Beaches—Erosion
　　　Shore erosion
　　xx Coast changes
　　　Erosion

169

Beach erosion *(Direct)* *(Continued)*
    Littoral drift
    Shore protection
Beach-flea *(QL444.A5)*
    xx Fleas
Beach-la-mar jargon *(PM7895.B4)*
    sa Pidgin English
    x Bêche-de-mer jargon
    xx Languages, Mixed
        Pidgin English
Beach mouse
    See Oldfield mouse
Beach plum
    xx Plum
Beach ridges *(Indirect)*
    x Fulls (Beaches)
    xx Beaches
Beachcombing *(Indirect)*
    xx Hobbies
        Treasure-trove
    — Juvenile literature
Beaches *(Indirect)* *(GB454.B3)*
    sa Bathing beaches
        Beach ridges
        Littoral drift
        Sand-dunes
        Seashore
    xx Seashore
    — Erosion
        See Beach erosion
    — Juvenile literature
    — Law and legislation *(Direct)*
Beachy Head, Battle of, 1690 *(DA86.8)*
    xx Europe—History—1648-1715
        Netherlands—History—1648-1714
Beacons *(Indirect)* *(VK1000-1246)*
    sa Light-ships
        Lighthouses
        Racon
        Radio beacons
    xx Aids to navigation
        Lighthouses
        Marine service
        Navigation
    — Contracts and specifications
Beading (Metalwork)
    xx Sheet-metal work
Beadles *(BX9079)*
    xx Church of Scotland—Clergy
        Church officers
        Sextons
Beads *(Art industries, NK3650; Technology,*
        TS2301.B4)
    sa Glass beads
        Magatama
        Rosary
Beads, Buddhist
    See Buddhist rosary
Beads (in religion, folk-lore, etc.)
    x Folk-lore of beads
    xx Religion, Primitive
Beadwork *(Art industries, NK3650;*
        Technology, TT860)
    sa Wampum belts
    x Indians of North America—Beadwork
    xx Arts and crafts movement
        Crocheting
        Embroidery
        Fancy work
        Knitting
        Weaving
    — Juvenile literature
Beagle B-206 (Transport planes)
    xx Transport planes
Beagle Expedition, 1831-1836 *(QH11)*
Beagles (Dogs) *(SF429.B3)*
    sa Beagling

Beagling
    sa Eton College Hunt
    xx Beagles (Dogs)
        Coursing
        Hunting
Beaked whales
    sa True's beaked whale
    x Bottlenosed whales
    xx Whales
Beaker cultures *(Indirect)* *(GN775.5.B4)*
    xx Bronze age
        Neolithic period
Beam, Balance
    See Balance beam
Beams
    See Girders
Beams, Atomic
    See Atomic beams
Beams, Box
    See Box beams
Beams, Composite
    See Composite construction
Beams, Concrete
    See Concrete beams
Beams, Electron
    See Electron beams
Beams, Laser
    See Laser beams
Beams, Particle
    See Particle beams
Beams, Prestressed concrete
    See Prestressed concrete beams
Beams, Wooden
    See Wooden beams
Bean beetle
    See Mexican bean beetle
Bean curd
    See Tofu
Bean ladybird
    See Mexican bean beetle
Bean leaf-beetle
    xx Beetles
Bean mosaic virus
    Example under Beans—Diseases and pests
Bean oil
    See Soy-bean oil
Bean thrips
Bean-weevil
    sa Broad-bean weevil
        Coffee-bean weevil
    xx Beetles
Beans *(Indirect)* *(Botany, QK495.L52;*
        Culture, SB327)
    sa Azuki bean
        Bonavist bean
        Broad bean
        Calabar bean
        Castor-bean
        Cookery (Beans)
        Cowpeas
        Florida velvet bean
        Kidney bean
        Lima bean
        Mung bean
        Scarlet runner bean
        Soy-bean
    xx Forage plants
    Example under Leguminosae
    — Disease and pest resistance
    — Diseases and pests *(Indirect)*
        (SB608.B3)
        sa names of diseases and pests, e.g.
            Bean mosaic virus; Mexican bean
            beetle
    — Fertilizers and manures
    — Field experiments
    — Harvesting
    — Irrigation

    — Marketing
    — Prices *(Direct)*
    — Storage
        sa Beans, Dried—Storage
        Example under Farm produce—Storage
    — Varieties
Beans, Canned
    x Canned beans
    xx Vegetables, Canned
Beans, Dried *(Indirect)*
    x Dried beans
    xx Vegetables, Dried
    — Marketing
    — Packaging
    — Storage
        xx Beans—Storage
    — Transportation
Bear-animalcules
    See Tardigrada
Bear Flag Revolt, 1846
    x Bear Flag War, 1846
    xx California—History—1846-1850
Bear Flag War, 1846
    See Bear Flag Revolt, 1846
Bear hunting *(SK295)*
    xx Bears
Bear-mice
    See Marmots
Bearcat (Fighter planes)
    x F8F (Fighter planes)
    xx Fighter planes
Beard *(GT2320; Dermatology, RL91)*
    sa Mustache lifters
    xx Hair
    — Anecdotes, facetiae, satire, etc.
Beard (in religion, folk-lore, etc.)
    sa Shaving—Moral and religious aspects
    x Folk-lore of beards
    xx Folk literature—Themes, motives
        Religion, Primitive
Bearded seal
    xx Seals (Animals)
Bearers of a flag of truce
    See Flags of truce
Bearing industry
    See Bearings (Machinery)—Trade and
        manufacture
Bearings, Fluid-film
    See Fluid-film bearings
Bearings, Gas-lubricated
    See Gas-lubricated bearings
Bearings (Machinery) *(TJ1061-1073)*
        Here are entered all works relating to the
        supports used in engineering, and
        more particularly in machinery, espe-
        cially for the moving parts.
    sa Aeroplanes—Bearings
        Automobiles—Bearings
        Ball-bearings
        Electric suspension
        Fluid-film bearings
        Friction
        Locomotives—Bearings
        Lubrication and lubricants
        Magnetic suspension
        Marine diesel motors—Bearings
        Motor vehicles—Bearings
        Nonmetallic bearings
        Pivot bearings
        Plastic bearings
        Roller bearings
        Rolling-mill machinery—Bearings
        Rubber bearings
        Turbogenerators—Bearings
        Wooden bearings
    x Bushings
        Journals (Machinery)
    xx Axles

Friction
Lubrication and lubricants
Machinery
Rolling contact
Tribology
— Design and construction
— — Programmed instruction
— Drawings
— Programmed instruction
— Quality control
— Standards *(Direct)*
— Tables, calculations, etc.
— Testing
— Trade and manufacture *(Direct)*
    x Bearing industry
— — Production control
Béarnais dialect *(PC3427.B)*
    xx Gascon dialect
    Provençal language
Bears *(QL737.C2; Bear-baiting, GV1105;*
    Hunting, SK295)
    sa Bear hunting
    Black bear
    Glacier bear
    Grizzly bear
    Polar bear
    Spectacled bear
— Behavior
— Caricatures and cartoons
— Food
— Juvenile literature
— Legends and stories *(QL795.B4)*
— Pictorial works
— Pictures, illustrations, etc.
Bears, Fossil *(QE882.C1)*
Bears (in religion, folk-lore, etc.)
    sa Teddy bears
    x Folk-lore of bears
    xx Religion, Primitive
Beasts
    See Bestiaries
    Domestic animals
    Zoology
Beat generation
    See Bohemianism
Beati immaculati (Music)
    See Psalms (Music)—119th Psalm
Beati omnes (Music)
    See Psalms (Music)—128th Psalm
Beati quorum (Music)
    See Psalms (Music)—32d Psalm
Beatific vision
    x Vision, Beatific
    xx Eschatology
    God
    Heaven
    Supernatural (Theology)
— History of doctrines
Beatification
    sa Blessed
    Canonization
    Heroic virtue
    xx Canonization
Beating (Wood-pulp)
    See Wood-pulp—Refining
Beatitudes *(BT382)*
    x Jesus Christ—Beatitudes
    xx Sermon on the mount
— Illustrations
    Example under Illustration of books
— Meditations
— Poetry
— Sermons
— Stories *(BT382)*
Beatniks
    See Bohemianism
Beatrix oryx
    See Arabian oryx

Beats
    See Bohemianism
Beatus vir, qui non abiit (Music)
    See Psalms (Music)—1st Psalm
Beatus vir, qui timet Dominum (Music)
    See Psalms (Music)—112th Psalm
Beaufort scale
    x Beaufort wind scale
    xx Winds—Measurement
Beaufort wind scale
    See Beaufort scale
Beaune-la-Rolande, Battle of, 1870
    (DC309.B4)
    xx Franco-German War, 1870-1871
Beauticians
    See Beauty operators
Beautification of cities and towns
    See Urban beautification
Beautification of the landscape
    See Landscape protection
Beautiful, The
    See Aesthetics
    Art—Philosophy
Beauty
    See Aesthetics
    Art—Philosophy
    Beauty, Personal
Beauty, Personal *(RA778)*
    sa Beauty contests
    Beauty culture
    Beauty shops
    Body-marking
    Charm
    Cosmetics
    Costume
    Hair
    Hand
    Skin
    Teeth
    Toilet
    x Beauty
    Complexion
    Grooming for women
    Grooming, Personal
    Personal beauty
    xx Beauty culture
    Beauty shops
    Cosmetics
    Face
    Hygiene
    Toilet
    Woman—Health and hygiene
— Early works to 1800
— Juvenile literature
Beauty, Personal, in literature
Beauty contests
    xx Beauty, Personal
Beauty culture *(TT950-979)*
    sa Beauty operators
    Beauty, Personal
    Beauty shops
    Cosmetics
    Hairdressing
    x Cosmetology
    xx Beauty, Personal
    Beauty shops
    Cosmetics
— Equipment and supplies
    See Beauty shops—Equipment and
    supplies
— Examinations, questions, etc.
— Juvenile literature
— Law and legislation
    See Beauty shops—Law and
    legislation
— Study and teaching *(Direct)*
— Vocational guidance

Beauty operators *(Direct)*
    sa Collective labor agreements—
    Hairdressing
    Wages—Beauty operators
    x Beauticians
    Cosmetologists
    Hairdressers
    xx Beauty culture
    Beauty shops
Beauty shops
    sa Beauty culture
    Beauty operators
    Beauty, Personal
    Cosmetics
    xx Beauty culture
    Beauty, Personal
— Accounting
— Designs and plans
— Equipment and supplies
    x Beauty culture—Equipment and
    supplies
— Law and legislation *(Direct)*
    x Beauty culture—Law and legislation
— Management
Beauvais
— Siege, 1472
Beauvais tapestry *(NK3049.B4)*
    xx Tapestry
Beaux
    See Dandies
Beaver (Transport planes)
    xx Transport planes
Beaver Dams, Battle of, 1813 *(E356.B3)*
Beaver Indians (Athapascan tribe)
    See Tsattine Indians
Beavers *(QL737.R6; Legends and stories,*
    QL795.B5)
    x Castor (Rodent)
    xx Rodentia
    Example under Fur-bearing animals
— Behavior
— Juvenile literature
Beavers, Fossil *(QE882.R6)*
Bebop music
    See Jazz music
Bêche-de-mer jargon
    See Beach-la-mar jargon
Bechterew's disease
    See Ankylosing spondylitis
Bechuana
    See Tswana (Bantu tribe)
Bechwana
    See Tswana (Bantu tribe)
Beckmann reaction
    See Beckmann rearrangement
Beckmann rearrangement
    x Beckmann reaction
Becquerel rays *(QC721)*
    x Rays, Becquerel
    xx Actinium
    Polonium
    Radiation
    Radioactivity
    Radium
Bed load
    x Bedload
    xx Sediment transport
— Measurement
    xx Stream measurements
Bed rugs
    See Coverlets
Bed-sores *(RD629)*
    x Decubitus
— Prevention
Bed-wetting
    See Urine—Incontinence
Bedamini (New Guinea people)
    xx Ethnology—New Guinea

Bedauye language
　　See Beja language
Bedawie language
　　See Beja language
Bedbugs　(QL523.C6; Household pests,
　　　TX325)
Bedclothes
　　See Bedding
Bedding
　　sa Blankets
　　　Coverlets
　　　Mattresses
　　　Pillowcases
　　　Pillows
　　　Sheets
　　x Bedclothes
　　xx Beds and bedsteads
　　　Home economics—Equipment and
　　　　supplies
　　　Household linens
Bedding (Horticulture)
　　See Gardening
Bedfordshire, Eng.
　— Gentry
　　　Example under reference from Gentry
Bedik (African people)
　　xx Ethnology—Senegal
Bedik language
Bedja language
　　See Beja language
Bedlington terriers　(SF429.B33)
　　xx Terriers
Bedload
　　See Bed load
Bedmaking
　　xx Beds and bedsteads
Bedouin law
　　See Law, Bedouin
Bedouins　(DS219.B4)
　　x Beduins
　　xx Arabs
　　　North Africans
　　Example under Nomads
Bedouins in Egypt, ⌐Syria, etc.⌐
Bedroom furniture　(Cabinet work,
　　　TT197.5.B4; Interior decoration,
　　　NK2117; Manufacture, TS880)
　　sa Beds and bedsteads
　　xx Furniture
Bedrooms
　　sa Children's rooms
　　　Sleeping customs
　　xx Architecture, Domestic
Beds and bedsteads
　　sa Bedding
　　　Bedmaking
　　　Hospital beds
　　xx Bedroom furniture
　— Costs
　— Juvenile literature
Beds and bedsteads in literature
Bedspreads
　　See Coverlets
Beduins
　　See Bedouins
Bee
　　See Bees
Bee breeding　(Indirect)　(SF531.5)
　　x Bees—Breeding
Bee culture　(Indirect)　(SF521-539)
　　sa Bees
　　　Honey
　　　Honey plants
　　x Apiculture
　　　Beekeeping
　　xx Bees
　　　Honey
　— Anecdotes, facetiae, satire, etc.

　— Early works to 1800
　— Equipment and supplies　(SF532-3)
　　　x Beehives
　— Juvenile literature
　— Laws and legislation　(Direct)
　— Pictorial works
　— Queen rearing
　　　x Queen bees
　　　　Queen rearing
　— Research　(Indirect)
　— Swarming
　　　See Bees—Swarming
Bee culture in art
　　See Bees in art
Bee hunting　(SF537)
　　x Bee trees
　　xx Bees
Bee-keepers' societies　(Indirect)　(SF521)
Bee milk
　　See Royal jelly
Bee stings
　　x Stings, Bee
　　xx Bee venom
　　　Bees
Bee trees
　　See Bee hunting
Bee venom
　　sa Bee stings
　　xx Insect venom
　— Physiological effect
　— Therapeutic use
Beech　(Botany, QK495.B56; Forestry,
　　　SD397.B4)
　— Diseases and pests
　　　sa Beech bark disease
Beech bark disease
　　xx Beech—Diseases and pests
Beechcraft (Aeroplanes)
　　xx Aeroplanes, Private
Beechcraft 17 (Aeroplanes)
　　xx Aeroplanes, Private
Beecher Island, Battle of, 1868　(E83.868)
　　xx Indians of North America—Wars—
　　　1868-1869
Beef　(Indirect)　(TX556.B4)
　　sa Cookery (Beef)
　　　Corned beef
　　xx Meat
　— Grading
　— Marketing
　— Prices　(Direct)
　— Transportation
Beef, Canned　(Indirect)
　　x Canned beef
　　xx Meat, Canned
Beef, Corned
　　See Corned beef
Beef, Dried
　　x Charqui
　　　Jerky
　　xx Meat industry and trade
Beef cattle　(Indirect)　(SF207)
　　sa Aberdeen-Angus cattle
　　　Charolais cattle
　　　Hereford cattle
　　　Shorthorn cattle
　　x Cattle, Beef
　　　Steers
　　xx Cattle
　— Diseases
　— Economic aspects　(Direct)
　— Equipment and supplies
　　　See Beef cattle housing and equipment
　— Feeding and feeds
　— Judging
　　　xx Stock-judging
　— Juvenile literature
　— Prices　(Direct)

　— Showing
　— Shrinkage
　　　x Beef cattle—Weight loss
　　　　Shrinkage of beef cattle
　　　　Weight loss of beef cattle
　　　xx Cattle—Physiology
　— Weight and measurement
　— Weight loss
　　　See Beef cattle—Shrinkage
Beef cattle breeding　(Indirect)　(SF207)
　　xx Cattle breeding
Beef cattle breeds　(SF207)
　　xx Cattle breeds
Beef cattle housing and equipment　(Indirect)
　　　(SF206)
　　x Beef cattle—Equipment and supplies
　　xx Cattle houses and equipment
Beef packers　(Beef trust, United States,
　　　HD2769.P3; Industry,
　　　HD9410-9429; Technology,
　　　TS1950-1975)
　　sa Packing-house products
　　　Stock-yards
　　xx Cattle trade
　　　Meat industry and trade
　　　Stock-yards
Beefmaster cattle　(SF199.B; Herd-books,
　　　SF193.B)
Beehive coke industry
　　See Coke industry
Beehives
　　See Bee culture—Equipment and supplies
Beekeeping
　　See Bee culture
Beembe language (Lake Tanganyika)
　　See Bembe language (Lake Tanganyika)
Beer　(Industry, HD9397; Technology,
　　　TP569-587)
　　sa Ale
　　　Brewing
　　　Cookery (Beer)
　　　Kvass
　　　Malt
　　　Malt-extracts
　　　Porter
　　　Rice beer
　　　Weiss beer
　　xx Alcoholic beverages
　　　Ale
　　　Brewing
　　　Brewing industry
　　　Malt liquors
　— Anecdotes, facetiae, satire, etc.
　— Law and legislation
　　　See Brewing industry—Law and
　　　　legislation
　— Prices　(Direct)
　— Taxation　(Direct)
　　　x Brewing industry—Taxation
　　　xx Liquor traffic—Taxation
　— Therapeutic use
Beer bottles　(Direct)
　　xx Bottles
Beer Hall Putsch, 1923
　　See Germany—History—Beer Hall Putsch,
　　　1923
Beer trays　(Direct)
　　xx Trays
Bees　(Indirect)　(Beekeeping, SF521-538;
　　　Entomology, QL568.A6)
　　sa Bee culture
　　　Bee hunting
　　　Bee stings
　　　Beeswax
　　　Bumblebees
　　　Carpenter bees
　　　Honey
　　　Honeycombs

172

Mason-bees
Royal jelly
Stingless bees
  x Aculeata
    Bee
    Honeybees
  xx Bee culture
    Honey
    Hymenoptera
    Insect societies
— Anatomy
— Behavior
— Breeding
    See Bee breeding
— Diseases (SF538)
    sa Foul brood, American
      Foul brood, European
— Feeding and feeds
— Juvenile literature
— Legends and stories
— Psychology
— Swarming
    x Bee culture—Swarming
      Swarming of bees
Bees, Folk-lore of
  See Folk-lore of bees
Bees, Stingless
  See Stingless bees
Bees (Cooperative gatherings) (Indirect)
  xx Agriculture, Cooperative
    Community life
    Cooperation
    Country life
    Manners and customs
    Rural conditions
    Social participation
Bees in art (N7660)
  x Bee culture in art
  xx Animal painting and illustration
Bees in literature
Beeswax (Indirect) (TP678)
  xx Bees
    Honeycombs
    Waxes
Beet
  See Beets and beet sugar
Beet juice
  xx Vegetable juices
— Therapeutic use
    xx Antineoplastic agents
Beet leaf-hopper
— Host plants
Beet pests (SB608.B4)
  sa names of pests, e.g. Dock false-worm;
    Leaf-spot; Sugar-beet crown-borer
  x Beets and beet sugar—Diseases and
    pests
  xx Beets and beet sugar
Beet seed (SB329)
  sa Sugar beet seed
  x Beets and beet sugar—Seed
  xx Vegetable seed
Beet yellows
  x Sugar-beet virus yellows
  xx Spinach—Diseases and pests
Beetle, Sawtoothed grain
  See Sawtoothed grain beetle
Beetles (Indirect) (QL571-597)
  sa Alfalfa weevil
    Ambrosia beetles
    Apple-tree weevil
    Archostemata
    Asiatic beetle
    Asparagus-beetle
    Bark-beetles
    Bark-weevil
    Bean leaf-beetle
    Bean-weevil

Black Hills beetle
Boll-weevil
Broad-nosed grain-weevil
Chestnut-weevil
Clover-leaf weevil
Cockchafers
Coffee-bean weevil
Cottonwood beetle
Cow-pea weevil
Cucumber-beetle
European chafer
Feather-wing beetles
Fireflies
Flea-beetles
Granary weevil
Green June beetle
Japanese beetle
Khapra beetle
Ladybirds
Larch case-bearer
Long-headed flour-beetle
Pales weevil
Palm-weevil
Palmetto-weevil
Pepper-weevil
Pine reproduction weevil
Potato-beetle
Rhinoceros beetle
Rice weevil
Sawtoothed grain beetle
Strawberry-weevil
Sugar-cane beetle
Tan-bark beetle
Tobacco-weevil
Vegetable weevil
Water-beetles
White-fringed beetle
White-pine weevil
  x Coleoptera
    Weevils
  xx Insects
— Anatomy
— Behavior
— Catalogs and collections (QL577)
— Host plants
— Identification
— Juvenile literature
Beetles, Fossil (QE832.C6)
  x Fossil beetles
  xx Insects, Fossil
Beets and beet sugar (Indirect) (Culture,
    SB219-221, SB329; Industry,
    HD9100-9119; Technology,
    TP390-391)
  sa Beet pests
    Cookery (Beets)
    Mangel-wurzel
    Sugar beet breeding
    Sugar-beet varieties
  x Beet
    Sugar-beet
  xx Sugar
    Sugar growing
— Analysis
— Costs
— Diseases and pests
    See Beet pests
— Fertilizers and manures
— Harvesting
— Irrigation
— Prices
— Seed
    See Beet seed
      Sugar beet seed
— Silage
    See Sugar-beet silage
— Storage
— Taxation

    See Sugar—Taxation
— Transportation
Beets as feed
  sa Sugar-beet silage
Beggar-weed
Beggars (Direct)
  x Mendicants
— Caricatures and cartoons
Beggars, The
  See Gueux
Beggars in art (N8217.B4)
Beggars in literature
Begging (Direct) (HV4480-4630; Pauperism
    and crime, HV6174)
  sa Tramps
    Vagrancy
  x Mendicancy
  xx Poor
    Tramps
    Vagrancy
Beggs method (TA650)
  xx Engineering models
    Structures, Theory of
Beghards (BX2975.B5)
  sa Beguines
    Bohemian Brethren
    Brethren of the Free Spirit
  xx Beguines
    Brethren of the Free Spirit
    Monasticism and religious orders
    Third orders
Beginner's all-purpose symbolic instruction
    code
  See Basic (Computer program language)
Beginning
  sa Birth (Philosophy)
    Causation
    Creation
    Space and time
  x Commencement
  xx Cosmology
    Creation
    Space and time
Beginning teachers
  See First year teachers
Begonia breeding (Indirect) (SB413.B4)
  x Begonias—Breeding
  xx Plant-breeding
Begonias (SB413.B4)
  Example under Foliage plants
— Breeding
    See Begonia breeding
— Therapeutic use
— Varieties
Beguinages (Indirect)
  xx Beguines
    Convents and nunneries
    Monasticism and religious orders for
      women
    Third orders
Beguines (BX4270.B5)
  sa Beghards
    Beguinages
    Brethren of the Free Spirit
  xx Beghards
    Brethren of the Free Spirit
    Monasticism and religious orders for
      women
    Third orders
Behari language
  See Bihari language
Beharis
  See Biharis
Behavior
  See Conduct of life
    Etiquette
Behavior, Good (Law)
  See Good behavior (Law)

Behavior, Instrumental
   See Operant behavior
Behavior, Operant
   See Operant behavior
Behavior, Verbal
   See Verbal behavior
Behavior (Psychology)
   See Animals, Habits and behavior of
      Human behavior
Behavior control, Electronic
   See Electronic behavior control
Behavior genetics
   xx Animals, Habits and behavior of
      Genetics
      Psychology
Behavior modification *(BF637.B4)*
   sa Behavior therapy
   xx Psychology, Applied
   — Programmed instruction
Behavior problems (Children)
   See Problem children
Behavior therapy *(RC489.B4)*
   sa Rational-emotive psychotherapy
   xx Behavior modification
      Psychotherapy
Behavioral models
   See Human behavior—Mathematical models
Behaviorism (Psychology) *(BF199)*
   sa Conditioned response
   xx Psychology
      Psychology, Physiological
Behçet's disease *(RC122.B4)*
   xx Blood-vessels—Diseases
      Eye—Diseases and defects
Behistun inscriptions
   See Achaemenian inscriptions
      Cuneiform inscriptions
      Old Persian inscriptions
Behosys
   x Beosis
      Kalios
Beidellite *(QE391.B)*
Being
   See Ontology
Beir (African people)
   See Murle (African people)
Beja (African people)
   xx Ethnology—Sudan
Beja language *(PJ2451-9)*
   x Bedauye language
      Bedawie language
      Bedja language
      Bishári dialect
      To-bedawie language
      Tu-bedawie language
   xx Cushitic languages
Bejel
   xx Syphilis
Bekoe
   See Batwa
Bektashi *(BP175.D4)*
   x Bektashites
   xx Dervishes
      Islamic sects
Bektashites
   See Bektashi
Bekwarra language
   xx Benue-Congo languages
Bel
   See Baal (Deity)
Bel (Tree)
   See Bael (Tree)
Bel canto *(MT845)*
   xx Singing—Methods
Belari
   See Lohars
Belemnites *(QE807.B4)*
Belfast

— Riots
Belfort, France
   — Siege, 1870-1871 *(DC305.92)*
      xx Franco-German War, 1870-1871
Belfort, Battle of, 1871 *(DC305.22)*
   xx Franco-German War, 1870-1871
Belfries
   See Towers
Belgae
Belgian almanacs
   See Almanacs, Belgian
Belgian aquatints
   See Aquatints, Belgian
Belgian artists
   See Artists, Belgian
Belgian book-plates
   See Book-plates, Belgian
Belgian cattle herders
   See Bouviers des Flandres
Belgian chicory
   See Belgian endive
Belgian draft horse *(SF293.B4)*
   xx Draft horses
Belgian endive *(Botany, QK495.C74; Culture,*
      SB351.E5)
   x Belgian chicory
      Endive, Belgian
      Endive, French
      French endive
      Witloof
   xx Chicory
Belgian engravers
   See Engravers, Belgian
Belgian Expedition to China, 1900 (Projected)
Belgian fiction (French) *(Collections,*
      PQ3848; History, PQ3832)
   Duplicate entry is made under French fic-
      tion—Belgian authors.
   Note under French fiction—Belgian authors
Belgian hare *(SF455)*
   xx Hares
Belgian literature *(Direct)* *(PQ3810-3858)*
   Comprises literature in Flemish, French,
      and Walloon.
   xx Flemish literature
      French literature
Belgian literature (Flemish)
   See Flemish literature
Belgian literature (French)
   See French literature—Belgian authors
Belgian literature (Walloon)
   See Walloon literature
Belgian malinois
   x Malinois sheepdog
Belgian missions
   See Missions, Belgian
Belgian newspapers *(History, etc.,*
      PN5261-9)
   sa Flemish newspapers
   x French newspapers (Belgian)
Belgian painting
   See Painting, Belgian
Belgian paleography
   See Paleography, Belgian
Belgian periodicals *(History, etc.,*
      PN5261-5270)
   sa Flemish periodicals
   x French periodicals (Belgian)
Belgian poetry
   Comprises poetry in Flemish, French,
      and Walloon.
   sa Walloon poetry
Belgian poetry (French)
   See French poetry—Belgian authors
Belgian posters
   See Posters, Belgian
Belgian property in Great Britain
Belgian prose literature

Belgian sheep dog *(SF429.B4)*
   x Groenendael sheepdog
Belgian students in the United States, [etc.]
Belgian tervuren
   See Tervuren
Belgian wit and humor *(Direct)*
      (PN6222.B4)
Belgian wit and humor, Pictorial
Belgians in Brazil, [Canada, Louisiana, etc.]
"Belgica" Expedition
   See Expédition antarctique belge,
      1897-1899
Belgium
— Commerce
—— United States
     Note under United States—Com-
      merce—Africa, [Belgium, China,
      etc.]
— History *(DH401-811)*
—— To 1555
—— 1555-1648
—— 1648-1794
—— 18th century
—— Revolution, 1789-1790
—— Invasion of 1792
—— 1794-1814
     sa Meenen, Belgium—Siege, 1794
—— Peasants' War, 1798 *(DH631)*
     x Peasants' War, 1798 (Belgium)
—— 1814-1830
—— Revolution, 1830-1839
—— 1830-1914
—— 1914-
—— German occupation, 1914-1918
     (D623.B4; DH682)
—— German occupation, 1940-1945
     Example under World War, 1939-
      1945—Collaborationists; World
      War, 1939-1945—Occupied ter-
      ritories
——— Poetry
— Neutrality
     x European War, 1914-1918—Belgian
      neutrality
      European War, 1914-1918—
      Neutrality of Belgium
      World War, 1939-1945—Neutrality
      of Belgium
     Example under Neutrality
— Registers
     Example under Yearbooks
Belgium in literature
Belgrad
— Siege, 1456
— Siege, 1521
     xx Turkey—History—1453-1683
— Siege, 1915
— Siege, 1944
     xx World War, 1939-1945—Campaigns
      —Yugoslavia
Belgrad, Bombardment of, 1862 *(DR386)*
Belgrad, Peace of, 1739 *(DR548)*
   xx Austro-Turkish War, 1737-1739
      Russo-Turkish War, 1736-1739
Belice question
   See British Honduras question
Belief and doubt *(Philosophy, BD215;*
      Psychology, BF773)
   Here are entered works treating the sub-
      ject from the philosophical standpoint.
      Works on religious belief are entered
      under the heading Faith.
   sa Agnosticism
      Error
      Evidence
      Irrationalism (Philosophy)
      Irreligion
      Rationalism

Scruples
Skepticism
Truth
  x Conviction
Doubt
Religious belief
  xx Agnosticism
Consciousness
Credulity
Emotions
Knowledge, Theory of
Philosophy
Psychology
Rationalism
Religion
Skepticism
Will
  Note under Faith
Belief and doubt in literature
Believers' church
  See Dissenters, Religious
Bell and Howell moving-picture camera
Bell-buoys
  See Buoys
Bell-founders *(Direct)* *(Antiquities,*
    CC200-250; Technology, TS583-9)
  xx Bells
Founding
Bell helicopter
Bell-lyra
  See Glockenspiel
Bell peppers
  See Peppers
Bell ringing
  See Change ringing
Handbell ringing
Bell System Telstar satellite
  See Project Telstar
Bell vireo
  x Bell's vireo
  xx Vireos
Bell X-1 (Supersonic planes)
  x X-1 (Bell supersonic plane)
  xx Supersonic planes
Bellabella Indians *(E99.B)*
  xx Indians of North America
Kwakiutl Indians
Bellacoola Indians
  xx Indians of North America
Salishan Indians
Belladonna *(RM666.B4)*
  sa Atropine
  xx Atropine
Mydriatics
  Example under Alkaloids; Materia medica;
Therapeutics
Bellamy system
  See Pressure pattern flying
Bellboys, Hotel
  See Hotel bellmen
Belle-Alliance, Battle of, 1815
  See Waterloo, Battle of, 1815
Belle coquette (Game) *(GV1017.B4)*
Belleau Wood, Battle of, 1918 *(D545.B4)*
  xx European War, 1914-1918—Campaigns
—France
Belleric myrobalan
  x Bahera
Myrobalan, Belleric
Belles-lettres
  See Literature
Bellevue intelligence scales
  See Wechsler adult intelligence scale
Bellhops, Hotel
  See Hotel bellmen
Belligerency *(JX4571-5187)*
  sa Combatants and noncombatants
(International law)

  xx War (International law)
Belligerent occupation
  See Military occupation
Bellinzone, Battle of, 1422
  See Arbedo, Battle of, 1422
Bellmen, Hotel
  See Hotel bellmen
Bellonese language
Bellows (Mechanical engineering)
  xx Couplings
Packing (Mechanical engineering)
Pipe-fittings
Pressure-gages
Sealing (Technology)
  — Standards
Bells *(Direct)* *(Antiquities, CC200-250;*
    Technology, TS583-9)
  sa Bell-founders
Carillons
Change ringing
Chimes
Electric bells
Handbell ringing
Handbells
Jaquemarts
  x Campanology
Church bells
  xx Liturgical objects
  — Collectors and collecting
  — Inscriptions *(CC200-250)*
    x Inscriptions on bells
  — Juvenile literature
  — Poetry
  — Private collections
Bell's palsy
  See Paralysis, Facial
Bell's vireo
  See Bell vireo
Bells, xylophone, string quartet with string
    orchestra *(M1105-6)*
  xx Sextets (Bells, xylophone, string
quartet)
String-orchestra music
  — Scores *(M1105)*
Belly dance
Belly dance music *(Indirect)*
Belote (Game) *(GV1295.B4)*
  x Clob-e-osh (Game)
Ka-La-Bre-Osh (Game)
Beloutchi language
  See Baluchi language
Below cost selling
  See Loss leaders
Belt buckles *(Indirect)*
  x Belt plates
  xx Belts (Clothing)
Buckles
Belt-clasps
  See Clasps
Belt conveyors
  See Conveying machinery
Belt industry
  See Belts and belting
Belts (Clothing)—Trade and
manufacture
Belt plates
  See Belt buckles
Belt toggles
  x Toggles, Belt
  xx Carving (Art industries)
Clothing and dress
Belted Galloway
  xx Galloway cattle
Belted kingfisher
  xx Kingfishers
Beltica camera
Belts, Indian
  See Wampum belts

Belts (Clothing)
  sa Belt buckles
  xx Clothing and dress
  — Trade and manufacture *(Direct)*
    (TS2301.B5)
    x Belt industry
Belts and belting *(TJ1100-1119)*
  sa Link-belting
Power transmission
  x Belt industry
Chain-belting
  xx Machinery
Power transmission
  — Maintenance and repair
  — Standards *(Direct)*
Beluga (Whale)
  See White whale
Belvedere, Battle of, 1944
  xx World War, 1939-1945—Campaigns—
Italy
Bemba (African tribe) *(DT963)*
  sa Ushi (African tribe)
  xx Bantus
  — Religion
Bemba language
  x Chibemba language
Wemba language
  xx Bantu languages
Bemba poetry *(PL8069.7)*
Bembe language (Lake Tanganyika)
  x Beembe language (Lake Tanganyika)
Ebembe language
Ibembe language
  xx Bantu languages
Bemis's Heights, Battle of, 1777
  See Saratoga campaign, 1777
Bena (African people)
  See Wabena
Bena-bena language
  x Benabena language
  xx Papuan languages
Benabena language
  See Bena-bena language
Benamee transactions
  See Benami transactions
Benami transactions
  sa Fraudulent conveyances (Hindu law)
  x Benamee transactions
Namartham
  xx Contracts (Hindu law)
Fraudulent conveyances (Hindu law)
Hindu law
Third parties (Hindu law)
Trusts and trustees (Hindu law)
Bench-marks *(Indirect)* *(TA610)*
  xx Leveling
Surveying
Benda language (Bantu)
  See Venda language
Bender gestalt test *(BF204.B4)*
  x Gestalt test
  xx Gestalt psychology
Mental tests
Personality tests
Bending
    Here are entered works dealing with
bending as a forming process. Works
on the bending behavior of materials
are entered under Flexure.
  sa Pipe bending
  xx Metal-work
  Note under Flexure
Bending machines
Bending moment
  xx Strains and stresses
Benedic, anima mea Domino, Domine Deus
(Music)
  See Psalms (Music)—104th Psalm

Benedic, anima mea Domino et omnia (Music)
  See Psalms (Music)—103d Psalm
Benedicam Dominum (Music)
  See Psalms (Music)—34th Psalm
Benedicks effect *(QC621)*
  sa Thomson effect
  xx Thermoelectricity
  Thomson effect
Benedictine drama
Benedictine nuns
  x Benedictines (Women)
  Nuns, Benedictine
  xx Benedictines
  Monasticism and religious orders for
    women
Benedictines *(BX3001-3055; Women,*
    BX4275-8)
  sa Benedictine nuns
  Camaldolites
  Cluniacs
  Tironensians
  Vallombrosans
  x Black Monks
  St. Benedict, Order of
  xx Cistercians
  Cluniacs
  Monasticism and religious orders
  — Missions *(BV2250)*
Benedictines, Cluniac
  See Cluniacs
Benedictines (Women)
  See Benedictine nuns
Benedictines in Austria, ₍France, Italy, etc.₎
  — Heraldry
Benediction *(BV197.B5; Catholic Church,*
    BX2048.B5)
  Here are entered works dealing with the
    act of blessing as a liturgical function,
    also works dealing with the blessing of
    various objects and persons, the so-
    called benedictions. Abstract works on
    blessing are entered under the heading
    Blessing and cursing.
  xx Blessing and cursing
  Consecration
Benediction of the Blessed Sacrament (Music)
    (M2150.4.B45)
Benedictionals
  sa Catholic Church. Liturgy and ritual.
    Benedictional
  xx Catholic Church. Liturgy and ritual.
    Benedictional
Benedictus
  xx Canticles
Benedictus Dominus (Music)
  See Psalms (Music)—144th Psalm
Benefices, Ecclesiastical *(BV775; Catholic*
    Church, BX1955)
  Here are entered works on benefices in
    general as well as in the Catholic
    Church.
  sa Chantries
  Clergy—Salaries, pensions, etc.
  Jus primariarum precum
  Patronage, Ecclesiastical
  subdivision Benefices *under names of*
    churches other than the Catholic
    Church, e.g. Church of England—
    Benefices
  x Catholic Church—Benefices
  Church benefices
  Ecclesiastical benefices
  Expectative graces
  Graces, Expectative
  Pluralism (Benefices)
  xx Catholic Church—Finance
  Church finance
  Church polity

Church property
Clergy
Clergy—Salaries, pensions, etc.
Benefices, Ecclesiastical (Canon law)
    (BX1939.B4)
  sa Excardination (Canon law)
  Incardination (Canon law)
  Patronage, Ecclesiastical (Canon law)
  xx Patronage, Ecclesiastical (Canon law)
  Example under Canon law
Beneficium competentiae
  See Exemption (Law)
Beneficium inventarii
  See Benefit of inventory
Beneficium separationis
  See Separation of patrimony
Benefit funds (Trade-union)
  See Welfare funds (Trade-union)
Benefit of clergy
  See Privilegium fori
Benefit of competency
  See Exemption (Law)
Benefit of inventory *(Direct)*
  x Beneficium inventarii
  Privilege of inventory
  xx Claims against decedents' estates
  Debtor and creditor
  Decedents' estates
  Inheritance and succession
Benefit of inventory (Roman law)
Benefit performances
  xx Fund raising
  Performing arts
Benefit societies
  See Friendly societies
Benefits, Unclaimed (Civil service pensions)
  See Civil service pensions—Unclaimed
    benefits
Benefits, Unjustified
  See Unjust enrichment
Benet-Mercié gun
  See Benet-Mercié machine-gun
Benet-Mercié machine-gun *(VF620.B4)*
  x Benet-Mercié gun
  Benet-Mercié machine rifle
  xx Hotchkiss machine-gun
  Machine-guns
Benet-Mercié machine rifle
  See Benet-Mercié machine-gun
Benevento in art
Benevolence
  sa Charity
  Kindness
  Poor
  xx Conduct of life
  Ethics
  Humanity
  Kindness
Benevolent institutions
  See Almshouses
  Asylums
  Blind—Institutional care
  Charities
  Children—Institutional care
  Deaf—Institutional care
  Hospitals
  Institutional care
  Woman—Institutional care
  subdivisions Benevolent and moral
    institutions and societies *and*
    Charities *under names of cities*
Benevolent societies
  See Charitable societies
  subdivision Benevolent and moral
    institutions and societies *under*
    names of cities, e.g. London—
    Benevolent and moral institutions
    and societies

Benga language *(PL8071-4)*
  xx Bantu languages
Bengal quince
  See Bael (Tree)
Bengali ballads and songs *(Direct)*
    (Collections, PK1716; History,
    PK1712)
Bengali drama *(Collections, PK1715; History,*
    PK1711)
Bengali drama (Tragedy)
Bengali fiction *(Direct)*
Bengali imprints *(Direct)*
Bengali Islamic prayers
  See Islamic prayers, Bengali
Bengali language *(PK1651-1695)*
  xx Indo-Aryan languages, Modern
Bengali literature *(Direct) (PK1700-1788)*
  xx Pakistan literature
  — Muslim authors
Bengali newspapers *(PN5378.B4-5)*
Bengali philology
Bengali poetry *(Collections, PK1714;*
    History, PK1710)
  sa Vaishnava poetry, Bengali
Bengali poetry (English)
  Duplicate entry is made under English
    poetry—Indic authors.
Bengali prose literature
Bengali Vaishnava poetry
  See Vaishnava poetry, Bengali
Bengali wit and humor
  xx Indic wit and humor
Bengalis
Bengalis in Delhi, ₍etc.₎
Benge language
  x Libenge language
  Mobenge language
  xx Bantu languages
Benguela language
  See Umbundu language
Benguetano language
  See Igorot language
Beni Marin dynasty *(DT319)*
  x Marinides
  Merinides
  xx Morocco—History—647-1516
Beni Meskine (Berber tribe)
  xx Berbers
  Ethnology—Morocco
Benin language
  See Bini language
Beniseed
  See Sesame
Benitoite *(QE391.B5)*
  xx Silicates
Benjamin (Tribe of Israel) *(DS113.5.B)*
  xx Jews
  Twelve tribes of Israel
Bennett's comet *(QB727.69)*
Bennington, Battle of, 1777 *(E241.B4)*
  x Walloomsac, N.Y., Battle of, 1777
  xx Burgoyne's Invasion, 1777
Bennington pottery
  x Pottery, Bennington
  xx Pottery, American
Benthos *(Indirect)*
  xx Aquatic biology
  Ocean bottom
Bentley automobile *(TL215.B)*
Bentonite *(Indirect) (TN948.B4)*
  x Gumbrin
Bentonite deposits *(Indirect)*
Benue-Congo languages
  sa Bantu languages
  Bekwarra language
  Birom language
  Efik language
  Jukun language

Tivi language
Yakö language
Benzaldehyde *(QD341.A6)*
Benzene *(QD341.H9)*
  sa Mills-Nixon effect
  x Benzol
  Example under Chemistry, Organic
  — Analysis
  — Physiological effect *(QP981.B)*
  — Spectra
Benzene, Amido-
  See Aniline
Benzene as fuel *(TP359.B4)*
  xx Fuel
    Liquid fuels
    Motor fuels
Benzene in the body *(QP801.B5)*
Benzidine dyes
  xx Dyes and dyeing
Benzoates
Benzoin *(QD341.K2)*
Benzol
  See Benzene
Beosis
  See Behosys
Beothikan Indians
  See Beothuk Indians
Beothuk Indians *(E99.B4)*
  x Beothikan Indians
    Beothukan Indians
    Red Indians of Newfoundland
  xx Indians of North America
Beothuk language *(PM695)*
  x Beothukan languages
Beothukan Indians
  See Beothuk Indians
Beothukan languages
  See Beothuk language
Bequests
  See Inheritance and succession
    Legacies
Berat gecesi
  See Laylat al-Barā'ah
Beraunite *(QE391.B)*
Berber languages *(PJ2340-2349;*
  PJ2369-2399)
  sa Baamarani dialect
    Guanche language
    Kabyle language
    Rif language
    Shilha language
    Siwa language
    Tamashek language
    Tamazight language
    Zenaga language
  x Libyan languages
  xx Hamitic languages
Berber literature
  x Libyan literature
Berberis
  See Barberries
Berbers *(GN649; DT193)*
  sa Ahansala
    Aït Atta (Berber tribe)
    Beni Meskine (Berber tribe)
    Celtiberi
    Chaamba
    Chaouia (Berber tribe)
    Guanches
    Hamites
    Hammudites
    Ikounka
    Kabyles
    Libyans
    Seksawa (Berber tribe)
    Tuaregs
  xx Celtiberi
    Hamites

Kabyles
Libyans
North Africans
Bereaved, Church work with the
  See Church work with the bereaved
Bereavement
  sa Consolation
    Grief
  x Loss of loved ones by death
  xx Consolation
    Death
  — Personal narratives
  — Psychological aspects
Berets *(GT2110)*
  xx Head-gear
Beretta submachine gun *(UF620.B45)*
  xx Machine-guns
Berezhany, Battle of, 1916-1917
  xx European War, 1914-1918—Campaigns
    —Eastern
Bergamot oil
  xx Citrus oils
    Perfumes
  Example under Essences and essential oils
  — Analysis
Bergen-op-Zoom
  — Siege, 1622 *(D267.B3)*
Bergmann's rule *(QH543)*
  xx Adaptation (Biology)
    Bioclimatology
    Body size
    Evolution
Bergylt
  See Rosefish
Beri-beri *(RC624)*
  x Kakké
Bericho (Asiatic people)
  See Doma (Asiatic people)
Bering Sea controversy
  x Fur-seal arbitration
  xx Fur trade
    Sealing—Law and legislation
Bering's Expedition, 1st, 1725-1730
  (G296.B4)
  xx Northwest coast of North America
  — Juvenile literature
Bering's Expedition, 2d, 1733-1743
  (G296.B4)
  — Juvenile literature
Berkeley, Calif.
  — Riots, 1969
Berkeley peerage claim
  Example under Peerage—Claims
Berkut eagle
  See Himalayan golden eagle
Berlin
  — Airlift
    See Berlin—Blockade, 1948-1949
  — Blockade, 1948-1949
    x Berlin airlift
    Berlin—Airlift
    Berlin blockade
    xx Berlin—History—Allied occupation,
      1945-
  — — Pictorial works
  — History
  — — Revolution, 1848-1849
    xx Germany—History—Revolution,
      1848-1849
  — — 1918-1945 *(DD879-880)*
  — — Allied occupation, 1945-
    sa Berlin—Blockade, 1948-1949
    Berlin question (1945-   )
    Berlin—Riot, June, 1953
    Berlin wall (1961-   )
  — International status
    sa Berlin question (1945-   )
    xx Berlin question (1945-   )

  — Riot, June, 1953
    xx Berlin—History—Allied occupation,
      1945-
  — Siege, 1945
    See Berlin, Battle of, 1945
Berlin, Battle of, 1945 *(D757.9)*
  x Berlin—Siege, 1945
  xx World War, 1939-1945—Campaigns—
    Germany
Berlin, Treaty of, 1878 *(D375.3)*
  xx Eastern question (Balkan)
    Russo-Turkish War, 1877-1878
  Example under International relations
Berlin airlift
  See Berlin—Blockade, 1948-1949
Berlin blockade
  See Berlin—Blockade, 1948-1949
Berlin crisis
  See Berlin question (1945-   )
Berlin in literature
Berlin porcelain *(NK4399.B4)*
  x Porcelain, Berlin
Berlin question (1945-   )
  sa Berlin—International status
    Berlin wall (1961-   )
  x Berlin crisis
  xx Berlin—History—Allied occupation,
    1945-
    Berlin—International status
    German reunification question (1949-
)
Berlin wall (1961-   )
  xx Berlin—History—Allied occupation,
    1945-
    Berlin question (1945-   )
  — Pictorial works
Berlin wool work
  See Canvas embroidery, Victorian
Berlin work
  See Canvas embroidery, Victorian
Bermuda . . .
  x Bermudian . . .
Bermuda grass
  x Bahama grass
    Devil grass
    Scutch grass
Bermudian . . .
  See Bermuda . . .
Bern (Canton) in art
Bern disputation, 1528
  xx Disputations, Religious
Bernoullian numbers *(QA246)*
  x Functions, Bernoulli's
    Numbers, Bernoullian
  xx Numerical functions
Bernstein polynomials
  x Polynomials, Bernstein
  xx Convergence
    Integrals
    Probabilities
    Series
Berom language
  See Birom language
Berouhi language
  See Brahui language
Berri
  See Zaghawa
Berries *(Indirect)* *(Culture, SB381-6)*
  sa Cookery (Berries)
    names of berries, e.g. Strawberries
  xx Fruit
    Fruit-culture
  — Composition
  — Diseases and pests
  — Harvesting
  — Varieties
Berries, Frozen *(TX828)*

Berseem
    xx Clover
       Forage plants
Berserkers *(DL65)*
Bertillon system *(HV6068)*
    x Criminal anthropometry
    xx Anthropometry
       Crime and criminals—Identification
       Fingerprints
Beryl *(Indirect)*
    xx Aluminum silicates
       Silicates
    Example under Silicate minerals
Beryllium *(QD181.B4)*
    x Glucinium
       Glucinum
    — Analysis
    — Isotopes
       x Beryllium isotopes
          Isotopic beryllium
    — — Spectra
    — Spectra
    — Toxicology *(RA1231.B4)*
Beryllium alloys
    sa Copper-beryllium alloys
       Copper-tin-beryllium alloys
Beryllium bronze
    xx Bronze
Beryllium compounds
Beryllium-copper alloys
    See Copper-beryllium alloys
Beryllium crystals
Beryllium industry *(Direct)*
    — Hygienic aspects *(RC965.B5)*
Beryllium isotopes
    See Beryllium—Isotopes
Beryllium ores *(Indirect)*
Beryllium organic compounds
    See Organoberyllium compounds
Beryllosodalite
    See Tugtupite
Bescommonconty Indians
    See Arosaguntacook Indians
Beseda (Dance) *(GV1796.B3)*
    xx Country-dance
Beseler Topcon camera
Besenyök
    See Petchenegs
Besm computer *(QA76.8.B4; Technology,*
    TK7889.B)
    xx Electronic digital computers
    — Memory systems
       Example under Computer storage devices
    — Programming *(QA76.8.B4)*
Besnier-Boeck disease
    See Sarcoidosis
Besnoitiosis *(SF810.B4)*
    x Globidiosis
    xx Veterinary protozoology
Bessarabia
    — History
    — — Tatarbunary Uprising, 1924
       x Tatarbunary Uprising, 1924
Bessarabia in literature
Bessel functions *(QA408)*
    sa Differential equations
       Hankel functions
       Harmonic analysis
       Harmonic functions
       Lommel functions
    x Cylindrical harmonics
       Functions, Besselian
    xx Harmonic analysis
       Harmonic functions
    Example under Functions, Transcendental
    — Computer programs
       Example under Computer programs

Bessel functions (Third kind)
    See Hankel functions
Bessemer furnace
    See Bessemer process
Bessemer process *(TN736-8)*
    x Bessemer furnace
       Thomas process
    xx Metallurgical furnaces
       Smelting
       Steel
    — Automation
    — Safety measures *(TN736)*
Best books
    See Bibliography—Best books
Best sellers
    sa Bibliography—Best books
    x Books—Best sellers
    xx Books and reading
Bestiality
    xx Sex
Bestiality (Law) *(Direct)*
    x Buggery
    xx Sex crimes
       Sodomy
Bestiaries
    sa Animal lore
    x Beasts
    xx Animal lore
       Fables
Bet Hillel and Bet Shammai
    See Beth Hillel and Beth Shammai
Bet Shammai and Bet Hillel
    See Beth Hillel and Beth Shammai
Beta decay
    sa Delayed neutrons
    x Decay, Beta
    xx Beta rays
       Radioisotopes—Decay
    — Tables, etc.
Beta functions
    See Functions, Beta
Beta particles
    See Beta rays
Beta ray spectrometry
    x Spectrometry, Beta ray
    xx Angular correlations (Nuclear physics)
       Beta rays
       Radiochemistry
       Spectrometer
       Spectrum analysis
Beta rays
    sa Beta decay
       Beta ray spectrometry
    x Beta particles
    xx Electrons
       Internal conversion (Nuclear physics)
       Ionizing radiation
       Radiation
       Radioactivity
    — Measurement
    — Physiological effect
    — Polarization
    — Scattering
Betatron *(QC787.B)*
    x Induction accelerator
    xx Electromagnetism
       Particle accelerators
Betatron oscillations *(QC786)*
    x Oscillations, Betatron
Betcherrygah
    See Budgerigars
Bété (African people)
    xx Ethnology—Ivory Coast
Bete language
    x Betegbo language
    xx Kwa languages
Betegbo language
    See Bete language

Betel nut *(Indirect)* *(Botany, QK495.P;*
    Pharmacy, RS165.B; Plant culture
    and horticulture, SB295.B)
    x Areca nut
       Pinang (Plant)
    xx Palms
    — Marketing
Beth Hillel and Beth Shammai *(BM501.25)*
    x Bet Hillel and Bet Shammai
       Bet Shammai and Bet Hillel
       Beth Shammai and Beth Hillel
       Hillelites
       Shammaites
    xx Tannaim
Beth Shammai and Beth Hillel
    See Beth Hillel and Beth Shammai
Bethe-Salpeter equation
    xx Particles (Nuclear physics)
       Quantum field theory
Bethel, Battle of, 1861
    See Big Bethel, Battle of, 1861
Bethlehem, Star of
    See Star of Bethlehem
Bethsaida, Blind man at (Miracle)
    See Opening of the eyes of one blind at
       Bethsaida (Miracle)
Beti (Bantu tribe)
    x Bati
    xx Bantus
Beti language
    See Bati language
BETKLA (Computer program)
Beton
    See Concrete
Betrayal of Christ
    See Jesus Christ—Betrayal
Betrothal *(GT2650)*
    sa Courtship
       Marriage
       Marriage customs and rites
    x Engagement
       Marriage, Promise of
    xx Contracts
       Courtship
       Marriage
    — Caricatures and cartoons
    — Law *(Direct)*
       sa Alienation of affections
          Breach of promise
       xx Breach of promise
          Marriage law
Betrothal (Byzantine law)
Betrothal (Canon law) *(BX1939.B)*
Betrothal (Islamic law) *(Direct)*
Betrothal (Roman law)
Betsileos
Betsimisaraka *(DT469.M264)*
    xx Malay race
Better-business bureaus
    xx Advertising
       Business
       Competition, Unfair
       Consumer protection
Betterment
    See Betterments
Betterment tax
    See Special assessments
Betterments *(Direct)*
    x Betterment
       Improvements (Real property)
    xx Negotiorum gestio
       Real property
Betting
    See Gambling
       Wagers
Betting systems
    See Gambling systems

Bevel-gearing
   See Gearing, Bevel
Beverages *(Bartenders' manuals, TX951;*
       Home economics, TX815-817;
       Technology, TP500-659;
       Therapeutics, RM238-257)
   sa Alcoholic beverages
      Bottling
      Carbonated beverages
      Coasters (for drinks)
      Mineral waters
      Soft drink industry
      names of beverages, e.g. Cocoa, Coffee,
        Tea
   x Drinks
   xx Diet
      Food
  — Costs
  — Early works to 1800
  — Law and legislation *(Direct)*
     sa Liquor laws
  — Packaging
     xx Bottling
  — Prices
  — Quality control
  — Standards *(Direct)*
  — Taxation *(Direct)*
     sa Liquor traffic—Taxation
Bewick wren
   x Bewick's wren
   xx Wrens
Bewick's wren
   See Bewick wren
Bezique *(GV1295.B5)*
Bezoar
   xx Calculi
BF 109 (Fighter planes)
   See Messerschmitt 109 (Fighter planes)
Bhaca (African tribe)
   x Amabaca
   xx Angoni
      Ethnology—Africa, South
Bhagavatas *(BL1245.B5)*
   x Bhagvatas
      Bhagvats
   xx Hindu sects
Bhagvatas
   See Bhagavatas
Bhagvats
   See Bhagavatas
Bhakti *(BL1215.B5)*
   x Bhakti-marga
   xx God—Worship and love
      Hinduism
Bhakti-marga
   See Bhakti
Bhakti yoga
   See Yoga, Bhakti
Bhang (Drug)
   x Bang
      Charas
      Churras
      Ganja
      Gunja
   xx Cannabis
      Narcotics
Bharat ratna *(CR6050)*
Bhatias
   x Bhatiyas
   xx Caste—India
      Caste—Pakistan
Bhatiyas
   See Bhatias
Bhikshu
   See Fakirs
Bhili language *(PK1800)*
   xx Indo-Aryan languages, Modern
Bhili literature *(Direct)*

Bhils *(DS432.B45)*
   sa Grasias
   xx Ethnology—India
      Grasias
      Mundas
      Untouchables
Bhojapuri language
   See Bhojpuri language
Bhojpuri fiction *(Direct)*
Bhojpuri language *(PK1825-1830)*
   sa Nagpuriā dialect
   x Bhojapuri language
Bhojpuri literature *(PK1827-8)*
Bhojpuri philology
Bhondas
   See Bondos
Bhoodan Movement
Bhotanta language
   See Tibetan language
Bhōtiā of Sikhim language
   See Dänjong-kä language
Bhubalia
   See Lohars
Bhuinhars
   See Bhuiyas
Bhuiyas *(DS485.O6)*
   sa Baigas
   x Bhuinhars
      Bhumias
      Bhuyas
   xx Mundas
Bhumia Baigas
   See Baigas
Bhumias
   See Bhuiyas
Bhutan . . .
   x Bhutanese . . .
Bhutan language
   See Tibetan language
Bhutanese . . .
   See Bhutan . . .
Bhuyas
   See Bhuiyas
Biacetylene
   See Acetylene
Biafran Conflict, 1967-1970
   See Nigeria—History—Civil War,
      1967-1970
Biami (Papuan people)
   xx Ethnology—Papua-New Guinea (Ter.)
      Papuans
Biangai language
Bias (Law) *(Direct)*
   sa Denial of justice
   xx Administrative discretion
      Denial of justice
      Rule of law
Bias seam binding
   See Seam binding
Bible
      This heading is used only with subdivi-
      sions.
   x Holy Scriptures
      Scriptures, Holy
   xx Hebrew literature
      History, Ancient
      Jewish literature
      Theology
   Example under Sacred books
  — Abridgments
  — Addresses, essays, lectures *(BS540)*
  — Adversary
     See Enemy in the Bible
  — Anecdotes, facetiae, satire, etc.
  — Animals
     See Bible—Natural history
  — Anthropology
     See Man (Theology)

Antiquities *(BS620)*
   sa Christian antiquities
      Ephod
      Fringes (Jewish cultus)
      Jews—Antiquities
      Musical instruments, Jewish
      Phylacteries
      subdivision Antiquities *under names*
        of Biblical countries and cities
   x Antiquities, Biblical
      Archaeology, Biblical
      Bible—Archaeology
      Biblical archaeology
      Monumental theology
   xx Jews—Antiquities
— — Juvenile literature
— Appreciation *(BS538)*
— Archaeology
     See Bible—Antiquities
— Astronomy *(BS655)*
   sa Star of Bethlehem
   xx Astronomy
— — Juvenile literature
— Atheism
     See Bible and atheism
— Atlases
     See Bible—Geography—Maps
— Authorship
— Bibliography *(Z7770-7772)*
      Here are entered works containing bib-
      liographies of texts of the Bible in
      two or more languages.
     Note under Bible—Collected works
— Biography *(BS570-580)*
   sa Apostles
      Brothers in the Bible
      Children in the Bible
      Fathers in the Bible
      Patriarchs (Bible)
      Prophets
      Women in the Bible
      names of individuals mentioned in
        the Bible, e.g. Mary, Virgin
   x Bible—Characters
      Biblical characters
— — Dictionaries, Juvenile *(BS539)*
— — Sermons *(BS571.5)*
— Birds
     See Bible—Natural history
— Botany
     See Bible—Natural history
— Brothers
     See Brothers in the Bible
— Canon *(BS465)*
— Canon, Catholic vs. Protestant *(BS465;*
     BS470)
     Note under Bible—Versions, Catholic vs.
     Protestant
— Cartoons, satire, etc.
— Cataloging
     See Cataloging of the Bible
— Catalogs
     See Bible. Manuscripts—Catalogs
     See Bible—Pictures, illustrations, etc.
     —Catalogs
— Catechisms, question-books *(BS612)*
      Here are entered catechisms and
      books with questions intended for
      juvenile use.
   sa Sunday-schools—Question-books
   xx Catechisms
      Sunday-schools—Question-books
— Chapters and verses
     See Bible—Numerical division
— Characters
     See Bible—Biography
— Children
     See Children in the Bible

Bible (Continued)
— Chronology (BS637)
    x Bible—History of Biblical events—
          Chronology
        Chronology, Biblical
— Codices
    See Bible. Manuscripts
— Coins
    See Bible—Numismatics
— Collected works (BS413-415)
        Here are entered collections of works
          on Biblical subjects (by one or more
          authors) too varied in character to
          admit of a specific subdivision. Col-
          lections of texts of the Bible are en-
          tered under the heading Bible—
          Bibliography.
— Colportage
    See Bible—Publication and
          distribution
— Commentaries (BS482-498)
    sa Catenae
        Scholia
    x Bible—Exegesis
        Bible—Interpretation
        Commentaries, Biblical
— Comparative studies
    Example under reference from Compara-
          tive studies
— Concordances (BS420-429)
    xx Concordances
— Concordances, English
    x Bible—Concordances, English—
          Authorized
— — American revised
— — Authorized
        See Bible—Concordances, English
— — Douai
— — Living Bible
— — Moffatt
— — New American Bible
— — New American standard
— — New World
— — Revised standard
— Concordances, French, [German, etc.]
— Copies, Curious
    x Bible—Curiosa
— Cosmology
    See Cosmology, Biblical
— Costume
    See Biblical costume
— Covenants
    See Covenants (Theology)—Biblical
          teaching
— Criticism, Form (New Testament,
          BS2377)
    sa Lists in the Bible
    x Bible—Form criticism
        Form criticism (Bible)
— Criticism, Higher
    See Bible—Criticism, interpretation,
          etc.
    See Bible—Introductions
— Criticism, interpretation, etc.
          (BS500-534)
    sa Bible as literature
        Colors in the Bible
        Modernist-fundamentalist
          controversy
        Sex in the Bible
    x Bible—Criticism, Higher
        Bible—Higher criticism
        Bible—Interpretation
        Bible—Literary criticism
        Biblical research
        Interpretation, Biblical
    xx Bible as literature
        Criticism

Note under Bible—Hermeneutics
— — Censorship
— — History (Direct)
    sa Antiochian school
    x Bible—Hermeneutics—History
— — — Early church, ca. 30-600
— — — Middle Ages, 600-1500
— — — Modern period, 1500-
— — — 16th century
— — — 17th century
— — — 18th century
— — — 19th century
— — — 20th century
— — Theory, methods, etc.
        See Bible—Hermeneutics
— Criticism, interpretation, etc., Jewish
        See Bible. O.T.—Criticism,
          interpretation, etc., Jewish
— Criticism, Textual (BS471)
    x Bible—Textual criticism
— Curiosa
    See Bible—Copies, Curious
    See Bible—Editions, Curious
        Bible—Miscellanea
— Devotional literature
— Dialogue
    See Dialogue in the Bible
— Dictionaries (BS440-443)
— Dictionaries, Juvenile
    xx Children's encyclopedias and
          dictionaries
— Drama
    See Bible as literature
    See Bible plays
        Mysteries and miracle-plays
— Dreams
    See Dreams in the Bible
— Economics (BS670)
    sa Christianity and economics
    x Christianity and economics—Biblical
          teaching
    xx Sociology, Biblical
— Editions, Curious
    x Bible—Curiosa
— Enemy
    See Enemy in the Bible
— Ethics (BS680.E)
    sa Sociology, Biblical
    xx Christian ethics
        Sociology, Biblical
— Ethnology (BS661)
    sa Lost tribes of Israel
    x Bible—Race problems
    xx Ethnology
        Man (Theology)
— Evidences, authority, etc. (BS480)
    sa Bible and tradition
        Bible—Quotations, Early
        Miracles
    x Bible—History of Biblical events—
          Sources
        Evidences of the Bible
    xx Apologetics
        Authority (Religion)
        Bible and tradition
        Bible—Inspiration
        Free thought
— — History of doctrines
— Examinations, questions, etc. (BS612)
— Exegesis
    See Bible—Hermeneutics
— Exegisis
    See Bible—Hermeneutics
— Farm life
    See Farm life in the Bible
— Fathers
    See Fathers in the Bible
— Festivals

    See Fasts and feasts
    See Passover
— Fiction
    See Bible—History of Biblical events
          —Fiction
— Fleeing
    See Fleeing in the Bible
— Folk-lore
    See Folk-lore—Jews
— Food
    See Food in the Bible
— Form criticism
    See Bible—Criticism, Form
— Gardens
    See Bible—Natural history
— Genealogy (BS569)
    sa Jesus Christ—Genealogy
— Geography (BS630-633; Asia,
          DS44-110)
    sa Ecclesiastical geography
        Mountains in the Bible
    x Geography, Biblical
    xx Atlases
        Ecclesiastical geography
— — Maps
    x Bible—Atlases
        Bible—Maps
— — — To 1800
— Geology
    See Bible and geology
— Handbooks, manuals, etc. (BS417)
— Harmonies (BS481)
— Hermeneutics (BS476)
        Here are entered works on the princi-
          ples of Biblical criticism. Critical
          works on the Bible are entered un-
          der Bible—Criticism, interpreta-
          tion, etc.
    sa Preunderstanding (Theology)
    x Bible—Criticism, interpretation, etc.
          —Theory, methods, etc.
        Bible—Exegesis
        Bible—Interpretation
        Hermeneutics, Biblical
— — History
        See Bible—Criticism, interpretation,
          etc.—History
— Hides and skins
    See Hides and skins in the Bible
— Hieroglyphic Bibles
    See Hieroglyphic Bibles
— Higher criticism
    See Bible—Criticism, interpretation,
          etc.
    See Bible—Introductions
— Historiography
        Here are entered works on the repre-
          sentation of historical events in the
          Bible.
    x Bible—History of Biblical events—
          Historiography
— History (Direct) (BS445-460)
    x Bible—Printing
— — Juvenile literature
— History Bibles
— History of Biblical events (BS635)
    x History, Biblical
    xx Palestine—History—To 70 A.D.
— — Chronology
        See Bible—Chronology
— — Fiction
    x Bible—Fiction
— — Historiography
        See Bible—Historiography
— — Juvenile literature
        See Bible stories
— — Poetry
    x Bible—Poetry

— — Sources

     See Bible—Evidences, authority,
       etc.

— History of contemporary events, etc.
     (BS635; Old Testament, BS1180,
     BS1197; New Testament,
     BS2410)

     xx Palestine—History—To 70 A.D.

— History of inter-testamental events
     See Judism—History—Post-exilic
       period, 586 B.C.-210 A.D.

— Homiletical use
     xx Bible—Use
       Preaching

— Homosexuality
     See Homosexuality in the Bible

— Hymnological use
     See Bible—Use in hymns

— Illustrations
     See Bible—Pictures, illustrations, etc.

— Indexes, Topical *(BS432)*

— Influence *(Direct) (BS472)*

— — Civilization, Occidental
     x Civilization, Occidental—Biblical
       influences

— Inspiration *(BS480)*
     sa Bible—Evidences, authority, etc.
       Inspiration
       Revelation
     x Bible—Revelation
     xx Inspiration

— — History of doctrines

— Interlinear translations

— Interpretation
     See Bible—Commentaries
     See Bible—Criticism, interpretation,
       etc.
       Bible—Hermeneutics

— Introductions *(BS474-5)*
     Here are entered works dealing with
     the origin, authorship, authenticity,
     general characteristics, contents,
     and aim of the different books of the
     Bible.
     x Bible—Criticism, Higher
       Bible—Higher criticism
       Bible—Literary criticism

— Juvenile literature *(BS539)*

— Juvenile poetry

— Language, style *(BS537)*
     sa Aramaic language
       Bible as literature
       Bible—Parables
       Greek language, Biblical
       Hebrew language
     xx Languages—Religious aspects

— Law
     See Jewish law
     See Law (Theology)

— Legends
     Here are entered works on legends in
     the whole Bible. Works on legends
     in the Old Testament are entered
     under the heading Legends, Jewish.
     Works on legends of the New Tes-
     tament are entered under the head-
     ing Bible. N.T.—Legends.
     sa Bible stories
     xx Bible stories

— Leprosy
     See Leprosy in the Bible

— Literary criticism
     See Bible as literature
     See Bible—Criticism, interpretation,
       etc.
     See Bible—Introductions

— Liturgical lessons, Dutch, [English, etc.]

— Liturgical use

---

  xx Bible—Use
     Liturgics
     Responsive worship

— Manuscripts
     See Bible. Manuscripts

— Maps
     See Bible—Geography—Maps

— Marginal readings

— Medicine, hygiene, etc. *(R135.5)*
     sa Healing in the Bible
     x Medicine, Biblical
     xx Christian Science
       Hygiene, Jewish

— Meditations *(BS483.5)*
     Example under Meditations

— Metallurgy

— Military history
     xx Military history, Ancient

— Mineralogy *(BS667)*

— Miracles
     See Jesus Christ—Miracles
     See Miracles

— Miscellanea *(BS534)*
     x Bible—Curiosa

— Monsters
     See Monsters in the Bible

— Music *(ML166)*
     Here are entered works on musical in-
     struments and music in the Bible
     (whole or parts) Works dealing with
     the singing of psalms in churches
     are entered under the heading Psal-
     mody.
     sa Music—History and criticism—To
       400
       Music—Jews
       Musical instruments, Jewish
     x Bible. O.T. Psalms—Music
     xx Music—History and criticism—To
       400
       Music—Jews
       Synagogue music—History and
       criticism

— Names
     sa God—Name
       Israel—Name
       Jesus Christ—Name
       Jews—Name
     x Biblical names
       Names, Biblical
     Example under Names

— Natural history *(BS660-667)*
     sa Nature in the Bible
       Nature—Religious interpretations
     x Animals in the Bible
       Bible—Animals
       Bible—Birds
       Bible—Botany
       Bible—Gardens
       Bible—Zoology
       Birds in the Bible
       Botany of the Bible
       Natural history, Biblical
       Plants in the Bible
       Zoology of the Bible

— — Juvenile literature

— Numbers
     See Numbers in the Bible

— Numerical division
     x Bible—Chapters and verses

— Numismatics *(CJ255)*
     x Bible—Coins
       Coins of the Bible
     xx Numismatics, Ancient

— Outlines, syllabi, etc.
     See Bible—Study—Outlines, syllabi,
       etc.

— Paleography

---

  xx Paleography

— Parables *(BS680.P3)*
     sa Jesus Christ—Parables
     x Parables, Biblical
       Parables, Christian
     xx Bible as literature
       Bible—Language, style
       Parables

— Paraphrases

— Paraphrases, English, [French, German,
     etc.]

— Pastoral theology
     See Pastoral theology—Biblical
       teaching

— Patristic quotations
     See Bible—Quotations, Early

— Periodicals *(BS410)*

— Philology
     See Greek language, Biblical
     See Hebrew language

— Philosophy *(BS645)*
     sa Philosophy, Jewish

— Picture Bibles *(BS560; N8020-8037;*
     Illuminated manuscripts,
     ND3355)
     Here are entered works, especially me-
     dieval works, containing pictorial
     illustrations exclusively, or with
     only short passages of text accom-
     panying the pictures. If pictures ac-
     company the complete text, the
     subdivision Pictures, illustrations,
     etc. is used.
     sa Hieroglyphic Bibles
     x Picture Bibles
     xx Christian art and symbolism
       Jesus Christ—Art

— Pictures, illustrations, etc. *(N8020-8185;*
     Juvenile, BS560)
     sa subdivision Art *under names of Bible*
     characters, and Biblical subjects,
     e.g. Jesus Christ—Art; Judgment
     Day—Art; *also subdivision*
     Pictures, illustrations, etc. *under*
     parts of the Bible, e.g. Bible.
     O.T.—Pictures, illustrations, etc.
     x Bible—Illustrations
     xx Christian art and symbolism
       Jesus Christ—Art
     Note under Bible—Picture Bibles

— — Catalogs
     x Bible—Catalogs

— — Juvenile literature

— Poetry
     See Bible—History of Biblical events
       —Poetry
       Hebrew poetry

— Political science
     x Bible and political science
       Political science and the Bible
     xx Political science
       Sociology, Biblical

— Poverty *(BS680.P47)*
     sa Poverty (Virtue)—Biblical teaching
     xx Poverty

— Prayers *(BV228-235)*
     sa Jesus Christ—Prayers
       Lord's prayer
       Prayer—Biblical teaching

— Printing
     See Bible—History
     See Bible—Publication and
       distribution

— Prophecies *(BS647-9; European War,*
     D524; Old Testament, BS1198;
     New Testament, BS2827)
     Subdivided by subject of prophecy, *e.g.*
     Bible—Prophecies—Negroes.

Bible
— Prophecies *(BS647-9; European War,
        D524; Old Testament, BS1198;
        New Testament, BS2827)*
        (Continued)
    sa Apocalyptic literature
        Jesus Christ—Prophecies
    xx Prophecies
        Example under Prophecies
— — Chronology
— — Messiah
        See Messiah—Prophecies
— — Negroes
        Example under Bible—Prophecies
— Psychology *(BS645)*
    sa Psychology, Religious
    x Psychology, Biblical
    xx Psychology, Religious
— Publication and distribution *(Direct)*
        (BV2369)
    sa Language question in the church
    x Bible—Colportage
        Bible—Printing
        Colportage
    xx Booksellers and bookselling—
        Colportage, subscription trade,
        etc.
        Language question in the church
        Missions
        Tract societies
— — Societies, etc. *(BV2369-2372)*
    x Bible societies
        Note under Bible—Societies, etc.
— Quotations, Early
        Here are entered works on quotations
        from the Bible found in early Chris-
        tian literature, and allusions and
        references thereto.
    x Bible—Patristic quotations
    xx Bible—Evidences, authority, etc.
        Christian literature, Early
— Race problems
        See Bible—Ethnology
— Reading *(BS617)*
— Reference editions
— Relation to the Koran
        See Koran—Relation to the Bible
— Revelation
        See Bible—Inspiration
— Rites and ceremonies
— Science
        See Bible and science
— Sermons
        Here are entered works containing ser-
        mons which are successively based
        on at least one whole book of the
        Bible, virtually forming a commen-
        tary in sermon form.
— Shepherds
        See Shepherds in the Bible
— Societies, etc.
        This heading is used for societies or-
        ganized for professional and schol-
        arly study of the Bible. For societies
        concerned with the publication and
        distribution of the Bible use the
        heading Bible—Publication and dis-
        tribution—Societies, etc.
— Sociology
        See Sociology, Biblical
— Stories
        See Bible stories
— Study *(Direct)* *(BS585-613)*
    sa Bible crafts
    x Bible—Teaching
    xx Religious education
        Sunday-schools
— — Biography *(BS501)*
    sa Theologians

— — Catholic Church *(BS587)*
        Here are entered works containing
        official decisions of the Catholic
        Church on the principles and
        methods to be observed in the
        study of the Bible.
— — Outlines, syllabi, etc. *(BS590-592)*
    x Bible—Outlines, syllabi, etc.
— — Text-books *(BS604-610)*
        Here are entered text-books of ele-
        mentary and high-school grade.
    sa Bible stories
        Sunday-schools—Question-books
— Symbolism
        See Symbolism in the Bible
— Teaching
        See Bible—Study
— Teachings
        See Bible—Theology
— Technology
        See Bible and technology
— Textual criticism
        See Bible—Criticism, Textual
— Theology *(BS543)*
        Here are entered works on the
        theology of the Bible, considered
        apart from the later theology of the
        church.
    sa Eschatology—Biblical teaching
        Jerusalem in the Bible
        Palestine in the Bible
        subdivision Biblical teaching *under
        subjects, e.g.* Church—Biblical
        teaching; Conversion—Biblical
        teaching; Family—Biblical
        teaching
    x Bible—Teachings
        Theology, Biblical
    xx Theology, Doctrinal
— Theophanies
        See Theophanies in the Bible
— Translating
    x Bible translating
        Bible—Versions—Theory, methods,
        etc.
— Translations
        See Bible—Versions
— Travel
        See Travel in the Bible
— Treaties
        See Treaties in the Bible
— Typology
        See Typology (Theology)
— Use
        Here are entered works that show how
        the Bible is applied to problems of
        doctrine and life, as well as works
        that indicate its purpose and func-
        tion.
    sa Bible—Homiletical use
        Bible—Liturgical use
        Bible—Use in hymns
— Use in hymns
    x Bible—Hymnological use
    xx Bible—Use
        Hymns
— Versions *(BS450-460)*
    sa Language question in the church
    x Bible translating
        Bible—Translations
    xx Language question in the church
        Languages—Religious aspects
— — Theory, methods, etc.
        See Bible—Translating
— Versions, Baptist
— Versions, Catholic *(BS453)*
    x Catholic Bibles

— Versions, Catholic vs. Protestant
        (BS470)
        Here are entered works contrasting
        Catholic and Protestant versions.
        Works dealing with the inclusion of
        the Apocrypha in the canon are en-
        tered under the heading Bible—
        Canon, Catholic vs. Protestant.
— Versions, Hussite
    x Hussite Bibles
— Versions, Jewish
        See Bible. O.T.—Versions, Jewish
— Visions
        See Visions in the Bible
— Weights and measures
        See Weights and measures, Jewish
— Women
        See Women in the Bible
— Zoology
        See Bible—Natural history
    x Bible—Codices
        Bible—Manuscripts
— Catalogs
    x Bible—Catalogs
— Facsimiles
Bible. N.T.
        This heading is used only with subdivi-
        sions.
— Criticism, interpretation, etc.
    sa Demythologization
        Rabbinical literature—Relation to
        the New Testament
        Example under reference from Higher
        criticism
— Gentiles
        See Gentiles in the New Testament
— Legends
        Note under Bible—Legends
— Relation to rabbinical literature
        See Rabbinical literature—Relation to
        the New Testament
Bible. N.T. Matthew
        This heading is used only with subdivi-
        sions.
— Criticism, interpretation, etc.
        Example under reference from Higher
        criticism
Bible. O.T.
        This heading is used only with subdivi-
        sions.
— Criticism, interpretation, etc.
        Note under Bible. O.T.—Criticism, in-
        terpretation, etc., Jewish
— Criticism, interpretation, etc., Jewish
        (Direct) *(BS1186)*
        Here are entered works dealing with
        Jewish Biblical criticism, interpre-
        tation, etc. Works of Biblical criti-
        cism, interpretation, etc. by Jewish
        authors are entered under Bible.
        O.T.—Criticism,   interpretation,
        etc.
    x Bible—Criticism, interpretation, etc.,
        Jewish
        Jewish Biblical criticism
    xx Jewish theology
— Gentiles
        See Gentiles in the Old Testament
— Legends
        See Legends, Jewish
— Mythology
        See Myth in the Old Testament
— Parables
    xx Parables, Jewish
— Pictures, illustrations, etc.
        Example under Bible—Pictures, illustra-
        tions, etc.
— Versions, Jewish

x Bible—Versions, Jewish
Jewish Bibles
Bible. O.T. Hexateuch
This heading is used only with subdivisions.
— Criticism, interpretation, etc.
Example under reference from Higher
criticism
Bible. O.T. Psalms
This heading is used only with subdivisions
— Music
See Bible—Music
Psalms (Music)
Bible and atheism
x Atheism and the Bible
Bible—Atheism
xx Christianity and atheism
Bible and Christian union *(BX9.5.B5)*
x Christian union and the Bible
Bible and evolution
x Evolution and the Bible
xx Bible and science
Evolution and religion
Bible and geology *(BS657)*
x Bible—Geology
Geology and Bible
Geology and religion
Geology, Biblical
Religion and geology
xx Bible and science
Bible and law
Here are entered works on the influence
of the Bible upon secular law. Works
on Biblical law are entered under the
heading Jewish law.
x Law and the Bible
Bible and political science
See Bible—Political science
Bible and science *(BS650-667)*
sa Bible and evolution
Bible and geology
Creation
Modernist-fundamentalist controversy
Nature—Religious interpretations
x Bible—Science
Science and the Bible
xx Religion and science
Bible and spiritualism *(BF1275.B5)*
xx Jesus Christ—Spiritualistic
interpretations
Bible and technology
x Bible—Technology
Technology and the Bible
xx Religion and science
Bible and temperance
See Temperance—Biblical arguments
Bible and the Koran
See Koran—Relation to the Bible
Bible and theosophy *(BP567)*
sa Jesus Christ—Theosophical
interpretations
x Theosophy and the Bible
Bible and tradition
sa Bible—Evidences, authority, etc.
Tradition (Theology)
x Tradition and the Bible
xx Bible—Evidences, authority, etc.
Tradition (Theology)
— History of doctrines
Bible as literature *(BS535)*
sa Bible—Criticism, interpretation, etc.
Bible—Parables
Religious literature
x Bible—Drama
Bible—Literary criticism
xx Bible—Criticism, interpretation, etc.
Bible—Language, style

Religious literature
Bible-Christian Church *(BX6510.B48)*
xx New Jerusalem Church
Bible Christians *(BX6510.B5)*
Bible colleges *(Indirect)* *(BV4019-4160)*
x Bible institutes (Colleges)
Bible schools
xx Religious education
Theological seminaries
Universities and colleges
— Accreditation
Bible crafts
xx Bible—Study
Creative activities and seat work
Handicraft
— Juvenile literature
Bible games and puzzles *(GV1507.B5)*
sa Games in religious education
x Bible puzzles
Games
Literary recreations
Puzzles
xx Crossword puzzles
Bible in literature *(General, PN49; Poetry:
general, PN1077)*
sa Religion in literature
xx Literature
Religion in literature
Bible in the schools
See Religion in the public schools
Bible institutes (Colleges)
See Bible colleges
Bible plays *(PN6120.R4)*
Here are entered works on the dramatization of Biblical events, collections of
such dramatizations, and such individual plays as are not entered under
the name of a principal character or
other specific heading.
sa Biblical costume
Hebrew drama
Liturgical drama
subdivision Drama *under names of
Biblical characters*
x Bible—Drama
Plays, Bible
xx Amateur theatricals
Children's plays
Mysteries and miracle-plays
Religious drama
Bible puzzles
See Bible games and puzzles
Bible schools
See Bible colleges
Bible societies
See Bible—Publication and distribution—
Societies, etc.
Bible stories *(BS546-559)*
sa Bible—Legends
x Bible—History of Biblical events—
Juvenile literature
Bible—Stories
xx Bible—Legends
Bible—Study—Text-books
Bible stories, English, [French, German, etc.]
Bible translating
See Bible—Translating
Bible—Versions
Bibles for the blind
See Blind, Bibles for the
Biblical anthropology
See Man (Theology)
Biblical Aramaic language
See Aramaic language
Biblical archaeology
See Bible—Antiquities
Biblical characters
See Bible—Biography

Biblical costume
sa Costume, Jewish
x Bible—Costume
Clothing and dress in the Bible
Costume, Biblical
xx Bible plays
Costume
Costume, Jewish
— Symbolism *(BS680.C65)*
xx Symbolism in the Bible
Biblical geology
See Bible and geology
Biblical Greek
See Greek language, Biblical
Biblical languages
See Languages—Religious aspects
Biblical law
See Jewish law
Biblical names
See Bible—Names
Biblical numerology
See Numbers in the Bible
Biblical research
See Bible—Criticism, interpretation, etc.
Bibliographers *(Z1001; Z1004)*
sa Area specialist bibliographers
Librarians
xx Librarians
Special librarians
— Correspondence, reminiscences, etc.
(Z1004)
Bibliographic Automation of Large Library
Operations Using a Time-sharing
System
See Ballots Project
Bibliographic classification
See Classification, Bibliographic
Bibliographic data in machine-readable form
See Machine-readable bibliographic data
Bibliographic information, Exchange of
See Exchange of bibliographic information
Bibliographical centers *(Z674.5)*
xx Catalogs, Union
Documentation
Libraries
Library cooperation
Bibliographical exhibitions *(Z121)*
Here is entered material on exhibitions
illustrating the history of the book and
book arts in general: writing, printing,
binding, illustration, collection and
preservation of books in libraries, etc.
sa Autographs—Exhibitions
Book industries and trade—Exhibitions
Bookbinding—Exhibitions
Illumination of books and manuscripts
—Exhibitions
Illustration of books—Exhibitions
Library exhibits
Manuscripts—Exhibitions
Printing—Exhibitions
x Bibliography—Exhibitions
Books—Exhibitions
xx Book industries and trade—Exhibitions
Bookbinding—Exhibitions
Illumination of books and manuscripts
—Exhibitions
Illustration of books—Exhibitions
Library exhibits
Manuscripts—Exhibitions
Printing—Exhibitions
Bibliographical journeys
See Literary journeys
Bibliographical searching
See Searching, Bibliographical
Bibliographical services *(Direct)* *(Z1008)*
sa Machine-readable bibliographic data
Translating services

Bibliographical services *(Direct)* *(Z1008)*
(Continued)
    xx Information services
Bibliographical societies *(Indirect)*
    sa Bibliography—Societies, etc.
    xx Bibliography—Societies, etc.
Bibliography *(Z1001-9000)*
    sa Abstracting and indexing services
      Anonyms and pseudonyms
      Archives
      Bio-bibliography
      Block-books
      Book collecting
      Bookbinding
      Books
      Books and reading
      Cataloging
      Catalogs
      Classification—Books
      Errors and blunders, Literary
      Exchange of bibliographic information
      Imaginary books and libraries
      Incunabula
      Indexes
      Indexing
      Information storage and retrieval
        systems
      Libraries
      Library science
      Literary forgeries and mystifications
      Livres à clef
      Manuscripts
      Margins in books
      Periodicals—Indexes
      Printing
      Reference books
      Searching, Bibliographical
      Titles of books
      Transmission of texts
      Unfinished books
      names of literatures, e.g. American
        literature; *and subdivision*
        Bibliography *under names of*
        persons, places and subjects; also
        subdivision Bibliography—
        Methodology *under specific subjects,*
        e.g. Medicine—Bibliography—
        Methodology; *and subdivision*
        Imprints *under names of countries,*
        states, cities, etc.
    xx Books
      Cataloging
      Documentation
      Library science
      Printing
  — **Best books** *(Z1035)*
    Subdivided by subject, *e.g.* Bibliogra-
      phy—Best books—Economics.
    sa Reference books—Bibliography
    x Appraisal of books
      Best books
      Bibliography, Critical
      Books—Appraisal
      Choice of books
      Evaluation of literature
      Literature—Evaluation
      Reading, Choice of
    xx Best sellers
      Book selection
      Books and reading
      Reference books
  — — Early works to 1800
  — — Economics
    Note under Bibliography—Best books
  — **Bibliography** *(Z1002)*
    Subdivided by subject, *e.g.* Bibliogra-
      phy—Bibliography—Botany, and
      by country, *e.g.* Bibliography—Bib-
      liography—America.

    sa Reference books—Bibliography
    x Bibliography of bibliographies
    xx Book selection
  — — Botany
    Note under Bibliography—Bibliogra-
      phy
  — — Rare books
    x Bibliography—Rare books—
      Bibliography

GEOGRAPHIC SUBDIVISIONS

  — — America
    Note under Bibliography—Bibliogra-
      phy
  — Books in library bindings
    See Bibliography—Library editions
  — Books issued in series *(Z1033.S5)*
    sa Bibliography—Children's books
      issued in series
  — Children's books issued in series
    xx Bibliography—Books issued in series
      Children's literature—Bibliography
  — Collections
  — Dictionaries *(Z1006)*
    sa Library science—Dictionaries
  — Early
    See subdivision Bibliography—Early
      under subjects, e.g. Botany—
      Bibliography—Early; English
      literature—Bibliography—Early
    The subdivision Bibliography—Early
      is used for bibliographies issued
      before 1800.
  — Early printed books
    sa Cataloging of early printed books
      Hand-printed Book Project
    x Early printed books
    xx Bibliography—Rare books
      Printing—History
  — — 15th century
    See Incunabula
  — — 16th century *(Z1014)*
  — — — Facsimiles *(Z241.3)*
  — — — Union lists
  — — 17th century
  — — 18th century

GENERAL SUBDIVISIONS

  — — Union lists
  — Editions
    sa Bibliography—Fine editions
      Bibliography—Library editions
      Bibliography—Paperback editions
      Transmission of texts
    x Editions
    xx Transmission of texts
  — Exhibitions
    See Bibliographical exhibitions
  — Fine editions *(Z1033.F5)*
    sa Printing—Specimens—Fine books
    x Books—Fine editions
      Deluxe editions
      Editions, Fine
      Fine editions
    xx Bibliography—Editions
      Bibliography—Rare books
  — First editions
    sa Literature—Bibliography—First
      editions
      subdivision Bibliography—First
      editions *under names of*
      literatures, e.g. American
      literature—Bibliography—First
      editions
    x Books—First editions
      Editions, First
      First editions
  — History *(Direct)*

  — Library editions *(Z1033.L6)*
    x Bibliography—Books in library
      bindings
      Bibliography—Publishers' library
      editions
      Books in library bindings
      Library bindings, Books in
      Library editions
      Publishers' library editions
    xx Bibliography—Editions
      Bookbinding
  — Limited editions
    sa Bibliography—Rare books
      Privately printed books
    x Books—Limited editions
      Editions, Limited
      Limited editions
    xx Bibliography—Rare books
      Privately printed books
  — Methodology
    See Bibliography—Theory, methods,
      etc.
  — Microscopic and miniature editions
    (Z1033.M6)
    sa Books—Sizes
      Diamond editions
      Editions, Diamond
      Editions, Microscopic
      Editions, Miniature
      Microscopic editions
      Miniature editions
      Pocket editions
    x Books—Microscopic editions
      Books—Miniature editions
      Miniature books
    xx Books—Format
      Books—Sizes
      Miniature objects
  — — Specimens
  — Out-of-print books
    See Out-of-print books
  — Paper-bound editions
    See Bibliography—Paperback editions
  — Paperback editions *(Z1033.P3)*
    sa Paperback wholesalers
      Paperbacks in education
    x Bibliography—Paper-bound editions
      Paper-bound editions
      Paperbacks
      Paperbound editions
    xx Bibliography—Editions
  — Photomechanical editions
    x Photomechanical editions
      Photoprints
  — Pirated editions
    See Copyright—Unauthorized reprints
  — Prohibited books
    See Prohibited books
  — Publishers' library editions
    See Bibliography—Library editions
  — Rare books
    sa Antiquarian booksellers
      Bibliography—Early printed books
      Bibliography—Fine editions
      Bibliography—Limited editions
      Books—Owners' marks
      Cataloging of rare books
      Illustrated books—Extra-illustrated
      Incunabula
      Manuscripts
      Vellum printed books
      subdivision Bibliography—First
      editions *under names of*
      literatures, e.g. English literature
      —Bibliography—First editions
    x Book rarities
      Books, Rare
      Early printed books

Rare books
  xx Antiquarian booksellers
     Bibliography—Limited editions
     Incunabula
— — Bibliography
      See Bibliography—Bibliography—
         Rare books
— — Juvenile literature
— Reference books
     See Reference books
— Reprint editions
     See Reprints (Publications)
— Societies, etc. (Z1008)
    sa Bibliographical societies
       Book clubs
    xx Bibliographical societies
       Book clubs
— Standards
— Terminology (Z1006)
— Theory, methods, etc.
    sa subdivision Bibliography—Theory,
       methods, etc. under specific
       subjects, e.g. Social sciences—
       Bibliography—Theory, methods,
       etc.
     x Bibliography—Methodology
— Universal catalogs (Z1011-1012)
    sa Bibliography, International
       Bibliography, Universal
     x Catalogs, Universal
       Universal catalogs
    xx Bibliography, Universal
— Vellum printed books
     See Vellum printed books
— Want lists
     See Books—Want lists
Bibliography, Critical
  See Bibliography—Best books
     Books and reading
     Criticism
     Literature—History and criticism
     subdivision History and criticism under
     names of literatures, e.g. American
     literature—History and criticism
Bibliography, International
  sa Bibliography, Universal
     Cataloging, Cooperative
   x Catalogs, Universal
     International bibliography
     Universal catalogs
  xx Bibliography, Universal
     Bibliography—Universal catalogs
     Cataloging, Cooperative
Bibliography, National (Direct)
     Here are entered works about national
     bibliographies in general. Lists of
     works published in a specific country
     are entered under the name of the
     country with subdivision Imprints, e.g.
     United States—Imprints. Lists of
     works about a particular country are
     entered under the name of the country
     with subdivision Bibliography, e.g.
     United States—Bibliography.
   x National bibliography
  xx Book registration, National
Bibliography, Official
  xx Book registration, National
Bibliography, Universal
  sa Bibliography, International
     Bibliography—Universal catalogs
     Cataloging, Cooperative
     Hand-printed Book Project
   x Catalogs, Universal
     Universal catalogs
  xx Bibliography, International
     Bibliography—Universal catalogs
     Cataloging, Cooperative

Bibliography of bibliographies
  See Bibliography—Bibliography
Bibliomania (Z992)
  sa Book clubs
     Book collecting
     Book thefts
     Women as book collectors
   x Bibliophily
  xx Book collecting
— Anecdotes, facetiae, satire, etc.
Bibliophily
  See Bibliomania
     Book collecting
Bibliothekarisch-analytisches System zur
  See BASIS-E (Information retrieval system)
Bibliotherapy
  xx Hospital libraries
     Reading, Psychology of
     Therapeutics
Bicameralism
  See Legislative bodies
Bichromatic harmonium (ML597)
   x Harmonium, Bichromatic
  xx Microtones
     Reed-organ
Bicknell's thrush (QL696.P2)
   x Gray-cheeked thrush, Bicknell's
  xx Thrushes
Bicol language
  See Bikol language
Bicolano language
  See Bikol language
Biculturalism (Indirect)
  xx Civilization
     Culture
— Canada
    xx Canada—English-French relations
Bicycle industry (Direct) (HD9999.B4-43)
— Advertising
     See Advertising—Bicycle industry
Bicycle insurance
  See Insurance, Bicycle
Bicycle polo (GV1059)
  xx Polo
Bicycle posters
  See Bicycles and tricycles—Posters
Bicycle racing (Direct) (GV1049)
  xx Cycling
     Racing
— Judging
    xx Sports officiating
Bicycle workers (Indirect) (HD8039.B48)
Bicycles, Military
  See Military cycling
Bicycles and tricycles (Sports and
     amusements, GV1041-1059;
     Technology, TL400-445; Trade,
     HD9999.B4-43)
  sa Cycling
     Cycling paths
     Minibikes
     Minicycles
     Motorcycles
     Water cycles
   x Tricycles
     Velocipedes
  xx Cycling
     Vehicles
— Juvenile literature
— Law and legislation
     See Cycling—Law and legislation
— Lighting
— Maintenance and repair
     x Bicycles and tricycles—Repairing
— — Juvenile literature
— Patents (TL437)
     Example under Patents
— Posters

  x Bicycle posters
  xx Advertising—Bicycle industry
— Registration
— Repairing
     See Bicycles and tricycles—
         Maintenance and repair
— Tires (TL425)
Bicyclic compounds
  xx Cyclic compounds
Bicycling
  See Cycling
Bid (The word)
  xx English language—Etymology
Bid'ah
  See Taqlīd
Bidding, Competitive
  See Contracts, Letting of
Bidjago
  See Bissagos
Bidjandjara language
  See Pitjandjara language
Bidjugos
  See Bissagos
Bidyogo
  See Bissagos
Biedermaier
  See Biedermeier
Biedermeier
   x Biedermaier
  xx German literature—19th century—
     History and criticism
Biedermeier (Art) (Direct)
  xx Art, Modern—19th century
Biedermeier style
  See Decoration and ornament—Biedermeier
     style
Biedl's syndrome
  See Laurence-Moon-Biedl syndrome
Biedma test
  See Wartegg-Biedma test
Biela's comet (QB723.B5)
Biella, Italy
— Flood, 1968
Biemond's syndrome
  See Laurence-Moon-Biedl syndrome
Biennials (Plants)
  xx Floriculture
     Flowers
     Plants, Cultivated
Big Bethel, Battle of, 1861 (E472.14)
   x Bethel, Battle of, 1861
Big Blue, Battle of the, 1864 (E477.16)
Big Bottom, Ohio
— Massacre, 1791
    xx Indians of North America—Wars—
       1790-1794
Big business (Direct)
  sa Competition
     Economies of scale
     Industrial concentration
     Industries, Size of
     Trusts, Industrial
   x Economic concentration
  xx Industrial management
     Industries, Size of
     Industry
Big Dipper
  See Ursa Major
Big game animals (Indirect)
  xx Game and game-birds
Big game fishing (Indirect) (SH457.5)
   x Deep-sea fishing
  xx Fishing
     Salt-water fishing
Big game hunting (Indirect)
  xx Hunting
— Juvenile literature

185

Big Hole, Battle of the, 1877
    xx Nez Percé Indians—Wars, 1877
Big-mouth bass fishing
    See Largemouth bass fishing
Big sagebrush
    xx Sagebrush
Big Tree, Treaty of, 1797
Big trefoil (Lotus uliginosus)
    See Lotus
Bigamy *(Direct)*
    sa Polygamy
    xx Impediments to marriage
        Marriage
        Marriage law
        Polygamy
        Sex and law
        Sex crimes
    Note under Polygamy
Bigamy (Canon law)
    xx Marriage (Canon law)
Bigarreau cherry
    See Sweet cherry
Bigeye tuna
    xx Tuna
Bigfoot
    See Sasquatch
Bighorn sheep
    xx Mountain sheep
    — Legends and stories
      — Juvenile literature
Bigotry
    See Toleration
Biguyduce Expedition, 1779
    See Penobscot Expedition, 1779
Bihari language *(PK1801-1831)*
    x Behari language
    xx Hindi language
        Indo-Aryan languages, Modern
        Magahi language
        Maithili language
Biharis
    x Beharis
    xx Ethnology—Bangladesh
        Ethnology—India
Bijas
    x Bijaskara
        Germ letters
    xx Alphabet (in religion, folk-lore, etc.)
        Hindu symbolism
        Mantras
Bijaskara
    See Bijas
Bikol language *(PL5581-4)*
    x Bicol language
        Bicolano language
        Vicol language
    xx Philippine languages
Bilaan language *(PL5595)*
    x Bilan language
    xx Philippine languages
Bilan language
    See Bilaan language
Bilbao, Spain
    — Siege, 1874
        xx Spain—History—Carlist War,
            1873-1876
    — Sieges, 1835, 1836
Bilbao Regatta, 1907
Bile *(QP197)*
    sa Biliary tract
        Bilious diseases and biliousness
        Bilirubin
        Cholagogues
        Ox-gall
    x Gall
    xx Body fluids
        Digestion
        Gall-bladder

Liver
Example under Physiology; Secretion
Bile acid metabolism
    xx Metabolism
Bile-ducts *(Comparative anatomy, QL867;*
        Diseases, RC849; Human anatomy,
        QM351; Surgical treatment,
        RD546-7)
    sa Ampulla of Vater
    x Ducts, Bile
        Gall-ducts
    xx Biliary tract
    — Diseases
        sa Bile-ducts—Obstructions
            Bile-ducts—Radiography
    — Obstructions
        xx Bile-ducts—Diseases
    — Radiography
        x Cholangiography
        xx Bile-ducts—Diseases
    — Surgery
      — — Complications and sequelae
Bile pigments *(QP197)*
    xx Animal pigments
        Hemoglobin
        Pyrrol
Bile salt metabolism
    xx Metabolism
Bile salts
    xx Salts
Bileki (Melanesian people)
    See Lakalai (Melanesian people)
Bilen language
    See Bilin language
Bilgo (Game) *(GV987)*
    xx Golf, Miniature
Bilharziasis
    See Schistosomiasis
Bilharziosis
    See Schistosomiasis
Biliary calculi
    See Calculi, Biliary
Biliary fistula
    See Fistula, Biliary
Biliary tract
    sa Bile-ducts
    xx Bile
    — Diseases
        sa Biliary tract—Radiography
            Fistula, Biliary
      — — Diagnosis
    — Radiography
        xx Biliary tract—Diseases
    — Surgery
Bilin language *(PJ2430)*
    sa Agau language
    x Bilen language
    xx Agau language
        Cushitic languages
        Hamitic languages
Bilinear forms
    See Forms, Bilinear
Bilingual education
    See Education, Bilingual
Bilingualism *(Indirect) (Mental tests,*
        LB1131)
    sa Education, Bilingual
    xx Language and languages
        Languages in contact
        Multilingualism
    — Psychological aspects
Bîlinî
    See Byliny
Bilious diseases and biliousness *(RC799-853)*
    sa Dyspepsia
        Jaundice
        Liver—Diseases
    xx Bile

Dyspepsia
    Intestines—Diseases
    Liver—Diseases
Bilirubin
    xx Bile
Bill (Anatomy) *(Birds, QL697)*
    xx Birds—Anatomy
Bill drafting *(Direct) (JF525; Great Britain,*
        JN608; United States, JK1106)
    sa Law—Language
        Reference legislation
    x Drafting of bills
        Legislation drafting
    xx Law—Language
        Legislation
    Note under Statutes
Bill of particulars
    See Bills of particulars
Bill of rights (U.S.)
    See United States. Constitution. 1st-10th
        amendments
Bill-posting *(HF5843)*
    sa Billboards
        Posters
        Signs and sign-boards
        Trade-unions—Bill-posting
    xx Advertising
        Advertising, Outdoor
        Posters
        Signs and sign-boards
    — Laws and regulations *(Direct)*
        (HF5843.5)
        xx Advertising laws
Billboards *(Direct)*
    xx Advertising, Outdoor
        Bill-posting
        Signs and sign-boards
    — Law and legislation *(Direct)*
        xx Advertising laws
Billeting of soldiers
    See Soldiers—Billeting
Billfishes
    See Swordfish
Billheads *(NE965)*
Billiards *(GV891)*
    Example under Games
Billiards, Pocket
    See Pool (Game)
Billies
    See Truncheons
Billing
    See Invoices
Bills, Legislative *(Direct)*
    sa Legislative calendars
        Resolutions, Legislative
    x Legislative bills
    xx Legislation
        Legislative histories
    — Digests
Bills, Private *(Direct)*
    sa Local laws
        subdivision Private bills *under names of*
            legislative bodies, e.g. Great Britain.
            Parliament—Private bills
    x Legislation, Private
        Private bills
        Private legislation
        Special legislation
    xx Legislation
        Parliamentary practice
Bills (Invoices)
    See Invoices
Bills and notes
    See Negotiable instruments
        Promissory notes
Bills of complaint (Canon law)
    See Complaints (Canon law)

Bills of credit
   See Letters of credit
      Negotiable instruments
Bills of exceptions
   See Exceptions (Law)
Bills of exchange *(Direct)*
   sa Acceptances
      Accommodation indorsements
      Checks
      Discount
      Foreign exchange
   x Exchange, Bills of
   xx Acceptances
      Banks and banking
      Drafts
      Money
      Negotiable instruments
   Notes under Acceptances; Drafts
   — Cases
   — — Digests
        See Bills of exchange—Digests
   — Digests
      x Bills of exchange—Cases—Digests
   — Examinations, questions, etc.
   — Programmed instruction
   — Taxation
      x Acceptances—Taxation
      Checks—Taxation
      Drafts—Taxation
      Negotiable instruments—Taxation
Bills of exchange (Canon law)
Bills of exchange (International law)
    (JX6289.B5)
   xx International law
Bills of fare
   See Menus
Bills of health
   x Certificates of health
      Health, Bills of
   xx Maritime law
      Quarantine
      Ship's papers
Bills of lading *(Direct)* *(HE2242)*
   x Affreightment
      Lading, Bills of
      Railroads—Bills of lading
   xx Commercial law
      Consular documents
      Contracts
      Contracts, Maritime
      Freight and freightage
      Interstate commerce
      Railroads—Freight
Bills of particulars *(Direct)*
   sa Set-off and counterclaim
   x Bill of particulars
   xx Actions and defenses
      Pleading
      Pre-trial procedure
      Set-off and counterclaim
Bills of peace
   x Peace, Bills of
   xx Equity
Bills of sale *(Direct)*
   sa Chattel mortgages
   xx Chattel mortgages
      Commercial documents
      Commercial law
      Sales
Biloxi Indians *(E99.B5)*
   xx Indians of North America
      Siouan Indians
Biloxi language *(PM702)*
   xx Siouan languages
Biluchi language
   See Baluchi language
Bilva
   See Bael (Tree)

Bimanese language *(PL5440)*
   xx Malay-Polynesian languages
Bimetal
   See Laminated metals
Bimetallism
   sa Austrian-German Monetary Union of
        1857
      Campaign literature, 1896
      Currency act of March 14, 1900
      Currency question
      Gold standard
      Latin Monetary Union
      Precious metals
      Quantity theory of money
      Silver
      Silver question
   x International bimetallism
   xx Coinage
      Currency question
      Gold standard
      Money
      Silver question
Bimlipatum jute
   See Ambary hemp
Bimoba language
   See Moba language
Bimorph cells
   See Bimorphs
Bimorphs *(QC595)*
   x Bimorph cells
   xx Direct energy conversion
      Pyro- and piezo-electricity
      Transducers
Bîn
   See Vina
Binandeli (Papuan people) *(DU740;*
       Anthropology, GN671.N5)
   x Orakaiva
Binandere language
   x Orokaiva language
   xx Papuan languages
Binary engines
   See Waste-heat engines
Binary forms
   See Forms, Binary
Binary-quaternary system
   See Binary system (Mathematics)
Binary scale
   See Binary system (Mathematics)
Binary stars
   See Stars, Double
Binary system (Mathematics)
   sa Error-correcting codes (Information
       theory)
   x Binary-quaternary system
      Binary scale
      Pair system
   xx Mathematics
      Numeration
   — Programmed instruction
Binary vapor systems
   See Steam power-plants—Binary vapor
       systems
Bination
   xx Mass
Bination (Canon law)
   xx Mass (Canon law)
Bindibu (Australian people)
   See Bindubi (Australian people)
Binding and loosing
   See Power of the keys
Binding energy
   sa Nuclear forces (Physics)
   x Nuclear binding energy
   xx Atoms
      Nuclear forces (Physics)
      Nuclear physics

Binding of books
   See Bookbinding
Binding sites (Biochemistry)
   x Active site (Biochemistry)
      Bonding sites (Biochemistry)
      Reactive site (Biochemistry)
   xx Biological chemistry
Binding twine
   See Twine
Bindubi (Australian people)
   x Bindibu (Australian people)
   xx Australian aborigines
Bindweed *(SB615.B5)*
Binet-Simon test *(LB1131)*
   sa Stanford-Binet test
   x Simon-Binet test
   xx Mental tests
Binet-Stanford test
   See Stanford-Binet test
Bingo
Bini (African people) *(DT515.42)*
   xx Ethnology—Nigeria
   — Juvenile literature
Bini language *(PL8077)*
   x Benin language
      Do language
      Edo language
   xx Kwa languages
Biniridjara (Australian people)
   See Piniridjara (Australian people)
Binjhals
   See Binjhwars
Binjhwaras
   See Binjhwars
Binjhwars *(DS432.B49)*
   x Binjhals
      Binjhwaras
   xx Ethnology—India
Binocular vision *(QP487)*
   xx Vision
Binoculars
   See Field-glasses
Binomial coefficients *(QA161.B48)*
   sa Pascal's triangle
   x Coefficients, Binomial
   xx Binomial theorem
      Combinations
   — Tables
Binomial equations
   See Equations, Binomial
Binomial theorem *(QA161)*
   sa Binomial coefficients
      Pascal's triangle
   xx Algebra
   — Problems, exercises, etc.
Bins *(TH4498)*
   xx Bulk solids handling
      Materials handling
      Stores or stock-room keeping
      Warehouses
Binumarien language
   xx Papuan languages
Bio-bibliography *(Z1010)*
   sa Authors
      subdivision Bio-bibliography *under*
        particular subjects and under names
        of countries, cities, etc., e.g. Botany
        —Bio-bibliography; France—
        Bio-bibliography; Königsberg—
        Bio-bibliography
   xx Authors
      Bibliography
      Biography
      Literature
Bioacoustics
   sa Animal sounds
      Hearing
      Nature sounds

Bioacoustics *(Continued)*
    Sound production by animals
    Sound—Psychological aspects
    Sound-waves—Physiological effect
    x Biological acoustics
    xx Sound
Bioassay
    See Biological assay
Bioastronautics
    See Space biology
       Space medicine
Biochemic medicine
    See Medicine, Biochemic
Biochemical engineering *(TP248.3)*
    sa Enzymes—Industrial applications
       Fermentation
       Fungi—Industrial applications
       Microbiological synthesis
    xx Biological chemistry
       Chemistry, Technical
Biochemical evolution
    See Chemical evolution
Biochemical genetics
    x Chemical genetics
    xx Biological chemistry
       Biosynthesis
       Molecular genetics
Biochemical memory transfer
    See Memory transfer
Biochemical oxygen demand
    sa Water—Dissolved oxygen
    x B.O.D.
       Biological oxygen demand
    xx Energy metabolism
       Sewage—Analysis
       Water—Analysis
       Water—Dissolved oxygen
       Water—Pollution
Biochemical systematics
    See Chemotaxonomy
Biochemical variation
    xx Variation (Biology)
Biochemistry
    See Biological chemistry
       Medicine, Biochemic
       Physiological chemistry
Biochemistry, Quantum
    See Quantum biochemistry
Biochemistry of soils
    See Soil biochemistry
Biochemists *(Direct)*
    sa Biological chemistry as a profession
    x Biological chemists
    xx Scientists
    — Biography
    — Correspondence, reminiscences, etc.
Biochemorphology *(QH659)*
    xx Biological chemistry
       Chemistry, Physical and theoretical
       Physiological chemistry
Biochromes
    See Pigments (Biology)
Bioclimatics
    See Bioclimatology
Bioclimatology *(Indirect)* *(QH543)*
    sa Acclimatization
       Bergmann's rule
       Climatology, Medical
       Crops and climate
       Frigorimeter
       Man—Influence of climate
       Phenology
    x Bioclimatics
       Biometeorology
    xx Biology
       Climatology
       Ecology
    — Research

    xx Biological research
    — Technique
Biocolloids *(Chemistry, QD549; Physiology,*
    QP525)
    xx Biological chemistry
       Colloids
Biocomputers
    See Conscious automata
Biodegradation *(Biochemistry, QP517.B5)*
    sa Sewage—Purification—Biological
       treatment
       Water—Purification—Biological
       treatment
    subdivision Biodegradation *under*
       names of particular substances, e.g.
       Insecticides—Biodegradation;
       Petroleum—Biodegradation
    x Biodeterioration
       Biological degradation
       Degradation, Biological
    xx Biological chemistry
       Decomposition (Chemistry)
       Microbiology
Biodeterioration
    See Biodegradation
Biodeterioration of materials
    See Materials—Biodeterioration
Biodynamics (Space flight)
    See Escape physiology (Space flight)
Bioenergetic psychotherapy *(RC489.B5)*
    xx Psychotherapy
Bioenergetics
    sa Energy metabolism
    xx Biological chemistry
       Energy budget (Geophysics)
       Metabolism
       Physiological chemistry
Bioengineering *(TA164)*
    sa Agricultural engineering
       Anthropometry
       Biological warfare
       Biomedical engineering
       Bionics
       Biosynthesis
       Biotelemetry
       Human engineering
       Life support systems (Space
       environment)
       Sanitary engineering
    x Biological engineering
       Life science engineering
    xx Biology
       Engineering
Biofeedback training
    x Visceral learning
    xx Biological control systems
       Feedback (Psychology)
       Operant conditioning
Bioflavonoids
    sa specific compounds of this group, e.g.
       Biotin; Hesperidin
    x Vitamin P
    xx Flavonoids
Biogan
    xx Antiseptics
Biogenesis
    See Life—Origin
Biogeochemical cycles
    sa Nitrogen—Fixation
    xx Biological chemistry
       Cycles
       Ecology
       Geochemistry
Biogeochemical prospecting
    x Botanical prospecting
       Geobotanical prospecting
    xx Geochemical prospecting
       Plant indicators

Biogeochemistry
    xx Biological chemistry
       Geochemistry
Biogeography
    See Geographical distribution of animals
       and plants
Biographical films
    xx Feature films
       Moving-pictures
Biography *(CT)*
    sa Anecdotes
       Autobiographies
       Autographs
       Bio-bibliography, *and subdivision*
       Bio-bibliography *under particular*
       subjects and under names of
       countries, cities, etc., e.g. Music—
       Bio-bibliography; Spain—
       Bio-bibliography
       Christian biography
       Classical biography
       Epitaphs
       Genealogy
       Heraldry
       Military biography
       Naval biography
       Obituaries
       Portraits
       Postage-stamps—Topics—Portraits
       Religious biography
       Table-talk
       Word portraits
    subdivision Biography *under particular*
       subjects and under names of
       countries, cities, etc., e.g. Actors—
       Biography; Boston—Biography;
       Indians of North America—
       Biography; Woman—Biography
    x History—Biography
       Memoirs
    xx Auxiliary sciences of history
       Genealogy
       History
    — To 500
       x Ancient biography
       Biography, Ancient
       History, Ancient—Biography
    — Middle Ages, 500-1500
       x Biography, Medieval
       Middle Ages—Biography
    — 11th century
       x Eleventh century—Biography
    — 15th century
       x Fifteenth century—Biography
    — 18th century
       x Eighteenth century—Biography
    — 19th century
       x Nineteenth century—Biography
    — 20th century
       x Twentieth century—Biography
    — — Portraits
       xx Portraits

    GENERAL SUBDIVISIONS

    — Anecdotes, facetiae, satire, etc.

    GENERAL SUBDIVISIONS

    — Anniversaries, etc.
       sa subdivision Anniversaries, etc. *under*
       names of individuals, e.g. Lincoln,
       Abraham, Pres. U.S., 1809-1865—
       Anniversaries, etc.
       xx Anniversaries

    GENERAL SUBDIVISIONS

    — Caricatures and cartoons

189

Biological products *(Public health, RA401;*
  Therapeutics, RM270-282)
  — Law and legislation *(Direct)*
  (Continued)
    xx Drugs—Laws and legislation
  — Standards
Biological research *(Indirect)*
  sa Bioclimatology—Research
    Biological physics—Research
    Biology, Experimental
    Biology—Methodology
    Biotelemetry
    Cell research
    Germfree life
    Marine biology—Research
    Microbiological research
    Molecular biology—Research
    Plankton research
    Protozoology—Research
    Radiobiology—Research
    Zoological research
  x Biology—Research
  xx Research
Biological rheology
  See Rheology (Biology)
Biological societies *(QH301)*
  sa Biology—Societies, etc. *[for*
      publications of biological and other
      societies in relation to biology]
  xx Societies
Biological specimens
  sa Diagnostic specimens
  xx Biological products
  — Collection and preservation
    xx Biology—Field work
  — — Juvenile literature
  — Plastic embedment
    x Plastic embedment (Biological
      specimens)
    xx Plastics
Biological structure
  See Morphology
Biological telemetry
  See Biotelemetry
Biological tracers
  See Tracers (Biology)
Biological transport
  sa Body fluid flow
    Secretion
  x Active transport
    Membrane transport
    Transport, Biological
  xx Body fluids
    Diffusion
    Osmosis
  — Mathematical models
Biological warfare *(UG447.8)*
  x Bacteria, Pathogenic—War use
    Bacterial warfare
    Bacteriological warfare
    CBR warfare
    Disease warfare
    Germ warfare
  xx Bioengineering
    Communicable diseases
    Military art and science
    Strategy
    Tactics
    War
  — Hygienic aspects
  — Safety measures
Biologicals
  See Biological products
Biologists *(Direct) (QH26)*
  sa Biology as a profession
    Ecologists
    Geneticists
    Marine biologists
    Microbiologists

    Zoologists
  xx Naturalists
    Scientists
  — Correspondence, reminiscences, etc.
Biology *(Indirect) (QH301-705)*
  sa Acclimatization
    Adaptation (Biology)
    Anatomy
    Aquatic biology
    Bioclimatology
    Bioengineering
    Biology, Experimental
    Biomathematics
    Biometry
    Botany
    Cells
    Classification—Books—Biology
    Color of animals
    Color of plants
    Communication in biology
    Convergence (Biology)
    Cryobiology
    Death (Biology)
    Desert biology
    Developmental biology
    Electronics in biology
    Electrophysiology
    Embryology
    Evolution
    Fertilization (Biology)
    Fresh-water biology
    Genetics
    Heredity
    Human biology
    Hybridization
    Information theory in biology
    Irritability
    Karyokinesis
    Life (Biology)
    Living fossils
    Marine biology
    Metabolism
    Microbiology
    Microscope and microscopy
    Mimicry (Biology)
    Morphogenesis
    Natural history
    Ontogeny
    Parasitology
    Parthenogenesis
    Photobiology
    Phylogeny
    Physiology
    Polarity (Biology)
    Protoplasm
    Psychobiology
    Radioactive tracers in biology
    Radiobiology
    Radioisotopes in biology
    Regeneration (Biology)
    Reproduction
    Seashore biology
    Sex (Biology)
    Soil biology
    Space biology
    Spontaneous generation
    Symbiosis
    Thermobiology
    Tracers (Biology)
    Ultrasonics in biology
    Variation (Biology)
    Vitalism
    Zoology
    headings beginning with the word
      Biological
  x Epigenesis
  xx Evolution
    Life (Biology)

    Life sciences
    Natural history
    Science
  — Abstracting and indexing
  — Apparatus and supplies
    See Biological apparatus and supplies
  — Atlases
  — Bibliography
    sa Biological literature
      Information storage and retrieval
        systems—Biology
    xx Biological literature
  — Bio-bibliography
  — Classification *(QH83)*
    sa Chemotaxonomy
      Homology (Biology)
      Immunotaxonomy
      Numerical taxonomy
      Species
    x Systematics (Biology)
      Taxonomy (Biology)
  — — Juvenile literature
  — Cultures
    See Cultures (Biology)
  — Early works to 1800 *(QH306)*
  — Ecology
    See Ecology
  — Electromechanical analogies
  — Examinations
  — Examinations, questions, etc.
  — Experiments
    sa Biology, Experimental
    xx Biology, Experimental
  — — Juvenile literature
  — Fellowships
    See Biology—Scholarships,
      fellowships, etc.
  — Field work
    sa Biological specimens—Collection and
      preservation
      Nature study
      Nature trails
    x Field biology
      Field work (Biology)
    xx Nature study
  — — Juvenile literature
  — Information services
    xx Communication in biology
  — Juvenile literature *(QH48)*
  — Laboratories
    See Biological laboratories
  — Laboratory manuals *(QH317)*
  — Mathematical models
    xx Biological models
      Biomathematics
  — Methodology
    sa Cultures (Biology)
    xx Biological research
      Biology, Experimental
  — Nomenclature
    sa Botany—Nomenclature
      Natural history—Nomenclature
      Zoology—Nomenclature
  — Periodicity
    sa Diel cycles
      Periodic diseases
      Photoperiodism
    x Biological clocks
      Biological cycles
      Biological periodicity
    xx Cycles
  — — Juvenile literature
  — Philosophy *(QH331)*
    sa Mechanism (Philosophy)
      Vitalism
    xx Vitalism
  — Pictorial works
  — Popular works

190

— Programmed instruction
— Punched card systems
    See Punched card systems—Biology
— Research
    See Biological research
— Scholarships, fellowships, etc. *(Direct)*
    x Biology fellowships
      Biology—Fellowships
      Biology scholarships
    xx Biology—Study and teaching
— Social aspects *(Direct)* *(QH333)*
— Societies, etc.
    xx Biological societies
— Statistical methods
    See Biometry
— Study and teaching *(Direct)*
    sa Biology—Scholarships, fellowships, etc.
— — Audio-visual aids
— Study and teaching (Elementary) *(Indirect)*
— Study and teaching (Higher) *(Indirect)*
— — Audio-visual aids
— Study and teaching (Secondary) *(Indirect)*
— Tables, etc. *(QH310)*
— Technique
    sa Isolation perfusion (Physiology)
— Terminology
    sa Botany—Terminology
      Natural history—Terminology
      Zoology—Terminology
— Vocational guidance
    See Biology as a profession
Biology, Economic
    sa Botany, Economic
      Zoology, Economic
    x Economic biology
Biology, Electronics in
    See Electronics in biology
Biology, Experimental
    sa Biology—Experiments
      Biology—Methodology
      Ovum implantation
      Zoology, Experimental
    x Experimental biology
    xx Biological research
      Biology
      Biology—Experiments
Biology, Molecular
    See Molecular biology
Biology as a profession *(QH314)*
    x Biology—Vocational guidance
    xx Biologists
Biology fellowships
    See Biology—Scholarships, fellowships, etc.
Biology in art
    xx Art
Biology scholarships
    See Biology—Scholarships, fellowships, etc.
Bioluminescence
    sa Bacteria, Luminous
      Fireflies
      Photophores
    x Animal luminescence
      Light production in animals and plants
      Luminescence, Animal
    xx Phosphorescence
— Juvenile literature
Biomagnetism
    See Magnetic fields—Physiological effect
Biomaterials
    See Biomedical materials
Biomathematics *(QH324)*
    sa Biology—Mathematical models
      Biometry
      Compartmental analysis
      Genetic algebras

Genetics—Mathematical models
    Information theory in biology
    Logits
    Medicine—Mathematical models
    xx Biology
      Biometry
      Mathematics
— Problems, exercises, etc.
— Research *(Direct)*
Biomechanics
    sa Animal mechanics
      Human mechanics
    x Biological mechanics
    xx Biological physics
      Mechanics
Biomedical engineering
    sa Biomedical materials
      Cardiovascular instruments, Implanted
      Electronics in biology
      Medical electronics
      Medical instruments and apparatus
      Myoelectric prosthesis
      Physiological apparatus
    x Engineering, Biomedical
      Engineering, Medical
      Medical engineering
    xx Bioengineering
      Biological physics
      Engineering
      Medicine
— Research *(Direct)*
Biomedical materials *(R857.M3)*
    sa Ceramics in medicine
      Prosthesis
    x Biomaterials
    xx Biomedical engineering
      Prosthesis
      Transplantation of organs, tissues, etc.
Biomes
    See Biotic communities
Biometeorology
    See Bioclimatology
Biometric research *(Direct)*
    x Biometry—Research
    xx Research
Biometrics
    See Biometry
Biometry *(Anthropology, GN51-59; Variation, QH401-5)*
    sa Biomathematics
      Entomology—Statistical methods
      Mathematical statistics
      Sampling (Statistics)
    x Biology—Statistical methods
      Biometrics
      Biostatistics
    xx Biology
      Biomathematics
      Heredity
      Mathematical statistics
      Sampling (Statistics)
      Statistics
— Computer programs
— Problems, exercises, etc.
— Research
    See Biometric research
— Tables, etc.
Biomicroscopy, Ocular
    See Ocular biomicroscopy

Bionics
    Here are entered works on applying the organizational principles of living organisms to the solution of engineering problems in general and, in particular, on considering living organisms as prototypes in dealing with the theory, circuitry and technology of information-processing electronic components or systems.
    sa Artificial intelligence
      Conscious automata
      Human information processing
      Optical data processing
    x Biotechnology
      Intellectronics
    xx Bioengineering
      Biological physics
      Cybernetics
      Simulation methods
      Systems engineering
— Juvenile literature
Bionomics
    See Ecology
Biopharmaceutics
    xx Pharmacology
      Pharmacy
Biophysical research
    See Biological physics—Research
Biophysics
    See Biological physics
Biopsy
    sa subdivision Biopsy *under subjects, e.g.* Kidneys—Biopsy
    xx Diagnosis
Biopsychology
    See Psychobiology
Biorheology
    See Rheology (Biology)
Biosciences
    See Life sciences
Bioscope
    See Moving-picture projection
Biosphere
    xx Atmosphere
      Earth
      Life (Biology)
Biostatistics
    See Biometry
Biosynthesis
    sa Adenosinetriphosphate synthesis
      Aldosterone synthesis
      Amino acid synthesis
      Biochemical genetics
      Chlorophyll synthesis
      Deoxyribose synthesis
      Enzyme synthesis
      Fatty acid synthesis
      Genetic regulation
      Glucose synthesis
      Glucuronic acid synthesis
      Glycogen synthesis
      Glycoprotein synthesis
      Hemoglobin synthesis
      Lipid synthesis
      Microbiological synthesis
      Nucleic acid synthesis
      Peptide synthesis
      Polysaccharide synthesis
      Protein biosynthesis
      Purine synthesis
      Ribonucleic acid synthesis
      Solanine synthesis
      Steroid hormone synthesis
      Virus-induced enzymes
      Vitamin synthesis
    xx Bioengineering
      Biological chemistry

Biosynthesis *(Continued)*
    Chemistry, Organic—Synthesis
    Microbial metabolites
    Physiological chemistry
Biotechnology
   See Bionics
    Human engineering
Biotelemetry
   sa Telemeter (Physiological apparatus)
   x Biological telemetry
    Telemetry, Biological
    Telemetry in biological research
   xx Bioengineering
    Biological research
    Electronic measurements
Biotic communities *(Indirect)*
   sa Animal societies
    Plant communities
   x Biomes
    Communities, Biotic
    Natural communities
   xx Ecology
  — Mathematical models
Biotin
   Example under Bioflavonoids
Biotite *(Indirect)*
   xx Mica
Biotite-granite
   See Mica
Biquadratic equations
   See Equations, Biquadratic
Bir Hacheim, Battle of, 1942
   See Bir Hakeim, Battle of, 1942
Bir Hakeim, Battle of, 1942 *(D766.93)*
   x Bir Hacheim, Battle of, 1942
   xx World War, 1939-1945—Campaigns—
    Libya
Bira (Bantu tribe)
   x Babira (Bantu tribe)
   xx Ethnology—Africa, Central
Birch *(Botany, QK495.B56; Forestry,*
    SD397.B5)
   sa Paper birch
  — Diseases and pests
    sa Birch leaf-mining sawfly
    Bronze birch borer
    Ribbed-cocoon-maker
Birch-bark canoes
   See Canoes and canoeing
    Indians of North America—Boats
Birch bark inscriptions
   See Bark inscriptions
Birch coccid
Birch Coulee, Battle of, 1862
   xx Indians of North America—Wars—
    1862-1865
Birch leaf-mining sawfly
   xx Birch—Diseases and pests
Birch-leaf skeletonizer
   See Ribbed-cocoon-maker
Birch partridges
   See Ruffed grouse
Birch reduction
   xx Reduction, Chemical
Bird attracting
   See Birds, Attracting of
Bird-banding *(Indirect) (QL677.5)*
   x Banding of birds
    Birds, Banding of
    Birds, Marking of
   xx Animal marking
    Birds—Migration
    Ornithological research
    Ornithology
  — Juvenile literature
Bird cages
   See Birdcages

Bird calls
   See Bird-song
Bird control *(Indirect) (SB995)*
   sa Airports—Bird control
    English sparrow—Control
   x Birds—Control
Bird control, Airport
   See Airports—Bird control
Bird Day
   xx Holidays
Bird dogs
   sa Pointers (Dogs)
    Retrievers
    Setters (Dogs)
   xx Hunting
    Hunting dogs
Bird feeders *(QL676.5)*
   xx Birds, Attracting of
    Birds—Food
  — Juvenile literature
Bird-houses *(QL676.5)*
   sa Dove-cotes
   xx Birds, Attracting of
    Birds—Eggs and nests
  — Juvenile literature
Bird hunting
   See Fowling
Bird-lice *(QL503.M2)*
   sa Anoplura
    Sheep lice
   x Mallophaga
   xx Anoplura
    Lice
    Neuroptera
Bird malaria
   See Malarial fever in birds
Bird names, Popular
   See Birds—Nomenclature (Popular)
Bird navigation *(QL698.8)*
   x Birds—Navigation
    Navigation by birds
   xx Animal navigation
Bird pests *(SB995)*
   x Birds as pests
   xx Birds, Injurious and beneficial
    Pests
Bird photography
   See Photography of birds
Bird populations
   x Populations, Bird
   xx Animal populations
    Birds—Behavior
    Birds—Geographical distribution
Bird seed
   See Birdseed
Bird-song *(QL698)*
   x Bird calls
   xx Animal sounds
    Nature sounds
   Note under Birds—Songs and music
  — Juvenile literature
  — Recording and reproducing
Bird watching *(Indirect)*
   x Birds—Study and teaching
   xx Wildlife watching
  — Juvenile literature
Birdcages
   x Bird cages
    Cages, Bird
Birds *(Indirect) (QL671-699)*
   sa Aviaries
    Flight
    Ornithology
    Pelecaniformes
    Postage-stamps—Topics—Birds
    State birds

    Cage-birds; Game and game-birds;
    Humming-birds; Water-birds; *and*
    similar headings
   xx Ornithology
    Vertebrates
  Example under Zoology
— Anatomy *(QL697)*
   sa Air-sacs (of birds)
    Bill (Anatomy)
    Feather tracts
    Feathers
    Gizzard
    Syrinx (of birds)
    Wings
    subdivision Birds *under* Digestive
    organs, Nervous system; *also*
    subdivision Anatomy *under names*
    of particular birds, e.g. Japanese
    quail—Anatomy
— Anecdotes, facetiae, satire, etc.
— Behavior
   sa Bird populations
    Birds—Eggs and nests
    Birds—Migration
    Imprinting (Psychology)
    Parasitic birds
    subdivision Behavior *under particular*
    birds, e.g. Ravens—Behavior
    Example under Animals, Habits and
    behavior of
— — Juvenile literature
— Catalogs and collections *(QL677)*
— Classification *(QL677)*
— Collection and preservation *(QL677.7)*
   sa Taxidermy
    Zoological specimens—Collection
    and preservation
   x Preservation (Natural history)
    Specimens, Preservation of
   xx Museums
    Natural history—Technique
    Taxidermy
    Zoological specimens—Collection
    and preservation
— Collisions with aeroplanes
   See Aeronautics—Accidents
— Control
   See Bird control
— Control at airports
   See Airports—Bird control
— Digestive organs
   See Digestive organs—Birds
— Diseases *(SF995)*
   sa Game and game-birds—Diseases
    Poultry—Diseases
    specific diseases of birds, e.g.
    Malarial fever in birds; Newcastle
    disease; Ornithosis
— Economic aspects
   See Birds, Injurious and beneficial
— Eggs and nests *(QL675)*
   sa Bird-houses
    Eggs—Incubation
    Eggshells
   x Birds—Nests
    Birds' nests
    Nests of birds
    Nidology
    Oology
   xx Birds—Behavior
    Eggs
    Nest building
— — Catalogs and collections
— — Identification
— — Juvenile literature
— Embryology
   See Embryology—Birds
— Evolution

— Flight
  See Flight
— Food *(QL698)*
  sa Bird feeders
    Birdseed
  xx Birds, Attracting of
— — Juvenile literature
— Generative organs
  See Generative organs—Birds
— Geographical distribution *(QL678-695)*
  sa Bird populations
  xx Zoogeography
— Identification
  x Identification of birds
— Juvenile literature *(QL676)*
— Legends and stories *(QL795.B57)*
  x Poultry—Legends and stories
— Migration *(QL698)*
  sa Bird-banding
  x Migration of birds
  xx Animal migration
    Birds—Behavior
    Phenology
— — Juvenile literature
— Navigation
  See Bird navigation
— Nervous system
  See Nervous system—Birds
— Nests
  See Birds—Eggs and nests
— Nomenclature *(QL677)*
  xx Zoology—Nomenclature
— Nomenclature (Popular) *(QL677)*
  x Bird names, Popular
  xx Zoology—Nomenclature (Popular)
— Parasites
  See Parasites—Birds
— Physiology *(QL698)*
  Example under Physiology, Comparative
— Pictorial works *(QL674)*
— Poetry
— Psychology
— Research
  See Ornithological research
— Societies, etc.
  xx Ornithological societies
— Songs and music *(M1977.B5; M1978.B5)*
    Here are entered compositions, both
    individual items and collections, for
    voices or instruments, having as
    their subject birds. Works on the
    calls or songs produced by birds are
    entered under Bird-song.
  x Topical songs (Birds)
— Study and teaching
  See Bird watching
    Ornithology—Study and teaching
— Tariff
  See Duty-free importation of birds
Birds, Aquatic
  See Water-birds
Birds, Attracting of *(QL676.5)*
  sa Bird feeders
    Bird-houses
    Birds—Food
  x Attracting birds
    Attracting of birds
    Bird attracting
  xx Birds, Protection of
Birds, Banding of
  See Bird-banding
Birds, Color of
  See Color of birds
Birds, Extinct
  sa Moa
    Rare birds
    names of extinct birds, e.g. Dodo

  x Extinct birds
  xx Extinct animals
Birds, Folk-lore of
  See Folk-lore of birds
Birds, Fossil *(QE871-5)*
  sa Coraciformes, Fossil
  x Fossil birds
  xx Paleontology
— Eggs *(QE875)*
  xx Eggs, Fossil
Birds, Injurious and beneficial *(Direct)*
  (SB995)
  sa Airports—Bird control
    Bird pests
    Birds of prey
  x Birds—Economic aspects
    Economic ornithology
    Ornithology, Economic
  xx Zoology, Economic
Birds, Marking of
  See Bird-banding
Birds, Ornamental
  sa Cage-birds
    Ducks
    Guinea-fowl
    Peafowl
    Pheasants
  x Ornamental birds
  xx Poultry
Birds, Parastic
  See Parastic birds
Birds, Photography of
  See Photography of birds
Birds, Protection of *(Direct) (Game-laws,*
  SK351-579; Periodicals, societies,
  etc., QL671)
  sa Audubon societies
    Birds, Attracting of
    Game protection
  x Migratory birds, Protection of
    Protection of birds
    Water-birds, Protection of
  xx Game protection
    Wildlife conservation
— Juvenile literature
— Law and legislation *(Direct)*
  xx Game-laws
    Wildlife conservation—Law and
    legislation
Birds, Rare
  See Rare birds
Birds (in numismatics)
Birds (in religion, folk-lore, etc.)
  See Folk-lore of birds
Birds as carriers of disease *(RA641.B5)*
  xx Communicable diseases
    Diseases—Transmission
Birds as pests
  See Bird pests
Birds in art *(N7665)*
  sa Goldfinches in art
  xx Animal painting and illustration
    Drawing—Instruction
Birds in literature *(Poetry, PN6110.B6)*
  sa Folk-lore of birds
  x Birds in poetry
  xx Animals in literature
    Folk-lore of birds
    Nature in literature
Birds in poetry
  See Birds in literature
Birds in the Bible
  See Bible—Natural history
Birds' nests
  See Birds—Eggs and nests
Birds of paradise *(QL696.P2)*
  x Paradise birds
  xx Passeriformes

— Pictorial works
Birds of prey *(Indirect) (QL696.A2)*
  sa Buzzards
    Eagles
    Falcons
    Goshawk
    Harriers
    Hawks
    Ospreys
    Owls
    Vultures
  xx Birds, Injurious and beneficial
    Predatory animals
— Identification
— Juvenile literature
— Legends and stories
— Pictorial works
Birdseed *(Indirect)*
  x Bird seed
  xx Birds—Food
Birgittines *(BX4285-8)*
  x Bridgettines
  xx Augustiniains
    Monasticism and religious orders
Biri language
  See Birri language
Birmingham, Eng.
— Industries
    Example under Industrial arts
— Riots, 1791
Birmingham, Battle of, 1643 *(DA415)*
Biro-Bidjan in literature
Birohi language
  See Brahui language
Birom language *(PL8078.B36)*
  x Berom language
    Bouroum language
    Burum language
  xx Benue-Congo languages
Birri language
  x Abiri language
    Ambili language
    Biri language
    Viri language
Birth
  See Childbirth
    Labor (Obstetrics)
    Parturition
Birth, Hour of
  x Hour of birth
  xx Vital statistics
Birth, Multiple *(RG696)*
  sa Quadruplets
    Triplets
    Twins
  x Multiple birth
    Plural births
  xx Obstetrics
    Parabiosis
    Quadruplets
    Triplets
    Twins
Birth, Premature
  See Infants (Premature)
Birth (in religion, folk-lore, etc.) *(GR450)*
  sa Churching of women
    Couvade
  x Folk-lore of birth
  xx Manners and customs
    Regeneration (in religion, folk-lore,
    etc.)
    Religion, Primitive
    Rites and ceremonies
Birth (Philosophy) *(BD443)*
  sa Fetus (Theology)
  xx Beginning
    Life
Birth announcements

Birth control *(Direct)* *(HQ763-6)*
  sa Abortion
    Conception—Prevention
    Family size
    PROJTARG (Computer program)
  x Contraception
    Family planning
    Planned parenthood
  xx Eugenics
    Family size
    Hygiene, Sexual
    Population
    Sexual ethics
  — Juvenile literature
  — Law and legislation *(Direct)*
    xx Crimes without victims
      Sex and law
  — Law and legislation (Jewish law)
    See Birth control (Jewish law)
  — Public opinion
  — Religious aspects
    xx Church and social problems
  — Catholic Church, [Islam, Protestant
      churches, etc.]
    x Catholic Church [Islam,
      Protestant churches, etc.] and
      birth control
  — Research *(Direct)*
  — Research grants *(Direct)*
  — Study and teaching *(Direct)*
  — Underdeveloped areas
    See Underdeveloped areas—Birth
      control
Birth control (Jewish law)
  x Birth control—Law and legislation
    (Jewish law)
Birth control and astrology
  See Astrology and birth control
Birth control clinics *(Direct)*
  x Family planning services
    Planned parenthood services
  xx Clinics
Birth defects
  See Deformities
Birth injuries
  xx Deformities
  — Complications and sequelae
Birth order
  sa Children, First-born
  x Ordinal position of children
    Sibling sequence
  xx Children
    Family
Birth records
  See Registers of births, etc.
Birth-stones *(GR805)*
  x Natal stones
  xx Birthdays
    Charms
    Gems (in religion, folk-lore, etc.)
Birthday books
  x Books, Birthday
  xx Birthdays
    Calendars
    Literary calendars
Birthdays
  sa Birth-stones
    Birthday books
    Fortune-telling by birthdays
  xx Days
  — Caricatures and cartoons
  — Songs and music *(M1977.B56;*
    M1978.B56)
Birthmark, Mongolian
  See Mongolian birthmark
Birthmarks
  xx Mole (Dermatology)
    Skin

Birthplaces *(Astrology, BF1729.B5)*
  xx Historic houses, etc.
Births, Registers of
  See Registers of births, etc.
Biruhi language
  See Brahui language
Bisa (African tribe) *(DT963.42)*
  xx Ethnology—Zambia
Bisa language
  x Wisa language
  xx Bantu languages
Bisa language (Mande)
  See Busa language
Bisaya language *(PL5621-9)*
  sa Cebú dialect
    Halaya dialect
    Haraya dialect
    Hiligaina dialect
    Samaro-Leytean dialect
  x Visayan language
  xx Hiligaina dialect
    Philippine languages
    Samaro-Leytean dialect
Bisayans (Philippine tribe)
  See Bisayas (Philippine tribe)
Bisayas (Philippine tribe) *(DS666.B)*
  x Bisayans (Philippine tribe)
    Visayas (Philippine tribe)
Biscayans
  See Basques
Biscuits *(TX769)*
Biscuits, English
  See Cookies
Bisected brain
  See Split brain
Bisexuality
  xx Hermaphroditism
    Homosexuality
    Sex (Psychology)
Bishári dialect
  See Beja language
Bishoprics
  See Dioceses
Bishops *(Indirect)*
  sa Apostolic succession
    Cathedraticum
    Chanceries, Diocesan
    Chapters, Cathedral, collegiate, etc.
    Chorepiscopi
    Church polity
    Conciliar theory
    Consecration of bishops
    Dioceses
    Episcopacy
    Investiture
    Metropolitans
    Ordination
    Popes—Primacy
    Rural deans
    Staff, Pastoral
    Vicars apostolic
    Vicars-general
    subdivision Bishops *under names of*
      denominations, e.g. Church of
      England—Bishops
  x Archbishops
    Clergy—Major orders
    Major orders
    Orders, Major
  xx Apostolic succession
    Catholic Church—Clergy
    Catholic Church—Government
    Christian biography
    Clergy
    Consecration of bishops
    Dioceses
    Episcopacy
    Investiture

    Popes—Primacy
    Vicars apostolic
  Note under Metropolitans
  — Appointment, call, and election
    xx Vocation, Ecclesiastical
  — Biblical teaching
  — Collegiality
    See Episcopacy
  — Consecration
    See Consecration of bishops
  — Residence
    Here are entered works dealing with
      the requirement that bishops reside
      in their dioceses.
    Example under Clergy—Residence
  — Temporal power
    xx Church and state
  — Titles
    Example under Titles of honor and nobil-
      ity

GEOGRAPHIC SUBDIVISIONS

  — England
    xx Church of England—Biography
    Church of England—Clergy
Bishops (Canon law) *(BX1939.B5)*
  sa Abbots (Canon law)
    Abbots nullius (Canon law)
    Administrators apostolic
    Consultors, Diocesan
    Jurisdiction (Canon law)
    Vicars capitular
  xx Jurisdiction (Canon law)
Bishop's ring
  x Pastoral ring
    Pontifical ring
  xx Rings (in religion, folk-lore, etc.)
    Symbolism in law
Bishop's-weed
  x Bishopweed
Bishopweed
  See Bishop's-weed
Bisio (Bantu tribe)
  x Bisiwo (Bantu tribe)
    Bujeba (Bantu tribe)
    Mabea (Bantu tribe)
    Mabi (Bantu tribe)
  xx Bantus
    Ethnology—Equatorial Guinea
Bisio language *(PL8078.B5)*
  x Bujeba language
    Mabea language
  xx Bantu languages
Bisiwo (Bantu tribe)
  See Bisio (Bantu tribe)
Bismarck Sea, Battle of, 1943
  xx World War, 1939-1945—Campaigns—
    New Guinea
Bismillah
  See Basmalah
Bismuth *(QD181.B5)*
  — Analysis
  — Isotopes
  — — Decay
  — Metallurgy *(TN799.B5)*
  — Therapeutic use *(RM666.B)*
Bismuth alloys
  sa Bismuth-antimony alloys
    Bismuth-cadmium alloys
    Copper-bismuth alloys
    Lead-bismuth alloys
    Uranium-bismuth alloys
Bismuth-antimony alloys
  x Antimony-bismuth alloys
  xx Antimony alloys
    Bismuth alloys
  — Electric properties

Bismuth-cadmium alloys
   x Cadmium-bismuth alloys
   xx Bismuth alloys
      Cadmium alloys
Bismuth-copper alloys
   See Copper-bismuth alloys
Bismuth crystals
Bismuth-lead alloys
   See Lead-bismuth alloys
Bismuth mines and mining *(Indirect)*
Bismuth ores *(Indirect)* *(TN490.B6)*
Bismuth organic compounds
   See Organobismuth compounds
Bismuth-uranium alloys
   See Uranium-bismuth alloys
Bison *(QL737.U5; Hunting, SK297)*
   xx Ruminantia
Bison, American
   sa Buffalo jump
   x American bison
      Buffalo, American
   Note under Buffaloes
Bison, European
   x Aurochs
      European bison
      Urochs
      Wisent
Bison, Fossil *(QE882.U3)*
Bissagos *(DT671.B58)*
   x Bidjago
      Bidjugos
      Bidyogo
Bisseni
   See Petchenegs
Bites, Venomous
   See Venom—Physiological effect
Bites and stings
   x Stings and bites
   xx Wounds
Bitola, Battle of, 1912
   xx Balkan Peninsula—History—War of
      1912-1913
Bits (Bridles)
   See Bridle
Bits (Drilling and boring)
   sa Augers
      Diamond bits
   x Drill bits
   xx Boring machinery
      Oil well drilling rigs
      Rock-drills
   — Standards *(Direct)*
   — Testing
Bitter pit
Bitter-rot
Bitterling
Bittern, European
   See European bittern
Bitters
   xx Mineral waters
Bitters bottles
   xx Bottles
   — Prices *(Direct)*
Bittersweet *(QK495.S7)*
   x Dulcamara
      Solanium dulcamara
Bitumen *(Indirect)* *(TN850)*
   sa Asphalt
      Bituminous materials
      Hydrocarbons
   xx Caustobioliths
      Hydrocarbons
   — Analysis
   — Geology *(Indirect)* *(TN850)*
      xx Geology
        Geology, Economic

Bituminous coal *(Fuel, TP325-6; Mining,*
   TN825)
   xx Coal
   — Analysis
   — Storage
Bituminous materials *(Indirect)* *(TE221)*
   sa Asphalt
      Asphalt cement
      Coal-tar
      Pavements, Bituminous
      Pitch
      Road materials
      Roofing, Bituminous
   xx Bitumen
      Building materials
      Road materials
   — Early works to 1800
   — Fatigue
   — Quality control
   — Safety measures
   — Testing
Bituminous pavements
   See Pavements, Bituminous
Bituminous roofing
   See Roofing, Bituminous
Biuret reaction *(QD305.A7)*
   x Pitrowsky reaction
Bivalves
   See Lamellibranchiata
Biwa *(ML1015.B55; ML1018.B55)*
   xx Lute
      Musical instruments, Japanese
Biwa and shakuhachi music
   See Shakuhachi and biwa music
Biyan language
   See Bassari language
Bizen pottery *(NK4168.B5)*
   x Kobizen pottery
      Pottery, Bizen
   xx Pottery, Japanese
Björkö, Treaty of, 1905 *(DK264)*
Bka'-rgyud-pa (Sect) *(BQ7669)*
   sa 'Brug-pa (Sect)
   x Kar-gyu (Sect)
      Kargyudpa
   xx Lamaist sects
Black *(QD441; TP913)*
   xx Dyes and dyeing
Black (in religion, folk-lore, etc.)
   x Folk-lore of the color black
   xx Religion, Primitive
Black Americans
   See Negroes
Black-and-white fantail
   See Willie wagtail
Black art
   See Witchcraft
Black basaltes *(NK4340.B5)*
   x Basaltes pottery
      Black pottery
      Black ware
Black bass *(SH681)*
   sa Largemouth bass
      Smallmouth bass
   xx Bass
   — Diseases and pests
Black bass fishing *(SH681)*
   sa Largemouth bass fishing
      Smallmouth bass fishing
   xx Bass fishing
      Fishing
Black bear
   sa Glacier bear
   xx Bears
   — Juvenile literature
   — Legends and stories
Black body radiation
   See Blackbody radiation

Black brant
   See Brent-goose
Black Brant rocket
   xx Atmosphere, Upper—Rocket
      observations
      Rockets, Sounding
Black bryony
Black bullhead
   x Bullhead, Black
      Horned pout
   xx Catfishes
Black-capped chickadee
   x Black-capped titmouse
      Black-throated titmouse
   xx Chickadees
Black-capped titmouse
   See Black-capped chickadee
Black-capped vireo
   xx Vireos
Black cardinals
      The thirteen cardinals who, because they
      refused to be amenable to the wishes of
      Napoléon I, were forbidden to wear
      red robes.
   x Cardinals, Black
Black Carib Indians *(F1505.2.C3)*
   sa St. Vincent—History—Carib War,
      1795-1796
   x Garif Indians
   xx Carib Indians
      Indians of Central America
      Indians of Central America—Mixed
        bloods
      Indians of the West Indies
      Negroes in Honduras
      Negroes in the West Indies
Black carpet beetle *(TX325)*
   xx Carpet beetles
Black chaff of wheat *(SB608.W5)*
   xx Wheat—Diseases and pests
Black cod
   See Sablefish
Black cotton soil
   x Black soil
      Cotton soil, Black
      Regur
   xx Soils
Black currant, European
   See European black currant
Black death *(RC171)*
   xx Epidemics
      Plague
   — Juvenile literature
Black dialect
   See Negro-English dialects
Black disease of sheep
   See Braxy
Black duck
   xx Ducks
   — Behavior
Black earth
   See Chernozem soils
Black-footed ferret *(QL737.C25)*
   x Ferret, Black-footed
   xx Weasels
   — Juvenile literature
Black Friars
   See Dominicans
Black grain-stem sawfly *(SB945.B48)*
Black grama grass
   x Woolly-foot grama grass
Black grouse
   x Blackcock
      Heathcock
   xx Grouse
Black hawk-eagle
   xx Eagles
Black Hawk purchase

Black Hawk War, 1832   *(E83.83)*
   sa Pecatonica River, Battle of, 1832
    x Illinois—History—Black Hawk War,
      1832
     United States—History—Black Hawk
      War, 1832
   xx Indians of North America—Wars—
      1815-1875
   — Juvenile literature
Black-headed gulls   *(QL696.L3)*
   xx Gulls
Black Hills beetle
   xx Beetles
Black holes (Astronomy)   *(QB843.B55)*
   x Frozen stars
   xx Gravitational collapse
     Stars
Black Hundreds (Russia)
Black in art
   xx Color
Black jack (Game)
   See Blackjack (Game)
Black Jews
   See Negro Jews
Black Knight rocket
   xx Rockets, Sounding
Black-lead
   See Graphite
Black light inspection
   See Penetrant inspection
Black locust
   See Locust (Tree)
Black lung
   See Lungs—Dust diseases
Black market   *(Direct)*
     Subdivided by commodity, *e.g.* Black
      market—Steel.
   x Gray market
   xx Commerce
     Price regulation
     Priorities, Industrial
     Rationing, Consumer
   — Steel
     xx Steel industry and trade
     Note under Black market
Black Mass
   See Satanism
Black militant organizations   *(Direct)*
   x Militant organizations, Black
   xx Black power
Black Monks
   See Benedictines
Black mullets
   sa Mullet fisheries
   x Mullets, Black
   xx Gray mullets
Black Muslims   *(Race question, E185.61;*
     Religion, BP221-3)
   x Nation of Islam
   xx Black nationalism
     Negro Muslims
     Negroes—Religion
     United States—Race question
   — Dietary laws
     x Dietary laws, Black Muslim
     xx Diet
   — Doctrinal and controversial works
        (BP222)
   — Education   *(Direct)*
Black nationalism   *(Direct)*
   sa Black Muslims
     Black power
     Ras Tafari movement
   x Black separatism
     Nationalism, Black
     Nationalism, Negro
     Nationalism—Negroes
     Separatism, Black

   xx Black power
     Negroes—Politics and suffrage
     Negroes—Race identity
Black-necked stilt
   x American stilt
     Black-winged stilt
Black oak   *(Botany, QK495.Q4; Forestry,*
     SD397.O12)
   x Dyers' oak
     Yellow-bark oak
   xx Oak
Black oak, California
   See California black oak
Black-outs
   See Blackouts in war
Black Panthers Trial, New York, 1970-1971
     x Bomb Conspiracy Trial, New York,
      1970-1971
     New York City Bomb Conspiracy Trial,
      1970-1971
Black people (United States)
   See Negroes
Black pepper (Spice)
   See Pepper (Spice)
Black pine leaf scale
Black pottery
   See Black basaltes
Black power   *(Direct)*
   sa Black militant organizations
     Black nationalism
   xx Black nationalism
     Negroes—Civil rights
     Negroes—Economic conditions
     Negroes—Politics and suffrage
Black quarter
   See Anthrax, Symptomatic
Black racer
   See Coluber constrictor
Black rhinoceros
   xx Rhinoceros
Black rot   *(SB741.B6)*
   sa Grapes—Diseases and pests
   Example under Grapes—Diseases and pests
Black sand   *(Indirect)*
   xx Sand
Black scab
   See Potato wart
Black scoter
   See Common scoter
Black separatism
   See Black nationalism
Black skimmer
   x Scissors bill
Black snake
   See Coluber constrictor
Black soil
   See Black cotton soil
Black spruce
   xx Spruce
   — Analysis
Black studies
   See Afro-American studies
Black swallowtail butterfly
Black-tailed deer
   See Mule deer
Black-tailed godwit
   x Godwit, Black-tailed
   xx Godwits
Black-tailed gull
   xx Gulls
Black-tailed jack-rabbit
   xx Jack-rabbits
Black-throated bunting
   See Dickcissel
Black-throated green warbler
   xx Wood warblers
Black-throated titmouse
   See Black-capped chickadee

Black-tongue
   x Canine blacktongue
     Canine pellagra
     Pellagra, Canine
   xx Dogs—Diseases
Black turpentine beetle
   x Turpentine beetles
Black Virgins
   x Virgins, Black
   xx Mary, Virgin—Art
     Mary, Virgin—Cultus
Black walnut, Eastern
   See Eastern black walnut
Black ware
   See Black basaltes
Black whale
   See Southern right whale
     Sperm whale
Black widow (Fighter planes)
   x F-15 (Fighter planes)
     FT-1 (Fighter planes)
     Northrop black widow (Fighter planes)
     P-61 (Fighter planes)
   xx Fighter planes
Black wildebeest
   See White-tailed gnu
Black willow
   xx Willows
Black-winged kite
Black-winged stilt
   See Black-necked stilt
Blackberries   *(SB386.B6)*
   — Diseases and pests
Blackbirds   *(QL696.P2)*
   sa European blackbird
     Mynahs
     Pale-eyed marsh blackbird
     Red-winged blackbird
     Tricolored blackbird
     Yellow-headed blackbird
   — Behavior
   — Juvenile literature
Blackboard drawing   *(NC865; Kindergarten,*
     LB1187)
   x Chalk drawing
   xx Chalk-talks
     Crayon drawing
     Drawing
     Drawing—Instruction
Blackboards
   x Chalkboards
   xx Schools—Furniture, equipment, etc.
Blackbody radiation   *(QC484)*
   sa Emissivity
   x Black body radiation
     Radiation, Blackbody
   xx Electric radiation
     Electromagnetic theory
     Emissivity
     Optics
     Thermodynamics
Blackcock
   See Black grouse
Blackeyed peas
   See Cow-peas
Blackfin tuna   *(QL638.S35)*
   xx Tuna
Blackfoot Indians
   See Siksika Indians
Blackfoot Indians (Dakota)
   See Sihasapa Indians
Blackfoot language
   See Siksika language
Blackfooted penguin
   See Jackass penguin
Blackjack (Game)   *(GV1295.B)*
   x Black jack (Game)
     Twenty-one (Game)

Van John (Game)
Vingt et un (Game)
  xx Gambling
Blackleg
  See Anthrax, Symptomatic
Blacklisting, Labor
  xx Discrimination in employment
Labor and laboring classes
Strikes and lockouts
Blacklisting of entertainers *(Direct)*
  x Entertainers, Blacklisting of
  xx Actors
Entertainers
Blacklists, Commercial
  x Commercial blacklists
  xx Commerce
Commercial policy
Competition, Unfair
Trading with the enemy
War—Economic aspects
Blackmail
  See Extortion
Blackouts, Electric power
  See Electric power failures
Blackouts in war
  x Black-outs
Dimouts
  xx Air defenses
Civil defense
Lighting
Blacksmithing *(Indirect) (TT218-223)*
  sa Carriage and wagon making
Forging
Horseshoeing
Ironwork
Welding
  xx Forging
Ironwork
— Tools and implements
  xx Tools
— — Standards
— Vocational guidance
  xx Blacksmiths
Blacksmiths *(Direct)*
  sa Blacksmithing—Vocational guidance
Horseshoers
Trade-unions—Blacksmiths
Blackwater (Disease of cattle)
  See Texas fever
Blackwater fever
  x Fever, Hemoglobinuric
Hemoglobinuric fever
  xx Leptospirosis
Malarial fever
Blacky pictures test
  xx Personality tests
Picture interpretation tests
Projective techniques
Bladder *(Comparative anatomy, QL872;
Human anatomy, QM411)*
  sa Pacemaker, Artificial (Bladder)
  xx Urinary organs
— Calculus
  See Calculi, Urinary
— Diseases *(RC919-923; Gynecology,
RG484-8)*
  sa Bladder—Perforation
Bladder—Radiography
Bladder—Sacculation
Fistula, Vesico-vaginal
Prostate gland—Diseases
Urinary stress incontinence
  xx Prostate gland—Diseases
  Example under Urinary organs—Dis-
eases
— Displacement *(RD581)*
  x Bladder—Prolapsus
Ectopia vesicae

— Exploration *(RC920)*
  x Cystoscopy
— Hernia
— Inflammation *(RC919)*
— Perforation *(RD581)*
  xx Bladder—Diseases
— Prolapsus
  See Bladder—Displacement
— Puncture and aspiration *(RD581)*
— Radiography
  x Cystography
  xx Bladder—Diseases
— — Atlases
— Rupture
— Sacculation *(RC919)*
  xx Bladder—Diseases
— Surgery *(RD581)*
  sa Lithotomy
Lithotrity
  x Cystotomy
— Tumors *(RD670)*
— — Chemotherapy
— Wounds and injuries
Bladder and bowel training
  See Bowel and bladder training
Bladder-worm
  See Hydatids
Bladdery fever
  See Pemphigus
Bladensburg, Battle of, 1814 *(E356.B5)*
  xx Washington, D.C.—History—Capture
by the British, 1814
Blades *(TJ267.B5)*
Here are entered general works on blades,
paddles or vanes which are parts of hy-
draulic and pneumatic mechanisms
such as propellers, water-wheels, tur-
bines, fans or compressors.
Works on cutting blades are entered un-
der the type of apparatus or the spe-
cific tool or weapon, *e.g.* Cutting ma-
chines, Knives, Swords.
  sa subdivision Blades *under names of
engines, e.g.* Aeroplanes—Turbojet
engines—Blades
  x Paddles (Hydraulic machinery)
Vanes (Mechanical engineering)
  xx Aerodynamics
Aerofoils
Fluid dynamics
Hydrodynamics
Mechanical engineering
Shells (Engineering)
Blanching
  See Bleaching
Blank-books
  xx Office equipment and supplies
Blank verse *(P311; English, PE5115)*
  xx Drama—Technique
English language—Versification
Poetry
Versification
Blankenese, Ger., in art
Blankets
  sa Electric blankets
Indians of North America—Textile
industry and fabrics
  xx Bedding
  Example under Textile industry and fabrics;
Weaving
Blanking (Metal-work)
  xx Sheet-metal work
Blanks in legal documents *(Direct)*
  xx Forgery
Fraud
Legal documents
Blantyre, Nyasaland
— Riot, Jan. 26, 1960

Blasphemy *(Direct) (Church law,
BV763.B6; Ethics, BJ1535.P95;
Moral theology, BV4627.B6)*
Here are entered works on blasphemy in
the legal and theological sense, "mali-
ciously reviling God or religion."
Works on profane language are en-
tered under Swearing. Works on judi-
cial or official oaths are entered under
Oaths.
  sa Commandments, Ten—Name of God
Liberty of the press
Prohibited books
Sacrilege
Trials (Blasphemy)
  xx Crimes without victims
Ecclesiastical law
Libel and slander
Liberty of speech
Liberty of the press
Offenses against religion
Prohibited books
Religious liberty
  Notes under Oaths; Swearing
Blasphemy (Greek law)
Blasphemy (Islam) *(BP167.3)*
  xx Islamic ethics
Blast disease of rice
  See Rice blast disease
Blast effect
  sa Impact
War damage to buildings
  subdivision Blast effect *under specific
subjects, e.g.* Atomic bomb—Blast
effect
  x Blast loads
Explosion loads
  xx Aerodynamic load
Building, Bombproof
Explosions
Impact
Shock (Mechanics)
Shock waves
Vibration
War damage to buildings
— Simulation methods *(TN279)*
Blast-furnaces *(TN677; Cast-iron,
TN713-718)*
  sa Cupola-furnaces
  xx Metallurgical furnaces
Smelting
Smelting furnaces
— Automatic control
— Combustion
— Cooling
— Design and construction
— Electric equipment
  xx Blast-furnaces—Equipment and
supplies
— Equipment and supplies
  sa Blast-furnaces—Electric equipment
— Fuel consumption
— Fuel systems
— Maintenance and repair
— Mathematical models
— Safety measures
— Safety regulations *(Direct)*
— Tables, calculations, etc. *(TN713)*
Blast loads
  See Blast effect
Blasting *(TN279)*
  sa Explosives
Mines, Military
Nuclear excavation
  xx Engineering
Explosives
Mines, Military
Mining engineering

Blasting *(TN279)* *(Continued)*
    Quarries and quarrying
    Stone
    Tunneling
  — Law and legislation
    See Explosives—Law and legislation
  — Problems, exercises, etc.
  — Safety measures
Blasting, Submarine *(TC191-2)*
  x Submarine blasting
  xx Hydraulic engineering
Blasting oil
  See Nitroglycerin
Blastocyst
  xx Placenta
Blastoidea
  sa Fissiculata
Blastomycetic dermatitis
  See Blastomycosis
Blastomycosis *(RC123.B6)*
  sa Coccidioidosis
  x Blastomycetic dermatitis
  xx Coccidioidosis
  Example under Skin—Diseases
Blattariae
  See Cockroaches
Blattoidea
  See Cockroaches
Blaubok
  See Blue antelope
Blazonry
  See Heraldry
Bleaching *(TP894)*
  sa Drying apparatus—Textile fabrics
    Dyes and dyeing
    Wood-pulp—Bleaching
  x Blanching
  xx Chemistry, Technical
    Cleaning
    Dyes and dyeing
    Textile industry and fabrics
  — Patents
Bleaching, Electric
  x Electric bleaching
Bleaching materials
  sa Bleaching powder
    Optical brighteners
  xx Chemicals
    Laundry
  — Patents
Bleaching powder
  x Lime, Chloride of
  xx Bleaching materials
Bleak (Fish)
Bleeding
  See Bloodletting
    Hemorrhage
Blended yarn
  x Textile fiber blends
    Textile fibers—Blends
  xx Yarn
Blenders (Cookery)
  xx Kitchen utensils
    Mixing machinery
Blending
  See Mixing
Blenheim, Battle of, 1704 *(D283.B6)*
  x Höchstädt, Battle of, 1704
  xx Spanish Succession, War of, 1701-1714
Blepharoptosis
  x Ptosis, Eyelid
  xx Eyelids—Diseases
Blepharospasm
  See Eyelids—Diseases
Blessed *(BX4650-4651)*
  xx Beatification
  — Portraits

Blessed water
  See Holy water
Blessing and cursing
  Here are entered works dealing with blessing in the abstract, also studies of the word "blessing." Works on the liturgical functions of blessing are entered under the heading Benediction.
  sa Barakah
    Excommunication
    Exorcism
  x Cursing and blessing
    Execration
    Imprecation
    Malediction
  xx Exorcism
    Incantations
    Polarity (in religion, folk-lore, etc.)
  Note under Benediction
Blessing and cursing in the Bible
Blessings, Table
  See Grace at meals
Blimps
  See Air-ships
Blind *(Direct)* *(Charities, HV1571-2349)*
  sa Artists, Blind
    Authors, Blind
    Blind-deaf
    Blind, Workers for the
    Blindness in literature
    Children, Blind
    Church work with the blind
    Missions to the blind
    Musicians, Blind
    Visually handicapped
  xx Physically handicapped
    Visually handicapped
  — Asylums
    See Blind—Institutional care
  — Biography *(HV1623-4)*
  — Education *(Direct)*
    sa Blind-deaf—Education
      Blind—Rehabilitation
      Blind—Travel
      Teachers of the blind
    x Education of the blind
      Visually handicapped children—Education
    xx Blind—Rehabilitation
      Children, Blind
      Vocational education
      Vocational guidance
    Example under Education
  — — Arithmetic, ₍Geography, Typewriting, etc.₎
  — — — Programmed instruction
  — — Reading
    See Blind—Printing and writing systems
  — Employment *(Direct)* *(HV1652-8)*
    sa Blind—Rehabilitation
    x Employment of the blind
    xx Blind—Rehabilitation
      Vocational rehabilitation
  — Institutional care *(Direct)*
    x Benevolent institutions
      Blind—Asylums
      Charitable institutions
      Homes (Institutions)
    xx Asylums
      Charities
      Charities, Medical
      Public welfare
  — Intelligence
    See Intelligence levels—Blind
  — Law and legislation *(Direct)*
    xx Charity laws and legislation
      Public welfare—Law

  — Mobility
    See Blind—Orientation and mobility
  — Orientation and mobility
    x Blind—Mobility
    xx Orientation
  — Pensions
    x Pensions for the blind
  — Personal narratives
  — Printing and writing systems *(HV1666-1698)*
    sa Braille music-notation
    x Blind—Education—Reading
      Braille system
      Moon system
      Moon's type for the blind
      New York point system
      Printing for the blind
    xx Braille music-notation
  — Psychology
  — Recreation
  — Rehabilitation *(Direct)*
    sa Blind—Education
      Blind—Employment
      Blind—Travel
    xx Blind—Education
      Blind—Employment
    Note under Rehabilitation
  — Research
  — Travel
    Here are entered works on the performance and adjustment of the blind in situations outside of the home involving walking or use of public vehicles, with or without the aid of canes, dogs or human guides.
    sa Guide dogs
    xx Blind—Education
      Blind—Rehabilitation
Blind, Apparatus for the *(HV1701)*
  sa Reading devices for the disabled
  x Apparatus for the blind
    Typewriters for the blind
  xx Reading devices for the disabled
    Self-help devices for the disabled
Blind, Bibles for the
  x Bibles for the blind
  xx Blind, Books for the
    Missions to the blind
Blind, Books for the
  sa Blind, Bibles for the
    Blind, Periodicals for the
    Sight-saving books
    Talking books
  x Books for the blind
    Braille books
  — Cataloging
    See Cataloging of books for the blind
  — Standards *(Direct)*
Blind, Cookery for the
  See Cookery for the blind
Blind, Libraries for the *(HV1721-1756; Z675.B6)*
  x Books for the blind
    Libraries for the blind
  xx Institution libraries
Blind, Maps for the
  sa subdivision Blind, Maps for the *under names of countries, regions, cities, etc.*
  x Maps for the blind
  xx Maps for the visually handicapped
Blind, Music for the *(HV1695; MT38)*
  sa Braille music-notation
  x Music for the blind
  xx Music
Blind, Periodicals for the
  x Periodicals for the blind
  xx Blind, Books for the

Blind, Physical education for the *(HV1767)*
    x Blind, Sports for the
        Physical education for the blind
        Sports for the blind
Blind, Poetry for the
    x Poetry for the blind
Blind, Sports for the
    See Blind, Physical education for the
Blind, Teachers of the
    See Teachers of the blind
Blind, Workers for the *(Direct)*
    sa Teachers of the blind
    xx Blind
    — Salaries, pensions, etc.
Blind authors
    See Authors, Blind
Blind children
    See Children, Blind
Blind-deaf
    x Deaf-blind
    xx Blind
        Deaf
        Physically handicapped
    — Education *(Direct)*
        xx Blind—Education
        Deaf—Education
    — Means of communication
    — Personal narratives
    — Rehabilitation *(Direct)*
Blind flying
    See Instrument flying
Blind gut
    See Cecum
Blind homemakers, Cookery for
    See Cookery for the blind
Blind landing
    See Ground controlled approach
        Instrument landing systems
Blind musicians
    See Musicians, Blind
Blind pilgrims (Game) *(GV1511.J4)*
Blind scholars
    See Scholars, Blind
Blind sculptors
    See Sculptors, Blind
Blind spot
    See Optic disc
Blind staggers
    See Selenosis
Blind teachers
    See Teachers, Blind
Blindness *(RE91)*
    sa Amblyopia
        Artificial vision
        Blindness in literature
        Color-blindness
        Conjunctivitis, Infantile
        Hemianopsia
        Snowblindness
    x Amaurosis
    xx Eye—Diseases and defects
        Vision
    — Genetic aspects
        x Congenital blindness
    — Prevention
Blindness, Feigned *(RA1146)*
    x Diseases, Feigned
        Feigned diseases
    xx Eye—Examination
        Malingering
Blindness in children
    See Children, Blind
Blindness in literature
    xx Blind
        Blindness
Blinds *(TH2276)*
    sa Window-shades
    x Window shutters

    xx Window-shades
        Windows
Blindspot
    See Optic disc
Bliss classification
    See Classification, Bibliographic
Blister rust
    sa Comandra blister rust
    x White-pine blister rust
    xx Rusts (Fungi)
    Example under Pine—Diseases and pests
Blister spot *(SB608.A6)*
Blisters
    x Vesication
    xx Counter-irritants
Blitzkrieg
    See Lightning war
Blizzards
    sa subdivision Blizzard *under names of*
        cities or localities, e.g. The West—
        Blizzard, 1949
    xx Storms
BLMC automobiles *(TL215.B23)*
    sa Austin automobile
        Austin-Healey automobile
        M.G. automobile
        Morris automobile
        Riley automobile
    x BMC automobiles
Bloat in animals
    x Hoven
Bloch constant
    x Constant, Bloch
    xx Functions of complex variables
Block anesthesia
    See Conduction anesthesia
Block booking
    xx Moving-pictures—Distribution
Block-books *(Z240-241)*
    sa Tile block-printing
        Wood-engraving
    x Xylography
    xx Bibliography
        Books
        Books—History—1400-1600
        Incunabula
        Printing—History
        Wood-engraving
    — Facsimiles
        sa Incunabula—Facsimiles
Block-books, Chinese, ⌈Japanese, etc.⌉
    x Chinese ⌈Japanese, etc.⌉ block-books
Block-books, Japanese
    sa Saga-bon
Block building (Education) *(LB1139.C7)*
    x Block play
    xx Creative activities and seat work
Block copolymers *(QD382.B5)*
    x Block polymers
    xx Polymers and polymerization
Block diagrams
    x Relief-maps
    xx Relief models
Block field
    See Felsenmeer
Block flute
    See Recorder (Musical instrument)
Block play
    See Block building (Education)
Block polymers
    See Block copolymers
Block-printing, Linoleum
    See Linoleum block-printing
Block-printing, Tile
    See Tile block-printing
Block-signal systems
    See Railroads—Signaling—Block system

Block trading *(Direct)*
    xx Stocks
Block wardens (Local government) *(Direct)*
    xx Local government
        Public opinion
Blockade *(JX5225)*
    sa Continental system of Napoleon
        Continuous voyages (International law)
        Contraband of war
        Embargo
        Navicert system
        Neutral trade with belligerents
        Search, Right of
        subdivision Blockades *under names of*
        wars
    xx Embargo
        Jurisdiction over ships at sea
        Naval art and science
        Neutral trade with belligerents
        Neutrality
        Sanctions (International law)
        War, Maritime (International law)
Blockade, Pacific *(JX4494)*
    x Pacific blockade
    xx Embargo
        War, Maritime (International law)
Blockade running
    See Blockade
Blockflute
    See Recorder (Musical instrument)
Blocking (Football)
    xx Football
Blocking groups (Chemistry)
    See Protective groups (Chemistry)
Blocking oscillators
    x Oscillators, Blocking
    xx Oscillators, Electric
Blons, Austria
    — Avalanche, 1954
Blood *(QP91-95)*
    sa Bacteremia
        Bacteriolysis
        Blood plasma
        Bloodletting
        Fibrinogen
        Hematopoiesis
        Hemolymph
        Hemolysis and hemolysins
        Hemorrhage
        Lipemia
        Oocytin
        Protein nitrogen
        Serum protein
    xx Anemia
        Body fluids
        Hematology
        Poultry industry—By-products
    — Agglutination *(Immunology, QR185;*
        Physiology, QP91)
        sa Blood groups
            Hemagglutinin
        x Hemagglutination
            Isoagglutination
            Isohemagglutination
            Sludged blood
        xx Agglutination
            Blood groups
            Diagnosis
    — Alcohol content
        See Blood alcohol
    — Analysis and chemistry *(Pathology,*
        RB145; Physiology, QP91-95)
        sa Abderhalden reaction
            Anoxemia
            Blood alcohol
            Blood—Sedimentation
            Blood sugar
            Glycolysis

Blood *(QP91-95)*
— Analysis and chemistry *(Pathology,*
        RB145; Physiology, QP91-95)
        (Continued)
    Hemoglobinometry
    Hypercapnia
    Hyperglycemia
    Porphyrinuria
  x Analysis of blood
    Blood chemistry
    Blood—Chemistry
    Examination of the blood
  xx Biological chemistry
    Medicine, Clinical—Laboratory
      manuals
    Physiological chemistry
  Example under Chemistry, Analytic
  Note under Blood—Examination
— Buffy coat *(QP91)*
  x Buffy coat
— Chemistry
  See Blood—Analysis and chemistry
— Circulation *(QP101)*
  sa Aorta
    Arteries
    Blood flow
    Blood pressure
    Blood-vessels
    Blood volume
    Blushing
    Cardiac catheterization
    Cardiovascular system
    Collateral circulation
    Heart
    Hemodynamics
    Microcirculation
    Peripheral circulation
    Plethora (Pathology)
    Plethysmography
    Pulmonary circulation
    Pulse
    Sphygmograph
    Veins
  x Circulation of the blood
  xx Arteries
    Blood pressure
    Blood-vessels
    Cardiovascular system
    Heart
    Physiology
    Veins
— Research
  See Cardiovascular research
— Circulation, Artificial *(QP101)*
  sa Perfusion pump (Heart)
  x Artificial blood circulation
    Artificial heart
    Extracorporeal circulation
    Extracorporeal perfusion
  xx Perfusion pump (Heart)
— — Complications and sequelae
— Circulation, Disorders of *(RC636)*
  sa Hypertension
    Hypotension
    Ischemia
  xx Cardiovascular system—Diseases
    Edema
    Embolism
    Heart—Diseases
    Shock
    Thrombosis
— Coagulation *(QP91)*
  sa Anticoagulants (Medicine)
    Blood coagulation factor XIII
    Blood coagulation tests
    Coagulase
    Dicumarol
    Fibrinolysis
    Thrombelastography

  x Coagulation of blood
  xx Coagulase
    Hemostasis
— Coagulation, Disorders of
  sa Disseminated intravascular
      coagulation
    Hemophilia
  x Coagulation disorders
  xx Hemorrhagic diseases
— Collection and preservation
  sa Frozen blood
  x Blood collection
    Blood preservation
    Collection of blood
  xx Blood banks
    Preservation of organs, tissues, etc.
— Color and coloring matter
  See Blood—Pigments
— Corpuscles and platelets *(QP91-95)*
  sa Blood cell count
    Blood platelets
    Erythrocytes
    Erythropoiesis
    Foà-Kurlov cells
    Leucocytes
  x Blood cells
— Dialysis
  See Hemodialysis
— Diseases *(RC636-643)*
  sa Agranulocytosis
    Blood platelet disorders
    Blood protein disorders
    Cold agglutinin syndrome
    Erythremia
    Erythroblastosis fetalis
    Erythrocyte disorders
    Hemochromatosis
    Hypergammaglobulinemia
    Hyperlipemia
    Hyperlipoproteinemia
    Leucopenia
    Methemoglobinemia
    Mononucleosis
    Pediatric hematology
    Piroplasmosis
  x Hematologic diseases
  xx Blood—Examination
    Hemochromatosis
  Example under reference from Diseases
    of the blood
— — Cases, clinical reports, statistics
— Examination *(RB145)*
  Here are entered treatises on the clinical examination of blood and on the
  diagnostic significance of blood
  changes in disease. *Cf.* Blood—
  Analysis and chemistry, for works
  on the technique and results of the
  chemical analysis of blood.
  sa Blood cell count
    Blood—Diseases
    Blood groups
    Blood—Sedimentation
    Evans blue
    Glycolysis
    Hematocrit
    Hemocytometer
  x Blood—Semiology
    Blood tests
    Examination of the blood
  xx Diagnosis
— Flow
  See Blood flow
— Freezing
  See Frozen blood
— Groups
  See Blood groups
— Jurisprudence

  See Forensic hematology
— Juvenile literature
— Mathematical models
— Parasites *(Parasitic diseases, RC226-248;*
      Pathogenic protozoa, QR251)
  x Parasites—Blood
  xx Medical parasitology
— Pigments *(QP91; RB145)*
  sa Hematoporphyrin
    Hemocyanin
    Hemoerythrin
    Hemoglobin
    Hemosiderin
  x Blood—Color and coloring matter
    Pigments (Blood)
  xx Animal pigments
— Plasma
  See Blood plasma
— Pressure
  See Blood pressure
— Sedimentation
  x Blood sedimentation
  xx Blood—Analysis and chemistry
    Blood—Examination
— Semiology
  See Blood—Examination
— Serum
  See Serum
— Tables, etc.
— Transfusion *(RM171)*
  sa Blood banks
    Blood donors
    Blood groups
    Blood plasma substitutes
    Compatibility testing (Hematology)
    Rh factor
  x Transfusion of blood
  xx Blood groups
    Surgery
— — Complications and sequelae
— — Moral and religious aspects *(Islam,*
      BP184.9.B5)
— — Social aspects *(Direct)*
— Transfusion, Intrauterine
  x Intrauterine blood transfusion
  xx Fetus—Diseases
— Transportation *(RM172)*
  sa Blood banks
  xx Blood banks
Blood, Frozen
  See Frozen blood
Blood, Gases in *(QP91)*
  sa Oximetry
  x Gases in the blood
Blood, Irradiated
  See Blood irradiation
Blood, Relics of the Precious
  See Precious Blood, Relics of the
Blood (in religion, folk-lore, etc.)
    (Comparative religion, BL570,
      BL600; Folk-lore, GR489)
  sa Blood accusation
    Blood brotherhood
    Blood covenant
    Lusalo
    Precious Blood, Relics of the
    Taurobolium
  x Folk-lore of blood
  xx Religion, Primitive
    Sacrifice
    Vendetta
Blood accusation *(BM717)*
  x Blood libel
    Murder, Ritual
    Ritual murder
  xx Blood (in religion, folk-lore, etc.)
    Jews—Persecutions
    Sacrifice, Human

Blood alcohol
    x Alcohol in blood
       Blood—Alcohol content
    xx Alcohol in the body
       Blood—Analysis and chemistry
Blood alcohol level
    See Alcohol in the body
Blood as food or medicine
Blood banks *(Direct)*
    sa Blood—Collection and preservation
       Blood—Transportation
    x Banked blood
    xx Blood plasma
       Blood—Transfusion
       Blood—Transportation
    — Economic aspects
    — Law and legislation *(Direct)*
    — Quality control
Blood-brain barrier
    x Brain-blood barrier
       Hematoencephalic barrier
    xx Brain—Blood-vessels
       Cerebrospinal fluid
Blood brotherhood *(GN491.5)*
    sa Blood covenant
    xx Blood covenant
       Blood (in religion, folk-lore, etc.)
       Society, Primitive
Blood cell count
    x Hemogram
    xx Blood—Corpuscles and platelets
       Blood—Examination
Blood cells
    See Blood—Corpuscles and platelets
Blood chemistry
    See Blood—Analysis and chemistry
Blood cholesterol
    x Serum cholesterol
    xx Blood lipids
       Cholesterol
Blood coagulation factor XIII
    x Fibrin stabilizing factor
       Laki-Lorand factor
    xx Blood—Coagulation
       Fibrin
Blood coagulation tests
    sa Thrombelastography
    xx Blood—Coagulation
Blood collection
    See Blood—Collection and preservation
Blood covenant
    sa Blood brotherhood
       Covenants (Religion)
    xx Blood brotherhood
       Blood (in religion, folk-lore, etc.)
       Covenants (Religion)
Blood donors
    xx Blood plasma
       Blood—Transfusion
    — Public opinion
Blood feuds
    See Vendetta
Blood flow
    sa Regional blood flow
    x Blood—Flow
    xx Blood—Circulation
       Body fluid flow
       Hemodynamics
    — Mathematical models
    — Measurement
       sa Plethysmography
Blood formation
    See Hematopoiesis
Blood groups *(QP91)*
    sa Blood—Agglutination
       Blood—Transfusion
       Paternity
       Rh factor

    x Blood—Groups
    xx Blood—Agglutination
       Blood—Examination
       Blood—Transfusion
       Heredity
       Paternity
    — Compatibility testing
       See Compatibility testing
          (Hematology)
    — Programmed instruction
Blood groups in animals *(QP98)*
    x Animal blood groups
Blood Indians
    See Kainah Indians
Blood, irradiation
    x Blood, Irradiated
       Irradiated blood
    xx Radiology, Medical
Blood libel
    See Blood accusation
Blood lipids *(QP99.3.L5)*
    sa Blood cholesterol
       Blood lipoproteins
    x Plasma lipids
       Serum lipids
    xx Lipids
    — Analysis
Blood lipoproteins *(QP99.3.L52)*
    x Plasma lipoproteins
       Serum lipoproteins
    xx Blood lipids
       Blood proteins
       Lipoproteins
Blood louse
    See Woolly apple aphid
Blood meal as feed
Blood money
    See Wergild
Blood of Jesus, Devotion to
    See Precious Blood, Devotion to
Blood pheasants *(QL696.G2)*
    xx Pheasants
Blood plasma
    sa Blood banks
       Blood donors
       Blood plasma substitutes
       Plasma proteins
       Plasmin
    x Blood—Plasma
       Blood substitutes
    xx Blood
       Serum
Blood plasma substitutes
    sa Dextran
       PVP
    x Blood substitutes
    xx Blood plasma
       Blood—Transfusion
Blood platelet disorders *(RC647.B5)*
    xx Blood—Diseases
Blood platelets
    sa Megakaryocytes
    x Thrombocytes
    xx Blood—Corpuscles and platelets
Blood preservation
    See Blood—Collection and preservation
Blood pressure
    sa Blood—Circulation
       Carotid sinus
       Central venous pressure
       Sphygmomanometer
       Venous pressure
    x Blood—Pressure
    xx Blood—Circulation
       Hemodynamics
       Pressure
    — Measurement
       sa Intravenous catheterization

       Ophthalmodynamometry
Blood pressure, High
    See Hypertension
Blood pressure, Low
    See Hypotension
Blood protein disorders *(RC647.B6)*
    xx Blood—Diseases
Blood proteins
    sa Blood lipoproteins
       Hemoglobin
       Myoglobin
       Plasma proteins
       Serum protein
Blood Purge, 1934
    See Germany—History—Great Blood
       Purge, 1934
Blood sedimentation
    See Blood—Sedimentation
Blood serum
    See Serum
Blood substitutes
    See Blood plasma
       Blood plasma substitutes
Blood sugar
    sa Glucose tolerance tests
       Hyperglycemia
       Hypoglycemia
    xx Blood—Analysis and chemistry
       Glucose
       Sugar in the body
Blood tests
    See Blood—Examination
Blood tumor
    See Hematoma
Blood vessel prosthesis
    xx Blood-vessels—Transplantation
       Prosthesis
Blood-vessels *(Comparative anatomy, QL835; Human anatomy, QM191)*
    sa Angiospasm
       Aorta
       Arteries
       Blood—Circulation
       Collateral circulation
       Ductus arteriosus
       Veins
       subdivision Blood-vessels *under organs and regions of the body, e.g.* Brain—Blood-vessels; Uterus—Blood-vessels
    x Vascular system
    xx Arteries
       Blood—Circulation
       Cardiovascular system
       Veins
    — Abnormities and deformities
    — Diseases *(RC691-700)*
       sa Aneurysms
       Angiomatosis
       Behçet's disease
       Diabetic angiopathies
       Peripheral vascular diseases
       Renal artery obstruction
       Scalenus anticus syndrome
       x Vascular diseases
    — — Diagnosis
       sa Angiocardiography
    — Grafts
       See Vascular grafts
    — Innervation
       Example under Nervous system
    — Permeability
    — Radiography
       See Angiography
    — Surgery *(RD598)*
    — — Atlases
    — — Complications and sequelae
    — Transplantation
       sa Blood vessel prosthesis

Blood-vessels, Brachial
    See Arm—Blood-vessels
Blood viscosity
    xx Hemodynamics
        Viscosity
Blood volume
    xx Blood—Circulation
        Hemodynamics
    — Measurement
Bloodhounds *(SF429.B6)*
    Example under Dog breeds
Bloodletting *(RM182)*
    sa Cupping
        Leeches
    x Bleeding
        Phlebotomy
        Venesection
    xx Blood
        Hemorrhage
        Medicine—Practice
        Plethora (Pathology)
        Surgery
Bloodroot *(Botany, QK495.S18; Materia*
       medica, RS165.S2)
Bloodsucking animals
    x Animals, Bloodsucking
    xx Parasites
        Pests
        Zoology, Economic
        Zoology, Medical
Bloody Assizes, 1685
    xx Monmouth's Rebellion, 1685
Bloody Brook, Battle of, 1675 *(E83.67)*
    xx King Philip's War, 1675-1676
Bloody murrain
    See Texas fever
Bloomer costume
    xx Clothing and dress
Blount Indians
    See Apalachicola Indians
Blouses
    sa T-shirts
    x Shirts, Women's
    xx Clothing and dress
Blow-flies
    See Blowflies
Blow outs, Oil well
    See Oil well blowouts
Blow-torches
Blow vipers
    See Hognose snakes
Blowers
    See Compressors
        Fans (Machinery)
Blowflies *(QL537.M7)*
    sa Screwworm
    x Blow-flies
    xx Flies
    Example under Diptera
Blowing adders
    See Hognose snakes
Blowing-engines
    See Fans (Machinery)
Blowouts, Oil well
    See Oil well blowouts
Blowpipe *(QD87)*
    sa Assaying
        Chemistry, Analytic—Qualitative
    xx Assaying
        Chemical apparatus
        Chemistry, Analytic—Qualitative
        Chemistry—Manipulation
        Metallurgical analysis
        Metals
        Mineralogy, Determinative
BLS
    See Bachelor of liberal studies
Blue

Blue and Gray Reunion, 1938
    See Gettysburg Reunion, 1938
Blue and white transfer ware *(NK4277)*
    x Flow blue china
        Transfer-printed ware in blue
    xx Transfer-printing
Blue antelope
    x Blaubok
    xx Antelopes
Blue baby
    See Tetralogy of Fallot
Blue crabs *(QL444.D3)*
    — Diseases
Blue dandelion
    See Chicory
Blue-footed booby *(QL696.P4)*
    xx Boobies (Birds)
    — Behavior
Blue-glass cure
    See Light, Colored
        Phototherapy
Blue goose *(QL696.A5)*
    x Chen caerulescens (Linnaeus)
    xx Geese
        Snow goose
Blue grama grass *(SB201.B5)*
    x Grama grass, Blue
Blue-grass
    sa Kentucky bluegrass
    x Bluegrass
Blue-gray gnatcatcher
    Example under Gnatcatchers
Blue grouse
    See Dusky grouse
Blue in art
    xx Art
        Color
Blue jay *(QL696.P2)*
    xx Jays
    — Juvenile literature
Blue jeans
    See Jeans (Clothing)
Blue language
    See Bolak
Blue laws
    See Sunday legislation
Blue-leaved mallee *(Botany, QK495.E86;*
       Culture, SD397.B)
    x Mallee, Blue-leaved
    xx Eucalyptus
Blue Licks, Battle of the, 1782 *(F454)*
    xx Huron Indians—Wars
        Indians of North America—Wars—
            1775-1783
Blue mold disease of apples
    See Apple blue mold
Blue mold of tobacco
    See Tobacco blue mold
Blue mountain tea
    See Sweet goldenrod
Blue-printing *(TR415; Industrial*
       reproduction, TR921)
    x Cyanotype
        Photography—Printing processes—
            Blue-printing
        Photography—Printing processes—
            Cyanotype
        Photography—Printing processes—
            Ferroprussiate
    xx Photography—Reproduction of plans,
        drawings, etc.
Blue-prints *(Mechanical drawing, T379)*
    x Blueprints
        Contact prints
        Mechanical drawings
    xx Engineering drawings
        Photocopying processes
    — Terminology

Blue racer
    See Coluber constrictor
Blue rot
    See Blue stain
Blue sailor (Plant)
    See Chicory
Blue sap stain
    See Blue stain
Blue shark *(QL638.95.C3)*
    x Great blue shark
Blue sky laws
    See Securities
Blue stain *(SB608.C7)*
    x Blue rot
        Blue sap stain
        Sap stain
    xx Wood-staining fungi
Blue Streak (Missile)
    See Blue Streak rocket
Blue Streak rocket
    x Blue Streak (Missile)
        Blue Streak satellite launcher
    xx Launch vehicles (Astronautics)
        Rockets (Aeronautics)
Blue Streak satellite launcher
    See Blue Streak rocket
Blue tongue
    See Bluetongue
Blue whale
    x Sibbald's rorqual
        Sulphurbottom
    xx Whales
    — Juvenile literature
Blue-winged teals *(QL696.A5)*
    x Teals, Blue-winged
    xx Ducks
Blueback herring *(QL638.C64)*
    x Herring, Blueback
Blueback salmon
    See Sockeye salmon
Blueberries *(Indirect)* *(SB386.B7)*
    — Harvesting
    — Marketing
    — Packing
    — Storage
    — Varieties
Blueberries, Dried
    x Dried blueberries
Bluebirds *(QL696.P2)*
    sa Eastern bluebird
Bluefin tuna
    xx Tuna
Bluefish
Bluegill *(QL638.C3)*
    xx Sunfishes
Bluegrass
    See Blue-grass
Bluegrass music *(Indirect)*
    xx Country music
        Fiddle tunes
        Music, Popular (Songs, etc.)
Bluehead chub *(QL638.C94)*
Blueprints
    See Blue-prints
Blues (Songs, etc.) *(Indirect)*
    x Soul music
    xx Jazz music
        Music, Popular (Songs, etc.)—United
            States
        Negro songs
        Negro spirituals
Bluethroat *(QL696.P2)*
Bluetongue
    x Blue tongue
Bluetongue virus
    xx Viruses
Blunders
    See Bulls, Colloquial

Errors and blunders, Literary
    Errors, Popular
Blunt Indians
    See Apalachicola Indians
Bluntnose minnow
    x Minnow, Bluntnose
Blushing *(QP401)*
    xx Blood—Circulation
Blushing in literature
BMC automobiles
    See BLMC automobiles
BMEWS
    See Ballistic missile early warning system
BMR
    See Basal metabolism
BMW automobile
BMW motorcycle *(TL448.B)*
BNB MARC
    See MARC System—Great Britain
Bo Tree
    See Bodhi Tree
Boa-constrictors *(QL666.O6)*
    Example under Snakes
Boa-ho
    See Bon (Tibetan religion)
Boar, Wild
    See Wild boar
Boar hunting
    See Wild boar
Board games *(GV1312)*
    sa specific games, e.g. Chess
    x Move games
    xx Games
Boarding homes
    See Rest homes
Boarding-houses
    See Hotels, taverns, etc.
Boarding schools *(Direct)*
    sa Private schools
    xx Private schools
    Residence and education
    Schools
Boards, Display
    See Display boards
Boards of directors
    See Directors of corporations
Boards of education
    See School boards
Boards of health
    See Health boards
Boards of supervision (Corporation law)
    See Directors of corporations
Boards of trade *(Indirect)* *(HF294; Serial*
    reports, etc., HF295-343)
    sa Industrial promotion
    x Chambers of commerce
    Trade, Boards of
    xx Commercial associations
    Trade and professional associations
    — Accounting *(HF5686.B36)*
Boards of zoning adjustment
    See Zoning boards
Boars
    sa Wild boar
    xx Swine
    — Juvenile literature
Boastfulness in literature
    sa Pride in literature
    x Braggarts in literature
    xx Pride in literature
Boat-building *(VM320-361)*
    sa Boats and boating
    Concrete boats
    Fiberglass boats
    Plastics in boat-building
    Ship-building
    Ship models
    Yacht-building

    xx Boats and boating
    Naval architecture
    Ship-building
    — Safety measures
Boat davits
    See Davits
Boat fittings
    See Boats and boating—Equipment and
    supplies
Boat handling
    See Boats and boating
Boat-houses *(NA6920)*
    xx Boats and boating
Boat jousting
    xx Aquatic sports
    Tournaments
Boat names
    sa Ship names
    xx Names
    Ship names
Boat-people (Chinese people)
    See Tanka (Chinese people)
Boat-racing
    See Motor-boat racing
    Rowing
    Yacht racing
Boat radio
    See Radio on boats
Boat trade
    See Boating industry
Boat trailers
    x Boats and boating—Trailers
    Trailer boating
    Trailerboating
    Trailers, Boat
    xx Automobiles—Trailers
    Trailers
Boat trains *(Direct)*
    xx Railroads—Passenger traffic
    Steamboat lines
Boating accidents
    See Boats and boating—Accidents and
    injuries
Boating for women
    x Yachting for women
    xx Boats and boating
Boating industry *(Direct)*
    sa Wages—Boating industry
    x Boat trade
    xx Boats and boating
    — Finance
Boatmen *(Direct)*
    sa Inland water transportation—
    Employees
    Merchant seamen
    Shipping
    xx Merchant seamen
    Shipping
    — Language (New words, slang, etc.)
Boatmen's songs
    xx Sailors' songs
    Songs
Boats, Aluminum
    See Aluminum boats
Boats, Concrete
    See Concrete boats
Boats, Jet-propelled
    See Jet boats
Boats, Submarine
    See Submarine boats
Boats (Small-boat service)
    See subdivision Small-boat service *under*
    navies, e.g. Great Britain. Navy—
    Small-boat service
Boats and boating *(Indirect)* *(GV771-836)*
    sa Aluminum boats
    Aquatic sports
    Boat-building

    Boat-houses
    Boating for women
    Boating industry
    Canal-boats
    Canoes and canoeing
    Catamarans
    Concrete boats
    Cookery, Marine
    Dhows
    Dories (Boats)
    Electric boats
    Eskimos—Boats
    Fiberglass boats
    Fishing boats
    Flatboats
    Glass bottom boats
    House-boats
    Hydrofoil boats
    Ice-boats
    Indians—Boats
    Indians of Central America—Boats
    Indians of North America—Boats
    Indians of South America—Boats
    Inflatable boats
    Launches
    Life-boats
    Marinas
    Motor-boats
    Rafting (Sports)
    Rowing
    Sailboats
    Sailing
    Scows
    Shantyboats and shantyboaters
    Ships
    Skiffs
    Steamboats
    Steel boats
    Submarine boats
    Torpedo-boats
    Trimarans
    Umiaks
    United States. Navy—Boats
    Vedette boats
    Work boats
    Yachts and yachting
    x Boat handling
    xx Aquatic sports
    Boat-building
    Locomotion
    Sailing
    Ship handling
    Ships
    — Accidents and injuries
    x Boating accidents
    Boats and boating—Injuries
    — Anecdotes, facetiae, satire, etc.
    — Equipment and supplies
    sa Electronics on boats
    Radio on boats
    x Boat fittings
    Fitting out of boats
    — Finance
    — Fires and fire prevention
    — Injuries
    See Boats and boating—Accidents and
    injuries
    — Juvenile literature
    — Law and legislation *(Direct)*
    — Maintenance and repair
    — Painting
    — Quotations, maxims, etc.
    — Radio
    See Radio on boats
    — Safety measures *(VK200)*
    — Tariff
    See Duty-free importation of boats
    — Taxation *(Direct)*

Boats and boating *(Indirect)* *(GV771-836)*
  (Continued)
  — Trailers
    See Boat trailers
Boatswains
  See United States. Navy—Boatswains
Boatswain's mates
  See United States. Navy—Boatswains
Boatswain's mates, Aviation
  See United States. Navy—Aviation
    boatswain's mates
Bob-white
  See Bobwhite
Bobangi language
  x Bubangi language
    Rebu language
  xx Bantu languages
Bobbin lace *(Indirect)* *(TT805)*
  sa Lace bobbins
  x Bone lace
    Pillow lace
  xx Lace and lace making
Bobbinet *(TS1580)*
Bobbinite *(TP290.B7)*
  xx Explosives
Bobbins (Lace)
  See Lace bobbins
Bobbins (Textile machinery)
  xx Reels (Textile machinery)
    Textile machinery
Bobcat
  xx Lynx
  — Legends and stories
Bobo (African people)
  x Bwa (African people)
    Bwawa (African people)
  xx Ethnology—Upper Volta
  — Rites and ceremonies
Bobo dialects *(PL8080)*
  x Bwamu dialect
  xx Gur languages
Bobolinks *(QL696.P2)*
Bobsledding
  See Coasting
Bobwhite
  x Bob-white
    Masked bobwhite
  xx Quails
  — Juvenile literature
Bocootawwonauke Indians
  xx Algonquian Indians
    Indians of North America
    Mound-builders
    Powhatan Indians
Boddhisattvas
  See Bodhisattvas
Bodenreform
  See Physiocrats
    Single tax
    Unearned increment
Bodhi
  See Enlightenment (Buddhism)
Bodhi-druma
  See Bodhi Tree
Bodhi Tree
  x Bo Tree
    Bodhi-druma
    Bodhirukkha
  xx Buddhist shrines
    Historic trees
Bodhidharma dolls *(Direct)*
  x Daruma dolls
  xx Art, Zen
    Dolls
    Folk art
  — Collectors and collecting *(Direct)*
Bodhirukkha
  See Bodhi Tree

Bodhisattas
  See Bodhisattvas
Bodhisattva bhūmis
  See Bodhisattva stages (Mahayana
    Buddhism)
Bodhisattva stages (Mahayana Buddhism)
  (BQ4330)
  x Bodhisattva bhūmis
    Fifty-two stages (Mahayana Buddhism)
    Ten stages (Mahayana Buddhism)
  xx Religious life (Mahayana Buddhism)
Bodhisattvahood
  See Buddhahood
Bodhisattvas
  x Boddhisattvas
    Bodhisattas
  xx Gods, Buddhist
Bodices
  xx Clothing and dress
Bodies, Geniculate
  See Geniculate bodies
Bodo languages *(PL3871-4)*
  sa Bara language
    Chutiya language
    Garo language
    Tipura language
  xx Garo language
    Tibeto-Burman languages
Body, Human
  sa Anatomy, Human
    Body image
    Man—Animal nature
    Mind and body
    Physiology
  x Human body
  xx Anatomy, Human
    Mind and body
    Physiology
    Psychology
    Self
  — Papal documents
    xx Christian ethics—Catholic authors
Body, Human, in literature
  xx Body and soul in literature
Body, Human (in religion, folk-lore, etc.)
  sa Body and soul in literature
  x Folk-lore of the body
  xx Body and soul in literature
    Religion, Primitive
Body and mind
  See Mind and body
Body and soul (Philosophy)
  See Mind and body
Body and soul (Theology)
  See Man (Theology)
Body and soul in literature
  Here are entered works dealing with the
    medieval legends and debates of the
    Body and Soul.
  sa Body, Human, in literature
    Body, Human (in religion, folk-lore,
    etc.)
  xx Body, Human (in religion, folk-lore,
    etc.)
    Dualism
    Mind and body
    Soul
Body build, Human
  See Somatotypes
Body composition
  sa Body weight
    Bone densitometry
  xx Anatomy
    Biological chemistry
    Body weight
Body constitution, Human
  See Man—Constitution

Body covering (Anatomy)
  sa Feathers
    Fur
    Hair
    Scales (Fishes)
    Shells
    Skin
  — Juvenile literature
Body fluid flow
  sa Blood flow
  xx Biological transport
    Fluid dynamics
    Rheology (Biology)
Body fluids *(QP90.5)*
  sa Amniotic liquid
    Bile
    Biological transport
    Blood
    Bronchi—Secretions
    Cerebrospinal fluid
    Dehydration in infants
    Digestive organs—Secretions
    Dropsy
    Extracellular fluid
    Extracellular space
    Exudates and transudates
    Fluid therapy
    Gastric juice
    Homeostasis
    Labyrinthine fluids
    Mucus
    Nose—Secretions
    Osmosis
    Pancreas—Secretions
    Perfusion (Physiology)
    Perspiration
    Saliva
    Semen
    Stomach—Secretions
    Synovia
    Urine
    Uterus—Secretions
    Water in the body
  x Animal fluids and humors
    Fluids and humors, Animal
  — Analysis
    xx Chemistry, Clinical
  — Mathematical models
  — Pressure
    sa Cerebrospinal fluid pressure
    xx Pressure
  — Programmed instruction
Body image
  x Image, Body
  xx Body, Human
    Perception
    Personality
    Psychology, Physiological
    Vision
Body-marking *(Direct)* *(GN418)*
  sa Tattooing
  xx Beauty, Personal
    Ethnology
    Manners and customs
Body mechanics
  See Posture
Body of revolution
  xx Aerodynamics
    Generation of geometric forms
    Revolutions (Descriptive geometry)
Body size
  Here are entered works on the influence
    of the size of the animal body upon its
    functioning, *e.g.* locomotion, metabo-
    lism, sense perception, etc.
  sa Anthropometry
    Bergmann's rule
  xx Anthropometry

Morphology (Animals)
Physiology, Comparative
— Juvenile literature
Body-snatching
  sa Exhumation
  x Resurrectionists (Body-snatchers)
  xx Criminal law
Body surfing
  See Surfing
Body temperature *(Diagnosis, RC75;*
      Physiology, QP135)
  sa Animal heat
    Antipyretics
    Fever
    Hypothermia
    Thermometers and thermometry,
      Medical
  x Temperature, Animal and human
    Temperature curve
  xx Animal heat
    Diagnosis
    Fever
    Medical thermography
    Physiology
    Thermometers and thermometry,
      Medical
  — Charts, diagrams, etc.
  — Regulation
    x Regulation of body temperature
    Thermoregulation
  — — Juvenile literature
  — — Mathematical models
Body types, Human
  See Somatotypes
Body water loss
  See Dehydration (Physiology)
Body weight
  sa Body composition
    Infants—Weight
  xx Anthropometry
    Body composition
    Weights and measures
Boeck's sarcoid
  See Sarcoidosis
Boehm flute
  See Flute
Boeing 707 (Jet transports)
  xx Jet transports
Boeing 720 (Jet transport) *(TL685.7)*
  xx Jet transports
Boeing 727 (Jet transports)
  xx Jet transports
Boeing 747 (Jet transports)
  xx Jet transports
Boeing airplanes
  sa Boeing P-26 (Fighter plane)
Boeing B-17
  See B-17 bomber
Boeing B-29
  See B-29 bomber
Boeing bombers
  sa B-17 bomber
    B-29 bomber
  x Boeing Fortresses (Bombers)
    Fortresses (Bombers)
  xx Bombers
Boeing Fortresses (Bombers)
  See Boeing bombers
Boeing P-26 (Fighter plane)
  x P-26 (Fighter plane)
    Peashooter (Fighter plane)
  xx Boeing airplanes
    Fighter planes
Boer students *(Direct)*
  x Students, Boer
Boer students in the Netherlands, ₍etc.₎
Boer War, 1880-1881
  See Transvaal—History—War of 1880-1881

Boer War, 1899-1902
  See South African War, 1899-1902
Boeroe language
  See Buru language
Boers *(DT888-944)*
  sa Africa, South—History—Great Trek,
    1836-1840
  x Africanders
    Afrikaanders
    Afrikanders
  xx Ethnology—Africa, South
Boers in the Argentine Republic, ₍the
    Netherlands, etc.₎
Bog-butter
Bog flora *(Indirect)* *(QK938.M3)*
  sa Marsh flora
    Pond flora
  x Flora
  xx Bogs
    Fresh-water flora
    Marsh flora
    Pond flora
Bogatyrs
  xx Byliny
    Heroes
Boghead coal
  See Torbanite
Bogomiles *(BX6510.B7)*
  xx Albigenses
    Sects, Medieval
Bogos
Bogotá
  — Riot, 1948
Bogs *(Indirect)*
  sa Bog flora
    Fens
    Marshes
    Moors and heaths
    Peat-bogs
  xx Drainage
    Fens
    Marshes
    Moors and heaths
    Waste lands
    Wetlands
Bohemia
  — History *(DB191-215)*
  — — To 1526
      sa Dürnkrut, Battle of, 1278
  — — 1403-1526
  — — 1526-
  — — 1526-1618
  — — 1618-1848
  — — Revolution, 1848 *(DB214)*
      xx Austria—History—Revolution,
        1848-1849
  — — 1848-1918
Bohemia in literature
  xx Czechoslovak Republic in literature
Bohemian Brethren *(BX4920-4921)*
  sa Moravians
  x Herrnhuter
  xx Beghards
    Moravians
  — Hymns
Bohemian Deists
  See Abrahamites (Bohemia)
Bohemian hymns, ₍language, newspapers, etc.₎
  See Czech language
    Czech newspapers
    Hymns, Czech
    similar headings
Bohemianism *(Direct)* *(American literature,*
    PS228.B6)
  sa Hippies
  x Beat generation
    Beatniks
    Beats

  xx Manners and customs
  — Caricatures and cartoons
Bohemians
  See Czechs
Bohon-upas
  See Upas
Boii *(D70)*
  x Boji
Boiken language
  sa Yangoru dialect
  x Boikin language
  xx Papuan languages
Boikin language
  See Boiken language
Boil
  See Furuncle
Boiler explosions
  See Kitchen-boiler explosions
    Steam-boiler explosions
Boiler insurance
  See Insurance, Boiler
Boiler-makers
  sa Trade-unions—Boiler-makers
  x Steam-boiler makers
Boiler-making industry *(Direct)*
  xx Boilers
  — Accidents
Boiler-plates *(TJ290-291)*
  xx Steam-boilers
Boiler-scale
  See Steam-boilers—Incrustations
Boiler water
  See Feed-water
Boilers *(Heating of buildings, TH7470-7476;*
    Hot water heating, TH7538;
    Steam-heating, TH7588)
  sa Autoclaves
    Boiler-making industry
    Feed-water
    Fuel
    Heating
    Injectors
    Locomotive boilers
    Pressure vessels
    Steam-boilers
  xx Heating
    Pressure vessels
  — Appraisal
    See Boilers—Valuation
  — Automatic control
  — Cleaning
  — Efficiencies
  — Safety measures
  — Testing
  — Valuation *(TJ288)*
    x Boilers—Appraisal
Boiling
  See Ebullition
Boiling, Film
  See Film boiling
Boiling, Nucleate
  See Nucleate boiling
Boiling (Cookery) *(TX685)*
  xx Cookery
Boiling-points *(QD518)*
  sa Azeotropes
    Distillation, Fractional
    Ebullition
  xx Chemistry, Physical and theoretical
    Molecular weights
    Solution (Chemistry)
    Temperature
    Thermochemistry
Boiling reactors
  See Boiling water reactors
Boiling water reactors *(TK9203.B6)*
  x Boiling reactors
    BORAX (Nuclear reactor)

Boiling water reactors *(TK9203.B6)*
(Continued)
  BWR
  xx Atomic power-plants
    Nuclear reactors
    Solid fuel reactors
    Steam power-plants
 — Mathematical models
 — Testing
Boji
 See Boii
Bolaang Mongondo language *(PL5291.Z9B)*
 xx Malayan languages
Bolak *(PM8101-9)*
 x Blue language
  Langue bleue (Artificial language)
 xx Languages, Artificial
Bolas
 sa Lasso
 xx Lasso
Boleko oil
 See Isano oil
Bolen test
 xx Cancer—Diagnosis
Boleros
  Here are entered collections of bolero music for various mediums. Individual boleros and collections of boleros for a specific medium are entered under the heading followed by specification of medium.
Boleros (Band) *(M1249; M1266)*
 xx Band music
Boleros (Guitar and piano) *(M276-7)*
 xx Guitar and piano music
Boleros (Orchestra) *(M1049; M1060)*
 xx Orchestral music
Boleros (Piano, 8 hands) *(M213)*
Boleros (Violoncello and piano) *(M230; M233)*
 xx Violoncello and piano music
Bolex moving-picture camera
 x Paillard moving-picture camera
Bolivia
 — History *(F3321-4)*
 — — To 1809
 — — Insurrection of Tupac-Amaru, 1780-1781
    See Peru—History—Insurrection of Tupac-Amaru, 1780-1781
 — — Wars of Independence, 1809-1825
   sa La Paz, Bolivia—History—Revolution, 1809
 — — 1825-
 — — 1825-1879
   sa Ingavi, Battle of, 1841
 — — Peru-Bolivian Confederation, 1836-1839
   See Peru—History—Peru-Bolivian Confederation, 1836-1839
 — — War with Chile, 1879-1884
   See War of the Pacific, 1879-1884
 — — 1879-1938
   sa Chaco War, 1932-1935
    War of the Pacific, 1879-1884
 — — 1938-
   sa Bolivia—History—Revolution, 1946
    Bolivia—History—Revolution, 1952
 — — Revolution, 1946
   xx Bolivia—History—1938-
 — — Revolution, 1952
   xx Bolivia—History—1938-
 — — Revolution, 1964
Bolivia (Game) *(GV1295.B6)*
 xx Canasta (Game)
Bolivian fiction *(History, PQ7812)*

Bolivian literature *(Direct) (PQ7801-7819)*
 xx Spanish American literature
Bolivian newspapers *(History, etc., PN5011-5015)*
Bolivian periodicals *(History, etc., PN5011-5015)*
Bolivian poetry *(Collections, PQ7814; History, PQ7810)*
Boll-weevil *(SB945.C8)*
 sa Kelep
 x Cotton boll-weevil
  Mexican boll-weevil
  Mexican cotton-boll weevil
 xx Beetles
 Example under Cotton—Diseases and pests; Insects, Injurious and beneficial; Pests
 — Control
   See Boll-weevil control
Boll-weevil control *(Indirect)*
 x Boll-weevil—Control
Bollandists *(BX4662)*
 sa Hagiography
 xx Jesuits
Bollworm
 See Corn earworm
Bologna
 — Riot, Nov. 21, 1920 *(DG571)*
 — Sepulchral monuments
   Example under Sepulchral monuments
Bolometer *(QC338)*
 xx Meteorological instruments
Bolsey camera
 Example under Miniature cameras
Bolshevism
 See Communism, *especially* Communism—Russia
Bolshevist self-criticism
 See Communist self-criticism
Bolted joints
 xx Bolts and nuts
  Joints (Engineering)
 — Testing
Bolting, Mine roof
 See Mine roof bolting
Boltonite
 See Forsterite
Bolts, Rock
 See Rock bolts
Bolts and nuts *(TJ1330)*
 sa Bolted joints
  Washers (for bolts and screws)
 x Nuts (Machinery)
 xx Carriage and wagon making
  Fastenings
  Hardware
  Joints (Engineering)
 Note under Machine parts
 — Drawing
   See Bolts and nuts—Drawings
 — Drawings
   x Bolts and nuts—Drawing
   xx Mechanical drawing
 — Standards *(Direct)*
 — Testing
Boltzmann transport equation
 See Transport theory
Bomarc (Missile)
 xx Surface-to-air missiles
 Example under Guided missiles
Bomb calorimeter
 xx Calorimeters and calorimetry
Bomb Conspiracy Trial, New York, 1970-1971
 See Black Panthers Trial, New York, 1970-1971
Bomb damage in industry
 See War damage, Industrial
Bomb damage to buildings
 See War damage to buildings

Bomb-proof building
 See Building, Bombproof
Bomb-proof construction
 See Building, Bombproof
Bomb racks
 xx Bombardment
  Bombers
  Bombs
Bomb reconnaissance
  Here are entered works on the location, identification, and application of safety measures as protection against unexploded bombs which have been set to detonate.
 xx Bombs
  Civil defense
Bomb shelters
 See Air raid shelters
  Atomic bomb shelters
Bomb-sights
 See Bombsights
Bombardment *(Indirect) (JX5117)*
 sa Atomic warfare
  Bomb racks
  Bombers
  Bombing, Aerial
  Bombsights
  subdivision Aerial operations *under names of wars, e.g.* World War, 1939-1945—Aerial operations; *also subdivision* Bombardment *under names of cities, e.g.* London—Bombardment, 1940
 xx Attack and defense (Military science)
  Coast defenses
  Sieges
  War
  War (International law)
  War, Maritime (International law)
Bombardment, Ion
 See Ion bombardment
Bombardment with particles
 See Collisions (Nuclear physics)
Bombardon
 See Tuba
Bombay
 — Riots, 1874
 — Riots, 1939
 — Textile General Strike, 1966
Bomber aeroplanes
 See Bombers
Bombers
 sa A-20 bomber
  B-17 bomber
  B-24 bomber
  B-29 bomber
  B-32 bomber
  B-36 bomber
  Boeing bombers
  Bomb racks
  Bombing, Aerial
  Devastator (Torpedo-bomber)
  Grumman Avenger (Bombers)
  Heinkel 111 (Bomber)
  Heinkel 177 (Bombers)
  Kamikaze aeroplanes
  Lancaster (Bombers)
  Messerschmitt 262 (Fighter planes)
  Mitchell bomber
  Mosquito (Bombers)
  Skyhawk bomber
  Skywarrior bomber
  Stuka (Bombers)
  Supersonic bombers
  Vigilante bomber
 x Bomber aeroplanes
 xx Aeroplanes, Military
  Bombardment

207

Bone black
　　See Animal charcoal
Bone carving　(Direct)　(NK6020)
　　sa Indians of Mexico—Bone carving
　　　Oracle bones
　　　Scrimshaws
　　xx Carving (Art industries)
　　　Paleography
　　　Writing—Materials and instruments
Bone conduction
　　xx Hearing
Bone densitometry
　　x Densitometry, Bone
　　xx Body composition
　　　Bones—Radiography
　　　Calcium in the body
Bone development
　　See Bone—Growth
Bone-grafting　(RD123)
　　sa Bone banks
　　x Bones—Transplantation
　　　Grafting of bone
　　　Osteoplasty
　　　Osteosynthesis
　　xx Bones—Surgery
　　　Homografts
　　　Surgery
　　　Surgery, Experimental
　　　Surgery, Plastic
　　　Transplantation of organs, tissues, etc.
Bone growth
　　See Bone—Growth
Bone implements　(Direct)
　　xx Archaeology
　　　Implements, utensils, etc.
　　　Industries, Primitive
Bone lace
　　See Bobbin lace
Bone marrow
　　See Marrow
Bone marrow derived cells
　　See B cells
Bone-meal　(Feed, SF99; Fertilizer, S659;
　　　Utilization of wastes, TP995)
　　xx Bone products
　　　Organic fertilizers
　　　Phosphatic fertilizers
Bone products
　　sa Animal charcoal
　　　Bone-meal
　　　Glue
　　　Phosphates
　　x Bones (Technology)
　　xx Animal charcoal
　　　Animal products
　　　Bones
　　　Glue
　　　Phosphates
Bone rattle
　　See Notched rattle
Bone regeneration
　　xx Regeneration (Biology)
Bone shark
　　See Basking shark
Bonefish
　　x Banana fish
　　　Ladyfish
Bonellein

Bones　(Animal, QL821; Human,
　　QM101-117)
　　Here are entered comprehensive and sys-
　　tematic works on the anatomy of the
　　bony structure of man and its articula-
　　tions; also comparative studies and dis-
　　cussions of bony structures of verte-
　　brate groups other than man. Works
　　on the comparative morphology, me-
　　chanics, etc. of the skeleton are en-
　　tered under the heading Skeleton.
　　Studies of skeletal remains are entered
　　under Anthropometry; Man, Prehis-
　　toric; etc.
　　sa Animal remains (Archaeology)
　　　Bone
　　　Bone products
　　　Callus
　　　Cartilage
　　　Cheek-bone
　　　Epiphysis
　　　Extremities (Anatomy)
　　　Facial bones
　　　Forensic osteology
　　　Fractures
　　　Humerus
　　　Hyoid bone
　　　Joints
　　　Ligaments
　　　Occipital bone
　　　Pelvis
　　　Ribs
　　　Skeleton
　　　Skull
　　　Spine
　　　Tibia
　　　Ulna
　　　Zygoma
　　x Osteology
　　xx Bone
　　　Fractures
　　　Musculoskeletal system
　　　Physiology
　　　Skeleton
　　Note under Skeleton
　—Abnormities and deformities
　　　(RD761-789)
　　　sa Laurence-Moon-Biedl syndrome
　—Atlases
　—Biopsy
　—Blood-vessels
　——Radiography
　　　x Bone angiography
　—Collection and preservation
　—Diseases　(RD684)
　　　sa Acrodystrophic neuropathy
　　　　Bones—Radiography
　　　　Exostosis
　　　　Fibrous dysplasia of bone
　　　　Fractures, Spontaneous
　　　　Necrosis
　　　　Osteal manifestations of general
　　　　　diseases
　　　　Osteitis deformans
　　　　Osteitis fibrosa
　　　　Osteomalacia
　　　　Osteomyelitis
　　　　Osteopetrosis
　　　　Osteoporosis
　　　　Osteopsathyrosis
　　　　Osteosclerosis
　　　　Perosis
　　　　X-rays
　——Genetic aspects
　—Innervation
　—Juvenile literature
　—Radiography
　　　sa Bone densitometry

　　xx Bones—Diseases
　—Surgery　(RD684)
　　　sa Bone-grafting
　　　　Osteoclasis
　　　　Osteotomy
　　　x Osteoplasty
　—Transplantation
　　　See Bone-grafting
　—Tuberculosis　(RC312.5.B)
　　　Example under Tuberculosis
　—Tumors　(RC280.B)
　　　sa Osteochondroma
　——Atlases
　——Diagnosis
　—Wounds and injuries
Bones (in religion, folk-lore, etc.)
　　x Folk-lore of bones
　　xx Religion, Primitive
Bones (Musical instrument)　(ML1040)
Bones (Technology)
　　See Bone products
Bongo　(ML1035)
　—Methods
　——Self-instruction　(MT662)
Bongo-Bagirmi languages
　　sa Bagirmi language
　　　Bongo language
　　　Kara language
　　　Kenga language
　　　Sara languages
　　　Yulu language
Bongo language
　　xx Bongo-Bagirmi languages
Bongu language　(PL6621.B7)
　　xx Papuan languages
Bonite Expedition, 1836-1837　(Q115)
Bonito
　　sa Pacific bonito
Bonito fisheries　(Indirect)　(SH351.B6)
　　xx Fisheries
　　　Mackerel fisheries
　　　Tuna fisheries
Bonjours, Les frères
　　See Fareinistes
Bonkei
　　xx Gardens, Miniature
Bonnō (Buddhism)
　　See Vice (Buddhism)
Bonny language
　　See Ijo language
Bons mots
　　See Wit and humor
Bonsai
　　sa Suiseki
　　x Bon-sai
　　　Dwarf trees
　　　Miniature trees
　　　Potted dwarf trees
　　xx Miniature plants
　　　Plants, Potted
Bonseki
　　See Suiseki
Bontoc Igorot (Philippine people)
　　See Bontoks (Philippine people)
Bontoks (Philippine people)
　　x Bontoc Igorot (Philippine people)
　　xx Ethnology—Philippine Islands
　　　Igorot
Bonus, Soldiers'
　　See Bounties, Military—[country
　　　subdivision], e.g. Bounties, Military
　　　—United States
　　　Pensions, Military—[country
　　　subdivision], e.g. Pensions, Military
　　　—United States
Bonus Expeditionary Force, 1932　(F199)
　—Juvenile literature
Bonus Expeditionary Force, 1933　(F199)

Bonus system *(Direct)* *(HD4928.B6)*
   Here are entered works on the distribution of money in the form of a bonus to employees as an outright gift or as a reward for outstanding efficiency or other achievement. Works on the sharing of all profits or a predetermined percentage of them among all employees are entered under Profit-sharing.
   sa Piece-work
   xx Incentives in industry
      Non-wage payments
      Piece-work
      Profit-sharing
      Wage payment systems
      Wages
   Note under Profit-sharing
Bony fishes
   See Osteichthyes
Booandik (Australian people)
   See Buandik (Australian people)
Boobies (Birds)
   sa Blue-footed booby
   xx Pelecaniformes
Booby traps (Military science)
   See Mines, Military
Boogie-woogie music
   See Piano music (Boogie woogie)
Book agents
   See Booksellers and bookselling—
      Colportage, subscription trade, etc.
Book automobiles
   See Bookmobiles
Book awards
   See Literary prizes
Book buying (Libraries)
   See Acquisitions (Libraries)
Book cases
   See Shelving (for books)
Book catalogs
   See Catalogs, Book
Book censorship
   See Censorship
Book clubs *(Direct)* *(Z549; Z1008)*
   sa Bibliography—Societies, etc.
      Group reading
   x Printing clubs
   xx Bibliography—Societies, etc.
      Bibliomania
      Book collectors
      Clubs
      Group reading
      Printing—Societies, etc.
      Societies
Book collecting *(Z987-997)*
   sa Antiquarian booksellers
      Bibliomania
      Book-plates
      Bookbinding—Armorial bindings
      Books—Owners' marks
      Libraries, Private
      Women as book collectors
   x Bibliophily
   xx Antiquarian booksellers
      Bibliography
      Bibliomania
      Book selection
      Books—Owners' marks
      Collectors and collecting
      Libraries, Private
Book collectors *(Direct)* *(Z989)*
   sa Book clubs
      Libraries, Private
      Women as book collectors

subdivisions Books and reading *and* Library *under names of individuals, e.g.* Napoléon I, Emperor of the French, 1769-1821—Books and reading; Washington, George, Pres. U.S., 1732-1799—Library
   xx Book selection
      Collectors and collecting
      Libraries, Private
   — Biography
   — Caricatures and cartoons
   — Correspondence, reminiscences, etc.
Book coupons *(Direct)*
   x Book tokens
      Coupons, Book
   xx Book industries and trade
      Booksellers and bookselling
Book coupons, UNESCO
   See UNESCO book coupons
Book covers
   sa Book jackets
   xx Bookbinding
      Design, Decorative
Book dedications
   See Dedications (in books)
Book design *(Z116.A3)*
   sa Gutenberg-Preis der Stadt Leipzig
      Printing, Practical—Make-up
   x Design, Book
   xx Book industries and trade
      Books—Format
      Printing, Practical—Make-up
Book digests
   See Books, Condensed
Book ends
Book exchanges
   See Exchanges, Literary and scientific
Book fairs
   See Book industries and trade—Exhibitions
Book illustration
   See Illustration of books
Book industries and trade *(Direct)* *(Z116-550)*
   sa Book coupons
      Book design
      Bookbinding
      Books—Statistics
      Booksellers and bookselling
      Imprints (in books)
      Newspaper agents
      Paper making and trade
      Printing
      Publishers and publishing
      Stationery
      UNESCO book coupons
   x Book trade
   xx Paper making and trade
      Printing
      Publishers and publishing
   — Accounting *(HF5686.B37)*
   — Anecdotes, facetiae, satire, etc.
   — Bibliography
   — — Theory, methods, etc.
   — Bio-bibliography
   — Biography
   — — Portraits
   — Code numbers
      x Code numbers (Book industries and trade)
   — Costs
   — Electronic data processing
      See Electronic data processing—Book industries and trade
   — Equipment and supplies
      x Booksellers and bookselling— Equipment and supplies
   — Exhibitions *(Z121)*
      sa Bibliographical exhibitions

      Bookbinding—Exhibitions
      Illustration of books—Exhibitions
      Printing—Exhibitions
      x Book fairs
         Books—Exhibitions
         Publishers and publishing— Exhibitions
      xx Bibliographical exhibitions
         Bookbinding—Exhibitions
         Illustration of books—Exhibitions
         Printing—Exhibitions
   — Heraldry
      xx Devices
         Printers' marks
      Example under Heraldry
   — Law
   — Safety measures
   — Standards
   — Tables and ready-reckoners
   — Underdeveloped areas
      See Underdeveloped areas—Book industries and trade
Book jackets
   xx Book covers
   — Exhibitions
Book lending
   See Inter-library loans
      Libraries—Circulation, loans
Book-making (Betting) *(SF331)*
   x Bookmaking (Betting)
   xx Gambling
      Horse race betting
   — Law and legislation *(Direct)*
   — Taxation *(Direct)*
Book margins
   See Margins in books
Book-marks
   See Books—Owners' marks
Book match covers
   See Matchcovers
Book numbers
   See Alphabeting
      Shelf-listing (Library science)
Book numbers, Publishers' standard
   See Publishers' standard book numbers
Book of common prayer
   See Church of England. Book of common prayer
      Protestant Episcopal Church in the U.S.A. Book of common prayer
Book of destinies
   See Book of life
Book of life
   x Book of destinies
      Destinies, Book of
      Life, Book of
   xx Predestination
      Salvation
Book of Mormon
   sa Nephites
   xx Mormons and Mormonism
   — Antiquities *(BX8627)*
      x Book of Mormon—Archaeology
   — Archaeology
      See Book of Mormon—Antiquities
   — Biography
   — Chronology
   — Concordances
   — Dictionaries
   — Genealogy
   — Geography
   — Indexes, Topical *(BX8627.A1)*
Book of Mormon stories *(BX8627.A2)*
Book-of-the-Month Club-College English Association award
Book ornamentation *(Z276)*
   sa Bookbinding—Ornamental bindings
      Endpapers

Book ornamentation *(Z276)*
(Continued)
 Fore-edge painting
 Printers' ornaments
 Type ornaments
 xx Bookbinding
 Printing
Book-plate designers *(Direct)*
 xx Artists
Book-plates *(Z993-6)*
 sa Bookbinding—Armorial bindings
 Books—Owners' marks
 Knights in book-plates
 Nude in book-plates
 Superexlibris
 Wine in book-plates
 x Bookplates
 Ex libris
 xx Book collecting
 Bookbinding—Armorial bindings
 Books—Owners' marks
 — Collectors and collecting
Book-plates, American, ₍Austrian, Belgian,
 etc.₎ *(Direct)*
 x American ₍Austrian, Belgian, etc.₎
 book-plates
Book-plates, Armorial
 See Book-plates, Heraldic
Book-plates, Artists' *(Direct)* *(Z993.15)*
 x Artists' book-plates
Book-plates, Children's
 x Children's book-plates
 Juvenile book-plates
Book-plates, Erotic *(Z994.5.N8)*
 sa Nude in book-plates
 x Erotic book-plates
 xx Erotic art
 Nude in book-plates
Book-plates, Heraldic *(Z994.5.H4)*
 x Armorial book-plates
 Book-plates, Armorial
 Heraldic book-plates
Book-plates, Imaginary *(Z995.5)*
 x Imaginary book-plates
Book-plates, Ladies'
 See Book-plates, Women's
Book-plates, Library
 x Library book-plates
Book-plates, Literary *(Z993.15)*
 x Literary book-plates
Book-plates, Medical *(Z994.5.M)*
 sa Book-plates, Pharmacists'
 Book-plates, Physicians'
 x Medical book-plates
 xx Book-plates, Pharmacists'
 Book-plates, Physicians'
Book-plates, Military
 x Military book-plates
Book-plates, Miniature *(Z995.6)*
 x Miniature book-plates
Book-plates, Pharmacists' *(Direct)*
 (Z993.15)
 sa Book-plates, Medical
 Book-plates, Physicians'
 x Pharmacists' book-plates
 xx Book-plates, Medical
 Book-plates, Physicians'
Book-plates, Physicians' *(Direct)* *(Z993.15)*
 sa Book-plates, Medical
 Book-plates, Pharmacists'
 x Physicians' book-plates
 xx Book-plates, Medical
 Book-plates, Pharmacists'
Book-plates, Scenic *(Z994.5.S3)*
 x Scenic book-plates
Book-plates, Women's *(Direct)* *(Z993.15)*
 x Book-plates, Ladies'
 Ladies' book-plates
 Women's book-plates

Book prices
 See Books—Prices
Book prizes
 See Literary prizes
Book rarities
 See Bibliography—Rare books
Book registration, National
 sa Bibliography, National
 Bibliography, Official
 Copyright
 xx Copyright
Book repairing
 See Bookbinding—Repairing
 Books—Conservation and restoration
Book reviewing *(PN98.B7)*
 Here are entered works on the technique
 of writing reviews. Collections of re-
 views are entered under the heading
 Books—Reviews and under subjects
 with subdivision Book reviews.
 sa Book talks
 x Newspapers—Sections, columns, etc.—
 Book section
 Reviewing (Books)
 xx Books—Reviews
 Note under Books—Reviews
Book reviews
 See Books—Reviews
Book sales
 See Books—Prices
 Booksellers and bookselling
Book selection *(Z689)*
 sa Bibliography—Best books
 Bibliography—Bibliography
 Book collecting
 Book collectors
 Books and reading
 Farmington plan
 Periodical selection
 Selection of nonbook materials
 x Books—Selection
 Choice of books
 Weeding (Books)
 xx Books and reading
 Periodical selection
 — Mathematical models
 — Study and teaching *(Direct)*
 Example under Library education
Book-sewing machines *(Z272)*
 xx Bookbinding machinery
 Sewing-machines
Book-shelves
 See Shelving (for books)
Book-stamps
 See Bookbinding—Stamped bindings
Book-study groups
 See Group reading
Book talks *(Direct)* *(Z716.3)*
 xx Book reviewing
 Public relations—Libraries
 Public speaking
Book thefts *(Z702)*
 x Libraries, Thefts from
 xx Bibliomania
Book titles
 See Titles of books
Book tokens
 See Book coupons
Book trade
 See Book industries and trade
 Booksellers and bookselling
 Publishers and publishing
Book-worms *(Z701)*
 sa Books—Conservation and restoration
 Books—Mutilation, defacement, etc.
 x Bookworms
 xx Books—Conservation and restoration

 Example under Insects, Injurious and benefi-
 cial
Bookbags
 See Schoolbags
Bookbinders *(Direct)* *(Z269-270)*
 sa Trade-unions—Bookbinders
 Wages—Bookbinders
 — Biography
 — Societies, etc. *(Z268)*
Bookbinders' Strike, London, 1901
 See London—Bookbinders' Strike, 1901
Bookbinding *(Direct)* *(Z266-275)*
 sa Bibliography—Library editions
 Book covers
 Book ornamentation
 Endpapers
 Marbling (Bookbinding)
 Pastedowns
 x Binding of books
 xx Arts and crafts movement
 Bibliography
 Book industries and trade
 Industrial arts
 Leather industry and trade
 Print finishing processes
 — Accounting
 — Armorial bindings
 sa Book-plates
 Books—Owners' marks
 Superexlibris
 x Armorial bookbindings
 xx Book collecting
 Book-plates
 Books—Owners' marks
 — Embossed bindings
 sa Bookbinding—Stamped bindings
 x Embossed bindings
 xx Bookbinding—Stamped bindings
 — Embroidered bindings
 — Estimates and costs
 — Exhibitions
 sa Bibliographical exhibitions
 Book industries and trade—
 Exhibitions
 xx Bibliographical exhibitions
 Book industries and trade—
 Exhibitions
 Example under Exhibitions
 — Facsimiles
 — Forgeries
 xx Literary forgeries and mystifications
 — Gilding *(Z271)*
 xx Gilding
 — Jeweled bindings
 x Jeweled bindings
 — Machinery
 See Bookbinding machinery
 — Marbling
 See Marbling (Bookbinding)
 — Materials, etc.
 — Mosaic bindings
 x Mosaic bindings
 — Ornamental bindings
 x Bookbinding, Ornamental
 xx Book ornamentation
 — Private collections *(Direct)*
 — Repairing
 x Book repairing
 Books—Repairing
 xx Books—Conservation and restoration
 — Specimens
 sa Portas
 — Stamped bindings
 sa Bookbinding—Embossed bindings
 x Book-stamps
 Stamped bindings
 xx Bookbinding—Embossed bindings
 — Standards

— England, [France, Germany, etc.]
    x English [French, German, etc.]
      bookbindings

Bookbinding, Islamic
    x Bookbinding, Muslim
      Islamic bookbinding
      Muslim bookbinding

Bookbinding, Muslim
    See Bookbinding, Islamic

Bookbinding, Ornamental
    See Bookbinding—Ornamental bindings

Bookbinding, Victorian
    x Victorian bookbinding

Bookbinding machinery
    sa Book-sewing machines
    x Bookbinding—Machinery
  — Appraisal
      See Bookbinding machinery—
        Valuation
  — Valuation
      x Bookbinding machinery—Appraisal

Bookcases
    See Shelving (for books)

Bookkeepers
    See Accountants

Bookkeeping *(HF5601-5689)*
    sa Accounting
      Auditing
      Average of accounts
      Business mathematics
      Calculating-machines
      Card system in business
      Cash registers
      Cost accounting
      Depreciation
      Financial statements
      Fiscal year
      Inventories
      Invoices
      Office equipment and supplies
      Single entry bookkeeping
      subdivision Accounting *under specific*
        industries, professions, trades, etc.
    x Double entry bookkeeping
    xx Accounting
      Business
      Business education
  — Examinations, questions, etc.
  — Machine methods
      See Bookkeeping machines
  — Programmed instruction
  — Study and teaching
      See Accounting—Study and teaching

Bookkeeping, Library *(Z683)*
    x Libraries—Bookkeeping
      Library bookkeeping

Bookkeeping machines *(Machines, HF5688;*
        Use, HF5679)
    x Bookkeeping—Machine methods
    xx Accounting machines
      Machine accounting

Bookmaking (Betting)
    See Book-making (Betting)

Bookmobiles *(Direct) (Z686)*
    x Book automobiles
    xx Libraries—Branches, delivery stations,
      etc.
      Libraries, Traveling
      Library extension
      Library fittings and supplies
  — Design and construction
  — Juvenile literature

Bookplates
    See Book-plates

Books
    sa Bibliography

Block-books
Cataloging
Chapter-headings
Classification—Books
Colophons
Copyright
Dedications (in books)
Illumination of books and manuscripts
Illustration of books
Imprints (in books)
Libraries
Literature
Manuscripts
Picture-books
Printing
Projected books
Publishers and publishing
Title-page
Titles of books
headings beginning with the word Book
  xx Bibliography
    Printing
    Publishers and publishing
— Anecdotes, facetiae, satire, etc.
— Appraisal
    See Bibliography—Best books
      Books and reading
      Criticism
      Literature—History and criticism
— Best sellers
    See Best sellers
— Care
    See Books—Conservation and
      restoration
— Censorship
    See Censorship
— Chapter-headings
    See Chapter-headings
— Conservation and restoration *(Z700-701)*
    sa Book-worms
      Bookbinding—Repairing
      Books—Disinfection
      Engravings—Conservation and
        restoration
      Manuscripts—Conservation and
        restoration
      Paper—Preservation
    x Book repairing
      Books—Care
      Books—Preservation
      Books—Repairing
      Books—Restoration
      Conservation of books
      Preservation of books
      Restoration of books
    xx Book-worms
      Books—Mutilation, defacement, etc.
      Engravings—Conservation and
        restoration
      Manuscripts—Conservation and
        restoration
— Dedications
    See Dedications (in books)
— Defacement
    See Books—Mutilation, defacement,
      etc.
— Desiderata
    See Books—Want lists
— Disinfection *(Z701)*
    sa Paper—Disinfection
    xx Books—Conservation and restoration
      Disinfection and disinfectants
— Exhibitions
    See Bibliographical exhibitions
      Book industries and trade—
        Exhibitions
      Printing—Exhibitions
— Fine editions

    See Bibliography—Fine editions
— First editions
    See Bibliography—First editions
      subdivision Bibliography—First
        editions *under* Literature *and*
        under names of literature, e.g.
        English literature—
          Bibliography—First editions
— Format
    sa Bibliography—Microscopic and
      miniature editions
      Book design
      Books—Sizes
    x Format of books
— History *(Direct) (Z4-8)*
    Duplicate entry is made under Print-
      ing—History for works including a
      significant contribution to the his-
      tory of printing.
    sa Printing—History
— — To 400 *(Z112)*
— — 400-1400 *(Z112)*
— — 1400-1600
      sa Block-books
      Incunabula

— — Juvenile literature
— Juvenile literature
— Limited editions
    See Bibliography—Limited editions
— Margins
    See Margins in books
— Microscopic editions
    See Bibliography—Microscopic and
      miniature editions
— Miniature editions
    See Bibliography—Microscopic and
      miniature editions
— Mutilation, defacement, etc. *(Z701)*
    sa Books—Conservation and restoration
      Manuscripts—Mutilation,
        defacement, etc.
    x Books—Defacement
      Defacement of books
      Mutilation of books
    xx Book-worms
      Manuscripts—Mutilation,
        defacement, etc.
— Owners' marks *(Z987-997; Z1033.A84)*
    sa Book collecting
      Book-plates
      Bookbinding—Armorial bindings
      Marginalia
      Superexlibris
    x Book-marks
    xx Autographs
      Bibliography—Rare books
      Book collecting
      Book-plates
      Bookbinding—Armorial bindings
      Devices
      Marginalia
— Packaging
— Pagination
    See Pagination
— Pictorial works
— Pirated editions
    See Copyright—Unauthorized reprints
— Poetry
    See Book verse
— Postal rates
    See Postal service—Book rates
— Preservation
    See Books—Conservation and
      restoration
— Prices *(Z1000)*
    sa Manuscripts—Prices

Books
— Prices *(Z1000)* *(Continued)*
   x Book prices
      Book sales
   xx Acquisitions (Libraries)
      Booksellers and bookselling
      Manuscripts—Prices
— Psychology *(Z1003)*
   sa Authors and readers
      Books and reading
— Quotations, maxims, etc. *(Z4.Z9)*
— Repairing
   See Bookbinding—Repairing
      Books—Conservation and
        restoration
— Reprints, Unauthorized
   See Copyright—Unauthorized reprints
— Restoration
   See Books—Conservation and
      restoration
— Reviews *(Direct)*
   Here are entered collections of re-
   views. Works on the technique of
   writing reviews are entered under
   the heading Book reviewing.
   sa Book reviewing
      Newspapers—Sections, columns, etc.
        —Reviews
      subdivision Book reviews *under*
        subjects
   x Book reviews
      Reviews
   xx Books and reading
      Criticism
   Note under Book reviewing
— Selection
   See Book selection
— Sizes
   sa Bibliography—Microscopic and
      miniature editions
   xx Bibliography—Microscopic and
      miniature editions
      Books—Format
— Statistics
   sa Library statistics
   xx Book industries and trade
      Library statistics
— Tariff
   See Tariff on books
— Want lists
   sa Antiquarian booksellers
      Out-of-print books
   x Bibliography—Want lists
      Books—Desiderata
      Books wanted, Lists of
      Want lists of books
   xx Acquisitions (Libraries)
      Antiquarian booksellers
      Out-of-print books
Books, Abridged
   See Books, Condensed
Books, Baby
   See Baby books
Books, Birthday
   See Birthday books
Books, Chained
   See Chained books
Books, Condemned
   See Condemned books
Books, Condensed *(PN6013.5)*
   x Abridged books
      Book digests
      Books, Abridged
      Condensed books
      Digests of books
   xx Literature—Collections
Books, Direct delivery of
   See Direct delivery of books

Books, Expurgated
   See Expurgated books
Books, Filmed
   See Film adaptations
Books, Fragmentary
   See Unfinished books
Books, Illustrated
   See Illustrated books
      Illustration of books
Books, Imaginary
   See Imaginary books and libraries
Books, Lending of
   See Inter-library loans
      Libraries—Circulation, loans
Books, Out-of-print
   See Out-of-print books
Books, Privately printed
   See Privately printed books
Books, Prohibited
   See Prohibited books
Books, Rare
   See Bibliography—Rare books
Books, Reference
   See Reference books
Books, Sacred
   See Sacred books
Books, Subscription
   See Booksellers and bookselling—
      Colportage, subscription trade, etc.
Books, Talking
   See Talking books
Books, Unfinished
   See Unfinished books
Books, Vellum printed
   See Vellum printed books
Books abroad, American
   See American books abroad
Books and reading *(Direct)* *(Z1003)*
   Here are entered works on the signifi-
   cance of books in man's life, his atti-
   tude toward, and interest in, reading
   books.
   sa Authors and readers
      Best sellers
      Bibliography—Best books *[for selected*
        lists and catalogs]
      Book selection
      Books—Reviews
      Classification—Books
      Fiction in libraries
      Group reading
      Libraries
      Literature
      Prohibited books
      Readability (Literary style)
      Readership surveys
      Reading interests
      Reference books
      Right to Read program
      Supplementary reading
      subdivision Books and reading *under*
        names of persons and classes of
        persons, e.g. Napoléon I, Emperor of
        the French, 1769-1821—Books and
        reading; Decembrists—Books and
        reading
   x Appraisal of books
      Bibliography, Critical
      Books—Appraisal
      Choice of books
      Evaluation of literature
      Literature—Evaluation
      Reading, Choice of
      Reading habits
   xx Authors and readers
      Bibliography
      Book selection
      Books—Psychology

      Education
      Group reading
      Literature
      Self-culture
   Note under Reading
— Caricatures and cartoons
— Moral and religious aspects
   See Literature and morals
— Quotations, maxims, etc.
Books and reading for children *(Direct)*
   Here are entered works on the attitude of
   children toward, and their interest in,
   reading books and the development of
   their interest by parents, teachers, and
   librarians. Works dealing with literature written for children are entered
   under Children's literature.
   sa Children's literature
      Children's reference books
   x Children—Books and reading
      Children, Books and reading for
      Reading interests of children
   xx Children's literature
      Libraries and schools
      Libraries, Children's
   Note under Children's literature
Books and reading for girls *(Direct)*
   x Girls—Books and reading
Books and reading for the aged *(Direct)*
   x Aged—Books and reading
Books and reading for youth *(Direct)*
   sa Children's reference books
   x Youth—Books and reading
— Censorship
Books for children
   See Children's literature
Books for mentally handicapped children
   See Mentally handicapped children, Books
      for
Books for physically handicapped children
   See Physically handicapped children, Books
      for
Books for retarded readers
   See Retarded readers, Books for
Books for sight saving
   See Sight-saving books
Books for slow learning children
   See Slow learning children, Books for
Books for socially handicapped children
   See Socially handicapped children, Books
      for
Books for the blind
   See Blind, Books for the
      Blind, Libraries for the
Books for the deaf
   See Deaf, Books for the
Books for the socially handicapped
   See Socially handicapped, Books for the
Books in art *(N8217.B6)*
   xx Art
Books in library bindings
   See Bibliography—Library editions
Books in literature
Books of hours
   See Hours, Books of
Books of knowledge
   See Encyclopedias and dictionaries
Books of prayer
   See Prayer-books
Books on microfilm *(Z265)*
   x Microfilm books
   xx Microfilms
Books on phonorecords
   See Talking books
Books on phonotapes
   See Talking books
Books wanted, Lists of
   See Books—Want lists

Booksellers and bookselling *(Direct)*
    (Z278-550)
  sa Antiquarian booksellers
    Book coupons
    Books—Prices
    Canvassing
    Catalogs, Booksellers'
    Copyright
    Publishers and publishing
    Remainders (Bookselling)
    Serial publication of books
    UNESCO book coupons
    Wages—Booksellers and bookselling
  x Book sales
    Book trade
  xx Book industries and trade
    Publishers and publishing
    Salesmen and salesmanship
  — Accounting
  — Auditing and inspection
  — Biography
  — Caricatures and cartoons
  — Colportage, subscription trade, etc.
    (HF5456.B7)
    sa Bible—Publication and distribution
      Christian literature—Publication and
        distribution
      Religious literature—Publication and
        distribution
    x Book agents
      Books, Subscription
      Booksellers and bookselling—
        Subscription trade
      Colportage
      Subscription book trade
    xx Canvassing
      Commercial travelers
      Peddlers and peddling
  — Equipment and supplies
    See Book industries and trade—
      Equipment and supplies
  — Inventories
  — Inventory control
    Example under Inventory control
  — Subscription trade
    See Booksellers and bookselling—
      Colportage, subscription trade,
      etc.
Booksellers' catalogs
  See Catalogs, Booksellers'
Bookworms
  See Book-worms
Boolean algebra
  See Algebra, Boolean
Boole's algebra
  See Algebra, Boolean
Boomerangs *(GN498.B6)*
  xx Arms and armor, Primitive
  — Juvenile literature
Booms, Gravity gradient
  See Gravity gradient booms
Booms, Oil spill
  See Oil spill booms
Boondei language
  See Bondei language
Boorishki language
  See Burushaski language
Booshuana
  See Tswana (Bantu tribe)
BOOST (Computer program)
Boosters
  See Locomotives—Boosters
Boot and shoe workers
  See Shoemakers
Boot-licking
  See Toadyism
Booths, Exhibit
  See Exhibitions—Booths

Boots and shoes *(Manners and customs,*
    GT2130)
  sa Athletic shoes
    Moccasins
    Orthopedic shoes
    Sabots
    Safety shoes
    Sandals
    Sneakers
  x Foot wear
    Footwear
    Lasts (Shoes)
    Shoes
  xx Leather industry and trade
  Example under Costume; Leather goods;
    Manufactures
  — Credit guides *(HF5585.B7)*
  — History *(Direct)* *(GT2130)*
  — Materials
  — — Testing
  — Prices
    xx Boots and shoes—Trade and
      manufacture
  — Repairing *(TS1023)*
    x Shoe repairing
  — — Accounting
  — Research *(Direct)*
  — Sizes
    xx Boots and shoes—Standards
    Example under reference from Sizes
  — Specifications
  — Standards
    sa Boots and shoes—Sizes
  — Tariff
    See Tariff on boots and shoes
  — Trade and manufacture *(Direct)*
    (HD9787; TS989-1025)
    sa Boots and shoes—Prices
      Leather
      Salesmen and salesmanship—Shoes
      Shoe machinery
      Shoemakers
      Strikes and lockouts—Shoe industry
      Wages—Shoe industry
    x Shoe industry and trade
  — — By-products
  — — Collective labor agreements
    See Collective labor agreements—
      Shoe industry
  — — Finance
  — — Labor productivity
  — — Management
  — — Mathematical models *(TS1020)*
  — — Quality control
  — — Safety measures
Boots and shoes, Felt *(TS1825)*
  x Felt boots
  — Standards *(Direct)*
Boots and shoes, Orthopedic
  See Orthopedic shoes
Boots and shoes, Rubber *(TS1910)*
  x Rubber boots and shoes
    Rubber footwear
  xx Rubber industry and trade
  — Tariff
    See Tariff on rubber footwear
Boots and shoes in art
  xx Art
Bootstrap theory (Nuclear physics)
  sa Form factor (Nuclear physics)
  xx Form factor (Nuclear physics)
    Particles (Nuclear physics)
Booty (International law) *(JX5295-5313)*
  sa Monetary gold confiscations
    Pillage
  x Captured property
  xx Confiscations
    Enemy property

    Military occupation
    Pillage
    Prizes
    Searches and seizures
    War (International law)
Booty (Islamic law) *(Direct)*
BOPTIC (Computer program)
Boquerón, Battle of, 1932 *(F2688.5)*
  x Batalla de Boquerón, 1932
    Fortín Boquerón, Battle of, 1932
  xx Chaco War, 1932-1935
Boquet River, Engagement at, 1814
Bor dialect
  xx Dinka language
Bora
  xx Winds
Bora language
  sa Witoto language
  xx Indians of South America—Languages
    Witoto language
Boracic acid
  See Boric acid
Boran (African people)
  xx Ethnology—Ethiopia
    Gallas
Boran dialect
  xx Galla language
Borani
  xx Hamites
Borates *(Indirect)* *(QD181.B1)*
Borax *(Indirect)* *(Mineral industries,*
    TN917; Trade, HD9660.B8)
  xx Canning and preserving
  — Physiological effect *(QP913.B1)*
BORAX (Nuclear reactor)
  See Boiling water reactors
Borax mines and mining *(Indirect)* *(TN917)*
Bordeaux
  — History
  — — Uprising, 1652-1653
    x Hormée, 1652-1653
      Ormaye, 1652-1653
      Ormée, 1652-1653
    xx Fronde
Bordeaux mixture *(SB952.P9)*
  xx Fungicides
  Example under Spraying
Bordeaux Raid, 1942 *(D774.B)*
  xx World War, 1939-1945—Naval
    operations
Border collies *(SF429.B64)*
  x Collies, Working
    Working collies
  xx Collies
Border life
  See Frontier and pioneer life
Border patrols *(Direct)*
  x Boundary patrols
    Frontier patrols
  xx Police
  — Dental care *(Direct)*
Border ruffians
  See United States—History—Civil War,
    1861-1865—Guerrillas
Border taxes
  See Drawbacks
    Tariff
Border terriers
  xx Terriers
Border traffic
  See Frontier workers
Border workers
  See Frontier workers
Borderers
  See United States—History—Civil War,
    1861-1865—Guerrillas
Borderline schizophrenia
  See Pseudoneurotic schizophrenia

Borders (Gardening)
    See Garden borders
Boredom
    xx Attention
        Fatigue, Mental
    — Anecdotes, facetiae, satire, etc.
Boredom in literature
Borers (Insects)
    sa names of boring insects, e.g. Apple-tree
        borers; Plum borer
    — Biological control   *(Indirect)*
        xx Borers (Insects)—Control
    — Control   *(Indirect)*
        sa Borers (Insects)—Biological control
    — Parasites
        See Parasites—Borers (Insects)
Bores (Tidal phenomena)   *(GC376)*
    x Tidal bores
    xx Natural disasters
        Tides
Borgward automobile
Bori (Cult)   *(BL2480.H3)*
    xx Hausas—Religion
Boric acid   *(Therapeutics, RM648.B)*
    x Boracic acid
    xx Canning and preserving
    — Physiological effect   *(QP913.B1)*
Borides   *(QD181.B1)*
    sa Rare earth borides
    Example under Chemistry, Inorganic
Boriding   *(TS695.3)*
    x Boron coating
    xx Diffusion coatings
Boring   *(Gas, oil, water, etc., TD410-412;*
        Mining, TN281)
        Here are entered works relating to the
        operation of cutting holes in earth or
        rock, whether carried on at the surface
        or in a mine, in order to determine the
        nature of the strata penetrated, or to
        furnish an outlet for water, oil, gas, etc.
        Material dealing with workshop opera-
        tions in metal, wood, etc. is entered
        under Drilling and boring.
    sa Artesian wells
        Core drilling
        Drill pipe
        Drilling muds
        Fusion piercing drilling
        Gas well drilling
        Oil well drilling
        Photography in boring
        Shaft sinking
        Underwater drilling
        Well drillers
        Wells
    x Diamond drilling
        Test boring
        Well-boring
    xx Artesian wells
        Engineering
        Gas, Natural
        Hydraulic engineering
        Mining engineering
        Petroleum
        Shaft sinking
        Tunneling
        Wells
    Note under Drilling and boring
    — Cold weather conditions
    — Standards
    — Tables, calculations, etc.
Boring barnacles
    See Acrothoracica
Boring machinery   *(Well digging, TD414)*
    sa Bits (Drilling and boring)
        Ice coring rigs
        Rock-drills

        Turbodrills
    xx Construction equipment
        Oil wells—Equipment and supplies
    — Automatic control   *(TN281)*
    — Cold weather operation
    — Electric driving
    — Maintenance and repair
    — Patents
    — Reliability
    — Specifications   *(TD414)*
    — Testing
    — Transmission devices   *(TN281)*
        xx Gearing
    — Vibration
Borings   *(Indirect)*
        Here are entered the results of boring op-
        erations conducted in various parts of
        the earth to determine the nature of
        the strata penetrated.
    sa Oil well logging
    x Deep borings
    xx Geology, Stratigraphic
Born approximation   *(QC794)*
    xx Approximation theory
        Quantum theory
        Scattering (Physics)
Borna's disease
    See Equine encephalomyelitis
Bornite   *(QE391.B)*
Bornmueller fir   *(Botany, QK495.P66;*
        Sylviculture, SB397.B58)
    xx Fir
Bornological spaces
    x Spaces, Bornological
    xx Linear topological spaces
Bornu language
    See Kanuri language
Boro Indians
    xx Indians of South America
Borodino, Battle of, 1812   *(DC235.5.B7)*
    — Juvenile literature
    — Museums
Boron   *(QD181.B1)*
    sa Ferroboron
        Soils—Boron content
    xx Nonmetals
    Example under Trace elements
    — Analysis
    — Isotopes
        x Boron isotopes
            Isotopic boron
    — — Decay
    — Physiological effect
    — Spectra
Boron as fuel
    x High energy fuels
    xx Jet planes—Fuel
        Rockets (Aeronautics)—Fuel
Boron coating
    See Boriding
Boron in soils
    See Soils—Boron content
Boron isotopes
    See Boron—Isotopes
Boron ores   *(Indirect)*
Boron organic compounds
    See Organoboron compounds
Boron steel
    xx Steel alloys
Bororo (African people)
    xx Ethnology—Sudan (Region)
        Fulahs
Bororo Indians
    xx Indians of South America
    — Fiction
Bororo language   *(PM5636)*
    xx Indians of South America—Languages

Borough-English (Law)
    xx Land tenure—Law
        Primogeniture
Boroughs   *(Indirect)*   *(JS261-7)*
    x Burghs
    xx Cities and towns
        Local government
        Municipal government
Boroughs, Parliamentary
    See Great Britain. Parliament. House of
        Commons—Election districts
Boroughs (Municipal subdivision)
    xx Municipal government
Borreliosis
    See Relapsing fever
Borstal system
    See Juvenile detention homes
Boruca Indians   *(F1545.2.B6)*
    x Brunca Indians
        Brunka Indians
    xx Indians of Central America
        Talamanca Indians
Boruca language   *(PM3539)*
    x Brunka language
    xx Indians of Central America—Languages
        Talamanca language
Borzoi
    See Russian wolf-hounds
Bose-Einstein gas
    x Bose gas
        Gas, Bose-Einstein
    xx Photons
        Quantum statistics
Bose-Einstein particles
    See Bosons
Bose gas
    See Bose-Einstein gas
Boshin War, 1868
    See Japan—History—Civil War, 1868
Bosjesmen
    See Bushmen
Bosnia and Herzegovina
    — History
    — — Rebellion of 1875
    — — 1878-1918
    — — 1918-
Bosons   *(QC721)*
    x Bose-Einstein particles
    xx Quantum statistics
Boss rule
    See Corruption (in politics)
Bosses (Architecture)
    xx Architecture
        Decoration and ornament, Architectural
Bossies tea
    See Rooibos tea
Bosso (African people)
    See Bozo (African people)
Boston
    — Biography
        Example under Biography
    — Cemeteries
        Example under Cemeteries
    — Census
        Example under Census
    — Charities
        Example under Poor; Woman—Charities
    — Description
    — — Guide-books
        Example   under   references   from
            Guide-books; Travel—Guide-
            books
    — — Juvenile literature
    — Directories
        Note under Directories
    — Galleries and museums
        Example under Museums
    — Garrison mob, 1835

214

— Genealogy
　　Example under reference from Family
　　histories
— History　*(F73)*
— — Colonial period, ca. 1600-1775
— — Revolution, 1775-1783
— — Anti-slavery movement, 1830-1863
— — 1865-

GENERAL SUBDIVISIONS

— — Juvenile literature
— Lodging-houses
　　Example under Lodging-houses
— Maps
　　Example under Maps
— Parks
　　Example under Parks
— Playgrounds
　　Example under Playgrounds
— Police
　　Example under Police
— Public schools
　　Note under Public schools
— Public works
　　Example under Civil engineering
　　Note under Art, Municipal
— Registers
　　Example under reference from Registers
— Siege, 1775-1776　*(E231)*
　　Note under Sieges
— Street cleaning
　　Example under Street cleaning
— Vacation schools
　　Example under Vacation schools
Boston.　Museum of Fine Arts
　Note under Art—Galleries and museums
Boston (Dance)
Boston (Game)
　See Solo whist
Boston bomber
　See A-20 bomber
Boston in literature
Boston Massacre, 1770　*(E215.4)*
— Juvenile literature
— Pictorial works
Boston Tea Party, 1773　*(E215.7)*
　xx Tea tax (American colonies)
— Juvenile literature
Boston terriers　*(SF429.B7)*
　xx Terriers
Bosworth Field, Battle of, 1485　*(DA260)*
Bot-flies
　See Botflies
Botanic gardens
　See Botanical gardens
Botanic medicine
　See Medicine, Botanic
Botanical apparatus　*(QK715)*
　xx Scientific apparatus and instruments
Botanical archaeology
　See Plant remains (Archaeology)
Botanical chemistry　*(QK861-6)*
　sa Hormones (Plants)
　　Plant pigments
　　Plants—Chemical analysis
　　Wood—Chemistry
　x Chemistry, Botanical
　　Phytochemistry
　　Plant chemistry
　xx Chemistry
　　Plants—Chemical analysis
— Laboratory manuals　*(QK861)*
Botanical collectors
　See Plant collectors
Botanical drug industry　*(Direct)*
　sa Botany, Medical
　x Medicinal plant industry
　　Vegetable drug industry

　xx Botany, Medical
　　Drug trade
Botanical gardens　*(Indirect)　(QK71-73)*
　sa Arboretums
　　names of gardens, e.g. Kew.　Royal
　　　Gardens
　x Botanic gardens
　xx Arboretums
　　Gardens
　　Parks
Botanical geography
　See Phytogeography
Botanical illustration　*(QK98.2)*
　x Illustration, Botanical
　xx Biological illustration
Botanical laboratories　*(QK78)*
　x Laboratories, Botanical
Botanical libraries
　x Libraries, Botanical
　xx Botany—Bibliography
Botanical literature
　xx Botany
　　Botany—Bibliography
Botanical museums　*(QK79)*
　sa Botany—Exhibitions
　　Botany—Type specimens
　　Herbaria
　xx Herbaria
　　Museums
　　Natural history museums
Botanical nomenclature
　See Botany—Nomenclature
Botanical prospecting
　See Biogeochemical prospecting
Botanical research　*(Direct)*
　sa Growth cabinets and rooms
　　Pasture research
　　Photosynthesis research
　　Plants, Protection of—Research
　x Botany—Research
　　Research, Botanical
　xx Botany
　　Research
Botanical societies　*(Indirect)　(QK1)*
　sa Botany—Societies, etc. *[for publications
　　of botanical and other societies in
　　relation to botany]*
　xx Societies
　Example under Learned institutions and socie-
　　ties; Scientific societies
Botanical specimens, Collection and
　　preservation of
　See Plants—Collection and preservation
Botanical surveys
　See Vegetation surveys
Botanists　*(Indirect)　(QK26-31)*
　sa Botany as a profession
　　Horticulturists
　　Plant collectors
　xx Botany—Bio-bibliography
　　Naturalists
　　Plant collectors
　　Scientists
— Biography　*(QK26-31)*
— Correspondence, reminiscences, etc.
— Directories
　　Note under Directories
Botany　*(Indirect)　(QK)*
　sa Acclimatization (Plants)
　　Aerial photography in botany
　　Alpine flora
　　Aquatic plants
　　Aromatic plants
　　Botanical literature
　　Botanical research
　　Bryology
　　Buds
　　Bulbs

　　Bulbs (Botany)
　　Carpel
　　Cave flora
　　Chimeras (Botany)
　　Climbing plants
　　Coenobic plants
　　Color of flowers
　　Color of plants
　　Corms
　　Desert flora
　　Ethnobotany
　　Fertilization of plants
　　Floriculture
　　Flowers
　　Fresh-water flora
　　Fruit
　　Grafting
　　Growth (Plants)
　　Herbaria
　　House plants
　　Hybridization, Vegetable
　　Insectivorous plants
　　Leaves
　　Marine flora
　　Microscope and microscopy
　　Mycology
　　Myrmecophilous plants
　　Paleobotany
　　Palynology
　　Parasitic plants
　　Phytogeography
　　Plants
　　Poisonous plants
　　Radioactive tracers in botany
　　Seedlings
　　Seeds
　　Shoots (Botany)
　　Shrubs
　　Trees
　　Tropical plants
　　Variation (Biology)
　　Vegetables
　　Vegetation and climate
　　Weeds
　　Woody plants
　　*divisions, classes, etc. of the vegetable
　　　kingdom, e.g.* Algae, Cryptogams,
　　　Ferns, Fungi, Lichens, Mosses,
　　　Phanerogams; *also headings
　　　beginning with the word* Plant; *and
　　　names of plants*
　x Botany—Phytography
　　Flora
　　Phytography
　　Phytology
　　Vascular plants
　　Vegetable kingdom
　xx Biology
　　Natural history
　　Nature study
　　Plants
　　Science
　Note under Cryptogams
— Analysis blanks　*(QK57)*
— Anatomy　*(QK641-707)*
　sa Abnormalities (Plants)
　　Bark
　　Botany—Morphology
　　Cambium
　　Flowers—Anatomy
　　Fruit—Anatomy
　　Inflorescence
　　Leaves—Anatomy
　　Lenticels
　　Plant cells and tissues
　　Prothallium
　　Roots (Botany)—Anatomy
　　Scales (Botany)

Botany *(Indirect) (QK)*
— Anatomy *(QK641-707)*
(Continued)
    Seeds—Anatomy
    Stems (Botany)
    Tendrils
    Trichomes
    Wood—Anatomy
  x Anatomy of plants
    Anatomy, Vegetable
    Botany—Histology
    Botany, Structural
    Botany—Structure
    Histology, Vegetable
    Plant anatomy
    Plant structure
    Plants—Anatomy
    Plants—Structure
    Structural botany
    Tissues, Vegetable
    Vegetable anatomy
    Vegetable histology
  xx Botany—Morphology
  Note under Histology
— — Atlases
— — Juvenile literature
— Bibliography *(Z5351-5360)*
  sa Botanical libraries
    Botanical literature
— — Early *(Z5352)*
    Example under reference from Bibliography—Early
— Bio-bibliography
  sa Botanists
  xx Bio-bibliography
— Catalogs and collections *(QK71-79)*
— Charts, diagrams, etc. *(QK55)*
— Classification *(QK91-95)*
  sa Botany—Type specimens
    Classification—Books—Botany
    Natural history—Classification
    Plants—Identification
  x Botany, Systematic
    Botany—Taxonomy
    Classification—Botany
    Classification—Plants
    Plant classification
    Plant taxonomy
    Plants—Classification
    Systematic botany
    Systematics (Botany)
    Taxonomy (Botany)
  Example under Classification
— — Research *(Direct)*
— — Statistical methods
  xx Numerical taxonomy
— Dictionaries
  Note under Encyclopedias and dictionaries; *and under reference from* Dictionaries
— Early works
  See Botany—Pre-Linnean works
— Ecology *(QK901-976)*
  sa Acclimatization (Plants)
    Allelopathy
    Burning of land
    Coastal flora
    Desert flora
    Epiphytes
    Forest ecology
    Forest influences
    Halophytes
    Insectivorous plants
    Island flora
    Mangrove swamps
    Parasitic plants
    Phenology
    Phreatophytes
    Phytogeography

    Plant communities
    Plant indicators
    Plant populations
    Plant-soil relationships
    Plant succession
    Plants, Effect of altitude on
    Plants—Hardiness
    Saprophytism
    Seeds—Dispersal
    Symbiosis
    Xerophytes
  x Botany—Oecology
    Plant ecology
    Plants—Ecology
    Plants—Oecology
  xx Acclimatization (Plants)
    Ecology
    Forest influences
— — Juvenile literature
— — Laboratory manuals
— — Statistical methods
— Electrophysiology
  See Electrophysiology of plants
— Embryology *(QK665)*
  sa Botany—Morphology
    Germination
    Plant morphogenesis
    Polyembryony
    Seeds
  x Embryology (Botany)
    Embryology, Vegetable
    Plant embryology
    Plants—Embryology
    Vegetable embryology
  xx Botany—Morphology
    Seeds
— Exhibitions
  xx Botanical museums
— Experiments
— — Juvenile literature
— Field work
  See Botany—Laboratory manuals
— Geographical distribution
  See Phytogeography
— Histology
  See Botany—Anatomy
    Plant cells and tissues
— Identification
  See Plants—Identification
— Juvenile literature *(QK49)*
— Laboratory manuals *(QK53)*
  x Botany—Field work
— Mapping
  See Vegetation mapping
— Maps
  See Phytogeography—Maps
— Methodology *(QK51)*
  sa Vegetation surveys
— Morphology *(QK641-669)*
  sa Abnormalities (Plants)
    Botany—Anatomy
    Botany—Embryology
    Flowers—Morphology
    Fruit—Morphology
    Involucre
    Lenticels
    Plant morphogenesis
    Prickles
    Seeds—Morphology
    Spines (Botany)
    Stele (Botany)
    Thorns
    Trichomes
  x Morphology (Plants)
    Plant morphology
    Plants—Morphology
  xx Botany—Anatomy
    Botany—Embryology

    Morphogenesis
— Nomenclators *(QK11)*
    Includes indexes of scientific names. Discussions of the principles involved in the application of botanical names are entered under Botany—Nomenclature.
  sa Plant names, Popular
  x Plant names, Scientific
  Example under reference from Nomenclators
  Note under Botany—Nomenclature
— Nomenclature *(QK96)*
    Cf. note under Botany—Nomenclators.
  sa Botany—Terminology
  x Botanical nomenclature
    Plant names, Scientific
    Plants—Nomenclature
  xx Biology—Nomenclature
    Botany—Terminology
    Natural history—Nomenclature
  Example under reference from Nomenclature
  Note under Botany—Nomenclators
— Nomenclature (Popular)
  See Plant names, Popular
— Oecology
  See Botany—Ecology
— Organography *(QK641-662)*
  sa Botany—Terminology
  x Organography
— Pathology
  See Plant diseases
— Physiology
  See Plant physiology
— Phytography
  See Botany
— Pictorial works *(QK98)*
  xx Natural history—Pictorial works
— Pre-Linnean works *(QK41)*
  sa Herbs
    Medicine, Medieval
  x Botany—Early works
    Herbals
  xx Botany, Medical
    Herbs
    Medicine, Medieval
    Natural history—Pre-Linnean works
— Research
  See Botanical research
— Societies, etc.
  xx Botanical societies
— Statistical methods
— Structure
  See Botany—Anatomy
— Surveying
  See Vegetation surveys
— Taxonomy
  See Botany—Classification
— Technique
— Teratology
  See Abnormalities (Plants)
— Terminology *(QK10)*
  sa Botany—Nomenclature
    Plant diseases—Terminology
  xx Biology—Terminology
    Botany—Nomenclature
    Botany—Organography
  Example under reference from Terminology
— Type specimens
  x Type specimens (Botany)
  xx Botanical museums
    Botany—Classification
    Herbaria
    Type specimens (Natural history)
— Variation *(QH406)*

sa Evolution
Fruit—Varieties
Island flora
Variation (Biology)
Variegation
Vegetables—Varieties
xx Mutation (Biology)
Plant genetics
Variation (Biology)
— Vocational guidance
See Botany as a profession

GEOGRAPHIC SUBDIVISIONS

— [local subdivision]
Note under Phytogeography

GEOGRAPHIC SUBDIVISIONS

— Antarctic regions
x Antarctic flora
Flora, Antarctic

GEOGRAPHIC SUBDIVISIONS

— Arctic regions
x Arctic flora
Flora, Arctic
Botany, Agricultural
See Botany, Economic
Botany, Economic *(Indirect) (SB107-9)*
sa Dye plants
Ethnobotany
Fiber plants
Forest products
Fungi—Economic aspects
Grain
Grasses
Honey plants
Oilseed plants
Plant introduction
Plants, Edible
Plants, Insecticidal
Poisonous plants
Rubber plants
Weeds
x Agricultural botany
Botany, Agricultural
Economic botany
Plants, Useful
xx Agriculture
Biology, Economic
— Juvenile literature
— Pictorial works
Botany, Experimental
x Experimental botany
Botany, Fossil
See Paleobotany
Botany, Medical *(Indirect)*
sa Ayahuasca
Botanical drug industry
Botany—Pre-Linnean works
Cannabis
Hay-fever plants
Herbs
Materia medica, Vegetable
Medicine, Botanic
Medicine, Medieval
Plants—Assimilation
x Herbals
Herbs—Therapeutic use
Medical botany
Medicinal plants
Plants, Medicinal
xx Botanical drug industry
Drugs
Materia medica, Vegetable
Medicine
Pharmacy
— Early works to 1800
— Pictorial works

Botany, Structural
See Botany—Anatomy
Botany, Systematic
See Botany—Classification
Botany as a profession
x Botany—Vocational guidance
xx Botanists
Botany in archaeology
See Plant remains (Archaeology)
Botany of the Bible
See Bible—Natural history
Botecudos
See Botocudo Indians
Botel Tobago language
See Yami language
Botflies
sa Sheep botfly
x Bot-flies
xx Flies
Bothwell Bridge, Battle of, 1679 *(DA804)*
Botocudo Indians *(F2520.1.B76)*
sa Shokleng Indians
x Aimores
Botocudos
xx Indians of South America
Kaingangue Indians
Shokleng Indians
Tapuya Indians
Botrytis blight of tulip
See Tulip fire
Botswana
— History
— — To 1966
— — 1966-
Bottle-charts *(GC235)*
x Charts, Bottle
xx Maps
Ocean currents
Bottle cutting
xx Cutting
Bottle feeding
x Nursing (Infant feeding)
xx Infants—Nutrition
Bottle gardens
See Glass gardens
Bottle makers' marks
See Bottles—Marks
Bottle tickets
See Wine labels
Bottle washing *(TP659)*
Bottle washing machines
xx Washing-machines
Bottled gas
See Liquefied petroleum gas
Bottlenosed dolphins *(QL737.C4)*
sa Atlantic bottlenosed dolphin
xx Dolphins
Bottlenosed whales
See Beaked whales
Bottles *(Direct) (Art, NK5440; Technology, TP866)*
sa Beer bottles
Bitters bottles
Cruets
Decanters
Ink bottles
Liquor bottles
Medicine bottles
Milk bottles
Miniature bottles
Poison bottles
Vinegar bottles
Water bottles
Wine bottles
x Flasks
xx Glass blowing and working
Glass containers
Glassware

— Collectors and collecting *(Direct)*
— — Caricatures and cartoons
— Conservation and restoration
x Conservation of bottles
Preservation of bottles
Restoration of bottles
— Marks
x Bottle makers' marks
Marks, Bottle makers'
— Private collections *(Direct)*
— Sterilization
Bottles, American, [etc.]
x American [etc.] bottles
Bottling *(TP659)*
sa Beverages—Packaging
Mineral waters
xx Beverages
Carbonated beverages
Soft drink industry
— Law and legislation *(Direct)*
Bottling machinery *(TP659)*
sa Carbonated beverages—Apparatus and supplies
Bottom deposits (Oceanography)
See Marine sediments
Bottom lands
See Alluvial plains
Bottom relief, Ocean
See Submarine topography
Bottomry and respondentia *(Direct)*
sa Ship mortgages
x Hypothecation
Respondentia
xx Contracts, Maritime
Insurance, Marine
Mortgages
Ship mortgages
Botulism *(RA1260)*
xx Clostridium diseases
Food poisoning
Example under Bacterial diseases
Boube language
See Bube language
Boudja (African tribe)
See Budja (African tribe)
Bouem language
See Lefana language
Bouffons, Guerre des
See Guerre des Bouffons
Bougies *(RC923)*
Bouguer anomalies
See Gravity anomalies
Bouity sect
See Bwiti sect
Boulders
sa Felsenmeer
Glaciers
Moraines
xx Felsenmeer
Geology
Geology, Stratigraphic—Pleistocene
Glaciers
Moraines
Sediments (Geology)
Boule (Game) *(GV1311.B6)*
xx Gambling
Boulgour
See Bulgur
Boulou language
See Bulu language
Bound Brook, Battle of, 1777 *(E241.B76)*
Boundaries *(International law, JX4111-4145; Theory of the state, JC323)*
sa Continental shelf
Ethnic barriers
Geopolitics
Uti possidetis (International law)

217

Boundaries *(International law, JX4111-4145;*
Theory of the state, JC323)
(Continued)
subdivision Boundaries *under names of*
countries, states, etc., e.g. United
States—Boundaries; United States—
Boundaries—Mexico; Mexico—
Boundaries—United States; *and*
subdivision Territorial questions
under names of wars, e.g. European
War, 1914-1918—Territorial
questions
 x Frontiers
  Geographical boundaries
  International boundaries
  Natural boundaries
  Political boundaries
 xx Geography
  Geography, Political
  Geopolitics
  History
  International law
  International relations
  Territorial waters
  Territory, National
Boundaries, State
 sa subdivision Boundaries *under names of*
  states, e.g. Texas—Boundaries;
  Virginia—Boundaries—Maryland;
  Maryland—Boundaries—Virginia
 x State boundaries
Boundaries (Estates) *(Direct)*
 sa Adjoining landowners
  Fences—Law
  Party walls
 x Estates, Boundaries of
  Landmarks (Boundaries)
 xx Adjoining landowners
  Fences—Law
  Real property
Boundary conditions (Differential equations)
 See Boundary value problems
Boundary layer *(Aeronautics, TL574.B6;*
Fluid dynamics, QA913)
 sa Film coefficients (Physics)
  Laminar flow
  Turbulent boundary layer
 xx Aerodynamics
  Fluid dynamics
 — Tables, calculations, etc.
Boundary layer (Meteorology)
 sa Planetary boundary layer
 xx Hydrodynamics
  Meteorology
Boundary layer control
 sa Aeroplanes—Control surfaces
  Vortex generators
 xx Aerofoils
  Aeroplanes—Control surfaces
  Drag (Aerodynamics)
  Fluid dynamics
Boundary layer noise
 sa Aeroplanes—Noise
 xx Aerodynamic noise
  Aeroplanes—Noise
  Noise
  Turbulence
Boundary patrols
 See Border patrols
Boundary stones, Babylonian
 x Babylonian boundary stones
  Kudurru inscriptions
 xx Cuneiform inscriptions
Boundary stones, Danish, ⌐Greek, Roman,
etc.⌐
 x Danish ⌐Greek, Roman, etc.⌐ boundary
  stones
Boundary traffic
 See Frontier workers

Boundary value problems
 sa Dirichlet problem
  Hypercircle method
  Initial value problems
  Neumann problem
  Sturm-Liouville equation
 x Boundary conditions (Differential
  equations)
 xx Differential equations
  Functions of complex variables
  Initial value problems
  Mathematical physics
 — Numerical solutions
Boundary waves (Oceanography)
 See Internal waves
Bounties *(Direct) (HD3641-6)*
 Here are entered works on payments
 made to business firms or individuals,
 calculated as a percentage of the value
 of the product grown or manufactured,
 or as a sum set for the performance of
 a stipulated act. Works on premiums
 awarded in competitions are entered
 under the heading Rewards (Prizes,
 etc.)
 sa Shipping bounties and subsidies
  Subsidies
 xx Commercial policy
  Economic policy
  Industry and state
  Subsidies
 Example under reference from Government
  regulation of commerce
Bounties, Military *(Indirect) (UB370-375)*
 sa Pensions, Military
  Prize money
  Recruiting and enlistment
 x Military bounties
  Scrip
 xx Pensions, Military
  Recruiting and enlistment
  Veterans
 — United States
  x Land scrip (United States)
   Mustering-out pay
   Scrip, Land (United States)
  xx United States. Army—Pay,
   allowances, etc.
  Example under references from Bonus,
   Soldiers'; Soldiers' bonus
Bouquetin *(Zoology, QL737.U5)*
 x Alpine ibex
  Alpine mountain goat
  Alpine wild goat
  Ibex
  Steinbock
 xx Goats
Bouquet's Expedition, 1763 *(E83.76)*
 sa Pontiac's Conspiracy, 1763-1765
 xx Pontiac's Conspiracy, 1763-1765
Bouquet's Expedition, 1764 *(E83.76)*
Bourbon Co., Ky.
 — Centennial celebrations, etc.
Bourbon whiskey
 See Whiskey
Bourbonne-les-Bains
 — Fire, 1717
Bourgeoisie
 See Middle classes
Bouro language
 See Buru language
Bouroum language
 See Birom language
Bourrée (Dance)

Bourrées
 Here are entered collections of bourrée
 music for various mediums. Individual
 bourrées and collections of bourrées
 for a specific medium are entered un-
 der the heading followed by specifica-
 tion of medium.
Bourrées (Harpsichord) *(M31)*
 xx Harpsichord music
Bourrées (Orchestra) *(M1048)*
 xx Orchestral music
Boussa language
 See Busa language
Boutan language
 See Tibetan language
Boutonneuse fever
 xx Rickettsial diseases
Bouviers des Flandres *(SF429.B73)*
 x Belgian cattle herders
Bouvines, Battle of, 1214 *(DC90)*
Bovine anatomy
 See Cattle—Anatomy
Bovine brucellosis
 See Brucellosis in cattle
Bovine fever
 See Texas fever
Bovine leukosis
 x Cattle leukemia
  Leukosis, Bovine
 xx Cattle—Diseases
  Leukemia in animals
Bovine malaria
 See Texas fever
Bovine mastitis
 See Mastitis
Bovine rhinotracheitis, Infectious
 See Infectious bovine rhinotracheitis
Bovine theileriasis
 See East Coast fever
Bovine tuberculosis
 See Tuberculosis in cattle
Bow (Music)
 See Stringed instruments, Bowed—Bow
Bow and arrow *(U877-8; Primitive,*
GN498.B78)
 sa Archery
  Arrow-heads
  Crossbow
  Hunting with bow and arrow
 x Arrows
 xx Archery
  Arms and armor, Primitive
  Indians of North America—Arms and
   armor
  Industries, Primitive
Bow hunting
 See Hunting with bow and arrow
Bow porcelain *(NK4399.B7)*
 x Porcelain, Bow
 Example under Porcelain
Bowed instruments
 See Stringed instruments, Bowed
Bowel, Large
 See Intestine, Large
Bowel and bladder training
 x Bladder and bowel training
 xx Defecation
  Urine—Secretion
Bower-birds
 See Bowerbirds
Bowerbirds *(QL696.P2)*
 x Bower-birds
 xx Passeriformes
 — Behavior
Bowfin
 sa Cookery (Bowfin)
Bowie knife
 xx Knives

Bowing of the head (Posture in worship)
   See Posture in worship
Bowling *(GV901-9)*
   x Tenpins
   xx Bowling games
   — Anecdotes, facetiae, satire, etc.
   — Apparatus and equipment
   — Pictorial works
Bowling, Duck pin
   x Duck pin bowling
     Duckpins
   xx Bowling games
Bowling alleys
   sa Pinsetters
   — Accounting
   — Fires and fire prevention
   — Maintenance and repair
Bowling games *(GV901-910.5)*
   sa Bowling
     Bowling, Duck pin
     Bowling on the green
     Ninepins
     Petanque
   xx Ball games
Bowling greens *(GV910)*
   xx Bowling on the green
     Lawns
Bowling on the green *(GV909)*
   sa Bowling greens
   x Bowls (Game)
     Lawn bowls
   xx Bowling games
   — Anecdotes, facetiae, satire, etc.
Bowls (Game)
   See Bowling on the green
Bowman's glands
   xx Nose—Anatomy
Bowmen
   See Archers
Box *(Botany, QK495.B9; Culture, SB435)*
   x Boxwood
   Example under Evergreens; Shrubs
   — Diseases and pests *(SB608.B)*
Box beams *(TA660.B4)*
   x Beams, Box
     Box girders
   xx Girders
Box girders
   See Box beams
Box irons
   See Irons (Pressing)
Box making *(TS900; Ready-reckoners, etc.,*
     HF5716.B6)
   sa Boxes
     Paper box industry
   xx Boxes
   — Standards
Box turtle
   xx Fresh-water turtles
Boxboard (Tree)
   See Ilomba
Boxers *(DS770-772)*
   sa China—History—1900
     Eastern question (Far East)
     Missions—China
     Paotingfu Massacre, 1900
     Peking—Siege, 1900
   — Indemnities *(DS771.5)*
     x United States—Boxer indemnity
       fund
   — Juvenile literature
Boxers (Dogs) *(SF429.B75)*
Boxes *(Trade, HD9999.B7)*
   sa Bandboxes
     Box making
     Cartons
     Crates
     Hatboxes

     Matchboxes
     Needlework boxes
     Paper box industry
     Silver boxes
     Trunks (Luggage)
   x Caskets
   xx Box making
     Containers
   — Collectors and collecting *(Direct)*
   — Juvenile literature
Boxes, Ornamental *(Direct)* *(NK3665)*
   x Caskets
     Ornamental boxes
Boxing *(Direct)* *(GV1115-1137)*
   sa Bag punching
   x Fighting
     Prize-fighting
     Pugilism
     Savate
     Sparring
   xx Athletics
     Self-defense
   — Accidents and injuries
     x Boxing accidents
       Boxing—Injuries
   — Biography
   — Injuries
     See Boxing—Accidents and injuries
   — Juvenile literature
   — Laws and regulations *(Direct)*
     (GV1116)
   — Moral and religious aspects *(GV1135)*
   — Pictorial works
   — Rules
     Example under Sports—Rules
Boxing accidents
   See Boxing—Accidents and injuries
Boxing stories *(GV1135)*
   xx Sports stories
Boxwood
   See Box
Boy-bishop *(BV50.H6)*
   xx Fasts and feasts
     Festivals
     Holy Innocents, Feast of the
Boy choir training
   See Choirboy training
Boy Scouts *(HS3313.B5-9)*
   sa Cub Scouts
     Explorers (Boy Scouts)
     Sea Scouts
     World War, 1939-1945—War work—
       Boy Scouts
   xx Boys
     Boys—Societies and clubs
     Scouts and scouting
   — Public relations
     x Public relations—Boy Scouts
     Example under Public relations
   — Songs and music
Boya (African people)
   See Longarim (African people)
Boyacá, Battle of, 1819
Boycott *(Direct)* *(HD5461)*
   sa Union label
   x Secondary boycotts
   xx Competition, Unfair
     Consumers' leagues
     Labor disputes
     Labor laws and legislation
     Passive resistance
     Strikes and lockouts
     Trade-unions
Boyne, Battle of the, 1690 *(DA945)*
Boys *(Care, HQ775; Ethics, BJ1641-8;*
     Protection, HV877)
   sa Adolescent boys
     Boy Scouts

     Children
     Church work with children
     Fathers and sons
     Mothers and sons
     Newsboys
     Newspaper carriers
     Sex instruction for boys
     Young men
     Youth
   subdivision Juvenile participants *under*
     names of wars, e.g. United States—
     History—Civil War, 1861-1865—
     Juvenile participants; World War,
     1939-1945—Juvenile participants
   xx Children
     Parent and child
     Young men
     Youth
   — Biography
     sa Biography—Juvenile literature
       Boys as soldiers
       Children—Biography
       Children in the Bible
     xx Children—Biography
   — Conduct of life *(BJ1641-8)*
   — Employment
     See Children—Employment
       Youth—Employment
   — Health and hygiene
     xx Hygiene
   — Portraits
     x Boys' portraits
     xx Children in art
       Children—Portraits
   — Prayer-books and devotions *(BV283.B7)*
     x Boys—Prayer-books and devotions—
       English
   — — English
     See Boys—Prayer-books and
       devotions
   — — French, ₍German, Italian, etc.₎
   — Religious life
   — Sexual behavior
   — Societies and clubs *(Direct)*
     (HS3301-3325; HV878)
     sa 4-H clubs
       Agricultural societies
       Boy Scouts
       Gangs
       Science clubs
       Young farmers' clubs
     x Boys' clubs
     xx Children's clubs
       Clubs
       Social settlements
       Societies
Boys anti-tank rifle
   xx Rifles
Boys as soldiers
   xx Boys—Biography
     Heroes
     Soldiers
Boys' clubs
   See Boys—Societies and clubs
Boys in literature
   See Children in literature
Boys in the Bible
   See Children in the Bible
Boys' portraits
   See Boys—Portraits
Boys' towns
   See Children—Institutional care
Boysenberries
Bozo (African people) *(DT547.42)*
   x Bosso (African people)
     Sorko (African people)
   xx Ethnology—Niger
     Mandingo (African people)

Bozo language
   xx Mande languages
Bracelets
   sa Bangle (Sikhism)
      Jewelry
      Watch bracelets
Braces, Orthopedic
   See Orthopedic braces
Brachial-basilar insufficiency syndrome
   See Subclavian steal syndrome
Brachial plexus *(Anatomy, QM471)*
   x Plexus, Brachial
   xx Nerves, Spinal
   — Surgery
Brachialgia
   x Arm pain
   xx Extremities, Upper—Diseases
Brachiation
   xx Animal locomotion
      Man—Attitude and movement
      Man—Origin
      Posture
Brachiopoda *(Indirect)* *(QL395-9)*
   sa Articulata
   xx Invertebrates
      Molluscoidea
   — Classification
Brachiopoda, Fossil *(QE796-7)*
   sa Articulata, Fossil
      Rhynchonellida, Fossil
      Spiriferida
   xx Paleontology
Brachistochrone
   xx Calculus of variations
      Control theory
      Curves
Brachycephaly *(GN71; GN131)*
   sa Hyperbrachycephaly
   x Isocephaly (Craniology)
   xx Craniology
Brachygraphy
   See Abbreviations
      Shorthand
Brachyura
   See Crabs
Brackish water biology
   See Marine biology
Brackish water fauna
   See Marine fauna
Brackish water flora
   See Marine flora
Brackish waters
   xx Sea-water
Bracteate coins
   xx Coins
Bracteates (Ornaments) *(Direct)*
      (NK7157-7161)
Braddock's Campaign, 1755 *(E199)*
   sa Monongahela, Battle of the, 1755
Bradsot
   See Braxy
Bradstreet's Expedition, 1764 *(E83.76)*
   xx Pontiac's Conspiracy, 1763-1765
Bradykinin
   See Kinins
Braggarts in literature
   See Boastfulness in literature
Brahma
   See Brahman
Brahma alphabet
   See Brahmi alphabet
Brahma knot
   See Sacred thread ceremony
Brāhma-samaj *(BL1260-1265)*
   sa Dev-samaj
   x Brahmasabba
      Brahmiyasamaj
      Brahmosomaj

   xx Hinduism
Brahman
   x Brahma
   xx Absolute, The
      Brahmanism
      God (Hinduism)
Brahman cattle
   See Zebus
Brahman mythology
   See Mythology, Hindu
      Vedas
Brāhmanas *(PK3002; PK3021; PK3321;*
      PK3421)
Brahmanical cord
   See Sacred thread ceremony
Brahmanism *(BL1100-1245)*
   sa Atonement (Brahmanism)
      Brahman
      Caste—India
      Hindu sects
      Hinduism
      Jains
      Salvation (Brahmanism)
      Saraswats
   xx Buddha and Buddhism
      Hinduism
      Religions
   — Relations
   — — Buddhism, [etc.]
   — Sacred books
Brahmans *(BL1215.B7)*
   sa Nambudiri
   x Brahmins
   xx Hindus
   — Anthropometry
Brahmans (Cattle)
   See Zebus
Brahmans in Bengal, [etc.]
Brahmas (Poultry) *(SF489.B8)*
Brahmasabba
   See Brahma-samaj
Brahmi alphabet *(PK119)*
   x Brahma alphabet
   xx Alphabet
      Indo-Aryan languages—Writing
Brahmins
   See Brahmans
Brahmiyasamaj
   See Brahma-samaj
Brahmosomaj
   See Brahma-samaj
Brahui language *(PL4621-4)*
   sa Dravidian languages
   x Berouhi language
      Birohi language
      Biruhi language
      Brohki language
   xx Dravidian languages
Brahui tribe
Braid *(Direct)*
   sa Braiding machinery
   x Plaiting
   xx Weaving
Braided rugs
   See Rugs, Braided
Braiding machinery *(TS1782.5)*
   xx Braid
      Textile machinery
Braidism
   See Hypnotism
Braille books
   See Blind, Books for the
Braille music-notation *(MT38)*
   sa Blind—Printing and writing systems
   xx Blind, Music for the
      Blind—Printing and writing systems
      Musical notation

Braille system
   See Blind—Printing and writing systems
Brain *(Anthropology, GN181-190;*
      Comparative anatomy, QL933-7;
      Human anatomy, QM455;
      Physiology, QP376-425)
   sa Basal ganglia
      Brain stem
      Cerebellum
      Cerebral cortex
      Cerebral dominance
      Cerebral ventricles
      Cerebrin
      Cerebrospinal fluid
      Choroid plexus
      Circumventricular organs
      Corpus callosum
      Corpus striatum
      Decerebrate rigidity
      Diencephalon
      Dreams
      Dura mater
      Frontal lobes
      Globus pallidus
      Head
      Hypothalamus
      Limbic system
      Medulla oblongata
      Memory
      Meninges
      Mesencephalon
      Mind and body
      Nervous system
      Neuropsychology
      Optic chiasm
      Optic lobes
      Organon vasculosum laminae terminalis
      Phrenology
      Pituitary body
      Pons Varolii
      Psychology
      Red nucleus
      Reticular formation
      Rhinencephalon
      Septum (Brain)
      Sleep
      Subthalamus
      Supraoptic nucleus
      Telencephalon
      Temporal lobes
      Thalamus
      Vestibular nuclei
   xx Central nervous system
      Craniology
      Head
      Nervous system
      Somatology
   Example under Anatomy, Comparative
   Note under Embryology, Human
   — Abnormities and deformities *(QL991;*
      Teratology, QM691)
      sa Anencephalus
         Cerebral palsy
         Paralysis, Spastic
   — Abscess *(RC394.A)*
   — Aging
      sa Cerebral arteriosclerosis
   — Analysis and chemistry
      See Brain chemistry
   — Anatomy
      sa Anterior commissure
   — Anemia *(RC394.A5)*
      sa Fatigue, Mental
         Neurasthenia
      xx Anemia
         Fatigue, Mental
         Neurasthenia
   — Atlases

— Blood-vessels
   sa Blood-brain barrier
     Intracranial aneurysms
     Meningeal artery
   x Cerebral circulation
   Example under Blood-vessels
— — Abnormities and deformities
— — Diseases
   See Cerebrovascular disease
— — Radiography
   x Cerebral angiography
   xx Angiography
— — Surgery
— Calcification
   xx Brain—Diseases
   Example under Calcification
— Cancer *(RC280.B7)*
   Example under Cancer
— Concussion *(RC394.C7)*
   x Cerebral concussion
     Concussion of the brain
   xx Brain—Wounds and injuries
— Congestion
   x Cerebral hyperemia
     Hyperemia, Cerebral
— Diseases *(RC386-394)*
   sa Acalculia
     Agraphia
     Alexia
     Amaurotic family idiocy
     Amnesia
     Aphasia
     Apoplexy
     Brain—Calcification
     Brain damage
     Brain—Radiography
     Cerebral arteriosclerosis
     Cerebral edema
     Cerebral palsy
     Cerebral sclerosis, Diffuse
     Cerebrovascular disease
     Cysticercosis, Cerebrospinal
     Encephalitis
     Fatigue, Mental
     Hepatolenticular degeneration
     Hydrocephalus
     Insanity
     Intracranial pressure
     Korsakoff's syndrome
     Leucodystrophy
     Nervous system—Diseases
     Paralysis, Spastic
     Presenile dementia
     Psychology, Pathological
     Sturge-Weber syndrome
     Thrombosis
     Wernicke's encephalopathy
   xx Central nervous system—Diseases
   Example under reference from Diseases
    of the brain
— — Diagnosis *(RC386.5)*
   sa Electroencephalography
     Encephalography
— — Homeopathic treatment *(RX281-301)*
— Duality
— Edema
   See Cerebral edema
— Electromechanical analogies
   xx Brain—Models
— Hemorrhage
   sa Apoplexy
     Subarachnoid hemorrhage
   Example under Hemorrhage
— Hernia
   See Encephalocele
— Hydatids
   xx Medical parasitology
— Infarction

   x Cerebral infarction
— Inflammation
   See Encephalitis
— Juvenile literature
— Localization of functions *(QP385)*
   sa Brain stimulation
     Electronic behavior control
     Phrenology
     Split brain
     Visual evoked response
   x Cerebral localization
     Localization of cerebral functions
   xx Phrenology
     Psychology, Physiological
— Mathematical models
   xx Brain—Models
— Models
   sa Brain—Electromechanical analogies
     Brain—Mathematical models
— Nomenclature
   See Brain—Terminology
— Puncture
   sa Spine—Puncture
   x Cisternal puncture
   xx Anesthesia
— Radiography
   sa Cisternography
   x Brain—X-ray examination
   xx Brain—Diseases
— — Atlases
— Research
   See Brain research
— Softening
   x Softening of the brain
— Surgery *(RD594)*
   sa Frontal lobotomy
     Psychosurgery
     Split brain
     Stereoencephalotomy
     Ventriculocisternostomy
   x Topectomy
   xx Head—Surgery
     Nervous system—Surgery
— — Cases, clinical reports, statistics
— Terminology
   x Brain—Nomenclature
— Tumors *(RD663)*
   sa Cerebellum—Tumors
     Intracranial tumors
     Meningioma
     Subdural hematoma
   xx Nervous system—Tumors
   Example under Tumors
— — Atlases
— — Diagnosis
— — Personal narratives
— Ventricles
   See Cerebral ventricles
— Weight *(Anthropology, GN181;*
    Comparative anatomy, QL933-7;
    Human anatomy, QM455)
— Wounds and injuries *(RD594)*
   sa Brain—Concussion
     Brain damage
     Trephining
   Example under Wounds; *and under reference from* Injuries
— — Complications and sequelae
— X-ray examination
   See Brain—Radiography
Brain bisection
   See Split brain
Brain-blood barrier
   See Blood-brain barrier
Brain chemistry
   x Brain—Analysis and chemistry
   xx Cerebrospinal fluid—Analysis and chemistry

   Neurochemistry
— Technique
Brain damage
   xx Brain—Diseases
     Brain—Wounds and injuries
— Diagnosis
Brain-damaged children
   x Brain-injured children
   xx Handicapped children
— Education *(Direct)*
   sa Teachers of brain-damaged children
— Juvenile literature
— Personal narratives
Brain-damaged children, Teachers of
   See Teachers of brain-damaged children
Brain drain *(Direct)*
   x Emigration and immigration of
    scientific and technical personnel
   xx Professions
     Scientists
Brain edema
   See Cerebral edema
Brain-injured children
   See Brain-damaged children
Brain research *(Direct)*
   x Brain—Research
   xx Neurology—Research
     Research
Brain stem
   xx Brain
— Anatomy
— Atlases
Brain stimulation
   x Intracranial stimulation
     Stimulation of the brain
   xx Brain—Localization of functions
Brain-washing *(BF633)*
   x Brainwashing
   xx Mental suggestion
     Will
Brainwashing
   See Brain-washing
Braising (Cookery) *(TX686)*
   x Braizing (Cookery)
   xx Cookery
Braizing (Cookery)
   See Braising (Cookery)
Braj bhākhā
   See Braj language
Braj bhāshā
   See Braj language
Braj language *(PK1961-4)*
   x Braj bhākhā
     Braj bhāshā
     Pingal language
   xx Hindi language
Braj philology
Brakes
   sa Air-brakes
     Friction materials
     Hydraulic brakes
     Magnetic brakes
     subdivision Brakes *under subjects, e.g.*
      Aeroplanes—Brakes; Electric
      railroads—Brakes
   xx Air-brakes
     Friction materials
     Railroads—Cars
Braking radiation
   See Bremsstrahlung
Brakna
   xx Ethnology—Mauritania
Bran
Bran beetle
   See Sawtoothed grain beetle
Bran bug
   See Sawtoothed grain beetle

Branch and bound algorithms
   xx Algorithms
      Network analysis (Planning)
      Programming (Mathematics)
Branch banks
   See Banks and banking—Branch banks
Branch dimorphism
   See Dimorphism (Plants)
Branch libraries
   See Libraries—Branches, delivery stations,
      etc.
Branch stores *(Direct)*
   sa Chain stores
   xx Branches (Business enterprises)
      Chain stores
      Retail trade
   — Taxation *(Direct)*
Branches (Business enterprises) *(Direct)*
   sa Banks and banking—Branch banks
      Branch stores
      Chain stores
   xx Business enterprises
   — Finance
   — Law and legislation *(Direct)*
Branchial arch
   sa Gills
   x Gill arch
   xx Fishes—Anatomy
      Gills
Branchial cleft fistula
   See Fistula, Branchial cleft
Branching (Botany)
   sa Pruning
   xx Stele (Botany)
Branching processes
   x Processes, Branching
   xx Stochastic processes
Branching ratios (Nuclear physics)
   xx Nuclear reactions
      Radioactivity
Branchiopoda *(QL444.B8)*
   sa Anostraca
      Conchostraca
      Notostraca
   x Phyllopoda
   xx Entomostraca
Branchiopoda, Fossil
   xx Crustacea, Fossil
Branchiostegal rays
   See Branchiostegals
Branchiostegals *(QL639)*
   x Branchiostegal rays
   xx Fishes—Anatomy
      Gills
      Hyoid bone
Brand management
   See Product management
Brand names
   See Business names
      Trade-marks
Branded merchandise *(Direct)*
   x Merchandise, Branded
      Proprietary articles
   xx Business names
      Trade-marks
Brandenburg
   — History *(DD491.B81-95)*
         Here is entered the history of the mar-
         gravate and electorate of Branden-
         burg up to the year 1640. The his-
         tory of the electorate of Branden-
         burg from 1640 to 1701 is entered
         under Prussia—History—1640-
         1740.
         Note under Prussia—History
Branding of cattle
   See Cattle—Marking

Branding of livestock
   See Livestock brands
Brandon, Manitoba
   — Packing-house Workers' Strike, 1960
      x Brandon Packers Strike, 1960
Brandon Packers Strike, 1960
   See Brandon, Manitoba—Packing-house
      Workers' Strike, 1960
Brands, Cattle
   See Cattle brands
Brands, Livestock
   See Livestock brands
Brands (Commerce)
   See Business names
      Trade-marks
Brandy *(Industry, HD9393; Technology,*
    TP599)
   sa Grappa
      Pisco
   x Cognac
   xx Distillation
      Wine and wine making
   Example under Alcohol; Liquors
   — Analysis
Brandy Station, Battle of, 1863 *(E475.51)*
   x Fleetwood, Battle of, 1863
Brandywine, Battle of, 1777 *(E241.B8)*
   sa Cooch's Bridge, Skirmish of, 1777
Brannerite *(Indirect)*
   x Absite
      Uraniferous leucoxene
   xx Uranium ores
Brass *(TS564-5)*
   sa Alloys
      Brasses
      Creep of brass
      Electrum
      Orichalc
   xx Alloys
      Electrum
      Zinc
   — Analysis
   — Cold working
      Example under Metals—Cold working
   — Corrosion
   — Creep
      See Creep of brass
   — Metallography
   — Metallurgy
   — Testing
   — Welding
Brass band music
   See Band music
Brass bands
   See Bands (Music)
Brass crystals
Brass forgings
   x Brass pressings
   xx Forging
Brass founding *(TS565)*
   sa Founding
      Metal-work
   xx Founding
Brass industry and trade *(Direct)*
    (HD9539.B7; TS564-5)
   sa Copper industry and trade
Brass ingots
   x Ingots, Brass
Brass instruments
   See Wind instruments
Brass plating *(TS692.B)*
   xx Electroplating
Brass pressings
   See Brass forgings
Brass rubbing *(Direct)*
   xx Brasses
      Rubbings

Brasses *(Indirect)* *(Art objects,*
    NK7800-7899; Sepulchral
    monuments, NB1840-1846)
   sa Brass rubbing
      Goldweights
      Horse brasses
   x Monumental brasses
      Sepulchral brasses
   xx Art
      Brass
      Epitaphs
      Inscriptions
      Sculpture
      Sepulchral monuments
      Tombs
Bratas
   xx Hinduism—Rituals
      Women, Hindu—Religious life
Bratslav Hasidim *(Direct)*
   xx Hasidism
Bråvalla, Battle of
   See Brávellir, Battle of
Brávellir, Battle of
   x Bråvalla, Battle of
Bravery
   See Courage
Bravos
   xx Crime and criminals
Braxy *(SF968)*
   x Black disease of sheep
      Bradsot
      Infectious necrotic hepatitis
   Example under Sheep—Diseases
Brazen serpent
   x Serpent, Brazen
   xx Jews—Antiquities
      Serpent worship
Braziers
   xx Heating
Brazil
   — History *(F2521-2538)*
     — To 1821
        sa Bandeiras
        xx Seven Reductions, War of the,
          1754-1756
     — 1500-1548
     — 1549-1762
        sa Bandeiras
     — French colony, 1555-1567
        sa Tamoio Confederation, 1554-1567
     — 1580-1640
     — Dutch Conquest, 1624-1654
        sa Guararapes, Battle of, 1648
          Guararapes, Battle of, 1649
          Tabocas, Battle of, 1643
      — Pictorial works
     — Guarani War, 1754-1756
        See Seven Reductions, War of the,
          1754-1756
     — 1763-1821
        sa Minas Gerais, Brazil—History—
          Revolution, 1789
      — Pictorial works
     — Revolution, 1789
        See Minas Gerais, Brazil—History
          —Revolution, 1789
     — 1822-
     — 1822-1889
      — Pictorial works
     — Revolution, 1842
     — 1889-
     — 1889-1930 *(F2537)*
        sa Brazil—History—Naval Revolt,
          1893-1894
     — Naval Revolt, 1893-1894
        xx Brazil—History—1889-1930
     — Conselheiro Insurrection, 1897
     — Naval Revolt, 1910

222

—— Revolution, 1924-1925
—— —— Naval operations
—— Revolution, 1930
—— —— 1930-1954 *(F2538)*
—— —— 1954-
—— Revolution, 1964
Brazil in art
Brazil in literature
Brazil nut *(SB401)*
   x Cream nut
     Pará nut
Brazil pine
   See Brazilian pine
Brazilian-Argentine War, 1825-1828
   See Argentine-Brazilian War, 1825-1828
Brazilian ballads and songs *(Collections, PQ9660; History, PQ9580)*
   sa Folk-songs, Brazilian
     National songs, Brazilian
     Songs, Brazilian
     War-songs, Brazilian
   xx Portuguese ballads and songs
Brazilian clover
   See Alfalfa
Brazilian concrete poetry
   See Concrete poetry, Brazilian
Brazilian essays *(Direct)*
Brazilian fiction *(Collections, PQ9675-6; History, PQ9597-9607)*
Brazilian gum
   See Angico gum
Brazilian literature *(PQ9500-9699)*
   x Portuguese literature—Brazil
   Example under America—Literatures
   — 19th century
   — 20th century
   — Negro authors
     x Negro literature (Brazilian)
Brazilian music
   See Music, Brazilian
Brazilian newspapers *(Direct) (History, etc., PN5021-9)*
Brazilian orations *(Direct)*
Brazilian pastoral drama
   See Pastoral drama, Brazilian
Brazilian periodicals *(Direct) (History, etc., PN5021-5030)*
Brazilian pine
   x Brazil pine
     Paraná pine
Brazilian poetry *(Direct) (Collections, PQ9649-9663; History, PQ9561-9581)*
   sa Concrete poetry, Brazilian
   — 20th century

GENERAL SUBDIVISIONS

   — Negro authors
     x Negro poetry (Brazilian)
Brazilian prose literature *(Collections, PQ9672-9687; History, PQ9597-9617)*
   — 20th century
Brazilian students in Europe, [France, the Czechoslovak Republic, etc.]
   xx Brazilians in Europe, [France, the Czechoslovak Republic, etc.]
Brazilian studies *(Direct)*
Brazilian wit and humor *(PN6222)*
Brazilians in Europe, [France, the Czechoslovak Republic, etc.]
   sa Brazilian students in Europe, [France, the Czechoslovak Republic, etc.]
Brazilians in literature
Brazing *(TT267)*
   sa Silver brazing
     Solder and soldering
     Vacuum brazing

subdivision Brazing *under specific subjects, e.g.* Aluminum—Brazing; Copper—Brazing; Ships—Brazing
   xx Metal-work
     Sealing (Technology)
     Solder and soldering
   — Patents
   — Testing
Breach of contract *(Direct)*
   x Non-performance (Law)
   xx Contracts
     Discharge of contracts
Breach of contract (Jewish law)
Breach of promise *(Direct) (HQ804)*
   sa Alienation of affections
     Betrothal—Law
   xx Betrothal—Law
     Marriage law
Breach of the peace *(Direct)*
   sa Affray
     Riots
   x Peace, Breach of
   xx Criminal law
     Riots
     Threats
Bread *(Bread making, TX769; Industry, HD9057)*
   sa Baking
     Bread in art
     Bread in literature
     Dough
     Flour
     Hot dog rolls
     Tortillas
   xx Baking
     Cookery
   Example under Baked products; Food
   — Bacteriology *(QR119)*
   — Juvenile literature
   — Laboratory manuals *(TX769)*
   — Prices *(Direct)*
   — Quality control
   — Quotations, maxims, etc.
   — Standards
   — Storage
   — Taxation *(Direct)*
Bread, Communion
   See Lord's Supper—Bread
Bread, Consecrated
   See Lord's Supper—Bread
Bread (in religion, folk-lore, etc.)
   sa Lord's Supper—Bread
     Matzos
   x Folk-lore of bread
   xx Food (in religion, folk-lore, etc.)
     Religion, Primitive
Bread dough craft *(Direct)*
   xx Dough
     Handicraft
   — Juvenile literature
Bread in art
   xx Art
     Bread
Bread in literature
   xx Bread
Bread molds (Baking) *(NK8490)*
   x Molds, Bread (Baking)
     Moulds, Bread (Baking)
Bread stamps (Liturgical objects)
   x Stamps, Bread (Liturgical objects)
   xx Christian art and symbolism
     Lord's Supper—Bread
Breadfruit *(Indirect) (SB379.B8)*
Breadstuffs
   See Flour
     Grain
     Wheat

Break-away luminaire supports
   See Roads—Lighting—Break-away supports
Break-away traffic sign supports
   See Traffic signs and signals—Break-away supports
Break crops
   See Rotation of crops
Breakage, shrinkage, etc. (Commerce)
     Works on breakage, shrinkage, etc. of individual products are entered under the headings for the products.
   x Commercial products—Breakage, shrinkage, etc.
     Commercial products—Shrinkage
     Shrinkage (Commerce)
   xx Freight and freightage
     Shipment of goods
Breakdown (Electricity)
   x Dielectric breakdown
     Electric breakdown
   xx Dielectrics
     Electric discharges
     Electric insulators and insulation
Breakers
   See Ocean waves
     Water waves
Breakfast foods
   See Cereals, Prepared
Breakfasts *(TX733)*
   sa Brunches
   xx Brunches
     Caterers and catering
     Cookery
     Menus
     Table
Breakwaters *(TC333)*
   sa Jetties
     Shore protection
   xx Civil engineering
     Engineering
     Harbors
     Hydraulic structures
     Jetties
     Marinas
     Sea-walls
     Shore protection
   — Patents *(TC333)*
Bream fishing *(SH691.B7)*
   xx Fishing
Breast *(QM495)*
   sa Milk, Human
   xx Mammary glands
   — Abnormities and deformities *(RG499)*
   — Cancer *(RC280.B8)*
     Example under Cancer
   —— Surgery
     x Breast—Surgery
   — Care and hygiene
     xx Hygiene
   — Diseases *(RG491-9; Puerperal state, RG861)*
     sa Lactation disorders
   — Examination
     sa Breast—Radiography
   — Radiography
     x Mammography
     xx Breast—Examination
   —— Atlases
   — Surgery
     sa Breast—Cancer—Surgery
   — Tuberculosis *(RC312.5.B7)*
   — Tumors *(RC280.B8)*
Breast feeding
   sa Lactation
     Milk, Human
     Wet-nurses
   x Nursing (Infant feeding)
   xx Infants—Nutrition

Breast feeding *(Continued)*
    Lactation
    Milk, Human
Breast in art *(N8217.B75)*
  xx Art
    Human figure in art
Breast-pump *(RG866)*
Breastbone
  See Sternum
Breastpins
  See Brooches
Breastplate of the High Priest *(BM657.B7)*
  xx Cultus, Jewish
    Ephod
    Jews—Antiquities
    Priests, Jewish—Vestments
Breath, Offensive
  xx Respiratory organs—Diseases
Breath and breathing (in religion, folk-lore, etc.)
  sa Ānāpānasmṛti
    Yoga, Haṭha
  x Breathing
    Folk-lore of breath and breathing
  xx Inspiration
    Religion, Primitive
    Respiration
    Soul
Breathing
  See Breath and breathing (in religion, folk-lore, etc.)
    Respiration
Breathing apparatus
  See Respirators
Breathing exercises
  sa Singing—Breathing exercises
  xx Hygiene
    Respiration
  — Therapeutic use
    x Respiration—Therapeutic use
Breccia *(Indirect)*
Breda
  — Siege, 1624-1625
Breda, Treaty of, 1667 *(D274.6)*
Breda machine-gun *(UF620.B)*
  xx Machine-guns
Breech delivery *(RG686)*
  x Breech presentation
  xx Labor, Complicated
Breech presentation
  See Breech delivery
Breechcloths
  sa Diapers
  x Breechclouts
  xx Clothing and dress, Primitive
Breechclouts
  See Breechcloths
Breeder reactors
  x Converter reactors
    Reactors, Breeder
  xx Fast reactors
    Nuclear reactors
Breeding *(S494)*
  sa Domestic animals
    Genetics
    Heredity
    Heterosis
    Hybridization
    Inbreeding
    Mendel's law
    Mutation breeding
    Plant-breeding
    Stock and stock-breeding
    breeding of particular groups of animals, e.g. Dog breeding; Homing pigeons—Breeding
  xx Genetics
    Inbreeding

— Statistical methods
Breeding behavior
  See Sexual behavior in animals
Breeding cycle
  See Sexual cycle
Breed's Hill, Battle of, 1775
  See Bunker Hill, Battle of, 1775
Breeds of cattle, ⌐dogs, horses, poultry, etc.⌐
  See Cattle ⌐Dog, Horse, Poultry, etc.⌐ breeds
Breeze, Sea
  See Sea breeze
Bregalnica, Battle of, 1913
  xx Balkan Peninsula—History—War of 1912-1913
Bregenz, Austria
  — Siege, 1647
    xx Thirty Years' War, 1618-1648
Brehon laws
  See Law, Celtic
    Law—Ireland
Breitenfeld, Battle of, 1631
  See Leipzig, Battle of, 1631
Bremsstrahlung *(QC484.3)*
  sa Cascade shower
  x Braking radiation
  xx Nuclear reactions
    Radiation
Bren machine-gun *(UF620.B57)*
  xx Machine-guns
Brenner Pass
  Example under Mountain passes; Valleys
Brent-goose
  x Black brant
  xx Geese
Brent-goose shooting
Brenta River
  — Flood, 1966
Breslau
  — Siege, 1945
    xx World War, 1939-1945—Campaigns —Germany
Brest
  — Siege, 1944
    xx World War, 1939-1945—France— Brest
Brest, White Russia
  — Siege, 1941
    xx World War, 1939-1945—Campaigns —Eastern
  — — Juvenile literature
  — — Pictorial works
Brest Expedition, 1694 *(DA86.8 1694)*
Brest Expedition, 1796-1797
  See French Expedition to Ireland, 1796-1797
Brest-Litovsk, Treaty of, Feb. 9, 1918 (Ukraine) *(D614.B5)*
  xx European War, 1914-1918—Treaties
Brest-Litovsk, Treaty of, Mar. 3, 1918 (Russia) *(D614.B6)*
  xx European War, 1914-1918—Treaties
Brethern of the Common Life
  See Brothers of the Common Life
Brethren, Plymouth
  See Plymouth Brethren
Brethren, United
  See Moravians
Brethren of Jesus
  See Jesus Christ—Brethren
Brethren of the Free Spirit
  sa Amalricians
    Beghards
    Beguines
    Libertines (Spirituals)
  x Brothers of the Free Spirit
    Free Spirit, Brethren of the
    Ortlibenses

  xx Adamites
    Amalricians
    Antinomianism
    Beghards
    Beguines
    Heresies and heretics—Middle Ages, 600-1500
    Pantheism
    Sects, Medieval
Brétigny, Treaty of, 1360 *(DC99.5.B7)*
  xx Hundred Years' War, 1339-1453
Breton Club
  See Jacobins
Breton drama *(Direct)*
Breton horse *(SF293.B7)*
Breton language *(PB2800-2849)*
  x Armoric language
  xx Celtic languages
Breton literature *(PB2856-2931)*
  x Armoric literature
  xx Celtic literature
Breton philology
Breton poetry *(Collections, PB2887; History, PB2858)*
Breton saints
  See Saints, Breton
Bretons *(DC611.B814-915)*
Breves, Papal
  See Briefs, Papal
Breviaries
  sa Catholic Church. Liturgy and ritual. Breviary
    Liturgies
    Rimed offices
  xx Catholic Church. Liturgy and ritual. Breviary
    Liturgies
    Prayer-books
Breweries *(Architecture, NA6420; Technology, TP569-587)*
  sa Brewery waste
  — Water-supply *(TP583)*
Brewers *(Direct)* *(TP573.5)*
  sa Brewery workers
  xx Brewery workers
Brewery waste
  xx Breweries
    Brewing
    Factory and trade waste
Brewery workers *(Direct)*
  sa Brewers
    Collective labor agreements—Brewing industry
    Trade-unions—Brewery workers
  xx Brewers
    Brewing industry
Brewing *(TP569-587)*
  sa Ale
    Beer
    Brewery waste
    Enzymes
    Liquors
    Malt
    Porter
  xx Beer
    Fermentation
    Liquors
  — Amateurs' manuals
  — Automation
  — Patents
Brewing industry *(Direct)* *(Economics, HD9397; Technology, TP569-587)*
  sa Ale
    Beer
    Brewery workers
    Porter
  x Alcoholic beverage industry
  xx Liquor traffic

Example under Chemistry, Technical
— Accidents
— Accounting *(HF5686.B5)*
— Collective labor agreements
    See Collective labor agreements—
        Brewing industry
— Equipment and supplies
— — Maintenance and repair
— Finance
— Law and legislation *(Direct)*
    x Beer—Law and legislation
    xx Liquor laws
— Mathematics
    See Business mathematics—Brewing
        industry
— Production standards
— Taxation
    See Beer—Taxation
— Technological innovations
Brewing of coffee
    See Coffee brewing
Bribery *(Direct)* *(HV6301-6321; Officials,*
    HV6306; Voters, HV6314)
    sa Judicial corruption
        Police corruption
    xx Competition, Unfair
        Corruption (in politics)
        Criminal law
        Elections—Corrupt practices
        White collar crimes
    Example under Misconduct in office
Bribri dialect *(PM3541)*
    sa Chibchan languages
    xx Chibchan languages
        Indians of Central America—Languages
Bribri Indians
    xx Indians of Central America
Bric-a-brac
    See Art objects
Brice's Crossroads, Battle of, 1864
    x Tishomingo Creek, Battle of, June 10,
        1864
Brick bridges
    See Bridges, Brick
Brick building
    See Building, Brick
Brick houses *(Direct)* *(NA7150)*
    sa Adobe houses
    x Houses, Brick
    xx Architecture, Domestic
        Building, Brick
        Dwellings
    Example under Buildings
Brick pavements
    See Pavements, Brick
Brick roads
    See Roads, Brick
Brick stamps
    x Stamps, Brick
    xx Brick trade
        Bricks
        Inscriptions
        Pottery—Marks
        Trade-marks
Brick trade *(Direct)* *(Economics, HD9605;*
    Periodicals and societies, TP785;
    Technology, TP827-842)
    sa Brick stamps
        Bricks
    xx Bricks
        Clay industries
Brick walls *(TH2243)*
    xx Bricks
        Walls
— Radiography
— Testing
Brick works
    See Brickworks

Bricklayers
    sa Bricklaying—Vocational guidance
    x Masons (Trade)
    xx Building trades
Bricklaying *(TH5501)*
    sa Masonry
    xx Bricks
        Building
        Masonry
— Accidents
— Cold weather conditions
— Safety measures
— Vocational guidance
    xx Bricklayers
Brickmakers *(Direct)*
    sa Wages—Brickmakers
    xx Brickmaking
Brickmaking *(Direct)* *(TP827-833)*
    sa Brickmakers
        Brickworks
        Kilns
    xx Kilns
— Safety measures
Brickmaking machinery *(TP829)*
Bricks *(Technology, TP827; Testing,*
    TA432-3)
    sa Brick stamps
        Brick trade
        Brick walls
        Bricklaying
        Clay
        Clinker brick
        Concrete face brick
        Fire-brick
        Glazed brick
        Hollow bricks
        Pressed brick
        Sand-lime brick
        Tiles
    xx Brick trade
        Building materials
        Clay
        Clay industries
    Note under Ceramics
— Defects
— Drying
— Prices *(Direct)*
— Standards
— Testing
— Transportation
Brickworks *(Direct)*
    x Brick works
    xx Brickmaking
— Pictorial works
Bridal books *(HQ746)*
    x Bride's books
    xx Weddings
Bridal bouquets
    xx Flower arrangement
        Weddings
Bridal customs
    See Marriage customs and rites
Bridal gowns
    See Wedding costume
Bride price *(GN480.1)*
    x Bride purchase
        Lobolo
    xx Dowry
        Marriage
Bride purchase
    See Bride price
Bride's books
    See Bridal books
Bridewell Prison, London
    Example under Prisons
Bridge (Game)
    See Bridge whist

Bridge approaches
    x Approaches, Bridge
    xx Roads
— Design and construction
Bridge circuits
    sa Wheatstone bridge
    x Bridges, Electric
        Circuits, Bridge
    xx Electric circuits
        Electric measurements
        Electronic circuits
        Electronic measurements
Bridge construction
    sa Bridges—Welding
        Cables
        Graphic statics
        Masonry
        Scaffolding
        Strains and stresses
    subdivision Design and construction
        under types of bridges, e.g. Bridges,
        Suspension—Design and
        construction
    x Bridges—Construction
— Safety measures
— Safety regulations *(Direct)*
Bridge failures
    x Bridges—Failure
        Collapse of bridges
    xx Structural stability
Bridge floors
    See Bridges—Floors
Bridge for three players
    See Three-handed bridge
Bridge lighting
    See Bridges—Lighting
Bridge lights (Navigation) *(VK1247-9)*
    xx Bridges
        Lighthouses
Bridge railings
    xx Bridges
Bridge whist *(GV1281)*
    sa Auction bridge
        Contract bridge
        Domino bridge
        Five-suit bridge
        Pirate bridge
        Poker-bridge
    x Bridge (Game)
    xx Whist
— Anecdotes, facetiae, satire, etc.
        (GV1281.5)
Bridges *(Indirect)* *(TG)*
    sa Arches
        Bridge lights (Navigation)
        Bridge railings
        Causeways
        Culverts
        Drawbridges
        Footbridges
        Girders
        Ice crossings
        Influence lines
        Military bridges
        Pontoon-bridges
        Railroad bridges
        Toll bridges
        Transporter-bridges
        Trusses
        Viaducts
    subdivision Bridges *under names of*
        rivers, cities, etc., e.g. New York
        (City)—Bridges; Washington, D.C.—
        Bridges—Arlington Memorial Bridge;
        and names of individual bridges not
        located in any city or town
    xx Civil engineering
        Engineering

Bridges *(Indirect)* *(TG)* *(Continued)*
    Girders
    Graphic statics
    Municipal engineering
    Transportation
    Trusses
    Viaducts
    Example under Structural engineering
  — Accidents *(TG470)*
    xx Disasters
  — Bailey construction
    See Bridges, Prefabricated
  — Bearings *(TG326)*
  — — Testing
  — Catalogs *(TG157)*
  — Construction
    See Bridge construction
  — Costs
    See Bridges—Estimates and costs
  — Decks
    See Bridges—Floors
  — Design *(TG300-301)*
    sa subdivision Design and construction
      under types of bridges, e.g.
      Bridges, Suspension—Design and
      construction
    Example under Structural design
  — — Mathematical models
  — Early works to 1800 *(TG144)*
  — Estimates and costs *(Direct)*
    x Bridges—Costs
  — Failure
    See Bridge failures
  — Floors *(TG325.6)*
    sa Bridges, Steel plate deck
    subdivision Floors *under special*
      types of bridges, e.g. Bridges,
      Concrete—Floors
    x Bridge floors
    Bridges—Decks
    Decks (Bridges)
    Floors (Bridges)
    xx Floors
  — — Joints
    xx Joints (Engineering)
  — Foundations and piers *(TG320)*
    sa Caissons
    Coffer-dams
    x Piers (Bridge)
    xx Caissons
    Coffer-dams
    Foundations
    Hydraulic structures
    Masonry
  — Ice control
    See Bridges—Snow and ice control
  — Juvenile literature
  — Law and legislation *(Direct)*
    xx Highway law
    Inland navigation—Laws and
      regulations
  — Lighting
    x Bridge lighting
    xx Municipal lighting
  — Live loads
    x Bridges—Moving loads
    Live loads (Bridges)
    Moving loads (Bridges)
    xx Bridges—Vibration
    Structural dynamics
  — — Tables, calculations, etc.
  — Maintenance and repair
    sa Bridges—Snow and ice control
    x Bridges—Repairing
  — — Costs
  — Models *(TG153)*
  — Moving loads
    See Bridges—Live loads

— Navigation clearances *(Direct)*
  x Navigation clearances (Bridges)
  Navigational clearances (Bridges)
  xx Bridges, Movable
  Inland navigation
— Pictorial works
— Popular works
— Repairing
  See Bridges—Maintenance and repair
— Snow and ice control
  x Bridges—Ice control
  Ice control on bridges
  Snow control on bridges
  xx Bridges—Maintenance and repair
  Slush on pavements, runways, etc.
  Snow removal
— — Safety measures *(TG153)*
— Specifications *(Direct)* *(TG310)*
— Surveying
— Tables, calculations, etc. *(TG151)*
— Testing *(TG305)*
— Trestles
  See Trestles
— Valuation
— Vibration
  sa Bridges—Live loads
  Example under Structural dynamics
— Welding
  xx Bridge construction
  Example under Welded steel structures
Bridges, Aluminum
  x Aluminum bridges
  xx Aluminum construction
Bridges, Arched *(TG327-340; TG410)*
  xx Arches
Bridges, Brick *(TG330)*
  x Brick bridges
Bridges, Cantilever *(TG385)*
  x Cantilever bridges
Bridges, Concrete *(TG335-340)*
  x Concrete bridges
  xx Concrete construction
— Design and construction
— Floors
  Example under Bridges—Floors
— — Maintenance and repair
— — Testing
— Joints
  xx Joints (Engineering)
— Maintenance and repair
  x Bridges, Concrete—Repairing
— Models
  Example under Engineering models
— Repairing
  See Bridges, Concrete—Maintenance
  and repair
— Standards *(Direct)*
— Tables, calculations, etc.
— Testing
Bridges, Continuous *(TG413)*
  x Continuous bridges
  xx Girders, Continuous
Bridges, Covered
  See Covered bridges
Bridges, Electric
  See Bridge circuits
Bridges, Ferry
  See Ferry-bridges
Bridges, Iron and steel
  sa Bridges, Plate-girder
  Bridges, Steel plate deck
  Eye-bars
  Iron, Structural
  Steel, Structural
  x Iron and steel bridges
  Steel and iron bridges
  xx Eye-bars
  Iron, Structural

  Steel, Structural
— Corrosion
— Design and construction
— Maintenance and repair
— Standards *(Direct)*
— Tables, calculations, etc.
Bridges, Masonry *(TG330)*
  x Masonry bridges
Bridges, Military
  See Military bridges
Bridges, Movable *(TG420)*
  sa Bridges—Navigation clearances
  Drawbridges
Bridges, Pile
  x Pile bridges
Bridges, Plate-girder
  x Plate-girder bridges
  xx Bridges, Iron and steel
  Plate girders
— Design and construction
Bridges, Pontoon
  See Pontoon-bridges
Bridges, Prefabricated *(TG418)*
  sa Military bridges
  x Bailey bridges
  Bridges—Bailey construction
  Prefabricated bridges
  xx Military bridges
Bridges, Railroad
  See Railroad bridges
Bridges, Steel plate deck *(TG416)*
  x Battledeck floor bridges
  Steel deck bridges
  Steel plate deck bridges
  xx Bridges—Floors
  Bridges, Iron and steel
  Plates, Iron and steel
— Design and construction
Bridges, Stone *(TG330)*
  x Stone bridges
  xx Building, Stone
Bridges, Suspension *(TG400)*
  sa Roofs, Suspension
  x Suspension bridges
  xx Roofs, Suspension
— Design and construction
  Example under Bridge construction;
    Bridges—Design
— Juvenile literature
Bridges, Toll
  See Toll bridges
Bridges, Tubular *(TG390)*
  x Tubular bridges
Bridges, Wooden *(TG365; TG375)*
  sa Covered bridges
  x Wooden bridges
Bridges (Dentistry)
  x Bridgework (Dentistry)
  xx Partial dentures
  Prosthodontics
Bridges (in numismatics) *(CJ161.B7)*
Bridges in art
  xx Art
Bridgettines
  See Birgittines
Bridgewater, Va.
— Flood, 1949
Bridgewater, Battle of, 1814
  See Lundy's Lane, Battle of, 1814
Bridgework (Dentistry)
  See Bridges (Dentistry)
Bridle *(SF309)*
  sa Curb-bit
  x Bits (Bridles)
  xx Harness
— Collectors and collecting *(Direct)*
Bridle paths
  See Trails

Brief test of literacy
  xx Mental tests
      Reading—Ability testing
Briefcases
  sa Schoolbags
  x Attaché cases
Briefhand
  See Shorthand
Briefs *(Direct)*
  xx Appellate procedure
      Legal composition
Briefs, Papal
  sa Rescripts, Papal
  x Breves, Papal
      Papal briefs
  xx Bulls, Papal
      Papal documents
      Rescripts, Papal
Brigands and robbers *(Direct)*
      (HV6441-6453)
  sa Bank robberies
      Bush-rangers
      Dacoits
      Haidamaks
      Klephts
      Megpunna
      Outcasts
      Outlaws
      Robbery
      Rogues and vagabonds
      Shifta
      Thieves
      Thugs
      Train robberies
  x Bandits
      Banditti
      Highwaymen
      Robbers
  xx Buccaneers
      Crime and criminals
      Larceny
      Outlaws
      Robbery
      Rogues and vagabonds
      Thieves
  — Juvenile literature
  — Personal narratives
Brigands and robbers in literature
  x Robbers in literature
  xx Crime in literature
Bright children
  See Gifted children
Brighteners, Optical
  See Optical brighteners
Brightness (Astronomy)
  See Photometry, Astronomical
Brighton, N.Y. (Township, Monroe Co.)
  — Fire, 1951
Brighton Run (Antique car race)
Bright's disease *(RC907)*
  sa Albuminuria
      Urine—Analysis and pathology
  xx Albuminuria
      Kidneys—Diseases
  Example under Urinary organs—Diseases
  — Homeopathic treatment *(RX356.B8)*
Brillouin zones *(Crystallography, QD939;*
      Physics, QC176)
  xx Crystals—Electric properties
      Energy-band theory of solids
      Wave mechanics
Brill's disease
  See Typhus fever
Brine
  See Salt
Brinell number
  See Brinell test

Brinell test *(TA407)*
  x Brinell number
  xx Hardness
      Metals—Testing
Brining
  See Salting of food
Briquet plants
  See Fuel-briquet plants
Briquets *(TP156.B7)*
      Here are entered general works on bri-
      quets and on briquetting of all classes
      of raw materials. Works on fuel bri-
      quets are entered under Briquets
      (Fuel)
  xx Compacting
Briquets (Fuel) *(TP323; TP327)*
  sa Agglomeration
      Fuel
      Mud fuel
  xx Coal
      Coal, Pulverized
      Fuel
      Lignite
      Mud fuel
  Note under Briquets
  — Early works to 1800
Briquetted hay
  See Pelleted hay
Brisk (Game) *(GV1511.B8)*
Brissa language *(PL8089)*
  sa Nzima language
      Tshi language
  x Aowin language
  xx Nzima language
      Tshi language
Brist (Game) *(GV1099)*
Bristle-tails
  See Thysanura
Bristlecone pine
  — Pictorial works
Bristles
  xx Hair
  — Grading
Bristoe Station, Battle of, 1863 *(E475.75)*
Bristol, Eng.
  — Riots, 1831 *(DA690.B8)*
  — Sieges, 1643, 1645
      xx Great Britain—History—Civil War,
          1642-1649
Bristol airplanes
Bristol porcelain *(NK4399.B75)*
  x Porcelain, Bristol
  xx Bristol pottery
Bristol pottery *(NK4088.B8)*
  sa Bristol porcelain
Britain, Battle of, 1940
  sa subdivision Bombardment *under names*
      of cities, e.g. London—
      Bombardment, 1940
  x Battle of Britain
  xx World War, 1939-1945—Aerial
      operations
  — Juvenile literature
British associations, institutions, etc.
  See Associations, institutions, etc., British
British automobiles
  See Automobiles, British
British banks and banking
  See Banks and banking, British
British church historians
  See Church historians, British
British Commonwealth of Nations
  See Commonwealth of Nations
British Dominions
  See Commonwealth of Nations
British-Dutch War . . .
  See Anglo-Dutch War . . .

British economic assistance
  See Economic assistance, British
British etchers
  See Etchers, British
British firearms
  See Firearms, British
British-French War . . .
  See Anglo-French War . . .
British goldsmithing
  See Goldsmithing, British
British Grand Prix Race *(GV1034.44.B)*
  xx Automobile racing
      Grand prix racing
British Honduras-Guatemala dispute
  See British Honduras question
British Honduras question *(F1449.B7)*
  x Belice question
      British Honduras-Guatemala dispute
      Guatemala-British Honduras dispute
  — Juvenile literature
British in Africa, ₍Egypt, India, etc.₎
  x English in Africa, ₍Egypt, India, etc.₎
  — Anecdotes, facetiae, satire, etc.
  — Juvenile literature
  — Sources
British in Central Asia
  See Eastern question (Central Asia)
British in foreign countries
  — Employment
British insurance companies
  See Insurance companies, British
British literature
  See English literature
      Irish literature
      Scottish literature
      Welsh literature
British marine painting
  See Marine painting, British
British military miniatures
  See Military miniatures, British
British miniature painters
  See Miniature painters, British
British missions
  See Missions, British
British mythology
  See Mythology, British
British newspapers
  See English newspapers
      Irish newspapers
      Scottish newspapers
      Welsh newspapers
British oak
  See English oak
British opinion of the United States
  See United States—Foreign opinion, British
British periodicals
  See English periodicals
      Irish periodicals
      Scottish periodicals
      Welsh periodicals
British physicists
  See Physicists, British
British pistols
  See Pistols, British
British poetry
  See English poetry
      Irish poetry
      Scottish poetry
      Welsh poetry
British pound
  See Pound, British
British propaganda
  See Propaganda, British
British property in foreign countries
  xx Alien property
British property in Poland, ₍the Czechoslovak
      Republic, Yugoslavia, etc.₎

British silver articles
   See Silver articles, British
British silver boxes
   See Silver boxes, British
British-Soviet treaty, 1942
   See Anglo-Russian treaty, 1942
British-Spanish War . . .
   See Anglo-Spanish War . . .
British students in the United States, [etc.]
British water-color painting
   See Water-color painting, British
British wit and humor
   See English wit and humor
Britons
   xx Celts
Brittany in literature
Brittany spaniels
   xx Spaniels
Brittle-stars
   See Ophiuroidea
Brittleness *(TA418.16)*
   sa Fracture of solids
     Notch effect
     subdivision Brittleness *under special*
      materials, e.g. Metals—Brittleness;
      Steel—Brittleness
   x Materials—Brittleness
   xx Fracture of solids
     Materials—Testing
     Plasticity
Broaches (Machinery)
   See Broaching machines
Broaching
   sa Broaching machines
   xx Broaching machines
     Drilling and boring
     Metal-cutting
   — Production standards
Broaching machines *(TJ1250)*
   sa Broaching
   x Broaches (Machinery)
   xx Broaching
     Drilling and boring machinery
     Metal-cutting
   — Design and construction *(TJ1250)*
   — Standards *(Direct)*
Broad bean
   x English bean
     Faba bean
     Horse bean
     Windsor bean
   xx Beans
   — Genetics
Broad bean as feed *(SF99.B7)*
Broad-bean weevil
   xx Bean-weevil
Broad Church Movement *(BX5117)*
   xx Church of England—Parties and
     movements
Broad mite
   Example under Mites
Broad-nosed grain weevil
   xx Beetles
Broadband amplifiers
   sa Distributed amplifiers
   x Wide-band amplifiers
Broadcasting
   See Radio broadcasting
Broadcasting, Educational
   See Educational broadcasting
Broadcasting, International
   See International broadcasting
Broadening, Collision
   See Collision broadening
Broadsides
   sa Playbills
     Proclamations
     Wall newspapers

   x Ballad-sheets
   xx Journalism
     Street literature
   — 15th and 16th centuries *(Z240.4)*
Broadway checkers *(GV1469.B7)*
   xx Checkers
Brocade *(Art, NK8900-8999)*
   xx Silk
Broccoli *(SB351.B7)*
   xx Cabbage
   — Varieties
Brochs
Broeders des Gemeenen Levens
   See Brothers of the Common Life
Brohki language
   See Brahui language
Broilers (Poultry)
   xx Poultry
Broiling *(TX687)*
   x Infra-red broiling
   xx Cookery
Brokage, Marriage
   See Marriage brokerage
Broken homes
   sa Children of divorced parents
   x Homes, Broken
   xx Divorce
     Family
     Father-separated children
     Home
Brokerage, Marriage
   See Marriage brokerage
Brokers *(Direct)* *(HF5421; Stockbrokers,*
     HG4621)
     Here are entered general works and
     works on stockbrokers and brokerage.
     Works dealing with other types of
     brokerage are entered under the name
     of the specific business, *e.g.* Insurance;
     Real estate business.
   sa Agency (Law)
     Commission-merchants
     Foreign-exchange brokers
     Over-the-counter markets
     Ship brokers
     Stock-exchange
   x Outside brokers
     Stock brokers
     Stockbrokers
   xx Agency (Law)
     Commerical law
     Investments
     Stock-exchange
     Wall Street
   — Accounting *(HF5686.B65)*
     x Stock-exchange—Accounting
   — Examinations, questions, etc.
   — Taxation *(Direct)*
Brokers, Marriage
   See Marriage brokerage
Brokers in public contracts, etc.
   x Intermediaries in public contracts, etc.
   xx Government purchasing
     Public administration
     Public contracts
Brokers' loans *(Direct)*
   x Call loans
   xx Bank loans
Brome-grass *(Culture, SB201.B8)*
   x Bromegrass
     Cheat (Grass)
     Chess (Grass)
     Rescue-grass
   xx Forage plants
   Example under Grasses
Bromegrass
   See Brome-grass

Bromegrass seed
   xx Grass seed
Bromelain
   See Bromelin
Bromelin
   x Bromelain
   xx Pineapple
Bromic acid *(Chemical technology, TP217.B;*
     Chemistry, QD181.B7)
Bromide ions
   xx Ions
Bromides
Bromides in the body *(QP535.B7)*
Bromination *(QP281.B7)*
Bromine *(QD181.B7)*
   xx Halogens
   — Isotopes
     x Bromine isotopes
      Isotopic bromine
   — — Decay
   — — Spectra
   — Spectra
Bromine isotopes
   See Bromine—Isotopes
Bromoform *(Chemistry, QD305.H6;*
     Physiological effects, QP915.B7;
     Therapeutics, RM666.B)
Brömsebro, Treaty of, 1541 *(DL703)*
Brömsebro, Treaty of, 1645 *(DL190)*
Bronchi *(QL854; QM257)*
   x Bronchia
   — Blood-vessels
   — — Radiography
   — Cancer *(RC280.B)*
   — Dilatation
     See Bronchiectasis
   — Diseases *(RC778)*
     sa Bronchi—Radiography
      Bronchial spasm
      Bronchiectasis
      Bronchodilator agents
      Bronchopneumonia
      Bronchopulmonary spirochaetosis
   — Exploration
   — Radiography
     x Bronchi—X-ray examination
     xx Bronchi—Diseases
     Example under Diagnosis, Radioscopic;
      Radiography
   — Secretions
     xx Body fluids
   — Tuberculosis
   — Tumors
   — X-ray examination
     See Bronchi—Radiography
Bronchia
   See Bronchi
Bronchial injections
   See Injections, Bronchial
Bronchial spasm
   sa Bronchoconstrictor agents
   xx Bronchi—Diseases
Bronchiectasia
   See Bronchiectasis
Bronchiectasis
   x Bronchi—Dilatation
     Bronchiectasia
   xx Bronchi—Diseases
   — Personal narratives
Bronchitis *(RC778)*
   sa Infectious bronchitis in poultry
   xx Cough
   Example under Medicine—Practice; Respira-
     tory organs—Diseases; Therapeutics
Bronchocele
   See Goiter
Bronchoconstrictor agents
   x Bronchospastic drugs

Drugs, Bronchoconstrictor
Drugs, Bronchospastic
xx Bronchial spasm
Bronchodilator agents
sa Adrenalin
x Bronchodilator drugs
Bronchospasmolytic drugs
Drugs, Bronchodilator
Drugs, Bronchospasmolytic
xx Bronchi—Diseases
Bronchodilator drugs
See Bronchodilator agents
Bronchopneumonia (RC772.B7)
xx Bronchi—Diseases
Pneumonia
Bronchopulmonary spirochaetosis (RC778)
x Bronchospirochaetosis
Castellani's bronchitis
Hemorrhagic bronchitis
Spirochaetosis, Bronchopulmonary
xx Bronchi—Diseases
Bronchoscope and bronchoscopy (RC778)
xx Endoscope and endoscopy
Lungs—Diseases
Bronchospasmolytic drugs
See Bronchodilator agents
Bronchospastic drugs
See Bronchoconstrictor agents
Bronchospirochaetosis
See Bronchopulmonary spirochaetosis
Bronchospirometry (RC734.B76)
xx Pulmonary function tests
Brong (African people)
See Abron (African people)
Bronze (Manufacture, TS570)
sa Aluminum bronze
Beryllium bronze
Bronzes
Founding
Lead bronze
Metal-work
Tungsten bronze
xx Copper alloys
Founding
Tin
Tin alloys
— Analysis (QD133)
— Corrosion
— Metallurgy
Bronze age (Indirect) (GN777-8)
sa Beaker cultures
Copper age
Iron age
Lausitz culture
x Prehistory
xx Copper age
Iron age
Man, Prehistoric
— Juvenile literature
Bronze birch borer (SB945.B)
xx Birch—Diseases and pests
Bronze coins
xx Coins
Bronze doors (Direct)
xx Art metal-work
Doors
Metal doors
Bronze doors, Byzantine (Direct)
x Byzantine bronze doors
Bronze founding
xx Founding
Bronze ingots
xx Ingots, Bronze
Bronzed cowbird
x Red-eyed cowbird
xx Cowbirds
Bronzed skin
See Addison's disease

Bronzes (Direct) (Art, NK7900-7999;
Technology, TS570)
x Figurines
Statuettes
xx Art
Art, Decorative
Art metal-work
Bronze
Decoration and ornament
Sculpture
Example under Art objects
— Catalogs
— Conservation and restoration
— Expertising
— Oriental [etc.] influences
— Private collections
Bronzes, Ancient
Bronzes, Baroque (Direct)
x Baroque bronzes
Bronzes, Byzantine
x Byzantine bronzes
Bronzes, Greek, [Italian, Japanese, etc.]
(Direct)
x Greek [Italian, Japanese, etc.] bronzes
Bronzes, Iberian
sa Bronzes, Portuguese
Bronzes, Spanish
x Iberian bronzes
Bronzes, Medieval (Direct)
Bronzes, Portuguese
x Portuguese bronzes
xx Bronzes, Iberian
Bronzes, Renaissance (Direct)
x Renaissance bronzes
Bronzes, Romanesque (Direct)
x Romanesque bronzes
Bronzes, Spanish
x Spanish bronzes
xx Bronzes, Iberian
Bronzing (TS715; TT380)
sa Metals—Coloring
xx Metals—Coloring
Plating
Example under Occupations, Dangerous
Brooches
sa Fibula (Archaeology)
x Breastpins
xx Fibula (Archaeology)
Jewelry
Brooders
See Incubators
Brooding
See Eggs—Incubation
Brook Farm (HX656.B8; American
philosophy, B905)
xx Cooperative societies
Transcendentalism (New England)
Brook stickleback (QL638.G27)
Brook trout
x Speckled trout
Squaretail
xx Trout
Brook trout fishing
xx Fishing
Trout fishing
Brooks' comet (QB723.B7)
Broom, Scotch
See Scotch broom
Broom, Spanish
See Spanish broom
Broom and brush industry (Direct)
(Economics, HD9999.B8;
HD9999.B84; Technology, TS2301)
sa Trade-unions—Broom and brush
industry
Wages—Broom and brush industry
x Brush industry
xx Brooms and brushes

— Collective labor agreements
See Collective labor agreements—
Broom and brush industry
Broom-corn (Botany, QK495.G74; Culture,
SB317.B8)
x Broom millet
Broomcorn
xx Sorghum
Broom millet
See Broom-corn
Broomcorn
See Broom-corn
Brooms and brushes (Direct) (TS2301.B8)
sa Broom and brush industry
Shaving-brushes
x Brushes
Brorsen's comet (I) (QB723.B8)
Brothels
See Prostitution
Brotherhood
See Brotherhoods
Brotherliness
Brotherhoods (BV950-970)
sa Brotherliness
Brothers (in religious orders,
congregations, etc.)
Gilds
Lay brothers
Monasticism and religious orders
x Brotherhood
xx Church societies
Men
Secret societies
Societies
Brotherliness (BV4647.B7)
x Brotherhood
xx Brotherhoods
Brothers, Lay
See Lay brothers
**Brothers (in religious orders, congregations,
etc.)** (BX2835)
x Monasticism and religious orders—
Brothers
Religious brothers
xx Brotherhoods
Monasticism and religious orders
Brothers and sisters
sa Twins
x Siblings
Sisters and brothers
xx Child study
Family
Twins
— Juvenile literature
**Brothers and sisters (in religion, folk-lore,
etc.)** (Folk-lore, GR473)
x Folk-lore of brothers and sisters
xx Religion, Primitive
Brothers in the Bible
x Bible—Brothers
xx Bible—Biography
Brothers of Jesus
See Jesus Christ—Brethren
Brothers of St. Francis Xavier
See Xaverian Brothers
Brothers of the Common Life (BX3070)
sa Devotio moderna
x Brethren of the Common Life
Broeders des Gemeenen Levens
Brüder des Gemeinsamen Lebens
xx Friends of God ("Gottesfreunde")
Monasticism and religious orders
Brothers of the Free Spirit
See Brethren of the Free Spirit
Brotherton Indians
xx Algonquian Indians
Indians of North America
Mahican Indians

Brotherton Indians *(Continued)*
    Mohegan Indians
    Montauk Indians
    Narraganset Indians
    Pequot Indians
    Stockbridge Indians
    Wappinger Indians
Broussaisism *(R733.B9)*
  xx Medicine
Brown bullhead
  x Bullhead, Brown
    Horned pout
  xx Catfishes
Brown coal
  See Lignite
Brown ear tick *(QL458.A2)*
Brown hare
  See European hare
Brown-headed chickadee
  x Acadian chickadee
  xx Chickadees
Brown Indian hemp
  See Ambary hemp
Brown lemming
  xx Lemmings
Brown pelican
  xx Pelicans
  — Juvenile literature
Brown rot
Brown rot of potato
  See Bacterial wilt of potato
Brown Swiss cattle
Brown-tail moth *(SB495.B9)*
  xx Moths
Brown trout
  xx Trout
Brown trout fishing
  xx Fishing
    Trout fishing
Brownian motion processes *(QA274.75)*
  x Wiener processes
  xx Brownian movements
    Markov processes
Brownian movements *(QC183)*
  sa Brownian motion processes
  xx Capillarity
    Liquids
    Matter—Properties
Brownie camera
  xx Kodak camera
Browning automatic pistol
  xx Browning firearms
    Pistols
Browning automatic rifle *(UD395.B8)*
  xx Browning firearms
    Rifles
Browning firearms
  sa Browning automatic pistol
    Browning automatic rifle
    Browning machine-gun
  xx Firearms
Browning machine-gun *(UF620.B)*
  xx Browning firearms
    Machine-guns
Brownists
  sa Pilgrim Fathers
  xx Congregationalism
    Pilgrim Fathers
    Puritans
Brownstown, Mich., Battle of, Aug. 5, 1812
    (E356.B8)
Brownstown, Mich., Battle of, Aug. 9, 1812
  See Monguagon, Mich., Battle of, Aug. 9,
    1812
Brownsville, Tex.
  — Riot, 1906 *(UB323.A4)*
Browse
  sa Chaparral

  xx Deer—Food
    Forage plants
Brucella vaccines
  See Brucellosis vaccines
Brucelliasis
  See Brucellosis
Brucellosis *(Direct)* *(QR201.B8)*
  x Brucelliasis
    Malta fever
    Undulant fever
  xx Zoonoses
  — Prevention
Brucellosis in cattle *(SF967.B7)*
  x Bang's disease
    Bovine brucellosis
    Contagious abortion
    Infectious abortion
  xx Abortion in animals
    Cattle—Diseases
    Communicable diseases in animals
Brucellosis in sheep
  x Ovine brucellosis
Brucellosis in swine *(SF971)*
Brucellosis vaccines *(QR189.5.B7)*
  x Brucella vaccines
Brucite *(Indirect)* *(QE391.B)*
Brüder des Gemeinsamen Lebens
  See Brothers of the Common Life
'Brug-pa (Sect) *(BQ7673)*
  x Dookpa
    Drukpa
    Dugpa
    Duk (Sect)
    Dukpa
  xx Bka'-rgyud-pa (Sect)
    Lamaist sects
  — Prayer-books and devotions
Brulé Indians *(E99.B8)*
  xx Dakota Indians
    Indians of North America
    Teton Indians
  — Pictorial works
Brunanburh, Battle of, 937 *(DA154.1)*
Brunca Indians
  See Boruca Indians
Brunches
  sa Breakfasts
    Luncheons
  xx Breakfasts
    Luncheons
Brunete, Battle of, 1937
  xx Spain—History—Civil War, 1936-1939
    —Campaigns and battles
Brunka Indians
  See Boruca Indians
Brunka language
  See Boruca language
Brünn
  — Siege, 1645 *(D276.B8)*
    xx Thirty Years' War, 1618-1648
Brunner's glands *(QL863; QM345)*
  x Glands of Brunner
Brunswick pottery *(NK4340.B7)*
  x Pottery, Brunswick
  xx Pottery, German
Brush
  xx Forests and forestry
  — Control
    See Brush control
Brush arc-light system *(TK4329.B)*
  xx Electric lighting, Arc
Brush control *(Indirect)* *(SB611-618)*
  sa Sagebrush—Control
  x Brush—Control
  xx Weed control
Brush drawing *(ND2460)*
  sa Pen drawing
    Sepia painting

    Sumie
  x Ink brushwork
    Wash drawing
  xx Drawing
    Pen drawing
    Sepia painting
Brush holders (Electrical engineering)
  xx Brushes, Electric
Brush industry
  See Broom and brush industry
Brush mouse
  xx Mice
Brush-tailed phalangers
  x Brush-tailed possums
    Vulpine phalangers
  xx Marsupialia
Brush-tailed possums
  See Brush-tailed phalangers
Brushes
  See Brooms and brushes
Brushes, Artists'
  See Artists' brushes
Brushes, Carbon *(TK2484)*
  sa Brushes, Electric
  x Carbon brushes
  xx Brushes, Electric
    Electric machinery
  — Tariff
    See Tariff on carbon brushes
Brushes, Electric *(TK2484)*
  sa Brush holders (Electrical engineering)
    Brushes, Carbon
  x Electric brushes
  xx Brushes, Carbon
    Commutation (Electricity)
    Electric machinery
Brusol, Treaty of, 1610 *(DC123.5)*
Brussels
  — History
  — — Insurrection, 1830
Brussels griffon *(SF429.B79)*
  x Griffon, Brussels
Brussels sprouts
  sa Cookery (Brussels sprouts)
  xx Cabbage
Brutalism (Architecture) *(Direct)*
  x Brutalist architecture
    New brutalism (Architecture)
  xx Architecture, Modern—20th century
Brutalist architecture
  See Brutalism (Architecture)
Brutality
  See Cruelty
Bryan Station, Ky.
  — Siege, 1782 *(F454)*
Bryology
  sa Bryophytes
    Mosses
  x Muscology
  xx Botany
    Bryophytes
Bryophyta
  See Bryophytes
Bryophytes *(Indirect)* *(QK533)*
  sa Bryology
    Liverworts
    Mosses
  x Bryophyta
  xx Bryology
    Cryptogams
  — Identification
Bryophytes, Fossil
Bryozoa
  See Polyzoa
Brzeziny, Battle of, 1914 *(D552.B7)*
  xx European War, 1914-1918—Campaigns
    —Eastern

Bu Indians
See Timbira Indians
Buandik (Australian people)
x Booandik (Australian people)
xx Australian aborigines
Buang language
Bubangi language
See Bobangi language
Bubble-cap plate towers
See Plate towers
Bubble chamber
xx Ionization chambers
Bubble gum
xx Chewing-gum
Bubbler (Fish)
See Fresh-water drum
Bubbles
xx Air
Gases
— Juvenile literature
Bube (African tribe)
x Bubi (African tribe)
Bubis (African tribe)
Ediya (African tribe)
xx Bantus
Bube language *(PL8091)*
x Adiyah language
Boube language
Bubi language
Ediya language
Fernandian language
xx Bantu languages
Bubi (African tribe)
See Bube (African tribe)
Bubi language
See Bube language
Bubis (African tribe)
See Bube (African tribe)
Buboes *(RC201)*
Bubonic plague
See Plague
Bubonidae
See Owls
Bubonocele
See Hernia
Buccaneers *(F2161; G535-7)*
sa Brigands and robbers
Filibusters
Pirates
Sea stories
x Filibusters (West Indian buccaneers)
Freebooters
xx Naval history
Pirates
Voyages and travels
— Juvenile literature
Bucchero (Pottery)
xx Pottery, Etruscan
Buchanites *(BX6510.B9)*
Bucharest
— Railroad Workers' Strike, February 1933
Bucharest, Treaty of, 1913 *(DR46.95)*
xx Balkan Peninsula—History—War of
1912-1913
Bucharest, Treaty of, 1918 *(D614.B8)*
xx European War, 1914-1918—Treaties
Buchenwald case, 1947
See War crime trials—Dachau—
Buchenwald case, 1947
Bucherer reaction
xx Chemical reactions
Buchmanism
See Oxford Group
Büchner-Preis
See Georg-Büchner-Preis
Bucket-shops
See Speculation

Buckets
See Pails
Buckeye (Training planes)
See T2J (Training planes)
Buckles *(Direct)*
sa Belt buckles
Shoe buckles
xx Clasps
Buckling (Mechanics) *(Mathematics, QA935;
Strength of materials, TA410;
Theory of structures, TG265)*
sa Structural stability
xx Deformations (Mechanics)
Plasticity
Strains and stresses
Buckling (Nuclear reactors)
See Nuclear reactors—Buckling
Bucknell University, Lewisburg, Pa.
— Gifts, legacies
Example under Legacies
Buckshot War, 1838 *(F153)*
x Harrisburg Insurrection, 1838
Buckthorn
sa Cascara
Frangula
xx Cascara
Frangula
— Diseases and pests
Buckwheat *(Indirect)* *(Culture, SB191.B9;
Trade, HD9049.B7-8)*
sa Cookery (Buckwheat)
Example under Agriculture
Bucolic literature
See Pastoral literature
Bucolic poetry
See Pastoral poetry
Bud-grafting
See Budding
Bud-moth
xx Moths
Buda
— Siege, 1684
— Siege, 1686
Budapest
— Siege, 1945 *(D765.562.B8)*
Buddha (The concept) *(BQ4180)*
x Buddhakāya (Buddhism)
Dharmakāya (Buddhism)
Nirmāṇakāya (Buddhism)
Sambhogakāya (Buddhism)
Tathāgata (Buddhism)
Trikāya (Buddhism)
xx Buddhist doctrines
Buddha and Buddhism *(Direct)*
sa Abhidharma
Ajivikas
Brahmanism
Buddhists
Caodaism
Communism and Buddhism
Cultus, Buddhist
Dharma (Buddhism)
Gods, Buddhist
Hayagrīva
Hell (Buddhism)
Hinayana Buddhism
Jains
Karma
Lamaism
Mahayana Buddhism
Meditation (Buddhism)
Miracles (Buddhism)
Monasteries, Buddhist
Nirvana
Ordination (Buddhism)
Pali literature
Parables, Buddhist
Perfection (Buddhism)

Philosophy, Buddhist
Preaching, Buddhist
Religious life (Buddhism)
Saddharma
Siddhas
Sociology, Buddhist
Stūpas
Tantric Buddhism
Tendai Buddhism
Theosophy
Women in Buddhism
Zen Buddhism
headings beginning with the words
Buddhism *and* Buddhist
x Buddhism
xx Hinduism
Religions
Theosophy
— Early Buddhism, ca. 486 B.C.-ca. 100
A.D.
x Early Buddhism
Original Buddhism
Primitive Buddhism
xx Buddhist doctrines
Philosophy, Buddhist
— — Introductions
— 20th century

GENERAL SUBDIVISIONS

— Anecdotes, facetiae, satire, etc.

GENERAL SUBDIVISIONS

— Biography *(BQ840-858)*
x Buddhist biography
Buddhists—Biography
xx Religious biography
— Catechisms and creeds *(BQ4170)*
— Charities *(Indirect)*
— Collections
sa Buddha and Buddhism—Sacred
books
— Confession (Liturgy)
See Confession (Liturgy)—Buddhism
— Controversial literature
— Dictionaries
x Buddhist doctrines—Dictionaries
— Discipline
sa Buddhist precepts
Five Precepts (Buddhism)
x Buddhist discipline
Vinaya
— Education
x Buddhist education
Buddhists—Education
— Essence, genius, nature
— History
— — To ca. 100 A.D.

GENERAL SUBDIVISIONS

— — Philosophy *(BQ282)*
xx History (Buddhism)
History—Philosophy
— Hymns
See Buddhist hymns
— Influence *(Direct)*
— Juvenile literature
— Liturgical objects
See Buddhist liturgical objects
— Miscellanea *(BQ4060)*
— Missions *(Indirect)* *(BL1478.9)*
Here are entered works on the spread
of Buddhism. Works on the spread
of Christianity among Buddhists
are entered under Missions to Bud-
dhists.
sa subdivision Missions *under names of*
individual Buddhist sects, e.g.
Shin (Sect)—Missions

231

Buddha and Buddhism *(Direct)*
(Continued)
— Natural history
— Origin
— Philosophy
   xx Buddhist doctrines
      Philosophy and religion
      Philosophy, Buddhist
      Religion—Philosophy
— Pictures, illustrations, etc.
— Prayer-books and devotions
   sa Buddhist prayers
   xx Buddhist liturgies
— Psychology
   sa Zen Buddhism—Psychology
   x Buddhist psychology
      Psychology, Buddhist
— Quotations, maxims, etc. *(BQ135)*
   x Maxims, Buddhist
— Relations
— — Christianity, ₁Islam, etc.₁
— Research
   See Buddhist research
— Rites and ceremonies
   See Buddhist rites and ceremonies
— Rituals
   sa Buddhist liturgies
      Chants (Buddhist)
      Funeral rites and ceremonies,
         Buddhist
      Memorial rites and ceremonies,
         Buddhist
      Omizutori
      Temples, Buddhist—Dedication
   subdivision Rituals *under names of*
      individual sects, e.g. Rinzai (Sect)
      —Rituals
   xx Buddhist rites and ceremonies
      Ritual
— Sacred books *(Pali literature,*
      PK4501-4681)
   xx Buddha and Buddhism—Collections
   Example under Sacred books
— — Language, style
— — Preservation *(Direct)*
   sa Kyōzuka
      Kyōzutsu
— — Quotations
— Sects
   See Buddhist sects
Buddhahood
   x Bodhisattvahood
      Buddhaship
Buddhakāya (Buddhism)
   See Buddha (The concept)
Buddhas *(BQ4670-4690)*
   xx Gods, Buddhist
Buddhaship
   See Buddahood
Buddhism
   See Buddha and Buddhism
Buddhism, Tantric
   See Tantric Buddhism
Buddhism and art *(Theology, BQ4570.A7)*
   x Art and Buddhism
   xx Art and religion
      Art, Buddhist
Buddhism and communism
   See Communism and Buddhism
Buddhism and economics
   sa Buddhist giving
   x Buddhist economics
      Economics and Buddhism
Buddhism and medicine
   See Medicine and Buddhism
Buddhism and politics *(BQ4570.S7)*
   x Politics and Buddhism
   xx Buddhism and state

Buddhism and race problems
   x Race problems and Buddhism
   xx Buddhism and social problems
Buddhism and science
   sa Medicine and Buddhism
   x Science and Buddhism
   xx Religion and science
Buddhism and social problems *(Direct)*
   sa Buddhism and race problems
   x Religion and social problems
      Social problems and Buddhism
   xx Religion and sociology
      Social history
      Social problems
Buddhism and state *(Direct)*
   sa Buddhism and politics
   x State and Buddhism
   xx Nationalism and religion
      Religion and state
— Nichiren (Sect)
   x Nichiren (Sect) and state
      Nichiren (Sect)—Relation to the
      state
Buddhism and war
   See War and Buddhism
Buddhism in literature
   xx Religion in literature
Buddhist almsgiving
   See Buddhist giving
Buddhist antiquities
   sa Kyōzutsu
   subdivision Antiquities, Buddhist *under*
      names of countries, cities, etc.
   x Antiquities, Buddhist
   xx Antiquities
Buddhist architecture
   See Architecture, Buddhist
Buddhist art
   See Art, Buddhist
Buddhist art and symbolism *(Direct)*
   (Buddhist art, N8193; Buddhist
   liturgical objects, NK1676; Buddhist
   painting, ND197; Non-Christian arts,
   NX676; Theology, BQ5100-5125)
   sa Mudrās (Buddhism)
   x Buddhist symbolism
      Symbolism, Buddhist
   xx Art, Buddhist
      Arts, Buddhist
      Symbolism
      Symbolism in art
Buddhist art objects
   See Art objects, Buddhist
Buddhist arts
   See Arts, Buddhist
Buddhist beads
   See Buddhist rosary
Buddhist biography
   See Buddha and Buddhism—Biography
Buddhist calendar
   See Calendar, Buddhist
Buddhist cave temples
   See Cave temples, Buddhist
Buddhist chants
   See Chants (Buddhist)
Buddhist civilization
   See Civilization, Buddhist
Buddhist convents and nunneries
   See Convents and nunneries, Buddhist
Buddhist converts
   x Converts, Buddhist
      Converts to Buddhism
   Note under Converts
Buddhist converts from Christianity
   x Converts from Christianity to
      Buddhism
Buddhist converts from Hinduism
   x Hindu converts to Buddhism

Buddhist converts to Christianity
   See Converts from Buddhism
Buddhist cosmogony
   See Cosmogony, Buddhist
Buddhist cosmology
   See Cosmology, Buddhist
Buddhist councils and synods
   x Buddhist synods
      Councils and synods, Buddhist
      Synods, Buddhist
Buddhist counseling
   See Pastoral counseling (Buddhism)
Buddhist cultus
   See Cultus, Buddhist
Buddhist demonology
   See Demonology, Buddhist
Buddhist devotional calendars
   x Devotional calendars—Buddhism
      Devotional calendars, Buddhist
— Shin (Sect), ₁etc.₁
Buddhist devotional literature
   sa Zen devotional literature
   x Devotional literature, Buddhist
   xx Buddhist literature
Buddhist devotional literature, Burmese, ₁etc.₁
   x Burmese ₁etc.₁ Buddhist devotional
      literature
Buddhist discipline
   See Buddha and Buddhism—Discipline
Buddhist doctrines *(Direct)*
   sa Buddha and Buddhism—Early
      Buddhism, ca. 486 B.C.-ca. 100 A.D.
      Buddha and Buddhism—Philosophy
      Chizan (Shingon sect)—Doctrines
      Compassion (Buddhism)
      Demonology, Buddhist
      Devotion (Buddhism)
      Dharma (Buddhism)
      Doubt (Buddhism)
      Eightfold Path
      Enlightenment (Buddhism)
      Enlightenment (Buddhism)—Requisites
      Eschatology, Buddhist
      Faith (Buddhism)
      Four Noble Truths
      Gotra (Buddhism)
      Heresies and heretics, Buddhist
      History (Buddhism)
      Impermanence (Buddhism)
      Kegon (Sect)—Doctrines
      Knowledge, Theory of (Buddhism)
      Lamaist doctrines
      Man (Buddhism)
      Middle Way (Buddhism)
      Moderation (Buddhism)
      Mudrās (Buddhism)
      Mysticism—Buddhism
      Nichiren (Sect)—Doctrines
      Peace (Buddhism)
      Pratītyasamutpāda
      Pratyaya
      Prayer (Buddhism)
      Pure Land Buddhism—Doctrines
      Reincarnation (Buddhism)
      Reward (Buddhism)
      Salvation (Buddhism)
      Satipaṭṭhāna (Buddhism)
      Shin (Sect)—Doctrines
      Shingon (Sect)—Doctrines
      Spirits (Buddhism)
      Sunyata
      Tathāgatagarbha (Buddhism)
      Tendai (Sect)—Doctrines
      Tenrikyō—Doctrines
      Truth (Buddhism)
      Vice (Buddhism)
      Vipaśyanā (Buddhism)
      Virtues (Buddhism)

Wisdom (Buddhism)
Wŏn Pulgyo (Sect)—Doctrines
  x Buddhist theology
  xx Philosophy, Buddhist
     Theology, Doctrinal
— Classification (BQ4175)
— Dictionaries
     See Buddha and Buddhism—
          Dictionaries
— Introductions
Buddhist economics
  See Buddhism and economics
Buddhist education
  See Buddha and Buddhism—Education
Buddhist epistemology
  See Knowledge, Theory of (Buddhism)
Buddhist ethics
  sa Ahiṃsā
     Buddhist etiquette
     Compassion (Buddhism)
     Virtues (Buddhism)
     Youth, Buddhist—Conduct of life
  x Ethics, Buddhist
  xx Religion and ethics
Buddhist etiquette (BJ2019.5.B8)
  x Buddhist temple etiquette
  xx Buddhist ethics
     Etiquette
Buddhist fasts and feasts
  See Fasts and feasts—Buddhism
Buddhist funeral rites and ceremonies
  See Funeral rites and ceremonies, Buddhist
Buddhist giving (BQ4420.G6)
  x Almsgiving, Buddhist
     Buddhist almsgiving
     Buddhist stewardship
     Dāna (Buddhism)
     Giving, Buddhist
     Stewardship, Buddhist
  xx Buddhism and economics
     Buddhist temple finance
     Religious life (Buddhism)
     Virtues (Buddhism)
Buddhist gods
  See Gods, Buddhist
Buddhist heresies and heretics
  See Heresies and heretics, Buddhist
Buddhist hermits (Indirect)
  xx Hermits
     Religious life (Buddhism)
Buddhist homiletics
  See Preaching, Buddhist
Buddhist hymns
  x Buddha and Buddhism—Hymns
     Hymns, Buddhist
Buddhist hymns, English, ⌐Japanese, etc.⌐
Buddhist idealism
  See Yogācāra (Buddhism)
Buddhist incantations
  x Incantations, Buddhist
Buddhist inscriptions
  See Inscriptions, Buddhist
Buddhist laity
  See Buddhist laymen
Buddhist laymen
  x Buddhist laity
     Lay Buddhists
     Upāsaka
     Upāsikā
  xx Laity
— Discipline (BQ5485-5530)
     sa Five Precepts (Buddhism)
Buddhist legends
  See Legends, Buddhist
Buddhist literature
  sa Buddhist devotional literature
     Zen literature
  xx Religious literature

Buddhist literature, Chinese, ⌐Tibetan, etc.⌐
Buddhist liturgical objects (Direct)
     (BQ5070-5075)
  sa Buddhist rosary
  x Buddha and Buddhism—Liturgical
     objects
  xx Cultus, Buddhist
     Liturgical objects
— Tantric Buddhism (BQ8924.5)
     x Tantric Buddhism—Buddhist
        liturgical objects
Buddhist liturgies
  sa Buddha and Buddhism—Prayer-books
     and devotions
     Lamaist liturgies
  x Liturgies—Buddhism
     Liturgies, Buddhist
  xx Buddha and Buddhism—Rituals
     Buddhist rites and ceremonies
Buddhist logic (BC25-26)
  sa Knowledge, Theory of (Buddhism)
  x Logic, Buddhist
  xx Philosophy, Buddhist
— Early works to 1800
Buddhist martyrs (Direct)
  x Martyrs, Buddhist
Buddhist medicine
  See Medicine, Buddhist
Buddhist meditations
  sa Lamaist meditations
  x Meditations, Buddhist
  xx Meditation (Buddhism)
Buddhist memorial rites and ceremonies
  See Memorial rites and ceremonies,
     Buddhist
Buddhist monasteries
  See Monasteries, Buddhist
Buddhist monasticism and religious orders
  See Monasticism and religious orders,
     Buddhist
Buddhist monks (Direct)
  xx Monasticism and religious orders,
     Buddhist
— Discipline (BQ6140)
Buddhist monks as soldiers
  xx Soldiers
Buddhist music
  See Music, Buddhist
Buddhist mythology
  See Mythology, Buddhist
Buddhist novices
  x Novices, Buddhist
     Srāmaṇera
     Srāmaṇerikā
  xx Monasticism and religious orders,
     Buddhist
     Novitiate
— Discipline (Female, BQ6155; Male,
     BQ6145)
Buddhist nuns (Direct)
  xx Convents and nunneries, Buddhist
     Nuns
— Biography (BQ855)
Buddhist ordination
  See Ordination (Buddhism)
Buddhist painting
  See Painting, Buddhist
Buddhist parables
  See Parables, Buddhist
Buddhist philosophical anthropology
  See Man (Buddhism)
Buddhist philosophy
  See Philosophy, Buddhist
Buddhist pilgrims and pilgrimages
  See Pilgrims and pilgrimages, Buddhist
Buddhist poetry (Direct)
  sa Zen poetry
  xx Religious poetry

Buddhist poetry, Korean, ⌐etc.⌐ (Direct)
  x Korean ⌐etc.⌐ Buddhist poetry
  xx Korean ⌐etc.⌐ poetry
Buddhist prayers
  x Prayers, Buddhist
  xx Buddha and Buddhism—Prayer-books
     and devotions
Buddhist preaching
  See Preaching, Buddhist
Buddhist precepts (BQ5485-5530)
  sa Five Precepts (Buddhism)
  x Eight Precepts (Buddhism)
     Ten Precepts (Buddhism)
  xx Buddha and Buddhism—Discipline
Buddhist priests
  See Priests, Buddhist
Buddhist psychology
  See Buddha and Buddhism—Psychology
Buddhist quotations
  See Quotations, Buddhist
Buddhist religious education
  See Religious education, Buddhist
Buddhist research (Direct)
  x Buddha and Buddhism—Research
  xx Research
Buddhist rites and ceremonies (Indirect)
     (BQ4965-5030)
  sa Buddha and Buddhism—Rituals
     Buddhist liturgies
  x Buddha and Buddhism—Rites and
     ceremonies
     Buddhists—Rites and ceremonies
  xx Rites and ceremonies
Buddhist rosary (Liturgical object,
     BQ5075.R7; Meditations,
     BQ5630.R6)
  x Beads, Buddhist
     Buddhist beads
     Juzu
     Rosary, Buddhist
  xx Buddhist liturgical objects
     Meditation (Buddhism)
     Prayer (Buddhism)
Buddhist saints
  See Saints, Buddhist
Buddhist scholars
  See Scholars, Buddhist
Buddhist sculpture
  See Sculpture, Buddhist
Buddhist sects (Direct)
  sa Buzan (Shingon sect)
     Chin'gakchong
     Chizan (Shingon sect)
     Fuju-fuse (Sect)
     Fuke (Sect)
     Heresies and heretics, Buddhist
     Hinayana Buddhism
     Ji (Sect)
     Kegon (Sect)
     Lamaist sects
     Mahāsāṅghikas
     Mahayana Buddhism
     Nichiren (Sect)
     Ramanya (Sect)
     Rinzai (Sect)
     Ritsu (Sect)
     San chieh (Sect)
     Sanron (Sect)
     Sarvāstivādins
     Shin (Sect)
     Shingon (Sect)
     Shugen (Sect)
     Tendai (Sect)
     Wŏn Pulgyo (Sect)
     Wŏnhyo (Sect)
  x Buddha and Buddhism—Sects
     Sects, Buddhist

Buddhist sermons
  sa Shin (Sect)—Sermons
  x Sermons, Buddhist
  xx Preaching, Buddhist
  — History and criticism
    See Preaching, Buddhist—History
Buddhist sermons, Chinese, ₍English,
  Japanese, etc.₎
Buddhist shrines   *(Direct)*
  sa Bodhi Tree
    Lamaist shrines
  x Shrines, Buddhist
Buddhist sociology
  See Sociology, Buddhist
Buddhist stewardship
  See Buddhist giving
Buddhist stories   *(Direct)*   *(BQ1031-1045)*
  sa Zen stories
  x Stories, Buddhist
Buddhist stories, Japanese, ₍etc.₎   *(Direct)*
  x Japanese ₍etc.₎ Buddhist stories
Buddhist symbolism
  See Buddhist art and symbolism
Buddhist synods
  See Buddhist councils and synods
Buddhist tales
  See Tales, Buddhist
Buddhist tantrism
  See Tantric Buddhism
Buddhist teachings
  See Dharma (Buddhism)
Buddhist temple etiquette
  See Buddhist etiquette
Buddhist temple finance   *(Direct)*
    (BQ5136-5139)
  sa Buddhist giving
  x Finance, Buddhist temple
    Temple finance, Buddhist
Buddhist temple records and registers
  See Temple records and registers, Buddhist
Buddhist temples
  See Temples, Buddhist
Buddhist theology
  See Buddhist doctrines
Buddhist virtues
  See Virtues (Buddhism)
Buddhist women
  See Women, Buddhist
Buddhist youth
  See Youth, Buddhist
Buddhists
  sa Missions to Buddhists
    Zen Buddhists
  xx Buddha and Buddhism
  — Biography
    See Buddha and Buddhism—
      Biography
  — Education
    See Buddha and Buddhism—
      Education
  — Persecutions   *(Direct)*
    xx Persecution
  — Rites and ceremonies
    See Buddhist rites and ceremonies
Buddhists in the United States, ₍Venezuela,
  etc.₎
Budding   *(SB125)*
  x Bud-grafting
  xx Grafting
    Plant propagation
    Reproduction, Asexual
Budgerigar breeding   *(SF473.B8)*
  x Budgerigars—Breeding
Budgerigars   *(SF473.B)*
  x Australian lovebird
    Betcherrygah
    Budgie birds
    Budgies

Budjeregar
  Canary parrot
  Grass parakeet
  Parakeet
  Parrakeet
  Shell parakeet
  Undulated parakeet
  Warbling grass parakeet
  Zebra parakeet
  xx Parrots
  — Breeding
    See Budgerigar breeding
  — Diseases
  — Feeding and feeds
  — Legends and stories
Budget   *(Direct)*   *(HJ2005-2199)*
  sa Capital budget
    Legislative auditing
    Local budgets
    Program budgeting
    Special funds
    subdivision Appropriations and
      expenditures *under names of*
      government departments, agencies,
      etc.
  xx Expenditures, Public
    Finance, Public
  — Programmed instruction

GEOGRAPHIC SUBDIVISIONS

  — United States
  — — States
    x State budgets
    xx Finance, Public—United States—
      States
Budget, Energy (Geophysics)
  See Energy budget (Geophysics)
Budget, Heat (Geophysics)
  See Heat budget (Geophysics)
Budget, Mass (Geophysics)
  See Mass budget (Geophysics)
Budget in business
  x Business budgeting
  xx Business
    Controllership
    Finance
  — Mathematical models
Budgets, County
  See County budgets
Budgets, Family
  See Budgets, Personal
    Home economics—Accounting
Budgets, Household
  See Home economics—Accounting
Budgets, Municipal
  See Municipal budgets
Budgets, Personal
  x Budgets, Family
    Personal budgets
  xx Cost and standard of living
    Finance, Personal
Budgets, School
  See School budgets
Budgets, Time
  See Time allocation
Budgie birds
  See Budgerigars
Budgies
  See Budgerigars
Budja (African tribe)   *(DT650)*
  x Boudja (African tribe)
    Bujia (African tribe)
  xx Ethnology—Zaire
Budjeregar
  See Budgerigars
Buds
  sa Shoots (Botany)
  xx Botany

  Shoots (Botany)
  — Juvenile literature
Buduma (African people)
  x Yedina (African people)
  xx Ethnology—Chad
    Ethnology—Niger
    Ethnology—Nigeria
Budworm, Corn
  See Spotted cucumber beetle
Buem language
  See Lefana language
Buena Vista, Battle of, 1847   *(E406.B9)*
Buenos Aires (Province) in literature
Buenos Aires in literature
Buerger's disease
  See Thromboangitis obliterans
Bufa, Cerro de la, Battle of, 1872
  See Zacatecas, Battle of, 1872
Buff-colored tomato weevil
  See Vegetable weevil
Buffalo
  — Commerce
  — Riot, 1967
Buffalo, American
  See Bison, American
Buffalo breeding   *(Indirect)*
  x Buffaloes—Breeding
  xx Stock and stock-breeding
Buffalo bugs
  See Carpet beetles
Buffalo carpet beetles
  See Carpet beetles
Buffalo Creek, W.Va.
  — Flood, 1972
Buffalo drive
  See Buffalo jump
Buffalo fish
Buffalo jump
  x Buffalo drive
  xx Bison, American
    Indians of North America—Hunting
Buffaloes   *(QL737.U5)*
    Here are entered works on the buffaloes
      of the eastern hemisphere. Not to be
      confused with Bison, American.
  sa Water buffalo
  x Gaur
    Seladang
  xx Ruminantia
  Example under Zoology
  — Breeding
    See Buffalo breeding
  — Diseases
    sa Hemorrhagic septicemia of cattle
  — Legends and stories   *(QL795.B)*
  — Physiology
Buffaloes (in religion, folk-lore, etc.)
  x Folk-lore of buffaloes
  xx Animals, Legends and stories of
    Religion, Primitive
Buffer solutions
  xx Acid-base equilibrium
    Hydrogen-ion concentration
    Ionic solutions
  — Tables
Buffet suppers
  See Suppers
Buffeting (Aerodynamics)
  x Aeroplanes—Buffeting
  xx Aerodynamics
    Turbulence
    Vibration (Aeronautics)
Buffing
  See Grinding and polishing
Bufflehead   *(QL696.A5)*
  xx Ducks
  — Behavior

Buffy coat
    See Blood—Buffy coat
Bugaku
    xx Gagaku
Bugatti automobile
Bugeyes (Boats) *(VM311.B8)*
    x Chesapeake Bay bugeyes
       Oyster dredgers
       Oyster fishing boats
    xx Fishing boats
       Sailboats
Buggery
    See Bestiality (Law)
       Sodomy
Bugi language
    See Buginese language
Buginese (Malay people)
    See Bugis (Malay people)
Buginese language *(PL5271)*
    sa Makasar language
       Malayan languages
    x Bugi language
    xx Makasar language
       Malayan languages
Bugis (Malay people)
    x Buginese (Malay people)
    xx Ethnology—Indonesia
Bugle *(ML960-961)*
    sa Trumpet
Bugle and drum corps
    x Drum and bugle corps
Bugle and drum music *(M1270)*
    x Drum and bugle music
    xx Percussion music
       Trumpet music
Bugle-calls
    sa Military calls
       Trumpet-calls
    xx Fanfares
       Hunting music
       Military calls
       Military music
       Signals and signaling
       Trumpet-calls
Bugonia *(Animal lore, QL89)*
    xx Animal lore
Bugotu language *(PL6225)*
    x Mahaga language
    xx Melanesian languages
Buhach
    See Pyrethrum
Buick automobile *(TL215.B)*
Builders' plant
    See Construction equipment
Building *(Direct) (TH)*
    Here are entered works dealing with the
    process of construction. Works on the
    construction business, including fi-
    nance, planning, management, and
    skills are entered under Construction
    industry. Works on types of labor in-
    volved are entered under the heading
    Building trades.
    sa Aluminum construction
       Arches
       Architecture
       Areaways
       Bricklaying
       Building fittings
       Building sites
       Building trades
       Buildings
       Carpentry
       Ceilings
       Chimneys
       Concrete construction
       Construction equipment
       Construction industry

Contractors' operations
Cornice work
Doors
Earth movements and building
Environmental engineering (Buildings)
Extraterrestrial bases
Finials
Floors
Folded plate structures
Foundations
Framing (Building)
Girders
Glass construction
Gutters
House construction
Industrialized building
Lathing
Lightweight construction
Masonry
Modular coordination (Architecture)
Moldings
Painting, Structural
Pisé
Prestressed construction
Rabitz construction
Roofs
Sanitary engineering
Sashes
Scaffolding
Shoring and underpinning
Skylights
Soil-cement construction
Space frame structures
Stair building
Struts (Engineering)
Tie-rods
Tile construction
Trusses
Underground construction
Underwater construction
Vaults (Architecture)
Walls
Windows
Wrecking
    x Architectural engineering
       Construction
       Engineering, Architectural
    xx Architecture
       Building trades
       Buildings
       Construction industry
       Structural design
       Structural engineering
       Technology
    Notes under Buildings; Construction industry
— Abstracts
— Accidents *(TH443)*
    sa Building failures
       subdivision Accidents *under specific*
       building operations, e.g. Roofing
       —Accidents
    x Construction industry—Accidents
— Accounting
    See Construction industry—
       Accounting
— Amateurs' manuals *(TH148)*
— Anecdotes, facetiae, satire, etc.
— Caricatures and cartoons
— Catalogs
— Classification
— Cold weather conditions
    Example under Cold
— Contracts and specifications *(Direct)*
    (TH425)
    sa Airports—Contracts and
       specifications
       Buildings—Mechanical equipment—
       Contracts and specifications

Contracts, Letting of
    Farm buildings—Contracts and
       specifications
    House construction—Contracts and
       specifications
    School buildings—Contracts and
       specifications
    x Building materials—Specifications
       Building—Specifications
       Construction industry—Contracts
       and specifications
    xx Building laws
       Contracts for work and labor
    Example under Contracts; Specifications
— Cost control
— Costs
    See Building—Estimates
— Details *(TH2031-3000)*
    x Buildings—Details
—— Drawings *(TH2031)*
— Early works to 1800
— Estimates *(Direct) (TH434-7)*
    x Building—Costs
       Building—Price books
       Construction industry—Estimates
       Quantity surveying
    xx Specifications
    Example under reference from Estimates
—— Problems, exercises, etc. *(TH435)*
— Examinations, questions, etc.
— Information services
— Inspection
    See Building inspection
— Juvenile literature
— Laboratory manuals
— Laws and regulations
    See Building laws
— Management
    See Construction industry—
       Management
— Materials
    See Building materials
— Modular coordination
    See Modular coordination
       (Architecture)
— Patents
— Pictures, illustrations, etc.
— Price books
    See Building—Estimates
— Prices *(Direct)*
    x Building prices
       Construction prices
— Problems, exercises, etc.
— Quality control
— Research
    See Building research
— Safety measures
    x Construction industry—Safety
       measures
— Specifications
    See Building—Contracts and
       specifications
— Study and teaching
    x Building trades—Study and teaching
—— Audio-visual aids
— Superintendence *(TH438)*
    x Building superintendence
    xx Construction industry—Management
—— Examinations, questions, etc.
— Tables, calculations, etc. *(TH151)*
    sa Strains and stresses
    Example under reference from Tables
       (Systematic lists)
— Technological innovations
    Example under Technological innova-
       tions
— Tools and implements
    sa Construction equipment

Building *(Direct) (TH)*
— Tools and implements *(Continued)*
    x Building tools and implements
    xx Construction equipment
      Tools
— — Drawing
    See Building—Tools and
        implements—Drawings
— — Drawings
    x Building—Tools and implements
      —Drawing
    xx Mechanical drawing
— — Patents
Building, Adobe
  sa Adobe houses
    Pisé
  x Adobe construction
  xx Earth houses
    Pisé
Building, Aluminum
  See Aluminum construction
Building, Bombproof *(TH1097)*
  sa Air raid shelters
    Atomic bomb shelters
    Blast effect
    War damage to buildings
  x Bomb-proof building
    Bomb-proof construction
    Bombproof building
    Bombproof construction
  xx Air defenses
    Air raid shelters
    Buildings—Protection
    Underground construction
Building, Brick *(TH1301)*
  sa Brick houses
  x Brick building
  xx Masonry
Building, Composite
  See Composite construction
Building, Concrete
  See Concrete construction
Building, Earthquake-proof
  See Earthquakes and building
Building, Fireproof *(TH1061-1093)*
  sa Fire-testing
    Fireproofing
    Insurance engineering
    Insurance, Fire
  x Fireproof building
  xx Building materials
    Buildings—Protection
    Fire prevention
    Insurance engineering
Building, House
  See House construction
Building, Ice and snow *(TH1431)*
  sa Igloos
  x Ice and snow building
  xx Ice
    Snow
Building, Iron and steel *(Building,*
    TH1610-1621; Engineering,
    TA684-5)
  sa Composite construction
    Electric lines—Poles and towers
    Iron, Structural
    Plates, Iron and steel
    Prestressed steel construction
    Roofing, Iron and steel
    Skyscrapers
    Steel piling
    Steel, Structural
    Structures, Theory of
    Welded steel structures
  x Architectural engineering
    Engineering, Architectural
    Iron and steel building

    Steel and iron building
  xx Girders
    Graphic statics
    Iron
    Iron, Structural
    Steel
    Steel, Structural
  Example under Structural engineering
— Details
— — Drawings
    xx Structural drawing
— Production standards
— Safety measures
— Standards *(Direct)*
— Tables, calculations, etc.
Building, Pisé
  See Pisé
Building, Plywood
  See Plywood construction
Building, Rammed earth
  See Pisé
Building, Stone *(TH1201)*
  sa Bridges, Stone
    Building stones
    Stone houses
  x Stone building
    Stone construction
  xx Building stones
Building, Stormproof
  x Storm-proof construction
  xx Buildings—Protection
    Storms
Building, Terra-cotta
  xx Terra-cotta
Building, Underground
  See Underground construction
Building, Welded steel
  See Welded steel structures
Building, Wooden
  sa Floors, Wooden
    Half-timbered houses
    Plywood construction
    Wooden beams
    Wooden-frame houses
— Joints
    See Timber joints
— Problems, exercises, etc.
— Standards *(Direct)*
— Tables, calculations, etc.
Building accidents, Liability for
  See Liability for building accidents
Building and loan associations *(Direct)*
    (HG2121-2156)
  x Building societies
    Cooperative building associations
    Loan associations
    Provident loan associations
    Savings and loan associations
  xx Banks and banking, Cooperative
    Cooperative societies
    Financial institutions
    Investments
    Loans, Personal
    Saving and thrift
    Savings-banks
— Accounting *(HF5686.B8)*
— Government guaranty of deposits
  xx Banks and banking—Government
    guaranty of deposits
— Law *(HG2131-5)*
— State supervision
— Tables, etc. *(HG2129)*
— Taxation *(Direct)*
Building as a profession
  xx Building trades
    Construction industry
Building block design
  See Unit construction

Building board
  See Fiberboard
    Wall board
Building codes
  See Building laws
Building contracts
  See Building—Contracts and specifications
Building damage prevention
  See Buildings—Protection
Building design
  See Architecture
Building designers *(Direct)*
  x Designers, Building
  xx Architects
Building deterioration, External
  See Weathering of buildings
Building dynamics
  See Structural dynamics
Building employees
  See Building-service employees
Building failures
  sa Buildings—Protection
  x Collapse of buildings
  xx Building—Accidents
    Disasters
— Pictorial works
Building fittings *(Catalogs, TH455, TH2055;*
    Maintenance, TH8901)
  sa Architectural ironwork
    Architectural metal-work
    Buildings—Mechanical equipment
    Door fittings
    Woodwork—Catalogs
  x Buildings—Fittings
    House fittings
  xx Architectural ironwork
    Architectural metal-work
    Building
    Hardware
    Woodwork—Catalogs
— Specifications *(Direct)*
Building gilds
Building guards
  See Watchmen
Building industry
  See Construction industry
Building inscriptions
  See Architectural inscriptions
Building inspection *(TH439)*
    Only general works are entered here.
    Works on building inspection in any
    particular country or locality are en-
    tered under Building laws—[local sub-
    division], *e.g.* Building laws—Phila-
    delphia.
  sa Building inspectors
  x Building—Inspection
    Inspection of buildings
  xx Building laws
— Examinations, questions, etc.
Building inspectors *(Direct)*
  xx Building inspection
    Building laws
Building laws *(Direct) (TH219-255)*
  sa Architects—Legal status, laws, etc.
    Building—Contracts and specifications
    Building inspection
    Building inspectors
    Building lines
    Building permits
    Buildings, Prefabricated—Law and
      legislation
    Construction industry—Law and
      legislation
    Elevators—Laws and regulations
    Fire-escapes
    Heating—Law and legislation
    Old age homes—Law and legislation

Party walls
School buildings—Law and legislation
Tenement-houses
Wrecking—Safety regulations
Zoning law
  x Architectural law and legislation
Architecture—Law and legislation
Building codes
Building—Laws and regulations
Law, Building
  xx Architects—Legal status, laws, etc.
Hurricane protection
Zoning law
— Criminal provisions
— Digests

— Philadelphia
  Note under Building inspection
Building leases *(Direct)*
  sa Superficies ₊for the equivalent concept
    in civil law systems₎
  x Ground leases
  xx Leases
  Superficies
— Forms
Building lines *(Direct)*
  xx Building laws
  Highway law
Building machinery
  See Construction equipment
Building machinery operators
  See Construction machinery operators
Building materials *(Direct) (TA401-492)*
  sa Aggregates (Building materials)
  Asbestos
  Bituminous materials
  Bricks
  Building, Fireproof
  Building materials industry
  Building papers
  Building stones
  Cement
  Ceramics
  Cob (Building material)
  Concrete
  Expanded metal
  Flooring
  Insulating materials
  Iron, Structural
  Pisé
  Plastics in building
  Reed (Building material)
  Reinforced concrete
  Shingles
  Slabs
  Steel, Structural
  Stone
  Stone, Artificial
  Strength of materials
  Structural engineering
  Stucco
  Tabby (Concrete)
  Terra-cotta
  Tiles
  Timber
  Wall board
  Wood
  x Building—Materials
  Buildings—Materials
  Structural materials
  xx Architecture
  Engineering
  Materials
Example under Materials
— Analysis
— Corrosion
— Density

— — Measurement
— Deterioration
— Moisture
— — Measurement
— Permeability
— Prices *(Direct)*
— Problems, exercises, etc. *(TA404.3)*
— Radiation effects
  See Building materials, Effect of
    radiation on
— Research *(Direct) (TA404.2)*
  xx Materials research
— Specifications
  See Building—Contracts and
    specifications
— Standards *(Direct)*
  xx Modular coordination (Architecture)
— Storage
— Tables, calculations, etc.
— Taxation *(Direct)*
— Testing *(TA401-492)*
  sa Fire-testing
  Example under Testing
— — Indexes
— — Laboratory manuals
— Thermal properties
  xx Building materials, Effect of
    temperature on
  Example under reference from Thermal
    properties of materials
— Trade-marks
— Transportation
Building materials, Effect of radiation on
  x Building materials—Radiation effects
  xx Radiation
Building materials, Effect of temperature on
  sa Building materials—Thermal properties
Building materials industry *(Direct)*
  sa Wages—Building materials industry
  xx Building materials
  Construction industry
— Accounting
— Auditing and inspection
— Automation
— Costs
— Dust control
— Electric equipment
— Equipment and supplies
— — Appraisal
  See Building materials industry—
    Equipment and supplies—
    Valuation
— — Patents
— — Valuation
  x Building materials industry—
    Equipment and supplies—
    Appraisal
— — Vibration
— Hygienic aspects
— Labor productivity
— Management
— Mathematical models *(TA403.6)*
— Production control
— Production standards
— Quality control
— Safety measures
— Safety regulations *(Direct)*
— Underdeveloped areas
  See Underdeveloped areas—Building
    materials industry
Building papers
  x Paper in building
  xx Building materials
  Dampness in buildings
  Paper products
— Standards
Building permits *(Direct)*
  xx Building laws

Building prices
  See Building—Prices
Building protection
  See Buildings—Protection
Building repair
  See Buildings—Repair and reconstruction
Building research *(Direct)*
  sa Heating research
  x Building—Research
  xx Research, Industrial
Building-service employees *(Direct)*
  sa Charwomen and cleaners
  Elevator operators
  Janitors
  Wages—Building-service employees
  Watchmen
  x Building employees
  xx Real estate management
— Collective labor agreements
  See Collective labor agreements—
    Building-service employees
Building sites *(Indirect)*
  sa Library sites
  School sites
  xx Building
  Surveying
— Fires and fire prevention *(TH9445.B8)*
— Lighting
— — Standards
— Water-supply
Building societies
  See Building and loan associations
Building standards
  See Standards, Engineering
Building stones *(Indirect) (TA426-8;
    TN950-973)*
  sa Building, Stone
  Masonry
  Pavements, Stone
  Quarries and quarrying
  Stone-cutting
  names of stones, e.g. Granite, Marble,
    Sandstone
  x Stone, Building
  xx Building materials
  Building, Stone
  Geology, Economic
  Masonry
  Quarries and quarrying
  Stone
— Juvenile literature
— Pictorial works
— Standards
— Testing *(TA427)*
Building superintendence
  See Building—Superintendence
Building superintendents
  See Janitors
Building tools and implements
  See Building—Tools and implements
Building trades *(Direct) (Economics,
    HD9715; Technology, TH)*
  Here are entered works limited to the
    skilled trades employed in building
    construction, *e.g.* carpentry, bricklay-
    ing. Works on all types of labor em-
    ployed in building construction, in-
    cluding skilled and unskilled workers,
    are entered under Construction work-
    ers.
  sa Building
  Building as a profession
  Collective labor agreements—
    Construction industry
  Construction industry
  Construction workers
  Trade-unions—Building trades
  Wages—Building trades

Building trades *(Direct) (Economics, HD9715; Technology, TH)*
  (Continued)
  Bricklayers; Carpenters; *and similar headings*
  x Trades
  xx Building
  Construction industry
  Construction industry—Employees
  Construction workers
  Example under reference from Unemployment, Seasonal
  Notes under Building; Construction industry; Construction workers
  — Accounting
    See Construction industry— Accounting
  — Caricatures and cartoons
  — Job descriptions
  — Retirement
  — Study and teaching
    See Building—Study and teaching
  — Vocational guidance
    x Construction industry—Vocational guidance
  — — Juvenile literature
Building weathering
  See Weathering of buildings
Buildings
  Here are entered general works on structures or edifices. Works on style, design, etc. are entered under Architecture. Works on the process of construction are entered under Building.
  sa Architecture
  Building
  Joint occupancy of buildings
  War damage to buildings
  names of particular types of buildings and construction, e.g. Archive buildings; Dwellings; Brick houses; Buildings, Prefabricated; *also subdivision* Buildings *under names of cities and names of institutions or groups of institutions; and subdivision* Diplomatic and consular service—Buildings *under names of countries*
  xx Architecture
  Building
  Example under Structural engineering
  — Acoustics
    See Architectural acoustics
  — Aerodynamics
    sa Ventilation
    Wind-pressure
  — Cleaning
    sa Bathrooms—Cleaning
    Industrial housekeeping
  — — Examinations, questions, etc.
  — Color
    See Color in architecture
  — Damage prevention
    See Buildings—Protection
  — Details
    See Architecture—Details
    Building—Details
  — Electric equipment
    xx Buildings—Mechanical equipment
  — — Fires and fire prevention
  — — Maintenance and repair
  — — Safety measures
  — Environmental engineering
    See Environmental engineering (Buildings)
  — Exterior walls
    See Exterior walls
  — Fittings
    See Building fittings

— Juvenile literature *(TH149)*
— Machinery
    See Buildings—Mechanical equipment
— Maintenance and repair
    See Buildings—Repair and reconstruction
— Materials
    See Building materials
— Mechanical equipment *(TH6010)*
    sa Buildings—Electric equipment
    x Buildings—Machinery
    Mechanical equipment of buildings
    xx Building fittings
    Machinery
— — Contracts and specifications
    x Buildings—Mechanical equipment —Specifications
    xx Building—Contracts and specifications
— — Maintenance and repair *(TH6013)*
— — Specifications
    See Buildings—Mechanical equipment—Contracts and specifications
— Models
    See Architectural models
— Protection *(TH9025-9615)*
    sa Building, Bombproof
    Building, Fireproof
    Building, Stormproof
    Buildings—Repair and reconstruction
    Dampness in buildings
    Earth movements and building
    Factories—Protection
    Lightning protection
    Weathering of buildings
    x Building damage prevention
    Building protection
    Buildings—Damage prevention
    Protection of buildings
    xx Building failures
— Repair and reconstruction
    sa Architecture—Conservation and restoration
    Church maintenance and repair
    x Building repair
    Buildings—Maintenance and repair
    Buildings, Reconstruction of
    Remodeling of buildings
    xx Architecture—Conservation and restoration
    Buildings—Protection
    Maintenance
    Repairing
— — Costs
— — Examinations, questions, etc.
— — Finance
    xx Housing—Finance
    Mortgages
— — Safety measures
— Testing
— Vibration
    xx Environmental engineering (Buildings)
— Weathering
    See Weathering of buildings
Buildings, Archive
  See Archive buildings
Buildings, Commercial
  See Mercantile buildings
    Office buildings
Buildings, Dampness in
  See Dampness in buildings
Buildings, Demountable
  See Buildings, Prefabricated
Buildings, Employees'
  See Employees' buildings and facilities

Buildings, Farm
  See Farm buildings
Buildings, Half-timbered
  See Half-timbered houses
Buildings, Historic
  See Historic houses, etc.
Buildings, Industrial
  See Industrial buildings
Buildings, Library
  See Library architecture
Buildings, Mercantile
  See Mercantile buildings
Buildings, Moving of
  See Moving of buildings, bridges, etc.
Buildings, Municipal
  See Municipal buildings
Buildings, Octagonal *(NA4160)*
Buildings, Office
  See Office buildings
Buildings, Packaged
  See Buildings, Prefabricated
Buildings, Plastic
  xx Air-supported structures
  Plastics
  Plastics in building
Buildings, Portable *(Architecture, NA8480; Building, TH1098)*
  x Houses, Portable
  Portable buildings
  xx Buildings, Prefabricated
Buildings, Prefabricated *(Direct) (Architecture, NA8480; Building, TH1098)*
  sa Buildings, Portable
  Modular construction
  Prefabricated apartment houses
  Prefabricated houses
  x Buildings, Demountable
  Buildings, Packaged
  Components construction
  Demountable buildings
  Packaged buildings
  Prefabricated buildings
  xx Industrialized building
  Example under Buildings
— Law and legislation *(Direct)*
    xx Building laws
— Reliability
Buildings, Public
  See Public buildings
    subdivision Public buildings *under names of countries, cities, etc.*
Buildings, Reconstruction of
  See Buildings—Repair and reconstruction
Buildings, Restoration of
  See Architecture—Conservation and restoration
Buildings, School
  See School buildings
Buildings, Sunday-school
  See Sunday-school buildings
Buildings in art
  Here are entered works on buildings as subjects depicted in the fine arts other than architecture.
  xx Art
Builsa (African tribe)
  x Bulo (African tribe)
  Bulsa (African tribe)
  Kanjaga (African tribe)
  xx Ethnology—Ghana
  Gurunsi (African people)
— Religion
Built-in furniture *(Cabinet work, TT197.5.B8; Design, NK2712)*
  x Furniture, Built-in
  xx Furniture

Built-in test equipment
　　See Automatic checkout equipment
Buin language
　　See Telei language
Bujeba (Bantu tribe)
　　See Bisio (Bantu tribe)
Bujeba language
　　See Bisio language
Bujia (African tribe)
　　See Budja (African tribe)
Bukidnon (Philippine people)
　　x Higaonan (Philippine people)
　　xx Ethnology—Mindanao
Bukuba language
　　See Bushongo language
Bukusu (Bantu tribe)
　　xx Bantus
　　　Ethnology—Kenya
Bukusu language
　　x Lubukusu language
　　xx Bantu languages
　　　Gisu language
Bulanda language
　　See Balante language
Bulavin Uprising, 1707-1709
　　See Russia—History—Bulavin Uprising,
　　　1707-1709
Bulb fly
　　See Narcissus bulb fly
Bulb industry *(Indirect)*
　　　Here are entered works on the technical
　　　and economic aspects of bulb culture
　　　and trade. Works on the growing of
　　　bulbs in private gardens or homes are
　　　entered under Bulbs.
　　x Bulbous and tuberous rooted plants
　　xx Bulbs
　　　Horticulture
Bulbous and tuberous rooted plants
　　See Bulb industry
　　　Bulbs
Bulbs *(Indirect) (SB425)*
　　sa Bulb industry
　　　Corms
　　x Bulbous and tuberous rooted plants
　　　Flowering bulbs
　　xx Botany
　　　Floriculture
　　　Gardening
　　　Horticulture
　　Note under Bulb industry
　　— Diseases and pests
　　　sa Narcissus bulb fly
　　— Pictorial works
　　— Storage
Bulbs (Botany)
　　xx Botany
Bulbuls
Bule
　　See Bulu language
Bulgaria
　　— History
　　— — To 1393
　　— — 1393-1878
　　　　sa Bulgaria—History—Peasant
　　　　　Uprising, 1850
　　　　　Bulgaria—History—Uprising,
　　　　　1876
　　　　　Russo-Turkish War, 1877-1878
　　— — Peasant Uprising, 1850
　　　　xx Bulgaria—History—1393-1878
　　— — Uprising, 1876
　　　　x Bulgarian Horrors, 1876
　　　　　Bulgarian Massacre, 1876
　　　　xx Bulgaria—History—1393-1878
　　— — 1878-1944
　　　　sa Bulgaria—History—June Uprising,
　　　　　1923

Bulgaria—History—September
　　Uprising, 1923
　　Kresnensko Uprising, 1878
　　Neuilly-sur-Seine, Treaty of, Nov.
　　　27, 1919 (Bulgaria)
　　Russo-Turkish War, 1877-1878
　　Serbo-Bulgarian War, 1885
— — June Uprising, 1923
　　xx Bulgaria—History—1878-1944
— — — Caricatures and cartoons
— — — September Uprising, 1923
　　xx Bulgaria—History—1878-1944
— — — Literature and the uprising
— — — Personal narratives
— — — Pictorial works
— — 1941-1944
— — 1944-
Bulgaria in literature
Bulgarian ballads and songs *(Collections,*
　　PG1010; Folk poetry, PG1021)
　　sa Folk-songs, Bulgarian
Bulgarian Church Slavic language
　　See Church Slavic language
Bulgarian drama
— 20th century
Bulgarian drama (Comedy) *(Collections,*
　　PG1022; History, PG1011)
Bulgarian essays *(Direct)*
Bulgarian fiction
Bulgarian Horrors, 1876
　　See Bulgaria—History—Uprising, 1876
Bulgarian imprints *(Direct)*
Bulgarian language *(PG801-993)*
　　xx Slavic languages, Southern
　　— To 1100
　　　See Church Slavic language
　　— Middle Bulgarian, 1100-1400
　　　(PG771-799)
Bulgarian literature *(PG1000-1158)*
　　sa Damaskini
　　xx Balkan Peninsula—Literatures
　　　Yugoslav literature
　　— Middle Bulgarian, 1100-1400
　　— 20th century
Bulgarian Massacre, 1876
　　See Bulgaria—History—Uprising, 1876
Bulgarian miniature paintings
　　See Miniature paintings, Bulgarian
Bulgarian mythology
　　See Mythology, Slavic
Bulgarian newspapers *(History, etc.,*
　　PN5355.B8)
Bulgarian periodicals *(History, etc.,*
　　PN5355.B8)
Bulgarian poetry *(Collections, PG1014,*
　　PG1021; History, PG1010)
　　— 20th century
Bulgarian property in Great Britain, [etc.]
Bulgarian prose literature *(Direct)*
Bulgarian question
　　See Eastern question (Balkan)
Bulgarian-Serbian War, 1885
　　See Serbo-Bulgarian War, 1885
Bulgarian wit and humor *(Direct)*
　　(Collections, PG1023; History,
　　PG1012)
　　　Here are entered collections from several
　　　authors and individual authors who
　　　have not written in other literary
　　　forms.
Bulgarian wit and humor, Pictorial *(Direct)*
Bulgarians *(Ethnography, DR64)*
　　xx Slavs, Southern
Bulgarians in Hungary, [Macedonia, etc.]
Bulge, Battle of the
　　See Ardennes, Battle of the, 1944-1945
Bulge forming
　　See Bulging (Metalwork)

Bulging (Metalwork) *(TS256)*
　　x Bulge forming
　　xx High energy forming
　　　High pressure (Technology)
　　　Metals—Cold working
Bulgur
　　x Arisah
　　　Boulgour
　　　Burghol
　　　Burghul
　　　Burgol
　　　Burgul
　　　Parboiled wheat
　　xx Wheat
　　— Patents
Bulk materials
　　See Bulk solids
Bulk milk tanks
　　See Milk tanks
Bulk sales *(Direct)*
　　x Bulk transfers
　　　Sales, Bulk
　　xx Debtor and creditor
　　　Fraudulent conveyances
　　　Sales
　　　Transfer (Law)
Bulk solids
　　sa Agglomeration
　　　Granular materials
　　　Powders
　　　special types of solids, e.g. Grain,
　　　　Gravel
　　x Bulk materials
　　　Particulate solids
　　xx Materials
　　　Particles
　　　Solids
　　— Sampling
Bulk solids flow
　　sa Fluidization
　　x Dry-solids flow
　　　Flow of bulk solids
　　　Solids flow, Bulk
　　xx Fluid dynamics
Bulk solids handling
　　sa Bins
　　　Coal-handling
　　　Earthwork
　　　Grain handling
　　　Ore handling
　　　Silos
　　x Handling of bulk solids
　　xx Conveying machinery
　　　Loading and unloading
　　　Materials handling
Bulk transfers
　　See Bulk sales
Bulked woven fabrics
　　See Textured woven fabrics
Bulkheads (Naval architecture) *(VM469)*
　　xx Naval architecture
　　　Ship-building
　　— Testing
Bull (in religion, folk-lore, etc.) *(Religion,*
　　BL443.B8)
　　sa Taurobolium
　　x Bulls (in religion, folk-lore, etc.)
　　　Folk-lore of bulls
　　xx Religion, Primitive
Bull, Golden
　　See Golden bull, 1356
Bull-fight stories
Bull-fighters *(GV1108)*
　　x Matadors
　　— Costume *(GV1108.2)*
Bull-fights *(Direct) (GV1107)*
　　sa Fighting bull
　　　Running the bulls

Bull-fights *(Direct)* *(GV1107)*
  (Continued)
      x Animal baiting
         Bull-fights—Spain
         Bullfights
         Fighting
      xx Animal fighting
         Fighting bull
   — Caricatures and cartoons
   — Early works to 1800
   — Law and legislation *(Direct)*
   — Pictorial works

GEOGRAPHIC SUBDIVISIONS

   — Spain
         See Bull-fights
Bull-fights in art *(N8250)*
      xx Sports in art
Bull-fights in literature
      xx Bulls in literature
Bull-fights in moving-pictures
      xx Moving-pictures
Bull of demarcation
      See Demarcation line of Alexander VI
Bull pup (Missile)
      x Bullpup (Missile)
Bull racing
      xx Racing
Bull Run, 1st Battle, 1861 *(E472.18)*
      x Manassas, Battles of
   — Juvenile literature
Bull Run, 2d Battle, 1862 *(E473.77)*
      x Groveton, Battle of, 1862
         Manassas, Battles of
Bull-terriers *(SF429.B8)*
      sa Staffordshire terriers
      xx Terriers
Bulla cruciata
      See Crusade bulls
Bulldogs *(SF429.B85)*
      sa French bulldogs
Bulldozers *(Road machinery, TE223)*
      xx Earthmoving machinery
         Road machinery
         Tracklaying vehicles
      Note under Tracklaying vehicles
   — Dynamics
   — Maintenance and repair
Buller's albatross
      xx Albatrosses
Bulletin boards *(LB1045)*
      sa Experience charts
      xx Display boards
         Employees, Reporting to
         Teaching—Aids and devices
         Visual education
Bulletin boards in religious education
      (BV1535.25)
      xx Religious education—Audio-visual aids
Bullets
      See Projectiles
Bullfights
      See Bull-fights
Bullfrog
      xx Frogs
   — Juvenile literature
Bullhead, Black
      See Black bullhead
Bullhead, Brown
      See Brown bullhead
Bullion
      See Precious metals
Bullockies
      xx Oxen
Bullock's oriole
      xx Orioles
Bullom language *(PL8093)*
      x Bulom language
         Sherbro language

Bullpup (Missile)
      See Bull pup (Missile)
Bulls
      sa Fighting bull
      xx Cattle
         Cattle breeding
   — Behavior
Bulls, Byzantine
      x Byzantine bulls
Bulls, Colloquial *(PN6231.B8)*
      x Blunders
         Bulls, Irish
         Colloquial bulls
         Irish bulls
      xx Irish wit and humor
         Wit and humor
Bulls, Crusade
      See Crusade bulls
Bulls, In Coena Domini
      See In Coena Domini bulls
Bulls, Irish
      See Bulls, Colloquial
         Irish wit and humor
Bulls, Papal
      sa Briefs, Papal
         Crusade bulls
         Encyclicals, Papal
         In Coena Domini bulls
         Rescripts, Papal
      x Papal bulls
         Popes—Bulls
      xx Exequatur (Ecclesiastical law)
         Papal documents
         Rescripts, Papal
      Note under Papal documents
   — Facsimiles
Bulls (in religion, folk-lore, etc.)
      See Bull (in religion, folk-lore, etc.)
Bulls and bears
      See Stock-exchange
Bull's Ferry, N.J., Engagement at, 1780
      (E241.B87)
Bulls in art
      xx Animals in art
         Art
Bulls in literature
      sa Bull-fights in literature
Bulo (African tribe)
      See Builsa (African tribe)
Bulom language
      See Bullom language
Bulsa (African tribe)
      See Builsa (African tribe)
Bultaco motorcycle *(TL448.B)*
Bulu (Bantu tribe)
Bulu language
      x Boulou language
         Bule
      xx Bantu languages
Bumbatana language
      See Bambatana language
Bumblebees *(QL568.A6)*
      x Humblebees
      xx Bees
Būn-sio dialect
      See Chinese language—Dialects—Hainan
Bunda language
      See Kimbundu language
Bundas
      See Bondos
Bundeli dialect *(PK1968)*
      x Bundelkhandi dialect
      xx Hindi language
Bundelkhandi dialect
      See Bundeli dialect
Bundle-branch block *(RC685.A65)*
      x Interventricular heart block
      xx Heart block

Bundles, Fiber (Mathematics)
      See Fiber bundles (Mathematics)
Bundles, Tangent
      See Tangent bundles
Bundling *(GT2651)*
      xx Courtship
Bundschuh Insurrections, 1493-1517
      (DD174.4)
      x Peasants' War, 1493-1517
Bungalows *(NA7571-2)*
      x Architecture, Rural
         Rural architecture
      xx Architecture, Domestic
         Cottages
         Dwellings
         Suburban homes
Bungee Indians
      See Chippewa Indians
Bungi Indians
      See Chippewa Indians
Bungo Ishigakibaru, Battle of, 1600
      See Ishigakibaru, Battle of, 1600
Bunion
      xx Toes—Abnormities and deformities
Bunker Hill, Battle of, 1775 *(E241.B9)*
      x Breed's Hill, Battle of, 1775
   — Juvenile literature
Bunkering stations
      See Coaling-stations
Bunsen burner
      xx Gas-burners
Bunt (Disease of wheat) *(SB608.W5)*
      Example under Wheat—Diseases and pests
Bunte salts
      xx Salts
Bunting (Cloth) *(TS1630)*
Bunun (Formosan people) *(DS895.F715)*
      xx Ethnology—Formosa
Bunyoro
      See Banyoro
Buoyancy, Positive
      See Buoyant ascent (Hydrodynamics)
Buoyant ascent (Hydrodynamics)
      x Buoyancy, Positive
         Buoyant-body water exit
      xx Hydrodynamics
Buoyant-body water exit
      See Buoyant ascent (Hydrodynamics)
Buoys *(Indirect)* *(VK1000-1246)*
      sa Oceanographic buoys
      x Bell-buoys
      xx Aids to navigation
         Marine service
         Navigation
Bur clover *(QK495.L52; SB205.B)*
      xx Clover
         Forage plants
         Legumes
   — Diseases and pests
Bur oak
      xx Oak
Burakumin
      See Eta
Burbot
      sa Cookery (Burbot)
Burbung
      xx Australian aborigines
Burden of proof *(Direct)*
      sa Res ipsa loquitur doctrine
      x Onus probandi
         Proof, Burden of
      xx Evidence (Law)
         Trial practice
Burden of proof (Roman law)
Burdock *(Arctium, QK495.A; Weeds, SB615.B)*
Bureaucracy
      sa Civil service

xx Civil service
Political science
Public administration
— Anecdotes, facetiae, satire, etc.
— Caricatures and cartoons
Bureaus, Scientific
See Scientific bureaus
Burettes *(QC104)*
Burgenland in literature
Burghol
See Bulgur
Burghs
See Boroughs
Burghul
See Bulgur
Burglar-alarms *(TK7251)*
sa Electric alarms
Electronic alarm systems
xx Burglary protection
Electric alarms
Electric apparatus and appliances
Electronic alarm systems
— Juvenile literature
Burglary *(Direct) (HV6646-6665)*
sa Trials (Burglary)
xx Criminal law
Larceny
Offenses against property
Thieves
Burglary insurance
See Insurance, Burglary
Burglary protection *(TH9701-9745)*
sa Burglar-alarms
Emergency lighting
Insurance, Burglary
Locks and keys
Safes
Vaults (Strong rooms)
Watchdogs
Watchmen
Window guards
x Protection against burglary
— Equipment and supplies
Burgol
See Bulgur
Burgoyne's Invasion, 1777 *(E233)*
sa Bennington, Battle of, 1777
Hubbardton, Battle of, 1777
Saratoga Campaign, 1777
St. Leger's Expedition, 1777
Stanwix, Fort, N.Y.—Siege, 1777
x Convention troops
xx Saratoga Campaign, 1777
Burgul
See Bulgur
Burgundian language *(PD1301)*
Burgundian law
See Law, Burgundian
Burgundians *(DC611.B771-9; Migrations, D149)*
Burial *(Ethnology, GN486; Manners and customs, GT3150-3390; Public health, RA625)*
sa Catacombs
Cemeteries
Cremation
Cryonics
Embalming
Epitaphs
Exhumation
Funeral rites and ceremonies
Indians of North America—Mortuary customs
Indians of South America—Mortuary customs
Mounds
Mummies
Sarcophagi

Sepulchral monuments
Ship burial
Tombs
Urn burial
x Burying-grounds
Graves
Interment
Mortuary customs
xx Dead
Hygiene, Public
Burial, Premature *(RA1063)*
sa Death, Apparent
xx Death, Apparent
Burial clubs
See Insurance, Burial
Burial customs
See Funeral rites and ceremonies
Burial insurance
See Insurance, Burial
Burial laws *(Direct)*
sa Cemeteries—Law and legislation
Cremation—Law and legislation
Exhumation—Law and legislation
Undertakers and undertaking—Law and legislation
x Law, Burial
Mortuary law
xx Cemeteries—Law and legislation
Dead bodies (Law)
Undertakers and undertaking—Law and legislation
Example under Public health laws
Burial laws (Canon law) *(BX1939.B8)*
Burial laws (Jewish law)
Burial laws (Roman law)
Burial of radioactive wastes
See Radioactive waste disposal in the ground
Burial service
See Funeral service
Burial statistics
See Mortality
Registers of births, etc.
Vital statistics
subdivision Statistics, Vital *under names of countries, cities, etc.*
Buriat drama *(Direct) (PL428)*
Buriat language *(PL427)*
sa Mongolian languages
xx Mongolian languages
Example under Mongolian philology
Buriat literature *(Direct) (PL428)*
Buriat poetry *(Direct) (PL428)*
Buriats *(DK759.B)*
xx Mongols
Buried cities
See Cities and towns, Ruined, extinct, etc.
Buried treasure
See Treasure-trove
Burishki language
See Burushaski language
Burke and Wills Expedition, 1860-1861 *(DU102)*
Burkitt tumor
See Burkitt's lymphoma
Burkitt's African lymphoma
See Burkitt's lymphoma
Burkitt's lymphoma
x African lymphoma
Burkitt tumor
Burkitt's African lymphoma
Burkitt's tumor
xx Lymphoma
Burkitt's tumor
See Burkitt's lymphoma
Burl
xx Wood
Burlap *(TS1735)*

Burlap craft *(TT880)*
xx Handicraft
— Juvenile literature
Burlesque (Literature) *(PN6149.B8)*
sa Farce
Grotesque
Parody
x Comic literature
Literature, Comic
Travesty
xx Comedy
Drama
Literature
Parody
Satire
Wit and humor
Note under Burlesques
Burlesque (Theater) *(PN1940-1949)*
sa Strip-tease
xx Amusements
Music-halls (Variety-theaters, cabarets, etc.)
Theater
Vaudeville
Note under Burlesques
Burlesques *(PN6231.B84)*
Here are entered collections of burlesque literature. Works on burlesque as a literary composition are entered under the heading Burlesque (Literature) Works on burlesque as a theatrical entertainment are entered under Burlesque (Theater)
sa Parodies
xx Parodies
Burma
— History
— — 1824-1948
sa Burmese War, 1824-1826
Burmese War, 1852
— — Japanese occupation, 1942-1945
— — 1945-
Burman language
See Burmese language
Burmese
xx Ethnology—Burma
Burmese Buddhist devotional literature
See Buddhist devotional literature, Burmese
Burmese Buddhist law
x Law, Burmese Buddhist
xx Hindu law
Law, Oriental
Burmese calendar
See Calendar, Burmese
Burmese cat *(SF449.B8)*
Burmese drama *(Direct) (Collections, PL3985; History, PL3981)*
Burmese fiction *(Direct)*
Burmese language *(PL3921-3969)*
x Burman language
xx Tibeto-Burman languages
Burmese literature *(PL3971-3999)*
Burmese poetry *(Direct)*
Burmese red jungle fowl
xx Jungle fowl
Burmese War, 1824-1826
x Anglo-Burmese War, 1824-1826
India—History—Burmese Wars, 1824-1852
xx Burma—History—1824-1948
Burmese War, 1852
x India—History—Burmese Wars, 1824-1852
xx Burma—History—1824-1948
Burmese wit and humor
Burners, Incense
See Incense burners and containers

Burning in effigy
See Executions in effigy
Burning-mirrors
 x Mirrors, Burning
Burning of land
 sa Prescribed burning
 Shifting cultivation
 x Land burning
 Land, Burning of
 xx Agriculture
 Botany—Ecology
 Land
 Prescribed burning
 Soils
Burning the dead
 See Cremation
Burnishing *(TJ1280)*
 xx Grinding and polishing
 Metals—Finishing
Burnishing, Diamond
 See Diamond burnishing
Burns and scalds *(RD131; Popular medicine, RC87)*
 x Scalds
 xx Accidents
 First aid in illness and injury
 — Complications and sequelae
 — Research
 xx Medical research
Burnside's Expedition to North Carolina, 1862 *(E473.3)*
Burnt offering
 See Sacrifice
Burnup, Fuel (Nuclear engineering)
 See Fuel burnup (Nuclear engineering)
Burr Conspiracy, 1805-1807 *(E334)*
 x United States—History—Burr Conspiracy, 1805-1807
Burr-Hamilton Duel
 x Hamilton-Burr Duel
 — Juvenile literature
Burros
 See Donkeys
Burroughs 220 dialect of ALGOL
 See BALGOL (Computer program language)
Burroughs B5700 (Computer) *(QA76.8.B)*
 xx Electronic digital computers
 — Programming
Burroughs B6700 (Computer) *(QA76.8.B)*
 xx Electronic digital computers
 — Programming
Burrowing animals
 xx Animals, Habits and behavior of
 Soil fauna
 Zoology—Ecology
 — Juvenile literature
Burrowing animals, Fossil
Burrowing barnacles
 See Acrothoracica
Bursa equivalent cells
 See B cells
Bursa Fabricii *(QL697)*
 x Bursa of Fabricius
Bursa of Fabricius
 See Bursa Fabricii
Bursa omentalis *(QL864; QM367)*
 xx Omentum
 Peritoneum
Bursa pharyngea
 See Pharyngeal bursa
Bursae mucosae *(QM485)*
 x Bursal synoviae
 xx Joints
 Synovial membranes
Bursae of hip *(Diseases, RC935.B8, RD688; Human anatomy, QM141)*
 xx Hip joint

Bursae of shoulder *(Diseases, RC935.B8, RD688; Human anatomy, QM141)*
 xx Shoulder joint
Bursae synoviae
 See Bursae mucosae
Bursaries
 See Scholarships
Bursitis *(RC935.B8)*
Bursts, Gas
 See Gas bursts
Bursts, Rock
 See Rock bursts
Buru language *(PL5281)*
 x Boeroe language
 Bouro language
 Masarete language
Burum language
 See Birom language
Burushaski language *(PL7501.B8)*
 sa Werchikwar dialect
 x Boorishki language
 Burishki language
 Khajuna language
Burusho *(DS485.H8)*
 x Hunzukuts
Burying-grounds
 See Burial
 Cemeteries
Bus bars
 See Bus conductors (Electricity)
Bus channels
 See Bus conductors (Electricity)
Bus conductors (Electricity) *(TK2821)*
 x Bus bars
 Bus channels
 Bus tubes (Electricity)
 Busbars
 Busways (Electricity)
 xx Electric conductors
 Electric networks
 Electric switchgear
Bus drivers
 See Motor bus drivers
Bus driving
 See Motor bus driving
Bus lines
 See Motor bus lines
Bus stations
 See Motor bus terminals
Bus terminals
 See Motor bus terminals
Bus tubes (Electricity)
 See Bus conductors (Electricity)
Busa language
 x Bisa language (Mande)
 Boussa language
 xx Mande languages
Busbars
 See Bus conductors (Electricity)
Busboys
 xx Restaurants, lunch rooms, etc.— Employees
Buses
 See Motor buses
 Omnibuses
Bush cinquefoil *(QK495.R78)*
Bush clover
 See Lespedeza
Bush-rangers *(Australia, HV6453.A73)*
 xx Brigands and robbers
 — Juvenile literature
Bush survival
 See Wilderness survival
Bushido
 xx Chivalry
 Ethics, Japanese
 National characteristics, Japanese
 Samurai

— Anecdotes, facetiae, satire, etc.
Bushings
 See Bearings (Machinery)
 Electric insulators and insulation
 Pipe-fittings
Bushman languages *(PL8101-4)*
 sa Hottentot language
 Kham language
 Sandawe language
 !Xū language
 x San languages
Bushmen *(Anthropology, GN660.B8; Folk-lore, GR360.B9; South Africa, DT763-4)*
 sa Tannekwe (African tribe)
 x Bosjesmen
 xx Ethnology—Africa, South
 Hottentots
Bushongo *(DT650)*
 xx Ethnology—Zaire
Bushongo language
 x Bakuba language
 Bukuba language
 Lukuba language
 xx Bantu languages
Bushwhackers
 See Guerrillas
Bushy Run, Battle of, 1763 *(E83.76)*
 xx Pontiac's Conspiracy, 1763-1765
Bushy-tailed wood rat
 xx Wood rats
Business *(HF5001-6201)*
 sa Accounting
 Advertising
 Applications for positions
 Better-business bureaus
 Bookkeeping
 Budget in business
 Business enterprises
 Business losses
 Business mathematics
 Business mortality
 Businessmen
 Card system in business
 Catalogs, Commercial
 Commerce
 Commercial law
 Commercial travelers
 Commission-merchants
 Competition
 Controllership
 Corporations
 Credit
 Customer relations
 Delivery of goods
 Department stores
 Entrepreneur
 Executives
 Expense accounts
 Financial statements
 Floor space, Industrial
 Good-will (in business, etc.)
 Industrial management
 Instalment plan
 Mail-order business
 Manufactures
 Marketing
 Markets
 Merchants
 Minority business enterprises
 Moving-pictures in industry
 New business enterprises
 Occupations
 Office management
 Organization charts
 Profit
 Promoters
 Purchasing

Railroads—Records and correspondence
Real estate business
Salesmen and salesmanship
Secretaries
Sex in business
Shipment of goods
Show-windows
Store fixtures
Success
Telephone in business
Trade-marks
Trading-stamps
Trust companies
Turnover (Business)
Warehouses
Wealth
Women in business
  x Business administration
    Trade
  xx Commerce
    Commercial law
    Economics
    Industrial management
    Management
    Success
— Abstracts
— Anecdotes, facetiae, satire, etc.
— Book reviews
— Calendars (HF5028)
    Example under Calendars
— Caricatures and cartoons
— Computer programs
— Fellowships
    See Business—Scholarships,
      fellowships, etc.
— Film catalogs
— Forms, blanks, etc. (HF5371)
    sa Business announcements
      Letterheads
      Manifold business forms industry
      Salesmen and salesmanship—
        Business forms
    x Accounting—Forms, blanks, etc.
      Forms (Business)
    xx Business records
    Example under reference from Forms,
      blanks, etc.
— Graphic methods (HA31)
— Information services
    sa Liability for credit information
— Mathematical models
    xx Business mathematics
— Periodicals
    sa House organs
— Programmed instruction
— Programming languages
    See Programming languages
      (Electronic computers)—
      Business
— Records
    See Business records
— Removal
    See Business relocation
— Scholarships, fellowships, etc. (Direct)
    x Business fellowships
      Business—Fellowships
      Business scholarships
    xx Business education
— Social aspects
    See Industry—Social aspects
— Study and teaching
    See Business education
— Subject headings
    See Subject headings—Business
— Taxation
    See Business tax
— Terms and phrases

Business, Choice of
  See Vocational guidance
Business administration
  See Business
Business agents (Trade-union)
  sa Grievance procedures
    Shop stewards
  xx Industrial relations
    Shop stewards
    Trade-unions
Business and government
  See Industry and state
Business and politics (Direct)
  x Politics and business
  xx Politics, Practical
— Anecdotes, facetiae, satire, etc.
Business and social problems
  See Industry—Social aspects
Business announcements
  x Announcements, Business
    Business etiquette—Stationery
    Commercial announcements
  xx Business—Forms, blanks, etc.
    Commercial correspondence
    Etiquette—Stationery
    Stationery
Business arithmetic
  See Business mathematics
Business autocodes
  See Programming languages (Electronic
    computers)—Business
Business budgeting
  See Budget in business
Business cards
  See Advertising cards
Business communication
  See Communication in management
Business consultants (Direct)
  x Consultants, Business
    Efficiency engineers
    Management consultants
  xx Consulting engineers
    Industrial management
Business corporations
  See Corporations
Business correspondence
  See Commercial correspondence
Business cycles (HB3711-3840)
  sa Business forecasting
    Depressions
    Economic forecasting
    Economic stabilization
    Multiplier (Economics)
    Stagnation (Economics)
  x Economic cycles
  xx Cycles
— Mathematical models
Business districts, Central
  See Central business districts
Business economics
  See Managerial economics
Business education (Indirect)
  (HF1101-1181)
  sa Accounting
    Bookkeeping
    Business—Scholarships, fellowships, etc.
    Business teachers
    Commercial law
    Distributive education
    Industrial tours
    Penmanship
    Secretaries
    Shorthand
    Typewriting
  x Business—Study and teaching
    Commercial education
    Commercial schools
    Education, Business

    Schools, Commercial
  xx Education
— Accreditation
— Audio-visual aids
— Curricula
— Examinations, questions, etc.
— Law and legislation (Direct)
    xx Educational law and legislation
— Problems, exercises, etc.
— Programmed instruction
— Research
— Teacher training
— Text-books
Business education graduates (Direct)
  xx College graduates
— Employment (Direct)
Business English
  See English language—Business English
Business enterprises (Direct)
    Here are entered works on business con-
    cerns as legal entities, as conceived in
    various legal systems, and known by
    such terms as "fonds de commerce";
    "Unternehmem"; "azienda" or "im-
    pressa"; "hacienda mercantil"; etc.,
    and for which (the accounting term
    "going concern" excepted) an ade-
    quate English equivalent is wanting.
  sa Branches (Business enterprises)
    Business enterprises, Foreign
    Business enterprises, Sale of
    International business enterprises
  x Enterprises
    Firms
  xx Business
    Commercial law
    Entrepreneur
    Universitates (Civil law)
— Digests
— Finance
— — Programmed instruction
— Mathematical models
— Registration and transfer (Direct)
    xx Non-contentious jurisdiction
      Publicity (Law)
      Recording and registration
      Transfer (Law)
— Taxation (Direct)
    sa Business tax
— Valuation (Direct)
Business enterprises, Foreign (Direct)
  sa Corporations, Foreign
    Investments, Foreign
  x Foreign business enterprises
  xx Aliens
    Business enterprises
Business enterprises, Government
  See Government business enterprises
Business enterprises, International
  See International business enterprises
Business enterprises, Minority
  See Minority business enterprises
Business enterprises, New
  See New business enterprises
Business enterprises, Sale of (Direct)
  x Sale of business enterprises
  xx Business enterprises
Business espionage
  See Business intelligence
Business ethics (HF5386; HF5391)
  sa Business etiquette
    Business intelligence
    Businessmen—Conduct of life
    Competition
    Courts of honor
    Honesty
    Honor
    Speculation

Business ethics *(HF5386; HF5391)*
   (Continued)
         Success
         Wealth, Ethics of
      x Commercial ethics
         Ethics, Commercial
      xx Conduct of life
         Ethics
         Honesty
         Honor
         Professional ethics
         Wealth, Ethics of
Business etiquette
      x Etiquette, Business
         Etiquette, Office
         Office etiquette
      xx Business ethics
         Etiquette
         Office management
   — Stationery
         See Business announcements
Business executives
   See Executives
Business failures
   See Bankruptcy
Business fellowships
   See Business—Scholarships, fellowships, etc.
Business forecasting
      sa Sales forecasting
         Tax revenue estimating
      x Forecasting, Business
      xx Business cycles
         Economic forecasting
Business games
   See Management games
Business insurance
   See Insurance, Business
      Insurance, Business life
Business intelligence
         Here are entered works on the systematic
         accumulation of information regarding
         business competitors and their pro-
         ducts, including trade secrets.
      sa Trade secrets
      x Business espionage
         Espionage, Business
         Industrial espionage
         Intelligence, Business
      xx Business ethics
         Competition, Unfair
         Industrial management
Business interns
   See Interns (Business)
Business interruption insurance
   See Insurance, Business interruption
Business law *(Direct)*
         Here are entered compilations which give
         in short compass "business law for
         business men." Works of a more scien-
         tific character, text-books, etc., are en-
         tered under Commercial law.
      sa Forms (Law)
      x Commercial law—Popular works
         Law, Business
      xx Commercial law
Business leases
   See Commercial leases
Business letters
   See Commercial correspondence
Business libraries *(Direct)* *(Z675.B8)*
      sa Commercial libraries
      x Libraries, Business
      xx Commercial libraries
      Example under Libraries
Business life insurance
   See Insurance, Business life
Business losses
      x Losses, Business
      xx Accounting

      Business
      Finance
      Industry
Business losses as tax deductions
   See Income tax—Deductions—Losses
Business machines
   See Electronic office machines
      Office equipment and supplies
Business mathematics
         Subdivided by industry or profession, *e.g.*
         Business mathematics—Brewing in-
         dustry.
      sa Business—Mathematical models
         Industrial management—Mathematical
         models
         Insurance—Mathematics
         Investments—Mathematics
         Marketing—Mathematical models
         Ready-reckoners
         Real estate business—Mathematics
         subdivision Tables, etc. *under economic*
         subjects; and subdivision Tables and
         ready-reckoners *under names of*
         industries
      x Arithmetic, Commercial
         Business arithmetic
         Commercial arithmetic
         Finance—Mathematics
         Mathematics, Business
         Mathematics of finance
      xx Accounting
         Bookkeeping
         Business
         Commerce
         Finance
         Mathematics
   — Agriculture
         See Agricultural mathematics
   — Brewing industry
      x Brewing industry—Mathematics
         Note under Business mathematics
   — Problems, exercises, etc.
   — Programmed instruction
   — Tables, etc.
Business men
   See Businessmen
Business mortality *(Direct)*
      sa Bankruptcy
      xx Business
         Industry
Business names *(Direct)*
      sa Branded merchandise
         Trade-marks
      x Brand names
         Brands (Commerce)
         Firm names
         Trade names
      xx Commercial law
         Industrial property
         Intangible property
         Names
         Trade-marks
Business patronage of the arts
   See Art patronage
Business psychology
   See Psychology, Industrial
Business records *(Direct)*
      sa Business—Forms, blanks, etc.
         specific types of business records, e.g.
         Financial statements; Inventories;
         Railroads—Records and
         correspondence
      x Business—Records
         Commercial records
         Corporations—Records and
         correspondence
         Office records
         Records, Business

      xx Archives
         Office management
      Example under Records
Business relocation *(Direct)*
      x Business—Removal
         Relocation of business
      xx Industries, Location of
Business-reply mail
   See Postal service—Business-reply mail
Business report writing *(HF5719)*
      xx Communication in management
         Report writing
Business research
   See Economic research
      Small business research
Business Russian
   See Russian language—Business Russian
Business scholarships
   See Business—Scholarships, fellowships, etc.
Business secrets
   See Trade secrets
Business Spanish
   See Spanish language—Business Spanish
Business stabilization
   See Economic stabilization
Business tax *(Direct)*
         Here are entered works on a form of tax,
         largely European, levied on commer-
         cial establishments by volume of busi-
         ness, such as the German "Gewerbe-
         steuer" or the French "Patentes."
      sa Artisans—Taxation
         Licenses
         Payroll tax
         Small business—Taxation
      x Business—Taxation
         Occupation tax
         Privilege tax
         Taxation of business
      xx Business enterprises—Taxation
         Licenses
         Taxation
   — Great Britain
      x Profits tax (Great Britain)
Business teachers *(Direct)*
      x Commercial teachers
         Teachers, Business
         Teachers, Commercial
      xx Business education
         Teachers
Business trusts
   See Massachusetts trusts
Business turnover
   See Turnover (Business)
Businessmen *(Direct)*
      sa Capitalists and financiers
         Merchants
      x Business men
      xx Business
         Commerce
         Industry
   — Biography
   — Caricatures and cartoons
   — Conduct of life
      xx Business ethics
   — Correspondence, reminiscences, etc.
   — Interviews
   — Pensions
   — Portraits
   — Prayer-books and devotions
         (BV4596.B8)
   — Religious life
Businessmen, Chinese, [etc.] *(Direct)*
      x Chinese [etc.] businessmen
Businessmen in literature
      x Merchants in literature
      xx Economics in literature

244

Businesswomen
  See Women in business
Busing of school children
  See School children—Transportation
Bussaco, Battle of, 1810 *(DC233.B8)*
  xx Peninsular War, 1807-1814
Bustards *(QL696.G8)*
  sa Houbara
Busts *(NB1300)*
  sa Masks (Sculpture)
    Portraits on gems
  xx Sculpture
Busways (Electricity)
  See Bus conductors (Electricity)
Busy work
  See Creative activities and seat work
Butadiine
  See Acetylene
Butadiyne
  See Acetylene
Butcher shops
  See Butchers
Butchering
  See Slaughtering and slaughter-houses
Butchers *(Direct)* *(HD9410-9429)*
  sa Meat cutting
    Trade-unions—Butchers
  x Butcher shops
  xx Meat industry and trade
  — Vocational guidance
Bute language
  See Mbum language
Butler's Indian Campaign, 1778
Butte, Battle of the, 1877
  x Tongue River, Battle of, 1877
    Wolf Mountain, Battle of, 1877
  xx Indians of North America—Wars—
    1866-1895
Butter *(Butter making, SF263-9; Trade,*
    HD9278)
  sa Butterfat
    Ghee
    Oleomargarine
  xx Dairying
    Milk
  Example under Dairy products; Oils and fats,
    Edible; Produce trade
  — Analysis and examination *(SF265)*
    xx Dairy products—Analysis and
      examination
  — Early works to 1800 *(SF263)*
  — Juvenile literature
  — Marketing
  — Packaging
  — Preservation *(SF263)*
    Example under Farm produce—Storage;
      Food—Preservation
  — Prices
  — Taxation *(Direct)*
Butter, Artificial
  See Oleomargarine
Butter factories
  See Creameries
Butter molds
  x Butter prints
    Molds, Butter
    Moulds, Butter
    Prints, Butter
Butter oil
  See Butterfat
Butter prints
  See Butter molds
Butter trade *(Direct)*
Butterfat
  sa Ghee
  x Butter oil
    Milk fat
  xx Butter

Oils and fats
Butterflies *(Indirect)* *(QL541-562)*
  sa Caterpillars
    Milkweed butterflies
    Monarch butterfly
    Queen butterfly
    Red admiral
    Viceroy butterfly
  x Lepidoptera diurna
    Rhopalocera
  xx Insects
    Lepidoptera
  — Behavior
  — Collection and preservation *(QL465)*
  — Identification
  — Juvenile literature
  — Nomenclature (Popular)
  — Pictorial works *(QL543)*
Butterflies, Fossil *(QE832.L5)*
  x Fossil butterflies
  xx Insects, Fossil
Butterflies in art
  xx Art
Butterfly dance
  xx Indians of North America—Dances
    Indians of North America—Rites and
      ceremonies
  — Juvenile literature
Butterfly-shell roofs
  See Roofs, Shell
Buttermilk *(Dairying, SF275.B8)*
Butternut (Nickname)
Butterscotch
  xx Confectionery
Buttocks
  x Derriere
    Gluteal region
  — Anecdotes, facetiae, satire, etc.
Buttocks (in religion, folk-lore, etc.)
  x Folk-lore of buttocks
  xx Religion, Primitive
Button industry *(Direct)*
  sa Pearl button industry
    Wages—Button industry
  xx Buttons
  — Accounting
Buttonholes
  xx Clothing and dress
    Sewing
Buttons *(Military science, UC487;*
    Technology, TS2301.B9; Trade,
    HD9969.B9)
  sa Button industry
    Pearl button industry
  xx Clothing and dress
    Fastenings
    Insignia
  — Collectors and collecting *(NK3670)*
Buttons, American, ⌐etc.¬
  x American ⌐etc.¬ buttons
Buttress dams *(TC547)*
  xx Concrete dams
    Dams
Butyl-chloral *(RM666.B9)*
  x Croton-chloral
Butyl rubber
  xx Rubber, Artificial
  — Prices *(Direct)*
Buwayhids *(DS288.6)*
  x Buyids
  xx Arabs
    Daylamites
    Iran—History—640-1500
    Mesopotamia—History—634-1534
Buxar, Battle of, 1764
Buy-make decisions
  See Make-or-buy decisions

Buy-or-make decisions
  See Make-or-buy decisions
Buyers' guides
  See Consumer education
    Marketing (Home economics)
    Shopping
    subdivision Directories *under particular*
      lines of business and industry
Buyids
  See Buwayhids
Buying
  See Purchasing
Buying, Automobile
  See Automobile purchasing
Buying, Industrial
  See Industrial procurement
Buzan (Shingon sect)
  xx Buddhist sects
    Shingon (Sect)
Buzi language
  See Loma language
Buzz bomb
  See V-1 bomb
Buzzards *(QL696.A2)*
  sa Honey buzzards
    Turkey buzzard
  xx Birds of prey
Bwa (African people)
  See Bobo (African people)
Bwaidoga language
  xx Melanesian languages
Bwaka (African people)
  See Gbaya (African people)
Bwamu dialect
  See Bobo dialects
Bwawa (African people)
  See Bobo (African people)
Bwem language
  See Lefana language
Bwine-Mukuni language
  See Lenje language
Bwiti sect *(BL2465)*
  x Bouity sect
    Mboeti sect
    Mbueti sect
  xx Negroes—Religion
BWR
  See Boiling water reactors
By-laws *(Direct)*
  x Bye-laws
    Bylaws
  xx Articles of incorporation
    Associations, institutions, etc.
    Corporation law
    Corporations
    Corporations, Nonprofit
    Unincorporated societies
By-laws, Municipal
  See Ordinances, Municipal
By-product coke industry
  See Coke industry
By-product coke plants
  See Coke plants
By-products
  See Waste products
    subdivision By-products *under*
      particular industries, e.g. Gas
      manufacture and works—
      By-products
Bye-laws
  See By-laws
Bygas
  See Baigas
Bylaws
  See By-laws
Byliny
  sa Bogatyrs
  x Bîlinî

Byliny *(Continued)*
   xx Chansons de geste
     Epic poetry, Russian
     Folk-songs, Russian
     Heldensage
     Russian ballads and songs
     Russian poetry
Bypasses, Highway
   See Highway bypasses
Byrd Antarctic Expedition, 1st, 1928-1930
   (G850 1928)
Byrd Antarctic Expedition, 2d, 1933-1935
   (G850 1933)
Byssinosis
   xx Lungs—Dust diseases
     Textile workers—Diseases and hygiene
Byzantine antiquities
   sa Christian antiquities
     subdivision Antiquities, Byzantine
       under names of countries, cities, etc.
    x Antiquities, Byzantine
   xx Antiquities
     Christian antiquities
Byzantine architecture
   See Architecture, Byzantine
Byzantine art
   See Art, Byzantine
Byzantine art objects
   See Art objects, Byzantine
Byzantine bronze doors
   See Bronze doors, Byzantine
Byzantine bronzes
   See Bronzes, Byzantine
Byzantine bulls
   See Bulls, Byzantine
Byzantine chant
   See Chants (Byzantine)
Byzantine chronology
   See Chronology, Byzantine
Byzantine cloisonné
   See Cloisonné, Byzantine
Byzantine decoration and ornament
   See Decoration and ornament, Byzantine
Byzantine drama *(PA5160)*
Byzantine ecclesiastical embroidery
   See Ecclesiastical embroidery, Byzantine
Byzantine emperors *(DF506)*
   xx Emperors
Byzantine Empire *(DF501-649)*
   x Eastern Empire
Byzantine empresses
   x Empresses, Byzantine
Byzantine enamel and enameling
   See Enamel and enameling, Byzantine
Byzantine glassware
   See Glassware, Byzantine
Byzantine icons
   See Icons, Byzantine
Byzantine illumination of books and
     manuscripts
   See Illumination of books and manuscripts,
     Byzantine
Byzantine jewelry
   See Jewelry, Byzantine
Byzantine law
   See Law, Byzantine
Byzantine letters
   sa Greek letters
   xx Greek letters
Byzantine literature *(Collections,*
   PA5170-5198; History,
   PA5101-5167)
   sa Christian literature, Byzantine
     Greek literature
   xx Greek literature
Byzantine mosaics
   See Mosaics, Byzantine

Byzantine mural painting and decoration
   See Mural painting and decoration,
     Byzantine
Byzantine music
   See Music, Byzantine
Byzantine painting
   See Painting, Byzantine
Byzantine paintings
   See Paintings, Byzantine
Byzantine poetry *(Collections, PA5180-5189;*
   History, PA5150-5155)
   sa Hymns, Greek
   xx Greek poetry
Byzantine portrait sculpture
   See Portrait sculpture, Byzantine
Byzantine portraits
   See Portraits, Byzantine
Byzantine pottery
   See Pottery, Byzantine
Byzantine scribes
   See Scribes, Byzantine
Byzantine sculpture
   See Sculpture, Byzantine
Byzantine studies *(Direct) (DF501-649)*
   sa Hellenism
Bzura River, Battle of, 1939 *(D765.2.B)*
   xx World War, 1939-1945—Campaigns—
     Poland
C-5A (Jet transports)
   xx Jet transports
C*-algebras
   sa Von Neumann algebras
   x Algebras, W
     W*-algebras
   xx Banach algebras
C-coefficient
   See Clebsch-Gordan coefficients
C.F.&I. clause
   See C.I.F. clause
C.I.F. clause
   sa Delivered pricing
   x C.F.&I. clause
     "Cost, insurance and freight"
   xx Commercial law
     Contracts, Maritime
     Delivered pricing
     Export sales
     Maritime law
     Risk
     Sales
     Shipment of goods
C.O.D. shipments
   sa Postal service—C.O.D. shipments
   x Cash on delivery shipments
     Collect on delivery shipments
   xx Payment
     Shipment of goods
Ca Gaba Indians
   See Kagaba Indians
Caá Guazú, Battle of, 1841
   x Caáguazú, Battle of
Caáguazú, Battle of
   See Caá Guazú, Battle of, 1841
Caapi
   See Ayahuasca
Caaygua Indians
   See Mbya Indians
Cab and omnibus service *(Direct)*
   (HE5601-5720)
   Here are entered works dealing with local
    passenger transportation by means of
    horse-drawn carriers. Works dealing
    with the corresponding automotive
    services are entered under Motor bus
    lines and Taxicabs.
   sa Coaching
     Motor bus lines
     Omnibuses

     Taxicabs
   x Cabs
     Hacks (Carriages)
     Omnibus service
   xx Carriages and carts
     Carriers
     Communication and traffic
     Motor bus lines
     Taxicabs
     Transportation
     Vehicles
Cabala *(Direct) (Jewish religion, BM525;*
   Occult sciences, BF1585-1623)
   sa Adam kadmon
     Gematria
     Hebrew language—Alphabet (in
       religion, folk-lore, etc.)
     Maggid (Cabala)
     Occult sciences
     Sabbathaians
     Symbolism of numbers
   x Cabbala
     Jews—Cabala
     Kabbala
     Qabalah
   xx Gematria
     Hebrew literature
     Jewish literature
     Judaism
     Magic
     Mysticism
     Occult sciences
Cabala and Christianity *(Direct) (BM525)*
   x Christianity and Cabala
   xx Christianity and other religions—
     Judaism
Cabanagem, Revolution of, 1835
   See Pará, Brazil (State)—History
Cabardan ballads and songs
   See Kabardian ballads and songs
Cabardan language
   See Kabardian language
Cabarets
   See Music-halls (Variety-theaters, cabarets,
     etc.)
Cabbage *(SB331)*
   sa Broccoli
     Brussels sprouts
     Cauliflower
     Chinese cabbage
     Cookery (Cabbage)
     Kale
     Sauerkraut
  — Disease and pest resistance
  — Diseases and pests *(SB608.C14)*
   sa Cabbage aphid
     Cabbage looper
     Cabbage maggot
     Cabbage web-worm
     Cabbage yellows
     Clubroot
  — Marketing
   Example under Vegetables—Marketing
  — Storage
  — Varieties
Cabbage aphid
   xx Cabbage—Diseases and pests
Cabbage black ring spot
   See Turnip mosaic virus
Cabbage fly
   See Cabbage maggot
Cabbage looper *(SB945.C)*
   xx Cabbage—Diseases and pests
Cabbage maggot *(SB608.C14)*
   x Cabbage fly
     Cabbage root fly
     Cabbage-root maggot
   xx Cabbage—Diseases and pests

— Control (Indirect)
Cabbage root fly
  See Cabbage maggot
Cabbage-root maggot
  See Cabbage maggot
Cabbage web-worm
  xx Cabbage—Diseases and pests
Cabbage yellows
  xx Cabbage—Diseases and pests
Cabbala
  See Cabala
Cabdriver robberies (Direct)
  xx Robbery
    Taxicabs
Cabin atmospheres (Space environment)
  See Space cabin atmospheres
Cabin Creek, 2d Battle, 1864
Cabinet government
  See Cabinet system
Cabinet officers (Indirect) (United States,
    JK610-616)
  sa Ministerial officers
    Prime ministers
  x Ministers of State
    Secretaries of State
  — Portraits, caricatures, etc.
  — Registers
Cabinet organ
  See Reed-organ
Cabinet system (Direct) (JF331-341)
  sa Coalition governments
    Ministerial responsibility
  x Cabinet government
    Parliamentary government
  xx Political science
    Representative government and
      representation
Cabinet-work (TT197)
  sa Furniture making
    Gluing
    Kitchen cabinets
    Loud-speaker cabinets
    Marquetry
    Veneers and veneering
    Woodwork
  xx Carpentry
    Furniture making
    Joinery
    Woodwork
  — Equipment and supplies
  — Juvenile literature
Cabinet-workers (Direct) (Industry,
    HD9773)
  sa Furniture workers
    Woodworkers
  xx Carpenters
    Furniture workers
    Joiners
    Woodworkers
  Example under Artisans
Cabins
  See Log cabins
Cabins, Aircraft
  See Aircraft cabins
Cabiri (BL313)
Cable code addresses
  See Telegraph code addresses
Cable codes
  See Cipher and telegraph codes
Cable directories
  See Cables, Submarine—Directories
Cable-laying ships
  See Cable ships
Cable railroads
  See Railroads, Cable
Cable sheathing
  See Electric cable sheathing

Cable ships (VM466.C3)
  x Cable-laying ships
    Cableships
  xx Cables, Submarine
    Ships
Cable television
  See Community antenna television
Cables (Manufacture, TS1784-7; Marine
    engineering, VM791)
  xx Bridge construction
    Power transmission
    Rope
    Wire rope
  — Vibration
Cables, Electric
  See Cables, Submarine
    Electric cables
    Telegraph cables
    Telephone cables
Cables, Submarine (Economics,
    HE7709-7741; Military art and
    science, UG607; Technology,
    TK5605-5681)
  sa Cable ships
    Telegraph cables
  x Cables, Electric
    Ocean cables
    Submarine cables
    Submarine telegraph
    Telegraph, Submarine
  xx Communication and traffic
    Electric cables
    Telecommunication
    Telegraph
  — Accounting
  — Code addresses
      See Telegraph code addresses
  — Directories (HE7710)
      x Cable directories
  — Laws and regulations (International law,
      HE7715)
      xx Telegraph—Laws and regulations
  — Rates

            GEOGRAPHIC SUBDIVISIONS

  — Atlantic (Economics, HE7725;
      Technology, TK5611)
      x Atlantic cable
  — — Juvenile literature
  — Pacific (Economics, HE7731;
      Technology, TK5613)
      x Pacific cable
Cableships
  See Cable ships
Cabooses (Railroads) (TF485)
  x Crummies
    Railroad cabooses
    Railroads—Cabooses
  xx Railroads—Cars
Cabotín prize
  xx Literary prizes
Cabrais
  See Kabre (African people)
Cabs
  See Cab and omnibus service
    Carriages and carts
    Taxicabs
Caca language
  See Cacán language
Cacán language
  x Caca language
    Cacana language
    Calchaqui language
    Catamareño language
    Kaka language
    Kakan language
    Kakana language
    Tucumaño language

  xx Indians of South America—Languages
    Kechua language
    Lule language
Cacana language
  See Cacán language
Cacao (Indirect) (SB267)
    Here are entered works on the cacao tree
      and its culture only. Works dealing
      with the commercial product are en-
      tered under Chocolate and Cocoa.
  sa Cacao shells
  x Chocolate-tree
  Note under Cocoa
  — Breeding
      See Cacao breeding
  — Diseases and pests (SB608.C17)
  — Fertilizers and manures (S667.C)
Cacao breeding (Indirect) (SB267)
  x Cacao—Breeding
  xx Plant-breeding
Cacao-butter (TP684.C2)
Cacao research
  xx Agricultural research
Cacao shells
  xx Cacao
    Materia medica, Vegetable
Cacao shells as feed
Cacchi Indians
  See Kekchi Indians
Cacchi language
  See Kekchi language
Cachalot
  See Sperm whale
Cachari language
  See Bara language
Cachets (Philately)
  See Postmarks
Cachiquel Indians
  See Cakchikel Indians
Cachiquel language
  See Cakchikel language
Cacomitl cat (QL737.C2)
Cactus (QK495.C11; Cattle food, SF99;
    Culture, SB317.C2, SB413.C12)
  sa Peyote
  xx Forage plants
    Succulent plants
  — Analysis
  — Identification
      x Identification of cactus
  — Juvenile literature
  — Pictorial works
Cactus wrens
  xx Wrens
  — Behavior
Cadang-cadang
  x Kadang-kadang
  xx Coconut-palm—Diseases and pests
Cadasters (Direct)
  xx Land
    Land titles—Registration and transfer
    Real property
    Surveying
Cadastral maps
  See Real property—Maps
Cadastral surveys
  See Real property
Cadaver in art
  xx Art
    Death—Art
Caddies
  See Caddying
Caddis-flies (Indirect) (QL516-519)
  x Trichoptera
  xx May-flies
    Neuroptera
  — Anatomy
  — Juvenile literature

Caddo Indians *(E99.C12)*
  sa Hasinai Indians
  xx Caddoan Indians
    Indians of North America
Caddo language *(PM721)*
  xx Caddoan languages
Caddoan Indians *(E99.C13)*
  sa Arikara Indians
    Caddo Indians
    Pawnee Indians
    Wichita Indians
  xx Indians of North America
  — Legends
Caddoan languages *(PM721)*
  sa Arikara language
    Caddo language
    Pawnee language
Caddying *(GV977)*
  x Caddies
  xx Golf
Cadence (Music) *(Harmony, ML444, MT50)*
  x Clausula
  xx Harmony
    Musical form
Cadenzas, Vocal
  See Vocal music—Cadenzas
Cade's Rebellion, 1450 *(DA257)*
  x Jack Cade's Rebellion
Cadihéos
  See Cadioéo Indians
Cadillac automobile
Cadioéo Indians *(F2520.1.C)*
  x Cadihéos
    Cadiques
    Kadieuéu Indians
  xx Guaycuru Indians
    Indians of South America
Cadiques
  See Cadioéo Indians
Cadis *(Direct)*
  x Kadis
    Qadis
  xx Judges (Islamic law)
Cadiz, Battle of, 1656 *(DA86.8 1656)*
Cadiz Expedition, 1587 *(DP402.C29)*
Cadiz Expedition, 1596 *(DP402.C29)*
Cadiz Expedition, 1625 *(DP402.C29)*
Cadmium *(Chemistry, QD181.C3; Mining, TN490.C2)*
  sa Plants, Effect of cadmium on
    Soils—Cadmium content
  — Analysis
  — Isotopes
    x Cadmium isotopes
      Isotopic cadmium
  — — Decay
  — — Spectra
  — Metallurgy *(TN799.C2)*
  — Spectra
Cadmium alloys
  sa Bismuth-cadmium alloys
    Cadmium-tin alloys
    Cadmium-zinc alloys
    Gold-cadmium alloys
    Lead-zinc-cadmium-tin alloys
    Magnesium-cadmium alloys
Cadmium-bismuth alloys
  See Bismuth-cadmium alloys
Cadmium crystals
Cadmium electrodes
  See Electrodes, Cadmium
Cadmium-gold alloys
  See Gold-cadmium alloys
Cadmium isotopes
  See Cadmium—Isotopes
Cadmium-magnesium alloys
  See Magnesium-cadmium alloys

Cadmium-nickel batteries
  See Nickel-cadmium batteries
Cadmium organic compounds
  See Organocadmium compounds
Cadmium plating
  xx Electroplating
Cadmium-tin alloys
  x Tin-cadmium alloys
  xx Cadmium alloys
    Tin alloys
Cadmium tungstate crystals
Cadmium-vapor electric lighting
  See Electric lighting, Cadmium vapor
Cadmium-zinc alloys
  x Zinc-cadmium alloys
  xx Cadmium alloys
    Zinc alloys
Cadoudal-Pichegru Conspiracy, 1803-1804 *(DC193.4)*
Caduceus *(BL457.C3)*
  xx Religion, Primitive
    Signs and symbols
Caecum
  See Cecum
Caen, Battle, of, 1944
  xx World War, 1939-1945—Campaigns—
    Normandy
Caenozoic period
  See Geology, Stratigraphic—Cenozoic
    Paleobotany—Cenozoic
    Paleontology—Cenozoic
Caesarean section
  See Cesarean section
Caesarism
  sa Imperialism
  xx Imperialism
Caesaropapism
  xx Church and state
Caesars
  See Roman emperors
Caesium
  See Cesium
Cafés
  See Hotels, taverns, etc.
    Restaurants, lunch rooms, etc.
Cafeterias
  See Restaurants, lunch rooms, etc.
    School lunchrooms, cafeterias, etc.
Caffeine
  xx Coffee
    Tea
  — Physiological effect
    x Physiological effect of caffeine
  — Therapeutic use
Cafirs
  See Kafirs (Kafiristan)
Cagaba Indians
  See Kagaba Indians
Cagaba language
  See Kagaba language
Cagancha, Battle of, 1839 *(F2726)*
  xx Uruguay—History—1830-1875
Cage-birds *(SF461)*
  sa Aviaries
    names of cage-birds, e.g. Canaries,
      Mocking-birds
  xx Birds, Ornamental
  Example under Birds
Cage inclusion compounds
  See Clathrate compounds
Cages, Bird
  See Birdcages
Caghnawaga Indians
  See Caughnawaga Indians
Cagots *(DC34.5.C3)*
  x Christianos
  xx Ethnology—France

Cahita Indians *(F1221.C3)*
  sa Mayo Indians
    Yaqui Indians
  xx Indians of Mexico
    Mayo Indians
    Piman Indians
    Yaqui Indians
Cahuilla Indians *(E99.C155)*
  x Coahuila Indians
    Cohuilla Indians
    Kawia Indians (Shoshoneans)
  xx Indians of North America
    Shoshonean Indians
  — Government relations
Cahuilla language *(PM731)*
  x Coahuila language
    Kawia language (Shoshone)
  xx Shoshonean languages
Cahuilla literature *(PM731)*
Caibate, Battle of, 1756 *(F2684)*
  x Caybate, Battle of, 1756
    Kaibate, Battle of, 1756
  xx Seven Reductions, War of the,
    1754-1756
Caigua Indians
  See Caingua Indians
Cain in literature
Cain complex *(RC563)*
  x Complexes (Psychology)
  xx Psychiatry
Caingangue Indians
  See Kaingangue Indians
Caingangue language
  See Kaingangue language
Caingua Indians *(F2230.2.C)*
  sa Mbya Indians
  x Caigua Indians
    Caiuás
    Cayuá Indians
    Kaingua Indians
    Kayuá Indians
  xx Guarani Indians
    Indians of South America
Cairn terriers *(SF429.C3)*
  xx Terriers
Cairns
  sa Mounds
Cairo
  — Fire, 1952
  — Riot, 1952
  — Siege, 1077
Caisson-disease *(RC103.C3)*
  sa Atmospheric pressure—Physiological
    effect
  x Compressed-air disease
    Decompression sickness
  xx Atmospheric pressure—Physiological
    effect
    Occupational diseases
  — Complications and sequelae
Caissons *(TC199)*
  sa Bridges—Foundations and piers
    Compressed air
    Foundations
    Pressure vessels
  xx Bridges—Foundations and piers
    Foundations
    Hydraulic structures
    Pressure vessels
Caiuás
  See Caingua Indians
Cakchi Indians
  See Kekchi Indians
Cakchi language
  See Kekchi language
Cakchikel Indians
  sa Quichés
  x Cachiquel Indians

Kacchiquel Indians
  xx Indians of Central America
     Mayas
     Quichés
Cakchikel language *(PM3576)*
  x Cachiquel language
     Kacchiquel language
  xx Indians of Central America—Languages
     Quichean languages
Cake *(TX771)*
  sa Cake decorating
     Cheesecake (Cookery)
     Cookies
     Doughnuts
     Pastry
  x Gingerbread
  xx Baking
     Cookery
     Pastry
  Example under Baked products
  — Juvenile literature
Cake decorating *(TX771)*
  sa Icings, Cake
  xx Cake
     Confectionery
     Icings, Cake
Cake icing
  See Icings, Cake
Calabar bean *(RS165.C)*
  x Ordeal bean
  xx Beans
Calabash tree
Calabrese
  See Strambotto
Calabrian literature
  See Italian literature—Calabria
Calais
  — Siege, 1346 *(DC98.5.C2)*
     xx Hundred Years' War, 1339-1453
  — Siege, 1558
Calais, Battle of, 1940 *(D756.5.C)*
  xx World War, 1939-1945—Campaigns—
     France
Calama, Battle of, 1879
  xx War of the Pacific, 1879-1884
Calamian language
  See Kalamian language
Calamiano language
  See Kalamian language
Calamin
Calamities
  See Disasters
Calandria (Dance) *(GV1796.C13)*
Calapooyan Indians
  See Kalapuyan Indians
Calcaneus
  See Heel bone
Calcareous algae
  See Coralline algae
Calcasieu Pass, Battle of, 1864
Calchaqui Indians *(F2823.C3)*
  sa Diaguita Indians
  xx Indians of South America
Calchaqui language
  See Cacán language
Calciferous glands
  xx Worms—Anatomy
Calcification
  sa Bone
     Calciphylaxis
     Calcium in the body
     Metabolism, Disorders of
     subdivision Calcification *under organs,
        etc. of the body, e.g.* Arteries—
        Calcification; Brain—Calcification;
        Lungs—Calcification
  xx Bone
     Calcium in the body

Metabolism, Disorders of
Calcimining *(TH8161)*
  x Kalsomining
  xx Painting, Industrial
     Plastering
Calcio fiorentino, Gioco del
  See Florentine football
Calciphylaxis
  xx Calcification
Calcite *(Indirect)* *(QE391.C2)*
Calcite crystals
Calcitonin
  x Thyrocalcitonin
  xx Thyroid hormones
Calcium *(Chemistry, QD181.C2;
     Physiological chemistry, QP535.C2)*
  sa Soils—Calcium content
  — Analysis
  — Isotopes
     x Radiocalcium
  — — Decay
  — Physiological effect *(QP913.C2;
     Therapeutics, RM666.C24)*
  — Spectra
Calcium alloys
  sa Magnesium-calcium-zinc alloys
Calcium carbide *(TP770)*
  — Storage
Calcium carbonate
  sa Aragonite
     Coccoliths
     Travertine
Calcium chloride
Calcium in soils
  See Soils—Calcium content
Calcium in the body *(QP535.C2)*
  sa Bone densitometry
     Calcification
     Calcium metabolism
  xx Calcification
     Deficiency diseases
  Example under Minerals in the body
  — Juvenile literature
Calcium metabolism
  xx Calcium in the body
     Metabolism
Calcium metabolism disorders
  sa Hypercalcemia
     Milk fever in animals
  xx Metabolism, Disorders of
Calcium oxalate
Calcium stearate
Calcium tungstate crystals
Calcium vapor in the sun
  See Sun—Flocculi
Calculating boards, Network
  See Electric network analyzers
Calculating-machines *(Bookkeeping,
     HF5688-9; Mechanical devices,
     QA75)*
     Here are entered works on calculators as
        well as all mechanical computers of
        pre-1945 vintage. Works on modern
        electronic computers first developed
        after 1945 are entered under Comput-
        ers.
  sa Accounting machines
     Analog computers
     Comptometers
     Computation laboratories
     Computers
     Cybernetics
     Digital counters
     Punched card systems
     Slide-rule
     Tabulating machines
  x Adding-machines
     Arithmetic, Mechanical

     Calculators
     Computing machines
     Mechanical arithmetic
  xx Bookkeeping
     Machine accounting
     Mathematical instruments
     Office equipment and supplies
     Office practice
     Tabulating machines
  Note under Computers
  — Appraisal
     See Calculating-machines—Valuation
  — Catalogs
  — Design and construction
  — Juvenile literature
  — Maintenance and repair
  — Problems, exercises, etc.
  — Terminology
  — Valuation
     x Calculating-machines—Appraisal
Calculators
  See Calculating-machines
     Ready-reckoners
Calculators, Satellite apparent position
  See Artificial satellites—Apparent position
     calculators
Calculi
  sa Bezoar
  x Calculus (Pathology)
Calculi, Biliary *(RC850; RD547)*
  x Biliary calculi
     Cholelithiasis
     Gall-bladder—Calculi
     Gall-stones
  — Psychosomatic aspects
  — Surgery
  — — Complications and sequelae
Calculi, Urinary *(RC921.V4; RD581)*
  sa Lithotomy
     Lithotrity
  x Bladder—Calculus
     Gravel (Pathology)
     Kidney stones
     Urinary calculi
     Urinary organs—Calculi
  xx Kidneys—Diseases
  — Early works to 1800
Calculus *(QA300-316)*
  sa Curvature
     Curves
     Differential equations
     Fourier series
     Functions
     Geometry, Infinitesimal
     Harmonic analysis
     Mathematical analysis
     Mean value theorems (Calculus)
     Nonlinear theories
     Surfaces
  x Analysis (Mathematics)
     Fluxions
     Infinitesimal calculus
     Limits (Mathematics)
  xx Functions
     Geometry, Infinitesimal
     Mathematical analysis
     Mathematics
  — Early works to 1800 *(QA302)*
  — Examinations, questions, etc.
  — Problems, exercises, etc.
  — Programmed instruction
Calculus, Absolute differential
  See Calculus of tensors
Calculus, Dental
  See Dental calculus
Calculus, Differential *(QA304-6)*
  x Differential calculus
  — Early works to 1800

Calculus, Differential *(QA304-6)*
(Continued)
— Programmed instruction
Calculus, Integral *(QA308-311)*
   sa Integrals
      Integrals, Generalized
   x Integral calculus
   xx Differential equations
— Early works to 1800
— Programmed instruction
Calculus, Operational *(QA432)*
   sa Laplace transformation
   x Operational calculus
   xx Differential equations
      Electric circuits
      Integral equations
— Problems, exercises, etc.
Calculus, Predicate
   See Predicate calculus
Calculus, Propositional
   See Propositional calculus
Calculus (Pathology)
   See Calculi
Calculus of differences
   See Difference equations
Calculus of operations *(QA253)*
   sa Algebras, Linear
   x Operations, Calculus of
   xx Algebra, Universal
      Algebras, Linear
Calculus of spinors
   See Spinor analysis
Calculus of tensors *(QA433)*
   sa Scalar field theory
      Spaces, Generalized
      Spinor analysis
      Tensor products
   x Absolute differential calculus
      Calculus, Absolute differential
      Tensor analysis
   xx Geometry, Differential
      Geometry, Infinitesimal
      Spinor analysis
      Vector analysis
— Problems, exercises, etc.
— Programmed instruction
Calculus of variations *(QA315-316)*
   sa Brachistochrone
      Convex domains
      Functional analysis
      Lagrangian functions
   x Isoperimetrical problems
      Variations, Calculus of
   xx Maxima and minima
Caldecott awards
   See Caldecott medal books
Caldecott medal books
   x Caldecott awards
   xx Illustrated books, Children's
      Literary prizes
Calderan, Battle of, 1514 *(DR504)*
   x Caldiran, Battle of, 1514
      Tschaldiran, Battle of, 1514
Caldiran, Battle of, 1514
   See Calderan, Battle of, 1514
Calendar *(CE73)*
   sa Chronology
      Church calendar
      Clog-almanacs
      Days
      Leap year
      Months
      Time
   x Computus
   xx Astronomy
      Chronology
      Chronology, Historical
— Early works to 1800
— History

— — Juvenile literature
— Juvenile literature
— Reform
   See Calendar reform
Calendar, Abnaki *(E99.A1)*
   x Abnaki calendar
      Abnaki Indians—Calendar
Calendar, Anglo-Saxon, [Burmese, Egyptian, etc.]
   x Anglo-Saxon [Burmese, Egyptian, etc.] calendar
Calendar, Arab
   See Calendar, Islamic
Calendar, Assyro-Babylonian *(CE33)*
   x Assyro-Babylonian calendar
      Babylonian calendar
Calendar, Aztec
   See Calendar, Mexican
Calendar, Buddhist *(CE38.5)*
   x Buddhist calendar
Calendar, Celtic
   x Celtic calendar
      Coligny calendar
      Gaulish calendar
Calendar, Ecclesiastical
   See Church calendar
Calendar, Germanic *(CE61.G3)*
   x Calendar, Scandinavian
      Germanic calendar
      Scandinavian calendar
Calendar, Gregorian *(CE76)*
   x Gregorian calendar
Calendar, Hebrew
   See Calendar, Jewish
Calendar, Islamic *(CE59)*
   x Calendar, Arab
      Calendar, Muslim
      Islamic calendar
      Muslim calendar
   Note under Religious calendars
Calendar, Jewish *(CE35)*
   sa Chronology, Jewish
      New moon (Judaism)
      Three Weeks (Jewish calendar)
      Tishri
   x Calendar, Hebrew
      Hebrew calendar
      Jewish calendar
   xx Chronology, Jewish
   Note under Religious calendars
Calendar, Julian *(CE75)*
   x Julian calendar
Calendar, Maya *(F1435.3.C14)*
   sa Calendar, Tarascan
      Calendar, Zapotec
   x Maya calendar
      Mayas—Calendar
   xx Mayas—Antiquities
Calendar, Mexican *(F1219.3.C2)*
   sa Calendar, Tarascan
      Calendar, Zapotec
   x Aztec calendar
      Calendar, Aztec
      Calendar stone of Mexico
      Mexican calendar
Calendar, Muslim
   See Calendar, Islamic
Calendar, Perpetual *(CE91-92)*
   x Perpetual almanac
      Perpetual calendar
Calendar, Religious
   See Religious calendars
Calendar, Republican *(CE77)*
   x Republican calendar
Calendar, Scandinavian
   See Calendar, Germanic
Calendar, Tarascan *(F1219.3.C2)*
   x Tarasco Indians—Calendar

   xx Calendar, Maya
      Calendar, Mexican
Calendar, Turkish
   Here are entered works on the old Turkish calendar, used by the Turks prior to their adoption of the Islamic calendar.
   x Turkish calendar
Calendar, Tzeltal *(F1435.3.C14)*
   x Tzeltal calendar
      Tzeltal Indians—Calendar
Calendar, Zapotec *(F1219.3.C2)*
   x Zapotec Indians—Calendar
   xx Calendar, Maya
      Calendar, Mexican
Calendar reform
   x Calendar—Reform
Calendar stone of Mexico
   See Calendar, Mexican
Calendar watches
   xx Astronomical clocks
      Clocks and watches
Calendaring of manuscripts
   See Cataloging of manuscripts
Calendars *(CE91; D11.5)*
   sa Almanacs
      Art calendars
      Birthday books
      Devotional calendars
      Music calendars
      subdivision Calendars *under subjects,*
        e.g. Business—Calendars
   x Annuals
      Dates, Books of
   xx Almanacs
      Chronology, Historical
      Yearbooks
— Juvenile literature
Calendars, Archival
   See Archives—Inventories, calendars, etc.
Calendars, Legislative
   See Legislative calendars
Calendars, Literary
   See Literary calendars
Calendars, Religious
   See Religious calendars
Calendars, Runic *(PD2014)*
   x Runic calendars
Calendering of plastics
   See Plastics—Calendering
Calenders (Paper making) *(TS1117)*
   xx Paper-making machinery
Calf
   See Calves
Calibration
   sa subdivision Calibration *under names of instruments, etc., e.g.* Rolls (Rolling-mills)—Calibration; Strain gages—Calibration
   xx Physical measurements
      Standardization
Calico engraving
   See Calico-printing
Calico-printing *(Direct)* *(TP930)*
   x Calico engraving
   xx Dyes and dyeing
      Printing
      Textile industry and fabrics
      Textile printing
Calico scallop *(QL430.7.P3)*
   xx Scallops
California
— Aerial photographs
   Example under Aerial photographs
— Description and travel
— — Views
      Example under reference from Scenery
— Gold discoveries *(F865)*

— — Juvenile literature
— History *(F856-870)*
— — To 1846
— — 1846-1850
    sa Bear Flag Revolt, 1846
        Kearny's Expedition, 1846
        Santa Clara, Battle of, 1847
        Temecula—Massacre, 1847
— — 1850-
— — 1850-1950
— — Civil War, 1861-1865 *(F497)*

California. University
— Sanitary affairs
    Example under reference from Sanitary
    affairs
    Note under School hygiene

California black oak *(Botany, QK495.F14;*
    Sylviculture, SD397.C33)
  x Black oak, California
     Kellogg's oak
  xx Oak

California buckeye

California condor
  xx Condors
— Juvenile literature
— Legends and stories

California cuckoo
  See Yellow-billed cuckoo

California gray whale
  See Pacific gray whale

California ground squirrel
  xx Ground-squirrels

California gull
  xx Gulls

California hagfish
  See Pacific hagfish

California halibut
  sa Halibut fisheries
  xx Halibut

California peach borer

California psychological inventory
  xx Personality tests

California quail
  x California valley quail
     Valley quail, California
  xx Quails

California Railroad Strike, 1894
    (HD5325.R12 1894.C2)

California sardine
  See Pacific sardine

California sea lion
  xx Eared seals

California valley quail
  See California quail

California vole
  xx Field mice

California white cedar
  See Incense cedar

California woodpecker *(QL696.P5)*
  xx Woodpeckers

Californite
  See Vesuvianite

Califs
  See Caliphs

Calipers *(TJ1313)*
  xx Measuring instruments
     Thickness measurement
— Standards
— Testing

Caliphate
  sa Caliphs
     Khilafat Movement
  x Khalifat
     Khilafat
  xx Caliphs
     Islam
     Kings and rulers

Caliphs *(Arabian, DS234-8)*
  sa Abbasids
     Caliphate
     Fatimites
     Hammudites
     Omayyads
  x Califs
     Khalifs
  xx Caliphate
     Kings and rulers
— Juvenile literature

Calisthenics
  See Callisthenics

Calixtines
  See Utraquists

Calking
  sa Sealing compounds
  x Caulking

Call loans
  See Brokers' loans

Calla *(SB413.C15)*
  x Calla-lily
  xx Lilies

Calla-lily
  See Calla

Callahuaya Indians
  xx Aymara Indians
     Indians of South America

Callahuaya language
  x Callawaya language
     Incan language
     Machchaj juyai language
  xx Aymara language
     Indians of South America—Languages

Callao
— Blockade, 1880
    xx War of the Pacific, 1879-1884
— Bombardment, 1866 *(F3447)*
— Siege, 1826
    xx Peru—History—War of
        Independence, 1820-1829

Callawaya language
  See Callahuaya language

Calligraphers *(Direct)*
  sa Copyists
  x Penmen
  xx Penmanship
     Writing
— Correspondence, reminiscences, etc.

Calligraphers, Muslim *(Direct)*
  x Muslim calligraphers

Calligraphers' marks
  x Marks, Calligraphers'
  xx Artists' marks

Calligraphic paintings
  See Letter-pictures

Calligraphy *(Z43-45)*
  xx Penmanship
     Writing
— Collectors and collecting *(Direct)*
— Competitions

Calligraphy, Arabic, ⌈**Chinese, German, etc.**⌉
    (Direct)

Calligraphy, Zen *(Direct)*
  x Zen calligraphy

Calling
  See Vocation

Calliope *(ML597)*
  xx Organ

Calliope music *(M175.C3)*
  x Merry-go-round music
  xx Organ music

Callisthenics *(GV481-508)*
  sa Dumb-bells
     Gymnastics
     Hoop exercises
     Indian clubs
     Musico-callisthenics

     Physical education and training
     Swedish gymnastics
  x Calisthenics
  xx Dumb-bells
     Exercise
     Gymnastics
     Hygiene
     Indian clubs
     Physical education and training
     Swedish gymnastics
— Juvenile literature

Callitype
  See Kallitype

Calls, Military
  See Military calls

Calls (Commerce)
  See Put and call transactions

Calls (for animals)
  sa Game calling (Hunting)

Callus *(QM569)*
  xx Bones
     Fractures

Callus (Botany) *(QK769)*

Calmar, Union of, 1397
  See Kalmar, Union of, 1397

Calmar War, 1611-1613
  See Kalmar War, 1611-1613

Calming of waves
  See Waves, Calming of

Calmuck language
  See Kalmuck language

Calmuck literature
  See Kalmuck literature

Calmucks
  See Kalmucks

Calomel *(RM666.M5)*

Caloosa Indians
  See Calusa Indians

Calor animalis
  See Animal heat

Caloric content of foods
  See Food—Caloric content

Caloric engines *(TJ765)*
  sa Stirling engines
  x Hot-air engines
  xx Engines

Calories (Food)
  See Food—Caloric content

Calorimeters and calorimetry *(QC291-7)*
  sa Animal heat
     Bomb calorimeter
     Cooling
     Heat—Laboratory manuals
     Heat of solution
     Respiration calorimeter
     Specific heat
  x Microcalorimetry
  xx Heat
     Thermometers and thermometry

Calorizing *(TS657)*
  xx Aluminum coating
     Diffusion coatings

Calotype *(TR395)*
  x Talbotype
  xx Photography

Cālukyas
  See Chalukyas

Calumet dance
  xx Indians of North America—Dances

Calumny
  See Libel and slander

Calusa Indians
  x Caloosa Indians
     Cape Florida Indians
     Kaloosas Indians
     Kalusa Indians
  xx Indians of North America

Calutron
    x Magnetic separators
    xx Electromagnets
       Isotope separation
       Isotopes
       Mass spectrometry
       Separators (Machines)
       Spectrograph
Calvaria *(QL822)*
    x Calvarium
    xx Skull
    — Tumors
Calvarial hyperostosis
    See Hyperostosis frontalis interna
Calvaries
    See Crosses
Calvarium
    See Calvaria
Calves *(Indirect) (SF205)*
    x Calf
    xx Cattle
       Cows
    — Diseases *(SF961-7)*
    — Economic aspects *(Direct)*
    — Feeding and feeds
       sa Milk as feed
    — Grading
    — Juvenile literature
    — Marketing
Calvinism *(Direct) (BX9401-9595)*
    sa Antinomianism
       Arminianism
       Congregationalism
       Covenants (Theology)
       Mercersburg theology
       Neonomianism
       New England theology
       Perseverance (Theology)
       Predestination
       Presbyterianism
       Puritans
       Zwinglianism
    xx Arminianism
       Congregationalism
       Puritans
       Reformation
       Reformed Church
       Theology
       Zwinglianism
    — Controversial literature
Calvinists
Calvinists in Brazil, [etc.]
Calvo clause
    See Calvo doctrine and clause
Calvo doctrine and clause *(JX5485.C2)*
    sa Drago doctrine
    x Calvo clause
    xx Aliens
       Claims
       Concessions
       Diplomatic protection
       Drago doctrine
       Investments, Foreign (International
          law)
Calypso (Game) *(GV1295.C)*
Calypso songs
    See Folk-songs—Trinidad
       Music, Popular (Songs, etc.)—Trinidad
Calyx (Botany)
    xx Flowers—Morphology
Cam
    See Chams
Čam language
    See Cham language
Camagüey, Cuba (Province)
    — Hurricane, 1932
       x Santa Cruz del Sur, Cuba—
          Hurricane, 1932

Camakoko language
    See Chamacoco language
Camaldolese
    See Camaldolites
Camaldolites *(BX3085.C; BX4290.C)*
    x Camaldolese
       Camaldulians
       Eremites
    xx Benedictines
       Hermits
Camaldolites in Italy
Camaldulians
    See Camaldolites
Camanche Indians
    See Comanche Indians
Camaro automobile *(TL215.C)*
    xx Chevrolet automobile
Camayura Indians
    See Kamaiurá Indians
Camba Lahuḷi dialect
    See Chamba Lahuḷi dialect
Camber (Aerofoils)
    xx Aerofoils
       Aeroplanes—Wings
Cambistry
    See Foreign exchange
       Money—Tables, etc.
       Weights and measures
Cambium *(QK707; QK725)*
    xx Botany—Anatomy
Cambium miner
Cambodian astronomy
    See Astronomy, Khmer
Cambodian language
    See Khmer language
Cambodian literature
    See Khmer literature
Cambodian manuscripts
    See Manuscripts, Khmer
Cambrai, League of, 1508 *(DG678.26)*
    x League of Cambrai, 1508
Cambrai, Battle of, 1917
    xx European War, 1914-1918—Campaigns
       —France
Cambrai, Treaty of, 1529 *(DC113.5)*
    x Ladies' peace
       Paix des dames
Cambrian period
    See Geology, Stratigraphic—Cambrian
       Paleobotany—Cambrian
       Paleontology—Cambrian
Cambric
    Example under Textile industry and fabrics
Cambridge. University
    — Prizes
       Example under Rewards (Prizes, etc.)
Cambridge, Eng., in literature
Cambridge Platonists *(B1133.C2)*
    x Platonists, Cambridge
Cambridge school of economics
    See Neoclassical school of economics
Cambrils
    — Siege, 1640
Camdella dynasty
    See Chandela dynasty
Camden, S.C., Battle of, 1780 *(E241.C17)*
Camel (Fighter planes)
    x Sopwith Camel (Fighter planes)
       Sopwith fighting biplane
    xx Fighter planes
Camellia *(Culture, SB413.C18)*
    — Breeding
       See Camellia breeding
    — Genetics
    — Pictorial works
    — Varieties
Camellia breeding
    x Camellia—Breeding

    xx Plant-breeding
Camellia in art
    xx Art
Camels *(QL737.U5; Animal industries,*
       SF249)
    x Dromedaries
    xx Domestic animals
       Ruminantia
    Example under Ungulata
    — Diseases *(SF979.C2)*
       sa Trypanosomiasis
    — Juvenile literature
Camels in art
    xx Art
Camembert cheese
Cameo glass *(Direct)*
    x Glass, Cameo
    xx Glassware
Cameo glass, English, [French, etc.] *(Direct)*
    x English [French, etc.] cameo glass
Cameo incrustation
    See Sulphides (Art)
Cameos *(Direct) (NK5720)*
    sa Gems
       Portraits on gems
       Sulphides (Art)
    xx Gems
       Glyptics
       Jewelry
       Portraits on gems
Camera obscura
Camera shutters
    x Shutters, Camera
Camera tubes, Television
    See Television camera tubes
Cameralism
    See Mercantile system
Cameras *(TR250-265)*
    sa Electric eye cameras
       Miniature cameras
       Moving-picture cameras
       Single-lens reflex cameras
       Twin-lens cameras
       View cameras
       individual makes of cameras, e.g.
          Ciro-flex camera, Exakta camera
    xx Photography
       Photography—Apparatus and supplies
    — Calibration
    — Collectors and collecting
    — Repairing
Cameron Clan
    Example under Clans and clan system
Cameroon fiction (French)
    See French fiction—Cameroon authors
Cameroon literature (French)
    See French literature—Cameroon authors
Cameroon poetry (French)
    See French poetry—Cameroon authors
Camillians
    x Fathers of the Good Death
Camino automobile
    See El Camino automobile
Camisards *(DC127.C3)*
    sa Huguenots in France
Camorra *(HV6453.I8)*
    sa Mafia
    xx Mafia
Camouflage (Biology)
    sa Color of animals
       Mimicry (Biology)
       Protective coloration (Biology)
    x Animal camouflage
    xx Animal defenses
       Color of animals
       Mimicry (Biology)
    — Juvenile literature

Camouflage (Military science) *(UG449;*
    V215)
  xx Military art and science
    Naval art and science
Camp administration
  See Camps—Administration
Camp cookery
  See Camps—Food service
    Outdoor cookery
Camp counselors *(GV198.C6)*
  x Camps—Counselors
    Counselors, Camp
Camp decoration
  See Camps—Decoration
Camp Fire Girls *(HS3353.C3)*
  xx Girls—Societies and clubs
Camp followers
  x Women camp followers
Camp layouts
  See Camp sites, facilities, etc.
Camp libraries
  See European War, 1914-1918—Libraries
    (in camps, etc.)
    War libraries
    World War, 1939-1945—Libraries
Camp maintenance
  See Camp sites, facilities, etc.
Camp management
  See Camps—Administration
Camp-meeting hymns
  See Revivals—Hymns
Camp-meetings *(BV3798-9; Methodist,*
    BX8475-6)
  sa Church camps
  x Campmeetings
  xx Evangelistic work
    Methodism
    Revivals
Camp nursing *(Indirect) (RT120.C3)*
  sa Camps—Safety measures
  x Camps—Nursing
  xx Camps—Safety measures
    Nurses and nursing
Camp sites, facilities, etc. *(Indirect)*
    (GV198.L3)
  x Camp layouts
    Camp maintenance
  xx Camping
    Camps
  — Design and construction
  — Law and legislation *(Direct)*
  — Sanitation
Camp sounds
  xx Camps
    Sounds
Camp stoves *(SK608)*
  x Stoves, Camp
  xx Camping—Outfits, supplies, etc.
    Outdoor cookery
Campa Indians *(F3430.1.C3)*
  x Ande Indians
    Anti Indians
  xx Indians of South America
  — Religion and mythology
Campa language *(PM5716)*
  x Ande language
    Anti language
  xx Arawakan languages
    Campa languages
    Indians of South America—Languages
Campa languages
  sa Campa language
    Nomatsiguenga language
  xx Arawakan languages
    Indians of South America—Languages
Campaign biography
  xx Biography (as a literary form)
    Campaign literature

    Politics, Practical
Campaign buttons
  See Campaign insignia
Campaign funds *(United States, JK1991-7)*
  sa Elections—[local subdivision]—
    Campaign funds, *e.g.* Elections—
    Philadelphia—Campaign funds
  x Assessments, Political
    Political assessments
    Political parties—Finance
  xx Corruption (in politics)
    Elections
    Politics, Practical
    United States—Officials and employees
    —Political activity
  Note under Elections—Campaign funds
Campaign insignia *(CJ5806)*
  x Campaign buttons
    Campaign pins
  xx Campaign paraphernalia
    Elections—United States
    Insignia
Campaign literature *(JK2251-2391)*
  By date, subdivided by party, and further
    by locality, *e.g.* Campaign literature,
    1900—Republican; Campaign litera-
    ture, 1856—Democratic—Pennsyl-
    vania.
  sa Campaign biography
    Political ballads and songs, American
  xx Political ballads and songs, American
    Politics, Practical
Campaign literature, 1856
  — Democratic
  — — Pennsylvania
    Note under Campaign literature
Campaign literature, 1896
  xx Bimetallism
Campaign literature, 1900
  — Republican
    Note under Campaign literature
Campaign management *(Direct)*
  xx Elections
    Management
    Politics, Practical
Campaign paraphernalia *(Direct)*
  sa Campaign insignia
  xx Elections
Campaign pins
  See Campaign insignia
Campaign songs *(Music, M1660-1665;*
    United States history, E)
  By date, subdivided by party, *e.g.* Cam-
    paign songs, 1840—Whig.
  sa Political ballads and songs, American
  xx American ballads and songs
    Political ballads and songs, American
    Songs, American
Campaign songs, 1840
  — Whig
    Note under Campaign songs
Campaigns, Advertising
  See Advertising campaigns
Campaigns, Presidential
  See Presidents—United States—Election
Campaldino, Battle of, 1289
Campanology
  See Bells
Campari
  See Police—Italy
Campbellites
  See Disciples of Christ
Campbell's Island, Battle of, 1814 *(E356.C2)*
Campbell's Station, Tenn., Battle of, 1863
Camperdown, Battle of, 1797 *(DA87.5 1797)*
  — Juvenile literature
Campers and coaches, Truck
  x Chassis-mounted coaches

    Coaches, Truck
    Pickup campers
    Pickup coaches
    Truck campers and coaches
  xx Motor-trucks
    Recreational vehicles
  — Maintenance and repair *(TL298)*
Campfire programs
  xx Amusements
    Camps
    Entertaining
Camphor *(QD416; Therapeutics,*
    RM666.C25)
  sa Camphoric acid
    Menthol
  xx Menthol
  — Physiological effect *(QP917.C2)*
Camphor industry and trade *(Direct)*
    (HD9675.C24)
Camphor tree
Camphoric acid *(QD341.A2)*
  xx Camphor
  — Physiological effect *(QP917.C2)*
Campi Bisenzio, Italy
  — Flood, 1966
Campi Palentini, Battle of, 1268
  See Tagliacozzo, Battle of, 1268
Campines *(SF489.C2)*
Camping *(Indirect) (SK601)*
  Here are entered works on the technique
    of camping. Works on camps with a
    definite program of activities are en-
    tered under the heading Camps.
  sa Backpacking
    Camp sites, facilities, etc.
    Camps
    Camps (Military)
    Outdoor cookery
    Outdoor life
    Snow camping
    Survival (after aeroplane accidents,
      shipwrecks, etc.)
    Tourist camps, hostels, etc.
    Wilderness survival
  xx Camps
    Fresh-air charity
    Hunting
    Outdoor education
    Outdoor life
    Outdoor recreation
  Note under Camps
  — Anecdotes, facetiae, satire, etc.
    (SK601-602)
  — Juvenile literature
  — Outfits, supplies, etc.
    sa Camp stoves
      Scientific expeditions—Equipment
        and supplies
      Tents
    xx Tents
  — Pictorial works
  — Prayer-books and devotions
    Subdivided by language.
  — Safety measures
  — Songs and music *(M1977.C3;*
    M1978.C3)
    xx Children's songs
Camping trailers
  xx Recreational vehicles
    Trailers
Campmeetings
  See Camp-meetings
Campo-Formio, Peace of, 1797 *(DC222.C3)*
Campo Grande, Battle of, 1869 *(F2687)*
  xx Paraguayan War, 1865-1870
Campo Grande, Battle of, 1933
  See Pampa Grande, Battle of, 1933

Campo Via, Battle of, 1933
  See Zenteno-Gondra, Battle of, 1933
Campos
  See Savannas
Camps *(Direct)* *(GV192-8)*
    Here are entered works on camps with a
    definite program of activities. Works
    on the technique of camping are en-
    tered under the heading Camping.
  sa Camp sites, facilities, etc.
    Camp sounds
    Campfire programs
    Camping
    Camps for the handicapped
    Church camps
    Day camps
    Dude ranches
    Labor camps
    Lumber camps
    Religious camps
    School camps
  x Organized camps
    Summer camps
  xx Camping
  Note under Camping
  — Accreditation *(GV198.A38)*
  — Administration *(GV198.A4)*
    x Camp administration
    Camp management
  — Counselors
    See Camp counselors
  — Decoration *(GV198.D4)*
    x Camp decoration
    xx Decoration and ornament
    Handicraft
  — Food service
    x Camp cookery
  — Nursing
    See Camp nursing
  — Psychological aspects
  — Safety measures
    sa Camp nursing
    xx Camp nursing
  — Safety regulations *(Direct)*
  — Vocational guidance
  — Water programs
    See Aquatic sports
Camps (Church)
  See Church camps
    Religious camps
Camps (Military) *(U180-185; UC400-405;*
    Camp making, UG365)
  sa Concentration camps
    Intrenchments
  x Castrametation
    Military camps
  xx Camping
    Military art and science
    Military field engineering
Camps for mentally handicapped children
  xx Camps for the handicapped
    Mentally handicapped children
Camps for the handicapped *(GV197.H3)*
  sa Camps for mentally handicapped
    children
  xx Camps
    Handicapped
Camps of instruction
  See Military training camps
Campus clergy
  See Chaplains, University and college
Campus cultures
  See Educational anthropology
Campus disorders
  See Student movements
    Student strikes
Campus ministers
  See Chaplains, University and college

Campus parking *(LB3253)*
  x Parking, Campus
  xx Automobile parking
    Universities and colleges—
    Administration
Campus planning *(Direct)*
  sa Campus size
    College facilities—Planning
    Education parks
  xx College facilities—Planning
    Educational planning
    School grounds
    Universities and colleges—Buildings
  — Mathematical models
Campus police
  x Police, Campus
    Universities and colleges—Police
  xx Police, Private
Campus size *(Direct)*
  x Size of campus
  xx Campus planning
    Universities and colleges—
    Administration
Campus stores
  See College stores
Cams *(TJ206)*
  xx Eccentrics (Machinery)
    Mechanical movements
    Rolling contact
  Note under Machine parts
  — Design and construction
Can-Am Road Race
  See Canadian-American Challenge Cup
Cana, Marriage in
  See Marriage in Cana (Miracle)
Canaanite drama
Canaanite language
  xx Syriac language, Palestinian
Canaanite literature
Canaanites *(DS121.4)*
  xx Ethnology—Palestine
Canada
  — Commerce
  — — United States
    Note under Reciprocity
  — Description and travel
  — — Guide-books
    Example under reference from Travel
    —Guide-books
  — — Juvenile literature
  — English-French relations
    sa Biculturalism—Canada
    Quebec (Province)—History—
    Autonomy and independence
    movements
    x Canada—French-English relations
    xx French-Canadians
  — Foreign relations
  — — United States
    Note under United States—Foreign
    relations—Canada, ₍France, Ja-
    pan, etc.₎
  — French-English relations
    See Canada—English-French relations
  — History *(F1001-1035)*
  — — To 1763 (New France)
    x New France—History
    Quebec (Province)—History—To
    1791
  — — — Historiography
  — — — Juvenile literature
  — — 1755-1763
  — — — Juvenile literature
  — — 1763-1791
    x Quebec (Province)—History—To
    1791
  — — 1763-1867
  — — 1775-1783

    x Quebec (Province)—History—To
    1791
  — — 1791-1841
  — — 19th century
  — — — Juvenile literature
  — — War of 1812
    See United States—History—War
    of 1812
  — — Rebellion, 1837-1838
    sa Saint-Denis, Que., Battle of, 1837
    x Papineau Rebellion
    Patriot War, 1837-1842
    Quebec (Province)—History—
    Rebellion, 1837-1838
    xx French-Canadians
  — — 1841-1867
  — — — Juvenile literature
  — — Fenian invasions, 1866-1870
    sa Fenians
  — — 1867-1914 *(F1033)*
  — — Rebellion, 1869-1870
    See Red River Rebellion,
    1869-1870
  — — Rebellion, 1885
    See Riel Rebellion, 1885
  — — 1914-1945
  — — — Sources
  — — 1945-
  — Lieutenant-governors
    Note under Lieutenant-governors
  — Relations (general) with the United States
    Note under United States—Relations
    (military) with Canada, ₍Europe,
    etc.₎
  — — Juvenile literature
  — Relations (military) with the United States
    Note under United States—Relations
    (military) with Canada, ₍Europe,
    etc.₎
  — Surveys
    Example under Topographical surveying
**Canada. Army. Seaforth Highlanders of
    Canada**
  Example under reference from Scottish regi-
    ments
**Cañada de la Cruz, Argentine Republic, Battle
    of, 1820**
  xx Argentine Republic—History—
    1817-1860
Cañada El Carmen, Battle of, 1934
  See El Carmen, Battle of, 1934
Canada goose *(QL696.A5)*
  xx Geese
  — Behavior
  — Juvenile literature
  — Legends and stories
Canada in art
Canadair Forty Four
  See Yukon (Transport planes)
Canadian-American Challenge Cup
  x Can-Am Road Race
  xx Automobile racing
  — Juvenile literature
Canadian Arctic Expedition, 1913-1918
Canadian ballads and songs *(Collections,
    PR9260; History, PR9180)*
  sa Ballads, Canadian
    Folk-songs, Canadian
    National songs, Canadian
    Songs, Canadian
Canadian clubs
  xx Clubs
Canadian dollar
  See Dollar, Canadian
Canadian drama *(Collections, PR9264-9270;
    History, PR9183-9195)*
  — 20th century

Canadian fiction *(Collections, PR9275-6; History, PR9197-9207)*
Canadian football *(GV948)*
  xx Football
Canadian glassware
  See Glassware, Canadian
Canadian intelligence test
  xx Mental tests
Canadian Invasion, 1775-1776 *(E231)*
  sa Quebec (City)—Siege, 1775-1776
  x Quebec Expedition, 1775
  — Juvenile literature
Canadian literature *(Direct) (Collections, PR9231-9293; History, PR9100-9221, PR9291-3)*
  sa French-Canadian literature
  x English literature—Canada
  Example under America—Literatures
  — Indian authors
    x Indian literature (Canadian)
Canadian newspapers *(Direct) (History, etc., PN4901-4919)*
Canadian Open Golf Championship Tournament, Winnipeg, 1952
  Note under Golf tournaments
Canadian orations *(Collections, PR9279; History, PR9209)*
Canadian periodicals *(Direct) (History, etc., PN4901-4920)*
Canadian poetry *(Collections, PR9249-9263; History, etc., PR9161-9181)*
  sa French-Canadian poetry
  — 20th century
Canadian prose literature *(Collections, PR9272-3; History, PR9197-9207)*
Canadian rice
  See Wild rice
Canadian silversmithing
  See Silversmithing, Canadian
Canadian Spy Trials, 1946
Canadian students in foreign countries
  xx Canadians in foreign countries
Canadian students in the United States, [etc.]
Canadian teachers in Africa, [etc.]
  x Teachers in Africa [etc.], Canadian
Canadian wit and humor, Pictorial *(Direct)*
Canadians
  sa French-Canadians
Canadians in foreign countries
  sa Alien labor, Canadian
    Canadian students in foreign countries
Canadians in Ohio, [Philadelphia, the United States, etc.]
Cañahua *(QK495.C46)*
  x Cañihua
Canaigre *(SB315.C3)*
Çanakkale pottery *(Direct) (NK4340.C3)*
  x Pottery, Çanakkale
  xx Pottery, Turkish
Canal aqueducts *(TC764)*
  xx Aqueducts
Canal-boats *(TC765)*
  sa Barges
    Gondolas
  xx Boats and boating
    Inland waterway vessels
    Work boats
  — Electric traction *(TC769)*
    x Electric traction canal-boats
    xx Towing
  — Inspection *(Indirect)*
  — Mechanical traction *(TC769)*
    xx Towing
  — Safety appliances
Canal rays *(QC711)*
  x Goldstein rays
    Positive rays
    Rays, Canal

  xx Cathode rays
Canals *(Indirect) (Economics: general, HE526; United States, HE395-6; Technology, TC601-791)*
  sa Embankments
    Intracoastal waterways
    Irrigation canals and flumes
    subdivision Canals *under names of cities, e.g.* Philadelphia—Canals; *and names of individual canals*
  xx Channels (Hydraulic engineering)
    Civil engineering
    Communication and traffic
    Engineering
    Hydraulic structures
    Inland navigation
    Intracoastal waterways
    Transportation
  — Cost of construction
  — Early works to 1800
  — Inclined planes *(TC763)*
  — Juvenile literature
  — Laws and regulations
  — Lifts *(TC763)*
  — Locks
    See Locks (Hydraulic engineering)
  — Pictorial works
  — Rates and tolls
    sa subdivision Rates and tolls *under names of individual waterways*
    x Canals—Tolls
    Rates and tolls
    xx Tolls
    Transportation—Rates
  — Steam-navigation *(TC769)*
    xx Steam-navigation
  — Tolls
    See Canals—Rates and tolls
Canals, Interoceanic *(Diplomatic history, JX1398-1403; Economics, HE528-545; Technology, TC601-791)*
  x Interoceanic canals
  — Juvenile literature
Canapés
  See Cookery (Appetizers)
Canard wings (Aeroplanes)
  See Aeroplanes—Wings, Canard
Canards (Journalism)
  xx Journalism
    Sensationalism in newspapers
Canarese language
  See Kannada language
Cañari Indians *(F3722.1.C2)*
  xx Indians of South America
Cañarian language *(PM5718.C5)*
  xx Indians of South America—Languages
Canarian language (Canary Islands)
  See Guanche language
Canarians
  See Canary Islanders
Canaries *(SF463)*
  sa Canary breeds
  Example under Cage-birds
  — Breeding
    See Canary breeding
  — Breeds
    See Canary breeds
Canarios
  See Canary Islanders
Canary breeding
  sa Canary breeds
  x Canaries—Breeding
Canary breeds
  x Canaries—Breeds
  xx Canaries
    Canary breeding

Canary Islanders
  x Canarians
    Canarios
Canary parrot
  See Budgerigars
Canasta (Game) *(GV1295.C2)*
  sa Bolivia (Game)
    Samba (Game)
  x Argentine rummy
    Basket rummy
  xx Rummy (Game)
Canberra, Australia, in art
Cancanai dialect
  See Kankanay dialect
Cancans
  Here are entered collections of cancan music for various mediums. Individual cancans and collections of cancans for a specific medium are entered under the heading followed by specification of medium.
Cancans (Orchestra) *(M1040; M1060)*
  xx Orchestral music
  — Scores *(M1048; M1060)*
Canceling machines
Cancellation of arrest records
  See Criminal registers—Cancellations
Cancellation of criminal records
  See Criminal registers—Cancellations
Cancellation of legal documents
  See Legal documents—Cancellation
Cancellation of negotiable instruments
  See Negotiable instruments—Cancellation
Cancellations (Philately) *(Direct)*
  sa Postmarks
  xx Postage-stamps
    Postmarks
Cancels (Printing)
  See Printing—Cancels
Cancer *(Direct) (RC261)*
  sa Adenocarcinoma
    Antineoplastic agents
    Carcinoembryonic antigens
    Carcinogenesis
    Carcinogens
    Kaposi's sarcoma
    Melanoblastoma
    Rhabdomyosarcoma
    Rodent ulcer
    Toxohormone
    Tumors in children
    subdivision Cancer *under names of organs and regions of the body, e.g.* Brain—Cancer; Breast—Cancer
  x Carcinoma
  xx Oncology
    Tumors
  — Age factors
    Example under Age factors in disease
  — Blood-vessels
    See Tumors—Blood-vessels
  — Chemotherapy
    sa Antineoplastic agents
    Example under Chemotherapy
  — Classification
    See Oncology—Classification
  — Complications and sequelae
  — Diagnosis
    sa Bolen test
  — Dietary aspects
    See Cancer—Nutritional aspects
  — Excision
    xx Chemosurgery
  — Genetic aspects
    Example under Heredity of disease
  — Hospitals
  — Immunological aspects
    Example under Immunology

Cancer *(Direct)* *(RC261)* *(Continued)*
— Juvenile literature
— Law and legislation *(Direct)*
   xx Medical laws and legislation
— Mortality
   Example under Mortality
— Nomenclature
   See Oncology—Nomenclature
— Nutritional aspects
   x Cancer—Dietary aspects
   Diet and cancer
   Nutrition and cancer
   Example under Diet in disease; Nutrition
— Origin
   See Carcinogenesis
— Palliative treatment
   x Palliative treatment of cancer
— Personal narratives
   See Cancer patients—Personal
     narratives
— Prevention
   sa Cancer education
— Psychological aspects
   Example under Medicine and psychology
— Psychosomatic aspects
— Radiotherapy
   Example under Radiotherapy
— — Charts, diagrams, etc.
— — Complications and sequelae
— Research
   See Cancer research
— Social aspects *(Direct)*
   xx Social medicine
— Study and teaching
   Here are entered works on cancer in-
   struction for medical personnel.
   Works on informing the public
   about cancer and its prevention are
   entered under Cancer education.
   Note under Cancer education
— Surgery
— Transplantation
   See Tumors—Transplantation
Cancer cells
   sa HeLa cells
   xx Cells
Cancer education
   Here are entered works on informing the
   public about cancer and its prevention.
   Works on cancer instruction for medi-
   cal personnel are entered under Can-
   cer—Study and teaching.
   xx Cancer—Prevention
   Health education
   Note under Cancer—Study and teaching
Cancer in children
   See Tumors in children
Cancer nursing *(RC266)*
   xx Nurses and nursing
Cancer patients
— Personal narratives
   x Cancer—Personal narratives
— Rehabilitation
Cancer research *(Direct)*
   x Cancer—Research
   xx Medical research
— Scholarships, fellowships, etc. *(Direct)*
Candelabra *(NK8360)*
Candelaria, Canary Islands, in art
Candella dynasty
   See Chandela dynasty
Candia
— Siege, 1667-1669 *(DR534.3-4)*
Candida infection
   See Candidiasis
Candidiasis
   sa Thrush (Mouth disease)
   x Candida infection

Candidosis
Moniliasis
Oidiomycosis
   xx Medical mycology
Candidosis
   See Candidiasis
Candleholders
   See Candlesticks
Candlemas *(BV50.C3)*
   sa Candles and lights
   Jesus Christ—Presentation
   x Feast of the Presentation of Jesus
     Christ
   Presentation of Jesus Christ, Feast of
     the
   Purification of the Blessed Virgin Mary,
     Feast of the
   xx Church year
   Churching of women
   Epiphany season
   Fasts and feasts
   Jesus Christ—Presentation
   Light and darkness (in religion,
     folk-lore, etc.)
   Mary, Virgin—Purification
Candlemas music *(M2078.C2)*
   xx Sacred vocal music
Candles *(TP993)*
   xx Lighting
— Juvenile literature
— Taxation *(Direct)*
Candles, Liturgical
   See Candles and lights
Candles (in religion, folk-lore, etc.)
   x Folk-lore of candles
   xx Religion, Primitive
Candles and lights *(BV196.C3; Catholic*
   Church, BX2308; Judaism,
   BM657.C3)
   Here are entered works on the use of can-
   dles and lights in religious worship.
   sa Hanukkah lamp
   Menorah
   x Candles, Liturgical
   Lights and candles
   Lights, Liturgical
   Liturgical candles
   xx Candlemas
   Fire (in religion, folk-lore, etc.)
   Light and darkness (in religion,
     folk-lore, etc.)
   Sacramentals
Candles and lights (Judaism)
   xx Liturgical objects—Judaism
Candlesticks *(Direct)*
   x Candleholders
   xx House furnishings
— Amateurs' manuals
Candombe (Dance) *(GV1796.C14)*
Candomblé (Cultus)
   See Umbanda (Cultus)
Candrella dynasty
   See Chandela dynasty
Candy
   See Confectionery
Candy containers, Glass
   See Glass candy containers
Cane sugar
   See Sugar
Canella Indians *(F2520.1.C)*
   xx Indians of South America
   Tapuya Indians
Canella language *(PM5719)*
   xx Indians of South America—Languages
   Tapuyan languages
Canephores *(NB169)*
Canes
   See Staffs (Sticks, canes, etc.)

Canichana language *(PM5723)*
   x Kanichana language
   xx Indians of South America—Languages
Canienga Indians
   See Mohawk Indians
Cañihua
   See Cañahua
Canine blacktongue
   See Black-tongue
Canine dirofilariasis
   See Canine heartworm disease
Canine distemper *(SF992.D5)*
   x Carré's disease
   xx Distemper
   Dogs—Diseases
Canine distemper virus
   x Carré's virus
   xx Medipest viruses
   Paramyxoviruses
Canine heartworm disease *(SF992.H4)*
   x Canine dirofilariasis
   Dog heartworm
   Heartworm disease in dogs
   xx Dogs—Diseases
Canine pellagra
   See Black-tongue
Caninefates
   x Cannanefates
   Cannenefates
   Canninefates
   xx Germanic tribes
Caning of chairs
   See Chair caning
Canker (Botany)
   See Canker (Plant disease)
Canker (Plant disease)
   x Canker (Botany)
   Example under Plant diseases
Canker-worms *(SB945.C33)*
   xx Caterpillars
Canna leaf-roller
   Example under Leaf-rollers
Cannabis *(Narcotic habit, RC568.C2;*
   Therapeutics, RM666.C26)
   Here are entered works on the descrip-
   tion, culture and use of Cannabis
   sativa as a drug plant. Works on Cannabis
   sativa as a fiber plant are entered under
   Hemp.
   sa Bhang (Drug)
   Hashish
   Marihuana
   xx Botany, Medical
   Hallucinogenic drugs
   Narcotics
   Note under Hemp
Cannae, Battle of, 216 B.C. *(DG247.3)*
   xx Punic War, 2d, 218-201 B.C.
Cannanefates
   See Caninefates
Canned beans
   See Beans, Canned
Canned beef
   See Beef, Canned
Canned corn
   See Maize, Canned
Canned crabs
   See Crabs, Canned
Canned fish
   See Fish, Canned
Canned fishery products
   See Fishery products, Canned
Canned foods
   See Food, Canned
Canned fruit
   See Fruit, Canned
Canned lobsters
   See Lobsters, Canned

Canned meat
    See Meat, Canned
Canned oysters
    See Oysters, Canned
Canned peas
    See Peas, Canned
Canned poultry
    See Poultry, Canned
Canned rice
    See Rice, Canned
Canned salmon
    See Salmon, Canned
Canned sardines
    See Sardines, Canned
Canned sweet potatoes
    See Sweet potatoes, Canned
Canned tomatoes
    See Tomatoes, Canned
Canned tuna
    See Tuna, Canned
Canned vegetables
    See Vegetables, Canned
Cannel coal (TN827)
    xx Coal
Cannenefates
    See Caninefates
Canneries (Direct) (TH4541)
    xx Canning and preserving
       Factories
       Food processing plants
    — Design and construction
    — Waste disposal (TD428.C3)
       xx Factory and trade waste
Cannery workers (Direct)
    sa Collective labor agreements—Canning
       industry
       Wages—Cannery workers
    xx Canning and preserving—Industry and
       trade
Cannibalism (GN409)
    x Anthropophagy
    xx Ethnology
       Society, Primitive
    — Anecdotes, facetiae, satire, etc.
Cannibalism (Animals) (QL756)
Cannikin Project
    x Project Cannikin
    xx Atomic weapons—Testing
       Underground nuclear explosions
Canninefates
    See Caninefates
Canning and preserving (TX599-613)
    sa Apple products
       Borax
       Boric acid
       Canneries
       Drying apparatus
       Food, Canned
       Food preservatives
       Salting of food
       subdivision Preservation under names
          of individual foods, e.g. Fishery
          products—Preservation; Fruit—
          Preservation; Mushrooms—
          Preservation
    x Pickling
       Preservation of vegetables
       Preserving
    xx Chemistry, Technical
       Cookery
       Drying apparatus—Food
       Food conservation
       Food—Preservation
    — Apparatus and supplies
    — — Collectors and collecting (Direct)
    — Automation
    — Industry and trade (Direct)
       sa Cannery workers

Salmon canning industry
    x Preserving and canning industry
    Example under Food industry and trade;
       Unemployment, Seasonal
— — Accidents
— — Collective labor agreements
       See Collective labor agreements—
          Canning industry
— — Costs
— — Law and legislation
       See Canning and preserving—Law
          and legislation
— — Management
— — Mathematical models
— — Safety measures
— — Standards (Direct)
— — Vocational guidance
— Juvenile literature
— Laboratory manuals
— Law and legislation (Direct)
    x Canning and preserving—Industry
       and trade—Law and legislation
    xx Food law and legislation
— Microbiology (TX603)
— Patents
— Tables, calculations, etc.
Cannizzaro reaction
    xx Aldehydes
       Chemical reactions
Cannon
    See Ordnance
Canoe birch
    See Paper birch
Canoe trips
    See Canoes and canoeing
Canoeing
    See Canoes and canoeing
Canoes and canoeing (Direct) (Ethnology,
       GN440.2; Sport, GV781-5)
    sa Indians of Central America—Boats
       Indians of North America—Boats
       Indians of South America—Boats
       Outrigger canoes
       White-water canoeing
    x Birch-bark canoes
       Canoe trips
       Canoeing
       Cayaks
       Kayaks
    xx Aquatic sports
       Boats and boating
— Pictorial works
Canon (Music) (History, ML448; Instruction,
       MT59)
    Here are entered works on the canon as
       a musical form. Music scores are en-
       tered under the heading Canons,
       fugues, etc.
    sa Fugue
    xx Counterpoint
       Fugue
       Musical form
Canon camera
Canon law
    sa Administrators apostolic
       Censures, Ecclesiastical
       Chancellors, Diocesan
       Church maintenance and repair
          (Ecclesiastical law)
       Church orders, Ancient
       Concordats
       Ecclesiastical courts
       Ecclesiastical law
       Legitimate ecclesiastical acts
       Manifestation of conscience
       Mass stipends
       Privileges and immunities, Ecclesiastical
       Rescripts, Papal

Vicars apostolic
Vicars capitular
Vicars-general
    special legal headings with Canon law
       added in parentheses, e.g. Benefices,
       Ecclesiastical (Canon law); Dioceses
       (Canon law)
    x Public law (Canon law)
    xx Catholic Church
       Church orders, Ancient
       Ecclesiastical law
       Rescripts, Papal
       Theology, Practical
Example under Law
— Early church, ca. 30-600 (BV761)
    xx Church history—Primitive and early
       church, ca. 30-600
— Conflict of laws
       See Conflict of laws (Canon law)
— History
    sa Glossators
— Interpretation and construction
    sa Epikeia
    Example under Law—Interpretation and
       construction
— Language
    xx Law—Language
— Philosophy
— Study and teaching (Direct)
Canon law, Eastern
    Here are entered works on the canon law
       of the Eastern churches, i.e., the Or-
       thodox Eastern, the Jacobite, and the
       Nestorian churches. Canon law of the
       Orthodox Eastern Church alone is en-
       tered under the heading Canon law,
       Orthodox Eastern. Canon law of the
       Eastern churches that recognize the
       supremacy of the Pope (oriental rites)
       is entered under the heading Canon
       law, Oriental.
    sa Marriage (Canon law, Eastern)
Canon law, Oriental
    Here are entered works on the canon law
       governing the oriental rites of the
       Catholic Church.
    sa Consanguinity (Canon law, Oriental)
       Impediments to marriage (Canon law,
          Oriental)
       Marriage (Canon law, Oriental)
       Monasticism and religious orders
          (Canon law, Oriental)
       Persons (Canon law, Oriental)
       Procedure (Canon law, Oriental)
    xx Catholic Church—Oriental rites
    Note under Canon law, Eastern
Canon law, Orthodox Eastern
    sa Nomocanon
       Church property (Canon law, Orthodox
          Eastern); Criminal law (Canon law,
          Orthodox Eastern); Marriage (Canon
          law, Orthodox Eastern); and similar
          headings
    x Orthodox Eastern Church—Law
    Note under Canon law, Eastern
Canon law, Protestant Episcopal
    sa Marriage (Canon law, Protestant
          Episcopal)
Canonesses (Catholic Church, BX4235-4250)
Canonical faculties
    See Faculties (Canon law)
Canonical precept
    See Precept (Canon law)
Canonization (Catholic Church, BX2330;
       Greek Church, BX576)
    sa Beatification
       Heroic virtue
       Saints

Canonization (Catholic Church, BX2330;
        Greek Church, BX576)
        (Continued)
    xx Beatification
        Rites and ceremonies
        Saints
Canonization sermons
    xx Sermons
Cañons
    See Canyons
Canons, Cathedral, collegiate, etc.
    sa Minor canons, Cathedral, collegiate,
        etc.
    x Canons, Secular
        Cathedral canons
        Church canons
        Residentiary canons
        Secular canons
    xx Chapters, Cathedral, collegiate, etc.
        Clergy
Canons, Minor
    See Minor canons, Cathedral, collegiate,
        etc.
Canons, Secular
    See Canons, Cathedral, collegiate, etc.
Canons, fugues, etc.
        Here are entered collections of miscel-
        laneous canons, fugues and similar
        compositions. Separate canons,
        fugues, etc. and collections of canons,
        fugues, etc. for a specific medium are
        entered under the heading followed by
        specification of medium.
    x Fugues
        Preludes and fugues
        Toccatas and fugues
    Notes under Canon (Music); Fugue
Canons, fugues, etc. (Accordion) (M175.A4)
    xx Accordion music
Canons, fugues, etc. (Accordion), Arranged
        (M175.A4)
Canons, fugues, etc. (Accordion ensemble)
    xx Accordion ensembles
Canons, fugues, etc. (Band) (M1245)
    xx Band music
Canons, fugues, etc. (Band), Arranged
        (M1258)
**Canons, fugues, etc. (Baritone, cornets (2),
        horn, trombone, tuba)** (M655-7)
    xx Wind sextets (Baritone, cornets (2),
        horn, trombone, tuba)
**Canons, fugues, etc. (Baritone, cornets (2),
        horn, trombone, tuba), Arranged**
        (M658-9)
Canons, fugues, etc. (Bassoon and oboe)
        (M288-9)
    xx Bassoon and oboe music
Canons, fugues, etc. (Bassoon, clarinet, flute)
        (M355-7)
    xx Wind trios (Bassoon, clarinet, flute)
**Canons, fugues, etc. (Bassoon, clarinet, flute,
        horn, oboe)** (M555-7)
    xx Wind quintets (Bassoon, clarinet, flute,
        horn, oboe)
**Canons, fugues, etc. (Bassoon, clarinet, flute,
        horn, oboe), Arranged** (M558-9)
**Canons, fugues, etc. (Bassoon, clarinet, flute,
        oboe)** (M455-7)
    xx Wind quartets (Bassoon, clarinet, flute,
        oboe)
**Canons, fugues, etc. (Bassoon, clarinet, flute,
        oboe), Arranged** (M458-9)
Canons, fugues, etc. (Bassoon, clarinet, oboe)
        (M355-7)
    xx Wind trios (Bassoon, clarinet, oboe)
**Canons, fugues, etc. (Bassoon, clarinet, oboe,
        piccolo)** (M455-7)
    xx Wind quartets (Bassoon, clarinet, oboe,
        piccolo)

Canons, fugues, etc. (Bassoons (4)) (M455-7)
    xx Wind quartets (Bassoons (4))
Canons, fugues, etc. (Chamber orchestra)
        (M1045)
    xx Chamber-orchestra music
— Scores (M1045)
**Canons, fugues, etc. (Chamber orchestra),
        Arranged** (M1060)
Canons, fugues, etc. (Clarinet and flute)
        (M288-9)
    xx Clarinet and flute music
Canons, fugues, etc. (Clarinet and piano)
        (M248-250)
    xx Clarinet and piano music
**Canons, fugues, etc. (Clarinet, violins (2),
        viola, violoncello)** (M560-562)
    xx Quintets (Clarinet, violins (2), viola,
        violoncello)
Canons, fugues, etc. (Clarinets (3)) (M355-7)
    xx Wind trios (Clarinets (3))
Canons, fugues, etc. (Clarinets (4)) (M455-7)
    xx Wind quartets (Clarinets (4))
Canons, fugues, etc. (Clarinets (4)), Arranged
        (M458-9)
Canons, fugues, etc. (Cornet, trombones (3))
        (M455-7)
    xx Wind quartets (Cornet, trombones (3))
**Canons, fugues, etc. (Cornet, trombones (3)),
        Arranged** (M458-9)
Canons, fugues, etc. (Flute and piano)
        (M240-242)
    xx Flute and piano music
Canons, fugues, etc. (Flute and violoncello)
        (M290-291)
    xx Flute and violoncello music
**Canons, fugues, etc. (Flute with string
        orchestra)** (M1105-6)
    xx Flute with string orchestra
Canons, fugues, etc. (Flutes (2)) (M288-9)
    xx Flute music (Flutes (2))
**Canons, fugues, etc. (Flutes (2) with string
        orchestra)** (M1105-6)
    xx Flutes (2) with string orchestra
— Scores (M1105)
Canons, fugues, etc. (Flutes (3)) (M355-7)
    xx Wind trios (Flutes (3))
Canons, fugues, etc. (Flutes (4)) (M455-7)
    xx Wind quartets (Flutes (4))
Canons, fugues, etc. (Glass harmonica)
        (M165)
    xx Glass-harmonica music
Canons, fugues, etc. (Guitar) (M125-7)
    xx Guitar music
Canons, fugues, etc. (Harpsichord) (M25)
    xx Harpsichord music
Canons, fugues, etc. (Harpsichord), Arranged
        (M32.8.M38)
**Canons, fugues, etc. (Harpsichord, flute,
        violins (2), violas (2), violoncellos
        (2))** (M820-822)
    xx Octets (Harpsichord, flute, violins (2),
        violas (2), violoncellos (2))
Canons, fugues, etc. (Harpsichord, violins (3))
        (M410-411; M412.2)
    xx Canons, fugues, etc. (Piano, violins (3))
        Quartets (Harpsichord, violins (3))
**Canons, fugues, etc. (Harpsichord, violins (3),
        viola da gamba)** (M510-512)
    xx Canons, fugues, etc. (Piano, violins (3),
        violoncello)
        Quintets (Harpsichord, violins (3), viola
        da gamba)
Canons, fugues, etc. (Harpsichords (2))
        (M214)
    xx Harpsichord music

**Canons, fugues, etc. (Horn, trombone,
        trumpets (2), tuba)** (M555-7)
    xx Wind quintets (Horn, trombone,
        trumpets (2), tuba)
**Canons, fugues, etc. (Horn, trombones (2),
        trumpets (2))** (M555-7)
    xx Wind quintets (Horn, trombones (2),
        trumpets (2))
**Canons, fugues, etc. (Horn, trombones (2),
        trumpets (2)), Arranged** (M558-9)
Canons, fugues, etc. (Instrumental ensemble)
    xx Instrumental ensembles
**Canons, fugues, etc. (Instrumental ensemble),
        Arranged**
Canons, fugues, etc. (Lute) (M140-141)
    xx Lute music
**Canons, fugues, etc. (Oboe with string
        orchestra)** (M1105-6)
    xx Oboe with string orchestra
Canons, fugues, etc. (Orchestra) (M1045;
        M1060)
    xx Orchestral music
Canons, fugues, etc. (Orchestra), Arranged
— Scores (M1060)
Canons, fugues, etc. (Organ) (M10)
    xx Organ music
Canons, fugues, etc. (Organ), Arranged
        (M12-13)
**Canons, fugues, etc. (Organ, baritone, cornets
        (2), trombone)** (M500-502)
    xx Quintets (Organ, baritone, cornets (2),
        trombone)
**Canons, fugues, etc. (Organ, violin, viola da
        gamba)** (M300-302)
    xx Trios (Organ, violin, viola da gamba)
**Canons, fugues, etc. (Organ, violins (2), viola
        da gamba)** (M400-402)
    xx Quartets (Organ, violins (2), viola da
        gamba)
Canons, fugues, etc. (Organ, viols (3))
        (M990)
    xx Quartets (Organ, viols (3))
Canons, fugues, etc. (Piano) (M20-22; M25)
    xx Piano music
Canons, fugues, etc. (Piano, 1 hand) (M26;
        M26.2)
    xx Piano music (1 hand)
Canons, fugues, etc. (Piano, 4 hands)
        (M200-201; M204)
    xx Piano music (4 hands)
**Canons, fugues, etc. (Piano, 4 hands),
        Arranged** (M211)
Canons, fugues, etc. (Piano), Arranged
**Canons, fugues, etc. (Piano, bells, cymbals,
        drums (2), kettledrums, triangle,
        xylophone)** (M835)
    xx Percussion music
        Piano music
        Xylophone music
Canons, fugues, etc. (Piano quartet)
        (M410-412)
    xx Piano quartets
Canons, fugues, etc. (Piano, violins (2))
        (M310-311; M312.4)
    xx Trios (Piano, violins (2))
Canons, fugues, etc. (Piano, violins (3))
        (M410-411; M412.2)
    sa Canons, fugues, etc. (Harpsichord,
        violins (3))
    xx Quartets (Piano, violins (3))
**Canons, fugues, etc. (Piano, violins (3),
        violoncello)** (M510-512)
    sa Canons, fugues, etc. (Harpsichord,
        violins (3), viola da gamba)
    xx Quintets (Piano, violins (3), violoncello)
Canons, fugues, etc. (Piano with orchestra)
        (M1010-1011)
    xx Piano with orchestra

Canons, fugues, etc. (Pianos (2)) *(M214)*
  xx Piano music (Pianos (2))
Canons, fugues, etc. (Pianos (2)), Arranged
  (M215)
Canons, fugues, etc. (Recorder and piano)
  (M240-242)
  xx Recorder and piano music
Canons, fugues, etc. (Recorder and piano),
  Arranged *(M243-4)*
Canons, fugues, etc. (Recorder, violin,
  violoncello) *(M360-362)*
  xx Trios (Recorder, violin, violoncello)
Canons, fugues, etc. (Recorders (2))
  (M288-9)
  xx Recorder music (Recorders (2))
Canons, fugues, etc. (Recorders (3))
  (M355-7)
  xx Wind trios (Recorders (3))
Canons, fugues, etc. (Recorders (3)), Arranged
  (M358-9)
Canons, fugues, etc. (Recorders (4))
  (M455-7)
  xx Wind quartets (Recorders (4))
Canons, fugues, etc. (Recorders (4)), Arranged
  (M458-9)
Canons, fugues, etc. (Recorders (5))
  (M555-7)
  xx Wind quintets (Recorders (5))
Canons, fugues, etc. (Recorders (5)), Arranged
  (M558-9)
Canons, fugues, etc. (Saxophones (3))
  (M355-7)
  xx Wind trios (Saxophones (3))
Canons, fugues, etc. (Saxophones (3), trumpet)
  (M455-7)
  xx Wind quartets (Saxophones (3),
    trumpet)
Canons, fugues, etc. (Saxophones (4))
  (M455-7)
  xx Wind quartets (Saxophones (4))
Canons, fugues, etc. (String ensemble)
  (M950-952)
  xx String ensembles
Canons, fugues, etc. (String orchestra)
  (M1145)
  xx String-orchestra music
Canons, fugues, etc. (String orchestra),
  Arranged *(M1160)*
Canons, fugues, etc. (String quartet)
  (M450-452)
  xx String quartets
Canons, fugues, etc. (String quartet), Arranged
  (M453-4)
Canons, fugues, etc. (String trio) *(M349-351)*
  xx String trios
Canons, fugues, etc. (String trio), Arranged
  (M352-3)
Canons, fugues, etc. (String trio with string
  orchestra) *(M1105-6)*
  xx String trio with string orchestra
—Scores *(M1105)*
Canons, fugues, etc. (Trombones (2), trumpets
  (2)) *(M455-7)*
  xx Wind quartets (Trombones (2),
    trumpets (2))
Canons, fugues, etc. (Trombones (2), trumpets
  (2)), Arranged *(M458-9)*
Canons, fugues, etc. (Trumpet with string
  orchestra) *(M1105-6)*
  xx Trumpet with string orchestra
—Scores and parts *(M1105)*
Canons, fugues, etc. (Viola) *(M47)*
  xx Viola music
Canons, fugues, etc. (Violas (2), violoncellos
  (2)) *(M450-451; M452.4)*
  xx String quartets (Violas (2), violoncellos
    (2))

Canons, fugues, etc. (Violin)
  xx Violin music
Canons, fugues, etc. (Violin and harpsichord)
  (M217-218; M221)
  xx Violin and harpsichord music
Canons, fugues, etc. (Violin and organ)
  (M182-4)
  xx Violin and organ music
Canons, fugues, etc. (Violin and piano)
  (M217-218; M221)
  xx Violin and piano music
Canons, fugues, etc. (Violin, viola, viola da
  gamba) *(M349-351)*
  xx String trios (Violin, viola, viola da
    gamba)
Canons, fugues, etc. (Violins (2), viola,
  violoncello, double bass)
  (M550-552)
  xx String quintets (Violins (2), viola,
    violoncello, double bass)
Canons, fugues, etc. (Violins (2), violas (2),
  violoncello) *(M550-552)*
  xx String quintets (Violins (2), violas (2),
    violoncello)
Canons, fugues, etc. (Violins (3)) *(M349-351)*
  xx String trios (Violins (3))
Canons, fugues, etc. (Violins (3), viola,
  violoncello) *(M550-552)*
  xx String quintets (Violins (3), viola,
    violoncello)
Canons, fugues, etc. (Violins (4), violas (2),
  violoncellos (2)) *(M850-852)*
  xx String octets (Violins (4), violas (2),
    violoncellos (2))
Canons, fugues, etc. (Violoncello and piano)
  (M229-230; M233)
  xx Violoncello and piano music
Canons, fugues, etc. (Violoncello and piano),
  Arranged *(M235-6)*
Canons, fugues, etc. (Violoncellos (4))
  xx String quartets (Violoncellos (4))
Canons, fugues, etc. (Viols (2)) *(M990)*
  xx Viol music (Viols (2))
Canons, fugues, etc. (Viols (3)) *(M990)*
  xx String trios (Viols (3))
Canons, fugues, etc. (Viols (4)) *(M990)*
  xx String quartets (Viols (4))
Canons, fugues, etc. (Viols (5)) *(M990)*
  xx String quintets (Viols (5))
Canons, fugues, etc. (Viols (6)) *(M990)*
  xx String sextets (Viols (6))
Canons, fugues, etc. (Viols (7)) *(M990)*
  xx String septets (Viols (7))
Canons, fugues, etc. (Vocal)
  sa Glees, catches, rounds, etc.
  xx Choruses
    Glees, catches, rounds, etc.
    Part-songs
    Vocal music
Canons, fugues, etc. (Wind ensemble)
  xx Wind ensembles
Canopus, Battle of, 1801
  See Alexandria, Battle of, 1801
Canopus, Decree of
  See Decree of Canopus
Cans
  See Containers
Cant *(English, PE3726)*
  sa Canting arms (Heraldry)
    Shelta
    Slang
    Swearing
  x Argot
    Crime and criminals—Language
  xx English language—Dialects
    Slang
Cantabrians
  xx Ethnology—Spain—Cantabria

Cantaloupe
  See Muskmelon
Cantata *(ML1500-1554; ML2400; ML3260)*
  xx Choral music
    Church music
    Musical form
    Oratorio
  Example under Vocal music—History and
    criticism
Cantatas
  Here are entered collections of sacred
    and secular cantatas for mixed voices
    or for various groups of voices (men's,
    mixed, women's) *Cf.* note under Op-
    eras.
  sa Choruses
    Solo cantatas
  xx Vocal music
—To 1800
— —Excerpts
— — —Scores
      x Cantatas—To 1800—Scores—
        Excerpts
— —Scores
— — —Excerpts
      See Cantatas—To 1800—
        Excerpts—Scores
Cantatas, Juvenile *(M1996; M2190)*
  x Children's cantatas
    Juvenile cantatas
  xx Cantatas, Sacred
    Cantatas, Secular
    Children's songs
Cantatas, Sacred *(M2020-2036)*
  Here are entered, with appropriate sub-
    divisions, sacred cantatas for mixed
    voices or collections of sacred cantatas
    for various groups of voices (men's,
    mixed, women's)
  sa Cantatas, Juvenile
    Pantomimes with music, Sacred
    Solo cantatas, Sacred
  x Sacred cantatas
  xx Sacred vocal music
—To 1800
— —Excerpts
— — —Vocal scores with organ *(M2027-8)*
      x Cantatas, Sacred—To 1800—
        Vocal scores with organ—
        Excerpts
— —Excerpts, Arranged
      xx Cantatas, Sacred—Excerpts,
        Arranged
— —Vocal scores with organ
— — —Excerpts
      See Cantatas, Sacred—To 1800
        —Excerpts—Vocal scores
        with organ

GENERAL SUBDIVISIONS

—Excerpts
— —Vocal scores with piano *(M2027-8)*
      x Cantatas, Sacred—Vocal scores
        with piano—Excerpts
—Excerpts, Arranged
      sa Cantatas, Sacred—To 1800—
        Excerpts, Arranged
—Vocal scores with piano
— —Excerpts
      See Cantatas, Sacred—Excerpts—
        Vocal scores with piano
—Vocal scores with pianos (2) *(M2023)*
Cantatas, Sacred (Equal voices)
—Vocal scores with organ
Cantatas, Sacred (Men's voices)
  (M2029-2032)
Cantatas, Sacred (Unison) *(M2101.5)*

259

Cantatas, Sacred (Women's voices)
    (M2033-6)
Cantatas, Secular *(M1530-1546)*
    Cf. note under Cantatas, Sacred.
    sa Cantatas, Juvenile
        Pantomimes with music
        Solo cantatas, Secular
    x Secular cantatas
    — To 1800
    —— Excerpts
    ——— Scores *(M1534)*
            x Cantatas, Secular—To 1800—
                Scores—Excerpts
    ——— Vocal scores with piano *(M1536-7)*
            x Cantatas, Secular—To 1800—
                Vocal scores with piano—
                Excerpts
    —— Excerpts, Arranged
        xx Cantatas, Secular—Excerpts,
            Arranged
    —— Scores *(M1530)*
    ——— Excerpts
            See Cantatas, Secular—To 1800
                —Excerpts—Scores
    —— Vocal scores with piano *(M1533)*
    ——— Excerpts
            See Cantatas, Secular—To 1800
                —Excerpts—Vocal scores
                with piano

GENERAL SUBDIVISIONS

    — Excerpts, Arranged
        sa Cantatas, Secular—To 1800—
            Excerpts, Arranged
Cantatas, Secular (Equal voices)
Cantatas, Secular (Men's voices)
    (M1538-1542)
Cantatas, Secular (Unison) *(M1609)*
Cantatas, Secular (Women's voices)
    (M1543-6)
**Cantatas, Secular (Women's voices) with brass
    ensemble** *(M1543.5; M1544-6)*
Cantate Domino canticum novum, cantate
    Domino (Music)
    See Psalms (Music)—96th Psalm
Cantate Domino canticum novum, laus eius
    (Music)
    See Psalms (Music)—149th Psalm
Cantate Domino canticum novum, quia
    mirabilia fecit (Music)
    See Psalms (Music)—98th Psalm
Cante flamenco
    See Flamenco music
Cante hondo
    See Flamenco
        Flamenco music
Canteen (British army) *(UC755.G7)*
    Note under Canteens (War-time, emergency,
        etc.)
Canteen (British navy) *(VC395.G7)*
    Note under Canteens (War-time, emergency,
        etc.)
Canteen (Canadian army) *(UC755.C2)*
    Note under Canteens (War-time, emergency,
        etc.)
Canteen (United States Army) *(UC753)*
    sa Post exchanges (United States Army)
    x United States. Army—Canteen
    xx Temperance
    Note under Canteens (War-time, emergency,
        etc.)
Canteens (Industrial)
    See Industrial feeding
Canteens (Recreation centers)
    See Recreation centers

Canteens (War-time, emergency, etc.)
    Here are entered works on temporary es-
    tablishments which provide members
    of the Armed Forces and, in emergen-
    cies, civilians with food and recreation.
    For military canteens use Canteen
    (British army); Canteen (British navy);
    Canteen (Canadian army); Canteen
    (United States Army); Post exchanges.
    Works dealing with employee lunch-
    rooms, sometimes called canteens, are
    entered under the heading Industrial
    feeding.
    xx Post exchanges
        Restaurants, lunch rooms, etc.
        Soldiers—Recreation
Cantelope
    See Muskmelon
Canterbury, Eng. (Diocese)
    Example under Church of England—Dioceses;
        Dioceses
    — History
        Example under Church of England—His-
            tory
Cantharides *(RM666.C27)*
    Example under Counter-irritants
Canticles
    sa Benedictus
        Hymns
        Nunc Dimittis
    xx Hymns
        Liturgies
Cantigny, Battle of, 1918 *(D545.C)*
    xx European War, 1914-1918—Campaigns
        —France
Cantilever bridges
    See Bridges, Cantilever
Cantillation
    sa Chants (Jewish)
        Music—Jews
    xx Chants (Jewish)
        Music—Jews
        Oral interpretation
    — Instruction and study *(MT860)*
Canting arms (Heraldry)
    x Allusive arms (Heraldry)
        Punning arms (Heraldry)
    xx Cant
        Heraldry
        Puns and punning
Canton, China
    — General Strike, 1925
Canton Forts, Battle of, 1856
    See Barrier Forts, Battle of, 1856
Cantonists *(DS135.R9)*
    xx Jews as soldiers
        Jews in Russia
        Russia. Armīā—Recruiting,
            enlistment, etc.
Cantors, Jewish *(BM658.2)*
    x Chazanim
        Chazzanim
        Ḥazanim
        Ḥazzanim
        Jewish cantors
    xx Cultus, Jewish
        Judaism—Functionaries
        Music—Jews
Cañute (Game)
Canvas
    sa names of articles manufactured, e.g.
        Awnings; Tents
Canvas embroidery *(TT778.C3)*
    x Bargello
        Canvas work (Needlepoint)
        Needlepoint canvas work
        Needlepoint embroidery
    xx Embroidery

    — Patterns
Canvas embroidery, Victorian *(Direct)*
    x Berlin wool work
        Berlin work
        Victorian canvas embroidery
Canvas priming
    x Priming, Canvas
Canvas sizing
    xx Sizing (Textile)
Canvas stretching
    xx Painting—Technique
Canvas work (Needlepoint)
    See Canvas embroidery
Canvasback
    xx Ducks
Canvassing *(HF5446-5456)*
    sa Booksellers and bookselling—
        Colportage, subscription trade, etc.
        Peddlers and peddling
    x Door-to-door selling
    xx Booksellers and bookselling
        Commercial agents
        Commercial travelers
        Peddlers and peddling
        Salesmen and salesmanship
    — Law and legislation *(Direct)*
Canvassing (Church work)
    sa Visitations (Church work)
        Visitations (Religious education)
    xx Social surveys
        Visitations (Church work)
        Visitations, Ecclesiastical
Canyons *(Indirect)*
    x Cañons
    xx Valleys
Canyons, Submarine
    See Submarine valleys
Canzone *(German, PT1241.C3; Italian,
    PQ4128.C6)*
Caodaism
    xx Buddha and Buddhism
        Spiritualism
        Taoism
Caoutchouc
    See Rubber
Cap clouds *(Indirect)* *(QC921)*
    x Cloud caps
    xx Clouds
        Weather, Influence of mountains on
Cap rock *(TN870.5)*
    xx Geology, Structural
        Petroleum—Geology
        Salt domes
Capacitor microphone
    See Electrostatic microphone
Capacitor motors *(TK2785)*
    x Electric motors, Capacitor
    xx Condensers (Electricity)
        Electric motors, Induction
Capacitors
    See Condensers (Electricity)
        Radio capacitors
Capacity, Industrial
    See Industrial capacity
Capacity (Law)
    See Capacity and disability
Capacity and disability *(Direct)*
    sa Age (Law)
        Civil death
        Guardian and ward
        Interdiction (Civil law)
        Married women
        Prisoners—Legal status, laws, etc.
        Prodigals (Law)
        Sick—Legal status, laws, etc.
    x Capacity (Law)
        Disability (Law)
        Incapacity (Law)

xx Age (Law)
    Children—Law
    Guardian and ward
    Insanity—Jurisprudence
    Interdiction (Civil law)
    Juristic acts
    Persons (Law)
    Prisoners—Legal status, laws, etc.
    Prodigals (Law)
    Sick—Legal status, laws, etc.
    Status (Law)

Capacity and disability (Islamic law)
    (Direct)

Capacity and disability (Roman-Dutch law)

Capacity and disability (Roman law)

Capanahua language
  x Capanawa language
  xx Indians of South America—Languages
    Panoan languages

Capanawa language
  See Capanahua language

Capaukoos (Papuan people)
  See Kapauku (Papuan people)

Cape coloured people
  See Colored people (South Africa)

Cape Dutch
  See Afrikaans language

Cape eagle owl
  xx Owls

Cape Florida Indians
  See Calusa Indians

Cape Indians
  See Makah Indians

Cape jasmine
  See Gardenia

Cape Matapan, Battle of, 1941
  See Matapan, Battle of, 1941

Cape of Good Hope
  — History
    sa Africa, South—History—Great Trek,
      1836-1840

Cape oryx
  See Gemsbok

Cape penguin
  See Jackass penguin

Cape periwinkle
  See Madagascar periwinkle

Capercaillie
  xx Grouse

Capes (Clothing)
  See Cloaks

Capillaries *(QL835; QM191; QP101)*
  — Diseases
  — Examination
  — Permeability

Capillarity *(QC183)*
  sa Brownian movements
    Electrocapillary phenomena
    Hydrostatics
    Jets
    Permeability
    Soil capillarity
    Splashes
    Surface chemistry
    Surface tension
  xx Matter—Properties
    Permeability
    Physics
    Splashes
    Surface chemistry
    Surface tension

Capitaine
  See Nile perch

Capital *(Direct) (Theory, HB501)*
  sa Banks and banking
    Capitalism
    Capitalists and financiers
    Human capital

    Interest and usury
    Investments
    Liquidity (Economics)
    Monopolies
    Profit
    Saving and investment
    Trusts, Industrial
    Venture capital
    Wealth
    Working capital
  xx Capitalism
    Economics
    Finance
    Income
    Labor and laboring classes
    Money
    Wealth
  — Accounting
    x Capital investments—Accounting
  — Mathematical models
  — Taxation
    See Capital levy
  — Underdeveloped areas
    See Underdeveloped areas—Capital

Capital and labor
  See Industrial relations

Capital budget *(Direct)*
  xx Budget
    Capital investments
  — Programmed instruction

Capital cities
  See Capitals (Cities)

Capital equipment
  See Industrial equipment

Capital exports
  See Foreign exchange
    Investments, Foreign

Capital flight tax *(Direct)*
  xx Capital levy
    Foreign exchange
    Taxation

Capital formation
  See Saving and investment

Capital gains tax *(Direct) (General,*
    HJ4639; United States, HJ4653.C3)
  sa Real property and taxation
  x Taxation of capital gains
  xx Capital levy
    Income tax
    Investments—Taxation
  — United States
    Note under Real property and taxation

Capital imports
  See Foreign exchange
    Investments, Foreign

Capital investments *(Direct) (HG4028.C4)*
  sa Art as an investment
    Capital budget
    Coins as an investment
    Investment tax credit
    Postage-stamps as an investment
    Replacement of industrial equipment
  x Plant and equipment investments
    Plant investments
  xx Investments
  — Accounting
    See Capital—Accounting
  — Mathematical models
    sa Acceleration principle (Economics)
  — Problems, exercises, etc.
  — Programmed instruction

Capital levy *(Direct) (HJ4132-3)*
  sa Capital flight tax
    Capital gains tax
    Property tax
  x Capital—Taxation
    Levy on capital
  xx Property tax

    Taxation

Capital output ratios
  See Capital productivity
    Cost effectiveness

Capital productivity *(Direct)*
  sa Aeroplane industry and trade—Capital
    productivity
    Agriculture—Capital productivity
    Furniture industry and trade—Capital
    productivity
    Labor productivity
  x Capital output ratios
    Productivity of capital
  xx Efficiency, Industrial
    Industrial productivity
    Labor productivity
    Machinery in industry
    Production (Economic theory)

Capital punishment *(Direct) (HV8694-9)*
  sa Crucifixion
    Electrocution
    Executions and executioners
    Garrote
    Guillotine
    Hanging
    Last meal before execution
    Stoning
  x Death penalty
  xx Criminal law
    Executions and executioners
    Punishment

Capital punishment (Germanic law)

Capital punishment (Islamic law) *(Direct)*

Capital punishment (Jewish law)

Capital punishment (Roman law)

Capital sins
  See Deadly sins

Capital stock *(Direct)*
  x Share capital
  xx Corporation law
    Corporations
    Stocks

Capitalis justiciarius
  See Justiciars (England)

Capitalism *(HB501)*
  sa Capital
    Christianity and economics
    Entrepreneur
    Technocracy
  xx Capital
    Capitalists and financiers
    Economics
    Entrepreneur
    Profit

Capitalism and Christianity
  See Christianity and capitalism

Capitalism and literature *(PN51)*
  x Literature and capitalism
  xx Literature and state

Capitalism and Protestantism
  See Protestantism and capitalism

Capitalists and financiers *(Direct)*
  sa Bondholders
    Capitalism
    Millionaires
    Stockholders
  x Financiers
    Investors
  xx Businessmen
    Capital
    Finance
    Millionaires
    Wealth
  — Correspondence, reminiscences, etc.
  — Jews
    x Capitalists and financiers, Jewish
      Jewish capitalists and financiers
  — Juvenile literature

Capitalists and financiers, Jewish
   See Capitalists and financiers—Jews

Capitalists and financiers in literature
   xx Economics in literature

Capitalization
   sa *subdivision* Capitalization *under names*
      of languages, e.g. English language—
      Capitalization

Capitalization (Finance)
   See Corporations—Finance
      Railroads—Finance
      Railroads—Valuation
      Securities
      Valuation

Capitalization societies
   See Face-amount certificate companies

Capitals (Architecture) *(Direct)*
   xx Architecture—Details
      Columns

Capitals (Architecture), Corinthian *(Direct)*
   x Corinthian capitals (Architecture)
   xx Architecture, Greek
      Columns, Corinthian

Capitals (Cities) *(G140; Political science,*
      JF1900; United States, E159)
   sa Capitols
      subdivision Capital *under names of*
      countries, and subdivision Capital
      and capitol under names of states
   x Capital cities
   xx Cities and towns
   — Juvenile literature

Capitol pages
   x Pages, Capitol
      Pages, Congressional
   xx United States. Congress—Officials and
      employees

Capitols *(Architecture, NA4410-4417)*
   sa *subdivision* Capital and capitol *under*
      names of states
   xx Architecture, Ancient
      Capitals (Cities)

Capitular vicars
   See Vicars capitular

Capitulations *(JX)*
   Agreements or conventions granting spe-
      cial privileges and rights of exterritori-
      ality to foreign governments, notably
      those granted by Turkey.
   sa Exterritoriality
   xx Exterritoriality

Capitulations, Military
   sa Prisoners of war
   x Military capitulations
      Surrender
   xx Military law
      Prisoners of war
      Sieges
      War (International law)

Capitulations, Military (Roman law)

Capo di Monte porcelain
   See Capodimonte porcelain

Capodimonte porcelain
   x Capo di Monte porcelain
      Porcelain, Capodimonte
   xx Porcelain, Italian

Capoeira (Dance)

Capons and caponizing *(SF499)*
   sa Castration
   xx Castration
      Poultry

Caporetto, Battle of, 1917
   xx European War, 1914-1918—Campaigns
      —Italo-Austrian

Capote Indians *(E99.C)*
   xx Indians of North America
      Ute Indians

Cappadocian inscriptions
   See Cuneiform inscriptions, Cappadocian

Cappadocian language *(P1003)*
   sa Cuneiform inscriptions, Cappadocian

Capri automobile
   xx Ford automobile

Caprifig
   See Fig
      Fig-insect

Capron
   See Nylon

Caps and gowns
   See Academic costume

Capsian culture
   xx Paleolithic period

Capstan *(VM811)*
   xx Anchors
      Deck machinery
      Hoisting machinery

Capsules (Pharmacy) *(RS201.C)*
   — Patents

Captains of ships
   See Shipmasters

Captive balloons
   See Balloons, Captive

Capture at sea *(JX5228)*
   sa Convoy
      Enemy property
      Privateering
      Prize law
      Ransom
   x Captured property
      Maritime capture
      Property captured at sea
   xx Enemy property
      Neutrality
      Postliminy
      Privateering
      Prize law
      Seizure of vessels and cargoes
      War (International law)
      War, Maritime (International law)
   Note under Enemy property

Captured property
   See Booty (International law)
      Capture at sea
      Enemy property

Capuchins *(BX3101-3155; Women,*
      BX4301-4)
   xx Franciscans
      Monasticism and religious orders
   — Missions *(BV2255)*

Capuchins in Central America, ₍France, Spain,
      etc.₎

Capuchins in literature

Capybaras
   x Carpincho
   xx Rodentia

Car axles *(TF386)*
   xx Axles
      Railroads—Cars

Car badges
   See Automobiles—Trade-marks

Car buying
   See Automobile purchasing

Car-couplings *(TF410)*
   xx Couplings
      Railroads—Cars
      Railroads—Safety appliances
   — Economic aspects
   — Maintenance and repair
   — Patents

Car fenders *(TF947)*
   x Fenders for street-cars
   xx Railroads—Cars
      Street-railroads—Safety appliances

Car heating
   See Railroads—Cars—Heating and
      ventilation

Car lighting
   See Railroads—Cars—Lighting

Car service (Freight)
   See Demurrage (Car service)
      Railroads—Freight
      Railroads—Freight-cars

Car sickness
   See Motion sickness

Car-springs *(TF391)*
   xx Railroads—Cars
      Springs (Mechanism)

Car trucks (Railroads) *(TF380)*
   xx Railroads—Cars
   — Drawings
   — Maintenance and repair

Car trusts *(Direct)* *(Finance, HG4971-7;*
      Railroads, HE1828, HE2236)
   xx Railroad law
      Railroad liens
      Railroads—Finance
      Sales, Conditional

Car tunnel kilns
   See Tunnel kilns

Car ventilation
   See Railroads—Cars—Heating and
      ventilation

Car washes *(Direct)*
   x Auto washes
      Carwashes
   xx Automobiles

Car-wheels *(TF383)*
   xx Railroads—Cars
      Wheels
   — Maintenance and repair *(TF383)*

Car workers
   See Railroads—Employees

Cara Indians
   sa Otavalo Indians
   xx Indians of South America

Caraate
   See Pinta

Carabao
   See Water buffalo

Carabobo, Battle of, 1821 *(F2324)*
   xx Venezuela—History—War of
      Independence, 1810-1823
   — Anniversaries, etc.

Caracas
   — Earthquake, 1812
   — Earthquake, 1967

Caracas in literature

Caraib Indians
   See Carib Indians

Caraib language
   See Carib language

Caraite manuscripts
   See Manuscripts, Karaite

Caraja Indians *(F2520.1.C)*
   x Carayás Indians
      Karajá Indians
   xx Indians of South America

Caraja language *(PM5741)*

Caramel *(TP380)*
   xx Coloring matter

Carancahua Indians
   See Karankawa Indians

Caranguiyo (Dance)

Cāraṇō
   See Charans

Carat (Unit of weight) *(QC106)*
   xx Metric system
      Standards of mass
   Example under Weights and measures

Caratheodory measure
   x Measure, Caratheodory

xx Algebra, Boolean
Measure theory
Caravan sites
See Trailer camps
Caravans
Caravans (Automobile trailers)
See Automobiles—Trailers
Caravans (Gipsy wagons)
See Wagons, Gipsy
Caravelle (Jet transports)
xx Jet transports
Carayás Indians
See Caraja Indians
Carbide cutting tools   *(TJ1186)*
x Carbide tools
Cutting tools, Carbide
Carbide tools
See Carbide cutting tools
Carbides   *(Manufacture, TP245.C4)*
sa Cementite
Silicon carbide
Example under Chemistry, Inorganic
Carbines
See Rifles
Carbohydrate metabolism   *(QP701)*
sa Phosphorylation
xx Carbohydrates in the body
Metabolism
Carbohydrates   *(Organic chemistry, QD321;*
Physiological chemistry, QP701)
sa Chitin
Dextran
Low-carbohydrate diet
names of compounds belonging to this
group, e.g. Cellulose, Dextrose,
Levulose, Pentoses
xx Physiological chemistry
Example under Chemistry, Organic
— Analysis
— Spectra
Carbohydrates in the body   *(QP701)*
sa Carbohydrate metabolism
xx Deficiency diseases
Metabolism
Carbolic acid   *(QD341.P5)*
sa Phenols
xx Phenols
Example under Chemicals
— Physiological effect   *(QP917.C)*
Note under Pharmacology
— Therapeutic use   *(RM666.C33)*
— Toxicology   *(RA1242.C2)*
Carbon   *(Chemical technology, TP245.C4;*
Chemistry, QD181.C1)
sa Charcoal
Coal
Coke
Decarburization of steel
Diamonds
Electric light carbons
Graphite
Plants, Effect of carbon on
Schungite
Soils—Carbon content
xx Nonmetals
— Analysis
— Isotopes   *(QD466.5.C1)*
sa Radiocarbon dating
x Carbon isotopes
Isotopic carbon
Radiocarbon
xx Radioactive tracers
Radioactivity
Example under Isotopes; Radioisotopes
— — Decay
— — Half-life
— — Spectra
— Manufacture   *(TK7725)*

— Spectra
— Testing
Carbon, Activated
x Activated carbon
Activated charcoal
Charcoal, Activated
xx Adsorption
Charcoal
— Patents
Carbon bisulphide
See Carbon disulphide
Carbon-black   *(TP951)*
x Acetylene black
— Optical properties
Carbon brushes
See Brushes, Carbon
Carbon compounds   *(QD248-449)*
Here are entered works dealing with spe-
cial groups of carbon compounds and
with their reactions. Comprehensive
works on organic chemistry, even
though they bear the title Carbon com-
pounds, are entered under Chemistry,
Organic.
xx Chemistry, Organic
— Spectra
Carbon copy
xx Copying processes
Typewriting
Carbon deposits in engines
See Combustion deposits in engines
Carbon dioxide   *(Chemistry, QD181.C1;*
Manufacture, TP244.C1)
sa Dry ice
Liquid carbon dioxide
x Carbonic acid
xx Gases, Asphyxiating and poisonous
Example under Refrigerants
— Analysis
— Physiological effect   *(QP913.C1)*
sa Hypercapnia
x Physiological effect of carbon
dioxide
— Tables, etc.
— Therapeutic use   *(RM666.C35)*
— Thermal properties
Carbon dioxide, Solid
See Dry ice
Carbon dioxide in the body
Carbon disulphide   *(QD181.C1; Labor*
hygiene, HD7265.C3)
x Carbon bisulphide
— Molecular rotation
— Physiological effect
— Toxicology
Carbon electrodes
See Electrodes, Carbon
Carbon fibers
sa Graphite fibers
x Fibers, Carbon
xx Inorganic fibers
Carbon in soils
See Soils—Carbon content
Carbon in the body   *(QP535.C1)*
Carbon isotopes
See Carbon—Isotopes
Carbon monoxide   *(QD181.C1; Physiology,*
QP913.C1; Toxicology,
RA1247.C17)
x Carbonic oxide
xx Gases, Asphyxiating and poisonous
— Molecular rotation
— Physiological effect
— Spectra
— Toxicology
Carbon paper
xx Paper

Carbon stars
See N stars
Carbon tetrachloride   *(QD181.C1)*
Carbonari   *(DG551-2; HS2394.C4)*
Carbonate minerals   *(QE389.61)*
x Minerals, Carbonate
xx Rocks, Carbonate
Carbonate rocks
See Rocks, Carbonate
Carbonated beverages   *(TP628-636)*
sa Bottling
Soft drink industry
x Carbonated drinks
Carbonated waters
Soda water
Soft drinks
xx Beverages
— Apparatus and supplies
sa Soda fountains
x Soda-water apparatus
xx Bottling machinery
Carbonated drinks
See Carbonated beverages
Carbonated waters
See Carbonated beverages
Mineral waters
Carbonates
sa Bastnaesite
Polycarbonates
Rocks, Carbonate
Soils—Carbonate content
Carbonates in soils
See Soils—Carbonate content
Carbonatites   *(Indirect)*
xx Rocks, Carbonate
Rocks, Igneous
Carbonic acid
See Carbon dioxide
Carbonic acid, Refrigerating
See Dry ice
Carbonic oxide
See Carbon monoxide
Carboniferous period
See Geology, Stratigraphic—Carboniferous
Paleobotany—Carboniferous
Paleontology—Carboniferous
Carbonium ions   *(QD305.C3)*
sa Radicals (Chemistry)
xx Ions
Carbonization   *(Chemical technology,*
TP156.C3)
sa Charcoal
Coal—Carbonization
Coal gasification
Coal gasification, Underground
Coal-tar products
Coke
Distillation, Destructive
xx Coal
Coke
Distillation, Destructive
Lignite
Carbons (Electric light)
See Electric light carbons
Carbonuria
xx Urine—Analysis and pathology
Carbonyl compounds
xx Oxo compounds
Carborundum
See Silicon carbide
Carbuncle   *(RL221)*
xx Pyoderma
Carbureters
See Carburetors

Carburetors *(TJ787)*
    sa subdivision Carburetors *under engines*
        or motors, e.g. Aeroplanes—Motors
          —Carburetors; Automobiles—Motors
          —Carburetors
    x Carbureters
      Carburettors
      Gas and oil engines—Carburetors
    xx Automobiles—Fuel systems
Carburettors
    See Carburetors
Carcinoembryonic antigens
    xx Antigens and antibodies
      Cancer
      Fetus
      Immunogenetics
Carcinogenesis
    sa Carcinogens
      Viral carcinogenesis
    x Cancer—Origin
      Tumorigenesis
    xx Cancer
Carcinogens
    xx Cancer
      Carcinogenesis
Carcinoid
    sa Malignant carcinoid syndrome
    x Argentaffinoma
      Chromaffinoma
    xx Tumors
Carcinoma
    See Cancer
      Tumors
Card catalogs (for libraries)
    See Catalogs, Card
Card games
    See Cards
      Musical card games
Card sharping
    See Cardsharping
Card system in business *(HF5736-5746)*
    sa Catalogs, Card
      Files and filing (Documents)
      Punched card systems
    x Indexes, Card
    xx Accounting
      Bookkeeping
      Business
      Catalogs, Card
      Files and filing (Documents)
      Office equipment and supplies
Card tricks *(GV1549)*
    sa Fortune-telling by cards
    x Cards—Tricks
    xx Conjuring
      Tricks
Card weaving *(TT848)*
    x Tablet weaving
    xx Handicraft
      Weaving
Cardamoms *(Direct) (Botany, QK495.Z;*
    Culture, SB307.C3; Therapeutics,
    RM666.C)
    — Marketing
Cardboard
    See Paperboard
Cardboard (Tree)
    See Ilomba
Cardia
    xx Esophagogastric junction
      Esophagus
      Stomach
    — Surgery
Cardiac arrest
    See Heart failure
Cardiac block
    See Heart block

Cardiac blood-vessels
    See Heart—Blood-vessels
Cardiac calcification
    See Heart—Calcification
Cardiac catheterization
    sa Catheters
    x Heart catheterization
    xx Blood—Circulation
      Heart—Diseases—Diagnosis
      Heart—Surgery
Cardiac conduction system
    See Heart conduction system
Cardiac diseases
    See Heart—Diseases
Cardiac function tests
    See Heart function tests
Cardiac glycosides
    xx Glycosides
Cardiac insufficiency
    See Heart failure
Cardiac massage
    x Heart—Massage
    xx Cardiac resuscitation
      Massage
Cardiac muscle
    See Heart—Muscle
Cardiac necrosis
    See Heart—Necrosis
Cardiac nerves
    See Heart—Innervation
Cardiac output *(QP113)*
    sa Hemodynamics
    xx Hemodynamics
Cardiac pacing
    See Pacemaker, Artificial (Heart)
Cardiac patients
    See Cardiacs
Cardiac resuscitation
    sa Cardiac massage
    xx Heart failure
      Resuscitation
Cardiacs
    sa Cookery for cardiacs
      Coronary care units
    x Cardiac patients
      Heart patients
    xx Heart—Diseases
    — Employment
      x Employment of cardiacs
    — Rehabilitation
      See Cardiovascular patient—
        Rehabilitation
Cardiff giant
    — Juvenile literature
Cardigan Welsh corgi
    See Welsh corgis
Cardinal-birds *(QL696.P2)*
    Example under Grosbeaks
    — Juvenile literature
    — Legends and stories
Cardinal points *(G108.5.C3)*
    sa Orientation (Religion)
    x Compass card
      Compass rose
      Points of the compass
    xx Compass
Cardinal protectors
    xx Catholic Church—Relations
      (diplomatic)
      Church and state—Catholic Church
      Monasticism and religious orders
      Nuncios, Papal
Cardinal virtues *(BV4645)*
    sa Temperance (Virtue)
    x Moral virtues
      Virtues, Cardinal
      Virtues, Moral
    xx Christian ethics

      Ethics
      Virtues
    — History of doctrines
Cardinals *(Direct) (Collected biography,*
    BX4663-5)
    xx Catholic Church—Clergy
      Catholic Curch—Government
      Christian biography
      Church polity
    — Bio-bibliography *(Z7838.C)*
    — Portraits *(BX4663-5)*
Cardinals, Black
    See Black cardinals
Carding *(TS1485)*
    sa Cotton carding
      Wool-carding
    xx Spinning
Carding-machines *(TS1487)*
    sa Combing machines
    xx Textile machinery
Cardiod *(QA567)*
    xx Curves, Quartic
Cardiography *(RC683)*
    sa Kinematocardiography
      Phonocardiography
      Ultrasonic cardiography
    xx Heart
      Heart—Diseases—Diagnosis
Cardiolipin
    xx Antigens and antibodies
Cardiological manifestations of general
    diseases
    x Cardiological symptoms of general
      diseases
    xx Cardiovascular system—Diseases
      Semiology
Cardiological symptoms of general diseases
    See Cardiological manifestations of general
      diseases
Cardiology
    sa Electronics in cardiology
      Heart—Diseases
      Pediatric cardiology
      Radioisotopes in cardiology
      Veterinary cardiology
    xx Heart—Diseases
      Internal medicine
    — Examinations, questions, etc.
    — Research
      x Heart—Diseases—Research
    — Terminology
      x Heart—Terminology
Cardiology, Experimental
    x Experimental cardiology
    xx Pathology, Experimental
      Physiology, Experimental
Cardiology, Forensic
    See Forensic cardiology
Cardioptosis
    See Heart—Displacement
Cardiospasm
    x Achalasia of the cardia
Cardiovascular agents
    sa Hydralazine
      Hypotensive agents
      Myocardial depressants
      Vasodilators
    x Cardiovascular drugs
      Drugs, Cardiovascular
Cardiovascular disease nursing
    sa Coronary care units
    xx Cardiovascular system—Diseases
      Nurses and nursing
Cardiovascular drugs
    See Cardiovascular agents
Cardiovascular instruments, Implanted
    x Implanted cardiovascular instruments
    xx Biomedical engineering

Medical electronics
Cardiovascular patient
This heading is used only with subdivisions.
— Rehabilitation
 x Cardiacs—Rehabilitation
Cardiovascular research *(Direct)*
 x Blood—Circulation—Research
 Cardiovascular system—Research
 xx Research
— Scholarships, fellowships, etc. *(Direct)*
 x Cardiovascular system—Diseases—
 Scholarships, fellowships, etc.
Cardiovascular services in hospitals
 See Hospitals—Cardiovascular services
Cardiovascular system *(Comparative anatomy, QL835-841; Human anatomy, QM178-197)*
 sa Blood—Circulation
 Blood-vessels
 Heart
 Nervous system, Vasomotor
 x Circulatory system
 Vascular system
 xx Blood—Circulation
— Abnormities and deformities
— Aging
— Diseases *(RC666-701)*
 sa Blood—Circulation, Disorders of
 Cardiological manifestations of general diseases
 Cardiovascular disease nursing
 Cardiovascular system—Radiography
 specific diseases, e.g. Varix
 x Vascular diseases
— — Atlases
— — Diagnosis
— — Dietary aspects
 See Cardiovascular system—
 Diseases—Nutritional aspects
— — Examinations, questions, etc.
— — Mortality
 xx Mortality
— — Nutritional aspects
 x Cardiovascular system—Diseases
 —Dietary aspects
 Diet and cardiovascular diseases
 Nutrition and cardiovascular diseases
 Example under Diet in disease; Nutrition
— — Prevention
— — Psychosomatic aspects
— — Scholarships, fellowships, etc.
 See Cardiovascular research—
 Scholarships, fellowships, etc.
— Examinations, questions, etc.
— Juvenile literature
— Mammals, [Reptiles, Vertebrates, etc.]
— Programmed instruction
— Radiography
 sa Radioisotopes in cardiology
 xx Cardiovascular system—Diseases
— — Programmed instruction
— Research
 See Cardiovascular research
— Surgery *(RD598)*
— — Complications and sequelae
— Syphilis
— Tuberculosis
 xx Tuberculosis
Cardiovascular system, Effect of radiation on the
 xx Radiation—Physiological effect
 Radioactivity—Physiological effect
Cardoon *(SB351.C)*

Cards *(GV1233-1299)*
 sa Baseball cards
 Cardsharping
 Fortune-telling by cards
 names of card games, e.g. Cribbage, Poker, Whist
 x Card games
 Playing-cards
 xx Amusements
 Gambling
 Games
— Art
— Collectors and collecting
— Exhibitions
— Law and legislation *(Direct)*
— Moral and religious aspects
— Private collections
— Taxation *(Direct)*
— Tricks
 See Card tricks
Cards, Advertising
 See Advertising cards
Cards, Catalog
 See Catalog cards
Cards, Greeting
 See Greeting cards
Cards, Holy
 See Holy cards
Cards, New Year
 See New Year cards
Cards, Visiting
 See Visiting-cards
Cardsharping *(GV1247)*
 x Card sharping
 Cheating at cards
 xx Cards
 Fraud
 Gambling
 Swindlers and swindling
Care of souls
 See Pastoral counseling
 Pastoral theology
Care of the sick
Here are entered works on various types of care, *e.g.* intensive, intermediate, long term, and home care including architectural planning, equipment, etc.
 sa Home nursing
 Hospitals
 Long-term care of the sick
 Nurses and nursing
 Terminal care
 x Sick, Care of
 xx Home nursing
 Hospitals
 Nurses and nursing
— Religious aspects
Care of the young (Animals)
 See Parental behavior in animals
Career education
 See Vocational education
Careers
 See Occupations
 Professions
 Vocational guidance
Careers in medicine
 See Medicine as a profession
Carelian language
 See Karelian language
Carga de Armiñon
 See Armiñon, Battle of, 1837
Cargo
 See Cargo handling
 subdivision Cargo *under subjects, e.g.*
 Helicopters—Cargo; Ships—Cargo
Cargo aircraft
 See Transport planes

Cargo cult
 See Cargo movement
Cargo dropping (Aeroplane)
 See Airdrop
Cargo gear
 See Cargo handling—Equipment
Cargo handling *(VK235)*
 sa Helicopters—Cargo
 Lighterage
 Stowage
 Unitized cargo systems
 x Cargo
 Stevedoring
 xx Inland waterway vessels—Cargo
 Loading and unloading
 Materials handling
 Ships—Cargo
— Equipment *(Shipboard, VM831; Wharves, TC370)*
 x Cargo gear
 xx Cranes, derricks, etc.
 Hoisting machinery
— Juvenile literature
— Labor productivity
— Production standards
— Safety measures
— Safety regulations *(Direct)*
Cargo movement
 sa Ras Tafari movement
 x Cargo cult
 xx Nationalism
 Nativistic movements
Cargo planes
 See Transport planes
Cargo preference *(Direct)*
 xx Merchant marine
 Shipping bounties and subsidies
Cargo ships
 See Merchant ships
Cargo vessels
 See Freighters
Cargoes, Seizure of
 See Seizure of vessels and cargoes
Carib Indians *(F2001)*
 sa Accawai Indians
 Apalai Indians
 Bakairi Indians
 Black Carib Indians
 Crichaná Indians
 Galibi Indians
 Ipurucotó Indians
 Macusi Indians
 Oyana Indians
 Trio Indians
 x Caraib Indians
 Charibbs
 Karinya Indians
 xx Indians of Central America
 Indians of South America
 Indians of the West Indies
— St. Vincent War, 1795-1796
 See St. Vincent—History—Carib War, 1795-1796

 GENERAL SUBDIVISIONS

— Juvenile literature
Carib language *(PM5756-9)*
 x Caraib language
 xx Cariban languages
 Indians of South America—Languages
Carib War, St. Vincent, 1795-1796
 See St. Vincent—History—Carib War, 1795-1796
Cariban languages *(PM5756-9)*
 sa Accawai language
 Arecuna language
 Bakairi language
 Carib language

Cariban languages *(PM5756-9)*
(Continued)
    Cuna language
    Galibi language
    Guaraúna language
    Hixkaryana language
    Kamarakoto language
    Macusi language
    Pemón dialects
    Taurepan language
    Tiriyó language
    Uaiuai language
  xx Accawai language
    Bakairi language
    Guaraúna language
    Indians of South America—Languages

Caribbean area
— Research
    See Caribbean studies

Caribbean literature

Caribbean studies *(Direct)*
  x Caribbean area—Research
  xx Research

Caribe
  x Piraña
    Piranha
— Control *(Indirect)*
  xx Fish control
    Predator control

Caribou *(Indirect)* *(QL737.U5)*
  sa Barren grounds caribou
    Reindeer
  x Rangifer
  xx Deer
    Reindeer
— Behavior

Caricature *(Direct)* *(NC1300-1763)*
  sa Caricatures and cartoons
    Grotesque
    Wit and humor
  xx Art
    Caricatures and cartoons
    Drawing
    Illustration of books
    Parody
    Satire

Caricatures and cartoons *(Direct)*
    (NC1300-1763)
  sa Caricature
    Cartoon captions
    Cartoonists
    Cartoons and children
    Comic books, strips, etc.
    Editorial cartoons
    Mazarinades
    Moving-picture cartoons
    Wit and humor, Pictorial
    subdivision Caricatures and cartoons
      under certain subjects, e.g. Marriage
      —Caricatures and cartoons; Triple
      Alliance, 1882—Caricatures and
      cartoons; *and subdivision* Humor,
      caricatures, etc. *under names of*
      wars, etc., e.g. European War,
      1914-1918—Humor, caricatures, etc.,
      and subdivisions Cartoons, satire,
      etc. *or* Portraits, caricatures, etc.
      under names of persons, e.g. Lincoln,
      Abraham, Pres. U.S., 1809-1865—
      Cartoons, satire, etc.; Napoléon I,
      Emperor of the French, 1769-1821—
      Portraits, caricatures, etc.
  x Cartoons
    Humorous illustrations
    Illustrations, Humorous
    Pictures, Humorous
  xx Caricature
    Pictures
    Portraits

    Wit and humor, Pictorial
— Competitions
— Marketing
— Psychological aspects

GEOGRAPHIC SUBDIVISIONS

— France, ₍Great Britain, etc.₎
  xx French ₍English, etc.₎ wit and
    humor, Pictorial

Caricaturists
  See Cartoonists

Carijó Indians
  See Fulnio Indians

Carillon music *(M172)*
  sa Carillon with band
    Carillon with orchestra
    Concertos (Carillon with band)
    Sonatas (Carillon)

Carillon with band *(M1205-6)*
  sa Concertos (Carillon with band)
  xx Carillon music
    Concertos (Carillon with band)

Carillon with orchestra *(M1038-9)*
  xx Carillon music
    Orchestral music

Carillons *(Direct)*
  sa Change ringing
    Handbell ringing
  xx Bells
    Church music
    Music

Cariri Indians
  See Kariri Indians

Cariri language
  See Kariri language

Carisoprodol
  x Soma (Drug)
  xx Muscle relaxants

Carleton's Invasion, 1776 *(E232)*
  sa Valcour Island, Battle of, 1776

Carlisle, Pa. United States Indian School
  Example under Indians of North America—
    Education; *and under reference from*
    Indians of North America—Schools

Carlism
  See Carlists

Carlist wars
  See Spain—History—Carlist War,
    1833-1840
    Spain—History—Carlist War,
    1873-1876

Carlists
  x Carlism

Carlovingian architecture
  See Architecture, Carlovingian

Carlovingian art
  See Art, Carlovingian

Carlovingian illumination of books and
    manuscripts
  See Illumination of books and manuscripts,
    Carlovingian

Carlovingian ivories
  See Ivories, Carlovingian

Carlovingian sculpture
  See Sculpture, Carlovingian

Carlovingians *(France, DC70-81; Germany,*
    DD129-134; Switzerland, DQ85-87)
  sa France—History—To 987
    Verdun, Treaty of, 843
  x Carolingians
  xx France—History—To 987

Carlowitz, Peace of, 1699 *(DB63)*
  xx Venice—History—Turkish Wars, 17th
    century

Carmathians
  See Karmathians

Carmelite nuns in Korea, ₍Mobile, Ala., etc.₎

Carmelites *(BX3201-3255; Women,*
    BX4321-4)
  x White Friars
  xx Friars
    Monasticism and religious orders
— Bio-bibliography *(Z7840.C2)*

Carmelites in Germany, ₍Scotland, etc.₎

Carnallite *(TN948.C34)*
  xx Halogens

Carnataca language
  See Kannada language

Carnatic music
  See Music, Karnatic

Carnation stem-rot

Carnations *(SB413.C3)*
  xx Pinks
  Example under Flowers
— Diseases and pests *(SB608.C3)*
— Handling
— Transportation

Carnations as feed *(SF99.C)*

Carnations in art
  xx Art
  Example under Flowers in art

Carnavalito (Dance) *(GV1796.C)*

Carnegie Foundation for the Advancement of
    Teaching
  Example under reference from Educational en-
    dowments

Carnegie Medal
  See Library Association Carnegie Medal

Carnifex Ferry, Battle of, 1861

Carnijó Indians
  See Fulnio Indians

Carnival *(GT4180-4299)*
  sa Masks
    Mumming
    subdivision Carnival *under names of*
      cities, e.g. Rome (City)—Carnival
  xx Masks

Carnival glass
  x Glass, Carnival
— Collectors and collecting

Carnival plays *(German literature, PT963.C3)*
  sa Mumming plays
  x Fastnachtspiele
    Plays, Medieval
  xx Drama
    Drama, Medieval
    Folk-drama
    German drama
    German drama (Comedy)

Carnival songs *(Italian literature, PQ4222.C4)*

Carnivals (Circus)
  See Amusement parks

Carnivora *(QL737.C2)*
  sa names of carnivorous animals
  xx Mammals
    Predatory animals

Carnivora, Fossil *(QE882.C1-4)*
  sa Wolverines, Fossil

Carnivorous plants
  See Insectivorous plants

Carnotite *(Indirect)* *(TN948.R3)*
  sa Radium
  xx Radium
    Uranium ores

Carob

Carob sugar
  xx Sugar

Carolina chickadee *(QL696.P2)*
  xx Chickadees
— Behavior

Carolina wren
  xx Wrens

Caroline Islands
— Papal arbitration, 1885

Caroline silver articles
　See Silver articles, Caroline
Caroline War, 1494-1496
　See Italy—History—Expedition of Charles
　　VIII, 1494-1496
Carolingian architecture
　See Architecture, Carlovingian
Carolingian art
　See Art, Carlovingian
Carolingian sculpture
　See Sculpture, Carlovingian
Carolingians
　See Carlovingians
Carols
　　Here are entered collections of carols ap-
　　propriate to one or more church sea-
　　sons and not restricted to one language
　　or nationality.
　x Christmas carols
　　Easter carols
　xx Christian poetry
　　Christmas music
　　Christmas—Poetry
　　Church music
　　Easter music
　　Easter—Poetry
　　Folk-songs
　　Hymns
　　Sacred vocal music
　　Songs
Carols, Argentine, ⌈Dutch, English, etc.⌉
　　May be subdivided by place, *e.g.* Carols,
　　French—Limousin.
　x Argentine ⌈Dutch, English, etc.⌉ carols
Carols, Bohemian
　See Carols, Czech
Carols, Czech
　x Carols, Bohemian
　　Czech carols
Carols, French
　— Limousin
　　Note under Carols, Argentine, ⌈Dutch,
　　English, etc.⌉
Carols (Instrumental settings)
　　The specification (Instrumental settings)
　　is also used after Carols with national
　　qualification.
Carotene
　See Carotin
Carotenoid metabolism
　xx Metabolism
Carotenoids
　See Carotinoids
Carotid artery　*(QL835; QM191)*
　xx Arteries
　— Abnormities and deformities
　— Excision　*(RD598)*
　— Ligature
　　xx Arteries—Ligature
　— Radiography
　— Surgery
Carotid canal　*(QL821; QM105)*
Carotid gland　*(Human anatomy, QM371;*
　　Physiology, QP187)
　sa Carotid sinus
　x Carotid glomus
　xx Carotid sinus
　　Nonchromaffin paraganglia
　— Tumors
Carotid glomus
　See Carotid gland
Carotid sinus
　sa Carotid gland
　xx Blood pressure
　　Carotid gland
Carotin　*(QK898.C)*
　sa Chromatographic analysis
　x Carotene

　xx Carotinoids
　　Chloroplast pigments
Carotinoids　*(QP671)*
　sa Carotin
　x Carotenoids
　xx Plant pigments
Carousel
　See Merry-go-round
Carp　*(QL638.C94; Culture, SH167.C3)*
　sa Cookery (Carp)
　xx Ostariophysi
　Example under Fishes
　— Pictorial works
Carp fisheries　*(Indirect)*　*(SH351.C3)*
　xx Fisheries
Carp fishing　*(SH691.C3)*
　xx Fishing
Carpal tunnel syndrome
　xx Median nerve—Wounds and injuries
Carpatho-Russians
　See Ruthenians
Carpatho-Ukrainians
　See Ruthenians
Carpel　*(QK659)*
　xx Botany
　　Plants—Reproduction
Carpenter ants
　xx Ants
Carpenter bees
　xx Bees
　— Juvenile literature
Carpenters　*(Direct)*
　sa Cabinet-workers
　　Joiners
　　Trade-unions—Carpenters
　　Wages—Carpenters
　　Woodworkers
　xx Building trades
　　Woodworkers
Carpenters' square　*(TH5619)*
　x Square (Instrument)
　　Steel square
　xx Carpentry—Tools
Carpentry　*(Economics, HD9773;*
　　Technology, TH5601-5691)
　sa Cabinet-work
　　Concrete construction—Formwork
　　Doors
　　Floors
　　Hand-railing
　　House framing
　　Joinery
　　Mitering
　　Moldings
　　Roofs
　　Rustic woodwork
　　Scaffolding
　　Stair building
　　Turning
　　Walls
　　Woodwork
　　Woodworking machinery
　xx Building
　　Joinery
　　Manual training
　　Woodwork
　— Accidents
　— Drafting
　　See Carpentry drafting
　— Estimates　*(TH5614-5615)*
　— Examinations, questions, etc.
　— Juvenile literature
　— Mathematics　*(TH5612)*
　　xx Shop mathematics
　— Tables, calculations, etc.　*(TH5608)*
　— Terminology
　— Tools　*(TH5618)*
　　sa Augers

　　Carpenters' square
　　Hammers
　　Lathes
　　Planes (Hand tools)
　　Saws
　xx Tools
　— Vocational guidance
　—— Juvenile literature
Carpentry drafting　*(TH5611)*
　x Carpentry—Drafting
　　Drafting, Carpentry
　xx Structural drawing
Carpet and rug industry
　See Rug and carpet industry
Carpet beetles
　sa Black carpet beetles
　x Buffalo bugs
　　Buffalo carpet beetles
　　Carpet bugs
Carpet bugs
　See Carpet beetles
Carpet industry
　See Rug and carpet industry
Carpet installation
　See Carpet laying
Carpet laying　*(TS1779.5)*
　x Carpet installation
　　Installation of carpets
　　Laying of carpets
　xx Carpets
Carpet manufacture
　See Carpets
Carpet-printing　*(TP931.C2)*
　xx Carpets
　　Printing
　　Textile printing
Carpetbag rule
　See Reconstruction
Carpets　*(Art, NK2775-2896; Technology,*
　　TS1772-6)
　sa Carpet laying
　　Carpet-printing
　　Moquette
　　Rug and carpet industry
　　Rugs
　　Weaving
　x Carpet manufacture
　xx Decoration and ornament
　　Floor coverings
　　House furnishings
　　Rugs
　Example under Textile industry and fabrics;
　　Weaving
　— Care
　— Costs
　　See Carpets—Estimates and costs
　— Estimates and costs
　　x Carpets—Costs
　— Private collections　*(NK2790)*
　— Tariff
　　See Tariff on carpets and rugs
　— Testing
Carpincho
　See Capybaras
Carpsucker, River
　See River carpsucker
Carpus
　sa Wrist
　xx Wrist
Carreras, Las, Battle of
　See Las Carreras, Battle of, 1849
Carré's disease
　See Canine distemper
Carré's virus
　See Canine distemper virus
Carriage and wagon making　*(Direct)*
　　(TS2001-2035)
　sa Axles

Carriage and wagon making *(Direct)*
(TS2001-2035) *(Continued)*
    Bolts and nuts
    Carriage industry
    Couplings
    Wheels
  x Wagon making
  xx Blacksmithing
    Carriage industry
— Accounting *(HF5686.C15)*
— Estimates
Carriage and wagon painting *(TS2030-2032)*
  sa Automobiles—Painting
    Japan gold-size
  x Wagon painting
  xx Painting, Industrial
Carriage industry *(Direct)* *(Economics,*
HD9999.C3; Technology,
TS2001-2035)
  sa Carriage and wagon making
    Trade-unions—Carriage industry
    Wages—Carriage industry
  xx Carriage and wagon making
Example under Manufactures
Carriage manufacturers and dealers *(Direct)*
Carriages and carts
  sa Ambulances
    Cab and omnibus service
    Coaching
    Handcarts
    Omnibuses
    Vehicles
  x Cabs
    Carts
    Coaches
    Hacks (Carriages)
  xx Transportation
    Vehicles
    Wagons
— Museums *(Direct)*
— Pictorial works
— Terminology
Carriages and carts in art
  xx Art
Carrier control systems *(TJ218)*
  x A-C carrier control systems
    Control systems, Carrier
  xx Automatic control
    Modulation (Electronics)
Carrier current telegraphy
  See Telegraph, Carrier current
Carrier current telephony
  See Telephone, Carrier current
Carrier flight decks
  See Aircraft carriers—Flight decks
Carrier Indians
  See Takulli Indians
Carrier language
  See Takulli language
Carrier pigeons
  See Homing pigeons
Carrier waves
  x Space charge waves
    Waves, Carrier
  xx Electromagnetic waves
    Modulation (Electronics)
Carriers *(Direct)*
  sa Aeronautics, Commercial—Law and
    legislation
    Bailments
    Cab and omnibus service
    Charter-parties
    Communication and traffic
    Contracts, Maritime
    Demurrage
    Express service
    Freight and freightage
    Freight forwarders

    Hire
    Interstate commerce
    Limited liability
    Maritime law
    Motor bus lines
    Motor buses—Law and legislation
    Postal service
    Railroad law
    Stoppage in transitu
    Storage and moving trade
    Taxicabs
    Transportation, Automotive—Laws and
      regulations
    Transportation—Laws and regulations
  x Common carriers
  xx Bailments
    Commercial law
    Contracts, Maritime
    Freight forwarders
    Hire
    Interstate commerce
    Limited liability
    Maritime law
    Public utilities
    Shipment of goods
    Trade regulation
    Transportation, Automotive—Laws and
      regulations
    Transportation—Laws and regulations
— Accounting
— Legal research
— Rates
    See Transportation—Rates
Carriers, Aircraft
  See Aircraft carriers
Carriers (Roman-Dutch law)
Carriers (Warships)
  See Aircraft carriers
Carries
  See Portages
Carrion crow
  xx Crows
Carrion's disease
  See Verruga peruana
Carrot fly
  See Carrot rust fly
Carrot rust fly
  x Carrot fly
  xx Carrots—Diseases and pests
Carrots *(SB211.C3)*
— Diseases and pests *(Indirect)*
    (SB608.C)
  sa Carrot rust fly
— Juvenile literature
— Prices *(Direct)* *(HD9235.C34-342)*
— Varieties
Carrots as feed
Carrousel
  See Merry-go-round
Carry-back of business losses
  See Income tax—Deductions—Losses
Carry-over business
  See Contango and backwardation
Carry-over of business losses
  See Income tax—Deductions—Losses
Carrying weights
  See Lifting and carrying
Cars, Armored (Tanks)
  See Tanks (Military science)
Cars, Railroad
  See Railroads—Cars
Cars (Automobiles)
  See Automobiles
Cars and car building
  See Railroads—Cars
    Railroads—Cars—Construction
    Railroads—Cars—Maintenance and
    repair

Carstone *(Indirect)*
  xx Sandstone
Cartagena, Colombia
— Siege, 1697 *(F2272)*
— Siege, 1741 *(F2272.5)*
    xx English West Indian Expedition,
      1739-1742
— Siege, 1815
    xx Colombia—History—War of
      Independence, 1810-1822
Cartago, Costa Rica
— Earthquake, 1910
Cartel for exchange of prisoners, 1862-1864
  See United States—History—Civil War,
    1861-1865—Prisoners, Exchange of
Cartels
  See Trusts, Industrial
Carthage
— History *(DT168-9)*
    sa Punic War, 1st, 264-241 B.C
    Punic War, 2d, 218-201 B.C.
    Punic wars
Carthaginian antiquities
  See Punic antiquities
Carthaginian gods
  See Gods, Punic
Carthaginians
  x Punics
  xx Phenicians
— Antiquities
    See Punic antiquities
Carthaginians in Spain, ₍etc.₎
Carthusian architecture
  See Architecture, Carthusian
Carthusians *(BX3301-3355)*
  x Chartreux, Ordre des
    Eremites
  xx Hermits
    Monasticism and religious orders
Carthusians in England, ₍France, etc.₎
Cartilage *(QM567)*
  sa Dysostosis
    Enchondroma
    Endochondral ossification
    Epiphysis
    Meniscus (Anatomy)
    Osteochondroma
    Xiphoid process
  x Gristle
  xx Bones
    Connective tissues
    Joints
    Ligaments
  Notes under Histology; Tissues
— Tumors
Cartographers *(United States, GA407; Other*
countries, GA473-1773)
  sa Cartography as a profession
Cartography *(Indirect)* *(GA101-1999)*
    Here are entered works on the general
    science of map-making, including map
    projection and the mapping of large
    areas. Works dealing with the mapping
    of small areas and the drawing of maps
    in elementary schools are entered un-
    der Map drawing. Works about the
    maps themselves are entered under
    Maps.
  sa Agricultural mapping
    Color in cartography
    Contours (Cartography)
    English language—Dialects—
      Cartography
    European War, 1914-1918—
      Cartography
    Forest mapping
    Geological mapping
    Geomorphological mapping

Grids (Cartography)
Map printing
Map-projection
Map scales
Maps, Military
Maps—Reproduction
Military topography
Mine maps
Nautical charts
Rectifiers (Photogrammetry)
Soil mapping
Stereoplanigraph
Topographical drawing
United States—History—Revolution,
1775-1783—Cartography
Vegetation mapping
World War, 1939-1945—Cartography
  x Chartography
  xx Geography, Mathematical
Map-projection
Maps
Surveying
Note under Map drawing
— Automation
— — Terminology
— Computer programs
  sa CORMAP (Computer program)
— Conventional signs
  See Maps—Symbols
— Conversion tables *(GA23)*
  xx Cartography—Tables, etc.
— Early works to 1800
— History
  x Maps—History
— Information services
— Juvenile literature
— Philosophy
— Symbols
  See Maps—Symbols
— Tables, etc.
  sa Cartography—Conversion tables
— Terminology
  See Maps—Terminology
— Vocational guidance
  See Cartography as a profession
Cartography, Primitive *(GN476.5)*
  sa Indians—Cartography
Cartography as a profession *(GA197.5)*
  x Cartography—Vocational guidance
  xx Cartographers
Cartomancy
  See Fortune-telling by cards
Cartometry
  xx Area measurement
Geography, Mathematical
Length measurement
Maps
Cartons *(Commerce, HF5770; Manufacture,*
TS1200)
  sa Egg carton craft
Paper box machinery
  x Paper boxes
  xx Boxes
Paper box industry
Paper containers
Paper products
Paperboard
Cartoon captions
  xx Caricatures and cartoons
— Marketing
Cartoonists *(Direct)*
  x Caricaturists
  xx Artists
Caricatures and cartoons
Wit and humor, Pictorial
— Biography
— Correspondence, reminiscences, etc.
— Interviews

Cartoons
  See Caricatures and cartoons
Cartoons, Editorial
  See Editorial cartoons
Cartoons and children *(LB1139.H8)*
  x Children and cartoons
  xx Caricatures and cartoons
Cartridge actuated devices
  See Propellant actuated devices
Cartridges *(UF740-745)*
  sa Handloading of ammunition
Propellant actuated devices
Shot (Pellets)
  xx Ammunition
Projectiles
— Patents
Cartridges, Phonograph
  See Phonograph cartridges
Carts
  See Carriages and carts
Cartularies
  sa Archives
Charters
Diplomatics
Terriers (Law)
  x Chartularies
  xx Archives
Manuscripts
Carvacrol *(RS165.C)*
Carving (Art industries)
  sa Belt toggles
Bone carving
Gem carving
Glyptics
Horn carving
Ivory carving
Leather carving
Netsukes
Scrimshaws
Stone carving
Wood-carving
  xx Art
Arts and crafts movement
Decoration and ornament
Design, Decorative
Sculpture
Carving (Meat, etc.) *(TX885)*
  xx Cookery
Dinners and dining
Meat cutting
Table
— Early works to 1800
Carwashes
  See Car washes
Caryatids *(NA3683)*
  xx Architecture—Details
Caryocinesis
  See Karyokinesis
Caryophyllidea *(QL391.P7)*
  xx Cestoda
Carzano, Battle of, 1917 *(D569.C)*
  xx European War, 1914-1918—Campaigns
—Italo-Austrian
Casablanca Massacre, 1907 *(DT324)*
  xx Morocco—History—20th century
Cascade converters *(TK2797)*
  x Converters, Electric
Electric converters
  xx Electric current converters
Rotary converters
Cascade shower *(QC490)*
  sa Cosmic ray showers
  x Shower, Cascade
  xx Bremsstrahlung
Nuclear physics
Pair production
— Tables, etc.

Cascade theory (Dynamics)
  See Cascades (Fluid dynamics)
Cascades (Fluid dynamics) *(TJ267.C3)*
  x Aerofoils in cascade
Cascade theory (Dynamics)
  xx Aerodynamics
Fluid dynamics
Cascara *(RM663.C37)*
  sa Buckthorn
  xx Buckthorn
Case
  See Grammar, Comparative and general—
Case
    subdivision Case *under names of*
languages and groups of languages
Case (Action)
  See Actions on the case
Case hardening
  x Cyaniding
Nitriding
  xx Cementation (Metallurgy)
Metals—Heat treatment
Steel—Heat treatment
Surface hardening
Case method
    Here are entered works on the use of re-
corded cases as a basis for instruction.
Case studies themselves are entered
under the appropriate subjects with
subdivision Case studies.
  xx Education
Case studies
  See Juvenile delinquency—Case studies
Surgery—Cases, clinical reports,
statistics
    subdivision Cases, clinical reports,
statistics *under medical topics, e.g.*
Leprosy—Cases, clinical reports,
statistics
    subdivision Case studies *under specific*
subjects, e.g. Insurance,
Unemployment—Case studies;
Juvenile delinquency—Case studies;
and subdivision Cases, clinical
reports, statistics *under medical*
topics, e.g. Leprosy—Cases, clinical
reports, statistics; Surgery—Cases,
clinical reports, statistics
Case work, Social
  See Social case work
Casein *(Chemical technology, TP248.C4;*
Chemistry of milk, SF253; Plastics,
TP986.C2)
  xx Milk proteins
  Example under Proteins
Casein painting *(ND2490)*
  xx Painting
Caseous lymphadenitis
  See Pseudotuberculosis
Caseros, Battle of, 1852 *(F2846)*
Cases, Miniature
  See Miniature cases
Cases of conscience
  See Casuistry
Cash flow
  sa Corporation reserves
  xx Corporations—Finance
Liquidity (Economics)
— Mathematical models
— Programmed instruction
Cash on delivery shipments
  See C.O.D. shipments
Cash position (Corporation finance)
  See Corporations—Cash position
Cash registers *(HF5531)*
  sa Cashiers
  xx Bookkeeping
Cashiers

Cash registers *(HF5531)* *(Continued)*
    Office equipment and supplies
    Point-of-sale systems industry
  — Maintenance and repair
     x Cash registers—Repairing
  — Repairing
     See Cash registers—Maintenance and
        repair
Cash takeover bid
  See Tender offers (Securities)
Cashew industry
  See Cashew nut industry
Cashew nut *(Indirect)* *(SB401)*
  — Marketing
Cashew nut industry *(Direct)*
    x Cashew industry
    Cashew trade
Cashew oil
  — Patents
Cashew trade
  See Cashew nut industry
Cashibo Indians *(F3430.1.C35)*
    xx Indians of South America
Cashiers
    sa Cash registers
    xx Cash registers
       Retail trade
  — Examinations, questions, etc.
Cashinaua language
  See Kashinaua language
Cashubian language
  See Kashubian language
Casidas
  See Qasidas
Casing, Oil well
  See Oil well casing
Caskets
  See Boxes
    Boxes, Ornamental
    Chests
Caskets (Coffins)
  See Coffins
Caspe declaration, 1412 *(DP131.6)*
    x Compromiso de Caspe
Cassava *(Indirect)* *(SB211.C3)*
    x Mandioca
  — Diseases and pests
Cassava as feed
Cassava as food
    xx Food
Cassegrain telescope
  See Telescope, Cassegrainian
Cassegrainian telescope
  See Telescope, Cassegrainian
Cassel, France, Battle of, 1328
    (DH801.F465)
Cassel, France, Battle of, 1677 *(D278.C)*
    xx Dutch War, 1672-1678
Casserole receipts *(TX693)*
    sa Stews
    xx Cookery
Cassette books
  See Talking books
Cassia *(Botany, QK495.L52; Forestry,*
    SD397.C34; Pharmacy, RS165.S4)
Cassiterite *(Indirect)* *(Metallurgy, TN793;*
    Tin ores, TN470-479)
Cassowaries *(QL696.C3)*
    xx Ratitae
Cassubian literature
  See Kashubian literature
Cast-iron *(Materials of engineering, TA474-5;*
    Metallurgy, TN710)
    sa Columns, Iron and steel
    Founding
    Iron-founding
    x Pig-iron
    xx Iron

Iron-founding
Iron industry and trade
— Analysis *(QD133)*
    xx Iron—Analysis
— Defects
— Electrometallurgy
— Fatigue
— Heat treatment
— Metallography
— Metallurgy
— — Mathematical models
— Specifications
— Standards
— Tables, calculations, etc.
— Testing *(TA475)*
— Welding
Cast-iron pipe
  See Pipe, Cast-iron
Cast stone
  See Stone, Cast
Castanet music *(M175.C35)*
    sa Castanets with chamber orchestra
    Quartets (Electronic harpsichord,
      castanets, percussion, violoncello)
Castanets *(MT720)*
Castanets with chamber orchestra *(M1038-9)*
    xx Castanet music
    Chamber-orchestra music
Castanets with chamber orchestra, Arranged
    (M1039.4.C35)
Castaways
  See Survival (after aeroplane accidents,
    shipwrecks, etc.)
Caste *(Indirect)* *(Anthropology, GN492.4;*
    India, DS422.C3; Social classes,
    HT713-725)
    sa Social classes
    xx Manners and customs
— Religious aspects *(Hinduism,*
    BL1215.C3)
— Ceylon
    sa Karavas
— India
    sa Agarwals
      Balahis
      Bauris
      Bhatias
      Charans
      Ethnology—India
      Ezhavas
      Jatavs
      Jats
      Kallans
      Kammas
      Khandelwals
      Lingayats
      Lohars
      Mahars
      Minas
      Moplahs
      Nadars
      Nairs
      Namasudras
      Nambudiri
      Okkaligas
      Patidars
      Saraswats
      Shudras
      Sikligars
      Ulladans
      Untouchables
      Vallabhachars
    xx Brahmanism
      Ethnology—India
      Hinduism
— Japan
    sa Eta
— Korea

    sa Pugok
— Pakistan
    sa Bhatias
Caste War of Yucatan, 1847-1855
  See Yucatan—History—Caste War,
    1847-1855
Castellani's bronchitis
  See Bronchopulmonary spirochaetosis
Castigatory
  See Cucking stool
Castile in art
Castile in literature
Castilian language
  See Spanish language
Casting
  See Founding
    Iron-founding
    Plaster casts
    Plastics—Molding
Casting, Centrifugal
  See Centrifugal casting
Casting, Continuous
  See Continuous casting
Casting, Steel
  See Steel founding
Casting (Chemical technology)
  See Molding (Chemical technology)
Casting (Fishing)
    sa Bait-casting
    Fly-casting
    Spin-fishing
    Tournament casting
    xx Fishing
Castings, Fossil
  See Coprolites
Castings, Metal
  See Metal castings
Castle (Chess)
  See Rook (Chess)
Castle-gammon (Game) *(GV1469.C3)*
Castles *(Indirect)* *(Architecture,*
    NA7710-7786; England,
    DA660-664; France, DC20, DC801;
    Germany, DD20; Italy, DG420;
    Spain, DP22)
    sa Moats
    Sandcastles
    x Châteaux
    Feudal castles
    xx Architecture
    Architecture, Medieval
    Fortification
— Anecdotes, facetiae, satire, etc.
— Guide-books
— Juvenile literature
— Legends
— — Juvenile literature
Castles (Gymnastics)
  See Pyramids (Gymnastics)
Castles (in heraldry)
Castles (in numismatics) *(CJ161.C3)*
    xx Numismatics
Castles in literature
Castor (Rodent)
  See Beavers
Castor-bean *(Indirect)* *(SB299.C3)*
    x Castor seed
    xx Beans
— Marketing
Castor-oil *(Chemical technology, TP684.C3;*
    Therapeutics, RM666.C375)
Castor-oil plant *(SB299.C3)*
Castor seed
  See Castor-bean
Castor semi-looper
Castrametation
  See Camps (Military)

Castrati *(History of vocal technique, ML1460; Voice culture, MT821)*
   sa Eunuchs
   xx Castration
      Singers
  — Biography
Castration *(Physiology, QP251-5; Social pathology, HV4989; Surgery, RD571; Veterinary medicine, SF889)*
   sa Capons and caponizing
      Castrati
      Skoptsi
      Spaying
   x Emasculation
   xx Capons and caponizing
      Spaying
      Veterinary surgery
Castration complex
   x Complexes (Psychology)
   xx Psychoanalysis
      Psychology, Pathological
      Sex (Psychology)
Castration of criminals and defectives *(Direct)*
   sa Sterilization of criminals and defectives
   xx Crime and criminals
      Delinquents
      Punishment
      Sterilization of criminals and defectives
Casts
      For construction *see* Plaster casts; for trade catalogs of casts from sculpture *see* Plaster casts—Catalogs; for catalogs of collections of casts from sculpture in galleries, museums, etc., *see* Sculpture—Catalogs; Sculpture—[local subdivision]—Catalogs; for casts of architectural subjects *see* Architectural casts.
   sa Prosthesis
   Notes under Plaster casts; Plaster casts—Catalogs
Casts, Surgical
   See Plaster casts, Surgical
Casual labor *(Direct) (HD5855-6)*
   sa Disguised unemployment
      Migrant labor
      Seasonal labor
      Seasonal variations (Economics)
   x Labor, Casual
   xx Labor and laboring classes
      Migrant labor
      Seasonal industries
      Seasonal variations (Economics)
      Unemployed
      Unemployment, Seasonal
Casualties, Disaster
   See Mass casualties
Casualties, Mass
   See Mass casualties
Casualties, War
   See War—Casualties (Statistics, etc.)
      subdivision Casualties (Statistics, etc.) *under names of wars*
Casualty insurance
   See Insurance, Casualty
Casuarina *(SD397.C)*
Casubian literature
   See Kashubian literature
Casuistry *(Catholic Church, BX1757-9; Ethics, BJ1440-1448)*
   sa Adiaphora
      Conscience
      Conscience, Examination of
      Ethical problems
      Pastoral counseling
      Probabilism
      Responsa

      Scruples
   x Cases of conscience
   xx Catholic Church—Discipline
      Christian ethics
      Conscience
      Ethics
      Scholasticism
Casus fortuitus
   See Accident (Casus fortuitus)
CAT
   See Children's apperception test
Cat, Domestic
   See Cats
Cat breeding *(Indirect) (SF447.5)*
   sa Cat breeds
   x Cats—Breeding
Cat breeds *(Indirect)*
   sa names of specific breeds, e.g. Angora cat, Siamese cat
   x Cats—Breeds
   xx Cat breeding
      Cats
  — Juvenile literature
Cat food
   See Cats—Food
Cat-mint
   See Catnip
Cat spruce
   See White spruce
Cat-thyme
Cat-worship
   See Cats (in religion, folk-lore, etc.)
Catabaptists
   See Anabaptists
Catabolism
   See Metabolism
Cataclastic rocks *(QE495)*
   xx Rocks
Catacombs *(Rome, DG807.4)*
   sa Christian art and symbolism
      Church history—Primitive and early church, ca. 30-600
   xx Burial
      Cemeteries
      Christian antiquities
      Christian art and symbolism
      Church history—Primitive and early church, ca. 30-600
      Tombs
  — Drama
Catalan ballads and songs *(Collections, PC3929; History, PC3913)*
   sa Folk-songs, Catalan
      Songs, Catalan
Catalan drama *(Direct) (Collections, PC3929.5; History, PC3915)*
   xx Spanish drama
Catalan farces *(Direct)*
   xx Spanish farces
Catalan fiction *(Direct) (Collections, PC3930; History, PC3917)*
Catalan imprints *(Direct)*
Catalan language *(PC3801-3899)*
   xx Spanish language
Catalan letters *(PC3930.L4)*
Catalan literature *(PC3901-3975)*
   xx Spanish literature
  — To 1500
  — 16th-18th centuries
  — 19th-20th centuries
  — — Phonotape catalogs
Catalan newspapers *(PN5311-5319)*
Catalan orations *(PC3930.O7)*
Catalan periodicals *(PN5311-5320)*
Catalan philology *(PC3801-3899)*
Catalan poetry *(Direct) (PC3913; PC3929)*
   xx Spanish poetry
  — To 1500

  — 16th-18th centuries
  — 19th-20th centuries
     GENERAL SUBDIVISIONS
  — Competitions
     sa Premi de poesia per a inèdits Mossèn Amadeu Oller
Catalans
   x Catalonians
Catalans in Greece
   See Spaniards in Greece
Catalans in Mexico, [Sicily, etc.]
Catalase *(Botany, QK896; Physiological chemistry, QP601)*
   xx Microbodies
Catalog card duplication
   See Catalog cards—Reproduction
Catalog card reproduction
   See Catalog cards—Reproduction
Catalog cards
   sa VSMF microfilm system
   x Cards, Catalog
   xx Cataloging
      Catalogs, Card
  — Duplication
     See Catalog cards—Reproduction
  — Reproduction
     x Catalog card duplication
      Catalog card reproduction
      Catalog cards—Duplication
      Duplication of catalog cards
      Reproduction of catalog cards
     xx Copying
Catalog cross references
   See Cross references (Cataloging)
Catalog use
   See Library catalogs and readers
Cataloging
   See Cataloging of religious literature
   sa Bibliography
      Catalog cards
      Classification—Books
      Colophons
      Cross references (Cataloging)
      Descriptive cataloging
      Errors and blunders, Literary
      Imprints (in books)
      Indexing
      Machine-readable bibliographic data
      Recataloging
      Searching, Bibliographical
      Subject cataloging
      Subject headings
   x Cataloguing
   xx Bibliography
      Books
      Catalogs, Card
      Documentation
      Library science
      Processing (Libraries)
  — Costs
  — Early works to 1900
  — Programmed instruction
  — Quotations, maxims, etc.
     sa Quotations, Buddhist
  — Standards *(Direct)*
Cataloging, Cooperative *(Z695)*
   sa Bibliography, International
      Bibliography, Universal
      Cataloging in publication
      Catalogs, Union
      Library cooperation
      National Program for Acquisitions and Cataloging
      Newspapers—Bibliography—Union lists
      Periodicals—Bibliography—Union lists
   x Cooperative cataloging
   xx Bibliography, International

xx Card system in business
   Library catalogs
Catalogs, Classed
   See Catalogs, Classified
Catalogs, Classified
   sa Classification—Books
   x Catalogs, Classed
      Catalogs, Systematic
      Classed catalogs
      Classified catalogs
   xx Catalogs, Subject
      Classification—Books
      Library catalogs
      Shelf-listing (Library science)
Catalogs, Classified (Dewey decimal)
Catalogs, Classified (Universal decimal)
Catalogs, College
   sa Catalogs, School
   x Catalogs, University
      College catalogs
      Universities and colleges—Catalogs
      University catalogs
   xx Catalogs, School
Catalogs, Commercial   *(HF5861-2)*
   sa Advertising, Direct-mail
   x Commercial catalogs
   xx Advertising
      Advertising, Direct-mail
      Business
      Manufactures
Catalogs, Dictionary
   sa Subject headings
   x Dictionary catalogs
   xx Library catalogs
Catalogs, Divided
   x Divided catalogs
   xx Library catalogs
Catalogs, Film
   See Moving-pictures—Catalogs
      subdivision Film catalogs *under specific
      subjects, e.g.* Geology—Film
      catalogs; Mental hygiene—Film
      catalogs
Catalogs, Library
   See Library catalogs
Catalogs, Publishers'   *(Indirect)*
   x Publishers' catalogs
   xx Publishers and publishing
   — Germany, [France, Italy, etc.]
      xx German [French, Italian, etc.]
         literature—Bibliography
Catalogs, School
   sa Catalogs, College
   x School catalogs
      Schools—Catalogs
   xx Catalogs, College
Catalogs, Sheaf   *(Z695)*
   x Leaf catalogs
      Loose-leaf catalogs
      Sheaf catalogs
   xx Catalogs, Card
      Library catalogs
Catalogs, Star
   See Stars—Catalogs
Catalogs, Subject   *(Z695)*
   sa Automatic indexing
      Catalogs, Classified
      Subject headings
   x Subject catalogs
   xx Library catalogs
Catalogs, Systematic
   See Catalogs, Classified
Catalogs, Union   *(Direct)   (Z695.83)*
   sa Bibliographical centers
      subdivision Bibliography—Union lists
      under subjects, e.g. Technology—
         Bibliography—Union lists
   x Library catalogs—Union catalogs

Union catalogs
   xx Cataloging, Cooperative
      Library catalogs
      Library cooperation
Catalogs, Universal
   See Bibliography, International
      Bibliography, Universal
      Bibliography—Universal catalogs
Catalogs, University
   See Catalogs, College
Catalogs in book form
   See Catalogs, Book
Cataloguing
   See Cataloging
Catalonia
   — History
   — — Autonomy and independence
         movements
         x Catalonia—History—Separatist
            movement
         Catalonia—Separatist movement
         Separatist movement in Catalonia
   — — Separatist movement
         See Catalonia—History—
            Autonomy and
            independence movements
   — Separatist movement
      See Catalonia—History—Autonomy
         and independence movements
Catalonians
   See Catalans
Catalpa   *(Botany, QK495.C35; Forestry,
            SD397.C35)*
Catalysis   *(QD501)*
   sa Catalysts
      Dehydrogenation
      Fluidization
      Heterogeneous catalysis
   xx Chemistry
      Chemistry, Physical and theoretical
      Surface chemistry
   — Mathematical models
Catalyst poisoning
   x Catalytic poisoning
      Poisoning of catalysts
Catalysts   *(QD501; Technology, TP159.C3)*
   sa Cobalt catalysts
      Copper catalysts
      Iron catalysts
      Manganese catalysts
      Metal catalysts
      Montmorillonite catalysts
      Nickel catalysts
      Palladium catalysts
      Platinum catalysts
      Platinum group catalysts
      Rhenium catalysts
      Silica-alumina catalysts
      Vanadium catalysts
      Ziegler-Natta catalysts
   x Catalytic agents
   xx Catalysis
      Chemical inhibitors
   — Analysis
   — Patents
   — Testing
Catalytic agents
   See Catalysts
Catalytic cracking   *(TP690.4)*
   xx Cracking process
Catalytic poisoning
   See Catalyst poisoning
Catalytic reforming
   sa Gasoline
   xx Petroleum—Refining
      Reforming, Catalytic
Catamarans   *(VM311.C3)*
   sa Multihull Transpacific Yacht Race

Trimarans
   xx Boats and boating
      Sailboats
Catamareño language
   See Cacán language
Catamounts
   See Pumas
Cataphoresis
   See Electrophoresis
Catapult   *(U875)*
   sa Ballista
Catapult seats (Aeroplanes)
   See Pilot ejection seats
Catapults (Aeronautics)   *(TL732)*
   xx Aeronautics
      Propellant actuated devices
Cataract   *(RE451)*
   xx Eye—Diseases and defects
   — Diagnosis
   — Surgery
   — — Complications and sequelae
Cataract, Battle of the, 1814
   See Lundy's Lane, Battle of, 1814
Cataracts
   See Waterfalls
Catarrh   *(RC741)*
   sa Cold (Disease)
   xx Cold (Disease)
      Nose—Diseases
   Example under Throat—Diseases
   — Homeopathic treatment   *(RX326.C2)*
Catarrh, Autumnal
   See Hay-fever
Catastral surveys
   See Real property
Catastrophes
   See Disasters
Catastrophes (Geology)   *(QE506)*
   sa Deluge
      Geology—History
Catastrophical, The   *(BD375)*
   sa Change
   xx Change
      Conversion
      Disasters
      Ontology
      Tragic, The
Catatonia
   x Katatonia
   xx Psychology, Pathological
      Psychomotor disorders
Catawba Indians   *(E99.C24)*
   x Kataba Indians
   xx Indians of North America
      Siouan Indians
Catawba language   *(PM751)*
   sa Siouan languages
   xx Siouan languages
Catawba literature   *(PM751)*
Catbird   *(QL696.P2)*
   — Pictorial works
   — — Juvenile literature
Catch crops
   See Cover crops
Catchers (Baseball)
   xx Baseball
   — Biography
   — — Juvenile literature
Catches
   See Glees, catches, rounds, etc.
Catching (Baseball)   *(GV872)*
   xx Baseball
Cateau-Cambrésis, Treaty of, 1559   *(DC114)*
Catechetical illustrations
   See Homiletical illustrations
Catechetical sermons
   x Sermons, Catechetical
   xx Catechetics

Catechetical sermons *(Continued)*
    Catechisms
    Religious education
    Sermons
Catechetics *(BV1474-5; Catholic Church,*
    BX1968; Lutheran Church, BX8070)
    Here are entered works dealing with the
    theory and method of catechizing, a
    means of imparting knowledge of the
    fundamental teachings of Christianity
    by question and answer.
    sa Catechetical sermons
       Catechisms
       Catechists
       Confirmation—Instruction and study
       First communion—Instruction and
         study
       Questioning
       Religious education
       subdivision Catechisms and creeds
         under names of Christian
         denominations, e.g. Catholic Church
         —Catechisms and creeds
    xx Catechisms
       Church—Teaching office
       Discussion
       Religious education
       Theology, Practical
    — Early church, ca. 30-600
       xx Church history—Primitive and early
         church, ca. 30-600

         GENERAL SUBDIVISIONS

    — Catholic Church
       x Christian doctrine (Catholic Church)
       Doctrine, Christian (Catholic
         Church)
       Teaching authority of the church

         GENERAL SUBDIVISIONS

    — Church of England, [Lutheran Church,
       etc.]
    — Papal documents
Catechetics (Canon law) *(BX1939.C3)*
    xx Church—Teaching office (Canon law)
Catechin
    x Catechuic acid
       Catechuin
    xx Catechu
       Kino
       Mahogany
Catechisms *(General, BT1030-1039;*
    Particular denominations, BX)
    sa Bible—Catechisms, question-books
       Catechetical sermons
       Catechetics
       Creeds
       Picture catechisms
       subdivision Catechisms and creeds
         under names of religions, sects, etc.,
         e.g. Catholic Church—Catechisms
         and creeds
    xx Catechetics
       Creeds
       Religious education
       Sunday-schools—Question-books
       Theology, Doctrinal
       Theology—Study and teaching
Catechisms, English, [French, German, etc.]
Catechists *(Direct)*
    xx Catechetics
       Religious education
Catechu *(Materia medica, RS165.C)*
    sa Catechin
Catechuic acid
    See Catechin
Catechuin
    See Catechin

Catechumens
    — Early church, ca. 30-600
       xx Church history—Primitive and early
         church, ca. 30-600
    — Middle Ages, 600-1500
       xx Church history—Middle Ages,
         600-1500
Categories, Abelian
    See Abelian categories
Categories (Mathematics)
    sa Abelian categories
       Functor theory
       Isomorphisms (Mathematics)
    xx Algebra, Homological
       Algebra, Universal
       Functor theory
       Groups, Theory of
       Logic, Symbolic and mathematical
       Topology
Categories (Philosophy) *(Logic, BC172;*
    Ontology, BD331-346)
    sa Dialectical materialism, Categories of
       Predicate (Logic)
       Quantity (Philosophy)
       Whole and parts (Philosophy)
    x Predicaments (Categories)
    xx Knowledge, Theory of
       Logic
       Ontology
       Predicate (Logic)
Categories of dialectical materialism
    See Dialectical materialism, Categories of
Categorization (Psychology)
    x Classification (Psychology)
    xx Abstraction
Catenae *(Bible commentaries, BS; Patristics,*
    BR63)
    xx Bible—Commentaries
       Christian literature, Early
Catenary *(QA835)*
    xx Curves, Plane
Caterers and catering *(TX901-921)*
    sa Breakfasts
       Desserts
       Dinners and dining
       Luncheons
       Menus
       Stewards
       Table
       Wages—Caterers
    xx Cookery
       Food service
       Menus
       Table
    — Accounting
    — Hygienic aspects *(RA601)*
    — Vocational guidance
Caterpillars
    sa Army-worms
       Canker-worms
       Cutworms
       Silkworms
       names of caterpillars, e.g. Alfalfa
         caterpillar, Florida fern caterpillar
    x Larvae—Lepidoptera
       Lepidoptera—Larvae
    xx Butterflies
       Larvae—Insects
       Lepidoptera
       Moths
    — Identification
    — Juvenile literature
    — Pictorial works
Catfishes *(QL638.S6)*
    sa Black bullhead
       Brown bullhead
       Channel catfish
       Gaff-topsails (Fishes)

    x Siluriformes
       Siluroidea
    xx Ostariophysi
    — Marketing *(HD9450-9469)*
Catfishes (in religion, folk-lore, etc.)
    x Folk-lore of catfishes
    xx Fish (in religion, folk-lore, etc.)
       Religion, Primitive
Catfishes in art
    xx Art
       Fishes in art
Catgut
    xx Animal gut industries
    — Prices *(Direct)*
Catgut sutures *(RD73.S8)*
    xx Ligature (Surgery)
       Sutures
Cathari
    See Albigenses
Catharists
    See Albigenses
Catharsis
    xx Emotions
       Psychoanalysis
       Tragedy
Cathartics
    See Purgatives
Cathedra
    See Chairs (Cathedra)
Cathedral canons
    See Canons, Cathedral, collegiate, etc.
Cathedral deans
    See Deans, Cathedral and collegiate
Cathedrals *(Indirect) (Architecture,*
    NA4830, NA5201-6113)
    sa Architecture, Gothic
       Chairs (Cathedra)
       Chapters, Cathedral, collegiate, etc.
       names of cathedrals
    x Religious art
    xx Abbeys
       Architecture
       Architecture, Gothic
       Architecture, Medieval
       Christian art and symbolism
       Church architecture
       Church of England
       Churches
       Dioceses
    — Juvenile literature
Cathedrals (Canon law)
    xx Church architecture (Canon law)
       Churches (Canon law)
Cathedraticum
    xx Bishops
       Catholic Church—Finance
Catheterization, Intravenous
    See Intravenous catheterization
Catheterization, Urinary
    See Urinary catheterization
Catheters *(RC923)*
    sa Arterial catheterization
    xx Cardiac catheterization
Cathetometers *(QC102)*
Cathlamet, Wash., in art
Cathlamet dialect *(PM753)*
    sa Chinookan languages
    x Kathlamet dialect
    xx Chinookan languages

Cathode ray oscillograph (*Electronics,*
TK7872; Radio, TK6565.C4)
Here are entered works on the instrument
combining a cathode ray oscilloscope
and a camera to produce a permanent
record of a waveform. Works on the
test instrument in which the variations
in an electrical quantity appear temporarily as a waveform on the
screen of a cathode ray tube are entered under Cathode ray oscilloscope.
sa Sampling oscilloscope
x Oscillograph, Cathode ray
Probes (Cathode ray oscillograph)
xx Cathode ray tubes
Electronic measurements
Oscillograph
Example under Electronic instruments; Recording instruments
Note under Cathode ray oscilloscope

Cathode ray oscilloscope (*TK7878.7*)
Here are entered works on the test instrument in which the variations in an
electrical quantity appear temporarily
as a visible waveform on the screen of
a cathode ray tube. Works on the instrument combining a cathode ray oscilloscope and a camera to produce a
permanent record of a waveform are
entered under Cathode ray oscillo-
graph.
sa Sampling oscilloscope
x Oscilloscope
xx Electric measurements
Electronic measurements
Note under Cathode ray oscillograph
Cathode ray picture tubes
See Television picture tubes
Cathode ray tube memory systems
(*TK7895.C3*)
xx Cathode ray tubes
Computer storage devices
Computers—Optical equipment
Electronic digital computers—Circuits
Storage tubes
Cathode ray tubes (*QC544.C3*)
sa Cathode ray oscillograph
Cathode ray tube memory systems
Cold cathode tubes
Flying spot scanners
Image iconoscope
Radar indicators
Storage tubes
Television camera tubes
Television picture tubes
xx Information display systems
Vacuum-tubes
— Patents
Cathode rays (*QC711*)
sa Canal rays
Cathodes
Electric discharges through gases
Electrons
X-rays
xx Cathodes
Electric discharges through gases
Electrons
Radiation
Radioactivity
X-rays
— Physiological effect
Cathode sputtering
See Sputtering (Physics)
Cathode sputtering (Plating process)
xx Metallic films
Sputtering (Physics)
Vapor-plating

Cathodes
sa Cathode rays
xx Cathode rays
Electrodes
Electron tubes
Cathodic protection
sa subdivision Cathodic protection *under*
subjects, e.g. Electric cables—
Cathodic protection; Pipe lines—
Cathodic protection
xx Corrosion and anti-corrosives
Electrolytic corrosion
— Automation
Catholic academies (*Direct*)
x Academies, Catholic
xx Forums (Discussion and debate)
Catholic action (*Direct*) (*BX2348*)
sa Christian democracy
Laity—Catholic Church
x Action, Catholic
Apostolate, Lay
Lay apostolate
xx Christian democracy
Church and social problems—Catholic
Church
Catholic adult education
See Catholic Church—Adult education
Catholic authors
sa Catholic historians
subdivision Catholic authors *under*
names of literatures, e.g. American
literature—Catholic authors
x Authors, Catholic
xx Catholic literature
— Biography
Catholic Bibles
See Bible—Versions, Catholic
Catholic Book Week
xx Catholic literature
Catholic Church (*BX801-4715*)
sa Anglo-Catholicism
Canon law
Councils and synods
Fasts and feasts
Inquisition
Oxford movement
Salvation outside the Catholic Church
subdivision Catholic Church *under*
subjects, e.g. Asceticism—Catholic
Church; World War, 1939-1945—
Catholic Church
x Roman Catholic Church
xx Papacy
Example under Christianity
— Adult education
x Catholic adult education
xx Adult education
Catholic Church—Education
— Anecdotes, facetiae, satire, etc.
— Apologetic works (*BX1750-1755;*
BX1780)
sa Press, Catholic
xx Apologetics
Example under Apologetics; *and under*
reference from Polemics
(Theology)
— Archdioceses
See Catholic Church—Dioceses
— Asceticism
See Asceticism—Catholic Church
— Benefices
See Benefices, Ecclesiastical
— Bibliography (*Z7837-7840*)
sa Catholic literature
Index librorum prohibitorum
— Bio-bibliography
— Biography (*BX4650-4705*)
Example under Theologians

— — Dictionaries
xx Catholic Church—Dictionaries
— Buildings
See Catholic institutions—Buildings
Churches, Catholic
— Caricatures and cartoons
— Catechisms and creeds (*BX1958-1968*)
Subdivided by language.
xx Creeds
Example under Catechetics; Catechisms
— — Charts, diagrams, etc.
— Ceremonies and practices (*BX1969*)
sa Catholic Church. Liturgy and ritual
—Rubrics
Enthronement of the Gospels
Example under Rites and ceremonies
— Charities (*HV530*)
sa Catholic Worker Movement
Example under Old age homes
— Clergy (*BX1912*)
sa Apostolic succession
Bishops
Cardinals
Clergy (Canon law)
Episcopacy
Ex-priests, Catholic
Priests
Privileges and immunities,
Ecclesiastical
Profession of faith
Retreats for clergy
Theological seminaries, Catholic
Vicars apostolic
xx Apostolic succession
Example under Clergy; Priests
— — Appointment, call, and election
Example under Clergy—Appoint-
ment, call, and election
— — Correspondence, reminiscences, etc.
Example under Clergy—Correspond-
ence, reminiscences, etc.
— — Deposition
sa Ex-priests, Catholic
Renunciation (Canon law)
x Deposition (Canon law)
xx Clergy—Deposition
Renunciation (Canon law)
— — Deprivation of the clerical garb
x Deprivation of the clerical garb
(Canon law)
Perpetual deprivation of the
clerical garb (Canon law)
Temporary deprivation of the
clerical garb (Canon law)
xx Clergy (Canon law)
Clergy—Costume
Punishment (Canon law)
— — Installation
xx Installation (Clergy)
— — Papal documents
— — Personality
See Catholic Church—Clergy—
Psychology
— — Pictures, illustrations, etc.
— — Psychology
x Catholic Church—Clergy—
Personality
— — Salaries, pensions, etc.
— Clergy (Oriental)
See Catholic Church—Oriental rites—
Clergy
— Clergy, Rating of
— Clergy, Training of (*BX900-920*)
Example under Clergy, Training of
— Collected works (*BX890*)
Example under Theology—Collected
works
Note under Papal documents

Catholic Church *(BX801-4715)*
(Continued)
— Confirmation
    See Confirmation—Catholic Church
— Converts
    See Converts, Catholic
— Dictionaries *(BX841)*
    sa Catholic Church—Biography—
      Dictionaries
    x Catholic Church—Encyclopedias
— Dictionaries, Juvenile *(BX841)*
    Note under Encyclopedias and dictionar-
      ies
— Dioceses *(BX1417-1691)*
    x Catholic Church—Archdioceses
— Diplomatic relations
    See Catholic Church—Relations
      (diplomatic)
— Diplomatic service *(JX1801-2)*
    sa Legates, Papal
      Nuncios, Papal
    xx Catholic Church—Relations
      (diplomatic)
      Diplomatic and consular service
— Directories *(BX845)*
— Discipline
    sa Casuistry
      Censures, Ecclesiastical
      Communicatio in sacris
      Denunciation (Canon law)
      Dispensations (Canon law)
      Excommunication
      Fasting—Dispensations
      Index librorum prohibitorum
      Indulgences
      Interdict (Canon law)
      Marriage (Canon law)
      Marriage—Dispensations
      Marriage, Mixed
      Obedience (Canon law)
      Penance
      Penitentials
      Profession of faith
      Secret societies and Catholic Church
      Ultramontanism
    xx Indulgences
    Example under Church discipline
— Doctrinal and controversial works
      (BX1749-1755)
    sa Anti-Catholicism
      Catholic Church—Teaching office
      Encyclicals, Papal
      Man (Theology)—Papal documents
    xx Anti-Catholicism
    Example under reference from Polemics
      (Theology)
— — Catholic authors *(BX1749-1755;*
      BX1780)
— — Debates, etc. *(BX1779)*
— — Protestant authors *(BX1760-1779)*
    sa Anti-clericalism
— Doctrinal and controversial works,
    Popular
— Education *(LC461-510; Church and*
    school, LC107-120; Jesuit, LB375,
    LC493)
    sa Catholic Church—Adult education
      Catholic high schools
      Catholic schools
      Catholic teachers
      Catholic universities and colleges
      Catholics—Scholarships, fellowships,
        etc.
      Church schools (Canon law)
      Educational law and legislation
        (Canon law)
      Lay teachers
      Mary, Virgin, and education

      Monasticism and religious orders—
        Education
      Theological seminaries, Catholic
      Vacation schools, Catholic
    names of dioceses used as local
      subdivision under Education, *e.g.*
      Education—Boston (Archdiocese);
      and names of individual Catholic
      educational institutions
    Note under Church and education
— — Papal documents
— — Societies, etc.
    xx Catholic Church—Societies, etc.
— Encyclopedias
    See Catholic Church—Dictionaries
— Exhibitions and museums *(BX840)*
    x Catholic Church—Museums
    Example under Religion—Exhibitions
      and museums
— Fasts and feasts
    See Fasts and feasts—Catholic Church
— Finance *(BX1950)*
    sa Benefices, Ecclesiastical
      Cathedraticum
      Fees, Ecclesiastical
      Investments (Canon law)
      Mass stipends
      Peter's pence
      Taxation, Papal
— Foreign relations
    See Catholic Church—Relations
      (diplomatic)
— Government *(BX1800-1915)*
    sa Bishops
      Cardinals
      Dioceses
      Investiture
      Legates, Papal
      Metropolitans
      Papacy
      Popes
      Vacancy of the Holy See
      Vicars apostolic
      Vicars-general
    x Public law (Canon law)
— Historiography *(BX938-9)*
    Example under Historiography
— History *(BX940-1749)*
    sa Councils and synods
      Counter Reformation
      Schism—Eastern and Western
        Church
      Schism, The Great Western,
        1378-1417
    names of councils, e.g. Constance,
      Council of, 1414-1418; Vatican
      Council, 1869-1870
— — Middle Ages, 600-1500
    See Church history—Middle Ages,
      600-1500
— — Modern period, 1500-
    sa Liberalism (Religion)—Catholic
      Church
    xx Church history—Modern period,
      1500-
— — 1965-

GENERAL SUBDIVISIONS

— — Historiography *(BX938)*
— — Juvenile literature *(BX948)*
— — Maps
— — Societies, etc.
    xx Catholic Church—Societies, etc.
— — Sources *(BX850-873)*
    Example under History—Sources
— Hymns *(BV360; BV467-510)*
    xx Catholic Church. Liturgy and
      ritual. Hymnary

— Infallibility
    sa Popes—Infallibility
    x Infallibility of the church
    xx Authority (Religion)
      Church—Infallibility
      Popes—Infallibility
— Influence
— Juvenile literature
— Liturgical movement
    See Liturgical movement—Catholic
      Church
— Marriage
    See Marriage—Catholic Church
— Medals
    See Medals, Devotional
— Membership
— Missions *(BV2130-2300)*
    sa Chinese rites
      Malabar rites
      Missions (Canon law)
      Monasticism and religious orders—
        Missions
    xx Jesuits—Missions
— — Congresses *(BV2160)*
— — Early works to 1800
    See Missions—Early works to 1800
— — Papal documents
— — Pictorial works
— — Pictures, illustrations, etc.
    xx Catholic Church—Pictures,
      illustrations, etc.
— — Societies, etc.
    xx Catholic Church—Societies, etc.
— Modernism
    See Modernism—Catholic Church
— Museums
    See Catholic Church—Exhibitions and
      museums
— Music
    See Church music—Catholic Church
— Mysticism
    See Mysticism—Catholic Church
— Name *(BX1753)*
    xx Sects—Names
    Example under Names
— Nobility
    See Nobility, Papal
— Oriental rites *(BX4710-4715)*
    sa Canon law, Oriental
      Patriarchs and patriarchate (Catholic
        Oriental)
— — Clergy
    x Catholic Church—Clergy
      (Oriental)
— Pastoral letters and charges *(BX874)*
— Pastoral theology
    See Pastoral theology—Catholic
      Church
— Periodicals *(BX801-6)*
    sa Press, Catholic
    x Catholic periodicals
— Pictures, illustrations, etc.
— Pictures, illustrations, etc.
    Here are entered pictorial works de-
      scriptive of the activities of the
      Catholic Church.
    sa Catholic Church—Missions—
      Pictures, illustrations, etc.
    subdivision Pictures, illustrations,
      etc. *under* Catholic Church in
      [country], *e.g.* Catholic Church in
      India—Pictures, illustrations, etc.
— Prayer-books and devotions
    (BX2000-2198)
    sa Hours, Books of
      Novenas
    Note under Family—Prayer-books and
      devotions

—— English, ₍French, German, etc.₎
— Relation to the state
　　See Church and state—Catholic
　　　Church
— Relations *(BX1781-8)*
　　sa Chair of Unity Octave
　　　Week of Prayer for Christian Unity
　　x Catholic Church—Relations
　　　(ecclesiastical)
—— Anglican Communion, ₍Lutheran
　　　Church, etc.₎
—— Buddhism
　　xx Christianity and other religions—
　　　Buddhism
—— Orthodox Eastern Church *(BX324.3)*
　　sa Schism, Acacian, 484-519
　　　Schism—Eastern and Western
　　　　Church
— Relations (Canon law)
— Relations (diplomatic) *(BX1790-1793;*
　　　History, BX850-1691;
　　　International law, JX1552;
　　　Legates, nuncios, BX1908)
　　sa Cardinal protectors
　　　Catholic Church—Diplomatic service
　　　Nuncios, Papal
　　x Catholic Church—Diplomatic
　　　relations
　　　Catholic Church—Foreign relations
　　xx International relations
—— Treaties *(BX850-1691; International*
　　　law, JX1552)
　　sa Concordats
— Relations (diplomatic) with Belgium,
　　　₍France, etc.₎
— Relations (ecclesiastical)
　　See Catholic Church—Relations
— Renewal
　　See Church renewal—Catholic Church
— Sacraments
　　See Sacraments—Catholic Church
— Sermons *(BX1756)*
　　sa Auto-da-fe sermons
— Societies, etc. *(BX808-817)*
　　　For international and American socie-
　　　ties, clerical, lay, or mixed, devoted
　　　to religious or non-religious activi-
　　　ties.
　　　For societies in countries other than
　　　the United States *see* Catholic
　　　Church in ₍country₎—Societies,
　　　etc., *e.g.* Catholic Church in Ger-
　　　many—Societies, etc.
　　sa Catholic Church—Education—
　　　Societies, etc.
　　　Catholic Church—History—
　　　Societies, etc.
　　　Catholic Church—Missions—
　　　Societies, etc.
　　　Confraternities
　　　Grail movement (Catholic)
　　　Kolping societies
　　　Monasticism and religious orders
　　　Monasticism and religious orders for
　　　　women
　　　Purgatorial societies
　　　Secular institutes
　　　Societies living in common without
　　　　vows
　　x Catholic Church in the United States
　　　—Societies, etc.
　　　Catholic societies
　　　Catholics—Societies, etc.
— Statistics
— Teaching office
　　x Magisterium ecclesiae
　　xx Authority (Religion)

Catholic Church—Doctrinal and
　　controversial works
Church—Infallibility
Church—Teaching office
— Terminology
— Traditionalist movement
　　See Catholic traditionalist movement
— Vacation schools
　　See Vacation schools, Catholic
— Women, Work with
　　See Church work with women—
　　　Catholic Church
— Work with women
　　See Church work with women—
　　　Catholic Church
— Work with youth
　　See Church work with youth—
　　　Catholic Church
— Yearbooks *(BX845)*
— Youth, Work with
　　See Church work with youth—
　　　Catholic Church
**Catholic Church.　Liturgy and ritual.
　　Antiphonary**
　　sa Antiphonaries (Music)
　　　Tonarius
　　xx Catholic Church.　Liturgy and ritual.
　　　Gradual
　　　Catholic Church.　Liturgy and ritual.
　　　Missal
Example under Service books (Music)
**Catholic Church.　Liturgy and ritual.
　　Benedictional**
　　sa Benedictionals
　　xx Benedictionals
**Catholic Church.　Liturgy and ritual.
　　Breviary *(BX2000)***
　　sa Breviaries
　　　Divine office
　　xx Breviaries
　　　Divine office
— Rubrics
　　xx Catholic Church.　Liturgy and ritual
　　　—Rubrics
**Catholic Church.　Liturgy and ritual.
　　Epistolary**
　　sa Epistolaries
**Catholic Church.　Liturgy and ritual.
　　Gradual**
　　sa Catholic Church.　Liturgy and ritual.
　　　Antiphonary
　　　Graduals (Music)
　　　Tonarius
　　x Graduale romanum
Catholic Church.　Liturgy and ritual.　Hours
　　sa Hours, Books of
**Catholic Church.　Liturgy and ritual.
　　Hymnary**
　　sa Catholic Church—Hymns
Catholic Church.　Liturgy and ritual.　Missal
　　(BX2015)
　　sa Catholic Church.　Liturgy and ritual.
　　　Antiphonary
　　　Catholic Church.　Liturgy and ritual.
　　　Troper
　　　Children's missals
　　　Dog Mass
　　　Labor Day Mass
　　　Masses
　　　Offertories
　　x Mass-books
　　xx Mass
　　　Missals
— Rubrics
　　xx Catholic Church.　Liturgy and ritual
　　　—Rubrics

**Catholic Church.　Liturgy and ritual.
　　Missal.　Masses for the dead**
　　sa Requiems
　　xx Prayers for the dead
**Catholic Church.　Liturgy and ritual.　Offices
　　for the dead**
　　xx Prayers for the dead
**Catholic Church.　Liturgy and ritual.
　　Psalter *(BX2033)***
　　sa Psalms (Music)
　　　Psalters
**Catholic Church.　Liturgy and ritual.　Ritual
　　(BX2035)**
**Catholic Church.　Liturgy and ritual.
　　Sacramentary**
　　sa Sacramentaries
　　xx Sacramentaries
**Catholic Church.　Liturgy and ritual.　Troper
　　(BX2043)**
　　xx Catholic Church.　Liturgy and ritual.
　　　Missal
**Catholic Church.　Liturgy and ritual.
　　Vesperals**
　　sa Vesperals (Music)
**Catholic Church.　Liturgy and ritual
　　(BX1970-2175)**
　　sa Altar prayers
　　　Baptism (Liturgy)
　　　Chants (Plain, Gregorian, etc.)
　　　Church music—Catholic Church
　　　Liturgical movement—Catholic Church
　　　Liturgics—Catholic Church
　　　Novenas
　　　Propers (Liturgy)
　　　Rimed offices
　　　Sacristans
　　　Sequences (Liturgy)
　　　Stations of the Cross
　　xx Church music—Catholic Church
　　　Liturgics—Catholic Church
Example under Liturgies; Ritual
— Calendar
　　Example under Church calendar
— Concordances
— Manuscripts *(BX1973)*
　　xx Liturgies—Manuscripts
— Papal documents
— Rubrics *(BX1971)*
　　sa Catholic Church.　Liturgy and
　　　ritual.　Breviary—Rubrics
　　　Catholic Church.　Liturgy and
　　　ritual.　Missal—Rubrics
　　xx Catholic Church—Ceremonies and
　　　practices
— Theology *(BX1970.A7-Z)*
　　x Theology, Liturgical
　　xx Theology, Catholic
**Catholic Church.　Liturgy and ritual.
　　Ambrosian rite**
　　x Ambrosian chant
**Catholic Church.　Liturgy and ritual.
　　Mozarabic rite**
　　x Mozarabic chant
Catholic Church and art *(The arts,*
　　　NX650.R4; Visual arts, N72.R4)
　　x Art and the Catholic Church
　　xx Art and religion
　　　Christian art and symbolism
Catholic Church and atheism
　　x Atheism and the Catholic Church
Catholic Church and birth control
　　See Birth control—Religious aspects—
　　　Catholic Church
Catholic Church and communism
　　See Communism and Christianity—Catholic
　　　Church
Catholic Church and fascism
　　See Fascism and the Catholic Church

Catholic Church and freemasonry
See Freemasons and Catholic Church
Catholic Church and humanism *(BX1397)*
   x Humanism and the Catholic Church
Catholic Church and labor
See Church and labor
Catholic Church and moving-pictures
See Moving-pictures and Catholic Church
Catholic Church and occult sciences *(Direct)*
   x Occult sciences and the Catholic
      Church
Catholic Church and philosophy
   x Philosophy and the Catholic Church
   xx Philosophy and religion
Catholic Church and salvation
See Salvation outside the Catholic Church
Catholic Church and secret societies
See Secret societies and Catholic Church
Catholic Church and social problems
See Church and social problems—Catholic
      Church
Catholic Church and socialism
See Socialism and Catholic Church
Catholic Church and spiritualism *(Direct)*
   x Spiritualism and the Catholic Church
Catholic Church and state
See Church and state—Catholic Church
**Catholic Church and the mentally
    handicapped**
   x Mentally handicapped and the Catholic
      Church
Catholic Church and theater
See Theater and Catholic Church
Catholic Church and world politics *(BX1793)*
   x World politics and the Catholic Church
   xx Christianity and international affairs
  — Papal documents
     x Christianity and international affairs
      —Papal documents
Catholic Church in Austria
   sa Josephinism
Catholic Church in Bavaria
   sa Concordat of 1924 (Bavaria)
Catholic Church in Boston, ₍Canada, Chile,
    etc.₎ *(BX1401-1691)*
   sa Catholics in Boston, ₍Canada, Chile,
      etc.₎
   , *for the missionary countries, names of
      religious orders operating in those
      countries, e.g. Catholic Church in
      the Philippine Islands see also
      Augustinians ₍Dominicans, etc.₎ in
      the Philippine Islands*
  — Adult education
  — Anniversaries, etc.
  — Education
  — Finance
  — Historiography
  — Pictorial works
Catholic Church in France
   sa Americanism (Catholic controversy)
      Fareinistes
      Louisets
      Nonjurors, French Catholic
      Priest workers
Catholic Church in Germany
   sa German Catholicism
  — History *(BX1536-1536.2)*
  — — 19th century
  — — 20th century
  — — 1933-1945
      sa Concordat of 1933 (Germany)
  — — 1945-
  — Societies, etc.
     Note under Catholic Church—Societies,
      etc.
Catholic Church in Great Britain
   sa Oath of allegiance, 1606

Catholic Church in India
  — Pictures, illustrations, etc.
     Example under Catholic Church—Pic-
      tures, illustrations, etc.
Catholic Church in Spain
   sa Concordat of 1962 (Spain)
Catholic Church in Switzerland
Catholic Church in the Philippine Islands
   xx Friars in the Philippine Islands
  Example under Catholic Church in Boston,
    ₍Canada, Chile, etc.₎
Catholic Church in the United States
   sa Americanism (Catholic controversy)
  — Foreign opinion
     x Foreign opinion of the Catholic
      Church in the United States
  — Societies, etc.
     See Catholic Church—Societies, etc.
Catholic Church music
  See Church music—Catholic Church
Catholic churches
  See Churches, Catholic
Catholic college students
  See College students, Catholic
Catholic converts
  See Converts, Catholic
Catholic criminals
   x Catholics as criminals
   xx Church and social problems—Catholic
      Church
      Crime and criminals
Catholic emancipation *(BX1492; Act,
    DA950.3)*
   sa Gordon Riots, 1780
   x Disabilities, Political (Great Britain)
      Emancipation, Catholic
      Political disabilities (Great Britain)
Catholic ex-priests
  See Ex-priests, Catholic
Catholic high schools *(Direct)*
   xx Catholic Church—Education
      High schools
  — Administration
     xx School management and organization
Catholic historians *(BX938-9)*
   x Historians, Catholic
   xx Catholic authors
Catholic hospitals
   xx Catholic institutions
      Hospitals
Catholic institutions *(Direct)*
   sa Catholic hospitals
   x Institutions, Catholic
  — Buildings
     x Catholic Church—Buildings
Catholic journalism
  See Journalism, Religious
     Press, Catholic
Catholic labor unions
  See Trade-unions, Catholic
Catholic League, 1609-1648
   xx Thirty Years' War, 1618-1648
Catholic learning and scholarship *(BX961.15)*
   sa Catholics as scientists
      Catholics—Intellectual life
   x Catholics—Learning and scholarship
      Learning and scholarship—Catholics
   xx Catholics—Intellectual life
      Learning and scholarship
Catholic libraries
  See Libraries, Catholic
Catholic literature
   sa Catholic authors
      Catholic Book Week
      Index librorum prohibitorum
      Press, Catholic

     subdivision Catholic authors *under
      names of literatures, e.g.* German
      literature—Catholic authors
   xx Catholic Church—Bibliography
      Christian literature
      Literature
  — Cataloging
     See Cataloging of Catholic literature
  — Publication and distribution
  — Subject headings
     See Subject headings—Catholic
      literature
Catholic movement (Anglican Communion)
  See Anglo-Catholicism
Catholic nonjurors, English
  See Nonjurors, English Catholic
Catholic nonjurors, French
  See Nonjurors, French Catholic
Catholic periodicals
  See Catholic Church—Periodicals
Catholic press
  See Press, Catholic
Catholic scholarships
  See Catholics—Scholarships, fellowships,
     etc.
Catholic schools *(Direct)*
   xx Catholic Church—Education
Catholic societies
  See Catholic Church—Societies, etc.
Catholic song-books
  See Song-books, Catholic
Catholic teachers *(Direct)*
   x Catholics as teachers
      Teachers, Catholic
   xx Catholic Church—Education
      Teachers
Catholic theological seminaries
  See Theological seminaries, Catholic
Catholic theology
  See Theology, Catholic
Catholic trade-unions
  See Trade-unions, Catholic
Catholic traditionalist movement
   x Catholic Church—Traditionalist
      movement
      Traditionalist movement, Catholic
Catholic Tübingen School
  See Tübingen School (Catholic theology)
Catholic universities and colleges *(Direct)*
   xx Catholic Church—Education
      Universities and colleges
  — Administration
  — Curricula
  — Entrance requirements
Catholic wit and humor
   xx Wit and humor
Catholic Worker Movement
   xx Catholic Church—Charities
      Church and social problems—Catholic
      Church
Catholicism
  See Catholicity
Catholicism, Old
  See Old Catholicism
Catholicity *(BX8-9)*
     Here are entered works emphasizing a
      unity and commonness of Christian
      ideas, thought, and belief, rather than
      of organization, the latter being repre-
      sented by the subject heading Chris-
      tian union.
   sa Church—Catholicity
      Ecumenical movement
   x Catholicism
   xx Anglo-Catholicism
      Christianity
      Theology, Doctrinal
Catholics

— Intellectual life (BX961.I5; United
    States, BX1407.I5)
    sa Catholic learning and scholarship
    xx Catholic learning and scholarship
— Learning and scholarship
    See Catholic learning and scholarship
— Scholarships, fellowships, etc. (Direct)
    x Catholic scholarships
    xx Catholic Church—Education
— Societies, etc.
    See Catholic Church—Societies, etc.
Catholics, Colored
  See Catholics, Negro
Catholics, Croatian, ₍Latvian, etc.₎
    Here are entered works on Catholics liv-
    ing outside their native country who
    use their native language in church ser-
    vices.
    x Croatian ₍Latvian, etc.₎ Catholics
Catholics, Croatian, ₍Latvian, etc.₎ in the
    United States
Catholics, Negro (United States, BX1407.N4)
    x Catholics, Colored
      Colored Catholics
      Negro Catholics
    xx Negroes—Religion
Catholics as criminals
  See Catholic criminals
Catholics as scientists
    Here are entered works on the attain-
    ments of Catholics as scientists. Works
    mainly biographical are entered under
    the heading Scientists, Catholic.
    xx Catholic learning and scholarship
      Scientists, Catholic
Catholics as teachers
  See Catholic teachers
Catholics in Boston, ₍Canada, Chile, etc.₎
    Here are entered works treating Cath-
    olics, not as an ecclesiastical body but
    as a distinct element or group in the
    population. Cf. Germans in the United
    States.
    xx Catholic Church in Boston, ₍Canada,
      Chile, etc.₎
Catholics in England
    x Recusants
Catholics in France
    sa Louisets
      Nonjurors, French Catholic
Catholics in Great Britain
    sa Oath of allegiance, 1606
Catholics in Lancashire, Eng.
    x Recusants
Catholics in literature
Catholics in non-Catholic countries
    xx Man—Migrations
      Minorities
Catio Indians
    xx Indians of South America
Catio language (PM5778)
    x Katio language
    xx Indians of South America—Languages
Cations (QD553)
Catnip (QK495.L15)
    x Cat-mint
Cato Street Conspiracy, 1820
Catoptromancy (BF1331)
    Here are entered works treating of divina-
    tion, etc., by interpretation of things
    seen in a reflecting surface or sub-
    stance. Duplicate entry is made under
    Crystal-gazing or Mirrors, Magic, as
    the case may be.
    sa Clairvoyance
      Crystal-gazing
      Divination
      Fortune-telling

      Magic
      Mirrors, Magic
    xx Clairvoyance
      Crystal-gazing
      Divination
      Fortune-telling
      Magic
      Mirrors, Magic
Catoquina Indians (F2520.1.C)
    x Catuquinarú Indians
    xx Indians of South America
Cats (SF441-9; Stories and anecdotes,
    QL795.C; Zoology, QL737.C2)
    sa Cat breeds
      Eyra
      Lynx
    x Cat, Domestic
    xx Domestic animals
Example under Pets
Note under Abnormalities (Animals)
— Anatomy
— Anecdotes, facetiae, satire, etc.
— Behavior
— Breeding
    See Cat breeding
— Breeds
    See Cat breeds
— Caricatures and cartoons
— Diseases (SF985)
— Food
    x Cat food
— Juvenile literature
— Legends and stories (General literature,
    PN6071.C3; PN6110.C3; Juvenile
    literature, PZ10.3; Zoology,
    QL795.C2)
— Literary collections
    Example under Literature—Collections
— Photography
    See Photography of cats
— Physiology
— Pictorial works (SF446)
— Pictures, illustrations, etc. (N7660;
    SF446)
    Example under Animal painting and illus-
    tration; Drawing—Instruction
— Psychology
— Quotations, maxims, etc.
— Songs and music
— Stud-books (SF443)
— Surgery
— Training
    xx Animals, Training of
Cats, Fossil (QE882.C1)
Cats (in religion, folk-lore, etc.) (Folk-lore,
    GR725; Religion, BL443.C3)
    x Cat-worship
      Folk-lore of cats
    xx Animals, Legends and stories of
      Religion, Primitive
Cats as laboratory animals
Cat's cradle
  See String-figures
Cats in art
    xx Art
— Juvenile literature
Cats in literature
Cattle (Indirect) (SF191-219)
    sa Beef cattle
      Bulls
      Calves
      Cattle breeds
      Cows
      Dairy cattle
      Draft animals
      Dual-purpose cattle
      Gayal
      Grazing

      Stock and stock-breeding
      Stock-ranges
      Veterinary medicine
      Veterinary obstetrics
    xx Agriculture
      Cows
      Domestic animals
      Oxen
      Ruminantia
Note under Cattle—Diseases
— Anatomy
    x Bovine anatomy
      Cows—Anatomy
    Example under Anatomy
— Behavior
— Breeding
    See Cattle breeding
— Breeds
    See Cattle breeds
— Dehorning
    See Dehorning
— Diseases (SF961-7)
    Works relating to diseases of cattle in
    a particular locality are entered
    here and also under Cattle—₍local
    subdivision₎ or Veterinary medicine
    —₍local subdivision₎ as the case
    may be.
    sa Abortion in animals
      Anaplasmosis
      Anthrax, Symptomatic
      Bovine leukosis
      Brucellosis in cattle
      East Coast fever
      Endocarditis
      Fescue foot
      Foot-and-mouth disease
      Heartwater
      Hemorrhagic septicemia of cattle
      Johne's disease
      Lameness in cattle
      Lumpy skin disease
      Milk fever in animals
      Mucosal diseases of cattle
      Pleuro-pneumonia
      Pulmonary adenomatosis
      Rinderpest
      Scab disease in cattle
      Scabies
      Stock inspection
      Texas fever
      Three-day sickness of cattle
      Trichomonas foetus
      Trypanosomiasis
      Tuberculosis in cattle
      Udder—Diseases
      Vaccinia
      X disease in cattle
    Example under Veterinary medicine
— — Terminology
— Economic aspects (Direct)
— Feeding and feeds
    Example under Animals, Food habits of
— — Economic aspects (Direct)
— Grading
— Grooming
    x Grooming of cattle
    xx Livestock exhibitions
— Herd-books (SF192-3)
    Here are entered all herd-books,
    whether general or special. Special
    herd-books are entered also under
    name of breed, e.g. Hereford cattle.
    x Herd books
— Judging
    xx Stock-judging
— Juvenile literature
— Lameness

Cattle *(Indirect)* *(SF191-219)*
  — Lameness *(Continued)*
    See Lameness in cattle
  — Legends and stories
  — Marketing
    See Cattle trade
  — Marking
    sa Cattle brands
      Earmarks
    x Branding of cattle
      Identification of cattle
  — Physiology
    sa Beef cattle—Shrinkage
    Example under Veterinary physiology
  — Transportation *(Railroads, HE2321.L7;*
      Ships, HE595.L7)
    sa Railroads—Livestock transportation
    xx Railroads—Livestock transportation
    Example under Transportation
Cattle, Beef
  See Beef cattle
Cattle barns
  See Cattle houses and equipment
Cattle brands *(Indirect)* *(SF101-3)*
  sa Earmarks
  x Brands, Cattle
  xx Cattle—Marking
    Livestock brands
  — Juvenile literature
  — Law and legislation *(Direct)*
Cattle breeders
  — Directories *(SF191.5)*
    x Cattle breeders' directories
Cattle breeders' directories
  See Cattle breeders—Directories
Cattle breeders' societies *(Indirect)* *(SF191)*
  xx Livestock associations
Cattle breeding *(Indirect)*
  sa Beef cattle breeding
    Bulls
    Cattle breeds
    Cow testing
    Dairy cattle breeding
    Dairying
  x Cattle—Breeding
  xx Stock and stock-breeding
Cattle breeds *(Indirect)* *(SF191-9)*
  Works on breeds of cattle in a specific
    locality are entered also under the
    heading Cattle—[local subdivision]
  sa Beef cattle breeds
    Dairy cattle breeds
    names of specific breeds, e.g.
      Aberdeen-Angus cattle, Hereford
      cattle
  x Breeds of cattle
    Cattle—Breeds
  xx Cattle
    Cattle breeding
  Example under Livestock breeds
Cattle dip
Cattle dog, Australian
  See Australian cattle dog
Cattle drives
  See Cattle trails
Cattle egret *(Agriculture, SB996.C3;*
    Zoology, QL696.C5)
  x Egret, Cattle
  xx Herons
Cattle grids
  See Cattle guards
Cattle grubs
  See Warble-flies
Cattle guards
  x Cattle grids
    Grids, Cattle
    Guards, Cattle
    Roads—Cattle guards

  xx Fences
    Roads—Accessories
Cattle houses and equipment *(Indirect)*
  sa Beef cattle housing and equipment
    Dairy barns
  x Cattle barns
  xx Animal housing
    Stables
Cattle insurance
  See Insurance, Agricultural—Livestock
Cattle leukemia
  See Bovine leukosis
Cattle lice
  xx Lice
Cattle markets
  See Stock-yards
Cattle pens
  xx Stock-yards
Cattle plague (Rinderpest)
  See Rinderpest
Cattle ranches
  See Ranches
Cattle-ranges
  See Stock-ranges
Cattle scab
  See Scab disease in cattle
Cattle stealing *(Direct)* *(HV6646-6665)*
  xx Larceny
    Thieves
Cattle-tick *(QL458.A2; SF593.T5)*
  x Fever-tick
  xx Texas fever
Cattle-tick fever
  See Texas fever
Cattle trade *(Direct)* *(HD9433)*
  sa Beef packers
    Cattle trails
    Cowboys
    Ranch life
    Stock-yards
  x Cattle—Marketing
  xx Animal industry
    Meat industry and trade
    Stock-ranges
  — Law and legislation
    See Animal industry—Law and
      legislation
  — Seasonal variations
  — Tables and ready-reckoners
    (HF5716.C2)
  — Taxation
    See Animal industry—Taxation
Cattle trails *(Indirect)*
  x Cattle drives
  xx Cattle trade
    Trails
Cattraeth, Battle of, ca. 600
Catuquinarú Indians
  See Catoquina Indians
CATV
  See Community antenna television
Caucasian languages *(PK9001-9201)*
  sa Abazin language
    Abkhazian language
    Adyghe language
    Agul language
    Akhwakh language
    Akkinski dialect
    Avaric language
    Balkar language
    Chamalal language
    Chechen language
    Circassian language
    Dargwa language
    Dido language
    Georgian language
    Ginukh dialect
    Ingush language

    Kartvelian languages
    Khinalugh language
    Kubachi dialect
    Lakh language
    Lezghian language
    Tabasaran language
    Tapanta dialect
    Tat language
    Tsakhur language
    Tsova-Tush language
    Ubykh language
    Udi language
Caucasian literature *(Direct)* *(Collections,*
    PK9040; History, PK9030)
Caucasian philology
  sa Georgian philology
  x Philology, Caucasian
Caucasian poetry *(Direct)* *(Collections,*
    PK9040; History, PK9030)
Caucasian race
  sa Aryans
    Mediterranean race
    Semites
    Teutonic race
  x Caucasians
    Caucasic race
    Caucasoid race
    White race
  xx Race
  Example under Anthropology; Ethnology
Caucasian rugs
  See Rugs, Caucasian
Caucasian whortleberry
Caucasians
  See Caucasian race
Caucasic race
  See Caucasian race
Caucasoid race
  See Caucasian race
Caucasus in literature
Cauchy problem
  xx Differential equations, Partial
  — Numerical solutions
    xx Numerical analysis
Caucus *(JF2085)*
  xx Legislative bodies
    Nominations for office
    Political conventions
    Politics, Practical
    Pre-legislative conferences
Caudata
  See Urodela
Caughley porcelain *(NK4399.C)*
  x Porcelain, Caughley
Caughnawaga Indians *(E99.C)*
  x Caghnawaga Indians
  xx Indians of North America
    Iroquoian Indians
    Iroquois Indians
    Mohawk Indians
    Oneida Indians
  — Legal status, laws, etc.
Cauliflower *(Culture, SB333)*
  xx Cabbage
  — Packaging
  — Varieties
Caulking
  See Calking
Caulk's Field, Battle of, 1814 *(E356.C3)*
Cauqui dialect
  x Jaqaru language
  xx Aymara language
Causa (Civil law)
  See Consideration (Law)
Causalgia
  xx Amputation
    Erythromelalgia
    Neuralgia

Pain
Causality
  See Causality (Physics)
  Causation
Causality (Physics) *(Nuclear reactions,*
    QC794; Philosophy of physics, QC6;
    Quantum field theory, QC174.5)
  sa Dispersion relations
  x Causality
  xx Heisenberg uncertainty principle
    Nuclear physics
    Physics—Philosophy
    Quantum theory
Causar
  See Pachisi
Causation *(BD530-595)*
  sa Necessity (Philosophy)
    Occasionalism
    Pratītyasamutpāda
    Proximate cause (Law)
    Sufficient reason
    Teleology
  x Causality
    Cause and effect
    Effect and cause
    Final cause
  xx Beginning
    God
    Metaphysics
    Necessity (Philosophy)
    Philosophy
    Teleology
Causative (Linguistics)
  xx Grammar, Comparative and general—
    Syntax
Cause, Proximate
  See Proximate cause (Law)
Cause and effect
  See Causation
Causeways *(Indirect)*
  xx Bridges
    Roads
Caustic eye injuries
  See Eye burns
Caustobioliths *(QE389.8)*
  sa Bitumen
    Coal
    Oil-shales
    Peat
    Petroleum
    Sapropelites
  xx Hydrocarbons
    Rocks
Cauterization
  See Cautery
Cautery
  x Cauterization
  xx Wounds
Cautio judicatum solvi
  See Security for costs
Cavalier King Charles spaniels *(SF429.C36)*
  xx Spaniels
Cavalletti
  xx Horse-training
    Jumping (Horsemanship)
Cavalry *(UE)*
  sa Cavalry pioneer troops
    Remount service
    France. Armée. Cavalerie; United
      States. Army. Cavalry; *and similar*
      headings
  — Pictorial works
  — Remounts *(UE460)*
    sa Remount service
    xx Remount service

Cavalry drill and tactics *(UE157-302)*
    Here are entered general works only.
    Works on the army of any particular
    country are entered under the name of
    the country with subheading Army.
    Cavalry—Drill and tactics, *e.g.* United
    States. Army. Cavalry—Drill and
    tactics.
  sa Skirmishing
  xx Drill and minor tactics
    Military art and science
    Tactics
Cavalry pioneer troops *(UE490)*
  xx Cavalry
    Pioneer troops
Cave architecture *(NA8455)*
  x Architecture, Cave
    Architecture, Grotto
    Grotto architecture
  xx Architecture
Cave churches *(Direct)* *(NA4910;*
    NA5201-6113)
  sa Cave temples
  x Monolithic churches
    Rock churches
  xx Cave temples
    Churches
Cave diving
  sa Marine caves
  x Diving, Cave
  xx Skin diving
    Speleology
    Underwater exploration
    Water, Underground
Cave-drawings *(Direct)* *(N5310)*
  sa Petroglyphs
  xx Mural painting and decoration
    Petroglyphs
    Picture-writing
    Rock paintings
  — Juvenile literature
Cave-dwellers *(GN783-4)*
  sa Pit-dwellers
    Tarahumare Indians
    Troglodytes
  xx Man, Prehistoric
  — Juvenile literature
Cave-dwellings *(GN783-4)*
  sa Earth houses
    Souterrains
  x Fogous
  xx Dwellings
  — Juvenile literature
Cave ecology *(QH541.5.C3)*
  xx Ecology
Cave fauna *(QL117)*
  x Fauna
  xx Zoology
  — Juvenile literature
Cave flora *(Indirect)* *(QK938.C3)*
  x Flora
  xx Botany
Cave temples *(Indirect)* *(NA4640-4641)*
  sa Cave churches
  xx Cave churches
    Temples
  — Conservation and restoration
Cave temples, Buddhist *(Direct)*
  x Buddhist cave temples
Cavernous sinus *(Diseases, RF421; Human*
    anatomy, QM505)
  x Sinus cavernosus
Caverns
  See Caves
Caves *(Indirect)* *(Physical geography,*
    GB601-8; Prehistoric archaeology,
    GN783-4)
  sa Hiding-places (Secret chambers, etc.)

    Lava tubes
    Marine caves
    Photography of caves
    Stalactites and stalagmites
    names of caves
  x Caverns
    Grottoes
  xx Speleology
  — Guide-books
  — Juvenile literature
  — Pictorial works
Caves (in religion, folk-lore, etc.) *(GR665)*
  x Folk-lore of caves
  xx Religion, Primitive
Caves in art
  xx Art
Caves in literature
Caviar
  xx Sturgeons
Cavina language
  See Cavineño language
Cavineño language *(PM7088)*
  x Cavina language
  xx Indians of South America—Languages
    Tacanan languages
Caving mining *(TN287)*
  xx Stoping (Mining)
Cavitation
  xx Hydrodynamics
    Ship propulsion
    Two-phase flow
    Wakes (Fluid dynamics)
Cavite, Battle of, 1898
  See Manila Bay, Battle of, 1898
Cavite Mutiny, 1872
  See Philippine Islands—History—Cavite
    Mutiny, 1872
Cavities (Aeroplanes)
  x Aeroplanes—Cavities
    Air inlets (Jet planes)
    Air intakes (Jet planes)
Cavity charges
  See Shaped charges
Caxinaua language
  See Kashinaua language
Cayaks
  See Canoes and canoeing
Cayapa Indians *(F3722.1.C3)*
  xx Indians of South America
Cayapo Indians *(F2520.1.C3)*
  sa Xikrin Indians
  x Kayapo Indians
  xx Indians of South America
    Tapuya Indians
  — Missions
Cayapo language *(PM5791)*
  x Kaiapo language
    Kayapo language
  xx Indians of South America—Languages
    Tapuyan languages
Caybate, Battle of, 1756
  See Caibate, Battle of, 1756
Cayley-Hamilton theorem
  x Hamilton-Cayley theorem
  xx Matrices
Cayuá Indians
  See Caingua Indians
Cayubaba language
  See Cayuvava language
Cayuga Indians *(E99.C3)*
  xx Indians of North America
    Iroquoian Indians
    Iroquois Indians
  — Government relations
Cayuse Indians *(E99.C)*
  sa Whitman Massacre, 1847
  xx Indians of North America

Cayuvava language
  x Cayubaba language
Cazcan Indians
  xx Indians of Mexico
CBR warfare
  See Atomic warfare
      Biological warfare
      Chemical warfare
CCI
  See College characteristics index
CCPM test
  See Constant choice perceptual maze test
CDC 3400 (Computer)
  xx Electronic digital computers
  — Programming
CDC 3600 (Computer)
  x Control Data 3600 (Computer)
  xx Electronic digital computers
  — Programming
CDC 6000 (Computer)
  xx Electronic digital computers
  — Programming
CDC 6400 (Computer)
  xx Electronic digital computers
  — Programming
CDC 6600 (Computer)
  x Control Data 6600 (Computer)
  xx Electronic digital computers
Ceboynas
  See Lucayan Indians
Cebú dialect (PL5649)
  x Cebuano (Bisaya dialect)
    Zebú dialect
  xx Bisaya language
     Philippine languages
Cebú literature (PL5649)
Cebuano (Bisaya dialect)
  See Cebú dialect
Cecidology
  See Galls (Botany)
Cecora, Battle of, 1620
  xx Turkey—History—1453-1683
Cecropia moth
  xx Moths
Cecum
  sa Appendix (Anatomy)
  x Blind gut
    Caecum
  xx Intestine, Large
  — Abnormities and deformities
  — Cancer
Cedar (Forestry, SD397.C4)
  sa Incense cedar
     Port Orford cedar
Cedar birds
  See Cedar waxwings
Cedar Creek, Battle of, 1864 (E477.33)
  x Middletown, Va., Battle of, 1864
  xx Shenandoah Valley Campaign,
     Aug.-Nov., 1864
Cedar Mountain, Battle of, 1862 (E473.76)
Cedar waxwings
  x Cedar birds
  xx Passeriformes
Cedynia, Battle of, 972
Cegiha language
  See Dhegiha language
Ceibo
  See Common coral tree
Ceilings (Architecture, NA2950; Building,
     TH2531; Decoration, NK2119)
  sa Mural painting and decoration
  xx Architecture—Details
     Building
  — Thermal properties
     xx Heat—Transmission
Ceilometer (QC923)
  x Cloud-height indicator

  xx Clouds
     Meteorological instruments
Celadonite
  xx Mica
Celaya, Battle of, 1915 (F1391.C3)
  xx Mexico—History—1910-1946
Celdal Indians
  See Tzeltal Indians
Celdal language
  See Tzeltal language
Celery (Culture, SB335)
  Example under Vegetables
  — Grading
  — Packing
Celery cabbage
  See Chinese cabbage
Celery-caterpillar
  Example under Vegetables—Diseases and
     pests
Celesta and harpsichord music (M284.C4;
     M285.C4)
  x Harpsichord and celesta music
Celesta and percussion music
  See Percussion and celesta music
Celesta, clarinet, harp with string orchestra
     (M1140-1141)
  sa Concertos (Celesta, clarinet, harp with
     string orchestra)
  xx Concertos (Celesta, clarinet, harp with
     string orchestra)
     String-orchestra music
     Trios (Celesta, clarinet, harp)
  — Scores (M1140)
Celesta music (M20-32)
  sa Nonets (Celesta, piano, clarinet, flute,
     horn, trombone, trumpet,
     violoncellos (2))
     Octets (Celesta, clarinets (2), flute,
     marimba, violin, violoncello, double
     bass)
     Octets (Celesta, harpsichord,
     reed-organ, vibraphone, violins (2),
     viola, violoncello)
     Octets (Celesta, piano, clarinet, flute,
     trumpet, percussion, double bass)
     Quartets (Celesta, flutes (2), percussion)
     Quartets (Celesta, saxophone, harp,
     percussion)
     Quintets (Celesta, flute, oboe, viola,
     violoncello)
     Quintets (Celesta, flutes (2), harps (2))
     Septets (Celesta, piano, harp,
     percussion, violin, violoncello)
     Sextets (Celesta, flute, oboe, saxophone,
     guitar, harp)
     Sextets (Celesta, harpsichord, violins
     (2), viola, violoncello)
     Trios (Celesta, clarinet, harp)
     Trios (Celesta, flute, violoncello)
Celestial globes
  See Globes, Celestial
Celestial mechanics
  See Mechanics, Celestial
Celestial messengers in literature
  See Divine messengers in literature
Celiac artery
  xx Arteries
  — Radiography
Celiac disease
  sa Gluten-free diet
  x Coeliac disease
  xx Diarrhea
Celiac plexus
  See Solar plexus
Celibacy (HQ800; Clergy, BV4390)
  sa Patarines
     Virginity
     Vows

  x Clerical celibacy
  xx Church discipline
     Clergy
     Marriage
     Monastic and religious life
     Monastic and religious life of women
     Virginity
Celioscopy
  See Abdomen—Examination
Cell, Voltaic
  See Electric batteries
Cell aggregation
  x Aggregation, Cell
Cell culture
  sa Cell lines
     Human cell culture
  x Culture of cells
  xx Cultures (Biology)
     Patholgy, Cellular
Cell culture, Effect of drugs on
  See Cells, Effect of drugs on
Cell cycle
  sa Cell proliferation
     Mitosis
  x Mitotic cycle
     Nuclear cycle (Cytology)
Cell differentiation
  sa Microbial differentiation
     Plant cell differentiation
  x Differentiation of cells
  xx Cytology
     Morphogenesis
     Plant cells and tissues
Cell division (QH605)
  sa Amitosis
     Cell proliferation
     Cytokinesis
     Karyokinesis
     Meiosis
     Mitosis
  xx Cell proliferation
  — Programmed instruction
Cell fractionation (QH585)
  x Fractionation of cells
  xx Cytology—Technique
     Separation (Technology)
Cell function
  See Cell physiology
Cell fusion
  See Cell hybridization
Cell hybridization (QH431)
  sa Somatic hybrids
  x Cell fusion
  xx Cytogenetics
Cell lines
  xx Cell culture
  — Catalogs and collections
Cell-mediated immunity
  See Cellular immunity
Cell membranes (QH601)
  sa Cells—Permeability
     Mitochondrial membranes
     Nuclear membranes
     Plasma membranes
  xx Membranes (Biology)
Cell metabolism
  sa Cellular control mechanisms
  xx Cellular control mechanisms
     Metabolism
  — Programmed instruction
Cell migration
  x Migration of cells
  xx Cytology
Cell motility
  See Cells—Motility
Cell nuclei (QH595)
  sa Anucleate cells
     Enucleation

282

Karyometry
Nuclear membranes
Nucleoids
Nucleolus
x Cell nucleus
Nucleus (Cells)
xx Cell organelles
Cell nucleolus
See Nucleolus
Cell nucleus
See Cell nuclei
Cell organelles
sa Cell nuclei
Endoplasmic reticulum
Golgi apparatus
Lysosomes
Mitochondria
Nucleolus
Plasma membranes
Plastids
Ribosomes
Spindle (Cell division)
x Organelles, Cell
Organoids, Cell
Cell physiology *(QH631)*
x Cell function
xx Cytology
Physiology
— Laboratory manuals
Cell populations *(QH587)*
sa Cell proliferation
x Populations, Cell
xx Cell proliferation
Cytology
Genetics
Cell proliferation
sa Cell division
Cell populations
x Cell renewal
Cellular proliferation
xx Cell cycle
Cell division
Cell populations
Cell recognition
See Cellular recognition
Cell regulation
See Cellular control mechanisms
Cell renewal
See Cell proliferation
Cell research *(Direct)*
x Cells—Research
Cytological research
Cytology—Research
xx Biological research
Research
Cell transformation
sa Bacterial transformation
x Culture alteration (Cytology)
Transformation of cells
xx Tissue culture
Cell walls
See Plant cell walls
Cell walls (Animals)
See Plasma membranes
Cell walls (Bacteria)
See Bacterial cell walls
Cellamare Conspiracy, 1718 *(DC132)*
Cellars
See Basements
Cellatron C8205 (Computer) *(QA76.8.C)*
xx Electronic digital computers
— Programming
Cellatron computer
xx Electronic digital computers
— Programming
Cello
See Violoncello

Cellophane *(TP986.C4)*
xx Cellulose
Viscose process
— Testing
Cells *(QH581-671)*
sa Anucleate cells
Astrocytes
Autolysis
Cancer cells
Centrosomes
Chloride cells
Chromatin
Chromatophores
Cilia and ciliary motion
Cytology
Cytoplasm
Embryology
Epithelium
Eukaryotic cells
Fertilization (Biology)
Fibroblasts
Germ cells
Histology
Immunocompetent cells
Irritability
Macrophages
Microbodies
Microsomes
Muscle cells
Osmosis
Pathology, Cellular
Pigments (Biology)
Plant cells and tissues
Protoplasm
Protoplasts
Protozoa
Purkinje cells
Regeneration (Biology)
Rejuvenescence (Botany)
Somatic hybrids
Turgor
Ultrastructure (Biology)
xx Biological physics
Biology
Cytology
Embryology
Histology
Ovum
Physiological chemistry
Physiology
Protoplasm
Regeneration (Biology)
Rejuvenescence (Botany)
Reproduction
— Juvenile literature
— Motility
sa Contractility (Biology)
x Cell motility
Motility of cells
xx Contractility (Biology)
— Permeability
x Plasma membranes—Permeability
xx Cell membranes
— Research
See Cell research
— Respiration
See Tissue respiration
Cells, Chromaffin
See Chromaffin cells
Cells, Effect of drugs on
x Cell culture, Effect of drugs on
Cellular pharmacology
Tissue culture, Effect of drugs on
xx Drugs—Physiological effect
Cells, Imaginal
See Imaginal disks
Cells of hermits
See Hermitages

Cellular concrete
See Lightweight concrete
Cellular control mechanisms *(QH604)*
Here are entered works on the various mechanisms of cellular control such as structural control, biochemical control, cell differentiation, etc. Works on the control of the type and rate of cellular processes by regulation of the activity of specific genes controlling individual biochemical reactions are entered under Genetic regulation.
sa Cell metabolism
Genetic regulation
x Cell regulation
xx Biological control systems
Cell metabolism
Note under Genetic regulation
Cellular glass
x Foam glass
Glass, Cellular
Glass, Foam
xx Foamed materials
Insulating materials
Cellular immunity *(QR185.C4)*
sa Immune complexes
x Cell-mediated immunity
Delayed hypersensitivity
Hypersensitivity, Delayed
xx Allergy
Immunity
Immunology
Cellular pathology
See Pathology, Cellular
Cellular pharmacology
See Cells, Effect of drugs on
Cellular plastics
See Plastic foams
Cellular proliferation
See Cell proliferation
Cellular recognition
x Cell recognition
Self-recognition (Immunology)
xx Immunology
Cellular respiration
See Tissue respiration
Cellular slime molds
See Acrasiales
Cellular therapy *(RM287)*
x Therapy, Cellular
xx Organotherapy
Therapeutics, Physiological
Transplantation of organs, tissues, etc.
Cellulitis
x Ethmyphytis
xx Connective tissues—Diseases
Pathology, Cellular
Celluloid *(TP986.C5)*
Example under Plastics
Cellulose *(Bacteriology, QR160; Botany, QK898.C35; Chemistry, QD321; Technology, TS1145)*
sa Cellophane
Cellulose industry
Dyes and dyeing—Cellulose
Hemicellulose
Nitrocellulose
Polysaccharides
Pyroxylin
Rayon
Viscose process
Wood—Chemistry
xx Polysaccharides
Wood—Chemistry
Example under Carbohydrates
— Analysis
— Drying
— Microbiology *(QR160)*

Cellulose *(Bacteriology, QR160; Botany,*
QK898.C35; Chemistry, QD321;
Technology, TS1145)
— Microbiology *(QR160)* *(Continued)*
   xx Wood—Microbiology
— Spectra
— Testing
Cellulose industry *(Direct)*
   xx Cellulose
Cellulose liquor
   See Sulphite liquor
Cellulose nitrates
   See Nitrocellulose
Celtiberi *(DP95)*
   sa Basques
      Berbers
   x Celtiberians
   xx Basques
      Berbers
      Iberians
Celtiberian alphabet *(CJ3194; CN)*
   xx Alphabet
Celtiberians
   See Celtiberi
Celtic . . .
   x Keltic . . .
Celtic architecture
   See Architecture, Celtic
Celtic calendar
   See Calendar, Celtic
Celtic Church *(BR748-9; BR794)*
   sa Culdees
Celtic folk-lore
   See Folk-lore, Celtic
Celtic languages *(PB1001-1095)*
   sa Breton language
      Cornish language
      Gaelic language
      Gaulish language
      Goidelic languages
      Irish language
      Manx language
      Welsh language
   xx Celtic philology
      Gaelic language
      Irish language
Celtic law
   See Law, Celtic
Celtic legends
   See Legends, Celtic
Celtic literature *(Celtic languages,*
PB1096-1100; English language,
PR8490-8499)
   sa Breton literature
      Cornish literature
      Gaelic literature
      Irish literature
      Scottish literature
      Welsh literature
   xx Celtic philology
      Irish literature
Celtic miniature painting
   See Miniature painting, Celtic
Celtic names
   See Names, Celtic
Celtic philology *(PB1001-1095)*
   sa Celtic languages
      Celtic literature
   xx Philology, Modern
Celtic poetry *(PB)*
Celtic poetry (English) *(PR8491; PR8496)*
   Duplicate entry is made under English
   poetry—Celtic authors.
   Note under English poetry—Celtic authors
Celts *(D70; GN549.C3; England,*
DA140-143; France, DC62-63)
   sa Alpine race
      Ambrones

Britons
Druids and Druidism
Galatians
Gauls
Latobici (Celtic people)
Picts
Welsh
   x Gaels
   xx Alpine race
      Aryans
      Galatians
      Gauls
Celts in Germany, ₍Italy, etc.₎
— Juvenile literature
Cemba (African people)
   See Bassari (African people)
Cembalo
   See Dulcimer
      Harpsichord
Cement *(Indirect) (Building, TH1461-1501;*
Economics, HD9622; Engineering,
TA680-683; Manufacture,
TP875-885; Mineral resources,
TN945; Properties, testing, etc.,
TA434-5)
   sa Adhesives
      Air-entraining cements
      Asbestos cement
      Asphalt cement
      Cement clinkers
      Cement coating
      Concrete
      Expanding cement
      Hydrocal
      Magnesia cement
      Pavements
      Portland cement
      Roman cement
      Slag cement
      Soil cement
      Steel Portland cement
   x Hydraulic cement
   xx Adhesives
      Building materials
      Ceramics
      Concrete
      Lime
      Masonry
      Plaster
      Pozzuolanas
— Additives
   x Cement admixtures
— — Patents
— Analysis *(TP882.3)*
— Corrosion
— Electric properties *(TA435)*
— Laboratory manuals
— Patents
— Pipe lines
— Prices
— Specifications *(Direct)*
— Standards *(Direct)*
— Storage
— Tariff
   See Tariff on cement
— Testing *(TA435)*
— Toxicology
— Transportation
Cement, Effect of temperature on
Cement admixtures
   See Cement—Additives
Cement clinkers *(TP881)*
   sa Clinker brick
   xx Cement
— Cooling
— Etching
   xx Etching
— Testing

Cement coating
   Here are entered works on the use of cement as a coating to protect other
   materials. Works on the protection of
   concrete from deterioration are entered under the heading Concrete
   coatings.
   xx Cement
      Coatings
      Protective coatings
   Note under Concrete coatings
Cement glands
   xx Invertebrates—Anatomy
Cement grout
   See Grout (Mortar)
Cement gun *(TA446)*
   sa Gunite
   xx Gunite
Cement industries *(Direct) (TP875-885)*
   sa Cement industry workers
      Portland cement industry
   xx Ceramic industries
— Accidents
— By-products
— Collective labor agreements
   See Collective labor agreements—
      Cement industries
— Labor productivity
— Management
— Safety measures
— Technological innovations
Cement industry workers *(Direct)*
   sa Collective labor agreements—Cement
      industries
      Trade-unions—Cement industry
      workers
      Wages—Cement industry workers
   xx Cement industries
Cement kilns *(TP881)*
   sa Kilns, Rotary
   xx Kilns
      Kilns, Rotary
— Maintenance and repair
Cement pipe and tile *(TP885.P5)*
   xx Pipe
— Standards
Cement plants *(Direct)*
— Automation
— Design and construction *(TH4541)*
— Dust control
— Equipment and supplies
— — Appraisal
   See Cement plants—Equipment
      and supplies—Valuation
— — Valuation
   x Cement plants—Equipment and
      supplies—Appraisal
— Hygienic aspects
Cement substance (Anatomy)
   See Ground substance (Anatomy)
Cementation (Metallurgy) *(TN734)*
   sa Case hardening
   xx Metallurgy
      Steel—Metallurgy
Cementation (Petrology)
   xx Geochemistry
      Petrology
      Sedimentation and deposition
Cementite *(TN756)*
   xx Carbides
Cements, Adhesive *(TP967-8)*
   sa Adhesives
   xx Adhesives
Cementum
   xx Teeth

Cemeteries *(Indirect)* *(RA626-630;*
Manners and customs, GT3320)
Includes works on the economic, hygienic, and similar aspects of modern cemeteries and burying-grounds. Works on tombs and mausoleums, mainly from the archaeological standpoint, are entered under Tombs. Material dealing with monuments and gravestones is entered under Sepulchral monuments.
  sa Catacombs
    Epitaphs
    Lanterns of the dead
    National cemeteries—United States
    Pet cemeteries
    Soldiers' bodies, Disposition of
    Tombs
    particular cemeteries, e.g. Mount Auburn Cemetery; Hampton, Va. National Cemetery; *and subdivision* Cemeteries *under names of cities, e.g.* Boston—Cemeteries
  x Burying-grounds
    Churchyards
    Graves
    Graveyards
  xx Burial
    Dead
    Hygiene, Public
    Sanitation
    Tombs
  — Consecration *(BV880)*
    x Consecration of cemeteries
    xx Church of England. Liturgy and ritual
      Dedication services
  — Landscape architecture
    xx Church gardens
      Landscape architecture
  — Law and legislation *(Direct)*
    sa Burial laws
    xx Burial laws
Cemeteries (Canon law)
  xx Sacred places (Canon law)
Cemeteries (Jewish law)
Cemeteries (Roman law)
Cemeteries in literature
  xx Death in literature
Cena, Ultima
  See Lord's Supper
Cenacolo
  See Lord's Supper
Cenosite *(Indirect)* *(QE391.C)*
Cenozoic period
  See Geology, Stratigraphic—Cenozoic
    Paleobotany—Cenozoic
    Paleontology—Cenozoic
Censers *(BV196.C)*
Censors, Roman *(DG83.5.C4)*
Censorship *(Direct)*
  sa Condemned books
    Expurgated books
    Index librorum prohibitorum
    Liberty of the press
    Prohibited books
    subdivision Censorship *under specific subjects, e.g.* European War, 1914-1918—Censorship; Radio—Censorship; Theater—Censorship
  x Book censorship
    Books—Censorship
    Intellectual freedom
  xx Church—Teaching office
    Condemned books
    Expurgated books
    Index librorum prohibitorum
    Liberty of the press

Literature and morals
    Literature, Immoral
    Prohibited books
Censorship (Canon law)
Censorship (Judaism) *(BM729.C4)*
  sa Approbations (Hebrew literature)
Censorship in libraries
  See Libraries—Censorship
Censorship of the press
  See Liberty of the press
    Press law
    Prohibited books
Censorship of the stage
  See Theater—Censorship
Censures, Ecclesiastical *(BX1939.C5)*
  sa Interdict (Canon law)
  xx Canon law
    Catholic Church—Discipline
    Punishment (Canon law)
Census *(Organization, HA37; Reports, by country, HA175-4010)*
  sa Indians of North America—Census
    Indians of South America—Census
    School census
    subdivision Census *under names of countries, cities, etc., e.g.* United States—Census; Boston—Census
  xx Population
    Statistics
    Vital statistics
  — Terminology
Census, School
  See School census
Census (Canon law)
Census districts *(Direct)*
  x Census tracts
    Enumeration districts
    Statistical districts
  xx Special districts
Census tracts
  See Census districts
Cent *(United States, CJ1836)*
  sa Half-cent
    Three-cent piece
  Example under Coins; Money
  — Errors
    x Diebreak errors, Liberty
      Liberty diebreak errors
    Example under Numismatics—Errors
Centaur program
  See Centaur rocket
Centaur rocket
  x Centaur program
  xx Liquid propellant rockets
Centaurs *(BL820.C)*
  xx Mythology, Classical
Centaurs in art
Centenarians *(Direct)*
  xx Longevity
    Old age
  — Portraits
Centennial celebrations
  See subdivision Centennial celebrations, etc. *under names of places and historic events, e.g.* Colorado—Centennial celebrations, etc.
Center of gravity
  See Center of mass
Center of mass *(QA839)*
  x Center of gravity
    Gravity, Center of
  xx Mass (Physics)
    Mechanics
Center parties *(Direct)*
  x Centrists
  xx Christian democracy
    Political parties
  — Europe

x Christian Democratic parties
Center punches
  x Centerpunches
  xx Drilling and boring
Centering of arches *(TH5591)*
  xx Arches
Centerless grinding
  xx Grinding and polishing
Centerpunches
  See Center punches
Centers for the performing arts *(Direct)* *(PN1585-9)*
  sa Auditoriums
    Music-halls
    Theaters
    names of individual centers, e.g. Lincoln Center for the Performing Arts, New York, United States. John F. Kennedy Center for the Performing Arts
  x Performing arts centers
  xx Performing arts
Centers of transportation
  See Terminals (Transportation)
Centipedes *(QL449)*
  x Chilopoda
  xx Myriapoda
Centos *(PN1475)*
  sa Pasticcio
  xx Macaronic literature
    Pasticcio
    Poetry
Central America
  sa Mercado Común Centroamericano countries
  — History *(F1436-8)*
  — — To 1821
  — — 1821-1951
  — — 1951-
Central American Common Market countries
  See Mercado Común Centroamericano countries
Central American fiction
Central American literature *(PQ7471-7539)*
  xx Spanish American literature
Central American periodicals
Central American poetry
Central Asian question
  See Eastern question (Central Asia)
Central banking
  See Banks and banking, Central
Central banks
  See Banks and banking, Central
Central business districts *(Direct)*
  x Business districts, Central
  xx Cities and towns—Planning
    Commerce
    Retail trade
Central Europe
  Here are entered works on the area included in the basins of the Danube, Elbe, and Rhine rivers.
  sa Danube Valley
    Europe, Eastern
  x Europe, Central
  xx Europe, Eastern
  Note under Europe, Eastern
Central heating plants
  See Heating from central stations
Central limit theorem
  xx Limit theorems (Probability theory)
Central nervous system
  sa Brain
    Extrapyramidal tracts
    Neural analyzers
    Spinal cord
  xx Nervous system
  — Aging

Central nervous system *(Continued)*
— Cancer
— Diseases
   sa Brain—Diseases
     Encephalomyelitis
     Jakob-Creutzfeldt disease
     Kernicterus
     Kuru
     Meningitis
     Meningoencephalitis
     Neurosyphilis
     Poliomyelitis
     Spinal cord—Diseases
— — Complications and sequelae
— — Diagnosis
— Surgery
— Tumors
— Wounds and injuries
Central philosophy (Buddhism)
   See Mādhyamika (Buddhism)
Central places *(Direct)*
   xx Cities and towns
Central processing (Libraries)
   See Centralized processing (Libraries)
Central service department (Hospitals)
   See Hospitals—Central service department
Central staging
   See Arena theater
Central station heating
   See Heating from central stations
Central venous pressure
   xx Blood pressure
     Venous pressure
— Programmed instruction
Centralization in government
   See Decentralization in government
Centralization in management
   See Decentralization in management
Centralization of libraries
   See Libraries—Centralization
Centralization of schools
   See Schools—Centralization
Centralized acquisitions (Libraries)
   See Acquisitions, Cooperative (Libraries)
Centralized processing (Libraries) *(Direct)*
   sa Acquisitions, Cooperative (Libraries)
     Cataloging, Cooperative
   x Central processing (Libraries)
   xx Libraries—Centralization
     Library cooperation
     Processing (Libraries)
Centralized purchasing (Libraries)
   See Acquisitions, Cooperative (Libraries)
Centralized traffic control (Railroads)
   See Railroads—Signaling—Centralized
     traffic control
Centrifugal casting
   x Casting, Centrifugal
   xx Founding
Centrifugal compressors
   See Compressors
Centrifugal force *(QC73)*
   sa Disks, Rotating
     Gravitation
   x Force, Centrifugal
   xx Gravitation
     Rotational motion
Centrifugal pumps *(TJ919)*
   x Pumps, Centrifugal
   xx Hydraulic machinery
     Pumping machinery
— Blades
— Design and construction
— Lubrication
— Testing
Centrifugal regulators
   See Governors (Machinery)

Centrifuges *(Chemistry, QD54.C4)*
   sa Human centrifuge
     Sedimentation analysis
     Zonal centrifuge
   x Ultracentrifuges
   xx Chemical apparatus
     Compacting
     Separators (Machines)
Centrioles
   xx Centrosomes
Centripetal force
   x Circular motion
     Force, Centripetal
   xx Motion
     Rotational motion
Centrists
   See Center parties
Centrosomes *(QH597)*
   sa Centrioles
   xx Cells
     Karyokinesis
Centurion's servant (Miracle)
Cepeda, Battle of, 1859 *(F2861)*
Cephalaematoma *(RD661)*
   xx Head—Tumors
     Tumors
Cephalin *(QP801.C)*
Cephalonia Massacre, 1943
   xx World War, 1939-1945—Atrocities
Cephalopoda *(Indirect)* *(QL430.2)*
   sa Octopoda
     Teuthidida
   xx Mollusks
— Anatomy
— Geographical distribution
— Identification
Cephalopoda, Fossil *(QE806-7)*
   sa Ammonoidea
     Endoceratoidea
     Sepiida, Fossil
   xx Mollusks, Fossil
Cepheids *(QB837)*
   xx Pulsating stars
Cer, Battle of, 1914
   xx European War, 1914-1918—Campaigns
     —Serbia
Ceramic coating
   sa Enamel and enameling
   x Coatings, Ceramic
   xx Coatings
     Protective coatings
Ceramic coloring
   See Color in the ceramic industries
Ceramic fibers
   x Fibers, Ceramic
     Fibrous ceramics
   xx Inorganic fibers
     Refractory materials
Ceramic industries *(Direct)*
   sa Cement industries
     Clay industries
     Color in the ceramic industries
     Glass manufacture
   xx Mineral industries
— Accounting
— Automation
— Equipment and supplies
— — Appraisal
     See Ceramic industries—Equipment
       and supplies—Valuation
— — Valuation
     x Ceramic industries—Equipment
       and supplies—Appraisal
— Hygienic aspects
— Labor productivity
— Management
— Materials
     See Ceramic materials

— Safety regulations *(Direct)*
— Tables, calculations, etc.
— Vocational guidance
Ceramic materials *(Indirect)*
   Works on individual materials are en-
   tered under the specific headings, *e.g.*
   Clay, Sand, Shale.
   sa Ceramic metals
     Electronic ceramics
   x Ceramic industries—Materials
     Ceramics—Materials
   xx Mines and mineral resources
— Analysis
— Corrosion
— Electric properties
— Radiation effects
     See Ceramic materials, Effect of
       radiation on
— Tables, calculations, etc.
— Testing
Ceramic materials, Effect of radiation on
   x Ceramic materials—Radiation effects
   xx Radiation
Ceramic metal electrodes
   See Electrodes, Ceramic metal
Ceramic-metal sealing
   See Ceramic to metal bonding
Ceramic metals
   sa Refractory transition metal compounds
   x Cermets
     Metallic ceramics
   xx Ceramic materials
     Heat resistant materials
     Powder metallurgy
— Analysis
— Standards
— Testing
— Welding
Ceramic research
   See Ceramics—Research
Ceramic sculpture *(Direct)*
   sa Terra-cottas
   xx Pottery
     Sculpture
— Technique
Ceramic technology
   See Ceramics
Ceramic to metal bonding
   x Ceramic-metal sealing
     Metal to ceramic bonding
   xx Metal bonding
     Sealing (Technology)
Ceramics
   Here are entered general works on the
   technology of fired earth products, or
   clay products intended for industrial
   and technical use. Works on earthenware, chinaware, and art objects are
   entered under Pottery or Pottery craft.
   Particular objects and types are entered under their specific names, *e.g.*
   Bricks; Pipe, Clay; Refractory materials; Tiles; Vases.
   sa Abrasives
     Cement
     Dies (Ceramics)
     Glass
     Glazes
     Glazing (Ceramics)
     Oxide ceramics
     Piezoelectric ceramics
     Pipe, Clay
     Pottery
     Pottery craft
     Refractory materials
     Slips (Ceramics)
     Tiles
   x Ceramic technology

Industrial ceramics
Keramics
xx Building materials
Chemistry, Technical
Clay
Mineral industries
— Analysis
— Coloring
See Color in the ceramic industries
— Cutting
See Ceramics cutting
— Defects
— Drying *(TP815)*
— Finishing
— Fracture *(TA430)*
xx Fracture of solids
— Laboratory manuals
— Materials
See Ceramic materials
— Popular works
— Pressing
— Research
x Ceramic research
— Standards
— Tables, calculations, etc.
— Testing
Ceramics, Dental
See Dentistry—Ceramics
Ceramics, Electronic
See Electronic ceramics
Ceramics (Art)
See Pottery
Ceramics cutting
x Ceramics—Cutting
xx Cutting
Ceramics in medicine *(R857.C4)*
xx Biomedical materials
Ceramics in the Talmud
Ceras
See Cheras
Cercle (Game) *(GV1017.C4)*
Cereal products
sa Cereals as food
Cereals, Prepared
Flour
Macaroni products
Meal
x Grain products
xx Grain
Cereal rusts *(SB741.R8)*
sa Wheat rusts
x Grain rusts
xx Grain—Diseases and pests
Rusts (Fungi)
Cereal smuts
xx Smuts
— Control *(Indirect)*
Cereal yellow dwarf virus
See Barley yellow dwarf virus
Cereals
See Grain
Cereals, Prepared *(TX395; TX557)*
x Breakfast foods
xx Cereal products
— Packaging
— Patents
Cereals as food *(TX393; TX557)*
sa Cookery (Cereals)
xx Cereal products
Food
Grain
Cerebellar nuclei
xx Cerebellum
Cerebellum *(QL937; QM455; QP379)*
sa Cerebellar nuclei
xx Brain
— Abscess *(RC394.A)*
— Diseases

— Tumors
sa Medulloblastoma
xx Brain—Tumors
Nervous system—Tumors
Cerebral angiography
See Brain—Blood-vessels—Radiography
Cerebral arteriosclerosis
xx Arteriosclerosis
Brain—Aging
Brain—Diseases
Cerebral circulation
See Brain—Blood-vessels
Cerebral concussion
See Brain—Concussion
Cerebral cortex
sa Hippocampus (Brain)
Motor cortex
Suprasylvian gyrus
x Cortex, Cerebral
xx Auditory pathways
Brain
— Surgery
Cerebral cysticercosis
See Cysticercosis, Cerebrospinal
Cerebral dominance
x Dominance, Cerebral
xx Brain
Cerebral edema *(RC394.E3)*
x Brain edema
Brain—Edema
xx Brain—Diseases
Edema
Cerebral embolism and thrombosis
x Cerebral thrombosis
xx Cerebrovascular disease
Embolism
Thromboembolism
Thrombosis
Cerebral ganglion
Cerebral hemorrhage
See Apoplexy
Cerebral hyperemia
See Brain—Congestion
Cerebral infarction
See Brain—Infarction
Cerebral ischemia
x Ischemia, Cerebral
xx Cerebrovascular disease
Cerebral localization
See Brain—Localization of functions
Cerebral palsied children
xx Paralytics
Physically handicapped children
— Education
— — Language arts, ₍etc.₎
— Home care
— Rehabilitation
Cerebral palsy *(Direct)* *(RC388)*
x Cerebral paralysis
Little's disease
Paralysis, Cerebral
xx Brain—Abnormities and deformities
Brain—Diseases
Paralysis
— Cases, clinical reports, statistics
— Genetic aspects
— Personal narratives
— Psychological aspects
— Research *(Direct)*
— Surgery
xx Orthopedic surgery
Cerebral paralysis
See Cerebral palsy
Cerebral peduncle
x Crura cerebri
Crus cerebri
Pedunculus cerebri
xx Mesencephalon

Cerebral sclerosis, Diffuse *(RJ496.C42)*
x Diffuse cerebral sclerosis
xx Brain—Diseases
Demyelination
Cerebral thrombosis
See Cerebral embolism and thrombosis
Cerebral ventricles
x Brain—Ventricles
xx Brain
Cerebrospinal fluid
— Tumors
Cerebrin *(QP801.C4)*
xx Brain
Physiological chemistry
Cerebropathia psychica toxaemica
See Korsakoff's syndrome
Cerebrorachidian fluid
See Cerebrospinal fluid
Cerebrospinal cysticercosis
See Cysticercosis, Cerebrospinal
Cerebrospinal fever
See Meningitis, Cerebrospinal
Cerebrospinal fluid *(QP375)*
sa Blood-brain barrier
Cerebral ventricles
Spine—Puncture
x Cerebrorachidian fluid
xx Body fluids
Brain
Spinal cord
— Analysis and chemistry
sa Brain chemistry
xx Biological chemistry
Medicine, Clinical—Laboratory
manuals
— Examination
— Pressure
See Cerebrospinal fluid pressure
Cerebrospinal fluid pressure
x Cerebrospinal fluid—Pressure
xx Body fluids—Pressure
— Measurement
Cerebrospinal meningitis
See Meningitis, Cerebrospinal
Cerebrovascular disease
sa Cerebral embolism and thrombosis
Cerebral ischemia
Sinus thrombosis
Stroke patients
Subclavian steal syndrome
x Brain—Blood-vessels—Diseases
Stroke
xx Brain—Diseases
— Cases, clinical reports, statistics
— Diagnosis
— Personal narratives
See Stroke patients—Personal
narratives
— Prevention
— Surgery
Ceremonial, Municipal
See Municipal ceremonial
Ceremonial purity
See Purity, Ritual
Ceremonies
See Etiquette
Manners and customs
Rites and ceremonies
Cerenkov radiation
See Cherenkov radiation
Ceres (Planet)
Ceresin *(TN857; TP695)*
sa Ozokerite
x Mineral wax
Wax, Mineral
Ceresole, Battle of, 1544
See Cérisoles, Battle of, 1544

Ceresole d'Alba, Battle of, 1544
   See Cérisoles, Battle of, 1544
Ceri Indians
   See Seri Indians
Cerianthidea *(QL377.C7)*
Cérisoles, Battle of, 1544
   x Ceresole, Battle of, 1544
     Ceresole d'Alba, Battle of, 1544
Cerium *(QD181.C4)*
   sa Sandell-Kolthoff reaction
   xx Bastnaesite
   Example under Rare earth metals
   — Isotopes
      x Cerium isotopes
        Isotopic cerium
   — — Decay
   — Spectra
Cerium alloys
Cerium group *(QD172.R2)*
   sa Bastnaesite
Cerium isotopes
   See Cerium—Isotopes
Cermets
   See Ceramic metals
Cerography
   x Wax printing
   xx Printing, Practical
Ceroplastic
   See Wax-modeling
Ceroptene
Cerro de la Bufa, Battle of, 1872
   See Zacatecas, Battle of, 1872
Certainty *(Epistemology, BD171; Logic,*
      BC171)
   sa Truth
   x Indubitability
   xx Knowledge, Theory of
     Logic
     Truth
Certainty of law
   See Legal certainty
Certamen Nacional de Investigaciones
     Visuales
   xx Art—Competitions
Certhiidae
   See Creepers
Certhiomorphae
   See Creepers
     Nuthatches
Certificates of airworthiness
   See Airworthiness certificates
Certificates of deposit *(Direct)*
   xx Bank deposits
     Negotiable instruments
Certificates of good conduct *(Direct)*
   sa Good behavior (Law)
   xx Criminal registers
Certificates of health
   See Bills of health
Certificates of incorporation *(Direct)*
   sa Charters
   x Incorporation, Certificates of
   xx Articles of incorporation
     Charters
     Corporation law
     Incorporation
Certificates of origin *(HJ6617)*
   xx Commerce
     Consular documents
     Drawbacks
     Marks of origin
     Tariff
Certificates of share
   See Stock certificates
Certificates of stock
   See Stock certificates
Certification, False
   See False certification

Certification of air lines
   See Air lines—Certification
Certification of architects
   See Architects—Certification
Certification of death
   See Death—Proof and certification
Certification of librarians
   See Librarians—Certification
Certification of psychiatric personnel
   See Psychiatric personnel—Certification
Certification of school superintendents and
     principals
   See School superintendents and principals—
     Certification
Certification of student counselors
   See Student counselors—Certification
Certification of teachers
   See Teachers—Certification
Certified mail
   See Postal service—United States—Certified
     mail
Certified public accountants
   See Accountants
Certiorari *(Direct)*
   xx Appellate procedure
     Extraordinary remedies
     Writs
Cerulein *(TP918.C)*
   x Coerulein
   xx Coal-tar colors
Ceruloplasmin
   xx Alpha globulin
     Fibrinolytic agents
Cerussite *(Lead ores, TN450-459;*
     Mineralogy, QE391.C)
Cervical rib syndrome
   See Scalenus anticus syndrome
Cervical vertebrae
   See Vertebrae, Cervical
Cervico-brachial neuralgia
   xx Neuralgia
Cervix uteri
   x Neck of the uterus
   xx Uterus
   — Cancer *(RC280.U8)*
   — — Diagnosis
   — Diseases *(RG310)*
   — — Diagnosis
   — Surgery
Cesarean section *(RG761)*
   sa Obstetrics—Surgery
   x Caesarean section
   xx Obstetrics—Surgery
Cesges de damis (Artificial language)
     (PM8125)
   x Numerical languages
   xx Languages, Artificial
Cesium *(Chemistry, QD181.C8)*
   x Caesium
   — Isotopes
      x Cesium isotopes
        Isotopic cesium
      xx Radioactive tracers
   — — Spectra
   — — Tables
   — Metallurgy
   — Radiation effects
     See Cesium, Effect of radiation on
   — Spectra
Cesium, Effect of radiation on
   x Cesium—Radiation effects
   xx Radiation
Cesium isotopes
   See Cesium—Isotopes
Cesium metabolism
   xx Metabolism
České Budějovice, Czechoslovak Republic, in
     literature

Çeşme, Battle of, 1770 *(DR553)*
   xx Russo-Turkish War, 1768-1774
Cessio bonorum
   See Assignments
     Assignments for benefit of creditors
     Assignments for benefit of creditors
       (Roman law)
     Bankruptcy
Cession of territory
   See Annexation (International law)
Cessna (Aeroplanes)
   xx Aeroplanes, Private
Cessna 150 (Private planes)
   xx Aeroplanes, Private
Cessna 180 (Private planes)
   xx Aeroplanes, Private
Cesspools *(TD775)*
Cestoda *(Indirect) (Zoology, QL391.C4)*
   sa Aporidea
     Caryophyllidea
     Gyrocotylidea
     Proteocephaloidea
     Tetrarhynchidea
   x Tapeworms
   xx Platyhelminthes
     Worms, Intestinal and parasitic
   Example under Parasites
   — Identification
   — Physiology
Cestus *(DE61.C35)*
Cetacea *(Indirect) (QL737.C4)*
   sa Dolphins
     River-dolphins
     Whales
   x Cete
     Cetomorpha
   xx Mammals
   Example under Zoology
   — Anatomy
     sa subdivision Cetacea *under* Digestive
       organs, Nervous system
   — Identification
   — Parasites
     See Parasites—Cetacea
Cetacea, Fossil *(QE882.C5)*
Cete
   See Cetacea
Cetomorpha
   See Cetacea
Cetra
   See English guitar
Ceuta in literature
Cewa dialect
   See Chewa dialect
Ceylon
   — History
   — — To 1505 *(DS489.6)*
   — — 1505-1948 *(DS489.7)*
   — — Rebellion, 1818
   — — 1948- *(DS489.8)*
   — — Rebellion, 1971
Ceylonese literature (English)
   See English literature—Ceylonese authors
Cha-cha (Dance)
Cha-chas
   Here are entered collections of cha-cha
     music for various mediums. Individual
     cha-chas and collections of cha-chas
     for a specific medium are entered un-
     der the heading followed by specifica-
     tion of medium.
Cha-chas (Dance orchestra)
   xx Dance-orchestra music
Cha-no-yu
   See Japanese tea ceremony
Cha-no-yu houses
   See Chashitsu (Japanese tearooms)

Chaamba *(DA346.C)*
  x Chambas
    Chanda
  xx Berbers
Chabad
  See Habad
Chabé (Artificial language) *(PM8128)*
  x Langue internationale naturelle
  xx Languages, Artificial
Chabiroe
  See Habiru
Chacabuco, Battle of, 1817 *(F3094)*
Chacarera (Dance) *(GV1796.C)*
Chachalaca
  — Legends and stories
Chacma baboon
  — Behavior
Chaco Boreal War, 1932-1935
  See Chaco War, 1932-1935
Chaco dispute
  See Chaco War, 1932-1935
Chaco War, 1932-1935 *(F2688.5)*
  sa Boquerón, Battle of, 1932
    El Carmen, Battle of, 1934
    Gondra, Battle of, 1933
    Nanawa, Battle of, 1933
    Nanawa, Battle of, 1933 (Jan. 20-24)
    Nanawa, Battle of, 1933 (July 4-6)
    Pampa Grande, Battle of, 1933
    Picuiba-Yrendagué, Battle of, 1934
    Strongest, Battle of, 1934
    Toledo, Battle of, 1933
    Villa Montes, Bolivia, Battle of, 1935
    Zenteno-Gondra, Battle of, 1933
  x Chaco Boreal War, 1932-1935
    Chaco dispute
  xx Bolivia—History—1879-1938
    Paraguay—History—1870-1938
  — Aerial operations
  — Communications
  — Hospitals, charities, etc.
  — Literature and the war
  — Medical and sanitary affairs
  — Personal narratives
  — Regimental histories *(Indirect)*
    Further subdivision by division, regiment, etc.
  — Supplies
Chacobo Indians *(F3320.2.C36)*
  xx Indians of South America
Chacobo language
  xx Indians of South America—Languages
    Panoan languages
Chaconne
  xx Musical form
Chaconnes
  Here are entered collections of chaconne music for various mediums. Individual chaconnes and collections of chaconnes for a specific medium are entered under the heading followed by specification of medium.
  x Ciacone
Chaconnes (Bassoon, clarinet, flute, horn, oboe) *(M555-7)*
  xx Wind quintets (Bassoon, clarinet, flute, horn, oboe)
Chaconnes (Clarinets (3)) *(M355-7)*
  xx Wind trios (Clarinets (3))
Chaconnes (Clarinets (3)), Arranged *(M358-9)*
Chaconnes (Harp) *(M115-117)*
  xx Harp music
Chaconnes (Harpsichord) *(M24)*
  xx Harpsichord music
Chaconnes (Harpsichord), Arranged *(M38)*
  xx Harpsichord music, Arranged

Chaconnes (Harpsichord, recorders (3)) *(M415-417)*
  xx Quartets (Harpsichord, recorders (3))
Chaconnes (Organ) *(M6-7; M11)*
  xx Organ music
Chaconnes (Piano) *(M25)*
  xx Piano music
Chaconnes (String orchestra) *(M1145)*
  xx String-orchestra music
Chaconnes (Tuba and piano) *(M264-5)*
  xx Tuba and piano music
Chaconnes (Viola and piano) *(M224-6)*
  xx Viola and piano music
Chaconnes (Violin) *(M40-42)*
  xx Violin music
Chaconnes (Violin and harpsichord) *(M217-218; M221)*
  xx Violin and harpsichord music
Chaconnes (Violin and organ) *(M182-4)*
  xx Violin and organ music
Chaconnes (Violin and organ), Arranged *(M185-6)*
  xx Violin and organ music
Chaconnes (Violin and piano) *(M217-218; M221)*
  xx Violin and piano music
Chaconnes (Violin with string orchestra) *(M1105-6)*
  xx Violin with string orchestra
Chaconnes (Violin with string orchestra), Arranged *(M1105-6)*
  — Scores *(M1105)*
Chaconnes (Violoncello and piano) *(M229-230; M233-6)*
  xx Violoncello and piano music
Chaconnes (Violoncello with chamber orchestra) *(M1016-1017)*
  xx Violoncello with chamber orchestra
  — Scores *(M1016)*
  — Solo with piano *(M1017)*
    xx Violoncello and piano music, Arranged
Chadic languages
  sa Afadic dialect
    Angas language
    Dangaleat language
    Gisiga language
    Hausa language
    Kunama language
    Mandara language
    Margi language
    Musgu language
    Ron language
    Tera language
  xx Afroasiatic languages
Chaeronea, Battle of, 338 B.C.
  xx Macedonia—History—To 168 B.C.
Chaetognatha *(Indirect)*
Chaetonotoidea *(QL391.G2)*
  xx Gastrotricha
Chaetopoda *(QL391.C7)*
  sa Archiannelida
    Myzostomaria
    Oligochaeta
    Polychaeta
  xx Annelida
Chaffinches
  xx Finches
Chafing-dish *(TX825)*
Chafing-dish receipts *(TX825)*
  sa Fondue
  xx Cookery
Chaga language *(PL8110.C3)*
  x Chagga language
    Djaga language
    Dschagga language
    Jagga language
    Tschagga language
  xx Bantu languages

    Wachaga
Chagas' disease
  x American trypanosomiasis
    Barbiero fever
    Cruz-Chagas disease
  xx Trypanosomiasis
Chagatai language
  See Jagataic language
Chagga language
  See Chaga language
Chaggas
  See Wachaga
Chahamanas *(DS451.8)*
  xx Rajputs
Chahta language
  See Choctaw language
Chaïka automobile
Chain banks *(Direct)*
  x Banks and banking—Chain banks
  xx Banks and banking
Chain-belting
  See Belts and belting
    Link-belting
Chain drive
  xx Chains
    Power transmission
  — Design and construction *(TJ1117)*
  — Tables, calculations, etc.
Chain indexing *(Z695.9)*
  xx Indexing
  — Programmed instruction
Chain reaction piles
  See Nuclear reactors
Chain saws
  xx Saws
  — Maintenance and repair
  — Vibration
Chain stores *(Direct)* *(HF5468)*
  sa Branch stores
    Chain stores, Voluntary
    Department stores
    Supermarkets
    Variety stores
  x Stores, Chain
  xx Branch stores
    Branches (Business enterprises)
    Department stores
    Retail trade
    Stores, Retail
    Variety stores
  — Accounting
  — Management
  — — Mathematical models
  — Taxation *(Direct)*
Chain stores, Cooperative
  See Chain stores, Voluntary
Chain stores, Voluntary *(Direct)*
  x Chain stores, Cooperative
    Cooperative chain stores
    Voluntary chain stores
  xx Chain stores
    Cooperation
    Retail trade
  — Finance
Chain-track vehicles
  See Tracklaying vehicles
Chained books
  x Books, Chained
Chains *(TS440; Testing, TA492.C6)*
  sa Chain drive
    Surveyors' chains
  xx Hoisting machinery
  — Fatigue
Chains, Equilibrium of
  See Equilibrium of chains
Chair caning *(TT199)*
  x Caning of chairs
  xx Chairs

Chair design
    x Chairs—Design
    xx Design
       Furniture design
Chair-makers (Direct)
    xx Chairs
       Furniture workers
Chair of Unity Octave (BX1786)
    x Church Unity Octave
    xx Catholic Church—Relations
       Christian union
       Prayer
Chairmen, Departmental (High schools)
    See Departmental chairmen (High schools)
Chairs (Direct) (Art industries, NK2715;
       Technology, TS880)
    sa Aeroplanes—Seats
       Chair caning
       Chair-makers
       Rocking chairs
       Wheelchairs
    x Seats
    xx Dining room furniture
       Furniture
   — Collectors and collecting
   — Design
       See Chair design
   — Juvenile literature
   — Private collections
Chairs (Cathedra)
    x Cathedra
    xx Cathedrals
       Christian antiquities
       Classical antiquities
       Thrones
Chairs (Sella) (DG79)
    x Sella curalis
       Sella (Roman antiquities)
    xx Classical antiquities
       Thrones
Chairs for the physically handicapped
    (TS885)
    sa Wheelchairs
    xx Physically handicapped
   — Testing
Chairs of state
    See Thrones
Chake Indians
    See Motilon Indians
Chakosi dialect
    See Anufo dialect
Chakras (Theosophy) (BP573.C5)
    xx Theosophy
Chakri dynasty
    x Rama dynasty
Chala language
    See Ron language
Chalastogastra
    See Symphyta
Chalcedon, Council of, 451 (BR225)
    x Council of Chalcedon, 451
Chalchihuitl (F1219)
    x Chalchuite
    xx Gems
Chalchuite
    See Chalchihuitl
Chalcid flies
    See Chalcid wasps
Chalcid wasps
    x Chalcid flies
       Chalcis flies
    xx Hymenoptera
Chalcidian League
    See Chalcidic League
Chalcidic League (DF85)
    x Chalcidian League
       League of Chalcidic Cities

Chalcis flies
    See Chalcid wasps
Chalcocite (QE391.C35)
Chalcodite (QE391.C)
Chalcopyrite (Copper ores, TN440-449)
Chaldaic language
    See Aramaic language
Chaldean astronomy
    See Astronomy, Assyro-Babylonian
Chaldean Church
    See Nestorian Church
Chaldean language
    See Aramaic language
Chaldee language
    See Aramaic language
Chaldian language
    See Cuneiform inscriptions, Vannic
       Vannic language
Chalices (Gold and silver plate,
       NK7215-7230)
    sa Grail
    x Communion-cups
    xx Christian antiquities
       Church plate
       Drinking vessels
       Liturgical objects
Chalicosis
    See Lungs—Dust diseases
Chaliza
    See Ḥalitsah
Chalk (Chemical technology, TP245.C3;
       Economics, HD9999.C36; Geology,
       QH471; Mineral resources,
       TN948.C5)
    x Whiting
Chalk drawing
    See Blackboard drawing
Chalk engraving
    See Graphotyping
Chalk figures
    See Hill figures
Chalk-talks (NC865; Pastoral theology,
       BV4227; Sunday-schools, BV1535)
    sa Blackboard drawing
Chalkboards
    See Blackboards
Challenge-reply systems (Radar)
    See Aeroplanes—IFF equipment
       Distance measuring equipment (Aircraft
       to ground station)
Challenger automobile (TL215.C)
    xx Dodge automobile
Challenger Expedition, 1872-1876 (G420.C4;
       Natural history, QH11; Science,
       Q115)
Example under Scientific expeditions
Chalukyas (DS451)
    x Cālukyas
       Salunkis
       Solankis
    xx India—History—324 B.C.—1000 A.D.
Chalumeau
    See Shawm
Cham language (PL4491)
    x Čam language
    xx Austroasiatic languages
       Malayan languages
Cham tribe
    See Chams
Chamacoco Indians (F2230.2.C5)
    x Chiamacoco Indians
    xx Indians of South America
       Zamucoan Indians
Chamacoco language
    x Camakoko language
       Ciamacoco language
    xx Zamucoan languages

Chamalal language (PK9201.C)
    x Hihatl language
       Tschamalal language
    xx Caucasian languages
Chamarrita (Dance)
    x Chimarrita (Dance)
Chamārs (DS422.C3)
Chamba Lahuḷi dialect (PL3801.C4)
    x Camba Lahuḷi dialect
    xx Tibeto-Burman languages
Chambas
    See Chaamba
Chamber music (Indirect) (M177-9)
    Here are entered miscellaneous collec-
      tions for various combinations of two,
      three, etc., solo instruments.
    Compositions for two solo instruments
      are entered under headings indicating
      the instruments involved, e.g. Flute
      music (Flutes (2)); Oboe and harpsi-
      chord music; Violin and viola music.
    Compositions for three, four, etc., solo in-
      struments are entered, as the case may
      be, under the headings: Trios, Quar-
      tets, Quintets, etc.; Instrumental en-
      sembles; Piano trios, ₍quartets, quin-
      tets₎; String trios, ₍quartets, quintets,
      etc.₎; String ensembles; Wind trios,
      ₍quartets, quintets, etc.₎; Wind ensem-
      bles.
    sa Monologues with music (Chamber
       music)
    xx Instrumental music
       Music
   — Analytical guides (MT140; MT145)
   — Dictionaries (ML102)
       Example under Music—Dictionaries
   — Discography (ML156.4.C4)
   — History and criticism (ML1100-1165)
       sa Chamber orchestra
          Ensemble playing
          Music in the home
          Orchestra
          String quartet
          String trio
       xx Chamber orchestra
Chamber orchestra (ML1200-1251)
    sa Chamber music—History and criticism
       Chamber-orchestra music
       Instrumentation and orchestration
    xx Chamber music—History and criticism
       Orchestra
Chamber-orchestra music (M1000-1049)
    Cf. note under Orchestral music.
    sa Accordion with chamber orchestra
       Balalaika with chamber orchestra
       Bassoon, clarinet, flute, horn, oboe with
          chamber orchestra
       Bassoon, clarinet, flute, oboe with
          chamber orchestra
       Bassoon, flute, horn, oboe with
          chamber orchestra
       Bassoon, oboe, violin, violoncello with
          chamber orchestra
       Bassoon with chamber orchestra
       Canons, fugues, etc. (Chamber
          orchestra)
       Castanets with chamber orchestra
       Clarinet and flute with chamber
          orchestra
       Clarinet with chamber orchestra
       Concerti grossi
       Concertos (Accordion with chamber
          orchestra)
       Concertos (Balalaika with chamber
          orchestra)
       Concertos (Bassoon, clarinet, flute,
          horn, oboe with chamber orchestra)

Concertos (Bassoon, clarinet, flute, oboe with chamber orchestra)

Concertos (Bassoon, flute, horn, oboe with chamber orchestra)

Concertos (Bassoon, oboe, violin, violoncello with chamber orchestra)

Concertos (Bassoon with chamber orchestra)

Concertos (Clarinet and flute with chamber orchestra)

Concertos (Clarinet with chamber orchestra)

Concertos (Domra with chamber orchestra)

Concertos (Double bass with chamber orchestra)

Concertos (English horn with chamber orchestra)

Concertos (Flute and oboe with chamber orchestra)

Concertos (Flute and trombone with chamber orchestra)

Concertos (Flute with chamber orchestra)

Concertos (Flutes (2) with chamber orchestra)

Concertos (Guitar with chamber orchestra)

Concertos (Guitars (2) with chamber orchestra)

Concertos (Harp with chamber orchestra)

Concertos (Harpsichord with chamber orchestra)

Concertos (Hurdy-gurdy with chamber orchestra)

Concertos (Jazz ensemble with chamber orchestra)

Concertos (Mouth-organ with chamber orchestra)

Concertos (Oboe and violin with chamber orchestra)

Concertos (Oboe with chamber orchestra)

Concertos (Organ with chamber orchestra)

Concertos (Percussion with chamber orchestra)

Concertos (Piano with chamber orchestra)

Concertos (Pianos (2) with chamber orchestra)

Concertos (Saxophone with chamber orchestra)

Concertos (Saxophones (4) with chamber orchestra)

Concertos (String quartet with chamber orchestra)

Concertos (Trombone with chamber orchestra)

Concertos (Trumpet with chamber orchestra)

Concertos (Viola d'amore with chamber orchestra)

Concertos (Viola with chamber orchestra)

Concertos (Violin and piano with chamber orchestra)

Concertos (Violin and viola with chamber orchestra)

Concertos (Violin with chamber orchestra)

Concertos (Violoncello with chamber orchestra)

Country-dances (Chamber orchestra)

Domra with chamber orchestra

Double bass with chamber orchestra

English horn with chamber orchestra

Flute and oboe with chamber orchestra

Flute and trombone with chamber orchestra

Flute with chamber orchestra

Flutes (2) with chamber orchestra

Galops (Chamber orchestra)

Guitar with chamber orchestra

Guitars (2) with chamber orchestra

Harp with chamber orchestra

Harpsichord with chamber orchestra

Hurdy-gurdy with chamber orchestra

Jazz ensemble with chamber orchestra

Marches (Chamber orchestra)

Monologues with music (Chamber orchestra)

Mouth-organ with chamber orchestra

Oboe and violin with chamber orchestra

Oboe with chamber orchestra

Organ with chamber orchestra

Overtures (Chamber orchestra)

Percussion with chamber orchestra

Piano with chamber orchestra

Pianos (2) with chamber orchestra

Polkas (Chamber orchestra)

Polonaises (Chamber orchestra)

Quadrilles (Chamber orchestra)

Salon-orchestra music

Saxophone with chamber orchestra

Saxophones (4) with chamber orchestra

String-orchestra music

String quartet with chamber orchestra

Suites (Chamber orchestra)

Symphonic poems (Chamber orchestra)

Symphonies (Chamber orchestra)

Trombone with chamber orchestra

Trumpet with chamber orchestra

Variations (Chamber orchestra)

Viola d'amore with chamber orchestra

Viola with chamber orchestra

Violin and piano with chamber orchestra

Violin and viola with chamber orchestra

Violin with chamber orchestra

Violins (2), viola with chamber orchestra

Violoncello with chamber orchestra

Violoncellos (2) with chamber orchestra

Waltzes (Chamber orchestra)

xx Chamber orchestra
   Instrumental music
   Orchestral music
   Salon-orchestra music
   String-orchestra music

Chamber-orchestra music, Arranged *(M1060-1075)*

Chamber pots *(Direct)* *(NK695.C5)*
   x Jordans
      Pots, Chamber
      Urinals (Vessels)
   xx House furnishings
      Sanitation, Household

Chambermaids, Hotel
   See Hotel maids

Chambers, Space
   See Space simulators

Chambers of commerce
   See Boards of trade

Chambers of rhetoric
   xx Literary societies

Chambersburg, Pa., Burning of, 1864 *(E476.66)*
   xx Maryland Campaign, June-Aug., 1864

Chameleons *(QL666.L2)*
   xx Lizards
   — Juvenile literature

Chamí Indians
   x Chamis

xx Indians of South America

Chamis
   See Chamí Indians

Chamois *(QL737.U5)*

Chamois hunting *(SK299)*

Chamorro language *(PL5295)*
   x Tjamoro language
   xx Malayan languages
      Micronesian languages

Chamosite *(Indirect)*
   xx Chlorites

Champagne, Battles of, 1914-1917 *(D545.C37)*
   xx European War, 1914-1918—Campaigns
      —France

Champagne (Wine) *(TP555)*
   xx Wine and wine making
   Example under Sparkling wines

Champas
   See Chams

Champerty
   See Maintenance and champerty

Champignons
   See Mushrooms

Champigny-sur-Marne, France, Battle of, 1870
   xx Franco-German War, 1870-1871

Champion of Champions International Sprint Race (Bicycle race) *(GV1049)*

Champion's Hill, Battle of, 1863 *(E475.26)*

Champlain, Lake, Battle of, 1609 *(F1030.1)*

Champlain, Lake, Battle of, 1814 *(E356.C)*
   sa Plattsburgh, N.Y., Battle of, 1814

Champlain tercentenary celebrations *(F1031.1)*
   x Lake Champlain Tercentenary Celebration, 1909

Champotón, Battle of, 1517
   xx Indians of Mexico—Wars
      Mexico—History—To 1519

Chams
   x Cam
      Cham tribe
      Champas
      Chiam tribe
      Tchames
   xx Malay race

Chamula Indians
   See Tzotzil Indians

Chamula language
   See Tzotzil language

Ch'an Buddhism
   See Zen Buddhism

Chana language
   sa Güenoa language

Chañabal language *(PM3601)*
   x Chanable language
      Chaneabal language
      Tojolabal language
   xx Indians of Mexico—Languages

Chanable language
   See Chañabal language

Chanca Indians *(F3430.1.C)*
   x Changa Indians
      Chanka Indians
   xx Indians of South America

Chance *(Cosmology, BD595; Logic, BC141; Mathematics, QA273)*
   sa Combinations
      Gambling systems
      Games of chance (Mathematics)
      Necessity (Philosophy)
      Probabilities
      Serendipity
   xx Fortune
      Necessity (Philosophy)
      Probabilities

Chance composition

Here are entered works dealing with compositions which have been created by chance methods or which may be performed in random or indeterminate style.

- x Aleatory music
  - Chance music
  - Music, Aleatory
  - Music, Chance
- xx Composition (Music)
  - Improvisation (Music)

Chance compositions

Here are entered works which have been composed by chance methods or which may be performed in random or indeterminate style. The heading is used as a second heading for those works having a specifically named medium of performance, *e.g.* 1. Piano music. 2. Chance compositions.

- x Aleatory music
  - Chance music
  - Music, Aleatory
  - Music, Chance
- xx Music

Chance in literature

Chance music

- *See* Chance composition
  - Chance compositions

Chancellors, Diocesan

- x Diocesan chancellors
- xx Canon law
  - Dioceses
  - Notaries (Canon law)

Chancellorsville, Battle of, 1863 *(E475.35)*

Chanceries, Diocesan *(Direct)*

- x Chanceries, Episcopal
  - Diocesan chanceries
  - Episcopal chanceries
- xx Bishops
  - Church polity
  - Dioceses

Chanceries, Episcopal

- *See* Chanceries, Diocesan

Chancery

- *See* Equity
  - Equity pleading and procedure

Chancery clerks (Mississippi) *(KFM7037.8.C5)*

Chancroid *(RC203.C5)*

- xx Hemophilus diseases

Chanda

- *See* Chaamba

Chandalar Kutchin Indians

- *See* Natsitkutchin Indians

Chandela dynasty *(Antiquities, DS416-419; History of India, DS451)*

- x Camdella dynasty
  - Candella dynasty
  - Candrella dynasty
  - Chandellas
- xx India—History—324 B.C.-1000 A.D.

Chandeliers *(Art, NK8360; Technology, TH7960-7970)*

- xx Interior decoration

Chandellas

- *See* Chandela dynasty

Chandi language

- *See* Ostiak language

Chané Indians

- sa Tereno Indians
- xx Indians of South America
  - Tereno Indians

Chaneabal language

- *See* Chañabal language

Changa Indians

- *See* Chanca Indians

Changari language

- xx Indo-Aryan languages, Modern

Changars

- x Chûbne

Changchih Incident, 1938

- *See* Changkufeng Incident, 1938

Change *(Ontology, BD373)*

- sa Catastrophical, The
  - Process philosophy
- xx Catastrophical, The
  - Ontology
- — Quotations, maxims, etc.

Change, Educational

- *See* Educational innovations

Change, Linguistic

- *See* Linguistic change

Change, Social

- *See* Social change

Change (Psychology)

- xx Psychology
  - Psychology, Applied
- — Mathematical models

Change in personality

- *See* Personality change

Change makers (Coins)

- *See* Coin changing machines

Change of attitude

- *See* Attitude change

Change of life in men

- *See* Climacteric

Change of life in women

- *See* Climacteric
  - Menopause

Change of sex

- x Sex change
  - Sex, Change of
  - Sex-role inversion
  - Transexualism
  - Transsexualism
- xx Generative organs
- — Personal narratives

Change of state (Physics) *(QC301-310)*

Change of voice

- *See* Voice, Change of

Change ringing *(MT710)*

- x Bell ringing
  - Chiming
- xx Bells
  - Carillons

Changga

- x Koryŏ kayo
  - Kyŏnggich'ega
  - Kyŏnggiyŏhaga
  - Pyŏlgokch'e
- xx Korean poetry

Ch'anggŭk

- x P'ansori
  - P'ansori sasŏl
- xx Opera, Korean

Changkaofeng Incident, 1938

- *See* Changkufeng Incident, 1938

Changku feng Incident, 1938

- *See* Changkufeng Incident, 1938

Changkufeng Incident, 1938 *(DS784)*

- x Changchih Incident, 1938
  - Changkaofeng Incident, 1938
  - Changku feng Incident, 1938
  - Hasang Incident, 1938
  - Hatsang Incident, 1938
  - Hazan Incident, 1938
  - Khasan Incident, 1938
- xx Russo-Japanese Border Conflicts, 1932-1941

Chank *(QL430.5.T85)*

Chanka Indians

- *See* Chanca Indians

Channel bass *(QL638.S34)*

- x Red drum

Redfish

Channel bass fishing

- xx Fishing

Channel catfish

- xx Catfishes

Channel catfish virus disease

- xx Fishes—Diseases and pests
  - Virus diseases

Channel improvements

- *See* Stream channelization

Channeling (Physics) *(QC176.8.C45)*

- xx Collisions (Nuclear physics)
  - Solids, Effect of radiation on
  - Wave mechanics

Channelization, Stream

- *See* Stream channelization

Channels (Hydraulic engineering) *(TC175)*

- sa Aqueducts
  - Canals
  - Flumes
  - Harbors
  - Lakes
  - Reservoirs
  - River channels
  - Sediment transport
  - Waterways
- xx Hydraulic engineering
  - Hydraulics
  - Hydrodynamics
  - Sediment transport

Chansons

- *See* French ballads and songs

Chansons, Polyphonic

Here are entered collections of chansons and separately published chansons of the 15th and 16th centuries. The heading is used only as a second heading, *e.g.* 1. Part-songs, French. 2. Chansons, Polyphonic.

- x Polyphonic chansons

Chansons de geste *(Collections, PQ1310; History, PQ201-3)*

- sa Byliny
- xx French poetry
  - Heldensage
  - Legends
  - Trouvères
- — Juvenile literature

Chantage

- *See* Extortion

Chanteys

- *See* Sailors' songs
  - Work-songs

Chantilly, Va., Battle of, 1862

- x Ox Hill, Battle of, 1862

Chanting

- *See* Chants (Anglican)
  - Chants (Buddhist)
  - Chants (Byzantine)
  - Chants (Hindu)
  - Chants (Jewish)
  - Chants (Plain, Gregorian, etc.)
  - Koran—Recitation
  - Vedas—Recitation

Chantries

- xx Benefices, Ecclesiastical
  - Chapels

Chants (Anglican)

- x Anglican chant
  - Chanting
  - Harmonized chant
- xx Church music—Protestant churches
  - Church of England. Liturgy and ritual
  - Oral interpretation
  - Protestant Episcopal Church in the U.S.A. Liturgy and ritual
  - Sacred vocal music
- — Accompaniment *(M14; MT190)*

— Instruction and study *(MT860)*
Chants (Buddhist)
  x Buddhist chants
    Chanting
  xx Buddha and Buddhism—Rituals
    Music, Buddhist
    Sacred vocal music
Chants (Byzantine)
  x Byzantine chant
    Chanting
  xx Church music—Orthodox Eastern
    Church
    Oral interpretation
Chants (Hindu) *(BL1226.2)*
  sa Hindu hymns
  x Chanting
    Hindu chant
  xx Hinduism—Rituals
    Oral interpretation
    Sacred vocal music
Chants (Jewish)
  sa Cantillation
    Songs, Sephardic
  x Chanting
    Jewish chant
  xx Cantillation
    Jews. Liturgy and ritual
    Music—Jews
    Oral interpretation
    Sacred vocal music
    Synagogue music
  — History and criticism *(ML3195)*
  — Instruction and study *(MT860)*
Chants (Plain, Gregorian, etc.)
  x Chanting
    Gregorian chant
    Plain chant
    Plain song
    Plainsong
  xx Catholic Church. Liturgy and ritual
    Church music—Catholic Church
    Liturgics
    Oral interpretation
    Sacred vocal music
  — Accompaniment *(M14; MT190)*
    sa Hymns—Accompaniment
    xx Hymns—Accompaniment
      Musical accompaniment
      Organ—Instruction and study
  — History and criticism *(ML3082)*
    sa Alleluia (Music)
    xx Music—History and criticism—
      Medieval, 400-1500
  — Instruction and study *(MT860)*
    sa Neumes
    xx Musical meter and rhythm
      Singing—Instruction and study
  — — To 1800
      xx Music—Theory—Medieval,
        400-1500
Chantys
  See Sailors' songs
    Work-songs
Chanukah
  See Hanukkah (Feast of Lights)
Chaos (Theology)
  xx Creation
    Theology, Doctrinal
Chaouia (Berber tribe)
  x Shawia (Berber tribe)
    Soaua (Berber tribe)
  xx Berbers
    Ethnology—Morocco
Chap-books *(General, PN970; English,*
    PR972-5)
  sa Comic books, strips, etc.
    Tracts
  x Jest-books

  xx Comic books, strips, etc.
    Folk literature
    Folk-lore
    Periodicals, Ephemeral
    Street literature
  — Illustrations
Chap-books, American, ₍French, etc.₎
    (American, PS472-8; French,
    PQ803-6)
  — Juvenile literature
Chap-books, Brazilian
  x Literatura de cordel
Chapa Indians
  See Shapra Indians
Chapanec Indians
  See Chiapanec Indians
Chapanec language
  See Chiapanec language
Chaparral *(Botany, QK149; Forestry,*
    SD397.C47)
  xx Browse
    Forests and forestry
    Trees
Chaparral cock
  See Road runner (Bird)
Chapel exercises
  See Universities and colleges—Chapel
    exercises
Chapel gardens
  See Church gardens
Chapels *(Indirect)* *(NA4870)*
  sa Chantries
    Church architecture
    Oratories
    Sepulchral chapels
    names of individual chapels, and
      subdivision Chapels *under names of*
      cities
  xx Church architecture
    Churches
Chapels, Court *(NA4870; NA5200-6113)*
  sa Chaplains, Court
  x Chapels royal
    Court chapels (Buildings)
Chapels (Music) *(Indirect)*
  sa Choirs (Music)
    Maîtrises
  x Chapels royal
    Music chapels
  xx Choirs (Music)
    Church music
    Orchestra
Chapels royal
  See Chapels, Court
    Chapels (Music)
Chaplains
  Here are entered comprehensive works
    on clergymen who are officially at-
    tached to the Armed Forces, to public
    bodies or institutions or to a family or
    court.
  For works limited to a specific type of
    chaplain, the heading is qualified by
    the functional adjective, *e.g.* Chap-
    lains, Hospital; Chaplains, Military.
  For works limited to chaplains of a par-
    ticular denomination, the name of the
    denomination is added as a subdivi-
    sion, *e.g.* Chaplains, Hospital—Cath-
    olic Church; Chaplains, Military—Lu-
    theran Church.
  Works limited to chaplains of a particular
    body or institution are entered under
    the name of the body with subdivision
    Chaplains, *e.g.* United States. Con-
    gress—Chaplains.
  sa Legislative bodies—Chaplains' prayers
  xx Clergy

Chaplains, Air Force
  See Chaplains, Military
Chaplains, Court *(Direct)*
  x Court chaplains
  xx Chapels, Court
Chaplains, Hospital
  x Hospital chaplains
    Hospitals—Chaplains
  Note under Chaplains
  — Catholic Church, ₍Lutheran Church, etc.₎
    Note under Chaplains
Chaplains, Industrial *(Direct)* *(BV2695.W6)*
  sa Priest workers
  x Industrial chaplains
  xx Church work
    Church work with skilled labor
    Evangelistic work
    Labor and laboring classes—Religious
      life
    Welfare work in industry
Chaplains, Military *(Direct)*
  x Air Force chaplains
    Chaplains, Air Force
    Chaplains, Naval
    Military chaplains
    Naval chaplains
  xx Church work with military personnel
  Note under Chaplains
  — Catholic Church, ₍Lutheran Church, etc.₎
    Duplicate entry is made under Chap-
      lains, Military—₍country₎
    Note under Chaplains
  — Wives
    x Military chaplains' wives
    xx Clergymen's wives
      Wives
Chaplains, Naval
  See Chaplains, Military
Chaplains, Police
  x Police chaplains
    Police—Chaplains
  — Correspondence, reminiscences, etc.
Chaplains, Prison *(Direct)*
  sa Prisons—Religious life
  x Prison chaplains
  — Correspondence, reminiscences, etc.
  — Shin (Sect)
    xx Shin (Sect)
Chaplains, School
  x School chaplains
  xx Chaplains, University and college
    Church work with students
Chaplains, University and college
  sa Chaplains, School
    Nuns in campus ministry
    Women in campus ministry
  x Campus clergy
    Campus ministers
    College chaplains
    University chaplains
  xx Church work with students
    Universities and colleges—Religion
Chaplains (Canon law)
Chaplains' prayers
  See Legislative bodies—Chaplains' prayers
Chappa *(RD631)*
Chapra Indians
  See Shapra Indians
Chapter-headings
  x Books—Chapter-headings
  xx Books
Chapter-house libraries
  See Fraternity libraries
Chapters, Cathedral, collegiate, etc.
    (Indirect)
  sa Canons, Cathedral, collegiate, etc.
    Minor canons, Cathedral, collegiate,
      etc.

Chapters, Cathedral, collegiate, etc.
    (Indirect) (Continued)
      Rural chapters
      Vicars capitular
    xx Bishops
      Cathedrals
      Dioceses
      Vicars capitular
Chapters, Cathedral, collegiate, etc. (Canon law) *(BX1939.C6)*
Chapters, General
    See General chapters
Chapters, Rural
    See Rural chapters
Chapultepec, Battle of, 1847
Char
    xx Coal
Character *(Character building, LC251-301; Ethics, BJ1518-1535; Psychology, BF818-839)*
    sa Conduct of life
      Nobility of character
      Temperament
    x Ethology
    xx Christian life
      Conduct of life
      Ethics
      Personality
      Temperament
      Virtue
Character, Sacramental
    See Sacramental character
Character education
    See Moral education
Character recognition devices, Optical
    See Optical character recognition devices
Character tests *(BF818-839)*
    sa Constant-choice perceptual maze test
      Personality tests
    x Psychological tests
      Tests, Character
      Will-temperament tests
    xx Educational tests and measurements
      Emotions
      Mental tests
      Personality tests
      Temperament
      Will
Characteristic classes
    x Classes, Characteristic
    xx Differential topology
Characteristic functions
    See Functions, Characteristic
Characteristics
    See Characters and characteristics
      National characteristics
Characterization (Conflict of laws)
    See Classification (Conflict of laws)
Characters and characteristics *(BF818-839)*
    sa Eccentrics and eccentricities
      Know-it-all persons
      Pedantry
      Phrenology
      Physiognomy
      Polarity (Psychology)
      Trait intercorrelations
      Typology (Psychology)
    x Characteristics
    xx Conduct of life
      Typology (Psychology)
    — Literary collections
Characters and characteristics in literature *(PN218; Drama, PN1689; Psychology, BF818-839)*
    sa Children in literature
      Clergy in literature
      Communists in literature
      Detectives in literature

      Dissenters in literature
      Drama—Technique
      Intellectuals in literature
      Jews in literature
      Lawyers in literature
      Livres à clef
      Master and servant in literature
      Men in literature
      Negroes in literature
      Nobility in literature
      Old age in literature
      Physicians in literature
      Pierrot
      Plots (Drama, novel, etc.)
      Women in literature
      Youth in literature
    subdivision Characters *under names of authors, e.g.* Shakespeare, William, 1564-1616—Characters
    x Literary characters
    xx Children in literature
      Drama
      Literature
      Plots (Drama, novel, etc.)
      Women in literature
Characters and characteristics in moving-pictures
    x Moving-picture characters
    xx Moving-pictures
Charades *(PN6369-6377)*
    xx Amateur theatricals
      Amusements
      Literary recreations
      Riddles
      Tableaux
Charadriiformes
    sa Avocets
      Gulls
      Kittiwake
      Lapwings
      Murres
      Oystercatcher
      Phalaropes
      Plovers
      Sandpipers
      Snipes
      Terns
      Turnstones
    x Waders (Birds)
Charans
    x Cāraṇō
    xx Caste—India
      Ethnology—India—Bombay (State)
      Minstrels
Charas
    See Bhang (Drug)
Charcoal *(Fuel, TP331; Heating, TH7423)*
    sa Carbon, Activated
    xx Carbon
      Carbonization
      Fuel
Charcoal, Activated
    See Carbon, Activated
Charcoal, Animal
    See Animal charcoal
Charcoal burners *(Direct)*
    x Charcoal makers
Charcoal-drawing *(NC850)*
    x Fusain (Art)
    xx Drawing
Charcoal kilns *(Indirect)*
    xx Kilns
Charcoal makers
    See Charcoal burners
Charcos
    xx Water-supply
Charcot joints
    x Charcot's joint

      Neuro-arthropathy
      Neurogenic arthropathy
      Neuropathic joint
    xx Joints—Diseases
Charcot's joint
    See Charcot joints
Charge, Nuclear
    See Nuclear charge
Charge account bank plans
    xx Banks and banking
      Consumer credit
      Retail trade
Charge and mass renormalization
    See Renormalization (Physics)
Charge conjugation parity violation
    See CP violation (Nuclear physics)
Charge exchange *(QC173)*
    x Exchange, Charge
    xx Collisions (Nuclear physics)
      Electrons—Capture
      Ions
Charge of the Light Brigade
    See Balaklava, Battle of, 1854
Charge transfer *(QC173)*
    x Transfer, Charge
    xx Collisions (Nuclear physics)
      Electrons
      Ion exchange
      Mass transfer
Charged particle accelerators
    See Particle accelerators
Charger automobile
    See Dodge Charger automobile
Chargers, Battery
    See Battery chargers
Charges, Police
    See Police charges
Charges and specifications (Courts-martial) *(Direct)*
    x Accusation
    xx Courts-martial and courts of inquiry
Charging systems (Libraries) *(Z714)*
    x Libraries—Charging systems
      Library charging systems
    xx Libraries—Circulation, loans
      Library science
Charibbs
    See Carib Indians
Chariots *(Chariot-racing, GV33)*
    xx Vehicles
Charismata
    See Gifts, Spiritual
Charismatic Movement
    See Pentecostalism
Charitable bequests *(Direct)*
    sa Charitable uses, trusts, and foundations
    x Pious bequests
      Pious legacies
      Religious bequests
      Religious legacies
    xx Charitable uses, trusts, and foundations
      Charities
      Charity laws and legislation
      Inheritance and succession
      Legacies
Charitable bequests (Canon law)
Charitable contributions as tax deductions
    See Corporations—Charitable contributions
      Income tax—Deductions—Charitable contributions
Charitable institutions
    See Almshouses
      Asylums
      Blind—Institutional care
      Charities
      Deaf—Institutional care
      Institutional care
      Orphans and orphan-asylums

Woman—Institutional care
  subdivisions Benevolent and moral
    institutions and societies *and*
    Charities *under names of cities*
Charitable institutions, Tort liability of
  See Tort liability of charitable organizations
Charitable societies *(HV1-4959)*
  sa Charities
    Charities—Societies, etc. *[for
      publications of charitable and other
      societies in relation to charity]*
    subdivision Benevolent and moral
      institutions and societies *under
      names of cities, e.g.* London—
      Benevolent and moral institutions
      and societies
  x Benevolent societies
    Humane societies
    Societies, Benevolent
  xx Charities
    Charity organization
    Societies
Charitable uses, trusts, and foundations
    (Direct)
    Here are entered works on the legal as-
      pects of the subject. General works on
      endowed institutions, endowment
      funds and donations to such funds are
      entered under the heading Endow-
      ments.
  sa Charitable bequests
    Cy pres doctrine
    Endowments
    Mortmain
    Pension trusts
    Religious trusts
  x Donations
    Endowed charities
    Foundations (Endowments)
    Trusts, Charitable
    Uses, Charitable
  xx Charitable bequests
    Charities
    Charity laws and legislation
    Endowments
    Juristic persons
    Trusts and trustees
    Uses (Law)
    Notes under Corporations, Nonprofit; Endow-
      ments
  — Taxation *(Direct)*
Charitable uses, trusts, and foundations
    (Canon law)
**Charitable uses, trusts, and foundations (Greek
    law)**
Charitable uses, trusts, and foundations
    (Hindu law)
Charitable uses, trusts, and foundations
    (Islamic law) *(Direct)*
  x Wakf
Charitable uses, trusts, and foundations
    (Roman-Dutch law) *(Direct)*
Charitable uses, trusts, and foundations
    (Roman law)
  x Piae causae
Charities *(Indirect)* *(HV1-4959)*
    Here are entered works on privately sup-
      ported welfare activities. Works on
      tax-supported activities are entered
      under Public welfare. Treatises on the
      methods employed in welfare work,
      public or private, are entered under So-
      cial service.
  sa Allotment of land
    Almshouses
    Asylums
    Bazaars, Charitable
    Blind—Institutional care

Charitable bequests
Charitable societies
Charitable uses, trusts, and foundations
Charity laws and legislation
Charity organization
Charity-schools
Child welfare
Church charities
Community organization
Corporations—Charitable contributions
Day nurseries
Deaf—Institutional care
Disaster relief
Dispensaries
Elberfeld system
Endowments
Food relief
Fresh-air charity
Friendly societies
Hospitals
Institutional care
International relief
Medical social work
Merchant seamen—Missions and
  charities
Monasteries
Old age homes
Orphans and orphan-asylums
Poor
Printers—Charities
Psychiatric social work
Public welfare
Ragged schools
Red Cross
Rehabilitation, Rural
Sisterhoods
Sisters of Charity
Social service
Social settlements
Social workers
Transients, Relief of
Travelers' aid societies
Unemployed
Woman—Charities
Woman—Institutional care
Women in charitable work
Work relief
Young women—Charities, protection,
  etc.
subdivisions Benevolent and moral
  institutions and societies, Charities,
  and Poor *under names of cities, e.g.*
  London—Benevolent and moral
  institutions and societies;
  Mülhausen—Charities; Baltimore—
  Poor; *also subdivision* Charities
  *under names of churches, ethnic and
  social groups, fraternal orders, etc.;
  and subdivision* Civilian relief *under
  names of wars, e.g.* World War,
  1939-1945—Civilian relief
  x Alms and almsgiving
  Benevolent institutions
  Charitable institutions
  Endowed charities
  Homes (Institutions)
  Institutions, Charitable and
    philanthropic
  Outdoor relief
  Philanthropy
  Poor relief
  Relief (Aid)
  Social welfare
  Welfare work
  xx Charitable societies
  Charity organization
  Endowments
  Poor

Poverty
Public welfare
Social problems
Social service
Sociology
Unemployed
Notes under Public welfare; Social service
— Accounting *(HF5686.C2-3)*
  xx Public institutions—Accounting
— Anecdotes, facetiae, satire, etc.
— Directories
    For directories of social agencies make
      duplicate entry under the heading
      Social service—Societies, etc.—
      Directories.
— Public relations
    See Public relations—Social service
— Societies, etc.
  xx Charitable societies
— Taxation
    See Church property—Taxation
      Corporations, Nonprofit—
        Taxation
      Income tax—Deductions—
        Charitable contributions
      Pension trusts—Taxation
Charities, Legal
  See Legal aid societies
Charities, Medical *(Indirect)* *(HV687-694;
    HV3000-3003; Hospitals,
    RA960-996)*
  sa Aged—Medical care
    Blind—Institutional care
    Children—Hospitals
    Deaf—Institutional care
    Dental clinics
    Diet-kitchens
    Dispensaries
    Epileptics—Hospitals
    Hospitals
    Incurables—Hospitals and asylums
    Leprosy—Hospitals
    Medical social work
    Psychiatric hospitals
    Tuberculosis—Hospitals and
      sanatoriums
    Voluntary health agencies
    subdivision Charities, Medical *under
      names of cities, e.g.* Philadelphia—
      Charities, Medical
  x Medical charities
    Socialized medicine
  xx Hygiene, Public
    Medical care
    Medical social work
    Medicine, Clinical
    Medicine, State
    Poor
    Note under Medical social work
— Research
Charities, Rural
  See Social service, Rural
Charity *(Moral theology, BV4639)*
  sa Altruism
    Humanity
    Kindness
    Love (Theology)
    Women in charitable work
  x Alms and almsgiving
  xx Benevolence
    Conduct of life
    Ethics
    Humanity
    Theological virtues
    Example under Virtues
— Quotations, maxims, etc.
Charity, Sisters of
  See Sisters of Charity

295

Charity in literature
Charity laws and legislation *(Direct)*
   (HV75-83)
      Here are entered works on the public regulation of private charities. Laws and regulations governing the administration of public charities are entered under Public welfare—Law.
   sa Almshouses—Law and legislation
      Asylums—Law and legislation
      Blind—Law and legislation
      Charitable bequests
      Charitable uses, trusts, and foundations
      Gleaning
      Old age homes—Law and legislation
      Poor laws
      Tort liability of charitable organizations
   x Law, Charity
   xx Charities
      Poor laws
Charity laws and legislation (Jewish law)
Charity organization *(HV40-69)*
   sa Charitable societies
      Charities
      Community welfare councils
      Federations, Financial (Social service)
      Social service exchanges
   x Philanthropy
   xx Charities
   Note under Social service
Charity-schools *(Indirect)* *(Great Britain, LC4096.G7)*
   sa Orphans and orphan-asylums
      Ragged schools
   xx Charities
      Child welfare
      Children—Institutional care
      Education
      Orphans and orphan-asylums
      Schools
Charlatans
   See Impostors and imposture
      Quacks and quackery
Charleston, S.C.
   — Fire, 1838
   — Fire, 1861
   — History
   — — War of 1812
   — Siege, 1780 *(E241.C4)*
   — Siege, 1863 *(E475.62)*
   — Slave insurrection, 1822
   — Tornado, 1761
Charleston (Dance) *(GV1796.C4)*
Charlie Chan films
   xx Moving-pictures
Charm *(BJ1609-1610)*
   xx Beauty, Personal
      Conduct of life
      Etiquette
      Hygiene
      Personality
      Success
      Woman
Charms *(Folk-lore, GR600)*
   sa Amulets
      Birth-stones
      Cramp-rings
      Evil eye
      Mandrake
      Talismans
   x Spells
   xx Amulets
      Demonology
      Evil eye
      Folk-lore
      Magic
      Superstition
      Talismans

      Witchcraft
Charms (Buddhism) *(BQ4570.A4)*
Charnwood-Cistercian pottery
   x Pottery, Charnwood-Cistercian
Charolais cattle
   x Charollais cattle
   xx Beef cattle
Charollais cattle
   See Charolais cattle
Charpentier's illusion
   See Autokinesis
Charqui
   See Beef, Dried
Charrua Indians *(F2230.2.C54)*
   xx Indians of South America
Charrua language *(PM5808.C5)*
   sa Güenoa language
Charter contracts, Air
   See Air charter contracts
Charter flight
   See Aeronautics, Commercial—Chartering
Charter-parties *(Direct)* *(Water transport, HE596)*
   sa Air charter contracts
      Lay days
   x Affreightment
      Chartering of ships
      Ship chartering
   xx Carriers
      Contracts, Maritime
      Freight and freightage
      Maritime law
Chartering of aeroplanes
   See Aeronautics, Commercial—Chartering
Chartering of ships
   See Charter-parties
Charters
   sa Archives
      Articles of incorporation
      Certificates of incorporation
      Corporations
      County charters
      Manuscripts
      Municipal charters
      subheading Charters *under names of American colonies, states, and cities, e.g.* Chicago. Charters; *and subdivision* Charters, grants, privileges *under foreign countries, cities, etc.*
   x Documents
   xx Archives
      Cartularies
      Certificates of incorporation
      Deeds
      Diplomatics
      History—Sources
      Incorporation
      Manuscripts
Charters, County
   See County charters
Charters, Municipal
   See Municipal charters
Chartism *(Economics, HD8396; English history, DA559.7)*
Chartography
   See Cartography
Chartreux, Ordre des
   See Carthusians
Charts, Aeronautical
   See Aeronautical charts
Charts, Astronautical
   See Astronautical charts
Charts, Astronomical
   See Astrographic catalog and chart
      Astronomy—Charts, diagrams, etc.
Charts, Bottle
   See Bottle-charts

Charts, Experience
   See Experience charts
Charts, Historical
   See Chronology, Historical—Charts
Charts, Nautical
   See Nautical charts
Chartularies
   See Cartularies
Charwomen and cleaners
   sa Janitors
      Trade-unions—Charwomen and cleaners
      Wages—Charwomen and cleaners
   x Scrubwomen
   xx Building-service employees
      Janitors
Chase, The
   See Hunting
Chashitsu (Japanese tearooms) *(Direct)*
   x Cha-no-yu houses
   xx Architecture, Sukiya
      Japanese tea ceremony
Chasidism
   See Hasidism
Chassis-mounted coaches
   See Campers and coaches, Truck
Chasta Indians *(E99.C48)*
   xx Athapascan Indians
      Indians of North America
Chastacosta language *(PM761)*
   xx Athapascan languages
Chastity *(Ethics, BJ1533.C4; Girdles of chastity, GT2810; Sociology, HQ; Theology, BV4647.C5)*
   sa Chastity belts
   xx Ethics
      Evangelical counsels
      Sexual ethics
   — Papal documents
Chastity, Vow of
   x Vow of chastity
   xx Evangelical counsels
      Monastic and religious life
      Monastic and religious life of women
      Vows
Chastity belts *(GT2810)*
   x Girdles of chastity
   xx Chastity
Chastity in literature
Chastushki
   xx Folk-songs, Russian
      Folk-songs, White Russian
      Russian poetry
Chasu language
   See Asu language
Château-Thierry, Battle of, 1918 *(D545.C4)*
   xx European War, 1914-1918—Campaigns —France
Châteaudun, France
   — Siege, 1870 *(DC309.C4)*
      xx Franco-German War, 1870-1871
Chateauguay, Battle of, 1813 *(E356.C4)*
Châteaux
   See Castles
Chatino language *(PM3616)*
Chattanooga, Battle of, 1863 *(E475.97)*
   sa Lookout Mountain, Battle of, 1863
      Missionary Ridge, Battle of, 1863
   xx Missionary Ridge, Battle of, 1863
Chattanooga Railroad Expedition, 1862 *(E473.55)*
   x Andrews' Raid, 1862
      Andrews' Railroad Raid
Chattel mortgages *(Direct)*
   sa Aircraft mortgages
      Bills of sale
      Liens

Pledges (Law)
  Sales, Conditional
  Ship mortgages
  Trust receipts
  x Agricultural warrants
    Hypothecation
    Warrants, Agricultural
  xx Bills of sale
    Commercial law
    Mortgages
    Personal property
    Pledges (Law)
    Sales, Conditional
    Security (Law)
  — Criminal provisions
Chattels
  See Personal property
Chatti
  See Hittites
Chauhan dynasties
Chaulmugra oil (*Physiological effects, QP915.C45; Therapeutics, RM666.C38*)
Chaulmugra tree
Chausar
  See Pachisi
Chautauquas (*LC6301.C4-6*)
  xx Education
    Lectures and lecturing
    Lyceums
    Theater
Chauvinism and jingoism
  sa Imperialism
    Militarism
  x Jingoism
  xx Imperialism
    Militarism
    Nationalism
    Patriotism
    Political ethics
Chavante-Akwẽ Indians
  See Akwẽ-Shavante Indians
Chavante language (*PM5809*)
Chawi language
  See Chayahuita language
Chayahuita language
  x Chawi language
    Chayawita language
  xx Indians of South America—Languages
Chayavada
  xx Hindi literature—20th century
    Hindi poetry—20th century
    Mysticism in literature
Chayawita language
  See Chayahuita language
Chayote (*SB351.C4*)
Chazanim
  See Cantors, Jewish
Chazars
  See Khazars
Chazzanim
  See Cantors, Jewish
Cheat (Grass)
  See Brome-grass
Cheating (Education)
  x Academic dishonesty
    Student cheating
    Student dishonesty
  xx Honesty
    Self-government (in education)
    Students—Conduct of life
  — Anecdotes, facetiae, satire, etc.
Cheating at cards
  See Cardsharping
Chebyshev approximation
  x Minimax approximation
    Tchebycheff approximation
  xx Approximation theory

— Computer programs
Chebyshev polynomials (*QA404.5*)
  x Functions, Chebyshev's
    Polynomials, Chebyshev
    Tchebycheff polynomials
  xx Chebyshev systems
    Orthogonal polynomials
Chebyshev systems
  sa Approximation theory
    Chebyshev polynomials
  x Tchebycheff systems
  xx Approximation theory
    Functions, Continuous
Chechehet language
  x Tšetšehet language
  xx Indians of South America—Languages
    Pampa language
Chechen (*DK34.C*)
  xx Ethnology—Caucasus
Chechen-Ingush A.S.S.R. in literature
Chechen language (*PK9201.C3*)
  x Tchetchen language
  xx Caucasian languages
Chechen literature (*Direct*) (*PK9201.C35*)
Chechen poetry (*Direct*)
Check off
  See Checkoff
Check pinochle (Game) (*GV1295.P6*)
  xx Penuchle (Game)
Check-rein (*HV4751*)
  xx Animals, Treatment of
    Driving
    Harness
Checker pool (*GV1469.C5*)
  x Pool checker
    Spanish pool
  xx Checkers
Checkered giant rabbits
  See American checkered giant rabbits
Checkers (*GV1461-3*)
  sa Broadway checkers
    Checker pool
  x Damen (Game)
    Draughts
  — Collections of games
  — Juvenile literature
Checkmate (Chess) (*GV1450.3*)
  xx Chess
Checkoff (*Direct*)
  x Check off
    Union dues checkoff
  xx Payroll deductions
    Trade-unions
    Union security
    Wages
Checks (*Direct*) (*HG1691-1700; Law, HF1259*)
  sa Bank float
    Clearinghouse
    Composite checks
    Currency exchanges (Domestic)
    Deposit banking
    Postal service—Postal checks
    Traveler's checks
  xx Banks and banking
    Bills of exchange
    Commercial law
    Deposit banking
    Drafts
    Negotiable instruments
  — Caricatures and cartoons
  — Cases
  — Criminal provisions
    xx Forgery
      Fraud
  — Digests
  — Examinations, questions, etc.
  — Taxation

    See Bills of exchange—Taxation
Checks (International law) (*JX6289.C5*)
Checkweighing (*HD4932.C5*)
  xx Piece-work
    Wages
Cheddar cheese
Cheder
  See Heder
Chedi era
  See Kalachuri dynasty
Cheek (*QM535*)
  xx Face
Cheek-bone (*QM105*)
  xx Bones
    Skull
Cheerfulness (*BJ1533.C5; Ethics, BJ1477-1486; Literary extracts, PN6071.O7*)
  sa Happiness
    Optimism
  x Gladness
  xx Conduct of life
    Contentment
    Ethics
    Happiness
    Optimism
Cheerleaders
  See Cheerleading
Cheerleading (*LB3635*)
  sa Cheers
  x Cheerleaders
  xx Cheers
Cheers (*School life, LB3635*)
  sa Cheerleading
  x College cheers
    Yells
  xx Cheerleading
Cheese (*Indirect*) (*SF271-3*)
  sa Cheese factories
    Cookery (Cheese)
  xx Dairying
    Milk
  Example under Food industry and trade
  — Bacteriology (*QR121*)
    sa Dairy bacteriology
      Milk—Bacteriology
    xx Bacteriology, Agricultural
      Dairy bacteriology
  — Juvenile literature
  — Packaging
  — Patents
  — Poetry
  — Prices
  — Storage (*TX612.C4*)
  — Taxation (*Direct*)
    x Cheese industry—Taxation
  — Varieties
    sa Montasio cheese
      Pecorino cheese
      specific varieties of cheese, e.g.
        Roquefort cheese
    x Cheeses
Cheese antennas
  See Microwave pillboxes
Cheese cake (Cookery)
  See Cheesecake (Cookery)
Cheese-cloth (*TS1580*)
Cheese factories
  xx Cheese
    Dairy plants
    Food processing plants
Cheese industry (*Direct*)
  — Law and legislation (*Direct*)
    xx Dairy laws
  — Taxation
    See Cheese—Taxation
Cheesecake (Cookery) (*TX773*)
  x Cheese cake (Cookery)

Cheesecake (Cookery) (TX773)
(Continued)
   xx Cake
      Cookery (Cheese)
Cheeses
   See Cheese—Varieties
Cheetahs (QL737.C2)
   x Cheetas
      Chetahs
      Chetas
      Chittahs
      Hunting-leopards
  — Behavior
  — Legends and stories
  — Pictorial works
Cheetas
   See Cheetahs
Chehalis Indians (E99.C49)
   xx Indians of North America
      Salishan Indians
Cheilostomata, Fossil
   x Chilostomata, Fossil
   xx Polyzoa, Fossil
Cheirognomy
   See Palmistry
Cheiromancy
   See Palmistry
Cheiroptera
   See Bats
Cheirosophy
   See Palmistry
Chelation therapy
   xx Metals in the body
      Therapeutics
Chelatometry
   See Complexometric titration
Chelsea, Battle of, 1775
Chelsea porcelain (NK4399.C5)
   x Porcelain, Chelsea
   Example under Porcelain
Cheltenham Gold Cup (SF359)
   xx Steeplechasing
Chemical abbreviations
   See Chemistry—Abbreviations
Chemical additives in food
   See Food additives
Chemical affinity (QD501)
   sa Chemical reaction, Rate of
      Valence (Theoretical chemistry)
   x Affinity, Chemical
   xx Chemistry, Physical and theoretical
      Reactivity (Chemistry)
Chemical analysis
   See Chemistry, Analytic
      subdivision Analysis under particular
         subjects, e.g. Water—Analysis
Chemical analysis of colors
   See Colors—Analysis
Chemical analysis of nuts
   See Nuts—Chemical composition
Chemical apparatus (QD53)
   sa Assaying apparatus
      Blowpipe
      Centrifuges
      Chemistry—Manipulation
      Electrochemical apparatus
      Glass blowing and working
      Lasers in chemistry
      Volumetric apparatus
   x Apparatus, Chemical
      Chemical instruments
      Chemistry—Apparatus
   xx Physical instruments
      Scientific apparatus and instruments
   Example under Instrument industry
  — Standards
     x Chemical engineering—Apparatus
        and supplies—Standards

Chemical bonds
   sa Electronegativity
      Mills-Nixon effect
      Molecular orbitals
      Overlap integral
   x Bonds, Chemical
   xx Chemistry, Physical and theoretical
      Overlap integral
      Quantum chemistry
      Valence (Theoretical chemistry)
  — Charts, diagrams, etc.
  — Tables, etc.
Chemical composition of nuts
   See Nuts—Chemical composition
Chemical composition of the earth
   See Geochemistry
Chemical denudation (QE581)
   x Denudation, Chemical
   xx Erosion
      Geochemistry
      Rivers
Chemical dosimetry (QD643.C5)
   x Chemical radiation dosimetry
   xx Radiation chemistry
      Radiation dosimetry
Chemical effects of radiation
   See Radiation chemistry
Chemical elements (QD466-7)
   sa Actinide elements
      Allotropy
      Atomic weights
      Nonmetals
      Periodic law
      Trace elements
      Valence (Theoretical chemistry)
   names of elements
   x Elements, Chemical
  — Juvenile literature
  — Purification
  — Spectra
Chemical embryology
   x Embryology, Chemical
   xx Biological chemistry
      Embryology
Chemical engineering (Direct) (TP155)
   sa Acids—Handling and transportation
      Chemical plants
      Chemical processes
      Chemistry, Technical
      Enzymes—Industrial applications
      Fluidization
      Geothermal engineering
      Leaching
      Mechanical engineering
      Metallurgy
      Mixing
      Molding (Chemical technology)
      Molecular sieves
      Moving-pictures in chemical
        engineering
      Protective atmospheres
      Recycle operations (Chemical
        technology)
      Zone melting
   x Chemistry, Industrial
      Engineering, Chemical
      Industrial chemistry
   xx Chemistry, Technical
      Engineering
      Mechanical engineering
      Metallurgy
  — Abstracts
  — Apparatus and supplies (TP157-9)
     sa Autoclaves
        Extraction apparatus
        Heat exchangers
        Packed towers
        Plate towers

        Separators (Machines)
     xx Autoclaves
        Chemical plants—Equipment and
         supplies
   — — Appraisal
      See Chemical engineering—
        Apparatus and supplies—
        Valuation
   — — Corrosion
   — — Design and construction
   — — Patents
   — — Prices
   — — Standards
      See Chemical apparatus—Standards
   — — Valuation (TP157)
      x Chemical engineering—Apparatus
        and supplies—Appraisal
  — Costs
  — Estimates
  — Examinations, questions, etc.
  — Graphic methods
  — Information services
  — Juvenile literature
  — Laboratory manuals
  — Mathematical models
  — Mathematics
  — Patents
  — Problems, exercises, etc. (TP168)
     xx Chemistry—Problems, exercises, etc.
  — Programmed instruction
  — Statistical methods
  — Study and teaching
  — — Audio-visual aids
  — Tables, calculations, etc.
  — Terminology
  — Translating
  — Vocational guidance
     See Chemical engineering as a
       profession
Chemical engineering as a profession
   (TP186)
   x Chemical engineering—Vocational
      guidance
Chemical engineering laboratories
   (TP165-183)
   sa Engineering experiment stations
   x Laboratories, Chemical engineering
   xx Chemical laboratories
      Chemistry, Technical—Research
      Engineering experiment stations
      Engineering laboratories
      Testing laboratories
Chemical engineering research (Direct)
   xx Engineering research
      Research
Chemical engineers (Direct) (TP139)
   sa Chemists
   xx Chemists
      Engineers
  — Biography
Chemical equations
   x Equations, Chemical
   xx Chemical reactions
      Chemistry—Notation
Chemical equilibrium (QD501)
   sa Linear free energy relationship
      Phase rule and equilibrium
   x Equilibrium, Chemical
   xx Chemistry, Physical and theoretical
      Phase rule and equilibrium
  — Computer programs
  — Mathematical models
  — Programmed instruction
  — Tables, etc.
Chemical evolution (QH325)
   x Biochemical evolution
      Evolution, Chemical
      Molecular evolution

xx Chemistry, Physical and theoretical
   Life—Origin
— Juvenile literature
Chemical fires
  See Chemicals—Fires and fire prevention
Chemical formulae
  See Chemistry—Notation
Chemical genetics
  See Biochemical genetics
Chemical geology
  See Geochemistry
    Mineralogical chemistry
    Mineralogy, Determinative
    Rocks—Analysis
Chemical harmonicon
  See Pyrophone
Chemical industries *(Direct)*
    (HD9650-9660)
    Here are entered works on industries
    based largely on chemical processes.
    Material dealing with the manufacture
    of chemicals as such is entered under
    Chemicals—Manufacture and indus-
    try.
  sa Chemical plants
    Chemical workers
    Oil industries
    Paint industry and trade
    names of specific industries, e.g. Soap
      trade, Paper making and trade
  x Industries, Chemical
  xx Chemicals—Manufacture and industry
    Chemistry, Technical
— Accidents
— Auditing and inspection
— Automation
— — Programmed instruction
— By-products
— Collective bargaining
    See Collective bargaining—Chemical
      industries
— Collective labor agreements
    See Collective labor agreements—
      Chemical industries
— Costs
— Defense measures
— Finance
— Fires and fire prevention
— Hygienic aspects
— Information services
— Job descriptions
— Labor productivity
— Law and legislation *(Direct)*
  sa Chemicals—Law and legislation
  xx Chemicals—Law and legislation
— Management
— Military aspects
    Example under Industrial mobilization;
      Military policy
— Patents
— Production standards
— Quality control
— Safety measures
— Safety regulations *(Direct)*
— Technological innovations
— Underdeveloped areas
    See Underdeveloped areas—Chemical
      industries
— Waste disposal *(TD899.C5)*
Chemical inhibitors
  sa Anti-freeze solutions
    Antioxidants
    Catalysts
    Corrosion and anti-corrosives
    Enzyme inhibitors
  x Inhibitors, Chemical
Chemical instruments
  See Chemical apparatus

Chemical kinetics
  See Chemical reaction, Rate of
Chemical labeling
  See Chemicals—Labeling
Chemical laboratories *(Direct) (QD51)*
  sa Atomic energy research—Laboratories
    Chemical engineering laboratories
    Radiochemical laboratories
  x Chemistry—Laboratories
    Laboratories, Chemical
  xx Testing laboratories
— Electric equipment
— Electronic equipment
— Safety measures
Chemical laboratory technicians *(Direct)*
    (TP186.5)
  xx Chemical workers
    Laboratory technicians
    Technologists
Chemical lasers
  xx Lasers
Chemical libraries *(Z675.C)*
  sa Information storage and retrieval
    systems—Chemistry
  x Libraries, Chemical
Chemical literature *(QD8.5)*
  sa Chemistry—Bibliography
  x Chemistry—Literature
  xx Chemistry—Bibliography
    Chemistry—History
Chemical literature searching
  See Information storage and retrieval
    systems—Chemistry
Chemical manipulation
  See Chemistry—Manipulation
Chemical memory transfer
  See Memory transfer
Chemical microscopy
  x Microscopy, Chemical
  xx Microscope and microscopy
Chemical models
  sa Atoms—Models
    Crystals—Models
    Molecules—Models
  x Chemistry—Models
    Models, Chemical
Chemical mutagenesis
  xx Mutagenesis
Chemical nomenclature
  See Chemistry—Nomenclature
Chemical oceanography *(GC98)*
    Subdivided by body of water, *e.g.* Chemi-
    cal oceanography—Arctic Ocean.
  sa Sea-water—Composition
    Water chemistry
  x Marine chemistry
  xx Geochemistry
    Oceanography
— Arctic Ocean
    Notes under Chemical oceanography;
      Sea-water—Composition
Chemical plants *(Direct) (TP155.5)*
  sa Plastics plants
  x Chemical works
  xx Chemical engineering
    Chemical industries
    Factories
— Air conditioning
— Automation
— Construction
    See Chemical plants—Design and
      construction
— Design and construction
    x Chemical plants—Construction
— Electric equipment
— Equipment and supplies
    sa Chemical engineering—Apparatus
      and supplies

— — Appraisal
    See Chemical plants—Equipment
      and supplies—Valuation
— — Corrosion
— — Drawings
— — Maintenance and repair
— — Reliability
— — Valuation
    x Chemical plants—Equipment and
      supplies—Appraisal
— Fires and fire prevention
— Heating and ventilation
— Maintenance and repair
— — Costs
— Management
— Mathematical models
— Pilot plants
— Pipe lines
— — Drawings
— Tables, calculations, etc.
— Waste disposal
— — Patents
— Water-supply
Chemical polishing of metals
  See Metals—Pickling
Chemical preservatives
  xx Food—Preservation
Chemical process control
  xx Process control
— Laboratory manuals
— Mathematical models
Chemical processes *(TP155.7)*
  sa Chemical reactions
  x Processes, Chemical
  xx Chemical engineering
    Chemical reactions
    Manufacturing processes
— Graphic methods
— Mathematical models
— Patents
— Problems, exercises, etc.
— Tables, calculations, etc.
Chemical radiation dosimetry
  See Chemical dosimetry
Chemical reaction, Conditions and laws of
    (QD501)
  sa Activity coefficients
    Linear free energy relationship
    Passivity (Chemistry)
    Reactivity (Chemistry)
  x Conditions and laws of chemical
    reaction
    Reaction, Conditions and laws of
      (Chemistry)
  xx Chemistry, Physical and theoretical
— Mathematical models
Chemical reaction, Kinetics of
  See Chemical reaction, Rate of
Chemical reaction, Rate of *(QD501)*
  sa Activity coefficients
    Linear free energy relationship
  x Chemical kinetics
    Chemical reaction, Kinetics of
    Reaction rate (Chemistry)
    Velocity of chemical reaction
  xx Chemical affinity
    Chemistry, Physical and theoretical
    Reactivity (Chemistry)
— Mathematical models
— Programmed instruction
— Tables, etc.
Chemical reactions *(QD73)*
  sa Abderhalden reaction
    Activity coefficients
    Acyloin reaction
    Addition reactions
    Alkali-aggregate reactions
    Alkylation

Chemical reactions *(QD73) (Continued)*
    Bucherer reaction
    Cannizzaro reaction
    Chemical equations
    Chemical processes
    Chemical reactors
    Chugaev reaction
    Darzens reaction
    Deamination
    Decarboxylation
    Delépine reaction
    Diazo reaction
    Diels-Alder reaction
    Elimination reactions
    Exchange reactions
    Friedel-Crafts reaction
    Gattermann reaction
    Gomberg-Bachmann reaction
    Hunsdiecker reaction
    Hydroxylation
    Ivanov reaction
    Jacobsen reaction
    Japp-Klingemann reaction
    Kolbe reaction
    Leuckart reaction
    Niementowski reaction
    Nitrosation
    Oxidation-reduction reaction
    Ozonization
    Perkin reaction
    Phosphorylation
    Prins reaction
    Reactivity (Chemistry)
    Rearrangements (Chemistry)
    Ring formation (Chemistry)
    Sandell-Kolthoff reaction
    Schiff reaction
    Schmidt reaction
    Sodium-water reaction
    Sommelet reaction
    Stephen reaction
    Steric hindrance
    Substitution reactions
    Szilard-Chalmers reaction
    Voigt reaction
    Wagner-Jauregg reaction
    Willgerodt reaction
    Wittig reaction
  x Reactions, Chemical
  xx Chemical processes
Chemical reactors
  x Reactors, Chemical
  xx Chemical reactions
    Chemistry, Technical
  — Mathematical models
Chemical reagents
  See Chemical tests and reagents
Chemical reduction
  See Reduction, Chemical
    Reduction, Electrolytic
Chemical research *(Indirect) (QD40)*
  sa Chemistry, Technical—Research
    Fertilizers and manures—Research
    Photochemical research
  x Chemistry—Research
  xx Research
Chemical societies *(Indirect) (QD1)*
  sa Chemistry—Societies, etc. *[for*
    publications of chemical and other
    societies in relation to chemistry]
  xx Societies
Chemical sterilization of insects
  See Insect chemosterilization
Chemical structure-biological activity
    relationship (Pharmacology)
  See Structure-activity relationship
    (Pharmacology)

Chemical symbols
  See Abbreviations
    Chemistry—Nomenclature
    Chemistry—Notation
Chemical taxonomy
  See Chemotaxonomy
Chemical technology
  See Chemistry, Technical
Chemical tests and reagents *(QD77)*
  sa Abderhalden reaction
    Fehling's solution
    Grignard reagents
    Indicators and test-papers
    Ozone
    Reinecke salt
    Schiff reaction
    Spot tests (Chemistry)
  x Chemical reagents
    Reagents, Chemical
  xx Indicators and test-papers
  — Specifications
  — Tables, etc.
Chemical warfare *(UG447)*
  sa Decontamination (from gases,
    chemicals, etc.)
    European War, 1914-1918—Chemistry
    Gases, Asphyxiating and poisonous—
      War use
    Smoke screens
    World War, 1939-1945—Chemistry
  x CBR warfare
    Chemistry in warfare
  xx Air defenses
    Air warfare
    Combustion
    Explosives, Military
    Gases, Asphyxiating and poisonous—
      War use
    Military art and science
    Strategy
    Tactics
    War
  — Hygienic aspects
  — Safety measures
    xx Civil defense
Chemical workers *(Direct)*
  sa Chemical laboratory technicians
    Chemists
    Collective bargaining—Chemical
      industries
    Collective labor agreements—Chemical
      industries
    Rubber industry workers
    Strikes and lockouts—Chemical
      workers
    Trade-unions—Chemical workers
    Wages—Chemical workers
  xx Chemical industries
    Chemicals—Manufacture and industry
  — Diseases and hygiene
Chemical works
  See Chemical plants
Chemicals
  sa Antifoaming agents
    Bleaching materials
    Drying agents
    Fire extinguishing agents
    Repellents
    Stabilizing agents
    groups of chemicals, e.g. Acids,
      Alkalies, Explosives; *and individual*
      chemical substances, e.g. Antimony,
      Barium, Carbolic acid
  — Deterioration
  — Fires and fire prevention
    x Chemical fires
  — Labeling
    x Chemical labeling

    xx Chemicals—Safety measures
  — Law and legislation *(Direct)*
    sa Chemical industries—Law and
      legislation
      Products liability—Chemical
      products
    x Chemicals—Safety regulations
    xx Chemical industries—Law and
      legislation
  — Manufacture and industry *(Direct)*
    (Economics, HD9650-9660;
    Technology, TP200-248)
    sa Chemical industries
      Chemical workers
      Chemistry, Technical
      Electrochemistry, Industrial
      specific chemical industries, e.g.
      Sulphuric acid industry
    xx Chemistry, Technical
    Example under Occupations, Dangerous
    Note under Chemical industries
  —— Accounting
  —— Collective bargaining
      See Collective bargaining—
        Chemical industries
  —— Collective labor agreements
      See Collective labor agreements—
        Chemical industries
  —— Costs
  —— Safety measures
      sa Chemicals—Safety measures
      xx Chemicals—Safety measures
  —— Underdeveloped areas
      See Underdeveloped areas—
        Chemical industries
  — Marketing
  — Patents *(TP210)*
  — Physiological effect
    sa Pharmacology
    xx Pharmacology
  — Prices *(Direct)*
  — Purification
  — Safety measures *(TP149)*
    sa Chemicals—Labeling
      Chemicals—Manufacture and
      industry—Safety measures
    xx Chemicals—Manufacture and
      industry—Safety measures
      Hazardous substances
  — Safety regulations
    See Chemicals—Law and legislation
  — Standards
  — Storage
  — Trade-marks
  — Transportation
    xx Tank trucks
Chemicals, Paper
  See Paper chemicals
Chemicals, Photographic
  See Photographic chemicals
Chemicals, Rubber
  See Rubber chemicals
Chemicals, Textile
  See Textile chemicals
Chemiculture
  See Hydroponics
Chemigraph
  xx Photomechanical processes
Chemiluminescence
  xx Luminescence
Chemiotaxis
  See Chemotaxis
Chemisorption
  xx Adsorption
CHEMIST (Computer program)

Chemistry *(QD)*

Here are entered only works treating of both organic and inorganic chemistry. Thus a book on inorganic and physical chemistry is not entered here, but under 1. Chemistry, Inorganic. 2. Chemistry, Physical and theoretical.

sa Acids
Agricultural chemistry
Alchemy
Assaying
Bases (Chemistry)
Biological chemistry
Botanical chemistry
Catalysis
Coacervation
Color
Combustion
Condensation
Cosmochemistry
Crystallization
Crystallography
Decomposition (Chemistry)
Dental chemistry
Dilution
Dissociation
Electrochemistry
Evaporation
Explosives
Fermentation
Fire
Foundry chemistry
Gases—Liquefaction
Geochemistry
Hot-atom chemistry
Immunochemistry
Liquid air
Masking (Chemistry)
Microchemistry
Pharmacy
Photochemistry
Photographic chemistry
Physiological chemistry
Poisons
Salts
Sanitary chemistry
Solution (Chemistry)
Spectrum analysis
Stereochemistry
Water chemistry
headings beginning with the word
Chemical
xx Science
— Abbreviations
x Chemical abbreviations
— Abstracting and indexing *(QD9)*
Example under Abstracting; Indexing
— Anecdotes, facetiae, satire, etc.
— Apparatus
See Chemical apparatus
— Bibliography *(Z5521-6)*
sa Chemical literature
xx Chemical literature
— — Catalogs
Example under Catalogs
— Bio-bibliography
x Chemists—Bio-bibliography
— Caricatures and cartoons
— Cataloging
See Cataloging of chemical literature
— Classification *(QD467)*
sa Punched card systems—Chemistry
— Computer programs
— Dictionaries, Juvenile
— Early works to 1800 *(QD27)*
— Electromechanical analogies
— Examinations
— Examinations, questions, etc. *(QD42)*

— Experiments *(QD43)*
x Chemistry—Lecture experiments
— — Juvenile literature
— Film catalogs *(QD40)*
— History *(Indirect) (QD11-18)*
sa Alchemy
Chemical literature
— Information services
— Juvenile literature *(QD35)*
— Laboratories
See Chemical laboratories
— Laboratory blanks *(QD45)*
— Laboratory manuals *(QD45)*
sa Chemistry, Clinical—Laboratory
manuals
Chemistry, Inorganic—Laboratory
manuals
Chemistry, Medical and
pharmaceutical—Laboratory
manuals
Chemistry, Organic—Laboratory
manuals
Glass blowing and working
Indicators and test-papers
Physiological chemistry—Laboratory
manuals
— Lecture experiments
See Chemistry—Experiments
— Literature
See Chemical literature
— Manipulation *(QD61)*
sa Blowpipe
Distillation, Fractional
Electric furnaces
Glass blowing and working
x Chemical manipulation
xx Chemical apparatus
Filters and filtration
— Mathematics
— Models
See Chemical models
— Nomenclature *(QD7)*
sa subdivision Nomenclature *under*
groups of compounds, e.g.
Hydrocarbons—Nomenclature
x Chemical nomenclature
Chemical symbols
— Notation *(QD7)*
sa Chemical equations
x Chemical formulae
Chemical symbols
Example under reference from Symbols
(in science, technology, etc.)
— — Programmed instruction
— Philosophy
— Phlogiston *(QD14; QD27)*
x Phlogiston
— Problems, exercises, etc. *(QD42)*
sa Chemical engineering—Problems,
exercises, etc.
x Stoichiometry
— Programmed instruction
— Punched card systems
See Punched card systems—Chemistry
— Research
See Chemical research
— Societies, etc.
xx Chemical societies
— Statistical methods
— Study and teaching *(QD40-45)*
— Study and teaching *(Direct)*
(QD40-45)
— — Audio-visual aids
— Study and teaching (Elementary)
— Study and teaching (Higher) *(Direct)*
— — Audio-visual aids
— Study and teaching (Secondary)
— Subject headings

See Subject headings—Chemistry
— Tables, etc. *(QD65)*
— Terminology
— Translating
Chemistry, Agricultural
See Agricultural chemistry
Chemistry, Analytic *(QD71-142)*
sa Archaeological chemistry
Chromatographic analysis
Colorimetric analysis
Electrolysis
Enzymatic analysis
Fluorimetry
Indicators and test-papers
Instrumental analysis
Iodometry
Metallurgical analysis
Mineralogy, Determinative
Phosphorimetry
Polarograph and polarography
Radioactivation analysis
Radiochemical analysis
Separation (Technology)
Spectrophotometry
subdivisions Analysis *and* Analysis and
chemistry *under special subjects, e.g.*
Gases—Analysis; Mercury—
Analysis; Rocks—Analysis; Blood—
Analysis and chemistry; Flour—
Analysis and chemistry
x Analysis (Chemistry)
Analytical chemistry
Chemical analysis
xx Metallurgical analysis
Mineralogy, Determinative
— Automation
— Laboratory manuals
— Qualitative *(QD81-95)*
sa Blowpipe
Spectrum analysis
Spot tests (Chemistry)
x Qualitative analysis
xx Blowpipe
— — Atlases
— Quantitative *(QD101-142)*
sa Distillation, Fractional
Electrochemical analysis
Heterometry
Thermogravimetry
Volumetric analysis
x Gravimetric analysis
Quantitative analysis
— Statistical methods
— Tables, etc.
Chemistry, Animal
See Physiological chemistry
Chemistry, Archaeological
See Archaeological chemistry
Chemistry, Biological
See Biological chemistry
Chemistry, Botanical
See Botanical chemistry
Chemistry, Clinical
sa Body fluids—Analysis
x Clinical chemistry
xx Chemistry, Medical and pharmaceutical
Pathology
— Automation
— Laboratory manuals
xx Chemistry—Laboratory manuals
— Notation
— Tables, etc.
Chemistry, Dairy
See Dairy bacteriology
Chemistry, Dental
See Dental chemistry

Chemistry, Forensic (HV8073; Medical
         jurisprudence, RA1057)
    sa Medical jurisprudence
       Poisons
     x Chemistry, Legal
       Forensic chemistry
       Legal chemistry
    xx Criminal investigation
       Medical jurisprudence
       Poisons
   — Laboratory manuals
Chemistry, Foundry
    See Foundry chemistry
Chemistry, Industrial
    See Chemical engineering
       Chemistry, Technical
Chemistry, Inorganic (QD151-199)
    sa Earths, Rare
       Electric furnaces
       Metals
       groups and classes of inorganic
         compounds, e.g. Acids, Inorganic;
         Alkalies; Borides; Carbides;
         Chlorides; Platinum group; Salts,
         Double
     x Inorganic chemistry
    Note under Chemistry
   — Laboratory manuals (QD45)
       xx Chemistry—Laboratory manuals
   — Nomenclature
   — Programmed instruction
   — Study and teaching
   — — Audio-visual aids
   — Synthesis
   — Tables (QD155.5)
Chemistry, Legal
    See Chemistry, Forensic
Chemistry, Medical and pharmaceutical
         (RS402-431)
    sa Chemistry, Clinical
       Disinfection and disinfectants
       Drugs
       Incompatibles (Pharmacy)
       Materia medica
       Medical technologists
       Pharmacy
       Poisonous plants
       Poisons
       Structure-activity relationship
         (Pharmacology)
     x Chemistry, Pathological
       Chemistry, Pharmaceutical
       Medical chemistry
       Pathological chemistry
       Pharmaceutical chemistry
    xx Medicine
       Pharmacology
       Pharmacy
       Physiological chemistry
       Therapeutics
   — Laboratory manuals (RS407)
       xx Chemistry—Laboratory manuals
          Pharmacy—Laboratory manuals
Chemistry, Metallurgic (QD133)
     x Metallurgic chemistry
    xx Chemistry, Technical
Chemistry, Mineralogical
    See Mineralogical chemistry
Chemistry, Nuclear
    See Nuclear chemistry
Chemistry, Organic (QD248-449)
    sa Carbon compounds
       Chemistry, Physical organic
       Condensation products (Chemistry)
       Etard's reaction
       Organic bases
       Organic geochemistry
       Organic water pollutants

Radicals (Chemistry)
Stereochemistry
Surface active agents
names of classes of organic compounds,
    e.g. Acids, Organic; Alcohols;
    Aldehydes; Alicyclic compounds;
    Alkaloids; Amines; Carbohydrates;
    Diazo compounds; Essences and
    essential oils; Esters; Ethers;
    Glucosides; Heterocyclic compounds;
    Ketones; Organometallic compounds;
    Proteins; Ptomaines; Sugars;
    Terpenes; and names of individual
    organic substances, e.g. Aniline,
    Benzene.
     x Organic chemistry
    xx Physiological chemistry
       Stereochemistry
Note under Carbon compounds
— Charts, diagrams, etc.
— Experiments (QD261)
— Laboratory manuals (QD261)
    xx Chemistry—Laboratory manuals
— Nomenclature (QD291)
— — Programmed instruction
— Programmed instruction
— Synthesis (QD262)
    sa Biosynthesis
       Kolbe reaction
       Perkin reaction
       Plastics
       Polymers and polymerization
       Quinoidation
       Synthetic products
     x Chemistry, Synthetic
       Synthetic chemistry
    xx Plastics
— Tables, etc. (QD291)
Chemistry, Pathological
    See Chemistry, Medical and pharmaceutical
       Physiological chemistry
Chemistry, Pharmaceutical
    See Chemistry, Medical and pharmaceutical
Chemistry, Photographic
    See Photographic chemistry
Chemistry, Physical and theoretical
         (QD453-651)
    sa Absorption
       Acids—Basicity
       Adsorption
       Allotropy
       Atomic mass
       Atomic theory
       Atomic volume
       Atomic weights
       Atoms
       Biochemorphology
       Boiling-points
       Catalysis
       Chemical affinity
       Chemical bonds
       Chemical equilibrium
       Chemical evolution
       Chemical reaction, Conditions and laws
         of
       Chemical reaction, Rate of
       Chemistry, Physical organic
       Colloids
       Coordination compounds
       Critical point
       Cryoscopy
       Crystallization
       Crystallography
       Dipole moments
       Dissociation
       Electrochemistry
       Electrolysis
       Electrolytes—Conductivity

Electronegativity
Equations of state
Flocculation
Gases—Liquefaction
Hydrogen bonding
Instrumental analysis
Ions—Migration and velocity
Isomerism
Liquid air
Mass transfer
Melting points
Molecular association
Molecular theory
Molecular weights
Nuclear chemistry
Nuclear physics
Nucleation
Periodic law
Phase rule and equilibrium
Photochemistry
Polymers and polymerization
Quantum chemistry
Quantum theory
Radiation chemistry
Radiochemistry
Solid state chemistry
Solubility
Solution (Chemistry)
Stereochemistry
Sulphur bonding
Surface chemistry
Thermochemistry
Thermodynamics
Valence (Theoretical chemistry)
Vapor density
Virial coefficients
     x Chemistry, Theoretical
       Physical chemistry
       Stoichiometry
       Theoretical chemistry
    xx Matter—Properties
       Nuclear physics
       Physics
       Quantum theory
       Stereochemistry
Note under Chemistry
— Abbreviations
— Charts, diagrams, etc.
— Examinations, questions, etc. (QD456)
— Graphic methods
— Laboratory manuals (QD457)
— Mathematics (QD455.3.M3)
— Notation (QD451.5)
— Problems, exercises, etc.
— Programmed instruction
— Terminology
Chemistry, Physical organic (QD476)
     x Physical organic chemistry
    xx Chemistry, Organic
       Chemistry, Physical and theoretical
— Experiments
— Problems, exercises, etc.
Chemistry, Physiological
    See Physiological chemistry
Chemistry, Quantum
    See Quantum chemistry
Chemistry, Sanitary
    See Sanitary chemistry
Chemistry, Soil
    See Soil chemistry
Chemistry, Solid state
    See Solid state chemistry
Chemistry, Surface
    See Surface chemistry
Chemistry, Synthetic
    See Chemistry, Organic—Synthesis
Chemistry, Technical (TP)
    sa Adulterations

302

Alloys
Animal products
Biochemical engineering
Bleaching
Canning and preserving
Ceramics
Chemical engineering
Chemical industries
Chemical reactors
Chemicals—Manufacture and industry
Chemistry, Metallurgic
Chemurgy
Cleaning compounds
Concrete—Chemistry
Corrosion and anti-corrosives
Cracking process
Distillation, Destructive
Drying agents
Electrochemistry
Extraction (Chemistry)
Flour—Analysis and chemistry
Food—Analysis
Gas chromatography—Industrial
    applications
Grain—Analysis and chemistry
Gums and resins
Gums and resins, Synthetic
High pressure (Technology)
Metallurgical analysis
Oxygen—Industrial applications
Photochemistry—Industrial applications
Radiochemistry—Industrial applications
Refrigerants
Rubber chemistry
Separation (Technology)
Synthetic products
Tanning
Textile chemistry
Waste products
Wine and wine making—Analysis
Wood—Chemistry
Workshop receipts
    particular industries and products, e.g.
      Alkali industry and trade; Brewing
      industry; Chlorine industry; Clay
      industries; Coal-tar products; Dyes
      and dyeing; Explosives; Gas
      manufacture and works; Paint;
      Perfumes
  x Chemical technology
    Chemistry, Industrial
    Industrial chemistry
    Technical chemistry
  xx Chemical engineering
    Chemicals—Manufacture and industry
    Metallurgy
    Technology
— Charts, diagrams, etc.
— Formulae, receipts, prescriptions
    (TP151)
— Laboratory manuals
— Problems, exercises, etc.
— Research   *(Direct) (TP165)*
  sa Chemical engineering laboratories
    Gas research
  xx Chemical research
    Research, Industrial
— Tables, etc.   *(TP151)*
Chemistry, Textile
  See Textile chemistry
Chemistry, Theoretical
  See Chemistry, Physical and theoretical
Chemistry as a profession
  sa Biological chemistry as a profession
    Chemists
  xx Chemists
Chemistry in warfare
  See Chemical warfare

Chemistry of concrete
  See Concrete—Chemistry
Chemistry of food
  See Food—Analysis
    Food—Composition
Chemists   *(Direct) (QD21-22)*
  sa Alchemists
    Chemical engineers
    Chemistry as a profession
    Pharmacists
  xx Chemical engineers
    Chemical workers
    Chemistry as a profession
    Scientists
  Note under Manpower
— Anecdotes, facetiae, satire, etc.
— Bio-bibliography
    See Chemistry—Bio-bibliography
— Biography
— — Juvenile literature
— Correspondence, reminiscences, etc.
— Fees
— Legal status, laws, etc.   *(Direct)*
Chemists, American, ⌈**British, French, etc.**⌉
  x American ⌈British, French, etc.⌉
    chemists
— Biography
— Correspondence, reminiscences, etc.
— Juvenile literature
Chemodectoma
  See Nonchromaffin paraganglioma
Chemoreceptors
  xx Sense-organs
Chemosphere   *(QC881)*
  sa Mesosphere
    Stratosphere
  xx Atmosphere, Upper
    Photochemistry
Chemostat
  xx Bacteriology—Apparatus and supplies
Chemosterilization of insects
  See Insect chemosterilization
Chemosurgery
  sa Cancer—Excision
  xx Surgery
Chemotaxis
  x Chemiotaxis
  xx Growth
    Physiological chemistry
Chemotaxonomy   *(QH83)*
  x Biochemical systematics
    Chemical taxonomy
  xx Biological chemistry
    Biology—Classification
    Phylogeny
Chemotherapy   *(RM663)*
  sa Anti-infective agents
    Antibiotics
    Anticholesteremic agents
    Antitubercular agents
    Antitussive agents
    Antiviral agents
    Immunosuppressive agents
    Lipotropic agents
    Psychopharmacology
    Pyrogens
    subdivision Chemotherapy *under*
      diseases, e.g. Cancer—Chemotherapy
  x Drug therapy
  xx Anti-infective agents
— Laboratory manuals
Chemurgics
  See Chemurgy
Chemurgy   *(TP371)*
  sa Synthetic products
  x Chemurgics
  xx Agricultural chemistry
    Agriculture

Chemistry, Technical
  Synthetic products
— Abstracts
Chen caerulescens (Linnaeus)
  See Blue goose
Chên k'ung Chiao   *(Direct) (BL1943.C5L6)*
  xx Religions
Cheng (Musical instrument)
  xx Musical instruments, Chinese
    Zither
Cheng music   *(M142.C49)*
  xx Zither music
Chengtu Incident, 1936
  xx Sino-Japanese Conflict, 1937-1945—
    Causes
Chenopodium oil   *(RM666.C38; RS165.C35)*
  x American wormseed-oil
    Wormseed-oil
Chepang language   *(PL3801.C5)*
  xx Tibeto-Burman languages
Chepewyan Indians
  See Chipewyan Indians
Cheras   *(DS451)*
  x Ceras
  xx India—History—To 324 B.C.
    Tamils
— Juvenile literature
Cheraw Indians   *(E99.C)*
  x Saura Indians
  xx Indians of North America
    Siouan Indians
Cheremis language
  See Cheremissian language
Cheremisses   *(DK34.C5)*
  sa Folk-lore, Cheremissian
  x Tcheremisses
  xx Ethnology—Russia
    Finno-Ugrians
Cheremissian drama   *(Direct) (Collections,*
    PH825; History, PH812)
Cheremissian fiction   *(Direct)*
Cheremissian language   *(PH801-7)*
  x Cheremis language
    Mari language
    Marii language
    Tcheremissian language
  xx Finno-Ugrian languages
Cheremissian literature   *(Direct)*
    (PH811-836)
Cheremissian philology
Cheremissian poetry   *(Direct) (Collections,*
    PH824; History, PH812)
Cheren, Battle of, 1941   *(D766.84)*
  x Keren, Battle of, 1941
  xx World War, 1939-1945—Campaigns—
    Africa, East
Cherenkov counters
  x Cherenkov detectors
  xx Cherenkov radiation
    Nuclear counters
Cherenkov detectors
  See Cherenkov counters
Cherenkov light
  See Cherenkov radiation
Cherenkov radiation   *(QC490)*
  sa Cherenkov counters
  x Cerenkov radiation
    Cherenkov light
  xx Optics
    Radiation
Cheribon agreement, 1946   *(DS644)*
  x Linggardjati agreement
Cherifs
  See Sherifs
Cheriton, Eng., Battle of, 1644   *(DA417)*
Cherkassy, Battle of, 1944
  xx World War, 1939-1945—Campaigns—
    Russia

Cherkess language
　　See Circassian language
Chernozem soils *(S598)*
　　x Black earth
　　xx Soils
Cherokee Indian Removal, 1838
　　See Cherokee Removal, 1838
Cherokee Indians *(E99.C5)*
　　sa Five Civilized Tribes
　　　Rechahecrian Indians
　　xx Five Civilized Tribes
　　　Indians of North America
　　　Iroquoian Indians
　　— Wars, 1759-1761　*(E83.759)*
　　　xx Indians of North America—Wars—
　　　　1750-1815
　　— Government relations
　　　sa Cherokee Removal, 1838
　　— Juvenile literature
　　— Land transfers
　　　sa Cherokee Removal, 1838
　　— Law
　　　　See Law, Cherokee
　　— Legal status, laws, etc.
　　　　Example under Indians—Legal status,
　　　　　laws, etc; Indians of North America
　　　　　—Legal status, laws, etc.
　　　　Note under Indians—Legal status, laws,
　　　　　etc.
　　— Registers
　　— Taxation
　　　　Example under Indians of North America
　　　　　—Taxation
Cherokee language　*(PM781-4)*
　　sa Iroquoian languages
　　xx Iroquoian languages
Cherokee law
　　See Law, Cherokee
Cherokee poetry
　　xx Indian poetry
　　　Poetry
Cherokee Removal, 1838
　　x Cherokee Indian Removal, 1838
　　　Trail of Tears, 1838
　　xx Cherokee Indians—Government
　　　　relations
　　　Cherokee Indians—Land transfers
Cherries, Flowering
　　See Flowering cherries
Cherry　*(Indirect)　(SB379.C5)*
　　sa Cookery (Cherries)
　　　Sour cherry
　　　Sweet cherry
　　Example under Fruit trees
　　— Diseases and pests　*(SB608.C43)*
　　　sa names of pests, e.g. Cherry fruit-fly
　　— Grading
　　— Harvesting
　　— Juvenile literature
　　— Marketing
　　— Prices　*(Direct)*
　　— Standards　*(Direct)*
　　— Storage
　　— Tariff
　　　　See Tariff on cherries
Cherry, Japanese
　　See Japanese flowering cherry
Cherry fruit-fly
　　Example under Cherry—Diseases and pests
Cherry fruit sawfly
　　Example under Sawflies
Cherry fruit worm
Cherry leaf-beetle　*(SB945.C45)*
Cherry plum　*(SB377)*
　　x Myrobalan plum
　　xx Plum
　　— Varieties
Cherry Valley, N.Y.

— Massacre, 1778
　　x Cherry Valley Massacre, 1778
— — Juvenile literature
Cherry Valley Massacre, 1778
　　See Cherry Valley, N.Y.—Massacre, 1778
Chert　*(QE391.C4)*
　　sa Novaculite
　　　Taconite
　　x Hornstone
　　　Rock-flint
　　xx Novaculite
Cherubim
　　See Angels
Chesapeake Bay
　　— Poetry
　　　　Note under Poetry of places
Chesapeake Bay bugeyes
　　See Bugeyes (Boats)
Chesapeake Bay dogs
　　See Chesapeake Bay retrievers
Chesapeake Bay retrievers　*(SF429.C4)*
　　x Chesapeake Bay dogs
　　xx Retrievers
Chesapeake-Leopard Affair, 1807　*(E357.3)*
Chesica　*(GV1469)*
Chess　*(GV1313-1457)*
　　sa Checkmate (Chess)
　　　Chess players, Rating of
　　　Chessmen
　　　King (Chess)
　　　Knight (Chess)
　　　Pawn (Chess)
　　　Rook (Chess)
　　xx Mathematical recreations
　　Example under Board games; Games
　　— Anecdotes, facetiae, satire, etc.
　　— Biography
　　— — Juvenile literature
　　— Collections of games　*(GV1452)*
　　　sa Chess—Tournaments
　　　x Chess games
　　— Combinations
　　　　See Chess—Middle games
　　— Congresses　*(GV1314)*
　　　　For chess congresses which are in ef-
　　　　fect tournaments use subdivision
　　　　Tournaments.
　　— Early works to 1800
　　— End games　*(GV1450.7)*
　　— Juvenile literature　*(GV1446)*
　　— Middle games　*(GV1450.3)*
　　　x Chess—Combinations
　　　　Chess—Sacrifices
　　— Openings　*(GV1450)*
　　　x Chess openings
　　— Pictorial works
　　— Problems
　　　　See Chess problems
　　— Programmed instruction
　　— Psychology　*(GV1448)*
　　— Rules　*(GV1457)*
　　— Sacrifices
　　　　See Chess—Middle games
　　— Terminology
　　— Tournaments　*(Direct)　(GV1455)*
　　　　Individual tournaments by date.
　　　xx Chess—Collections of games
　　— Variants　*(GV1458)*
　　　sa Chinese chess
　　　　Military chess
　　　　Shogi
Chess (Grass)
　　See Brome-grass
Chess games
　　See Chess—Collections of games
Chess men
　　See Chessmen

Chess openings
　　See Chess—Openings
Chess players, Rating of
　　x Rating of chess players
　　xx Chess
Chess problems　*(GV1451)*
　　sa Fairy chess
　　x Chess—Problems
Chessmen　*(NK9990.C4)*
　　sa King (Chess)
　　　Knight (Chess)
　　　Pawn (Chess)
　　　Rook (Chess)
　　x Chess men
　　xx Chess
Chest
　　sa Aorta
　　　Heart
　　　Lungs
　　　Mediastinum
　　　Pericardium
　　　Pleura
　　　Respiratory organs
　　x Thorax
　　xx Respiratory organs
　　　Viscera
　　— Abnormities and deformities　*(RD766)*
　　— Diseases　*(RC941)*
　　　sa Chest—Radiography
　　　　Tuberculosis
　　　xx Heart—Diseases
　　　　Lungs—Diseases
　　　　Pleura—Diseases
　　　　Respiratory organs—Diseases
　　— — Cases, clinical reports, statistics
　　— — Diagnosis　*(RC941)*
　　　sa Auscultation
　　　　Percussion
　　　x Chest—Exploration
　　　xx Auscultation
　　— — Eclectic treatment　*(RV293)*
　　— — Homeopathic treatment　*(RX360)*
　　— Exploration
　　　　See Chest—Diseases—Diagnosis
　　— Paracentesis　*(RD536)*
　　　x Thoracentesis
　　　xx Aspiration and aspirators
　　　Example under Paracentesis
　　— Radiography
　　　xx Chest—Diseases
　　— — Programmed instruction
　　— Surgery　*(RD536)*
　　　x Thoracic surgery
　　　Example under Surgery, Operative
　　— Tumors　*(RC280.C; RD667)*
　　— Wounds and injuries　*(RD536)*
　　　Example under Surgery; Traumatism;
　　　　Wounds; *and under reference from*
　　　　Injuries
　　— — Mathematical models
Chest weights　*(GV515)*
　　x Pulley weights
　　xx Gymnastics
Chester White swine　*(SF393.C5)*
　　Example under Swine breeds
Chestnut　*(Indirect)　(SD397.C5)*
　　Example under Nuts
　　— Disease and pest resistance
　　— Diseases and pests　*(SB608.C45)*
　　　sa names of pests, e.g. Chestnut-borer
Chestnut-blight　*(SB608.C45)*
Chestnut-borer　*(SB608.C45)*
　　Example under Chestnut—Diseases and pests
Chestnut-collared swift
　　xx Swifts
Chestnut Hill, Battle of, 1777　*(E241.C52)*
Chestnut oak　*(SD397.O12)*
　　xx Oak

Chestnut-sided warbler
  xx Wood warblers
Chestnut-weevil *(SB608.C45)*
  xx Beetles
  Example under Nuts—Diseases and pests
Chests *(Direct)* *(Art, NK2725;*
    Cabinet-work, TT197)
  x Caskets
    Coffers
  xx Dining room furniture
    Furniture
  — Juvenile literature
Chetahs
  See Cheetahs
Chetas
  See Cheetahs
Chetco Indians *(E99.C526)*
  x Chetkoe Indians
  xx Athapascan Indians
    Indians of North America
Chetkoe Indians
  See Chetco Indians
Chevelle automobile *(TL215.C)*
  xx Chevrolet automobile
Cheviot sheep *(SF375)*
Chevrolet automobile *(TL215.C5)*
  sa Camaro automobile
    Chevelle automobile
    Chevy II automobile
    Corvair automobile
    Corvette automobile
    El Camino automobile
    Monte Carlo automobile
    Nova automobile
    Vega automobile
  Example under Automobiles
Chevrons *(UC530-535)*
  xx Uniforms, Military
Chevy Chase, Battle of, 1388
  See Otterburn, Battle of, 1388
Chevy II automobile *(TL215.C)*
  xx Chevrolet automobile
Chewa (African tribe)
  x Maravi (African tribe)
  xx Ethnology—Malawi
Chewa dialect *(PL8110.C5)*
  sa Nyanja language
  x Cewa dialect
    Chichewa dialect
  xx Bantu languages
    Nyanja language
Chewing
  See Mastication
Chewing-gum
  sa Bubble gum
Cheyenne Indians *(E99.C53)*
  xx Algonquian Indians
    Indians of North America
  — Juvenile literature
  — Pictorial works
  — Wars
    sa Fetterman Fight, 1866
  — Wars, 1864 *(E83.863)*
    sa Sand Creek, Battle of, 1864
  — Wars, 1876 *(E83.866)*
    sa Dakota Indians—Wars, 1876
      Little Big Horn, Battle of the, 1876
    xx Dakota Indians—Wars, 1876
      Indians of North America—Wars—
      1866-1895
Cheyenne language *(PM795)*
  xx Algonquian languages
Cheyenne law
  See Law, Cheyenne
Chi-chifundi dialect
  See Cifundi dialect
Chi language
  See Tshi language

Chi Rho monogram
  See Chi Rho symbol
Chi Rho symbol *(BV168.C4)*
  x Chi Rho monogram
    Chirho symbol
    Chrismon
    Christogram
  xx Monograms
    Symbolism
Chi-square test
  xx Statistical hypothesis testing
  — Programmed instruction
Chi-Tonga language
  See Tonga language (Nyasa)
Chi-yao language
  See Yao language
Chiam tribe
  See Chams
Chiamacoco Indians
  See Chamacoco Indians
Ch'iang people *(DS731.C)*
  xx Ethnology—China—Szechwan
Chianti wine *(TP559.I8)*
  xx Wine and wine making
Chiapanec Indians *(F1221.C5)*
  x Chapanec Indians
    Chiapas Indians
  xx Indians of Mexico
Chiapanec language *(PM3618)*
  x Chapanec language
Chiapas Indians
  See Chiapanec Indians
Chiaroscuro *(NC755)*
  sa Light in art
  x Clairobscur
  xx Art—Technique
    Color prints
    Light in art
    Painting—Technique
    Wood-engraving
Chibcha calendar
  See Calendar, Chibcha
Chibcha Indians *(F2270.2.C4)*
  sa Guaymi Indians
    Ijca Indians
    Muzo Indians
    Tunebo Indians
  x Moscas
    Muiscas
    Muysca Indians
  xx Indians of South America
  — Legends
Chibcha language *(PM5811)*
  xx Chibchan languages
    Indians of South America—Languages
Chibchan languages *(PM5811)*
  sa Bribri dialect
    Chibcha language
    Kagaba language
    Talamanca language
    Terraba language
  xx Bribri dialect
    Indians of South America—Languages
Chibemba language
  See Bemba language
Chicachas Indians
  See Chickasaw Indians
Chicago
  — Bathing beaches
    Example under Bathing beaches
  — Fire, 1871
  — — Juvenile literature
  — — Pictorial works
  — Fire, 1866
  — Foreign population
    Example under reference from Foreign-
    ers

  — Haymarket Square Riot, 1886
    (HX846.C4)
    x Haymarket Square Riot, 1886
  — — Juvenile literature
  — History *(F548)*
  — — To 1875
  — — — Juvenile literature
  — — Civil War, 1861-1865 *(F548.4)*
  — — 1875-
  — Libraries
    Example under Libraries
  — Lighting
    Example under Lighting; Municipal light-
      ing; Street-lighting
  — Manufactures
    Example under Manufactures
  — Massacre, 1812 *(E356.C53)*
    x Fort Dearborn Massacre, 1812
    Example under Massacres
  — Riot, 1919
  — Riot, April 1968
  — Riot, August 1968
  — Stock-yards
    Example under Stock-yards
Chicago. Charters
  Example under Charters; Municipal charters
Chicago. Municipal Court
  Example under Municipal courts
Chicago. University
  — Curricula
    Example under Education—Curricula;
      and under references from Courses
      of study; Curricula (Courses of
      study); Study, Courses of
  — Faculty
    Example under Universities and colleges
      —Faculty; *and under reference*
      from Faculty (Education)
Chicago. World's Columbian Exposition,
  1893
  Example under Exhibitions; *and under refer-*
    ence from International exhibitions
Chicago (Game)
  See Chicago bridge (Game)
Chicago bridge (Game)
  x Chicago (Game)
  xx Contract bridge
Chicago in literature
Chicago-Lambeth Quadrilateral
  See Lambeth Quadrilateral
Chicago Strike, 1894 *(HD5325.R12 1894.C5)*
  x American Railway Union Strike, 1894
    Pullman Strike, 1894
Chicanery
  See Deception
Chicanery (International law)
  xx International law
Chicanery (Islamic law) *(Direct)*
Chicanery (Law) *(Direct)*
  sa Evasion (Law)
  xx Evasion (Law)
    Torts
Chicano literature
  See American literature—Mexican
    American authors
Chicanos
  See Mexican Americans
Chicasa Indians
  See Chickasaw Indians
Chich
  See Chick-pea
Chich-pea
  See Chick-pea
Chicha (Liquor)
Chichacha Indians
  See Chickasaw Indians
Chichewa dialect
  See Chewa dialect

Chichibu Peasant Uprising, 1884 *(DS882.5)*
— Pictorial works
Chichimeca-Jonaz Indians *(F1221.C53)*
   x Jonaz-Chichimeca Indians
     Meco Indians
   xx Chichimecs
     Indians of Mexico
Chichimecs *(F1219)*
   sa Chichimeca-Jonaz Indians
   xx Indians of Mexico
Chick bronchitis, Infectious
   See Infectious bronchitis in poultry
Chick embryo
   xx Embryology—Birds
     Poultry
— Atlases
— Juvenile literature
Chick-pea *(Indirect)*
   x Chich
     Chich-pea
     Dwarf pea
     Garavance
     Gram (Legume)
   xx Legumes
Chickadees *(QL696.P2)*
   sa Black-capped chickadee
     Brown-headed chickadee
     Carolina chickadee
Chickamauga, Battle of, 1863 *(E475.81)*
Chickasaw Indians *(E99.C55)*
   sa Five Civilized Tribes
   x Chicachas Indians
     Chicasa Indians
     Chichacha Indians
     Chickesaw Indians
     Chikasaw Indians
   xx Five Civilized Tribes
     Indians of North America
     Muskhogean Indians
— Government relations
— Land tenure
— Law
     See Law, Chickasaw
— Legal status, laws, etc.
— Tribal citizenship
     xx Law, Chickasaw
     Example under reference from Citizen-
       ship, Tribal; Tribal citizenship
     Example under Indians of North America
       —Citizenship; *and under references*
       from Citizenship, Tribal; Tribal citi-
       zenship
     Note under Indians of North America—
       Citizenship
— Wars, 1739-1740 *(E83.739)*
     xx Indians of North America—Wars—
       1600-1750
Chickasaw language
   xx Muskhogean languages
Chickasaw law
   See Law, Chickasaw
Chicken cholera *(SF995)*
   xx Poultry—Diseases
Chicken coops
   See Poultry houses and equipment
Chicken-mite *(SF995)*
Chicken-pox *(RJ406.C4)*
   sa Varicella-zoster virus
   x Varicella
   xx Herpesvirus diseases
   Example under Children—Diseases
— Juvenile literature
Chicken-pox in poultry *(SF995)*
   x Fowl pox
   xx Poultry—Diseases
Chicken-pox virus
   See Varicella-zoster virus

Chickens
   See Poultry
Chickens (in religion, folk-lore, etc.)
   x Folk-lore of chickens
   xx Religion, Primitive
Chickesaw Indians
   See Chickasaw Indians
Chicle-gum *(SB289-291)*
Chicory *(Indirect)* *(Agriculture, SB211.C5;*
     Vegetables, SB351.C5)
   sa Belgian endive
   x Blue dandelion
     Blue sailor (Plant)
     Coffee weed
     Succory
Chief justices
   See Judges
Chief Rabbinate *(Direct)*
   xx Judaism
     Rabbis
Chien ware
   See Chien yao ware
Chien yao ware
   x Chien ware
     Temmoku ware
   xx Pottery, Chinese
Chievitz's organ
   x Juxtaoral organ
   xx Parotid glands
Chifundi dialect
   See Cifundi dialect
Chiga (Bantu tribe)
   xx Ethnology—Uganda
Chiga language
   See Kiga language
Chigga
   See Chigoe
Chiggers (Mites) *(QL458.A2)*
   x Jiggers (Mites)
     Trombiculinae
— Control *(Indirect)*
     xx Mite control
Chiglit language
   See Kopagmiut language
Chigoe *(Fleas, QL503.A7; Mites, QL458.A2)*
   x Chigga
     Jigger
Chigogo language
   See Gogo language
Chihamba
   xx Ndembu (African tribe)—Rites and
     ceremonies
     Religion, Primitive
Chihuahua dogs *(SF429.C45)*
Chihuahua Expedition, 1846-1847
   See Doniphan's Expedition, 1846-1847
Chikasaw Indians
   See Chickasaw Indians
Chil-way-uk dialect
   See Chilliwack dialect
Chilblains *(RL271)*
   xx Cold—Physiological effect
     Frostbite
Chilcotin Indians
   See Tsilkotin Indians
Child abuse
   See Cruelty to children
Child analysis
   x Child psychoanalysis
   xx Child psychotherapy
     Psychoanalysis
— Cases, clinical reports, statistics
Child and father
   See Father and child
Child and mother
   See Mother and child
Child and parent
   See Parent and child

Child birth
   See Childbirth
Child care centers
   See Child welfare
     Day nurseries
     Foster day care
Child development
   See Child study
     Children—Growth
Child discipline
   See Discipline of children
Child endowment
   See Family allowances
Child feeding behavior
   See Children—Nutrition—Psychological
     aspects
Child guidance centers
   See Child guidance clinics
Child guidance clinics *(Direct)*
   x Child guidance centers
   xx Child psychiatry
     Child study
     Child welfare
     Juvenile delinquency
     Problem children
     Psychiatric social work
Child health
   See Child welfare
     Children—Care and hygiene
Child insurance
   See Insurance, Child
Child Jesus, Devotion to
   See Holy Childhood, Devotion to
Child labor
   See Children—Employment
     Youth—Employment
Child labor in literature
   xx Children—Employment
     Children in literature
     Youth in literature
Child marriage *(Direct)*
   x Marriage, Child
   xx Marriage
Child mental health *(Indirect)* *(RJ111)*
   sa Child psychiatry
   x Pediatric mental health
   xx Child psychiatry
     Child study
     Mental hygiene
— Evaluation *(Indirect)* *(RJ111)*
Child minders
   See Foster day care
Child molesting
   xx Pedophilia
     Sex crimes
Child placing
   See Adoption
     Foster home care
Child psychiatry *(Indirect)* *(RJ499)*
   sa Adolescent psychiatry
     Child guidance clinics
     Child mental health
     Child psychotherapy
     Children of the mentally ill
     Mentally handicapped children
     Mentally ill children
     Schizophrenia in children
     School phobia
   x Pediatric psychiatry
     Psychiatry, Child
   xx Child mental health
     Child study
     Pediatric neurology
     Psychiatry
— Cases, clinical reports, statistics
— Classification
     xx Nosology
— Juvenile literature

Child psychoanalysis
  See Child analysis
Child psychology
  See Child study
Child psychotherapy
  sa Child analysis
     Play therapy
  xx Child psychiatry
     Psychotherapy
  — Cases, clinical reports, statistics
  — Residential treatment
       x Residential treatment of disturbed
            children
      xx Children—Institutional care
Child rearing
  See Children—Management
Child research
  See Children—Research
Child study *(LB1101-1139; Child in the
     family, HQ771-785; Child life,
     HQ781-5; Child psychology, BF721;
     Somatology, GN63)*
  sa Adolescence
     Adolescent psychology
     Aggressiveness (Child psychology)
     Anxiety (Child psychology)
     Brothers and sisters
     Child guidance clinics
     Child mental health
     Child psychiatry
     Childishness
     Children, Adopted—Testing
     Children and animals
     Children and death
     Children and strangers
     Children, First-born
     Children's accidents
     Children's dreams
     Children's questions and answers
     Cognition (Child psychology)
     Comic books and children
     Creative ability (Child psychology)
     Critical periods (Biology)
     Curiosity (Child psychology)
     Discipline of children
     Education, Preschool
     Educational psychology
     Emotional problems of children
     Exceptional children
     Father-separated children
     Fear (Child psychology)
     Frustration (Child psychology)
     Geometry concept
     Gesell incomplete man test
     Handicapped children
     Head banging
     Imprinting (Psychology)
     Jealousy (Child psychology)
     Kindergarten
     Libraries, Children's
     Mental tests
     Moving-pictures and children
     Moving-pictures in child study
     Only child
     Parent and child
     Parents' and teachers' associations
     Passivity (Child psychology)
     Perception (Child psychology)
     Play
     Playmates
     Prejudices and antipathies (Child
       psychology)
     Problem children
     Problem solving (Child psychology)
     Psychical research and children
     Radio and children
     Reasoning (Child psychology)
     Self-control (Child psychology)

Sick children—Psychology
     Television and children
     Underachievers
     Wechsler intelligence scale for children
     World test
  x Child development
     Child psychology
     Pedology (Child study)
     Psychology, Child
  xx Children
     Developmental psychology
     Education
     Educational psychology
     Genetic psychology
     Kindergarten
     Psychology
     Teaching
  — Cases, clinical reports, statistics
       x Children—Cases, clinical reports,
            statistics
  — Forms, blanks, etc.
  — Juvenile literature
  — Methodology
  — — Examinations, questions, etc.
Child suicide
  See Children—Suicidal behavior
Child vagrants
  See Children, Vagrant
Child welfare *(Direct)* *(HV701-1420)*
     A work dealing with charities for children
       in a given city is entered here and also
       under city, subdivision Charities, *e.g.*
       1. Child welfare—Edinburgh. 2. Edin-
       burgh—Charities.
  sa Abandoned children
     Charity-schools
     Child guidance clinics
     Children—Hospitals
     Children—Institutional care
     Children—Law
     Children, Vagrant
     Cruelty to children
     Day nurseries
     Foster day care
     Foster home care
     Foundlings
     Fresh-air charity
     Juvenile delinquency
     Maternal and infant welfare
     Milk depots
     Mothers' pensions
     Orphans and orphan-asylums
     Play schools
     Playgrounds
     Runaway children
     Unmarried fathers
     Visiting housekeepers
  x A.D.C.
     Aid to dependent children
     Child care centers
     Child health
     Children—Charities
     Children—Protection
     Humane societies
     Protection of children
  xx Charities
     Children—Hospitals
     Juvenile delinquency
     Mothers' pensions
     Orphans and orphan-asylums
     Poor
     Public welfare
     Social work with children
     Social work with youth
  — Forms, blanks, etc.
  — Information services
     Example under Information services
  — Juvenile literature

— Law and legislation
     See Children—Law
  — Outlines, syllabi, etc.
  — Public opinion
  — Research
     xx Social service—Research
  — Terminology

  — Edinburgh
     Note under Child welfare
Childbirth
     Here are entered works on human birth.
       Technical works on the process of la-
       bor and delivery are entered under the
       heading Labor (Obstetrics) Works on
       the system of psychological prepara-
       tion for childbirth, referred to as
       "natural childbirth," are entered under
       the heading Childbirth—Psychology.
  x Birth
     Child birth
  xx Labor (Obstetrics)
     Obstetrics
     Parturition
  — Cases, clinical reports, statistics
  — Juvenile literature
  — Psychology *(RG661)*
       x Childbirth, Natural
            Natural childbirth
      xx Psychology, Applied
          Note under Childbirth
Childbirth, Natural
  See Childbirth—Psychology
Childbirth in literature
Childermas
  See Holy Innocents, Feast of the
Childhood, Holy
  See Holy Childhood, Devotion to
Childhood of Jesus, Devotion to
  See Holy Childhood, Devotion to
Childishness
  sa Infantilism
  xx Age (Psychology)
     Child study
     Infantilism
     Psychology, Physiological
Children *(HQ750-789)*
  sa Abandoned children
     Birth order
     Boys
     Child study
     Church work with children
     City children
     Comic books and children
     Day nurseries
     Domestic education
     Education of children
     Eskimos—Children
     Etiquette for children and youth
     Exceptional children
     Girls
     Heredity
     Hindu children
     Indians of Central America—Children
     Indians of Mexico—Children
     Indians of North America—Children
     Infants
     Jewish children
     Kindergarten
     Maoris—Children
     Moving-pictures and children
     Muslim children
     Negro children
     Newspapers and children
     Oriental children
     Play
     Playgrounds

Children *(HQ750-789)* *(Continued)*
    Prenatal influences
    Radio and children
    Radio programs for children
    Runaway children
    Social work with children
    Stepchildren
    Television and children
    Television programs for children
    Vietnamese Conflict, 1961- —
        Children
    World War, 1939-1945—Children
    Youth
  x Pedology (Child study)
  xx Boys
    Family
    Girls
    Infants
    Youth
— Accidents
  See Children's accidents
— Anecdotes and sayings *(PN6328.C5)*
  sa Wit and humor, Juvenile
  x Children's sayings
    Sayings
  xx Anecdotes
— Asylums
  See Children—Institutional care
— Biblical teaching
  sa Children in the Bible
  xx Children in the Bible
— Biography *(CT107; CT145; etc.)*
  sa Biography—Juvenile literature
    Boys—Biography
    Children in Africa, ₍the United
      States, etc.₎—Biography
    Children in the Bible
    Girls—Biography
    Presidents—United States—Children
  xx Biography—Juvenile literature
    Boys—Biography
    Girls—Biography
— Books and reading
  See Books and reading for children
— Care and hygiene *(RJ61; RJ101)*
  sa Baby sitters
    Children—Diseases
    Children—Medical examinations
    Children—Nutrition
    Children—Preparation for medical
      care
    Children—Sleep
    Community health services for
      children
    Health education
    Infants—Care and hygiene
    Nurses and nursing
    Pediatric nursing
    Physical education for children
    School children—Food
    School hygiene
    School nurses
    Sports for children
  x Child health
    Children—Health
    Children—Hygiene
    Health of children
  xx Hygiene
    Nurses and nursing
    Pediatrics
— — Juvenile literature
— Caricatures and cartoons
— Cases, clinical reports, statistics
  See Child study—Cases, clinical
      reports, statistics
— Charities
  See Child welfare
— Clothing

  See Children's clothing
— Clubs
  See Children's clubs
— Conduct of life *(BJ1631-8)*
— — Juvenile literature
— Constitution
  x Physical constitution of children
  xx Children—Growth
    Man—Constitution
— Conversion to Christianity *(BV4925-6)*
  xx Children—Religious life
    Conversion
    Infant baptism
    Infant salvation
— Costume *(GT1730)*
  sa Children's clothing
  x Children's costume
  xx Children's clothing
    Costume
— — Juvenile literature
— Crying
  See Crying
— Death and future state *(BV4907)*
  sa Infant salvation
  x Death of children
  xx Future life
    Infant salvation
— Dental care *(Direct)*
  Here are entered works on plans and
    facilities for the dental care of chil-
    dren. Works on the technical as-
    pects of children's dentistry are en-
    tered under Pedodontia.
  xx Pedodontia
  Note under Pedodontia
— Discipline
  See Discipline of children
— Diseases *(RJ)*
  sa Children—Hospitals
    Corpulence in children
    Dentition
    Glycogenosis
    Infants—Diseases
    Pediatric allergy
    Pediatric hematology
    Pediatric nursing
    Pediatric periodontia
    Tuberculosis in children
    Tumors in children
    names of diseases, e.g. Chicken-pox,
      Whooping-cough
  x Children's diseases
    Diseases of children
  xx Children—Care and hygiene
    Medicine—Practice
    Pediatrics
— — Classification
  xx Nosology
— — Diagnosis *(RJ50)*
  sa Pediatric radiology
  x Pediatric diagnosis
  xx Diagnosis
— — Eclectic treatment *(RV375-7)*
— — Film catalogs
— — Genetic aspects
— — Homeopathic treatment *(RX501-531)*
  Example under Homeopathy
— — Prevention
  x Preventive pediatrics
— — Research
  See Pediatric research
— — Statistics
— Education
  See Education of children
— Employment *(Direct)* *(HD6228-6250)*
  sa Apprentices
    Child labor in literature
    Chimney-sweeps

    High school students—Employment
    Hours of labor
    Labor supply
    Newsboys
    Newspaper carriers
    Night work
    Student employment
    Sweating system
    Youth—Employment
  x Boys—Employment
    Child labor
    Employment of children
    Girls—Employment
    Labor and laboring classes—Child
      labor
    Working-girls
  xx Age and employment
    Children—Law
    Education, Compulsory
    Factory system
    Hours of labor
    Labor and laboring classes
    Labor laws and legislation
    Labor supply
    Night work
    School attendance
    Social problems
— — Juvenile literature
— Etiquette
  See Etiquette for children and youth
— Exhibitions
— Food
  See Children—Nutrition
— Growth *(RJ131)*
  sa Children—Constitution
    Prader-Willi syndrome
  x Child development
  Example under Growth
— — Juvenile literature
— — Programmed instruction
— — Testing
  x Developmental testing
  xx Developmental psychobiology
— Health
  See Children—Care and hygiene
— Hospital care
  xx Children—Institutional care
    Hospital care
— Hospitals *(Indirect)* *(RJ27-28)*
  sa Child welfare
    Hospital schools
    individual hospitals for children, e.g.
      Philadelphia. Children's Hospital
  x Children's hospitals
  xx Charities, Medical
    Child welfare
    Children—Diseases
    Hospitals
    Sanatoriums
— Hours of labor
  See Hours of labor
— Hygiene
  See Children—Care and hygiene
— Institutional care *(Direct)*
  sa Almshouses
    Asylums
    Charity-schools
    Child psychotherapy—Residential
      treatment
    Children—Hospital care
    Day nurseries
    Foster day care
    Foster home care
    Fresh-air charity
    Housemothers
    Junior republics
    Orphans and orphan-asylums
    Ragged schools

Reformatories
x Benevolent institutions
Boys' towns
Children—Asylums
Children's homes
Children's villages
Foster care, Institutional
Homes (Institutions)
xx Child welfare
Foster home care
— — Costs
— — Research (Direct)
— Language (LB1139.L3)
sa Aphasic children
Children—Writing
Communicative disorders in children
Illinois test of psycholinguistic
abilities
Physically handicapped children—
Language
x Children—Vocabulary
xx Language and languages
Speech
Vocabulary
— — Juvenile literature
— Law (Direct) (HV721-739)
sa Abandoned children—Law and
legislation
Adoption
Capacity and disability
Children—Employment
Children (Hindu law)
Children (International law)
Children (Jewish law)
Children (Roman-Dutch law)
Children (Roman law)
Children's rights
Crippled children—Law and
legislation
Curfew
Exceptional children—Law and
legislation
Gifts to minors
Guardian and ward
Handicapped children—Law and
legislation
Illegitimacy
Juvenile courts
Juvenile delinquency
Mentally handicapped children—
Law and legislation
Orphans and orphan-asylums—Law
and legislation
Parent and child (Law)
Physically handicapped children—
Law and legislation
Stepchildren
Unborn children (Law)
x Child welfare—Law and legislation
Infants—Law
Minors (Law)
Youth—Law and legislation
xx Child welfare
Children's rights
Domestic relations
Parent and child (Law)
— — Criminal provisions
— — Popular works
— Management (HQ769-780)
sa Baby sitters
Children and strangers
Children—Nutrition—Psychological
aspects
Children—Preparation for medical
care
Children's allowances
Children's questions and answers
Cruelty to children

Discipline of children
Governesses
Moral education
Play schools
Problem children
Toilet training
x Child rearing
Children—Training
Training of children
xx Domestic education
Parent and child
— — Anecdotes, facetiae, satire, etc.
— — Film catalogs
— — Juvenile literature
— — Personal narratives
— — Programmed instruction
— — Quotations, maxims, etc.
— — Study and teaching
x Parent and child—Study and
teaching
— Medical examinations
x Medical inspection in schools
School children—Medical
examinations
xx Children—Care and hygiene
School hygiene
Example under Periodic health examina-
tions; and under reference from
Medical examinations
— Mortality (HB1323.C5)
sa Infants—Mortality
Insurance, Child
x Infant mortality
Mortuary statistics
xx Mortality
Population
— Nutrition (RJ206)
sa Infants—Nutrition
School children—Food
x Children—Food
Nutrition of children
xx Children—Care and hygiene
— — Psychological aspects
x Child feeding behavior
Children's eating habits
Children's food habits
xx Appetite
Children—Management
Food habits
School children—Food
— Paraphernalia
See Children's paraphernalia
— Periodicals
— Photography
See Photography of children
— Pictorial works
sa Children—Portraits
— Poetry
— Portraits (N7640-7649)
sa Boys—Portraits
Girls—Portraits
x Children's portraits
xx Children in art
Children—Pictorial works
Photography of children
— Prayer-books and devotions (BV4870)
sa Children's missals
x Children—Prayer-books and
devotions—English
Prayers for children
— — 1961-

GENERAL SUBDIVISIONS

— — English
See Children—Prayer-books and
devotions

GENERAL SUBDIVISIONS

— — French, ⌐German, Italian, etc.⌐
— Prayer-books and devotions, Jewish
See Jewish children—Prayer-books
and devotions
— Preparation for dental care
See Children—Preparation for medical
care
— Preparation for medical care
x Children—Preparation for dental
care
xx Children—Care and hygiene
Children—Management
— — Juvenile literature (R130.5)
— Protection
See Child welfare
— Quotations, maxims, etc.
— Recreation
See Amusements
Creative activities and seat work
Games
— Religious life (BV4560-4579;
Conversion, BV4925-6)
sa Children—Conversion to Christianity
Confession of children
Lord's Supper—Admission age
Example under Christian life; and under
reference from Religious life
— — Anecdotes, facetiae, satire, etc.
— Religious life (Hinduism)
See Hindu children—Religious life
— Religious life (Islam)
See Muslim children—Religious life
— Research (Direct) (HQ768.8)
x Child research
— Rooms
See Children's rooms
— Sleep
xx Children—Care and hygiene
Sleep
— Societies and clubs
See Children's clubs
— Sports
See Sports for children
— Statistical methods
— Statistics
Works which deal with Statistics of
children in a particular country or
locality are entered here and also
under name of country, etc., with
subdivision Statistics, Vital, e.g. 1.
Children—Statistics. 2. United
States—Statistics, Vital.
— Suicidal behavior
x Child suicide
xx Suicide
— Surgery (RD137)
sa Infants (Newborn)—Surgery
Orthopedia
Pediatric orthopedia
x Pediatric surgery
Surgery, Pediatric
xx Surgery
— Training
See Children—Management
— Transportation
See School children—Transportation
— Vocabulary
See Children—Language
— Wounds and injuries
xx Pediatrics
— Writing (LB1139.W)
xx Children—Language
Writing
Children, Abandoned
See Abandoned children

309

Children, Abnormal and backward
   See Exceptional children
      Handicapped children
Children, Adopted *(Direct)*
   x Adopted children
   xx Adoption
      Foster home care
  — Testing
     xx Child study
     Example under Mental tests
Children, Aphasic
   See Aphasic children
Children, Atypical
   See Exceptional children
Children, Backward
   See Mentally handicapped children
      Slow learning children
Children, Blind *(Direct)*
   sa Blind—Education
      Vision disorders in children
      Visually handicapped children
   x Blind children
      Blindness in children
   xx Blind
      Physically handicapped children
      Vision disorders in children
  — Ability testing
Children, Books and reading for
   See Books and reading for children
Children, Cruelty to
   See Cruelty to children
Children, Deaf
   sa Deaf—Means of communication
   x Deaf children
      Deafness in children
      Hard-of-hearing children
      Hearing-impaired children
      Hypoacoustic children
   xx Deaf
      Hearing disorders in children
      Physically handicapped children
  — Education
     See Deaf—Education
  — Family relationships
  — Juvenile literature
  — Language
     xx Language and languages
      Speech
  — Recreation
Children, Exceptional
   See Exceptional children
Children, First-born *(HQ754.F5)*
   sa Primogeniture
      Redemption of the first-born
   x Eldest child
      First-born children
   xx Birth order
      Child study
      Infants
      Primogeniture
Children, Folk-lore of
   See Folk-lore of children
Children, Foreign
   See Children in foreign countries
Children, Hindu
   See Hindu children
Children, Islamic
   See Muslim children
Children, Jewish
   See Jewish children
Children, Mexican American
   See Mexican American children
Children, Muslim
   See Muslim children
Children, Negro
   See Negro children
Children, Oriental
   See Oriental children

Children, Photography of
   See Photography of children
Children, Preaching to
   See Preaching to children
Children, Retarded
   See Mentally handicapped children
      Slow learning children
Children, Runaway
   See Runaway children
Children, Sick
   See Sick children
Children, Vagrant *(Direct)*
   sa Runaway children
   x Child vagrants
      Vagrant children
   xx Child welfare
      Juvenile delinquency
      Tramps
      Vagrancy
Children (Christian theology) *(BT705)*
   xx Man (Theology)
      Theology, Doctrinal
Children (Hindu law)
   xx Children—Law
Children (International law)
   xx Children—Law
      International law
Children (Islamic law)
Children (Jewish law)
   xx Children—Law
Children (Roman-Dutch law)
   xx Children—Law
Children (Roman law)
   xx Children—Law
Children and alcohol
   See Alcohol and children
Children and animals *(BF723.A45)*
   x Animals and children
   xx Child study
Children and cartoons
   See Cartoons and children
Children and comic books
   See Comic books and children
Children and dancing
   See Dancing and children
Children and death
   sa Youth and death
   x Death and children
   xx Child study
      Death
      Death—Psychology
Children and erotica
   x Erotica and children
   xx Erotic literature
      Literature, Immoral
Children and folk-lore
   See Folk-lore and children
Children and mass media
   See Mass media and children
Children and moving-pictures
   See Moving-pictures and children
Children and newspapers
   See Newspapers and children
Children and poetry
   See Poetry and children
Children and politics *(HQ784.P5)*
   x Politics and children
Children and psychical research
   See Psychical research and children
Children and radio
   See Radio and children
Children and strangers
   x Strangers and children
   xx Child study
      Children—Management
Children and television
   See Television and children

Children and the performing arts
   See Performing arts and children
Children and traffic safety
   See Traffic safety and children
Children as actors *(PN2071.C; PN3157;*
      PN3171)
   sa Drama in education
   xx Actors
      Drama in education
      Gifted children
  — Juvenile literature
Children as artists *(N352)*
   sa Children in art
      Children's art
      Finger painting
      Folk art
   xx Children in art
      Children's art
      Folk art
      Gifted children
Children as authors *(Child study, BF723.A8;*
      Literature, PN171.C5)
   sa Children in literature
   x Children as poets
   xx Authors
      Authorship
      Children in literature
      Gifted children
   Notes under Children's literature; Children's
      writings
Children as collectors
   xx Collectors and collecting
Children as consumers
   See Youth as consumers
Children as musicians *(ML83)*
   sa Rhythm bands and orchestras
   xx Gifted children
      Musicians
Children as poets
   See Children as authors
Children as soldiers
   See United States—History—Civil War,
      1861-1865—Juvenile participants
      World War, 1939-1945—Juvenile
      participants
Children as witnesses *(Direct)*
   xx Evidence (Law)
      Psychology, Forensic
      Witnesses
Children in Africa
  — Biography
     xx Children—Biography
     Example under Autobiographies
  — Juvenile literature
Children in art *(N7640-7649)*
   sa Boys—Portraits
      Children as artists
      Children—Portraits
      Girls—Portraits
      Photography of children
   xx Art
      Children as artists
      Figure drawing
   Example under Figure drawing
  — Juvenile literature
Children in cities
   See City children
Children in classical antiquity *(DE61.C4)*
Children in Egypt, ₍Greece, Spain, etc.₎
  — Biography
  — — Juvenile literature
  — Juvenile literature
  — Pictorial works
Children in foreign countries *(G570)*
   x Children, Foreign
  — Pictorial works
  — — Juvenile literature

Children in literature
  sa Characters and characteristics in
      literature
    Child labor in literature
    Children as authors
    Youth in literature
  x Boys in literature
    Children in poetry
  xx Characters and characteristics in
      literature
    Children as authors
    Literature
    Youth in literature
Children in motion pictures
  xx Moving-pictures
  Note under Moving-pictures—Plots, themes,
    etc.
Children in poetry
  See Children in literature
Children in the Bible *(BS576-8; New
    Testament, BS2446)*
  sa Children—Biblical teaching
  x Bible—Children
    Boys in the Bible
    Girls in the Bible
  xx Bible—Biography
    Biography—Juvenile literature
    Boys—Biography
    Children—Biblical teaching
    Children—Biography
    Girls—Biography
Children in the United States
  sa Mexican American children
    Presidents—United States—Children
  — Biography
    xx Children—Biography
Children of alcoholic parents
  xx Alcoholism
    Parent and child
Children of alien laborers *(Direct)*
  xx Alien labor
  — Education *(Direct)*
Children of divorced parents
  sa Father-separated children
  xx Broken homes
    Divorce
    Parent and child
    Single-parent family
  — Juvenile literature
Children of God
  sa God—Fatherhood
    Kingdom of God
    People of God
  x God, Children of
  xx God—Fatherhood
    Mystical union
Children of God (Movement) *(BV4487.C5)*
  xx Jesus People
    Youth—Religious life
Children of immigrants *(Direct)*
  x First generation children
    Immigrants' children
  xx Emigration and immigration
  — Education *(Direct)*
  —— Language arts, [etc.]
Children of migrant laborers
  xx Migrant labor
  — Education *(Direct) (LC5151-3)*
    Example under Education; Education of
      children
Children of military personnel
  x Dependents of military personnel
    Families of military personnel
    Military children
    Military dependents
    Military families
  xx Soldiers

Children of missionaries
  xx Missionaries
  — Education
Children of the mentally ill
  xx Child psychiatry
    Mentally ill
Children of the rich
  x Rich children
    Wealthy children
  xx Wealth
  — Personality
    See Children of the rich—Psychology
  — Psychology
    x Children of the rich—Personality
Children of working mothers
  xx Mothers—Employment
Children separated from their fathers
  See Father-separated children
Children's accidents
  sa Traffic safety and children
  x Children—Accidents
  xx Accidents
    Child study
Children's allowances
  x Allowances, Children's
  xx Children—Management
    Finance, Personal
    Money
    Saving and thrift
Children's almanacs
  See Almanacs, Children's
Children's apperception test *(BF698.8.C4)*
  x CAT
  xx Apperception—Testing
    Projective techniques
Children's art *(Direct) (N352)*
    Here are entered collections of art pro-
      duced by children under fifteen years
      of age and or below the ninth grade in
      school.
  sa Children as artists
  xx Children as artists
Children's belongings
  See Children's paraphernalia
Children's book-plates
  See Book-plates, Children's
Children's books
  See Children's literature
    Illustrated books, Children's
Children's cantatas
  See Cantatas, Juvenile
Children's Christian literature
  See Christian literature for children
Children's clothing *(TT635)*
  sa Children—Costume
    Infants—Clothing
  x Children—Clothing
  xx Children—Costume
    Children's paraphernalia
    Clothing and dress
  — Pattern design *(TT640)*
    x Pattern cutting (Clothing)
      Pattern drafting (Clothing)
      Patterns (Clothing)
    xx Costume design
      Garment cutting
      Tailoring—Pattern design
  — Prices
Children's clubs
  sa Boys—Societies and clubs
    Girls—Societies and clubs
  x Children—Clubs
    Children—Societies and clubs
  — Juvenile literature
Children's communion
  See Infant communion
    Lord's Supper—Admission age

Children's costume
  See Children—Costume
Children's courts
  See Juvenile courts
Children's Crusade, 1212 *(D169)*
  xx Crusades
Children's dances
  See Dancing—Children's dances
Children's diseases
  See Children—Diseases
Children's drama
  See Children's plays
Children's dreams
  xx Child study
    Dreams
  — Pictorial works
Children's eating habits
  See Children—Nutrition—Psychological
    aspects
Children's encyclopedias and dictionaries
    (AG1-91)
  sa Bible—Dictionaries, Juvenile
    Natural history—Dictionaries, Juvenile
    Science—Dictionaries, Juvenile
  x Juvenile dictionaries
    Juvenile encyclopedias
  xx Children's literature
    Children's reference books
    Encyclopedias and dictionaries
**Children's encyclopedias and dictionaries,
    Dutch,** [**French, German, etc.**]
Children's etiquette
  See Etiquette for children and youth
Children's films
    Here are entered individual fiction films
      which are produced primarily for chil-
      dren.
  x Juvenile films
  xx Moving-pictures
    Moving-pictures for children
  Note under Moving-pictures for children
  — History and criticism
    Note under Moving-pictures for children
Children's food habits
  See Children—Nutrition—Psychological
    aspects
Children's furniture
  sa Cradles
  x Furniture, Children's
  xx Children's paraphernalia
    Children's rooms
    Furniture
    Miniature furniture
    Nurseries—Equipment and supplies
Children's gardens *(SB457)*
    Here are entered books on gardens for
      children. Books on gardening written
      for children are entered under the
      heading Gardening—Juvenile litera-
      ture.
  sa Gardening—Juvenile literature
    School gardens
  xx Gardening
    Gardening—Juvenile literature
    Gardens
Children's homes
  See Children—Institutional care
Children's hospitals
  See Children—Hospitals
Children's illustrated books
  See Illustrated books, Children's
Children's librarians *(Direct) (Z718.1)*
  xx Libraries, Children's
Children's libraries
  See Libraries, Children's
    School libraries

Children's literature *(PZ5-90)*

Here are entered works dealing with literature written for children. Works dealing with the attitude of children toward, and their interest in, reading books and the development of their interest by parents, teachers, and librarians are entered under Books and reading for children. Literary works written by children are entered under Children's writings. Discussions of their works are entered under Children as authors.

sa Books and reading for children
Children's encyclopedias and dictionaries
Children's plays
Children's poetry
Children's stories
Christian literature for children
Fairy tales
Fiction in libraries
Hieroglyphic Bibles
High interest-low vocabulary books
Illustrated books, Children's
Libraries and schools
Libraries, Children's
Library Association Carnegie Medal
Mentally handicapped children, Books for
Newbery medal books
Physically handicapped children, Books for
Picture-books for children
Slow learning children, Books for
Socially handicapped children, Books for
Story-telling
Sunday-school literature
Talking books for children
William Allen White children's book award
subdivision Juvenile literature *under particular subjects, e.g.* Astronomy—Juvenile literature
x Books for children
Children's books
Juvenile literature
xx Books and reading for children
Children's paraphernalia
Fiction in libraries
Libraries and schools
Libraries, Children's
Literature
School libraries
Sunday-school literature
Note under Books and reading for children
— Bibliography *(Z1037)*
sa Bibliography—Children's books issued in series
School libraries
— Book reviews
— Cataloging
See Cataloging of children's literature
— Film adaptations
— History and criticism *(PN1009)*
— Moral and religious aspects
xx Literature and morals
— Publishing *(Direct)*
— Subject headings
See Subject headings—Children's literature
— Technique
sa New literates, Writing for
xx Authorship

Children's literature, French, ⌈Italian, etc.⌉ *(Direct)*
x French ⌈Italian, etc.⌉ children's literature
— Stories, plots, etc.
— Technique
Children's missals *(Catholic, BX2015.A55)*
x Missals for children
xx Catholic Church.   Liturgy and ritual. Missal
Children—Prayer-books and devotions
Children's museums *(AM8)*
sa Museums and schools
x Museums, Children's
Museums for children
xx Education of children
Museums
Museums and schools
Children's music (Piano, ⌈Violin, etc.⌉)
See Piano ⌈Violin, etc.⌉ music, Juvenile
Children's opera
See Opera, Juvenile
Children's operas
See Operas, Juvenile
Children's oratorios *(M2190)*
x Juvenile oratorios
Oratorios, Juvenile
xx Children's songs
Oratorios
Children's paraphernalia *(Direct)*
sa Children's clothing
Children's furniture
Children's literature
Games
Illustrated books, Children's
Toys
x Children—Paraphernalia
Children's belongings
Paraphernalia, Children's
— Collectors and collecting *(Direct)*
Children's parties *(GV1203)*
sa Pinatas
x Parties for children
xx Amusements
Entertaining
Games
Children's periodicals *(History, PN4835)*
x Periodicals, Juvenile
xx Press, Juvenile
Children's periodicals, French, ⌈German, etc.⌉
xx French ⌈German, etc.⌉ periodicals
Children's plays *(PN6120.A4-5)*
Here are entered collections of plays for children and works on such plays. Works on amateur theatricals, if not limited to children's plays, are entered under the heading Amateur theatricals.
sa Bible plays
x Children's drama
Plays for children
School plays
xx Amateur theatricals
Children's literature
Drama
Theater
Note under Amateur theatricals
— Presentation, etc. *(Direct)* *(PN3157)*
x Children's theater
Children's plays, French, ⌈Spanish, etc.⌉
Children's poetry *(PN6110.C4; PZ8.3)*
sa Children's songs
Lullabies
Nursery rhymes
Poetry in mathematics education
Tongue twisters
subdivision Juvenile poetry *under specific subjects*

x Juvenile poetry
Poetry for children
xx Children's literature
Poetry
— Authorship
xx Poetics
— Indexes
Children's poetry, English, ⌈French, Italian, etc.⌉ *(Direct)*
x English ⌈French, Italian, etc.⌉ children's poetry
xx English ⌈French, Italian, etc.⌉ poetry
Children's portraits
See Children—Portraits
Children's press
See Press, Juvenile
Children's questions and answers
x Questions and answers, Children's
xx Child study
Children—Management
Questions and answers
Children's reference books *(Z1037.1)*
sa Children's encyclopedias and dictionaries
x Juvenile reference books
Reference books for children
xx Books and reading for children
Books and reading for youth
Reference books
— Examinations, questions, etc.
Children's rights
sa Children—Law
x Rights of children
xx Children—Law
Civil rights
Children's rooms
sa Children's furniture
Nurseries
x Children—Rooms
Rooms, Children's
xx Architecture, Domestic
Bedrooms
Dwellings
Children's sayings
See Children—Anecdotes and sayings
Children's self-conceptions test
x CSC test
xx Mental tests
Children's sermons *(BV4315)*
xx Preaching to children
Sermons
Note under Story sermons
— Outlines
Children's sermons, Jewish *(BM743)*
x Jewish children's sermons
Jewish sermons for children
xx Sermons, Jewish
Children's songs *(Music, M1990-1998; Singing games, GV1215)*
Here are entered general collections and collections of American and English songs for children.
sa Camping—Songs and music
Cantatas, Juvenile
Children's oratorios
Games with music
Kindergarten—Music
Lullabies
Nursery rhymes
Nursery schools—Music
Operas, Juvenile
Sunday-schools—Hymns
xx Children's poetry
School song-books
Songs
Children's songs, Argentine, ⌈German, Swiss, etc.⌉

Children's songs, Belgian
  sa Children's songs, Flemish
Children's songs, Flemish
  xx Children's songs, Belgian
Children's songs, Hebrew
  See Children's songs, Jewish
Children's songs, Jewish
  x Children's songs, Hebrew
    Children's songs, Yiddish
Children's songs, Yiddish
  See Children's songs, Jewish
Children's stories *(Collections, PZ5-90)*
  sa Christian life—Stories
    Fairy tales
    Missionary stories
    Story-telling
  x Stories
  xx Children's literature
    Fiction
  — Discography
  — Technique
    xx Authorship
      Fiction—Technique
Children's stories, Afrikaans, [etc.] *(Direct)*
  x Afrikaans [etc.] children's stories
  xx Afrikaans [etc.] fiction
Children's stories, Hebrew
  xx Hebrew literature
Children's theater
  See Children's plays—Presentation, etc.
Children's villages
  See Children—Institutional care
Children's writings *(Collections, PN6066)*
    Here are entered collections and in-
    dividual works written by children un-
    der fifteen years of age and/or below
    the ninth grade in school. Discussions
    of such literature are entered under
    Children as authors.
  sa Negro children's writings
    School prose
    School verse
  Note under Children's literature
Children's writings, American, [English, etc.]
  x American [English, etc.] children's
    writings
Children's zoos *(Indirect) (QL76)*
  xx Zoological gardens
Chile
  — Antiquities
  — History *(F3081-3098)*
  — — To 1565
  — — To 1810
  — — 1565-1810
  — — 1810-
  — — War of Independence, 1810-1824
    sa Rancagua, Battle of, 1814
  — — 1824-1920
    sa War of the Pacific, 1879-1884
  — — War with Peru, 1836-1839
    See Peru—History—Peru-Bolivian
      Confederation, 1836-1839
  — — Insurrection of 1851
  — — Insurrection of 1859
  — — War with Spain, 1865-1866
    x Peru—History—War with Spain,
      1865-1866
  — — War with Bolivia, 1879-1884
    See War of the Pacific, 1879-1884
  — — War with Peru, 1879-1884
    See War of the Pacific, 1879-1884
  — — Revolution, 1891
  — — 1920-
  — Tidal wave, 1960
Chilean ballads and songs *(Collections,*
  PQ8060-8061; History,
  PQ7979-7980)

Chilean clover
  See Alfalfa
Chilean drama *(Collections, PQ8064-8070;*
  History, PQ7997-8007)
Chilean fiction *(Collections, PQ8075-6;*
  History, PQ7997-8007)
  — 20th century
Chilean letters *(Collections, PQ8081;*
  History, PQ8011)
Chilean literature *(Direct) (PQ7900-8099)*
  xx Spanish American literature
  — 20th century
Chilean newspapers *(History, etc.,*
  PN5041-9)
Chilean periodicals *(History, etc.,*
  PN5041-5050)
Chilean poetry *(Collections, PQ8049-8063;*
  History, PQ7961-7981)
  — 20th century
Chilean wit and humor *(PN6222.C)*
Chileans in Brazil, [California, etc.]
Chili *(Indirect)*
  x Chilli
    Hot pepper
  — Marketing
Chili con carne
  xx Cookery (Meat)
Chiliasm
  See Millennium
Chilindre
  See Cylinder (Timepiece)
Chilkat Indians *(E99.C552)*
  xx Indians of North America
    Tlingit Indians
Chillán, Chile
  — Earthquake, 1939
Chilli
  See Chili
Chillicothe, Ohio
  — Fire, 1852
Chilliwack dialect *(PM803)*
  x Chil-way-uk dialect
    Chillwayuk dialect
  xx Cowichan languages
    Salishan languages
Chills and fever
  See Malarial fever
Chillwayuk dialect
  See Chilliwack dialect
Chilopoda
  See Centipedes
Chilostomata, Fossil
  See Cheilostomata, Fossil
Chilula Indians *(E99.C553)*
  xx Athapascan Indians
    Indians of North America
Chilula language *(PM805)*
  xx Athapascan languages
Chimaera (Genetics)
  See Mosaicism
Chimaerae
  See Chimaeriformes
Chimaeriformes *(Indirect) (QL638.7)*
  x Chimaerae
    Holocephali
  xx Elasmobranchii
Chimariko Indians *(E99.C56)*
  xx Indians of North America
Chimariko language *(PM821)*
Chimarrita (Dance)
  See Chamarrita (Dance)
Chimbu (New Guinea people)
  x Kuman (New Guinea people)
  xx Ethnology—New Guinea
Chimbu language
  x Kuman language (New Guinea)
    Kumanugu language
  xx Papuan languages

Chimbunda language
  See Mbunda language (Zambia)
Chime music *(M172)*
  sa Quartets, [Trios, etc.] *followed by*
    specifications which include chimes
Chimera (Genetics)
  See Mosaicism
Chimeras (Botany) *(QH406)*
  xx Botany
Chimes
  sa Clock music
  xx Bells
    Music
Chiming
  See Change ringing
Chiming clock selections
  See Clock music
Chimmesyan Indians *(E99.C)*
  sa Niska Indians
    Tsimshian Indians
  xx Indians of North America
Chimmesyan languages *(PM831)*
  sa Niska language
    Tsimshian language
  x Chimsyan languages
    Zimshīan languages
  xx Niska language
    Tsimshian language
Chimney-money
  See Hearth-money
Chimney plumes
  See Smoke plumes
Chimney swallow
  See Chimney swift
Chimney-sweeps *(HD8039.C49)*
  xx Children—Employment
  — Legal status, laws, etc. *(Direct)*
Chimney swift *(QL696.A)*
  x Chimney swallow
    Swallow, Chimney
  xx Swifts
  — Juvenile literature
Chimneypieces
  See Fireplaces
    Mantels
Chimneys *(Direct) (TH2281-4;*
  Architecture, NA3040; Power-plants,
  TH4591)
  sa Fireplaces
    Flues
  x Smokestacks
  xx Architecture—Details
    Building
    Fireplaces
    Flues
    Heating
    Smoke prevention
    Ventilation
  — Maintenance and repair
Chimpanzees *(QL737.P9)*
  xx Apes
  — Anatomy
  — — Atlases
  — Behavior
  — Juvenile literature
  — Legends and stories
  — Physiology
  — Psychology
Chimsyan languages
  See Chimmesyan languages
Chimu Indians *(F3430.1.C)*
  xx Indians of South America
    Yunca Indians
Chimu language *(PM5813)*
  xx Indians of South America—Languages
Chin *(QM535)*
  xx Face
  — Surgery

Ch'in (Musical instrument) *(ML1015-1018)*
   xx Musical instruments, Chinese
      Zither
Ch'in dynasty, 221-207 B.C.
   See China—History—Ch'in dynasty,
      221-207 B.C.
Chin languages *(PL3891-4)*
   sa Khyang language
      Kuki-Chin languages
      Lai language
      Siyin language
      Tibeto-Burman languages
      Tiddim Chin dialect
   x Shu languages
      Zho languages
   xx Khyang language
      Kuki-Chin languages
      Tibeto-Burman languages
Chin law
   See Law, Chin
Ch'in music *(M142.C5)*
Chin tribes
   sa Hakas (Tribe)
      Kukis
China
   — Commerce
     — United States
        Note under United States—Com-
           merce—Africa, ₍Belgium, China,
           etc.₎
   — History *(DS701-796)*
     x Chinese question
     — To 1766 B.C.
     — To 1643
     — Shang dynasty, 1766-1122 B.C.
       x Shang dynasty, 1766-1122 B.C.
     — 1766 B.C.-220 A.D.
      — Anecdotes, facetiae, satire, etc.
     — Chou dynasty, 1122-221 B.C.
       x Chou dynasty, 1122-221 B.C.
     — Warring States, 403-221 B.C.
        (DS747.2)
     — Ch'in dynasty, 221-207 B.C.
       x Ch'in dynasty, 221-207 B.C.
      — Anecdotes, facetiae, satire, etc.
     — Han dynasty, 202 B.C.-220 A.D.
        (DS748)
       x Han dynasty
      — Anecdotes, facetiae, satire, etc.
     — Three kingdoms, 220-265 *(DS748.2)*
      — Anecdotes, facetiae, satire, etc.
     — 220-618
     — Chin dynasty, 265-419
     — Southern and northern dynasties,
       317-589 *(DS748.5)*
     — Northern Wei dynasty, 386-534
        (DS748.6)
       x Northern Wei dynasty
        T'o pa dynasty
        Toba Tatars
        Wei dynasty, Northern
        Yuan Wei dynasty
     — Sui dynasty, 581-618
     — T'ang dynasty, 618-907
     — Five dynasties, 907-960
     — Sung dynasty, 960-1279
      sa Khitan Mongols
      — Anecdotes, facetiae, satire, etc.
     — Yuan dynasty, 1260-1368
     — Ming dynasty, 1368-1644
     — Tatar Conquest, 1643-1644
      xx Manchus
       Tatars
     — Ch'ing dynasty, 1644-1912
      sa Manchus
      xx Manchus
      — Examinations, questions, etc.
      — 19th century

   sa Barrier Forts, Battle of, 1856
      Nien Rebellion, 1853-1868
      Taiping Rebellion, 1850-1864
   — — — Miscellanea
   — — War of 1840-1842
     sa Nanking, Treaty of, 1842
     x Opium War, 1840-1842
   — — Foreign intervention, 1857-1861
     sa Taiping Rebellion, 1850-1864
   — — 1862-1899
   — — Kuang-hsü, 1875-1908
   — — War with Japan, 1894-1895
     See Chinese-Japanese War,
       1894-1895
   — — Reform movement, 1898
   — — 1900
   — — 1900-
     xx Boxers
   — — Hsüang-t'ung, 1908-1912
   — — Revolution, 1911-1912
   — — — Juvenile literature
   — — — Pictorial works
   — — 1912-1937
     sa Long March, 1934-1935
   — — Republic, 1912-1949
   — — Revolution, 1913
   — — Northern Expedition, 1926-1928
     x Northern Expedition, 1926-1928
   — — Tsinan Incident, 1928 *(DS777.49)*
     x Tsinan Incident, 1928
   — — 1937-1945
     sa Sino-Japanese Conflict, 1937-1945
     xx Sino-Japanese Conflict, 1937-1945
   — — 1945-
   — — Civil War, 1945-1949
   — — — Personal narratives
   — — 1949-

      GENERAL SUBDIVISIONS

   — — Invasions
     x Invasions of China
China (Porcelain)
   See Porcelain
China-clay
   See Kaolin
China fairings *(Direct)*
   xx Porcelain
China fairings, Victorian *(Direct)*
   x Victorian china fairings
China in art
China in literature
China-Japan War, 1894-1895
   See Chinese-Japanese War, 1894-1895
China painting *(NK4605)*
   x Porcelain painting
   xx Arts and crafts movement
      Color in the ceramic industries
      Decoration and ornament
      Painting
      Porcelain
   — Subjects
     See China painting—Themes, motives
   — Themes, motives
     x China painting—Subjects
China Relief Expedition, 1900-1901
     (DS770-772)
China trade art *(Direct)*
   x Chinese export art
      Export art, Chinese
China trade porcelain *(Direct)*
   x Chinese export porcelain
      East India porcelain
      Export porcelain, Chinese
      Lowestoft, Oriental
      Oriental Lowestoft
      Porcelain, China trade
      Porcelain, East India
   xx Porcelain, Chinese

China wood-oil
   See Tung-oil
China wood-oil tree
   See Tung tree
Chinacrin
   See Atabrine
Chinampas *(Mexican horticulture, SB87.M6)*
Chinantec Indians *(F1221.C56)*
   x Cinantec Indians
      Tenez Indians
      Teutecas Indians
      Zinantec Indians
   xx Indians of Mexico
Chinantecan languages *(PM3630)*
   sa Proto-Chinantec language
   xx Indians of Mexico—Languages
Chinaware
   See Porcelain
      Pottery
Chinch-bugs *(SB945.C5)*
   sa False chinch bug
   xx Heteroptera
   Example under Grain—Diseases and pests
Chinchasuyu dialect *(PM5814.C3)*
   x Tšintšaysuyu dialect
Chinchilla rabbits *(SF455)*
   Example under Rabbit breeds
Chinchillas *(QL737.R6)*
   xx Rodentia
   — Diseases
Chinchona
   See Cinchona
Chincoteague pony *(SF315.2.C4)*
   xx Ponies
Chindau language *(PL8110.C)*
   x Cindau language
      Ndau language
      Sofala language
      Vandau language
   xx Bantu languages
Chinese
   sa Tokhari
   Example under Orientals
   — Anthropometry
     sa Chinese—Craniology
   — Craniology
     xx Chinese—Anthropometry
   — Origin *(GN635.C5)*
Chinese astronomy
   See Astronomy, Chinese
Chinese block-books
   See Block-books, Chinese
Chinese businessmen
   See Businessmen, Chinese
Chinese cabbage *(SB351.C)*
   x Celery cabbage
      Pak-choi
      Petsai
   xx Cabbage
Chinese characters
   x Chinese language—Alphabet
      Chinese language—Orthography and
       spelling
      Chinese logographs
   xx Chinese language—Writing
   — Anecdotes, facetiae, satire, etc.
Chinese chess *(GV1458.C5)*
   x Hsiang chi (Game)
   xx Chess—Variants
Chinese chronology
   See Chronology, Chinese
Chinese classics
   x Chinese literature—To 210 B.C.
   — Study and teaching *(Direct)*
     (PL2461.Z9)
Chinese cloisonné
   See Cloisonné, Chinese

Chinese cosmogony
   See Cosmogony, Chinese
Chinese diaries *(Collections, PL2611)*
Chinese document writing
   See Document writing, Chinese
Chinese drama *(History, PL2934-5; Theater,*
     PN2870-2878; Translations,
     PL3277.E5, etc.)
   sa San ch'ü
  — 20th century
Chinese essays
   sa Chinese examination essays
Chinese examination essays
   xx Chinese essays
Chinese export art
   See China trade art
Chinese export porcelain
   See China trade porcelain
Chinese fiction *(Collections, PL2625-2653;*
     History, PL2415-2443; Translations,
     PL2656.E8, etc.)
  — 20th century
Chinese flower arrangement
   See Flower arrangement, Chinese
Chinese-French War, 1884-1885 *(DS549)*
   x Chino-French War, 1884-1885
    Franco-Chinese War, 1884-1885
    Sino-French War, 1884-1885
Chinese gold articles
   See Gold articles, Chinese
Chinese imprints *(Direct)*
Chinese in Brazil, ₍Guyana, South Africa, etc.₎
   x Coolie labor
    Labor, Coolie
   xx Contract labor
  — Citizenship
  — Economic conditions
  — Juvenile literature
  — Legal status, laws, etc.
Chinese in Canada
   xx Deportation
Chinese in foreign countries
   sa Chinese teachers in foreign countries
Chinese in the United States
   xx Deportation
  — Juvenile literature
  — Legal status, laws, etc.
Chinese-Indian Border Dispute, 1957-
   See Sino-Indian Border Dispute, 1957-
Chinese inscriptions
   See Inscriptions, Chinese
Chinese intelligence
   See Intelligence levels—Chinese
Chinese-Japanese Conflict, 1937-1945
   See Sino-Japanese Conflict, 1937-1945
Chinese-Japanese War, 1894-1895 *(DS765-7)*
   x China—History—War with Japan,
     1894-1895
    China-Japan War, 1894-1895
    Chino-Japanese War, 1894-1895
    Japan—History—War with China,
     1894-1895
    Japanese-Chinese War, 1894-1895
    Sino-Japanese War, 1894-1895
   xx Eastern question (Far East)
  — Causes *(DS765)*
  — Diplomatic history
  — Medical and sanitary affairs *(UH302*
     1894)
  — Personal narratives
  — Personal narratives, Japanese, ₍etc.₎
  — Pictorial works
Chinese jewelry
   See Jewelry, Chinese
Chinese junks
   See Junks
Chinese lacquer and lacquering
   See Lacquer and lacquering, Chinese

Chinese language *(PL1001-2239)*
   xx Indochinese languages
  — Alphabet
     See Chinese characters
  — Archaic Chinese *(PL2241-5)*
    x Ancient Chinese language
     Archaic Chinese language
  — Dialects
  — — Hainan *(PL1841)*
    x Būn-sio dialect
     Hailam dialect
  — — Hakka
    x Hakka dialect
  — Machine translating
    xx Chinese language—Translating
  — Orthography and spelling
     See Chinese characters
      Chinese language—Transliteration
  — Reform
     Example under reference from Language
      reform
  — Translating
    sa Chinese language—Machine
     translating
     Kunten
    Example under Translating and interpret-
     ing
  — Transliteration
    x Chinese language—Orthography and
     spelling
    Example under reference from Romani-
     zation (Linguistics)
  — Writing
    sa Chinese characters
     Document writing, Chinese
    x Ideography
  — Writing, Cursive
    x Grass writing
  — Writing, Li style
    x "Clerkly" style writing
     Li-shu
Chinese layerage
   See Air layering
Chinese letters
Chinese literature *(PL2501-3299)*
  — To 210 B.C.
     See Chinese classics
  — 20th century

GENERAL SUBDIVISIONS

  — Buddhist authors
  — Cataloging
     See Cataloging of Chinese literature
  — Japanese authors
    x Japanese literature (Chinese)
Chinese logographs
   See Chinese characters
Chinese lute
   See P'i p'a
Chinese medicine
   See Medicine, Chinese
Chinese mirrors
   See Mirrors, Chinese
Chinese national characteristics
   See National characteristics, Chinese
Chinese newspapers *(Direct) (History, etc.,*
     PN5361-9)
Chinese oil tree
   See Tung tree
Chinese painted enamel
   See Painted enamel, Chinese
Chinese periodicals *(PN5361-5370)*
Chinese philology
Chinese philosophy
   See Philosophy, Chinese

Chinese poetry *(Direct) (Collections,*
    PL2517-2543; History,
    PL2306-2333)
   sa Fu
    Revolutionary poetry, Chinese
    San ch'ü
    Tz'u
  — 20th century

GENERAL SUBDIVISIONS

  — Japanese authors
    x Japanese poetry (Chinese)

GENERAL SUBDIVISIONS

  — Korean authors
    x Korean poetry (Chinese)
Chinese porcelain
   See Porcelain, Chinese
Chinese pottery
   See Pottery, Chinese
Chinese property in foreign countries
Chinese prose literature
   sa Fu
Chinese question
   See China—History
    Eastern question (Far East)
Chinese rites
    Here are entered works dealing with the
     controversy concerning the participa-
     tion of Christian converts in Chinese
     rites and ceremonies.
   sa Malabar rites
   x Rites, Chinese
   xx Catholic Church—Missions
    Malabar rites
Chinese sculpture
   See Sculpture, Chinese
Chinese shadows
   See Shadow pantomimes and plays
Chinese silk
   See Silk, Chinese
Chinese snuff boxes and bottles
   See Snuff boxes and bottles, Chinese
Chinese soldiers' writings
   See Soldiers' writings, Chinese
Chinese students in France, ₍the United
    States, etc.₎
Chinese studies *(Direct) (PL1001-1095)*
   sa Sinologists
Chinese sugar-cane
   See Sorgo
Chinese tallow tree
   See Tallow tree
Chinese teachers in foreign countries
   xx Chinese in foreign countries
Chinese trade porcelain
   See Porcelain, Chinese
Chinese typewriters
   See Typewriters, Chinese
Chinese vases
   See Vases, Chinese
Chinese white dolphin *(QL737.C432)*
Chinese wit and humor *(PN6222,C5)*
Chinese wood-oil tree
   See Tung tree
Ch'ing ch'ü
   See San ch'ü
Ching-p'o language *(PL3311.C5)*
Chin'gakchong
   xx Buddhist sects
Chingpaw language
   See Kachin language
Chingpaws
   See Kachin tribes
Chinidine
   See Quinidine
Chinioidina
   See Quinoidine

Chino-French War, 1884-1885
  See Chinese-French War, 1884-1885
Chino-Japanese War, 1894-1895
  See Chinese-Japanese War, 1894-1895
Chino language
  See Shona language
Chinoidine
  See Quinoidine
Chinone
  See Quinone
Chinook Indians *(E99.C57)*
  sa Clackamas Indians
  xx Chinookan Indians
     Indians of North America
Chinook jargon *(PM846-9)*
  sa Chinook language
     Chinookan languages
  xx Chinook language
     Chinookan languages
Chinook language *(PM841-4)*
  sa Chinook jargon
     Chinookan languages
  xx Chinook jargon
     Chinookan languages
  — Texts
Chinook salmon
  x King salmon
     Quinnat
  xx Pacific salmon
     Salmon
  — Juvenile literature
Chinookan Indians
  sa Chinook Indians
     Clackamas Indians
     Multnomah Indians
     Shoto Indians
  xx Indians of North America
Chinookan languages *(PM841-4)*
  sa Cathlamet dialect
     Chinook jargon
     Chinook language
     Tlakluit language
     Wasco language
  xx Cathlamet dialect
     Chinook jargon
     Chinook language
Chins, Japanese (Dogs)
  See Japanese spaniels
Chintz *(Art, NK8800-8899)*
Chinyanja language
  See Nyanja language
Chios, Battle of, 1657 *(DR534.5.C5)*
Chios, Battle of, 1694 *(DR539)*
Chip disposal (Metal-cutting)
  See Metal-cutting—Chip disposal
Chipaya Indians
Chipboard
  See Particle board
Chipewyan Indians *(E99.C59)*
  x Chepewyan Indians
  xx Athapascan Indians
     Indians of North America
  — Legends
Chipewyan language *(PM850.C2)*
  sa Athapascan languages
  x Chippewyan language
     Montagnais (Athapascan) language
  xx Athapascan languages
Chipmunks *(QL737.R6)*
  — Juvenile literature
  — Legends and stories *(Juvenile, PZ10.3; Zoology, QL795.C)*
Chipmunks as pets *(SF459.C5)*
Chippendale style
  See Decoration and ornament—
     Chippendale style
Chippers (Woodworking machinery)
Chippewa, Battle of, 1814 *(E356.C55)*

Chippewa Indians *(E99.C6)*
  sa Missisauga Indians
  x Bungee Indians
     Bungi Indians
     Chippeway Indians
     Ochipawa Indians
     Ojibwa Indians
     Otchipwe Indians
     Salteaux Indians
     Saulteaux Indians
     Sauteux Indians
  xx Algonquian Indians
     Indians of North America
  — Government relations
  — — Juvenile literature
  — Juvenile literature
  — Land tenure
  — Legal status, laws, etc.
  — Legends
  — Treaties
     sa Old Crossing treaty, 1863
  — Wars, 1898 *(E83.895)*
Chippewa language *(PM851-4)*
  sa Algonquian languages
  x Ojibwa language
     Otchipwe language
     Sauteux language
  xx Algonquian languages
     Indians of North America—Languages
Chippewa poetry
  xx Indian poetry
     Poetry
Chippeway Indians
  See Chippewa Indians
Chippewyan language
  See Chipewyan language
Chips, Wood
  See Wood chips
Chip'yŏng-ni, Battle of, 1951
  xx Korean War, 1950-1953
  — Juvenile literature
Chiquito Indians *(F3320.2.C)*
  sa Manacica Indians
  xx Indians of South America
Chiquito language *(PM5816)*
  xx Indians of South America—Languages
Chirho symbol
  See Chi Rho symbol
Chiricahua Indians
  See Apache Indians
Chiriguano Indians *(F3320.2.C4)*
  xx Indians of South America
     Tupi Indians
Chiriguano language *(PM5817.C2)*
Chiripá Indians
  xx Guarani Indians
     Indians of South America
Chirognomy
  See Palmistry
Chirography
  See Penmanship
     Writing
Chiromancy
  See Palmistry
Chiroplast *(MT221)*
  xx Piano—Instruction and study
Chiropodists *(Direct)*
  x Podiatrists
  xx Chiropody
  — Legal status, laws, etc.
     See Chiropody—Law and legislation
Chiropody *(RD563)*
  sa Chiropodists
     Foot—Care and hygiene
     Nails, Ingrowing
  x Podiatry
  xx Foot—Care and hygiene
     Foot—Surgery

     Toes
  — Formulae, receipts, prescriptions
  — Law and legislation *(Direct)*
     x Chiropodists—Legal status, laws, etc.
  — Vocational guidance
     See Chiropody as a profession
Chiropody as a profession
  x Chiropody—Vocational guidance
Chiropractic *(Indirect)* *(RM730)*
  sa Chiropractors
     Naturopathy
     Spondylotherapy
  xx Massage
     Medicine
     Medicine—Practice
     Osteopathy
     Spondylotherapy
     Therapeutics, Physiological
  — Examinations, questions, etc.
  — Law and legislation *(Direct)*
     x Chiropractors—Legal status, laws, etc.
Chiropractic as a profession
Chiropractic clinics *(Indirect)* *(RZ242)*
  xx Clinics
  — Design and construction
Chiropractors *(Direct)*
  xx Chiropractic
  — Legal status, laws, etc.
     See Chiropractic—Law and legislation
Chiroptera
  See Bats
Chirosophy
  See Palmistry
Chirotherapy
  See Massage
Chisels
  x Gouges (Woodworking)
  Note under Wood-cutting tools
  — Safety measures *(TJ1201.C)*
Ch'itan
  See Khitan Mongols
Chitimacha Indians *(E99.C7)*
  x Chitimachan Indians
     Shetimasha Indians
  xx Indians of North America
  — Religion and mythology
Chitimacha language *(PM861)*
Chitimachan Indians
  See Chitimacha Indians
Chitin *(Chemistry, QD321; Physiological chemistry, QP701)*
  xx Carbohydrates
     Cuticle
     Physiological chemistry
Chitons *(QL430.1)*
  x Polyplacophora
  xx Amphineura
Chittahs
  See Cheetahs
Chittoriya Lohars
  See Lohars
Chivalrie (Game) *(GV1017.C5)*
Chivalry *(CR)*
  sa Bushido
     Civilization, Medieval
     Courtly love
     Courts of love
     Crusades
     Feudalism
     Heraldry
     Honor
     Hwarangdo
     Knights and knighthood
     Pages, Medieval
     Tournaments
  xx Civilization, Medieval
     Courtly love

Crusades
Feudalism
Heraldry
Knights and knighthood
Manners and customs
Middle Ages—History
Orders of knighthood and chivalry
— Romances
See Romances
Chivalry in literature
Chizan (Shingon sect)
xx Buddhist sects
Shingon (Sect)
— Doctrines
xx Buddhist doctrines
Chlamydia infections (RC124.5)
xx Rickettsial diseases
— Diagnosis
Chlamydophoridae
See Armadillos
CHLOE scanner
xx Optical scanners
Chloracetic acids
See Chloroacetic acids
Chloral (Therapeutics, RM666.C4)
x Chloral-hydrate
xx Narcotics
— Physiological effect
Chloral habit (HV5813)
xx Narcotic habit
Chloral-hydrate
See Chloral
Chloramphenicol
See Chloromycetin
Chlorates (QD181.C5)
Chlordan (SB952.C4)
x Chlordane
— Toxicology (RA1242.C4)
Chlordane
See Chlordan
Chloride cells
x Chloride secreting cells
Keys-Willmer cells
Salt secreting cells
xx Cells
Fishes—Anatomy
Gills
Osmoregulation
Chloride secreting cells
See Chloride cells
Chlorides (Chemistry, QD181.C5;
Disinfectants, RE766.C4-5;
Physiological chemistry, QD535.C5)
sa specific chlorides, e.g. Cuprous chloride
Example under Chemistry, Inorganic
— Physiological effect (QP913.C5)
sa Plants, Effect of chlorides on
— Spectra
— Therapeutic use (RM666.C5)
Chlorides in the body (QP535.C5)
Chlorinated rubber
See Rubber, Chlorinated
Chlorination (Chemistry, QD281.C5;
Metallurgy, TN765)
sa Rubber, Chlorinated
x Chlorine process
xx Gold—Metallurgy
Silver—Metallurgy
Tin—Metallurgy
Chlorination of sewage
See Sewage—Purification—Chlorination
Chlorination of water
See Water—Purification—Chlorination
Chlorine (QD181.C5)
sa Liquid chlorine
Soils—Chlorine content
x Oxymuriatic acid
xx Halogens

— Effect on plants
See Plants, Effect of chlorine on
— Physiological effect
— Safety measures
— Spectra
— Toxicology
— Transportation
Chlorine and derivatives as disinfectants
(RA766.C4)
xx Disinfection and disinfectants
Chlorine compounds
sa Organochlorine compounds
Chlorine in soils
See Soils—Chlorine content
Chlorine industry (Chemical technology,
TP245.C5; Trade, HD9660.C)
Example under Chemistry, Technical
— Accounting
Chlorine organic compounds
See Organochlorine compounds
Chlorine process
See Chlorination
Chlorite minerals (Indirect)
Chlorites (QD181.C5; Mineralogy,
QE389.62)
sa Chamosite
Chlormadinone
x Lormin
xx Progestational hormones
Chloroacetic acids (QD305.A2)
x Chloracetic acids
xx Acetic acid
Chloroform (Anesthetics, RD86.C5;
Chemistry, QD305.H6)
xx Anesthetics
— Physiological effect (QP915.C6)
sa Plants, Effect of chloroform on
— Spectra
— Toxicology
Chloroleukemia
See Chloroma
Chloroma (RC643)
x Chloroleukemia
Chlorosarcoma
Green cancer
Chloromycetin
x Chloramphenicol
xx Antibiotics
Chlorophyceae
sa Desmidiales
Ulotrichales
x Green algae
xx Algae
Chlorophyll (QK898.C5)
sa Chlorosis (Plants)
Porphyrin and porphyrin compounds
xx Chloroplast pigments
Chloroplasts
Plant pigments
Plants—Chemical analysis
— Analysis
sa Primary productivity (Biology)—
Measurement
xx Primary productivity (Biology)—
Measurement
— Juvenile literature
— Physiological effect
— Spectra
— Therapeutic use
Chlorophyll synthesis
xx Biosynthesis
Chlorophyllin
xx Plant pigments
Chloroplast membranes
xx Chloroplasts
Membranes (Biology)
Chloroplast pigments
sa Carotin

Chlorophyll
xx Chloroplasts
Plant pigments
Chloroplastids
See Chloroplasts
Chloroplasts
sa Chlorophyll
Chloroplast membranes
Chloroplast pigments
Chromatophores
x Chloroplastids
xx Chromatophores
Plastids
Chloroplatinic acid (QD181.P8)
xx Platinum
Chlorosarcoma
See Chloroma
Chlorosis (RC641)
x Greensickness
Chlorosis (Plants)
xx Chlorophyll
Deficiency diseases in plants
Plants—Assimilation
Chlorpromazine
x Thorazine
Chlysty
See Khlysty
Chocho language (PM3641)
x Chuchona language
xx Indians of Mexico—Languages
Popolocan languages
Choco Indians
xx Indians of Central America
Indians of South America
— Religion and mythology
— Social life and customs
Choco language (PM5817.C4)
x Cholo language
Epera speech
Sambu dialect
xx Indians of South America—Languages
Chocolate (Chemical technology, TP638-640;
Therapeutics, RM241; Trade,
HD9200)
sa Cocoa
Cookery (Chocolate)
xx Cocoa
Note under Cacao
— Early works to 1800
— Law and legislation (Direct)
— Processing
See Chocolate processing
— Tariff
See Tariff on chocolate
— Taxation (Direct)
Chocolate industry (Direct) (Economics,
HD9999.C; Technology, TP640)
xx Confectionery
— Accounting
Chocolate processing (Indirect) (TP640)
x Chocolate—Processing
— Patents
Chocolate-tree
See Cacao
Choctaw hymns
See Hymns, Choctaw
Choctaw Indians (E99.C8)
sa Five Civilized Tribes
xx Five Civilized Tribes
Indians of North America
Muskhogean Indians
— Government relations
— Juvenile literature
— Land tenure
— Law
See Law, Choctaw
— Legal status, laws, etc.
— Tribal citizenship

Choctaw Indians *(E99.C8)*
— Tribal citizenship *(Continued)*
    xx Law, Choctaw
Choctaw language *(PM871-4)*
    sa Muskhogean languages
    x Chahta language
    xx Muskhogean languages
Choctaw law
    See Law, Choctaw
Chodhris *(DS432.C53)*
    x Chodras
    xx Ethnology—India
Chodras
    See Chodhris
Choice, Axiom of
    See Axiom of choice
Choice (Psychology)
    sa Commitment (Psychology)
    Decision-making
    Dissonance (Psychology)
    Edwards personal preference schedule
    Prisoner's dilemma game
    Risk-taking (Psychology)
    xx Decision-making
    Psychology
Choice by lot *(BF1779.L6)*
    sa Divination
    Oracles
    x Lot, Choice by
    xx Divination
    Fortune-telling
    Oracles
Choice of books
    See Bibliography—Best books
    Book selection
    Books and reading
Choice of college
    See College, Choice of
Choice of nonbook materials
    See Selection of nonbook materials
Choice of periodicals
    See Periodical selection
Choice of profession
    See Vocational guidance
Choice of school
    See School, Choice of
Choice of transportation
    x Modal choice in transportation
    Modal split (Transportation)
    Transportation, Choice of
    xx Traffic estimation
    Traffic surveys
    Transportation
— Mathematical models
Choice of vocational school
    See Vocational school, Choice of
Choir books
    See Service books (Music)
Choir boy training
    See Choirboy training
Choir boys
    See Choirboys
Choir-screens
    See Screens (Church decoration)
Choir-stalls *(Direct)* *(NA5075)*
    x Misereres (Seats)
    Stalls, Choir
    xx Church decoration and ornament
    Church furniture
Choirboy training *(MT915)*
    x Boy choir training
    Choir boy training
    xx Choirs (Music)
    Choral singing, Juvenile
— Manuals, text-books, etc. *(MT915)*
Choirboys
    sa Seises
    x Choir boys

xx Singers
Choirs (Music) *(Instruction, MT88)*
    sa Chapels (Music)
    Choirboy training
    Choral music
    Choral singing
    Choral societies
    Conducting, Choral
    Maîtrises
    xx Chapels (Music)
    Choral music
    Choral singing
    Choral societies
    Church music
    Conducting, Choral
Chōjirō pottery *(NK4168.K87)*
    x Pottery, Chōjirō
    xx Pottery, Japanese
    Raku pottery
Chokwe (Bantu tribe) *(DT611.42)*
    x Bachokwe (Bantu tribe)
    Kioko (Bantu tribe)
    Quioco (Bantu tribe)
    Tshokwe (Bantu tribe)
    xx Bantus
    Ethnology—Angola
— Religion
Chokwe language *(PL8113)*
    x Cibokwe language
    Cokwe language
    Jok language
    Katchokue language
    Kiokwe language
    Quioco language
    Tutchokue language
    xx Bantu languages
Chol language
    See Choltí language
Cholagogues
    xx Bile
    Gastrointestinal agents
    Liver
Cholam
    See Durra
Cholangiography
    See Bile-ducts—Radiography
Cholas
    x Colas
    xx India—History—324 B.C.—1000 A.D.
    Tamils
Cholecystitis *(RC853.C5)*
    xx Gall-bladder—Diseases
Cholein
    See Choline
Cholelithiasis
    See Calculi, Biliary
Cholera, Asiatic *(Direct)* *(RC126-134)*
    sa Cholera spirillum
    Vibrio comma
    x Asiatic cholera
    Example under Epidemics; Tropics—Diseases
        and hygiene
— Diagnosis
— Homeopathic treatment *(RX226.C5)*
— Immunological aspects
— Prevention *(RA644.C3)*
— Preventive inoculation *(RM761)*
— Research
Cholera infantum *(RJ456.C)*
    sa Diarrhea
    xx Diarrhea
    Summer diseases
Cholera morbus *(RC809)*
Cholera spirillum *(QR201.C5)*
    xx Cholera, Asiatic
Cholesteremia
    See Hypercholesteremia

Cholesterin
    See Cholesterol
Cholesterol *(Chemistry, QD416;*
    Physiological chemistry, QP801.C5)
    sa Blood cholesterol
    x Cholesterin
Cholesterol, Dietary
    See Low-cholesterol diet
Cholesterol inhibitors
    See Anticholesteremic agents
Cholesterol metabolism *(QP801.C5)*
    sa Hypercholesteremia
    xx Metabolism
Choline *(Chemistry, QD416; Physiological*
    chemistry, QP801.C55)
    x Cholein
Cholinergic agents
    See Parasympathomimetic agents
Cholinergic blocking agents
    See Parasympatholytic agents
Cholinesterase inhibitors
    x Anticholinesterase agents
    xx Parasympathomimetic agents
— Toxicology
Cholinolytic agents
    See Parasympatholytic agents
Cholo language
    See Choco language
Choltí language *(PM3649)*
    x Chol language
    xx Mayan languages
Choluteca language
    See Mangue language
Cholym Tatars
    See Chulyma Tatars
Chondal language
    See Chontal language
Chondrichthyes, Fossil
Chondriosomes
    See Mitochondria
Chondrites (Meteorites) *(QE395)*
    sa Chondrules
    x Chondritic meteorites
    xx Chondrules
    Meteorites
Chondritic meteorites
    See Chondrites (Meteorites)
Chondroblastoma
    xx Connective tissues—Tumors
Chondrodite *(QE391.C6)*
Chondrodystrophia foetalis
    See Rickets, Fetal
Chondroectodermal dysplasia
    See Ellis-van Creveld syndrome
Chondrostei, Fossil
Chondrules
    sa Chondrites (Meteorites)
    xx Chondrites (Meteorites)
Chonek Indians
    See Tzoneca Indians
Ch'ongch'on-gang, Battle of, 1950
    (DS918.2.C4)
    xx Korean War, 1950-1953
Ch'ŏnji Taean'gyo *(BL2240.C6)*
Chono Indians *(F2986)*
    x Chonoan Indians
    xx Indians of South America
Chonoan Indians
    See Chono Indians
Ch'ŏnt'ae (Sect)
    See Tendai (Sect)
Chontal Indians *(F1221.C)*
    xx Indians of Mexico
Chontal language *(PM3651)*
    x Chondal language
    Tequistlateca language
    xx Indians of Mexico—Languages

Chontaquiro Indians
    See Piro Indians (Peru)
Chontaquiro language
    See Chuntaquiro language
Chope language
    See Chopi language
Chopi (African tribe)
    sa Valenge (African tribe)
    x Bachopi (African tribe)
        Muchopi (African tribe)
    xx Bantus
        Valenge (African tribe)
Chopi language *(PL8115)*
    x Chope language
        Hlengwe language
        Lenge language
        Shilenge language
        Si-tswa language
        Silenge language
        Xilenge language
    xx Bantu languages
Choppers
    See Forage harvesting machinery
Choptank Indians
    xx Indians of North America
    — Land transfers
Chopunnish Indians
    See Nez Percé Indians
Chora language
    See Cora language
Choral conducting
    See Conducting, Choral
Choral music *(Indirect) (History: general,*
        ML1500-1554; sacred,
        ML2900-3275; secular,
        ML2400-2770)
    Here are entered works on choral music.
    Collections of sacred and secular cho-
    ral compositions are entered under the
    heading Choruses.
    sa Cantata
        Choirs (Music)
        Choral singing
        Choral societies
        Conducting, Choral
        Madrigal
        Motet
        Part-song
    x Music, Choral
    xx Choirs (Music)
        Choral societies
        Church music
        Music
        Vocal music—History and criticism
    Note under Choruses
Choral reading
    See Choral speaking
Choral recitations *(PN4305.C4)*
    xx Choral speaking
        Recitations
Choral singing *(Direct) (MT875)*
    sa Choirs (Music)
        Choral societies
        Conducting, Choral
    x Singing, Choral
    xx Choirs (Music)
        Choral music
        Conducting, Choral
        Singing
    — Diction *(MT875)*
        xx Singing—Diction
    — Instruction and study *(MT898-945)*
    — Interpretation (Phrasing, dynamics, etc.)
        (MT875)
Choral singing, Juvenile *(MT898-945)*
    sa Choirboy training
    xx School song-books

Choral societies *(Direct) (ML25-28; MT88)*
    sa Choirs (Music)
        Choral music
        Community music
    x Singing societies
    xx Choirs (Music)
        Choral music
        Choral singing
        Musical societies
Choral societies, German *(ML26-28)*
Choral speaking *(PN4193.C5)*
    sa Choral recitations
    x Choral reading
        Speaking choirs
        Unison speaking
    xx Drama—Chorus
        Elocution
Choral vicars
    See Minor canons, Cathedral, collegiate,
        etc.
Chorale *(Catholic, ML3084;*
        Nondenominational, ML3265;
        Protestant, ML3184)
    sa Chorale prelude
    xx Chorale prelude
        Church music
        Church music—Lutheran Church
        Hymn tunes
        Hymns, German
        Lutheran Church—Hymns
        Musical form
Chorale prelude
    sa Chorale
    xx Chorale
        Hymns, German
        Musical form
Chorale preludes
    Here are entered compositions originally
    written or arranged for organ. Similar
    compositions written for media other
    than organ receive the heading Cho-
    rale preludes, followed by specification
    of medium, *e.g.* Chorale preludes (Or-
    chestra)
    sa Chorales
    xx Chorales
        Organ music
Chorale preludes (Band) *(M1245; M1258)*
    xx Band music
Chorale preludes (Harpsichord)
    xx Harpsichord music
Chorale preludes (Instrumental ensemble)
    xx Instrumental ensembles
Chorale preludes (Oboe and organ)
        (M182-6)
    xx Oboe and organ music
Chorale preludes (Orchestra) *(M1045;*
        M1060)
    xx Orchestral music
    Note under Chorale preludes
Chorale preludes (Organ, horns (2), trombone,
        trumpets (2)) *(M600-602)*
    xx Sextets (Organ, horns (2), trombone,
        trumpets (2))
Chorale preludes (Piano)
    xx Piano music
Chorale preludes (Piano and organ)
        (M182-6)
    xx Piano and organ music
Chorale preludes (Pianos (2)) *(M214-215)*
    xx Piano music (Pianos (2))
Chorale preludes (String orchestra) *(M1145;*
        M1160)
    xx String-orchestra music
    — Scores and parts *(M1145; M1160)*

Chorale preludes (Trombones (2), trumpets
        (2)) *(M455-7)*
    xx Wind quartets (Trombones (2),
        trumpets (2))
Chorale preludes (Trumpet and organ)
        (M182-6)
    xx Trumpet and organ music
Chorale preludes (Violin and piano)
        (M217-218; M221-3)
    xx Violin and piano music
Chorale preludes (Violoncello and piano)
        (M229-230; M233-6)
    xx Violoncello and piano music
Chorales
    sa Chorale preludes
    xx Chorale preludes
        Choruses, Sacred
        Hymns, German
        Lutheran Church—Hymns
        Sacred vocal music
        Tune-books
    — Analytical guides
Chorales (Instrumental settings)
Chordata *(QL605-7)*
    sa Protochordates
        Tunicata
        Vertebrates
Chordata, Fossil
Chordeumida *(Indirect) (QL449)*
    xx Millepeds
Chorea *(RC389)*
    sa Athetosis
        Hereditary chorea
    x St. Vitus's dance
    xx Movement disorders
Chorea, Epidemic *(RC389)*
    sa Hysteria, Epidemic
    x Dancing mania
        Epidemic chorea
    xx Hysteria, Epidemic
Choreography
    sa Ballet
        Dance notation
    xx Ballet
        Dancing
Chorepiscopi *(BX1939.R8)*
    x Rural bishops
    xx Archdeacons
        Bishops
        Dioceses
        Rural deans
Choresmian language
    See Khorezmi language
Chorioallantois
    sa Chorion
    xx Fetal membranes
Choriocarcinoma
    xx Trophoblastic tumors
Choriomeningitis, Lymphocytic
    See Lymphocytic choriomeningitis
Chorion *(QL977; QM611)*
    xx Chorioallantois
        Fetal membranes
    — Tumors *(RG591)*
Chorionic gonadotropins
    xx Gonadotropin
Chorionitis
    See Scleroderma (Disease)
Chorioretinitis
    xx Eye—Diseases and defects
Choroid *(QL949; QM511)*
    sa Tapetum lucidum
    xx Eye
    — Diseases *(RE551-661)*
        x Choroiditis
        xx Eye—Diseases and defects
Choroid plexus *(QL937; QM455)*
    x Plexus, Choroid

Choroid plexus   (QL937; QM455)
(Continued)
   xx Brain
Choroiditis
   See Choroid—Diseases
Chorotega Indians
   See Mangue Indians
Chorotega language
   See Mangue language
Chorotegans
   See Mangue Indians
Chorotes Indians
   See Choroti Indians
Choroti Indians   (F3320.2.C)
   x Chorotes Indians
     Yofuaha Indians
   xx Indians of South America
Choroti language   (PM5817.C7)
   x Yofuaha language
Chorros Blancos, Battle of, 1820
   xx Colombia—History—War of
     Independence, 1810-1822
Chorti Indians   (F1465.2.C5)
   xx Indians of Central America
     Mayas
Chorti language   (PM3661)
   xx Indians of Central America—Languages
Chorus, Dawn (Radio meteorology)
   See Dawn chorus (Radio meteorology)
Chorus (Drama)
   See Drama—Chorus
     Drama—Chorus (Greek drama)
Choruses   (M1495)
     Here are entered collections of sacred
     and secular choral compositions, for
     various groups of voices (men's,
     mixed, women's), both accompanied
     and unaccompanied. Works on cho-
     ruses are entered under the heading
     Choral music.
   sa Canons, fugues, etc. (Vocal)
     Part-songs
     Song-books
   xx Cantatas
     Madrigals (Music)
     Part-songs
     Vocal music
   Note under Choral music
Choruses, Sacred   (M2060)
     Here are entered collections of sacred
     choral compositions, for various
     groups of voices (men's, mixed, wo-
     men's), both accompanied and unac-
     companied.
   sa Chorales
     Part-songs, Sacred
     Sacred duets
     Sacred nonets
     Sacred octets
     Sacred quartets
     Sacred quintets
     Sacred septets
     Sacred sextets
     Sacred trios
     Service books (Music)
   x Sacred choruses
   xx Anthems
     Motets
     Part-songs, Sacred
     Sacred songs
     Sacred vocal music
Choruses, Sacred (Changing voices)
Choruses, Sacred (Equal voices)   (M2060)
Choruses, Sacred (Equal voices) with
     instr. ensemble   (M2021)
Choruses, Sacred (Equal voices, 2 pts.) with
     organ   (M2064.2; M2074.2)
Choruses, Sacred (Equal voices, 2 pts.) with
     piano   (M2064.2; M2074.2)

Choruses, Sacred (Equal voices, 2 pts.) with
     trumpets (2)   (M2064.2; M2074.2)
Choruses, Sacred (Equal voices, 3 pts.)
     (M2060)
Choruses, Sacred (Equal voices, 3 pts.),
     Unaccompanied   (M2084.3;
     M2094.3)
Choruses, Sacred (Equal voices, 3 pts.) with
     organ   (M2064.3; M2074.3)
Choruses, Sacred (Equal voices, 3 pts.) with
     piano   (M2064.3; M2074.3)
Choruses, Sacred (Equal voices, 4 pts.) with
     organ   (M2064.4; M2074.4)
Choruses, Sacred (Equal voices),
     Unaccompanied   (M2084)
Choruses, Sacred (Men's voices)   (M2060)
Choruses, Sacred (Men's voices, 2 pts.) with
     instr. ensemble   (M2029)
Choruses, Sacred (Men's voices, 2 pts.) with
     organ   (M2063.2; M2073.2)
Choruses, Sacred (Men's voices, 3 pts.),
     Unaccompanied   (M2083.3;
     M2093.3)
Choruses, Sacred (Men's voices, 3 pts.) with
     instr. ensemble   (M2029)
Choruses, Sacred (Men's voices, 3 pts.) with
     orchestra   (M2029-2032)
   — Scores   (M2029)
Choruses, Sacred (Men's voices, 3 pts.) with
     organ   (M2063.3; M2073.3)
Choruses, Sacred (Men's voices, 4 pts.)
     (M2060)
Choruses, Sacred (Men's voices, 4 pts.),
     Unaccompanied   (M2083.4;
     M2093.4)
Choruses, Sacred (Men's voices, 4 pts.) with
     band
   — Parts   (M2029)
Choruses, Sacred (Men's voices, 4 pts.) with
     instr. ensemble   (M2029)
Choruses, Sacred (Men's voices, 4 pts.) with
     orchestra
   — Vocal scores with organ   (M2030)
     xx Choruses, Sacred (Men's voices, 4
      pts.) with organ
Choruses, Sacred (Men's voices, 4 pts.) with
     organ   (M2063.4; M2073.4)
   sa Choruses, Sacred (Men's voices, 4 pts.)
     with orchestra—Vocal scores with
     organ
Choruses, Sacred (Men's voices, 4 pts.) with
     piano   (M2063.4; M2073.4)
Choruses, Sacred (Men's voices, 4 pts.) with
     piano, 4 hands   (M2063.4;
     M2073.4)
Choruses, Sacred (Men's voices, 6 pts.) with
     orchestra   (M2029)
   — Scores   (M2029)
Choruses, Sacred (Men's voices, 7 pts.) with
     orchestra
   — Vocal scores with piano   (M2030)
     xx Choruses, Sacred (Men's voices, 7
      pts.) with piano
Choruses, Sacred (Men's voices, 7 pts.) with
     piano   (M2063.6; M2073.6)
   sa Choruses, Sacred (Men's voices, 7 pts.)
     with orchestra—Vocal scores with
     piano
Choruses, Sacred (Men's voices, 12 pts.) with
     orchestra
   — Scores   (M2029)
Choruses, Sacred (Men's voices),
     Unaccompanied   (M2083)
Choruses, Sacred (Men's voices) with instr.
     ensemble   (M2029)
Choruses, Sacred (Men's voices) with organ
     (M2063; M2073)
Choruses, Sacred (Mixed voices)   (M2060)

Choruses, Sacred (Mixed voices, 2 pts.)
     (M2060)
Choruses, Sacred (Mixed voices, 2 pts.) with
     handbells   (M2021)
Choruses, Sacred (Mixed voices, 2 pts.) with
     organ   (M2062.2; M2072.2)
Choruses, Sacred (Mixed voices, 3 pts.)
     (M2060)
Choruses, Sacred (Mixed voices, 3 pts.),
     Unaccompanied   (M2082.3;
     M2092.3)
Choruses, Sacred (Mixed voices, 3 pts.) with
     band
   — Scores   (M2103.3)
Choruses, Sacred (Mixed voices, 3 pts.) with
     harpsichord   (M2062.3; M2072.3)
Choruses, Sacred (Mixed voices, 3 pts.) with
     instr. ensemble   (M2021)
Choruses, Sacred (Mixed voices, 3 pts.) with
     orchestra
   — To 1800
    — —Scores   (M2020)
   — Scores   (M2020)
Choruses, Sacred (Mixed voices, 3 pts.) with
     organ   (M2062.3; M2072.3)
Choruses, Sacred (Mixed voices, 3 pts.) with
     piano   (M2062.3; M2072.3)
Choruses, Sacred (Mixed voices, 4 pts.)
     (M2060)
Choruses, Sacred (Mixed voices, 4 pts.),
     Unaccompanied   (M2082.4;
     M2092.4)
   — To 1800
   Note under Motets
Choruses, Sacred (Mixed voices, 4 pts.) with
     band
   — Scores (reduced) and parts   (M2021)
   — Scores (reduced) and parts (instrumental)
     (M2021)
   — Vocal scores with organ   (M2023)
     xx Choruses, Sacred (Mixed voices, 4
      pts.) with organ
Choruses, Sacred (Mixed voices, 4 pts.) with
     chamber orchestra
   — Scores   (M2021)
   — Vocal scores with piano   (M2023)
     xx Choruses, Sacred (Mixed voices, 4
      pts.) with piano
Choruses, Sacred (Mixed voices, 4 pts.) with
     guitar   (M2062.4; M2072.4)
Choruses, Sacred (Mixed voices, 4 pts.) with
     instr. ensemble   (M2021)
Choruses, Sacred (Mixed voices, 4 pts.) with
     orchestra
   — To 1800
    — —Scores   (M2020)
     xx Choruses, Sacred (Mixed voices, 4
      pts.) with piano
   — Scores   (M2020)
   — Vocal scores with organ   (M2023)
     xx Choruses, Sacred (Mixed voices, 4
      pts.) with organ
   — Vocal scores with piano   (M2023)
     xx Choruses, Sacred (Mixed voices, 4
      pts.) with piano
Choruses, Sacred (Mixed voices, 4 pts.) with
     orchestra and organ
   — Scores   (M2020)
   — Vocal scores with piano   (M2023)
     xx Choruses, Sacred (Mixed voices, 4
      pts.) with piano
Choruses, Sacred (Mixed voices, 4 pts.) with
     orchestra and piano
   — Vocal scores with piano   (M2023)
     xx Choruses, Sacred (Mixed voices, 4
      pts.) with piano

Choruses, Sacred (Mixed voices, 4 pts.) with
   organ *(M2062.4; M2072.4)*
   sa Choruses, Sacred (Mixed voices, 4 pts.)
     with string orchestra—To 1800—
     Vocal scores with organ
    Choruses, Sacred (Mixed voices, 4 pts.)
     with orchestra—Vocal scores with
     organ
    Choruses, Sacred (Mixed voices, 4 pts.)
     with band—Vocal scores with organ
Choruses, Sacred (Mixed voices, 4 pts.) with
   piano *(M2062.4; M2072.4)*
   sa Choruses, Sacred (Mixed voices, 4 pts.)
     with orchestra and organ—Vocal
     scores with piano
    Choruses, Sacred (Mixed voices, 4 pts.)
     with orchestra—Vocal scores with
     piano
    Choruses, Sacred (Mixed voices, 4 pts.)
     with string orchestra and piano—
     Vocal scores with piano
    Choruses, Sacred (Mixed voices, 4 pts.)
     with string orchestra—Vocal scores
     with piano
    Choruses, Sacred (Mixed voices, 4 pts.)
     with orchestra—To 1800—Vocal
     scores with piano
    Choruses, Sacred (Mixed voices, 4 pts.)
     with orchestra and piano—Vocal
     scores with piano
    Choruses, Sacred (Mixed voices, 4 pts.)
     with chamber orchestra—Vocal
     scores with piano
Choruses, Sacred (Mixed voices, 4 pts.) with
   piano and organ *(M2062.4;
   M2072.4)*
Choruses, Sacred (Mixed voices, 4 pts.) with
   pianos (2) *(M2062.4; M2072.4)*
Choruses, Sacred (Mixed voices, 4 pts.) with
   string orchestra
  —To 1800
  ——Vocal scores with organ *(M2023)*
     xx Choruses, Sacred (Mixed voices, 4
      pts.) with organ
  —Vocal scores with piano *(M2023)*
     xx Choruses, Sacred (Mixed voices, 4
      pts.) with piano
Choruses, Sacred (Mixed voices, 4 pts.) with
   string orchestra and organ
  —Scores *(M2021)*
Choruses, Sacred (Mixed voices, 4 pts.) with
   string orchestra and piano
   (M2021; M2023)
  —Scores *(M2021)*
  —Vocal scores with piano *(M2023)*
     xx Choruses, Sacred (Mixed voices, 4
      pts.) with piano
Choruses, Sacred (Mixed voices, 4 pts.) with
   trumpets (2) and organ *(M2062.4;
   M2072.4)*
Choruses, Sacred (Mixed voices, 5 pts.),
   Unaccompanied *(M2082.5;
   M2092.5)*
Choruses, Sacred (Mixed voices, 5 pts.) with
   chamber orchestra *(M2021)*
  —To 1800
  ——Scores
Choruses, Sacred (Mixed voices, 5 pts.) with
   instr. ensemble *(M2021)*
Choruses, Sacred (Mixed voices, 5 pts.) with
   orchestra
  —To 1800
    Note under Anthems
  ——Scores *(M2020)*
  —Vocal scores with piano *(M2023)*
     xx Choruses, Sacred (Mixed voices, 5
      pts.) with piano

Choruses, Sacred (Mixed voices, 5 pts.) with
   organ *(M2062.5; M2072.5)*
Choruses, Sacred (Mixed voices, 5 pts.) with
   piano *(M2062.5; M2072.5)*
   sa Choruses, Sacred (Mixed voices, 5 pts.)
     with orchestra—Vocal scores with
     piano
Choruses, Sacred (Mixed voices, 5 pts.) with
   string orchestra *(M2021)*
Choruses, Sacred (Mixed voices, 6 pts.),
   Unaccompanied *(M2082.6;
   M2092.6)*
Choruses, Sacred (Mixed voices, 6 pts.) with
   band
  —Scores and parts *(M2021)*
Choruses, Sacred (Mixed voices, 6 pts.) with
   instr. ensemble *(M2021)*
Choruses, Sacred (Mixed voices, 6 pts.) with
   orchestra
  —Scores (reduced) *(M2020)*
  —Scores (reduced) and parts *(M2020)*
  —Vocal scores with 2 pianos *(M2023)*
     xx Choruses, Sacred (Mixed voices, 6
      pts.) with 2 pianos
  —Vocal scores with organ *(M2023)*
     xx Choruses, Sacred (Mixed voices, 6
      pts.) with organ
  —Vocal scores with piano *(M2023)*
     xx Choruses, Sacred (Mixed voices, 6
      pts.) with piano
Choruses, Sacred (Mixed voices, 6 pts.) with
   organ *(M2062.6; M2072.6)*
   sa Choruses, Sacred (Mixed voices, 6 pts.)
     with orchestra—Vocal scores with
     organ
Choruses, Sacred (Mixed voices, 6 pts.) with
   piano *(M2062.6; M2072.6)*
   sa Choruses, Sacred (Mixed voices, 6 pts.)
     with orchestra—Vocal scores with
     piano
    Choruses, Sacred (Mixed voices, 6 pts.)
     with string orchestra—To 1800—
     Vocal scores with piano
Choruses, Sacred (Mixed voices, 6 pts.) with
   pianos (2) *(M2062.6; M2072.6)*
   sa Choruses, Sacred (Mixed voices, 6 pts.)
     with orchestra—Vocal scores with
     pianos (2)
Choruses, Sacred (Mixed voices, 6 pts.) with
   string orchestra
  —To 1800
  ——Vocal scores with piano *(M2023)*
     xx Choruses, Sacred (Mixed voices, 6
      pts.) with piano
  ——Vocal scores with piano *(M2023)*
Choruses, Sacred (Mixed voices, 7 pts.),
   Unaccompanied *(M2082.6;
   M2092.6)*
Choruses, Sacred (Mixed voices, 7 pts.) with
   band *(M2021)*
  —Vocal scores with piano *(M2023)*
     xx Choruses, Sacred (Mixed voices, 7
      pts.) with piano
Choruses, Sacred (Mixed voices, 7 pts.) with
   chamber orchestra
  —Vocal scores with piano *(M2023)*
     xx Choruses, Sacred (Mixed voices, 7
      pts.) with piano
Choruses, Sacred (Mixed voices, 7 pts.) with
   instr. ensemble *(M2021)*
Choruses, Sacred (Mixed voices, 7 pts.) with
   orchestra
  —Vocal scores with piano *(M2023)*
     xx Choruses, Sacred (Mixed voices, 7
      pts.) with piano
Choruses, Sacred (Mixed voices, 7 pts.) with
   organ *(M2062.6; M2072.6)*

Choruses, Sacred (Mixed voices, 7 pts.) with
   piano *(M2062.6; M2072.6)*
   sa Choruses, Sacred (Mixed voices, 7 pts.)
     with orchestra—Vocal scores with
     piano
    Choruses, Sacred (Mixed voices, 7 pts.)
     with chamber orchestra—Vocal
     scores with piano
    Choruses, Sacred (Mixed voices, 7 pts.)
     with band—Vocal scores with piano
Choruses, Sacred (Mixed voices, 8 pts.),
   Unaccompanied *(M2082.6;
   M2092.6)*
Choruses, Sacred (Mixed voices, 8 pts.) with
   band
  —Scores (reduced) and parts *(M2021)*
Choruses, Sacred (Mixed voices, 8 pts.) with
   chamber orchestra
  —Vocal scores with piano *(M2023)*
     xx Choruses, Sacred (Mixed voices, 8
      pts.) with piano
Choruses, Sacred (Mixed voices, 8 pts.) with
   instr. ensemble *(M2021)*
Choruses, Sacred (Mixed voices, 8 pts.) with
   orchestra
  —To 1800
  ——Scores *(M2020)*
  —Scores *(M2020)*
  —Scores (reduced) and parts *(M2020)*
  —Vocal scores *(M2022)*
  —Vocal scores with piano *(M2023)*
     xx Choruses, Sacred (Mixed voices, 8
      pts.) with piano
  —Vocal scores with pianos (2) *(M2023)*
     xx Choruses, Sacred (Mixed voices, 8
      pts.) with pianos (2)
Choruses, Sacred (Mixed voices, 8 pts.) with
   orchestra and organ *(M2020)*
  —Vocal scores with piano *(M2023)*
Choruses, Sacred (Mixed voices, 8 pts.) with
   organ *(M2062.6; M2072.6)*
Choruses, Sacred (Mixed voices, 8 pts.) with
   piano *(M2062.6; M2072.6)*
   sa Choruses, Sacred (Mixed voices, 8 pts.)
     with chamber orchestra—Vocal
     scores with piano
    Choruses, Sacred (Mixed voices, 8 pts.)
     with orchestra—Vocal scores with
     piano
    Choruses, Sacred (Mixed voices, 8 pts.)
     with string orchestra and organ—
     Vocal scores with piano
Choruses, Sacred (Mixed voices, 8 pts.) with
   piano, 4 hands *(M2062.6;
   M2072.6)*
Choruses, Sacred (Mixed voices, 8 pts.) with
   pianos (2) *(M2062.6; M2072.6)*
   sa Choruses, Sacred (Mixed voices, 8 pts.)
     with orchestra—Vocal scores with
     pianos (2)
Choruses, Sacred (Mixed voices, 8 pts.) with
   string orchestra
  —Scores *(M2021)*
Choruses, Sacred (Mixed voices, 8 pts.) with
   string orchestra and organ
     xx Choruses, Sacred (Mixed voices, 8 pts.)
     with piano
  —Vocal scores with piano *(M2023)*
Choruses, Sacred (Mixed voices, 9 pts.),
   Unaccompanied *(M2082.6;
   M2092.6)*
Choruses, Sacred (Mixed voices, 9 pts.) with
   orchestra
  —Vocal scores with piano *(M2023)*
     xx Choruses, Sacred (Mixed voices, 9
      pts.) with piano

Choruses, Sacred (Mixed voices, 9 pts.) with
    piano (M2062.6; M2072.6)
    sa Choruses, Sacred (Mixed voices, 9 pts.)
        with orchestra—Vocal scores with
        piano
Choruses, Sacred (Mixed voices, 10 pts.) with
    orchestra (M2020-2023)
    —Scores (M2020)
Choruses, Sacred (Mixed voices, 10 pts.) with
    organ (M2062.6; M2072.6)
Choruses, Sacred (Mixed voices, 11 pts.) with
    band (M2021; M2023)
    —Scores (M2021)
Choruses, Sacred (Mixed voices, 11 pts.) with
    orchestra (M2020)
    —Vocal scores with piano (M2023)
Choruses, Sacred (Mixed voices, 12 pts.),
    Unaccompanied (M2082.6;
    M2092.6)
Choruses, Sacred (Mixed voices, 12 pts.) with
    organ (M2062.6; M2072.6)
Choruses, Sacred (Mixed voices, 13 pts.),
    Unaccompanied (M2082.6;
    M2092.6)
Choruses, Sacred (Mixed voices, 13 pts.) with
    instr. ensemble (M2021)
Choruses, Sacred (Mixed voices, 13 pts.) with
    organ (M2062.6; M2072.6)
Choruses, Sacred (Mixed voices, 14 pts.) with
    instr. ensemble (M2021)
Choruses, Sacred (Mixed voices, 15 pts.) with
    organ (M2062.6; M2072.6)
Choruses, Sacred (Mixed voices, 16 pts.),
    Unaccompanied (M2082.6;
    M2092.6)
Choruses, Sacred (Mixed voices, 16 pts.) with
    instr. ensemble (M2021)
Choruses, Sacred (Mixed voices, 16 pts.) with
    orchestra
    —Vocal scores with piano (M2023)
        xx Choruses, Sacred (Mixed voices, 16
            pts.) with piano
Choruses, Sacred (Mixed voices, 16 pts.) with
    organ (M2062.6; M2072.6)
Choruses, Sacred (Mixed voices, 16 pts.) with
    piano (M2062.6; M2072.6)
    sa Choruses, Sacred (Mixed voices, 16
        pts.) with orchestra—Vocal scores
        with piano
Choruses, Sacred (Mixed voices, 24 pts.) with
    organ (M2062.6; M2072.6)
Choruses, Sacred (Mixed voices),
    Unaccompanied (M2082)
Choruses, Sacred (Mixed voices) with band
    (M2021)
Choruses, Sacred (Mixed voices) with instr.
    ensemble (M2021)
Choruses, Sacred (Mixed voices) with jazz
    ensemble (M2021)
    xx Jazz ensembles
Choruses, Sacred (Mixed voices) with
    orchestra
    —To 1800
    ——Scores (M2020)
    ——Vocal scores with organ (M2023)
        xx Choruses, Sacred (Mixed voices)
            with organ
    ——Vocal scores with piano (M2023)
        xx Choruses, Sacred (Mixed voices)
            with piano
Choruses, Sacred (Mixed voices) with
    orchestra and organ
Choruses, Sacred (Mixed voices) with organ
    (M2062)
    sa Choruses, Sacred (Mixed voices) with
        orchestra—To 1800—Vocal scores
        with organ

Choruses, Sacred (Mixed voices) with
    string orchestra—To 1800—Vocal
    scores with organ
Choruses, Sacred (Mixed voices) with
    percussion (M2021)
Choruses, Sacred (Mixed voices) with piano
    (M2062)
    sa Choruses, Sacred (Mixed voices) with
        orchestra—To 1800—Vocal scores
        with piano
Choruses, Sacred (Mixed voices) with string
    orchestra
    —To 1800
    ——Scores (M2021)
    ——Vocal scores with organ (M2023)
        xx Choruses, Sacred (Mixed voices)
            with organ
Choruses, Sacred (Mixed voices) with string
    orchestra and organs (2) (M2021)
    —To 1800
    ——Scores (M2021)
Choruses, Sacred (Mixed voices) with various
    acc. (M2060)
Choruses, Sacred, Unaccompanied (M2081)
Choruses, Sacred (Unison) (M2101.5)
Choruses, Sacred (Unison) with guitar
    (M2101.5)
Choruses, Sacred (Unison) with instr.
    ensemble (M2101.5)
Choruses, Sacred (Unison) with oboe and
    organ (M2101.5)
Choruses, Sacred (Unison) with orchestra
    —Scores (M2101.5)
Choruses, Sacred (Unison) with organ
    (M2101.5)
Choruses, Sacred (Unison) with piano
    (M2101.5)
    sa Choruses, Sacred (Unison) with string
        orchestra—Vocal scores with piano
Choruses, Sacred (Unison) with string
    ensemble (M2101.5)
Choruses, Sacred (Unison) with string
    orchestra
    —Vocal scores with piano (M2101.5)
        xx Choruses, Sacred (Unison) with
            piano
Choruses, Sacred, with orchestra
    sa Sacred monologues with music (Chorus
        with orchestra)
    —To 1800
    ——Scores
Choruses, Sacred, with organ (M2061)
    sa Sacred monologues with music (Chorus
        with orchestra)—Vocal scores with
        organ
Choruses, Sacred, with piano (M2061)
    sa Sacred monologues with music (Chorus
        with orchestra)—Vocal scores with
        piano
Choruses, Sacred (Women's voices) (M2060)
Choruses, Sacred (Women's voices, 2 pts.),
    Unaccompanied (M2084.2;
    M2094.2)
Choruses, Sacred (Women's voices, 2 pts.)
    with instr. ensemble (M2033)
Choruses, Sacred (Women's voices, 2 pts.)
    with orchestra
    —To 1800
    ——Vocal scores with organ (M2034)
        xx Choruses, Sacred (Women's
            voices, 2 pts.) with organ
Choruses, Sacred (Women's voices, 2 pts.)
    with organ (M2064.2; M2074.2)
    sa Choruses, Sacred (Women's voices, 2
        pts.) with orchestra—To 1800—
        Vocal scores with organ

Choruses, Sacred (Women's voices, 2 pts.)
    with piano (M2064.2; M2074.2)
    sa Choruses, Sacred (Women's voices, 2
        pts.) with string orchestra—Vocal
        scores with piano
Choruses, Sacred (Women's voices, 2 pts.)
    with string orchestra
    —Scores (M2033)
    —Vocal scores with piano (M2034)
        xx Choruses, Sacred (Women's voices, 2
            pts.) with piano
Choruses, Sacred (Women's voices, 3 pts.)
    (M2060)
Choruses, Sacred (Women's voices, 3 pts.),
    Unaccompanied (M2084.3;
    M2094.3)
Choruses, Sacred (Women's voices, 3 pts.)
    with flute and piano (M2064.3;
    M2074.3)
Choruses, Sacred (Women's voices, 3 pts.)
    with harp (M2064.3; M2074.3)
Choruses, Sacred (Women's voices, 3 pts.)
    with instr. ensemble (M2033)
Choruses, Sacred (Women's voices, 3 pts.)
    with orchestra
    —Scores (M2033)
    —Vocal scores (M2034)
Choruses, Sacred (Women's voices, 3 pts.)
    with organ (M2064.3; M2074.3)
Choruses, Sacred (Women's voices, 3 pts.)
    with piano (M2064.3; M2074.3)
Choruses, Sacred (Women's voices, 3 pts.)
    with string orchestra
    —Scores (M2033)
Choruses, Sacred (Women's voices, 4 pts.)
    (M2060)
Choruses, Sacred (Women's voices, 4 pts.),
    Unaccompanied (M2084.4;
    M2094.4)
Choruses, Sacred (Women's voices, 4 pts.)
    with chamber orchestra (M2033)
    —Vocal scores with piano (M2034)
        xx Choruses, Sacred (Women's voices, 4
            pts.) with piano
Choruses, Sacred (Women's voices, 4 pts.)
    with instr. ensemble (M2033)
Choruses, Sacred (Women's voices, 4 pts.)
    with orchestra
    —To 1800
    ——Scores (M2033)
    —Scores (M2033)
Choruses, Sacred (Women's voices, 4 pts.)
    with organ (M2064.4; M2074.4)
Choruses, Sacred (Women's voices, 4 pts.)
    with piano (M2064.4; M2074.4)
    sa Choruses, Sacred (Women's voices, 4
        pts.) with chamber orchestra—Vocal
        scores with piano
Choruses, Sacred (Women's voices, 4 pts.)
    with string orchestra
    —Scores (M2033)
    —Vocal scores (M2034)
Choruses, Sacred (Women's voices, 5 pts.),
    Unaccompanied (M2084.5;
    M2094.5)
Choruses, Sacred (Women's voices, 5 pts.)
    with instr. ensemble (M2033)
Choruses, Sacred (Women's voices, 5 pts.)
    with orchestra (M2033-6)
    —Vocal scores (M2034)
Choruses, Sacred (Women's voices, 6 pts.)
    with orchestra
    —Scores (M2033)
Choruses, Sacred (Women's voices, 6 pts.)
    with piano (M2064.6; M2074.6)
Choruses, Sacred (Women's voices, 7 pts.)
    with instr. ensemble (M2033)

Choruses, Sacred (Women's voices, 8 pts.),
Unaccompanied (M2084.6;
M2094.6)
Choruses, Sacred (Women's voices),
Unaccompanied (M2084)
Choruses, Sacred (Women's voices) with instr.
ensemble (M2033)
Choruses, Sacred (Women's voices) with organ
(M2064)
Choruses, Sacred (Women's voices) with piano
(M2064)
Choruses, Secular (M1547)
Here are entered collections of secular
choral compositions, for various
groups of voices (men's, mixed, wo-
men's), both accompanied and unac-
companied.
sa Part-songs
Song-books
Vocal duets
Vocal nonets
Vocal octets
Vocal quartets
Vocal quintets
Vocal septets
Vocal sextets
Vocal trios
x Secular choruses
xx Madrigals (Music)
Part-songs
Choruses, Secular (Children's voices)
(M1546.5; M1997-8)
Choruses, Secular (Children's voices) with
instrumental ensemble (M1546.5;
M1997-8)
Choruses, Secular (Equal voices, 2 pts.) with
chamber orchestra (M1543-6)
Choruses, Secular (Equal voices, 2 pts.) with
piano (M1551.2; M1572)
Choruses, Secular (Equal voices, 3 pts.),
Unaccompanied (M1581.3; M1603)
Choruses, Secular (Equal voices, 3 pts.) with
instrumental ensemble (M1531;
M1539; M1543.5)
Choruses, Secular (Equal voices, 3 pts.) with
orchestra (M1543-6)
— Vocal scores with piano (M1544)
xx Choruses, Secular (Equal voices, 3
pts.) with piano
Choruses, Secular (Equal voices, 3 pts.) with
piano
sa Choruses, Secular (Equal voices, 3 pts.)
with orchestra—Vocal scores with
piano
Choruses, Secular (Equal voices),
Unaccompanied (M1581)
Choruses, Secular (Men's voices) (M1547)
Choruses, Secular (Men's voices, 2 pts.) with
orchestra
— Vocal scores with piano (M1540)
xx Choruses, Secular (Men's voices, 2
pts.) with piano
Choruses, Secular (Men's voices, 2 pts.) with
piano (M1550.2; M1562)
sa Choruses, Secular (Men's voices, 2 pts.)
with orchestra—Vocal scores with
piano
Choruses, Secular (Men's voices, 3 pts.),
Unaccompanied (M1580.3; M1593)
Choruses, Secular (Men's voices, 3 pts.) with
band
— Vocal scores with piano (M1540)
xx Choruses, Secular (Men's voices, 3
pts.) with piano
Choruses, Secular (Men's voices, 3 pts.) with
percussion (M1539)

Choruses, Secular (Men's voices, 3 pts.) with
piano (M1550.3; M1563)
sa Choruses, Secular (Men's voices, 3 pts.)
with band—Vocal scores with piano
Choruses, Secular (Men's voices, 3 pts.) with
violin (M1550.3; M1563)
Choruses, Secular (Men's voices, 4 pts.)
(M1547)
Choruses, Secular (Men's voices, 4 pts.),
Unaccompanied (M1580.4; M1594)
Choruses, Secular (Men's voices, 4 pts.) with
band
— Scores (reduced) and parts (M1539)
— Vocal scores with piano (M1540)
xx Choruses, Secular (Men's voices, 4
pts.) with piano
Choruses, Secular (Men's voices, 4 pts.) with
instr. ensemble (M1539)
Choruses, Secular (Men's voices, 4 pts.) with
orchestra
— Parts (vocal) (M1540)
— Scores (reduced) and parts (M1538)
— Vocal scores with piano (M1540)
xx Choruses, Secular (Men's voices, 4
pts.) with piano
Choruses, Secular (Men's voices, 4 pts.) with
percussion instruments (M1539)
Choruses, Secular (Men's voices, 4 pts.) with
piano (M1550.4; M1564)
sa Choruses, Secular (Men's voices, 4 pts.)
with string orchestra—Vocal scores
with piano
Choruses, Secular (Men's voices, 4 pts.)
with band—Vocal scores with piano
Choruses, Secular (Men's voices, 4 pts.)
with orchestra—Vocal scores with
piano
Choruses, Secular (Men's voices, 4 pts.) with
piano, 4 hands (M1550.4; M1564)
Choruses, Secular (Men's voices, 4 pts.) with
piano and reed-organ (M1550.4;
M1564)
Choruses, Secular (Men's voices, 4 pts.) with
pianos (2) (M1550.4; M1564)
Choruses, Secular (Men's voices, 4 pts.) with
string orchestra
— Vocal scores with piano (M1540)
xx Choruses, Secular (Men's voices, 4
pts.) with piano
Choruses, Secular (Men's voices, 5 pts.),
Unaccompanied (M1580.5; M1595)
Choruses, Secular (Men's voices, 5 pts.) with
orchestra (M1538-1542)
— Vocal scores with piano (M1540)
Choruses, Secular (Men's voices, 6 pts.),
Unaccompanied (M1580.6; M1596)
Choruses, Secular (Men's voices, 6 pts.) with
band
— Scores (M1539)
Choruses, Secular (Men's voices, 6 pts.) with
piano (M1550.6; M1566)
Choruses, Secular (Men's voices, 8 pts.),
Unaccompanied (M1580.6; M1596)
Choruses, Secular (Men's voices, 8 pts.) with
instr. ensemble (M1539)
Choruses, Secular (Men's voices, 8 pts.) with
orchestra (M1538-1542)
— Vocal scores with piano (M1540)
xx Choruses, Secular (Men's voices, 8
pts.) with piano
Choruses, Secular (Men's voices, 8 pts.) with
piano (M1550.6; M1566)
sa Choruses, Secular (Men's voices, 8 pts.)
with string orchestra—Vocal scores
with piano
Choruses, Secular (Men's voices, 8 pts.)
with orchestra—Vocal scores with
piano

Choruses, Secular (Men's voices, 8 pts.) with
string orchestra
— Vocal scores with piano (M1540)
xx Choruses, Secular (Men's voices, 8
pts.) with piano
Choruses, Secular (Men's voices),
Unaccompanied (M1580)
Choruses, Secular (Men's voices) with
accordion (M1550)
Choruses, Secular (Men's voices) with band
(M1539)
Choruses, Secular (Men's voices) with piano
(M1550)
Choruses, Secular (Men's voices) with piano, 4
hands (M1550)
Choruses, Secular (Mixed voices) (M1547)
Choruses, Secular (Mixed voices, 2 pts.) with
instr. ensemble (M1531)
Choruses, Secular (Mixed voices, 2 pts.) with
piano (M1549.2; M1552)
Choruses, Secular (Mixed voices, 3 pts.),
Unaccompanied (M1579.3; M1583)
Choruses, Secular (Mixed voices, 3 pts.) with
instr. ensemble (M1531)
Choruses, Secular (Mixed voices, 3 pts.) with
orchestra
— Scores (M1530)
— Vocal scores with piano (M1533)
xx Choruses, Secular (Mixed voices, 3
pts.) with piano
Choruses, Secular (Mixed voices, 3 pts.) with
piano (M1549.3; M1553)
sa Choruses, Secular (Mixed voices, 3
pts.) with orchestra—Vocal scores
with piano
Choruses, Secular (Mixed voices, 3 pts.) with
piano, 4 hands (M1549.3; M1553)
Choruses, Secular (Mixed voices, 3 pts.) with
string orchestra
— Scores (M1531)
Choruses, Secular (Mixed voices, 4 pts.)
(M1547)
Choruses, Secular (Mixed voices, 4 pts.),
Unaccompanied (M1579.4; M1584)
Choruses, Secular (Mixed voices, 4 pts.) with
band
— Scores (reduced) and parts (M1531)
— Vocal scores with piano (M1533)
xx Choruses, Secular (Mixed voices, 4
pts.) with piano
Choruses, Secular (Mixed voices, 4 pts.) with
chamber orchestra
— Vocal scores with piano (M1533)
xx Choruses, Secular (Mixed voices, 4
pts.) with piano
Choruses, Secular (Mixed voices, 4 pts.) with
guitar (M1549.4; M1554)
Choruses, Secular (Mixed voices, 4 pts.) with
instr. ensemble (M1531)
Choruses, Secular (Mixed voices, 4 pts.) with
orchestra
— Scores (M1530)
— Scores and parts (M1530)
— Scores (reduced) and parts (M1530)
— Scores (reduced) and parts (instrumental)
(M1530)
— Vocal scores (M1532)
— Vocal scores with piano (M1533)
xx Choruses, Secular (Mixed voices, 4
pts.) with piano
— Vocal scores with piano and parts
(instrumental) (M1533)
Choruses, Secular (Mixed voices, 4 pts.) with
organ (M1549.4; M1554)
Choruses, Secular (Mixed voices, 4 pts.) with
percussion instruments (M1531)

Choruses, Secular (Mixed voices, 4 pts.) with
  piano   (M1549.4; M1554)
  sa Choruses, Secular (Mixed voices, 4
    pts.) with band—Vocal scores with
    piano
  Choruses, Secular (Mixed voices, 4
    pts.) with string orchestra—Vocal
    scores with piano
  Choruses, Secular (Mixed voices, 4
    pts.) with orchestra—Vocal scores
    with piano
  Choruses, Secular (Mixed voices, 4
    pts.) with chamber orchestra—Vocal
    scores with piano
Choruses, Secular (Mixed voices, 4 pts.) with
  piano, 4 hands   (M1549.4; M1554)
Choruses, Secular (Mixed voices, 4 pts.) with
  pianos (2)   (M1549.4; M1554)
Choruses, Secular (Mixed voices, 4 pts.) with
  string orchestra
  — Scores   (M1531)
  — Vocal scores with piano   (M1533)
    xx Choruses, Secular (Mixed voices, 4
      pts.) with piano
Choruses, Secular (Mixed voices, 5 pts.),
  Unaccompanied   (M1579.5; M1585)
Choruses, Secular (Mixed voices, 5 pts.) with
  chamber orchestra
  — Vocal scores with piano   (M1533)
    sa Choruses, Secular (Mixed voices, 5
      pts.) with piano
Choruses, Secular (Mixed voices, 5 pts.) with
  dance orchestra   (M1531)
  — Scores (reduced)   (M1531)
Choruses, Secular (Mixed voices, 5 pts.) with
  flute   (M1549.5; M1555)
Choruses, Secular (Mixed voices, 5 pts.) with
  instr. ensemble   (M1531)
Choruses, Secular (Mixed voices, 5 pts.) with
  orchestra
  — Scores   (M1530)
  — Vocal scores with piano   (M1533)
    xx Choruses, Secular (Mixed voices, 5
      pts.) with piano
  — Vocal scores with piano (4 hands)
    (M1533)
    xx Choruses, Secular (Mixed voices, 5
      pts.) with piano, 4 hands
  — Vocal scores with piano and trumpets
    (M1533)
Choruses, Secular (Mixed voices, 5 pts.) with
  percussion instruments   (M1531)
Choruses, Secular (Mixed voices, 5 pts.) with
  piano   (M1549.5; M1555)
  sa Choruses, Secular (Mixed voices, 5
    pts.) with chamber orchestra—Vocal
    scores with piano
  Choruses, Secular (Mixed voices, 5
    pts.) with orchestra—Vocal scores
    with piano
Choruses, Secular (Mixed voices, 5 pts.) with
  piano, 4 hands   (M1549.5; M1555)
  sa Choruses, Secular (Mixed voices, 5
    pts.) with orchestra—Vocal scores
    with piano (4 hands)
Choruses, Secular (Mixed voices, 5 pts.) with
  string orchestra
  — Vocal scores   (M1531)
Choruses, Secular (Mixed voices, 6 pts.),
  Unaccompanied   (M1579.6; M1586)
Choruses, Secular (Mixed voices, 6 pts.) with
  band
  — Vocal scores with piano   (M1533)
    xx Choruses, Secular (Mixed voices, 6
      pts.) with piano
Choruses, Secular (Mixed voices, 6 pts.) with
  chamber orchestra
  — Scores   (M1531)

Choruses, Secular (Mixed voices, 6 pts.) with
  instr. ensemble   (M1531)
Choruses, Secular (Mixed voices, 6 pts.) with
  orchestra
  — Scores   (M1530)
  — Vocal scores with piano   (M1533)
    xx Choruses, Secular (Mixed voices, 6
      pts.) with piano
Choruses, Secular (Mixed voices, 6 pts.) with
  organ   (M1549.6; M1556)
Choruses, Secular (Mixed voices, 6 pts.) with
  percussion instruments   (M1531)
Choruses, Secular (Mixed voices, 6 pts.) with
  piano   (M1549.6; M1556)
  sa Choruses, Secular (Mixed voices, 6
    pts.) with orchestra—Vocal scores
    with piano
  Choruses, Secular (Mixed voices, 6
    pts.) with band—Vocal scores with
    piano
Choruses, Secular (Mixed voices, 6 pts.) with
  piano, 4 hands   (M1549.6; M1556)
Choruses, Secular (Mixed voices, 7 pts.),
  Unaccompanied   (M1579.6; M1586)
Choruses, Secular (Mixed voices, 7 pts.) with
  chamber orchestra   (M1531)
Choruses, Secular (Mixed voices, 7 pts.) with
  instr. ensemble   (M1531)
Choruses, Secular (Mixed voices, 7 pts.) with
  orchestra
  — Vocal scores with piano   (M1533)
    xx Choruses, Secular (Mixed voices, 7
      pts.) with piano
Choruses, Secular (Mixed voices, 7 pts.) with
  piano   (M1549.6; M1556)
  sa Choruses, Secular (Mixed voices, 7
    pts.) with orchestra—Vocal scores
    with piano
Choruses, Secular (Mixed voices, 7 pts.) with
  string orchestra   (M1531)
  — Vocal scores with piano   (M1533)
Choruses, Secular (Mixed voices, 8 pts.),
  Unaccompanied   (M1579.6; M1586)
Choruses, Secular (Mixed voices, 8 pts.) with
  band
  — Scores (reduced) and parts (instrumental)
    (M1531)
Choruses, Secular (Mixed voices, 8 pts.) with
  chamber orchestra
  — Vocal scores with piano   (M1533)
    xx Choruses, Secular (Mixed voices, 8
      pts.) with piano
    xx Choruses, Secular (Mixed voices, 8
      pts.) with piano
Choruses, Secular (Mixed voices, 8 pts.) with
  harp   (M1549.6; M1556)
Choruses, Secular (Mixed voices, 8 pts.) with
  horn   (M1549.6; M1556)
Choruses, Secular (Mixed voices, 8 pts.) with
  instr. ensemble   (M1531)
Choruses, Secular (Mixed voices, 8 pts.) with
  orchestra
  — Scores   (M1530)
  — Scores and parts (instrumental)   (M1530)
  — Vocal scores   (M1532)
  — Vocal scores with piano   (M1533)
    xx Choruses, Secular (Mixed voices, 8
      pts.) with piano
  — Vocal scores with pianos (2)   (M1533)
Choruses, Secular (Mixed voices, 8 pts.) with
  percussion instruments   (M1531)
Choruses, Secular (Mixed voices, 8 pts.) with
  piano   (M1549.6; M1556)
  sa Choruses, Secular (Mixed voices, 8
    pts.) with chamber orchestra—Vocal
    scores with piano

Choruses, Secular (Mixed voices, 8
  pts.) with chamber orchestra—Vocal
  scores with pianos (2)
Choruses, Secular (Mixed voices, 8
  pts.) with orchestra—Vocal scores
  with piano
Choruses, Secular (Mixed voices, 8
  pts.) with orchestra—Vocal scores
  with pianos (2)
Choruses, Secular (Mixed voices, 8
  pts.) with string orchestra—Vocal
  scores with piano
Choruses, Secular (Mixed voices, 8 pts.) with
  piano, 4 hands   (M1549.6; M1556)
Choruses, Secular (Mixed voices, 8 pts.) with
  string orchestra   (M1531)
  — Vocal scores with piano   (M1533)
    xx Choruses, Secular (Mixed voices, 8
      pts.) with piano
Choruses, Secular (Mixed voices, 8 pts.) with
  violoncello   (M1531)
Choruses, Secular (Mixed voices, 9 pts.),
  Unaccompanied   (M1579.6; M1586)
Choruses, Secular (Mixed voices, 9 pts.) with
  instr. ensemble   (M1531)
Choruses, Secular (Mixed voices, 9 pts.) with
  orchestra
  — Scores   (M1530)
  — Scores (reduced)   (M1530)
Choruses, Secular (Mixed voices, 9 pts.) with
  organ   (M1549.6; M1556)
Choruses, Secular (Mixed voices, 10 pts.),
  Unaccompanied   (M1579.6; M1586)
Choruses, Secular (Mixed voices, 10 pts.) with
  instrumental ensemble   (M1531)
Choruses, Secular (Mixed voices, 10 pts.) with
  orchestra
  — Scores (reduced)   (M1530)
Choruses, Secular (Mixed voices, 11 pts.) with
  band   (M1531-33.3)
  — Vocal scores   (M1532)
Choruses, Secular (Mixed voices, 11 pts.) with
  orchestra   (M1530-1530.3;
  M1532-4)
  — Vocal scores with piano   (M1533)
    xx Choruses, Secular (Mixed voices, 11
      pts.) with piano
Choruses, Secular (Mixed voices, 11 pts.) with
  piano   (M1549.6; M1556)
  sa Choruses, Secular (Mixed voices, 11
    pts.) with orchestra—Vocal scores
    with piano
Choruses, Secular (Mixed voices, 12 pts.),
  Unaccompanied   (M1579.6; M1586)
Choruses, Secular (Mixed voices, 12 pts.) with
  orchestra
  — Vocal scores with piano   (M1533)
    xx Choruses, Secular (Mixed voices, 12
      pts.) with piano
Choruses, Secular (Mixed voices, 12 pts.) with
  piano   (M1549.6; M1556)
  sa Choruses, Secular (Mixed voices, 12
    pts.) with orchestra—Vocal scores
    with piano
  Choruses, Secular (Mixed voices, 12
    pts.) with string orchestra—Vocal
    scores with piano
Choruses, Secular (Mixed voices, 12 pts.) with
  string orchestra   (M1531-4)
  — Vocal scores with piano   (M1533)
    xx Choruses, Secular (Mixed voices, 12
      pts.) with piano
Choruses, Secular (Mixed voices, 14 pts.) with
  flute   (M1579.7; M1587)
Choruses, Secular (Mixed voices, 16 parts),
  Unaccompanied   (M1579.6; M1586)
Choruses, Secular (Mixed voices, 16 pts.) with
  instr. ensemble   (M1531)

Choruses, Secular (Mixed voices, 20 pts.) with orchestra (M1530-1537)
— Scores (M1530)
Choruses, Secular (Mixed voices, 24 pts.) with instr. ensemble (M1531)
Choruses, Secular (Mixed voices, 28 pts.) with instr. ensemble (M1531)
Choruses, Secular (Mixed voices, 32 pts.) with orchestra (M1530-1537)
— Scores (M1530)
Choruses, Secular (Mixed voices, 32 pts.) with percussion instruments (M1531)
Choruses, Secular (Mixed voices), Unaccompanied (M1579)
Choruses, Secular (Mixed voices) with clarinet (M1531)
Choruses, Secular (Mixed voices) with instr. ensemble (M1531)
Choruses, Secular (Mixed voices) with kayakeum (M1549)
Choruses, Secular (Mixed voices) with orchestra (M1530)
Choruses, Secular (Mixed voices) with orchestra and organ
Choruses, Secular (Mixed voices) with orchestra and piano
Choruses, Secular (Mixed voices) with piano (M1549)
Choruses, Secular, Unaccompanied (M1578)
Choruses, Secular (Unison) (M1609)
Choruses, Secular (Unison) with band
— Vocal scores with piano (M1609)
    xx Choruses, Secular (Unison) with piano
Choruses, Secular (Unison) with chamber orchestra (M1609)
Choruses, Secular (Unison) with instr. ensemble (M1609)
Choruses, Secular (Unison) with orchestra
— Parts (vocal) (M1609)
— Vocal scores with piano (M1609)
    xx Choruses, Secular (Unison) with piano
Choruses, Secular (Unison) with piano (M1609)
sa Choruses, Secular (Unison) with band—Vocal scores with piano
    Choruses, Secular (Unison) with orchestra—Vocal scores with piano
    Choruses, Secular (Unison) with string orchestra—Vocal scores with piano
Choruses, Secular (Unison) with string orchestra
— Vocal scores with piano (M1609)
    xx Choruses, Secular (Unison) with piano
Choruses, Secular, with accordion (M1548)
Choruses, Secular, with band (M1531)
— Scores and parts (M1531)
Choruses, Secular, with piano (M1548)
sa Galops (Chorus with piano)
    Waltzes (Chorus with piano)
Choruses, Secular, with piano, 4 hands (M1548)
sa Waltzes (Chorus with piano, 4 hands)
Choruses, Secular (Women's voices) (M1547)
Choruses, Secular (Women's voices, 2 pts.), Unaccompanied (M1581.2; M1602)
Choruses, Secular (Women's voices, 2 pts.) with chamber orchestra (M1543.5)
— Vocal scores with piano (M1544)
    xx Choruses, Secular (Women's voices, 2 pts.) with piano
Choruses, Secular (Women's voices, 2 pts.) with instr. ensemble (M1543.5)
Choruses, Secular (Women's voices, 2 pts.) with orchestra
— Scores (M1543)

— Vocal scores with piano (M1544)
    xx Choruses, Secular (Women's voices, 2 pts.) with piano
Choruses, Secular (Women's voices, 2 pts.) with piano (M1551.2; M1572)
sa Choruses, Secular (Women's voices, 2 pts.) with chamber orchestra—Vocal scores with piano
    Choruses, Secular (Women's voices, 2 pts.) with orchestra—Vocal scores with piano
Choruses, Secular (Women's voices, 2 pts.) with string orchestra
— Scores (M1543.5)
Choruses, Secular (Women's voices, 2 pts.) with violoncello (M1543.5)
Choruses, Secular (Women's voices, 3 pts.), Unaccompanied (M1581.3; M1603)
Choruses, Secular (Women's voices, 3 pts.) with band (M1543.5)
— Scores and parts (instrumental) (M1543.5)
Choruses, Secular (Women's voices, 3 pts.) with chamber orchestra
— Scores (M1543.5)
Choruses, Secular (Women's voices, 3 pts.) with harp (M1551.3; M1573)
Choruses, Secular (Women's voices, 3 pts.) with instr. ensemble (M1543.5)
Choruses, Secular (Women's voices, 3 pts.) with orchestra
— Vocal scores with piano (M1544)
    xx Choruses, Secular (Women's voices, 3 pts.) with piano
Choruses, Secular (Women's voices, 3 pts.) with piano (M1551.3; M1573)
sa Choruses, Secular (Women's voices, 3 pts.) with string orchestra—Vocal scores with piano
    Choruses, Secular (Women's voices, 3 pts.) with orchestra—Vocal scores with piano
Choruses, Secular (Women's voices, 3 pts.) with piano, 4 hands (M1551.3; M1573)
Choruses, Secular (Women's voices, 3 pts.) with pianos (2)
Choruses, Secular (Women's voices, 3 pts.) with string orchestra
— Vocal scores with piano (M1544)
    xx Choruses, Secular (Women's voices, 3 pts.) with piano
Choruses, Secular (Women's voices, 4 pts.), Unaccompanied (M1581.4; M1604)
Choruses, Secular (Women's voices, 4 pts.) with chamber orchestra
— Vocal scores with organ (M1544)
    xx Choruses, Secular (Women's voices, 4 pts.) with organ
— Vocal scores with piano (M1544)
    xx Choruses, Secular (Women's voices, 4 pts.) with piano
Choruses, Secular (Women's voices, 4 pts.) with harp and piano
Choruses, Secular (Women's voices, 4 pts.) with horns (4) (M1543.5)
Choruses, Secular (Women's voices, 4 pts.) with instr. ensemble (M1543.5)
Choruses, Secular (Women's voices, 4 pts.) with orchestra
— Scores and parts (M1543)
— Scores and parts (instrumental) (M1543)
— Vocal scores with piano (M1544)
    xx Choruses, Secular (Women's voices, 4 pts.) with piano

Choruses, Secular (Women's voices, 4 pts.) with organ (M1551.4; M1574)
sa Choruses, Secular (Women's voices, 4 pts.) with chamber orchestra—Vocal scores with organ
Choruses, Secular (Women's voices, 4 pts.) with piano (M1551.4; M1574)
sa Choruses, Secular (Women's voices, 4 pts.) with chamber orchestra—Vocal scores with piano
    Choruses, Secular (Women's voices, 4 pts.) with orchestra—Vocal scores with piano
    Choruses, Secular (Women's voices, 4 pts.) with string orchestra—Vocal scores with piano
Choruses, Secular (Women's voices, 4 pts.) with piano, 4 hands
Choruses, Secular (Women's voices, 4 pts.) with string orchestra
— Vocal scores with piano (M1544)
    xx Choruses, Secular (Women's voices, 4 pts.) with piano
Choruses, Secular (Women's voices, 5 pts.), Unaccompanied (M1581.5; M1605)
Choruses, Secular (Women's voices, 5 pts.) with piano (M1551.5; M1575)
Choruses, Secular (Women's voices, 6 pts.), Unaccompanied (M1581.6; M1606)
Choruses, Secular (Women's voices, 6 pts.) with orchestra
— Vocal scores with piano (M1544)
    xx Choruses, Secular (Women's voices, 6 pts.) with piano
Choruses, Secular (Women's voices, 6 pts.) with piano (M1551.6; M1576)
sa Choruses, Secular (Women's voices, 6 pts.) with orchestra—Vocal scores with piano
Choruses, Secular (Women's voices, 7 parts) with orchestra (M1543-4)
Choruses, Secular (Women's voices, 8 pts.) with orchestra
— Vocal scores (M1544)
— Vocal scores with piano (M1544)
    xx Choruses, Secular (Women's voices, 8 pts.) with piano
Choruses, Secular (Women's voices, 8 pts.) with piano (M1551.6; M1576)
sa Choruses, Secular (Women's voices, 8 pts.) with orchestra—Vocal scores with piano
Choruses, Secular (Women's voices, 10 pts.) with orchestra (M1543-6)
— Scores (M1543)
Choruses, Secular (Women's voices, 10 pts.) with piano, 4 hands (M1551.6; M1576)
Choruses, Secular (Women's voices, 18 pts.) with instr. ensemble (M1543.5)
Choruses, Secular (Women's voices), Unaccompanied (M1581)
Choruses, Secular (Women's voices) with chamber orchestra (M1543-6)
— Scores (M1543)
Choruses, Secular (Women's voices) with instrumental ensemble (M1543.5)
Choruses, Secular (Women's voices) with piano (M1551)
sa Choruses, Secular (Women's voices) with string orchestra—Vocal scores with piano
Choruses, Secular (Women's voices) with string orchestra
— Vocal scores with piano (M1544)
    xx Choruses, Secular (Women's voices) with piano
Choruses, Unaccompanied (M1495)

Choruses (Equal voices) (M1495)
Choruses (Men's voices) (M1495)
Choruses (Men's voices, 3 pts.) with piano
    (M1495)
Choruses (Men's voices, 4 pts.) (M1495)
Choruses (Men's voices, 4 pts.),
    Unaccompanied (M1495)
Choruses (Men's voices, 4 pts.) with piano
    (M1495)
Choruses (Men's voices), Unaccompanied
    (M1495)
Choruses (Men's voices) with piano (M1495)
Choruses (Mixed voices) (M1495)
Choruses (Mixed voices, 3 pts.) (M1495)
Choruses (Mixed voices, 3 pts.) with piano
    (M1495)
Choruses (Mixed voices, 4 pts.) (M1495)
Choruses (Mixed voices, 4 pts.),
    Unaccompanied (M1495)
Choruses (Mixed voices, 4 pts.) with piano
    (M1495)
Choruses (Mixed voices), Unaccompanied
    (M1495)
Choruses (Mixed voices) with piano (M1495)
Choruses (Unison) (M1495)
Choruses (Unison) with piano (M1495)
Choruses (Women's voices) (M1495)
Choruses (Women's voices, 2 pts.) with piano
    (M1495)
Choruses (Women's voices, 3 pts.),
    Unaccompanied (M1495)
Choruses (Women's voices, 3 pts.) with piano
    (M1495)
Choruses (Women's voices), Unaccompanied
    (M1495)
Choruses (Women's voices) with piano
    (M1495)
Choruses with chamber orchestra
    sa Monologues with music (Choruses with
        chamber orchestra)
Choruses with instrumental ensemble
    sa Monologues with music (Chorus with
        instrumental ensemble)
Choruses with orchestra
    sa Monologues with music (Chorus with
        orchestra)
       Polkas (Chorus with orchestra)
       Waltzes (Chorus with orchestra)
Choruses with piano (M1495)
    sa Monologues with music (Chorus with
        piano)
Choruses with piano, 4 hands (M1495)
    sa Monologues with music (Choruses with
        piano, 4 hands)
Chosen people (Jews)
    See Jews—Election, Doctrine of
Choses
    See Personal property
Choses in action (Direct)
    sa Assignments
       Negotiable instruments
    xx Actions and defenses
       Intangible property
       Property
       Things (Law)
Chota Nagpur, India
    — History
    — — Insurrection, 1831-1832
         x Kol Insurrection, 1831-1832
        xx India—History—British
           occupation, 1765-1947
Chotscho
    x Qara-Chôdscha
       Qara Khôja
    xx Uigurs
Chou dynasty, 1122-221 B.C.
    See China—History—Chou dynasty,
       1122-221 B.C.

Chouans (DC218.5)
    sa Vendean War, 1793-1800
    xx Vendean War, 1793-1800
Chow chows (Dogs) (SF429.C5)
Chozars
    See Khazars
Chrau language
    xx Mon-Khmer languages
Chremonidean War
    See Greece—History—Chremonidean War,
       267-262 B.C.
Chrestomathies
    See Anthologies
       Readers [for readers in the English
          language]
       subdivision Readers under names of
          other languages
Chrismon
    See Chi Rho symbol
Christ
    See Jesus Christ
Christ the King, Feast of
    See Jesus Christ the King, Feast of
Christening
    See Baptism
Christensenite
    See Tridymite
Christian Alexandrian school
    See Alexandrian school, Christian
Christian antiquities (Direct) (BR130-133)
    sa Ampullas, Coronation
       Architecture, Gothic
       Byzantine antiquities
       Catacombs
       Chairs (Cathedra)
       Chalices
       Christian art and symbolism
       Church architecture
       Church furniture
       Church vestments
       Crosses
       Fasts and feasts
       Fonts
       Heraldry, Sacred
       Relics and reliquaries
       Sarcophagi
       Sepulchral monuments
       Staff, Pastoral
    x Antiquities, Christian
       Antiquities, Ecclesiastical
       Archaeology, Christian
       Christian archaeology
       Church antiquities
       Ecclesiastical antiquities
       Monumental theology
    xx Antiquities
       Bible—Antiquities
       Byzantine antiquities
       Christian art and symbolism
    — Pictures, illustrations, etc.
Christian archaeology
    See Christian antiquities
Christian art and symbolism (N7810-8185;
       Theology, BV150-168)
    Works on Christian art in a particular
       country or locality are entered under
       1. Christian art and symbolism. 2. Art
       —[local subdivision]
    sa Altarpieces
       Art and religion
       Art, Early Christian
       Bible—Picture Bibles
       Bible—Pictures, illustrations, etc.
       Bread stamps (Liturgical objects)
       Catacombs
       Cathedrals
       Catholic Church and art
       Christian antiquities

       Church architecture
       Church decoration and ornament
       Church furniture
       Church vestments
       Crib in Christian art and tradition
       Crosses
       Custodials
       Dove [Eagle, Fish, Goldfinch, Triangle,
         etc.] (in religion, folk-lore, etc.)
       Ecclesiastical embroidery
       Emblems
       Flabella
       Fonts
       Heraldry, Sacred
       Holy cards
       Holy Spirit—Symbolism
       Hours, Books of
       Icons
       Illumination of books and manuscripts
       Image (Theology)
       Jewish art and symbolism
       Liturgical objects
       Monastic and religious life in art
       Mosaics
       Nimbus (Art)
       Orientation (Religion)
       Orthodox Eastern Church and art
       Paradise in art
       Pectoral cross
       Pietà
       Relics and reliquaries
       Religious articles
       Sarcophagi
       Screens (Church decoration)
       Ship models (Church decoration)
       Soul in art
       Staff, Pastoral
       Symbolism in the Bible
       Symbolism of numbers
       Temple of God
       Tree of life
       subdivision Art under subjects, e.g.
         Jesus Christ—Art; Saints—Art
    x Art, Christian
       Art, Ecclesiastical
       Christian symbolism
       Ecclesiastical art
       Iconography
       Painting, Religious
       Religious art
       Religious painting
       Religious sculpture
       Sacred art
       Sculpture, Religious
    xx Archaeology
       Art
       Art and religion
       Catacombs
       Christian antiquities
       Church decoration and ornament
       Crosses
       Emblems
       Jesus Christ—Art
       Liturgics
       Mysticism
       Saints—Art
       Soul in art
       Symbolism
       Symbolism in art
       Theology, Practical
    — Juvenile literature
    — Private collections
    — Roman [etc.] influences
Christian art and symbolism (Canon law)
    (BX1939)
Christian atheism
    See Death of God theology

Christian biography *(BR1690-1725)*
 sa Abbots
  Apostles
  Apostolic Fathers
  Bishops
  Cardinals
  Clergy
  Fathers of the church
  Hagiography
  Hermits
  Martyrs
  Missionaries
  Monasticism and religious orders
  Pilgrim Fathers
  Popes
  Puritans
  Reformers
  Saints
  Theologians
 x Christian life—Biography
  Christianity—Biography
  Christians—Biography
  Church biography
  Ecclesiastical biography
 xx Biography
  Martyrs
  Religious biography
  Theologians
 — Juvenile literature
Christian Brethren
 See Plymouth Brethren
Christian Catholicism
 See Old Catholicism
Christian civilization
 See Civilization, Christian
Christian coffee house
 See Coffee house ministry
Christian colleges
 See Church colleges
Christian communication
 See Communication (Theology)
Christian converts
 See Converts
Christian democracy
 sa Catholic action
  Center parties
  Church and labor
  Socialism, Christian
  Trade-unions, Catholic
 xx Catholic action
  Church and social problems—Catholic
   Church
  Social policy
  Sociology, Christian (Catholic)
Christian Democratic parties
 See Center parties—Europe
Christian devotional calendars
 See Devotional calendars
Christian devotional literature
 See Devotional literature
Christian doctrine
 See Theology, Doctrinal
Christian doctrine (Catholic Church)
 See Catechetics—Catholic Church
Christian drama *(Direct)*
 xx Christian literature
  Drama
  Religious drama
 — Presentation, etc.
Christian drama, American, ₍**English, etc.**₎
  (Direct)
 x American ₍English, etc.₎ Christian
  drama
 xx American ₍English, etc.₎ drama
Christian education
 See Religious education
Christian ethics *(BJ1190-1278)*
 sa Adiaphora

Bible—Ethics
Cardinal virtues
Casuistry
Christian life
Christianity and economics
Commandments of the church
Commandments, Ten
Conscience, Examination of
Epikeia
Escape (Ethics)
Evangelical counsels
Fear of God
Golden rule
Guilt
Human acts
Jesus Christ—Ethics
Law and gospel
Love (Theology)
Merit (Christianity)
Pastoral medicine
Pastoral psychology
Perfection
Probabilism
Scruples
Sin
Sin, Venial
Sins
Social ethics
Vices
Virtues
 subdivision Ethics *under names of*
  Christian theologians, e.g.
  Augustinus, Aurelius, Saint, Bp. of
  Hippo—Ethics; *also subdivision*
  Moral and religious aspects *under*
  specific subjects, e.g. Amusements—
  Moral and religious aspects; Dancing
  —Moral and religious aspects;
  Fiction—Moral and religious aspects
 x Christian ethics—Modern period
  Ethical theology
  Ethics, Christian
  Moral theology
  Theology, Ethical
  Theology, Moral
 xx Christian life
  Ethics
  Religion and ethics
  Social ethics
  Theology, Doctrinal
— Early church, ca. 30-600 *(BJ1212)*
 xx Church history—Primitive and early
  church, ca. 30-600
— Middle Ages, 600-1500 *(BJ1217)*
— Modern period, 1500-
 See Christian ethics

  GENERAL SUBDIVISIONS

— Anglican authors, ₍Catholic authors, etc.₎
 x Moral theology
  Theology, Moral

  GENERAL SUBDIVISIONS

— Catholic authors
 sa Body, Human—Papal documents
  Pastoral medicine—Catholic Church
  Virtue, Infused

  GENERAL SUBDIVISIONS

— Comparative studies
— Controversial literature
— Juvenile literature
— Methodology *(BJ1200)*
Christian etiquette
 See Church etiquette
Christian evidences
 See Apologetics

Christian existentialism
 See Christianity and existentialism
Christian fiction
 xx Fiction
Christian flags
 See Church pennants
Christian giving *(BV772)*
  Here are entered works that deal with the
   duty of a Christian to contribute of his
   means to the support of church and
   charity.
 sa Stewardship, Christian
 x Giving, Christian
 xx Church finance
 Note under Stewardship, Christian
— Juvenile literature
— Stories
Christian hymns
 See Hymns
Christian Indians (Moravians)
 See Moravian Indians
Christian labor unions
 See Trade-unions, Catholic
Christian leadership *(BV652.1)*
 sa Church officers
 x Church leadership
  Lay leadership
 xx Church work
  Leadership
  Religious education
Christian legends
 See Legends, Christian
Christian life *(BV4500-4595)*
 sa Asceticism
  Character
  Christian ethics
  Commitment to the church
  Conduct of life
  Conversion
  Devotional exercises
  Faith
  Monastic and religious life
  Monastic and religious life of women
  Peace of mind
  Perfection
  Piety
  Prayer
  Religious education
  Religiousness
  Revivals
  Sanctification
  Spiritual life
  Stewardship, Christian
  Witness bearing (Christianity)
  subdivision Religious life *under classes*
   of persons and institutions, e.g.
   Children—Religious life
 x Discipleship
  Religious life (Christianity)
 xx Asceticism
  Christian ethics
  Conduct of life
  Ethics
  Spiritual life
  Theology, Practical
— Early church, ca. 30-600
— Middle Ages, 600-1500
— 1960-

  GENERAL SUBDIVISIONS

— Anecdotes, facetiae, satire, etc.
— Anglican authors, ₍Catholic authors, etc.₎
— Biblical teaching
 xx Life—Biblical teaching

  GENERAL SUBDIVISIONS

— Biography
 See Christian biography

Christian life *(BV4500-4595)*
(Continued)

GENERAL SUBDIVISIONS

— Caricatures and cartoons
— Drama
— Pictures, illustrations, etc. *(BV4515)*
    xx Homiletical illustrations
— Poetry
— Quotations, maxims, etc. *(BV4513)*
— Stories *(BV4515)*
    sa Rural churches—Stories
    x Devotional stories
    xx Children's stories
       Homiletical illustrations
       Parables
    Example under Fiction; *and under refer-*
    ence from Stories
— Study and teaching
Christian literature
  sa Catholic literature
    Christian drama
    Christian poetry
    Devotional literature
  xx Literature
    Religious literature
— Publication and distribution
    xx Booksellers and bookselling—
       Colportage, subscription trade,
       etc.
— Stories, plots, etc.
Christian literature, American, [English, etc.]
  (Direct)
  xx American [English, etc.] literature
Christian literature, Byzantine *(Direct)*
  xx Byzantine literature
Christian literature, Early
    Here with the specification (Collections)
    or (Selections: Extracts, etc.) are en-
    tered writings of Christian authors to
    the time of Gregory the Great in the
    West and John of Damascus in the
    East.
    Works about those early Christians com-
    monly known as Fathers of the church
    are entered under the heading Fathers
    of the church.
  sa Apologetics—Early church, ca. 30-600
    Apostolic Fathers
    Baptism—History—Early church, ca.
       30-600—Sources
    Bible—Quotations, Early
    Catenae
    Christian poetry, Early
    Church history—Primitive and early
       church, ca. 30-600—Sources
    Church orders, Ancient
    Fathers of the church
    Hymns, Early Christian
    Jesus Christ—Biography—Apocryphal
       and legendary literature
    Jesus Christ—Trial—Apocryphal and
       legendary literature
    Latin literature, Medieval and modern
    Literature, Medieval
    Liturgies, Early Christian
    Lord's Supper—Early works to 600
    Martyrologies
    Penance—History—Early church, ca.
       30-600—Sources
    Prayers, Early Christian
    Scholia
    Sermons, Early Christian
    Theology—Collected works—Early
       church, ca. 30-600
  x Early Christian literature
  xx Church history—Primitive and early
       church, ca. 30-600—Sources
    Latin literature, Medieval and modern

Literature
Note under Fathers of the church
— Concordances
    x Apostolic Fathers—Concordances
    Fathers of the church—
       Concordances
— Greek authors, [Latin authors, Syriac
    authors, etc.]
— Indexes, Topical
— Manuscripts
Christian literature, Early (Collections)
Note under Theology—Collections
Christian literature for children
  x Children's Christian literature
  xx Children's literature
Christian ministry
See Clergy—Office
Christian names
See Names, Personal
Christian perfection
See Perfection
Christian poetry
  sa Carols
    Hymns
  x Christianity—Poetry
  xx Christian literature
    Hymns
    Poetry
    Religious poetry
Christian poetry, American, [Dutch, etc.]
  (Direct)
  x American [Dutch, etc.] Christian
    poetry
  xx American [Dutch, etc.] poetry
Christian poetry, Early *(Latin, PA6124)*
  x Early Christian poetry
  xx Christian literature, Early
Christian poetry, English
— Middle English (1100-1500)
— Early modern, 1500-1700
— 18th century
— 19th century
Christian priesthood
See Priesthood
Christian Science *(Direct)* *(BX6901-6997)*
  sa Bible—Medicine, hygiene, etc.
    Faith-cure
    Jewish Science
    Mental healing
  x Divine healing
    Mind-cure
  xx Faith-cure
    Medicine and religion
    Mental healing
Note under Church of Christ, Scientist
— Legal aspects *(BX6953)*
    xx Medical laws and legislation
Christian Science, Jewish
See Jewish Science
Christian Science churches
See Churches, Christian Science
Christian socialism
See Socialism, Christian
Christian sociology
See Sociology, Christian
Christian stewardship
See Stewardship, Christian
Christian symbolism
See Christian art and symbolism
Christian theologians
See Theologians
Christian union *(Direct)* *(BX1-9)*
  sa Chair of Unity Octave
    Communicatio in sacris
    Community churches
    Disputations, Religious
    Ecumenical movement
    Federated churches

Intercommunion
Interdenominational cooperation
Lambeth Quadrilateral
Local church councils
Mary, Virgin, and Christian union
Open pulpit
Ratisbon, Colloquy of, 1541
Ratisbon, Colloquy of, 1546
Simultaneum
Syncretistic controversy
Unionism (Religion)
Week of Prayer for Christian Unity
  x Christianity—Union between churches
    Church unity
    Irenics
  xx Church
    Ecumenical movement
Note under Catholicity
— Anglican Communion, [Catholic Church,
    Orthodox Eastern Church, etc.]
    x Ecumenical movement—Anglican
       Communion, [Catholic Church,
       Orthodox Eastern Church, etc.]
— Biblical teaching
— Controversial literature
    See Ecumenical movement—
       Controversial literature
— Prayer-books and devotions
— Sermons
Christian union and baptism
See Baptism and Christian union
Christian union and church polity
See Church polity and Christian union
Christian union and episcopacy
See Episcopacy and Christian union
Christian union and missions
See Missions and Christian union
Christian union and pastoral theology
See Pastoral theology and Christian union
Christian union and religious education
See Religious education and Christian union
Christian union and sacraments
See Sacraments and Christian union
Christian union and the Bible
See Bible and Christian union
Christian union and the Lord's Supper
See Lord's Supper and Christian union
Christian year
See Church year
Christiana, Pa.
— Riot, 1851 *(E450)*
    xx Fugitive slave law of 1850
       Slavery in the United States—
       Fugitive slaves
Christianity *(Direct)* *(BR1-129)*
  sa Catholicity
    Church
    Civilization, Christian
    Councils and synods
    Deism
    Ecumenical movement
    God
    Jesus Christ
    Miracles
    Missions
    Protestantism
    Reformation
    Socialism, Christian
    Sociology, Christian
    Theism
    Theology
    Women in Christianity
  headings beginning with the words
    Christian *and* Church; *and names of*
    Christian *churches and sects, e.g.*
    Catholic Church, Lutheran Church
    Huguenots
  xx Church

Deism
God
Jesus Christ
Religions
Theism
Theology
— Early church, ca. 30-600   *(BR165;*
        BS2410-2413)
— Middle Ages, 600-1500   *(BR250-275)*
— — Sources
— 16th century   *(BR280)*
— 17th century   *(BR120; BR440)*
— 18th century   *(BR120; BR470)*
— 19th century   *(BR121-5; BR477)*
— 20th century   *(BR121-5; BR479)*
    sa Death of God theology
— Anecdotes, facetiae, satire, etc.
        (PN6231.C35)
— Apologetic works
    See Apologetics
— Apostolic basis
    See Church—Apostolicity
— Biography
    See Christian biography
— Catholicity
    See Church—Catholicity
— Controversial literature   *(BL2700-2790)*
    sa Agnosticism
        Atheism
        Christianity and religious humanism
        Free thought
        Jesus Christ—Rationalistic
            interpretations
        Rationalism
        Secularism
    Example under reference from Polemics
        (Theology)
— Essence, genius, nature   *(BR120-123)*
    sa Demythologization
— Evidences
    See Apologetics
— History
    See Church history
— Influence   *(Direct)*
— Juvenile literature   *(BR125.5)*
— Miscellanea
— Origin
    sa Church—Foundation
    x Christianity—Sources
    xx Church—Foundation
— Philosophy   *(BR100)*
    sa Philosophical theology
        Transcendence of God
    x Theology—Philosophy
    xx Philosophy
        Philosophy and religion
        Religion—Philosophy
        Theology, Doctrinal
— Poetry
    See Christian poetry
— Polity
    See Church polity
— Psychology   *(BR100)*
    xx Bible—Psychology
        Conversion
        Psychology, Religious
— Renewal
    See Church renewal
— Sources
    See Christianity—Origin
— Terminology
— — Anecdotes, facetiae, satire, etc.
— Union between churches
    See Christian union
— Universality
    See Church—Catholicity
Christianity and agriculture
    sa Rural churches

    x Agriculture and Christianity
    xx Sociology, Christian
        Sociology, Rural
Christianity and antisemitism
    x Antisemitism and Christianity
    xx Christianity and other religions—
        Judaism
Christianity and atheism   *(BR128.A8)*
    sa Bible and atheism
        Communism and Christianity
    x Atheism and Christianity
Christianity and Cabala
    See Cabala and Christianity
Christianity and capitalism   *(BR115.C3)*
    sa Protestantism and capitalism
    x Capitalism and Christianity
    xx Christianity and economics
Christianity and communication
    See Communication (Theology)
Christianity and communism
    See Communism and Christianity
Christianity and culture   *(BR115.C8)*
    x Culture and Christianity
    xx Civilization, Christian
        Religion and culture
— Early church, ca. 30-600
    xx Church history—Primitive and early
        church, ca. 30-600
Christianity and democracy   *(Direct)*
        (BR115.P7)
    x Democracy and Christianity
    xx Christianity and politics
Christianity and economics   *(BR115.E3)*
    sa Christianity and capitalism
        Church and labor
        Communism and Christianity
        Property—Moral and religious aspects
        Protestantism and capitalism
        Religion and labor
        Socialism, Christian
        Sociology, Christian
        Stewardship, Christian
    x Economics and Christianity
    xx Bible—Economics
        Capitalism
        Christian ethics
        Church and labor
        Church and the world
        Communism and religion
        Economics
        Socialism and religion
        Socialism, Christian
        Sociology, Christian
        Stewardship, Christian
        Wealth, Ethics of
— Biblical teaching
    See Bible—Economics
Christianity and evolution
    See Evolution and Christianity
Christianity and existentialism
    x Christian existentialism
        Existentialism and Christianity
Christianity and international affairs
        (BR115.I7)
    sa Catholic Church and world politics
        Church and underdeveloped areas
        Friends, Society of, and world politics
    x Church and international affairs
        International affairs and Christianity
    xx Church and social problems
        Church and the world
        Religion and international affairs
        World politics
— Papal documents
    See Catholic Church and world
        politics—Papal documents
Christianity and law
    See Religion and law

Christianity and literature
    x Literature and Christianity
    xx Religion and literature
Christianity and magic   *(BR115.M25)*
    x Magic and Christianity
    xx Christianity and superstition
Christianity and medicine
    See Medicine and religion
Christianity and occult sciences   *(Direct)*
    x Occult sciences and Christianity
Christianity and other religions   *(General,*
        BR127)
    sa Christianity and religious humanism
        Paganism
    x Syncretism (Christianity)
Note under Religions—Relations
— Assyro-Babylonian
— Buddhism   *(BR128.B8)*
    sa Catholic Church—Relations—
        Buddhism
        Christianity and other religions—
        Nichiren (Sect)
        Christianity and other religions—Zen
        Buddhism
        Jesus Christ—Buddhist
        interpretations
        Missions to Buddhists
— Celtic
— Chinese
— Confucianism
    sa Missions to Confucians
— Cornish
— Dionysia
— Druidism
— Egyptian
— Ethical culture movement
— Germanic
— Greek
— Hinayana Buddhism   *(BQ7276.C5)*
— Hinduism   *(BR128.H5)*
    sa Jesus Christ—Hindu interpretations
        Missions to Hindus
— Iranian
— Islam   *(BP172)*
    sa Islamic literature—Christian
        interpretations
        Jesus Christ—Islamic interpretations
        Koran—Relation to the Bible
        Mary, Virgin—Islamic interpretations
        Missions to Muslims
— Japanese
— Judaism   *(BM535)*
    sa Cabala and Christianity
        Christianity and antisemitism
        Jesus Christ—Biography—Sources,
        Jewish
        Mary, Virgin—Jewish interpretations
        Missions to Jews
        Rabbinical literature—History and
        criticism, Christian
        Rabbinical literature—Relation to
        the New Testament
— Juvenile literature
— Lamaism
— Mithraism
— Nichiren (Sect)
    xx Christianity and other religions—
        Buddhism
— Norse
— Roman
— Shin (Sect)   *(BQ8719.4.C5)*
— Shinto
— Sikhism   *(BR128.S6)*
— Taoism
— Zen Buddhism
    xx Christianity and other religions—
        Buddhism
— Zoroastrianism

Christianity and philosophy
   See Philosophy and religion
Christianity and politics *(BR115.P7)*
   sa Christianity and democracy
      Church and international organization
      Clergy—Political activity
   x Politics and Christianity
   xx Church and state
      Church and the world
      Religion and politics
Christianity and progress *(BR115.P77)*
   x Progress and Christianity
   xx Sociology, Christian
Christianity and psychical research
      (BR115.P85)
   x Psychical research and Christianity
Christianity and religious humanism
   xx Christianity and other religions
      Christianity—Controversial literature
      Humanism, Religious
Christianity and revolution
   See Revolution (Theology)
Christianity and science
   See Religion and science
Christianity and superstition *(BR115.S85)*
   sa Christianity and magic
   x Superstition and Christianity
Christianity and the world
   See Church and the world
Christianity and war
   See War and religion
Christianity in literature *(PN49)*
   sa Lord's Supper in literature
      Trinity in literature
   xx Religion in literature
Christianity in the Midrash
   sa Christianity in the Talmud
   xx Christianity in the Talmud
      Midrash
Christianity in the Talmud
   sa Christianity in the Midrash
   xx Christianity in the Midrash
      Talmud
Christianos
   See Cagots
Christians
  — Biography
     See Christian biography
  — Name
Christians, Jewish
   See Jewish Christians
Christians and Moors, Dance of
   See Moros y Cristianos (Dance)
Christians in Africa, ₍**Syria, Turkey, etc.**₎
  — Ceremonies and practices
     Example under Rites and ceremonies
  — Legal status, laws, etc.
Christians in literature
Christians of St. John
   See Mandaeans
Christmas *(Indirect)* *(GT4985)*
   sa Christmas decorations
      Epiphany season
      Jesus Christ—Nativity
   x Christmas books
   xx Church year
      Fasts and feasts
      Holidays
      Jesus Christ—Nativity
   Example under Days; *and under reference*
     from Religious festivals
  — Anecdotes, facetiae, satire, etc.
  — Caricatures and cartoons
  — Controversial literature
  — Drama
     See Christmas plays
  — Juvenile literature
  — Literary collections

— Meditations
— Pictorial works
— Poetry *(PN6110.C5)*
   sa Carols
   x Christmas poetry
   xx Hymns
   Example under Poetry
— Prayer-books and devotions
     Subdivided by language.
— Quotations, maxims, etc.
— Songs and music
     See Christmas music
— Sounds
     See Christmas sounds
Christmas books
   See Christmas
      Christmas plays
      Christmas stories
      Gift-books (Annuals, etc.)
Christmas cards *(NC1860)*
   sa Greeting cards
  — Juvenile literature
Christmas carols
   See Carols
Christmas cookery
   xx Cookery
  — Juvenile literature
Christmas decorations *(Indirect)*
   sa Christmas trees
      Pinatas
   xx Christmas
      Holiday decorations
  — Safety measures
Christmas music
   sa Carols
   x Christmas—Songs and music
   xx Church music
      Holidays—Songs and music
      Music
      Sacred vocal music
Christmas plates *(Direct)*
   xx Plates (Tableware)
Christmas plays *(PN6120.C5)*
   sa Crib in Christian art and tradition
      Mumming plays
   x Christmas books
      Christmas—Drama
      Plays, Christmas
   xx Drama
      Jesus Christ—Drama
      Religious drama
Christmas plays, Medieval *(PN2159.C)*
   x Plays, Medieval
   xx Drama, Medieval
      Religious drama
Christmas poetry
   See Christmas—Poetry
Christmas seals
   See Seals (Christmas, etc.)
Christmas sermons *(BV4257)*
   x Jesus Christ—Nativity—Sermons
   xx Sermons
Christmas service
     Here are entered works containing orders
      of worship for a Christmas service.
   xx Liturgies
Christmas sounds
   x Christmas—Sounds
   xx Sounds
Christmas star
   See Star of Bethlehem
Christmas stories *(PN6071.C6)*
   x Christmas books
Christmas trees *(GT4985)*
   xx Christmas decorations
      Folk-lore of trees
  — Juvenile literature
  — Marketing

Christogram
   See Chi Rho symbol
Christology
   See Jesus Christ
Chromaffin cells
   sa Aortic paraganglia
   x Cells, Chromaffin
   xx Adrenal glands
      Nervous system, Sympathetic
Chromaffinoma
   See Carcinoid
Chromammines
   See Chromium-ammonium compounds
Chromatic aberration (Optics)
   See Achromatism
      Lenses
Chromatic alteration (Music)
   x Alteration, Chromatic
      Musica ficta
   xx Harmony
      Music—Instruction and study
      Music—Theory
Chromatics
   See Color
Chromatin *(QH599)*
   sa Sex chromatin
   xx Cells
Chromatographic analysis
   sa Gas chromatography
      Gel permeation chromatography
      Liquid chromatography
      Paper chromatography
      Thin layer chromatography
   x Analysis, Chromatographic
   xx Biological chemistry
      Carotin
      Chemistry, Analytic
      Colorimetric analysis
      Dyes and dyeing—Chemistry
      Separation (Technology)
  — Apparatus and supplies
  — — Maintenance and repair
  — Laboratory manuals
  — Tables
Chromatography, Gel permeation
   See Gel permeation chromatography
Chromatography, Thin layer
   See Thin layer chromatography
Chromatophores *(QL767)*
   sa Animal pigments
      Chloroplasts
      Melanophores
      Plant pigments
   x Pigment cells
   xx Animal pigments
      Cells
      Chloroplasts
      Plant pigments
      Plastids
      Protoplasm
Chrome-manganese steel
   x Chromium-manganese steel
   xx Chrome steel
      Chromium alloys
      Manganese alloys
      Manganese steel
Chrome-nickel steel
   sa Steel, Heat resistant
      Steel, Stainless
   x Chromium-nickel steel
   xx Chrome steel
      Chromium alloys
      Nickel alloys
      Nickel steel
      Steel alloys
  — Corrosion
  — Welding

Chrome steel *(Metallurgy, TN757.C5;*
  Testing, TA479.C5)
  sa Chrome-manganese steel
    Chrome-nickel steel
    Chromium-molybdenum steel
    Steel, Stainless
  xx Steel
  — Testing
Chrome-vanadium steel *(Construction,*
  TA479; Metallurgy, TN575)
  xx Steel
Chrome-yellow *(TP936)*
Chromicyanides *(QD181.C7)*
Chromite *(Indirect) (TN490.C4)*
  xx Chromium ores
    Spinel group
Chromium *(QD181.C7)*
  — Analysis
  — Isotopes
    x Radioactive chromium
      Radiochromium
    xx Radioactive tracers
  — — Spectra
  — Spectra
  — Toxicology
Chromium alloys *(TA490)*
  sa Aluminum-chromium alloys
    Chrome-manganese steel
    Chrome-nickel steel
    Chromium-cobalt-nickel-molybdenum
      alloys
    Chromium-copper alloys
    Chromium-copper-nickel alloys
    Chromium-iron alloys
    Chromium-iron-nickel alloys
    Chromium-iron-silicon alloys
    Chromium-molybdenum steel
    Chromium-tellurium alloys
    Gold-chromium alloys
    Nickel-chromium alloys
    Nickel-chromium-aluminum alloys
  — Corrosion
  — Magnetic properties
Chromium-aluminum alloys
  See Aluminum-chromium alloys
Chromium-ammonium compounds
  x Chromammines
  xx Ammonium compounds
    Chromium compounds
  Example under Metal-ammonia compounds
Chromium-cobalt-nickel-molybdenum alloys
  x Quaternary alloys
    Super alloys
  xx Chromium alloys
    Cobalt alloys
    Heat resistant alloys
    Molybdenum alloys
    Nickel alloys
Chromium compounds
  sa Chromium-ammonium compounds
Chromium-copper alloys
  x Copper-chromium alloys
  xx Chromium alloys
    Copper alloys
Chromium-copper-nickel alloys
  xx Chromium alloys
    Copper alloys
    Nickel alloys
Chromium films *(QC176.84.E5)*
  xx Metallic films
  — Optical properties *(QC176.84.E5)*
Chromium-gold alloys
  See Gold-chromium alloys
Chromium in animal nutrition *(SF98.C45)*
  xx Feeding
Chromium-iron alloys
  x Iron-chromium alloys
  xx Chromium alloys

— Testing
Chromium-iron-nickel alloys
  sa Inconel
  x Nickel-chromium-iron alloys
  xx Chromium alloys
    Nickel alloys
  — Analysis
Chromium-iron-silicon alloys
  xx Chromium alloys
    Silicon alloys
Chromium-manganese steel
  See Chrome-manganese steel
Chromium-molybdenum steel
  xx Chrome steel
    Chromium alloys
    Molybdenum alloys
    Steel alloys
    Steel, Stainless
Chromium-nickel alloys
  See Nickel-chromium alloys
Chromium-nickel steel
  See Chrome-nickel steel
Chromium ores *(Indirect) (TN490.C4)*
  sa Chromite
  — Analysis
Chromium organic compounds
  See Organochromium compounds
Chromium-plating *(TS692.C4)*
  xx Electroplating
    Plating
  — Automation *(TS692.C4)*
Chromium-tellurium alloys
  x Tellurium-chromium alloys
  xx Chromium alloys
    Tellurium alloys
  — Electric properties
Chromium wire
  xx Wire
  — Testing
Chromizing
  xx Diffusion coatings
Chromogen *(QK899)*
  xx Color of plants
Chromolithographs *(NE2520-2529)*
  xx Chromolithography
    Engravings
Chromolithography *(NE2500-2529)*
  sa Chromolithographs
    Color-printing
    Color prints
    Lithography
  xx Color-printing
    Color prints
    Lithography
Chromophone
  See Harmony—Mechanical aids
Chromophotography
  See Color photography
Chromosomal aberrations
  See Chromosome abnormalities
Chromosome abnormalities
  sa Human chromosome abnormalities
    Karyotypes
    Trisomy
  x Chromosomal aberrations
    Chromosome anomalies
  xx Chromosomes
    Karyotypes
    Mutation (Biology)
Chromosome anomalies
  See Chromosome abnormalities
Chromosome mapping
  sa Linkage (Genetics)
  x Gene mapping
  xx Linkage (Genetics)
Chromosome numbers
  sa Aneuploidy
    Haploidy

    Polyploidy
  xx Chromosomes
Chromosome theory
  See Chromosomes
Chromosomes *(QH605)*
  sa Allelomorphism
    Chromosome abnormalities
    Chromosome numbers
    Crossing over (Genetics)
    Genetic recombination
    Genetics
    Giant chromosomes
    Human chromosomes
    Karyokinesis
    Karyotypes
    Linkage (Genetics)
    Sex chromosomes
    Translocation (Genetics)
    Trisomy
  x Chromosome theory
  xx Crossing over (Genetics)
    Genetics
    Heredity
    Karyokinesis
    Linkage (Genetics)
  — Laboratory manuals
Chromosphere, Solar
  See Solar chromosphere
Chromospheres, Stellar
  See Stellar chromospheres
Chromospheric eruptions
  See Solar flares
Chromoxylography
  See Color prints
Chronic alcoholic delirium
  See Korsakoff's syndrome
Chronic diseases *(Direct) (Pathology,*
  RB156; Public health, RA973.5)
  sa Chronically ill
  x Diseases, Chronic
  — Diagnosis
  — Prevention
  — Psychological aspects
    xx Medicine, Psychosomatic
      Sick—Psychology
Chronic lymphocytic leukemia
  See Lymphocytic leukemia
Chronically ill *(Direct)*
  xx Chronic diseases
    Sick
  — Care and treatment *(Direct)*
    sa Hospitals—Home care programs
Chronically ill children *(Direct)*
  xx Pediatrics
  — Education *(Direct)*
Chronicle history (Drama)
  See Historical drama
Chronicle play
  See Historical drama
Chronograms *(Z1121)*
  sa Anagrams
  xx Anagrams
    Chronology
    Inscriptions
    Medals
    Puzzles
Chronograph *(Astronomical instruments,*
  QB107; Ballistic instruments,
  UF830-840)
  sa Le Boulengé chronograph
    Photochronograph
  xx Astronomical clocks
    Astronomical instruments
    Time measurements
Chronology *(CE)*
  sa Almanacs
    Calendar
    Chronograms

Chronology *(CE)* *(Continued)*
    Clocks and watches
    Day
    Dendrochronology
    Geological time
    Months
    Night
    Radioactive dating
    Time
    Week
    x Eras
       Hours (Time)
    xx Almanacs
       Astronomy
       Auxiliary sciences of history
       Calendar
       History
       History, Ancient
       Time
    — Juvenile literature
Chronology, Assyro-Babylonian *(CE33)*
    x Assyro-Babylonian chronology
       Chronology, Sumerian
Chronology, Aztec
    See Chronology, Mexican
Chronology, Biblical
    See Bible—Chronology
Chronology, Byzantine, ₍Chinese, Egyptian, etc.₎
    x Byzantine ₍Chinese, Egyptian, etc.₎ chronology
Chronology, Ecclesiastical *(CE81)*
    sa Church calendar
    x Church chronology
       Church history—Chronology
       Ecclesiastical chronology
    xx Church calendar
       Fasts and feasts
    — Charts
Chronology, Greek *(CE42)*
    x Greek chronology
    — Tables *(CE42)*
Chronology, Hebrew
    See Chronology, Jewish
Chronology, Historical *(D11)*
    sa Calendar
       Calendars
       History, Ancient—Chronology
       History—Yearbooks
       Stone age—Chronology
       subdivision History—Chronology *under names of countries, cities, etc., e.g.* France—History—Chronology; London—History—Chronology
    x Annals
       Dates
       Historical chronology
       History—Chronology
       History, Modern—Chronology
       World history—Chronology
    — Charts *(D11)*
       x Charts, Historical
          Historical charts
    — Tables *(D11)*
Chronology, Islamic
    x Chronology, Muslim
       Islamic chronology
       Muslim chronology
Chronology, Jewish
    sa Calendar, Jewish
       Jews—History—Chronology
    x Chronology, Hebrew
       Hebrew chronology
       Jewish chronology
    xx Calendar, Jewish
       Jews—History—Chronology
Chronology, Maya *(F1435)*
    x Chronology, Yucatecan

    Katun
    Maya chronology
    Yucatecan chronology
    xx Chronology, Mexican
Chronology, Mexican
    sa Chronology, Maya
    x Aztec chronology
       Chronology, Aztec
       Mexican chronology
Chronology, Muslim
    See Chronology, Islamic
Chronology, Oriental
    x Oriental chronology
    — Terminology
       x Era names
          Reign names
Chronology, Roman *(CE46)*
    sa Secular games
    x Roman chronology
Chronology, Spanish *(CE61.S)*
    sa Spanish Era (Chronology)
    x Spanish chronology
Chronology, Stone age
    See Stone age—Chronology
Chronology, Sumerian
    See Chronology, Assyro-Babylonian
Chronology, Yucatecan
    See Chronology, Maya
Chronometer *(QB107)*
    xx Astronomical clocks
       Clocks and watches
       Horology
       Time measurements
Chronometer (Music)
    See Metronome
Chronometry, Mental
    See Time perception
Chronophotography
    See Cinematography
Chronothermal medicine
    See Medicine, Chronothermal
Chronothermalism
    See Medicine, Chronothermal
Chrysanthemum leaf miner *(QL537.A4; Agricultural pest, SB945.C)*
    xx Leaf-miners
    — Control *(Indirect)*
Chrysanthemums *(SB413.C55)*
    Example under Floriculture
    — Diseases and pests *(Indirect)*
    — Handling
    — Varieties
Chrysanthemums in art
    xx Art
Chrysarobin *(RS165.C)*
Chryselephantine sculpture
    See Sculpture, Chryselephantine
Chrysler automobile
Chrysler Corporation Slowdown Strike, 1939
    Note under Strikes and lockouts
Chrysler's Farm, Ont., Battle of, 1813
Chrysolite *(QE391.C)*
    sa Forsterite
    x Olivin
    xx Refractory materials
Chrysophyceae *(QK569.C63)*
    xx Algae
Chrysotile
    xx Serpentine
Chrystocrenes
    See Rock glaciers
Ch'üan chen chiao *(BL1943.C55)*
Chuana language
    See Sechuana language
Chuang language *(PL4251.C4)*
    xx Tai languages
Chuang literature *(Direct)*

Chûbne
    See Changars
Chuchona language
    See Chocho language
Chuchuhuasha *(RS165.C28)*
Chucks *(TJ1219)*
    sa Collets
    xx Collets
Chudnof, Russia, Battle of, 1660 *(DK121)*
Chuetas
    x Maranos in Majorca
       Maranos in Puerto Rico
    xx Ethnology—Majorca
       Ethnology—Puerto Rico
Chuf dialect
    See Khuf dialect
Chufa
Chugach Eskimos *(F915)*
    xx Eskimos
Chugaev reaction
    xx Chemical reactions
Chūgan shisō
    See Mādhyamika (Buddhism)
Chukar partridge
    x Chukor partridge
    xx Partridges
Chukchi *(DK759.C)*
Chukchi language *(PM41-44)*
    x Tchuktchi language
       Tuski language
    xx Hyperborean languages
Chukor partridge
    See Chukar partridge
Chulo
    See Coatis
Chultunes *(F1435.1.C)*
    xx Mayas—Antiquities
       Water-storage
Chulupí language *(PM5817.C8)*
    x Ashluslay language
Chulyma Tatars
    x Cholym Tatars
       Meletski Tatars
    xx Ethnology—Siberia
       Tatars
Chum salmon
    x Dog salmon
    xx Pacific salmon
       Salmon
Chumash Indians
    See Chumashan Indians
Chumash language
    See Chumashan language
Chumashan Indians *(E99.C)*
    x Chumash Indians
    xx Indians of North America
    — Art
Chumashan language *(PM891)*
    x Chumash language
Ch'ung chia (Tribe)
    See Pu-i (Tribe)
Chungli dialect
    See Ao language
Chuntaquiro Indians
    See Piro Indians (Peru)
Chuntaquiro language *(PM5818)*
    x Chontaquiro language
       Piro (Arawakan) language
       Simirenchi language
    xx Arawakan languages
       Indians of South America—Languages
Chupacho Indians
    xx Indians of South America
Chur, Switzerland
    — Fire, 1674
Church *(BV590-640)*
    sa Christian union
       Christianity

Communion of saints
Ecumenical movement
Jesus Christ—Mystical body
Language question in the church
Mary, Virgin, and the church
Mission of the church
Priesthood, Universal
Salvation outside the Catholic Church
Salvation outside the church
  x Ecclesiastical theology
    Theology, Ecclesiastical
  xx Christianity
    People of God
    Theology
— Apostolicity   (BV601.2)
  x Apostolicity
    Christianity—Apostolic basis
  xx Church—Marks
— Authority   (BT91)
  sa Liberty of speech in the church
  xx Authority (Religion)
— — History of doctrines
— Biblical teaching
    Example under Bible—Theology
— Catholicity   (BV601.3)
  x Christianity—Catholicity
    Christianity—Universality
  xx Catholicity
    Church—Marks
— Credibility
  xx Authority (Religion)
— Foundation
  sa Christianity—Origin
    Pentecost
    Popes—Primacy
  x Jesus Christ—Foundation of the
    church
  xx Christianity—Origin
    Holy Spirit
    Jesus Christ—Mystical body
    Papacy
— History of doctrines
— — Early church, ca. 30-600
    Example under Theology, Doctrinal—
    History—Early church, ca. 30-
    600
— — Middle Ages, 600-1500
    Example under Theology, Doctrinal—
    History—Middle Ages, 600-
    1500
— — 16th century
— — 18th century
— — 19th century
— — 20th century
    xx Ecumenical movement
— Holiness
  xx Church—Marks
    Holiness
— Infallibility
  sa Catholic Church—Infallibility
    Catholic Church—Teaching office
    Church—Teaching office
    Popes—Infallibility
  x Infallibility of the church
  xx Church—Teaching office
— Juvenile literature
— Marks
  sa Church—Apostolicity
    Church—Catholicity
    Church—Holiness
    Church—Unity
  x Church—Notes
    Marks of the church
    Notes of the church
— Meditations
— Mission
    See Mission of the church
— Necessity

— Non-institutional forms
    See Non-institutional churches
— Notes
    See Church—Marks
— Papal documents   (BX1746)
— Pictorial works
— Public opinion
— Purpose
    See Mission of the church
— Reform
    See Church renewal
— Renewal
    See Church renewal
— Sermons
— Teaching office
  sa Catechetics
    Catholic Church—Teaching office
    Censorship
    Church and education
    Church—Infallibility
    Missions
    Preaching
    Profession of faith
    Prohibited books
    Religious education
    Theological seminaries
  x Teaching office of the church
  xx Authority (Religion)
    Church—Infallibility
— — History of doctrines
— Teaching office (Canon law)
  sa Catechetics (Canon law)
    Preaching (Canon law)
    Profession of faith (Canon law)
    Prohibited books (Canon law)
    Religious education (Canon law)
    Theological seminaries (Canon law)
— Unity
  sa Intercommunion
  xx Church—Marks
— Visibility
Church, Apostolic
    See Church history—Primitive and early
    church, ca. 30-600
Church (The word)   (PE1599.C)
  xx English language—Etymology
Church accounting
    See Church finance—Accounting
Church administration
    See Church management
Church administration, Indigenous
    See Indigenous church administration
Church and college   (LC383)
  sa Church and education
    Church colleges
    Education and state
    Universities and colleges—Religion
  x College and church
    Education and church
  xx Church and education
    Church colleges
    Education
    Education, Higher
    Religious education
    Universities and colleges
Church and college in Great Britain, ₍India,
    the United States, etc.₎   (History of
    education, LA; Religion and
    education, LC321-629)
Church and cremation   (Direct)   (BT826.4)
  x Cremation and the church
Church and economics
  sa Church and industry

Church and education   (Church education,
    LC351-629; History of education,
    LA91-131; Separation of church and
    schools, LC107-120)
    Here are entered treatises on the relation
    of the church to education in general,
    and works on the history of the part
    that the church has taken in secular
    education. Works limited to a particu-
    lar denomination are entered under
    that denomination, with subdivision
    Education, e.g. Catholic Church—
    Education; Presbyterian Church in the
    U.S.A.—Education.
    Works on the history and theory of reli-
    gious education are entered under
    Religious education.
  sa Church and college
    Church schools
    Missions—Educational work
    Religion in the public schools
    Teaching, Freedom of
    Theology—Study and teaching
  x Education and church
    Education and religion
    Religion and education
  xx Church and college
    Church and state
    Church—Teaching office
    Education
    Religious education
    Teaching, Freedom of
    Theology—Study and teaching
  Note under Religious education
Church and education in Connecticut, ₍Italy,
    the United States, etc.₎
Church and industry   (BV628)
  x Industry and the church
  xx Christianity and economics
    Church and labor
    Church and social problems
    Sociology, Christian
Church and international affairs
    See Christianity and international affairs
Church and international organization
  x International organization and the
    church
  xx Christianity and politics
    Church and social problems
    Church and state
    International organization
— Catholic Church
Church and labor   (Direct)   (HD6338)
  sa Christianity and economics
    Church and industry
    Church and social problems
    Judaism and labor
    Labor Day Mass
    Labor supply—Religious aspects
    Priest workers
    Trade-unions, Catholic
    Work (Theology)
  x Catholic Church and labor
    Labor and the church
  xx Christian democracy
    Christianity and economics
    Church and social problems
    Labor and laboring classes
    Religion and labor
Church and leisure
  sa Recreation in church work
  x Leisure and the church
Church and moving-pictures, Catholic
    See Moving-pictures and Catholic Church
Church and race problems   (Direct)
  sa Segregation—Religious aspects
  x Integrated churches
    Race problems and the church

Church and race problems *(Direct)*
(Continued)
  xx Church and social problems
    Race problems
  — Sermons *(BT734.2)*
Church and refugee problems *(Direct)*
    (HV645)
  sa Church work with refugees
  x Refugee problems and the church
  xx Church and social problems
    Population transfers
Church and slavery
  See Slavery and the church
Church and social problems *(Direct)*
    (HN30-39)
    Here are entered works dealing with the
      orgin and treatment of social problems
      from the point of view of the church.
      The relationship of this heading to
      Sociology, Christian, is that of con-
      crete to abstract, practice to theory,
      and works to which these headings are
      appropriate are classified respectively
      in social reform or theology. Works
      covering both aspects are entered un-
      der the one heading which more nearly
      expresses the primary interest of the
      work. Works dealing with problems
      arising in the foreign mission field have
      duplicate entry under Missions, For-
      eign, or, if localized, under Missions,
      subdivided by place.
  sa Birth control—Religious aspects
    Christianity and international affairs
    Church and industry
    Church and international organization
    Church and labor
    Church and race problems
    Church and refugee problems
    Church charities
    Civilization, Christian
    Interdenominational cooperation
    Judaism and social problems
    Non church-affiliated people
    Slavery and the church
    Socialism, Christian
    Sociology, Christian
  x Religion and social problems
    Social problems and the church
  xx Church and labor
    Church and the world
    Church work
    Civilization, Christian
    Religion and sociology
    Social history
    Social problems
    Social service
    Socialism, Christian
    Sociology, Christian
  Note under Sociology, Christian
  — Anglican Communion, ₍Catholic Church,
      Lutheran Church, etc.₎
  — Catholic Church
    sa Catholic action
      Catholic criminals
      Catholic Worker Movement
      Christian democracy
      Kolping societies
      Priest workers
      Socialism and Catholic Church
      Sociology, Rural (Catholic)
      Trade-unions, Catholic
    x Catholic Church and social problems
  — — Papal documents

        GEOGRAPHIC SUBDIVISIONS

  — France
    sa Priest workers

Church and society
  See Church and the world
Church and state *(General, BV629-631;*
      Political theory, JC510-514)
  sa Anti-clericalism
    Appeal as from an abuse
    Asylum, Right of
    Bishops—Temporal power
    Caesaropapism
    Christianity and politics
    Church and education
    Church and international organization
    Church lands
    Church polity
    Church property
    Church representation
    Concordats
    Ecclesiastical law
    Established churches
    Government, Resistance to
    Investiture
    Liberty of conscience
    Monasteries and state
    Nationalism and religion
    Patronage, Ecclesiastical
    Penal laws (against nonconformists)
    Popes—Temporal power
    Religion and state
    Religion in the public schools
    Religious education—Law and
      legislation
    Religious liberty
    Secularization
    Taxation, Exemption from
  x State and church
  xx Church history
    Church polity
    Investiture
    Nationalism and religion
    Political science
    Popes—Temporal power
    Religion and state
    Religious liberty
  — Biblical teaching
  — Catholic Church *(BX1790-1793)*
    sa Cardinal protectors
      Church and state in France, ₍Italy,
        etc.₎
      Fascism and the Catholic Church
      Translatio imperii
    x Catholic Church and state
      Catholic Church—Relation to the
        state
  — — Papal documents
  — Church of England *(BX5157)*
    sa Church and state in Great Britain
    x Church of England—Relation to the
      state
    xx Church and state in Great Britain
  — Lutheran Church
    x Lutheran Church and state
      Lutheran Church—Relation to the
        state
  — Mormonism
    sa Kingdom of God (Mormonism)
    x Mormons and Mormonism—
      Relation to the state
  — Presbyterian Church
    x Presbyterian Church and state
      Presbyterian Church—Relation to
        the state
  — Sermons
Church and state in Austria
  sa Josephinism
Church and state in Bavaria
  sa Concordat of 1924 (Bavaria)
Church and state in England
  See Church and state in Great Britain

Church and state in Europe
  sa Holy Roman Empire
Church and state in France *(Church history,*
      BR840-849)
  sa Gallicanism
    Pragmatic sanction of Charles VII,
      1438
  xx Church and state—Catholic Church
  — 20th century *(BR846)*
Church and state in Germany *(Church*
      history, BR850-859)
  — 19th century
    sa Kulturkampf
  — 20th century *(BR856)*
  — 1933-1945 *(BR856)*
  — 1945-
Church and state in Great Britain *(Church*
      history, BR740-759; Church of
      England, BX5157)
    Here are entered works dealing not only
      with church and state in England,
      Scotland and Ireland, or in any two of
      them, but also works dealing with Eng-
      land alone.
  sa Church and state—Church of England
    Church of England—Bishops—
      Temporal power
    Church of England—Establishment and
      disestablishment
    Conventicle act, 1670
    Oath of allegiance, 1606
    Puritans
    Royal supremacy (Church of England)
  x Church and state in England
  xx Church and state—Church of England
    Church of England
Church and state in Ireland
  sa Church of Ireland—Establishment and
    disestablishment
Church and state in Italy, ₍Mexico, Spain,
    etc.₎
  xx Church and state—Catholic Church
Church and state in New England
Church and state in Russia *(BR930-939)*
  — 1917-
Church and state in Scotland
  sa Church of Scotland—Establishment and
    disestablishment
Church and state in Sweden
  sa Konventikelplakatet, 1726
Church and state in Wales
  sa Church in Wales—Establishment and
    disestablishment
Church and the poor *(BV639.P6)*
  x Poor and the church
Church and the press *(Direct) (PN4756)*
    Subdivided by denomination.
  x Press and the church
  xx Public relations—Churches
Church and the world *(BR115.W6)*
    Here are entered works on the position
      and responsibilities of the Christian
      church in a secular society.
  sa Christianity and economics
    Christianity and international affairs
    Christianity and politics
    Church and social problems
    Church and underdeveloped areas
    History (Theology)
    Kingdom of God
    Sociology, Christian
  x Christianity and the world
    Church and society
    Society and the church
    World and the church
    Worldliness (Theology)
  xx Mission of the church
  — Biblical teaching

Church and travel   (G156.5.C5)
  x Travel and the church
Church and underdeveloped areas   (Direct)
      (BR115.U6)
  x Underdeveloped areas and the church
  xx Christianity and international affairs
     Church and the world
Church and war
  See War and religion
Church anniversaries   (BV652.9)
  x Church centennial celebrations
     Churches—Anniversaries
     Churches—Centennial celebrations
  xx Anniversaries
Church announcements   (Direct)
  sa Church bulletins
  xx Advertising—Churches
     Church work
     Oral communication
Church antiquities
  See Christian antiquities
Church architecture   (Direct)
      (NA4790-6113)
  sa Abbeys
     Architecture and religion
     Architecture, Cistercian
     Architecture, Gothic
     Architecture, Jesuit
     Basilicas
     Cathedrals
     Chapels
     Church decoration and ornament
     Crossing (Architecture)
     Crypts
     Jaquemarts
     Lich-gates
     Liturgy and architecture
     Mosques
     Narthex
     Orientation (Architecture)
     Orientation (Religion)
     Spires
     Sunday-school buildings
     Temples
     Towers
     Vaults (Architecture)
  x Architecture, Church
     Architecture, Ecclesiastical
     Church buildings
     Ecclesiastical architecture
     Religious art
     Rood-lofts
  xx Architecture
     Architecture and religion
     Architecture, Gothic
     Chapels
     Christian antiquities
     Christian art and symbolism
     Churches
  — Conservation and restoration
     x Church architecture—Restoration
  — Designs and plans   (NA4810-4811)
     xx Church facilities—Planning
  — Details
     xx Architecture—Details
  — Philosophy
  — Restoration
     See Church architecture—
        Conservation and restoration
Church architecture (Canon law)
  sa Cathedrals (Canon law)
Church attendance   (BV652; BV4523)
  sa Public worship
     United States.   Navy—Religious life
  x Attendance, Church
     Church-going
  xx Pastoral theology
     Public worship

Worship
— Juvenile literature
— Law and legislation   (Direct)
     sa Church attendance (Canon law)
     xx Ecclesiastical law
Church attendance (Canon law)
      (BX1939.C63)
  xx Church attendance—Law and
     legislation
Church bells
  See Bells
Church benefices
  See Benefices, Ecclesiastical
Church biography
  See Christian biography
Church buildings
  See Church architecture
     Churches
Church bulletins
  xx Advertising—Churches
     Church announcements
Church calendar   (CE81-83)
  sa Chronology, Ecclesiastical
     Church year
     Fasts and feasts
     Saints—Calendar
     subheading Liturgy and ritual—
        Calendar under particular church
        bodies, e.g. Catholic Church.
        Liturgy and ritual—Calendar
  x Calendar, Ecclesiastical
     Computus ecclesiasticus
     Ecclesiastical calendar
     Heortology
  xx Calendar
     Chronology, Ecclesiastical
     Fasts and feasts
     Saints
Notes under Church year; Religious calendars
— Comparative studies
     See Religious calendars
Church camps   (Direct) (BV1650)
  sa Religious camps
  x Camps (Church)
  xx Camp-meetings
     Camps
     Church work with children
     Church work with youth
     Vacation schools, Religious
Church canons
  See Canons, Cathedral, collegiate, etc.
Church centennial celebrations
  See Church anniversaries
Church charities   (HV530)
  sa subdivision Charities under church
     denominations, e.g. Methodist
     Episcopal Church—Charities
  x Religious social work
  xx Charities
     Church and social problems
     Church finance
Church chronology
  See Chronology, Ecclesiastical
Church colleges   (Indirect) (LC427-629)
  sa Church and college
  x Christian colleges
     Church-related colleges
     Denominational colleges
  xx Church and college
     Church schools
     Universities and colleges
Church commandments
  See Commandments of the church
Church commitment
  See Commitment to the church
Church committees
     Subdivided by denomination.
  sa Parish councils

  x Parish committees
  xx Church management
     Committees
Church correspondence   (BV652)
  x Correspondence
  xx Church work
     Letter-writing
Church costume
  See Church vestments
Church councils
  See Councils and synods
Church councils, Local
  See Local church councils
Church counseling centers
  See Pastoral counseling centers
Church courts
  See Ecclesiastical courts
Church decoration and ornament   (Indirect)
      (NA5000; NK2190)
  sa Altarpieces
     Altars
     Aumbries
     Choir-stalls
     Christian art and symbolism
     Church furniture
     Flower arrangement in churches
     Fonts
     Glass painting and staining
     Liturgical objects
     Mosaics
     Mural painting and decoration
     Sacrament houses
     Screens (Church decoration)
     Ship models (Church decoration)
  x Church ornament
     Ecclesiastical decoration and ornament
  xx Christian art and symbolism
     Church architecture
     Churches
     Decoration and ornament
     Interior decoration
     Religious articles
Church dedication   (BV880; Catholic Church,
      BX2302)
  sa Corner stones, Laying of
     Patron saints
  x Consecration of churches
     Dedication of churches
  xx Church of England.   Liturgy and ritual
     Dedication services
     Rites and ceremonies
Church dedication (Canon law)   (BX1939.C)
Church dedication sermons   (BV4258)
  xx Sermons
Church desecration
  See Sacrilege
Church discipline
  sa Absolution
     Asceticism
     Celibacy
     Confession
     Confessors
     Conscience, Examination of
     Dispensations
     Easter duties
     Ecclesiastical courts
     Evangelical counsels
     Excommunication
     Indulgences
     Inquisition
     Marriage, Mixed
     Monasticism and religious orders—
        Discipline
     Penance
     Purgatory
     Simony
     Visitations, Ecclesiastical

Church discipline (Continued)
    subdivision Discipline *under church*
      denominations, e.g. Catholic Church
      —Discipline; Church of England—
      Discipline
    x Discipline, Ecclesiastical
      Ecclesiastical discipline
    xx Church membership
      Church polity
      Disciplinary power
      Ecclesiastical courts
      Excommunication
      Penance
  — Early church, ca. 30-600 *(BV648)*
    sa Church orders, Ancient
    xx Church history—Primitive and early
      church, ca. 30-600
      Church orders, Ancient

Church doors *(Direct) (NA4950)*
  xx Doors
Church embroidery
  See Ecclesiastical embroidery
Church entertainments *(BV1620-1643)*
  sa Recreation in church work
  x Church sociables
    Entertainments
  xx Amusements
Church etiquette *(BJ2018-2019)*
  sa Clergy—Etiquette
  x Christian etiquette
    Church protocol
    Etiquette, Christian
    Etiquette, Church
    Protocol, Church
  xx Church work
    Clergy—Etiquette
Church extension
  See Missions, Home
Church fabric
  See Church maintenance and repair
Church facilities
  — Planning
    sa Church architecture—Designs and
      plans
    x Planning, Church facilities
Church fairs
  See Bazaars, Charitable
Church fathers
  See Fathers of the church
Church federations, Local
  See Local church councils
Church festivals
  See Fasts and feasts
Church finance *(Direct) (BV770-777)*
  Here are entered works dealing with the
    solicitation of funds for church work,
    their administration and the account-
    ing for them.
  sa Annates
    Benefices, Ecclesiastical
    Christian giving
    Church charities
    Church fund raising
    Church lands
    Church property
    Church purchasing
    Church tax
    Church work—Forms, blanks, etc.
    Churchwardens' accounts
    Clergy—Salaries, pensions, etc.
    Easter dues
    Fees, Ecclesiastical
    Pews and pew rights
    Stewardship, Christian
    Taxation, Exemption from
    Tithes

    subdivision Finance *under church*
      denominations, and under special
      topics, e.g. Church of England—
      Finance; Missions—Finance
  x Finance, Church
  xx Annates
    Church management
    Church polity
    Finance
  Note under Stewardship, Christian
  — Early church, ca. 30-600
    xx Church history—Primitive and early
      church, ca. 30-600

GENERAL SUBDIVISIONS

  — Accounting
    x Church accounting
Church flags
  See Church pennants
Church flower arrangement
  See Flower arrangement in churches
Church fund raising *(BV772.5)*
  x Churches—Fund raising
  xx Church finance
    Fund raising
Church furniture *(NA5050-5090)*
  sa Altarpieces
    Altars
    Aumbries
    Choir-stalls
    Confessionals (Architecture)
    Fonts
    Kneelers (Church furniture)
    Pulpits
    Sacrament houses
    Screens (Church decoration)
    Tabernacle (Church furniture)
  x Ecclesiastical furniture
  xx Christian antiquities
    Christian art and symbolism
    Church decoration and ornament
    Furniture
Church gardens
  sa Cemeteries—Landscape architecture
  x Chapel gardens
    Churches—Gardens
    Liturgical gardens
  xx Gardens
    Landscape gardening
Church-going
  See Church attendance
Church goods
  See Church supplies
Church government
  See Church polity
Church group work
  sa Church meetings
    Prayer groups
  x Group work, Church
    Parish group work
  xx Church societies
    Church work
    Communication (Theology)
    Social group work
    Young people's meetings (Church
      work)
Church group work with young adults
    (BV4446)
  xx Church work with young adults
Church group work with youth *(BV4447)*
  xx Church work with youth
Church growth *(BV652.25)*
  xx Evangelistic work
    Missions
Church historians *(BR139)*
  x Historians, Church
  xx Church history—Historiography
    Historians

Church historians, British, [German, etc.]
  x British [German, etc.] church historians
  — Correspondence, reminiscences, etc.
Church history *(BR)*
  sa Abbeys
    Church and state
    Convents and nunneries
    Councils and synods
    Creeds
    Dioceses
    Ecclesiastical geography
    Episcopacy
    Fathers of the church
    Inquisition
    Language question in the church
    Martyrs
    Miracles
    Missions
    Monasticism and religious orders
    Papacy
    Persecution
    Popes
    Protestant churches
    Protestantism
    Reformation
    Revivals
    Sects
    Sisterhoods
    headings beginning with the word
      Christian; *names of denominations,*
      sects, churches, councils, etc.; and
      subdivision Church history *under*
      names of countries, cities, etc.
  x Christianity—History
    Ecclesiastical history
    History, Church
    History, Ecclesiastical
    Religious history
  xx History
    Theology
  — Primitive and early church, ca. 30-600
      (BR160-240)
    sa Alexandrian school, Christian
      Alogi
      Antiochian school
      Apologetics—Early church, ca.
        30-600
      Apostles
      Apostolic Fathers
      Arianism
      Asceticism—Early church, ca.
        30-600
      Baptism—History—Early church, ca.
        30-600
      Catacombs
      Catechetics—Early church, ca.
        30-600
      Catechumens—Early church, ca.
        30-600
      Christian ethics—Early church, ca.
        30-600
      Christianity and culture—Early
        church, ca. 30-600
      Church discipline—Early church, ca.
        30-600
      Church finance—Early church, ca.
        30-600
      Church history—4th century
      Church history—6th century
      Church orders, Ancient
      Church polity—Early church, ca.
        30-600
      Ebionism
      Edict of Milan, 313
      Elkesaites
      Eunomianism
      Fathers of the church

Funeral rites and ceremonies, Early
Christian
Heresies and heretics—Early church,
ca. 30-600
Infant baptism—Early church, ca.
30-600
Jewish Christians—Early church, ca.
30-600
Monasticism and religious orders—
Early church, ca. 30-600
Montanism
Mysticism—Early church, ca. 30-600
Neoplatonism
Persecution—Early church, ca.
30-600
Religious education—History—Early
church, ca. 30-600
Religious thought—To 600
Sabellianism
Schism, Acacian, 484-519
Seven churches
Theology, Doctrinal—History—Early
church, ca. 30-600
Tradition (Theology)—Early church,
ca. 30-600
War and religion—Early church, ca.
30-600
Women in Christianity—Early
church, ca. 30-600
x Apostolic Church
Church, Apostolic
Primitive and early church
Primitive Christianity
xx Catacombs
Church orders, Ancient
Fathers of the church
— — Juvenile literature
— — Pictures, illustrations, etc.
— — Sources
sa Christian literature, Early
xx Christian literature, Early
— 4th century   (BR205)
xx Church history—Primitive and early
church, ca. 30-600
— 6th century
xx Church history—Primitive and early
church, ca. 30-600
— Middle Ages, 600-1500   (BR160-270)
sa Albigenses
Apologetics—Middle Ages, 600-1500
Asceticism—Middle Ages, 600-1500
Catechumens—Middle Ages,
600-1500
Church history—11th century
Church history—12th century
Crusades
Inquisition
Monasticism and religious orders—
Middle Ages, 600-1500
Mysticism—Middle Ages, 600-1500
Papacy
Patarines
Popes—Temporal power
Reformation—Early movements
Religious thought—Middle Ages,
600-1500
Schism, The Great Western,
1378-1417
Waldenses
x Catholic Church—History—Middle
Ages, 600-1500
xx Middle Ages
— — Pictures, illustrations, etc.
— 11th century
xx Church history—Middle Ages,
600-1500
— 12th century

xx Church history—Middle Ages,
600-1500
— 13th century
— Modern period, 1500-   (BR290)
sa Catholic Church—History—Modern
period, 1500-
Counter-Reformation
Liberalism (Religion)—Catholic
Church
Missions—History
Protestantism—History
Reformation
Religious thought—Modern period,
1500-
Sects
xx Counter-Reformation
Reformation
Sects
— Reformation, 1517-1648
See Reformation
— 17th century   (BR440)
sa Syncretistic controversy
— 18th century   (BR470)
sa Evangelical Revival
— 19th century   (BR477)
— 20th century   (BR479)
— 1945-

GENERAL SUBDIVISIONS

— Atlases
See Ecclesiastical geography—Maps

GENERAL SUBDIVISIONS

— Chronology
See Chronology, Ecclesiastical

GENERAL SUBDIVISIONS

— Historiography   (BR138; Catholic
Church, BX938)
sa Church historians
— Juvenile literature
— Maps
See Ecclesiastical geography—Maps
— Philosophy   (BR138)
xx History—Philosophy
— Pictures, illustrations, etc.   (BR154)
— Sources
sa Church records and registers
Church in art
xx Art
Church in literature   (PN56.C)
Church in Wales
sa Church of England in Wales
— Establishment and disestablishment
xx Church and state in Wales
Church kneelers (Furniture)
See Kneelers (Church furniture)
Church lands   (Indirect)   (HD101-1130)
sa Parsonages
x Glebes
xx Church and state
Church finance
Church property
Ecclesiastical law
Land
Land grants
Land tenure
Mortmain
Public lands
— Philippine Islands
x Friars in the Philippine Islands
Church Latin
See Latin language—Church Latin
Church law
See Ecclesiastical law
Church leadership
See Christian leadership

Church libraries
See Libraries, Church
Church maintenance and repair
x Church fabric
Churches—Maintenance and repair
Fabrica ecclesiae
xx Buildings—Repair and reconstruction
Church management
Church maintenance and repair (Canon law)
See Church maintenance and repair
(Ecclesiastical law)
**Church maintenance and repair (Ecclesiastical
law)**   (Direct)
x Church maintenance and repair (Canon
law)
xx Canon law
Ecclesiastical law
Church management   (BV652)
sa Advertising—Churches
Church committees
Church finance
Church maintenance and repair
Churches—Location
Group ministry
Parish councils
Public relations—Churches
x Church administration
Churches—Administration
Churches—Management
Parish administration
Parish management
xx Church work
Institution management
Church meetings   (BV652.15)
x Meetings, Church
xx Church group work
Church membership   (BV820)
sa Baptism
Baptism and church membership
Church discipline
Close and open communion
Commitment to the church
Confirmation
Covenants (Church polity)
Lord's Supper
Non church-affiliated people
xx Church polity
Confirmation
Intercommunion
Priesthood, Universal
Church membership and baptism
See Baptism and church membership
Church music   (Indirect)   (Aesthetics,
ML3869; History, ML178,
ML3000-3190, ML3270; Instruction
and study, MT88, MT860-865,
MT915)
Here are entered works on church music
and on sacred vocal music in general.
Sacred vocal compositions are entered
under the heading Sacred vocal music
and headings referred to under that
heading.
Subdivided, when desirable, by denomi-
nation as well as by locality, e.g. 1.
Church music—Church of England. 2.
Church music—England.
sa Advent music
Anthem
Ascension Day music
Cantata
Carillons
Carols
Chapels (Music)
Choirs (Music)
Choral music
Chorale
Christmas music

337

Church music *(Indirect)* *(Aesthetics,*
ML3869; History, ML178,
ML3000-3190, ML3270; Instruction
and study, MT88, MT860-865,
MT915) *(Continued)*
    Conducting, Choral
    Easter music
    Epiphany music
    Funeral music
    Hymns
    Mass (Music)
    Motet
    Music in churches
    Oratorio
    Organ music
    Passion music—History and criticism
    Psalmody
    Religion and music
    Sequences (Liturgy)
    Wedding music
  x Music, Religious
    Music, Sacred
    Religious music
    Sacred music
  xx Devotional exercises
    Liturgics
    Music
    Music in churches
    Psalmody
    Religion and music
  Note under Sacred vocal music
— Almanacs, yearbooks, etc. *(ML13-21)*
  x Church music—Yearbooks
— Anglican Communion
  sa Church music—Church of England
    Church music—Protestant Episcopal
    Church in the U.S.A.
— Catholic Church
  sa Catholic Church. Liturgy and ritual
    Chants (Plain, Gregorian, etc.)
    Mass (Music)
    Motet
    Tonarius
  x Catholic Church music
    Catholic Church—Music
  xx Catholic Church. Liturgy and ritual
— — Congresses
    See Music—Congresses
— — History and criticism
  sa Maîtrises
— Catholic Church (Byzantine rite)
    (ML3060)
  xx Church music—Orthodox Eastern
    Church
— Choruses and choir books
    See Service books (Music)
— Church of England *(ML3166)*
  sa Church of England. Liturgy and
    ritual
  xx Church music—Anglican
    Communion
    Church music—Protestant Episcopal
    Church in the U.S.A.
  Note under Church music
— Congresses
    See Music—Congresses
— Greek Church
    See Church music—Orthodox Eastern
    Church
— History and criticism
  sa Music—History and criticism—
    Medieval, 400-1500
    Organ—History
— Lutheran Church *(ML3168)*
  sa Chorale
— Orthodox Eastern Church *(ML3060)*
  sa Chants (Byzantine)

Church music—Catholic Church
    (Byzantine rite)
  x Church music—Greek Church
— Protestant churches *(ML3100-3188)*
  sa Chants (Anglican)
  Example under Protestant churches
— Protestant Episcopal Church in the U.S.A.
    (ML3166)
  sa Church music—Church of England
  xx Church music—Anglican
    Communion
— Service books
    See Service books (Music)
— Societies, etc. *(ML128)*
    Here are entered works about societies
    for the cultivation of church music
    and the publications of such socie-
    ties.
  xx Musical societies
— Yearbooks
    See Church music—Almanacs,
    yearbooks, etc.

GEOGRAPHIC SUBDIVISIONS

— England *(ML2931)*
    Note under Church music
— France *(ML2927)*
  sa Maîtrises
Church music (Canon law)
Church-night services *(BV28)*
  sa Evening-service music
    Vespers
  x Midweek services
    Week-night services
  xx Church work
    Prayer-meetings
    Public worship
    Vespers
Church of Abyssinia
    See Ethiopic Church
Church of Christ, Scientist *(BX6901-6996)*
    Here are entered official publications of
    the church, including hymn-books,
    etc. Other works about the church are
    entered under Christian Science.
Church of Christ of Latter-Day Saints
    See Church of Jesus Christ of Latter-Day
    Saints
    Mormons and Mormonism
Church of England. Book of common prayer
    (BX5145)
  x Book of common prayer
  xx Church of England. Liturgy and ritual
    Prayer-books
  Example under Liturgies; Ritual
— Sermons
Church of England. Book of common prayer.
    Psalter
  sa Psalters
Church of England *(BX5011-5199)*
  sa Anglo-Catholicism
    Cathedrals
    Church and state in Great Britain
    Dissenters, Religious—England
    Episcopacy
    Marprelate controversy
    Nonjurors
    Oxford movement
    Puritans
  x Anglican Church
    England, Church of
    Episcopal Church
  xx Puritans
— Anecdotes, facetiae, satire, etc.
— Benefices *(BX5165)*
  xx Church of England—Government
  Example under Benefices, Ecclesiastical
— Biography *(BX5197-9)*

  sa Bishops—England
    Church of England—Clergy
— Bishops *(BX5176-8)*
  Example under Bishops
— — Salaries, pensions, etc.
— — Temporal power *(BX5176)*
  xx Church and state in Great Britain
    Church of England—Government
— Caricatures and cartoons
— Catechisms and creeds *(BX5139)*
  sa Church of England. Articles of
    religion
— Ceremonies and practices
— Clergy *(BX5175-5180)*
  sa Anglican orders
    Apostolic succession
    Bishops—England
    Clergy—England
    Episcopacy
    Proctors (Church of England)
  xx Apostolic succession
    Church of England—Biography
  Example under Clergy; Priests
— — Correspondence, reminiscences, etc.
— Clergy, Training of
— Constitution
    See Church of England—Government
— Continuity
    See Continuity of the church—
    Anglican Communion
— Converts
    See Converts, Anglican
— Dioceses *(BX5106-7)*
  sa names of dioceses, e.g. Canterbury,
    Eng. (Diocese); Salisbury, Eng.
    (Diocese)
  Example under Dioceses
— Discipline *(BX5150-5155)*
  Example under Church discipline
— Doctrinal and controversial works
    (BX5130-5132)
— — Debates, etc.
— Education *(LC582-3)*
— Episcopal charges
    See Church of England—Pastoral
    letters and charges
— Establishment and disestablishment
    (BX5157)
  xx Church and state in Great Britain
— Evangelical party
    See Evangelicalism—Church of
    England
— Fasts and feasts
    See Fasts and feasts—Church of
    England
— Finance *(BX5157-5165)*
  Example under Church finance
— Government *(BX5150-5182)*
  sa Church of England—Benefices
    Church of England—Bishops—
    Temporal power
    Royal supremacy (Church of
    England)
  x Church of England—Constitution
  Example under Church polity
— History *(BX5051-5101)*
  sa subdivision History *under names of*
    dioceses, e.g. Canterbury, Eng.
    (Diocese)—History
— Hymns *(BV370)*
— Marriage
    See Marriage—Church of England
— Membership
— Missions *(BV2500)*
  Example under Missions
— Modernism
    See Modernism —Church of England
— Movements

See Church of England—Parties and
movements
— Parish missions
See Parish missions—Anglican
Communion
— Parties and movements (BX5115-5126)
sa Anglo-Catholicism
Broad Church Movement
Evangelicalism—Church of England
Modernism—Church of England
x Church of England—Movements
— Pastoral letters and charges (BX5034)
x Church of England—Episcopal
charges
Example under Visitation sermons;
Visitations, Ecclesiastical; and un-
der references from Episcopal
charges; Pastoral letters and
charges
— Prayer-books and devotions
— Proctors
See Proctors (Church of England)
— Relation to the state
See Church and state—Church of
England
— Relations
— — Catholic Church
— Sermons (BX5133)
Church of England. Articles of religion
(BX5137)
x Articles, Thirty-nine
Thirty-nine articles
xx Church of England—Catechisms and
creeds
Church of England. Liturgy and ritual
(BX5141-7)
sa Cemeteries—Consecration
Chants (Anglican)
Church dedication
Church of England. Book of common
prayer
xx Church music—Church of England
Church of England. Liturgy and ritual.
Coronation service (DA112)
Church of England in America (BX5881)
Here are entered works which deal with
the English church in America as a
whole, or in several colonies. Works
limited to the church in one or two
colonies are entered under Church of
England in Connecticut, [Maryland,
etc.] See also Protestant Episcopal
Church in the U.S.A. (established as
such in 1789, formerly the "Church of
England in America")
Note under Protestant Episcopal Church in the
U.S.A.
— Clergy, Loyalist
x Clergy, Loyalist
xx American loyalists
Church of England in Connecticut, [Maryland,
etc.]
Note under Church of England in America
Church of England in Ireland
See Church of Ireland
Church of England in Scotland
See Episcopal Church in Scotland
Church of England in Wales
xx Church in Wales
Church of Ethiopia
See Ethiopic Church
Church of God (Direct) (BX7020)
Here are entered works on the various
religious bodies using the words
"Church of God" in their name.
sa Holiness churches
xx Holiness churches
Pentecostal churches

Church of Ireland (BX5410-5595)
x Church of England in Ireland
Episcopal Church
Established Church of Ireland
— Clergy
— — Correspondence, reminiscences, etc.
— Establishment and disestablishment
(BX5550)
x Church and state in Ireland
— Government
Church of Jesus Christ of Latter-Day Saints
(BX8601-8695)
Here are entered works dealing with the
church as distinct from the other bran-
ches or sects of Mormonism. Works of
a general nature are entered under the
heading Mormons and Mormonism,
with appropriate subdivisions if neces-
sary.
x Church of Christ of Latter-Day Saints
xx Mormons and Mormonism
Church of Scotland (BX9075-9)
sa Covenanters
Presbyterian Church
Presbyterianism
— Charities
— Clergy
sa Beadles
— — Salaries, pensions, etc.
— Establishment and disestablishment
(BX9078)
xx Church and state in Scotland
Church of the Brethren (BX7801-7843)
x Dompelaers
Dunkards
Dunkers
German Baptist Brethren
Tunkers
xx Anabaptists
Baptists
Church of the New Jerusalem
See New Jerusalem Church
Church officers (BV705)
sa Beadles
Church secretaries
Church ushers
Deacons
District superintendents (Methodist)
Elders (Church officers)
Installation service (Church officers)
Ophphikia
Sextons
x Church staff
xx Christian leadership
Church polity
Church work
Church orders
xx Liturgies
Church orders, Ancient (BV761.A1-5)
Here are entered works dealing with one
or more of a group of closely related
early compositions containing rules
and regulations, usages and practices
governing the discipline, cult (liturgy
and ritual) and management of church
affairs in general, which were believed
to have been formulated by the apostles. They are prominent among the
sources of liturgy and of the later compilations of canon law, with which they
are not to be confused.
sa Canon law
Church discipline—Early church, ca.
30-600
Church history—Primitive and early
church, ca. 30-600
Church polity—Early church, ca.
30-600

Liturgies, Early Christian
Theology, Doctrinal—History—Early
church, ca. 30-600
xx Canon law
Christian literature, Early
Church discipline—Early church, ca.
30-600
Church history—Primitive and early
church, ca. 30-600
Church polity—Early church, ca.
30-600
Liturgies, Early Christian
Theology, Doctrinal—History—Early
church, ca. 30-600
Church orders, Lutheran
x Lutheran church orders
Church orders, Protestant
x Protestant church orders
Church orders, Reformed
x Reformed Church orders
Church ornament
See Church decoration and ornament
Church parking
See Churches—Parking facilities
Church pennants (Christian art and
symbolism, BV168.F5)
x Christian flags
Church flags
Pennants, Church
xx Flags
Liturgical objects
Church plate (Direct) (NK7100-7215)
sa Ampullas, Coronation
Chalices
Custodials
Monstrances
x Communion plate
xx Liturgical objects
Plate
Church plate, American (NK7112; NK7215)
Church polity (BV646-651)
sa Baptism and church membership
Benefices, Ecclesiastical
Cardinals
Chanceries, Diocesan
Church and state
Church discipline
Church finance
Church membership
Church officers
Church property
Clergy
Congregationalism
Covenants (Church polity)
Dioceses
Ecclesiastical law
Episcopacy
Indigenous church administration
Institutionalism (Religion)
Investiture
Laity
Larger parishes
Liberty of conscience
Local church councils
Methodism
Patronage, Ecclesiastical
Pews and pew rights
Presbyterianism
Puritans
Simultaneum
Sunday
subdivision Government under church
denominations, e.g. Church of
England—Government
x Christianity—Polity
Church government
Ecclesiastical polity
Polity, Ecclesiastical

Church polity (BV646-651) (Continued)
  xx Bishops
    Church and state
    Theology, Practical
  Note under Polity (Religion)
  — Early church, ca. 30-600 (BV648)
    sa Church orders, Ancient
      xx Church history—Primitive and early
        church, ca. 30-600
        Church orders, Ancient
  — Comparative studies
    See Polity (Religion)
Church polity and Christian union
    (BX9.5.C5)
  x Christian union and church polity
Church precepts
  See Commandments of the church
Church property (Indirect) (BV775-7)
  sa Benefices, Ecclesiastical
    Church lands
    Convents and nunneries
    Monasteries
    Parsonages
    Patronage, Ecclesiastical
    Pews and pew rights
    Privileges and immunities, Ecclesiastical
    Secularization
  x Property, Church
  xx Church and state
    Church finance
    Church polity
    Ecclesiastical law
    Property
  — Maintenance and repair
  — Taxation (Direct)
    sa Corporations, Religious—Taxation
      Taxation, Exemption from
    x Charities—Taxation
    xx Corporations, Nonprofit—Taxation
      Property tax
      Real property tax
      Taxation, Exemption from
Church property (Canon law) (BX1939.C66)
  sa Mortgages (Canon law)
Church property (Canon law, Orthodox
    Eastern)
  xx Canon law, Orthodox Eastern
Church protocol
  See Church etiquette
Church public relations
  See Public relations—Churches
Church publicity (Direct)
  sa Advertising—Churches
  xx Public relations—Churches
    Publicity
Church purchasing (BV652.75)
  xx Church finance
    Purchasing
Church rates (Church of England, BX5165)
  sa Church tax
  xx Church tax
    Churchwardens' accounts
Church records and registers (Direct)
  sa Archives, Diocesan
    Baptismal certificates
    Church statistics
    Registers of births, etc.
    Temple records and registers
  x Church registers
    Ecclesiastical records and registers
    Ecclesiastical registers
    Parish registers
  xx Archives
    Church history—Sources
    Registers of births, etc.
    Temple records and registers
Church records on microfilm
  xx Microfilms

Church reform
  See Church renewal
Church registers
  See Church records and registers
    Registers of births, etc.
Church-related colleges
  See Church colleges
Church renewal (BV600)
  sa Counter-Reformation
    Mission of the church
    Reformation
  x Christianity—Renewal
    Church reform
    Church—Reform
    Church—Renewal
    Reform of the church
    Renewal of the church
  xx Theology, Practical
  — Catholic Church, [etc.]
    x Catholic Church [etc.]—Renewal
Church representation (Direct)
  xx Church and state
    Ecclesiastical law
Church schools (Indirect) (LC427-629)
  Here are entered works dealing with elementary and secondary schools whose
  pupils receive their entire education
  under church auspices, control, or support. Works dealing with the schools of
  a particular denomination are entered
  under that denomination with subdivision Education, e.g. Presbyterian
  Church in the U.S.A.—Education.
  sa Church colleges
    Vacation schools, Religious
  x Denominational schools
    Diocesan schools
    Parish schools
    Parochial schools
    Schools, Denominational
    Schools, Parochial
  xx Church and education
    Private schools
    Religious education
    Schools
  — Curricula
  — Finance
    x School finance
      Tuition
  — Law and legislation (Direct)
    sa Church schools (Canon law)
    xx Educational law and legislation
Church schools, Week-day
  See Week-day church schools
Church schools (Canon law) (BX1939.S35)
  xx Catholic Church—Education
    Church schools—Law and legislation
Church secretaries (BV705)
  xx Church officers
    Church work
    Office management
    Secretaries
Church settlements
  See Social settlements
Church Slavic language (PG601-698)
  x Bulgarian Church Slavic language
    Bulgarian language—To 1100
    Old Bulgarian language
    Old Church Slavic language
    Old Slovenian language
    Serbian Church Slavic language
    Slovenian language (Old)
Church Slavic literature (PG701-5)
Church Slavic poetry (Direct)
Church sociables
  See Church entertainments
Church societies (BV900-1450)
  sa Altar gilds

    Brotherhoods
    Church group work
  xx Societies
    Theology, Practical
Church societies (Canon law) (BX1939.C)
Church staff
  See Church officers
Church statistics (Indirect)
  sa Church work—Forms, blanks, etc.
    Ecclesiastical geography
  x Churches—Statistical methods
    Ecclesiastical statistics
  xx Church records and registers
    Ecclesiastical geography
    Statistics
Church supplies (HF5035.C3; TS2301.C5)
  x Church goods
    Ecclesiastical supplies
    Goods, Ecclesiastical
    Supplies, Ecclesiastical
Church tax (Direct)
  Here are entered works on taxes levied by
    the state for the support of the estab-
    lished church or of recognized reli-
    gious bodies.
  sa Church rates
    Tithes
  xx Church finance
    Church rates
    Taxation
    Tithes
Church towers
  See Towers
Church unity
  See Christian union
Church Unity Octave
  See Chair of Unity Octave
Church ushers (BV705)
  xx Church officers
    Church work
    Ushers
Church vacation schools
  See Vacation schools, Religious
Church vestments (BV167; Catholic Church,
    BX1925; Church of England,
    BX5180; Monastic, BX2790)
  sa Altar-cloths
    Clergy—Costume
    Colors, Liturgical
    Cope
    Monasticism and religious orders—
      Habit
    Sacristans
    Scapulars
    Staff, Pastoral
  x Church costume
    Ecclesiastical costume
    Ecclesiastical vestments
    Vestments
  xx Christian antiquities
    Christian art and symbolism
    Clergy—Costume
    Costume
    Embroidery
    Liturgical objects
    Liturgics
  Note under Clergy—Costume
Church wardens' accounts
  See Churchwardens' accounts
Church work (BV4400-4470)
  Subdivided by denomination.
  sa Chaplains, Industrial
    Christian leadership
    Church and social problems
    Church announcements
    Church correspondence
    Church etiquette
    Church group work

Church management
Church-night services
Church officers
Church secretaries
Church ushers
City churches
City clergy
City missions
Deaconesses
Evangelistic work
Fish movement (Christianity)
Indigenous church administration
Institutional missions
Institutionalism (Religion)
Interdenominational cooperation
Local church councils
Mass media in religion
Missions
Office practice in churches
Parish houses
Parish missions
Pastoral counseling
Pastoral psychology
Pastoral theology
Public relations—Churches
Recreation in church work
Revivals
Rural churches
Rural clergy
Suburban churches
Sunday-schools
Telephone in church work
Visitations (Church work)
Women in church work
   x Church work with adults
   Institutional church
   Ministry
  xx Parishes
   Pastoral theology
   Theology, Practical
— Audio-visual aids
   xx Religious education—Audio-visual
      aids
— Forms, blanks, etc. *(Catholic Church,*
    BX1947; Church finance, BV773;
    Ministry, BV707)
   xx Church finance
   Church statistics
   Registers of births, etc.
— Vocational guidance
   See Church work as a profession
Church work, Rural
  See Rural churches
Church work as a profession *(BV683)*
   x Church work—Vocational guidance
   Religion as a profession
  xx Vocation, Ecclesiastical
Church work with adults
  See Church work
   Church work with men
   Church work with women
Church work with alcoholics *(Direct)*
  xx Alcoholics
Church work with apartment dwellers
  xx Apartment houses
   City churches
Church work with boys
  See Church work with children
Church work with children *(Direct)*
    (BV639.C4)
  sa Church camps
   Preaching to children
   x Church work with boys
   Church work with girls
  xx Boys
   Children
   Girls
   Social work with children

Church work with criminals *(Direct)*
    (BV4464.7)
  sa Church work with juvenile delinquents
   Prisons—Missions and charities
  xx Rehabilitation of criminals
Church work with employed women
  xx Woman—Employment
Church work with exceptional children
  xx Exceptional children
Church work with families *(Direct)*
    (BV4438)
  xx Family
Church work with foreigners *(Immigrants,*
    BV639.I4)
   x Foreigners, Church work with
Church work with girls
  See Church work with children
Church work with homosexuals *(Direct)*
  xx Homosexuality
Church work with juvenile delinquents
    (BV4464.5)
  xx Church work with criminals
   Church work with youth
   Juvenile delinquency
   Social work with delinquents and
    criminals
Church work with men
  sa Men in church work
   x Church work with adults
  xx Men in church work
Church work with mentally handicapped
   children
  xx Mentally handicapped children
Church work with migrant labor *(Direct)*
  xx Migrant labor
Church work with military personnel
    (BV4457)
  sa Chaplains, Military
  xx Soldiers—Religious life
Church work with minorities
  xx Minorities
Church work with narcotic addicts
  xx Narcotic addicts
Church work with prisoners of war
  xx Prisoners of war
Church work with problem children
    (BV4464)
  xx Juvenile delinquency
   Problem children
   Social work with delinquents and
    criminals
Church work with prostitutes
  xx Prostitution
Church work with refugees
  xx Church and refugee problems
   Refugees
Church work with sick children *(BV4460)*
  xx Pastoral medicine
   Sick children
Church work with single people *(BV639.S5)*
  xx Single people
Church work with skilled labor *(Direct)*
  sa Chaplains, Industrial
  xx Skilled labor
Church work with students *(BV1610)*
  sa Chaplains, School
   Chaplains, University and college
  xx Students
Church work with the aged *(BV4435)*
  xx Aged
   Aged—Religious life
Church work with the bereaved *(BV4330)*
  sa Funeral service
   x Bereaved, Church work with the
  xx Grief
Church work with the blind
  xx Blind

Church work with the deaf *(BV4463)*
  xx Deaf
Church work with the handicapped
  xx Handicapped
Church work with the insane
  See Church work with the mentally ill
Church work with the mentally handicapped
    (BV4461)
  xx Mentally handicapped
Church work with the mentally ill
   x Church work with the insane
  xx Mentally ill—Care and treatment
   Pastoral medicine
Church work with the sick *(Direct)*
    (BV4335; BV4460; Catholic Church,
    BX2347.8.S5)
   Works on church work with the sick by
    other than Christian denominations
    are entered under Visiting the sick fol-
    lowed by the names of the religious
    community in parentheses, *e.g.* Visit-
    ing the sick (Judaism)
  sa Pastoral medicine
   x Visiting the sick (Christianity)
  xx Pastoral medicine
   Sick
Church work with tourists, travelers, etc.
   x Tourists, Church work with
  xx Travelers
Church work with veterans
  xx Soldiers—Religious life
   Veterans
Church work with women *(Direct)*
    (BV4445)
  sa Women in church work
   x Church work with adults
  xx Woman
   Women and religion
   Women in church work
— Catholic Church *(BX2347.8.W6)*
   x Catholic Church—Women, Work
    with
   Catholic Church—Work with women
Church work with young adults *(BV4446)*
  sa Church group work with young adults
   x Church work with young married
    couples
   Young married couples
  xx Young adults
Church work with young married couples
  See Church work with young adults
Church work with youth *(Direct)* *(BV4447)*
  sa Church camps
   Church group work with youth
   Church work with juvenile delinquents
   Coffee house ministry
   Preaching to youth
  xx Social work with youth
   Youth
— Catholic Church *(BX2390.Y7)*
   x Catholic Church—Work with youth
   Catholic Church—Youth, Work with
— Lutheran Church
   x Lutheran Church—Work with youth
   Lutheran Church—Youth, Work
    with
— Personal narratives
Church year *(BV30)*
   Here are entered works on the Christian
    festivals with their cycles, as making
    up the Christian or church year. Works
    on the origin of festivals and fasts are
    entered under Fasts and feasts. Works
    containing computations for finding
    these days are entered under Church
    calendar.
  sa All Saints Day
   Ascension Day

Church year *(BV30)* *(Continued)*
  Assumption of the Blessed Virgin
    Mary, Feast of the
  Candlemas
  Christmas
  Easter
  Epiphany season
  Good Friday
  Holy Innocents, Feast of the
  Holy Week
  Immaculate Conception, Feast of the
  Jesus Christ the King, Feast of
  Lent
  Mary, Virgin—Feasts
  Palm Sunday
  Pentecost festival
  Pentecost season
  Presentation of the Blessed Virgin
    Mary, Feast of the
  Quinquagesima Sunday
  Sacred Heart, Feast of the
  Visitation festival
  x Christian year
  Ecclesiastical year
  Heortology
  Liturgical year
  Year, Church
  xx Church calendar
  Fasts and feasts
  Liturgics
  Theology, Practical
— Anecdotes, facetiae, satire, etc.
— Meditations *(Catholic, BX2170.C55)*
  xx Devotional calendars
— Prayer-books and devotions
Church year sermons
  sa Festival-day sermons
  xx Sermons
Churches *(Indirect)* *(Architecture,*
    NA4790-6113)
  sa Baptisteries
  Cathedrals
  Cave churches
  Chapels
  Church architecture
  Church decoration and ornament
  Corner stones, Laying of
  Larger parishes
  Mountain churches
  Negro churches
  Oratories
  Parish houses
  Parishes
  Parsonages
  Patron saints
  names of individual churches; and
    subdivision Churches *under names of*
    cities
  x Church buildings
  xx Religious and ecclesiastical institutions
— Administration
  See Church management
— Anniversaries
  See Church anniversaries
— Centennial celebrations
  See Church anniversaries
— Fund raising
  See Church fund raising
— Gardens
  See Church gardens
— Guide-books
— Interdenominational use *(Direct)*
    (BV636)

  Here are entered works on the sepa-
    rate use of a single church building
    by separate denominational groups.
    Duplicate entry is made, if appro-
    priate, under Churches, Anglican
    [etc.]
  x Churches, Sharing of
  Churches—Sharing of facilities
  Sharing of churches
  xx Interdenominational cooperation
— Juvenile literature
— Libraries
  See Libraries, Church
— Location
  xx Church management
  Cities and towns—Planning
— Maintenance and repair
  See Church maintenance and repair
— Management
  See Church management
— Parking facilities
  x Church parking
  xx Automobile parking
— Pictorial works
— Public relations
  See Public relations—Churches
— Secular use *(Direct)*
  x Secular use of churches
— Sharing of facilities
  See Churches—Interdenominational
    use
— Statistical methods
  See Church statistics
— Terminology
Churches, Anglican *(NA4821.A)*
  Here are entered works dealing with An-
    glican church buildings.
  x Anglican churches
  Churches, Episcopal
  Churches, Protestant Episcopal
  Episcopal churches
  Protestant Episcopal churches
  Note under Churches—Interdenominational
    use
Churches, Avant-garde
  See Non-institutional churches
Churches, Baptist *(NA4821.B)*
  Here are entered works dealing with Bap-
    tist church buildings.
  x Baptist churches
Churches, Catholic *(Direct)* *(NA4820;*
    Architecture, NA5200-6113)
  Here are entered works dealing with
    Catholic church buildings.
  x Catholic Church—Buildings
  Catholic churches
Churches, Christian Science
  Here are entered works dealing with
    Christian Science church buildings.
  x Christian Science churches
Churches, City
  See City churches
Churches, Community
  See Community churches
Churches, Country
  See Rural churches
Churches, Episcopal
  See Churches, Anglican
Churches, Federated
  See Federated churches
Churches, Friend *(Direct)*
  Here are entered works dealing with the
    meeting-houses or churches of the So-
    ciety of Friends.
  x Friend churches
  Friend meeting-houses
  Meeting-houses, Friend
  xx Friends, Society of

Churches, Lutheran *(Direct)* *(NA4821.L8)*
  Here are entered works dealing with Lu-
    theran church buildings.
  x Lutheran churches
Churches, Methodist
  Here are entered works dealing with
    Methodist church buildings.
  x Methodist churches
Churches, Mormon
  Here are entered works dealing with
    Mormon church buildings.
  x Mormon churches
Churches, Negro
  See Negro churches
Churches, Non-institutional
  See Non-institutional churches
Churches, Nondenominational
  See Independent churches
Churches, Orthodox Eastern *(Indirect)*
  Here are entered works dealing with Or-
    thodox Eastern church buildings.
  x Orthodox Eastern churches
Churches, Presbyterian *(NA4821.P)*
  Here are entered works dealing with Pres-
    byterian church buildings.
  x Presbyterian churches
Churches, Protestant *(Architecture,*
    NA5200-6113)
  Here are entered works dealing with Prot-
    estant church buildings. Works dealing
    with the organizations worshiping in
    such buildings are entered under Prot-
    estant churches.
Churches, Protestant Episcopal
  See Churches, Anglican
Churches, Reformed *(NA4821.R)*
  Here are entered works dealing with Re-
    formed church buildings.
  x Reformed churches
Churches, Rural
  See Rural churches
Churches, Sharing of
  See Churches—Interdenominational use
Churches, Simultaneous
  See Simultaneum
Churches, Suburban
  See Suburban churches
Churches, Town
  See City churches
Churches, Undenominational
  See Community churches
  Independent churches
Churches, United
  See Community churches
Churches, Urban
  See City churches
Churches *(Canon law)* *(BX1939.C)*
  sa Cathedrals (Canon law)
  Oratories (Canon law)
  xx Sacred places (Canon law)
Churches in art
  xx Art
Churching of women *(Direct)*
  sa Candlemas
  xx Birth (in religion, folk-lore, etc.)
  Mothers—Religious life
  Purity, Ritual
Churchwardens' accounts *(CS436; DA690)*
  sa Church rates
  x Church wardens' accounts
  xx Church finance
Churchyards
  See Cemeteries
Churras
  See Bhang (Drug)
Churubusco, Battle of, 1847 *(E406.C5)*
Chūshingura Incident, 1703
  See Forty seven Rōnin

Chutiya language (PL4001.C7)
  xx Bodo languages
Chutney industry (Direct)
Chuvak language
  See Chuvashian language
Chuvashes (DK34.C)
  xx Ethnology—Russia
Chuvashian fiction (Direct)
Chuvashian language (PL381-4)
  x Chuvak language
    Shuvak language
    Tchuvak language
    Tchuvashian language
  xx Altaic languages
Chuvashian literature (Direct)
Chuvashian philology
Chuvashian poetry (Direct) (Collections,
    PL384.A2; History, PL383.5)
Chuvashian wit and humor (Direct)
Chwana language
  See Sechuana language
Chwee language
  See Tshi language
Chyle (Blood-making, QP91; Digestion,
    QP165)
  xx Absorption (Physiology)
    Lymphatics
Chymotrypsin (QP601)
Ci-Renje language
  See Lenje language
Ci-Tonga language
  See Tonga language (Zambesi)
Ci-venda language
  See Venda language
Ciacone
  See Chaconnes
Ciamacoco language
  See Chamacoco language
Cibokwe language
  See Chokwe language
Ciboney Indians (F1769)
  x Siboney Indians
  xx Indians of the West Indies
Cicada (QL523.C5)
  sa Periodical cicada
  xx Homoptera
  — Juvenile literature
Cicada, Fossil
Cicada, Periodical
  See Periodical cicada
Cicatrices (RL621)
  x Scars
  xx Granulation tissue
    Surgery
Cicero, Ill.
  — Riots, 1951
Ciceronian notes
  See Tironian notes
Ciceronianism (PA6346)
  xx Humanism
    Learning and scholarship
Ciciliana
  See Strambotto
Cidaroidea
  xx Sea-urchins
Cider (Economics, HD9398; Technology,
    TP563)
  sa Apple juice
    Cookery (Cider)
    Wine and wine making
  xx Apple juice
    Fruit wines
Cielito (Dance)
Cifundi dialect
  x Chi-chifundi dialect
    Chifundi dialect
  xx Swahili language

Ciga language
  See Kiga language
Cigar bands and labels (Indirect)
  x Cigar labels
  xx Cigars
    Labels
    Smoking paraphernalia
Cigar case-bearer
Cigar labels
  See Cigar bands and labels
Cigar lighters (TS2280)
  x Cigarette lighters
    Lighters, Cigar
  xx Smoking paraphernalia
Cigar makers (Direct)
  sa Trade-unions—Tobacco workers
Cigar manufacture and trade (Direct)
    (Economics, HD9149.C48-5;
    Technology, TS2260)
  xx Tobacco manufacture and trade
  — Trade-marks
Cigar smoke
  xx Smoke
Cigar tax (Direct)
  xx Tobacco—Taxation
Cigarets
  See Cigarettes
Cigarette beetle
  x Tobacco beetle
Cigarette cards (NE965)
  xx Advertising cards
    Smoking paraphernalia
  — Collectors and collecting (NE965)
  — — Juvenile literature
Cigarette filters (TS2260)
  x Filter tips
  xx Filters and filtration
Cigarette habit (HV5740-5745)
  xx Cigarettes
    Smoking
    Tobacco habit
    Tobacco—Physiological effect
  — Anecdotes, facetiae, satire, etc.
Cigarette labeling
  See Cigarettes—Labeling
Cigarette lighters
  See Cigar lighters
Cigarette manufacture and trade (Direct)
    (Economics, HD9149.C39-42;
    Technology, TS2260)
  xx Cigarettes
    Tobacco manufacture and trade
  — Equipment and supplies
  — Trade-marks
Cigarette package labels (Direct)
    (NC1883.5-6)
  xx Cigarettes—Labeling
    Labels
    Packaging
    Smoking paraphernalia
Cigarette paper
  xx Cigarettes
    Paper
    Smoking paraphernalia
  — Taxation (Direct)
  xx Cigarette tax
Cigarette smoke
  xx Cigarettes
    Smoke
Cigarette tax (Direct)
  sa Cigarette paper—Taxation
  xx Cigarettes
    Tobacco—Taxation
Cigarettes
  sa Cigarette habit
    Cigarette manufacture and trade
    Cigarette paper
    Cigarette smoke

Cigarette tax
  x Cigarets
  xx Smoking
    Tobacco
  — Labeling (Direct)
    sa Cigarette package labels
    x Cigarette labeling
  — Patents
Cigars (TS2260)
  sa Cigar bands and labels
Ciguatera
  See Poisonous fishes
Cilia and ciliary motion (QL852; QP311)
  sa Epithelium
    Flagella (Microbiology)
  xx Cells
    Epithelium
Ciliary body
  xx Eye
Ciliary ganglion
  xx Optic nerve
Ciliata (QL368.C5)
  sa Astomida
  xx Infusoria
    Protozoa
  — Anatomy
  — Behavior
  — Identification
Cilicia
  — History
  — — Armenian Kingdom, 1080-1375
      x Cilician Kingdom, 1080-1375
        Little Armenia, Kingdom of,
        1080-1375
        New Armenia, Kingdom of,
        1080-1375
      xx Armenia—History—
        Turkic-Mongol domination,
        1045-1522
Cilician Kingdom, 1080-1375
  See Cilicia—History—Armenian Kingdom,
    1080-1375
Cilowe (Bantu people)
  See Lomwe (Bantu people)
Cimambwe language
  See Mambwe language
Cimbalom (ML1015-1018)
  x Cymbalom
  xx Dulcimer
Cimbalom and piano music (M282.C5;
    M283.C5)
  x Piano and cimbalom music
Cimbalom and violin music
  See Violin and cimbalom music
Cimbalom music (M142.C)
  sa Quartets (Cimbalom, violin, viola,
    double bass)
Cimbalom with orchestra (M1037.4.C54)
  sa Concertos (Cimbalom)
  xx Concertos (Cimbalom)
Cimbri (DG255.5)
  xx Germanic tribes
Cimmerians
Cinantec Indians
  See Chinantec Indians
Cinantec language
  See Chinantec language
Cincari
  See Arumanians
Cinch (Game)
  See Pedro (Game)

Cinchona *(Indirect)* *(Botany, QK495.C57;*
Culture, SB295.C5; Pharmacy,
RS165.C3; Therapeutics,
RM666.C53)
Here are entered works on the group of
plants producing quinine and on the
pharmacology, therapeutic uses, etc. of
the bark. *See also* the names of its al-
kaloids, *e.g.* Quinine, Cinchonidine,
etc.
sa Quinidine
x Chinchona
Jesuits' bark
Peruvian bark
Yellow bark
xx Quinine
— Diseases and pests
Cinchonidine *(Chemistry, QD421;*
Therapeutics, RM666.C54)
Note under Cinchona
Cincinnati
— Riot, 1884
Cinclidae
See Dippers (Birds)
Cinco de Mayo, Battle of, 1862 *(F1233)*
Cinco de Mayo (Mexican holiday)
x Fifth of May (Mexican holiday)
xx Puebla, Mexico (City)—Siege, 1862
Cindau language
See Chindau language
Cinder blocks *(Building, TH1491)*
x Cinder concrete blocks
xx Concrete blocks
Cinder concrete blocks
See Cinder blocks
Cineangiography
xx Angiography
Cinematography, Medical
Cinefluorography
xx Cinematography, Medical
Radiology, Medical
Cinema
See Moving-pictures
Cinemascope
See Wide-screen processes
(Cinematography)
Cinematograph film
See Moving-picture film
Cinematographers
x Moving-picture cameramen
xx Photographers
— Correspondence, reminiscences, etc.
Cinematographic film
See Moving-picture film
Cinematography *(TR845-899)*
Here are entered works on photographic
processes only. Works on operation,
management, etc. of moving-pictures
are entered under Moving-pictures.
sa Amateur moving-pictures
Cinematography, Trick
Color cinematography
Front-screen projection
Kineto-phonograph
Kinetograph
Kinetoscope
Microcinematography
Moving-picture cameras
Moving-picture film
Moving-pictures, Three-dimensional
Sports cinematography
Television film
United States. Navy—Photographers
Wide-screen processes
(Cinematography)
x Chronophotography
Photography—Animated pictures
Photography—Moving-pictures

xx Photography
Photography, Instantaneous
Note under Moving-pictures
— Apparatus and supplies
— Automation
— Competitions
xx Moving-pictures—Competitions
— Electronic equipment
— Exposure
xx Photography—Exposure
— Failures *(TR899)*
— Industrial applications
See Cinematography, Industrial
— Juvenile literature
— Lighting
x Moving-pictures—Lighting
— Printing processes
xx Cinematography—Processing
— Processing *(TR886.2)*
sa Cinematography—Printing processes
— — Automatic control
— Safety measures
— Scientific applications *(TR893)*
sa Cinematography, High-speed
Photography, Time-lapse
Wildlife cinematography
x Moving-pictures—Scientific
applications
xx Photography—Scientific applications
— Standards
— Study and teaching *(TR852)*
Cinematography, Abstract
x Abstract cinematography
xx Experimental films
Cinematography, High-speed
x High-speed cinematography
xx Cinematography—Scientific applications
Cinematography, Industrial
x Cinematography—Industrial
applications
Industrial cinematography
Cinematography, Medical
sa Cineangiography
Cinefluorography
x Medical cinematography
Cinematography, Stereoscopic
See Moving-pictures, Three-dimensional
Cinematography, Submarine
sa Photography, Submarine
x Submarine cinematography
Underwater cinematography
xx Photography, Submarine
Cinematography, Trick
sa Photography, Trick
x Trick cinematography
xx Cinematography
Photography, Trick
Cinematography, Wide-screen
See Wide-screen processes
(Cinematography)
Cinematography, Wildlife
See Wildlife cinematography
Cinematomicrography
See Microcinematography
Cinemicrography
See Microcinematography
Cinephotomicrography
See Microcinematography
Cinerama
See Wide-screen processes
(Cinematography)
Cinerary urns
See Urns
Cingalese
See Sinhalese
Cinnabar *(Mineral industries, TN490.M;*
Mineralogy, QE391.C)
xx Mercury ores

Cinnamon *(Indirect)* *(Culture, SB307.C;*
Food, TX407.C)
xx Bark
Example under Condiments; Spices
Cinquille (Game)
See Quintille (Game)
Cionorrhaphy
See Palate—Surgery
CIP program
See Cataloging in publication
Cipher and telegraph codes *(HE7669-7679;*
Commercial codes, HE7676-7;
Foreign languages, HE7678)
Subdivided by subject, *e.g.* Cipher and
telegraph codes—Astronomy; Cipher
and telegraph codes—Bankers and
brokers.
sa Morse code
Telegraph code addresses
Translingua script
Weather telegraphy
x Cable codes
Codes, Telegraph
Telegraph codes
Telegraph—Codes
xx Ciphers
Commerce
Signs and symbols
Telegraph
— Astronomy
xx Astronomy—Observations
Note under Cipher and telegraph codes
— Bankers and brokers
Note under Cipher and telegraph codes
— Meteorology *(QC872)*
x Meteorology—Cipher and telegraph
codes
xx Weather telegraphy
— Psychological aspects
— Railroads
x Railroads—Cipher and telegraph
codes
xx Railroads
Cipher stories
See Code and cipher stories
Ciphers *(Z103-4)*
sa Abbreviations
Cipher and telegraph codes
Code names
Cryptography
Telegraph
Writing
x Codes
Contractions
xx Abbreviations
Code names
Cryptography
Signs and symbols
Symbolism
Writing
— Early works to 1800 *(Z103.5)*
— Juvenile literature
Ciphers (Lettering)
See Monograms
Circadian rhythm
See Diel cycles
Circassian language *(PK9201.C5)*
sa Adyghe language
x Cherkess language
xx Adyghe language
Caucasian languages
Circassians
sa Adyghe
— Religion
Circassians in Israel, [etc.]
Circle *(Analytic geometry, QA557; Plane*
geometry, QA484)
sa Inversions (Geometry)

xx Curves, Plane
Geometry, Plane
Sphere
— Juvenile literature
Circle, Vertical
See Vertical circle
Circle (in religion, folk-lore, etc.) *(BL604.C)*
sa Mandala
Wheels (in religion, folk-lore, etc.)
Yin Yang symbol
x Folk-lore of circles
xx Religion, Primitive
Circle-squaring *(QA467)*
sa Pi
x Quadrature of the circle
Squaring of the circle
xx Geometry—Problems, Famous
Pi
Circles of the triangle
See Triangle
Circuit-breakers, Electric
See Electric circuit-breakers
Circuit courts *(Direct)*
Works on individual circuit courts are entered under the official heading for the court, e.g. *United States. Circuit Court (1st Circuit)*
x Courts, Circuit
xx Courts—United States
Circuit riding
See Itinerancy (Church polity)
Circuits, Bridge
See Bridge circuits
Circuits, Electric
See Electric circuits
Circuits, Hydraulic
See Hydraulic circuits
Circuits, Integrated
See Integrated circuits
Circuits, Microwave
See Microwave circuits
Circular functions
See Trigonometrical functions
Circular letters
xx Advertising, Direct-mail
Letter-writing
Circular motion
See Centripetal force
Circular saws
sa Planer saws
Radial saws
xx Saws
— Maintenance and repair
— Standards
Circular velocity of money
sa Credit
Inflation (Finance)
Multiplier (Economics)
Quantity theory of money
x Money, Circular velocity of
xx Credit
Money
Multiplier (Economics)
Quantity theory of money
Circulars, Advertising
See Advertising fliers
Circulation, Pulmonary
See Pulmonary circulation
Circulation, Regional
See Regional blood flow
Circulation of newspapers
See Newspaper circulation
Circulation of periodicals
See Periodicals—Circulation
Circulation of the blood
See Blood—Circulation
Circulatory system
See Cardiovascular system

Circulin
xx Antibiotics
Circumcellians
See Circumcellions
Circumcellions *(BT1365)*
x Agonists
Circumcellians
xx Donatists
Heresies and heretics—Early church, ca. 30-600
Sects, Medieval
Circumcision *(Ethnology, GN484; Surgery, RD590)*
sa Clitoridectomy
Infibulation
Phimosis
xx Initiations (in religion, folk-lore, etc.)
Judaism
Phimosis
Circumnavigation
See Voyages around the world
Circumstance ethics
See Situation ethics
Circumstantial evidence
See Evidence, Circumstantial
Circumventricular organs
sa Neurohypophysis
xx Brain
Circus *(Indirect)* *(GV1801-1837)*
sa Acrobats and acrobatism
Amateur circus
Amusement parks
Animals, Training of
Hippodrome
Wild west shows
xx Amusements
Hippodrome
— Biography
— — Juvenile literature
— Juvenile literature
— Pictorial works
Circus animals *(Indirect)* *(GV1829)*
xx Animals
— Juvenile literature
— Legends and stories
Circus collecting
See Wild animal collecting
Circus in art
xx Art
Circus theater
See Arena theater
Cire-perdue process
See Precision casting
Ciro-flex camera *(TR263.C)*
Example under Cameras
Cirrhipedia
See Cirripedia
Cirrhosis hepatis
See Liver—Cirrhosis
Cirrhosis of the liver
See Liver—Cirrhosis
Cirripedia *(Indirect)* *(QL444.C5)*
sa Acrothoracica
x Barnacles
Cirrhipedia
xx Crustacea
Entomostraca
Cistercian architecture
See Architecture, Cistercian
Cistercian art
See Art, Cistercian
Cistercian illumination of books and manuscripts
See Illumination of books and manuscripts, Cistercian
Cistercian nuns
x Cistercians (Women)
Nuns, Cistercian

xx Cistercians
Monasticism and religious orders for women
Cistercians *(BX3401-3455)*
sa Benedictines
Cistercian nuns
Trappists
individual Cistercian abbeys
xx Monasticism and religious orders
Trappists
Cistercians (Women)
See Cistercian nuns
Cistercians in Belgium, ⌈England, France, etc.⌉
Cisternal puncture
See Brain—Puncture
Cisternography
xx Brain—Radiography
Citara
See Cithara
Sitar
Citation indexes
xx Indexes
Citation of legal authorities *(Direct)*
Here are entered works on the method of citing legal authorities. Compilations of legal citations such as citation books are entered under the heading Annotations and citations (Law)
x Legal citations
xx Annotations and citations (Law)
Legal authorities
Legal research
Citations (Law)
See Annotations and citations (Law)
Cithara *(ML760)*
sa Lyre-guitar
x Citara
Kithara
xx Cithern
Musical instruments, Greek
Cithern *(ML760)*
sa Cithara
English guitar
Zither
xx Guitar
Zither
Cithern music *(M142.C5)*
Cities, Imaginary
See Geographical myths
Cities and towns *(Indirect)* *(HT101-381; Influence on crime, HV6177; Local government, JS)*
Here are entered statistical and descriptive works (sociological and topographic) on the cities and towns of one or more countries, and works on the city problem. Under the heading Municipal government are entered theoretical and practical works on that topic; under Municipal corporations, formal legal treatises and collections of statutes; under Local government, works on local government not municipal. Individual forms are entered under Boroughs, Villages, Garden cities, etc. *Cf.* notes under Local government, Municipal corporations, Municipal government.
sa Art, Municipal
Boroughs
Capitals (Cities)
Central places
Community
Company towns
Cries
Education, Urban
Garden cities
Markets

Cities and towns *(Indirect)* *(HT101-381;*
    Influence on crime, HV6177; Local
    government, JS) *(Continued)*
    Parks
    Plazas
    Sociology, Urban
    Streets
    Tenement-houses
    University towns
    Urbanization
    Villages
    headings beginning with the words
      City, Municipal *and* Urban
  x Geography, Urban
    Municipalities
    Towns
    Urban areas
    Urban geography
    Urbanism
  xx Geography, Political
    Local government
    Sociology
    Sociology, Urban
  Notes under Municipal corporations; Munici-
    pal government
— Beautification
    See Urban beautification
— Biblical teaching
— Civic improvement *(JS93-99; Societies:*
    United States, JS302-3)
  sa Community art projects
    Community centers
    Community organization
    Municipal buildings
    Urban beautification
    Urban renewal
    subdivision Civic improvement *under*
      names of cities and towns, e.g.
      Washington, D.C.—Civic
      improvement
  x Civic improvement
    Civic planning
    Municipal improvements
— Economic aspects
    See Urban economics
— Growth *(City problem, HT371;*
    Statistics, HB2161-2370)
  sa Agricultural colonies
    Annexation (County government)
    Annexation (Municipal government)
    Land subdivision
    Metropolitan areas
    Residential mobility
    Suburbs
  x Cities and towns, Movement to
  xx Migration, Internal
    Population
    Vital statistics
  Example under Growth
— — Mathematical models
— Juvenile literature
— Law and legislation
    See Municipal corporations
— Lighting
    See Municipal lighting
    Street-lighting
— Maps
— Mathematical models
— Planning *(Direct)* *(NA9000-9284)*
    When subdivided by place, refer from
    the place with subdivision City
    planning.
  sa Art, Municipal
    Central business districts
    City planners
    Classification—Books—City planning
    Community development
    Flood damage prevention

    Garden cities
    Housing
    Indians—City planning
    Industries, Location of
    Labor and laboring classes—
      Dwellings
    Land subdivision
    Municipal services
    Open spaces
    Parks
    Playgrounds
    Regional planning
    Slums
    Social surveys
    Space (Architecture)
    Store location
    Suburbs
    Traffic surveys
    Urban beautification
    Urban renewal
    Urban transportation
    Zoning
    Churches—Location; Factories—
      Location; *and similar headings;*
      and subdivisions Public buildings
      and Public works *under names of*
      cities and towns, e.g. Columbus,
      Ohio—Public works
  x City planning
    Civic planning
    Model cities
    Planning, City
    Redevelopment, Urban
    Slum clearance
    Town planning
    Urban design
    Urban development
    Urban planning
  xx Art, Municipal
    Community development
    Garden cities
    Labor and laboring classes—
      Dwellings
    Land
    Municipal engineering
    Regional planning
    Tenement-houses
    Urban renewal
  Note under Urban renewal
— — 1945-

GENERAL SUBDIVISIONS

— — Anecdotes, facetiae, satire, etc.

GENERAL SUBDIVISIONS

— — Bibliography
  sa Information storage and retrieval
    systems—Cities and towns—
    Planning

GENERAL SUBDIVISIONS

— — Caricatures and cartoons

GENERAL SUBDIVISIONS

— — Early works to 1870

GENERAL SUBDIVISIONS

— — Electronic data processing
    See Electronic data processing—
    City planning

GENERAL SUBDIVISIONS

— — Examinations, questions, etc.

GENERAL SUBDIVISIONS

— — Hygienic aspects *(NA9050)*
  xx Hygiene, Public
— — Information services

  — — Juvenile literature
  — — Law and legislation
    See City planning and
      redevelopment law
  — — Mathematical models
  — — Public opinion
  — — Research *(Direct)*
    xx Municipal research
  — — Simulation methods
  — — Statistical services
  — — Study and teaching *(Direct)*
  — — Terminology
  — — Underdeveloped areas
    See Underdeveloped areas—City
      planning
  — — Vocational guidance *(NA9013)*
    x City planning as a profession
  — — Zone system
    See Zoning
— Public opinion
— Public relations
    See Public relations—Municipal
      government
— Religious life
    x City and town life—Religious aspects
    xx City churches
    Example under reference from Religious
      life
— Research
    See Municipal research
— Simulation methods
— Sounds
    See City sounds
— Study and teaching *(Direct)*
— — Audio-visual aids
— Subject headings
    See Subject headings—Cities and
      towns
— Surveying
    See Surveying
— Terminology
— Views
— — Juvenile literature
Cities and towns, Ancient
  xx Geography, Ancient
Cities and towns, Islamic *(Indirect)*
  x Cities and towns, Muslim
    Islamic cities and towns
    Muslim cities and towns
  xx Sociology, Islamic
Cities and towns, Medieval *(D134)*
Cities and towns, Movement to
  See Cities and towns—Growth
    Rural-urban migration
    Urbanization
Cities and towns, Muslim
  See Cities and towns, Islamic
Cities and towns, Ruined, extinct, etc.
    (Indirect)
  sa Excavations (Archaeology)
  x Buried cities
    Extinct cities
    Ghost towns
    Sunken cities
— Pictorial works
Cities and towns in art
  xx Art
— Juvenile literature
Cities and towns in literature *(PN56.C;*
    American fiction, PS374.C5; English
    fiction, PR830.C; Fiction,
    PN3448.C5)
  sa Poetry of places
    names of individual cities and towns,
      e.g. London in literature
  x Villages in literature
  xx Literary landmarks
    Poetry of places

Cities of refuge
  See Asylum, Right of—Biblical teaching
Citizen associations
  See Citizens' associations
Citizen lawsuits
  See Citizen suits (Civil procedure)
Citizen participation in anti-poverty programs
  See Economic assistance, Domestic—
    Citizen participation
Citizen participation in community health
    services
  See Community health services—Citizen
    participation
Citizen participation in crime prevention
  See Crime prevention—Citizen participation
Citizen participation in environmental
    protection
  See Environmental protection—Citizen
    participation
Citizen participation in highway planning
  See Highway planning—Citizen
    participation
Citizen participation in medical policy
  See Medical policy—Citizen participation
Citizen participation in regional planning
  See Regional planning—Citizen
    participation
Citizen participation in urban renewal
  See Urban renewal—Citizen participation
Citizen participation in urban transportation
    policy
  See Urban transportation policy—Citizen
    participation
Citizen participation in water resources
    development
  See Water resources development—Citizen
    participation
Citizen suits (Civil procedure) *(Direct)*
  sa Class actions (Civil procedure)
    Popular actions
  x Citizen lawsuits
    Citizens' actions
    Private attorney general
  xx Actions and defenses
    Class actions (Civil procedure)
    Popular actions
Citizens' actions
  See Citizen suits (Civil procedure)
Citizens' advisory committees in education
    (LC220)
  sa Citizens' advisory committees in
    vocational education
    Parents' advisory committees in
    education
  x Advisory committees in education
    Citizens' committees in education
  xx Community and school
    School boards
Citizens' advisory committees in science
    (Indirect)
  x Advisory committees in science
    Citizens' committees in science
  xx Science and state
Citizens' advisory committees in technology
    (Indirect)
  x Advisory committees in technology
    Citizens' committees in technology
  xx Technology and state
Citizens' advisory committees in vocational
    education
  xx Citizens' advisory committees in
    education
Citizens' associations *(Direct)*
  sa Crime prevention—Citizen participation
    Regional planning—Citizen
    participation
    Urban renewal—Citizen participation
  x Citizen associations

Taxpayers' associations
Citizens band radio
  See Citizens radio service
Citizens' committees in education
  See Citizens' advisory committees in
    education
Citizens' committees in science
  See Citizens' advisory committees in
    science
Citizens' committees in technology
  See Citizens' advisory committees in
    technology
Citizen's defender
  See Ombudsman
Citizens radio service *(Direct)*
  sa Citizens radio service (Class D)
    Mobile radio stations
    Models and modelmaking—Radio
    control systems
    Radio control
  x Citizens band radio
  xx Mobile radio stations
    Radio control
    Radio, Short wave
Citizens radio service (Class D)
  sa Mobile radio stations
  x Personal radiotelephone
    Private radiotelephone
  xx Citizens radio service
    Microwave communication systems
    Radiotelephone
Citizenship *(Direct) (JF800-823; Education*
    for, LC1091; United States,
    JK1751-1788)
  sa Aliens
    Allegiance
    Americanization
    Citizenship as point of contact (Conflict
    of laws)
    Civics
    Corporations—Nationality
    Deportation
    Domicile
    Expatriation
    Freemen
    Honorary citizenship
    Indians of North America—Citizenship
    Married women—Nationality
    Naturalization
    Patriotism
    Political rights
    Self-determination, National
    Statelessness
    Suffrage
  x Nationality (Citizenship)
  xx Aliens
    Allegiance
    Civics
    Constitutional law
    Deportation
    Domicile
    Expatriation
    Naturalization
    Political rights
    Political science
  — Conflict of laws
    See Conflict of laws—Citizenship
  — Juvenile literature *(United States,*
    JK1759)
  — Quotations, maxims, etc.

GEOGRAPHIC SUBDIVISIONS

  — Germany
    x Nuremberg laws
Citizenship, Loss of *(Direct)*
  sa Expatriation
    Political rights, Loss of
    Statelessness

  x Denaturalization
    Loss of citizenship
  xx Political rights, Loss of
Citizenship, Tribal
  See subdivision Tribal citizenship *under*
    names of Indian tribes, e.g.
    Chickasaw Indians—Tribal
    citizenship
Citizenship (International law)
  sa Dual nationality
    Option of nationality
  xx International law
Citizenship (Islamic law)
Citizenship as point of contact (Conflict of
    laws) *(Direct)*
  xx Citizenship
    Conflict of laws
    Points of contact (Conflict of laws)
Citric acid cycle
  See Krebs cycle
Citric acid in the body
Citroën automobile *(TL215.C)*
  sa Ami 6 automobile
    Ami 8 automobile
Citron *(SB369)*
  x Ethrog
    Etrog
  xx Citrus fruits
Citron (Jewish cultus)
  xx Cultus, Jewish
    Sukkoth
Citronella-oil *(Indirect)*
Citrus black fly *(SB945.B45)*
Citrus canker *(SB741.C5)*
  Example under Citrus fruits—Diseases and
    pests
Citrus fruit by-products
  See Citrus fruits—By-products
Citrus fruit industry *(Direct)*
  x Citrus industry
    Citrus trade
  xx Citrus fruits
    Fruit trade
  — Law and legislation *(Direct)*
Citrus fruit irrigation
  See Citrus fruits—Irrigation
Citrus fruit pulp, Dried
  See Dried citrus pulp
Citrus fruit research
  See Citrus fruits—Research
Citrus fruits *(Indirect) (Culture, SB369)*
  sa Citron
    Citrus fruit industry
    Cookery (Citrus fruits)
    Grapefruit
    Lemon
    Lime (Tree)
    Orange
    Tangelo
    Tangerine
  xx Fruit
    Tropical fruit
  — Accounting
  — Analysis *(QK866.C59)*
  — By-products *(SB369; TP506)*
    sa Alcohol
      Citrus oils
      Dried citrus pulp
      Lime oil
      Pectin
    x Citrus fruit by-products
      Citrus products
  — Cooperative marketing
    xx Citrus fruits—Marketing
  — Diseases and pests *(Indirect)*
    (SB608.C5)
    sa Citrus fruits—Storage—Diseases and
      injuries

Citrus fruits *(Indirect)* *(Culture, SB369)*
— Diseases and pests *(Indirect)*
  (SB608.C5) *(Continued)*
    names of diseases and pests, e.g.
      Citrus canker, Mediterranean
      fruit-fly, Mottle-leaf
— Fertilizers and manures
— Harvesting
— Irrigation
  x Citrus fruit irrigation
— Marketing
  sa Citrus fruits—Cooperative marketing
  Example under Fruit—Marketing
— Packing
— Precooling
— Prices
— Research
  x Citrus fruit research
  xx Agricultural research
— Standards *(Direct)*
— Storage
  Example under Fruit—Storage
— — Diseases and injuries
    xx Citrus fruits—Diseases and pests
      Farm produce—Storage—Diseases
      and injuries
— Transportation
  Example under Fruit—Transportation
Citrus industry
  See Citrus fruit industry
Citrus oils *(TP959.C54)*
  sa Bergamot oil
    Orange-oil
  xx Citrus fruits—By-products
    Essences and essential oils
Citrus products
  See Citrus fruits—By-products
Citrus pulp as feed
  See Dried citrus pulp
Citrus rust mite *(SB945.C)*
  Example under Mites
Citrus scab
  See Sour orange scab
Citrus thrips *(SB608.C5)*
Citrus trade
  See Citrus fruit industry
Cittamātra
  See Vijñaptimātratā
City and state, Relation of
  See Municipal home rule
City and town life *(Indirect)*
  sa Indians of North America—Urban
    residence
  x City life
    Town life
    Urban life
  xx Sociology, Urban
— Juvenile literature
— Juvenile poetry
— Literary collections
— Religious aspects
  See Cities and towns—Religious life
— Sounds
  See City sounds
City and town life in literature
City attorneys *(Direct)*
  x Attorneys, Municipal
    City solicitors
    Corporation counsels, Municipal
    Corporation lawyers, Municipal
    Municipal law officers
    Town counsels
  xx Government attorneys
    Lawyers
    Municipal corporations
City attorneys' opinions *(Direct)*
  xx Advisory opinions

City beautification
  See Urban beautification
City children *(HT206)*
  x Children in cities
  xx Children
— Juvenile literature
— Pictorial works
City churches *(Direct)* *(BV637)*
  sa Church work with apartment dwellers
    Cities and towns—Religious life
    City clergy
    City missions
    Suburban churches
  x Churches, City
    Churches, Town
    Churches, Urban
    Town churches
    Urban churches
    Urbanization—Religious aspects
  xx Church work
    City clergy
    Suburban churches
City clergy *(Indirect)* *(BV637.5)*
  sa City churches
  x Clergy, City
    Clergy, Urban
    Ministry, Urban
    Urban clergy
    Urban ministry
  xx Church work
    City churches
    Clergy
    Pastoral theology
City councilmen *(Direct)*
  x Aldermen
    Councilmen, City
  xx Municipal government
— Pensions
City driving
  See Automobile driving in cities
City fauna
  See Urban fauna
City-federal relations
  See Federal-city relations
City government
  See Municipal government
City income tax
  See Income tax, Municipal
City laws
  See Town laws
City life
  See City and town life
City lighting
  See Municipal lighting
City manager
  See Municipal government by city manager
City missions *(Direct)*
  sa Institutional missions
  x Missions, City
  xx Church work
    City churches
    Missions, Home
City noise *(Direct)* *(TD891-3)*
  sa Airport noise
    Noise control
    Traffic noise
  x Urban noise
  xx Noise
    Noise pollution
City ordinances
  See Ordinances, Municipal
City planners *(Direct)* *(NA9080)*
  x Town planners
    Urbanists
  xx Architects
    Cities and towns—Planning
City planning
  See Cities and towns—Planning

City planning and redevelopment law
  (Direct)
  sa Housing—Law and legislation
    Land subdivision—Law and legislation
    Regional planning—Law and legislation
    Zoning law
  x Cities and towns—Planning—Law and
    legislation
    City planning law
    Slum clearance law
    Town planning law
    Urban renewal—Law and legislation
  xx Regional planning—Law and legislation
— Cases
— Digests
City planning and the press
  x Press and city planning
City planning as a profession
  See Cities and towns—Planning—
    Vocational guidance
City planning law
  See City planning and redevelopment law
City schools
  See Urban schools
City solicitors
  See City attorneys
City sounds
  sa Waterfront sounds
  x Cities and towns—Sounds
    City and town life—Sounds
  xx Sounds
City surveying
  See Surveying
City traffic *(Direct)*
  sa Pedestrians
    Traffic noise
  x Street traffic
    Traffic, City
    Urban traffic
  xx Communication and traffic
    Streets
    Traffic engineering
    Traffic surveys
    Urban transportation
— Environmental aspects *(Direct)*
City transit
  See Local transit
City transportation
  See Urban transportation
City walls *(Indirect)*
  sa subdivision Walls *under names of cities,*
    etc.
  xx Fortification
    Walls
City wildlife
  See Urban fauna
Ciudad de Barcelona prizes
  x Barcelona prizes
  xx Literary prizes
Civic action of Armed Forces
  See Armed Forces—Civic action
Civic art
  See Art, Municipal
Civic centers *(Indirect)*
  sa Municipal buildings
    Public buildings
    names of individual civic centers, e.g.
      Washington, D.C. Municipal
      Center
  x Municipal centers
  xx Municipal buildings
    Public buildings
Civic ceremonial
  See Municipal ceremonial
Civic improvement
  See Cities and towns—Civic improvement

subdivision Civic improvement *under names of cities and towns, e.g.* Washington, D.C.—Civic improvement

Civic planning
   See Cities and towns—Civic improvement
   Cities and towns—Planning

Civic rights
   See Political rights

Civic theater
   See Theater, Municipal

Civics
   sa Americanization
      Citizenship
      Civil rights
      Germanization
      Patriotism
      Political ethics
      Political rights
   x Civics, American
   xx Citizenship
      Political ethics
      Political science
      Social ethics
      Social sciences
   — Film catalogs

Civics, American
   See Civics

Civics, British, ₍French, etc.₎
   — Juvenile literature

Civics, Russian
   xx Communism—Russia

Civil aeronautics
   See Aeronautics, Commercial
   Private flying

Civil aviation
   See Aeronautics, Commercial
   Private flying

Civil death
   sa Absence and presumption of death
      Attainder
      Infamy (Law)
      Outlawry
      Prisoners—Legal status, laws, etc.
   xx Absence and presumption of death
      Attainder
      Capacity and disability
      Civil rights
      Infamy (Law)
      Prisioners—Legal status, laws, etc.

Civil defense *(UA926-9)*
   sa Air defenses, Civil
      Air raid shelters
      Air raid wardens
      Air raid warning systems
      Aircraft spotting
      Atomic bomb—Safety measures
      Atomic bomb shelters
      Auxiliary police
      Blackouts in war
      Bomb reconnaissance
      Chemical warfare—Safety measures
      Decontamination (from gases, chemicals, etc.)
      Disaster relief
      Emergency clothing supply
      Emergency communication systems
      Emergency food supply
      Emergency housing
      Emergency transportation
      Emergency water supply
      Evacuation of civilians
      Industry—Defense measures
      Mass casualties
      Panic
      Rescue work
      Rest centers (Disaster relief)
      Telegraph—Defense measures

Telephone—Defense measures
World War, 1939-1945—Evacuation of civilians
subdivision Civil defense *under names of countries, cities, etc., e.g.* Great Britain—Civil defense
   x Civilian defense
     Defense, Civil
     World War, 1939-1945—Civil defense
   xx Air defenses
     Attack and defense (Military science)
     Disaster relief
     Military art and science
     War damage, Industrial
   Notes under Air defenses; War—Protection of civilians
   — Abbreviations
   — Equipment and supplies
     sa Disaster hospitals
     xx Survival and emergency equipment
   — Psychological aspects

Civil disobedience
   See Government, Resistance to

Civil disorders
   See Riots

Civil engineering *(Direct) (TA)*
   sa Aqueducts
      Arches
      Breakwaters
      Bridges
      Canals
      Coffer-dams
      Construction equipment
      Curves in engineering
      Docks
      Drainage
      Dredging
      Earthwork
      Embankments
      Excavation
      Extraterrestrial bases
      Foundations
      Guy anchors
      Harbors
      Highway engineering
      Hydraulic engineering
      Marine engineering
      Masonry
      Mechanical engineering
      Military engineering
      Mining engineering
      Piers
      Piling (Civil engineering)
      Public works
      Railroad engineering
      Railroads—Construction
      Reclamation of land
      Rivers
      Roads
      Sanitary engineering
      Snowsheds
      Soil freezing
      Steel, Structural
      Streets
      Strength of materials
      Structural dynamics
      Structural engineering
      Surveying
      Tunnels
      United States. Navy—Engineering aids
      Walls
      Water-supply engineering
      Wharves
     subdivision Public works *under names of countries, cities, etc., e.g.* France—Public works; Boston—Public works

   x Engineering, Civil
   xx Engineering
   — Abbreviations *(TA11)*
   — Bibliography
     sa Civil engineering literature
   — Cold weather conditions
     sa Ice excavation
     Ice tunneling
     Example under Engineering—Cold weather conditions
   — Contracts and specifications *(Direct) (TA180-182)*
   — Early works to 1850 *(TA144)*
   — Estimates and costs
     See Engineering—Estimates and costs
   — Examinations, questions, etc.
   — Juvenile literature
   — Literature
     See Civil engineering literature
   — Management
     See Engineering—Management
   — Notation *(TA11)*
     x Civil engineering symbols
   — Pictorial works
   — Popular works
   — Problems, exercises, etc. *(TA151)*
   — Research *(Direct)*
     xx Engineering research
   — Safety measures
   — Study and teaching
     See Engineering—Study and teaching
   — Tables, calculations, etc.

Civil engineering as a profession
   See Engineering as a profession

Civil engineering literature *(TA10)*
   x Civil engineering—Literature
   xx Civil engineering—Bibliography

Civil engineering symbols
   See Civil engineering—Notation

Civil engineers *(Direct)*
   sa Highway engineers
   xx Engineers
   — Legal status, laws, etc. *(Direct)*
     xx Engineering law
   — Salaries, pensions, etc.

Civil engineers, American, ₍etc.₎
   x American ₍etc.₎ civil engineers
   — Biography

Civil functions
   See subdivision Civil functions *under subjects, e.g.* United States. Army. Corps of Engineers—Civil functions

Civil government
   See Political science
   For compends, text-books, etc. with special reference to the United States *see* United States—Politics and government—Handbooks, manuals, etc.

Civil law *(Direct)*
   sa Condicio juris
      Conditions (Law)
      Declaration of intention
      Duress (Law)
      Fungibles
      Infamy (Law)
      Interest (Law)
      Liability (Law)
      Novation
      Nullity
      Obligations (Law)
      Reconciliation (Law)
      Rescission (Law)
      Restitutio in integrum
      Roman-Dutch law
      Roman law
      Unjust enrichment
      Usufruct

Civil law (Direct) (Continued)
>special legal headings with Civil law
>>added in parentheses, e.g. Delegation
>>(Civil law); Interdict (Civil law)
>>x Law, Civil
>>xx Roman law
>>Note under Civil law systems
>— Classification
>>x Classification—Civil law
>— Codification
>— Digests
>— International unification
>>x International unification of civil law
>>International unification of private
>>>law
>>Unification of civil law
>>Unification of private law
>>Example under reference from International unification of law
>— Interpretation and construction
>— Popular works
>— Sources

>>GEOGRAPHIC SUBDIVISIONS

>— Rome
>>See Roman law
Civil law (Adat law)
>See Adat law
Civil law (Islamic law)
>See Islamic law
Civil law (Jewish law)
>See Jewish law
Civil law (Roman-Dutch law)
>See Roman-Dutch law
Civil law (Roman law)
>See Roman law
Civil law systems
>Here are entered works on the legal systems derived from Roman law. Material on the laws of one or several states or nations regulating all the private relations of citizens to each other are entered under the heading Civil law.
>sa subdivision Roman influence under names of legal systems or under the law of a particular jurisdiction, e.g. Common law—Roman influence; Law—Brazil—Roman influence
>xx Roman law
>>Roman law—Influence
Civil liberty
>See Liberty
Civil list (Direct)
>sa Appanage
>xx Appanage
>>Civil service
>>Finance, Public
>>Kings and rulers
>>Pensions
Civil marriage (HQ1006)
>Here are entered general treatises only. Discussions of civil marriage in various countries are entered under Marriage law with country subdivision.
>xx Marriage
Civil-military relations
>See Civil supremacy over the military
>>Militarism
>>Sociology, Military
Civil obedience
>See Government, Resistance to
Civil procedure (Direct)
>sa Acquiescence (Law)
>>Actions and defenses
>>Admissions (Law)
>>Agricultural courts and procedure
>>Amparo (Writ)

>>Appellate procedure
>>Arbitration and award
>>Attachment and garnishment
>>Class actions (Civil procedure)
>>Code pleading
>>Complaints (Civil procedure)
>>Compromise (Law)
>>Conciliation (Civil procedure)
>>Contumacy
>>Costs (Law)
>>Default (Law)
>>Defense (Civil procedure)
>>Dismissal and nonsuit
>>Divorce suits
>>Equity pleading and procedure
>>Exceptions (Law)
>>Executions (Law)
>>Extraordinary remedies
>>Injunctions
>>Instructions to juries
>>Intervention (Civil procedure)
>>Joinder of issue
>>Judgments
>>Judicial assistance
>>Jury
>>Law and fact
>>Legal advertising
>>Matrimonial actions
>>Motions (Law)
>>New matter (Civil procedure)
>>New trials
>>Nisi prius
>>Non-contentious jurisdiction
>>Notice (Law)
>>Parties to actions
>>Pleading
>>Pre-trial procedure
>>Prejudicial actions
>>Probate law and practice
>>Process
>>Prohibition (Writ)
>>Provisional remedies
>>Remedies (Law)
>>Security for costs
>>Set-off and counterclaim
>>Small claims courts
>>Summary proceedings
>>Supplementary proceedings
>>Terms of court
>>Time (Law)
>>Trial practice
>>Venue
>xx Actions and defenses
>>Appellate procedure
>>Courts
>>Procedure (Law)
>>Trial practice
>— Codification
>— Digests
>— Forms
>>Note under Formalities (Law)
>— Interpretation and construction
>— Legal research

>>GEOGRAPHIC SUBDIVISIONS

>— Rome
>>See Civil procedure (Roman law)
Civil procedure (Adat law)
>Example under Adat law
Civil procedure (Ancient law)
Civil procedure (Canon law) (BX1939.C664)
>sa Lis pendens (Canon law)
>>Matrimonial actions (Canon law)
>xx Procedure (Canon law)
Civil procedure (Greek law)
Civil procedure (International law) (JX6601-6625)
>sa Judgments, Foreign

>>Judicial assistance
>xx International law
>Note under Judicial assistance
Civil procedure (Islamic law)
>sa Matrimonial actions (Islamic law)
Civil procedure (Jewish law)
Civil procedure (Roman-Dutch law)
Civil procedure (Roman law)
>sa Addicere (The word)
>>Contumacy (Roman law)
>>Recuperatores (Roman law)
>x Civil procedure—Rome
Civil procedure (Saxon law)
Civil remedies
>See Remedies (Law)
Civil rights (Direct)
>sa Assembly, Right of
>>Children's rights
>>Civil death
>>Detention of persons
>>Due process of law
>>Equality before the law
>>Free choice of employment
>>Freedom of association
>>Freedom of information
>>Freedom of movement
>>Habeas corpus
>>Indians of North America—Civil rights
>>Jews—Legal status, laws, etc.
>>Liberty
>>Liberty of contract
>>Liberty of speech
>>Liberty of the press
>>Natural law
>>Negroes—Civil rights
>>Petition, Right of
>>Political rights
>>Race discrimination—Law and legislation
>>Religious liberty
>>Right of property
>>Right to counsel
>>Right to education
>>Searches and seizures
>>Speedy trial
>>Teaching, Freedom of
>x Human rights
>>Rights, Civil
>xx Civics
>>Constitutional law
>>Discrimination
>>Liberty
>>Personality (Law)
>>Political science
>— Caricatures and cartoons
>— Juvenile literature
>— Underdeveloped areas
>>See Underdeveloped areas—Civil rights
Civil rights (International law)
>xx International law
Civil rights (Islamic law)
Civil rights (Jewish law)
Civil rights workers (Direct)
>xx Negroes—Civil rights
>— Correspondence, reminiscences, etc.

Civil service *(Direct)* *(JF1321-1671;*
  Colonial, JV443-5; Municipal,
  JS148-163; State labor,
  HD8011-8023; United States,
  JK631-901; Other countries, JN-JQ)
  Here are entered works on career government service and the laws governing it.
  Works on government service, including that by political appointment or
  employment contract, are entered under the name of the country state, or
  city, with the subdivision Officials and
  employees. Works on personnel of a
  specific government agency are entered under the name of that agency,
  with the subdivision Officials and employees.
  sa Administrative law
    Applications for office
    Bureaucracy
    Civil list
    Civil service pensioners
    Collective bargaining—Government
      employees
    Collective labor agreements—Municipal
      employees
    Correctional personnel
    Employee-management relations in
      government
    Government business enterprises—
      Employees
    Local officials and employees
    Misconduct in office
    Municipal officials and employees
    Public officers
    Strikes and lockouts—Civil service
    Trade-unions—Government employees
    Uniforms, Civil
    Women in the civil service
    subdivision Officials and employees—
      Appointment, qualifications, tenure,
      etc. *under names of countries, cities,*
      etc., e.g. United States—Officials and
      employees—Appointment,
      qualifications, tenure, etc.
  x Administration
    Government employees
    Office, Tenure of
    Tenure of office
  xx Administrative law
    Bureaucracy
    Political science
    Public administration
    Public officers
  — Anecdotes, facetiae, satire, etc.
  — Colonies
    See Civil service, Colonial
  — Ethics
    See Civil service ethics
  — Examinations *(United States, JK716)*
    sa subdivision Officials and employees
      —Examinations *under names of*
      cities and towns
    x Civil service examinations
      Competitive examinations
    xx Examinations
  — Examinations, questions, etc.
  — Political activity
    Here are entered general works on pol-
    itical activities of civil servants.
    Works limited to particular locali-
    ties are entered under names of
    countries, cities, etc. with subdivi-
    sion Officials and employees—Poli-
    tical activity.
    x Government employees' political
      activities
    xx Public administration

— Positions
    See Civil service positions
— Recruiting
    See Civil service recruiting
— Salaries
    Here are entered general works on
    civil service salaries. Works limited
    to particular localities are entered
    under the name of the country, city,
    etc., with subdivision Officials and
    employees—Salaries, allowances,
    etc. *e.g.* United States—Officials
    and employees—Salaries, allow-
    ances, etc. Works limited to specific
    departments or institutions are en-
    tered under the name of the depart-
    ment or institution, with subdivi-
    sion Appointments, promotions, sa-
    laries, etc., *e.g.* United States.
    Dept. of Agriculture—Appoint-
    ments, promotions, salaries, etc.
— Study and teaching *(Direct)*
    sa Interns (Civil service)
— Subject headings
    See Subject headings—Civil service
— Supplementary employment
    xx Conflict of interests (Public office)
    Example under Supplementary employ-
    ment
— Underdeveloped areas
    See Underdeveloped areas—Civil
    service
— Veterans' preference *(Direct)*
    x Veteran preference
      Veterans' preference
    xx Veterans—Employment
— Vocational guidance
    See Civil service positions

    GEOGRAPHIC SUBDIVISIONS

— ⌐country⌐
— — Colonies
    Note under Civil service, Colonial

    GEOGRAPHIC SUBDIVISIONS

— United States
    x United States—Civil service

    GEOGRAPHIC SUBDIVISIONS

— — States
Civil service, Colonial
    Here are entered general and compara-
    tive works only. Works on civil service
    of the colonies of an individual country
    are entered under the heading Civil
    service with subdivision ⌐country⌐—
    Colonies. Works dealing with a spe-
    cific colony are entered under the
    same heading, subdivided by the name
    of the colony.
    x Civil service—Colonies
      Colonial civil service
      Colonies—Civil service
      Colonies—Officials and employees
Civil service, International
    See International officials and employees
Civil service, Municipal
    See Municipal officials and employees
Civil service ethics
    x Civil service—Ethics
    xx Political ethics
Civil service examinations
    See Civil service—Examinations
Civil service interns
    See Interns (Civil service)
Civil service jobs
    See Civil service positions

Civil service pensioners *(Direct)*
    sa Civil service pensions
    x Pensioners, Civil service
      Retired government officials and
      employees
    xx Civil service
      Civil service retirement
— United States
    xx United States—Officials and
      employees, Retired
Civil service pensions *(Direct)* *(JF1671;*
    United States, JK791)
    sa Survivors' benefits
      subdivision Officials and employees—
      Pensions *under names of particular*
      departments, e.g. United States.
      Federal Bureau of Investigation—
      Officials and employees—Pensions;
      also subdivision Pensions *and*
      Salaries, pensions, etc., *under names*
      of industries, professions, etc., e.g.
      Lawyers—Pensions; Teachers—
      Salaries, pensions, etc.
    x Pensions, Civil
      Retirement pensions
    xx Civil service pensioners
      Civil service retirement
      Old age pensions
      Pensions
— Cost-of-living adjustments *(Direct)*
    x Cost-of-living pension adjustments
— Finance
— Tables and ready-reckoners
— Taxation *(Direct)*
— Unclaimed benefits
    x Benefits, Unclaimed (Civil service
      pensions)
      Unclaimed benefits of civil service
      pensions

    GEOGRAPHIC SUBDIVISIONS

— United States
    x United States—Pensions, Civil
      service

    GEOGRAPHIC SUBDIVISIONS

— — States
Civil service positions *(Direct)*
    sa subdivision Positions *under names of*
      individual government departments
      or agencies, e.g. United States. War
      Dept.—Positions
    x Civil service jobs
      Civil service—Positions
      Civil service—Vocational guidance
      Government jobs
      Government positions
    xx Occupations
— Classification
    sa subdivision Officials and employees
      —Salaries, allowances, etc. *under*
      names of countries, states, cities,
      or individual government agencies
— Juvenile literature
Civil service recruiting *(Direct)*
    x Civil service—Recruiting
    xx Recruiting of employees
Civil service reform *(United States,*
    JK681-699)
    sa Corruption (in politics)
      Patronage, Political
    x Merit system
      Spoils system
    xx Patronage, Political
Civil service retirement *(Direct)*
    sa Civil service pensioners
      Civil service pensions
    xx Retirement

Civil supremacy over the military *(Direct)*
  x Civil-military relations
    Civilian control of the military
    Military and civilian power
    Military-civil relations
    Supremacy of the civil authority
  xx Constitutional law
    Executive power
    Legislative power
    Sociology, Military
Civil uniforms
  See Uniforms, Civil
Civil war *(International law, JX4541)*
  sa Insurgency
  x Rebellions
  xx Government, Resistance to
    International law
    Revolutions
    War
  — Great Britain
    See Great Britain—History—Civil
      War, 1642-1649
  — United States
    See United States—History—Civil
      War, 1861-1865
Civil wrongs
  See Torts
Civilian control of the military
  See Civil supremacy over the military
Civilian defense
  See Civil defense
Civilians, Evacuation of
  See Evacuation of civilians
Civilization *(CB; HM101)*
    Includes works treating of culture or civil-
    ization in general. Literature dealing
    with the culture of peoples and races
    ordinarily classed as civilized and not
    confined to one country are entered
    under the headings Civilization,
    Greek; Civilization, Germanic; Civili-
    zation, Homeric; etc.
    Works on the civilization of a single coun-
    try are entered under the name of the
    country with the subdivision Civiliza-
    tion, *e.g.* United States—Civilization
    Works treating of the culture of uncivil-
    ized tribes are entered under the name
    of the tribe.
    Works treating of the impact of one civili-
    zation upon another are entered under
    the civilization affected with appropri-
    ate subdivision, *e.g.* Japan—Civiliza-
    tion—Occidental influences.
  sa Acculturation
    Animals and civilization
    Anthropology
    Archaeology
    Art
    Astronautics and civilization
    Biculturalism
    Culture
    Education
    Ethics
    Ethnology
    Humanism
    Inventions
    Learning and scholarship
    Manners and customs
    Migrations of nations
    Personality and culture
    Popular culture
    Progress
    Religion and culture
    Religions
    Renaissance
    Social evolution
    Social problems
    Social sciences
    Society, Primitive
    Technology and civilization
    War and civilization
  xx Anthropology
    Auxiliary sciences of history
    Culture
    Ethnology
    History
    History—Philosophy
    Humanism
    Political science
    Progress
    Social problems
    Sociology
  — Historiography *(CB15)*
  — History
    sa Civilization, Medieval
      Civilization, Modern
  — — Juvenile literature
  — Italian, ₍Jewish, Portuguese, etc.₎
    influences
  — Juvenile literature
  — Philosophy *(CB19)*
    sa Philosophical anthropology
  — Pictorial works
Civilization, Aegean
  sa Civilization, Mycenaean
    Minoans
  x Aegean civilization
Civilization, American
  See America—Civilization ₍*for works*
      dealing with the western hemisphere
      in modern times₎
    Indians—Culture *and names of*
      individual tribes, etc. ₍for works
      dealing with ancient American
      civilization₎
    Latin America—Civilization ₍*for works*
      dealing with Latin America in
      general₎
    United States—Civilization ₍*for works*
      limited to the United States₎
Civilization, Ancient *(CB311)*
  sa Protohistory
    Science, Ancient
  xx History, Ancient
  — Historiography
  — Pictorial works
  — Juvenile literature
Civilization, Anglo-Saxon, ₍Phenician, etc.₎
  x Anglo-Saxon ₍Phenician, etc.₎
    civilization
  — Anecdotes, facetiae, satire, etc.
  — Programmed instruction
Civilization, Arab *(DS215)*
  sa Civilization, Islamic
    Jews—Civilization—Arab influences
  x Arab civilization
  xx Civilization, Islamic
    Civilization, Semitic
    Saracens
  — Greek influences
  — Iranian influences
  — Occidental influences
    xx Civilization, Occidental
Civilization, Aryan *(CB201-231; GN539)*
  sa Aryans
  x Aryan civilization
Civilization, Assyro-Babylonian *(DS70.7)*
  sa Cuneiform inscriptions
    Cuneiform writing
    Sumerians
  x Assyro-Babylonian civilization
    Babylonian civilization
    Civilization, Babylonian
Civilization, Babylonian
  See Civilization, Assyro-Babylonian
Civilization, Baroque
  x Baroque civilization
Civilization, Buddhist *(CB255)*
  x Buddhist civilization
  xx Civilization, Oriental
Civilization, Christian *(BR115.C5)*
  sa Christianity and culture
    Church and social problems
  x Christian civilization
  xx Christianity
    Church and social problems
Civilization, Comparative
  See Comparative civilization
Civilization, Dravidian *(DS425)*
  sa Mundas
  x Dravidian civilization
Civilization, Etruscan
  See Etruscans
Civilization, Germanic *(CB213-214)*
  x Germanic civilization
    Germanic tribes—Civilization
    Teutonic civilization
  Note under Civilization
Civilization, Greco-Roman
    Here are entered works on the fusion of
    Greek and Roman civilizations after
    the Roman conquest of Greece ca. 140
    B.C. The heading is not synonymous
    with classical civilization. Works on
    classical civilization are entered under
    Rome—Civilization and/or Civiliza-
    tion, Greek.
  x Greco-Roman civilization
  xx Civilization, Greek
Civilization, Greek *(DF75-129)*
  sa Civilization, Greco-Roman
    Civilization, Homeric
    Hellenism
  x Greece—Civilization
    Greek civilization
  Notes under Civilization; Civilization, Greco-
    Roman
  — Juvenile literature
Civilization, Hindu *(DS423-5)*
  x Civilization, Vedic
    Hindu civilization
    Vedic civilization
  xx Hinduism
Civilization, Hispanic *(CB226)*
  sa Latin America—Civilization
    Spain—Civilization
  x Civilization, Spanish
    Hispanic civilization
    Spanish civilization
Civilization, Homeric *(PA4037)*
  x Homeric civilization
  xx Civilization, Greek
  Note under Civilization
Civilization, Indian
  See Indians—Culture
Civilization, Islamic *(D199.3; India, DS427)*
  sa Civilization, Arab
    Civilization, Occidental—Islamic
      influences
  x Civilization, Muslim
    Islamic civilization
    Muslim civilization
  xx Civilization, Arab
  Note under Islam
  — Greek influences
  — Occidental influences
  — Pictorial works
Civilization, Jewish
  See Jews—Civilization
Civilization, Latin
  sa subdivision Civilization—Latin
    influences *under names of countries*
  x Latin civilization

Civilization, Medieval *(CB351-5)*
- sa Art, Medieval
    Chivalry
    Education, Medieval
    Feudalism
    Middle Ages
    Military religious orders
    Monasticism and religious orders
    Ordeal
    Renaissance
    Science, Medieval
    Travel, Medieval
- xx Chivalry
    Civilization—History
    Middle Ages
    Middle Ages—History
    Renaissance
— Jewish influences
    xx Jews—Civilization
— Juvenile literature

Civilization, Minoan
  See Minoans
Civilization, Modern *(CB357-425)*
- sa Detribalization
    History, Modern
    Renaissance
- x Modern civilization
- xx Civilization—History
    History, Modern
    Renaissance
— 18th century *(CB411)*
    xx Eighteenth century
— 19th century *(CB415-417)*
    xx Nineteenth century
— — Juvenile literature
— 20th century *(CB425-7)*
    xx Twentieth century
— — English influences
— — 1950-
— — Anecdotes, facetiae, satire, etc.
— — Juvenile literature
— — Pictorial works

GENERAL SUBDIVISIONS

— Juvenile literature

GENERAL SUBDIVISIONS

— Latin influences

GENERAL SUBDIVISIONS

— Roman influences
Civilization, Muslim
  See Civilization, Islamic
Civilization, Mycenaean
- x Mycenaean civilization
- xx Civilization, Aegean
— Egyptian ₍Semitic, etc.₎ influences
Civilization, Occidental *(CB245)*
- sa Architecture, Japanese—Occidental
      influences
    Civilization, Arab—Occidental
      influences
    Eurasianism
- x Civilization, Western
    Occidental civilization
    Western civilization
- xx Occidental studies
— Biblical influences
    See Bible—Influence—Civilization,
      Occidental
— Islamic influences
    x Civilization, Occidental—Muslim
      influences
    xx Civilization, Islamic
— Muslim influences
    See Civilization, Occidental—Islamic
      influences
— Oriental influences

See East and West
Civilization, Oriental *(CB253)*
- sa Civilization, Buddhist
    Eurasianism
    Philosophy, Ancient—Oriental
      influences
- x Oriental civilization
- xx Oriental studies
— Occidental influences
    See East and West
Civilization, Pagan *(CB151)*
- sa Civilization, Secular
- x Pagan civilization
- xx Civilization, Secular
    Paganism
Civilization, Pre-Columbian
  See Indians—Culture
Civilization, Secular
- sa Civilization, Pagan
- xx Civilization, Pagan
    Secularism
Civilization, Semitic *(CB241)*
- sa Civilization, Arab
    Jews—Civilization
- x Semitic civilization
— Parthian influences
    xx Parthians
— Roman influences
Civilization, Slavic
- sa Slavophilism
- x Slavic civilization
— Byzantine influences
Civilization, Spanish
  See Civilization, Hispanic
    Spain—Civilization
Civilization, Sumerian
  See Sumerians
Civilization, Vedic
  See Civilization, Hindu
Civilization, Villanovan
- x Villanovan civilization
Civilization, Western
  See Civilization, Occidental
Civilization and aeronautics
  See Aeronautics and civilization
Civilization and astronautics
  See Astronautics and civilization
Civilization and computers
  See Computers and civilization
Civilization and machinery
  See Technology and civilization
Civilization and personality
  See Personality and culture
Civilization and science
  See Science and civilization
Civilization and technology
  See Technology and civilization
Civilization and war
  See War and civilization
Clackama Indians
  See Clackamas Indians
Clackamas Indians
- x Clackama Indians
- xx Chinook Indians
    Chinookan Indians
    Indians of North America
Claco
  See Tlaco
Cladding
  See Metal cladding
Cladocera *(Indirect)* *(QL444.C6)*
- x Water-fleas
- xx Crustacea
    Entomostraca
Cladocera, Fossil
- xx Crustacea, Fossil
    Entomostraca, Fossil

Claiakwat Indians
  See Clayoquot Indians
Claim associations
  See Land claim associations
Claims *(HJ8903-8963; United States,*
      International law, JX238)
- sa Alabama claims
    Calvo doctrine and clause
    Drago doctrine
    Exhaustion of local remedies
      (International law)
    French spoliation claims
    Government liability (International law)
    Military occupation damages
    Restitution and indemnification claims
      (1933-   )
    Spanish Florida claims
    subdivision Claims *under names of*
      wars, e.g. United States—History—
      Civil War, 1861-1865—Claims; *and*
      under names of countries, cities, etc.,
      e.g. United States—Claims; *also*
      under names of claimants (countries,
      states, cities, individuals, etc.)
      subdivision Claims vs. ₍name of
      country or party against which
      claims are brought₎, e.g. Maryland—
      Claims vs. United States
- x International claims
    Private claims
    War claims
- xx Finance, Public
    Government liability (International law)
    International law
    War
Claims, Adjustment of
  See Insurance, Accident ₍Fire, etc.₎—
      Adjustment of claims
    Insurance—Adjustment of claims
Claims, Freight
  See Freight and freightage—Claims
Claims, Revalorization of
  See Revalorization of debts
Claims against decedents' estates *(Direct)*
- sa Benefit of inventory
    Separation of patrimony
- x Ancestral debts
    Debts of decedents' estates
- xx Debtor and creditor
    Decedents' estates
    Executors and administrators
    Inheritance and succession
    Probate law and practice
— Sources
Claims against decedents' estates (Canon law)
Claims against decedents' estates (Roman law)
Clairaudience *(BF1338)*
- xx Clairvoyance
    Psychical research
Clairobscur
  See Chiaroscuro
Clairvoyance *(BF1325)*
- sa Catoptromancy
    Clairaudience
    Crystal-gazing
    Divination
    Extrasensory perception
    Fortune-telling
    Hypnotism
    Mind-reading
    Psychometry (Occult sciences)
    Second sight
    Thought-transference
    Trance
- xx Animal magnetism
    Catoptromancy
    Divination
    Fortune-telling

Clairvoyance (BF1325) (Continued)
   Mind-reading
   Occult sciences
   Psychical research
   Psychometry (Occult sciences)
   Second sight
   Thought-transference
Claisen condensation (QD319)
   sa Claisen rearrangement
   xx Claisen rearrangement
   Condensation products (Chemistry)
Claisen rearrangement
   sa Claisen condensation
   xx Claisen condensation
   Ethers
   Rearrangements (Chemistry)
Clallam Indians (E99.C82)
   x Klallam Indians
   xx Indians of North America
   Salishan Indians
Clallam language (PM895)
   xx Salishan languages
Clam fisheries (Indirect) (SH373)
   xx Clams
   Shellfish fisheries
   — Equipment and supplies
Clam shrimps
   See Conchostraca
Clamcoët Indians
   See Karankawa Indians
Clamps (Joinery)
   xx Joinery
Clams (QL430.6-7)
   sa Clam fisheries
   Toheroa
   xx Lamellibranchiata
   Example under Sea food
Clan gods (Shinto)
   See Tutelaries (Shinto)
Clandestine literature
   See Underground literature
Clandestine marriages (Canon law)
   See Clandestinity (Canon law)
Clandestinity (Canon law)
   x Clandestine marriages (Canon law)
   xx Marriage (Canon law)
Clans and clan system (Direct) (JC20-45;
      Ethnology, GN492)
   sa Gipsies—Scotland
   Kinship
   Society, Primitive
   Tartans
   Tribes and tribal system
   names of clans, e.g. Cameron Clan;
      MacGregor Clan
   x Highland clans
   Scottish clans
   xx Family
   Feudalism
   Kinship
   Political science
   Society, Primitive
   Tribes and tribal system
Clapham Sect
   xx Evangelicalism—Church of England
   Slavery in Great Britain—Anti-slavery
      movements
Clares, Poor
   See Poor Clares
Claret (TP548-559)
   xx Wine and wine making
Clarification of liquids
   See Liquids—Clarification
Clarifiers, Sewage
   See Sewage clarifiers
Clarinet (History and construction,
      ML945-8)
   sa Basset horn

   x Clarionet
   Primer clarinet
— Fingering charts
   Example under Tabulature (Musical no-
      tation)
— Methods (MT382)
— — Self-instruction (MT388)
      x Clarinet—Self-instruction
— Methods (Jazz) (MT382)
— Orchestra studies (MT386)
   xx Clarinet—Studies and exercises
— Self-instruction
   See Clarinet—Methods—
      Self-instruction
— Studies and exercises (MT385)
   sa Clarinet—Orchestra studies
Clarinet, English horn, flute, oboe with string
      orchestra (M1105-6)
   sa Concertos (Clarinet, English horn, flute,
      oboe with string orchestra)
   Suites (Clarinet, English horn, flute,
      oboe with string orchestra)
   xx Concertos (Clarinet, English horn, flute,
      oboe with string orchestra)
   String-orchestra music
   Wind quartets (Clarinet, English horn,
      flute, oboe)
Clarinet and bassoon music
   See Bassoon and clarinet music
Clarinet and double-bass music (M290-291)
   x Double-bass and clarinet music
Clarinet and flute music (M288-9)
   sa Canons, fugues, etc. (Clarinet and flute)
   Clarinet and flute with chamber
      orchestra
   Clarinet and flute with string orchestra
   Concertos (Clarinet and flute with
      chamber orchestra)
   Concertos (Clarinet and flute with
      string orchestra)
   Sonatas (Clarinet and flute)
   Suites (Clarinet and flute)
   Variations (Clarinet and flute)
   x Flute and clarinet music
Clarinet and flute music, Juvenile (M1410)
Clarinet and flute with chamber orchestra
      (M1040-1041)
   sa Concertos (Clarinet and flute with
      chamber orchestra)
   Suites (Clarinet and flute with chamber
      orchestra)
   xx Chamber-orchestra music
   Clarinet and flute music
   Concertos (Clarinet and flute with
      chamber orchestra)
Clarinet and flute with string orchestra
      (M1105-6)
   sa Concertos (Clarinet and flute with
      string orchestra)
   Suites (Clarinet and flute with string
      orchestra)
   xx Clarinet and flute music
   Concertos (Clarinet and flute with
      string orchestra)
   String-orchestra music
— Scores (M1105)
Clarinet and guitar music (M296-7)
   x Guitar and clarinet music
Clarinet and guitar music, Arranged
      (M296-7)
Clarinet and harp music (M296-7)
   sa Clarinet and harp with string orchestra
   Concertos (Clarinet and harp with
      string orchestra)
   x Harp and clarinet music

Clarinet and harp with string orchestra
      (M1105-6)
   sa Concertos (Clarinet and harp with
      string orchestra)
   x Harp and clarinet with string orchestra
   xx Clarinet and harp music
   Concertos (Clarinet and harp with
      string orchestra)
   String-orchestra music
Clarinet and horn music (M288-9)
   sa Variations (Clarinet and horn)
   x Horn and clarinet music
Clarinet and oboe music (M288-9)
   sa Clarinet and oboe with orchestra
   Concertos (Clarinet and oboe)
   Suites (Clarinet and oboe)
   x Oboe and clarinet music
Clarinet and oboe with orchestra
      (M1040-1041)
   sa Concertos (Clarinet and oboe)
   xx Clarinet and oboe music
   Concertos (Clarinet and oboe)
   Orchestral music
— Scores (M1040-1041)
Clarinet and percussion music (M298)
   x Percussion and clarinet music
Clarinet and piano music (M248-250)
   sa Canons, fugues, etc. (Clarinet and
      piano)
   Marches (Clarinet and piano)
   Minuets (Clarinet and piano)
   Sonatas (Clarinet and piano)
   Suites (Clarinet and piano)
   Variations (Clarinet and piano)
   x Piano and clarinet music
Clarinet and piano music, Arranged
      (M251-2)
   sa Clarinet with chamber orchestra—Solo
      with piano
   Clarinet with orchestra—Solo with
      piano
   Clarinet with string orchestra—Solo
      with piano
   Concertos (Clarinet)—Solo with piano
   Concertos (Clarinet with band)—Solo
      with piano
   Concertos (Clarinet with chamber
      orchestra)—Solo with piano
   Concertos (Clarinet with string
      orchestra), Arranged—Solo with
      piano
   Concertos (Clarinet with string
      orchestra)—Solo with piano
   Suites (Clarinet with orchestra)—Solo
      with piano
   Suites (Clarinet with string orchestra)—
      Solo with piano
   Variations (Clarinet with orchestra)—
      Solo with piano
Clarinet and piano music, Arranged (Jazz)
   See Clarinet and piano music (Jazz)
Clarinet and piano music (Jazz) (M248-252)
   x Clarinet and piano music, Arranged
      (Jazz)
Clarinet and tuba music (M288-9)
   x Tuba and clarinet music
Clarinet and vibraphone music (M298)
   sa Clarinet and vibraphone with string
      orchestra
   Concertos (Clarinet and vibraphone
      with string orchestra)
   x Vibraphone and clarinet music
Clarinet and vibraphone with string orchestra
      (M1105-6)
   sa Concertos (Clarinet and vibraphone
      with string orchestra)
   xx Clarinet and vibraphone music

Concertos (Clarinet and vibraphone
 with string orchestra)
 String-orchestra music
Clarinet and violin music *(M290-291)*
 sa Clarinet and violin with orchestra
 Clarinet and violin with string orchestra
 Concertos (Clarinet and violin)
 Concertos (Clarinet and violin with
  string orchestra)
 Suites (Clarinet and violin)
 x Violin and clarinet music
Clarinet and violin music, Arranged
 (M290-291)
Clarinet and violin with orchestra
 (M1040-1041)
 sa Concertos (Clarinet and violin)
 xx Clarinet and violin music
 Concertos (Clarinet and violin)
Clarinet and violin with string orchestra
 (M1105-6)
 sa Concertos (Clarinet and violin with
  string orchestra)
 xx Clarinet and violin music
 Concertos (Clarinet and violin with
  string orchestra)
 String-orchestra music
— Scores *(M1105)*
Clarinet and violoncello music
 sa Clarinet and violoncello with orchestra
 Concertos (Clarinet and violoncello)
 Sonatas (Clarinet and violoncello)
 Suites (Clarinet and violoncello)
 x Violoncello and clarinet music
Clarinet and violoncello with orchestra
 (M1040-1041)
 sa Concertos (Clarinet and violoncello)
 xx Clarinet and violoncello music
 Concertos (Clarinet and violoncello)
 Orchestral music
Clarinet, flute, harp with string orchestra
 (M1105-6)
 sa Concertos (Clarinet, flute, harp with
  string orchestra)
 xx Concertos (Clarinet, flute, harp with
  string orchestra)
 String-orchestra music
 Trios (Clarinet, flute, harp)
— Scores and parts *(M1105)*
Clarinet, flute, oboe with string orchestra
 (M1105-6)
 sa Concertos (Clarinet, flute, oboe with
  string orchestra)
 xx Concertos (Clarinet, flute, oboe with
  string orchestra)
 String-orchestra music
 Wind trios (Clarinet, flute, oboe)
— Scores *(M1105)*
Clarinet, flute, trumpet with string orchestra
 (M1105-6)
 sa Concertos (Clarinet, flute, trumpet with
  string orchestra)
 Suites (Clarinet, flute, trumpet with
  string orchestra)
 xx Concertos (Clarinet, flute, trumpet with
  string orchestra)
 String-orchestra music
 Wind trios (Clarinet, flute, trumpet)
**Clarinet, harp, violin, violoncello with string
 orchestra** *(M1105)*
 sa Concertos (Clarinet, harp, violin,
  violoncello with string orchestra)
 xx Concertos (Clarinet, harp, violin,
  violoncello with string orchestra)
 Quartets (Clarinet, harp, violin,
  violoncello)
 String-orchestra music
— Scores *(M1105)*

Clarinet music *(M70-72)*
 sa Clarinet with band
 Clarinet with chamber orchestra
 Clarinet with dance orchestra
 Clarinet with jazz ensemble
 Clarinet with orchestra
 Clarinet with string orchestra
 Concertos (Clarinet)
 Concertos (Clarinet with band)
 Concertos (Clarinet with chamber
  orchestra)
 Concertos (Clarinet with dance
  orchestra)
 Concertos (Clarinet with jazz ensemble)
 Concertos (Clarinet with string
  orchestra)
 Recorded accompaniments (Clarinet)
 Sonatas (Clarinet)
 Suites (Clarinet)
 Quartets, ⌈Trios, etc.⌉, Wind quartets,
  ⌈trios, etc.⌉ *followed by specifications
  which include the clarinet*
Clarinet music, Arranged *(M73-74)*
Clarinet music (Clarinets (2)) *(M288-9)*
 sa Clarinets (2) with orchestra
 Clarinets (2) with string orchestra
 Concertos (Clarinets (2))
 Sonatas (Clarinets (2))
 Suites (Clarinets (2))
Clarinet music (Clarinets (2)), Arranged
 (M288-9)
Clarinet music (Clarinets (3))
 See Wind trios (Clarinets (3))
Clarinet music (Clarinets (4))
 See Wind quartets (Clarinets (4))
Clarinet music (Clarinets (5))
 See Wind quintets (Clarinets (5))
Clarinet music (Clarinets (6))
 See Wind sextets (Clarinets (6))
Clarinet music (Clarinets (8))
 See Wind octets (Clarinets (8))
Clarinet players
 See Clarinetists
**Clarinet, trombone, trumpet with string
 orchestra** *(M1105-6)*
 sa Concertos (Clarinet, trombone, trumpet
  with string orchestra)
 xx Concertos (Clarinet, trombone, trumpet
  with string orchestra)
 String-orchestra music
 Wind trios (Clarinet, trombone,
  trumpet)
Clarinet with band *(M1205)*
 sa Concertos (Clarinet with band)
 xx Band music
 Clarinet music
 Concertos (Clarinet with band)
Clarinet with brass ensemble *(M955-9)*
Clarinet with chamber orchestra *(M1024-5)*
 sa Concertos (Clarinet with chamber
  orchestra)
 Rondos (Clarinet with chamber
  orchestra)
 xx Chamber-orchestra music
 Clarinet music
 Concertos (Clarinet with chamber
  orchestra)
— Solo with piano *(M1025)*
 xx Clarinet and piano music, Arranged
Clarinet with chamber orchestra, Arranged
 (M1024-5)
— Scores *(M1024)*
Clarinet with dance orchestra *(M1353)*
 sa Concertos (Clarinet with dance
  orchestra)
 xx Clarinet music
 Concertos (Clarinet with dance
  orchestra)

Dance-orchestra music
Clarinet with instr. ensemble
 sa Concertos (Clarinet with instr.
  ensemble)
 xx Instrumental ensembles
Clarinet with jazz ensemble *(M955-7)*
 sa Concertos (Clarinet with jazz ensemble)
 xx Clarinet music
 Concertos (Clarinet with jazz ensemble)
 Jazz ensembles
Clarinet with orchestra *(M1024-5)*
 sa Concertos (Clarinet)
 Suites (Clarinet with orchestra)
 Variations (Clarinet with orchestra)
 xx Clarinet music
 Concertos (Clarinet)
 Orchestral music
— Solo with piano *(M1025)*
 xx Clarinet and piano music, Arranged
Clarinet with string orchestra *(M1105-6)*
 sa Concertos (Clarinet with string
  orchestra)
 Suites (Clarinet with string orchestra)
 Variations (Clarinet with string
  orchestra)
 xx Clarinet music
 Concertos (Clarinet with string
  orchestra)
 String-orchestra music
— Solo with piano *(M1106)*
 xx Clarinet and piano music, Arranged
Clarinetists
 x Clarinet players
Clarinets (2) with orchestra *(M1024-5)*
 sa Concertos (Clarinets (2))
 x Two clarinets with orchestra
 xx Clarinet music (Clarinets (2))
 Concertos (Clarinets (2))
 Orchestral music
— Scores *(M1024)*
Clarinets (2) with string orchestra
 (M1024-5)
 sa Suites (Clarinets (2) with string
  orchestra)
 xx Clarinet music (Clarinets (2))
Clarinets (3) with string orchestra
 (M1124-5)
 xx String-orchestra music
 Wind trios (Clarinets (3))
— Scores *(M1105)*
Clarinets (4) with string orchestra
 (M1105-6)
 sa Concertos (Clarinets (4) with string
  orchestra)
 Suites (Clarinets (4) with string
  orchestra)
 x Four clarinets with string orchestra
 xx Concertos (Clarinets (4) with string
  orchestra)
 String-orchestra music
 Suites (Clarinets (4) with string
  orchestra)
 Wind quartets (Clarinets (4))
— Scores *(M1105)*
Clarionet
 See Clarinet
Clarisses
 See Poor Clares
Clark's Expedition against Detroit, 1781
 (E237)
 xx Shawnee Indians
Clark's Expedition to the Illinois, 1778-1779
 (E234)
— Juvenile literature
CLASP (Computer program language)
 x Computer language for aeronautics and
  space programming

CLASP (Computer program language)
  (Continued)
    xx Electronic data processing—
        Aeronautics
Clasps
    sa Buckles
       Fibula (Archaeology)
    x Belt-clasps
    xx Fastenings
       Fibula (Archaeology)
Class actions (Civil procedure) *(Direct)*
    sa Citizen suits (Civil procedure)
       Parties to actions
    xx Actions and defenses
       Citizen suits (Civil procedure)
       Civil procedure
       Parties to actions
Class conflict
  See Social conflict
Class distinction
  See Social classes
Class field theory
    xx Algebraic number theory
Class length
  See Class periods
Class meetings, Methodist *(BX8346)*
    x Methodist class meetings
    xx Methodist Church—Government
       Prayer-meetings
Class oriented ring associated language
  See CORAL (Computer program language)
Class periods
    x Class length
       Length of classes
Class schedules
  See Schedules, School
Class size *(LB3013)*
    sa Double shifts (Public schools)
    x Teacher-pupil ratio
    xx Double shifts (Public schools)
       School management and organization
       School size
       Teaching
Class struggle
  See Social conflict
Classed catalogs
  See Catalogs, Classified
Classes, Characteristic
  See Characteristic classes
Classes, Social
  See Social classes
Classes (Mathematics)
  See Set theory
Classet Indians
  See Makah Indians
Classical antiquities *(DE; Greece, DF;*
    Rome, DG)
    sa Archaeology
       Art, Greek
       Art objects, Classical
       Art, Roman
       Chairs (Cathedra)
       Chairs (Sella)
       Classical philology
       Gems
       Musical instruments
       Mythology, Classical
       Numismatics, Greek
       Numismatics, Roman
       Pottery, Greek
       Pottery, Roman
       Tripods
       Vases
    subdivision Antiquities *under names of*
       countries, e.g. Greece—Antiquities
    x Antiquities, Classical
       Antiquities, Grecian
       Antiquities, Roman
       Archaeology, Classical

Classical archaeology
    Roman antiquities
    xx Antiquities
       Archaeological museums and
         collections
       Art, Ancient
       Classical philology
       Sculpture, Ancient
  — Destruction and pillage
  — Dictionaries
    See Classical dictionaries
  — Juvenile literature
Classical antiquities in art
    xx Art
Classical archaeology
  See Classical antiquities
Classical arts
  See Arts, Classical
Classical atlases
  See Classical geography
Classical biography *(DE7)*
    sa Greece—Biography
       Rome—Biography
    xx Biography
Classical dancing
  See Modern dancing
Classical dictionaries *(DE5)*
    x Classical antiquities—Dictionaries
       Dictionaries, Classical
    xx History, Ancient
Classical drama *(Collections, PA3461-6;*
    History and criticism, PA3024-9)
    sa Greek drama
       Latin drama
    x Drama, Classical
    xx Drama
Classical drama (Comedy)
Classical education *(LC1001-1021)*
    Here are entered works dealing with clas-
      sical education in general, its history,
      its value as compared with the study of
      science, etc. Treatises on the study of
      Greek language and literature and
      Latin language and literature in
      schools and colleges are entered under
      Greek language—Study and teaching,
      Greek literature—Study and teaching,
      Latin language—Study and teaching,
      Latin literature—Study and teaching.
    sa Education, Humanistic
       Humanism
       Humanities
       Universities and colleges
    x Education, Classical
    xx Education
       Education, Higher
       Education, Humanistic
       Humanism
       Humanities
       Universities and colleges
Classical epic poetry
  See Epic poetry, Classical
Classical fiction *(Direct)*
    sa Greek fiction
       Latin fiction
Classical field theory
  See Field theory (Physics)
Classical geography *(DE23-31; G87)*
    sa Geography, Ancient
    x Classical atlases
       Geography, Classical
       Geography—Early works
    xx Geography
       Geography, Historical
  Note under Geography, Ancient
  — Maps
    x Atlases, Historical
       Historical atlases

       History—Atlases
       Maps, Historical
       War maps
Classical languages
    sa Greek language
       Latin language
    x Dead languages
       Languages, Classical
  — Study and teaching *(Direct)*
Classical letters
    sa Greek letters
       Latin letters
Classical literature *(Collections,*
    PA3301-3671; History and criticism,
    PA3001-3045)
    sa Greek literature
       Latin literature
    x Literature, Classical
    xx Greek literature
       Latin literature
       Literature
       Literature, Ancient
  — Appreciation *(PA3013)*
  — Bibliography
  — — Union lists
Classical love poetry
  See Love poetry, Classical
Classical mythology
  See Mythology, Classical
Classical orations
    sa Greek orations
       Latin orations
    xx Orations
Classical papyri
  See Manuscripts, Classical (Papyri)
Classical pastoral poetry
  See Pastoral poetry, Classical
Classical philology *(PA1-199)*
    Here are entered treatises on the theory,
      methods and history of classical schol-
      arship.
    sa Classical antiquities
       Classicists
       Greek language
       Greek literature
       Greek philology
       Hellenism
       Humanism
       Latin language
       Latin literature
       Latin philology
    x Philology, Classical
    xx Classical antiquities
       Greek language
       Greek literature
       Greek philology
       Humanism
       Latin language
       Latin literature
       Latin philology
    Example under Philology
  — Biography
    See Philologists
Classical poetry *(Collections, PA3431-3459;*
    History and criticism, PA3019-3022)
    sa Epic poetry, Classical
       Love poetry, Classical
       Pastoral poetry, Classical
    xx Poetry
       Poetry, Ancient
Classical wit and humor
    sa Greek wit and humor
       Latin wit and humor
    x Wit and humor, Classical
    xx Wit and humor, Ancient
Classicism *(PN56.C6)*
    sa Hellenism
       Neoclassicism (Literature)

x Pseudo-classicism
xx Aesthetics
Classicism in art
　sa Neoclassicism (Architecture)
　　Neoclassicism (Art)
　xx Art
Classicism in music
　xx Music—History and criticism—18th
　　century
　　Music—Philosophy and aesthetics
　　Style, Musical
Classicists *(Direct)* *(PA83-85)*
　　Here are entered works on scholars spe-
　　cializing in the study of Greek and
　　Latin cultures.
　x Hellenists
　　Latinists
　xx Classical philology
　　Scholars
Classics, Anonymous (Cataloging)
　See Cataloging of anonymous classics
Classification
　sa Classification of sciences
　　Information storage and retrieval
　　systems
　　subdivision Classification *under names*
　　of special subjects, e.g. Botany—
　　Classification; Language and
　　languages—Classification; Stars—
　　Classification
　x Knowledge, Classification of
—Archives
　x Archives—Classification
—Books *(Z696-7)*
　　Subdivided by subject, *e.g.* Classifica-
　　tion—Books—Agriculture; Classifi-
　　cation—Books—Belgium.
　sa Catalogs, Classified
　　Classification, BBK
　　Classification, Bibliographic
　　Classification, Colon
　　Classification, Decimal
　　Classification, Dewey decimal
　　Classification, Expansive
　　Classification, Faceted
　　Classification, Library of Congress
　　Classification, Universal decimal
　　Reclassification (Libraries)
　x Libraries—Arrangement of books on
　　shelves
　　Libraries—Classification
　　Library classification
　xx Bibliography
　　Books
　　Books and reading
　　Cataloging
　　Catalogs, Classified
　　Documentation
　　Library science
　　Processing (Libraries)
　　Subject cataloging
　　Subject headings
——Aeronautics
　　sa Classification—Books—Space
　　　flight
　　xx Aeronautics
——Agriculture
　　Note under Classification—Books
——Aluminum
　　xx Aluminum
　　　Classification—Books—Metallurgy
——Atomic energy
　　xx Atomic energy
——Biology
　　xx Biology
——Botany
　　xx Botany—Classification
——City planning

——Cities and towns—Planning
——Copying processes
　　xx Copying processes
——Culture
　　xx Culture
——Education
　　xx Education
——Engineering
　　xx Engineering
——Geography
　　xx Geography
——Geology
　　xx Geology
——Hydrology
　　xx Hydrology
——Industrial management
　　xx Industrial management
——Law
　　xx Law—Classification
——Library science
　　xx Library science
——Materials
　　xx Materials
——Medicine
　　xx Medicine
——Metal-work
　　xx Metal-work
——Metallurgy
　　sa Classification—Books—Aluminum
　　xx Metallurgy
——Meteorology
　　xx Meteorology
——Microscope and microscopy
　　xx Microscope and microscopy
——Military art and science
　　xx Military art and science
——Municipal government
　　xx Municipal government
——Natural history
　　xx Natural history—Classification
——Naval art and science
　　xx Naval art and science
——Paleontology
　　xx Paleontology
——Physics
　　xx Physics
——Physiology
　　xx Physiology
——Railroads
　　xx Railroads
——Sewage disposal
　　xx Sewage disposal
——Space flight
　　xx Classification—Books—
　　　Aeronautics
　　　Space flight
——Technology
　　xx Industrial arts
　　　Technology
——Telecommunication
　　xx Telecommunication
——Terminology
——Therapeutics
　　xx Therapeutics
——Zoology
　　xx Zoology—Classification

GEOGRAPHIC SUBDIVISIONS

——Belgium
　　Note under Classification—Books
—Botany
　　See Botany—Classification
—Civil law
　　See Civil law—Classification
—Correspondence *(Business, HF5736)*
—Diseases
　　See Nosology
—Drawings *(Z697.D)*

　x Drawings—Classification
—International law
　　See International law—Classification
—Law
　　See Law—Classification
—Manuscripts *(Z697.M; Catalogs, Z6621)*
　x Manuscripts—Classification
—Maps *(Z697.M)*
　x Maps—Classification
—Minerals
　　See Mineralogy—Classification
—Moving-pictures
　　Example under Moving-pictures
—Music *(ML111)*
　x Music—Classification
—Natural history
　　See Natural history—Classification
—Phonorecords *(Z697.P)*
　x Phonorecords—Classification
—Phonotapes
　x Phonotapes—Classification
—Photographs *(Z697.P)*
　sa Classification—Slides (Photography)
　x Photographs—Classification
—Pictures
　x Pictures—Classification
—Plants
　　See Botany—Classification
—Programmed instruction
—Religions
　　See Religions—Classification
—Roman law
　　See Roman law—Classification
—Slides (Photography)
　　Subdivided by subject, *e.g.* Classifica-
　　tion—Slides (Photography)—Ar-
　　chitecture.
　x Slides (Photography)—Classification
　xx Classification—Photographs
　　Slides (Photography)
——Architecture
　　Note under Classification—Slides
　　　(Photography)
——Transportation
—Stars
　　See Stars—Classification
—Zoology
　　See Zoology—Classification
Classification, Analytico-synthetic
　See Classification, Faceted
Classification, BBK
　x BBK classification
　　Classification,
　　Bibliothecal-bibliographical
　xx Classification—Books
Classification, Bibliographic *(Z696.B6-639)*
　x Bibliographic classification
　　Bliss classification
　xx Classification—Books
Classification, Bibliothecal-bibliographical
　See Classification, BBK
Classification, Colon
　x Colon classification
　xx Classification—Books
　　Classification, Faceted
Classification, Décasépel
　x Décasépel classification
　xx Documentation
Classification, Decimal *(Z696)*
　sa Classification, Dewey decimal
　　Classification, Universal decimal
　x Decimal classification
　xx Classification—Books
Classification, Dewey decimal
　x Dewey decimal classification
　xx Classification—Books
　　Classification, Decimal
—Programmed instruction

357

Classification, Expansive *(Z696)*
  x Cutter classification
    Expansive classification
  xx Classification—Books
Classification, Faceted
  sa Classification, Colon
  x Analytico-synthetic classification
    Classification, Analytico-synthetic
    Faceted classification
  xx Classification—Books
Classification, Library of Congress *(Z696)*
  x Library of Congress classification
  xx Classification—Books
  — Programmed instruction
Classification, Primitive *(GN470)*
    Here are entered works on the systematic
    division of the universe into groups,
    classes, or families by primitive peo-
    ples.
  x Folk classification
    Popular classification
    Primitive classification
  xx Philosophy, Primitive
Classification, Universal decimal
  x Universal decimal classification
  xx Classification—Books
    Classification, Decimal
  — Programmed instruction
Classification (Conflict of laws)
  x Characterization (Conflict of laws)
    Qualification (Conflict of laws)
  xx Conflict of laws
    Law—Classification
Classification (Psychology)
  See Categorization (Psychology)
Classification of crimes *(Direct)*
  x Crimes, Classification of
    Offenses, Classification of
  xx Criminal law
Classification of land
  See Land—Classification
Classification of risks
  See Insurance, Fire—Classification of risks
Classification of school children
  See Ability grouping in education
Classification of sciences *(Q177;
    Methodology, BD240-241)*
  sa Numerical taxonomy
  x Knowledge, Classification of
    Science—Classification
    Sciences, Classification of
  xx Classification
    Methodology
    Science—Methodology
  — Juvenile literature
Classification theory (Statistics)
  See Discriminant analysis
Classification yards
  See Railroads—Yards
Classified advertising
  See Advertising, Classified
Classified catalogs
  See Catalogs, Classified
Classified defense information
  See Defense information, Classified
Classified documents
  See Security classification (Government
    documents)
Classified information
  See Security classification (Government
    documents)
Classroom management *(LB3011)*
  xx School discipline
    School management and organization
    Teaching
Classroom observation
  See Observation (Educational method)

Classroom recitation
  See Recitation (Education)
Classroom simulators *(LB1731)*
  xx Education—Simulation methods
    Student teaching
    Synthetic training devices
Classroom utilization
  x Space utilization (Education)
  xx Universities and colleges—Buildings
Classrooms, Windowless
  See Windowless classrooms
Clathrate compounds
  x Cage inclusion compounds
    Clathrate inclusion compounds
    Clathrates
  xx Complex compounds
    Molecular sieves
Clathrate inclusion compounds
  See Clathrate compounds
Clathrates
  See Clathrate compounds
Clatset Indians
  See Makah Indians
Clauses
  See Grammar, Comparative and general—
    Clauses
    subdivision Clauses *under names of
      languages and groups of languages*
Claustrophobia
  xx Fear
Clausula
  See Cadence (Music)
Clausula rebus sic stantibus
  See Rebus sic stantibus clause
Clavacin *(RD96.C)*
  xx Antiseptics
Clavecin
  See Harpsichord
Clavicembalo
  See Harpsichord
Clavichord *(ML651; Tuning, MT165)*
  xx Piano
  — Instruction and study *(MT252)*
Clavichord makers *(ML651)*
  xx Musical instruments—Makers
Clavichord music *(M20-39)*
  sa Sonatas (Clavichord)
    Suites (Clavichord)
  xx Piano music
  — History and criticism *(ML700-742)*
Clavichord music, Arranged *(M32.8-38.5)*
Clavichord music (4 hands) *(M200-204;
    M207-211)*
  xx Piano music (4 hands)
Clavicle *(QL821; QM101)*
  sa Shoulder girdle
  x Collarbone
  Example under Skeleton
  — Abnormities and deformities *(RD684)*
  — Fracture *(RD101)*
  — Surgery
Clavicylinder *(ML1055)*
  x Euphonium (Chladni's)
Clavioline *(ML1092)*
  xx Musical instruments, Electronic
Clavioline music *(M175.C54)*
  sa Septets (Piano, guitar, clavioline,
    musical saw, percussion, vibraphone,
    xylophone)
Claviorganum *(ML651)*
  xx Harpsichord
    Organ
Claviorganum music *(M6-13)*
  xx Harpsichord music
    Organ music
Claws
  See Nails (Anatomy)

Clay *(Indirect) (Geology, QE471; Mineral
    resources, TN941-3; Technology,
    TP811)*
  sa Agglomeration
    Argillite
    Bricks
    Ceramics
    Fire-clay
    Illite
    Kaolin
    Marl
    Modeling
    Montmorillonite
    Palygorskite
    Particles
    Pipe, Clay
  xx Aluminum silicates
    Bricks
    Sediments (Geology)
    Soils
  Note under Ceramic materials
  — Analysis
    x Clay minerals—Analysis
  — Laboratory manuals *(TP815)*
  — Moisture
  — — Mathematical models
  — Testing
  — Therapeutic use *(RM737)*
Clay industries *(Direct) (Economics,
    HD9590-9600; Mineral resources,
    TN941.3; Technology, TP785-842)*
  sa Brick trade
    Bricks
    Pottery
    Tiles
    Wages—Clay industries
  xx Ceramic industries
  Example under Chemistry, Technical
  — Accidents
  — Drying
  — Equipment and supplies
  — Juvenile literature
  — Safety measures
  — Tariff
    See Tariff on clay products
Clay minerals *(Indirect)*
  sa names of individual clay minerals, e.g.
    Kaolinite; Vermiculite
  x Minerals, Clay
  Example under Silicate minerals
  — Analysis
    See Clay—Analysis
  — Nomenclature
Clay modeling
  See Modeling
Clay pipe
  See Pipe, Clay
Clay tablets
  sa Cuneiform inscriptions
  xx Cuneiform inscriptions
Clay tobacco-pipes *(Direct)*
  xx Tobacco-pipes
Clay tobacco-pipes, French, [etc.] *(Direct)*
  x French [etc.] clay tobacco-pipes
Clayoquot Indians *(E99.C83)*
  x Claiakwat Indians
    Ilaoquatsh Indians
    Klahoquaht Indians
    Tlaoquatsh Indians
  xx Indians of North America
    Nootka Indians
Clayton-Bulwer treaty, 1850 *(F1438)*
Clean and unclean
  See Purity, Ritual
Clean rooms *(TH7694)*
  sa Laminar flow clean rooms
  x Clean work stations
    Factories—Clean rooms

Rooms, Clean
White rooms
  xx Contamination (Technology)
Dust—Removal
Environmental engineering (Buildings)
Factories—Air conditioning
Factories—Heating and ventilation
— Microbiology
Clean speech
  xx Conduct of life
Clean work stations
  See Clean rooms
Cleaning   *(TP895; TP932; Garments, TP909)*
  sa Bleaching
Cleaning compounds
Dry cleaning
Dry-cleaning machines
Dyes and dyeing
House cleaning
Laundry
Metal cleaning
Mops and mopsticks
Scouring compounds
Soap
Spotting (Cleaning)
Street cleaning
Ultrasonic cleaning
Vacuum cleaning
Washing powders
  subdivision Cleaning *under subjects,*
    e.g. Cotton—Cleaning; Tank-vessels
    —Cleaning
  xx Contamination (Technology)
Cleaning and dyeing industry   *(Direct)*
    (Garment cleaning, TP932; Garment
    dyeing, TP909)
  sa Dry cleaning
Rug cleaning
Strikes and lockouts—Cleaning and
    dyeing industry
Wages—Cleaning and dyeing industry
  x Cleaning industry
  xx Dry cleaning
Dyes and dyeing
— Accounting
— Juvenile literature
— Law and legislation   *(Direct)*
— Public opinion
— Safety measures
Cleaning compounds   *(TP932)*
  sa Detergents, Synthetic
Paint removers
Scouring compounds
Soap
Washing powders
  x Cleaning preparations
Cleansers (Compounds)
  xx Chemistry, Technical
Cleaning
Soap
— Analysis
— Fires and fire prevention
— Labeling   *(Direct)*
— Packaging
— Patents
— Physiological effect
— Testing
Cleaning industry
  See Cleaning and dyeing industry
Cleaning machinery and appliances   *(TP932)*
  sa Dry-cleaning machines
Drying apparatus—Textile fabrics
Dust—Removal
Exhaust systems
  xx Contamination (Technology)
Dust—Removal
Home economics

Cleaning preparations
  See Cleaning compounds
Cleanliness
  See Baths
    Hygiene
    Sanitation
Cleanliness, Ritual
  See Purity, Ritual
Cleansers
  See Washing powders
Cleansers (Compounds)
  See Cleaning compounds
Cleansing of the leper (Miracle)
Cleansing of the ten lepers (Miracle)
  See Healing of the ten lepers (Miracle)
Clear air turbulence   *(QC880)*
  xx Atmosphere, Upper
    Atmospheric turbulence
    Jet stream
    Vertical wind shear
Clear-cutting   *(Indirect)*
  sa Cut-over lands
  x Clearcutting
    Deforestation
    Forest clearcutting
    Timber clearcutting
  xx Clearing of land
    Forest management
    Lumbering
Clearance sales
  See Special sales
Clearances (Electric railroads)
  See Electric railroads—Clearances
Clearcutting
  See Clear-cutting
Clearing, International
  See International clearing
Clearing agreements
  See International clearing
Clearing factor
  See Lipoprotein lipase
Clearing-house
  See Clearinghouse
Clearing of land   *(Indirect)   (S607)*
    Here are entered works on the removal of
    timber, bushes, etc. Works on general
    reclamation and on drainage and irri-
    gation are entered under Reclamation
    of land.
  sa Clear-cutting
    Explosives in agriculture
    Shifting cultivation
  x Land clearing
  xx Agriculture
    Cut-over lands
    Land
    Reclamation of land
    Waste lands
Clearing of securities   *(Direct)*
  x Clearing of stocks
    Securities, Clearing of
    Stock clearing
  xx Clearinghouse
    Securities
    Stocks
Clearing of stocks
  See Clearing of securities
Clearinghouse
  sa Clearing of securities
    individual clearinghouses
  x Clearing-house
  xx Banks and banking
    Checks
Cleavage (Crystallography)
  See subdivision Cleavage *under names of*
    crystals, e.g. Mica crystals—Cleavage
Cleavage of rocks
  See Rocks—Cleavage

Clebsch-Gordan coefficients
  sa Racah coefficients
  xx Racah coefficients
Clebsch-Gordon coefficients
  x C-coefficient
    Coefficients, Clebsch-Gordan
    Vector-coupling coefficient
    Wigner coefficient
  xx Angular momentum (Nuclear physics)
    Quantum theory
    Vector analysis
Cleft lip
  See Harelip
Cleft palate
  x Palate, Cleft
— Psychological aspects
  xx Sick—Psychology
Cleistogamy
  xx Fertilization of plants
    Flowers
Clematis   *(Botany, QK495.C62; Culture,*
    SB413.C6)
Clemmensen reaction
  See Clemmensen reduction
Clemmensen reduction
  x Clemmensen reaction
  xx Reduction, Chemical
Cleptomania
  See Kleptomania
Clergy   *(Indirect)   (BV659-685)*
  sa Benefices, Ecclesiastical
    Bishops
    Canons, Cathedral, collegiate, etc.
    Celibacy
    Chaplains
    City clergy
    Clericalism
    Confessors
    Confidential communications—Clergy
    Counseling for clergy
    Deacons
    Deans, Cathedral and collegiate
    Directors of religious education
    Elders (Church officers)
    Ex-clergy
    Fees, Ecclesiastical
    Minor canons, Cathedral, collegiate,
      etc.
    Monasticism and religious orders
    Ordination
    Pastoral theology
    Patronage, Ecclesiastical
    Priests
    Privileges and immunities, Ecclesiastical
    Rabbis
    Rural clergy
    Spiritual directors
    Theologians
    Tonsure
    Vicars, Parochial
    Vows
  subdivision Clergy *under church*
    denominations, e.g. Catholic Church
    —Clergy; Church of England—
    Clergy
  x Clergy—Major orders
    Major orders
    Ministers of the gospel
    Orders, Major
    Pastors
    Rectors
  xx Christian biography
    Church polity
    Pastoral theology
    Priests
    Theology, Practical
— Anecdotes, facetiae, satire, etc.

Clergy *(Indirect)* *(BV659-685)*
(Continued)
— Appointment, call, and election
    (BV4012)
    sa Missionaries—Appointment, call,
      and election
      Vocation (in religious orders,
        congregations, etc.)
      subdivision Clergy—Appointment,
        call, and election *under church*
        denominations, e.g. Catholic
        Church—Clergy—Appointment,
        call, and election
    x Clergy—Vocation
      Religion as a profession
    xx Vocation, Ecclesiastical
— — Middle Ages
— Autographs
— Biblical teaching
— Caricatures and cartoons
— Conferences
    See Clergy conferences
— Confidential communications
    See Confidential communications—
      Clergy
— Correspondence, reminiscences, etc.
    sa subdivision Clergy—Correspondence,
      reminiscences, etc. *under*
      particular denominations, e.g.
      Catholic Church—Clergy—
      Correspondence, reminiscences,
      etc.
— Costume
    Here are entered works on the cos-
    tume worn by the clergy in daily life
    and on the street. Works on the cos-
    tume worn at liturgical functions
    are entered under the heading
    Church vestments.
    sa Catholic Church—Clergy—
      Deprivation of the clerical garb
      Church vestments
      Monasticism and religious orders—
        Habit
    x Clerical costume
      Clerical dress
      Clerical habit
      Costume, Clerical
      Costume, Ecclesiastical
      Dress, Clerical
      Dress, Ecclesiastical
      Ecclesiastical costume
      Ecclesiastical dress
      Ecclesiastical habit
      Habit, Clerical
      Habit, Ecclesiastical
    xx Church vestments
      Monasticism and religious orders—
        Habit
— Deposition
    sa Catholic Church—Clergy—
      Deposition
— Education
    See Clergy, Training of
      Theological seminaries
— Etiquette *(BV4012)*
    sa Church etiquette
    x Clerical etiquette
      Etiquette, Clerical
    xx Church etiquette
— Families
    See Clergymen's families
— Finance, Personal *(BV4397)*
    x Clergy—Personal finance
      Personal finance for clergymen
    xx Finance, Personal
— Installation
    See Installation (Clergy)
— Language (New words, slang, etc.)

— Libraries
    See Libraries, Private
— Major orders
    See Bishops
      Clergy
— Minor orders
    sa Altar boys
— Office
    x Christian ministry
      Ecclesiastical office
      Holy orders
      Ministry
      Office, Ecclesiastical
      Sacred ministry
— Personal finance
    See Clergy—Finance, Personal
— Political activity *(BV4327)*
    xx Christianity and politics
      Politics, Practical
— Post-ordination training *(BV4165)*
    x Post-ordination training
    xx Clergy, Training of
      Theology—Study and teaching
— Prayer-books and devotions
— — English, [French, German, etc.]
— Pretheological education
    See Pretheological education
— Psychology
    xx Psychology, Religious
— Public relations
    See Public relations—Clergy
— Religious life
    sa Retreats for clergy
      Spiritual direction
— Residence
    sa subdivision Residence *under special*
      classes of clergymen, e.g. Bishops
      —Residence
    x Residence, Clerical
— Retirement *(BV4382)*
    xx Clergy—Salaries, pensions, etc.
    Example under Retirement
— Salaries, pensions, etc. *(BV4380-4382;*
    Catholic, BX1950)
    sa Benefices, Ecclesiastical
      Clergy—Retirement
      subdivision Clergy—Salaries,
        pensions, etc. *under church*
        denominations
    x Ecclesiastical pensions
      Pensions, Ecclesiastical
    xx Benefices, Ecclesiastical
      Church finance
— Taxation *(Direct)*
— Vocation
    See Clergy—Appointment, call, and
      election

GEOGRAPHIC SUBDIVISIONS

— England
    xx Church of England—Clergy
Clergy, City
    See City clergy
Clergy, Country
    See Rural clergy
Clergy, Indigenous
    See Native clergy
Clergy, Itinerant
    See Itinerancy (Church polity)
Clergy, Loyalist
    See Church of England in America—
      Clergy, Loyalist
Clergy, Native
    See Native clergy
Clergy, Negro
    See Negro clergy
Clergy, Privilege of
    See Privilegium fori

Clergy, Rating of
    sa subdivision Clergy, Rating of *under*
      church denominations, e.g.
      Methodist Church—Clergy, Rating
      of
    x Clergymen, Rating of
      Efficiency rating
      Rating of clergymen
      Service rating
    xx Ability—Testing
Clergy, Rural
    See Rural clergy
Clergy, Training of *(BV4019-4160)*
    sa Clergy—Post-ordination training
      Seminary extension
      Theology—Study and teaching
      subdivision Clergy, Training of *under*
        church denominations, e.g. Catholic
        Church—Clergy, Training of
    x Clergy—Education
      Training of clergymen
    xx Theology—Study and teaching
Clergy, Urban
    See City clergy
Clergy (Canon law) *(BX1939.C665)*
    sa Catholic Church—Clergy—Deprivation
      of the clerical garb
      Excardination (Canon law)
      Incardination (Canon law)
      Irregularities (Canon law)
      Parishes (Canon law)
      Profession of faith (Canon law)
      Vicars, Parochial (Canon law)
    x Priests (Canon law)
    xx Catholic Church—Clergy
Clergy (Canon law, Orthodox Eastern)
Clergy conferences
    x Clergy—Conferences
      Clerical conferences
      Conferences
      Pastoral conferences
    xx Councils and synods
Clergy conferences (Canon law)
    (BX1939.C69)
Clergy dropouts
    See Ex-clergy
Clergy in literature *(English literature,*
    PR151.C7; German literature,
    PT151.C7)
    sa Clergymen as authors
    x Priests in literature
    xx Characters and characteristics in
      literature
Clergy in moving-pictures
    xx Moving-pictures
Clergymen, Rating of
    See Clergy, Rating of
Clergymen as authors *(PN171.C; PR120.C;*
    etc.)
    x Ministers as authors
      Ministers as writers
      Priests as authors
      Priests as writers
    xx Clergy in literature
Clergymen's families *(BV4396)*
    sa Clergymen's wives
    x Clergy—Families
    xx Clergymen's wives
Clergymen's wives *(BV4395)*
    sa Chaplains, Military—Wives
      Clergymen's families
    xx Clergymen's families
      Wives
      Women in church work
— Religious life
Clerical ability and aptitude tests
    x Clerical tests
      Clerks—Ability testing

xx Ability—Testing
Clerical celibacy
   See Celibacy
Clerical conferences
   See Clergy conferences
Clerical costume
   See Clergy—Costume
Clerical dress
   See Clergy—Costume
Clerical employees
   See Clerks
Clerical etiquette
   See Clergy—Etiquette
Clerical habit
   See Clergy—Costume
Clerical medicine
   See Pastoral medicine
Clerical occupations
   x Clerks—Vocational guidance
   xx Clerks
Clerical psychology
   See Pastoral psychology
Clerical tests
   See Clerical ability and aptitude tests
Clericalism
   xx Clergy
      Priests
Clerk (The word)
Clerkenwell Riot, 1833
   See London—Riot, 1833
"Clerkly" style writing
   See Chinese language—Writing, Li style
Clerks *(Direct)* *(HF5501; Aid to,*
      HV3165-3173; Mercantile clerks,
      HD8039.M4)
   sa Bank employees
      Clerical occupations
      Clerks (Retail trade)
      Office practice
      Receptionists
      Trade-unions—Clerks
   x Clerical employees
      Commercial employees
      Employees, Clerical
      Office employees
      White collar workers
   xx Commercial law
      Office practice
   — Ability testing
      See Clerical ability and aptitude tests
   — Anecdotes, facetiae, satire, etc.
   — Collective bargaining
      See Collective bargaining—Clerks
   — Collective labor agreements
      See Collective labor agreements—
         Clerks
   — Diseases and hygiene
   — Job descriptions
   — Salaries, pensions, etc. *(HF5549)*
      x Wages—Clerks
   — Vocational guidance
      See Clerical occupations
Clerks (Retail trade) *(Direct)*
   Here are entered works on sales personnel in retail establishments, their work,
   employment conditions and legal
   status. Works on the technique of
   salesmanship and the occupation of
   salesman in general are entered under
   the heading Salesmen and salesmanship.
   sa Drugstore employees
      Salesmen and salesmanship
      Service shopping
      Strikes and lockouts—Retail trade
      Trade-unions—Clerks (Retail trade)
      Wages—Clerks (Retail trade)
   x Clerks (Salesmen)

      Retail clerks
      Sales clerks
      Stores, Retail—Employees
   xx Clerks
      Salesmen and salesmanship
   Note under Salesmen and salesmanship
   — Juvenile literature
   — Programmed instruction
   — Vocational guidance
Clerks (Salesmen)
   See Clerks (Retail trade)
Clerks of court *(Direct)*
   x Court clerks
      Justices' clerks
      Prothonotaries
   xx Courts—Officials and employees
   — Correspondence, reminiscences, etc.
Clerks of the counties (Great Britain)
   sa Clerks of the peace (Great Britain)
   x Clerks of the county councils
      County clerks (Great Britain)
   xx Clerks of the peace (Great Britain)
Clerks of the county councils
   See Clerks of the counties (Great Britain)
Clerks of the peace (Great Britain)
   sa Clerks of the counties
   xx Clerks of the counties (Great Britain)
Clermont, Council of, 1095 *(First Crusade,*
      D161)
   x Council of Clermont, 1095
Clesian tablet
   x Tablet, Clesian
      Tavola clesiana
Cleveland
   — History
   — — Civil War, 1861-1865
   — Riot, 1968
Client-centered counseling
   See Client-centered psychotherapy
Client-centered psychotherapy *(RC481)*
   x Client-centered counseling
      Client-centered therapy
      Counseling, Client-centered
      Counseling, Nondirective
      Nondirective counseling
      Nondirective psychotherapy
      Nondirective therapy
      Rogerian psychotherapy
      Therapy, Client-centered
      Therapy, Nondirective
   xx Psychotherapy
Client-centered therapy
   See Client-centered psychotherapy
Clientela
   See Patron and client
Cliff-dwellers *(E99.P9)*
   xx Indians of North America
      Pueblo Indians
Cliff-dwellings *(Indirect)* *(America, E61;*
      Southwest, E78.S7)
   xx Archaeology
      Dwellings
      Pueblo Indians—Antiquities
      Pueblos
   — Pictorial works
Clifford algebras
   x Algebras, Clifford
   xx Algebras, Linear
Climacteric
   sa Menopause
   x Change of life in men
      Change of life in women
   xx Menopause
Climate
   See Climatology
      subdivision Climate *under names of*
      countries, cities, etc.

Climate, Influence of
   See Architecture and climate
      Man—Influence of climate
Climate and architecture
   See Architecture and climate
Climate and soils
   See Soils and climate
Climatic changes *(Indirect)* *(QC981)*
   sa Paleoclimatology
   x Climatic fluctuations
   xx Climatology
Climatic classification
   sa Moisture index
   xx Climatology
Climatic factors
   See subdivision Climatic factors *under*
      subjects, e.g. Air conditioning—
      Climatic factors; Cooling towers—
      Climatic factors
Climatic fluctuations
   See Climatic changes
Climatic geomorphology *(Indirect)*
   xx Climatology
      Geomorphology
Climatological maps
   See Climatology—Charts, diagrams, etc.
Climatology *(QC981-999)*
   sa Architecture and climate
      Atmospheric circulation
      Atmospheric pressure
      Atmospheric temperature
      Bioclimatology
      Climatic changes
      Climatic classification
      Climatic geomorphology
      Dendrochronology
      Evaporation (Meteorology)
      Forest influences
      Man—Influence of climate
      Mesoclimatology
      Meteorology
      Microclimatology
      Numerical weather forecasting
      Paleoclimatology
      Rain and rainfall
      Seasons
      Soils and climate
      Statistical weather forecasting
      Synoptic climatology
      Temperature inversions
      Urban climatology
      Vegetation and climate
      Weather
      World Weather Watch
   subdivision Climate *under names of*
      countries, cities, etc., e.g. United
      States—Climate; Colorado—Climate;
      also subdivision Climatic factors
      under subjects, e.g. Air conditioning
      —Climatic factors; Cooling towers—
      Climatic factors
   x Climate
   xx Earth
      Earth sciences
      Meteorology
      Physical geography
      Weather
   — Charts, diagrams, etc.
      x Climatological maps
         Maps, Climatological
   — Computer programs *(QC981)*
   — Juvenile literature
   — Mathematical models
   — Statistical methods
   — Tables, etc.
Climatology, Agricultural
   See Crops and climate

Climatology, Medical   (RA791-954)
  sa Altitude, Influence of
    Health resorts, watering-places, etc.
    Hygiene
    Man—Influence of climate
    Medical geography
    Open-air treatment
    Sea air
    Seasonal variations (Diseases)
    Solar radiation—Physiological effect
    Summer diseases
    Tropics—Diseases and hygiene ·
  x Medical climatology
  xx Bioclimatology
    Hygiene
    Man—Influence of climate
    Medical geography
    Medicine
    Therapeutics, Physiological
Climatology, Phenological
  See Phenology
Climb and bank indicators
  See Artificial horizons (Aeronautical
    instruments)
Climbing plants   (Botany, QK773; Culture,
    SB427)
  sa Climbing roses
    Kudzu
    Ornamental climbing plants
  x Vines
  xx Botany
    Gardening
    Plants
    Woody plants
  Example under Floriculture
Climbing roses   (SB411)
  xx Climbing plants
    Roses
Clinic managers
  xx Clinics
    Group medical practice
Clinical assistants
  See Physicians' assistants
Clinical chemistry
  See Chemistry, Clinical
Clinical endocrinology
  sa Laurence-Moon-Biedl syndrome
    Pediatric endocrinology
  xx Endocrinology
Clinical enzymology
  x Enzymology, Clinical
  xx Enzymes
    Medicine, Clinical
Clinical genetics
  See Medical genetics
Clinical laboratory technicians
  See Medical technologists
Clinical medicine
  See Medicine, Clinical
Clinical parasitology
  See Medical parasitology
Clinical pastoral training
  See Pastoral psychology—Study and
    teaching
Clinical physiology
  See Physiology, Pathological
Clinical psychology
  sa Four picture test
    Interns (Clinical psychology)
    Minnesota multiphasic personality
      inventory
    Neuroses—Diagnosis
    Photographs—Psychological aspects
    Thematic apperception test
  x Diagnostic psychological testing
    Psychology, Clinical
  xx Mental tests
    Nervous system—Diseases—Diagnosis

Personality, Disorders of
    Psychiatry
    Psychology, Applied
    Psychology, Pathological
Clinical psychology as a profession
Clinical radiology
  See Radiology, Medical
Clinical records
  See Medical records
Clinical thermometers
  See Thermometers and thermometry,
    Medical
Clinics   (Direct)
    Here are entered works dealing with insti-
    tutions for treatment of non-resident
    patients.
  sa Birth control clinics
    Chiropractic clinics
    Clinic managers
    Dental clinics
    Group medical practice
    Narcotic clinics
    Psychiatric clinics
    Speech clinics
  x Medical clinics
  xx Community health services
    Group medical practice
    Health facilities
    Hospitals
    Medical centers
    Medicine—Practice
  — Design and construction
  — Juvenile literature
Clinics, Dental
  See Dental clinics
Clinker brick   (TP832.C5)
  xx Bricks
    Cement clinkers
Clinometer   (TA579)
Clinoptilolite   (Indirect)
  xx Zeolites
Clinostat   (QK771)
Clinton, Iowa
  — Flood, 1965
Clintonite
Clipper-ships   (VK; VM)
  xx Merchant ships
    Ships
  — Juvenile literature
Clipping bureaus   (AG500-551)
  x Newspaper clipping bureaus
  xx Clippings (Books, newspapers, etc.)
Clipping of dogs
  See Dog grooming
Clippings (Books, newspapers, etc.)   (Z691;
    Z697.C6)
  sa Clipping bureaus
    Libraries, Package
    Newspaper office libraries
    Vertical files (Libraries)
  x Cuttings
    Newspaper clippings
    Press clippings
  xx Newspaper office libraries
    Newspapers
    Scrap-books
    Vertical files (Libraries)
Clitellata
  See Leeches
    Oligochaeta
Clitoridectomy
  xx Circumcision
    Gynecology, Operative
Cloaca (Zoology)   (QL871)
  sa Rectum
  xx Generative organs
    Genito-urinary organs
    Rectum

Cloaks   (Dressmaking, TT530; Economics,
    HD9940)
  x Capes (Clothing)
  xx Clothing and dress
Clob-e-osh (Game)
  See Belote (Game)
Cloche gardening   (SB127)
  xx Forcing (Plants)
    Gardening
    Horticulture
Clock and watch makers   (Direct) (Art,
    NK7486-7497; Technology,
    TS542-3)
  x Watch makers
  xx Jewelers
  — Legal status, laws, etc.   (Direct)
Clock and watch making   (Direct)
    (Economics, HD9999.C6;
    Technology, TS540-549)
  sa Clocks and watches
  x Watch making
  xx Clocks and watches
  Example under Technology
  — Machinery   (TS546)
  — — Appraisal
    See Clock and watch making—
      Machinery—Valuation
  — — Valuation   (TS546)
    x Clock and watch making—
      Machinery—Appraisal
  — Military aspects
    Example under Industrial mobilization;
      Military policy
  — Quality control   (TS548)
  — Safety measures
  — Vocational guidance
    x Clock and watch making as a
      profession
Clock and watch making as a profession
  See Clock and watch making—Vocational
    guidance
Clock chimes selections
  See Clock music
Clock music
  x Chiming clock selections
    Clock chimes selections
    Music, Clock
  xx Chimes
Clock paradox
  See Time dilatation
Clock radios
  xx Radio—Receivers and reception
Clock-towers
  See Towers
Clocks, Astronomical
  See Astronomical clocks
Clocks, Atomic
  See Atomic clocks
Clocks, Real-time
  See Real-time clocks (Computers)
Clocks and watches   (Direct) (Art,
    NK7480-7499; Economics,
    HD9999.C6; Technology,
    TS540-549)
  sa Astronomical clocks
    Atomic clocks
    Balance cocks
    Calendar watches
    Chronometer
    Clock and watch making
    Time clocks
    Time measurements
    Tower-clocks
    Watch keys
  x Watches
  xx Chronology
    Clock and watch making
    Hall-marks

Horology
House furnishings
Time measurements
— Adjusting
     See Clocks and watches—Repairing
          and adjusting
— Catalogs
— Collectors and collecting
— Drawing
     See Clocks and watches—Drawings
— Drawings
     x Clocks and watches—Drawing
     xx Mechanical drawing
— Escapements *(TS545)*
     x Escapements
— Jewels
     x Upjeweling
— Juvenile literature
— Museums
— Patents
— Poetry
— Prices *(Direct)*
— Private collections *(NK7483)*
— Regulation
     See Clocks and watches—Repairing
          and adjusting
— Repairing and adjusting *(TS547)*
     x Clocks and watches—Adjusting
          Clocks and watches—Regulation
          Watch repairing
     xx Repairing
— — Production standards
— Standards
— Tariff
     See Tariff on clocks
          Tariff on watches
— Testing
— Trade-marks
Clocks and watches, American, ⌈Swiss, etc.⌉
     (Direct)
     x American ⌈Swiss, etc.⌉ clocks and
          watches
Clocks and watches, Electric *(TS547)*
     x Clocks and watches, Electronic
          Electric clocks and watches
          Electronic clocks and watches
     xx Electric apparatus and appliances
          Electronic apparatus and appliances
— Repairing and adjusting
Clocks and watches, Electronic
     See Clocks and watches, Electric
Clocks and watches in art *(N8217.C4)*
     xx Art
Clog-almanacs *(CE89)*
     xx Calendar
Clog-dance music
     xx Dance music
Clog-dancing *(GV1793)*
     sa Tap dancing
     xx Dancing
          Tap dancing
Cloisonné *(NK5010-5015)*
     x Shippo
     xx Art metal-work
          Enamel and enameling
          Pottery
Cloisonné, Byzantine *(Direct)*
     x Byzantine cloisonné
Cloisonné, Chinese, ⌈Japanese, etc.⌉ *(Direct)*
     x Chinese ⌈Japanese, etc.⌉ cloisonné
Cloisters
     See Convents and nunneries
          Enclosure (Monasticism)
          Monasteries
Clonorchiasis *(RC139)*
Clontarf, Battle of, 1014 *(DA932.6)*
Close and open communion *(BV820)*
     sa Intercommunion

x Close communion
     Communion, Close
     Communion, Open
     Mixed communion
     Open communion
     Strict communion
xx Church membership
     Intercommunion
     Lord's Supper
     Sacraments
Close communion
     See Close and open communion
Close corporations *(Direct)*
     sa Family corporations
          Stock purchase agreements (Close
               corporations)
     x Closed corporations
     xx Corporation law
          Corporations
— Appraisal
     See Close corporations—Valuation
— Finance
— Taxation *(Direct)*
— Valuation
     x Close corporations—Appraisal
Close range photography
     See Photography, Close-up
Close rolls
     See Close writs
Close-up photography
     See Photography, Close-up
Close writs
     x Close rolls
Closed Brethren
     See Plymouth Brethren
Closed circuit respiratory systems (Space
     environment)
     See Closed respiratory systems (Space
          environment)
Closed-circuit television *(TK6680)*
     sa Industrial television
          Military television
          Television in education
          Television in police work
     x Television, Closed-circuit
     xx Intercommunication systems
          Microwave communication systems
          Television
          Television in education
Note under Television
— Patents
— Repairing
Closed collections in archives
     See Restricted collections in archives
Closed corporations
     See Close corporations
Closed cycle ecological systems
     See Closed ecological systems
Closed cycle ecological systems (Space
     environment)
     See Closed ecological systems (Space
          environment)
Closed ecological systems
     x Closed cycle ecological systems
          Ecological systems, Closed
     xx Human ecology
**Closed ecological systems (Space
     environment)**
     sa Closed respiratory systems (Space
          environment)
     x Closed cycle ecological systems (Space
          environment)
          Ecological systems, Closed (Space
          environment)
     xx Life support systems (Space
          environment)

**Closed respiratory systems (Space
     environment)**
     sa Artificial atmospheres (Space
          environment)
     x Closed circuit respiratory systems
          (Space environment)
     xx Closed ecological systems (Space
          environment)
          Pressure breathing
          Respiration
Closed road course
     See Racetracks (Automobile racing)
Closed sea (Mare clausum)
     See Freedom of the seas
Closed shelves in libraries
     See Open and closed shelves
Closed shop
     See Open and closed shop
Closed stacks in libraries
     See Open and closed shelves
Closets
     See Clothes closets
          Linen closets
          Water-closets
Closing costs
     See Settlement costs
Clostridium diseases
     sa Botulism
          Gas gangrene
          Tetanus
     x Clostridium infections
     xx Bacterial diseases
Clostridium infections
     See Clostridium diseases
Closure (Parliamentary practice)
     See Cloture
Closure operators
     x Operators, Closure
     xx Lattice theory
Cloth
     See Inflammable textiles
          Textile industry and fabrics
Cloth, Glass
     See Glass cloth
Cloth of gold
     x Gold, Cloth of
Cloth of Gold, Field of, 1520
     See Field of Cloth of Gold, 1520
Cloth of silver
     x Silver, Cloth of
Clothes closets
     x Closets
     xx Dwellings
          Storage in the home
Clothes designers
     See Costume designers
Clothes driers
     See Clothes dryers
Clothes dryers
     x Clothes driers
          Dryers, Clothes
     xx Drying apparatus
Clothes moths
     xx Moths
Clothespins
     xx Laundry
Clothiers
     See Clothing trade
Clothing
     See Clothing and dress
Clothing, Cold weather
     x Arctic clothing
          Cold weather clothing
     xx Clothing, Protective
          Insulation (Heat)
Clothing, Doll
     See Doll clothes

Clothing, Fur
   See Fur garments
Clothing, Industrial
   See Work clothes
Clothing, Leather
   See Leather garments
Clothing, Men's
   See Men's clothing
Clothing, Protective *(HD7395.C5)*
   sa Clothing, Cold weather
      Clothing, Waterproof
      Pressure suits
      Safety goggles
      Safety hats
      Safety shoes
   x Protective clothing
      Safety clothing
   xx Aircraft survival equipment
      Clothing and dress
      Industrial safety
      Occupations, Dangerous—Safety
        appliances
      Work clothes
  — Standards *(Direct)*
Clothing, Waterproof
   x Waterproof clothing
   xx Clothing, Protective
Clothing and dress *(GT500-2350; Domestic*
    economy, TX340; Ethnology,
    GN418-419; Hygiene, RA779;
    Theory, design, TT507)
   Here are entered works dealing with
   clothing as a covering for the body and
   works on the art of dress. Descriptive
   and historical works on the costumes
   of particular countries, nations, or
   periods are entered under Costume.
   sa Aprons
      Belt toggles
      Belts (Clothing)
      Bloomer costume
      Blouses
      Bodices
      Buttonholes
      Buttons
      Children's clothing
      Cloaks
      Clothing and dress measurements
      Clothing, Protective
      Coats
      Collars
      Corset
      Costume
      Costume design
      Darts (Clothing)
      Décolletage
      Dress accessories
      Dressmaking
      Emergency clothing supply
      Fashion
      Fashion as a profession
      Fashion shows
      Fur garments
      Garment cutting
      Handbags
      Handkerchiefs
      Hats
      Hosiery
      Interfacings (Clothing)
      Jeans (Clothing)
      Leather garments
      Livery
      Men's clothing
      Models, Fashion
      Negroes—Clothing and dress
      Newspapers—Sections, columns, etc.—
        Fashion
      Overalls

      Passementerie
      Pockets
      Raincoats
      Riding habit
      Saris
      Scarves
      Seams (Sewing)
      Shawls
      Skirts
      Sleeves
      Sport clothes
      Stoles (Clothing)
      Sweaters
      Tailoring
      Toilet
      Trousers
      Underwear
      Uniforms
      Vests
      Waists
      Work clothes
   x Clothing
      Dress
      Woman—Dress
   xx Costume
      Fashion
      Manners and customs
      Woman—Health and hygiene
  Note under Costume
  — Care
    sa Clothing and dress—Repairing
      Knit goods—Repairing
    xx Home economics
  — Caricatures and cartoons
  — Cleaning
    See Dry cleaning
      Laundry
  — Hygienic aspects *(Direct)* *(RA779)*
    xx Woman—Health and hygiene
  — Juvenile literature
  — Laws and regulations
    See Sumptuary laws
  — Physiological aspects
    x Physiological aspects of clothing and
      dress
  — Psychology *(GT521)*
    x Psychology of clothing
      Psychology of dress
  — Repairing *(TT720-730)*
    sa Reweaving
    xx Clothing and dress—Care
  — Tariff
    See Tariff on clothing
  — Terminology
Clothing and dress, Primitive
   sa Breechcloths
Clothing and dress in art
   See Costume in art
Clothing and dress in the Bible
   See Biblical costume
Clothing and dress measurements
   x Measurements of women's clothing
      Sizes of women's clothing
   xx Clothing and dress
  — Tables, calculations, etc.
Clothing factories *(Direct)* *(TT498)*
   x Garment factories
   xx Factories
  — Automation
  — Design and construction *(TH4522)*
  — Electric equipment
  — Equipment and supplies
    — Appraisal
      See Clothing factories—Equipment
        and supplies—Valuation
    — Laboratory manuals
    — Valuation *(TT498)*

    x Clothing factories—Equipment
      and supplies—Appraisal
Clothing trade *(Direct)* *(Economics,*
    HD9940; Manufacture, TT490-695)
   sa Fashion as a profession
      Hosiery industry
      Men's furnishing goods
      Salesmen and salesmanship—Clothing
      Shirts, Men's
      Tailoring
      Tailors
      Underwear industry
   x Clothiers
   xx Sweating system
      Tailors
  — Accounting
  — Anecdotes, facetiae, satire, etc.
  — Collective bargaining
    See Collective bargaining—Clothing
      industry
  — Collective labor agreements
    See Collective labor agreements—
      Clothing industry
  — Costs
  — Defense measures
  — Finance
  — Hygienic aspects
  — Job descriptions
    Example under Job descriptions
  — Juvenile literature
  — Labor productivity
  — Management
  — Pictorial works
  — Prices
  — Production standards
  — Quality control
  — Safety measures
  — Seasonal variations
  — Standards *(Direct)*
  — Taxation *(Direct)*
  — Vocational guidance
    xx Clothing workers
Clothing workers *(Direct)*
   sa Clothing trade—Vocational guidance
      Collective bargaining—Clothing
        industry
      Collective labor agreements—Clothing
        industry
      Sweating system
      Tailors
      Trade-unions—Clothing workers
      Wages—Clothing workers
   x Garment workers
   xx Sweating system
  — Diseases and hygiene
Cloture
   x Closure (Parliamentary practice)
      Limitation of debate
   xx Legislative bodies—Freedom of debate
      Parliamentary practice
Cloud caps
   See Cap clouds
Cloud chamber
   x Expansion chamber
      Wilson chamber
      Wilson cloud chamber
   xx Ionization chambers
      Ions
Cloud electrification *(QC921.6.E4)*
   x Electrification of clouds
   xx Atmospheric electricity
      Cloud physics
Cloud-height indicator
   See Ceilometer
Cloud modification
   See Weather control
Cloud physics *(QC921.5)*
   sa Atmospheric nucleation

Cloud electrification
Condensation
Precipitation (Meteorology)
xx Clouds
Cloud seeding
See Rain-making
Clouded leopard *(QL737.C2)*
x Clouded tiger
Felis nebulosa
Neofelis nebulosa
xx Leopards
Clouded tiger
See Clouded leopard
Clouds *(Direct) (QC921-3)*
sa Artificial clouds
Cap clouds
Ceilometer
Cloud physics
Condensation trails
Cumulonimbus
Cumulus
Nephanalysis (Meteorology)
Noctilucent clouds
Photography of clouds
Weather control
xx Meteorology
— Atlases
— Charts, diagrams, etc.
— Juvenile literature
— Photographs
— Photographs from space
xx Meteorological satellites
Example under Space photography
— Pictorial works
Clouds, Magellanic
See Magellanic Clouds
Clouds in art
xx Art
Clouds in literature
Clove *(Indirect)*
Example under Condiments
Clove trade *(Direct)*
Clover *(Indirect) (SB205.C64)*
sa Alsike clover
Berseem
Bur clover
Crimson clover
Dodder
Red clover
Rose clover
Strawberry clover
Subterranean clover
Sweet clover
White clover
xx Forage plants
— Diseases and pests *(SB608.C55)*
sa *names of pests, e.g.* Clover aphids,
Clover-root curculio
— Harvesting
— Identification
— Pictorial works
— Tariff
See Tariff on clover seed
— Varieties
Clover, Crimson
See Crimson clover
Clover, Subterranean
See Subterranean clover
Clover aphids
xx Clover—Diseases and pests
Clover as feed
Clover-leaf weevil
xx Beetles
Clover-root curculio
xx Clover—Diseases and pests
Clover-seed chalcis-fly
Clover-worm
xx Moths

Cloverleaf (Highway engineering)
See Roads—Interchanges and intersections
Clowning
See Clowns
Clowns *(Circus clowns, GV1811; Drama, PN1955)*
sa Comedians
Pierrot
x Clowning
xx Comedians
Entertainers
Fools and jesters
— Juvenile literature
Clowns (in religion, folk-lore, etc.)
x Folk-lore of clowns
Clowns in art
xx Art
Clowns in literature
Cloze procedure
xx Association of ideas
Comprehension
Reading
Club foot
See Clubfoot
Club-house libraries
See Fraternity libraries
Club-houses *(Direct) (NA7910-7970)*
sa Fishing lodges
Hunting lodges
xx Architecture
— Electric equipment
Club-mosses *(QK524.L9)*
x Lycopodium
Clubfoot
x Club foot
Talipes
xx Foot—Abnormities and deformities
Clubroot *(SB733)*
xx Cabbage—Diseases and pests
Clubs *(Political, JF2101; Social, HS2501-3200)*
sa Athletic clubs
Book clubs
Boys—Societies and clubs
Canadian clubs
Girls—Societies and clubs
Political clubs
Riding clubs
Science clubs
Science fiction societies
Social group work
Societies
Woman—Societies and clubs
Working-men's clubs
Working-women's clubs
subdivision Clubs *under names of cities, countries, regions, etc., e.g.* New York (City)—Clubs; *and names of individual clubs, e.g.* Grolier Club, New York; Jacobins
xx Associations, institutions, etc.
Societies
— Accounting *(HF5686.C45)*
— Law and legislation *(Direct)*
xx Corporation law
Unincorporated societies
Clubs, Art
See Art—Societies
Clubs, Burial
See Insurance, Burial
Clubs, Musical
See Musical societies
Clugniacs
See Cluniacs
Cluniac architecture
See Architecture, Cluniac
Cluniac art
See Art, Cluniac

Cluniacs *(BX3460-3470)*
sa Benedictines
x Benedictines, Cluniac
Clugniacs
Cluny, Order of
xx Benedictines
Monasticism and religious orders
— Rules
Cluniacs in England, ⌈**France, Switzerland, etc.**⌉
Cluny, Order of
See Cluniacs
Clupeiformes *(QL637.9.C4)*
sa Anchovies
xx Osteichthyes
Cluster analysis
xx Correlation (Statistics)
Multivariate analysis
— Computer programs
Cluster-pine *(Botany, QK495.P66; Forestry, SD397.P)*
x Star-pine
— Diseases and pests
Cluster set theory
xx Functions
Set theory
Topology
Clustering of particles
See Agglomeration
Coagulation
Clutches (Machinery) *(TJ1074)*
sa Couplings
Magnetic clutches
subdivision Clutches *under subjects, e.g.*
Automobiles—Clutches;
Motor-trucks—Clutches
x Friction clutches
xx Couplings
Gearing
Machinery
— Standards
Cluttering (Speech pathology) *(RC424.5)*
x Agitophasia
Paraphrasia praeceps
Tachyphemia
xx Speech, Disorders of
Clydesdale horse *(SF293.C)*
xx Draft horses
Example under Horse breeds
Clymeniida *(QE807.C65)*
xx Ammonoidea
Cnidae
See Nematocysts
Cnidocysts
See Nematocysts
Co-authorship (Copyright)
See Copyright (Joint tenancy)
Co-eds
See Women college students
Co-heirs *(Direct)*
sa Accretion (Law)
Distribution of decedents' estates
Partition of decedents' estates
x Joint heirs
xx Decedents' estates
Inheritance and succession
Co-ministry
See Group ministry
Co-ownership
See Joint tenancy
Coacervation
xx Chemistry
Coach dogs
See Dalmatian dogs
Coaches
See Carriages and carts
Coaching

Coaches, Truck
    See Campers and coaches, Truck
Coaches (Athletics)
    sa Coaching (Athletics)
        Football coaches
    xx Coaching (Athletics)
    — Certification *(Direct)*
        xx Coaches (Athletics)—Legal status,
            laws, etc.
    — Legal status, laws, etc. *(Direct)*
        sa Coaches (Athletics)—Certification
    — Salaries, pensions, etc.
Coaching *(Indirect) (SF305-7)*
    sa Driving
        Roads
    x Coaches
        Riding
        Stagecoach lines
        Stagecoaches
    xx Cab and omnibus service
        Carriages and carts
        Driving
        Horsemanship
        Locomotion
        Vehicles
    — Time-tables
Coaching (Athletics) *(GV711)*
    sa Baseball coaching
        Baseball managing
        Basketball coaching
        Coaches (Athletics)
        Football coaching
        Hockey coaching
        Moving-pictures in sports
        Soccer coaching
        Track-athletics coaching
    xx Athletics
        Coaches (Athletics)
        College sports
        Physical education and training
        Sports
Coaching in art
Coagulase
    sa Blood—Coagulation
    xx Blood—Coagulation
Coagulation
    sa Agglomeration
        Gelation
        Precipitation (Chemistry)
        Sonic coagulation
    x Clustering of particles
    xx Agglomeration
        Colloids
        Flocculation
        Precipitation (Chemistry)
        Suspensions (Chemistry)
Coagulation, Sonic
    See Sonic coagulation
Coagulation disorders
    See Blood—Coagulation, Disorders of
Coagulation of blood
    See Blood—Coagulation
Coahuila Indians
    See Cahuilla Indians
Coahuila language
    See Cahuilla language
Coahuiltecan languages
    See Coahuilteco language
        Pakawan languages
Coahuilteco language *(PM3681)*
    x Coahuiltecan languages
    xx Pakawan languages
Coal *(Indirect) (Economics, HD9540-9559;*
        Mining, TN800-834)
    sa Anthracite coal
        Bituminous coal
        Briquets (Fuel)
        Cannel coal

Carbonization
    Char
    Coal mines and mining
    Coal-tar industry
    Coaling
    Coaling-stations
    Coke
    Coke industry
    Lignite
    Sapropelites
    x Coal lands
    xx Carbon
        Caustobioliths
        Fuel
        Geology, Economic
        Lignite
— Analysis *(TP325-9)*
    Example under Sampling
— Carbonization
    x Low temperature carbonization of
        coal
    xx Carbonization
        Coal—Testing
        Coke
— — Pilot plants
— Combustion
    See Combustion
— Drying
— Examinations, questions, etc.
— Gasification
    See Coal gasification
— Geology *(Indirect)*
    x Coal geology
    xx Geology
        Geology, Economic
— Grading
— Liquefaction
    See Coal liquefaction
— Maps
— Microbiology
— Moisture
— Optical properties
— Pipe lines
    x Coal slurry pipe lines
    xx Coal—Transportation
— Prices *(Direct)*
— Spectra
— Standards *(Direct)*
— Storage
    Example under reference from Storage
— Sulphur content
    xx Sulphur
— Tables, calculations, etc.
— Taxation *(Direct)*
    x Coal taxation
        Coal trade—Taxation
— Testing *(TP325-9)*
    sa Coal—Carbonization
    xx Coal research
— Thermal properties
— Transportation *(HE595.C6; HE2321.C6)*
    sa Coal—Pipe lines
    x Coal transportation
— — Costs
— Weathering
    See Coal-weathering
Coal, Pulverized *(TP328)*
    sa Briquets (Fuel)
        Fly ash
        Fuel, Colloidal
    x Pulverized coal
Coal-carrying vessels *(VM401)*
    xx Merchant ships
        Ships
Coal-gas
    See Gas
Coal gasification *(Direct) (TP759)*
    x Coal—Gasification

Gasification of coal
    xx Carbonization
        Distillation, Destructive
        Gas manufacture and works
        Gas-producers
    — Water-supply
Coal gasification, Underground *(Direct)*
    (TP759)
    x Gasification of coal, Underground
        Underground gasification of coal
    xx Carbonization
        Coal mines and mining
        Gas manufacture and works
Coal geology
    See Coal—Geology
Coal-handling *(TH4471)*
    xx Bulk solids handling
Coal-handling machinery *(TJ1405)*
    sa Conveying machinery
    xx Conveying machinery
    — Patents
Coal hydrogenation
    See Coal liquefaction
Coal lands
    See Coal
Coal leases *(Direct)*
    xx Mining leases
Coal liquefaction *(Direct)*
    x Coal hydrogenation
        Coal—Liquefaction
        Fischer-Tropsch process
        Liquefaction of coal
    xx Hydrogenation
        Liquid fuels
        Petroleum, Synthetic
    — Patents
    — Water-supply
Coal mine waste
    xx Coal mines and mining
        Factory and trade waste
Coal-miners *(Direct) (HD8039.M62)*
    sa Collective bargaining—Coal mining
        industry
        Collective labor agreements—Coal
            mining industry
        Trade-unions—Coal-miners
        Wages—Coal-miners
        Women coal-miners
    xx Miners
    Example under Labor and laboring classes; *and*
        under reference from Laborers
    — Anecdotes, facetiae, satire, etc.
    — Diseases and hygiene *(Diseases,*
        RC964-5; Hygiene, RA787; Labor
        hygiene, HD7269.M6)
        sa Nystagmus
    — Pensions
    — Personal narratives
    — Pictorial works
Coal mines and mining *(Indirect)*
    (TN800-834)
    sa Barrier pillars
        Coal gasification, Underground
        Coal mine waste
        Radio in mining
        Strikes and lockouts—Coal mining
        headings beginning with the words
        Mine *and* Mining
    xx Coal
    Example under Mines and mineral resources
    — Accidents *(TN311-319)*
        sa Mine explosions
            Mine fires
            names of specific coal mine
            accidents, e.g. Monongah Mines
            Disaster, Monongah, W.Va., 1907
        xx Mine accidents
        Example under Accidents

— Accounting (HF5686.M6)
— Auditing and inspection
— Automation
— Collective bargaining
   See Collective bargaining—Coal
      mining industry
— Collective labor agreements
   See Collective labor agreements—Coal
      mining industry
— Costs
— Dust control
   xx Mine dusts
— Electric equipment
   xx Electricity in mining
— — Reliability
— Electronic equipment
— Equipment and supplies
— — Appraisal
   See Coal mines and mining—
      Equipment and supplies—
      Valuation
— — Corrosion (TN803)
— — Valuation (TN803)
   x Coal mines and mining—
      Equipment and supplies—
      Appraisal
— Explosives (TN803)
   xx Explosives
— Finance
— Fires and fire prevention
— Government ownership (Direct)
   x Government ownership of coal
      mines
   Example under Government ownership
— Job descriptions
— Labor productivity
   Example under Labor productivity
— Law and legislation (Direct)
   xx Mining law
— Management
— Mathematical models
— Patents
   xx Mining engineering—Patents
— Problems, exercises, etc.
— Production standards
— Research
— Safety measures (TN295)
   x Safety measures
   Example under Mine safety; Occupa-
      tions, Dangerous—Safety appli-
      ances
— Safety regulations (Direct)
   Example under Mine safety—Law and
      legislation
— Taxation (Direct)
— Valuation (TN803)
— Vocational guidance
— Water-supply
Coal-mining machinery (TN813-814)
— Hydraulic drive
— Maintenance and repair
— Patents
— Reliability
— Safety measures
— Transmission devices
   x Transmissions, Coal-mining
      machinery
   xx Gearing
      Power transmission
Coal money (Celtic antiquities, DA140;
      Dorset, DA670.D7)
   xx Money, Primitive
Coal-oil
   See Kerosene
      Petroleum
Coal preparation (TN816)
   sa Coal washing
   xx Coal washing

— Problems, exercises, etc.
— Safety measures
— Tables, calculations, etc.
Coal preparation plants (Direct)
   sa Fuel-briquet plants
— Automation
— Electric equipment
— Equipment and supplies
— — Reliability
— Labor productivity (TN816)
— Management
Coal research (Direct)
   sa Coal—Testing
   xx Fuel research
      Research, Industrial
Coal slurry pipe lines
   See Coal—Pipe lines
Coal-tar (TP953)
   xx Bituminous materials
      Tar
— Analysis
— Testing (TP953)
Coal-tar colors (TP914)
   sa Alizarin
      Aniline black
      Cerulein
      Coloring matter
      Dyes and dyeing
      Gallein
      Naphthazarin
      Rose bengal
   x Aniline colors
   xx Coloring matter
      Colors
      Dyes and dyeing
— Physiological effect (QP971)
— Safety measures
— Toxicology (RA1242.C7)
Coal-tar industry (Direct) (HD9660.C6-63)
   xx Coal
      Coke industry
      Petroleum industry and trade
— Automation
— Equipment and supplies
Coal-tar products (TP953)
   sa Distillation, Destructive
      Gas
      Mineral oils
      Oils and fats
      Tar acids
   x Products, Coal-tar
   xx Carbonization
      Distillation, Destructive
      Gas
      Petroleum products
   Example under Chemistry, Technical
— Analysis
— Quality control
— Testing (TP953)
Coal taxation
   See Coal—Taxation
Coal trade (Direct) (HD9540-9559)
   xx Fuel trade
— Accounting (HF5686.C48)
— Finance
— Military aspects
— Records and correspondence
— Tables and ready-reckoners
      (HF5716.C4)
— Taxation
   See Coal—Taxation
Coal transportation
   See Coal—Transportation
Coal washing (TN816)
   sa Coal preparation
   xx Coal preparation
— Mathematical models (TN816)

Coal-weathering (TN817)
   x Coal—Weathering
      Weathering of coal
   xx Weathering
Coaling (International law, JX5244.C5;
      Navigation, VK361)
   xx Coal
Coaling-stations (Indirect) (V240)
   sa Navy-yards and naval stations
   x Bunkering stations
      Stations, Coaling
   xx Coal
      Navies
      Navy-yards and naval stations
Coalition (Social sciences)
   sa Coalition governments
   xx Power (Social sciences)
      Social groups
      Social sciences
Coalition governments (Direct)
   sa Popular fronts
   xx Cabinet system
      Coalition (Social sciences)
      Political parties
      Politics, Practical
Coalport porcelain (NK4399.C)
   x Porcelain, Coalport
Coanda effect
   xx Convex surfaces
      Jets—Fluid dynamics
Coarctation of the aorta
   See Aortic coarctation
Coarse fish control
   See Fish control
Coarseness in literature
   See Vulgarity in literature
Coast artillery
   See Artillery, Coast
Coast changes (Hydraulic engineering,
      TC330-345; Physical geography,
      GB451-460)
   sa Beach erosion
      Scour and fill (Geomorphology)
      Shore-lines
      Shore protection
   x Shore erosion
   xx Beach erosion
      Coasts
      Erosion
      Littoral drift
      Physical geography
      Seashore
      Shore-lines
      Shore protection
   Note under Beach erosion
Coast defenses (UG410-448)
   sa Artillery, Coast
      Bombardment
      Floating batteries
      Mines, Military
      Ordnance, Coast
      subdivision Coast defenses under names
         of countries, e.g. Great Britain—
         Coast defenses
   x Defenses, Coast
      Harbor defenses
      Seacoast defenses
   xx Attack and defense (Military science)
      Fortification
      Military engineering
Coast-guard (Gt. Brit.) (HJ6897; Naval
      science, VG55.G7)
Coast guns
   See Ordnance, Coast
Coast-pilot guides
   See Pilot guides
Coast protection
   See Shore protection

Coast protective works
  See Shore protection
Coast radio stations
  See Marine radio stations
Coastal flora (Indirect) (QK938.C6)
  sa Halophytes
    Marine flora
  x Flora
    Littoral flora
    Seashore flora
    Shore flora
  xx Botany—Ecology
    Coasts
    Marine flora
    Seashore biology
Coastal signals
  See Signals and signaling
Coasters (for drinks)
  xx Beverages
Coasting (GV855)
  sa Tobogganing
  x Bobsledding
    Sledding
  xx Tobogganing
    Winter sports
Coasts (Indirect) (Physical geography,
      GB451-460)
  sa Bays
    Coast changes
    Coastal flora
    Estuaries
    Fjords
    Littoral drift
    Marine caves
    Ocean waves
    Seashore
    Shore protection
    Storm surges
    Terraces (Geology)
    Territorial waters
    Tidal flats
  xx Oceanography
    Seashore
    Shore-lines
    Shore protection
  — Juvenile literature (GB451)
  — Pictorial works
  — Recreational use
    sa Aquatic sports
    xx Aquatic sports
      Outdoor recreation
  — Terminology
Coastwise navigation (Indirect) (United
      States, HE751-3)
    Here are entered works on the movement
      of shipping along the coast and on the
      improvement of such routes by dredg-
      ing or otherwise where the operations
      are not limited to a single harbor.
  sa Coastwise shipping
    Intracoastal waterways
  xx Coastwise shipping
    Hydrography
    Merchant marine
    Navigation
    Shipping
    Transportation
  — Law and legislation (Direct)
    xx Maritime law
Coastwise shipping (Direct)
  sa Coastwise navigation
    Intercoastal shipping
  x Shipping, Coastwise
    Water transportation, Coastal
  xx Coastwise navigation
    Commerce
    Intercoastal shipping
    Merchant marine

Shipping
  Transportation
Notes under Intracoastal waterways; Shipping
  — Law and legislation (Direct)
    xx Commercial law
      Maritime law
  — Rates
Coat, Holy
  See Holy Coat
Coat color of animals
  See Color of animals
Coated fabrics (TS1512)
  sa Waterproofing of fabrics
  x Coated textiles
    Coatings, Textile
    Fabrics, Coated
    Soil-resistant fabrics
    Textile coatings
  xx Coatings
    Protective coatings
    Textile industry and fabrics
Coated paper
  See Paper coatings
Coated textiles
  See Coated fabrics
Coatimundi
  See Coatis
Coating, Electrophoretic
  See Electrophoretic deposition
Coating, Metal
  See Metal coating
Coating, Plastic
  See Plastic coating
Coating compositions
  See Protective coatings
Coating processes (TP156.C57)
  sa Coatings
    Enamel and enameling
    Finishes and finishing
    Laminated materials
    Plating
    Sealing (Technology)
    Spraying
    Waterproofing
  x Surface coating processes
  xx Coatings
    Surfaces (Technology)
Coatings
  sa Cement coating
    Ceramic coating
    Coated fabrics
    Coating processes
    Concrete coatings
    Edible coatings
    Enamel and enameling
    Epoxy coatings
    Finishes and finishing
    Lacquer and lacquering
    Metal coating
    Paint
    Plastic coating
    Plastic coatings
    Protective coatings
    Thin films
    Varnish and varnishing
  x Surface coatings
  xx Coating processes
    Materials
    Surfaces (Technology)
    Thin films
  — Thermal properties
  — — Tables
Coatings, Ceramic
  See Ceramic coating
Coatings, Diffusion
  See Diffusion coatings
Coatings, Epoxy
  See Epoxy coatings

Coatings, Protective
  See Protective coatings
Coatings, Textile
  See Coated fabrics
Coatis
  x Chulo
    Coatimundi
  — Behavior
Coats (TT530-535; TT595-600)
  x Jackets
    Overcoats
  xx Clothing and dress
    Tailoring
  Example under Costume; Men's clothing
  — Juvenile literature
Coats of arms
  See Devices
    Heraldry
Coaxial cables
  x Coaxial lines
  xx Electric cables
Coaxial lines
  See Coaxial cables
Cob, White-eared
  See White-eared kob
Cob (Building material) (TH1421)
  xx Building materials
Cobalt (Chemistry, QD181.C6)
  sa Soils—Cobalt content
  — Analysis
  — Effect on plants
    See Plants, Effect of cobalt on
  — Isotopes
    x Radiocobalt
  — — Tables
  — — Therapeutic use
    xx Radiotherapy
  — Magnetic properties
  — Physiological effect
    sa Plants, Effect of cobalt on
  — Spectra
  — Thermal properties
Cobalt alloys
  sa Chromium-cobalt-nickel-molybdenum
      alloys
    Cobalt-nickel alloys
    Cobalt-nickel-silicon alloys
    Copper-cobalt-manganese alloys
    Gold-cobalt alloys
    Iron-cobalt alloys
    Iron-nickel-cobalt alloys
    Tungsten carbide-cobalt alloys
    Tungsten-cobalt alloys
    Vanadium permendur
Cobalt amines
  See Cobalt-ammonium compounds
Cobalt-ammonium compounds (QD181.C6)
  x Ammonium cobalt bases
    Cobalt amines
Cobalt catalysts
  xx Catalysts
Cobalt-gold alloys
  See Gold-cobalt alloys
Cobalt in soils
  See Soils—Cobalt content
Cobalt in the body
Cobalt industry (Direct)
  xx Mineral industries
Cobalt-iron alloys
  See Iron-cobalt alloys
Cobalt mines and mining (Indirect)
      (TN490.C6)
Cobalt-nickel alloys
  x Nickel-cobalt alloys
  xx Cobalt alloys
    Nickel alloys
Cobalt-nickel-silicon alloys
  xx Cobalt alloys

Nickel alloys
Silicon alloys
Cobalt ores *(Indirect)*
Cobalt organic compounds
  See Organocobalt compounds
Cobalt-tungsten alloys
  See Tungsten-cobalt alloys
Cobalt-tungsten carbide alloys
  See Tungsten carbide-cobalt alloys
Cobaría Indians
  xx Indians of South America
    Tunebo Indians
Cobbeos Indians
  See Cubeo Indians
Cobitidae
  See Loaches
COBOL (Computer program language)
  (HF5548.5.C2)
  sa IDS (Computer program language)
  x Common business oriented language
  xx English language
  Example under Programming languages (Electronic computers)
  — Problems, exercises, etc.
  — Programmed instruction
Cobordism theory
  xx Differential topology
Cobra automobile
  xx Ford automobile
Coca *(Therapeutics, RM666.C)*
Coca language *(PM3686)*
  xx Indians of Mexico—Languages
Cocaine *(Anesthetics, RD86.C6;*
    Physiological effect, QP921.C7)
  xx Local anesthesia
    Narcotics
  — Toxicology *(RA1238.C7)*
Cocaine habit *(HV5810)*
  xx Narcotic habit
Cocama Indians *(Peru, F3430.1.C)*
  x Kokama Indians
    Ucayale Indians
  xx Indians of South America
    Tupi Indians
Cocama language *(PM5823)*
  x Ucayale language
  xx Indians of South America—Languages
Coccidae
  See Scale-insects
Coccidia
  sa Coccidiosis
  xx Coccidiosis
    Protozoa
Coccidioidal granuloma
  See Coccidioidosis
Coccidioidomycosis
  See Coccidioidosis
Coccidioidosis
  sa Blastomycosis
  x Coccidioidal granuloma
    Coccidioidomycosis
  xx Blastomycosis
Coccidiosis *(Cattle diseases, SF967.C6;*
    Veterinary medicine, SF792)
  sa Coccidia
  xx Coccidia
    Medical protozoology
Coccinellidae
  See Ladybirds
Coccoliths
  xx Calcium carbonate
    Marine sediments
Coccoliths, Fossil
Cocculin
  See Picrotoxin
Coccygeal gland *(Human anatomy, QM371;*
    Physiology, QP187)
  x Gland of Luschka

— Diseases *(Tumors, RD672)*
Coccyx *(QM111)*
  xx Spine
  — Tumors
    See Sacrococcygeal region—Tumors
Coccyzus
  See Cuckoos
Cochin bantams *(SF489.C)*
  xx Bantams
Cochineal *(SF561)*
  xx Dyes and dyeing
Cochise culture
  xx Paleo-Indians
Cochiti Indians *(E99.C84)*
  xx Indians of North America
    Keresan Indians
Cochlea
  xx Labyrinth (Ear)
  — Blood-vessels
  — Diseases
  — Electromechanical analogies
  — Innervation
Cochlear nucleus
  xx Auditory pathways
Cock-fighting *(Indirect)* *(SF503)*
  x Animal baiting
    Fighting
  xx Animal fighting
Cockateels *(Animal culture, SF473.C;*
    Zoology, QL696.P7)
  x Cockatiels
  xx Parrots
Cockatiels
  See Cockateels
Cockchafers *(QL596.S3)*
  x Dor-bug
  xx Beetles
  — Biological control
Cocker spaniels *(SF429.C55)*
  xx Spaniels
  — Juvenile literature
Cockle fisheries *(Indirect)*
  xx Shellfish fisheries
Cockpits, Pressurized
  See Aeroplanes—Pressurization
Cockroaches *(Indirect)* *(QL508.B6)*
  x Blattariae
    Blattoidea
  xx Orthoptera
  Example under Household pests
  — Anatomy
  — Control
  — Juvenile literature
  — Resistance to insecticides
Cockroaches, Fossil *(QE832.O7)*
  xx Orthoptera, Fossil
Cockroaches as carriers of disease
    (RC641.C6)
  xx Communicable diseases
    Insects as carriers of disease
Cocksfoot grass
  See Orchard grass
Cockspur coral tree
  See Common coral tree
Cocktails *(TX951)*
  xx Alcoholic beverages
Cocoa *(Indirect)* *(Beverages, TX817.C5;*
    Manufacture, TP640; Sources,
    TX415; Therapeutics, RM241;
    Trade, HD9200)
  Here are entered works on the commercial product. Works on the cacao tree and its culture are entered under the heading Cacao.
  sa Chocolate
  xx Chocolate
  Example under Beverages
  Note under Cacao

— Processing
  See Cocoa processing
— Tariff
  See Tariff on chocolate
Cocoa processing *(Indirect)* *(TP640)*
  sa Cocoa syrup
  x Cocoa—Processing
  — Patents
Cocoa syrup
  xx Cocoa processing
Cocoa trade *(Direct)*
  — Law and legislation *(Direct)*
  — Mathematical models
Cocobolo *(SD397.C6)*
Cocomaricopa Indians
  See Maricopa Indians
Coconut *(Indirect)* *(Culture, SB401;*
    Economics, HD9259.C6; Oils,
    TP684.C7)
  sa Coconut industry
    Coir
    Copra
  xx Copra
  — Tariff
    See Tariff on coconuts
Coconut industry *(Direct)*
    (HD9259.C58-62)
  x Coconut trade
  xx Coconut
    Fruit-trade
Coconut oil
  — Standards *(Direct)*
Coconut-palm *(Indirect)* *(SB401)*
  xx Oilseed plants
    Palms
  — Diseases and pests *(Indirect)*
    (SB608.C58)
    sa Cadang-cadang
  — Fertilizers and manures
Coconut trade
  See Coconut industry
Cocoons
  x Pupal cases
  xx Insects—Development
Cocopa Indians *(E99.C)*
  xx Indians of Mexico
    Indians of North America
    Yuman Indians
Cod-fisheries *(Indirect)* *(SH351.C5)*
  xx Fisheries
Cod-liver oil *(RM666.C6)*
Cod oil
  See Rosin-oil
Code and cipher stories
  x Cipher stories
    Code stories
    Cryptogram stories
  xx Detective and mystery stories
Code Ari (Artificial language) *(PM8129)*
  xx Languages, Artificial
Code names
  sa Acronyms
    Ciphers
  x Names, Code
  xx Abbreviations
    Ciphers
    Names
Code numbers (Book industries and trade)
  See Book industries and trade—Code
    numbers
Code numbers (Education)
  See Education—Code numbers
Code numbers (Information storage and retrieval)
  See Information storage and retrieval
    systems—Code numbers
Code pleading *(Direct)*
  xx Civil procedure

Code pleading *(Direct)* *(Continued)*
    Pleading
Code remedies
    See Remedies (Law)
Code stories
    See Code and cipher stories
Code words (Information storage and retrieval)
    See Information storage and retrieval
        systems—Code words
Codeine *(RS165.C6)*
    sa Dihydrocodeine
Codes
    See Ciphers
Codes, Error-correcting
    See Error-correcting codes (Information
        theory)
Codes, Telegraph
    See Cipher and telegraph codes
Codes for punched card systems
    See Punched card systems
Codetermination (Industrial relations)
    See Employees' representation in
        management
Codfish *(QL638.G2; Fisheries, SH351.C5)*
    sa Atlantic cod
        Cookery (Codfish)
        Klipfish
        Norway pout
        Pacific cod
    x Saith
    xx Gadiformes
    — Diseases and pests
Codicils
    See Wills
Codification of law
    See Law—Codification
Coding theory
    sa Error-correcting codes (Information
        theory)
        Programming (Electronic computers)
        Rate distortion theory
    xx Data compression (Telecommunication)
        Digital electronics
        Information theory
        Machine theory
        Programming (Electronic computers)
        Signal theory (Telecommunication)
    — Programmed instruction
Codling-moth *(SB945.C7)*
    xx Moths
    Example under Fruit—Diseases and pests
Codo (Unit of measure)
    See Cubit
Coeducation *(Indirect)* *(LC1601)*
    sa Education
        Education of women
    x Girls—Education
    xx Education
        Education of women
        Universities and colleges
Coefficient of concordance
    xx Correlation (Statistics)
Coefficient of elasticity
    See Elasticity (Economics)
Coefficient of expansion
    See Expansion (Heat)
        Expansion of liquids
        Expansion of solids
Coefficients, Binomial
    See Binomial coefficients
Coefficients, Clebsch-Gordan
    See Clebsch-Gordan coefficients
Coefficients, Racah
    See Racah coefficients
Coelacanth *(QL638.L26)*
    — Juvenile literature
Coelacanthiformes

Coelenterata *(Indirect)* *(QL375-9; Fossil,
    QE777-9)*
    sa Alcyonaria
        Anthozoa
        Corals
        Hydromedusae
        Hydrozoa
        Medusae
        Sponges
        Zoantharia
    x Polyps
        Radiata
        Zoophyta
    xx Animal colonies
        Corals
        Invertebrates
    — Anatomy *(QL378)*
        sa Nematocysts
Coelenterata, Fossil *(QE777)*
    Example under Invertebrates, Fossil
Coeli enarrant (Music)
    See Psalms (Music)—19th Psalm
Coeliac disease
    See Celiac disease
Coelostat *(QB97)*
    x Siderostat
    xx Astronomical instruments
Coena Domini bulls
    See In Coena Domini bulls
Coenobic plants *(Algae, QK565)*
    xx Algae
        Botany
        Colonies (Biology)
        Fungi
        Myxomycetes
        Plants
        Unicellular organisms
Coenzymes
    sa Flavins
    xx Enzymes
Coercion (Law)
    See Duress (Law)
Coerulein
    See Cerulein
Coeur d'Alene Indians
    See Skitswish Indians
Coeur d'Alene Strike, 1899 *(HD5325.M8
    1899.C4)*
Coexistence
    See World politics—1945-
        Russia—Foreign relations—United
        States; United States—Foreign
        relations—Russia; *and similar
        headings*
Coffee *(Indirect)* *(Adulteration, TX583;
    Chemical technology, TP645;
    Culture, SB269; Manners and
    customs, GT2918; Sources, TX415;
    Therapeutics, RM246)*
    sa Caffeine
        Cookery (Coffee)
        Soluble coffee
    xx Cookery
    Example under Beverages; Tropical crops
    — Analysis
    — Costs
    — Diseases and pests *(SB608.C6)*
        sa Coffee anthracnose
            Coffee berry borer
            Coffee leaf rust
    — Early works to 1800
    — Fertilizers and manures
        x Fertilizers and manures for coffee
        Example under Fertilizers and manures
    — Grading
    — Harvesting
    — Juvenile literature
    — Law and legislation *(Direct)*

    x Coffee trade—Law and legislation
    — Physiological effect
    — Prices
    — Processing
        See Coffee processing
    — Tables, etc. *(HF5716.C5)*
    — Tariff
        See Tariff on coffee
    — Taxation *(Direct)* *(HD9199)*
    — Therapeutic use
    — Transportation
Coffee anthracnose
    x Coffee berry disease
    xx Anthracnose
        Coffee—Diseases and pests
Coffee-bean weevil
    xx Bean-weevil
        Beetles
Coffee berry borer *(SB608.C6)*
    xx Coffee—Diseases and pests
Coffee berry disease
    See Coffee anthracnose
Coffee breaks
    See Rest periods
Coffee brewing
    x Brewing of coffee
    xx Cookery (Coffee)
Coffee-house management *(Direct)*
    x Coffee-houses—Management
    xx Hotel management
        Restaurant management
Coffee house ministry *(BV4377)*
    x Christian coffee house
        Ministry, Coffee house
    xx Church work with youth
        Evangelistic work
Coffee-houses *(Indirect)* *(NA7855;
    TX901-910)*
    x Coffeehouses
    xx Hotels, taverns, etc.
        Restaurants, lunch rooms, etc.
    — Management
        See Coffee-house management
Coffee in literature
Coffee leaf-miner
    xx Leaf-miners
Coffee leaf rust *(SB608.C6)*
    xx Coffee—Diseases and pests
Coffee making paraphernalia *(Direct)*
    (TX657)
    x Paraphernalia, Coffee making
    xx Cookery (Coffee)
Coffee plantation workers *(Direct)*
    x Coffee workers
Coffee processing *(TP645; Air pollution,
    TD888.C6)*
    x Coffee—Processing
    Example under Food industry and trade
    — Patents
Coffee research
    xx Agricultural research
Coffee trade *(Direct)* *(HD9195; HD9199)*
    — Accounting
    — Law and legislation
        See Coffee—Law and legislation
Coffee waste *(Trade waste, TD899)*
    xx Factory and trade waste
Coffee weed
    See Chicory
Coffee workers
    See Coffee plantation workers
Coffeehouses
    See Coffee-houses
Coffer-dams *(TC198)*
    sa Bridges—Foundations and piers
    xx Bridges—Foundations and piers
        Civil engineering
        Dams

Foundations
    Hydraulic structures
Coffers
  See Chests
Coffin industry *(Direct)*
  sa Wages—Coffin makers
  xx Coffins
Coffins *(Manufacture, TS2301.U5)*
  sa Coffin industry
  x Caskets (Coffins)
  xx Sarcophagi
Cog railroads
  See Rack-railroads
Cog-wheels
  See Gearing
Cognac
  See Brandy
Cognac (Mark of origin)
  xx Marks of origin
Cognition *(BF311)*
  sa Awareness
    Cognitive balance
    Field dependence (Psychology)
    Knowledge, Theory of
    Perception
    Risk-taking (Psychology)
    Three-dimensional test of visualization
      skills
  xx Knowledge, Theory of
    Perception
    Psychology
    Thought and thinking
  — Ability testing
Cognition (Child psychology)
  sa Human information processing (Child
    psychology)
  xx Child study
  — Juvenile literature
Cognitive balance
  xx Cognition
    Dissonance (Psychology)
Cognitive dissonance
  See Dissonance (Psychology)
Cohanim
  Here are entered works dealing with the
    hereditary religious privileges and re-
    sponsibilities in Jewish law and prac-
    tice of the descendants of the priests of
    the Temple in Jerusalem since 70
    A.D., the year of its destruction.
    Works dealing with the priests during
    the Temple period are entered under
    Priests, Jewish.
  x Cohen (Cohanim)
    Kohanim
    Kohen (Cohanim)
  xx Jews—Rites and ceremonies
    Priests, Jewish
  Note under Priests, Jewish
Cohen (Cohanim)
  See Cohanim
Coherence (Optics) *(QC403)*
  x Coherence of light
    Optical coherence
  xx Optics
Coherence of light
  See Coherence (Optics)
Coherent light communication systems
  See Laser communication systems
Coherent radar *(TK6592.C6)*
  sa Side-looking radar
  x Holographic radar
  xx Holography
    Microwaves
    Radar
Coherer *(Physics, QC665; Technology,*
    TK5863)
  sa Telegraph, Wireless

  xx Electric apparatus and appliances
    Electric waves
    Telegraph, Wireless
Cohesion *(QC183)*
  sa Adhesion
    Plasticity
    Wetting agents
  xx Adhesion
Coho fishing
  See Silver salmon fishing
Coho salmon
  See Silver salmon
Cohomology theory
  See Homology theory
Cohonina culture
Cohuilla Indians
  See Cahuilla Indians
Coiffure
  See Hairdressing
Coils, Electric
  See Electric coils
Coin banks *(NK4698)*
  x Banks, Coin
    Mechanical banks
    Penny banks
Coin changers
  See Coin changing machines
Coin changing machines
  x Change makers (Coins)
    Coin changers
    Currency changers (Coins)
    Money changing machines (Coins)
Coin collecting
  See Numismatics—Collectors and collecting
Coin dealers *(Direct)*
  x Numismatics—Dealers
Coin hoards *(Direct)*
  x Hoards
  xx Coins
    Numismatics
Coin operated laundries
  See Laundries, Self-service
Coin operated lockers
  x Lockers, Coin operated
Coin operated machines
  See Dry-cleaning machines
    Jukeboxes
    Laundries, Self-service
    Pinball machines
    Slot machines
    Vending machines
Coin redemption fund *(Speeches in Congress,*
    etc., 1895-1896, HG532)
  xx Silver question
Coin tricks *(GV1559)*
  xx Conjuring
    Tricks
Coinage *(Indirect)* *(General, HG261-315;*
    United States, HG551-566; Other
    countries, HG651-1490)
  sa Adulterated coins
    Bimetallism
    Commemorative coins
    Currency question
    Gold
    Gold—Standards of fineness
    Legal tender
    Mints
    Money
    Quantity theory of money
    Silver question
    Silver—Standards of fineness
  xx Gold
    Mints
    Money
    Silver
    Silver question
  — Juvenile literature

  — United States
    x United States—Coinage
Coinage, International *(HG381-395)*
  x International coinage
    International money
    Money, International
  xx Currency question
    Monetary unions
    Money
Coinage of words
  See Words, New
Coining, Illicit
  See Counterfeits and counterfeiting
Coins *(CJ)*
  Here are entered lists of coins, specimens,
    etc. Works dealing with coins, medals,
    tokens, etc., collectively, also works
    dealing with coins alone are entered
    under the heading Numismatics.
  sa Adulterated coins
    Bracteate coins
    Bronze coins
    Coin hoards
    Commemorative coins
    Copper coins
    Gold coins
    Obsidional coins
    Pattern coins
    Porcelain coins
    Proof coins
    Silver coins
    Tokens
    names of coins, e.g. Cent, Dollar,
      Guinea (Coin), Shilling, Sou marqué
  xx Money
  Note under Numismatics
  — Cleaning
  — Collectors and collecting
    See Numismatics—Collectors and
      collecting
  — Dictionaries
    See Numismatics—Dictionaries
  — Preservation
  — Prices
    sa Coins as an investment
  — Private collections
    See Numismatics—Private collections
Coins, Ancient *(CJ201-1397)*
Coins, Arab, [**Austrian, French, etc.**] *(Direct)*
  Here are entered works on local mints as
    well as on coin hoards limited to spe-
    cific coinages.
  x Arab [Austrian, French, etc.] coins
  — Juvenile literature
Coins, British
  sa Coins, English
    Sixpence
  xx Coins, English
Coins, Byzantine
  sa Scyphate coins
Coins, Cufic
  x Cufic coins
    Kufic coins
Coins, English
  sa Coins, British
    Maundy coins
    Penny, English
  xx Coins, British
Coins, Foreign *(Direct)*
  x Foreign coins
Coins, Islamic
  sa Coins, Omayyad
    Dirham (Coin)
  x Coins, Muslim
    Islamic coins
    Muslim coins

Coins, Jewish
   sa Numismatics—Jews
Coins, Medieval *(Direct)* *(CJ1601-1715)*
   sa Tremissis
Coins, Muslim
   See Coins, Islamic
Coins, Omayyad *(CJ3421)*
   x Omayyad coins
   xx Coins, Islamic
Coins, Oriental *(CJ3430-3890; Ancient,*
      CJ1301-1397)
   x Oriental coins
Coins, Oscan
   x Oscan coins
Coins, Papal *(CJ2928.P3)*
   x Papal coins
Coins, Roman
   sa Denarius (Coin)
      Follis (Coin)
Coins, Runic
   x Runic coins
   xx Runes
Coins, Spanish
   sa Croat (Coin)
      Piece of eight
Coins as an investment
   xx Capital investments
      Coins—Prices
      Numismatics—Collectors and collecting
Coins of the Bible
   See Bible—Numismatics
Coir
   xx Coconut
      Fibers
Coir industry *(Direct)* *(HD9156.C3-63)*
Coir industry workers *(Direct)*
      (HD8039.C64)
Coke *(Economics, HD9559.C68; Technology,*
      TP336)
   sa Carbonization
      Coal—Carbonization
      Petroleum coke
   xx Carbon
      Carbonization
      Coal
      Fuel
      Fuel trade
   — Grading
   — Quenching
   — Standards *(Direct)*
   — Testing
Coke industry *(Direct)* *(HD9559.C68-7)*
   sa Coal-tar industry
      Coke plants
      Gas industry
   x Beehive coke industry
      By-product coke industry
   xx Coal
      Gas industry
   — Automation
   — By-products
      xx Factory and trade waste
   — — Analysis
   — — Production control
   — Costs *(TP336)*
   — Electric equipment
   — Equipment and supplies *(TP336)*
   — — Appraisal
      See Coke industry—Equipment and
         supplies—Valuation
   — — Valuation
      x Coke industry—Equipment and
         supplies—Appraisal
   — Production control
   — Quality control
   — Safety measures
   — Safety regulations *(Direct)*
   — Water-supply

Coke-oven gas
   xx Coke-ovens
Coke-ovens *(TP336)*
   sa Coke-oven gas
   — Maintenance and repair
Coke plants *(Direct)*
   x By-product coke plants
   xx Coke industry
   — Design and construction *(TH4541)*
   — Equipment and supplies
Cokwe language
   See Chokwe language
Col di Lana, Battle of, 1916
   xx European War, 1914-1918—Campaigns
         —Italo-Austrian
Cola
   See Cola-nut
Cola-nut *(Pharmacy, RS165.C64)*
   x Cola
      Kola-nut
Colas
   See Cholas
Colchester, Eng.
   — Siege, 1648 *(DA415)*
Cold
   sa Cryobiology
      Heat
      Low temperature research
      Low temperatures
      Metals at low temperatures
      Refrigeration and refrigerating
         machinery
      Temperature
      Winter
   subdivisions Cold weather conditions
      and Cold weather operation *under*
      subjects, e.g. Airports—Cold weather
      conditions; Building—Cold weather
      conditions; Aeroplanes—Cold
      weather operation; Diesel motor—
      Cold weather operation
   xx Heat
      Low temperature research
      Low temperatures
      Temperature
   — Physiological effect *(QP82)*
      sa Arctic medicine
         Chilblains
         Cold adaptation
         Cold—Therapeutic use
         Plants, Effect of cold on
         Temperature—Physiological effect
      xx Cryobiology
         Temperature—Physiological effect
   — Therapeutic use *(RM863)*
      sa Cryosurgery
         Dry ice—Therapeutic use
      x Crymotherapy
         Cryotherapy
      xx Cold—Physiological effect
Cold (Disease) *(RF361)*
   sa Catarrh
      Cough
      Influenza
      Rhinoviruses
   x Common cold
   xx Catarrh
      Cough
   — Homeopathic treatment *(RX326.C6)*
   — Prevention
      x Cold prevention (Medicine)
   — Psychosomatic aspects
Cold adaptation
   x Adaptation to cold
   xx Adaptation (Biology)
      Cold—Physiological effect
   — Juvenile literature

Cold agglutinin syndrome *(RC647.C6)*
   xx Agglutinins
      Blood—Diseases
Cold Bath Fields Riot, 1833
   See London—Riot, 1833
Cold cathode counter tubes
   See Cold cathode tubes
Cold cathode counters
   See Cold cathode tubes
Cold cathode tubes *(TK7872.C3)*
   x Cold cathode counter tubes
      Cold cathode counters
      Counter tubes
      Counting tubes
      Decade counter tubes
   xx Cathode ray tubes
      Electric discharges through gases
      Electron tubes
      Electronic circuits
      Electronics
      Nuclear counters
      Vacuum-tubes
Cold cookery
   See Cookery (Cold dishes)
Cold dishes
   See Cookery (Cold dishes)
Cold flow
   See Creep of metals
Cold-frames *(Flower culture, SB415;*
      Vegetable culture, SB352)
   sa Wardian cases
   xx Floriculture
      Gardening
      Greenhouses
      Horticulture
      Vegetable gardening
Cold Harbor, Battle of, 1864 *(E476.52)*
Cold prevention (Medicine)
   See Cold (Disease)—Prevention
Cold regions
   sa Frozen ground
      Patterned ground
      Polar regions
Cold resistance of plants
   See Plants—Frost resistance
Cold storage *(Direct)* *(TP493)*
   sa Cold-storage lockers
      Compressed air
      Eggs—Preservation
      Farm produce—Storage
      Fishery products—Preservation
      Meat industry and trade
      Refrigeration and refrigerating
         machinery
      Refrigerator-cars
   x Storage
   xx Farm produce—Storage
      Food—Preservation
      Meat industry and trade
      Refrigeration and refrigerating
         machinery
      Refrigerators
   — Hygienic aspects
      xx Ptomaine poisoning
   — Insulation *(TP493)*
      xx Insulation (Heat)
Cold-storage lockers *(TP493.5)*
   sa Home freezers
   x Frozen-food lockers
   xx Cold storage
      Food, Frozen
      Home freezers
      Refrigeration and refrigerating
         machinery
   — Accounting
Cold-storage lockers, Cooperative
   See Cooperative cold-storage lockers

Cold storage on shipboard *(VM485)*
    sa Marine refrigeration
    x Ships—Cold storage
    xx Marine refrigeration
Cold War
    See World politics—1945-
Cold waves (Hairdressing)
    See Permanent waving
Cold weather clothing
    See Clothing, Cold weather
Cold weather conditions
    See subdivision Cold weather conditions
        under subjects, e.g. Mining
        engineering—Cold weather
        conditions
Cold weather conditions (Engineering)
    See Engineering—Cold weather conditions
Cold weather medicine
    See Arctic medicine
Cold weather operation (Helicopters)
    See Helicopters—Cold weather operation
Cold weather operations (Military)
    See Transportation, Military—Cold weather
        conditions
        Winter warfare
Cold weather photography
    See Photography—Cold weather conditions
Cold welding
    x Welding, Cold
    xx Metals—Cold working
        Pressure welding
        Welding
Cold working of metals
    See Metals—Cold working
Colemanite *(QE391.C; TN948.C7)*
Coleoptera
    See Beetles
Colibacillosis
Coliberti
    See Colliberts
Colic *(RC809; Diseases of children, RJ456.C)*
Coligny calendar
    See Calendar, Celtic
Colima warbler
    xx Wood warblers
Colimastitis
    See Mastitis
Colinae
    See Quails
Colitis *(RC862.C6)*
    sa Ulcerative colitis
    x Colon (Anatomy)—Inflammation
        Colonitis
    xx Colon (Anatomy)—Diseases
    — Psychosomatic aspects
Colla Indians *(Peru, F3430.1.C6)*
    x Collagua Indians
        Kolla Indians
    xx Aymara Indians
        Indians of South America
Collaboration in literature
    See Authorship—Collaboration
Collaborationists
    See Treason
        World War, 1939-1945—
        Collaborationists
Collage
    xx Art
        Assemblage (Art)
        Found objects (Art)
        Handicraft
    — Juvenile literature
Collagen
    sa Connective tissues
        Hide powder
    x Collogen
    xx Connective tissues

Collagen diseases
    sa Arthritis deformans
        Arthritis deformans in children
        Infectious arthritis
        Lupus erythematosus
        Rheumatic fever
        Scleroderma (Disease)
    x Collagenosis
        Diffuse collagen disease
    xx Connective tissues—Diseases
Collagenosis
    See Collagen diseases
Collages
    sa Fabric pictures
        Pressed flower pictures
Collages, American, ⌈French, etc.⌉
    x American ⌈French, etc.⌉ collages
Collagua Indians
    See Colla Indians
Collapse, Gravitational
    See Gravitational collapse
Collapse of bridges
    See Bridge failures
Collapse of buildings
    See Building failures
Collapse of dams
    See Dam failures
Collapse of the lungs
    See Atelectasis
        Collapse therapy
Collapse therapy
    sa Pneumothorax, Artificial
    x Collapse of the lungs
        Lungs—Collapse
    xx Surgery, Operative
Collapsible luminaire supports
    See Roads—Lighting—Break-away supports
Collapsible traffic sign supports
    See Traffic signs and signals—Break-away
        supports
Collar (in heraldry) *(CR41.C5)*
    Example under Heraldry
Collarbone
    See Clavicle
Collared dove
    xx Pigeons
Collared lemming
    x Greenland collared lemming
    xx Lemmings
Collared peccary *(QL737.U59)*
    xx Peccaries
    — Juvenile literature
Collars
    xx Clothing and dress
Collateral circulation
    xx Blood—Circulation
        Blood-vessels
Collateral loans
    See Lombard loans
        Pawnbroking
Colle, Battle of, 1269
    See Colle di Val d'Elsa, Italy, Battle of,
        1269
Colle di Val d'Elsa, Italy, Battle of, 1269
    x Colle, Battle of, 1269
    xx Florence—History—To 1421
        Guelfs and Ghibellines
Collect on delivery shipments
    See C.O.D. shipments
Collecting
    See Collectors and collecting
Collecting of accounts *(HF5556-9)*
    sa Collection agencies
        Postal service—Collection of notes, etc.
    x Accounts, Collecting of
        Collection letters
        Collection of accounts
    xx Accounts current

        Accounts receivable
        Commercial law
        Credit
        Credit management
        Debt
Collection agencies *(Direct)*
    xx Collecting of accounts
Collection laws *(Direct)* *(HF5556-9)*
    sa Poor debtor's oath
    xx Commercial law
    — Forms
Collection laws (Jewish law)
Collection letters
    See Collecting of accounts
Collection of accounts
    See Collecting of accounts
Collection of blood
    See Blood—Collection and preservation
Collective agreements
    See Collective labor agreements
Collective bargaining *(Direct)*
    sa Arbitration, Industrial
        Collective bargaining unit
        Collective labor agreements
        Employees' representation in
            management
        Labor contract
        Mediation and conciliation, Industrial
        Strikes and lockouts
        Trade-unions
    x Bargaining
    xx Arbitration, Industrial
        Employees' representation in
            management
        Industrial relations
        Labor and laboring classes
        Labor contract
        Labor disputes
        Negotiation
        Strikes and lockouts
        Trade-unions
    Example under Industrial relations
    — Aeronautics *(Direct)*
        x Aeronautics, Commercial—Collective
            bargaining
            Air lines—Collective bargaining
            Collective bargaining—Air lines
        xx Air lines—Employees
    — Aeroplane industry *(Direct)*
        x Aeroplane industry and trade—
            Collective bargaining
        xx Aeroplane industry workers
    — Air lines
        See Collective bargaining—
            Aeronautics
    — Automobile industry *(Direct)*
        x Aeroplane industry and trade—
            Collective bargaining
        xx Automobile industry workers
    — Banks and banking *(Direct)*
        x Banks and banking—Collective
            bargaining
        xx Bank employees
    — Chemical industries *(Direct)*
        x Chemical industries—Collective
            bargaining
            Chemicals—Manufacture and
            industry—Collective bargaining
        xx Chemical workers
    — Civil service
        See Collective bargaining—
            Government employees
    — Clerks *(Direct)*
        x Clerks—Collective bargaining
    — Clothing industry *(Direct)*
        x Clothing trade—Collective
            bargaining
        xx Clothing workers

Collective bargaining *(Direct)*
(Continued)
— Coal mining industry *(Direct)*
  x Coal mines and mining—Collective
    bargaining
  xx Coal-miners
— College employees *(Direct)*
  x Universities and colleges—
    Employees—Collective bargaining
  xx Wages—College employees
— College teachers *(Direct)*
  x College teachers—Collective
    bargaining
— Construction industry *(Direct)*
  x Construction industry—Collective
    bargaining
— Cotton manufacture *(Direct)*
  x Cotton manufacture—Collective
    bargaining
— Electric industries *(Direct)*
  x Electric industries—Collective
    bargaining
  xx Electric industry workers
— Electric utilities *(Direct)*
  x Electric utilities—Collective
    bargaining
  xx Electric industry workers
— Engineers *(Direct)*
  x Engineers—Collective bargaining
— Fisheries *(Direct)*
  x Fisheries—Collective bargaining
  xx Fishermen
— Foundrymen *(Direct)*
  x Foundrymen—Collective bargaining
— Government business enterprises
    (Direct)
  x Government business enterprises—
    Collective bargaining
— Government employees *(Direct)*
  sa Collective bargaining—Municipal
    employees
  x Collective bargaining—Civil service
  xx Civil service
    Employee-management relations in
    government
  Example under reference from Govern-
    ment employees
— Highway transport workers *(Direct)*
  x Highway transport workers—
    Collective bargaining
— Hospitals *(Direct)*
  x Hospitals—Collective bargaining
  xx Hospitals—Staff
— Iron industry *(Direct)*
  x Iron industry and trade—Collective
    bargaining
  xx Iron and steel workers
— Journalists *(Direct)*
  x Collective bargaining—Newspapers
    Journalists—Collective bargaining
    Newspapers—Collective bargaining
— Librarians *(Direct)*
  x Librarians—Collective bargaining
— Longshoremen *(Direct)*
  x Longshoremen—Collective
    bargaining
— Mathematical models
— Meat industry *(Direct)*
  x Meat industry and trade—Collective
    bargaining
— Merchant marine *(Direct)*
  x Merchant marine—Collective
    bargaining
  xx Merchant seamen
— Mining industry *(Direct)*
  x Mining industry and finance—
    Collective bargaining
  xx Miners
— Motor bus lines *(Direct)*

  x Motor bus lines—Collective
    bargaining
— Moving-picture industry *(Direct)*
  x Moving-picture industry—Collective
    bargaining
— Municipal employees *(Direct)*
  x Municipal officials and employees—
    Collective bargaining
  xx Collective bargaining—Government
    employees
— Newspapers
  See Collective bargaining—Journalists
— Nonferrous metal industries *(Direct)*
  x Nonferrous metal industries—
    Collective bargaining
— Nurses *(Direct)*
  x Nurses and nursing—Collective
    bargaining
— Paper industry *(Direct)*
  x Paper making and trade—Collective
    bargaining
  xx Paper industry workers
— Petroleum industry *(Direct)*
  x Petroleum industry and trade—
    Collective bargaining
  xx Petroleum workers
— Printing industry *(Direct)*
  x Printing industry—Collective
    bargaining
  xx Printers
— Professions *(Direct)*
  x Professions—Collective bargaining
— Radio broadcasting *(Direct)*
  x Radio broadcasting—Collective
    bargaining
— Railroads *(Direct)*
  x Railroads—Collective bargaining
  xx Railroad construction workers
    Railroads—Employees
— Research *(Direct)*
— Rubber industry *(Direct)*
  x Rubber industry and trade—
    Collective bargaining
— Skilled labor *(Direct)*
  x Skilled labor—Collective bargaining
— Steel industry *(Direct)*
  x Steel industry and trade—Collective
    bargaining
  xx Iron and steel workers
— Teachers *(Direct)* *(LB2842)*
  x Teachers—Collective bargaining
— Telegraphers *(Direct)*
  x Telegraphers—Collective bargaining
— Television broadcasting *(Direct)*
  x Television broadcasting—Collective
    bargaining
— Textile industry *(Direct)*
  x Textile industry and fabrics—
    Collective bargaining
  xx Textile workers
— Transportation *(Direct)*
  x Transportation—Collective
    bargaining

Collective bargaining unit *(Direct)*
  xx Collective bargaining
    Trade-unions
Collective education *(Direct)* *(LB1029.C5)*
  Here are entered works dealing with the
  educational problems peculiar to the
  collective settlements (Kibbutzim) in
  Israel or elsewhere.
  x Collective settlements—Education
    Education, Collective
  xx Education—Experimental methods
Collective farms *(Direct)*
  sa Collective settlements
  xx Agriculture, Cooperative
    Collective settlements

  State farms
— Accounting
  xx Agriculture—Accounting
— Auditing and inspection
  Example under Auditing
— Costs
  xx Agriculture—Costs
— Finance
  sa Collective farms—Income
    distribution
— Income distribution
  xx Collective farms—Finance
    Hours of labor
— Insurance *(Direct)*
  xx Insurance
— Labor productivity
  See Agriculture—Labor productivity
— Law and legislation *(Direct)*
  xx Agricultural laws and legislation
— Management
  xx Farm management
— Officials and employees
— — Pensions
    See Collective farms—Pensions
— Pensions *(Direct)*
  x Collective farms—Officials and
    employees—Pensions
  xx Agricultural laborers—Pensions
    Farmers—Pensions
— Taxation *(Direct)*
  xx Cooperative societies—Taxation
Collective labor agreements *(Direct)*
  sa Open and closed shop
  x Collective agreements
    Labor agreements
    Trade agreements (Labor)
    Union agreements
  xx Collective bargaining
    Labor contract
    Trade-unions
— Abrasives industry *(Direct)*
  x Abrasives industry—Collective labor
    agreements
— Aeronautics *(Direct)*
  x Aeronautics, Commercial—Collective
    labor agreements
    Air lines—Collective labor
    agreements
    Collective labor agreements—Air
    lines
  xx Air lines—Employees
— Aeroplane industry *(Direct)*
  x Aeroplane industry and trade—
    Collective labor agreements
  xx Aeroplane industry workers
— Agricultural machine industry *(Direct)*
  x Agricultural machinery—Trade and
    manufacture—Collective labor
    agreements
— Agriculture *(Direct)*
  x Agriculture—Collective labor
    agreements
  xx Agricultural laborers
— Air lines
  See Collective labor agreements—
    Aeronautics
— Aluminum industry *(Direct)*
  x Aluminum industry and trade—
    Collective labor agreements
— Artificial flower industry *(Direct)*
  x Artificial flower industry—Collective
    labor agreements
— Automobile industry *(Direct)*
  x Automobile industry and trade—
    Collective labor agreements
  xx Automobile industry workers
— Banks and banking *(Direct)*

x Banks and banking—Collective labor
   agreements
xx Bank employees
— Boots and shoes
— — Trade and manufacture
      See Collective labor agreements—
         Shoe industry
— Brewing industry   (Direct)
   x Brewing industry—Collective labor
      agreements
   xx Brewery workers
— Broom and brush industry   (Direct)
   x Broom and brush industry—
      Collective labor agreements
— Building-service employees   (Direct)
   x Building-service employees—
      Collective labor agreements
— Building trades
      See Collective labor agreements—
         Construction industry
— Canning industry   (Direct)
   x Canning and preserving—Industry
      and trade—Collective labor
      agreements
   xx Cannery workers
— Cement industries   (Direct)
   x Cement industries—Collective labor
      agreements
   xx Cement industry workers
— Chemical industries   (Direct)
   x Chemical industries—Collective
      labor agreements
      Chemicals—Manufacture and
         industry—Collective labor
         agreements
   xx Chemical workers
— Clerks   (Direct)
   x Clerks—Collective labor agreements
— Clothing industry   (Direct)
   x Clothing trade—Collective labor
      agreements
   xx Clothing workers
— Coal mining industry   (Direct)
   x Coal mines and mining—Collective
      labor agreements
   xx Coal-miners
— Commercial agents   (Direct)
   sa Collective labor agreements—
      Commercial travelers
   x Commercial agents—Collective labor
      agreements
— Commercial travelers   (Direct)
   x Commercial travelers—Collective
      labor agreements
   xx Collective labor agreements—
      Commercial agents
— Confectioners   (Direct)
   x Confectioners—Collective labor
      agreements
   xx Collective labor agreements—Food
      industry
— Construction industry   (Direct)
   sa Collective labor agreements—Stone
      industry and trade
   x Collective labor agreements—
      Building trades
      Collective labor agreements—
         Stone-masons
      Construction industry—Collective
         labor agreements
   xx Building trades
      Construction workers
      Stone-masons
— Cork industry   (Direct)
   x Cork industry—Collective labor
      agreements
— Dairying   (Direct)

x Dairying—Collective labor
   agreements
— Distilling industries   (Direct)
   x Distilling industries—Collective labor
      agreements
— Education   (Direct)   (LB2831.5)
   x Education—Collective labor
      agreements
   xx Educators
      Teachers
— Electric industries   (Direct)
   x Electric industries—Collective labor
      agreements
   xx Electric industry workers
— Engineers   (Direct)
   x Engineers—Collective labor
      agreements
   xx Engineers—Legal status, laws, etc.
— Escalator clauses
      See Wages—Cost-of-living
         adjustments
— Executives   (Direct)
   x Executives—Collective labor
      agreements
— Fisheries   (Direct)
   x Fisheries—Collective labor
      agreements
   xx Fishermen
— Food industry   (Direct)
   sa Collective labor agreements—
      Confectioners
   x Food industry and trade—Collective
      labor agreements
   xx Food industry and trade—Employees
— Food service   (Direct)
   x Food service—Collective labor
      agreements
   xx Food service employees
— Furniture industry   (Direct)
   x Furniture industry and trade—
      Collective labor agreements
— Glass manufacture   (Direct)
   x Glass manufacture—Collective labor
      agreements
   xx Glass-workers
— Government business enterprises
      (Direct)
   sa Collective labor agreements—
      Municipal employees
   x Government business enterprises—
      Collective labor agreements
   xx Public utilities—Employees
— Government employees   (Direct)
   Example under reference from Govern-
      ment employees
— Hairdressing   (Direct)
   x Hairdressing—Collective labor
      agreements
   xx Beauty operators
— Hosiery industry   (Direct)
   x Hosiery industry—Collective labor
      agreements
— Hospitals   (Direct)
   sa Collective labor agreements—
      Medical personnel
      Collective labor agreements—
         Physicians
   x Hospitals—Collective labor
      agreements
   xx Collective labor agreements—
      Medical personnel
      Collective labor agreements—
         Physicians
— Hotels, taverns, etc.   (Direct)
   x Hotels, taverns, etc.—Collective
      labor agreements
— Inland navigation

See Collective labor agreements—
   Inland water transportation
— Inland water transportation   (Direct)
   x Collective labor agreements—Inland
      navigation
      Inland navigation—Collective labor
         agreements
      Inland water transportation—
         Collective labor agreements
   xx Inland water transportation—
      Employees
      Merchant seamen
— Insurance companies   (Direct)
   x Insurance companies—Collective
      labor agreements
   xx Insurance companies—Employees
— Iron industry   (Direct)
   x Iron industry and trade—Collective
      labor agreements
   xx Iron and steel workers
— Janitors   (Direct)
   x Janitors—Collective labor
      agreements
— Journalists   (Direct)
   x Collective labor agreements—
      Newspapers
      Journalists—Collective labor
         agreements
      Newspapers—Collective labor
         agreements
— Knit goods industry   (Direct)
   x Knit goods industry—Collective
      labor agreements
— Leather industry   (Direct)
   x Leather industry and trade—
      Collective labor agreements
   xx Leather workers
— Local transit   (Direct)
   x Local transit—Collective labor
      agreements
   xx Transport workers
— Lumber trade   (Direct)
   x Lumber trade—Collective labor
      agreements
   xx Lumbermen
— Machine industry   (Direct)
   x Machinery—Trade and manufacture
      —Collective labor agreements
— Meat industry   (Direct)
   x Meat industry and trade—Collective
      labor agreements
   xx Packing-house workers
— Medical personnel   (Direct)
   sa Collective labor agreements—
      Hospitals
      Wages—Medical personnel
   x Medical personnel—Collective labor
      agreements
   xx Collective labor agreements—
      Hospitals
— Merchant marine   (Direct)
   x Merchant marine—Collective labor
      agreements
   xx Merchant seamen
— Messengers   (Direct)
   x Messengers—Collective labor
      agreements
— Metal industry   (Direct)
   x Metal trade—Collective labor
      agreements
   xx Metal-workers
— Mining industry   (Direct)
   x Mining industry and finance—
      Collective labor agreements
   xx Miners
— Moving-picture industry   (Direct)
   x Moving-picture industry—Collective
      labor agreements

Collective labor agreements *(Direct)*
— Moving-picture industry *(Direct)*
  (Continued)
    xx Moving-picture industry—Employees
— Municipal employees *(Direct)*
    xx Civil service
      Collective labor agreements—
        Government business enterprises
      Municipal officials and employees
— Newspapers
    See Collective labor agreements—
      Journalists
— Oil industries *(Direct)*
    x Oil industries—Collective labor
      agreements
    xx Petroleum workers
— Opera chorus singers *(Direct)*
    x Opera chorus singers—Collective
      labor agreements
— Optical trade *(Direct)*
    x Optical trade—Collective labor
      agreements
    xx Opticians
— Paper box industry *(Direct)*
    x Paper box industry—Collective labor
      agreements
— Paper industry *(Direct)*
    x Paper making and trade—Collective
      labor agreements
    xx Paper industry workers
— Petroleum industry *(Direct)*
    x Petroleum industry and trade—
      Collective labor agreements
    xx Petroleum workers
— Pharmacists *(Direct)*
    x Pharmacists—Collective labor
      agreements
— Physicians *(Direct)*
    sa Collective labor agreements—
      Hospitals
      Physicians—Salaries, pensions, etc.
    x Physicians—Collective labor
      agreements
    xx Collective labor agreements—
      Hospitals
      Physicians—Salaries, pensions, etc.
— Plastics industry *(Direct)*
    x Plastics industry and trade—
      Collective labor agreements
— Printing industry *(Direct)*
    x Printing industry—Collective labor
      agreements
    xx Printers
— Professions *(Direct)*
    x Professions—Collective labor
      agreements
— Programmed instruction
— Railroads *(Direct)*
    x Railroads—Collective labor
      agreements
    xx Railroad construction workers
      Railroads—Employees
— Refuse collectors *(Direct)*
    x Refuse and refuse disposal—
      Collective labor agreements
      Refuse collectors—Collective labor
        agreements
— Retail trade *(Direct)*
    x Retail trade—Collective labor
      agreements
— Sanitation workers *(Direct)*
    x Sanitation workers—Collective labor
      agreements
— Shoe industry *(Direct)*
    x Boots and shoes—Trade and
      manufacture—Collective labor
        agreements

Collective labor agreements—Boots
    and shoes—Trade and
    manufacture
    xx Shoemakers
— Soft drink industry *(Direct)*
    x Soft drink industry—Collective labor
      agreements
— Stagehands *(Direct)*
    x Stagehands—Collective labor
      agreements
— Steel industry *(Direct)*
    x Steel industry and trade—Collective
      labor agreements
    xx Iron and steel workers
— Stone industry and trade *(Direct)*
    x Stone industry and trade—Collective
      labor agreements
    xx Collective labor agreements—
      Construction industry
— Stone-masons
    See Collective labor agreements—
      Construction industry
— Street-railroads *(Direct)*
    x Street-railroads—Collective labor
      agreements
    xx Street-railroads—Employees
— Sugar industry *(Direct)*
    x Sugar—Manufacture and refining—
      Collective labor agreements
      Sugar trade—Collective labor
        agreements
    xx Sugar refinery workers
      Sugar workers
— Surveyors *(Direct)*
    x Surveyors—Collective labor
      agreements
— Textile industry *(Direct)*
    x Textile industry and fabrics—
      Collective labor agreements
    xx Textile workers
— Tobacco industry *(Direct)*
    x Tobacco manufacture and trade—
      Collective labor agreements
    xx Tobacco workers
— Transport workers *(Direct)*
    x Transport workers—Collective labor
      agreements
— Trucking industry *(Direct)*
    x Transportation, Automotive—
      Collective labor agreements
    xx Highway transport workers
— Undertakers and undertaking *(Direct)*
    x Undertakers and undertaking—
      Collective labor agreements
— Watchmen *(Direct)*
    x Watchmen—Collective labor
      agreements
— Wine making *(Direct)*
    x Wine and wine making—Collective
      labor agreements
— Wood-pulp industry *(Direct)*
    x Wood-pulp industry—Collective
      labor agreements
— Woodworking industries *(Direct)*
    x Woodworking industries—Collective
      labor agreements
    xx Woodworkers
— Wool trade and industry *(Direct)*
    x Wool trade and industry—Collective
      labor agreements
Collective psychotherapy
  See Group psychotherapy
Collective security
  See Security, International
Collective settlements *(Direct)*
    sa Collective farms
      Harmonists
      Jansonists

names of particular communities, e.g.
    Hopedale Community
    x Communal settlements
      Communistic settlements
    xx Collective farms
      Communism
      Cooperation
      Socialism
— Accounting
— Anecdotes, facetiae, satire, etc.
— Education
    See Collective education
— Juvenile literature
— Law and legislation *(Direct)*
    xx Agricultural laws and legislation
— Mathematical models
— Organization and administration
— Pictorial works
— Religious life
Collectivism *(HX)*
    sa Communism
      Fascism
      Government ownership
      Individualism
      Socialism
      Totalitarianism
    xx Individualism
      Totalitarianism
Collectors and collecting *(AM200-501)*
    sa Book collecting
      Book collectors
      Children as collectors
      Hobbies
      Men as collectors
      Phonorecord collecting
      Plant collectors
    subdivisions Collectors and collecting
      and Collection and preservation
      under names of objects collected,
      e.g. Postage-stamps—Collectors and
        collecting; Zoological specimens—
        Collection and preservation
    x Antiques
      Collecting
    xx Art
— Anecdotes, facetiae, satire, etc.
— Marks
    See Collectors' marks
Collectors' marks *(N8380)*
    x Collectors and collecting—Marks
      Marks, Collectors'
Collects
    xx Propers (Liturgy)
— Meditations
College, Choice of *(LB2350.5)*
    x Choice of college
      Universities and colleges—Selection
College administrator placement
  See College administrators—Selection and
    appointment
College administrator selection
  See College administrators—Selection and
    appointment
College administrators *(Direct)*
    sa College presidents
      College student personnel
        administrators
      Deans (in schools)
      Departmental chairmen (Universities)
    x College officials
      University administrators
      University officials
    xx Universities and colleges—
      Administration
— Appointment
    See College administrators—Selection
      and appointment
— Salaries, pensions, etc. *(LB2331.68)*

— Selection and appointment
   x College administrator placement
      College administrator selection
      College administrators—
         Appointment
   xx Universities and colleges—
      Administration

College administrators, Training of *(Direct)*

College admission officers
   x Admission officers, College
      University admission officers
   xx Universities and colleges—Admission

College admissions
   See Universities and colleges—Admission

College and church
   See Church and college

College and community
   See Community and college

College and school drama *(History and criticism, PN3175-3191)*
   Subdivided by college or university.
   sa College theater
      Drama festivals
      Drama in education
   x College drama
      College plays
      College theatricals
      Drama, Academic
      Plays, College
      School drama
      School plays
      Theatricals, College
      University drama
   xx Acting
      Amateur theatricals
      Drama
      Drama in education
      Student activities
— Competitions

College and school journalism *(LB3621; Amateur journalism, PN4825-4830)*
   sa College and school periodicals
      School yearbooks
   x College journalism
      School journalism
      Student journalism
   xx Amateur journalism
      Journalism
      Student activities
— Law and legislation *(Direct)*
   xx Educational law and legislation
      Press law

College and school periodicals
   sa Scholarly periodicals
   x College periodicals
      School periodicals
      Student periodicals
      Students' periodicals
   xx College and school journalism
      Periodicals
      Scholarly periodicals

College annuals
   See School yearbooks

College athletics
   See Athletics
      College sports
      Track-athletics

College attendance *(Indirect) (LC148)*
   sa College dropouts
   x Academic probation
      Probation, Academic
      School attendance—College
      University attendance

College autonomy
   See University autonomy

College bookstores
   See College stores

College buildings
   See Universities and colleges—Buildings

College catalogs
   See Catalogs, College

College chaplains
   See Chaplains, University and college

College characteristics index
   x CCI

College cheers
   See Cheers

College colors
   See School colors

College communities
   See University towns

College community centers
   See Student unions

College cooperation
   See University cooperation

College costs *(LB2342)*
   sa Student aid
      Student loan funds
   x College education costs
      Student expenditures
      Tuition
   xx Education—Finance
      Universities and colleges—Finance

College credits
   See School credits

College degrees
   See Degrees, Academic

College departmental libraries
   See Libraries, University and college—
      Departmental libraries

College discipline *(Direct)*
   x Discipline, College
      University discipline
   xx School discipline
      Self-government (in education)
      Universities and colleges—
         Administration

College drama
   See College and school drama

College dropouts *(Direct)*
   x University dropouts
   xx College attendance
      Dropouts
      Personnel service in higher education

College education costs
   See College costs

College employees
   See Universities and colleges—Employees

College Entrance Examination Board English composition test
   See English composition test

College entrance requirements
   See Universities and colleges—Entrance
      requirements
      subdivision Entrance requirements
      under names of universities and
      colleges, e.g. Harvard University—
      Entrance requirements

College environment
   x Environment, College
      University environment

College etiquette
   See Student etiquette

College facilities *(Direct)*
   x University facilities
   xx School facilities
— Community use
   See College facilities—Extended use
— Extended use *(Direct)*
   x College facilities—Community use
      Community use of college facilities
      Extended use of college facilities
— Planning *(Direct)*
   sa Campus planning
   x Universities and colleges—Planning

   xx Campus planning
      Educational planning

College faculty
   See College teachers
      Universities and colleges—Faculty

College fraternities
   See Greek letter societies
      Students' societies

College freshmen *(Direct)*
   sa subdivision Freshmen *under names of*
      universities, colleges, etc.
   x Freshmen, College
   xx College students
— Health and hygiene
   xx School hygiene
— Religious life

College freshmen orientation
   See College student orientation

College gowns
   See Academic costume

College graduates *(Direct)*
   Here are entered works on college graduates as a socio-economic group. Works on college graduates in relation to their alma maters are entered under Universities and colleges—Alumni.
   sa Business education graduates
      Teachers college graduates
      Universities and colleges—Alumni
      Women college graduates
   x University graduates
   xx Professions
      Universities and colleges—Alumni
— Biography
— Employment *(Direct)*

College housing
   See Student housing

College humor
   See College wit and humor

College investments
   See University investments

College journalism
   See College and school journalism

College-level examinations
   Here are entered works on examinations designed to evaluate nontraditional college-level education, specifically including independent study and correspondence work. Works on examinations in colleges are entered under Universities and colleges—Examinations.
   xx School credits—Outside work
      Students, Transfer of
      Universities and colleges—
         Examinations

College librarians *(Direct) (Z675.U5)*
   x Academic librarians
      Librarians, University
      University librarians
   xx Librarians
— Job descriptions
— Salaries, pensions, etc. *(Direct)*

College libraries
   See Libraries, University and college

College life
   See College students

College officials
   See College administrators

College operas, revues, etc. *(M1504)*
   Subdivided by college or university.
   sa Operatic scenes
   x College revues
      Collegiate shows
   xx Musical revues, comedies, etc.
      Operas
      Operatic scenes

College orations *(United States, PS663.C7)*
    Subdivided by college or university.
    sa School orations
    xx American orations
        School orations
    Example under Students
College periodicals
    See College and school periodicals
College personnel management
    x Universities and colleges—Personnel
        management
        University personnel management
    xx School personnel management
        Universities and colleges—
        Administration
College plays
    See College and school drama
College poetry
    See College verse
College presidents *(Direct)*
    sa subdivision Presidents *under names of*
        universities, colleges, etc.
    x Presidents, College
        University presidents
    xx College administrators
        Universities and colleges—
        Administration
  — Biography
College presses
    See University presses
College prose
    Subdivided by college or university.
    xx School prose
College prose, English, [**French, Russian, etc.**]
    (Direct)
College publicity *(Direct)*
    xx Public relations—Universities and
        colleges
        School publicity
College qualification test
    See Selective service college qualification
        test
College radio stations
    See Radio stations
College rank
    See Universities and colleges—Evaluation
College readers
    Here are entered selections of reading
    material in the English language, liter-
    ary as well as non-literary, compiled
    for teaching rhetoric, comprehension
    and related topics on the college level.
    General literary selections are entered
    under appropriate literature headings,
    e.g. American literature.
    x University readers
    xx American literature
        English literature
        Literature
        Readers
    Note under Readers
College registrars *(LB2341)*
    x Registrars, College
    xx Student registration
        Universities and colleges—Admission
College revues
    See College operas, revues, etc.
College seniors
    x Seniors, College
    xx College students
College sermons
    See Universities and colleges—Sermons
College settlements
    See Social settlements
College sites
    See School sites
College songs
    See Students' songs

College sports
    sa Baseball
        Coaching (Athletics)
        Football
        Intramural sports
        Jumping
        Rowing
        Soccer
        Sports
        Track-athletics
        Vaulting
        subdivision Athletics *under names of*
        colleges, universities, etc., e.g.
        Harvard University—Athletics
    x College athletics
        Universities and colleges—Athletics
        Universities and colleges—Sports
    xx Amusements
        Athletics
        Physical education and training
        School sports
        Sports
        Student activities
  — Administration
        See College sports—Organization and
        administration
  — Economic aspects *(Direct)*
  — Law and legislation *(Direct)*
  — Organization and administration
    x College sports—Administration
  — Philosophy
    See Sports—Philosophy
  — Records *(GV741)*
College stamps
    x University stamps
    xx Postage-stamps
College stores *(Direct)*
    x Campus stores
        College bookstores
    xx Retail trade
College stories *(PZ1-7)*
    xx Fiction
College student mobility *(Direct)* *(LA230)*
    x Migration of college students
    xx Student mobility
College student orientation
    x College freshmen orientation
        College students—Orientation
        Orientation (College students)
    xx Study, Method of
College student personnel administrators
    xx College administrators
        Personnel service in higher education—
        Administration
College student personnel administrators,
    Training of *(Direct)*
College student self-government
    See Self-government (in higher education)
College students *(Direct)*
    sa College freshmen
        College seniors
        Graduate students
        Teachers college students
        Women college students
        subdivision Students *under names of*
        universities, colleges, etc.
    x College life
        Undergraduates
        Universities and colleges—Students
        University students
  — Anecdotes, facetiae, satire, etc.
  — Attitudes
    xx Attitude (Psychology)
  — Caricatures and cartoons
  — Conduct of life
    xx Student ethics
  — Correspondence, reminiscences, etc.
  — Health and hygiene

    xx School hygiene
  — Missionary activity
    See College students in missionary
        work
  — Orientation
    See College student orientation
  — Personal narratives
  — Personality
    See College students—Psychology
  — Pictorial works
  — Political activity
    x New Left
    xx Politics, Practical
  — — Pictorial works
  — Prayer-books and devotions
  — Psychology
    x College students—Personality
  — Recreation
  — Religious life
    sa College students in missionary work
  — Sexual behavior *(HQ35.2)*
  — Social and economic status
    See College students' socio-economic
        status
  — Suicidal behavior
    xx Suicide
  — Transportation *(Direct)*
    x Commuting college students
        Student transportation, College
College students, Catholic *(Direct)*
    x Catholic college students
  — Religious life
College students, Jewish
    xx Students, Jewish
  — Religious life
College students, Negro *(Direct)*
    x Negro college students
    xx Negroes—Education
  — Books and reading
  — Fellowships
    See College students, Negro—
        Scholarships, fellowships, etc.
  — Political activity
    xx Politics, Practical
  — Religious life
  — Scholarships, fellowships, etc. *(Direct)*
    x College students, Negro—
        Fellowships
College students in missionary work
    x College students—Missionary activity
    xx College students—Religious life
        Missions
College students' socio-economic status
    (Direct)
    x College students—Social and economic
        status
    xx Students' socio-economic status
College teacher aides
    See Graduate teaching assistants
College teacher assistants
    See Graduate teaching assistants
College teacher mobility *(LB2335.3)*
    x Mobility
College teachers *(Direct)* *(LB1778)*
    sa Agricultural colleges—Faculty
        Communist college teachers
        Graduate teaching assistants
        Junior colleges—Faculty
        Library schools—Faculty
        Medical colleges—Faculty
        Negro college teachers
        Universities and colleges—Faculty
        Women as college teachers
    x College faculty
        Faculty (Education)
        Instructors
        Professors
        Universities and colleges—Teachers

University teachers
  xx Teachers
    Universities and colleges—Faculty
— Appointment
    See College teachers—Selection and
      appointment
— Collective bargaining
    See Collective bargaining—College
      teachers
— Correspondence, reminiscences, etc.
— Incentive awards
    xx College teachers—Salaries, pensions,
      etc.
      Rewards (Prizes, etc.)
— Leaves of absence
    x Sabbatical leave
— Legal status, laws, etc. *(Direct)*
— Political activity
    xx Politics, Practical
— Recruiting *(Direct)*
— Registers
— Religious life
— Salaries, pensions, etc. *(LB2334)*
    sa College teachers—Incentive awards
— Selection and appointment
    x College teachers—Appointment
— Supply and demand *(Direct)*
— Taxation *(Direct)*
— Tenure *(Direct)*
— Work load *(LB2331)*
    x Faculty work load
College teachers, Part-time
  x Part-time college teachers
  xx Teachers, Part-time
College teachers, Professional ethics for
  x College teaching ethics
  xx Professional ethics
College teachers, Rating of
College teachers, Training of *(Indirect)*
  xx Teachers, Training of
College teachers as artists
  xx Art in universities and colleges
    Artists
College teachers as authors
  x Authors, College
    Authors, University
  xx Authors
    Teachers as authors
College teaching *(LB2331)*
  sa Seminars
  x University teaching
  xx Teaching
— Vocational guidance
    See College teaching as a profession
College teaching as a profession *(Direct)*
  x College teaching—Vocational guidance
    University teaching as a profession
  xx Teaching as a profession
— Juvenile literature
College teaching ethics
  See College teachers, Professional ethics for
College theater *(Direct)*
  x College theatricals
    Theatricals, College
    University theater
  xx Amateur theatricals
    College and school drama
    Student activities
    Theater
    Theater—Little theater movement
College theatricals
  See College and school drama
    College theater
College towns
  See University towns
College trustees *(LB2341)*
  sa Junior college trustees
  x Trustees, College

Universities and colleges—Trustees
University trustees
  xx Universities and colleges—
    Administration
College unions
  See Student unions
College verse *(PN6110.C7)*
  Subdivided by college or university.
  sa School verse
    Students' songs
  x College poetry
  xx Poetry
    School verse
    Students' songs
College verse, English, [French, Russian, etc.]
  (Direct)
  x English [French, Russian, etc.] college
    verse
  xx English [French, Russian, etc.] poetry
College wit and humor
  x College humor
  xx Wit and humor
College yearbooks
  See School yearbooks
Colleges
  See Universities and colleges
Colleges, Small
  See Small colleges
Colleges for women
  See Women's colleges
Collegiality of bishops
  See Episcopacy
Collegiate church deans
  See Deans, Cathedral and collegiate
Collegiate shows
  See College operas, revues, etc.
Collembola *(Indirect) (QL503.C6)*
Collet chucks
  See Collets
Collets
  sa Chucks
  x Collet chucks
    Draw-in collets
    Spring collets
  xx Chucks
    Jigs and fixtures
Colliberts *(HT731)*
  x Coliberti
Collies *(SF429.C6)*
  sa Border collies
  Example under Dog breeds
Collies, Working
  See Border collies
Collineation *(QA601)*
Collins Expedition, 1878-1879 *(HE2930.M2)*
Collinsville, Australia
— Powerhouse Construction Project
    Lockout, 1967
Collision broadening *(QC454)*
  sa Doppler effect
  x Broadening, Collision
  xx Spectrum analysis
Collisional excitation *(QC173)*
  x Excitation, Collisional
  xx Collisions (Nuclear physics)
    Scattering (Physics)
Collisions, Aircraft
  See Aeronautics—Accidents
Collisions, Automobile
  See Traffic accidents
Collisions, Railroad
  See Railroads—Accidents
Collisions (Nuclear physics)
  sa Channeling (Physics)
    Charge exchange
    Charge transfer
    Collisional excitation
    Compton effect

Cross sections (Nuclear physics)
Inelastic cross sections
Ion bombardment
Ionization
Neutron cross sections
Nuclear reactions
Radiation
Scattering (Physics)
Secondary electron emission
Sputtering (Physics)
Stopping power (Nuclear physics)
names of particles, e.g. Electrons,
    Neutrons, Protons
  x Bombardment with particles
    Electron collisions
    Impact phenomena (Nuclear physics)
    Nuclear collisions
  xx Ionization
    Nuclear physics
    Particles (Nuclear physics)
    Radiation
Collisions at sea *(International law, JX4434)*
  sa Liability for marine accidents
    Rule of the road at sea
    Salvage
    Shipwrecks
    names of ships
  xx Disasters
    Marine accidents
    Maritime law
    Navigation
    Rule of the road at sea
    Salvage
    Shipwrecks
— Prevention *(VK371-8)*
  sa Ships' lights
  xx Merchant marine—Signaling
    Ships' lights
    Signals and signaling
— — Problems, exercises, etc.
Collodion *(TS1145)*
Collodion process *(TR390)*
  x Wet collodion process
    Wet plate process
Collogen
  See Collagen
Colloidal fuel
  See Fuel, Colloidal
Colloids *(Chemistry, QD549; Physiology,*
  QP525)
  sa Azeotropes
    Biocolloids
    Coagulation
    Dialysis
    Foam
    Gelation
    Metallic soaps
    Micelles
    Particles
    Rheology
    Sephadex
    Soil colloids
    Thixotropy
  x Dispersoids
    Gels
    Sols
  xx Amorphous substances
    Chemistry, Physical and theoretical
    Diffusion
    Matter—Properties
    Micelles
    Particles
    Rheology
    Solution (Chemistry)
    Surface chemistry
— Electric properties
— Problems, exercises, etc.
— Programmed instruction

Colloids (Chemistry, QD549; Physiology,
    QP525) (Continued)
— Radiation effects
        See Colloids, Effect of radiation on
Colloids, Effect of radiation on
    x Colloids, Irradiated
        Colloids—Radiation effects
        Radiation—Effect on colloids
    xx Radiation
Colloids, Irradiated
    See Colloids, Effect of radiation on
Colloquial bulls
    See Bulls, Colloquial
Colloquial English
    See English language—Conversation and
        phrase books
        English language—Spoken English
Colloquial Latin
    See Latin language, Colloquial
Colloquies, Religious
    See Disputations, Religious
Colloquy of Ratisbon, 1541
    See Ratisbon, Colloquy of, 1541
Colloquy of Ratisbon, 1546
    See Ratisbon, Colloquy of, 1546
Collotype (TR930)
    sa Heliotype
    xx Photography
        Photomechanical processes
Colmar, Battle of, 1945
    xx World War, 1939-1945—Campaigns—
        France (1944-1945)
Colobognatha (Millepeds, QL449)
    xx Myriapoda
Cologne (Toilet water)
    See Eau de Cologne
Cologne water
    See Eau de Cologne
Colombia
— History (F2251-2277)
— — To 1810
— — Insurrection of the Comuneros, 1781
        sa Venezuela—History—Insurrection
            of the Comuneros, 1781
        xx Venezuela—History—Insurrection
            of the Comuneros, 1781
— — 1810-
— — War of Independence, 1810-1822
        sa Cartagena, Colombia—Siege, 1815
            Chorros Blancos, Battle of, 1820
            Juanambú River, Battle of the,
                1814
            Pantano de Vargas, Battle of,
                1819
— — — Anniversaries, etc.
— — 1822-1832
— — 1832-1886
— — 1886-1903 (F2276.5)
        sa Colombia—History—Revolution,
            1899-1903
— — Revolution, 1899-1903 (F2276.5)
        sa Palonegro, Battle of, 1900
        xx Colombia—History—1886-1903
— — 1903-1946 (F2277)
— — 1946- (F2278)
— — Poetry
        Note under Poetry of places
Colombian drama (Direct)
Colombian fiction (Direct) (Collections,
    PQ8176.F3; History, PQ8172)
— 20th century
Colombian literature (Direct)
    (PQ8160-8179)
    xx Spanish American literature
— 20th century
Colombian maxims
    See Maxims, Colombian

Colombian newspapers (History, etc.,
    PN5051-5)
Colombian periodicals (History, etc.,
    PN5051-5)
Colombian-Peruvian asylum case
    x Peruvian-Colombian asylum case
    xx Asylum, Right of—Cases
        Extradition—Cases
Colombian poetry (Direct) (Collections,
    PQ8174; History, PQ8170)
— 20th century
Colombian prose literature (Collections,
    PQ8176; History, PQ8172)
Colombian students in the United States,
    ⌈etc.⌉
Colombians in the United States, ⌈etc.⌉
Colombo plan
    See Economic assistance in Southeastern
        Asia
        Technical assistance in Southeastern
            Asia
Colon (Anatomy) (QL863; QM345)
    xx Intestine, Large
— Cancer (RC280.C)
— Diseases (RC860)
        sa Colitis
            Diverticulitis
            Megacolon
            Proctosigmoidoscopy
        xx Proctology
— Inflammation
        See Colitis
— Radiography
— Surgery
        sa Colostomy
Colon (Punctuation)
    sa Semicolon
    xx Punctuation
Colon classification
    See Classification, Colon
Colonate (HD139.C7)
    sa Serfdom
Colonial affairs
    See Colonies
Colonial agents
    x Agents, Colonial
    xx Diplomatic and consular service
Colonial agricultural laws
    See Agricultural laws and legislation,
        Colonial
Colonial American art industries and trade
    See Art industries and trade, Early
        American
Colonial animals
    See Animal colonies
Colonial architecture
    See Architecture, Colonial
Colonial armies
    See Armies, Colonial
Colonial art
    See Art, Colonial
Colonial banks and banking
    See Banks and banking, Colonial
Colonial civil service
    See Civil service, Colonial
Colonial companies (HF481-491)
    sa names of individual companies
    x Commercial companies
        Companies, Colonial
        Merchant companies
    xx Colonization
        Commerce
Colonial education
    See Education, Colonial
Colonial forestry law
    See Forestry law and legislation, Colonial
Colonial irrigation laws
    See Irrigation laws, Colonial

Colonial labor laws and legislation
    See Labor laws and legislation, Colonial
Colonial law
    See Colonies—Law
Colonial mining law
    See Mining law, Colonial
Colonial painting
    See Painting, Colonial
Colonial railroad law
    See Railroad law, Colonial
Colonial railroads
    See Railroads, Colonial
Colonial real property
    See Real property, Colonial
Colonial research
    See Colonies—Research
Colonial silversmithing
    See Silversmithing, Colonial
Colonial wars
    See United States—History—Colonial
        period, ca. 1600-1775
Colonialism
    See Colonies
        Imperialism
        World politics
Coloniality (Zoology)
    See Animal colonies
Colonic irrigation
    See Enema
Colonies (JV)
    This heading, as well as the subdivision
        Colonies under country, may also be
        subdivided by any subdivision regu-
        larly used under names of countries,
        e.g. Colonies—Commerce; Great Brit-
        ain—Colonies—Commerce. Any sub-
        ject subdivided by country may also be
        further subdivided by the addition of
        the subdivision Colonies, e.g. Postage-
        stamps—France—Colonies.
    sa Agricultural colonies
        Colonies in Africa, ⌈America, Asia,
            etc.⌉ ⌈for works about colonies of
            various countries in a particular area⌉
        Colonization
        Emigration and immigration
        Land settlement
        Penal colonies
        Protectorates
        subdivision Colonies under names of
            countries, e.g. France—Colonies
    x Anti-colonialism
        Colonial affairs
        Colonialism
        Dependencies
        Nonselfgoverning territories
    xx Colonization
    Note under Colonization
— Administration (JV412-485)
        sa Military government of dependencies
            subdivision Colonies—
                Administration under names of
                countries, e.g. France—Colonies—
                Administration
        xx Administrative law
— Agricultural laws and legislation
        See Agricultural laws and legislation,
            Colonial
— Armies
        See Armies, Colonial
— Civil service
        See Civil service, Colonial
— Commerce
        Example under Colonies
— Economic conditions

380

sa *subdivision* Colonies—Economic
  conditions *under names of*
  countries, e.g. Great Britain—
  Colonies—Economic conditions
— Education
  See Education, Colonial
— Educational law and legislation
  See Educational law and legislation,
  Colonial
— Finance *(HJ240; Budgets, HJ2025;*
  Debts, HJ8043-5; Tariffs,
  HF1723)
  Here are entered general works on
  colonial finance, private or public.
  Works on finance in colonies of in-
  dividual countries are entered un-
  der the headings Finance, or Fi-
  nance, Public, subdivided by coun-
  try—Colonies. Works on finance of
  a specific colony are entered under
  the same headings, subdivided by
  the name of the colony.
  sa Grants-in-aid, Colonial
  Example under Finance
— Forestry law and legislation
  See Forestry law and legislation,
  Colonial
— Grants-in-aid
  See Grants-in-aid, Colonial
— Historiography
— International law
  See Colonies (International law)
— Irrigation laws
  See Irrigation laws, Colonial
— Labor laws and legislation
  See Labor laws and legislation,
  Colonial
— Law
  Here are entered general and compara-
  tive works on colonial law. Works
  on the colonial law of a particular
  country are entered under Law—
  [local subdivision]—Colonies.
  Works on the law of any particular
  colony are entered under the head-
  ing Law, subdivided by the name of
  that colony, *e.g.* Law—Nigeria.
  x Colonial law
  Law, Colonial
— Mining law
  See Mining law, Colonial
— Officials and employees
  See Civil service, Colonial
— Railroad law
  See Railroad law, Colonial
— Railroads
  See Railroads, Colonial
— Real property
  See Real property, Colonial
— Research
  x Colonial research
Colonies (Biology) *(QH549)*
  sa Animal colonies
  Animal populations
  Coenobic plants
  Plant populations
  xx Ecology
Colonies (International law) *(JX4027)*
  x Colonies—International law
  xx International law
Colonies in Africa, [America, Asia, etc.]
  xx Colonies
Colonies in literature
Colonitis
  See Colitis

Colonization *(United States, HD171-179;*
  Other countries, HD301-1130)
  Here are entered works on the policy of
  settling immigrants or nationals in
  colonial areas. Works on migration
  from one country to another are entered under Emigration and immigration. Works on migration within a
  country are entered under Migration,
  Internal. Works on general colonial
  policy, including land settlement, are
  entered under Colonies.
  sa Agricultural colonies
  Colonial companies
  Colonies
  Emigration and immigration
  Land grants
  Migration, Internal
  Penal colonies
  Public lands
  subdivision Colonization *under names*
  of countries, regions, etc., e.g. Africa
  —Colonization; *and under names of*
  classes of persons, e.g. Epileptics—
  Colonization; Negroes—Colonization
  xx Colonies
  Emigration and immigration
  Land settlement
  Note under Agricultural colonies
Colonization, Mennonite
  See Mennonites—Colonization
Colonization of Negroes
  See Negroes—Colonization
Colophons *(Z242.C7)*
  sa Imprints (in books)
  Incipits
  Title-page
  xx Books
  Cataloging
  Imprints (in books)
  Incunabula
  Printing—History
  Title-page
Colophons of manuscripts *(Z110.C6)*
  x Manuscripts—Colophons
Color *(Art, ND1279-1286; Physics, QC495)*
  sa Black in art
  Blue in art
  Color in advertising
  Colors
  Dyes and dyeing
  Music and color
  Reading—Color aids
  White in art
  x Chromatics
  xx Aesthetics
  Chemistry
  Colors
  Light
  Optics
  Painting
  Photometry
— Juvenile literature
— Measurement
  See Colorimetry
— Physiological effect
  xx Light—Physiological effect
  Phototherapy
— Psychology *(BF789.C7; Psychology of*
  vision, BF241)
  sa Color pyramid test
  Lüscher test
  x Psychology of color
  xx Color-hearing
  Color-sense
— Study and teaching
  sa Coloring for children
  Painting books

— Terminology
  sa Color guides
  Colors, Words for
  x Colors—Terminology
  xx Color guides
Color and form recognition test
  xx Color-sense
  Form perception
  Mental tests
Color and music
  See Music and color
Color-blindness *(RE921)*
  sa Color-sense
  x Color discrimination
  xx Blindness
  Color-sense
  Eye—Diseases and defects
  Vision
— Genetic aspects
Color-blindness in children *(Indirect)*
  x Color vision disorders in children
  xx Pediatric ophthalmology
Color centers
  x F centers
  xx Crystal lattices
  Crystals—Defects
  Dislocations in crystals
  Point defects
Color cinematography *(TR853)*
  sa Color moving-pictures
  xx Cinematography
  Color moving-pictures
  Color photography
Color discrimination
  See Color-blindness
  Color-sense
Color-etchings
  See Color prints
Color fastness (Textiles)
  See Colorfastness (Textiles)
Color-field painting *(Direct)*
  x Color painting (Painting style)
  xx Abstract expressionism
  Concrete art
  Painting, Modern—20th century
Color guides
  sa Color—Terminology
  xx Color—Terminology
Color-hearing *(BF497)*
  sa Color—Psychology
  Color-sense
  Music and color
  Perception
  Synesthesia
  Words in color
  xx Color-sense
  Perception
  Psychology
  Senses and sensation
  Synesthesia
Color in advertising *(HF5839)*
  sa Packaging
  Show-windows
  Signs and sign-boards
  x Advertising, Color in
  xx Advertising
  Color
  Commercial art
Color in architecture *(NA2795)*
  x Architectural polychromy
  Buildings—Color
  Color in building
  xx Architecture
  Interior decoration
  Polychromy
Color in art
  xx Art

Color in building
  See Color in architecture
Color in cartography
  sa Four-color problem
  x Hypsometric colors
  xx Cartography
Color in gardening
  sa Color of flowers
  xx Color of flowers
    Gardening
    Plants, Ornamental
Color in heraldry
  xx Heraldry
Color in industry
  xx Industry
Color in interior decoration
  xx Interior decoration
    Polychromy
Color in postage-stamps
  See Postage-stamps—Color
Color in sculpture
  See Polychromy
Color in the ceramic industries *(TP823)*
  sa China painting
    Engobes
    Glass painting and staining
    Glazes
  x Ceramic coloring
    Ceramics—Coloring
    Coloring of ceramics
    Pottery—Coloring
  xx Ceramic industries
    Decoration and ornament
Color in the textile industries *(Design,*
    TS1475; Dyeing, TP892)
  sa Dyes and dyeing
  xx Dyes and dyeing
    Textile industry and fabrics
    Textile printing
Color measurement
  See Colorimetry
Color moving-pictures
  sa Color cinematography
  x Colored moving-pictures
    Technicolor pictures
  xx Color cinematography
    Moving-pictures
Color-music
  See Music and color
Color of animals *(QL767)*
  sa Animal pigments
    Camouflage (Biology)
    Color of birds
    Color of fishes
    Color of insects
    Color of reptiles
    Melanism
    Melanosis
    Mimicry (Biology)
    Protective coloration (Biology)
  x Animal coloration
    Animals, Color of
    Coat color of animals
    Pigmentation
  xx Animal pigments
    Biology
    Camouflage (Biology)
    Color-variation (Biology)
    Evolution
    Melanophores
    Mimicry (Biology)
    Variation (Biology)
    Zoology
  — Juvenile literature
Color of birds *(QL698)*
  x Birds, Color of
  xx Color of animals
    Variation (Biology)

Color of fishes *(QL639)*
  x Fishes—Color
  xx Color of animals
Color of flowers *(Ecology, QK926;*
    Nomenclature, QK669)
  sa Anthocyanidins
    Anthocyanin
    Color in gardening
    Variegation
  xx Botany
    Color in gardening
    Color of plants
    Flowers
    Variation (Biology)
Color of food
  sa Color of fruit
    Color of meat
    Coloring matter in food
  x Food color
    Food—Color
Color of fruit *(QK899)*
  x Fruit—Color
  xx Color of food
    Color of plants
Color of insects *(QL496)*
  x Insects—Color
    Insects, Color of
  xx Color of animals
    Variation (Biology)
Color of leaves *(QK899)*
  sa Variegation
  x Leaves, Color of
  xx Color of plants
    Variation (Biology)
Color of man *(GN197)*
  sa Albinos and albinism
    Hair
    Indians—Color
    Melanism
  x Complexion
    Pigmentation
    Skin, Color of
  xx Albinos and albinism
    Anthropology
    Color-variation (Biology)
    Ethnology
    Evolution
    Man
    Man—Influence of environment
    Negro race
    Skin
    Somatology
  — Juvenile literature
Color of meat
  x Meat—Color
  xx Color of food
Color of plants *(QK899)*
  sa Chromogen
    Color of flowers
    Color of fruit
    Color of leaves
    Plant pigments
    Variegation
  x Plants—Color
  xx Biology
    Botany
    Color-variation (Biology)
    Evolution
    Plant pigments
    Plants
    Variation (Biology)
Color of reptiles *(QL699)*
  x Reptiles—Color
  xx Color of animals
Color of soils
  x Soils—Color
    Soils, Color of

Color of stars
  See Stars—Color
Color of wood
  x Wood—Color
Color painting (Painting style)
  See Color-field painting
Color perception
  See Color-sense
Color photography *(TR510-525)*
  sa Color cinematography
    Color sensitometry (Photography)
    Hillotype
  x Chromophotography
    Heliochromy
    Photography, Color
  xx Photography
  — Autochrome process *(TR510)*
  — Developing and developers
    xx Photographic chemicals
    Example under Color photography—
      Processing
  — Lippmann process *(TR525)*
    x Lippmann process
  — Printing processes
    x Color prints (Photography)
    xx Photography—Printing processes
    Example under Color photography—
      Processing
  — Processing *(TR530)*
    sa special color photographic processes,
      e.g. Color photography—
      Developing and developers; Color
      photography—Printing processes
  — Three-color process *(TR520)*
    x Three-color process
    xx Color-printing
    Photoengraving
Color-printing *(Z258)*
    Here are entered general works on typo-
    graphic printing in color, that is, works
    for the practical printer. Works dealing
    with the printing of engravings in color
    are entered under Color prints.
  sa Chromolithography
    Color photography—Three-color
      process
    Color separation
    Electronics in color printing
    Rubrication
    Screen process printing
    Serigraphy
  xx Chromolithography
    Printing, Practical
  Note under Color prints
Color prints *(NE1850-1879)*
    Here are entered works on pictures
    printed in color from engraved metal,
    wood, or stone. Works dealing with
    color work in its relation to practical
    printing are entered under Color-print-
    ing.
  sa Chiaroscuro
    Chromolithography
    Linoleum block-printing
    Serigraphs (Prints)
    Sporting prints
    Tile block-printing
  x Chromoxylography
    Color etchings
    Paintings—Color reproductions
    Wood-engravings, Colored
  xx Chromolithography
    Engravings
  Note under Color-printing
  — Private collections *(Direct)*
Color prints, English, ₍French, etc.₎ *(Direct)*
  x English ₍French, etc.₎ color prints

Color prints (Photography)
See Color photography—Printing processes
Color pyramid test *(BF698.8.C6)*
  x Farbpyramidentest
  xx Color—Psychology
    Projective techniques
Color-sense *(QP481)*
  sa Color and form recognition test
    Color-blindness
    Color-hearing
    Color—Psychology
    Retina
  x Color discrimination
    Color perception
  xx Color-blindness
    Color-hearing
    Optics, Physiological
    Psychology, Physiological
    Retina
    Senses and sensation
    Vision
  — Genetic aspects
    Example under Genetics
Color sensitometry (Photography) *(TR515)*
  xx Color photography
    Photographic sensitometry
Color separation
  xx Color-printing
Color slides
  See Slides (Photography)
Color television *(TK6670)*
  x Television, Color
  xx Television
  — Apparatus and supplies
  — — Testing
  — Juvenile literature
  — Receivers and reception
    x Color television receivers
  — Repairing *(TK6670)*
Color television receivers
  See Color television—Receivers and
    reception
Color-variation (Biology) *(QH401-8)*
  sa Color of animals
    Color of man
    Color of plants
    Mimicry (Biology)
  xx Variation (Biology)
Color vision disorders in children
  See Color-blindness in children
Colorado
  — Centennial celebrations, etc.
    Example under Anniversaries; *and under*
      reference from Centennial celebra-
      tions
  — Climate
    Example under Climatology
  — History *(F771-781)*
  — — To 1876
  — — Civil War, 1861-1865 *(E498)*
  — — 1876-1950
  — — 1951-
Colorado beetle
  See Potato-beetle
Colorado Indians (Ecuador) *(F3722.1.C)*
  x Saccha Indians
    Tsatchela Indians
  xx Indians of South America
Colorado River
  — Water-rights
    Example under Water-rights
Colorado-Zuñi Expedition, 1851
  See Zuñi-Colorado Expedition, 1851
Coloration, Protective (Biology)
  See Protective coloration (Biology)
Colorature
  See Embellishment (Vocal music)

Colored Baptists
  See Baptists, Negro
Colored Catholics
  See Catholics, Negro
Colored Disciples of Christ
  See Disciples of Christ, Negro
Colored glass
  See Glass, Colored
Colored Lutherans
  See Lutherans, Negro
Colored mammies
  See Mammies
Colored Methodist Episcopal Church
    (BX8460-8469)
  xx Methodist Episcopal Church
Colored Methodists
  See Methodists, Negro
Colored Mormons
  See Mormons and Mormonism, Negro
Colored moving-pictures
  See Color moving-pictures
Colored people (South Africa)
    Here are entered works dealing with the
      problems of that element in the popu-
      lation of South Africa which consists
      of crosses between Europeans and
      Bantus, Hottentots, Malays, etc.
  x Cape coloured people
    Coloured persons (South Africa)
  xx Miscegenation
  — Education
  — Employment
Colored people (United States)
  See Negroes
Colored Presbyterians
  See Presbyterians, Negro
Colored refugees
  See Slavery in the United States—Fugitive
    slaves
Colorfastness (Textiles)
  x Color fastness (Textiles)
    Fastness of color (Textiles)
  xx Dyes and dyeing—Textile fibers
    Textile industry and fabrics
Colorimetric analysis
  sa Chromatographic analysis
  xx Chemistry, Analytic
    Colorimetry
Colorimetry *(QC495; Chemical analysis,*
    QD113)
  sa Colorimetric analysis
  x Color measurement
    Color—Measurement
  xx Mensuration
  — Problems, exercises, etc.
  — Tables, etc.
Coloring books
  See Painting books
Coloring for children *(LB1187-8)*
  sa Painting books
  xx Color—Study and teaching
Coloring matter *(Dyes, TP910-925; Paints,*
    pigments, etc., TP936)
  sa Caramel
    Coal-tar colors
    Dyes and dyeing
    Pigments
  x Colorings
  xx Coal-tar colors
    Dyes and dyeing
    Pigments
Coloring matter in food *(TX571.C7)*
  x Dyes and dyeing—Food
  xx Color of food
    Food
  — Specifications *(Direct)*
Coloring of ceramics
  See Color in the ceramic industries

Coloring of metals
  See Metals—Coloring
Coloring of photographs
  See Photographs—Coloring
Coloring of plastics
  See Plastics—Coloring
Coloring of transparencies
  See Transparencies—Coloring
Colorings
  See Coloring matter
Colorpoint cat *(SF449.C6)*
  x Long-haired siamese cat
  xx Siamese cat
Colors *(Artists' pigments, ND1510; Color in*
    painting, ND1279-1286; Industrial
    painting, TT310-324; Physics,
    QC495)
  sa Coal-tar colors
    Color
    Structural colors
    Symbolism of colors
    names of colors, e.g. Purple, Yellow
  xx Color
  — Analysis *(QC495)*
    x Analysis of colors
    Chemical analysis of colors
  — Juvenile literature
  — Terminology
    See Color—Terminology
Colors, Liturgical *(BV165)*
  x Liturgical colors
  xx Church vestments
    Symbolism of colors
Colors, School
  See School colors
Colors, Words for
  x Words for colors
  xx Color—Terminology
Colors (Flags)
  See Flags
Colors in literature
  sa Colors in the Bible
Colors in the Bible *(BS680.C55)*
  xx Bible—Criticism, interpretation, etc.
    Colors in literature
Colostomy
  xx Colon (Anatomy)—Surgery
Colostrum *(QP246)*
  xx Milk, Human
Coloured persons (South Africa)
  See Colored people (South Africa)
Colpahuaico, Battle of, 1824 *(F3446)*
  xx Peru—History—War of Independence,
    1820-1829
Colportage
  See Bible—Publication and distribution
    Booksellers and bookselling—
      Colportage, subscription trade, etc.
Colposcope
  xx Endoscope and endoscopy
Colposcopy
  xx Endoscope and endoscopy
  — Atlases
Colt automatic machine-gun *(UF620.C6)*
  xx Colt firearms
    Machine-guns
Colt automobile
  See Dodge Colt automobile
Colt firearms
  sa Colt automatic machine-gun
    Colt revolver
  xx Firearms
Colt Galant automobile
  x Galant automobile
Colt revolver
  xx Colt firearms
    Revolvers
Coltsfoot

Coluber constrictor
   x Black racer
      Black snake
      Blue racer
      North American black snake
Columbae
   See Pigeons
Columbates
   See Niobates
Columbia, S.C., Burning of, 1865 *(E477.75)*
   xx Sherman's March through the Carolinas
Columbia Co., Pa.
   — Tornado, 1890
Columbia driver judgment test
   xx Automobile drivers' tests
Columbia Indians
   See Sinkiuse-Columbia Indians
Columbia University
   — Graduate students
      Example under Graduate students
Columbia University. School of Law.
      Blackstone Moot Court
   Example under Moot courts
Columbidae
   See Pigeons
Columbium
   See Niobium
Columbium ores
   See Niobium ores
Columbus, Miss.
   — History
   — —Civil War, 1861-1865
Columbus, Ohio
   — Public works
      Example under Cities and towns—Planning
Columbus Day *(E120)*
   xx Holidays
   — Juvenile literature
Columbus test *(BF698.8.C64)*
   xx Picture interpretation tests
      Projective techniques
      Social maturity scales
Columella auris *(QL948; QM507)*
   xx Ear
Columns *(Direct)* *(Building, TH2252-3;*
      Testing, TA492.C7)
   sa Bases (Architecture)
      Capitals (Architecture)
      Half-columns
   x Pillars
   xx Architecture
Columns, Concrete *(TA681-3; Testing,*
      TA439-445)
   x Concrete columns
   xx Concrete construction
   — Fatigue
      xx Concrete—Fatigue
   — Tables, calculations, etc.
   — Testing
Columns, Corinthian *(NA2860)*
   sa Capitals (Architecture), Corinthian
   x Corinthian columns
   xx Architecture, Greek
Columns, Doric *(NA2860)*
   x Doric columns
   xx Architecture, Greek
Columns, Ionic *(NA2860)*
   x Ionic columns
   xx Architecture, Greek
Columns, Iron and steel *(Building,*
      TH1610-1625; Testing, TA492.C7)
   x Iron and steel columns
      Steel and iron columns
   xx Cast-iron
      Iron, Structural
      Steel, Structural
   Example under Structural design

Columns, Packed
   See Packed towers
Columns, Plate
   See Plate towers
Columns, Wooden *(TH2252-3)*
   x Wooden columns
Colville Indians *(E99.C)*
   xx Indians of North America
      Salishan Indians
   — Legal status, laws, etc.
Colymbidae
   See Divers (Birds)
Colza
   See Rape (Plant)
Colza-oil
   See Rape-oil
Coma *(RC383.C6)*
   sa Diabetic coma
      Loss of consciousness
      Stupor
   xx Stupor
Coma, Hepatic
   See Hepatic coma
Coman language
   See Kipchak language
Comanche Indians *(E99.C85)*
   x Camanche Indians
      Commanche Indians
   xx Indians of North America
      Numic Indians
      Shoshonean Indians
   — Juvenile literature
Comanche language *(PM921)*
   sa Shoshonean languages
   xx Numic languages
      Shoshonean languages
Comandra blister rust
   xx Blister rust
Comans
   See Kipchak
Comas Solá's comet *(QB723.C)*
Comb filters
   xx Electric filters
Comb racks
Combat
   sa Battles
      Dueling
      Hand-to-hand fighting
      Wager of battle
   x Fighting
   xx Dueling
      Wager of battle
   — Physiological aspects
      x Physiological aspects of combat
      xx Stress (Physiology)
   — Psychological aspects
      xx Psychology, Military
Combat, Trial by
   See Wager of battle
Combat rations
   See Operational rations (Military supplies)
Combat television
   See Military television
Combat vehicles
   See Armored vehicles, Military
Combatants and noncombatants (International
      law)
   sa Guerillas (International law)
      Levies en masse
   x Noncombatants (International law)
   xx Armed Forces
      Belligerency
      Military law
      War (International law)
Combate de Armiñon
   See Armiñon, Battle of, 1837
Combativeness
   See Fighting (Psychology)

Combination of grades
   xx Education—Curricula
      Educational acceleration
Combinations *(Mathematics, QA165)*
   sa Binomial coefficients
      Probabilities
   xx Algebra
      Chance
      Combinatorial analysis
      Mathematics
      Permutations
   — Problems, exercises, etc.
Combinations, Industrial
   See Trusts, Industrial
Combinations in restraint of trade
   See Monopolies
      Restraint of trade
      Trusts, Industrial
Combinations of labor
   See Strikes and lockouts
Combinatorial analysis *(QA164)*
   sa Combinations
      Combinatorial geometry
      Difference sets
      Graph theory
      Matroids
      Permutations
   xx Algebra
      Mathematical analysis
   — Problems, exercises, etc.
Combinatorial geometry *(QA167)*
   x Geometry, Combinatorial
   xx Combinatorial analysis
Combinatorial topology
   sa Discontinuous groups
   xx Complexes
      Topology
Combinatory logic
   x Logic, Combinatory
   xx Logic, Symbolic and mathematical
Combined hydroelectric and steam power
      systems
   See Hydrothermal electric power systems
Combined operations (Military science)
   See Amphibious warfare
      Landing operations
      Unified operations (Military science)
Combined sewers *(Indirect)*
   xx Sewerage
Combined training (Horsemanship)
   See Three-day event (Horsemanship)
Combines (Agricultural machinery) *(S699)*
   xx Harvesting machinery
      Threshing machines
   — Electric equipment
   — Hydraulic equipment
   — Maintenance and repair
   — Motors
   — Transportation
Combing machines
   xx Carding-machines
      Textile machinery
Combs *(HD9999.C7)*
   xx Costume
Combustible liquids
   See Inflammable liquids
Combustion *(QD516)*
   sa Chemical warfare
      Fire
      Flame
      Fuel
      Greek fire
      Heat
      Propellants
      Smoke
   subdivision Combustion *under subjects,*
      e.g. Diesel motor—Combustion; Gas
      and oil engines—Combustion

x Coal—Combustion
xx Chemistry
Fire
Heat
Smoke
Thermochemistry
— Measurement
— — Laboratory manuals
— Programmed instruction
— Research
See Combustion research
— Tables, etc. (QD516)
Combustion, Heat of
See Heat of combustion
Combustion, Spontaneous (Coal storage,
TN817; Fire prevention, TH9198;
Mine accidents, TN313-315)
x Spontaneous combustion
xx Mine fires
Combustion, Spontaneous human (RA1171)
x Spontaneous human combustion
Combustion, Theory of (QD516)
Combustion deposits in engines
x Carbon deposits in engines
xx Engines
Fuel
Combustion engineering (TJ254.5)
xx Heat engineering
Combustion gases
sa Automobile exhaust gas
Flue gases
xx Gases
— Analysis
— Tables, calculations, etc.
Combustion research
x Combustion—Research
xx Research
Comechingone Indians (Argentine Republic,
F2823.C)
xx Indians of South America
Comedians (Direct)
sa Clowns
xx Actors
Clowns
Entertainers
— Biography
— Vocational guidance
Comedians, British
See Comedians, English
Comedians, English
x Comedians, British
Comedy (Collections, PN6147-9; History,
PN1920-1929)
sa Burlesque (Literature)
Comedy films
Comic, The
Commedia dell' arte
Farce
Grotesque
Tragicomedy
French drama (Comedy); Greek drama
(Comedy); Italian drama (Comedy);
and similar headings
x Comic literature
Literature, Comic
xx Drama
Wit and humor
Comedy films
sa names of individual comedians in
moving-pictures
x Moving-picture comedies
xx Comedy
Farce
Feature films
Moving-picture cartoons
Moving-picture plays
Moving-pictures

Comet (Jet transports) (TL686.D4)
x Comet jet liner
De Havilland Comet
xx Jet transports
Comet jet liner
See Comet (Jet transports)
Comets (QB721-732)
Subdivided by date, e.g. Comets—1835.
Periodic comets are entered under the
name of the discoverer, e.g. Halley's
comet.
xx Astronomy
Solar system
— 1835
Note under Comets

GENERAL SUBDIVISIONS

— Atlases
xx Astronomy—Charts, diagrams, etc.

GENERAL SUBDIVISIONS

— Juvenile literature

GENERAL SUBDIVISIONS

— Orbits (QB357)
xx Mechanics, Celestial
Orbits
— Spectra
— Tables (QB722)
Comeya Indians
See Kamia Indians
Comfort, Standard of
See Cost and standard of living
Comfort stations
See Public comfort stations
subdivision Public comfort stations
under names of cities, e.g. New York
(City)—Public comfort stations
Comic, The (BH301.C7)
x Ludicrous, The
Ridiculous, The
xx Comedy
Wit and humor
Comic books and children
x Children and comic books
Comic books and youth
Youth and comic books
xx Child study
Children
Comic books, strips, etc.
Comic books and youth
See Comic books and children
Comic books, strips, etc.
sa Chap-books
Comic books and children
Newspapers—Sections, columns, etc.—
Comics
Sex—Comic books, strips, etc.
x Comic strips
Comics
Funnies
xx Caricatures and cartoons
Chap-books
Wit and humor, Pictorial
— Biography
sa Comic books, strips, etc.—French—
Biography
— Dialogue
— French
x French comic books, strips, etc.
xx French wit and humor, Pictorial
— — Biography
xx Comic books, strips, etc.—
Biography
— Moral and religious aspects
— Prices (Direct)
— Subjects

See Comic books, strips, etc.—
Themes, motives
— Themes, motives
x Comic books, strips, etc.—Subjects
Comic literature
See Burlesque (Literature)
Comedy
Commedia dell' arte
Farce
Parody
Satire
subdivision Parodies, travesties, etc.
under names of prominent authors,
e.g. Shakespeare, William, 1564-1616
—Parodies, travesties, etc.
Comic opera
See Opera
Operetta
Zarzuela
Comic songs
See Humorous songs
Comic strips
See Comic books, strips, etc.
Comics
See Comic books, strips, etc.
COMIT (Computer program language)
Comites Palatii
See Counts palatine
Comity of nations (JX4081)
x Courtesy of nations
International courtesy
Nations, Comity of
xx International law
International relations
Comma
xx Punctuation
Commanche Indians
See Comanche Indians
Commandments, Six hundred and thirteen
(BM520.8)
sa Azharot
x Mizwahs, Six hundred and thirteen
Precepts, Six hundred and thirteen
Six hundred and thirteen
commandments
Taryag mizwot
xx Commandments (Judaism)
Jewish law
Judaism
Commandments, Six hundred and thirteen
(Samaritan)
xx Samaritans—Religion
Commandments, Ten (Moral theology,
BV4655-4710; Texts, BS1281-5)
sa Evangelical counsels
Revelation on Sinai
x Decalogue
Ten commandments
xx Christian ethics
Commandments (Judaism)
Jewish law
Judaism
— Adultery
xx Adultery
— Art
— Blasphemy
See Commandments, Ten—Name of
God
— Covetousness
xx Avarice
— Early works to 1800
— False witness
xx Oaths
Perjury
Witnesses
— God
xx God
— Images

Commandments, Ten *(Moral theology,*
BV4655-4710; Texts, BS1281-5)
— Images *(Continued)*
   sa Photography (Jewish law)
   xx Idols and images
— Juvenile literature *(BV4656)*
— Meditations
— Murder
   xx Murder
— Name of God
   x Commandments, Ten—Blasphemy
   xx Blasphemy
      God—Name
— Numerical division
— Other gods
   xx Idols and images—Worship
— Parents
   xx Obedience
      Parent and child
— Sabbath
   xx Sabbath
      Sunday
— Summary
   See Summary of the Law (Theology)
— Theft
   xx Larceny
      Robbery
      Thieves
Commandments (Judaism)
  sa Commandments, Six hundred and
     thirteen
     Commandments, Ten
     Revelation on Sinai
  x Mitsvot
     Precepts (Judaism)
  xx Jewish law
Commandments of the church *(BV4720)*
   Here are entered works dealing with certain precepts of the church, disciplinary rather than doctrinal in character,
   e.g. to observe Sundays and fast days,
   to pay tithes, to go to confession, etc.
   If used for any church other than the
   Catholic, the name of the denomination is added as a subdivision.
  sa Easter duties
  x Church commandments
     Church precepts
     Precepts of the church
  xx Christian ethics
— Meditations
Commands (Logic) *(BC199.C5)*
  x Imperatives (Logic)
  xx Logic
Commedia dell' arte *(Collections, PQ4236-8;*
     History, PQ4155-9)
  sa Improvisation (Acting)
     Pierrot
  x Comic literature
     Literature, Comic
  xx Acting
     Comedy
     Farce
     Improvisation (Acting)
     Italian drama (Comedy)
— Pictorial works
Commemoration of saints
  See Saints—Commemoration
Commemoration of the faithful departed
  See Saints—Commemoration
Commemorations
  See Anniversaries
     Memorials
Commemorative coins *(Direct)*
  xx Coinage
     Coins
Commemorative plates *(Direct)*
  xx Commemorative porcelain

Commemorative pottery
Plates (Tableware)
Commemorative porcelain *(Direct)*
  sa Commemorative plates
  xx Porcelain
Commemorative postage stamps *(Direct)*
  x Postage-stamps—Topics—
     Commemoratives
  xx Postage-stamps
Commemorative pottery *(Direct)*
  sa Commemorative plates
  xx Pottery
Commemorative volumes
  See Festschriften
Commencement
  See Beginning
Commencement addresses
  See Baccalaureate addresses
Commensalism
  xx Symbiosis
Commentaries, Biblical
  See Bible—Commentaries
Commentators
  See Journalists
Commentators (Liturgy)
  See Mass commentators
Commerce *(HF; Commercial customs,*
     GT6010-6050; Primitive,
     GN436-440)
  sa Balance of trade
     Black market
     Blacklists, Commercial
     Business
     Business mathematics
     Businessmen
     Central business districts
     Certificates of origin
     Cipher and telegraph codes
     Coastwise shipping
     Colonial companies
     Commission-merchants
     Communication and traffic
     Competition, International
     Contraband of war
     Customs unions
     Delivery of goods
     Distribution (Economic theory)
     East-West trade (1945-   )
     Exchange
     Export credit
     Export marketing
     Export sales
     Foreign exchange
     Foreign licensing agreements
     Freight and freightage
     Geography, Commercial
     Geography, Economic
     Government trading
     Harbors
     Indians of Central America—
       Commerce
     Indians of North America—Commerce
     Indians of the West Indies—Commerce
     Inland navigation
     Inland water transportation
     Insurance, Marine
     International business enterprises
     Interstate commerce
     Investments, Foreign
     Maritime law
     Markets
     Merchant marine
     Merchants
     Money
     Monopolies
     Neutral trade with belligerents
     Neutrality
     Outlet stores

Ports of entry
Prices
Purchasing
Restraint of trade
Retail trade
Samples (Commerce)
Shipment of goods
Shipping
Smuggling
Sterling area
Trade-marks
Trade missions
Trade routes
Transit, International
Transportation
Underdeveloped areas—Commerce
Usages of trade
Warehouses
Wholesale trade
subdivision Commerce *under names of*
  countries, cities, etc.; subdivision
  Finance, commerce, confiscations,
  etc. *under names of wars; also names*
  of articles of commerce, e.g. Cotton,
  Leather, Lumber; *and headings*
  beginning with the word Commercial
x Exports
  Foreign commerce
  Foreign trade
  Imports
  International trade
  Trade
xx Business
  Communication and traffic
  Economics
  Exchange
  Finance
  Manufactures
  Space in economics
  Transportation
— Abbreviations
— Acronyms
— History
  xx Industry—History
— — Juvenile literature
— Information services
  sa subdivision Commerce—Information
    services *under names of countries,*
    cities, etc., e.g. New York (City)
    —Commerce—Information
    services
— Mathematical models
— Problems, exercises, etc.
— Psychological aspects
— Statistical methods
  See Commercial statistics
— Statistics
  See Commercial statistics
— Terminology *(HF1002)*
— Vocational guidance
Commerce, Prehistoric *(GN799.C45)*
  x Prehistoric commerce
Commerce clause (United States.
   Constitution)
  See Interstate commerce
Commercial aeronautics
  See Aeronautics, Commercial
Commercial agents *(Direct)*
  sa Agency (Law)
     Canvassing
     Commercial travelers
     Commission merchants
     Compradors
     Concert agents
     Literary agents
     Salesmen and salesmanship
     Theatrical agencies
     Travel agents

subdivision Agents *under names of businesses, etc., e.g.* Insurance— Agents
    x Agents, Commercial
    xx Agency (Law)
    Note under Foreign propagandists in the United States
— Accounting
— Collective labor agreements
    See Collective labor agreements— Commercial agents
— Salaries, commissions, etc.
— Taxation   *(Direct)*
Commercial agents, American, [**French, etc.**] *(Direct)*
Commercial announcements
  See Business announcements
Commercial arbitration
  See Arbitration and award
Commercial arbitration, International
  See Arbitration and award, International
Commercial arbitration agreements
  See Arbitration agreements, Commercial
Commercial arithmetic
  See Business mathematics
Commercial art   *(Direct)* *(NC997)*
    sa Art and industry
    Color in advertising
    Photography, Advertising
    x Advertising art
    Advertising, Art in
    Advertising, Pictorial
    Art, Commercial
    Art in advertising
    Commercial design
    xx Advertising
    Art
    Art and industry
    Drawing—Instruction
    Posters
— Printing   *(Z257)*
    sa Pictures—Printing
    xx Pictures—Printing
    Printing
— Vocational guidance
    See Commercial art as a profession
Commercial art as a profession
    x Commercial art—Vocational guidance
    xx Commercial artists
Commercial artists   *(Direct)*
    sa Commercial art as a profession
    xx Artists
— Interviews
Commercial associations   *(Direct)* *(HF294-343)*
    sa Boards of trade
    x Commercial organizations
    xx Societies
Commercial attachés   *(Direct)*
    x Attachés
    xx Diplomatic and consular service
Commercial attachés, American, [**French, etc.**] *(Direct)*
Commercial aviation
  See Aeronautics, Commercial
Commercial blacklists
  See Blacklists, Commercial
Commercial buildings
  See Mercantile buildings
    Office buildings
Commercial catalogs
  See Catalogs, Commercial
Commercial companies
  See Colonial companies
Commercial condominium
  See Condominium (Office buildings)
Commercial corners
  See Monopolies

Speculation
Stock-exchange
Trusts, Industrial
Commercial correspondence   *(HF5721-5733)*
    sa Adjustment letters
    Advertising, Direct-mail
    Business announcements
    English language—Business English
    Form letters
    Letter services
    Letterheads
    Sales letters
    x Business correspondence
    Business letters
    Correspondence
    xx Letter-writing
    Office practice
— Copying processes
    See Copying processes
— Programmed instruction
Commercial correspondence, French, [**German, Spanish, etc.**]
Commercial courts   *(Direct)* *(HF1221-2)*
    sa Arbitration and award, International
    xx Commercial law
    Courts
Commercial credit
  See Credit
Commercial credit companies
  See Commercial finance companies
    Instalment plan
Commercial crimes   *(Direct)*
    sa Competition, Unfair
    Fraud
    Monopolies
    Price regulation
    Restraint of trade
    Trusts, Industrial—Law
    Usury laws
    Weights and measures—Law and legislation
    White collar crimes
    x Crimes, Commercial
    Offenses affecting the public trade
    xx Criminal law
    Trade regulation
    White collar crimes
Commercial crises
  See Depressions
Commercial design
  See Commercial art
Commercial documents   *(Direct)*
    sa Bills of sale
    Consular documents
    Interim certificates
    Invoices
    Legal documents
    Negotiable instruments
    Stock certificates
    x Documents, Commercial
    xx Legal documents
— Forms
Commercial education
  See Business education
Commercial employees
  See Clerks
Commercial ethics
  See Business ethics
Commercial finance companies   *(Direct)*
    x Accounts receivable finance companies
    Commercial credit companies
    Credit companies
    Finance companies, Commercial
    Instalment credit companies
    Sales-finance companies
    xx Accounts receivable
    Credit
    Financial institutions

Instalment plan
Inventories
— Accounting   *(HF5686.C495)*
Commercial fishing
  See Fisheries
Commercial geography
  See Geography, Commercial
Commercial journalism
  See Journalism, Commercial
Commercial law   *(Direct)* *(HF1201-1400)*
    sa Accounting—Law
    Accounts current
    Admiralty
    Agency (Law)
    Arbitration and award
    Arbitration and award, International
    Assignments
    Attachment and garnishment
    Auctions
    Bailments
    Banking law
    Bankruptcy
    Bills of lading
    Bills of sale
    Brokers
    Business enterprises
    Business law
    Business names
    C.I.F. clause
    Carriers
    Chattel mortgages
    Checks
    Clerks
    Coastwise shipping—Law and legislation
    Collecting of accounts
    Collection laws
    Commercial courts
    Commission merchants
    Competition, Unfair
    Contracts
    Contracts, Maritime
    Conveyancing
    Corporation law
    Customer relations (Law)
    Debt
    Debtor and creditor
    Deeds
    Delivery orders
    F.O.B. clause
    Food law and legislation
    Foreign exchange
    Foreign trade regulation
    Forms (Law)
    Freight forwarders
    Insurance law
    Invoices
    Joint adventures
    Landlord and tenant
    Law merchant
    Leases
    Licenses
    Liens
    Limited liability
    Liquidation
    Maritime law
    Marketing—Law and legislation
    Moratorium
    Mortgages
    Negotiable instruments
    Partnership
    Payment
    Personal property
    Promissory notes
    Real property
    Receipts (Acknowledgments)
    Receivers
    Restraint of trade

Commercial law *(Direct) (HF1201-1400)*
(Continued)
    Sales
    Sales, Conditional
    Security (Law)
    Statute of frauds
    Suretyship and guaranty
    Trade-marks
    Trade regulation
    Trading with the enemy
    Trust companies
    Trusts and trustees
    Trusts, Industrial—Law
    Usury laws
    Vendors and purchasers
    Warehouses
    Warranty
  x Law, Commercial
    Mercantile law
  xx Business
    Business education
    Law merchant
    Maritime law
Note under Business law
— Codification
— Interpretation and construction
— Popular works
    See Business law
— Programmed instruction

GEOGRAPHIC SUBDIVISIONS

— United States
    x United States—Commercial law
Commercial law (Adat law) *(Direct)*
Commercial law (Islamic law) *(Direct)*
Commercial law (Lübeck law)
  Example under Lübeck law
Commercial leases *(Direct)*
  sa Leased departments, concessions, etc.
  x Business leases
  xx Landlord and tenant
    Leases
Commercial libraries *(Direct) (Z675.C7)*
  sa Business libraries
  x Libraries, Commercial
  xx Business libraries
Commercial missions
  See Trade missions
Commercial motor vehicles
  See Commercial vehicles
Commercial museums *(HF61)*
  xx Museums
Commercial organizations
  See Commercial associations
Commercial paper
  See Negotiable instruments
Commercial photography
  See Photography, Commercial
Commercial policy *(HF1401-1650)*
  sa Autarchy
    Blacklists, Commercial
    Bounties
    Commercial treaties
    Commodity control
    Competition, Unfair
    Currency convertibility
    Customs unions
    Dumping (Commercial policy)
    Export controls
    Export credit
    Export premiums
    Favored nation clause
    Foreign exchange—Law
    Foreign trade promotion
    Foreign trade regulation
    Free ports and zones
    Free trade and protection
    Government trading
    Import quotas

    Reciprocity
    Shipping bounties and subsidies
    Subsidies
    Tariff
    subdivision Commercial policy *under*
      names of countries, e.g. France—
      Commercial policy; Italy—
      Commercial policy
  x Foreign trade policy
    Government regulation of commerce
    Trade barriers
    World economics
  xx Blacklists, Commercial
    Economic policy
    Industry and state
    International economic relations
Commercial products *(Indirect)*
    (HF1041-1051)
  sa Animal products
    Commodity control
    Commodity exchanges
    Display of merchandise
    Durable goods, Consumer
    Forest products
    Geography, Commercial
    Geography, Economic
    Luxuries
    Manufactures
    Marine resources
    New products
    Raw materials
    Substitute products
    Surplus commodities
    Synthetic products
    names of individual products
  x Merchandise
    Products, Commercial
  xx Commodity exchanges
    Natural resources
    Substitute products
— Breakage, shrinkage, etc.
    See Breakage, shrinkage, etc.
      (Commerce)
— Classification
    sa Freight and freightage—
      Classification
      Tariff—Terminology and
      classification
— Examinations, questions, etc.
— Grading
    See Grading
— Mathematical models
— Safety measures
    See Product safety
— Shrinkage
    See Breakage, shrinkage, etc.
      (Commerce)
— Specifications
— Standards *(Direct)*
— Terminology
— Testing
—— Laboratory manuals
Commercial ratings
  See Credit guides
Commercial records
  See Business records
Commercial routes
  See Trade routes
Commercial schools
  See Business education
Commercial secrets
  See Trade secrets

Commercial statistics *(Serial documents,*
    HF91-293; Theory and method,
    HF1016-1017; United States,
    HF3001-6; Other countries,
    HF3211-4040 (1))
  sa subdivision Commerce *under names of*
    countries, cities, etc., e.g. France—
    Commerce; London—Commerce
  x Commerce—Statistical methods
    Commerce—Statistics
  xx Statistics
— Problems, exercises, etc.
Commercial teachers
  See Business teachers
Commercial travelers *(Direct) (HF5441-4)*
  sa Automobiles, Company
    Booksellers and bookselling—
      Colportage, subscription trade, etc.
    Canvassing
    Peddlers and peddling
    Trade-unions—Commercial travelers
  x Drummers
    Salesmen, Traveling
    Travelers, Commercial
    Traveling salesmen
  xx Agency (Law)
    Business
    Commercial agents
    Commission merchants
    Salesmen and salesmanship
— Anecdotes, facetiae, satire, etc.
— Collective labor agreements
    See Collective labor agreements—
      Commercial travelers
— Correspondence, reminiscences, etc.
— Salaries, commissions, etc.
— Taxation *(Direct)*
Commercial travelers, British, [**German, etc.**]
Commercial treaties *(HF1721-1733)*
  sa Favored nation clause
    Reciprocity
    subdivision Commercial treaties *under*
      names of countries, e.g. Great
      Britain—Commercial treaties
  x Trade agreements (Commerce)
  xx Commercial policy
    Competition, International
    Foreign trade regulation
    Reciprocity
    Tariff
    Treaties
Commercial trusts
  See Trusts, Industrial
Commercial vehicles
  sa Motor buses
    Motor-trucks
  x Commercial motor vehicles
  xx Automobiles
    Motor vehicles
    Transportation, Automotive
    Vehicles
Commercial vehicles, American, [**British, etc.**]
Commercials, Radio
  See Radio advertising
Commercials, Television
  See Television advertising
Comminution
  See Size reduction of materials
Commissariat
  See Armies—Commissariat
    subdivision Commissariat *under armies,*
      e.g. Italy. Esercito—Commissariat;
      United States. Army—
      Commissariat
Commission government
  See Municipal government by commission
Commission government with city manager
  See Municipal government by city manager

Commission merchants *(Direct)* *(HF5421-6)*
  sa Aestimatum
    Commercial travelers
    Commodity exchanges
    Compradors
    Manufacturers' agents
  x Factors
  xx Agency (Law)
    Brokers
    Business
    Commerce
    Commercial agents
    Commercial law
    Commodity exchanges
    Merchants
    Wholesale trade
— Taxation *(Direct)*
Commissioners of deeds *(Direct)*
  xx Deeds
Commissioners of supply (Scotland)
  xx Real property tax—Scotland
Commissions, Art
  See Art commissions
Commissions, Independent regulatory
  See Independent regulatory commissions
Commissions, Library
  See Library commissions
Commissions, Public service
  See Public service commissions
Commissions of array *(English military history, DA60)*
  x Array, Commissions of
  xx Military service, Compulsory—Great Britain
Commissions of inquiry
  See Governmental investigations
Commissions of inquiry, International *(JX1971)*
  x International commissions of inquiry
  xx Arbitration, International
    International relations
    Peaceful change (International relations)
Commissions of the federal government
  See Executive advisory bodies
    Independent regulatory commissions
Commissoria lex (Foreclosure of pledge)
  See Pledges (Law)
Commissoria lex (Rescission)
  See Rescission (Law)
    Resolution (Civil law)
    Sales, Conditional
Commissure, Anterior
  See Anterior commissure
Commitment (Psychology) *(BF619)*
  xx Choice (Psychology)
Commitment to the church
  x Church commitment
  xx Christian life
    Church membership
Committees
  sa Church committees
    Legislative bodies—Committees
    Party committees
  xx Associations, institutions, etc.
    Meetings
    Parliamentary practice
— Anecdotes, facetiae, satire, etc.
Committees in management
  See Management committees
Commodates
  See Loans for use
Commodities, Surplus
  See Surplus commodities
Commodities clause
  See Railroad law—United States

Commodity control
    Works on the control of individual commodities are entered under the name of the commodity, *e.g.* Rubber industry and trade; Wheat trade.
  xx Commercial policy
    Commercial products
    Raw materials
Commodity dollar
  x Compensated dollar
    Dollar, Commodity
    Neutral money
    Stabilized dollar
Commodity exchanges *(Direct)* *(HG6046)*
    Here are entered works on commodity exchanges in general. Works on exchanges dealing in a single commodity or class of commodities, *e.g.* cotton, grain, tobacco are entered under Cotton trade, Grain trade, etc.
  sa Arbitrage
    Commercial products
    Commission merchants
    Hedging (Finance)
    Marketing
    Markets
    Produce trade
    Put and call transactions
    Speculation
  x Exchanges, Commodity
    Exchanges, Produce
    Futures
    Produce exchanges
  xx Commercial products
    Commission merchants
    Marketing
    Markets
    Produce trade
    Speculation
Common business languages
  See Programming languages (Electronic computers)—Business
Common business oriented language
  See COBOL (Computer program language)
Common carriers
  See Carriers
Common cold
  See Cold (Disease)
Common cold viruses
  See Rhinoviruses
Common coral tree
  x Ceibo
    Cockspur coral tree
    Coral tree, Common
    Seibo
Common cormorant
  See Great cormorant
Common currencies
  See Monetary unions
Common lands
  See Commons
Common law *(Direct)*
  sa Customary law
    Judge-made law
    Law—Codification
    Law—Great Britain—History and criticism
    Law—United States—History and criticism
  x Anglo-American law
    Law, Anglo-American
  xx Customary law
Example under Law
— Roman influence
  x Roman law—Influence—Common law
  xx Roman law—History
Example under Civil law systems

Note under Roman law—Influence
Common law marriage *(Direct)*
  xx Marriage
    Marriage law
Common law pleading
  See Pleading
Common life
  See Monasticism and religious orders—Common life
Common loon *(QL696.G33)*
Common market countries
  See European Economic Community countries
Common oystercatcher
  See Oystercatcher
Common schools
  See Public schools
Common scoter
  x Black scoter
    Scoter, Black
    Scoter, Common
  xx Ducks
Common sense
  x Horse sense
  xx Judgment
    Knowledge, Theory of
    Prudence
    Reason
Common Slavic
  See Proto-Slavic language
Common snipe
  See Wilson's snipe
Common Statistics Tabulating Language
  See COST (Computer program language)
Commonplace-books *(PN6245-6; Authors' aids, PN245)*
  sa Handbooks, vade-mecums, etc.
  x Adversaria
Commonplace-books (Law)
  See Lawyers—Handbooks, manuals, etc.
Commonplaces
  See Terms and phrases
Commons *(Direct)* *(HD1286-9)*
  sa Mark
    Mir
    Parks
    Pasture, Right of
    Village communities
    Zadruga
  x Common lands
  xx Land tenure
    Public lands
    Real property
    Village communities
Commons, Student
  See Student unions
Commons (Social order)
  See Estates (Social orders)
    Labor and laboring classes
    Middle classes
    Plebs (Rome)
    Proletariat
Commonwealth, The
  See Political science
    Republics
    State, The
Commonwealth of England
  See Great Britain—History—Commonwealth and Protectorate, 1649-1660
Commonwealth of Nations *(Direct)*
    Here are entered works dealing with the United Kingdom and the self-governing dominions. If the British colonies are included the subject Great Britain and Great Britain—Colonies should be used as main heading or local subdivision.

389

Commonwealth of Nations   (Direct)
(Continued)
    sa Great Britain—Colonies
       Imperial federation
    x British Commonwealth of Nations
       British Dominions
       Dominions, British
    xx Great Britain
       Great Britain—Colonies
       Imperial federation
— Armed Forces
— — Scottish regiments
       Example under reference from Scottish regiments
— International status
— Juvenile literature
— Race question
Commonwealth of Nations fiction (English)
    See English fiction—Commonwealth of
       Nations authors
Commonwealth of Nations literature (English)
    See English literature—Commonwealth of
       Nations authors
Communal settlements
    See Collective settlements
Commune de Paris, 1871
    See Paris—History—Commune, 1871
Communes (China)   (Direct)
— Accounting   (S567)
    xx Agriculture—Accounting
— Juvenile literature
Communicable disease nursing   (RT95)
    xx Communicable diseases
       Nurses and nursing
Communicable diseases   (Direct)
    (Miscellaneous preventive measures,
    RA769; Practice of medicine,
    RC111-216; Public hygiene,
    RA643-4)
    sa Airborne infection
       Animals as carriers of disease
       Bacteria, Pathogenic
       Bacterial diseases
       Bacteriology
       Biological warfare
       Birds as carriers of disease
       Cockroaches as carriers of disease
       Communicable disease nursing
       Diseases—Reporting
       Diseases—Transmission
       Disinfection and disinfectants
       Dogs as carriers of disease
       Dust
       Epidemics
       Epidemiology
       Fish as carriers of disease
       Fleas as carriers of disease
       Flies as carriers of disease
       Focal infection
       Fumigation
       Gasteropoda as carriers of disease
       Germ theory of disease
       Ground-squirrels as carriers of disease
       Immunity
       Inoculation
       Insects as carriers of disease
       Lice as carriers of disease
       Mites as carriers of disease
       Mosquitoes
       Quarantine
       Rats as carriers of disease
       Rickettsial diseases
       Rodents as carriers of disease
       Soil pollution
       Ticks as carriers of disease
       Urinary tract infections
       Vaccination
       Virus diseases
       Worms as carriers of disease

       Zoonoses
       names of communicable diseases, e.g. Q
         fever
    x Contagion and contagious diseases
       Contagious diseases
       Diseases, Communicable
       Diseases, Contagious
       Diseases, Infectious
       Infectious diseases
    xx Air—Microbiology
       Diseases—Causes and theories of
         causation
       Diseases—Reporting
       Diseases—Transmission
       Epidemics
       Hygiene, Public
       Immunity
       Infection
       Medicine—Practice
       Quarantine
       Soil pollution
— Cases, clinical reports, statistics
— Examinations, questions, etc.
— Homeopathic treatment
— Hospitals   (Direct)
    x Isolation (Hospital care)
       Isolation hospitals
       Lazarettos
       Pesthouses
— Immunological aspects
— Juvenile literature
— Law and legislation
    See Public health laws
— Prevention
    sa Medicine, Preventive
Communicable diseases in animals
    sa Brucellosis in cattle
       Pseudorabies
       Theileriosis
       Veterinary immunology
       Wildlife diseases
       Zoonoses
    x Epidemics in animals
       Epizootic diseases
    xx Veterinary medicine
— Diagnosis
    xx Diagnosis
— Law and legislation
    See Veterinary hygiene—Law and
       legislation
Communicable diseases in children
    xx Pediatrics
Communicatio in sacris
    Here are entered works dealing with the
    participation of Catholics with non-
    Catholics in prayer and other forms of
    worship. For the corresponding term
    used among Lutherans *see* Unionism
    (Religion)
    sa Simultaneum
       Unionism (Religion)
    x Communication in worship
    xx Catholic Church—Discipline
       Christian union
       Indifferentism (Religion)
       Intercommunion
       Sects
       Unionism (Religion)
Note under Unionism (Religion)

Communication   (Direct) (P90)
    Here are entered works on human com-
    munication, including both the pri-
    mary techniques of language, pictures,
    etc., and the secondary techniques
    which facilitate the process, such as
    the press and radio. Works dealing
    predominantly with the modern means
    of mass communication are entered
    under Mass media. Works dealing with
    individual means of communication
    are entered under the headings Lan-
    guage and languages, Printing, Tele-
    communication, etc. Works dealing
    collectively with the industries con-
    cerned are entered under the heading
    Communication and traffic.
    sa Communication and traffic
       Communications research
       Cybernetics
       Diffusion of innovations
       Information science
       Information theory
       Intercultural communication
       Knowledge, Sociology of
       Language and languages
       Language arts
       Leaflets dropped from aircraft
       Mass media
       Nonverbal communication
       Oral communication
       Persuasion (Psychology)
       Popular culture
       Science news
       Self-disclosure
       Semantics (Philosophy)
       Symbolism in communication
       Visual aids
    x Mass communication
    xx Language and languages
       Semantics (Philosophy)
       Sociology
— Audio-visual aids
— Biography
— Caricatures and cartoons
— Content analysis
    See Content analysis
       (Communication)
— Information services
— Juvenile literature
— Mathematical models
— Methodology
    sa Communication in science
       Communication in the social
         sciences
       Communication—Study and teaching
       Content analysis (Communication)
    xx Communication—Study and teaching
       Communications research
— Pictorial works
— Programmed instruction
— Psychological aspects
    xx Interpersonal relations
— — Juvenile literature
— Research
    See Communications research
— Social aspects   (Direct)
— Study and teaching
    sa Communication—Methodology
    xx Communication—Methodology
— Underdeveloped areas
    See Underdeveloped areas—
       Communication
— Vocational guidance
Communication, Administrative
    See Communication in management
Communication, Business
    See Communication in management

Communication, Employee
   See Communication in personnel
      management
Communication, Industrial
   See Communication in management
Communication, Intercultural
   See Intercultural communication
Communication, Primitive *(Transportation,*
   GN438; Social life and customs,
   GN488.3)
Communication (Theology) *(BV4319)*
   sa Church group work
      Evangelistic work
      Image (Theology)
      Mass media in religion
      Missions
      Preaching
      Public relations—Churches
      Radio in religion
      Religious education
      Television in religion
      Witness bearing (Christianity)
   x Christian communication
      Christianity and communication
      Word (Theology)
   xx Demythologization
      Evangelistic work
      Missions
      Pastoral theology
      Preaching
Communication among animals
   See Animal communication
Communication and traffic *(Indirect) (HE;*
   Primitive, GN38)
   Here are entered works dealing collectively with the communications industries. Works dealing with individual
   means of communication are entered
   under the headings Radio broadcasting, Shipping, Telecommunication,
   etc. Works dealing collectively with
   the modern means of mass communication are entered under Mass media.
   sa Aeronautics
      Air travel
      Cab and omnibus service
      Cables, Submarine
      Canals
      City traffic
      Commerce
      Communications, Military
      Express service
      Harbors
      Inland navigation
      Mass media
      Messengers
      Motor bus lines
      Motor buses
      Ocean travel
      Postal service
      Radio
      Railroads
      Roads
      Route surveying
      Shipping
      Street-railroads
      Taxicabs
      Telecommunication
      Telegraph
      Telephone
      Trade routes
      Traffic engineering
      Traffic regulations
      Traffic surveys
      Transportation
   x Mass communication
      Traffic
   xx Carriers

      Commerce
      Communication
      Economics
      Locomotion
      Transportation
   Note under Communication
   — Acronyms
   — Employees
      sa Trade-unions—Communication and
         traffic
   — Examinations, questions, etc.
   — Finance
   — Information services
   — International cooperation
   — Juvenile literature
   — Law and legislation   *(Direct)*
      xx Trade regulation
   — Terminology
Communication arts
   See Language arts
Communication in agriculture *(S494.5.C6)*
   sa Agricultural libraries
      Agriculture—Information services
   x Agricultural communication
   xx Agriculture
      Communication of technical
         information
Communication in anthropogeography
   xx Anthropo-geography
      Communication in science
Communication in biology
   sa Biology—Information services
   xx Biology
      Communication in science
Communication in dentistry
   x Dental communication
   xx Communication in medicine
      Dentistry
Communication in education *(Direct)*
   sa Communication in technical education
      Communication in vocational education
      Education—Information services
      Educational publishing
      Pedagogical libraries
   xx Education
      Interaction analysis in education
Communication in industry
   See Communication in management
Communication in lumbering *(SD538)*
   xx Lumbering
Communication in management
   sa Automatic data collection systems
      Business report writing
      Communication in personnel
         management
   x Administrative communication
      Business communication
      Communication, Administrative
      Communication, Business
      Communication in industry
      Communication, Industrial
      Industrial communication
   xx Industrial management
      Personnel management
Communication in mechanical engineering
   xx Communication of technical
        information
      Mechanical engineering
Communication in medicine *(R118)*
   sa Communication in dentistry
      Health education
      Medical libraries
      Medical writing
      Medicine—Information services
   x Health communication
      Medical communication
      Medicine, Communication in
   xx Communication in science

Communication in personnel management
   (HF5549.5.C6)
   sa Employees, Reporting to
   x Communication, Employee
      Employee communication
   xx Communication in management
      Personnel management
Communication in psychology *(BF76.7)*
   xx Communication in science
Communication in research
   See Communication in science
Communication in science *(Q223)*
   sa Communication in anthropogeography
      Communication in biology
      Communication in medicine
      Communication in psychology
      Communication of technical
         information
      Science clubs
      Science—Information services
      Science news
      Scientific libraries
   x Communication in research
      Science communication
      Science, Communication in
      Science information
      Scientific communications
   xx Communication—Methodology
      Research
      Science—Information services
      Science—Methodology
Communication in sex
   xx Sex
Communication in technical education
   xx Communication in education
      Technical education
Communication in technology
   See Communication of technical
      information
Communication in the social sciences
   xx Communication—Methodology
      Social science research
      Social sciences—Methodology
Communication in vocational education
   xx Communication in education
      Vocational education
Communication in worship
   See Communicatio in sacris
Communication of technical information
   sa Communication in agriculture
      Communication in mechanical
         engineering
      Technical correspondence
      Technical libraries
      Technical literature
      Technical writing
      Technology—Documentation
      Technology—Information services
      Technology—Translating services
   x Communication in technology
      Technical communication
      Technical information, Communication
        of
   xx Communication in science
Communication research
   See Communications research
Communication satellites
   See Artificial satellites in
      telecommunication
Communication skills (Elementary education)
   See English language—Study and teaching
      (Elementary)
Communication systems, Optical (Laser-based)
   See Laser communication systems
Communication theory
   See Information theory
Communication with the dead
   See Spiritualism

Communications, Confidential
　　See Confidential communications
Communications, Highway
　　See Highway communications
Communications, Military *(UA940-945)*
　　sa Aeroplanes—IFF equipment
　　　Electronic data processing—Military
　　　　intelligence
　　　European War, 1914-1918—
　　　　Communications
　　　Military telegraph
　　　Military telephone
　　　Military television
　　　Mobile communication systems
　　　Radio, Military
　　　Signals and signaling
　　　Transportation, Military
　　　United States—History—Civil War,
　　　　1861-1865—Communications
　　　World War, 1939-1945—
　　　　Communications
　　　subdivision Communication systems
　　　　under armies, navies, etc., e.g.
　　　　United States. Navy—
　　　　Communication systems
　　x Communications, Naval
　　　Military communications
　　　Naval communications
　　xx Communication and traffic
Communications, Naval
　　See Communications, Military
Communications, Police
　　See Police communication systems
Communications, Railroad
　　See Railroads—Communication systems
Communications-relay satellites
　　See Artificial satellites in
　　　telecommunication
Communications research
　　sa Communication—Methodology
　　　Content analysis (Communication)
　　x Communication research
　　　Communication—Research
　　xx Communication
Communications workers
　　See Telecommunication—Employees
Communicative disorders
　　x Disorders of communication
　　xx Deaf—Means of communication
　　　Speech, Disorders of
　　— Rehabilitation
Communicative disorders in children
　　sa Hearing disorders in children
　　　Speech disorders in children
　　　Vision disorders in children
　　x Disorders of communication in children
　　xx Children—Language
Communion
　　See Lord's Supper
Communion, Close
　　See Close and open communion
Communion, First
　　See First communion
Communion, Infant
　　See Infant communion
Communion, Open
　　See Close and open communion
Communion bread
　　See Lord's Supper—Bread
Communion-cups
　　See Chalices
Communion in both elements
　　See Lord's Supper—Communion in both
　　　elements
Communion of saints *(BT972)*
　　xx Apostles' Creed
　　　Church
　　　Jesus Christ—Mystical body

Saints
　　Theology, Doctrinal
— History of doctrines
Communion plate
　　See Church plate
Communion sermons *(BV4257.5)*
　　Here are entered sermons preached at, or
　　　in preparation for, a communion ser-
　　　vice. Sermons on the Lord's Supper it-
　　　self are entered under Lord's Supper—
　　　Sermons.
　　xx Sermons
　　Note under Lord's Supper—Sermons
Communion-service music *(M2016.5; M2017;*
　　　M2017.2)
　　sa Masses
　　xx Lord's Supper (Liturgy)
　　　Masses
　　　Sacred vocal music
Communion tokens
　　See Tokens, Communion
Communion wine
　　See Lord's Supper—Wine
Communism *(Indirect) (HX626-795)*
　　sa Anti-communist movements
　　　Collective settlements
　　　Communist lawyers
　　　Communist parties
　　　Communist revisionism
　　　Communist state
　　　Communist strategy
　　　Communists
　　　Dictatorship of the proletariat
　　　Harmonists
　　　Jansonists
　　　Labadists
　　　Land, Nationalization of
　　　Marxian economics
　　　Mir
　　　Nationalism and socialism
　　　Propaganda, Anti-communist
　　　Propaganda, Communist
　　　Shakers
　　　Socialism
　　　Socialism and youth
　　　Trade-unions and communism
　　　Tribes and tribal system
　　　Village communities
　　　Women and socialism
　　x Bolshevism
　　　Maoism
　　　Marxism
　　xx Collectivism
　　　Individualism
　　　Political science
　　　Socialism
　　　Totalitarianism
　　　Village communities
— 1945-
　　x New Left

　　　GENERAL SUBDIVISIONS

— Anecdotes, facetiae, satire, etc.

　　　GENERAL SUBDIVISIONS

— Historiography

　　　GENERAL SUBDIVISIONS

— History

　　　GENERAL SUBDIVISIONS

—— Pictorial works

　　　GENERAL SUBDIVISIONS

— Jews
　　sa Communism and Judaism
　　　Communism and Zionism

　　　GENERAL SUBDIVISIONS

— Juvenile literature

　　　GENERAL SUBDIVISIONS

— Miscellaneous *(HX87)*
— Pictorial works
— Songs and music
— Study and teaching *(Direct)*
—— Audio-visual aids

　　　GEOGRAPHIC SUBDIVISIONS

— Germany
—— Underground literature
　　xx Underground literature

　　　GEOGRAPHIC SUBDIVISIONS

— Russia
　　sa Civics, Russian
　　x Bolshevism

　　　GEOGRAPHIC SUBDIVISIONS

— United States
—— 1917-
　　sa Communism in education

　　　GEOGRAPHIC SUBDIVISIONS

——— Juvenile literature
Communism and architecture
　　x Architecture and communism
Communism and art
　　sa Communist aesthetics
　　　Socialist realism in art
　　x Art and communism
Communism and Buddhism
　　x Buddhism and communism
　　xx Buddha and Buddhism
　　　Sociology, Buddhist
Communism and Christianity *(Direct)*
　　x Christianity and communism
　　xx Christianity and atheism
　　　Christianity and economics
　　　Communism and religion
— Catholic Church *(Direct) (BX1396.4)*
　　sa Socialism and Catholic Church
　　x Catholic Church and communism
　　　Communism and the Catholic
　　　　Church
　　xx Socialism and Catholic Church
Communism and culture
　　x Culture and communism
Communism and education *(HX526)*
　　Here are entered works on the position of
　　　education in communist ideology.
　　　Works on communist indoctrination in
　　　all phases of education are entered un-
　　　der Communist education.
　　x Education and communism
　　Note under Communist education
Communism and family *(HX546)*
　　x Family and communism
Communism and intellectuals
　　x Intellectuals and communism
Communism and Islam
　　x Islam and communism
Communism and Judaism
　　x Judaism and communism
　　xx Communism and religion
　　　Communism—Jews
　　　Judaism
　　　Sociology, Jewish
Communism and law
　　See Law and socialism
Communism and libraries
　　See Libraries and communism
Communism and literature
　　sa Communism and satire
　　　Socialist realism in literature

x Literature and communism
Communism and medicine *(HX550.M4)*
  x Medicine and communism
Communism and moving-pictures
    (HX550.M65)
  x Moving-pictures and communism
Communism and music
  x Music and communism
Communism and property
  See Property and socialism
Communism and religion *(HX536; Catholic*
    Church, BX1396.4)
  sa Christianity and economics
    Communism and Christianity
    Communism and Judaism
    Communists (Canon law)
    Religion and economics
    Socialism and Catholic Church
  x Religion and communism
  xx Socialism and Catholic Church
Communism and satire
  x Satire and communism
  xx Communism and literature
Communism and social sciences *(Direct)*
    (HX541.5)
  x Social sciences and communism
Communism and society
  x Marxian sociology
    Society and communism
  xx Sociology
Communism and the Catholic Church
  See Communism and Christianity—Catholic
    Church
Communism and trade-unions
  See Trade-unions and communism
Communism and youth
  See Socialism and youth
Communism and Zionism
  x Zionism and communism
  xx Communism—Jews
    Zionism
Communism in education
  xx Communism—United States—1917-
    Education—United States
Communism in literature
  sa Socialist realism in literature
  xx Politics in literature
Communist aesthetics
  x Aesthetics, Communist
  xx Communism and art
Communist college teachers *(Direct)*
  xx College teachers
    Communists
Communist countries *(D847)*
  sa People's democracies
  x Iron curtain lands
    Russian satellites
    Soviet bloc
  xx People's democracies
  — Anecdotes, facetiae, satire, etc.
  — Juvenile literature
  — Literatures
  — Propaganda
    See Propaganda, Communist
Communist education *(Direct)*
  Here are entered works on communist in-
    doctrination in all phases of education.
    Works on the position of education in
    communist ideology are entered under
    Communism and education.
  x Education, Communist
  Note under Communism and education
Communist ethics *(BJ1390)*
  sa Socialist ethics
    Totalitarian ethics
  x Ethics, Communist
  xx Ethics
    Social ethics

    Socialist ethics
    Totalitarian ethics
  — Juvenile literature
Communist Insurrection, Malayan, 1948-1960
  See Malaya—History—Malayan
    Emergency, 1948-1960
Communist journalism
  See Journalism, Communist
Communist lawyers *(Direct)*
  xx Communism
    Communists
    Lawyers
Communist Leaders' Trial, New York, 1949
  See Communist Trial, New York, 1949
Communist parties
  sa Popular fronts
  xx Communism
    Political parties
  — Purges
    See Communist party purges
Communist party purges
  sa subdivision Purges *under names of*
    communist parties, e.g.
    Kommunisticheskaia partia
    Sovetskogo Soiuza—Purges
  x Communist parties—Purges
    Purges (Communist parties)
  xx Political purges
Communist press
  See Press, Communist
Communist propaganda
  See Propaganda, Communist
Communist revisionism
  x Revisionism, Communist
  xx Communism
Communist self-criticism
  x Bolshevist self-criticism
    Criticism, Communist
    Self-criticism, Communist
    Self-examination
  xx Discussion
Communist state
  sa Dictatorship of the proletariat
    People's democracies
    Soviets
  x State, Communist
  xx Communism
    Dictatorship of the proletariat
    People's democracies
    Socialism
    Soviets
    State, The
Communist strategy
  x Strategy, Communist
  xx Communism
    World politics—1945-
Communist teachers *(Direct)*
  xx Communists
    Teachers
  — Biography
Communist Trial, Cologne, 1852
Communist Trial, New York, 1949
  x Communist Leaders' Trial, New York,
    1949
    Trial of Communist Leaders, New
    York, 1949
Communist Trial, Seoul, Korea, 1968
  x Trial of Communists, Seoul, Korea,
    1968
Communist trials *(Direct)*
  xx Trials (Sedition)
    Trials (Treason)
Communistic settlements
  See Collective settlements
Communists *(Direct)*
  sa Communist college teachers
    Communist lawyers
    Communist teachers

  xx Communism
  — Correspondence, reminiscences, etc.
Communists, Negro
  x Negro communists
Communists (Canon law)
  xx Communism and religion
Communists in literature
  xx Characters and characteristics in
    literature
Communities, Biotic
  See Biotic communities
Community
  Here are entered works on geographically
    defined social units within a larger so-
    ciety, served by an aggregate of institu-
    tions, economically self-sufficient, and
    characterized by close contacts and
    common interests and activities.
  sa Community life
    Community organization
  xx Cities and towns
    Sociology
    Sociology, Rural
Community and architects
  See Architects and community
Community and college *(Direct)* *(LC237)*
  x College and community
    Town and gown
    University and community
  xx Community and school
Community and hospital
  See Hospital and community
Community and libraries
  See Libraries and community
Community and Negro teachers
  See Negro teachers and the community
Community and school *(Direct)* *(LC215)*
  Here are entered works on ways in which
    the community at large, as distinct
    from government, may aid the school
    program.
  sa Citizens' advisory committees in
    education
    Community and college
    Community schools
    Negro teachers and the community
    Parents' and teachers' associations
    School excursions
    Teachers and community
  x School and community
  xx Community life
    Education and state
Community and teachers
  See Teachers and community
Community antenna television *(Direct)*
  x Cable television
    CATV
  xx Television relay systems
  — Law and legislation *(Direct)*
Community art centers
  See Art centers
Community art projects *(Direct)*
  sa Community music
  x Art projects, Community
    Neighborhood art projects
  xx Art
    Cities and towns—Civic improvement
Community centers *(Direct)*
  sa Art centers
    Mosques as community centers
    Playgrounds
    Recreation
    Recreation centers
    School facilities—Extended use
    Student unions
  x Play centers
    School buildings—Community use
    Schools as social centers

Community centers *(Direct)*
  (Continued)
      Social centers
    xx Cities and towns—Civic improvement
      Community life
      Community organization
      Playgrounds
      Recreation
      School facilities—Extended use
      Social problems
      Social settlements
  — Costs
  — Fires and fire prevention
Community centers, Jewish
    x Jewish community centers
    xx Jews—Social life and customs
Community centers, Mobile
    x Mobile community centers
Community centers for employees
    See Employees' buildings and facilities
Community chests
    See Federations, Financial (Social service)
Community churches *(BV636)*
      Here are entered works dealing with local
      churches that aim to serve their com-
      munity without having any denomina-
      tional affiliations. Works on the type of
      community church which is a federa-
      tion of two or more denominational
      churches united for local worship but
      with each unit retaining its denomina-
      tional affiliation are entered under
      Federated churches.
    sa Independent churches
      Larger parishes
    x Churches, Community
      Churches, Undenominational
      Churches, United
      Undenominational churches
      Union churches
      United churches
    xx Christian union
      Independent churches
      Interdenominational cooperation
      Larger parishes
      Rural churches
    Note under Federated churches
Community college libraries
    See Municipal university and college
      libraries
Community colleges
    See Municipal universities and colleges
Community councils
    See Community organization
Community dental services *(Direct)*
    sa Dental public health
    xx Community health services
      Dental care
      Dental public health
Community development *(Direct)*
      Here are entered works on the basic de-
      velopment of either underdeveloped
      areas or of deprived regions of more
      advanced countries, emphasizing im-
      provements in the standard of living
      and the active participation of the local
      peoples in the programs set up.
    sa Agricultural extension work
      Cities and towns—Planning
      Factories—Location
      Fundamental education
      Industries, Location of
      Radio in community development
      Rehabilitation, Rural
      Technical assistance
      Youth volunteers in community
        development
    x Rural economic development
    xx Agricultural extension work

      Cities and towns—Planning
      Community life
      Economic assistance, Domestic
      Rehabilitation, Rural
      Social change
      Sociology, Rural
      Technical assistance
      Underdeveloped areas
      Villages
  — Audio-visual aids
  — Research *(Direct)*
    xx Social science research
  — Study and teaching *(Direct)*
Community forests *(Direct)* *(SD561-668)*
    xx Forests and forestry
Community health services *(Direct)*
    sa Clinics
      Community dental services
    xx Hygiene, Public
  — Citizen participation
    x Citizen participation in community
      health services
  — Finance
Community health services for children
      (Direct)
    xx Children—Care and hygiene
      Hygiene, Public
Community junior colleges
    See Municipal junior colleges
Community leadership
    xx Community life
      Community power
      Leadership
Community life *(HM131)*
    sa Bees (Cooperative gatherings)
      Community and school
      Community centers
      Community development
      Community leadership
      Community organization
      Hospital and community
      Libraries and community
      Neighborhood
      Social isolation
      Social participation
    xx Associations, institutions, etc.
      Community
      Human ecology
  — Juvenile literature
  — Research
  — Simulation methods
Community mental health service use
    See Community mental health services—
      Utilization
Community mental health services *(Direct)*
    sa Crisis intervention (Psychiatry)
    xx Hygiene, Public
      Mental health services
      Mental hygiene
  — Administration
    xx Health services administration
  — Finance
  — Utilization
    x Community mental health service
      use
      Utilization of community mental
      health services
Community music *(M1997.C5; History and*
      criticism, ML2500-2770; Instruction,
      MT875)
    sa Music as recreation
      Music in the army
      Music Week
      Playground music
    x Music, Community
      Singing, Community
    xx Choral societies
      Community art projects

      Music Week
Community newspapers *(Direct)*
    x Neighborhood newspapers
      Newspapers, Community
Community organization
    sa Community centers
      Community power
      Community welfare councils
      Federations, Financial (Social service)
      Local government
      Urban renewal
    x Community councils
    xx Charities
      Cities and towns—Civic improvement
      Community
      Community life
      Public welfare
      Recreation
      Social service
      Urban renewal
  — Law and legislation *(Direct)*
    xx Municipal corporations
Community plays, etc. *(PN3203-5)*
    x Plays, Community
Community power
    sa Community leadership
    xx Community organization
      Elite (Social sciences)
      Local government
      Power (Social sciences)
      Sociology, Urban
Community property *(Direct)*
    sa Separate property
    xx Husband and wife
      Marriage law
  — Taxation *(Direct)*
    xx Husband and wife—Taxation
Community property (Frankish law)
Community psychiatry
    See Social psychiatry
Community psychology
    xx Psychology, Applied
      Social psychology
Community schools *(Direct)* *(LB2820)*
    x Neighborhood schools
      Schools, Community
      Schools, Neighborhood
    xx Community and school
      Schools—Centralization
      Urban schools
  — Administration
Community song-books
    See Song-books
Community surveys
    See Social surveys
Community theater
    See Theater—Little theater movement
Community use of college facilities
    See College facilities—Extended use
Community use of school facilities
    See School facilities—Extended use
Community welfare councils *(Direct)*
    x Health and welfare federations
      Social planning councils
      Welfare councils
      Welfare federations
    xx Charity organization
      Community organization
Commutation (Electricity)
    sa Brushes, Electric
    x Commutators
    xx Electric machinery
Commutation rates (Railroads)
    See Railroads—Fares—Special rates
Commutative algebra
    x Algebra, Commutative
Commutative groups
    See Abelian groups

394

Commutative law (Mathematics)
  xx Mathematics
Commutative rings
  sa Radical theory
  xx Rings (Algebra)
Commutators
  See Commutation (Electricity)
Commuting (Direct)
  sa Railroads—Commuting traffic
  xx Labor and laboring classes
    Transportation
    Urban transportation
  — Public opinion
Commuting college students
  See College students—Transportation
Comopoda
  See Lamellibranchiata
Compact automobiles
  See Automobiles, Compact
Compact cars
  See Automobiles, Compact
Compact spaces, Locally
  See Locally compact spaces
Compactification, Stone-Čech
  See Stone-Čech compactification
Compacting
  sa Agglomeration
    Briquets
    Centrifuges
    Extrusion (Metals)
    Powder metallurgy
    Pressed brick
    Soil stabilization
    Vibratory compacting
    Wood, Compressed
  x Compaction
    Compressing of granular materials
  xx Compressibility
    Extrusion (Metals)
    Granular materials
    Powders
Compaction
  See Compacting
Compaction of soils
  See Soil stabilization
Compaction of soils and plants
  See Plants, Effect of soil compaction on
Compacts, Interstate
  See Interstate agreements
Compagnie de Saint-Sulpice
  See Sulpicians
Compagnonnages (HD6464-6)
  xx Apprentices
    Gilds
    Journeymen's societies
    Labor and laboring classes
    Trade-unions
Companies
  See Corporations
    Partnership
Companies, Colonial
  See Colonial companies
Companies, Holding
  See Holding companies
Companies, Insurance
  See Insurance companies
Companies, One-man
  See One-man companies
Companies, Private
  See Private companies
Companies, Stock
  See Stock companies
Companies, Subsidiary
  See Subsidiary corporations
Companies, Trust
  See Trust companies
Companion crops (S603.5)
  x Intercropping

  xx Field crops
    Rotation of crops
    Vegetable gardening
Companionate marriage
  See Marriage, Companionate
Companions of Muḥammad, the prophet
    (BP136.46)
  sa Ansar
  x Ṣaḥāba
Companionship
  See Fellowship
Company aeroplanes
  See Aeroplanes, Company
Company automobiles
  See Automobiles, Company
Company cars
  See Automobiles, Company
Company insurance
  See Insurance, Business
Company law
  See Corporation law
Company magazines
  See Employees' magazines, handbooks, etc.
Company meetings
  See Corporate meetings
Company police
  See Police, Private
Company publications
  See Employees' magazines, handbooks, etc.
Company reports
  See Corporation reports
Company secretaries
  See Corporation secretaries
Company stores
  x Industrial stores
  xx Company towns
    Retail trade
Company towns (Direct)
    Here are entered works on communities
    in which all or the major portion of the
    property and businesses are owned by
    one industry. Works on housing prov-
    ided by an industry to its employees
    are entered under Industrial housing.
  sa Company stores
  xx Cities and towns
    Industrial relations
  Note under Industrial housing
Company unions (Direct) (HD6490.C6)
  xx Employees' representation in
      management
    Independent unions
    Industrial relations
    Trade-unions
Company vacations
  See Vacations, Employee
Comparative anatomy
  See Anatomy, Comparative
Comparative civilization
  x Civilization, Comparative
Comparative economic systems
  See Comparative economics
Comparative economics
  x Comparative economic systems
    Economics, Comparative
  xx Economic policy
    Economics
Comparative education (LA126-133)
  sa Intercultural education
  x Education, Comparative
  xx Education—History
    Teachers, Training of
Comparative endocrinology
  See Endocrinology, Comparative
Comparative ethics
  See Ethics, Comparative

Comparative government
  sa subdivision Politics and government
      under names of countries, cities, etc.
  x Government, Comparative
  xx Political science
  — Study and teaching (Direct)
Comparative grammar
  See Grammar, Comparative and general
Comparative jurisprudence
  See Comparative law
Comparative law
    Here are entered works on the compari-
    son of various systems of law as a
    method of legal study and research.
    Comparative studies of individual legal
    topics or branches of the law are en-
    tered under the respective headings
    applying to these subjects.
  sa Ethnological jurisprudence
    Law—History and criticism
  x Comparative jurisprudence
    Comparative legislation
    Jurisprudence, Comparative
    Law, Comparative
    Legislation, Comparative
  xx Law—History and criticism
  — Study and teaching (Direct)
Comparative legislation
  See Comparative law
Comparative librarianship
  x International librarianship
    Librarianship, Comparative
  xx International education
    Library science
Comparative linguistics
  See Grammar, Comparative and general
    Language and languages
Comparative literature
  See Literature, Comparative
Comparative morphology
  See Anatomy, Comparative
    Morphology
Comparative negligence
  See Negligence, Comparative
Comparative pathology
  See Pathology, Comparative
Comparative philology
  See Philology, Comparative
Comparative philosophy
  See Philosophy, Comparative
Comparative physiology
  See Physiology, Comparative
Comparative psychology
  See Psychology, Comparative
Comparative religion
  See Religions
Comparative semantics
  See Semantics, Comparative
Comparative studies
  See subdivision Comparative studies under
    individual works and subjects in the
    field of religion, e.g. Bible—
    Comparative studies; Creeds—
    Comparative studies
Comparative symbolics
  See Creeds—Comparative studies
Comparison (Grammar)
  x Grammar, Comparative and general—
    Comparison
Comparison (Philosophy)
  xx Philosophy
Comparison (Psychology) (BF441)
  sa Identity
  xx Attention
    Consciousness
    Knowledge, Theory of
    Psychology

Compartmental analysis (Biology)
   xx Biomathematics
      Tracers (Biology)
Compass *(VK577; Deviation, QC849)*
   sa Cardinal points
      Magnetic ranges
      Magnetism, Terrestrial
      Radio compass
   x Deviation of the compass
      Magnetic needle
      Mariner's compass
      Variation of the compass
   xx Magnetic ranges
      Magnetism
      Magnetism, Terrestrial
   Example under Navigation
Compass, Gyroscopic
   See Gyro compass
Compass, Radio
   See Radio compass
Compass, Solar
   See Solar compass
Compass, Surveyor's
   See Surveyor's compass
COMPASS (Computer program language)
   x Comprehensive Assemblage (Computer
      program language)
Compass card
   See Cardinal points
Compass rose
   See Cardinal points
Compasses (Mathematical instruments)
   xx Drawing instruments
      Measuring instruments
Compassion (Buddhism) *(BQ4360)*
   x Jihi
      Karunā
      Loving kindness (Buddhism)
      Maitrī
      Mettā
   xx Buddhist doctrines
      Buddhist ethics
Compassion (Ethics)
   See Sympathy
Compatibility testing (Hematology)
   x Blood groups—Compatibility testing
   xx Blood—Transfusion
      Immunohematology
Compatible time-sharing system (Electronic
      computers)
   x MIT time-sharing system (Electronic
      computers)
   xx Electronic data processing
      Time-sharing computer systems
Compensated dollar
   See Commodity dollar
Compensating circuits
   See Equalizers (Electronics)
Compensating-powder *(TP290.C7)*
   xx Explosives
      Gunpowder
Compensation
   See Pensions
      Wages
Compensation, Deferred
   See Deferred compensation
Compensation, Dismissal
   See Wages—Dismissal wage
Compensation (Civil law)
   See Set-off and counterclaim
Compensation (Islamic law) *(Direct)*
Compensation (Law) *(Direct)*
   sa Damages
      Indemnity
      Workmen's compensation
   — Cases
Compensation (Physiology)
   See Adaptation (Physiology)

Compensation (Psychology)
   xx Defense mechanisms (Psychology)
Compensation (Roman law)
Compensation for judicial error *(Direct)*
   xx Criminal justice, Administration of
      Government liability
      Judicial error
Compensation for victims of crime
   See Reparation
Compensation neuroses
   See Traumatic neuroses
Compensatory education *(Direct)*
   x Education, Compensatory
   xx Cultural lag
      Education
   — Evaluation
Compensatory motion
   See Irritability
Compensatory spending
   See Deficit financing
Competence (Legal authority)
   See Competent authority
Competent authority *(Direct)*
   sa Administrative procedure
      Jurisdiction
   x Competence (Legal authority)
   xx Public officers
Competition *(Commercial, HF1436;*
      Industrial, HD41)
   sa Conglomerate corporations
      Government competition
      Industrial concentration
      Laissez-faire
      Monopolies
      Oligopolies
      Open price system
      Second best, Theory of
      Struggle
      Supply and demand
      Trusts, Industrial
   xx Big business
      Business
      Business ethics
      Conglomerate corporations
      Economics
      Industrial concentration
      Laissez-faire
      Monopolies
      Open price system
      Supply and demand
      Trusts, Industrial
   — Mathematical models
Competition, Government
   See Government competition
Competition, International
   sa Commercial treaties
      International cooperation
      War—Economic aspects
   x International competition
      World economics
   xx Commerce
      International relations
      War—Economic aspects
   — Mathematical models
Competition, Socialist
   See Socialist competition
Competition, Unfair *(Direct)* *(HD3625-6)*
   sa Advertising laws
      Better-business bureaus
      Blacklists, Commercial
      Boycott
      Bribery
      Business intelligence
      Design protection
      Dumping (Commercial policy)
      Marks of origin
      Patents
      Price cutting

      Price discrimination
      Price policy
      Price regulation
      Rebates
      Restraint of trade
      Slogans—Law and legislation
      Special sales
      Trade-marks
      Trade secrets
   x Fair trade
      Unfair competition
      Unfair trade practices
   xx Advertising laws
      Commercial crimes
      Commercial law
      Commercial policy
      Criminal law
      Industrial laws and legislation
      Industrial property
      Patent laws and legislation
      Price policy
      Restraint of trade
      Torts
      Trade regulation
   — Conflict of laws
      See Conflict of laws—Competition,
         Unfair
   — Examinations, questions, etc.
   — Forms

      GEOGRAPHIC SUBDIVISIONS

   — United States
      sa Basing-point system
Competition, Unfair (Jewish law)
Competition (Psychology)
   xx Conflict (Psychology)
      Interpersonal relations
      Motivation (Psychology)
Competition angling
   See Tournament fishing
Competitions
   See Rewards (Prizes, etc.)
      School contests
      subdivision Competitions *under specific*
         subjects, e.g. Architecture—
         Competitions, Poetry—Competitions
Competitive antagonists (Metabolism)
   See Antimetabolites
Competitive behavior, Employee
   See Employee competitive behavior
Competitive bidding
   See Contracts, Letting of
Competitive examinations
   See Civil service—Examinations
      Examinations
Compiling (Electronic computers)
   sa AMOS (Computer program)
      Assembling (Electronic computers)
   xx Assembling (Electronic computers)
      Electronic data processing
      Electronic digital computers—
         Programming
      Translators (Computer programs)
Complaints (Canon law)
   x Bills of complaint (Canon law)
   xx Ecclesiastical courts
Complaints (Civil procedure) *(Direct)*
   x Declaration (Common law pleading)
   xx Actions and defenses
      Civil procedure
      Pleading
Complaints (Criminal procedure) *(Direct)*
   sa Informers
      Private prosecutors
      Simulation of crimes
   xx Actions and defenses
      Criminal procedure
      Private prosecutors

— Forms
Complaints (Military law) *(Direct)*
   x Grievance procedures (Military law)
   xx Military law
Complaints (Retail trade)
   x Adjustments (Retail trade)
      Consumer complaints
      Customer complaints
   xx Adjustment letters
      Consumers
      Customer relations
      Retail trade
Complancha
   See Laments
Complement deflection
   See Complement fixation
Complement deviation
   See Complement fixation
Complement fixation *(QR185)*
   x Complement deflection
      Complement deviation
   xx Complements (Immunity)
      Diagnosis
      Tuberculosis—Diagnosis
Complementarity (Physics) *(QC174.5)*
   xx Quantum theory
Complementary genes
   See Complementation (Genetics)
Complementation (Genetics)
   x Complementary genes
      Genes, Complementary
   xx Allelomorphism
      Genetics
Complements (Immunity) *(QR185)*
   sa Complement fixation
      Immune complexes
      Phytoalexin
   x Alexins
   xx Immune complexes
      Immunity
Complete denture, Lower
   See Mandibular prosthesis
Complete dentures
   x Dentures, Complete
      Full dentures
   xx Prosthodontics
— Atlases
Complex compounds
   sa Clathrate compounds
      Complex ions
      Complexometric titration
      Coordination compounds
      Crystal field theory
      Hydrates
      Ligand field theory
   xx Complex ions
      Masking (Chemistry)
— Magnetic properties
— Spectra
— Tables, etc.
Complex ions
   sa Complex compounds
      Transition metals
   xx Complex compounds
      Ions
Complex manifolds
   sa Almost complex manifolds
   xx Analytic spaces
      Manifolds (Mathematics)
Complex numbers
   See Numbers, Complex
Complexes *(QA608)*
   sa Combinatorial topology
      CW complexes
   x Linear complexes
   xx Algebras, Linear
      Coordinates
      Geometry

Line geometry
   Transformations (Mathematics)
Complexes (Psychology)
   See Cain complex
      Castration complex
      Oedipus complex
Compleximetry
   See Complexometric titration
Complexion
   See Beauty, Personal
      Color of man
      Cosmetics
Complexometric titration
   x Chelatometry
      Compleximetry
   xx Complex compounds
      Volumetric analysis
Complication experiments (Psychology)
   xx Psychology, Physiological
      Time perception
Compline music *(Catholic liturgical music,*
   M2149.5.C6)
Componential analysis in anthropology
   (GN34.3.C6)
   xx Anthropology
      Semantics
Components construction
   See Buildings, Prefabricated
Composers *(Direct)* *(Biography: collective,*
   ML390; individual, ML410)
   sa Women composers
   x Music—Biography
   xx Musicians
— Autographs *(ML93-98)*
   Example under Graphology
— Biography
— Caricatures and cartoons
— Correspondence, reminiscences, etc.
   See Musicians—Correspondence,
      reminiscences, etc.
— Dictionaries
   See Music—Bio-bibliography
— Juvenile literature
— Portraits *(ML87-88)*
Composers, American, ⌜Dutch, French, etc.⌝
   x American ⌜Dutch, French, etc.⌝
      composers
— Juvenile literature
Composers, Bohemian
   See Composers, Czech
Composers, Czech
   x Composers, Bohemian
Composers, Women
   See Women composers
Composing-machines
   See Type-setting machines
Composing stick *(Z249)*
   xx Printing machinery and supplies
      Type-setting
Composite beams
   See Composite construction
Composite building
   See Composite construction
Composite checks *(Direct)*
   xx Checks
      Payrolls
Composite construction
   sa Pavements, Composite
   x Beams, Composite
      Building, Composite
      Composite beams
      Composite building
      Composite girders
      Girders, Composite
   xx Building, Iron and steel
      Composite materials
      Concrete construction
      Concrete slabs

— Fatigue
   xx Materials—Fatigue
— Tables
Composite girders
   See Composite construction
Composite materials
   sa Composite construction
      Fibrous composites
      Laminated materials
      Metallic composites
      Plastic-impregnated wood
   x Multiphase materials
      Reinforced solids
      Solids, Reinforced
      Two phase materials
   xx Materials
— Electric properties
— Mathematical models
— Testing
Composite pavements
   See Pavements, Composite
Composite photography
   See Photography, Composite
Composites, Fibrous
   See Fibrous composites
Composition (Art) *(N7430)*
   sa Architecture—Composition, proportion,
      etc.
      Human figure in art
      Painting
      Proportion (Art)
      Texture (Art)
   x Art—Composition
   xx Art
      Painting
      Proportion (Art)
Composition (Law) *(Direct)*
   sa Assignments for benefit of creditors
      Compromise (Law)
   xx Accord and satisfaction
      Bankruptcy
      Compromise (Law)
      Debtor and creditor
      Extinguishment of debts
Composition (Music) *(History, ML430-455;*
   Instruction, MT40-67)
   sa Chance composition
      Counterpoint
      Ground bass
      Harmony
      Imitation (in music)
      Instrumentation and orchestration
      Melody
      Music, Popular (Songs, etc.)—Writing
      and publishing
      Musical accompaniment
      Musical form
      Musical revue, comedy, etc.—Writing
      and publishing
      Symmetrical inversion (Music)
   x Music—Composition
      Musical composition
   xx Music
      Music—Instruction and study
      Music—Theory
— Mechanical aids
   sa Computer composition
Composition (Photography) *(TR179)*
   x Photographic composition
      Photography—Composition
   xx Photography
Composition (Printing)
   See Type-setting
Composition (Rhetoric)
   See Letter-writing
      Rhetoric

Composition (Rhetoric)   *(Continued)*
    subdivision Composition and exercises
    under names of languages, e.g.
      English language—Composition and
      exercises
Composition (Roman law)
Compost
  sa Humus
    Wood waste as mulch, soil conditioner,
      etc.
  x Indore process
  xx Agricultural wastes
    Fertilizers and manures
    Garden fertilizers
    Humus
    Organic fertilizers
    Sanitary landfills
    Soils
Compound centrifugal force
  See Coriolis force
Compound E
  See Cortisone
Compound eye
  xx Eye
Compound F
  See Hydrocortisone
Compound microscope   *(QH212.C6)*
  xx Microscope and microscopy
Compound nucleus   *(QC794)*
  sa Nuclear physics
    Nuclear reactions
  x Nucleus, Compound
  xx Nuclear physics
    Nuclear reactions
Compound offenses   *(Direct)*
    Here are entered works on the legal prob-
    lems, mainly in continental European
    law, resulting from the violation of sev-
    eral laws by one act, or the violations
    of one law by several acts, or on crimes
    which are characterized by a number
    of successive or simultaneous in-
    dividual violations. Here belong the le-
    gal concepts of "concours d'infrac-
    tion" in French; "Verbrechenskonkur-
    renz," "fortgesetztes Verbrechen,"
    etc. in German; "concorso di reati,"
    "reato continuato," etc. in Italian; and
    "concurrencia de delitos," "delito con-
    tinuado," etc. in Spanish.
  sa Joinder of offenses
  x Merger (Criminal law)
    Offenses, Compound
  xx Criminal law
    Joinder of offenses
Compound offenses (Jewish law)
Compound offenses (Roman-Dutch law)
Compound offenses (Roman law)
Compounds, Unsaturated   *(QD305; QD341)*
Compradors   *(Direct)*
  xx Commercial agents
    Commission merchants
Comprehension   *(BF325)*
  sa Apperception
    Cloze procedure
    Learning, Psychology of
    Listening
    Memory
    Reading comprehension
  x Understanding
  xx Apperception
    Knowledge, Theory of
    Learning, Psychology of
    Memory
  — Testing
    xx Ability—Testing

**Comprehensive Assemblage (Computer
    program language)**
  See COMPASS (Computer program
    language)
Comprehensive high schools   *(Direct)*
  x Cosmopolitan high schools
  xx High schools
Compressed air   *(Technology, TJ981-1009)*
  sa Air-engines
    Air lift pumps
    Pneumatic machinery
    Pneumatic tools
    Pneumatic-tube transportation
    Pressure vessels
  x Air, Compressed
    Pneumatic transmission
  xx Air-compressors
    Air-engines
    Caissons
    Cold storage
    Foundations
    Pneumatics
    Power (Mechanics)
    Pressure vessels
  — Safety measures
  — Therapeutic use   *(RM827)*
    sa Hyperbaric oxygenation
Compressed-air disease
  See Caisson-disease
Compressed-air railroads
  See Railroads, Compressed-air
Compressed-air starters
  See Aeroplanes—Motors—Starting devices
Compressed gas
  See Gases, Compressed
Compressed-gas automobiles
  See Automobiles—Motors
    (Compressed-gas)
Compressed gas containers
  See Gas cylinders
Compressed gas cylinders, Tariff on
  See Tariff on compressed gas cylinders
Compressed speech   *(Direct)*
  x Time compressed speech
  xx Speech
Compressed water
  sa Pressurized water reactors
  x Water, Compressed
  xx Water
Compressed wood
  See Wood, Compressed
Compressibility   *(Liquids, QC284)*
  sa Compacting
    Elasticity
    Ground-cushion phenomenon
    Mach number
    Shock waves
  x Liquids—Compressibility
  xx High pressure (Science)
    Hydrostatics
    Matter—Properties
    Physics
    Pressure
  — Computer programs   *(QC281)*
  — Tables, etc.
Compressibility of soils test
  See Soil consolidation test
Compressing machinery
  See Compressors
Compressing of granular materials
  See Compacting
Compression of wood
  See Wood, Compressed
Compressometers   *(Textile testing, TS1449)*
Compressors   *(TJ990-992)*
  sa Air-compressors
    Gas, Natural—Pipe lines—Compressor
    stations

    Marine compressors
    Petroleum—Pipe lines—Compressor
    stations
    Refrigeration and refrigerating
    machinery
    Superchargers
    Turboblowers
  x Axial flow compressors
    Blowers
    Centrifugal compressors
    Compressing machinery
    Exhausters
  xx Refrigeration and refrigerating
    machinery
    Turbomachines
  — Aerodynamics   *(TJ267.5.C5)*
    Example under Aerodynamics
  — Appraisal
    See Compressors—Valuation
  — Automatic control
  — Blades   *(TJ990)*
    x Rotor blades (Compressors)
    Stator blades (Compressors)
  — — Vibration
    xx Compressors—Vibration
  — Catalogs
  — Design and construction
  — Dynamics
  — Lubrication
  — Maintenance and repair
  — Reliability   *(TJ990)*
  — Safety appliances
  — Safety measures
  — Testing
  — Valuation   *(TJ990)*
    x Compressors—Appraisal
  — Vibration
    sa Compressors—Blades—Vibration
Compressors, Air
  See Air-compressors
Compressors, Supersonic
  See Supersonic compressors
Compromise (Arbitration agreement)
  See Arbitration agreements, Commercial
Compromise (Canon law)
Compromise (Ethics)   *(BJ1430-1438)*
  sa Perfection (Ethics)
  xx Ethics
    Perfection (Ethics)
Compromise (Law)   *(Direct)*
  sa Arbitration and award
    Composition (Law)
    Consent decrees
    Tax compromises
  x Settlement out of court
    Transactio
    Transaction (Civil law)
  xx Accord and satisfaction
    Arbitration and award
    Civil procedure
    Composition (Law)
    Contracts
    Debtor and creditor
    Extinguishment of debts
  — Forms
Compromise (Roman law)
Compromise of 1850   *(E423)*
  sa Fugitive slave law of 1850
    Slavery in the United States
  x Onmibus bill, 1850
  xx Slavery in the United States
Compromises, Tax
  See Tax compromises
Compromiso de Caspe
  See Caspe declaration, 1412
Comptometers   *(QA75)*
  xx Calculating-machines

Compton effect
    xx Collisions (Nuclear physics)
        Electrons
        Photons
Comptrollership
    See Controllership
Compulsion
    See Duress (Law)
Compulsion (Psychology)
    See Obsessive-compulsive neuroses
Compulsory education
    See Education, Compulsory
Compulsory labor
    See Forced labor
Compulsory licensing of patents *(Direct)*
    xx Patent laws and legislation
        Patent licenses
        Patents and government-developed
           inventions
Compulsory loans
    See Forced loans
Compulsory military service
    See Military service, Compulsory
Compulsory non-military service
    See Service, Compulsory non-military
Compulsory school attendance
    See Education, Compulsory
        Educational law and legislation
        School attendance
Compulsory voting
    See Voting, Compulsory
Computability theory
    See Recursive functions
Computable functions
    See Recursive functions
Computation laboratories *(Direct)* *(QA74)*
    x Computer centers
        Computer laboratories
        Computing laboratories
        Mathematics—Laboratories
        Numerical analysis laboratories
    xx Calculating-machines
        Computers
        Numerical calculations
Computational linguistics
    See Language data processing
        Mathematical linguistics
        Programming languages (Electronic
           computers)
COMPUTE (Computer program)
    xx Time-sharing computer systems
Computer-aided systems for command
    See Electronic data processing—Tactics
Computer animation
    sa Animation (Cinematography)
    x Animated cartoons by computer
        Animation, Computer
        Computer-assisted film making
    xx Computer drawing
        Moving-picture cartoons
Computer arithmetic and logic units
    x Arithmetic and logic units, Computer
    xx Electronic digital computers—Circuits
Computer-assisted film making
    See Computer animation
Computer-assisted instruction *(Indirect)*
    x Electronic data processing in
        programmed instruction
    xx Educational technology
        Electronic data processing—Education
        Electronic digital computers
        Programmed instruction
    — Computer programs
Computer centers
    See Computation laboratories
        Data processing service centers
        Electronic data processing departments

Computer circuits
    See Computers—Circuits
Computer composition
    sa Computer music
    xx Composition (Music)—Mechanical aids
        Computer music
        Computer sound processing
Computer control
    See Automation
Computer department security measures
    See Electronic data processing departments
        —Security measures
Computer drawing
        Here are entered works on the use of
        computer graphics to create artistic
        designs. Works on the technique for
        producing line drawings, including
        particularly engineering drawings, by
        use of current digital computing and
        plotting equipment are entered under
        Computer graphics.
    sa Computer animation
    xx Drawing
    Note under Computer graphics
Computer engineering *(TK7885-7895)*
    x Computers—Design and construction
    — Programmed instruction
Computer grading and marking (Students)
    See Electronic data processing—Grading
        and marking (Students)
Computer graphics *(T385)*
        Here are entered works on the technique
        for producing line drawings, including
        particularly engineering drawings, by
        use of current digital computing and
        plotting equipment. Works on the use
        of computer graphics to create artistic
        designs are entered under Computer
        drawing.
    sa Digital incremental plotters
        GRAIL (Electronic computer system)
        GRASS (Electronic computer system)
        POGO (Computer program)
        VIEW (Computer program)
    x Automatic drafting
        Electronic data processing—
           Engineering graphics
        Electronic data processing—Mechanical
           drawing
        Graphic data processing
        Graphics, Computer
    xx Electronic data processing—
           Engineering design
        Electronic digital computers
        Engineering graphics
    Note under Computer drawing
Computer industry *(Direct)*
    sa Computers
Computer input-output equipment
    sa Analog-to-digital converters
        Automatic speech recognition
        Computer output microfilm devices
        Computer storage devices
        Computers—Optical equipment
        Data tape drives
        Information display systems
        Modems
        Printers (Data processing systems)
        Punched card systems
        Reading machines (Data processing
           equipment)
    x Computers—Input-output equipment
        Data terminals (Computers)
        Electronic analog computers—
           Input-output equipment
        Electronic digital computers—
           Input-output equipment
        Input equipment (Computers)

        Input-output equipment (Computers)
        Output equipment (Computers)
        Terminals, Data (Computers)
    — Programmed instruction
Computer insurance
    See Insurance, Computer
Computer laboratories
    See Computation laboratories
Computer language for aeronautics and space
        programming
    See CLASP (Computer program language)
Computer languages
    See Programming languages (Electronic
        computers)
Computer leases *(Direct)*
    sa Data processing service centers
    xx Data processing service centers
        Industrial equipment leases
        Leases
Computer memory systems
    See Computer storage devices
Computer music
    sa Computer composition
    x Music, Computer
        Tape-recorder music
    xx Computer composition
        Electronic music
        Music
        Technology and the arts
Computer output microfilm devices
        (TK7887.8.C6)
    x Microfilm devices, Computer output
    xx Computer input-output equipment
        Computers—Optical equipment
Computer program languages
    See Programming languages (Electronic
        computers)
Computer program testing
    See Computer programs—Testing
Computer programming
    See Programming (Electronic computers)
Computer programming as a profession
    See Programming (Electronic computers)—
        Vocational guidance
Computer programming management
    x Programming management (Electronic
        computers)
    xx Electronic data processing departments
        Management
        Programming (Electronic computers)
Computer programs
    sa subdivision Computer programs *under*
        subjects, e.g. Bessel functions—
        Computer programs; *and names of*
        computer programs, e.g. GAT
        (Computer program)
    x Computer software
        Programs, Computer
        Software, Computer
    xx Electronic digital computers—
        Programming
        Programming (Electronic computers)
    — Debugging
        See Debugging in computer science
    — Patents
    — Reliability
    — Testing
        sa Debugging in computer science
        x Computer program testing
        xx Debugging in computer science
Computer reliability
    See Computers—Reliability
Computer science literature *(Direct)*
    (QA76)
Computer security measures
    See Electronic data processing departments
        —Security measures

Computer simulation   *(QA76)*
    sa Digital computer simulation
     x Simulation, Computer
    xx Electromechanical analogies
         Mathematical models
         Simulation methods
Computer simulation, Digital
    See Digital computer simulation
Computer software
    See Computer programs
         Programming (Electronic computers)
         Programming languages (Electronic
           computers)
         and similar headings
Computer software insurance
    See Insurance, Computer
Computer sorting
    See Sorting (Electronic computers)
Computer sound processing
    sa Computer composition
     x Sound processing, Computer
    xx Electronic digital computers
         Sound
Computer storage devices
    sa Associative storage
         Cathode ray tube memory systems
         Data tapes
         Magnetic memory
           (Calculating-machines)
         Microfilm aperture card systems
         Punched card systems
         Read-only storage
         subdivision Memory systems *under
           names of individual computers, e.g.*
           Besm computer—Memory systems
     x Computer memory systems
         Computers—Memory systems
         Computers—Storage devices
         Electronic digital computers—Memory
           systems
         Storage devices, Computer
    xx Computer input-output equipment
Computer translating
    See Machine translating
Computer typesetting
    See Computerized typesetting
Computerized typesetting
    sa LEFT (Computer program language)
         PAGE-1 (Electronic computer system)
         ULTRA-X (Computer program
           language)
     x Automated typesetting
         Computer typesetting
         Electronic data processing—Typesetting
    xx Electronic data processing—Book
           industries and trade
         Type-setting
    — Costs
    — Terminology
Computers   *(Mathematics, QA76-76.3;
           Electrical engineering,
           TK7885-7895)*
         Here are entered works on modern elec-
         tronic computers first developed after
         1945. Works on calculators, as well as
         all mechanical computers of pre-1945
         vintage, are entered under Calculat-
         ing-machines.
    sa Airborne computers
         Computation laboratories
         Correlators
         Electronic analog computers
         Electronic data processing
         Electronic digital computers
         Hybrid computers
         Information storage and retrieval
           systems
         Miniature computers

         *headings beginning with the word
           Computer*
     x Automatic computers
         Automatic data processors
         Computers, Electronic
         Computing machines (Computers)
         Electronic brains
         Electronic calculating-machines
         Electronic computers
    xx Calculating-machines
         Computer industry
         Cybernetics
         Electronic apparatus and appliances
         Electronic office machines
         Information storage and retrieval
           systems
         Machine theory
    Note under Calculating-machines
    — Abbreviations
    — Amateurs' manuals
    — Anecdotes, facetiae, satire, etc.
    — Appraisal
         See Computers—Valuation
    — Caricatures and cartoons
    — Circuits
         x Computer circuits
        xx Electronic circuits
    — — Quality control
    — Design and construction
         See Computer engineering
    — Fires and fire prevention
    — Input-output equipment
         See Computer input-output equipment
    — Juvenile literature
    — Law and legislation   *(Direct)*
    — Memory systems
         See Computer storage devices
    — Moral and regious aspects
    — Notation
    — Optical equipment
         sa Cathode ray tube memory systems
              Computer output microfilm devices
              Information display systems
              Optical character recognition devices
              Optical data processing
        xx Computer input-output equipment
              Optical data processing
              Optical instruments
              Photoelectronic devices
    — Patents
    — Popular works
    — Print-out equipment
         See Printers (Data processing systems)
    — Printers
         See Printers (Data processing systems)
    — Programming
         See Programming (Electronic
           computers)
    — Reliability
         x Computer reliability
    — Storage devices
         See Computer storage devices
    — Terminology
    — Valuation
         x Computers—Appraisal
    — Vocational guidance
    — — Juvenile literature
Computers, Density altitude
    See Density altitude computers
Computers, Electronic
    See Computers
Computers, Electronic analog
    See Electronic analog computers
Computers, Electronic digital
    See Electronic digital computers
Computers, Hybrid
    See Hybrid computers

Computers and civilization
     x Civilization and computers
Computing laboratories
    See Computation laboratories
Computing machines
    See Calculating-machines
Computing machines (Computers)
    See Computers
Computing tables
    See Ready-reckoners
Computus
    See Calendar
Computus ecclesiasticus
    See Church calendar
Comradeship   *(BJ1533.C56)*
    sa Fellowship
Concani language
    See Konkani language
Concealed writing
    See Writing, Invisible
Concelebration   *(Catholic Church, BX2231.5)*
    xx Lord's Supper—Celebration
         Mass—Celebration
Concentrated milk
    See Milk, Concentrated
Concentrated study   *(LB1029.C55)*
     x Immersion technique (Education)
         Intensive programs in education
         Total immersion technique (Education)
    xx Education—Experimental methods
         Project method in teaching
         Study, Method of
Concentration
    See Attention
Concentration, Industrial
    See Industrial concentration
Concentration, Stress
    See Stress concentration
Concentration camps   *(Indirect)*
    sa Cuba—History—Revolution, 1895-1898
         Political prisoners
         subdivision Concentration camps *under
           certain wars, e.g.* South African War,
           1899-1902—Concentration camps;
           *also names of individual
           concentration camps, e.g.*
           Argelès-sur-Mer (Concentration
           camp); Dachau (Concentration
           camp)
     x Detention camps
         Internment camps
    xx Camps (Military)
         Detention of persons
         Political crimes and offenses
         Prisoners of war
         World War, 1939-1945—Prisoners and
           prisons
    — Pictorial works
    — Psychological aspects
        xx Prison psychology
Concentration camps in literature
Concentration cells   *(Electrochemistry,
           QD568; Physics, QC603)*
    xx Electric batteries
Concentration functions
     x Functions, Concentration
    xx Convergence
         Functions of real variables
         Measure theory
         Probabilities
Concentration of schools
    See Schools—Centralization
Concept art
    See Conceptual art
Concept formation
    See Concepts
Concept learning
    xx Learning, Psychology of

Conception (Gynecology, RG136;
    Reproduction, QP251-281)
— Prevention (RG136; Limitation of
    offspring, HQ763-6;
    Neo-Malthusianism, HB875)
    sa Contraceptives
        Eugenics
        Hygiene, Sexual
        Malthusianism
        Population
        Sexual ethics
        Sterilization (Birth control)
    x Contraception
    xx Birth control
        Fertility, Effect of drugs on
        Hygiene, Sexual
— — Juvenile literature
Conception of geometry
    See Geometry concept
Concepts
    sa Example
        Ideals (Psychology)
    x Concept formation
    xx Abstraction
        Knowledge, Theory of
        Perception
        Psychology
Conceptual art (Direct) (The arts,
    NX600.C6; Visual arts, N6494.C63)
    x Art, Conceptual
        Art povera
        Arte povera
        Concept art
        Language art (Fine arts)
        Possible art
        Post-object art
    xx Art, Modern—20th century
Conceptualism (B731)
    sa Nominalism
        Realism
    xx Nominalism
        Realism
        Scholasticism
        Universals (Philosophy)
Concert agents
    sa Impresarios
    x Concerts—Agents
    xx Commercial agents
        Impresarios
Concert halls
    See Music-halls
Concert of Europe
    x European concert
    xx Great powers
        International organization
Concerti grossi (M1040-1041)
    Cf. note under Orchestral music.
    sa Concertos
    xx Chamber-orchestra music
        Concertos
        Orchestral music
        String-orchestra music
— Analytical guides (MT125; MT130)
— Solos with piano (M1041; M1106)
Concerti grossi, Arranged (M1040-1041)
Concerti grossi arranged for band (M1257)
    xx Band music, Arranged
— Scores (reduced) and parts
Concerti grossi arranged for organ (M12-13)
    xx Organ music, Arranged
Concerti grossi arranged for piano (M37)
    xx Piano music, Arranged
Concerti grossi arranged for piano (4 hands)
    (M210)
    xx Piano music (4 hands), Arranged
Concerti grossi arranged for piano (Pianos
    (2)) (M215)
    xx Piano music (Pianos (2)), Arranged

Concerti grossi arranged for string orchestra
    (M1160)
    xx String-orchestra music, Arranged
— Scores (M1160)
Concertina (ML1055.C6)
    sa Accordion
        Bandonion
    xx Accordion
        Bandonion
Concertina and guitar music
    sa Potpourris (Concertina and guitar)
    x Guitar and concertina music
Concertina music (M154)
Concerto (History, ML1263)
    xx Musical form
Concerto (Organ) (ML1263)
    xx Organ music—History and criticism
Concerto (Piano) (ML1263)
    xx Piano music—History and criticism
Concerto (Violin) (ML1263)
    xx Violin music—History and criticism
Concerto (Violoncello) (ML1263)
    xx Violoncello music—History and
        criticism
Concerto grosso (ML448)
    xx Musical form
Concertos (M1004.5-1041)
    Here are entered collections of miscel-
    laneous concertos for various instru-
    ments. Concertos for particular instru-
    ments, both collections and separates,
    are entered under the headings Con-
    certos (Piano), Concertos (Violin), etc.
    Where the accompanying medium is
    other than full orchestra, headings
    such as Concertos (Flute with string
    orchestra), Concertos (Trumpet with
    band) are used. Cf. note under Orches-
    tral music.
    sa Concerti grossi
    xx Concerti grossi
        Orchestral music
Concertos (Accordion) (M1039.4.A)
    sa Accordion with orchestra
    xx Accordion music
        Accordion with orchestra
— Solo with piano (M1039.4.A3)
    xx Accordion and piano music
Concertos (Accordion with chamber orchestra)
    (M1039.4.A3)
    sa Accordion with chamber orchestra
    xx Accordion music
        Accordion with chamber orchestra
        Chamber-orchestra music
— Solo with piano (M1039.4.A3)
Concertos (Accordion with plectral ensemble)
    (M1360)
    sa Accordion with plectral ensemble
    xx Accordion music
        Accordion with plectral ensemble
        Plectral ensembles
— Scores (M1360)
Concertos (Accordion with string orchestra)
    (M1040-1041)
    sa Accordion with string orchestra
    xx Accordion music
        Accordion with string orchestra
        String-orchestra music
— Scores (M1105)
Concertos (Balalaika with chamber orchestra)
    (M1037.4.B3)
    sa Balalaika with chamber orchestra
    xx Balalaika music
        Balalaika with chamber orchestra
        Chamber-orchestra music
— Scores (M1037.4.B3)
Concertos (Band) (M1203)
    xx Band music

Concertos (Baritone with string orchestra)
    (M1134.B37; M1135.B37)
    sa Baritone with string orchestra
    xx Baritone music
        Baritone with string orchestra
Concertos (Bassoon) (M1026-7)
    sa Bassoon with orchestra
    xx Bassoon music
        Bassoon with orchestra
— Cadenzas (M1004.7; M1026.5)
— Solo with piano (M1027)
    xx Bassoon and piano music, Arranged
Concertos (Bassoon and clarinet)
    (M1040-1041)
    sa Bassoon and clarinet with orchestra
    xx Bassoon and clarinet music
        Bassoon and clarinet with orchestra
— Solos with piano (M1041)
    xx Trios (Piano, bassoon, clarinet),
        Arranged
Concertos (Bassoon and clarinet with string
    orchestra) (M1105-6)
    sa Bassoon and clarinet with string
        orchestra
    xx Bassoon and clarinet music
        Bassoon and clarinet with string
        orchestra
        String-orchestra music
Concertos (Bassoon and flute with string
    orchestra) (M1140-1141)
    sa Bassoon and flute with string orchestra
    xx Bassoon and flute music
        Bassoon and flute with string orchestra
Concertos (Bassoon and oboe) (M1040-1041)
    sa Bassoon and oboe with orchestra
    xx Bassoon and oboe music
        Bassoon and oboe with orchestra
Concertos (Bassoon and oboe with string
    orchestra) (M1105-6)
    sa Bassoon and oboe with string orchestra
    xx Bassoon and oboe music
        Bassoon and oboe with string orchestra
        String-orchestra music
— Solos with piano (M1106)
    xx Trios (Piano, bassoon, oboe),
        Arranged
Concertos (Bassoon and piccolo with string
    orchestra) (M1105-6)
    sa Bassoon and piccolo with string
        orchestra
    xx Bassoon and piccolo music
        Bassoon and piccolo with string
        orchestra
        String-orchestra music
— Scores (M1105)
Concertos (Bassoon and recorder with string
    orchestra) (M1105-6)
    sa Bassoon and recorder with string
        orchestra
    xx Bassoon and recorder music
        Bassoon and recorder with string
        orchestra
        String-orchestra music
Concertos (Bassoon and trumpet with string
    orchestra) (M1105-6)
    sa Bassoon and trumpet with string
        orchestra
    xx Bassoon and trumpet music
        Bassoon and trumpet with string
        orchestra
        String-orchestra music
— Solos with piano (M1106)
    xx Trios (Piano, bassoon, trumpet),
        Arranged
Concertos (Bassoon and violin with string
    orchestra) (M1105-6)
    sa Bassoon and violin with string orchestra
    xx Bassoon and violin music

Concertos (Bassoon and violin with string
    orchestra) (M1105-6)
      (Continued)
      Bassoon and violin with string orchestra
      String-orchestra music
  — Solos with piano (M1106)
      xx Trios (Piano, bassoon, violin),
          Arranged
Concertos (Bassoon, clarinet, English horn,
    flute) (M1040-1041)
    sa Bassoon, clarinet, English horn, flute
       with orchestra
    xx Bassoon, clarinet, English horn, flute
       with orchestra
      Orchestral music
      Wind quartets (Bassoon, clarinet,
       English horn, flute)
  — Solos with piano (M1041)
      xx Quintets (Piano, bassoon, clarinet,
          English horn, flute), Arranged
Concertos (Bassoon, clarinet, flute, horn,
    oboe) (M1040-1041)
    sa Bassoon, clarinet, flute, horn, oboe with
       orchestra
    xx Bassoon, clarinet, flute, horn, oboe with
       orchestra
      Wind quintets (Bassoon, clarinet, flute,
       horn, oboe)
  — Scores (M1040)
Concertos (Bassoon, clarinet, flute, horn, oboe
    with band) (M1205-6)
    sa Bassoon, clarinet, flute, horn, oboe with
       band
    xx Band music
      Bassoon, clarinet, flute, horn, oboe with
       band
      Wind quintets (Bassoon, clarinet, flute,
       horn, oboe)
  — Scores and parts (M1205)
Concertos (Bassoon, clarinet, flute, horn, oboe
    with chamber orchestra)
    (M1040-1041)
    sa Bassoon, clarinet, flute, horn, oboe with
       chamber orchestra
    xx Bassoon, clarinet, flute, horn, oboe with
       chamber orchestra
      Chamber-orchestra music
      Wind quintets (Bassoon, clarinet, flute,
       horn, oboe)
Concertos (Bassoon, clarinet, flute, horn, oboe
    with string orchestra) (M1105-6)
    sa Bassoon, clarinet, flute, horn, oboe with
       string orchestra
    xx Bassoon, clarinet, flute, horn, oboe with
       string orchestra
      String-orchestra music
      Wind quintets (Bassoon, clarinet, flute,
       horn, oboe)
  — Solos with piano (M1106)
      xx Sextets (Piano, bassoon, clarinet,
          flute, horn, oboe), Arranged
Concertos (Bassoon, clarinet, flute, horn,
    violoncello with string orchestra)
    (M1105-6)
    sa Bassoon, clarinet, flute, horn,
       violoncello with string orchestra
    xx Bassoon, clarinet, flute, horn,
       violoncello with string orchestra
      Quintets (Bassoon, clarinet, flute, horn,
       violoncello)
      String-orchestra music
Concertos (Bassoon, clarinet, flute, oboe,
    harp) (M1040-1041)
    sa Bassoon, clarinet, flute, oboe, harp with
       orchestra
    xx Bassoon, clarinet, flute, oboe, harp with
       orchestra
      Quintets (Bassoon, clarinet, flute, oboe,
       harp)

— Scores (M1040)
Concertos (Bassoon, clarinet, flute, oboe,
    violins (2), viola, violoncello with
    string orchestra) (M1105-6)
    xx Bassoon, clarinet, flute, oboe, violins
       (2), viola, violoncello with string
       orchestra
    sa Bassoon, clarinet, flute, oboe, violins
       (2), viola, violoncello with string
       orchestra
    xx Octets (Bassoon, clarinet, flute, oboe,
       violins (2), viola, violoncello)
      String-orchestra music
Concertos (Bassoon, clarinet, flute, oboe with
    chamber orchestra) (M1040-1041)
    sa Bassoon, clarinet, flute, oboe with
       chamber orchestra
    xx Bassoon, clarinet, flute, oboe with
       chamber orchestra
      Chamber-orchestra music
      Wind quartets (Bassoon, clarinet, flute,
       oboe)
Concertos (Bassoon, clarinet, flute, oboe with
    string orchestra) (M1105-6)
    sa Bassoon, clarinet, flute, oboe with string
       orchestra
    xx Bassoon, clarinet, flute, oboe with string
       orchestra
      String-orchestra music
      Wind quartets (Bassoon, clarinet, flute,
       oboe)
  — Scores (M1105-6)
Concertos (Bassoon, clarinet, flute, trumpet
    with string orchestra) (M1105-6)
    sa Bassoon, clarinet, flute, trumpet with
       string orchestra
    xx Bassoon, clarinet, flute, trumpet with
       string orchestra
      String-orchestra music
      Wind quartets (Bassoon, clarinet, flute,
       trumpet)
Concertos (Bassoon, clarinet, flute with string
    orchestra) (M1105-6)
    sa Bassoon, clarinet, flute with string
       orchestra
    xx Bassoon, clarinet, flute with string
       orchestra
Concertos (Bassoon, clarinet, horn, oboe)
    (M1040-1041)
    sa Bassoon, clarinet, horn, oboe with
       orchestra
    xx Bassoon, clarinet, horn, oboe with
       orchestra
      Wind quartets (Bassoon, clarinet, horn,
       oboe)
  — To 1800
  — — Scores (M1040)
  — — Solos with piano (M1041)
      xx Quintets (Piano, bassoon, clarinet,
          horn, oboe), Arranged
Concertos (Bassoon, clarinet, horn, oboe with
    string orchestra) (M1140-1)
    sa Bassoon, clarinet, horn, oboe with
       string orchestra
    xx Bassoon, clarinet, horn, oboe with
       string orchestra
      String-orchestra music
      Wind quartets (Bassoon, clarinet, horn,
       oboe)
  — Scores (M1105-6)
Concertos (Bassoon, clarinet, oboe with string
    orchestra) (M1105-6)
    sa Bassoon, clarinet, oboe with string
       orchestra
    xx Bassoon, clarinet, oboe with string
       orchestra
      String-orchestra music
      Wind trios (Bassoon, clarinet, oboe)

Concertos (Bassoon, clarinet, trumpet)
    (M1040-1041)
    sa Bassoon, clarinet, trumpet with
       orchestra
    xx Bassoon, clarinet, trumpet with
       orchestra
      Wind trios (Bassoon, clarinet, trumpet)
  — Scores (M1040)
Concertos (Bassoon, flute, horn, oboe)
    (M1040-1041)
    sa Bassoon, flute, horn, oboe with
       orchestra
    xx Bassoon, flute, horn, oboe with
       orchestra
      Wind quartets (Bassoon, flute, horn,
       oboe)
  — Solos with piano (M1041)
      xx Quintets (Piano, bassoon, flute, horn,
          oboe), Arranged
Concertos (Bassoon, flute, horn, oboe),
    Arranged (M1040-1041)
Concertos (Bassoon, flute, horn, oboe, trumpet
    with string orchestra)
    (M1140-1141)
    sa Bassoon, flute, horn, oboe, trumpet
       with string orchestra
    xx Bassoon, flute, horn, oboe, trumpet
       with string orchestra
      String-orchestra music
      Wind quintets (Bassoon, flute, horn,
       oboe, trumpet)
Concertos (Bassoon, flute, horn, oboe with
    chamber orchestra) (M1040-1041)
    sa Bassoon, flute, horn, oboe with
       chamber orchestra
    xx Bassoon, flute, horn, oboe with
       chamber orchestra
      Chamber-orchestra music
      Wind quartets (Bassoon, flute, horn,
       oboe)
Concertos (Bassoon, flute, horn, oboe with
    string orchestra) (M1105-6)
    sa Bassoon, flute, horn, oboe with string
       orchestra
    xx Bassoon, flute, horn, oboe with string
       orchestra
      String-orchestra music
      Wind quartets (Bassoon, flute, horn,
       oboe)
Concertos (Bassoon, horn, trumpet, double
    bass) (M1040-1041)
    sa Bassoon, horn, trumpet, double bass
       with orchestra
    xx Bassoon, horn, trumpet, double bass
       with orchestra
      Quartets (Bassoon, horn, trumpet,
       double bass)
Concertos (Bassoon, oboe, trumpet with string
    orchestra) (M1105-6)
    sa Bassoon, oboe, trumpet with string
       orchestra
    xx Bassoon, oboe, trumpet with string
       orchestra
      String-orchestra music
      Wind trios (Bassoon, oboe, trumpet)
Concertos (Bassoon, oboe, violin, violoncello)
    (M1040-1041)
    sa Bassoon, oboe, violin, violoncello with
       orchestra
    xx Bassoon, oboe, violin, violoncello with
       orchestra
      Quartets (Bassoon, oboe, violin,
       violoncello)
Concertos (Bassoon, oboe, violin, violoncello
    with chamber orchestra)
    (M1040-1041)
    sa Bassoon, oboe, violin, violoncello with
       chamber orchestra

xx Bassoon, oboe, violin, violoncello with
   chamber orchestra
   Chamber-orchestra music
   Quartets (Bassoon, oboe, violin,
   violoncello)
Concertos (Bassoon with band) *(M1205-6)*
sa Bassoon with band
xx Band music
   Bassoon music
   Bassoon with band
Concertos (Bassoon with chamber orchestra)
   (M1026-7)
sa Bassoon with chamber orchestra
xx Bassoon music
   Bassoon with chamber orchestra
   Chamber-orchestra music
— Scores *(M1026)*
Concertos (Bassoon with string orchestra)
   (M1105-6)
sa Bassoon with string orchestra
xx Bassoon music
   Bassoon with string orchestra
   String-orchestra music
— Solo with piano *(M1106)*
   xx Bassoon and piano music, Arranged
**Concertos (Bassoon with string orchestra),
   Arranged** *(M1105-6)*
— Solo with piano *(M1106)*
   xx Bassoon and piano music, Arranged
Concertos (Carillon with band) *(M1205-6)*
sa Carillon with band
xx Carillon music
   Carillon with band
**Concertos (Celesta, clarinet, harp with string
   orchestra)** *(M1140-1141)*
sa Celesta, clarinet, harp with string
   orchestra
xx Celesta, clarinet, harp with string
   orchestra
   String-orchestra music
   Trios (Celesta, clarinet, harp)
Concertos (Cimbalom) *(M1037.4.C54)*
sa Cimbalom with orchestra
xx Cimbalom with orchestra
Concertos (Clarinet) *(M1024-5)*
sa Clarinet with orchestra
xx Clarinet music
   Clarinet with orchestra
— Solo with piano *(M1025)*
   xx Clarinet and piano music, Arranged
**Concertos (Clarinet and flute with chamber
   orchestra)** *(M1040-1041)*
sa Clarinet and flute with chamber
   orchestra
xx Chamber-orchestra music
   Clarinet and flute music
   Clarinet and flute with chamber
   orchestra
**Concertos (Clarinet and flute with string
   orchestra)**
sa Clarinet and flute with string orchestra
xx Clarinet and flute music
   Clarinet and flute with string orchestra
   String-orchestra music
**Concertos (Clarinet and harp with string
   orchestra)** *(M1105-6)*
sa Clarinet and harp with string orchestra
xx Clarinet and harp music
   Clarinet and harp with string orchestra
   String-orchestra music
Concertos (Clarinet and oboe) *(M1040-1041)*
sa Clarinet and oboe with orchestra
xx Clarinet and oboe music
   Clarinet and oboe with orchestra
   Orchestral music

**Concertos (Clarinet and vibraphone with
   string orchestra)** *(M1105-6)*
sa Clarinet and vibraphone with string
   orchestra
xx Clarinet and vibraphone music
   Clarinet and vibraphone with string
   orchestra
   String-orchestra music
— Scores *(M1105)*
Concertos (Clarinet and violin)
   (M1040-1041)
sa Clarinet and violin with orchestra
xx Clarinet and violin music
   Clarinet and violin with orchestra
**Concertos (Clarinet and violin with string
   orchestra)** *(M1105-6)*
sa Clarinet and violin with string orchestra
xx Clarinet and violin music
   Clarinet and violin with string orchestra
   String-orchestra music
Concertos (Clarinet and violoncello)
   (M1040-1041)
sa Clarinet and violoncello with orchestra
xx Clarinet and violoncello music
   Clarinet and violoncello with orchestra
**Concertos (Clarinet, English horn, flute, oboe
   with string orchestra)** *(M1105-6)*
sa Clarinet, English horn, flute, oboe with
   string orchestra
xx Clarinet, English horn, flute, oboe with
   string orchestra
   String-orchestra music
   Wind quartets (Clarinet, English horn,
   flute, oboe)
**Concertos (Clarinet, flute, harp with string
   orchestra)** *(M1105-6)*
sa Clarinet, flute, harp with string
   orchestra
xx Clarinet, flute, harp with string
   orchestra
   String-orchestra music
   Trios (Clarinet, flute, harp)
**Concertos (Clarinet, flute, oboe with string
   orchestra)** *(M1105-6)*
sa Clarinet, flute, oboe with string
   orchestra
xx Clarinet, flute, oboe with string
   orchestra
   String-orchestra music
   Wind trios (Clarinet, flute, oboe)
**Concertos (Clarinet, flute, trumpet with string
   orchestra)** *(M1105-6)*
sa Clarinet, flute, trumpet with string
   orchestra
xx Clarinet, flute, trumpet with string
   orchestra
   String-orchestra music
   Wind trios (Clarinet, flute, trumpet)
**Concertos (Clarinet, harp, violin, violoncello
   with string orchestra)** *(M1105)*
sa Clarinet, harp, violin, violoncello with
   string orchestra
xx Clarinet, harp, violin, violoncello with
   string orchestra
   Quartets (Clarinet, harp, violin,
   violoncello)
   String-orchestra music
**Concertos (Clarinet, trombone, trumpet with
   string orchestra)** *(M1105-6)*
sa Clarinet, trombone, trumpet with string
   orchestra
xx Clarinet, trombone, trumpet with string
   orchestra
   String-orchestra music
   Wind trios (Clarinet, trombone,
   trumpet)
— Scores *(M1105)*
— Solos with piano *(M1106)*

xx Quartets (Piano, clarinet, trombone,
   trumpet), Arranged
Concertos (Clarinet with band) *(M1205)*
sa Clarinet with band
xx Band music
   Clarinet music
   Clarinet with band
— Solo with piano *(M1205)*
   xx Clarinet and piano music, Arranged
Concertos (Clarinet with chamber orchestra)
   (M1024-5)
sa Clarinet with chamber orchestra
xx Chamber-orchestra music
   Clarinet music
   Clarinet with chamber orchestra
— Solo with piano *(M1025)*
   xx Clarinet and piano music, Arranged
Concertos (Clarinet with dance orchestra)
   (M1353)
sa Clarinet with dance orchestra
xx Clarinet music
   Clarinet with dance orchestra
   Dance-orchestra music
— Scores *(M1353)*
Concertos (Clarinet with instr. ensemble)
xx Clarinet with instr. ensemble
   Instrumental ensembles
Concertos (Clarinet with jazz ensemble)
   (M955-7)
sa Clarinet with jazz ensemble
xx Clarinet music
   Clarinet with jazz ensemble
   Jazz ensembles
Concertos (Clarinet with string orchestra)
   (M1105-6)
sa Clarinet with string orchestra
xx Clarinet music
   Clarinet with string orchestra
   String-orchestra music
— Solo with piano *(M1106)*
   xx Clarinet and piano music, Arranged
**Concertos (Clarinet with string orchestra),
   Arranged** *(M1105-6)*
— Solo with piano *(M1106)*
   xx Clarinet and piano music, Arranged
Concertos (Clarinets (2)) *(M1024-5)*
sa Clarinets (2) with orchestra
xx Clarinet music (Clarinets (2))
   Clarinets (2) with orchestra
   Orchestral music
Concertos (Clarinets (4) with string orchestra)
   (M1124-5)
sa Clarinets (4) with string orchestra
xx Clarinets (4) with string orchestra
   String-orchestra music
   Wind quartets (Clarinets (4))
Concertos (Cornet) *(M1030-1031)*
sa Concertos (Trumpet)
   Cornet with orchestra
xx Concertos (Trumpet)
   Cornet music
   Cornet with orchestra
Concertos (Cornet and trumpet)
   (M1040-1041)
sa Cornet and trumpet with orchestra
xx Cornet and trumpet music
   Cornet and trumpet with orchestra
Concertos (Cornet with band) *(M1205)*
sa Cornet with band
xx Band music
   Cornet music
   Cornet with band
Concertos (Cornets (4) with band)
   (M1205-6)
sa Cornets (4) with band
xx Band music
   Cornets (4) with band
   Wind quartets (Cornets (4))

Concertos (Dance orchestra) (M1356)
  xx Dance-orchestra music
Concertos (Domra) (M1037.4.D64)
  sa Domra with orchestra
  xx Domra music
     Domra with orchestra
  —Solo with piano (M1037.4.D64)
     xx Domra and piano music, Arranged
Concertos (Domra with chamber orchestra)
     (M1037.4.D64)
  sa Domra with chamber orchestra
  xx Chamber-orchestra music
     Domra music
     Domra with chamber orchestra
  —Solo with piano (M1037.4.D64)
     xx Domra with piano music, Arranged
Concertos (Double bass) (M1018)
  sa Double bass with orchestra
  xx Double-bass music
     Double bass with orchestra
  —Solo with piano (M1018)
     xx Double-bass and piano music,
        Arranged
Concertos (Double bass), Arranged (M1018)
  —Solo with piano (M1018)
     xx Double-bass and piano music,
        Arranged
Concertos (Double bass with band)
     (M1205-6)
  sa Double bass with band
  xx Band music
     Double-bass music
     Double bass with band
  —Solo with piano (M1206)
     xx Double-bass and piano music,
        Arranged
Concertos (Double bass with chamber
     orchestra) (M1018)
  sa Double bass with chamber orchestra
  xx Chamber-orchestra music
     Double-bass music
     Double bass with chamber orchestra
Concertos (Double bass with string orchestra)
     (M1105-6)
  sa Double bass with string orchestra
  xx Double-bass music
     Double bass with string orchestra
     String-orchestra music
  —Solo with piano (M1106)
     xx Double-bass and piano music,
        Arranged
Concertos (English horn) (M1034.E5;
     M1035.E5)
  sa English horn with orchestra
  xx English-horn music
     English horn with orchestra
Concertos (English horn and flute with string
     orchestra) (M1105-6)
  sa English horn and flute with string
     orchestra
  xx English horn and flute music
     English horn and flute with string
        orchestra
     String-orchestra music
  —Solos with piano (M1106)
     xx Trios (Piano, English horn, flute),
        Arranged
Concertos (English horn and harp with string
     orchestra) (M1105-6)
  sa English horn and harp with string
     orchestra
  xx English horn and harp music
     English horn and harp with string
        orchestra
     String-orchestra music

Concertos (English horn and oboe with string
     orchestra) (M1105-6)
  sa English horn and oboe with string
     orchestra
  xx English horn and oboe music
     English horn and oboe with string
        orchestra
     String-orchestra music
Concertos (English horn and trumpet with
     string orchestra) (M1105-6)
  sa English horn and trumpet with string
     orchestra
  xx English horn and trumpet music
     English horn and trumpet with string
        orchestra
     String-orchestra music
Concertos (English horn with chamber
     orchestra) (M1034-5)
  sa English horn with chamber orchestra
  xx Chamber-orchestra music
     English-horn music
     English horn with chamber orchestra
  —Scores (M1034)
Concertos (English horn with string orchestra)
     (M1105-6)
  sa English horn with string orchestra
  xx English-horn music
     English horn with string orchestra
     String-orchestra music
  —Scores (M1105)
  —Solo with piano (M1106)
     xx English horn and piano music,
        Arranged
Concertos (English horns (2)) (M1134.E5;
     M1135.E5)
  sa English horns (2) with string orchestra
  xx English-horn music (English horns (2))
Concertos (English horns (2)) with string
     orchestra (M1134.E5; M1135.E5)
  sa English horns (2) with string orchestra
  xx English-horn music (English horns (2))
     English horns (2) with string orchestra
     String-orchestra music
Concertos (Euphonium and horns (4) with
     band) (M1205)
  sa Euphonium and horns (4) with band
  xx Euphonium and horns (4) with band
Concertos (Flute) (M1020-1021)
  sa Concertos (Recorder)
     Flute with orchestra
  xx Flute music
     Flute with orchestra
  —Cadenzas (M1004.7; M1020.5)
  —Solo with piano (M1021)
     xx Flute and piano music, Arranged
Concertos (Flute and harp) (M1040-1041)
  sa Flute and harp with orchestra
  xx Flute and harp music
     Flute and harp with orchestra
  —To 1800
  ——Solos with piano (M1041)
     xx Trios (Piano, flute, harp),
        Arranged
Concertos (Flute and harp with string
     orchestra) (M1105-6)
  sa Flute and harp with string orchestra
  xx Flute and harp music
     Flute and harp with string orchestra
     String-orchestra music
Concertos (Flute and harpsichord with string
     orchestra) (M1105-6)
  sa Flute and harpsichord with string
     orchestra
  xx Flute and harpsichord music
     Flute and harpsichord with string
        orchestra
     String-orchestra music
  —Scores (M1105)

Concertos (Flute and horn with string
     orchestra) (M1105-6)
  sa Flute and horn with string orchestra
  xx Flute and horn music
     Flute and horn with string orchestra
     String-orchestra music
  —Solos with piano (M1106)
     xx Trios (Piano, flute, horn), Arranged
Concertos (Flute and oboe) (M1040-1041)
  sa Flute and oboe with orchestra
  xx Flute and oboe music
     Flute and oboe with orchestra
Concertos (Flute and oboe with chamber
     orchestra) (M1040-1041)
  sa Flute and oboe with chamber orchestra
  xx Chamber-orchestra music
     Flute and oboe music
     Flute and oboe with chamber orchestra
Concertos (Flute and oboe with chamber
     orchestra), Arranged
     (M1040-1041)
Concertos (Flute and oboe with string
     orchestra) (M1105-6)
  sa Flute and oboe with string orchestra
  xx Flute and oboe music
     Flute and oboe with string orchestra
     String-orchestra music
Concertos (Flute and percussion with string
     orchestra) (M1105-6)
  sa Flute and percussion with string
     orchestra
  xx Flute and percussion music
     Flute and percussion with string
        orchestra
     String-orchestra music
  —Scores (M1105)
Concertos (Flute and piano with string
     orchestra) (M1105-6)
  sa Flute and piano with string orchestra
  xx Flute and piano music
     Flute and piano with string orchestra
     String-orchestra music
Concertos (Flute and recorder with string
     orchestra) (M1105-6)
  sa Flute and recorder with string orchestra
  xx Flute and recorder music
     Flute and recorder with string orchestra
     String-orchestra music
Concertos (Flute and trombone with chamber
     orchestra) (M1040-1041)
  sa Flute and trombone with chamber
     orchestra
  xx Chamber-orchestra music
     Flute and trombone music
     Flute and trombone with chamber
        orchestra
Concertos (Flute and trumpet with string
     orchestra) (M1105-6)
  sa Flute and trumpet with string orchestra
  xx Flute and trumpet music
     Flute and trumpet with string orchestra
     String-orchestra music
Concertos (Flute and viola d'amore with string
     orchestra) (M1105-6)
  sa Flute and viola d'amore with string
     orchestra
  xx Flute and viola d'amore music
     Flute and viola d'amore with string
        orchestra
     String-orchestra music
Concertos (Flute and viola d'amore with string
     orchestra), Arranged (M1105-6)
  —Solos with piano (M1106)
     xx Trios (Piano, flute, viola d'amore),
        Arranged
Concertos (Flute and violin) (M1040-1041)
  sa Flute and violin with orchestra
  xx Flute and violin music

Flute and violin with orchestra
— Solos with piano *(M1041)*
  xx Trios (Piano, flute, violin), Arranged
**Concertos (Flute and violin with string
  orchestra)** *(M1105-6)*
  sa Flute and violin with string orchestra
  xx Flute and violin music
  Flute and violin with string orchestra
  String-orchestra music
**Concertos (Flute and violoncello with string
  orchestra)** *(M1105-6)*
  sa Flute and violoncello with string
    orchestra
  xx Flute and violoncello music
  Flute and violoncello with string
    orchestra
  String-orchestra music
Concertos (Flute), Arranged *(M1020-1021)*
  — Parts *(M1020)*
**Concertos (Flute, horn, harp with string
  orchestra)** *(M1105-6)*
  sa Flute, horn, harp with string orchestra
  xx Flute, horn, harp with string orchestra
  String-orchestra music
  Trios (Flute, horn, harp)
  — Scores *(M1105)*
**Concertos (Flute, kettledrums, violin with
  string orchestra)** *(M1140-1141)*
  sa Flute, kettledrums, violin with string
    orchestra
  xx Flute, kettledrums, violin with string
    orchestra
  String-orchestra music
  Trios (Flute, kettledrums, violin)
**Concertos (Flute, oboe d'amore, viola d'amore
  with string orchestra)** *(M1105-6)*
  sa Flute, oboe d'amore, viola d'amore with
    string orchestra
  xx Flute, oboe d'amore, viola d'amore with
    string orchestra
  String-orchestra music
  Trios (Flute, oboe d'amore, viola
    d'amore)
**Concertos (Flute, oboe, trumpet with string
  orchestra)** *(M1105-6)*
  sa Flute, oboe, trumpet with string
    orchestra
  xx Flute, oboe, trumpet with string
    orchestra
  String-orchestra music
  Wind trios (Flute, oboe, trumpet)
Concertos (Flute, oboe, violin, violoncello)
  (M1105-6)
  sa Flute, oboe, violin, violoncello with
    orchestra
  xx Flute, oboe, violin, violoncello with
    orchestra
  Quartets (Flute, oboe, violin,
    violoncello)
**Concertos (Flute, saxophone, harp with string
  orchestra)** *(M1105-6)*
  sa Flute, saxophone, harp with string
    orchestra
  xx Flute, saxophone, harp with string
    orchestra
  String-orchestra music
  Trios (Flute, saxophone, harp)
**Concertos (Flute, viola, violoncello with string
  orchestra)** *(M1105-6)*
  sa Flute, viola, violoncello with string
    orchestra
  xx Flute, viola, violoncello with string
    orchestra
  String-orchestra music
  Trios (Flute, viola, violoncello)
  — Scores *(M1105)*
Concertos (Flute with band) *(M1205-6)*
  sa Flute with band

  xx Band music
  Flute music
  Flute with band
Concertos (Flute with chamber orchestra)
  (M1020-1021)
  sa Flute with chamber orchestra
  xx Chamber-orchestra music
  Flute music
  Flute with chamber orchestra
  — Solo with piano *(M1021)*
    xx Flute and piano music, Arranged
Concertos (Flute with instrumental ensemble)
  sa Flute with instrumental ensemble
  xx Flute with instrumental ensemble
Concertos (Flute with string orchestra)
  (M1105-6)
  sa Flute with string orchestra
  xx Flute music
  Flute with string orchestra
  String-orchestra music
  Note under Concertos
  — To 1800
  —— Solo with piano *(M1106)*
    xx Flute and piano music, Arranged
  — Solo with piano *(M1106)*
    xx Flute and piano music, Arranged
**Concertos (Flute with string orchestra),
  Arranged** *(M1105-6)*
  — To 1800
  —— Solo with piano *(M1106)*
    xx Flute and piano music, Arranged
  — Solo with piano *(M1106)*
    xx Flute and piano music, Arranged
Concertos (Flute with wind ensemble)
  (M955-7)
  sa Flute with wind ensemble
  xx Flute music
  Flute with wind ensemble
  Wind ensembles
Concertos (Flutes (2)) *(M1020-1021)*
  sa Flutes (2) with orchestra
  xx Flute music (Flutes (2))
  Flutes (2) with orchestra
  — To 1800
  —— Scores *(M1020)*
  —— Solos with piano *(M1021)*
    xx Trios (Piano, flutes (2)), Arranged
**Concertos (Flutes (2), glockenspiel with string
  orchestra)** *(M1105-6)*
  sa Flutes (2), glockenspiel with string
    orchestra
  xx Flutes (2), glockenspiel with string
    orchestra
  String-orchestra music
  Trios (Flutes (2), glockenspiel)
  — Scores *(M1105)*
**Concertos (Flutes (2), marimba with string
  orchestra)** *(M1105-6)*
  sa Flutes (2), marimba with string
    orchestra
  xx Flutes (2), marimba with string
    orchestra
  String-orchestra music
  Trios (Flutes (2), marimba)
Concertos (Flutes (2) with chamber orchestra)
  (M1020-1021)
  sa Flutes (2) with chamber orchestra
  xx Chamber-orchestra music
  Flute music (Flutes (2))
  Flutes (2) with chamber orchestra
**Concertos (Flutes (2) with chamber
  orchestra), Arranged**
  (M1020-1021)
  — Parts *(M1020-1021)*
Concertos (Flutes (2) with string orchestra)
  (M1105-6)
  sa Flutes (2) with string orchestra
  xx Flute music (Flutes (2))

  Flutes (2) with string orchestra
  String-orchestra music
Concertos (Flutes (3) and harp)
  (M1040-1041)
  sa Flutes (3) and harp with orchestra
  xx Flutes (3) and harp with orchestra
Concertos (Flutes (3) with band) *(M1205-6)*
  sa Flutes (3) with band
  xx Band music
  Flutes (3) with band
  Wind trios (Flutes (3))
Concertos (Flutes (3) with string orchestra)
  (M1120-1)
  sa Flutes (3) with string orchestra
  xx Flutes (3) with string orchestra
  String-orchestra music
  Wind trios (Flutes (3))
Concertos (Flutes (4) with band) *(M1205-6)*
  sa Flutes (4) with band
  xx Band music
  Flutes (4) with band
  Wind quartets (Flutes (4))
Concertos (Glockenspiel with string orchestra)
  (M1105-6)
  sa Glockenspiel with string orchestra
  xx Glockenspiel music
  Glockenspiel with string orchestra
  String-orchestra music
  — Scores *(M1105)*
Concertos (Guitar) *(M1037.4.G8)*
  sa Guitar with orchestra
  xx Guitar music
  Guitar with orchestra
  — Parts
  — Solo with piano *(M1037.4.G8)*
    xx Guitar and piano music, Arranged
Concertos (Guitar), Arranged *(M1037.4.G8)*
  — Solo with piano *(M1037.4.G8)*
    xx Guitar and piano music, Arranged
Concertos (Guitar with chamber orchestra)
  (M1037.4.G8)
  sa Guitar with chamber orchestra
  xx Chamber-orchestra music
  Guitar music
  Guitar with chamber orchestra
  — Solo with piano *(M1037.4.G8)*
    xx Guitar and piano music, Arranged
Concertos (Guitar with string orchestra)
  (M1105-6)
  sa Guitar with string orchestra
  xx Guitar music
  Guitar with string orchestra
  String-orchestra music
**Concertos (Guitar with string orchestra),
  Arranged** *(M1105-6)*
Concertos (Guitars (2)) *(M1037.4.G8)*
  sa Guitars (2) with orchestra
  xx Guitar music (Guitars (2))
  Guitars (2) with orchestra
**Concertos (Guitars (2) with chamber
  orchestra)** *(M1037.4.G8)*
  sa Guitars (2) with chamber orchestra
  xx Chamber-orchestra music
  Guitar music (Guitars (2))
  Guitars (2) with chamber orchestra
**Concertos (Guitars (2) with chamber
  orchestra), Arranged**
  (M1037.4.G8)
Concertos (Guitars (4)) *(M1037.4.G8)*
  sa Guitars (4) with orchestra
  xx Guitars (4) with orchestra
  Quartets (Guitars (4))
Concertos (Harp) *(M1036-7)*
  sa Harp with orchestra
  xx Harp music
  Harp with orchestra
  — Solo with piano *(M1037)*
    xx Harp and piano music, Arranged

Concertos (Harp and lute) *(M1040-1041)*
  sa Harp and lute with orchestra
  xx Harp and lute music
    Harp and lute with orchestra
Concertos (Harp and organ with string orchestra) *(M1105-6)*
  sa Harp and organ with string orchestra
  xx Harp and organ with string orchestra
Concertos (Harp and percussion with string orchestra) *(M1105-6)*
  sa Harp and percussion with string orchestra
  xx Harp and percussion music
    Harp and percussion with string orchestra
    String-orchestra music
Concertos (Harp and piano) *(M1040-1041)*
  sa Harp and piano with orchestra
  xx Harp and piano music
    Harp and piano with orchestra
Concertos (Harp and viola with string orchestra) *(M1105-6)*
  sa Harp and viola with string orchestra
  xx Harp and viola music
    Harp and viola with string orchestra
    String-orchestra music
Concertos (Harp), Arranged *(M1036-7)*
Concertos (Harp, harpsichord, piano with string orchestra) *(M1105-6)*
  sa Harp, harpsichord, piano with string orchestra
  xx Harp, harpsichord, piano with string orchestra
    String-orchestra music
    Trios (Harp, harpsichord, piano)
  — Scores
Concertos (Harp, violin, violoncello) *(M1040-1041)*
  sa Harp, violin, violoncello with orchestra
  xx Harp, violin, violoncello with orchestra
    Trios (Harp, violin, violoncello)
Concertos (Harp with chamber orchestra) *(M1036-7)*
  sa Harp with chamber orchestra
  xx Chamber-orchestra music
    Harp music
    Harp with chamber orchestra
  — Scores *(M1036)*
Concertos (Harp with instr. ensemble)
  sa Harp with instr. ensemble
  xx Harp music
    Harp with instr. ensemble
    Instrumental ensembles
Concertos (Harp with string orchestra) *(M1105-6)*
  sa Harp with string orchestra
  xx Harp music
    Harp with string orchestra
    String-orchestra music
Concertos (Harp with string orchestra), Arranged *(M1105-6)*
  — Solo with piano *(M1106)*
    xx Harp and piano music, Arranged
Concertos (Harpischord, flute, harp with string orchestra) *(M1105-6)*
  sa Harpsichord, flute, harp with string orchestra
  xx Harpsichord, flute, harp with string orchestra
    String-orchestra music
    Trios (Harpsichord, flute, harp)
Concertos (Harps (2)) *(M1036-7)*
  sa Harps (2) with orchestra
  xx Harp music (Harps (2))
    Harps (2) with orchestra
Concertos (Harps (2) with string orchestra) *(M1105-6)*
  sa Harps (2) with string orchestra

Concertos (Harpsichord) *(M1010-1011)*
  sa Harpsichord with orchestra
  xx Concertos (Piano)
    Harpsichord music
    Harpsichord with orchestra
  — To 1800
  —— 2-harpsichord scores
    See Concertos (Harpsichord)—To 1800—2-piano scores
  —— 2-piano scores *(M1011)*
    x Concertos (Harpsichord)—To 1800—2-harpsichord scores
    xx Piano music (Pianos (2)), Arranged
Concertos (Harpsichord and piano) *(M1010-1011)*
  sa Harpsichord and piano with orchestra
  xx Harpsichord and piano music
    Harpsichord and piano with orchestra
Concertos (Harpsichord and piano with dance orchestra) *(M1353)*
  sa Harpsichord and piano with dance orchestra
  xx Dance-orchestra music
    Harpsichord and piano music
    Harpsichord and piano with dance orchestra
Concertos (Harpsichord), Arranged *(M1010-1011)*
Concertos (Harpsichord, flute, oboe with string orchestra) *(M1105-6)*
  sa Harpsichord, flute, oboe with string orchestra
  xx Harpsichord, flute, oboe with string orchestra
    String-orchestra music
    Trios (Harpsichord, flute, oboe)
Concertos (Harpsichord, flute, violin with string orchestra) *(M1105-6)*
  sa Harpsichord, flute, violin with string orchestra
  xx Harpsichord, flute, violin with string orchestra
    String-orchestra music
    Trios (Harpsichord, flute, violin)
  — To 1800
  —— Scores *(M1105)*
Concertos (Harpsichord, flutes (2) with string orchestra) *(M1105-6)*
  sa Harpsichord, flutes (2) with string orchestra
  xx Harpsichord, flutes (2) with string orchestra
    String-orchestra music
    Trios (Harpsichord, flutes (2))
  — Scores
Concertos (Harpsichord, piano, violin) *(M1040-1041)*
  sa Harpsichord, piano, violin with orchestra
  xx Harpsichord, piano, violin with orchestra
Concertos (Harpsichord with chamber orchestra) *(M1010-1011)*
  sa Harpsichord with chamber orchestra
  xx Chamber-orchestra music
    Harpsichord music
    Harpsichord with chamber orchestra
  — Scores *(M1010)*
Concertos (Harpsichord with instrumental ensemble)
  sa Harpsichord with instrumental ensemble
  xx Harpsichord music

    Harpsichord with instrumental ensemble
    Instrumental ensembles
Concertos (Harpsichord with string orchestra) *(M1105-6)*
  sa Harpsichord with string orchestra
  xx Harpsichord music
    Harpsichord with string orchestra
    String-orchestra music
  — To 1800
  —— 2-piano scores *(M1106)*
    xx Piano music (Pianos (2)), Arranged
Concertos (Harpsichord with string orchestra), Arranged *(M1105-6)*
Concertos (Harpsichords (2)) *(M1010-1011)*
  sa Harpsichords (2) with orchestra
  xx Harpsichord music (Harpsichords (2))
    Harpsichords (2) with orchestra
  — To 1800
  —— Parts *(M1010-1011)*
Concertos (Harpsichords (2) with string orchestra) *(M1105-6)*
  sa Harpsichords (2) with string orchestra
  xx Harpsichord music (Harpsichords (2))
    Harpsichords (2) with string orchestra
    String-orchestra music
Concertos (Harpsichords (2) with string orchestra), Arranged *(M1105-6)*
Concertos (Harpsichords (3) with string orchestra) *(M1105-6)*
  sa Harpsichords (3) with string orchestra
  xx Harpsichord music (Harpsichords (3))
    Harpsichords (3) with string orchestra
    String-orchestra music
Concertos (Harpsichords (4)) *(M1010-1011)*
  sa Harpsichords (4) with orchestra
  xx Harpsichord music (Harpsichords (4))
    Harpsichords (4) with orchestra
Concertos (Harpsichords (4)), Arranged *(M1010-1011)*
Concertos (Harpsichords (4) with string orchestra) *(M1105-6)*
  sa Harpsichords (4) with string orchestra
  xx Harpsichord music (Harpsichords (4))
    Harpsichords (4) with string orchestra
    String-orchestra music
Concertos (Horn) *(M1028-9)*
  sa Horn with orchestra
  xx Horn music
    Horn with orchestra
  — Solo with piano *(M1029)*
    xx Horn and piano music, Arranged
Concertos (Horn, trombones (2), trumpets (2) with string orchestra) *(M1105-6)*
  sa Horn, trombones (2), trumpets (2) with string orchestra
  xx Horn, trombones (2), trumpets (2) with string orchestra
    String-orchestra music
  — Scores *(M1105)*
Concertos (Horn with band) *(M1205)*
  sa Horn with band
  xx Band music
    Horn music
    Horn with band
  — Scores *(M1205)*
Concertos (Horn with band), Arranged *(M1257)*
  — Scores *(M1257)*
Concertos (Horn with chamber orchestra) *(M1028-9)*
  sa Horn with chamber orchestra
  xx Horn music
    Horn with chamber orchestra
Concertos (Horn with string orchestra) *(M1105-6)*
  sa Horn with string orchestra

xx Horn music
    Horn with string orchestra
    String-orchestra music
— To 1800
—— Solo with piano *(M1106)*
    xx Horn and piano music, Arranged
— Scores *(M1105)*
— Solo with piano *(M1106)*
    xx Horn and piano music, Arranged
Concertos (Horn with string orchestra),
    Arranged *(M1105-6)*
— Scores *(M1105)*
Concertos (Horns (2)) *(M1028-9)*
  sa Horns (2) with orchestra
  xx Horn music (Horns (2))
    Horns (2) with orchestra
— Solos with piano *(M1029)*
Concertos (Horns (2) and oboes (2) with
    string orchestra) *(M1140-1141)*
  sa Horns (2) and oboes (2) with string
    orchestra
  xx Horns (2) and oboes (2) with string
    orchestra
Concertos (Horns (2) with string orchestra)
    (M1105-6)
  sa Horns (2) with string orchestra
  xx Horn music (Horns (2))
    Horns (2) with string orchestra
    String-orchestra music
Concertos (Horns (3)) *(M1028-9)*
  sa Horns (3) with orchestra
  xx Horns (3) with orchestra
    Wind trios (Horns (3))
Concertos (Horns (3) with band) *(M1205)*
  sa Horns (3) with band
    Wind trios (Horns (3)) with band
  xx Band music
    Horns (3) with band
    Wind trios (Horns (3))
    Wind trios (Horns (3)) with band
Concertos (Horns (4)) *(M1028-9)*
  sa Horns (4) with orchestra
  xx Horns (4) with orchestra
    Wind quartets (Horns (4))
Concertos (Horns (4)), Arranged *(M1028-9)*
Concertos (Horns (4) with band) *(M1205)*
  sa Horns (4) with band
    Wind quartets (Horns (4)) with band
  xx Band music
    Horns (4) with band
    Wind quartets (Horns (4))
    Wind quartets (Horns (4)) with band
Concertos (Hurdy-gurdies (2))
    (M1039.4.H87)
  sa Hurdy-gurdies (2) with orchestra
  xx Hurdy-gurdies (2) with orchestra
    Hurdy-gurdy music (Hurdy-gurdies (2))
Concertos (Hurdy-gurdies (2) with instr.
    ensemble)
  sa Hurdy-gurdies (2) with instr. ensemble
  xx Hurdy-gurdies (2) with instr. ensemble
    Hurdy-gurdy music (Hurdy-gurdies (2))
    Instrumental ensembles
Concertos (Hurdy-gurdy with chamber
    orchestra) *(M1039.4.H87)*
  sa Hurdy-gurdy with chamber orchestra
  xx Chamber-orchestra music
    Hurdy-gurdy music
    Hurdy-gurdy with chamber orchestra
Concertos (Hurdy-gurdy with chamber
    orchestra), Arranged
    (M1039.4.H87)
Concertos (Jazz ensemble) *(M1040-1041)*
  sa Jazz ensemble with orchestra
  xx Jazz ensemble with orchestra
    Jazz ensembles

Concertos (Jazz ensemble with chamber
    orchestra) *(M1040-1041)*
  sa Jazz ensemble with chamber orchestra
  xx Chamber-orchestra music
    Jazz ensemble with chamber orchestra
    Jazz ensembles
Concertos (Jazz octet) *(M1040-1041)*
  sa Jazz octet with orchestra
    Jazz octets
  xx Jazz octet with orchestra
    Jazz octets
    Orchestral music
Concertos (Jazz quartet) *(M1040-1041)*
  sa Jazz quartet with orchestra
  xx Jazz quartet with orchestra
    Jazz quartets
    Orchestral music
Concertos (Jazz quintet) *(M1040-1041)*
  sa Jazz quintet with orchestra
  xx Jazz quintet with orchestra
    Jazz quintets
Concertos (Jazz trio) *(M1040-1041)*
  sa Jazz trio with orchestra
  xx Jazz trio with orchestra
    Jazz trios
Concertos (Kettledrums) *(M1038-9)*
  sa Kettledrums with orchestra
  xx Kettledrum music
    Kettledrums with orchestra
— Solo with piano *(M1039)*
  xx Kettledrum and piano music,
    Arranged
Concertos (Kettledrums and piano with string
    orchestra) *(M1140-1141)*
  sa Kettledrums and piano with string
    orchestra
  xx Kettledrum and piano music
    Kettledrums and piano with string
    orchestra
Concertos (Kettledrums with band) *(M1205)*
  sa Kettledrums with band
  xx Kettledrum music
    Kettledrums with band
Concertos (Kettledrums with string ensemble)
    (M985)
  sa Kettledrums with string ensemble
  xx Kettledrum music
    Kettledrums with string ensemble
Concertos (Koto) *(M1037.4.K68)*
  sa Koto with orchestra
  xx Koto music
    Koto with orchestra
— Scores *(M1037.4.K68)*
Concertos (Lute with string orchestra)
    (M1105-6)
  sa Lute with string orchestra
  xx Lute music
    Lute with string orchestra
    String-orchestra music
Concertos (Mandolin) *(M1037.4.M3)*
  sa Mandolin with orchestra
  xx Mandolin music
    Mandolin with orchestra
— Solo with piano *(M1037.4.M3)*
  xx Mandolin and piano music,
    Arranged
Concertos (Mandolin), Arranged
    (M1037.4.M3)
Concertos (Mandolin with string orchestra)
    (M1105-6)
  sa Mandolin with string orchestra
  xx Mandolin music
    Mandolin with string orchestra
    String-orchestra music
— To1800
—— Scores *(M1105)*

Concertos (Mandolins (2) with string
    orchestra) *(M1105-6)*
  sa Mandolins (2) with string orchestra
  xx Mandolin music (Mandolins (2))
    Mandolins (2) with string orchestra
    String-orchestra music
— To 1800
—— Solos with piano *(M1106)*
    xx Trios (Piano, mandolins (2)),
    Arranged
— To 1800
—— Scores *(M1105)*
Concertos (Marimba) *(M1039.4.M3)*
  sa Marimba with orchestra
  xx Marimba music
    Marimba with orchestra
— Solo with piano *(M1039.4)*
  xx Marimba and piano music, Arranged
Concertos (Mouth-organ) *(M1039.4.M6)*
  sa Mouth-organ with orchestra
  xx Mouth-organ music
    Mouth-organ with orchestra
— Solo with piano *(M1039.4.M6)*
  xx Mouth-organ and piano music,
    Arranged
Concertos (Mouth-organ with chamber
    orchestra) *(M1039.4.M6)*
  sa Mouth-organ with chamber orchestra
  xx Chamber-orchestra music
    Mouth-organ music
    Mouth-organ with chamber orchestra
— Scores *(M1039.4.M6)*
Concertos (Mouth-organ with string orchestra)
    (M1105-6)
  sa Mouth-organ with string orchestra
  xx Mouth-organ music
    Mouth-organ with string orchestra
    String-orchestra music
Concertos (Oboe) *(M1022-3)*
  sa Oboe with orchestra
  xx Oboe music
    Oboe with orchestra
— Solo with piano *(M1023)*
  xx Oboe and piano music, Arranged
Concertos (Oboe and harp) *(M1040-1041)*
  sa Oboe and harp with orchestra
  xx Oboe and harp music
    Oboe and harp with orchestra
— Scores *(M1040)*
Concertos (Oboe and harp with string
    orchestra) *(M1105-6)*
  sa Oboe and harp with string orchestra
  xx Oboe and harp music
    Oboe and harp with string orchestra
    String-orchestra music
Concertos (Oboe and harpsichord with string
    orchestra) *(M1105-6)*
  sa Oboe and harpsichord with string
    orchestra
  xx Oboe and harpsichord music
    Oboe and harpsichord with string
    orchestra
    String-orchestra music
Concertos (Oboe and harpsichord with string
    orchestra), Arranged *(M1105-6)*
— Scores *(M1105)*
Concertos (Oboe and recorder with string
    orchestra) *(M1105-6)*
  sa Oboe and recorder with string orchestra
  xx Oboe and recorder music
    Oboe and recorder with string orchestra
    String-orchestra music
Concertos (Oboe and trumpet with string
    orchestra) *(M1105-6)*
  sa Oboe and trumpet with string orchestra
  xx Oboe and trumpet music
    Oboe and trumpet with string orchestra
    String-orchestra music

Concertos (Oboe and trumpet with string orchestra), Arranged *(M1105-6)*
Concertos (Oboe and viola with string orchestra) *(M1105-6)*
   sa Oboe and viola with string orchestra
   xx Oboe and viola music
      Oboe and viola with string orchestra
      String-orchestra music
  — Scores *(M1105)*
Concertos (Oboe and violin) *(M1040-1041)*
   sa Oboe and violin with orchestra
   xx Oboe and violin music
      Oboe and violin with orchestra
Concertos (Oboe and violin), Arranged *(M1040-1041)*
Concertos (Oboe and violin with chamber orchestra) *(M1040-1041)*
   sa Oboe and violin with chamber orchestra
   xx Chamber-orchestra music
      Oboe and violin music
      Oboe and violin with chamber orchestra
  — Scores *(M1040)*
Concertos (Oboe and violin with string orchestra) *(M1105-6)*
   sa Oboe and violin with string orchestra
   xx Oboe and violin music
      Oboe and violin with string orchestra
      String-orchestra music
  — To 1800
  — — Scores
Concertos (Oboe and violin with string orchestra), Arranged *(M1105-6)*
Concertos (Oboe), Arranged *(M1022-3)*
  — Solo with piano *(M1023)*
    xx Oboe and piano music, Arranged
Concertos (Oboe d'amore) *(M1034.O26; M1035.O26)*
   sa Oboe d'amore with orchestra
   xx Oboe d'amore music
      Oboe d'amore with orchestra
      Orchestral music
  — Solo with piano *(M1035.O26)*
    xx Oboe d'amore and piano music, Arranged
Concertos (Oboe d'amore with string orchestra) *(M1105-6)*
   sa Oboe d'amore with string orchestra
   xx Oboe d'amore music
      Oboe d'amore with string orchestra
      String-orchestra music
Concertos (Oboe d'amore with string orchestra), Arranged *(M1105-6)*
Concertos (Oboe, violin, violoncello) *(M1040-1041)*
   sa Oboe, violin, violoncello with orchestra
   xx Oboe, violin, violoncello with orchestra
      Trios (Oboe, violin, violoncello)
Concertos (Oboe, violin, violoncello with string orchestra) *(M1105-6)*
   sa Oboe, violin, violoncello with string orchestra
   xx Oboe, violin, violoncello with string orchestra
      String-orchestra music
      Trios (Oboe, violin, violoncello)
Concertos (Oboe with band) *(M1205-6)*
   sa Oboe with band
   xx Band music
      Oboe music
      Oboe with band
  — Scores *(M1205)*
Concertos (Oboe with chamber orchestra) *(M1022-3)*
   sa Oboe with chamber orchestra
   xx Chamber-orchestra music
      Oboe music

Oboe with chamber orchestra
  — Solo with piano *(M1023)*
    xx Oboe and piano music, Arranged
Concertos (Oboe with instr. ensemble)
   sa Oboe with instr. ensemble
   xx Instrumental ensembles
      Oboe music
      Oboe with instr. ensemble
Concertos (Oboe with string ensemble) *(M960-962)*
   sa Oboe with string ensemble
   xx Oboe music
      Oboe with string ensemble
      String ensembles
Concertos (Oboe with string orchestra) *(M1105-6)*
   sa Oboe with string orchestra
   xx Oboe music
      Oboe with string orchestra
      String-orchestra music
  — Solo with piano *(M1106)*
    xx Oboe and piano music, Arranged
Concertos (Oboe with string orchestra), Arranged *(M1105-6)*
  — Scores *(M1105)*
Concertos (Oboes (2) and trumpet with string orchestra) *(M1105-6)*
   sa Oboes (2) and trumpet with string orchestra
   xx Oboes (2) and trumpet with string orchestra
      String-orchestra music
      Wind trios (Oboes (2), trumpet)
Concertos (Oboes (2) with string orchestra) *(M1105-6)*
   sa Oboes (2) with string orchestra
   xx Oboe music (Oboes (2))
      Oboes (2) with string orchestra
      String-orchestra music
  — To 1800
  — — Scores
Concertos (Ondes Martenot) *(M1039.4.O5)*
   sa Ondes Martenot with orchestra
   xx Ondes Martenot music
      Ondes Martenot with orchestra
  — Scores *(M1039.4.O5)*
Concertos (Ondes Martenot with string orchestra) *(M1105-6)*
   sa Ondes Martenot with string orchestra
   xx Ondes Martenot music
      Ondes Martenot with string orchestra
      String-orchestra music
  — Solo with piano *(M1106)*
    xx Ondes Martenot and piano music, Arranged
Concertos (Organ) *(M1105-6)*
   sa Organ with orchestra
   xx Organ music
      Organ with orchestra
  — Parts *(M1005)*
  — Parts (solo) *(M1005)*
  — Solo with piano *(M1006)*
    xx Piano and organ music, Arranged
Concertos (Organ, harp, kettledrums with string orchestra) *(M1105-6)*
   sa Organ, harp, kettledrums with string orchestra
   xx Organ, harp, kettledrums with string orchestra
      String-orchestra music
      Trios (Organ, harp, kettledrums)
  — Scores *(M1105)*
Concertos (Organ with band) *(M1205)*
   sa Organ with band
   xx Band music
      Organ music
      Organ with band

Concertos (Organ with brass ensemble)
   sa Organ with brass ensemble
   xx Organ with brass ensemble
Concertos (Organ with chamber orchestra) *(M1005-6)*
   sa Organ with chamber orchestra
   xx Chamber-orchestra music
      Organ music
      Organ with chamber orchestra
Concertos (Organ with string orchestra) *(M1105-6)*
   sa Organ with string orchestra
   xx Organ music
      Organ with string orchestra
      String-orchestra music
  — Solo with piano *(M1106)*
    xx Piano and organ music, Arranged
Concertos (Organ with string orchestra), Arranged *(M1105-6)*
Concertos (Organ with wind ensemble)
   sa Organ with wind ensemble
   xx Organ music
      Organ with wind ensemble
      Wind ensembles
Concertos (Organs (3)) *(M1005-6)*
   sa Organs (3) with orchestra
   xx Organ music (Organs (3))
      Organs (3) with orchestra
Concertos (Percussion) *(M1038-9)*
   sa Percussion with orchestra
   xx Percussion music
      Percussion with orchestra
  — Solo with piano *(M1039)*
    xx Percussion and piano music, Arranged
Concertos (Percussion and organ with string orchestra) *(M1105-6)*
   sa Percussion and organ with string orchestra
   xx Percussion and organ with string orchestra
Concertos (Percussion and piano with string orchestra) *(M1105-6)*
   sa Percussion and piano with string orchestra
   xx Percussion and piano music
      Percussion and piano with string orchestra
      String-orchestra music
Concertos (Percussion with band) *(M1205-6)*
   sa Percussion with band
   xx Band music
      Percussion music
      Percussion with band
  — Scores *(M1205)*
Concertos (Percussion with chamber orchestra) *(M1038-9)*
   sa Percussion with chamber orchestra
   xx Chamber-orchestra music
      Percussion music
      Percussion with chamber orchestra
  — Solos with piano *(M1039)*
    xx Percussion and piano music, Arranged
Concertos (Percussion with jazz ensemble) *(M985)*
   sa Percussion with jazz ensemble
   xx Jazz ensembles
      Percussion music
      Percussion with jazz ensemble
Concertos (Percussion with string orchestra) *(M1105-6)*
   sa Percussion with string orchestra
   xx Percussion music
      Percussion with string orchestra
      String-orchestra music
Concertos (Piano) *(M1010-1011)*
   sa Concertos (Harpsichord)

Piano with orchestra
  xx Piano music
    Piano with orchestra
Note under Concertos
— To 1800
—— 2-piano scores *(M1011)*
    xx Piano music (Pianos (2)),
      Arranged
——— Excerpts
      See Concertos (Piano)—To 1800
          —Excerpts—2-piano
          scores
—— Excerpts
——— 2-piano scores *(M1011)*
    x Concertos (Piano)—To 1800—
      2-piano scores—Excerpts
    xx Piano music (Pianos (2)),
      Arranged
— 2-piano scores *(M1011)*
    xx Piano music (Pianos (2)), Arranged
—— Excerpts
    See Concertos (Piano)—Excerpts—
      2-piano scores
— Cadenzas *(M1004.7; M1010.5)*
— Excerpts
—— 2-piano scores *(M1011)*
    x Concertos (Piano)—2-piano scores
      —Excerpts
    xx Piano music (Pianos (2)),
      Arranged
— Excerpts, Arranged
— Parts (solo) *(M1010)*
Concertos (Piano, 1 hand) *(M1010-1011)*
  sa Piano (1 hand) with orchestra
  xx Piano (1 hand) with orchestra
    Piano music (1 hand)
— 2-piano scores *(M1011)*
    xx Piano music (Pianos (2)), Arranged
Concertos (Piano, 4 hands) *(M1010-1011)*
  sa Piano (4 hands) with orchestra
  xx Piano (4 hands) with orchestra
    Piano music (4 hands)
— 3-piano scores *(M1011)*
    xx Piano music (Pianos (3)), Arranged
Concertos (Piano), Arranged *(M1010-1011)*
Concertos (Piano, flute, viola with string orchestra) *(M1105-6)*
  sa Piano, flute, viola with string orchestra
  xx Piano, flute, viola with string orchestra
    String-orchestra music
    Trios (Piano, flute, viola)
— Scores *(M1105)*
Concertos (Piano, flute, violin with string orchestra) *(M1105-6)*
  sa Piano, flute, violin with string orchestra
  xx Piano, flute, violin with string orchestra
    String-orchestra music
    Trios (Piano, flute, violin)
— To 1800
—— Scores *(M1105)*
Concertos (Piano, oboe, trumpet, violin, double bass with string orchestra) *(M1105-6)*
  sa Piano, oboe, trumpet, violin, double bass with string orchestra
  xx Piano, oboe, trumpet, violin, double bass with string orchestra
    Quintets (Piano, oboe, trumpet, violin, double bass)
    String-orchestra music
— Scores
Concertos (Piano trio) *(M1040-1041)*
  sa Piano trio with orchestra
  xx Piano trio with orchestra
    Piano trios
— Scores *(M1040)*

Concertos (Piano trio with string orchestra) *(M1105-6)*
  sa Piano trio with string orchestra
  xx Piano trio with string orchestra
    Piano trios
    String-orchestra music
— Scores *(M1105)*
Concertos (Piano, trumpet, vibraphone, double bass) *(M1040-1041)*
  sa Piano, trumpet, vibraphone, double bass with orchestra
  xx Orchestral music
    Piano, trumpet, vibraphone, double bass with orchestra
    Quartets (Piano, trumpet, vibraphone, double bass)
— Scores *(M1040)*
Concertos (Piano, trumpet, viola) *(M1040-1041)*
  sa Piano, trumpet, viola with orchestra
  xx Piano, trumpet, viola with orchestra
    Trios (Piano, trumpet, viola)
Concertos (Piano, trumpets (3) with string orchestra) *(M1105-6)*
  sa Piano, trumpets (3) with string orchestra
  xx Piano, trumpets (3) with string orchestra
    Quartets (Piano, trumpets (3))
    String-orchestra music
Concertos (Piano, violins (2) with string orchestra) *(M1105-6)*
  sa Piano, violins (2) with string orchestra
  xx Piano, violins (2) with string orchestra
    String-orchestra music
    Trios (Piano, violins (2))
Concertos (Piano with band) *(M1205)*
  sa Piano with band
  xx Band music
    Piano music
    Piano with band
— 2-piano scores *(M1205)*
    xx Piano music (Pianos (2)), Arranged
Concertos (Piano with band), Arranged *(M1257)*
Concertos (Piano with brass ensemble) *(M917)*
  sa Piano with brass ensemble
  xx Piano with brass ensemble
Concertos (Piano with chamber orchestra) *(M1010-1011)*
  sa Piano with chamber orchestra
  xx Chamber-orchestra music
    Piano music
    Piano with chamber orchestra
— 2-piano scores *(M1011)*
    xx Piano music (Pianos (2)), Arranged
Concertos (Piano with dance orchestra) *(M1353)*
  sa Piano with dance orchestra
  xx Dance-orchestra music
    Piano music
    Piano with dance orchestra
— Scores *(M1353)*
Concertos (Piano with instrumental ensemble)
  sa Piano with instrumental ensemble
  xx Instrumental ensembles
    Piano music
    Piano with instrumental ensemble
Concertos (Piano with percussion ensemble)
  sa Piano with percussion ensemble
  xx Piano music
    Piano with percussion ensemble
Concertos (Piano with salon orchestra) *(M1353)*
  sa Piano with salon orchestra
  xx Piano music
    Piano with salon orchestra

Salon-orchestra music
Concertos (Piano with string ensemble) *(M910-912)*
  sa Piano with string ensemble
  xx Piano music
    Piano with string ensemble
    String ensembles
Concertos (Piano with string orchestra) *(M1105-6)*
  sa Piano with string orchestra
  xx Piano music
    Piano with string orchestra
    String-orchestra music
— To 1800
—— 2-piano scores *(M1106)*
    xx Piano music (Pianos (2)),
      Arranged
—— Scores and parts *(M1105)*
— 2-piano scores *(M1106)*
    xx Piano music (Pianos (2)), Arranged
Concertos (Piano with string orchestra), Arranged *(M1105-6)*
— 2-piano scores *(M1106)*
Concertos (Piano with wind ensemble)
  sa Piano with wind ensemble
  xx Piano music
    Piano with wind ensemble
    Wind ensembles
Concertos (Pianos (2)) *(M1010-1011)*
  sa Pianos (2) with orchestra
  xx Piano music (2 pianos)
    Pianos (2) with orchestra
— 3-piano scores *(M1011)*
    xx Piano music (Pianos (3)), Arranged
Concertos (Pianos (2)), Arranged *(M1010-1011)*
Concertos (Pianos (2) with band) *(M1205-6)*
  sa Pianos (2) with band
  xx Piano music (Pianos (2))
    Pianos (2) with band
Concertos (Pianos (2) with chamber orchestra) *(M1010-1011)*
  sa Pianos (2) with chamber orchestra
  xx Chamber-orchestra music
    Piano music (Pianos (2))
    Pianos (2) with chamber orchestra
— 3-piano scores *(M1011)*
    xx Piano music (Pianos (3)), Arranged
Concertos (Pianos (2) with string orchestra) *(M1105-6)*
  sa Pianos (2) with string orchestra
  xx Piano music (Pianos (2))
    Pianos (2) with string orchestra
    String-orchestra music
Concertos (Pianos (3)) *(M1010-1011)*
  sa Pianos (3) with orchestra
  xx Piano music (Pianos (3))
    Pianos (3) with orchestra
Concertos (Pianos (3) with string orchestra)
  sa Pianos (3) with string orchestra
  xx Piano music (Pianos (3))
    Pianos (3) with string orchestra
    String-orchestra music
— Parts
Concertos (Piccolo with string orchestra) *(M1105-6)*
  sa Piccolo with string orchestra
  xx Piccolo music
    Piccolo with string orchestra
    String-orchestra music
Concertos (Piccolo with string orchestra), Arranged *(M1105-6)*
— Solo with piano *(M1106)*
    xx Piccolo and piano music, Arranged
Concertos (Piccolos (2)) *(M1020-1021)*
  sa Piccolos (2) with orchestra
  xx Piccolo music (Piccolos (2))
    Piccolos (2) with orchestra

Concertos (Recorder) (M1020-1021)
    sa Recorder with orchestra
    xx Concertos (Flute)
        Recorder music
        Recorder with orchestra
Concertos (Recorder and trumpet with string
    orchestra) (M1105-6)
    sa Recorder and trumpet with string
        orchestra
    xx Recorder and trumpet music
        Recorder and trumpet with string
        orchestra
        String-orchestra music
Concertos (Recorder and viola da gamba with
    string orchestra) (M1105-6)
    sa Recorder and viola da gamba with
        string orchestra
    xx Recorder and viola da gamba music
        Recorder and viola da gamba with
        string orchestra
        String-orchestra music
  — To 1800
  —— Solos with piano (M1106)
    xx Trios (Piano, recorder, viola da
        gamba), Arranged
Concertos (Recorder and violin with string
    orchestra) (M1105-6)
    sa Recorder and violin with string
        orchestra
    xx Recorder and violin music
        Recorder and violin with string
        orchestra
        String-orchestra music
  — To 1800
  —— Solos with piano (M1106)
    xx Trios (Piano, recorder, violin),
        Arranged
Concertos (Recorder), Arranged
    (M1020-1021)
Concertos (Recorder with string orchestra)
    (M1105-6)
    sa Recorder with string orchestra
    xx Recorder music
        Recorder with string orchestra
        String-orchestra music
  — To 1800
  —— Solo with piano (M1106)
    xx Recorder with piano music,
        Arranged
Concertos (Recorder with string orchestra),
    Arranged (M1105-6)
Concertos (Recorders (2)) (M1020-1021)
    sa Recorders (2) with orchestra
    xx Recorder music (Recorders (2))
        Recorders (2) with orchestra
  — Scores (M1020)
Concertos (Recorders (2) with string
    orchestra) (M1105-6)
    sa Recorders (2) with string orchestra
    xx Recorder music (Recorders (2))
        Recorders (2) with string orchestra
        String-orchestra music
  — To 1800
  —— Scores
Concertos (Recorders (3) with string
    orchestra) (M1120-1)
    sa Recorders (3) with string orchestra
    xx Recorders (3) with string orchestra
        String-orchestra music
        Wind trios (Recorders (3))
  — Scores (M1105)
Concertos (Recorders (6) with string
    orchestra) (M1105-6)
    sa Recorders (6) with string orchestra
    xx Recorders (6) with string orchestra
        String-orchestra music
        Wind sextets (Recorders (6))
  — Scores (M1105)

Concertos (Saxophone) (M1034-5)
    sa Saxophone with orchestra
    xx Saxophone music
        Saxophone with orchestra
  — Excerpts
  —— Solo with piano (M1035)
    x Concertos (Saxophone)—Solo
        with piano—Excerpts
    xx Saxophone and piano music,
        Arranged
  — Solo with piano (M1035)
    xx Saxophone and piano music,
        Arranged
  —— Excerpts
    See Concertos (Saxophone)—
        Excerpts—Solo with piano
Concertos (Saxophone and piano)
    (M1040-1041)
    sa Saxophone and piano with orchestra
    xx Saxophone and piano music
        Saxophone and piano with orchestra
  — Scores (M1040)
Concertos (Saxophone and trumpet with string
    orchestra) (M1140-1141)
    sa Saxophone and trumpet with string
        orchestra
    xx Saxophone and trumpet music
        Saxophone and trumpet with string
        orchestra
Concertos (Saxophone with band) (M1205-6)
    sa Saxophone with band
    xx Band music
        Saxophone music
        Saxophone with band
Concertos (Saxophone with chamber
    orchestra) (M1034-5)
    sa Saxophone with chamber orchestra
    xx Chamber-orchestra music
        Saxophone music
        Saxophone with chamber orchestra
Concertos (Saxophone with dance orchestra)
    (M1353)
    sa Saxophone with dance orchestra
    xx Dance-orchestra music
        Saxophone music
        Saxophone with dance orchestra
  — Scores (M1353)
Concertos (Saxophone with string orchestra)
    (M1105-6)
    sa Saxophone with string orchestra
    xx Saxophone music
        Saxophone with string orchestra
        String-orchestra music
  — Solo with piano (M1106)
    xx Saxophone and piano music,
        Arranged
Concertos (Saxophones (4) with chamber
    orchestra) (M1034-5)
    sa Saxophones (4) with chamber orchestra
    xx Chamber-orchestra music
        Saxophones (4) with chamber orchestra
        Wind quartets (Saxophones (4))
Concertos (Saxophones (4) with string
    orchestra) (M1134.S4; M1135.S4)
    sa Saxophones (4) with string orchestra
    xx Saxophones (4) with string orchestra
        String-orchestra music
        Wind quartets (Saxophones (4))
  — Scores (M1105)
Concertos (Shakuhachi and biwa)
    (M1040-1041)
    sa Shakuhachi and biwa with orchestra
    xx Shakuhachi and biwa music
        Shakuhachi and biwa with orchestra
Concertos (Sitar) (M1037.4.S58)
    sa Sitar with orchestra
    xx Sitar music
        Sitar with orchestra

Concertos (String quartet) (M1040-1041)
    sa String quartet with orchestra
    xx String quartet with orchestra
        String quartets
Concertos (String quartet), Arranged
    (M1040-1041)
  — Solos with piano (M1041)
    xx Piano quintets, Arranged
Concertos (String quartet with band)
    (M1205-6)
    sa String quartet with band
    xx Band music
        String quartet with band
        String quartets
  — Scores (M1205)
Concertos (String quartet with chamber
    orchestra) (M1040-1041)
    sa String quartet with chamber orchestra
    xx Chamber-orchestra music
        String quartet with chamber orchestra
        String quartets
  — Scores (M1040)
Concertos (String quartet with string
    orchestra) (M1105-6)
    sa String quartet with string orchestra
    xx String-orchestra music
        String quartet with string orchestra
        String quartets
Concertos (String trio) (M1040-1041)
    sa String trio with orchestra
    xx String trio with orchestra
        String trios
Concertos (String trio with string orchestra)
    (M1105-6)
    sa String trio with string orchestra
    xx String-orchestra music
        String trio with string orchestra
        String trios
Concertos (Tar) (M1037.4.T3)
    xx Tar music
  — Solo with piano (M1037.4.T3)
    xx Tar and piano music, Arranged
Concertos (Trautonium) (M1039.4.T)
    sa Trautonium with orchestra
    xx Trautonium music
        Trautonium with orchestra
Concertos (Trombone) (M1032-3)
    sa Trombone with orchestra
    xx Trombone music
        Trombone with orchestra
  — Solo with piano (M1033)
    xx Trombone and piano music,
        Arranged
Concertos (Trombone and kettledrums with
    string orchestra) (M1105-6)
    sa Trombone and kettledrums with string
        orchestra
    xx String-orchestra music
        Trombone and kettledrums with string
        orchestra
        Trombone and percussion music
Concertos (Trombone and trumpet with band)
    (M1205-6)
    sa Trombone and trumpet with band
    xx Band music
        Trombone and trumpet music
        Trombone and trumpet with band
Concertos (Trombone and trumpet with string
    orchestra) (M1105-6)
    sa Trombone and trumpet with string
        orchestra
    xx String-orchestra music
        Trombone and trumpet music
        Trombone and trumpet with string
        orchestra
  — Solos with piano (M1106)
    xx Trios (Piano, trombone, trumpet),
        Arranged

Concertos (Trombone with band) *(M1205)*
  sa Trombone with band
  xx Band music
    Trombone music
    Trombone with band
  — Scores and parts *(M1205)*
  — Solo with piano *(M1206)*
    xx Trombone and piano music,
      Arranged
Concertos (Trombone with chamber orchestra)
    (M1032-3)
  sa Trombone with chamber orchestra
  xx Chamber-orchestra music
    Trombone music
    Trombone with chamber orchestra
Concertos (Trombone with string orchestra)
    (M1105-6)
  sa Trombone with string orchestra
  xx String-orchestra music
    Trombone music
    Trombone with string orchestra
  — Scores *(M1105)*
  — Solo with piano *(M1106)*
    xx Trombone and piano music,
      Arranged
**Concertos (Trombones (3), trumpets (3) with
    band)** *(M1205-6)*
  sa Trombones (3), trumpets (3) with band
  xx Trombones (3), trumpets (3) with band
Concertos (Trombones (3) with band)
    (M1205-6)
  sa Trombones (3) with band
  xx Band music
    Trombones (3) with band
    Wind trios (Trombones (3))
  — Scores and parts *(M1205)*
Concertos (Trombones (4) with band)
    (M1205)
  sa Trombones (4) with band
  xx Band music
    Trombones (4) with band
    Wind quartets (Trombones (4))
Concertos (Trumpet) *(M1030-1031)*
  sa Concertos (Cornet)
    Trumpet with orchestra
  xx Concertos (Cornet)
    Trumpet music
    Trumpet with orchestra
  — To 1800
  —— Solo with piano *(M1031)*
      xx Trumpet and piano music,
        Arranged
  — Solo with piano *(M1031)*
    xx Trumpet and piano music, Arranged
Concertos (Trumpet and piano)
    (M1040-1041)
  sa Trumpet and piano with orchestra
  xx Trumpet and piano music
    Trumpet and piano with orchestra
**Concertos (Trumpet and piano with string
    orchestra)** *(M1105-6)*
  sa Trumpet and piano with string
    orchestra
  xx String-orchestra music
    Trumpet and piano music
    Trumpet and piano with string
      orchestra
  — Solos with piano *(M1106)*
    xx Trios (Pianos (2), trumpet),
      Arranged
**Concertos (Trumpet and violin with string
    orchestra)** *(M1105-6)*
  sa Trumpet and violin with string
    orchestra
  xx String-orchestra music
    Trumpet and violin music
    Trumpet and violin with string
      orchestra

**Concertos (Trumpet and violin with string
    orchestra), Arranged** *(M1105-6)*
Concertos (Trumpet), Arranged
    (M1030-1031)
**Concertos (Trumpet, harp, chimes with string
    orchestra)** *(M1105-6)*
  sa Trumpet, harp, chimes with string
    orchestra
  xx String-orchestra music
    Trios (Trumpet, harp, chimes)
    Trumpet, harp, chimes with string
      orchestra
Concertos (Trumpet with band) *(M1205)*
  sa Trumpet with band
  xx Band music
    Trumpet music
    Trumpet with band
  Note under Concertos
Concertos (Trumpet with band), Arranged
    (M1257)
Concertos (Trumpet with chamber orchestra)
    (M1030-1031)
  sa Trumpet with chamber orchestra
  xx Chamber-orchestra music
    Trumpet music
    Trumpet with chamber orchestra
  —— Solo with piano *(M1031)*
      xx Trumpet and piano music,
        Arranged
  — Scores *(M1030)*
  — Solo with piano *(M1031)*
    xx Trumpet and piano music, Arranged
  — To 1800
Concertos (Trumpet with dance orchestra)
    (M1353)
  sa Trumpet with dance orchestra
  xx Dance-orchestra music
    Trumpet music
    Trumpet with dance orchestra
Concertos (Trumpet with instr. ensemble)
  sa Trumpet with instr. ensemble
  xx Instrumental ensembles
    Trumpet music
    Trumpet with instr. ensemble
Concertos (Trumpet with string orchestra)
    (M1105-6)
  sa Trumpet with string orchestra
  xx String-orchestra music
    Trumpet music
    Trumpet with string orchestra
  — Solo with piano *(M1106)*
    xx Trumpet and piano music, Arranged
**Concertos (Trumpet with string orchestra),
    Arranged** *(M1105-6)*
**Concertos (Trumpets (2) with string
    orchestra)** *(M1105-6)*
  sa Trumpets (2) with string orchestra
  xx String-orchestra music
    Trumpet music (Trumpets (2))
    Trumpets (2) with string orchestra
  — To 1800
  —— Solos with piano
      xx Trios (Piano, trumpets (2)),
        Arranged
**Concertos (Trumpets (2) with string
    orchestra), Arranged** *(M1105-6)*
Concertos (Trumpets (3) with band)
    (M1205-6)
  sa Trumpets (3) with band
  xx Band music
    Trumpets (3) with band
    Wind trios (Trumpets (3))
**Concertos (Trumpets (3) with string
    orchestra)** *(M1130-1131)*
  sa Trumpets (3) with string orchestra
  xx Trumpets (3) with string orchestra

**Concertos (Trumpets (4) with string
    orchestra)** *(M1130-1131)*
  sa Trumpets (4) with string orchestra
  xx Trumpets (4) with string orchestra
**Concertos (Trumpets (8) with string
    orchestra)** *(M1130-1131)*
  sa Trumpets (8) with string orchestra
  xx Trumpets (8) with string orchestra
Concertos (Tuba) *(M1034-5)*
  sa Tuba with orchestra
  xx Tuba music
    Tuba with orchestra
  — Solo with piano *(M1035)*
    xx Tuba and piano music, Arranged
Concertos (Tuba with band) *(M1205)*
  sa Tuba with band
  xx Band music
    Tuba music
    Tuba with band
Concertos (Tuba with string orchestra)
    (M1105-6)
  sa Tuba with string orchestra
  xx String-orchestra music
    Tuba music
    Tuba with string orchestra
  — Solo with piano *(M1106)*
    xx Tuba and piano music, Arranged
Concertos (Vibraphone) *(M1039.4.X9)*
  sa Vibraphone with orchestra
  xx Vibraphone music
    Vibraphone with orchestra
  — Scores and parts *(M1039.4.X9)*
Concertos (Viola) *(M1014-1015)*
  sa Viola with orchestra
  xx Viola music
    Viola with orchestra
  — To 1800
  —— Solo with piano *(M1015)*
      xx Viola and piano music, Arranged
  — Solo with piano *(M1015)*
    xx Viola and piano music, Arranged
Concertos (Viola and double bass)
    (M1040-1041)
  sa Viola and double bass with orchestra
  xx Viola and double-bass music
    Viola and double bass with orchestra
**Concertos (Viola and harpsichord with string
    orchestra)** *(M1105-6)*
  sa Viola and harpsichord with string
    orchestra
  xx String-orchestra music
    Viola and harpsichord music
    Viola and harpsichord with string
      orchestra
**Concertos (Viola and harpsichord with string
    orchestra), Arranged** *(M1105-6)*
**Concertos (Viola and organ with string
    orchestra)** *(M1105-6)*
  sa Viola and organ with string orchestra
  xx String-orchestra music
    Viola and organ music
    Viola and organ with string orchestra
**Concertos (Viola and organ with string
    orchestra), Arranged** *(M1105-6)*
Concertos (Viola and piano) *(M1040-1041)*
  sa Viola and piano with orchestra
  xx Viola and piano music
    Viola and piano with orchestra
  — Scores *(M1040)*
Concertos (Viola and piano with band)
    (M1205-6)
  sa Viola and piano with band
  xx Band music
    Viola and piano music
    Viola and piano with band
  — Scores *(M1205)*

Concertos (Viola and piano with string
    orchestra) (M1105-6)
    sa Viola and piano with string orchestra
    xx String-orchestra music
        Viola and piano music
        Viola and piano with string orchestra
Concertos (Viola), Arranged (M1014-1015)
— Solo with piano (M1015)
    xx Viola and piano music, Arranged
Concertos (Viola da gamba) (M1019)
    sa Viola da gamba with orchestra
    xx Viola da gamba music
        Viola da gamba with orchestra
Concertos (Viola da gamba with string
    orchestra) (M1105-6)
    sa Viola da gamba with string orchestra
    xx String-orchestra music
        Viola da gamba music
        Viola da gamba with string orchestra
— To 1800
—— Scores (M1105)
Concertos (Viola d'amore) (M1019)
    sa Viola d'amore with orchestra
    xx Viola d'amore music
        Viola d'amore with orchestra
— To 1800
—— Solo with piano (M1019)
    xx Viola d'amore and piano music,
        Arranged
Concertos (Viola d'amore and lute with string
    orchestra) (M1105-6)
    sa Viola d'amore and lute with string
        orchestra
    xx String-orchestra music
        Viola d'amore and lute music
        Viola d'amore and lute with string
        orchestra
Concertos (Viola d'amore with chamber
    orchestra) (M1019)
    sa Viola d'amore with chamber orchestra
    xx Chamber-orchestra music
        Viola d'amore music
        Viola d'amore with chamber orchestra
Concertos (Viola d'amore with string
    orchestra) (M1105-6)
    sa Viola d'amore with string orchestra
    xx String-orchestra music
        Viola d'amore music
        Viola d'amore with string orchestra
— To 1800
—— Solo with piano (M1106)
    xx Viola d'amore and piano music,
        Arranged
Concertos (Viola with band) (M1205-6)
    xx Viola with band
Concertos (Viola with chamber orchestra)
    (M1014-1015)
    sa Viola with chamber orchestra
    xx Chamber-orchestra music
        Viola music
        Viola with chamber orchestra
— Solo with piano (M1015)
    xx Viola and piano music, Arranged
Concertos (Viola with string ensemble)
    xx String ensembles
        Viola music
        Viola with string ensemble
Concertos (Viola with string orchestra)
    (M1105-6)
    sa Viola with string orchestra
    xx String-orchestra music
        Viola music
        Viola with string orchestra
— To 1800
—— Scores and parts (M1105)
Concertos (Viola with string orchestra),
    Arranged (M1105-6)
— Solo with piano (M1106)

xx Viola and piano music, Arranged
Concertos (Violas (2) with string orchestra)
    (M1114-1115)
    sa Violas (2) with string orchestra
    xx Viola music (Violas (2))
        Violas (2) with string orchestra
Concertos (Violin) (M1012-1013)
    sa Violin with orchestra
    xx Violin music
        Violin with orchestra
    Note under Concertos
— To 1800
—— Solo with piano (M1013)
    xx Violin and piano music, Arranged
— Analysis, appreciation
— Cadenzas (M1004.7; M1012.5)
— Excerpts
—— Solo with piano (M1013)
    xx Violin and piano music, Arranged
— Excerpts, Arranged
— Solo with piano (M1013)
    xx Violin and piano music, Arranged
Concertos (Violin and double bass)
    (M1040-1041)
    sa Violin and double bass with orchestra
    xx Violin and double bass with orchestra
Concertos (Violin and double bass with string
    orchestra) (M1140-1141)
    sa Violin and double bass with string
        orchestra
    xx Violin and double-bass music
        Violin and double bass with string
        orchestra
Concertos (Violin and harp) (M1040-1041)
    sa Violin and harp with orchestra
    xx Violin and harp music
        Violin and harp with orchestra
Concertos (Violin and harpsichord)
    (M1040-1041)
    sa Violin and harpsichord with orchestra
    xx Concertos (Violin and piano)
        Violin and harpsichord music
        Violin and harpsichord with orchestra
Concertos (Violin and harpsichord with string
    orchestra) (M1105-6)
    sa Violin and harpsichord with string
        orchestra
    xx String-orchestra music
        Violin and harpsichord music
        Violin and harpsichord with string
        orchestra
— Scores (M1105)
Concertos (Violin and organ with string
    orchestra) (M1105-6)
    sa Violin and organ with string orchestra
    xx String-orchestra music
        Violin and organ music
        Violin and organ with string orchestra
— Scores (M1105)
Concertos (Violin and piano) (M1040-1041)
    sa Concertos (Violin and harpsichord)
        Violin and piano with orchestra
    xx Violin and piano music
        Violin and piano with orchestra
— Solos with piano (M1041)
    xx Trios (Pianos (2), violin), Arranged
Concertos (Violin and piano with chamber
    orchestra) (M1040-1041)
    sa Violin and piano with chamber
        orchestra
    xx Chamber-orchestra music
        Violin and piano music
        Violin and piano with chamber
        orchestra
— Scores (M1040)
— Solos with piano (M1041)
    xx Trios (Pianos (2), violin), Arranged

Concertos (Violin and piano with string
    orchestra) (M1105-6)
    sa Violin and piano with string orchestra
    xx String-orchestra music
        Violin and piano music
        Violin and piano with string orchestra
— Solos with piano (M1106)
    xx Trios (Pianos (2), violin), Arranged
Concertos (Violin and viola) (M1040-1041)
    sa Violin and viola with orchestra
    xx Violin and viola music
        Violin and viola with orchestra
Concertos (Violin and viola with chamber
    orchestra) (M1040-1041)
    sa Violin and viola with chamber orchestra
    xx Chamber-orchestra music
        Violin and viola music
        Violin and viola with chamber orchestra
— Solos with piano (M1041)
    xx Trios (Piano, violin, viola), Arranged
Concertos (Violin and viola with string
    orchestra) (M1105-6)
    sa Violin and viola with string orchestra
    xx String-orchestra music
        Violin and viola music
        Violin and viola with string orchestra
Concertos (Violin and violoncello)
    (M1040-1041)
    sa Violin and violoncello with orchestra
    xx Violin and violoncello music
        Violin and violoncello with orchestra
— Excerpts
—— Solos with piano (M1041)
    xx Piano trios, Arranged
— Solos with piano (M1041)
    xx Piano trios, Arranged
Concertos (Violin and violoncello with
    chamber orchestra) (M1040-1041)
    sa Violin and violoncello with chamber
        orchestra
    xx Violin and violoncello music
        Violin and violoncello with chamber
        orchestra
— Solos with piano (M1041)
    xx Piano trios, Arranged
Concertos (Violin and violoncello with instr.
    ensemble) (M985)
    sa Violin and violoncello with instr.
        ensemble
    xx Instrumental ensembles
        Violin and violoncello music
        Violin and violoncello with instr.
        ensemble
Concertos (Violin and violoncello with string
    orchestra) (M1105-6)
    sa Violin and violoncello with string
        orchestra
    xx String-orchestra music
        Violin and violoncello music
        Violin and violoncello with string
        orchestra
Concertos (Violin), Arranged (M1012-1013)
— Solo with piano (M1013)
    xx Violin and piano music, Arranged
Concertos (Violin with band) (M1205-6)
    sa Violin with band
    xx Band music
        Violin music
        Violin with band
Concertos (Violin with chamber orchestra)
    (M1012-1013)
    sa Violin with chamber orchestra
    xx Chamber-orchestra music
        Violin music
        Violin with chamber orchestra
— Solo with piano (M1013)
    xx Violin and piano music, Arranged

Concertos (Violin with instr. ensemble)
  sa Violin with instr. ensemble
  xx Instrumental ensembles
    Violin music
    Violin with instr. ensemble
Concertos (Violin with percussion ensemble)
  sa Violin with percussion ensemble
  xx Percussion ensembles
    Violin music
    Violin with percussion ensemble
Concertos (Violin with string ensemble)
  sa Violin with string ensemble
  xx String ensembles
    Violin music
    Violin with string ensemble
Concertos (Violin with string orchestra)
  (M1105-6)
  sa Violin with string orchestra
  xx String-orchestra music
    Violin music
    Violin with string orchestra
  — To 1800
  —— Excerpts
  ——— Solo with piano
      x Concertos (Violin with string
        orchestra)—To 1800—Solo
        with piano—Excerpts
      xx Violin and piano music,
        Arranged
  —— Solo with piano
  ——— Excerpts
      See Concertos (Violin with
        string orchestra)—To
        1800—Excerpts—Solo
        with piano

    GENERAL SUBDIVISIONS

  — Solo with piano *(M1106)*
    xx Violin and piano music, Arranged
Concertos (Violin with string orchestra),
  Arranged *(M1105-6)*
  — Solo with piano *(M1106)*
    xx Violin and piano music, Arranged
Concertos (Violins (2)) *(M1012-1013)*
  sa Violins (2) with orchestra
  xx Violin music (Violins (2))
    Violins (2) with orchestra
  — Solos with piano *(M1013)*
    xx Trios (Piano, violins (2)), Arranged
Concertos (Violins (2) and viola with chamber
  orchestra) *(M1040-1041)*
  sa Violins (2), viola with chamber
    orchestra
  xx Violins (2), viola with chamber
    orchestra
Concertos (Violins (2), viola) *(M1040-1041)*
  sa Violins (2), viola with orchestra
  xx String trios (Violins (2), viola)
    Violins (2), viola with orchestra
Concertos (Violins (2) with string orchestra)
  (M1105-6)
  sa Violins (2) with string orchestra
  xx String-orchestra music
    Violin music (Violins (2))
    Violins (2) with string orchestra
Concertos (Violins (2) with string orchestra),
  Arranged
  — Solos with piano *(M1106)*
    xx Trios (Piano, violins (2)), Arranged
Concertos (Violins (3)) *(M1012-1013)*
  sa Violins (3) with orchestra
  xx String trios (Violins (3))
    Violins (3) with orchestra
  — Scores *(M1012)*
  — Solos with piano *(M1013)*
    xx Quartets (Piano, violins (3)),
      Arranged

Concertos (Violins (3), viola, violoncello with
  string orchestra) *(M1105-6)*
  sa Violins (3), viola, violoncello with
    string orchestra
  xx String-orchestra music
    String quintets (Violins (3), viola,
      violoncello)
    Violins (3), viola, violoncello with
      string orchestra
  — Scores *(M1105)*
Concertos (Violins (3) with string orchestra)
  (M1105-6)
  sa Violins (3) with string orchestra
  xx String-orchestra music
    String trios (Violins (3))
    Violins (3) with string orchestra
Concertos (Violins (3) with string orchestra),
  Arranged *(M1105-6a)*
  — Scores and parts *(M1105)*
  — Solos with piano *(M1106)*
    xx Quartets (Piano, violins (3)),
      Arranged
Concertos (Violins (4) with string orchestra)
  (M1105 -6)
  sa Violins (4) with string orchestra
  xx String-orchestra music
    String quartets (Violins (4))
    Violins (4) with string orchestra
  — Solos with piano *(M1106)*
    xx Quintets (Piano, violins (4)),
      Arranged
Concertos (Violoncello) *(M1016-1017)*
  sa Violoncello with orchestra
  xx Violoncello music
    Violoncello with orchestra
  — Analysis, appreciation
  — Excerpts
  —— Solo with piano *(M1017)*
      x Concertos (Violoncello)—Solo
        with piano—Excerpts
      xx Violoncello and piano music,
        Arranged
  — Solo with piano *(M1017)*
    xx Violoncello and piano music,
      Arranged
  —— Excerpts
      See Concertos (Violoncello)—
        Excerpts—Solo with piano
Concertos (Violoncello and harp with string
  orchestra) *(M1105-6)*
  sa Violoncello and harp with string
    orchestra
  xx String-orchestra music
    Violoncello and harp music
    Violoncello and harp with string
      orchestra
Concertos (Violoncello), Arranged
  (M1016-1017)
  — Solo with piano *(M1017)*
    xx Violoncello and piano music,
      Arranged
Concertos (Violoncello piccolo with string
  orchestra) *(M1105-6)*
  sa Violoncello piccolo with string
    orchestra
  xx String-orchestra music
    Violoncello piccolo music
    Violoncello piccolo with string
      orchestra
  — To 1800
  —— Scores *(M1105)*
Concertos (Violoncello with band)
  (M1205-6)
  sa Violoncello with band
  xx Band music
    Violoncello music
    Violoncello with band
  — Scores *(M1205)*

Concertos (Violoncello with chamber
  orchestra) *(M1016-1017)*
  sa Violoncello with chamber orchestra
  xx Chamber-orchestra music
    Violoncello music
    Violoncello with chamber orchestra
  — Solo with piano *(M1017)*
    xx Violoncello and piano music,
      Arranged
Concertos (Violoncello with instr. ensemble)
  sa Violoncello with instr. ensemble
  xx Instrumental ensembles
    Violoncello music
    Violoncello with instr. ensemble
Concertos (Violoncello with string orchestra)
  (M1105-6)
  sa Violoncello with string orchestra
  xx String-orchestra music
    Violoncello music
    Violoncello with string orchestra
  — Solo with piano *(M1106)*
    xx Violoncello and piano music,
      Arranged
Concertos (Violoncello with string orchestra),
  Arranged *(M1105-6)*
  — Solo with piano *(M1106)*
    xx Violoncello and piano music,
      Arranged
Concertos (Violoncellos (2)) *(M1016-1017)*
  sa Violoncellos (2) with chamber orchestra
    Violoncellos (2) with orchestra
  xx Violoncellos (2) with orchestra
Concertos (Violoncellos (2) with string
  orchestra) *(M1105-6)*
  sa Violoncellos (2) with string orchestra
  xx String-orchestra music
    Violoncello music (Violoncellos (2))
    Violoncellos (2) with string orchestra
Concertos (Violoncellos (3)) *(M1016-1017)*
  sa Violoncellos (3) with orchestra
  xx String trios (3 violoncellos)
    Violoncellos (3) with orchestra
Concertos (Xylophone) *(M1038-9)*
  sa Xylophone with orchestra
  xx Xylophone music
    Xylophone with orchestra
Concertos (Yang ch'in with orchestra)
  (M1039.4.Y35)
  sa Yang ch'in with orchestra
  xx Yang ch'in music
    Yang ch'in with orchestra
Concerts *(Direct)*
  sa Music festivals
    Music—Performance
  xx Amusements
    Music
    Music festivals
    Music—Performance
  Example under Performing arts
  — Agents
    See Concert agents
  — Program building
    x Program building (Music)
  — Programs *(ML25.7; ML40-44)*
    sa Operas—Programs
    x Programs, Concert
Concessions *(Direct)*
  sa Calvo doctrine and clause
    Licenses
    Mines and mineral resources
    Mining law
    Municipal franchises
    Petroleum law and legislation
    Railroad law
    Railroads
  xx Administrative law
    Industry and state
    Licenses

Concessions (Direct) (Continued)
    Municipal franchises
    — Taxation (Direct)
Concessions, Leased
    See Leased departments, concessions, etc.
Concessions (Amusements, etc.) (Direct)
Conchifera
    See Lamellibranchiata
Conchinamine (QP921.Q4)
Conchinine
    See Quinidine
Conchology
    See Mollusks
        Shells
Conchostraca
    x Clam shrimps
    xx Branchiopoda
Conciliar theory
    Here are entered works dealing with the
      relative authority of the Pope and
      church councils.
    sa Councils and synods
    x Conciliarism
    xx Authority (Religion)
        Bishops
        Councils and synods
        Gallicanism
        Popes
        Popes—Infallibility
Conciliarism
    See Conciliar theory
Conciliation, Industrial
    See Mediation and conciliation, Industrial
Conciliation, International
    See Mediation, International
Conciliation (Civil procedure) (Direct)
    xx Civil procedure
Conclaves, Papal
    See Popes—Election
Concord (BV4647.C)
Concord, Battle of, 1775 (E241.C7)
Concordances
    sa Indexes
        subdivision Concordances under Bible;
        and under anonymous classics and
        names of authors, e.g. Pearl (Middle
        English poem)—Concordances;
        Shakespeare, William, 1564-1616—
        Concordances; Shakespeare, William,
        1564 -1616. Sonnets—
        Concordances
Concordat of 1122 (Holy Roman Empire)
    See Concordat of Worms, 1122
Concordat of 1448 (Holy Roman Empire)
    See Concordat of Vienna, 1448
Concordat of 1516 (France)
Concordat of 1753 (Spain)
Concordat of 1801 (France)
    sa Louisets
Concordat of 1817 (Bavaria)
Concordat of 1818 (Naples)
Concordat of 1841 (Sardinia)
Concordat of 1851 (Spain)
Concordat of 1851 (Tuscany)
Concordat of 1855 (Austria)
Concordat of 1857 (Portugal)
Concordat of 1860 (Haiti)
Concordat of 1862 (Ecuador)
Concordat of 1862 (Venezuela)
Concordat of 1881 (Ecuador)
Concordat of 1886 (Portugal)
Concordat of 1887 (Colombia)
Concordat of 1914 (Serbia)
Concordat of 1922 (Latvia)
Concordat of 1924 (Bavaria)
    xx Catholic Church in Bavaria
        Church and state in Bavaria
Concordat of 1925 (Poland)

Concordat of 1927 (Lithuania)
Concordat of 1927 (Rumania)
Concordat of 1929 (Italy)
    x Lateran pact, 1929
    — Anecdotes, facetiae, satire, etc.
Concordat of 1929 (Prussia)
Concordat of 1932 (Baden)
Concordat of 1933 (Austria)
Concordat of 1933 (Germany)
    xx Catholic Church in Germany—History
        —1933-1945
Concordat of 1940 (Portugal)
Concordat of 1953 (Spain)
Concordat of 1962 (Spain)
    xx Catholic Church in Spain
Concordat of Vienna, 1448
    x Concordat of 1448 (Holy Roman
      Empire)
      Vienna, Concordat of, 1448
Concordat of Worms, 1122
    x Concordat of 1122 (Holy Roman
      Empire)
      Worms, Concordat of, 1122
    xx Investiture
    — Sources
Concordats (BX1401-1691; BX1790)
    xx Canon law
        Catholic Church—Relations
          (diplomatic)—Treaties
        Church and state
        Ecclesiastical law
        International law
        International relations
        Treaties
Concorde (Jet transports)
    xx Supersonic transport planes
Concrete (TA439-446)
    sa Asphalt
        Asphalt concrete
        Cement
        Concrete mixers
        Concrete products
        Creep of concrete
        Frost resistant concrete
        Gunite
        Heat resistant concrete
        Lightweight concrete
        Pavements
        Precast concrete
        Prestressed concrete
        Ready-mixed concrete
        Reinforced concrete
        Resin concrete
        Sand-lime products
        Stone, Artificial
        Stone, Cast
        Sulphate-resistant concrete
        Tabby (Concrete)
        Vacuum concrete process
        Vibrated concrete
    x Beton
    xx Building materials
        Cement
        Foundations
        Masonry
        Plaster
        Stone, Artificial
    — Additives
      x Concrete admixtures
    — — Patents (TP881)
    — Air entrainment
      See Lightweight concrete
    — Analysis
      See Concrete—Chemistry
    — Chemistry
      sa Alkali-aggregate reactions
        Concrete—Corrosion
        Concrete—Curing

      x Chemistry of concrete
        Concrete—Analysis
        Concrete chemistry
      xx Chemistry, Technical
    — Contraction
      See Concrete—Expansion and
        contraction
    — Cooling
    — Corrosion (TA440)
      xx Concrete—Chemistry
      Example under Corrosion and anti-corro-
        sives
    — Cracking
      sa Pavements, Asphalt concrete—
        Cracking
      x Cracking of concrete
      xx Concrete—Defects
    — Creep
      See Creep of concrete
    — Curing
      x Concrete curing
        Concrete, Curing of
        Curing of concrete
      xx Concrete—Chemistry
        Concrete construction
      Example under Curing
    — — Safety measures
    — Defects
      sa Alkali-aggregate reactions
        Concrete construction—
          Deterioration
        Concrete—Cracking
      xx Alkali-aggregate reactions
    — Deterioration
      x Deterioration of concrete
    — Expansion and contraction
      sa Concrete, Effect of temperature on
        Expansive concrete
      x Concrete—Contraction
        Concrete—Shrinkage
        Contraction of concrete
        Expansion of concrete
        Shrinkage of concrete
      xx Concrete, Effect of temperature on
        Concrete—Testing
        Expansion of solids
    — Fatigue
      sa Columns, Concrete—Fatigue
        Concrete beams—Fatigue
      x Fatigue of concrete
      xx Concrete—Testing
      Example under Materials—Fatigue
    — Finishing
      x Concrete finishes
        Concrete surface finishes
      xx Concrete construction—Formwork
        Finishes and finishing
        Grinding and polishing
    — Freezing and thawing
      See Frost resistant concrete
    — Juvenile literature
    — Moisture
    — Patents
    — Permeability
    — Pipe lines
    — Protective coatings
      See Concrete coatings
    — Pump placing (TA682.45)
      x Concrete, Pumped
        Concrete pumping
        Pumped concrete
        Pumping of concrete
    — Quality control
    — Radiography (TA440)
    — Research
      See Concrete research
    — Shrinkage

See Concrete—Expansion and
contraction
— Specifications
— Standards *(Direct)*
— Tables, calculations, etc.
— Testing *(TA440)*
sa Concrete construction—Testing
Concrete—Expansion and
contraction
Concrete—Fatigue
Example under Strength of materials
— — Laboratory manuals
— — Patents *(TA440)*
— Thermal properties
— Transportation
— Vibration
See Vibrated concrete
Concrete, Air-entrained
See Lightweight concrete
Concrete, Asphalt
See Asphalt concrete
Concrete, Curing of
See Concrete—Curing
Concrete, Effect of temperature on
sa Concrete—Expansion and contraction
Frost resistant concrete
Heat resistant concrete
xx Concrete—Expansion and contraction
Frost resistant concrete
Heat resistant concrete
Concrete, Expanding
See Expansive concrete
Concrete, Expansive
See Expansive concrete
Concrete, Frost resistant
See Frost resistant concrete
Concrete, Heat resistant
See Heat resistant concrete
Concrete, Lightweight
See Lightweight concrete
Concrete, Precast
See Precast concrete
Concrete, Premixed
See Ready-mixed concrete
Concrete, Prestressed
See Prestressed concrete
Concrete, Pumped
See Concrete—Pump placing
Concrete, Ready-mixed
See Ready-mixed concrete
Concrete, Reinforced
See Reinforced concrete
Concrete, Self-stressed
See Expansive concrete
Concrete, Vibrated
See Vibrated concrete
Concrete (Philosophy) *(BD332)*
xx Existentialism
Ontology
Reality
Concrete admixtures
See Concrete—Additives
Concrete arches
See Arches, Concrete
Concrete art *(Direct)*
sa Color-field painting
Concrete poetry
Constructivism (Art)
Optical art
x Art, Concrete
xx Art, Abstract
Art, Modern—20th century
Concrete as art material
x Concrete in art
xx Artists' materials
Concrete beams
sa Prestressed concrete beams
x Beams, Concrete

Concrete girders
xx Concrete products
Girders
— Fatigue
xx Concrete—Fatigue
— Testing
— Transportation
Concrete blocks *(TP885.C7; TH1491)*
sa Cinder blocks
Concrete slabs
xx Concrete products
Concrete slabs
— Testing
— Transportation
Concrete boats
x Boats, Concrete
Reinforced concrete boats
xx Boat-building
Boats and boating
Concrete bridges
See Bridges, Concrete
Concrete building
See Concrete construction
Concrete chemistry
See Concrete—Chemistry
Concrete coatings
Here are entered works on the protection
of concrete from deterioration. Works
on the use of cement as a coating to
protect other materials are entered un-
der the heading Cement coating.
x Concrete—Protective coatings
xx Coatings
Protective coatings
Note under Cement coating
— Patents *(TA440)*
— Testing
Concrete columns
See Columns, Concrete
Concrete construction *(TA680-683; Building,
TH1461-1501)*
sa Arches, Concrete
Bridges, Concrete
Columns, Concrete
Composite construction
Concrete—Curing
Concrete dams
Concrete houses
Concrete piling
Concrete products
Concrete walls
Flooring, Concrete
Floors, Concrete
Grouting
Pavements, Concrete
Pipe, Concrete
Precast concrete construction
Prestressed concrete
Prestressed concrete construction
Reinforced concrete construction
Roads, Concrete
Sewers, Concrete
Ships, Concrete
Underwater concrete construction
Vibrated concrete
x Building, Concrete
Concrete building
Construction, Concrete
xx Architecture
Building
Example under Structural engineering
— Cold weather conditions
— Contracts and specifications *(Direct)*
— Deterioration
xx Concrete—Defects
— Estimates *(TA681)*
— Formwork *(TA681)*
sa Concrete—Finishing

x Forms (Concrete construction)
xx Carpentry
— Hinges
sa Concrete construction—Joints
x Concrete hinges
Construction hinges (Concrete)
Reinforced concrete construction—
Hinges
xx Concrete construction—Joints
Hinges
— Joints
sa Concrete construction—Hinges
Roads, Concrete—Joints
x Concrete joints
Construction joints (Concrete)
Reinforced concrete construction—
Joints
xx Concrete construction—Hinges
Joints (Engineering)
— — Testing
— Maintenance and repair
— Models
— Problems, exercises, etc.
— Quality control
— Safety measures
— Study and teaching
— — Audio-visual aids
— Tables, calculations, etc. *(TA682)*
— Testing
xx Concrete—Testing
— Translations
Example under Translations
— Vacuum process
See Vacuum concrete process
Concrete construction, Precast
See Precast concrete construction
Concrete construction, Prefabricated
See Precast concrete construction
Concrete construction, Submarine
See Underwater concrete construction
Concrete construction, Tilt-up
See Precast concrete construction
Concrete curing
See Concrete—Curing
Concrete cutting
x Cutting of concrete
Concrete dams *(Direct)*
sa Arch dams
Buttress dams
x Dams, Concrete
xx Concrete construction
Dams
— Foundations *(TC547)*
xx Foundations
Concrete face brick *(TP832.C)*
xx Bricks
Concrete products
Concrete finishes
See Concrete—Finishing
Concrete flooring
See Flooring, Concrete
Concrete footings
x Footings, Concrete
xx Foundations
— Testing
Concrete girders
See Concrete beams
Concrete hinges
See Concrete construction—Hinges
Concrete houses *(NA7160)*
x Houses, Concrete
xx Architecture, Domestic
Concrete construction
Dwellings
Example under House construction
— Heating and ventilation
— Hygienic aspects

Concrete in art
  See Concrete as art material
Concrete inserts
  x Inserts, Concrete
  — Testing
Concrete intelligence
  See Mechanical ability
Concrete joints
  See Concrete construction—Joints
Concrete mixers
  xx Concrete
    Mixing machinery
Concrete music
    Here are entered works in which the sounds produced were originally recorded on magnetic tape from natural sounds and subsequently rearranged or altered. The heading is used as a second heading when the tape is used with a specifically named medium or performance, *e.g.* 1. Quintets (Clarinet, flute, harp, viola, violoncello) 2. Concrete music.
  sa Electronic music
    Monologues with music (Concrete music)
    Quartets (Concrete music)
    Suites (Concrete music)
    Variations (Concrete music)
  x Music, Concrete
    Tape-recorder music
  xx Electronic music
    Music
Concrete pavements
  See Pavements, Concrete
Concrete piling *(TA787)*
  xx Concrete construction
    Piling (Civil engineering)
  — Tables, calculations, etc.
  — Testing
Concrete pipe
  See Pipe, Concrete
Concrete plants *(Direct)*
  — Accidents
  — Automation
  — Design and construction
  — Electric equipment
  — Equipment and supplies
  —— Drawing
      See Concrete plants—Equipment and supplies—Drawings
  —— Drawings
      x Concrete plants—Equipment and supplies—Drawing
      xx Mechanical drawing
  —— Vibration
  — Heating and ventilation
  — Hygienic aspects *(RC965.C4)*
  — Management
  — Noise
  — Safety measures
Concrete poetry
  x Visual poetry
  xx Concrete art
    Letter-pictures
    Poetry
Concrete poetry, Brazilian, [Portuguese, etc.] *(Direct)*
  x Brazilian [Portuguese, etc.] concrete poetry
  xx Brazilian [Portuguese, etc.] poetry
Concrete products *(TP885)*
  sa Concrete beams
    Concrete blocks
    Concrete face brick
    Concrete slabs
    Pipe, Concrete
    Sewers, Concrete

  xx Concrete
    Concrete construction
  — Costs
  — Standards *(Direct)*
Concrete products industry *(Direct)*
  — Costs
  — Labor productivity
Concrete pumping
  See Concrete—Pump placing
Concrete research *(Direct)*
  x Concrete—Research
  xx Research
Concrete roads
  See Roads, Concrete
Concrete roofing
  See Roofing, Concrete
Concrete sewers
  See Sewers, Concrete
Concrete ships
  See Ships, Concrete
Concrete slabs
  sa Composite construction
    Concrete blocks
  x Slabs, Concrete
  xx Concrete blocks
    Concrete products
    Slabs
    Stone, Artificial
  — Defects
  — Electromechanical analogies
      Example under Electromechanical analogies
  — Programmed instruction
  — Tables, calculations, etc.
  — Testing
  — Transportation
Concrete surface finishes
  See Concrete—Finishing
Concrete trusses
  See Trusses, Concrete
Concrete walls
  xx Concrete construction
    Walls
  — Specifications *(Direct)*
  — Testing
Concretions *(QE581)*
  sa Geodes
  xx Sedimentary structures
Concubinage *(Direct)*
  sa Free love
  xx Free love
    Marriage
    Marriage law
Concubinage (Roman law)
Concurrent powers
  See Exclusive and concurrent legislative powers
Concussion of the brain
  See Brain—Concussion
Condemnation of land
  See Eminent domain
Condemned books *(Z1019-1020)*
  sa Censorship
    Expurgated books
    Index librorum prohibitorum
    Liberty of the press
    Prohibited books
  x Books, Condemned
  xx Censorship
    Expurgated books
    Liberty of the press
    Prohibited books
Condemned societies
  x Prohibited societies
  xx Societies
Condemned societies (Canon law) *(BX1939.C8)*

Condensate oil wells
  x Corrosive oil wells
    Distillate oil wells
    Gas-condensate wells
    Sour oil wells
  xx Gas, Natural
    Oil wells
Condensation *(Meteorology, QC918)*
  sa Glaze (Meteorology)
    Moisture
  xx Atmospheric nucleation
    Chemistry
    Cloud physics
Condensation (Meteorology)
  See Condensation trails
Condensation and expansion, Thermal
  See Expansion (Heat)
Condensation control in buildings
  See Dampness in buildings
Condensation products (Chemistry) *(QD341; QD391)*
  sa Aldol condensation
    Claisen condensation
    Perkin reaction
    Phenolic resins
    Plastics
    Polyesters
    Polymers and polymerization
    Schiff bases
  xx Chemistry, Organic
    Plastics
    Polymers and polymerization
Condensation trails *(TL557.C7)*
  x Aeroplanes—Condensation trails
    Condensation (Meteorology)
    Contrails
    Vapor trails
  xx Aeronautics
    Clouds
    Meteorology in aeronautics
Condensed books
  See Books, Condensed
Condensed degenerate gases
  See Superfluidity
Condensed milk
  See Milk, Condensed
Condenser microphone
  See Electrostatic microphone
Condensers (Electricity) *(QC587)*
  sa Capacitor motors
    Dielectric amplifiers
    Radio capacitors
  x Capacitors
    Electric capacitors
    Electric condensers
    Electrolytic capacitors
    Electrolytic condensers
  xx Electric apparatus and appliances
    Electric capacity
    Electrostatics
    Induction coils
    Induction (Electricity)
    Tank circuits
  — Standards
  — Tariff
      See Tariff on electric condensers
  — Testing
Condensers (Steam) *(TJ557-565)*
  xx Steam-engines
  — Testing
Condensers (Vapors and gases) *(TP363)*
  x Vapor condensers
Condicio juris *(Direct)*
  x Conditio juris
  xx Civil law
    Nullity
    Roman law
Condición (Dance) *(GV1796.C57)*

Condictio
   See Unjust enrichment (Roman law)
Condiments *(Agriculture, SB305-7; Cookery,*
      TX819; Manners and customs,
      GT2870)
   sa Spices
     names of condiments, e.g. Cinnamon,
      Clove, Pepper (Spice)
   xx Cookery
     Food
     Spices
   — Analysis
   — Juvenile literature
Conditio juris
   See Condicio juris
Condition (Buddhism)
   See Pratyaya
Conditional reflexes
   See Conditioned response
Conditional response
   See Conditioned response
Conditional sales
   See Sales, Conditional
Conditional statements (Logic)
   See Conditionals (Logic)
Conditionalism
   See Annihilationism
Conditionality (Buddhism)
   See Pratītyasamutpāda
Conditionals (Logic) *(BC199.C56)*
   sa Counterfactuals (Logic)
   x Conditional statements (Logic)
   xx Grammar, Comparative and general
     Logic
Conditioned emotional response
   See Emotional conditioning
Conditioned eyelid response
   See Eyelid conditioning
Conditioned immortality
   See Annihilationism
Conditioned operant response
   See Operant conditioning
Conditioned reflexes
   See Conditioned response
Conditioned response *(BF319)*
   sa Aversive stimuli
     Emotional conditioning
     Extinction (Psychology)
     Eyelid conditioning
     Habituation (Neuropsychology)
     Operant behavior
     Operant conditioning
     Reinforcement (Psychology)
     Stimulus generalization
     Stimulus satiation
     Substitution (Psychology)
     Verbal behavior
     Verbal conditioning
   x Conditional reflexes
     Conditional response
     Conditioned reflexes
   xx Association of ideas
     Behaviorism (Psychology)
     Habituation (Neuropsychology)
     Learning, Psychology of
     Psychology, Physiological
     Reflexes
Conditioning, Instrumental
   See Operant conditioning
Conditioning, Operant
   See Operant conditioning
Conditions, Immoral (Law)
   See Immoral conditions (Law)
Conditions (Jewish law)
Conditions (Law) *(Direct)*
   sa Expectancies (Law)
     Immoral conditions (Law)
     Indemnity against liability

Modus (Civil law)
     Resolution (Civil law)
   xx Civil law
     Contracts
     Modus (Civil law)
Conditions (Roman law)
Conditions and laws of chemical reaction
   See Chemical reaction, Conditions and laws
     of
Condolence, Etiquette of
   See Etiquette
Condominium (Housing) *(Direct)*
   sa Apartment houses, Cooperative
   x Condominium (Real property)
     Cotenancy
     Horizontal property
     Property, Horizontal
   xx Apartment houses, Cooperative
     Joint tenancy
     Real property
   — Cases
   — — Digests
      See Condominium (Housing)—
       Digests
   — Digests
     x Condominium (Housing)—Cases—
      Digests
   — Public opinion
Condominium (International law)
   (JX4068.C7)
   xx International law
     Sovereignty
Condominium (Office buildings) *(Direct)*
   x Commercial condominium
     Condominium (Real property)
     Cotenancy
     Horizontal property
     Property, Horizontal
   xx Joint tenancy
     Office buildings
     Real property
Condominium (Real property)
   See Condominium (Housing)
     Condominium (Office buildings)
Condoms
   xx Contraceptives
     Venereal diseases—Prevention
Condors *(QL696.A2)*
   sa California condor
Condottieri *(DG532-7)*
   xx Mercenary troops
     Soldiers of fortune
   — Portraits
Conduct, Disorderly
   See Disorderly conduct
Conduct in courtrooms
   See Conduct of court proceedings
Conduct of court proceedings *(Direct)*
   sa Contempt of court
   x Conduct in courtrooms
     Court proceedings, Conduct of
     Courtroom decorum
     Courtroom proceedings
     Decorum in court
     Legal decorum
     Photographing of court proceedings
     Radio broadcasting of court
      proceedings
     Television broadcasting of court
      proceedings
   xx Legal etiquette
     Procedure (Law)
     Publicity (Law)
Conduct of life *(BJ1545-1695)*
   sa Altruism
     Anger
     Avarice
     Benevolence

     Business ethics
     Character
     Characters and characteristics
     Charity
     Charm
     Cheerfulness
     Christian life
     Clean speech
     Contentment
     Courage
     Courtesy
     Culture
     Duty
     Egoism
     Ethics
     Etiquette
     Euthenics
     Fairness
     Family life education
     Fellowship
     Filial piety
     Forgiveness
     Friendship
     Gratitude
     Habit
     Honesty
     Honor
     Humanity
     Hypocrisy
     Ingratitude
     Interpersonal relations
     Justice
     Kindness
     Love
     Loyalty
     Maxims
     Obedience
     Patience
     Patriotism
     Preparedness
     Pride and vanity
     Prudence
     Reliability
     Respect
     Right and wrong
     Self-control
     Self-culture
     Self-respect
     Sharing
     Simplicity
     Spiritual life
     Sportsmanship
     Success
     Sympathy
     Temperance
     Truthfulness and falsehood
     Vices
     Virtue
     Virtues
     Worry
     subdivision Conduct of life *under*
      names of classes of persons, e.g.
      Youth—Conduct of life
   x Behavior
     Ethics, Practical
     Morals
   xx Character
     Christian life
     Courtesy
     Duty
     Ethics
     Life
     Success
     Young men
     Young women
     Youth
   — Dictionaries
   — Early works to 1900

Conduct of life *(BJ1545-1695)*
(Continued)
— Public opinion
— Quotations, maxims, etc. *(BJ1548)*
Conductimetric analysis
See Conductometric analysis
Conducting *(History, ML457; Instruction, MT85)*
Here are entered works on orchestral conducting or a combination of orchestral and choral conducting. Works restricted to choral conducting are entered under the heading Conducting, Choral.
sa Bands (Music)
Conducting, Choral
Conductors (Music)
Music—Performance
Orchestra
Rehearsals (Music)
xx Bands (Music)
Conductors (Music)
Music—Instruction and study
Music—Performance
Orchestra
Rehearsals (Music)
— Juvenile literature
Conducting, Choral *(History, ML457; Instruction, MT85)*
sa Choirs (Music)
Choral singing
Conductors (Music)
x Choral conducting
xx Choirs (Music)
Choral music
Choral singing
Church music
Conducting
Conductors (Music)
Note under Conducting
Conducting system of the heart
See Heart conduction system
Conduction anesthesia *(RD85.C6)*
x Anesthesia, Conduction
Block anesthesia
Nerve-block anesthesia
Perineural anesthesia
Regional anesthesia
xx Anesthesia
Conduction of heat
See Heat—Conduction
Conduction system of the heart
See Heart conduction system
Conductive rubber
See Rubber—Electric properties
Conductive system of the heart
See Heart conduction system
Conductivity, Electric
See Electric conductivity
Conductivity of electrolytes
See Electrolytes—Conductivity
Conductometric analysis *(QD115)*
x Amperometric analysis
Conductimetric analysis
Titration, Conductometric
xx Electrochemical analysis
Conductors, Electric
See Electric conductors
Conductors, Railroad
See Railroad conductors
Conductors (Music) *(Biography: collective, ML402; individual, ML422)*
sa Conducting
Conducting, Choral
x Bandmasters
Music—Biography
Music conductors
xx Conducting
Conducting, Choral

Musicians
Orchestra
— Biography
— Juvenile literature
Conduits
See Aqueducts
Electric conduits
Condurango
See Cundurango
Condyle of the mandible
See Mandibular condyle
Cone *(QA491; QA521; QA561)*
xx Geometry, Descriptive
Geometry, Solid
Cone propulsion (Boats)
See Jet boat engines
Conelrad
x Control of electromagnetic radiation
Plan for control of electromagnetic radiation
xx Air raid warning systems
United States—Civil defense
Conestoga Indians *(E99.C87)*
sa Susquehanna Indians
xx Indians of North America
Iroquoian Indians
Susquehanna Indians
Confectioners *(Economics, HD9999.C72)*
sa Wages—Confectioners
— Collective labor agreements
See Collective labor agreements—Confectioners
Confectionery *(Direct) (Candy-making, TX783-799; Industry, HD9999.C72)*
sa Butterscotch
Cake decorating
Chocolate industry
Halvah
Ice cream, ices, etc.
Nougats
Snack foods
x Candy
xx Cookery
Ice cream, ices, etc.
— Accounting *(HF5686.C63)*
— Analysis
— Appliances, utensils, etc. *(TX793)*
— — Maintenance and repair
— — — Patents
— — Patents
— Costs
— Early works to 1800
— Juvenile literature
— Law and legislation *(Direct)*
— Packaging
Example under Packaging
— Patents
— Quality control
— Standards *(Direct)*
— Tables, calculations, etc.
Confederacies
See Confederation of states
Confederate Memorial Day
See Memorial Day, Confederate
Confederate music
See United States—Civil War, 1861-1865—Songs and music—Confederate States
Confederate propaganda
See Propaganda, Confederate
Confederate States of America
sa United States—History—Civil War, 1861-1865
— Appropriations and expenditures
— Bio-bibliography
— Biography *(E467)*
— Claims *(HJ8943)*
— Commerce *(HF3027.6; HF3153)*

— Copyright
See Copyright—Confederate States of America
— Cotton trade
See Cotton trade—Confederate States of America
— Courts-martial and courts of inquiry
See Courts-martial and courts of inquiry—Confederate States of America
— Debts, Public
See Debts, Public—Confederate States of America
— Defenses *(UA580-585)*
— Diplomatic and consular service
— Economic conditions *(E487)*
— Executive departments *(JK9720-9770)*
— Foreign population *(E487)*
— Foreign relations *(E469; E487-8)*
— — France, ₍Great Britain₎
— Government publications
— History *(E487-8)*
x Southern States—History—Civil War, 1861-1865
— — Juvenile literature
— — Museums
— — Periodicals *(E482)*
— — Pictorial works
— — Societies, etc. *(E483)*
— — Sources *(E467.1; E484)*
— History, Military *(E470; E545)*
— History, Naval *(E591-600)*
— Hospitals, charities, etc. *(E621-5)*
— Industries *(HC105.6)*
— Money
See Money—Confederate States of America
— Music
See United States—History—Civil War, 1861-1865—Songs and music—Confederate States
— Naval education
See Naval education—Confederate States of America
— Officials and employees
— — Salaries, allowances, etc.
— Patents
See Patents—Confederate States of America
— Politics and government *(JK9661-9993)*
— Railroads
See Railroads—Confederate States of America
— Regimental histories
See United States—History—Civil War, 1861-1865—Regimental histories
— Registers *(JK9663)*
— Religion *(BR535; E650)*
— Seal *(CD5610)*
— Secret service
See United States—History—Civil War, 1861-1865—Secret Service—Confederate States
— Social conditions *(E487)*
— Social life and customs *(E487)*
— Soldiers' monuments
See Soldiers' monuments—Southern States
— Songs and music
See United States—History—Civil War, 1861-1865—Songs and music—Confederate States
— Tariff
See Tariff—Confederate States of America
— Taxation

See Taxation—Confederate States of
America
— Text-books
See Text-books—Confederate States
of America
— Warehouses
See Warehouses—Confederate States
of America
Confederate States of America. Army
(UA580-585)
— Appointments and retirements
(UB414.5)
— Appropriations and expenditures
(UA583.5)
— Chaplains (E546.7)
— Commissariat (UC85-86)
— Field service (U173.5)
— Firearms (UD383.5)
— Guard duty (U193.5)
— Handbooks, manuals, etc. (U113.5)
— Medals, badges, decorations, etc.
(UB433.5)
— Negro troops (E585.N3)
— Officers
— — Correspondence, reminiscences, etc.
— Ordnance and ordnance stores (UF23.5;
UF153.5)
— Pay, allowances, etc. (UC87)
— Prisons (E611-612)
— Promotions (UB414.5)
— Recruiting, enlistment, etc. (UB343.5)
sa United States—History—Civil War,
1861-1865—Conscientious
objectors
— Registers (E548)
x United States—History—Civil War,
1861-1865—Registers, lists, etc.—
Confederate States
— Regulations (UB504.5)
— Sanitary affairs (UH224)
— Supplies and stores (UC85-88)
— Surgeons
— — Correspondence, reminiscences, etc.
— Transportation (UC86)
— Uniforms (UC483.5)
**Confederate States of America. Army.
Artillery** (E546.6)
— Drill and tactics (UF160.5)
**Confederate States of America. Army.
Cavalry** (E546.5)
— Drill and tactics (UE160.5)
**Confederate States of America. Army.
Infantry** (E546.4; UD153.5)
— Drill and tactics (UD160.5)
Confederate States of America. Constitution
(JK9679)
Confederate States of America. Navy
(E591-600)
— Appointments and retirements
— History (E591-600)
— — Juvenile literature
— Officers
— — Correspondence, reminiscences, etc.
— Ordnance and ordnance stores (VF23.5)
— Pay, allowances, etc.
— Recruiting, enlistment, etc.
— Registers (V11.C8)
— Regulations (VB369.5)
— Supplies and stores
— Uniforms
Confederation of states
x Confederacies
xx Federal government
Conference committees, Legislative
See Legislative conference committees
Conference lines
See Shipping conferences

Conference of Ratisbon, 1541
See Ratisbon, Colloquy of, 1541
Conference of Ratisbon, 1546
See Ratisbon, Colloquy of, 1546
Conference reporting to parents
See Parent-teacher conferences
Conference rooms (Indirect)
x Meeting rooms
xx Congresses and conventions
Conferences
See Clergy conferences
Congresses and conventions
Forums (Discussion and debate)
Meetings
Conferences, Pre-legislative
See Pre-legislative conferences
Confession (BV845-7; Catholic Church,
BX2262-7; Church of England,
BX5149.C6; Protestant Episcopal
Church, BX5949.C6)
sa Absolution
Confidential communications
Confidential communications—Clergy
Conscience, Examination of
Easter duties
Forgiveness of sin
Penance
Penitentials
Sin
x Auricular confession
Confession—Catholic Church
xx Absolution
Church discipline
Forgiveness of sin
Penance
— Catholic Church
See Confession
— Frequency of confession
— Judaism (BM723.7)
xx Judaism
— Juvenile literature
— Orthodox Eastern Church
x Orthodox Eastern Church—
Confession
— Psychology
xx Psychology, Religious
Confession, Seal of
See Seal of confession
Confession (Canon law)
sa Seal of confession
Confession (Frankish law)
Confession (Jewish law)
Confession (Law) (Direct)
sa Admissions (Law)
Self-incrimination
xx Criminal procedure
Evidence, Criminal
Evidence (Law)
Confession (Liturgy)
— Buddhism, [etc.]
x Buddha and Buddhism, [etc.]—
Confession (Liturgy)
Confession (Roman law)
Confession in literature (PN56.C67)
Confession of children
xx Children—Religious life
Confession of judgment (Direct)
xx Judgments
Pleading
Confessionals (Architecture) (Direct)
(NA5095.C)
xx Church furniture
Confessions of faith
See Creeds
Confessors (BV845; BX2262-7)
sa Spiritual directors
xx Church discipline
Clergy

Penance
Confessors (Canon law) (BX1939.C7)
sa Solicitation (Canon law)
Confidant in literature
Confidence (BJ1533.C6)
sa Trust (Psychology)
xx Ethics
Trust (Psychology)
Confidential communications (Direct)
sa Official secrets
Privacy, Right of
Self-incrimination
x Communications, Confidential
Privileged communications
(Confidential communications)
Professional secrets
Secrets, Professional
xx Confession
Criminal law
Evidence (Law)
Legal ethics
Objections (Evidence)
Personality (Law)
Privacy, Right of
Professional ethics
Secrecy (Law)
— Banking (Direct)
x Banks and banking—Confidential
communications
xx Banks and banking
— Clergy (Direct)
sa Seal of confession
x Clergy—Confidential
communications
xx Clergy
Confession
— Lawyers (Direct)
x Attorney-client privilege
Lawyer-client privilege
Lawyers—Confidential
communications
xx Attorney and client
Legal ethics
— Notaries (Direct)
x Notaries—Confidential
communications
xx Legal ethics
— Physicians (Direct)
x Doctor-patient privilege
Patient-physician privilege
Physician-patient privilege
Physicians—Confidential
communications
xx Medical ethics
Medical laws and legislation
— Press (Direct)
x Newsman's privilege
Press—Confidential communications
xx Journalistic ethics
Press law
Reporters and reporting
— Social case work (Direct)
xx Social case work
— Student counselors (Direct)
x Student counselors—Confidential
communications
— Taxation (Direct)
x Taxation—Confidential
communications
Configuration (Psychology)
See Gestalt psychology
Configuration space
sa Configurations
Wave function
x Space, Configuration
xx Configurations
Dynamics of a particle
Wave function

x Partnership—Conflict of laws
— Patents   *(Direct)*
    x Patent laws and legislation—Conflict
      of laws
— Performance   *(Direct)*
    x Performance (Law)—Conflict of laws
— Possession   *(Direct)*
    x Possession (Law)—Conflict of laws
— Public policy   *(Direct)*
    x Public policy (Law)—Conflict of
      laws
— Retroactivity   *(Direct)*
    x Retroactive laws—Conflict of laws
— Roman law
    See Conflict of laws (Roman law)
— Social insurance
    See Conflict of laws—Insurance,
      Social
— Study and teaching   *(Direct)*
— Taxation   *(Direct)*
    sa Taxation, Double
    x Taxation—Conflict of laws
    xx Taxation, Double
— Unfair competition
    See Conflict of laws—Competition,
      Unfair

GEOGRAPHIC SUBDIVISIONS

— Mexico
— — States
Conflict of laws (Canon law)
    x Canon law—Conflict of laws
    Conflict of laws—Canon law
Conflict of laws (Roman law)
    x Conflict of laws—Roman law
    Roman law—Conflict of laws
Conflicting interest (Agency)
    See Conflict of interests (Agency)
Conformal invariants
    x Invariants, Conformal
    xx Conformal mapping
    Functions of complex variables
Conformal mapping   *(QA360; QA646)*
    sa Conformal invariants
    Moment spaces
    Quasiconformal mappings
    x Conformal representation of surfaces
    Mapping, Conformal
    Transformation, Conformal
    xx Surfaces, Representation of
    Transformations (Mathematics)
Conformal representation of surfaces
    See Conformal mapping
    Surfaces, Representation of
Conformational analysis
    x Analysis, Conformational
    xx Molecular rotation
Conformity
    sa Deviant behavior
    Dissenters
    Individuality
    Influence (Psychology)
    Persuasion (Psychology)
    Social values
    x Nonconformity
    Rebels (Social psychology)
    Social conformity
    xx Attitude (Psychology)
    Deviant behavior
    Individuality
    Influence (Psychology)
    Liberty
    Social acceptance
— Anecdotes, facetiae, satire, etc.
— Mathematical models
Conformity (Religion)
    See Dissenters, Religious

Conformity as a theme in literature
    See Conformity in literature
Conformity in literature
    x Conformity as a theme in literature
Confraternities   *(Catholic Church, BX808-9)*
    sa Disciplinati
    Gilds
    Purgatorial societies
    x Sodalities
    xx Catholic Church—Societies, etc.
    Monasticism and religious orders
Confraternities (Canon law)
Confrides, Spain
— Earthquake, 1949
Confucian converts to Christianity
    See Converts from Confucianism
Confucian ethics
    x Ethics, Confucian
    xx Ethics, Chinese
Confucian memorial rites and ceremonies
    See Memorial rites and ceremonies,
      Confucian
Confucian parables
    See Parables, Confucian
Confucian philosophy
    See Philosophy, Confucian
Confucian shrines   *(Direct)*
    x Shrines, Confucian
Confucian sociology
    See Sociology, Confucian
Confucian temples
    See Temples, Confucian
Confucianism   *(Direct) (BL1830-1875)*
    sa Confucianists
    Neo-Confucianism
    Parables, Confucian
    Philosophy, Confucian
    Sociology, Confucian
    Temples, Confucian
    Yōmeigaku
    headings beginning with the word
      Confucian
    xx Religions
— 20th century

GENERAL SUBDIVISIONS

— Relations

GENERAL SUBDIVISIONS

— — Christianity, [Taoism, etc.]

GENERAL SUBDIVISIONS

— Rituals
    sa Memorial rites and ceremonies,
      Confucian
Confucianism and economics   *(Direct)*
    x Economics and Confucianism
    xx Sociology, Confucian
Confucianism and state   *(Direct)*
    x State and Confucianism
    xx Nationalism and religion
    Religion and state
Confucianism and world politics
    x World politics and Confucianism
Confucianists
    xx Confucianism
    Philosophy, Confucian
Confucianists in Korea, [etc.]
— Biography
Confusion of debts
    See Confusion of rights
Confusion of goods   *(Direct)*
    sa Accession (Law)
    Specification (Civil law)
    x Goods, Confusion of
    xx Accession (Law)
    Acquisition of property
    Specification (Civil law)

Confusion of rights   *(Direct)*
    x Confusion of debts
    Debts, Confusion of
    Merger of rights
    Rights, Confusion of
    Rights, Merger of
    xx Contracts
    Extinguishment of debts
Confusion of rights (Roman law)
Confusion of titles
    See Merger of estates
Confusion of tongues   *(P101)*
    x Tongues, Confusion of
    xx Language and languages
Conga (Dance)   *(GV1796.C)*
Congadas
    xx Folk-songs, Brazilian
    Negroes in Brazil
Congenital arthromyodysplasia
    See Arthrogryposis
Congenital blindness
    See Blindness—Genetic aspects
Congenital deafness
    See Deafness—Genetic aspects
Congenital glaucoma
    See Glaucoma in children
Congenital heart disease
    See Heart—Abnormities and deformities
Congenital malformations
    See Deformities
Congenital nervous system diseases
    See Nervous system—Abnormities and
      deformities
Congestion of the lungs
    See Lungs—Congestion
Congestive heart failure   *(RC685.C53)*
    xx Heart—Diseases
    Heart failure
Conglomerate   *(Indirect) (QE471)*
    xx Rocks, Sedimentary
Conglomerate corporations   *(Direct)*
    (HD2756)
    sa Competition
    x Conglomerate mergers
    Corporations, Conglomerate
    Mergers, Conglomerate
    xx Competition
    Consolidation and merger of
      corporations
    Corporations
    Industrial concentration
Conglomerate mergers
    See Conglomerate corporations
Conglutination
    xx Immunity
— History
— — To 1908
— — 1908-1960
— — 1960-
— — — Pictorial works
Congo language   *(PL8401-4)*
    x Embomma language
    Fioti language
    Fyoti language
    Gimbala language
    Ki-kongo language
    Kifioti language
    Kikwango language
    KiLari language
    Kingala language
    Kituba language
    Laadi language
    Lari language
    Malemba language
    Manukutuba language
    Mbala language
    Mbochi language
    Mboma language

Congo language (PL8401-4) (Continued)
xx Bantu languages
Congo poetry (French)
See French poetry—Congo authors
Congo red
xx Azo dyes
— Therapeutic use
Congo wit and humor, Pictorial
Congregation in animals
See Herding behavior in animals
Congregational churches (BX7101-7260)
— Catechisms and creeds
— Clergy
— — Correspondence, reminiscences, etc.
— Doctrinal and controversial works
— Government
— Sermons
Congregational churches in California,
⌐Connecticut, etc.⌐ (BX7133-7228)
Congregationalism (BX7101-7260)
sa Antinomianism
Brownists
Calvinism
Covenants (Church polity)
Dissenters, Religious
New England theology
Presbyterianism
Puritans
Unitarianism
x Independency (Church polity)
xx Calvinism
Church polity
Dissenters, Religious
Puritans
Congregationalists, Finnish, ⌐German, etc.⌐
Here are entered works on Congregation-
alists living outside of their native
country who use their native language
in church services.
Congresses and conventions (Direct) (AS)
sa Conference rooms
International organization
Treaties
names of particular congresses; and
subdivision Congresses under
particular subjects
x Conferences
Conventions (Congresses)
International conferences, congresses
and conventions
xx Intellectual cooperation
International cooperation
International relations
Treaties
— Economic aspects (Direct)
— Terminology
Congresses and conventions (Cataloging)
See Cataloging of society publications
Congressional hearings
See Legislative hearings—United States
Congressional investigations
See Governmental investigations—United
States
Congressional Medal of Honor
See Medal of Honor
Congressional reform
See United States. Congress—Reform
Congressional secretaries
xx Office practice in government
Secretaries
United States. Congress—Officials and
employees
— Handbooks, manuals, etc.
Congressmen
See Legislators—United States
Congruences (Geometry) (QA608)
xx Geometry
Geometry, Differential

Mathematics
Similarity (Geometry)
Congruences and residues (QA242-4)
sa Fermat's theorem
Numbers, Theory of
x Quadratic residues
Residues
xx Algebra
Fermat's theorem
Mathematics
Numbers, Theory of
Coniagui (African people)
See Koniagui (African people)
Conic projection (Cartography)
See Conical projection (Cartography)
Conic sections (Analytic geometry, QA559;
Plane geometry, QA485)
sa Curves
Ellipse
Geometry, Analytic
Hyperbola
Parabola
xx Curves, Plane
Ellipse
Geometry, Analytic
Geometry, Plane
Mathematics
Parabola
— Problems, exercises, etc.
Conical projection (Cartography)
x Conic projection (Cartography)
xx Map-projection
Conical waves
See Head waves
Conics, Spherical (QA561)
x Spherical conics
xx Curves on surfaces
Conidia (Fungi, QK601)
Conifer seed
sa Norway spruce—Seed
x Coniferae—Seed
Coniferous seed
xx Seeds
Coniferae (Botany, QK495.C75; Fossil,
QE977; Ornamental, SB437.5.C6;
Sylviculture, SD397.C7)
sa Evergreens
individual varieties and species, e.g.
Pine, Longleaf pine, White pine
xx Evergreens
Gymnosperms
— By-products
— Diseases and pests (Indirect)
(SB608.C7)
sa names of specific diseases and pests,
e.g. Red turpentine beetle
— Fertilizers and manures (S667.C)
— Genetics
— Identification
— Juvenile literature
— Seed
See Conifer seed
Coniferous seed
See Conifer seed
Coniine
See Conine
Conine (RM666.C)
x Coniine
Conium (Pharmacy, RS165.C; Therapeutics,
RM666.C)
x Hemlock (Materia medica)
Conjecture
See Prediction (Logic)
Conjugation (Biology)
xx Reproduction
Conjunctiva (QL949; QM511)
xx Eye
— Diseases (RE310-326)

sa Conjunctivitis
Eye—Inflammation
Keratoconjunctivitis sicca
Pterygium
x Egyptian ophthalmia
Ophthalmia
xx Conjunctivitis
Eye—Diseases and defects
Eye—Inflammation
— Tumors
Conjunctivitis (RE321)
sa Conjunctiva—Diseases
xx Conjunctiva—Diseases
Eye—Diseases and defects
Eye—Inflammation
Conjunctivitis, Granular
sa Epitheliosis
x Granular lids
Lids, Granular
Trachoma
Conjunctivitis, Infantile (RJ296)
x Infantile conjunctivitis
Ophthalmia neonatorum
xx Blindness
Gonorrhea
Conjuração mineira, 1789
See Minas Gerais, Brazil—History—
Revolution, 1789
Conjuring (GV1541-1561)
Here are entered works on modern ("par-
lor") magic, legerdemain, prestidigita-
tion, etc. Works dealing with occult
science ("supernatural" arts) are en-
tered under the heading Magic.
sa Card tricks
Coin tricks
Fire-eating
Jugglers and juggling
Magic
Medicine-man
Tricks
x Legerdemain
Prestidigitation
Sleight of hand
xx Amusements
Hallucinations and illusions
Jugglers and juggling
Magic
Occult sciences
Tricks
— Apparatus and supplies
— — Catalogs (GV1561)
— Cataloging
See Cataloging of magic literature
— Early works to 1800 (GV1546)
— Juvenile literature (GV1548)
CONMIN (Computer program)
xx Mathematical optimization
Conn organ music
See Electronic organ music (Conn
registration)
Connecticut
— History (F91-100)
— — Colonial period, ca. 1600-1775
— — — Juvenile literature
— — French and Indian War, 1755-1763
(E199)
— — Revolution, 1775-1783 (E263.C5)
sa New London, Conn.—History—
Burning by the British, 1781
— — 1775-1865
— — War of 1812 (E359.5.C7)
— — Civil War, 1861-1865 (E499)
Connecting factors (Conflict of laws)
See Points of contact (Conflict of laws)
Connecting system of the heart
See Heart conduction system

Connections (Mathematics)
    xx Geometry, Differential
Connective tissues *(QM563)*
    sa Adipose tissues
        Bone
        Cartilage
        Collagen
        Elastic tissue
        Fasciae (Anatomy)
        Fibroblasts
        Ground substance (Anatomy)
        Mesenchyme
    x Areolar tissue
    xx Collagen
        Elastic tissue
        Musculoskeletal system
        Tissues
    Note under Histology
  — Aging
  — Development
    See Connective tissues—Growth
  — Diseases
    sa Cellulitis
        Collagen diseases
        Mast cell disease
  — — Genetic aspects
  — Growth
    x Connective tissues—Development
  — Transplantation
  — Tumors
    sa Chondroblastoma
Connemara pony *(SF315.2.C6)*
    xx Ponies
Connexes *(QA608)*
Conn's disease
    See Hyperaldosteronism
Connsonata organ music
    See Electronic organ music (Conn
        registration)
Conodonts *(QE899)*
Conoy Indians *(E99.C873)*
    xx Algonquian Indians
        Indians of North America
Conquest, Right of
    sa Military occupation
        Territory, National
    x Right of conquest
    xx International law
        Military occupation
        Territory, National
Conquien
    See Cooncan
Conquista (Dance)
    See Moros y Cristianos (Dance)
Conquistadors
    See America—Discovery and exploration—
        Spanish
Consanguinity *(Direct) (Consanguineous*
      marriages, HQ1026; Degeneration,
      HV4981; Statistics, HB1113.R38)
    sa Inbreeding
        Incest
        Kinship
    x Intermarriage
        Marriage—Prohibited degrees
    xx Eugenics
        Heredity
        Impediments to marriage
        Inbreeding
        Kinship
Consanguinity (Canon law)
Consanguinity (Canon law, Oriental)
    xx Canon law, Oriental
Consanguinity (Canon law, Orthodox Eastern)
Consanguinity (Hindu law)
    x Sapindaship
Consanguinity (Islamic law) *(Direct)*
Consanguinity (Jewish law)

Consanguinity (Roman law)
Conscience *(Ethics, BJ1471; Theology,*
    BV4615)
    sa Casuistry
        Free will and determinism
        Guilt
        Liberty of conscience
        Super-ego
    xx Casuistry
        Duty
        Ethics
  — Biblical teaching *(BS2545.C58)*
  — History of doctrines
Conscience, Examination of *(BX2377)*
    sa Scruples
    x Examination of conscience
        Self-examination
    xx Casuistry
        Christian ethics
        Church discipline
        Confession
        Penance
        Sin
Conscience, Manifestation of
    See Manifestation of conscience
Conscience in literature
Conscientious objectors *(Indirect)*
    (UB341-2)
    sa Pacifism
        subdivision Conscientious objectors
        under names of wars, e.g. United
        States—History—Civil War,
        1861-1865—Conscientious objectors;
        World War, 1939-1945—
        Conscientious objectors
    xx Liberty of conscience
        Military service, Compulsory
        Pacifism
        War and religion
  — Law and legislation *(Direct)*
  — Personal narratives
Conscious automata *(Q325)*
    sa Perceptrons
    x Artificial consciousness
        Biocomputers
        Electronic brains
        Intelligent machines
        Mechanical brains
        Synthetic consciousness
    xx Automata
        Bionics
        Consciousness
        Cybernetics
        Perceptrons
Consciousness *(Physiology, QP411;*
    Psychology, BF311-315)
    sa Automatism
        Belief and doubt
        Comparison (Psychology)
        Conscious automata
        Gestalt psychology
        Immanence (Philosophy)
        Individuality
        Intuition
        Intuition (Psychology)
        Knowledge, Theory of
        Panpsychism
        Personality
        Reaction-time
        Self
        Subconsciousness
    xx Apperception
        Mind and body
        Perception
        Philosophy
        Psychology
        Self
        Spirit

        Subconsciousness
Consciousness, Loss of
    See Loss of consciousness
Consciousness, Multiple
    See Personality, Disorders of
Consciousness-expanding drugs
    See Hallucinogenic drugs
Conscript labor
    See Contract labor
        Forced labor
        Service, Compulsory non-military
        World War, 1939-1945—Conscript
        labor
Conscription, Military
    See Military service, Compulsory
Consecrated bread
    See Lord's Supper—Bread
Consecration *(Christian life, BV4501)*
    sa Benediction
    xx Holiness
Consecration of bishops *(Catholic Church,*
    BX2304)
    sa Bishops
        Investiture
    x Bishops—Consecration
    xx Bishops
        Investiture
        Ordination
Consecration of cemeteries
    See Cemeteries—Consecration
Consecration of churches
    See Church dedication
Consecration of virgins *(BX2305)*
    x Virgins, Consecration of
    xx Monasticism and religious orders for
        women
Consecration programs
    See Dedication services
Consecration services
    See Dedication services
Consensus (Social sciences)
    sa Authority
        Decision-making
        Democracy
        Legitimacy of governments
        Power (Social sciences)
        Social contract
    xx Authority
        Decision-making
        Power (Social sciences)
Consent (Canon law)
Consent (Law) *(Direct)*
    sa Acquiescence (Law)
        Age of consent
        Declaration of intention
        Marriage—Parental consent
        Mistake (Law)
        Silence (Law)
    xx Declaration of intention
        Justification (Law)
Consent decrees *(Direct)*
    xx Compromise (Law)
        Equity pleading and procedure
Conservation (Psychology)
    sa Conservation of space (Psychology)
        Conservation of substance (Psychology)
    xx Judgment
        Memory
        Perception
Conservation education
    See Conservation of natural resources—
        Study and teaching
        Natural resources—Study and teaching
        and similar headings
Conservation laws (Physics)
    sa Parity nonconservation
        Symmetry (Physics)
    xx Physics

Conservation methods, Museum
    See Museum conservation methods
Conservation of art objects
    See Art objects—Conservation and
        restoration
Conservation of books
    See Books—Conservation and restoration
Conservation of bottles
    See Bottles—Conservation and restoration
Conservation of buildings
    See Architecture—Conservation and
        restoration
Conservation of energy
    See Force and energy
Conservation of energy resources
    See Energy conservation
Conservation of engravings
    See Engravings—Conservation and
        restoration
Conservation of food
    See Food conservation
Conservation of forests
    See Forest conservation
Conservation of leather work
    See Leather work—Conservation and
        restoration
Conservation of manuscripts
    See Manuscripts—Conservation and
        restoration
Conservation of marine resources
    See Marine resources conservation
Conservation of mineral resources
    See Mineral resources conservation
Conservation of monuments
    See Monuments—Preservation
Conservation of mural painting and decoration
    See Mural painting and decoration—
        Conservation and restoration
Conservation of natural monuments
    See Natural monuments
Conservation of natural resources *(Indirect)*
    (S900-949)
    sa Energy conservation
        Estuarine area conservation
        Forest conservation
        Human ecology
        Marine resources conservation
        Mineral resources conservation
        Nature conservation
        Reclamation of land
        Recycling (Waste, etc.)
        Soil conservation
        Water conservation
        Wildlife conservation
    x Conservation of resources
        Resource management
    xx Ecology
        Environmental policy
        Environmental protection
        Human ecology
        Natural resources
    — Juvenile literature
    — Religious aspects
    — Research grants *(Direct)*
    — Study and teaching *(Indirect)*
        x Conservation education
        Environmental education
        Environmental studies
    —— Audio-visual aids *(S946)*
    — Vocational guidance
Conservation of nature
    See Nature conservation
Conservation of paintings
    See Paintings—Conservation and restoration
Conservation of petroleum
    See Petroleum conservation

Conservation of photographs
    See Photographs—Conservation and
        restoration
Conservation of power resources
    See Energy conservation
Conservation of prints
    See Prints—Conservation and restoration
Conservation of resources
    See Conservation of natural resources
Conservation of sculpture
    See Sculpture—Conservation and
        restoration
Conservation of space (Psychology)
    x Space, Conservation of (Psychology)
    xx Conservation of substance (Psychology)
        Conservation (Psychology)
        Psychology
        Space-perception
Conservation of substance (Psychology)
    sa Conservation of space (Psychology)
    x Substance, Conservation of
        (Psychology)
    xx Conservation (Psychology)
Conservation of textiles
    See Textile industry and fabrics—
        Conservation and restoration
Conservation of the soil
    See Soil conservation
Conservation of water
    See Water conservation
Conservation of water-colors
    See Paintings—Conservation and restoration
Conservation of wildlife
    See Wildlife conservation
Conservationists *(Indirect) (S926)*
    sa Ecologists
Conservatism *(Direct)*
    sa Authoritarianism
    xx Political science
        Social sciences
        Sociology
    — Public opinion
Conservatism and literature
    x Literature and conservatism
    xx Literature
        Politics in literature
Conservative Judaism *(BM197.5)*
    x Judaism, Conservative
    xx Jewish sects
Conservative Party (Gt. Brit.) *(JN1129.C7)*
    sa Tories, English
    x Unionist Party (Gt. Brit.)
    xx Tories, English
    — Party work
Conservatories
    See Greenhouses
Conservatories of music *(ML3795; MT1-5)*
    Here are entered works on conservatories
    in general and also those of a particular
    country. Works dealing with the con-
    servatories of a particular city are en-
    tered under the name of the city with
    subdivision Conservatories of music.
    sa Maîtrises
    x Music conservatories
        Music—Conservatories
        Music schools
    xx Music
        Music—Instruction and study
        Schools
Conservators
    See Conservatorships
Conservatorships *(Direct)*
    sa Guardian and ward
    x Conservators
    xx Guardian and ward
Considerateness
    See Thoughtfulness

Consideration (Law) *(Direct)*
    sa Contracts, Gratuitous
        Motive (Law)
    x Causa (Civil law)
    xx Contracts
        Motive (Law)
Consideration (Roman-Dutch law)
Consignation *(Direct)*
    sa Deposits (Law)
        Escrows
    xx Contracts
        Debtor and creditor
        Deposits (Law)
        Payment
    Note under Deposits (Law)
    — Forms
Consignment sale shops *(Direct)*
    sa Swap shops
    xx Secondhand trade
        Stores, Retail
        Swap shops
Consilium principis
    xx Roman emperors
Consol navigation
    x Consolan navigation
        Sonne navigation
    xx Aeronautical radio stations
        Electronics in aeronautics
        Electronics in navigation
        Radio in navigation
Consolan navigation
    See Consol navigation
Consolation *(BV4900-4908)*
    sa Bereavement
        Peace of mind
    xx Bereavement
        Grief
        Loneliness
        Suffering
    — Early works to 1800
Consolation (Greek religion)
Consolation (Islam)
    xx Religious life (Islam)
Consolation (Judaism) *(BM729.C6)*
Consolidated income tax returns
    See Corporations—Taxation—Consolidated
        returns
Consolidated returns
    See Corporations—Taxation—Consolidated
        returns
Consolidated tax returns
    See Corporations—Taxation—Consolidated
        returns
Consolidation and merger of corporations
    (Direct)
    sa Bank mergers
        Conglomerate corporations
        Corporate reorganizations
        Industrial concentration
        Railroads—Consolidation
        Trusts, Industrial
        subdivision Consolidation *under*
        industries, e.g. Transportation—
        Consolidation
    x Amalgamation of corporations
        Corporate mergers
        Corporations—Consolidation
        Corporations—Merger
        Fusion of corporations
        Merger of corporations
    xx Corporate reorganizations
        Corporation law
        Industrial concentration
        Trusts, Industrial
    — Accounting
    — Taxation *(Direct)*
        xx Corporations—Taxation

Consolidation of land holdings *(Direct)*
 (Economics, HD1481; Law, K)
   x Amalgamation of land
    Land consolidation
    Land—Consolidation
   xx Agricultural laws and legislation
    Land tenure
    Real property
Consolidation of local governments
   See Metropolitan government
Consolidation of schools
   See Schools—Centralization
Consolidation of soil
   See Soil consolidation
Consonants
   sa Grammar, Comparative and general—
    Phonology
    subdivision Consonants *under names of
     languages and groups of languages*
   xx Phonetics
Consortium (Finance)
   See Syndicates (Finance)
Conspiracies *(Direct)* *(HV6275)*
   xx Crime and criminals
    History
    Political crimes and offenses
    Subversive activities
    Treason
Conspiracy *(Direct)*
   sa Racketeering
    Trials (Conspiracy)
   xx Criminal law
    Racketeering
    Torts
Conspiracy of Pontiac
   See Pontiac's Conspiracy, 1763-1765
Constables *(Direct)* *(HV7981)*
   sa Police, Rural
   xx Peace officers
    Police
    Police, Rural
    Process
Constance, Council of, 1414-1418 *(BX830
  1414)*
   x Council of Constance, 1414-1418
   Example under Catholic Church—History
Constance, Lake of, in literature
Constance, Treaty of, 1153
Constance, Treaty of, 1183 *(DD149.7)*
Constancy *(BJ1533.C67)*
Constant, Bloch
   See Bloch constant
Constant, Solar
   See Solar constant
Constant-choice perceptual maze test
   x CCPM test
   xx Character tests
    Maze tests
    Mental tests
Constantine, Algeria (City)
  — Siege, 1837
Constantine, Donation of
   See Donation of Constantine
Constantinople
   See Istanbul
Constantinople, Council of, 1st, 381 *(BR215)*
Constantinople, Council of, 2d, 553 *(BR230)*
Constantinopolitan Creed *(BT1003.C6)*
   x Nicene-Constantinopolitan Creed
   xx Creeds
    Nicene Creed
Constants, Astronomical
   See Astronomical constants
Constants, Ionization
   See Ionization constants
Constellation (Transport planes)
   x Lockheed Constellation (Transport
    planes)

   xx Transport planes
Constellations *(QB802; Popular works,
  QB63)*
   sa Stars
    names of constellations, e.g. Ursa Major
   xx Astronomy
    Stars
  — Juvenile literature
Constipation *(RC861)*
   sa Auto-intoxication
    Digestion
    Dyspepsia
   xx Intestines—Diseases
  — Homeopathic treatment *(RX336.C)*
Constituent power *(Direct)*
   xx Constitutional law
    Legislative power
Constitution, Human
   See Man—Constitution
Constitution (Philosophy)
   xx Philosophy
Constitution of matter
   See Matter—Constitution
Constitutional amendments
   sa Constitutions, State—Amendments
    subdivision Amendments *under
     constitutions of individual countries,
     e.g.* United States. Constitution—
     Amendments
   x Amendments, Constitutional
    Constitutions—Amendments
   xx Constitutional law
Constitutional conventions *(Direct)*
  *(General, JF71-99; United States,
  JK301)*
   x Conventions, Constitutional
  — Rules and practice *(Direct)*
Constitutional diseases *(RC251-320; Diseases
  of children, RJ390-399)*
   sa Man—Constitution
   x Diseases, Constitutional
   xx Diathesis
  — Dosimetric treatment
    xx Medicine, Dosimetric
  — Research *(Direct)*
Constitutional history *(J-JQ)*
   sa Democracy
    Monarchy
    Political science
    Representative government and
     representation
    Republics
    subdivision Constitutional history *under
     names of countries, states, etc., e.g.*
     Great Britain—Constitutional
     history; New York (State)—
     Constitutional history
   x Constitutional history, Modern
    Constitutional law—History
    History, Constitutional
   xx Constitutions
    History
    Political science
Constitutional history, Ancient
Constitutional history, Medieval
Constitutional history, Modern
   See Constitutional history
Constitutional law *(J-JQ)*
   sa Act of state
    Administrative law
    Amparo (Writ)
    Citizenship
    Civil rights
    Civil supremacy over the military
    Constituent power
    Constitutional amendments
    De facto doctrine
    Delegation of powers

    Democracy
    Due process of law
    Eminent domain
    Equality before the law
    Exclusive and concurrent legislative
     powers
    Executive power
    Federal government
    Federal-state controversies
    Government liability
    Habeas corpus
    Incompatibility of offices
    Injunctions
    International and municipal law
    Interstate controversies
    Judicial power
    Judicial review
    Law—Interpretation and construction
    Legislation
    Legislative bodies
    Legislative power
    Martial law
    Monarchy
    Natural law
    People (Constitutional law)
    Police power
    Political rights
    Privileges and immunities
    Proportional representation
    Public domain
    Referendum
    Representative government and
     representation
    Republics
    Retroactive laws
    Rule of law
    Separation of powers
    Sovereignty
    Suffrage
    Taxing power
    Treaty-making power
    Vested rights
    Veto
    War and emergency powers
    subdivision Constitutional law *under
     names of countries, e.g.* United
     States—Constitutional law
   x Constitutional limitations
    Law, Constitutional
    Limitations, Constitutional
   xx Administrative law
    Constitutions
    Political science
    Public law
   Example under Law
  — Cases
    sa subdivision Consitutional law—Cases
     under names of countries, e.g.
     United States—Constitutional law
     —Cases
  — Compends
  — Digests
    sa subdivision Constitutional law—
     Digests *under names of countries,
     e.g.* United States—Constitutional
     law—Digests
  — History
    See Constitutional history
  — Interpretation and construction
    sa Implied powers (Constitutional law)
     subdivision Constitutional law—
      Interpretation and construction
      under names of countries
  — Terms and phrases
    Example under Legal maxims
Constitutional law (Islamic law)
Constitutional limitations
   See Constitutional law

Constitutional limitations *(Continued)*
　subdivision Constitutional law *under*
　　names of countries
Constitutions *(J-JQ)*
　sa Constitutional history
　　Constitutional law
　　Preambles (Law)
　　Representative government and
　　　representation
　　subheading Constitution *under names*
　　　of countries, states, etc., e.g. United
　　　States. Constitution
　xx Political science
　　Representative government and
　　　representation
　— Amendments
　　See Constitutional amendments
Constitutions, State *(Direct) (JK18-19;*
　　JK2413-2428)
　sa subheading Constitution *under names*
　　of states, e.g. Massachusetts.
　　Constitution
　x State constitutions
　xx Political science
　　State governments
　　Statehood (American politics)
　— Amendments
　　xx Constitutional amendments
　— Sources
Constitutum possessorium
　xx Acquisition of property
　　Fiducia
　　Possession (Law)
　　Security (Law)
Construct state (Grammar)
　See subdivision Noun *under names of*
　　languages and groups of languages
Construction
　See Architecture
　　Building
　　Engineering
Construction, Concrete
　See Concrete construction
Construction, House
　See House construction
Construction, Lightweight
　See Lightweight construction
Construction, Modular
　See Modular construction
Construction, Plywood
　See Plywood construction
Construction, Prestressed
　See Prestressed construction
Construction, Soil-cement
　See Soil-cement construction
Construction, Welded steel
　See Welded steel structures
Construction (Philosophy)
　xx Philosophy
Construction and interpretation (Law)
　See Law—Interpretation and construction
Construction and interpretation of statutes
　See Law—Interpretation and construction
Construction block principle
　See Unit construction
Construction camps
　See Labor camps
Construction equipment *(Direct) (TH900)*
　sa Boring machinery
　　Building—Tools and implements
　　Earthmoving machinery
　　Excavating machinery
　　Hoisting machinery
　　Public works equipment
　　Pumping machinery
　　Road machinery
　　Scrapers (Earthmoving machinery)
　x Builders' plant

　　Building machinery
　　Construction industry—Equipment and
　　　supplies
　　Construction machinery
　xx Building
　　Building—Tools and implements
　　Civil engineering
　　Earthmoving machinery
　　Machinery
　— Classification
　— Cold weather operation
　— Cost of operation
　— Costs
　— Design and construction
　— Drawing
　　See Construction equipment—
　　　Drawings
　— Drawings
　　x Construction equipment—Drawing
　　xx Mechanical drawing
　— Electric driving
　— Electric equipment
　— — Maintenance and repair
　— Examinations, questions, etc.
　— Fuel
　— Hydraulic drive
　— Juvenile literature
　— Lubrication
　— Maintenance and repair
　　x Construction equipment—Repairing
　— — Costs
　— — Laboratory manuals *(TH900)*
　— — Production standards
　— Noise
　— Prices
　— Problems, exercises, etc. *(TH900)*
　— Production standards
　— Rate-books
　— Repairing
　　See Construction equipment—
　　　Maintenance and repair
　— Safety measures
　— Standards *(Direct)*
　— Testing
　— Trade and manufacture *(Direct)*
　— Transmission devices
　　xx Gearing
　— Vibration
　— Welding
Construction equipment operators
　See Construction machinery operators
Construction hinges (Concrete)
　See Concrete construction—Hinges
Construction industry *(Direct)*
　　Here are entered works dealing compre-
　　hensively with the construction busi-
　　ness, including finance, planning, man-
　　agement, and skills. Works on types of
　　labor involved are entered under the
　　heading Building trades. Works on the
　　process of construction are entered un-
　　der Building.
　sa Building
　　Building as a profession
　　Building materials industry
　　Building trades
　　Contractors' operations
　　Modular construction industry
　　Wrecking
　x Building industry
　xx Building
　　Building trades
Example under reference from Industries
Note under Building
　— Accidents
　　See Building—Accidents
　— Accounting
　　x Building—Accounting

　　Building trades—Accounting
　　Contractors' operations—Accounting
　— Auditing and inspection
　— Automation
　— Collective bargaining
　　See Collective bargaining—
　　　Construction industry
　— Collective labor agreements
　　See Collective labor agreements—
　　　Construction industry
　— Communication systems
　　xx Telecommunication
　— Contracts and specifications
　　See Building—Contracts and
　　　specifications
　— Costs
　— Employees
　　sa Building trades
　　　Construction workers
　— Equipment and supplies
　　See Construction equipment
　— Estimates
　　See Building—Estimates
　— Finance
　— Forms, blanks, etc.
　— Hygienic aspects *(Direct)*
　— Information services
　— Labor productivity
　— Law and legislation *(Direct)*
　　xx Building laws
　— Management
　　sa Building—Superintendence
　　　Industrialized building
　　x Building—Management
　— Mathematical models
　— Noise control
　— Prices *(Direct)*
　— Problems, exercises, etc.
　— Production standards
　— Public opinion
　— Safety measures
　　See Building—Safety measures
　— Safety regulations *(Direct)*
　— Seasonal variations
　— Standards
　— Statistical methods
　— Statistical services
　— Taxation *(Direct)*
　— Underdeveloped areas
　　See Underdeveloped areas—
　　　Construction industry
　— Vocational guidance
　　See Building trades—Vocational
　　　guidance
Construction joints (Concrete)
　See Concrete construction—Joints
Construction machinery
　See Construction equipment
Construction machinery operators
　x Building machinery operators
　　Construction equipment operators
　xx Construction workers
Construction of roads
　See Road construction
Construction prices
　See Building—Prices
Construction workers *(Direct)*
　　Here are entered works on all types of
　　labor employed in building construc-
　　tion, including skilled and unskilled
　　workers. Works limited to the skilled
　　trades employed in building construc-
　　tion, *e.g.* carpentry, bricklaying, are
　　entered under Building trades.
　sa Building trades
　　Collective labor agreements—
　　　Construction industry
　　Construction machinery operators

Strikes and lockouts—Construction
workers
Trade-unions—Construction workers
Wages—Construction workers
xx Building trades
Construction industry—Employees
Note under Building trades
— Diseases and hygiene
— Retirement
Constructive mathematics
sa Intuitionistic mathematics
x Mathematics, Constructive
xx Logic, Symbolic and mathematical
Constructivism (Architecture) *(Direct)*
xx Architecture, Modern—20th century
Constructivism (Art) *(Direct)*
sa Minimal sculpture
xx Art, Modern—20th century
Concrete art
Constructivism (Russian literature)
xx Futurism
Russian literature—20th century—
History and criticism
Russian poetry—20th century—History
and criticism
Consubstantiation
See Lord's Supper—Real presence
Consuetudo (Roman law)
See Customary law (Roman law)
Consul automobile
xx Ford automobile
Consular documents *(HF5773.C7)*
sa Bills of lading
Certificates of origin
Consular invoices
xx Commercial documents
Consular law
Shipment of goods
Consular fees
See Fees, Consular
Consular invoices
x Invoices, Consular
xx Consular documents
Invoices
Consular jurisdiction *(JX1698)*
sa Diplomatic privileges and immunities
particular cases, e.g. Emilio Rondanini
(Ship)
x Jurisdiction, Consular
xx Consular law
Consuls
Courts
Diplomatic and consular service
Exterritoriality
Consular law *(JX1625-1894)*
Here are entered works on the legal status
of foreign consuls and the legal aspects
of consular service in general. Works
on the law governing the consular service of an individual country are entered under the name of that country
with the subdivision Diplomatic and
consular service.
sa Consular documents
Consular jurisdiction
x Law, Consular
xx Consuls
Diplomatic and consular service
International law
— Codification

Consular reports *(Indirect)* *(HC1-8)*
Sets of reports, with their indexes, are en-
tered under the above heading with
country subdivision, and also under
name of country, subdivisions Com-
merce and Manufactures, *e.g.* 1. Consular reports—United States. 2. United
States—Commerce. 3. United States—
Manufactures.
x Reports, Consular
xx Diplomatic and consular service
Manufactures
— United States
x United States—Consular reports
Note under Consular reports
Consular service
See Diplomatic and consular service
Consulates
See Diplomatic and consular service
Consuls *(JX1625-1894)*
sa Consular jurisdiction
Consular law
subdivision Diplomatic and consular
service *under names of countries*
xx Diplomatic and consular service
Diplomats
International law
International relations
Consuls, Roman *(DG83.5.C7)*
x Roman consuls
Consultants, Business
See Business consultants
Consultants, Curriculum
See Curriculum consultants
Consultants, Educational
See Educational consultants
Consultants, Engineering
See Consulting engineers
Consultants, Government
See Government consultants
Consultants, Library
See Library consultants
Consultants, Medical
See Medical consultants
Consultants, Public relations
See Public relations consultants
Consultants, Social insurance
See Social insurance consultants
Consultation, Medical
See Medical consultation
Consultation, Psychiatric
See Psychiatric consultation
Consulting engineers *(Direct)*
sa Business consultants
particular types of engineers, e.g.
Mining engineers
x Consultants, Engineering
xx Engineers
— Fees
— Salaries, pensions, etc. *(Direct)*
Consultors, Diocesan *(Canon law,*
BX1939.C73)
x Diocesan consultors
xx Bishops (Canon law)
Dioceses (Canon law)
Consumer advertising
See Advertising
Consumer behavior
See Consumers
Consumer complaints
See Complaints (Retail trade)

Consumer credit *(Direct)*
Here are entered works on the economic
aspects and methods of instalment or
deferred-payment financing in gen-
eral. Works dealing with specific meth-
ods of consumer credit are entered un-
der Loans, Personal; Instalment plan;
etc.
sa Charge account bank plans
Credit cards
Finance charges
Instalment plan
Insurance, Group creditors
Loans, Personal
x Credit, Consumer
xx Banks and banking
Credit
Finance, Personal
— Anecdotes, facetiae, satire, etc.
— Forms
— Law and legislation *(Direct)*
xx Consumer protection—Law and
legislation
— Mathematical models
Consumer durable goods
See Durable goods, Consumer
Consumer education *(TX335)*
Here are entered works on the selection
and most efficient use of consumer
goods and services, as well as works on
means and methods of educating the
consumer.
sa Consumers
Consumption (Economics)
Home economics
Marketing (Home economics)
Shopping
Unit pricing
specific consumer problems, e.g. Food
adulteration and inspection;
Instalment plan; Labels
x Buyers' guides
Shoppers' guides
xx Consumer protection
Consumers
Consumers' leagues
Consumption (Economics)
Home economics
Marketing (Home economics)
Purchasing
Rationing, Consumer
Shopping
Notes under Consumers; Consumption (Eco-
nomics); Marketing (Home econom-
ics)
— Juvenile literature
— Teacher training
Consumer loans
See Loans, Personal
Consumer organizations
See Consumer panels
Cooperative societies
Consumer panels *(Direct)*
x Consumer organizations
xx Consumers
Consumers' preferences
Market surveys
Marketing research
Consumer price index
See Cost and standard of living
Consumer protection *(Direct)*
Here are entered works dealing collec-
tively with various governmental and
private activities which guard the con-
suming public against dangers to its
health, safety, or economic well-being.
sa Product safety
Quality of products

427

Consumer protection *(Direct)*
(Continued)
   Banks and banking—Government
    guaranty of deposits; Better-business
    bureaus; Consumer eudcation; Durgs
    —Adulteration and analysis; Food
    adulteration and inspection;
    Insurance—State supervision; *and*
    similar headings
 xx Consumers
 — Law and legislation *(Direct)*
  sa Consumer credit—Law and
   legislation
   Drugs—Laws and legislation
   Food law and legislation
   Labels—Law and legislation
   Packaging—Law and legislation
   Trade regulation
  xx Trade regulation
 — — Popular works
 — Public opinion
 — Vocational guidance
Consumer protection (Jewish law)
Consumer rationing
 See Rationing, Consumer
Consumers *(Direct)*
  Here are entered works on consumer
   behavior. Consumers' guides are en-
   tered under Consumer education.
   Works on the economic theory of con-
   sumption are entered under Consump-
   tion (Economics)
 sa Aged as consumers
  Bantus as consumers
  Complaints (Retail trade)
  Consumer education
  Consumer panels
  Consumer protection
  Consumers' leagues
  Consumers' preferences
  Consumption (Economics)
  Consumption (Economics)—Surveys
  Cooperation
  Durable goods, Consumer
  Farmers as consumers
  Men consumers
  Negroes as consumers
  Spanish Americans as consumers
  Women as consumers
  Youth as consumers
 x Consumer behavior
 xx Consumer education
  Consumers' leagues
  Marketing
  Marketing (Home economics)
  Purchasing
  Shopping
 Notes under Consumption (Economics); Mar-
  keting (Home economics)
 — Juvenile literature
 — Mathematical models
 — Public opinion
Consumers' goods
 See Manufactures
Consumers' leagues *(Cooperation,*
  HD3271-3570; Labor, HD6951-7)
  Here are entered works on the organiza-
   tion of retail purchasers seeking to im-
   prove working conditions. Consumers'
   cooperatives and similar organiza-
   tions, concerned primarily with the
   problem of distribution, are entered
   under Cooperative societies.
 sa Boycott
  Consumer education
  Consumers
  Sweating system
 xx Consumers
  Cooperative societies

  Labor and laboring classes
  Sweating system
  Welfare work in industry
Consumers' preferences *(Direct)*
 sa Consumer panels
 xx Consumers
  Market surveys
Consumption
 See Tuberculosis
Consumption (Economics) *(Direct)*
  (HB801-845)
  Works designed to inform and educate
   the consumer are entered under the
   heading Consumer education. Works
   on consumer behavior are entered un-
   der the heading Consumers.
 sa Consumer education
  Marketing
  Prices
  Purchasing power
  Rationing, Consumer
  Social credit
  Substitution (Economics)
  Supply and demand
 xx Consumer education
  Consumers
  Economics
  Income
  Luxury
  Supply and demand
  Wealth
 Notes under Consumers; Consumption (Eco-
  nomics)—Surveys
 — Juvenile literature
 — Mathematical models
 — Surveys
   Here are entered works on the tech-
    niques employed. Surveys of con-
    sumption in particular areas are en-
    tered under Consumption (Eco-
    nomics) with local subdivision.
  sa Cost and standard of living
   Market surveys
  xx Consumers
 — Taxation
   See Taxation of articles of
    consumption
Consumption coagulopathy
 See Disseminated intravascular coagulation
Consumptive use
 See Evapotranspiration
Contact angle *(QC183)*
 xx Fluid mechanics
  Surface chemistry
Contact dermatitis *(RC592)*
 x Dermatitis, Contact
  Dermatitis venenata
 xx Allergy
  Skin—Inflammation
Contact lenses *(RE977.C6)*
 x Lenses, Contact
 xx Eyeglasses
  Lenses
 — Patents
Contact prints
 See Blue-prints
  Lumiprints
Contact transformations *(QA385)*
 x Tangential transformations
  Transformations, Contact
  Transformations, Tangential
 xx Transformations (Mathematics)
Contact vernaculars
 See Languages, Mixed
Contactors, Electric
 See Electric contactors
Contacts, Electric
 See Electric contacts

Contaflex camera
 xx Zeiss cameras
Contagion and contagious diseases
 See Communicable diseases
Contagious abortion
 See Brucellosis in cattle
Contagious diseases
 See Communicable diseases
Contagious ecthyma *(Indirect)* *(SF969.C)*
 x Contagious pustular stomatitis
  Ecthyma, Contagious
  Pustular stomatitis, Contagious
  Scabby mouth
  Sore mouth
 xx Virus diseases
Contagious pustular stomatitis
 See Contagious ecthyma
Container cargo
 See Unitized cargo systems
Container gardening *(SB418)*
 sa Glass gardens
  Hanging plants
  House plants
 x Pot plant gardening
 xx Gardening
Container industry *(Direct)*
 sa Paper box industry
  Wages—Container industry
 xx Package goods industry
  Packaging
  Packing for shipment
 — Labor productivity
 — Sanitation
Container-ship operations
 See Unitized cargo systems
Container ships
 xx Containerization
  Freighters
  Merchant ships
 — Registers *(Direct)*
Containerization *(TA1215)*
 sa Container ships
  Unitized cargo systems
 x Intermodal transportation
 xx Containers
  Freight and freightage
 — Juvenile literature
Containers *(TS2301.C8)*
 sa Bagging
  Barrels
  Baskets
  Boxes
  Containerization
  Crates
  Drums (Containers)
  Flowerpots
  Food containers
  Gas cylinders
  Glass candy containers
  Glass containers
  Incense burners and containers
  Packaging
  Paper bags
  Paper containers
  Parfleches
  Plastic containers
  Schoolbags
  Sealing (Technology)
  Tin cans
  Tin containers
  subdivision Containers *under subjects,*
   e.g. Milk—Containers
 x Cans
 xx Packaging
  Packing for shipment
 — Accounting
 — Juvenile literature
 — Law and legislation *(Direct)*

— Standards
— Tariff
    See Duty-free importation of
        containers
— Testing
Containers, Paper
  See Paper containers
Containers, Pressurized
  See Pressure packaging
     Pressure vessels
Contaminants, Organic water
  See Organic water pollutants
Contaminated food
  See Food contamination
Contamination, Milk
  See Milk contamination
Contamination (Technology)
  sa Clean rooms
     Cleaning
     Cleaning machinery and appliances
     Culture contamination (Biology)
     Decontamination (from gases,
       chemicals, etc.)
     Dust control
     Filters and filtration
     Food contamination
     Fume control
     Pollution
     Protective coverings
     Radioactive decontamination
     Sterilization
  x Impurities (Technology)
     Industrial contamination
     Particulate contamination in industry
  xx Aerosols
     Dust
     Factory sanitation
Contamination of biological cultures and
    culture media
  See Culture contamination (Biology)
Contamination of environment
  See Pollution
Contango and backwardation *(Direct)*
  x Backwardation
     Carry-over business
     Continuation business
  xx Contracts, Aleatory
     Speculation
     Stock-exchange
Contarex camera
  xx Single-lens reflex cameras
Contax camera
  xx Zeiss cameras
Contemplation *(BV5091.C7)*
  sa Devotion
     Meditation
     Recollection (Theology)
  xx Devotion
     Meditation
     Mystical union
     Mysticism
     Prayer
Contemplation (Hinduism)
  See Samadhi
Contemplation (Jainism)
  See Samadhi (Jainism)
Contemplative orders *(Men, BX2810;*
    Women, BX4230)
  xx Monasticism and religious orders
Contemporaneity
  See Contemporary, The
Contemporary, The *(BD640)*
  x Contemporaneity
  xx Time
Contemporary art
  See Art, Modern—20th century
Contemporary painting
  See Painting, Modern—20th century

Contemporary sculpture
  See Sculpture, Modern—20th century
Contempt of Congress
  See Contempt of legislative bodies—United
    States
Contempt of court *(Direct) (United States,*
    JK1543)
  sa Contumacy
     Outlawry
  x Court, Contempt of
  xx Conduct of court proceedings
     Courts
     Crime and the press
     Criminal law
     Newspaper court reporting
Contempt of legislative bodies *(Direct)*
  sa Trials (Contempt of legislative bodies)
  — United States
    x Contempt of Congress
Contempt of the world
  See Asceticism
Content-addressed storage
  See Associative storage
Content analysis (Communication) *(P93)*
     Here are entered works dealing with the
     methods of interpreting and summa-
     rizing the essential points of any kind
     of communication, oral, written, or
     printed. Works dealing with such sum-
     maries in individual subject fields are
     entered under the subject, *e.g.* a con-
     tent analysis of American periodicals
     under American periodicals.
  sa Abstracting
     Subject cataloging
  x Analysis of content (Communication)
     Communication—Content analysis
     Subject analysis
  xx Communication—Methodology
     Communications research
Contentiousness
  See Quarreling
Contentment *(Ethics, BJ1533.C7; Theology,*
    BV4647.C7)
  sa Cheerfulness
     Happiness
  x Gladness
  xx Conduct of life
     Ethics
     Happiness
  — Quotations, maxims, etc.
Contested elections *(JF1083)*
     Here are entered only general works. Col-
     lections confined to a particular coun-
     try or state, or works dealing with a
     single case, are entered under the legis-
     lative body of that country or state,
     with subdivision Contested elections,
     e.g. United States. Congress.
     House—Contested elections
  x Elections, Contested
Contests, Prize, in advertising
  See Prize contests in advertising
Contextual ethics
  See Situation ethics
Contiguous zones (Maritime law) *(Direct)*
    (JX4144)
  sa Territorial waters
  x High seas, Jurisdiction over
  xx Maritime law
     Territorial waters
Continental drift
  sa Gondwana (Geology)
     Paleomagnetism
     Plate tectonics
     Tethys (Paleogeography)
  x Drift, Continental
     Drifting of continents

  xx Continents
     Gondwana (Geology)
     Paleogeography
     Paleogeophysics
     Paleomagnetism
     Plate tectonics
     Tethys (Paleogeography)
  — Juvenile literature
Continental margins *(Direct) (GC84-84.2)*
  sa Continental shelf
  x Margins, Continental
  xx Continents
Continental money
  See Money—United States—History—
    Colonial period, ca. 1600-1775
Continental shelf
  sa Territorial waters
  xx Boundaries
     Continental margins
     Ocean bottom (Maritime law)
     Submerged lands
     Territorial waters
  — Economic aspects *(Direct)*
    xx Marine resources
  — Juvenile literature
Continental system of Napoleon *(HF1532;*
    HF1543; etc.)
  sa Orders in council
  x Napoleon, Continental system of
  xx Blockade
     France—History—Consulate and
      Empire, 1799-1815
     Orders in council
Continents *(GB423)*
  sa Continental drift
     Continental margins
  xx Geology
     Geophysics
     Physical geography
  — Juvenile literature
Contingent fees
  See Lawyers—Fees
Contingent remainders
  See Remainders (Estates)
Contingentia futura (Logic)
  See Future contingents (Logic)
Contingents, Future (Logic)
  See Future contingents (Logic)
Continuation, Analytic
  See Analytic continuation
Continuation business
  See Contango and backwardation
Continuation schools
  See Evening and continuation schools
Continued fractions
  See Fractions, Continued
Continuing education centers *(Direct)*
  x Education centers, Continuing
  xx Adult education
     Evening and continuation schools
     Universities and colleges—Graduate
      work
Continuing legal education
  See Law—Study and teaching (Continuing
    education)
Continuity *(Mathematics, QA9; Philosophy,*
    B105.C5; Physics, QC6)
  x Continuum
  xx Mathematics—Philosophy
Continuity of the church
  — Anglican Communion *(BX5056)*
    sa Anglican orders
    x Anglican Communion—Continuity
     Church of England—Continuity
Continuo
  See *Continuo* used as part of the
    specification of medium in headings,
    e.g.

Continuo and bassoon music
   See Bassoon and continuo music
Continuous bridges
   See Bridges, Continuous
Continuous casting
   x Casting, Continuous
   xx Founding
      Metal castings
   — Patents
   — Safety measures
Continuous degrees, Doctrine of
   See Degrees, Doctrine of
Continuous functions
   See Functions, Continuous
Continuous girders
   See Girders, Continuous
Continuous groups
   See Groups, Continuous
Continuous kilns
   See Tunnel kilns
Continuous rails (Railroads)
   See Railroads—Continuous rails
Continuous voyages (International law)
      (JX5234)
   sa Contraband of war
      Rule of 1756 (International law)
   x Voyages, Continuous (International
      law)
   xx Blockade
      Contraband of war
      Neutral trade with belligerents
      Prize law
      War, Maritime (International law)
Continuum
   See Continuity
Continuum mechanics *(QA808.2)*
   sa Elastic solids
      Field theory (Physics)
      Fluid mechanics
      Magnetohydrodynamics
      Sound
      Thermoelasticity
      Viscoelasticity
   x Mechanics of continua
   xx Deformations (Mechanics)
      Elasticity
      Field theory (Physics)
      Mechanics, Analytic
   — Problems, exercises, etc.
Continuum physics
   See Field theory (Physics)
Contorniates *(CJ5665)*
Contortae
   x Gentianales
   xx Dicotyledons
Contortion
   See Acrobats and acrobatism
Contour farming
   xx Soil conservation
      Tillage
Contour lines (Cartography)
   See Contours (Cartography)
Contours (Cartography)
   x Contour lines (Cartography)
      Isohypse
      Map contours
   xx Altitudes
      Cartography
      Topographic maps
Contraband of war *(JX5231-2)*
   sa Continuous voyages (International law)
      Navicert system
      Neutral trade with belligerents
      Trent Affair, Nov. 8, 1861
      Unneutral service
   x European War, 1914-1918—Contraband
      of war

      Requisitions (of neutral vessels and
         cargoes)
      Ships, Requisition of
   xx Blockade
      Commerce
      Continuous voyages (International law)
      Jurisdiction over ships at sea
      Neutral trade with belligerents
      Neutrality
      Prize law
      Search, Right of
      Seizure of vessels and cargoes
      Unneutral service
      War, Maritime (International law)
Contraband trade
   See Smuggling
Contraception
   See Birth control
      Conception—Prevention
Contraceptives
   sa Condoms
      Diaphragms, Vaginal
      Intrauterine contraceptives
      Oral contraceptives
   xx Conception—Prevention
Contraceptives, Oral
   See Oral contraceptives
Contract, Form of
   See Form of contract
Contract, Freedom of
   See Liberty of contract
Contract, Liberty of
   See Liberty of contract
Contract-acceptance trials of ships
   See Ship trials
Contract bridge *(GV1282.3)*
   sa Chicago bridge (Game)
      Duplicate contract bridge
      Five-suit bridge
      Ghoulie
      Squeeze (Contract bridge)
      Three-handed bridge
      World contract bridge championship
   xx Auction bridge
      Bridge whist
   — Anecdotes, facetiae, satire, etc.
   — Collections of games
   — Programmed instruction
Contract clause (United States. Constitution)
   xx Exclusive and concurrent legislative
      powers—United States
      United States—Constitutional law
Contract labor *(Indirect) (HD4871-5)*
   sa Indentured servants
      Padrone system
      Peonage
      Service, Compulsory non-military
      Slavery
      Chinese in Brazil, [Guyana, South
         Africa, etc.]
   x Conscript labor
   xx Forced labor
      Labor and laboring classes
      Labor laws and legislation, Colonial
      Native labor
      Padrone system
      Peonage
      Service, Compulsory non-military
      Slave labor
Contract penuchle *(GV1295.P6)*
Contract research
   See Research and development contracts
      Research, Industrial

Contract system (Labor) *(Direct)*
   Here are entered works on the employment, by one entrepreneur, of laborers
   under contract with another entrepreneur or contractor, and on the lending of labor forces by one employer to
   another. Works on the private employment of convicts are entered under the
   heading Convict labor.
   sa Convict labor
   xx Labor contract
Contractile vacuole
   xx Contractility (Biology)
Contractility (Biology)
   sa Cells—Motility
      Contractile vacuole
      Muscle contraction
      Muscle—Motility
   xx Cells—Motility
      Muscle—Motility
Contraction-crack polygons
   See Ice-wedge polygons
Contraction of concrete
   See Concrete—Expansion and contraction
Contractions
   See Abbreviations
      Ciphers
      Paleography
Contractions (Topology)
   xx Topological spaces
      Topology
Contractors *(Direct) (T12; TA12-13;*
      TH12-13)
   sa Electric contracting
      Labor contractors
      Taxation of public contractors
   — Insurance requirements
      x Contractors' insurance
         Insurance, Contractors'
Contractors, Independent
   See Independent contractors
Contractors, Labor
   See Labor contractors
Contractors' insurance
   See Contractors—Insurance requirements
Contractors' operations *(TA201-210)*
   xx Building
      Construction industry
   — Accounting
      See Construction industry—
         Accounting
Contracts *(Direct) (Commercial law,*
      HF1253-5; Subcontracting,
      HD2381-5)
   sa Accessory obligations
      Accident (Casus fortuitus)
      Aestimatum
      Agency (Law)
      Air charter contracts
      Artists' contracts
      Authentication
      Authors and publishers
      Bailments
      Betrothal
      Bills of lading
      Breach of contract
      Compromise (Law)
      Conditions (Law)
      Confusion of rights
      Consideration (Law)
      Consignation
      Contracts, Agricultural
      Contracts, Aleatory
      Contracts for work and labor
      Contracts, Gratuitous
      Contracts, Joint and several
      Contracts, Maritime
      Contracts, Preliminary

Contracts to make wills
Cost-plus contracts
Covenants
Debtor and creditor
Declaratory acts
Deeds
Delegation (Civil law)
Delivery of goods (Law)
Discharge of contracts
Earnest
Escalator clause
Extinguishment of debts
Form of contract
Gold clause
Illegal contracts
Immoral contracts
Impossibility of performance
Instalment contracts
Insurance policies
Juristic acts
Labor contract
Leases
Legalization
Lesion (Law)
Liability (Law)
Liberty of contract
Mandate (Contract)
Master and servant
Maturities
Mortgages
Natural obligations
Negotiable instruments
Negotiorum gestio
Novation
Offer and acceptance
Option (Contract)
Partnership
Penalties, Contractual
Performance contracts
Performance (Law)
Pledges (Law)
Pre-emption
Priorities of claims and liens
Public contracts
Quasi contracts
Real contracts (Civil law)
Rebus sic stantibus clause
Reformation of instruments
Rescission (Law)
Research and development contracts
Resolution (Civil law)
Restitutio in integrum
Reward (Law)
Sales
Simulation (Civil law)
Specific performance
Standardized terms of contract
Third parties (Law)
Undue influence
Unjust enrichment
Valuta clause
Vis major (Civil law)
    subdivision Contracts and specifications
      under particular subjects, e.g.
      Building—Contracts and
      specifications; Engineering—
      Contracts and specifications
 x Agreements
   Contractual limitations
   Limitations, Contractual
xx Commercial law
   Juristic acts
   Liberty of contract
   Obligations (Law)
Example under Law
Note under Debt
— Conflict of laws
   See Conflict of laws—Contracts

— Examinations, questions, etc.
— Forms
  xx Forms (Law)
— Interpretation and construction
— Programmed instruction
Contracts, Agricultural *(Direct)*
 sa Agriculture, Cooperative
   Farm tenancy
   Métayer system
 x Agricultural contracts
 xx Agricultural laws and legislation
   Contracts
   Land tenure—Law
Contracts, Aleatory *(Direct)*
 sa Annuities
   Contango and backwardation
   Gambling
   Insurance law
   Speculation
   Wagers
 x Aleatory contracts
 xx Contracts
   Speculation
Contracts, Aleatory (Jewish law)
Contracts, Artists'
 See Artists' contracts
Contracts, Government
 See Public contracts
Contracts, Gratuitous *(Direct)*
 sa Fraudulent conveyances
   Gifts
 x Gratuitous contracts
 xx Consideration (Law)
   Contracts
Contracts, Gratuitous (Roman law)
Contracts, Illegal
 See Illegal contracts
Contracts, Immoral
 See Immoral contracts
Contracts, Insurance
 See Insurance policies
Contracts, Joint and several *(Direct)*
 x Joint and several contracts
 xx Contracts
   Correality and solidarity
Contracts, Letting of *(Direct) (Competitive*
   system, HD2365; Public contracts,
   HD3858-3860)
 sa Subcontracting
 x Bidding, Competitive
   Competitive bidding
   Letting of contracts
 xx Building—Contracts and specifications
   Public works
— Cases
—— Digests
    See Contracts, Letting of—Digests
— Digests
  x Contracts, Letting of—Cases—
    Digests
Contracts, Maritime *(Direct)*
 sa Average (Maritime law)
   Bills of lading
   Bottomry and respondentia
   C.I.F. clause
   Carriers
   Charter-parties
   Export sales
   F.O.B. clause
   Freight and freightage
   Insurance, Marine
   Jettison
   Liens
   Ocean freight forwarders
   Pilots and pilotage
   Salvage
 x Maritime contracts
 xx Carriers

   Commercial law
   Contracts
   Maritime law
   Shipping
Contracts, Preliminary *(Direct)*
 x Preliminary agreements
   Preliminary contracts
 xx Contracts
Contracts, Public
 See Public contracts
Contracts, Real
 See Real contracts (Civil law)
Contracts, Revalorization of
 See Revalorization of debts
Contracts, Standard
 See Standardized terms of contract
Contracts, Uniform
 See Standardized terms of contract
Contracts (Canon law)
Contracts (Frankish law)
 xx Law, Frankish
Contracts (Germanic law)
Contracts (Greek law)
Contracts (Hindu law)
 sa Benami transactions
Contracts (International law)
   Here are entered works on international
    law dealing with private contractual
    obligations. Works on obligations be-
    tween states are entered under the
    heading International obligations.
    Works on contracts in private interna-
    tional law are entered under the head-
    ing Conflict of laws—Contracts.
 sa Conflict of laws—Contracts
 x Contracts and peace treaties
   Peace treaties and contracts
 xx Conflict of laws—Contracts
   International and municipal law
Contracts (Islamic law)
 sa Option (Contract law, Islamic)
Contracts (Jewish law)
 sa Deeds, Jewish
 Example under Jewish law
Contracts (Roman-Dutch law)
 Example under Roman-Dutch law
Contracts (Roman law)
 sa Mandate (Contract law, Roman)
— Forms
Contracts and peace treaties
 See Contracts (International law)
Contracts contra bonos mores
 See Immoral contracts
Contracts for work and labor *(Direct)*
 sa Building—Contracts and specifications
   Independent contractors
 x Contracts for work, labor, and materials
   Work and labor, Contracts for
 xx Contracts
   Hire
   Independent contractors
   Sales
Contracts for work and labor (Jewish law)
Contracts for work, labor, and materials
 See Contracts for work and labor
Contracts of adhesion
 See Standardized terms of contract
Contracts to devise or bequeath
 See Contracts to make wills
Contracts to make wills *(Direct)*
 x Contracts to devise or bequeath
 xx Contracts
   Inheritance and succession
   Wills
Contractual limitations
 See Contracts
Contractual penalties
 See Penalties, Contractual

Contracture (Pathology)
    sa Dupuytren's contracture
    xx Muscles—Diseases
        Spasms
Contractus aestimatorius
    See Aestimatum
Contradance
    See Country-dance
Contradances
    See Country-dances
Contradiction *(Dialectical materialism,*
        B809.833; Logic, BC199.C6)
    xx Philosophy
Contrahomology theory
    See Homology theory
Contrails
    See Condensation trails
Contrariety
    See Opposition, Theory of
Contrariety (in religion, folk-lore, etc.)
    See Polarity (in religion, folk-lore, etc.)
Contrary-to-fact conditional
    See Counterfactuals (Logic)
Contrast enema
    See Barium enema
Contrast media
    x Radiopaque diagnostic agents
    xx Radiography
    — Toxicology
Contraventions (Criminal law) *(Direct)*
        "In the codes of various European coun-
        tries . . . the lowest class of offenses,
        constituted by those punishable in po-
        lice courts."—Webster.
        Term used for a multitude of offenses
        over which magistrates have an exclu-
        sive summary jurisdiction, and for
        which there is no brief designation in
        Anglo-American legal nomenclature.
        — *Cf.* Bouvier, Law dictionary, 8th
        ed., 1914, under Misdemeanor.
    sa Police magistrates
        Vagrancy
    xx Criminal law
        Police magistrates
Contre-bass de viol
    See Violone
Contributions, Military
    See Requisitions, Military
Contributory negligence
    See Negligence, Contributory
Contrition
    See Penance
        Repentance
Control, Inventory
    See Inventory control
Control, Production
    See Production control
Control (Psychology)
    sa Electronic behavior control
    x Power (Psychology)
    xx Emotions
        Frustration
        Psychology
        Senses and sensation
Control biophysics
    See Biological control systems
Control boards (Electrical engineering)
    x Control consoles
        Control panels
    xx Automatic control
Control consoles
    See Control boards (Electrical engineering)
Control Data 3600 (Computer)
    See CDC 3600 (Computer)
Control Data 6600 (Computer)
    See CDC 6600 (Computer)

Control engineering
    See Automatic control
Control equipment
    See Automatic control
Control of dust
    See Dust control
Control of electromagnetic radiation
    See Conelrad
Control of evaporation
    See Evaporation control
Control of fumes
    See Fume control
Control of industrial processes
    See Process control
Control of metabolism
    See Metabolic regulation
Control of pests
    See Pest control
Control of temperature
    See Temperature control
Control panels
    See Control boards (Electrical engineering)
Control systems, Biological
    See Biological control systems
Control systems, Carrier
    See Carrier control systems
Control systems (Flight)
    See Flight control
Control systems of aeroplanes, ₍artificial
        satellites, rocket engines, etc.₎
    See Aeroplanes ₍Artificial satellites, Rocket
        engines, etc.₎—Control systems
Control theory *(QA402.3)*
    sa Automatic control
        Biological control systems
        Brachistochrone
        Kalman filtering
        Transfer functions
    xx Dynamics
        Machine theory
        System analysis
    — Computer programs
    — Problems, exercises, etc.
Control tower display systems
    See Airports—Traffic control—Display
        systems
Control towers (Airports)
    See Airports—Control towers
Controlled access highways
    See Express highways
Controlled atmospheres (Industrial processes)
    See Protective atmospheres
Controlled atmospheres (Space environment)
    See Artificial atmospheres (Space
        environment)
Controlled fusion
    sa Fusion reactors
        Plasma confinement
    x Controlled thermonuclear reactions
        Fusion reactions, Controlled
        Nuclear fusion, Controlled
        Thermonuclear reactions, Controlled
    xx Atomic power
        Direct energy conversion
        Nuclear fusion
        Space vehicles—Propulsion systems
    — Indexes
    — Popular works
    — Research *(Direct)*
Controlled fusion reactors
    See Fusion reactors
Controlled reading
    See Developmental reading
Controlled thermonuclear reactions
    See Controlled fusion
Controlled thermonuclear reactors
    See Fusion reactors

Controllers, Electric
    See Electric controllers
Controllership *(HF5550)*
    sa Accounting
        Auditing
        Budget in business
        Credit managers
    x Comptrollership
    xx Business
        Finance
        Industrial management
Controversies, Interstate
    See Interstate controversies
Controversies between the United States and a
        State
    See Federal-state controversies
Contumacy *(Direct)*
    sa Default (Law)
        Fugitives from justice
        Judgments by default
    xx Civil procedure
        Contempt of court
        Criminal procedure
        Default (Law)
Contumacy (Canon law)
Contumacy (Roman law)
    sa Default (Roman law)
    xx Civil procedure (Roman law)
        Criminal procedure (Roman law)
        Default (Roman law)
Conundrums
    See Riddles
Conurbations
    See Metropolitan areas
Convalescence *(Amusements, GV1231)*
    sa Hospitals, Convalescent
        Invalids
        Nursing homes
    xx Hospitals, Convalescent
        Invalids
        Nurses and nursing
Convection, Gravitational
    See Density currents
Convection (Meteorology) *(QC880)*
    xx Atmospheric circulation
        Dynamic meteorology
        Heat—Convection
Convection of heat
    See Heat—Convection
Conventicle act, 1670
    xx Assembly, Right of
        Church and state in Great Britain
        Dissenters, Religious—England
Conventicle act, 1726
    See Konventikelplakatet, 1726
Convention (Philosophy) *(B809.15)*
    xx Philosophy
Convention troops
    See Burgoyne's Invasion, 1777
Conventional persons
    See Juristic persons
Conventional signs (Topography)
    See Topographical drawing—Conventional
        signs
Conventions, Constitutional
    See Constitutional conventions
Conventions, Pan-American
    See Pan-American treaties and conventions
Conventions, Political
    See Political conventions
Conventions, Postal
    See Postal conventions
Conventions, Sales
    See Sales meetings
Conventions (Congresses)
    See Congresses and conventions
Conventions (Treaties)
    See Treaties

Convents and nunneries *(Indirect)* *(Catholic Church, BX4200-4560)*
  sa Abbeys
    Beguinages
    Enclosure (Monasticism)
    Monasteries
    Monasticism and religious orders for women
    Mothers general
    Nuns
    Priories
    Secularization
  x Cloisters
    Nunneries
  xx Abbeys
    Church history
    Church property
    Monasteries
    Monasticism and religious orders for women
    Sisterhoods
Convents and nunneries, Buddhist *(Direct)*
  sa Buddhist nuns
  x Buddhist convents and nunneries
  xx Monasteries, Buddhist
Convergence *(Mathematical series, QA295)*
  sa Asymptotic expansions
    Bernstein polynomials
    Concentration functions
    Law of large numbers
    Nets (Mathematics)
  xx Functions
Convergence (Biology)
  xx Biology
    Phylogeny
Conversation *(BJ2120-2128)*
  sa Discussion
    Imaginary conversations
    Table-talk
  x Talking
  xx Etiquette
    Language and languages
Conversation piece (Portrait painting) *(Direct)*
  xx Genre painting
    Portrait painting
Conversion *(General, BV4912-4950; Psychology, BR110; Theology, BT780)*
  sa Catastrophical, The
    Children—Conversion to Christianity
    Converts
    Grace (Theology)
    Jews—Conversion to Christianity
    Regeneration (Theology)
    Repentance
    Salvation
  xx Christian life
    Evangelistic work
    Regeneration (Theology)
    Theology, Doctrinal
  — Biblical teaching
    Example under Bible—Theology
  — Comparative studies *(BL639)*
  — Early works to 1800
  — Popular works
  — Psychology
    xx Psychology, Religious
Conversion (Law)
  See Trover and conversion
Conversion (Psychoanalysis)
  xx Defense mechanisms (Psychology)
    Mind and body
Conversion of saline waters
  See Saline water conversion
Conversion of waste products
  See Recycling (Waste, etc.)
    Salvage (Waste, etc.)

Conversion tables
  See subdivision Conversion tables *under subjects, e.g.* Metric system—Conversion tables; Time—Conversion tables
Convert making
  See Evangelistic work
Converter reactors
  See Breeder reactors
Converters, Digital-to-analog
  See Digital-to-analog converters
Converters, Electric
  See Cascade converters
    Electric current converters
    Rotary converters
Converters, Synchronous
  See Rotary converters
Converters, Thermionic
  See Thermionic converters
Convertibility of currency
  See Currency convertibility
Convertible aircraft
  See Convertiplanes
Convertible bonds *(Direct)*
  sa Convertible preferred stocks
  x Bonds, Convertible
  xx Bonds
Convertible preferred stocks *(Direct)*
  x Preferred stocks, Convertible
    Stocks, Convertible
  xx Convertible bonds
    Preferred stocks
Convertiplanes *(TL685)*
  x Convertible aircraft
  xx Aeroplanes
    Helicopters
    Vertically rising aeroplanes
  — Juvenile literature
Converts *(BV4930-4935)*
  Here are entered works on converts to Christianity; for persons affiliating upon conversion with a particular denomination prefer Converts, Anglican, ₍Catholic, Mormon, etc.₎ Works emphasizing the religion from which conversion to Christianity takes place are entered under such headings as Converts from Buddhism; Converts from Judaism.
  Works on converts to Judaism are entered under Proselytes and proselyting, Jewish.
  Works on converts to other religions are entered under Buddhist ₍Muslim, etc.₎ converts.
  Works emphasizing the religion from which conversion to non-Christian religions takes place are entered under such headings as Muslim converts from Christianity; Proselytes and proselyting, Jewish—Converts from Christianity.
  sa Penitents
  x Christian converts
    Converts to Christianity
  xx Conversion
Converts, Anglican *(Church of England, BX5197-9; Protestant Episcopal Church, BX5990-5995)*
  Here are entered works on persons who previously had no religious affiliations, or who had been affiliated with a non-Anglican Christian body, or a non-Christian body.
  x Anglican converts
    Church of England—Converts
    Protestant Episcopal Church in the U.S.A.—Converts

  xx Converts, Protestant
  Note under Converts
Converts, Baptist
  x Baptist converts
    Baptists—Converts
  xx Converts, Protestant
Converts, Buddhist
  See Buddhist converts
Converts, Catholic *(BX4668)*
  sa Converts (Canon law)
  x Catholic Church—Converts
    Catholic converts
  Note under Converts
Converts, Friend
  x Friend converts
    Friends, Society of—Converts
Converts, Islamic
  See Muslim converts
Converts, Mennonite *(BX8141)*
  x Mennonite converts
    Mennonites—Converts
Converts, Mormon
  x Mormon converts
  xx Mormons and Mormonism
  Note under Converts
Converts, Muslim
  See Muslim converts
Converts, Orthodox Eastern
  x Orthodox Eastern Church—Converts
    Orthodox Eastern converts
Converts, Protestant
  sa Converts, Anglican, ₍Baptist, etc.₎
    Nicodemites
  x Protestant converts
    Protestantism—Converts
Converts, Reformed Church
  x Reformed Church converts
    Reformed Church—Converts
Converts, Seventh-Day Adventist
  x Seventh-Day Adventist converts
    Seventh-Day Adventists—Converts
Converts (Canon law)
  xx Converts, Catholic
Converts from Buddhism
  x Buddhist converts to Christianity
    Converts to Christianity from Buddhism
  xx Missions to Buddhists
  Note under Converts
Converts from Christianity to Buddhism
  See Buddhist converts from Christianity
Converts from Christianity to Islam
  See Muslim converts from Christianity
Converts from Christianity to Judaism
  See Proselytes and proselyting, Jewish—Converts from Christianity
Converts from Confucianism
  x Confucian converts to Christianity
    Converts to Christianity from Confucianism
  xx Missions to Confucians
Converts from Hinduism
  x Converts to Christianity from Hinduism
    Hindu converts to Christianity
  xx Missions to Hindus
Converts from Islam *(BV2626.3-4)*
  x Converts to Christianity from Islam
    Islamic converts to Christianity
    Muslim converts to Christianity
  xx Missions to Muslims
Converts from Judaism *(BV2619-2623)*
  x Converts to Christianity from Judaism
    Jewish converts to Christianity
    Jews—Converts to Christianity
  xx Jewish Christians
    Missions to Jews
  Note under Converts

Converts from Shinto
  x Converts to Christianity from Shinto
    Shinto converts to Christianity
Converts to Buddhism
  See Buddhist converts
Converts to Christianity
  See Converts
Converts to Christianity from Buddhism
  See Converts from Buddhism
Converts to Christianity from Confucianism
  See Converts from Confucianism
Converts to Christianity from Hinduism
  See Converts from Hinduism
Converts to Christianity from Islam
  See Converts from Islam
Converts to Christianity from Judaism
  See Converts from Judaism
Converts to Christianity from Shinto
  See Converts from Shinto
Converts to Islam
  See Muslim converts
Converts to Judaism
  See Proselytes and proselyting, Jewish
Convex areas
  See Convex surfaces
Convex bodies
  sa Convex surfaces
  xx Convex domains
    Convex surfaces
    Geometry, Differential
Convex domains
  sa Convex bodies
    Convex surfaces
  x Convex regions
    Convexity
  xx Calculus of variations
    Geometry, Differential
    Groups of points
Convex functions (QA331.5)
  x Functions, Convex
  xx Functions of real variables
Convex programming
  xx Programming (Mathematics)
Convex regions
  See Convex domains
Convex surfaces
  sa Coanda effect
    Convex bodies
  x Convex areas
  xx Convex bodies
    Convex domains
    Geometry, Differential
    Surfaces
Convexity
  See Convex domains
Conveyancing (Direct) (Forms, HF1243)
  sa Abstracts of title
    Acknowledgments
    Deeds
    Forms (Law)
    Land titles
    Leases
    Mortgages
    Settlements (Law)
    Title companies
    Title examinations
    Worthier title
  xx Abstracts of title
    Acknowledgments
    Commercial law
    Deeds
    Forms (Law)
    Land tenure—Law
    Land titles
    Legal composition
    Mortgages
    Real property
    Vendors and purchasers

— Costs
  See Settlement costs
Conveyancing (Jewish law)
Conveyancing (Roman law)
Conveying machinery (TJ1350-1353;
      TJ1385-1418)
  sa Bulk solids handling
    Coal-handling machinery
    Feed mechanisms
    Fork lift trucks
    Grain handling
    Hoisting machinery
    Hydraulic conveying
    Industrial electric trucks
    Mining machinery
    Monorail conveyors
    Passenger conveyors
    Pneumatic-tube transportation
    Screw conveyors
    Vibrating conveyors
    Wire-rope transportation
  x Belt conveyors
    Conveyors
  xx Coal-handling machinery
    Feed mechanisms
    Hoisting machinery
    Materials handling
    Railroads, Industrial
— Appraisal
  See Conveying machinery—Valuation
— Automatic control
— Construction
  See Conveying machinery—Design
      and construction
— Design and construction
  x Conveying machinery—Construction
— Drawing
  See Conveying machinery—Drawings
— Drawings
  x Conveying machinery—Drawing
  xx Mechanical drawing
— Dynamics (TJ1390)
— Electric driving
— Electric equipment
— Fires and fire prevention
— Maintenance and repair
  x Conveying machinery—Repairing
— Repairing
  See Conveying machinery—
      Maintenance and repair
— Safety measures
— Safety regulations (Direct)
— Standards (Direct)
— Tables, calculations, etc.
— Terminology (TJ1350)
— Valuation (TJ1390)
  x Conveying machinery—Appraisal
Conveyors
  See Conveying machinery
Conveyors, Auger
  See Screw conveyors
Conveyors, Monorail
  See Monorail conveyors
Conveyors, Passenger
  See Passenger conveyors
Conveyors, Screw
  See Screw conveyors
Convict labor (Indirect) (HV8888-8931)
  sa Peonage
  x Lease system
    Prison industries
    Prison labor
  xx Contract system (Labor)
    Crime and criminals
    Forced labor
    Labor and laboring classes
    Peonage
    Prisoners

    Prisons
  Note under Contract system (Labor)
Convict ships
  sa subdivision Exiles under names of
      countries, e.g. Tasmania—Exiles
  xx Penal colonies
    Sailing ships
Conviction
  See Belief and doubt
    Truth
Convictions, Alternative
  See Alternative convictions
Convicts
  See Prisoners
Convolution transforms
  See Convolutions (Mathematics)
Convolutions (Mathematics)
  x Convolution transforms
    Transformations, Convolution
  xx Distribution (Probability theory)
    Functions
    Integrals
    Transformations (Mathematics)
Convolvulin
  See Jalap
Convoy (JX5268)
  xx Capture at sea
    Search, Right of
    War, Maritime (International law)
— Cold weather conditions
Convulsion therapy
  See Shock therapy
Convulsionaries (BX4732)
  x Convulsionists
  xx Jansenists
Convulsionists
  See Convulsionaries
Convulsions
  sa Anticonvulsants
    Epilepsy
    Pregnancy, Complications of
    Puerperal convulsions
    Spasms
    Tetanus
  x Eclampsia
  xx Epilepsy
    Spasms
— Homeopathic treatment (RX301.C7)
Cooch-grass
  See Quitch-grass
Cooch's Bridge, Skirmish of, 1777
      (E241.C73)
  xx Brandywine, Battle of, 1777
Cook-books
  See Cookery
Cook-books for the blind
  See Cookery for the blind
Cook Co., Ill.
— Politics and government
  Note under County government
Cookbooks
  See Cookery
Cookbooks for the blind
  See Cookery for the blind
Cookers, Fireless
  See Fireless cookers
Cookery (TX645-840)
  sa Aladdin oven
    Baking
    Boiling (Cookery)
    Braising (Cookery)
    Bread
    Breakfasts
    Broiling
    Cake
    Canning and preserving
    Carving (Meat, etc.)
    Casserole receipts

Caterers and catering
Chafing-dish receipts
Christmas cookery
Coffee
Condiments
Confectionery
Cooking schools
Desserts
Diet
Dinners and dining
Electric cookery
Fireless cookers
Flavoring essences
Food
Frying
Gastronomy
Jelly
Lenten menus
Luncheons
Menus
Mixers (Cookery)
Outdoor cookery
Pancakes, waffles, etc.
Paper bag cookery
Pastry
Pizza
Pressure cookery
Roasting (Cookery)
Salads
Sandwiches
Sauces
Soufflés
Soups
Steaming (Cookery)
Stews
Stocks (Cookery)
Suppers
Table
Tempura
Tortillas
   x Cook-books
      Cookbooks
  xx Diet
     Dinners and dining
     Food
     Gastronomy
     Home economics
     Table
Note under Receipts
— Anecdotes, facetiae, satire, etc.
— Caricatures and cartoons
— Competitions
— Early works to 1800 *(TX703-713;*
    TX727)
— Examinations, questions, etc.
— Exhibitions *(TX346)*
— Forms, blanks, etc.
— Garnishes and garnishing
     See Cookery (Garnishes)
— Juvenile literature *(TX652.5)*
— Laboratory manuals *(TX663)*
— Pictorial works
— Study and teaching (Preschool) *(Direct)*
— Terminology
— Vocational guidance
Cookery, Algerian *(TX725.A)*
  xx Cookery, Arab
Cookery, American *(TX715; Before 1801,*
  TX703)
     Subdivided by states or sections, *e.g.*
     Cookery, American—Virginia.
— Virginia
     Note under Cookery, American
Cookery, Amish
  See Cookery, Mennonite
Cookery, Arab *(TX725)*
  sa Cookery, Algerian
     Cookery, Egyptian

Cookery, Syrian
Cookery, Argentine, ⌜Chinese, etc.⌝
— Early works to 1800
Cookery, Balkan *(TX725)*
  sa Cookery, Bulgarian
     Cookery, Croatian
     Cookery, Greek
     Cookery, Moldavian
     Cookery, Romanian
     Cookery, Serbian
     Cookery, Turkish
Cookery, Barbecue
  See Barbecue cookery
Cookery, Bulgarian
  xx Cookery, Balkan
Cookery, Camp
  See Outdoor cookery
Cookery, Canadian
  sa Cookery, French-Canadian
Cookery, Cold
  See Cookery (Cold dishes)
Cookery, Croatian
  sa Cookery, Serbian
  xx Cookery, Balkan
     Cookery, Serbian
     Cookery, Yugoslav
Cookery, Danish
  xx Cookery, Scandinavian
Cookery, Egyptian
  xx Cookery, Arab
Cookery, Fireless
  See Fireless cookers
Cookery, French-Canadian
  xx Cookery, Canadian
Cookery, Greek
  xx Cookery, Balkan
Cookery, Hebrew
  See Cookery, Jewish
Cookery, Indonesian
  sa Cookery, Javanese
Cookery, International *(TX725)*
  x International cookery
Cookery, Iranian
  sa Cookery, Tajik
Cookery, Javanese
  xx Cookery, Indonesian
Cookery, Jewish
  sa Jews—Dietary laws
  x Cookery, Hebrew
Cookery, Marine *(VC370-375; VK224)*
  sa Cookery, Military
  x Cookery, Naval
     Cookery on ships
     Marine cookery
     Naval cookery
  xx Boats and boating
     Cookery, Military
Cookery, Mennonite
  x Amish cookery
     Cookery, Amish
     Mennonite cookery
Cookery, Microwave
  See Microwave cookery
Cookery, Military *(UC720-735)*
  sa Cookery, Marine
  x Military cookery
  xx Armies—Commissariat
     Cookery, Marine
Cookery, Moldavian
  xx Cookery, Balkan
Cookery, Moravian
  x Moravian cookery
Cookery, Naval
  See Cookery, Marine
Cookery, Negro
  x Negro cookery
Cookery, Norwegian
  xx Cookery, Scandinavian

Cookery, Outdoor
  See Outdoor cookery
Cookery, Philippine *(TX725)*
  sa Cookery, Tagalog
Cookery, Romanian
  xx Cookery, Balkan
Cookery, Russian
  sa Cookery, Tajik
     Cookery, Uzbek
     Cookery, White Russian
Cookery, Scandinavian
  sa Cookery, Danish, ⌜Norwegian, Swedish⌝
Cookery, Serbian
  sa Cookery, Croatian
  xx Cookery, Balkan
     Cookery, Croatian
     Cookery, Yugoslav
Cookery, Shaker
  x Shaker cookery
Cookery, Slovenian
  xx Cookery, Yugoslav
Cookery, Swedish
  xx Cookery, Scandinavian
Cookery, Syrian
  xx Cookery, Arab
Cookery, Tagalog *(TX725)*
  xx Cookery, Philippine
Cookery, Tajik
  xx Cookery, Iranian
     Cookery, Russian
Cookery, Tropical *(Before 1800, TX713;*
    1800 to date, TX725)
  x Tropical cookery
Cookery, Turkish
  xx Cookery, Balkan
Cookery, Uzbek
  xx Cookery, Russian
Cookery, White Russian
  xx Cookery, Russian
Cookery, Yoga
  x Yoga cookery
Cookery, Yugoslav *(TX723.5.Y8)*
  sa Cookery, Croatian
     Cookery, Serbian
     Cookery, Slovenian
Cookery (Anchovies) *(TX747)*
  xx Anchovies
     Cookery (Fish)
Cookery (Appetizers) *(TX740)*
  x Appetizers
     Canapés
     Hors d'oeuvres
Cookery (Apples) *(TX813.A6)*
  xx Apple
Cookery (Apricots) *(TX813.A64)*
  xx Apricot
Cookery (Artichokes) *(TX803.A7)*
  xx Artichokes
Cookery (Asparagus)
  xx Asparagus
Cookery (Avocado) *(TX813.A9)*
  xx Avocado
Cookery (Baby foods) *(TX740)*
  xx Cookery (Canned foods)
Cookery (Bacon)
  xx Bacon
Cookery (Bananas)
  xx Banana
     Cookery (Fruit)
Cookery (Beans)
  xx Beans
Cookery (Beef)
  sa Cookery (Veal)
  x Cookery (Ground beef)
     Cookery (Hamburger)
     Hamburger
  xx Beef
     Cookery (Meat)

Cookery (Beer) *(TX726.3)*
  xx Beer
    Cookery (Liquors)
Cookery (Beets)
  xx Beets and beet sugar
Cookery (Berries)
  xx Berries
Cookery (Bowfin) *(TX747)*
  xx Bowfin
    Cookery (Fish)
Cookery (Brussels sprouts) *(TX803.B)*
  xx Brussels sprouts
Cookery (Buckwheat)
  xx Buckwheat
Cookery (Burbot) *(TX747)*
  xx Burbot
    Cookery (Fish)
Cookery (Buttermilk)
  See Cookery (Sour cream and milk)
Cookery (Cabbage)
  xx Cabbage
Cookery (Canned foods) *(TX821)*
  sa Cookery (Baby foods)
  xx Food, Canned
Cookery (Carp) *(TX747)*
  xx Carp
    Cookery (Fish)
Cookery (Cereals) *(TX808-9)*
  xx Cereals as food
Cookery (Cheese) *(TX759)*
  sa Cheesecake (Cookery)
    Cookery (Cottage cheese)
    Fondue
  xx Cheese
    Cookery (Dairy products)
Cookery (Cherries)
  xx Cherry
Cookery (Chicken)
  xx Cookery (Poultry)
    Poultry
Cookery (Chocolate)
  xx Chocolate
Cookery (Cider)
  xx Cider
    Cookery (Wine)
Cookery (Citrus fruits) *(TX813.C5)*
  sa Cookery (Grapefruit)
    Cookery (Tangerines)
  xx Citrus fruits
Cookery (Codfish) *(TX747)*
  xx Codfish
    Cookery (Fish)
Cookery (Coffee) *(TX819.C6)*
  sa Coffee brewing
    Coffee making paraphernalia
  xx Coffee
Cookery (Cold dishes) *(TX830)*
  sa Mousses
  x Cold cookery
    Cold dishes
    Cookery, Cold
Cookery (Corn)
  See Cookery (Maize)
Cookery (Cottage cheese)
  xx Cookery (Cheese)
    Cottage cheese
Cookery (Cottonseed meal) *(TX809.C8)*
  xx Cottonseed meal
Cookery (Cranberries) *(TX813.C7)*
  xx Cranberries
Cookery (Curry) *(TX749)*
Cookery (Dairy products) *(TX759)*
  sa Cookery (Cheese)
    Cookery (Milk)
    Cookery (Sour cream and milk)
    Cookery (Yogurt)
  — Juvenile literature

Cookery (Dates) *(TX813.D5)*
  xx Date
Cookery (Dried eggs)
  See Cookery (Eggs)
Cookery (Dried foods)
  xx Food, Dried
Cookery (Ducks)
  xx Cookery (Poultry)
    Ducks
Cookery (Eels) *(TX747)*
  xx Cookery (Fish)
    Eels
Cookery (Eggs) *(TX745)*
  sa Eggs as food
  x Cookery (Dried eggs)
    Omelets
  xx Eggs
Cookery (Entrées) *(TX740)*
  x Entrées
Cookery (Figs) *(TX813.F5)*
  xx Fig
Cookery (Fish) *(TX747)*
  sa Barbecue cookery
    Cookery (Anchovies)
    Cookery (Bowfin)
    Cookery (Burbot)
    Cookery (Carp)
    Cookery (Codfish)
    Cookery (Eels)
    Cookery (Grayfish)
    Cookery (Groupers)
    Cookery (Haddock)
    Cookery (Herring)
    Cookery (Mackerel)
    Cookery (Pollock)
    Cookery (Salmon)
    Cookery (Sardines)
    Cookery (Sharks)
    Cookery (Tile-fish)
    Cookery (Trout)
    Cookery (Tuna)
    Lenten menus
  xx Cookery (Sea food)
    Fish as food
Cookery (Flowers) *(TX814.5.F5)*
  sa Cookery (Roses)
  x Flower cookery
  xx Flowers
Cookery (Frankfurters)
  x Cookery (Hot dogs)
  xx Cookery (Sausages)
Cookery (Frogs) *(TX749)*
  xx Frogs
Cookery (Frozen foods) *(TX828)*
  x Frozen food cookery
  xx Food, Frozen
Cookery (Fruit) *(TX811-813)*
  sa Cookery (Bananas)
    Cookery (Pears)
    Cookery (Roselle)
    Jam
    Jelly
  xx Fruit
  — Early works to 1800
  — Juvenile literature
Cookery (Game)
  sa Cookery (Venison)
  xx Cookery (Meat)
    Cookery (Wild foods)
    Game and game-birds
Cookery (Garlic) *(TX819.G3)*
  xx Garlic
Cookery (Garnishes) *(TX652)*
  sa Cookery (Relishes)
  x Cookery—Garnishes and garnishing
    Decoration of food
    Food decoration
    Garnishes in cookery

Cookery (Gelatin) *(TX814.5.G4)*
  xx Gelatin
Cookery (Grapefruit)
  xx Cookery (Citrus fruits)
    Grapefruit
Cookery (Grayfish) *(TX747)*
  xx Cookery (Fish)
    Grayfish
Cookery (Ground beef)
  See Cookery (Beef)
Cookery (Groupers) *(TX747)*
  xx Cookery (Fish)
    Groupers
Cookery (Haddock) *(TX747)*
  xx Cookery (Fish)
    Haddock
Cookery (Ham)
  xx Cookery (Meat)
    Ham
Cookery (Hamburger)
  See Cookery (Beef)
Cookery (Herbs)
  sa Cookery (Roselle)
  xx Herbs
  — Early works to 1800
Cookery (Herring)
  xx Cookery (Fish)
    Herring
Cookery (Honey) *(TX560.H7)*
  x Honey cookery
  xx Honey
  — Juvenile literature
Cookery (Hot dogs)
  See Cookery (Frankfurters)
Cookery (Lamb and mutton)
  x Cookery (Mutton)
  xx Cookery (Meat)
    Lamb (Meat)
    Mutton
Cookery (Leeks) *(TX803.L4)*
  xx Leeks
Cookery (Lemons) *(TX813.L4)*
  xx Lemon
Cookery (Lentils)
  xx Lentils
Cookery (Liquors) *(TX726)*
  sa Cookery (Beer)
    Cookery (Rum)
    Cookery (Wine)
  x Cookery (Spirits, Alcoholic)
Cookery (Lobsters) *(TX753)*
  xx Lobsters
Cookery (Macaroni) *(TX809.M)*
  x Cookery (Noodles)
    Cookery (Spaghetti)
    Cookery (Vermicelli)
  xx Macaroni products
Cookery (Mackerel) *(TX747)*
  xx Cookery (Fish)
    Mackerel
Cookery (Maize) *(TX809.M2)*
  x Cookery (Corn)
  xx Maize
Cookery (Mangos)
  xx Mango
Cookery (Maple sugar and syrup)
  x Cookery (Maple syrup)
  xx Maple sugar
    Maple syrup
Cookery (Maple syrup)
  See Cookery (Maple sugar and syrup)
Cookery (Marihuana) *(TX819.M25)*
  xx Marihuana
Cookery (Meat) *(TX749)*
  sa Barbecue cookery
    Chili con carne
    Cookery (Beef)
    Cookery (Game)

Cookery (Ham)
Cookery (Lamb and mutton)
Cookery (Pork)
Cookery (Sausages)
Meat, Smoked
Pâtés (Cookery)
xx Meat
— Juvenile literature
Cookery (Milk)
xx Cookery (Dairy products)
Milk
Cookery (Mushrooms) *(TX804)*
xx Mushrooms
Cookery (Mutton)
See Cookery (Lamb and mutton)
Cookery (Noodles)
See Cookery (Macaroni)
Cookery (Nuts) *(TX814)*
xx Nuts
Cookery (Olives) *(TX813.O)*
xx Olive
Cookery (Onions)
xx Onions
Cookery (Oranges) *(TX813.O6)*
xx Orange
Cookery (Oysters) *(TX753)*
xx Cookery (Sea food)
Oysters
Cookery (Peaches)
xx Peach
Cookery (Peanuts) *(TX803.P35)*
xx Peanuts
Cookery (Pears)
xx Cookery (Fruit)
Pear
Cookery (Peas) *(TX803.P4)*
xx Peas
Cookery (Pecans) *(TX814)*
xx Pecan
Cookery (Pepper) *(TX819.P3)*
xx Pepper (Spice)
Cookery (Pineapples)
xx Pineapple
Cookery (Plums) *(TX813.P55)*
xx Plum
Cookery (Pollock) *(TX747)*
xx Cookery (Fish)
Cookery (Pork) *(TX749)*
xx Cookery (Meat)
Pork
Cookery (Potatoes) *(TX803.P8)*
sa Potato chips
Potato products
xx Potatoes
Cookery (Poultry) *(TX749)*
sa Cookery (Chicken)
Cookery (Ducks)
Cookery (Turkeys)
Poultry as food
x Poultry cookery
xx Poultry
Cookery (Rabbits) *(TX749)*
xx Rabbits
Cookery (Raisins)
xx Raisins
Cookery (Relishes) *(TX819)*
x Relishes
xx Cookery (Garnishes)
Cookery (Rice) *(TX809.R5)*
xx Rice
Cookery (Roselle) *(TX814.5.R58)*
xx Cookery (Fruit)
Cookery (Herbs)
Roselle
Cookery (Roses) *(TX814.5.R6)*
xx Cookery (Flowers)
Roses

Cookery (Rum) *(TX726)*
xx Cookery (Liquors)
Rum
Cookery (Salmon) *(TX747)*
xx Cookery (Fish)
Salmon
Cookery (Sardines) *(TX747)*
xx Cookery (Fish)
Sardines
Cookery (Sausages)
sa Cookery (Frankfurters)
xx Cookery (Meat)
Sausages
Cookery (Sea food)
sa Cookery (Fish)
Cookery (Oysters)
Cookery (Shellfish)
Cookery (Shrimp)
xx Sea food
Cookery (Sharks) *(TX747)*
xx Cookery (Fish)
Sharks
Cookery (Shellfish) *(TX753)*
sa Cookery (Shrimp)
xx Cookery (Sea food)
Shellfish
Cookery (Shrimp) *(TX753)*
xx Cookery (Sea food)
Cookery (Shellfish)
Shrimps
Cookery (Smoked foods) *(TX835)*
x Food, Smoked
Smoked foods cookery
Cookery (Sour cream and milk) *(TX759)*
x Cookery (Buttermilk)
Cookery (Sour milk)
xx Cookery (Dairy products)
Cream
Milk
Sour cream
Cookery (Sour milk)
See Cookery (Sour cream and milk)
Cookery (Soy-beans)
xx Soy-bean
Cookery (Spaghetti)
See Cookery (Macaroni)
Cookery (Spirits, Alcoholic)
See Cookery (Liquors)
Cookery (Sprouts) *(TX801)*
xx Cookery (Vegetables)
Cookery (Squash) *(TX803.S67)*
xx Squash
Cookery (Strawberries) *(TX813.S9)*
xx Strawberries
Cookery (Sweet potatoes)
sa Sweet potato flakes
xx Sweet potatoes
Cookery (Syrups)
xx Syrups
Cookery (Tangerines)
xx Cookery (Citrus fruits)
Tangerine
Cookery (Tea)
sa Tea making paraphernalia
xx Tea
Cookery (Tile-fish) *(TX747)*
xx Cookery (Fish)
Tile-fish
Cookery (Tomatoes)
xx Tomatoes
Cookery (Trout) *(TX747)*
xx Cookery (Fish)
Trout
Cookery (Truffles) *(TX804.5)*
xx Truffles
Cookery (Tuna)
xx Cookery (Fish)

Cookery (Turkeys)
xx Cookery (Poultry)
Turkeys
Cookery (Veal)
xx Cookery (Beef)
Veal
Cookery (Vegetables) *(TX801-3)*
sa Cookery (Sprouts)
xx Vegetables
Vegetarianism
— Early works to 1800
Cookery (Venison)
xx Cookery (Game)
Venison
Cookery (Vermicelli)
See Cookery (Macaroni)
Cookery (Whale meat)
xx Whales
Cookery (Wild foods)
sa Cookery (Game)
xx Food, Wild
Outdoor cookery
Cookery (Wine) *(TX726)*
sa Cookery (Cider)
xx Cookery (Liquors)
Wine and wine making
Cookery (Yogurt)
xx Cookery (Dairy products)
Yogurt
Cookery for allergics *(RM221.A6)*
xx Allergy
Cookery for the sick
Cookery for arthritics *(RM221.A7)*
xx Arthritis
Cookery for the sick
Cookery for cardiacs
sa Salt-free diet
xx Cardiacs
Cookery for the sick
Salt-free diet
Cookery for diabetics
sa Diabetes—Nutritional aspects
Sugar-free diet
x Diabetic cookery
Diabetic diet
xx Cookery for the sick
Diabetes
Diabetes—Nutritional aspects
Diet in disease
Sugar-free diet
Cookery for hypoglycemics *(RM221.H9)*
xx Cookery for the sick
Hypoglycemia
Cookery for institutions, etc. *(TX820)*
Here are entered works dealing solely
with culinary problems of quantity
feeding. Works on the quantity prepa-
ration and service of food to those eat-
ing away from home are entered under
Food service.
x Quantity cookery
xx Food service
Note under Food service
Cookery for the blind
x Blind, Cookery for the
Blind homemakers, Cookery for
Cook-books for the blind
Cookbooks for the blind
Cookery for the physically handicapped
xx Physically handicapped—Rehabilitation
Self-help devices for the disabled
Cookery for the sick *(RM219)*
sa Cookery for allergics
Cookery for arthritics
Cookery for cardiacs
Cookery for diabetics
Cookery for hypoglycemics
Diet-kitchens

Cookery for the sick *(RM219)*
(Continued)
    Low-fat diet
    Salt-free diet
    Sugar-free diet
    Wheat-free diet
  x Food for invalids
    Invalid cookery
  xx Diet in disease
    Nurses and nursing
    Sick
Cookery in literature
Cookery on ships
  See Cookery, Marine
Cookies *(TX772)*
  sa Cooky molds
  x Biscuits, English
  xx Cake
    Cooky molds
  Example under Baked products
  — Juvenile literature
Cooking banana
  See Plantain banana
Cooking schools *(TX661-9)*
  xx Cookery
    Schools
Cooking utensils
  See Kitchen utensils
Cooks *(Direct)* *(TX649)*
  — Biography
  — Correspondence, reminiscences, etc.
  — Interviews
Cooks in literature
Cook's Mills, Battle of, 1814 *(E356.C74)*
Cooky cutters
  See Cooky molds
Cooky molds
  sa Cookies
  x Cooky cutters
  xx Cookies
Cool stars *(QB843.C6)*
  x Late-type stars
  xx Stars
Cooley's anemia
  See Thalassemia
Coolie labor
  See Chinese in Brazil, [Guyana, South
    Africa, etc.]
Cooling *(QC331)*
  sa Adiabatic demagnetization
    Germanium—Quenching
    Iron—Quenching
    Metals—Quenching
    Precooling
    Steel—Quenching
  subdivision Cooling *under subjects, e.g.*
    Aeroplanes—Electronic equipment—
      Cooling; Gas and oil engines—
      Cooling; Vacuum-tubes—Cooling
  xx Calorimeters and calorimetry
    Heat—Radiation and absorption
Cooling appliances
  See Refrigeration and refrigerating
    machinery
Cooling of aircraft engines
  See Aeroplanes—Motors—Cooling
Cooling of automobile engines
  See Automobiles—Motors—Cooling
Cooling of food
  See Food—Cooling
Cooling of marine engines
  See Marine engines—Cooling
Cooling of vegetables
  See Vegetables—Cooling
Cooling ponds
  — Climatic factors
Cooling stresses
  See Residual stresses

Cooling towers *(TJ563)*
  xx Evaporating appliances
    Refrigeration and refrigerating
      machinery
  — Climatic factors
    x Cooling towers and climate
      Cooling towers and weather
    xx Atmospheric temperature
      Humidity
      Winds
    Example under Climatology; *and under*
      reference from Climatic factors
  — Design and construction
  — Testing *(TJ563)*
Cooling towers and climate
  See Cooling towers—Climatic factors
Cooling towers and weather
  See Cooling towers—Climatic factors
Coon hunting *(SK341.C6)*
  x Raccoon hunting
  xx Raccoons
Cooncan *(GV1295.C6)*
  x Conquien
    Rum (Game)
Cooperage
  See Coopers and cooperage
Cooperation *(Indirect)* *(HD2951-3570;*
    Cooperative business, HF5431-6)
  Here are entered works on the theory and
    history of cooperation and the cooper-
    ative movement. Works dealing
    specifically with the nature and organi-
    zation of cooperative enterprises and
    the laws governing them are entered
    under Cooperative societies.
  sa Agriculture, Cooperative
    Banks and banking, Cooperative
    Bees (Cooperative gatherings)
    Chain stores, Voluntary
    Collective settlements
    Cooperative societies
    Fedritive movement
    Fisheries, Cooperative
    Housing, Cooperative
    International cooperation
    Motor bus lines, Cooperative
    Mutualism
    Plenocracy
    Profit-sharing
    Savings-banks
    Solidarity
    Trade-unions
  x Cooperative distribution
    Cooperative production
    Distribution, Cooperative
    Production, Cooperative
  xx Associations, institutions, etc.
    Consumers
    Economics
    Profit-sharing
  Note under Cooperative societies
  — Accounting
    See Cooperative societies—
      Accounting
  — Finance
    See Cooperative societies—Finance
  — Personal narratives
  — Research *(Direct)*
  — Societies, etc.
    xx Cooperative societies
  — Statistics
    See Cooperative societies—Statistics
  — Study and teaching *(Direct)*
  — — Audio-visual aids
  — Terminology
  — Underdeveloped areas
    See Underdeveloped areas—
      Cooperation

Cooperation, Agricultural
  See Agriculture, Cooperative
Cooperation, Intellectual
  See Intellectual cooperation
Cooperation, Interchurch
  See Interdenominational cooperation
Cooperation, Interdenominational
  See Interdenominational cooperation
Cooperation, International
  See International cooperation
Cooperation, Interstate
  See Interstate agreements
Cooperation, Library
  See Library cooperation
Cooperation, Medical
  See Medical cooperation
Cooperative advertising
  x Advertising, Cooperative
  xx Advertising
Cooperative agriculture
  See Agriculture, Cooperative
Cooperative apartment houses
  See Apartment houses, Cooperative
Cooperative associations
  See Cooperative societies
Cooperative banks
  See Banks and banking, Cooperative
Cooperative building associations
  See Building and loan associations
Cooperative cataloging
  See Cataloging, Cooperative
Cooperative chain stores
  See Chain stores, Voluntary
Cooperative cold-storage lockers
  x Cold-storage lockers, Cooperative
  xx Agriculture, Cooperative
Cooperative credit associations, Agricultural
  See Agricultural cooperative credit
    associations
Cooperative distribution
  See Cooperation
    Cooperative societies
Cooperative education
  See Education, Cooperative
Cooperative fisheries
  See Fisheries, Cooperative
Cooperative housing
  See Housing, Cooperative
Cooperative marketing of farm produce
    (Indirect)
  sa Cooperative marketing of livestock
    subdivision Cooperative marketing
      under names of products, e.g. Apple
      —Cooperative marketing
  xx Agriculture, Cooperative
    Farm produce—Marketing
  — Law and legislation *(Direct)*
    xx Agricultural laws and legislation
Cooperative marketing of fish
  See Fishes—Cooperative marketing
Cooperative marketing of livestock *(Indirect)*
  sa Livestock associations
    Swine—Cooperative marketing
  x Domestic animals—Cooperative
    marketing
  xx Agriculture, Cooperative
    Cooperative marketing of farm produce
    Marketing of livestock
Cooperative marketing of petroleum products
  See Petroleum products—Cooperative
    marketing
Cooperative motor bus lines
  See Motor bus lines, Cooperative
Cooperative nursery schools *(LB1140)*
  xx Nursery schools
    Parent and child
Cooperative operation of oil fields
  See Unit operation of oil fields

Cooperative production
    See Cooperation
        Cooperative societies
Cooperative societies *(Direct)*
    Here are entered works dealing specifi-
    cally with the nature and organization
    of cooperative enterprises and the laws
    governing them. Works on the theory
    and history of cooperation and the
    cooperative movement are entered un-
    der the heading Cooperation.
    sa Agricultural cooperative credit
        associations
        Apartment houses, Cooperative
        Banks and banking, Cooperative
        Brook Farm
        Building and loan associations
        Consumers' leagues
        Cooperation—Societies, etc. *[for*
          publications of cooperative and other
          societies in relation to cooperation]
        Federations, Financial (Social service)
        Motor bus lines, Cooperative
        Rochdale system
        Student cooperatives
        Women in cooperative societies
    x Consumer organizations
        Cooperative associations
        Cooperative distribution
        Cooperative production
        Cooperative stores
        Distribution, Cooperative
        Production, Cooperative
        Societies, Cooperative
        Stores, Cooperative
    xx Cooperation
        Corporations
        Societies
        Work relief
    Note under Cooperation
    — Accounting
        x Cooperation—Accounting
    — — Problems, exercises, etc
    — Auditing and inspection
    — Finance
        sa Underdeveloped areas—Cooperative
          societies—Finance
        x Cooperation—Finance
        xx Corporations—Finance
    — Law
        xx Corporation law
    — Management
    — Officials and employees
    — Pictorial works
    — Statistics
        x Cooperation—Statistics
    — Taxation   *(Direct)*
        sa Collective farms—Taxation
        xx Corporations, Nonprofit—Taxation
    — Underdeveloped areas
        See Underdeveloped areas—
          Cooperative societies
Cooperative societies, Agricultural
    See Agriculture, Cooperative
Cooperative societies meetings
    xx Meetings
Cooperative stores
    See Cooperative societies
Cooperativeness
Coopers and cooperage *(Direct)* *(TS840;*
    TS890; Trade, HD9750-9769;
    Wages, HD4966.C82)
    sa Barrels
        Staves and stave trade
        Trade-unions—Coopers and cooperage
    x Cooperage
    xx Barrels
    — Accidents

Cooptation *(Direct)*
    xx Associations, institutions, etc.
        Election law
        Elections
Coordinate indexing *(Z695.9)*
    xx Indexing
Coordinates *(Analytic geometry, QA556;*
    Spherical astronomy, QB147)
    sa Complexes
        Grids (Cartography)
    xx Geometry, Analytic
        Geometry, Differential
        Mathematics
        Surfaces
    — Tables
Coordinates, Curvilinear
    x Curvilinear coordinates
Coordinates, Elliptic
    x Elliptic coordinates
Coordinates, Oblique
    x Oblique coordinates
Coordinates, Polar *(QA556)*
    sa Euler angles
    x Polar coordinates
Coordinates, Tangential
    x Tangential coordinates
Coordinates, Tetrahedral
    x Tetrahedral coordinates
Coordinates, Trilinear
    x Trilinear coordinates
Coordination compounds
    sa Crystal field theory
        Ligand field theory
    xx Chemistry, Physical and theoretical
        Complex compounds
        Sequestration (Chemistry)
    — Magnetic properties
    — Spectra
Coordination of industrial designs
    See Industrial design coordination
Coorg language
    See Kodagu language
Coos Indians *(E99.C874)*
    x Kusan Indians
    xx Indians of North America
Coos language *(PM1611)*
    sa Kusan languages
    x Kaus language
        Kwokwoos language
Cootenai Indians
    See Kutenai Indians
Cootenai language
    See Kutenai language
Coots *(QL696.G8)*
    xx Rails (Birds)
        Waterfowl
Copaiba *(RS165.C8)*
    x Copaiva
    — Physiological effect   *(QP981.C7)*
Copaiva
    See Copaiba
Copal *(TP938)*
    x Gum-copal
    xx Varnish and varnishing
    Example under Gums and resins
Cope
    xx Church vestments
Copeck
    See Kopeck
Copenhagen
    — Bombardment by the English, 1807
        xx Denmark—History—1660-1814
    — Siege, 1658-1660   *(DL192)*
Copenhagen, Battle of, 1801   *(DL199.3)*
    xx Great Britain—History—1800-1837
Copenhagen in literature
Copenhagen porcelain *(NK4399.C6)*
    x Porcelain, Copenhagen

Copepoda *(Indirect)* *(QL444.C7; Fossil,*
    QE817.C7)
    sa Cyclopoida
    xx Crustacea
        Entomostraca
    — Geographical distribution
Copiers
    See Copying machines
Copla *(PQ6096.C6)*
    Cf. note under Coplas.
Coplas *(PQ6209.C6)*
    Here are entered collections of coplas.
    Works dealing with the copla as a liter-
    ary form are entered under the heading
    Copla.
    xx Folk-songs, Spanish
        Poetry
        Spanish poetry
Copper *(Chemistry, QD181.C9)*
    sa Copper foil
        Creep of copper
        Soils—Copper content
    — Acoustic properties
    — Analysis   *(QD137.C6)*
        Example under Metallurgical analysis
    — Assaying
    — Biodeterioration
    — Brazing
        Example under Brazing
    — — Programmed instruction
    — Brittleness
    — Cold working
    — Coloring
        sa Copper enameling
        xx Metals—Coloring
    — Corrosion
        sa Patina of metals
    — Creep
        See Creep of copper
    — Decay
    — Density
    — Dipole moments
    — Electric properties
    — Electrometallurgy   *(TN870)*
        Example under Electrometallurgy
    — Fatigue
    — Isotopes
    — — Half-life
    — Magnetic properties
    — Metallography   *(TN693.C9)*
    — Metallurgy   *(TN780)*
        sa Ziervogel process
        Example under Metallurgy
    — — Juvenile literature
    — Molecular rotation
    — Optical properties
    — Permeability
    — Physiological effect   *(QP913.C9)*
        sa Plants, Effect of copper on
    — Prices   *(Direct)*
    — Purification
    — Quenching
    — Radiation effects
        See Copper, Effect of radiation on
    — Reactivity
    — Spectra
    — Standards   *(Direct)*
    — Tariff
        See Tariff on copper
    — Therapeutic use
    — Thermal properties
    — — Tables
    — Toxicology   *(RA1231.C7)*
    — Welding   *(TS227)*
        x Copper welding
        Example under Welded joints; Welding
Copper, Effect of radiation on
    x Copper, Irradiated

Copper, Effect of radiation on
(Continued)
    Copper—Radiation effects
    Radiation—Effect on copper
  xx Radiation
Copper, Irradiated
  See Copper, Effect of radiation on
Copper, Powdered
  See Copper powder
Copper age *(Indirect)* *(GN777-8)*
  sa Archaeology
    Bronze age
  xx Archaeology
    Bronze age
Copper alloys *(Manufacture, TS650;*
    Metallography, TN693.C9;
    Properties, testing, etc., TA490)
  sa Aluminum-copper alloys
    Aluminum-copper-magnesium alloys
    Bronze
    Chromium-copper alloys
    Chromium-copper-nickel alloys
    Copper-arsenic alloys
    Copper-beryllium alloys
    Copper-bismuth alloys
    Copper-cobalt-manganese alloys
    Copper ferrite
    Copper-lead alloys
    Copper-magnesium alloys
    Copper-magnesium-silicon alloys
    Copper-nickel alloys
    Copper-nickel-tin alloys
    Copper-nickel-zinc alloys
    Copper steel
    Copper-tin alloys
    Copper-tin-beryllium alloys
    Copper-tin-magnesium alloys
    Copper-titanium-zinc alloys
    Copper-zinc alloys
    Copper-zirconium alloys
    Gold-copper alloys
    Iron-copper alloys
    Lead bronze
    Manganese-copper alloys
    Nickel silver
    Platinum-copper alloys
    Silver-bearing copper
    Silver-copper alloys
  xx Alloys
  — Brazing
  — Corrosion
    sa Patina of metals
  — Metallography
  — Standards
  — Welding
Copper-aluminum alloys
  See Aluminum-copper alloys
Copper-arsenic alloys
  x Arsenic-copper alloys
  xx Arsenic
    Copper alloys
  — Analysis
Copper arsenite
  See Paris green
Copper articles *(Direct)*
  x Copper work
    Copperwork
  xx Coppersmithing
  — Collectors and collecting *(Direct)*
Copper articles, Italian, [Swedish, etc.]
    (Direct)
  x Italian [Swedish, etc.] copper articles
Copper articles, Medieval *(Direct)*
Copper-beryllium alloys
  x Beryllium-copper alloys
  xx Beryllium alloys
    Copper alloys
Copper-bismuth alloys
  x Bismuth-copper alloys

  xx Bismuth alloys
    Copper alloys
Copper castings
  xx Copper founding
    Metal castings
  — Radiography
Copper catalysts
  xx Catalysts
Copper-chromium alloys
  See Chromium-copper alloys
Copper-cobalt-manganese alloys
  xx Cobalt alloys
    Copper alloys
    Manganese alloys
Copper coins
  xx Coins
Copper compounds *(QD181.C9)*
  xx Fertilizers and manures
  — Thermal properties
  — — Tables
Copper crystals
  — Radiation effects
    See Copper crystals, Effect of
      radiation on
Copper crystals, Effect of radiation on
  x Copper crystals—Radiation effects
  xx Radiation
Copper deficiency disease
  See Hypocupremia
Copper enameling
  xx Copper—Coloring
    Enamel and enameling
Copper engraving
  See Engraving
Copper ferrite
  xx Copper alloys
    Ferrite
    Magnetic materials
Copper foil
  xx Copper
    Metal foils
  — Radiation effects
    See Copper foil, Effect of radiation on
Copper foil, Effect of radiation on
  x Copper foil—Radiation effects
  xx Radiation
Copper founding
  sa Copper castings
  xx Founding
Copper-gold alloys
  See Gold-copper alloys
Copper in soils
  See Soils—Copper content
Copper in the body
  sa Copper metabolism
    Hypocupremia
Copper industry and trade *(Direct)*
    (HD9539.C5-7)
  xx Brass industry and trade
  — Government ownership *(Direct)*
  — Labor productivity
  — Taxation *(Direct)*
  — Technological innovations
  — Underdeveloped areas
    See Underdeveloped areas—Copper
      industry and trade
  — Waste disposal *(TD899.M45)*
Copper ions
  xx Ions
Copper-iron alloys
  See Iron-copper alloys
Copper-iron-tin sulphide
  See Stannite
Copper-lead alloys
  x Lead-copper alloys
  xx Copper alloys
    Lead alloys

Copper-magnesium alloys
  x Magnesium-copper alloys
  xx Copper alloys
    Magnesium alloys
Copper-magnesium-silicon alloys
  xx Copper alloys
    Magnesium alloys
    Silicon alloys
Copper-manganese alloys
  See Manganese-copper alloys
Copper metabolism *(QP535.C9)*
  xx Copper in the body
    Metabolism
Copper miners *(Direct)*
  sa Wages—Copper miners
  xx Copper mines and mining
    Miners
Copper Miners' Strike, Noranda, Que.,
  1953-1954
  See Noranda, Que.—Copper Miners' Strike,
    1953-1954
Copper Miners' Strike, Zambia, 1935
Copper Miners' Strike, Zambia, 1940
Copper mines and mining *(Indirect)*
    (TN440-449)
  sa Copper miners
    Strikes and lockouts—Copper mining
  — Juvenile literature
  — Pictorial works
Copper-nickel alloys
  x Nickel-copper alloys
  xx Copper alloys
    Nickel alloys
Copper-nickel-tin alloys
  xx Copper alloys
    Nickel alloys
    Tin alloys
Copper-nickel-zinc alloys *(Manufacture,*
    TS650; Metallography, TN690;
    Strength and testing, TA490)
  sa Nickel silver
  xx Copper alloys
    Nickel alloys
    Zinc alloys
Copper ores *(Indirect)* *(TN440-449)*
  Example under Ore-deposits; Ores
  — Analysis
Copper organic compounds
  See Organocopper compounds
Copper pipe
  See Pipe, Copper
Copper plating *(TS692.C6)*
  xx Electroplating
Copper-platinum alloys
  See Platinum-copper alloys
Copper powder
  x Copper, Powdered
    Powdered copper
  xx Metal powders
Copper roofing
  See Roofing, Copper
Copper salts *(QD181.C9)*
  xx Salts
  — Physiological effect *(QP913.C9)*
Copper silicates
  xx Silicates
Copper-silver alloys
  See Silver-copper alloys
Copper steel *(TA479.C7)*
  xx Copper alloys
    Steel
Copper-tin alloys
  x Tin-copper alloys
  xx Copper alloys
    Tin alloys
Copper-tin-beryllium alloys
  xx Beryllium alloys
    Copper alloys

Tin alloys

Copper-tin-magnesium alloys
   xx Copper alloys
      Magnesium alloys
      Tin alloys
Copper-titanium-zinc alloys
   xx Copper alloys
      Titanium alloys
      Zinc alloys
Copper tubes
   See Tubes, Copper
Copper tubing
   See Tubes, Copper
Copper welding
   See Copper—Welding
Copper wire
   xx Wire
Copper work
   See Copper articles
Copper-zinc alloys
   x Zinc-copper alloys
   xx Copper alloys
      Zinc alloys
  — Fatigue
  — Spectra
Copper-zirconium alloys
   x Zirconium-copper alloys
   xx Copper alloys
      Zirconium alloys
Copperhead (Nickname)
Copperheads
   xx Pit-vipers
Coppermine Apache Indians
   See Mimbreño Indians
Copperplate printing
   See Engravings—Printing
      Plate-printing
Coppersmithing *(Direct)*
   sa Copper articles
   xx Art metal-work
      Metal-work
Copperwork
   See Copper articles
Copra *(SB401)*
   sa Coconut
   xx Coconut
Coprolites
   x Castings, Fossil
      Excrement, Fossil
      Feces, Fossil
      Fossil excrement
      Fossil feces
   xx Paleontology
Coptic Church *(BX130-139)*
   sa Ethiopic Church
      Monasteries, Coptic
  — Relations
  — — Buddhism, ⌐Catholic Church, Islam,
      etc.⌐
Coptic Church in Jerusalem, ⌐etc.⌐
     (BX134.5.A-Z)
Coptic language *(PJ2001-2187)*
   xx Afroasiatic languages
      Egyptian language
  — Papyri
     x Coptic papyri
       Papyri, Coptic
     xx Manuscripts (Papyri)
Coptic literature *(PJ2190-2199)*
Coptic literature (Arabic)
   See Arabic literature—Coptic authors
Coptic magic
   See Magic, Coptic
Coptic monasteries
   See Monasteries, Coptic
Coptic monasticism and religious orders
   See Monasticism and religious orders,
      Coptic

Coptic papyri
   See Coptic language—Papyri
Coptic philology
Coptic processional crosses
   See Processional crosses, Coptic
Copts *(DT72.C7)*
   xx Egyptians
      Ethnology—Egypt
  — Education
Copy, Advertising
   See Advertising copy
Copy-books
   See Penmanship—Copy-books
      Writing
Copy-reading
   x Copyreading
   xx Editing
      Journalism
Copy writers *(Direct)*
   xx Advertising copy
Copy writing
   See Advertising copy
Copyhold
   xx Land tenure—Law
      Manors
      Real property
Copying
   sa Catalog cards—Reproduction
      Copying processes
      Manuscripts—Reproduction
      Maps—Reproduction
      Pictures—Copying
      Tripiṭaka—Copying
      Water-marks—Reproduction
   xx Copying processes
Copying machines
   x Copiers
      Duplicating machines
   xx Copying processes
      Office equipment and supplies
Copying machines (Machine-tools)
Copying processes *(Z48)*
   sa Carbon copy
      Classification—Books—Copying
       processes
      Copying
      Copying machines
      Fluid copying processes
      Hectograph
      Mimeograph
      Multigraph
      Photocopying processes
      Signature writing machines
      Thermography (Copying process)
   x Autographic processes
      Commercial correspondence—Copying
       processes
      Duplicating processes
      Manifolding
      Reproduction processes
      Reprography
      Typewriting—Copying processes
      Writing—Copying processes
   xx Copying
      Documentation
      Letter services
  — Costs *(Direct)*
  — Vocational guidance
Copyists
   sa Pecia
   xx Calligraphers
      Diplomatics
      Manuscripts
      Paleography
Copyreading
   See Copy-reading
Copyright *(Direct) (Z551-656)*
   sa Authors and publishers

      Authorship—Collaboration
      Book registration, National
      Copyright licenses
      Design protection
      Domaine public payant
      Legal deposit (of books, etc.)
      Patent laws and legislation
      Public domain (Copyright law)
      Slogans—Law and legislation
      Trade-marks
   x Intellectual property
      Literary property
      Property, Literary
   xx Authors and publishers
      Authorship
      Book registration, National
      Books
      Booksellers and bookselling
      Genealogy—Law and legislation
      Intangible property
      Literature
      Patent laws and legislation
      Publishers and publishing
      Trade regulation
  — Adaptations *(Direct)*
     x Adaptations (Copyright)
       Arrangement (Music)—Copyright
       Copyright—Musical arrangements
  — Addresses
     See Copyright—Lectures, sermons,
       etc.
  — Advertisements *(Direct) (Z656.A)*
  — Architecture *(Direct) (Z654)*
  — Art *(Direct) (Z654)*
     sa Copyright—Droit de suite
     x Art—Copyright
     xx Law and art
  — Artistic performance *(Direct) (Z650)*
      Here are entered works treating of the
       intellectual property of actors,
       musicians and other performing art-
       ists in their performance. Works on
       the protection of authors and com-
       posers against unauthorized per-
       formance of their works are entered
       under the heading Copyright—Per-
       forming rights.
     x Performing artists, Legal rights of
       Radio and copyright
     xx Copyright—Drama
       Copyright—Moving-pictures
       Copyright—Music
       Copyright—Neighboring rights
     Note under Copyright—Performing
       rights
  — Assignment
     See Copyright—Transfer
  — Broadcasting rights *(Direct)*
     x Copyright and radio
       Copyright and television
       Copyright—Radio rights
       Copyright—Television rights
       Radio and copyright
       Television and copyright
     xx Copyright—Drama
       Copyright—Music
       Copyright—Performing rights
  — Cases
     x Copyright infringement—Cases
  — Computer programs *(Direct)*
     xx Copyright and electronic data
       processing
  — Criminal provisions
     See Copyright infringement
  — Depository copies
     See Legal deposit (of books, etc.)
  — Designs
     See Design protection

Copyright *(Direct)* *(Z551-656)*
(Continued)
— Drama *(Direct)* *(Z652.D7)*
    sa Copyright—Artistic performance
        Copyright—Broadcasting rights
        Copyright—Performing rights
    x Drama—Copyright
        Play-right
        Stage-right
    xx Theater
        Theater—Laws and regulations
— Droit de suite *(Direct)*
    x Droit de suite (Copyright)
    xx Copyright—Art
— Duration *(Direct)*
    x Copyright—Renewal
        Duration of copyright
        Renewal of copyright
— Editing *(Direct)*
— Employees
    See Copyright, Employees'
— Examinations, questions, etc.
— Fair use
    See Fair use (Copyright)
— Government employees
    See Copyright, Government
        employees'
— Government information
    See Copyright—Official information
— Lectures, sermons, etc. *(Direct)*
    x Copyright—Addresses
        Copyright—Sermons
        Lectures and lecturing—Copyright
        Sermons—Copyright
        Speeches, addresses, etc.—Copyright
— Lending rights
    See Public lending rights (of authors)
— Letters *(Direct)* *(Z652.L4)*
— Licenses
    See Copyright licenses
— Manufacturing clause
    x Copyright—United States—
        Manufacturing clause
        Manufacturing clause (Copyright
        law)
    xx Copyright—United States
— Maps *(Direct)* *(Z656.M3)*
— Moral rights *(Direct)* *(Z649.M6)*
    Here are entered works on the legal
    protection of the personal, non-
    pecuniary rights of authors and art-
    ists.
    x Moral rights (Copyright law)
    xx Personality (Law)
— Moving-pictures *(Direct)* *(Z655)*
    sa Copyright—Artistic performance
    x Moving-pictures—Copyright
    xx Moving-pictures—Law
— Moving-pictures, Talking *(Direct)*
    (Z655.3)
— Music *(Direct)* *(Z653)*
    sa Copyright—Artistic performance
        Copyright—Broadcasting rights
        Copyright—Performing rights
        Musicians—Legal status, laws, etc.
    x Music—Copyright
— Musical arrangements
    See Copyright—Adaptations
— Neighboring rights *(Direct)*
    sa Copyright—Artistic performance
    x Neighboring rights (Copyright)
        Rights called neighboring on
        copyrights
— Newspaper articles *(Direct)* *(Z652.N4)*
    xx Journalism
        Press law
— Official information *(Direct)*
    sa Copyright, Government employees'
    x Copyright—Government information

Government information—Copyright
    xx Copyright, Government employees'
— Performing rights *(Direct)*
    Here are entered works on the protec-
    tion of authors and composers
    against unauthorized performance
    of their works. Works treating of
    the intellectual property of actors,
    musicians and other performing art-
    ists in their performance are en-
    tered under the heading Copyright
    —Artistic performance.
    sa Copyright—Broadcasting rights
    x Performing rights (Copyright)
    xx Copyright—Drama
        Copyright—Music
    Note under Copyright—Artistic perform-
    ance
— Phonorecords *(Direct)*
— Photographs *(Direct)* *(Z654)*
    x Photographs—Copyright
— Popular works
— Public domain
    See Public domain (Copyright law)
— Public lending rights
    See Public lending rights (of authors)
— Radio rights
    See Copyright—Broadcasting rights
— Renewal
    See Copyright—Duration
— Royalties *(Direct)*
    x Royalties (Copyright)
— Sculpture *(Direct)* *(Z654)*
    x Sculpture—Copyright
— Sermons
    See Copyright—Lectures, sermons,
        etc.
— Taxation *(Direct)*
    x Taxation of royalties
    xx Income tax
— Television rights
    See Copyright—Broadcasting rights
— Titles *(Direct)* *(Z649.T5)*
    xx Title-page
        Titles of books
— Transfer *(Direct)* *(Z649.T7)*
    x Copyright—Assignment
        Transfer of copyright
— Translations *(Direct)* *(Z649.T8)*
— Unauthorized reprints *(Direct)*
    x Bibliography—Pirated editions
        Books—Pirated editions
        Books—Reprints, Unauthorized
        Editions, Pirated
        Literary piracy
        Piracy, Literary
        Pirated editions
        Reprints, Unauthorized
        Unauthorized reprints
    xx Copyright infringement
        Privately printed books
        Torts

GEOGRAPHIC SUBDIVISIONS

— Confederate States of America
    x Confederate States of America—
        Copyright

GEOGRAPHIC SUBDIVISIONS

— United States
    sa Copyright—Manufacturing clause
    x United States—Copyright

GEOGRAPHIC SUBDIVISIONS

— — Manufacturing clause
    See Copyright—Manufacturing
        clause

Copyright, Employees' *(Direct)*
    sa Copyright, Government employees'
    x Copyright—Employees
        Employees' copyright
Copyright, Government employees' *(Direct)*
    sa Copyright—Official information
    x Copyright—Government employees
    xx Copyright, Employees'
        Copyright—Official information
Copyright, International *(Z552)*
    x International copyright
Copyright, Perpetual *(Direct)* *(Z551)*
Copyright (Canon law)
Copyright (Jewish law)
Copyright (Joint tenancy) *(Direct)*
    x Co-authorship (Copyright)
    xx Authorship—Collaboration
        Joint tenancy
Copyright (Roman law)
Copyright and audio-visual education
    (Direct)
    x Audio-visual education and copyright
    xx Copyright infringement
        Fair use (Copyright)
Copyright and electronic data processing
    (Direct)
    sa Copyright—Computer programs
    x Electronic data processing and
        copyright
    xx Copyright infringement
        Fair use (Copyright)
Copyright and radio
    See Copyright—Broadcasting rights
Copyright and television
    See Copyright—Broadcasting rights
Copyright deposit
    See Legal deposit (of books, etc.)
Copyright infringement *(Direct)*
    sa Copyright and audio-visual education
        Copyright and electronic data
        processing
        Copyright—Unauthorized reprints
        Fair use (Copyright)
        Plagiarism
    x Copyright—Criminal provisions
        Infringement of copyright
    xx Industrial property—Criminal
        provisions
— Cases
    See Copyright—Cases
Copyright licenses *(Direct)*
    x Copyright—Licenses
    xx Copyright
        Licenses
Coq gaulois (Heraldic device) *(CR542)*
    Example under Devices; Heraldry
Cor pulmonale
    x Pulmonary heart disease
    xx Heart—Diseases
        Lungs—Diseases
Cora Indians *(F1220; F1221.C)*
    sa Huichol Indians
    x Coras
        Nayarit Indians
        Nayerits
    xx Huichol Indians
        Indians of Mexico
        Piman Indians
— Legends *(F1220)*
— Religion and mythology *(F1220)*
Cora language *(PM3711)*
    x Chora language
        Nayarita language
    xx Piman languages
Cora literature *(Direct)*
Cora poetry *(Direct)*
Coracan millet
    See Ragi

Coraciae
   See Coraciiformes
Coraciiformes, Fossil *(QE872.C8)*
   x Coraciiformes, Fossil
   xx Birds, Fossil
Coraciiformes *(QL696.C7)*
   sa Hoopoes
      Hornbills
      Kingfishers
   x Coraciae
      Picariae
Coraciiformes, Fossil
   See Coraciiformes, Fossil
CORAL (Computer program language)
   x Class oriented ring associated language
Coral fisheries *(Indirect)* *(SH399.C6)*
   xx Fisheries
Coral industry and trade *(Direct)*
      (HD9747)
Coral reef ecology *(Indirect)* *(QH541.5.C7)*
   xx Coral reefs and islands
      Marine ecology
   — Juvenile literature
Coral reef fauna *(Indirect)* *(QL125)*
   xx Coral reefs and islands
      Marine fauna
   — Behavior
   — Pictorial works
Coral reefs and islands *(QE565)*
   sa Coral reef ecology
      Coral reef fauna
      Reefs
      names of coral reefs and islands
   x Atolls
   xx Geology
      Islands
      Reefs
   — Juvenile literature
Coral Sea, Battle of the, 1942 *(D774.C)*
   xx World War, 1939-1945—Naval
      operations
Coral tree, Common
   See Common coral tree
Coralline algae
   x Calcareous algae
      Nullipores
   xx Algae
Corals *(Indirect)* *(QL377.C5-7)*
   sa Coelenterata
      Madreporaria
      Marine fauna
      Zoantharia
   x Lithophytes
   xx Anthozoa
      Coelenterata
      Zoantharia
   — Juvenile literature
   — Therapeutic use *(RS85-86)*
Corals, Fossil *(QE778)*
   sa Madreporaria, Fossil
Corals in art
   xx Art
Coram nobis, Writ of error
   See Writ of error coram nobis
Coranna language
   See Korana language
Corannas
   See Korana (African people)
Coras
   See Cora Indians
Corbels *(NA2960)*
   xx Architecture—Details
Corbino effect *(QC611)*
Corcoran Gallery of Art, Washington, D.C.
   Example under reference from Picture-galler-
      ies
   Note under Art—Galleries and museums
Cord automobile

Cord grass
   xx Xerophytes
Cordage *(Manufacture, TS1784-5; Trade,
      HD9999.C73)*
   sa Fibers
      Knots and splices
      Rope
      String
      Twine
   xx Hemp
      Rope
   — Juvenile literature
Cordaitales *(QE978)*
   xx Gymnosperms, Fossil
Corded culture
   See Corded Ware culture
Corded Ware culture *(Indirect)*
      (GN776.2.C6)
   x Battle-ax cultures
      Corded culture
   xx Europe—Antiquities
      Neolithic period—Europe
Cordeliers (Monastic order)
   See Franciscans in France
Cordials (Liquor)
   See Liqueurs
Cordierite *(Indirect)* *(TN948.C75)*
   x Dichroite
      Iolite
   xx Silicates
      Urtite
Córdoba, Argentine Republic
   — Riot, 1969
Cordova Rebellion, 1839
   xx Texas—History—Republic, 1836-1846
Cordovan leather
   See Leather work
Corduroy
Core curriculum
   See Education—Curricula
Core drilling
   x Core drills
   xx Boring
   — Automation
   — Standards
Core drills
   See Core drilling
Core makers
   See Coremakers
Core materials
   x Materials, Core
   xx Coremaking
      Molding materials
Coredemption
   See Mary, Virgin—Coredemption
Coregoninae
   See Whitefishes
Coremakers *(Direct)*
   sa Iron molders
   x Core makers
   xx Foundries
      Iron molders
Coremaking
   sa Core materials
   x Cores (Founding)
   xx Molding (Founding)
   — Production standards
Cores (Founding)
   See Coremaking
Corfu
   — History
   — — Italian occupation, 1923 *(DF847;
      DF901.C7)*
Corfu, Declaration of, 1917
   x Declaration of Corfu, 1917
   xx European War, 1914-1918—Congresses,
      conferences, etc.

Corfu Channel case
   xx Government liability (International law)
      —Cases
Corgis, Welsh
   See Welsh corgis
Coriander *(Botany, QK495.U48; Culture,
      SB307.C; Trade, HD9210)*
   — Seed
      See Coriander seed
Coriander fruit
   See Coriander seed
Coriander seed *(Indirect)*
   x Coriander fruit
      Coriander—Seed
   xx Seeds
Corina
   See Limba
Corinth, Miss.
   — Siege, 1862 *(E473.56)*
Corinth, Miss., Battle of, 1862 *(E474.44)*
Corinthian capitals (Architecture)
   See Capitals (Architecture), Corinthian
Corinthian columns
   See Columns, Corinthian
Corinthian League *(DF233.2)*
Corinthian raisins
   See Currant grapes
Coriolis force *(QC880.4.C65)*
   x Compound centrifugal force
      Deflecting force
   xx Dynamic meteorology
      Earth—Rotation
Coritani *(DA141)*
   x Coritavi
Coritavi
   See Coritani
Cork *(Building materials, TA455.C6;
      Manufacture, TS908; Plant anatomy,
      QK648; Trade, HD9769.C73)*
Cork craft *(TT190.5)*
   xx Handicraft
   — Juvenile literature
Cork industry *(Direct)*
   — Collective labor agreements
      See Collective labor agreements—
         Cork industry
Cork-tree *(SD397.C79)*
   sa Amur cork tree
   xx Oak
   — Varieties
Corkwood
   See Balsa wood
Corliss steam-engine *(TJ485.C5)*
   xx Steam-engines
Corliss valve-gear *(TJ548.C8)*
   x Valve-gears
CORMAP (Computer program)
   xx Cartography—Computer programs
Cormorants *(QL696.S6)*
   sa Double-crested cormorant
      Great cormorant
   xx Sea birds
Corms
   xx Botany
      Bulbs
      Floriculture
      Gardening
Corn
   See Grain
      Maize
Corn, Canned
   See Maize, Canned
Corn, Indian
   See Maize
Corn, Sweet
   See Sweet corn
Corn borer, European
   See European corn borer

Corn borer, Southern
  See Southern corn borer
Corn borer, Southwestern
  See Southwestern corn borer
Corn cobs
  See Corncobs
Corn crake
  See Corncrake
Corn earworm
  x Bollworm
    Cotton bollworm
    Tobacco budworm
    Tomato fruitworm
    Vetchworm
  — Control *(Indirect)*
Corn harvesting machinery
  See Corn picking machinery
Corn husk craft
  See Cornhusk craft
Corn laws (Great Britain)
Corn leaf-beetle *(SB945.C73)*
Corn machinery *(Indirect)*
  sa Corn picking machinery
    Corn planters (Machines)
  x Maize—Machinery
  xx Agricultural machinery
Corn maidens' dance
  xx Indians of North America—Dances
    Indians of North America—Religion
      and mythology
Corn meal
  sa Tortillas
  x Indian meal
  xx Maize
Corn oil
Corn oil cake
  See Corn oil meal
Corn oil meal
  x Corn oil cake
Corn oil meal as feed
Corn palaces *(Sioux City, F269.S6)*
Corn paper
  See Paper, Maize
Corn pickers (Machines)
  See Corn picking machinery
Corn picking machinery *(S695)*
  x Corn harvesting machinery
    Corn pickers (Machines)
    Mechanical corn pickers
  xx Corn machinery
    Harvesting machinery
    Maize—Harvesting
  — Maintenance and repair
Corn planters (Machines)
  x Maize planters
    Planters, Corn
  xx Agricultural machinery
    Corn machinery
Corn products industry *(Direct)*
  xx Maize
  — Accounting
Corn root-aphis *(SB945.C75)*
  xx Maize—Diseases and pests
Corn root-rot
  See Root-rot of maize
Corn rootworm, Northern
  See Northern corn rootworm
Corn rootworm, Southern
  See Spotted cucumber beetle
Corn shuck craft
  See Cornhusk craft
Corn silage
  x Maize silage
    Maize—Silage
  xx Maize as feed
Corn-stalk borer *(SB945.C77)*
Corn-stalk disease
  See Hemorrhagic septicemia of cattle

Corn-stalks *(TP966.C7)*
  x Cornstalks
  xx Maize
Corn-starch *(Chemistry, QD321; Food
      values, TX558.S8; Industry, TP415)*
  xx Glucose industry
    Starch
Corn sugar
  See Maize sugar
Corn syrup
Corn trade
  See Grain trade
    Maize
Corncobs *(TP996.C6)*
  x Corn cobs
  xx Maize
Corncrake
  x Corn crake
    European land rail
    Land rail, European
  xx Rails (Birds)
Cornea *(QL949; QM511)*
  sa Epithelium
    Eye banks
  xx Eye
  — Diseases *(RE336)*
    sa Keratoconjunctivitis sicca
    x Keratomalacia
    xx Eye—Diseases and defects
  — Preservation
    x Corneal preservation
    xx Preservation of organs, tissues, etc.
  — Surgery
  — Tattooing
    x Corneal tattooing
      Tattooing of the cornea
    xx Eye—Surgery
  — Transplantation
    x Corneal transplant
    xx Eye—Surgery
      Example under Transplantation of or-
        gans, tissues, etc.
  — Ulcers *(RE340)*
Corneal preservation
  See Cornea—Preservation
Corneal tattooing
  See Cornea—Tattooing
Corneal transplant
  See Cornea—Transplantation
Corned beef
  x Beef, Corned
  xx Beef
    Salting of food
Cornell University
  — Description
  — — Views
      Example under Views
Cornemuse
  See Bagpipe
Corner stone laying
  See Corner stones, Laying of
Corner stones, Laying of
  x Corner stone laying
    Foundation stones, Laying of
    Laying of corner stones
    Stones, Corner, Laying of
    Stones, Foundation, Laying of
  xx Church dedication
    Churches
    Public buildings
    Rites and ceremonies
Corners, Commercial
  See Monopolies
    Speculation
    Stock-exchange
    Trusts, Industrial

Cornet *(History and construction,
      ML960-961)*
  sa Trumpet
  xx Trumpet
  — Orchestra studies *(MT446)*
    xx Cornet—Studies and exercises
  — Studies and exercises *(MT445)*
    sa Cornet—Orchestra studies
Cornet and baritone music
  See Baritone and cornet music
Cornet and piano music *(M260-261)*
  sa Sonatas (Cornet and piano)
    Suites (Cornet and piano)
  x Piano and cornet music
Cornet and piano music, Arranged
      (M260-261)
  sa Cornet with band—Solo with piano
Cornet and piano music (Jazz) *(M260-261)*
Cornet and trumpet music *(M288-9)*
  sa Concertos (Cornet and trumpet)
    Cornet and trumpet with orchestra
  x Trumpet and cornet music
Cornet and trumpet with orchestra
      (M1040-1041)
  sa Concertos (Cornet and trumpet)
  xx Concertos (Cornet and trumpet)
    Cornet and trumpet music
    Orchestral music
Cornet and trumpet with orchestra, Arranged
      (M1040-1041)
Cornet music *(M85-89)*
  sa Concertos (Cornet)
    Concertos (Cornet with band)
    Cornet with band
    Cornet with orchestra
    Quartets, ₍Trios, etc.₎, Wind quartets,
      ₍trios, etc.₎ *followed by specifications
      which include the cornet*
Cornet music, Arranged (Jazz)
  See Cornet music (Jazz)
Cornet music (Cornets (2)) *(M288-9)*
Cornet music (Cornets (4))
  See Wind quartets (Cornets (4))
Cornet music (Jazz) *(M85-89)*
  x Cornet music, Arranged (Jazz)
Cornet with band *(M1205)*
  sa Concertos (Cornet with band)
  xx Band music
    Concertos (Cornet with band)
    Cornet music
  — Solo with piano *(M1205)*
    xx Cornet and piano music, Arranged
Cornet with orchestra *(M1030-1031)*
  sa Concertos (Cornet)
  xx Concertos (Cornet)
    Cornet music
    Orchestral music
Cornet with orchestra, Arranged
      (M1030-1031)
Cornets (4) with band *(M1205-6)*
  sa Concertos (Cornets (4) with band)
  x Four cornets with band
  xx Band music
    Concertos (Cornets (4) with band)
    Wind quartets (4 cornets)
Cornets (4) with band, Arranged *(M1257)*
  — Scores and parts *(M1257)*
Cornhusk craft *(TT878)*
  x Corn husk craft
    Corn shuck craft
    Cornshuck craft
  xx Handicraft
Cornice work *(TH2482)*
  xx Building
Cornices *(Architecture, NA2960; Building,
      TH2482)*
  xx Architecture—Details
Corning, N.Y.

— Flood, 1972
Cornish
  x Cornishmen
Cornish drama *(Collections, PB2569; History and criticism, PB2552)*
Cornish fowl *(SF489.C6)*
Cornish in America, [etc.]
Cornish language *(PB2501-2549)*
  xx Celtic languages
Cornish literature *(Collections, PB2563-2621; History and criticism, PB2551-4)*
  xx Celtic literature
Cornish Rex cat
  See Rex cat
Cornishmen
  See Cornish
Cornshuck craft
  See Cornhusk craft
Cornstalks
  See Corn-stalks
Cornu ammonis
  See Hippocampus (Brain)
Cornua cutanea
  See Horns, Cutaneous
Cornwall, Eng.
— Blizzard, 1891
Cornwall, Eng. in art
Coro, Venezuela
— History
—— Revolution, 1533
    xx Venezuela—History—To 1556
Corolla automobile
  See Toyota Corolla automobile
Corona, Solar
  See Sun—Corona
Corona, Stellar
  See Stars—Corona
Corona (Electricity) *(QC643)*
Corona Mark II automobile
  See Toyota Corona Mark II automobile
Coronary arteries
  xx Arteries
    Heart—Blood-vessels
— Diseases
    See Coronary heart disease
— Innervation
— Radiography
    xx Angiography
Coronary artheriosclerosis
  See Coronary heart disease
Coronary care units *(RA975.5.C6)*
  xx Cardiacs
    Cardiovascular disease nursing
    Hospital care
    Hospitals—Cardiovascular services
    Hospitals—Construction
    Intensive care units
Coronary heart disease *(RC685.C6)*
  x Coronary arteries—Diseases
    Coronary artheriosclerosis
    Coronary thrombosis
  xx Heart—Diseases
— Programmed instruction
— Research *(Direct)*
    xx Heart—Diseases—Research
— Surgery
Coronary thrombosis
  See Coronary heart disease
Coronation ampullas
  See Ampullas, Coronation
Coronation Safari
  See East African Safari Rally
Coronation sermons
  xx Sermons
Coronation stone
  See Stone of Scone

Coronations *(Indirect) (Institutional history, JC391; Manners and customs, GT5050; England, DA111-112; France, DC33; Germany, DD61.8; Italy, DG441-450; Medieval, D127; Russia, DK32; Scotland, DA773; Spain, DP48)*
  sa Ampullas, Coronation
    Durbars
    subdivision Coronation *under names of rulers, e.g.* Napoléon I, Emperor of the French, 1769-1821—Coronation
  xx Crowns
    Kings and rulers
    Pageants
    Rites and ceremonies
— Great Britain
    sa Stone of Scone
Coronel, Battle of, 1914 *(D582.F2)*
  xx European War, 1914-1918—Naval operations
Coroners *(Direct)*
  sa Forensic pathology
    Medical examiners (Law)
  x Inquests, Coroners'
  xx Criminal justice, Administration of
    Death—Causes
    Forensic pathology
    Medical examiners (Law)
— Correspondence, reminiscences, etc.
Corporal (Missile)
  Example under Ballistic missiles
Corporal punishment *(Direct) (Penology, HV8609; Schools, LB3025)*
  sa Flagellants and flagellation
    School discipline
  x Flagellation
    Flogging
    Whipping
  xx Punishment
    School discipline
Corporal works of mercy *(BV4647.M4)*
  x Mercy, Corporal works of
    Works of mercy, Corporal
  xx Good works (Theology)
Corporate debt *(HG4028.D3)*
  xx Corporations—Finance
    Debt
Corporate design coordination
  See Industrial design coordination
Corporate divestiture *(Direct)*
  x Corporations—Divestiture
    Divestiture, Corporate
    Divestment, Corporate
  xx Corporate reorganizations
Corporate entry (Cataloging) *(Z695.8)*
  sa Cataloging of government publications
    Cataloging of society publications
  x Cataloging of corporate entries
  xx Cataloging of government publications
    Descriptive cataloging
Corporate finance
  See Corporations—Finance
Corporate image and design
  See Industrial design coordination
Corporate insurance
  See Insurance, Business
Corporate insurance departments
  See Insurance departments
Corporate law departments
  See Corporate legal departments
Corporate legal departments *(Direct)*
  x Corporate law departments
    Law departments, Corporate
    Legal departments, Corporate
  xx Corporation law
    Law offices
    Lawyers

Practice of law
Corporate meetings *(Direct)*
  sa Corporate minutes
    Stockholders' meetings
  x Company meetings
    Corporation meetings
    Corporations—Meetings
    Meetings, Corporate
  xx Corporation law
    Corporations
    Directors of corporations
    Stockholders' meetings
Corporate mergers
  See Consolidation and merger of corporations
Corporate minutes *(Direct)*
  x Minutes, Corporate
  xx Corporate meetings
Corporate practice of law
  See Legal service corporations
Corporate practice of medicine
  See Medical corporations
Corporate profits *(Direct)*
  xx Corporations—Finance
    Profit
Corporate reorganizations *(Direct)*
  sa Bankruptcy
    Consolidation and merger of corporations
    Corporate divestiture
  x Corporations—Reorganization
    Reorganization of corporations
  xx Bankruptcy
    Consolidation and merger of corporations
    Corporation law
    Corporations
    Corporations—Finance
— Taxation *(Direct)*
Corporate reserves
  See Corporation reserves
Corporate secretaries
  See Corporation secretaries
Corporate state *(Economic history, HD3611-3616; Fascism, JC481)*
    Here are entered works on systems of government organized on the basis of functional representation. Works on the government of a particular corporate state are entered under name of country with subdivision Politics and government. *Cf.* note under Trade and professional associations.
  sa Fascism
    Functional representation
    Gild socialism
    Trade and professional associations
  x Corporations (Corporate state)
    Corporatism
    Corporative state
    Corporativism
    State, Corporate
  xx Fascism
    Functional representation
    Gild socialism
    Industry and state
    Political science
    Syndicalism
    Trade-unions
Corporate style
  See Industrial design coordination
Corporation accounting
  See Corporations—Accounting
Corporation act, 1661
  sa Test act, 1673
  x Disabilities, Political (Great Britain)
    Political disabilities (Great Britain)
    Test act, 1661

Corporation act, 1661 *(Continued)*
  xx Test act, 1673
Corporation counsels, Municipal
  See City attorneys
Corporation courts
  See Municipal courts
Corporation directors
  See Directors of corporations
Corporation executives
  See Executives
Corporation farms
  See Farm corporations
Corporation finance
  See Corporations—Finance
Corporation income tax
  See Corporations—Taxation
Corporation law *(Direct)*
  sa Articles of incorporation
    Bank service corporations
    Bonds
    By-laws
    Capital stock
    Certificates of incorporation
    Close corporations
    Clubs—Law and legislation
    Consolidation and merger of
      corporations
    Cooperative societies—Law
    Corporate legal departments
    Corporate meetings
    Corporate reorganizations
    Corporations, Foreign
    Corporations, International
    Corporations—Nationality
    Corporations, Nonprofit
    Corporations, Religious
    De facto corporations
    Directors of corporations
    Disregard of corporate entity
    Domicile of corporations
    Family corporations
    Farm corporations
    Incorporation
    Limited partnership
    Liquidation
    Massachusetts trusts
    Mining corporations
    Minority stockholders
    One-man companies
    Private companies
    Professional corporations
    Public service commissions
    Public utilities
    Railroad law
    Securities
    Stockholders
    Stocks
    Subsidiary corporations
    Trusts, Industrial
    Ultra vires
    Unincorporated societies
  x Company law
    Corporations—Laws and legislation
    Law, Corporation
  xx Commercial law
    Corporations
    Juristic persons
    Monopolies
    Partnership
    Public utilities
    Trusts, Industrial—Law
  Note under Public utilities
— Cases
— — Digests
      See Corporation law—Digests
— Conflict of laws
      See Conflict of laws—Corporations
— Criminal provisions

    Example under Criminal law
— Digests
    x Corporation law—Cases—Digests
— Domicile
    See Domicile of corporations
— Forms
— Popular works

GEOGRAPHIC SUBDIVISIONS

— United States
— — Forms
      Note under Forms (Law)
Corporation law (Greek law)
Corporation law (Islamic law)
Corporation law (Roman law)
  sa Universitates (Civil law)
  xx Universitates (Civil law)
Corporation lawyers, Municipal
  See City attorneys
Corporation meetings
  See Corporate meetings
Corporation reports
  sa Financial statements
  x Annual reports, Corporate
    Company reports
    Reports, Corporation
  xx Report writing
— Anecdotes, facetiae, satire, etc.
Corporation reserves *(Direct)*
  sa Amortization
    Depreciation
    Insurance—Reserves
    Sinking-funds
  x Corporate reserves
    Corporations—Reserves
    Reserve funds, Corporation
    Reserves, Corporation
  xx Amortization
    Cash flow
    Corporations—Accounting
    Corporations—Finance
    Reserves (Accounting)
    Sinking-funds
— Taxation *(Direct)*
    xx Corporations—Taxation
Corporation secretaries *(Direct)*
  x Company secretaries
    Corporate secretaries
  xx Corporations
    Secretaries
Corporation tax
  See Corporations—Taxation
Corporations *(Direct) (Finance,
    HG4001-4280; Theory and policy,
    HD2709-2930)*
    Here are entered works on business as-
      sociations organized as legal persons.
  sa Bank service corporations
    Bonds
    By-laws
    Capital stock
    Close corporations
    Conglomerate corporations
    Cooperative societies
    Corporate meetings
    Corporate reorganizations
    Corporation law
    Corporation secretaries
    Directors of corporations
    Domicile of corporations
    Farm corporations
    Holding companies
    International business enterprises
    Massachusetts trusts
    Mining corporations
    Municipal corporations
    Municipal franchises
    One-man companies

    Private companies
    Professional corporations
    Promoters
    Public service commissions
    Public utilities
    Securities
    Stock companies
    Stock ownership
    Stockholders
    Stocks
    Subsidiary corporations
    Trust companies
    Trusts, Industrial
  x Business corporations
    Companies
    Corporations, Business
    Limited companies
    Public corporations
    Stock corporations
  xx Business
    Charters
    Public utilities
    Stock companies
    Stocks
    Trusts, Industrial
Example under Associations, institutions, etc.
Note under Public utilities
— Accounting *(HF5686.C7)*
    sa Corporation reserves
      Surplus (Accounting)
    x Corporation accounting
    Example under Accounting
— — Examinations, questions, etc.
— Auditing
    Example under Auditing
— Cash position
    sa Small business—Cash position
    x Cash position (Corporation finance)
    xx Corporations—Finance
— — Mathematical models
— Charitable contributions *(Direct)*
    x Charitable contributions as tax
      deductions
    xx Charities
      Corporations—Taxation
— Consolidation
    See Consolidation and merger of
      corporations
— Criminal liability
    See Criminal liability of juristic
      persons
— Divestiture
    See Corporate divestiture
— Domicile
    See Domicile of corporations
— Finance *(HG4001-4280)*
    sa Cash flow
      Cooperative societies—Finance
      Corporate debt
      Corporate profits
      Corporate reorganizations
      Corporation reserves
      Corporations—Cash position
      Corporations—Taxation
      Corporations—Valuation
      Dividends
      Securities, Privately placed
      Self-financing
      Tender offers (Securities)
    x Capitalization (Finance)
      Corporate finance
      Corporation finance
    Example under Finance
— — Examinations, questions, etc.
      (HG4026)
— — Mathematical models
— Insurance departments
      See Insurance departments

446

— Juvenile literature
— Laws and legislation
    See Corporation law
— Meetings
    See Corporate meetings
— Merger
    See Consolidation and merger of corporations
— Nationality
    sa Corporations, Foreign
    x Juristic persons—Nationality
    xx Citizenship
       Conflict of laws—Corporations
       Corporation law
       Corporations, Foreign
       Domicile of corporations
— Records and correspondence
    See Business records
— Reorganization
    See Corporate reorganizations
— Reserves
    See Corporation reserves
— State supervision
— Taxation   *(HD2753)*
    sa Consolidation and merger of corporations—Taxation
       Corporation reserves—Taxation
       Corporations—Charitable contributions
       Undistributed profits tax
    x Corporation income tax
       Corporation tax
       Federal corporation tax
       Franchises, Taxation of
       Taxation of franchises
    xx Corporations—Finance
       Corporations—Valuation
    Example under Taxation
— — Consolidated returns
    x Consolidated income tax returns
       Consolidated returns
       Consolidated tax returns
       Income tax—Consolidated returns
       Tax returns, Consolidated
    xx Tax returns
— Tort liability
    See Tort liability of corporations
— Valuation   *(United States, HD2781)*
    sa Corporations—Taxation
       Mining industry and finance—Valuation
       Public utilities—Valuation
       Railroads—Valuation
    x Stocks—Valuation
    xx Corporations—Finance
    Note under Valuation
— — Mathematical models

Corporations, American, ₍French, etc.₎   *(Direct)*
    Here are entered works on foreign corporations chartered by nationals of individual countries. Works on foreign corporations in general are entered under the heading Corporations, Foreign.
— Charitable contributions
— Finance
— Taxation   *(Direct)*

Corporations, Business
    See Corporations
Corporations, Conglomerate
    See Conglomerate corporations
Corporations, Ecclesiastical
    See Corporations, Religious

Corporations, Foreign   *(Direct)*
    Here are entered works on the legal status of corporations of foreign nationality in a given country. Works on the law of a state of the United States governing corporations doing business in that state, are entered under the above heading subdivided by the state in which they are doing business. Works treating of United States state laws collectively are entered under the heading Corporations, Foreign—United States —States.
    sa Corporations, International
       Corporations—Nationality
       Insurance companies, Foreign
    x Foreign corporations
       Juristic persons, Foreign
    xx Aliens
       Business enterprises, Foreign
       Corporation law
       Corporations, International
       Corporations—Nationality
       International business enterprises
       Investments, Foreign
    Note under Corporations, American, ₍French, etc.₎
— Taxation   *(Direct)*
    xx Income tax—Foreign income
       Taxation of aliens

GEOGRAPHIC SUBDIVISIONS

— United States
    Here are entered works on the legal status of corporations of foreign nationality in the United States. Works treating of United States state laws governing domestic corporations "doing business in other states," collectively, are entered under the heading Corporations, Foreign—United States—States.

GEOGRAPHIC SUBDIVISIONS

— — States
    Notes under Corporations, Foreign; Corporations, Foreign—United States

Corporations, Government   *(Direct)*
    (HD3850; United States, HD3881-8; Other countries, HD4001-4420)
    sa Government business enterprises
       Government competition
    x Authorities, Public
       Government corporations
       Government-owned corporations
       Public authorities
    xx Government business enterprises
       Government ownership
       Juristic persons
— Accounting
— Auditing and inspection
    See Government business enterprises —Auditing and inspection
— Employees
— Finance
    xx Finance, Public
— Research
— Taxation   *(Direct)*

Corporations, International
    sa Corporations, Foreign
    x International corporations
       Multinational corporations
    xx Corporation law
       Corporations, Foreign
— Tort liability
    See Tort liability of charitable organizations

Tort liability of corporations
Corporations, Medical
    See Medical corporations
Corporations, Membership
    See Corporations, Nonprofit
Corporations, Nonprofit   *(Direct)*
    Here are entered works on the law of incorporated associations established for other than business purposes. Works on corporations established to administer endowment funds are entered under the heading Charitable uses, trusts, and foundations.
    sa By-laws
       Unincorporated societies
    x Associations (Law)
       Corporations, Membership
       Membership corporations
       Nonprofit corporations
    xx Corporation law
       Juristic persons
       Unincorporated societies
— Accounting
— Discipline
— Forms
— Registration and transfer   *(Direct)*
— Taxation   *(Direct)*
    sa Church property—Taxation
       Cooperative societies—Taxation
       Taxation, Exemption from
       Universities and colleges—Taxation
    x Charities—Taxation
    xx Taxation, Exemption from
Corporations, Nonprofit (Roman law)
Corporations, Professional
    See Professional corporations
Corporations, Religious   *(Indirect)   (BV765)*
    x Corporations, Ecclesiastical
       Ecclesiastical corporations
       Religious corporations
    xx Corporation law
       Ecclesiastical law
       Sects
— Taxation   *(Direct)*
    xx Church property—Taxation
Corporations, Religious (Canon law)
    (BX1939.C75)
Corporations, Subsidiary
    See Subsidiary corporations
Corporations (Corporate state)
    See Corporate state
       Trade and professional associations
Corporatism
    See Corporate state
Corporative state
    See Corporate state
Corporativism
    See Corporate state
Corpulence   *(RC628)*
    sa Obese-hyperglycemic syndrome
       Prader-Willi syndrome
       Reducing
    x Obesity
    xx Fat
— Anecdotes, facetiae, satire, etc.
— Control
    See Reducing
— Psychological aspects
    sa Leanness—Psychological aspects
    xx Leanness—Psychological aspects
       Psychology
Corpulence in art
    xx Art
Corpulence in children   *(RJ399.C6)*
    xx Children—Diseases
— Juvenile literature
Corpus callosum
    xx Brain

Corpus Christi, Argentine Republic, Battle of, 1536 *(F2841)*
Corpus Christi festival *(BV63)*
Corpus criminis
   See Corpus delicti
Corpus delicti *(Direct)*
   x Corpus criminis
   xx Criminal law
Corpus geniculatum
   See Geniculate bodies
Corpus luteum *(QL881; QM421; QP261)*
   sa Ovulation
      Progesterone
   xx Graafian follicle
      Ovaries
      Ovulation
Corpus luteum hormone
   See Progesterone
Corpus striatum
   xx Basal ganglia
      Brain
Corpus subthalamicum
   See Subthalamus
Corpuscular theory of light
   See Light, Corpuscular theory of
Corpuscular theory of matter
   See Electrons
      Matter—Constitution
Correality and solidarity *(Direct)*
   sa Contracts, Joint and several
      Joint tortfeasors
   x "Joint and several"
      Solidarity (Civil law)
   xx Debtor and creditor
      Obligations (Law)
Correality and solidarity (Greek law)
Correality and solidarity (Roman law)
Correcting circuits
   See Equalizers (Electronics)
Correction officer
   See Correctional personnel
Correctional employees
   See Correctional personnel
Correctional institutions *(Direct)*
   sa Criminal courts
      Halfway houses
      Juvenile courts
      Juvenile detention homes
      Penal colonies
      Prisons
      Reformatories for women
      Workhouses
   x Corrections institutions
      Penal institutions
   xx Corrections
      Public institutions
   — Design and construction
Correctional law *(Direct)*
   sa Prisoners—Legal status, laws, etc.
      Prisons—Laws and regulations
      Sentences (Criminal procedure)
   xx Corrections
      Criminal law
      Criminal procedure
      Punishment
Correctional personnel *(Direct)*
   sa Parole officers
      Prison wardens
      Prisons—Officials and employees
      Probation officers
   x Correction officer
      Correctional employees
      Corrections employees
   xx Civil service
      Corrections
Correctional services
   See Corrections

Corrections *(Direct)*
   sa Correctional institutions
      Correctional law
      Correctional personnel
      Imprisonment
      Interviewing in corrections
      Pardon
      Parole
      Police services for juveniles
      Probation
      Punishment
      Rehabilitation of criminals
      Rehabilitation of juvenile delinquents
      Social work with delinquents and criminals
      Volunteer workers in corrections
      Work release of prisoners
   x Correctional services
      Penology
   xx Criminal justice, Administration of
   — Examinations, questions, etc.
   — Research *(Direct)*
Corrections employees
   See Correctional personnel
Corrections institutions
   See Correctional institutions
Corrective teaching
   See Remedial teaching
Correlation, Stratigraphic
   See Stratigraphic correlation
Correlation (Statistics) *(Mathematics, QA273-281; Statistics, HA33)*
   sa Autocorrelation (Statistics)
      Cluster analysis
      Coefficient of concordance
      Correlators
      Factor analysis
      Frequency curves
      Latent structure analysis
      Multicollinearity
   xx Errors, Theory of
      Least squares
      Mathematical statistics
      Probabilities
      Regression analysis
      Statistics
      Statistics—Graphic methods
Correlation analysis (Chemistry)
   See Linear free energy relationship
Correlation equation (Chemistry)
   See Linear free energy relationship
Correlation meter
   See Correlators
Correlation of forces
   See Force and energy
Correlators
   x Correlation meter
   xx Computers
      Correlation (Statistics)
Correspondence
   See Church correspondence
      Commercial correspondence
      Genealogical correspondence
      Government correspondence
      International correspondence
      Legal correspondence
      Letter-writing
      Letters
      Love-letters
Correspondence, Diplomatic
   See Diplomatic documents
Correspondence, Legal
   See Legal correspondence

Correspondence files
   See subdivision Records and correspondence *under specific subjects, e.g.* Railroads—Records and correspondence; United States. Army—Records and correspondence
Correspondence schools and courses *(Direct)* *(LC5901-6101; Business schools, HF1116, HF1133; Technology, T172)*
   sa Singing—Methods—Self-instruction
      subdivision Self-instruction *under names of languages; and subdivision* Methods—Self-instruction *under names of musical instruments*
   x Home education
      Home study courses
      Self-instruction
      "Teach yourself" courses
   xx Education
      Schools
      Technical education
      University extension
   — Anecdotes, facetiae, satire, etc.
   — Law and legislation *(Direct)*
      xx Educational law and legislation
Correspondences, Doctrine of *(BX8727)*
   x Doctrine of correspondences
   xx Analogy (Religion)
Correspondent banks
   See Banks and banking—Correspondent banks
Correspondents, Foreign
   See Foreign correspondents
Corridos *(Collections, PQ7260; History, PQ7180)*
   xx Folk-songs, Mexican
      Mexican ballads and songs
Corriedale sheep *(SF373.C)*
Corrosion, Electrolytic
   See Electrolytic corrosion
Corrosion and anti-corrosives *(TA462; TA467)*
   sa Acids—Handling and transportation
      Aluminum coating
      Cathodic protection
      Corrosion resistant materials
      Electrolytic corrosion
      Faolite
      Fretting corrosion
      Metals—Pickling
      Paint
      Phosphate coating
      Protective coatings
      Sea-water corrosion
      Soil corrosion
      Stress corrosion
      Waterproofing
      Zinc coating
      subdivision Corrosion *under subjects, e.g.* Aluminum—Corrosion; Concrete—Corrosion; Steam-boilers—Corrosion
   x Anti-corrosive paint
      Atmospheric corrosion
      Metal corrosion
      Metals—Corrosion
      Rust
      Rustless coatings
   xx Chemical inhibitors
      Chemistry, Technical
      Materials—Deterioration
      Metallic surfaces
      Paint
      Protective coatings
      Waterproofing
      Weathering
   — Laboratory manuals

— Maps
— Problems, exercises, etc.
— Research
    xx Research, Industrial
— Tables, calculations, etc.
Corrosion resistant materials
  xx Corrosion and anti-corrosives
— Standards
Corrosive oil wells
  See Condensate oil wells
Corrugated board
  See Corrugated paperboard
Corrugated paperboard *(TS1138)*
  x Corrugated board
  xx Paper
    Paperboard
— Testing
Corrugated sheet-metal
  See Sheet-metal, Corrugated
Corruption, Judicial
  See Judicial corruption
Corruption, Police
  See Police corruption
Corruption (in politics) *(Direct)* *(JF1081;*
    By country, JK-JQ; Municipal, etc.,
    JS)
  sa Bribery
    Campaign funds
    Elections—Corrupt practices
    Lobbying
    Misconduct in office
  x Boss rule
    Graft (in politics)
    Political scandals
    Spoils system
  xx Civil service reform
    Conflict of interests (Public office)
    Misconduct in office
    Patronage, Political
    Political crimes and offenses
    Political ethics
    Politics, Practical
— Anecdotes, facetiae, satire, etc.
Corruption (in politics) in literature
  x Political corruption in literature
Corsages
  xx Flower arrangement
Corsair (Fighter planes) *(TL686.C45)*
  x F4U (Fighter planes)
  xx Fighter planes
Corsairs
  See Pirates
    Privateering
Corset *(Costume, GT2075; Hygiene, RA779;*
    Manufacture, TT677)
  xx Clothing and dress
    Foundation garments
    Underwear
— Tariff
    See Tariff on corsets
Corset industry *(Direct)*
  sa Wages—Corset industry
  xx Foundation garment industry
Corsetry
  See Foundation garments
Corsica
— History *(DC611.C8-839)*
— — To 1347
— — Genoese domination, 1347-1768
— — 16th century
— — 18th century
— — French domination, 1768-1794
— — French Revolution, 1789-1793
— — British occupation, 1794-1796
— — 1796-
Corsica in literature

Corsican literature *(Italian dialects,*
    PC1796-9)
    Comprises literature in both French and
    Corsican dialect.
  xx French literature
    Italian literature—Corsica
Corsican pine
  See Austrian pine
Corsicans *(DC611.C8-839)*
Corsicans in the Barbary States, [etc.]
Corte de Justicia Centroamericana, Cartago,
    Costa Rica
  Example under International courts
Cortex, Cerebral
  See Cerebral cortex
Cortical evoked potential
  See Visual evoked response
Corticoids
  See Adrenocortical hormones
Corticosteroids
  See Adrenocortical hormones
Corticosterone
  xx Adrenocortical hormones
    Cortin
Corticotrophic hormones
  See ACTH
Corticotropin
  See ACTH
Cortin *(QP187)*
  sa Corticosterone
  xx Hormones
Cortina automobile
  xx Ford automobile
Corti's organ
  x Organ of Corti
  xx Labyrinth (Ear)
    Neural receptors
Cortisol
  See Hydrocortisone
Cortisone
  sa ACTH
    Hydrocortisone
  x Compound E
    Cortone
  xx Adrenocortical hormones
Cortone
  See Cortisone
Coruña, Battle of, 1809 *(DC233.C7)*
  xx Peninsular War, 1807-1814
Corundum *(Indirect)* *(Mineral resources,*
    TN948.C8; Mineralogy, QE391.C9)
  sa Emery
    Rubies
— Spectra
Corvair automobile
  xx Automobiles, Compact
    Chevrolet automobile
Corvée *(HJ5951-7)*
  xx Highway law
    Road construction workers
    Roads
    Service, Compulsory non-military
    Tax collection
    Taxation
Corvette automobile *(TL215.C)*
  xx Chevrolet automobile
Corvette Stingray automobile *(TL215.C63)*
  x Stingray automobile
Corwith Expedition, 1895 *(F1376)*
Corybantes
  xx Cultus, Greek
    Priests, Greek
Coshatta Indians
  See Koasati Indians
Cosmetes
  xx Archons
    Ephebia
— Portraits

Cosmetics *(Manners and customs, GT2340;*
    Manufacture, TP983; Toilet, RA778)
  sa Beauty culture
    Beauty, Personal
    Cosmetics industry
    Hair preparations
    Ointments
    Perfumes
    Toilet
    Toilet preparations
  x Complexion
    Make-up (Cosmetics)
  xx Beauty culture
    Beauty, Personal
    Beauty shops
    Costume
    Toilet
    Toilet preparations
    Woman—Health and hygiene
— Analysis
— Early works to 1800
— Law and legislation *(Direct)*
— Microbiology
— Packaging
— Patents
— Standards *(Direct)*
— Taxation
    See Toilet preparations—Taxation
— Testing
— Toxicology
— Trade-marks
Cosmetics industry *(Direct)*
  sa Salesmen and salesmanship—Cosmetics
  xx Cosmetics
— Equipment and supplies
Cosmetologists
  See Beauty operators
Cosmetology
  See Beauty culture
Cosmic chemistry
  See Cosmochemistry
Cosmic dust *(QB791)*
  x Dust, Cosmic
  xx Interstellar matter
Cosmic electrodynamics *(QC809.E55;*
    Astrophysics, QB461)
  sa Magnetohydrodynamics
  xx Astrophysics
    Cosmic physics
    Electrodynamics
    Electromagnetic theory
    Magnetohydrodynamics
Cosmic harmony
  See Harmony of the spheres
Cosmic noise *(QC809.C6)*
  xx Radio astronomy
    Radio meteorology
    Radio noise
— Charts, diagrams, etc.
Cosmic physics *(QC801-8; Meteorology,*
    QC883)
  sa Astrophysics
    Auroras
    Cosmic electrodynamics
    Magnetic fields (Cosmic physics)
    Magnetism, Terrestrial
    Magnetohydrodynamics
    Solar wind
    Van Allen radiation belts
  xx Physics
    Space sciences
  Note under Space sciences
Cosmic ray showers *(QC485)*
  x Cosmic showers
    Showers, Cosmic
  xx Cascade shower
    Ionization
    Pair production

Cosmic rays *(QC485)*
    sa Forbush decreases
        Mesons
        Positrons
        Solar cosmic rays
        Van Allen radiation belts
    x Millikan rays
    xx Extraterrestrial radiation
        Ionizing radiation
        Nuclear physics
        Radioactivity
        Space environment
  — Juvenile literature
  — Observations
  — Physiological effect
  — Tables, etc.
Cosmic renewal
    See Regeneration (in religion, folk-lore,
        etc.)
Cosmic showers
    See Cosmic ray showers
Cosmobiology
    See Space biology
Cosmochemistry *(QB450)*
    x Cosmic chemistry
        Space chemistry
    xx Chemistry
        Space sciences
Cosmogony *(QB981; Geological, QE506)*
    sa Creation
        Interstellar matter
        Meteoritic hypothesis
        Nebulae
        Nebular hypothesis
        Universe, Destruction of
    x Universe
    xx Astronomy
        Earth
        Nebular hypothesis
  — Early works to 1800
Cosmogony, Ancient
Cosmogony, Babylonian, ⌈Chinese, etc.⌉
    x Babylonian ⌈Chinese, etc.⌉ cosmogony
Cosmogony, Biblical
    See Creation
Cosmogony, Buddhist
    sa Matter (Buddhism)
    x Buddhist cosmogony
    xx Philosophy, Buddhist
Cosmogony, Glacial
    sa Glacial epoch
    x Glacial cosmogony
    xx Glacial epoch
Cosmography
    sa Geography
    x Universe
    xx Earth
        Geography, Mathematical
Cosmology *(BD493-708)*
    sa Astronomy
        Astronomy—Philosophy
        Beginning
        Creation
        Earth
        Eternal return
        Harmony of the spheres
        Kinematic relativity
        Life on other planets
        Microcosm and macrocosm
        Monadology
        Nebular hypothesis
        Philosophy
        Philosophy of nature
        Planets—Origin
        Plurality of worlds
        Religion and astronautics
        Space sciences
        Teleology

        Theosophy
    x Universe
    xx Astronomy—Philosophy
        Creation
        Deism
        Earth
        Metaphysics
        Philosophy
        Philosophy of nature
  — Early works to 1800
Cosmology, Biblical *(BS651)*
    sa Creation
    x Bible—Cosmology
    xx Creation
Cosmology, Buddhist
    x Buddhist cosmology
    xx Philosophy, Buddhist
Cosmology, Hindu *(B132.C)*
    x Hindu cosmology
    xx Philosophy, Hindu
Cosmology, Islamic *(B745.C6)*
    sa Islam and astronautics
    x Cosmology, Muslim
        Islamic cosmology
        Muslim cosmology
    xx Philosophy, Islamic
Cosmology, Jewish *(B157.C)*
    x Jewish cosmology
    xx Philosophy, Jewish
Cosmology, Muslim
    See Cosmology, Islamic
Cosmology in literature
Cosmonauts
    See Astronauts
Cosmopolitan high schools
    See Comprehensive high schools
Cosmopolitanism
    See Internationalism
Cosmoramas
    sa Cycloramas
        Diorama
        Panoramas
    xx Cycloramas
        Diorama
        Panoramas
Cossacks *(Ethnography, DK35)*
    sa Hetmans
        Zaporogians
    x Cozacks
  — Historiography
Cossacks, Dnieperian
    See Zaporogians
Cossacks in literature
Cost *(HB199; Crises, HB3719)*
    sa Costs, Industrial
        Markup
        Prices
        Value
        subdivisions Cost of construction, Cost
          of operation, Costs, *and* Estimates
          and costs *under specific subjects, e.g.*
          Railroads—Cost of construction;
          Railroads—Cost of operation;
          Research, Industrial—Costs;
          Engineering—Estimates and costs
    x Costs
        Costs (Economics)
    xx Costs, Industrial
        Economics
    Note under reference from Estimates
  — Accounting
        See Cost accounting
COST (Computer program language)
    x Common Statistics Tabulating Language
Cost accounting *(HF5686.C8)*
    x Cost—Accounting
        Managerial accounting
    xx Accounting

        Bookkeeping
        Cost control
        Costs, Industrial
  — Problems, exercises, etc.
  — Programmed instruction
Cost and standard of living *(Direct)*
        (HD6977-7080)
    sa Budgets, Personal
        Discretionary income
        Family allowances
        Food prices
        Home economics—Accounting
        Luxury
        Prices
        Purchasing power
        Rent
        Saving and thrift
        Wages
    x Comfort, Standard of
        Consumer price index
        Cost of living
        Food, Cost of
        Household expenses
        Living, Cost of
        Living, Standard of
        Standard of living
    xx Consumption (Economics)—Surveys
        Economics
        Home economics
        Labor and laboring classes
        Luxury
        Poor
        Prices
        Purchasing power
        Saving and thrift
        Social problems
        Wages
        Wealth
  — Mathematical models
  — Public opinion
  — Research
Cost benefit analysis
    See Cost effectiveness
Cost control
    sa Cost accounting
        Value analysis (Cost control)
        subdivision Cost control *under specific*
          subjects, e.g. Lumbering—Cost
          control
    x Cost reduction
    xx Costs, Industrial
  — Graphic methods
Cost effectiveness
    sa Value analysis (Cost control)
    x Capital output ratios
        Cost benefit analysis
    xx Costs, Industrial
        Engineering economy
        Engineering—Estimates and costs
        Value analysis (Cost control)
  — Mathematical models
"Cost, insurance and freight"
    See C.I.F. clause
Cost mark system
    See Price marks
Cost of armies
    See Armies, Cost of
Cost of dental care
    See Dental care, Cost of
Cost of living
    See Cost and standard of living
Cost-of-living pension adjustments
    See Civil service pensions—Cost-of-living
        adjustments
        Old age pensions—Cost-of-living
        adjustments
Cost-of-living wage adjustments
    See Wages—Cost-of-living adjustments

Cost of medical care
   See Medical care, Cost of
Cost of navies
   See Navies, Cost of
Cost of war
   See War, Cost of
Cost-plus contracts *(Direct)*
   xx Contracts
Cost reduction
   See Cost control
Costa Rica
   — History *(F1541-1557)*
   — — To 1821
   — — 1821-1948
       sa Rivas, Battle of, 1856
           Santa Rosa, Battle of, 1856
   — — 1948-
Costa Rican drama *(Direct)*
Costa Rican essays *(Direct)*
Costa Rican literature *(PQ7480-7489)*
Costa Rican poetry *(Collections, PQ7486;*
   History, PQ7482)
Costa Rican wit and humor *(Direct)*
Costanoan language *(PM971)*
Costen's syndrome
   xx Temporomandibular joint—Diseases
Costs
   See Cost
Costs, Industrial *(Direct)*
   sa Cost
      Cost accounting
      Cost control
      Cost effectiveness
      Economies of scale
      Expense accounts
      Labor costs
      Make-or-buy decisions
      Manufactures—Costs
      Marketing—Costs
      Overhead costs
      Prices
      subdivisions Cost of construction, Cost
       of operation, Costs, Estimates and
       costs, *under specific subjects, e.g.*
       Railroads—Cost of construction;
       Railroads—Cost of operation;
       Ship-building—Costs; Engineering—
       Estimates and costs
    x Industrial costs
      Industry—Costs
    xx Cost
      Industrial engineering
      Industry
   — Mathematical models
Costs, Labor
   See Labor costs
Costs, Social
   See Externalities (Economics)
Costs (Canon law)
Costs (Economics)
   See Cost
Costs (Law) *(Direct)*
   sa Bailiffs—Fees
      Fees, Administrative
      Fines (Penalties)
      In forma pauperis
      Insurance, Litigation
      Lawyers—Fees
      Notaries—Fees
      Security for costs
      Trusts and trustees—Fees
      Witnesses—Fees
      subdivision Costs *under individual legal*
       procedures, e.g. Divorce—Costs;
       Probate law and practice—Costs
    x Fee system (Taxation)
      Fees (Law)
      Fees, Legal

Legal fees
   xx Actions and defenses
      Civil procedure
      Fees, Administrative
      Fees, Professional
Costume *(Indirect) (Manners and customs,*
   GT500-2370)
   Here are entered descriptive and historical works on modes or customs of
   dress among various nations and at different periods, including styles peculiar to particular professions or classes
   of people or to a particular character;
   also works on fancy costume and dress
   for the theater and special occasions,
   e.g. court receptions, carnivals, mas-
   querades, etc. General works treating
   the subject from the standpoint of
   utility and works on the art of dress are
   entered under Clothing and dress.
   sa Academic costume
      Allegorical costume
      Arms and armor
      Biblical costume
      Children—Costume
      Church vestments
      Clothing and dress
      Combs
      Cosmetics
      Décolletage
      Doll clothes
      Dressmaking
      Fans
      Fashion
      Handkerchiefs
      Head-gear
      Impersonators, Female
      Impersonators, Male
      Indians of North America—Costume
       and adornment
      Jewelry
      Livery
      Make-up, Theatrical
      Men's clothing
      Millinery
      Monasticism and religious orders,
       Buddhist—Habit
      Monasticism and religious orders—
       Habit
      Sashes (Costume)
      Toilet
      Umbrellas and parasols
      Uniforms
      Veils
      Wedding costume
      Wigs
      subdivision Costume *under particular*
       classes of people, etc., e.g. Physicians
       —Costume; *and individual articles of*
       apparel, e.g. Boots and shoes, Coats,
       Hosiery
    x Acting—Costume
      Costume, Theatrical
      Fancy dress
      Folk costume
      Moving-pictures—Costume
      Stage costume
      Style in dress
      Theater—Costume
      Theatrical costume
      Woman—Dress
    xx Art
      Beauty, Personal
      Clothing and dress
      Ethnology
      Fashion
      Hairdressing
      Head-gear

      Manners and customs
      Toilet
      Uniforms
   Note under Clothing and dress
   — Caricatures and cartoons
   — Conservation and restoration
     xx Museum techniques
   — History
   — — To 500 *(GT530-560)*
      x Costume, Ancient
   — — Medieval, 500-1500 *(GT575)*
      x Costume, Medieval
   — — 15th century
   — — 16th century *(GT585)*
   — — 17th century *(GT585)*
   — — 18th century *(GT585)*
   — — 19th century *(GT595)*
   — — 20th century *(GT596)*
   — — Juvenile literature
   — Juvenile literature
   — Laws and regulations
     See Sumptuary laws
   — Museums
     See Costume museums
   — Pictorial works
   — Private collections
     xx Costume museums
   — Terminology

       GEOGRAPHIC SUBDIVISIONS

   — Greece
     x Greek costume
Costume, Ancient
   See Costume—History—To 500
Costume, Arab, ₍Oriental, Slavic, etc.₎
   (Direct)
   x Arab ₍Oriental, Slavic, etc.₎ costume
Costume, Biblical
   See Biblical costume
Costume, Clerical
   See Clergy—Costume
Costume, Ecclesiastical
   See Clergy—Costume
Costume, Islamic *(BP190.5.C6)*
   x Costume, Muslim
      Islamic costume
      Muslim costume
Costume, Jewish *(GT540)*
   sa Biblical costume
      Priests, Jewish—Vestments
      Shaatnez
    x Jewish costume
      Jews—Clothing and dress
    xx Biblical costume
Costume, Medieval
   See Costume—History—Medieval,
     500-1500
Costume, Military
   See Uniforms, Military
     subdivision Uniforms *under armies,*
      navies, etc. e.g. United States.
      Army—Uniforms; United States.
      Navy—Uniforms
Costume, Muslim
   See Costume, Islamic
Costume, Theatrical
   See Costume
Costume design *(TT507)*
   sa Children's clothing—Pattern design
      Dressmaking—Pattern design
      Shirts, Men's—Pattern design
      Tailoring—Pattern design
    x Dress design
      Fashion design
    xx Clothing and dress
      Design
      Fashion
   — Vocational guidance

Costume design (TT507)
— Vocational guidance (Continued)
    x Costume design as a profession
    xx Fashion as a profession
Costume design as a profession
  See Costume design—Vocational guidance
Costume designers (Direct)
    x Clothes designers
      Couturiers
      Dress designers
      Fashion designers
    xx Fashion as a profession
— Biography (TT505)
Costume in art
    x Clothing and dress in art
    xx Art
Costume museums
    sa Costume—Private collections
    x Costume—Museums
Cot death
  See Sudden death in infants
Cotenancy
  See Condominium (Housing)
      Condominium (Office buildings)
      Joint tenancy
Cotillion
  See German (Dance)
      Quadrille (Dance)
Cotillions
    Here are entered collections of cotillion
    music for various mediums. Individual
    cotillions and collections of cotillions
    for a specific medium are entered un-
    der the heading followed by specifica-
    tion of medium.
Cotillions (Piano) (M30)
    xx Piano music
Cottage cheese
    sa Cookery (Cottage cheese)
    x Dutch cheese
      Smearcase
— Marketing
Cottage industries (Direct)
    Here are entered works on industries car-
    ried on in the home by a self-employed
    worker and his family, often with the
    aid of a few apprentices. Works on in-
    dustries carried on in the home for an
    outside employer are entered under
    the heading Home labor.
    sa Artisans
      Home labor
    x Village industries
    xx Artisans
      Home labor
      Industry
      Small business
— Taxation (Direct)
Cottages (NA7551-5)
    sa Architecture, Domestic
      Bungalows
      Country homes
      Suburban homes
    x Architecture, Rural
      Rural architecture
    xx Architecture, Domestic
      Dwellings
      Farm buildings
      Housing, Rural
      Labor and laboring classes—Dwellings
      Suburban homes
Cottages, Summer
  See Summer homes
Cottoidei
  See Mail-cheeked fishes

Cotton (Indirect) (Agriculture, SB245-252;
    Botany, QK495.M27; Fibers,
    TS1542)
    sa Cotton fabrics
      Cotton textiles
      Decrystallized cotton
      Fibers
      Khaki
      Linters
    xx Fibers
      Oilseed plants
Example under Commerce; Fiber plants; Field
    crops; Textile fibers
— Cleaning
    Example under Cleaning
— Cooperative marketing
    xx Cotton—Marketing
— Diseases and pests (Indirect)
    (SB608.C8)
    sa names of pests, e.g. Boll-weevil,
      Cotton-worm
    x Cotton pests
    Example under Agricultural pests
— Drying
— Fertilizers and manures
— Genetics
— Grading (TS1542; Economics,
    HD9070-9089)
    Example under Grading
— Harvesting
    See Cotton picking
— Irrigation
    x Cotton irrigation
    xx Cotton growing
    Example under Irrigation
— Juvenile literature
— Marketing
    sa Cotton—Cooperative marketing
— Moisture
    Example under Moisture
— Prices (Direct)
    xx Cotton trade
— Research
    See Cotton research
— Sampling
    Example under Sampling
— Storage
— — Costs
— Tables, etc. (HF5716.C6)
— Taxation (Direct) (HD9070.8)
— Testing
— Trade-marks
— Transportation
— Varieties
    x Cotton varieties
— Water requirements
— Weed control (Indirect)
— Weights and measures (United States,
    HD9076)
Cotton bagging
  See Bagging
Cotton baling (SB252)
    x Baling of cotton
    xx Baling
      Cotton handling
— Patents
Cotton boll-weevil
  See Boll-weevil
Cotton bollworm
  See Corn earworm
Cotton breeding (SB249)
    xx Cotton growing
      Plant-breeding
Cotton carding (TS1578)
    xx Carding
      Cotton manufacture
      Cotton spinning

Cotton combing (TS1578)
    xx Cotton manufacture
Cotton dyeing
  See Dyes and dyeing—Cotton
Cotton fabrics
    sa Typewriter ribbons
    xx Cotton
      Cotton textiles
      Textile industry and fabrics
— Cleaning
— Preservation
    x Preservation of cotton fabrics
    xx Cotton finishing
— Quality control
    See Cotton manufacture—Quality
      control
— Standards
Cotton fabrics, Effect of light on
    xx Textile chemistry
Cotton famine, 1861-1864 (Great Britain,
    HD9881.5)
Cotton finishing (TS1580)
    sa Cotton fabrics—Preservation
      Mercerization
    xx Cotton manufacture
      Finishes and finishing
      Textile finishing
— Quality control
    See Cotton manufacture—Quality
      control
Cotton ginning
  See Cotton gins and ginning
Cotton gins and ginning (SB252; TS1585)
    sa Wages—Cotton ginning
    x Cotton ginning
      Gin (Cotton machinery)
    xx Cotton machinery
— Accidents
— Costs
— Fires and fire prevention (TH9445.C7)
— Waste disposal
Cotton growing (Indirect) (Agriculture,
    SB245-252; Economics,
    HD9070-9089)
    sa Cotton breeding
      Cotton—Irrigation
      Cotton picking
— Accounting
— Costs
— Equipment and supplies
— Labor productivity
— Law and legislation (Direct)
Cotton handling
    sa Cotton baling
    x Handling of cotton
Cotton-harvesting machinery
  See Cotton-picking machinery
Cotton hosiery
  See Hosiery, Cotton
Cotton irrigation
  See Cotton—Irrigation
Cotton leaf curl (SB608.C)
Cotton leaf-roller
    xx Leaf-rollers
Cotton machinery (TS1583)
    sa Cotton gins and ginning
      Cotton-picking machinery
      Cotton planters (Machines)
      Looms
      Spinning machinery
      Textile machinery
    xx Cotton manufacture
      Textile machinery
— Design and construction (TS1583)
— Safety appliances (TS1583)
    Example under Industrial safety
Cotton manufacture (Direct) (TS1550-1590)
    sa Cotton carding

Councils and synods *(Direct) (General,*
    BV710) (Continued)
        Popes—Primacy
        Religious gatherings
    x Church councils
        Synods
    xx Catholic Church
        Catholic Church—History
        Christianity
        Church history
        Conciliar theory
        Popes—Primacy
        Religious gatherings
Councils and synods, Buddhist
    See Buddhist councils and synods
Councils and synods, Diocesan *(Direct)*
    x Diocesan councils and synods
        Diocesan synods
Councils and synods, Diocesan (Canon law)
Councils and synods, Ecumenical
    sa names of councils and synods, e.g.
        Vatican Council, 1869-1870
    x Ecumenical councils and synods
        Oecumenical councils and synods
Councils and synods, Jewish
    See Jewish councils and synods
Councils and synods, Parish
    See Parish councils
Councils and synods, Plenary
    x Plenary councils and synods
Councils and synods, Plenary (Canon law)
Councils and synods, Provincial
    x Provincial councils and synods
Councils and synods, Provincial (Canon law)
Councils and synods (Canon law)
    (BX1939.C78)
        Here are entered works on the organiza-
        tion and authority of councils and syn-
        ods as treated in canon law.
Councils and synods (Canon law, Eastern)
Councils and synods in art
    xx Art
Counseling *(Direct)*
    sa Employee counseling
        Genetic counseling
        Group counseling
        Interviewing
        Marriage counseling
        Pastoral counseling
        Personnel service in education
        Rehabilitation counseling
        Social case work
        Television in counseling
        Vocational guidance
    xx Family life education
        Interviewing
        Personnel service in education
        Psychology, Applied
        Social case work
        Vocational guidance
    — Vocational guidance
        See Counseling as a profession
Counseling, Buddhist
    See Pastoral counseling (Buddhism)
Counseling, Client-centered
    See Client-centered psychotherapy
Counseling, Employee
    See Employee counseling
Counseling, Nondirective
    See Client-centered psychotherapy
Counseling, Pastoral
    See Pastoral counseling
Counseling, Rabbinical
    See Pastoral counseling (Judaism)
Counseling as a profession
    x Counseling—Vocational guidance
Counseling centers, Pastoral
    See Pastoral counseling centers

Counseling for clergy *(BV4398.5)*
        Here are entered works on the clergy as
        recipients of counseling. Works on the
        clergyman as the counselor are entered
        under Pastoral counseling.
    xx Clergy
        Priests
    Note under Pastoral counseling
Counseling in literature
Counselor-parent relationships
    See Parent-student counselor relationships
Counselor-teacher relationships
    See Teacher-counselor relationships
Counselors, Camp
    See Camp counselors
Counselors, Residence
    See Residence counselors
Counselors, Student
    See Student counselors
Counsels, Evangelical
    See Evangelical counsels
Counsels, Public relations
    See Public relations consultants
Counter-irritants
    sa Acupuncture
        Baunscheidtism
        Blisters
        Cupping
        Moxa
        names of individual drugs, e.g.
        Cantharides, Iodine
    xx Irritation
        Materia medica
        Therapeutics
        Therapeutics, Cutaneous and external
Counter-Reformation *(Indirect) (History:*
    general, D220-271; Germany,
    DD176-189; Church history, BR430)
    sa Church history—Modern period, 1500-
        Jesuits
        Reformation
        Thirty Years' War, 1618-1648
        Trent, Council of, 1545-1563
    x Anti-Reformation
    xx Catholic Church—History
        Church history—Modern period, 1500-
        Church renewal
        Reformation
        Trent, Council of, 1545-1563
    — Historiography
Counter tubes
    See Cold cathode tubes
Counterclaim
    See Set-off and counterclaim
Counterfactual conditionals
    See Counterfactuals (Logic)
Counterfactuals (Logic) *(BC199.C66)*
    x Contrary-to-fact conditional
        Counterfactual conditionals
    xx Conditionals (Logic)
        Logic
Counterfeits and counterfeiting *(Direct)*
    (HG335-341; Counterfeit detectors,
    United States, HG641-5)
    sa Bank-notes—Forgeries
        Reproduction of money, documents,
        etc.—Law and legislation
        World War, 1939-1945—Counterfeit
        money
    x Coining, Illicit
        Illicit coining
    xx Criminal law
        Forgery
        Money
Counterglow *(QC976.C7)*
    x Gegenschein
    xx Astronomy
        Atmosphere

        Geophysics
        Meteorological optics
        Zodiacal light
Counterinsurgency
    See Insurgency
Counterintelligence
    See Intelligence service
Countermark (Numismatics)
    See Counterstamp (Numismatics)
Counterpart funds *(Direct)*
    xx Economic assistance, American
Counterpoint *(History, ML446; Instruction,*
    MT55)
    sa Canon (Music)
        Descants
        Fugue
        Organum
    xx Composition (Music)
        Music
        Music—Instruction and study
        Music—Theory
Counterrevolutions *(Direct) (JC492)*
    xx Revolutions
Counters, Digital
    See Digital counters
Counters, Proportional
    See Proportional counters
Countersignature (Constitutional law)
    See Ministerial responsibility
Counterstamp (Numismatics)
    x Countermark (Numismatics)
    xx Numismatics
Countervailing duties
    See Antidumping duties
Counting
    See Numeration
Counting devices, Digital
    See Digital counters
Counting-out rhymes *(GR485)*
    x Counting rhymes
        Folk-lore of numbers
        Number rhymes
    xx Folk-lore
        Nursery rhymes
Counting rhymes
    See Counting-out rhymes
Counting tubes
    See Cold cathode tubes
        Geiger-Müller counters
        Ionization chambers
Country and western music
    See Country music
Country churches
    See Rural churches
Country clergy
    See Rural clergy
Country-dance *(GV1763)*
        Here are entered works about the coun-
        try-dance. Country-dance music is en-
        tered under the heading Country-
        dances.
    sa Beseda (Dance)
    x Contradance
        Longways dance
Country-dances
        Here are entered collections of country-
        dance music for various mediums. In-
        dividual country-dances and collec-
        tions of country-dances for a specific
        medium are entered under the heading
        followed by specification of medium.
    x Contradances
    Note under Country-dance
Country-dances (Accordion ensemble)
    (M1362)
    xx Accordion ensembles
Country-dances (Band) *(M1248)*
    xx Band music

— Scores and parts *(M1248)*
Country-dances (Bassoon, clarinet, flute, oboe) *(M455-9)*
  xx Wind quartets (Bassoon, clarinet, flute, oboe)
Country-dances (Bassoons (2), horns (2), oboes (2)) *(M655-7)*
  xx Wind sextets (Bassoons (2), horns (2), oboes (2))
Country-dances (Chamber orchestra) *(M1048; M1060)*
  xx Chamber-orchestra music
— Scores
Country-dances (Clarinets (4)) *(M455-9)*
  xx Wind quartets (Clarinets (4))
Country-dances (Flute, violins (2), violoncello) *(M463-4)*
  xx Quartets (Flute, violins (2), violoncello)
Country-dances (Harpsichord) *(M31; M32.8)*
  xx Harpsichord music
Country-dances (Orchestra) *(M1048; M1060)*
  xx Orchestral music
— Scores and parts
— Scores (reduced) and parts
Country-dances (Piano) *(M31; M32.8)*
  xx Piano music
Country-dances (Piano, recorders (2)) *(M315-319)*
  xx Trios (Piano, recorders (2))
Country-dances (String orchestra) *(M1145; M1160)*
  xx String-orchestra music
Country-dances (Violin) *(M40-44)*
  xx Violin music
Country-dances (Violin and harpsichord) *(M217-218; M221-3)*
  xx Violin and harpsichord music
Country-dances (Violin and piano) *(M217-218; M221-3)*
  xx Violin and piano music
Country-dances (Violins (2)) *(M286-7)*
  xx Violin music (Violins (2))
Country-dances (Violins (2), violoncello) *(M349-353)*
  xx String trios (Violins (2), violoncello)
Country-dances (Violins (3)) *(M349-353)*
  xx String trios (Violins (3))
Country homes *(Direct) (TH4850)*
  sa Farmhouses
    Summer homes
  x Architecture, Rural
    Rural architecture
  xx Architecture, Domestic
    Cottages
    Dwellings
    Housing, Rural
    Summer homes
Country life *(Indirect) (S521; Manners and customs, GT3470; Social groups, HT401-485)*
  Here are entered popular or literary works on living in the country. Descriptive studies on living conditions in the country are entered under the heading Rural conditions. Studies or treatises on the theory of social organization in rural districts and communities are entered under the heading Sociology, Rural.
  sa Agricultural societies
    Bees (Cooperative gatherings)
    Country life in literature
    Farm life
    Farmers
    Home economics, Rural
    Mountain life
    Outdoor life

    Part-time farming
    Pastoral poetry
    Rural conditions
    Rural youth
    Sociology, Rural
  x Rural life
  xx Farm life
    Outdoor life
    Rural conditions
    Sociology, Rural
  Notes under Rural conditions; Sociology, Rural
— Anecdotes, facetiae, satire, etc.
— Gift-books
— Juvenile literature
— Pictorial works *(S521)*
— Poetry *(PN6110.C8)*
— Sounds
    See Country sounds
Country life in art *(N8217.C65)*
  xx Art
Country life in literature
  sa Farm life in literature
    Pastoral literature
  xx Country life
    Pastoral literature
Country life in motion pictures
  xx Moving-pictures
Country ministry
  See Rural clergy
Country music *(Indirect)*
  sa Bluegrass music
    Fiddle tunes
    Hillbilly musicians
  x Country and western music
    Gospel music
    Hillbilly music
    Western and country music
  xx Folk music
    Music, Popular (Songs, etc.)
Country schools
  See Rural schools
Country sounds
  sa Farm sounds
  x Country life—Sounds
  xx Sounds
Country stores
  See General stores
Counts palatine
  x Comites Palatii
County agents
  See County agricultural agents
County agricultural agents *(S533-4)*
  x County agents
  xx Agricultural education
    Agricultural extension work
County annexation
  See Annexation (County government)
County attorneys *(Direct)*
  x Attorneys, County
    County counsels
    County law officers
    County solicitors
  xx County officials and employees
    Government attorneys
    Lawyers
County budgets *(Direct)*
  x Budgets, County
  xx Local budgets
County charters *(Direct)*
  sa charters of American counties, e.g. Montgomery Co., Md. Charters
  x Charters, County
  xx Charters
    County government
County clerks (Great Britain)
  See Clerks of the counties (Great Britain)

County colleges (English)
  See Municipal universities and colleges
County counsels
  See County attorneys
County courts *(Direct)*
    Works on individual courts are entered under the official heading for the court, *e.g.* North Carolina. County Court (Onslow Co.)
  x Courts, County
  xx Courts
County finance
  See Local finance
County government *(Direct) (General, JS261-7; Great Britain, JS3260; United States, JS411-414, JS451)*
    Here are entered works on county government in general, and on county government in the United States as a whole. Works on the government of individual counties are entered under the name of the county, with subdivision Politics and government, *e.g.* Cook Co., Ill.—Politics and government.
  sa Annexation (County government)
    County charters
    County manager government
  xx Local government
  Note under Local government
— Records and correspondence
    x County records
    xx Public records

  GEOGRAPHIC SUBDIVISIONS

— ⌜local subdivision⌝
— — Registers
      Example under reference from Registers
County law officers
  See County attorneys
County libraries
  See Libraries, County
County manager government *(Direct)*
  xx County government
County officers
  See County officials and employees
County officials and employees *(Direct)*
  sa County attorneys
    Ordinaries
  x County officers
    Town officers
  xx Local officials and employees
— Salaries, allowances, etc. *(Direct)*
County records
  See County government—Records and correspondence
County school systems *(Indirect) (LB2813)*
  sa Intermediate service units (Education)
    School supervision, County
  xx Public schools
    School management and organization
County solicitors
  See County attorneys
Coup d'état of 1851
  See France—History—Coup d'état, 1851
Coupled mode theory
  sa Jahn-Teller effect
  x Coupled modes, Theory of
    Coupled systems
  xx Oscillations
    Vibration
    Wave-motion, Theory of
Coupled modes, Theory of
  See Coupled mode theory
Coupled systems
  See Coupled mode theory

Couples (Mechanics)
    See Forces and couples
Couplets
    sa Renku
    xx Poetry
Coupling constants *(QC721)*
    xx Particles (Nuclear physics)
Couplings *(Machinery, TJ183)*
    sa Bellows (Mechanical engineering)
       Car-couplings
       Clutches (Machinery)
       Hydraulic couplings
       Universal joints (Mechanics)
    xx Carriage and wagon making
       Clutches (Machinery)
       Gearing
       Machinery
Coupon ballot *(JK2217)*
    x Ballot, Coupon
    xx Ballot
Coupons, Book
    See Book coupons
Coups d'état *(JC494)*
    xx Government, Resistance to
       History
       Political science
       Revolutions
Courage *(BJ1533.C8)*
    sa Fear
       Fortitude
       Heroes
       Morale
       Timidity
    x Bravery
       Heroism
    xx Conduct of life
       Ethics
       Fear
       Heroes
    — Juvenile literature
    — Quotations, maxims, etc.
Courage in art
    xx Art
Courante
    xx Musical form
Courantes
    Here are entered collections of courante
      music for various mediums. Individual
      courantes and collections of courantes
      for a specific medium are entered un-
      der the heading followed by specifica-
      tion of medium.
Courantes (Bassoon, clarinet, flute, oboe)
    (M455-9)
    xx Wind quartets (Bassoon, clarinet, flute,
      oboe)
Couriers, Diplomatic
    See Diplomatic couriers
Cours d'amour
    See Courts of love
Course computers
    See Course-line computers
Course indicators
    See Course-line computers
Course-line computers *(TL696.C8)*
    sa Pictorial course computer
    x Course computers
       Course indicators
    xx Aeronautical instruments
       Electronics in aeronautics
       Navigation (Aeronautics)
Courses of study
    See Education—Curricula
       Education—[local subdivision]—
         Curricula

      subdivision Curricula *under specific*
      types of education or school, and
      under names of individual schools,
      e.g. Technical education—Curricula;
      High schools—Curricula; Library
      schools—Curricula; Chicago.
      University—Curricula *For works on*
      the curriculum of a special
      denomination, sect, or order, see
      name of denomination, etc. with
      subdivision Education. *For course of*
      study in a particular subject, see
      subdivision Study and teaching
      under subject. (Exceptions:
      subdivision Instruction *under*
      Drawing; Instruction and study
      under Confirmation, First
      communion, *and all headings in the*
      field of music)
Coursing *(SK291)*
    sa Beagling
    xx Hares
       Hounds
       Hunting
Coursing (Racing)
    See Dog racing
Court, Contempt of
    See Contempt of court
Court, Terms of
    See Terms of court
Court administration *(Direct)*
    x Court management
       Courts—Administration
    xx Management
Court and courtiers
    See Courts and courtiers
Court baron
    See Courts baron and courts leet
Court bonds
    See Judicial bonds
Court calendars *(Direct)*
    x Court dockets
       Trial-dockets
    xx Court records
Court chapels (Buildings)
    See Chapels, Court
Court chaplains
    See Chaplains, Court
Court clerks
    See Clerks of court
Court congestion and delay *(Direct)*
    sa Speedy trial
    x Court delay
    xx Courts
       Justice, Administration of
       Speedy trial
Court delay
    See Court congestion and delay
Court dockets
    See Court calendars
Court epic, German *(PT203)*
    x German court epic
    xx Epic poetry, German
       German poetry—Middle High German,
       1050-1500
Court favorites
    See Favorites, Royal
Court fools
    See Fools and jesters
Court-houses *(Direct) (Architecture,*
    NA4470-4477)
    sa names of particular court buildings, e.g.
      Washington, D.C. United States
      Courthouse for the District of
      Columbia
    xx Public buildings
    — Designs and plans

    — Heating and ventilation *(TH7392.C;*
      TH7684.C8)
    — Pictorial works
Court leet
    See Courts baron and courts leet
Court management
    See Court administration
Court marshals
    See United States marshals
Court martial
    See Courts-martial and courts of inquiry
Court martial defenses
    See Defense (Courts-martial)
Court martial trials
    See Trials (Military offenses)
Court-noué
    x Roncet
Court officers
    See Courts—Officials and employees
Court officials and employees
    See Courts—Officials and employees
Court-plaster
Court proceedings, Conduct of
    See Conduct of court proceedings
Court records *(Direct)*
    sa Court calendars
       Criminal registers
       Probate records
    x Records of court
    xx Archives
       Evidence (Law)
       Public records
    — Destruction and reconstruction *(Direct)*
       x Court records—Reconstruction
         Destruction of court records
         Reconstruction of court records
    — Preservation
    — Reconstruction
       See Court records—Destruction and
         reconstruction
Court reporting
    See Law reporting
Court reporting (by newspapers)
    See Newspaper court reporting
Court reports
    See Law reports, digests, etc.
Court rules *(Direct)*
    sa Pleading
    x Rules of court
    xx Courts
       Procedure (Law)
Court vacations
    See Terms of court
Courtesans
    xx Courts and courtiers
       Prostitutes
Courtesans, French, [Japanese, etc.]
    x French [Japanese, etc.] courtesans
    — Correspondence, reminiscences, etc.
Courtesans in literature
Courtesy *(BJ1533.C9; Conduct of life,*
    BJ1520-1688)
    sa Conduct of life
       Etiquette
    x Manners
       Politeness
    xx Conduct of life
       Ethics
       Etiquette
Courtesy of nations
    See Comity of nations
Courtiers
    See Courts and courtiers
Courting
    See Courtship
Courtly love *(GT2620)*
    sa Chivalry
       Courts of love

Love
Minnesingers
Troubadours
Trouvères
  x Love, Courtly
  xx Chivalry
    Courts of love
    Love
    Minnesingers
    Troubadours
    Trouvères
  — Anecdotes, facetiae, satire, etc.
Courtrai, Battle of, 1302
  x Battle of the Spurs
Courtroom decorum
  See Conduct of court proceedings
Courtroom drama
  xx Drama
Courtroom proceedings
  See Conduct of court proceedings
Courts (Direct) (JF700-723; By country,
      JK-JQ; Colonial, JV471)
  sa Administrative courts
    Admiralty
    Agricultural courts and procedure
    Appellate courts
    Appellate procedure
    Arbitration and award
    Civil procedure
    Commercial courts
    Consular jurisdiction
    Contempt of court
    County courts
    Court congestion and delay
    Court rules
    Courts baron and courts leet
    Courts-martial and courts of inquiry
    Courts of last resort
    Criminal courts
    Criminal procedure
    District courts
    Domestic relations courts
    Ecclesiastical courts
    Fehmic courts
    Feudal courts
    Indians of North America—Courts
    Judges
    Judgments
    Judicial councils
    Judicial power
    Judicial review
    Jurisdiction
    Jury
    Justice, Administration of
    Juvenile courts
    Labor courts
    Legislative bodies as courts
    Municipal courts
    Psychology, Forensic
    Small claims courts
    Terms of court
    Traffic courts
    Venue
    Vigilance committees
  x Judiciary
  xx Judges
    Judicial districts
    Judicial power
    Jurisdiction
    Justice, Administration of
    Law
    Procedure (Law)
  — Accounting
  — Administration
    See Court administration
  — Finance
  — Officials and employees
    sa Auditors (Civil procedure)

Bailiffs
Clerks of court
Judges
Masters in chancery
Ordinaries
Viewers (Law)
  x Court officers
    Court officials and employees
    Judicial officers
  Example under reference from Officials
    and employees
— Statistics
  See Judicial statistics

GEOGRAPHIC SUBDIVISIONS

— Rome
  sa Recuperatores (Roman law)
  x Courts (Roman law)

GEOGRAPHIC SUBDIVISIONS

— United States
  sa Circuit courts
  x United States—Courts
    United States—Judiciary

GEOGRAPHIC SUBDIVISIONS

— — Juvenile literature
— — States
    x Judiciary, State
Courts, Administrative
  See Administrative courts
Courts, Church
  See Ecclesiastical courts
Courts, Circuit
  See Circuit courts
Courts, County
  See County courts
Courts, Criminal
  See Criminal courts
Courts, District
  See District courts
Courts, Ecclesiastical
  See Ecclesiastical courts
Courts, Industrial
  See Labor courts
Courts, International
  See International courts
Courts, Islamic (Direct)
  x Courts (Islamic law)
    Courts, Muslim
    Islamic courts
    Muslim courts
    Sharia courts
Courts, Jewish
  sa Rabbinical courts
  x Jewish courts
    Jews—Courts
  xx Jewish law
Courts, Labor
  See Labor courts
Courts, Manorial
  See Manorial courts
Courts, Municipal
  See Municipal courts
Courts, Muslim
  See Courts, Islamic
Courts, Rabbinical
  See Rabbinical courts
Courts (Islamic law)
  See Courts, Islamic
Courts (Roman law)
  See Courts—Rome
Courts and courtiers (Court life,
      GT3510-3530)
  sa Courtesans
    Education of princes
    Favorites, Royal
    Fools and jesters

Heralds
Kings and rulers
Precedence
Princes
Princesses
Queens
subdivision Court and courtiers *under*
  names of countries, e.g. France—
  Court and courtiers
  x Court and courtiers
    Courtiers
  xx Favorites, Royal
    Kings and rulers
    Manners and customs
    Queens
— Costume
— Language
  xx Language and languages
Courts and courtiers in art
  xx Art
Courts and courtiers in literature
Courts baron and courts leet
  sa Manorial courts
  x Court baron
    Court leet
  xx Courts
    Manorial courts
Courts-martial and courts of inquiry (Direct)
      (Military, UB850-867; Naval,
      VB800-815)
  sa Charges and specifications
    (Courts-martial)
    Law officers (Courts-martial)
    Military courts
    Trials (Military offenses)
  x Court martial
    Courts of inquiry
    Inquiry, Courts of
    Military justice
    Military tribunals
  xx Courts
    Criminal courts
    Criminal justice, Administration of
    Criminal procedure
    Martial law
    Military law
    Naval law
    Trial practice
Note under Military courts
— Law officers
    See Law officers (Courts-martial)

GEOGRAPHIC SUBDIVISIONS

— Confederate States of America
  x Confederate States of America—
    Courts-martial and courts of
    inquiry

GEOGRAPHIC SUBDIVISIONS

— United States
  x United States. Army—
    Courts-martial and courts of
    inquiry
    United States—Courts-martial and
    courts of inquiry
    United States. Navy—
    Courts-martial and courts of
    inquiry

Courts of honor *(Direct) (K; Military, UB880)*

Here are entered works on (1) tribunals formed from members of an officers' corps to decide questions of honor arising among its members; (2) tribunals formed from members of certain vocational groups to investigate and judge actions of other members of such groups with regard to their professional or business ethics.

  x Honor, Courts of
  xx Business ethics
     Honor
     Legal ethics
     Medical ethics
Courts of inquiry
  See Courts-martial and courts of inquiry
Courts of last resort *(Direct)*
  sa Appellate courts
    names of individual supreme courts, e.g.
     United States. Supreme Court
  x Last resort, Courts of
     Supreme courts
  xx Appellate procedure
     Courts
Courts of love *(GT3600; Provence, DC611.P961)*
  sa Courtly love
     Troubadours
  x Cours d'amour
     Love, Courts of
  xx Chivalry
     Courtly love
     Troubadours
Courts of ordinary
  See Probate courts
Courts of probate
  See Probate courts
Courts of Stannaries
  See Stannary courts
Courtship *(Manners and customs, GT2650; Sociology, HQ801)*
  sa Betrothal
     Bundling
     Dating (Social customs)
     Love
     Love-letters
     Marriage
  x Courting
  xx Betrothal
     Love
     Love-letters
     Marriage
  — Anecdotes, facetiae, satire, etc.
Courtship (Animal behavior)
  See Courtship of animals
Courtship in literature
  See Love in literature
Courtship of animals
  sa Sex recognition (Zoology)
  x Animal courtship
     Courtship (Animal behavior)
     Mating behavior
  xx Animals, Habits and behavior of
     Sexual behavior in animals
  — Juvenile literature
Courtyards *(Indirect)*
  sa subdivision Courtyards *under names of cities, etc.*
Coushatta Indians
  See Koasati Indians
Couturiers
  See Costume designers
Couvade *(GT2460)*
  xx Birth (in religion, folk-lore, etc.)
     Ethnology

Covellin *(Copper ores, TN440-449; Metallurgy, TN780)*
Covenant of grace
  See Covenants (Theology)
Covenant of works
  See Covenants (Theology)
Covenant theology
  See Covenants (Theology)
Covenanters *(BX9081-2)*
  sa Presbyterianism
     Rullion Green, Battle of, 1666
     Solemn league and covenant
  x Covenants (Church history)
  xx Church of Scotland
Covenanters in the United States *(E184.C8)*
Covenants *(Direct)*
  sa Real covenants
  xx Contracts
     Deeds
Covenants (Church history)
  See Covenanters
     Solemn league and covenant
Covenants (Church polity) *(General, BT1010; Congregational, BX7235-6; Presbyterian, BX9183)*

Here are entered covenants as expressions of church polity, creeds, membership, etc.

  x Half-way covenant
  xx Church membership
     Church polity
     Congregationalism
     Creeds
Covenants (Jewish theology) *(BM612.5)*
Covenants (Religion) *(BL617)*

Here are entered works dealing with covenants in various religions, especially primitive. Material dealing with that use of the covenant idea which makes it the organizing principle of a theological system is entered under Covenants (Theology)

  sa Blood covenant
  x Salt covenant
     Threshold covenant
  xx Blood covenant
     Religion, Primitive
     Rites and ceremonies
     Symbolism
Covenants (Theology) *(BT155)*

Here are entered works which give the covenant idea a central importance not elsewhere assigned to it, and use it as the organizing principle of an entire theological system describing the relations of God and man under the form of a covenant of works and a covenant of grace.

  sa Dispensationalism
     Grace (Theology)
     Salvation
     Typology (Theology)
  x Covenant of grace
     Covenant of works
     Covenant theology
     Federal theology
     Theology, Covenant
     Theology, Federal
  xx Calvinism
     Grace (Theology)
     Kingdom of God
     Salvation
     Theology, Doctrinal
     Typology (Theology)
  Note under Covenants (Religion)
  — Biblical teaching *(BS680.C67)*
    x Bible—Covenants
  — Sermons

Covenants running with land
  See Real covenants
Cover crops *(Indirect)*
  sa Green manuring
     Legumes
     Soil conservation
  x Catch crops
  xx Field crops
     Legumes
     Soil conservation
Cover plants
  See Ground cover plants
Covered bridges
  x Bridges, Covered
  xx Bridges, Wooden
Coverings, Protective
  See Protective coverings
Coverlets *(Direct) (Art, NK9100-9199; Technology, TT835)*
  x Bed rugs
     Bedspreads
     Quilts
  xx Bedding
     Interior decoration
     Quilting
Coverlets, American, [English, etc.] *(Direct)*
  x American [English, etc.] coverlets
Covers (Philately)
  sa Postage-stamps
     Postmarks
     Stamped envelopes
  x Envelopes (Philately)
     First-day covers
  xx Envelopes (Stationery)
     Postage-stamps
     Postmarks
Coverture
  See Married woman
Covetousness
  See Avarice
Cow
  See Cows
Cow barns
  See Dairy barns
Cow-bells *(CC260)*
Cow-birds
  See Cowbirds
Cow Creek Indians
  See Umpqua Indians
Cow-pea curculio *(SB945.C)*
Cow-pea weevil *(SB945.C)*
  xx Beetles
Cow-peas *(SB205.C8)*
  x Blackeyed peas
     Cowpeas
     Southern peas
  xx Beans
     Forage plants
     Peas
Cow testing

Here are entered works on the testing of dairy cows by weighing their milk over a definite period and determining its fat content. Works dealing with testing of cows for tuberculosis are entered under Tuberculosis in cattle.

  xx Cattle breeding
     Cows
     Dairying
Cow testing associations
  xx Agricultural societies
     Dairying
Cowage
  See Cowhage
Cowbirds *(QL696.P2)*
  sa Bronzed cowbird
  x Cow-birds

Cowboy slang
    See Cowboys—Language (New words,
        slang, etc.)
Cowboys (F596)
    sa Gauchos
        Negroes as cowboys
        Ranch life
        Rodeos
    x Herdsmen
        Vaqueros
    xx Cattle trade
        Frontier and pioneer life
        Gauchos
        Horsemen
        Ranch life
        Stock-ranges
    — Anecdotes, facetiae, satire, etc.
    — Caricatures and cartoons
    — Juvenile literature
    — Language (New words, slang, etc.)
        (PE3727.C6)
        x Cowboy slang
        Example under Language and languages;
            Slang; Words, New
    — Poetry (American, PS595.C6)
    — Songs and music (Literature, PS595.C6;
        Music, M1629-1630)
        xx Music, Popular (Songs), etc.)—United
            States
        Example under Songs
Cowboys in art (N8217.C75)
    xx Art
Cowboys in literature
Cowhage
    x Cowage
        Cowitch
    xx Worms, Intestinal and parasitic
Cowichan Indians (E99.C875)
    sa Stalo Indians
    xx Indians of North America
Cowichan languages
    sa Chilliwack dialect
        Salishan languages
        Stalo language
Cowitch
    See Cowhage
Cowl flaps
    See Aeroplanes—Motors—Cowlings
Cowlings (Aeroplanes)
    See Aeroplanes—Motors—Cowlings
Cowpeas
    See Cow-peas
Cowpens, Battle of, 1781 (E241.C9)
Cowper's glands (Comparative anatomy,
    QL876-881; Human anatomy,
    QM416-421; Physiology, QP257,
    QP265)
    x Mery's glands
    Example under Glands
    — Diseases
Cowpox
    See Vaccinia
Cowries (Ethnology, GN436.2; Mollusca,
    QL430.5.C77)
Cowries, Fossil
Cows (SF191-219)
    sa Calves
        Cattle
        Cow testing
        Dairying
        Heifers
        Milk production
        particular breeds of cattle, e.g. Ayrshire
            cattle, Hereford cattle
    x Cow
    xx Cattle
        Dairying
        Domestic animals

    — Anatomy
        See Cattle—Anatomy
    — Caricatures and cartoons
    — Diseases
    — Feeding and feeds
        See Dairy cattle—Feeding and feeds
    — Juvenile literature
    — Legends and stories
Cows (in religion, folk-lore, etc.)
    x Folk-lore of cows
    xx Animals, Legends and stories of
        Religion, Primitive
Coxa plana
    See Legg-Calvé-Perthes disease
Coxalgia
    See Hip joint—Diseases
Coxsackie virus
    xx Enteroviruses
        Poliomyelitis
        Viruses
Coyotes (Indirect) (QL737.C2)
    xx Wolves
    Example under Predatory animals
    — Behavior
    — Control (Indirect) (SB994.C)
        xx Mammal control
    — Juvenile literature
Coyotes, Fossil
Coypou
    See Coypu
Coypu
    x Coypou
        Nutria
    — Control (Indirect) (SB994.C82)
    — Diseases
Coypus as laboratory animals
Cozacks
    See Cossacks
CP violation (Nuclear physics)
    x Charge conjugation parity violation
        Violation, Charge conjugation parity
    xx Particles (Nuclear physics)
        Symmetry (Physics)
Crab apple
    See Crabapple
Crab-eating macaque
    See Kra
Crab fisheries (Indirect) (SH380)
    xx Fisheries
        Shellfish fisheries
Crab grass
    See Crabgrass
Crab meat
    xx Crabs
Crab Nebula
    xx Nebulae
Crab spiders
    xx Spiders
Crabapple
    x Crab apple
    xx Apple
Crabgrass
    x Crab grass
Crabgrass, Spreading
    See Pangolagrass
Crabs (Indirect) (QL444.D3)
    sa Crab meat
        Dungeness crab
        Fiddler-crabs
        Ghost crabs
        Glass-crabs
        Hermit-crabs
        Sand-crabs
        Tanner crabs
    x Brachyura
    xx Crustacea
        Decapoda (Crustacea)
    — Behavior

    Example under Crustacea—Behavior
    — Classification
    — Juvenile literature
Crabs, Canned
    x Canned crabs
    xx Fishery products, Canned
Crabs, Fossil (QE817.D3)
    xx Crustacea, Fossil
        Decapoda (Crustacea), Fossil
Cracking of asphalt concrete pavements
    See Pavements, Asphalt concrete—Cracking
Cracking of concrete
    See Concrete—Cracking
Cracking process (Gasoline, TP692.2)
    sa Catalytic cracking
        Fluidization
        Gasoline
        Oil gas
    x Petroleum cracking
        Petroleum—Cracking
    xx Chemistry, Technical
        Distillation, Destructive
        Hydrocarbons
        Petroleum—Refining
    — Problems, exercises, etc.
Crackle
    x Craquelé
    xx Glassware
        Lacquer and lacquering
        Pottery
Cracovians (Mathematics)
    See Matrices
Cradle songs
    See Lullabies
Cradles (Ethnology, GN415.C8)
    xx Children's furniture
Crafts (Handicrafts)
    See Handicraft
Craho Indians (F2520.1.C67)
    x Kraho Indians
    xx Indians of South America
        Timbira Indians
Crâmignons (GV1796.C)
Cramming
    See Study, Method of
Cramp, Telegraphers'
    See Telegraphers' cramp
Cramp, Writers'
    See Writers' cramp
Cramp-rings (R133)
    xx Charms
        Medicine, Magic, mystic, and spagiric
        Rings
Cranberries (SB383)
    sa Cookery (Cranberries)
    — Cooperative marketing
    — Diseases and pests (SB608.C87)
        sa names of pests, e.g. Cranberry
            root-worm
    — Storage
    — Water requirements
Cranberries, Frozen
    Example under Fruit, Frozen
Cranberry fire-worm (SB608.C87)
    xx Moths
Cranberry-girdler
Cranberry root-worm
    Example under Cranberries—Diseases and
        pests
Cranberry span-worm
Crane-flies (QL537.T6)
    xx Flies
Crane-flies, Winter
    See Winter crane-flies
Cranes, Whooping
    See Whooping cranes
Cranes (Birds) (QL696.G8)
    sa Sandhill crane

459

Cranes (Birds) *(QL696.G8)* *(Continued)*
   Whooping cranes
Cranes (in religion, folk-lore, etc.)
   x Folk-lore of cranes
   xx Religion, Primitive
Cranes, derricks, etc. *(TJ1363-5)*
   sa Cargo handling—Equipment
      Davits
      Electric cranes
      Floating cranes
      Gantry cranes
      Oil well drilling rigs
      Tower cranes
      Truck-mounted cranes
   x Derricks
   xx Hoisting machinery
   — Automation
   — Brakes
   — Design and construction
   — Dynamics
   — Electric driving
   — Electric equipment
   — Hydraulic drive
   — Juvenile literature
   — Law and legislation   *(Direct)*
      x Cranes, derricks, etc.—Safety
         regulations
   — Maintenance and repair
   — Mathematical models   *(TJ1363)*
   — Reliability
   — Safety measures
   — Safety regulations
      See Cranes, derricks, etc.—Law and
         legislation
   — Tables, etc.
Craney Island, Battle of, 1813   *(E356.C8)*
Cranial hyperostosis
   See Hyperostosis frontalis interna
Cranial nerves
   See Nerves, Cranial
Cranial neuralgia
   See Neuralgia, Cranial
Cranial osteoporosis
   See Craniotabes
Cranial sutures   *(Anthropology, GN131;*
         Comparative anatomy, QL821;
         Human anatomy, QM105)
   x Skull, Sutures of
      Sutures, Cranial
   xx Craniology
      Skull
Craniology   *(Indirect)*   *(GN71-131)*
      Here are entered works dealing with
      skulls from an anthropological, archa-
      eological, or ethnological point of
      view. Strictly anatomical and patho-
      logical literature is entered under
      Skull. Treatises on methods of measur-
      ing the skull are entered under Crani-
      ometry.
   sa Brachycephaly
      Brain
      Cranial sutures
      Craniophore
      Dolichocephaly
      Hyperbrachycephaly
      Indians of North America—Craniology
      Jaws
      Man, Prehistoric
      Microcephaly
      Occipital bone
      Phrenology
      Pituitary fossa
      Prognathism
      Sagittal curve
      Skull—Abnormities and deformities
      Skull—Artificial deformities
   x Cranium

   xx Anthropology
      Anthropometry
      Man
      Skull
      Skull—Abnormities and deformities
      Skull—Artificial deformities
      Somatology
   — Jews
      See Jews—Craniology
   — Lapps
      See Lapps—Craniology
   — Negroes
      See Negroes—Craniology

            GEOGRAPHIC SUBDIVISIONS

   — New Guinea
      xx Papuans
Craniometry   *(GN71-131)*
   sa Anthropometry
   x Cranium
   xx Anthropometry
      Skull
   Note under Craniology
Craniophore   *(GN72)*
   xx Craniology
Craniotabes   *(RJ546.C)*
   x Cranial osteoporosis
   xx Infants—Diseases
      Skull—Diseases
Craniotomy   *(RG781)*
   xx Obstetrics—Surgery
Cranium
   See Craniology
      Craniometry
      Skull
Crank books
   See Eccentric literature
Cranks
   See Eccentrics and eccentricities
Cranks and crankshafts
   xx Shafting
   — Maintenance and repair
   — Vibration
Crannogs
   See Lake-dwellers and lake-dwellings—
      Ireland
Crao Indians
   xx Indians of South America
Crapette (Game)
   See Russian bank (Game)
Crappie
   sa White crappie
   xx Sunfishes
Craps (Game)   *(GV1303)*
Craquelé
   See Crackle
Crash injuries
   x Injuries, Crash
   xx Accidents
      Automotive medicine
      Impact—Physiological effect
      Wounds
   — Research
      See Crash injury research
Crash injury research   *(Direct)*
   x Crash injuries—Research
   xx Research
Cratering, Nuclear
   See Nuclear excavation
Craters, Crypto-explosion
   See Cryptoexplosion structures
Craters, Lunar
   See Lunar craters
Craters, Meteorite
   See Meteorite craters
Crates   *(TS900)*
   xx Boxes
      Containers

Crau (African people)
   See Kru (African people)
Cravats
   See Neckties
Crawford's Indian Campaign, 1782   *(E238)*
   xx Huron Indians—Wars
      Indians of North America—1775-1783
Crawl spaces
   xx Attics
      Basements
Crawler tractors
      Here are entered works on tractors which
      travel on endless belt treads instead of
      wheels.
   x Track-type tractors
      Tracklaying tractors
      Tractors, Crawler
   xx Tracklaying vehicles
      Tractors
   Note under Tracklaying vehicles
   — Dynamics
   — Maintenance and repair
   — Parts
   — Transmission devices, Automatic
Crawling and creeping
   x Creeping
   xx Animal locomotion
      Infants
   — Therapeutic use
Crayfish   *(Indirect)*   *(QL444.D3)*
   xx Crustacea
   — Anatomy
Crayfish, Sea
   See Spiny lobsters
Crayfish culture   *(Indirect)*
   xx Shellfish culture
Crayfish fisheries   *(Indirect)*
   xx Shellfish fisheries
Crayon drawing   *(NC855-875)*
   sa Blackboard drawing
      Pastel drawing
   xx Drawing
      Pastel drawing
      Portrait painting
   — Juvenile literature
Crayon drawings   *(NC855-875)*
   x Drawings, Crayon
   xx Drawings
      Pastels
Crayon engraving
   xx Engraving
Crayon manner
   See Stipple engraving
Crayons
   xx Drawing materials
Cream   *(SF251-262)*
   sa Cookery (Sour cream and milk)
      Milk
      Sour cream
   xx Dairying
      Milk
   — Marketing
Cream, Fermented
   See Sour cream
Cream cheese   *(SF272.C)*
Cream nut
   See Brazil nut
Cream of tartar   *(Baking powders, etc.,*
      TX409; Therapeutics, RM666.C)
   x Potassium bitartrate
Cream sauce
   x White sauce
   xx Sauces
Cream-separators   *(SF247)*
   x Separators, Cream
   xx Dairying
      Milk
      Separators (Machines)

Creameries *(SF266)*
  sa Dairying
  x Butter factories
  xx Dairy plants
    Dairying
    Food processing plants
    Milk
  — Apparatus and supplies *(SF247)*
  — — Cleaning
  — Automation
Creamery waste
  See Dairy waste
Crease-resistant fabrics
  x Fabrics, Crease-resistant
    Permanent-press fabrics
  xx Creasing of textiles
    Textile industry and fabrics
Creasing of textiles
  sa Crease-resistant fabrics
    Pressing of garments
  x Permanent creasing of textiles
    Textile creasing
  xx Textile industry and fabrics
Creatine *(QP801.C8)*
  sa Creatinuria
  x Kreatine
Creatine metabolism
  xx Metabolism
Creatinine *(QP801.C8)*
Creatinuria
  xx Creatine
    Urine—Analysis and pathology
Creation *(Bible, BS651; Comparative religion, BL224-5)*
  sa Beginning
    Chaos (Theology)
    Cosmology
    Cosmology, Biblical
    Deluge
    Earth
    Evolution
    Geology
    God
    Jesus Christ—Primacy
    Man
    Nebular hypothesis
  x Cosmogony, Biblical
  xx Beginning
    Bible and science
    Cosmogony
    Cosmology
    Cosmology, Biblical
    Earth
    Evolution
    Geology
    God
    Man
    Natural theology
    Nebular hypothesis
    Philosophy
    Religion and science
    Teleology
  — Art *(N8180)*
  — Biblical teaching
  — — Juvenile literature
  — Comparative studies *(BL325.C7)*
  — Early works to 1800 *(BL224)*
  — History of doctrines
  — Miscellanea
  — Poetry
  — Sermons
Creation (Islam) *(BP166.23)*
Creation (Literary, artistic, etc.) *(BF408)*
  sa Creative ability
    Creative thinking (Education)
    Creative writing
    Creativity in literature
    Inspiration

Originality
    Planning
    Research—Psychological aspects
  x Creativeness
    Creativity
  xx Art
    Creative ability
    Genius
    Imagination
    Inspiration
    Intellect
    Inventions
    Literature
    Originality
  — Ability testing
    See Creative ability—Testing
Creation as a theme in literature
  See Creation in literature
Creation in literature
  x Creation as a theme in literature
Creative ability
  sa Creation (Literary, artistic, etc.)
    Creative thinking (Education)
    Originality
  x Creativeness
    Creativity
  xx Ability
    Creation (Literary, artistic, etc.)
    Creative thinking (Education)
    Genius
    Imagination
    Inspiration
  — Testing *(Bibliography, Z7204.C8)*
    sa Prediction of creative ability
      Remote associates test
    x Creation (Literary, artistic, etc.)—
      Ability testing
    xx Ability—Testing
Creative ability (Child psychology) *(BF723.C7)*
  xx Child study
Creative activities and seat work *(GV1201; LB1537)*
  sa Activity programs in education
    Bible crafts
    Block building (Education)
    Paper work
    Sand tables
  x Busy work
    Children—Recreation
    Occupations and busy work
    Seat work
  xx Activity programs in education
    Amusements
    Education, Primary
    Handicraft
    Kindergarten
Creative thinking (Education) *(Educational psychology, LB1062; Psychology, BF408)*
  sa Creative ability
  x Creativity (Education)
  xx Creation (Literary, artistic, etc.)
    Creative ability
  — Juvenile literature
  — Testing
    xx Educational tests and measurements
Creative writing *(PN173-198)*
  x Writing (Authorship)
  xx Authorship
    Creation (Literary, artistic, etc.)
Creative writing (Elementary education) *(LB1576)*
Creative writing (Higher education) *(PN173-198)*
Creative writing (Secondary education) *(LB1631)*

Creativeness
  See Creation (Literary, artistic, etc.)
    Creative ability
Creativity
  See Creation (Literary, artistic, etc.)
    Creative ability
Creativity (Education)
  See Creative thinking (Education)
Creativity as a theme in literature
  See Creativity in literature
Creativity in literature
  x Creativity as a theme in literature
  xx Creation (Literary, artistic, etc.)
Crèches (Day nurseries)
  See Day nurseries
Crécy, Battle of, 1346 *(DC98.5.C8)*
  xx Hundred Years' War, 1339-1453
Credibility
  See Truthfulness and falsehood
Credit *(Direct)* *(Practice, HF5565-5585; Theory, HG3701-3781)*
  sa Acceptances
    Accounts current
    Accounts receivable
    Agricultural credit
    Banks and banking
    Circular velocity of money
    Collecting of accounts
    Commercial finance companies
    Consumer credit
    Credit bureaus
    Credit departments
    Credit management
    Credit managers
    Debt
    Debts, Public
    Development credit corporations
    Export credit
    Finance charges
    Forest credit
    Industrial loan associations
    Instalment plan
    Insurance, Credit
    Liquidity (Economics)
    Loans
    Moratorium
    Open market operations
    Promissory notes
    Trust receipts
  x Commercial credit
  xx Banks and banking
    Business
    Circular velocity of money
    Debt
    Economics
    Finance
    Monetary policy
    Money
  — Examinations, questions, etc.
  — Information services
    See Credit bureaus
  — Mathematical models
  — Problems, exercises, etc.
Credit, Agricultural
  See Agricultural credit
Credit, Consumer
  See Consumer credit
Credit, Export
  See Export credit
Credit, Forest
  See Forest credit
Credit, Letters of
  See Letters of credit
Credit, Social
  See Social credit
Credit administration
  See Credit management

Credit bureaus *(Direct)*
> Here are entered works on agencies organized to furnish credit information, as well as on the credit information activities of banks, chambers of commerce, and similar agencies.
>
> *sa* Credit guides
> Liability for credit information
> *x* Credit information services
> Credit—Information services
> Mercantile agencies
> *xx* Credit

Credit cards *(Direct)*
> *xx* Consumer credit
> Point-of-sale systems industry

Credit companies
> *See* Commercial finance companies
> Instalment plan

Credit cooperatives
> *See* Banks and banking, Cooperative

Credit departments *(Direct)*
> *sa* Credit managers
> *xx* Credit
> Credit management

Credit executives
> *See* Credit managers

Crédit foncier
> *See* Agricultural credit

Credit guides *(Direct)* *(HF5571-8)*
> Here are entered: 1) general credit guides, 2) credit guides of particular locality, *e.g.* Credit guides—Chicago, 3) credit guides of a particular trade. Credit guides of a trade are entered also under the trade, *e.g.* 1. Credit guides. 2. Lumber trade—Credit guides. or 1. Credit guides—United States. 2. Lumber trade—United States—Credit guides.
>
> *x* Commercial ratings
> *xx* Credit bureaus
> — Chicago
> > *Note under* Credit guides
> — United States
> > *Note under* Credit guides

Credit information, Liability for
> *See* Liability for credit information

Credit information services
> *See* Credit bureaus

Credit insurance
> *See* Insurance, Credit

Credit management *(Direct)*
> *sa* Collecting of accounts
> Credit departments
> Credit managers
> *x* Credit administration
> *xx* Credit
> Management
> — Vocational guidance
> > *See* Credit management as a profession

Credit management as a profession
> *x* Credit management—Vocational guidance

Credit managers *(Direct)*
> *x* Credit executives
> Credit men
> *xx* Controllership
> Credit
> Credit departments
> Credit management
> Office management

Credit men
> *See* Credit managers

Credit unions
> *See* Banks and banking, Cooperative

Creditor
> *See* Debtor and creditor

Creditors' bills *(Direct)*
> *sa* Debtor and creditor
> Fraudulent conveyances
> *xx* Bankruptcy
> Debtor and creditor
> Equity
> Executions (Law)
> Fraudulent conveyances

Creditors group insurance
> *See* Insurance, Group creditors

Credits, School
> *See* School credits

Credo (Music) *(M2079.L3; M2099.L3)*
> *x* Nicene Creed (Music)

Credulity *(BF773)*
> *sa* Belief and doubt
> Errors, Popular
> Faith
> Superstition

Cree hymns
> *See* Hymns, Cree

Cree Indians *(E99.C88)*
> *xx* Algonquian Indians
> Indians of North America
> — Legends

Cree language *(PM986-9)*
> *sa* Algonquian languages
> *x* Cris language
> Knistenaux language
> Knisteneux language
> Maskegon dialect
> *xx* Algonquian languages

Creed, Thirteen articles of (Judaism)
> *See* Thirteen articles of faith (Judaism)

Creeds *(General, BT990-999; By denomination, BX)*
> *sa* Apostles' Creed
> Athanasian Creed
> Catechisms
> Constantinopolitan Creed
> Covenants (Church polity)
> Nicene Creed
> Rule of faith
> *subdivision* Catechisms and creeds under names of religions, sects, etc., *e.g.* Catholic Church—Catechisms and creeds
> *x* Confessions of faith
> Faith, Confessions of
> Symbolics
> *xx* Catechisms
> Church history
> Theology, Doctrinal
> — Comparative studies *(BT990)*
> > *x* Comparative symbolics
> > *Example under reference from* Comparative studies
> — Subscription
> > *sa* Profession of faith

Creeds, Ecumenical *(BT990)*
> Here are entered works that combine in one study the Apostles', Nicene, and Athanasian creeds.

Creeds, Jewish
> *sa* Thirteen articles of faith (Judaism)
> *x* Jewish creeds
> *xx* Jewish theology

Creek Indians *(E99.C9)*
> *sa* Creek War, 1813-1814
> Creek War, 1836
> Five Civilized Tribes
> Seminole War, 1st, 1817-1818
> Seminole War, 2d, 1835-1842
> St. Augustine Expedition, 1740
> Yuchi Indians
> *x* Maskoki Indians
> Muscogee Indians
> Muskogee Indians
> Muskoki Indians
> Yamacraw Indians
> *xx* Five Civilized Tribes
> Indians of North America
> Muskhogean Indians
> — Government relations
> — Legal status, laws, etc.
> — Religion and mythology
> — Tribal government

Creek language *(PM991)*
> *sa* Hitchiti language
> Muskhogean languages
> *x* Maskoki language
> Muscogee language
> Muskoki language
> *xx* Hitchiti language
> Muskhogean languages

Creek War, 1813-1814 *(E83.813)*
> *sa* Horse Shoe, Battle of the, 1814
> Tennessee militiamen, Execution of, 1815
> *xx* Creek Indians
> Indians of North America—Wars—1812-1815

Creek War, 1836 *(E83.836)*
> *x* Alabama—History—Creek War, 1836
> *xx* Creek Indians
> Indians of North America—Wars—1815-1875
> Seminole War, 2d, 1835-1842

Creep of aluminum *(TA480.A6)*
> *x* Aluminum—Creep
> *xx* Aluminum

Creep of brass
> *x* Brass—Creep
> *xx* Brass

Creep of concrete
> *x* Concrete—Creep
> *xx* Concrete
> Creep of materials
> Deformations (Mechanics)
> Rheology

Creep of copper *(TA480.C7)*
> *x* Copper—Creep
> *xx* Copper

Creep of lead *(TL480.L)*
> *x* Lead—Creep
> *xx* Lead

Creep of magnesium *(TA480.M)*
> *x* Magnesium—Creep
> *xx* Magnesium

Creep of materials
> *sa* Creep of concrete
> Creep of metals
> Creep of plastics
> Creep of rocks
> Creep of soil
> Creep of wood
> Stress relaxation
> *x* Materials—Creep
> *xx* Deformations (Mechanics)
> Fracture of solids
> Materials—Dynamic testing
> Plasticity
> Strength of materials
> Stress relaxation
> — Mathematical models *(TA418.22)*

Creep of metals *(TA460)*
> *sa* Nimonic alloys
> *x* Cold flow
> Metallic creep
> Metals—Creep
> *xx* Creep of materials
> Deformations (Mechanics)
> Dislocations in metals
> Metals—Fracture
> Rheology
> — Charts, diagrams, etc.

Creep of molybdenum (*TA480.M*)
   x Molybdenum—Creep
   xx Molybdenum
Creep of plastics (*TA455.P5*)
   x Plastics—Creep
   xx Creep of materials
     Deformations (Mechanics)
     Rheology
Creep of rhenium
   xx Rhenium
Creep of rocks
   x Rocks—Creep
   xx Creep of materials
     Rock mechanics
Creep of soil
   sa Soil consolidation
     Solifluction
   x Slow flowage
   xx Creep of materials
     Mass-wasting
     Rheology
     Soil mechanics
     Solifluction
Creep of steel (*TA473*)
   xx Steel
Creep of titanium (*TA480.T*)
   x Titanium—Creep
   xx Titanium
Creep of wood (*TA420*)
   x Wood—Creep
   xx Creep of materials
     Wood
Creeper lanes
   x Slow-moving lanes
   xx Roads
Creepers (*QL696.P2*)
   x Certhiidae
     Certhiomorphae
Creeping
   See Crawling and creeping
Cremation (*RA631-7; Manners and customs, GT3330*)
   sa Dead
     Funeral rites and ceremonies
     Urn burial
   x Burning the dead
     Crematories
     Mortuary customs
   xx Burial
     Dead
     Funeral rites and ceremonies
     Hygiene, Public
     Incineration
     Sanitation
   — Law and legislation (*Direct*)
     xx Burial laws
   — Moral and religious aspects (*BT826.4*)
Cremation (Jewish law)
Cremation and the church
   See Church and cremation
Crematories
   See Cremation
Cremona
   — Siege, 1702
Cremona transformations (*QA602*)
   sa Geometry, Algebraic
     Transformations (Mathematics)
     Transformations, Quadratic
   xx Geometry, Algebraic
     Transformations (Mathematics)
     Transformations, Quadratic
Creole dialects (*Indirect*) (*PM7831-7875*)
   sa Negro-Danish dialects
     Negro-English dialects
   x Dialects
   xx Languages, Mixed
Creole tales
   See Tales, Creole

Creoles (*Louisiana, F380.C9*)
   xx Miscegenation
Creolin (*RA766.C9*)
   xx Disinfection and disinfectants
Creosote (*Chemical technology, TP248.C; Therapeutics, RM666.C8*)
   x Kreosote
   Example under Wood preservatives
Creosote bush
Crepe
   xx Silk manufacture and trade
Crepe paper (*TS1109*)
   xx Paper
     Paper products
     Paper work
Crêpes (Cookery)
   See Pancakes, waffles, etc.
Crepuscule
   See Twilight
Cresol (*Chemical technology, TP248.C67; Chemistry, QD341.P5*)
   x Kresol
Crested lark (*QL696.P2*)
   xx Larks
Crested wheat grass
   See Wheat grass, Crested
Crests (*CR55-57*)
   sa Heraldry
   xx Heraldry
Cretaceous period
   See Geology, Stratigraphic—Cretaceous
     Paleobotany—Cretaceous
     Paleontology—Cretaceous
Cretans
   sa Minoans
Cretans in the United States
Crete
   — History (*Ancient, DF261.C8; Modern, DF901.C78-89*)
   — — Insurrection of 1866-1868
   — — Insurrection of 1889
   — — Massacre of 1896
Cretinism (*RC657*)
   sa Goiter
     Myxedema
   xx Goiter
     Idiocy
     Myxedema
     Thyroid gland—Diseases
Crewel embroidery
   See Crewelwork
Crewelwork (*TT776.C7*)
   x Crewel embroidery
   xx Embroidery
Crib death
   See Sudden death in infants
Crib in Christian art and tradition (*Art, N8180*)
   sa Santos (Art)
   x Manger in Christian art and tradition
   xx Christian art and symbolism
     Christmas plays
Cribbage (*GV1295.C9*)
   Example under Cards
Cribriform plate (*QM505*)
   xx Nose
Cribwork (*TC197*)
   xx Foundations
     Hydraulic structures
Crichaná Indians (*F2519-2520.1.C*)
   xx Carib Indians
     Indians of South America
Cricket (*Direct*) (*GV911-925*)
   sa Cricket grounds
     Wicket
   xx Wicket
   Example under School sports
   — Anecdotes, facetiae, satire, etc.

   — Poetry
   — Terminology
Cricket automobile (*TL215.C7*)
   x Avenger automobile
   xx Plymouth automobile
Cricket grounds (*GV927*)
   xx Cricket
Cricket in art
   xx Art
Cricket stories
   xx Sports stories
Crickets (*QL508.G8*)
   sa Mole-crickets
     Tree crickets
   x Oecanthinae
   xx Orthoptera
   — Behavior
   — Juvenile literature
Cricopharyngeal sphincter
   See Pharyngoesophageal sphincter
Cries (*GT3450*)
   sa Battle-cries
     Peddlers and peddling
     subdivision Cries *under names of cities, e.g.* London—Cries
   x Street cries
     Street songs
   xx Cities and towns
     Manners and customs
     Sounds
     Street music and musicians
Crime and age (*HV6163*)
   sa Juvenile delinquency
   x Age and crime
   xx Crime and criminals
Crime and alcoholism
   See Alcoholism and crime
Crime and criminals (*Direct*) (*HV6001-9920; Manners and customs, GT6550-6715*)
   sa Alcoholism and crime
     Anarchism and anarchists
     Assassination
     Assassins
     Atrocities
     Automobile thieves
     Bravos
     Brigands and robbers
     Castration of criminals and defectives
     Catholic criminals
     Conspiracies
     Convict labor
     Crime and age
     Crime and superstition
     Crime and the press
     Crime and weather
     Crime in literature
     Crime prevention
     Crimes without victims
     Criminologists
     Dacoits
     Degeneration
     Delinquent women
     Delinquents
     Drug abuse and crime
     Education and crime
     Education of prisoners
     Fugitives from justice
     Gangs
     Hoodlums
     Hypnotism and crime
     Illegitimacy and crime
     Impostors and imposture
     Indians of North America—Crime
     Insane, Criminal and dangerous
     Insanity, Moral
     Jewish criminals
     Juvenile delinquency

Crime and criminals (Direct)
          (HV6001-9920; Manners and
          customs, GT6550-6715)
          (Continued)
        Kleptomania
        Mafia
        Mentally handicapped and crime
        Molly Maguires
        Narcotics and crime
        Negro criminals
        Occasional criminals
        Organized crime
        Outlaws
        Parapsychology and crime
        Penal colonies
        Pimps
        Pirates
        Police
        Prison psychology
        Prisoners
        Prisoners, Transportation of
        Prisons
        Prostitution
        Racketeering
        Recidivists
        Reformatories
        Regicides
        Rehabilitation of criminals
        Rogues and vagabonds
        Rural crimes
        Social work with delinquents and
          criminals
        Sterilization of criminals and defectives
        Suburban crimes
        Swindlers and swindling
        Thieves
        Thugs
        Tongs (Secret societies)
        Tramps
        Vice
        Victims of crimes
        Vigilance committees
        War and crime
        War criminals
        White collar crimes
        headings beginning with the word
          Criminal
    x   Criminals
        Criminology
    xx Criminal justice, Administration of
        Degeneration
        Delinquents
        Deviant behavior
        Ethics
        Social ethics
        Social problems
        Sociology
        Vice
  — Anecdotes, facetiae, satire, etc.
  — Biography (HV6245-8; Great Britain,
          HV6945; United States, HV6785)
  — Classification
  — Identification (HV6065-6079)
    sa Bertillon system
        Fingerprints
        Palmprints
        Photography, Legal
    x   Identification of criminals
    xx Criminal investigation
        Evidence, Criminal
        Photography, Legal
  — Language
        See Cant
  — Mathematical models
  — Public opinion
  — Research (Direct)
  — Songs and music (M1977.C7;
          M1978.C7)
  — Statistical methods

        See Criminal statistics
  — Statistics
        See Criminal statistics
  — Stories
        See Crime stories
  — Underdeveloped areas
        See Underdeveloped areas—Crime
          and criminals
Crime and criminals, Sexual
    See Sex crimes
Crime and drug abuse
    See Drug abuse and crime
Crime and education
    See Education and crime
Crime and hypnotism
    See Hypnotism and crime
Crime and illegitimacy
    See Illegitimacy and crime
Crime and insanity
    See Insane, Criminal and dangerous
Crime and narcotics
    See Narcotics and crime
Crime and parapsychology
    See Parapsychology and crime
Crime and superstition
    x   Superstition and crime
    xx Crime and criminals
        Criminal anthropology
        Superstition
Crime and the mentally handicapped
    See Mentally handicapped and crime
Crime and the press
    sa Contempt of court
        Newspaper court reporting
    x   Press and crime
        Trial reporting
        Trials in the press
    xx Crime and criminals
        Journalism
        Newspaper court reporting
        Press law
Crime and war
    See War and crime
Crime and weather
    x   Weather and crime
    xx Crime and criminals
        Weather—Mental and physiological
          effects
Crime d'amour
    See Crime passionnel
Crime detection
    See Criminal investigation
Crime in literature (HV6249)
    sa Brigands and robbers in literature
        Detectives in literature
        Picaresque literature
        Rogues and vagabonds
        individual crimes in literature, e.g.
          Extortion in literature
    x   Literature, Crime in
    xx Crime and criminals
Crime in transportation
    See Crimes aboard aircraft
        Train robberies
Crime of passion
    See Crime passionnel
Crime passionnel (Direct) (HV6053; K)
    sa Trials (Crime passionnel)
        Uxoricide
    x   Crime d'amour
        Crime of passion
    xx Extenuating circumstances
        Homicide
Crime photography
    See Photography, Legal
Crime prevention (Direct)
    sa Criminal psychology
        Education and crime

        Electronics in crime prevention
        Informers
        Sterilization of criminals and defectives
        Surety of the peace
    x   Prevention of crime
    xx Crime and criminals
        Criminal anthropology
  — Citizen participation
    x   Citizen participation in crime
          prevention
    xx Citizens' associations
  — Equipment and supplies
  — Public opinion
  — Youth participation
    x   Youth participation in crime
          prevention
        Youth patrols (Crime prevention)
Crime prevention surveys
        Here are entered works on the methods
        and techniques of security and crime
        prevention surveys.
    x   Security surveys (Crime prevention)
Crime statistics
    See Criminal statistics
Crime stories
    sa Detective and mystery stories
    x   Crime and criminals—Stories
    xx Detective and mystery stories
        Fiction
Crime stories, American, [etc.] (Direct)
    x   American [etc.] crime stories
    xx American [etc.] fiction
Crime syndicates
    See Gangs
        Organized crime
        Racketeering
Crimea in art
Crimean War, 1853-1856 (Russia,
          DK214-215; Turkey, DR567)
    sa Alma, Battle of the, 1854
        Balaklava, Battle of, 1854
        Eastern question (Balkan)
        Inkermann, Battle of, 1854
        Kars, Turkey (City)—Siege, 1855
        Oltenitza, Battle of, 1853
        Petropavlovsk-Kamchatskiy, Battle of,
          1854
        Sevastopol—Seige, 1854-1855
        Silistria—Siege, 1854
        Sinop, Battle of, 1853
    x   France—History—Crimean War,
          1853-1856
        Great Britain—History—Crimean War,
          1853-1856
        Russo-Turkish War, 1853-1856
    xx Eastern question (Balkan)
  — Causes (DK215)
  — Diplomatic history (DK215)
  — Fiction
  — Hospitals, charities, etc.
        Example under Nurses and nursing; War
          —Relief of sick and wounded
  — Influence and results
  — Juvenile literature
  — Maps
        Example under War maps
  — Medical and sanitary affairs
  — Personal narratives
  — Pictorial works
  — Poetry
  — Sermons
  — Women
Crimen laesae majestatic
    See Lese majesty
Crimes, Classification of
    See Classification of crimes
Crimes, Commercial
    See Commercial crimes

Crimes, Insurance
   See Insurance crimes
Crimes, Military
   See Military offenses
Crimes, Naval
   See Naval offenses
Crimes, Political
   See Political crimes and offenses
Crimes, Religious
   See Offenses against religion
Crimes, Rural
   See Rural crimes
Crimes, Suburban
   See Suburban crimes
Crimes aboard aircraft *(Direct)*
   sa Hijacking of aircraft
   x Crime in transportation
   xx Aeronautics—Laws and regulations
      Offenses against public safety
Crimes against humanity
   sa Deportation
      Forced labor
      Genocide
      Murder
      Trials (Crimes against humanity)
      War crimes
   xx Criminal law
      International offenses
Crimes against humanity, German
Crimes against peace
   sa Aggression (International law)
   x Incitement to war
      Peace, Crimes against
      Propaganda, War
      War, Incitement to
      War propaganda
   xx Criminal law
      International offenses
      Peace
      War (International law)
Crimes against property
   See Offenses against property
Crimes against public safety
   See Offenses against public safety
Crimes against religion
   See Offenses against religion
Crimes against socialist property
   See Offenses against socialist property
Crimes against the person
   See Offenses against the person
Crimes and misdemeanors
   See Criminal law
Crimes without victims *(Direct)*
   sa Birth control—Law and legislation
      Blasphemy
      Drug abuse
      Drunkenness (Criminal law)
      Gambling
      Incest
      Narcotic laws
      Obscenity (Law)
      Prostitution
      Sodomy
      Vagrancy
   x Morals offenses
      Non-victim crimes
      Offenses against public morality
      Victimless crimes
   xx Crime and criminals
      Criminal law
      Moral conditions
Criminal act *(Direct)*
   sa Criminal attempt
      Omission, Criminal
      Preparation (Criminal law)
   xx Criminal law
Criminal anthropology *(HV6001-6197)*
   sa Crime and superstition

Crime prevention
Criminal behavior, Prediction of
Criminal psychology
Prisoners—Examination
War and crime
   x Anthropology, Criminal
      Criminal anthropometry
   xx Anthropometry
— Research
Criminal anthropometry
   See Anthropometry
      Bertillon system
      Criminal anthropology
Criminal assault
   See Rape
Criminal attempt *(Direct)*
   sa Aberratio ictus
      Preparation (Criminal law)
   x Attempt, Criminal
   xx Criminal act
      Preparation (Criminal law)
Criminal attempt (Canon law)
Criminal attempt (Greek law)
Criminal attempt (Saxon law)
Criminal behavior, Prediction of
   sa Jesness inventory
   x Delinquency prediction
      Prediction of criminal behavior
   xx Criminal anthropology
      Criminal psychology
      Juvenile delinquency
      Prediction (Psychology)
Criminal courts *(Direct)*
   sa Courts-martial and courts of inquiry
      Criminal procedure
      Fehmic courts
      Judgments, Criminal
      Jury
      Justices of the peace
      Juvenile courts
      Police magistrates
      Traffic courts
   x Courts, Criminal
   xx Correctional institutions
      Courts
      Criminal justice, Administration of
      Criminal procedure
— Statistics
      See Criminal statistics
Criminal defenses
   See Defense (Criminal procedure)
Criminal evidence
   See Evidence, Criminal
Criminal insane
   See Insane, Criminal and dangerous
Criminal intent *(Direct)*
   sa Aberratio ictus
      Mistake (Criminal law)
      Premeditation (Law)
   x Dolus (Criminal law)
      Intent, Criminal
      Mens rea
   xx Guilt (Law)
Criminal intent (Jewish law)
Criminal investigation *(Direct)* *(HV8073)*
   sa Arson investigation
      Automobile theft investigation
      Chemistry, Forensic
      Crime and criminals—Identification
      Detectives
      Eavesdropping
      Electronics in criminal investigation
      Evidence, Criminal
      Forensic ballistics
      Fraud investigation
      Homicide investigation
      Informers
      Legal documents—Identification

Lie detectors and detection
Medical jurisprudence
Missing persons
Palmprints
Photography, Legal
Police charges
Police questioning
Public prosecutors
Typewriting—Identification
Wire-tapping
Writing—Identification
   x Crime detection
   xx Criminal justice, Administration of
      Detectives
      Governmental investigations
      Investigations
      Police
   Note under Investigations
— International cooperation
— Juvenile literature
Criminal judgments
   See Judgments, Criminal
Criminal jurisdiction *(Direct)*
   Here are entered works on the problem of
   territorial limitation of criminal law
   (Droit pénal international; Interna-
   tionales Strafrecht) and on the conflict
   of jurisdictions in the administration of
   criminal law.
   x Conflict of criminal jurisdiction
      Conflict of laws—Criminal law
      Conflict of laws—Criminal procedure
      Criminal law—Conflict of laws
      Criminal law, International
      Criminal procedure—Conflict of laws
      Exterritorial crime
      International criminal law
   xx Conflict of laws
      Criminal law
      Criminal procedure
      Jurisdiction
   Note under International offenses
Criminal justice, Administration of *(Direct)*
   sa Amnesty
      Arrest
      Bail
      Compensation for judicial error
      Coroners
      Corrections
      Courts-martial and courts of inquiry
      Crime and criminals
      Criminal courts
      Criminal investigation
      Criminal law
      Criminal procedure
      Impeachments
      Imprisonment
      Judicial error
      Juvenile courts
      Juvenile delinquency
      Law enforcement
      Lynching
      Medical examiners (Law)
      Pardon
      Parole
      Police
      Preventive detention
      Prisons
      Probation
      Prosecution
      Public prosecutors
      Punishment
      Rehabilitation of criminals
   x Administration of criminal justice
   xx Criminal law
      Justice, Administration of
— Citizen participation
— Economic aspects *(Direct)*

Criminal justice, Administration of (Direct)
  (Continued)
  — Public opinion
  — Statistics
      See Criminal statistics
  — Study and teaching (Direct)
      sa Interns (Criminal justice
            administration)
Criminal justice, Errors of
    See Judicial error
Criminal justice interns
    See Interns (Criminal justice administration)
Criminal law (Direct)
    sa Abduction
       Abortion
       Accomplices
       Adultery
       Affray
       Aggravating circumstances
       Arson
       Assault and battery
       Body-snatching
       Breach of the peace
       Bribery
       Burglary
       Capital punishment
       Classification of crimes
       Commercial crimes
       Competition, Unfair
       Compound offenses
       Confidential communications
       Conspiracy
       Contempt of court
       Contraventions (Criminal law)
       Corpus delicti
       Correctional law
       Counterfeits and counterfeiting
       Crimes against humanity
       Crimes against peace
       Crimes without victims
       Criminal act
       Criminal jurisdiction
       Criminal justice, Administration of
       Criminal liability
       Criminal procedure
       Criminal syndicalism
       Disorderly conduct
       Drunkenness (Criminal law)
       Dueling
       Duress (Law)
       Elections—Corrupt practices
       Embezzlement
       Escape (Law)
       Ex post facto laws
       Executions and executioners
       Executions in effigy
       Exposure (Criminal law)
       Extenuating circumstances
       False testimony
       Fines (Penalties)
       Flagrans crimen
       Forgery
       Fraud
       Gambling
       Guilt (Law)
       Hamsocn
       Homicide
       Illegality
       Indeterminate sentence
       Infamy (Law)
       Infanticide
       Insurance crimes
       International offenses
       Justification (Law)
       Kidnapping
       Larceny
       Libel and slander
       Limitation of actions (Criminal law)
       Lotteries

       Maintenance and champerty
       Malicious mischief
       Military offenses
       Misconduct in office
       Misprision
       Mistake (Criminal law)
       Murder
       Naval offenses
       Obscenity (Law)
       Offenses against property
       Offenses against public safety
       Offenses against religion
       Offenses against socialist property
       Offenses against the person
       Official secrets
       Omission, Criminal
       Pardon
       Parole
       Perjury
       Pimps
       Poisoning
       Political crimes and offenses
       Preparation (Criminal law)
       Prevarication (Law)
       Principals (Criminal law)
       Prisons—Laws and regulations
       Probation
       Proximate cause (Law)
       Punishment
       Racketeering
       Ransom
       Rape
       Recidivists
       Reparation
       Resisting an officer
       Riots
       Robbery
       Sanctions, Administrative
       Sedition
       Self-defense (Law)
       Sex crimes
       Shanghaiing
       Simulation of crimes
       Smuggling
       Sovereignty, Violation of
       Suicide
       Tax evasion
       Traffic violations
       Treason
       Unauthorized use
       Unlawful entry
       Vagrancy
       Wife beating
    subdivision Criminal provisions under
       legal topics, e.g. Corporation law—
       Criminal provisions
    x Crimes and misdemeanors
       Felony
       Law, Criminal
       Misdemeanors (Law)
       Penal codes
       Penal law
    xx Criminal justice, Administration of
       Criminal procedure
       Pleas of the crown
       Public law
       Punishment
Example under Law
  — Cases
  — — Digests
        See Criminal law—Digests
  — Conflict of laws
        See Criminal jurisdiction
  — Digests
      x Criminal law—Cases—Digests
  — Examinations, questions, etc.
  — Interpretation and construction

      Example under Law—Interpretation and
        construction
  — Juvenile literature
  — Legal research
  — Pleading and practice
      See Criminal procedure
  — Statistics
      See Criminal statistics
  — Study and teaching (Direct)
  — Terms and phrases

      GEOGRAPHIC SUBDIVISIONS

  — Rome
      See Criminal law (Roman law)
Criminal law, International
    See Criminal jurisdiction
       International offenses
Criminal law (Adat law) (Direct)
Criminal law (Burgundian law)
    Example under Law, Burgundian
Criminal law (Byzantine law)
Criminal law (Canon law)
    sa Accomplices (Canon law)
       Denunciation (Canon law)
Criminal law (Canon law, Orthodox Eastern)
    sa Adultery (Canon law, Orthodox
         Eastern)
    xx Canon law, Orthodox Eastern
Criminal law (Frankish law)
Criminal law (Germanic law)
  — Sources
Criminal law (Greek law)
Criminal law (Islamic law)
Criminal law (Jewish law)
Criminal law (Lombard law)
    xx Law, Lombard
Criminal law (Primitive law) (Direct)
Criminal law (Roman-Dutch law)
    Example under Roman-Dutch law
Criminal law (Roman law)
    x Criminal law—Rome
Criminal law (Saxon law)
Criminal liability (Direct)
    sa Aggravating circumstances
       Drunkenness (Criminal law)
       Duress (Law)
       Extenuating circumstances
       Guilt (Law)
       Ignorance (Law)
       Mistake (Criminal law)
       Necessity (Law)
       Proximate cause (Law)
       Respondeat superior
    x Accountability
       Criminal responsibility
       Liability, Criminal
       Responsibility, Criminal
    xx Criminal law
       Insane, Criminal and dangerous
       Insanity—Jurisprudence
       Liability (Law)
Criminal liability (Canon law)
Criminal liability (International law)
    xx International law
       International offenses
Criminal liability (Islamic law)
Criminal liability (Jewish law)
Criminal liability (Roman law)
Criminal liability of juristic persons (Direct)
    x Corporations—Criminal liability
       Juristic persons—Criminal liability
    xx Juristic persons
Criminal negligence
    See Negligence, Criminal
Criminal omission
    See Omission, Criminal
Criminal procedure (Direct)
    sa Acquittals

Alternative convictions
Amparo (Writ)
Appellate procedure
Arrest
Bail
Complaints (Criminal procedure)
Confession (Law)
Contumacy
Correctional law
Courts-martial and courts of inquiry
Criminal courts
Criminal jurisdiction
Criminal law
Criminal registers
Default (Law)
Defense (Criminal procedure)
Double jeopardy
Evidence, Circumstantial
Evidence, Criminal
Executions and executioners
Extradition
Flagrans crimen
Fugitives from justice
Grand jury
Habeas corpus
Indeterminate sentence
Indictments
Informations
Instructions to juries
Joinder of offenses
Judgments
Judgments, Criminal
Judicial assistance
Jury
Justices of the peace
Law and fact
Motions (Law)
New trials
Ordeal
Outlawry
Parole
Pleading (Criminal procedure)
Pleas (Criminal procedure)
Police charges
Prejudicial actions
Preliminary examinations (Criminal
    procedure)
Private prosecutors
Privileges and immunities
Probation
Prosecution
Psychology, Forensic
Public defenders
Public prosecutors
Reformatio in pejus
Searches and seizures
Sentences (Criminal procedure)
Speedy trial
Summary proceedings
Surety of the peace
Torture
Trial practice
Trials
Venue
Wager of battle
Writs
  x Criminal law—Pleading and practice
 xx Appellate procedure
    Courts
    Criminal courts
    Criminal justice, Administration of
    Criminal law
    Procedure (Law)
    Public law
    Trial practice
— Conflict of laws
    See Criminal jurisdiction
— Costs

— Examinations, questions, etc.
— Forms
— Interpretation and construction
— Juvenile literature
— Programmed instruction
— Statistics
    See Criminal statistics

GEOGRAPHIC SUBDIVISIONS

— Rome
    See Criminal procedure (Roman law)
Criminal procedure (Canon law)
  sa Precept (Canon law)
  xx Procedure (Canon law)
Criminal procedure (Germanic law)
Criminal procedure (International law)
  xx International law
    International offenses
Criminal procedure (Islamic law)
Criminal procedure (Jewish law)
Criminal procedure (Roman law)
  sa Contumacy (Roman law)
  x Criminal procedure—Rome
Criminal procedure (Saxon law)
Criminal psychology *(HV6080-6113)*
  sa Anonymous letters
    Criminal behavior, Prediction of
    Forensic psychiatry
    Hypnotism and crime
    Occasional criminals
    Oppression (Psychology)
    Prison psychology
    Prisoners—Examination
    Psychology, Forensic
    Psychology, Pathological
    Sex crimes
  x Psychology, Criminal
  xx Crime prevention
    Criminal anthropology
    Law—Psychology
    Psychology, Forensic
    Psychology, Pathological
Criminal records
  See Criminal registers
Criminal registers *(Direct)*
  sa Certificates of good conduct
  x Arrest records
    Criminal records
    Registers, Criminal
    Registration of criminals
  xx Court records
    Criminal procedure
    Criminal statistics
    Recording and registration
— Cancellations *(Direct)*
  x Cancellation of arrest records
    Cancellation of criminal records
Criminal responsibility
  See Criminal liability
Criminal statistics *(Direct) (Criminal*
    classes, HV6208; Documents,
    HV7245-7400; Monographs,
    HV7415)
  sa Criminal registers
    Military offenses—Statistics
    Prison sentences—Statistics
    Prisons—Statistics
    Violent deaths
  x Crime and criminals—Statistical
    methods
    Crime and criminals—Statistics
    Crime statistics
    Criminal courts—Statistics
    Criminal justice, Administration of—
      Statistics
    Criminal law—Statistics
    Criminal procedure—Statistics
  xx Judicial statistics

    Statistics
Criminal syndicalism *(Direct)*
  sa Sabotage
  xx Criminal law
    Direct action
    Labor laws and legislation
    Sabotage
    Subversive activities
    Syndicalism
Criminals
  See Crime and criminals
Criminals, Rehabilitation of
  See Rehabilitation of criminals
Criminologists
  xx Crime and criminals
Criminology
  See Crime and criminals
Crimiso, Battle of, 339 B.C.
  See Crimissus, Battle of, 339 B.C.
Crimissus, Battle of, 339 B.C.
  x Crimiso, Battle of, 339 B.C.
Crimping of textiles *(TS1487.7)*
  xx Textile industry and fabrics
Crimson clover
  x Clover, Crimson
  xx Clover
Crinoidea *(Indirect) (QL384.C8)*
  xx Echinodermata
Crinoidea, Fossil *(QE782)*
  sa Millericrinida, Fossil
  xx Pelmatozoa, Fossil
Crinoline *(GT2075)*
  x Farthingale
  xx Underwear
Crinothene
  See Polyethylene
Criollo horse *(SF293.C)*
Cripple Creek Strike, 1893 *(HD5325)*
Cripple Creek Strike, 1903-1904
    (HD5325.M8 1903.C)
  Example under Strikes and lockouts
Crippled children *(Direct)*
  sa Orthopedic apparatus
    Pediatric orthopedia
  xx Pediatric orthopedia
    Physically handicapped children
— Education
— Institutional care *(Direct)*
— Law and legislation *(Direct)*
  xx Children—Law
— Recreation
— Rehabilitation
Cripples
  See Physically handicapped
Cripples, War
  See Veterans, Disabled
Cris language
  See Cree language
Crisca Indians
  See Akwě-Shavante Indians
Crises, Commercial
  See Depressions
Crises and critical days (Pathology) *(RB153)*
  xx Pathology
Crisis intervention (Psychiatry)
  x Emergency mental health services
  xx Community mental health services
    Psychotherapy
Crisis theology
  See Dialectical theology
Cristero Rebellion, 1926-1929
  xx Mexico—History—1910-1946
Cristianos y Moros (Dance)
  See Moros y Cristianos (Dance)
Cristobalite
  xx Silica
Criterion (Theory of knowledge) *(BD182)*
  xx Knowledge, Theory of

Critical flicker frequency
    See Flicker fusion
Critical materials
    See Strategic materials
Critical micelle concentration
    xx Micelles
        Solution (Chemistry)
    — Tables, etc.
Critical path analysis
    xx Network analysis (Planning)
    — Problems, exercises, etc.
    — Programmed instruction
Critical periods (Biology)
    sa Imprinting (Psychology)
        Puberty
    xx Child study
        Developmental biology
        Developmental psychobiology
        Genetic psychology
Critical point *(QC307)*
    sa Phase rule and equilibrium
    x Point, Critical
    xx Chemistry, Physical and theoretical
        Equations of state
        Matter—Properties
        Phase rule and equilibrium
Criticality (Nuclear engineering) *(TK9153)*
    xx Nuclear engineering
        Nuclear fuels
        Nuclear physics
Criticism *(Direct) (Aesthetics, BH39-41; Literary criticism, PN75-99)*
    Here are entered works on the principles of criticism in general and of literary criticism in particular. Criticism in a specific field is entered under the appropriate heading, *e.g.* Art criticism; English literature—History and criticism; English poetry—History and criticism; Literature—History and criticism; Music—History and criticism
    sa Aesthetics
        Art criticism
        Bible—Criticism, interpretation, etc.
        Books—Reviews
        Drama—History and criticism
        Dramatic criticism
        Hermeneutics
        Literature—History and criticism
        Moving-picture criticism
        Music—History and criticism
        Musical criticism
        Newspapers—Sections, columns, etc.—Reviews
        Poetry—History and criticism
        Radio criticism
        Style, Literary
        Television criticism
        subdivision History and criticism *under names of literatures, e.g.* Spanish literature—History and criticism; *and subdivision* Criticism and interpretation *under names of prominent authors*
    x Appraisal of books
        Bibliography, Critical
        Books—Appraisal
        Evaluation of literature
        Literary criticism
        Literature—Evaluation
    xx Aesthetics
        Literature
        Rhetoric
        Style, Literary
    Note under Literature—History and criticism
Criticism, Communist
    See Communist self-criticism

Criticism, Textual *(P47; PA47; etc.)*
    sa Structuralism (Literary analysis)
        subdivision Criticism, Textual *under individual authors and literatures, e.g.* Shakespeare, William, 1564-1616 —Criticism, Textual; Greek literature —Criticism, Textual
    x Textual criticism
    xx Editing
Criticism (Philosophy) *(B809.3)*
    xx Philosophy
Crixá Indians
    See Akwẽ-Shavante Indians
Cro-Magnon man
    sa Aurignacian culture
    xx Aurignacian culture
        Fossil man
Croaker, Atlantic
    See Atlantic croaker
Croat (Coin)
    xx Coins, Spanish
Croatan Indians
    See Lumbee Indians
Croatia
    — History
    — — Peasant Uprising, 1573
        sa Slovenia—History—Peasant Uprising, 1573
        xx Slovenia—History—Peasant Uprising, 1573
    — — Uprising of 1573 *(DB378)*
Croatian-American newspapers
    xx Croatian newspapers
Croatian ballads and songs *(PG1464)*
    sa Folk-songs, Croatian
    xx Yugoslav ballads and songs
Croatian Catholics
    See Catholics, Croatian
Croatian drama *(Direct) (Collections, PG1615; History, PG1611)*
    xx Yugoslav drama
Croatian drama (Comedy)
Croatian essays *(Direct)*
    xx Yugoslav essays
Croatian fiction *(Direct) (Collections, PG1616; History, PG1612)*
    sa Croatian prose literature
    — 20th century
Croatian language
    See Serbo-Croatian language
Croatian literature *(PG1600-1798)*
    xx Yugoslav literature
    — 20th century

GENERAL SUBDIVISIONS

    — Muslim authors
        x Muslim Croatian literature
Croatian literature in foreign countries
Croatian newspapers *(Direct)*
    sa Croatian-American newspapers
    xx Yugoslav newspapers
Croatian periodicals
    sa Serbian periodicals
    xx Serbian periodicals
        Yugoslav periodicals
Croatian philology
    See Serbo-Croatian philology
Croatian poetry *(Direct) (Collections, PG1614; History, PG1610)*
    sa Croatian poetry in foreign countries
    — 20th century
Croatian poetry in foreign countries
    xx Croatian poetry
Croatian prose literature *(Direct) (Collections, PG1616; History, PG1612)*
    xx Croatian fiction

Croatians
    See Croats
Croato-Hungarian Compromise, 1868
    x Hungarian-Croatian Compromise, 1868
Croato-Serbian language
    See Serbo-Croatian language
Croats *(Austria, DB33-34; Croatia, DB361-379; Yugoslavia, DR364-7)*
    sa Dalmatians
    x Croatians
        Serbo-Croatians
    xx Yugoslavs
Croats in Canada, [the United States, etc.]
Croats in foreign countries
Crobo (African tribe)
    See Krobo (African tribe)
Crocheting *(TT820-825)*
    sa Beadwork
        Doilies
        Hairpin lace
        Lace and lace making
        Sweaters
    xx Fancy work
    — Juvenile literature
    — Patterns
Crocheting machines *(TT685)*
Crocidolite
    See Riebeckite
Crockery
    See Pottery
Crocodiles *(QL666.C9)*
    — Juvenile literature
Crocodiles, Fossil *(QE862.C8)*
    xx Reptiles, Fossil
Crocodiles (in religion, folk-lore, etc.)
    x Folk-lore of crocodiles
    xx Religion, Primitive
Crofters *(HD1511.G66)*
    xx Farm tenancy—Great Britain
        Landlord and tenant—Great Britain
Crohn's disease
    See Regional ileitis
Croix de guerre (France) *(UB435.F)*
    xx France. Armée—Medals, badges, decorations, etc.
Crombec
Cromlechs *(GN790-792)*
    sa Dolmens
        Menhirs
    x Stone circles
    xx Archaeology
        Megalithic monuments
        Menhirs
Croo monkey
    See Kra
Crooked Billet, Battle of the, 1778 *(E241.C94)*
Crooning
Crop estimating
    See Agricultural estimating and reporting
Crop insurance
    See Insurance, Agricultural—Crops
Crop reporting
    See Agricultural estimating and reporting
Crop reports
    See Agriculture—[country subdivision]—Statistics
        Agriculture—Statistics
Crop residue tillage
    See Stubble mulching
Crop rotation
    See Rotation of crops
Crop statistics
    See Agriculture—Statistics
Crop yields
    sa Agricultural estimating and reporting
        Agriculture—Statistics
        Crops and climate

particular crops, e.g. Barley
  x Crops
  xx Agricultural estimating and reporting
    Agriculture
    Agriculture—Statistics
    Crops and climate
  — Mathematical models
Crop zones *(Indirect)* *(S439)*
  sa Alpine regions
    Arid regions
    Life zones
    Soils—Classification
  x Zones, Crop
  xx Agricultural geography
    Crops and climate
    Life zones
Cropland adjustment program
  See Farm production quotas
Cropland conversion program *(Direct)*
  xx Agriculture and state—United States
    Soil conservation—United States
Cropping, Double
  See Double cropping
Cropping systems *(Indirect)*
  sa Double cropping
    Rotation of crops
Crops
  See Agriculture
    Crop yields
    Field crops
    Plants, Cultivated
Crops, Rotation of
  See Rotation of crops
Crops and climate *(Indirect)* *(S600)*
  sa Crop yields
    Crop zones
    Meteorology, Agricultural
    Plants—Frost resistance
    Vegetation and climate
  x Agricultural climatology
    Climatology, Agricultural
  xx Agricultural ecology
    Agricultural physics
    Agriculture
    Bioclimatology
    Crop yields
    Meteorology, Agricultural
    Phenology
  — Mathematical models
  — Statistical methods
Croquet *(GV931-5)*
Crosier
  See Staff, Pastoral
Cross
  See Holy Cross
Cross, Pectoral
  See Pectoral cross
Cross, Sign of the *(BV197.S5; Catholic*
    Church, BX2048.S5)
  x Sign of the cross
  xx Crosses
    Liturgics
    Rites and ceremonies
Cross-connections (Plumbing) *(TH6523)*
  sa Backsiphonage (Plumbing)
  x Backflow connections
    Interconnection (Plumbing)
  xx Backsiphonage (Plumbing)
    Plumbing
    Water—Pollution
Cross-country running
  See Running
Cross-country skiing *(Direct)* *(GV854.9.C7)*
  xx Skis and skiing
  — Juvenile literature
Cross-examination *(Direct)*
  xx Examination of witnesses

Cross-field generators
  See Rotating amplifiers
Cross infection
  x Hospital infections
  xx Hospitals—Hygiene
    Infection
Cross of Lorraine
  x Lorraine, Cross of
  xx Crosses
    Crosses (in heraldry)
Cross references (Cataloging) *(Z693-5)*
  x Catalog cross references
    References (Cataloging)
    Syndetic structure (Cataloging)
  xx Cataloging
    Indexing
    Subject headings
Cross section fluctuations (Nuclear physics)
    (QC794)
  x Fluctuations, Cross section (Nuclear
    physics)
  xx Cross sections (Nuclear physics)
    Nuclear excitation
    Nuclear reactions
Cross sections, Elastic
  See Elastic cross sections
Cross sections, Inelastic
  See Inelastic cross sections
Cross sections, Neutron
  See Neutron cross sections
Cross sections (Nuclear physics)
    (QC794.6.C7)
  sa Cross section fluctuations (Nuclear
    physics)
    Elastic cross sections
    Inelastic cross sections
  x Nuclear cross sections
  xx Collisions (Nuclear physics)
  — Tables
Cross-stitch *(TT771)*
  sa Samplers
  xx Embroidery
    Needlework
  — Patterns
Cross talk
  See Crosstalk
Cross-word puzzles
  See Crossword puzzles
Crossbills *(QL696.P2)*
Crossbow *(U878)*
  xx Bow and arrow
Crosscut saws *(TJ1233)*
  xx Saws
  — Maintenance and repair
Crosses *(Indirect)* *(Antiquities, CC300-350;*
    Christian art and symbolism, BV160;
    Comparative religion, BL640.C7;
    Relics, etc., BT465; Theology,
    BT453)
  sa Christian art and symbolism
    Cross of Lorraine
    Cross, Sign of the
    Crosses (in heraldry)
    Crucifixion
    Pectoral cross
    Processional crosses
    Red cross (Symbol)
    Swastika
    Symbolism
  x Calvaries
  xx Christian antiquities
    Christian art and symbolism
    Crucifixion
    Jesus Christ
    Liturgical objects
    Sepulchral monuments
    Signs and symbols
    Symbolism

  — Cultus *(BX2310.C7)*
    x Veneration of the Cross
  — Legends
  — Pictorial works
  — Terminology
Crosses (in heraldry) *(CR41.C7)*
  sa Cross of Lorraine
  xx Crosses
Crossing (Architecture)
  xx Church architecture
Crossing over (Genetics)
  sa Chromosomes
  xx Chromosomes
    Genetic recombination
    Genetics
    Heredity
    Translocation (Genetics)
Crossings, Railroad
  See Railroads—Crossings
Crossroads Africa
  x Operation Crossroads Africa
Crosstalk
  x Cross talk
  xx Electro-acoustics
    Radio
    Telecommunication
    Telephone
Crossword puzzles *(GV1507.C7)*
  sa Bible games and puzzles
    Word games
  x Cross-word puzzles
  xx Literary recreations
    Puzzles
    Word games
  — Dictionaries
    See Crossword puzzles—Glossaries,
      vocabularies, etc.
  — Glossaries, vocabularies, etc.
    (GV1507.C7)
    x Crossword puzzles—Dictionaries
    xx English language—Glossaries,
      vocabularies, etc.
Crotalus
  See Rattlesnakes
Crotalus (Materia medica) *(RS163.C;*
    Homeopathy, RX615.C)
Crotin *(QP941)*
  xx Croton tiglium
Croton Aqueduct
  Example under Aqueducts
Croton-chloral
  See Butyl-chloral
Croton Dam
  Example under Dams
Croton oil
  Example under Purgatives
Croton tiglium *(RM666.C9)*
  sa Crotin
Crotonic acid *(QD305.A2)*
Croup *(RC746)*
  x Cynanche trachealis
    Membranous croup
  Example under Respiratory organs—Diseases
Crow blackbirds
  See Purple grackle
Crow hunting *(SK325.C7)*
  xx Crows
Crow Indians *(E99.C92)*
  x Absahrokee Indians
    Absaroka Indians
  xx Hidatsa Indians
    Indians of North America
    Siouan Indians
Crowd (Musical instrument) *(ML1015-1018)*
  x Crwth
Crowding stress
  xx Personal space
    Social behavior in animals

Crowding stress *(Continued)*
    Stress (Physiology)
    — Juvenile literature
Crowds *(HM281-3)*
    sa Demonstrations
      Mobs
      Riot control
      Riots
      Spectator control
    xx Mobs
      Riots
      Social psychology
      Sociology
Crown (Coin) *(Silver, CJ2485)*
Crown-gall disease *(SB741.C9)*
    Example under Apple—Diseases and pests
Crown jewels *(Indirect)* *(NK7400-7419)*
    sa Ampullas, Coronation
      Crowns
      Regalia (Insignia)
    x Jewels
    xx Gems
      Jewelry
      Regalia (Insignia)
Crown lands *(Direct)*
    sa Public lands
      subdivision Public lands *under names of*
        countries, states, etc.
    x Demesne, Royal
      Royal demesne
    xx Public lands
      Regalia
Crown of Italy, Order of the
    See Order of the Crown of Italy
Crown Point, N.Y.
    — Capture, 1775
Crown Point Expedition, 1755 *(E199)*
    sa George, Lake, Battle of, 1755
Crown proceedings
    See Government liability—Great Britain
Crown vetch
    See Axseed
Crowns *(CR4480)*
    sa Coronations
      Iron Crown of Lombardy
      Tiara, Papal
    xx Crown jewels
      Regalia (Insignia)
Crowns (Dentistry)
    xx Partial dentures
      Prosthodontics
Crowns (in heraldry)
Crown's extent
    See Extent (Writ)
Crownvetch
    See Axseed
Crows *(QL696.P2)*
    sa Carrion crow
      Crow hunting
      Hooded crow
    — Juvenile literature
    — Legends and stories
    — Pictorial works
Crozier
    See Staff, Pastoral
Crucibles *(QD54.C; TN677; TP159.C)*
Crucifixion *(HV8569)*
    sa Crosses
    xx Capital punishment
      Crosses
      Execution and executioners
Crucifixion of Christ
    See Jesus Christ—Crucifixion
Cruciform wings (Aeroplanes)
    See Aeroplanes—Wings, Cruciform
Cruelty *(BJ1535.C)*
    sa Animals, Treatment of
      Atrocities

    x Brutality
    xx Ethics
Cruelty, Legal
    See Legal cruelty
Cruelty, Matrimonial
    See Legal cruelty
Cruelty in literature
Cruelty to children *(Direct)*
    sa Discipline of children
    x Battered child syndrome
      Child abuse
      Children, Cruelty to
    xx Child welfare
      Children—Management
      Parent and child
Cruelty to the aged *(Direct)*
    sa Aged, Killing of the
    x Mistreatment of the aged
    xx Aged
Cruets *(Direct)* *(NK5440.C75)*
    xx Bottles
      Pitchers
Cruisers (Warships)
    xx Warships
    — Pictorial works
Crummies
    See Cabooses (Railroads)
Crura cerebri
    See Cerebral peduncle
Crus cerebri
    See Cerebral peduncle
Crusade bulls
    Here are assembled texts of and critical
    works on the many bulls issued by the
    popes granting indulgences and other
    benefits to participants in the Crusades
    and, by extension down to present
    times, to other persons, especially in
    the Hispanic world.
    x Bulla cruciata
      Bulls, Crusade
      Cruzada, Bula de
    xx Bulls, Papal
      Crusades
      Crusades—Finance
      Indulgences
Crusades *(D151-173)*
    sa Children's Crusade, 1212
      Chivalry
      Crusade bulls
      Jerusalem—History—Latin kingdom,
        1099-1244
      Latin Orient
      Templars
    xx Chivalry
      Church history—Middle Ages,
        600-1500
      Latin Orient
      Middle Ages—History
      Palestine—History—638-1917
      Saracens
    — First, 1096-1099 *(D161)*
    — Second, 1147-1149 *(D162)*
    — Third, 1189-1192 *(D163)*
    — Later, 13th, 14th, and 15th centuries
      (D171-2)
    — Fourth, 1202-1204 *(D164)*
      sa Istanbul—Siege, 1203-1204
        Latin Orient
      xx Istanbul—Siege, 1203-1204
        Latin Empire, 1204-1261
        Latin Orient
    — Fifth, 1218-1221 *(D165)*
    — Sixth, 1228-1229 *(D166)*
    — Seventh, 1248-1250 *(D167)*
      sa Mansura, Battle of, 1250
    — Eighth, 1270 *(D168)*
    — Fiction

    — Finance
      sa Crusade bulls
    — Historiography
    — Influence *(D157-160)*
    — Juvenile literature *(D158)*
    — Music
      See Crusades—Songs and music
    — Poetry
    — Songs and music
      x Crusades—Music
Crushed stone
    See Stone, Crushed
Crushed stone industry *(Direct)*
    xx Stone, Crushed
      Stone industry and trade
    — Dust control
    — Employees *(Direct)*
      sa Wages—Crushed stone industry
    — Equipment and supplies
Crushing machinery *(TJ1345)*
    sa Milling machinery
    xx Milling machinery
    — Appraisal
      See Crushing machinery—Valuation
    — Design and construction
    — Valuation *(TJ1345)*
      x Crushing machinery—Appraisal
Crustacea *(Indirect)* *(QL435-445)*
    sa Amphipoda
      Arthrostraca
      Cirripedia
      Cladocera
      Copepoda
      Crabs
      Crayfish
      Cumacea
      Cyclopoida
      Decapoda (Crustacea)
      Entomostraca
      Isopoda
      Leptostraca
      Lobsters
      Malacostraca
      Ostracoda
      Schizopoda
      Thoracostraca
    xx Arthropoda
      Invertebrates
      Shellfish
    — Anatomy *(QL445)*
      sa subdivision Crustacea *under*
        Digestive organs, Nervous system
    — Behavior
      sa subdivision Behavior *under names of*
        particular crustacea, e.g. Crabs—
        Behavior
      xx Animals, Habits and behavior of
    — Catalogs and collections
    — Development
    — Diseases and pests *(SH175)*
    — Embryology
      See Embryology—Crustacea
    — Geographical distribution
    — Identification
    — Larvae
      See Larvae—Crustacea
    — Physiology *(QL445)*
Crustacea, Fossil *(QE816-817)*
    sa Branchiopoda, Fossil
      Cladocera, Fossil
      Crabs
      Entomostraca, Fossil
      Fossil
      Malacostraca, Fossil
Crutch walking
    See Crutches
Crutches *(RD756)*
    x Crutch walking

xx Orthopedic apparatus
Physically handicapped
Cruz-Chagas disease
See Chagas' disease
Cruzada, Bula de
See Crusade bulls
Crwth
See Crowd (Musical instrument)
Crying *(HQ748.C)*
sa Weepers (Mourners)
x Children—Crying
Infants—Crying
Weeping
xx Emotions
Grief
Crying (in religion, folk-lore, etc.)
x Folk-lore of crying
xx Religion, Primitive
Crying in art
xx Art
Crymotherapy
See Cold—Therapeutic use
Cryobiology
sa Cold—Physiological effect
Freeze-drying
Hypothermia
Plants, Effect of cold on
Psychrotrophic organisms
x Freezing
Low temperature biology
xx Biology
Cold
Low temperatures
Cryoconite
xx Mineralogy
Cryogenic engineering
See Low temperature engineering
Cryogenic gyroscopes
xx Gyroscope
Low temperature engineering
Superconductors
Cryogenic interment
See Cryonics
Cryogenic surgery
See Cryosurgery
Cryogenics
See Low temperature engineering
Low temperature research
Low temperatures
Refrigeration and refrigerating
machinery
Cryolite *(TN948.C)*
Cryonics
x Cryogenic interment
Freezing of human bodies
Human cold storage
xx Burial
Resuscitation
Cryopedology
sa Aerial photography in cryopedology
Aeronautics in cryopedology
Frozen ground
xx Frost
Geodynamics
Physical geography
Cryophorus *(QC303)*
Cryoscopy *(QD545)*
sa Molecular weights
Solution (Chemistry)
Supercooling
x Freezing points of solutions
xx Chemistry, Physical and theoretical
Molecular weights
Solution (Chemistry)
Supercooling
Cryostat *(QC278)*
Cryosurgery
x Cryogenic surgery

xx Cold—Therapeutic use
Surgery
Cryotherapy
See Cold—Therapeutic use
Cryotrons
x Superconductive devices
xx Electronics
Superconductors
Cryptanalysis
See Cryptography
Cryptesthesia
See Extrasensory perception
Crypto-explosion craters
See Cryptoexplosion structures
Cryptobiosis *(QH331)*
sa Anhydrobiosis
Dormancy in plants
Seeds
Spores (Botany)
x Abiosis
Anabiosis
Latent life
Life, Latent
xx Dormancy (Biology)
Life (Biology)
Cryptobiotic organisms
See Cryptozoa
Cryptococcosis
See Torulosis
Cryptoexplosion structures *(Indirect)*
   (QE613)
x Craters, Crypto-explosion
Crypto-explosion craters
Cryptoexplosive structures
Cryptovolcanic structures
Structures, Cryptoexplosion
xx Geology, Structural
Meteorites
Volcanism
Cryptoexplosive structures
See Cryptoexplosion structures
Cryptogams *(QK505-635)*
Works on the cryptogamic flora of a par-
ticular country or locality are entered
under 1. Cryptogams. 2. Botany—[lo-
cal subdivision]
sa Algae
Bryophytes
Ferns
Fungi
Lichens
Mosses
x Acrogens
Nonvascular plants
Protophyta
xx Ferns
Plants
Example under Botany
Cryptogams, Vascular
See Pteridophyta
Cryptogram stories
See Code and cipher stories
Cryptography *(Z103-4)*
sa Alphabet (in religion, folk-lore, etc.)
Ciphers
World War, 1939-1945—Cryptography
x Cryptanalysis
Cryptology
Secret writing
Steganography
xx Ciphers
Signs and symbols
Symbolism
Writing
— Early works to 1800 *(Z103)*
— Juvenile literature
— Terminology

Cryptology
See Cryptography
Cryptorchis
See Testicle—Abnormities and deformities
Cryptostomata *(QE799.C7)*
xx Gymnolaemata, Fossil
Cryptovolcanic structures
See Cryptoexplosion structures
Cryptozoa *(Indirect)*
x Cryptobiotic organisms
xx Invertebrates
— Juvenile literature
Crypts *(Direct)* *(Architecture, NA2880;*
   Building, TH2150-2160)
xx Church architecture
Tombs
Crypturi
See Tinamiformes
Crystal detectors
x Crystal rectifiers
Detectors, Crystal
xx Crystals
Electric current rectifiers
Electronic apparatus and appliances
Radio detectors
Radio—Rectifiers
Semiconductors
Crystal devices, Liquid
See Liquid crystal devices
Crystal diodes
See Diodes, Semiconductor
Crystal field theory
sa Jahn-Teller effect
Ligand field theory
xx Complex compounds
Coordination compounds
Transition metals
Crystal-gazing *(BF1331)*
sa Catoptromancy
x Crystal-vision
xx Catoptromancy
Clairvoyance
Divination
Fortune-telling
Hypnotism
Magic
Mirrors, Magic
Occult sciences
Second sight
Superstition
Thought-transference
Crystal growth
See Crystals—Growth
Crystal lattices
sa Color centers
Lattice gas
x Crystals—Lattices
xx Crystallography, Mathematical
Lattice theory
— Charts, diagrams, etc.
— Tables, etc.
Crystal mixers
xx Diodes, Semiconductor
Crystal optics *(QD941)*
sa Universal stage (Optical instrument)
x Crystals—Optical properties
Optical crystallography
xx Crystallography
Optics, Physical
Crystal Palace, Hyde Park, London
Example under Exhibition buildings
Crystal rectifiers
See Crystal detectors
Crystal texture
See Texture (Crystallography)
Crystal-vision
See Crystal-gazing

Crystalline lens *(Comparative anatomy,*
   QL949; Diseases, RE401-461;
   Human anatomy, QM511)
   sa Aphakia
   x Lens, Crystalline
   xx Eye
   — Diseases *(RE401)*
      xx Eye—Diseases and defects
Crystalline rocks
   See Rocks, Crystalline
Crystalline texture
   See Texture (Crystallography)
Crystallization *(QD901-999; Supersaturated*
      solutions, QD548)
   sa Epitaxy
      Solidification
      Solutions, Solid
      Solutions, Supersaturated
      Zone melting
      subdivision Growth *under* Crystals *and*
         under names of particular types of
         crystals, e.g. Metal crystals—Growth
   xx Chemistry
      Chemistry, Physical and theoretical
      Separation (Technology)
Crystallization, Water of *(QD951)*
   x Water of crystallization
   xx Water of hydration
Crystallographers *(QD903.5-6)*
Crystallography *(QD901-999)*
   sa Anisotropy
      Asterism (Crystallography)
      Crystal optics
      Crystals
      Dislocations in crystals
      Geology
      Mineralogy
      Oscillators, Crystal
      Phonons
      Polymorphism (Crystallography)
      Pyro- and piezo-electricity
      Solid state chemistry
      Texture (Crystallography)
      X-ray crystallography
      names of minerals, e.g. Feldspar
   xx Chemistry
      Chemistry, Physical and theoretical
      Geology
      Geometry, Solid
      Mineralogy
      Petrology
      Rocks
      Science
      Solid state chemistry
   — Apparatus and supplies
   — Early works to 1800 *(QD904)*
   — History *(Indirect)*
   — Juvenile literature
   — Laboratory manuals
   — Pictorial works
   — Problems, exercises, etc.
   — Tables, etc.
Crystallography, Mathematical *(QD911-915)*
   sa Crystal lattices
      Crystals—Mathematical models
      Energy-band theory of solids
      Lattice theory
      Symmetry groups
   x Crystallometry
      Mathematical crystallography
   xx Crystals—Mathematical models
      Groups, Theory of
      Lattice theory
Crystallography, X-ray
   See X-ray crystallography
Crystalloids (Botany) *(QK899)*
   x Protein crystals
   xx Plant cells and tissues

Crystallometry
   See Crystallography, Mathematical
Crystals
   sa Annealing of crystals
      Crystal detectors
      Dislocations in crystals
      Domain structure
      Germanium diodes
      Oscillators, Crystal
      Powders
      Semiconductors
      names of particular types of crystals,
         e.g. Ionic crystals; Metal crystals;
         Quartz crystals
   xx Crystallography
      Powders
      Solids
   — Defects
      sa Color centers
         Point defects
   — Electric properties
      sa Brillouin zones
         Ferroelectricity
   — Growth *(QD921)*
      sa Epitaxy
      x Crystal growth
      xx Crystallization
   — — Laboratory manuals
   — — Mathematical models
   — Juvenile literature
   — Lattices
      See Crystal lattices
   — Magnetic properties *(QD940)*
   — — Tables, etc.
   — Mathematical models
      sa Crystallography, Mathematical
      xx Crystallography, Mathematical
   — Models
      xx Chemical models
   — Optical properties
      See Crystal optics
   — Pictorial works
   — Radiation effects
      See Crystals, Effect of radiation on
   — Spectra
   — Tables, etc.
   — Texture
      See Texture (Crystallography)
   — Thermal properties
Crystals, Dislocations in
   See Dislocations in crystals
Crystals, Effect of radiation on
   x Crystals, Irradiated
      Crystals—Radiation effects
      Radiation—Effect on crystals
   xx Radiation
Crystals, Irradiated
   See Crystals, Effect of radiation on
Crystals, Liquid
   See Liquid crystals
Crystolon
   See Silicon carbide
Csakan
   See Czakan
CSC test
   See Children's self-conceptions test
CTC system (Railroads)
   See Railroads—Signaling—Centralized
      traffic control
Ctenophora *(Indirect)* *(QL380)*
   xx Invertebrates
Ctenophora (Coelenterata) *(QL377.C8)*
Ctenostomata *(QL398.C8)*
Ctesiphon, Battle of, 1915. *(D568.5)*
   xx European War, 1914-1918—Campaigns
      —Turkey and the Near East—
      Mesopotamia
Cuando (Dance) *(GV1796.C)*

Cuanhama
   See Kuanyama (African tribe)
Cuanhama language
   See Kuanyama language
Cuatro puertorriqueño *(ML1015-1018)*
   xx Musical instruments, Puerto Rican
   — Methods *(MT648)*
Cub Scouts
   sa Webelos
   xx Boy Scouts
Cuba
   — Diplomatic and consular service
   — — Fees
         Example under Fees, Consular
   — History *(F1751-1849)*
   — — To 1810
   — — British occupation, 1762-1763
   — — 1810-1899
   — — Black Eagle Conspiracy, 1830
   — — Negro Conspiracy, 1844
   — — Insurrection, 1849-1851
         x Cuban expeditions, 1849-1851
            Lopez expeditions to Cuba
         xx Filibusters
   — — Insurrection, 1868-1878
   — — 1878-1895
   — — 1895-
   — — Revolution, 1895-1898
         sa Cuban question—1895-1898
            San Pedro, Battle of, 1896
            Santiago Campaign, 1898
         xx Concentration camps
            Cuban question—1895-1898
   — — — Campaigns and battles
   — — — Foreign participants
   — — — Medical and sanitary affairs
   — — — Personal narratives
   — — — Registers, lists, etc.
   — — — Registers of dead
   — — 1899-1906
   — — American occupation, 1906-1909
         x Cuban intervention, 1906-1909
   — — 1909-1933
   — — Revolution, 1933
   — — 1933-1959
   — — — Juvenile literature
   — — 1959-
         sa Cuba—History—Invasion, 1961
            Cuban Missile Crisis, Oct. 1962
   — — — Juvenile literature
   — — Invasion, 1961
         x Bay of Pigs invasion
            Cuban invasion, 1961
            Girón, Playa Invasion, 1961
            Operation Pluto
            Pluto, Operation
         xx Cuba—History—1959-
   — — — Personal narratives
   — Hurricane, 1844
   — Hurricane, 1846
   — Hurricane, 1926
Cuba in literature
Cuban ballads and songs
   sa Folk-songs, Cuban
      National songs, Cuban
      Songs, Cuban
   xx Spanish American ballads and songs
Cuban drama *(Collections, PQ7386.D7;*
      History, PQ7381)
Cuban essays *(Collections, PQ7386.E;*
      History, PQ7382)
Cuban expeditions, 1849-1851
   See Cuba—History—Insurrection,
      1849-1851
Cuban fiction *(Collections, PQ7386.F;*
      History, PQ7382)
   — 20th century

Cuban intervention, 1906-1909
  See Cuba—History—American occupation, 1906-1909
Cuban invasion, 1961
  See Cuba—History—Invasion, 1961
Cuban literature *(PQ7370-7389)*
  xx Spanish American literature
  — 20th century *(Collections, PQ7383; History, PQ7378)*
Cuban Missile Crisis, Oct. 1962
  xx Cuba—History—1959-
Cuban newspapers *(Direct)* *(History, etc., PN4931-9)*
Cuban orations *(Collections, PQ7386.O; History, PQ7382)*
Cuban periodicals *(History, etc., PN4931-4940)*
Cuban poetry *(Direct)* *(Collections, PQ7384; History, PQ7380)*
  — 19th century
  — 20th century *(Collections, PQ7384; History, PQ7380)*
Cuban prose literature *(Collections, PQ7386.P7; History, PQ7382)*
Cuban question
  — To 1895 *(F1783-5)*
  — 1895-1898 *(F1786; United States political history, E721)*
    sa Cuba—History—Revolution, 1895-1898
    xx Cuba—History—Revolution, 1895-1898
  — — Speeches in Congress
Cuban students in the United States, [etc.]
Cuban wit and humor *(PN6222.C8)*
Cuban wit and humor, Pictorial
Cubans
Cubans in Florida, [Key West, etc.]
Cube
  xx Geometry, Solid
Cube, Duplication of *(QA469)*
  x Delian problem
    Duplication of the cube
  xx Geometry—Problems, Famous
Cube in art
  xx Art
Cube root *(QA119; Tables, QA49)*
  sa Roots, Numerical
  xx Arithmetic
Cubebs *(RS165.C9)*
Cubeo Indians
  x Cobbeos Indians
    Kobena Indians
  xx Indians of South America
Cubic curves
  See Curves, Cubic
Cubic equations
  See Equations, Cubic
Cubic measurement
  See Volume (Cubic content)
Cubic saltpeter
  See Saltpeter, Chile
Cubic surfaces
  See Surfaces, Cubic
Cubism *(Direct)*
  sa Post-impressionism (Art)
    Purism (Art)
  xx Aesthetics
    Art
    Art, Modern—20th century
    Modernism (Art)
    Painting
    Post-impressionism (Art)
Cubit
  x Codo (Unit of measure)
    Hasta (Unit of measure)
    Hath (Unit of measure)
  Example under Weights and measures

Cuchan Indians
  See Yuma Indians
Cucking stool *(HV8626)*
  x Castigatory
    Ducking stool
    Trebuchet (Punishment)
    Tumbrel (Punishment)
  xx Punishment
Cuckolds
  xx Adultery
    Free love
Cuckoos *(QL696.C5)*
  sa European cuckoo
    Road runner (Bird)
    Yellow-billed cuckoo
  x Coccyzus
    Cuculidae
  — Behavior
Cuckoos (in religion, folk-lore, etc.)
  x Folk-lore of cuckoos
  xx Religion, Primitive
Cuculidae
  See Cuckoos
Cucumber beetle, Spotted
  See Spotted cucumber beetle
Cucumber beetle, Striped
  See Striped cucumber beetle
Cucumber mosaic virus
  Example under Cucumbers—Diseases and pests
Cucumbers *(Indirect)* *(SB337)*
  — Disease and pest resistance
  — Diseases and pests
    sa names of diseases and pests, e.g. Cucumber mosaic virus; Spotted cucumber beetle
  — Marketing
Cueca (Dance) *(GV1796.C)*
  sa Zamacueca (Dance)
Cuesta escarpments
  See Cuestas
Cuestas *(Indirect)* *(GB571-9)*
  x Cuesta escarpments
    Hogbacks
  xx Plains
Cufic coins
  See Coins, Cufic
Cufic paleography
  See Paleography, Arabic (Cufic)
Cuicatec language *(PM3731)*
  xx Indians of Mexico—Languages
    Mixtec language
Cuichana Indians
  See Yuma Indians
Cuicurús
  See Kuikuru Indians
Cuitlateco language *(PM3738)*
  x Teco language
  xx Indians of Mexico—Languages
Cuitlatecos
  See Teco Indians
Cul-de-sac streets *(TE279)*
  x Dead-end streets
    Streets, Cul-de-sac
  — Design and construction
Culdees *(BR747)*
  xx Celtic Church
    Monasticism and religious orders
Culdocentesis
  xx Pelvis—Examination
Culina language
  x Culino language
  xx Arawakan languages
    Indians of South America—Languages
Culino language
  See Culina language
Cull tree felling *(Indirect)*
  x Felling cull trees

    xx Lumbering
      Tree felling
  — Costs
Cullar
  See Kallans
Culloden, Battle of, 1746 *(DA814.5)*
Culpeper's Rebellion, 1677-1679
  xx North Carolina—History—Colonial period, ca. 1600-1775
Cult *(BL600)*
  sa Ritual
  xx Cultus
    Religion
    Ritual
    Worship
Culteranismo
  See Gongorism
Cultism
  See Gongorism
Cultivated pearls
  See Cultured pearls
Cultivated plants
  See Plants, Cultivated
Cultivation, Shifting
  See Shifting cultivation
Cultivation of soils
  See Tillage
Cultivation of vacant lots
  See Working-men's gardens
Cultivators *(Mechanical engineering and machinery, TJ1482)*
  xx Agricultural machinery
Cults, Messianic
  See Nativistic movements
Cults, Prophetistic
  See Nativistic movements
Cultural activities of libraries
  See Libraries—Cultural programs
Cultural anthropology
  See Ethnology
Cultural assimilation
  See Assimilation (Sociology)
Cultural change
  See Social change
Cultural diffusion
  See Culture diffusion
Cultural evolution
  See Social change
    Social evolution
Cultural exchange programs
  See Cultural relations
    Exchange of persons programs
    Intellectual cooperation
Cultural lag *(HM101)*
  sa Compensatory education
  x Culture lag
    Lag, Cultural
  xx Culture
    Progress
    Social change
    Social evolution
Cultural programs in libraries
  See Libraries—Cultural programs
Cultural property, Protection of *(Direct)*
  sa subdivisions Conservation and restoration, Preservation, *or other appropriate subdivisions under types of cultural property or individual objects, e.g.* Art objects—Conservation and restoration; Monuments—Preservation
  x Art treasures, Protection of
    Protection of cultural property
    War damage to cultural property
  xx Disasters
  — Law and legislation *(Direct)*
  — — Criminal provisions

Cultural property, Protection of (International law)
    sa Art treasures in war
    xx War (International law)
Cultural relations
    sa Exchange of persons programs
       subdivision Relations (general) *under
        names of countries, e.g.* United
        States—Relations (general) with
        Latin America
    x Cultural exchange programs
      Intercultural relations
    xx Intellectual cooperation
      International relations
Cultural relativism *(GN405)*
    sa Ethnocentrism
    x Relativism, Cultural
    xx Ethnology
      Ethnopsychology
      Relativity
Culturally deprived
    See Socially handicapped
Culturally deprived children
    See Socially handicapped children
Culturally disadvantaged
    See Socially handicapped
Culturally handicapped
    See Socially handicapped
Culturally handicapped children
    See Socially handicapped children
Culture *(CB; Primitive, GN400-406;*
        Sociology, HM101)
    sa Acculturation
      Biculturalism
      Civilization
      Cultural lag
      Culture diffusion
      Education
      Educational anthropology
      Humanism
      Intellectual life
      Intercultural communication
      Learning and scholarship
      Personality and culture
      Philistinism
      Popular culture
      Self-culture
      Social evolution
      Subculture
    xx Civilization
      Conduct of life
      Education
      Historical sociology
      Humanism
      Learning and scholarship
    — Juvenile literature
Culture, Evolution of
    See Social evolution
Culture, Formal
    See Formal discipline
Culture, Popular
    See Popular culture
Culture alteration (Cytology)
    See Cell transformation
Culture and Christianity
    See Christianity and culture
Culture and communism
    See Communism and culture
Culture and education
    See Educational anthropology
Culture and personality
    See Personality and culture
Culture and religion
    See Religion and culture
Culture conflict *(BF740)*
    sa Interracial marriage
      Marriage, Mixed
      Miscegenation

      North and south
      Race problems
    x Conflict of cultures
    xx Ethnopsychology
      Genetic psychology
      Psychology, Pathological
Culture contact
    See Acculturation
Culture contamination (Biology)
    x Contamination of biological cultures
      and culture media
    xx Asepsis and antisepsis
      Contamination (Technology)
      Cultures (Biology)
Culture diffusion
    sa Diffusion of innovations
    x Cultural diffusion
    xx Culture
      Social change
Culture lag
    See Cultural lag
Culture media (Biology)
    x Nutrient media (Biology)
    xx Cultures (Biology)
    — Sterilization
Culture of cells
    See Cell culture
Culture of tissues
    See Tissue culture
Cultured pearls
    x Cultivated pearls
    xx Pearl industry and trade
      Pearls
Cultures (Biology)
    sa Cell culture
      Culture contamination (Biology)
      Culture media (Biology)
      Tissue culture
      subdivision Cultures and culture media
        under special subjects, e.g.
        Bacteriology—Cultures and culture
        media
    x Biology—Cultures
    xx Biology—Methodology
Cultus *(Direct) (BL550-620)*
    sa Cult
      Emperor worship
      Evocation
      Fertility cults
      Foot washing (Rite)
      Kings and rulers (in religion, folk-lore,
        etc.)
      Liturgics
      Lustrations
      Orientation (Religion)
      Posture in worship
      Religious calendars
      Ritual
      Sacred groves
      Shrines
      subdivision Cultus *under names of
        individual saints, e.g.* Mary, Virgin—
        Cultus
    xx Mysteries, Religious
      Mythology
      Religion
      Religion, Primitive
      Rites and ceremonies
      Sacrifice
      Worship
Cultus, Alexandrian *(BL2443)*
**Cultus, Assyro-Babylonian, [Egyptian, Hindu,
    etc.]**
    x Assyro-Babylonian [Egyptian, Hindu,
      etc.] cultus
Cultus, Buddhist
    sa Buddhist liturgical objects
      Mandala (Buddhism)

    x Buddhist cultus
    xx Buddha and Buddhism
Cultus, Disparity of
    See Marriage, Mixed
Cultus, Greek *(DF122)*
    sa Bacchantes
      Corybantes
      Delphian oracle
      Dionysia
      Eleusinian mysteries
      Oracles, Greek
    x Greek cultus
    xx Mythology, Greek
Cultus, Hindu
    sa Mandala
      Sacrifice (Hinduism)
Cultus, Islamic *(Direct)*
    sa Sacrifice (Islam)
      Saints, Muslim—Cultus
    x Cultus, Muslim
      Islamic cultus
      Muslim cultus
    xx Islamic religious practice
Cultus, Japanese
    sa Emperor worship, Japanese
    x Japanese cultus
Cultus, Jewish *(BM)*
    sa Ark of the Covenant
      Ark of the law
      Breastplate of the High Priest
      Cantors, Jewish
      Citron (Jewish cultus)
      Ephod
      Fringes (Jewish cultus)
      Hanukkah lamp
      Jews. Liturgy and ritual
      Judaism
      Liturgical objects—Judaism
      Lulab (Jewish cultus)
      Menorah
      Mezuzah
      Myrtle (Jewish cultus)
      Phylacteries
      Sacrifice (Judaism)
      Tabernacle
      Tallith
      Willow (Jewish cultus)
      Worship (Judaism)
    x Jewish cultus
    xx Jews. Liturgy and ritual
      Judaism
Cultus, Muslim
    See Cultus, Islamic
Cultus, Roman *(History, DG123-4; Religion,
      BL800-820)*
    sa Augustales
      Bacchanalia
      Emperor worship, Roman
      Lupercalia
      Priests, Roman
      Regifugium
      Ver sacrum
      Vestals
    x Roman cultus
Cultus, Sikh
    x Sikh cultus
Cultus, Sumerian
    See Sumerians
Cultus (Canon law)
Culverts *(Indirect) (Railroads, TF282;
      Roads, TE213)*
    xx Arches
      Bridges
      Hydraulic structures
      Railroads—Construction
      Railroads—Earthwork
      Roads—Accessories
    — Contracts and specifications *(Direct)*

— Corrosion
— Design and construction
— Maintenance and repair
Cum invocarem (Music)
  See Psalms (Music)—4th Psalm
Cumacea *(QL444.C9)*
  xx Crustacea
    Malacostraca
Cuman language
  See Kipchak language
Cumana Indians *(F2319)*
  x Cumanagoto Indians
  xx Indians of South America
Cumana language *(PM5876)*
  xx Indians of South America—Languages
Cumanagoto Indians
  See Cumana Indians
Cumans
  See Kipchak
Cumarins
  See Coumarins
Cumberland disease
  See Anthrax
Cumberland Gap, Battle of, 1862 *(E473.52)*
Cumberland Gap, Tenn., in literature
Cumenol *(QD305.A4)*
Cumol *(QD341.P5)*
Cumulative voting
  See Proportional representation
Cumulonimbus
  x Thunderclouds
  xx Clouds
Cumulus
  xx Clouds
— Mathematical models *(QC921.5)*
Cuna Indians *(F1565.2.C8)*
  x San Blas Indians
    Tule Indians
  xx Indians of Central America
Cuna language *(PM3743)*
  xx Cariban languages
Cuna poetry *(Direct)* *(PM3743.7)*
Cunama language
  See Kunama language
Cunamas
  See Kunamas
Cundurango *(RS165.C67)*
  x Condurango
Cuneiform inscriptions *(CN; PJ; PK)*
    Here are entered collections and speci-
    mens of cuneiform inscriptions, espe-
    cially of Assyro-Babylonian inscrip-
    tions, also transliterated texts, criti-
    cisms, explanations, etc. Cuneiform
    (notably Babylonian) literature pre-
    served on clay tablets is entered under
    the heading Assyro-Babylonian lan-
    guage—Texts.
  sa Achaemenian inscriptions
    Assyro-Babylonian language—Texts
    Assyro-Babylonian literature
    Boundary stones, Babylonian
    Clay tablets
    Cuneiform writing
    Elamite language
    Old Persian inscriptions
    Shemshāra tablets
    Sumerian language—Texts
    Tell-el-Amarna tablets
    Ugaritic language
    Vannic language
  x Assyro-Babylonian inscriptions
    Babylonian inscriptions
    Behistun inscriptions
    Inscriptions, Assyrian
    Inscriptions, Babylonian
    Inscriptions, Behistun
    Inscriptions, Cuneiform

  xx Achaemenian inscriptions
    Assyro-Babylonian literature
    Civilization, Assyro-Babylonian
    Clay tablets
    Cuneiform writing
    Elamite language
    Old Persian inscriptions
Cuneiform inscriptions, Cappadocian
  x Cappadocian inscriptions
  xx Cappadocian language
Cuneiform inscriptions, Elamite *(P943)*
  sa Elamite language
  x Inscriptions, Elamite
  xx Elamite language
Cuneiform inscriptions, Persian
  See Old Persian inscriptions
Cuneiform inscriptions, Sumerian
    (PJ4051-4075)
  x Sumerian cuneiform inscriptions
Cuneiform inscriptions, Vannic *(P959)*
  x Chaldian language
    Inscriptions, Vannic
    Vannic inscriptions
Cuneiform writing *(PJ3191-3225)*
  sa Achaemenian inscriptions
    Cuneiform inscriptions
    Old Persian language—Writing
  x Sumerian syllabaries
    Syllabaries, Assyro-Babylonian
    Syllabaries, Sumerian
  xx Achaemenian inscriptions
    Alphabet
    Civilization, Assyro-Babylonian
    Cuneiform inscriptions
    Elamite language
    Inscriptions
    Paleography
    Writing
Cunnilingus
  xx Sex
Cunza language
  See Atacamenian language
Cup fungi
  See Discomycetes
Cup plates *(Glassware, NK5440.C8)*
  xx Glassware
Cup-shaped coins
  See Scyphate coins
Cupboards *(Art, NK2725; Cabinet-making,*
    TT197)
  xx Dining room furniture
    Furniture
Cupid *(BL820.C)*
— Art *(N7760)*
— Juvenile literature
Cupid in literature
Cupisnique Indians *(F3430.1.C8)*
  xx Indians of South America
Cupola-furnaces *(TS231)*
  xx Blast-furnaces
    Founding
    Iron-founding
    Metallurgical furnaces
— Automation
Cupolas
  See Domes
Cupping *(RM184)*
  sa Hemospasia
  xx Bloodletting
    Counter-irritants
    Hemospasia
    Therapeutics, Cutaneous and external
Cuprammonium silk
  See Rayon
Cuprous chloride *(QD181.C9)*
  Example under Chlorides
Cups, Mustache
  See Mustache cups

Cups and saucers
  See Drinking cups
Curara
  See Curare
Curare *(Pharmacology, QP921.C8;*
    Therapeutics, RM666.C94)
  sa Tubocurarine
  x Curara
    Curari
    Intocostrin
  xx Anesthetics
— Physiological effect
Curari
  See Curare
Curators
  See Museum directors
Curb-bit *(SF309)*
  xx Animals, Treatment of
    Bridle
    Harness
Curbs
  xx Pavements
— Tables, calculations, etc.
Cure of souls
  See Pastoral counseling
    Pastoral theology
Curetes *(BL820.C7)*
  xx Demonology
    Mythology
    Mythology, Classical
Curette *(RG109.C8)*
  xx Surgical instruments and apparatus
Curfew *(Direct)*
  xx Children—Law
Curing *(TP156.C8)*
  sa Drying
    Weathering
    subdivision Curing *under specific*
      subjects, e.g. Concrete—Curing
  xx Drying
    Weathering
— Patents
Curing of concrete
  See Concrete—Curing
Curiosa, Literary
  See Literary curiosa
Curiosities and wonders *(AG240-243)*
  sa Disasters
    Eccentrics and eccentricities
    Literary curiosa
    Monsters
    Seven Wonders of the World
    subdivision Miscellanea *under subjects*
      for curiosities and wonders of special
      topics, e.g. Aeronautics—Miscellanea
  x Enigmas
    Oddities
    Wonders
— Early works to 1900
— Juvenile literature
Curiosity *(BF323.C8)*
  sa Wonder
  x Exploratory behavior
    Inquisitiveness
  xx Interest (Psychology)
Curiosity (Child psychology)
  xx Child study
Curium *(QD181.C55)*
  xx Radioactive substances
Curlew bug *(SB608.G6)*
Curlews *(QL696.L7)*
  sa Eskimo curlew
  xx Shore birds
Curling *(GV845)*
  xx Winter sports
Curly coated retrievers *(SF429.C8)*
  xx Retrievers

Curly-top (*Beet diseases. SB608.B4*)
Example under Virus diseases of plants
Curragh Incident, 1914
See Curragh Mutiny, 1914
Curragh Mutiny, 1914
  x Curragh Incident, 1914
  xx Home rule (Ireland)
Currant grapes (*SB399*)
  sa Raisins
  x Corinthian raisins
    Zante currants
  xx Grapes
    Raisins
Currants (*SB386.C9*)
  sa European black currant
  — Diseases and pests
  — Varieties
Currency
  See Money
Currency, Occupation
  See Occupation currency
Currency act of March 14, 1900 (*Speeches in Congress, HG534*)
  xx Bimetallism
    Silver question
Currency changers (Coins)
  See Coin changing machines
Currency convertibility
  x Convertibility of currency
  xx Commercial policy
    Currency question
    Foreign exchange
    Gold standard
    Industrial management and inflation
    Money
Currency devaluation
  See Currency question
Currency exchanges (Domestic) (*Direct*)
    Here are entered works on enterprises engaged in the business of cashing checks, drafts, money orders, etc. for a fee.
  xx Checks
    Negotiable instruments
Currency question (*Direct*) (*United States, HG501-538; Other countries, HG651-1490 (5-9) or (2-4)*)
  sa Banks and banking, Central
    Bimetallism
    Coinage, International
    Currency convertibility
    Deflation (Finance)
    Finance
    Finance, Public
    Foreign exchange problem
    French franc area
    Gold
    Gold clause
    Gold standard
    Hoarding of money
    Industrial management and inflation
    Inflation (Finance)
    Legal tender
    Monetary policy
    Monetary unions
    Money
    Open market operations
    Paper money
    Pound, British—Devaluation
    Pound, Israeli—Devaluation
    Precious metals
    Purchasing power
    Revalorization of debts
    Revalorization of insurance
    Rupee, Indian—Devaluation
    Silver
    Silver question
    Social credit

    Sterling area
    Valuta clause
  x Currency devaluation
    Devaluation of currency
    Fiat money
    Free coinage
    Monetary question
    Scrip
  xx Bimetallism
    Coinage
    Finance
    Finance, Public
    Gold
    Inflation (Finance)
    Legal tender
    Money
    Silver question
  — Congresses
    See Money—Congresses
  — Underdeveloped areas
    See Underdeveloped areas—Currency question

    GEOGRAPHIC SUBDIVISIONS

  — United States
    sa Dollar, American—Devaluation
    x Specie payments
      United States—Currency question
Currende
Current algebra
  See Algebra of currents
Current balance (Electric meter)
  xx Amperes
    Balance
    Electric meters
Current events
    Here are entered works on the study and teaching of current events. Accounts, discussions, etc. of the events themselves, issued serially or covering a stated year, are entered under the headings History—Periodicals; History—Yearbooks.
  xx History, Modern—Study and teaching
Current events and the stock-exchange
  See Stock-exchange and current events
Current noise (Electricity) (*QC176.8.E4*)
  x Noise, Current
  xx Electric noise
    Energy-band theory of solids
    Semiconductors
Currents, Alternating
  See Electric currents, Alternating
Currents, Density
  See Density currents
Currents, Direct
  See Electric currents, Direct
Currents, Electric
  See Electric currents
Currents, Oceanic
  See Ocean currents
Currents, Suspension
  See Turbidity currents
Currents, Turbidity
  See Turbidity currents
Curricula (Courses of study)
  See Education—Curricula
    Education—[local subdivision]—Curricula

subdivision Curricula *under specific types of education or school, and under names of individual schools, e.g.* Technical education—Curricula; High schools—Curricula; Library schools—Curricula; Chicago. University—Curricula *For works on the curriculum of a special denomination, sect, or order, see name of denomination, etc. with subdivision* Education. *For course of study in a particular subject, see subdivision* Study and teaching *under subject.* (*Exceptions: subdivision* Instruction *under* Drawing; Instruction and study *under* Confirmation, First communion, *and all headings in the field of music*)
Curriculum change (*Direct*)
  x Instructional change
  xx Curriculum planning
    Education—Curricula
Curriculum consultants
  x Consultants, Curriculum
  xx Education—Curricula
    School management and organization
Curriculum development
  See Curriculum planning
Curriculum enrichment
  xx Education—Curricula
Curriculum laboratories
  x Laboratories, Curriculum
  xx Education—Curricula
    Regional educational laboratories
    School libraries
Curriculum planning (*Direct*)
  sa Curriculum change
    Interdisciplinary approach in education
  x Curriculum development
    Planning, Curriculum
  xx Education—Curricula
Cursillo movement (*BX2375*)
  sa Retreats
  x Movement, Cursillo
  xx Retreats
Cursing and blessing
  See Blessing and cursing
Cursolari, Battle of, 1571
  See Lepanto, Battle of, 1571
Curtain hooks, Tariff on
  See Tariff on curtain hooks
Curtain walls (*TH2231*)
  sa Metal curtain walls
  x Enclosure walls
    Window walls
  xx Exterior walls
Curtains
  See Drapery
Curtains, Air
  See Air curtains
Curtains (in religion, folk-lore, etc.)
  x Folk-lore of curtains
    Veils (in religion, folk-lore, etc.)
  xx Religion, Primitive
Curtall
  See Bassoon
Curtesy (*Direct*)
  sa Dower
    Election (Wills)
  xx Dower
    Husband and wife
    Inheritance and succession
Curtiss Hawk (Fighter planes)
  sa P-40 (Fighter planes)
  xx Fighter planes
Curtiss Warhawk
  See P-40 (Fighter planes)

Curupaity, Battle of, 1866 *(F2687)*
    xx Paraguayan War, 1865-1870
Curvature
    sa Surfaces of constant curvature
    xx Calculus
        Curves
        Surfaces
Curve, Lumbar
    See Lumbar curve
Curve fitting
    sa CURVES (Computer program)
        EXPOSUM (Computer program)
        Least squares
        Statistics—Graphic methods
    x Fitting, Curve
    xx Least squares
        Numerical analysis
        Statistics—Graphic methods
    — Computer programs
Curved surfaces
    See Surfaces
Curves
    sa Brachistochrone
        Curvature
        Curves in engineering
        Envelopes (Geometry)
        Frequency curves
        Involutes (Mathematics)
        Quaternions
        Railroads—Curves and turnouts
        Roulettes (Geometry)
    xx Calculus
        Conic sections
        Geometry
        Geometry, Analytic
        Geometry, Differential
        Geometry, Enumerative
        Mathematics
    Example under Locus (Mathematics)
    — Juvenile literature
    — Rectification and quadrature *(QA626)*
        x Quadrature of curves
            Rectification of curves
Curves, Algebraic
    sa Geometry, Algebraic
    x Algebraic curves
    xx Geometry, Algebraic
Curves, Cubic
    x Cubic curves
Curves, Isothermic
    x Isothermic curves
Curves, Jordan
    x Curves, Simple
        Jordan curves
    xx Curves on surfaces
        Topology
Curves, Knotted
    See Curves of double curvature
Curves, Logarithmic
    x Logarithmic curves
Curves, Orthogonal *(QA567)*
    x Orthogonal curves
Curves, Parallel
    x Parallel curves
Curves, Pedal
    x Pedal curves
Curves, Plane
    sa Asymptotes
        Catenary
        Circle
        Conic sections
        Cyclodes
        Cycloids
        Lissajous' curves
        Pentacardioid
    x Higher plane curves
        Plane curves

Curves, Quartic *(QA565-7)*
    sa Cardioid
    x Quartic curves
Curves, Quintic *(QA565-7)*
    x Quintic curves
Curves, R
    See R-curves
Curves, Resistance
    See R-curves
Curves, Simple
    See Curves, Jordan
Curves, Transcendental *(QA628)*
    x Transcendental curves
CURVES (Computer program)
    xx Curve fitting
Curves in engineering *(Railroads, TF216-217;*
        Roads, TE153)
    sa Railroads—Curves and turnouts
    x Transition curve
    xx Civil engineering
        Curves
        Engineering
    — Tables
Curves of double curvature *(QA581)*
    x Curves, Knotted
        Double curvature, Curves of
        Knotted curves
Curves on surfaces *(QA643)*
    sa Conics, Spherical
        Curves, Jordan
    x Surfaces, Curves on
Curvilinear coordinates
    See Coordinates, Curvilinear
Curzon Line
Cushing's syndrome
    xx Adrenal cortex—Diseases
        Metabolism, Disorders of
Cushion materials
    See Cushioning materials
Cushion star
    xx Starfishes
Cushioning materials *(TS198.6.C8)*
    sa Cushions
        Excelsior
    x Cushion materials
        Impact limiter
    xx Cushions
        Packing for shipment
        Shock (Mechanics)
Cushions
    sa Cushioning materials
        Pillows
    xx Cushioning materials
        House furnishings
        Pillows
Cushites *(GN545)*
    sa Konso (African people)
    xx Hamites
Cushitic languages *(PJ2401-2413)*
    sa Afar language
        Agau language
        Beja language
        Bilin language
        Galla language
        Iraqw language
        Kemant language
        Mocha language
        Quara language
        Saho language
        Sidama language
        Somali language
    xx Hamitic languages
    Note under Ethiopian languages
Cussey, Battle of, 1870 *(DC309.C8)*
Custard glass
    x Glass, Custard
    xx Glassware

Custodials *(Direct)*
    xx Christian art and symbolism
        Church plate
        Relics and reliquaries
Custodian-engineers
    See Janitors
Custodians
    See Janitors
Custodians, School
    See School custodians
Custodianship accounts *(Direct)*
    x Customers' securities (Banking)
    xx Banks and banking
        Trust companies
    Example under Banking law
Custom-house
    See Customs administration
Customary law *(Direct)*
    sa Common law
        Law merchant
        Time immemorial (Law)
        Town laws
        Usages of trade
    x Customs (Law)
        Usage and custom (Law)
    xx Common law
        Time immemorial (Law)
    — Sources
        sa Custumals
Customary law (Canon law) *(BX1939.C85)*
Customary law (Greek law)
Customary law (Islamic law)
Customary law (Roman law)
    x Consuetudo (Roman law)
Customer complaints
    See Complaints (Retail trade)
Customer relations
    sa Complaints (Retail trade)
        Customer service
    x Defective products
    xx Business
        Public relations
Customer relations (Law) *(Direct)*
    xx Commercial law
Customer service
    x Service (in industry)
        Technical service
    xx Customer relations
        Durable goods, Consumer
        Marketing
Customers' securities (Banking)
    See Custodianship accounts
Customhouse brokers *(Direct)*
    sa Ocean freight forwarders
    x Customs brokers
    xx Ocean freight forwarders
Customs, Social
    See Manners and customs
        Indians—Social life and customs; Jews
            —Social life and customs; *and*
            similar headings; and subdivision
            Social life and customs *under names*
            of countries, cities, etc.
Customs (Law)
    See Customary law
        Usages of trade
Customs (Tariff)
    See Tariff
Customs administration *(Indirect)*
        (HJ6603-7380)
    sa Bonded warehouses and goods
        Customs administration and tourists
        Customs appraisal
        Customs courts
        Duty-free importation
        International travel regulations
        Ports of entry
        Smuggling

Customs administration *(Indirect)*
  (HJ6603-7380) (Continued)
    Tariff
    names of individual custom houses, e.g.
      United States. Custom House, New
      York
    x Custom-house
    xx Finance, Public
      Foreign trade regulation
      Tariff
— Study and teaching *(Direct)*

— United States
    x United States—Custom-house
    Note under Tariff—Law
Customs administration and tourists *(Direct)*
    x Tourists and customs administration
    xx Customs administration
      Duty-free importation
      International travel regulations
      Tourist trade
      Travel
Customs appraisal *(Direct)*
    x Appraisal (Customs administration)
      Customs valuation
    xx Customs administration
      Valuation
Customs brokers
    See Customhouse brokers
Customs classification
    See Tariff—Terminology and classification
Customs courts *(Direct)*
    sa Tax courts
    x Revenue courts
    xx Administrative courts
      Customs administration
      Tax courts
Customs duties
    See Tariff
Customs duties, Internal
    See Octroi
Customs exemptions
    See Customs privileges
      Duty-free importation
Customs nomenclature
    See Tariff—Terminology and classification
Customs of trade
    See Usages of trade
Customs privileges *(Direct)*
    x Customs exemptions
      Tariff, Exemption from
      Tariff exemptions
    xx Diplomatic privileges and immunities
      Duty-free importation
Customs unions *(HF1713)*
    x Free trade areas
      Tariff unions
    xx Commerce
      Commercial policy
      International economic integration
      Second best, Theory of
      Tariff
Customs valuation
    See Customs appraisal
Custozza, Battle of, 1848 *(DG553.5.C8)*
    xx Austro-Sardinian War, 1848-1849
Custozza, Battle of, 1866 *(DG558)*
    xx Austro-Italian War, 1866
      Austro-Prussian War, 1866
Custumals
    sa Town laws
    xx Customary law—Sources
      Law—Sources
      Town laws
Cut flowers
    sa Flower arrangement
    xx Floriculture

  Flowers
— Storage
— Tariff
    See Tariff on cut flowers
— Transportation
Cut glass *(Direct) (TP861)*
    sa Glass, Ornamental
      Sand-blast
    x Glass, Cut
    xx Glassware
— Collectors and collecting
Cut glass, American, [English, etc.]
    x American [English, etc.] cut glass
— Prices
Cut-outs, Electric
    See Electric cut-outs
Cut-over lands *(Direct)*
    sa Clearing of land
    x Logged-off lands
    xx Clear-cutting
      Forests and forestry
      Lumbering
      Reclamation of land
      Waste lands
Cut-throat trout
    See Cutthroat trout
Cutaneous diseases
    See Skin—Diseases
Cutaneous glands *(QL943; QM491; QP221)*
    x Glands, Cutaneous
    xx Skin
Cutaneous horns
    See Horns, Cutaneous
Cutaneous leishmaniasis
    See Leishmaniasis, Cutaneous
Cutaneous manifestations of general diseases
    sa Dermatomyositis
      Pruritus
      Xanthoma
    x Cutaneous symptoms of general
      diseases
    xx Semiology
      Skin—Diseases
Cutaneous nerves
    See Skin—Innervation
Cutaneous symptoms of general diseases
    See Cutaneous manifestations of general
      diseases
Cutaneous tests
    See Skin tests
Cutaneous therapeutics
    See Therapeutics, Cutaneous and external
Cutch-grass
    See Quitch-grass
Cutgana Indians
    See Yuma Indians
Cuticle
    sa Chitin
      Plant cuticle
    xx Skin
Cutin
    xx Plant cuticle
Cutis
    See Skin
Cutlers *(Gilds, England, HD6461.C9)*
    sa Knifesmiths
Cutlery *(Direct) (TS380)*
    sa Knives
      Tableware
    xx Hardware
      Tableware
      Tools
Cutlery trade *(Direct)*
    sa Wages—Cutlery trade
Cutter classification
    See Classification, Expansive
Cutthroat trout
    x Cut-throat trout

    xx Trout
Cutting
    sa Bottle cutting
      Ceramics cutting
      Garment cutting
      Gem cutting
      Laser beam cutting
      Metal-cutting
      Plastics cutting
      Saws
      Turning
    x Materials cutting
      Materials—Cutting
Cutting, Laser beam
    See Laser beam cutting
Cutting fluids
    See Metal-working lubricants
Cutting lubricants
    See Metal-working lubricants
Cutting machines *(TJ1230)*
    sa Electric cutting machinery
      Metal-cutting tools
      Wood-cutting tools
    xx Metal-cutting
    Notes under Blades; Metal-cutting tools
— Standards
Cutting of concrete
    See Concrete cutting
Cutting of gems
    See Gem cutting
Cutting of metals
    See Metal-cutting
Cutting of plastics
    See Plastics cutting
Cutting tools, Carbide
    See Carbide cutting tools
Cuttings
    See Clippings (Books, newspapers, etc.)
Cuttings, Plant
    See Plant cuttings
Cuttlefish, Fossil
    See Sepiida, Fossil
Cutworms *(SB945.C92)*
    xx Caterpillars
      Moths
CW complexes
    xx Algebraic topology
      Complexes
Cy pres doctrine
    xx Charitable uses, trusts, and foundations
      Equity
      Law—Interpretation and construction
      Perpetuities
      Wills
Cyanacetic ether *(QD305.E7)*
Cyanamid *(S651)*
    xx Fertilizers and manures
Cyanide process *(TN767)*
    xx Electrometallurgy
      Gold—Metallurgy
      Metallurgy
Cyanides *(Chemistry, QD181.C15;
      Manufacture, TP248.C9)*
— Analysis
— Spectra
— Toxicology *(RA1242.H9)*
Cyaniding
    See Case hardening
Cyanite *(Indirect) (TN948.C95)*
    x Rhoetzite
    xx Silicates
Cyanocitta
    See Jays
Cyanocobalamine
    sa Intrinsic factor (Physiology)
    xx Vitamins
— Patents

Cyanocobalamine deficiency
   x Vitamin B12 deficiency
   xx Vitamin B deficiency
Cyanogen compounds *(QD181.C15)*
  — Analysis
Cyanophyta *(Indirect)*
   xx Algae
Cyanosis *(RC669)*
Cyanotype
  See Blue-printing
Cybernetics
   sa Biological control systems
     Bionics
     Computers
     Conscious automata
     Information theory
     Information theory in aesthetics
     Information theory in psychology
     Perceptrons
     Self-organizing systems
     System analysis
     Systems engineering
   x Mechanical brains
   xx Automatic control
     Calculating-machines
     Communication
     Electronics
     System theory
  — Juvenile literature
  — Research *(Direct)* *(Q317)*
Cycadales, Fossil
Cycadofilices *(QE973)*
   sa Pteridospermae
Cyclamates
   xx Nonnutritive sweeteners
  — Specifications *(Direct)*
Cyclamen *(Botany, QK495.P; Culture, SB413.C)*
Cyclamen mite *(SB945.M65)*
   xx Gerbera—Diseases and pests
Cycle, Hydrologic
  See Hydrologic cycle
Cycle-cars *(TL390)*
   xx Automobiles
     Motorcycles
Cycles *(Philosophy, B105.C9; History, D16.9; Science, Q176)*
   sa Biogeochemical cycles
     Biology—Periodicity
     Business cycles
     Eternal return
     Geology—Periodicity
     Hydrologic cycle
     Hydrometeorology—Periodicity
     Oscillations
     Rhythm
     Runoff—Periodicity
     Solar cycle
     Time
     Vibration
     Waves
   x Cyclic theory
     Periodicity
   xx Philosophy
     Rhythm
     Time
Cycles, Motor
  See Motorcycles
Cycles, Song
  See Song cycles
Cyclic compounds
   sa Bicyclic compounds
     Cycloparaffins
     Heterocyclic compounds
Cyclic theory
  See Cycles
Cyclide *(QA603)*

Cycling *(Direct)* *(GV1041-1059)*
   sa Bicycle racing
     Bicycles and tricycles
     Cycling paths
     Military cycling
     Motorcycling
   x Bicycling
   xx Bicycles and tricycles
     Highway law
     Locomotion
     Track-athletics
  — Anecdotes, facetiae, satire, etc.
  — Juvenile literature
  — Law and legislation *(Direct)*
     x Bicycles and tricycles—Law and
       legislation
     xx Traffic regulations
  — Records *(GV1053)*
  — Safety measures
  — — Juvenile literature
Cycling paths *(Direct)*
   xx Bicycles and tricycles
     Cycling
     Roads
     Streets
Cyclists *(GV1041-1059)*
   sa Cyclists' tests
  — Costume
Cyclists' tests *(Direct)*
   xx Automobile drivers' tests
     Cyclists
Cyclitols
   xx Alcohols
Cyclization (Chemistry)
  See Ring formation (Chemistry)
Cyclo-aliphatic compounds
  See Alicyclic compounds
Cycloaddition
  See Ring formation (Chemistry)
Cycloalkanes
  See Cycloparaffins
Cyclodes *(QA623)*
   xx Curves, Plane
     Kinematic geometry
Cyclodialysis
   xx Eye—Surgery
     Glaucoma
Cycloidal propellers *(VM757.C9)*
   x Vertical axis propeller
     Voith-Schneider propeller
   xx Propellers
Cycloids *(QA623)*
   x Trochoids
   xx Curves, Plane
     Roulettes (Geometry)
Cycloids, Mixed (Chemistry)
  See Heterocyclic compounds
Cyclomorphosis
   xx Metamorphosis
     Zoology—Variation
Cyclone forecasting *(QC951)*
   x Forecasting, Cyclone
   xx Weather forecasting
Cyclone tracks *(Indirect)* *(QC941)*
   x Tracks, Cyclone
Cyclones *(QC941-951)*
     Works on the cyclonic storms of the West
      Indies are entered under Hurricanes;
      those of the China seas and the Philip-
      pines under Typhoons.
   sa Storms
   headings beginning with the word
     Cyclone
   xx Hurricanes
     Meteorology
     Storms
     Tornadoes
     Typhoons

     Winds
Cyclones (Chemical technology)
  See Separators (Machines)
Cyclones (Machines)
  See Separators (Machines)
Cyclonometer *(QC951)*
   xx Meteorological instruments
Cycloparaffins
   x Cycloalkanes
   xx Cyclic compounds
     Paraffins
Cyclopean remains
  See Megalithic monuments
Cyclopedias
  See Encyclopedias and dictionaries
Cyclopia
  See Eye—Abnormities and deformities
Cyclopidea
  See Cyclopoida
Cyclopoida *(QL444.C73)*
   x Cyclopidea
   xx Copepoda
     Crustacea
Cycloramas *(ND2880)*
   sa Cosmoramas
     Diorama
     Panoramas
   xx Cosmoramas
     Diorama
     Panoramas
Cyclotomy *(QA245)*
   sa Equations, Abelian
   x Equations, Cyclotomic
   xx Equations, Abelian
     Numbers, Theory of
Cyclotron *(QC544)*
   sa Synchrocyclotron
     Synchrotron
   x Magnetic resonance accelerator
   xx Atoms
     Nuclear magnetic resonance
     Nuclear physics
     Particle accelerators
     Transmutation (Chemistry)
Cyclotron resonance
   x Resonance, Cyclotron
   xx Energy-band theory of solids
     Magnetism
     Quantum electrodynamics
Cylinder (Mathematics) *(QA491)*
   xx Geometry, Solid
     Surfaces
Cylinder (Timepiece) *(QB214)*
   x Chilindre
   xx Sun-dials
Cylinder recordings
  See Phonocylinders
Cylinder records
  See Phonocylinders
Cylinder seals *(CD5344)*
   x Cylindrical seals
     Roll seals
   xx Seals (Numismatics)
Cylinders *(Aircraft engines, TL702.C9; Automobile motors, TL210; Compressed gases, TP243; Strength and testing, TA492.C9)*
   sa Gas cylinders
   subdivision Cylinders *under engines or motors, e.g.* Steam-engines—Cylinders; Aeroplanes—Motors—Cylinders
  — Plastic properties
     xx Plasticity
  — Standards
  — Tables, calculations, etc.
  — Testing
  — Vibration

Cylindric algebras
  x Algebras, Cylindric
    Cylindrical algebras
  xx Logic, Symbolic and mathematical
Cylindrical algebras
  See Cylindric algebras
Cylindrical harmonics
  See Bessel functions
Cylindrical projection (Cartography)
  xx Map-projection
Cylindrical seals
  See Cylinder seals
Cylindrical shell roofs
  See Roofs, Shell
Cylindroid *(QA841)*
  sa Screws, Theory of
Cymbalom
  See Cimbalom
Cymbals *(ML1040)*
Cymene *(QD341.H9)*
Cymograph
  See Kymograph
Cymri
  See Welsh
Cymric language
  See Welsh language
Cymry
  See Welsh
Cynanche maligna
  See Angina maligna
Cynanche trachealis
  See Croup
Cynicism *(B508)*
  sa Irony
Cynipidae
  See Gall-flies
Cynthia silk moth
  See Ailanthus moth
Cynurenic acid *(Physiological chemistry,*
    QP801.C9)
  xx Urine
Cypress *(Botany, QK495.C97; Building*
    materials, TA419; Forestry,
    SD397.C9; Plant pathology,
    SB608.C9; Religion, BL444)
  Example under Lumber
  — Juvenile literature
Cyprian War, 1570-1571 *(DR515-516)*
  sa Lepanto, Battle of, 1571
  x Holy League (Venice, Spain, and the
    Pope) 1570-1571
Cypriniformes
  xx Ostariophysi
    Osteichthyes
Cyprinodontes *(QL638.C95)*
  x Cyprinodontiformes
    Microcyprini
Cyprinodontiformes
  See Cyprinodontes
Cypriote syllabary *(PA567.S3)*
  xx Alphabet
    Hittites
Cypriotes
Cyprus in literature
Cypselidae
  See Swifts
Cypseliformes
  See Apodiformes
Cyrillic alphabet *(PG92)*
  xx Alphabet
    Slavic languages—Alphabet
Cystic fibrosis
  x Fibrosis, Cystic
    Mucoviscidosis
  xx Glands—Diseases
    Lungs—Diseases
  — Personal narratives
  — Psychological aspects

  xx Sick—Psychology
Cysticercosis
  xx Taenia
Cysticercosis, Cerebrospinal
  x Cerebral cysticercosis
    Cerebrospinal cysticercosis
  xx Brain—Diseases
Cystinosis
  x Lignac's disease
  xx Renal tubular transport, Disorders of
Cystinuria
  xx Renal tubular transport, Disorders of
    Urine—Analysis and pathology
Cystocarp *(QK569.R4)*
Cystography
  See Bladder—Radiography
Cystoscopy
  See Bladder—Exploration
Cystotomy
  See Bladder—Surgery
Cysts *(RD676-7)*
  sa Odontogenic cysts
    Pancreatic cysts
    Perineurial cysts, Sacral
    Pilonidal cyst
    Tumors
    subdivision Cysts *under subjects, e.g.*
      Esophagus—Cysts
  xx Tumors
  — Surgery
Cytherian atmosphere
  See Venus (Planet)—Atmosphere
Cytisine *(Chemistry, QD421; Physiological*
    effect, QP921.C)
  x Baptitoxine
    Laburnine
    Sophorine
    Ulexine
  xx Antiseptics
    Diuretics and diuresis
Cytochemistry *(QH611)*
  sa Histochemistry
  xx Biological chemistry
    Cytology
    Histochemistry
  — Technique
Cytochrome c
  xx Hemoproteins
    Pigments (Biology)
    Tissue respiration
Cytodiagnosis
  See Diagnosis, Cytologic
Cytogenetics
  sa Cell hybridization
    Cytoplasmic inheritance
    Nucleic acid hybridization
  xx Cytology
    Genetics
Cytokinesis *(QH605)*
  xx Cell division
    Cytoplasm
Cytologic diagnosis
  See Diagnosis, Cytologic
Cytological research
  See Cell research
Cytology
  sa Cell differentiation
    Cell migration
    Cell physiology
    Cell populations
    Cells
    Cytochemistry
    Cytogenetics
    Exfoliative cytology
    Plant cells and tissues
    Radioactive tracers in cytology
  xx Cells
  — Atlases

  — Experiments
  — Laboratory manuals
  — Mathematical models
  — Programmed instruction
  — Research
    See Cell research
  — Statistical methods
  — Technique
    sa Cell fractionation
      Enucleation
      Fixation (Histology)
      Karyometry
      Micrurgy
      Nucleic acid hybridization
Cytomegalic inclusion disease *(Direct)*
  x Inclusion disease, Cytomegalic
  xx Cytomegaloviruses
    Fetus—Diseases
    Virus diseases
Cytomegaloviruses
  sa Cytomegalic inclusion disease
  xx Viruses
Cytopathology
  See Pathology, Cellular
Cytoplasm *(QH591)*
  sa Cytokinesis
  xx Cells
    Protoplasm
Cytoplasmic bodies, type I
  See Microbodies
Cytoplasmic heredity
  See Cytoplasmic inheritance
Cytoplasmic inheritance
  sa Cytoplasmic male sterility
    Plasmids
  x Cytoplasmic heredity
  xx Cytogenetics
    Heredity
    Protoplasm
Cytoplasmic male sterility *(QK827)*
  xx Cytoplasmic inheritance
    Sterility in plants
Cytoplasmic polyhedrosis virus *(QR360)*
  xx Viruses
Cytotoxic drugs
  See Antineoplastic agents
Cytotoxin
  See Serum
Czakan
  x Csakan
  xx Flute
    Recorder (Musical instrument)
Czakan and piano music *(M240-242)*
  sa Ländler (Czakan and piano)
  x Piano and czakan music
Czardas
  Here are entered collections of czarda
  music for various mediums. Individual
  czardas and collections of czardas for
  a specific medium are entered under
  the heading followed by specification
  of medium.
Czardas (Band) *(M1248; M1264)*
  xx Band music
  — Scores (reduced) and parts
Czardas (Orchestra) *(M1048; M1060)*
  xx Orchestral music
  — Scores *(M1048; M1060)*
Czech-American literature *(PG5050-5069)*
  x American literature (Czech)
  xx Czech literature
Czech-American newspapers *(PN4885)*
  xx American newspapers
    Czech newspapers
Czech ballads and songs *(PG5008; PG5015;*
    PG5025)
  sa Folk-songs, Czech
    Songs, Czech

Czech carols
  See Carols, Czech
Czech drama
  sa Verse drama, Czech
Czech drama (Comedy) *(Direct)*
Czech fiction *(Collections, PG5029; History, PG5011)*
  sa Short stories, Czech
Czech film posters
  See Film posters, Czech
Czech folk-lore
  See Folk-lore, Czech
Czech hymns
  See Hymns, Czech
Czech imprints *(Direct)*
Czech language *(PG4771)*
  x Bohemian language
  xx Slavic languages, Western
  — To 1500
    x Czech language—Old Czech

      GENERAL SUBDIVISIONS

  — Old Czech
    See Czech language—To 1500

      GENERAL SUBDIVISIONS

  — Primers
    See Primers, Czech
Czech language in Slovakia, ₍etc.₎
Czech legends
  See Legends, Czech
Czech letters
Czech literature *(PG5000-5198)*
  sa Czech-American literature
  — 19th century
  — 20th century

      GENERAL SUBDIVISIONS

  — Catholic authors
Czech literature in foreign countries
Czech manuscripts
  See Manuscripts, Czech
Czech medals
  See Medals, Czech
Czech mythology
  See Mythology, Slavic
Czech newspapers *(History, etc., PN5168)*
  sa Czech-American newspapers
  x Bohemian newspapers
Czech periodicals *(History, etc., PN5168)*
Czech periodicals in foreign countries
Czech philology *(PG4001-4771)*
  x Philology, Bohemian
    Philology, Czech
  — Terminology
Czech poetry *(Collections, PG5025; History, PG5008)*
  sa Czech poetry in foreign countries
  — 20th century
Czech poetry (German)
  See German poetry—Czech authors
Czech poetry in foreign countries
  xx Czech poetry
Czech prose literature *(Collections, PG5029; History, PG5010)*
Czech refugees
  See Refugees, Czech
Czech wit and humor
Czechoslovak-Polish Confederation (Proposed)
  x Polish-Czechoslovak Confederation (Proposed)
  xx European federation
Czechoslovak property in the United States
Czechoslovak Republic
  — History
  — — 1918-1938
  — — 1938-1945
  — — — Pictorial works

  — — 1945-
  — — Coup d'état, 1948
  — — — Juvenile literature
  — — Intervention, 1968-
    x Russian intervention in the Czechoslovak Republic, 1968-
    Soviet invasion of the Czechoslovak Republic, 1968-
    Warsaw Pact intervention in the Czechoslovak Republic, 1968-
  — — — Caricatures and cartoons
  — — — Foreign public opinion
  — — — Juvenile literature
  — — — Pictorial works
Czechoslovak Republic in literature
  sa Bohemia in literature
Czechs *(DB47-48; DB191-217)*
  x Bohemians
Czechs in Pennsylvania, ₍the United States, etc.₎
  — Intellectual life
  — Juvenile literature
  — Religious life
Czestochowa, Poland
  — Siege, 1655
Częstochowa trials, 1945-1950
  See War crime trials—Częstochowa, Poland, 1945-1950
D-amplifiers
  See Distributed amplifiers
D Day
  See World War, 1939-1945—Campaigns—Normandy
D layer
  See D region
D region
  x D layer
  xx Ionosphere
Dabida dialect *(PL8707.95.D)*
  x Kidawida dialect
  xx Taita language
Dace, European
  See European dace
Dachau (Concentration camp)
  Example under Concentration camps
Dachshund *(SF429.D25)*
  sa Miniature dachshund
  x Badger-dogs, German
  — Pictorial works
Dacian language *(P1006)*
  xx Romanian language
Dacians *(Direct) (D90.D)*
  xx Ethnology—Romania
Daco-Romanian dialect
  See Romanian language
Dacoits *(HV6453.I6)*
  x Dakoits
  xx Brigands and robbers
    Crime and criminals
Dacron
  xx Textile fibers, Synthetic
Dacron dyeing
  See Dyes and dyeing—Dacron
Dacrycystitis
  See Dacryocystitis
Dacryocystitis
  x Dacrycystitis
  xx Lacrimal organs—Diseases
Dacryocystorhinostomy
  x Dacryocystorhinotomy
  xx Eye—Surgery
    Nose—Surgery
Dacryocystorhinotomy
  See Dacryocystorhinostomy
Dactylography
  See Fingerprints
Dactylology
  See Deaf—Means of communication

Dactyloscopy
  See Fingerprints
Dactyls, Double
  See Double dactyls
Dadaism
  sa Assemblage (Art)
    Letter-pictures
    Pop art
  xx Aesthetics
    Art, Modern—20th century
    Expressionism
    Literature, Modern—20th century—History and criticism
    Modernism (Art)
    Post-impressionism (Art)
    Surrealism
Dade's Battle, 1835 *(E83.835)*
  xx Seminole War, 2d, 1835-1842
Dādūpanthīs *(BL1245.D25)*
  xx Hindu sects
Daf automobile
Daffodil fly
  See Narcissus bulb fly
Daffodils *(SB413.D12)*
  x Narcissus
  — Diseases and pests
    sa Narcissus bulb fly
  — Fertilizers and manures
  — Varieties
Dafla language *(PL4001.D2)*
  xx Tibeto-Burman languages
Daflas
  xx Ethnology—India—North East Frontier Agency
  — Religion
  — Rites and ceremonies
Daga language
  See Dimuga language
Dagaaba (African tribe)
  See Dagari (African tribe)
Dagaba (African tribe)
  See Dagari (African tribe)
Dagari (African tribe)
  x Dagaaba (African tribe)
    Dagaba (African tribe)
    Dagarti (African tribe)
    Dagati (African tribe)
    Lodagaa (African tribe)
  xx Ethnology—Ghana
    Lobi (African tribe)
Dagari language
  x Dagati language
  xx Mossi languages
Dagarti (African tribe)
  See Dagari (African tribe)
Dagati (African tribe)
  See Dagari (African tribe)
Dagati language
  See Dagari language
Dagbamba (African people)
  See Dagomba (African people)
Dagbane language
  See Dagomba language
Dagga
  See Hashish
Daggatuns *(DT346.D)*
Daggers *(Art, NK6805)*
  sa Saxes
  xx Arms and armor
Daggers, German, ₍Scottish, etc.₎ *(Direct)*
  x German ₍Scottish, etc.₎ daggers
Daggers, Malay
  x Krises
Daghestan in literature
Daghestan literature *(PK9051)*
  sa Ingush literature
Daghestan poetry *(PK9051)*
Dagmar automobile

Dagobas
See Stūpas
Dagomba (African people)
  x Dagbamba (African people)
  xx Ethnology—Ghana
  — Kings and rulers
Dagomba language
  x Dagbane language
  xx Mossi languages
Dagsexe language
  See Tucano language
Daguerreotype *(TR365)*
  xx Photography
    Photography—Early works to 1850
Dagur language *(PL431.D3)*
  x Dahur language
    Daure language
  xx Mongolian languages
Dahceie language
  See Tucano language
Dahlgren's Raid
  See Kilpatrick-Dahlgren Raid, 1864
Dahlia mosaic virus
  x Stunt of dahlias
  xx Dahlias—Diseases and pests
Dahlias *(SB413.D13)*
  Example under Floriculture
  — Diseases and pests
    sa Dahlia mosaic virus
Dahoman language
Dahomeyans
Dahur language
  See Dagur language
Dahurian larch
  xx Larch
Dai (African people)
  See Day (African people)
Daijō-sai
  See Ōnie no Matsuri
Daily activity cycles
  See Diel cycles
Daily Mail Transatlantic Air Race, 1969
  x New York-London Air Race, 1969
  xx Aeronautics—Flights
    Aeroplane racing
Daily Mirror World Cup Rally, 1970
  x London-Mexico City World Cup Rally, 1970
    World Cup Rally, 1970
  xx Automobile racing
    Automobile rallies
Daily offices
  See Divine office
Daily readings (Spiritual exercises)
  See Devotional calendars
Daily vacation Bible schools
  See Vacation schools, Religious
Daimio
  See Daimyo
Daimler automobile *(TL215.D3)*
Daimyo
  x Daimio
  xx Feudalism—Japan
  — Correspondence, reminiscences, etc.
  — Succession
  — — Anecdotes, facetiae, satire, etc.
Dairies
  See Dairy plants
    Dairying
    Milk plants
Dairy
  See Dairy plants
    Dairying
    Milk plants
Dairy bacteriology *(QR121)*
  sa Bacteriology, Agricultural
    Cheese—Bacteriology
    Milk—Bacteriology

    Milk—Sterilization
  x Chemistry, Dairy
  xx Bacteriology, Agricultural
    Cheese—Bacteriology
    Dairy microbiology
    Dairying
    Milk—Bacteriology
  — Laboratory manuals
  — Technique
Dairy barns *(Indirect)* *(Architecture, NA8230; Building, TH4930)*
  sa Stables
  x Cow barns
  xx Barns
    Cattle houses and equipment
    Farm buildings
    Stables
  — Heating and ventilation
Dairy cattle *(Indirect)* *(SF208)*
  sa Guernsey cattle
    Holstein-Friesian cattle
    Jersey cattle
    Jeverland cattle
    Milk production
    Red Danish cattle
  x Milch cattle
  xx Cattle
    Dairying
  — Diseases
  — Feeding and feeds
    x Cows—Feeding and feeds
  — Judging
    xx Stock-judging
  — Showing
Dairy cattle breeding *(Indirect)* *(SF208)*
  xx Cattle breeding
Dairy cattle breeds *(SF208)*
  xx Cattle breeds
Dairy chemistry
  See Dairy products—Analysis and examination
Dairy engineers
  See Dairy scientists
Dairy industry
  See Dairying
Dairy inspection *(Direct)* *(SF255)*
  sa Dairy products—Analysis and examination
    Milk—Analysis and examination
    Milk hygiene
  x Milk inspection
  xx Dairy laws
    Dairying
Dairy journalism
  See Journalism, Agricultural
Dairy laws *(Direct)* *(HD9000.9; HD9275)*
  sa Cheese industry—Law and legislation
    Dairy inspection
    Ice cream, ices, etc.—Law and legislation
    Milk, Concentrated—Law and legislation
    Products liability—Dairy products
  x Dairying—Laws and legislation
    Law, Dairy
    Milk hygiene—Law and legislation
    Milk—Law and legislation
    Milk trade—Law and legislation
  xx Dairying
  Example under Public health laws
Dairy machinery
  See Dairying—Apparatus and supplies
Dairy microbiology *(Indirect)* *(QR121)*
  sa Dairy bacteriology
  xx Microbiology
Dairy plants *(Direct)* *(SF247)*
  sa Cheese factories
    Creameries

    Dairy waste
    Dairy workers
    Milk plants
  x Dairies
    Dairy
    Dairy products plants
  xx Dairying
    Factories
    Food processing plants
  — Automation
  — Design and construction
  — Equipment and supplies
  — — Cleaning
  — Hygienic aspects
  — Maintenance and repair
  — — Costs
  — Noise control
  — Safety measures
  — Sanitation
Dairy products *(Direct)* *(HD9275)*
  sa Dairying
    Egg products industry
    individual products, e.g. Butter, Milk
  x Milk products
    Products, Dairy
  xx Animal products
    Dairying
    Produce trade
  Example under Animal food
  — Analysis and examination *(SF253)*
    sa Butter—Analysis and examination
    x Dairy chemistry
      Dairy products—Composition
      Dairy products—Testing
    xx Agricultural chemistry
      Dairy inspection
  — Composition
    See Dairy products—Analysis and examination
  — Cooperative marketing
    xx Dairy products—Marketing
  — Costs
  — Marketing *(Dairy industry, SF261; Economics, HD9275)*
    sa Dairy products—Cooperative marketing
    xx Farm produce—Marketing
  — Packaging
  — Prices *(Direct)*
  — Products liability
    See Products liability—Dairy products
  — Standards
  — Storage
  — Testing
    See Dairy products—Analysis and examination
  — Transportation *(HE2321.D25)*
Dairy products plants
  See Dairy plants
Dairy research *(Indirect)*
  sa Dairying—Economic aspects—Research
  x Dairying—Research
  xx Agricultural research
    Research, Industrial
Dairy schools *(SF241-5)*
  xx Agricultural education
    Dairying
    Schools
Dairy scientists *(Indirect)* *(SF229)*
  x Dairy engineers
  xx Scientists
Dairy waste
  x Creamery waste
  xx Agricultural wastes
    Dairy plants
    Factory and trade waste
Dairy workers *(Direct)*
  sa Strikes and lockouts—Dairying

Wages—Dairy workers
  xx Dairy plants
      Milk plants
      Milk trade
Dairying *(Indirect) (SF221-275)*
  sa Butter
      Cheese
      Cow testing
      Cow testing associations
      Cows
      Cream
      Cream-separators
      Creameries
      Dairy bacteriology
      Dairy cattle
      Dairy inspection
      Dairy laws
      Dairy plants
      Dairy products
      Dairy schools
      Milk
      Milk plants
      Milk production
      Milking machines
      Plastics in dairying
      Radioisotopes in dairying
      Strikes and lockouts—Dairying
      Veterinary hygiene
  x Dairies
      Dairy
      Dairy industry
  xx Agriculture
      Animal industry
      Bacteriology, Agricultural
      Cattle breeding
      Cows
      Creameries
      Dairy products
      Home economics
      Veterinary hygiene
  Note under Milk production
  — Accounting *(SF261)*
    Example under Accounting; Auditing
  — Apparatus and supplies *(SF247)*
    x Dairy machinery
      Dairying—Equipment and supplies
  — — Maintenance and repair
  — Collective labor agreements
    See Collective labor agreements—
      Dairying
  — Costs
  — Economic aspects *(Indirect)*
  — — Research *(Direct)*
    xx Dairy research
  — Equipment and supplies
    See Dairying—Apparatus and supplies
  — Finance
  — Job descriptions
  — Juvenile literature
  — Labor productivity
  — Laboratory manuals *(SF253)*
  — Laws and legislation
    See Dairy laws
  — Mathematical models
  — Patents
  — Production standards
  — Research
    See Dairy research
  — Study and teaching *(Direct) (SF241-5)*
  — — Audio-visual aids
  — Tables and ready-reckoners *(SF240)*
  — Vocational guidance
    x Dairying as a profession
Dairying as a profession
  See Dairying—Vocational guidance
Daisies *(SB413.D)*
  sa Gerbera

Dajak language
  See Dyak language
Dajo, Mount, Battle of, 1906 *(DS685)*
  xx Moros
Dakar, Battle of, 1940
  xx World War, 1939-1945—Africa,
      French-speaking West—Dakar
Dakhini Hindi dialect
  See Hindi language—Dialects—Deccan
Dakhmas
  See Dokhmas
Dakkhini Hindi dialect
  See Hindi language—Dialects—Deccan
Dakoits
  See Dacoits
Dakota Indians *(E99.D1)*
  sa Brulé Indians
      Hunkpapa Indians
      Kiyuksa Indians
      Mdewakanton Indians
      Miniconjou Indians
      Oglala Indians
      Oneota Indians (Great Plains)
      Oohenonpa Indians
      Oto Indians
      Sans Arc Indians
      Santee Indians
      Saone Indians
      Sihasapa Indians
      Sisseton Indians
      Teton Indians
      Wahpekute Indians
      Wahpeton Indians
      Yanktonai Indians
  x Nadowessioux Indians
      Naudowessie Indians
      Nawdowissnee Indians
      Sioux Indians
      Wahpakoota Sioux Indians
  xx Indians of North America
      Siouan Indians
  — Art
  — Economic conditions
  — Government relations
    Example under Indians of North America
      —Government relations; Native
      races
  — Land transfers
    Example under Indians of North America
      —Land transfers
  — Legends
  — Missions
    Example under reference from Missions,
      Indian
  — Poetry
    Example under Indians of North America
      —Poetry
  — Religion and mythology
  — Social life and customs
  — Treaties, 1805
  — Treaties, 1841
  — Treaties, 1851
  — Tribal government
  — Wars
    sa Fetterman Fight, 1866
      Lake of the Woods Massacre, 1736
    Example under Indians of North America
      —Wars
  — Wars, 1862-1865 *(E83.86)*
    sa Wood Lake, Battle of, 1862
    xx Indians of North America—Wars—
      1862-1865
  — — Juvenile literature
  — Wars, 1876 *(E83.876)*
    sa Cheyenne Indians—Wars, 1876
      Little Big Horn, Battle of the, 1876
    xx Cheyenne Indians—Wars, 1876

      Indians of North America—Wars,
      1866-1895
  — Wars, 1890-1891 *(E83.89)*
    sa Wounded Knee Creek, Battle of,
      1890
    xx Indians of North America—Wars—
      1866-1895
  — — Juvenile literature
Dakota language *(PM1021-4)*
  sa Santee dialect
      Siouan languages
      Yankton dialect
  x Sioux language
  xx Santee dialect
      Siouan languages
      Yankton dialect
Dakota poetry
  xx Indian poetry
      Poetry
Dakyū
  See Polo, Japanese
Dalecarlia, Sweden, in literature
D'Alembertian operator
  x Alembertian operator
      Operator, D'Alembertian
  xx Differential equations, Partial
Dall sheep
  xx Mountain sheep
Dalmatian dogs *(SF429.D3)*
  x Coach dogs
      Danish dogs
      Fire dogs
Dalmatian drama *(Direct)*
Dalmatian drama (Comedy)
Dalmatian language (Romance) *(PC890)*
  sa Romance languages
      Vegliote dialect
  x Dalmatico language
  xx Vegliote dialect
Dalmatian language (Slavic)
  See Serbo-Croatian language
Dalmatian literature *(Croatian,*
      PG1640-1658)
  xx Yugoslav literature
Dalmatian poetry *(Collections, PG1654;*
      History, PG1650)
Dalmatian prose literature *(Direct)*
Dalmatians
  xx Croats
      Yugoslavs
Dalmatico language
  See Dalmatian language (Romance)
Dalton laboratory plan *(LB1029.L3)*
  x Dalton plan
  xx Education of children
      Teaching
Dalton plan
  See Dalton laboratory plan
Dam failures *(Indirect)*
  x Collapse of dams
      Dams—Failure
  xx Disasters
Dam safety
  xx Dams
      Industrial safety
  — Law and legislation *(Direct)*
Damage control (Warships) *(V810)*
  sa Ships—Fires and fire prevention
      Ships—Maintenance and repair
  x Battle damage repair (Warships)
      Warships—Damage control
      Warships—Emergency repair
  xx Ships—Maintenance and repair
Damages *(Direct)*
  sa Death by wrongful act
      Exemplary damages
      Indemnity
      Liquidated damages

Damages *(Direct)* *(Continued)*
    Negligence
    Negligence, Contributory
    Penalties, Contractual
    x Injuries (Law)
    Measure of damages
    xx Accident law
    Compensation (Law)
    Death by wrongful act
    Interest (Law)
    Negligence
    Obligations (Law)
    Personal injuries
    Set-off and counterclaim
    Torts
  — Taxation *(Direct)*
    xx Income tax
Damages, Exemplary
  See Exemplary damages
Damages (Jewish law)
Damages (Roman law)
Damaras
  See Hereros
    Hill Damaras
Damascene work
  See Damascening
Damascening *(NK6676)*
    x Damascene work
    xx Arms and armor
    Art industries and trade
    Art metal-work
Damascus
  — Siege, 633 *(DS99.D3)*
Damascus, Treaty of, 1936
  See Franco-Syrian treaty, 1936
Damask roses *(Indirect)*
    xx Roses
  — Diseases and pests
Damask weaving
    xx Weaving
Damaskini
    xx Bulgarian literature
    Macedonian literature
Damen (Game)
  See Checkers
Damietta
  — Siege, 1218-1219 *(D165)*
Damping, Landau
  See Landau damping
Damping (Mechanics) *(Engineering, TA355;*
    Mathematics, QA935)
    sa Electric waves—Damping
    Internal friction
    Shock (Mechanics)
    Sound-waves—Damping
    Vibration (Aeronautics)—Damping
    subdivision Shock absorbers *under*
      subjects, e.g. Automobiles—Shock
      absorbers
    xx Oscillations
    Vibration
    Waves
Damping-off diseases *(SB741.D3)*
Dampness in buildings *(TH9031)*
    sa Air conditioning
    Building papers
    Ventilation
    x Buildings, Dampness in
    Condensation control in buildings
    Moisture control in buildings
    xx Air conditioning
    Buildings—Protection
    Exterior walls
    Ventilation
    Waterproofing
  — Standards
  — Tables, calculations, etc.

Dams *(Direct)* *(TC540-549)*
  sa Barrages
    Buttress dams
    Coffer-dams
    Concrete dams
    Dam safety
    Earth dams
    Earth pressure
    Fishways
    Flood dams and reservoirs
    Retaining walls
    Sluice gates
    Spillways
    particular dams, e.g. Croton Dam
    xx Barrages
    Dikes (Engineering)
    Earth pressure
    Earthwork
    Engineering
    Hydraulic structures
    Irrigation
    Rivers
    Water-power
    Water-storage
    Water-supply
    Weirs
  — Design and construction *(TC540)*
  — Drawings
    Example under Structural drawing
  — Estimates *(Direct)*
  — Failure
    See Dam failures
  — Foundations
    xx Foundations
  — Juvenile literature
  — Models
    xx Hydraulic models
  — Registers
  — Surveying
    xx Surveying
Dams, Arch
  See Arch dams
Dams, Concrete
  See Concrete dams
Dams (Horses)
  See Mares
Damsel flies
    xx Odonata
Dan (African people)
  See Gere (African people)
Dan language
    x Gere language
    Gio language
    Mebe language
    Yabuba language
    xx Mande languages
Dāna (Buddhism)
  See Buddhist giving
Danakil language
  See Afar language
Danbury, Conn.
  — Burning by the British, 1777
Dance band
  See Dance orchestra
Dance bands
  See Dance orchestras
Dance equipment
  See Dancing—Apparatus and equipment
Dance etiquette *(BJ2043)*
    xx Dancing
    Etiquette
Dance festivals
    x Ballet festivals
    xx Art festivals
    Festivals

Dance music *(Indirect)* *(M1450-1459)*
    Here are entered collections of miscel-
    laneous dance music. Music for in-
    dividual dances is entered under dance
    form followed by specification of
    medium, *e.g.* Polkas (Accordion);
    Waltzes (Orchestra)
    If the collection is for a medium other
    than piano, additional heading is used
    for the medium, *e.g.* 1. Dance music. 2.
    Violin and piano music.
    sa Ballet dance music
    Clog-dance music
    Dance-orchestra music
    Folk dance music
    xx Dancing
    Instrumental music
    Music
    Piano music
  — History and criticism *(ML3400-3451)*
    sa Instrumentation and orchestration
      (Dance orchestra)
    Jazz music
Dance music, American, ₍French, German,
  etc.₎
Dance notation *(GV1587)*
    xx Choreography
    Movement notation
Dance of death *(N7720; Block-books,*
    Z241.D17)
    x Danse macabre
    Death, Dance of
Dance orchestra *(ML1200; MT733)*
    sa Dance orchestras
    Instrumentation and orchestration
      (Dance orchestra)
    x Dance band
    School dance band
    xx Bands (Music)
    Orchestra
Dance-orchestra music *(M1350)*
    Cf. note under Orchestral music.
    sa Cha-chas (Dance orchestra)
    Clarinet with dance orchestra
    Concertos (Clarinet with dance
      orchestra)
    Concertos (Dance orchestra)
    Concertos (Harpsichord and piano with
      dance orchestra)
    Concertos (Piano with dance orchestra)
    Concertos (Saxophone with dance
      orchestra)
    Concertos (Trumpet with dance
      orchestra)
    Fox trots (Dance orchestra)
    Harpsichord and piano with dance
      orchestra
    Jazz ensembles
    Merengues (Dance orchestra)
    Overtures (Dance orchestra)
    Pasodobles (Dance orchestra)
    Piano with dance orchestra
    Saxophone with dance orchestra
    Suites (Dance orchestra)
    Trumpet with dance orchestra
    Variations (Dance orchestra)
    Waltzes (Dance orchestra)
    xx Band music
    Dance music
    Instrumental music
    Jazz ensembles
    Orchestral music
Dance orchestras *(Indirect)*
    x Dance bands
    xx Dance orchestra
    Music
    Music—Performance

Dance parties

Here are entered works dealing with informal dances. Works concerned with formal dances are entered under Balls (Parties)

   sa Balls (Parties)
       Television dance parties
   x Dances
   xx Balls (Parties)
       Dancing
       Entertaining
   Note under Balls (Parties)

Dance production *(GV1782)*
   sa Dancing—Stage-setting and scenery
   x Ballet production
       Ballet—Production and direction
       Dancing—Production and direction
   xx Theater—Production and direction

Dance psychotherapy
   See Dance therapy

Dance therapy *(RC489.D)*
   sa Tarantella
   x Dance psychotherapy
       Dancing—Therapeutic use
   xx Recreational therapy

Dancers
   x Ballet dancers
   xx Artists
       Dancing
       Entertainers
   — Biography
   — Caricatures and cartoons

Dancers, Women
   See Women dancers

Dances
   See Balls (Parties)
       Dance parties
       Dancing—Children's dances
       names of specific types of dances, e.g.
          Quadrille (Dance), Waltz

Dancing *(Indirect) (GV1580-1799;*
      Primitive, GN463)
   sa Ballet
       Ballroom dancing
       Balls (Parties)
       Choreography
       Clog-dancing
       Dance etiquette
       Dance music
       Dance parties
       Dancers
       Folk dancing
       Jazz dance
       Jitterbug dancing
       Modern dance
       Music in physical education
       Musico-callisthenics
       Play-party
       Purpose (Dancing)
       Rock and roll dancing
       Round dancing
       Shakespeare, William, 1564-1616—
          Dancing
       Square dancing
       Tap dancing
       names of dances, e.g. Quadrille
          (Dance), Waltz
   xx Amusements
       Balls (Parties)
   — Aesthetics
      See Dancing—Philosophy
   — Apparatus and equipment *(GV1600)*
      x Dance equipment
   — Children's dances *(GV1799)*
      x Children's dances
       Dances
      xx Dancing and children
       Games

— Dictionaries
— Early works to 1800 *(GV1590)*
— Jews
   x Jews—Dancing
— Juvenile literature
— Libraries and museums
   See Music libraries
       Music museums
— Moral and religious aspects
      (GV1740-1741)
   xx Dancing (in religion, folk-lore, etc.)
   Example under Christian ethics
— Philosophy
   x Dancing—Aesthetics
   xx Aesthetics
— Pictorial works *(GV1595)*
— Political aspects
— Production and direction
   See Dance production
— Psychological aspects
— Stage-setting and scenery
   x Stage scenery
       Stage-setting
       Staging
   xx Dance production
— Terminology
— Therapeutic use
   See Dance therapy
— Vocational guidance
   x Dancing as a profession

Dancing, Ballet
   See Ballet dancing

Dancing (in religion, folk-lore, etc.) *(BL605)*
   sa Dancing—Moral and religious aspects
       Folk dancing
       Indians of Central America—Dances
       Indians of North America—Dances
       Kagura
       Religious dance, Modern
       Seises
   x Folk-lore of dancing
   xx Jews—Antiquities
       Religion, Primitive
       Rites and ceremonies

Dancing and children
   sa Dancing—Children's dances
   x Children and dancing

Dancing as a profession
   See Dancing—Vocational guidance

Dancing in art *(N8217.D)*
   sa Ballet in art
   xx Art

Dancing in literature

Dancing in moving-pictures, television, etc.
      (GV1779)

Here are entered works dealing with professional dancing in moving-pictures and television shows. Works dealing with telecast dance parties are entered under Television dance parties.

   sa Ballet in moving-pictures, television, etc.
   x Dancing in television
       Moving-pictures and dancing
       Television and dancing
   xx Moving-pictures
       Television
   Note under Television dance parties

Dancing in religious education
   xx Religious dance, Modern
       Religious education

Dancing in television
   See Dancing in moving-pictures, television, etc.

Dancing mania
   See Chorea, Epidemic

Dancing mice *(QL737.R6)*
   x Waltzing mice
   xx Mice
   — Psychology

Dandelion powdery mildew *(SB733)*

Dandelions *(Botany, QK495.T2)*
   sa Kok-saghyz
   Example under Greens, Edible
   — Juvenile literature

Dandie (Dog)
   See Dandie Dinmont terrier

Dandie Dinmont terrier *(SF429.D33)*
   x Dandie (Dog)
       Pepper and mustard terrier
   xx Terriers

Dandies *(Biography, CT9985-6)*
   x Beaux
       Dandyism
       Dudes

Dandies in literature

Dandruff *(RL91)*
   xx Scalp—Diseases
       Skin—Diseases

Dandyism
   See Dandies

Danes
   xx Scandinavians
   — Anecdotes, facetiae, satire, etc.

Danes in England, ₍France, Scotland, etc.₎

Dangadi language
   See Thangatti language

Dangaleat language
   xx Chadic languages

Dangarik language
   See Phalura language

Dangati language
   See Thangatti language

Dangerous goods
   See Hazardous substances

Dangerous materials
   See Hazardous substances

Dangerous occupations
   See Occupations, Dangerous

Danggadi language
   See Thangatti language

Dangme language
   See Adangme language

Dani (New Guinea people)
   sa Missions to Dani (New Guinea people)
   x Ndani (New Guinea people)
   xx Ethnology—New Guinea

Dani language *(PL6265.Z9)*

Danilo culture
   xx Man, Prehistoric
       Neolithic period

Danish agricultural assistance
   See Agricultural assistance, Danish

Danish-American literature
   x American literature (Danish)
   xx Danish literature

Danish ballads and songs *(Collections,*
      PT7990; History, PT7791)
   sa Ballads, Danish
       Folk-songs, Danish
       National songs, Danish
       Songs, Danish

Danish Baptists
   See Baptists, Danish

Danish boundary stones
   See Boundary stones, Danish

Danish dogs
   See Dalmatian dogs

Danish drama *(Direct) (Collections,*
      PT7999-8020; History,
      PT7800-7832)
— 20th century

Danish essays
 Here are entered collections of essays by
  several authors.
Danish fiction *(Collections, PT8022-4;*
  History, PT7835-7862)
Danish hymns
 See Hymns, Danish
Danish language *(PD3001-3929)*
 x Dano-Norwegian language
 xx Germanic languages
  Norwegian language
  Scandinavian languages
 Example under Germanic philology
 — To 1500 *(PD3771-8)*
  x Danish language—Old Danish
 — Old Danish
  See Danish language—To 1500
Danish letters *(PT7866; PT8030)*
Danish literature *(Direct) (Collections,*
  PT7915-8046; History,
  PT7601-7910)
 sa Danish-American literature
 xx Scandinavian literature
 Example under Germanic philology
 — To 1500 *(PT7721-7737)*
 — 19th century
 — 20th century
Danish Lutherans
 See Lutherans, Danish
Danish matchbox labels
 See Matchbox labels, Danish
Danish Mormons
 See Mormons and Mormonism, Danish
Danish mythology
 See Mythology, Norse
Danish-Negro dialect
 See Negro-Danish dialect
Danish newspapers *(History, etc., PN5281-9)*
Danish periodicals *(History, etc.,*
  PN5281-5290)
Danish philology *(Direct)*
 xx Scandinavian philology
Danish photographers
 See Photographers, Danish
Danish poetry *(Collections, PT7975-7994;*
  History, etc., PT7770-7795)
 — 17th century
 — 18th century
Danish property in Great Britain, [etc.]
Danish prose literature *(Collections,*
  PT8021-4; History, PT7835-7862)
 — 19th century
 — 20th century
Danish proverbs
 See Proverbs, Danish
Danish sculpture
 See Sculpture, Danish
Danish wit and humor *(Direct)*
 Here are entered collections from several
  authors and individual authors who
  have not written in other literary
  forms.
Danites *(BX8601-8695)*
 xx Mormons and Mormonism
Dänjong-kä language *(PL3651.D2)*
 x Bhōtiā of Sikkim language
  Dé-jong ké language
  Dēnjong-ké language
  Sikkim-Bhutia language
Dankali language
 See Afar language
Danlos syndrome
 See Ehlers-Danlos syndrome
Dano-Norwegian language
 See Danish language
  Norwegian language
Dano-Swedish War, 1643-1645 *(DL190)*
 sa Fehmarn, Battle of, 1644

 x Denmark—History—Dano-Swedish
  Wars, 1643-1660
  Sweden—History—Dano-Swedish
  Wars, 1643-1660
Dano-Swedish Wars, 1657-1660 *(DL192)*
 sa Roskilde, Denmark, Peace of, 1658
  Sound, Battle of the, 1658
  Swedish-Dutch War, 1658-1659
 x Denmark—History—Dano-Swedish
  Wars, 1643-1660
  Sveco-Danish Wars, 1657-1660
  Sweden—History—Dano-Swedish
  Wars, 1643-1660
  Swedish-Danish Wars, 1657-1660
Danse macabre
 See Dance of death
Danube River
 — Navigation
 — — Laws and regulations
  Example under Inland navigation—
   Laws and regulations
 — Regulation
  Example under Rivers—Regulation
Danube Valley
 xx Central Europe
Dar Banda
 See Banda (African people)
Darbyites
 See Plymouth Brethren
Dardanelles, Battle of the, 1656
  (DR534.5.D3)
Dardannelles Campaign, 1915
 See European War, 1914-1918—Campaigns
  —Turkey and the Near East—
  Gallipoli
Dardic languages
 See Pisacha languages
Dardu languages
 See Pisacha languages
Dargari language *(PL7101.D3)*
 x Targari language
  Tarkarri language
  Thargari language
 xx Australian languages
Darghi language
 See Dargwa language
Dargin language
 See Dargwa language
Dargwa language *(PK9201.D3)*
 x Darghi language
  Dargin language
 xx Caucasian languages
 — Dialects
 — — Kubachi
  See Kubachi dialect
Dari language
 See Kabuli-Persian language
Daribi
 x Migaru Page Daribi
  Mikaru
 xx Ethnology—New Guinea
Darien Expedition, 1870 *(TC788)*
Darier's disease
 See Keratosis
Dark Ages
 See Europe—History—392-814
  Middle Ages
Dark rooms
 See Photography—Studios and dark rooms
Darkness and light in literature
 See Light and darkness in literature
Darkness in the Bible
 See Light and darkness in the Bible
Darkroom technique in photography
 See Photography—Processing
Darkroom technique in radiography
 See Radiography—Processing

Darkrooms, Photographic
 See Photography—Studios and dark rooms
Dart automobile
 See Dodge Dart automobile
Dart boards
 xx Darts (Game)
Dart Herald (Transport planes) *(TL686.H)*
 xx Transport planes
 — Juvenile literature
Darters (Fishes) *(QL638.P4)*
 sa Slough darter
Darts (Clothing)
 xx Clothing and dress
  Sewing
Darts (Game)
 sa Dart boards
Daruma dolls
 See Bodhidharma dolls
Darwinism
 See Evolution
Darzens reaction
 xx Chemical reactions
Dasahara
 See Dasara
Dasara *(BL1213.D)*
 x Dasahara
  Dussera
 Example under Fasts and feasts—Hinduism
Dase language
 See Tucano language
Dash (Punctuation)
 xx Punctuation
Dassault Mirage (Fighter planes)
 See Mirage (Fighter planes)
Dasypodidae
 See Armadillos
Data archives
 See Data libraries
Data centers
 See Data libraries
Data collection systems, Automatic
 See Automatic data collection systems
Data compression (Telecommunication)
 sa Coding theory
  Pulse-code modulation
  Television bandwidth compression
  Vocoder
 xx Data transmission systems
Data display systems
 See Information display systems
Data files
 See Data libraries
  Files and filing (Documents)
Data libraries *(Direct)*
 sa Information storage and retrieval
  systems
 x Data archives
  Data centers
  Data files
  Libraries, Data
 xx Information services
  Information storage and retrieval
  systems
Data processing
 See Electronic data processing
  Information storage and retrieval
  systems
  Punched card systems
Data processing service centers *(Direct)*
 sa Computer leases
  Time-sharing computer systems
 x Computer centers
  Electronic data processing service
  centers
 xx Computer leases
  Electronic data processing
  Electronic data processing departments

Data Reconfiguration Service (Computer program)
  See DRS (Computer program)
Data Retrieval Language (Computer program language
  See DRL (Computer program language)
Data smoothing filters
  See Digital filters (Mathematics)
Data storage and retrieval systems
  See Information storage and retrieval systems
Data tape drives *(TK7887.55)*
  x Tape drives
    Tape transport
  xx Computer input-output equipment
Data tapes
  sa Magnetic tapes
  x Magnetic recordings (Data storage)
    Magnetic tape files
    Magnetic tape recordkeeping
    Punched tapes
    Tape files
    Tape recordings (Data storage)
  xx Computer storage devices
    Electronic data processing
    Files and filing (Documents)
    Information storage and retrieval systems
    Magnetic tapes
    Programming (Electronic computers)
Data terminals (Computers)
  See Computer input-output equipment
DATA-TEXT (Computer program language)
Data transmission systems
  sa Automatic data collection systems
    Automatic picture transmission
    Data compression (Telecommunication)
    Facsimile transmission
    Information networks
    Library information networks
    Modems
    Telemeter
    Teletype
  x Transmission of data
  xx Electronic data processing
    Information theory
    Telecommunication
  — Mathematical models
  — Patents
  — Testing
Date *(Indirect)* *(As food, TX558.D35; Cultivation, SB364)*
  sa Cookery (Dates)
  xx Date-palm
  — Diseases and pests
    See Date-palm—Diseases and pests
  — Marketing
  — Tariff
    See Tariff on dates
  — Varieties
    See Date-palm—Varieties
Date etiquette
  See Dating (Social customs)
Date line, International
  See International date line
Date-palm *(Indirect)* *(SB364)*
  sa Date
  xx Palms
  — Diseases and pests
    x Date—Diseases and pests
  — Varieties
    x Date—Varieties
Date-palm fiber industry *(Direct)*
  (TS1747.D3)
Date stone
  See Datolite
Date stones (Building)

Date-sugar *(TF393)*
  xx Sugar
Dates
  See Chronology, Historical
Dates, Books of
  See Calendars
Dating, Potassium-argon
  See Potassium-argon dating
Dating, Radioactive
  See Radioactive dating
Dating, Radiocarbon
  See Radiocarbon dating
Dating, Tritium
  See Tritium dating
Dating, Uranium-lead
  See Uranium-lead dating
Dating (Social customs)
  x Date etiquette
    Dating etiquette
  xx Courtship
    Etiquette
    Sexual ethics
  — Anecdotes, facetiae, satire, etc.
  — Juvenile literature
Dating etiquette
  See Dating (Social customs)
Dating of meteorites
  See Meteorites—Age
Dating of milk
  See Milk dating
Dating of pottery
  See Pottery dating
Dating of rocks
  See Geological time
Dating of stemware
  See Stemware dating
Datio in solutum
  See Accord and satisfaction (Roman law)
Dation in payment
  See Accord and satisfaction
Datolite *(QE391.D)*
  x Date stone
  xx Mineralogy
    Zeolites
Datsun automobile
Datura *(Pharmacy, RS165.D2; Therapeutics, RM666.D3)*
  x Jamestown weed
Daughters
  sa Fathers and daughters
    Mothers and daughters
  xx Girls
  — Caricatures and cartoons
Daughters and fathers
  See Fathers and daughters
Daughters and mothers
  See Mothers and daughters
Daunii *(DG225.D3)*
  xx Ethnology—Italy
Daure language
  See Dagur language
Davenport, Iowa
  — Flood, 1965
Davenport porcelain
  x Porcelain, Davenport
  xx Porcelain, English
Davenport pottery
  x Pottery, Davenport
  xx Pottery, English
David Georgians
  See Davidists
Davidists
  x David Georgians
David's shield
  See Magen David
Davis cup *(GV999)*
  x International lawn tennis championship
  xx Tennis

Davits *(VM831; Boat lowering, VM801)*
  x Anchor davits
    Boat davits
    Hatch davits
  xx Cranes, derricks, etc.
    Ships—Equipment and supplies
Da'wā (Islamic law)
  See Actions and defenses (Islamic law)
Da'wah (Islam) *(BP170.85)*
  x Evangelistic work (Islam)
    Islam—Evangelistic work
  xx Islam—Missions
Dawn (in religion, folk-lore, etc.) *(Folk-lore, GR930; Hinduism, BL1215.D3; Mythology, BL325.D)*
  x Folk-lore of dawn
  xx Mythology
    Religion, Primitive
Dawn chorus (Radio meteorology) *(QC973)*
  sa Hiss (Radio meteorology)
    Whistlers (Radio meteorology)
  x Chorus, Dawn (Radio meteorology)
  xx Electric interference
    Ionosphere
    Radio meteorology
    Radio noise
  — Tables, etc.
Dawn in literature
Daxsea language
  See Tucano language
Day
  sa Night
  xx Chronology
    Time
Day (African people)
  x Dai (African people)
    Sara Dai (African people)
  xx Ethnology—Chad
Day airglow
  See Airglow
Day camps
  sa Play schools
  xx Camps
    Play schools
Day care
  See Day nurseries
    Foster day care
Day care aides *(Direct)*
  xx Day nurseries
  — In-service training *(Direct)*
Day dreams
  See Fantasy
Day lilies
  x Daylilies
Day nurseries *(Direct)* *(HV851-861)*
  sa Day care aides
    Foster day care
    Nursery schools
    Play schools
  x Child care centers
    Crèches (Day nurseries)
    Day care
    Nurseries, Day
  xx Architecture and youth
    Charities
    Child welfare
    Children
    Children—Institutional care
    Foster day care
    Nursery schools
    Public welfare
    Social settlements
    Woman—Charities
  — Costs
  — Equipment and supplies
  — Federal aid
    See Federal aid to day nurseries
  — Finance

Day nurseries *(Direct)* *(HV851-861)*
— Finance *(Continued)*
   sa Federal aid to day nurseries
— Law and legislation *(Direct)*
— Licenses *(Direct)*
Day of Atonement (Jewish holiday)
  See Yom Kippur
Day of Jehovah *(BS1199.D3)*
  x Day of the Lord
     Day of Yahveh
     Jehovah, Day of
     Lord, Day of the
     Yahveh, Day of
  xx Judgment Day—Biblical teaching
     Kingdom of God—Biblical teaching
Day of Judgment
  See Judgment Day
Day of the Lord
  See Day of Jehovah
Day of Yahveh
  See Day of Jehovah
Day release (Great Britain)
  See Education, Cooperative
Dayak language
  See Dyak language
Dayaks
  See Dyaks
Dayflower *(QK495.C73)*
Dayflower in literature
Daylamites
  sa Buwayhids
  xx Ethnology—Iran
Daylight
  xx Lighting
— Measurement
— Tables, etc.
Daylight saving *(HN49.D3)*
  xx Hours of labor
     Time—Systems and standards
— Law and legislation *(Direct)*
    Note under Time (Law)
Daylilies
  See Day lilies
Dayr al Qamar, Lebanon, Massacre of, 1860
  xx Maronites
Days *(Folk-lore, GR930)*
  sa Anniversaries
     Birthdays
     Fasts and feasts
     Festivals
     Holidays
     Leap year
     Promotion of special events
     Sunday
     names of special days, e.g. Christmas,
       Flag Day, Halloween, Memorial Day
  x Days of the week
     Folk-lore of days
     Hours (Time)
  xx Anniversaries
     Calendar
     Horology
— Juvenile literature
Days of the week
  See Days
Dayton, Ohio
— Flood, 1913
—— Juvenile literature
Daza (African people)
  x Toubou (African people)
  xx Ethnology—Africa, West
Daza language *(PL8121.D5)*
  x Dazza language
     Toubou language
     Tubu language
Dazza language
  See Daza language

DC-10 (Jet transport)
  See McDonnell Douglas DC-10 (Jet
    transport)
Dciriku language
  See Diriku language
DCL (Electronic computer system)
  x Demographic Computer Library
DDT (Insecticide)
  sa Plants, Effect of DDT on
  xx Ethanes
— Physiological effect
— Toxicology *(RA1242.D35)*
De Dion-Bouton automobile
De facto corporations *(Direct)*
  xx Corporation law
     De facto doctrine
     Incorporation
De facto doctrine
  sa De facto corporations
     Quo warranto
     Recognition (International law)
     State succession
  x De facto doctrine (International law)
     De facto government
  xx Administrative law
     Constitutional law
     Executive power
     Government liability
     Military occupation
     Municipal corporations
     Recognition (International law)
     Revolutions
     State succession
De facto doctrine (International law)
  See De facto doctrine
     Military occupation
     Recognition (International law)
De facto government
  See De facto doctrine
     Recognition (International law)
De Havilland Comet
  See Comet (Jet transports)
De-icing of aeroplanes
  See Aeroplanes—Ice prevention
Dé-jong ké language
  See Dänjong-kä language
De Jur moving-picture camera
De Lange's syndrome
  xx Deformities
     Mental deficiency
De profundis (Music)
  See Psalms (Music)—130th Psalm
De Quervain's disease
  See Tenosynovitis
Deaconesses *(Direct)* *(BV4423-5)*
  sa Deacons
  xx Church work
     Deacons
     Nurses and nursing
     Sisterhoods
     Women in charitable work
— Salaries, pensions, etc.
Deacons *(BV680; Catholic Church, BX1912)*
  sa Deaconesses
  x Diaconate
  xx Church officers
     Clergy
     Deaconesses
— Public opinion
Dead *(Disposition of, RA619-640; Folk-lore,*
    GR455; Manners and customs,
    GT3150-3390)
  sa Burial
     Cemeteries
     Cremation
     Dokhmas
     Embalming
     Epitaphs

     Funeral rites and ceremonies
     Lanterns of the dead
     Monuments
     Mounds
     Obituaries
     Scaffold burial
     Sepulchral monuments
     Tombs
     Undertakers and undertaking
     Urn burial
  x Mortuary customs
  xx Cremation
     Death
     Funeral rites and ceremonies
— Commemoration
  See Saints—Commemoration
— Identification *(RA1055)*
  x Identification of the dead
— Law and legislation
  See Dead bodies (Law)
Dead, Baptism for the
  See Baptism for the dead
Dead, Communication with the
  See Spiritualism
Dead, Lanterns of the
  See Lanterns of the dead
Dead, Prayers for the
  See Prayers for the dead
Dead, Worship of the
  See Ancestor worship
Dead (in religion, folk-lore, etc.)
    (Comparative religion, BL470;
    Egyptian religion, BL2443; Folk-lore,
    GR455)
  sa Ancestor worship
     Saints—Commemoration
  x Folk-lore of the dead
  xx Religion, Primitive
Dead animals, Disposal of
  See Dead animals, Removal and disposal of
Dead animals, Removal and disposal of
    (Direct) *(SF757)*
  sa Pet cemeteries
  x Animal bodies, Disposal of
     Dead animals, Disposal of
     Disposal of dead animals
     Removal of dead animals
  xx Veterinary hygiene
Dead bodies (Canon law, Eastern)
Dead bodies (Germanic law)
Dead bodies (Greek law)
Dead bodies (Jewish law)
Dead bodies (Law) *(Direct)*
  sa Autopsy
     Burial laws
  x Dead—Law and legislation
Dead-end streets
  See Cul-de-sac streets
Dead languages
  See Classical languages
     Extinct languages
Dead reckoning (Navigation)
  sa Inertial navigation
     Inertial navigation (Aeronautics)
  xx Navigation
Deadeyes
  xx Masts and rigging
Deadly sins *(BV4626-7)*
  sa Anger
     Avarice
     Envy
     Gluttony
     Laziness
     Pride and vanity
     Sadness
     Sin, Mortal
  x Capital sins
     Seven capital sins

Seven deadly sins
  Sins, Capital
  Sins, Deadly
  xx Sin, Mortal
  Sins
  — Sermons
Deadly sins in art
  xx Art
Deadman anchors
  See Guy anchors
Deaerators
  xx Feed-water purification
  Water—Aeration
Deaf *(Direct) (RF320; Charities,*
    HV2350-2990)
  sa Blind-deaf
  Children, Deaf
  Church work with the deaf
  x Deaf and dumb
  Deaf-mutes
  Dumb (Deaf-mutes)
  xx Physically handicapped
  — Asylums
    See Deaf—Institutional care
  — Education *(Direct)*
    sa Blind-deaf—Education
    Teachers of the deaf
    x Children, Deaf—Education
    Education of the deaf
    xx Vocational education
    Vocational guidance
  — — English language, ꜒Physical education,
    Religion, etc.꜓
  — — Speech
    See Deaf—Means of
      communication
  — Employment *(Direct)*
    xx Vocational rehabilitation
  — Institutional care *(Direct)*
    x Benevolent institutions
    Charitable institutions
    Deaf—Asylums
    Homes (Institutions)
    xx Asylums
    Charities
    Charities, Medical
    Public welfare
  — Intelligence
    See Intelligence levels—Deaf
  — Marriage *(HQ1040)*
    x Marriage of the deaf
    xx Eugenics
    Heredity, Human
    Marriage
  — Means of communication
      (HV2471-2500)
    sa Communicative disorders
    Lipreading
    x Dactylology
    Deaf—Education—Speech
    Deaf—Sign language
    Finger alphabet
    Gesture language
    Manual alphabets
    Speech-reading
    xx Children, Deaf
    Sign language
  — Personal narratives
  — Rehabilitation *(Direct)*
  — — Research *(Direct)*
  — Research *(Direct)*
  — Sign language
    See Deaf—Means of communication
Deaf, Books for the *(Bibliography,*
    Z1039.D4)
  x Books for the deaf
Deaf, Libraries for the
  x Libraries for the deaf

Deaf, Teachers of the
  See Teachers of the deaf
Deaf and dumb
  See Deaf
Deaf as athletes
  x Deaf in athletics
  xx Athletes
Deaf as authors *(PN171.D)*
Deaf-blind
  See Blind-deaf
Deaf children
  See Children, Deaf
Deaf in athletics
  See Deaf as athletes
Deaf in folk-lore *(GR950.D)*
  x Folk-lore of the deaf
Deaf-mutes
  See Deaf
Deafness *(RF290-310)*
  sa Ear
  Hearing
  Hearing aids
  Ménière's disease
  Otosclerosis
  xx Audiology
  Ear—Diseases
  Hearing
  Hearing disorders
  — Genetic aspects
    sa Alport's syndrome
    x Congenital deafness
  — Psychological aspects
Deafness in children
  See Children, Deaf
Dealer aids
  x Dealer help
  Dealer training
  xx Marketing
  Retail trade
  Sales promotion
  Salesmen and salesmanship
Dealer help
  See Dealer aids
Dealer training
  See Dealer aids
Deamination
  sa Amines
  xx Amines
  Chemical reactions
  Elimination reactions
Deaneries (Buildings)
  See Parsonages
Deans, Cathedral and collegiate *(Direct)*
  x Cathedral deans
  Collegiate church deans
  xx Clergy
Deans, Rural
  See Rural deans
Deans (in schools) *(Direct) (Education of*
    women, LC1567; Higher education,
    LB2341)
  sa Deans of women
  x Student advisers
  xx College administrators
  Educators
  Personnel service in education
  Teachers
  — Biography
  — Correspondence, reminiscences, etc.
Deans of girls
  See Deans of women
Deans of women
  x Deans of girls
  Women deans
  xx Deans (in schools)

Death *(Cytology, QH671; Folk-lore, GR455;*
    Manners and customs,
    GT3150-3390; Medical
    jurisprudence, RA1063; Philosophy,
    BD444; Physiology, QP87; Proof of,
    in life insurance, HG8896; Statistics,
    HB1321-1530; Theology, BT825)
  sa Annihilationism
  Bereavement
  Children and death
  Dead
  Future life
  Future punishment
  Heaven
  Hell
  Intermediate state
  Martyrdom
  Mortality
  Terminal care
  Translation to heaven
  xx Eschatology
  Intermediate state
  Life
  — Anecdotes, facetiae, satire, etc.
  — Art *(N8217.D5)*
    sa Cadaver in art
    x Death in art
  — Biblical teaching
  — Caricatures and cartoons
  — Causes *(Medical jurisprudence, RA1063)*
    sa Asphyxia
    Autopsy
    Coroners
    Drowning
    Medical examiners (Law)
    Mortality
    Old age
    Sudden death
    Suicide
    Temperature—Physiological effect
    Violent deaths
    Vital statistics
    xx Autopsy
    Vital statistics
  — — Nomenclature
  — Comparative studies
  — Drama
  — Early works to 1800
  — Juvenile literature
  — Meditations *(BT825)*
    Example under Meditations
  — Poetry
  — Proof and certification *(Direct) (State*
    medicine, RA405)
    sa Absence and presumption of death
    Medical examiners (Law)
    x Certification of death
    xx Absence and presumption of death
    Insurance, Life
  — Proof and certification (Canon law)
    (BX1939)
  — Psychology
    sa Children and death
    Youth and death
  — Quotations, maxims, etc.
  — Sermons
Death, Apparent *(First aid, RC87-88;*
    Medical jurisprudence, RA1063;
    New-born infants, RJ255)
  sa Burial, Premature
  Drowning, Restoration from
  Resuscitation
  xx Burial, Premature
Death, Dance of
  See Dance of death
Death, Declaration of
  See Absence and presumption of death

Death, Last letters before
   See Last letters before death
Death, Power over
   See Life and death, Power over
Death, Presumption of
   See Absence and presumption of death
Death, Sudden
   See Sudden death
Death (African religion)
Death (Biology) *(QH559)*
   sa Mortality
      Rigor mortis
      Violent deaths
   xx Biology
      Life (Biology)
      Mortality
Death (Buddhism) *(BQ4487)*
   xx Eschatology, Buddhist
Death (Egyptian religion) *(BL2450.D)*
   xx Eschatology, Egyptian
Death (Hinduism) *(BL1215.D4)*
   sa Mṛtyuñjaya homa
   xx Eschatology, Hindu
Death (Islam)
   xx Eschatology, Islamic
   — Koranic teaching *(BP134.D35)*
Death (Judaism) *(BM635.4)*
   xx Eschatology, Jewish
Death and children
   See Children and death
Death and youth
   See Youth and death
Death by wrongful act *(Direct)*
   sa Damages
   xx Damages
      Homicide
      Torts
Death-duties
   See Inheritance and transfer tax
Death in art
   See Death—Art
Death in literature *(PN56.D; English*
      literature, PR149.D)
   sa Cemeteries in literature
Death in motion pictures
   xx Moving-pictures
   Note under Moving-pictures—Plots, themes,
      etc.
Death in music
   xx Funeral music
      Music
      Program music
      Symbolism in music
Death-masks
   See Masks (Sculpture)
Death notices
   See Obituaries
Death of children
   See Children—Death and future state
Death of God theology *(BT83.5)*
   sa Secularization (Theology)
   x Atheism, Christian
      Christian atheism
      God is dead theology
      Theothanasia
      Theothanatology
   xx Christianity—20th century
      Theology—20th century
Death penalty
   See Capital punishment
Death rate
   See Mortality
      Vital statistics
Deathbed hallucinations
   x Deathbed visions
   xx Hallucinations and illusions
Deathbed marriage *(Direct)*
   x Marriage in danger of death

   xx Marriage law
Deathbed marriage (Canon law)
   xx Marriage (Canon law)
      Marriage—Dispensations
Deathbed visions
   See Deathbed hallucinations
Deathbed words
   See Last words
Deaths, Registers of
   See Registers of births, etc.
Debar, Yugoslavia
   — Earthquake, 1967
Debarkers (Woodworking machinery)
   See Barkers (Woodworking machinery)
Debarking
   See Bark peeling
Debates, Religious
   See Disputations, Religious
Debates and debating *(PN4181-4191)*
   sa Discussion
      Forums (Discussion and debate)
      Oratory
      Parliamentary practice
      Public speaking
      Radio addresses, debates, etc.
   x Argumentation
      Speaking
   xx Discussion
      Elocution
      Oratory
      Public speaking
      Rhetoric
Debentures
   See Bonds
Debility
Deblin, Poland
   — Siege, 1914-1915
      xx European War, 1914-1918—
         Campaigns—Poland
Debt *(Direct)*
   Here are entered economic and statistical
      works on: 1) internal private debts, 2)
      both internal and external private
      debts, 3) both internal private and pub-
      lic debts, 4) internal and external pri-
      vate and public debts. Legal works on
      debts are entered under the headings
      Contracts and Debtor and creditor. *Cf.*
      notes under Debts, External and
      Debts, Public.
   sa Bankruptcy
      Collecting of accounts
      Corporate debt
      Credit
      Debts, External
      Moratorium
   xx Commercial law
      Credit
      Economics
   Notes under Debtor and creditor; Debts, Ex-
      ternal; Debts, Public
Debt, Imprisonment for *(Indirect)*
      (HV8650-8651)
   x Imprisonment for debt
   xx Imprisonment
Debt, Imprisonment for (Jewish law)
Debt, Servitude for
   See Peonage
Debt, Writ of
   See Writ of debt
Debtor and creditor *(Direct)*
   Cf. note under Debt.
   sa Abandonment (Maritime law)
      Accounts current
      Assignments
      Assignments for benefit of creditors
      Attachment and garnishment
      Bankruptcy

      Benefit of inventory
      Bulk sales
      Claims against decedents' estates
      Composition (Law)
      Compromise (Law)
      Consignation
      Correality and solidarity
      Creditors' bills
      Delegation (Civil law)
      Escalator clause
      Executions (Law)
      Expromission
      Extinguishment of debts
      Fraudulent conveyances
      Gold clause
      Liens
      Moratorium
      Novation
      Payment
      Performance (Law)
      Poor debtor's oath
      Priorities of claims and liens
      Receipts (Acknowledgments)
      Remission (Civil law)
      Revalorization of debts
      Security (Law)
      Separation of patrimony
      Subrogation
      Valuta clause
   x Creditor
   xx Commercial law
      Contracts
      Creditors' bills
      Fraudulent conveyances
      Liens
      Obligations (Law)
      Payment
      Security (Law)
   Note under Debt
   — Popular works
Debtor and creditor (Hindu law) *(Direct)*
Debtor and creditor (Islamic law) *(Direct)*
Debtor and creditor (Jewish law)
Debtor and creditor (Roman law)
Debts, Confusion of
   See Confusion of rights
Debts, External *(Direct)*
   Here are entered works on public and or
      private debts owed to foreign credi-
      tors. Works dealing with both internal
      and external debts are entered under
      the heading Debt unless they are lim-
      ited to the discussion of public debts
      only, in which case the subject heading
      Debts, Public is assigned. *Cf.* notes un-
      der Debt; Debts, Public.
   sa Drago doctrine
      Loans, Foreign
   x Debts, International
      External debts
      International debts
   xx Debt
      Debts, Public
      International finance
      Investments, Foreign
   Notes under Debt; Debts, Public
   — Mathematical models
   — Underdeveloped areas
      See Underdeveloped areas—Debts,
         External
Debts, Extinguishment of
   See Extinguishment of debts
Debts, International
   See Debts, External

Debts, Public *(Direct)* *(HJ8003-8897)*
Here are entered works on internal public debts as well as works on both internal and external public debts. Works dealing with external public debts only are entered under the heading Debts, External. *Cf.* notes under Debt; Debts, External.
- *sa* Bonds
  Debts, External
  European War, 1914-1918—Finance
  Forced loans
  Repudiation
  Sinking-funds
  State bankruptcy
  War, Cost of
- *x* National debts
  Public debts
- *xx* Bonds
  Credit
  Economics
  Finance, Public
  Loans
- *Notes under* Debt; Debts, External
- — Accounting
  - *xx* Finance, Public—Accounting
- — Public opinion

  GEOGRAPHIC SUBDIVISIONS

- — Confederate States of America
  - *x* Confederate States of America—Debts, Public
Debts, Revalorization of
See Revalorization of debts
Debts of decedents' estates
See Claims against decedents' estates
Debugging in computer science
- *sa* Computer programs—Testing
- *x* Computer programs—Debugging
  Troubleshooting in computer science
- *xx* Computer programs—Testing
  Electronic data processing
  Electronic digital computers—Programming
Decade counter tubes
See Cold cathode tubes
Decadence
See Degeneration
Decadence (Literary movement) *(PN56.D45)*
- *xx* Literature, Modern—19th century—History and criticism
Decadence as a theme in literature
See Decadence in literature
Decadence in literature
- *x* Decadence as a theme in literature
Decalcomania *(NK9510)*
Decalogue
See Commandments, Ten
Decanter labels
See Wine labels
Decanters *(Direct)*
- *xx* Bottles
  Liquor bottles
  Pottery
- — Private collections *(Direct)*
Decapoda (Crustacea) *(Indirect)* *(QL444.D3)*
- *sa* Crabs
  Lobsters
  Shrimps
  Spiny lobsters
- *xx* Crustacea
  Malacostraca
Decapoda (Crustacea), Fossil *(QE817.D3)*
- *sa* Crabs, Fossil
Decarboxylation
- *xx* Chemical reactions
  Elimination reactions

Decarburization of steel
- *xx* Carbon
  Steel—Heat treatment
Décasépel classification
See Classification, Décasépel
Decasyllable
Decathlon *(GV1060.7)*
- *xx* Track-athletics
Decay, Alpha
See Alpha decay
Decay, Beta
See Beta decay
Decay, Gamma
See Gamma decay
Decay, Radioactive
See subdivision Decay *under radioactive substances, e.g.* Fission products—Decay; Radium—Decay
Decca navigation *(VK560)*
- *xx* Electronics in aeronautics
  Electronics in navigation
  Hyperbolic navigation
Deccan hemp
See Ambary hemp
Deceased wife's sister, Marriage with
See Marriage with deceased wife's sister
Decedents' estates *(Direct)*
- *sa* Benefit of inventory
  Claims against decedents' estates
  Co-heirs
  Decedents' family maintenance
  Distribution of decedents' estates
  Estates, Unclaimed
  Executors and administrators
  Inventories of decedents' estates
  Partition of decedents' estates
  Sale of decedents' estates
  Separation of patrimony
  Widow's allowance
  Widow's share
  subdivision Estate *under names of deceased persons*
- *x* Estates of decedents
- *xx* Estates (Law)
  Inheritance and succession
  Probate law and practice
  Wills
- — Cases
  For individual cases *see* subdivision Estate under names of deceased persons.
- — Taxation *(Direct)*
  - *xx* Inheritance and transfer tax
Decedents' estates (Roman law)
Decedents' family maintenance *(Direct)*
- *x* Family maintenance
- *xx* Decedents' estates
  Inheritance and succession
  Legitime
  Widow's allowance
  Wills
Deceit
See Deception
  Fraud
Deceit in literature
See Deception in literature
Deceleration
See Acceleration (Mechanics)
December
- — Juvenile literature
December ninth movement *(DS775)*
Decembrists
- *sa* Russia—History—Conspiracy of December, 1825
- *x* Dekabrists
- *xx* Russia—History—Conspiracy of December, 1825
- — Books and reading

Example under Books and reading
Decennalia
See Roman emperors
  Rome—History—Chronology
Decentralization in education
See Schools—Decentralization
Decentralization in government *(Direct)*
- *sa* Administrative and political divisions
  Federal government
  Local government
  Public administration
- *x* Centralization in government
  Government centralization
  Government decentralization
- *xx* Federal government
  Local government
  Political science
  Public administration
Decentralization in management *(Direct)*
- *x* Centralization in management
- *xx* Management
Decentralization in schools
See Schools—Decentralization
Deception
- *sa* Fraud
- *x* Chicanery
  Deceit
  Subterfuge
- — Terminology
Deception in literature
- *x* Deceit in literature
  Guile in literature
Decerebrate rigidity
- *x* Rigidity, Decerebrate
- *xx* Brain
Decibels *(TK381)*
- *xx* Sound—Measurement
Decidability theory
See Gödel's theorem
Decimal classification
See Classification, Decimal
Decimal fractions
See Fractions, Decimal
Decimal system *(International coinage, HG393; Weights and measures, QC91-94)*
- *sa* Duodecimal system
  Quinary system
- *xx* Arithmetic
  Duodecimal system
  Numeration
  Weights and measures
- — Conversion tables
- — Juvenile literature
- — Programmed instruction
Decimas *(Collections, PQ6209; History, PQ6096)*
- *xx* Spanish poetry
Decimeter waves
- *x* Waves, Decimeter
- *xx* Microwaves
Decision (Ethics)
See Decision-making (Ethics)
Decision (Psychology)
See Decision-making
Decision logic tables
- *x* Decision tables
  Logic structure tables
- *xx* Decision-making
  Graphic methods
- — Computer programs
Decision-making
Here are entered general works on the process of arriving at decisions for action, including the attempts to formulate a general theory based on mathematical analysis and psychological experiment.

Decision-making *(Continued)*
 sa Choice (Psychology)
  Consensus (Social sciences)
  Decision logic tables
  Dilemma
  Electronic data processing—Tactics
  Make-or-buy decisions
  Management games
  Risk-taking (Psychology)
  Statistical decision
 x Decision processes
  Decision (Psychology)
 xx Choice (Psychology)
  Consensus (Social sciences)
  Estimation theory
  Game theory
  Policy sciences
 — Mathematical models
  xx Mathematical optimization
   Psychology—Mathematical models
   Psychometrics
 — Programmed instruction
Decision-making, Judicial
 See Judicial process
Decision-making (Ethics) *(BJ1468.5)*
 x Decision (Ethics)
  Ethics of decision-making
  Freedom of decision (Ethics)
 xx Ethics
  Free will and determinism
 — Juvenile literature
Decision-making in architecture
 xx Architectural practice
  Architecture
Decision-making in literature
Decision-making in school management
 sa Teacher participation in administration
  Teacher participation in curriculum
   planning
  Teacher-participation in personnel
   service
 xx School management and organization
 — Mathematical models
Decision problems
 See Statistical decision
Decision processes
 See Decision-making
Decision tables
 See Decision logic tables
Deck-cargo
 See Ships—Cargo
Deck machinery *(VM781)*
 sa Capstan
  Windlasses
 xx Machinery
  Marine engineering
 — Electric driving
 — Hydraulic drive
 — Maintenance and repair
Decke (Geology)
 See Nappes (Geology)
Decks (Architecture, Domestic) *(TH4970)*
 x Sun decks (Architecture)
  Terraces (Architecture)
 xx Architecture, Domestic
  Landscape architecture
  Patios
  Porches
  Roofs
 — Pictorial works
Decks (Bridges)
 See Bridges—Floors
Declamation
 See Elocution
  Orations
  Recitations
Declamation, Musical
 See Monologues with music

Musical accentuation
Declaration (Common law pleading)
 See Complaints (Civil procedure)
Declaration of Corfu, 1917
 See Corfu, Declaration of, 1917
Declaration of death
 See Absence and presumption of death
Declaration of intention *(Direct)*
 sa Consent (Law)
  Mistake (Law)
  Motive (Law)
  Rescission (Law)
  Reward (Law)
  Silence (Law)
  Simulation (Civil law)
  Undue influence
 x Declarations (Law)
  Expression of intention
  Intention, Declaration of
 xx Civil law
  Consent (Law)
  Juristic acts
Declaration of London, 1909
 See London, Declaration of, 1909
Declaration of Paris, 1856
 See Paris, Declaration of, 1856
Declaration of war
 See War, Declaration of
Declarations (Law)
 See Declaration of intention
  Pleading
Declaratory acts *(Direct)*
 sa Judgments, Declaratory
 xx Contracts
  Juristic acts
Declaratory judgments
 See Judgments, Declaratory
Décolletage
 x Décolleté
  Low-cut neckline
  Low-necked dress
 xx Clothing and dress
  Costume
Décolleté
 See Décolletage
Decomposed prisoner's dilemma game
 See Prisoner's dilemma game
Decomposition (Chemistry)
 sa Biodegradation
  Dissociation
 xx Chemistry
  Dissociation
Decomposition method *(QA402.2)*
 x Method, Decomposition
 xx Operations research
  Programming (Mathematics)
  System analysis
Decompression, Abdominal
 See Abdominal decompression
Decompression (Physiology)
 xx Atmospheric pressure—Physiological
   effect
  Diving, Submarine
  Space medicine
Decompression sickness
 See Caisson-disease
Decontamination (from gases, chemicals, etc.)
 sa Food contamination
 xx Chemical warfare
  Civil defense
  Contamination (Technology)
  Gases, Asphyxiating and poisonous—
   War use
Decontamination (from radioactive substances)
 See Radioactive decontamination
Decoration, Fore-edge
 See Fore-edge painting

Decoration, Graffito
 See Graffito decoration
Decoration, Interior
 See Interior decoration
Decoration and ornament *(Indirect)*
  (NK1160-1590)
 sa Alphabets
  Arabesques
  Art, African, [Italian, Spanish, etc.]
  Art, Decorative
  Art objects
  Bas-relief
  Bronzes
  Camps—Decoration
  Carpets
  Carving (Art industries)
  China painting
  Church decoration and ornament
  Color in the ceramic industries
  Decorative balls
  Decoupage
  Design
  Design, Decorative
  Devices
  Driftwood arrangement
  Egg decoration
  Embroidery
  Enamel and enameling
  Fancy work
  Figureheads of ships
  Flower arrangement
  Fore-edge painting
  Fretwork
  Friezes
  Furniture
  Garden ornaments and furniture
  Gems
  Gesso
  Glass painting and staining
  Graffito decoration
  Heraldry, Ornamental
  Holiday decorations
  Hours, Books of
  Illumination of books and manuscripts
  Illustration of books
  Interior decoration
  Ironwork
  Jewelry
  Lead-work
  Leather work
  Lettering
  Library decoration
  Marquetry
  Metal-work
  Moldings
  Monograms
  Mosaics
  Mural painting and decoration
  New Year decorations, etc.
  Nose ornaments
  Ornamental rocks
  Painting
  Party decorations
  Plants in art
  Pottery
  School decoration
  Scrolls (Decorative design)
  Sculpture
  Show-windows
  Stencil work
  Street decoration
  Stucco
  Sword guards
  Table setting and decoration
  Tapestry
  Terra-cotta
  Textile design
  Tray painting

Vase-painting
Wood-carving
  x Arts, Decorative
    Decorative arts
    Nature in ornament
    Ornament
    Painting, Decorative
  xx Arabesques
    Art
    Art, Decorative
    Arts and crafts movement
    Design, Decorative
  — 1900 style
    See Decoration and ornament—Art
        nouveau
  — Art deco
    See Art deco
  — Art nouveau
    x Decoration and ornament—1900
        style
    xx Art nouveau
  — Biedermeier style
    x Biedermeier style
  — Chippendale style
    x Chippendale style
  — Directoire style *(NK1940)*
    x Directoire style
  — Empire style *(NK1370)*
  — Federal style
    x Federal style
  — Georgian style
    x Georgian style (Decoration and
        ornament)
  — Louis-Philippe style
  — Louis XIII style
  — Louis XIV style *(NK1350)*
  — Louis XV style *(NK1355)*
  — Louis XVI style *(NK1360)*
  — Napoléon III style
    See Decoration and ornament—
        Second Empire style
  — Neoclassicism
    xx Neoclassicism (Art)
  — Queen Anne style
    x Queen Anne style
  — Regency style
  — Restoration style
  — Second Empire style
    x Decoration and ornament—
        Napoléon III style
  — Subject headings
    See Subject headings—Decoration and
        ornament
  — Victorian style
Decoration and ornament, Ancient
    (NK1180-1250)
Decoration and ornament, Anglo-Saxon,
    [**French, German, etc.**] *(Direct)*
    x Anglo-Saxon [French, German, etc.]
        decoration and ornament
  — Pictorial works
Decoration and ornament, Architectural
    (Direct) (NA3310-3950)
    sa Fore-edge painting
        Metopes
        Stone carving
    x Architectural decoration and ornament
        Architecture—Decoration and
            ornament
        Stonework, Decorative
    xx Architectural design
        Architecture
        Exterior walls
Decoration and ornament, Baroque *(Direct)*
    (NK1345)
    sa Furniture, Baroque
    x Baroque decoration and ornament

Decoration and ornament, Byzantine
    (NK1265)
    x Byzantine decoration and ornament
Decoration and ornament, Georgian
    (Transcaucasia) *(Direct)*
    x Georgian decoration and ornament
        (Transcaucasia)
Decoration and ornament, Gothic *(NK1295)*
    x Gothic decoration and ornament
    xx Architecture, Gothic
Decoration and ornament, Hindu *(Direct)*
    x Hindu decoration and ornament
Decoration and ornament, Islamic *(Direct)*
    (NK1270-1275)
    x Decoration and ornament, Muslim
        Islamic decoration and ornament
        Muslim decoration and ornament
Decoration and ornament, Jacobean
    (NK1443)
    x Jacobean decoration and ornament
Decoration and ornament, Medieval
    (NK1260-1295)
Decoration and ornament, Merovingian
    (Direct)
    x Merovingian decoration and ornament
Decoration and ornament, Muslim
    See Decoration and ornament, Islamic
Decoration and ornament, Primitive
    (NK1177)
Decoration and ornament, Renaissance
    (NK1330-1339)
    x Renaissance decoration and ornament
Decoration and ornament, Rococo *(Direct)*
    (NK1355)
    sa Furniture, Rococo
    x Rococo decoration and ornament
Decoration and ornament, Romanesque
    (NK1285)
    x Romanesque decoration and ornament
Decoration and ornament, Rustic *(Direct)*
    x Rustic decoration and ornament
Decoration Day
    See Memorial Day
Decoration of food
    See Cookery (Garnishes)
Decorations, Holiday
    See Holiday decorations
Decorations of honor *(Indirect)*
    (CR4501-6305; Military,
    UB430-435)
    sa Heraldry
        Insignia
        Medals
        Orders of knighthood and chivalry
        particular medals, e.g. Dufferin medals;
        and subdivision Medals, badges,
            decorations, etc. *under armies,*
            navies, etc., e.g. United States.
            Army—Medals, badges, decorations,
            etc.
    x Badges of honor
        Honor, Decorations of
    xx Heraldry
        Insignia
        Military paraphernalia
        Orders of knighthood and chivalry—
            Insignia
    — Collectors and collecting
    — Law and legislation *(Direct)*
Decorations of honor, Academic
    (LB2381-2391)
    sa Degrees, Academic
    x Academic decorations of honor
    xx Degrees, Academic
        Learned institutions and societies
Decorations of honor, Papal *(CR5547-5577)* ·
    sa Golden rose (Papal award)
    x Papal decorations of honor

Decorative art
    See Art, Decorative
Decorative arts
    See Art, Decorative
        Art industries and trade
        Arts and crafts movement
        Decoration and ornament
        Design, Decorative
        Interior decoration
        the specific subjects referred to under
            these headings
Decorative balls *(TT896.8)*
    x Balls, Decorative
    xx Decoration and ornament
        Handicraft
Decorative design
    See Design, Decorative
Decorative design, Miniature
    See Miniature decorative design
Decorative lighting
    See Lighting, Architectural and decorative
Decorative metal-work
    See Art metal-work
Decorum in court
    See Conduct of court proceedings
Decoupage
    sa Potichomania
    xx Decoration and ornament
        Design, Decorative
        Paper work
    — Juvenile literature
Decoys (Hunting) *(SK335)*
    xx Duck shooting
        Fowling
        Game and game-birds
        Hunting
    — Pictorial works
Decree laws
    See Delegated legislation
Decree of Canopus *(DT62.S8; PJ1531.C)*
    x Canopus, Decree of
Decremeter *(QL544.D4)*
    xx Electric waves
        Telegraph, Wireless
Decrystallized cotton *(TS1580)*
    xx Cotton
        Cotton manufacture
Decubitus
    See Bed-sores
Dedekind sums
    x Sums, Dedekind
    xx Numbers, Theory of
Dedication, Feast of
    See Hanukkah (Feast of Lights)
Dedication of churches
    See Church dedication
Dedication programs
    See Dedication services
Dedication services *(BV199.D4)*
    sa Cemeteries—Consecration
        Church dedication
        Synagogue dedication services
        Temples, Buddhist—Dedication
    x Consecration programs
        Consecration services
        Dedication programs
        Programs, Consecration
        Programs, Dedication
        Services, Consecration
        Services, Dedication
    xx Liturgies
        Worship programs
Dedication to public use *(Direct)*
    xx Highway law
        Public use
        Real property
Dedications (in books) *(PN171.D4)*
    x Book dedications

Dedications (in books) *(PN171.D4)*
  (Continued)
      Books—Dedications
    xx Authorship
      Books
Deduction (Logic)
  See Logic
Deductive logic
  See Logic
Deeds *(Direct)*
  sa Abstracts of title
      Acknowledgments
      Charters
      Commissioners of deeds
      Conveyancing
      Covenants
      Land titles
      Mortgages
      Real property
      Torrens system
      Vendors and purchasers
  x Documents
      Indentures
  xx Abstracts of title
      Acknowledgments
      Commercial law
      Contracts
      Conveyancing
      Land titles
      Real property
      Vendors and purchasers
  Example under Legal instruments
Deeds, Jewish
  x Jewish deeds
      Starrs
  xx Contracts (Jewish law)
Deeds of trust *(Direct)*
  xx Housing—Finance
      Mortgages
      Securities
      Trust indentures
      Trusts and trustees
Deep borings
  See Borings
Deep diving vehicles
  See Oceanographic submersibles
Deep drawing (Metal-work) *(TS250)*
  x Metals—Deep drawing
  xx Drawing (Metal-work)
      Metals—Cold working
      Sheet-metal work
  — Automation
Deep fat fryers
  See Fryers, Deep fat
Deep-ocean drilling ships
  See Deep-sea drilling ships
Deep-sea deposits
  See Marine sediments
Deep Sea Drilling Project
  x Project, Deep Sea Drilling
  xx Marine sediments
      Submarine geology
      Underwater drilling
Deep-sea drilling ships *(VM453)*
  sa Underwater drilling
  x Deep-ocean drilling ships
      Drilling platforms
      Ocean drilling ships
      Oceanic drilling ships
  xx Oceanographic research ships
      Underwater drilling
Deep-sea exploration
  See Deep-sea sounding
      Marine biology
      Marine fauna
      Marine flora
Deep-sea fishes
  See Fishes, Deep-sea

Deep-sea fishing
  See Big game fishing
      Salt-water fishing
Deep-sea instrument stations
  See Oceanographic research stations
Deep-sea manganese nodules
  See Manganese nodules
Deep-sea mining
  See Ocean mining
Deep-sea moorings
  x Moorings, Deep-sea
      Oceanographic research stations—
        Anchorage
  xx Anchorage
      Oceanographic buoys
Deep-sea research vessels
  See Oceanographic submersibles
Deep-sea sounding *(GC75-78)*
    Subdivided by locality, *e.g.* Deep-sea
      sounding—Atlantic Ocean.
  sa Bathometer
      Echo sounding
      Sea-water
      Submarine topography
  x Deep-sea exploration
      Sea soundings
  xx Sounding and soundings
  — Atlantic Ocean
    Note under Deep-sea sounding
Deep-sea temperature *(GC161-177)*
    Subdivided by locality, *e.g.* Deep-sea
      temperature—Pacific Ocean.
  sa Ocean temperature
  x Sea-water—Temperature
  xx Ocean temperature
      Temperature
  — Pacific Ocean
    Note under Deep-sea temperature
Deep-sea zone
  See Abyssal zone
Deep space probes
  See Space probes
Deep submergence vehicles
  See Oceanographic submersibles
Deep-water drilling
  See Underwater drilling
Deep-water drilling (Petroleum)
  See Oil well drilling, Submarine
Deepavali
  See Divali
Deer *(Indirect)* *(QL737.U5)*
  sa Antelopes
      Caribou
      Elk
      Fallow deer
      Mouse-deer
      Mule deer
      Musk-deer
      Red deer
      Reindeer
      Roe-deer
      Sika deer
      Venison
      White-tailed deer
  xx Ruminantia
  Example under Game and game-birds; Un-
    gulata
  — Anatomy
  — Behavior
  — Diseases
  — Food
    sa Browse
    Example under Animals, Food habits of
  — Juvenile literature
  — Legends and stories
Deer, Fossil *(QE882.U3)*
Deer (in religion, folk-lore, etc.) *(GR730.D4)*
  x Folk-lore of deer

  xx Religion, Primitive
Deer flies
  See Deerflies
Deer-hounds *(SF429.D4)*
  x Scotch deer-hounds
      Stag-hounds
  Example under Hounds
Deer hunting *(Indirect)* *(SK301)*
  sa Mule deer hunting
      Red deer hunting
      White-tailed deer hunting
  Example under Hunting
Deer in art
  xx Art
Deerflies
  x Deer flies
  xx Horseflies
  — Control *(Indirect)*
Defacement of books
  See Books—Mutilation, defacement, etc.
Defacement of manuscripts
  See Manuscripts—Mutilation, defacement,
    etc.
Defalcation
  See Embezzlement
Defamation
  See Libel and slander
Default (Law) *(Direct)*
  sa Contumacy
      Judgments by default
  xx Civil procedure
      Contumacy
      Criminal procedure
Default (Roman law)
  sa Contumacy (Roman law)
  xx Contumacy (Roman law)
Default judgments
  See Judgments by default
Defeasible fees *(Direct)*
  xx Estates (Law)
      Real property
Defeat (Psychology)
  xx Emotions
Defecation *(QP156)*
  sa Bowel and bladder training
      Elimination behavior
      Feces
  xx Eliminative behavior
      Feces
      Intestines
Defectionists
  See Turncoats
Defective and delinquent classes
  See Delinquents
      Handicapped
Defective hearing
  See Hearing disorders
Defective manufactures
  See Manufactures—Defects
Defective products
  See Customer relations
      Products liability
    subdivision Defects *under subjects*
Defective speech
  See Speech, Disorders of
Defective vision
  See Vision disorders
Defectives
  See Delinquents
      Handicapped
Defectors
  See Turncoats
Defects
  See subdivision Defects *under subjects, e.g.*
    Glass—Defects; Leather—Defects;
    Steel—Defects; Wood—Defects
Defects, Point
  See Point defects

Defects in manufactures
    See Manufactures—Defects

Defence (Game) *(GV1469.D3)*

Defender of the bond
    See Defender of the marriage bond

Defender of the marriage bond
    sa Promoters of justice (Canon law)
    x Defender of the bond
    xx Divorce (Canon law)
        Marriage—Annulment (Canon law)
        Marriage (Canon law)
        Matrimonial actions (Canon law)
        Promoters of justice (Canon law)

Defenders, Public
    See Public defenders

Defense, Civil
    See Civil defense

Defense, Perceptual
    See Perceptual defense

Defense (Civil procedure) *(Direct)*
    x Defense (Law)
    xx Actions and defenses
        Civil procedure
        Trial practice

Defense (Courts-martial) *(Direct)*
    x Court martial defenses
    xx Defense (Criminal procedure)

Defense (Criminal procedure) *(Direct)*
    sa Alibi
        Defense (Courts-martial)
        Public defenders
        Right to counsel
    x Criminal defenses
        Defense (Law)
        Defenses, Criminal
    xx Actions and defenses
        Criminal procedure
        Due process of law

Defense (Law)
    See Actions and defenses
        Defense (Civil procedure)
        Defense (Criminal procedure)

Defense (Military science)
    See Attack and defense (Military science)

Defense contracts *(Direct)*
    sa Renegotiation of government contracts
        Research and development contracts
        subdivision Procurement *under armies,*
          navies, etc., e.g. United States.
          Army—Procurement
    x Military contracts
        War contracts
    xx Public contracts
    — Accounting
    — Price policy *(Direct)*
        xx Price policy

Defense economics
    See Disarmament—Economic aspects
        War—Economic aspects

Defense information, Classified *(Direct)*
    sa Atomic weapons information
        Security classification (Government
          documents)
    x Classified defense information
        Military secrets
        Secret defense information
        Secrets, Military
    xx Espionage
        Military policy
        Official secrets

Defense materials system
    See Priorities, Industrial—United States

Defense measures
    See subdivision Defense measures *under*
      subjects, e.g. Gas industry—Defense
      measures; Petroleum industry and
      trade—Defense measures; Telegraph
      —Defense measures; Telephone—
      Defense measures

Defense mechanism test
    xx Personality tests

Defense mechanisms (Physiology)
    See Defense reaction (Physiology)

Defense mechanisms (Psychology)
    sa Compensation (Psychology)
        Conversion (Psychoanalysis)
        Denial (Psychology)
        Displacement (Psychology)
        Fantasy
        Identification (Psychology)
        Projection (Psychology)
        Regression (Psychology)
        Repression (Psychology)
        Sublimation
    x Mechanisms of defense
        Mental mechanisms
    xx Adjustment (Psychology)
        Psychoanalysis

Defense mechanisms (Zoology)
    See Animal defenses
        Animal weapons

Defense mechanisms of animals
    See Animal defenses
        Animal weapons

Defense reaction (Physiology)
    x Defense mechanisms (Physiology)
    xx Physiology

Defense research
    See Military research

Defenses
    See Industrial mobilization

Defenses, Air
    See Air defenses

Defenses, Coast
    See Coast defenses

Defenses, Criminal
    See Defense (Criminal procedure)

Defenses, National
    See subdivision Defenses *under names of*
      countries, e.g. Great
      Britain-Defenses

Defenses, Radar
    See Radar defense networks

Defensive basketball
    See Basketball—Defense

Defensive football
    See Football—Defense

Defensiveness (Psychology)
    sa Aggressiveness (Psychology)
    xx Aggressiveness (Psychology)
        Anxiety

Deference
    See Respect

Deferred compensation *(Direct)*
    x Compensation, Deferred
    xx Wages
    — Taxation *(Direct)*
        xx Income tax
        Tax planning

Deferred rebates
    See Shipping—Rates

Defibrators *(TS1176.6.E7)*
    xx Wood-pulp industry—Equipment and
      supplies
    — Reliability *(TS1176.6.E7)*

Defibrination syndrome
    See Disseminated intravascular coagulation

Deficiency appropriation bills
    See United States—Appropriations and
      expenditures

Deficiency diseases *(RC620-632)*
    sa Ariboflavinosis
        Avitaminosis
        Beri-beri
        Calcium in the body
        Carbohydrates in the body
        Diet
        Kwashiorkor
        Magnesium deficiency diseases
        Malnutrition
        Metabolism
        Minerals in the body
        Nutrition
        Pellagra
        Pigmentation disorders
        Potassium deficiency diseases
        Protein deficiency
        Pyridoxine deficiency diseases
        Rickets
        Trace elements in nutrition
        Vitamins
        Zinc deficiency diseases
    x Diseases, Deficiency
    xx Diet
        Malnutrition
        Metabolism
        Nutrition
        Nutrition disorders
        Vitamins
    — Diagnosis

Deficiency diseases in domestic animals
      (SF780.5)
    sa Grass tetany
        Hypocupremia
        Milk fever in animals
    xx Veterinary medicine

Deficiency diseases in plants *(SB742-3)*
    sa Chlorosis (Plants)
    xx Fertilizers and manures
        Plant diseases
        Plants, Effect of minerals on
        Plants—Nutrition

Deficiency diseases in poultry
    sa Perosis
    xx Poultry—Diseases

Deficit financing *(Direct)*
    x Compensatory spending
        Deficit spending
    xx Finance, Public
        Full employment policies

Deficit spending
    See Deficit financing

Defilements (Buddhism)
    See Vice (Buddhism)

Definability
    See Definition (Logic)

Definition (Logic) *(BC199.D4)*
    sa Semantics (Philosophy)
    x Definability
        Undefinability
    xx Logic
        Meaning (Psychology)
        Predicate (Logic)
        Semantics
        Thought and thinking

Deflation (Finance) *(Direct)*
    xx Currency question
        Depressions
        Economic policy
        Finance
        Money
        Prices

Deflecting force
    See Coriolis force

Defloration *(GN479)*
    sa Jus primae noctis
    xx Marriage customs and rites
        Virginity

Defoaming agents
　　See Antifoaming agents
Defoliation *(QK763)*
　　sa Abscission (Botany)
　　x Leaves—Shedding
　　　Leaves, Shedding of
　　　Shedding of leaves
　　xx Abscission (Botany)
　　　Leaves
　　　Phenology
Deforestation
　　See Clear-cutting
Deformable potential
　　See Deformation potential
Deformation, Rock
　　See Rock deformation
Deformation of surfaces
　　See Surfaces, Deformation of
Deformation potential *(QC612.P6)*
　　x Deformable potential
　　　Potential, Deformation
　　xx Lattice theory
　　　Potential barrier
Deformations, Continuous
　　See Homotopy theory
Deformations (Mechanics) *(Strains and*
　　　　stresses, TG265)
　　sa Buckling (Mechanics)
　　　Continuum mechanics
　　　Creep of concrete
　　　Creep of materials
　　　Creep of metals
　　　Creep of plastics
　　　Dislocations in crystals
　　　Dislocations in metals
　　　Extensometer
　　　Fracture of solids
　　　Plasticity
　　　Residual stresses
　　　Rheology
　　　Rock deformation
　　　Shear (Mechanics)
　　　Strains and stresses
　　　Torsion
　　xx Elastic solids
　　　Mechanics
　　　Rheology
　　　Strains and stresses
Deformities *(Human anatomy, QM691-9;*
　　　　Somatic anthropology, GN68-69.8)
　　sa Birth injuries
　　　De Lange's syndrome
　　　Dwarfs
　　　Ellis-van Creveld syndrome
　　　Fistula, Tracheoesophageal
　　　Giants
　　　Medicine and art
　　　Monsters
　　　Phocomelus
　　　Siamese twins
　　　subdivision Abnormities and
　　　　deformities *under names of organs,*
　　　　regions and systems of the body, e.g.
　　　　Eye—Abnormities and deformities;
　　　　Head—Abnormities and deformities;
　　　　Nervous system—Abnormities and
　　　　deformities
　　x Abnormalities
　　　Birth defects
　　　Congenital malformations
　　　Freaks
　　　Human curiosities
　　　Malformations
　　　Teratology
　　xx Monsters
　　　Mutilation
　　　Orthopedia
　　　Self-mutilation

Surgery
　　Surgery, Primitive
— Causes and theories of causation
　　sa Teratogenic agents
— Classification
— Genetic aspects
　　sa Dysraphia
— Intrauterine diagnosis
　　x Fetus—Abnormities and deformities
　　　—Diagnosis
　　xx Fetus—Abnormities and deformities
　　　Fetus—Diseases—Diagnosis
Deformities, Artificial *(Ethnology, GN477.6)*
　　sa Self-mutilation
　　　subdivision Abnormities and
　　　　deformities *under names of organs*
　　　　and regions of the body
　　x Artificial deformities
Degassing of metals *(TN673)*
　　sa Deoxidizing of metals
　　x Metals—Degassing
　　xx Gases in metals
Degaussing *(VM479)*
　　xx Magnetism of ships
　　　Mines, Submarine
Degema language
　　xx Kwa languages
Degenerate gases, Condensed
　　See Superfluidity
Degeneration *(Biology, QH556; Criminology,*
　　　　HV4961-4998; Sociology, HM111)
　　sa Crime and criminals
　　　Delinquents
　　　Insanity
　　　Insanity, Moral
　　x Decadence
　　xx Crime and criminals
　　　Delinquents
　　　Eugenics
　　　Evolution
　　　Heredity, Human
　　　Sociology
　　　Vice
Degeneration, Fatty
　　sa Fatty liver
　　　Heart, Fatty
　　x Fatty degeneration
　　xx Heart, Fatty
　　Note under Degeneration (Pathology)
Degeneration, Hepatolenticular
　　See Hepatolenticular degeneration
Degeneration (Pathology)
　　　Here are entered works on pathological
　　　degeneration in general. Special
　　　material is entered under the specific
　　　variety, *e.g.* Degeneration, Fatty.
Degeneration of the retina
　　See Retinal degeneration
Deglutition *(QP311)*
　　x Swallowing
　　xx Esophagus
　　　Throat
Degradation, Biological
　　See Biodegradation
Degree days *(Direct) (Heating, TH7225;*
　　　　Petroleum trade, HD9566)
　　xx Atmospheric temperature
　　　Fuel trade
　　　Heating
　　　Industry and weather
Degree mills
　　See Diploma mills
Degrees, Academic *(Indirect)*
　　　　(LB2381-2391)
　　sa Decorations of honor, Academic

　　　names of specific degrees, e.g. Bachelor
　　　　of arts degree; Doctor of philosophy
　　　　degree; *also subdivision* Degrees
　　　　for lists of degrees awarded by
　　　　individual institutions under names
　　　　of institutions, e.g. Harvard
　　　　University—Degrees
　　x Academic degrees
　　　College degrees
　　　Doctors' degrees
　　　Honorary degrees
　　　Titles of degree
　　　University degrees
　　xx Decorations of honor, Academic
　　　Education, Higher
　　　Scholars
　　　Titles of honor and nobility
　　　Universities and colleges
— Abbreviations
— Law and legislation *(Direct)*
Degrees, Doctrine of
　　x Continuous degrees, Doctrine of
　　　Discrete degrees, Doctrine of
　　　Doctrine of degrees
　　xx New Jerusalem Church—Doctrinal and
　　　controversial works
Degrees of latitude and longitude
　　See Geodesy
　　　Latitude
　　　Longitude
Degtiarev machine-gun
　　x Degtyarev machine-gun
　　xx Machine-guns
Degtyarev machine-gun
　　See Degtiarev machine-gun
Dehorning *(SF912)*
　　x Cattle—Dehorning
　　　Horns, Removal of
　　xx Veterinary surgery
Dehu language *(PL6253.Z9D47)*
　　x Lifou language
　　　Lifu language
　　　Miny language
　　xx Melanesian languages
Dehydrated foods
　　See Food, Dried
Dehydrated fruit
　　See Fruit, Dried
Dehydrated milk
　　See Milk, Dried
Dehydrated vegetables
　　See Vegetables, Dried
Dehydrating agents
　　See Drying agents
Dehydration (Physiology)
　　x Body water loss
　　xx Metabolism, Disorders of
Dehydration in infants
　　xx Body fluids
　　　Infants—Diseases
　　　Infants—Mortality
Dehydration of food
　　See Food—Drying
Dehydrofrozen food
　　See Food, Frozen
Dehydrogenases
　　sa Flavoproteins
— Analysis
Dehydrogenation
　　xx Catalysis
　　　Elimination reactions
　　　Reduction, Chemical
Dei gratia (in royal titles)
　　xx Kings and rulers
　　　Titles of honor and nobility
Dei language
　　See Kissi language

Deification
See Apotheosis
Deism (BL2700-2790)
  sa Atheism
    Christianity
    Cosmology
    Free thought
    God
    Positivism
    Rationalism
    Theism
  xx Atheism
    Christianity
    God
    Pantheism
    Rationalism
    Religion
    Theism
    Theology
  — Biography
Deists, Bohemian
  See Abrahamites (Bohemia)
Deities
  See Gods
Dejection
  See Depression, Mental
Dekabrists
  See Decembrists
Deke automobile
  See DKW automobile
Delage automobile (TL215.D)
Delavan's comet (QB723.D)
Delaware
  — History (F161-175)
  — — Colonial period, ca. 1600-1775
  — — Revolution, 1775-1783 (E263.D3)
  — — War of 1812 (E359.5.D3)
  — — Civil War, 1861-1865 (E500)
  — Juvenile literature
Delaware Indians (E99.D2)
  sa Hackensack Indians
    Indians of North America—Wars—
      1790-1794
    Moravian Indians
  x Lenape Indians
    Lenni Lenape
    Linapi
  xx Algonquian Indians
    Indians of North America
  — Government relations
  — Juvenile literature
  — Missions
  — Names
    Example under Indians of North America
      —Names
Delaware language (PM1031-4)
  sa Algonquian languages
  x Lenape language
    Lenni Lenape language
  xx Algonquian languages
    Munsee language
Delaware River estuary
  Example under Estuaries
Delaware River watershed
  Example under Watersheds—[local subdivi-
    sion]
Delay circuits
  See Delay lines
Delay devices
  See Delay lines
Delay lines
  x Artificial delay lines
    Delay circuits
    Delay devices
    Time-delay networks
  xx Automatic control
    Automatic timers
    Electric waves

    Electronics
    Waves
Delayage (Car service)
  See Demurrage (Car service)
Delayed-action preparations (RS201.D4)
  x Prolonged-action preparations
    Prolonged-release drugs
    Sustained-release drugs
Delayed hypersensitivity
  See Cellular immunity
Delayed neutrons
  xx Beta decay
    Neutrons
    Nuclear fission
Delayed protons
  xx Nuclear fission
    Protons
Deleage's disease
  See Myotonia atrophica
Delegated legislation (Direct)
  sa Executive orders
    War and emergency legislation
  x Administrative regulations
    Administrative rules
    Decree laws
    Delegation of legislative power
    Quasi-legislation
    Regulations, Administrative
    Rules, Administrative
  xx Delegation of powers
    Executive power
    Legislation
    Legislative power
    Separation of powers
Delegating of authority
  See Delegation of authority
Delegation (Civil law) (Direct)
  sa Expromission
    Negotiable instruments
    Suretyship and guaranty
  xx Contracts
    Debtor and creditor
    Extinguishment of debts
    Novation
    Suretyship and guaranty
  Example under Civil law
  — Conflict of laws
    See Conflict of laws—Delegation
Delegation of authority
  x Authority, Delegation of
    Delegating of authority
  xx Executive ability
    Industrial management
    Management
Delegation of legislative power
  See Delegated legislation
Delegation of powers (Direct) (JF225;
    JK-JQ)
  sa Delegated legislation
    Judicial review
    Separation of powers
    War and emergency powers
  x Powers, Delegation of
  xx Administrative law
    Constitutional law
    Executive power
    Judicial power
    Legislative power
    Political science
    Separation of powers
Delegation of powers (Canon law)
  xx Jurisdiction (Canon law)
Delépine reaction
  xx Chemical reactions
Delfin (Training planes)
  x L-29 (Training planes)
  xx Jet planes
    Training planes

Delft in art
Delft in literature
Delft ware (NK4295)
  Example under Pottery
Delhi
  — Siege, 1857 (DS478)
    xx India—History—Sepoy Rebellion,
      1857-1858
Delhi boil
  See Leishmaniasis, Cutaneous
Delian League, First, 5th century, B.C.
  (DF227.5)
Delian League, Second, 4th century, B.C.
  (DF231.2)
Delian problem
  See Cube, Duplication of
Delicatessen
  xx Food industry and trade
Delinquency, Juvenile
  See Juvenile delinquency
Delinquency prediction
  See Criminal behavior, Prediction of
Delinquent classes
  See Delinquents
Delinquent girls (Direct)
  sa Delinquent women
    Unmarried mothers
  x Girls as criminals
    Girls, Delinquent
  xx Delinquent women
    Delinquents
    Girls
    Juvenile delinquency
Delinquent women (Direct) (HV6046)
  sa Delinquent girls
    Reformatories for women
  x Female offenders
    Woman—Crime
    Women as criminals
    Women, Delinquent
    Women delinquents
    Women offenders
  xx Crime and criminals
    Delinquent girls
    Woman—Social and moral questions
Delinquents (Direct)
  sa Castration of criminals and defectives
    Crime and criminals
    Degeneration
    Delinquent girls
    Education and crime
    Heredity, Human
    Idiocy
    Incorrigibles (Juvenile delinquency)
    Inefficiency, Intellectual
    Insanity
    Juvenile delinquency
    Problem children
    Social work with delinquents and
      criminals
    Vice
  x Defective and delinquent classes
    Defectives
    Delinquent classes
  xx Crime and criminals
    Degeneration
    Handicapped
    Heredity, Human
    Social problems
  — Education
    sa Education of prisoners
Delirium (RC48; RC106; RC610, etc.)
Delirium tremens (RC368)
  xx Alcoholic psychoses
Delivered pricing
  sa Basing-point system
    C.I.F. clause
  x Freight-absorption system

Delivered pricing *(Continued)*
  xx C.I.F. clause
Delivery (Transfer of possession)
  See Delivery of goods (Law)
Delivery of goods *(HF5761-5780)*
  sa Airdrop
    Shipment of goods
  x Store delivery services
  xx Business
    Commerce
    Shipment of goods
    Transportation
  — Programmed instruction
Delivery of goods (Law) *(Direct)*
  x Delivery (Transfer of possession)
  xx Contracts
    Performance (Law)
    Sales
Delivery orders *(Direct)*
  xx Commercial law
Della Cruscans (English writers) *(PR1219)*
Delphian oracle *(DF261.D35)*
  x Delphic oracle
  xx Cultus, Greek
    Oracles, Greek
Delphic oracle
  See Delphian oracle
Delphinium
  x Larkspur
  Example under Stock poisoning plants
Delsarte system *(GV463; PN4157)*
  sa Expression
  xx Elocution
    Expression
    Physical education and training
Delta (Jet planes)
  See Fairey Delta (Jet planes)
Delta Kappa Epsilon
  Example under Greek letter societies
Delta modulation
  xx Pulse-code modulation
Delta plan, Netherlands
  x Deltaplan
Delta rays *(QC721)*
  sa Alpha rays
  xx Alpha rays
    Electrons
    Radiation
    Radioactivity
Delta wings (Aeroplanes)
  See Aeroplanes—Wings, Triangular
Deltaplan
  See Delta plan, Netherlands
Deltas
  sa Alluvial plains
    subdivision Delta *under names of*
      rivers, e.g. Mississippi River—Delta
  xx Alluvial plains
    Rivers
Deltatheridia
  xx Insectivora, Fossil
Deluge *(Bible, BS658; Geology, QE507)*
  sa Noah's ark
  x Flood, Biblical
  xx Catastrophes (Geology)
    Creation
    Earth
    Geology
  — Comparative studies *(BL325.D4)*
  — Juvenile literature
Deluge (Hinduism) *(BL1215.D45)*
  x Flood (Hinduism)
  xx Hinduism
Deluge in art
  xx Art
Deluge in literature
Delusional insanity
  See Paranoia

Delusions
  See Errors, Popular
    Hallucinations and illusions
    Impostors and imposture
    Medical delusions
    Superstition
    Swindlers and swindling
    Witchcraft
Delusions (Buddhism)
  See Vice (Buddhism)
Deluxe editions
  See Bibliography—Fine editions
Demagnetization, Adiabatic
  See Adiabatic demagnetization
Demand and supply
  See Supply and demand
Demarcation line of Alexander VI *(E123)*
  x Bull of demarcation
    Line of demarcation of Alexander VI
Deme *(Ancient Greece, JC75.D)*
Dementia
  sa Schizophrenia
  xx Insanity
Dementia, Presenile
  See Presenile dementia
Dementia praecox
  See Schizophrenia
Demerol
  See Isonipecaine
Demesne, Royal
  See Crown lands
Demianov rearrangement
  See Demjanov rearrangement
Demilunes of Heidenhain
  See Salivary glands
Demineralization of saline waters
  See Saline water conversion
Demjanov rearrangement
  x Demianov rearrangement
    Demjanow rearrangement
    Demyanov rearrangement
  xx Rearrangements (Chemistry)
Demjanow rearrangement
  See Demjanov rearrangement
Demobilization
  See subdivision Demobilization *and*
    Mobilization *under armies, navies,*
    etc., e.g. United States. Army—
    Demobilization
Democracy *(JC421-458)*
  sa Aristocracy
    Despotism
    Equality
    Federal government
    Liberty
    Middle classes
    Monarchy
    Referendum
    Representative government and
      representation
    Republics
    Socialism
    Suffrage
  x Self-government
  xx Aristocracy
    Consensus (Social sciences)
    Constitutional history
    Constitutional law
    Despotism
    Equality
    Federal government
    Monarchy
    Political science
    Representative government and
      representation
    Republics
  — Juvenile literature
  — Public opinion

  — Songs and music
Democracy and Christianity
  See Christianity and democracy
Democracy in education
  See Self-government (in education)
Democratic Party *(JK2311-2319)*
  Subdivided by locality, *e.g.* Democratic
    Party. Connecticut.
  Example under Political parties
Democratic Party. Connecticut
  Note under Democratic Party
Demodulators
  See Radio detectors
Demogorgon (Roman deity) in literature
Demographers *(Direct)*
  x Population specialists
  xx Demography
Demographic Computer Library
  See DCL (Electronic computer system)
Demography *(HB881-3700)*
  sa Demographers
    Fertility, Human
    Geopolitics
    Mortality
    Population
    Population forecasting
    Vital statistics
    War—Casualties (Statistics, etc.)
    subdivision Population *under names of*
      countries, e.g. France—Population
  xx Economics
    Geopolitics
    Population
    Vital statistics
  — Mathematical models
  — Methodology
  — Problems, exercises, etc.
  — Research grants *(Direct)*
  — Study and teaching *(Direct)*
Demolition, Military *(UG370)*
  x Military demolition
  xx Explosives, Military
    Military art and science
    Military field engineering
    Obstacles (Military science)
Demolition derbies, Automobile
  See Auto demolition derbies
Demon automobile
  See Dodge Demon automobile
Demoniac possession *(New Testament,*
    BS2545.D5; Occult sciences,
    BF1555)
  sa Demonomania
    Satanism
    Spirit possession
  x Possession, Demoniac
  xx Demonomania
    Hysteria
    Satanism
    Spirit possession
Demoniac possession in art
Demonology *(Comparative religion, BL480;*
    Folk-lore, GR525-540; Occult
    sciences, BF1501-1561; Theology,
    BT975)
  sa Amulets
    Apparitions
    Charms
    Curetes
    Demonomania
    Devil
    Devil-worship
    Discernment of spirits
    Evil eye
    Exorcism
    Jinn
    Magic
    Occult sciences

Poltergeists
Satanism
Superman
Superstition
Witchcraft
x Demonology, Christian
Demonology—Comparative studies
Evil spirits
xx Apparitions
Devil
Devil-worship
Exorcism
Ghosts
Occult sciences
Spirits
Superstition
Witchcraft
— Biblical teaching
— Comparative studies
See Demonology
Demonology, Buddhist
x Buddhist demonology
xx Buddhist doctrines
Demonology, Indic
Spirits (Buddhism)
Demonology, Christian
See Demonology
Demonology, French, [Germanic, etc.]
(BL660-2630)
x French [Germanic, etc.] demonology
Demonology, Indic
sa Demonology, Buddhist
x Indic demonology
Demonology, Islamic (BP166.89)
x Demonology, Muslim
Islamic demonology
Muslim demonology
xx Spirits (Islam)
Demonology, Lamaist
x Lamaist demonology
xx Lamaism
Demonology, Muslim
See Demonology, Islamic
Demonomania (RC616)
sa Demoniac possession
Exorcism
Witchcraft
x Demonopathy
xx Demoniac possession
Demonology
Hysteria
Witchcraft
Demonopathy
See Demonomania
Demonstration, False (Law)
See False demonstration (Law)
Demonstration centers in education (Direct)
sa Laboratory schools
x Educational workshops
xx Educational innovations
Laboratory schools
Regional educational laboratories
Teachers, Training of
Teaching demonstrations
Demonstration schools
See Laboratory schools
Demonstration teaching
See Teaching demonstrations
Demonstrations (Indirect)
Here are entered works on large public
gatherings, marches, etc., organized
for non-violent protest or affirmation,
even though incidental disturbances or
incipient rioting may occur.
sa Riots
x Public demonstrations
xx Crowds
Public meetings

Riots
Demonstrative evidence
See Evidence, Demonstrative
Demospongea
See Demospongiae
Demospongia
See Demospongiae
Demospongiae (Indirect)
sa Poecilosclerida
x Demospongea
Demospongia
xx Sponges
Demospongiae, Fossil (QE775)
Demotic inscriptions
See Egyptian language—Inscriptions
Demotic writing
See Egyptian language—Papyri, Demotic
Egyptian language—Writing, Demotic
Demountable buildings
See Buildings, Prefabricated
Demountable houses
See Prefabricated houses
Demurrage
sa Lay days
xx Carriers
Freight and freightage
Lay days
Shipping
Demurrage (Car service) (HE1826)
x Car service (Freight)
Delayage (Car service)
Freight-car service
xx Railroads—Freight
Demurrer
See Pleading
Demyanov rearrangement
See Demjanov rearrangement
Demyelination
sa Cerebral sclerosis, Diffuse
Encephalomyelitis
Multiple sclerosis
xx Nervous system—Diseases
Demythologization (BS2378)
Here are entered works dealing with a
method of New Testament interpreta-
tion proposed first by Rudolf Bult-
mann. To demythologize is to translate
the "Mythological" discourse of the
New Testament into existential (or an-
thropological) terminology.
sa Communication (Theology)
Myth
Myth in the Old Testament
xx Bible. N.T.—Criticism, interpretation,
etc.
Christianity—Essence, genius, nature
Eschatology
Existentialism
History—Philosophy
Myth
Mythology
Ontology
Denarius (Coin)
xx Coins, Roman
Denarius Sancti Petri
See Peter's pence
Denaturalization
See Citizenship, Loss of
Denatured alcohol
See Alcohol, Denatured
Denazification (D802.G3)
x Germany—Denazification
xx Germany—History—Allied occupation,
1945-
Germany—Politics and government—
1945-
Nationalsozialistische Deutsche
Arbeiter-Partei

Reconstruction (1939-1951)—Germany
Denca language
See Dinka language
Dendi dialect
xx Songhai language
Dendrites
xx Neurons
Dendrochronology (Direct) (QC883)
sa Meteorology—Periodicity
Rain and rainfall
x Dendroclimatology
Tree-ring analysis
Tree-ring hydrology
xx Archaeology—Methodology
Chronology
Climatology
Meteorology—Periodicity
Paleoclimatology
Rain and rainfall
Tree-rings
Dendroclimatology
See Dendrochronology
Dendrology
See Trees
Dendrometer (SD555)
xx Forests and forestry—Mensuration
Déné Indians
See Tinne Indians
Denervation
xx Nervous system—Surgery
Denghil Tepe, Siege of, 1880-1881
See Geok-Tepe—Siege, 1880-1881
Dengue (RC137)
sa Three-day sickness of cattle
xx Hemorrhagic fever
— Prevention
Denial (Psychology)
xx Defense mechanisms (Psychology)
Denial of justice (Direct) (General, K;
International law, JX4263.D45)
sa Bias (Law)
Exhaustion of local remedies
(International law)
x Justice, Denial of
xx Administrative responsibility
Bias (Law)
Diplomatic protection
Government liability
International law
Jurisdiction
Justice, Administration of
Misconduct in office
Denial of justice (Germanic law)
Denial of self
See Self-denial
Denim (TS1580)
sa Jeans (Clothing)
Denitrification
See Nitrification
Dēnjong-ké language
See Dänjong-kä language
Denka language
See Dinka language
Denmark
— History (DL101-291)
— — To 1241
— — 1241-1397
— — 1241-1660
— — 1397-1448
sa Kalmar, Union of, 1397
— — 1448-1660
sa Hemmingstedt, Battle of, 1500
— — The Count's War, 1534-1536
— — Coup d'état, 1536
— — Northern Seven Years' War, 1563-1570
See Northern Seven Years' War,
1563-1570
— — Dano-Swedish Wars, 1643-1660

Denmark
— History *(DL101-291)*
— — Dano-Swedish Wars, 1643-1660
(Continued)
    See Dano-Swedish Wars,
        1643-1645
        Dano-Swedish Wars,
        1657-1660
— — Coup d'état, 1660
— — 1660-1814
    sa Copenhagen—Bombardment by
        the English, 1807
— — Coup d'état, 1784
— — 1789-1900
— — 19th century
— — War of 1807-1814
— — 1814-1849
— — 1849-1866
    sa Schleswig-Holstein question
        Schleswig-Holstein War,
        1848-1850
        Schleswig-Holstein War, 1864
— — 1900-
— — German occupation, 1940-1945
    x German occupation of Denmark,
        1940-1945
— — — Foreign public opinion
— — — Juvenile literature
Denmark in art
Denmark in literature
Dennewitz, Battle of, 1813
    xx Napoléon I, Emperor of the French,
        1769-1821—Campaigns of
        1813-1814
Denning's comet *(QB723.D4)*
Denominational colleges
    See Church colleges
Denominational schools
    See Church schools
Denominations, Religious
    See Religions
        Sects
        particular denominations and sects
Denominative
    See Grammar, Comparative and general—
        Denominative
        subdivision Denominative *under names*
        of languages and groups of languages
Dense plasma focus *(QC718.5.D38)*
    x Plasma focus
    xx Plasma (Ionized gases)
Densified wood
    See Wood, Compressed
Densitometer (Meteorological instrument)
    (QC880)
    xx Atmospheric density
        Meteorological instruments
— Calibration
Densitometry, Bone
    See Bone densitometry
Density
    See Sea-water—Density
        Specific gravity
        subdivision Density *under subjects, e.g.*
        Earth—Density; Sea-water—Density
Density, Atmospheric
    See Atmospheric density
Density, Electric
    See Electric charge and distribution
Density altitude computers *(TL557.D4)*
    x Computers, Density altitude
        Pressure altitude computers
        Pressure height computers
    xx Aeronautical instruments
        Atmospheric pressure
        Atmospheric temperature
        Meteorological instruments
        Meteorology in aeronautics

Density currents
    sa Turbidity currents
    x Convection, Gravitational
        Currents, Density
        Gravitational convection
    xx Jets
        Mixing
        Turbulence
Dental amalgams
    xx Amalgams
        Dental materials
        Fillings (Dentistry)
Dental anatomy
    See Teeth
Dental anesthesia
    See Anesthesia in dentistry
Dental arch
    xx Mandible
        Maxilla
— Atlases
Dental assistants *(Direct)*
    xx Allied health personnel
        Dental hygienists
Dental bacteriology
    See Mouth—Bacteriology
Dental calculus
    x Calculus, Dental
    xx Dental deposits
Dental care *(Direct)*
    sa Community dental services
        Insurance, Dental
        subdivision Dental care *under specific*
        subjects, e.g. Aged—Dental care;
        Sick—Dental care
    xx Medical care
Dental care, Cost of *(Direct)*
    x Cost of dental care
    xx Medical care, Cost of
    Note under Dental economics
Dental care, Military
    See United States—Armed Forces—Dental
        care
Dental care, Prepaid
    See Insurance, Dental
Dental caries
    xx Teeth—Diseases
— Prevention
    xx Teeth—Care and hygiene
— Research
    See Dental caries research
Dental caries research
    x Dental caries—Research
    xx Dental research
        Research
Dental ceramics
    See Dentistry—Ceramics
Dental chemistry *(RK290)*
    sa Dental materials
    x Chemistry, Dental
    xx Chemistry
Dental clinics *(Direct) (RK3)*
    sa Group dental practice
    x Clinics, Dental
        Dentistry—Clinics
    xx Charities, Medical
        Clinics
— Design and construction *(RK3)*
Dental colleges
    See Dental schools
Dental communication
    See Communication in dentistry
Dental deposits
    sa Dental calculus
        Dental plaques
    x Deposits, Dental
    xx Teeth—Diseases
— Examination

Dental economics *(Direct)*
    Here are entered works on the economic
        aspects of dental service from the point
        of view of both the dentist and the pub-
        lic. Works on special aspects of dental
        economics are entered under specific
        headings, *e.g.* Dental care, Cost of.
    sa Group dental practice
    xx Medical economics
— Public opinion
Dental enamel
    See Enamel, Dental
Dental ethics
    xx Medical ethics
Dental fees *(Direct)*
    sa Medical fees
    x Dentistry—Fees
        Dentists—Fees
    xx Dentists—Salaries, pensions, etc.
        Fees, Professional
        Medical economics
        Medical fees
Dental fillings
    See Fillings (Dentistry)
Dental focal infection
    See Focal infection, Dental
Dental group practice
    See Group dental practice
Dental health and nutrition
    See Nutrition and dental health
Dental health education *(Direct)*
    x Teeth—Care and hygiene—Study and
        teaching
    xx Dentistry—Study and teaching
        Health education
        School hygiene
Dental hygiene
    Here are entered works on dental hygiene
        as practiced by dental hygienists.
        Works on dental hygiene for the lay-
        man are entered under Teeth—Care
        and hygiene.
    xx Teeth—Care and hygiene
    Note under Teeth—Care and hygiene
— Examinations, questions, etc.
Dental hygienists *(Direct)*
    sa Dental assistants
        Dental technicians
    xx Allied health personnel
        Dental technicians
        Dentists
Dental implantation
    See Implant dentures
Dental impression materials *(RK658)*
    sa Plaster casts, Dental
    x Impression materials, Dental
    xx Dental materials
        Plaster casts, Dental
Dental instruments and apparatus *(RK681-6)*
    sa Dental materials
        Orthodontic appliances
        Universal appliance (Dentistry)
    x Dental supplies
        Instruments, Dental
— Catalogs
— Sterilization
    Example under Sterilization
Dental insurance
    See Insurance, Dental
Dental jurisprudence *(Direct) (RA1062)*
    x Dentistry, Forensic
        Dentistry—Jurisprudence
        Forensic dentistry
        Jurisprudence, Dental
    xx Medical jurisprudence
Dental laboratories
    x Laboratories, Dental
    xx Medical laboratories

— Management
Dental laws and legislation *(Direct)*
    (RK4-15)
    x Dentists—Legal status, laws, etc.
    Law, Dental
— Programmed instruction
Dental libraries *(Z675.D3)*
    x Libraries, Dental
Dental materia medica
    See Materia medica, Dental
Dental materials *(RK652.5)*
    sa Acrylic resins
        Dental amalgams
        Dental impression materials
    xx Dental chemistry
        Dental instruments and apparatus
— Programmed instruction
— Specifications
Dental medicine
    See Teeth—Diseases
        Therapeutics, Dental
Dental metallurgy
    See Dentistry—Metallurgy
Dental nerve
    See Alveolar nerve
Dental nerves
    See Teeth—Innervation
Dental orthopedics
    See Orthodontia
Dental pathology
    See Teeth—Diseases
Dental personnel
    xx Medical personnel
— Salaries, pensions, etc.
Dental pharmacology *(Indirect)* *(RK701)*
    sa Materia medica, Dental
    xx Materia medica, Dental
        Pharmacology
Dental photography
    See Photography, Dental
Dental pins *(RK667.P5)*
Dental plaques
    x Plaques, Dental
    xx Dental deposits
        Mouth—Bacteriology
Dental plaster casts
    See Plaster casts, Dental
Dental prosthesis
    See Prosthodontics
Dental public health *(Direct)*
    sa Community dental services
    x Dentistry in public health
        Public health dentistry
    xx Community dental services
        Hygiene, Public
    Note under Dental surveys
— Law and legislation *(Direct)*
— Programmed instruction
Dental pulp
    sa Dentin
    x Pulp, Dental
    xx Dentin
        Teeth
Dental research *(Direct)* *(RK80)*
    sa Dental caries research
    x Dentistry—Research
    xx Medical research
        Research
Dental schools *(Direct)*
    x Dental colleges
    xx Dentistry—Study and teaching
— Entrance examinations
    xx Dentistry—Examinations, questions,
        etc.
— Entrance requirements
Dental service in hospitals
    See Hospital dental service

Dental supplies
    See Dental instruments and apparatus
Dental surgery
    See Dentistry, Operative
Dental surveys
    Here are entered works on the techniques
    employed, and reports, etc. of in-
    dividual surveys; the latter are entered
    also under the heading Dental public
    health, subdivided by the name of a
    country or other place concerned.
    xx Surveys
Dental technicians *(Direct)*
    sa Dental hygienists
    xx Allied health personnel
        Dental hygienists
        Dentistry—Ceramics
        Prosthodontics
Dental therapeutics
    See Therapeutics, Dental
Dentifrices
    x Tooth paste
        Toothpaste
    xx Teeth—Care and hygiene
        Toilet preparations
— Packaging
Dentin
    sa Dental pulp
    xx Dental pulp
        Teeth
— Spectra
Dentistry *(Indirect)* *(RK)*
    sa Communication in dentistry
        Diagnosis, Radioscopic
        Electricity in dentistry
        Hypnotism in dentistry
        Indians of Mexico—Dentistry
        Industrial dentistry
        Mouth
        Occlusion (Dentistry)
        Orthodontia
        Pedodontia
        Periodontia
        Preventive dentistry
        Prosthodontics
        Teeth
        Television in dentistry
        Therapeutics, Dental
        Veterinary dentistry
        headings beginning with the word
            Dental
    xx Medicine
        Teeth
— Ability testing
— Accounting
— Atlases
— Caricatures and cartoons *(NC1763.D3)*
— Ceramics *(RK655)*
    sa Dental technicians
    x Ceramics, Dental
        Dental ceramics
— Clinics
    See Dental clinics
— Early works to 1800 *(RK50)*
— Examinations, questions, etc. *(RK57)*
    sa Dental schools—Entrance
        examinations
— Fees
    See Dental fees
— Film catalogs
— History *(Indirect)*
— International cooperation
— Jurisprudence
    See Dental jurisprudence
— Juvenile literature
— Laboratory manuals *(RK652)*
— Metallurgy *(RK653)*
    x Dental metallurgy

Metallurgy, Dental
— Pictorial works
— Popular works *(RK61)*
— Practice *(RK58)*
    sa Group dental practice
        Orthodontia—Practice
— Psychological aspects *(RK53)*
    x Dentistry, Psychosomatic
        Psychosomatic dentistry
— Research
    See Dental research
— Scholarships, fellowships, etc.
— Study and teaching *(Direct)*
    (RK71-231)
    sa Dental health education
        Dental schools
        Moving-pictures in dentistry
— Subject headings
    See Subject headings—Dentistry
— Terminology
Dentistry, Forensic
    See Dental jurisprudence
Dentistry, Military
    sa Dentistry, Naval
        Veterans—Dental care
    x Military dentistry
    xx Medicine, Military
        Surgery, Military
Dentistry, Naval
    x Naval dentistry
    xx Dentistry, Military
Dentistry, Operative *(RK501-555)*
    sa Anesthesia in dentistry
        Fillings (Dentistry)
        Inlays (Dentistry)
        Teeth—Abnormities and deformities
        Teeth—Extraction
        Teeth—Transplantation
    x Dental surgery
        Operative dentistry
        Surgery, Dental
    xx Teeth—Extraction
— Atlases
Dentistry, Preventive
    See Preventive dentistry
Dentistry, Prosthetic
    See Prosthodontics
Dentistry, Psychosomatic
    See Dentistry—Psychological aspects
Dentistry, Talmudic
    See Talmud—Medicine, hygiene, etc.
Dentistry, Veterinary
    See Veterinary dentistry
Dentistry and nutrition
    See Nutrition and dental health
Dentistry as a profession *(RK60)*
    xx Dentists
Dentistry in art *(N8217.D6)*
    xx Art
Dentistry in public health
    See Dental public health
Dentists *(Direct)* *(RK)*
    sa Dental hygienists
        Dentistry as a profession
        Negro dentists
        Orthodontists
        Periodontists
    xx Medical personnel
— Correspondence, reminiscences, etc.
        (Biography: collective, RK41;
        individual, RK43)
— Diseases and hygiene
— Fees
    See Dental fees
— Juvenile literature
— Legal status, laws, etc.
    See Dental laws and legislation
— Pensions

Dentists *(Direct) (RK)*
— Pensions *(Continued)*
    See Dentists—Salaries, pensions, etc.
— Salaries, pensions, etc.
    sa Dental fees
    x Dentists—Pensions
— Taxation *(Direct)*
Dentition *(Direct) (Anthropology, GN209;*
    Children, RK285)
    sa Teeth
    x Teething
    xx Children—Diseases
       Teeth
    Note under Teeth
Dentures, Complete
    See Complete dentures
Dentures, Partial
    See Partial dentures
Denudation, Chemical
    See Chemical denudation
Denunciation (Canon law)
    x Denuntiatio evangelica
       Denuntiatio judicialis
       Evangelical denunciation
    xx Catholic Church—Discipline
       Criminal law (Canon law)
Denuntiatio evangelica
    See Denunciation (Canon law)
Denuntiatio judicialis
    See Denunciation (Canon law)
Denver. Juvenile Court of the City and
    County of Denver
    Example under Juvenile courts
Deodorization
    xx Odor control
       Odors
Deontic logic *(BC145)*
    x Logic, Deontic
    xx Duty
       Modality (Logic)
Deontological proof of God
    See God—Proof, Moral
Deontology
    See Duty
       Ethics
Deoxidizing of metals *(TN673)*
    x Metals—Deoxidizing
       Metals, Deoxidizing of
    xx Degassing of metals
       Gases in metals
Deoxy . . .
    x Desoxy . . .
Deoxy sugars
    xx Sugars
Deoxyribonucleic acid repair
    x Repair mechanisms in DNA
    xx Radiogenetics
Deoxyribose synthesis
    xx Biosynthesis
Department chairmen (High schools)
    See Departmental chairmen (High schools)
Department chairmen (Universities)
    See Departmental chairmen (Universities)
Department stores *(Direct) (HF5461-5;*
    Employees, HD7515; Taxation,
    HJ5669.D3)
    sa Chain stores
       Store detectives
       Variety stores
    x Stores, Department
    xx Business
       Chain stores
       Mercantile buildings
       Retail trade
       Stores, Retail
       Variety stores
— Accounting *(HF5686.D5)*
— Employees *(Direct)*

sa Department stores—Vocational
    guidance
— — Juvenile literature
— Job descriptions
— Juvenile literature
— Law and legislation *(Direct)*
— Seasonal variations
— Taxation *(Direct)*
— Vocational guidance
    xx Department stores—Employees
Departmental chairmen (Colleges)
    See Departmental chairmen (Universities)
Departmental chairmen (High schools)
    (Direct)
    x Chairmen, Departmental (High schools)
       Department chairmen (High schools)
       Heads of departments (High schools)
    xx High schools—Administration
Departmental chairmen (Universities)
    (Direct)
    x Department chairmen (Universities)
       Departmental chairmen (Colleges)
    xx College administrators
       Universities and colleges—
       Administration
Departmental libraries in universities
    See Libraries, University and college—
       Departmental libraries
Departmental salaries
    See subdivision Officials and employees—
       Salaries, allowances, etc. *under*
       names of countries, cities, etc., e.g.
       United States—Officials and
       employees—Salaries, allowances, etc.
       and subdivision Appointments,
       promotions, salaries, etc. *under*
       names of departments or institutions,
       e.g. United States. Dept. of
       Agriculture—Appointments,
       promotions, salaries, etc.
Departmental system of teaching
    See Teaching, Departmental system of
Depas
    x Depas amphikypellon
    xx Drinking vessels
       Vases, Greek
— Classification
Depas amphikypellon
    See Depas
Dependability
    See Reliability
Dependencies
    See Colonies
Dependency (Psychology)
    xx Interpersonal relations
Dependent origination (Buddhism)
    See Pratītyasamutpāda
Dependents of military personnel
    See Air Force wives
       Army wives
       Children of military personnel
       Marine Corps wives
       Navy wives
Depersonalization
    x Identity, Loss of
       Loss of identity
    xx Personality, Disorders of
Depilation
    See Hair, Removal of
Depletion allowances *(Direct)*
    xx Tax deductions
Depolarization of muons
    See Muons—Depolarization
Depolarizing agents, Neuromuscular
    See Neuromuscular depolarizing agents
Depolarizing muscle relaxants
    See Neuromuscular depolarizing agents

Deportation *(Direct) (International law,*
    JX4261)
    sa Aliens
       Asylum, Right of
       Citizenship
       Exiles
       Expatriation
       Extradition
       Self-determination, National
       Chinese in Canada; Chinese in the
       United States; Japanese in the
       United States; *and similar headings;*
       also subdivision Emigration and
       immigration *under names of*
       countries, e.g. United States—
       Emigration and immigration
    x Expulsion
    xx Aliens
       Citizenship
       Crimes against humanity
       Emigration and immigration law
       Exiles
       Expatriation
       Extradition
Deposit banking *(Direct)*
    sa Bank deposits
       Checks
       Public depositaries
       Savings-banks
    x Banks and banking, Deposit
    xx Banks and banking
       Checks
Deposit insurance
    See Insurance, Deposit
Deposit libraries
    See Libraries, Storage
Deposit of books
    See Legal deposit (of books, etc.)
Depositaries, Public
    See Public depositaries
Depositaries for public moneys
    See Public depositaries
Deposition, Electrophoretic
    See Electrophoretic deposition
Deposition (Canon law)
    See Catholic Church—Clergy—Deposition
Deposition and sedimentation
    See Sedimentation and deposition
Depositions *(Direct)*
    xx Affidavits
       Evidence (Law)
       Witnesses
Depositories, Night (Banking)
    See Banks and banking—Night and curb
       depositories
Depositories, Public
    See Public depositaries
Depository copies
    See Legal deposit (of books, etc.)
Depository libraries
    See Libraries, Depository
Deposits, Bank
    See Bank deposits
Deposits, Deep-sea
    See Marine sediments
Deposits, Dental
    See Dental deposits
Deposits, Hydrothermal
    See Hydrothermal deposits
Deposits (Law) *(Direct)*
    Here are entered general works and also
    those specifically on naked bailments
    of goods to be kept for the depositors.
    Deposits in the sense of payment to
    bind a bargain are entered under the
    heading Earnest. Deposits paid into a
    court to discharge an obligation are en-
    tered under the heading Consignation.

sa Bailments
    Consignation
    Earnest
    Escrows
xx Bailments
    Consignation
    Pledges (Law)
    Real contracts (Civil law)
    Security (Law)
Deposits (Roman-Dutch law)
Deposits (Roman law)
Depots (Transportation)
   See Terminals (Transportation)
Depravity
   See Sin, Original
Depreciation *(HF5681.D5)*
  sa Depreciation allowances
    Economic life (of economic goods)
    Replacement of industrial equipment
  x Obsolescence (Accounting)
  xx Accounting
    Bookkeeping
    Corporation reserves
    Economic life (of economic goods)
    Reserves (Accounting)
  — Tables, etc.
Depreciation allowances *(Direct)*
  sa Amortization deductions
    Investment tax credit
  xx Depreciation
    Tax deductions
Depressants
   See Sedatives
Depressed classes of India
   See Untouchables
Depression, Mental *(BF173)*
  sa Antidepressants
    Manic-depressive psychoses
  x Dejection
    Depressive psychoses
    Mental depression
  xx Insanity
    Manic-depressive psychoses
    Melancholia
    Neurasthenia
    Neuroses
    Psychology, Pathological
  — Personal narratives
  — Physiological aspects
Depression glass
  x Glass, Depression
  xx Glassware
Depressions *(HB3711-3840)*
    Subdivided by date and, if world wide,
    may be further subdivided by country,
    e.g.   Depressions—1929—United
    States.
  sa Deflation (Finance)
  x Commercial crises
    Crises, Commercial
    Economic depressions
    Panics
  xx Business cycles
    Economics
    Overproduction
  — 1929
  — — Pictorial works

      GEOGRAPHIC SUBDIVISIONS

  — — United States
    Note under Depressions

      GEOGRAPHIC SUBDIVISIONS

  — — — Juvenile literature
  — — — Songs and music
Depressive psychoses
   See Depression, Mental

Deprivation, Maternal
   See Maternal deprivation
Deprivation, Sensory
   See Sensory deprivation
Deprivation, Sleep
   See Sleep deprivation
Deprivation (Psychology)
  x Loss (Psychology)
  xx Psychology
Deprivation of the clerical garb (Canon law)
   See Catholic Church—Clergy—Deprivation
    of the clerical garb
Depth (Philosophy) *(B105.D37)*
  x Profoundness (Philosophy)
    Profundity (Philosophy)
  xx Philosophy
Depth-area-duration (Hydrometeorology)
  x Depth-duration-area
    (Hydrometeorology)
  xx Hydrometeorology
    Precipitation (Meteorology)—
      Measurement
    Storms
Depth charges *(VF509)*
  xx Anti-submarine warfare
    Ordnance, Naval
Depth-duration-area (Hydrometeorology)
   See Depth-area-duration
    (Hydrometeorology)
Depth gage *(TJ1166)*
  xx Gages
Depth perception
  x Distance perception
  xx Space-perception
Derailments
   See Railroads—Accidents
Derby porcelain *(NK4399.D4)*
  x Porcelain, Derby
Dereliction (Civil law)
   See Abandonment of property
Derelicts *(VK1297)*
  sa Wreck
  xx Navigation
    Wreck
Derham (Coin)
   See Dirham (Coin)
Dermabrasion
  xx Skin—Surgery
Dermaptera *(Indirect) (QL510)*
  sa European earwig
  x Earwigs
  xx Insects
  — Catalogs and collections
Dermatitis
   See Skin—Inflammation
Dermatitis, Contact
   See Contact dermatitis
Dermatitis herpetiformis
  x Duhring's disease
Dermatitis venenata
   See Contact dermatitis
Dermatoglyphics *(QL941)*
  sa Fingerprints
    Palmprints
  xx Fingerprints
  — Genetic aspects
    xx Human genetics
Dermatologic agents
  x Drugs, Dermatologic
  xx Dermatology
Dermatologic nursing *(Indirect) (RL125)*
  xx Nurses and nursing
Dermatologists
  xx Dermatology
Dermatology *(RL; Eclectic medicine,*
    RV381-391; Homeopathy,
    RX561-581)
  sa Dermatologic agents

    Dermatologists
    Pediatric dermatology
    Radioisotopes in dermatology
    Skin—Diseases
  — Apparatus and instruments
    xx Surgical instruments and apparatus
    Example under Medical instruments and
      apparatus
  — Atlases
    x Skin—Diseases—Atlases
  — Examinations, questions, etc.
  — Formulae, receipts, prescriptions
    Example under Medicine—Formulae, re-
      ceipts, prescriptions
  — Jurisprudence
    See Forensic dermatology
  — Technique
  — Terminology
Dermatology, Forensic
   See Forensic dermatology
Dermatology, Veterinary
   See Veterinary dermatology
Dermatomycosis *(RL765)*
Dermatomyositis
  xx Cutaneous manifestations of general
    diseases
    Myositis
Dermatoneurosis
   See Neurocutaneous disorders
Dermatophytes *(RL765)*
  xx Fungi
    Skin—Diseases
Dermatosclerosis
   See Scleroderma (Disease)
Derricks
   See Cranes, derricks, etc.
Derriere
   See Buttocks
Dervishes *(BP175.D4)*
  sa Bektashi
    Fakirs
  xx Islam
    Sufism
  — Pictures, illustrations, etc.
Des Chutes
   See Wyam Indians
Des Moines
  — Politics and government
    Example under Municipal government by
      commission
Des Moines plan of city government
   See Municipal government by commission
    Municipal government—Iowa
Desalination of water
   See Saline water conversion
Desalinization of water
   See Saline water conversion
Desalting of petroleum
   See Petroleum—Refining—Desalting
Desalting of water
   See Saline water conversion
Desana Indians
  x Winá Indians
  xx Indians of South America
Descaling
  sa Steel—Pickling
  x Incrustation removal
    Industrial scale removal
    Scale removal
  xx Metal cleaning
  — Patents
Descants
  xx Counterpoint
Descent
   See Genealogy
    Heredity
Descent and distribution
   See Distribution of decedents' estates

Descent and distribution *(Continued)*
    Inheritance and succession
Descents
    See Inheritance and succession
Description (Philosophy) *(B105.D4)*
    xx Philosophy
Description (Rhetoric) *(PN45; English
       language, PE1427; English literature,
       PR1285)*
    x Descriptive writing
    xx Rhetoric
Descriptive cataloging *(Z694)*
    sa Corporate entry (Cataloging)
       Titles of books
    xx Cataloging
    — Problems, exercises, etc.
    — Programmed instruction
Descriptive geometry
    See Geometry, Descriptive
Descriptive writing
    See Description (Rhetoric)
Desecration
    See Sacrilege
Desegregation
    See Segregation
Desegregation, Faculty
    See Faculty integration
Desegregation in education
    See School integration
Desegregation in higher education
    See Segregation in higher education
Desemers
    See Steelyards
Desert biology *(Indirect)* *(QH88)*
    sa Desert ecology
       Desert fauna
       Desert flora
    xx Biology
       Natural history
    — Juvenile literature
Desert ecology *(Indirect)* *(QH541.5.D4)*
    xx Desert biology
       Ecology
    — Juvenile literature
Desert fauna *(QL116)*
    x Fauna
    xx Desert biology
       Zoology
    — Juvenile literature
    — Physiology
Desert flora *(Indirect)* *(QK922; QK938.D4)*
    sa Succulent plants
    x Flora
    xx Botany
       Botany—Ecology
       Desert biology
       Succulent plants
    — Pictorial works
Desert locust *(Economic entomology,
       SB945.L7; Insects, QL508.A2)*
    xx Locusts
    — Biological control *(Indirect)*
       (SB945.L7)
       xx Desert locust—Control
       Example under Insect control—Biologi-
          cal control
    — Control *(Indirect)* *(SB945.L7)*
       sa Desert locust—Biological control
       Example under Insect control; *and under
          reference from* Extermination
Desert research *(Direct)*
    x Deserts—Research
    xx Research
Desert soils
    xx Soils
Desert survival
    xx Survival (after aeroplane accidents,
       shipwrecks, etc.)

Desert warfare
    xx Military art and science
       Strategy
       Tactics
       War
Desert whale
    See Pacific gray whale
Desert wood rat
    xx Wood rats
Desertion, Military *(Direct)* *(UB788)*
    sa subdivision Desertions *under names of
       individual wars and conflicts, e.g.
       Vietnamese Conflict, 1961-   —
       Desertions*
    x Military desertion
    xx Military offenses
    — Personal narratives

GEOGRAPHIC SUBDIVISIONS

    — United States
       x United States. Army—Desertions
Desertion, Naval *(Direct)* *(VB870-875)*
    x Naval desertion
    xx Naval offenses
    — United States
       x United States. Navy—Desertions
Desertion and non-support *(Direct)*
       (Marriage law, HQ805)
    sa Husband and wife
       Parent and child (Law)
    x Abandonment of family
       Non-support
    xx Divorce
       Domestic relations
       Husband and wife
       Support (Domestic relations)
Desertion and non-support (Jewish law)
    sa Agunah
Deserts *(Indirect)* *(GB611-618)*
    sa Oases
       *headings beginning with the word
          Desert*
    xx Arid regions
       Plains
       Steppes
    — Juvenile literature
    — Pictorial works
    — Research
       See Desert research
    — Terminology
Deserts (in religion, folk-lore, etc.)
    sa Wilderness (Theology)
    x Folk-lore of deserts
    xx Religion, Primitive
       Wilderness (Theology)
Desiccants
    See Drying agents
Desiccated foods
    See Food, Dried
Desiccation of food
    See Food—Drying
Design *(Direct)* *(Decoration, NK1160-1590;
       Drawing, NC703)*
    sa Architectural design
       Chair design
       Costume design
       Furniture design
       Kaleidoscope
       Paper money design
       Pattern-making
       Postage-stamp design
       Textile design
    xx Decoration and ornament
       Geometrical drawing
       Manual training
       Pattern-making
    — Copyright
       See Design protection

    — Juvenile literature
Design, Architectural
    See Architectural design
Design, Book
    See Book design
Design, Decorative *(Direct)* *(NK1160-1590)*
    sa Art, Decorative
       Book covers
       Carving (Art industries)
       Decoration and ornament
       Decoupage
       Drawing
       Glass, Ornamental
       Heraldry, Ornamental
       Hex signs
       Illumination of books and manuscripts
       Lettering
       Miniature decorative design
       Scrolls (Decorative design)
       Tapestry
       Textile design
       Tole painting
    x Arts, Decorative
       Decorative arts
       Decorative design
       Ornamental design
    xx Art
       Art, Decorative
       Arts and crafts movement
       Decoration and ornament
       Drawing
    — Animal forms *(NK1555)*
       x Animal forms in design
       Nature in ornament
       xx Animal painting and illustration
       Animals in art
    — Chinese [etc.] influences
    — Plant forms *(NK1560-1565)*
       x Designs, Floral
       Floral design
       Nature in ornament
       Plant forms in design
       xx Flowers in art
       Plants in art
    — Subjects
       See Design, Decorative—Themes,
          motives
    — Themes, motives
       x Design, Decorative—Subjects
Design, Engineering
    See Engineering design
Design, Industrial *(Direct)*
    sa Engineering design
       Engineering models
       Environmental engineering
       Human engineering
       Industrial design coordination
       Industrial designers
       Mechanical drawing
       Unit construction
       Value analysis (Cost control)
    x Industrial design
    xx Mechanical drawing
       New products
    — Awards
       xx Rewards (Prizes, etc.)
    — Classification
    — Juvenile literature
    — Management
       x Industrial design departments
    — Pictorial works
    — Production standards
    — Vocational guidance
       xx Industrial designers
Design, Magazine
    See Magazine design
Design, Postage-stamp
    See Postage-stamp design

Design, Theatrical
   See Theaters—Stage-setting and scenery
Design (Philosophy)
   See Teleology
Design (Typography)
   See Printing, Practical—Make-up
Design coordination, Industrial
   See Industrial design coordination
Design of experiments
   See Experimental design
Design of work systems
   See Work design
Design patents
   See Design protection
Design perception
   See Pattern perception
Design protection *(Direct)*
   x Copyright—Designs
      Design—Copyright
      Design patents
   xx Competition, Unfair
      Copyright
      Industrial design coordination
      Industrial property
      Patent laws and legislation
Design protection (International law)
   xx International law
Designed genetic change
   See Genetic engineering
Designers, Building
   See Building designers
Designers, Industrial
   See Industrial designers
Designs, Architectural
   See Architecture—Designs and plans
Designs, Floral
   See Design, Decorative—Plant forms
Designs (Industrial publicity)
   See Industrial design coordination
Designs for typing
   See Art typing
Desilting basins
   xx Hydraulic structures
      Irrigation canals and flumes
Desire *(BF575.D4)*
   x Appetency
   xx Emotions
      Will
Desire for God
   x God, Desire for
   xx God—Knowableness
      Man (Theology)
      Supernatural (Theology)
Desks *(Indirect)* *(Cabinet work,*
      TT197.5.D4; Manufacture, TS880)
   xx Furniture
      Office furniture
      Schools—Furniture, equipment, etc.
      Tables
Desmidiales *(QK569.D48)*
   x Desmids
   xx Chlorophyceae
Desmids
   See Desmidiales
Desmocytes
   See Fibroblasts
Desmoscolecida *(QL391.N4)*
   xx Nematoda
Desmostylia *(QE882.D45)*
   xx Mammals, Fossil
Desoxy . . .
   See Deoxy . . .
Despair
   sa Hope
   xx Hope
Despair in literature
Despotism *(JC375-392)*
   sa Authority

Democracy
Dictators
Kings and rulers
Monarchy
   x Absolutism
      Abuse of power
      Tyranny
   xx Authoritarianism
      Authority
      Democracy
      Dictators
      Kings and rulers
      Monarchy
      Political science
Desserts *(TX773)*
   sa Mousses
   xx Caterers and catering
      Cookery
      Dinners and dining
      Table
   — Early works to 1800
Desserts, Frozen
   sa Ice cream, ices, etc.
      Mellorine
   xx Food, Frozen
Destinies, Book of
   See Book of life
Destiny
   See Fate and fatalism
Destiny, Spear of
   See Holy Lance
Destitution
   See Poverty
Destriau effect
   See Electroluminescence
Destroyer escorts
   x Escort destroyers
   xx Anti-submarine warfare
      Warships
Destroyers (Warships) *(V825)*
   sa Anti-submarine warfare
   xx Anti-submarine warfare
      Warships
   — Juvenile literature
   — Manning
   — Pictorial works
Destruction of court records
   See Court records—Destruction and
      reconstruction
Destruction of legal documents
   See Legal documents—Destruction and
      reconstruction
Destruction of property
   See Malicious mischief
      Sabotage
      Vandalism
Destruction of the Jews (1939-1945)
   See Holocaust, Jewish (1939-1945)
Destruction of the universe
   See Universe, Destruction of
Destructive distillation
   See Distillation, Destructive
Destructors, Refuse
   See Incinerators
Desulphuration
   x Desulphurization
   xx Elimination reactions
      Sulphuration
Desulphurization
   See Desulphuration
Detachment of the retina
   See Retinal detachment
Details, Architectural
   See Architecture—Details
Detection of atomic weapons tests
   See Atomic weapons—Testing—Detection
Detection of fish
   See Fish detection

Detection of tunnels
   See Tunnel detection
Detection of underground nuclear explosions
   See Underground nuclear explosions—
      Detection
Detective and mystery films
   xx Feature films
      Moving-pictures
   — History and criticism
Detective and mystery plays *(Collections,*
      PN6120.M9)
   x Mystery plays (Modern)
   xx Drama
Detective and mystery plays, American,
      ᵣEnglish, etc.ᵧ *(Direct)*
   x American ᵣEnglish, etc.ᵧ detective plays
      American ᵣEnglish, etc.ᵧ mystery plays
   xx American ᵣEnglish, etc.ᵧ drama
Detective and mystery stories *(Collections,*
      PZ1-3; History, PN3448.D4)
   sa Code and cipher stories
      Crime stories
      Ghost stories
      Horror tales
   x Mystery stories
   xx Adventure stories
      Crime stories
      Fiction
   — Technique *(PN3383.D4)*
      xx Fiction—Technique
Detective and mystery stories, German,
      ᵣRussian, etc.ᵧ
   x German ᵣRussian, etc.ᵧ detective stories
      German ᵣRussian, etc.ᵧ mystery stories
   xx German ᵣRussian, etc.ᵧ fiction
Detectives *(Direct)* *(Police, HV7551-8077;*
      Private, HV8081-8099)
   sa Criminal investigation
      House detectives
      Police
      Police, Private
      Secret service
      Store detectives
      Watchmen
   xx Criminal investigation
      Police
      Secret service
   — Correspondence, reminiscences, etc.
Detectives in literature
   xx Characters and characteristics in
      literature
      Crime in literature
Detectors, Crystal
   See Crystal detectors
Detectors, Neutron
   See Neutron counters
Detectors, Proximity
   See Proximity detectors
Detectors, Radio
   See Radio detectors
Detention, Preventive
   See Preventive detention
Detention camps
   See Concentration camps
Detention homes, Juvenile
   See Juvenile detention homes
Detention of persons *(Direct)*
   sa Arrest
      Concentration camps
      Habeas corpus
      Imprisonment
      Juvenile detention homes
      Preventive detention
      Reformatories
      Workhouses
   xx Civil rights

Detergent pollution of rivers, lakes, etc.
(Indirect) (TD427.D4)
  xx Detergents, Synthetic
    Water—Pollution
Detergent pollution of the sea
  xx Detergents, Synthetic
    Marine pollution
Detergents, Synthetic
  sa Detergent pollution of rivers, lakes, etc.
    Detergent pollution of the sea
    Synthetic detergents industry
  x Synthetic detergents
  xx Cleaning compounds
    Soap
    Surface active agents
  — Biodegradation
  — Patents
  — Quality control
  — Testing
  — Toxicology   (RA1242.D4)
Deterioration of buildings, External
  See Weathering of buildings
Deterioration of concrete
  See Concrete—Deterioration
Deterioration of materials
  See Materials—Deterioration
Deterioration of microfilms
  See Microfilms—Deterioration
Deterioration of paper
  See Paper—Deterioration
Deterioration of plastics
  See Plastics—Deterioration
Deterioration of polymeric materials
  See Polymers and polymerization—
    Deterioration
Deterioration of wood
  See Wood—Deterioration
Determinants   (QA191)
  sa Wronskian determinant
  x Resultants
  xx Algebra
    Mathematics
  — Problems, exercises, etc.
Determinative mineralogy
  See Mineralogy, Determinative
Determinism and indeterminism
  See Free will and determinism
Deterrence (Strategy)   (U162.6)
  xx Attack and defense (Military science)
    Military policy
    Psychology, Military
    Strategy
  — Mathematical models
Detonations
  See Acoustic phenomena in nature
Detonators
Detoxyl
Detribalization
  xx Acculturation
    Civilization, Modern
    Tribes and tribal system
    Urbanization
Detroit
  — Riot, 1863
  — Riot, 1943
  — Riot, 1967
  — Siege, 1712   (E197)
    xx United States—History—Queen
      Anne's War, 1702-1713
  — Siege, 1763   (E83.76)
    sa Pontiac's Conspiracy, 1763-1765
    xx Pontiac's Conspiracy, 1763-1765
  — Surrender to the British, 1812
      (E356.D4)
Detroit plan
  See Working-men's gardens
Deus, Deus meus respice in me (Music)
  See Psalms (Music)—22d Psalm

Deus ex machina
  xx Drama—Technique
Deus, in adjutorium (Music)
  See Psalms (Music)—70th Psalm
Deus in nomine tuo (Music)
  See Psalms (Music)—54th Psalm
Deus misereatur (Music)
  See Psalms (Music)—67th Psalm
Deus noster refugium (Music)
  See Psalms (Music)—46th Psalm
Deus, quis similis (Music)
  See Psalms (Music)—83d Psalm
Deuterium   (QD181.H1)
  sa Deuterons
  xx Hydrogen—Isotopes
  — Physiological effect
Deuterium ions
  xx Ions
  — Scattering
Deuterium oxide   (QD181.H1)
  sa Heavy water reactors
  x Heavy water
    Water, Heavy
  — Spectra
Deuteron scattering
  See Deuterons—Scattering
Deuterons
  xx Atoms
    Deuterium
    Nuclear physics
  — Scattering   (QC721)
    x Deuteron scattering
    Example under Scattering (Physics)
  — Spectra
**Deutsch-Österreichischer Münz-Verein von
  1857**
  See Austrian-German Monetary Union of
    1857
Deutscher Kunstpreis der Jugend
  xx Art—Competitions
Deutschkatholizismus
  See German Catholicism
Dev-samaj   (BL1226)
  xx Brahma-samaj
    Hinduism
Devaluation of currency
  See Currency question
Devanagari alphabet   (PK119)
  sa Type and type-founding—Devanagari
    type
  xx Alphabet
    Indic languages—Alphabet
**Devanagari alphabet (in religion, folk-lore,
  etc.)**
  x Folk-lore of the Devanagari alphabet
  xx Alphabet (in religion, folk-lore, etc.)
    Religion, Primitive
Devanagari type
  See Type and type-founding—Devanagari
    type
Devanagari typewriters
  See Typewriters, Devanagari
Devastator (Torpedo-bomber)   (TL685.3)
  x TBD-1
  xx Bombers
    Douglas airplanes
Developing countries
  See Underdeveloped areas
Development
  See Embryology
    Evolution
    Growth
Development banks   (Direct) (HG4517)
  xx Banks and banking
    Economic development
    Investment banking
Development charges
  See Special assessments

Development credit corporations   (Direct)
  sa Small business investment companies
  xx Banks and banking
    Credit
    Small business—Finance
    Small business investment companies
Development education
  See Acculturation
Development reading
  See Developmental reading
Developmental biology
  sa Aging
    Critical periods (Biology)
    Developmental genetics
    Developmental psychobiology
    Embryology
    Growth
    Ontogeny
  xx Biology
    Embryology
    Growth
    Ontogeny
  — Laboratory manuals
  — Technique
Developmental dyslexia
  See Reading disability
Developmental genetics
  xx Developmental biology
    Embryology
    Genetics
    Growth
Developmental neurology
  xx Neurology
  — Mathematical models
Developmental psychobiology
  sa Children—Growth—Testing
    Critical periods (Biology)
    Developmental psychology
  xx Developmental biology
    Psychobiology
Developmental psychology
    Here are entered works on the psycholog-
    ical development of the individual
    from infancy to old age. Works on the
    evolutionary psychology of man in
    terms of origin and development,
    whether in the individual or in the spe-
    cies, are entered under Genetic psy-
    chology.
  sa Age (Psychology)
    Child study
    Maturation (Psychology)
  xx Developmental psychobiology
    Psychology
  Note under Genetic psychology
Developmental reading   (LB1050.5)
    Here are entered studies on the improve-
    ment of reading under controlled con-
    ditions.
  sa Rapid reading
    Reading films
  x Accelerated reading
    Controlled reading
    Development reading
    Reading, Developmental
  xx Reading, Psychology of
    Reading—Remedial teaching
Developmental testing
  See Children—Growth—Testing
Deventer, Surrender of, 1587   (DH199.D4)
Deviancy
  See Deviant behavior
Deviant behavior
  sa Conformity
    Crime and criminals
    Social adjustment
  x Deviancy
    Social deviance

xx Conformity
    Social adjustment
Deviation, Sexual
  See Sexual deviation
Deviation of the compass
  See Compass
Devices *(Heraldry, CR67-69)*
  sa Book industries and trade—Heraldry
    Books—Owners' marks
    Emblems
    Heraldry
    House marks
    Insignia
    Mottoes
    Printers' marks
    Symbolism
    individual devices, e.g. Coq gaulois
      (Heraldic device), Eagle (in
      heraldry), Fleur-de-lis, Snake devices
      (American colonies)
  x Arms, Coats of
    Coats of arms
  xx Decoration and ornament
    Emblems
    Emblems, National
    Heraldry
    Insignia
    Mottoes
    Proverbs
    Signs and symbols
    Symbolism
Devil *(Comparative religion, BL480;*
    Demonology, BF1546-1561;
    Theology, BT980-981)
  sa Demonology
    Satanism
  x Satan
  xx Demonology
    Enemy in the Bible
    Folk-lore
    Theology, Doctrinal
  — Anecdotes, facetiae, satire, etc.
  — Art *(N8140)*
  — Biblical teaching *(Old Testament,*
    BS1199.D)
  — Drama
  — History of doctrines
  — Koranic teaching *(BP134.D43)*
  — Meditations
Devil dance *(GV1641.B6)*
Devil grass
  See Bermuda grass
Devil in literature *(PN57.D4)*
Devil-worship *(Comparative religion, BL480;*
    Demonology, BF1546-1550)
  sa Demonology
    Occult sciences
    Satanism
    Yezidis
  xx Demonology
    Worship
Devilfish
  See Octopus
Devolution, War of, 1667-1668 *(D275-6)*
  x Franco-Spanish War, 1667-1668
    French-Spanish War, 1667-1668
    Spanish-French War, 1667-1668
    War of Devolution, 1667-1668
Devon, Eng.
  — Blizzard, 1891
Devon, Eng., in literature
Devon cattle *(SF199.D5; Herd-books,*
    SF193.D5)
Devon Rex cat
  See Rex cat
Devonian period
  See Geology, Stratigraphic—Devonian
    Paleobotany—Devonian

Paleontology—Devonian
Devotio moderna *(BR270)*
  Here are entered works on the medieval
  movement initiated by Gerard Groote,
  which resulted in the founding of the
  Brothers of the Common Life and the
  Windesheim Congregation of Augus-
  tinian Canons.
  x New Devotion
  xx Brothers of the Common Life
    Humanism
    Mysticism—Middle Ages, 600-1500
    Reformation—Early movements
    Renaissance
Devotion *(BV4815)*
  sa Contemplation
    Devotional exercises
    Prayer
    Worship
  xx Contemplation
    Mysticism
    Spiritual life
Devotion (Buddhism) *(BQ5595-5630)*
  xx Buddhist doctrines
    Spiritual life (Buddhism)
Devotion to the Holy Name
  See Holy Name, Devotion to
Devotional calendars *(BV4810-4812)*
  sa Church year—Meditations
  x Christian devotional calendars
    Daily readings (Spiritual exercises)
    Devotional exercises (Daily readings)
    Devotional yearbooks
  xx Calendars
  — Baptists, ⌈Catholic Church, Lutheran
    Church, etc.⌉
  — Buddhism
    See Buddhist devotional calendars
  — Hinduism
    See Hindu devotional calendars
  — Islam
    See Islamic devotional calendars
  — Judaism
    See Jewish devotional calendars
Devotional calendars, Buddhist
  See Buddhist devotional calendars
Devotional calendars, Hindu
  See Hindu devotional calendars
Devotional calendars, Islamic
  See Islamic devotional calendars
Devotional calendars, Jewish
  See Jewish devotional calendars
Devotional calendars, Muslim
  See Islamic devotional calendars
Devotional exercises *(BV4800-4870; By*
    denomination, BX)
  sa Church music
    Hymns
    Hymns—Devotional use
    Liturgies
    Lord's prayer
    Lord's Supper
    Meditations
    Prayer
    Prayer-books
    Responsive worship
  x Devotional theology
    Devotions
    Exercises, Devotional
    Theology, Devotional
  xx Christian life
    Devotion
    Prayer
    Theology, Practical
    Worship
Devotional exercises (Daily readings)
  See Devotional calendars

Devotional literature *(BV4800-4895; Catholic*
    Church, BX2177-2198)
  sa Primers (Prayer-books)
    subdivision Devotional literature *under*
      specific subjects, e.g. Providence and
      government of God—Devotional
      literature
  x Christian devotional literature
    Devotional literature, English
    Devotional theology
    Theology, Devotional
  xx Christian literature
    Theology, Practical
Devotional literature, Buddhist
  See Buddhist devotional literature
Devotional literature, English
  See Devotional literature
Devotional literature, French, ⌈German,
    Italian, etc.⌉
Devotional literature, Hindu
  See Hindu devotional literature
Devotional literature, Islamic
  See Islamic devotional literature
Devotional literature, Jaina
  See Jaina devotional literature
Devotional literature, Jewish
  See Jewish devotional literature
Devotional literature, Muslim
  See Islamic devotional literature
Devotional literature, Sikh
  See Sikh devotional literature
Devotional medals
  See Medals, Devotional
Devotional pictures
  See Holy cards
Devotional stories
  See Christian life—Stories
Devotional theology
  See Devotional exercises
    Devotional literature
    Meditations
    Prayers
    subdivision Prayer-books and devotions
      under names of Christian
      denominations, religious orders, etc.
Devotional yearbooks
  See Devotional calendars
Devotions
  See Devotional exercises
Dew *(QC929.D5)*
  xx Meteorology
    Water
Dew line
  See Distant early warning system
Dew-ponds *(TD395)*
Dewali
  See Divali
Dewar flasks *(QD535)*
  sa Thermos bottles
Dewatering, Electroosmotic
  See Electroosmotic dewatering
Dewaxing of petroleum
  See Petroleum—Refining—Dewaxing
Dewaxing of shale oils
  See Shale oils—Refining—Dewaxing
Dewbow *(QC976.R2)*
  xx Meteorological optics
    Rainbow
Dewey Celebration, New York, Sept. 28-30,
    1899 *(F128.5)*
Dewey decimal classification
  See Classification, Dewey decimal
DEWS
  See Distant early warning system
Dexter cattle
  x Dexter Kerry cattle
Dexter Kerry cattle
  See Dexter cattle

Dexterity
    See Motor ability
Dextran
    sa Sephadex
    x Fermentation gum
    xx Blood plasma substitutes
        Carbohydrates
        Glucose
        Sugar—Manufacture and refining—
           By-products
Dextrine *(Chemistry, QD321; Manufacture,*
    TP417)
    xx Polysaccharides
Dextrose *(Chemistry, QD321; Manufacture,*
    TP414; Therapeutics, RM666.D45)
    Example under Carbohydrates
Dhamma (Buddhism)
    See Dharma (Buddhism)
Dharma *(B132.D5)*
    xx Hindu law
        Hinduism
        Philosophy, Hindu
Dharma (Buddhism)
    x Buddhist teachings
        Dhamma (Buddhism)
    xx Buddha and Buddhism
        Buddhist doctrines
Dharma cult
    See Dharmaṭhākura
Dharmakāya (Buddhism)
    See Buddha (The concept)
Dharmaṭhākura
    x Dharma cult
    xx Hindu sects
Dheds *(DS422.C3)*
Dhegiha Indians *(E99.D)*
    sa Kansa Indians
        Omaha Indians
        Osage Indians
        Ponca Indians
        Quapaw Indians
    xx Indians of North America
        Siouan Indians
Dhegiha language *(PM1058)*
    sa Siouan languages
    x Cegiha language
    xx Siouan languages
Dhimal dialect *(PL3801.D5)*
    sa Tibeto-Burman languages
Dhimmis
    xx Aliens (Islamic law)
        Status (Islamic law)
Dho Alur
    See Alur language
Dhows *(VM371)*
    x Lateens
    xx Boats and boating
        Sailing ships
Dhurwas
    xx Ethnology—India—Bastar
Dhyāna (Meditation)
    See Meditation (Buddhism)
        Meditation (Hinduism)
Dhyāna (Sect)
    See Zen Buddhism
Di-kele language
    See Kele language
Día de las Américas
    See Pan American Day
Diabantite *(QE391.D)*
Diabase *(Indirect)* *(QE461)*
    x Dolerite
    xx Rocks, Igneous
Diabetes *(Direct)* *(RC658.5; RC660-662)*
    sa Acetonemia
        Alloxan
        Antidiabetics
        Cookery for diabetics

        Glycosuria
        Hemochromatosis
        Insulin shock
        headings beginning with the word
           Diabetic
    xx Glands, Ductless—Diseases
        Metabolism, Disorders of
  — Complications and sequelae
    Example under Diseases—Complications
        and sequelae
  — Diagnosis
    sa Glucose tolerance tests
  — Dietary aspects
    See Diabetes—Nutritional aspects
  — Genetic aspects
  — Juvenile literature
  — Mortality
  — Nutritional aspects
    sa Cookery for diabetics
    x Diabetes—Dietary aspects
        Diet and diabetes
        Nutrition and diabetes
    xx Cookery for diabetics
  — Oral therapy
  — Personal narratives
  — Prevention
  — Programmed instruction
  — Psychological aspects
  — Psychosomatic aspects
  — Research
    x Diabetes research
    xx Medical research
Diabetes in children *(RJ420.D5)*
    xx Pediatrics
Diabetes in pregnancy *(RG580.D5)*
    xx Pregnancy, Complications of
Diabetes research
    See Diabetes—Research
Diabetic angiopathies *(RC700.D5)*
    xx Blood-vessels—Diseases
Diabetic coma
    xx Coma
Diabetic cookery
    See Cookery for diabetics
Diabetic diet
    See Cookery for diabetics
Diabetic nephropathies
    xx Kidneys—Diseases
Diabetic neuropathies
Diabetic retinopathy *(RE661.D5)*
    xx Retina—Diseases
Diabetics
    This heading is used only with subdivi-
        sions.
  — Employment
    x Employment of diabetics
  — Rehabilitation
Diablo (Game) *(GV1216)*
Diacetylene
    See Acetylene
Diaconate
    See Deacons
Diadochi
    See Macedonia—History—Diadochi,
        323-276 B.C.
Diaeresis (Philosophy)
    x Dieresis (Philosophy)
    xx Philosophy, Ancient
Diagenesis *(Indirect)*
    xx Geology, Structural
        Mineralogy
        Rocks, Sedimentary
Diagnosis *(Laboratory methods, RB37-55;*
    Practice of medicine, RC71-78)
    sa Abdominal pain
        Auscultation
        Biopsy
        Blood—Agglutination

        Blood—Examination
        Body temperature
        Children—Diseases—Diagnosis
        Communicable diseases in animals—
           Diagnosis
        Complement fixation
        Diagnosis, Cytologic
        Diagnosis, Differential
        Diagnosis, Fluoroscopic
        Diagnosis, Radioscopic
        Diagnosis, Surgical
        Diagnostic specimens
        Electrodiagnosis
        Function tests (Medicine)
        Infants—Diseases—Diagnosis
        Lymphatics—Puncture
        Medical history taking
        Medical logic
        Medical screening
        Medical thermography
        Medicine, Clinical
        Microscopy, Medical
        Obstetrics—Diagnosis
        Orthopedia—Diagnosis
        Pain
        Pathology
        Percussion
        Physical diagnosis
        Prognosis
        Pulse
        Radiesthesia
        Radioisotopes in medical diagnosis
        Reflexes
        Serum diagnosis
        Sternum—Puncture
        Thermography (Medicine)
        Thermometers and thermometry,
           Medical
        Tremor
        Urine—Analysis and pathology
        Veterinary medicine—Diagnosis
        Woman—Diseases—Diagnosis
    subdivision Diseases—Diagnosis *under*
        names of organs and regions of the
        body, e.g. Lungs—Diseases—
        Diagnosis; *and subdivision* Diagnosis
        under particular diseases, e.g.
        Tuberculosis—Diagnosis
    x Examinations, Medical
        Medical examinations
        Symptoms
    xx Medicine, Clinical
        Medicine—Practice
        Pathology
        Prognosis
        Semiology
  — Programmed instruction
  — Statistical methods
Diagnosis, Cytologic
    sa Exfoliative cytology
        Medical genetics—Technique
    x Cytodiagnosis
        Cytologic diagnosis
    xx Diagnosis
  — Automation
    x Automated cell identification
Diagnosis, Differential *(RC71.5)*
    sa Facial manifestations of general
        diseases
        Veterinary medicine—Diagnosis,
        Differential
    x Differential diagnosis
    xx Diagnosis
Diagnosis, Fluoroscopic
    x Fluoroscopic diagnosis
    xx Diagnosis
        X-rays

Diagnosis, Obstetrical
   See Obstetrics—Diagnosis
Diagnosis, Otolaryngological
   See Otolaryngology—Diagnosis
Diagnosis, Radioscopic *(RC78)*
   sa Angiocardiography
     Angiography
     Encephalography
     Pediatric radiology
     Pneumomediastinum
     Pneumoperitoneum, Artificial
     Radiologists
     X-rays
     X-rays in obstetrics
     subdivision Radiography *under names*
       of organs, e.g. Bronchi—Radiography
   x Radiodiagnosis
     Radioscopic diagnosis
     Roentgenology, Diagnostic
     X-ray diagnosis
   xx Dentistry
     Diagnosis
     Electrodiagnosis
     Hospitals—Radiological services
     Radiography
     Radiology, Medical
     X-rays
   — Atlases
   — Cases, clinical reports, statistics
   — Complications and sequelae
   — Research
      See Diagnostic radiologic research
Diagnosis, Surgical *(RD35)*
   sa Electrodiagnosis
   x Surgery—Diagnosis
     Surgical diagnosis
   xx Diagnosis
Diagnosis, Ultrasonic
   sa Ultrasonic cardiography
     Ultrasonic encephalography
   x Diagnostic ultrasonics
     Ultrasonic diagnosis
     Ultrasonography
   xx Ultrasonics in medicine
Diagnosis, Urinary
   See Urine—Analysis and pathology
Diagnosis, Veterinary
   See Veterinary medicine—Diagnosis
Diagnostic psychological testing
   See Clinical psychology
Diagnostic radioisotopes
   See Radioisotopes in medical diagnosis
Diagnostic radiologic research *(Direct)*
   x Diagnosis, Radioscopic—Research
   xx Medical research
     Research
Diagnostic specimens
   x Medical specimens
     Specimens, Diagnostic
   xx Biological specimens
     Diagnosis
   — Collection and preservation
Diagnostic ultrasonics
   See Diagnosis, Ultrasonic
Diagnostics, Plasma
   See Plasma diagnostics
Diagram, Petrofabric
   See Petrofabric diagram
Diagrams, Grotrian
   See Grotrian diagrams
Diagrams, Logic
   See Logic diagrams
Diagrams, Statistical
   See Statistics—Charts, tables, etc.
     Statistics—Graphic methods
Diagrams, Weight (Nuclear physics)
   See Weight diagrams (Nuclear physics)

Diaguita Indians *(F2823.D5)*
   xx Calchaqui Indians
     Indians of South America
Diakonia (Theology)
   See Service (Theology)
Dial gage
   See Dial indicator
Dial indicator *(TJ1166)*
   x Dial gage
   xx Gages
Dial telephone
   See Telephone, Dial
Dialectic
   sa Polarity (Philosophy)
     Transcendence of God
   xx Polarity (Philosophy)
Dialectic (Logic)
   See Logic
Dialectic (Religion)
   See Dialectical theology
     Polarity (in religion, folk-lore, etc.)
Dialectical materialism *(B809.8)*
   sa Historical materialism
     Reflection (Dialectical materialism)
   x Materialism, Dialectical
   xx Socialism
   — Examinations, questions, etc.
Dialectical materialism, Categories of
   x Categories of dialectical materialism
   xx Categories (Philosophy)
Dialectical materialism, Laws of
   x Laws of dialectical materialism
Dialectical theology *(BT78)*
   sa Neo-orthodoxy
   x Barthianism
     Crisis theology
     Dialectic (Religion)
     Theology, Crisis
   xx Theology, Doctrinal
Dialectology
   sa subdivision Dialectology *under names*
     of languages and groups of
     languages, e.g. English language—
     Dialectology
   x Dialects
     Language and languages—Dialects
Dialects
   See Creole dialects
     Dialectology
     Franco-Provençal dialects
     Gallo-Italian dialects
     Grammar, Comparative and general
     Italic languages and dialects
     Languages, Mixed
     names of particular dialects, e.g.
       Gallegan dialect, Gascon dialect; *and*
       subdivisions Dialects, Idioms,
       corrections, errors, *and*
       Provincialisms *under names of*
       languages or groups of languages,
       e.g. Greek language—Dialects;
       Romance languages—Dialects;
       English language—Idioms,
       corrections, errors; Spanish language
       —Provincialisms
Dialing *(QB215)*
   sa Sun-dials
   x Dialling
   xx Sun-dials
   — Early works to 1800
Dialling
   See Dialing
Dialogue *(PN1551; English literature, PR618)*
   sa Drama
     Monologue
     Stichomythia
   xx Drama
   Note under Dialogues

Dialogue in the Bible
   x Bible—Dialogue
Dialogue sermons *(BV4307.D5)*
   x Sermon dialogues
   xx Sermons
Dialogues *(PN4290-4291)*
     Here are entered collections of dialogues
       in the English language. Works on dia-
       logue are entered under the heading
       Dialogue.
   sa Imaginary conversations
   xx Recitations
   — Indexes
Dialogues, French, ₍**German, etc.**₎
Dialysis
   sa Electrodialysis
     Hemodialysis
     Saline water conversion—Piezodialysis
       process
   xx Colloids
     Diffusion
     Filters and filtration
     Osmosis
Diamagnetism *(QC771)*
   xx Magnetism
Diamond-back moth *(SB945.D)*
   xx Moths
   — Biological control *(Indirect)*
       (SB945.D5)
     xx Diamond-back moth—Control
   — Control *(Indirect)* *(SB945.D5)*
     sa Diamond-back moth—Biological
       control
Diamond bits *(TN871.5)*
   xx Bits (Drilling and boring)
     Rock-drills
Diamond burnishing
   x Burnishing, Diamond
   xx Metals—Finishing
Diamond crystals
   sa Diamonds, Artificial
Diamond cutters *(Direct)*
   sa Trade-unions—Diamond cutters
   xx Diamond cutting industry
Diamond cutting
   xx Gem cutting
Diamond cutting industry *(Direct)*
   sa Diamond cutters
   xx Diamond industry and trade
Diamond deposits *(Indirect)* *(Mineralogy,*
     QE393; Mineral industries,
     TN990-994)
Diamond drilling
   See Boring
     Rock-drills
     Sullivan diamond drill
Diamond editions
   See Bibliography—Microscopic and
     miniature editions
Diamond industry and trade *(Direct)*
     (HD9677)
   sa Diamond cutting industry
     Diamond mines and mining
Diamond Island, Lake George, Skirmish at,
     1777 *(E233)*
Diamond mines and mining *(Indirect)*
     (TN990-994)
   xx Diamond industry and trade
   — Police
     xx Police, Private
Diamond Necklace Affair *(DC137.15)*
Diamond powder
   — Testing
Diamond rattlesnake
   See Eastern diamondback rattlesnake
     Western diamondback rattlesnake
Diamond skin disease
   See Swine erysipelas

Diamond smuggling
  xx Smuggling
Diamond tools
  See Diamonds, Industrial
Diamond wheels
  xx Diamonds, Industrial
    Grinding wheels
    Wheels
  — Standards (Direct)
Diamondback rattlesnake
  See Eastern diamondback rattlesnake
    Western diamondback rattlesnake
Diamondback terrapin
  x Terrapin, Diamondback
  xx Fresh water turtles
Diamonds (Art, NK7660; Mineralogy,
    QE393; Technology, TS753)
  sa Gems
    Precious stones
    headings beginning with the word
      Diamond
  xx Carbon
  Example under Precious stones
  — Juvenile literature
  — Radiation effects
    See Diamonds, Effect of radiation on
Diamonds, Artificial (TP873.5.D5)
  x Artificial diamonds
    Synthetic diamonds
  xx Diamond crystals
    Diamonds, Industrial
  Example under Precious stones, Artificial
  — Testing
Diamonds, Effect of radiation on
  x Diamonds, Irradiated
    Diamonds—Radiation effects
    Radiation—Effect on diamonds
  xx Radiation
Diamonds, Industrial (Direct) (Tools,
    TJ1193)
  sa Diamond wheels
    Diamonds, Artificial
    Sullivan diamond drill
  x Diamond tools
  xx Tools
  — Patents
  — Standards (Direct)
  — Trade-marks
Diamonds, Irradiated
  See Diamonds, Effect of radiation on
Dian dialect
  See Dyan dialect
DIANA-2 (Electronic computer system)
Dianetics
  sa Scientology
  xx Mental hygiene
    Psychoanalysis
    Psychotherapy
    Scientology
Dianthus
  See Pinks
Diapause
  xx Dormancy (Biology)
    Insects—Metamorphosis
Diapensiales
  xx Angiosperms
Diaper service (Direct)
  xx Laundry industry
Diapers
  xx Breechcloths
Diaphoresis and diaphoretics (RM551)
  sa Perspiration
  xx Therapeutics
Diaphragm (Comparative anatomy, QL851;
    Human anatomy, QM265;
    Physiology, QP121)
  sa Voice
  xx Respiratory organs

  Voice
— Hernia (RD621)
  sa Hiatal hernia
— Innervation
— Radiography
— Tumors
Diaphragms, Vaginal
  x Vaginal diaphragms
  xx Contraceptives
Diaphragms (Mechanical devices)
  sa Pressure-gages
    Pressure—Measurement
  xx Fluid mechanics
    Mechanical engineering
    Pressure
— Patents
Diapir fold
  See Diapirs
Diapiric structures
  See Diapirs
Diapirs (Indirect) (QE606)
  sa Salt domes
  x Diapir fold
    Diapiric structures
    Piercement fold
  xx Domes (Geology)
    Folds (Geology)
Diaries (PN4390; English literature, PR908,
    PR1330)
  sa American [English, French, etc.] diaries
    Autobiographies
  xx Autobiographies
Diaries (Blank-books) (CT9999)
Diarrhea (RC811; Children's diseases,
    RJ456.D5; Homeopathic treatment,
    RX336.D5)
  sa Celiac disease
    Cholera infantum
    Scours
    Sprue
    Summer diseases
  xx Cholera infantum
    Intestines—Diseases
    Summer diseases
— Bacteriology (QR201.D4)
  xx Bacteriology, Medical
— Diagnosis
Diaspora
  See Israel and the Diaspora
Diaspora of the Jews
  See Jews—Diaspora
Diaspore clay (Indirect)
Diastase (Botany, QK896; Physiological
    chemistry, QP601)
  x Amylase
    Ptyalin
  xx Physiological chemistry
  Example under Enzymes
Diathermy (RM874)
  sa Electrocoagulation
    Fever therapy
  xx Electrotherapeutics
    Thermotherapy
Diathesis (RB151; RC251)
  sa Constitutional diseases
    Temperament
  xx Diseases—Causes and theories of
      causation
    Temperament
Diatomaceous earth (TN948.D5)
  x Diatomite
    Fossil dust
    Infusorial earth
    Kieselguhr
  xx Filters and filtration
Diatomales
  See Diatoms

Diatomite
  See Diatomaceous earth
Diatoms (Indirect) (QK569.D54)
  x Bacillariophyceae
    Bacillariophyta
    Diatomales
  xx Algae
    Phytoplankton
Diatoms, Fossil
Diau Indians
  See Trio Indians
Diawara (African people)
  x Djawara (African people)
  xx Ethnology—Sudan (Region)
Diazo compounds (QD305.A9; QD341.A9)
  sa Diazo reaction
    Resazurin
  Example under Chemistry, Organic
Diazo print
  See Diazotype
Diazo reaction
  xx Chemical reactions
    Diazo compounds
Diazoresorcinol
  See Resazurin
Diazotype
  x Diazo print
    Dyeline
    White print
    Whiteprint
  xx Photocopying processes
Dibenamine
  x Dibenzylamine
  xx Amines
    Sympatholytic agents
Dibenzylamine
  See Dibenamine
Dibranchiata (QL430.2)
  xx Mollusks
Dice (GV1303)
  sa Fortune-telling by dice
    Rugby (Dice game)
  xx Gambling
Dichroism (QC446.D)
  x Pleochroism
  xx Polarization (Light)
Dichroite
  See Cordierite
Dichroscope (QC373.D)
Dickcissel
  x Black-throated bunting
  xx Passeriformes
Dickinson-Jackson Duel
  See Jackson-Dickinson Duel
Dickite (QE391.D)
Dicotyledons (Plant anatomy, QK671)
  sa Contortae
    Geraniales
    Guttiferales
    Ranales
    Rutales
  xx Angiosperms
Dicotyledons, Fossil (QE983)
  xx Paleobotany
Dicotyles
  See Peccaries
Dictagraph
  See Dictograph
Dictaphone
  See Dictating machines
Dictating machines (HF5548)
  x Dictaphone
  xx Office equipment and supplies
Dictation (Educational method)
    (LB1029.D5)
  xx Teaching
Dictation (Office practice)
  sa Shorthand

xx Shorthand
Dictators *(JC495)*
   sa Despotism
      Heads of state
      Totalitarianism
   x Tyrants
   xx Despotism
      Kings and rulers
      Totalitarianism
   — Biography
   — — Juvenile literature
   — Juvenile literature
Dictatorship of the proletariat
   sa Communist state
   xx Communism
      Communist state
      Proletariat
      Totalitarianism
Dictatypy
   See Stenotypy
Diction
   sa Elocution
      Singing—Diction
      Style, Literary
      Vocabulary
      subdivision Diction *under names of*
      languages, e.g. English language—
      Diction
   xx Elocution
      Reading
      Rhetoric
      Speech
      Style, Literary
Dictionaries
   See Encyclopedias and dictionaries
      Dictionaries of a particular language or
      subject are entered under the language
      or subject with subdivisions Dictionar-
      ies, Dictionaries, Juvenile or, in the
      case of countries, cities, etc. or ethnic
      groups, Dictionaries and ency-
      clopedias, *e.g.* English language—Dic-
      tionaries; English language—Dictio-
      naries, Juvenile; Botany—Dictionar-
      ies; France—Dictionaries and ency-
      clopedias; Jews—Dictionaries and
      encyclopedias.
Dictionaries, Classical
   See Classical dictionaries
Dictionaries, Picture
   See Picture dictionaries
Dictionaries, Polyglot *(P361)*
   sa Language and languages—Glossaries,
      vocabularies, etc.
      subdivision Dictionaries—Polyglot
      under names of languages, e.g.
      English language—Dictionaries—
      Polyglot
   x Polyglot dictionaries
   xx Encyclopedias and dictionaries
      Language and languages—Dictionaries
Dictionary catalogs
   See Catalogs, Dictionary
Dictograph *(HF5548)*
   x Dictagraph
   xx Office equipment and supplies
Dicumarol
   xx Blood—Coagulation
      Sweet clover
Didactic drama *(Direct)*
   xx Drama
Didactic drama, American, ₍etc.₎ *(Direct)*
   x American ₍etc.₎ didactic drama
   xx American ₍etc.₎ drama
Didactic literature *(PN605.D6)*
   sa Exempla
   x Literature, Didactic
   xx Literature

      Literature and morals
Didactic literature, French, ₍German, etc.₎
Didactic poetry *(History, etc., PN1401)*
   xx Poetry
Didactic poetry, French, ₍Italian, etc.₎
   (Direct)
   x French ₍Italian, etc.₎ didactic poetry
   xx French ₍Italian, etc.₎ poetry
Didactics
   See Teaching
Didinga (African people)
   xx Ethnology—Sudan
Dido language
   x Tsez language
   xx Caucasian languages
Didymium *(QD181.N4)*
   xx Bastnaesite
Die-casting *(TS239)*
   xx Dies (Metal-working)
      Founding
   — Automatic control
   — Costs
Die-casting industry *(Direct)*
   xx Foundries
Die castings
   xx Metal castings
   — Inspection
      xx Engineering inspection
   — Marketing
Die makers
   See Tool and die makers
Diebreak errors, Liberty
   See Cent—Errors
Diegueño Indians *(E99.D5)*
   sa Kamia Indians
   xx Indians of North America
      Yuman Indians
   — Religion and mythology
Diegueño language *(PM1071)*
   xx Yuman languages
Diel cycles
   x Circadian rhythm
      Daily activity cycles
   xx Biology—Periodicity
   — Mathematical models
Dielectric amplifiers
   x Amplifiers, Dielectric
   xx Condensers (Electricity)
      Dielectrics
Dielectric breakdown
   See Breakdown (Electricity)
Dielectric heating
   x Heating, Dielectric
   xx Dielectrics
      Electric heating
Dielectric loss
   xx Dielectrics
Dielectric relaxation *(QC585)*
   sa Polarization (Electricity)
   x Relaxation, Dielectric
   xx Dielectrics
      Polarization (Electricity)
Dielectric resonator
   See Dielectric wave guides
Dielectric wave guides
   x Dielectric resonator
      H-guide
      Sandwich wave guides
   xx Wave guides
Dielectrics *(QC585)*
   sa Breakdown (Electricity)
      Dielectric amplifiers
      Dielectric heating
      Dielectric loss
      Dielectric relaxation
      Dipole moments
      Electrets
      Electric insulators and insulation

      Ferroelectricity
      Hysteresis loop
      Kerr effect
      Microwave heating
   xx Electric engineering—Materials
      Electric insulators and insulation
      Exciton theory
   — Magnetic properties
   — Optical properties
   — Patents *(TK3421)*
   — Radiation effects
      See Dielectrics, Effect of radiation on
   — Research *(Direct)*
      x Dielectrics research
   — Spectra
   — — Tables, etc.
   — Testing
Dielectrics, Effect of radiation on
   x Dielectrics, Irradiated
      Dielectrics—Radiation effects
      Electric insulators and insulation, Effect
      of radiation on
      Radiation—Effect on electric insulators
      and insulation
      Radiation—Effect on materials
   xx Radiation
Dielectrics, Irradiated
   See Dielectrics, Effect of radiation on
Dielectrics research
   See Dielectrics—Research
Diels-Alder reaction
   xx Chemical reactions
Dien Bien Phu, Vietnam, Battle of, 1954
      (DS553.3.D5)
   xx Indochina, French—History—
      Indochinese War, 1946-1954—
      Campaigns
   — Juvenile literature
Diencephalon
   sa Subthalamus
      Thalamus
   xx Brain
Dieppe Raid, 1942 *(D756.5.D5)*
   xx World War, 1939-1945—Naval
      operations
Dieresis (Philosophy)
   See Diaeresis (Philosophy)
Dies, Blanking and piercing
   See Punching machinery
Dies (Ceramics)
   x Dry press molds
   xx Ceramics
Dies (Metal-working) *(TS253)*
   sa Die-casting
      Eye-bars
      Punching machinery
      Tool and die industry
   xx Forging
      Metal stamping
      Punching machinery
   — Drawing
      See Dies (Metal-working)—Drawings
   — Drawings
      x Dies (Metal-working)—Drawing
      xx Mechanical drawing
   — Standards *(Direct)*
   — Tariff
      See Tariff on dies
   — Thermal properties
Dies (Screw-cutting)
   See Taps and dies
Dies and taps
   See Taps and dies
Dies irae (Music)
   xx Sacred vocal music
      Sequences (Music)
Diesel-electric locomotives
   See Diesel locomotives

Diesel electric power-plants
    x Power-plants, Diesel electric
    xx Electric power-plants
    — Automation
    — Reliability
Diesel engine
    See Diesel motor
Diesel exhaust gas
    See Diesel motor exhaust gas
Diesel fuels *(TP343)*
    x Diesel motor—Fuel
       Diesel oil
    xx Motor fuels
    — Taxation   *(Direct)*
Diesel locomotives *(TJ619)*
    sa Railroads—Dieselization
    x Diesel-electric locomotives
    xx Locomotives
       Railroads—Dieselization
    — Automatic control
    — Climatic factors
    — Cold weather operation
    — Compressors   *(TJ669.C6)*
       xx Air-compressors
    — Cooling
    — Design and construction
    — Electric equipment
    — — Cooling
    — — Design and construction   *(TJ619)*
    — Equipment and supplies   *(TJ619)*
    — Fuel consumption
    — Hydraulic drive
       xx Oil hydraulic machinery
       Example under Fluid power technology;
         and under reference from Hydrau-
         lic drive
    — Inspection   *(TJ619)*
    — Juvenile literature
    — Lubrication
    — Maintenance and repair
    — Reliability
    — Springs and suspension
    — Technological innovations
    — Testing
    — Transmission devices
       xx Gearing
    — Welding
Diesel motor *(TJ795)*
    sa Marine diesel motors
       subdivision Motors (Diesel) *under*
         subjects, e.g. Aeroplanes—Motors
         (Diesel)
    x Diesel engine
    xx Gas and oil engines
       Marine engines
       Motors
    — Automatic control
    — Bearings
    — Cold weather operation
       Example under Cold
    — Combustion
       Example under Combustion
    — Cooling
       sa Marine engines—Cooling
    — Cylinders
    — Design
    — Drawing
       See Diesel motor—Drawings
    — Drawings
       x Diesel motor—Drawing
       xx Mechanical drawing
    — Exhaust gas
       See Diesel motor exhaust gas
    — Fuel
       See Diesel fuels
    — Fuel systems
       xx Fuel pumps
    — — Maintenance and repair

— — Reliability   *(TJ797)*
— — Testing
— Lubrication
— Maintenance and repair
— Models   *(TJ795)*
— Noise
— Oil filters
    xx Filters and filtration
       Oil filters
— Parts
    xx Machine parts
— Soundproofing
— Starting
— Superchargers
    Example under Superchargers
— Testing
— Valves
— Vibration
Diesel motor exhaust gas
    x Diesel exhaust gas
       Diesel motor—Exhaust gas
       Exhaust gas (Diesel)
    xx Automobile exhaust gas
       Gases
    — Analysis
    — Physiological effect
Diesel motor industry *(Direct)*
    — Quality control
Diesel oil
    See Diesel fuels
Dieselization of railroads
    See Railroads—Dieselization
Diet *(Indirect)* *(Food values, TX551-560;*
      Nutrition, QP141; Therapeutics,
      RM214-259)
    sa Animal food
       Beverages
       Black Muslims—Dietary laws
       Cookery
       Deficiency diseases
       Dietitians
       Food
       Food, Dietetic
       Food habits
       Food, Raw
       Gastronomy
       Jews—Dietary laws
       Menus
       Monasticism and religious orders—
         Dietary rules
       Muslims—Dietary laws
       Newspapers—Sections, columns, etc.—
         Food
       Nutrition
       Reducing diets
       School children—Food
       Therapeutics, Physiological
       Vegetarianism
    x Dietetics
    xx Appetite
       Cookery
       Deficiency diseases
       Digestion
       Food
       Food habits
       Hygiene
       Nutrition
    Example under Therapeutics, Physiological
    — Early works to 1800   *(RM215)*
    — Mathematical models
    — Meditations
Diet, Low-calorie
    See Low-calorie diet
Diet, Low-carbohydrate
    See Low-carbohydrate diet
Diet, Low-fat
    See Low-fat diet

Diet, Low-sugar
    See Sugar-free diet
Diet, Wheat-free
    See Wheat-free diet
Diet and anemia
    See Anemia—Nutritional aspects
Diet and arteriosclerosis
    See Arteriosclerosis—Nutritional aspects
Diet and arthritis
    See Arthritis—Nutritional aspects
Diet and cancer
    See Cancer—Nutritional aspects
Diet and cardiovascular diseases
    See Cardiovascular system—Diseases—
       Nutritional aspects
Diet and diabetes
    See Diabetes—Nutritional aspects
Diet and goiter
    See Goiter—Nutritional aspects
Diet and gout
    See Gout—Nutritional aspects
Diet and heart disease
    See Heart—Diseases—Nutritional aspects
Diet and intellect
    See Intellect—Nutritional aspects
Diet and kidney diseases
    See Kidneys—Diseases—Nutritional aspects
Diet and mental illness
    See Mental illness—Nutritional aspects
Diet and tumors
    See Tumors—Nutritional aspects
Diet in disease *(RM214-259)*
    sa Cookery for diabetics
       Cookery for the sick
       Diet in veterinary medicine
       Dietitians
       Food, Artificial
       Food, Dietetic
       Gluten-free diet
       Grapes—Therapeutic use
       Ketogenic diet
       Low-cholesterol diet
       Low-fat diet
       Low-protein diet
       Salt-free diet
       Sugar-free diet
       Wheat-free diet
       subdivision Nutritional aspects *under*
         diseases, e.g. Cancer—Nutritional
         aspects; Cardiovascular system—
         Diseases—Nutritional aspects
    x Diet therapy
       Dietetics
       Disease, Diet in
    xx Nurses and nursing
       Sick
       Therapeutics
       Therapeutics, Physiological
    Example under Therapeutics, Physiological
Diet in veterinary medicine
    x Veterinary nutrition
    xx Diet in disease
       Feeding
       Veterinary medicine
Diet-kitchens *(HV694)*
    xx Charities, Medical
       Cookery for the sick
       Food relief
       Sick
Diet of Augsburg, 1518
    See Augsburg, Diet of, 1518
Diet of Augsburg, 1530
    See Augsburg, Diet of, 1530
Diet of Augsburg, 1548
    See Augsburg, Diet of 1548
Diet of Ratisbon, 1532
    See Ratisbon, Diet of, 1532

Diet of Ratisbon, 1640-1641
  See Ratisbon, Diet of, 1640-1641
Diet of Ratisbon, 1653-1654
  See Ratisbon, Diet of, 1653-1654
Diet of Spires, 1526
  See Spires, Diet of, 1526
Diet of Spires, 1529
  See Spires, Diet of, 1529
Diet of Worms, 1521
  See Worms, Diet of, 1521
Diet therapy
  See Diet in disease
Dietaries *(Food values, TX551-560;*
      Therapeutics, RM214-261)
  sa Food
  xx Food
Dietary departments of hospitals, etc.
  See Hospitals—Food service
Dietary laws, Black Muslim
  See Black Muslims—Dietary laws
Dietary laws, Islamic
  See Muslims—Dietary laws
Dietary laws, Jewish
  See Jews—Dietary laws
Dietary laws, Muslim
  See Muslims—Dietary laws
Dietary laws, Sikh
  See Sikhs—Dietary laws
Dietary proteins
  See Low-protein diet
Dietetic food
  See Food, Dietetic
Dietetics
  See Diet
      Diet in disease
      Nutrition
Dieting
  See Reducing
Dieting for weight loss
  See Reducing diets
Dietists
  See Dietitians
Dietitians *(RM214-218)*
  x Dietists
  xx Diet
      Diet in disease
      Nurses and nursing
  — Vocational guidance
      xx Home economics as a profession
Diffeomorphisms
  xx Differential topology
Difference (Philosophy)
  xx Philosophy
Difference (Psychology) *(BF697)*
  sa Polarity (Psychology)
      Variability (Psychometrics)
  xx Psychology
Difference algebra
  See Algebra, Difference
Difference amplifiers
  See Differential amplifiers
Difference-differential equations
  See Differential-difference equations
Difference equations *(QA431)*
  sa Algebra, Difference
      Asymptotic expansions
      Differential-difference equations
      Nets (Mathematics)
  x Calculus of differences
      Differences, Calculus of
      Equations, Difference
      Finite differences
  — Numerical solutions
      xx Numerical analysis
Difference fields
  See Algebra, Difference
Difference sets
  x Sets, Difference

  xx Combinatorial analysis
Differences, Calculus of
  See Difference equations
Differentiable manifolds
  sa Tangent bundles
  xx Manifolds (Mathematics)
Differentiable mappings
  x Mappings, Differentiable
  xx Differential topology
Differential algebra
  See Algebra, Differential
Differential amplifiers *(TK7871.58.D46)*
  x Difference amplifiers
Differential analyzers, Electronic
  See Electronic differential analyzers
Differential calculus
  See Calculus, Differential
Differential diagnosis
  See Diagnosis, Differential
Differential-difference equations *(QA373)*
  x Difference-differential equations
  xx Difference equations
      Differential equations
      Functional equations
Differential equations *(QA371-7)*
  sa Algebra, Differential
      Boundary value problems
      Calculus, Integral
      Calculus, Operational
      Differential-difference equations
      Differential operators
      Eikonal equation
      Electronic differential analyzers
      Existence theorems
      Functional differential equations
      Functions
      Green's functions
      Groups, Continuous
      Initial value problems
      Inverse problems (Differential
        equations)
      Lagrange equations
      Laplace transformation
      Liapunov functions
      Potential, Theory of
      Stochastic differential equations
      Sturm-Liouville equation
      Surfaces
      Transformations, Infinitesimal
      Weber functions
      Wronskian determinant
  x Equations, Differential
  xx Bessel functions
      Calculus
  — Numerical solutions
      sa Error functions
        Hermite polynomials
        Lamé polynomials
        Runge-Kutta formulas
        Sommerfeld polynomial method
      xx Numerical calculations
        Perturbation (Mathematics)
  —— Computer programs
  — Problems, exercises, etc. *(QA371-7)*
  — Programmed instruction
Differential equations, Elliptic
  x Elliptic differential equations
      Elliptic partial differential equations
      Linear elliptic differential equations
  xx Differential equations, Linear
      Differential equations, Partial
  — Numerical solutions
Differential equations, Functional
  See Functional differential equations
Differential equations, Hyperbolic
  x Hyperbolic differential equations
  xx Differential equations, Partial
  — Numerical solutions *(QA377)*

  xx Numerical analysis
Differential equations, Linear *(QA372-7)*
  sa Airy functions
      Differential equations, Elliptic
  x Linear differential equations
  — Numerical solutions
      xx Numerical calculations
  — Programmed instruction
Differential equations, Nonlinear
  sa Duffing equations
  x Nonlinear differential equations
  xx Nonlinear theories
  — Numerical solutions
      sa Averaging method (Differential
        equations)
      xx Numerical analysis
Differential equations, Parabolic
  x Parabolic differential equations
      Parabolic partial differential equations
  xx Differential equations, Partial
Differential equations, Partial *(QA374-7)*
  sa Cauchy problem
      D'Alembertian operator
      Differential equations, Elliptic
      Differential equations, Hyperbolic
      Differential equations, Parabolic
      Dirac equation
      Fokker-Planck equation
      Harmonic functions
      Hodograph equations
      Laplacian operator
      Maxwell equations
      Navier-Stokes equations
      Neumann problem
      Operator equations
      Schrödinger equation
      Wave equation
  x Functions, Potential
      Partial differential equations
      Potential functions
  — Numerical solutions
      xx Numerical calculations
  — Problems, exercises, etc.
  — Programmed instruction
Differential fields
  See Algebra, Differential
Differential forms *(QA381)*
  x Forms, Differential
  xx Geometry, Differential
      Groups, Continuous
Differential games
  x Games, Differential
  xx Game theory
Differential geometry
  See Geometry, Differential
Differential invariants *(QA381)*
  sa Transformations (Mathematics)
  x Invariants, Differential
  xx Groups, Continuous
Differential operators
  sa Hamiltonian operator
      Partial differential operators
      Schrödinger operator
  x Operators, Differential
  xx Differential equations
      Operator theory
Differential relays *(TK2861)*
  xx Electric relays
Differential staffing of schools
  See Differentiated teaching staffs
Differential thermal analysis
  See Thermal analysis
Differential thermal curves
  See Thermal analysis
Differential topology *(QA612)*
  sa Characteristic classes
      Cobordism theory
      Diffeomorphisms

Differential topology (QA612)
(Continued)
    Differentiable mappings
    Foliations (Mathematics)
    Global analysis (Mathematics)
  xx Geometry, Differential
    Topology
Differential values inventory
  x Personal values inventories
  xx Mental tests
Differentiated teaching assignments
  See Differentiated teaching staffs
Differentiated teaching staffs (LB1029.D55)
  x Differential staffing of schools
    Differentiated teaching assignments
    Staff differentiation in schools
    Teaching staffs, Differentiated
  xx Teaching
Differentiation of cells
  See Cell differentiation
Difficulty of ascent
  See Mountains—Difficulty of ascent
Diffraction (QC415)
  sa Apodization
    Eriometer
    Holography
    subdivision Diffraction *under subjects,*
      e.g. Electric waves—Diffraction;
      Neutrons—Diffraction; X-rays—
      Diffraction
  xx Light
    Optics
Diffraction gratings
  sa Moiré method
  x Gratings, Diffraction
  xx Optical instruments
    Spectroscope
    Spectrum analysis—Instruments
Diffractometer, X-ray
  See X-ray diffractometer
Diffuse cerebral sclerosis
  See Cerebral sclerosis, Diffuse
Diffuse collagen disease
  See Collagen diseases
Diffuse sky radiation
  See Atmospheric radiation
Diffusers
  sa Aeroplanes—Ramjet engines—Diffusers
    Aeroplanes—Turbojet engines—
      Diffusers
    Supersonic diffusers
  xx Fluid dynamics
    Mechanical engineering
  — Aerodynamics (Turbines, TJ267.5.D4)
Diffusion (Chemistry, QD543; Physics,
    QC185)
  sa Biological transport
    Colloids
    Dialysis
    Extraction (Chemistry)
    Film coefficients (Physics)
    Gases
    Kirkendall effect
    Light—Scattering
    Mass transfer
    Matter—Properties
    Packed towers
    Plasma diffusion
    Turbulent diffusion (Meteorology)
  x Gases—Diffusion
    Liquids—Diffusion
  xx Matter—Properties
    Packed towers
    Physics
    Separation (Technology)
    Solution (Chemistry)
    Solutions, Solid
  — Mathematical models
  — Tables, etc.

Diffusion bonding (Metals)
  sa Metal cladding
  x Bonding, Diffusion (Metals)
    Solid state bonding (Metals)
  xx Metal bonding
    Pressure welding
Diffusion coatings
  sa Boriding
    Calorizing
    Chromizing
    Siliconizing (Metallurgy)
    Sulphonitriding
  x Coatings, Diffusion
    Metals—Diffusion coatings
  xx Metallic surfaces
    Protective coatings
    Surface hardening
Diffusion of innovations
  sa Technology transfer
  x Innovations, Diffusion of
  xx Acculturation
    Communication
    Culture diffusion
    Technological innovations
  — Mathematical models
Diffusion processes (QA274.75)
  xx Markov processes
Diffusivity, Thermal
  See Thermal diffusivity
Digaru language
  See Taraon language
Digesters (Chemical engineering)
  See Autoclaves
Digestion (Physiology, QP145-156)
  sa Auto-intoxication
    Bile
    Diet
    Digestive ferments
    Digestive organs
    Dyspepsia
    Enzymes
    Food
    Gastric juice
    Gastrointestinal motility
    Intestinal absorption
    Mastication
    Metabolism, Disorders of
    Nutrition
  xx Absorption (Physiology)
    Constipation
    Nutrition
    Pancreas—Secretions
    Physiological chemistry
    Physiology
    Stomach
  — Early works to 1800
  — Examinations, questions, etc.
  — Juvenile literature
Digestive ferments
  sa Pancreas—Secretions
    Pancreopepsine
    Papain
    Pepsin
    Rennet
    Trypsin
  x Ferments
  xx Digestion
    Enzymes
    Fermentation
    Pancreas—Secretions
Digestive organs (Comparative anatomy,
    QL856-867; Human anatomy,
    QM301-353)
  sa names of individual organs, e.g.
    Intestines, Pancreas, Stomach
  xx Alimentary canal
    Digestion
    Stomach

  — Abnormities and deformities
  — Amphibians, ₍Birds, Fishes, etc.₎
    Works on the digestive organs of a par-
    ticular class, order, family, genus, or
    species are entered under Digestive
    organs, subdivided by the larger
    zoological groups only. When the
    monograph treats of one of the
    smaller divisions, additional entry is
    made under the special subject, *e.g.*
    1. Digestive organs—Amphibians.
    2. Frogs.
  x Amphibians ₍Birds, Fishes, etc.₎—
    Digestive organs
  xx Amphibians ₍Birds, Fishes, etc.₎—
    Anatomy
  — Bacteriology (QR171)
  — Blood-vessels
    x Alimentary canal—Blood-vessels
  —— Radiography (RC804.A5)
    x Gastrointestinal angiography
  — Cancer (RC280.D)
  — Diseases (RC799-869)
    sa Alimentary canal—Inflammation
      Alimentary canal—Obstructions
      Digestive organs—Radiography
      Gastrointestinal agents
      names of specific diseases, e.g.
        Gastroesophageal reflux; *and*
        subdivision Diseases *under names*
        of individual organs, e.g. Stomach
        —Diseases
    x Alimentary canal—Diseases
    xx Intestines—Diseases
  —— Diagnosis (RC803-4)
  —— Homeopathic treatment (RX331-6)
  — Examinations, questions, etc.
  — Exploration
  — Foreign bodies
  — Innervation
    x Alimentary canal—Innervation
  — Microbiology
  — Programmed instruction
  — Radiography
    xx Digestive organs—Diseases
  — Secretions
    xx Body fluids
  — Surgery (RD540; RD547)
  — Syphilis
  — Ulcers
Digestive organs, Effect of radiation on the
  xx Radiation—Physiological effect
Digests of books
  See Books, Condensed
Digests of cases (Law)
  See Law reports, digests, etc.
Diggers
  See Levellers
Digging machines
  See Excavating machinery
Digital circuits
  See Digital electronics
Digital computer circuits
  See Electronic digital computers—Circuits
Digital computer simulation
  sa Artificial intelligence
    ECSS (Computer program language)
    GASP (Computer program language)
    GPSS (Computer program language)
    SIMSCRIPT (Computer program
      language)
  x Computer simulation, Digital
    Digital simulation
    Electronic data processing—
      Mathematical models
  xx Computer simulation
    Electronic digital computers
    Mathematical models

Simulation methods
— Problems, exercises, etc.
Digital computers, Electronic
   See Electronic digital computers
Digital counters
   Here are entered works on mechanical,
   electromechanical or electronic dis-
   crete-state counting devices operating
   on any given number base, consisting
   of any combination of sensing, ac-
   cumulating and readout elements, and
   being used as components in meters,
   automata and control systems. Works
   on manual or other counters for arithmetic processes are entered under the
   specific name, *e.g.* Abacus, or under
   the subject, Mathematical instruments. Works on devices which detect
   and measure radiation are entered under Nuclear counters or the specific
   name, *e.g.* Scintillation counters.
   x Automatic counting devices
      Counters, Digital
      Counting devices, Digital
   xx Calculating-machines
      Digital electronics
      Measuring instruments
Digital differential analyzers, Electronic
   See Electronic differential analyzers
Digital electronics *(TK7868.D5)*
   sa Analog-to-digital converters
      Coding theory
      Digital counters
      Digital filters (Mathematics)
      Digital-to-analog converters
      Electronic digital computers—Circuits
      Pulse-code modulation
      Switching theory
   x Digital circuits
   xx Electronics
   — Laboratory manuals
Digital filters (Mathematics)
   x Data smoothing filters
      Filters, Digital (Mathematics)
      Linear digital filters (Mathematics)
      Linear filters (Mathematics)
      Numerical filters
      Smoothing filters (Mathematics)
   xx Digital electronics
      Fourier transformations
      Functional analysis
      Numerical analysis
      Numerical calculations
Digital incremental plotters
   x Plotters, Digital incremental
   xx Computer graphics
      Digital-to-analog converters
      Electronic digital computers
Digital simulation
   See Digital computer simulation
Digital-to-analog converters
   sa Digital incremental plotters
      XY plotters
   x Converters, Digital-to-analog
   xx Digital electronics
      Hybrid computers
Digitalis *(Pharmacy, RS165.D5;*
      Therapeutics, RM666.D5)
   — Physiological effect
   — Toxicology
Dignity *(BV4647.D)*
   xx Honor
Digo language
   x KiDigo language
   xx Bantu languages
      Nika language
Digression (Rhetoric)
   xx Rhetoric

Dihydrocodeine
   x Paracodin
   xx Codeine
Dijmjhna Expedition, 1882-1883
Dijon
   — Siege, 1513
   — Siege, 1870-1871   *(DC305.7)*
      xx Franco-German War, 1870-1871
Dike districts
   See Levee districts
Dikes (Engineering) *(TC337)*
   sa Dams
      Earthwork
      Embankments
      Jetties
      Reclamation of land
      Sea-walls
      Shore protection
   x Dykes
   xx Earthwork
      Embankments
      Engineering
      Flood dams and reservoirs
      Hydraulic structures
      Levees
      Marshes, Tide
      Reclamation of land
      Sea-walls
      Shore protection
Dikes (Geology) *(Indirect)* *(QE611)*
   sa Aplite
   x Dykes
   xx Intrusions (Geology)
      Volcanism
Diketones
   See Ketones
Dilapidations
   sa Waste (Law)
   xx Adjoining landowners
      Ecclesiastical law
      Landlord and tenant
      Real property
      Torts
      Waste (Law)
Dilatation of time
   See Time dilatation
Dilation of time
   See Time dilatation
Dilatometer *(QC100.5-111; QC281-6)*
Dilemma *(BC185)*
   xx Decision-making
      Logic
      Syllogism
Dilettantism *(BH301.D5)*
   xx Aesthetics
Dilexi, quoniam (Music)
   See Psalms (Music)—116th Psalm
Diligam te Domine (Music)
   See Psalms (Music)—18th Psalm
Dill
   xx Herbs
Dilogarithms *(QA351)*
   xx Functions, Transcendental
      Integrals
      Logarithms
Dilpok language *(PM8161-4)*
Dilution
   xx Chemistry
Dime novels *(PS374.D5)*
   xx American fiction
      Fiction
Dime novels, German
   x Groschenromane
   xx German fiction
Dimension theory (Topology)
   xx Topology
Dimensional analysis
   sa Dimensionless numbers

Engineering mathematics
   Engineering models
   Structural frames—Models
   xx Engineering mathematics
      Mathematical physics
      Physical measurements
   — Computer programs
Dimensionless groups
   See Dimensionless numbers
Dimensionless numbers
   sa special dimensionless numbers, e.g.
      Mach number, Reynolds number
   x Dimensionless groups
      Groups, Dimensionless
      Nondimensional numbers
      Numbers, Dimensionless
      Numbers, Nondimensional
   xx Dimensional analysis
Dimensions
   sa Length measurement
   xx Physical measurements
      Units
Dimethyl
   See Ethanes
Dimini ware
Diminishing returns
   x Law of diminishing returns
   xx Agriculture—Economic aspects
      Economics
Dimitrov prizes
   xx Literary prizes
Dimorphism (Animals)
   sa Sexual dimorphism (Animals)
   xx Morphology (Animals)
Dimorphism (Plants) *(QK671)*
   sa Sexual dimorphism (Plants)
   x Branch dimorphism
   xx Plants
Dimouts
   See Blackouts in war
Dimuga language
   x Daga language
   xx Papuan languages
Dīn-i Ilāhī *(BP195.D5-52)*
   x Dīn Ilāhī
   xx Islamic sects
Dīn Ilāhī
   See Dīn-i Ilāhī
Dinar
Dinaric race
   x Adriatic race
   xx Ethnology—Italy
      Ethnology—Yugoslavia
Ding an sich
   x Thing-in-itself
   xx Knowledge, Theory of
      Ontology
      Reality
Dingaan's Day
   xx Holidays
Dingal language *(PK2461-9)*
   sa Shekhawati dialect
   x Marwari language
   xx Indo-Aryan languages, Modern
      Rajasthani language
Dingal poetry *(Direct)* *(PK2476)*
Dingley bill
   See Dingley tariff
Dingley tariff *(Discussion, HF1755-6;*
      Schedules, HJ6085)
   x Dingley bill
   Example under Tariff
Dingo
   — Control   *(Indirect)*
      xx Predator control
Dining
   See Dinners and dining

Dining cars
　　See Railroads—Dining-car service
Dining etiquette
　　See Table etiquette
Dining room etiquette
　　See Table etiquette
Dining room furniture　*(Cabinet work,*
　　　TT197.5.D5; Interior decoration,
　　　NK2117; Manufacture, TS880)
　　sa Chairs
　　　Chests
　　　Cupboards
　　　Tables
　　xx Dining rooms
　　　Furniture
　　— Catalogs
Dining rooms　*(Domestic science, TX855-9;*
　　　House decoration, NK2117)
　　sa Dining room furniture
　　xx Architecture, Domestic
　　　Dinners and dining
　　　Dwellings
Dinka (Nilotic tribe)
　　xx Ethnology—Sudan
　　　Nilotic tribes
　　— Religion
Dinka language　*(PL8131)*
　　sa Bor dialect
　　　Padang dialect
　　x Denca language
　　　Denka language
　　xx Nilotic languages
Dinka law
　　See Law, Dinka
Dinners and dining　*(Direct)*　*(TX737)*
　　sa Carving (Meat, etc.)
　　　Cookery
　　　Desserts
　　　Dining rooms
　　　Drinking customs
　　　Food
　　　Gastronomy
　　　Menus
　　　Table
　　x Banquets
　　　Dining
　　　Eating
　　xx Caterers and catering
　　　Cookery
　　　Entertaining
　　　Etiquette
　　　Gastronomy
　　　Menus
　　　Table
Dinners and dining in art
　　xx Art
Dinocerata　*(QE882.U8)*
Dinoflagellata
　　x Dinoflagellida
　　xx Flagellata
Dinoflagellida
　　See Dinoflagellata
Dinornithiformes
　　See Moa
Dinosauria　*(QE862.D5)*
　　xx Reptiles, Fossil
　　— Anecdotes, facetiae, satire, etc.
　　— Food　*(QE862.D5)*
　　— — Juvenile literature
　　— Juvenile literature
Dinwiddie, Battle of, 1865　*(E477.67)*
Diocesan archives
　　See Archives, Diocesan
Diocesan chancellors
　　See Chancellors, Diocesan
Diocesan chanceries
　　See Chanceries, Diocesan

Diocesan consultors
　　See Consultors, Diocesan
Diocesan councils and synods
　　See Councils and synods, Diocesan
Diocesan schools
　　See Church schools
Diocesan synods
　　See Councils and synods, Diocesan
Dioceses　*(Direct)*
　　sa Archdeacons
　　　Bishops
　　　Cathedrals
　　　Chancellors, Diocesan
　　　Chanceries, Diocesan
　　　Chapters, Cathedral, collegiate, etc.
　　　Chorepiscopi
　　　Rural chapters
　　　Rural deans
　　　subdivision Dioceses *under names of*
　　　　church bodies, e.g. Church of
　　　　England—Dioceses; *and names of*
　　　　dioceses, e.g. Canterbury, Eng.
　　　　(Diocese)
　　x Archbishoprics
　　　Bishoprics
　　xx Bishops
　　　Catholic Church—Government
　　　Church history
　　　Church polity
　　　Ecclesiastical geography
　　　Episcopacy
　　　Vicars-general
Dioceses (Canon law)　*(BX1939.D55)*
　　sa Administrators apostolic
　　　Consultors, Diocesan
　　　Vicars capitular
　　Example under Canon law
Diodes
　　sa Germanium diodes
　　　Silicon diodes
　　　Varactors
　　xx Gas tubes
　　　Vacuum-tubes
Diodes, Crystal
　　See Diodes, Semiconductor
Diodes, Double-base
　　See Unijunction transistors
Diodes, Electron-tube
　　sa Kenotrons
　　x Electron-tube diodes
　　　Vacuum-tube diodes
　　xx Electron tubes
Diodes, Semiconductor
　　sa Crystal mixers
　　　Tunnel diodes
　　　Varistors
　　　Zener diodes
　　x Crystal diodes
　　　Diodes, Crystal
　　　Semiconductor diodes
　　xx Semiconductors
　　— Reliability
Diodontomorphi
　　See Tetraodontiformes
Diola (African people)
　　xx Ethnology—Senegal
Diola language　*(PL8134)*
　　x Dyola language
　　　Yola language
Diomedeidae
　　See Albatrosses
Dionysia　*(BL820.B2; Greek antiquities,*
　　　DF123; Greek drama, PA3203)
　　sa Bacchantes
　　　Greek drama (Satyr play)
　　x Orphic mysteries
　　　Orphism
　　xx Cultus, Greek

Diophantine analysis　*(QA242)*
　　sa Distribution modulo one
　　　Forms, Quadratic
　　　Numbers, Theory of
　　　Series, Farey
　　x Equations, Indeterminate
　　　Indeterminate analysis
　　xx Algebra
　　　Forms, Quadratic
　　　Numbers, Theory of
　　— Tables, etc.
Dioptrics
　　See Refraction
Diorama　*(Painting, ND2880)*
　　sa Cosmoramas
　　　Cycloramas
　　　Panoramas
　　xx Cosmoramas
　　　Cycloramas
　　　Panoramas
Diorite　*(Indirect)*　*(QE461)*
　　xx Rocks, Igneous
Diosmosis　*(QD543)*
　　sa Growth (Plants)
　　xx Growth (Plants)
　　　Osmosis
Diotocardia
　　See Archaeogastropoda
Diour language
　　See Dyur language
Dip net fishing
　　See Lift net fishing
Dip of the horizon
　　See Horizon, Dip of
Dipavali
　　See Divali
Diphtheria　*(Direct)*　*(RC138)*
　　— Bacteriology　*(QR201.D5)*
　　— Biochemic treatment　*(RC138)*
　　— Compilations and sequelae
　　　sa Diphtheric polyneuritis
　　— Homeopathic treatment　*(RX226.D6)*
　　　Example under Homeopathy
　　— Hospitals　*(RC138)*
　　　Example under Hospitals
　　— Mortality
　　— Prevention　*(RA644.D6)*
　　　sa Diphtheria—Preventive inoculation
　　— Preventive inoculation
　　　x Diphtheria—Vaccination
　　　xx Diphtheria—Prevention
　　— Vaccination
　　　See Diphtheria—Preventive
　　　　inoculation
Diphtheria antitoxin
　　Example under Serumtherapy; Toxins and an-
　　　titoxins
Diphtheric polyneuritis
　　x Diphtheritic paralysis
　　　Polyneuritis, Diphtheric
　　xx Diphtheria—Complications and
　　　sequelae
　　　Neuritis, Multiple
Diphtheritic paralysis
　　See Diphtheric polyneuritis
Dipleidoscope　*(QB213)*
Diploetic vein
　　See Diploic vein
Diploic vein
　　x Diploetic vein
Diploma factories
　　See Diploma mills
Diploma mills　*(LB2388)*
　　x Degree mills
　　　Diploma factories
　　xx Fraud
　　　Universities and colleges

Diplomacy *(JX1621-1894)*
  sa Diplomatic and consular service
   Diplomatic documents
   Diplomatic etiquette
   Diplomatic gifts
   Diplomatic negotiations in international
    disputes
   Diplomatic protests
   Diplomats
   Notification (International relations)
   Treaties
   Ultimatums
   subdivision Foreign relations *under
    names of countries, e.g. United
    States—Foreign relations*
  xx Diplomatic and consular service
   History
   International relations
  — Anecdotes, facetiae, satire, etc.
  — Language *(JX1677)*
    x International language
     Language, International
    xx Language, Universal
     Languages—Political aspects
Diplomatic and consular service
    (JX1621-1894)
   Subdivision Diplomatic and consular ser-
    vice may be subdivided by country,
    e.g. Italy—Diplomatic and consular
    service—United States
  sa Agricultural attachés
   Ambassadors
   Catholic Church—Diplomatic service
   Colonial agents
   Commercial attachés
   Consular jurisdiction
   Consular law
   Consular reports
   Consuls
   Diplomacy
   Diplomatic couriers
   Diplomatic documents
   Diplomatic gifts
   Diplomatic privileges and immunities
   Diplomatic protection
   Diplomats
   Diplomats' wives
   Embassy buildings
   Exterritoriality
   Fees, Consular
   Foreign offices
   Foreign propagandists in the United
    States
   Labor attachés
   Legates, Papal
   Military attachés
   Nuncios, Papal
   subdivision Diplomatic and consular
    service *under names of countries,
    e.g.* France—Diplomatic and
    consular service
  x Consular service
   Consulates
   Embassies
   Foreign service
   Legations
   Ministers (Diplomatic agents)
  xx Diplomacy
   Diplomats
   Government missions
   International law
   International relations
  — Accounting
  — Anecdotes, facetiae, satire, etc.
  — Fees
    See Fees, Consular
  — Registers, lists, etc. *(JX1705-1894)*

   Here are entered registers of diplo-
    matic and consular officials of vari-
    ous countries stationed abroad in
    several countries. Registers of dip-
    lomatic and consular officials of
    various countries stationed in a spe-
    cific country are entered under the
    heading Diplomatic and consular
    service in Great Britain, ₍Italy, etc.₎
    Registers of diplomatic and consu-
    lar officials of a specific country are
    entered under the name of the
    country with subdivision Diplo-
    matic and consular service—Regis-
    ters.
    x Diplomatic lists
**Diplomatic and consular service in Great
   Britain, ₍Italy, etc.₎**
   Note under Diplomatic and consular service—
    Registers, lists, etc.
Diplomatic correspondence
   See Diplomatic documents
Diplomatic couriers
   x Couriers, Diplomatic
   xx Diplomatic and consular service
  — Correspondence, reminiscences, etc.
Diplomatic documents
   Here are entered works on the nature and
    handling of diplomatic correspond-
    ence in general and under the aspect of
    international law. Collections of diplo-
    matic papers are entered under the
    subject to which they refer. Manuals
    on the diplomatic correspondence of a
    particular country are entered under
    the foreign office of that country with
    subdivision Records and correspond-
    ence, *e.g.* United States. Dept. of
    State—Records and correspondence.
   x Correspondence, Diplomatic
    Diplomatic correspondence
    Diplomatic papers
    Documents, Diplomatic
   xx Diplomacy
    Diplomatic and consular service
    International law
    International relations
Diplomatic etiquette *(Direct) (JX1678-9)*
   sa Precedence
   x Diplomatic protocol
    Protocol, Diplomatic
   xx Diplomacy
    Etiquette
Diplomatic gifts *(JX1683.G5)*
   xx Diplomacy
    Diplomatic and consular service
    Gifts
Diplomatic immunities
   See Diplomatic privileges and immunities
Diplomatic lists
   See Diplomatic and consular service—
    Registers, lists, etc.
**Diplomatic negotiations in international
   disputes** *(JX4473)*
   x Negotiations in international disputes
   xx Arbitration, International
    Diplomacy
    International relations
    Pacific settlement of international
     disputes
Diplomatic papers
   See Diplomatic documents
Diplomatic privileges and immunities
    (JX1671-2)
   sa Customs privileges
    International agencies—Privileges and
     immunities

   subdivision Privileges and immunities
    *under names of individual
    international organizations and under
    names of countries with subdivision
    Diplomatic and consular service, e.g.*
    Inter- national Labor Office—
    Privileges and immunities; United
    Nations—Privileges and immunities;
    United States—Diplomatic and
    consular service—Privileges and
    immunites
   x Diplomatic immunities
   xx Ambassadors
    Consular jurisdiction
    Diplomatic and consular service
    Exterritoriality
    Immunities of foreign states
    Privileges and immunities
Diplomatic protection *(JX4263.P7-8)*
   sa Calvo doctrine and clause
    Denial of justice
    Diplomatic protests
    Exhaustion of local remedies
     (International law)
    Intervention (International law)
   x Protection of citizens abroad
   xx Aliens
    Diplomatic and consular service
    International law
    International relations
Diplomatic protests
   x Diplomatic representations
    Protests, Diplomatic
    Representations, Diplomatic
   xx Diplomacy
    Diplomatic protection
    International law
Diplomatic protocol
   See Diplomatic etiquette
Diplomatic representations
   See Diplomatic protests
Diplomatics *(Direct) (CD1-724)*
   sa Archives
    Charters
    Copyists
    Document writing, Chinese
    Formularies (Diplomatics)
    Manuscripts
    Manuscripts—Facsimiles
    Paleography
    Seals (Numismatics)
    Signatures (Writing)
    Tironian notes
   x Documents
   xx Archives
    Auxiliary sciences of history
    Cartularies
    Historiography
    History
    History—Sources
    Manuscripts
    Manuscripts—Facsimiles
    Paleography
Diplomatics, Latin, ₍Turkish, etc.₎ *(Direct)*
   x Latin ₍Turkish, etc.₎ diplomatics
Diplomats *(Direct) (JX1621-1894)*
   sa Ambassadors
    Consuls
    Diplomatic and consular service
    Legates, Papal
    Nuncios, Papal
    Women as diplomats
   xx Diplomacy
    Diplomatic and consular service
    International law
    International relations
    Statesmen
  — Anecdotes, facetiae, satire, etc.

Diplomats *(Direct)* *(JX1621-1894)*
(Continued)
— Biography
— Correspondence, reminiscences, etc.
Diplomats' wives
   xx Diplomatic and consular service
      Wives
Diplopoda
   See Millepeds
Diploporita *(QE783.D5)*
Dipole moments
   sa Quadrupole moments
      subdivision Dipole moments *under names of substances and groups of substances, e.g.* Formaldehyde—Dipole moments; Vapors—Dipole moments
   x Electric dipole moments
   xx Chemistry, Physical and theoretical
      Dielectrics
      Matter—Constitution
      Molecules
      Polarization (Electricity)
      Quadrupole moments
— Tables, etc.
Dipper (Constellation)
   See Ursa Major
Dippers (Birds) *(QL696.P2)*
   x Cinclidae
      Water ouzels
Dipping fluids *(SF918.D5)*
Dipping-needle *(QC819)*
   xx Magnetic instruments
Dipsomania
   See Alcoholism
Diptera *(Indirect)* *(QL531-8)*
   sa Fleas
      Flies
      particular kinds of flies, gnats, etc., e.g. Blowflies, Hessian flies, Mosquitoes
   x Antliata
      Midges
   xx Insects
— Classification
— Identification
— Juvenile literature
Diptera, Fossil *(QE832.D6)*
Diptychs
   sa Tablets (Paleography)
   xx Tablets (Paleography)
Dirac equation *(QC174.45)*
   xx Differential equations, Partial
      Quantum field theory
      Wave equation
Direct action *(Strikes, HD5306)*
   sa Criminal syndicalism
      General strike
      Government, Resistance to
      Sabotage
      Terrorism
   xx Anarchism and anarchists
      Strikes and lockouts
      Syndicalism
      Trade-unions
Direct advertising
   See Advertising, Direct-mail
Direct book delivery
   See Direct delivery of books
Direct cell division
   See Amitosis
Direct currency machinery
   See Dynamos—Direct current
      Electric machinery—Direct current
      Electric motors, Direct current
Direct current amplifiers *(TK7871.58.D5)*
   x Amplifiers, Direct current
Direct current power distribution
   See Electric power distribution—Direct current

Direct currents
   See Electric currents, Direct
Direct delivery of books *(Direct)* *(Z712)*
   x Books, Direct delivery of
      Direct book delivery
      Home delivery of books
      Library service, Mail
      Mail delivery of books
      Mail library service
   xx Libraries—Branches, delivery stations, etc.
      Libraries—Circulation, loans
      Library extension
Direct discourse in literature
   x Discourse, Direct, in literature
Direct distance dialing (Telephone)
   See Telephone, Dial
Direct energy conversion *(TK2896)*
   sa Bimorphs
      Controlled fusion
      Electric power production from chemical action
      Electrohydrodynamic generators
      Fuel cells
      Ion rockets
      Magnetohydrodynamic generators
      Microwave heating
      Nuclear rockets
      Photoelectric cells
      Plasma rockets
      Solar batteries
      Thermionic converters
      Thermionic emission
      Thermoelectric apparatus and appliances
      Thermoelectric generators
   x Direct generation of electricity
      Energy conversion, Direct
   xx Electric power production
      Energy transfer
Direct generation of electricity
   See Direct energy conversion
Direct legislation
   See Referendum
Direct-mail advertising
   See Advertising, Direct-mail
Direct placement (Securities)
   See Securities, Privately placed
Direct primaries
   See Primaries
Direct taxation
   See Income tax
      Taxation
Directed numbers
   See Signed numbers
Directed study
   See Supervised study
Directing (Theater)
   See Theater—Production and direction
Direction, Sense of
   See Orientation
Direction, Spiritual
   See Spiritual direction
Direction finders, Radio
   See Radio direction finders
Direction finding by simultaneous lobing
   See Monopulse radar
Directoire style
   See Decoration and ornament—Directoire style
Directories *(AY2001)*
   This is a subject, not a form heading, *i.e.* it covers only the history, description, and bibliography of directories and directory-making. For form headings *see* subdivision Directories under names of places and subjects, *e.g.* Boston—Directories; Botanists—Directories.

   sa subdivision Social registers *under names of cities*
Directories, Medical
   See Physicians—[local subdivision]—Directories, e.g. Physicians—Chicago—Directories
Directors, Moving-picture
   See Moving-picture producers and directors
Directors, Spiritual
   See Spiritual directors
Directors of corporations *(Direct)* *(HD2745; K)*
   sa Bank directors
      Corporate meetings
      Insider trading in securities
   x Boards of directors
      Boards of supervision (Corporation law)
      Corporation directors
   xx Corporation law
      Corporations
— Salaries, pensions, etc. *(Direct)*
Directors of museums
   See Museum directors
Directors of religious education *(BV1531)*
   Here are entered works dealing with full-time, paid, and professionally trained officers in charge of the religious education program of the local church. Material dealing with the work of lay Sunday-school superintendents is entered under Sunday-school superintendents.
   sa Sunday-school superintendents
   x Ministers of religious education
   xx Clergy
      Religious education
      Religious education as a profession
      Sunday-school superintendents
Directory, French, 1795-1799
   See France—History—Revolution, 1795-1799
Dirges
   xx Funeral hymns
Dirham (Coin)
   x Derham (Coin)
      Dirhem (Coin)
   xx Coins, Islamic
Dirhem (Coin)
   See Dirham (Coin)
Dirichlet integrals
   See Integrals, Dirichlet
Dirichlet problem *(QA425)*
   xx Boundary value problems
      Potential, Theory of
— Numerical solutions
      xx Numerical analysis
Dirichlet series
   See Series, Dirichlet
Dirico language
   See Diriku language
Dirigible balloons
   See Air-ships
Diriko language
   See Diriku language
Diriku language *(PL8135)*
   x Dciriku language
      Dirico language
      Diriko language
      Gciriku language
      Mbogedu language
   xx Bantu languages
Dirt-eating
   See Pica (Pathology)
Dirt roads
   See Roads, Earth
Dirty songs
   See Bawdy songs

Disabilities, Political (Great Britain)
    See Catholic emancipation
        Corporation Act, 1661
        Dissenters, Religious—England
        Oath of Allegiance, 1601
        Test Act, 1673
Disability, Reading
    See Reading disability
Disability (Law)
    See Capacity and disability
Disability evaluation *(Direct)*
    sa Industrial accidents
        Insurance, Accident
        Pensions, Medical examinations for
    x Disability rating
        Estimation of disability
        Evaluation of disability
        Incapacity, Estimation of
    xx Handicapped
        Industrial accidents
        Insurance, Accident
        Insurance, Employers' liability
        Medicine, Industrial
        Medicine, Military
        Old age pensions
        Pensions, Military
Disability insurance
    See Insurance, Disability
Disability rating
    See Disability evaluation
Disabled
    See Handicapped
Disabled sailors
    See Veterans, Disabled
Disabled soldiers
    See Veterans, Disabled
Disabled vehicles on express highways
    x Stalled vehicles on express highways
    xx Express highways
        Motor vehicles
        Traffic engineering
Disabled veterans
    See Veterans, Disabled
Disallowance of legislation *(Direct)*
    x Reservation of legislation
    xx Legislation
        Repeal of legislation
        Veto
Disarmament *(JX1974)*
    sa Arbitration, International
        Armies, Cost of
        Atomic weapons and disarmament
        Militarism
        Navies, Cost of
        Peace
        Sea-power
        Security, International
        War, Cost of
    x Arms control
        Limitation of armament
        Military power
    xx Arbitration, International
        Armaments
        Armies
        International relations
        Militarism
        Military art and science
        Navies
        Peace
        Sea-power
        Security, International
        War
        War, Cost of
    — Control and inspection
        See Disarmament—Inspection
    — Economic aspects *(Direct)* *(HC65)*
        x Defense economics
    — Inspection *(UA12.5)*

    x Disarmament—Control and
            inspection
        Inspection for disarmament
        Inspection of disarmament
    — Mathematical models
Disarmament and atomic weapons
    See Atomic weapons and disarmament
Disaster casualties
    See Mass casualties
Disaster hospitals
    x Hospitals, Disaster
        Packaged disaster hospitals
    xx Civil defense—Equipment and supplies
        Emergency medical services
Disaster insurance
    See Insurance, Disaster
Disaster nursing *(RT108)*
    sa Emergency nursing
    xx Emergency medical services
        Emergency nursing
        Nurses and nursing
Disaster relief *(Direct)* *(HV553-5)*
    sa Civil defense
        Emergency clothing supply
        Emergency communication systems
        Emergency food supply
        Emergency housing
        Emergency medical services
        Emergency transportation
        Emergency water supply
        Evacuation of civilians
        Food relief
        Hurricane protection
        Insurance, Disaster
        Rest centers (Disaster relief)
    x Emergency relief
    xx Assistance in emergencies
        Charities
        Civil defense
        Hurricane protection
        International relief
        Public welfare
    — Public opinion
    — Research
        x Disaster research
Disaster research
    See Disaster relief—Research
Disasters *(Direct)*
    sa Accidents
        Bridges—Accidents
        Building failures
        Catastrophical, The
        Collisions at sea
        Cultural property, Protection of
        Dam failures
        Fires
        Gas, Natural—Pipe line failures
        Hazardous geographic environments
        Mine accidents
        Natural disasters
        Panic
        Railroads—Accidents
        Shipwrecks
        Steamboat disasters
        Submarine disasters
        Theaters—Accidents
        particular disasters, e.g. Galveston—
            Storm, 1900; Messina—Earthquake,
            1908; San Francisco—Earthquake
            and fire, 1906
    x Calamities
        Catastrophes
    xx Accidents
        Curiosities and wonders
        Hazardous geographic environments
    — Psychological aspects *(BF789.D5; Child
            study, BF723.D5)*
    — — Testing

    — Public opinion
    — Religious interpretations
        xx Theodicy
Disbudding *(SB125)*
    xx Pruning
Disc, Optic
    See Optic disc
Disc electrophoresis
    See Zone electrophoresis
Disc jockeys *(Direct)*
    xx Radio announcing
Discernment of spirits *(BV5083)*
    x Spirits, Discernment of
    xx Demonology
        Experience (Religion)
        Psychology, Religious
Discernment of spirits (Islam) *(BP166.89)*
    xx Spirits (Islam)
Discharge, Military
    See Military discharge
Discharge benefits
    See Wages—Dismissal wage
Discharge gratuities, Prison
    See Prison release gratuities
Discharge of contracts *(Direct)*
    sa Accord and satisfaction
        Arbitration and award
        Breach of contract
        Impossibility of performance
        Legal documents—Cancellation
        Novation
        Performance (Law)
        Rescission (Law)
        Waiver
    xx Contracts
Discharges (Electricity)
    See Electric discharges
Disciples, Twelve
    See Apostles
Disciples of Christ *(Direct)* *(BX7301-7343)*
    x Campbellites
    — Clergy
    — — Correspondence, reminiscences, etc.
    — Government
    — Hymns *(BV397)*
    — Missions *(BV2532)*
    — Sermons
Disciples of Christ, Negro
    x Colored Disciples of Christ
        Negro Disciples of Christ
    xx Negroes—Religion
Disciples of St. John
    See Mandaeans
Discipleship
    See Christian life
Disciplinary power *(Direct)*
    sa Church discipline
        Military discipline
        Municipal officials and employees—
            Discipline
        Parent and child (Law)
        School discipline
        subdivisions Discipline *under church
            denominations, and* Officials and
            employees—Discipline *under names
            of countries*
Disciplinati
    xx Confraternities
        Flagellants and flagellation
Discipline, College
    See College discipline
Discipline, Ecclesiastical
    See Church discipline
Discipline, Formal
    See Formal discipline
Discipline, Industrial
    See Labor discipline

Discipline, Labor
See Labor discipline
Discipline, Mental
See Mental discipline
Discipline, Military
See Military discipline
Discipline, Naval
See Naval discipline
Discipline, Prison
See Prison discipline
Discipline, School
See School discipline
Discipline of children
sa Discipline of infants
School discipline
x Child discipline
Children—Discipline
Punishment of children
xx Child study
Children—Management
Cruelty to children
Punishment
Discipline of infants
x Infants—Discipline
xx Discipline of children
Disclosing official secrets
See Official secrets
Disclosure in accounting
xx Accounting
Auditing
Financial statements
Discography
See Phonorecords—Catalogs and collections
subdivision Discography *under names of individual composers, types of music, and other subjects*
Discomycetes *(QK623.D6)*
x Cup fungi
Inoperculates
Operculates
xx Ascomycetes
Fungi
Discontent
Discontent in literature
Discontinuous functions
See Functions, Discontinuous
Discontinuous groups
sa Kleinian groups
xx Combinatorial topology
Functions of complex variables
Groups, Theory of
Discophora (Coelenterata) *(QL377.S4)*
xx Hydromedusae
Discosorida *(QE807.N4)*
xx Nautiloidea, Fossil
Discotheques
sa subdivision Discotheques *under names of cities*
xx Music-halls (Variety-theaters, cabarets, etc.)
Discount *(Direct) (Banking, HG1651-4; Business, HF5553; Law, K)*
sa Acceptances
Prime rate
x Bank discount
xx Acceptances
Banking law
Banks and banking
Bills of exchange
Interest and usury
Price policy
Rebates
— Tables, etc. *(HG1654)*
Discount (Rebate)
See Rebates
Discount dealers
See Discount houses (Retail trade)
Discount houses (Retail trade) *(Direct)*
sa Outlet stores
x Discount dealers
Discount stores
xx Price cutting
Rebates
Retail trade
Discount stores
See Discount houses (Retail trade)
Discounts, Employee
See Employee discounts
Discourse, Direct, in literature
See Direct discourse in literature
Discourse, Indirect, in literature
See Indirect discourse in literature
Discourse analysis *(P301)*
x Discourse grammar
Text grammar
xx Semantics
Semiotics
Discourse grammar
See Discourse analysis
Discourses
See Lectures and lecturing
Orations
Speeches, addresses, etc.
Discoverer (Artificial satellite) *(TL796.5.U6D)*
x Project Discoverer
xx Artificial satellites
— Juvenile literature
Discoverers
See Discoveries (in geography)
Explorers
Discoveries, Maritime
See Discoveries (in geography)
Discoveries (in geography) *(G80-99; G220-420; Polar regions, G575-890)*
sa Antarctic regions
Arctic regions
Explorers
Geography—15th-16th centuries
Geography—17th-18th centuries
Geography—History
Northeast Passage
Northwest coast of North America
Northwest Passage
Scientific expeditions
Voyages and travels
subdivisions Discovery and exploration, Description and travel, *and* Exploring expeditions *under names of countries, e.g.* America—Discovery and exploration; Asia—Description and travel; Spain—Exploring expeditions
x Discoverers
Discoveries, Maritime
Maritime discoveries
Navigators
xx Adventure and adventurers
Explorers
Geography
Geography—15th-16th centuries
Geography—17th-18th centuries
Geography—History
History
Voyages and travels
— American, [Belgian, Dutch, etc.]
Discoveries (in science)
See Industrial arts
Inventions
Patents
Science
Discovery, Learning by
See Learning by discovery
Discovery (Law) *(Direct)*
sa Interrogatories
xx Equity pleading and procedure
Discrete degrees, Doctrine of
See Degrees, Doctrine of
Discrete-time systems *(QA402)*
sa Feedback control systems
x Sampled-data systems
xx System analysis
Discretion *(Ethics, BJ1533.D5; Moral theology, BV4647.D6)*
Discretion, Administrative
See Administrative discretion
Discretion, Judicial
See Judicial discretion
Discretion (Law)
See Administrative discretion
Judicial discretion
Discretion of court
See Judicial discretion
Discretionary income *(Direct)*
Here are entered works on that part of personal income above that obligated for fixed expenses such as rent, food, insurance, etc. which is available for either saving or spending.
xx Cost and standard of living
Income
Discriminant analysis *(QA278.65)*
x Analysis, Discriminant
Classification theory (Statistics)
Discrimination theory (Statistics)
xx Multivariate analysis
— Computer programs
Discrimination *(Direct)*
Here are entered general works on social discrimination based on race, religion, sex, social minority status, or other factors.
sa Civil rights
Discrimination in education
Discrimination in employment
Discrimination in housing
Discrimination in public accommodations
Minorities
Race discrimination
Segregation
Toleration
xx Assimilation (Sociology)
Minorities
Race problems
Social problems
Social psychology
Toleration
Discrimination, Racial
See Race discrimination
Discrimination in education *(Direct)*
sa Segregation in education
x Educational discrimination
xx Discrimination
Race discrimination
Race problems in school management
Segregation in education
— Law and legislation *(Direct)*
xx Educational law and legislation
Right to education
Discrimination in employment *(Direct) (HD4903)*
sa Age and employment
Blacklisting, Labor
Equal pay for equal work
Ex-convicts, Employment of
Trade-unions—Negro membership
subdivision Employment *under names of social or racial groups, e.g.* Negroes—Employment; Woman—Employment
x Employment discrimination
Fair employment practice

Job discrimination
  xx Discrimination
       Labor and laboring classes
       Personnel management
       Race discrimination
       Right to labor
  Note under Race discrimination
— Law and legislation *(Direct)*
     xx Labor laws and legislation
— Mathematical models
Discrimination in housing *(Direct)*
  sa Jews—Segregation
       Negroes—Housing
  x Fair housing
       Housing, Discrimination in
       Open housing
       Segregation in housing
  xx Discrimination
       Housing
       Race discrimination
— Law and legislation *(Direct)*
     sa Real covenants
     xx Real covenants
— Mathematical models
Discrimination in public accommodations
       (Direct)
  sa Segregation in transportation
  x Public accommodations, Discrimination
       in
       Segregation in public accommodations
  xx Discrimination
       Race discrimination
— Law and legislation *(Direct)*
Discrimination in sports
  See Segregation in sports
Discrimination in transportation
  See Segregation in transportation
Discrimination learning
  xx Transfer of training
Discrimination theory (Statistics)
  See Discriminant analysis
Discriminators, Frequency
  See Frequency discriminators
Discs
  See Phonorecords
Discus (Fish) *(SF458.D5)*
  x Pompadour fish
Discus throwing
  xx Weight throwing
Discussion
  sa Catechetics
       Communist self-criticism
       Debates and debating
       Forums (Discussion and debate)
       Meetings
       Negotiation
  x Group discussion
  xx Conversation
       Debates and debating
       Leadership
       Meetings
Discussion in religious education *(BV1534.5)*
       Here are entered works on discussion as
         a technique in religious education and
         aids and materials to be used by reli-
         gious education discussion groups.
  xx Religious education
Disease, Diet in
  See Diet in disease
Disease (Pathology)
  See Pathology
Disease germs
  See Bacteria, Pathogenic
       Germ theory of disease
Disease resistance of plants
  See Plants—Disease and pest resistance
Disease transmission
  See Diseases—Transmission

Disease warfare
  See Biological warfare
Diseases
       This heading is used only with subdivi-
         sions.
— Causes and theories of causation
       (RB151)
     sa Accidents
          Auto-intoxication
          Bacteria, Pathogenic
          Communicable diseases
          Diathesis
          Diseases in twins
          Environmentally induced diseases
          Germ theory of disease
          Heredity
          Infection
          Metaplasia
          Temperament
          Traumatism
     x Aetiology
          Etiology
     xx Germ theory of disease
          Medicine
          Pathology
— Classification
     See Nosology
— Complications and sequelae *(RB127)*
     sa Adhesions
          subdivision Complications and
            sequelae *under names of diseases,
            surgery, etc., e.g.* Diabetes—
            Complications and sequelae;
            Surgery—Complications and
            sequelae; Anesthesia—
            Complications and sequelae
     x Diseases—Sequelae
— Environmental aspects
     See Environmentally induced diseases
— Juvenile literature
— Nomenclature *(RB115)*
— Prevention
     See Medicine, Preventive
— Reporting *(Direct)*
     sa Communicable diseases
     x Morbidity reporting
          Registration of diseases
          Reporting of diseases
     xx Communicable diseases
          Hygiene, Public
          Medical statistics
          Medicine
          Public health laws
— Sequelae
     See Diseases—Complications and
          sequelae
— Transmission
     sa Animals as carriers of disease
          Birds as carriers of disease
          Communicable diseases
          Fish as carriers of disease
          Insects as carriers of disease
          Virus-vector relationships
          Worms as carriers of disease
          subdivision Transmission *under
            names of specific diseases, e.g.*
            Poliomyelitis—Transmission
     x Disease transmission
          Transmission of diseases
     xx Communicable diseases
          Epidemiology
Diseases, Chronic
  See Chronic diseases
Diseases, Communicable
  See Communicable diseases
Diseases, Constitutional
  See Constitutional diseases

Diseases, Contagious
  See Communicable diseases
Diseases, Deficiency
  See Deficiency diseases
Diseases, Feigned
  See Blindness, Feigned
       Malingering
Diseases, Hemorrhagic
  See Hemorrhagic diseases
Diseases, Hereditary
  See Heredity of disease
Diseases, Iatrogenic
  See Iatrogenic diseases
Diseases, Incurable
  See Incurable diseases
Diseases, Infectious
  See Communicable diseases
Diseases, Mental
  See Mental illness
       Psychology, Pathological
       Psychoses
Diseases, Occupational
  See Occupational diseases
Diseases, Periodic
  See Periodic diseases
Diseases, Summer
  See Summer diseases
Diseases, Tropical
  See Tropics—Diseases and hygiene
Diseases in twins
  xx Diseases—Causes and theories of
       causation
       Twins
Diseases of animals
  See Veterinary medicine
Diseases of children
  See Children—Diseases
       Infants—Diseases
Diseases of occupations
  See Occupational diseases
Diseases of plants
  See Plant diseases
Diseases of the blood, ₍brain, heart, etc.₎
  See subdivision Diseases *under specific
       subjects, e.g.* Blood—Diseases; Brain
       —Diseases
Diseases of women
  See Woman—Diseases
Disembarkation
  See Landing operations
Disgerminoma
  xx Generative organs—Cancer
Disguised unemployment
  x Hidden unemployment
       Unemployment, Disguised
       Unemployment, Hidden
  xx Agricultural laborers
       Casual labor
       Underdeveloped areas—Unemployed
       Unemployed
       Unemployment, Seasonal
— Mathematical models
Dish gardening
  See Gardens, Miniature
Dishonesty
  See Honesty
Dishwashers
  See Dishwashing machines
Dishwashing
  sa Dishwashing machines
  xx Home economics
Dishwashing machines *(TX657.D6)*
  x Dishwashers
  xx Dishwashing
       Kitchen utensils
— Patents
Disinfection and disinfectants *(RA761-6)*
  sa Aeroplanes—Disinfection

Disinfection and disinfectants *(RA761-6)*
(Continued)
   Air—Purification
   Ammonium compounds as disinfectants
   Antiseptics
   Books—Disinfection
   Chlorine and derivatives as
    disinfectants
   Creolin
   Formaldehyde
   Fumigation
   Health facilities—Disinfection
   Heat as a disinfectant
   Hospitals—Disinfection
   Hydrazine
   Hydrocyanic acid
   Hydrogen peroxide
   Lime as a disinfectant
   Lysoform
   Poultry houses and equipment—
    Disinfection
   Refrigeration as a disinfectant
   Ships—Disinfection
   Soil disinfection
   Steam as a disinfectant
   Sterilization
   Washing powders
   subdivision Disinfection *under*
    individual substances, e.g. Fertilizers
    and manures—Disinfection
  x Germicides
  xx Antiseptics
   Bacteriology
   Chemistry, Medical and pharmaceutical
   Communicable diseases
   Fumigation
   Hygiene
   Hygiene, Public
   Putrefaction
   Sanitation
 — Testing
Disinheritance *(Direct)*
  sa Legitime
  xx Inheritance and succession
   Wills
Disinheritance (Greek law)
Disinheritance (Roman law)
Disinterment
 See Exhumation
Disk-seal tubes
  x Lighthouse tubes
   Megatrons
   Planar grid tubes
  xx Microwave tubes
Disks, Imaginal
 See Imaginal disks
Disks, Rotating
  sa Gas-turbine disks
   Steam-turbine disks
  x Rotating disks
  xx Centrifugal force
   Plates (Engineering)
   Rotational motion (Rigid dynamics)
   Strains and stresses
   Wheels
 — Testing
 — Thermal properties
Disks (Mechanics)
 See Plates (Engineering)
Dislocation theory
 See Dislocations in crystals
  Dislocations in metals
Dislocations *(RD106)*
  sa subdivision Dislocation *under organs*
   and parts of the body, e.g. Hip joint
   —Dislocation; Thumb—Dislocation
  x Joints—Dislocation
   Luxations

Dislocations (Crystals)
 See Dislocations in crystals
Dislocations (Metals)
 See Dislocations in metals
Dislocations in crystals *(QD945)*
  sa Color centers
   Dislocations in metals
   Point defects
   Strengthening mechanisms in solids
  x Crystals, Dislocations in
   Dislocation theory
   Dislocations (Crystals)
  xx Crystallography
   Crystals
   Deformations (Mechanics)
   Plasticity
Dislocations in metals *(TN690)*
  sa Creep of metals
  x Dislocation theory
   Dislocations (Metals)
  xx Deformations (Mechanics)
   Dislocations in crystals
   Physical metallurgy
   Plasticity
Dismemberment of nations
  sa Secession
   State succession
  xx International law
   Secession
   Sovereignty
   State succession
Dismissal and nonsuit *(Direct)*
  x Nonsuit
  xx Civil procedure
   Judgments
Dismissal of employees
 See Employees, Dismissal of
Dismissal of executives
 See Executives, Dismissal of
Dismissal of supervisors
 See Supervisors, Dismissal of
Dismissal wage
 See Wages—Dismissal wage
Disorderly conduct *(Direct)*
  x Conduct, Disorderly
  xx Criminal law
Disorders of communication
 See Communicative disorders
Disorders of communication in children
 See Communicative disorders in children
Disorders of hearing
 See Hearing disorders
Disorders of locomotion
 See Locomotion, Disordered
Disorders of nutrition
 See Nutrition disorders
Disorders of perception
 See Perception, Disorders of
Disorders of personality
 See Personality, Disorders of
Disorders of sleep
 See Sleep disorders
Disorders of speech
 See Speech, Disorders of
Disparity of cultus
 See Marriage, Mixed
Dispensaries *(Indirect)* *(RA960-993)*
  sa Hospitals
   Nervous system—Diseases—
    Dispensaries
   Throat—Diseases—Dispensaries
   subdivision Dispensaries *under names*
    of cities, e.g. Paris—Dispensaries
  xx Charities
   Charities, Medical
   Hospitals
   Public welfare

Dispensaries, Homeopathic
 See Homeopathy—Hospitals and
  dispensaries
Dispensaries, Ophthalmic and aural *(RE3)*
  x Ophthalmic and aural dispensaries
  xx Ear—Diseases
   Eye—Diseases and defects
Dispensational theology
 See Dispensationalism
Dispensationalism *(BT157)*
  x Dispensational theology
   Theology, Dispensational
  xx Covenants (Theology)
   Eschatology
   Millennium
   Plymouth Brethren
   Theology, Doctrinal
Dispensations
  sa Epikeia
   Fasting—Dispensations
   Marriage—Dispensations
  xx Church discipline
Dispensations (Canon law) *(BX1939.D6)*
  xx Catholic Church—Discipline
   Church discipline
Dispensations (Law) *(Direct)*
  sa Administrative discretion
Dispensatories *(RS151)*
  sa Medicine—Formulae, receipts,
   prescriptions
   Pharmacopoeias
  xx Drugs
   Medicine—Formulae, receipts,
    prescriptions
   Pharmacopoeias
   Pharmacy
Dispensatories, Eclectic *(RV431)*
  x Eclectic dispensatories
  xx Medicine, Eclectic
Dispersion *(QC431-5)*
  sa Achromatism
   Suspensions (Chemistry)
  xx Optics
Dispersion, Plasma
 See Plasma diffusion
Dispersion analysis
 See Particle size determination
Dispersion hardening
 See Dispersion strengthening
Dispersion of the Jews
 See Jews—Diaspora
Dispersion relations
  sa Plasma (Ionized gases)
  xx Causality (Physics)
   Nuclear physics
   Quantum theory
Dispersion strengthening
  sa Precipitation hardening
  x Dispersion hardening
  xx Physical metallurgy
   Powder metallurgy
   Precipitation hardening
   Strengthening mechanisms in solids
Dispersoids
 See Colloids
Displaced persons (World War, 1939-1945)
 See World War, 1939-1945—Displaced
  persons
  names of individual camps, e.g.
   Schleissheim (Displaced persons
   camp)
Displacement (Psychology)
  xx Defense mechanisms (Psychology)
   Human behavior
   Psychology, Pathological
   Sublimation
Displacement (Ships) *(VM157)*
  sa Tonnage

x Ships—Displacement
xx Naval architecture
— Juvenile literature
Displacement activity (Animal behavior)
　xx Animals, Habits and behavior of
Displacement reactions
　See Substitution reactions
Display boards
　sa Bulletin boards
　x Boards, Display
　xx Exhibitions
　　Signs and sign-boards
Display figures
　See Models, Fashion
Display of merchandise (HF5845-9)
　sa Packaging
　　Show-windows
　　Showrooms
　　names of articles manufactured, e.g.
　　　Dry-goods, Hosiery; also names of
　　　industries and trades, e.g. Hosiery
　　　industry, Jewelry trade
　x Merchandise, Display of
　xx Advertising
　　Advertising, Point-of-sale
　　Commercial products
　　Retail trade
　　Sales promotion
　　Show-windows
　　Showrooms
Display systems, Information
　See Information display systems
Display techniques
　See Museum techniques
Display type
　See Printing—Specimens
　　Type and type-founding—Display type
Displays in education (LB1043.6)
　x Educational displays
　xx Exhibitions
Disposal of dead animals
　See Dead animals, Removal and disposal of
Disposal of refuse
　See Refuse and refuse disposal
Dispossession
　See Eviction
Disputations, Religious
　sa Bern disputation, 1528
　　Lausanne disputation, 1536
　　Leipzig disputation, 1519
　　Marburg conference, 1529
　　Ratisbon, Colloquy of, 1541
　　Ratisbon, Colloquy of, 1546
　　Tortosa disputation, 1413-1414
　x Colloquies, Religious
　　Debates, Religious
　　Disputations, Theological
　　Religious colloquies
　　Religious debates
　　Religious disputations
　　Theological disputations
　　Theology—Disputations
　xx Christian union
　　Councils and synods
　　Religion
　　Theology
Disputations, Theological
　See Disputations, Religious
Disputes, Labor
　See Labor disputes
Disputing
　See Quarreling
Disqualification of judges (Direct)
　xx Judges
Disregard of corporate entity (Direct)
　x Disregarding corporate entity
　xx Corporation law

Disregarding corporate entity
　See Disregard of corporate entity
Dissecting microscope (QH212.D5)
　xx Microscope and microscopy
Dissection (Comparative anatomy, QL812;
　　Human anatomy, QM34-39)
　sa Anatomy, Comparative—Laboratory
　　manuals
　　Anatomy, Human—Laboratory manuals
　　Human dissection
　　Pithing (Zoology)
　　Veterinary anatomy—Laboratory
　　manuals
　　Veterinary dissection
　　Vivisection
　　Zoology—Laboratory manuals
　xx Anatomy
　　Anatomy, Comparative—Laboratory
　　manuals
　　Surgery
　　Zoology—Laboratory manuals
Disseminated intravascular coagulation
　　(RC647.D5)
　x Consumption coagulopathy
　　Defibrination syndrome
　xx Blood—Coagulation, Disorders of
Disseminated vasculomyelinopathy
　See Allergic encephalomyelitis
Dissemination of information, Selective
　See Selective dissemination of information
Dissenters (Direct)
　sa Dissenters, Religious
　x Nonconformists
　　Rebels (Social psychology)
　xx Conformity
— Juvenile literature
— Literary collections
Dissenters, Religious (Direct)
　sa Congregationalism
　　Methodism
　　Nicodemites
　　Penal laws (against nonconformists)
　　Presbyterianism
　x Believers' church
　　Conformity (Religion)
　　Free churches
　　Nonconformists, Religious
　　Nonconformity (Religion)
　　Protestant dissenters
　　Separatism (Religion)
　xx Congregationalism
　　Dissenters
　　Established churches
　　Liberty of conscience
　　Sects
— England (BX5200-5207)
　sa Conventicle act, 1670
　　Presbyterian Church of England
　　Seekers (Sect)
　x Disabilities, Political (Great Britain)
　　Political disabilities (Great Britain)
　xx Church of England
Dissenters in literature
　xx Characters and characteristics in
　　literature
Dissenting opinions (Direct)
　xx Judicial opinions
　　Law reports, digests, etc.
Dissertations, Academic (Indirect)
　　(Preparation, LB2369)
　Here are entered works relating to theses,
　inaugural dissertations ("Habilita-
　tionsschriften"), dissertations accom-
　panying programs ("Programmab-
　handlungen, Schulschriften, Gelegen-
　heitsschriften"), etc.

　sa subdivision Dissertations under names
　　of individual universities and
　　colleges, e.g. Harvard University—
　　Dissertations
　x Academic dissertations
　　Programs, Academic
　　Theses
　　Thesis writing
　xx Universities and colleges
— Abstracts
　xx Abstracts

　　　GEOGRAPHIC SUBDIVISIONS

— United States
　x American dissertations
　　Dissertations, American
Dissertations, American
　See Dissertations, Academic—United States
Dissociation (QD517; Electrolysis, QD561)
　sa Acidity function
　　Decomposition (Chemistry)
　xx Chemistry
　　Chemistry, Physical and theoretical
　　Decomposition (Chemistry)
　　Thermochemistry
— Tables, etc.
Dissociation of personality
　See Personality, Disorders of
Dissolute persons in literature
　See Libertines in literature
Dissolved oxygen in water
　See Water—Dissolved oxygen
Dissonance (Psychology)
　sa Cognitive balance
　x Cognitive dissonance
　xx Adaptability (Psychology)
　　Choice (Psychology)
　　Motivation (Psychology)
　　Social psychology
Distaff (Spinning) (Direct)
　xx Spinning
Distal ileitis
　See Regional ileitis
Distance, Zenith
　See Zenith distance
Distance geometry (QA613)
　x Abstract metrics
　　Metric topology
　xx Metric spaces
　　Topology
**Distance measuring equipment (Aircraft to
　　ground station)** (TL696.D65)
　x Aeroplanes—Distance measuring
　　equipment
　　Challenge-reply systems (Radar)
　　DME
　　Interrogator-transpondor systems
　　Narrow-band DME
　　Pulse multiplex DME
　xx Aeronautical instruments
　　Air traffic control
　　Distances—Measurement
　　Instrument landing systems
　　Omnirange system
　　Radar in aeronautics
— Standards (Direct)
Distance perception
　See Depth perception
Distances
　sa Railroads—Distances, etc.
　　subdivision Distances, etc. under names
　　of countries, cities, etc., e.g. United
　　States—Distances, etc.; London—
　　Distances, etc.
— Measurement (Physics, QC102;
　　Surveying, TA601)
　sa Distance measuring equipment
　　(Aircraft to ground station)

Distances
— Measurement *(Physics, QC102;*
Surveying, TA601)
(Continued)
Geodimeter
Map scales
Range-finding
Telemeter
Tellurometer
x Measurement of distances
— — Tables *(TA601)*
— Tables, etc. *(Aeronautics, TL551;*
Automobiling, GV1024-5;
Geography, G109-110; Naval
ordnance, VF550; Navigation,
VK799; Ordnance, UF857)
Here are entered general works not
confined to any one locality. Works
on distances in a particular country
or locality are entered under name
of country, city, etc., with subdivi-
sion Distances, etc.
sa Time-rate-distance tables
Roads—[local subdivision], *e.g.*
Roads—England; Roads—London
and vicinity
x Tables of distances
xx Geography—Tables, etc.
Roads
Distant early warning system *(Direct)*
x Dew line
DEWS
Early warning systems
xx Air defenses, Military
Radar defense networks
Distemper *(SF991)*
sa Canine distemper
Distillate oil wells
See Condensate oil wells
Distillation *(QD63.D6; TP156.D5)*
sa Alcohol
Alcoholometer
Azeotropes
Brandy
Distillation apparatus
Distillation, Molecular
Distilleries
Essences and essential oils
Liquors
Rum
Solar stills
Water, Distilled
Water—Purification—Distillation
process
Wood distillation
x Rectification of spirits
xx Alcohol
Liquors
Packed towers
Separation (Technology)
— Tables, calculations, etc.
Distillation, Destructive
sa Carbonization
Coal gasification
Coal-tar products
Cracking process
Gas
Mineral oils
Oils and fats
Oxo process
Petroleum
x Destructive distillation
xx Carbonization
Chemistry, Technical
Coal-tar products
Gas
Petroleum
Distillation, Fractional *(QD526)*
sa Distillation, Molecular

Plate towers
x Fractional distillation
xx Boiling-points
Chemistry, Analytic—Quantitative
Chemistry—Manipulation
Plate towers
Thermochemistry
Distillation, Molecular
sa Molecular stills
x Molecular distillation
xx Distillation
Distillation, Fractional
Distillation apparatus
sa Plate towers
Solar stills
x Distilling apparatus
Stills
xx Distillation
— Taxation *(Direct)*
xx Liquor traffic—Taxation
Distillation of sea-water
See Sea-water, Distillation of
Distillation process, Flash (Saline water
conversion)
See Saline water conversion—Flash
distillation process
Distillation process (Saline water conversion)
See Saline water conversion—Distillation
process
Distillation process (Water purification)
See Water—Purification—Distillation
process
Distilled water
See Water, Distilled
Distilleries
x Stills
xx Distillation
Distilling industries
— Fires and fire prevention *(TH9445.D5)*
— Law and legislation *(Direct)*
sa Distilling, Illicit
xx Alcohol—Law and legislation
Alcohol—Taxation
Liquor laws
Liquor traffic—Taxation
Distillers by-products as feed
See Distillers feeds
Distillers feeds *(SF99.D5)*
x Distillers by-products as feed
Distillers grains as feed
Draff
xx Distilling industries—By-products
Feeds
Distillers grains as feed
See Distillers feeds
Distillery by-products
See Distilling industries—By-products
Distillery warehouses *(Direct) (United*
States, HJ5020)
xx Bonded warehouses and goods
Internal revenue
Liquor traffic—Taxation
Warehouses
Distilling, Illicit *(United States, HJ5021)*
x Illicit distilling
Moonshining
xx Distilleries—Law and legislation
Liquor traffic—Taxation
Distilling apparatus
See Distillation apparatus
Distilling industries *(Direct) (Economics,*
HD9390-9395; Technology,
TP589-618)
sa Distilleries
Liquor traffic
x Alcoholic beverage industry
Licensed beverage industry
Liquor industry

xx Alcohol
Liquor traffic
— Automation
— By-products
sa Distillers feeds
x Distillery by-products
xx Factory and trade waste
— — Storage
— Collective labor agreements
See Collective labor agreements—
Distilling industries
— Equipment and supplies
— — Maintenance and repair
— Job descriptions
— Safety measures
— Taxation
See Liquor traffic—Taxation
Distomatosis *(RC139)*
sa Fasciola and fascioliasis
Liver flukes
Trematoda
x Distomiasis
Liver-rot
xx Liver flukes
Trematoda
Distomiasis
See Distomatosis
Distress (Law) *(Direct)*
sa Landlord and tenant
xx Executions (Law)
Landlord and tenant
Remedies (Law)
Self-help (Law)
Distress (Roman law)
Distress signals
xx Signals and signaling
Distributed amplifiers
x D-amplifiers
xx Amplifiers, Vacuum-tube
Broadband amplifiers
Distributed lags (Economics)
xx Econometrics
Estimation theory
Distribution, Cooperative
See Cooperation
Cooperative societies
Distribution (Economic theory) *(HB771)*
sa Interest and usury
Profit
Rent
Wages
xx Commerce
Income
Wealth
Distribution (Functional analysis)
See Distributions, Theory of (Functional
analysis)
Distribution (Probability theory) *(QA273)*
sa Convolutions (Mathematics)
Frequency curves
Gaussian processes
Poisson distribution
Statistical hypothesis testing
Weibull distribution
x Distribution functions
Frequency distribution
xx Functions, Characteristic
Probabilities
— Tables, etc.
Distribution functions
See Distribution (Probability theory)
Distribution modulo one
xx Diophantine analysis
Numbers, Theory of
Sequences (Mathematics)
Distribution of decedents' estates *(Direct)*
sa Partition of decedents' estates
x Descent and distribution

xx Co-heirs
Decedents' estates
Executors and administrators
Inheritance and succession
Partition of decedents' estates
Probate law and practice
Distribution of decedents' estates (Islamic law)
Distribution of goods, Physical
See Physical distribution of goods
Distribution of income
See Income
Distribution of seed by the government
See Seed distribution
Distribution of values theory
See Value distribution theory
Distribution of wealth
See Wealth
Distributions, Theory of (Functional analysis)
sa Hyperfunctions
x Distribution (Functional analysis)
Functions, Generalized
Generalized functions
xx Functional analysis
Functions
Linear topological spaces
Distributive education *(Direct)* *(HF5415)*
x Education, Distributive
xx Business education
Marketing
Retail trade
Salesmen and salesmanship
Distributive law (Mathematics)
xx Mathematics
District air conditioning
See Air conditioning from central stations
District courts *(Direct)*
Works on individual district courts are entered under the official heading for the court, *e.g.* United States. District Court. California (Northern District)
x Courts, District
xx Courts
District heating
See Heating from central stations
District libraries
See Libraries, Regional
District nurses
See Nurses and nursing
District of Columbia
— History
See Washington, D.C.—History
District superintendents (Methodist)
xx Church officers
Methodist Church—Clergy
Methodist Church—Government
Districting (in city planning)
See Zoning
Districts, Special
See Special districts
Ditch, Battle of the, 627 *(DS232)*
x al-Khandaq, Battle of, 627
Ditchers
See Trenching machinery
Ditches *(Agriculture, S621; Land drainage, TC970)*
sa Grassed waterways
xx Drainage
Ditching of aircraft
See Aeroplanes—Ditching
Dithionates *(QD181.S1)*
Dithyramb *(Greek poetry, PA3118.D5)*
xx Greek poetry
Lyric poetry
Diu, India
— Siege, 1539 and 1545 *(DS485.D5)*

Diur language
See Dyur language
Diuretics and diuresis *(RM375-7)*
sa Cytisine
xx Kidneys
Urine
Diuretin *(RM666.D6)*
Diurnal infra-red albedo variations
See Infra-red albedo—Diurnal variation
Diurnal variation (Infra-red albedo)
See Infra-red albedo—Diurnal variation
Diurnal variation (Terrestrial magnetism)
See Magnetism, Terrestrial—Diurnal variation
Divali *(BL1213.D5)*
x Deepavali
Dewali
Dipavali
Diwali
Divergent series
See Series, Divergent
Divers *(Direct)*
sa Diving
Diving, Submarine
xx Diving
Diving, Submarine
— Legal status, laws, etc. *(Direct)*
— Medical examinations
Divers (Birds) *(QL696.P9)*
sa Pygopodes
x Colymbidae
Diversification in industry *(Direct)*
x Product diversification
xx Interindustry economics
Diversity receivers and reception (Radio)
See Radio—Receivers and reception—Diversity systems
Diverticulitis
xx Colon (Anatomy)—Diseases
Dives and Lazarus (Parable) *(BT378.D5)*
x Lazarus and Dives
Rich man and Lazarus (Parable)
xx Poor—Biblical teaching
Wealth—Biblical teaching
Divestiture, Corporate
See Corporate divestiture
Divestment, Corporate
See Corporate divestiture
Divided catalogs
See Catalogs, Divided
Dividends *(Direct)*
x Stock dividends
xx Corporations—Finance
Stocks
— Tables, etc.
See Stocks—Tables, etc.
— Taxation *(Direct)*
xx Income tax
Dividing-engine
Divination *(Direct)* *(Comparative religion, BL613; Occult sciences, BF1745-1779)*
sa Astrology
Catoptromancy
Choice by lot
Clairvoyance
Crystal-gazing
Divining-rod
Dreams
Feng-shui
Fortune-telling
Fortune-telling by birthdays
Fortune-telling by cards
Fortune-telling by dice
Fortune-telling by fingerprints
Fortune-telling by names
Fortune-telling by tea leaves
Geomancy

Ifa
Occult sciences
Omens
Oracle bones
Oracles
Palmistry
Prophecies
Second sight
Sibyls
Superstition
x Augury
Soothsaying
xx Catoptromancy
Choice by lot
Clairvoyance
Fortune-telling
Geomancy
Magic
Mirrors, Magic
Occult sciences
Omens
Oracles
Prophecies
Second sight
Supernatural
Superstition
— Controversial literature
— Juvenile literature
Divine glory
See Glory of God
Divine healing
See Christian Science
Faith-cure
Miracles
Divine immanence
See Immanence of God
Divine messengers in literature
x Celestial messengers in literature
xx Angels
Messengers in literature
Divine office
sa Catholic Church. Liturgy and ritual. Breviary
Lauds
Rimed offices
Vespers
x Daily offices
Office, Divine
xx Catholic Church. Liturgy and ritual. Breviary
Prayer
Divine office (Canon law)
Divine right of kings *(JC389)*
sa Emperor worship
Kings and rulers (in religion, folk-lore, etc.)
Prerogative, Royal
x Higher law
Kings, Divine right of
xx Authority
Kings and rulers
Kings and rulers—Succession
Monarchy
Political science
Prerogative, Royal
Divine transcendence
See Transcendence of God
Diving *(Aquatic sports, GV837)*
sa Divers
Swimming
xx Divers
Swimming
— Juvenile literature
Diving, Cave
See Cave diving
Diving, Skin
See Skin diving

Diving, Submarine *(VM981-9; Submarine construction, TC183)*
  sa Bathyscaphe
    Decompression (Physiology)
    Divers
    Diving-bells
    Diving suits
    Manned undersea research stations
    Skin diving
    Underwater demolition teams
    Underwater exploration
    Underwater welding and cutting
  x Submarine diving
  xx Divers
    Ocean
    Oceanography
  — Equipment and supplies
    xx Ocean engineering
  — Juvenile literature
  — Law and legislation *(Direct)*
    xx Fishery law and legislation
      Wreck
  — Physiological aspects
    x Physiological aspects of submarine
      diving
  — Safety measures *(VM981)*
Diving-bells *(VM987)*
  xx Diving, Submarine
    Oceanographic submersibles
Diving suits
  x Scaphanders
  xx Diving, Submarine
    Skin diving—Equipment and supplies
Divining-rod *(BF1628)*
  sa Radiesthesia
    Springs (in religion, folk-lore, etc.)
  x Dowsing
    Water witching
  xx Divination
    Folk-lore
    Springs
    Springs (in religion, folk-lore, etc.)
    Water (in religion, folk-lore, etc.)
    Water, Underground
Divinity of Christ
  See Jesus Christ—Divinity
Division *(Arithmetic, QA115)*
  xx Arithmetic
  — Juvenile literature
  — Problems, exercises, etc.
  — Tables *(QA49)*
    x Tables, Mathematical
    xx Mathematics—Tables, etc.
Division of labor *(HD51)*
  sa Machinery in industry
  x Labor, Division of
  xx Economics
    Labor and laboring classes
    Machinery in industry
Division of powers
  See Federal government
    Separation of powers
Division of words
  See Syllabication
Divisionism
  See Neo-impressionism (Art)
Divorce *(Direct) (HQ811-960)*
  sa Alienation of affections
    Alimony
    Broken homes
    Children of divorced parents
    Desertion and non-support
    Divorce suits
    Divorcees
    Legal cruelty
    Marriage—Annulment
    Remarriage
    Separation (Law)

    Trials (Divorce)
  xx Ethics
    Family
    Husband and wife
    Marriage
    Marriage—Annulment
    Marriage law
    Separation (Law)
    Social problems
    Woman—Social and moral questions
  — Anecdotes, facetiae, satire, etc.
  — Biblical teaching *(HQ824)*
  — Conflict of laws
    See Conflict of laws—Divorce
  — Costs
    x Divorce costs
    Example under Costs (Law)
  — Domicile
    See Domicile in domestic relations
  — Juvenile literature
  — Personal narratives
Divorce (Ancient law)
Example under Law, Ancient
Divorce (Canon law) *(HQ1024)*
  sa Defender of the marriage bond
    Marriage—Annulment (Canon law)
    Separation (Canon law)
  x Pauline privilege
    Privilegium Paulinum
  xx Marriage (Canon law)
    Separation (Canon law)
Divorce (Canon law, Orthodox Eastern)
  xx Marriage (Canon law, Orthodox
    Eastern)
Divorce (Hindu law)
Divorce (Islamic law) *(Direct)*
Divorce (Jewish law)
  sa Agunah
  x Jews—Divorce
  xx Agunah
Divorce (Roman-Dutch law)
Divorce (Roman law)
Divorce (Yoruba law)
Divorce a mensa et thoro
  See Separation (Law)
Divorce costs
  See Divorce—Costs
Divorce from bed and board
  See Separation (Law)
Divorce in literature
  xx Social problems in literature
Divorce practice
  See Divorce suits
Divorce proceedings
  See Divorce suits
Divorce suits *(Direct)*
  x Divorce practice
    Divorce proceedings
  xx Civil procedure
    Divorce
    Matrimonial actions
Divorce suits (Canon law)
  xx Matrimonial actions (Canon law)
Divorced persons
  See Divorcees
Divorcees
  sa Single-parent family
  x Divorced persons
  xx Divorce
    Single-parent family
    Single people
    Single women
  — Personal narratives *(HQ814-819)*
Diwali
  See Divali
Dixi, Custodiam (Music)
  See Psalms (Music)—39th Psalm

Dixit Dominus (Music)
  See Psalms (Music)—110th Psalm
Dixit injustus (Music)
  See Psalms (Music)—36th Psalm
Dixmude, Battle of, 1914
  See Yser, Battle of the, 1914
Dizziness
  See Vertigo
Djaga language
  See Chaga language
Djahmiyya
  See al-Jahmīyah
Djarai
  See Jarai
Djawara (African people)
  See Diawara (African people)
Djedji dialect
  See Fon dialect
Djimini (African people)
  x Dyimini (African people)
    Gimini (African people)
    Jimini (African people)
  xx Ethnology—Ivory Coast
Djiong
  See Moso (Tribe)
Djirbal language
  x Djirubal language
    Dyirbal language
    Tjirbal language
  xx Australian languages
Djirubal language
  See Djirbal language
Djo language
  See Ijo language
Djore-Xikrin Indians
  See Xikrin Indians
Djuka tribe *(F2431.N3)*
  xx Ethnology—Surinam
DKW automobile
  x Deke automobile
DL-ASEDC (Electronic computer system)
  x Dynamic language-application system
    for the evaluation of data collections
  xx Electronic data processing
DME
  See Distance measuring equipment (Aircraft
    to ground station)
Dnepr computer
  xx Electronic digital computers
Dnieper River Campaign, 1943
  See World War, 1939-1945—Campaigns—
    Dnieper River
Dnipro computer
  x UMShN computer
  xx Electronic digital computers
Do 335 (Fighter planes)
  See Pfeil (Fighter planes)
Do-it-yourself work
    Do-it-yourself manuals in specific fields
    are entered under the name of the ac-
    tivity, *e.g.* House painting, Interior
    decoration.
  xx Industrial arts
Do language
  See Bini language
Dobermann pinschers *(SF429.P5)*
  x Pinschers, Dobermann
  — Legends and stories
Doblons
  See Doubloons
Dobro *(ML1015-1018)*
  xx Guitar
  — Methods *(MT599.D6)*
Dobrudja in literature
Dobu language *(PL6621.D6)*
  x Dobuan language
  xx Papuan languages

Dobuan language
  See Dobu language
Docimasia pulmonum *(RA1065)*
  xx Fetus
    Lungs
    Medical jurisprudence
    Respiration
Dock false-worm *(SB945.D7)*
  Example under Beet pests
Dock hands
  See Longshoremen
Dock warrants
  See Warehouse receipts
Docks *(Indirect) (Construction, TC355-365;*
    Docking facilities, VK361-5; Port
    guides, regulations, etc., HE951-3;
    Transportation and communication,
    HE551-9)
  sa Dry-docks
    Harbors
    Wharves
    subdivision Docks *under names of*
      cities and towns, e.g. London—
      Docks
  xx Civil engineering
    Engineering
    Harbors
    Hydraulic structures
    Marinas
    Wharves
  — Fenders
    See Fenders for docks, piers, etc.
  — Juvenile literature
  — Safety measures
Dockyards
  See Navy-yards and naval stations
Doctor of education degree
  x Education, Doctor of
Doctor of jurisprudence degree
  See Doctor of laws degree
Doctor of laws degree
  x Doctor of jurisprudence degree
    Jurisprudence, Doctor of
    Law, Doctor of
Doctor of philosophy degree *(LB2386)*
  x Philosophy, Doctor of
  Example under Degrees, Academic
Doctor-patient privilege
  See Confidential communications—
    Physicians
Doctor-patient relationship
  See Physician and patient
Doctors
  See Physicians
Doctors' degrees
  See Degrees, Academic
Doctors in art
  See Medicine and art
Doctors of the church *(BX4669)*
  xx Fathers of the church
    Saints
    Theologians
Doctrinal anthropology
  See Man (Theology)
Doctrinal development
  See Dogma, Development of
Doctrinal theology
  See Theology, Doctrinal
Doctrine, Christian (Catholic Church)
  See Catechetics—Catholic Church
Doctrine, Development of
  See Dogma, Development of
Doctrine of correspondences
  See Correspondences, Doctrine of
Doctrine of degrees
  See Degrees, Doctrine of
Doctrine of worthier title
  See Worthier title

Doctrines
  See Dogma
    Theology, Doctrinal
Document copying
  See Photocopying processes
Document files
  See subdivision Records and
    correspondence *under specific*
    subjects, e.g. Railroads—Records and
    correspondence; United States.
    Army—Records and correspondence
Document writing, Chinese
  x Chinese document writing
  xx Chinese language—Writing
    Diplomatics
Documentary evidence
  See Evidence, Documentary
Documentary films
  See Moving-pictures, Documentary
Documentary moving-pictures
  See Moving-pictures, Documentary
Documentary photography
  See Photography, Documentary
Documentary television programs *(Direct)*
  x Television programs, Documentary
  xx Moving-pictures, Documentary
Documentation
  sa Abstracting
    Abstracting and indexing services
    Archives
    Bibliographical centers
    Bibliography
    Cataloging
    Classification—Books
    Classification, Décasépel
    Copying processes
    Files and filing (Documents)
    Indexing
    Information services
    Information storage and retrieval
      systems
    Library science
    MINSK-ARDIS (Information retrieval
      system)
    Museums
    Photocopying processes
    SESAM (Information retrieval system)
    SMART (Information retrieval system)
    Translating services
    subdivision Documentation *under*
      subjects, e.g. Agriculture—
      Documentation
  xx Information science
    Information services
  — Standards
  — Terminology
Documentation in electronic data processing
  See Electronic data processing
    documentation
Documents
  See Archives
    Charters
    Deeds
    Diplomatics
    Government publications
    Legal documents
    Municipal documents
Documents, Commercial
  See Commercial documents
Documents, Diplomatic
  See Diplomatic documents
Documents, Identification of
  See Legal documents—Identification
Documents, Legal
  See Legal documents
Documents, Papal
  See Papal documents

Documents, Printing of *(Z264.5)*
  x Printing—Documents
  xx Printing, Practical
Documents in electronic data processing
  See Electronic data processing
    documentation
Documents in microform
  sa Documents on microform
  xx Microforms
Documents librarians *(Direct)*
  xx Librarians
    Special librarians
Documents on microfilm *(Z265)*
  sa SESAM (Information retrieval system)
  x Archival material on microfilm
  xx Documents in microform
    Microfilms
  — Law and legislation *(Direct)*
Dodder *(QK495.C98)*
  xx Clover
  Example under Parasitic plants
  — Diseases and pests
Dodge automobile *(TL215.D6)*
  sa Challenger automobile
    Dodge Colt automobile
    Dodge Dart automobile
    Dodge Demon automobile
Dodge Charger automobile
  x Charger automobile
Dodge Colt automobile *(TL215.D)*
  x Colt automobile
  xx Dodge automobile
Dodge Dart automobile *(TL215.D)*
  x Dart automobile
  xx Dodge automobile
Dodge Demon automobile *(TL215.D)*
  x Demon automobile
  xx Dodge automobile
Dodo *(QE872.C7)*
  Example under Birds, Extinct
Dodos (African tribe)
  See Dodoth (African tribe)
Dodosi (African tribe)
  See Dodoth (African tribe)
Dodoth (African tribe)
  x Dodos (African tribe)
    Dodosi (African tribe)
    Dodotho (African tribe)
  xx Ethnology—Uganda
    Nilo-Hamitic tribes
Dodotho (African tribe)
  See Dodoth (African tribe)
Dog
  See Dogs
Dog breeders' societies *(SF421)*
Dog breeding
  sa Dog breeds
  x Dogs—Breeding
  Example under Breeding
Dog breeds *(Indirect)*
  sa names of specific breeds, e.g.
    Bloodhounds, Collies, Siberian
    huskies
  x Breeds of dogs
    Dogs—Breeds
  xx Dog breeding
    Dogs
  — Juvenile literature
Dog-fighting *(GV1109)*
  x Animal baiting
    Fighting
  xx Animal fighting
Dog food
  See Dogs—Food
Dog grooming
  x Clipping of dogs
    Dogs—Clipping
    Dogs—Grooming

Dog grooming *(Continued)*
    Dogs—Trimming
    Grooming of dogs
    Trimming of dogs
    xx Dog-shows
Dog guides
    See Guide dogs
Dog heartworm
    See Canine heartworm disease
Dog licenses
    See Dogs—Taxation
Dog Mass *(BX2015.5.H)*
    xx Catholic Church. Liturgy and ritual.
        Missal
        Dogs (in religion, folk-lore, etc.)
        Hunting (in religion, folk-lore, etc.)
Dog racing *(Indirect) (SF440)*
    sa Greyhounds
    x Coursing (Racing)
    xx Racing
Dog Rib Indians
    See Thlingchadinne Indians
Dog salmon
    See Chum salmon
Dog-shows *(SF425)*
    sa Dog grooming
        Dogs—Judging
        Dogs—Showing
        Field trials
    x Dogs—Exhibitions
    xx Pet shows
Dog stories
    See Dogs—Legends and stories
Dogari dialect
    See Dogri dialect
Dogfish *(QL638.9)*
    x Dogshark
    xx Sharks
    — Anatomy
Dogger Bank, Battle of the, 1915 *(D582.D6)*
    xx European War, 1914-1918—Naval
        operations
Doggerel
    xx Humorous poetry
        Poetry
Dogma *(BT19-33)*
    Here are entered works on dogma in the
        abstract. Works on the Christian dog-
        mas are entered under Theology, Doc-
        trinal.
    sa Apostasy
        Indifferentism (Religion)
        Rule of faith
    x Doctrines
    xx Apostasy
        Theology, Doctrinal
Dogma, Development of
    sa Theology, Doctrinal—History
    x Doctrinal development
        Doctrine, Development of
    xx Theology, Doctrinal—History
Dogmatic theology
    See Theology, Doctrinal
Dogmatism
    x Authoritarianism (Psychology)
        Authority (Psychology)
    xx Attitude (Psychology)
        Rigidity (Psychology)
        Thought and thinking
    — Testing
Dogo language
    See Dogon language
Dogom language
    See Dogon language
Dogon language
    x Dogo language
        Dogom language
        Habe language

    Tombo language
    xx Gur languages
Dogons (African people)
    x Habe (African people)
    xx Ethnology—Mali
    — Religion
Dogra dialect
    See Dogri dialect
Dogri dialect *(PK2645-8)*
    x Dogari dialect
        Dogra dialect
    xx Panjabi language
Dogri drama *(Direct) (Collections,*
    PK2648.A2; History and criticism,
    PK2647.5)
Dogri fiction *(Direct)*
Dogri literature *(Direct) (PK2647-8)*
Dogri poetry *(Direct)*
Dogrib Indians
    See Thlingchadinne Indians
Dogs *(Indirect) (SF421-439; Folk-lore,*
    GR720; Manners and customs,
    GT5890; Zoology, QL737.C2)
    sa Dog breeds
        Hunting dogs
        Working dogs
    x Dog
    xx Domestic animals
    Example under Pets
    — Anatomy
    — — Atlases
    — Anecdotes, facetiae, satire, etc.
    — Behavior
    — Breeding
        See Dog breeding
    — Breeds
        See Dog breeds
    — Caricatures and cartoons
    — Clipping
        See Dog grooming
    — Diseases *(SF991)*
        sa Black-tongue
            Canine distemper
            Canine heartworm disease
    — Early works to 1800
    — Exhibitions
        See Dog-shows
    — Food
        x Dog food
    — Grooming
        See Dog grooming
    — Judging
        xx Dog-shows
    — Juvenile literature
    — Laws and legislation *(Direct)*
        (SF437-9)
    — Legends and stories *(QL795.D6)*
        x Dog stories
        xx Animals, Legends and stories of
    — Photography
        See Photography of dogs
    — Physiology *(QP)*
    — Pictorial works *(SF430)*
    — Pictures, illustrations, etc. *(N7660;*
        SF430)
    — Poetry *(PN6110.D)*
    — Psychology
    — Quotations, maxims, etc.
    — Showing
        xx Dog-shows
    — — Juvenile literature
    — Stud-books *(SF423)*
        x Stud-books
    — Surgery
        Example under Veterinary surgery
    — Taxation *(Direct) (HJ5791-2)*
        x Dog licenses
            Licensing of dogs

    — Training *(SF431)*
        xx Animals, Training of
            Game and game-birds
    — Trimming
        See Dog grooming
Dogs, Fossil *(QE882.C1)*
Dogs, War use of *(UH100)*
    sa subdivision Dogs *under names of*
        individual wars
    x War, Use of dogs in
    xx Animals, War use of
    — Juvenile literature
Dogs (in religion, folk-lore, etc.) *(Folk-lore,*
    GR720; Religion, BL325.A6)
    sa Dog Mass
    x Folk-lore of dogs
    xx Religion, Primitive
Dogs as carriers of disease *(RA641.D6)*
    xx Animals as carriers of disease
        Communicable diseases
Dogs as laboratory animals
    xx Laboratory animals
Dogs in art
    xx Art
Dogs in literature
Dogs in moving-pictures
    xx Moving-pictures
Dogshark
    See Dogfish
Dogwood *(Botany, QK495.C785; Materia*
    medica, RS165.C85)
    sa Flowering dogwood
Dogwood, Poison
    See Poison-sumac
Dohema language
    See Eudeve language
Dohme language
    See Eudeve language
Doilies *(TT751; TT775; TT825)*
    xx Crocheting
        Embroidery
        Lace and lace making
Dok- en Werf-Maatschappij Wilton-Fijenoord
    Strike, 1965
Dokhmas *(GT3350)*
    x Dakhmas
        Exposure of the dead
        Towers of silence
    xx Dead
        Funeral rites and ceremonies
        Zoroastrianism
Dolantin
    See Isonipecaine
Dolce Stil nuovo
    See Italian poetry—To 1400
Dolder scale
    xx Social maturity scales
        Vineland social maturity scale
Doleantie
    xx Nederlandse Hervormde Kerk—Parties
        and movements
Dolerite
    See Diabase
Dolichocephaly *(GN71-72)*
    xx Craniology
Doll artists
    See Dollmakers
Doll clothes
    x Clothing, Doll
        Dolls' clothes
    xx Costume
        Dolls
        Dressmaking
        Sewing
        Soft toy making
    — Juvenile literature

Doll furniture *(Direct)* *(Handicrafts, TT175.5)*
   x Furniture—Models
   xx Doll-houses
      Miniature furniture
   — Juvenile literature
Doll-houses *(Indirect)* *(Art museums, NK495; Play, GV1219; Toy manufacture, TS2301.T7)*
   sa Doll furniture
      Miniature rooms
   x Miniature houses
   xx Miniature objects
      Miniature rooms
   — Juvenile literature
Doll makers
   See Dollmakers
Doll making
   See Dollmaking
Doll marks
   See Dolls—Trade-marks
Dollar *(CJ; HG)*
   sa Piece of eight
      Taler
   xx Silver question
   Example under Coins; Money
Dollar, American
   x American dollar
   xx Money—United States
   — Devaluation
      x Dollar devaluation (United States)
      xx Currency question—United States
Dollar, American (Coin)
   x American dollar (Coin)
Dollar, Canadian
   x Canadian dollar
Dollar, Commodity
   See Commodity dollar
Dollar-a-year men
   See Without-compensation personnel
Dollar devaluation (United States)
   See Dollar, American—Devaluation
Dollar mark
   See Dollar sign
Dollar sign *(CJ161.D6)*
   x Dollar mark
   xx Numismatics
Dollmakers *(Direct)*
   x Doll artists
      Doll makers
   xx Dolls
Dollmaking
   sa Dolls—Repairing
      Paper doll making
   x Doll making
   xx Dolls
   — Amateurs' manuals
   — Juvenile literature
Dolls *(GV1219; Art museums, NK495; Manufacture, TS2301.T7)*
   sa Bodhidharma dolls
      Doll clothes
      Dollmakers
      Dollmaking
   x Figurines
   xx Toys
   — Collectors and collecting
   — Juvenile literature
   — Patents
   — Pictorial works
   — Psychological aspects
   — Repairing
      xx Dollmaking
   — Trade-marks
      x Doll marks
Dolls, American, [Japanese, etc.]
   — Trade-marks

Dolls, Japanese
   sa Kokeshi dolls
Dolls, Kokeshi
   See Kokeshi dolls
Dolls (in religion, folk-lore, etc.)
   sa Katcinas
   x Folk-lore of dolls
   xx Idols and images
      Religion, Primitive
Dolls' clothes
   See Doll clothes
Dolly Varden (Trout)
   xx Trout
Dolmens *(GN790-792)*
   sa Menhirs
   xx Cromlechs
      Megalithic monuments
      Menhirs
Dolomite *(Indirect)* *(Building stones, TN967; Minerals, QE391.D6; Petrology, QE471)*
   xx Evaporites
      Rocks, Carbonate
Dolors of Our Lady, Devotion to
   See Sorrows of the Blessed Virgin Mary, Devotion to.
Dolphin (in religion, folk-lore, etc.)
   x Folk-lore of dolphins
   xx Dolphins
      Fish (in religion, folk-lore, etc.)
      Religion, Primitive
Dolphins *(Indirect)* *(QL737.C4)*
   sa Bottlenosed dolphins
      Dolphin (in religion, folk-lore, etc.)
      False killer whale
      Killer whale
      Pigmy killer whale
      Porpoises
   xx Cetacea
      Porpoises
   — Behavior
   — Juvenile literature
Dolphins, Fossil *(QE882.C5)*
Dolus (Byzantine law)
Dolus (Canon law)
Dolus (Civil law) *(Direct)*
   sa Bad faith (Law)
      Fraud
      Negligence
      Rescission (Law)
   xx Fraud
      Guilt (Law)
      Liability (Law)
      Negligence
      Simulation (Civil law)
Dolus (Criminal law)
   See Criminal intent
Dolus (Islamic law)
Dom dialects
   sa Golin dialect
      Marigl dialect
   xx Papuan languages
Doma (Asiatic people)
   x Bericho (Asiatic people)
   xx Ethnology—Hunza
Domain, Eminent
   See Eminent domain
Domain, Public
   See Public domain
Domain configuration
   See Domain structure
Domain structure
   x Domain configuration
      Ferromagnetic domain
      Magnetic domain
   xx Crystals
      Ferroelectricity
      Ferromagnetism

Domaine public payant *(Direct)*
   x Kulturabgabe
      Kulturpfennig
   xx Copyright
      State encouragement of science, literature, and art—Law and legislation
Domains, Siegel
   See Siegel domains
Dombra
   See Domra
Domes *(Direct)* *(Architecture, NA2890; Building, TH2170)*
   sa Geodesic domes
      Roofs
      Roofs, Shell
   x Cupolas
   xx Architecture—Details
      Roofs
Domes, Observatory
   See Observatory domes
Domes (Geology) *(Indirect)*
   sa Diapirs
      Salt domes
   xx Geology, Structural
Domesday book *(DA190)*
   x Doomsday book
Domestic animals *(Indirect)* *(Animal industry, SF; Ethnology, GN426; Manners and customs, GT5870-5895)*
   sa Animals, Treatment of
      Camels
      Cats
      Cattle
      Cows
      Dogs
      Domestication
      Draft animals
      Feral livestock
      Goats
      Horses
      Indians of North America—Domestic animals
      Pets
      Pounds
      Quarantine, Veterinary
      Reindeer
      Sheep
      Stock and stock-breeding
      Swine
   x Animal husbandry
      Animals, Domestic
      Beasts
      Farm animals
      Livestock
   xx Agriculture
      Animal culture
      Animal industry
      Animal introduction
      Breeding
      Domestication
      Pets
      Veterinary medicine
      Zoology
      Zoology, Economic
   — Age *(SF869)*
      Example under Age
   — Age determination
      Example under Age determination (Zoology)
   — Anatomy
      See Veterinary anatomy
   — Behavior
   — Brands
      See Livestock brands
   — Cooperative marketing

Domestic animals *(Indirect)* *(Animal industry, SF; Ethnology, GN426; Manners and customs, GT5870-5895)*
  — Cooperative marketing *(Continued)*
    See Cooperative marketing of livestock
  — Costs
    See Stock and stock-breeding—Costs
  — Diseases
    See Veterinary medicine
  — Grading
    xx Marketing of livestock
  — History
    x Domestic animals—Origin
  — — Juvenile literature
  — Housing
    See Animal housing
  — Juvenile literature
  — Law
    Here are entered general works only. The laws of a particular country or state relating to domestic animals are entered under Domestic animals—[local subdivision]—Law, *e.g.* Domestic animals—Maryland—Law.
    sa Animal industry—Law and legislation
      Liability for animals
      Veterinary jurisprudence
    xx Animal industry—Law and legislation
  — Legends and stories
  — Marketing
    See Marketing of livestock
  — Names
  — Nomenclature (Popular)
  — Origin
    See Domestic animals—History
  — Parasites
    See Parasites—Domestic animals
  — Physiology
    See Veterinary physiology
  — Pictorial works
    xx Animal pictures
  — Prices *(Direct)*
  — Radiation effects
    See Domestic animals, Effect of radiation on
  — Taxation
  — Transportation *(Quarantine, SF998)*
    Example under Animals—Transportation
  — Maryland
  — — Law
    Note under Domestic animals—Law

Domestic animals, Effect of radiation on *(SF757.8)*
  x Domestic animals—Radiation effects
    Radiation—Effect on domestic animals
    Stock and stock-breeding—Radiation effects
  xx Radiation—Physiological effect
    Radioisotopes in agriculture
Domestic appliances
  See Household appliances
Domestic architecture
  See Architecture, Domestic
Domestic capacity measures, Tariff on
  See Tariff on domestic capacity measures
Domestic economy
  See Home economics
Domestic education *(Direct)* *(LC37)*
  sa Children—Management
    Education of women
    Governesses
    Tutors and tutoring

  x Home education
  xx Children
    Education
    Family
Domestic electric apparatus
  See Household appliances, Electric
Domestic engineering *(TD; TH; TX298)*
  sa Dwellings—Air conditioning
    Dwellings—Heating and ventilation
    Dwellings—Lighting
    Home accidents
    Plumbing
    Refrigerators
    Sanitation, Household
  xx Dwellings
  — Costs
  — Equipment and supplies
  — Tables, calculations, etc.
Domestic jurisdiction
  See Jurisdiction (International law)
Domestic relations *(Direct)*
  sa Affinity (Law)
    Children—Law
    Desertion and non-support
    Domicile in domestic relations
    Family
    Guardian and ward
    Husband and wife
    Joint family
    Marriage law
    Parent and child (Law)
  x Family law
    Family—Law
  xx Family
    Marriage
    Persons (Law)
    Sex and law
  — Cases
  — — Digests
      See Domestic relations—Digests
  — Criminal provisions
  — Digests
    x Domestic relations—Cases—Digests
  — Domicile
    See Domicile in domestic relations
  — Forms
Domestic relations (Adat law) *(Direct)*
  Example under Adat law
Domestic relations (Byzantine law)
Domestic relations (Canon law)
Domestic relations (Celtic law)
Domestic relations (Germanic law)
  Example under Law, Germanic
Domestic relations (Greek law)
  Example under Law, Greek
Domestic relations (Islamic law)
  sa Support (Domestic relations law, Islamic)
Domestic relations (Jewish law)
Domestic relations (Kgatla law)
  Example under Law, Kgatla
Domestic relations (Primitive law) *(Direct)*
  Example under Law, Primitive
Domestic relations (Roman law)
Domestic relations (Tswana law)
Domestic relations (Visigothic law)
Domestic relations courts *(Direct)*
  x Family courts
  xx Courts
    Juvenile courts
Domestic science
  See Home economics
Domestic service
  See Servants
Domestic supplies
  See Household supplies

Domestication *(S494; SB123; Agriculture, SF41; Manners and customs, GT5870-5899)*
  sa Animals, Training of
    Domestic animals
    Plants, Cultivated
  x Animals, Domestication of
  xx Animals, Training of
    Domestic animals
Domestics
  See Servants
Domicile *(Direct)* *(International law, JX4241)*
  sa Citizenship
    Domicile as point of contact (Conflict of laws)
    Domicile in domestic relations
    Domicile in public welfare
    Domicile in taxation
    Domicile of corporations
    Freedom of movement
  x Residence (Law)
  xx Citizenship
    Conflict of laws
Domicile (Canon law) *(BX1939.D65)*
  x Quasi-domicile (Canon law)
Domicile (Jewish law)
Domicile (Roman law)
Domicile as point of contact (Conflict of laws) *(Direct)*
  xx Conflict of laws
    Domicile
    Points of contact (Conflict of laws)
Domicile in domestic relations *(Direct)*
  x Adoption—Domicile
    Divorce—Domicile
    Domestic relations—Domicile
    Guardian and ward—Domicile
    Marriage law—Domicile
    Matrimonial domicile
    Parent and child (Law)—Domicile
  xx Domestic relations
    Domicile
Domicile in public welfare *(Direct)*
  sa Warning out (Law)
  x Public welfare—Domicile
    Settlement law (Public welfare)
  xx Domicile
    Poor laws
    Public welfare
    Transients, Relief of
Domicile in taxation *(Direct)*
  x Taxation—Domicile
  xx Domicile
    Taxation
Domicile of corporations *(Direct)*
  sa Corporations—Nationality
  x Corporation law—Domicile
    Corporations—Domicile
  xx Corporation law
    Corporations
    Domicile
Dominance, Cerebral
  See Cerebral dominance
Dominance organization in animals
  See Social hierarchy in animals
Dominator (Bomber)
  See B-32 bomber
Domine, Dominus noster (Music)
  See Psalms (Music)—8th Psalm
Domine, exaudi orationem meam, auribus percipe (Music)
  See Psalms (Music)—143d Psalm
Domine, exaudi orationem meam, et clamor meus (Music)
  See Psalms (Music)—102d Psalm

Domine, ne in furore tuo arguas me, neque in
    ira tua corripias me, miserere mei
      Domine (Music)
    See Psalms (Music)—6th Psalm
Domine, non est (Music)
    See Psalms (Music)—131st Psalm
Domine, refugium (Music)
    See Psalms (Music)—90th Psalm
Domini est terra (Music)
    See Psalms (Music)—24th Psalm
Dominica, Battle of, 1782 *(E271)*
    x Martinique, Battle of, 1782
      Rodney's Victory, April 1782
Dominical letters *(CE85)*
Dominican ballads and songs *(Collections,*
    PQ7406; History, PQ7402)
    sa Ballads, Dominican
      Folk-songs, Dominican
      National songs, Dominican
      Songs, Dominican
Dominican drama
Dominican fiction *(Direct)*
Dominican literature *(PQ7400-7409)*
    — 20th century
Dominican periodicals
Dominican poetry *(Collections, PQ7406;*
    History, PQ7402)
Dominican Republic
    — History
    — — To 1844 *(F1938.3)*
    — — 1844-1930 *(F1938.4)*
        sa Las Carreras, Battle of, 1849
    — — American occupation, 1916-1924
            (F1938.45)
    — — 1930- *(F1938.5)*
    — — 1930-1961 *(F1938.5)*
    — — 1961- *(F1938.55)*
Dominicans *(BX3501-3555; Women,*
    BX4341-4)
    x Black Friars
      Friars, Black
      Friars preachers
      Jacobins (Dominicans)
      Preaching friars
      Predicadores
      St. Dominic, Order of
    xx Friars
      Monasticism and religious orders
    — Bio-bibliography *(Z7840.D7)*
    — Biography
    — Manuscripts
    — Missions
    — Spiritual life *(BX3503)*
Dominicans in China, ₍Ecuador, France, etc.₎
    Cf. reference from Catholic Church in
      Boston, ₍Canada, Chile, etc.₎
Dominicans in France
    x Jacobins (Dominicans)
Dominion Day (Canada)
Dominion of the sea
    See Maritime law
      Sea-power
Dominions, British
    See Commonwealth of Nations
Domino bridge *(GV1468)*
    xx Bridge whist
      Dominoes
Dominoes *(GV1467)*
    sa Domino bridge
    Example under Games
Dominus illuminatio (Music)
    See Psalms (Music)—27th Psalm
Dominus regit me (Music)
    See Psalms (Music)—23d Psalm
Dominus regnavit, decorem indutus est (Music)
    See Psalms (Music)—93d Psalm
Dompago dialect
    xx Gur languages

Dompelaers
    See Church of the Brethren
Domra *(ML1015-1018)*
    x Dombra
    xx Balalaika
      Lute
    — Methods
    — — Self-instruction *(MT643)*
    — Studies and exercises *(MT643.3)*
      xx Domra music
Domra and piano music *(M282-3)*
    sa Sonatas (Domra and piano)
    x Piano and domra music
Domra and piano music, Arranged *(M282-3)*
    sa Concertos (Domra)—Solo with piano
      Concertos (Domra with chamber
        orchestra)—Solo with piano
Domra music *(M142.D6)*
    sa Concertos (Domra)
      Concertos (Domra with chamber
        orchestra)
      Domra—Studies and exercises
      Domra with chamber orchestra
      Domra with orchestra
    xx Balalaika music
      Lute music
Domra with chamber orchestra
    (M1037.4.D64)
    sa Concertos (Domra with chamber
        orchestra)
    xx Chamber-orchestra music
      Concertos (Domra with chamber
        orchestra)
      Domra music
Domra with orchestra *(M1037.4.D64)*
    sa Concertos (Domra)
    xx Concertos (Domra)
      Domra music
      Orchestral music
Donatio mortis causa
    See Gifts causa mortis
Donation of Constantine *(BX875.D6-7)*
    x Constantine, Donation of
Donation of Pepin *(DD126.5)*
    x Pepin, Donation of
    xx Popes—Temporal power
Donations
    See Charitable uses, trusts, and foundations
      Endowments
      Gifts
Donati's comet *(QB723.D)*
Donatists *(BT1370)*
    sa Circumcellions
Donauwörth, Ger., in literature
Donelson, Fort, Battle of, 1862 *(E472.97)*
Doniphan's Expedition, 1846-1847 *(E405.2)*
    x Chihuahua Expedition, 1846-1847
    — Juvenile literature
Donkeys *(Indirect) (SF361)*
    sa Mules
    x Ass, Domestic
      Asses
      Burros
    — Juvenile literature
    — Law and legislation *(Direct)*
    — Legends and stories
Donkeys (in religion, folk-lore, etc.)
    x Folk-lore of donkeys
    xx Religion, Primitive
Donner Party *(F868.N5)*
    xx Overland journeys to the Pacific
Donner Pass
    — Blizzard, 1952
        See Sierra Nevada Mountains—
          Blizzard, 1952
Donovanosis
    See Granuloma venereum

Donuts
    See Doughnuts
Doodles *(NC915.D6)*
    xx Drawings
Dookpa
    See 'Brug-pa (Sect)
Doomsday
    See Judgment Day
Doomsday book
    See Domesday book
Door fittings *(TH2279)*
    xx Building fittings
      Doors
      Hardware
Door knockers
    x Doorknockers
      Knockers, Door
Door porters
    See Dummy board figures
Door-to-door selling
    See Canvassing
      Peddlers and peddling
Doorknockers
    See Door knockers
Doormen, Hotel
    See Hotel doormen
Doors *(Direct) (Building, TH2278)*
    sa Air curtains
      Bronze doors
      Church doors
      Door fittings
      Doorways
      Garage doors
      Glass doors, Sliding
      Grilles
      Mechanically-operated doors
      Metal doors
      Screen doors
    xx Building
      Carpentry
    Example under Millwork (Woodwork)
    — Standards
    — Tables and ready-reckoners *(HF5716.D)*
Doors, Automobile
    See Automobiles—Doors
Doors, Metal
    See Metal doors
Doorways *(Direct) (NA3010)*
    sa Porches
    x Portals
    xx Architecture—Details
      Doors
      Porches
Doorways, Renaissance *(Direct)*
    x Renaissance doorways
Doping in sports
    xx Drugs
      Sports
      Sports medicine
Doppler effect
    sa Doppler radar
    x Doppler shift
    xx Collision broadening
      Frequencies of oscillating systems
      Light
      Radiation
      Sound-waves
      Waves
Doppler radar *(TK6592.D6)*
    xx Doppler effect
      Radar
Doppler shift
    See Doppler effect
Doppler velocimeter, Laser
    See Laser Doppler velocimeter
Dor-bug
    See Cockchafers

Doraskean languages *(PM3753)*
  xx Indians of Central America—Languages
Dorians *(DF251)*
Doric columns
  See Columns, Doric
Dories (Boats)
  xx Boats and boating
  Fishing boats
Dorkings *(SF489.D7)*
Dormancy (Biology)
  sa Cryptobiosis
  Diapause
  Dormancy in insects
  Dormancy in plants
  Hibernation
  Spores (Bacteria)
  xx Life (Biology)
  Metabolism
Dormancy in insects
  xx Dormancy (Biology)
  Insects—Physiology
Dormancy in plants
  xx Cryptobiosis
  Dormancy (Biology)
  Plant physiology
  Seeds
Dormant partners *(Direct)*
  x Partners, Dormant
  Partnership, Dormant
  Silent partners
  Sleeping partners
  xx Partnership
  — Taxation *(Direct)*
Dormice
  sa Edible dormouse
  Garden dormouse
  Hazel mouse
  xx Mice
Dormitories *(Direct)* *(LB3227)*
  x Halls of residence
  Residence halls
  xx Residence and education
  School buildings
  Student housing
  Universities and colleges—Buildings
  — Administration
  — Designs and plans *(NA6602.D6)*
  — Equipment and supplies
    See Dormitories—Furniture,
      equipment, etc.
  — Fires and fire prevention *(TH9445.D6)*
  — Furniture, equipment, etc.
    x Dormitories—Equipment and
      supplies
    Dormitory furniture
    Dormitory supplies
    xx Furniture
  — Staff
    sa Housemothers
    Residence counselors
    x Residence hall staff
    Resident assistants (Dormitories)
Dormitory furniture
  See Dormitories—Furniture, equipment, etc.
Dormitory supplies
  See Dormitories—Furniture, equipment, etc.
Dormouse, Edible
  See Edible dormouse
Dormouse, Garden
  See Garden dormouse
Dornach, Battle of, 1499 *(DQ107.S8)*
  xx Swabian War, 1499
Dornier Do 335 (Fighter planes)
  See Pfeil (Fighter planes)
Dorobo (African people) *(DT429)*
  x Andorobo
  Ogiek
  Torobo

Wandorobo
  xx Ethnology—Africa, East
  Nilo-Hamitic tribes
Dorr Rebellion, 1842 *(F83.4)*
Dory (Fish) *(QL638.Z4)*
  x John-dory
Dos
  See Dowry
Dosage of drugs
  See Drugs—Dosage
Dosimeters *(QC795.5)*
  sa Nuclear counters
  xx Nuclear counters
  Radiation dosimetry
  Radioactivity—Instruments
Dosimetric medicine
  See Medicine, Dosimetric
Dosimetry
  See Drugs—Dosage
  Radiation dosimetry
Dosimetry, Photographic
  See Photographic dosimetry
Dosiology
  See Drugs—Dosage
Dothideales *(QK623.D74)*
  x Dothiorales
  Pseudosphaeriales
  xx Ascomycetes
Dothiorales
  See Dothideales
Dots (Art)
  sa Dotted prints (Engravings)
  Neo-impressionism (Art)
  xx Art
Dotted prints (Engravings) *(NE440)*
  xx Dots (Art)
  Engraving
  Engravings
  Stipple engravings
Dotterel *(QL696.C43)*
  — Behavior
Douai
  — Siege, 1667
Double-base diodes
  See Unijunction transistors
Double bass *(ML920-925)*
  x Bass viol
  — Orchestra studies *(MT331)*
    xx Double bass—Studies and exercises
  — Studies and exercises *(MT330)*
    sa Double bass—Orchestra studies
Double-bass and bassoon music
  See Bassoon and double-bass music
Double-bass and clarinet music
  See Clarinet and double-bass music
Double-bass and flute music
  See Flute and double-bass music
Double-bass and guitar music *(M237-8)*
  sa Suites (Double bass and guitar)
  x Guitar and double-bass music
Double-bass and piano music *(M237-8)*
  sa Sonatas (Double bass and piano)
  Suites (Double bass and piano)
  Variations (Double bass and piano)
  x Piano and double-bass music
Double-bass and piano music, Arranged
    (M237-8)
  sa Concertos (Double bass), Arranged—
    Solo with piano
  Concertos (Double bass)—Solo with
    piano
  Concertos (Double bass with band)—
    Solo with piano
  Concertos (Double bass with string
    orchestra)—Solo with piano
  Double bass with orchestra—Solo with
    piano

Suites (Double bass with orchestra)—
    Solo with piano
  Variations (Double bass with string
    orchestra)—Solo with piano
Double-bass and piano music (Jazz)
Double-bass and saxophone music
  See Saxophone and double-bass music
Double-bass and trombone music
  See Trombone and double-bass music
Double-bass and viola d'amore music
  See Viola d'amore and double-bass music
Double-bass and viola music
  See Viola and double-bass music
Double-bass and violin music
  See Violin and double-bass music
Double-bass makers *(ML404)*
  xx Musical instruments—Makers
Double-bass music *(M55-57)*
  sa Concertos (Double bass)
  Concertos (Double bass with band)
  Concertos (Double bass with chamber
    orchestra)
  Concertos (Double bass with string
    orchestra)
  Double bass with band
  Double bass with chamber orchestra
  Double bass with orchestra
  Double bass with string ensemble
  Double bass with string orchestra
  String ensembles
  Suites (Double bass)
  Variations (Double bass)
  Quartets, ⌈Trios, etc.⌉, String quartets,
    ⌈trios, etc.⌉ *followed by specifications*
    which include the double bass
Double-bass music (Double basses (2))
    (M286-7)
Double-bass music (Double basses (3))
  See String trios (Double basses (3))
Double-bass music (Double basses (4))
  See String quartets (Double basses (4))
Double-bass players
  See Violinists, violoncellists, etc.
Double-bass viol
  See Violone
Double bass with band *(M1205-6)*
  sa Concertos (Double bass with band)
  xx Band music
  Concertos (Double bass with band)
  Double-bass music
  — Scores *(M1205)*
Double bass with chamber orchestra
    (M1018)
  sa Concertos (Double bass with chamber
    orchestra)
  xx Chamber-orchestra music
  Concertos (Double bass with chamber
    orchestra)
  Double-bass music
Double bass with orchestra *(M1018)*
  sa Concertos (Double bass)
  Suites (Double bass with orchestra)
  xx Concertos (Double bass)
  Double-bass music
  Orchestral music
  — Solo with piano *(M1018)*
    xx Double-bass and piano music,
      Arranged
Double bass with string ensemble
  xx Double-bass music
  String ensembles
Double bass with string orchestra *(M1105-6)*
  sa Concertos (Double bass with string
    orchestra)
  Variations (Double bass with string
    orchestra)
  xx Concertos (Double bass with string
    orchestra)

Double-bass music
  String-orchestra music
Double consciousness
  See Personality, Disorders of
Double-crested cormorant
  xx Cormorants
Double cropping *(Indirect)* *(S603.7)*
  x Cropping, Double
  xx Cropping systems
    Field crops
Double-crostics *(GV1507.D65)*
  xx Acrostics
    Literary recreations
    Puzzles
Double curvature, Curves of
  See Curves of double curvature
Double dactyls
  x Dactyls, Double
  xx Poetry
Double descent (Kinship) *(GN480)*
  xx Kinship
Double employment
  See Supplementary employment
Double entry bookkeeping
  See Bookkeeping
Double glazing, Sealed
  See Sealed double glazing
Double integrals
  See Integrals, Multiple
Double jeopardy *(Direct)*
  x Former jeopardy
    Jeopardy, Double
    Ne bis in idem
    Non bis in idem
  xx Criminal procedure
    Due process of law
    Prosecution
Double layer, Electric
  See Electric double layer
Double layer potential
  See Zeta potential
Double nationality
  See Dual nationality
Double penuchle *(GV1295.P6)*
  xx Penuchle (Game)
Double quartets
  See String octets (Violins (4), violas (2),
    violoncellos (2))
Double refraction
  See Refraction, Double
Double salts
  See Salts, Double
    the respective metals or basic radicals
Double shifts (Public schools) *(Direct)*
  sa Class size
    Platoon schools
  xx Class size
    Platoon schools
    School management and organization
Double stars
  See Stars, Double
Double taxation
  See Taxation, Double
Double taxation conventions
  See Taxation, Double—Treaties
Double truth theory
  xx Knowledge, Theory of
    Theology
Doubles (Tennis)
  See Tennis—Doubles
Doubles in literature
Doubloons *(CJ3188)*
  x Doblons
    Onza de oro
Doubt
  See Belief and doubt
Doubt (Buddhism) *(BQ4430.D)*
  x Kankhā (Buddhism)

Vicikicchā (Buddhism)
Vicikitsā (Buddhism)
  xx Buddhist doctrines
    Faith (Buddhism)
Dough *(TX769)*
  sa Bread dough craft
  xx Baking
    Bread
    Flour
Doughnuts
  x Donuts
  xx Cake
    Pastry
Douglas airplanes
  sa Devastator (Torpedo-bomber)
    Douglas transport planes
    McDonnell Douglas airplanes
    Skystreak (Supersonic planes)
Douglas D-558 Skystreak
  See Skystreak (Supersonic planes)
Douglas fir *(Building materials, TA419-420;*
    Forestry, SD397.D7)
  x Oregon pine
  xx Fir
  — Diseases and pests
    sa *particular diseases and pests, e.g.*
      Douglas fir beetle
Douglas-fir bark-beetle
  See Douglas fir beetle
Douglas fir beetle
  x Douglas-fir bark-beetle
  xx Bark-beetles
  Example under Douglas fir—Diseases and
    pests
Douglas fir pitch moth *(SB608.F4)*
  xx Moths
Douglas-fir tussock moth
  x Tussock moth, Douglas-fir
  xx Fir—Diseases and pests
    Moths
Douglas skyraider
  See Skyraider (Fighter planes)
Douglas transport planes *(TL686.D65)*
  xx Douglas airplanes
    Transport planes
Doukhobors
  See Dukhobors
Douma language
  See Aduma language
Doumbou language
  See Ndumu language
Dourine *(SF959.D6)*
  xx Horses—Diseases
Dove, White-winged
  See White-winged dove
Dove (in religion, folk-lore, etc.) *(Religion,*
    BV168.D6)
  x Doves
    Folk-lore of doves
  xx Christian art and symbolism
    Holy Spirit—Art
    Mythology
    Religion, Primitive
Dove (Transport planes)
  xx Transport planes
Dove-cotes *(Direct)* *(NA8370)*
  xx Bird-houses
Dove shooting
  See Pigeon shooting
Doves
  See Dove (in religion, folk-lore, etc.)
    Pigeons
Dowels
Dower *(Direct)*
  sa Curtesy
    Election (Wills)
    Legitime
    Settlements (Law)

Widow's share
  x Present-value tables
    Widow's terce
    Widow's third
  xx Curtesy
    Freedom of testation
    Husband and wife
    Inheritance and succession
    Legitime
    Marriage law
    Real property
    Settlements (Law)
Dower (Byzantine law)
Dower (Greek law)
Dower (Jewish law)
  sa Ketuba
Dower (Roman law)
Down
  See Feathers
Downs, Battle of the, 1639 *(DH206.D6)*
  xx Netherlands—History—Wars of
    Independence, 1556-1648
Down's syndrome
  See Mongolism
Downwash (Aerodynamics) *(TL574.D6)*
  xx Aerodynamics
    Aerofoils
Downy mildew
  sa Tobacco blue mold
Downy mildew of lettuce *(SB608.L523)*
  xx Lettuce—Diseases and pests
Dowry *(Direct)* *(HQ1017)*
  sa Bride price
  x Dos
  xx Husband and wife
    Marriage law
  — Taxation *(Direct)*
Dowry (Canon law) *(BX1939.D)*
  xx Monasticism and religious orders
    (Canon law)
Dowry (Germanic law)
Dowry (Greek law)
Dowry (Islamic law) *(Direct)*
Dowry (Oriental law)
  Example under Law, Oriental
Dowry (Roman law)
Dowry insurance
  See Insurance, Marriage endowment
Dowsing
  See Divining-rod
Doxology *(BV194.D)*
  sa Old Hundredth (Tune)
Dozen system
  See Duodecimal system
Dózsa Uprising, 1514
  — Pictorial works
Drachma
  sa Tetradrachma
Draff
  See Distillers feeds
Draft, Mechanical
  See Mechanical draft
Draft, Military
  See Military service, Compulsory
Draft animals *(Indirect)* *(SF78)*
  sa Draft horses
    specific animals used for draft purposes,
      e.g. Mules, Oxen
  x Draught animals
  xx Cattle
    Domestic animals
Draft-gear *(Railroad cars, TF413)*
Draft horses *(SF311)*
  sa Belgian draft horse
    Clydesdale horse
    Jura horse
    Percheron horse
    Shire horse

Draft horses *(SF311)* *(Continued)*
    Suffolk horse
    xx Draft animals
        Horses
Draft Riot, 1863 *(F128.44)*
    x New York (City)—Draft Riot, 1863
    xx Military service, Compulsory
    Example under Riots
Draft tubes
    xx Hydraulic structures
        Hydraulic turbines
        Tubes
Drafting, Aircraft
    See Aircraft drafting
Drafting, Automotive
    See Automotive drafting
Drafting, Carpentry
    See Carpentry drafting
Drafting, Electric
    See Electric drafting
Drafting, Electronic
    See Electronic drafting
Drafting, Mechanical
    See Mechanical drawing
Drafting, Naval
    See Naval drafting
Drafting, Plumbing
    See Plumbing drafting
Drafting, Ship
    See Naval drafting
Drafting of bills
    See Bill drafting
Drafting-room practice
    See Drawing-room practice
Drafts *(Direct)* *(HF1215.7, United States; Other countries, HF1277-1400)*
    Here are entered works dealing in general with orders for the payment of money drawn by one party on another, and including non-negotiable instruments such as postal money-orders, cashier's checks, "Anweisungen," etc. Works on bills of exchange both foreign and domestic are entered under the heading Bills of exchange.
    sa Acceptances
        Bills of exchange
        Checks
        Letters of credit
        Negotiable instruments
        Promissory notes
        Traveler's checks
    x Bank drafts
    xx Negotiable instruments
    — Taxation
        See Bills of exchange—Taxation
Draftsmen, Naval
    See United States. Navy—Draftsmen
Drag (Aerodynamics)
    sa Boundary layer control
        Lift (Aerodynamics)
        Skin friction (Aerodynamics)
    x Aerodynamic forces
    xx Aerodynamic load
        Aerodynamics
        Aeroplanes
        Air resistance
        Lift (Aerodynamics)
    — Tables, calculations, etc.
Drag racing *(GV1029.3)*
    xx Automobile racing
    — Juvenile literature
Drago doctrine *(International relations, JX1393.D8)*
    sa Calvo doctrine and clause
    xx Aliens
        Calvo doctrine and clause
        Claims

Debts, External
    International law
    Intervention (International law)
    Investments, Foreign (International law)
    Monroe doctrine
Dragomen
    xx Arabic language—Translating
        Turkish language—Translating
Dragon boat festival
Dragonflies *(Indirect)*
    xx Odonata
    — Anatomy
    — Juvenile literature
    — Legends and stories
Dragonflies (in religion, folk-lore, etc.)
    x Folk-lore of dragonflies
    xx Religion, Primitive
    Example under Folk-lore of insects
Dragonnades *(DC127)*
    xx Persecution
Dragons *(GR830.D7)*
    sa Animal lore
        Animals, Mythical
        Monsters
    xx Animal lore
        Animals, Mythical
        Folk-lore
        Monsters
    — Legends and stories
Dragon's blood *(Pharmacy, RS165.D7; Pigments, TP936)*
Dragons in art
    xx Art
Dragons in literature
Drags (Hydrography) *(VK594)*
    x Sweeps (Hydrography)
        Wire drags (Hydrography)
        Wire sweeps (Hydrography)
    xx Hydrographic surveying
        Hydrography
Drain-gages *(S594)*
    xx Gages
Drain-tiles *(TP839; Testing, TA447)*
    xx Tiles
Drainage *(Indirect)* *(Agriculture, S621; Economics, HD1681-3; Engineering, TC970-978; Physical geography, GB906)*
    Here are entered only works relating to land drainage, as distinguished from sewerage and house drainage.
    sa Airport drainage
        Bogs
        Ditches
        Fens
        Grassed waterways
        Marshes
        Mine drainage
        Moors and heaths
        Railroad drainage
        Relief wells
        Reservoir drawdown
        Runoff
        Sewerage
        Storm sewers
    x Land drainage
    xx Agricultural engineering
        Agriculture
        Civil engineering
        Engineering
        Hydraulic engineering
        Marshes, Tide
        Municipal engineering
        Reclamation of land
        Sanitary engineering
        Sewerage
        Soil moisture

        Soil percolation
        Soils
        Waste lands
    — Graphic methods
    — Mathematical models
    — Tables, calculations, etc.
Drainage, House *(TD913; Plumbing, TH6571-6675; Rural sanitation, TD929)*
    sa Plumbing
        Roof drainage
        Sanitary engineering
        Septic tanks
        Sewerage
    x House drainage
    xx House construction
        Plumbing
        Sanitation, Household
    — Law and legislation
        See Sewerage—Law and legislation
    — Tables, calculations, etc.
Drainage, Road
    See Road drainage
Drainage, Roof
    See Roof drainage
Drainage, Surgical
    x Surgical drainage
    — Programmed instruction
Drainage assessment
    See Drainage tax
Drainage districts *(Direct)*
    xx Special districts
Drainage laws *(Direct)* *(HD1681-3)*
    sa Drainage tax
    x Law, Drainage
    xx Reclamation of land—Law and legislation
        Water—Laws and legislation
Drainage of mines
    See Mine drainage
Drainage rates
    See Drainage tax
Drainage research
    xx Agricultural research
        Engineering research
Drainage tax *(Direct)*
    x Drainage assessment
        Drainage rates
    xx Drainage laws
        Local taxation
Drains, Sand
    See Sand drains
Drama *(PN1600-1861)*
    Here are entered works dealing with the subject of the drama in general. Works on the history and criticism of the drama are entered under Drama—History and criticism. *Cf.* note under the heading Literature.
    sa Acting
        Ballet
        Burlesque (Literature)
        Carnival plays
        Characters and characteristics in literature
        Children's plays
        Christian drama
        Christmas plays
        Classical drama
        College and school drama
        Comedy
        Courtroom drama
        Detective and mystery plays
        Dialogue
        Didactic drama
        Dramatic criticism
        Dramatists
        Farce

Folk-drama
Ghost plays
Hindu drama
Historical drama
Indian drama
Interludes
Jesuit drama
Masques
Melodrama
Monologue
Moralities
Mysteries and miracle-plays
Negro drama
One-act plays
Opera
Pantomime
Passion-plays
Pastoral drama
Plots (Drama, novel, etc.)
Political plays
Prologues and epilogues
Psychodrama
Puppets and puppet-plays
Religion in drama
Religious drama
Stage adaptations
Television plays
Theater
Tragedy
Tragicomedy
Verse drama
English ₍French, German, etc.₎ drama;
and subdivision Drama under names
of famous persons and special
subjects, e.g. Easter—Drama; France
—History—Revolution, 1789-1799—
Drama; Indians of North America—
Drama
  x Drama, Modern
    Plays
    Stage
  xx Acting
    Dialogue
    Literature
    Theater
Example under Literary form
Note under Theater
— 15th and 16th centuries
    x Drama, Modern
— 17th century   (PN1831)
    x Drama, Modern
— 18th century   (PN1841)
    x Drama, Modern
— 19th century   (PN1851)
    x Drama, Modern
— 20th century   (PN1861)
    sa Living newspaper
    x Drama, Modern
— — Stories, plots, etc.

GENERAL SUBDIVISIONS

— Addresses, essays, lectures   (PN1621-3)
    Here are entered single addresses, es-
    says, and lectures, as well as collec-
    tions by one or more authors. For
    collections covering the subject sys-
    tematically and comprehensively,
    prefer the subdivision History and
    criticism.
— Bio-bibliography   (Z5781-5)
— Biography
    See Dramatists
— Chorus
    sa Choral speaking
    x Chorus (Drama)
— Chorus (Greek drama)   (PA3136)
    x Chorus (Drama)
      Greek drama—Chorus

— Collections   (PN6110.5-6120)
    x Drama—Selections
— Competitions
— Copyright
    See Copyright—Drama
— Dictionaries   (PN1625)
— History and criticism   (PN1720-1861)
    sa Music—Almanacs, yearbooks, etc.
      Theater—₍local subdivision₎, e.g.
        Theater—Paris; Theater—United
        States
    xx Criticism
    Notes under Drama; Dramatic criticism
— Indexes
— Outlines, syllabi, etc.   (PN1731)
— Periodicals   (PN1600-1609)
— Plot
    See Plots (Drama, novel, etc.)
— Selections
    See Drama—Collections
— Societies, etc.   (PN1611-1619)
— Stories, plots, etc.
    Note under Plots (Drama, novel, etc.)
— Study and teaching   (PN1701)
    sa Drama in education
— Technique   (PN1660-1691)
    sa Blank verse
      Deus ex machina
      Dramatic unities
      Farce—Technique
      Moving-picture plays—Technique
      Play within a play
      Playwriting
      Radio plays—Technique
      Stage directions
      Television plays—Technique
    x Dramaturgy
    xx Authorship
      Characters and characteristics in
        literature
      Playwriting
      Radio plays—Technique
Drama, Academic
    See College and school drama
Drama, Classical
    See Classical drama
Drama, Historical
    See Historical drama
Drama, Liturgical
    See Liturgical drama
Drama, Medieval   (PN1751)
    sa Carnival plays
      Christmas plays, Medieval
      Liturgical drama
      Moralities
      Mysteries and miracle-plays
      Passion-plays
    x Plays, Medieval
    xx Easter—Drama
      Moralities
      Mysteries and miracle-plays
Drama, Modern
    See Drama
      Drama—15th and 16th centuries
      Drama—17th century
      Drama—18th century
      Drama—19th century
      Drama—20th century
Drama, Oriental
    See Oriental drama
Drama, Primitive   (GN464)
Drama, Religious
    See Religious drama
Drama and liturgy
    See Liturgy and drama
Drama festivals
    x Theater festivals
    xx Amateur theatricals

Art festivals
College and school drama
Festivals
Drama in education   (PN3171)
    sa Acting
      Children as actors
      College and school drama
      Puppets and puppet-plays in education
      Religious drama
      Schools—Exercises and recreations
      Theater
    xx Acting
      Children as actors
      College and school drama
      Drama—Study and teaching
      Education
      Play
      Schools—Exercises and recreations
Drama in religious education   (BV1534.4)
    xx Religious education
Dramatic criticism   (Direct)   (PN1707)
    Here are entered works on criticism of
    the drama as presented on the stage.
    Collections of reviews of dramatic per-
    formances are entered under Theater
    —Reviews. Works on criticism of the
    drama as a literary form are entered
    under Drama—History and criticism.
    sa Moving-picture criticism
      Newspapers—Sections, columns, etc.—
        Reviews
      Radio criticism
      Television criticism
    x Theater criticism
    xx Criticism
      Drama
      Theater
Dramatic education
    See Acting—Study and teaching
Dramatic films
    See Feature films
Dramatic music
    See Ballad opera
      Music in theaters
      Music, Incidental
      Musical revue, comedy, etc.
      Opera
      Operetta
      Singspiel
      Zarzuela
Dramatic plots
    See Plots (Drama, novel, etc.)
Dramatic unities
    x Unities, Dramatic
      Unity, Dramatic
    xx Drama—Technique
Dramatists   (PN1720-1861)
    sa Librettists
      Women dramatists
    x Drama—Biography
      Playwrights
    xx Drama
      Litterateurs
      Poets
    Example under Authors; Writers
— Correspondence, reminiscences, etc.
— Interviews
Dramatists, English, ₍French, German, etc.₎
    Cf. note under Authors, American, ₍Eng-
    lish, French, etc.₎
    x English ₍French, German, etc.₎ drama
      —Biography
Dramaturgy
    See Drama—Technique
Drames à clef
    See Livres à clef
Dramshops
    See Hotels, taverns, etc.

Dramshops *(Continued)*
  Liquor traffic
Drang nach Osten *(DD119.2)*
  sa Germans in Poland, ⌈Russia, etc.⌉
    Teutonic Knights
  xx Imperialism
    Pangermanism
Drapery *(TT390; Upholstery, NK3195;*
    Window displays, HF5849.D6)
  x Curtains
  xx Household linens
    Interior decoration
    Upholstery
Drapery in art *(NC775)*
  xx Art
Draught, Mechanical
  See Mechanical draft
Draught animals
  See Draft animals
Draught of fishes (Miracle)
  See Miraculous draught of fishes (Miracle)
Draughts
  See Checkers
Dravidian civilization
  See Civilization, Dravidian
Dravidian languages *(PL4601-4794)*
  sa Badaga dialect
    Brahui language
    Gondi language
    Kannada language
    Kodagu language
    Kolami language
    Konda language
    Koraga language
    Kota language
    Kui language
    Kurukh language
    Malayalam language
    Parji language
    Pengo language
    Tamil language
    Telugu language
    Toda language
    Tulu language
  xx Badaga dialect
    Brahui language
    Gondi language
    Indic languages
    Kodagu language
    Kui language
    Kurukh language
    Malayalam language
    Telegu language
    Toda language
Dravidian literature *(Direct)*
Dravidian mythology
  See Mythology, Dravidian
Dravidian philology *(PL4601)*
Dravidian poetry *(Collections, PL4906;*
    History, PL4902)
Dravidians
  xx Ethnology—India
Draw-a-man test
  x Goodenough draw-a-man test
  xx Draw-a-person test
    Projective techniques
Draw-a-person test *(BF698.8.D7)*
  sa Draw-a-man test
  xx Projective techniques
Draw-in collets
  See Collets
Draw-poker
  See Poker
Drawbacks *(HF1715-1718)*
  sa Certificates of origin
    Dumping (Commercial policy)
  x Border taxes
    Rebates of duties

  Tariff rebates
  xx Tariff
Drawbenches
  See Metal-drawing machinery
Drawbridges *(TG420)*
  xx Bridges
    Bridges, Movable
Drawdown, Reservoir
  See Reservoir drawdown
Drawing *(Direct) (NC)*
  sa Anatomy, Artistic
    Architectural drawing
    Blackboard drawing
    Brush drawing
    Caricature
    Charcoal-drawing
    Computer drawing
    Crayon drawing
    Design, Decorative
    Drawing books
    Drawing, Psychology of
    Drawings
    Fashion drawing
    Figure drawing
    Geometrical drawing
    Graphic methods
    Human figure in art
    Illustration of books
    Landscape drawing
    Map drawing
    Mechanical drawing
    Military sketching
    Painting
    Pastel drawing
    Pen drawing
    Pencil drawing
    Perspective
    Portrait drawing
    Projection
    Proportion (Art)
    Shades and shadows
    Topographical drawing
  x Sketching
  xx Art
    Design, Decorative
    Graphic arts
    Illustration of books
    Manual training
    Perspective
— Competitions
  sa Edwin-Scharff-Preis
— Examinations, questions, etc.
— Instruction *(NC390-670; Public schools,*
    NC610-635)
  sa Airbrush art
    Art schools
    Birds in art
    Blackboard drawing
    Commercial art
    Scratchboard drawing
    special subjects of instruction, e.g.
      Figure drawing; Flower painting
      and illustration; Trees in art; *also*
      subdivision Pictures, illustrations,
      etc. *under names of animals, e.g.*
      Cats—Pictures, illustrations, etc.
  x Drawing—Study and teaching
    Drawing—Technique
    Example under references from Courses
      of study; Curricula (Courses of
      study); Study, Courses of
— — Juvenile literature
— Quotations, maxims, etc.
— Scientific applications
  sa Archaeological illustration
    Scientific illustration
  xx Scientific illustration
— Study and teaching

  See Drawing—Instruction
— Subjects
  See Drawing—Themes, motives
— Technique
  See Drawing—Instruction
— Themes, motives
  x Drawing—Subjects
Drawing, Aircraft
  See Aircraft drafting
Drawing, Architectural
  See Architectural drawing
Drawing, Automotive
  See Automotive drafting
Drawing, Baroque *(Direct)*
  x Baroque drawing
Drawing, French, ⌈German, Italian, etc.⌉
    (Direct)
  x French ⌈German, Italian, etc.⌉ drawing
Drawing, Naval
  See Naval drafting
Drawing, Psychology of *(BF456.D7; Child*
    study, BF723.D7)
  sa Graphology
    Tree test
  xx Drawing
    Graphology
    Psychology
Drawing, Rococo *(Direct)*
  x Rococo drawing
Drawing, Structural
  See Structural drawing
Drawing (Metal-work)
  sa Deep drawing (Metal-work)
    Metal-drawing machinery
    Wiredrawing
  xx Forging
    Metal stamping
— Terminology
Drawing books
  xx Drawing
Drawing instruments *(N8530-8540;*
    Mechanical drawing, T375-7)
  Here are entered works describing the in-
    struments employed in drawing, their
    use and care. Catalogs of such instru-
    ments and other drawing materials are
    entered under Drawing materials—
    Catalogs.
  sa Compasses (Mathematical instruments)
    Mechanical drawing
    Rulers (Instruments)
  x Instruments, Drawing
  xx Mathematical instruments
Drawing materials
  sa Crayons
— Catalogs *(N8540; Mechanical drawing,*
    T377)
  sa Artists' materials
  Note under Drawing instruments
Drawing-room practice *(Mechanical drawing,*
    T352; Mechanical engineering,
    TJ227)
  sa Engineering drawings
    Microfilm aperture card systems—
      Engineering drawings
  x Drafting-room practice
  xx Mechanical drawing
— Automation
Drawings *(Direct) (NC)*
  sa Crayon drawings
    Doodles
    Engineering drawings
    Engravings
    Etchings
    Graffiti
    Lithographs
    Pastels
    Rubbings

xx Drawing
— Catalogs *(NC37-38)*
>Here are entered dealers' and general sales catalogs. Catalogs of exhibitions are entered under Drawings—Exhibitions. For catalogs of private collections use the heading Drawings—Private collections.

— Classification
>*See* Classification—Drawings

— Conservation and restoration
— Exhibitions *(NC15)*
>*Note under* Drawings—Catalogs

— Prices
>*sa* Art—Catalogs
>Art—Prices

— Private collections *(NC30-33)*
>*Note under* Drawings—Catalogs

Drawings, American, ₍Dutch, Flemish, etc.₎ *(Direct)*
>*x* American ₍Dutch, Flemish, etc.₎ drawings

Drawings, Crayon
>*See* Crayon drawings

Drawings, Engineering
>*See* Engineering drawings

Drawings, Gothic *(Direct)*
>*x* Gothic drawings

Drawings, Hindu *(Direct)*
>*x* Hindu drawings

Drawings, Medieval *(Direct)*
Drawings, Renaissance *(Direct)*
>*x* Renaissance drawings

Drawings, Shaker *(Direct)*
>*x* Shaker drawings

Drawn-work *(TT785-791)*
>*sa* Hardanger needlework
>*xx* Fancy work
>Needlework

— Patterns *(TT785-791)*
Dreadnoughts
>*See* Battleships

Dreams *(BF1074-1099)*
>*sa* Children's dreams
>Fantasy
>Nightmares
>Psychoanalysis
>Sex in dreams
>Sleep
>Somnambulism
>Symbolism (Psychology)
>*x* Oneiromancy
>*xx* Brain
>Divination
>Fortune-telling
>Mind and body
>Omens
>Psychical research
>Psychoanalysis
>Sleep
>Sleep disorders
>Subconsciousness
>Superstition
>Visions

— Caricatures and cartoons
— Juvenile literature
— Physiological aspects *(QP426)*
— Pictorial works
Dreams in literature
Dreams in the Bible *(BF1099.B5)*
>*x* Bible—Dreams

Dredgers
>*See* Dredges

Dredges *(TC188)*
>*sa* Dredging
>*x* Dredgers
>Dredging machinery
>*xx* Dredging

Earthwork
Excavating machinery
Hydraulic mining
Work boats
— Automatic control *(TC188)*
— Electric equipment *(TC188)*
— Maintenance and repair *(TC188)*
Dredging *(TC187-8)*
>*sa* Dredges
>Manganese mines and mining, Submarine
>*xx* Civil engineering
>Dredges
>Engineering
>Harbors
>Hydraulic engineering
>Manganese mines and mining, Submarine

— Tables, calculations, etc.
Dredging (Biology) *(QH61-63)*
>*sa* Marine biology
>Marine fauna
>Marine flora
>*xx* Marine biology
>Marine fauna
>Marine sediments
>Natural history—Technique
>Zoological specimens—Collection and preservation

Dredging (Gold mining)
>*See* Gold dredging

Dredging machinery
>*See* Dredges

Drei Zinnen, Battles of
>*See* Tre Cime di Lavaredo, Battles of, 1915-1917

Dreikaiserbund, 1872
>*See* Three Emperors' League, 1872

Dreikaiserbund, 1881
>*See* Three Emperors' League, 1881

Drentsche patrijshond *(SF429.D7)*
>*x* Dutch spaniel
>*xx* Spaniels

Drepanocytic anemia
>*See* Sickle cell anemia

Dresden
— History
— — Revolution, 1848-1849
Dresden, Battle of, 1813 *(DC236.7.D8)*
Dresden, Peace of, 1745 *(DD407.5)*
Dresden porcelain *(NK4380)*
>*sa* Meissen porcelain
>*x* Porcelain, Dresden
>*xx* Meissen porcelain
>*Example under* Porcelain

Dress
>*See* Clothing and dress

Dress, Clerical
>*See* Clergy—Costume

Dress, Ecclesiastical
>*See* Clergy—Costume

Dress accessories *(TT560)*
>*x* Accessories (Dress)
>*xx* Clothing and dress
>Millinery

— Juvenile literature
Dress design
>*See* Costume design

Dress designers
>*See* Costume designers

Dressage
>*xx* Horse-training
>Horsemanship
>Horses—Paces, gaits, etc.

— Pictorial works
Dressing of game
>*See* Game and game-birds, Dressing of

Dressing of ores
>*See* Ore-dressing

Dressing of poultry
>*See* Poultry, Dressing of

Dressing of rabbits
>*See* Rabbits, Dressing of

Dressings (Surgery)
>*See* Bandages and bandaging
>Splints (Surgery)
>Wounds—Treatment

Dressmakers *(Direct)*
>*sa* Wages—Dressmakers

Dressmaking *(TT500-560; Economics, HD9942)*
>*sa* Doll clothes
>Dressmaking materials
>Needlework
>Newspapers—Sections, columns, etc.—Fashion
>Sewing
>Tailoring (Women's)
>*xx* Clothing and dress
>Costume
>Fashion
>Needlework
>Sewing
>Tailoring (Women's)
>*Example under* Woman—Employment

— Accounting *(HF5686.D)*
— Juvenile literature
— Pattern books
>*x* Fashion books
>Pattern books (Clothing)
>Patterns (Clothing)
>*xx* Fashion

— Pattern design
>*sa* Garment cutting
>Kimonos—Pattern design
>*x* Pattern cutting (Clothing)
>Pattern drafting (Clothing)
>Patterns (Clothing)
>*xx* Costume design
>Garment cutting
>Tailoring—Pattern design

— Periodicals
— Study and teaching
— — Audio-visual aids
— Tables, calculations, etc.
— Teacher training
Dressmaking materials
>*xx* Dressmaking

Dreyse machine-gun *(UF620.D)*
>*xx* Machine-guns

Dried beans
>*See* Beans, Dried

Dried blueberries
>*See* Blueberries, Dried

Dried citrus pulp
>*x* Citrus fruit pulp, Dried
>Citrus pulp as feed
>*xx* Citrus fruits—By-products
>Feeds

Dried fish
>*See* Fish, Dried

Dried fishery products
>*See* Fishery products, Dried

Dried flower arrangement *(Indirect)*
(SB449.3.D7)
>*sa* Pressed flower pictures
>*x* Dried plant material arrangement
>*xx* Everlasting flowers
>Flower arrangement
>Flowers—Drying

Dried foods
>*See* Food, Dried

Dried fruit
>*See* Fruit, Dried

Dried milk
    See Milk, Dried
Dried peas
    See Peas, Dried
Dried plant material arrangement
    See Dried flower arrangement
Dried vegetables
    See Vegetables, Dried
Driers *(TP937.7)*
    Here are entered works limited to driers used in paints, varnishes, etc. Material on driers used to exhaust moisture is entered under the heading Drying agents. Works dealing with the apparatus used in drying operations are entered under the heading Drying apparatus.
    sa Drying oils
    xx Drying agents
Drift *(QE697)*
    sa Glaciers
        Moraines
        Valley trains
    x Glacial drift
    xx Geology
        Glacial epoch
        Moraines
Drift, Continental
    See Continental drift
Drift, Ionospheric
    See Ionospheric drift
Drift, Littoral
    See Littoral drift
Drift of sea ice
    See Sea ice drift
Drifting ice stations
    sa Arlis II (Drifting ice station)
        Ice islands
    x Floating ice stations
        Ice stations, Drifting
    xx Geophysical research
        Ice islands
        Oceanographic research stations
        Sea ice
Drifting of continents
    See Continental drift
Driftwood arrangement
    xx Decoration and ornament
        Flower arrangement
Drill (Agricultural implement) *(S687-9)*
    x Seeding machinery
    xx Agricultural machinery
        Sowing
Drill (not military) *(GV1797)*
    sa Flag-waving (Exercise)
    xx Physical education and training
Drill and minor tactics
    Here are entered general works, including works for home guards, boy scouts, bands, etc. Manuals, handbooks, and regulations intended for the army of a particular country are entered under the name of the country, with subheading Army. Artillery ₍Cavalry, Infantry₎—Drill and tactics, *e.g.* United States. Army. Artillery—Drill and tactics.
    sa Artillery drill and tactics
        Baton twirling
        Cavalry drill and tactics
        Drum majorettes
        Drum majors
        Infantry drill and tactics
        Military art and science
        Night fighting (Military science)
        Street fighting (Military science)
        Tactics
    x Military drill

Minor tactics
    Soldiers—Drill
    xx Military art and science
        Tactics
Drill bits
    See Bits (Drilling and boring)
Drill pipe
    x Drill rod
    xx Boring
        Oil well drilling rigs
        Pipe
    — Maintenance and repair
    —— Safety measures *(TN871.5)*
Drill presses *(TJ1260)*
    xx Drilling and boring machinery
        Metal-working machinery
Drill rod
    See Drill pipe
Drilling, Gas well
    See Gas well drilling
Drilling, Oil well
    See Oil well drilling
Drilling, Underwater
    See Underwater drilling
Drilling and boring *(Machine-shop practice, TJ1160; Primitive man, GN447.D7)*
    Here are entered works relating to the drilling and boring of holes in metal, wood, and other materials, as carried on in workshops, etc., for building and constructive purposes. Works relating to the operation of cutting holes in earth or rocks, in order to determine the nature of the strata penetrated, or to furnish an outlet for water, oil, or gas are entered under Boring.
    sa Broaching
        Center punches
    Note under Boring
    — Computer programs *(TJ1260)*
    — Production standards
    — Safety measures
    — Tables and ready-reckoners
Drilling and boring machinery *(Machine tools, TJ1260-1270)*
    sa Broaching machines
        Drill presses
        Rock-drills
        Twist drills
    — Drawing
        See Drilling and boring machinery—Drawings
    — Drawings
        x Drilling and boring machinery—Drawing
        xx Mechanical drawing
    — Electric equipment
    — Maintenance and repair
    — Numerical control
Drilling fluids
    See Drilling muds
Drilling muds
    x Drilling fluids
        Fluids, Drilling
        Mud-laden fluids
        Muds, Drilling
        Oil well drilling fluids
        Oil well drilling muds
        Petroleum—Drilling fluids
    xx Boring
        Excavation
        Oil well drilling
        Soil stabilization
    — Additives *(TN871.2)*
Drilling platforms
    See Artificial islands
        Deep-sea drilling ships

Drilling rigs, Oil well
    See Oil well drilling rigs
Drina, Battles of the, 1914
    xx European War, 1914-1918—Campaigns —Serbia
Drink offerings
    See Libations
Drink question
    See Liquor problem
Drinker respirator
    See Iron lung
Drinking and airplane accidents *(Direct)*
    x Aeroplane accidents and drinking
        Alcoholism and airplane accidents
    xx Aeronautics—Accidents
        Alcohol—Physiological effect
        Drunkenness (Criminal law)
Drinking and Jews
    See Alcohol and Jews
Drinking and Negroes
    See Alcohol and Negroes
Drinking and traffic accidents *(Direct)*
    Here are entered works on the relation between alcoholic intoxication and traffic accidents. Works on drunk driving as a criminal offense are entered under Drunk driving.
    sa Drunk driving
    x Alcoholism and traffic accidents
        Drunken drivers
        Drunkenness and traffic accidents
        Traffic accidents and alcoholism
    xx Alcohol—Physiological effect
        Automobile drivers
        Traffic accidents
    Notes under Drunk driving; Human behavior
Drinking and women
    See Alcohol and women
Drinking and youth
    See Alcohol and youth
Drinking cups *(Art objects, NK4895; Gold and silver plate, NK7100-7230; Manners and customs, GT2940-2947)*
    sa Mustache cups
    x Cups and saucers
    xx Drinking vessels
    — Hygienic aspects *(RA642)*
        xx Hygiene, Public
    — Private collections *(Direct)*
Drinking customs *(Direct) (GT2850-2930)*
    sa Drinks and drinking (in religion, folk-lore, etc.)
        Japanese tea ceremony
        Toasts
    x Healths, Drinking of
    xx Dinners and dining
        Manners and customs
    — Anecdotes, facetiae, satire, etc.
    — Caricatures and cartoons
    — Terminology
Drinking fountains *(NA9420; Hygiene, RA642)*
    xx Fountains
Drinking horns
    See Drinking vessels
Drinking in art
    xx Art
Drinking in literature
    sa Temperance—Drama
        Temperance—Poetry
        Wine in literature
Drinking on aircraft
    xx Aeronautics—Safety measures
        Liquor problem
Drinking songs *(PN6237)*
    sa Students' songs
    xx Songs

Students' songs
Drinking vessels *(Direct)* *(NK4895)*
  sa Chalices
    Depas
    Drinking cups
    Steins
  x Drinking horns
    Goblets
    Mazers (Drinking bowls)
    Quaichs
  — Prices *(Direct)*
  — Private collections *(Direct)*
Drinking vessels, English, ⌐Scottish, etc.⌐
    (Direct)
  x English ⌐Scottish, etc.⌐ drinking vessels
Drinking water *(Indirect)*
  x Potable water
  xx Fresh water
    Water
  — Law and legislation *(Direct)*
    xx Water—Laws and legislation
  — Standards *(Direct)*
    x Drinking water standards
    xx Water—Composition
      Water-supply
Drinking water standards
  See Drinking water—Standards
Drinks
  See Beverages
    Drinks and drinking (in religion,
      folk-lore, etc.)
    Liquors
Drinks and drinking (in religion, folk-lore,
    etc.)
  sa Libations
  x Drinks
    Folk-lore of drinking
  xx Drinking customs
    Libations
    Religion, Primitive
    Sacred meals
Drio Indians
  See Trio Indians
Drip irrigation
  See Trickle irrigation
Drip stones
  See Stalactites and stalagmites
Dripstones
  See Stalactites and stalagmites
Drive-in banking
  x Drive-up banking
  xx Banks and banking
Drive-in theaters
  xx Moving-picture theaters
Drive-up banking
  See Drive-in banking
Drive whist *(GV1291.D7)*
  xx Whist
Driver education
  See Automobile driver education
Drivers, Automobile
  See Automobile drivers
Drivers' licenses, Automobile
  See Automobile drivers' licenses
Drivers' tests, Automobile
  See Automobile drivers' tests
Driveways *(TE279.3)*
  xx Pavements
    Roads
    Streets
  — Contracts and specifications *(Direct)*
Driving *(SF305)*
  sa Check-rein
    Coaching
    Horses
  x Riding
  xx Coaching
    Horsemanship

Locomotion
Driving, Automobile
  See Automobile driving
Driving, Motor bus
  See Motor bus driving
Driving, Motor-truck
  See Motor-truck driving
Driving, Motor vehicle
  See Motor vehicle driving
Driving, Tractor
  See Tractor driving
Driving tests, Automobile
  See Automobile drivers' tests
Driving under the influence of alcohol
  See Drunk driving
DRL (Computer program language)
  x Data Retrieval Language (Computer
    program language)
  xx Information storage and retrieval
    systems
Drogheda
  — Siege, 1641-1642 *(DA943)*
Drogheda, Statute of
  See Poynings' law
Droit d'aubaine *(JX6505)*
  xx Alien property—France
    Aliens
    Inheritance and succession
Droit de banalité
  See Banality (Law)
Droit de suite (Copyright)
  See Copyright—Droit de suite
Droit du seigneur
  See Jus primae noctis
Droit féodal
  See Feudal law
Drolls *(English drama, PR1251)*
  xx Farces
Dromaeidae
  See Emus
Dromaeognathae
  See Tinamiformes
Dromedaries
  See Camels
Drone aircraft
  x Aeroplanes, Drone
    Pilotless aircraft
    Remotely piloted aircraft
  xx Aeroplanes
Droop Mountain, Battle of, 1863 *(E475.76)*
Drop foot
  xx Foot—Diseases
Drop-forging
  See Forging
Drop-outs
  See Dropouts
Drop shipments
  xx Mail-order business
    Shipment of goods
    Wholesale trade
Drop tests (Chemistry)
  See Spot tests (Chemistry)
Drop word lists in automatic indexing
  See Exclusion lists in automatic indexing
Dropout behavior, Prediction of
  x Prediction of dropout behavior
  xx Educational anthropology
    Educational sociology
    Prediction (Psychology)
Dropouts *(Direct)* *(LC142-8)*
  sa Adult education dropouts
    College dropouts
    Elementary school dropouts
    High school dropouts
    Negro dropouts
  x Drop-outs
    School dropouts
  xx Personnel service in education

School attendance
    Youth
  — Employment *(Direct)*
Dropping mercury electrodes
  See Electrodes, Dropping mercury
Drops *(QC183)*
  sa Atomization
  xx Fluids
Dropsy *(RB144)*
  xx Body fluids
Dropsy, Abdominal
  See Ascites
Droughts *(Direct)* *(QC929.D8)*
  sa Dust storms
    Plants—Drought resistance
    Rain and rainfall
  xx Meteorology
    Rain and rainfall
    Water-supply
  — Charts, diagrams, etc.
  — Statistical methods
Drowning *(Legal medicine, RA1076)*
  sa Life-preservers
    Life-saving
    Swimming
  xx Accidents
    Asphyxia
    Death—Causes
    Violent deaths
  — Psychological aspects
Drowning, Restoration from *(RC88)*
  sa Artificial respiration
    First aid in illness and injury
  x Restoration from drowning
  xx Artificial respiration
    Death, Apparent
    First aid in illness and injury
    Life-saving
DRS (Computer program) *(QA76.6)*
  x Data Reconfiguration Service
    (Computer program)
Drug abuse *(Direct)* *(HV5800-5840)*
    Here are entered works on the misuse of
    drugs in a broad sense, such as aspirin,
    bromides, caffeine, sedatives, alcohol,
    LSD, marihuana, and narcotics.
    Works limited to addiction to narcot-
    ics such as opium, morphine, codeine
    and heroin, are entered under Nar-
    cotic habit.
  sa Aerosol sniffing
    Alcoholism
    Drugs and infants
    Drugs and sex
    Drugs and youth
    Glue-sniffing
    Hallucinogenic drugs
    Marihuana
    Narcotic habit
    Stimulants
  x Drug addiction
    Drug habit
  xx Crimes without victims
  — Information services
  — Juvenile literature
  — Personal narratives
    x Drugs and youth—Personal
      narratives
  — Pictorial works
  — Programmed instruction
  — Research *(Direct)*
  — Study and teaching *(Direct)*
  — — Audio-visual aids
  — Treatment *(Direct)*
  — — Juvenile literature
Drug abuse and automobile drivers *(Direct)*
    (HE5620.D65)
  x Automobile drivers and drug abuse

Drug abuse and automobile drivers *(Direct)*
    (HE5620.D65) *(Continued)*
        Automobile driving and drug abuse
Drug abuse and crime *(Direct)*
    sa Drugs—Laws and legislation
    x Crime and drug abuse
    xx Crime and criminals
Drug abuse and employment
    x Employment and drug abuse
    xx Personnel management
Drug abuse and military personnel
    See Drugs and military personnel
Drug addiction
    See Drug abuse
        Narcotic habit
Drug addicts
    See Narcotic addicts
Drug adulteration
    See Drugs—Adulteration and analysis
Drug allergy
    sa Drug-exanthems
    xx Allergy
        Drugs—Side effects
Drug antagonism
    xx Drug interactions
        Pharmacology
Drug benefit plans
    See Insurance, Pharmaceutical services
Drug degradation
    See Drug stability
Drug-eruptions
    See Drug-exanthems
Drug-exanthems
    x Drug-eruptions
    xx Drug allergy
        Pharmacology
        Skin—Diseases
Drug factories *(Direct)* *(TH4541)*
    x Pharmaceutical plants
    xx Factories
  — Maintenance and repair
    — — Costs
Drug habit
    See Drug abuse
        Narcotic habit
Drug-induced disease
    See Drugs—Side effects
Drug industry
    See Drug trade
Drug insurance
    See Insurance, Pharmaceutical services
Drug interactions *(Indirect)* *(RM302)*
    sa Drug antagonism
        Drug synergism
        Drugs—Side effects
    xx Drugs—Side effects
Drug metabolism
    xx Metabolism
        Pharmacology
Drug receptors
    x Receptors, Drug
    xx Pharmacology
Drug research
    See Pharmaceutical research
Drug resistance
    x Resistance to drugs
    xx Pharmacology
Drug resistance in micro-organisms
    sa R factors
    x Antibiotics resistance in
        micro-organisms
        Bacterial resistance to antibiotics
        Microbial drug resistance
        Resistance to drugs in micro-organisms
    xx Micro-organisms, Effect of drugs on
        Microbial genetics
        Pharmacology

Drug stability
    x Drug degradation
        Stability, Drug
    xx Pharmacology
Drug stores
    See Drugstores
Drug synergism
    xx Drug interactions
        Pharmacology
Drug therapy
    See Chemotherapy
Drug toxicity
    See Drugs—Toxicology
Drug trade *(Direct)* *(Business,*
    HF6201.D4-6; Economics,
    HD9665-9675)
    sa Botanical drug industry
        Drugstores
        Pharmacists
        Prescription pricing
        Vitamin industry
    x Drug industry
        Pharmaceutical industry
  — Accounting
  — Employees
  — Hygienic aspects
  — Law and legislation
      See Drugs—Laws and legislation
          Pharmacy—Laws and legislation
  — Management
  — Quality control
  — Statistical methods
  — Technological innovations
        (HD9665-9675)
Druggists
    See Pharmacists
Drugs *(Pharmacology, QP905-981;*
    Pharmacy, RS; Therapeutics, RM)
    sa Botany, Medical
        Dispensatories
        Doping in sports
        Materia medica
        Medicine—Formulae, receipts,
          prescriptions
        Pharmacognosy
        Pharmacology
        Pharmacy
        Poisons
        headings beginning with the word
          Drug; *also particular drugs and*
          groups of drugs, e.g. Narcotics,
          Stimulants
    xx Chemistry, Medical and pharmaceutical
        Materia medica
        Pharmacology
        Pharmacopoeias
        Pharmacy
        Therapeutics
  — Adulteration and analysis
        (Pharmaceutical chemistry,
        RS421-431)
        Here are entered treatises and text-
          books on methods of analyzing
          drugs and detecting adulterations,
          laboratory reports of tests, lists of
          adulterated articles, and reports of
          state and other drug commissions.
    x Drug adulteration
    xx Adulterations
        Consumer protection
  — Catalogs *(RS355-6)*
  — Classification
  — Dosage
    x Dosage of drugs
        Dosimetry
        Dosiology
        Posology
    xx Materia medica

  — Juvenile literature
    x Materia medica—Juvenile literature
        Pharmacy—Juvenile literature
  — Labeling *(Direct)*
  — Laws and legislation *(Direct)*
        (HD9665.7; Food and drug laws,
        HD9000.9)
        Here are entered general treatises on
          the legal regulation of strength,
          purity, etc., of drugs, together with
          collected and separate laws.
    sa Biological products—Law and
        legislation
        Medicines, Patent, proprietary, etc.
        —Law and legislation
        Narcotic laws
        Products liability—Drugs
    x Drug trade—Law and legislation
    xx Consumer protection—Law and
        legislation
        Drug abuse and crime
        Narcotic laws
    Example under Public health laws
    Note under Drugs—Standards
  — Marketing
  — Microbiology
    xx Sanitary microbiology
  — Packaging
    sa Edible coatings
  — Patents
  — Physiological effect
    sa Cells, Effect of drugs on
        Drugs and sex
        Drugs—Side effects
        Fertility, Effect of drugs on
        Fetus, Effect of drugs on the
        Hangover cures
        Micro-organisms, Effect of drugs on
  — Preservation *(RS159)*
  — Prices and sale *(HD9665-9675)*
  — Products liability
    See Products liability—Drugs
  — Psychological aspects
  — Purification
  — Research
    See Pharmaceutical research
  — Safety measures
  — Side effects
    sa Drug allergy
        Drug interactions
        Drugs—Toxicology
    x Drug-induced disease
        Side effects of drugs
    xx Drug interactions
        Drugs—Physiological effect
        Iatrogenic diseases
  — Spectra
    Example under Absorption spectra
  — Standards *(RS189)*
        Here are entered technical reports,
          etc., establishing grades, quality,
          degree of purity and strength. Pure
          food and drug laws are entered un-
          der the heading Drugs—Laws and
          legislation.
    sa Biological assay
    Example under Standardization; *and un-*
    der reference from Standards
  — Taxation *(Direct)*
  — Toxicology
    sa Narcotics—Physiological effect—
        Genetic aspects
        Ototoxic agents
    x Drug toxicity
    xx Drugs—Side effects
Drugs, Antineoplastic
    See Antineoplastic agents

Drugs, Antitubercular
  See Antitubercular agents
Drugs, Antitussive
  See Antitussive agents
Drugs, Antiviral
  See Antiviral agents
Drugs, Bronchoconstrictor
  See Bronchoconstrictor agents
Drugs, Bronchodilator
  See Bronchodilator agents
Drugs, Bronchospasmolytic
  See Bronchodilator agents
Drugs, Bronchospastic
  See Bronchoconstrictor agents
Drugs, Cardiovascular
  See Cardiovascular agents
Drugs, Cytotoxic
  See Antineoplastic agents
Drugs, Dermatologic
  See Dermatologic agents
Drugs, Gastrointestinal
  See Gastrointestinal agents
Drugs, Muscle relaxant
  See Muscle relaxants
Drugs, Radiation-protective
  See Radiation-protective agents
Drugs, Radioprotective
  See Radiation-protective agents
Drugs, Synthetic
  See Synthetic drugs
Drugs and infants *(Direct)*
  x Infants and drugs
  xx Drug abuse
Drugs and military personnel *(Direct)*
  x Drug abuse and military personnel
    Military personnel and drugs
Drugs and sex
  sa Aphrodisiacs
    Fertility, Effect of drugs on
  x Sex and drugs
  xx Drug abuse
    Drugs—Physiological effect
Drugs and youth *(Direct)*
  sa Alcohol and youth
    Narcotics and youth
    Smoking and youth
  x Youth and drugs
  xx Drug abuse
  — Juvenile literature
  — Personal narratives
      See Drug abuse—Personal narratives
  — Pictorial works
Drugs by mouth
  See Oral medication
Drugs in animal feeds
  See Medicated feeds
Drugstore employees *(Direct)*
      (HD8039.D7)
  sa Wages—Drugstore employees
  x Drugstores—Employees
  xx Clerks (Retail trade)
Drugstores *(Direct)*
  sa Hospital pharmacies
  x Drug stores
    Pharmacies
  xx Drug trade
    Stores, Retail
  — Accounting
  — Employees
      See Drugstore employees
  — Inventories
  — Management
  — Taxation *(Direct)*
  — Valuation
Druids and Druidism *(BL910)*
  sa Bards and bardism
    Folk-lore of trees
    Mythology, Celtic

  xx Celts
    Religions
Drukpa
  See 'Brug-pa (Sect)
Drum *(ML1035; Primitive, GN467.D8)*
  sa Kettledrum
    Mridanga
    Pung (Drum)
    Stone drum
    Tambourin
    Tupan
  x Bass drum
    Side drum
    Snare drum
  xx Kettledrum
  Example under Percussion instruments
  — Studies and exercises (Rock) *(MT662.3)*
    xx Rock music
Drum, Fresh-water
  See Fresh-water drum
Drum (in religion, folk-lore, etc.)
  x Folk-lore of the drum
  xx Religion, Primitive
Drum and bagpipe music
  See Bagpipe and drum music
Drum and bugle-calls
  See Military calls
Drum and bugle corps
  See Bugle and drum corps
Drum and bugle music
  See Bugle and drum music
Drum and fife music
  See Fife and drum music
Drum and guitar music
  See Guitar and drum music
Drum and trumpet music
  See Trumpet and drum music
Drum language
  xx Music, Primitive
    Signals and signaling
Drum majorettes *(GV1797)*
  x Majorettes
  xx Drill and minor tactics
Drum majoring *(MT733.5)*
  sa Baton twirling
  xx Baton twirling
Drum majors *(Direct)* *(MT733.5)*
  xx Bands (Music)
    Drill and minor tactics
Drum music
  See Percussion music
Drumlins *(QE697)*
  xx Glacial epoch
Drummers
  See Commercial travelers
Drums (Containers)
  x Oil drums
    Steel drums
  xx Containers
  — Labeling *(Direct)*
  — Storage
Drunk driving *(Direct)*
      Here are entered works on drunk driving
      as a criminal offense. Works on the
      relation between alcoholic intoxica-
      tion and traffic accidents are entered
      under Drinking and traffic accidents.
  x Driving under the influence of alcohol
    Drunken drivers
  xx Drinking and traffic accidents
    Drunkenness (Criminal law)
    Traffic violations
  Note under Drinking and traffic accidents
  — Digests
Drunkards
  See Alcoholics
Drunken drivers
  See Drinking and traffic accidents

Drunk driving
Drunkenness
  See Alcoholism
    Liquor problem
    Temperance
Drunkenness (Canon law)
Drunkenness (Criminal law) *(Direct)*
      Here are entered works on alcoholic in-
      toxication as a criminal offense or as a
      factor of criminal liability. Works on
      the relation between alcoholism and
      criminal behavior or the incidence of
      crime are entered under the heading
      Alcoholism and crime.
  sa Alcoholism and crime
    Drinking and airplane accidents
    Drunk driving
  x Inebriety
    Intoxication
  xx Alcoholism and crime
    Crimes without victims
    Criminal law
    Criminal liability
  Note under Alcoholism and crime
Drunkenness (Roman law)
Drunkenness and traffic accidents
  See Drinking and traffic accidents
Drunkenness testing
  See Alcohol in the body
Druses *(DS94.8.D8; Religion, BL1695)*
  x Druzes
  xx Religions
    Shiites
Druses in Israel, [etc.]
  — Education
  — Pictorial works
Druzes
  See Druses
Drvar, Battle of, 1944
  xx World War, 1939-1945—Campaigns—
    Yugoslavia
Dry cleaning *(TP932)*
  sa Cleaning and dyeing industry
  x Clothing and dress—Cleaning
  xx Cleaning
    Cleaning and dyeing industry
  — Patents
  — Vocational guidance
Dry-cleaning machines
  x Coin operated machines
    Self-service dry-cleaning machines
  xx Cleaning
    Cleaning machinery and appliances
  — Appraisal
      See Dry-cleaning machines—
        Valuation
  — Electric driving
  — Valuation
      x Dry-cleaning machines—Appraisal
Dry-docks *(TC361)*
  sa Marine railways
  x Graving-docks
  xx Docks
  — Design and construction
  — Patents *(TC361)*
Dry farming *(Indirect)* *(SB110)*
  x Dryland farming
    Farming, Dry
  xx Agriculture
    Arid regions agriculture
    Irrigation
    Tillage
Dry film lubricants
  See Solid lubricants
Dry-goods *(Direct)* *(Economics,*
      HD9950-9969; Manufacture,
      TS1760-1768)
  sa Textile industry and fabrics

Dry-goods *(Direct)* *(Economics, HD9950-9969; Manufacture, TS1760-1768)* *(Continued)*
    Variety stores
    particular classes of goods, e.g. Hosiery, Knit goods
    xx Textile industry and fabrics
    Example under Display of merchandise
  — Accounting *(HF5686.D)*
  — Tables, etc. *(HF5716.D8)*
Dry ice *(TP492.8)*
    x Carbon dioxide, Solid
    Carbonic acid, Refrigerating
    xx Carbon dioxide
    Ice
    Ice industry
    Refrigeration and refrigerating machinery
  — Therapeutic use
    xx Cold—Therapeutic use
Dry paintings
    See Sandpaintings
Dry-point *(NE2220-2225)*
    xx Engraving
    Etching
Dry-points
    xx Engravings
    Etchings
Dry-points, American, [etc.] *(Direct)*
    x American [etc.] dry-points
Dry press molds
    See Dies (Ceramics)
Dry-rot *(TA422)*
    sa Wood—Preservation
    xx Timber
    Wood—Deterioration
Dry-solids flow
    See Bulk solids flow
Dryads *(BL820.D)*
    x Wood nymphs
    xx Folk-lore
    Mythology
    Superstition
Dryers, Clothes
    See Clothes dryers
Dryfe Sands, Battle of, 1593
Drying
    sa Curing
    Drying agents
    Efflorescence
    Spray drying
    subdivision Drying *under specific subjects, e.g.* Biological products—Drying; Forage plants—Drying
    xx Curing
    Evaporation
  — Juvenile literature
Drying agents
    sa Driers
    Molecular sieves
    x Dehydrating agents
    Desiccants
    xx Chemicals
    Chemistry, Technical
    Drying
    Note under Driers
  — Patents
Drying apparatus *(TP363)*
    sa Clothes dryers
    Freeze-drying
    Infra-red drying apparatus
    Kilns
    xx Canning and preserving
    Kilns
    Note under Driers
  — Automatic control
  — Design and construction
  — Food *(TX609)*

    sa Canning and preserving
    Food, Dried
    Vegetables—Evaporation
    xx Food—Preservation
    Vegetables—Evaporation
  — Grain
    See Grain—Drying
  — Textile fabrics
    x Drying-room
    xx Bleaching
    Cleaning machinery and appliances
    Dyes and dyeing
    Textile industry and fabrics
Drying of fruit
    See Fruit—Drying
Drying of vegetables
    See Vegetables—Evaporation
Drying oils *(TP937.7)*
    sa Linseed-oil
    Oiticica oil
    Soy-bean oil
    Tung-oil
    xx Driers
    Oils and fats
    Paint materials
    Protective coatings
Drying-room
    See Drying apparatus—Textile fabrics
Dryland farming
    See Arid regions agriculture
    Dry farming
Dschagga language
    See Chaga language
Dschaggas
    See Wachaga
Dual (Grammar)
    See Grammar, Comparative and general—Number
    subdivision Number *under names of languages and groups of languages*
Dual allegiance
    See Dual nationality
Dual Alliance, 1879
    x Alliance, Dual, 1879
    xx Austria—History—1867-1918
    Germany—History—1871-1918
Dual citizenship
    See Dual nationality
Dual employment
    See Supplementary employment
Dual enrollment *(Direct)*
    Here are entered works on an arrangement whereby a student regularly and concurrently attends a public school part time and a nonpublic school part time.
    x Dual school enrollment
    Enrollment, Dual
    Shared-time education
    xx School attendance
Dual nationality *(JX4231.D7)*
    sa Conflict of laws—Citizenship
    x Double nationality
    Dual allegiance
    Dual citizenship
    Nationality, Dual
    Nationality, Plural
    Plural nationality
    xx Allegiance
    Citizenship (International law)
    Conflict of laws
    Conflict of laws—Citizenship
    Naturalization
Dual-purpose cattle *(Indirect)* *(SF211)*
    xx Cattle
Dual school enrollment
    See Dual enrollment

Duala language *(PL8141)*
    x Dualla language
    xx Bantu languages
Dualism *(B812; Ontology, BD331; Systems, B851-4695)*
    sa Body and soul in literature
    Idealism
    Materialism
    Mind and body
    Monism
    Occasionalism
    Realism
    Soul
    xx Idealism
    Materialism
    Monism
    Occasionalism
    Philosophy
    Realism
Dualism (Religion) *(BL218)*
    xx Religion
Dualla language
    See Duala language
Dubbing of moving-pictures
    x Moving-pictures—Dubbing
    xx Moving-pictures, Talking
    Translating and interpreting
Dublin
  — Riots, 1913
  — Riots, 1914
Dubrovnik, Yugoslavia
  — Earthquake, 1667
Ducat
    x Sequin
    Zecchino
Duchies *(Direct)*
    x Dukedoms
    xx Feudalism
    Nobility
Duck (Textile) *(TS1580)*
  — Tariff
    See Tariff on duck
Duck hawk
    See Peregrine falcon
Duck hunting
    See Duck shooting
Duck pin bowling
    See Bowling, Duck pin
Duck plague
    x Duck virus enteritis
    xx Poultry—Diseases
    Virus diseases
Duck plague virus
    xx Viruses
Duck shooting *(SK333.D8)*
    sa Decoys (Hunting)
    x Duck hunting
    xx Fowling
    Waterfowl shooting
    Example under Hunting
  — Anecdotes, facetiae, satire, etc.
Duck stamps
    x Migratory bird hunting stamps
Duck virus enteritis
    See Duck plague
Duckbill
    See Platypus
Ducking stool
    See Cucking stool
Duckmole
    See Platypus
Duckpins
    See Bowling, Duck pin
Ducks *(QL696.A5; Breeding, SF505)*
    sa Black duck
    Blue-winged teals
    Bufflehead
    Canvasback

Common scoter
Cookery (Ducks)
Fulvous tree duck
Game and game-birds
Labrador duck
Mallard
Mandarin duck
Old-squaw
Pochard
Ring-necked duck
Ruddy shelduck
Shelduck
Torrent ducks
Tufted duck
Wood-duck
  xx Birds, Ornamental
  Poultry
  Waterfowl
— Feeding and feeds
  x Ducks—Food
— Food
  See Ducks—Feeding and feeds
— Identification
— Juvenile literature
— Legends and stories
Ducks as pets *(SF459.D8)*
Duct, Pancreatic
  See Pancreatic duct
Ducted fans
  sa Gas-turbines
  xx Fans (Machinery)
Ductility of metals
  See Metals—Ductility
  subdivision Ductility *under particular*
    metals, e.g. Steel—Ductility
Ductless glands
  See Glands, Ductless
Ducts, Air
  See Air ducts
Ducts, Bile
  See Bile-ducts
Ductus arteriosus
  x Ductus Botalli
  xx Aorta
  Blood-vessels
  Fetus
Ductus Botalli
  See Ductus arteriosus
Duda *(ML980)*
  x Polish bagpipe
  xx Bagpipe
Duda music *(M145)*
Dude ranches *(SK601)*
  xx Camps
  Farms—Recreational use
  Outdoor recreation
  Ranch life
  Resorts
Dudes
  See Dandies
Dudley Indians *(E99.D8)*
  xx Indians of North America
Dudley's Defeat, 1813 *(E356.D8)*
Due process of law *(Direct) (United States,*
    JK1548.D; JL-JQ; K)
  sa Defense (Criminal procedure)
  Double jeopardy
  Ex post facto laws
  Retroactive laws
  Right to counsel
  xx Civil rights
  Constitutional law
  Equality before the law
  Justice
  Justice, Administration of
  Rule of law
  Note under Equality before the law

Dueling *(Direct) (Code, CR4571-4595)*
  sa Combat
  Fencing
  Wager of battle
  x Duels
  Fighting
  xx Combat
  Criminal law
  Ethics
  Fencing
  Honor
  Manners and customs
  Wager of battle
Dueling in literature
Duels
  See Dueling
Duesenberg automobile *(TL215.D8)*
Duets
  See Percussion music
  Piano music (4 hands)
  Sacred duets
  Vocal duets
  Bassoon and piano music *and similar*
    headings for combinations of two
    different solo instruments; and Flute
    music (Flutes (2)) *and similar*
    headings for combinations of two
    identical solo instruments
Duets (Unspecified instruments)
Duette
  x Six hundred (Game)
Dufferin medals
  xx Medals
  Example under Decorations of honor
Duffing equations *(QA372)*
  x Equations, Duffing
  xx Differential equations, Nonlinear
Dugpa
  See 'Brug-pa (Sect)
Duhring's disease
  See Dermatitis herpetiformis
Duk (Sect)
  See 'Brug-pa (Sect)
Duke of Edinburgh's award
Dukedoms
  See Duchies
Dukhobors *(BX7433)*
  x Doukhobors
  Example under Refugees, Religious
Dukla Pass, Battle of, 1944
  xx World War, 1939-1945—Campaigns—
    Eastern
Dukpa
  See 'Brug-pa (Sect)
Dukwalli
  See Wolf ritual
Dulcamara
  See Bittersweet
Dulcimer *(ML1015-1018)*
  sa Cimbalom
  Gusli
  Kantele (Musical instrument)
  Kokle
  Santūr
  Yang ch'in
  x Appalachian dulcimer
  Cembalo
Dulcimer and guitar music *(M292-3)*
  x Guitar and dulcimer music
Dulcimer music *(M142.D8)*
Dulia
  See Saints—Cultus
Dulien language
  See Lushei language
Duma language
  See Aduma language
Dumaki language *(PK1837)*
  xx Indo-Aryan languages, Modern

Dumb (Deaf-mutes)
  See Deaf
Dumb-bells *(GV487)*
  sa Callisthenics
  xx Callisthenics
  Gymnastics
  Example under Physical education and training
Dumlupınar, Battle of, 1922
  xx Greco-Turkish War, 1921-1922
  Turkey—History—Revolution,
    1918-1923
Dummer's War
  See Eastern Indians, Wars with, 1722-1726
Dummy board figures *(NK9955.D8)*
  x Door porters
  Figurines
  Fireboards
  Picture boards
  Silent companions
Dummy warships
  xx Warships
Dump cars *(Mine railroads, TN342;*
    Railroads, TF470)
  xx Mine railroads—Cars
  Railroads—Cars
Dump trucks *(TL230)*
  x Dumpers (Motor trucks)
  xx Dumping appliances
  Motor-trucks
— Cold weather operation
— Maintenance and repair
— Parts
Dumpers (Motor trucks)
  See Dump trucks
Dumping (Commercial policy) *(HF1425)*
  sa Antidumping duties
  Price cutting
  xx Commercial policy
  Competition, Unfair
  Drawbacks
  Export premiums
  Price cutting
  Shipping bounties and subsidies
Dumping appliances *(TJ1418)*
  sa Dump trucks
Dumping reactions
  See Dumping syndrome
Dumping stomach
  See Dumping syndrome
Dumping syndrome
  x Dumping reactions
  Dumping stomach
  xx Postgastrectomy syndromes
Dumy
  xx Folk-songs
Dumy, Polish
  xx Folk-songs, Polish
  Polish ballads and songs
Dumy, Ukrainian
  xx Folk-songs, Ukrainian
Duna (Papuan people)
  xx Ethnology—Papua-New Guinea (Ter.)
Dune buggies *(TL236.7)*
  xx All terrain vehicles
  Motor vehicles
— Juvenile literature
Dune buggy racing *(GV1029.9.D8)*
  xx Automobile racing
— Juvenile literature
Dunes
  See Sand-dunes
Dunes, Battle of the, 1658 *(DC124.45)*
  x Dunkirk, France, Battle of, 1658
Dunfermline, Scot.   Weavers' Incorporation
  Example under Gilds
Dungan language *(PL3801.D9)*
  xx Indochinese languages

Dungans
    xx Ethnology—Turkestan
Dungeness crab
    xx Crabs
Dungeons
    See Prisons
Dungri-Grasias
    See Grasias
Dunite (Indirect) (QE461)
Dunkards
    See Church of the Brethren
Dunkers
    See Church of the Brethren
Dunkirk, France
    — Siege, 1793 (DS220.5)
Dunkirk, France, Battle of, 1658
    See Dunes, Battle of the, 1658
Dunkirk, France, Battle of, 1940
        (D756.5.D8)
    xx World War, 1939-1945—Campaigns—
        France
    — Songs and music
        xx World War, 1939-1945—Songs and
            music
Dunmore's Expedition, 1774 (E83.77)
    xx Indians of North America—Wars—
        1750-1815
    — Registers, lists, etc.
Dunmow flitch
    x Flitch of Dunmow
    xx Bacon
Dunsīan language
    See Tung-hsiang language
Duodecimal system (QA141.5)
    sa Decimal system
    x Dozen system
    xx Arithmetic
        Decimal system
        Numeration
        Weights and measures
    — Tables, etc.
Duodenum (Comparative anatomy, QL863;
        Human anatomy, QM345;
        Physiology, QP156)
    xx Intestine, Small
    — Abnormities and deformities
    — Cancer
    — Diseases
        sa Duodenum—Radiography
    — Intubation
    — Radiography (RC804.R6)
        xx Duodenum—Diseases
    — Surgery
        sa Esophagoduodenostomy
    — Ulcers
    — Wounds and injuries
Duplicate auction bridge (GV1282)
    xx Auction bridge
        Contract bridge
Duplicate contract bridge (GV1282.3)
Duplicate whist (GV1283)
    xx Whist
Duplicates in libraries (Z689)
    x Libraries—Duplicate books
        Library duplicates
    xx Exchanges, Literary and scientific
Duplicating machines
    See Copying machines
Duplicating processes
    See Copying processes
Duplicating services
    See Letter services
Duplication of catalog cards
    See Catalog cards—Reproduction
Duplication of the cube
    See Cube, Duplication of
Dupuytren's contraction
    See Dupuytren's contracture

Dupuytren's contracture
    x Dupuytren's contraction
    xx Contracture (Pathology)
        Fingers—Abnormities and deformities
        Toes—Abnormities and deformities
Dura mater
    xx Brain
        Spinal cord
    — Abscess
    — Diseases
Durable goods, Consumer
    sa Customer service
    x Consumer durable goods
    xx Commercial products
        Consumers
    — Prices (Direct)
Duralumin (Materials of construction:
        general, TA480.A6; aeronautics,
        TL699.D9)
    xx Aluminum-copper alloys
Duramold
    xx Aeroplanes—Materials
        Plastics
Duration, Intuition of
    See Time perception
Duration of copyright
    See Copyright—Duration
Durazzo, Battle of, 48 B.C. (DG266)
    xx Rome—History—Civil War, 49-48 B.C.
Durazzo, Battle of, 1918 (United States.
        Navy, D589.U6)
    xx European War, 1914-1918—Naval
        operations
Durban, Natal
    — Riots, 1949
Durbars (Direct) (DS422; DS480; DS480.3;
        etc.)
        Subdivided by place and date, e.g. Dur-
            bars—Delhi, 1903.
    xx Coronations
    — Delhi, 1903
        Note under Durbars
Duress (Canon law)
Duress (Islamic law)
Duress (Jewish law)
Duress (Law) (Direct)
    sa Necessity (Law)
        Respondeat superior
        Threats
    x Coercion (Law)
        Compulsion
    xx Civil law
        Criminal law
        Criminal liability
        Necessity (Law)
        Threats
        Torts
        Undue influence
Duress (Roman law)
Durham cattle
    See Polled Durham cattle
        Shorthorn cattle
Durmast oak
    xx Oak
Dürnkrut, Battle of, 1278
    xx Austria—History—1273-1519
        Bohemia—History—To 1526
Dürnstein, Battle of, 1805 (DC227.5.D8)
Duroc Jersey swine (SF393.D9)
Durra (Indirect) (Botany, QK495.G74;
        Culture, SB191.S7)
    x Cholam
        Feterita
        Indian millet
        Jowar
        Juar
        Millet, Indian
    xx Sorghum

— Marketing
Durum wheat (Indirect)
    x Macaroni wheat
    xx Wheat
    — Disease and pest resistance
    — Diseases and pests
Duryea automobile
    — Juvenile literature
Dusky-footed wood rat
    xx Wood rats
Dusky grouse
    x Blue grouse
        Richardson grouse
    xx Grouse
    — Behavior
Düsseldorfer Malerschule
    xx Painting, Modern—19th century
Dussera
    See Dasara
Dust (Atmosphere, QC882; Labor hygiene,
        HD7264)
    sa Contamination (Technology)
        Fly ash
        Mine dusts
        Soot
    xx Air—Pollution
        Communicable diseases
        Particles
    — Bacteriology
        See Dust—Microbiology
    — Electric properties
    — Explosions
        See Dust explosion
    — Measurement
        x Dust counting
    — Microbiology (QR101)
        x Dust—Bacteriology
        xx Sanitary microbiology
    — Prevention (TE221)
        sa Air filters
        xx Dust control
            Roads—Maintenance and repair
            Roads, Oiled
    — Removal (TH7692-8)
        sa Clean rooms
            Cleaning machinery and appliances
            Electrostatic precipitation
            Exhaust systems
            Gases—Cleaning
            Vacuum cleaning
        x Dust extraction
        xx Cleaning machinery and appliances
            Dust control
            Hygiene, Public
            Sanitary engineering
            Ventilation
    — Thermal properties
Dust, Cosmic
    See Cosmic dust
Dust, Radioactive
    See Radioactive fallout
Dust control
    sa Dust—Prevention
        Dust—Removal
        subdivision Dust control under specific
            industries and plants, e.g. Foundries
            —Dust control
    x Control of dust
    xx Air—Pollution
        Contamination (Technology)
Dust counting
    See Dust—Measurement
Dust devils (QC958)
    xx Dust storms
        Dynamic meteorology
Dust diseases
    See Lungs—Dust diseases

Dust explosion *(HD7262)*
    x Dust—Explosions
       Explosions, Dust
    xx Accidents
       Explosions
       Industrial accidents
       Mine dusts
Dust extraction
    See Dust—Removal
Dust-fall *(QC929.S5)*
    x Dust showers
    xx Meteorology
Dust showers
    See Dust-fall
Dust storms *(QC958)*
    sa Dust devils
    xx Droughts
       Erosion
       Storms
       Wind erosion
Dusting
    See Sweeping and dusting
Dusting, Electrostatic
    See Electrostatic dusting
Dusting in agriculture
    See Spraying and dusting in agriculture
Dustmops
    See Mops and mopsticks
Dusun language
    xx Malayan languages
Dusuns *(DS646.33)*
    xx Ethnology—Borneo
Dutch almanacs
    See Almanacs, Dutch
Dutch Argentine cattle
    See Holando-Argentino cattle
Dutch ballads and songs *(Collections,*
       PT5480; History, PT5239)
    sa Ballads, Dutch
       Folk-songs, Dutch
       National songs, Dutch
       Songs, Dutch
Dutch carols
    See Carols, Dutch
Dutch cheese
    See Cottage cheese
Dutch Christian poetry
    See Christian poetry, Dutch
Dutch clover
    See White clover
Dutch composers
    See Composers, Dutch
Dutch drama *(Collections, PT5490-5515;*
       History, etc., PT5250-5295)
    — 19th century
    — 20th century
Dutch drawings
    See Drawings, Dutch
Dutch elm disease *(SB608.E)*
    x Elm blight
    xx Elm—Diseases and pests
Dutch-English War
    See Anglo-Dutch War
Dutch erotic stories
    See Erotic stories, Dutch
Dutch essays *(Direct) (PT5539)*
    Here are entered collections of essays by
       several authors.
Dutch etchers
    See Etchers, Dutch
Dutch etchings
    See Etchings, Dutch
Dutch ethical movement
    See Ethical movement (Dutch Reformed
       Church)
Dutch farces *(Direct)*

Dutch fiction *(Collections, PT5520-5530;*
       History, etc., PT5320-5336)
    sa Erotic stories, Dutch
Dutch furniture
    See Furniture, Dutch
Dutch genre painting
    See Genre painting, Dutch
Dutch genre paintings
    See Genre paintings, Dutch
Dutch in Africa, ⌈**Japan, New York (City),**
    etc.⌉
    — Juvenile literature
Dutch landscape painting
    See Landscape painting, Dutch
Dutch language *(PF1-979)*
    sa Flemish language
    xx Flemish language
       Germanic languages
       Low German language
    Example under Germanic philology
    — To 1500 *(PF771-8)*
       x Low German language—Old Low
         German, 750-1050
         Old Low Franconian language
    — Business Dutch
    — Dialects
    — — Africa, South
         Note under Afrikaans language
    — Dictionaries
       sa Picture dictionaries, Dutch
Dutch letters *(Direct)*
Dutch literature *(Direct) (Collections,*
       PT5400-5547; History, etc.,
       PT5001-5395)
    sa Flemish literature
    Example under Germanic literature; Germanic
       philology
    Note under Flemish literature
    — To 1500 *(PT5121-5137)*
    — 1500-1800 *(PT5141-5165)*
    — 19th century *(PT5170-5175)*
    — 20th century *(PT5180-5185)*
    — Bio-bibliography
    — Catholic authors
    — Jewish authors
       x Jewish literature (Dutch)
Dutch majolica
    See Majolica, Dutch
Dutch-marked rabbits
    See Dutch rabbits
Dutch newspapers *(Direct) (History, etc.,*
       PN5251-9)
Dutch orations *(Collections, PT5535;*
       History, PT5340)
Dutch painting
    See Painting, Dutch
Dutch panel painting
    See Panel painting, Dutch
Dutch periodicals *(History, etc.,*
       PN5251-5260)
Dutch philology *(PF1-979)*
    xx Germanic philology
Dutch poetry *(Direct) (Collections,*
       PT5470-5488; History, etc.,
       PT5201-5245)
    sa Christian poetry, Dutch
       Quatrains, Dutch
       Religious poetry, Dutch
    — To 1500 *(Collections, PT5425-5435;*
       History, PT5131-4)
    — 1500-1800 *(Collections, PT5477;*
       History, PT5215-5222)
       sa Gueux—Songs and music
    — 19th century *(Collections, PT5478;*
       History, PT5225-7)
    — 20th century *(Collections, PT5478;*
       History, PT5230-5232)

Dutch property in Great Britain, ⌈**the United**
    States, etc.⌉
Dutch prose literature
    — 20th century
Dutch quatrains
    See Quatrains, Dutch
Dutch rabbits
    x Dutch-marked rabbits
    xx Rabbits
Dutch religious poetry
    See Religious poetry, Dutch
Dutch self-portraits
    See Self-portraits, Dutch
Dutch spaniel
    See Drentsche patrijshond
Dutch standard (Sugar testing)
    See Sugar—Analysis and testing
Dutch still-life painting
    See Still-life painting, Dutch
Dutch students in Geneva, ⌈**Germany, etc.**⌉
Dutch studies *(Direct)*
Dutch-Swedish War, 1658-1659
    See Swedish-Dutch War, 1658-1659
Dutch tiles
    See Tiles, Dutch
Dutch War, 1672-1678 *(D277-8)*
    sa Cassell, France, Battle of, 1677
       Maastricht—Siege, 1673
       Nijmegen, Peace of, 1678-1679
       Schooneveld, Battle of, 1673
       Seneffe, Battle of, 1674
       Tobago, Battle of, 1677
    x Anglo-Dutch War, 1672-1674
    xx Europe—History—1648-1715
       Great Britain—History—Restoration,
         1660-1688
       Netherlands—History—1648-1714
    — Naval operations
Dutch wit and humor *(PT5346; PT5541;*
       Minor collections, PN6222.N38)
    Here are entered collections from several
       authors and individual authors who
       have not written in other literary
       forms.
Dutch wood-engravers
    See Wood-engravers, Dutch
Duties
    See Octroi
       Tariff
       Taxation
Duty *(BJ1450-1458)*
    sa Conduct of life
       Conscience
       Deontic logic
       Ethics
       Vocation
    x Deontology
       Obligation
    xx Conduct of life
       Ethics
       Responsibility
Duty-free entry
    See Duty-free importation
Duty-free exportation of goods in transit
    See Duty-free transit
Duty-free importation *(Direct)*
    sa Customs administration and tourists
       Customs privileges
    x Customs exemptions
       Duty-free entry
       Tariff, Exemption from
       Tariff exemptions
    xx Customs administration
       Tariff
Duty-free importation of aircraft *(Direct)*
    x Aeroplanes—Tariff
Duty-free importation of animals *(Direct)*
    x Animals—Tariff

Duty-free importation of automobiles
   (Direct)
   xx Tariff on automobiles
Duty-free importation of birds   *(Direct)*
   x Birds—Tariff
Duty-free importation of boats   *(Direct)*
   x Boats and boating—Tariff
Duty-free importation of containers *(Direct)*
   x Containers—Tariff
Duty-free importation of copper   *(Direct)*
   xx Tariff on copper
Duty-free importation of goods in transit
   See Duty-free transit
Duty-free importation of machinery   *(Direct)*
   x Machinery—Tariff
Duty-free importation of medical equipment
   (Direct)
   x Duty-free importation of surgical
     equipment
   xx Duty-free importation of scientific
     equipment
     Tariff on medical instruments and
      apparatus
     Tariff on surgical instruments and
      apparatus
Duty-free importation of pallets   *(Direct)*
   x Pallets (Shipping, storage, etc.)—Tariff
Duty-free importation of relief supplies
   (Direct)
   xx International relief
Duty-free importation of samples   *(Direct)*
   x Samples (Commerce)—Tariff
     Tariff on samples
Duty-free importation of scientific equipment
   (Direct)
   sa Duty-free importation of medical
     equipment
   xx Tariff on scientific apparatus and
     instruments
Duty-free importation of surgical equipment
   See Duty-free importation of medical
     equipment
Duty-free importation of wrapping materials
   (Direct)
   x Wrapping materials—Tariff
Duty-free transit   *(Direct)*
   x Duty-free exportation of goods in
     transit
     Duty-free importation of goods in
     transit
     Goods in transit, Tariff on
     Merchandise in transit, Tariff on
   xx Free ports and zones
     Tariff—Law
Dvaita (Sankhya)
   See Sankhya
Dvaita (Vedanta)
   xx Hinduism
     Pantheism
     Philosophy, Hindu
     Vedanta
Dwamish Indians   *(E99.D9)*
   xx Indians of North America
Dwarf conifers
   x Dwarf trees
Dwarf elm
   See Siberian elm
Dwarf fruit trees   *(SB357.5)*
   x Dwarf trees
   xx Fruit-culture
     Fruit trees
     Trees
Dwarf mistletoe
   x American mistletoe
     Dwarfmistletoe
   xx Mistletoe
Dwarf novae   *(QB843.D85)*
   x Novae, Dwarf

   xx Dwarf stars
     Stars, Variable
Dwarf pea
   See Chick-pea
Dwarf stars
   sa Dwarf novae
     Red dwarfs
     White dwarfs
   x Low-luminosity stars
   xx Stars
Dwarf trees
   See Bonsai
     Dwarf conifers
     Dwarf fruit trees
Dwarf vegetables
   See Midget vegetables
Dwarfism
   xx Growth disorders
Dwarfmistletoe
   See Dwarf mistletoe
Dwarfs   *(Ethnography, GN681; Folk-lore,*
   GR555; Somatology, GN69.3-5)
   sa Pygmies
   x Midgets
   xx Deformities
     Folk-lore
     Monsters
     Pygmies
   — Personal narratives   *(GN69.5)*
Dwarfs in art
   xx Art
Dwarfs in literature
Dwelling-terraces
   See Terrace houses
Dwellings *(Direct) (Architecture,*
   NA7100-7566; Building: popular
   works, TH148; Building
   maintenance, TH8901; Domestic
   economy, TX301-339; Economics,
   HD1341; Folk-lore, GR490;
   Manners and customs, GT170-384)
   General works and works on dwellings in
    the United States are entered under
    this heading without subdivision.
    Works on dwellings in other countries
    are entered under Dwellings—⌜coun-
    try subdivision⌝, *e.g.* Dwellings—
    Greece.
   sa Adobe houses
     Apartment houses
     Architecture, Domestic
     Attics
     Bathrooms
     Brick houses
     Bungalows
     Cave-dwellings
     Children's rooms
     Cliff-dwellings
     Clothes closets
     Concrete houses
     Cottages
     Country homes
     Dining rooms
     Domestic engineering
     Earth houses
     Farmhouses
     Fishing lodges
     Grass huts
     House construction
     Igloos
     Indians—Dwellings
     Indians of Central America—Dwellings
     Indians of North America—Dwellings
     Labor and laboring classes—Dwellings
     Lake-dwellers and lake-dwellings
     Log cabins
     Mobile homes
     Pit houses

     Prefabricated houses
     Recreation rooms
     Row houses
     Single story houses
     Sod houses
     Solar houses
     Stone houses
     Suburban homes
     Summer homes
     Tree-dwellings
     Yurts
   x Houses
     Residences
   Example under Buildings
   — Air conditioning
     x Home air conditioning
     xx Domestic engineering
   — Caricatures and cartoons
   — Costs
     See Dwellings—Estimates and costs
   — Estimates and costs
     x Dwellings—Costs
   — Fires and fire prevention   *(TH9445.D9)*
   — Heating and ventilation
     x Dwellings—Ventilation
     xx Domestic engineering
   — — Law and legislation
     See Heating—Law and legislation
   — Juvenile literature
   — Layout
     See Room layout (Dwellings)
   — Lighting
     xx Domestic engineering
   — Maintenance and repair
     xx House construction
     Example under Maintenance
   — Prices   *(Direct)*
   — Psychological aspects
     xx Man—Influence of environment
   — Religious aspects   *(GN414.A1)*
   — Remodeling
     sa Kitchens—Remodeling
     x Remodeling (Architecture)
     Remodeling of dwellings
     xx House construction
   — — Costs   *(Direct) (TH4816)*
   — Sounds
     See Household sounds
   — Testing   *(TH4811)*
   — Transportation
   — Ventilation
     See Dwellings—Heating and
      ventilation

    GEOGRAPHIC SUBDIVISIONS

   — Greece
     Note under Dwellings
Dwellings (in religion, folk-lore, etc.)
   x Folk-lore of dwellings
   xx Religion, Primitive
Dwellings in literature
Dyabarma (African people)
   See Zarma (African people)
Dyak language   *(PL5301-4)*
   sa Maanyan language
     Ngadju dialect
   x Dajak language
     Dayak language
   xx Malayan languages
Dyaks   *(DS646.32.D9)*
   sa Ibans (Bornean people)
     Maanyans (Bornean people)
     Missions to Dyaks
   x Dayaks
   xx Ethnology—Borneo
     Malay race
   — Pictorial works
   — Religion

Dyan dialect
  x Dian dialect
  xx Lobi dialects
Dye industry *(Direct)*
  x Dyestuffs industry
Dye plants *(Indirect)* *(SB285-7)*
  sa Lichens
    Logwood
    Safflower
    Turmeric
  xx Botany, Economic
    Dyes and dyeing
    Plants
Dyeing
  See Dyes and dyeing
Dyeing machinery
  See Dyes and dyeing—Apparatus
Dyeline
  See Diazotype
Dyerma (African people)
  See Zarma (African people)
Dyers' oak
  See Black oak
Dyes and dyeing *(Economics, HD9999.D8-9;*
    Technology, TP897-929)
  sa Auxochromes
    Azo dyes
    Batik
    Benzidine dyes
    Black
    Bleaching
    Calico-printing
    Cleaning and dyeing industry
    Coal-tar colors
    Cochineal
    Color in the textile industries
    Coloring matter
    Drying apparatus—Textile fabrics
    Dye plants
    Fluorescein
    Henna
    Indigo
    Khaki
    Madder
    Optical brighteners
    Prussian blue
    Purple
    Quercetin
    Quercitron-bark
    Reactive dyes
    Rossing-machines
    Sulphide dyes
    Sumac
    Thiazine dyes
    Tie-dyeing
  x Dyeing
    Tinctorial substances
  xx Bleaching
    Cleaning
    Coal-tar colors
    Color
    Color in the textile industries
    Coloring matter
    Pigments
    Textile industry and fabrics
  Example under Chemistry, Technical
  — Analysis
  — Apparatus *(TP893)*
    x Dyeing machinery
    xx Textile machinery
  — Automation
  — Cellulose
    xx Cellulose
  — Chemistry *(TP893)*
    sa Chromatographic analysis
    Textile chemistry
    x Dyestuffs
  — Cotton *(TP930)*

    x Cotton dyeing
  — Dacron
    x Dacron dyeing
  — Early works to 1800
  — Feathers
    x Feather dyeing
    xx Feathers
  — Food
    See Coloring matter in food
  — Fur
    See Fur—Dressing and dyeing
  — Glass fibers
    x Glass fibers—Dyeing
  — Hair
    See Hair—Dyeing and bleaching
      Hair dyes
  — Hides and skins
    See Hides and skins—Dressing and
      dyeing
  — Hosiery
    x Hosiery dyeing
      Hosiery—Dyeing
  — Knit goods
    x Knit goods—Dyeing
    xx Knit goods—Finishing
  — Laboratory manuals
  — Leather
    x Leather dyeing
    xx Leather industry and trade
  — Nylon
    x Nylon dyeing
  — Paper *(TS1109)*
    xx Paper making and trade
  — Plastics
    x Plastics—Dyeing
  — Prices *(Direct)*
  — Rayon
    x Rayon dyeing
  — Rubber goods
    x Rubber goods—Dyeing
  — Safety measures
  — Silk *(TP901)*
    x Silk dyeing
  — Standards
  — Tables, calculations, etc.
  — Tariff
    See Tariff on dyestuffs
  — Textile fibers
    sa Colorfastness (Textiles)
    x Textile fibers—Dyeing
    xx Textile chemicals
  — Textile fibers, Synthetic
    x Textile fibers, Synthetic—Dyeing
  — — Patents
  — Waste disposal
  — Wool *(TP899)*
    x Wool dyeing
    xx Wool
      Woolen and worsted finishing
      Woolen and worsted manufacture
Dyes and dyeing, Domestic *(TP909)*
Dyestuffs
  See Dyes and dyeing—Chemistry
    Tariff on dyestuffs
Dyestuffs industry
  See Dye industry
Dyimini (African people)
  See Djimini (African people)
Dying patient
  See Terminal care
Dying words
  See Last words
Dyirbal language
  See Djirbal language
Dykes
  See Dikes (Engineering)
    Dikes (Geology)

Dynamic display systems
  See Information display systems
Dynamic language-application system for the
    evaluation of data collections
  See DL-ASEDC (Electronic computer
    system)
Dynamic loading (Materials)
  See Materials—Dynamic testing
Dynamic loads (Pavements)
  See Pavements—Live loads
Dynamic meteorology
  sa Anticyclones
    Atmospheric thermodynamics
    Convection (Meteorology)
    Coriolis force
    Dust devils
    Hurricanes—Kinetic energy
    Hydrodynamic weather forecasting
    Vertical wind shear
  xx Meteorology
    Turbulence
    Winds
  — Problems, exercises, etc.
Dynamic models (Computer program language)
  See DYNAMO (Computer program
    language)
Dynamic programming
  xx Mathematical optimization
    Programming (Mathematics)
    Systems engineering
  — Problems, exercises, etc.
Dynamic short range weather forecasting
  See Hydrodynamic short range weather
    forecasting
Dynamic testing (Materials)
  See Materials—Dynamic testing
Dynamic weather forecasting
  See Hydrodynamic weather forecasting
Dynamics *(QA845-871)*
  sa Aerodynamics
    Astrodynamics
    Control theory
    Electrodynamics
    Force and energy
    Hydrodynamics
    Irreversible processes
    Kinematics
    Lagrangian functions
    Machinery, Dynamics of
    Materials—Dynamic testing
    Matter
    Mechanics
    Motion
    Perturbation (Mathematics)
    Physics
    Plasma dynamics
    Problem of two bodies
    Quantum theory
    Rotational motion
    Stability
    Statics
    Thermodynamics
    Transients (Dynamics)
    subdivision Dynamics *under subjects,*
      e.g. Motor vehicles—Dynamics
  x Kinetics
  xx Force and energy
    Mathematics
    Mechanics
    Mechanics, Analytic
    Physics
    Statics
  — Computer programs
  — Early works to 1800
  — Problems, exercises, etc.
  — Programmed instruction
  — Statistical methods

Dynamics, Molecular
   See Molecular dynamics
Dynamics, Rigid *(QA861-3)*
   sa Gyroscope
      Moments of inertia
      Rotational motion (Rigid dynamics)
      Screws, Theory of
      Top
   x Rigid dynamics
Dynamics, Structural
   See Structural dynamics
Dynamics, Topological
   See Topological dynamics
Dynamics (Music)
   See Music—Interpretation (Phrasing,
      dynamics, etc.)
Dynamics and statics (Social sciences)
   See Statics and dynamics (Social sciences)
Dynamics of a particle *(QA851-5)*
   sa Configuration space
      Law of areas (Mechanics)
   x Particle, Dynamics of a
Dynamite *(TP285)*
   xx Explosives
DYNAMO (Computer program language)
      (HF5548)
   x Dynamic models (Computer program
      language)
   xx Industrial management—Mathematical
      models
   Example under Programming languages (Elec-
      tronic computers)
Dynamo tenders' manuals *(TK2184)*
Dynamometer *(TJ1053)*
   x Ergometer
Dynamos *(TK2411-2491)*
   sa Armatures
      Automobiles—Electric generators
      Gramme dynamos
      Magneto-electric machines
      Turbogenerators
   x Electric generators
      Generators, Electric
   xx Electric apparatus and appliances
      Electric machinery
      Motors
   — Alternating current *(TK2761-5)*
      x Alternating current dynamos
         Alternating current generators
         Alternators, Electric
         Electric alternators
      xx Electric machinery—Alternating
         current
   — Amateurs' manuals *(TK9911)*
   — Cooling
   — Design and construction *(TK2435)*
   — Direct current *(TK2661-5)*
      sa Rotating amplifiers
      x Direct current machinery
      xx Electric machinery—Direct current
   — Erecting work
   — Field coils *(TK2475)*
   — Maintenance and repair
   — Protection
   — Testing *(TK2433)*
DYNFOR (Computer program language)
Dyola language
   See Diola language
Dysautonomia
   x Familial dysautonomia
DYSEAC computer
   See Seac computer
Dysentery *(RC140)*
   sa Amebiasis
      Shigellosis
      Swine dysentery
   xx Intestines—Diseases
   — Complications and sequelae

Dysgraphia
   See Agraphia
Dyshidrosis
   See Pompholyx (Disease)
Dyslalia
   xx Aphasia
      Lisping
      Speech, Disorders of
      Stuttering
Dyslexia
   sa Alexia
   xx Alexia
Dyslexia, Developmental
   See Reading disability
Dysmenorrhea *(RG181)*
   xx Menstruation disorders
Dysostosis *(RJ320.D9)*
   xx Cartilage
      Fetus—Diseases
Dyspepsia *(RC829)*
   sa Bilious diseases and biliousness
      Pancreas—Secretions
      Pepsin
   x Indigestion
   xx Bilious diseases and biliousness
      Constipation
      Digestion
      Stomach—Diseases
   — Homeopathic treatment *(RX336.D9)*
Dyspnoea
   xx Respiration
Dysprosium
Dysraphia *(RC362)*
   sa Anencephalus
      Spina bifida
      Syringomyelia
   x Dysraphic states
      Status dysraphicus
   xx Deformities—Genetic aspects
      Nervous system—Abnormities and
         deformities
Dysraphic states
   See Dysraphia
Dystonia
   xx Muscles—Diseases
Dystonia musculorum deformans
   x Oppenheim-Ziehen disease
      Ziehen-Oppenheim disease
   xx Movement disorders
      Muscles—Diseases
Dystrophia myotonica
   See Myotonia atrophica
Dystrophy *(RB149)*
   sa Muscular dystrophy
   — Psychosomatic aspects
Dystrophy, Retinal
   See Retinal degeneration
Dyur language *(PL8143)*
   x Diour language
      Diur language
      Dzur language
      Giur language
      Jur language
      Luo language
   xx Nilotic languages
      Shilluk language
Dzalamo (African people)
   See Wazaramo (African people)
Dzema language
   See Maba language
Dzilio language
   See Bari language
Dzo language
   See Ijo language
Dzur language
   See Dyur language
Džurdžin language
   See Ju-chên language

Eagle (Ampulla)
   See Ampullas, Coronation
Eagle (in heraldry) *(CR41.E2; France,*
      CR542)
   xx Devices
   Example under Heraldry
Eagle (in religion, folk-lore, etc.)
      (Mythology, BL325.E3)
   x Folk-lore of eagles
   xx Christian art and symbolism
      Religion, Primitive
Eagle dance *(E98.D2)*
   xx Indians of North America—Dances
Eagle in art
   xx Art
Eagle owl *(QL696.S8)*
   xx Owls
Eagles *(QL696.A2)*
   sa Bald eagle
      Black hawk-eagle
      Golden eagle
      Himalayan golden eagle
      Lammergeier
      Sea eagles
   xx Birds of prey
   — Behavior
   — Juvenile literature
   — Pictorial works
Eagles, Fossil
Ear *(Comparative anatomy, QL948; Human*
      anatomy, QM507; Physiology,
      QP461-471)
   sa Basilar membrane
      Columella auris
      Fenestra rotunda
      Hearing
      Labyrinth (Ear)
      Middle ear
      Otocysts
      Otoliths
      Otosclerosis
      Semicircular canals
      Stapedius muscle
      Tensor tympani muscle
      Tympanal organ
   x Otology
   xx Auditory pathways
      Deafness
      Head
      Hearing
   Example under Sense-organs
   — Abnormities and deformities
   — Anatomy
      Example under Anatomy
   — Blood-vessels
   — Care and hygiene *(RF135)*
   — Diseases *(RF1-320)*
      sa Alport's syndrome
         Deafness
         Dispensaries, Ophthalmic and aural
         Ear—Radiography
         Hearing disorders
         Hospitals, Ophthalmic and aural
         Mastoid process—Diseases
         Otosclerosis
         Ototoxic agents
         Tinnitus
      x Otitis
      xx Otolaryngology
   — — Diagnosis *(RF123)*
      sa Vestibular function tests
   — — Homeopathic treatment *(RX441-6)*
   — Fungi *(RF190)*
      x Fungous ear diseases
         Otomycosis
      Example under Medical mycology
   — Juvenile literature
   — Physiology

See Hearing
— Radiography
    xx Ear—Diseases
— Surgery   *(RF126)*
    xx Otolaryngology, Operative
        Surgery, Orificial
—— Atlases
— Tumors   *(RC280.E2)*
Ear, nose, and throat nursing
  See Otolaryngological nursing
Ear ossicles
  sa Malleus (Ear)
  xx Middle ear
— Diseases
— Surgery
— Transplantation
    xx Surgery, Plastic
Ear plugs (Whales)
  xx Whales
Ear-rings   *(Art, NK7300-7399; Manufacture,*
    TS740-759)
  xx Jewelry
Ear-shells
  See Abalones
Ear-stones
  See Otoliths
Ear tick, Spinose
  See Spinose ear tick
Ear training   *(MT35)*
  sa Musical dictation
  xx Music—Instruction and study
    Musical dictation
— Programmed instruction
Eared seals
  sa California sea lion
    Guadalupe fur seal
    Northern fur seal
    Sea lions
    South African fur seal
    Southern fur seals
  xx Seals (Animals)
Eared seals, Fossil   *(QE882.P5)*
Early American art industries and trade
  See Art industries and trade, Early
    American
Early Buddhism
  See Buddha and Buddhism—Early
    Buddhism, ca. 486 B.C.-ca. 100 A.D.
Early Christian . . .
  x Early church . . .
Early Christian architecture
  See Architecture, Early Christian
Early Christian art
  See Art, Early Christian
Early Christian art metal-work
  See Art metal-work, Early Christian
Early Christian art objects
  See Art objects, Early Christian
Early Christian funeral rites and ceremonies
  See Funeral rites and ceremonies, Early
    Christian
Early Christian glassware
  See Glassware, Early Christian
Early Christian hymns
  See Hymns, Early Christian
Early Christian literature
  See Christian literature, Early
Early Christian liturgies
  See Liturgies, Early Christian
Early Christian mosaics
  See Mosaics, Early Christian
Early Christian mural painting and decoration
  See Mural painting and decoration, Early
    Christian
Early Christian painting
  See Painting, Early Christian
Early Christian paintings
  See Paintings, Early Christian

Early Christian poetry
  See Christian poetry, Early
Early Christian pottery
  See Pottery, Early Christian
Early Christian prayers
  See Prayers, Early Christian
Early Christian sarcophagi
  See Sarcophagi, Early Christian
Early Christian sculpture
  See Sculpture, Early Christian
Early Christian sermons
  See Sermons, Early Christian
Early church . . .
  See Early Christian . . .
Early Gothic Art
  See Art, Gothic—Early Gothic
Early man
  See Fossil man
Early man in the Americas
  See Paleo-Indians
Early marriage
  See Teen-age marriage
Early printed books
  See Bibliography—Early printed books
    Bibliography—Rare books
    Incunabula
Early Renaissance art
  See Art, Renaissance—Early Renaissance
Early warning systems
  See Ballistic missile early warning system
    Distant early warning system
Early's Invasion of Maryland and
    Pennsylvania, 1864
  See Maryland Campaign, June-Aug., 1864
Earmarks
  xx Cattle brands
    Cattle—Marking
Earnest   *(Direct)*
  sa Penalties, Contractual
  x Arrha
  xx Contracts
    Deposits (Law)
    Penalties, Contractual
    Sales
    Security (Law)
  Note under Deposits (Law)
Earnest (Greek law)
Earnest (Roman law)
Earth   *(Earth as planet, QB631; Physical*
    history, QE501)
  sa Antarctic regions
    Arctic regions
    Astronomical geography
    Atmosphere
    Biosphere
    Climatology
    Cosmogony
    Cosmography
    Cosmology
    Cosmology
    Creation
    Deluge
    Earthquakes
    End of the world (Astronomy)
    Geodesy
    Geography
    Geology
    Geophysics
    Glacial epoch
    Latitude
    Longitude
    Magnetism, Terrestrial
    Meteorology
    Ocean
    Oceanography
    Physical geography
  xx Astronomy
    Cosmology

    Creation
    Geology
    Physical geography
    Solar system
— Age   *(QE508)*
  sa Geological time
  xx Geological time
  Example under Age
— Chemical composition
  See Geochemistry
— Core
  xx Earth—Internal structure
— Crust
  sa Mohole project
    Plate tectonics
    Upper mantle project
  xx Earth—Internal structure
    Earth—Surface
—— Juvenile literature
— Curiosa and miscellany   *(QB638)*
— Density   *(QB341)*
  xx Gravitation
    Pendulum
  Example under reference from Density
— Figure   *(QB281-3)*
  sa Arc measures
    Area measurement
    Attractions of ellipsoids
    Geodesy
    Isostasy
    Rotating masses of fluid
  x Figure of the earth
  xx Geodesy
    Gravity
—— Juvenile literature
— Internal structure   *(QE509)*
  sa Earth—Core
    Earth—Crust
    Earth—Mantle
    Mohorovicic discontinuity
    Upper mantle project
— Juvenile literature
— Magnetism
  See Magnetism, Terrestrial
— Mantle
  sa Mohole project
    Plate tectonics
    Upper mantle project
  xx Earth—Internal structure
—— Popular works
— Maps
  See World maps
— Mass
  xx Mass (Physics)
— Mathematical models
— Orbit
  sa Astronomical unit
  xx Astronomical unit
— Origin   *(QB631)*
— Photographs from space   *(QB637)*
— Programmed instruction
— Radiation
  See Terrestrial radiation
— Rotation   *(QB633)*
  sa Coriolis force
    Foucault's pendulum
  x Rotation of the earth
  xx Foucault's pendulum
    Pendulum
—— Juvenile literature
— Surface   *(QE511)*
  sa Albedo
    Earth—Crust
—— Juvenile literature
— Temperature
  See Earth temperature
Earth, Effect of man on
  See Man—Influence on nature

Earth, Medical and surgical uses of
   See Earths, Medical and surgical uses of
Earth, Rammed
   See Pisé
Earth (in religion, folk-lore, etc.) *(Folk-lore,*
       GR655; Nature-worship, BL435)
   x Earth-worship
     Folk-lore of the earth
   xx Religion, Primitive
Earth currents *(Indirect)*
   sa Geomagnetic micropulsations
   x Telluric currents
   xx Electric currents, Vagrant
     Geophysics
     Magnetism, Terrestrial
Earth dams *(Direct) (TC543)*
   x Hydraulic fill dams
     Rockfill dams
   xx Dams
     Embankments
  — Tables, calculations, etc.
  — Thermal properties *(TC543)*
Earth fills
   See Fills (Earthwork)
Earth houses *(GN783)*
   sa Building, Adobe
     Pisé
     Sod houses
   x Earth lodges
     Earthen houses
   xx Architecture, Domestic
     Cave-dwellings
     Dwellings
Earth lodges
   See Earth houses
Earth movements *(Indirect) (GB481-8)*
   sa Earth tides
     Lahars
     Subsidences (Earth movements)
   xx Geophysics
     Natural disasters
     Physical geography
     Seismology
Earth movements and building *(TH1094)*
   sa Earthquakes and building
   x Subsidences and building
   xx Building
     Buildings—Protection
Earth moving machinery
   See Earthmoving machinery
Earth-nut oil
   See Peanut oil
Earth oscillations
   See Free earth oscillations
Earth pillars
   See Earth pyramids
Earth pressure *(TA765)*
   sa Dams
     Retaining walls
     Underground construction
   xx Dams
     Earthwork
     Pressure
     Retaining walls
  — Measurement
  — Tables, calculations, etc. *(TA765)*
Earth pyramids *(Indirect)*
   x Earth pillars
     Pyramids, Earth
   xx Geomorphology
Earth radiation
   See Terrestrial radiation
Earth resistance *(QC809.E15)*
   x Earth resistivity
     Resistance, Earth
     Resistivity, Earth
   xx Electric prospecting
     Electric resistance

Geophysics
Earth resistivity
   See Earth resistance
Earth roads
   See Roads, Earth
Earth satellites
   See Artificial satellites
Earth science instruments *(QE49.5)*
   x Instruments, Earth science
   xx Physical instruments
Earth science research *(Direct)*
   x Earth sciences—Research
   xx Research
Earth sciences *(Indirect)*
   sa Aeronautics in earth sciences
     Astronautics in earth sciences
     Atmosphere
     Climatology
     Electronics in earth sciences
     Geochemistry
     Geography
     Geology
     Geophysics
     Hydrology
     Meteorology
     Oceanography
   x Geoscience
  — Documentation
  — Experiments
  — Juvenile literature
  — Popular works
  — Research
     See Earth science research
  — Statistical methods
  — Study and teaching *(Direct)*
  —— Audio-visual aids *(QE43)*
Earth sciences and state *(Indirect)*
   x State and earth sciences
   xx Science and state
Earth scientists *(Indirect)*
   sa Geographers
     Geologists
     Meteorologists
     Oceanographers
   xx Scientists
Earth stations (Satellite telecommunication)
     (Direct)
   x Artificial satellites in
     telecommunication—Earth stations
     Artificial satellites in
     telecommunication—Ground stations
     Ground stations (Satellite
     telecommunication)
   xx Artificial satellites in
     telecommunication
     Ground support systems (Astronautics)
Earth temperature *(Indirect) (QC907)*
   sa Geothermal resources
     Heat budget (Geophysics)
   x Earth—Temperature
     Ground temperature
   xx Meteorology
     Solar radiation
     Temperature
Earth tides *(Indirect)*
   xx Earth movements
     Geophysics
     Tides
  — Computer programs
  — Observations
Earth-worship
   See Earth (in religion, folk-lore, etc.)
Earthen houses
   See Earth houses
Earthenware
   See Pottery
Earthenware stoves
   See Stoves, Earthenware

Earthmovers
   See Earthmoving machinery
Earthmoving machinery *(TA725)*
   sa Bulldozers
     Construction equipment
     Excavating machinery
     Graders (Earthmoving machinery)
     Road machinery
     Scrapers (Earthmoving machinery)
     Soil stabilization—Equipment and
       supplies
   x Earth moving machinery
     Earthmovers
   xx Construction equipment
     Earthwork
     Road machinery
  — Automatic control
  — Design and construction
  — Drawing
     See Earthmoving machinery—
       Drawings
  — Drawings
     x Earthmoving machinery—Drawing
     xx Mechanical drawing
  — Dynamics
  — Fuel consumption
  — Hydraulic equipment
  — Juvenile literature
  — Maintenance and repair
  —— Laboratory manuals *(TA725)*
  — Noise
Earthmoving machinery operators *(Indirect)*
  — Vocational guidance
     xx Engineering as a profession
  —— Juvenile literature
Earthquake insurance
   See Insurance, Earthquake
Earthquake intensity
   x Intensity, Earthquake
     Seismic intensity
   xx Earthquakes
Earthquake prediction
   x Earthquakes—Prediction
     Prediction, Earthquake
Earthquake simulators
   x Simulators, Earthquake
Earthquake sounds
Earthquakes *(Indirect) (QE531-541;*
      Magnetic effects, QC843)
   sa Earthquake intensity
     Microseisms
     Seismic waves
     Seismology
     Seismometry
     Tidal waves
   subdivision Earthquake *under names of*
     cities, e.g. Messina—Earthquake,
     1908
   xx Earth
     Geodynamics
     Geology
     Natural disasters
     Physical geography
     Seismology
     Seismometry
  — Juvenile literature
  — Measurement
     See Seismometry
  — Prediction
     See Earthquake prediction
  — Religious interpretations
     x Earthquakes—Sermons
     Example under Theodicy
  — Research
     See Seismological research
  — Sermons
     See Earthquakes—Religious
       interpretations

Earthquakes and atomic power-plants
    x Atomic power-plants, Earthquake-proof
    xx Earthquakes and building
Earthquakes and building *(TH1095)*
    sa Earthquakes and atomic power-plants
    x Building, Earthquake-proof
    xx Earth movements and building
       Structural dynamics
  — Safety regulations *(Direct)*
  — Tables, calculations, etc.
Earthquakes and hydraulic structures
    (TC181)
    xx Hydraulic structures
       Structural dynamics
Earthquakes and railroads *(Indirect)*
    x Railroads and earthquakes
    xx Natural disasters and railroads
       Structural dynamics
Earths, Medical and surgical uses of
    (Antiseptics, RD96.E2)
    sa Baths, Moor and mud
    x Earth, Medical and surgical uses of
    xx Surgery, Aseptic and antiseptic
Earths, Rare *(Indirect)* *(QD172.R2)*
    sa Rare earth industry
       Rare earth metals
       kinds of rare earths, e.g. Yttrium earths
    x Rare earths
    xx Chemistry, Inorganic
       Metals
       Rare earth metals
  — Spectra
Earthwork *(TA715-770)*
    Here are entered all works relating to
    earthwork in engineering operations.
    Earthwork fortifications are entered
    also under the heading Fortification.
    Treatises on early and prehistoric earth-
    work remains are entered under Earth-
    works (Archaeology)
    sa Dams
       Dikes (Engineering)
       Dredges
       Earth pressure
       Earthmoving machinery
       Embankments
       Excavation
       Fills (Earthwork)
       Fortification
       Foundations
       Hydraulic filling
       Railroads—Earthwork
       Retaining walls
       Shafts (Excavations)
       Soil mechanics
       Tunneling
       Underground construction
    xx Bulk solids handling
       Civil engineering
       Dikes (Engineering)
       Engineering
       Excavation
       Fortification
       Foundations
       Military engineering
  Note under Earthworks (Archaeology)
  — Cold weather conditions
  — Early works to 1800
  — Estimates and costs *(Direct)*
  — Law and legislation *(Direct)*
    x Excavation—Law and legislation
  — Problems, exercises, etc.
  — Production standards
  — Safety measures
  — Tables, calculations, etc. *(TA721)*

Earthworks (Archaeology) *(Indirect)*
    (GN789)
    Here are entered all works relating to
    earthwork remains of an archaeologi-
    cal character. Engineering operations
    and their results are entered under the
    heading Earthwork.
    sa Fortification, Primitive
       Mounds
    xx Archaeology
       Excavations (Archaeology)
       Mounds
  Note under Earthwork
Earthworm culture
    xx Earthworms
Earthworms *(QL391.O4)*
    Here are entered works on the common
    earthworm (Lumbricus terrestris).
    Works on earthworms as a group are
    entered under Opisthopora or the ap-
    propriate lesser taxon.
    sa Earthworm culture
    xx Annelida
       Soil biology
       Soil fauna
       Worms
  Note under Opisthopora
  — Anatomy
  — Juvenile literature
Earwigs
    See Dermaptera
Easels
    xx Artists' materials
Easements
    See Servitudes
Easements, Avigation
    See Avigation easements
East
    sa Latin Orient
       Levant
       Near East
    x Orient
East (Far East) *(DS501-519)*
    x Far East
  — Historical geography
    Note under Geography, Historical
East (Near East)
    See Near East
East Africa Federation
    x Federation of East Africa
East African Coast fever
    See East Coast fever
East African Safari Rally *(GV1034.84.E)*
    x Coronation Safari
       Safari Rally, East African
    xx Automobile racing
       Automobile rallies
East African swine fever
    See African swine fever
East and West *(CB251)*
    Here are entered works on both accultu-
    ration and cultural conflict between
    Oriental and Occidental civilizations.
    sa Eastern question
       Intercultural communication
       Occidentals in Oriental art
       Philosophy, Comparative
    x Civilization, Occidental—Oriental
       influences
       Civilization, Oriental—Occidental
       influences
       Orient and Occident
       West and East
    xx Acculturation
       Eastern question
       Eurasianism
  — Juvenile literature

East Armenian language
    See Armenian language, Modern—East
       Armenian
East Asia co-prosperity sphere
    See Greater East Asia co-prosperity sphere
East Cameroon fiction (French)
    See French fiction—Cameroon authors
East Cameroon literature (French)
    See French literature—Cameroon authors
East Cameroon poetry (French)
    See French poetry—Cameroon authors
       French poetry—East Cameroon authors
East Coast fever *(SF967.E)*
    x Bovine theileriasis
       East African Coast fever
    xx Cattle—Diseases
       Theileriosis
       Ticks as carriers of disease
East Europe
    See Europe, Eastern
East European studies *(Direct)*
    x Europe, Eastern, studies
East Friesian sheep
East Goths
    See Goths
East India porcelain
    See China trade porcelain
East Indian authors, [poets, etc.]
    See Authors [Poets, etc.], Indic
East Indian literature
    See Indic literature
East Indian orations (English)
    See English orations—Indic authors
East Indian philosophy
    See Philosophy, East Indian
East Indian refugees
    See Refugees, East Indian
East Indian students in foreign countries
    xx East Indians in foreign countries
East Indian students in Great Britain, [the
    United States, etc.]
East Indians
    sa Hindus
    x Indians, East
    xx Hindus
  Example under Orientals
East Indians in foreign countries
    sa East Indian students in foreign
       countries
East Indians in Natal, [South Africa, etc.]
  — Biography
  — Education
  — Juvenile literature
  — Legal status, laws, etc.
East Prussian horse
    See Trakehner horse
East Siberian laika
East Syrian Church
    See Nestorian Church
East Syrians
    See Assyrians
East-West trade (1945-   )
    xx Commerce
       Europe—Commerce
       International economic relations
Easter *(Indirect)* *(BV55;Church calendar,*
    CE83; Manners and customs,
    GT4935)
    sa Jesus Christ—Resurrection
       Paschal mystery
       Quartodecimans
    xx Church year
       Fasts and feasts
       Holy Week
       Jesus Christ—Resurrection
       Lent
  Example under references from Ecclesiastical
    fasts and feasts; Religious festivals

Easter *(Indirect)* *(BV55;Church calendar,*
CE83; Manners and customs,
GT4935) *(Continued)*
— Art
— Drama *(PN6120.E2)*
sa Drama, Medieval
Mysteries and miracle-plays
xx Jesus Christ—Drama
Religious drama
Example under Drama
— Hymns
See Easter hymns
— Poetry *(PN6110.E2)*
sa Carols
Easter hymns
— Prayer-books and devotions
x Easter—Prayer-books and devotions
—English
—— English
See Easter—Prayer-books and
devotions
— Sermons *(BV4259)*
— Songs and music
See Easter music
— Stories
See Easter stories
Easter carols
See Carols
Easter dues
x Easter offerings
xx Church finance
Tithes
Easter duties
xx Church discipline
Commandments of the church
Confession
Lord's Supper
Easter eggs
x Eggs, Easter
xx Egg decoration
Painting
Easter hymns
x Easter—Hymns
xx Easter music
Easter—Poetry
Hymns
Easter music
sa Carols
Easter hymns
x Easter—Songs and music
xx Church music
Holidays—Songs and music
Music
Sacred vocal music
Easter offerings
See Easter dues
Easter Rebellion, 1916
See Ireland—History—Sinn Fein Rebellion,
1916
Easter seals
See Seals (Christmas, etc.)
Easter service
xx Liturgies
Easter stories
x Easter—Stories
Eastern black walnut
x Black walnut, Eastern
xx Walnut
Eastern bluebird *(QL696.P2)*
xx Bluebirds
— Behavior
Eastern church theology
See Theology, Eastern church
Eastern churches *(BX100-189)*
sa Monophysites
Nestorian Church
Orthodox Eastern Church
xx Sects

Eastern diamond rattlesnake
See Eastern diamondback rattlesnake
Eastern diamondback rattlesnake
x Diamond rattlesnake
Diamondback rattlesnake
Eastern diamond rattlesnake
xx Rattlesnakes
Eastern Empire
See Byzantine Empire
Eastern encephalitis
See Equine encephalomyelitis
Eastern equine encephalomyelitis
See Equine encephalomyelitis
Eastern Europe
See Europe, Eastern
Eastern gall rust
xx Rusts (Fungi)
Eastern hognose snake
xx Hognose snakes
Eastern Indians, Wars with, 1722-1726
(E83.72)
sa Pigwacket Fight, 1725
x Dummer's War
Wars with the Eastern Indians,
1722-1726
xx Indians of North America—Wars—
1600-1750
Eastern Orthodox
See Orthodox (Orthodox Eastern Church)
Eastern Orthodox Church
See Orthodox Eastern Church
Eastern oyster
See American oyster
Eastern pipistrelle
Eastern question *(General history, D371-3;*
19th century, D374-5; 20th century,
D461-9)
sa East and West
World politics
xx East and West
World politics
Eastern question (Balkan) *(History, D374-7,*
D461-9; International law, JX1319)
sa Balkan Entente, 1934-
Balkan Peninsula—History—War of
1912-1913
Berlin, Treaty of, 1878
Crimean War, 1853-1856
Macedonian question
Russians in Asia Minor
Russo-Turkish War, 1828-1829
Russo-Turkish War, 1877-1878
San Stefano, Treaty of, 1878
Straits question
Turco-Italian War, 1911-1912
Young-Turkish Party
Yugoslavs
x Balkan question
Bulgarian question
xx Crimean War, 1853-1856
Macedonian question
Eastern question (Central Asia) *(D378)*
sa Afghan wars
British in Central Asia
Russians in Central Asia
Russo-Khivan Expedition, 1873
x Central Asian question
Eastern question (Far East) *(History,*
DS515-519; International law,
JX1321)
sa Chinese-Japanese War, 1894-1895
Pan-Pacific relations
Portsmouth, Treaty of, 1905
Russo-Japanese War, 1904-1905
Yellow peril
x Chinese question
Far Eastern question
Open door policy (Far East)

xx Boxers
Pan-Pacific relations
Yellow peril
— Juvenile literature
Eastern ribbonsnake
x Ribbonsnake, Eastern
xx Garter snakes
Eastern Schism
See Schism—Eastern and Western Church
Eastern Slavic languages
See Slavic languages, Eastern
Eastern tent caterpillar *(SB945.E)*
x Apple-tree tent caterpillar
xx Moths
Tent-caterpillars
— Control *(Indirect)*
Eastern white pine
See White pine
Eastern wood pewee
See Wood pewee
Eastern wood rat
xx Wood rats
Eastern Woodland Indians
See Woodland Indians
Eating
See Dinners and dining
Gastronomy
Table
Eating utensils
See Tableware
Eau de Cologne
x Cologne (Toilet water)
Cologne water
xx Perfumes
Eavesdropping *(Direct)*
sa Wire-tapping
x Electronic bugging
Electronic eavesdropping
Electronic listening devices
Interception of communications,
Unauthorized
Listening devices, Unauthorized use of
Unauthorized interception of
communications
xx Criminal investigation
Electronics in criminal investigation
Evidence, Criminal
Evidence (Law)
Privacy, Right of
Wire-tapping
Ebelsberg, Battle of, 1809
xx Napoléon I, Emperor of the French,
1769-1821—German and Austrian
Campaign, 1809
Ebembe language
See Bembe language (Lake Tanganyika)
Ebino-chō, Japan
— Earthquake, 1968
Ebionism *(BT1375)*
sa Jewish Christians—Early church, ca.
30-600
x Ebionites
xx Church history—Primitive and early
church, ca. 30-600
Jewish Christians—Early church, ca.
30-600
Ebionites
See Ebionism
Ebon language
See Marshall language
Ebonite
See Rubber
Ebridians
See Ebriida
Ebriedians
See Ebriida
Ebriida
x Ebridians

552

Ebriedians
  xx Flagellata
    Marine plankton
Ebriida, Fossil
Ebro River, Battle of the, 1938
  xx Spain—History—Civil War, 1936-1939
    —Campaigns and battles
Ebstein's anomaly
  xx Heart—Abnormities and deformities
Ebullition *(QC304)*
  sa Film boiling
    Nucleate boiling
  x Boiling
  xx Boiling-points
    Vapors
Écarté (Game) *(GV1295.E3)*
Ecaudata
  See Anura
Eccard telephone
  See Telephone—Eccard system
Ecce nunc (Music)
  See Psalms (Music)—134th Psalm
Ecce, quam bonum (Music)
  See Psalms (Music)—133d Psalm
Eccentric literature
    Here are entered works on literary pro-
    ducts written by cranks, and eccentric
    in character. Works on eccentrics as
    fictional characters are entered under
    the heading Eccentrics in literature.
  x Crank books
    Literature, Eccentric
  xx Literary curiosa
  Note under Eccentrics in literature
Eccentricities
  See Eccentrics and eccentricities
Eccentrics (Machinery) *(TJ543)*
  sa Cams
Eccentrics and eccentricities *(Biography,*
    CT9990-9991)
  sa Eccentrics in literature
    Hermits
    Insanity
    Recluses
  x Cranks
    Eccentricities
    Fixed ideas
  xx Characters and characteristics
    Curiosities and wonders
    Insanity
Eccentrics in literature
    Here are entered works on eccentrics as
    fictional characters. Works on literary
    products written by cranks, and eccen-
    tric in character, are entered under the
    heading Eccentric literature.
  xx Eccentrics and eccentricities
  Note under Eccentric literature
Ecclesiastical acts, Legitimate
  See Legitimate ecclesiastical acts
Ecclesiastical antiquities
  See Christian antiquities
Ecclesiastical architecture
  See Church architecture
Ecclesiastical art
  See Christian art and symbolism
Ecclesiastical benefices
  See Benefices, Ecclesiastical
Ecclesiastical biography
  See Christian biography
Ecclesiastical calendar
  See Church calendar
Ecclesiastical chronology
  See Chronology, Ecclesiastical
Ecclesiastical corporations
  See Corporations, Religious
Ecclesiastical costume
  See Church vestments

Clergy—Costume
    Monasticism and religious orders—
      Habit
Ecclesiastical courts *(Direct)*
  sa Appeal as from an abuse
    Church discipline
    Complaints (Canon law)
    Privilegium fori
    Promoters of justice (Canon law)
  x Church courts
    Courts, Church
    Courts, Ecclesiastical
    Ecclesiastical tribunals
    Tribunals, Ecclesiastical
  xx Canon law
    Church discipline
    Courts
    Ecclesiastical law
Ecclesiastical decoration and ornament
  See Church decoration and ornament
Ecclesiastical discipline
  See Church discipline
Ecclesiastical divisions
  See Ecclesiastical geography
Ecclesiastical dress
  See Clergy—Costume
Ecclesiastical embroidery *(Direct)*
  x Church embroidery
  xx Christian art and symbolism
    Embroidery
Ecclesiastical embroidery, Baroque *(Direct)*
  x Baroque ecclesiastical embroidery
Ecclesiastical embroidery, Byzantine *(Direct)*
  x Byzantine ecclesiastical embroidery
Ecclesiastical embroidery, English, [etc.]
    (Direct)
  x English [etc.] ecclesiastical embroidery
Ecclesiastical fasts and feasts
  See Fasts and feasts
    names of special fasts and feasts, e.g.
      Easter, Lent
Ecclesiastical fees
  See Fees, Ecclesiastical
Ecclesiastical furniture
  See Church furniture
Ecclesiastical geography *(Indirect)*
    (BR97-99)
    Here are entered works dealing with the
    geographical expansion of the Chris-
    tian religion and its creeds, sects, or-
    ders, monasteries, shrines, etc., and
    also with its territorial organization
    into patriarchates, dioceses, provinces,
    national churches, etc.
  sa Bible—Geography
    Church statistics
    Dioceses
    Geography, Historical
  x Ecclesiastical divisions
    Geography, Ecclesiastical
  xx Bible—Geography
    Church history
    Church statistics
    Geography
    Geography, Historical
    Religion and geography
  — Maps *(BR98)*
    x Church history—Atlases
      Church history—Maps
Ecclesiastical habit
  See Clergy—Costume
Ecclesiastical history
  See Church history
Ecclesiastical immunity
  See Privileges and immunities, Ecclesiastical
Ecclesiastical institutions
  See Religious and ecclesiastical institutions

Ecclesiastical languages
  See Languages—Religious aspects
Ecclesiastical law *(Direct) (BV759-763)*
  sa Asylum, Right of
    Blasphemy
    Canon law
    Church attendance—Law and
      legislation
    Church lands
    Church maintenance and repair
      (Ecclesiastical law)
    Church property
    Church representation
    Concordats
    Corporations, Religious
    Dilapidations
    Ecclesiastical courts
    Established churches
    Exequatur (Ecclesiastical law)
    Penal laws (against nonconformists)
    Pews and pew rights
    Privileges and immunities, Ecclesiastical
    Religious education—Law and
      legislation
    Simony
    Simultaneum
    Sunday legislation
    Tithes
    subdivision Government *under*
      denominations, e.g. Presbyterian
      Church—Government
  x Church law
    Law, Ecclesiastical
  xx Canon law
    Church and state
    Church polity
    Theology, Practical
  Note under Religious law and legislation
  — Interpretation and construction
Ecclesiastical office
  See Clergy—Office
Ecclesiastical patronage
  See Patronage, Ecclesiastical
Ecclesiastical pensions
  See Clergy—Salaries, pensions, etc.
Ecclesiastical polity
  See Church polity
Ecclesiastical privileges
  See Privileges and immunities, Ecclesiastical
Ecclesiastical processions
  See Processions, Ecclesiastical
Ecclesiastical records and registers
  See Church records and registers
Ecclesiastical registers
  See Church records and registers
Ecclesiastical rites and ceremonies
  See Liturgies
    Rites and ceremonies
    Sacraments
    particular rites and ceremonies, e.g.
      Funeral rites and ceremonies; Lord's
      Supper
Ecclesiastical statistics
  See Church statistics
Ecclesiastical supplies
  See Church supplies
Ecclesiastical theology
  See Church
    headings beginning with the words
      Church *and* Ecclesiastical
Ecclesiastical tribunals
  See Ecclesiastical courts
Ecclesiastical vestments
  See Church vestments
Ecclesiastical visitations
  See Visitations, Ecclesiastical
Ecclesiastical vocation
  See Vocation, Ecclesiastical

Ecclesiastical year
   See Church year
Ecdysis
   sa Ecdysone
   x Molting in arthropods and reptiles
      Moulting in arthropods and reptiles
   xx Arthropoda—Physiology
      Ecdysone
      Insects—Development
      Molting
      Myriapoda—Development
      Reptiles—Physiology
Ecdysone
   sa Ecdysis
   xx Ecdysis
      Hormones
Echea
   See Vases, Acoustic
Echeia
   See Vases, Acoustic
Echeloot language
   See Tlakluit language
Echinococciasis
   See Echinococcosis
Echinococcosis *(SF810.H8)*
   x Echinococciasis
      Hydatid disease
Echinodermata *(Indirect) (QL381-5)*
   sa Crinoidea
      Holothurians
      Ophiuroidea
      Pelmatozoa
      Sea-urchins
      Starfishes
   x Radiata
      Zoophyta
   xx Invertebrates
   — Identification
   — Physiology
Echinodermata, Fossil *(QE781-3)*
   sa Holothurians, Fossil
      Stylophora
Echinoidea
   See Sea-urchins
Echiuroidea *(Indirect) (QL391.G5)*
   xx Gephyrea
Echo *(QC233)*
   xx Acoustic phenomena in nature
      Sound
   — Juvenile literature
Echo cardiography
   See Ultrasonic cardiography
Echo encephalography
   See Ultrasonic encephalography
Echo project
   See Project Echo
Echo ranging
   See Sonar
Echo scattering layers *(Indirect)*
   x Scattering layers, Echo
      Sonic scattering layers
      Sound scattering layers
   xx Echo sounding
      Marine fauna
      Sonar in fishing
Echo sounders
   See Echo sounding
Echo sounding *(Navigation, VK584;*
      Oceanography, GC78.E)
   sa Echo scattering layers
   x Echo sounders
      Sonic sounding
   xx Deep-sea sounding
      Sounding and soundings
      Underwater acoustics
Echo sounding in fisheries
   See Echo sounding in fishing

Echo sounding in fishing *(Indirect)*
   (SH344.23.E3)
   x Echo sounding in fisheries
   xx Fish detection
ECHO viruses
   x Echoviruses
      Enteric cytopathogenic human orphan
        viruses
   xx Enteroviruses
      Viruses
Echolocation (Physiology)
   xx Animal orientation
      Hearing
      Orientation
      Sonar
Echoviruses
   See ECHO viruses
Eclampsia
   See Convulsions
Eclampsia puerperalis
   See Puerperal convulsions
Eclectic dispensatories
   See Dispensatories, Eclectic
Eclectic medicine
   See Medicine, Eclectic
Eclectic obstetrics
   See Obstetrics, Eclectic
Eclectic surgery
   See Surgery, Eclectic
Eclipses *(Calculation and prediction, QB175)*
   sa Occultations
      Transits
   xx Astronomy
      Astronomy, Spherical and practical
      Occultations
      Transits
Eclipses, Lunar *(QB579)*
   Subdivided by date, *e.g.* Eclipses, Lunar
      —1866.
   x Lunar eclipses
      Moon—Eclipses
   — 1866
      Note under Eclipses, Lunar
Eclipses, Solar *(QB541-551)*
   Subdivided by date, *e.g.* Eclipses, Solar—
      1854.
   x Solar eclipses
   xx Sun
   — 1854
      Note under Eclipses, Solar

GENERAL SUBDIVISIONS

   — Juvenile literature *(QB541)*
Eclipses, Solar (in religion, folk-lore, etc.)
   x Folk-lore of solar eclipses
   xx Religion, Primitive
Eclipsing binaries *(QB821-9)*
   x Eclipsing double stars
      Eclipsing variables
   xx Stars, Double
      Stars, Variable
   — Atlases *(QB821)*
   — Spectra
   — Tables, etc.
Eclipsing double stars
   See Eclipsing binaries
Eclipsing variables
   See Eclipsing binaries
Ecliptic *(QB171)*
   xx Astronomy, Spherical and practical
Eclogite *(QE461)*
   x Eklogite
Eclogues
   See Pastoral poetry
Ecological genetics
   xx Ecology
      Genetics

Ecological research *(Direct)*
   sa Research natural areas
   x Ecology—Research
   xx Research
   — Law and legislation *(Direct)*
Ecological succession
   sa Plant succession
   x Succession, Ecological
   — Juvenile literature
Ecological systems, Closed
   See Closed ecological systems
Ecological systems, Closed (Space
      environment)
   See Closed ecological systems (Space
      environment)
Ecologists *(Direct)*
   xx Biologists
      Conservationists
      Naturalists
      Scientists
Ecology *(Indirect) (QH540-541)*
   sa Agricultural ecology
      Animal populations
      Aquatic ecology
      Bioclimatology
      Biogeochemical cycles
      Biological productivity
      Biotic communities
      Botany—Ecology
      Cave ecology
      Colonies (Biology)
      Conservation of natural resources
      Desert ecology
      Ecological genetics
      Fire ecology
      Food chains (Ecology)
      Forest ecology
      Fresh-water ecology
      Geographical distribution of animals
        and plants
      Grassland ecology
      Heath ecology
      Hot spring ecology
      Human ecology
      Indicators (Biology)
      Island ecology
      Jungle ecology
      Marine ecology
      Marsh ecology
      Meadow ecology
      Microbial ecology
      Microclimatology
      Mountain ecology
      Paleoecology
      Prairie ecology
      Predation (Biology)
      Radioecology
      Seashore ecology
      Soil ecology
      Swamp ecology
      Tundra ecology
      Wetland ecology
      Zoology—Ecology
      headings beginning with the word
        Ecological
   x Balance of nature
      Biology—Ecology
      Bionomics
      Environment
      Oecology
   — Authorship
   — Caricatures and cartoons
   — Examinations, questions, etc.
   — Experiments
   — — Juvenile literature
   — Juvenile literature
   — Laboratory manuals
   — Mathematical models

— Methodology
— Programmed instruction
— Research
 See Ecological research
— Study and teaching
 sa National environmental study areas
 x Environmental education
— — Audio-visual aids
— Technique
— Terminology
— Vocational guidance
Ecology, Human
 See Human ecology
Ecology, Social
 See Human ecology
Econometrics
 sa Distributed lags (Economics)
  Economics, Mathematical
  Information theory in economics
  Statistics
 x Economic statistics
 xx Economics, Mathematical
  Statistics
Economic anthropology
 See Economics, Primitive
Economic assistance
 Here are entered works on international
 economic aid given in the form of tech-
 nical assistance, loans, gifts, or relief
 grants.
 sa European Economic Community—
  Economic assistance
  Exchanges of patents and technical
   information
  International relief
  Lend-lease operations (1941-1945)
  Loans
  Reconstruction (1939-1951)
  Technical assistance
  United Nations—Economic assistance
  World War, 1939-1945—Civilian relief
 x Aid to developing countries
  Aid to underdeveloped areas
  Assistance to underdeveloped areas
  Economic assistance in underdeveloped
   areas
  Foreign aid program
  Foreign assistance
  Grants-in-aid, International
  International grants-in-aid
  Underdeveloped areas—Economic
   assistance
 xx Economic policy
  Government missions
  International cooperation
  International economic relations
  Reconstruction (1939-1951)
— Caricatures and cartoons
— Information services *(Direct)*
— Public opinion
Economic assistance, American *(Direct)*
 sa Counterpart funds
  Offshore procurement program, 1951-
  United States—Foreign relations—Law
   and legislation
 x Economic assistance, American—
   Europe
  Marshall plan
 xx Mutual security program, 1951-
— Europe
 See Economic assistance, American
Economic assistance, British, ₍**French, etc.**₎
  (Direct)
 x British ₍French, etc.₎ economic
   assistance
— Public opinion
Economic assistance, Domestic *(Direct)*
 sa Community development

Endowments—Program-related
 investments
Government lending
Grants-in-aid
Negative income tax
Public works
Subsidies
Unemployed
Work relief
 x Anti-poverty programs
 xx Economic policy
  Grants-in-aid
  Unemployed
— Citizen participation
 x Citizen participation in anti-poverty
  programs
— Law and legislation *(Direct)*
— — United States
 x Anti-poverty legislation (United
  States)

GEOGRAPHIC SUBDIVISIONS

— United States
 x Anti-poverty program (United
  States)
Economic assistance in Asia, ₍**India, etc.**₎
Economic assistance in Latin America
 sa Alliance for progress
Economic assistance in Southeastern Asia
 x Colombo plan
Economic assistance in underdeveloped areas
 See Economic assistance
Economic biology
 See Biology, Economic
Economic botany
 See Botany, Economic
Economic concentration
 See Big business
  Industrial concentration
  Oligopolies
  Trusts, Industrial
Economic conditions
 See Economic history
  subdivision Economic conditions *under*
  names of countries, regions, cities,
  etc.
Economic councils *(Direct) (HD3611)*
 Here are entered works dealing with plan-
 ning or advisory councils. Works deal-
 ing with administrative councils are
 entered under Administrative eco-
 nomic councils.
 sa Administrative economic councils
 x Councils, Economic
 Note under Administrative economic councils
Economic councils, Administrative
 See Administrative economic councils
Economic cycles
 See Business cycles
Economic depressions
 See Depressions
Economic development
 Here are entered general works on the
 theory and policy of economic development. Works restricted to a particu-
 lar area are entered under the name of
 the area with subdivisions Economic
 conditions, Economic policy, or In-
 dustries.
 sa Development banks
  Industrial productivity centers
  Industrialization
  Saving and investment
  Underdeveloped areas
 x Economic growth
 xx Economic policy
  Economics
  Statics and dynamics (Social sciences)

— Biography
— Mathematical models
— Research *(Direct)*
— Simulation methods
— Social aspects
 Here are entered works which discuss
 social parameters or elements,
 within the theory of economic de-
 velopment, which may cause social
 change. Social resultants of eco-
 nomic development are entered un-
 der: Social history; ₍Country₎—So-
 cial conditions; or Social change.
 xx Social change
  Social history
Economic entomology
 See Insects, Injurious and beneficial
Economic equilibrium
 See Equilibrium (Economics)
Economic forecasting
 sa Business forecasting
  Economic indicators
  Employment forecasting
  Income forecasting
 x Forecasting, Economic
 xx Business cycles
  Economics
— Mathematical models
— Methodology
Economic geography
 See Geography, Economic
Economic geology
 See Geology, Economic
Economic growth
 See Economic development
  subdivision Economic conditions *under*
  names of countries, regions, cities,
  etc.
Economic history
 sa Automation—Economic aspects
  Industry—History
  subdivision Economic conditions *under*
  names of countries, regions, cities,
  etc.
 x Economic conditions
  History, Economic
 xx Economics
— To 1500
— Medieval, 500-1500
— 15th century
— 16th century
— 1600-1750
— — Historiography
— 1750-1918
— — Historiography
— 20th century
— 1918-
— 1918-1945
— 1945-
— — Examinations, questions, etc.

GENERAL SUBDIVISIONS

— Chronology
— Historiography
— Information services
 sa subdivision Economic conditions—
  Information services *under names*
  of countries, regions, cities, etc.

GENERAL SUBDIVISIONS

— Methodology
Economic indicators *(Direct)*
 xx Economic forecasting
— Underdeveloped areas
 See Underdeveloped areas—Economic
  indicators
Economic integration, International
 See International economic integration

555

Economic lag
   x Lag, Economic
   xx Economics
      Supply and demand
Economic life (of economic goods)
   sa Depreciation
      Replacement of industrial equipment
   x Life, Economic
   xx Depreciation
Economic lot size
      Here are entered works on the number of
      units of material or of a manufactured
      item that can be purchased or pro-
      duced within the lowest unit-cost
      range.
   x Batch size determination
      Lot size determination
      Production lot size
      Size of economic lot
   xx Inventory control
Economic multiplier
   See Multiplier (Economics)
Economic nationalism
   See Economic policy
Economic ornithology
   See Birds, Injurious and beneficial
Economic planning
   See Economic policy
      subdivision Economic policy *under*
      names of countries, e.g. United
      States—Economic policy
Economic poisons
   See Pesticides
Economic policy *(HD82-85; By country, HC,*
      HF1401-2580; By industry, HD)
   sa Agriculture and state
      Autarchy
      Bounties
      Commercial policy
      Comparative economics
      Deflation (Finance)
      Economic assistance
      Economic assistance, Domestic
      Economic development
      Economic security
      Economic stabilization
      Economic zoning
      Fiscal policy
      Free trade and protection
      Full employment policies
      Government lending
      Government ownership
      Government spending policy
      Industrial laws and legislation
      Industrial mobilization
      Industrialization
      Industry and state
      Inflation (Finance)
      International economic relations
      Labor policy
      Labor supply
      Laissez-faire
      Land reform
      Manpower policy
      Mercantile system
      Monetary policy
      Municipal ownership
      National security
      Physiocrats
      Priorities, Industrial
      Sanctions (International law)
      Social policy
      Subsidies
      Tariff
      Technical assistance
      Underdeveloped areas—Economic
         policy
      Unemployed

      Wage-price policy
      Welfare economics
      Welfare state
   subdivision Economic policy *under*
      names of countries, regions, cities,
      etc.
   x Economic nationalism
      Economic planning
      National planning
      Planning, Economic
      Planning, National
      Planning, State
      Public policy
      State planning
      World economics
   xx Economics
      Industry and state
      National security
      Reciprocity
      Social policy
   — Book reviews
   — Mathematical models
Economic policy, Foreign
   See International economic relations
Economic relations, Foreign
   See International economic relations
Economic research *(Direct)*
   sa Economic surveys
      Education—Economic aspects—
         Research
      Farm management research
      Market surveys
   x Business research
      Economics—Research
   xx Research
Economic sanctions
   See Sanctions (International law)
Economic security *(Direct)*
   sa Family allowances
      Full employment policies
      Guaranteed annual income
      Insurance, Social
      Negative income tax
      Old age pensions
      Public welfare
      Wages—Annual wage
      Wages—Minimum wage
   x Security, Economic
   xx Economic policy
      Social policy
      Welfare economics
Economic self-sufficiency
   See Autarchy
Economic stabilization *(HB3730)*
   x Business stabilization
      Stabilization, Economic
   xx Business cycles
      Economic policy
   — Mathematical models
Economic statistics
   See Econometrics
      Economics, Mathematical
      Statistics
Economic surveys
      Here are entered works on the techniques
      employed. The surveys themselves are
      entered under the area surveyed fol-
      lowed by the subdivision Economic
      conditions.
   sa Market surveys
   x Surveys, Economic
   xx Economic research
      Social surveys
Economic theory
   See Economics
Economic union
   See International economic integration

Economic zoning *(Direct)*
   x Zoning, Economic
   xx Administrative and political divisions
      Economic policy
      Statistics
   — Mathematical models
Economic zoology
   See Zoology, Economic
Economics *(HB)*
   sa Austrian school of economists
      Balance of trade
      Banks and banking
      Business
      Capital
      Capitalism
      Christianity and economics
      Commerce
      Communication and traffic
      Comparative economics
      Competition
      Consumption (Economics)
      Cooperation
      Cost
      Cost and standard of living
      Credit
      Debt
      Debts, Public
      Demography
      Depressions
      Diminishing returns
      Division of labor
      Economic development
      Economic forecasting
      Economic history
      Economic lag
      Economic policy
      Economists
      Elasticity (Economics)
      Employment (Economic theory)
      Entrepreneur
      Equilibrium (Economics)
      Exchange
      Externalities (Economics)
      Factory system
      Finance
      Finance, Public
      Free trade and protection
      Government ownership
      Gross national product
      Income
      Index numbers (Economics)
      Individualism
      Industry
      Institutional economics
      Interest and usury
      Keynesian economics
      Labor and laboring classes
      Labor economics
      Laissez-faire
      Land
      Leisure class
      Luxury
      Macroeconomics
      Managerial economics
      Manufactures
      Marginal productivity
      Marginal utility
      Marxian economics
      Mercantile system
      Microeconomics
      Money
      Monopolies
      Multiplier (Economics)
      Mutualism
      Neoclassical school of economics
      Over-production
      Physiocrats
      Plenocracy

Population
Prices
Profit
Property
Rent
Rent (Economic theory)
Risk
Saving and investment
Saving and thrift
Self-interest
Socialism
Space in economics
Speculation
Stagnation (Economics)
Statics and dynamics (Social sciences)
Statistics
Substitution (Economics)
Sumptuary laws
Supply and demand
Tariff
Taxation
Time and economic reactions
Transportation
Trusts, Industrial
Unearned increment
Urban economics
Value
Wages
Waste (Economics)
Wealth
Welfare economics
   subdivision Economic aspects *under*
     special subjects, e.g. Agriculture—
     Economic aspects
x Economic theory
   Political economy
— Ability testing
— Anecdotes, facetiae, satire, etc.
— Bibliography
— — Theory, methods, etc.
— Examinations, questions, etc.
— Graphic methods   *(HB71)*
— History *(Indirect)* *(HB75-125)*
— — To 1800 *(HB77-83)*
— — 19th century *(HB85)*
— — 20th century *(HB87)*
— Information services *(Direct)*
— Juvenile literature *(HB171.7)*
— Mathematical models
   sa Agriculture—Economic aspects—
     Mathematical models
   subdivision Economic conditions—
     Mathematical models *under*
     names of countries, regions, cities,
     etc., e.g. United States—
     Economic conditions—
     Mathematical models
   xx Economics, Mathematical
— Methodology *(HB71)*
   sa Economics, Mathematical
— Miscellanea
— Problems, exercises, etc.
— Programmed instruction
— Psychological aspects
   Example under Psychology, Applied
— Quotations, maxims, etc.
— Research
   See Economic research
— Study and teaching *(Direct)*
— Study and teaching (Elementary)
    (Direct)
— Study and teaching (Primary) *(Direct)*
— Study and teaching (Secondary) *(Direct)*
— Subject headings
   See Subject headings—Economics
— Terminology
— Text-books
— Translating

— Vocational guidance
   x Economics, Vocational opportunities
     in
   Example under Vocational guidance
Economics, Comparative
   See Comparative economics
Economics, International
   See International economic relations
Economics, Mathematical   *(HB)*
   sa Econometrics
     Economics—Mathematical models
     Interindustry economics
   x Economic statistics
     Mathematical economics
   xx Econometrics
     Economics—Methodology
     Mathematics
Economics, Medical
   See Medical economics
Economics, Primitive   *(GN489)*
   x Economic anthropology
     Finance, Primitive
   xx Society, Primitive
Economics, Vocational opportunities in
   See Economics—Vocational guidance
Economics and Buddhism
   See Buddhism and economics
Economics and Christianity
   See Christianity and economics
Economics and Confucianism
   See Confucianism and economics
Economics and Islam
   See Islam and economics
Economics and religion
   See Religion and economics
Economics in literature
   sa Businessmen in literature
     Capitalists and financiers in literature
     Industry in literature
     Labor and laboring classes in literature
     Money in literature
Economics of scale
   xx Industries, Size of
Economics of war
   See War, Cost of
     War—Economic aspects
Economies of scale
   x Economies of size
     Scale, Economies of
     Size, Economies of
   xx Big business
     Costs, Industrial
     Farms Size of
     Industries, Size of
Economies of size
   See Economies of scale
Economists *(Direct)*
   sa Austrian school of economists
     Physiocrats
     Women as economists
   xx Economics
— Correspondence, reminiscences, etc.
— Legal status, laws, etc. *(Direct)*
Economists, American, ⸢Austrian, British, etc.⸣
   x American ⸢Austrian, British, etc.⸣
     economists
Economists, Austrian
   sa Austrian school of economists
   x Austrian economists
Economy
   See Saving and thrift
Economy, Engineering
   See Engineering economy
Economy (Orthodox Eastern theology)
   xx Theology, Eastern church
Ecrehos and Minquiers case
   See Minquiers and Ecrehos case

ECSS (Computer program language)
   x Extendable computer system simulator
   xx Digital computer simulation
Ecstasy *(Comparative religion, BL626;*
    Christianity, BV5091.E3;
    Spiritualism, BF1321)
   sa Enthusiasm
     Hysteria
     Trance
   xx Hysteria
     Subconsciousness
     Trance
Ecstasy (Hinduism)
   xx Mysticism—Hinduism
Ecstasy (Judaism)
Ecthyma, Contagious
   See Contagious ecthyma
Ectognatha
   See Thysanura
Ectopia vesicae
   See Bladder—Displacement
Ectopic pregnancy
   See Pregnancy, Ectopic
Ectotrophi
   See Thysanura
Ecuador
— History   *(F3701-3799)*
— — To 1809
— — Wars of Independence, 1809-1830
— — 1830-
— — 1830-1895
— — Revolution, 1895
— — 1895-1944
     sa Zarumilla, Battle of, 1941
— — 1944-
Ecuadorian drama *(Direct)*
Ecuadorian essays *(Direct)*
Ecuadorian literature *(PQ8200-8219)*
   xx Spanish American literature
Ecuadorian newspapers *(History, etc.,*
    PN5066-9)
Ecuadorian orations *(PQ8216.O)*
Ecuadorian periodicals *(History, etc.,*
    PN5066-5070)
Ecuadorian poetry *(Direct)* *(Collections,*
    PQ8214; History, PQ8210)
Ecumenical councils and synods
   See Councils and synods, Ecumenical
Ecumenical movement
   sa Christian union
     Church—History of doctrines—20th
      century
     Intercommunion
     Local church councils
     Missions—Cooperative movement
   x Movement, Ecumenical
   xx Catholicity
     Christian union
     Christianity
     Church
— Anglican Communion, ⸢Catholic Church,
     Orthodox Eastern Church, etc.⸣
   See Christian union—Anglican
     Communion, ⸢Catholic Church,
     Orthodox Eastern Church, etc.⸣
— Controversial literature
   x Christian union—Controversial
     literature
Eczema *(RL251)*
   sa Pompholyx (Disease)
   Example under Skin—Diseases
— Psychosomatic aspects
Eddas *(Elder Edda, PT7233-7241; Younger*
    Edda, PT7312-7314)
   xx Icelandic and Old Norse literature
     Icelandic and Old Norse poetry
     Poetry
     Scandinavian literature

Eddies
　　sa Vortex-motion
　　xx Fluid dynamics
　　　　Turbulence
Eddy currents (Electric)　*(TK2271)*
　　xx Electric currents
Eddy diffusion (Meteorology)
　　See Turbulent diffusion (Meteorology)
Eddy flux
　　x Turbulent flux
Eddystone language
　　See Mandegusu language
Edelweiss
　　xx Alpine flora
Edema　*(RB144; Infantile, RJ268)*
　　sa Angioneurotic edema
　　　　Blood—Circulation, Disorders of
　　　　Cerebral edema
　　　　Lymphedema
　　　　Pulmonary edema
　　x Oedema
Eden　*(BS1237)*
　　sa Tree of life
Edenkoben
　　— Siege, 1794
Edentata　*(QL737.E2)*
　　sa Armadillos
　　　　Sloths
　　xx Mammals
Edentata, Fossil　*(QE882.E2)*
　　sa Armadillos, Fossil
　　　　Sloths, Fossil
Edible coatings　*(TP436.E)*
　　xx Coatings
　　　　Drugs—Packaging
　　　　Food additives
　　　　Food—Packaging
　　— Patents
Edible dormouse
　　x Dormouse, Edible
　　xx Dormice
Edible frog
　　xx Frogs
Edible fungi
　　See Mushrooms, Edible
　　　　Truffles
Edible mushrooms
　　See Mushrooms, Edible
Edible oils and fats
　　See Oils and fats, Edible
Edible plants
　　See Plants, Edible
Edible snails
　　See Snails, Edible
Edict of Milan, 313　*(BR180)*
　　x Milan, Edict of
　　xx Church history—Primitive and early
　　　　church, ca. 30-600
Edict of Nantes　*(BR845)*
　　sa France—History—Wars of the
　　　　Huguenots, 1562-1598
　　x Nantes, Edict of
　　xx France—History—Wars of the
　　　　Huguenots, 1562-1598
　　　　Huguenots in France
Edict of restitution, 1629　*(D267.E3)*
　　x Restitution, Edict of
　　xx Thirty Years' War, 1618-1648
Ediles
　　See Aediles
Edinburgh
　　— Charities
　　　　Note under Child welfare
　　— Gilds
　　　　Example under Gilds
Edipus complex
　　See Oedipus complex
Edirne, Turkey (City)

— Siege, 1912-1913　*(DR46.9)*
　　xx Balkan Peninsula—History—War of
　　　　1912-1913
Edison effect
　　See Thermionic emission
Editing　*(PN162)*
　　　　Here are entered works on the editing of
　　　　books and texts. Works dealing with
　　　　the editing of newspapers, etc. are en-
　　　　tered under Journalism.
　　sa Authorship—Handbooks, manuals, etc.
　　　　Copy-reading
　　　　Criticism, Textual
　　　　LEFT (Computer program language)
　　　　Manuscripts—Editing
　　　　Moving-pictures—Editing
　　　　Music—Editing
　　　　Printing, Practical—Style manuals
　　xx Authorship
　　　　Journalism
Editions
　　See Bibliography—Editions
Editions, Diamond
　　See Bibliography—Microscopic and
　　　　miniature editions
Editions, Fine
　　See Bibliography—Fine editions
Editions, First
　　See Bibliography—First editions
　　　　subdivision Bibliography—First editions
　　　　under Literature *and under names of*
　　　　literatures, e.g. English literature—
　　　　Bibliography—First editions
Editions, Limited
　　See Bibliography—Limited editions
Editions, Microscopic
　　See Bibliography—Microscopic and
　　　　miniature editions
Editions, Miniature
　　See Bibliography—Microscopic and
　　　　miniature editions
Editions, Pirated
　　See Copyright—Unauthorized reprints
Editorial cartoons　*(Direct)*
　　x Cartoons, Editorial
　　xx Caricatures and cartoons
　　　　Editorials
　　　　Wit and humor, Pictorial
Editorial writing
　　See Editorials
Editorials
　　sa Editorial cartoons
　　x Editorial writing
　　xx Journalism
Editors (Journalism)
　　See Journalists
Edixa camera
Ediya (African tribe)
　　See Bube (African tribe)
Ediya language
　　See Bube language
Edo language
　　See Bini language
Edomites　*(DS110.E)*
Educability
　　xx Education
　　　　Learning, Psychology of
Education　*(Indirect) (L)*
　　sa Ability grouping in education
　　　　Adult education
　　　　Agricultural education
　　　　Area studies
　　　　Books and reading
　　　　Business education
　　　　Case method
　　　　Charity-schools
　　　　Chautauquas
　　　　Child study

Church and college
Church and education
Classical education
Classification—Books—Education
Coeducation
Communication in education
Compensatory education
Correspondence schools and courses
Culture
Domestic education
Drama in education
Educability
Education and state
Education of children
Education of princes
Education of princesses
Education of prisoners
Education of the aged
Education of women
Educators
Evening and continuation schools
Examinations
Foreign study
Formal discipline
Fundamental education
General semantics
Group work in education
High schools
Home and school
Howard plan
Humane education
Illiteracy
Inefficiency, Intellectual
International education
Learning and scholarship
Learning, Psychology of
Libraries
Library education
Lyceums
Manual training
Mental discipline
Military education
Mining schools and education
Monitorial system of education
Moral education
Moving-pictures in education
Music in education
Nature study
Naval education
Open-air schools
Overpressure (Education)
Paperbacks in education
Parents' and teachers' associations
Pedantry
Phonograph in education
Physical education and training
Pictures in education
Platoon schools
Postage-stamps in education
Printing, Practical, in education
Private schools
Professional education
Public schools
Radio in education
Ragged schools
Religious education
Religious education of adolescent boys
Religious education of adolescents
Religious education of young people
Role playing
Rural schools
Scholarships
School city, state, etc.
Schools, *and references under that*
　　heading
Self-culture
Self-government (in education)
Socialization

Students
Study, Method of
Suburban schools
Summer schools
Teachers
Teaching
Technical education
Telephone in education
Television in education
Universities and colleges
University extension
Vacation schools
Video tapes in education
Vocational education
Youth
    subdivision Education *under names of denominations, sects, orders, etc., e.g.* Jesuits—Education; *and under special classes of people and various social groups, e.g.* Blind—Education; Mentally handicapped children—Education; Children of migrant laborers—Education; *also subdivision* Study and teaching *under special subjects, e.g.* Science—Study and teaching; *and headings beginning with the word* Educational
  x Human resource development
    Instruction
    Pedagogy
  xx Civilization
    Coeducation
    Culture
    Learning and scholarship
    Mental discipline
    Schools
    Teaching
  Note under Social surveys
— Medieval, 500-1500
    See Education, Medieval
— 1945-1964
— 1965-
    sa International Education Year, 1970
— — Chronology

GENERAL SUBDIVISIONS

— Abbreviations
— Aims and objectives   *(Essays, LB41)*
    sa Educational accountability
    Educational equalization
    Educational planning
    Educational sociology
    x Educational aims and objectives
    xx Educational sociology
— Bibliography   *(Z5811-5819)*
    sa Educational literature
    Pedagogical libraries
    xx Educational literature
— Broadcasting
    See Educational broadcasting
— Caricatures and cartoons
— Code numbers
    x Code numbers (Education)
— Collective labor agreements
    See Collective labor agreements—Education
— Colonies
    See Education, Colonial
    Note under Education, Colonial
— Congresses
    x Educational workshops
    Workshops in education
    Example under reference from Workshops (Seminars)
— Costs
    Here are entered works on institutional costs in the field of education.
    x School costs

    xx Education—Finance
    Schools—Accounting
— Curricula   *(Colleges and universities, LB2361-5; Elementary schools, LB1570-1571; Secondary schools, LB1628-9)*
    Works on the curriculum of a particular denomination, sect, or order are entered under name of denomination, etc. with subdivision Education, and also under Education—[local subdivision]—Curricula, when confined to a given country, state, or city.
    Curriculum studies confined to the public or private schools of one city or county have duplicate entry as follows: 1. Education—Wisconsin—Madison. 2. Education—Wisconsin—Curricula.
    sa Articulation (Education)
    Combination of grades
    Curriculum change
    Curriculum consultants
    Curriculum enrichment
    Curriculum laboratories
    Curriculum planning
    Lesson planning
    Schedules, School
    Student evaluation of curriculum
    Teacher participation in curriculum planning
    subdivision Curricula *under local subdivisions of* Education, *e.g.* Education—Massachusetts—Curricula; *also under heading* Universities and colleges, *and local subdivisions, e.g.* Universities and colleges—Curricula; Universities and colleges—United States—Curricula; *and under specific types of education or school and under names of individual schools, e.g.* Technical education—Curricula; High schools—Curricula; Library schools—Curricula; Chicago. University—Curricula
    x Core curriculum
    Courses of study
    Curricula (Courses of study)
    Schools—Curricula
    Study, Courses of
— Early works to 1800
— Economic aspects   *(Direct)*
    sa Education—Finance
    Teachers' socio-economic status
— — Research   *(Direct)*
    xx Economic research
    Educational research
— Electronic data processing
    See Electronic data processing—Education
— Exhibitions and museums
    sa Educational exhibits, Traveling
    x School exhibits
— Experimental methods   *(LB1026-7)*
    sa Activity programs in education
    Collective education
    Concentrated study
    Educational innovations
    Eight-Year Study
    Free schools
    Imprinting (Psychology)
    Jena plan
    Mental tests
    Nongraded schools
    Open plan schools

    School camps
    x Experimental methods in education
    xx Educational innovations
— Federal aid
    See Federal aid to education
— Finance   *(LB2824-2830)*
    sa College costs
    Education—Costs
    Educational vouchers
    Federal aid to education
    School bonds
    School purchasing
    Student activities—Accounting
    x Public schools—Finance
    School finance
    School taxes
    Schools—Finance
    Taxes, School
    Tuition
    xx Education—Economic aspects
    Public schools—Business management
— — Accounting
— Graduate work   *(LB2372.E3)*
    Here are entered works dealing with advanced professional study in the field of education.
    x Graduate study in education
    Graduate work in education
    Teachers—Graduate work
    xx Education—Study and teaching
— Graphic methods   *(LB2846)*
— Historiography
— History
    sa Comparative education
    Educational literature
    x Teaching—History
— — To 1500
    See Education, Ancient
— — Medieval, 500-1500
    See Education, Medieval

GENERAL SUBDIVISIONS

— — Juvenile literature
— — Pictorial works
— Information services   *(Direct)*
    xx Communication in education
— Integration
    See School integration
— Juvenile literature
— Mathematical models
— Personnel service
    See Personnel service in adult education
    Personnel service in elementary education
    Personnel service in higher education
    Personnel service in secondary education
— Philosophy   *(LB125-875)*
    sa Educational anthropology
    Humor in education
    x Philosophy of teaching
— — 1965-
— Psychology
    See Educational psychology
— Publishing
    See Educational publishing
— Punched card systems
    See Punched card systems—Education
— Quotations, maxims, etc.
— Research
    See Educational research
— Segregation
    See Segregation in education
— Simulation methods   *(LB1029.S53)*
    sa Classroom simulators

Education *(Indirect)* *(L)*
— Simulation methods *(LB1029.S53)*
   (Continued)
      Educational games
      Microteaching
      Simulated environment (Teaching
         method)
— Societies, etc.
   xx Educational associations
— Standards
   x Standards and standardization in
      education
— State aid
   See State aid to education
— States, New
   See States, New—Education
— Statistical methods
   See Educational statistics
— Statistics *(Serial documents, L111-791;*
      Theory, LB2846)
— Study and teaching *(Direct)*
      Here are entered works dealing with
         the study and teaching of education
         as a science.
      sa Education—Graduate work
      x Pedagogy
      Note under Teachers, Training of
— Subject headings
   See Subject headings—Education
— Terminology *(LB15)*
— Underdeveloped areas
   See Underdeveloped areas—Education

GEOGRAPHIC SUBDIVISIONS

— ₍country₎
— Arabia
   Note under Education, Arabic

GEOGRAPHIC SUBDIVISIONS

— Boston (Archdiocese)
   Example under Catholic Church—Edu-
      cation

GEOGRAPHIC SUBDIVISIONS

— Greece, Ancient
   See Education, Greek

GEOGRAPHIC SUBDIVISIONS

— Greece, Modern
   x Education, Greek (Modern)

GEOGRAPHIC SUBDIVISIONS

— Ireland
   x Irish university question

GEOGRAPHIC SUBDIVISIONS

— Levant
   Note under Education, Arabic

GEOGRAPHIC SUBDIVISIONS

— Massachusetts
— — Curricula
   Example under Education—Curricula

GEOGRAPHIC SUBDIVISIONS

— — Statistics
   Note under Educational statistics

GEOGRAPHIC SUBDIVISIONS

— United States
   sa Communism in education

GEOGRAPHIC SUBDIVISIONS

— — Directories
   Example under references from
      School directories; Schools—
      Directories

GEOGRAPHIC SUBDIVISIONS

— Wisconsin
— — Curricula
   Note under Education—Curricula

GEOGRAPHIC SUBDIVISIONS

— — Madison
   Note under Education—Curricula
Education, Agricultural
   See Agricultural education
Education, Ancient
   x Education—History—To 1500
Education, Art
   See Art—Study and teaching
Education, Bilingual *(Direct)*
      (LC3701-3743)
   x Bilingual education
   xx Bilingualism
      Intercultural education
      Minorities—Education
Education, Business
   See Business education
Education, Character
   See Moral education
Education, Christian
   See Religious education
Education, Classical
   See Classical education
Education, Collective
   See Collective education
Education, Colonial
      Here are entered general and compara-
         tive works only. Works on education
         in the colonies of an individual country
         are entered under the heading Educa-
         tion with subdivision ₍country₎—Colo-
         nies. Works dealing with a specific
         colony are entered under the heading
         Education, subdivided by the name of
         the colony.
   x Colonial education
      Colonies—Education
      Education—Colonies
      Native races—Education
Education, Communist
   See Communist education
Education, Comparative
   See Comparative education
Education, Compensatory
   See Compensatory education
Education, Compulsory *(Indirect)*
      (LC129-139)
   sa Children—Employment
      Educational law and legislation
      Evening and continuation schools
      Right to education
      School attendance
      School census
   x Compulsory education
      Compulsory school attendance
   xx Educational law and legislation
      School attendance
Education, Cooperative *(Direct)*
      (LB1029.C6)
      Here are entered works dealing with the
         plan of instruction under which stu-
         dents spend alternating periods in
         school and in a practical occupation.
   sa Field work (Educational method)
   x Cooperative education
      Day release (Great Britain)
      Study-work plan
      Work experience
      Work-study plan
   xx Apprentices
      Field work (Educational method)
      Industry and education

Vocational education
— Audio-visual aids
Education, Distributive
   See Distributive education
Education, Doctor of
   See Doctor of education degree
Education, Domestic
   See Domestic education
Education, Elementary *(Direct)*
      (LB1555-1601)
   sa Eighth grade (Education)
      Elementary education of adults
      Elementary school teaching
      Elementary schools
      Fifth grade (Education)
      Global method of teaching
      Radio in elementary education
      School supervision, Elementary
      Seventh grade (Education)
      Sixth grade (Education)
      Television in elementary education
   x Elementary education
   xx Education of children
— 1945-
— 1965-

GENERAL SUBDIVISIONS

— Aims and objectives
— Audio-visual aids
— Curricula
— Personnel service
   See Personnel service in elementary
      education

GENERAL SUBDIVISIONS

— Research *(Direct)*
   xx Educational research
Education, Ethical
   See Moral education
      Religious education
Education, Greek *(LA75)*
   x Education—Greece, Ancient
      Greek education
— Athens, ₍Sparta, etc.₎
Education, Greek (Modern)
   See Education—Greece, Modern
Education, Higher *(Direct)*
   sa Church and college
      Classical education
      Degrees, Academic
      Eight-Year Study
      Federal aid to higher education
      Higher education and state
      Higher education of women
      Junior colleges
      Moving-pictures in higher education
      Professional education
      Radio in higher education
      Seminars
      Technical education
      Television in higher education
      Universities and colleges
      Universities and colleges—Graduate
         work
      University extension
      Women's colleges
   x Higher education
   xx Universities and colleges
— 1945-
— 1965-
— — Curricula

GENERAL SUBDIVISIONS

— Aims and objectives
   x Educational aims and objectives

GENERAL SUBDIVISIONS

— Audio-visual aids

— Costs
— Curricula
— Personnel service
    See Personnel service in higher
       education

GENERAL SUBDIVISIONS

— Research
    x Institutional research (Education)
      Research in higher education
    xx Educational research

GENERAL SUBDIVISIONS

— Segregation
    See Segregation in higher education

GENERAL SUBDIVISIONS

— State aid
    See State aid to higher education

GENERAL SUBDIVISIONS

— Terminology
    See Universities and colleges—
      Terminology

Education, Humane
  See Humane education

Education, Humanistic *(Direct)*
    (LC1001-1021; Renaissance,
    LA106-8)
  sa Classical education
    Humanism
  x Education, Liberal
    Humanistic education
    Liberal education
  xx Classical education
    Humanities

Education, Humor in
  See Humor in education

Education, Industrial
  See Manual training
    Technical education

Education, Intercultural
  See Intercultural education

Education, International
  See International education

Education, Islamic
  See Islam—Education

Education, Liberal
  See Education, Humanistic

Education, Medieval *(LA85-98)*
  sa Education of women, Medieval
    Monasticism and religious orders
    Universities and colleges—Europe,
      [France, etc.]
  x Education—History—Medieval,
    500-1500
    Medieval education
    Seven liberal arts
  xx Civilization, Medieval
    Middle Ages
— Finance

Education, Military
  See Military education

Education, Mining
  See Mining schools and education

Education, Moral
  See Moral education

Education, Musical
  See Music—Instruction and study

Education, Muslim
  See Islam—Education

Education, Naval
  See Naval education

Education, Outdoor
  See Outdoor education

Education, Physical
  See Physical education and training

Education, Premedical
  See Premedical education

Education, Preschool *(Direct)* *(LB1140)*
  sa Agazzi method of teaching
    Kindergarten
    Nursery schools
    Religious education of preschool
      children
    Television in preschool education
  x Infant education
    Preschool education
  xx Child study
    Education of children
    Kindergarten
    Nursery schools
— 1945-
— 1965-   *(LB1140.2)*
— Audio-visual aids
— Curricula
— Finance
— Teacher training

Education, Primary *(Direct)* *(LB1501-1547)*
  sa Creative activities and seat work
    First grade (Education)
    Fourth grade (Education)
    Readiness for school
    School supervision, Primary
    Second grade (Education)
    Third grade (Education)
  x Primary education
  xx Education of children
— 1945-

GENERAL SUBDIVISIONS

— Audio-visual aids
— Curricula

Education, Primitive *(Indirect)* *(GN488.5)*
  sa Initiations (in religion, folk-lore, etc.)
    subdivision Education *under names of*
      races, etc., e.g. Indians—Education

Education, Professional
  See Professional education

Education, Religious
  See Religious education

Education, Rural *(Direct)* *(LC5146-8)*
  sa Rural schools
  x Rural education
  xx Rural schools

Education, Scientific
  See Science—Study and teaching

Education, Secondary *(Direct)*
  sa Eight-Year Study
    Eleventh grade (Education)
    Evening and continuation schools
    Folk high schools
    High schools
    High schools—Postgraduate work
    Howard Plan
    Junior high schools
    Middle schools
    Ninth grade (Education)
    Private schools
    Public schools
    Public schools, Endowed (Great
      Britain)
    School supervision, Secondary
    Tenth grade (Education)
    Thirteenth grade (Education)
    Twelfth grade (Education)
  x High school education
    Secondary education
    Secondary schools
  xx High schools
— 1945-
— — Curricula
— 1965-
— — Curricula

GENERAL SUBDIVISIONS

— Aims and objectives
    x Educational aims and objectives

GENERAL SUBDIVISIONS

— Audio-visual aids
— Costs
— Economic aspects *(Direct)*
— Personnel service
    See Personnel service in secondary
      education

GENERAL SUBDIVISIONS

— Research *(Direct)*
    xx Educational research

Education, Technical
  See Technical education

Education, Theological
  See Religious education
    Theology—Study and teaching

Education, Urban *(Direct)* *(LC5101-5143)*
  sa Schools—Decentralization
  x Urban education
  xx Cities and towns
— Finance *(Direct)*

Education, Visual
  See Visual education

Education, Vocational
  See Vocational education

Education and anthropology
  See Educational anthropology

Education and church
  See Church and college
    Church and education

Education and communism
  See Communism and education

Education and crime *(Direct)* *(HV6166)*
  sa Education of prisoners
    Illiteracy
  x Crime and education
  xx Crime and criminals
    Crime prevention
    Delinquents
    Illiteracy

Education and folk-lore
  See Folk-lore and education

Education and heredity *(LC201)*
  xx Educational psychology
    Heredity, Human

Education and industry
  See Industry and education

Education and journalism
  See Journalism and education

Education and libraries
  See Libraries and education

Education and nationalism
  See Nationalism and education

Education and politics
  See Politics and education

Education and religion
  See Church and education

Education and residence
  See Residence and education

Education and socialism
  See Socialism and education

Education and sociology
  See Educational sociology

Education and state *(Indirect)* *(LC71-188)*
  sa Adult education and state
    Art and state
    Art commissions
    Community and school
    Endowment of research
    Endowments
    Federal aid to adult education
    Federal aid to education
    Federal aid to higher education

Education and state *(Indirect)* *(LC71-188)*
  (Continued)
      Federal aid to vocational education
      Higher education and state
      Nationalism and education
      Politics and education
      Right to education
      Scholarships
      State aid to education
      State encouragement of science,
        literature, and art
      State supervision of teaching
      Theater and state
   x Educational policy
      State and education
   xx Church and college
      Education
      Endowment of research
      Nationalism and education
      Social policy
Education and travel
  See Student travel
Education and war
  See War and education
Education as a profession
  xx Educators
Education as a theme in art
  See Education in art
Education centers
  See Education parks
Education centers, Continuing
  See Continuing education centers
Education for librarianship
  See Library education
Education in art *(N8217.E3)*
  x Education as a theme in art
    Schools in art
  xx Art
Education in literature *(PN56.E; Schools in*
    American literature, PS169.S4;
    Schools in fiction, PN3448.S4)
  x Schools in literature
Education of adults
  See Adult education
Education of aristocrats
  See Upper classes—Education
Education of children
      Works confined to a particular locality
        are entered here and also under Edu-
        cation—[local subdivision]
  sa Children's museums
    Dalton laboratory plan
    Education, Elementary
    Education, Preschool
    Education, Primary
    Euthenics
    Montessori method of education
    Object-teaching
    Physical education for children
    Platoon schools
    Project method in teaching
    Religious education of children
    School social work
    subdivision Education *under various*
      social groups, e.g. Children of
      migrant laborers—Education
  x Children—Education
  xx Children
    Education
    Teaching
  — Curricula
Education of criminals
  See Education of prisoners
Education of girls
  See Education of women
Education of princes *(LC4929-4949; Political*
    theory, JC393)
  sa Political ethics
    Political science

    State, The
  x Kings and rulers—Education
    Princes, Education of
  xx Courts and courtiers
    Education
    Kings and rulers—Duties
    Political science
    Upper classes—Education
Education of princesses
  x Princesses—Education
  xx Education
Education of prisoners *(HV8875-8883)*
  x Education of criminals
    Prison schools
    Prisoners—Education
    Prisoners, Education of
  xx Crime and criminals
    Delinquents—Education
    Education
    Education and crime
    Prisoners
    Prisons
    Reformatories
Education of the aged
  x Aged—Education
  xx Adult education
    Education
Education of the blind
  See Blind—Education
Education of the deaf
  See Deaf—Education
Education of veterans
  See Veterans—Education
Education of women *(Indirect)*
    (LC1401-2571)
  sa Adult education of women
    Coeducation
    Health education of women
    Howard Plan
    Vocational education of women
    Women college students
    Women, Muslim—Education
    Women's colleges
  x Education of girls
    Girls—Education
    Woman—Education
    Women's education
  xx Coeducation
    Domestic education
    Education
    Girls
    Young women
Education of women, Medieval *(LC1707)*
  xx Education, Medieval
Education of workers
  See Labor and laboring classes—Education
Education parks *(LB3220)*
  x Education centers
    Education plazas
    Educational centers
    Educational parks
    Educational plazas
  xx Campus planning
    School facilities
Education plazas
  See Education parks
Education vouchers
  See Educational vouchers
Education Week
  See American Education Week
Education Year, 1970
  See International Education Year, 1970
Educational acceleration
  sa Advanced placement programs
    (Education)
    Combination of grades
  x Acceleration in education
    Intensive programs in education

  xx Ability
    Ability grouping in education
    Gifted children
    School management and organization
Educational accountability *(Direct)*
  sa Performance contracts in education
  x Accountability in education
    Educational program evaluation
    Evaluation research in education
    Program evaluation in education
  xx Education—Aims and objectives
    School management and organization
Educational administration
  See School management and organization
    Universities and colleges—
      Administration
    subdivision Administration *under*
      Universities and colleges—[local
      subdivision], *e.g.* Universities and
      colleges—United States—
      Administration
Educational aims and objectives
  See Education—Aims and objectives
    Education, Higher—Aims and
      objectives
    Education, Secondary—Aims and
      objectives
Educational anthropology
  sa Dropout behavior, Prediction of
  x Campus cultures
    Culture and education
    Education and anthropology
  xx Anthropology
    Culture
    Education—Philosophy
Educational aspirations
  See Student aspirations
Educational assistance
    Here are entered works on international
      aid to education given to under-
      developed areas in the form of techni-
      cal assistance.
  sa Educational exchanges
  x Foreign aid to education
    Foreign educational aid
  xx Educational exchanges
    Technical assistance
    Underdeveloped areas—Education
Educational assistance, American *(Direct)*
  x University contract programs
Educational associations *(Indirect)* *(L10-97)*
  sa Education—Societies, etc. *[for*
    publications of educational and other
    societies in relation to education]
    Parents' and teachers' associations
    Teachers' unions
    names of individual educational
      organizations
  x Educational societies
  xx Societies
    Teachers
Educational broadcasting *(Direct)*
    (LB1044.8)
  x Broadcasting, Educational
    Education—Broadcasting
  xx Radio in education
    Television in education
Educational broadcasting in adult education
    (Direct)
  xx Radio in adult education
    Television in adult education
Educational centers
  See Education parks
Educational change
  See Educational innovations
Educational consultants *(Direct)*
  x Consultants, Educational

Educational cooperation
   See University cooperation
Educational discrimination
   See Discrimination in education
Educational displays
   See Displays in education
Educational endowments
   See Endowment of research
      Endowments
      names of specific endowments, e.g.
        Carnegie Foundation for the
        Advancement of Teaching

Educational equalization *(Direct)*
   sa Right to education
   x Equal educational opportunity
     Equalization, Educational
   xx Education—Aims and objectives

Educational exchanges *(Direct) (LB2283-5)*
   Here are entered works dealing with international exchanges of educational personnel (students, educators, research scholars, specialists, etc.) supplies, and materials.
   sa Educational assistance
     Exchange of persons programs
     International farm youth exchange project
     Students, Interchange of
     Teachers, Interchange of
   x Exchanges, Educational
     International educational exchanges
   xx Educational assistance
     Exchange of persons programs
     Intellectual cooperation

Educational exhibits, Traveling *(LC6691)*
   sa Art—Exhibitions, Traveling
   x Traveling educational exhibits
   xx Education—Exhibits and museums
Educational facilities
   See School facilities

Educational fund raising
   xx Endowments
     Fund raising
     Universities and colleges—Finance

Educational games *(LB1029.G3; Play, GV1480)*
   x Instructive games
   xx Education—Simulation methods
     Games
     Puzzles
     Recreation
   — Juvenile literature
Educational guidance
   See Personnel service in education

Educational innovations *(Direct) (LB1027)*
   sa Demonstration centers in education
     Education—Experimental methods
     Educational technology
     Regional educational laboratories
   x Change, Educational
     Educational change
     Innovations, Educational
     Technological change in education
   xx Education—Experimental methods
     Educational planning
   — Evaluation
Educational journalism
   See Journalism, Educational
Educational land use
   See School lands

Educational law and legislation *(Direct) (LB2503-2797)*
   sa Adult education—Law and legislation
     Business education—Law and legislation
     Church schools—Law and legislation
     College and school journalism—Law and legislation

Correspondence schools and courses—Law and legislation
Discrimination in education—Law and legislation
Education, Compulsory
Elementary school teachers—Legal status, laws, etc.
Federal aid to education
Federal aid to private schools
Health education—Law and legislation
High school principals—Legal status, laws, etc.
High school teachers—Legal status, laws, etc.
International education—Law and legislation
Junior high school principals—Legal status, laws, etc.
Liability for school accidents
Library legislation
Medical education—Law and legislation
Municipal universities and colleges—Law and legislation
Nursery school teachers—Legal status, laws, etc.
Nursery schools—Law and legislation
Parents' advisory committees in education
Parents' and teachers' associations—Law and legislation
Private schools—Law and legislation
Religious education—Law and legislation
Right to education
School discipline
School employees—Legal status, laws, etc.
School management and organization
School management and organization—Law and legislation
School psychologists—Legal status, laws, etc.
School superintendents and principals—Legal status, laws, etc.
Segregation in education—Law and legislation
Social work education—Law and legislation
State aid to education
State aid to private schools
Student activities—Law and legislation
Student counselors—Law and legislation
Students—Legal status, laws, etc.
Summer schools—Law and legislation
Teachers colleges—Law and legislation
Teachers—Legal status, laws, etc.
Teachers of exceptional children—Legal status, laws, etc.
Teachers of handicapped children—Legal status, laws, etc.
Teachers, Training of—Law and legislation
Technical education—Law and legislation
Universities and colleges—Law and legislation
Vacation schools—Law and legislation
Vocational education—Law and legislation
Vocational teachers—Legal status, laws, etc.
   x Compulsory school attendance
     Law, Educational
     School law
     Schools—Law and legislation
   xx Education, Compulsory
     Public institutions—Law and legislation

School attendance
— Cases
— — Digests
     See Educational law and legislation —Digests
— Colonies
     See Educational law and legislation, Colonial
— Digests
   x Educational law and legislation—Cases—Digests
— Popular works
— Research

GEOGRAPHIC SUBDIVISIONS

— ₍country₎
— — Colonies
     Note under Educational law and legislation, Colonial

GEOGRAPHIC SUBDIVISIONS

— United States
— — States

Educational law and legislation, Colonial
   Here are entered general and comparative works only. Works on educational law and legislation of the colonies of an individual country are entered under the heading Educational law and legislation with subdivision ₍country₎—Colonies. Works dealing with a specific colony are entered under the same heading, subdivided by the name of the colony.
   x Colonies—Educational law and legislation
     Educational law and legislation—Colonies
     Native races—Education—Law and legislation

Educational law and legislation (Canon law)
   sa Universities and colleges (Canon law)
   xx Catholic Church—Education

Educational law and legislation (Jewish law)
Educational libraries
   See Pedagogical libraries

Educational literature
   sa Education—Bibliography
   xx Education—Bibliography
     Education—History
Educational measurements
   See Educational tests and measurements
Educational media
   See Teaching—Aids and devices
Educational media, Cataloging of
   See Cataloging of educational media
Educational media personnel
   See Instructional materials personnel
Educational missions
   See Missions—Educational work
Educational parks
   See Education parks
Educational performance contracts
   See Performance contracts in education
Educational photography
   See Photography in education

Educational planning *(Direct)*
   sa Campus planning
     College facilities—Planning
     Educational innovations
     Elementary school facilities—Planning
     High school facilities—Planning
     Junior high school facilities—Planning
     School facilities—Planning
     School management and organization
     Vocational education facilities—Planning
     Vocational education planning

Educational planning (Direct)
(Continued)
   x Educational program
     Planning, Educational
   xx Education—Aims and objectives
   — Mathematical models
   — Statistical methods
     xx Educational statistics
Educational plazas
   See Education parks
Educational policy
   See Education and state
Educational program
   See Educational planning
Educational program evaluation
   See Educational accountability
Educational psychology (LB1051-1091)
   sa Ability grouping in education
     Abstraction
     Achievement motivation
     Apperception
     Attention
     Automobile driver education—
       Psychological aspects
     Child study
     Education and heredity
     English language—Study and teaching
       —Psychological aspects
     Formal discipline
     Imagination
     Intelligence levels
     Interest (Psychology)
     Learning, Psychology of
     Listening
     Memory
     Mental tests
     Perception
     Psychology, Applied
     Rewards and punishments in education
     School psychologists
     Students—Psychology
     Subconsciousness
     Thought and thinking
     Transfer of training
   x Education—Psychology
     Psychology, Educational
   xx Child study
     Psychology
     Teaching
   — Programmed instruction
   — Terminology
Educational publicity
   See School publicity
Educational publishing (Direct) (Z286.E)
   x Education—Publishing
   xx Communication in education
     Publishers and publishing
Educational radio stations (Direct)
   xx Radio in education
     Radio stations
   — Law and legislation (Direct)
     xx Radio—Laws and regulations
Educational reports (Direct)
   sa School reports
   x Reports, Educational
   xx Educational research
Educational research (Direct) (LB1028)
   sa Agricultural education—Research
     Education—Economic aspects—
       Research
     Education, Elementary—Research
     Education, Higher—Research
     Education, Secondary—Research
     Educational reports
     Gifted children—Education—Research
     Handicapped children—Education—
       Research
     Regional educational laboratories
   x Education—Research

   xx Research
   — Administration
     See Educational research—
       Management
   — Information services
   — Management (LB1028.2)
     x Educational research—
       Administration
Educational secretaries
   See School secretaries
Educational societies
   See Educational associations
Educational sociology (Direct) (LC71-245)
   sa Dropout behavior, Prediction of
     Education—Aims and objectives
     Negroes—Education
     School environment
     Socially handicapped children—
       Education
     Socially handicapped—Education
     Students' socio-economic status
     Teachers' socio-economic status
     Technical education—Social aspects
   x Education and sociology
     Social problems in education
     Society and education
     Sociology, Educational
   xx Education—Aims and objectives
     Sociology
Educational statistics (LB2846)
   Here are entered works on the compilation and study of statistics in the field
   of education. Collections of these statistics are entered under the appropriate heading with subdivision Statistics,
   e.g. Education—Massachusetts—Statistics; Harvard University—Statistics;
   Junior colleges—Statistics.
   sa Educational planning—Statistical
     methods
   x Education—Statistical methods
   xx Statistics
Educational surveys (LB2823)
   Here are entered works on the technique
   of conducting school surveys, evaluating school efficiency, etc. Specific surveys are entered under the name of the
   school or subject surveyed.
   sa Adult education—Evaluation
     Elementary schools—Evaluation
     Laboratory schools—Evaluation
     School districts—Evaluation
   x Evaluation of schools
     Instructional systems analysis
     School evaluation
     School surveys
     Self-evaluation of schools
     Surveys, Educational
   xx Social surveys
Educational technology (Direct) (LB1028.3)
   sa Audio-visual education
     Computer-assisted instruction
     Electronic data processing—Education
     Programmed instruction
     Teaching—Aids and devices
     Teaching machines
   x Instructional technology
     Technology, Educational
   xx Educational innovations
     Teaching—Aids and devices
Educational television
   See Television in education
Educational television stations (Direct)
   sa Television in education
   xx Television in education
     Television stations
   — Finance
   — Law and legislation (Direct)

   xx Television—Law and legislation
Educational tests and measurements (Direct)
   (LB3051)
   sa Ability—Testing
     Character tests
     Creative thinking (Education)—Testing
     Examinations
     Grading and marking (Students)
     High school placement test
     Iowa tests of educational development
     Mental tests
     Personality tests
     Sociometry
     Spelling ability—Testing
     Students, Rating of
     Wisconsin tests of testimony and
       reasoning assessment
   x Educational measurements
     Tests and measurements in education
   xx Examinations
     Mental tests
     Psychometrics
     Students, Rating of
   Note under Students, Rating of
   — Examinations, questions, etc.
   — Programmed instruction
Educational Timesharing System (Electronic
   computer system)
   See ETS (Electronic computer system)
Educational toys
   x Instructive toys
     Teaching toys
   xx Toys
Educational transparencies
   See Transparencies in education
Educational vouchers (Direct)
   x Education vouchers
     Vouchers, Educational
   xx Education—Finance
Educational workshops
   See Demonstration centers in education
     Education—Congresses
     Teachers' workshops
Educators (Direct) (Biography,
   LA2301-2397; Theories and systems,
   LB51-875)
   sa Collective labor agreements—Education
     Deans (in schools)
     Education as a profession
     Teachers
   x Faculty (Education)
   xx Education
     Teachers
   — Anecdotes, facetiae, satire, etc.
   — Biography
   — Interviews
Educators, Islamic
   See Educators, Muslim
Educators, Jewish (BM88; LB75)
   x Jews as educators
Educators, Muslim
   x Educators, Islamic
     Islamic educators
     Muslim educators
   xx Islam—Biography
Eductors (Pumps)
   See Ejector pumps
Edwardian art objects
   See Art objects, Edwardian
Edwards personal preference schedule
   x EPPS
   xx Choice (Psychology)
     Personality tests
Edwin-Scharff-Preis
   xx Drawing—Competitions
Ee ja nai ka Uprising, 1867
   x Eejanaika Uprising, 1867

xx Japan—History—Restoration,
    1853-1870
    Shinto—History—To 1868
Eejanaika Uprising, 1867
  See Ee ja nai ka Uprising, 1867
Eel fisheries *(Indirect) (SH351.E4)*
  xx Eels
    Fisheries
Eel fishing *(SH691.E4)*
  xx Eels
    Fishing
Eels *(QL638.A55)*
  sa Cookery (Eels)
    Eel fisheries
    Eel fishing
    Morays
  x Apodal fishes
    Apodes
    Fishes, Apodal
    Leptocephalidae
  — Juvenile literature
Eels, Electric
  See Electric eel
Eels, Smoked
  x Smoked eel
  xx Fish, Smoked
Eelworms
  See Nematoda
Efate language *(PL6231)*
  sa Melanesian languages
  x Fate language
    Vate language
  xx Melanesian languages
Effect and cause
  See Causation
Effect of praise
  See Praise
Effective mass (Physics) *(QC176.8.E4)*
  xx Energy-band theory of solids
    Free electron theory of metals
    Mass (Physics)
Effective range (Nuclear physics)
    (QC794.6.S3)
  x Range, Effective (Nuclear physics)
  xx Potential scattering
Effectiveness and validity of law
  x Validity and effectiveness of law
  xx International law
    Jurisprudence
Effectiveness and validity of law (Roman law)
Effervescent wines
  See Sparkling wines
Efficiency, Feed utilization
  See Feed utilization efficiency
Efficiency, Industrial *(T58)*
  sa Capital productivity
    Industrial engineering
    Industrial productivity
    Labor productivity
    Mechanization
    Performance
    Socialist competition
    Stakhanov movement
    Work measurement
  x Industrial efficiency
  xx Industrial management
    Industry
  — Study and teaching
  — Terminology
Efficiency, Mechanical
  See Mechanical efficiency
Efficiency, Personal
  See Success
Efficiency engineers
  See Business consultants
Efficiency rating
  See Clergy, Rating of
    Employees, Rating of

    Executives, Rating of
    Soldiers, Rating of
    Supervisors, Rating of
    Teachers, Rating of
Effigies
  xx Portraits
    Sculpture
Effigies, Sepulchral
  See Sepulchral monuments
Effigies (in religion, folk-lore, etc.)
  x Folk-lore of effigies
  xx Religion, Primitive
Effigy, Executions in
  See Executions in effigy
Efflorescence
  xx Drying
    Surface chemistry
Effort
  See Struggle
Effusions, Pleural
  See Pleural effusions
Efik (African people)
  xx Ethnology—Nigeria
Efik language *(PL8147)*
  xx Benue-Congo languages
Egba (African tribe)
  xx Ethnology—Nigeria
    Yorubas
  — Juvenile literature
Egg (Biology)
  See Embryology
Egg carton craft
  xx Cartons
    Handicraft
  — Juvenile literature
Egg-cups
  See Eggcups
Egg decoration *(TT896.7)*
  sa Easter eggs
  xx Decoration and ornament
    Handicraft
  — Juvenile literature
Egg Harbor, N.J., Skirmish of, 1778
  See Little Egg Harbor, N.J., Skirmish of,
    1778
Egg inspection *(Indirect)*
  x Eggs—Examination
    Eggs—Inspection
  xx Poultry inspection
Egg-plant *(SB351.E5)*
  — Diseases and pests *(SB608.E2)*
Egg-plant lace-bug *(SB608.E2)*
Egg-plant tortoise beetle *(SB608.E2)*
Egg processing *(Indirect)*
  sa Eggs, Dried
    Eggs, Frozen
    Eggs—Preservation
  x Eggs—Processing
  — Patents
Egg products industry *(Direct)*
  xx Dairy products
    Egg trade
    Eggs
  — Equipment and supplies
Egg trade *(Direct)*
  sa Egg products industry
    Eggs—Prices
  xx Poultry industry
  — Law and legislation
    See Eggs—Law and legislation
  — Seasonal variations
    Example under Seasonal variations (Economics)
Eggcups *(Art, NK9990.E5)*
  x Egg-cups
Eggs *(Indirect) (SF490; Egg trade,*
    HD9284)
  sa Birds—Eggs and nests

    Cookery (Eggs)
    Egg products industry
    Eggshells
    subdivision Eggs *under subjects, e.g.*
      Fishes—Eggs; Reptiles—Eggs
  Example under Animal food; Produce trade
  — Cleaning
  — Cooperative marketing
    xx Eggs—Marketing
  — Examination
    See Egg inspection
  — Fertility
    See Eggs—Hatchability
  — Grading
    x Eggs—Quality
      Eggs—Standardization
  — — Mathematical models
  — Hatchability
    x Eggs—Fertility
      Fertility of eggs
      Hatchability of eggs
    xx Eggs—Incubation
  — Hatching
    See Eggs—Incubation
  — Incubation *(SF495)*
    sa Eggs—Hatchability
      Incubators
    x Brooding
      Eggs—Hatching
      Hatching of eggs
      Incubation of eggs
    xx Birds—Eggs and nests
      Embryology—Birds
      Poultry breeding
  — Inspection
    See Egg inspection
  — Juvenile literature
  — Law and legislation *(Direct)*
    x Egg trade—Law and legislation
  — Marketing
    sa Eggs—Cooperative marketing
    Example under Farm produce—Marketing
  — Packing
    Example under Packing for shipment
  — Preservation *(SF501)*
    sa Eggs, Frozen
      Eggs—Storage
    xx Cold storage
      Egg processing
    Example under Farm produce—Storage
  — Prices *(Direct)*
    xx Egg trade
    Example under Prices
  — Processing
    See Egg processing
  — Production *(SF487-8)*
    sa Poultry
    xx Poultry
  — Quality
    See Eggs—Grading
  — Standardization
    See Eggs—Grading
  — Storage
    xx Eggs—Preservation
  — Tariff
    See Tariff on eggs
Eggs, Dried
  x Powdered eggs
  xx Egg processing
    Food, Dried
Eggs, Easter
  See Easter eggs
Eggs, Fossil *(QE841)*
  sa Birds, Fossil—Eggs
  x Fossil eggs
  xx Vertebrates, Fossil

Eggs, Frozen
    xx Egg processing
        Eggs—Preservation
        Food, Frozen
Eggs (in religion, folk-lore, etc.) *(GR735)*
    x Folk-lore of eggs
    xx Folk-lore of birds
        Religion, Primitive
Eggs as food
    xx Cookery (Eggs)
        Food
Eggs in art
    xx Art
Eggshell craft
    xx Eggshells
        Handicraft
  — Juvenile literature
Eggshells
    sa Eggshell craft
    xx Birds—Eggs and nests
        Eggs
Ego (Psychology)
    sa Ego-ideal
        Identity (Psychology)
        Regression (Psychology)
        Super-ego
    xx Identity (Psychology)
        Personality
        Psychoanalysis
        Psychology
        Self
        Super-ego
Ego-ideal
    xx Ego (Psychology)
        Self-perception
        Self-realization
Ego strength
    xx Personality
Egoism *(BJ1474)*
    sa Altruism
        Avarice
        Self-interest
        Self-love (Psychology)
    xx Altruism
        Avarice
        Conduct of life
        Ethics
        Hedonism
        Philosophy
        Self-interest
EGPS (Computer program language)
      (QA76.5)
    x Extended general purpose simulator
Egret, Cattle
  See Cattle egret
Egrets
  See Herons
Egtved disease
  See Viral hemorrhagic septicemia
Egypt
  — History *(DT43-154)*
  — — To 332 B.C.
      sa Hyksos
      Example under reference from Prehis-
        tory
  — — To 640 A.D.
  — — 332-30 B.C.
      sa Alexandrine War, 48-47 B.C.
  — — Greco-Roman period, 332 B.C.-640
      A.D.
  — — 30 B.C.-640 A.D.
  — — 640-1250
      sa Ayyubids
        Fatimites
        Ikhshidids
        Tulunids
  — — 640-1882
  — — Invasion of Saint Louis, 1249

  — — 1250-1517
      sa Mamelukes
  — — — Historiography
  — — 1517-1882
      sa Ridania, Battle of, 1517
  — — 1798-
  — — French occupation, 1798-1801
  — — 19th century
  — — British occupation, 1882-1936
      sa Gordon Relief Expedition,
        1884-1885
  — — 1919-
  — — Insurrection, 1919
      xx Egypt—History—1919-
  — — 1919-
      sa Egypt—History—Insurrection,
        1919
  — — 1952- *(DT107.83)*
  — — Intervention, 1956
      sa Sinai Campaign, 1956
      x Anglo-French intervention in
        Egypt, 1956
        Israel-Arab War, 1956
  — — — Humor, caricatures, etc.
  — — — Personal narratives
  — — — Sources
  — Kings and rulers
      sa Pharaohs
      Example under Kings and rulers
Egypt in literature
Egyptian amulets
  See Amulets, Egyptian
Egyptian architecture
  See Architecture—Egypt
      Architecture, Egyptian
Egyptian art metal-work
  See Art metal-work, Egyptian
Egyptian art objects
  See Art objects, Egyptian
Egyptian ballads and songs *(PJ1487;*
      Translations, PJ1945)
    sa Folk-songs, Egyptian
Egyptian calendar
  See Calendar, Egyptian
Egyptian chronology
  See Chronology, Egyptian
Egyptian cultus
  See Cultus, Egyptian
Egyptian drama *(PJ1571; Translations,*
      PJ1947)
Egyptian embroidery
  See Embroidery, Egyptian
Egyptian eschatology
  See Eschatology, Egyptian
Egyptian fasts and feasts
  See Fasts and feasts—Egyptian religion
Egyptian fiction *(PJ1487; Translations,*
      PJ1949)
Egyptian gods
  See Gods, Egyptian
Egyptian henna
  See Henna
Egyptian hieroglyphics
  See Egyptian language—Writing,
      Hieroglyphic
Egyptian jewelry
  See Jewelry, Egyptian
Egyptian language *(PJ1001-1479)*
    sa Coptic language
    xx Afroasiatic languages
  — Inscriptions *(PJ1501-1819)*
      x Demotic inscriptions
        Hieratic inscriptions
        Inscriptions, Demotic
        Inscriptions, Egyptian
        Inscriptions, Hieratic
      xx Inscriptions, Hieroglyphic
        Stele (Archaeology)

  — Papyri *(PJ1501-1921)*
      x Egyptian papyri
        Papyri, Egyptian
      xx Manuscripts (Papyri)
  — Papyri, Demotic *(PJ1809-1921)*
      x Demotic writing
        Manuscripts, Demotic (Papyri)
  — Papyri, Hieratic
      x Hieratic writing
        Manuscripts, Hieratic (Papyri)
  — Writing *(PJ1051-1109)*
      Note under Writing
  — Writing, Demotic *(PJ1107)*
      x Demotic writing
  — Writing, Hieratic *(PJ1105)*
      x Hieratic writing
  — Writing, Hieroglyphic *(PJ1091-7)*
      x Egyptian hieroglyphics
        Hieroglyphics, Egyptian
Egyptian letters *(PJ1487; Translations,*
      PJ1947)
Egyptian librarians
  See Librarians, Egyptian
Egyptian literature *(Collections,*
      PJ1501-1989; History, PJ1481-8)
    sa Arabic literature—Egypt
Egyptian magic
  See Magic, Egyptian
Egyptian medicine
  See Medicine, Egyptian
Egyptian mythology
  See Mythology, Egyptian
Egyptian newspapers *(Direct)*
Egyptian ophthalmia
  See Conjunctiva—Diseases
Egyptian oracles
  See Oracles, Egyptian
Egyptian papyri
  See Egyptian language—Papyri
Egyptian periodicals *(Direct) (History,*
      PN5499.E4)
Egyptian plagues
  See Plagues of Egypt
Egyptian poetry *(Direct)*
Egyptian rings
  See Rings, Egyptian
Egyptian sibyl
  See Babylonian sibyl
Egyptian students in foreign countries
Egyptian studies
  See Egyptology
Egyptian tapestry
  See Tapestry, Egyptian
Egyptian temples
  See Temples, Egyptian
Egyptian-Turkish Conflict, 1831-1840
  See Turco-Egyptian Conflict, 1831-1840
Egyptian wit and humor *(Direct)*
Egyptians *(DT61; DT71)*
    sa Copts
    xx Ethnology—Egypt
  — Anthropometry
Egyptians in Asia
Egyptologists
  See Egyptology
Egyptology *(Archaeology and history,*
      DT57-154; Language and literature,
      PJ1001-1989)
    Here are entered works dealing with the
    study of the languages, antiquities, etc.
    of Egypt in a general and comprehen-
    sive way, *e.g.* scope, methods, history,
    and kindred subjects.
    x Egyptian studies
      Egyptologists
    xx Oriental studies
  — Juvenile literature
Ehime, Japan, in literature

Eḥkili language
   See Šḥauri language
Ehlers-Danlos syndrome *(RC580.E35)*
   x Danlos syndrome
   xx Medical genetics
Eichsfeld, Ger.
   — History
    — — Revolution, 1848-1849
       xx Germany—History—Revolution,
          1848-1849
Eider
Eidetic imagery *(BF367)*
   sa Eidetic parents test
   x Imagery, Eidetic
   xx After-images
     Imagery (Psychology)
     Memory
     Psychology
Eidetic parents test *(BF698.8.E47)*
   xx Eidetic imagery
     Parent and child
Eifel in art
Eigenvalues
   sa Sommerfeld polynomial method
   xx Matrices
Eigenvectors
   xx Matrices
     Vector spaces
Eight (Group of artists)
   See Ashcan School
Eight (The number)
   xx Symbolism of numbers
Eight card redrawing test
   xx Personality tests
     Projective techniques
Eight-hour movement *(HD5106-5250)*
   xx Hours of labor
Eight-man football
   xx Football
Eight Precepts (Buddhism)
   See Buddhist precepts
Eight trumpets with string orchestra
   See Trumpets (8) with string orchestra
Eight-Year Study *(LB1026)*
   xx Articulation (Education)
     Education—Experimental methods
     Education, Higher
     Education, Secondary
Eighteenth century
   sa Civilization, Modern—18th century
     Enlightenment
   xx History, Modern—18th century
   — Biography
      See Biography—18th century
Eightfold Path
   sa Nirvana
   x Eightfold Way (Buddhism)
   xx Buddhist doctrines
     Four Noble Truths
Eightfold Way (Buddhism)
   See Eightfold Path
Eightfold way (Nuclear physics)
   sa Nuclear spin
   x Unitary symmetry
   xx Groups, Theory of
     Particles (Nuclear physics)
Eighth grade (Education)
   xx Education, Elementary
Eighty-eight (Game)
   See Hachi-ju-hachi (Game)
Eikonal equation
   xx Differential equations
     Optics, Geometrical
Eikons
   See Ikons
Eikyoku
   See Enkyoku

Eilenberg-Moore spectral sequences
   x Spectral sequences, Eilenberg-Moore
   xx Algebraic topology
     Sequences (Mathematics)
     Spectral theory (Mathematics)
Einsatzgruppen Trial, Nuremberg, 1947-1948
   See War crime trials—Nuremberg—
      Einsatzgruppen case, 1947-1948
Einstein unified field theory
   See Unified field theories
Eisenstein series
   x Series, Eisenstein
   xx Functions, Automorphic
     Functions of several complex variables
Ejection (Psychology) *(BF311)*
   sa Anthropomorphism
     Gestalt psychology
     Perception
   xx Knowledge, Theory of
     Perception
     Psychology
Ejection seats (Aeroplanes)
   See Pilot ejection seats
Ejectment *(Direct)*
   sa Adverse possession
     Land titles
   x Mesne profits
   xx Actions and defenses
     Adverse possession
     Land titles
     Possessory actions
     Real property
Ejectment (Roman law)
Ejector pumps *(TJ901)*
   x Eductors (Pumps)
     Ejectors (Pumps)
   xx Jet pumps
Ejector seats (Aeroplanes)
   See Pilot ejection seats
Ejectors (Jet propulsion)
   See Short take-off and landing aircraft—Jet
     propulsion—Ejectors
     Vertically rising aeroplanes—Jet
     propulsion—Ejectors
Ejectors (Pumps)
   See Ejector pumps
Ejo language
   See Ijo language
Ekagi language
   See Kapauku language
Ekajuk language
   xx Ekoi languages
Ekari (Papuan people)
   See Kapauku (Papuan people)
Ekari language
   See Kapauku language
Ekaw language
   See Kaw language
Ekegusii language
   See Gusii language
Eklogite
   See Eclogite
Ekoi *(GN653)*
Ekoi languages *(PL8152)*
   sa Ekajuk language
   x Ekoid languages
   xx Bantu languages
Ekoid languages
   See Ekoi languages
El Alamein, Battle of, 1942
   See al 'Alamayn, Battle of, 1942
El Bruch, Spain, Battle of, 1808
   xx Peninsular War, 1807-1814
El Camino automobile
   x Camino automobile
   xx Chevrolet automobile
El Caney, Battle of, 1898 *(E717.1)*

El Carmen, Battle of, 1934
   x Cañada El Carmen, Battle of, 1934
   xx Chaco War, 1932-1935
El Dorado *(E121)*
El Ebano, Battle of, 1915 *(F1234)*
   xx Mexico—History—1910-1946
Elaeococca oil
   See Tung-oil
Elamite language *(P943)*
   sa Achaemenian inscriptions
     Cuneiform inscriptions
     Cuneiform inscriptions, Elamite
     Cuneiform writing
   x Amardic language
     Anzanic language
     Susian language
   xx Cuneiform inscriptions
     Cuneiform inscriptions, Elamite
Elands *(QL737.U5)*
   xx Antelopes
Elands, Fossil *(QE882.U3)*
Elasmobranchii *(QL638.7-9)*
   sa Chimaeriformes
     Plagiostomi
Elasmobranchii, Fossil
Elastic analysis (Theory of structures)
   xx Elasticity
     Structures, Theory of
Elastic cross sections *(QC794.6.C7)*
   sa Inelastic cross sections
   x Cross sections, Elastic
   xx Cross sections (Nuclear physics)
     Inelastic cross sections
Elastic fabrics
   sa Stretch woven fabrics
   x Elastic webbing
   xx Rubber
     Stretch woven fabrics
Elastic plates and shells *(QA935)*
     Here are entered works on the mathematical
     theories of elasticity in plates
     and shells. Theoretical and technical
     works on plates and shells as engineer-
     ing structures are entered under Plates
     (Engineering) and Shells (Engineer-
     ing)
   sa Plates (Engineering)
     Shells (Engineering)
   x Elastic shells
     Plates, Elastic
     Shells, Elastic
   xx Elastic waves
     Elasticity
     Plasticity
   Notes under Plates (Engineering); Shells (En-
     gineering)
   — Tables, etc.
Elastic rods and wires *(QA935)*
     Here are entered works on mathematical
     theories of elasticity in rods and wires.
     Theoretical and technical works on
     rods and wires as members of engi-
     neering structures are entered under
     Bars (Engineering) and Wire.
   sa Bars (Engineering)
     Wire
   x Rods
   xx Elastic waves
     Elasticity
   Note under Bars (Engineering)
Elastic shells
   See Elastic plates and shells
Elastic solids *(QA935; QC191; TG265)*
   sa Deformations (Mechanics)
     Internal friction
     Strains and stresses
     Torsion
     Vibration

Elastic solids *(QA935; QC191; TG265)*
  (Continued)
    xx Continuum mechanics
      Elastic waves
      Mechanics
      Solids
      Statics
  — Models *(QC191)*
  — Thermal properties
    See Thermoelasticity
Elastic tissue *(QM563)*
  sa Connective tissues
  xx Connective tissues
    Tissues
Elastic waves *(QA935; Geophysics,*
    QC809.E5; Seismology, QE539;
    Solids, QC191)
  sa Aeroelasticity
    Elastic plates and shells
    Elastic rods and wires
    Elastic solids
    Head waves
    Hydroelasticity
    Internal friction
    Microseisms
    Rayleigh waves
    Seismic waves
    Stress waves
    Underground nuclear explosions
  xx Elasticity
    Underground nuclear explosions
    Vibration
    Waves
  — Diffraction
Elastic webbing
  See Elastic fabrics
Elasticity *(Mathematical theory, QA931-5;*
    Physics, QC191)
  sa Aeroelasticity
    Continuum mechanics
    Elastic analysis (Theory of structures)
    Elastic plates and shells
    Elastic rods and wires
    Elastic waves
    Hydroelasticity
    Hypercircle method
    Hysteresis
    Photoelasticity
    Plasticity
    Plates (Engineering)
    Rheology
    Shear (Mechanics)
    Shells (Engineering)
    Strains and stresses
    Strength of materials
    Thermoelasticity
    Viscoelasticity
  x Young's modulus
  xx Compressibility
    Flexure
    Impact
    Mathematical physics
    Matter—Properties
    Mechanics
    Mechanics, Analytic
    Physics
    Rheology
    Statics
    Strains and stresses
    Strength of materials
  — Electromechanical analogies
  — Problems, exercises, etc.
  — Tables, etc.
Elasticity, Coefficient of
  See Elasticity (Economics)
Elasticity (Economics)
  x Coefficient of elasticity
    Elasticity, Coefficient of
  xx Economics

Elastomeric materials
  See Elastomers
Elastomers
  sa Plastics
    Plastisols
    Rubber
  x Elastomeric materials
  xx Plastics
    Polymers and polymerization
    Rubber
  — Molding
  — Radiation effects
    See Elastomers, Effect of radiation on
  — Testing
Elastomers, Effect of radiation on
  x Elastomers, Irradiated
    Elastomers—Radiation effects
    Radiation—Effect on elastomers
  xx Radiation
Elastomers, Irradiated
  See Elastomers, Effect of radiation on
Elation *(BF575.E)*
  xx Emotions
Elbe River in art
Elbe Slavs
  See Polabian Slavs
Elberfeld system *(HV57)*
  xx Charities
    Friendly visiting
Elbow *(QM131)*
  Example under Joints
  — Fracture
  — Surgery
    x Excision of elbow
  — Wounds and injuries
Elbow-stones *(GN799.E)*
  xx Indians of the West Indies—Antiquities
Elchesaites
  See Elkesaites
Elchingen, Battle of, 1805 *(DC227.5.E6)*
  xx Austria—History—1789-1815
    Napoléon I, Emperor of the French,
      1769-1821—German and Austrian
      Campaign, 1805
Elders (Church officers)
  x Presbyters
  xx Church officers
    Clergy
Eldest child
  See Children, First-born
Élé dialect
  See Lele dialect
Eleatics *(B196)*
  xx Philosophy, Ancient
Election (Theology) *(BT810)*
  sa Jews—Election, Doctrine of
    Particularism (Theology)
    Perseverance (Theology)
    Predestination
    Semi-Pelagianism
  xx Predestination
    Theology, Doctrinal
  — Biblical teaching
  — History of doctrines *(BT809)*
  — Sermons
Election (Wills) *(Direct)*
  xx Curtesy
    Dower
    Inheritance and succession
    Probate law and practice
    Renunciation of inheritance
    Wills
Election Day
  xx Holidays—United States
Election districts *(Direct)*
  sa Apportionment (Election law)
    Gerrymander

    subdivision Election districts *under*
      names of legislative bodies, e.g.
      Great Britain. Parliament. House
      of Commons—Election districts
  x Legislative districts
  xx Administrative and political divisions
    Apportionment (Election law)
    Election law
    Elections
    Representative government and
      representation
Election finance
  See Elections—Campaign funds
Election forecasting *(Direct)*
  x Forecasting, Election
    Straw votes
  xx Elections
    Public opinion polls
Election law *(Direct) (JF825-831; United*
    States, JK1961-3)
  sa Cooptation
    Election districts
    Electioneering—Law and legislation
    Elections—Corrupt practices
    Literacy tests (Election law)
    Local elections
    Nominations for office
    Primaries
    School elections—Law and legislation
    Suffrage
    Voters, Registration of
    Voting, Absent
    Voting-machines—Law and legislation
  x Law, Election
  Note under Local elections
  — Criminal provisions
    See Elections—Corrupt practices
  — Digests
Election law (Canon law) *(BX1930.E4)*
Election law (Roman law)
Election of Israel
  See Jews—Election, Doctrine of
Election sermons *(BV4260)*
  — Connecticut, ₍Massachusetts, New
    Hampshire, etc.₎
Election statistics
  See Elections—Statistics
Electioneering *(Direct)*
  sa Advertising, Political
    Radio in politics
    Telephone in politics
    Television in politics
  xx Elections
    Politics, Practical
  — Law and legislation *(Direct)*
    xx Election law
  — — Digests
Elections *(Direct) (JF1001-1191; United*
    States, JK1951-2246, JK2700-9595)
  sa Australian ballot
    Ballot
    Ballot-box
    Campaign funds
    Campaign management
    Campaign paraphernalia
    Cooptation
    Election districts
    Election forecasting
    Electioneering
    Elections, Nonpartisan
    Indians of North America—Suffrage
    Local elections
    Majorities
    Mexican Americans—Politics and
      suffrage
    Negroes—Politics and suffrage
    Nominations for office
    Plebiscite

Preferential ballot
Presidents—United States—Election
Primaries
Proportional representation
Referendum
Representative government and
representation
School elections
Soldiers—Suffrage
Suffrage
Voters, Registration of
Voting
Voting, Absent
Voting, Compulsory
Voting-machines
Voting, Plural
Voting research
Woman—Suffrage
  subdivision Elections *under names of
    legislative bodies of countries, states,
    etc., e.g.* Great Britain. Parliament
    —Elections
 x Franchise
   Polls
 xx Plebiscite
   Political science
   Politics, Practical
   Representative government and
     representation
Note under Local elections
— Anecdotes, facetiae, satire, etc.
— Campaign funds
      General works on the collection and
      disbursement of campaign funds
      and on the levying of political as-
      sessments on civil employees of the
      government are entered under the
      heading Campaign funds.
      Works on the campaign funds of a par-
      ticular state or locality are entered
      under the heading Elections—⌈lo-
      cal subdivision⌉—Campaign funds.
   x Election finance
— Corrupt practices *(JF1081-5; JK1994-7;*
     JK2241-6; Great Britain,
     JN1081-1097)
   x Election law—Criminal provisions
   xx Bribery
     Corruption (in politics)
     Criminal law
     Election law
     Political crimes and offenses
— Public opinion
— Statistics
   x Election statistics
— Underdeveloped areas
     See Underdeveloped areas—Elections

      GEOGRAPHIC SUBDIVISIONS

— Philadelphia
— — Campaign funds
     Example under Campaign funds

      GEOGRAPHIC SUBDIVISIONS

— United States
   sa Campaign insignia
   x United States—Elections
   xx Presidents—United States

      GEOGRAPHIC SUBDIVISIONS

— — Caricatures and cartoons
— — Juvenile literature
Elections, Contested
  See Contested elections

subdivision Contested elections *under
    names of legislative bodies of
    countries, states, etc., e.g.* United
    States. Congress. House—
    Contested elections
Elections, Local
  See Local elections
Elections, Municipal
  See Local elections
Elections, Nonpartisan
   x Nonpartisan elections
   xx Elections
     Local elections
Elections, Primary
  See Primaries
Elections in literature
Electoral college
  See Presidents—United States—Election
Electors (Kurfürsten) *(JN3250.C83)*
   sa Golden bull, 1356
   xx Holy Roman Empire—Kings and rulers
Electra (Turboprop transports)
   x Electra turboprop liner
     Lockheed Electra
     Turboprop transports
   xx Jet transports
     Lockheed airplanes
Electra in literature
Electra turboprop liner
  See Electra (Turboprop transports)
Electrets
   xx Dielectrics
     Electromagnetism
     Polarization (Electricity)
— Patents
Electric accidents
  See Electricity, Injuries from
Electric accounting machines
  See Accounting machines
Electric action of points *(QC701-3)*
   sa Electric discharges
     Electric leakage
     Electrostatics
   xx Electric discharges
     Electric leakage
     Electrostatics
Electric alarms *(TK7241-7271)*
   sa Burglar-alarms
     Fire-alarms
   xx Burglar-alarms
     Electric apparatus and appliances
     Fire-alarms
Electric alternators
  See Dynamos—Alternating current
Electric analogies in mechanics
  See Electromechanical analogies
Electric anesthesia *(RD86.E4)*
   x Anesthesia (Electric)
     Electroanesthesia
     Electronarcosis
   xx Electrophysiology
     Electrotherapeutics
Electric annunciators *(TK7201-7221)*
   xx Electric apparatus and appliances
Electric apparatus and appliances *(Electric
     industries, TK; Medical apparatus,
     RM889; Scientific apparatus,
     QC543-4)*
   sa Armatures
     Burglar-alarms
     Clocks and watches, Electric
     Coherer
     Condensers (Electricity)
     Dynamos
     Electrodynamometer
     Electromagnets
     Electrometer
     Electrophorus

     Electroscope
     Electrotherapeutics—Apparatus and
       instruments
     Fire-alarms
     Fluxmeter
     Galvanometer
     Gas—Electric ignition
     Household appliances, Electric
     Induction coils
     Magneto-electric machines
     Oscillators, Electric
     Outlet boxes (Electric engineering)
     Phonic wheel
     Potentiometer
     Pumping machinery, Electric
     Quality factor meters
     Recording instruments
     Remote control
     Spark-plugs
     Storage batteries
     Telecommunication—Apparatus and
       supplies
     Transducers
     Electric alarms; Electric annunciators;
       Electric resistors; *and similar
       headings beginning with the word*
       Electric
   x Apparatus, Electric
     Appliances, Electric
     Electric appliances
     Electric engineering—Apparatus and
       appliances
     Electricity—Apparatus and appliances
     Instruments, Electric
   xx Electric engineering
     Physical instruments
     Scientific apparatus and instruments
— Amateurs' manuals *(TK9900-9971)*
   x Household appliances, Electric—
       Amateurs' manuals
— — Juvenile literature
— Appraisal
     See Electric apparatus and appliances
       —Valuation
— Catalogs *(Electric industries, TK455;
       Scientific apparatus, QC543-4)*
   sa Electric lighting—Catalogs of
       supplies, etc.
     Electric railroads—Equipment and
       supplies—Catalogs
   x Electric engineering—Catalogs of
       supplies, etc.
     Electricity—Catalogs of supplies, etc.
— Design and construction
— Deterioration
— Drawing
     See Electric drafting
— Drawings
   xx Electric drafting
— Fires and fire prevention
   xx Fire prevention
— Juvenile literature
— Maintenance and repair
— — Costs
— Patents *(TK257)*
— Prices *(Direct)*
— Protection
   sa Electric fuses
     Lightning-arresters
     Overvoltage
     Shielding (Electricity)
     Short circuits
     Transients (Electricity)
   x Electric protective apparatus
     Protection, Electric
   xx Electric engineering
     Electric switchgear
— Reliability

Electric apparatus and appliances *(Electric industries, TK; Medical apparatus, RM889; Scientific apparatus, QC543-4)* *(Continued)*
— Safety measures
— Standards
— Storage
— Testing *(TK401)*
— Transportation
— Tropical conditions
— Valuation
    x Electric apparatus and appliances—Appraisal
Electric apparatus and appliances, Domestic
    See Household appliances, Electric
Electric apparatus and appliances, Explosionproof
    sa Electric controllers, Explosionproof
    x Explosionproof electric apparatus and appliances
Electric apparatus and appliances (Jewish law)
    xx Prohibited work (Jewish law)
Electric appliances
    See Electric apparatus and appliances
Electric arc *(QC705)*
    sa Arc spectra
        Mercury arc
    x Arc, Electric
        Voltaic arc
    xx Electric lamps, Arc
        Electric spark
Electric arc welding
    See Electric welding
Electric armatures
    See Armatures
Electric automobiles
    See Automobiles, Electric
Electric baths
    See Baths, Electric
Electric batteries *(QC603-5)*
    sa Atomic batteries
        Concentration cells
        Fuel cells
        Selenium cells
        Solar batteries
        Standard cells
        Storage batteries
        Thermopiles
    x Batteries, Electric
        Cell, Voltaic
        Galvanic batteries
        Primary batteries
        Voltaic cell
    xx Electrochemistry
        Storage batteries
        Thermopiles
— Juvenile literature
— Patents
— Standards
Electric bearings
    See Electric suspension
Electric bells *(TK7108-7118)*
    xx Bells
Electric blankets
    xx Blankets
        Household appliances, Electric
— Testing
Electric bleaching
    See Bleaching, Electric
Electric boats *(VM345)*
    xx Boats and boating
        Electricity in transportation
Electric breakdown
    See Breakdown (Electricity)
Electric brushes
    See Brushes, Electric

Electric cable industry
    See Electric wire and cable industry
Electric cable sheathing
    x Cable sheathing
        Sheathed cables
    xx Electric cables
— Corrosion
Electric cables *(TK3301-3351)*
    sa Cables, Submarine
        Coaxial cables
        Electric cable sheathing
        Electric conduits
        Electric lines
        Electric wire
        Electric wire and cable industry
        Electric wiring
        Telegraph cables
        Telephone cables
    x Cables, Electric
    xx Electric conductors
        Electric lines
        Electric wire
        Electric wiring
— Cathodic protection
    xx Electric cables—Corrosion
    Example under Cathodic protection
— Computer programs
— Corrosion
    sa Electric cables—Cathodic protection
— Joints
    xx Electric connectors
        Joints (Engineering)
— Plastic insulation
    x Plastic insulation of electric cables
    xx Electric insulators and insulation
        Plastics
— Reliability
— Standards
— Testing *(TK3307)*
— Thermal properties
— Trade-marks
Electric capacitors
    See Condensers (Electricity)
Electric capacity *(QC589)*
    sa Condensers (Electricity)
    xx Electrostatics
— Programmed instruction
Electric charge and distribution *(QC581)*
    sa Magnetostatics
        Renormalization (Physics)
        Space charge
    x Density, Electric
        Electric density
    xx Electric discharges
        Electrostatics
        Induction (Electricity)
Electric circuit-breakers *(TK2842)*
    sa Electric relays
        Short circuits
    x Circuit-breakers, Electric
— Pictorial works
— Standards
— Testing
Electric circuits *(QC601; Electric engineering, TK3001-3226)*
    sa Bridge circuits
        Calculus, Operational
        Electric fault location
        Electric filters
        Electric networks
        Electronic circuits
        Magnetic circuits
        Printed circuits
        Radar circuits
        Radio circuits
        Short circuits
        Vacuum-tube circuits
        Volta effect

    x Circuits, Electric
    xx Electric lines
— Juvenile literature
— Problems, exercises, etc.
— Programmed instruction
Electric clocks and watches
    See Clocks and watches, Electric
Electric coils *(Electric engineering, TK2391; Physics, QC544.C7; Radio, TK6565.C6)*
    x Coils, Electric
    xx Magnetic circuits
        Tank circuits
Electric communication
    See Telecommunication
Electric condensers
    See Condensers (Electricity)
Electric conductivity *(QC607-611)*
    sa Electrolytes—Conductivity
        Photoconductivity
        Photoelectricity
        Plasma (Ionized gases)—Conductivity
        Semiconductors
        Semimetals
        Superconductivity
        Tunneling (Physics)
    x Conductivity, Electric
    xx Free electron theory of metals
Electric conductors *(Engineering, TK3301-3351; Physics, QC611)*
    sa Bus conductors (Electricity)
        Electric cables
        Electric resistors
        Electric wire
        Microwave wiring
        Radio, Short wave
        Wave guides
    x Conductors, Electric
Electric conduits *(TK3261)*
    x Conduits
    xx Electric cables
        Electric lines
        Electric power distribution
        Electric wiring
        Telephone lines
Electric connectors
    sa Electric cables—Joints
        Electric contacts
    x Plugs (Electricity)
        Sockets, Electric
    xx Electric contactors
— Standards
Electric contactors *(TK2861)*
    Here are entered works on devices for repeatedly establishing and interrupting an electric power circuit. Works on the conducting part of a relay, switch, circuit-breaker, connector, contactor, etc., which coacts with another conducting part to make or break a circuit are entered under Electric contacts.
    sa Electric connectors
        Electric resistors
        Ohmic contacts
    x Contactors, Electric
        Plugs (Electricity)
        Sockets, Electric
    xx Electric relays
        Electric switchgear
    Note under Electric contacts
— Lubrication
— Patents
— Standards
— Testing

Electric contacts *(TK2821)*

> Here are entered works on the conducting part of a relay, switch, circuit-breaker, connector, contactor, etc., which coacts with another conducting part to make or break a circuit. Works on devices for repeatedly establishing and interrupting an electric power circuit are entered under Electric contactors.

  x Contacts, Electric
  xx Electric connectors
    Electric switchgear
  Note under Electric contactors

Electric contracting *(Direct)*
  sa Electricians
  xx Contractors
    Electric industries

Electric control, Remote
  See Remote control

Electric controllers *(TK2851; Electric railroads, TF930)*
  sa Ballasts (Electricity)
    Electric reactors
    Electric rheostats
    Magnetic amplifiers
    Remote control
    Rotating amplifiers
    Voltage regulators
  x Controllers, Electric
  xx Automatic control
    Electric machinery
    Electric rheostats
  — Standards *(Direct)*

Electric controllers, Explosionproof
  x Explosionproof electric controllers
  xx Electric apparatus and appliances, Explosionproof

Electric converters
  See Cascade converters
    Electric current converters
    Rotary converters

Electric cookery *(TX827)*
  sa Microwave cookery
    Stoves, Electric
  xx Cookery

Electric cranes *(TJ1363-5)*
  xx Cranes, derricks, etc.
  — Brakes
  — Juvenile literature
  — Maintenance and repair
  — Safety measures

Electric current converters *(TK2796)*
  sa Cascade converters
    Electric inverters
    Frequency changers
    Klystrons
    Rotary converters
  x Converters, Electric
    Electric converters
  xx Electric machinery
  — Mathematical models
  — Noise

Electric current rectifiers *(TK2798)*
  sa Aluminum cell
    Crystal detectors
    Junction transistors
    Kenotrons
    Mercury-arc rectifiers
    Radio—Rectifiers
    Selenium rectifiers
    Semiconductor rectifiers
    Silicon-controlled rectifiers
    Silicon rectifiers
    Thyristors
  x Rectifiers (Electric)
    Rectifiers, Electric current
  xx Electric transformers

Semiconductors
— Electromechanical analogies

Electric currents *(QC601-641)*
  sa Eddy currents (Electric)
    Electric fault location
    Electric measurements
    Electric noise
    Electric transformers
    Galvanomagnetic effects
    Hall effect
    Pinch effect (Physics)
    Short circuits
    Transients (Electricity)
  x Currents, Electric
    Electric potential
    Potential, Electric
  — Grounding *(TK3227)*
    x Electric power distribution—Grounding
      Grounding (Electricity)
  — — Patents
  — Heating effects *(QC623)*
  — Juvenile literature

Electric currents, Alternating *(Engineering, TK1141-1168; Theory, QC641)*
  sa Impedance (Electricity)
    Reactance (Electricity)
  x Alternating currents
    Currents, Alternating
  — Polyphase *(TK1161)*
    x Polyphase currents
  — — Computer programs
  — Programmed instruction
  — Single-phase *(TK1145)*
  — Two-phase *(TK1151)*

Electric currents, Direct
  sa Electric machinery—Direct current
    Electric power distribution—Direct current
  x Currents, Direct
    Direct currents
  — Programmed instruction

Electric currents, Vagrant *(Electric engineering, TK3255; Electric railroads, TF912)*
  sa Earth currents
    Electrolytic corrosion

Electric cut-outs *(TK2846)*
  x Cut-outs, Electric
  xx Electric switchgear
  — Standards

Electric cutting machinery *(TK4660.5)*
  x Electric spark cutting
  xx Cutting machines
    Electric machinery
    Metal-working machinery
  — Automatic control

Electric density
  See Electric charge and distribution

Electric dipole moments
  See Dipole moments

Electric discharge lamps
  See Electric discharge lighting

Electric discharge lighting *(TK4381-4383)*
  sa Electric lighting, Cadmium vapor
    Electric lighting, Mercury vapor
    Electric lighting, Sodium vapor
    Fluorescent lighting
    Neon lamps
  x Electric discharge lamps
  xx Electric discharges through gases
    Electric lighting

Electric discharge machining
  See Electric metal-cutting

Electric discharges *(QC701-715)*
  sa Breakdown (Electricity)
    Electric action of points
    Electric charge and distribution

    Electric spark
    Exploding wire phenomena
    Photoelectricity
  x Discharges (Electricity)
    Electricity—Discharges
  xx Electric action of points
    Electrostatics
    Nuclear physics
    Photoelectricity
  — Detection
    xx Electric testing

Electric discharges through gases *(QC711)*
  sa Afterglow (Physics)
    Cathode rays
    Cold cathode tubes
    Electric discharge lighting
    Electron tubes
    Electrons—Emission
    Induction (Electricity)
    Ionization of gases
    Mercury arc
    Plasma (Ionized gases)
    Thyratrons
    Vacuum
    Vacuum-tubes
    X-rays
  x Electricity—Discharges through gases
    Gases, Electric discharges through
  xx Cathode rays
    Electrons
    Ions
    Vacuum
    Vacuum-tubes

Electric double layer
  sa Zeta potential
  x Double layer, Electric
    Helmholtz double layer
  xx Electrochemistry

Electric drafting *(TK431)*
  sa Automatic control—Drawings
    Electric apparatus and appliances—Drawings
    Electric machinery—Drawing
    Electric wiring—Diagrams
    Electronic drafting
  x Drafting, Electric
    Electric apparatus and appliances—Drawing
    Electric engineering—Drafting
  xx Mechanical drawing
  — Problems, exercises, etc.

Electric driving *(TK4058)*
  sa subdivision Electric driving *under subjects, e.g.* Machine-tools—Electric driving; Printing-press—Electric driving
  xx Electric machinery
    Electric power
    Power transmission
  — Automatic control
  — Electromechanical analogies
  — Laboratory manuals
  — Patents
  — Problems, exercises, etc.

Electric eel *(QL638.G9)*
  x Eels, Electric
  xx Electric organs in fishes

Electric engineering *(Direct) (TK)*
  sa Electric apparatus and appliances
    Electric apparatus and appliances—Protection
    Electric lighting
    Electric lines—Models
    Electric machinery
    Electric network analyzers
    Electric power distribution
    Electric power production
    Electric power systems

Electric engineering *(Direct)* *(TK)*
(Continued)
    Electric railroads
    Electricity in astronautics
    Electricity in building
    Electricity in military engineering
    Electricity in mining
    Electrification
    Electro-acoustics
    Electromechanical devices
    Geothermal engineering
    High voltages
    Magnetic devices
    Radio
    Telegraph
    Telephone
  x Electricity—Transmission
    Engineering, Electrical
  xx Engineering
    Machinery
    Mechanical engineering
    Technology
  Note under Electric utilities
— Abbreviations
— Amateurs' manuals *(TK9901)*
— Apparatus and appliances
    See Electric apparatus and appliances
— Catalogs of supplies, etc.
    See Electric apparatus and appliances
      —Catalogs
    Electric lighting—Catalogs of
      supplies, etc.
    Electric railroads—Equipment and
      supplies—Catalogs
— Contracts and specifications *(Direct)*
    (TK425)
— Drafting
    See Electric drafting
— Estimates *(TK435)*
— Examinations, questions, etc. *(TK169)*
— Graphic methods
  xx Electric engineering—Tables,
    calculations, etc.
— Information services
— Insurance requirements *(TK260; Wiring,*
    TK3275)
  xx Electric wiring—Insurance
    requirements
    Insurance, Fire—Risks
— Juvenile literature *(TK148)*
— Laboratory manuals *(TK147)*
  xx Electric testing
    Electricity—Laboratory manuals
— Laws and legislation *(Direct)*
    (TK215-255)
  sa Electric engineering—Safety
    regulations
  x Electricity—Laws and legislation
  xx Telegraph—Laws and regulations
    Telephone—Laws and regulations
— Materials
  sa Dielectrics
    Electronics—Materials
    Plastics in electric engineering
    Semiconductors
    Steel, Electrical
    Telecommunication—Materials
    Thermoelectric materials
— — Testing
— — — Laboratory manuals
— Mathematics
  x Electric engineering mathematics
  xx Engineering mathematics
— Museums and collections *(TK6)*
— Notation
    Example under reference from Symbols
      (in science, technology, etc.)
— Popular works *(TK148)*
— Problems, exercises, etc. *(TK168)*

— Production standards
— Programmed instruction
— Research *(Direct)*
— Safety measures *(TK152)*
  x Safety measures
— Safety regulations *(Direct)*
  xx Electric engineering—Laws and
    legislation
— Simulation methods
— Standards *(Direct)*
    Example under Standardization; *and un-*
    der reference from Standards
— Statistics
— Tables, calculations, etc. *(TK151)*
  sa Electric engineering—Graphic
    methods
— Terminology *(TK9)*
— Tools and implements
  xx Tools

Electric engineering as a profession *(TK159)*
  sa Electric industries—Vocational
    guidance
  xx Electric industries—Vocational
    guidance

Electric engineering mathematics
    See Electric engineering—Mathematics

Electric engineers *(Direct)*
  xx Engineers
— Correspondence, reminiscences, etc.
— Salaries, pensions, etc. *(Direct)*

Electric equipment of automobiles
    See Automobiles—Electric equipment

Electric eye cameras
  sa individual makes of electric eye
    cameras, e.g. Fujica camera
  xx Cameras
    Photoelectric cells
    Photography—Electronic equipment

Electric fault location
  sa Short circuits
  x Fault location (Electrical engineering)
  xx Electric circuits
    Electric currents
    Short circuits

Electric fences *(Agricultural engineering,*
    S723)
  • *xx* Electric wire
    Fences

Electric fields *(QC661)*
  sa Electromagnetic fields
  xx Electromagnetic fields
    Field theory (Physics)
— Physiological effect
— Simulation methods

Electric filters *(QC661; Radio, TK6565.F5)*
  sa Comb filters
    Equalizers (Electronics)
    Microwave filters
    Radio filters
    Sound analyzers
  x Electric wave filters
    Wave filters, Electric
  xx Electric circuits
    Electric networks
    Signal theory (Telecommunication)
— Noise
— Tables, calculations, etc.

Electric fishes
    See Electric organs in fishes

Electric fishing
  x Electrofishing
    Fishing, Electric
  xx Fisheries
    Fisheries—Equipment and supplies
    Fishing
— Safety measures

Electric furnaces *(Chemistry, QD157,*
    QD277; Electric engineering,
    TK4661; Metallurgy, TN681-7;
    Metallurgy of iron and steel, TN706)
  sa Electric kilns
    Electron beam furnaces
  xx Chemistry, Inorganic
    Chemistry—Manipulation
    Electric heating
    Furnaces
— Appraisal
    See Electric furnaces—Valuation
— Automatic control
— Design and construction
— Materials
— Mathematical models *(TN687)*
— Protective atmospheres
  xx Protective atmospheres
— Standards
— Tables, calculations, etc.
— Valuation
  x Electric furnaces—Appraisal

Electric fuses *(TK3511; Switchboards,*
    TK2846)
  sa Fuses (Ordnance)
  x Fuses, Electric
  xx Electric apparatus and appliances—
    Protection
— Programmed instruction
— Standards

Electric gages
  xx Electric measurements
    Gages
— Testing

Electric generators
    See Dynamos

Electric heating *(TK4601-4661)*
  sa Dielectric heating
    Electric furnaces
    Electric water heaters
    Induction heating
    Infra-red heating
    Infra-red rays—Industrial applications
    Microwave heating
    Resistance heating
  xx Heating

Electric household appliances
    See Household appliances, Electric

Electric ignition of gas
    See Gas—Electric ignition

Electric ignition of vapors
    See Vapors—Electric ignition

Electric impedance plethysmography
    See Impedance plethysmography

Electric industrial trucks
    See Industrial electric trucks

Electric industries *(Direct) (Economics,*
    HD9685-9697; Technology, TK)
  sa Electric contracting
    Electric industry workers
    Electric machinery industry
    Electric utilities
    Electric wire and cable industry
    Electrochemistry, Industrial
    Electronic industries
    individual electric articles and
      industries, e.g. Household appliances,
      Electric; Radio industry and trade
  x Industries, Electric
  xx Electrification
— Accounting *(HF5686.E3)*
— Automation
— Collective bargaining
    See Collective bargaining—Electric
      industries
— Collective labor agreements
    See Collective labor agreements—
      Electric industries

— Employees
  See Electric industry workers
— Equipment and supplies
— Exhibitions *(TK6)*
  x Electricity—Exhibitions
    Exhibitions, Electrical
— Finance *(HG4029.E4)*
— Fires and fire prevention
— Hygienic aspects
— Labor productivity
— Management
— Production control
— Production standards
— Quality control
— Safety measures
— Safety regulations *(Direct)*
— Subcontracting *(Direct)*
— Taxation
— Trade-marks
— Vocational guidance
  sa Electric engineering as a profession
  xx Electric engineering as a profession
Electric industry workers *(Direct)*
  sa Collective bargaining—Electric
    industries
    Collective bargaining—Electric utilites
    Collective labor agreements—Electric
      industries
    Electricians
    Electronic technicians
    Trade-unions—Electric industry
      workers
    Trade-unions—Electricians
    Wages—Electric industry workers
  x Electric industries—Employees
    Electric utilities—Employees
    Electric workers
  xx Electric industries
    Electric utilities
— Job descriptions
Electric instrument transformers *(TK2794)*
  x Instrument transformers, Electric
  xx Electric transformers
— Testing *(TK2794)*
Electric insulators and insulation
    *(Engineering, TK3331-3441; Physics,
    QC611)*
  sa Breakdown (Electricity)
    Dielectrics
    Electric cables—Plastic insulation
    Electric wire, Insulated
    Electronic apparatus and appliances—
      Plastic embedment
    Insulating oils
    Insulating paper
    Insulating varnish
    Vulcanized fiber
  x Bushings
    Insulation (Electric)
  xx Dielectrics
    Electric resistance
    Insulating materials
— Cold weather conditions
— Collectors and collecting
— Defects
— Deterioration
— Laboratory manuals
— Moisture
— Prices *(Direct)*
— Standards
— Testing *(TK3431)*
Electric insulators and insulation, Effect of
    radiation on
  See Dielectrics, Effect of radiation on
Electric interference
  sa Dawn chorus (Radio meteorology)
    Hiss (Radio meteorology)
    Radar—Interference

Radio—Interference
    Television—Interference
  x Interference (Electricity)
  xx Electric noise
Electric inverters *(Electric engineering,
    TK2699; Electronics, TK7872.I65)*
  x Inverters, Electric
  xx Electric current converters
Electric irons
  x Irons, Electric
  xx Household appliances, Electric
    Irons (Pressing)
    Pressing of garments
Electric kilns *(TP841)*
  x Kilns, Electric
  xx Electric furnaces
    Kilns
Electric laboratories *(Engineering,
    TK411-415; Physics, QC541)*
  x Electricity—Laboratories
    Laboratories, Electric
  xx Electric testing
    Physical laboratories
    Testing laboratories
— Apparatus and supplies
Electric lamp industry *(Direct)*
Electric lamps *(TK4310-4399)*
  sa Electric lighting
    Germicidal lamps
  x Glow-lamps
  xx Electric lighting
    Lamps
— Amateurs' manuals *(TK9921)*
— Prices *(Direct)*
— Standards
Electric lamps, Arc *(TK4321-4335)*
  sa Electric arc
    Electric lighting, Arc
  x Arc lamps
  xx Electric lighting, Arc
Electric lamps, Fluorescent
  See Fluorescent lamps
Electric lamps, Incandescent *(TK4351-4367)*
  sa Electric lighting, Incandescent
    Iodine incandescent lamps
    Neon lamps
    Nernst lamp
    Tantalum lamp
    Tungsten lamp
  x Incandescent lamps
  xx Electric lighting, Incandescent
    Neon lamps
— Filaments *(TK4365)*
  x Filaments for electric lamps
— Patents
— Testing *(TK4367)*
Electric lamps, Portable *(Mining, TN307)*
  x Portable electric lamps
  xx Mine lighting
Electric leakage *(QC702)*
  sa Electric action of points
  xx Electric action of points
Electric levitation
  See Electric suspension
Electric light
  See Electric lighting
    Photometry
    Phototherapy
Electric light, Candle power of *(TK4175)*
Electric light and power industry
  See Electric utilities
Electric light carbons *(Manufacture, TK7725;
    Use, TK4335)*
  x Carbons (Electric light)
  xx Carbon
Electric light fixtures *(TH7960-7967)*
Electric light in photography
  See Photography—Artificial light

Photography—Portraits—Lighting and
    posing
Electric light plants *(Direct)*
    (TK4201-4238)
— Contracts and specifications *(TK4181)*
Electric lighting *(Direct) (TK4131-4399)*
  sa Electric discharge lighting
    Electric lamps
    Electric utilities
    Emergency lighting
    Floodlighting
    Garden lighting
    Library architecture—Lighting
    Lighting, Architectural and decorative
    Neon lamps
    Printing plants—Lighting
    Railroads—Cars—Lighting
  x Electric light
    Light, Electric
  xx Electric engineering
    Electric lamps
    Lighting
    Neon lamps
  Note under Electric utilities
— Accounting
  See Electric utilities—Accounting
— Amateurs' manuals *(TK9921)*
— Catalogs of supplies, etc. *(TK4195-8)*
  x Electric engineering—Catalogs of
    supplies, etc.
  xx Electric apparatus and appliances—
    Catalogs
— Contracts and specifications *(TK4181)*
— Early works to 1870 *(TK4160)*
— Installation *(TK4255)*
  sa Electric lighting—Wiring
  xx Electric wiring
— Insurance requirements *(TK3275)*
  xx Electric wiring
    Electric wiring—Insurance
      requirements
— Laboratory manuals
— Machinery *(TK4241)*
— Materials *(TK4169)*
— Rates
  See Electric utilities—Rates
— Safety measures *(TK152)*
— Tables, calculations, etc.
— Wiring *(TK4255)*
  x Wiring, Electric
  xx Electric lighting—Installation
    Electric wiring
Electric lighting, Arc *(TK4311-4335)*
  sa Brush arc-light system
    Electric lamps, Arc
  x Arc light
  xx Electric lamps, Arc
Electric lighting, Cadmium vapor *(TK4381)*
  x Cadmium-vapor electric lighting
  xx Electric discharge lighting
Electric lighting, Fluorescent
  See Fluorescent lighting
Electric lighting, Incandescent
    (TK4341-4367)
  sa Electric lamps, Incandescent
  x Incandescent electric lighting
    Incandescent lighting
  xx Electric lamps, Incandescent
Electric lighting, Mercury vapor *(TK4381)*
  x Mercury electric light
  xx Electric discharge lighting
Electric lighting, Sodium vapor *(TK4381)*
  x Sodium-vapor light
  xx Electric discharge lighting
Electric lighting of ships *(VM493)*
  sa Electricity on ships
  xx Electricity on ships
    Ships—Lighting

Electric lighting of ships *(VM493)*
(Continued)
    Ships' lights
Electric lines *(TK3201-3261)*
    Here are entered works on general trans-
      mission systems, their construction
      and properties.
  sa Electric cables
    Electric circuits
    Electric conduits
    Electric networks
    Electric wiring
    Telegraph lines
    Telephone lines
  x Electric power transmission
    Electricity—Distribution
    Electricity—Transmission
    Power transmission, Electric
  xx Electric cables
    Electric power distribution
  Note under Electric wiring
— Environmental aspects *(Direct)*
— Estimates *(Direct)*
— Ice prevention
  x Ice on electric lines
    Icing of electric lines
  xx Ice prevention
— Law and legislation *(Direct)*
— Models *(TK3226)*
  x Model networks
  xx Electric engineering
    Electric power distribution
— Overhead *(TK3231-3248)*
  x Overhead electric lines
    Overhead power lines
— — Corrosion
— — Right of way
    x Right of way (Overhead electric
      lines)
— — Safety measures
— — Testing *(TK3207)*
— Poles and towers *(TK3242-3)*
  x Electric lines—Towers and poles
    Poles, Electric line
  xx Building, Iron and steel
    Towers
    Wood poles
— — Corrosion
— — Standards
— — Transportation
— Problems, exercises, etc.
— Protection
— Repairing
— Safety measures
— Testing *(TK3207; TK3307)*
  xx Electric testing
— Towers and poles
  See Electric lines—Poles and towers
— Underground *(TK3251-3261)*
  x Underground lines (Trolleys)
— — Corrosion
Electric locomotives *(TF975)*
  sa Railroad motor-cars
    Railroads—Electrification
  xx Electric railroads—Rolling-stock
    Locomotives
    Railroads—Electrification
  Note under Railroads—Electric equipment
— Batteries
— Brakes
— Cooling
— Dynamics
— Electric equipment
— — Drawings
— Gearing
  See Electric locomotives—
      Transmission devices
— Juvenile literature
— Maintenance and repair

  x Electric locomotives—Repairs
  xx Electric railroads—Maintenance and
    repair
— — Production standards
— Mathematical models
— Repairs
  See Electric locomotives—
      Maintenance and repair
— Springs and suspension
— Testing
— Transmission devices
  x Electric locomotives—Gearing
  xx Gearing
Electric logging (Oil wells)
  See Oil well logging, Electric
Electric machinery *(TK2000-2799)*
  sa Brushes, Carbon '
    Brushes, Electric
    Commutation (Electricity)
    Dynamos
    Electric controllers
    Electric current converters
    Electric cutting machinery
    Electric driving
    Electric motors
    Electric transformers
    Electricity in mining
    Oscillators, Electric
  xx Electric engineering
    Electromechanical devices
    Machinery
  Note under Electric machines
— Alternating current *(TK2711-2799)*
  sa Dynamos—Alternating current
    Electric machinery, Synchronous
    Phase converters
  x Alternating current machinery
— Appraisal
  See Electric machinery—Valuation
— Cooling *(TK2189)*
— Design and construction *(TK2331)*
— Direct current *(TK2611-2699)*
  sa Dynamos—Direct current
    Electric motors, Direct current
  x Direct current machinery
  xx Electric currents, Direct
— — Design and construction *(TK2625)*
— — Problems, exercises, etc.
— Drawing *(TK2325)*
  xx Electric drafting
— Dynamics
— Laboratory manuals
— Maintenance and repair *(TK2189)*
— Mathematical models
— Motive power *(TK2081)*
— Noise
— Packing
— Patents *(TK257)*
— Polyphase *(TK2745)*
  x Polyphase currents
— Prices *(Direct)*
— Problems, exercises, etc.
— Protection
— Regulation *(TK2851)*
— Reliability
— Safety measures
— Standards *(TK2311)*
— Storage
— Tables, calculations, etc.
— Testing *(TK401; TK2316)*
  xx Electric testing
— Transportation
— Valuation
  x Electric machinery—Appraisal
— Vibration
— Windings
— — Maintenance and repair

Electric machinery, Explosionproof
  x Explosionproof electric machinery
Electric machinery, Synchronous *(TK2731)*
  sa Electric motors, Synchronous
    Synchros
  xx Electric machinery—Alternating
    current
— Programmed instruction
Electric machinery industry *(Direct)*
  xx Electric industries
    Machinery—Trade and manufacture
— Automation
— Employees
— Equipment and supplies
— Management
— Mathematical models
— Prices *(Direct)*
— Safety measures
Electric machines *(QC573)*
  Here are entered works on machines for
    generating static electricity by friction
    or induction. Material dealing with
    dynamo-electric machinery is entered
    under Electric machinery.
  x Electricity, Static
    Influence machines
    Static electricity
  xx Electrostatic apparatus and appliances
    Electrostatics
    Electrotherapeutics—Apparatus and
      instruments
Electric machining
  See Electric metal-cutting
Electric measurements *(Electric engineering,*
    TK275-399; Physics, QC535)
  sa Bridge circuits
    Cathode ray oscilloscope
    Electric gages
    Electric meters
    Electric testing
    Electronic measurements
    Fluxmeter
    Galvanometer
    Inductance
    Mutual inductance
    Oil well logging, Electric
    Photoelectric measurements
    Radio measurements
    Self-inductance
    Strain gages
    Wheatstone bridge
  x Measurements, Electric
  xx Electric currents
    Electric testing
    Electricity—Laboratory manuals
    Electromagnetic measurements
    Electronic measurements
    Galvanometer
    Ohm's law
    Physical measurements
    Weights and measures
— Laboratory manuals
— Law and legislation *(Direct)*
— Problems, exercises, etc.
— Statistical methods
Electric-mechanical devices
  See Electromechanical devices
Electric membrane process of desalinization
  See Saline water conversion—
      Electrodialysis process
Electric metal-cutting
  sa Plasma arc cutting
  x Electric discharge machining
    Electric machining
    Electric spark machining
    Spark-erosion machining
  xx Metal-cutting

Electric meters *(TK301-399)*
sa Ammeter
  Current balance (Electric meter)
  Frequency meters
  Ohmmeter
  Phasemeter
  Ratiometer (Electric meter)
  Spectrum analyzers
  Voltmeter
  Voltohmmeter
  Watt-hour meter
  Wattmeter
x Meters, Electric
xx Electric measurements
— Repairing
— Standards
— Testing
Electric meters, Recording *(TK393)*
— Standards *(Direct)*
Electric motors *(TK2511-2541; Alternating current, TK2781-9; Direct current, TK2681; Use, TK4055-8)*
sa Armatures
  Automobiles, Electric
  Electric propulsion
  Electric railway motors
  Electric transformers
  Electric vehicles
  Electricity in mining
  Frequency changers
  Industrial electric trucks
  Stepping motors
  Trolley buses—Motors
xx Electric machinery
  Motors
— Amateurs' manuals *(TK9911)*
— Design and construction *(TK2435)*
— — Juvenile literature
— Lubrication
— Prices *(Direct)*
— Protection
— Reliability
— Repairing *(TK4057; Electric railways, TF935)*
— Rewinding
  See Electric motors—Windings
— Safety measures
— Standards
— Starting devices *(TK2541)*
— — Standards *(Direct)*
— Testing *(TK2433)*
  xx Electric testing
— Vibration
— Windings *(TK2474-7)*
  sa Electric motors, Alternating current —Windings
  Electric motors, Induction— Windings
  Electric transformers—Windings
  x Electric motors—Rewinding
  Rewinding of electric motors
  Windings (Electric motors)
  xx Armatures
Electric motors, Alternating current *(TK2781-9)*
sa Electric motors, Induction
  Electric motors, Polyphase
  Electric motors, Synchronous
— Maintenance and repair
— Windings
  sa Electric motors, Induction— Windings
  xx Electric motors—Windings
Electric motors, Asynchronous
  See Electric motors, Induction
Electric motors, Capacitor
  See Capacitor motors

Electric motors, Direct current *(TK2681)*
x Direct current machinery
xx Electric machinery—Direct current
— Maintenance and repair
Electric motors, Fractional horsepower *(TK2537)*
x Fractional horsepower electric motors
Electric motors, Induction *(TK2785)*
sa Capacitor motors
  Squirrel cage motors
x Asynchronous electric motors
  Electric motors, Asynchronous
  Induction motors
xx Electric motors, Alternating current
— Maintenance and repair
— Mathematical models
— Reliability
— Safety appliances
— Testing
— Windings
  xx Electric motors, Alternating current —Windings
  Electric motors—Windings
Electric motors, Polyphase *(TK2785)*
xx Electric motors, Alternating current
Electric motors, Reluctance
  See Reluctance motors
Electric motors, Repulsion *(TK2789)*
Electric motors, Series-wound
x Series-wound electric motors
Electric motors, Synchronous *(TK2787)*
sa Reluctance motors
x Synchronous motors
xx Electric machinery, Synchronous
  Electric motors, Alternating current
— Reliability
Electric musical instruments
  See Musical instruments, Electronic
Electric network analyzers *(TK3001; Alternating current, TK3141; Direct current, TK3111)*
x Calculating boards, Network
  Electric power distribution—Network analyzers
  Model networks
  Network analyzers
xx Electric engineering
  Electric power distribution
  Electromechanical analogies
  Electronic analog computers
Electric networks *(TK3226)*
sa Bus conductors (Electricity)
  Electric filters
  Equalizers (Electronics)
  Gyrators
  Switching theory
x Network theory
  Networks, Electric
xx Electric circuits
  Electric lines
  Electric power distribution
  System analysis
— Computer programs
— Laboratory manuals
— Problems, exercises, etc.
— Programmed instruction
Electric noise
sa Current noise (Electricity)
  Electric interference
  Electronic noise
  Telephone—Noise
x Noise, Electric
xx Electric currents
  Electronic noise
  Oscillations
Electric organs in fishes *(QP348)*
sa Electric eel
x Electric fishes

Fishes, Electric
xx Electrophysiology
  Fishes—Anatomy
Electric organs in insects *(QP348)*
xx Electrophysiology
  Insects
Electric oscillators
  See Oscillators, Electric
Electric potential
  See Electric currents
  Electromotive force
  Electrostatics
  Potential, Theory of
Electric power *(Distribution, TK3001-3511; Machinery, TK2000-2941; Production, TK1001-1831; Uses, TK4001-9971)*
sa Electric driving
  Electronic apparatus and appliances— Power supply
  Telephone—Power supply
xx Electrification
  Power (Mechanics)
  Power resources
Note under Electric utilities
— Costs
  See Electric utilities—Costs
— Interruptions
  See Electric power failures
— Juvenile literature
— Law and legislation
  See Electric utilities—Law and legislation
— Rates
  See Electric utilities—Rates
— Statistics *(Direct)*
  xx Electric utilities—Statistics
— Tables, calculations, etc.
— Taxation
  See Electric utilities—Taxation
— Terminology
Electric power development
  See Electrification
Electric power distribution *(Direct)* *(TK3001-3511)*
sa Electric conduits
  Electric lines
  Electric lines—Models
  Electric network analyzers
  Electric networks
  Electric substations
  Electric wiring
  Interconnected electric utility systems
  Interconnected electric utility systems —Automation
  Rural electrification
x Electric power transmission
  Electricity—Distribution
  Electricity—Transmission
  Power distribution, Electric
  Power transmission, Electric
xx Electric engineering
  Electric power systems
  Electrification
  Power transmission
  Water-power electric plants
— Alternating current *(TK3141-3171)*
— Automation
— Communication systems *(TK3091)*
— Costs
— Direct current *(TK3111)*
  x Direct current power distribution
  xx Electric currents, Direct
— Grounding
  See Electric currents—Grounding
— High tension *(TK3144)*
  x High-tension power distribution
— — Computer programs

Electric power distribution *(Direct)*
    (TK3001-3511)
  — High tension *(TK3144)*
  (Continued)
  — — Safety appliances
  — Juvenile literature
  — Mathematical models
  — Multiphase *(TK3158)*
  — Network analyzers
    See Electric network analyzers
  — Polycyclic *(TK3159)*
  — Problems, exercises, etc.
  — Reliability
  — Tables, calculations, etc.
Electric power factor *(TK153)*
  x Power factor, Electric
Electric power failures *(TK3091)*
  x Blackouts, Electric power
    Electric power interruptions
    Electric power—Interruptions
    Power blackouts
    Power failures
Electric power in mining
  See Electricity in mining
Electric power industry
  See Electric utilities
Electric power interruptions
  See Electric power failures
Electric power-plants *(Direct)*
    (TK1191-1831)
  sa Atomic power-plants
    Diesel electric power-plants
    Electric railroads—Substations
    Interconnected electric utility systems
    Power (Mechanics)—Statistics
    Telephone—Power-plants
    Water-power electric plants
  x Power-plants, Electric
  — Automation
  — Combined hydroelectric and steam
    See Hydrothermal electric power
      systems
  — Communication systems
  — Contracts and specifications *(TK1191)*
  — Costs
  — Design and construction
  — — Safety measures
  — Dust control
  — Environmental aspects *(Direct)*
    (TD195.E4)
    xx Environmental engineering
      Pollution
  — Equipment and supplies
  — — Maintenance and repair
  — — Protection
  — Fires and fire prevention *(TH9445.E4)*
  — Fuel consumption
  — Heating and ventilation
    x Electric power-plants—Ventilation
  — Juvenile literature
  — Lighting
  — Load
    sa Interconnected electric utility
      systems—Automation
    x Load (Electric power)
  — — Electromechanical analogies
  — — Mathematical models
  — Location
  — Management *(TK1811)*
  — Protection
  — Reliability
  — Safety regulations *(Direct)*
  — Testing *(TK1831)*
    xx Electric testing
  — Valuation
  — Ventilation
    See Electric power-plants—Heating
      and ventilation
  — Water-supply

Electric power-plants, Portable
  x Portable electric power-plants
  — Safety measures
Electric power pooling
  See Interconnected electric utility systems
Electric power production *(TK1001-1831)*
  sa Direct energy conversion
    Electric railroads—Current supply
    Electronic apparatus and appliances—
      Current supply
    Hydrothermal electric power systems
    Radio—Current supply
    Telecommunication—Current supply
    Telegraph—Current supply
    Telephone—Current supply
  x Power production, Electric
  xx Electric engineering
    Electric power systems
    Electrification
    Water-power electric plants
**Electric power production from chemical
    action** *(TK2901)*
  sa Fuel cells
  xx Direct energy conversion
Electric power system stability
  x Stability of electric power systems
  xx Transients (Electricity)
Electric power systems *(Direct)*
    Here are entered works on the complex
      assemblage of equipment and circuits
      for generating, transmitting, trans-
      forming, and distributing electric en-
      ergy.
  sa Electric power distribution
    Electric power production
    Interconnected electric utility systems
  xx Electric engineering
  — Automation
  — Communication systems
    xx Telecommunication
  — Design and construction
  — Electromechanical analogies
  — Management
  — — Forms
  — Mathematical models
  — Protection
    sa Protective relays
  — Reliability
  — Safety measures
  — Terminology
Electric power transmission
  See Electric lines
    Electric power distribution
Electric precipitation
  See Electrostatic precipitation
Electric properties, Lunar
  See Moon—Electric properties
Electric properties of materials
  See subdivision Electric properties *under
    names of particular materials or
    substances, e.g.* Ice—Electric
    properties; Marble—Electric
    properties
Electric propulsion
  xx Electric motors
Electric propulsion of space vehicles
  See Space vehicles—Electric propulsion
    systems
Electric prospecting
  sa Earth resistance
  x Geo-electric prospecting
    Prospecting—Electric methods
  xx Prospecting—Geophysical methods
  — Charts, diagrams, etc.
  — Equipment and supplies
  — Problems, exercises, etc.
  — Tables, calculations, etc.

Electric protective apparatus
  See Electric apparatus and appliances—
    Protection
Electric pumps
  See Pumping machinery, Electric
Electric radiation *(QC483)*
  sa Blackbody radiation
  x Radiation, Electric
Electric railroads *(Indirect) (TF855-1124;
    Interurban, HE5351-5600;
    Street-railroads, HE4201-5300)*
    For general works only. Works on electric
      street-railroads in a particular locality
      are entered under Street-railroads—
      [local subdivision]
  sa Electric railway motors
    Railroads—Electrification
    Street-railroads
    Trolley buses
  x Electric street-railroads
    Railroads, Electric
  xx Electric engineering
    Electricity in transportation
    Public utilities
    Railroads
    Railroads—Electrification
    Street-railroads
    Transportation
  — Accidents
    x Railway accidents
  — Accounting *(HE4351)*
  — Automation
  — Brakes *(TF949.B7)*
    Example under Brakes
  — Cars *(TF920-949)*
    sa Electric railroads—Rolling-stock
    x Street-cars
      Street-railroads—Cars
    xx Electric railroads—Rolling-stock
      Railroads—Cars
  — — Catalogs
  — — Equipment and supplies
  — — Maintenance and repair
    xx Electric railroads—Maintenance
      and repair
  — — — Production standards
  — — Models
  — — Museums
    x Trolley museums
    Example under Transportation mu-
      seums
  — — Pictorial works
  — — Sounds
    xx Railroad sounds
      Sounds
  — Clearances
    x Clearances (Electric railroads)
    xx Electric railroads—Wires and wiring
  — Communication systems
    xx Telecommunication
  — Construction *(TF863-900)*
  — Contracts and specifications *(Direct)*
    (TF857)
  — Cost of construction *(TF857)*
  — Current supply
    xx Electric power production
  — Electromechanical analogies
  — Electronic equipment
    xx Electric railroads—Equipment and
      supplies
    Electronic apparatus and appliances
  — — Reliability
  — Employees *(Street-railroads, HE4311;
    Trade-union periodicals,
    HD6350.S8)*
  — Equipment and supplies *(TF920-952)*
    sa Electric railroads—Electronic
      equipment

—— Catalogs *(TF952)*
    x Electric engineering—Catalogs of
        supplies, etc.
    xx Electric apparatus and appliances
        —Catalogs
—— Protection
— Finance *(HE4351)*
— Freight *(TF970)*
    x Street-railroads—Freight
    xx Freight and freightage
— Juvenile literature
— Law *(Direct)*
    xx Railroad law
— Maintenance and repair
    sa Electric locomotives—Maintenance
        and repair
        Electric railroads—Cars—
        Maintenance and repair
—— Production standards
— Management *(TF960-962)*
— Mathematical models
— Models *(TF197)*
— Motormen's manuals *(TF965)*
— Motors
    See Electric railway motors
— Pantograph
    x Pantograph (Current collector)
— Rails *(TF872)*
    x Rails (Railroads)
—— Welding
— Rolling-stock
    sa Electric locomotives
        Electric railroads—Cars
    x Rolling-stock
    xx Electric railroads—Cars
—— Electric equipment
—— Reliability
— Safety measures
— Safety regulations *(Direct)*
— Signaling
—— Block system
— Standards *(Direct)*
— Substations *(TF863)*
    xx Electric power-plants
— Switches
    x Switches, Electric railroad
    xx Railroads—Switches
— Testing *(TF857)*
    xx Electric testing
— Third rail *(TF890)*
    x Third-rail railroads
— Train speed
    x Train speed
— Trains
— Trolley-wheels *(TF885)*
    x Trolley-wheels
    xx Wheels
— Wires and wiring *(TF880-900)*
    sa Electric railroads—Clearances
    x Wiring, Electric
    xx Electric wiring
—— Standards *(Direct)*
Electric railroads, Miniature *(TF857)*
    x Miniature electric railroads
    xx Miniature objects
Electric railway motors *(TF935)*
    x Electric railroads—Motors
        Street railway motors
    xx Electric motors
        Electric railroads
        Motors
— Design and construction
— Maintenance and repair
— Testing
— Windings
Electric razors
    See Electric shavers

Electric reactors *(TK2851)*
    sa Magnetic amplifiers
    x Reactors, Electric
    xx Electric controllers
        Reactance (Electricity)
— Standards *(Direct)*
Electric relays
    sa Differential relays
        Electric contactors
        Protective relays
        Static relays
        Telephone relays
    x Relays, Electric
    xx Electric circuit-breakers
        Electric switchgear
— Problems, exercises, etc.
— Standards
— Testing
Electric resistance *(QC611)*
    sa Earth resistance
        Electric insulators and insulation
        Electric resistors
        Electrolytes—Conductivity
        Impedance (Electricity)
        Magnetoresistance
        Photoelectricity
        Reactance (Electricity)
        Wheatstone bridge
    x Resistance, Electric
    xx Impedance (Electricity)
        Photoelectricity
        Reactance (Electricity)
Electric resistance heating
    See Resistance heating
Electric resistors *(Electric machinery,*
    TK2851; Radio, TK6565.R)
    sa Ballasts (Electricity)
        Electrodes
        Radio resistors
        Strain gages
        Thermistors
        Varistors
        Voltage dividers
    x Resistors, Electric
    xx Electric apparatus and appliances
        Electric conductors
        Electric contactors
        Electric resistance
        Electrodes
— Calibration
— Patents
— Standards
Electric resonators *(Electric waves, QC655;*
    Radio, TK6565.R43)
    sa Radio resonators
    x Resonators, Electric
Electric rheostats *(TK2851)*
    sa Electric controllers
    x Rheostats, Electric
    xx Electric controllers
— Standards *(Direct)*
Electric rocket engines *(TL783.5)*
    sa Arc-jet rocket engines
        Ion rockets
        Photon rockets
        Plasma rockets
        Space vehicles—Electric propulsion
        systems
    x Electric rocket propulsion
    xx Magnetohydrodynamic generators
        Particle accelerators
        Rocket engines
— Design and construction
Electric rocket propulsion
    See Electric rocket engines
Electric sensing zone method
    See Coulter principle

Electric shavers *(TT967)*
    x Electric razors
        Shavers, Electric
    xx Razors
        Shaving
— Maintenance and repair
Electric ship propulsion
    See Ship propulsion, Electric
Electric shock
    sa Electricity, Injuries from
        Electrocution
    xx Electricity, Injuries from
        Electrocution
        Electrotherapeutics
        Shock
Electric shock therapy *(RC485)*
    x Electroconvulsive shock therapy
        Electroshock therapy
    xx Shock therapy
Electric signal theory
    See Signal theory (Telecommunication)
Electric signs *(TK4399.S6)*
    x Signs (Advertising)
    xx Signs and sign-boards
        Street signs
Electric slag process
    See Electroslag process
Electric space vehicles
    See Space vehicles—Electric propulsion
        systems
Electric spark *(QC703)*
    sa Electric arc
        Lichtenberg figures
    x Spark, Electric
    xx Electric discharges
        Sparks
Electric spark cutting
    See Electric cutting machinery
Electric spark machining
    See Electric metal-cutting
Electric standards *(QC537)*
    x Standards, Electric
    xx Electric units
        Weights and measures
Electric steel
    See Steel, Electrical
Electric stimulation
    x Stimulation, Electric
    xx Electricity in medicine
        Electrotherapeutics
Electric stoves
    See Stoves, Electric
Electric street-railroads
    See Electric railroads
        Street-railroads
Electric substations *(TK1751)*
    sa Street-railroads—Electric substations
    x Stations, Electric (Substations)
        Substations, Electric
    xx Electric power distribution
— Charts, diagrams, etc.
— Lighting
Electric surge
    See Transients (Electricity)
Electric suspension
    x Electric bearings
        Electric levitation
        Suspension, Electric
    xx Bearings (Machinery)
Electric switches
    See Electric switchgear
Electric switchgear *(TK2821-2846)*
    sa Bus conductors (Electricity)
        Electric apparatus and appliances—
        Protection
        Electric contactors
        Electric contacts
        Electric cut-outs

Electric switchgear *(TK2821-2846)*
  (Continued)
        Electric relays
        Mercury switches
        Static relays
        Switching theory
        Telephone switchboards
        Thyristors
        Vacuum switches
    x Electric switches
        Switches, Electric
  — Testing
Electric telegraph
  See Telegraph
Electric testing *(TK401)*
    sa Electric discharges—Detection
        Electric engineering—Laboratory
          manuals
        Electric laboratories
        Electric measurements
        Electricity—Laboratory manuals
        subdivision Testing *under* Electric lines,
          Electric machinery, Electric motors,
          Electric power-plants, Electric
          railroads, Electric transformers,
          Electric wire, *and* Electric wire,
          Insulated
    xx Electric measurements
        Electricity—Laboratory manuals
        Testing
Electric thermometry
  See Thermometers and thermometry
Electric tools, Portable
  See Power tools
Electric toys *(TK9971)*
    xx Toys
Electric traction canal-boats
  See Canal-boats—Electric traction
Electric tractors, Industrial
  See Industrial electric trucks
Electric transformers *(TK2551)*
    sa Aluminum cell
        Electric current rectifiers
        Electric instrument transformers
        Electronic transformers
        Radio transformers
        Television transformers
        Vibrator transformers
    x Transformers, Electric
    xx Electric currents
        Electric machinery
        Electric motors
  — Cooling
  — Design and construction
  — Marketing
  — Noise
  — Patents
  — Problems, exercises, etc.
  — Reliability
  — Repairing
  — Testing *(TK2551)*
      xx Electric testing
  — Transportation
  — Vibration
  — Windings
      xx Electric motors—Windings
Electric transformers, Explosionproof
        (TK2794)
    x Explosionproof electric transformers
Electric transient phenomena
  See Transients (Electricity)
Electric trucks, Industrial
  See Industrial electric trucks
Electric units *(QC536)*
    sa Electric standards
    x Farad
    xx Units

Electric utilities *(Direct)* *(HD9685)*
        Here are entered economic works on the
        sale and distribution of electricity for
        lighting and power purposes. Techni-
        cal works are entered under Electric
        engineering; Electric lighting; Electric
        power; etc.
    sa Electric industry workers
        Electrification
        Interconnected electric utility systems
        Rural electrification
    x Electric light and power industry
        Electric power industry
    xx Electric industries
        Public utilities
  — Accidents
  — Accounting
      x Electric lighting—Accounting
  — Collective bargaining
      See Collective bargaining—Electric
            utilities
  — Costs
      x Electric power—Costs
  — Defense measures *(UA929.95.E4)*
  — Employees
      See Electric industry workers
  — Finance
  — Government ownership *(Direct)*
      x Government ownership of electric
            utilities
  — Labor productivity
  — Law and legislation *(Direct)*
      x Electric power—Law and legislation
  — Management *(Direct)*
  — Mathematical models
  — Rates
      x Electric lighting—Rates
        Electric power—Rates
  — Research *(Direct)*
      xx Research, Industrial
  — Statistics
      sa Electric power—Statistics
  — Taxation *(Direct)*
      x Electric power—Taxation
      xx Public utilities—Taxation
Electric utility systems, Interconnected
  See Interconnected electric utility systems
Electric valves
  See Electron tubes
Electric vehicles
    sa Automobiles, Electric
        Industrial electric trucks
    x Vehicles, Electric
    xx Electric motors
        Electricity in transportation
        Motor vehicles
  — Standards *(Direct)*
Electric water heaters *(TH6561.5)*
    xx Electric heating
        Household appliances, Electric
        Water heaters
Electric wave filters
  See Electric filters
Electric waves *(QC661-5)*
    sa Coherer
        Decremeter
        Delay lines
        Electromagnetic waves
        Electrooptics
        Microwaves
        Radio measurements
        Radio, Short wave
        Radio waves
        Signal theory (Telecommunication)
        Telegraph, Wireless
        Telephone, Wireless
        Transients (Electricity)
        Wave guides

    x Hertzian waves
    xx Electromagnetic theory
        Electromagnetic waves
        Interference (Light)
        Telegraph, Wireless
        Waves
  — Damping *(QC665)*
      xx Damping (Mechanics)
  — Diffraction
      Example under Diffraction
  — Scattering
Electric welding *(TK4660)*
    sa Electroslag welding
    x Arc welding
        Electric arc welding
        Resistance welding
        Spot welding
    xx Welding
  — Automation *(TK4660)*
      x Automatic welding
  — Costs
      See Electric welding—Estimates and
            costs
  — Equipment and supplies
  — — Appraisal
      See Electric welding—Equipment
            and supplies—Valuation
  — — Maintenance and repair
  — — Valuation
      x Electric welding—Equipment and
            supplies—Appraisal
  — Estimates and costs *(Direct)*
      x Electric welding—Costs
  — Handbooks, manuals, etc.
  — Hygienic aspects
      See Welding—Hygienic aspects
  — Patents
  — Production standards
      Example under Production standards
  — Quality control
  — Safety measures
      See Welding—Safety measures
  — Standards
  — Tables, calculations, etc.
Electric well logging
  See Oil well logging, Electric
Electric wire *(TK3301-3351)*
    sa Electric cables
        Electric fences
        Electric wire and cable industry
        Telegraph wire
        Telephone wire
    xx Electric cables
        Electric conductors
        Wire
  — Corrosion
  — Standards *(TK3307)*
  — Testing *(TK3307)*
      xx Electric testing
  — Trade-marks
Electric wire, Insulated *(TK3331-3351)*
    xx Electric insulators and insulation
  — Patents
  — Testing *(TK3335)*
      xx Electric testing
Electric wire and cable industry *(Direct)*
    x Electric cable industry
    xx Electric cables
        Electric industries
        Electric wire
  — Automation
  — Production control
Electric wiring *(TK3201-3285)*
        Works on the design and construction of
        general transmission systems are en-
        tered under Electric lines.
    sa Aeroplanes—Electric wiring
        Automobiles—Electric wiring

Electric cables
Electric conduits
Electric lighting—Installation
Electric lighting—Insurance
  requirements
Electric lighting—Wiring
Electric railroads—Wires and wiring
Lightning-arresters
Outlet boxes (Electric engineering)
Street-railroads—Wires and wiring
Telegraph lines
Telephone lines
Trolley buses—Wires and wiring
  x Wiring, Electric
  xx Electric cables
  Electric lines
  Electric power distribution
— Diagrams *(TK3205)*
  xx Electric drafting
— Estimates *(TK435)*
— Insurance requirements *(TK3275)*
  sa Electric engineering—Insurance
    requirements
  Electric lighting—Insurance
    requirements
— Problems, exercises, etc.
— Production standards
— Safety measures *(TK152; Indoor wiring,
    TK3275)*
— Tables, calculations, etc. *(TK3205)*
Electric wiring, Interior *(TK3271-3285)*
— Amateurs' manuals
— Diagrams *(TK3285)*
Electric workers
  See Electric industry workers
Electrical . . .
  See Electric . . .
Electrically exploded wires
  See Exploding wire phenomena
Electrically propelled space vehicles
  See Space vehicles—Electric propulsion
    systems
Electricians *(Direct) (Physics, QC514-515;
    Technology, TK139-140)*
  sa Trade-unions—Electric industry
    workers
  Trade-unions—Electricians
  Wages—Electricians
  xx Electric contracting
  Electric industry workers
— Licenses *(Direct)*
Electricity *(QC501-721)*
  sa Atmospheric electricity
  Electrons
  Hall effect
  High voltages
  Impedance (Electricity)
  Induction (Electricity)
  Lightning
  Magnetism
  Radioactivity
  Reactance (Electricity)
  Telegraph
  Telephone
  Thermoelectricity
  Thomson effect
  X-rays
    headings beginning with Electric *and*
      Electro
  x Galvanism
  xx Magnetism
  Mathematical physics
  Physics
— Accidents
    See Electricity, Injuries from
— Apparatus and appliances
    See Electric apparatus and appliances
— Bibliography *(Z5831-5)*

— — Catalogs
    Example under Catalogs
— Catalogs of supplies, etc.
    See Electric apparatus and appliances
      —Catalogs
— Discharges
    See Electric discharges
— Discharges through gases
    See Electric discharges through gases
— Distribution
    See Electric lines
— Early works to 1850 *(QC516-517)*
— Effect on plants
    See Plants, Effect of electricity on
— Examinations, questions, etc.
— Exhibitions
    See Electric industries—Exhibitions
— Experiments *(Popular works, QC527;
      Study and teaching, QC533-4)*
  xx Physics—Experiments
— — Juvenile literature
— Juvenile literature *(QC527)*
— Laboratories
    See Electric laboratories
— Laboratory manuals *(QC534)*
  sa Electric engineering—Laboratory
      manuals
  Electric measurements
  Electric testing
  xx Electric testing
— Laws and legislation
    See Electric engineering—Laws and
      legislation
— Mechanical analogies
    See Electromechanical analogies
— Notation
— Physiological effect
  sa Electrophysiology
  xx Electrophysiology
— Problems, exercises, etc. *(QC532)*
— Programmed instruction
— Religious aspects *(BL265.E6)*
  xx Religion and science
— Study and teaching (Secondary)
— Tables, etc. *(QC529)*
— Transmission
    See Electric engineering
      Electric lines
      Electric power distribution
Electricity, Animal
  See Electrophysiology
Electricity, Atmospheric
  See Atmospheric electricity
Electricity, Injuries from *(Direct) (Medical
      jurisprudence, RA1091; Treatment,
      RD96.5)*
  sa Electric shock
  x Electric accidents
  Electricity—Accidents
  Injuries from electricity
  xx Accidents
  Electric shock
  Electrophysiology
  Electrotherapeutics
  Industrial accidents
  Lightning
  Wounds
Electricity, Medical
  See Electrotherapeutics
Electricity, Piezo-
  See Pyro- and piezo-electricity
Electricity, Pyro-
  See Pyro- and piezo-electricity
Electricity, Static
  See Electric machines
  Electrostatics
Electricity in aeronautics *(TL690-691)*
  sa Aeroplanes—Electric equipment

Electronics in aeronautics
  xx Aeronautics
  Electricity in transportation
Electricity in agriculture *(TK4018)*
  sa Agricultural engineering
  Agricultural machinery—Electric
    equipment
  Electricity in forestry
  Electrohorticulture
  Farm buildings—Lighting
  xx Agricultural engineering
  Agricultural machinery
  Agriculture
  Farm mechanization
  Rural electrification
— Laboratory manuals
Electricity in astronautics
  sa Astrionics
  Ground support systems (Astronautics)
  Space stations—Electric equipment
  Space vehicles—Electric equipment
  x Astronautics, Electricity in
  xx Electric engineering
Electricity in building
  xx Electric engineering
Electricity in dentistry
  xx Dentistry
  Electrotherapeutics
Electricity in forestry
  xx Electricity in agriculture
Electricity in horticulture
  See Electrohorticulture
Electricity in medicine
  sa Electric stimulation
  Electrotherapeutics
  xx Medicine
Electricity in military engineering *(UG480)*
  xx Electric engineering
  Military engineering
Electricity in mining *(TN343)*
  sa Coal mines and mining—Electric
    equipment
  Mine lighting
  Mining engineering
  Mining machinery—Electric equipment
  x Electric power in mining
  Mining, Electric
  xx Electric engineering
  Electric machinery
  Electric motors
  Mining engineering
  Mining machinery
— Laboratory manuals
— Problems, exercises, etc.
Electricity in petroleum engineering
  xx Petroleum engineering
Electricity in surgery
  See Electrosurgery
Electricity in transportation
  sa Automobiles—Electric equipment
  Electric boats
  Electric railroads
  Electric vehicles
  Electricity in aeronautics
  Electricity on ships
  Motor buses—Electric equipment
  Railroads—Electric equipment
  Railroads—Electrification
  Subways—Electric equipment
  xx Transportation
— Juvenile literature
Electricity on ships *(VM471-9)*
  sa Electric lighting of ships
  River boats—Electric equipment
  Ship propulsion, Electric
  subdivision Electric installations *under
    navies, e.g.* United States. Navy—
    Electric installations

Electricity on ships *(VM471-9)*
   (Continued)
      x Ships, Electricity on
      xx Electric lighting of ships
         Electricity in transportation
         Marine engineering
         Naval architecture
      — Mathematical models
      — Safety measures
Electrification *(Direct)*
   sa Electric industries
      Electric power
      Electric power distribution
      Electric power production
      Railroads—Electrification
      Rural electrification
   x Electric power development
   xx Electric engineering
      Electric utilities
   — Pictorial works
Electrification, Rural
   See Rural electrification
Electrification of clouds
   See Cloud electrification
Electrification of railroads
   See Railroads—Electrification
Electro-acoustics *(TK5981)*
   sa Crosstalk
      Electroacoustic transducers
      Intercommunication systems
      Magnetic recorders and recording
      Musical instruments, Electronic
      Phonograph
      Vocoder
      Voder
   xx Acoustical engineering
      Architectural acoustics
      Electric engineering
      Music—Acoustics and physics
      Musical instruments, Electronic
      Phonograph
      Radio
      Sound
Electro-optical shutters
   See Kerr cell shutters
Electro-osmosis
   sa Electroosmotic dewatering
   x Electroendosmosis
      Electrosmosis
   xx Electrolysis
      Osmosis
Electroacoustic transducers
   sa Hydrophone
      Ultrasonic transducers
   xx Electro-acoustics
      Transducers
Electroanesthesia
   See Electric anesthesia
Electrobiology
   See Electrophysiology
Electrocapillary phenomena *(QC577)*
   xx Capillarity
Electrocardiography *(Medicine, RC683.5.E5)*
   sa Electrokymography
      Vectorcardiography
   xx Electrodiagnosis
      Heart—Diseases—Diagnosis
   — Cases, clinical reports, statistics
   — Programmed instruction
Electrochemical analysis *(QD115)*
   sa Conductometric analysis
      Coulometry
      Polarograph and polarography
      Voltammetry
   x Analysis, Electrochemical
      Analysis, Electrolytic
      Electrolytic analysis
   xx Chemistry, Analytic—Quantitative
      Electrochemistry

Electrolysis
Electrochemical apparatus
   sa Potentiostat
      Solions
   x Apparatus, Electrochemical
      Electrochemical instruments
   xx Chemical apparatus
      Electrochemistry
Electrochemical corrosion
   See Electrolytic corrosion
Electrochemical cutting
   sa Electrolytic grinding
   xx Metal-cutting
Electrochemical instruments
   See Electrochemical apparatus
Electrochemistry *(Organic chemistry,*
      QD273; Physical and theoretical
      chemistry, QD553-585)
   sa Electric batteries
      Electric double layer
      Electrochemical analysis
      Electrochemical apparatus
      Electroforming
      Electrolysis
      Electrometallurgy
      Electrophoresis
      Electroplating
      Electrotyping
      Fuel cells
      Magnetochemistry
      Petroleum products—Antistatic
         additives
      Reduction, Electrolytic
   xx Chemistry
      Chemistry, Physical and theoretical
      Chemistry, Technical
   — Laboratory manuals *(QD557)*
   — Popular works
   — Problems, exercises, etc.
   — Tables, etc. *(QD65)*
Electrochemistry, Industrial *(TP250-261)*
   sa Electrostatic precipitation
   x Industrial electrochemistry
   xx Chemicals—Manufacture and industry
      Electric industries
   — Quality control
   — Safety measures
Electrocoagulation
   xx Diathermy
Electroconvulsive shock therapy
   See Electric shock therapy
Electrocution *(HV8696)*
   sa Electric shock
   xx Capital punishment
      Electric shock
      Execution and executioners
Electrodeposition of alloys
   See Alloy plating
Electrodeposition of metals
   See Electroforming
      Electroplating
Electrodermal response
   See Galvanic skin response
Electrodes
   sa Cathodes
      Electric resistors
      Electron tubes—Grids
      Vacuum-tubes—Grids
   xx Electric resistors
   — Prices
   — Standards
Electrodes, Alkali metal
   x Alkali metal electrodes
Electrodes, Amalgam
   x Amalgam electrodes
   xx Electrodes, Mercury
Electrodes, Cadmium
   x Cadmium electrodes

Electrodes, Carbon *(TK7725)*
   x Carbon electrodes
Electrodes, Ceramic metal
   x Ceramic metal electrodes
Electrodes, Dropping mercury *(QD571)*
   x Dropping mercury electrodes
      Mercury dropping electrodes
   xx Electrodes, Mercury
Electrodes, Glass *(Electrochemistry, QD561)*
   x Glass electrodes
Electrodes, Iron
   x Iron electrodes
Electrodes, Mercury
   sa Electrodes, Amalgam
      Electrodes, Dropping mercury
   x Mercury electrodes
Electrodes, Nickel
   x Nickel electrodes
Electrodes, Oxide
   x Oxide electrodes
Electrodes, Oxygen
   x Oxygen electrodes
Electrodes, Palladium
   x Palladium electrodes
Electrodes, Platinum
   x Platinum electrodes
Electrodes, Zinc
   x Zinc electrodes
Electrodiagnosis *(RC77)*
   sa Diagnosis, Radioscopic
      Electrocardiography
      Electroencephalography
      Electromyography
   xx Diagnosis
      Diagnosis, Surgical
Electrodialysis
   sa Ion-permeable membranes
      Saline water conversion—
         Electrodialysis process
      Sewage—Purification—Electrodialysis
         process
   xx Dialysis
      Ion-permeable membranes
   — Electromechanical analogies
Electrodynamics *(QC631-645)*
   sa Cosmic electrodynamics
      Electrohydrodynamics
      Electromechanical devices
      Field-coupled surface waves
      Inductance
      Ion flow dynamics
      Magnetohydrodynamics
      Mutual inductance
      Self-inductance
      Vacuum polarization
      Wave mechanics
   xx Dynamics
   — Problems, exercises, etc.
Electrodynamics, Quantum
   See Quantum electrodynamics
Electrodynamometer *(QC544.E3)*
   xx Electric apparatus and appliances
   — Calibration *(QC544.E3)*
Electroencephalography
   sa Visual evoked response
   xx Brain—Diseases—Diagnosis
      Electrodiagnosis
      Electrophysiology
      Encephalography
      Visual evoked response
   — Mathematical models
Electroendosmosis
   See Electro-osmosis
Electrofishing
   See Electric fishing
Electrofluiddynamic generators
   See Electrohydrodynamic generators

Electrofluidynamics
  See Electrohydrodynamics
Electroforming
  sa Electroplating
     Electrotyping
  x Electrodeposition of metals
  xx Electrochemistry
     Electrometallurgy
     Electroplating
Electrogalvanizing
  See Zinc plating
Electrogasdynamic generators
  See Electrohydrodynamic generators
Electrogasdynamics
  See Electrohydrodynamics
Electrogastrography *(RC804.E4)*
  xx Electrophysiology
     Stomach—Diseases—Diagnosis
Electrohomeopathy *(RM891)*
  xx Homeopathy
Electrohorticulture *(SB139)*
  sa Plants, Effect of electricity on
  x Electricity in horticulture
  xx Electricity in agriculture
     Gardening
     Horticulture
Electrohydrodynamic generators *(TK2975)*
  x Electrofluiddynamic generators
     Electrogasdynamic generators
  xx Direct energy conversion
Electrohydrodynamics *(QC631)*
  x Electrofluidynamics
     Electrogasdynamics
  xx Electrodynamics
     Fluid dynamics
     Hydrodynamics
Electrohysterography
  xx Electrophysiology
     Labor (Obstetrics)
Electrojet, Equatorial
  See Equatorial electrojet
Electrokinetic potential
  See Zeta potential
Electrokymography
  xx Electrocardiography
     Heart—Diseases—Diagnosis
Electroless plating
  x Nonelectrolytic plating
  xx Metal coating
     Plating
  — Patents
Electroluminesence
  sa Image intensifiers
  x Destriau effect
  xx Light
     Luminescence
     Semiconductors
Electrolysis *(QD553-585)*
  sa Electro-osmosis
     Electrochemical analysis
     Electrolytes—Conductivity
     Electrolytic cells
     Electrolytic corrosion
     Electrolytic polishing
     Electrometallurgy
     Ions
     Kolbe reaction
     Overvoltage
     Oxidation, Electrolytic
     Sugar—Manufacture and refining—
       Electrolysis
     Voltameter
  xx Chemistry, Analytic
     Chemistry, Physical and theoretical
     Electrochemistry
     Ions
     Solution (Chemistry)
  — Automation

— Equipment and supplies
Electrolysis in medicine *(RM886)*
  x Medicine, Electrolysis in
  xx Electrotherapeutics
Electrolysis in surgery *(RD33.5)*
  sa Electrosurgery
     Hair, Removal of
  xx Electrotherapeutics
     Surgery
Electrolysis of water
  See Water—Electrolysis
Electrolyte metabolism
  xx Metabolism
  — Programmed instruction
Electrolyte solutions
  sa Plating baths
  x Polyelectrolyte solutions
     Solutions, Electrolyte
  xx Electrolytes
     Solution (Chemistry)
  — Programmed instruction
  — Tables
Electrolyte therapy
  xx Electrolytes
     Therapeutics
Electrolytes *(Colloids, QD549; Electrolysis,*
     QD553-585; Solutions, QD541-3)
  sa Activity coefficients
     Electrolyte solutions
     Electrolyte therapy
  — Analysis
  — Conductivity *(QD565)*
     x Conductivity of electrolytes
     xx Chemistry, Physical and theoretical
       Electric conductivity
       Electric resistance
       Electrolysis
  — Tables, etc.
  — Thermal properties
Electrolytic analysis
  See Electrochemical analysis
Electrolytic capacitors
  See Condensers (Electricity)
Electrolytic cells
  x Electrolyzers
  xx Electrolysis
Electrolytic condensers
  See Condensers (Electricity)
Electrolytic corrosion *(Electric engineering,*
     TK3255; Electric railroads, TF912;
     Water-mains, pipes, etc., TD491)
  sa Cathodic protection
     Gas-pipes—Corrosion
     Soil corrosion
  x Corrosion, Electrolytic
     Electrochemical corrosion
     Galvanic corrosion
  xx Corrosion and anti-corrosives
     Electric currents, Vagrant
     Electrolysis
     Gas-pipes
     Water-pipes
Electrolytic grinding
  xx Electrochemical cutting
     Grinding and polishing
Electrolytic oxidation
  See Oxidation, Electrolytic
Electrolytic pickling of metals
  See Metals—Pickling
Electrolytic polishing
  x Electropolishing
  xx Electrolysis
     Grinding and polishing
     Metals—Finishing
Electrolytic reduction
  See Reduction, Electrolytic
Electrolyzers
  See Electrolytic cells

Electromagnetic brakes
  See Magnetic brakes
Electromagnetic clutches
  See Magnetic clutches
Electromagnetic compatibility
  See Radio—Interference
Electromagnetic fields
  sa Electric fields
     Electromagnetic mass shift
     Electromagnetic waves
     Plasma instabilities
     Plasma stability
  x Fields, Electromagnetic
  xx Electric fields
     Electromagnetic theory
     Electromagnetic waves
     Field theory (Physics)
     Magnetic fields
  — Physiological effect
  — Problems, exercises, etc.
Electromagnetic interactions *(QC794)*
  x Interactions, Electromagnetic
  xx Nuclear reactions
Electromagnetic lenses
  xx Electron optics
     Lenses
     Magnetic lenses
Electromagnetic machines
  See Magneto-electric machines
Electromagnetic mass shift *(QC721)*
  x Mass shift, Electromagnetic
     Shift, Electromagnetic mass
  xx Electromagnetic fields
     Mass (Physics)
     Particles (Nuclear physics)
Electromagnetic measurements
  sa Electric measurements
     Electronic measurements
     Gamma rays—Measurement
     Photoelectric measurements
     Photometry
     Radiation—Measurement
     Radio measurements
  x Measurements, Electromagnetic
  xx Electromagnetic theory
     Radiation—Measurement
Electromagnetic pumps
  x Induction pumps
     Pumps, Electromagnetic
  xx Pumping machinery, Electric
Electromagnetic screens
  See Shielding (Electricity)
Electromagnetic shields
  See Shielding (Electricity)
Electromagnetic theory *(QC661-675)*
  sa Blackbody radiation
     Cosmic electrodynamics
     Electric waves
     Electromagnetic fields
     Electromagnetic measurements
     Electromagnetic waves
     Electrons
     Field theory (Physics)
     Internal conversion (Nuclear physics)
     Light
     Magneto-optics
     Maxwell equations
     Nuclear induction
     Optics, Physical
     Quadrupole moments
     Quantum electrodynamics
     Unified field theories
  x Light, Electromagnetic theory of
  xx Electrons
     Field theory (Physics)
     Light, Wave theory of
     Magnetism
     Magneto-optics

Electromagnetic theory *(QC661-675)*
  (Continued)
    Optics, Physical
Electromagnetic waves
  sa Carrier waves
    Electric waves
    Electromagnetic fields
    Gamma rays
    Heat
    Infra-red rays
    Light
    Microwaves
    Photoabsorption
    Radio waves
    Ultra-violet rays
    Wave guides
    X-rays
  x Waves, Electromagnetic
  xx Electric waves
    Electromagnetic fields
    Electromagnetic theory
    Radiation
  — Diffraction
  — Physiological effect
  — Polarization
    sa Polarization (Light)
  — Scattering
    sa Mie scattering
  — — Mathematical models
  — — Tables, etc.
  — Tables, etc.
Electromagnetism *(QC760)*
  sa Betatron
    Electrets
    Gases, Ionized
    Inductance
    Magnetic materials
    Magneto-electric machines
    Magneto-ionic theory
    Magnetohydrodynamics
    Magnetostatics
    Masers
    Mutual inductance
    Self-inductance
    Vacuum polarization
  xx Magnetic induction
    Magnetism
  — Physiological effect
  — Problems, exercises, etc.
Electromagnetism in medicine *(RZ422)*
  x Medicine, Electromagnetism in
  xx Electrotherapeutics
Electromagnets *(QC760)*
  sa Calutron
    Lifting magnets
    Magnetic induction
    Magneto-electric machines
    Superconducting magnets
  x Magnet winding
  xx Electric apparatus and appliances
    Magnetic induction
    Magnetism
    Magnets
  — Standards *(Direct)*
Electromechanical analogies
  Here are entered general works on the
  method of solving problems by electrical or mechanical analogies as well as
  its application to either mechanics or
  electricity.
  sa Computer simulation
    Electric network analyzers
    subdivision Electromechanical analogies
      under subjects, e.g. Concrete slabs—
      Electromechanical analogies
  x Analogies, Electromechanical
    Electric analogies in mechanics
    Electricity—Mechanical analogies
    Mechanical analogies in electricity

    Mechanics—Electric analogies
  xx Engineering models
    Mechanics
    Simulation methods
Electromechanical components
  See Electromechanical devices
Electromechanical devices
  Here are entered works on electric generators, motors, transducers, sensing instruments, microphones, and similar
  devices, which convert electrical energy into mechanical energy, or the reverse, and which normally function as
  components of larger systems, *e.g.*
  electric power systems, information
  systems, control systems, etc.
  sa Electric machinery
    Transducers
  x Electric-mechanical devices
    Electromechanical components
  xx Electric engineering
    Electrodynamics
    Mechanical engineering
Electrometallurgy *(TN681-7)*
  Here are entered works on electric smelting and refining, or electrolytic separation of metals. Works on electrodeposition of metals are entered under
  Electroplating.
  sa Cyanide process
    Electroforming
    Electroplating
    Electroslag process
    Electrotyping
    Vacuum metallurgy
    subdivision Electrometallurgy *under*
      names of metals, e.g. Copper—
      Electrometallurgy
  x Galvanoplasty
  xx Electrochemistry
    Electrolysis
    Electroplating
    Electrotyping
    Metallurgy
    Smelting
  — Equipment and supplies
Electrometer *(QC544.E4)*
  xx Electric apparatus and appliances
Electromicturation
  See Pacemaker, Artificial (Bladder)
Electromotive force *(QC618; Electrolysis,*
  QD561)
  sa Activity coefficients
    Polarograph and polarography
  x Electric potential
    Force, Electromotive
    Potential, Electric
Electromyography
  xx Electrodiagnosis
Electron beam cutting
  xx Electron beams
    Electron beams—Industrial applications
    Metal-cutting
Electron beam furnaces
  x Electron beam melting
  xx Electric furnaces
    Electron beams—Industrial applications
    Metallurgical furnaces
Electron beam melting
  See Electron beam furnaces
Electron beam recording
  See Thermoplastic recording
Electron beam welding
  xx Electron beams
    Electron beams—Industrial applications
    Welding
  — Automation
  — Equipment and supplies

  — Patents
Electron beams
  sa Electron beam cutting
    Electron beam welding
    Electron gun
    Thermoplastic recording
    Velocity modulation
  x Beams, Electron
  xx Electron optics
    Electronics
    Particle beams
  — Industrial applications
    sa Electron beam cutting
      Electron beam furnaces
      Electron beam welding
      Electron gun
Electron capture
  See Electrons—Capture
Electron collisions
  See Collisions (Nuclear physics)
Electron density, Ionospheric
  See Ionospheric electron density
Electron diffraction
  See Electrons—Diffraction
Electron emission
  See Electrons—Emission
Electron gas
  sa Free electron theory of metals
  x Fermi gas
  xx Electrons
  — Electric properties
Electron gun *(TK7872.E45)*
  xx Electron beams
    Electron beams—Industrial applications
    Electron tubes
Electron-hole pair theory
  See Exciton theory
Electron image converter tubes
  See Image converters
Electron metallography
  xx Metallography
  — Technique
Electron microscope
  sa Scanning electron microscope
  x Electron microscopy
  xx Electron optics
    Image intensifiers
    Microscope and microscopy
  — Technique
Electron microscopy
  See Electron microscope
Electron multipliers
  See Photoelectric multipliers
Electron optics *(QC447)*
  sa Electromagnetic lenses
    Electron beams
    Electron microscope
    Electronics
    Electrostatic lenses
    Image converters
    Image iconoscope
    Image intensifiers
    Ion flow dynamics
    Magnetic lenses
    Microwave lenses
    Quantum electronics
    Television camera tubes
  x Electronic optics
    Optics, Electronic
  xx Optics
Electron paramagnetic resonance
  sa Hyperfine interactions
  x Electron resonance
    Electron spin resonance
    Paramagnetic resonance, Electronic
  xx Electrons
    Magnetic resonance
    Paramagnetism

Resonance
Spectrum analysis
Electron precipitation (QC809.R3)
  x Precipitation, Electron
  xx Magnetic fields (Cosmic physics)
    Van Allen radiation belts
Electron probes
  See Probes (Electronic instruments)
Electron resonance
  See Electron paramagnetic resonance
Electron scattering
  See Electrons—Scattering
Electron spectroscopy
  x Electron spectroscopy for chemical
    analysis
    ESCA
  xx Electrons—Emission
    X-rays
Electron spectroscopy for chemical analysis
  See Electron spectroscopy
Electron spin resonance
  See Electron paramagnetic resonance
Electron-tube circuits
  See Electronic circuits
Electron-tube diodes
  See Diodes, Electron-tube
Electron tubes
  sa Cathodes
    Cold cathode tubes
    Diodes, Electron-tube
    Electron gun
    Electronic circuits
    Gas tubes
    Germanium diodes
    Image converters
    Image intensifiers
    Masers
    Microwave tubes
    Oscillators, Crystal
    Thyratrons
    Vacuum-tubes
    X-ray tubes
  x Electric valves
    Valves, Electric
  xx Electric discharges through gases
    Electronic circuits
    Electronics
    Vacuum-tubes
  Example under Electronic industries
— Brazing
— Grids
    x Grids (Electronics)
    xx Electrodes
— Materials (TK7872.V3)
    xx Electronics—Materials
— Packing
— Patents
— Problems, exercises, etc.
— Programmed instruction
— Reliability
— Standards
— Testing
— Thermionic emission
    xx Thermionic emission
— Welding
Electron work function
  sa Electrons—Emission
    Field emission
    Photoelectricity
    Thermionic emission
  x Electronic work function
    Work function, Electron
  xx Electrons—Emission
    Metals, Effect of temperature on
    Photoelectricity
Electronarcosis
  See Electric anesthesia

Electronegativity
  xx Atoms
    Chemical bonds
    Chemistry, Physical and theoretical
Electronic addressing machines
  x Addressing machines, Electronic
  xx Electronic office machines
Electronic alarm systems
  sa Burglar-alarms
  x Intrusion alarm systems
  xx Burglar-alarms
    Electronic apparatus and appliances
Electronic amplifiers
  See Amplifiers (Electronics)
Electronic analog computers (QA76)
  sa Electric network analyzers
    Field plotters
    Function generators (Electronic analog
      computers)
    Reac computer
    USM-1 computer
  x Analog calculating-machines
    Computers, Electronic analog
  xx Analog computers
    Computers
    Hybrid computers
— Circuits
    x Analog computer circuits
    xx Electronic circuits
— Design and construction (TK7888)
— Input-output equipment
    See Computer input-output equipment
— Laboratory manuals
— Memory systems
— Problems, exercises, etc.
— Programming
    xx Programming (Electronic computers)
— Testing
Electronic apparatus and appliances
    (TK7870)
  sa Aeroplanes—Electronic equipment
    Antennas (Electronics)
    Auditoriums—Electronic sound control
    Automobiles—Electronic equipment
    Clocks and watches, Electric
    Computers
    Crystal detectors
    Electric railroads—Electronic
      equipment
    Electronic alarm systems
    Electronic control
    Electronic instruments
    Electronic navigation equipment
      industry
    Electronic office machines
    Electronic toys
    Electronics on boats
    Industrial electronics
    Intercommunication systems
    Liquid level indicators
    Metal detectors
    Microwave wiring
    Miniature electronic equipment
    Photoelectronic devices
    Photography—Electronic equipment
    Printed circuits
    Proximity detectors
    Railroads—Electronic equipment
    Railroads—Models—Electronic
      equipment
    Rate gyroscopes
    Rockets (Aeronautics)—Electronic
      equipment
    Space vehicles—Electronic equipment
    Storage tubes
    Telecommunication—Apparatus and
      supplies
    Theaters—Electronic sound control

    Thyratrons
    Transducers
    Traveling-wave tubes
    United States. Navy—Electronic
      installations
  x Electronics—Apparatus and appliances
  xx Electronic instruments
    Electronics
    Physical instruments
    Scientific apparatus and instruments
— Catalogs (TK7870)
— Cleaning (TK7870)
— Cooling
— Current supply
    xx Electric power production
— Design and construction
    sa Electronic apparatus and appliances
      —Unit construction
— Drawing
    See Electronic drafting
— Maintenance and repair
— — Programmed instruction
— Packaging
— Patents
— Plastic embedment
    x Encapsulation (Electronics)
      Plastic embedment (Electronics)
      Plastic packaging (Electronics)
      Potting (Electronics)
    xx Electric insulators and insulation
      Electronics—Materials
      Plastic coating
      Plastics
— Power supply
    xx Electric power
— Protection
— Radiation effects
    See Electronic apparatus and
      appliances, Effect of radiation
      on
— Reliability
    Example under Reliability (Engineering)
— Specifications
— Standards (Direct)
— Testing
    sa Probes (Electronic instruments)
      Signal generators
— — Programmed instruction
— Unit construction
    x Project Tinkertoy
    xx Electronic apparatus and appliances
      —Design and construction
    Example under Unit construction
— Vibration
**Electronic apparatus and appliances, Effect of
    radiation on**
  x Electronic apparatus and appliances—
    Radiation effects
    Radiation—Effect on electronic
      apparatus and appliances
  xx Radiation
Electronic behavior control (BF210)
  x Behavior control, Electronic
  xx Brain—Localization of functions
    Control (Psychology)
    Human behavior
    Physiology, Experimental
    Psychology, Experimental
Electronic brains
  See Artificial intelligence
    Computers
    Conscious automata
Electronic bugging
  See Eavesdropping
    Electronics in criminal investigation
    Electronics in espionage
Electronic calculating-machines
  See Computers

583

Electronic cameras
  sa Television cameras
  x Electronic moving-picture cameras
  xx Electronography
     Moving-picture cameras
     Photography—Electronic equipment
     Television cameras
Electronic ceramics *(TK7872.C4)*
  x Ceramics, Electronic
  xx Ceramic materials
     Electronics—Materials
Electronic circuit design
  x Electronic circuits—Design
  — Computer programs
Electronic circuits
  sa Bridge circuits
     Cold cathode tubes
     Computers—Circuits
     Electron tubes
     Electronic analog computers—Circuits
     Electronic digital computers—Circuits
     Integrated circuits
     Miniature computers—Circuits
     Mixing circuits
     Printed circuits
     Semiconductors
     Static relays
     Transistor circuits
     Trigger circuits
  x Electron-tube circuits
  xx Electric circuits
     Electron tubes
     Electronics
  — Design
       See Electronic circuit design
  — Maintenance and repair
  — Noise
     x Noisy circuits
     Example under Electronic noise
  — Problems, exercises, etc.
Electronic clocks and watches
  See Clocks and watches, Electric
Electronic computer programming
  See Programming (Electronic computers)
Electronic computers
  See Computers
Electronic control
  sa Guided missiles—Electronic equipment
     Machine-tools—Numerical control
     Milling-machines—Numerical control
     Radio control
     Static relays
  xx Electronic apparatus and appliances
     Governors (Machinery)
     Industrial electronics
     Remote control
     Servomechanisms
Electronic countermeasures *(UG485)*
  sa Radar confusion reflectors
  xx Electronics in military engineering
Electronic data processing
     Subdivided by subject, *e.g.* Electronic data processing—Road construction; Electronic data processing—Steel industry and trade; Electronic data processing—Traffic engineering.
  sa Analog-to-digital converters
     Artificial intelligence
     Assembling (Electronic computers)
     AUTOSATE
     Compatible time-sharing system (Electronic computers)
     Compiling (Electronic computers)
     Data processing service centers
     Data tapes
     Data transmission systems
     Debugging in computer science

     DL-ASEDC (Electronic computer system)
     Language data processing
     List processing (Electronic computers)
     Machine-tools—Numerical control
     Magnacard data processing system
     Microfilm aperture card systems
     Multiprogramming (Electronic computers)
     Office practice—Automation
     On-line data processing
     Optical data processing
     Parallel processing (Electronic computers)
     Programming (Electronic computers)
     Programming languages (Electronic computers)
     Pulse frequency modulation
     Real-time data processing
     Sorting (Electronic computers)
  x Automatic data processing
     Data processing
     Integrated data processing
  xx Computers
     Information science
     Information storage and retrieval systems
     Machine theory
     Office practice—Automation
  — Abbreviations
  — Acronyms
  — Aeronautics
     sa CLASP (Computer program language)
        Radar air traffic control systems
        ROCKET (Computer program)
  — Air lines
  — — Reservations
        x Air lines—Reservations—Electronic data processing
        xx Real-time data processing
  — Anecdotes, facetiae, satire, etc.
  — Astronautics
     sa ROCKET (Computer program)
  — Banks and banking
     sa Bank service corporations
     x Banks and banking—Electronic data processing
     xx Banks and banking—Equipment and supplies
  — Biography
  — Book industries and trade
     sa Computerized typesetting
     x Book industries and trade—Electronic data processing
  — City planning
     x Cities and towns—Planning—Electronic data processing
  — Civil engineering
     sa Electronic data processing—Structures, Theory of
        ICES (Electronic computer system)
  — Costs
  — Documents
     See Electronic data processing documentation
  — Education *(Direct)*
     sa Computer-assisted instruction
     x Education—Electronic data processing
     xx Educational technology
  — Engineering design
     sa Computer graphics
     x Engineering design—Electronic data processing
  — Engineering graphics
     See Computer graphics
  — English language

     Example under Language data processing
  — Finance, Public
     sa AUNTIE (Computer system)
     x Finance, Public—Electronic data processing
  — Grading and marking (Students)
     x Computer grading and marking (Students)
        Grading and marking (Students)—Electronic data processing
  — Historical research
     x Historical research—Electronic data processing
        History—Sources—Electronic data processing
  — Investments
     sa Electronic data processing—Stocks
     x Investments—Electronic data processing
  — Juvenile literature
  — Language and languages
     See Language data processing
  — Mathematical models
     See Digital computer simulation
  — Mathematical physics
     See Electronic data processing—Physics
  — Mechanical drawing
     See Computer graphics
  — Military intelligence
     x Military information systems
        Military intelligence—Electronic data processing
     xx Communications, Military
  — Petroleum geology
     x Petroleum—Geology—Electronic data processing
  — Physics
     x Electronic data processing—Mathematical physics
        Physics—Electronic data processing
     xx Mathematical physics
  — Popular works
  — Psychology
     x Psychology—Electronic data processing
     xx Psychology—Methodology
  — Public administration
     x Public administration—Electronic data processing
     xx Public administration—Automation
  — Records
     See Electronic data processing documentation
  — Research
     See Electronic data processing in research
  — Road construction
     x Road construction—Electronic data processing
     Note under Electronic data processing
  — Schools
     x Schools—Electronic data processing
     xx School management and organization
  — Standards *(Direct)*
  — Steel industry and trade
     x Steel industry and trade—Electronic data processing
     Note under Electronic data processing
  — Stocks
     x Stocks—Electronic data processing
     xx Electronic data processing—Investments
  — Structures, Theory of
     x Structures, Theory of—Electronic data processing
     xx Electronic data processing—Civil engineering

584

— Tactics
    x Computer-aided systems for
        command
      Tactics—Electronic data processing
    xx Decision-making
— Terminology
— Traffic engineering
    x Traffic engineering—Electronic data
      processing
    Note under Electronic data processing
— Typesetting
    See Computerized typesetting
— Vocational guidance
    Here are entered works on guidance
    toward a career in the field of elec-
    tronic data processing. Works on
    the use of electronic data process-
    ing techniques in the field of voca-
    tional guidance are entered under
    the heading Electronic data proc-
    essing in vocational guidance.
    sa Electronic data processing personnel
    xx Electronic data processing personnel
— — Juvenile literature
Electronic data processing and copyright
    See Copyright and electronic data
      processing

Electronic data processing departments
    sa Computer programming management
      Data processing service centers
    x Computer centers
— Auditing
— Fires and fire prevention
    xx Electronic data processing
      departments—Security measures
— Management
— Security measures
    sa Electronic data processing
      departments—Fires and fire
      prevention
    x Computer department security
      measures
      Computer security measures

Electronic data processing documentation
    Here are entered works on the content,
    structure, and form of records or docu-
    ments which describe the design, de-
    velopment, and operation of electronic
    data processing undertakings.
    x Documentation in electronic data
      processing
      Documents in electronic data
      processing
      Electronic data processing—Documents
      Electronic data processing—Records
    xx Records
Electronic data processing in programmed
    instruction
    See Computer-assisted instruction

Electronic data processing in research
    x Electronic data processing—Research
      Research—Electronic data processing

**Electronic data processing in vocational
    guidance**
    xx Vocational guidance
    Note under Electronic data processing—Voca-
      tional guidance

Electronic data processing personnel *(Direct)*
    sa Electronic data processing—Vocational
      guidance
    xx Electronic data processing—Vocational
      guidance
— Salaries, pensions, etc.
Electronic data processing service centers
    See Data processing service centers
Electronic data processing system printers
    See Printers (Data processing systems)

Electronic differential analyzers
    (Mathematics, QA76)
    x Differential analyzers, Electronic
      Digital differential analyzers, Electronic
    xx Differential equations
Electronic digital computers
    sa Aragats computer
      ARITMA computer
      ATE 80 (Computer)
      ATLAS (Computer)
      Besm computer
      Burroughs B5700 (Computer)
      Burroughs B6700 (Computer)
      CDC 3400 (Computer)
      CDC 3600 (Computer)
      CDC 6000 (Computer)
      CDC 6400 (Computer)
      CDC 6600 (Computer)
      Cellatron C8205 (Computer)
      Cellatron computer
      Computer-assisted instruction
      Computer graphics
      Computer sound processing
      Digital computer simulation
      Digital incremental plotters
      Dnepr computer
      Dnipro computer
      Elliott computer
      Ermeth computer
      Error-correcting codes (Information
        theory)
      GE 600 series (Computers)
      GIER (Computer)
      IBM 1130 (Computer)
      IBM 1401 (Computer)
      IBM 1440 (Computer)
      IBM 1620 (Computer)
      IBM 1800 (Computer)
      IBM 360 (Computer)
      IBM 370 (Computer)
      IBM 3965 (Computer)
      IBM 650 (Computer)
      IBM 7030 (Computer)
      IBM 7040 (Computer)
      IBM 7044 (Computer)
      IBM 7090 (Computer)
      IBM 7094 (Computer)
      IBM System/3 (Computer)
      Illiac computer
      INAC (Computer)
      ISS 714 (Computer)
      JOHNNIAC computer
      Kiev computer
      Leo computer
      MACC-7/S (Computer)
      Miniature computers
      Minsk computer
      Mir computer
      Nairi computer
      ODRA computer
      PDP-11 (Computer)
      PDP-8 (Computer)
      Pegasus computer
      Promin' computer
      Random number generators
      RC 4000 (Computer)
      RCA 301 (Computer)
      Real-time clocks (Computers)
      ROBOTRON (Computer)
      RPC 4000 (Computer)
      Seac computer
      Sequential machine theory
      Sesm computer
      Setun' computer
      Soemtron 381 (Computer)
      SPEAC (Computer)
      Strela computer
      Swac computer

      Time-sharing computer systems
      Titan (Computer)
      United States. Air Force translator
      Univac computer
      Ural computer
      Wisc computer
      ZPA 6000 (Computer)
      ZRA 1 (Computer)
    x Automatic digital computers
      Computers, Electronic digital
      Digital computers, Electronic
    xx Computers
      Hybrid computers
      Sequential machine theory
— Amateurs' manuals
— Circuits *(TK7888.3)*
    sa Cathode ray tube memory systems
      Computer arithmetic and logic units
      Parametrons
    x Digital computer circuits
    xx Digital electronics
      Electronic circuits
— — Noise
— — Programmed instruction
— Costs
— Design and construction
— Evaluation
— — Statistical methods
— Input-output equipment
    See Computer input-output equipment
— Juvenile literature
— Laboratory manuals
— Maintenance and repair
    x Electronic digital computers—
      Repairing
— — Costs *(TK7888.3)*
— Memory systems
    See Computer storage devices
— Patents
— Problems, exercises, etc.
— Programmed instruction
— Programming *(QA76.5)*
    sa Assembling (Electronic computers)
      Compiling (Electronic computers)
      Computer programs
      Debugging in computer science
      Floating-point arithmetic
      GAT (Computer program)
      GRAIL (Electronic computer
        system)
      ICES (Electronic computer system)
      List processing (Electronic
        computers)
      Microprogramming
      Multiprogramming (Electronic
        computers)
      Parallel processing (Electronic
        computers)
      Programming languages (Electronic
        computers)—Business
      ROCKET (Computer program)
      Sorting (Electronic computers)
      subdivision Programming *under*
        specific computers, e.g. Univac
        computer—Programming
    xx Programming (Electronic computers)
— — Problems, exercises, etc.
— — Programmed instruction
— — Psychological aspects
— — Standards *(Direct)*
— Registers
— Reliability
— Repairing
    See Electronic digital computers—
      Maintenance and repair
— Terminology
— Testing

Electronic drafting *(TK7866)*
  sa Electronics—Diagrams
  x Drafting, Electronic
    Electronic apparatus and appliances—
      Drawing
    Electronics—Drafting
  xx Electric drafting
    Mechanical drawing
Electronic eavesdropping
  See Eavesdropping
Electronic equipment, Miniature
  See Miniature electronic equipment
Electronic games
  See Electronic toys
Electronic harpsichord *(ML697)*
  x Harpsichord, Electronic
  xx Musical instruments, Electronic
Electronic harpsichord music *(M20-32)*
  sa Quartets (Electronic harpsichord,
    castanets, percussion, violoncello)
Electronic industries *(Direct)*
  sa names of individual industries and
    products, e.g. Radio industry and
    trade; Electron tubes
  xx Electric industries
    Electronics
  — Automation *(TK7870)*
    Example under Automation
  — Costs
  — Equipment and supplies
  — — Appraisal
    See Electronic industries—
      Equipment and supplies—
      Valuation
  — — Valuation
    x Electronic industries—Equipment
      and supplies—Appraisal
  — Management
  — Quality control
  — Safety regulations *(Direct)*
  — Vocational guidance
Electronic industry workers *(Direct)*
  sa Wages—Electronic industry workers
Electronic instruments *(TK7870)*
  sa Astronautical instruments
    Automatic checkout equipment
    Electronic apparatus and appliances
    Electronic measurements
    Electronics in surveying
    specific electronic instruments, e.g.
      Cathode ray oscillograph;
      Vacuum-tube voltmeter
  x Instruments, Electronic
  xx Electronic apparatus and appliances
    Electronics
    Engineering instruments
    Industrial electronics
  — Maintenance and repair
Electronic level gages
  See Liquid level indicators
Electronic listening devices
  See Eavesdropping
    Electronics in criminal investigation
    Electronics in espionage
Electronic measurements *(Electronics,*
    TK7882.M; Physics, QC535)
  sa Aerospace telemetry
    Biotelemetry
    Bridge circuits
    Cathode ray oscillograph
    Cathode ray oscilloscope
    Electric measurements
    Ionization chambers
    Microwave measurements
    Pulse height analyzers
    Radio measurements
    Telemeter
    Telemeter (Physiological apparatus)

    Vacuum-tube voltmeter
  x Measurements, Electronic
  xx Electric measurements
    Electromagnetic measurements
    Electronic instruments
  — Laboratory manuals
Electronic moving-picture cameras
  See Electronic cameras
Electronic music
    Here are entered works in which the
    sounds produced were originally re-
    corded on magnetic tape from elec-
    tronic instruments, or from a combina-
    tion of electronic instruments and
    other sources, and subsequently rear-
    ranged or altered, or performed live.
    The heading is used as a medium of
    performance after the names of spe-
    cific forms, *e.g.* 1. Suites (Electronic
    music) It is used as a second heading
    when a tape recording is used with
    specifically named conventional in-
    struments, *e.g.* 1. Quintets (Clarinet,
    flute, harp, viola, violoncello) 2. Elec-
    tronic music.
  sa Computer music
    Concrete music
    Songs (High voice) with electronic
      music
    Suites (Electronic music)
    Symphonies (Electronic music)
  x Electrophonic music
    Music, Electronic
    Synthesizer music
    Tape-recorder music
  xx Concrete music
    Music
    Technology and the arts
Electronic musical instruments
  See Musical instruments, Electronic
Electronic navigation
  See Electronics in navigation
Electronic navigation equipment industry
    (Direct)
  xx Electronic apparatus and appliances
    Electronics in navigation
Electronic noise
  sa Electric noise
    Radio noise
    subdivision Noise *under names of*
      electronic devices, e.g. Electronic
      circuits—Noise; Transistors—Noise
  x Noise, Electronic
  xx Electric noise
    Signal theory (Telecommunication)
Electronic office machines
  sa Computers
    Electronic addressing machines
    Office practice—Automation
  x Business machines
    Office machines
  xx Electronic apparatus and appliances
    Office equipment and supplies
    Office practice—Automation
Electronic optics
  See Electron optics
Electronic organ *(ML597)*
  sa Allen organ
    Baldwin organ
    Hammond organ
    Minshall-Estey organ
    Silvertone organ
    Welte-Lichtton-Orgel
    Wurlitzer organ
  x Organ, Electronic
  xx Musical instruments, Electronic
    Organ
  — Construction *(ML597)*

  — Registration *(MT192)*
    x Registration (Electronic organ)
  — Repairing *(ML597)*
Electronic organ music *(M14.8; M14.85)*
  xx Organ music
    Organ music, Arranged
Electronic organ music (Conn registration)
    (M14.8; M14.85)
  x Conn organ music
    Connsonata organ music
Electronic organ music (Hammond
    registration) *(M14.8; M14.85)*
  x Hammond organ music
Electronic organ music (Silvertone
    registration) *(M14.8; M14.85)*
  x Silvertone organ music
Electronic organ music (Thomas registration)
    (M14.8; M14.85)
  x Thomas organ music
Electronic photography
  See Electronography
Electronic piano *(ML697)*
  x Piano, Electronic
  xx Musical instruments, Electronic
  — Instruction and study *(MT250)*
Electronic potentiostat
  See Potentiostat
Electronic probes
  See Probes (Electronic instruments)
Electronic pulse techniques
  See Pulse techniques (Electronics)
Electronic surveying
  See Electronics in surveying
Electronic technicians
  x Technicians, Electronic
  xx Electric industry workers
    Technologists
Electronic toys
  x Electronic games
  xx Electronic apparatus and appliances
    Toys
Electronic traffic controls
  x Traffic signs and signals, Electronic
  xx Electronics in transportation
    Highway communications
    Traffic safety
    Traffic signs and signals
Electronic transformers *(TK7872.T)*
  xx Electric transformers
    Electronics
Electronic translating
  See Machine translating
Electronic translating machines
  See Translating machines
Electronic work function
  See Electron work function
    Electrons—Emission
Electronics *(TK7800-7882)*
  sa Amplifiers (Electronics)
    Astrionics
    Cold cathode tubes
    Cryotrons
    Cybernetics
    Delay lines
    Digital electronics
    Electron beams
    Electron tubes
    Electronic apparatus and appliances
    Electronic circuits
    Electronic industries
    Electronic instruments
    Electronic transformers
    Electronics in aeronautics
    Electronics in agriculture
    Electronics in biology
    Electronics in geophysics
    Electronics in military engineering
    Electronics in navigation

Facsimile transmission
Feedback (Electronics)
High-fidelity sound systems
Industrial electronics
Masks (Electronics)
Medical electronics
Microelectronics
Microwave circuits
Miniature electronic equipment
Modulation (Electronics)
Oscillators, Crystal
Particle accelerators
Pulse techniques (Electronics)
Quantum electronics
Radioisotopes in electronics
Semiconductors
Shielding (Electricity)
Thermoelectric apparatus and
    appliances
Transistors
  xx Electron optics
     Electrons
     Vacuum-tubes
— Abbreviations
— Amateurs' manuals
— Apparatus and appliances
    See Electronic apparatus and
       appliances
— Caricatures and cartoons
— Diagrams
    xx Electronic drafting
— Drafting
    See Electronic drafting
— Experiments
— Graphic methods *(TK7825)*
    sa Smith charts
    xx Electronics—Tables, calculations,
       etc.
— Information services
    sa Information storage and retrieval
       systems—Electronics
    xx Electronics libraries
— Juvenile literature
— Laboratory manuals
— Materials *(TK7835)*
    sa Electron tubes—Materials
      Electronic apparatus and appliances
        —Plastic embedment
      Electronic ceramics
      Radar—Materials
      Radio—Materials
      Semiconductors
      Superconductors
      Telecommunication—Materials
    xx Electric engineering—Materials
— — Analysis
— Mathematics
    x Electronics mathematics
    xx Engineering mathematics
      Mathematical physics
— — Programmed instruction
— Notation
— Popular works *(TK7819)*
— Problems, exercises, etc.
— Programmed instruction
— Research *(TK7855)*
    xx Research, Industrial
— Safety measures
— Tables, calculations, etc.
    sa Electronics—Graphic methods
— Technique
— Terminology
Electronics as a profession *(TK7845)*
  sa Radio as a profession
    Television as a profession
Electronics in aeronautics *(TL695)*
  sa Aeronautical instruments—Display
     systems

    Aeronautics—Communication systems
    Aeroplanes—Electronic equipment
    Aerospace telemetry
    Aids to air navigation
    Air traffic control—Equipment and
      supplies
    Airborne computers
    Airports—Traffic control—Display
      systems
    Astrionics
    Consol navigation
    Course-line computers
    Decca navigation
    Hyperbolic navigation
    Instrument landing systems
    Landing aids (Aeronautics)
    Loran
    Omnirange system
    Radar in aeronautics
    Radio in aeronautics
    Rockets (Aeronautics)—Electronic
      equipment
  x Aeronautics, Electronics in
    Avionics
  xx Aeronautics
    Aids to air navigation
    Air traffic control
    Electricity in aeronautics
    Electronics
    Electronics in transportation
    Landing aids (Aeronautics)
    Navigation (Aeronautics)
— Juvenile literature
Electronics in agriculture
  x Agriculture, Electronics in
  xx Agriculture
    Electronics
Electronics in astronautics
  See Astrionics
Electronics in aviation
Electronics in biology
  x Biological electronics
    Biology, Electronics in
  xx Biological physics
    Biology
    Biomedical engineering
    Electronics
Electronics in cardiology
  xx Cardiology
    Medical electronics
Electronics in clinical medicine
  xx Medical electronics
    Medicine, Clinical
Electronics in color printing *(Z258)*
  xx Color-printing
    Electronics in printing
Electronics in crime prevention
  xx Crime prevention
Electronics in criminal investigation
  sa Eavesdropping
  x Electronic bugging
    Electronic listening devices
  xx Criminal investigation
Electronics in earth sciences
  sa Electronics in geophysics
  x Geoscience electronics
  xx Earth sciences
Electronics in espionage
  x Electronic bugging
    Electronic listening devices
  xx Espionage—Equipment and supplies
Electronics in geodesy
  See Electronics in surveying
Electronics in geophysics
  x Geophysics, Electronics in
  xx Electronics
    Electronics in earth sciences
    Geophysics

Electronics in industry
  See Industrial electronics
Electronics in medicine
  See Medical electronics
Electronics in military engineering *(UG485)*
  sa Electronic countermeasures
    Military art and science—Automation
    Radio, Military
  xx Electronics
    Military art and science—Automation
    Military engineering
Electronics in navigation *(VK560)*
  sa Artificial satellites in navigation
    Consol navigation
    Decca navigation
    Electronic navigation equipment
      industry
    Hyperbolic navigation
    Loran
    Loran charts
    Radar in navigation
    Radio in navigation
    Raydist
    Sonar
    United States. Navy—Electronic
      installations
  x Electronic navigation
    Navigation, Electronics in
  xx Aids to navigation
    Electronics
    Electronics in transportation
    Navigation
Electronics in photogrammetry
  xx Photogrammetry
Electronics in printing
  sa Electronics in color printing
  xx Printing machinery and supplies
Electronics in psychiatry
  x Psychoelectronics
  xx Medical electronics
    Psychiatry
Electronics in rocketry *(TL784.E4)*
  x Rocketry, Electronics in
Electronics in sanitary engineering *(TH6025)*
  xx Sanitary engineering
Electronics in surveying *(Geodetic surveying,*
       QB301; Plane surveying, TA595)
  sa Radar in surveying
    names of particular instruments, e.g.
    Tellurometer
  x Electronic surveying
    Electronics in geodesy
  xx Electronic instruments
    Geodesy
    Surveying
Electronics in transportation
  sa Electronic traffic controls
    Electronics in aeronautics
    Electronics in navigation
  xx Transportation
Electronics libraries *(Direct)* *(Z675.E4)*
  sa Electronics—Information services
    Information storage and retrieval
      systems—Electronics
  x Libraries, Electronics
  xx Engineering libraries
Electronics literature searching
  See Information storage and retrieval
      systems—Electronics
Electronics mathematics
  See Electronics—Mathematics
Electronics on boats *(VM325)*
  x Marine electronic equipment
    Small boat electronics
  xx Boats and boating—Equipment and
      supplies
    Electronic apparatus and appliances
— Amateurs' manuals

Electronium *(ML1092)*
   x Elektronium
Electronium music *(M175.E4)*
   sa Quartets (Electronium, piano,
       percussion, viola)
Electronography
   sa Electronic cameras
      Image intensifiers
   x Electronic photography
      Photography, Electronic
   xx Electrooptical photography
      Image intensifiers
      Phototypesetting
Electrons *(QC721)*
   sa Atomic orbitals
      Auger effect
      Beta rays
      Cathode rays
      Charge transfer
      Compton effect
      Delta rays
      Electric discharges through gases
      Electromagnetic theory
      Electron gas
      Electron paramagnetic resonance
      Electronics
      Energy-band theory of solids
      Exciton theory
      Fermi surfaces
      Free electron theory of metals
      Internal conversion (Nuclear physics)
      Ion acoustic waves
      Ionospheric electron density
      Ions
      Mesons
      Molecular orbitals
      Neutrons
      Photoelectricity
      Plasma (Ionized gases)
      Polarons
      Positron annihilation
      Positronium
      Positrons
      Project Argus
      Protons
      Quantum electrodynamics
      Space charge
      Spin-lattice relaxation
      Sporadic E (Ionosphere)
      Vacuum polarization
   x Corpuscular theory of matter
   xx Atoms
      Cathode rays
      Electricity
      Electromagnetic theory
      Ions
      Magneto-optics
      Matter—Constitution
      Neutrons
      Physics
      Positrons
      Protons
      Radioactivity
   Example under Collisions (Nuclear physics);
      Particles (Nuclear physics)
   — Capture
      sa Charge exchange
      x Electron capture
      xx Nuclear physics
   — — Tables, etc.
   — Diffraction *(QC721)*
      x Electron diffraction
   — — Tables, etc.
   — Emission
      sa Electron spectroscopy
      Electron work function
      Field emission
      Photoelectricity

Secondary electron emission
      Thermionic emission
   x Electron emission
      Electronic work function
      Emission of electrons
      Work function, Electronic
   xx Electric discharges through gases
      Electron work function
      Free electron theory of metals
      Internal conversion (Nuclear
        physics)
   — Juvenile literature
   — Physiological effect
   — Polarization *(QC793.5.E628)*
   — Scattering *(QC721)*
      x Electron scattering
   — Tables, etc.
Electrons, Thermal
   See Thermal electrons
Electronystagmography
   xx Nystagmus
Electrooptical devices *(TA1750)*
   xx Electrooptics
Electrooptical photography
   sa Electronography
   x Photoelectronic image devices
      Photography, Electrooptical
   xx Electrooptics
      Photoelectronic devices
      Photography
Electrooptics
   sa Electrooptical devices
      Electrooptical photography
      Kerr effect
      Light modulators
      Liquid crystal devices
      Stark effect
   xx Electric waves
      Optics
Electroosmotic dewatering *(TA710)*
   x Dewatering, Electroosmotic
   xx Electro-osmosis
      Soil stabilization
Electrophonic music
   See Electronic music
Electrophonic musical instruments
   See Musical instruments, Electronic
Electrophoresis
   sa Electrophoretic deposition
      Immunoelectrophoresis
      Paper electrophoresis
      Zone electrophoresis
   x Cataphoresis
   xx Electrochemistry
      Separation (Technology)
Electrophoretic coating
   See Electrophoretic deposition
Electrophoretic deposition
   x Coating, Electrophoretic
      Deposition, Electrophoretic
      Electrophoretic coating
   xx Electrophoresis
      Painting, Industrial
   — Patents
Electrophorus *(QC544.E6)*
   xx Electric apparatus and appliances
Electrophotography *(TR1035-1045)*
   sa Electrostatic printing
      Ferromagnetography
      Thermoplastic recording
   xx Photocopying processes
      Photoelectronic devices
      Photography
      Photomechanical processes
   — Equipment and supplies
Electrophysiology *(QP341-8)*
   sa Electric anesthesia
      Electric organs in fishes

Electric organs in insects
      Electricity, Injuries from
      Electricity—Physiological effect
      Electroencephalography
      Electrogastrography
      Electrohysterography
      Galvanic skin response
      Impedance plethysmography
      Muscle
      Nerves
      Visual evoked response
   x Animal electricity
      Electricity, Animal
      Electrobiology
   xx Biology
      Electricity—Physiological effect
      Neurology
      Physiology
   — Experiments
   — Mathematical models
   — Research
   — Technique
Electrophysiology of plants *(QK845)*
   x Botany—Electrophysiology
      Plants—Electrophysiology
   xx Plant physiology
Electropism
   See Galvanotropism
Electroplating *(TS670-692)*
   sa Alloy plating
      Aluminum coating
      Brass plating
      Cadmium plating
      Chromium-plating
      Copper plating
      Electroforming
      Electrometallurgy
      Iron plating
      Lead plating
      Metals—Finishing
      Metals—Pickling
      Plating baths
      Zinc coating
      Zinc plating
   x Electrodeposition of metals
      Galvanoplasty
   xx Electrochemistry
      Electroforming
      Electrometallurgy
      Gilding
      Metal-work
      Plating
      Silver-plating
      Silvering
   — Automation
   — Costs
   — Equipment and supplies
   — Laboratory manuals
   — Mathematical models
   — Quality control
   — Safety measures
   — Tables, calculations, etc.
   — Testing
   — Vocational guidance
   — Waste disposal
Electroplating baths
   See Plating baths
Electroplating solutions
   See Plating baths
Electropolishing
   See Electrolytic polishing
Electroretinography
   xx Eye—Examination
Electroscope
   xx Electric apparatus and appliances
Electroshock therapy
   See Electric shock therapy

Electroslag casting
  See Electroslag process
Electroslag melting
  See Electroslag process
Electroslag process
  x Electric slag process
    Electroslag casting
    Electroslag melting
    Electroslag refining process
  xx Electrometallurgy
    Slag
Electroslag refining process
  See Electroslag process
Electroslag welding *(TK4660)*
  xx Electric welding
Electrosmosis
  See Electro-osmosis
Electrostatic apparatus and appliances
  sa Electric machines
  xx Electrostatics
Electrostatic atomization
  xx Atomization
Electrostatic dusting *(Indirect)* *(SB953)*
  x Dusting, Electrostatic
  xx Spraying and dusting in agriculture
Electrostatic lenses
  xx Electron optics
    Lenses
    Magnetic lenses
Electrostatic microphone *(TK5986)*
  x Capacitor microphone
    Condenser microphone
    Microphone, Electrostatic
  xx Electrostatics
    Microphone
Electrostatic precipitation *(TP156.P7)*
  x Electric precipitation
  xx Dust—Removal
    Electrochemistry, Industrial
    Electrostatics
    Precipitation (Chemistry)
  — Safety measures
Electrostatic printing
  sa Xerography
  x Printing, Electrostatic
  xx Electrophotography
    Electrostatics
    Photocopying processes
    Printing, Practical
Electrostatic propulsion systems
  See Ion rockets
    Plasma rockets
Electrostatic separation
  See Electrostatic separators
Electrostatic separators *(TP156.E5)*
  x Electrostatic separation
    Separators, Electrostatic
  xx Electrostatics
    Ore-dressing
    Particles
    Separators (Machines)
  — Maintenance and repair
Electrostatic spray painting
  See Spray painting, Electrostatic
Electrostatic storage tubes
  See Storage tubes
Electrostatics *(QC571-595)*
  sa Antistatic agents (Textiles)
    Condensers (Electricity)
    Electric action of points
    Electric capacity
    Electric charge and distribution
    Electric discharges
    Electric machines
    Electrostatic apparatus and appliances
    Electrostatic microphone
    Electrostatic precipitation
    Electrostatic printing

Electrostatic separators
  Electrotherapeutics
  Induction (Electricity)
  Kerr effect
  Petroleum products—Antistatic
    additives
  Potential, Theory of
  x Electric potential
    Electricity, Static
    Potential, Electric
    Static electricity
  xx Electric action of points
    Statics
  — Experiments
  — Juvenile literature
  — Patents
Electrosurgery *(RD33.5)*
  x Electricity in surgery
    Galvanosurgery
  xx Electrolysis in surgery
    Electrotherapeutics
    Surgery
Electrotherapeutics *(RM869-890)*
  sa Baths, Electric
    Diathermy
    Electric anesthesia
    Electric shock
    Electric stimulation
    Electricity in dentistry
    Electricity, Injuries from
    Electrolysis in medicine
    Electrolysis in surgery
    Electromagnetism in medicine
    Electrosurgery
    Radiotherapy
    Spondylotherapy
    Vibration (Therapeutics)
  x Electricity, Medical
    Faradization
    Medical electricity
  xx Electricity in medicine
    Electrostatics
    Massage
    Medicine—Practice
    Physical therapy
    Therapeutics, Physiological
  — Apparatus and instruments *(RM889)*
    sa Electric machines
    xx Electric apparatus and appliances
  — Laboratory manuals *(RM873)*
Electrothermal rocket engines
  See Arc-jet rocket engines
Electrotyping *(Z252)*
  sa Electrometallurgy
    Glyphography
    Stereotyping
  x Galvanoplastic process
    Galvanoplasty
  xx Electrochemistry
    Electroforming
    Electrometallurgy
    Glyphography
    Printing, Practical
    Stereotyping
Electrum
  sa Brass
  xx Brass
Elegiac poetry *(PN1389)*
  sa Laments
  x Elegies
    Lamentations
  xx Poetry
Elegiac poetry, French, ₍Italian, etc.₎
  (Direct)
  x French ₍Italian, etc.₎ elegiac poetry
  xx French ₍Italian, etc.₎ poetry
Elegies
  See Elegiac poetry

Eleidin *(Comparative anatomy of stomach,*
    QL862; Histology, QM561)
Elektronium
  See Electronium
Elema (Papuan people) *(DU740)*
  sa Toaripi (Papuan people)
  xx Papuans
  — Religion
Elementary adult education
  See Elementary education of adults
Elementary education
  See Education, Elementary
Elementary education for adults
  See Elementary education of adults
Elementary education of adults
  sa Reading (Adult education)
  x Adult elementary education
    Elementary adult education
    Elementary education for adults
  xx Adult education
    Education, Elementary
    Illiteracy
Elementary particles (Physics)
  See Particles (Nuclear physics)
Elementary school . . .
  x Grade school . . .
Elementary school administration *(Direct)*
    (LB2822.5)
  xx School management and organization
Elementary school buildings *(Direct)*
  xx Elementary school facilities
    School buildings
Elementary school counselors *(Direct)*
  xx Personnel service in elementary
    education
    Student counselors
Elementary school dropouts *(Direct)*
  xx Dropouts
    Personnel service in elementary
    education
    School attendance
Elementary school facilities *(Direct)*
  sa Elementary school buildings
  xx School facilities
  — Planning *(Direct)*
    xx Educational planning
Elementary school principals *(Direct)*
    (LB2822.5)
  xx School superintendents and principals
  — Appointment
    See Elementary school principals—
      Selection and appointment
  — Biography
  — Correspondence, reminiscences, etc.
  — In-service training
  — Selection and appointment
    x Elementary school principals—
      Appointment
Elementary school principals, Training of
    (Direct)
  xx School superintendents and principals,
    Training of
Elementary school students
  See School children
Elementary school students' socio-economic
    status *(Direct)* *(LC208)*
  xx Students' socio-economic status
Elementary school teachers *(Direct)*
  x Teachers, Elementary school
  xx Teachers
  — Appointment
    See Elementary school teachers—
      Selection and appointment
  — Certification *(Direct)*
    xx Elementary school teachers—Legal
      status, laws, etc.
  — In-service training *(Direct)*

Elementary school teachers (Direct)
— In-service training (Direct)
      (Continued)
      xx Elementary school teachers, Training
         of
— Legal status, laws, etc. (Direct)
   sa Elementary school teachers—
      Certification
   xx Educational law and legislation
— Pensions
   See Elementary school teachers—
      Salaries, pensions, etc.
— Personality
   See Elementary school teachers—
      Psychology
— Psychology
   x Elementary school teachers—
      Personality
— Recruiting (Direct)
— Salaries, pensions, etc.
   x Elementary school teachers—
      Pensions
— Selection and appointment
   x Elementary school teachers—
      Appointment
Elementary school teachers, Rating of
Elementary school teachers, Self-rating of
Elementary school teachers, Training of
      (Direct)
   sa Elementary school teachers—In-service
      training
Elementary school teaching
   xx Education, Elementary
      Teaching
Elementary schools (Indirect)
   sa Middle schools
      Negro elementary schools
   xx Education, Elementary
      Schools
— Accreditation
— Evaluation
   x Evaluation of elementary schools
   xx Educational surveys
— Safety measures
Elements, Chemical
   See Chemical elements
Elements, Inert
   See Gases, Rare
Elements, Nonmetallic
   See Nonmetals
Elephant (in heraldry) (CR41.E6)
   Example under Heraldry
Elephant (in numismatics) (CJ161.E5)
Elephant hunting (Indirect) (SK305.E3)
   xx Elephants
Elephant seal, Northern
   See Northern elephant seal
Elephant seals (QL737.P64)
   sa Northern elephant seal
      Southern elephant seal
   xx Seals (Animals)
Elephant shrews (QL737.I5)
Elephant shrews, Fossil (QE882.I5)
Elephantiasis (RC142.5)
   xx Lymphatics—Diseases
      Lymphedema
Elephants (QL737.U8)
   sa African elephant
      Elephant hunting
      Indian elephant
— Anecdotes, facetiae, satire, etc.
— Behavior
— Diseases
— Juvenile literature
— Legends and stories (QL795.E4)
   xx Animals, Legends and stories of
— Pictorial works
— Pictures, illustrations, etc.
Elephants, Fossil (QE882.U7)

Elephants in art
   xx Art
Elephas primigenius
   See Mammoth
Eleusinian mysteries (BL795.E5)
   xx Cultus, Greek
      Mysteries, Religious
Eleuth language
   See Aleut language
Elevated railroads
   See Railroads, Elevated
Elevated temperatures
   See High temperatures
Elevations
   See Altitudes
      subdivision Altitudes under names of
      countries, states, etc.
Elevator operators
   xx Building-service employees
Elevators (TJ1370-1380)
   sa Elevators, Private residence
   x Hydraulic elevators
      Lifts
   xx Hoisting machinery
— Laws and regulations (Direct)
   xx Building laws
— Maintenance and repair
— Standards
— Tables, calculations, etc.
Elevators, Automatic
   x Automatic elevators
      Self-controlled elevators
      Self-service elevators
Elevators, Automatic (Jewish law)
   xx Prohibited work (Jewish law)
Elevators, Grain
   See Grain elevators
Elevators, Private residence (TJ1374)
   x Inclined passenger lifts
      Private elevators
      Private residence elevators
   xx Elevators
Elevators (Aeroplanes) (TL677.E6)
   xx Aerofoils
      Aeroplanes—Control surfaces
      Aeroplanes—Tail surfaces
      Lift (Aerodynamics)
Eleventh century
   xx Middle Ages—History
— Biography
      See Biography—11th century
Eleventh grade (Education)
   x Junior class (High school)
   xx Education, Secondary
Elf owl
   xx Owls
Elgeyo (African tribe) (DT434.E;
      Ethnography, DT429)
   xx Ethnology—Kenya
Elgin marbles (NB92)
Elijah the Prophet's Day (Orthodox Eastern
      Church, BX376.5.E4)
   xx Fasts and feasts
Elimination (QA192)
   x Resultants
   xx Algebra
Elimination reactions (Organic chemistry,
      QD281.E4)
   sa Deamination
      Decarboxylation
      Dehydrogenation
      Desulphuration
   xx Chemical reactions
Eliminative behavior
   sa Defecation
      Urine—Secretion
   xx Animals, Habits and behavior of
      Defecation

      Urine—Secretion
Elite (Social sciences)
   sa Community power
   x Elites (Social sciences)
   xx Leadership
      Power (Social sciences)
      Social classes
      Social groups
Elite (Social sciences) in literature
Elites (Social sciences)
   See Elite (Social sciences)
Elixir of life (GR605)
   sa Alchemy
   x Life, Elixir of
   xx Alchemy
      Folk-lore
      Medicine, Medieval
Elixirs (RS201.E4)
Elizabeth, N.J., Battle of, 1780 (E241.E39)
Elizabeth City, N.C.
— Capture, 1862 (E473.3)
Elizabethtown, N.C., Battle of, 1781
      (E241.E4)
Elk (Indirect) (QL737.U5)
   sa Roosevelt elk
      Tule elk
   x American elk
      Elk, American
      Wapiti
   xx Deer
Elk, American
   See Elk
Elk, European
   See Moose
Elk hunting (Indirect) (SK301)
Elkesaites (BT1377)
   x Elechesaites
   xx Church history—Primitive and early
      church, ca. 30-600
      Jewish Christians—Early church, ca.
      30-600
Elkhounds
   See Norwegian elkhounds
Ellice language (PL6431)
   x Funafuti language
   xx Polynesian languages
Elliott computer
   xx Electronic digital computers
— Programming
Ellipse (QA485; QA559)
   sa Conic sections
   xx Conic sections
— Juvenile literature
Ellipsoid (Analytic geometry, QA561;
      Attractions and potential, QA827)
   sa Functions, Spheroidal
   xx Quadrics
      Surfaces
Ellipsoidal harmonics
   See Lamé's functions
Ellipsoids, Attractions of
   See Attractions of ellipsoids
Ellipsometry (QC443)
   xx Polariscope
      Polarization (Light)
      Surfaces (Technology)
      Thin films
— Tables
Elliptic coordinates
   See Coordinates, Elliptic
Elliptic differential equations
   See Differential equations, Elliptic
Elliptic functions
   See Functions, Elliptic
Elliptic partial differential equations
   See Differential equations, Elliptic
Ellis-van Creveld syndrome (RG629.E4)
   x Chondroectodermal dysplasia

xx Deformities
Elm *(Botany, QK495.U4)*
   sa American elm
      Siberian elm
   Example under Trees
   — Diseases and pests *(Indirect)*
          (SB608.E5)
      sa Dutch elm disease
         Elm leaf-beetle
         Elm mosaic virus
         Elm phloem necrosis
      x American elm—Diseases and pests
      Example under Trees—Diseases and
         pests
Elm, Fossil
Elm blight
   See Dutch elm disease
Elm leaf-beetle *(SB608.E5)*
   xx Elm—Diseases and pests
Elm mosaic virus
   xx Elm—Diseases and pests
Elm phloem necrosis
   x Phloem necrosis of elms
   xx Elm—Diseases and pests
   Example under Virus diseases of plants
Elm spanworm
Elmoran
   See Masai
Elocution *(PN4071-4197)*
   sa Acting
      Choral speaking
      Debates and debating
      Delsarte system
      Diction
      Expression
      Gesture
      Lectures and lecturing
      Oral reading
      Oratory
      Preaching
      Reading
      Singing—Diction
      Ventriloquism
      Voice
      Voice culture
   x Declamation
      Speaking
   xx Diction
      Eloquence
      Expression
      Language and languages
      Oratory
      Reading
      Rhetoric
      Voice
Elocutionists *(PN4059)*
   sa Orators
Elopiformes *(QL637.9.E4)*
   xx Osteichthyes
Eloquence *(PN4001-4173)*
   sa Elocution
      Expression
      Oratory
   xx Oratory
Eluvium
   xx Sediments (Geology)
Elvas, Linhas de, Battle of, 1659 *(DP635)*
   x Linhas de Elvas, Battle of, 1659
Elves
   See Fairies
Elysian fields
   See Elysium
Elysium *(Greek mythology, BL795.E6)*
   sa Future life
      Heaven
      Paradise
   x Elysian fields
      Paradise (Greek mythology)

   xx Eschatology, Greco-Roman
Emaciation
   See Leanness
Emanation (Radioactive substances)
   See Radon
Emancipation, Catholic
   See Catholic emancipation
Emancipation of slaves
   See Emancipation proclamation
      Slavery—Emancipation
      Slavery in the United States—
         Emancipation
Emancipation of the serfs, Russia, 1851
   See Serfdom—Russia
Emancipation of women
   See Woman—Rights of women
Emancipation proclamation *(E453)*
   x Emancipation of slaves
      Slaves, Emancipation of
   xx Slavery in the United States—
      Emancipation
   — Centennial celebrations, etc.
   — Juvenile literature
   — Poetry
Emanon
   See Radon
Emasculation
   See Castration
Embalming *(RA622-3; Manners and customs,*
        GT3340)
   sa Mummies
      Post-mortem plastic surgery
   x Mortuary customs
   xx Burial
      Dead
      Mummies
      Undertakers and undertaking
   — Law and legislation *(Direct)*
Embankments *(TA760-770; Canals, TC759;*
        Coasts, TC337; Rivers, TC533)
   sa Dikes (Engineering)
      Earth dams
      Levees
      Retaining walls
      Rock slopes
      Sea-walls
      Shore protection
   xx Canals
      Civil engineering
      Dikes (Engineering)
      Earthwork
      Fills (Earthwork)
      Hydraulic structures
      Rivers
      Shore protection
      Slopes (Soil mechanics)
   — Charts, diagrams, etc.
   — Safety regulations *(Direct)*
Embargo *(International law, JX4491)*
   sa Blockade
      Blockade, Pacific
      Reprisals
   x European War, 1914-1918—Embargoes
   xx Blockade
      International law
      Sanctions (International law)
      War, Maritime (International law)
Embargo, 1807-1809 *(E336.5; HF3027.1)*
Embarkation (Military science)
   x Embarkation of troops
   xx Transports
Embarkation of troops
   See Embarkation (Military science)
Embarrassment
   xx Self-consciousness
Embassies
   See Ambassadors
      Diplomatic and consular service

   Embassy buildings
Embassy buildings *(Direct)* *(NA4440-4447)*
   x Embassies
   xx Diplomatic and consular service
      Public buildings
Embeddings, Topological
   See Topological imbeddings
Embeddings (Mathematics) *(Algebraic*
        geometry, QA564)
   sa Topological imbeddings
   x Imbeddings (Mathematics)
   xx Geometry, Algebraic
Embellishment (Music) *(MT80)*
   sa Music—Performance
      Variation (Music)
   x Ornaments (Music)
   xx Music—Instruction and study
      Musical notation
      Variation (Music)
Embellishment (Vocal music) *(MT80)*
   sa Music—Performance
   x Coloratura
   xx Fioriture
      Music—Instruction and study
      Ornaments (Music)
      Vocal music—History and criticism
Ember-day menus
   See Lenten menus
Ember days
   xx Fasts and feasts
Embezzlement *(Direct)* *(HV6675-6685)*
   sa Trials (Embezzlement)
   x Defalcation
   xx Criminal law
      Larceny
      Offenses against property
      White collar crimes
Embiotocidae
   See Surf-fishes
Emblem books
   xx Illustrated books
Emblem books, German, ₜetc.₎
   x German ₜetc.₎ emblem books
Emblems *(Art, N7740; Christianity,*
        BV150-155; Comparative religion,
        BL603; Heraldry, CR; Literature,
        PN6349-6358)
   sa Christian art and symbolism
      Devices
      Fasces
      Industrial design coordination
      Insignia
      Maces, Ceremonial
      Mottoes
      Railroads—Freight-cars—Markings
      Regalia (Insignia)
      Society emblems
      Symbolism
      Trade-union emblems
      United Nations—Emblem and flag
      headings beginning with the word
         Emblem
   xx Christian art and symbolism
      Devices
      Heraldry
      Signs and symbols
      Symbolism
Emblems, National *(Direct)*
   sa Devices
      Flags
      Heraldry
      Insignia
      National flowers
      National songs
      Seals (Numismatics)
   x National emblems
   xx Flags
      Heraldry

Emblems, National *(Direct) (Continued)*
    Insignia
    Seals (Numismatics)
  — Juvenile literature
Emblems, State *(Direct)*
    x State emblems
  — Juvenile literature
Embolism *(RC691)*
    sa Amniotic fluid embolism
    Blood—Circulation, Disorders of
    Cerebral embolism and thrombosis
    Fat embolism
    Infarction
    Pulmonary embolism
    Thromboembolism
    xx Arterial occlusions
Embomma language
  See Congo language
Embossed bindings
  See Bookbinding—Embossed bindings
Embossing (Metal-work) *(TS213)*
    xx Metal-work
    Metals—Finishing
    Surfaces (Technology)
Embossing (Typography) *(Z256)*
    x Printing, Practical—Embossing
    xx Printing, Practical
Embossing of glass
  See Glass embossing
Embroidery *(Direct) (Art, NK9200-9310;*
    Manufacture, TS1783; Needlework,
    TT770-777; Trade, HD9935)
    sa Beadwork
    Canvas embroidery
    Church vestments
    Crewelwork
    Cross-stitch
    Doilies
    Ecclesiastical embroidery
    Fabric pictures
    Hardanger needlework
    Leather embroidery
    Needlework
    Punched work
    Samplers
    xx Art, Decorative
    Arts and crafts movement
    Decoration and ornament
    Fancy work
    Needlework
    Sewing
  — Collectors and collecting *(Direct)*
  — Juvenile literature
  — Patterns *(TT753-5; TT770-773)*
    x Patterns for embroidery
Embroidery, Egyptian, [English, Turkish, etc.]
    x Egyptian [English, Turkish, etc.]
    embroidery
Embroidery, English
    sa Hastings embroidery
Embroidery, Georgian *(Direct)*
    x Georgian embroidery
Embroidery, Indian
  See Indians of North America—Embroidery
Embroidery, Machine *(TS1783)*
    x Machine embroidery
Embroidery, Medieval *(Direct)*
Embroidery, Oriental *(NK9272-9285)*
    x Oriental embroidery
Embroidery, Stuart *(Direct)*
    x Stuart embroidery
Embroidery, Tudor *(Direct)*
    x Tudor embroidery
Embroidery industry *(Direct) (HD9935)*
    sa Wages—Embroidery industry
    xx Textile industry and fabrics
Embryogeny
  See Embryology

Embryology *(QL951-973)*
    sa Amniotic liquid
    Cells
    Chemical embryology
    Developmental biology
    Developmental genetics
    Embryology, Experimental
    Fertilization (Biology)
    Fetus
    Gametes
    Gametogenesis
    Gastrulation
    Genetics
    Germ cells
    Germinal layers
    Graafian follicle
    Metamorphosis
    Morphogenesis
    Myogenesis
    Neoteny
    Neural tube
    Ontogeny
    Ovoviviparity
    Ovulation
    Ovum
    Parablast
    Paroöphoron
    Placenta
    Polyembryony
    Protoplasm
    Reproduction
    Tumors, Embryonal
    x Development
    Egg (Biology)
    Embryogeny
    Epigenesis
    Zoology—Embryology
    xx Biology
    Cells
    Developmental biology
    Evolution
    Morphology (Animals)
    Protoplasm
    Reproduction
    Zoology
  — Abstracts
  — Atlases *(QL956)*
  — Birds
    sa Chick embryo
    Eggs—Incubation
  — Birds, [Crustacea, Insects, etc.]
    Works on the embryology of a special
    class, order, family, genus, or spe-
    cies are entered under Embryology,
    subdivided by the larger zoological
    groups only. When the monograph
    treats of one of the smaller divi-
    sions, additional entry is made un-
    der the special subject, *e.g.* 1. Em-
    bryology—Crustacea. 2. Lobsters.
    x Birds [Crustacea, Insects, etc.]—
    Embryology
  — — Juvenile literature
  — Charts, diagrams, etc.
  — Cultures and culture media
  — Fishes
    xx Fishes—Development
  — Laboratory manuals *(QL957)*
  — Technique
  — Terminology *(QL952)*
Embryology, Chemical
  See Chemical embryology
Embryology, Experimental *(QL961)*
    x Experimental embryology
    xx Embryology
  — Technique

Embryology, Human *(QM601-611)*
    Works on the fetal development of a spe-
    cial organ of the body have duplicate
    entry, *e.g.* 1. Heart. 2. Embryology,
    Human.
    x Human embryology
    xx Human biology
    Human reproduction
  — Atlases
  — Juvenile literature
  — Laboratory manuals
  — Research *(Direct)*
Embryology, Vegetable
  See Botany—Embryology
Embryology, Veterinary
  See Veterinary embryology
Embryology (Botany)
  See Botany—Embryology
Embryotomy, Veterinary
  See Veterinary obstetrics
Embu (Bantu people) *(DT434.E242)*
    x Waembu (Bantu people)
    xx Bantus
    Ethnology—Kenya
Embu language
    xx Bantu languages
Emerald mines and mining *(Indirect)*
    (TN997.E5)
Emeralds *(Mineralogy, QE394.E;*
    Technology, TS755.E5)
    Example under Precious stones
Emergencies
  See Accidents
    First aid in illness and injury
Emergencies, Assistance in
  See Assistance in emergencies
Emergencies, Medical
  See Accidents
    First aid in illness and injury
    Medical emergencies
Emergency assistance
  See Assistance in emergencies
Emergency clothing supply
    xx Civil defense
    Clothing and dress
    Disaster relief
Emergency communication systems
    sa Radio
    Telephone
    Tornado warning systems
    xx Civil defense
    Disaster relief
    Telecommunication
Emergency equipment
  See Survival and emergency equipment
Emergency facilities, Amortization of
  See Amortization deductions
Emergency food supply *(Direct)*
    sa Food relief
    x Stockpiling of food supplies
    xx Civil defense
    Disaster relief
    Emergency mass feeding
    Food relief
    Food supply
  — Law and legislation *(Direct)*
    xx War and emergency legislation
Emergency housing *(Direct)*
    xx Civil defense
    Disaster relief
    Housing
Emergency kits
  See Survival and emergency equipment
Emergency landings (over water)
  See Aeroplanes—Ditching
Emergency legislation
  See War and emergency legislation

Emergency lighting
    x Lighting, Emergency
    xx Burglary protection
        Electric lighting
        Lighting
Emergency mass feeding *(TX946)*
    sa Emergency food supply
    x Mass feeding
    xx Food relief
        Food service
Emergency medical care
    See Emergency medical services
Emergency medical services *(Direct)*
    (RA645.5-7)
    sa Disaster hospitals
        Disaster nursing
        Hospitals—Emergency service
        subdivisions Ambulance service *and*
            Hospitals—Emergency service *under*
            names of cities
    x Emergency medical care
        Mass casualties—Treatment
    xx Disaster relief
        First aid in illness and injury
        Medical emergencies
    — Cases, clinical reports, statistics
Emergency mental health services
    See Crisis intervention (Psychiatry)
Emergency nursing
    sa Disaster nursing
    xx Disaster nursing
        Medical emergencies
        Nurses and nursing
Emergency powers
    See Executive power
        War and emergency powers
Emergency rations
    See Survival and emergency rations
Emergency relief
    See Disaster relief
Emergency rooms
    See Hospitals—Emergency service
Emergency services in hospitals
    See Hospitals—Emergency service
Emergency transportation
    xx Civil defense
        Disaster relief
        Transportation
    — Mathematical models
Emergency water supply *(Direct)*
    xx Civil defense
        Disaster relief
        Water-supply
    — Law and legislation *(Direct)*
        xx War and emergency legislation
Emery *(TN936)*
    xx Corundum
Emery-wheels *(TJ1290)*
    xx Grinding and polishing
        Wheels
Emesis
    See Vomiting
Emetics *(RM359)*
    sa Apomorphine
        Ipecacuanha
    xx Gastrointestinal agents
        Materia medica
Emetine *(RM666.E5; Dentistry, RK701)*
    — Physiological effect
Emigrant remittances *(Direct)*
    x Immigrant remittances
        Remittances, Emigrant
    xx Foreign exchange—Law
Emigrants' narratives
    See United States—Emigration and
        immigration—Personal narratives

Emigrants' reminiscences
    See United States—Emigration and
        immigration—Personal narratives
Emigration and immigration *(JV6001-9500)*
    sa Agricultural colonies
        Alien labor
        Aliens
        Anthropo-geography
        Assimilation (Sociology)
        Children of immigrants
        Colonization
        Frontier workers
        Immigrants in literature
        Man—Migrations
        Migration, Internal
        Naturalization
        Population transfers
        Ports of entry
        Refugees
        Repatriation
        subdivision Emigration and immigration
            under names of countries, cities, etc.;
            and names of special nationalities,
            e.g. Italians in the United States,
            Japanese in San Francisco
    x Foreign population
        Immigrants
        Immigration
        Population, Foreign
    xx Assimilation (Sociology)
        Colonies
        Colonization
        Race problems
        Social problems
    Notes under Colonization; Man—Migrations;
        Migrations of nations
    — Economic aspects *(Direct)*
    — Juvenile literature
    — Psychological aspects
        sa Refugees, Political—Psychology
        xx Assimilation (Sociology)
            Social psychology
    — Religious aspects
        xx Refugees, Religious
Emigration and immigration law *(Direct)*
    sa Admission of nonimmigrants
        Deportation
        Exit permits (Emigration)
        Freedom of movement
        Refugees, Political—Legal status, laws,
            etc.
        Repatriation
    x Immigration law
        Law, Emigration
        Law, Immigration
    xx International travel regulations
        Refugees, Political—Legal status, laws,
            etc.
    — Popular works

            GEOGRAPHIC SUBDIVISIONS

    — United States
        x United States—Emigration and
            immigration law
Emigration and immigration of scientific and
    technical personnel
    See Brain drain
Émigrés *(DC158.1-17)*
    sa France—History—Revolution,
        1789-1799
        Refugees, Political
        French in Russia; French in the United
            States; *and similar headings*
    xx Refugees, Political
Emilio Rondanini (Ship) *(JX598.E7)*
    Example under Consular jurisdiction; Exter-
        ritoriality

Eminent domain *(Direct)* *(HD1261-5;*
    Public works, HD3865-6)
    sa Angary, Right of
        Government liability
        Public servitudes
        Public use
    x Condemnation of land
        Domain, Eminent
        Expropriation
        Land, Condemnation of
    xx Angary, Right of
        Constitutional law
        Government purchasing of real
            property
        Land
        Police power
        Property
        Railroad law
        Railroads
        Real property
        Right of property
    — Cases
Eminent domain (International law)
    x Nationalization of alien property
    xx Alien property
        International law
    — Cases
        sa Sabbatino case
Eminent domain (Roman law)
EMIS (Information retrieval system)
    (Z699.5.A5)
    x Extension Management Information
        System
    xx Management information systems
Emission, Acoustic
    See Acoustic emission
Emission, Field
    See Field emission
Emission, Secondary electron
    See Secondary electron emission
Emission, Synchrotron
    See Synchrotron radiation
Emission, Thermionic
    See Thermionic emission
Emission control devices (Motor vehicles)
    See Motor vehicles—Pollution control
        devices
Emission of electrons
    See Electrons—Emission
Emission of positrons
    See Positrons—Emission
Emission spectroscopy *(QC454)*
    x Spectroscopy, Emission
    xx Spectrum analysis
Emissive power
    See Emissivity
Emissivity
    sa Blackbody radiation
    x Emissive power
    xx Blackbody radiation
        Radiation
    — Measurement
Emmanuel movement *(RZ400)*
    sa Medicine and religion
    xx Medicine and religion
        Mental healing
        Mind and body
Emmenagogues *(RM521)*
    sa Menstruation
    xx Menstruation
Emmental cheese
    See Swiss cheese
Emmenthaler cheese
    See Swiss cheese
Emmy awards
    xx Television broadcasting—Awards
Emotional conditioning
    x Conditioned emotional response

Emotional conditioning *(Continued)*
    xx Conditioned response
       Emotions
Emotional maturity
    x Maturity, Emotional
    xx Emotions
       Genetic psychology
       Maturation (Psychology)
Emotional problems of children *(LB1139.E)*
    xx Child study
       Emotions
Emotionally disturbed children
    See Mentally ill children
       Problem children
Emotions *(BF511-593)*
    sa Affect (Psychology)
       Ambivalence
       Anger
       Anxiety
       Attitude (Psychology)
       Avoidance (Psychology)
       Awe
       Bashfulness
       Belief and doubt
       Catharsis
       Character tests
       Control (Psychology)
       Crying
       Defeat (Psychology)
       Desire
       Elation
       Emotional conditioning
       Emotional maturity
       Emotional problems of children
       Empathy
       Envy
       Escape (Psychology)
       Facial expression
       Fear
       Frustration
       Grief
       Hate
       Horror
       Impulse
       Intimacy (Psychology)
       Jealousy
       Joy
       Laughter
       Love
       Melancholy
       Pain
       Pathognomy
       Pleasure
       Prejudices and antipathies
       Rigidity (Psychology)
       Shame
       Surprise
       Sympathy
       Temperament
       Timidity
       Transference (Psychology)
       Wonder
       Worry
    x Feelings
       Passions
    xx Affect (Psychology)
       Pathognomy
       Psychology
       Psychology, Physiological
       Temperament
    — Biblical teaching
    — Early works to 1850
    — Juvenile literature
Emotions in art
    xx Art
Emotions in literature
    sa Anxiety in literature
       Fear in literature

       Frustration in literature
Emotive-rational psychotherapy
    See Rational-emotive psychotherapy
Empathy *(BF575.E55)*
    xx Attitude (Psychology)
       Emotions
       Prejudices and antipathies
       Social psychology
       Sympathy
Emperor penguin
    xx Penguins
    — Juvenile literature
Emperor system (Japan)
    See Emperor worship, Japanese
Emperor worship *(BL465)*
    x Worship, Emperor
    xx Apotheosis
       Cultus
       Divine right of kings
       Kings and rulers (in religion, folk-lore,
          etc.)
Emperor worship, Japanese
    sa Tennō (Sect)
    x Emperor system (Japan)
       Japan—Emperors—Cultus
       Japanese emperor worship
       Tennō system (Japan)
    xx Cultus, Japanese
Emperor worship, Roman *(DG124)*
    x Roman emperor worship
       Roman emperors—Cultus
    xx Cultus, Roman
       Rome—Kings and rulers
Emperors *(D107)*
    sa Apotheosis
       Byzantine emperors
       Japan—Emperors
       Roman emperors
       subdivision Kings and rulers *under*
          names of countries
    x Rulers
       Sovereigns
    xx Apotheosis
       Kings and rulers
       Monarchy
Emperors as poets
    See Kings and rulers as poets
Emphysema, Pulmonary *(RC776)*
    x Pulmonary emphysema
    xx Lungs—Diseases
Emphyteusis *(Direct)*
    xx Leases
Emphyteusis (Roman law)
Empire, Islamic
    See Islamic Empire
Empire Day *(DA18)*
    xx Holidays
Empirical argument
    See God—Proof, Empirical
Empirical theology *(BT83.53)*
    x Theology, Empirical
    xx Empiricism
       Theology, Doctrinal
Empiricism *(B816)*
    sa Empirical theology
       Realism
    xx Experience
       Knowledge, Theory of
       Rationalism
Employee absenteeism
    See Absenteeism (Labor)
Employee benefits
    See Non-wage payments
Employee communication
    See Communication in personnel
       management
Employee competitive behavior
    sa Incentives in industry

       Socialist competition
    x Competitive behavior, Employee
    xx Employee morale
       Incentives in industry
       Personnel management
       Psychology, Industrial
Employee counseling
    x Counseling, Employee
       Industrial counseling
    xx Counseling
       Industrial relations
       Personnel management
       Welfare work in industry
Employee discounts *(Direct)* *(HD4928.E4)*
    x Discounts, Employee
    xx Non-wage payments
       Wages—Clerks (Retail trade)
Employee-employer relations
    See Industrial relations
Employee food service
    See Industrial feeding
Employee housing
    See Industrial housing
Employee incentives
    See Incentives in industry
Employee induction
    x Employee orientation
    xx Employees, Training of
       Personnel management
Employee maintenance
    x Maintenance, Employee
       Quarters-subsistence-laundry allowances
    xx Wages
Employee-management relations in
        government *(Direct)*
    sa Collective bargaining—Government
       employees
    x Management-employee relations in
       government
    xx Civil service
       Industrial relations
Employee morale
    sa Employee competitive behavior
       Incentives in industry
       Job satisfaction
    x Industrial morale
       Morale, Employee
    xx Morale
       Personnel management
       Psychology, Industrial
Employee orientation
    See Employee induction
Employee ownership *(Direct)*
       (Profit-sharing, HD2970-3110;
       Stockholders, HD2781.S7)
    x Stock ownership for employees
    xx Employees' representation in
       management
       Incentives in industry
       Profit-sharing
       Stock ownership
Employee pension trusts
    See Pension trusts
Employee recreation
    See Industrial recreation
Employee rules *(Direct)*
    sa Featherbedding (Industrial relations)
       Psychiatric hospitals—Employee rules
    x Rules for employees
       Shop rules
       Work rules
    xx Labor discipline
       Labor laws and legislation
       Personnel management
Employee seniority
    See Seniority, Employee
Employee suggestions
    See Suggestion systems

Employee training directors   (Direct)
  x Training officers
  xx Employees, Training of
Employee turnover
  See Labor turnover
Employee vacations
  See Vacations, Employee
Employees, Clerical
  See Clerks
Employees, Dismissal of   (Direct) (HD7813)
  sa Employees, Reinstatement of
    Employees, Suspension of
    Executives, Dismissal of
    Exit interviews
    High school teachers—Tenure
    Layoff systems
    Supervisors, Dismissal of
    Teachers—Tenure
    Temporary employment
    Wages—Dismissal wage
  x Dismissal of employees
    Notice of dismissal
    Termination of employment
  xx Labor and laboring classes
    Labor contract
    Labor laws and legislation
    Master and servant
    Personnel management
    Temporary employment
    Wages—Dismissal wage
  — Anecdotes, facetiae, satire, etc.
Employees, Identification of
  See Labor passports
Employees, Probationary   (Direct)
  x Probationary employees
  xx Labor and laboring classes
    Labor contract
Employees, Rating of   (T60.R)
  sa Ability—Testing
    Executives, Rating of
    Performance standards
    Supervisors, Rating of
    Teachers, Rating of
  x Efficiency rating
    Performance rating (of employees)
    Rating of employees
    Service rating
  xx Ability—Testing
    Labor and laboring classes
    Personnel management
    Teachers, Rating of
  — Programmed instruction
  — Terminology
Employees, Recruiting of
  See Recruiting of employees
Employees, Reinstatement of   (Direct)
  x Reinstatement of employees
  xx Employees, Dismissal of
    Labor contract
    Personnel management
Employees, Relocation of   (Direct)
    Here are entered works on the transfer of
    employees by their companies to
    another geographical location. Works
    on the transfer of employees from one
    department or position to another
    within the same company, within the
    same geographical location are entered
    under Employees, Transfer of.
  sa Employees, Transfer of
  x Relocation of employees
  xx Employees, Transfer of
    Labor mobility
    Personnel management
  Note under Employees, Transfer of
Employees, Reporting to
  sa Bulletin boards
    Employees' magazines, handbooks, etc.

  x Reporting to employees
  xx Communication in personnel
      management
    Industrial relations
    Personnel management
Employees, Resignation of   (Direct)
  sa Exit interviews
    High school teachers—Tenure
  x Quits
    Resignation of employees
    Termination of employment
  xx Labor contract
    Labor mobility
    Labor turnover
Employees, Supervision of
  See Supervision of employees
Employees, Suspension of   (Direct)
  x Suspension of employees
  xx Employees, Dismissal of
    Labor contract
    Labor laws and legislation
    Master and servant
    Personnel management
Employees, Training of   (Direct)
    (HF5549.5.T7; T58)
    Works on employee training in specific
    industries, etc. have duplicate entry
    under the name of the industry, etc.
  sa Apprentices
    Employee induction
    Employee training directors
    Executives, Training of
    Hospitals—Staff—In-service training
    Industrial tours
    Interns (Business)
    Interns (Civil service)
    Learners, Industrial
    Moving-pictures in industry
    Paraprofessionals in social service—
      In-service training
    Public health personnel—In-service
      training
    Retraining, Occupational
    Social workers—In-service training
    Technical education
    Training manuals
  x In-service training
    Training of employees
    Training within industry
    Vestibule schools
  xx Apprentices
    Occupational training
    Personnel management
    Technical education
  Notes under Occupational training; Vocational
      education
  — Audio-visual aids
  — Costs
  — Evaluation
  — Law and legislation   (Direct)
  — Programmed instruction
Employees, Transfer of   (Direct)
    Here are entered works on the transfer of
    employees from one department or po-
    sition to another within the same com-
    pany, within the same geographical lo-
    cation. Works dealing with the transfer
    of employees by their companies to
    another geographical location are en-
    tered under Employees, Relocation of.
  sa Employees, Relocation of
  x Transfer of employees
  xx Employees, Relocation of
    Personnel management
  Note under Employees, Relocation of
Employees' buildings and facilities   (NA6598)
  sa Restaurants, lunch rooms, etc.
  x Buildings, Employees'

    Community centers for employees
    Employees' service buildings
    Personnel buildings
    Service buildings, Employees'
    Welfare buildings in industry
  xx Factories
    Industrial buildings
    Office buildings
    Welfare work in industry
Employees' copyright
  See Copyright, Employees'
Employees' handbooks
  See Employees' magazines, handbooks, etc.
Employees' inventions
  See Inventions, Employees'
Employees' magazines, handbooks, etc.
    (Direct)
    Here are entered works devoted exclu-
    sively or mainly to employees' affairs
    and interests.
    Works treating of the history, purpose,
    preparation, value, etc. of periodical
    publications published by individual
    business concerns to disseminate in-
    formation promoting their interests
    and success are entered under the
    heading House organs.
  x Company magazines
    Company publications
    Employees' handbooks
    Employees' manuals
    Factory press
    House organs, Interior
    Shop papers
  xx Employees, Reporting to
    Industrial relations
    Journalism, Technical
    Labor and laboring classes—Periodicals
    Personnel management
  Note under House organs
Employees' manuals
  See Employees' magazines, handbooks, etc.
Employees' representation in management
    (Direct) (HD5650-5659)
  sa Collective bargaining
    Company unions
    Employee ownership
    Shop stewards
    Works councils
  x Codetermination (Industrial relations)
    Labor representation in regulation of
      industry
    Management, Employees'
      representation in
  xx Collective bargaining
    Industrial relations
    Industry
    Labor and laboring classes
  Example under Industrial relations
Employees' service buildings
  See Employees' buildings and facilities
Employees' vacations
  See Vacations, Employee
Employer-employee relations
  See Industrial relations
Employer identification numbers   (Direct)
  xx Tax administration and procedure
Employers' associations   (Indirect)
    (HD6350-6940)
  sa Gilds
    Trade and professional associations
  x Associations, Employers'
  xx Gilds
    Societies
    Trade and professional associations
Employers' liability   (Direct)
    (HD7814-7816)
  sa Factories—Safety appliances

Employers' liability *(Direct)*
            (HD7814-7816) *(Continued)*
      Factory inspection
      Independent contractors
      Industrial accidents
      Industrial safety—Law and legislation
      Insurance, Employers' liability
      Occupational diseases
      Occupations, Dangerous
      Personal injuries
      Safety appliances
      Workmen's compensation
   x Injuries (Law)
      Liability, Employers'
      Tort liability of employers
   xx Accident law
      Accidents
      Factories—Safety appliances
      Factory inspection
      Factory laws and legislation
      Independent contractors
      Industrial accidents
      Liability (Law)
      Master and servant
      Negligence
      Occupations, Dangerous
      Personal injuries
      Strict liability
      Workmen's compensation
   — Terminology
   — War risks *(Direct)*
      xx War and emergency legislation

            GEOGRAPHIC SUBDIVISIONS

   — United States
      xx Interstate commerce
Employers' liability insurance
   See Insurance, Employers' liability
Employment, Free choice of
   See Free choice of employment
Employment, Part-time
   See Part-time employment
Employment, Seniority in
   See Seniority, Employee
Employment, Summer
   See Summer employment
Employment, Supplementary
   See Supplementary employment
Employment, Temporary
   See Temporary employment
Employment (Economic theory) *(HB301)*
   sa Job vacancies
      Labor supply
      Manpower policy
   xx Economics
   — Mathematical models
Employment agencies *(Direct)*
            (HD5861-6000)
   sa Hiring halls
      Job vacancies
      Labor contractors
      Labor supply
      Teacher placement agencies
   x Agencies, Employment
      Employment exchanges
      Employment offices
      Labor exchanges
   xx Full employment policies
      Labor and laboring classes
      Labor supply
      Labor turnover
      Personnel management
      Recruiting of employees
      Unemployed
Employment and age
   See Age and employment
Employment and alcoholism
   See Alcoholism and employment

Employment and drug abuse
   See Drug abuse and employment
Employment and homosexuality
   See Homosexuality and employment
Employment discrimination
   See Discrimination in employment
Employment exchanges
   See Employment agencies
Employment forecasting *(Direct)*
   sa Labor supply
   x Forecasting, Employment
   xx Economic forecasting
      Labor supply
   — Mathematical models
Employment in foreign countries
   See Americans in foreign countries—
            Employment
      similar headings
Employment interviewing *(HF5549.5.I6)*
   sa Exit interviews
   xx Applications for positions
      Interviewing
      Recruiting of employees
Employment management
   See Personnel management
Employment of cardiacs
   See Cardiacs—Employment
Employment of children
   See Children—Employment
Employment of diabetics
   See Diabetics—Employment
Employment of ex-convicts
   See Ex-convicts, Employment of
Employment of students
   See Student employment
Employment of the blind
   See Blind—Employment
Employment of the mentally ill
   See Mentally ill—Employment
Employment of the physically handicapped
   See Physically handicapped—Employment
Employment of veterans
   See Veterans—Employment
Employment of war victims
   See War victims—Employment
Employment of wives
   See Wives—Employment
Employment of women
   See Woman—Employment
Employment of youth
   See Youth—Employment
Employment offices
   See Employment agencies
Employment opportunities
   See Job vacancies
Employment references *(Direct)*
   x Letters of recommendation
      Recommendations for positions
      References, Employment
   xx Applications for positions
      Master and servant
      Personnel management
Employment stabilization *(Direct)*
   sa Full employment policies
      Wages—Annual wage
   x Stabilization of employment
   xx Full employment policies
      Industrial management
      Labor turnover
      Personnel management
      Unemployed
      Unemployment, Seasonal
Employment tax
   See Payroll tax
Employment tests *(Direct)*
   sa Occupational aptitude tests
   xx Occupational aptitude tests
      Personnel management

Empresses, Byzantine
   See Byzantine empresses
Empresses, Japanese
   See Japan—Empresses
Empresses, Roman
   See Roman empresses
Empresses, Russian
   See Russian empresses
Empresses, Turkish
   See Turkish empresses
Emptiness (Sunyata)
   See Sunyata
Empyema *(RC742; Children's diseases,
            RJ436.E5)*
   sa Pleurisy
   xx Pleurisy
Empyrean
   xx Heaven
Emulsin *(QP601)*
Emulsion paint
   xx Paint
Emulsion polymerization
   See Addition polymerization
Emulsions *(Chemical engineering, TP156.E6;
            Pharmacy, RS201.E5; Physics,
            QC183)*
   sa Photographic emulsions
   xx Mixtures
      Pharmacy
      Separation (Technology)
Emulsions, Nuclear
   See Nuclear emulsions
Emus *(QL696.C3)*
   x Dromaeidae
   xx Ratitae
EMW automobile
En ventre sa mère
   See Unborn children (Law)
Enamel, Dental
   x Dental enamel
      Tooth enamel
   xx Teeth
   — Spectra
Enamel and enameling *(Direct) (Art,
            NK5000-5015; Pottery, TP812)*
   sa Cloisonné
      Copper enameling
      Painted enamel
   x Enamels
      Porcelain enamels
   xx Art, Decorative
      Arts and crafts movement
      Ceramic coating
      Coating processes
      Coatings
      Decoration and ornament
      Jewelry making
      Metals—Finishing
   — Defects
   — Laboratory manuals
   — Testing
Enamel and enameling, Byzantine *(Direct)*
   x Byzantine enamel and enameling
Enamel and enameling, English, ⌐**German,
      etc.**⌐
Enamel and enameling, Islamic
   x Enamel and enameling, Muslim
      Islamic enamel and enameling
      Muslim enamel and enameling
Enamel and enameling, Muslim
   See Enamel and enameling, Islamic
Enamel and enameling, Renaissance *(Direct)*
   x Renaissance enamel and enameling
Enamel paints
   See Paint
      Painting, Industrial
      Varnish and varnishing

Enameled ware *(TS700-705)*
  sa Agate ware
      Transfer-printing
  xx Iron industry and trade
  — Collectors and collecting *(Direct)*
  — Standards
Enamels
  See Enamel and enameling
Enargite *(TN780)*
Encapsulation, Particle
  See Microencapsulation
Encapsulation (Electronics)
  See Electronic apparatus and appliances—
      Plastic embedment
Encaustic painting *(ND2480)*
  x Wax-painting
  xx Mural painting and decoration
      Painting
      Painting, Ancient
Encephalitides
  See Encephalitis
Encephalitis
  sa Encephalomyelitis
  x Brain—Inflammation
      Encephalitides
  xx Brain—Diseases
Encephalitis, Epidemic
  sa Encephalitis, Tick-borne
      Equine encephalomyelitis
      Japanese encephalitis
      St. Louis encephalitis
  x Encephalitis lethargica
      Epidemic encephalitis
Encephalitis, Hemorrhagic
  See Hemorrhagic encephalitis
Encephalitis, Postvaccinal
  x Postvaccinal encephalitis
Encephalitis, St. Louis
  See St. Louis encephalitis
Encephalitis, Tick-borne
  sa Tick-borne encephalitis viruses
  x Tick-borne encephalitis
  xx Encephalitis, Epidemic
Encephalitis lethargica
  See Encephalitis, Epidemic
Encephalitis Type B
  See Japanese encephalitis
Encephalitis viruses, Tick-borne
  See Tick-borne encephalitis viruses
Encephalocele *(QM691)*
  sa Meningo-encephalocele
  x Brain—Hernia
  xx Skull—Abnormities and deformities
Encephalography *(RC386.5)*
  sa Electroencephalography
      Pneumoencephalography
      Rheoencephalography
      Ultrasonic encephalography
  xx Brain—Diseases—Diagnosis
      Diagnosis, Radioscopic
      Radiography
Encephalomyelitis
  sa Allergic encephalomyelitis
      Avian encephalomyelitis
      Equine encephalomyelitis
      Teschen disease
  x Meningo-encephalomyelitis
      Myelinoclasia
      Perivenous demyelination
  xx Central nervous system—Diseases
      Demyelination
      Encephalitis
Encephalomyelitis, Avian
  See Avian encephalomyelitis
Enchondroma
  xx Cartilage
Encke's comet *(QB723.E3)*

Enclaves in granite
  See Granite—Inclusions
Enclosure (Canon law)
Enclosure (Monasticism)
  x Cloisters
  xx Convents and nunneries
      Monasteries
      Monasticism and religious orders
      Monasticism and religious orders for
        women
Enclosure walls
  See Curtain walls
Enclosures
  See Inclosures
Encomiendas (Latin America) *(F1411;*
      HD464)
  xx Indians, Treatment of—Latin America
Encounter groups
  See Group relations training
Encroachment, Saltwater
  See Saltwater encroachment
Enculturation
  See Socialization
Encumbrances (Law) *(Direct)*
  sa Liens
      Mortgages
      Real covenants
      Rent charges
      Restraints on alienation
      Servitudes
  x Incumbrances (Law)
  xx Real property
Encyclicals, Papal *(Collections, BX860)*
  x Papal encyclicals
  xx Bulls, Papal
      Catholic Church—Doctrinal and
        controversial works
      Papal documents
Encyclopedias and dictionaries *(AE; AG)*
  Encyclopedias and dictionaries of a par-
    ticular subject are entered under the
    subject with subdivisions Dictionaries,
    Dictionaries, Juvenile or, in the case of
    countries, cities, etc. or ethnic groups,
    Dictionaries and encyclopedias, *e.g.*
    Botany—Dictionaries; Catholic
    Church—Dictionaries, Juvenile;
    France—Dictionaries and ency-
    clopedias; Jews—Dictionaries and en-
    cyclopedias.
  sa Children's encyclopedias and
      dictionaries
      Dictionaries, Polyglot
      Handbooks, vade-mecums, etc.
      Lexicography
      Picture dictionaries
      Questions and answers
      Thesauri
      Women's encyclopedias and
        dictionaries
  x Books of knowledge
      Cyclopedias
      Dictionaries
      Knowledge, Books of
      Subject dictionaries
  xx Reference books
  — Authorship
  — Early works to 1600
  — History and criticism
    xx Lexicography
  — Illustrations
    See Picture dictionaries, Dutch,
      [English, etc.]
Encyclopedias and dictionaries, Danish,
    [Romanian, Spanish, etc.]
Encyclopedists *(B1911)*
  xx French literature
Encystment (Zoology) *(Protozoa, QL369)*

End of the earth (Astronomy)
  See End of the world (Astronomy)
End of the world *(Astronomy, QB638.8;*
    Theology, BT875-6)
  Here are entered works dealing not only
    with the Judgment Day, but also with
    preceding events, signs, fulfilments of
    prophecies, etc.
  sa Antichrist
      Judgment Day
      One thousand, A.D.
      Universe, Destruction of
  x World, End of the
  xx Eschatology
  — Art
  — Early works to 1800
End of the world (Astronomy) *(QB638.8)*
  x End of the earth (Astronomy)
  xx Earth
  — Juvenile literature *(QB638.8)*
End of the world (Islam)
  sa Judgment Day (Islam)
  xx Eschatology, Islamic
End of the world in literature
End papers
  See Endpapers
End play (Football) *(GV951.25)*
  xx Football
Endangered species
  See Rare animals
Endarteritis
Endeavor
  See Struggle
Endecasyllable
  See Hendecasyllable
Endemic dental fluorosis
  See Mottled enamel
Endermic medication *(RM151)*
  x Endermic method
      Endermosis
  xx Therapeutics
Endermic method
  See Endermic medication
Endermosis
  See Endermic medication
Endive, Belgian
  See Belgian endive
Endive, French
  See Belgian endive
Endleaf
  See Endpapers
Endless punishment
  See Future punishment
      Hell
Endlichite *(QE391.E5)*
Endocarditis *(RC685.E5)*
  xx Cattle—Diseases
      Heart—Diseases
Endoceratoidea
  xx Cephalopoda, Fossil
Endochondral ossification
  xx Bone
      Cartilage
Endocrine diagnosis
  See Glands, Ductless—Diseases—Diagnosis
Endocrine diseases
  See Glands, Ductless—Diseases
Endocrine genetics
  xx Endocrinology
      Genetics
Endocrine glands
  See Glands, Ductless
Endocrine gynecology
  sa Sexual cycle of women
  x Gynecologic endocrinology
  xx Endocrinology
      Gynecology

Endocrine obstetrics
See Obstetrical endocrinology
Endocrine therapy
See Hormone therapy
Endocrines
See Endocrinology
Endocrinological gastroenterology
See Gastrointestinal hormones
Endocrinology (Medicine, RC648-665; Physiology, QP187)
sa Clinical endocrinology
Endocrine genetics
Endocrine gynecology
Glands, Ductless
Gonadotropin
Hormone receptors
Hormones
Hormones, Sex
Neuroendocrinology
Obstetrical endocrinology
Organotherapy
Ovaries
Pancreas
Parathyroid glands
Pediatric endocrinology
Pineal body
Pituitary body
Premenstrual syndrome
Rejuvenation
Schering award
Testicle
Thymus gland
Thyroid gland
Veterinary endocrinology
x Endocrines
xx Hormones
Internal medicine
Neurosecretion
Organotherapy
— Abstracts
— Atlases
— Cases, clinical reports, statistics
— Formulae, receipts, prescriptions
— Psychosomatic aspects
x Psychoendocrinology
xx Medicine, Psychosomatic
Neuroendocrinology
— Statistical methods
— Technique
Endocrinology, Comparative (Anatomy, QL868; Physiology, QP187)
x Comparative endocrinology
xx Physiology, Comparative
Endocrinology, Experimental
x Experimental endocrinology
Endodontia
See Endodontics
Endodontics (RK351)
x Endodontia
xx Teeth—Diseases
— Atlases
Endogamy and exogamy (GN480.3)
sa Totemism
x Exogamy
xx Marriage
Endolymphatic hydrops
See Ménière's disease
Endometriosis (RG301)
x Adenomyosis
Endometrium—Inflammation
xx Uterus—Diseases
Uterus—Tumors
Woman—Diseases
Endometrium
xx Mucous membrane
Uterus
— Cancer
— — Diagnosis

— Diseases
— — Diagnosis
— Inflammation
See Endometriosis
Endoplasmic reticulum (QH603.E6)
xx Cell organelles
Endorsements
See Indorsements
Endoscope and endoscopy (RF476, RF514; Special, RC786, RC864, RC872, etc.)
sa Arthroscopy
Bronchoscope and bronchoscopy
Colposcope
Colposcopy
Laparoscopy
xx Genito-urinary organs—Diseases
Endothelioma
xx Tumors
Endothelium (QM562)
Endotoxin
xx Bacteria
Endotoxin shock
See Septic shock
Endotracheal anesthesia
See Intratracheal anesthesia
Endowed charities
See Charitable uses, trusts, and foundations
Charities
Endowments
Endowment insurance
See Insurance, Life—Endowment policies
Endowment of research (Indirect) (LB2336-7; Q181)
sa Education and state
Engineering and state
Research institutes
Scholarships
Science and state
State encouragement of science, literature, and art
Technology and state
x Educational endowments
Philanthropy
Research, Endowment of
xx Education and state
Endowments
Intellectual cooperation
Research—Finance
State encouragement of science, literature, and art
Endowments (Direct) (Charities, HV16-25; Higher education, LB2336-7)
Here are entered general works on endowed institutions, endowment funds and donations to such funds. Works on the legal structure of endowments are entered under the heading Charitable uses, trusts, and foundations.
sa Charitable uses, trusts, and foundations
Charities
Educational fund raising
Endowment of research
Libraries—Gifts, legacies
Music—Endowments
University investments
subdivision Endowments under names of individual institutions
x Donations
Educational endowments
Endowed charities
Foundations (Endowments)
Hospital endowments
Philanthropy
School endowments
xx Charitable uses, trusts, and foundations
Charities
Education and state

Note under Charitable uses, trusts, and foundations
— Employees
See Endowments—Officials and employees
— Officials and employees
x Endowments—Employees
— Program-related investments
x Program-related investments of endowments
Social investments
xx Economic assistance, Domestic
Institutional investments
— Public relations
See Public relations—Endowments
Endpapers (Z272)
sa Marbling (Bookbinding)
Pastedowns
x End papers
Endleaf
Endsheet
Flyleaf
xx Book ornamentation
Bookbinding
Endrumpf
See Peneplains
Ends and means (BJ84.E5)
x Means and ends
xx Ethics
Philosophy
Endsheet
See Endpapers
Endurance, Physical
See Physical fitness
Enema (RM163)
sa Barium enema
x Colonic irrigation
Intestinal irrigation
xx Irrigation (Medicine)
Enemy aliens
See Aliens
Enemy in the Bible
sa Devil
x Adversary in the Bible
Bible—Adversary
Bible—Enemy
Enemy property
Here are entered general works on the treatment of enemy property taken on land, either captured in the field or seized and confiscated (or administered) elsewhere. Works dealing with property taken at sea are entered under Capture at sea.
sa Alien property
Booty (International law)
Capture at sea
European War, 1914-1918— Confiscations and contributions
Military occupation damages
Requisitions, Military
Trading with the enemy
World War, 1939-1945—Confiscations and contributions
x Captured property
xx Alien property
Capture at sea
Military occupation
Requisitions, Military
Trading with the enemy
War (International law)
Energy
See Force and energy
Energy, Vital
See Vital force
Energy-band theory of solids
sa Brillouin zones
Current noise (Electricity)

Cyclotron resonance
Effective mass (Physics)
Energy gap (Physics)
Fermi surfaces
Free electron theory of metals
Hartree-Fock approximation
  x Band theory of solids
  xx Crystallography, Mathematical
Electrons
Exciton theory
Molecules
Quantum theory
Solids
Wave mechanics
Energy budget (Geophysics)
  sa Atmospheric radiation
Bioenergetics
Heat budget (Geophysics)
Hydrologic cycle
Ocean-atmosphere interaction
Terrestrial radiation
  x Budget, Energy (Geophysics)
  xx Atmospheric radiation
Force and energy
Geophysics
Solar radiation
Terrestrial radiation
Transport theory
Energy conservation *(Indirect) (TJ163.3-4)*
Here are entered general works on the
conservation of all forms of energy.
Works on the conservation of a spe-
cific form of energy are entered under
that form, *e.g.* Petroleum conserva-
tion. Works on the conservation of en-
ergy as a physical concept are entered
under Force and energy.
  sa Petroleum conservation
Recycling (Waste, etc.)
Waste heat
  x Conservation of energy resources
Conservation of power resources
  xx Conservation of natural resources
Power resources
Recycling (Waste, etc.)
Energy conversion, Direct
  See Direct energy conversion
Energy distribution, Spectral
  See Spectral energy distribution
Energy gap (Physics) *(QC176.8.E4)*
  x Gap, Energy
  xx Energy-band theory of solids
Photoconductivity
Solids
Energy levels (Quantum mechanics)
  sa Jahn-Teller effect
Level-crossing spectroscopy
Nuclear excitation
Triplet state
  x Energy states
  xx Nuclear excitation
Nuclear physics
Quantum theory
  — Charts, diagrams, etc.
  — Tables, etc.
Energy metabolism
  sa Basal metabolism
Biochemical oxygen demand
  xx Bioenergetics
Metabolism
  — Terminology
Energy of immersion
  See Heat of wetting
Energy research
  See Power resources—Research
Energy resources
  See Power resources

Energy states
  See Energy levels (Quantum mechanics)
Energy transfer
  sa Direct energy conversion
Heat—Transmission
  xx Force and energy
Transport theory
  — Tables
Enets people
  See Entsy
Enfidaville, Battle of, 1943
  x Takrouna, Battle of, 1943
  xx World War, 1939-1945—Campaigns—
Tunisia
Enfield rifle *(UD395.E)*
  xx Rifles
Enforcement measures (International law)
  See Sanctions (International law)
Enforcement of law
  See Law enforcement
Enga (New Guinea people)
  x Mae-Enga
  xx Ethnology—New Guinea
Enga language
  x Tsaga language
  xx Papuan languages
Engagement
  See Betrothal
Engelmann spruce *(SD397.E5)*
  xx Spruce
  — Diseases and pests
      sa Engelmann spruce beetle
Engelmann spruce beetle
  xx Engelmann spruce—Diseases and pests
Engenni language
  xx Kwa languages
Engine nacelles (Aeroplane)
  See Aeroplanes—Nacelles
Engineering *(Direct) (TA; Economics,*
        HD9680-9712)
  sa Agricultural engineering
Aqueducts
Arches
Architecture
Bioengineering
Biomedical engineering
Blasting
Boring
Breakwaters
Bridges
Building materials
Canals
Chemical engineering
Civil engineering
Classification—Books—Engineering
Curves in engineering
Dams
Dikes (Engineering)
Docks
Drainage
Dredging
Earthwork
Electric engineering
Engineering meteorology
Engineering models
Engineers
Engines
Environmental engineering
Fillets (Engineering)
Forestry engineering
Gas engineering
Girders
Harbors
Hydraulic engineering
Industrial engineering
Irrigation
Joints (Engineering)
Low temperature engineering

Machinery
Maintainability (Engineering)
Marine engineering
Masonry
Mechanical drawing
Mechanical engineering
Mechanics
Mensuration
Military engineering
Mining engineering
Municipal engineering
Nuclear engineering
Ocean engineering
Photography in engineering
Plant engineering
Railroad engineering
Railroads—Construction
Reclamation of land
Reliability (Engineering)
Reservoirs
Rivers
Roads
Sanitary engineering
Sea-walls
Statics
Steam engineering
Steam-engines
Strength of materials
Structural engineering
Subways
Surveying
Systems engineering
Tolerance (Engineering)
Tunneling
Ventilation
Walls
Water-supply engineering
  x Construction
  xx Industrial arts
Mechanics
Technology
  — Abbreviations
  — Ability testing
  — Abstracting and indexing
  — Accounting *(TA185)*
  — Authorship
      See Technical writing
  — Bibliography
      sa Engineering literature
  — Classification
  — Cold weather conditions
      sa subdivision Cold weather conditions
         under specific engineering
         subjects, e.g. Civil engineering—
         Cold weather conditions; Strip
         mining—Cold weather conditions
      x Cold weather conditions
         (Engineering)
      xx Engineering meteorology
  — Computer programs
  — Congresses *(TA5)*
  — Contracts and specifications *(Direct)*
      (TA180-182)
      xx Engineering law
      Example under Contracts
  — Design
      See Engineering design
  — Electromechanical analogies
  — Estimates and costs *(Direct) (TA183)*
      sa Cost effectiveness
         Engineering economy
         Mechanical engineering—Estimates
           and costs
      x Civil engineering—Estimates and
         costs
      Example under Cost; Costs, Industrial;
         and under reference from Estimates
  — Examinations, questions, etc. *(TA159)*

Engineering *(Direct)* *(TA; Economics,*
  HD9680-9712)
— Examinations, questions, etc. *(TA159)*
  (Continued)
    Note under Questions and answers
— Exhibitions *(TA6)*
    x Exhibitions, Engineering
— Experiments
— Fellowships
    See Engineering—Scholarships,
      fellowships, etc.
— Geology
    See Engineering geology
— Graphic methods *(TA337)*
    Here are entered works on the use of
    scales, graph papers, graphs, nomo-
    graphs and similar graphic devices
    in engineering computation. Works
    on the preparation of drawings for
    use in the design of engineering pro-
    ducts, and in the computation, anal-
    ysis and presentation of engineering
    data, including mechanical draw-
    ings, freehand sketches and graph-
    ical constructions, are entered un-
    der Engineering graphics.
    xx Engineering graphics
      Engineering mathematics
    Note under Engineering graphics
— Indexes *(Z5851)*
    Example under Indexes
— Information services
— Juvenile literature
— Law and legislation
    See Engineering law
— Literature
    See Engineering literature
— Management *(TA190)*
    x Civil engineering—Management
      Structural engineering—Management
    Example under Management
— Manuscripts
— Materials
    See Materials
— Methodology
— Models
    See Engineering models
— Notation *(TA11)*
    x Engineering symbols
— Periodicals
    Example under Periodicals
— — Indexes
    Example under Periodicals—Indexes
— Philosophy
— Pictorial works
— Popular works *(TA148)*
— Problems, exercises, etc.
— Production standards *(TA183)*
— Programmed instruction *(T65.5.P7)*
— Research
    See Engineering research
— Research grants *(Direct)*
    x Engineering research—Research
      grants
— Safety measures
— Scholarships, fellowships, etc. *(Direct)*
    x Engineering fellowships
      Engineering—Fellowships
      Engineering scholarships
    xx Engineering—Study and teaching
— Societies, etc.
    xx Engineering societies
— Statistical methods *(TA340)*
    x Engineering statistics
    xx Engineering mathematics
    Example under Statistics; *and under ref-*
      erence from Statistical methods
— Study and teaching *(Direct)* *(T61-173)*

    sa Engineering—Scholarships,
      fellowships, etc.
      Engineering schools
      Engineering students
    x Civil engineering—Study and
      teaching
    xx Vocational education
    Example under Technical education
— — Law and legislation *(Direct)*
— Supplies *(T12-13)*
— Tables, calculations, etc. *(TA151)*
— Teacher training *(Direct)*
— Terminology *(T9)*
— Tools and implements *(TA213-215)*
    sa Public works equipment
    xx Tools
— — Rate-books
Engineering, Agricultural
    See Agricultural engineering
Engineering, Architectural
    See Building
      Building, Iron and steel
      Strains and stresses
      Strength of materials
      Structures, Theory of
Engineering, Biomedical
    See Biomedical engineering
Engineering, Chemical
    See Chemical engineering
Engineering, Civil
    See Civil engineering
Engineering, Electrical
    See Electric engineering
Engineering, Genetic
    See Genetic engineering
Engineering, Hydraulic
    See Hydraulic engineering
Engineering, Industrial
    See Industrial engineering
Engineering, Irrigation
    See Irrigation engineering
Engineering, Marine
    See Marine engineering
Engineering, Mechanical
    See Mechanical engineering
      Mechanics, Applied
Engineering, Medical
    See Biomedical engineering
Engineering, Military
    See Military engineering
Engineering, Mining
    See Mining engineering
Engineering, Municipal
    See Municipal engineering
Engineering, Railroad
    See Railroad engineering
Engineering, Sanitary
    See Sanitary engineering
Engineering, Steam
    See Steam engineering
Engineering, Structural
    See Structural engineering
Engineering, Traffic
    See Traffic engineering
Engineering, Water-supply
    See Water-supply engineering
Engineering aids, Naval
    See United States. Navy—Engineering
      aids
Engineering analysis
    See Engineering mathematics
Engineering and state *(Indirect)*
    x State and engineering
    xx Endowment of research
      Technology and state
Engineering as a profession *(TA157)*
    sa Earthmoving machinery operators—
      Vocational guidance

    x Civil engineering as a profession
    xx Engineers
Engineering cybernetics
    See Automation
Engineering design *(TA174)*
    sa Materials
      Strains and stresses
      Structural design
      Systems engineering
      subdivisions Design *and* Design and
        construction *under special subjects,*
        e.g. Machinery—Design; Aeroplanes
        —Design and construction
    x Design, Engineering
      Engineering—Design
    xx Design, Industrial
      Strains and stresses
— Electronic data processing
    See Electronic data processing—
      Engineering design
— Management
Engineering drawing
    See Mechanical drawing
Engineering drawings
    sa Blue-prints
      Files and filing (Documents)—
        Engineering drawings
      Microfilm aperture card systems—
        Engineering drawings
    x Drawings, Engineering
      Mechanical drawings
      Technical drawings
    xx Drawing-room practice
      Drawings
      Mechanical drawing
      Structural drawing
      Technical literature
Engineering economics
    See Engineering economy
Engineering economy *(Direct)*
    Here are entered works on the quantita-
    tive evaluation of engineering alterna-
    tives in terms of worth and cost.
    sa Cost effectiveness
      Replacement of industrial equipment
    x Economy, Engineering
      Engineering economics
    xx Engineering—Estimates and costs
      Industrial engineering
— Problems, exercises, etc.
Engineering ethics *(TA157)*
    x Ethics, Engineering
    xx Ethics
      Professional ethics
Engineering experiment stations
    (TA416-417)
    sa Chemical engineering laboratories
      Engineering laboratories
      Research, Industrial
      Testing laboratories
    x Stations, Engineering experiment
    xx Chemical engineering laboratories
      Engineering laboratories
      Research, Industrial
      Testing laboratories
Engineering fellowships
    See Engineering—Scholarships, fellowships,
      etc.
Engineering geology *(Indirect)*
    (Engineering, TA705; Geology,
    QE33; Mining engineering, TN260)
    sa Radioisotopes in engineering geology
      Rock mechanics
      Soil-surveys—Geophysical methods
    x Engineering—Geology
    xx Geology, Economic
      Rock mechanics
— Equipment and supplies

— Field work
— — Safety measures
— Instruments
    x Instruments, Engineering geology
— Mathematics
    xx Engineering mathematics
— Problems, exercises, etc.
— Research   *(Direct)*
    xx Engineering research
    Geological research

Engineering graphics
    Here are entered works on the preparation of drawings for use in the design of engineering products, and in the computation, analysis and presentation of engineering data, including mechanical drawings, freehand sketches and graphical constructions. Works on the use of scales, graph papers, graphs, nomographs and similar graphic devices in engineering computation are entered under Engineering—Graphic methods.
  sa Computer graphics
    Engineering—Graphic methods
  x Graphics, Engineering
  xx Geometry, Descriptive
    Mechanical drawing
  Note under Engineering—Graphic methods
— Programmed instruction
— Study and teaching
— — Audio-visual aids
Engineering inspection   *(TA190)*
  sa Die castings—Inspection
    Non-destructive testing
    Nuclear pressure vessels—Inspection
    Optical tooling
  x Inspection, Engineering
  xx Quality control
— Psychological aspects
Engineering instruments   *(TA165)*
  sa Automatic control
    Automatic timers
    Electronic instruments
    Instrument industry
    Instrument manufacture
    Leak detectors
    Machinery, Automatic
    Remote control
    Surveying—Instruments
    Weld thermal simulators
  x Instruments, Engineering
  xx Scientific apparatus and instruments
— Maintenance and repair
— — Costs   *(TA165)*
— Patents
— Standards
— Testing
Engineering laboratories   *(Direct)*
    (TA416-417)
  sa Chemical engineering laboratories
    Engineering experiment stations
    Hydraulic laboratories
    Testing laboratories
    Thermodynamics laboratories
  x Laboratories, Engineering
    Laboratories, Mechanical
    Mechanical laboratories
  xx Engineering experiment stations
    Engineering research
    Testing laboratories
— Equipment and supplies
Engineering law   *(Direct)* *(TA221-324)*
  sa Civil engineers—Legal status, laws, etc.
    Engineering—Contracts and specifications
    Engineers—Legal status, laws, etc.
    Heat engineering—Safety regulations

  x Architectural law and legislation
    Architecture—Law and legislation
    Engineering—Law and legislation
    Law, Engineering
  xx Architects—Legal status, laws, etc.
    Engineers—Legal status, laws, etc.
Engineering libraries   *(Z675.E6)*
  sa Electronics libraries
    Information storage and retrieval systems—Electronics
    Information storage and retrieval systems—Engineering
    Information storage and retrieval systems—Materials
    Information storage and retrieval systems—Metallurgy
    Technical libraries
  x Libraries, Engineering
  xx Technical libraries
  Example under Libraries, Special
Engineering literature   *(TA10)*
  x Engineering—Literature
  xx Engineering—Bibliography
Engineering literature searching
  See Information storage and retrieval systems—Engineering
Engineering materials
  See Materials
Engineering mathematics
  sa Dimensional analysis
    Electric engineering—Mathematics
    Electronics—Mathematics
    Engineering geology—Mathematics
    Engineering—Graphic methods
    Engineering—Statistical methods
    Industrial engineering—Mathematics
    Mechanics, Applied
    Structures, Theory of
  x Engineering analysis
  xx Dimensional analysis
    Mathematical analysis
    Mathematical physics
    Mathematics
— Formulae
— Programmed instruction
Engineering meteorology   *(TA197)*
  sa Aeroplanes—Climatic factors
    Atomic energy and meteorology
    Engineering—Cold weather conditions
    Environmental engineering
    Heating—Climatic factors
    Ice prevention
    Industry and weather
    Meteorology in aeronautics
    Wind-pressure
  x Meteorology in engineering
  xx Engineering
    Meteorology
    Weather
Engineering models   *(TA177)*
  sa Acoustic models
    Beggs method
    Electromechanical analogies
    Hydraulic models
    Models (Patents)
    Pilot plants
    Ship models
  subdivision Models *under particular subjects, e.g.* Bridges, Concrete—Models; Machinery—Models
  x Engineering—Models
    Similitude in engineering
  xx Design, Industrial
    Dimensional analysis
    Engineering
    Mechanics, Applied
    Models and modelmaking

Engineering research   *(Indirect)*
  sa Chemical engineering research
    Civil engineering—Research
    Drainage research
    Engineering geology—Research
    Engineering laboratories
    Frozen ground research
    Heating research
    Hydraulic engineering—Research
    Packaging research
    Research, Industrial
    Sanitary engineering—Research
    Structural engineering—Research
    Welding research
  x Engineering—Research
    Research, Engineering
  xx Research
    Research, Industrial
— International cooperation
— Research grants
    See Engineering—Research grants
Engineering scholarships
  See Engineering—Scholarships, fellowships, etc.
Engineering schools   *(Direct)*
  x Schools of engineering
  xx Engineering—Study and teaching
— Buildings
— Entrance examinations
Engineering secretaries
  sa Technical shorthand
  xx Secretaries
Engineering services marketing   *(Direct)*
  xx Sales promotion
Engineering societies   *(Indirect)* *(TA1-4)*
  sa Engineering—Societies, etc. *[for publications of engineering and other societies in relation to engineering]*
  xx Societies
Engineering standards
  See Standards, Engineering
Engineering statistics
  See Engineering—Statistical methods
Engineering students   *(Direct)*
  xx Engineering—Study and teaching
    Students
— Political activity
    xx Politics, Practical
Engineering teachers   *(Direct)*
  xx Teachers
— Salaries, pensions, etc.
Engineering test reactors
  x ETR
    Reactors, Engineering test
  xx Nuclear reactors
    Nuclear reactors—Materials—Testing
Engineering tolerances
  See Tolerance (Engineering)
Engineers   *(Direct)* *(Biography, TA139-140)*
  sa Aeronautical engineers
    Automobile engineers
    Chemical engineers
    Civil engineers
    Consulting engineers
    Electric engineers
    Engineering as a profession
    Highway engineers
    Industrial engineers
    Inventors
    Locomotive engineers
    Marine engineers
    Mechanical engineers
    Military engineers
    Mining engineers
    Petroleum engineers
    Safety engineers
    Sanitary engineers
    Technologists

Engineers (Direct) (Biography, TA139-140)
(Continued)
    Water-supply engineers
    Women engineers
    xx Engineering
       Inventors
— Biography
— Collective bargaining
    See Collective bargaining—Engineers
— Collective labor agreements
    See Collective labor agreements—
        Engineers
— Correspondence, reminiscences, etc.
— Employment (Direct)
— Fees
    xx Engineers—Salaries, pensions, etc.
— Legal status, laws, etc. (Direct)
    sa Collective labor agreements—
       Engineers
       Engineering law
    xx Engineering law
— Recruiting
— Salaries, pensions, etc. (Direct)
    sa Engineers—Fees
Engineers, Jewish
    x Jews as engineers
Engines (TJ250-255)
    sa Air-engines
       Caloric engines
       Combustion deposits in engines
       Farm engines
       Fire-engines
       Free piston engines
       Fuel
       Gas and oil engines
       Heat-engines
       Horsepower (Mechanics)
       Locomotives
       Marine engines
       Motors
       Pistons
       Portable engines
       Pumping machinery
       Steam-boilers
       Steam-engines
       Traction-engines
       Tractors
       Turbines
       Waste-heat engines
       Water-pressure engines
    xx Engineering
       Machinery
— Juvenile literature
— Terminology
— Testing
England
— History
    See Great Britain—History
England, Church of
    See Church of England
England in art
England in literature (PN56)
England-Spiel
    See Englandspiel
Englandspiel
    x England-Spiel
       Nordpol-Spiel
    xx World War, 1939-1945—
       Collaborationists
English alabaster sculpture
    See Alabaster sculpture, English
English arms and armor
    See Arms and armor, English
English as a foreign language
    See English language—Study and teaching
       —Foreign students
English as a second language
    See English language—Study and teaching
       —Foreign students

English authors
    See Authors, English
English ballads and songs (Direct)
    (Collections, PR1181-8; History,
    PR507)
    Here are entered collections of ballads
    and songs which contain the words but
    not the music; also, with subdivision
    History and criticism, general works
    and those dealing with the literary as-
    pects of the subject.
    Collections including both words and mu-
    sic, and works treating chiefly of the
    music, take the heading Ballads, Eng-
    lish, or Songs, English.
    sa Ballad operas
       Ballads, English
       Folk-songs, English
       National songs, English
       Political ballads and songs, English
       Songs, English
       War-songs, English
    Notes under Ballads; Songs, American, [Eng-
       lish, French, etc.]
English bean
    See Broad bean
English bookbindings
    See Bookbinding—England
English cameo glass
    See Cameo glass, English
English carols
    See Carols, English
English Catholic nonjurors
    See Nonjurors, English Catholic
English children's poetry
    See Children's poetry, English
English children's writings
    See Children's writings, English
English Christian drama
    See Christian drama, English
English college verse
    See College verse, English
English color prints
    See Color prints, English
English composition test
    x College Entrance Examination Board
       English composition test
    xx English language—Composition and
       exercises
       English language—Examinations
English coverlets
    See Coverlets, English
English cut glass
    See Cut glass, English
English detective plays
    See Detective and mystery plays, English
English diaries (Collections, PR1330;
    History, PR908)
    xx Diaries
— Irish authors (Collections, PR8880;
    History, PR8810)
    x Irish diaries (English)
— Scottish authors (Collections, PR8680;
    History, PR8610)
    x Scottish diaries (English)
English drama (Collections, PR1241-1273)
    sa Ballad opera
       Christian drama, English
       Detective and mystery plays, English
       Historical drama, English
       Moralities, English
       Mysteries and miracle-plays, English
       One-act plays, English
       Prologues and epilogues
       Verse drama, English
    xx Drama
    Note under Theater

— To 1500 (Collections, PR1260; History,
    PR641-4)
    Note under Mysteries and miracle-plays,
       English, [French, German, etc.]
— Early modern and Elizabethan, 1500-1600
    (Collections, PR1262-3; History,
    PR646-658)
    xx Historical drama
— Restoration, 1660-1700 (Collections,
    PR1265-6; History, PR691-8)
— 18th century (Collections, PR1269;
    History, PR701-719)
— 19th century (Collections, PR1271;
    History, PR721-734)
— 20th century (Collections, PR1272;
    History, PR736-9)
— Addresses, essays, lectures (PR627)
    Cf. note under English literature—Ad-
    dresses, essays, lectures.
— African authors
    x African drama (English)
— Bio-bibliography (Z2014.D7)
— Biography
    See Dramatists, English
— Dictionaries (PR623)
— Examinations, questions, etc.
— Guyanese authors
    x Guyanese drama (English)
— History and criticism (PR621-739)
— Irish authors (Collections, PR8864-8870;
    History, PR8783-8795)
    Duplicate entry is made under Irish
       drama (English)
    Note under Irish drama (English)
— New Guinea authors
    x New Guinea drama (English)
— Outlines, syllabi, etc.
    See English literature—Outlines,
       syllabi, etc.
— Scottish authors (Collections,
    PR8664-8670; History,
    PR8583-8595)
    Duplicate entry is made under Scottish
       drama.
    Note under Scottish drama
— Sources (PR625)
— Stories, plots, etc. (PR635.P5)
    Example under reference from Stories
— Study and teaching
    See English literature—Study and
       teaching
— Translations from foreign literature
— Translations from French, [German, etc.]
    Duplicate entry is made under French
       [German, etc.] drama—Transla-
       tions into English.
— Translations into French, [German, etc.]
    Duplicate entry is made under French
       [German, etc.] drama—Transla-
       tions from English.
— Welsh authors (Collections,
    PR8970-8976; History, PR8933-4)
    Duplicate entry is made under Welsh
       drama.
    Note under Welsh drama
— Africa, South
    See South African drama (English)
— Philippine Islands
    See Philippine drama (English)
English drama (Comedy) (Collections,
    PR1248; History, PR631)
    sa Ballad opera
— Restoration, 1660-1700 (Collections,
    PR698.C6; History, PR1266)
English drama (Tragedy) (Collections,
    PR1257; History, PR633)
English drinking vessels
    See Drinking vessels, English

English ecclesiastical embroidery
   See Ecclesiastical embroidery, English
English Electric (BAC) Lightning
   See BAC Lightning (Fighter plane)
English embroidery
   See Embroidery, English
English engraving
   See Engraving, English
English epigrams
   See Epigrams, English
English essays *(Collections, PR1361-9;*
   History, PR921-7)
     Here are entered collections of essays by
     several authors.
   xx Essays
  — Philippine Islands
    See Philippine essays (English)
English fairy poetry
   See Fairy poetry, English
English fantastic fiction
   See Fantastic fiction, English
English farces *(Direct)*
English fiction *(Collections, PZ1)*
   sa Fantastic fiction, English
      Historical fiction, English
      Short stories, English
   xx Fiction
  — Middle English, 1100-1500 *(Collections,*
    PR1119-1120; History,
    PR251-297)
  — Early modern, 1500-1700 *(Collections,*
    PR1293-5; History, PR767-9)
  — 18th century *(Collections, PR1297;*
    History, PR769)
  — 19th century *(Collections, PR1301-4;*
    History, PR771-789)
  — — Illustrations
  — 20th century *(History, PR881-8)*
  — Addresses, essays, lectures *(PR824)*
    Cf. note under English literature—Ad-
    dresses, essays, lectures.
  — Bio-bibliography *(Z2010)*
  — Biography
    See Authors, English
      Novelists, English
  — Book reviews
  — Commonwealth of Nations authors
    x Commonwealth of Nations fiction
     (English)
  — Examinations, questions, etc.
  — History and criticism *(PR821-888)*
  — Indic authors
    x Indic fiction (English)
  — Irish authors *(Collections, PR8875-6;*
    History, PR8797-8807)
     Duplicate entry is made under Irish
     fiction (English)
    Note under Irish fiction (English)
  — Nigerian authors
    x Nigerian fiction (English)
  — Outlines, syllabi, etc.
    See English literature—Outlines,
     syllabi, etc.
  — Philippine authors
    See Philippine fiction (English)
  — Scottish authors *(Collections, PR8675-6;*
    History, PR8597-8607)
     Duplicate entry is made under Scottish
     fiction.
    Note under Scottish fiction
  — Stories, plots, etc.
  — Study and teaching
    See English literature—Study and
     teaching
  — Translations from French, ₍German, etc.₎
     Duplicate entry is made under French
     ₍German, etc.₎ fiction—Transla-
     tions into English.

  — Translations into French, ₍German, etc.₎
     Duplicate entry is made under French
     ₍German, etc.₎ fiction—Transla-
     tions from English.
  — Welsh authors
    x Welsh fiction (English)
  — West Indian authors
    x West Indian fiction (English)

GEOGRAPHIC SUBDIVISIONS

  — Africa, South
    See South African fiction (English)

GEOGRAPHIC SUBDIVISIONS

  — New Zealand
    See New Zealand fiction
English folk music
   See Folk music, English
English folk-songs
   See Folk-songs, English
English furniture
   See Furniture, English
English graphic arts
   See Graphic arts, English
English guitar *(ML1015-1018)*
   x Cetra
   xx Cithern
     Guitar
English guitar music *(M142.E5)*
English horn *(ML940-941)*
   sa Oboe
   xx Oboe
  — Orchestra studies *(MT376)*
    xx English horn—Studies and exercises
  — Studies and exercises *(MT376)*
    sa English horn—Orchestra studies
English-horn and bassoon music
   See Bassoon and English-horn music
English horn and flute music *(M288-9)*
   sa Concertos (English horn and flute with
     string orchestra)
     English horn and flute with string
     orchestra
   x Flute and English-horn music
   xx English-horn music
     Flute music
English horn and flute with string orchestra
   (M1105-6)
   sa Concertos (English horn and flute with
     string orchestra)
   xx Concertos (English horn and flute with
     string orchestra)
     English horn and flute music
     String-orchestra music
English horn and harp music *(M296-7)*
   sa Concertos (English horn and harp with
     string orchestra)
     English horn and harp with string
     orchestra
   x Harp and English horn music
English horn and harp with string orchestra
   (M1105-6)
   sa Concertos (English horn and harp with
     string orchestra)
   xx Concertos (English horn and harp with
     string orchestra)
     English horn and harp music
     String-orchestra music
  — Scores and parts *(M1105)*
English horn and harpsichord music
   (M246.2)
   x Harpsichord and English horn music
English horn and oboe music *(M288-9)*
   sa Concertos (English horn and oboe with
     string orchestra)
     English horn and oboe with string
     orchestra
   x Oboe and English horn music

English horn and oboe with string orchestra
   (M1105-6)
   sa Concertos (English horn and oboe with
     string orchestra)
   xx Concertos (English horn and oboe with
     string orchestra)
     English horn and oboe music
     String-orchestra music
  — Scores *(M1105)*
English horn and organ music *(M182-4)*
   x Organ and English-horn music
English horn and piano music *(M246.2)*
   sa Sonatas (English horn and piano)
   x Piano and English horn music
English horn and piano music, Arranged
   (M246.2)
   sa Concertos (English horn with string
     orchestra)—Solo with piano
     English horn with string orchestra—
     Solo with piano
English horn and trumpet music *(M288-9)*
   sa Concertos (English horn and trumpet
     with string orchestra)
     English horn and trumpet with string
     orchestra
   x Trumpet and English horn music
English horn and trumpet with string
   orchestra *(M1105-6)*
   sa Concertos (English horn and trumpet
     with string orchestra)
   xx Concertos (English horn and trumpet
     with string orchestra)
     English horn and trumpet music
     String-orchestra music
  — Solos with piano *(M1106)*
    xx Trios (Piano, English horn, trumpet),
     Arranged
English horn and violoncello music
   (M290-291)
   x Violoncello and English horn music
English-horn music *(M110.E5)*
   sa Bassoon and English-horn music
     Concertos (English horn)
     Concertos (English horn with chamber
     orchestra)
     Concertos (English horn with string
     orchestra)
     English horn and flute music
     English horn with chamber orchestra
     English horn with orchestra
     English horn with string orchestra
     Quartets, ₍Trios, etc.₎, Wind quartets,
     ₍trios, etc.₎ *followed by specifications*
     which include the English horn
English-horn music (English horns (2))
   (M288-9)
   sa Concertos (English horns (2)) with
     string orchestra
     English horns (2) with string orchestra
English horn with chamber orchestra
   (M1034-5)
   sa Concertos (English horn with chamber
     orchestra)
   xx Chamber-orchestra music
     Concertos (English horn with chamber
     orchestra)
     English-horn music
English horn with orchestra *(M1034.E5;*
   M1035.E5)
   sa Concertos (English horn)
   xx Concertos (English horn)
     English-horn music
     Orchestral music
  — Scores and parts *(M1034.E)*
English horn with string orchestra
   (M1105-6)
   sa Concertos (English horn with string
     orchestra)

English horn with string orchestra
    (M1105-6) *(Continued)*
    xx Concertos (English horn with string
        orchestra)
        English-horn music
        String-orchestra music
    — Solo with piano
        xx English horn and piano music,
          Arranged
English horns (2) with string orchestra
    (M1134.E5; M1135.E5)
    sa Concertos (English horns (2)) with
        string orchestra
    xx Concertos (English horns (2)) with
        string orchestra
        English-horn music (English horns (2))
        String-orchestra music
English humorous poetry
    See Humorous poetry, English
English hymns
    See Hymns, English
English illumination of books and manuscripts
    See Illumination of books and manuscripts,
        English
English imprints *(Direct)*
    Here are entered works on publications in
        the English language regardless of
        place of origin. Imprints of a specific
        place are entered under the subdivi-
        sion Imprints under names of coun-
        tries, states, cities, etc., *e.g.* United
        States—Imprints.
    x Imprints (Publications)
English in Africa, ₍Egypt, India, etc.₎
    See British in Africa, ₍Egypt, India, etc.₎
English in Ireland
English interludes
    See Interludes, English
English language *(PE1001-3729)*
    sa Basic English
        COBOL (Computer program language)
        SIMSCRIPT (Computer program
          language)
    xx Germanic languages
    Example under Germanic philology; Language
        and languages
    — To 1100
        See Anglo-Saxon language
    — Middle English, 1100-1500 *(PE501-685)*
        x Middle English
          Old English language
    — Semantics
    — Early modern, 1500-1700
        (PE1079-1081)
    — — Foreign elements
    — — — French, ₍etc.₎
    — 18th century *(PE1083)*
    — 20th century

       GENERAL SUBDIVISIONS

    — Abbreviations
        See Abbreviations, English

       GENERAL SUBDIVISIONS

    — Ability testing
    — Accents and accentuation
        x English language—Stress

       GENERAL SUBDIVISIONS

    — Accidence
        See English language—Inflection

       GENERAL SUBDIVISIONS

    — Acronyms
        See Acronyms

       GENERAL SUBDIVISIONS

    — Adjective

    — Adverb
    — — Position
        See English language—Word order

       GENERAL SUBDIVISIONS

    — Alphabet
        Here are entered works on the script of
        the English language, also elemen-
        tary works on the script and pro-
        nunciation of the sounds repre-
        sented in the English alphabet.
        sa Initial teaching alphabet
        Unifon alphabet

       GENERAL SUBDIVISIONS

    — — Juvenile literature
    — Alphabet (in religion, folk-lore, etc.)
        xx Alphabet (in religion, folk-lore, etc.)

       GENERAL SUBDIVISIONS

    — Americanisms
        See Americanisms

       GENERAL SUBDIVISIONS

    — Analogy
    — Analysis and parsing
        See English language—Grammar

       GENERAL SUBDIVISIONS

    — Antonyms
        See English language—Synonyms and
        antonyms

       GENERAL SUBDIVISIONS

    — Apheresis
    — Article
    — Audio-visual instruction
        Here are entered phonorecords and
        films as media of language instruc-
        tion.
        sa English language—Films for French
        speakers
        English language—Films for Spanish
        speakers
        xx English language—Study and
        teaching
        Example under Audio-visual education;
        Filmstrips;   Moving-pictures;
        Phonorecords

       GENERAL SUBDIVISIONS

    — Auxiliary verbs
        xx English language—Verb

       GENERAL SUBDIVISIONS

    — Bibliography
        See English philology—Bibliography

       GENERAL SUBDIVISIONS

    — Business English *(PE1115)*
        x Business English
        xx Commercial correspondence
    — — Programmed instruction
    — Capitalization
        Example under Capitalization
    — Case
    — Chrestomathies
        See Readers
    — Clauses
    — Comparison
    — Composition and exercises

    Here are entered works of an elemen-
        tary character containing exercises
        in, and treatises on English compo-
        sition. More advanced works on
        English composition are entered
        under the headings English lan-
        guage—Rhetoric and English lan-
        guage—Style.
    sa English composition test
        English language—Exercises for
        dictation
        English language—Grammar
        English language—Text-books for
        foreigners
    x English language—Exercises
    xx English language—Rhetoric
    Example under Rhetoric; *and under ref-*
        erence from Composition (Rheto-
        ric)
    — — Juvenile literature
    — — Programmed instruction
        See English language—Programmed
        instruction
    — Compound words
    — Conditional sentences
        See English language—Mood
        English language—Sentences
    — Conjugation
        See English language—Inflection
        English language—Verb
    — Conjunctions
    — Consonants
    — Contraction
    — Conversation and phrase books
        x Colloquial English
        Spoken English
    — — French, ₍Italian, etc.₎
    — — Polyglot
    — Conversation and phrase books (for
        soldiers, etc.)
    — Declension
    — Diagraming
        See English language—Grammar
    — Dialectology
        Example under Dialectology
    — Dialects *(Direct)*
        sa Americanisms
        Cant
        English language—Provincialisms
        Pidgin English
    — — Anecdotes, facetiae, satire, etc.
    — — Cartography
        sa English language—Dialects—
        Maps
        xx Cartography
    — — Glossaries, vocabularies, etc.
    — — Lexicology
    — — Maps
        xx English language—Dialects—
        Cartography
    — — Negro
        See Negro-English dialects
    — — Phonetics
        xx English language—Phonetics
    — — Texts

       GEOGRAPHIC SUBDIVISIONS

    — — United States
        See English language in the United
        States—Dialects—₍local
        subdivision₎
    — Diction
        Example under Diction
    — Dictionaries
        sa Picture dictionaries, English

subdivisions Etymology—
  Dictionaries; Glossaries,
  vocabularies, etc.; Idioms,
  corrections, errors; Rime—
  Dictionaries; Synonyms and
  antonyms; Terms and phrases
  under English language
  Note under reference from Dictionaries
— — Early works to 1700
— — French, [Italian, etc.]
— — History and criticism
  See English language—
  Lexicography
— — Polyglot
  Example under Dictionaries, Polyglot;
  Polyglot glossaries, phrase
  books, etc.
— — Study and teaching
— Dictionaries, Juvenile
  Note under reference from Dictionaries
— — Hebrew, [Italian, etc.]
— Diminutives
— Diphthongs
  xx English language—Phonetics
  English language—Vowels
— Elision
— Ellipsis
— Epithets
  See Epithets
— Eponyms *(PE1583)*
  xx English language—Etymology
  Example under Eponyms
— Errors
  See English language—Idioms,
  corrections, errors
— Etymology
  sa English language—Eponyms
  English language—Obsolete words
  Words, Obscene—English
  Bid (The word); Church (The word)
  and similar headings
  x English language—Word history
  xx English language—History
  Example under Semantics; *and under reference from* Etymology
— — Anecdotes, facetiae, satire, etc.
— — Dictionaries
  xx English language—Dictionaries
— — Juvenile literature
— — Names
  xx Names, English
— — — Juvenile literature
— — Popular works
— Examinations
  sa English composition test
— Examinations, questions, etc.
  Example under reference from Foreign
  language testing; Language testing
  Note under Examinations
— Exercises
  See English language—Composition
  and exercises
— Exercises for dictation
  xx English language—Composition and
  exercises
  English language—Orthography and
  spelling
— Fellowships
  See English language—Scholarships,
  fellowships, etc.
— Figures of speech
  See Figures of speech
— Films for French speakers
  xx English language—Audio-visual
  instruction
— Films for Spanish speakers
  xx English language—Audio-visual
  instruction

— Foreign elements
  Example under Language and languages
  —Foreign elements; *and under reference from* Etymology
— — French
  sa English language—Gallicisms
— — French, [Greek, Latin, etc.]
— Foreign words and phrases
  sa Aureate terms
— — Arabic, [Italian, etc.]
— — Dictionaries
— — French
  See English language—Gallicisms
— — Juvenile literature
— Gallicisms
  x English language—Foreign words
  and phrases—French
  xx English language—Foreign elements
  —French
  Example under Gallicisms
— Gender
— Generative grammar
  See English language—Grammar,
  Generative
— Gerund
— Glossaries, vocabularies, etc.
  sa Anagrams—Glossaries, vocabularies,
  etc.
  Crossword puzzles—Glossaries,
  vocabularies, etc.
  x English language—Vocabularies
  xx English language—Dictionaries
— — Juvenile literature
— — Polyglot
— Government jargon
  x Federal prose
  Gobbledygook
  Officialese
  Whitehallese
  xx English language—Idioms,
  corrections, errors
  Example under references from Government jargon; Official jargon
— Grammar
  sa English language—Text-books for
  foreigners
  English language—Usage
  x English language—Analysis and
  parsing
  English language—Diagraming
  English language—Parsing
  xx English language—Composition and
  exercises
  Example under Text-books; *and under
  reference from* Grammar
— — 1500-1800
— — 1800-1870
— — 1870-1950 *(PE1111)*
— — 1950- *(PE1112)*
— — Outlines, syllabi, etc.
  xx English language—Outlines,
  syllabi, etc.
— — Programmed instruction
  See English language—Programmed
  instruction
— — Study and teaching *(PE1065)*
  xx English language—Study and
  teaching
— — Terminology
— Grammar, Comparative
— — Exercises
— — French, [Latin, etc.]
— Grammar, Generative
  x English language—Generative
  grammar
  Example under Generative grammar
— Grammar, Historical
— Hiatus

— History
  sa English language—Etymology
— — Juvenile literature
— Homonyms
— — Juvenile literature
— Honorific
— Idioms, corrections, errors
  sa English language—Government
  jargon
  English language—Usage
  x English language—Errors
  xx English language—Dictionaries
  Example under Errors and blunders, Literary; *and under reference from*
  Dialects
— Indirect discourse
  Example under reference from Indirect
  discourse
— Infinitive
— Infinitive, Split
  See English language—Word order
— Inflection
  x English language—Accidence
  English language—Conjugation
  English language—Morphology
— Interjections
— Interrogative
— Intonation
— Lexicography
  x English language—Dictionaries—
  History and criticism
— Lexicology
  See Lexicology
— Liturgical use
  See Liturgical language—English
— Machine translating
  xx English language—Translating
— Maps
— Metrics and rhythmics
  See English language—Rhythm
  English language—Style
  English language—Versification
— Modality
  Example under Modality (Linguistics)
— Monosyllables
  Example under Monosyllables
— Mood
  x English language—Conditional
  sentences
  English language—Subjunctive
— Morphology
  See English language—Inflection
  English language—Word
  formation
— Names
  See Names, English
— Negatives
— Noun
— Number
— Numerals
— Obscene words
  See Words, Obscene—English *Better don't !*
— Obsolete words
  xx English language—Etymology
— Orthography and spelling
  sa English language—Exercises for
  dictation
  Spellers
  Spelling ability
  Spelling reform
  x English language—Spelling
  Example under references from Orthography; Spelling
— — Anecdotes, facetiae, satire, etc.
— — Juvenile literature
— — Programmed instruction
— Outlines, syllabi, etc.

English language *(PE1001-3729)*
— Outlines, syllabi, etc. *(Continued)*
   sa English language—Grammar—
      Outlines, syllabi, etc.
     English language—Rhetoric—
      Outlines, syllabi, etc.
— Paraphrase
— Paronyms
— Parsing
   See English language—Grammar
— Participle
— Particles
— Parts of speech
   Example under Parts of speech
— Periodicals
— Periphrastic verbs
   See English language—Verb
— Phonemics
   Example under Phonemics
— Phonetic transcriptions
— Phonetics
   sa English language—Dialects—
     Phonetics
     English language—Diphthongs
     Reading (Elementary)—Phonetic
      method
   xx Reading (Elementary)
—— Juvenile literature
— Phonology
   Here are entered works on the history
    of sounds or letters and the laws
    which govern their changes.
   Example under Phonetics; *and under reference from* Phonology
— Phonorecords for foreign speakers
— Phraseology
   Example under Phraseology
— Phrases and terms
   See English language—Terms and
    phrases
— Prefixes
   See English language—Suffixes and
    prefixes
— Prepositions
— Primers
   See Primers
— Programmed instruction
   x English language—Composition and
    exercises—Programmed
    instruction
    English language—Grammar—
    Programmed instruction
   xx English language—Self-instruction
— Pronoun
— Pronunciation
   Here are entered works on the pronun-
    ciation of words (as distinct from
    that of particular sounds or letters)
    especially with reference to best us-
    age.
   Example under reference from Orthoepy
—— Juvenile literature
— Pronunciation by foreigners
   x Foreign accent
— Prosody
   See English language—Versification
— Provincialisms *(Direct)*
   xx English language—Dialects
— Punctuation
   Example under Punctuation
— Quantity
— Quotations, maxims, etc.

Here are entered quotations and other
short sentences or sayings about the
English language. General collections of quotations and other such
material in the English language or
from English sources are entered
under Quotations, English; Epi-
grams, English; and similar head-
ings.
— Readers
   See Readers
— Reduplication
— Reform
— Remedial teaching
   x Remedial English
   xx Remedial teaching
— Reverse indexes
   Example under Reverse indexes
— Rhetoric
   sa English language—Composition and
    exercises
    English language—Style
    Exposition (Rhetoric)
   Note under English language—Composi-
    tion and exercises
——— Early works to 1800
——— Outlines, syllabi, etc.
   xx English language—Outlines,
    syllabi, etc.
——— Programmed instruction
— Rhythm
   x English language—Metrics and
    rhythmics
   xx English language—Versification
   Example under Rhythm
— Rime
   Example under Rime
——— Dictionaries
   xx English language—Dictionaries
— Scholarships, fellowships, etc. *(Direct)*
   x English language fellowships
    English language—Fellowships
    English language scholarships
   xx English language—Study and
    teaching
— Scientific English
   See English language—Technical
    English
— Self-instruction
   sa English language—Programmed
    instruction
— Semantics
   x English language—Semasiology
   Example under Semantics
——— Programmed instruction
— Semasiology
   See English language—Semantics
— Sentences
   x English language—Conditional
    sentences
— Slang
   sa Pidgin English
    Pig Latin
    Words, Obscene—English
   Example under Slang
——— Dictionaries
— Societies, etc.
   See English philology—Societies, etc.
— Spellers
   See Spellers
— Spelling
   See English language—Orthography
    and spelling
— Spelling reform
   See Spelling reform
— Split infinitive
   See English language—Word order
— Spoken English

   x Colloquial English
    Spoken English
— Stress
   See English language—Accents and
    accentuation
— Study and teaching
   Here are entered general works, and
    those dealing with the teaching of
    the language to native English
    speakers. Works on study by per-
    sons with other linguistic back-
    grounds are further subdivided by
    the subdivisions French students,
    Spanish students, etc., general
    works by the subdivision Foreign
    students, *e.g.* English language—
    Study and teaching—French ₍Span-
    ish, etc.₎ students; English language
    —Study and teaching—Foreign
    students. If foreign students in an
    area, continent, etc. with different
    native languages are involved, local
    subdivision may be used, *e.g.* Eng-
    lish language—Study and teaching
    —Asia, Southeastern.
   sa English language—Audio-visual
    instruction
    English language—Grammar—Study
    and teaching
    English language—Remedial
    teaching
    English language—Scholarships,
    fellowships, etc.
    English language—Teacher training
——— Audio-visual aids
——— Foreign students
   x English as a foreign language
    English as a second language
   Note under English language—Study
    and teaching
——— French ₍Spanish, etc.₎ students
   Note under English language—Study
    and teaching
——— Negro students
   xx Negroes—Education
——— Psychological aspects
   xx Educational psychology

GEOGRAPHIC SUBDIVISIONS

——— Asia, Southeastern
   Note under English language—Study
    and teaching
— Study and teaching (Elementary)
   (LB1576)
   x Communication skills (Elementary
    education)
— Study and teaching (Higher)
——— Foreign students
— Study and teaching (Primary) *(Direct)*
   (LB1524-8)
— Study and teaching (Secondary) *(Direct)*
   (LB1631)
——— German ₍etc.₎ students
— Style
   sa Aureate terms
   x English language—Metrics and
    rhythmics
    English literature—Style
   xx English language—Rhetoric
   Example under Style, Literary
   Note under English language—Composi-
    tion and exercises
— Subjunctive
   See English language—Mood
— Substitution
— Suffixes and prefixes
   x English language—Prefixes
— Syllabication

— Synonyms and antonymns
  Example under Thesauri
— Synonyms and antonyms *(PE1591)*
  x English language—Antonyms
  xx English language—Dictionaries
  Example under Synonyms; *and under reference from* Antonyms
— — Juvenile literature
— Syntax
  Example under reference from Syntax
— Teacher training
  xx English language—Study and teaching
— Technical English
  x English language—Scientific English
  Scientific English
  Technical English
  xx Technical writing
  Technology—Language
— Tense
— Terms and phrases
  sa Aureate terms
  x English language—Phrases and terms
  xx English language—Dictionaries
  Example under Terms and phrases
— Text-books
— Text-books for foreigners
  xx English language—Composition and exercises
  English language—Grammar
  Example under Text-books
— — German, ₍Italian, Spanish, etc.₎
  (PE1128-1130)
— Translating
  sa English language—Machine translating
— Translating into French, ₍German, etc.₎
— Transliteration into Korean, ₍Russian, etc.₎
— Usage
  xx English language—Grammar
  English language—Idioms, corrections, errors
— Verb
  sa English language—Auxiliary verbs
  English language—Voice
  x English language—Conjugation
  English language—Periphrastic verbs
— — Tables, lists, etc.
— Verbals
— Versification
  sa Blank verse
  English language—Rhythm
  Free verse
  Heroic verse, English
  x English language—Metrics and rhythmics
  English language—Prosody
  Example under Versification
— Vocabularies
  See English language—Glossaries, vocabularies, etc.
— Vocabulary
  See Vocabulary
— Voice
  xx English language—Verb
— Vowel gradation
— Vowels
  sa English language—Diphthongs
  Example under Vowels
— Word formation
  x English language—Morphology
— Word frequency
  xx Vocabulary

Example under Language and languages—Word frequency; Mathematical linguistics; *and under references from* Frequency counts of words; Frequency word lists; Word counts; Word frequency
— Word history
  See English language—Etymology
— Word order
  x English language—Adverb—Position
  English language—Infinitive, Split
  English language—Split infinitive
  Example under references from Language and languages—Word order; Word order
English language fellowships
  See English language—Scholarships, fellowships, etc.
English language in Australia
  x Australian English
English language in foreign countries *(PE2751)*
English language in India, ₍the Philippine Islands, etc.₎
— Anecdotes, facetiae, satire, etc.
— Juvenile literature
— Terms and phrases
English language in the United States
  Here are entered works dealing with the English language in the United States as a whole, its history, structure, orthography, pronunciation, etc., with appropriate subdivisions as used under English language. Works limited to the usage of words and idiomatic expressions peculiar to the United States are entered under Americanisms.
  sa Americanisms
  Negroes—Language
  x American English
  American language
  Note under Americanisms
— Dialects
— — Juvenile literature

  GEOGRAPHIC SUBDIVISIONS

— — ₍local subdivision₎
  x English language—Dialects—United States
  Note under Americanisms
English language scholarships
  See English language—Scholarships, fellowships, etc.
English laudatory poetry
  See Laudatory poetry, English
English leather work
  See Leather work, English
English letters *(Collections, PR1341-9; History, PR911-917)*
  xx Letters
English literature *(Direct) (Collections, PR1101-1149)*
  sa Christian literature, English
  College readers
  x British literature
  Example under Authors; Germanic literature; Germanic philology; Literature
— To 1100
  See Anglo-Saxon literature
— Middle English, 1100-1500 *(Collections, PR1119-1131; History, PR251-369)*
  sa Sermons, English—Middle English, 1100-1500
  x Middle English
  Old English literature
— — Modernized versions

— Early modern, 1500-1700 *(Collections, PR1119-1131; History, PR401-439)*
— 18th century *(Collections, PR1134-9; History, PR441-9)*
  Note under Readers
— 19th century *(Collections, PR1143-5; History, PR451-469)*
— 20th century *(Collections, PR1149; History, PR471-9)*
— Addresses, essays, lectures *(PR99-101)*
  Here are entered single addresses, essays, and lectures, as well as collections by one or more authors. For collections covering the subject systematically and comprehensively, prefer the subdivision History and criticism.
  Note under English poetry—Addresses, essays, lectures
— African authors
  x African literature (English)
— — Interviews
— Anecdotes, facetiae, satire, etc.
— Appreciation *(Direct)*
— Bibliography *(Z2001-2029)*
  sa Catalogs, Publishers'—Great Britain
— — Catalogs *(Z2029)*
— — Early *(Z2002; Z2012)*
  For bibliographies issued before 1800.
  Example under reference from Bibliography—Early
— — First editions *(Z2014.F5)*
  x Authors, English—First editions
  Example under Bibliography—Rare books; *and under references from* Books—First editions; Editions, First; First editions
— Bio-bibliography *(Z2010-2014)*
  Note under Authors, American, ₍English, French, etc.₎
— Biography
  See Authors, English—Biography
— Catholic authors *(Collections, PR1110.C3; Collections of poetry, PR1195.C4)*
  x English poetry—Catholic authors
— Ceylonese authors
  x Ceylonese literature (English)
— Commonwealth of Nations authors
  x Commonwealth of Nations literature (English)
— Criticism, Textual
— Dictionaries *(PR19)*
— Discography
— Examinations, questions, etc. *(PR87)*
— Explication
  Example under reference from Explication, Literary; Explication de texte; Exposition, Literary; Interpretation, Literary
— Ghanaian authors
  x Ghanaian literature (English)
— Guyanese authors
  x Guyanese literature (English)
— History and criticism *(PR1-978)*
  Note under Criticism
— — Theory, etc.
— Indexes
— Indic authors *(PR9700-9799)*
  For literature by native Indian authors. Works on literature by English residents of India are entered under Anglo-Indian literature.
  xx Anglo-Indian literature
— Irish authors *(Collections, PR8831-8893; History, PR8700-8821)*

English literature (Direct) (Collections,
    PR1101-1149)
— Irish authors (Collections, PR8831-8893;
    History, PR8700-8821)
    (Continued)
    Duplicate entry is made under Irish lit-
    erature (English)
    Note under Irish literature (English)
— Jamaican authors
    x Jamaican literature (English)
— Japanese authors (PR9900.J)
    Duplicate entry is made under Japa-
    nese literature (English)
    Note under Japanese literature (English)
— Jewish authors
    Duplicate entry is made under Jewish
    literature (English)
    Note under Jewish literature (English)
— Kenyan authors
    x Kenyan literature (English)
— Liberian authors
    x Liberian literature (English)
— Malawi authors
    x Malawi literature (English)
— Nigerian authors
    x Nigerian literature (English)
— Outlines, syllabi, etc. (PR87)
    x English drama—Outlines, syllabi,
    etc.
    English fiction—Outlines, syllabi,
    etc.
    English poetry—Outlines, syllabi,
    etc.
— Pictorial works
— Scottish authors (Collections,
    PR8631-8693; History,
    PR8500-8621)
    Duplicate entry is made under Scottish
    literature.
    Note under Scottish literature
— Study and teaching (Direct) (PR31-55)
    x English drama—Study and teaching
    English poetry—Study and teaching
— — Audio-visual aids
— Style
    See English language—Style
— Translations from French, ₍German, etc.₎
    Duplicate entry is made under French
    ₍German, etc.₎ literature—Transla-
    tions into English.
— Translations into French, ₍German, etc.₎
    Duplicate entry is made under French
    ₍German, etc.₎ literature—Transla-
    tions from English.
— Ugandan authors
    x Ugandan literature (English)
— Welsh authors
    x Welsh literature (English)

    GEOGRAPHIC SUBDIVISIONS

— Africa, South
    See South African literature (English)

    GEOGRAPHIC SUBDIVISIONS

— Australia
    See Australian literature

    GEOGRAPHIC SUBDIVISIONS

— Canada
    See Canadian literature

    GEOGRAPHIC SUBDIVISIONS

— New Zealand
    See New Zealand literature

    GEOGRAPHIC SUBDIVISIONS

— Philippine Islands
    See Philippine literature (English)

English logicians
    See Logicians, English
English love poetry
    See Love poetry, English
English madrigals (Music)
    See Madrigals (Music), English
English military music
    See Military music, English
English musicians
    See Musicians, English
English mystery plays
    See Detective and mystery plays, English
English names
    See Names, English
English narrative poetry
    See Narrative poetry, English
English newspapers (Direct) (History,
    PN5111-5129)
    x British newspapers
    xx Newspapers
— Circulation
    sa Readership surveys
    xx Newspaper circulation
— Directories (Z6956.E5)
— Irish (History, PN5141-9)
    Duplicate entry is made under Irish
    newspapers (English)
    Note under Irish newspapers (English)
— Language
— Scottish (History, PN5131-9)
    Duplicate entry is made under Scottish
    newspapers.
    Note under Scottish newspapers
— Sections, columns, etc.
    xx Newspapers—Sections, columns, etc.

    GEOGRAPHIC SUBDIVISIONS

— New Zealand
    See New Zealand newspapers
English newspapers in foreign countries
English nonsense literature
    See Nonsense literature, English
English oak
    x British oak
    xx Oak
English opera
    See Opera, English
English orations (Collections, PR1321-9;
    History, PR901-7)
    Here are entered only collections of ora-
    tions by several authors.
    xx Orations
— Indic authors
    x East Indian orations (English)
    Indic orations (English)
— Irish authors (Collections, PR8879;
    History, PR8809)
    x Irish orations (English)
English paleography
    See Paleography, English
English papier-mâché
    See Papier-mâché, English
English part-songs
    See Part-songs, English
English pastoral poetry
    See Pastoral poetry, English
English patriotic poetry
    See Patriotic poetry, English
English penny
    See Penny, English
English periodicals (Direct) (History, etc.,
    PN5111-5130)
    x British periodicals
    xx Periodicals
    Note under Periodicals
— Circulation
    sa Readership surveys
    xx Periodicals—Circulation

— Directories (Z6956.E5)
— Irish (History, PN5141-5150)
    Duplicate entry is made under Irish
    periodicals (English)
    Note under Irish periodicals (English)
— Scottish (History, PN5131-5140)
    Duplicate entry is made under Scottish
    periodicals.
    Note under Scottish periodicals
English philology (PE)
    x Philology, English
    xx Germanic philology
    Philology, Modern
    Example under Philology
— Bibliography (Z2015)
    x English language—Bibliography
— Societies, etc.
    x English language—Societies, etc.
— Teacher training
— Text-books
English poetry (Direct) (Collections,
    PR1171-1227; History, PR500-609)
    sa Children's poetry, English
    College verse, English
    Epigrams, English
    Fairy poetry, English
    Haiku, English
    Humorous poetry, English
    Laudatory poetry, English
    Narrative poetry, English
    Pastoral poetry, English
    Patriotic poetry, English
    Political poetry, English
    Religious poetry, English
    Sonnets, English
    Waka, English
    x British poetry
    xx Poetry
    Note under Lyric poetry
— To 1100
    See Anglo-Saxon poetry
— Middle English, 1100-1500 (Collections,
    PR1203; History, PR311-369)
— — Modernized versions (PR1203-4)
— Early modern, 1500-1700 (Collections,
    PR1204-1213; History,
    PR521-549)
— 18th century (Collections, PR1215-1219;
    History, PR551-579)
— 19th century (Collections, PR1221-4;
    History, PR581-599)
— — Book reviews
— 20th century (Collections, PR1224-7;
    History, PR601-9)
— Addresses, essays, lectures
    Cf. note under English literature—Ad-
    dresses, essays, lectures.
    Example under Essays
— African authors
    x African poetry (English)
— Bibliography (Z2014.P7)
— — First editions (Z2014.P7)
— Bio-bibliography (Z2014.P7)
— Catholic authors
    See English literature—Catholic
    authors
— Celtic authors (PR8491; PR8496)
    Duplicate entry is made under Celtic
    poetry (English)
    Note under Celtic poetry (English)
— Criticism, Textual
— Dictionaries (Recitations, PN4321)
— Examinations, questions, etc.
— Explication
    Example under reference from Explica-
    tion, Literary; Explication de texte;
    Exposition, Literary; Interpreta-
    tion, Literary

608

— Ghanaian authors
  x Ghanaian poetry (English)
— History and criticism *(PR500-609)*
  Note under Criticism
— Indexes
— Indic authors *(Collections,*
    PR9755-9769; History,
    PR9726-9732)
    For poetry by native Indic authors.
    Works on poetry by English resi-
    dents of India are entered under the
    heading Anglo-Indian poetry.
  xx Anglo-Indian poetry
  Note under Bengali poetry (English)
— Irish authors *(Collections, PR8849-8863;*
    History, PR8761-8781)
    Duplicate entry is made under Irish
    poetry (English)
  Notes under Irish ballads and songs (Eng-
    lish); Irish poetry (English)
— Japanese authors *(PR9900.J)*
    Duplicate entry is made under Japa-
    nese literature (English)
  Note under Japanese literature (English)
— Memorizing *(Selections, PN6110.M4;*
    Study of literature, PR33-35)
— Musical settings
— Negro authors
  x Negro poetry (English)
— Outlines, syllabi, etc.
    See English literature—Outlines,
    syllabi, etc.
— Papuan authors
  x Papuan poetry (English)
— Paraphrases, tales, etc. *(PR1180)*
    Example under Tales; *and under refer-*
    ence from Paraphrases
— Scottish authors *(Collections,*
    PR8649-8663; History,
    PR8561-8581)
    Duplicate entry is made under Scottish
    poetry.
    Note under Scottish poetry
— Stories, plots, etc.
— Study and teaching
    See English literature—Study and
    teaching
— Translations from foreign literature
    Note under Translations
— Translations from French, [German, etc.]
    Duplicate entry is made under French
    [German, etc.] poetry—Transla-
    tions into English.
— Translations into French, [German, etc.]
    Duplicate entry is made under French
    [German, etc.] poetry—Transla-
    tions from English.
— Ugandan authors
  x Ugandan poetry (English)
— Welsh authors *(Collections,*
    PR8955-8969; History,
    PR8926-8932)
  x Welsh poetry (English)
— West Indian authors
  x West Indian poetry (English)
— Zambian authors
  x Zambian poetry (English)

GEOGRAPHIC SUBDIVISIONS

— Africa, South
    See South African poetry (English)

GEOGRAPHIC SUBDIVISIONS

— New Zealand
    See New Zealand poetry
English poets
  See Poets, English

English political satire
  See Political satire, English
English porcelain
  See Porcelain, English
English pound
  See Pound, British
English propaganda
  See Propaganda, British
English prose literature *(Direct)*
    (Collections, PR1281-1307; History,
    PR751-975)
— Early modern, 1500-1700 *(Collections,*
    PR1293-5; History, PR767-9)
— 18th century *(Collections, PR1297;*
    History, PR769)
— 19th century *(Collections, PR1301-4;*
    History, PR771-788)
— 20th century *(Collections, PR1307;*
    History, PR801-8)
— African authors
  x African prose literature (English)
— Memorizing *(PR33-35)*
— Scottish authors *(Collections,*
    PR8672-8687; History,
    PR8597-8607)
    Duplicate entry is made under Scottish
    prose literature.
    Note under Scottish prose literature
— Africa, South
    See South African prose literature
    (English)
English religious poetry
  See Religious poetry, English
English romances
  See Romances, English
English satire
  See Satire, English
English school certificate examination
  See High school equivalency examination
English setters *(SF429.E5)*
  xx Setters (Dogs)
English silverware
  See Silverware, English
English slipware
  See Slipware, English
English songs
  See Songs, English
English sonnets
  See Sonnets, English
English sparrow
  x House sparrow
  xx Sparrows
— Control *(Indirect) (SB996.S7)*
  xx Bird control
— Juvenile literature
English sporting prints
  See Sporting prints, English
English springer spaniels *(SF429.E7)*
  x Springer spaniels, English
    Springers, English
  xx Spaniels
English waka
  See Waka, English
English war-songs
  See War-songs, English
English West Indian Expedition, 1654-1655
    (F1621)
English West Indian Expedition, 1695
    (F1621)
English West Indian Expedition, 1739-1742
    (F2272.5)
  sa Cartagena, Colombia—Siege, 1741
  xx Austrian Succession, War of, 1740-1748
English West Indian Expedition, 1759
    (F2151)
English West Indian Expedition, 1793-1794
    (F1621)

English West Indian Expedition, 1795-1796
    (F1621)
  xx Guyana—History—To 1803
English wit and humor *(Collections,*
    PN6173-5; History, PR931-7)
    Here are entered collections from several
    authors and individual authors who
    have not written in other literary
    forms.
  sa Humorous poetry, English
  x British wit and humor
  xx Wit and humor
English wit and humor, Pictorial
    (NC1470-1479)
  sa Caricatures and cartoons—Great Britain
  xx Wit and humor, Pictorial
English wood-engravers
  See Wood-engravers, English
English wood-engraving
  See Wood-engraving, English
Engobes *(TP823)*
  xx Color in the ceramic industries
    Glazes
    Paste
    Pottery
Engraved glass *(Direct)*
  x Glass, Engraved
  xx Glass engraving
    Glass, Ornamental
    Glassware
Engraved portraits
  See Portrait prints
Engraver beetles
  See Bark-beetles
Engravers *(Direct) (Collective, NE800;*
    Individual, NE501-794, NE805)
  sa Etchers
    Medalists
    Mezzotinters
    Stipple engravers
    Women engravers
    Wood-engravers
  x Metal engravers
  xx Artists
    Printmakers
— Autographs
— Correspondence, reminiscences, etc.
Engravers, American, [Belgian, French, etc.]
    (Direct)
  x American [Belgian, French, etc.]
    engravers
Engravers' marks *(NE820)*
  sa Artists' marks
  x Marks, Engravers'
  xx Artists' marks
Engraving *(Direct) (NE)*
  sa Aquatint
    Bank-notes
    Crayon engraving
    Dotted prints (Engravings)
    Dry-point
    Engravings
    Etching
    Gems
    Glass engraving
    Glyptics
    Graphotyping
    Linoleum block-printing
    Mezzotint engraving
    Monotype (Engraving)
    Nature-printing and nature-prints
    Niello
    Photoengraving
    Prints in paste
    Stipple engraving
    Tile block-printing
    Wood-engraving
  x Copper engraving

Engraving *(Direct) (NE) (Continued)*
    Line-engraving
    Siderography
    Steel-engraving
    xx Art
    Etching
    Graphic arts
    Illustration of books
    Prints
  — Competitions
  — Early works to 1800 *(NE440-480)*
  — Technique
    sa Postage-stamp printing
  — — Juvenile literature
Engraving, American, ₍**English, etc.**₎ *(Direct)*
  x American ₍English, etc.₎ engraving
Engraving, Renaissance *(NE440)*
Engraving (Metal-work) *(NE2700-2710)*
    xx Art metal-work
    Goldsmithing
    Jewelry making
    Metal-work
    Silversmithing
Engraving machines *(NE2720)*
Engravings *(Direct) (NE)*
    sa Chromolithographs
    Color prints
    Dotted prints (Engravings)
    Dry-points
    Etchings
    Illustrated books
    Photogravures
    Prints in paste
    Rotogravures
    Sporting prints
    Stipple engravings
    Wood-engravings
    xx Drawings
    Engraving
    Etchings
    Pictures
  — Cataloging
    See Cataloging of engravings
  — Catalogs
    Here are entered dealers' and general
    sales catalogs. Catalogs of exhibi-
    tions are entered under Engravings
    —Exhibitions. Catalogs of private
    collections are entered under the
    heading Engravings—Private col-
    lections.
    Example under Catalogs
  — Collectors and collecting *(NE880-885)*
  — Conservation and restoration *(NE380)*
    sa Books—Conservation and restoration
    Manuscripts—Conservation and
    restoration
    x Conservation of engravings
    Engravings—Preservation
    Engravings—Restoration
    Preservation of engravings
    Restoration of engravings
    xx Books—Conservation and restoration
    Manuscripts—Conservation and
    restoration
  — Exhibitions
    Note under Engravings—Catalogs
  — Preservation
    See Engravings—Conservation and
    restoration
  — Prices *(NE85)*
    xx Art—Prices
    Example under Prices
  — Printing *(NE2800-2890)*
    sa Postage-stamp printing
    Wood-engravings—Printing
    x Copperplate printing
    Printing, Copperplate

    xx Pictures—Printing
    Plate-printing
    Printing
  — — Specimens
    xx Printing—Specimens
  — Private collections *(NE57-59)*
    Note under Engravings—Catalogs
  — Restoration
    See Engravings—Conservation and
    restoration
Engravings, Baroque *(Direct)*
  x Baroque engravings
Engravings, Chinese, ₍**Italian, etc.**₎ *(Direct)*
  x Chinese ₍Italian, etc.₎ engravings
Engravings, Jewish
  x Jewish engravings
Engravings, Renaissance *(Direct)*
  x Renaissance engravings
Engrossing
  See Monopolies
Enharmonic organ
  See Organ
Enhydrinae
  See Sea-otters
Enigmas
  See Curiosities and wonders
  Riddles
Eniwa case
Enkyoku *(Collections, PL761; History,*
  PL731)
  x Eikyoku
  xx Japanese ballads and songs
Enlightenment *(B2621)*
    Here are entered works dealing with en-
    lightenment in the sense of the intel-
    lectual movement of the 18th century
    (German *Afklärung*) When the work
    deals with the movement in a particu-
    lar country or city, duplicate entry is
    made under name of place, with sub-
    division Intellectual life.
    sa Haskalah
    xx Eighteenth century
    Illuminati
    Philosophy, Modern—18th century
    Rationalism
Enlightenment (Buddhism)
  x Awakening (Buddhism)
  Bodhi
  Illumination (Buddhism)
  xx Buddhist doctrines
  Nirvana
  Salvation (Buddhism)
  — Requisites
    sa Satipaṭṭhāna (Buddhism)
    x Enlightenment (Buddhism)—
    Thirty-seven
    Bodhipakkhiya-dhammas
    xx Buddhist doctrines
  — Thirty-seven Bodhipakkhiya-dhammas
    See Enlightenment (Buddhism)—
    Requisites
Enlightenment (Turkish religious movement)
  See Nurculuk
Enlightenment (Zen Buddhism)
  x Satori
  xx Zen Buddhism
Enlistment
  See Foreign enlistment
  Recruiting and enlistment
  subdivision Recruiting, enlistment, etc.
  under armies, navies, etc., e.g. Italy.
  Esercito—Recruiting, enlistment,
  etc.
Enriched food
  See Food, Enriched
Enrichment, Unjust
  See Unjust enrichment

Enrollment, Dual
  See Dual enrollment
Ensemble playing *(MT728)*
  xx Chamber music—History and criticism
Ensembles (Mathematics)
  See Set theory
Ensembles (Music)
  See Instrumental ensembles
  Jazz ensembles
  Percussion ensembles
  String ensembles
  Vocal ensembles
  Wind ensembles
Ensiform process
  See Xiphoid process
Ensigns
  See Flags
Ensilage *(SB195)*
  sa Silos
  Sugar-beet silage
  names of specific silages, e.g. Alfalfa
  silage
  x Silage
  xx Agriculture
  Feeds
  Forage plants
  Silos
  — Handling
    See Silage handling
  — Moisture
Ensilage machinery
  See Silage machinery
Ensol
  xx Enzymes
Enstatite *(QE391.E6)*
Entail *(Direct)*
  sa Fideicommissum
  Heirlooms
  Shelley's case, Rule in
  x Estate tail
  Limitations (Law)
  xx Fideicommissum
  Inheritance and succession
  Land tenure
  Primogeniture
  Restraints on alienation
Entail (Frankish law)
Entail (Lübeck law)
Entente, Baltic, 1934-
  See Baltic Entente, 1934-
Entente, Little, 1920-1939
  See Little Entente, 1920-1939
Entente, Triple, 1907
  See Triple Entente, 1907
Enteric-coated tablets
  x Tablets, Enteric-coated
  xx Tablets (Medicine)
Enteric cytopathogenic human orphan viruses
  See ECHO viruses
Enteric fever
  See Typhoid fever
Enteric infections
  See Intestines—Bacteriology
Enteritis *(RC862.E5)*
  sa Regional enteritis
  xx Intestines—Diseases
Enteritis, Regional
  See Regional enteritis
Enterobacterial vaccines *(QR189.5.E53)*
Enterobiasis
  See Oxyuriasis
Enterokinase
  sa Trypsin
  Trypsinogen
  xx Pancreas—Secretions
Enteropneusta *(QL612)*
  xx Hemichordata

Enteroptosis *(RC862)*
  xx Intestines—Diseases
Enterotoxemia
  x Infectious enterotoxemia
    Overeating disease of sheep
    Ovine enterotoxemia
    Pulpy kidney disease
Enteroviruses
  sa Coxsackie virus
    ECHO viruses
    Poliovirus
    Reoviruses
  xx Viruses
Enterprises
  See Business enterprises
    Entrepreneur
Entertainers *(Direct)*
  sa Actors
    Blacklisting of entertainers
    Clowns
    Comedians
    Dancers
    Geishas
    Magicians
    Masters of ceremonies
    Musicians
    Negro entertainers
  x Performing artists
    Show-men
  xx Artists
  — Biography
  — — Juvenile literature
  — Correspondence, reminiscences, etc.
  — Legal status, laws, etc. *(Direct)*
  — Portraits
Entertainers, Blacklisting of
  See Blacklisting of entertainers
Entertainers, Women *(Direct)*
  — Biography
Entertaining *(Amusements, GV1470-1561;*
    Cookery, menus, etc., TX731-9;
    Dining-room service, TX851-885;
    Etiquette, BJ2021-2038)
  sa Amusements
    Balls (Parties)
    Campfire programs
    Children's parties
    Dance parties
    Dinners and dining
    Etiquette
    Games
    Hospitality
    Luncheons
    Party decorations
    Showers (Parties)
    Suppers
  x Guests
    Parties
  xx Amusements
    Etiquette
    Home economics
  — Caricatures and cartoons
Entertainments
  See Amusements
    Church entertainments
Enthalpy *(QC318)*
  x Heat content
    Heat function
  xx Thermodynamics
  — Charts, diagrams, etc.
Enthronement of the Gospels
  x Gospels enthroned
  xx Catholic Church—Ceremonies and
    practices
    Rites and ceremonies
Enthusiasm *(Psychology, BF575.E6; Religion,*
    BR112)
  sa Sacramentarians

  xx Ecstasy
    Fanaticism
    Inspiration
    Mysticism
    Psychology, Religious
    Revivals
Enthusiasts (Messalians)
  See Messalians
Enthymeme (Logic)
  xx Logic
    Syllogism
Entire functions
  See Functions, Entire
Entirety, Tenancy by the
  See Tenancy by the entirety
Entomological research *(Indirect)*
  sa Insect cages
  x Entomology—Research
    Insects—Research
    Research, Entomological
  xx Entomology
    Research
Entomologists *(Direct) (Bibliography,*
    Z5856; Biography, QL26-31)
  xx Naturalists
    Scientists
    Zoologists
  — Biography
  — Correspondence, reminiscences, etc.
Entomology *(Indirect)*
  sa Entomological research
    Insects
    Radioactive tracers in entomology
  xx Insects
    Zoology
  — Abstracts
  — Collected works
    x Insects—Collected works
  — Congresses
    x Insects—Congresses
  — Cultures and culture media
    See Insect rearing
  — Early works to 1800
  — Laboratory manuals
    x Insects—Laboratory manuals
  — Nomenclature
  — Research
    See Entomological research
  — Societies, etc.
    x Insects—Society publications
  — Statistical methods
    xx Biometry
  — Terminology
Entomology, Economic
  See Insects, Injurious and beneficial
Entomology, Veterinary
  See Veterinary entomology
Entomostraca *(QL444.E6)*
  sa Branchiopoda
    Cirripedia
    Cladocera
    Copepoda
    Mystacocarida
    Otracoda
  xx Crustacea
Entomostraca, Fossil
  sa Cladocera, Fossil
  xx Crustacea, Fossil
Entoprocta
  x Kamptozoa
Entozoa
  See Worms, Intestinal and parasitic
Entr'acte music *(M1510-1518; History,*
    ML2000)
  sa Tonadilla
  x Act-tune
  xx Music, Incidental
    Overture

Entrance examinations
  See subdivision Examinations *under*
    Universities and colleges; *and*
    subdivision Entrance examinations
    under headings for professional
    schools, e.g. Law schools—Entrance
    examinations
Entrance halls *(Indirect)*
  x Foyers
    Vestibules
  xx Architecture
    Halls
Entrance requirements
  See subdivision Entrance requirements
    under types of schools and names of
    individual schools, e.g. High schools
    —Entrance requirements; Harvard
    University—Entrance requirements
Entrées
  See Cookery (Entrées)
Entremés *(PQ6127.E6)*
  sa Tonadilla
  x Entremets
  xx Farce
    Interludes, Spanish
    Spanish drama—Classical period,
      1500-1700
    Spanish drama (Comedy)
    Spanish farces
Entremets
  See Entremés
Entrenchments
  See Intrenchments
Entrepreneur *(HB601)*
  sa Business enterprises
    Capitalism
    New business enterprises
    Profit
  x Enterprises
  xx Business
    Capitalism
    Economics
    Industry
    Profit
    Self-employed
Entropy
  xx Heat
    Thermodynamics
Entry into planetary atmospheres
  See Space vehicles—Atmospheric entry
Entsy
  x Enets people
  xx Ethnology—Russia
    Samoyeds
Enucleation
  xx Cell nuclei
    Cytology—Technique
Enumeration districts
  See Census districts
Enumerations in the Bible
  See Lists in the Bible
Enuresis
  See Urine—Incontinence
Envelopes, Addressing of
  x Addressing of envelopes
  xx Envelopes (Stationery)
    Letter services
Envelopes (Geometry) *(QA621)*
  xx Curves
    Geometry
    Surfaces
Envelopes (Philately)
  See Covers (Philately)
Envelopes (Stationery)
  sa Covers (Philately)
    Envelopes, Addressing of
    Stamped envelopes
  xx Stationery

Environment
  See Acclimatization
  Adaptation (Biology)
  Anthropo-geography
  Ecology
  Euthenics
  Human ecology
  Man—Influence of environment
  Man—Influence on nature
  Nature and nurture
  subdivision Environmental aspects
    under special subjects, e.g.
    Agricultural chemicals—
    Environmental aspects; Atomic
    power-plants—Environmental
    aspects; *and headings beginning with
    the word* Environmental
Environment, College
  See College environment
Environment, High school
  See High school environment
Environment, Human
  See Human ecology
Environment, School
  See School environment
Environment, Space
  See Space environment
Environment (Art) *(Direct)*
  xx Art, Modern—20th century
  Assemblage (Art)
Environment and mass media
  See Mass media and the environment
Environment and state
  See Environmental policy
Environment simulation (Teaching method)
  See Simulated environment (Teaching
    method)
Environment testing
  See Environmental testing
Environmental control
  See Environmental engineering
  Environmental law
  Environmental policy
Environmental education
  See Conservation of natural resources—
    Study and teaching
  Ecology—Study and teaching
  Human ecology—Study and teaching
Environmental effects
  See Environmental engineering
Environmental engineering
  sa Electric power-plants—Environmental
    aspects
  Environmental health
  Environmental policy
  Environmental protection
  Environmental testing
  Extraterrestrial bases
  Human engineering
  Life support systems (Space
    environment)
  Motor-trucks—Environmental aspects
  Noise control
  Petroleum chemicals industry—
    Environmental aspects
  Pollution
  Sanitary engineering
  Space simulators
  subdivision Influence of environment
    under subjects, e.g. United States.
    Army—Ordnance and ordnance
    stores—Influence of environment
  x Environmental control
  Environmental effects
  Environmental management
  Environmental stresses
  xx Design, Industrial
  Engineering

Engineering meteorology
  Environmental health
  Environmental protection
  Pollution
  Testing
— Computer programs
— Information services *(Direct)*
— Research *(Direct)*
— Research grants *(Direct)*
— Vocational guidance
    See Environmental engineering as a
      profession
Environmental engineering (Buildings)
  sa Air conditioning
  Architectural acoustics
  Buildings—Vibration
  Clean rooms
  Heating
  Interior decoration
  Lighting
  Sanitation, Household
  Ventilation
  x Buildings—Environmental engineering
  xx Architecture
  Building
  Sanitation, Household
— Problems, exercises, etc.
— Tables, calculations, etc.
Environmental engineering as a profession
  x Environmental engineering—Vocational
    guidance
Environmental health *(Indirect)*
  sa Air—Pollution
  Environmental engineering
  Environmentally induced diseases
  Industrial hygiene
  Soil pollution
  Water—Pollution
  xx Environmental engineering
  Hygiene, Public
  Man—Influence of environment
— International cooperation
Environmental health engineering
  See Sanitary engineering
Environmental laboratories *(Direct)*
  (TD178.8)
  x Laboratories, Environmental
Environmental law *(Direct)*
  sa Air—Pollution—Law and legislation
  Marine pollution—Law and legislation
  Natural resources—Law and legislation
  Noise control—Law and legislation
  Refuse and refuse disposal—Law and
    legislation
  Shore protection—Law and legislation
  Water—Pollution—Law and legislation
  x Environmental control
  Environmental management
  xx Environmental policy
  Environmental protection
— Cases
— — Digests
    See Environmental law—Digests
— Criminal provisions
— Digests
    x Environmental law—Cases—Digests
Environmental law (Jewish law)
Environmental management
  See Environmental engineering
  Environmental law
  Environmental policy
Environmental policy *(Direct) (HC68)*
  sa Conservation of natural resources
  Environmental law
  Environmental protection
  Human ecology
  Man—Influence on nature
  Pollution

  x Environment and state
  Environmental control
  Environmental management
  Public policy
  State and environment
  xx Environmental engineering
  Environmental protection
  Human ecology
  Man—Influence on nature
— Finance
— Juvenile literature
— Mathematical models
— Public opinion
— Research
    See Environmental policy research
Environmental policy research *(Direct)*
  x Environmental policy—Research
  xx Research
Environmental pollution
  See Pollution
Environmental protection *(Direct)*
  sa Air quality management
  Conservation of natural resources
  Environmental engineering
  Environmental law
  Environmental policy
  Landscape protection
  Strip mining—Environmental aspects
  Water resources development—
    Environmental aspects
  x Protection of environment
  xx Environmental engineering
  Environmental policy
— Citizen participation
    x Citizen participation in
      environmental protection
    xx Social action
— Information services *(Direct)*
— International cooperation
— Juvenile literature
— Mathematical models
— Public opinion
— Research *(Direct)*
— Terminology
— Vocational guidance
— — Juvenile literature
Environmental radioactivity
  See Radioactive pollution
  Radioecology
Environmental simulation (Teaching method)
  See Simulated environment (Teaching
    method)
Environmental stresses
  See Environmental engineering
Environmental studies
  See Conservation of natural resources—
    Study and teaching
  Human ecology—Study and teaching
Environmental study areas, National
  See National environmental study areas
Environmental testing *(TA171)*
  sa Space vehicles—Equipment and
    supplies—Environmental testing
  x Environment testing
  xx Environmental engineering
  Testing
Environmentally induced diseases *(RB152)*
  x Diseases—Environmental aspects
  xx Diseases—Causes and theories of
    causation
  Environmental health
  Medical geography
Environments, Hazardous geographic
  See Hazardous geographic environments
Environs
  See subdivision Suburbs and environs *under
    names of cities and towns*

612

Envy *(BF575.E6)*
  sa Jealousy
  xx Deadly sins
    Emotions
    Jealousy
Enzheim, Battle of, 1674 *(D278.E6)*
Enzymatic analysis
  xx Biological chemistry
    Chemistry, Analytic
    Enzymes
  — Laboratory manuals
Enzyme antagonists
  See Enzyme inhibitors
Enzyme inhibitors
  sa Antifibrinolytic agents
    Antimetabolites
    Mingin
    Trasylol
  x Antagonists, Enzyme
    Enzyme antagonists
    Enzymes—Antagonists
    Inhibitors, Enzyme
    Metabolic inhibitors
  xx Chemical inhibitors
    Enzymes
Enzyme synthesis
  xx Biosynthesis
  — Mathematical models
Enzymes *(QP601)*
  sa Abderhalden reaction
    Autolysis
    Clinical enzymology
    Coenzymes
    Digestive ferments
    Ensol
    Enzymatic analysis
    Enzyme inhibitors
    Fermentation
    Fibrinolysis
    Fibrinolytic agents
    Isoenzymes
    Lipolysis
    Malt
    Metabolic regulation
    Pancreas—Secretions
    Rennet
    Virus-induced enzymes
    names of enzymes, e.g. Diastase,
      Pepsin, Zymase
  x Ferments
    Soluble ferments
  xx Brewing
    Digestion
    Fermentation
    Metabolic regulation
    Pancreas—Secretions
    Physiological chemistry
  — Analysis
  — Antagonists
    See Enzyme inhibitors
  — Classification
  — Industrial applications
    xx Biochemical engineering
      Chemical engineering
  — — Patents
  — Juvenile literature
  — Mathematical models
  — Nomenclature
  — Radiation effects
    See Enzymes, Effect of radiation on
  — Specifications *(Direct)*
  — Therapeutic use
  — Toxicology
Enzymes, Effect of radiation on
  x Enzymes—Radiation effects
  xx Radiation—Physiological effect
Enzymology, Clinical
  See Clinical enzymology

Eocene period
  See Geology, Stratigraphic—Eocene
    Paleobotany—Eocene
    Paleontology—Eocene
Eolian harp
  See Aeolian harp
Eolithic period
  See Stone age
Eoliths *(GN775-6)*
  xx Stone age
Eonism
  See Transvestism
Eosin *(QD441)*
Eosinophiles *(Hematology, RB145;*
    Physiology of the blood, QP95)
  xx Leucocytes
Epera speech
  See Choco language
Ephebia *(DF95)*
  sa Cosmetes
Ephebic oath
  xx Oaths
Ephedrine *(QD421)*
Ephemera, Printed
  See Printed ephemera
Ephemeral fever
  See Three-day sickness of cattle
Ephemeral periodicals
  See Periodicals, Ephemeral
Ephemeral printing
  See Printed ephemera
Ephemeral streams *(Indirect)*
  x Streams, Ephemeral
  xx Rivers
Ephemerida
  See May-flies
Ephemerides *(QB7-9)*
  sa Moon—Ephemerides
    Nautical almanacs
    Planets—Ephemerides
    Planets, Minor—Ephemerides
    Pluto (Planet)—Ephemerides
    Satellites—Jupiter, ₍Mars, Saturn, etc.₎
      —Ephemerides
    Schwassmann-Wachmann's comet (I)
    Stars, Double—Ephemerides
    Stars—Ephemerides
  x Astronomy—Ephemerides
    Solar system—Ephemerides
  xx Nautical almanacs
Ephemeroptera
  See May-flies
Ephesus, Council of, 431 *(BR220)*
Ephod *(BM657.E7)*
  sa Breastplate of the High Priest
  xx Bible—Antiquities
    Cultus, Jewish
    Jews—Antiquities
    Priests, Jewish—Vestments
Ephrata Community *(F159.E6)*
Ephthalite language
  x Hephthalite language
  xx Iranian languages
Ephthalites
  x Aptal
    Haptal
    Hephthalites
    White Huns
  xx Huns
    Yüeh-chih
Epic literature
  x Literature, Epic
  xx Literature
Epic literature, Irish, ₍White Russian, etc.₎
  x Irish ₍White Russian, etc.₎ literature,
    Epic

Epic poetry *(Collections, PN6110.E6;*
    History, PN689-690, PN1301-1333)
  sa Narrative poetry
    Rhapsody
    Romances
  x Heroic poetry
  xx Narrative poetry
    Poetry
    Rhapsody
  — Criticism, Textual
  — Paraphrases, tales, etc.
Epic poetry, Classical *(Direct)*
  x Classical epic poetry
  xx Classical poetry
Epic poetry, Finnish, ₍French, Germanic, etc.₎
    (Direct)
  x Finnish ₍French, Germanic, etc.₎ epic
    poetry
  xx Finnish ₍French, Germanic, etc.₎ poetry
Epic poetry, German
  sa Court epic, German
Epic poetry, Russian
  sa Byliny
Epic poetry, Vedic
  See Vedic poetry
Epicyclic gearing
  See Gearing, Planetary
Epicycloids and hypocycloids *(QA623)*
  x Hypocycloids
    Trochoids
  xx Roulettes (Geometry)
Epidemic chorea
  See Chorea, Epidemic
Epidemic encephalitis
  See Encephalitis, Epidemic
Epidemic hepatitis
  See Hepatitis, Infectious
Epidemic hysteria
  See Hysteria, Epidemic
Epidemic tremor
  See Avian encephalomyelitis
Epidemics *(Direct) (RA649-653)*
  sa Black death
    Communicable diseases
    Quarantine
    names of communicable diseases, e.g.
      Cholera, Asiatic; Yellow fever
  x Pestilences
  xx Communicable diseases
    Epidemiology
    Hygiene, Public
  — Boston
    Note under Medical geography
Epidemics, Mental
  See Hysteria, Epidemic
Epidemics in animals
  See Communicable diseases in animals
Epidemiological research
  x Epidemiology—Research
  xx Research
Epidemiology *(RA651)*
  sa Diseases—Transmission
    Epidemics
    Medical record linkage
  xx Communicable diseases
  — Research
    See Epidemiological research
  — Statistical methods
  — Technique *(RA652.4)*
Epidermis *(Comparative anatomy, QL941;*
    Histology, QM561; Human anatomy,
    QM484; Physiology, QP88)
  sa Keratinization
  xx Skin
Epidermolysis bullosa
  x Acantholysis bullosa
    Goldscheider's disease
    Köbner's disease

Epididymis
— Abnormities and deformities
Epididymite *(Indirect)*
Epidote *(QE391.E8)*
  sa Allanite
Epidural anesthesia
  See Peridural anesthesia
Epie language
  See Atisa language
Epigenesis
  See Biology
    Embryology
    Evolution
    Life—Origin
Epiglottis *(Comparative anatomy, QL853; Human anatomy, QM255)*
Epigram
  Note under Epigrams
Epigrams *(PN6279-6288; Poetry, PN1441)*
    Here are entered collections of epigrams. Works dealing with the epigram as a literary form are entered under the heading Epigram.
  sa Aphorisms and apothegms
    Maxims
    Proverbs
    Quotations
    Table-talk
    Toasts
    subdivision Quotations, maxims, etc. *under subjects, e.g.* Politics, Practical —Quotations, maxims, etc.
  x Ana
    Sayings
  xx Aphorisms and apothegms
    Poetry
    Proverbs
    Wit and humor
Epigrams, English
  Note under English language—Quotations, maxims, etc.
Epigrams, English, ⌜French, Japanese, etc.⌝ *(Direct)*
  x English ⌜French, Japanese, etc.⌝ epigrams
  xx English ⌜French, Japanese, etc.⌝ poetry
Epigraphy
  See Inscriptions
Epikeia
  x Epikia
    Epiky
  xx Canon law—Interpretation and construction
    Christian ethics
    Dispensations
Epikia
  See Epikeia
Epiky
  See Epikeia
Epilepsy *(RC372-4)*
  sa Convulsions
    Spasms
    Traumatic epilepsy
  xx Convulsions
    Idiocy
    Insanity
    Spasms
— Early works to 1800
— Genetic aspects
— Surgery
Epileptics
— Care and treatment *(Direct)*
— Colonization
    Example under Colonization
— Employment
— Hospitals
  xx Charities, Medical
    Hospitals

— Laws and legislation *(Direct)*
  xx Mental health laws
— Personal narratives
— Rehabilitation *(Direct)*
Epilogues
  See Prologues and epilogues
Epimenidean paradox
  See Liar paradox
Épinal, Battle of, 1870 *(DC309.E8)*
  xx Franco-German War, 1870-1871
Epinephrin
  See Adrenalin
Epiphanies
Epiphanies in literature
Epiphanism *(B817)*
  sa Existentialism
  xx Existentialism
    Philosophy
Epiphany *(BV50.E7)*
  sa Magi
  x Twelfth day
    Twelfth night
  xx Fasts and feasts
    Jesus Christ—Nativity
— Art
— Drama
— Meditations
— Sermons
— Songs and music
    See Epiphany music
Epiphany music
  x Epiphany—Songs and music
  xx Church music
    Music
    Sacred vocal music
Epiphany season *(BV50.E7)*
  sa Candlemas
  x Sundays after Epiphany
  xx Christmas
    Church year
Epiphysis *(Human anatomy, QM569; Zoology, QL821)*
  sa *subdivision* Epiphysis *under specific subjects, e.g.* Femur—Epiphysis
  xx Bones
    Cartilage
Epiphytes *(QK922)*
  x Air plants
  xx Botany—Ecology
    Plant physiology
Episcopacy *(BV669-670; Church of England, BX5176)*
  sa Anglican orders
    Apostolic succession
    Bishops
    Dioceses
    Methodism
  x Bishops—Collegiality
    Collegiality of bishops
  xx Apostolic succession
    Bishops
    Catholic Church—Clergy
    Church history
    Church of England
    Church of England—Clergy
    Church polity
    Priesthood
— History of doctrines
Episcopacy and Christian union
  x Christian union and episcopacy
Episcopal chanceries
  See Chanceries, Diocesan
Episcopal charges
  See *subdivision* Pastoral letters and charges *under names of church bodies which are episcopal in polity, e.g.* Church of England—Pastoral letters and charges

Episcopal Church
  See Church of England
    Church of Ireland
    Episcopal Church in Scotland
    Protestant Episcopal Church in the U.S.A.
Episcopal Church in Scotland *(BX5210-5393)*
  x Church of England in Scotland
    Episcopal Church
Episcopal churches
  See Churches, Anglican
Episcopalians *(BX5800-5997)*
Episcopalians, Negro *(BX5979-5980)*
Episcopalians in Brookline, Mass., ⌜Chicago, etc.⌝
Episiotomy
  xx Labor, Complicated
Episomes
  sa Bacteriophage lambda
    Plasmids
  xx Bacterial genetics
    Molecular genetics
    Plasmids
Epistaxis
  See Nosebleed
Epistemology
  See Knowledge, Theory of
Epistolaries
  xx Catholic Church. Liturgy and ritual. Epistolary
    Lectionaries
Epistolary fiction *(PN3448.E6)*
  xx Fiction
Epistropeus
  See Axis (Vertebra)
Epitaphs *(Direct) (General collections, PN6288.5-6298; Poetry, PN1441; Local: United States, F; Greek and Latin, CN; Other, CS)*
  sa Brasses
    Sepulchral monuments
  x Graves
  xx Archaeology
    Biography
    Burial
    Cemeteries
    Dead
    Inscriptions
    Tombs
Epitaxy
  xx Crystallization
    Crystals—Growth
Epithalamia *(English, PR1195.E6)*
  x Wedding publications
  xx Love poetry
Epithelial cells
  See Exfoliative cytology
Epitheliosis
  xx Conjunctivitis, Granular
    Eye—Diseases and defects
Epithelium *(QM561)*
  sa Cilia and ciliary motion
    Exfoliative cytology
    Hair follicles
    Lamina epithelialis
    Mesothelium
    Mucous membrane
  xx Cells
    Cilia and ciliary motion
    Cornea
  Note under Histology

Epithets *(PE1447)*

Here are entered works on general and English epithets. Works on epithets in other languages are entered under the name of the language with subdivision Epithets, *e.g.* Latin language—Epithets.

sa Names

Nicknames

x English language—Epithets

xx Names

Nicknames

Epizoa

See Parasites

Epizootic diseases

See Communicable diseases in animals

names of diseases, e.g. Epizootic lymphangitis

Epizootic lymphangitis *(SF809.E)*

sa Glanders

x Farcy (Lymphangitis)

xx Glanders

Horses—Diseases

Example under reference from Epizootic diseases

Eponyms

sa subdivision Eponyms *under names of languages and groups of languages, e.g.* English language—Eponyms

x People words

Words from personal names

Epoöphoron

See Parovarium

Epoxides

See Epoxy compounds

Epoxy-asphalt concrete pavements

See Pavements, Epoxy-asphalt concrete

Epoxy coatings

x Coatings, Epoxy

xx Coatings

Epoxy resins

Plastic coating

Epoxy compounds

x Epoxides

xx Epoxy resins

Ethers

— Analysis

— Patents

— Testing

Epoxy resins *(TP986.E6)*

sa Epoxy coatings

Epoxy compounds

Pavements, Epoxy-asphalt concrete

xx Gums and resins, Synthetic

Plastics

— Electric properties

— Radiation effects

See Epoxy resins, Effect of radiation on

— Testing

Epoxy resins, Effect of radiation on

x Epoxy resins—Radiation effects

xx Radiation

EPPS

See Edwards personal preference schedule

EPSILON (Computer program language)

Equal educational opportunity

See Educational equalization

Equal pay for equal work *(Direct)*

xx Discrimination in employment

Wages

Woman—Employment

Equal protection of the law

See Equality before the law—United States

Equality *(Political science, JC575-8; Sociology, HM146)*

sa Aristocracy

Democracy

Individualism

Liberty

Social classes

Social justice

Socialism

x Inequality

Social equality

xx Democracy

Liberty

Political science

Socialism

Sociology

Equality before the law *(Direct) (JC578; United States, JK1001; K)*

Here are entered discussions of the principle of just legislation and administration of justice, and its application in various constitutional systems.

Works on the doctrine of equal protection of the law are entered under the heading Equality before the law—United States. Works on the doctrine of due process of law are entered under the heading Due process of law.

sa Due process of law

Race discrimination—Law and legislation

United States. Constitution. 14th amendment

xx Civil rights

Constitutional law

Justice

— Biblical teaching

xx Jewish law

GEOGRAPHIC SUBDIVISIONS

— United States

x Equal protection of the law

Note under Equality before the law

Equality of states *(JX4003)*

sa Great powers

xx Great powers

International law

Sovereignty

Equalization, Educational

See Educational equalization

Equalizers (Electronics) *(TK7872.E7)*

x Attenuation equalizers

Compensating circuits

Correcting circuits

xx Electric filters

Electric networks

Equation, Fokker-Planck

See Fokker-Planck equation

Equation, Schrödinger

See Schrödinger equation

Equation of payments

See Average of accounts

Equation of time

See Time, Equation of

Equations *(QA211-218)*

xx Algebra

Mathematics

— Numerical solutions *(QA218)*

sa Algebra—Graphic methods

xx Algebra—Graphic methods

Equations, Abelian *(QA215)*

sa Cyclotomy

x Abelian equations

xx Cyclotomy

Equations, Binomial *(QA245)*

x Binomial equations

Equations, Biquadratic *(QA215)*

x Biquadratic equations

Equations, Chemical

See Chemical equations

Equations, Cubic *(QA215)*

x Cubic equations

Equations, Cyclotomic

See Cyclotomy

Equations, Difference

See Difference equations

Equations, Differential

See Differential equations

Equations, Duffing

See Duffing equations

Equations, Euler-Lagrange

See Lagrange equations

Equations, Functional

See Functional equations

Equations, Hodograph

See Hodograph equations

Equations, Indeterminate

See Diophantine analysis

Equations, Integral

See Integral equations

Equations, Lagrange

See Lagrange equations

Equations, Maxwell

See Maxwell equations

Equations, Navier-Stokes

See Navier-Stokes equations

Equations, Operator

See Operator equations

Equations, Quadratic *(QA161)*

x Quadratic equations

Equations, Quartic *(QA215)*

x Quartic equations

Equations, Quintic *(QA215)*

x Quintic equations

Equations, Roots of *(QA212)*

sa Root-locus method

x Roots of equations

Equations, Sextic *(QA215)*

x Sextic equations

Equations, Simultaneous *(QA195)*

x Simultaneous equations

Equations, Theory of *(QA211-218)*

sa Galois theory

Groups, Theory of

Symmetric functions

x Theory of equations

Equations, Volterra

See Volterra equations

Equations of motion *(QC122-168)*

sa Lagrange equations

x Motion equations

xx Lagrange equations

Mechanics

Equations of state

sa Critical point

Virial coefficients

xx Chemistry, Physical and theoretical

Matter—Properties

Equator (in religion, folk-lore, etc.)

See Shellbacks

Equatorial electrojet

x Electrojet, Equatorial

xx Atmospheric electricity

Ionospheric drift

Magnetism, Terrestrial

Equatorial orbits (Artificial satellites)

See Artificial satellites—Equatorial orbits

Equatorial satellites

See Artificial satellites—Equatorial orbits

Equestrian clubs

See Riding clubs

Equestrian order (Athens)

x Knights, Athenian

Equestrian order (Rome) *(DG83.3)*

x Equites (Rome)

Knights, Roman

Equestrian statues

See Statues

Equestrianism

See Horsemanship

Equilibrium *(Analytical mechanics,*
    QA821-835; Physics, QC131)
  sa Irreversible processes
    Phase rule and equilibrium
    Stability
    Statics
    Virtual work
  xx Stability
    Statics
Equilibrium, Chemical
  See Chemical equilibrium
Equilibrium, Ionic
  See Ionic equilibrium
Equilibrium, Thermal
  See Heat
    Thermodynamics
Equilibrium, Vapor-liquid
  See Vapor-liquid equilibrium
Equilibrium (Economics) *(HB145)*
  x Economic equilibrium
    General equilibrium (Economics)
    Partial equilibrium (Economics)
  xx Economics
    Statics and dynamics (Social sciences)
Equilibrium (Physiology) *(QP471)*
  sa Labyrinth (Ear)
    Man—Attitude and movement
    Vertigo
  x Balance (Physiology)
  xx Labyrinth (Ear)
    Vertigo
Equilibrium (Social sciences)
  See Statics and dynamics (Social sciences)
Equilibrium of chains *(QA835)*
  x Chains, Equilibrium of
    Strings, Equilibrium of
Equilibrium of flexible surfaces *(QA835)*
  x Flexible surfaces, Equilibrium of
    Surfaces, Flexible (Statics)
Equilibrium theory of tides
  See Tides
Equine babesiasis
  See Equine piroplasmosis
Equine biliary fever
  See Equine piroplasmosis
Equine encephalomyelitis
  x Borna's disease
    Eastern encephalitis
    Eastern equine encephalomyelitis
    Equine viral encephalitis
    Infectious equine encephalomyelitis
    Western encephalitis
    Western equine encephalomyelitis
  xx Encephalitis, Epidemic
    Encephalomyelitis
    Horses—Diseases
    Sleeping-sickness
Equine infectious anemia *(SF959.A6)*
  x Equine malarial fever
    Swamp fever, Equine
    Vallee's disease
  xx Horses—Diseases
    Infectious anemia
Equine influenza
  x Newmarket cough
    Pinkeye in horses
    Shipping fever of horses
  xx Horses—Diseases
    Influenza
Equine influenza vaccines
  xx Influenza vaccines
    Vaccination of animals
Equine malaria
  See Equine piroplasmosis
Equine malarial fever
  See Equine infectious anemia
Equine piroplasmosis *(SF959.P)*
  x Equine babesiasis
    Equine biliary fever
    Equine malaria
    Horse tick fever
    Piroplasmosis, Equine
  xx Horses—Diseases
Equine tuberculosis
  See Tuberculosis in horses
Equine viral encephalitis
  See Equine encephalomyelitis
Equinox, Vernal
  See Vernal equinox
Equipment, Capital
  See Industrial equipment
Equipment, Industrial
  See Industrial equipment
Equipment, Pollution control
  See Pollution control equipment
Equipment, Public works
  See Public works equipment
Equipment leasing
  See Industrial equipment leases
Equipollence, Mathematical *(QA556.5)*
  x Mathematical equipollence
Equiprobabilism
  See Probabilism
Equisetophyta
  xx Pteridophyta
Equitable remedies *(Direct)*
  sa Extraordinary remedies
    Injunctions
    Rescission (Law)
    Specific performance
  x Relief (Law)
    Specific relief
  xx Equity
    Equity pleading and procedure
    Extraordinary remedies
    Judicial review of administrative acts
    Remedies (Law)
Equitation
  See Horsemanship
Equites (Rome)
  See Equestrian order (Rome)
Equity *(Direct)*
  sa Bills of peace
    Creditors' bills
    Cy pres doctrine
    Equitable remedies
    Equity pleading and procedure
    Estoppel
    Extraordinary remedies
    Receivers
    Reformation of instruments
    Subrogation
    Trusts and trustees
  x Chancery
  xx Actions and defenses
    Trusts and trustees
Equity (Canon law)
Equity (Frankish law)
Equity (International law)
  xx International law
Equity (Roman law)
  x Aequitas
Equity pleading and procedure *(Direct)*
  sa Consent decrees
    Discovery (Law)
    Equitable remedies
    Masters in chancery
    Receivers
    Referees
  x Chancery
  xx Civil procedure
    Equity
    Pleading
    Procedure (Law)
    Trial practice
Equity pleading and procedure (Greek law)

Equivalence, Rational (Algebraic geometry)
  See Rational equivalence (Algebraic
    geometry)
Equivalence classes (Set theory)
  xx Set theory
Equivalency examination, High school
  See High school equivalency examination
Era names
  See Chronology, Oriental—Terminology
Eradiation
  See Terrestrial radiation
Eranian languages
  See Iranian languages
Eranian literature
  See Iranian literature
Eranian philology
  See Iranian philology
Eras
  See Chronology
Erbium *(QD181.E6)*
  — Isotopes
  — — Spectra
Erckel francolin *(Culture, SF510.P3;*
    Hunting, SK325.P3; Zoology,
    QL696.G27)
  x Erckel's francolin
  xx Francolins
Erckel's francolin
  See Erckel francolin
Eremites
  See Augustinians
    Camaldolites
    Carthusians
    Hermits
Eremitic life
  xx Hermits
    Monastic and religious life
Eremitic life in literature
Erepsin *(QP601)*
Ergodic theory *(QA614)*
  x Ergodic transformations
  xx Groups, Continuous
    Mathematical physics
    Measure theory
    Transformations (Mathematics)
Ergodic transformations
  See Ergodic theory
Ergograph *(QP321)*
Ergometer
  See Dynamometer
Ergonometrics
  See Work measurement
Ergonomics
  See Human engineering
Ergot *(Experimental pharmacology,*
    QP921.E6; Pharmacy, RS165.E7;
    Therapeutics, RM666.E8)
  x Rye smut
    Spurred rye
  — Toxicology
Eria silk moth
  See Ailanthus moth
Eria silkworm
  See Ailanthus moth
Erie, Fort
  — Siege, 1814 *(E356.E5)*
Erie, Lake, Battle of, 1813 *(E356.E6)*
  — Juvenile literature
Erie Canal in literature
Erie Indians *(E99.E5)*
Erie School District
  Example under Special districts
Eriometer *(Optics, QC373.E)*
  xx Diffraction
    Optical instruments
Eripe me, Domine (Music)
  See Psalms (Music)—140th Psalm

Eristics (Greek philosophy)
　　See Megarians (Greek philosophy)
Erlang traffic formula
　　See Queuing theory
Ermeth computer　*(QA76.8.E7)*
　　xx Electronic digital computers
Ermines
　　See Weasels
Erokh (African tribe)
　　See Wambulu (African tribe)
Eromanga language　*(PL6271)*
　　x Erromanga language
　　xx Melanesian languages
Erosion　*(Indirect)*　*(QE571-597)*
　　sa Aeroplanes—Rain erosion
　　　Beach erosion
　　　Chemical denudation
　　　Coast changes
　　　Dust storms
　　　Geomorphology
　　　Glacial erosion
　　　Glaciers
　　　Karst
　　　Planation
　　　Potholes
　　　Runoff
　　　Scour and fill (Geomorphology)
　　　Sediment transport
　　　Sedimentation and deposition
　　　Sinkholes
　　　Soil erosion
　　　Solifluction
　　　Valleys
　　　Weathering
　　　Wind erosion
　　x Geologic erosion
　　xx Geology
　　　Geomorphology
　　　Glaciers
　　　Physical geography
　　　Physical geology
　　　Rivers
　　　Sedimentation and deposition
　　　Soil conservation
　　　Valleys
　　　Water
　　　Weathering
　　— Juvenile literature
　　— Measurement　*(QE571)*
Erosion control
　　See Soil conservation
Erosion control research
　　See Soil conservation—Research
Erosion of metals　*(TA460)*
　　sa Aeroplanes—Rain erosion
　　x Metals—Erosion
　　xx Materials—Deterioration
　　　Weathering
Erotic art　*(Direct)*　*(Visual arts, N8217.E6)*
　　sa Art and morals
　　　Book-plates, Erotic
　　　Love in art
　　　Nude in art
　　　Photography, Erotic
　　x Art, Erotic
　　　Art, Immoral
　　　Sex in art
　　xx Art
　　　Art and morals
　　　Erotica
　　— Law and legislation
　　　　See Obscenity (Law)
Erotic book-plates
　　See Book-plates, Erotic
　　　Nude in book-plates
Erotic films
　　sa Sex in moving-pictures
　　x Moving-pictures, Erotic

　　xx Erotica
　　　Moving-pictures
　　　Sex in moving-pictures
　　— History and criticism
Erotic literature　*(HQ450-471)*
　　sa Children and erotica
　　　Liberty of the press
　　　Literature, Immoral
　　　Love in literature
　　　Love-letters
　　　Obscenity (Law)
　　　Sex in literature
　　x Literature, Erotic
　　xx Erotica
　　　Literature
　　　Literature, Immoral
　　　Love in literature
　　— History and criticism
　　　　xx Liberty of the press
Erotic photography
　　See Photography, Erotic
Erotic poetry
　　xx Erotica
　　　Poetry
Erotic poetry, French, ₍German, etc.₎
　　　　(Direct)
　　x French ₍German, etc.₎ erotic poetry
　　xx French ₍German, etc.₎ poetry
Erotic proverbs　*(Direct)*
　　xx Proverbs
Erotic stories
　　xx Fiction
Erotic stories, Dutch, ₍etc.₎　*(Direct)*
　　x Dutch ₍etc.₎ erotic stories
　　xx Dutch ₍etc.₎ fiction
Erotic symbolism
　　See Sex symbolism
Erotica
　　sa Erotic art
　　　Erotic films
　　　Erotic literature
　　　Erotic poetry
　　　Literature, Immoral
　　　Obscenity (Law)
　　　Photography, Erotic
　　　Sex in moving-pictures
　　　Sex in the performing arts
　　　Sex symbolism
Erotica and children
　　See Children and erotica
Erotica and youth
　　See Youth and erotica
ERP (European recovery program)
　　See Reconstruction (1939-1951)—Europe
Errata (in books)
　　x Errors, Printing
　　　Misprints
　　　Printing errors
　　　Typographical errors
　　xx Transmission of texts
Erromanga language
　　See Eromanga language
Error　*(BD171)*
　　xx Belief and doubt
　　　Knowledge, Theory of
　　　Relativity
　　　Truth
　　　Truthfulness and falsehood
Error, Writ of
　　See Writ of error
Error (Criminal law)
　　See Mistake (Criminal law)
Error (Law)
　　See Mistake (Law)
Error-correcting codes (Information theory)
　　sa Pulse frequency modulation
　　x Codes, Error-correcting
　　　Error-detecting codes

　　　Forbidden-combination check
　　　Self-checking codes
　　xx Artificial intelligence
　　　Automatic checkout equipment
　　　Automatic control
　　　Binary system (Mathematics)
　　　Coding theory
　　　Electronic digital computers
　　　Information theory
　　　Telecommunication
Error-detecting codes
　　See Error-correcting codes (Information
　　　theory)
Error function integrals
　　See Error functions
Error functions
　　x Error function integrals
　　　Functions, Error
　　　Gauss error function
　　　Integral error function
　　xx Differential equations—Numerical
　　　solutions
　　　Integrals, Definite
　　　Mathematical physics
　　　Probabilities
Errors
　　　Here are entered works on errors of judg-
　　　ment, errors of observation, etc. (as,
　　　for example, in experimental psy-
　　　chology) and on errors of too general
　　　a nature to be covered by more specific
　　　headings, such as Errors, Popular; Er-
　　　rors, Scientific; etc.
　　sa Fallibility
　　x Mistakes
　　xx Fallibility
Errors, Logical
　　See Fallacies (Logic)
Errors, Numismatic
　　See Numismatics—Errors
Errors, Popular　*(AZ999)*
　　sa History—Errors, inventions, etc.
　　　Medical delusions
　　　Superstition
　　x Blunders
　　　Delusions
　　　Mistakes
　　　Popular errors
　　xx Credulity
　　　Superstition
　　Note under Errors
Errors, Printing
　　See Errata (in books)
Errors, Scientific
　　x Mistakes
　　　Scientific errors
　　Note under Errors
Errors, Theory of　*(QA275)*
　　sa Correlation (Statistics)
　　　Graphic methods
　　　Least squares
　　　Probabilities
　　　Roundoff errors
　　　Sampling (Statistics)
　　x Theory of errors
　　xx Astronomy—Observations
　　　Mathematical statistics
　　　Mathematics
　　　Physical measurements
　　　Probabilities
　　　Sampling (Statistics)
　　　Triangulation
Errors and blunders, Literary　*(PN6231.B8)*
　　sa Literary forgeries and mystifications
　　　subdivision Idioms, corrections, errors
　　　　under names of languages, e.g.
　　　　English language—Idioms,
　　　　corrections, errors

Errors and blunders, Literary *(PN6231.B8)*
  (Continued)
    x Anachronisms, Literary
      Blunders
      Literary anachronisms
      Literary blunders
      Literary errors and blunders
      Mistakes
    xx Bibliography
      Cataloging
      Literature
Errors of criminal justice
  See Judicial error
Ersatz
  See Substitute products
Erse
  See Gaelic language
    Irish language
Erub
  See Eruv
Eructavit cor meum (Music)
  See Psalms (Music)—45th Psalm
Erudition
  See Learning and scholarship
Eruptive fever
  See Exanthemata
Eruptive rocks
  See Rocks, Igneous
Eruv
  x Erub
  xx Jewish law—Interpretation and
    construction
    Sabbath (Jewish law)
Erysipelas *(RC142)*
  xx Pyoderma
  Example under Exanthemata
Erythremia
  x Erythrocythemia
    Polycythemia
    Vaquez's disease
  xx Altitude, Influence of
    Blood—Diseases
Erythroblastosis fetalis
  x Erythroblastosis neonatorum
    Fetal erythroblastosis
  xx Blood—Diseases
    Fetus—Diseases
    Rh factor
  Example under Infants (Newborn)—Diseases
  — Prevention
Erythroblastosis neonatorum
  See Erythroblastosis fetalis .
Erythrocyte disorders *(RC647.E7)*
  xx Blood—Diseases
Erythrocytes
  sa Heinz bodies
    Hematocrit
    Reticulocytes
  x Red blood cells
    Red blood corpuscles
  xx Blood—Corpuscles and platelets
Erythrocythemia
  See Erythremia
Erythroedema
  See Acrodynia
Erythromelalgia
  sa Causalgia
  xx Neuralgia
Erythromycin
  xx Antibiotics
Erythropoiesis
  sa Erythropoietin
  xx Blood—Corpuscles and platelets
Erythropoietin
  xx Erythropoiesis
Erzya dialect *(PH778.E8)*
  xx Mordvinian language
Es (Ionosphere)
  See Sporadic E (Ionosphere)

Esaki diodes
  See Tunnel diodes
Esbjerg in art
ESCA
  See Electron spectroscopy
Escalade of Geneva, 1602
  See Geneva—Siege, 1602
Escalator clause *(Direct)*
  sa Gold clause
    Valuta clause
  xx Contracts
    Debtor and creditor
    Inflation (Finance)
    Payment
Escalator clause (Wages)
  See Wages—Cost-of-living adjustments
Escalators *(TJ1376)*
  xx Staircases
  — Law and legislation *(Direct)*
Escape (Ethics)
  xx Christian ethics
    Ethics
Escape (Law) *(Direct)*
  xx Criminal law
    Fugitives from justice
Escape (Psychology)
  sa Avoidance (Psychology)
    Wilderness (Theology)
  xx Anxiety
    Avoidance (Psychology)
    Emotions
    Psychology, Physiological
Escape in literature
Escape physiology (Space flight)
  x Biodynamics (Space flight)
  xx Space biology
    Space medicine
Escapements
  See Clocks and watches—Escapements
Escapes *(Prisons, HV8657-8)*
  sa Survival and emergency equipment
  x Prison escapes
  xx Adventure and adventurers
    Fugitives from justice
    Prisoners
    Prisons
  — Juvenile literature
Escargots
  See Snails, Edible
Escharotics
  sa names of individual escharotics, e.g.
    Nitric acid
Eschatology *(Comparative religion,*
    BL500-547; Theology, BT819-890)
  sa Annihilationism
    Antichrist
    Apocalyptic literature
    Beatific vision
    Death
    Demythologization
    Dispensationalism
    End of the world
    Future life
    Future punishment
    Heaven
    Heavenly recognition
    Hell
    Immortality
    Intermediate state
    Judgment Day
    Kingdom of God
    Limbo
    Millennium
    Nirvana
    Paradise
    Particular judgment (Theology)
    Probation after death
    Purgatory

    Resurrection
    Second Advent
    Time (Theology)
    Translation to heaven
    Universe, Destruction of
  x Last things (Theology)
  xx Intermediate state
    Theology, Doctrinal
  — Biblical teaching
    xx Bible—Theology
  — Comparative studies
  — Early works to 1800 *(Doctrinal*
      theology, BT820)
  — History of doctrines
  — — Early church, ca. 30-600
  — — Middle Ages, 600-1500
  — — 20th century *(BT819.5)*
  — Meditations
  — Miscellanea
  — Sermons
Eschatology, Ancient
Eschatology, Assyro-Babylonian, [Egyptian,
    etc.]
  x Assyro-Babylonian [Egyptian, etc.]
    eschatology
Eschatology, Buddhist
  sa Death (Buddhism)
    Future life (Buddhism)
    Immortality (Buddhism)
    Saddharmavipralopa
    Western Paradise (Buddhism)
  xx Buddhist doctrines
Eschatology, Egyptian
  sa Death (Egyptian religion)
Eschatology, Greco-Roman
  sa Elysium
  x Greco-Roman eschatology
Eschatology, Hindu
  sa Death (Hinduism)
    Future life (Hinduism)
  x Hindu eschatology
Eschatology, Islamic *(BP166.8)*
  sa Death (Islam)
    End of the world (Islam)
    Future life (Islam)
    Future punishment (Islam)
    Hell (Islam)
    Intercession (Islam)
    Intermediate state (Islam)
    Judgment Day (Islam)
    Mahdism
    Paradise (Islam)
    Resurrection (Islam)
  x Eschatology, Muslim
    Islamic eschatology
    Muslim eschatology
  xx Islamic theology
  — Koranic teaching
Eschatology, Jewish
  sa Death (Judaism)
    Hell (Judaism)
    Immortality (Judaism)
    Messianic era (Judaism)
Eschatology, Muslim
  See Eschatology, Islamic
Eschatology, Shinto
  x Shinto eschatology
Eschatology in literature
Escheat *(Direct)*
  xx Bona vacantia
    Estates (Law)
    Estates, Unclaimed
    Forfeiture
    Inheritance and succession
    Reversion
Escherichia coli infections
  xx Bacteriology, Medical
    Intestines—Bacteriology

Lungs—Bacteriology
Escondido (Dance)
Escort automobile *(TL215.E)*
  xx Ford automobile
Escort destroyers
  See Destroyer escorts
Escrows *(Direct)*
  xx Consignation
      Deposits (Law)
      Legal instruments
Escuage
  See Scutage
Escutcheons *(CR91-93)*
  x Shields (Heraldry)
  xx Heraldry
Ese Ejja language
  xx Indians of South America—Languages
Esira language
  See Shira language
Eskar *(QE578)*
  x Esker
      Kames
  xx Geology, Structural
Esker
  See Eskar
Eskimauan Indians
  See Eskimos
Eskimo children
  See Eskimos—Children
Eskimo curlew
  xx Curlews
Eskimo dogs *(SF429.E8)*
Eskimo language *(PM61-64)*
  sa Aglemiut dialect
  x Greenlandic language
  xx Hyperborean languages
Eskimo language, Asiatic
  See Yuit language
Eskimo literature
  xx United States—Literatures
Eskimo music
  See Eskimos—Music
Eskimo newspapers
Eskimo poetry *(PM64)*
Eskimo poetry (American)
  See American poetry—Eskimo authors
Eskimos *(Indirect)* *(E99.E7)*
  sa Aleuts
      Chugach Eskimos
      Igloos
      Kaniagmiut (Eskimo tribe)
      Nunamiut (Eskimo tribe)
      Ugalakmiut Indians
  x Eskimauan Indians
      Esquimaux
      Innuit
      Inuit
  xx Arctic races
      Indians of North America
  — Amusements
      See Eskimos—Games
  — Anthropometry
      x Anthropometry—Eskimos
  — Antiquities
  — Art
      xx Art, Primitive
  — — Juvenile literature
  — Boats
      sa Umiaks
      xx Boats and boating
          Indians of North America—Boats
  — Children
      x Eskimo children
      xx Children
  — Costume and adornment
  — Dances
  — Economic conditions
  — Education *(E99.E7)*

— Fishing
— Folk-lore
    See Folk-lore, Eskimo
— Food
— Games
    x Eskimos—Amusements
        Eskimos—Recreations
        Eskimos—Sports
— Health and hygiene *(Direct)*
— Hunting
— Implements
— Legends
— Music *(ML3560)*
    sa Folk-songs, Eskimo
    x Eskimo music
        Music, Eskimo
— Pictorial works
— Psychology
— Recreations
        See Eskimos—Games
— Religion and mythology
— Rites and ceremonies
— Sports
        See Eskimos—Games
— Urban residence
— Writing
Esophageal hernia
  See Hiatal hernia
Esophageal motility
  xx Esophagus
Esophageal speech
  xx Speech
Esophagoduodenostomy
  xx Duodenum—Surgery
      Esophagus—Surgery
Esophagogastric junction
  sa Cardia
  x Gastroesophageal junction
  xx Esophagus
      Stomach
Esophagojejunostomy
  xx Esophagus—Surgery
      Jejunostomy
Esophagoplasty
  xx Esophagus—Surgery
Esophagus *(Comparative anatomy, QL861;*
      Human anatomy, QM331;
      Physiology, QP146)
  sa Cardia
      Deglutition
      Esophageal motility
      Esophagogastric junction
      Pharyngoesophageal sphincter
  x Oesophagus
  xx Throat
— Abnormities and deformities
— Cancer *(RC280)*
— Cysts
      Example under Cysts
— Diseases *(RC815.7)*
    sa Esophagus—Radiography
        names of specific diseases, e.g.
            Gastroesophageal reflux
— — Atlases
— Diverticula *(RC815.7)*
— Exploration *(RC815.7)*
— Foreign bodies *(RF545)*
— Innervation
— Intubation
— Radiography
    xx Esophagus—Diseases
— Surgery *(RD516)*
    sa Esophagoduodenostomy
        Esophagojejunostomy
        Esophagoplasty
— Tumors
— Wounds and injuries

Esopus Indians *(E99.E8)*
  xx Algonquian Indians
      Indians of North America
      Munsee Indians
  — Wars, 1655-1660 *(E83.655)*
      xx Indians of North America—Wars—
          1600-1750
  — Wars, 1663-1664 *(E83.663)*
      xx Indians of North America—Wars—
          1600-1750
Esopus language
  See Munsee language
Esoteric Buddhism
  See Tantric Buddhism
Espaliers
  x Fruit trees, Training of
  xx Landscape gardening
      Plants, Ornamental
Esparto *(Grasses, QK495.G74; Paper*
      making, TS1109)
  xx Grasses
Esperanto *(PM8201-8298)*
  xx Languages, Artificial
Esperanto fiction *(Direct)*
Esperanto imprints *(Direct)*
Esperanto literature *(Direct)*
Esperanto poetry *(Direct)*
Esperanto prose literature *(Direct)*
Espingoles
  xx Firearms
Espionage *(Direct)*
  sa Defense information, Classified
      Ninjutsu
      Spies
      Trials (Espionage)
  xx Intelligence service
      Secret service
      Sovereignty, Violation of
      Subversive activities
— Anecdotes, facetiae, satire, etc.
— Equipment and supplies
    sa Electronics in espionage
— Juvenile literature
Espionage, Business
  See Business intelligence
Espionage, Japanese, ⌜Polish, Russian, etc.⌝
      (Direct)
Espionage stories
  See Spy stories
ESPL (Computer program language)
Esquimaux
  See Eskimos
Essay *(PN4500)*
      Here are entered works on the essay as a
          literary form. Collections of essays are
          entered under the heading Essays.
  x Literary sketch
      Sketch, Literary
Essays *(PN6141-5)*
  sa English essays; French essays; *and*
          similar headings; and subdivision
          Addresses, essays, lectures *under*
          particular subjects, e.g. English
          poetry—Addresses, essays, lectures
  xx Literature
  Note under Essay
Esselene language
  See Esselenian language
Esselenian language *(PM1137)*
  x Esselene language
Essence (Philosophy)
  xx Philosophy
      Substance (Philosophy)
Essences and essential oils *(Chemical*
      technology, TP958; Chemistry,
      QD416)
  sa Aromatic plants
      Citrus oils

Essences and essential oils *(Chemical technology, TP958; Chemistry, QD416)* *(Continued)*
    Flavoring essences
    Incense
    Perfumes
    Plants, Effect of essential oils on
    names of essences and essential oils,
      e.g. Attar of roses, Bergamot oil
    x Aromatic plant products
      Essential oils
      Oils, Essential
      Vegetable oils
      Volatile oils
    xx Aromatic plants
      Distillation
      Flavoring essences
      Oils and fats
      Oils and fats, Edible
      Terpenes
    Example under Chemistry, Organic
    — Analysis
    — Spectra
    — Therapeutic use
      xx Materia medica, Vegetable
Essenes *(BM175.E8)*
    sa Qumran community
      Zealots (Jewish party)
    xx Jewish sects
Essential fatty acids
    x Fatty acids, Essential
    xx Acids, Fatty
    — Therapeutic use
Essential oils
    See Essences and essential oils
Essex swine *(SF393.E7)*
Essling, Battle of, 1809
    See Aspern, Battle of, 1809
Esslingen, Battle of, 1809
    See Aspern, Battle of, 1809
Established Church of Ireland
    See Church of Ireland
Established churches *(Direct)*
    (Ecclesiastical aspects, BV633)
    sa Dissenters, Religious
    x National churches
      State churches
      State religion
    xx Church and state
      Ecclesiastical law
      Religion and state
Estate planning *(Direct)*
    sa Estate settlement costs
      Estates (Law)
      Inheritance and transfer tax
      Insurance
      Investments
      Tax planning
      Taxation
      Trusts and trustees
    xx Estates (Law)
      Finance, Personal
      Tax planning
Estate settlement costs
    xx Estate planning
      Inheritance and succession
Estate tail
    See Entail
Estate tax
    See Inheritance and transfer tax
Estates, Administration of
    See Administration of estates
Estates, Boundaries of
    See Boundaries (Estates)
Estates, Unclaimed *(Direct)* *(CS23)*
    sa Escheat
    x Property, Unclaimed
      Unclaimed estates

      Unclaimed property
    xx Bona vacantia
      Decedents' estates
      Inheritance and succession
Estates (Law) *(Direct)*
    sa Decedents' estates
      Defeasible fees
      Escheat
      Estate planning
      Executory interests
      Future interests
      Merger of estates
      Possessory interests in land
      Remainders (Estates)
      Reversion
      Shelley's case, Rule in
    x Limitations (Law)
    xx Estate planning
      Inheritance and succession
      Probate law and practice
      Real property
    — Accounting
    — Cases
Estates (Social orders) *(Direct)*
    sa Feudalism
      Legislative bodies
      Ministerials
      Social classes
    x Commons (Social order)
    xx Feudalism
    — Rome
      sa Plebs (Rome)
Estates in expectancy
    See Expectancies (Law)
Estates of decedents
    See Decedents' estates
Esterification *(QD305.A2; QD341.A2)*
Esters *(QD305.A2; QD341.A2)*
    sa Polyesters
    Example under Chemistry, Organic
    — Spectra
Esther, Feast of
    See Purim (Feast of Esther)
Esthetics
    See Aesthetics
Esthonian . . .
    See Estonian . . .
Estill's Defeat, 1782 *(F454)*
Estimates
    See subdivisions Estimates *and* Estimates
      and costs *under technical subjects,*
      e.g. Building—Estimates;
      Engineering—Estimates and costs
    Cf. Cost.
Estimation of disability
    See Disability evaluation
Estimation theory *(QA276.8)*
    sa Decision-making
      Distributed lags (Economics)
      Fix-point estimation
      Kalman filtering
      Multicollinearity
    xx Least squares
      Mathematical statistics
      Stochastic processes
    — Computer programs
    — Juvenile literature
Estonia
    — History
    — — Revolution of 1905
    — — War of Independence, 1918-1920
    — — — Regimental histories
    — — 1918-1940
    — — — Pictorial works
    — — — Communist Coup, 1924
    — — — Russian occupation, 1940-1941
    — — — Personal narratives
    — — German occupation, 1941-1944

    - — — 1944-
Estonian . . .
    x Esthonian . . .
Estonian ballads and songs *(PH641; PH651; PH663)*
    sa Folk-songs, Estonian
Estonian drama *(Direct)* *(Collections, PH663; History, PH632)*
Estonian fiction *(Direct)*
Estonian imprints *(Direct)*
Estonian language *(PH601-629)*
    xx Finnish languages
      Finno-Ugrian languages
Estonian literature *(PH631-688)*
Estonian mythology
    See Mythology, Finno-Ugrian
Estonian newspapers *(PN5355.E8)*
Estonian periodicals *(PN5355.E8)*
Estonian poetry in foreign countries
Estonian wit and humor, Pictorial
Estonians *(DK511.E4-8; Craniology, GN103.E8)*
    xx Finno-Ugrians
Estoppel *(Direct)*
    sa Evidence (Law)
      Judgments
      Res judicata
      Waiver
    xx Actions and defenses
      Equity
      Evidence (Law)
      Res judicata
Estrada doctrine
    See Recognition (International law)
Estrangement (Philosophy)
    See Alienation (Philosophy)
Estrangement (Social psychology)
    See Alienation (Social psychology)
Estrays
    See Pounds
Estrogen
    sa Coumestrol
    — Analysis *(QP801.H7)*
    — Physiological effect
    — Therapeutic use
      xx Hormone therapy
Estrous cycle
    See Estrus
Estruation
    See Estrus
Estrum
    See Estrus
Estrus
    x Estrous cycle
      Estruation
      Estrum
      Heat in animals
      Oestrum
      Oestrus
      Rut
    xx Ovulation
      Reproduction
      Sex (Biology)
      Sexual cycle
      Sexual instinct
Estuaries *(Indirect)*
    sa Bays
      Estuarine area conservation
      Estuarine ecology
      Estuarine oceanography
      names of estuaries of specific rivers, etc., e.g. Delaware River estuary
    xx Bays
      Coasts
      Rivers
      Tides
    — Computer programs
    — Mathematical models

Estuarine area conservation *(Indirect)*
  xx Conservation of natural resources
      Estuaries
      Wetlands
Estuarine biology *(Indirect)*
  xx Aquatic biology
Estuarine ecology *(Indirect) (QH541.5.E8)*
  xx Estuaries
      Estuarine oceanography
      Marine ecology
  — Juvenile literature
Estuarine fisheries
  xx Fisheries
Estuarine oceanography *(GC96-7)*
      Works on estuarine oceanography of a
        particular locality are entered under
        the heading Oceanography subdivided
        by locality, *e.g.* Oceanography—
        Chesapeake Bay.
  sa Estuarine ecology
      Estuarine sediments
  xx Estuaries
      Oceanography
Estuarine pollution *(Indirect)*
  xx Marine pollution
Estuarine sediments *(Indirect)*
  xx Estuarine oceanography
      Marine sediments
      Sediments (Geology)
Eta
  x Burakumin
  xx Caste—Japan
  — Economic conditions
  — Education
  — Personal narratives
Etard's reaction *(QD281.O9)*
  xx Chemistry, Organic
Etchants
  See Etching reagents
Etchaottine Indians
  See Slave Indians
Etchareottine Indians
  See Slave Indians
Etcheetee language
  See Hitchiti language
Etchemin Indians
  See Malecite Indians
Etchemin language
  See Malecite language
Etchers *(NE2110-2115)*
  sa Stipple engravers
  xx Artists
      Engravers
      Printmakers
Etchers, British, ₍Dutch, French, etc.₎
      (Direct)
  x British ₍Dutch, French, etc.₎ etchers
Etching *(Direct) (NE1940-2210)*
  sa Aquatint
      Cement clinkers—Etching
      Dry-point
      Engraving
      Etchings
      Glass etching
      Metals—Finishing
      Pyrography
      Semiconductors—Etching
      Stipple engraving
      Zincography
  xx Art
      Engraving
      Prints
  — Competitions
  — Technique *(NE2120-2130)*
Etching reagents
  x Etchants
Etchings *(Direct) (NE1940-2210)*
  sa Dry-points

      Engravings
      Stipple engravings
  xx Drawings
      Engravings
      Etching
      Pictures
  — Catalogs
      Here are entered dealers' and general
        sales catalogs. Catalogs of exhibi-
        tions are entered under Etchings—
        Exhibitions. Catalogs of private col-
        lections are entered under the head-
        ing Etchings—Private collections.
  — Exhibitions *(NE1950-1955)*
      Note under Etchings—Catalogs
  — Prices
  — Private collections *(NE1945)*
      Note under Etchings—Catalogs
Etchings, Dutch, ₍French, etc.₎ *(Direct)*
  x Dutch ₍French, etc.₎ etchings
Etchita language
  See Hitchiti language
Eternal life
  See Future life
Eternal punishment
  See Future punishment
      Hell
Eternal recurrence
  See Eternal return
Eternal return
  x Eternal recurrence
  xx Cosmology
      Cycles
      Eternity
Eternity *(BT910-911)*
      Here are entered works on the philosoph-
        ical concept of eternity. Eschatological
        works are entered under the heading
        Future life.
  sa Eternal return
      Future life
      Time (Theology)
  xx Future life
      Infinite
  — Quotations, maxims, etc.
Ethanes *(QD305.H6)*
  sa DDT (Insecticide)
      Halothane
  x Dimethyl
  xx Paraffins
  — Molecular rotation
Ethanol
  See Alcohol
Ethenyl
  See Vinyl polymers
Ether *(QD305.E7)*
  sa Aether
Ether (Anesthetic) *(RD79-86)*
  xx Anesthetics
  — Physiological effect *(RD86.E8)*
      sa Plants, Effect of ether on
Ether (of space) *(QC177)*
  sa Interstellar matter
  xx Gravitation
      Matter—Constitution
      Physics
      Space and time
      Space sciences
      Waves
Etherification *(QD281.E8)*
Ethers *(QD305.E7; QD341.E7)*
  sa Claisen rearrangement
      Epoxy compounds
  Example under Chemistry, Organic
  — Spectra
Ethical culture movement *(BJ10.E8)*
Ethical education
  See Moral education

      Religious education
Ethical movement (Dutch Reformed Church)
      Here are entered works dealing with a
        theological—not a moral—movement
        which originated about 1853 with
        Daniel Chantepie de la Saussaye. It
        emphasized the personal nature of reli-
        gion as against contemporary rational
        and humanistic theories.
  x Dutch ethical movement
      Ethische richting
  xx Nederlandse Hervormde Kerk—Parties
      and movements
Ethical problems
  xx Casuistry
      Ethics
      Responsa
Ethical relativism
  sa Ethics, Evolutionary
  x Relativism, Ethical
      Relativity (Ethics)
  xx Ethics
      Ethics, Evolutionary
Ethical theology
  See Christian ethics
Ethical wills
  See Wills, Ethical
Ethics *(BJ)*
  sa Actors, Professional ethics for
      Altruism
      Anger
      Animals, Treatment of
      Art and morals
      Asceticism
      Avarice
      Benevolence
      Business ethics
      Cardinal virtues
      Casuistry
      Character
      Charity
      Chastity
      Cheerfulness
      Christian ethics
      Christian life
      Communist ethics
      Compromise (Ethics)
      Conduct of life
      Confidence
      Conscience
      Contentment
      Courage
      Courtesy
      Crime and criminals
      Cruelty
      Decision-making (Ethics)
      Divorce
      Dueling
      Duty
      Egoism
      Ends and means
      Engineering ethics
      Escape (Ethics)
      Ethical problems
      Ethical relativism
      Etiquette
      Example
      Existential ethics
      Fairness
      Fellowship
      Filial piety
      Free will and determinism
      Friendship
      Gambling
      God—Proof, Moral
      Good and evil
      Gratitude
      Guilt

Ethics *(BJ) (Continued)*
  Habit
  Happiness
  Hedonism
  Honesty
  Honor
  Humanistic ethics
  Humanity
  Hunting—Moral and religious aspects
  Hypocrisy
  Indifferentism (Ethics)
  Influence (Psychology)
  Ingratitude
  Journalistic ethics
  Judgment (Ethics)
  Justice
  Kindness
  Legal ethics
  Librarians, Professional ethics for
  Life and death, Power over
  Literature and morals
  Love
  Loyalty
  Machiavellianism (Psychology)
  Medical ethics
  Mental reservation
  Mercy
  Military ethics
  Moral education
  Moral rearmament
  Music and morals
  Natural law
  Nursing ethics
  Obedience
  Patience
  Patriotism
  Peace
  Perfection (Ethics)
  Pleasure
  Police ethics
  Political ethics
  Popularity
  Power (Philosophy)
  Pride and vanity
  Probabilism
  Professional ethics
  Promises
  Prudence
  Religious ethics
  Responsibility
  Reward (Ethics)
  Right and wrong
  Secularism
  Self-denial
  Self-interest
  Self-realization
  Self-respect
  Self-sacrifice
  Sexual ethics
  Simplicity
  Sin
  Sins
  Situation ethics
  Social ethics
  Social problems
  Socialist ethics
  Spiritual life
  Spirituality
  Stoics
  Student ethics
  Sublimation
  Success
  Suicide
  Sunday
  Swearing
  Sympathy
  Teachers, Professional ethics for
  Temperance

  Temptation
  Totalitarian ethics
  Truthfulness and falsehood
  Utilitarianism
  Vice
  Vices
  Virtue
  Virtue, Infused
  Virtues
  Virtues (Buddhism)
  Vocation
  War
  Wealth, Ethics of
  Will
  Woman—Social and moral questions
  Worth
  subdivision Moral and religious aspects
      under specific subjects, e.g.
      Amusements—Moral and religious
      aspects; *also subdivision* Ethics
      under names of philosophers
    x Deontology
    Ethics, Practical
    Ethology
    Moral philosophy
    Morality
    Morals
    Philosophy, Moral
    Science, Moral
   xx Civilization
    Conduct of life
    Duty
    Life
    Natural law
    Philosophy
    Theology
    Virtue
  — History *(Indirect) (BJ71-1185)*
  — Juvenile literature
Ethics, Buddhist
    See Buddhist ethics
Ethics, Chinese
    sa Confucian ethics
Ethics, Chinese, [Germanic, Greek, etc.]
  — Quotations, maxims, etc.
Ethics, Christian
    See Christian ethics
Ethics, Circumstance
    See Situation ethics
Ethics, Commercial
    See Business ethics
Ethics, Communist
    See Communist ethics
Ethics, Comparative *(BJ69)*
    x Comparative ethics
   xx Philosophy, Comparative
Ethics, Confucian
    See Confucian ethics
Ethics, Contextual
    See Situation ethics
Ethics, Engineering
    See Engineering ethics
Ethics, Evolutionary *(BJ1298-1335)*
    sa Ethical relativism
    x Ethics, Naturalistic
    Evolutionary ethics
    Naturalistic ethics
   xx Ethical relativism
    Evolution
Ethics, Existential
    See Existential ethics
Ethics, Gnostic
    See Gnostic ethics
Ethics, Hindu
    See Hindu ethics
Ethics, Humanistic
    See Humanistic ethics

Ethics, Indian
    See Indians of North America—Ethics
Ethics, Islamic
    See Islamic ethics
Ethics, Jaina
    See Jaina ethics
Ethics, Japanese
    sa Bushido
    Shingaku
Ethics, Jewish
    sa Jewish etiquette
    Jewish way of life
    Merit (Jewish theology)
    Musar movement
    Reconciliation (Judaism)
    Sin (Judaism)
    Wills, Ethical
    subdivision Conduct of life *under*
        special groups of Jews, e.g. Youth,
        Jewish—Conduct of life
    x Jewish ethics
    Jews—Ethics
   xx Religion and ethics
  — Sermons
        Example under Sermons, Jewish
Ethics, Journalistic
    See Journalistic ethics
Ethics, Judicial
    See Judicial ethics
Ethics, Korean
    sa Hwarangdo
Ethics, Legal
    See Legal ethics
Ethics, Literary
    See Literary ethics
Ethics, Medical
    See Medical ethics
Ethics, Medieval *(BJ231-255)*
Ethics, Military
    See Military ethics
Ethics, Modern *(BJ301-977)*
    x Modern ethics
  — 20th century *(BJ319)*
Ethics, Muslim
    See Islamic ethics
Ethics, Naturalistic
    See Ethics, Evolutionary
Ethics, Police
    See Police ethics
Ethics, Political
    See Political ethics
Ethics, Positivist *(BJ1365-1385)*
    x Positivist ethics
   xx Positivism
Ethics, Practical
    See Conduct of life
    Ethics
Ethics, Primitive
Ethics, Religious
    See Religious ethics
Ethics, Sexual
    See Sexual ethics
Ethics, Sikh
    See Sikh ethics
Ethics, Situation
    See Situation ethics
Ethics, Social
    See Social ethics
Ethics, Socialist
    See Socialist ethics
Ethics, Totalitarian
    See Totalitarian ethics
Ethics and astronautics
    See Astronautics and ethics
Ethics and law
    See Law and ethics
Ethics and religion
    See Religion and ethics

Ethics and science
  See Science and ethics
Ethics and social sciences
  See Social sciences and ethics
Ethics and technology
  See Technology and ethics
Ethics and the arts
  See Arts and morals
Ethics of decision-making
  See Decision-making (Ethics)
Ethics of wealth
  See Wealth, Ethics of
Ethiopia
— History
—— To 1490 *(DT383)*
—— 1490-1889 *(DT384-6)*
—— 1889- *(DT387)*
— Languages
    Note under Ethiopian langauges
Ethiopian-Italian War, 1895-1896
  See Italo-Ethiopian War, 1895-1896
Ethiopian-Italian War, 1935-1936
  See Italo-Ethiopian War, 1935-1936
Ethiopian languages *(PJ8991-9)*
    Here are entered works on the Semitic
    languages of Ethiopia. Works on the
    Hamitic languages of Ethiopia are en-
    tered under Cushitic languages. Gen-
    eral works on the languages of Ethi-
    opia are entered under Ethiopia—Lan-
    guages.
  sa Amharic language
    Ethiopic language
    Gurage language
    Harari language
    Tigré language
    Tigriña language
  xx Semitic languages
Ethiopian literature *(Direct)*
Ethiopian poetry
Ethiopian studies *(Direct)*
Ethiopians *(DT380)*
  sa Amharas
Ethiopic . . .
  x Aethiopic . . .
Ethiopic Church *(BX140-149)*
  x Abyssinian Church
    Church of Abyssinia
    Church of Ethiopia
  xx Coptic Church
    Monophysites
Ethiopic language *(PJ9001-9085)*
  x Geez language
  xx Ethiopian languages
Ethiopic literature *(PJ9090-9101)*
Ethiopic manuscripts
  See Manuscripts, Ethiopic
Ethiopic philology
Ethische richting
  See Ethical movement (Dutch Reformed
    Church)
Ethmyphytis
  See Cellulitis
Ethnic attitudes
  sa Race awareness
  xx Attitude (Psychology)
    Minorities
    Race awareness
Ethnic attitudes in literature
Ethnic barriers *(JX4115-4181)*
  xx Boundaries
    Ethnology
    Man—Migrations
Ethnic group names
  See Names, Ethnological
Ethnic groups
  See Minorities
    Race problems

Ethnic journalism
  See Ethnic press
Ethnic press *(Direct)*
  x Ethnic journalism
    Journalism, Ethnic
  xx Minorities
    Press
Ethnic psychology
  See Ethnopsychology
Ethnic revivals
  See Nativistic movements
Ethnic wit and humor *(Direct)*
  sa subdivision Anecdotes, facetiae, satire,
    etc. *under* National characteristics,
    Chinese, ₍French, Russian, etc.₎ *and*
    under names of particular ethnic and
    national groups, e.g. Jews—
    Anecdotes, facetiae, satire, etc.;
    Scotch—Anecdotes, facetiae, satire,
    etc.
  x Aliens—Anecdotes, facetiae, satire, etc.
    Minorities—Anecdotes, facetiae, satire,
    etc.
    National characteristics—Anecdotes,
    facetiae, satire, etc.
  xx Wit and humor
Ethnobotany *(Indirect)*
    Works on the ethnobotany of particular
    ethnic groups or tribes are entered
    here and also under the name of the
    ethnic group or tribe, with subdivision
    if necessary, *e.g.* Indians of North
    America—Food.
  xx Botany
    Botany, Economic
    Ethnology
    Plant lore
Ethnocentrism
  xx Cultural relativism
    Ethnopsychology
    Nationalism
    Prejudices and antipathies
    Race
Ethnography
  See Ethnology
Ethnological jurisprudence
  sa Law, Primitive
  x Jurisprudence, Ethnological
  xx Comparative law
    Law, Primitive
Ethnological museums and collections
    (Indirect) (GN35-41)
  sa Indians of Mexico—Museums
    Indians of North America—Museums
  x Folk-lore—Museums
  xx Anthropological museums and
    collections
    Museums
Ethnological names
  See Names, Ethnological
Ethnology *(Indirect) (GN)*
  sa Acculturation
    Anthropo-geography
    Anthropometry
    Archaeology
    Arms and armor, Primitive
    Art, Primitive
    Bible—Ethnology
    Body-marking
    Cannibalism
    Civilization
    Color of man
    Costume
    Couvade
    Cultural relativism
    Ethnic barriers
    Ethnobotany
    Ethnomusicology

    Ethnopsychology
    Ethnozoology
    Folk-lore
    Head-hunters
    Industries, Primitive
    Kinship
    Language and languages
    Man—Migrations
    Man, Prehistoric
    Man, Primitive
    Manners and customs
    Moving-pictures in ethnology
    Music, Primitive
    Musical instruments, Primitive
    Native races
    Nativistic movements
    Navigation, Primitive
    Outcasts
    Pariahs
    Race problems
    Religion, Primitive
    Sacrifice
    Socialization
    Society, Primitive
    Structural anthropology
    Tattooing
    Totemism
    Tree-dwellings
    names of races, tribes, and peoples, e.g.
    Aryans, Caucasian race, Hopi
    Indians, Indians, Negroes; *and*
    subdivision Social life and customs
    under names of countries
  x Aborigines
    Cultural anthropology
    Ethnography
    Geographical distribution of man
    Races of man
  xx Anthropology
    Archaeology
    Civilization
    Geography
    History
    Man
    Man, Primitive
    Native races
    Science
    Somatology
— Book reviews
— Classification
— Juvenile literature *(GN31; GN330;*
    GN406)
— Methodology
    sa Interviewing in ethnology
    Photography in ethnology
— Names
    See Names, Ethnological
— Philosophy
    sa Noble savage
— Pictorial works
— Vocational guidance
    See Ethnology as a profession

    GEOGRAPHIC SUBDIVISIONS

— Afghanistan
    sa Hazāras
    Pushtuns

    GEOGRAPHIC SUBDIVISIONS

— Africa
    xx Negro race

    GEOGRAPHIC SUBDIVISIONS

— Africa, Central
    sa Abron (African people)
    Bira (Bantu tribe)
    Mamvu (African tribe)
    Sonyo (African tribe)

Ethnology *(Indirect)* *(GN)*
(Continued)

— Africa, East
   sa Dorobo (African people)
      Kipsigis
      Luo (Nilotic tribe)
      Makonde (Bantu tribe)
      Nika (Bantu tribe)
      Nilo-Hamitic tribes
      Taita (Bantu tribe)
      Tindiga (African people)

— Africa, French-speaking West
   sa Jaawambe (African people)
      Komo (Secret order)
      Soninke (African people)

— Africa, South
   sa Bhaca (African tribe)
      Boers
      Bushmen
      Ghoya (Bantu tribe)
      Mamabolo (Bantu people)
      Mashona
      Pedi (Basuto tribe)
      Phalaborwa (Bantu tribe)
      Tswana (Bantu tribe)
      Venda (Bantu tribe)
      Xosa

— Africa, Southern
   sa Nguni

— Africa, Southwest
   sa Bondelswarts (African tribe)
      Kuanyama (African tribe)
      Sambyu (Bantu tribe)

— Africa, West
   sa Abron (African people)
      Bassari (African people)
      Daza (African people)
      Gbaya (African people)
      Kru (African people)
      Lobi (African people)
      Nyanga (African people)
      Toma (African tribe)

— Angola
   sa Chokwe (Bantu tribe)
      Hanya (Bantu tribe)
      Kuanyama (African tribe)
      Luenas (Bantu tribe)
      Mbundu (Bantu tribe)
      Mwila (Bantu people)
      Vatwa (African people)

— Arctic regions
   See Arctic races

— Asia
   sa Asians

— Asia, Central
   sa Karluks
      Oghuz

— Asia Minor
   sa Kaskans

— Asia, Southeastern
   sa Karens
      Mon (Southeast-Asiatic people)

— Assam
   sa Abors
      Apa Tanis

— Australia
   sa Australian aborigines

— Balkan Peninsula
   sa Arumanians
      Gagauzi

— Bangladesh
   sa Arakanese in East Pakistan
      Biharis
      Namasudras

— Barotseland
   sa Lozi (African tribe)

— Bismarck Archipelago
   sa Tangas (Melanesian people)

— Borneo
   sa Dusuns
      Dyaks
      Ibans (Bornean people)

— Botswana
   sa Tannekwe (African tribe)

— Bougainville Island
   sa Nasioi (Melanesian people)

— Burma
   sa Burmese
      Khamtis
      Padaungs
      Wa (Burmese people)

— Burundi
   sa Barundi
      Batutsi
      Batwa

— Cameroon
   sa Bakossi (Bantu people)
      Bangangte
      Banyang (Bantu tribe)
      Evuzok (Bantu people)
      Kotoko (African people)
      Nso (African people)

— Cameroons
   sa Bakwiri (African people)
      Bamun (African tribe)

Bangwa (African people)

— Carpathian Mountains
   sa Huculs
      Lemki

— Caucasus
   sa Abkhazians
      Archi
      Balkarians
      Chechen
      Ingush
      Kabardians
      Karachaevs
      Kumyks
      Laz
      Lezghians
      Mingrelians
      Svanetians

— Celebes
   sa Minahasa (Indonesian people)

— Central African Republic
   sa Langbas (African people)
      Ngbaka (Lobaye)
      Nzakara (African people)

— Central America
   x Indians of Central America—
      Ethnology

— Chad
   sa Buduma (African people)
      Day (African people)
      Hadjerai (African tribe)
      Kotoko (African people)
      Mbaï (African people)
      Sara (African tribe)
      Zaghawa

— China
   sa Min-chia
      Monguors
      Tanka (Chinese people)

— — Kweichow (Province)
   sa Pu-i (Tribe)

— — Szechwan
   sa Ch'iang people

— — Yünnan (Province)
   sa Moso (Tribe)

— Colombia
   sa Andaqui Indians

— Congo
   sa Lunda (Bantu tribe)

— Congo (Brazzaville)
   sa Bateke (Bantu people)
      Mbete (African people)

Ethnology *(Indirect) (GN)*

GEOGRAPHIC SUBDIVISIONS

— India

GEOGRAPHIC SUBDIVISIONS

— — Punjab *(Continued)*
    Od (Punjab tribe)
    Sansis

GEOGRAPHIC SUBDIVISIONS

— — Rajasthan
   sa Lohars

GEOGRAPHIC SUBDIVISIONS

— — West Bengal
   sa Koras
    Lodhas

GEOGRAPHIC SUBDIVISIONS

— Indochina, French
   sa Moi (Southeast-Asiatic people)
    Rade (Indochinese tribe)

GEOGRAPHIC SUBDIVISIONS

— Indonesia
   sa Bugis (Malay people)
    Gayos (Indonesian people)
    Kubu (Indonesian people)
    Kurai (Indonesian people)
    Maanyans (Bornean people)
    Mandobo
    Menangkabau (Indonesian people)
    Pakpak (Indonesian people)
    Simelungun (Indonesian people)
    Sundanese (Indonesian people)

GEOGRAPHIC SUBDIVISIONS

— — Irian Barat
   sa Kaowerawédj (Papuan people)
    Kapauku (Papuan people)
    Marind tribes
    Mejprat (Papuan people)

GEOGRAPHIC SUBDIVISIONS

— Iran
   sa Baseri tribe
    Daylamites
    Iranians
    Kashkai tribe
    Papis

GEOGRAPHIC SUBDIVISIONS

— Italy
   sa Daunii
    Dinaric race
    Friulians
    Marsi
    Messapii
    Samnites
    Siculi
    Vestini
    Villanovans

GEOGRAPHIC SUBDIVISIONS

— Ivory Coast
   sa Alagya (African people)
    Baoulé (African people)
    Bété (African people)
    Djimini (African people)
    Gere (African people)
    Guro (African people)
    Ouobé (African tribe)
    Tura (African people)

GEOGRAPHIC SUBDIVISIONS

— Japan
   sa Ainu

GEOGRAPHIC SUBDIVISIONS

— Java
   sa Badui (Indonesian tribe)
    Tenggerese

GEOGRAPHIC SUBDIVISIONS

— Kamchatka
   sa Kamchadals

GEOGRAPHIC SUBDIVISIONS

— Kenya
   sa Bajun (African people)
    Baluyia (Bantu tribe)
    Bukusu (Bantu tribe)
    Elgeyo (African tribe)
    Embu (Bantu people)
    Giryama (Bantu tribe)
    Gusii (Bantu tribe)
    Ik (African people)
    Kipsigis
    Meru (African tribe)
    Nandi (African tribe)
    Njemps (African people)
    Pokomo (Bantu tribe)
    Samburu
    Sapiny (African tribe)
    Tiriki (Bantu tribe)
    Turkana (African tribe)
    Wanga (Bantu tribe)

GEOGRAPHIC SUBDIVISIONS

— Laos
   sa Miao people

GEOGRAPHIC SUBDIVISIONS

— Latvia
   sa Livonians

GEOGRAPHIC SUBDIVISIONS

— Liberia
   sa Gbandi (African people)
    Gere (African people)
    Grebo (African tribe)

GEOGRAPHIC SUBDIVISIONS

— Lithuania
   sa Yatvyags

GEOGRAPHIC SUBDIVISIONS

— Madagascar
   sa Antemoro (Madagascan people)
    Bara (Madagascan tribe)

GEOGRAPHIC SUBDIVISIONS

— Majorca
   sa Chuetas

GEOGRAPHIC SUBDIVISIONS

— Malawi
   sa Angoni
    Chewa (African tribe)
    Lomwe (Bantu people)
    Ngonde (African tribe)
    Tumbuka (African tribe)

GEOGRAPHIC SUBDIVISIONS

— Malay Archipelago
   sa Bajau (Malay people)

GEOGRAPHIC SUBDIVISIONS

— Malaya
   sa Sakai

GEOGRAPHIC SUBDIVISIONS

— Malaysia
   sa Jah Hut (Malaysian people)
    Jakun (Malayan people)

Timoguns (Bornean people)

GEOGRAPHIC SUBDIVISIONS

— Mali
   sa Dogons (African people)
    Senufo (African people)

GEOGRAPHIC SUBDIVISIONS

— Manchuria
   sa Golds
    Ju-chên (Tribe)

GEOGRAPHIC SUBDIVISIONS

— Mauritania
   sa Brakna

GEOGRAPHIC SUBDIVISIONS

— Melanesia
   sa Melanesians

GEOGRAPHIC SUBDIVISIONS

— Melville Island (Timor Sea)
   sa Tiwi (Melville Island people)

GEOGRAPHIC SUBDIVISIONS

— Mesopotamia
   sa Habiru

GEOGRAPHIC SUBDIVISIONS

— Mexico
   x Indians of Mexico—Ethnology

GEOGRAPHIC SUBDIVISIONS

— Mindanao
   sa Bukidnon (Philippine people)
    Manobos (Philippine people)

GEOGRAPHIC SUBDIVISIONS

— Morocco
   sa Ahansala
    Aït Atta (Berber tribe)
    Beni Meskine (Berber tribe)
    Chaouia (Berber tribe)
    Ikounka
    Seksawa (Berber tribe)
    Tekna

GEOGRAPHIC SUBDIVISIONS

— Mozambique
   sa Barwe (African people)
    Lomwe (Bantu people)

GEOGRAPHIC SUBDIVISIONS

— Natal
   sa Fingos
    Makhanyas (Zulu tribe)

GEOGRAPHIC SUBDIVISIONS

— Nepal
   sa Gurkhas
    Gurungs
    Licchavis (Asian people)
    Limbus (Asian people)
    Magars
    Newars
    Sherpas

GEOGRAPHIC SUBDIVISIONS

— New Britain (Island)
   sa Lakalai (Melanesian people)
    Maenge (Melanesian people)
    Tolai (Melanesian people)

GEOGRAPHIC SUBDIVISIONS

— New Guinea
   sa Abelam (New Guinea tribe)
    Asmat
    Bedamini (New Guinea people)

Chimbu (New Guinea people)
Dani (New Guinea people)
Daribi
Enga (New Guinea people)
Garia (New Guinea tribe)
Gende (Papuan people)
Gururumba (New Guinea tribe)
Huli (Papuan people)
Jaqai
Kukukuku (Papuan people)
Kumas (New Guinea tribe)
Mbowamb
Motu (New Guinea tribe)
Muiu (New Guinea tribe)
Tsembaga Maring

GEOGRAPHIC SUBDIVISIONS

— New Guinea (Ter.)
   sa Kanake (New Guinea people)
      Kawelka (New Guinea people)
      Maring (New Guinea people)
      Tshuosh (New Guinea tribe)

GEOGRAPHIC SUBDIVISIONS

— New Ireland (Island)
   sa Pala (Melanesian people)

GEOGRAPHIC SUBDIVISIONS

— New Zealand
   sa Ngaitahu (Maori tribe)

GEOGRAPHIC SUBDIVISIONS

— Niger
   sa Bozo (African people)
      Buduma (African people)
      Mawri (African people)
      Wogo (African tribe)
      Zarma (African people)

GEOGRAPHIC SUBDIVISIONS

— Nigeria
   sa Anang (African tribe)
      Bachama (African people)
      Bariba (African tribe)
      Bini (African people)
      Buduma (African people)
      Efik (African people)
      Egba (African tribe)
      Gade (African tribe)
      Gwari (African tribe)
      Igara (African tribe)
      Ijo (African people)
      Jekri (African people)
      Kagoro (African tribe)
      Kaleri tribe
      Kanuri
      Kapsiki (African people)
      Koro (African tribe)
      Kotoko (African people)
      Maguzawa (African people)
      Moba (African people)
      Nupe (African people)
      Sobo (African people)
      Tivi (African people)
      Ubium (African people)
      Yorubas

GEOGRAPHIC SUBDIVISIONS

— North America
   x Indians of North America—
      Ethnology

GEOGRAPHIC SUBDIVISIONS

— Nubia
   sa Nuba (African people)

GEOGRAPHIC SUBDIVISIONS

— Ocean Island

   sa Banabans (Oceanian people)

GEOGRAPHIC SUBDIVISIONS

— Pakistan
   sa Khattaks

GEOGRAPHIC SUBDIVISIONS

— Palestine
   sa Canaanites
      Gibeonites

GEOGRAPHIC SUBDIVISIONS

— Papua
   sa Toaripi (Papuan people)

GEOGRAPHIC SUBDIVISIONS

— Papua-New Guinea (Ter.)
   sa Biami (Papuan people)
      Duna (Papuan people)
      Huri (Papuan people)
      Massim (Melanesian people)
      Me'udana (Melanesian people)

GEOGRAPHIC SUBDIVISIONS

— Philippine Islands
   sa Bontoks (Philippine people)
      Gaddang (Philippine people)
      Hanunóo
      Kalingas
      Kenney
      Magindanaos (Philippine people)
      Mamanuas (Philippine tribe)
      Moros
      Samals (Philippine people)
      Tasaday (Philippine people)
      Tausugs

GEOGRAPHIC SUBDIVISIONS

——— Panay Island
      sa Sulod (Philippine people)

GEOGRAPHIC SUBDIVISIONS

— Poland
   sa Kurpie
      Lasowiacy
      Yatvyags

GEOGRAPHIC SUBDIVISIONS

— Puerto Rico
   sa Chuetas

GEOGRAPHIC SUBDIVISIONS

— Rambi Island, Fiji Islands
   sa Banabans (Oceanian people)

GEOGRAPHIC SUBDIVISIONS

— Rhodesia, Southern
   sa Barwe (African people)
      Karanga (African people)
      Mashona
      Tangwena (African people)

GEOGRAPHIC SUBDIVISIONS

— Romania
   sa Dacians
      Moti (Romanian people)

GEOGRAPHIC SUBDIVISIONS

— Rotuma Island
   sa Rotumans

GEOGRAPHIC SUBDIVISIONS

— Ruanda-Urundi
   sa Bahutu

GEOGRAPHIC SUBDIVISIONS

— Russia
   sa Adyghe

Cheremisses
Chuvashes
Entsy
Ingrians
Karelians
Kazan Tatars
Merya (Finnish tribe)
Nentsy
Nganasani
Ostiaks
Roxolani
Syryenians
Usun
Veps
Voguls
Votes (People)
Votiaks

GEOGRAPHIC SUBDIVISIONS

— Rwanda
   sa Barundi
      Batutsi
      Batwa

GEOGRAPHIC SUBDIVISIONS

— Ryukyu Islands
   sa Ryukyuans

GEOGRAPHIC SUBDIVISIONS

— Sahara
   sa Aït Atta (Berber tribe)
      Mekhadma
      Ouled Naïl

GEOGRAPHIC SUBDIVISIONS

— Senegal
   sa Badyaranké (African people)
      Bedik (African people)
      Diola (African people)
      Lebou (African people)
      Wolofs

GEOGRAPHIC SUBDIVISIONS

— Siberia
   sa Chulyma Tatars
      Gilyaks
      Golds
      Karagasses
      Kets
      Khakassians
      Kyzyl Tatars
      Nigidals
      Olcha
      Oroches
      Udekhe
      Yukaghir

GEOGRAPHIC SUBDIVISIONS

— Sierra Leone
   sa Limba (African tribe)

GEOGRAPHIC SUBDIVISIONS

— Solomon Islands
   sa Baegu (Melanesian people)
      Siuai (Papuan people)

GEOGRAPHIC SUBDIVISIONS

— South America
   x Indians of South America—
      Ethnology

GEOGRAPHIC SUBDIVISIONS

— South Asia
   sa Pushtuns

GEOGRAPHIC SUBDIVISIONS

— Soviet Central Asia
   sa Kara-Kalpaks

Ethnology *(Indirect) (GN)*
(Continued)

Subculture
Totalitarianism—Psychology
subdivision Psychology *under names of races and other ethnic groups, e.g.*
Negroes—Psychology
x Ethnic psychology
Folk-psychology
National psychology
Psychological anthropology
Psychology—Comparative studies
Psychology, Ethnic
Psychology, National
Psychology, Racial
Race psychology
xx Anthropology
Ethnology
Man, Primitive
National characteristics
Psychology
Social psychology
Sociology
Ethnozoology *(Indirect)*
Works on the ethnozoology of particular ethnic groups or tribes are entered here and also under the name of the ethnic group or tribe, with subdivision if necessary, *e.g.* Indians of North America—Food.
xx Animal lore
Ethnology
Zoology
Zoology, Economic
Ethology
See Animals, Habits and behavior of
Character
Ethics
Ethopoeia
Ethrog
See Citron
Ethyl alcohol
See Alcohol
Ethyl bromide *(Anesthetics, RD86.E85; Therapeutics, RM666.B8; Toxicology, RA1247.E68)*
Ethyl chloride *(RD86.E86)*
Ethyl tannate *(QD341.A2)*
xx Tannates
Ethylene alcohol
See Glycols
Ethylene crystals
Ethylene glycol
See Glycols
Ethylene-propylene rubber *(TS1925)*
x Rubber, Ethylene-propylene
xx Rubber, Artificial
Etiolation *(QK757)*
xx Plant physiology
Etiology
See Diseases—Causes and theories of causation
Etiquette *(Indirect)* *(BJ1801-2193)*
sa Academic etiquette
Air Force wives
Army wives
Bar mitzvah etiquette
Buddhist etiquette
Business etiquette
Charm
Conversation
Courtesy
Dance etiquette
Dating (Social customs)
Dinners and dining
Diplomatic etiquette
Entertaining
Etiquette for children and youth
Etiquette for men
Etiquette for women

Forms of address
Hospitality
Letter-writing
Manners and customs
Marine Corps wives
Military ceremonies, honors, and salutes
Mourning etiquette
Naval ceremonies, honors, and salutes
Navy wives
Non-commissioned officers' wives
Officers' wives
Precedence
Salutations
Social secretaries
Student etiquette
Table etiquette
Telephone etiquette
Travel etiquette
Wedding etiquette
subdivision Social life and customs *under names of countries*
x Behavior
Ceremonies
Condolence, Etiquette of
Guests
Manners
Politeness
Usages
xx Conduct of life
Courtesy
Entertaining
Ethics
Manners and customs
— Anecdotes, facetiae, satire, etc. *(PN6231.E8)*
— Juvenile films
Example under Moving-pictures for children
— Pictorial works
— Stationery *(BJ2081-2095)*
sa Business announcements
Visiting-cards
xx Stationery
Etiquette, Business
See Business etiquette
Etiquette, Christian
See Church etiquette
Etiquette, Church
See Church etiquette
Etiquette, Clerical
See Clergy—Etiquette
Etiquette, Islamic
See Islamic etiquette
Etiquette, Jewish
See Jewish etiquette
Etiquette, Legal
See Legal etiquette
Etiquette, Medieval (to 1600) *(BJ1821; BJ1871; BJ1921; BJ1981; etc.)*
Etiquette, Mosque
See Mosque etiquette
Etiquette, Muslim
See Islamic etiquette
Etiquette, Office
See Business etiquette
Etiquette, Synagogue
See Synagogue etiquette
Etiquette, Telephone
See Telephone etiquette
Etiquette for children and youth
x Children—Etiquette
Children's etiquette
Etiquette for youth
Youth etiquette
Youth—Etiquette
xx Children
Etiquette

Youth
Etiquette for men *(American, BJ1855)*
x Men's etiquette
xx Etiquette
Etiquette for women *(Direct) (American, BJ1856)*
x Women's etiquette
xx Etiquette
Etiquette for youth
See Etiquette for children and youth
Etiquettes
See Labels
Eton College Hunt
xx Beagling
ETR
See Engineering test reactors
Etrog
See Citron
Etrurians
See Etruscans
Etruscan gems
See Gems, Etruscan
Etruscan language *(PA2400-2409)*
xx Italic languages and dialects
Etruscan medicine
See Medicine, Etruscan
Etruscan mirrors
See Mirrors, Etruscan
Etruscan rings
See Rings, Etruscan
Etruscan studies *(Direct) (DG223)*
x Etruscology
Etruscan temples
See Temples, Etruscan
Etruscan urns
See Urns, Etruscan
Etruscan vases
See Vases, Etruscan
Etruscans
x Civilization, Etruscan
Etrurians
— Origin
— Religion
Etruscology
See Etruscan studies
ETS (Electronic computer system)
x Educational Timesharing System (Electronic computer system)
xx Time-sharing computer systems
Ettchaottine Indians
See Slave Indians
Etymology
See Language and languages—Etymology
subdivisions Etymology, Foreign elements *and* Semantics *under particular languages or groups of cognate languages, e.g.* Aryan languages—Etymology; English language—Etymology; English language—Foreign elements; French language—Semantics
Euahlayi tribe
xx Australian aborigines
Eucalyptus *(Indirect) (Botany, QK495.E86; Culture, SD397.E8)*
sa Blue-leaved mallee
Green mallee
x Mallee
Red-gum (Tree)
— Identification
— Pictorial works
Eucalyptus oil
Eucaryotic cells
See Eukaryotic cells
Eucharist
See Lord's Supper
Euchites
See Messalians

Euchre *(GV1249)*
    sa Progressive euchre
Euclid's algorithm
    See Algorithms
Euclid's Elements *(QA451)*
    Here are entered text-books based on Eu-
    clid's Elementa. Greek texts and trans-
    lations are entered under the headings
    Mathematics, Greek; Geometry—
    Early works to 1800.
    sa Geometry
    xx Geometry
        Geometry, Plane
Eudemonism
    See Hedonism
Eudeve language *(PM1171)*
    sa Opata language
    x Batuco language
      Dohema language
      Dohme language
      Hegue language
      Heve language
Eudidymite *(Indirect)*
Eudiometer
    xx Gases—Analysis
Eudolat
    See Isonipecaine
Eugenics *(HQ750-799)*
    sa Atavism
      Birth control
      Consanguinity
      Deaf—Marriage
      Degeneration
      Euthenics
      Family size
      Fathers
      Genetics
      Heredity
      Heredity, Human
      Malthusianism
      Mentally handicapped—Marriage
      Mothers
      Premarital examinations
      Sterilization of criminals and defectives
    x Homiculture
      Race improvement
    xx Conception—Prevention
      Euthenics
      Family
      Family size
      Heredity
      Population
      Sex—Cause and determination
      Social problems
Eugubine tables *(PA2461)*
    xx Inscriptions, Oscan-Umbrian
Euhemerism *(Religions, BL42)*
Eukaryotic cells
    x Eucaryotic cells
    xx Cells
Eulenburg's disease
    See Myotonia cogenita
Euler angles
    xx Angle
      Coordinates, Polar
Euler-Lagrange equations
    See Lagrange equations
Euler's numbers *(QA246)*
    x Numbers, Euler's
Eulittoral zonation
    See Intertidal zonation
Eulogies
    xx Orations
      Speeches, addresses, etc.
Eulogistic poetry
    See Laudatory poetry
Eulysite *(QE461)*

Eunomianism *(Arianism, BT1350)*
    x Anomaeans
      Eunomians
    xx Arianism
      Church history—Primitive and early
        church, ca. 30-600
      Heresies and heretics—Early church,
        ca. 30-600
      Theology, Doctrinal—History—Early
        church, ca. 30-600
Eunomians
    See Eunomianism
Eunuchs *(HQ449)*
    xx Castrati
Eupatheoscope *(QC271)*
    sa Thermometers and thermometry
    xx Thermometers and thermometry
Euphemism
    sa subdivision Euphemism *under names of*
      languages
Euphonium *(ML965-8)*
    sa Baritone (Musical instrument)
      Trombone
    xx Baritone (Musical instrument)
      Trombone
Euphonium (Chladni's)
    See Clavicylinder
Euphonium and horns (4) with band
    sa Concertos (Euphonium and horns (4)
      with band)
    xx Concertos (Euphonium and horns (4)
      with band)
Euphonium music *(M90-92)*
    sa Quartets, [Trios, etc.], Wind quartets
      [trios, etc.] *followed by specifications*
      which include the euphonium
Euphuism *(PR427; Lyly, PR2659.L9;*
      Shakespeare, PR2955.L8)
    sa Aureate terms
    xx Aureate terms
      Baroque literature
Eurasian hedgehog
    See European hedgehog
Eurasianism
    sa East and West
    xx Civilization, Occidental
      Civilization, Oriental
Eurasians *(India, DS430)*
    sa Anglo-Indians
    xx Miscegenation
Eurasians in Indonesia, [etc.]
Eurika language
    See Koriki language
Euro-bond market
    xx Bonds
      Foreign exchange
      International finance
Euro-dollar market
    xx Banks and banking, International
      Foreign exchange
      International finance
Eurolengo
    xx Languages, Artificial
Europa Cup (Soccer) *(GV943.5)*
    x Europacup (Soccer)
    xx Soccer
Europacup (Soccer)
    See Europa Cup (Soccer)
Europe
    sa Council of Europe countries
      Europe, Eastern
      European Economic Community
        countries
      European Free Trade Association
        countries
— Antiquities
    sa Corded Ware culture
— Commerce

    sa East-West trade (1945-   )
— Defenses
    sa Military assistance
— Economic integration
    x European common market (1955-
)
    Example under International economic
      integration
—— Juvenile literature
— History *(D101-725)*
—— To 476
—— 392-814
    sa Migrations of nations
      Rome—History—Empire, 284-476
    x Dark Ages
    xx Middle Ages—History
      Rome—History—Empire, 284-476
—— 476-1492
    sa Middle Ages—History
      Twelfth [Thirteenth, Fourteenth,
      Fifteenth] century
    xx Middle Ages—History
—— 1492-
—— 1492-1517
—— 1492-1648
——— Examinations, questions, etc.
——— Juvenile literature
—— 1517-1648
    sa Pavia, Battle of, 1525
      Thirty Years' War, 1618-1648
      Vaucelles, Truce of, 1556
    xx Reformation
—— 17th century
—— 1648-1715
    sa Beachy Head, Battle of, 1690
      Dutch War, 1672-1678
—— 1648-1789
    sa Seven Years' War, 1756-1763
——— Juvenile literature
—— 18th century
—— 1789-1815
    sa Second Coalition, War of the,
      1798-1801
    x Napoleonic Wars
    xx Peninsular War, 1807-1814
——— Juvenile literature
—— 1789-1900
    x Europe—History—19th century
——— Juvenile literature
——— Pictorial works
—— 19th century
    See Europe—History—1789-1900
—— 1815-1848
——— Historiography
—— 1815-1871
—— 1848-1849
    sa Poland—History—Revolution of
      1848
    xx Revolutions
—— 1848-1871
—— 1871-1918
—— 20th century
——— Juvenile literature
——— Pictorial works
—— 1918-1945
—— 1945-
— Industries
— Information services
    Example under Industry—Informa-
      tion services
— Languages
    Example under Language and languages
— Politics
    sa European federation
    Note under International relations
— Relations (military) with the United States

Note under United States—Relations (military) with Canada, ⌐Europe, etc.⌐

Europe, Central
    See Central Europe

Europe, Eastern
    Here are entered works on the area east of the Oder and Neisse rivers extending south to the Adriatic. This concept, based on political and economic developments, is not to be confused with the older geographical limitations of Eastern Europe to the region east of the Baltic Sea and the Carpathian Mountains or with the heading Central Europe, defined as the area included in the basins of the Danube, Elbe, and Rhine rivers.
    sa Central Europe
    x East Europe
       Eastern Europe
    xx Central Europe
       Europe

Europe, Eastern
    sa Slavic countries

Europe, Eastern, studies
    See East European studies

Europe in art

Europe in literature

European apple sucker
    See Apple sucker

European beech

European bison
    See Bison, European

European bittern *(QL696.A7)*
    x Bittern, European
    xx Herons

European black currant *(SB386.C9)*
    x Black currant, European
    xx Currants
    — Diseases and pests

European blackbird
    x Merl
    xx Blackbirds
       Thrushes

European canker

European chafer
    xx Beetles
    Example under Field crops—Diseases and pests

European common market (1955-   )
    See Europe—Economic integration
       European Economic Community

European common market countries
    See European Economic Community countries

European concert
    See Concert of Europe

European cooperation
    Here are entered works on cooperation in all fields of activity. Works on political cooperation are entered under the heading European federation.
    xx International cooperation

European cormorant
    See Great cormorant

European corn borer *(SB945.E75; Maize pests, SB608.M2)*
    x Corn borer, European
    — Biological control

European cuckoo *(QL696.C5)*
    xx Cuckoos
    — Behavior

European dace *(QL638.C94; SH351.D3)*
    x Dace, European

European earwig
    xx Dermaptera

European Economic Community
    x European common market (1955-)
    Example under International economic integration
    — Budget
       See European Economic Community —Finance
    — Economic assistance
       xx Economic assistance
          International cooperation
    — Finance
       x European Economic Community— Budget
    — Juvenile literature

European Economic Community countries
    x Common market countries
       European common market countries
    xx Europe

European elk
    See Moose

European federation *(D1060)*
    sa Czechoslovak-Polish Confederation (Proposed)
    x European union
       Federation of Europe
       Pan Europa movement
       Paneuropean federation
       United States of Europe (Proposed)
    xx Europe—Politics
       Federal government
       Regionalism (International organization)
    Note under European cooperation
    — Caricatures and cartoons
    — Chronology
    — Pictorial works

European flounder
    See Plaice

European foul brood
    See Foul brood, European

European Free Trade Association countries
    xx Europe

European green alder
    x Green alder
    xx Alder

European hare *(SF455.E)*
    x Brown hare
    xx Hares

European hedgehog *(QL737.I53)*
    x Eurasian hedgehog
    xx Hedgehogs

European hornbeam
    x Hornbeam, European
       Yoke elm

European land rail
    See Corncrake

European larch
    xx Larch

European mistletoe
    xx Mistletoe
    — Therapeutic use

European newspapers

European nightjar

European Payments Union
    Example under Monetary unions

European periodicals

European pilchard *(QL638.C64)*
    x European sardine
       Pilchard, European
    xx Sardines

European polecat *(QL737.C25)*
    sa Ferrets
    x Polecat, European
    xx Ferrets

European recovery program
    See Reconstruction (1939-1951)—Europe

European red mite
    x Fruit tree red spider

European sardine
    See European pilchard

European spruce sawfly *(SB945.E)*
    Example under Sawflies; Spruce—Diseases and pests

European studies *(Direct)*

European union
    See European federation

European War, 1914-1918 *(Indirect)*
    (D501-680)
    x United States—History—European War, 1914-1918
       War of 1914
       World War, 1914-1918
    xx History, Modern—20th century
    — Addresses, sermons, etc. *(D523-5)*
    — Aerial operations *(D600-607)*
    — Aerial operations, American, ⌐British, etc.⌐
    — American propaganda
       See Propaganda, American
    — Anecdotes *(D526; D570.9; D640)*
    — Anniversaries, etc.
    — Armistices *(D641)*
    — Art and the war *(N6491)*
       xx Art treasures in war
    — Atrocities *(D625-6)*
       sa Armenian massacres, 1915-1923
          European War, 1914-1918— Destruction and pillage
          War crime trials—Leipzig, 1921
       xx War (International law)
       Example under War crimes
    — Autographs *(D503)*
    — Battle-fields *(D528)*
    — — Guide-books *(D528)*
       sa individual battles, campaigns, sieges
       x European War, 1914-1918— Guide-books
    — Belgian neutrality
       See Belgium—Neutrality
    — Biography *(Collections, D507)*
    — Blockades *(D580-581)*
    — British propaganda
       See Propaganda, British
    — Campaigns *(D529-569)*
       x European War, 1914-1918—Tactical history
       Example under Battles
    — — Africa *(D575-6; DT779.5)*
    — — — Cameroons *(D576.C3)*
    — — — German Southwest *(D576.G5)*
    — — — Southwest
    — — — Tanganyika
    — — — Togoland *(D576.T7)*
    — — Alps
       See European War, 1914-1918— Campaigns—Italo-Austrian
    — — Alsace *(D545.A55)*
       sa Neufchâteau, Battle of, 1914
    — — Balkan Peninsula *(D560-565)*
       x European War, 1914-1918— Campaigns—Macedonia
    — — Belgium *(D541-2)*
       sa Antwerp—Siege, 1914
          Houthulst, Battle of, 1918
          Kemmel, Battles of, 1918
          Langemarck, Battle of, 1914
          Liége—Siege, 1914
          Yser, Battle of the, 1914
       x European War, 1914-1918— Campaigns—Flanders
    — — Dardanelles
       See European War, 1914-1918— Campaigns—Turkey and the Near East—Gallipoli
    — — Eastern *(D550-558)*
       sa Berezhany, Battle of, 1916-1917

European War, 1914-1918 *(Indirect)*
   (D501-680)
— Campaigns *(D529-569)*
— — Eastern *(D550-558)* *(Continued)*
      Brzeziny, Battle of, 1914
      Jarosławice, Battle of, 1914
      Komarów, Battle of, 1914
      Lemberg, Battle of, 1914
      Limanova, Battle of, 1914
      Łódź, Battle of, 1914
      Masurenland, Battles of,
        1914-1915
      Širvintà, Battle of, 1914
      Tannenberg, Battle of, 1914
      Zborov, Battle of, 1917
— — Far East *(D520.O8)*
    sa Tsingtao, China—Siege, 1914
— — Flanders
    See European War, 1914-1918—
        Campaigns—Belgium
— — France *(D544-5; D548)*
    sa Aisne, Battle of the, 1914
       Aisne, Battle of the, 1917
       Aisne, Battle of the, 1918
       Amiens, Battle of, 1918
       Argonne, Battle of the, 1915
       Argonne, Battle of the, 1918
       Arras, Battle of, 1917
       Belleau Wood, Battle of, 1918
       Cambrai, Battle of, 1917
       Cantigny, Battle of, 1918
       Champagne, Battles of, 1914-1917
       Château-Thierry, Battle of, 1918
       Lys, Battle of the, 1918
       Marne, 2d Battle of the, 1918
       Marne, Battle of the, 1914
       Maubeuge, France—Siege, 1914
       Mons, Battle of, 1914
       Seicheprey, Battle of, 1918
       Somme, 2d Battle of the, 1918
       Somme, Battle of the, 1916
       St. Mihiel, Battle of, 1918
       Verdun, Battle of, 1914
       Verdun, Battle of, 1916
       Vimy Ridge, Battle of, 1917
— — Italo-Austrian *(D569)*
    sa Caporetto, Battle of, 1917
       Carzano, Battle of, 1917
       Col di Lana, Battle of, 1916
       Gorizia, Battle of, 1916
       Isonzo, Battles of the, 1915-1917
       Monte Cimone, Battle of, 1916
       Monte Novegno, Battle of, 1916
       Monte Piano, Battles of,
         1915-1917
       Montello, Battle of, 1918
       Ortigara, Battle of, 1917
       Pasubio, Battles of, 1916-1918
       Piave, 1st Battle of the, 1917
       Piave, 2d Battle of the, 1918
       Pozzuolo del Friuli, Battle of,
         1917
       Tre Cime di Lavaredo, Battles of,
         1915-1917
       Vittorio Veneto, Battle of, 1918
    x European War, 1914-1918—
        Campaigns—Alps
— — Lorraine *(D545.L)*
— — Macedonia
    See European War, 1914-1918—
        Campaigns—Balkan
         Peninsula
       European War, 1914-1918—
        Campaigns—Serbia
— — New Guinea, German *(D578.N4)*
— — Poland *(D551-2)*
    sa Deblin, Poland—Siege, 1914-1915
       Lvov—Siege, 1918-1919

       Przemysl—Siege, 1914
       Przemysl—Siege, 1915
— — Romania *(D565)*
    sa Mărăşeşti, Romania, Battle of,
       1917
— — Serbia *(D561-2)*
    sa Cer, Battle of, 1914
       Drina, Battles of the, 1914
    x European War, 1914-1918—
       Campaigns—Macedonia
— — Turkey and the Near East *(D566-8)*
    sa Jebel Mūsa, Syria, Defense of,
       1915
— — — Caucasus *(D567.C3)*
— — — Egypt *(D568.2)*
— — — Gallipoli *(D568.3)*
    x Dardanelles Campaign, 1915
       European War, 1914-1918—
        Campaigns—Dardanelles
       Gallipoli Campaign, 1915
— — — — Juvenile literature
— — — Iran *(D568.8)*
— — — Mesopotamia *(D568.5)*
    sa Ctesiphon, Battle of, 1915
       Kut el Amara—Siege,
         1915-1916
— — — Palestine *(D568.7)*
    sa Gaza, Battles of, 1917
       Jewish Legion
— — Western *(D530-549)*
    sa Ypres, 1st Battle of, 1914
       Ypres, 2d Battle of, 1915
       Ypres, 3d Battle of, 1917
— — — Juvenile literature
— Cartography
    sa European War, 1914-1918—Maps
    xx Cartography
— Cartoons
    See European War, 1914-1918—
        Humor, caricatures, etc.
       European War, 1914-1918—
        Iconography
— Casualties (Statistics, etc.) *(D609)*
    x European War, 1914-1918—Statistics
       of dead, wounded, etc.
    Example under Vital statistics
— Catholic Church *(D622)*
    xx War and religion
— Causes *(D511-520)*
    Here are entered treatises, pamphlets,
      and popular controversial literature
      on the causes of the war, responsi-
      bility for the war, etc.
    xx European War, 1914-1918—Sources
— Cavalry operations *(D529.4)*
— Censorship *(Indirect)* *(D631-3)*
    Example under Censorship
— Charities
    See European War, 1914-1918—
        Hospitals, charities, etc.
       Red Cross
— Chemistry *(D639.S2)*
    xx Chemical warfare
— Children *(D639.C4)*
— Chronology *(D522.5)*
— Civilian relief *(Indirect)*
    xx European War, 1914-1918—
       Hospitals, charities, etc.
— Claims *(JX5326)*
— Commerce
    See European War, 1914-1918—
        Economic aspects
       Search, Right of
— Communications
    xx Communications, Military
— Confiscations and contributions
    (Indirect) *(JX5295-5313)*

For works on seizure of property on
    land and sea by belligerents, forced
    contributions from cities, etc.
    sa European War, 1914-1918—
       Destruction and pillage
    xx Confiscations
       Enemy property
       Requisitions, Military
       War (International law)
— Congresses, conferences, etc. *(D504)*
    sa Corfu, Declaration of, 1917
— Conscientious objectors *(Direct)*
— Construction
    See European War, 1914-1918—
        Engineering and construction
— Contraband of war
    See Contraband of war
— Correspondents
    See European War, 1914-1918—
        Journalists
— Deportations from Belgium *(D639.D5)*
    x Expulsion
— Deportations from France *(D639.D5)*
    x Expulsion
— Deportations from Lithuania *(D639.D5)*
— Deportations from Turkey and the Near
    East *(D639.D5)*
— Deportations of Armenians *(D639.D5)*
— Destruction and pillage
    x European War, 1914-1918—Pillage
    xx European War, 1914-1918—
       Atrocities
       European War, 1914-1918—
        Confiscations and contributions
— Dictionaries *(D510)*
— Diplomatic history *(D505; D610-621)*
    Here are entered collections of docu-
      ments, diplomatic correspondence,
      etc., general and special (including
      "White papers" and the like) and
      treatises entitled "Diplomatic his-
      tory," "Documentary history," etc.
      Cf. note under European War,
      1914-1918—Sources
    sa European War, 1914-1918—
       Historiography
    xx European War, 1914-1918—
       Historiography
       European War, 1914-1918—Sources
    Note under European War, 1914-1918—
       Sources
— Dogs
— Drama
— Economic aspects *(Indirect)* *(D635;*
    HC56; United States, HC106.2)
    Here are entered works on the condi-
      tion and prospects of commerce
      and industry as affected by the war.
    sa European War, 1914-1918—Finance
       European War, 1914-1918—Supplies
    x European War, 1914-1918—
       Commerce
       European War, 1914-1918—
        Embargoes
    xx European War, 1914-1918—Finance
       Reconstruction (1914-1939)
    Example under Profiteering; War—Eco-
       nomic aspects
— Education and the war
    xx War and education
— Embargoes
    See Embargo
       European War, 1914-1918—
        Economic aspects
— Engineering and construction *(D529.7)*
    x European War, 1914-1918—
       Construction
    xx Military engineering

— English propaganda
    See Propaganda, British
— Fiction
— Finance *(Indirect) (D635; HJ236;*
        United States, HJ257)
    sa European War, 1914-1918—
        Economic aspects
    xx Debts, Public
        European War, 1914-1918—
            Economic aspects
— Food question *(Indirect) (HD9000.6;*
        United States, HD9006)
    xx European War, 1914-1918—Supplies
        Food supply
    Note under Food conservation
— French propaganda
    See Propaganda, French
— Gas warfare
    See Gases, Asphyxiating and
        poisonous—War use
— German propaganda
    See Propaganda, German
— Gift-books
— Guerrillas
    See European War, 1914-1918—
        Underground movements
— Guide-books
    See European War, 1914-1918—
        Battle-fields—Guide-books
— Historiography *(D522.42)*
    sa European War, 1914-1918—
        Diplomatic history
    xx European War, 1914-1918—
        Diplomatic history
— Hospitals, charities, etc. *(D628-9;*
        D637-8)
    sa European War, 1914-1918—Civilian
        relief
    x European War, 1914-1918—
        Charities
        European War, 1914-1918—Nurses
            and nursing
    Example under International relief
    Note under European War, 1914-1918—
        Women's work
— Humor, caricatures, etc. *(D526)*
    x European War, 1914-1918—
        Cartoons
    Example under Caricatures and cartoons
— Iconography *(D503; German medals,*
        CJ6170)
    x European War, 1914-1918—
        Cartoons
        European War, 1914-1918—Medals,
            badges, decorations, etc.
        European War, 1914-1918—Views
— Indians
    xx Indians of North America as soldiers
— Influence and results *(D512-520)*
        Here are entered general works and
        works on two or more countries.
        Works limited to a particular coun-
        try are entered under European
        War, 1914-1918—ᵣcountry subdivi-
        sion₁, *e.g.* European War, 1914-
        1918—France.
    x European War, 1914-1918—Politics,
        psychology, etc.
— Internment camps
    See European War, 1914-1918—
        Prisoners and prisons
— Inventions
    See Inventions
— Jews *(D639.J4)*
    sa Jewish Legion
— Journalists *(D631-3)*
    x European War, 1914-1918—
        Correspondents

— Juvenile literature *(D522.7)*
— Language (New words, slang, etc.)
        (D523; PC3747.S7; PE3727.S7)
    x Trench language (European War)
— Law and legislation *(Indirect) (D505;*
        D635)
    sa Trading with the enemy
    x War legislation (1914-1918)
    xx War and emergency legislation
— Libraries (in camps, etc.) *(Z675.W2)*
    x Camp libraries
        Libraries, Camp
        Libraries, Soldiers'
        Soldiers' libraries
— Literary collections
— Literature and the war
    xx War and literature
— Maps
    xx European War, 1914-1918—
        Cartography
— Medals, badges, decorations, etc.
    See European War, 1914-1918—
        Iconography
        subdivision Medals, badges,
        decorations, etc. *under armies,*
        navies, etc., e.g. United States.
        Army—Medals, badges,
        decorations, etc.
— Medical and sanitary affairs *(D628-9)*
    x European War, 1914-1918—Sanitary
        affairs
    Example under War—Medical aspects
— Military supplies
    See European War, 1914-1918—
        Supplies
— Mines, Submarine
    See European War, 1914-1918—Naval
        operations—Submarine
— Miscellanea *(D525; D640)*
— Moral aspects *(D524; D639.M6;*
        D639.S3)
    xx Moral conditions
— Museums *(D503)*
    Example under Museums
— Music
    See European War, 1914-1918—Songs
        and music
— Muslims
    xx Muslims
— Naval operations *(D580-589)*
    sa Coronel, Battle of, 1914
        Dogger Bank, Battle of the, 1915
        Durazzo, Battle of, 1918
        Falkland Islands, Battle of the, 1914
        Helgoland, Battle of, 1914
        Jutland, Battle of, 1916
        Submarine chasers
        Zeebrugge-Ostend raids, 1918
        names of ships
    xx Armed merchant ships
— — Submarine *(D590-595)*
    x European War, 1914-1918—
        Mines, Submarine
        European War, 1914-1918—
        Submarine operations
— Naval operations, American, ᵣBritish,
        French, etc.₁
— Negroes *(D639.N4)*
    xx Negroes as soldiers
— — Juvenile literature
— Neutrality of Belgium, ᵣItaly, the United
        States, etc.₁
        See Belgium ᵣItaly, United States,
        etc.₁—Neutrality
— Numismatics *(CJ)*
    xx Numismatics
— Nurses and nursing

    See European War, 1914-1918—
        Hospitals, charities, etc.
        European War, 1914-1918—
        Women's work
— Ordnance
    See *subdivision* Ordnance and
        ordnance stores *under armies*
        and navies
— Outlines, syllabi, etc. *(D522.5)*
— Peace *(D613)*
    sa League of Nations
— Pensions
    See Pensions, Military
— Periodicals *(D501)*
— Personal narratives *(D640)*
    xx European War, 1914-1918—Sources
— Personal narratives, French, ᵣGerman,
        etc.₁
        Here are entered narratives of officers,
        private soldiers, etc. belonging to
        one of the nations at war. When
        limited to a special subject, dupli-
        cate entry is made under subject.
— — Juvenile literature
— Physics
— Pictorial works *(D522; D527)*
    x European War, 1914-1918—Views
— Pigeons
    xx Homing pigeons
— Pillage
    See European War, 1914-1918—
        Destruction and pillage
— Poetry
    x European War, 1914-1918—
        War-songs
— Politics, psychology, etc.
    See European War, 1914-1918—
        Influence and results
— Portraits *(D507)*
— Postal service *(D635)*
        Here are entered works on the postal
        service as affected by or related to
        the war, with duplicate entry under
        Postal service—ᵣcountry subdivi-
        sion₁ Ordinary routine publications
        (reports, etc.), even if containing
        some reference to war conditions,
        are entered only under Postal ser-
        vice—ᵣcountry subdivision₁
— Posters
— Prisoners and prisons *(D627)*
    x European War, 1914-1918—
        Internment camps
— Prisoners and prisons, French, ᵣGerman,
        etc.₁
— Prizes, etc. *(JX5245-5266)*
— Propaganda *(D639.P6-7; D619.3)*
    sa Propaganda, French, ᵣGerman, etc.₁
    x War propaganda
— Prophecies *(D524)*
— Public opinion
        Here are entered only works dealing
        expressly with public opinion, not
        works on politics, etc.
    xx Public opinion
— Railroads
    See European War, 1914-1918—
        Transportation
        Railroads—ᵣlocal subdivision₁
— Reconstruction
    See Reconstruction (1914-1939)
— Recruiting, enlistment, etc.
    See *subdivision* Recruiting, enlistment,
        etc.—European War,
        1914-1918 *under armies and*
        navies, e.g. France. Armée—
        Recruiting, enlistment, etc.—
        European War, 1914-1918

European War, 1914-1918 *(Indirect)*
(D501-680) *(Continued)*
— Refugees *(D637-8)*
    sa Russia—History—Revolution,
        1917-1921—Refugees
— Regimental histories *(Indirect)*
— Registers, lists, etc. *(D609)*
    x European War, 1914-1918—Statistics
        of dead, wounded, etc.
— Registers of dead *(D609)*
    sa Soldiers' bodies, Disposition of
    x European War, 1914-1918—Statistics
        of dead, wounded, etc.
— Religious aspects *(D524; D639.R4)*
— Reparations *(D648-9)*
    sa Bank for International Settlements
    x Reparations (European War,
        1914-1918)
    Example under Reparations
— Resistance movements
    See European War, 1914-1918—
        Underground movements
— Russian propaganda
    See Propaganda, Russian
— Sanitary affairs
    See European War, 1914-1918—
        Medical and sanitary affairs
— Science *(D639.S2)*
— Secret service *(Indirect) (D639.S7)*
    Example under Secret service
— Societies, etc. *(D502; United States,*
    D570.A1)
— Soldiers' bodies, Disposition of
    See Soldiers' bodies, Disposition of
— Songs and music *(M1646)*
    x European War, 1914-1918—Music
    European War, 1914-1918—
        War-songs
— Sounds
    xx Sounds
— Sources *(D505)*
    Here are entered official and other re-
    cords, contributions to military,
    political, financial and economic
    history, etc. Collections limited to,
    or consisting largely of, diplomatic
    correspondence, state papers,
    negotiations, etc. are entered under
    the subdivision Diplomatic history.
    Cf. note under that heading.
    sa European War, 1914-1918—Causes
    European War, 1914-1918—
        Diplomatic history
    European War, 1914-1918—Personal
        narratives
    Note under European War, 1914-1918—
        Diplomatic history
— Statistics
— Statistics of dead, wounded, etc.
    See European War, 1914-1918—
        Casualties (Statistics, etc.)
    European War, 1914-1918—
        Registers, lists, etc.
    European War, 1914-1918—
        Registers of dead
— Subject headings
    See Subject headings—European War,
        1914-1918
— Submarine operations
    See European War, 1914-1918—Naval
        operations—Submarine
— Supplies *(D639.S9)*
    sa European War, 1914-1918—Food
        question
    x European War, 1914-1918—Military
        supplies
    European War, 1914-1918—War
        materials

    xx European War, 1914-1918—
        Economic aspects
    Military supplies
    Example under Munitions
— Tactical history
    See European War, 1914-1918—
        Campaigns
— Technology *(D639.S2)*
— Territorial questions *(Indirect)*
    (D650.T4; D651)
    sa Adriatic question
    Mandates
    Example under Boundaries
— Theater and the war *(D639.T; By*
    country, PN2220-3035)
— Transportation *(D639.T8; United States,*
    D570.72-3)
    Here are entered general works and
    works on railroads in the war.
    x European War, 1914-1918—
        Railroads
— Treaties *(D610-614; D642-651)*
    sa Brest-Litovsk, Treaty of, Feb. 9,
        1918 (Ukraine)
    Brest-Litovsk, Treaty of, Mar. 3,
        1918 (Russia)
    Bucharest, Treaty of, 1918
    London, Treaty of, 1915
    Neuilly-sur-Seine, Treaty of, Nov.
        27, 1919 (Bulgaria)
    Sèvres, Treaty of, 1920
    St. Germain, Treaty of, Sept. 10,
        1919 (Austria)
    St. Germain, Treaty of, Sept. 10,
        1919 (Czechoslovak Republic)
    St. Germain, Treaty of, Sept. 10,
        1919 (Serbia)
    Trianon, Treaty of, June 4, 1920
        (Hungary)
    Versailles, Treaty of, June 28, 1919
        (Germany)
— Underground literature
    xx Literature
    Underground literature
— Underground movements *(Direct)*
    x European War, 1914-1918—
        Guerrillas
    European War, 1914-1918—
        Resistance movements
    Resistance movements (European
        War, 1914-1918)
    Underground movements (European
        War, 1914-1918)
    xx Guerrillas
    Spies
— Veterinary service *(UH650-655)*
— Views
    See European War, 1914-1918—
        Iconography
    European War, 1914-1918—
        Pictorial works
— War materials
    See European War, 1914-1918—
        Supplies
— War-songs
    See European War, 1914-1918—
        Poetry
    European War, 1914-1918—Songs
        and music
— War work *(D637-9)*
    x War work
— — Boy Scouts *(D639.B; Great Britain,*
    D547.B7)
— — Christian Scientists *(D639.C5)*
— — Colleges
    See European War, 1914-1918—
        War work—Schools

— — Friends, Society of *(BX7747; D637.8;*
    D639.F9)
— — Knights of Columbus *(D622)*
— — Mennonites *(BX8116; D639.M)*
— — Red Cross
    xx Red Cross
    War—Relief of sick and wounded
— — Salvation Army *(D639.S15)*
— — Schools *(D639.E2-6)*
    x European War, 1914-1918—War
        work—Colleges
— — Seventh-Day Adventists *(BX6154;*
    D639.S)
— — Y.M.C.A. *(D639.Y7)*
    xx Young Men's Christian
        Associations
— — Y.W.C.A. *(D639.Y7)*
    xx Young Women's Christian
        Associations
— Women's work *(D639.W7)*
    For general works only. Prefer Euro-
    pean War, 1914-1918—Hospitals,
    charities, etc., and similar headings.
    sa Yeomen (F)
    x European War, 1914-1918—Nurses
        and nursing
European War, 1914-1918, in motion pictures
    xx Moving-pictures
European War, 1939-1945
    See World War, 1939-1945
European wheat sawfly
    See European wheat-stem sawfly
European wheat-stem sawfly *(SB608.W5)*
    x European wheat sawfly
European wildcat
    x Wild cat, European
    Wildcat, European
Europeans in Africa, [Egypt, etc.]
Europium *(QD181.E8)*
— Isotopes
    x Europium isotopes
    Isotopic europium
Europium isotopes
    See Europium—Isotopes
Eurypterida *(QE823.E8)*
    xx Arachnida
Euskara language
    See Basque language
Eustachian tube *(Comparative anatomy,*
    QL948; Human anatomy, QM507;
    Physiology, QP461)
    xx Middle ear
Eutaw Springs, Battle of, 1781 *(E241.E)*
Euthanasia *(Direct) (R726)*
    sa Aged, Killing of the
    Insane, Killing of the
    Trials (Euthanasia)
    x Mercy death
    xx Homicide
    Medical ethics
Euthenics *(HN64)*
    sa Eugenics
    x Environment
    Race improvement
    xx Conduct of life
    Education of children
    Eugenics
    Man—Influence of environment
    Moral education
    Social problems
Eutrophication *(Indirect)*
    sa Water bloom
    Water—Pollution
    xx Lakes
    Limnology
    Plants—Nutrition
    Water—Pollution

Eutychians *(BT1380)*
  xx Monophysites
Euxenite *(QE391.E)*
Evacuation, Civilian
  See Evacuation of civilians
Evacuation Day, Nov. 25, 1783 *(E239)*
Evacuation of civilians
  sa subdivision Evacuation of civilians
        under names of wars, e.g. World
        War, 1939-1945—Evacuation of
        civilians
    x Civilians, Evacuation of
        Evacuation, Civilian
    xx Civil defense
        Disaster relief
        Traffic engineering
Evacuation of hospitals
  See Hospital evacuation
Evaluation, Job
  See Job evaluation
Evaluation of disability
  See Disability evaluation
Evaluation of elementary schools
  See Elementary schools—Evaluation
Evaluation of literature
  See Bibliography—Best books
        Books and reading
        Criticism
        Literature—History and criticism
Evaluation of public libraries
  See Public libraries—Evaluation
Evaluation of school districts
  See School districts—Evaluation
Evaluation of schools
  See Educational surveys
Evaluation of social action programs
  See Evaluation research (Social action
        programs)
Evaluation of universities and colleges
  See Universities and colleges—Evaluation
Evaluation research (Social action programs)
        (Direct)
    x Evaluation of social action programs
        Evaluative research (Social action
        programs)
    xx Social action
        Social science research
        Social service—Research
Evaluation research in education
  See Educational accountability
Evaluative research (Social action programs)
  See Evaluation research (Social action
        programs)
Evangelaries
  See Evangeliaries
Evangeliaries
    x Evangelaries
        Evangelistaries
    xx Lectionaries
Evangelical academies *(Direct)*
        (BV4487.E9)
    x Academies, Evangelical
    xx Forums (Discussion and debate)
Evangelical counsels
        Here are entered works dealing with the
        evangelical counsels of poverty, chas-
        tity, and obedience which are recom-
        mended towards achieving perfection
        over and above the Ten command-
        ments.
    sa Chastity
        Chastity, Vow of
        Monastic and religious life
        Monastic and religious life of women
        Obedience
        Obedience, Vow of
        Poverty
        Poverty (Virtue)

Poverty, Vow of
    x Counsels, Evangelical
    xx Christian ethics
        Church discipline
        Commandments, Ten
        Monastic and religious life
        Monastic and religious life of women
        Perfection (Catholic)
Evangelical denunciation
  See Denunciation (Canon law)
Evangelical religion
  See Evangelicalism
Evangelical Revival *(Great Britain, BR758)*
    sa Evangelicalism
        Evangelicalism—Church of England
        Great Awakening
        Methodism
    x Revival, Evangelical
    xx Church history—18th century
        Evangelicalism
        Great Awakening
Evangelicalism *(Direct)*
    sa Evangelical Revival
        Fundamentalism
        Pietism
        Radstockism
    x Evangelical religion
        Protestantism, Evangelical
    xx Evangelical Revival
        Fundamentalism
        Pietism
        Protestantism
  —Church of England *(BX5125)*
    sa Clapham Sect
        Keswick movement
    x Church of England—Evangelical
        Party
    xx Church of England—Parties and
        movements
        Evangelical Revival
  —Protestant Episcopal Church in the U.S.A.
        (BX5925)
Evangelism
  See Evangelistic work
Evangelistaries
  See Evangeliaries
Evangelistic sermons *(BV3797)*
    x Revival sermons
        Sermons, Revival
    xx Sermons
Evangelistic work *(Direct)* *(BV3750-3799)*
    sa Camp-meetings
        Chaplains, Industrial
        Church growth
        Coffee house ministry
        Communication (Theology)
        Conversion
        Institutional missions
        Jesus Christ—Evangelistic methods
        Missions
        Parish missions
        Revivals
        Salvation Army
        Visitations (Religious education)
        Witness bearing (Christianity)
    x Convert making
        Evangelism
        Revival (Religion)
    xx Church work
        Communication (Theology)
        Missions
        Revivals
        Theology, Practical
        Witness bearing (Christianity)
  —Juvenile literature
Evangelistic work (Islam)
  See Da'wah (Islam)

Evangelists *(Indirect)* *(BV3780-3785)*
    x Revivalists
  —Correspondence, reminiscences, etc.
Evangelists (Bible)
    xx Apostles
  —Art
Evans blue
    xx Blood—Examination
Evansite *(QE391.E9)*
Evaporated milk
  See Milk, Evaporated
Evaporating appliances *(TP363)*
    sa Cooling towers
  —Automatic control
  —Design and construction
  —Electromechanical analogies
Evaporation *(Physics, QC304)*
    sa Drying
        Evaporation control
        Film boiling
    xx Chemistry
        Meteorology
        Moisture
        Physics
        Vapors
        Weather
Evaporation, Latent heat of *(QC304)*
    x Latent heat of evaporation
Evaporation (Meteorology) *(Direct)*
        (QC915-917)
    sa Evaporative power
        Evapotranspiration
    x Evaporation measurements
    xx Climatology
        Evapotranspiration
        Humidity
        Meteorology
        Water-supply
Evaporation capacity
  See Evaporative power
Evaporation control
    sa Reservoirs—Evaporation control
    x Control of evaporation
    xx Evaporation
Evaporation measurements
  See Evaporation (Meteorology)
Evaporation of food
  See Food—Drying
Evaporation of fruit
  See Fruit—Drying
Evaporation of vegetables
  See Vegetables—Evaporation
Evaporation power
  See Evaporative power
Evaporation process, Flash (Saline water
        conversion)
  See Saline water conversion—Flash
        distillation process
Evaporative capacity
  See Evaporative power
Evaporative power *(Direct)* *(QC915)*
    x Evaporation capacity
        Evaporation power
        Evaporative capacity
        Evaporativity
        Potential evaporation
    xx Evaporation (Meteorology)
  —Charts, diagrams, etc.
Evaporativity
  See Evaporative power
Evaporites *(Indirect)*
    sa Anhydrite
        Dolomite
        Gypsum
        Limestone
        Salt
    xx Rocks, Sedimentary

Evapotranspiration *(Indirect)*
  sa Evaporation (Meteorology)
    Plants—Transpiration
    Plants—Water requirements
  x Consumptive use
  xx Evaporation (Meteorology)
    Plants—Transpiration
    Plants—Water requirements
    Water-supply
  — Measurement
Evasion, Fiscal
  See Tax evasion
Evasion (Islamic law)
Evasion (Law) *(Direct)*
  sa Chicanery (Law)
    Lacunae in law
    Tax evasion
  x Actio in fraudem legis
    In fraudem legis
  xx Chicanery (Law)
    Lacunae in law
    Simulation (Civil law)
Even language
  See Lamut language
Evening and continuation schools *(Indirect)*
  (LC5501-5560)
  sa Continuing education centers
    subdivision Evening and continuation
    schools *under names of cities, e.g.*
    London—Evening and continuation
    schools
  x Continuation schools
    Evening colleges
    Evening schools
    Factory schools
    Night schools
  xx Education
    Education, Compulsory
    Education, Secondary
    Public schools
    Schools
    Technical education
Evening colleges
  See Evening and continuation schools
Evening schools
  See Evening and continuation schools
Evening-service music
  sa Magnificat (Music)
    Vespers (Music)
  xx Church-night services
    Prayer-meetings
    Sacred vocal music
    Sunday-evening services
    Vespers (Music)
Evenki
  See Tunguses
Evenki language
  See Tungus language
Everglade kite *(QL696.A2)*
Evergreens *(Indirect) (Culture, SB435)*
  sa Coniferae
    Ornamental evergreens
    names of evergreen shrubs and trees,
    e.g. Box, Pine, Rhododendron
  xx Coniferae
    Hedges
    Shrubs
    Trees
    Woody plants
Everlasting flowers *(SB447)*
  sa Dried flower arrangement
  x Flowers, Everlasting
    Immortelle
  xx Flowers
Everlasting punishment
  See Future punishment
    Hell

Eviction *(Direct)*
  sa Forcible entry and detainer
    Rent control
  x Dispossession
  xx Landlord and tenant
    Leases
  — Popular works
Eviction (Roman law)
  See Warranty (Roman law)
Eviction control
  See Rent control
Evidence *(Logic, BC171-3; Psychology,*
    BF761-8)
  sa Interviewing
    Prediction (Logic)
    Psychology, Applied
    Psychology, Forensic
  x Proof
  xx Belief and doubt
    Faith
    Logic
    Philosophy
    Truth
Evidence, Circumstantial *(Direct)*
  sa Res ipsa loquitur doctrine
  x Circumstantial evidence
    Evidence, Presumptive
    Presumptive evidence
  xx Criminal procedure
    Evidence, Criminal
    Evidence (Law)
    Presumptions (Law)
Evidence, Criminal *(Direct)*
  sa Confession (Law)
    Crime and criminals—Identification
    Eavesdropping
    Evidence, Circumstantial
    Flagrans crimen
    Forensic ballistics
    Lie detectors and detection
    Police questioning
    Self-incrimination
    Torture
    Typewriting—Identification
    Wire-tapping
    Writing—Identification
  x Criminal evidence
  xx Criminal investigation
    Criminal procedure
    Evidence (Law)
Evidence, Criminal (Frankish law)
Evidence, Criminal (Islamic law)
Evidence, Demonstrative *(Direct)*
  x Demonstrative evidence
  xx Evidence, Expert
Evidence, Documentary *(Direct)*
  sa Affidavits
    Legal documents—Destruction and
    reconstruction
    Legal documents—Identification
  x Documentary evidence
  xx Evidence (Law)
    Legal documents
Evidence, Documentary (Islamic law)
Evidence, Expert *(Direct)*
  sa Evidence, Demonstrative
    Forensic ballistics
    Typewriting—Identification
    Writing—Identification
  x Expert evidence
    Opinion evidence
  xx Evidence (Law)
    Witnesses
Evidence, Expert (Canon law)
Evidence, Expert (Roman law)
Evidence, Hearsay *(Direct)*
  x Hearsay evidence
  xx Evidence (Law)

    Objections (Evidence)
    Witnesses
Evidence, Presumptive
  See Evidence, Circumstantial
    Presumptions (Law)
Evidence, Prima facie *(Direct)*
  x Prima facie evidence
  xx Evidence (Law)
Evidence, Real *(Direct)*
  x Real evidence
  xx Evidence (Law)
Evidence (Canon law)
Evidence (Canon law, Orthodox Eastern)
Evidence (Islamic law)
Evidence (Jewish law)
Evidence (Law) *(Direct)*
  sa Admissions (Law)
    Affidavits
    Burden of proof
    Children as witnesses
    Confession (Law)
    Confidential communications
    Court records
    Depositions
    Eavesdropping
    Estoppel
    Evidence, Circumstantial
    Evidence, Criminal
    Evidence, Documentary
    Evidence, Expert
    Evidence, Hearsay
    Evidence, Prima facie
    Evidence, Real
    Examination of witnesses
    Foreign law, Pleading and proof of
    Forensic ballistics
    Judicial notice
    Law and fact
    Letters rogatory
    Medical jurisprudence
    Objections (Evidence)
    Ordeal
    Presumptions (Law)
    Psychology, Forensic
    Reputation (Law)
    Summation (Law)
    Typewriting—Identification
    Wire-tapping
    Witnesses
    Writing—Identification
  x Extrinsic evidence
    Parol evidence
    Trial evidence
  xx Actions and defenses
    Estoppel
    Judicial process
    Psychology, Forensic
    Trial practice
  — Conflict of laws
    See Conflict of laws—Evidence
  — Examinations, questions, etc.
Evidence (Lombard law)
  xx Law, Lombard
Evidence (Roman-Dutch law)
Evidence (Roman law)
Evidences, Christian
  See Apologetics
Evidences of Christianity
  See Apologetics
Evidences of the Bible
  See Bible—Evidences, authority, etc.
Evil
  See Good and evil
Evil, Non-resistance to *(Religion, BR115.W2;*
    Social pathology, HV8686;
    Sociology, HM278)
  sa Government, Resistance to
    Pacifism

x Non-resistance to evil
xx Pacifism
Evil eye *(BF1553; Folk-lore, GR590)*
  sa Charms
    Eye (in religion, folk-lore, etc.)
    Superstition
    Witchcraft
  x Jettatura
  xx Charms
    Demonology
    Eye in literature
    Eye (in religion, folk-lore, etc.)
    Folk-lore
    Superstition
    Witchcraft
Evil in literature
  xx Good and evil
Evil spirits
  See Demonology
Eviya (African people) *(DT546.142)*
  x Moviya (African people)
  xx Ethnology—Gabon
Evocation
  xx Cultus
    Religion
Evoked occipital potential
  See Visual evoked response
Evoked response, Visual
  See Visual evoked response
Evolution *(QH361-371; Paleontology,*
    QE721; Philosophy, B818)
  sa Adaptation (Biology)
    Anatomy, Comparative
    Bergmann's rule
    Biology
    Color of animals
    Color of man
    Color of plants
    Creation
    Degeneration
    Embryology
    Ethics, Evolutionary
    Genetic psychology
    Genetics
    Heredity
    Holism
    Homology (Biology)
    Human evolution
    Island fauna
    Island flora
    Isolating mechanisms
    Life—Origin
    Living fossils
    Man—Influence of environment
    Man—Origin
    Mendel's law
    Mimicry (Biology)
    Missing link
    Modernist-fundamentalist controversy
    Natural selection
    Ontogeny
    Origin of species
    Phylogeny
    Plants—Evolution
    Social evolution
    Stars—Evolution
    Teleology
    Variation (Biology)
  x Darwinism
    Development
    Epigenesis
  xx Biology
    Botany—Variation
    Creation
    Genetics
    Heredity
    Man—Origin
    Mutation (Biology)

    Natural selection
    Ontogeny
    Philosophy, Modern
    Phylogeny
    Teleology
    Transmutation of animals
    Variation (Biology)
    Zoology
    Zoology—Variation
  — Juvenile literature
  — Mathematics
  — Pictorial works
Evolution, Chemical
  See Chemical evolution
Evolution, Galactic
  See Galaxies—Evolution
Evolution, Stellar
  See Stars—Evolution
Evolution and Christianity *(BT712)*
  x Christianity and evolution
  xx Evolution and religion
    Religion and science
Evolution and Judaism *(BM538.E8)*
  x Judaism and evolution
  xx Evolution and religion
    Judaism and science
Evolution and religion *(BL263)*
  sa Bible and evolution
    Evolution and Christianity
    Evolution and Judaism
  x Religion and evolution
  xx Religion and science
Evolution and the Bible
  See Bible and evolution
Evolutionary ethics
  See Ethics, Evolutionary
Evolutionary psychology
  See Genetic psychology
Evuzok (Bantu people)
  xx Bantus
    Ethnology—Cameroon
Ewage language
  xx Papuan languages
Ewe (African people) *(DT500)*
Ewe language *(PL8161-4)*
  sa Aja dialect
    Fon dialect
    Mina dialect
  xx Kwa languages
Ewe law
  See Law, Ewe
Ewes
  sa Sheep milk
  xx Sheep
Ewondo language
  x Jaunde language
    Yaunde language
  xx Bantu languages
EWP
  See Exploding wire phenomena
Ex-Catholic priests
  See Ex-priests, Catholic
Ex-clergy *(Indirect) (BV672.5)*
  sa Ex-priests, Catholic
  x Clergy dropouts
    Ex-pastors
    Former clergy
  xx Clergy
Ex-convicts, Employment of *(Direct)*
    (HV9288)
  x Employment of ex-convicts
  xx Discrimination in employment
    Rehabilitation of criminals
Ex dock clause *(Direct)*
  x Ex pier clause
    Ex quay clause
  xx Export sales

Ex libris
  See Book-plates
Ex-nuns *(Direct)*
  sa Nuns
  xx Monastic and religious life of women
    Monasticism and religious orders for
      women
    Nuns
  — Personal narratives
Ex-pastors
  See Ex-clergy
Ex pier clause
  See Ex dock clause
Ex post facto laws *(Direct)*
  x Nulla poena sine lege doctrine
    Nullum crimen sine lege doctrine
  xx Criminal law
    Due process of law
    Retroactive laws
    Rule of law
Ex post facto laws (Canon law)
Ex-priests, Catholic
  x Catholic ex-priests
    Ex-Catholic priests
  xx Catholic Church—Clergy
    Catholic Church—Clergy—Deposition
    Ex-clergy
  — Personal narratives
Ex quay clause
  See Ex dock clause
Ex-service men
  See Veterans
Ex-votos
  See Votive offerings
Exa camera
Exact (Philosophy)
  x Exactitude (Philosophy)
    Exactness (Philosophy)
  xx Philosophy
Exact test, Fisher
  See Fisher exact test
Exactitude (Philosophy)
  See Exact (Philosophy)
Exactness (Philosophy)
  See Exact (Philosophy)
Exakta camera
  Example under Cameras
Exaltabo te, Deus (Music)
  See Psalms (Music)—145th Psalm
Exaltabo te, Domine (Music)
  See Psalms (Music)—30th Psalm
Examination of conscience
  See Conscience, Examination of
Examination of mines
  See Mine examination
Examination of the blood
  See Blood—Analysis and chemistry
    Blood—Examination
Examination of witnesses *(Direct)*
  sa Cross-examination
    Objections (Evidence)
  xx Evidence (Law)
    Trial practice
    Witnesses
Examinations *(Direct) (College, LB2353,*
    LB2367; Professional courses,
    LC1070-1071; School, LB3051-3060;
    Teachers, LB1763-5)
  Here are entered works on examinations
    in general, *e.g.* discussions on the value
    of examinations, statistics, history, and
    similar general topics.
  SPECIAL TOPICS

Examinations *(Direct)* *(College, LB2353, LB2367; Professional courses, LC1070-1071; School, LB3051-3060; Teachers, LB1763-5)* *(Continued)*

1. Lower schools.—General works on examinations, whether for teachers or pupils, are entered under Examinations. Compilations of questions and answers for such examinations are entered under Examinations—Questions; when confined to a single country, state, or city, the subdivision Questions is added to the local subdivision, *e.g.* Examinations—Ohio—Questions. Compilations limited to a county are entered under state subdivision.

2. Universities and colleges.—Works on examinations in universities and colleges as well as compilations of questions and answers for these examinations, are entered under Universities and colleges, with subdivision Examinations. If limited to a single country, state, or city, the subdivision Examinations is added to the local subdivision, *e.g.* Universities and colleges—United States—Examinations.

   Works limited to a specific college or university are entered under that college or university, with subdivision Examinations, *e.g.* Harvard University—Examinations. If limited to a specific branch of study, that branch is added as a further subdivision, *e.g.* Universities and colleges—Wisconsin—Examinations—English; Harvard University—Examinations—Mathematics, and duplicate entry is made under the specific subject.

3. Universities and colleges—Entrance requirements.—Works in which the requirements for admission to college or university are stated or discussed are entered under the heading Universities and colleges—Entrance requirements, subdivided in the same manner as Examinations, *e.g.* Universities and colleges—Entrance requirements; Universities and colleges—Austria—Entrance requirements; Pennsylvania. University—Entrance requirements; Smith College—Entrance requirements—Mathematics. Compilations of questions and answers for entrance examinations are entered under the subdivision Examinations.

4. Professional schools—Entrance requirements.—Works in which the requirements for admission to professional schools are stated or discussed are entered under the heading for the pertinent category of professional schools with subdivision Entrance requirements, *e.g.* Medical colleges—Entrance requirements. Compilations of questions and answers for entrance examinations in professional schools are entered under the subdivision Entrance examinations, *e.g.* Law schools—Entrance examinations.

5. Particular branches of study.—Compilations of questions and answers for examinations in a particular branch of study are entered under the specific subject, *e.g.* English language—Examinations, questions, etc.; Law—United States—Examinations, questions, etc.; Medicine—Examinations, questions, etc. General discussions, including the rules governing these examinations, are entered either under the appropriate phrase, *e.g.* Law examinations, or under the subject with subdivison Examinations, *e.g.* Accounting—Examinations.

    sa Civil service—Examinations
        Educational tests and measurements
        Multiple-choice examinations
        Test anxiety
        True-false examinations
        subdivision Examinations *under armies and navies, e.g.* France. Armée—Examinations
    x Achievement tests
        Competitive examinations
        Teachers—Examinations
        Tests
    xx Education
        Educational tests and measurements
        Questions and answers
        Teaching
    Notes under Examinations—Questions; Universities and colleges—Entrance requirements; Universities and colleges—Examinations
— Audio-visual aids
— Questions *(LB3051-9)*
    Cf. note under Examinations.
    sa High school equivalency examination
        International baccalaureate
        Mental tests
    Note under Examinations
— Ohio
— — Questions
    Note under Examinations
— United States
    sa National teacher examinations
Examinations, Medical
    See Diagnosis
        Insurance, Accident [Health, Life]—Medical examinations
        Pensions, Medical examinations for
        Premarital examinations
        Examinations in medicine are entered under Medicine—Examinations, questions, etc.
Examinations, Preparation for
    See Study, Method of
Examinations before trial
    See Preliminary examinations (Criminal procedure)
Examinations of land titles
    See Title examinations
Examinations of titles to land
    See Title examinations
Examiners (Administrative procedure) *(Direct)*
    x Hearing examiners
        Trial examiners
    xx Administrative courts
        Administrative procedure
Example
    sa Exempla
        Ideals (Psychology)
        Influence (Psychology)
    x Model
        Pattern
    xx Authority

        Concepts
        Ethics
        Exempla
        Ideals (Psychology)
        Imitation
        Influence (Psychology)
Exanthemata *(RC106)*
    sa Fever
        names of eruptive diseases, e.g.
        Erysipelas, Measles
    x Eruptive fever
        Fever, Eruptive
    xx Fever
EXAPT (Computer program language)
Excardination (Canon law) *(BX1939.E)*
    sa Incardination (Canon law)
    xx Benefices, Ecclesiastical (Canon law)
        Clergy (Canon law)
        Incardination (Canon law)
Excavating machinery *(TA735-747)*
    sa Dredges
        Power shovels
        Rock-drills
        Steam-shovels
        Trenching machinery
    x Digging machines
    xx Construction equipment
        Earthmoving machinery
— Apparatus and supplies
— — Catalogs
— Automatic control
— Bearings
— Cold weather operation *(TA735)*
— Design and construction
— Drawing
    See Excavating machinery—Drawings
— Drawings
    x Excavating machinery—Drawing
    xx Mechanical drawing
— Dynamics
— Electric driving
— Electric equipment
— Hydraulic drive
— Juvenile literature
— Lubrication
— Maintenance and repair
— Reliability
— Testing
Excavation *(Building, TH5101; Engineering, TA730-747)*
    sa Drilling muds
        Earthwork
        Ice excavation
        Nuclear excavation
        Railroads—Earthwork
        Shafts (Excavations)
        Spoil banks
        Stoping (Mining)
        Tunneling
    xx Civil engineering
        Earthwork
        Tunneling
— Estimates *(Direct)*
— Laboratory manuals
— Law and legislation
    See Earthwork—Law and legislation
— Safety measures
— Tables, calculations, etc. *(TA721)*
Excavations (Archaeology) *(Indirect)* *(CC75; CC165)*
    sa Archaeological expeditions
        Archaeological surveying
        Archaeology
        Earthworks (Archaeology)
    x Ruins
    xx Archaeology
        Cities and towns, Ruined, extinct, etc.
— Juvenile literature

Exclusion, Right of *(BX1805)*
  (Continued)
      Jus exclusivae
      Right of exclusion
    xx Popes—Election
      Veto
Exclusion lists in automatic indexing
      (Z695.92)
    x Drop word lists in automatic indexing
      Noise word lists in automatic indexing
      Non-significant words in automatic
        indexing
      Stop lists in automatic indexing
      Stop word lists in automatic indexing
    xx Automatic indexing
      Subject headings
Exclusiva
  See Exclusion, Right of
Exclusive and concurrent legislative powers
      (Direct)
    x Concurrent powers
      Exclusive powers
      Federal-state concurrent legislative
        powers
      Legislative powers, Exclusive and
        concurrent
      Pre-emption of legislative power
    xx Constitutional law
      Federal government
      Legislation
      Legislative power
      State governments
  — United States
      sa Contract clause (United States.
        Constitution)
Exclusive Brethren
  See Plymouth Brethren
Exclusive licenses *(Direct)*
    sa Foreign licensing agreements
    xx Foreign licensing agreements
      Licenses
      Monopolies
      Restraint of trade
Exclusive powers
  See Exclusive and concurrent legislative
      powers
Excommunication *(Catholic Church,*
      BX2275)
    sa Church discipline
      Interdict (Canon law)
    x Anathema
      Expulsion
    xx Blessing and cursing
      Catholic Church—Discipline
      Church discipline
      Interdict (Canon law)
  — Biblical teaching
Excommunication (Canon law) *(BX1939.E8)*
Excommunication (Jewish law) *(BM720.E9)*
    x Ḥerem
    xx Jews—Social life and customs
Excrement, Fossil
  See Coprolites
Excretion *(QP159; QP211)*
    sa Excretory organs
      Feces
      Nitrogen excretion
      Oxalic acid—Excretion
      Perspiration
      Secretion
      Urinary organs
      Urine
    xx Physiology
      Secretion
  — Juvenile literature
Excretion (in religion, folk-lore, etc.)
    sa Feces (in religion, folk-lore, etc.)
      Scatology
      Urine (in religion, folk-lore, etc.)

    x Folk-lore of excretion
    xx Religion, Primitive
Excretory organs *(QL872)*
    xx Excretion
Excursion boats *(Direct)*
    xx Ships
  — Registers *(Direct)*
      Example under Ship registers
Execration
  See Blessing and cursing
Execution in effigy
  See Executions in effigy
Execution of Tennessee militiamen, 1815
  See Tennessee militiamen, Execution of,
      1815
Execution sermons *(BV4262)*
      Here are entered sermons preached at the
        execution of criminals.
    xx Sermons
Executions (Administrative law) *(Direct)*
    xx Administrative law
Executions (Ancient law)
Executions (Canon law)
Executions (International law)
    xx International law
      Sanctions (International law)
Executions (Islamic law)
Executions (Law) *(Direct)*
    sa Attachment and garnishment
      Creditors' bills
      Distress (Law)
      Exemption (Law)
      Extent (Writ)
      Foreclosure
      Judicial sales
      Poor debtor's oath
      Supplementary proceedings
      Tax-sales
    xx Civil procedure
      Debtor and creditor
      Judgments
      Writs
  — Cases
  — — Digests
      See Executions (Law)—Digests
  — Conflict of laws
      See Conflict of laws—Executions
  — Digests
    x Executions (Law)—Cases—Digests
Executions (Roman law)
Executions and executioners *(Direct)*
      (HV8551-3)
    sa Capital punishment
      Crucifixion
      Electrocution
      Executions in effigy
      Guillotine
      Hanging
      Last meal before execution
      Stoning
    xx Capital punishment
      Criminal law
      Criminal procedure
  — Personal narratives
Executions by effigy
  See Executions in effigy
Executions in effigy *(Direct)*
    x Burning in effigy
      Effigy, Executions in
      Execution in effigy
      Executions by effigy
      Hanging in effigy
    xx Criminal law
      Executions and executioners
      Fugitives from justice
      Punishment
Executive ability *(HF5500)*
    sa Ability

      Delegation of authority
      Leadership
      Management
      Personnel management
      Planning
    x Ability, Executive
      Administrative ability
    xx Ability
      Executives
      Management
  — Testing
    x Executives—Ability testing
Executive advisory bodies *(Direct)*
    x Administrative advisory bodies
      Advisory bodies, Executive
      Commissions of the federal government
      Government advisory boards
    xx Administrative agencies
      Administrative law
      Public administration
Executive agencies
  See Administrative agencies
Executive agreements
    sa subdivison Foreign relations—Executive
        agreements *under names of*
        countries, e.g. United States—
        Foreign relations—Executive
        agreements
    xx Executive power
      International law
      International relations
      Treaties
Executive compensation
  See Executives—Salaries, pensions, etc.
Executive departments
  See Administrative agencies
      subdivision Executive departments
        under names of countries, cities, etc.
Executive impoundment of appropriated funds
      (Direct)
    x Appropriated funds, Executive
        impoundment of
      Impoundment of appropriated funds,
        Executive
    xx Executive power
      Expenditures, Public
      Legislative power
      Separation of powers
Executive investigations
  See Governmental investigations
Executive orders *(Direct)*
    xx Delegated legislation
      Executive power
Executive power *(Direct) (JF251-314;*
      United States, JK501-901; Other
      countries, JN-JQ)
    sa Civil supremacy over the military
      De facto doctrine
      Delegated legislation
      Delegation of powers
      Executive agreements
      Executive impoundment of
        appropriated funds
      Executive orders
      Executive privilege (Government
        information)
      Heads of state
      Implied powers (Constitutional law)
      Initiative, Right of
      Judicial review
      Monarchy
      Pardon
      Prerogative, Royal
      Presidents
      Prime ministers
      Promulgation (Law)
      Separation of powers
      Treaty-making power

Veto
War and emergency powers
subdivisions Foreign relations—Treaties
and Officials and employees—
Appointments, qualifications, tenure,
etc. *under names of countries*
x Emergency powers
Power, Executive
xx Constitutional law
Implied powers (Constitutional law)
Political science
Presidents
— United States
x Presidents—United States—Powers
— — States
sa subdivision Governors—Powers
and duties *under names of*
individual states, e.g. Louisiana
—Governors—Powers and
duties
Executive power (Canon law)
Executive privilege (Government information)
(Direct)
sa Government and the press
x Government secrecy
Legislative right to information from
executive agencies
Secrecy in government
xx Executive power
Freedom of information
Government information
Governmental investigations
Official secrets
Separation of powers
Executives *(Direct)*
sa Arts administrators
Executive ability
Foremen
Government executives
Middle managers
Personnel management
Women executives
x Business executives
Corporation executives
xx Business
Industrial management
Management
Personnel management
— Ability testing
See Executive ability—Testing
— Anecdotes, facetiae, satire, etc.
— Books and reading
— Caricatures and cartoons
— Collective labor agreements
See Collective labor agreements—
Executives
— Correspondence, reminiscences, etc.
— Health programs
xx Men—Health and hygiene
Welfare work in industry
Example under reference from Health
programs
— Information services
— Language
xx Language and languages
— Portraits, caricatures, etc.
— Recruiting
— Retirement
— Salaries, pensions, etc. *(Direct)*
sa Expense accounts
x Executive compensation
xx Wages
— — Accounting
xx Wages—Accounting
— Taxation *(Direct)*
— Training
See Executives, Training of

Executives, Dismissal of *(Direct)*
x Dismissal of executives
xx Employees, Dismissal of
Executives, Rating of
x Efficiency rating
Rating of executives
xx Ability—Testing
Employees, Rating of
Personnel management
Executives, Training of *(Direct)*
x Executives—Training
Training of executives
xx Employees, Training of
Industrial management
Personnel management
— Audio-visual aids
Executives' wives
xx Wives
Executors and administrators *(Direct)*
sa Claims against decedents' estates
Distribution of decedents' estates
Partition of decedents' estates
Probate law and practice
Trusts and trustees
Widow's allowance
x Administrators and executors
xx Decedents' estates
Guardian and ward
Inheritance and succession
Probate law and practice
Trusts and trustees
Wills
Note under Administration of estates
— Accounting *(HF5686.E9)*
— Fees
xx Lawyers—Fees
Probate law and practice—Costs
Executors and administrators (Islamic law)
Executory interests *(Direct)*
sa Expectancies (Law)
xx Estates (Law)
Expectancies (Law)
Future interests
Real property
Remainders (Estates)
Exempla *(BV4224)*
sa Allegories
Example
Fables
First communion—Stories
Homiletical illustrations
Ideals (Psychology)
Influence (Psychology)
Legends
Parables
Short stories
Tales
xx Anecdotes
Didactic literature
Example
Homiletical illustrations
Tales
Exempla, Islamic
x Exempla, Muslim
Islamic exempla
Muslim exempla
xx Homiletical illustrations, Islamic
Islamic devotional literature
Religious life (Islam)
Exempla, Muslim
See Exempla, Islamic
Exemplary damages *(Direct)*
x Damages, Exemplary
Punitive damages
Retributive damages
Smart money
Vindictive damages
xx Damages

Exemption (Canon law) *(BX1939.E)*
xx Privileges and immunities, Ecclesiastical
Exemption (Law) *(Direct)*
sa Homestead law
Wages—Exemption
x Beneficium competentiae
Benefit of competency
xx Executions (Law)
Exemption from military service
See Military service, Compulsory
Exemption from taxation
See Taxation, Exemption from
Exequatur (Ecclesiastical law) *(Direct)*
sa Bulls, Papal
x Regium placet
xx Ecclesiastical law
Exercise *(GV461-547; Hygiene, RA781;*
Physiology, QP301; Therapeutics,
RM721)
sa Callisthenics
Gymnastics
Isometric exercise
Muscle strength
Physical education and training
Physical fitness
Reducing exercises
Yoga, Haṭha
particular types of exercise, e.g.
Fencing, Rowing, Running
x Warm-up
xx Hygiene
Physical education and training
— Anecdotes, facetiae, satire, etc.
— Early works to 1800
— Juvenile literature
— Physiological effect
Exercise for women
xx Woman—Health and hygiene
Exercise therapy
See Gymnastics, Medical
Exercises, Devotional
See Devotional exercises
Exercises, Spiritual
See Spiritual exercises
Exercitor maris
See Ship's husbands
Exercitor navis
See Ship's husbands
Exfoliative cytology
sa Vaginal smears
x Epithelial cells
Goblet cells
xx Cytology
Diagnosis, Cytologic
Epithelium
— Atlases
— Technique
Exhaust control devices (Motor vehicles)
See Motor vehicles—Pollution control
devices
Exhaust emissions (Aircraft)
See Aircraft exhaust emissions
Exhaust gas (Automobile)
See Automobile exhaust gas
Exhaust gas (Diesel)
See Diesel motor exhaust gas
Exhaust gas analysis
See Automobile exhaust gas—Analysis
Exhaust mufflers
See Gas and oil engines—Mufflers
Exhaust systems *(TJ960)*
sa Air ducts
Fans (Machinery)
xx Cleaning machinery and appliances
Dust—Removal
Factories—Heating and ventilation
Factory sanitation
— Drawings

Exhausters
    See Compressors
        Fans (Machinery)
Exhaustion
    See Fatigue
Exhaustion of administrative remedies
        (Direct)
    xx Administrative courts
        Administrative remedies
        Judicial review of administrative acts
Exhaustion of local remedies (International
    law)
    x Local redress rule (International law)
        Local remedy rule (International law)
    xx Claims
        Denial of justice
        Diplomatic protection
        Government liability (International law)
        International law
Exhibition booths
    See Exhibitions—Booths
Exhibition buildings *(NA6750)*
    sa subdivsion Buildings *under names of*
        exhibitions, e.g. Philadelphia.
        Centennial Exhibition, 1876—
        Buildings; *also names of particular*
        exhibtion buildings, e.g. Crystal
        Palace, Hyde Park, London
    x Exposition buildings
        Fair buildings
    xx Architecture
Exhibitionism *(Social pathology, HQ79)*
    Works on the criminal manifestation of
    exhibitionism are entered under the
    heading Indecent exposure.
    sa Indecent exposure
    xx Sex
Exhibitions *(T391-999)*
    sa Agricultural exhibitions
        Display boards
        Displays in education
        Fairs
        Flower shows
        Livestock exhibitions
        Museum techniques
        particular exhibitions, e.g. Chicago.
        World's Columbian Exposition,
        1893; *and subdivision* Exhibitions
        under names of cities, e.g. New York
        (City)—Exhibitions; *and under*
        special subjects, e.g. Bookbinding—
        Exhibitions
    x Exhibits
        Expositions
        Industrial arts—Exhibitions
        Industrial exhibitions
        International exhibitions
        Technology—Exhibitions
        World's fairs
    xx Fairs
        Sales promotion
    — Booths
        x Booths, Exhibit
            Exhibition booths
    — Classification of exhibits *(T396-7)*
    — Equipment and supplies
    — Juvenile literature
    — Law and legislation *(Direct)*
Exhibitions, Agricultural
    See Agricultural exhibitions
Exhibitions, Electrical
    See Electric industries—Exhibitions
Exhibitions, Engineering
    See Engineering—Exhibitions
Exhibitions, Livestock
    See Livestock exhibitions
Exhibitions (International law)
    xx International law

Exhibits
    See Exhibitions
Exhumation *(RA637)*
    x Disinterment
    xx Autopsy
        Body-snatching
        Burial
    — Law and legislation *(Direct)*
        xx Burial laws
Exhumation (Jewish law)
Exilarchate
Exiles *(Biography, CT105; International law,*
    JX4261)
    sa Deportation
        Expatriation
        Governments in exile
        Penal colonies
        Refugees
        Refugees, Political
        subdivision Exiles *under names of*
        certain countries, e.g. Siberia—
        Exiles; Tasmania—Exiles
    xx Deportation
        Penal colonies
        Refugees, Political
Exiles (Roman law)
Existence theorems *(QA371)*
    xx Differential equations
        Mathematical physics
Existential ethics
    sa Situation ethics
    x Ethics, Existential
    xx Ethics
        Existentialism
Existential psychology
    x Psychology, Existential
    xx Existentialism
        Phenomenology
        Psychiatry
        Psychoanalysis
Existentialism *(Modern philosophy, B819)*
    sa Concrete (Philosophy)
        Demythologization
        Epiphanism
        Existential ethics
        Existential psychology
        Relationism
    x Existenzphilosophie
    xx Epiphanism
        Ontology
        Phenomenology
        Philosophy, Modern
        Relationism
        Self
    — Anecdotes, facetiae, satire, etc.
Existentialism and Christianity
    See Christianity and existentialism
Existentialism in literature
    xx Philosophy in literature
Existenzphilosophie
    See Existentialism
Exit interviews
    x Termination interviews
    xx Employees, Dismissal of
        Employees, Resignation of
        Employment interviewing
Exit permits (Emigration)
    xx Emigration and immigration law
Exmoor pony
    xx Ponies
Exo-condensation
    See Ring formation (Chemistry)
Exobiology
    See Life on other planets
        Space biology
Exocoetus
    See Flying-fish
Exocrine glands *(QP187.7)*

Exodus, The
    x Exodus (Biblical event)
        Jews—Exodus
    xx Jews—History—To1200 B.C.
    — Art
    — History of doctrines
    — Juvenile literature
    — Typology
        xx Typology (Theology)
Exodus (Biblical event)
    See Exodus, The
Exodus, The
    — Biblical teaching *(BS680.E9)*
Exogamy
    See Endogamy and exogamy
Exophthalmic goiter
    See Graves' disease
Exophthalmos *(RE715.E9)*
    xx Eye—Diseases and defects
        Graves' disease
Exorcism *(BF1559; Folk-lore, GR540;*
    Religion, BX2340)
    sa Blessing and cursing
        Demonology
        Witchcraft
    xx Blessing and cursing
        Demonology
        Demonomania
        Superstition
        Witchcraft
Exostosis *(RD608)*
    xx Bones—Diseases
Exoticism in art
    x Art, Exotic
    xx Art
Exoticism in literature
    sa Robinsonades
        Utopias in literature
        Voyages, Imaginary
    xx Robinsonades
        Utopias
        Voyages, Imaginary
Expandable space structures *(TL940)*
    sa Balloons
        Project Echo
    x Inflatable space structures
        Pliant space structures
        Space structures, Expandable
    xx Air-supported structures
        Artificial satellites
        Balloons
        Space stations
        Space vehicles
Expandable structures
    See Air-supported structures
Expanded metal
    xx Building materials
        Sheet-metal work
Expanding cement
    xx Cement
Expansion (Game) *(GV1299.E9)*
Expansion (Heat) *(QC281-6)*
    sa Expansion of gases
        Thermal stresses
    x Coefficient of expansion
        Condensation and expansion, Thermal
        Thermal expansion
    xx Heat
        Physics
    — Measurement
    — Tables, etc.
Expansion (United States politics)
    See Imperialism
        subdivsions Colonial question, Foreign
        relations—War of 1898, *and*
        Territorial expansion *under* United
        States

Expansion chamber
  See Cloud chamber
Expansion joints
  sa Rocket engines—Expansion joints
  xx Joints (Engineering)
Expansion of concrete
  See Concrete—Expansion and contraction
Expansion of gases
  x Gases—Expansion
    Gases, Expansion of
  xx Expansion (Heat)
    Heat
Expansion of liquids *(QC284)*
  x Coefficient of expansion
    Liquids—Expansion
  xx Heat
Expansion of solids *(QC282)*
  sa Concrete—Expansion and contraction
    Standards of length
    Thermal stresses
  x Coefficient of expansion
  xx Heat
    Solids
    Standards of length
Expansive classification
  See Classification, Expansive
Expansive concrete *(TA439)*
  x Concrete, Expanding
    Concrete, Expansive
    Concrete, Self-stressed
    Expanding concrete
    Self-stressed concrete
  xx Concrete—Expansion and contraction
Expatriation *(Direct) (JX4226)*
  sa Citizenship
    Deportation
    Naturalization
    Statelessness
  xx Aliens
    Citizenship
    Citizenship, Loss of
    Deportation
    Exiles
    International law
    Naturalization
    Statelessness
Expectancies (Law) *(Direct)*
  sa Executory interests
    Future interests
    Remainders (Estates)
    Reversion
  x Estates in expectancy
    Expectant estates
  xx Conditions (Law)
    Executory interests
    Future interests
Expectant estates
  See Expectancies (Law)
Expectation (Psychology)
  xx Motivation (Psychology)
Expectative graces
  See Benefices, Ecclesiastical
Expectorants *(RM390)*
Expédition antarctique belge, 1897-1899
    (G850)
  x "Belgica" Expedition
Expedition of the Thousand
  See Italy—History—War of 1860-1861
Expeditions, Antarctic
  See Antarctic regions
    names of expeditions, e.g. United States
      Exploring Expedition, 1838-1842;
      and names of ships
Expeditions, Archaeological
  See Archaeological expeditions
Expeditions, Arctic
  See Arctic regions

names of expeditions, e.g. Grinnell
    Expedition, 1st, 1850-1851; *and*
    names of ships
Expeditions, Sacred
  See Parish missions
Expeditions, Scientific
  See Scientific expeditions
Expenditure tax
  See Spendings tax
Expenditures, Public
  sa Budget
    Executive impoundment of
      appropriated funds
    Government spending policy
    Special funds
    subdivision Appropriations and
      expenditures *under names of*
      countries, states, etc.
  x Appropriations and expenditures
    Government expenditures
    Public expenditures
  xx Finance, Public
    Government spending policy
    Public administration
  — Classification
  — Research *(Direct)*
Expense accounts
  sa Income tax—Deductions—Expenses
  xx Business
    Costs, Industrial
    Executives—Salaries, pensions, etc.
    Sales management
Expense accounts and taxation *(Direct)*
  x Taxation and expense accounts
  xx Income tax—Deductions—Expenses
Expenses as tax deductions
  See Income tax—Deductions—Expenses
Experience
  sa Adaptability (Psychology)
    Empiricism
    Facts (Philosophy)
    God—Proof, Empirical
    Immanence (Philosophy)
    Pragmatism
    Wisdom
  xx Knowledge, Theory of
    Philosophy
    Pragmatism
    Psychology
    Reality
  — Quotations, maxims, etc.
Experience (Religion) *(Conversion,*
    BV4912-4915; Philosophy and
    Christianity, BR110; Psychology of
    religion, BL53)
  sa Discernment of spirits
    God—Proof, Empirical
    Inner Light
    Mystique of sin
  x Religious experience
  xx Authority (Religion)
    Psychology, Religious
Experience (Religion) and hallucinogenic drugs
  See Hallucinogenic drugs and religious
    experience
Experience charts *(LB1045)*
  x Charts, Experience
  xx Bulletin boards
    Teaching—Aids and devices
Experiential world inventory
  xx Personality tests
    Thought and thinking
Experimental animals
  See Laboratory animals
Experimental biology
  See Biology, Experimental
Experimental botany
  See Botany, Experimental

Experimental cardiology
  See Cardiology, Experimental
Experimental design
  sa Analysis of variance
    Factorial experiment designs
    Response surfaces (Statistics)
  x Design of experiments
    Statistical design
  xx Analysis of variance
    Mathematical optimization
    Research
    Science—Experiments
    Science—Methodology
    Statistical decision
    Statistics
  — Programmed instruction
Experimental embryology
  See Embryology, Experimental
Experimental endocrinology
  See Endocrinology, Experimental
Experimental farms
  See Agricultural experiment stations
Experimental films *(PN1995.9.E96)*
  sa Cinematography, Abstract
  x Avant-garde films
    Moving-pictures, Experimental
    Personal films
    Underground films
  xx Moving-pictures
Experimental leukemia
  See Leukemia, Experimental
Experimental medicine
  See Medicine, Experimental
Experimental methods in education
  See Education—Experimental methods
Experimental oncology
  See Oncology, Experimental
Experimental pathology
  See Pathology, Experimental
Experimental phonetics
  See Phonetics, Experimental
Experimental physiology
  See Physiology, Experimental
Experimental plants
  See Pilot plants
Experimental psychiatry
  See Psychiatric research
Experimental psychology
  See Psychology, Experimental
Experimental roads
  See Roads, Experimental
Experimental surgery
  See Surgery, Experimental
Experimental theater
  x Avant-garde theater
  xx Theater
Experimental therapeutics
  See Therapeutics, Experimental
Experimental toxicology
  See Toxicology, Experimental
Experimental zoology
  See Zoology, Experimental
Experimentation on man, Medical
  See Human experimentation in medicine
Experimentation on man, Psychological
  See Human experimentation in psychology
Experimenter effects in psychological research
  See Psychological research, Experimenter
    effects in
Expert evidence
  See Evidence, Expert
Expertising
  See subdivision Expertising *under subjects,*
    e.g. Art—Expertising
Expertising, X-ray
  xx Art—Expertising
    X-rays

Expiration of rights
   See Lapse (Law)
Explication, Literary
   See subdivision Explication *under specific*
      literatures, e.g. English literature—
      Explication; English poetry—
      Explication
Explication de texte
   See subdivision Explication *under specific*
      literatures, e.g. English literature—
      Explication; English poetry—
      Explication
Exploded wire phenomena
   See Exploding wire phenomena
Exploding wire phenomena *(QC703)*
   sa Photography, High-speed
   x Electrically exploded wires
      EWP
      Exploded wire phenomena
      Wire explosions, Electric
   xx Electric discharges
      Plasma (Ionized gases)
      Pulse techniques (Electronics)
      Wire
Exploration, Submarine
   See Underwater exploration
Exploration, Underwater
   See Underwater exploration
Exploration of space
   See Outer space—Exploration
Exploratory behavior
   See Curiosity
Exploratory fishing *(Indirect)* *(SH343.5)*
   xx Fisheries—Research
      Fishery resources
      Fishes
      Oceanographic research
Explorer (Artificial satellite)
   xx Artificial satellites
   — Orbits
      Example under Artificial satellites—Or-
      bits
Explorers *(G80-890)*
   sa Discoveries (in geography)
      Travelers
      Voyages and travels
      subdivisions Description and travel *and*
      Discovery and exploration *under*
      names of continents, countries, etc.
   x Discoverers
      Navigators
      Voyagers
   xx Adventure and adventurers
      Discoveries (in geography)
      Heroes
      Travelers
      Voyages and travels
   — Anecdotes, facetiae, satire, etc.
   — Juvenile literature
Explorers, American, [Dutch, Swedish, etc.]
   x American [Dutch, Swedish, etc.]
      explorers
   — Juvenile literature
Explorers, Women
   x Women explorers
Explorers (Boy Scouts)
   x Venture Scouts
   xx Boy Scouts
   — Juvenile litrearure
Explosion insurance
   See Insurance, Explosion
Explosion loads
   See Blast effect
Explosionproof electric apparatus and
      appliances
   See Electric apparatus and appliances,
      Explosionproof

Explosionproof electric controllers
   See Electric controllers, Explosionproof
Explosionproof electric machinery
   See Electric machinery, Explosionproof
Explosionproof electric transformers
   See Electric transformers, Explosionproof
Explosions *(Chemistry, QD516)*
   sa Blast effect
      Dust explosion
      Insurance, Explosion
      Kitchen-boiler explosions
      Nuclear explosions
      Project Plowshare
      Shock waves
      Steam-boiler explosions
      Underwater explosions
      subdivision Explosion *under names of*
      cities, etc.
   xx Accidents
   — Computer programs
   — Physiological effect
Explosions, Dust
   See Dust explosion
Explosions, Underground nuclear
   See Underground nuclear explosions
Explosions, Underwater
   See Underwater explosions
Explosions in mines
   See Mine explosions
Explosive actuators
   See Propellant actuated devices
Explosive forming
   sa Extrusion (Metals)
      Sheet-metal work
   x Metals—Explosive forming
   xx Explosives
      Forging
      High energy forming
Explosive welding
   xx Welding
Explosives *(Economics, HD9663;*
      Technology, TP268-299)
   sa Ammunition
      Blasting
      Bobbinite
      Coal mines and mining—Explosives
      Compensating-powder
      Dynamite
      Explosive forming
      Guncotton
      Gunpowder
      Liquid oxygen
      Melinite
      Mines, Military
      Nitroglycerin
      Propellant actuated devices
      Propellants
      Shaped charges
      Torpedoes
   xx Blasting
      Chemistry
      Gunnery
      Nitrocellulose
      Shooting, Military
   Example under Chemicals; Chemistry, Techni-
      cal
   — Juvenile literature
   — Law and legislation *(Direct)* *(TP297-9)*
      sa Explosives, Military—Safety
         regulations
      x Blasting—Law and legislation
         Explosives—Safety regulations
      xx Firearms—Laws and regulations
         Mine safety—Law and legislation
         Safety regulations
      Note under Safety regulations
   — Patents
   — Problems, exercises, etc.

— Safety measures *(TP297)*
   xx Hazardous substances
— Safety regulations
   See Explosives—Law and legislation
— Storage
— Testing *(TP271)*
— Transportation *(Railroads, HE2321.E8)*
   sa Transportation, Military
   xx Railroads—Accidents
      Transportation, Military
   Example under Shipment of goods
Explosives, Military *(TP268-299)*
   sa Chemical warfare
      Demolition, Military
      Greek fire
      Incendiary bombs
      Melinite
      Mines, Military
      Torpedoes
   x Military explosives
   xx Torpedoes
— Safety regulations *(Direct)*
   xx Explosives—Law and legislation
Explosives in agriculture *(S679)*
   xx Agriculture
      Clearing of land
Explosives in astronautics
   xx Astronautics
Explosives in forestry
   xx Forests and forestry
Explosives in lumbering
   xx Lumbering
Explosives industry *(Direct)*
   sa Wages—Explosives industry
Exponential functions
   See Functions, Exponential
Exponential measurements
   See subdivision Exponential measurements
      under subjects, e.g. Heavy water
      reactors—Exponential measurements
Exponents (Algebra)
   sa Functions, Exponential
      Roots, Numerical
   x Power (Algebra)
   — Programmed instruction
Export and import controls
   See Foreign trade regulation
Export art, Chinese
   See China trade art
Export associations
   For associations of American exporters
      set up under the Webb-Pomerene act.
   x Webb-Pomerene associations
   xx United States—Commercial policy
Export controls *(Direct)*
   x Export licenses
      Licenses, Export
   xx Commercial policy
      Foreign trade promotion
      Foreign trade regulation
      Free trade and protection
Export credit *(Direct)*
   sa Insurance, Export credit
   x Credit, Export
   xx Commerce
      Commercial policy
      Credit
      Foreign trade promotion
Export credit guarantees
   See Insurance, Export credit
Export credit insurance
   See Insurance, Export credit
Export duties *(Direct)*
   xx Tariff
Export duties on canned fruit *(Direct)*
   xx Tariff on fruit
Export duties on coffee *(Direct)*
   xx Tariff on coffee

Export duties on dried fruit *(Direct)*
    xx Tariff on fruit
Export duties on eggs *(Direct)*
    xx Tariff on eggs
Export duties on rice *(Direct)*
    xx Tariff on rice
Export duties on tea *(Direct)*
    xx Tariff on tea
Export insurance
    See Insurance, Inland marine
Export licenses
    See Export controls
Export marketing
    xx Commerce
        Marketing
Export porcelain, Chinese
    See China trade porcelain
Export premiums *(Direct)* *(HF2701)*
    sa Dumping (Commercial policy)
        Shipping bounties and subsidies
    x Premiums, Export
    xx Commercial policy
        Foreign trade promotion
        Shipping bounties and subsidies
        Subsidies
Export promotion
    See Foreign trade promotion
Export sales *(Direct)*
    sa C.I.F. clause
        Ex dock clause
        F.O.B. clause
        Foreign trade promotion
    x International sales
        Sales, Export
        Sales, International
    xx Commerce
        Contracts, Maritime
        Sales
    — Examinations, questions, etc.
    — Forms
Export trade promotion
    See Foreign trade promotion
Exports
    See Commerce
        Tariff
Exposition, Literary
    See subdivision Explication *under specific*
        literatures, e.g. English literature—
        Explication; English poetry—
        Explication
Exposition (Rhetoric) *(English, PE1429)*
    Here are entered works on expository
    writing in English rhetoric. Works on
    expository writing in other languages
    are entered under the name of the lan-
    guage with subdivision Rhetoric, *e.g.*
    French language—Rhetoric.
    x Expository writing
    xx English language—Rhetoric
        Rhetoric
Exposition buildings
    See Exhibition buildings
Expositions
    See Exhibitions
Expository writing
    See Exposition (Rhetoric)
EXPOSUM (Computer program)
    xx Curve fitting
Exposure (Criminal law) *(Direct)*
    x Exposure of child
    xx Criminal law
        Offenses against the person
Exposure of child
    See Exposure (Criminal law)
Exposure of person
    See Indecent exposure
Exposure of the dead
    See Dokhmas

    Scaffold burial
Express highways *(Direct)*
    sa Automobile driving on highways
        Disabled vehicles on express highways
        Highway bypasses
        Highway relocation
        Park districts
        Toll roads
        names of individual express highways,
           e.g. Garden State Parkway
    x Controlled access highways
        Express roads
        Expressways
        Freeways
        Limited access highways
        Motorways
        Parkways
        Superhighways
        Turnpikes (Modern)
    xx Roads
        Toll roads
        Traffic engineering
    — Airspace utilization *(HE355.8)*
        x Airspace over highways
           Freeway airspace utilization
        xx Roads—Right of way—Multiple use
    — Communication systems
        xx Highway communications
           Telecommunication
    — Design
    — Economic aspects *(Direct)*
    — Estimates and costs
    — Juvenile literature
    — Law and legislation *(Direct)*
        xx Highway law
    — Medians
        See Median strips
    — Pictorial works
    — Public opinion
    — Right of way
        See Roads—Right of way
Express roads
    See Express highways
Express service *(Direct)* *(HE5880-5990)*
    sa Aeronautics, Commercial—Freight
        Parcel-post stamps
    x Railroads—Express service
    xx Carriers
        Communication and traffic
        Railroads
        Transportation
    — Employees *(Direct)*
        sa Trade-unions—Express service
    — Money-orders
    — Taxation *(Direct)*

        GEOGRAPHIC SUBDIVISIONS

    — United States
        sa Pony express
Express trusts
    xx Trusts and trustees
Expression *(Emotions, BF585-593; Oratory,*
        PN4155-4165)
    sa Acting
        Delsarte system
        Elocution
        Facial expression
        Nonverbal communication
        Rhetoric
    xx Acting
        Delsarte system
        Elocution
        Eloquence
        Nonverbal communication
        Reading
        Rhetoric
Expression (Philosophy) *(B105.E95)*
    xx Philosophy

Expression of intention
    See Declaration of intention
Expressionism *(Aesthetics, BH301.E9)*
    sa Dadaism
        Surrealism
Expressionism (Art) *(Direct)* *(ND1265)*
    sa Abstract expressionism
        Post-impressionism (Art)
    xx Aesthetics
        Art
        Art, Modern—20th century
        Modernism (Art)
        Painting
        Post-impressionism (Art)
        Sculpture
Expressways
    See Express highways
Expromission *(Direct)*
    xx Debtor and creditor
        Delegation (Civil law)
        Novation
Expropriation
    See Eminent domain
Expulsion
    See Deportation
        Excommunication
        Penal colonies
        European War, 1914-1918—
           Deportations from Belgium;
           European War, 1914-1918—
           Deportations from France; United
           States—Emigration and immigration;
           World War, 1939-1945—
           Deportations from Latvia; *and*
           similar headings
Expulsion of students
    See Student expulsion
Expunging resolutions, 1834-1837 *(E384.7)*
Expurgated books *(Z1019-1020)*
    sa Censorship
        Condemned books
        Index librorum prohibitorum
        Liberty of the press
        Printing—Cancels
        Prohibited books
    x Books, Expurgated
    xx Censorship
        Condemned books
        Liberty of the press
        Printing—Cancels
        Prohibited books
    — Specimens
Extemporaneous preaching
    See Preaching, Extemporaneous
Extemporaneous speaking
    x Impromptu speaking
        Oratory, Extemporaneous
        Speaking
    xx Public speaking
        Speech
Extemporization (Music)
    See Improvisation (Music)
Extendable computer system simulator
    See ECSS (Computer program language)
Extended care facilities *(Indirect)*
    (RA975.5.E9)
    sa Nursing homes
    x Long-term care facilities
    xx Hospitals
        Long-term care of the sick
    — Administration
    — Food service
Extended general purpose simulator
    See EGPS (Computer program language)
Extended range forecasting
    See Long-range weather forecasting
Extended range forecasts
    See Long-range weather forecasts

Extended use of college facilities
  See College facilities—Extended use
Extended use of school facilities
  See School facilities—Extended use
Extension, Seminary
  See Seminary extension
Extension (Logic)
  xx Logic
Extension (Philosophy)
  xx Philosophy
Extension fields (Mathematics)
  See Field extensions (Mathematics)
Extension Management Information System
  See EMIS (Information retrieval system)
Extension research, Agricultural
  See Agricultural extension work—Research
Extension work, Agricultural
  See Agricultural extension work
Extensometer *(TA413)*
  xx Deformations (Mechanics)
Extent (Writ) *(Direct)*
  x Crown's extent
    Extent in aid
    Extent in chief
  xx Executions (Law)
    Writs
Extent in aid
  See Extent (Writ)
Extent in chief
  See Extent (Writ)
Extents, Manorial
  See Manorial extents
Extenuating circumstances *(Direct)*
  sa Aggravating circumstances
    Crime passionnel
  x Extenuation (Law)
    Mitigation (Law)
  xx Aggravating circumstances
    Criminal law
    Criminal liability
Extenuation (Law)
  See Extenuating circumstances
Exterior ballistics
  See Ballistics, Exterior
Exterior walls *(TH2235)*
  sa Curtain walls
    Dampness in buildings
    Decoration and ornament, Architectural
    Façades
    Weathering of buildings
  x Buildings—Exterior walls
    External walls
  xx Walls
  — Testing
  — Thermal properties
    sa Insulation (Heat)
    xx Heat—Transmission
      Insulation (Heat)
  — — Tables
Extermination
  See Insect control; Pest control; *and similar
    headings; and subdivision* Control
    under subjects, e.g. Desert locust—
    Control; Wolves—Control
Extermination, Jewish (1939-1945)
  See Holocaust, Jewish (1939-1945)
External debts
  See Debts, External
External economies and diseconomies
  See Externalities (Economics)
External walls
  See Exterior walls
Externalities (Economics)
  x Costs, Social
    External economies and diseconomies
    Social costs
  xx Economics
    Waste (Economics)

Exterritorial crime
  See Criminal jurisdiction
Exterritoriality *(JX1671-2; JX4175)*
  sa Capitulations
    Consular jurisdiction
    Diplomatic privileges and immunities
    Government vessels
    Privileges and immunities
    specific instances, e.g. Emilio
      Rondanini (Ship)
  x Extraterritoriality
    Jurisdiction, Exterritorial
  xx Capitulations
    Diplomatic and consular service
    Immunities of foreign states
    International law
Extinct animals *(Indirect) (QL88)*
  sa Birds, Extinct
    Paleontology
    Rare animals
  x Animals, Extinct
  xx Paleontology
    Rare animals
    Zoology
Extinct birds
  See Birds, Extinct
Extinct cities
  See Cities and towns, Ruined, extinct, etc.
Extinct languages
  sa Alphabet
    Writing
    *names of particular extinct languages,
      e.g.* Hittite language; Sumerian
      language
  x Dead languages
  xx Alphabet
    Language and languages
    Writing
Extinction, Interstellar
  See Interstellar reddening
Extinction (Psychology) *(BF319.5.E9)*
  sa Habituation (Neuropsychology)
    Reinforcement (Psychology)
  xx Conditioned response
    Habituation (Neuropsychology)
    Psychology, Physiological
Extinguishers, Fire
  See Fire extinguishers
Extinguishment of debts *(Direct)*
  sa Composition (Law)
    Compromise (Law)
    Confusion of rights
    Delegation (Civil law)
    Limitation of actions
    Novation
    Payment
    Performance (Law)
    Rebus sic stantibus clause
    Remission (Civil law)
    Rescission (Law)
    Resolution (Civil law)
    Set-off and counterclaim
    Vis major (Civil law)
  x Debts, Extinguishment of
  xx Contracts
    Debtor and creditor
Extinguishment of debts (Roman law)
  x Acceptilation
Extortion *(Direct)*
  sa Racketeering
    Threats
    Trials (Extortion)
  x Blackmail
    Chantage
  xx Offenses against property
    Racketeering
    Threats
    Undue influence

Extortion (Roman law)
Extortion in literature
  Example under Crime in literature
Extra-curricular activities
  See Student activities
Extra-illustrated books
  See Illustrated books—Extra-illustrated
Extra-oral medication
  See Parenteral therapy
Extra-vehicular space suits
  See Extravehicular space suits
Extracellular fluid
  xx Body fluids
Extracellular fluid space
  See Extracellular space
Extracellular space
  x Extracellular fluid space
  xx Body fluids
Extracorporeal circulation
  See Blood—Circulation, Artificial
Extracorporeal perfusion
  See Blood—Circulation, Artificial
Extraction, Obstetrical
  See Obstetrical extraction
Extraction (Chemistry) *(TP156.E8)*
  xx Chemistry, Technical
    Diffusion
    Packed towers
    Separation (Technology)
    Solution (Chemistry)
Extraction apparatus
  x Extractors (Chemical engineering)
  xx Chemical engineering—Apparatus and
    supplies
Extractors (Chemical engineering)
  See Extraction apparatus
Extracts *(Pharmacy, RS201.E9)*
  sa Pantocrine
  xx Materia medica
Extradition *(Direct) (International,
    JX4275-4399; Interstate, JF781)*
  sa Asylum, Right of
    Deportation
    Political crimes and offenses
  xx Asylum, Right of
    Criminal procedure
    Deportation
    International law
    Judicial assistance
    Political crimes and offenses
  — Cases
    sa Colombian-Peruvian asylum case
Extradural anesthesia
  See Peridural anesthesia
Extragalactic nebulae
  See Galaxies
Extraordinary remedies *(Direct)*
  sa Amparo (Writ)
    Certiorari
    Equitable remedies
    Habeas corpus
    Injunctions
    Mandamus
    Quo warranto
    Receivers
  x Special proceedings
  xx Actions and defenses
    Civil procedure
    Equitable remedies
    Equity
    Judicial review of administrative acts
    Remedies (Law)
Extrapyramidal tracts
  xx Central nervous system
Extrasensory perception
  x Cryptesthesia
    Perception, Extrasensory
  xx Clairvoyance

Psychical research
Second sight
— Juvenile literature
Extraterrestrial bases
sa Lunar bases
x Space construction engineering
xx Building
Civil engineering
Environmental engineering
Life support systems (Space
environment)
Outer space—Exploration
Extraterrestrial environment
See Space environment
Extraterrestrial life
See Life on other planets
Extraterrestrial radiation
sa Albedo
Cosmic rays
Solar radiation
Stars—Radiation
Terrestrial radiation
Van Allen radiation belts
x Space radiation
xx Radiation
Solar radiation
Space environment
Terrestrial radiation
Extraterritorial powers of municipalities
See Municipal powers and services beyond
corporate limits
Extraterritoriality
See Exterritoriality
Extravehicular activity (Manned space flight)
x Space vehicles—Extravehicular activity
Space walk
Walking in space
xx Manned space flight
Extravehicular space suits
x Extra-vehicular space suits
Full-pressure suits (Space environment)
Orbital space suits
Portable life support systems (Space
environment)
xx Pressure suits
Space suits
Extraversion
sa Introversion
Maudsley personality inventory
Self-disclosure
x Extroversion
xx Introversion
Psychology
— Testing
Extreme and mean ratio
See Golden section
Extreme unction *(BX2290)*
x Last rites (Sacraments)
Last sacraments
Unction, Extreme
xx Oil (in religion, folk-lore, etc.)
Sacraments
Extreme unction (Canon law)
Extremities, Lower *(QL950.7; QM549)*
— Abnormities and deformities *(RD781-9)*
— Blood-vessels
— — Surgery
— Diseases *(RC951)*
sa Extremities, Lower—Radiography
Paraplegia
— Fractures
Example under Fractures
— — Complications and sequelae
— Paralysis
See Paraplegia
— Radiography
xx Extremities, Lower—Diseases
— Wounds and injuries

Extremities, Upper
— Abnormities and deformities
— Blood-vessels
— — Radiography
— Diseases
sa Brachialgia
Extremities, Upper—Radiography
— Innervation
— Radiography
xx Extremities, Upper—Diseases
— Surgery *(RD557-9)*
— Wounds and injuries
Extremities (Anatomy) *(Comparative*
anatomy: general, QL950.7; muscles,
QL831; skeleton, QL821; Human
anatomy: general, QM548-9;
muscles, QM165; skeleton, QM117)
sa Arm
Leg
x Limbs (Anatomy)
xx Anatomy, Human
Bones
Skeleton
— Blood-vessels
— — Abnormities and deformities
— — Diseases
sa Extremities (Anatomy)—
Blood-vessels—Radiography
— — Radiography
xx Extremities (Anatomy)—
Blood-vessels—Diseases
— — Surgery
— Diseases
— — Diagnosis
— Fractures *(RD101)*
— Innervation
— Paralysis
See Tetraplegia
— Surgery
— Transplantation
— Wounds and injuries
Extrinsic evidence
See Evidence (Law)
Extroversion
See Extraversion
Extrusion (Metals) *(TS255)*
sa Compacting
Hydrostatic extrusion
x Metals—Extrusion
xx Compacting
Explosive forming
Extrusion process
Forging
Metal-working machinery
Metals
Extrusion (Plastics)
xx Extrusion process
Extrusion process *(TJ1450)*
sa Extrusion (Metals)
Extrusion (Plastics)
xx Manufacturing processes
Power presses
Exudates and transudates
xx Body fluids
Exudation (Botany)
sa Gums and resins
Plants—Transpiration
xx Plant physiology
Exultate Deo (Music)
See Psalms (Music)—81st Psalm
Exultate, justi (Music)
See Psalms (Music)—33d Psalm
Eye *(Comparative anatomy, QL949; Human*
anatomy, QM511; Physiology,
QP475-495)
sa Aqueous humor
Choroid
Ciliary body

Compound eye
Conjunctiva
Cornea
Crystalline lens
Eye (in religion, folk-lore, etc.)
Fundus oculi
Intraocular pressure
Iris (Eye)
Lacrimal organs
Optic chiasm
Optic nerve
Pupil (Eye)
Retina
Sclera
Uvea
Vision
Visual pigments
Vitreous humor
x Eyes
xx Anatomy, Comparative
Head
Ophthalmology
Optics, Physiological
Photoreceptors
Vision
Example under Sense-organs
— Abnormities and deformities *(QM691)*
sa Aphakia
Astigmatism
x Cyclopia
Monophthalmia
Example under Abnormalities (Animals);
Deformities
— Accommodation and refraction
(Pathology, RE925-939;
Physiology, QP476)
sa Optometry
Orthoptics
x Ametropia
Refraction of the eye
xx Optometrists
Optometry
— — Programmed instruction
— Adaptation
x Ocular adaptation
xx Adaptation (Physiology)
— Aging
— Anatomy
— Atlases
— Bacteriology *(QR171)*
Example under Bacteria, Pathogenic
— Blood-vessels
— — Diseases *(RE720)*
xx Eye—Diseases and defects
— — Radiography
xx Angiography
— Care and hygiene *(RE51)*
sa Eye—Protection
x Sight-saving
— Diseases and defects *(RE)*
sa Alport's syndrome
Amblyopia
Astigmatism
Behçet's disease
Blindness
Cataract
Chorioretinitis
Choroid—Diseases
Color-blindness
Conjunctiva—Diseases
Conjunctivitis
Cornea—Diseases
Crystalline lens—Diseases
Dispensaries, Ophthalmic and aural
Epitheliosis
Exophthalmos
Eye—Blood-vessels—Diseases
Eye—Radiography

Eye (Comparative anatomy, QL949; Human
        anatomy, QM511; Physiology,
        QP475-495)
    — Diseases and defects (RE)
      (Continued)
            Eye—Xerosis
            Eyelids—Diseases
            Eyestrain
            Glaucoma
            Heterophoria
            Hospitals, Ophthalmic and aural
            Hyperopia
            Iridocyclitis
            Iritis
            Light coagulation
            Myopia
            Norrie's disease
            Nystagmus
            Ocular manifestations of general
                diseases
            Oculomotor paralysis
            Ophthalmic nursing
            Ophthalmology
            Optic nerve—Diseases
            Retina—Diseases
            Retrolental fibroplasia
            Rhinosporidiosis
            Strabismus
            Therapeutics, Opthalmological
            Veterinary opthalmology
            Vision disorders
            Vitreous humor—Diseases
        xx Therapeutics, Ophthalmological
    — — Atlases
    — — Diagnosis
    — — — Atlases
    — — Early works to 1800
          See Ophthalmology—Early works
            to 1800
    — — Genetic aspects
    — — Homeopathic treatment (RX401-431)
    — — Movements
          sa Autokinesis
    — Examination (RE75-79)
          sa Blindness, Feigned
            Electroretinography
            Gonioscopy
            Ocular biomicroscopy
            Ophthalmoscope and
                ophthalmoscopy
            Perimetry
            Phorometer
            Skiascopy
          x Ophthalmometry
            Vision screening
          xx Optometrists
    — Foreign bodies (RE835)
          xx Eye—Surgery
          Example under Foreign bodies (Surgery)
    — Fungi
          x Fungous eye diseases
    — Hospitals
          See Hospitals, Ophthalmic and aural
    — Inflammation (RE96)
          sa Conjunctiva—Diseases
            Conjunctivitis
          x Ophthalmia
          xx Conjunctiva—Diseases
          Example under Inflammation
    — Innervation
    — Juvenile literature
    — Movements (Pathology, RE731;
          Physiology, QP476)
          sa Oculomotor paralysis
    — Muscles (Diseases, RE731)
          xx Muscles
    — — Anomalies (RE906)
    — — — Surgery
    — Paralysis (RE760)

    — Periodicals
          See Ophthalmology—Periodicals
    — Protection
          sa Safety goggles
            subdivisions Safety appliances and
                Safety measures under particular
                industries and occupations, e.g.
                Welding—Safety measures
          x Eye protection
          xx Accidents—Prevention
            Eye—Care and hygiene
    — Quotations, maxims, etc.
    — Radiography
          xx Eye—Diseases and defects
    — Surgery (RE80-87)
          sa Cornea—Tattooing
            Cornea—Transplantation
            Cyclodialysis
            Dacryocystorhinostomy
            Eye banks
            Eye—Foreign bodies
            Eyelids—Surgery
            Iridectomy
            Retina—Surgery
    — — Complications and sequelae
    — Syphilis (RE201.7.E9)
    — Transplantation
          Example under Transplantation of or-
            gans, tissues, etc.
    — Tumors (RC280.E9)
    — Wounds and injuries (RE831)
          sa Eye burns
    — Xerosis
          x Xerosis of the eye
          xx Eye—Diseases and defects
            Vitamin A deficiency
Eye, Instruments and apparatus for (RE)
      sa Tonometers
      x Apparatus, Ophthalmological
        Instruments, Ophthalmological
        Ophthalmological instruments and
            apparatus
      xx Scientific apparatus and instruments
        Surgical instruments and apparatus
Eye, Parietal (QL949)
      x Leydig's organ
        Parietal eye
        Pineal eye
      xx Pineal body
Eye (in religion, folk-lore, etc.)
      sa Evil eye
      x Folk-lore of the eye
      xx Evil eye
        Eye
        Religion, Primitive
Eye (Physiognomy)
      xx Physiognomy
Eye banks
      xx Cornea
        Eye—Surgery
Eye-bars (Manufacture, TS350; Materials of
        engineering, TA492.E)
      xx Bridges, Iron and steel
        Dies (Metal-working)
        Forging
        Punching machinery
Eye burns
      x Caustic eye injuries
      xx Eye—Wounds and injuries
Eye fatigue
      See Eyestrain
Eye in art (N8217.E9)
      xx Art
Eye in literature (PN56.E9)
      sa Evil eye
Eye protection
      See Eye—Protection
Eye-sockets (GN131)

    — Cancer
    — Diseases
          sa Eye-sockets—Radiography
    — Fracture
    — Radiography
          xx Eye-sockets—Diseases
    — — Atlases
    — Surgery
    — Tumors
Eyeglass frames
      xx Eyeglasses
Eyeglasses (RE940-981; Costume, GT2370)
      sa Contact lenses
        Eyeglass frames
        Lenses
        Sun glasses
      x Spectacles
      xx Opticians
        Optometrists
    — Juvenile literature
Eyeglasses in art
      xx Art
Eyegrounds
      See Fundus oculi
Eyelashes (QM488)
      xx Hair
Eyelets (Metal-work)
      x Grommets (Metal-work)
      xx Metal-work
Eyelid conditioning
      x Conditioned eyelid response
      xx Conditioned response
        Eyelids
Eyelids (Comparative anatomy, QL949;
        Human anatomy, QM511)
      sa Eyelid conditioning
        Meibomian glands
    — Diseases (RE121-155)
          sa Blepharoptosis
            Hordeolum
          x Blepharospasm
          xx Eye—Diseases and defects
    — Surgery
          xx Eye—Surgery
    — Tumors
Eyelin
Eyes
      See Eye
Eyes, Artificial (RE986)
      x Artificial eyes
      xx Prosthesis
Eyestrain (RE48; RE51)
      sa Asthenopia
      x Eye fatigue
      xx Asthenopia
        Eye—Diseases and defects
Eylau, Battle of, 1807
      See Preussisch-Eylau, Battle of, 1807
Eyo language
      See Yoruba language
Eyra (QL737.C2)
      xx Cats
Eysenck personality inventory
      See Maudsley personality inventory
Ezhavas (DS432.E95)
      xx Caste—India
        Ethnology—India
F-4 (Fighter planes)
      See Phantom (Fighter planes)
F-15 (Fighter planes)
      See Black widow (Fighter planes)
F-51 (Fighter planes)
      See Mustang (Fighter planes)
F-86 planes
      See Sabre (Jet fighter planes)
F-104 (Fighter plane)
      See Starfighter (Fighter plane)

F-105 fighter plane
See Thunderchief (Fighter planes)
F-111 (Fighter planes)
  x TFX (Fighter planes)
  xx Fighter planes
F centers
See Color centers
F.D. (Jet planes)
See Fairey Delta (Jet planes)
F layer
See F region
F.O.B. clause
  x "Free on board"
  xx Basing-point system
  Commercial law
  Contracts, Maritime
  Export sales
  Maritime law
  Risk
  Sales
  Shipment of goods
F region *(Indirect)* *(QC879)*
  x F layer
  xx Ionosphere
F.T.S.
See Federal Telecommunications System
F4D fighter plane
See Skyray fighter plane
F4U (Fighter planes)
See Corsair (Fighter planes)
F8F (Fighter planes)
See Bearcat (Fighter planes)
Faba bean
See Broad bean
Fables *(PN980-994; PZ8.2; PZ14.2; etc.)*
  sa Allegories
  Animals, Legends and stories of
  Bestiaries
  Folk-lore
  Gesta Romanorum
  Parables
  xx Allegories
  Animals, Legends and stories of
  Exempla
  Fiction
  Folk-lore
  Homiletical illustrations
  Legends
  Literature
  Parables
  Tales
  — Illustrations
  — Juvenile literature
Fables, Classical
  sa Fables, Greek
  Fables, Latin
Fables, French, ⌐German, Italian, etc.¬
Fables, Greek
  xx Fables, Classical
Fables, Latin
  xx Fables, Classical
Fabric pictures *(NK9315)*
  xx Collages
  Embroidery
  Needlework
Fabric shops *(Direct)*
  x Piece goods shops
  Yard goods shops
  xx Retail trade
  Textile industry and fabrics
Fabrica ecclesiae
See Church maintenance and repair
Fabrics, Bulked woven
See Textured woven fabrics
Fabrics, Coated
See Coated fabrics
Fabrics, Crease-resistant
See Crease-resistant fabrics

Fabrics, Fireproofing of
See Fireproofing of fabrics
Fabrics, Laminated
See Laminated fabrics
Fabrics, Nonwoven
See Nonwoven fabrics
Fabrics, Stretch woven
See Stretch woven fabrics
Fabrics, Synthetic
See Synthetic fabrics
Fabrics, Textured woven
See Textured woven fabrics
Fabrics, Waterproofing of
See Waterproofing of fabrics
Fabrique nationale automatic rifles
  x ABL automatic rifles
  FN automatic rifles
  xx Rifles
Façades *(Direct)* *(NA2840-2841)*
  xx Architecture—Details
  Exterior walls
Face *(Comparative anatomy, QL950.5;*
      Dermatology, RL87; Drawing,
      NC770; Human anatomy, QM535)
  sa Beauty, Personal
  Cheek
  Chin
  Mouth
  Nose
  Pathognomy
  Physiognomy
  xx Figure drawing
  Head
  Pathognomy
  Physiognomy
  — Abnormities and deformities *(RD763)*
  — Cancer
  — Diseases
    sa Facial pain
    Rosacea
  — — Atlases
  — — Diagnosis
  — — — Atlases
  — Expression
    See Facial expression
  — Fractures
  — Innervation
  — Muscles
    See Facial muscles
  — Surgery *(RD523-7)*
  — Wounds and injuries *(RD523)*
Face-amount certificate companies *(Direct)*
  x Capitalization societies
  Face-amount installment certificate
    companies
  Sociedades de capitalización
  Sociétés de capitalisation
  Sparversicherung
  xx Investment trusts
  Saving and thrift
Face-amount installment certificate companies
See Face-amount certificate companies
Face fly
  xx Flies
  — Control *(Indirect)*
Face in art
  xx Art
Face of God
See God—Face
Face urns
See Urns
Faceted classification
See Classification, Faceted
Facetiae
See Wit and humor
Facial bones
  xx Bones
  — Fractures

— Growth
Facial expression
  x Face—Expression
  xx Emotions
  Expression
  Physiognomy
  — Terminology
Facial manifestations of general diseases
  x Facial symptoms of general diseases
  xx Diagnosis, Differential
  — Atlases
Facial muscles
  x Face—Muscles
  xx Muscles
Facial nerve
  xx Nerves, Cranial
  — Surgery
Facial neuralgia
See Neuralgia, Facial
Facial pain
  sa Neuralgia, Facial
  xx Face—Diseases
  Head—Diseases
Facial paralysis
See Paralysis, Facial
Facial symptoms of general diseases
See Facial manifestations of general
    diseases
Facies, Stratigraphic
See Facies (Geology)
Facies (Geology) *(Indirect)*
  sa Lithofacies
  x Facies, Stratigraphic
  Stratigraphic facies
  xx Geology, Stratigraphic
  Petrology
  — Analysis
Facilitatory tract
See Reticular formation
Facility layout
See Plant layout
Facsimile, Radio
See Radio facsimile
Facsimile transmission *(TK6710)*
  sa Radio facsimile
  Ultrafax
  x Fax
  Remote facsimile duplicator
  Telefax
  xx Data transmission systems
  Electronics
  Telecommunication
Facsimiles
  sa Radio facsimile
  Reproduction of money, documents,
    etc.
  subdivision Facsimiles *under specific*
    subjects, e.g. Autographs—
    Facsimiles; Incunabula—Facsimiles;
    Posters—Facsimiles
Fact and law
See Law and fact
Factice, Tariff on
See Tariff on factice
Factor analysis
  sa Factorial experiment designs
  Psychology—Mathematical models
  x Analysis, Factorial
  Factorial analysis
  xx Correlation (Statistics)
  Mental tests
  Psychometrics
Factor tables *(QA51)*
  x Prime factors
  Tables, Mathematical
  xx Mathematics—Tables, etc.
  Numbers, Prime
  Numbers, Theory of

Factor tables (QA51) (Continued)
    Ready-reckoners
Factorial analysis
    See Factor analysis
Factorial designs
    See Factorial experiment designs
Factorial experiment designs
    x Factorial designs
    xx Experimental design
    Factor analysis
Factories (Direct) (Architecture,
    NA6400-6510; Building,
    TH4511-4541; Junior labor,
    HD6270; Model, HD7406-7510;
    Social conditions, HD6974; Women
    in, HD6068)
    sa Aeroplane factories
    Canneries
    Chemical plants
    Clothing factories
    Dairy plants
    Drug factories
    Employees' buildings and facilities
    Food processing plants
    Glass factories
    Macaroni factories
    Metallurgical plants
    Mills and mill-work
    Pilot plants
    Plant shutdowns
    Sugar factories
    Textile factories
    Workshops
    headings beginning with the word
        Factory
    x Factory buildings
    Industrial plants
    Mills (Buildings)
    Plants, Industrial
    xx Architecture
    Factory system
    Industrial buildings
    Mills and mill-work
    Technology
    Workshops
— Accounting (HF5686.M3)
    sa Manufactures—Accounting
    xx Manufactures—Accounting
— Air conditioning (TH7684.F2)
    sa Clean rooms
    Example under Air conditioning
— Clean rooms
    See Clean rooms
— Cost of operation (TS155)
— Design and construction (TH4511;
    TS155)
    sa Floor space, Industrial
    Plant layout
    x Factory construction
    Factory design
    Plant design
    Example under Structural design
— Electric equipment
    sa Industrial electronics
— Electronic equipment
    See Industrial electronics
— Equipment and supplies (TH4511)
    xx Industrial equipment
— Fires and fire prevention (TH9445)
    Example under Fire prevention
— Heating and ventilation (TH7392.M6;
    TH7684.F2)
    sa Clean rooms
    Exhaust systems
    Metallurgical plants—Heating and
        ventilation
    x Factories—Ventilation
    xx Factory sanitation

    Example under Heating; Ventilation
— Inspection
    See Factory inspection
— Law and legislation
    See Factory laws and legislation
— Layout
    See Plant layout
— Lighting (TH7975.F2; Electric lighting,
    TK4399.F2)
    x Factory lighting
    Industrial lighting
    Example under Lighting
— Location (T56)
    sa Industrial sites
    Industries, Location of
    x Location of factories
    xx Cities and towns—Planning
    Community development
    Industries, Location of
— Maintenance and repair
    See Plant maintenance
— Management
    See Factory management
— Noise
    See Industrial noise
— Protection
    sa Food industry and trade—Defense
        measures
    Gas industry—Defense measures
    Industry—Security measures
    Mineral industries—Defense
        measures
    Petroleum industry and trade—
        Defense measures
    Underground factories
    War damage, Industrial
    x Factory protection
    √ Industrial plant protection
    xx Buildings—Protection
    Police, Private
    War damage, Industrial
— — Equipment and supplies
— Safety appliances (HD7273)
    sa Employers' liability
    xx Employers' liability
— Safety measures
    xx Factory sanitation
    Industrial hygiene
    Example under Industrial safety
— Sanitation
    See Factory sanitation
— Taxation (Direct)
— Toilet facilities
    x Toilet facilities in factories
    xx Factory sanitation
    Water-closets
— Valuation (TH4511)
— Ventilation
    See Factories—Heating and
        ventilation
— Vocational guidance
Factories, Underground
    See Underground factories
Factoring (Finance)
    See Accounts receivable
Factors
    See Commission merchants
    Manufacturers' agents
Factors (Algebra) (Algebraic expressions,
    QA161; Numbers, QA242)
    sa Perfect numbers
    xx Algebra
    Mathematics
Factory and trade waste (Indirect)
    (TD897-9)
    sa Agricultural wastes
    Animal waste
    Brewery waste

    Canneries—Waste disposal
    Coal mine waste
    Coffee waste
    Coke industry—By-products
    Dairy waste
    Distilling industries—By-products
    Flock
    Flue gases
    Petroleum waste
    Pollution
    Potato waste
    Refuse and refuse disposal
    Saline water conversion plants—Waste
        disposal
    Tanning—Waste disposal
    Textile waste
    Waste disposal in the ground
    Waste disposal in the ocean
    Waste products
    Water reuse
    Wood-pulp industry—Waste disposal
    x Factory waste
    Industrial wastes
    Solid waste management
    Trades-waste
    Waste, Disposal of
    xx Plant engineering
    Pollution
    Refuse and refuse disposal
    Waste products
— Analysis
— Mathematical models
— Research (Direct)
    xx Research, Industrial
— — Mathematical models
Factory buildings
    See Factories
Factory canteens
    See Industrial feeding
Factory construction
    See Factories—Design and construction
Factory costs
    See Manufactures—Costs
Factory data acquisition systems, Automatic
    See Automatic data collection systems
Factory design
    See Factories—Design and construction
Factory housekeeping
    See Industrial housekeeping
Factory inspection (Indirect)
    (HD3656-3790)
    sa Employers' liability
    Industrial accidents
    Labor inspection
    Occupational diseases
    x Factories—Inspection
    Inspection of factories
    xx Employers' liability
    Factory laws and legislation
    Factory system
    Labor and laboring classes
    Labor inspection
    Occupations, Dangerous
Factory laws and legislation (Direct)
    (HD3621-7)
    sa Employers' liability
    Factory inspection
    Industrial accidents
    Industrial hygiene—Law and legislation
    Industrial safety—Law and legislation
    Labor laws and legislation
    x Factories—Law and legislation
    Law, Factory
    Law, Industrial
    xx Factory system
    Industrial hygiene—Law and legislation
    Industrial laws and legislation
    Industrial safety—Law and legislation

Labor laws and legislation
  Example under Legislation
Factory layout
  See Plant layout
Factory libraries *(Z675.F3)*
  x Libraries, Factory
  xx Labor and laboring classes—Education
Factory lighting
  See Factories—Lighting
Factory management *(Direct)* *(TS155)*
  sa Assembly-line methods
    Foremen
    Industrial engineering
    Industrial project management
    Office management
    Personnel management
    Plant engineering
    Production control
    Production engineering
    Quality control
    Stakhanov movement
  x Factories—Management
    Management of factories
    Shop management
  xx Industrial management
    Management
    Personnel management
  Note under Industrial management
  — Forms, blanks, etc.
  — Mathematical models
Factory monitoring systems, Automatic
  See Automatic data collection systems
Factory noise
  See Industrial noise
Factory outlets
  See Outlet stores
Factory press
  See Employees' magazines, handbooks, etc.
Factory protection
  See Factories—Protection
Factory sanitation *(TD895)*
  sa Contamination (Technology)
    Exhaust systems
    Factories—Heating and ventilation
    Factories—Safety measures
    Factories—Toilet facilities
    Food industry and trade—Sanitation
    Industrial housekeeping
  x Factories—Sanitation
  xx Industrial hygiene
    Plant engineering
    Sanitation
  — Law and legislation
    See Industrial hygiene—Law and
      legislation
Factory schools
  See Evening and continuation schools
Factory sites
  See Industrial sites
Factory system *(Indirect)* *(HD2351-6)*
  sa Children—Employment
    Factories
    Factory inspection
    Factory laws and legislation
    Woman—Employment
  xx Economics
    Industry—History
    Labor and laboring classes
    Machinery in industry
    Manufactures
Factory tours
  See Industrial tours
Factory waste
  See Factory and trade waste
Facts (Philosophy)
  xx Experience
    Philosophy

Faculties, Canonical
  See Faculties (Canon law)
Faculties (Canon law) *(BX1939.F3)*
  sa Absolution (Canon law)
  x Canonical faculties
    Faculties, Canonical
Faculties (Church of England)
Faculty (Education)
  See College teachers
    Educators
    Junior colleges—Faculty
    Municipal junior colleges—Faculty
    Teachers
    Universities and colleges—Faculty
    subdivision Faculty *under names of
      specific universities, etc., e.g.*
      Chicago. University—Faculty
Faculty advisors
  xx Personnel service in higher education
    Student counselors
Faculty integration *(Direct)*
  x Desegregation, Faculty
    Integration, Faculty
    Teachers—Integration
  xx School integration
Faculty participation in administration
  See Teacher participation in administration
Faculty-principal relationships
  See Teacher-principal relationships
Faculty work load
  See College teachers—Work load
    Teachers—Work load
Fados *(M1781-2)*
  xx Folk-songs, Portuguese
Faience
  See Pottery
Failure (in business)
  See Bankruptcy
Failure (Psychology)
  xx Success
  — Anecdotes, facetiae, satire, etc.
Failure (Psychology) in literature
Failure of metals
  See Metals—Fracture
Failure of solids
  See Fracture of solids
Failure to assist in emergencies
  See Assistance in emergencies
Fainting
  See Syncope (Pathology)
Fair buildings
  See Exhibition buildings
Fair employment practice
  See Discrimination in employment
Fair housing
  See Discrimination in housing
Fair Oaks, Battle of, 1862 *(E473.65)*
  x Seven Pines, Battle of, 1862
  xx Peninsular Campaign, 1862
Fair trade
  See Competition, Unfair
    Price maintenance
Fair trade (Tariff)
  See Free trade and protection
    Reciprocity
Fair use (Copyright) *(Direct)*
  sa Copyright and audio-visual education
    Copyright and electronic data
      processing
    Photocopying processes—Fair use
      (Copyright)
  x Copyright—Fair use
  xx Copyright infringement
Fairey Delta (Jet planes)
  x Delta (Jet planes)
    F.D. (Jet planes)
  xx Jet planes
    Supersonic planes

Fairies *(Folk-lore, GR550; Occultism,
    BF552)*
  sa Tengu
  x Elves
    Gnomes
    Goblins
  xx Folk-lore
    Superstition
  — Juvenile literature
Fairings *(Direct)*
  xx Fairs
    Souvenirs (Keepsakes)
Fairlane automobile *(TL215.F)*
  xx Ford automobile
Fairness *(BJ1533.F2)*
  sa Justice
  xx Conduct of life
    Ethics
    Justice
Fairs *(Charity fairs, HV544; Manners and
    customs, GT4580-4699; Markets,
    HF5470-5475; Street fairs, HF5481)*
  sa Agricultural exhibitions
    Bazaars, Charitable
    Bazaars, Oriental
    Exhibitions
    Fairings
    Markets
    subdivision Fairs *under names of
      countries, cities, etc., e.g.* Lyons—
      Fairs; *and names of particular fairs*
  x Trade fairs
  xx Exhibitions
    Foreign trade promotion
    Manners and customs
    Markets
  — Juvenile literature
  — Law and legislation *(Direct)*
Fairs in art
  xx Art
Fairy chess *(GV1451.2)*
  xx Chess problems
Fairy lamps *(NK5440.F3)*
  xx Lamps
Fairy plays *(Juvenile, PN6120.A4-5)*
  x Plays, Fairy
Fairy poetry *(PN6110.F3)*
  xx Fairies
    Fairy tales
    Poetry
Fairy poetry, English, [etc.] *(Direct)*
  x English [etc.] fairy poetry
  xx English [etc.] poetry
Fairy primrose *(SB413.P7)*
  xx Primroses
  — Varieties
Fairy tales *(Folk-lore, GR550; History and
    criticism, PN3437; Juvenile works,
    PZ8, PZ14, PZ24; Occultism,
    BF1552)*
  sa Folk-lore
  xx Children's literature
    Children's stories
    Fiction
    Folk literature
    Folk-lore
    Legends
    Literature
  — Anecdotes, facetiae, satire, etc.
  — Classification *(GR550; Z5983.F17)*

Fairy tales *(Folk-lore, GR550; History and criticism, PN3437; Juvenile works, PZ8, PZ14, PZ24; Occultism, BF1552)*
— Classification *(GR550; Z5983.F17)* (Continued)
  Here are entered lists of fairy tales, or their types, themes, motives, variants, etc., compiled with the aim of arranging them in certain clearly defined groups, also treaties discussing the principles upon which systems of classification may be based. Whenever desirable, additional entry is made under Folk-lore —Classifciation.
  sa Literature, Comparative—Themes, motives
  Plots (Drama, novel, etc.)
  x Fairy tales—Themes, motives
  Fairy tales—Types
  xx Literature, Comparative—Themes, motives
  Plots (Drama, novel, etc.)
— Dictionaries *(GR550)*
— Illustrations
— Indexes
— Moral and religious aspects
— Readers
  See Readers—Fairy tales
— Themes, motives
  See Fairy tales—Classification
— Types
  See Fairy tales—Classification
Faith *(Moral theology, BV4637; Theology, BT770-772)*
  Here are entered works on religious faith and doubt. Works on belief and doubt from the philosophical standpoint are entered under the heading Belief and doubt.
  sa Agnosticism
  Apostasy
  Atheism
  Evidence
  Faith and reason
  Hope
  Rule of faith
  Salvation
  Sanctification
  Skepticism
  Trust in God
  Truth (Theology)
  x Religious belief
  Theological belief
  xx Belief and doubt
  Christian life
  Credulity
  Justification
  Religion
  Spiritual life
  Theological virtues
  Theology, Doctrinal
  Trust in God
— Biblical teaching
— Early works to 1800
— History of doctrines
— Juvenile literature
— Meditations
— Psychology
  xx Psychology, Religious
— Quotations, maxims, etc.
Faith, Confessions of
  See Creeds
Faith, Profession of
  See Profession of faith
Faith, Rule of
  See Rule of faith

Faith, Thirteen articles of (Judaism)
  See Thirteen articles of faith (Judaism)
Faith (Buddhism)
  sa Doubt (Buddhism)
  xx Buddhist doctrines
Faith (Islam) *(BP166.78)*
  xx Islamic theology
  Salvation (Islam)
— Psychology
  xx Islam—Psychology
  Psychology, Religious
Faith (Judaism) *(BM729.F3)*
Faith and justification
  See Justification
Faith and reason *(BT50)*
  Here are entered works on the proper limits, differences, similarities, and interaction of the knowledge attained through faith and that attained through reason. Works more general in scope are entered under Philosophy and religion, or Religion and science.
  x Logic and faith
  Reason and faith
  xx Apologetics
  Faith
  Knowledge, Theory of (Religion)
  Philosophy and religion
  Rationalism
  Reason
  Religion and science
— History of doctrines
Faith-cure *(BT732.5; Medical aspects, RZ400-401)*
  sa Christian Science
  Healing gods
  Incubation (in religion, folk-lore, etc.)
  Jewish Science
  Magnetic healing
  Medicine, Magic, mystic, and spagiric
  Mental healing
  Miracles
  Therapeutics, Suggestive
  x Divine healing
  Faith healing
  Mind-cure
  Spiritual healing
  xx Christian Science
  Healing (in religion, folk-lore, etc.)
  Medicine and religion
  Mental healing
  Mind and body
  Subconsciousness
  Therapeutics, Suggestive
— Law and legislation *(Direct)*
  xx Medical laws and legislation
— Personal narratives
Faith-cure and spiritualism *(BF1275.F3)*
  x Spiritualism and faith-cure
Faith healing
  See Faith-cure
Faith, hope and charity
  See Theological virtues
Faith in literature
Fakirs *(BL2015.F2)*
  x Bhikshu
  Faqirs
  xx Asceticism
  Dervishes
  Yoga
Falaise Gap, Battle of, 1944
  xx World War, 1939-1945—Campaigns— Normandy
Falashas *(Ethiopia, DT380; Jews, DS135.E75)*
  x Fenjas
  Foggara
  Kaila

xx Jews
Falcidian law
  See Legitime
Falcon, Peregrine
  See Peregrine falcon
Falcon (Missile)
  x Air-to-air missiles
  Anti-aircraft missiles
  Falcon missiles
Falcon missiles
  See Falcon (Missile)
Falconry *(Indirect) (SK321)*
  sa Fowling
  x Hawking
  xx Fowling
  Game and game-birds
  Hunting
— Early works to 1800
— Juvenile literature
Falcons *(QL696.A2)*
  sa Bat falcon
  Gyrfalcon
  Lesser kestrel
  Peregrine falcon
  xx Birds of prey
— Behavior
Fali (African people)
  xx Ethnology—East Cameroon
Falicaine
  xx Anesthetics
Faliscan language *(PA2530)*
  xx Italic languages and dialects
Falkland Islands, Battle of the, 1914 *(D582.F2)*
  xx European War, 1914-1918—Naval operations
Fall
  See Autumn
Fall army-worms *(SB945.A8)*
  x Grassworm
  xx Army-worms
Fall of man *(BT710)*
  sa Good and evil
  Paradise
  Sin
  Sin, Original
  x Man, Fall of
  xx Man (Theology)
  Sin
  Sin, Original
  Temptation
  Theology, Doctrinal
— History of doctrines
Fall of man in literature
Fall River, Mass.
— Textile Workers' Strike, 1875
  x Fall River Strike, 1875
Fall River Indians
  See Pocasset Indians
Fall River Strike, 1875
  See Fall River, Mass.—Textile Workers' Strike, 1875
Fallacies (Logic) *(BC175)*
  x Errors, Logical
  Sophistry (Logic)
  xx Judgment (Logic)
  Logic
  Reasoning
Fallibility
  sa Errors
  xx Errors
  Philosophical anthropology
Falling-stars
  See Meteors
Fallopian tubes *(Comparative anatomy, QL881; Gynecology, RG421-433; Human anatomy, QM421)*
— Innervation

— Motility
  x Motility of the Fallopian tube
— Radiography
— Surgery
Fallot's tetralogy
  See Tetralogy of Fallot
Fallout, Radioactive
  See Radioactive fallout
Fallout shelters
  See Atomic bomb shelters
Fallow
  See Fallowing
Fallow deer
  xx Deer
Fallowing
  sa Shifting cultivation
     Soil fertility
  x Fallow
  xx Rotation of crops
     Soil fertility
     Tillage
Falls (Accidents) (Direct)
  xx Accidents
     Impact—Physiological effect
Falls Fight, 1676 (E83.67)
  xx King Philip's War, 1675-1676
Falsa demonstratio
  See False demonstration (Law)
False brinelling
  See Fretting corrosion
False certification (Direct)
  x Certification, False
  xx Forgery
     Fraud
     Legal documents
     Misconduct in office
False chinch bug
  xx Chinch-bugs
False demonstration (Law) (Direct)
  x Demonstration, False (Law)
     Falsa demonstratio
  xx Mistake (Law)
False imprisonment (Direct)
  sa Trials (False imprisonment)
  x Abuse of process
     Imprisonment, False
     Wrongful imprisonment
  xx Imprisonment
     Malicious prosecution
     Offenses against the person
     Torts
False killer whale
  x Killer whale, False
  xx Dolphins
     Whales
False Messiahs
  See Pseudo-Messiahs
False personation (Direct)
  sa Impersonating an officer
  x Impersonation (Law)
  xx Fraud
     Impersonation
False saffron
  See Safflower
False spider mites
  x Spider mites, False
False swearing
  See Perjury
False testimony (Direct)
  sa Perjury
  x False witness
  xx Criminal law
     Perjury
     Witnesses
False white rainbow
  See Fogbow
False wireworm (SB945.F)

False witness
  See False testimony
Falsehood
  See Truthfulness and falsehood
Falven language
  See Kipchak language
Fama publica
  See Reputation (Law)
Famagusta, Cyprus
  — Siege, 1571 (DS54.7)
Familial dysautonomia
  See Dysautonomia
Familial Mediterranean fever
  See Periodic peritonitis
Families of military personnel
  See Air Force wives
     Army wives
     Children of military personnel
     Marine Corps wives
     Navy wives
Families of royal descent
  See Royal descent, Families of
Familists (BX7575)
  x Family of Love (Religious sect)
Family (Direct) (HQ; Manners and
     customs, GT2420; Primitive,
     GN478-486)
  sa Aunts
     Birth order
     Broken homes
     Brothers and sisters
     Children
     Church work with families
     Clans and clan system
     Divorce
     Domestic education
     Domestic relations
     Eugenics
     Family life education
     Family life surveys
     Family size
     Fathers
     Fathers-in-law
     Foster day care
     Foster home care
     Grandparents
     Heredity, Human
     Home
     Jewish families
     Joint family
     Kinship
     Marriage
     Master and servant
     Matriarchy
     Mothers
     Mothers-in-law
     Negro families
     Only child
     Parent and child
     Polygamy
     Problem family
     Rural families
     Single-parent family
     Tribes and tribal system
     Twins
     Widows
     Woman
     subdivision Family relationships under
        classes of persons representing social
        or medical pathology, e.g.
        Schizophrenics—Family relationships
  x Patriarchy
  xx Domestic relations
     Home
     Kinship
     Marriage
     Matriarchy
     Sociology

     Woman
  — Anecdotes, facetiae, satire, etc.
  — Biblical teaching (BS680.F3)
     sa Fathers in the Bible
     Example under Bible—Theology
  — Caricatures and cartoons
  — Juvenile literature
  — Koranic teaching (BP134.F25)
  — Law
     See Domestic relations
  — Papal documents (BX2351)
  — Pictorial works
  — Prayer-books and devotions (BV255-9;
        Catholic, BX2170.F3)
        Here are entered prayer-books and de-
        votional exercises intended for
        family worship. For any denomina-
        tional aspect duplicate entry is
        made under the name of the
        denomination, with subdivision
        Prayer-books and devotions, e.g.
        Catholic Church—Prayer-books
        and devotions.
     x Family—Prayer-books and devotions
        —English
     Example under Prayer-books
  — — English
     See Family—Prayer-books and
        devotions
  — — French, [German, Italian, etc.]
  — Public opinion
  — Recreation
     See Family recreation
  — Religious life (BV4526)
     x Family worship
  — — Sermons
  — — — Outlines (BV4526)
  — Religious life (Buddhism)
     Example under Religious life (Buddhism)
  — Religious life (Hinduism) (BL1228.3.F3)
     Example under Religious life (Hinduism)
  — Religious life (Islam) (BP188.3.F3)
     Example under Religious life (Islam)
  — Religious life (Judaism)
     xx Jewish way of life
  — Research
     See Family research
  — Terminology
     See Kinship—Terminology
Family, Holy
  See Jesus Christ—Family
Family allowances (Direct) (Social welfare,
     HV697-700; Wages and social
     insurance, HD4925)
  sa subdivison Pay, allowances, etc. under
        armies, navies, etc., e.g. United
        States. Army—Pay, allowances,
        etc.; and subdivison Officials and
        employees—Salaries, allowances, etc.
        under countries, cities, etc.
  x Allowances, Family
     Child endowment
     Family endowment
     Family wages
  xx Cost and standard of living
     Economic security
     Mothers' pensions
     Wages
Family allowances (Inheritance and succession)
  See Widow's allowance
Family and communism
  See Communism and family
Family archives (Indirect) (CD)
     Forms and blanks for recording family
        data are entered under Family records.
  sa subdivision Archives under names of
        individual families
  x Archives, Family

Family archives *(Indirect)* *(CD)*
  (Continued)
    xx Family records
Family associations
  See Genealogy—Societies, etc.
Family budgets
  See Home economics—Accounting
Family case work
  See Family social work
Family corporations *(Direct)*
    x Family enterprises
    xx Close corporations
      Corporation law
  — Taxation *(Direct)*
Family courts
  See Domestic relations courts
    Juvenile courts
Family endowment
  See Family allowances
Family enterprises
  See Family corporations
Family farm operating agreements
  See Father-son farm operating agreements
Family farms *(Indirect)*
    xx Agriculture
      Farms
  — Management
    xx Farm management
Family festivals *(Direct)*
    xx Festivals
Family fun
  See Family recreation
Family group therapy
  See Family psychotherapy
Family histories
  See subdivsion Genealogy *under countries,
    cities, etc., e.g.* United States—
    Genealogy; Boston—Genealogy; *and
    individual families, e.g.* Lincoln
    family
Family in art
    xx Art
Family in literature
    xx Marriage in literature
Family law
  See Domestic relations
Family life education
    sa Counseling
      Finance, Personal
      Home economics
      Interpersonal relations
      Marriage counseling
      Sex instruction
    xx Conduct of life
      Family
      Family social work
      Marriage
  — Curricula
Family life surveys
    xx Family
      Home
      Social surveys
Family maintenance
  See Decedents' family maintenance
Family medicine
    xx Social medicine
  — Programmed instruction
Family of Love (Religious sect)
  See Familists
Family planning
  See Birth control
Family planning services
  See Birth control clinics
Family provision
  See Legitime
Family psychotherapy *(Indirect)*
    x Family group therapy
      Family therapy
    xx Group psychotherapy

— Cases, clinical reports, statistics
Family records *(CS24)*
    sa Family archives
  Note under Family archives
Family recreation *(GV182.8)*
    x Family fun
      Family—Recreation
    xx Amusements
      Games
      Recreation
Family research *(Direct)*
    Here are entered works on the history,
      programs, methodology, etc. of family
      studies from the sociological or ethno-
      logical point of view.
    x Family—Research
    xx Research
Family size
    sa Birth control
      Eugenics
    xx Birth control
      Eugenics
      Family
      Social problems
  — Juvenile literature
  — Mathematical models
Family social work *(Indirect)*
    sa Family life education
      Marriage counseling
    x Family case work
    xx Social case work
Family therapy
  See Family psychotherapy
Family wages
  See Family allowances
Family worship
  See Family—Religious life
Famine compact, 1765 *(HC275)*
Famines *(General, HC63; By country,
      HC95-695; Relief agencies, HV630)*
    sa subdivision Famines *under names of
      certain countries, e.g.* India—
      Famines; Ireland—Famines
    xx Food supply
      Starvation
Famous people, Voices of
  See Voices of famous people
Famous problems (in geometry)
  See Geometry—Problems, Famous
Fan (African people) *(Ethnology, GN655.F3)*
    x Fang (African people)
      Mpangwe
      Oshibas
      Pahouin
      Pahuins
      Pamue
      Pangwe
  — Legal status, laws, etc.
  — Religion *(BL2480.F)*
Fan-in-wing aircraft
    sa Short take-off and landing aircraft
      Vertically rising aeroplanes
    xx Aeroplanes
      Aeroplanes—Wings
      Lift fans
Fan language *(PL8167.F3)*
    x Makē language
      Pamue language
    xx Bantu languages
Fan magazines
  See Moving-pictures—Periodicals
Fan painting *(Direct)*
    xx Fans
      Painting
Fan painting, Japanese, [etc.]
    x Japanese [etc.] fan painting
Fan paintings *(Direct)*
    xx Paintings

Fan paintings, Japanese, [etc.] *(Direct)*
    x Japanese [etc.] fan paintings
Fanagalo
  See Fanakalo
Fanakalo *(PM7895.F3)*
    x Fanagalo
      Fanekalo
      Isi-Lololo
      Isi-Piki
      Kitchen Kaffir
      Pidgin Kaffir
    xx Languages, Mixed
Fanariots
  See Phanariots
Fanaticism *(Psychology, BF575.F16;
      Religion, BR114)*
    sa Asceticism
      Enthusiasm
    x Intolerance
Fancy dress
  See Costume
Fancy work *(TT740-897)*
    sa Appliqué
      Artificial flowers
      Beadwork
      Crocheting
      Drawn-work
      Embroidery
      Hooking
      Knitting
      Lace and lace making
      Needlework
      Netting
      Patchwork
      Pressed flower pictures
      Quilting
    xx Decoration and ornament
      Needlework
      Sewing
Fandangos
    Here are entered collections of fandangos
      for various mediums. Separate fandan-
      gos and collections of fandangos for a
      specific medium are entered under the
      heading followed by specification of
      medium.
Fanekalo
  See Fanakalo
Fanfare for Europe Festival
Fanfares *(M1270)*
    sa Bugle-calls
      Military calls
      Trumpet-calls
    xx Band music
      Military calls
      Military music
      Trumpet-calls
Fang (African people)
  See Fan (African people)
Fanning-mills *(S699)*
    x Winnowing-machines
    xx Agricultural machinery
      Threshing machines
Fans *(Direct)* *(Art, NK4870; Manners and
      customs, GT2150)*
    sa Fan painting
      Flabella
    xx Costume
Fans, Electric
  See Fans (Machinery)
Fans, Lift
  See Lift fans
Fans, Mechanical
  See Fans (Machinery)
Fans (in religion, folk-lore, etc.)
    x Folk-lore of fans
    xx Religion, Primitive

Fans (Machinery)
  sa Ducted fans
    Lift fans
    Punkas
  x Blowers
    Blowing-engines
    Exhausters
    Fans, Electric
    Fans, Mechanical
  xx Exhaust systems
    Heating
    Pneumatic-tube transportation
    Ventilation
  — Appraisal
    See Fans (Machinery)—Valuation
  — Automation
  — Noise
  — Problems, exercises, etc.
  — Testing
  — Valuation
    x Fans (Machinery)—Appraisal
Fans in art
  xx Art
Fantasia *(ML448)*
  xx Musical form
Fantastic, The (Aesthetics) *(BH301.F3)*
  xx Aesthetics
Fantastic fiction
  sa Ghost stories
    Science fiction
    Supernatural in literature
  xx Fiction
    Literature
    Supernatural in literature
Fantastic fiction, American, ⌐English, etc.⌐
    (Direct)
  x American ⌐English, etc.⌐ fantastic
    fiction
  xx American ⌐English, etc.⌐ fiction
Fantastic films
  sa Supernatural in moving-pictures
  x Moving-pictures—Fantastic films
  xx Feature films
    Supernatural in moving-pictures
Fantastic literature *(Direct)*
  sa Supernatural in literature
  xx Literature
    Supernatural in literature
Fantastic poetry *(Direct)*
  xx Poetry
Fantasy
  x Day dreams
  xx Autism
    Defense mechanisms (Psychology)
    Dreams
    Imagination
    Psychology, Pathological
    Visions
Fante language
  See Fanti language
Fanti language *(PL8167.F4)*
  sa Tshi language
  x Fante language
    Fantsi language
  xx Akan language
    Kwa languages
    Tshi language
  — Phonetic transcriptions
Fanti poetry *(Direct)*
Fantig dialect
  See Lonwolwol dialect
Fanting dialect
  See Lonwolwol dialect
Fantis *(DT511; GN655.F)*
  sa Akans (African people)
  xx Akans (African people)
    Ashantis
    Ethnology—Ghana

Fantsi language
  See Fanti language
Fanzines
  xx Little magazines
Faolite
  xx Corrosion and anti-corrosives
FAP (Computer program language)
  x Fortran assembly program (Computer
    program language)
  xx FORTRAN (Computer program
    language)
Faqirs
  See Fakirs
Far East
  See East (Far East)
Far Eastern question
  See Eastern question (Far East)
Far ultraviolet spectroscopy
  See Vacuum ultraviolet spectroscopy
Farad
  See Electric units
Faraday effect
  xx Magneto-optics
  — Charts, diagrams, etc.
Faradization
  See Electrotherapeutics
Farbpyramidentest
  See Color pyramid test
Farce *(PN1940-1949)*
  Here are entered works on the farce as a
    literary form. Collections of farces are
    entered under the heading Farces.
  sa Comedy films
    Commedia dell' arte
    Entremés
  x Comic literature
    Literature, Comic
  xx Burlesque (Literature)
    Comedy
    Drama
  — Technique
    xx Drama—Technique
Farces *(Collections, PN6120.F3)*
  sa Drolls
    French farces; German farces; Spanish
    farces; *and similar headings*
Farcy (Glanders)
  See Glanders
Farcy (Lymphangitis)
  See Epizootic lymphangitis
Fare, Bills of
  See Menus
Fareinistes *(BX7577.F3)*
  x Bonjours, Les frères
  xx Catholic Church in France
    Flagellants and flagellation
    Jansenists
Farewell sermons
  xx Sermons
Farey sequences
  See Series, Farey
Farey series
  See Series, Farey
Farinaceous products
  See Starch
Farm accounting
  See Agriculture—Accounting
Farm animals
  See Domestic animals
    Stock and stock-breeding
Farm buildings *(Indirect) (Architecture,*
    NA8200-8260)
  sa Agricultural engineering
    Architecture, Domestic
    Barns
    Cottages
    Dairy barns
    Farmhouses

    Livestock housing
    Poultry houses and equipment
    Sheep houses and equipment
    Silos
    Stables
    Swine houses and equipment
  x Architecture, Rural
    Buildings, Farm
    Rural architecture
  xx Agricultural engineering
    Agriculture
    Architecture
    Architecture, Domestic
    Housing, Rural
    Livestock housing
  — Air conditioning
  — Contracts and specifications *(Direct)*
    xx Building—Contracts and
      specifications
  — Fires and fire prevention
  — Heating and ventilation *(TH7392.F)*
    x Farm buildings—Ventilation
  — Lighting
    xx Electricity in agriculture
  — Maintenance and repair
  — Tables, calculations, etc.
  — Valuation *(HD1393)*
  — Ventilation
    See Farm buildings—Heating and
      ventilation
Farm corporations *(Direct)*
  x Agricultural corporations
    Corporation farms
    Farms, Incorporated
    Incorporated farms
  xx Agricultural laws and legislation
    Corporation law
    Corporations
    Farm management
Farm crops
  See Field crops
Farm design
  See Farm layout
Farm engines *(TJ712)*
  sa Agricultural engineering
  xx Agricultural machinery
    Engines
    Steam-engines
  — Testing
Farm equipment *(S675)*
  sa Agricultural engineering
    Agricultural implements
    Agricultural instruments
    Agricultural machinery
    Feeding—Equipment and supplies
    Gardening—Equipment and supplies
    Haying equipment
    Stock and stock-breeding—Equipment
      and supplies
  x Agricultural supplies
    Farm supplies
  xx Agricultural engineering
    Agricultural machinery
  — Automation
Farm equipment operators
  See Agricultural machinery operators
Farm families
  See Rural families
Farm forestry
  See Wood-lots
Farm houses
  See Farmhouses
Farm implements
  See Agricultural implements
Farm income *(Direct)*
  sa Agricultural prices
  xx Agricultural prices
    Agriculture—Economic aspects

Farm income *(Direct) (Continued)*
  Income
Farm input industries
  See Farm supply industries
Farm laborers
  See Agricultural laborers
Farm law *(Direct) (United States,*
  HD185-6)
    Here are entered compilations on the law
      of the farm for the use of farmers.
      Works of a more general character are
      entered under Agricultural laws and
      legislation.
  x Law, Farm
  xx Agricultural laws and legislation
Farm layout *(Indirect) (S563)*
  x Farm design
    Farm planning
    Farms—Design
  xx Farm management
Farm life *(Indirect) (Popular works, S521;*
  Sociology, HT421)
  sa Country life
    Farm life in literature
    Home economics, Rural
    Rural conditions
    Rural youth
    Sociology, Rural
  x Rural life
  xx Agriculture
    Country life
    Farmers
    Rural conditions
    Sociology, Rural
  — Anecdotes, facetiae, satire, etc.
      (PN6231.C65)
  — Juvenile literature
  — Pictorial works
  — Sounds
      See Farm sounds
Farm life clubs
  See Agricultural societies
Farm life in art
  xx Art
    Genre (Art)
    Peasants in art
Farm life in literature
  xx Country life in literature
    Farm life
    Peasants in literature
Farm life in moving-pictures
  xx Moving-pictures
Farm life in the Bible
  x Bible—Farm life
Farm location
  See Farms, Location of
Farm machinery
  See Agricultural machinery
Farm management *(Indirect) (S560-575)*
  sa Agriculture—Accounting
    Agriculture—Safety measures
    Collective farms—Management
    Family farms—Management
    Farm corporations
    Farm layout
    Farm mechanization
    Farm risks
    Farms, Size of
    State farms—Management
  x Farm organization
  xx Agriculture
    Agriculture—Economic aspects
    Farmers
    Farms
    Land tenure
    Management
  — Mathematical models
    x Agricultural production functions

Production functions, Agricultural
— Problems, exercises, etc.
— Records and correspondence
    x Farm records
— Research
    See Farm management research
— Simulation methods
— Vocational guidance
    See Farm management as a profession
Farm management as a profession *(Indirect)*
  (S562.5)
  x Farm management—Vocational
    guidance
  xx Agriculture as a profession
Farm management research
  x Farm management—Research
  xx Agricultural research
    Economic research
Farm manure *(S655)*
  sa Manure gases
    Manure handling
    Poultry manure
  x Barnyard manure
    Farm waste
    Farmyard manure
  xx Agricultural wastes
    Animal waste
    Fertilizers and manures
    Organic fertilizers
  — Storage
Farm manure as feed
Farm mechanics
  See Agricultural engineering
Farm mechanization *(Direct)*
  sa Electricity in agriculture
  x Agricultural mechanization
    Mechanization, Agricultural
    Mechanization in agriculture
    Mechanized farming
    Power farming
  xx Agricultural machinery
    Farm management
    Machinery in industry
  — Costs
  — Mathematical models
  — Underdeveloped areas
      See Underdeveloped areas—Farm
        mechanization
Farm mechanization, Cooperative *(Indirect)*
  sa Machine-tractor stations
  xx Agriculture, Cooperative
  — Law and legislation *(Direct)*
      xx Agricultural laws and legislation
Farm operating agreements, Father and son
  See Father-son farm operating agreements
Farm organization
  See Farm management
Farm ownership *(Direct)*
  sa Farm partnership
  xx Farms
    Home ownership
    Land tenure
Farm partnership *(Direct)*
  xx Farm ownership
    Partnership
Farm planning
  See Farm layout
Farm ponds *(Indirect)*
  x Ponds, Farm
  xx Ponds
  — Juvenile literature
Farm population
  See Rural population
Farm produce *(Indirect) (Agriculture, S-SB;*
  Economics, HD9000-9019)
  sa Field crops
    Food industry and trade
    Produce trade

Surplus agricultural commodities
  x Agricultural commodities
    Agricultural products
    Produce
  xx Agriculture
    Food
    Food industry and trade
    Produce trade
    Raw materials
— Advertising
    See Advertising—Farm produce
— Grading
    sa Vegetables—Grading
    Example under Grading
    Note under Agricultural processing
— Juvenile literature
— Labeling
— Marketing *(S571; Economics,*
    HD9000.6; HD9006, etc.)
    Here are entered works on the market-
      ing of farm produce from the point
      of view of the farmer.
    Works on the marketing of unproc-
      essed agricultural and other com-
      modities from the point of view of
      the commodity dealer are entered
      under the heading Produce trade.
    Works on the marketing of processed
      food products are entered under the
      heading Food industry and trade.
    sa Cooperative marketing of farm
      produce
    Dairy products—Marketing
    Fiars prices
    Marketing of livestock
    Roadside marketing
    Vegetable trade
    Vegetables—Marketing
    subdivision Marketing *under specific*
      commodities, e.g. Eggs—
      Marketing; Peach—Marketing
    x Agricultural marketing
    Food trade
    Marketing of farm produce
    xx Agricultural prices
    Agriculture—Economic aspects
    Prices
    Vegetable trade
    Example under Marketing
    Notes under Food industry and trade;
      Produce trade
— — Outlines, syllabi, etc.
— — Research
— — Statistical methods
— Packaging
— Precooling
    See Precooling
— Processing
    See Agricultural processing
— Research
— Storage *(SB129; Economics, HD9000.9)*
    sa Cold storage
    Food—Storage
    Grain—Storage
    Vegetables—Storage
    subdivision Preservation *under food*
      products, e.g. Butter—
      Preservation; Eggs—Preservation;
      and subdivision Storage *under*
      specific commodities, e.g. Beans—
      Storage
    x Stored products
    xx Cold storage
    Food—Storage
    Example under reference from Storage
— — Diseases and injuries
    sa Citrus fruits—Storage—Diseases
      and injuries

Food storage pests
    Grain—Storage—Diseases and
      injuries
    Vegetables—Storage—Diseases
      and injuries
    x Storage and transportation
      diseases and injuries
    xx Agricultural pests
    Fungi in agriculture
    Insects, Injurious and beneficial
— Surpluses
    See Surplus agricultural commodities
— Tariff
    See Tariff on farm produce
— Taxation *(Direct)* *(HD9000.8-9019)*
    xx Agriculture—Taxation
— Transportation *(S571)*
    sa Fruit—Transportation
    Plant quarantine
    Poultry—Transportation
    Vegetables—Transportation
    xx Plant quarantine
    Example under Shipment of goods;
      Transportation
— — Diseases and injuries
    x Storage and transportation
      diseases and injuries
    xx Agricultural pests
    Fungi in agriculture
    Insects, Injurious and beneficial

GEOGRAPHIC SUBDIVISIONS

— ₍local subdivision₎
Farm production quotas *(Direct)*
    x Agricultural production quotas
    Cropland adjustment program
    xx Agricultural administration
    Agricultural laws and legislation
    Agriculture and state
— Public opinion
Farm records
    See Farm management—Records and
      correspondence
Farm rents *(Direct)*
    x Rent, Farm
    xx Agriculture—Economic aspects
    Farm tenancy
    Farms
    Rent
Farm risks
    x Risks, Farm
    xx Agriculture
    Farm management
    Insurance, Agricultural
Farm roads *(Direct)* *(TE229.2)*
    x Roads, Farm
    xx Agricultural engineering
    Private roads
Farm shops *(Indirect)* *(S676)*
    sa Agricultural machinery—Maintenance
      and repair
    x Farm workshops
    xx Machine-shops
    Workshops
— Safety measures
Farm size
    See Farms, Size of
Farm sounds
    x Farm life—Sounds
    Farms—Sounds
    xx Country sounds
    Sounds
Farm supplies
    See Farm equipment
Farm supply industries *(Direct)* *(HD9475)*
    sa Agricultural machinery

specific farm supply industries, e.g.
    Agricultural machinery—Trade and
      manufacture; Fertilizer industry;
      Flour and feed trade
    x Farm input industries
    xx Agricultural industries
Farm surpluses
    See Surplus agricultural commodities
Farm tenancy *(Direct)*
    sa Farm rents
    Landlord and tenant
    Métayer system
    x Leases, Usufructuary
    Tenant farming
    Usufructuary leases
    xx Contracts, Agricultural
    Farms
    Land tenure—Law
    Landlord and tenant
— Economic aspects *(Direct)* *(HD1511)*
    xx Agriculture—Economic aspects
    Land tenure
— — United States
    sa Share-cropping

GEOGRAPHIC SUBDIVISIONS

— Great Britain
    sa Crofters
Farm tenancy (Greek law)
Farm tools
    See Agricultural implements
Farm trailers
    xx Agricultural machinery
    Trailers
Farm waste
    See Animal waste
    Farm manure
Farm wood-lots
    See Wood-lots
Farm woodlands
    See Wood-lots
Farm workers
    See Agricultural laborers
Farm workshops
    See Farm shops
Farm youth exchange project, International
    See International farm youth exchange
      project
Farmers *(Indirect)*
    sa Agricultural laborers
    Farm life
    Farm management
    Peasantry
    Rural population
    xx Agriculture
    Agriculturists
    Country life
    Peasantry
    Sociology, Rural
Note under Rural population
— Biography
— Correspondence, reminiscences, etc.
— Language (New words, slang, etc.)
— Pensions *(Direct)*
    sa Collective farms—Pensions
— Political activity
    xx Politics, Practical
— Prayer-books and devotions
— — English, ₍French, German, etc.₎
— Religious life *(BV4596.F)*
— Supplementary employment
— — Personal narratives
Farmers as consumers *(Direct)*
    xx Consumers
Farmers' cooperatives
    See Agricultural cooperative credit
      associations
    Agriculture, Cooperative

Farmers' institutes *(Indirect)*
    x Institutes, Farmers'
    xx Agricultural education
    Agricultural extension work
    Agricultural societies
    Agriculture
Farmers' organizations
    See Agricultural societies
Farmers' wives *(Direct)*
    xx Wives
    Women in agriculture
— Employment *(Direct)*
Farmhouses *(Indirect)* *(Architecture,*
    NA8210; Building, TH4920)
    x Farm houses
    xx Architecture, Domestic
    Country homes
    Dwellings
    Farm buildings
— Air conditioning
— Heating and ventilation
Farming
    See Agriculture
Farming, Dry
    See Dry farming
Farming, Part-time
    See Part-time farming
Farming of taxes
    See Taxes, Farming of
Farming on shares
    See Métayer system
    Share-cropping
Farmington Mine Disaster, Farmington,
    W.Va., 1968
Farmington plan
    xx Acquisitions, Cooperative (Libraries)
    Acquisitions (Libraries)
    Book selection
    Library cooperation
Farms *(Indirect)* *(S560-575; Large,*
    HD1471; Small, HD1476)
    sa Family farms
    Farm management
    Farm ownership
    Farm rents
    Farm tenancy
    Plantations
    Ranches
    Sheep ranches
    State farms
    xx Agriculture
    Land
    Real property
— Accounting
    See Agriculture—Accounting
— Classification
— Design
    See Farm layout
— Recreational use *(Direct)*
    sa Dude ranches
    xx Agriculture—Economic aspects
    Outdoor recreation
    Tourist trade
    Vacations
— Sounds
    See Farm sounds
— Valuation *(Direct)* *(HD1393)*
    x Land valuation
    Land—Valuation
    Valuation of land
Farms, Experimental
    See Agricultural experiment stations
Farms, Incorporated
    See Farm corporations
Farms, Location of *(Indirect)*
    x Farm location
    Location of farms
    xx Agriculture

Farms, Location of *(Indirect)*
  (Continued)
    Land
Farms, Size of *(Indirect)*
  sa Economies of scale
  x Farm size
    Size of farms
  xx Agriculture—Economic aspects
    Farm management
Farmville, Va., Battle of, 1865 *(E477.67)*
Farmyard manure
  See Farm manure
Faro
  xx Gambling
Faroese ballads and songs *(Collections, PT7594; History, PT7590)*
  sa Ballads, Faroese
    Folk-songs, Faroese
Faroese dialect *(PD2483)*
  xx Icelandic and Old Norse languages
    Scandinavian languages
  — Texts *(PD2483)*
    xx Icelandic and Old Norse literature
Faroese literature *(PT7581-7599)*
  xx Scandinavian literature
Faroese philology
Faroese poetry *(Collections, PT7594; History, PT7590)*
Farrapos
  See Rio Grande do Sul, Brazil (State)—History—Revolution of the Farrapos, 1835-1845
Farriery
  See Horses
    Horseshoeing
    Veterinary medicine
    Veterinary surgery
Farsightedness
  See Hyperopia
Farthingale
  See Crinoline
Fasces
  xx Emblems
    Rome—Antiquities
    Rome—Officials and employees—Medals, badges, decorations, etc.
Fasciae (Anatomy) *(QM563)*
  xx Connective tissues
Fasciations
  See Abnormalities (Plants)
Fasciola and fascioliasis
  x Fascioliasis
    Fasciolosis
    Liver-rot
  xx Distomatosis
    Liver flukes
Fascioliasis
  See Fasciola and fascioliasis
Fasciolosis
  See Fasciola and fascioliasis
Fascism *(Indirect)* *(JC481; Italy, DG571)*
  sa Corporate state
    National socialism
    Synarchism
    Totalitarianism
  x Neo-fascism
  xx Authoritarianism
    Collectivism
    Corporate state
    National socialism
    Synarchism
    Totalitarianism
  — Argentine Republic
    x Justicialism
      Peronism
  — Brazil
    x Integralismo
  — Germany

Here are entered works on post-World War II fascist and neo-Nazi movements. Works on fascism in Germany during the Nazi regime are entered under the heading National socialism.
    x Neo-Nazism
    xx National socialism
  — Italy
    sa Partito nazionale fascista
Fascism and literature
  x Literature and fascism
  xx Politics in literature
Fascism and the Catholic Church
  x Catholic Church and fascism
  xx Church and state—Catholic Church
Fashion *(GT500-2370; TT500-645)*
  sa Clothing and dress
    Costume
    Costume design
    Dressmaking
    Dressmaking—Pattern books
    Men's clothing
    Tailoring
  x Style in dress
  xx Clothing and dress
    Costume
  — Authorship
    See Fashion writing
  — Pictorial works
  — Quotations, maxims, etc.
Fashion and art *(GT529.A7)*
  x Art and fashion
Fashion as a profession *(TT507)*
  sa Costume design—Vocational guidance
    Costume designers
    Fashion writing as a profession
  xx Clothing and dress
    Clothing trade
  — Juvenile literature
Fashion books
  See Dressmaking—Pattern books
Fashion design
  See Costume design
Fashion designers
  See Costume designers
Fashion drawing *(TT509)*
  xx Drawing
Fashion models
  See Models, Fashion
Fashion photography *(TR679)*
  x Photography, Fashion
  xx Photography, Advertising
Fashion shows *(TT502)*
  x Style shows
  xx Advertising—Clothing and dress
    Clothing and dress
Fashion writing *(TT503.5)*
  sa Newspapers—Sections, columns, etc.—Fashion
  x Fashion—Authorship
  xx Authorship
  — Vocational guidance
    See Fashion writing as a profession
Fashion writing as a profession
  x Fashion writing—Vocational guidance
  xx Fashion as a profession
  — Juvenile literature
Fashionable society
  See Upper classes
Fashoda Crisis, 1898
  xx Sudan—History—1862-1899
Fast-day menus
  See Lenten menus
Fast-day sermons *(BV4270)*
  xx Fasts and feasts
    Sermons

Fast days
  See Fasts and feasts
Fast neutrons
  xx Neutrons
  — Capture *(QC721)*
  — Measurement *(QC721)*
  — Spectra *(QC721)*
  — — Charts, diagrams, etc.
Fast pulsed reactors
  See Pulsed reactors
Fast reactors
  sa Breeder reactors
  xx Nuclear reactors
Fast-response data processing
  See Real-time data processing
Fasteners
  See Fastenings
    Zippers
Fastenings *(Trade, HD9999.F3-33)*
  sa Bolts and nuts
    Buttons
    Clasps
    Hooks and eyes
    Keys and keyways (Machinery)
    Locks and keys
    Pins (Engineering)
    Retaining rings
    Rivets and riveting
    Screws
    Sealing (Technology)
    Steel straps
    Zippers
  x Fasteners
    Snap fastenings
  xx Joints (Engineering)
    Manufacturing processes
  — Drawing
    See Fastenings—Drawings
  — Drawings
    x Fastenings—Drawing
    xx Mechanical drawing
  — Juvenile literature
  — Standards *(Direct)*
  — Tables, calculations, etc.
Faster reading
  See Rapid reading
Fasting *(RM226-8; Asceticism, BV5055)*
  sa Fasts and feasts
  x Abstinence
  xx Asceticism
    Penance
  — Dispensations *(Catholic eucharist, BX2225)*
    xx Catholic Church—Discipline
      Dispensations
Fasting (Canon law) *(BX1939.F35)*
Fasting (Hinduism) *(BL1215.F3)*
  xx Asceticism—Hinduism
Fasting (Islam) *(BP179)*
  xx Pillars of Islam
  — Koranic teaching *(BP134.F3)*
Fasting (Judaism)
  xx Asceticism—Judaism
Fastnachtspiele
  See Carnival plays
Fastness of color (Textiles)
  See Colorfastness (Textiles)

Fasts and feasts *(Indirect) (Christianity, BV30-135; Church calendar, CE81; Comparative religion, BL590; Manners and customs, GT3930-4995)*

Here without subdivision are entered works on religious fasts and feasts in general and on Christian fasts and feasts; also general works on fasts and feasts in the United States. The heading may also be divided by religious body or non-Christian religion, *e.g.* Fasts and feasts—Catholic Church, [Judaism, etc.]

sa Agape
  All Saints' Day
  All Souls' Day
  Ascension Day
  Assumption of the Blessed Virgin Mary, Feast of the
  Boy-bishop
  Candlemas
  Christmas
  Chronology, Ecclesiastical
  Church calendar
  Church year
  Easter
  Elijah the Prophet's Day
  Ember days
  Epiphany
  Fast-day sermons
  Festival-day sermons
  Festivals
  Good Friday
  Holidays
  Holy Innocents, Feast of the
  Immaculate Conception, Feast of the
  Jesus Christ the King, Feast of
  Lent
  Love feasts
  Mary, Virgin—Feasts
  Maundy Thursday
  Palm Sunday
  Pentecost festival
  Presentation of the Blessed Virgin Mary, Feast of the
  Quinquagesima Sunday
  Sacred Heart, Feast of the
  Sacred meals
  Sunday
  Thanksgiving Day
  Vigils (Liturgy)
  Visitation festival
  subdivision Festivals, etc. *under names of cities, towns, etc.; and subdivision* Religious life and customs *under names of countries, states, cities, etc., e.g.* Germany—Religious life and customs
x Bible—Festivals
  Church festivals
  Ecclesiastical fasts and feasts
  Fast days
  Feasts
  Heortology
  Holy days
  Religious festivals
xx Catholic Church
  Christian antiquities
  Church calendar
  Days
  Fasting
  Festivals
  Holidays
  Liturgics
  Rites and ceremonies
  Sacred meals
  Theology, Practical

Note under Church year
— Buddhism *(Direct)*
  sa names of individual fasts and feasts, e.g. Uposatha Day
  x Buddhist fasts and feasts
— Catholic Church, [Church of England, Presbyterian Church, etc.]
  x Catholic Church [Church of England, Presbyterian Church, etc.]—Fasts and feasts
  Note under Fasts and feasts
— Egyptian religion
  x Egyptian fasts and feasts
— Greek religion
  sa Religious calendars—Greek religion
  x Greek fasts and feasts
— Hinduism *(BL1212)*
  sa names of individual fasts and feasts, e.g. Dasara
  x Fasts and feasts, Hindu
    Hindu fasts and feasts
  xx Hinduism
—— Juvenile literature
— Islam *(BP186)*
  sa names of individual fasts and feasts, e.g. Ramadan
  x Fasts and feasts, Islamic
    Fasts and feasts, Muslim
    Islamic fasts and feasts
    Muslim fasts and feasts
  xx Islamic religious practice
— Jews
  See Fasts and feasts—Judaism
— Judaism
  sa Festival-day sermons, Jewish
    Religious calendars—Judaism
    Sefirah period
    names of individual fasts and feasts, e.g. Rosh ha-Shanah; Sukkoth
  x Fasts and feasts, Jewish
    Fasts and feasts—Jews
    Festivals—Jews
    Holidays, Jewish
    Holidays—Jews
    Jewish fasts anf feasts
    Jewish holidays
    Jews—Fasts and feasts
    Jews—Festivals
  xx Judaism
  Note under Fasts and feasts
—— Juvenile literature
—— Pictures, illustrations, etc.
— Meditations
— Samaritan religion *(BM970)*
  x Samaritan fasts and feasts
  xx Samaritans—Religion
Fasts and feasts, Hindu, [Islamic, Jewish, etc.]
  See Fasts and feasts—Hinduism, [Islam, Judaism, etc.]
Fasts and feasts, Muslim
  See Fasts and feasts—Islam
Fasu language
  xx Papuan languages
Fat *(Physiological chemistry, QP751)*
  Here is entered material on fat in its relation to the animal organism. Works on the technological aspects of fats in general are entered under the heading Oils and fats.
  sa Adipocere
    Corpulence
    Fat metabolism
    Lipemia
    Low-fat diet
    Steapsin
  x Fats
  xx Absorption (Physiology)
    Physiological chemistry

Note under Oils and fats
Fat embolism
  xx Embolism
Fat metabolism *(QP751)*
  xx Fat
    Metabolism
Fat necrosis *(RB149)*
Fat-rumped sheep
Fat-tailed sheep *(SF373.F3)*
Fat tissue
  See Adipose tissues
Fatalism
  See Fate and fatalism
Fate and fatalism *(Ethics, BJ1460-1468; Philosophy, BD411; Religion, BL235)*
  sa Free will and determinism
    Necessity (Philosophy)
    Occasionalism
    Predestination
  x Destiny
    Fatalism
  xx Fortune
    Necessity (Philosophy)
    Philosophy
— Quotations, maxims, etc.
Fate and fatalism (Islam) *(BP166.3)*
  sa Free will and determinism (Islam)
    Predestination (Islam)
    Trust in God (Islam)
  xx Free will and determinism (Islam)
    Islamic theology
Fate and fatalism in literature
Fate language
  See Efate language
Father and child
  sa Father-separated children
    Fathers and daughters
    Fathers and sons
  x Child and father
    Father-child relationship
  xx Parent and child
— Pictorial works
—— Juvenile literature
Father and son farm operating agreements
  See Father-son farm operating agreements
Father-child relationship
  See Father and child
Father-in-law
  See Fathers-in-law
Father-search in literature *(PN57.F25)*
  xx Recognition in literature
Father-separated children *(BF723.F3)*
  sa Broken homes
  x Children separated from their fathers
  xx Child study
    Children of divorced parents
    Father and child
    Parent and child
    Single-parent family
Father-son farm operating agreements
  x Family farm operating agreements
    Farm operating agreements, Father and son
    Father and son farm operating agreements
Fatherhood (Theology)
  sa God—Fatherhood
  xx Theology, Doctrinal
Fatherland (Theology)
  See Homeland (Theology)
Fathers *(Eugenics, HQ756)*
  sa Father's Day
    Grandparents
    Parent and child
  xx Eugenics
    Family
    Parent and child

Fathers *(Eugenics, HQ756)* *(Continued)*
  — Anecdotes, facetiae, satire, etc.
  — Biblical teaching
    See Fathers in the Bible
  — Biography
  — — Juvenile literature
  — Caricatures and cartoons
  — Juvenile literature
  — Literary collections
  — Poetry
  — Quotations, maxims, etc.
  — Religious life
Fathers, Apostolic
  See Apostolic Fathers
Fathers, Unmarried
  See Unmarried fathers
Fathers and daughters
  x Daughters and fathers
  xx Daughters
    Father and child
    Girls
  — Anecdotes, facetiae, satire, etc.
  — Juvenile literature
Fathers and sons
  x Sons and fathers
  xx Boys
    Father and child
Fathers and sons in literature
Father's Day *(HQ756)*
  xx Fathers
  — Exercises, recitations, etc.
    Example under Recitations
  — Songs and music
Fathers-in-law
  x Father-in-law
  xx Family
Fathers in literature
  sa Fathers in the Bible
Fathers in the Bible *(BS579.F3)*
  x Bible—Fathers
    Fathers—Biblical teaching
  xx Bible—Biography
    Family—Biblical teaching
    Fathers in literature
Fathers of the church *(Collective biography,*
    BR1705; Patrology, BR60-67)
    Here are entered works on the life and
    thought of the "Fathers of the
    church," a term that embraces the
    leaders of the early church to the time
    of Gregory the Great in the West and
    John of Damascus in the East. Occa-
    sionally, especially in comprehensive
    works, this time limit has not been
    strictly observed.
    Works on the writings of these men are
    entered under the heading Christian
    literature, Early.
  sa Apostolic fathers
    Christian literature, Early
    Church history—Primitive and early
      church, ca. 30-600
    Doctors of the church
    Martyrs
    Persecution
    Saints
  x Church fathers
    Patristics
    Philosophy, Patristic
  xx Christian biography
    Christian literature, Early
    Church history
    Church history—Primitive and early
      church, ca. 30-600
    Saints
  Note under Christian literature, Early
  — Bio-bibliography *(Z7791)*
  — Biography

  — Concordances
    See Christian literature, Early—
      Concordances
  — Dictionaries
Fathers of the church, Armenian, ⌐Ethiopic,
    Greek, Latin, etc.⌐
Fathers of the Good Death
  See Camillians
Fatigue *(Educational hygiene, LB3431;*
    Educational psychology, LB1075;
    Muscle, QP321; Psychology, BF481)
  sa Rest
    Rest periods
  x Exhaustion
    Weariness
  xx Biological physics
    Occupational diseases
    Physiology
    Rest
Fatigue, Mental *(Mental hygiene, RA788;*
    Nervous diseases, popular works,
    RC351; Physiology, QP421;
    Psychology, BF481)
  sa After-images
    Boredom
    Brain—Anemia
    Inefficiency, Intellectual
    Neurasthenia
    Overpressure (Education)
  x Mental exhaustion
    Mental fatigue
    Mental overwork
    Overwork, Mental
  xx Attention
    Brain—Anemia
    Brain—Diseases
    Inefficiency, Intellectual
    Mental hygiene
    Mind and body
    Neurasthenia
    Psychology, Pathological
    Psychology, Physiological
    Work
Fatigue of airframes
  See Airframes—Fatigue
Fatigue of concrete
  See Concrete—Fatigue
Fatigue of materials
  See Materials—Fatigue
Fatigue of metals
  See Metals—Fatigue
    subdivision Fatigue *under particular*
      metals, e.g. Steel—Fatigue
Fatigue of rocks
  See Rocks—Fatigue
Fatigue of welded joints
  See Welded joints—Fatigue
Fatigue testing
  See Fatigue testing machines
    Materials—Fatigue
Fatigue testing machines *(TA413)*
  x Fatigue testing
  xx Metals—Fatigue
    Testing-machines
  — Automatic control *(TA413)*
Fatimites *(DT173)*
  xx Caliphs
    Egypt—History—640-1250
    Ismailites
Fats
  See Fat
    Oils and fats
Fatty acid metabolism
  xx Acids, Fatty
    Metabolism
Fatty acid synthesis
  xx Acids, Fatty
    Biosynthesis

Fatty acids
  See Acids, Fatty
Fatty acids, Essential
  See Essential fatty acids
Fatty degeneration
  See Degeneration, Fatty
Fatty heart
  See Heart, Fatty
Fatty liver *(RC848.F3)*
  xx Degeneration, Fatty
    Liver—Diseases
Fatty tissue
  See Adipose tissues
Fatwās
  x Futwas
  xx Advisory opinions (Islamic law)
    Islamic law—Sources
Fault location (Electrical engineering)
  See Electric fault location
Fault troughs
  See Grabens (Geology)
Faultfinding *(BJ1535.F3)*
Faults (Geology) *(QE606)*
  sa Nappes (Geology)
    Rifts (Geology)
  xx Geology, Structural
Fauna
  See Cave fauna
    Desert fauna
    Forest fauna
    Fresh-water fauna
    Island fauna
    Jungle fauna
    Marine fauna
    Zoology
Fauna, Prehistoric
  See Paleontology
Fauves (School of art)
  See Fauvism
Fauvism *(Direct)*
  x Fauves (School of art)
  xx Art, Modern—20th century
    Modernism (Art)
    Painting, French
    Post-impressionism (Art)
Favism
  xx Allergy
    Hemolytic anemia
Favored nation clause *(HF1721-1733)*
  x Most favored nation clause
  xx Commercial policy
    Commercial treaties
    Free trade and protection
    Reciprocity
    Tariff
Favorites, Royal *(D107.7)*
  sa Courts and courtiers
    Fools and jesters
    subdivision Court and courtiers *under*
      names of countries, e.g. France—
      Court and courtiers
  x Court favorites
    Royal favorites
  xx Courts and courtiers
Favus *(RL770)*
Fawning
  See Toadyism
Fax
  See Facsimile transmission
Fayence
  See Pottery
Faye's comet *(QB723.F2)*
Fayum portraits
  See Mummy portraits
Fca language
  See Balante language

Fear *(Child study, BF723.F4; Psychology, BF575.F2)*
>   *sa* Agoraphobia
>   Anxiety
>   Bashfulness
>   Claustrophobia
>   Courage
>   Horror
>   Hysteria (Social psychology)
>   Panic
>   Peace of mind
>   Phobias
>   School phobia
>   Stage fright
>   Timidity
>   *xx* Anxiety
>   Courage
>   Emotions
>   Horror
>   Nervous system—Diseases
>   — Juvenile literature

Fear (Child psychology)
>   *xx* Child study

Fear in literature
>   *sa* Hypochondria in literature
>   *xx* Emotions in literature

Fear of flying
>   *x* Flying, Fear of
>   *xx* Aeronautics—Psycholgy

Fear of God
>   *x* Fear of the Lord
>   God—Fear
>   God, Fear of
>   *xx* Christian ethics
>   Gifts, Spiritual
>   God
>   God—Worship and love
>   — Biblical teaching

Fear of God (Judaism)
>   *xx* God (Judaism)

Fear of the Lord
>   *See* Fear of God

Feast-day sermons
>   *See* Festival-day sermons

Feast of Dedication
>   *See* Hanukkah (Feast of Lights)

Feast of Esther
>   *See* Purim (Feast of Esther)

Feast of Fools
>   *See* Fools, Feast of

Feast of Jesus Christ the King
>   *See* Jesus Christ the King, Feast of

Feast of kingship (Shinto rite)
>   *See* Ōnie no Matsuri

Feast of Lights
>   *See* Hanukkah (Feast of Lights)

Feast of Rejoicing over the Law
>   *See* Simḥat Torah

Feast of St. Martin
>   *See* St. Martin's Day

Feast of Tabernacles
>   *See* Sukkoth

Feast of the Assumption of the Blessed Virgin
>   Mary
>   *See* Assumption of the Blessed Virgin
>   Mary, Feast of the

Feast of the Holy Innocents
>   *See* Holy Innocents, Feast of the

Feast of the Immaculate Conception
>   *See* Immaculate Conception, Feast of the

Feast of the Maccabees
>   *See* Hanukkah (Feast of Lights)

Feast of the Presentation of Jesus Christ
>   *See* Candlemas

Feast of the Presentation of the Blessed Virgin
>   Mary
>   *See* Presentation of the Blessed Virgin
>   Mary, Feast of the

Feast of the Sacred Heart
>   *See* Sacred Heart, Feast of the

Feast of the Three Hierarchs
>   *See* Three Hierarchs, Feast of the

Feast of Weeks
>   *See* Shavu'oth (Feast of Weeks)

Feasts
>   *See* Fasts and feasts

Feather dyeing
>   *See* Dyes and dyeing—Feathers

Feather flowers *(TT891)*
>   *xx* Artificial flowers
>   Feather-work

Feather industry *(Direct)* *(HD9999.F4)*
>   *sa* Wages—Feather industry
>   *xx* Feathers

Feather tracts
>   *x* Pterylae
>   Pterylography
>   Pterylosis
>   *xx* Birds—Anatomy
>   Feathers

Feather-wing beetles
>   *xx* Beetles

Feather-work *(Indirect)* *(Primitive, GN434.F3)*
>   *sa* Feather flowers

Featherbedding (Industrial relations)
>   *sa* Railroads—Full crew rules
>   *xx* Employee rules
>   Industrial relations
>   Labor and laboring classes

Feathers *(QL697)*
>   *sa* Dyes and dyeing—Feathers
>   Feather industry
>   Feather tracts
>   Molting
>   *x* Down
>   *xx* Birds—Anatomy
>   Body covering (Anatomy)
>   Poultry industry—By-products
>   — Identification
>   — Juvenile literature

Feature films
>   Here are entered individual full-length
>   fiction films with a running time of 60
>   minutes or more.
>   *sa* Animal films
>   Biographical films
>   Comedy films
>   Detective and mystery films
>   Fantastic films
>   Gangster films
>   Historical films
>   Horror films
>   Musical revues, comedies, etc.
>   Religious films
>   Samurai films
>   Science fiction films
>   Short films
>   Spy films
>   War films
>   Western films
>   *x* Dramatic films
>   Theatrical films
>   *xx* Moving-pictures

February 26 Incident, 1936
>   *See* Japan—History—February 26 Incident,
>   1936

Fecal incontinence
>   *See* Feces—Incontinence

Fecanes
>   *See* Fingos

Feces *(QP159)*
>   *sa* Defecation
>   Meconium
>   *xx* Defecation
>   Excretion

>   Physiological chemistry
>   — Analysis *(RB49)*
>   — Bacteriology *(QR171)*
>   — Incontinence
>   *x* Fecal incontinence

Feces, Fossil
>   *See* Coprolites

Feces (in religion, folk-lore, etc.)
>   *x* Folk-lore of feces
>   *xx* Excretion (in religion, folk-lore, etc.)
>   Religion, Primitive

Fechner's law *(Psychology, BF237)*
>   *x* Weber-Fechner law
>   *xx* Mind and body
>   Psychology, Physiological
>   Senses and sensation

Fecundity
>   *See* Fertility

Fedayeen
>   *sa* al Karāmah, Jordan, Battle of, 1968
>   *x* Fidā'iyun
>   *xx* Israel-Arab Border Conflicts, 1949-
>   — Personal narratives
>   — Pictorial works

Federal aid to adult education *(Direct)*
>   *x* Adult education—Federal aid
>   *xx* Adult education—Finance
>   Adult education—Law and legislation
>   Education and state

Federal aid to day nurseries *(Direct)*
>   *x* Day nurseries—Federal aid
>   *xx* Day nurseries—Finance

Federal aid to education *(Direct)* *(LB2825)*
>   *sa* Federal aid to libraries
>   Federal aid to private schools
>   *x* Education—Federal aid
>   Federal grants for education
>   *xx* Education and state
>   Education—Finance
>   Educational law and legislation
>   Grants-in-aid

Federal aid to higher education *(Direct)*
>   *xx* Education and state
>   Education, Higher
>   Higher education and state
>   Universities and colleges—Finance

Federal aid to hospitals *(Direct)*
>   *x* Hospitals—Federal aid
>   *xx* Grants-in-aid
>   Hospitals—Finance
>   Hospitals—Laws and legislation

Federal aid to law enforcement agencies
>   *(Direct)*
>   *xx* Grants-in-aid
>   Law enforcement

Federal aid to libraries *(Direct)*
>   *x* Libraries—Federal aid
>   *xx* Federal aid to education
>   Grants-in-aid
>   Libraries and state
>   Library finance
>   Library legislation

Federal aid to outdoor recreation *(Direct)*
>   *x* Outdoor recreation—Federal aid
>   *xx* Grants-in-aid
>   Outdoor recreation—Finance
>   Outdoor recreation—Law and
>   legislation

Federal aid to private schools *(Direct)*
>   *sa* State aid to private schools
>   *x* Federal grants for private schools
>   *xx* Educational law and legislation
>   Federal aid to education
>   Private schools
>   State aid to private schools

Federal aid to the arts *(Direct)*
>   *x* Art—Federal aid
>   Arts—Federal aid

Federal aid to the arts   *(Direct)*
   (Continued)
         Federal grants for art
         Federal grants for the arts
      xx Art and state
         Art—Finance
         Arts—Finance
         Grants-in-aid
         State encouragement of science,
            literature, and art
         Subsidies
Federal aid to transportation   *(Direct)*
      x Federal grants for transportation
         Transportation—Federal aid
      xx Grants-in-aid
         Transportation and state
         Transportation—Finance
         Transportation—Laws and regulations
Federal aid to vocational education   *(Direct)*
      x Federal grants for vocational education
         Vocational education—Federal aid
      xx Education and state
         Vocational education—Finance
         Vocational education—Law and
            legislation
Federal areas within states   *(Direct)*
      x Federal enclaves
      xx Federal government
Federal-city relations   *(Direct)*
      x City-federal relations
         Federal-municipal relations
         Urban-federal relations
      xx Federal government
         Municipal government
Federal communications services
      See Federal Telecommunications System
Federal corporation tax
      See Corporations—Taxation
Federal enclaves
      See Federal areas within states
Federal funds market (United States)
      xx Federal Reserve banks
Federal government   *(Direct)*   *(JC355;*
            Federal and state relations,
            JF751-786)
      sa Confederation of states
         Decentralization in government
         Democracy
         European federation
         Exclusive and concurrent legislative
            powers
         Federal areas within states
         Federal-city relations
         Federal-state controversies
         Grants-in-aid
         Imperial federation
         Intergovernmental fiscal relations
         Intergovernmental tax relations
         Interstate controversies
         Interstate relations
         Intervention (Federal government)
         Latin American federation
         Legislative power
         State governments
         State rights
         subheading Constitution *and subdivsion*
            Politics and government *under*
            names of federal states, e.g.
            Australia. Constitution; United
            States. Constitution; Australia—
            Politics and government; United
            States—Politics and government
      x Division of powers
         Federal-state relations
         Federalism
      xx Constitutional law
         Decentralization in government
         Democracy
         Legislative power

         Political science
         Republics
         State governments
      Note under Separation of powers
      — Information services
         xx Government information
Federal grants
      See Grants-in-aid
Federal grants for art
      See Federal aid to the arts
Federal grants for education
      See Federal aid to education
Federal grants for private schools
      See Federal aid to private schools
Federal grants for the arts
      See Federal aid to the arts
Federal grants for transportation
      See Federal aid to transportation
Federal grants for vocational education
      See Federal aid to vocational education
Federal home loan banks   *(HG3729.U4-5)*
      x Home loan banks
      xx Banks and banking
Federal incorporation
      See Incorporation
Federal intervention
      See Intervention (Federal government)
Federal land banks   *(HG2051.U5)*
Federal libraries
      See Libraries, Governmental,
            administrative, etc.
Federal loyalty-security program, 1947-
      See Loyalty-security program, 1947-
Federal-municipal relations
      See Federal-city relations
Federal Party   *(JK2300-2309)*
         Subdivided by locality *e.g.* Federal Party.
            Massachusetts.
      x Federalists (U.S.)
Federal prose
      See English language—Government jargon
Federal questionnaires
      See Government questionnaires
Federal Reserve banks   *(HG2559-2565)*
      sa Federal funds market (United States)
      xx Banks of issue—United States
      Example under Banks and banking, Central
Federal revenue sharing
      See Intergovernmental fiscal relations
         Intergovernmental tax relations
Federal-state concurrent legislative powers
      See Exclusive and concurrent legislative
            powers
Federal-state controversies   *(Direct)*
      x Controversies between the United
            States and a State
         Federal-state disputes
      xx Constitutional law
         Federal government
Federal-state disputes
      See Federal-state controversies
Federal-state fiscal relations
      See Intergovernmental fiscal relations
Federal-state relations
      See Federal government
Federal-state tax relations
      See Intergovernmental tax relations
Federal style
      See Decoration and ornament—Federal
            style
Federal Telecommunications System
      x F.T.S.
         Federal communications services
         United States—Executive departments
            —Communication systems
Federal theology
      See Covenants (Theology)

Federalism
      See Federal government
The Federalist
      — Authorship
         Note under Authorship
Federalists (U.S.)
      See Federal party
Federated churches   *(BV636)*
         Here are entered works dealing with local
            churches formed by the federation of
            two or more denominational churches,
            united for local worship but with each
            unit retaining its denominational af-
            filiation. Works on the type of local
            church whose aim is to serve all in a
            community but which has no denomi-
            national affiliation are entered under
            Community churches.
      sa Larger parishes
      x Churches, Federated
      xx Christian union
         Interdenominational cooperation
         Larger parishes
         Rural churches
      Note under Community churches
Federation, Imperial
      See Imperial federation
Federation, International
      See International organization
Federation of East Africa
      See East Africa Federation
Federation of Europe
      See European federation
Federation of Latin America
      See Latin American federation
Federations, Financial (Social service)
            (HV40-41; United States: local,
            HV99; national HV97)
      x Community chests
         Federations for charity and
            philanthropy
         Financial federations
         Welfare federations
      xx Charity organization
         Community organization
         Cooperative societies
         Fund raising
         Social service
Federations, Local church
      See Local church councils
Federations for charity and philanthropy
      See Federations, Financial (Social service)
Fedritive movement   *(HD2961)*
      xx Cooperation
Fee system (Taxation)
      See Cost (Law)
         Fees, Administrative
         Internal revenue
         Stamp-duties
         Taxation
         subdivsion Officials and employees—
            Salaries, allowances, etc. *under*
            names of countries, etc., e.g. United
            States—Officials and employees—
            Salaries, allowances, etc.
Feeble-minded
      See Mentally handicapped
Feeblemindedness
      See Mental deficiency
Feed
      See Feeds
Feed additive residues   *(Indirect)*
            (RA1270.F4)
      xx Food contamination
         Toxicology
Feed additives   *(Indirect)*   *(SF98.A2)*
      sa Lysine in animal nutrition
         Medicated feeds

x Feeds—Additives
— Prices *(Direct)*
Feed conversion efficiency
See Feed utilization efficiency
Feed grain program
xx Agriculture and state—United States
Feed-grinders *(S709)*
xx Agricultural machinery
Feed heads
See Risers (Founding)
Feed industry and trade
See Flour and feed trade
Feed mechanisms
sa Conveying machinery
xx Conveying machinery
Machinery
Feed mills *(Direct)* *(TS2158)*
xx Flour and feed trade
Milling machinery
— Costs
— Equipment and supplies
— — Appraisal
See Feed mills—Equipment and
supplies—Valuation
— — Maintenance and repair
— — Valuation *(TS2158)*
x Feed mills—Equipment and
supplies—Appraisal
— Fires and fire prevention
— Laboratory manuals *(TS2158)*
— Management *(TS2158)*
— — Problems, exercises, etc. *(TS2158)*
— Production standards *(TS2158)*
Feed processing
x Feeds—Processing
xx Agricultural processing
Feed pumps
See Feed-water pumps
Feed research *(Direct)*
x Feeds—Research
xx Research
Feed trade
See Flour and feed trade
Feed utilization efficiency
sa *subdivision* Feed utilization efficiency
under names of animals or groups of
animals, e.g. Poultry—Feed
utilization efficiency
x Efficiency, Feed utilization
Feed conversion efficiency
Meat production efficiency
xx Feeding
Feeds
Feed-water *(TJ375-387)*
sa Steam accumulators
x Boiler water
xx Boilers
Steam-boilers
Steam-boilers—Incrustations
Water
Feed-water heaters *(TJ381-3)*
Feed-water pumps *(TJ385)*
x Feed pumps
Pumps, Feed-water
xx Pumping machinery
Feed-water purification *(TJ379)*
sa Deaerators
Water—Softening
xx Steam-boilers—Incrustations
Water—Purification
Note under Water—Softening
Feedback (Electronics) *(TK7835)*
sa Feedback oscillators
xx Amplifiers, Vacuum-tube
Electronics
Feedback control systems
Vacuum-tube circuits

Feedback (Psychology) *(BF319.5.F4)*
sa Biofeedback training
xx Learning, Psychology of
Reinforcement (Psychology)
Feedback amplifiers *(TK7871.2)*
Feedback control systems *(TJ216)*
sa Adaptive control systems
Biological control systems
Feedback (Electronics)
Man-machine systems—Manual control
Root-locus method
Servomechanisms
xx Adaptive control systems
Automatic control
Automation
Discrete-time systems
— Mathematical models
Feedback oscillators *(TK7872.O7)*
x Oscillators, Feedback
xx Feedback (Electronics)
Oscillators, Electric
Feeder air lines
See Air lines, Local service
Feeders
See Risers (Founding)
Feeders, Liquid
See Liquid feeders
Feedheads
See Risers (Founding)
Feeding
sa Amino acids in animal nutrition
Ammonia in animal nutrition
Antibiotics in animal nutrition
Ascorbic acid in animal nutrition
Chromium in animal nutrition
Diet in veterinary medicine
Feed utilization efficiency
Feedlots
Feeds
Lysine in animal nutrition
Minerals in animal nutrition
Nitrogen in animal nutrition
Phosphorus in animal nutrition
Proteins in animal nutrition
Radioisotopes in animal nutrition
Selenium in animal nutrition
Vitamins in animal nutrition
subdivision Feeding and feeds *under*
names of animals and groups of
animals, e.g. Horses—Feeding and
feeds; Poultry—Feeding and feeds
x Animal nutrition
xx Feeds
Nutrition
Stock and stock-breeding
— Economic aspects *(Direct)*
— Equipment and supplies
xx Farm equipment
— Examinations, questions, etc.
— Mathematical models
— Tables, calculations, etc.
Feeding, Artificial
See Artificial feeding
Feeding behavior
See Animals, Food habits of
Feeding of the five thousand (Miracle)
x Five thousand, Feeding of the (Miracle)
— Juvenile literature
Feeding programs (Space flight)
See Menus for space flight
Feeding stuffs
See Feeds
Feedlots *(Indirect)*
xx Feeding
— Economic aspects *(Direct)*
— Waste disposal
Feeds *(Indirect)*
sa Distillers feeds

Dried citrus pulp
Ensilage
Feed utilization efficiency
Feeding
Forage
Forage plants
Pelleted feed
Poultry industry—By-products
Grain as feed; Molasses as feed; *and*
similar headings; and subdivision
Feeding and feeds *under names of*
animals and groups of animals, e.g.
Horses—Feeding and feeds; Poultry
—Feeding and feeds
x Feed
Feeding stuffs
Fodder
xx Feeding
Nutrition
Stock and stock-breeding
— Additives
See Feed additives
— Amino acid content
See Amino acids in animal nutrition
— Ammonia content
See Ammonia in animal nutrition
— Analysis *(SF97)*
xx Agricultural chemistry
— — Laboratory manuals
— Composition *(Indirect)*
— Disinfection *(RA761)*
— Drying
— Grading
x Feeds—Standards
— Law and legislation *(Direct)*
— Marketing
xx Flour and feed trade
— Microbiology
— Mineral content
See Minerals in animal nutrition
— Patents
— Prices
— Processing
See Feed processing
— Protein content
See Proteins in animal nutrition
— Research
See Feed research
— Standards
See Feeds—Grading
— Storage
— Tables, calculations, etc.
— Transportation
— — Rates
— Weight and measurement
Feeds, Antenna
See Antenna feeds
Feeling
See Perception
Touch
Feelings
See Emotions
Fees, Administrative *(Direct)*
sa Costs (Law)
Fees, Consular
Harbors—Port charges
Stamp-duties
Tonnage fees
x Administrative fees
Fee system (Taxation)
xx Administrative law
Costs (Law)
Stamp-duties
Fees, Adult education
See Adult education fees
Fees, Bank
See Banks and banking—Service charges

Fees, Consular
    sa subdivision Diplomatic and consular
        service—Fees *under names of*
        countries, e.g. Cuba—Diplomatic and
        consular service—Fees
    x Consular fees
        Diplomatic and consular service—Fees
    xx Diplomatic and consular service
        Fees, Administrative
Fees, Ecclesiastical *(Canon law, BX1939.F)*
    sa Annates
        Mass stipends
        Tithes
    xx Catholic Church—Finance
        Church finance
        Clergy
        Clergy—Salaries, pensions, etc.
Fees, Legal
    See Costs (Law)
        Lawyers—Fees
Fees, Medical
    See Medical fees
Fees, Professional *(Direct)*
    sa Costs (Law)
        Dental fees
        Medical fees
        subdivision Fees *under names of*
        professional groups, e.g. Architects—
        Fees; Lawyers—Fees
    x Professional fees
Fees (Law)
    See Costs (Law)
        Lawyers—Fees
Feet
    See Foot
Feet, Washing of
    See Foot washing (Rite)
Feet of fines
    See Fines and recoveries
Feet washing
    See Foot washing (Rite)
Fehling's solution *(QD321; TP382)*
    xx Chemical tests and reagents
Fehmarn, Battle of, 1644 *(DL190)*
    xx Dano-Swedish War, 1643-1645
Fehmic courts *(JN3269)*
    x Vehmgerichte
    xx Courts
        Criminal courts
Fehrbellin, Battle of, 1675 *(DD394.3)*
Feigned diseases
    See Blindness, Feigned
        Malingering
Felata
    See Fulahs
Feldshers
    See Physicians' assistants
Feldspar *(Indirect)* *(QE391.F3)*
    sa Adularia
        Albite
        Anorthosite
        Plagioclase
    Example under Crystallography; Mineralogy
Felis marmorata
    See Marbled cat
Felis nebulosa
    See Clouded leopard
Felis pardalis
    See Ocelots
Fellans
    See Fulahs
Fellatio
    xx Sex
Felling cull trees
    See Cull tree felling
Fellowship
    x Companionship
    xx Comradeship

Conduct of life
    Ethics
    Friendship
    Social ethics
Fellowship (Judaism) *(BM720.F4)*
    xx Sociology, Jewish
Fellowships
    See Scholarships
        subdivision Scholarships, fellowships,
        etc. *under subjects, e.g.* Medicine—
        Scholarships, fellowships, etc.
Felon (Disease)
    x Whitlow
Felony
    See Criminal law
Felsenmeer *(Indirect)*
    sa Boulders
    x Block field
        Stone field
    xx Boulders
Felt *(TS1825)*
    sa Hatter's fur
        Paper-making felts
Felt (in religion, folk-lore, etc.)
    x Folk-lore of felt
Felt boots
    See Boots and shoes, Felt
Felt work
    x Feltwork
    xx Handicraft
    — Juvenile literature
Feltrinelli prize
Felts (Paper-making)
    See Paper-making felts
Feltwork
    See Felt work
Female
    See Woman
Female alcoholism
    See Alcohol and women
Female drinking
    See Alcohol and women
Female impersonators
    See Impersonators, Female
Female offenders
    See Delinquent women
Female sex hormone
    See Hormones, Sex
Female sterility
    See Sterility, Female
Female sterilization
    See Sterilization of women
Feminine health
    See Woman—Health and hygiene
Feminine psychology
    See Woman—Psychology
Femininity (Psychology)
    xx Sex (Psychology)
        Woman—Psychology
Feminism
    See Woman
        Woman—Social and moral questions
Femoral artery
    x Femur—Artery
    xx Arteries
Femoral epiphysis
    See Femur—Epiphysis
Femoral hernia
    xx Hernia
Femoral nerve
    — Surgery
Femoral vein *(Anatomy, Comparative,*
        QL835; Anatomy, Human, QM191)
    Example under Veins
Femur *(Anatomy, Comparative, QL821;*
        Anatomy, Human, QM117)
    sa Iliofemoral joint
    x Thighbone

    xx Leg
  — Abnormities and deformities
  — Artery
    See Femoral artery
  — Diseases
    sa Femur—Radiography
        Idiopathic femoral necrosis
  — Epiphysis
    x Femoral epiphysis
    Example under Epiphysis
  — Fracture *(RD101)*
  — Radiography
    xx Femur—Diseases
  — Surgery
  — Wounds and injuries
Femur neck
  — Fracture
Fences *(NA8390-8392; Agriculture, S723-5)*
    sa Cattle guards
        Electric fences
        Gates
        Hedges
        Roads—Guard fences
        Snow fences
        Wire fencing
    xx Hedges
  — Law *(Direct)*
    sa Boundaries (Estates)
    xx Boundaries (Estates)
Fences (Receivers of stolen goods)
    See Receiving stolen goods
Fencing *(U860-863)*
    sa Dueling
        Kendo
        Sabers
        Single-stick
        Stage fencing
        Swordplay
        Swordsmen
    x Fighting
    xx Athletics
        Dueling
        Swords
    Example under Exercise; Physical education
        and training
  — Early works to 1800
Fencing, Oriental
    x Oriental fencing
Fencing in art *(N8217.F4)*
    xx Art
Fenders, Automobile
    See Automobiles—Fenders
Fenders for automobiles
    See Automobiles—Fenders
Fenders for docks, piers, etc.
    sa Ships—Fenders
    x Docks—Fenders
        Piers—Fenders
    xx Harbors
Fenders for street-cars
    See Car fenders
Fenestra rotunda *(QL948; QM507; QP461)*
    xx Ear
Feng-shui *(BF1779.F4)*
    xx Divination
        Geomancy
Fenians *(DA954)*
    xx Canada—History—Fenian invasions,
        1866-1870
        Home rule (Ireland)
        Ireland—History—1837-1901
        Irish question
Fenite *(Indirect)* *(QE475)*
    xx Rocks, Igneous
Fenjas
    See Falashas
Fennecs *(QL737.C22)*
    xx Foxes

— Legends and stories
Fennel
Fens *(England, DA670.F33)*
  sa Bogs
    Marshes
    Moors and heaths
    Reclamation of land
    Waste lands
  xx Bogs
    Drainage
    Marshes
    Moors and heaths
    Waste lands
    Wetlands
Feral animals
  See Feral livestock
Feral livestock *(Indirect)*
  x Animals, Feral
    Feral animals
    Livestock, Feral
    Wild livestock
  xx Domestic animals
    Stock and stock-breeding
Ferberite *(QE391.F4)*
  sa Tungsten
  xx Tungsten
Fermat's theorem *(QA244)*
  sa Congruences and residues
  xx Congruences and residues
Fermentation *(Fermentation industries,*
    TP500-618; Micro-organisms,
    QR151; Physiological chemistry,
    QP601; Plant physiology, QK896)
    Here are entered comprehensive works
    and general works on special topics,
    e.g. technical mycology.
    Works on particular groups of micro-
    organisms involved in fermentation
    are entered under Bacteria; Molds
    (Botany); Yeast.
  sa Bacteriology
    Brewing
    Digestive ferments
    Enzymes
    Putrefaction
    Sugars
    Urine—Fermentation and ferments
    Wine and wine making
  x Ferments
  xx Bacteria
    Bacteriology
    Biochemical engineering
    Chemistry
    Enzymes
    Microbiological synthesis
    Putrefaction
    Wine and wine making
  — Apparatus and supplies
  — Patents *(TP506)*
Fermentation gum
  See Dextran
Fermentation tube *(QR66)*
  xx Bacteriology—Technique
Fermented cream
  See Sour cream
Ferments
  See Digestive ferments
    Enzymes
    Fermentation
Fermi-Dirac particles
  See Fermions
Fermi gas
  See Electron gas
Fermi surfaces *(QC176)*
  x Surfaces, Fermi
  xx Electrons
    Energy-band theory of solids
    Free electron theory of metals

    Quantum statistics
Fermions
  x Fermi-Dirac particles
  xx Quantum statistics
Fern allies
  See Pteridophyta
Fernandian language
  See Bube language
Fernico
  See Iron-nickel-cobalt alloys
Ferns *(Indirect) (QK520-532; Culture,*
    SB429)
  sa Cryptogams
  x Acrogens
    Filicineae
  xx Botany
    Cryptogams
    Foliage plants
    Pteridophyta
  — Anatomy *(QK521)*
    Example under Anatomy
  — Diseases and pests
  — Identification
  — Juvenile literature
  — Pictorial works
Ferns, Fossil *(QE961)*
  xx Paleobotany
Feroge languages
Ferrant Pegasus computer
  See Pegasus computer
Ferrara
  — Earthquake, 1571
Ferrara-Florence, Council of, 1438-1439
    (BX830 1438)
Ferrari automobile
Ferrates
  See Ferrites (Magnetic materials)
Ferret, Black-footed
  See Black-footed ferret
Ferrets *(Rat-catching, SB994.R2; Zoology,*
    QL737.C2)
  sa European polecat
    Weasels
  xx European polecat
    Weasels
Ferrets as laboratory animals
Ferric hydrates
  See Ferric hydroxides
Ferric hydroxides *(QD181.F4)*
  x Ferric hydrates
Ferric nitrate *(QD181.F4)*
  x Nitrate of iron
Ferric salts *(QD181.F4)*
  xx Salts
Ferrierite *(Indirect) (QE391.F45)*
Ferries *(Indirect) (HE5751-5870)*
  sa Train ferries
    subdivision Ferries *under names of*
    cities or towns, e.g. New York (City)
    —Ferries
  xx River boats
    Transportation
    Work boats
  — Access roads *(Direct)*
    x Access roads to ferries
    xx Roads
  — Juvenile literature
  — Law and legislation *(Direct)*
    xx Highway law
    Inland navigation—Laws and
    regulations
Ferrimagnetism
  xx Magnetism
Ferrite *(Metallography, TN693.I7)*
  sa Copper ferrite
    Ferrites (Magnetic materials)
  xx Ferrites (Magnetic materials)

Ferrite isolators *(TK7872.F4)*
  x Isolators, Ferrite
  xx Wave guides
Ferrites (Magnetic materials)
  sa Ferrite
    Orthoferrites
    Yttrium iron garnet
  x Ferrates
  xx Ferrite
    Gyrators
    Magnetic materials
  — Analysis
  — Heat treatment
  — Patents *(TK7871.15.F4)*
  — Testing
  — Thermal properties
Ferro-vanadium
  See Ferrovanadium
Ferroboron
  xx Boron
  — Analysis
Ferroelectric crystals
  sa Ferroelectric storage cells
  x Ferroelectrics
Ferroelectric effect
  See Ferroelectricity
Ferroelectric storage cells
  x Memory devices
  xx Ferroelectric crystals
Ferroelectricity *(QC595)*
  sa Domain structure
  x Ferroelectric effect
    Seignette-electricity
  xx Crystals—Electric properties
    Dielectrics
    Polarization (Electricity)
    Pyro- and piezo- electricity
Ferroelectrics
  See Ferroelectric crystals
Ferrography (Photomechanical process)
  See Ferromagnetography
Ferromagnetic domain
  See Domain structure
Ferromagnetic resonance
  x Resonance, Ferromagnetic
  xx Ferromagnetism
    Magnetic resonance
Ferromagnetism
  sa Antiferromagnetism
    Barkhausen effect
    Domain structure
    Ferromagnetic resonance
    Ising model
    Magnetization
    Spin waves
  xx Magnetism
Ferromagnetography
  x Ferrography (Photomechanical process)
    Magnetography (Photomechanical
    process)
  xx Electrophotography
    Photomechanical processes
Ferromanganese *(TN757.F3)*
  xx Iron-manganese alloys
  — Analysis
Ferrosilicon *(TN757.F4)*
  x Silicon-iron
  xx Iron-silicon alloys
    Silicon steel
Ferrotitanium alloys
  See Titanium-iron alloys
Ferrotungsten
  xx Iron-tungsten alloys
  — Analysis
Ferrotype
  See Tintype
Ferrous metal industries
  See Iron industry and trade

Ferrous metal industries *(Continued)*
　　Steel industry and trade
Ferrous salts *(QD181.F4)*
　　xx Salts
Ferrous sulphate *(QD181.F4)*
　　x Iron sulphate
Ferrovanadium
　　x Ferro-vanadium
　　xx Vanadium alloys
Ferry-bridges *(TG435)*
　　x Bridges, Ferry
Fertility *(Physiology, QP273)*
　　sa Heterosis
　　x Fecundity
　　xx Reproduction
　　　Sterility
Fertility, Effect of drugs on
　　sa Conception—Prevention
　　　Oral contraceptives
　　xx Drugs and sex
　　　Drugs—Physiological effect
　　　Pharmacology
Fertility, Human *(Physiological*
　　　anthropology, GN241; Physiology,
　　　QP273; Statistics, HB903.F4)
　　sa PROJTARG (Computer program)
　　　subdivsion Population *under names of*
　　　countries, e.g. United States—
　　　Population
　　x Human fertility
　　xx Demography
　　　Sterility
　　　Vital statistics
　　— Mathematical models
Fertility cults *(Direct)*
　　xx Cultus
　　　Mysteries, Religious
Fertility of eggs
　　See Eggs—Hatchability
Fertilization (Biology) *(QH485)*
　　x Amphimixis
　　xx Biology
　　　Cells
　　　Embryology
　　　Physiology
　　　Reproduction
　　— Atlases
Fertilization of plants *(Pollination, QK926;*
　　　Sexual reproduction, QK827)
　　sa Cleistogamy
　　　Heterostylism
　　　Pollen—Dispersal
　　　Pollen tube
　　x Pollination
　　xx Botany
　　　Flowers
　　　Plant physiology
　　　Plants
　　　Plants—Reproduction
Fertilization of plants by insects *(QK926)*
　　x Insect pollenizers
　　　Pollination by insects
　　xx Insect-plant relationships
　　　Insects
　　　Insects, Injurious and beneficial
Fertilizer industry *(Direct)*
　　sa Wages—Fertilizer industry
　　　names of individual fertilizers, e.g.
　　　Guano, Nitrates
　　x Fertilizers and manures—Industry and
　　　trade
　　xx Nitrogen industries
　　Example under Farm supply industries
　　— Accidents
　　— Employees
　　— Equipment and supplies
　　— — Corrosion
　　— Hygienic aspects

— Management
— Mathematical models
— Underdeveloped areas
　　See Underdeveloped areas—Fertilizer
　　　industry
— Waste disposal *(TD899.F47)*
Fertilizer research
　　See Fertilizers and manures—Research
Fertilizer spreaders
　　x Spreaders of fertilizers
　　xx Agricultural machinery
　　　Fertilizers and manures
Fertilizers and manures *(Indirect)*
　　　(Agriculture, S631-667; Manufacture,
　　　TP963; Trade, HD9483)
　　sa Aerial fertilizing
　　　Agricultural chemistry
　　　Ashes (Fertilizer)
　　　Compost
　　　Copper compounds
　　　Cyanamid
　　　Deficiency diseases in plants
　　　Farm manure
　　　Fertilizer spreaders
　　　Fish-scrap fertilizer
　　　Forest soils—Fertilization
　　　Garden fertilizers
　　　Green manuring
　　　Guano
　　　Gypsum
　　　Humus
　　　Lime
　　　Liming of soils
　　　Liquid fertilizers and manures
　　　Manure gases
　　　Marl
　　　Night soil
　　　Nitrates
　　　Nitrification
　　　Nitrogen fertilizers
　　　Oil cake
　　　Organic fertilizers
　　　Peat
　　　Phosphate industry
　　　Phosphates
　　　Phosphatic fertilizers
　　　Potassium fertilizers
　　　Sewage irrigation
　　　Soil fertility
　　　Wood waste as mulch, soil conditioner,
　　　　etc.
　　　Ammonia as fertilizer; Sewage as
　　　　fertilizer; *and similar headings; and*
　　　　subdivision Fertilizers and manures
　　　　under names of crops, e.g. Coffee—
　　　　Fertilizers and manures; Potatoes—
　　　　Fertilizers and manures
　　x Manures
　　xx Agricultural chemicals
　　　Agricultural chemistry
　　　Agriculture
　　　Soil inoculation
　　　Soils
　　— Analysis *(S639)*
　　— Disinfection *(S635)*
　　　Example under Disinfection and disin-
　　　　fectants
　　— Economic aspects *(Direct)*
　　— Industry and trade
　　　See Fertilizer industry
　　— Law and legislation *(Direct)*
　　— Mathematical models
　　— Patents
　　— Preservation and storage *(S635)*
　　　xx Agricultural engineering
　　— Prices *(Direct)*
　　— Research
　　　x Fertilizer research

　　xx Agricultural research
　　　Chemical research
　　　Research, Industrial
— Standards
— Tables and ready-reckoners
　　　(HF5716.F3)
— Tariff
　　See Tariff on fertilizers
— Toxicology
— Transportation
Fertilizers and manures for coffee, ₍potatoes,
　　etc.₎
　　See Coffee ₍Potatoes, etc.₎—Fertilizers and
　　　manures
Fertilizers and manures in forestry
　　See Forest soils—Fertilization
Fescue foot
　　xx Cattle—Diseases
Festival-day sermons *(BV4254.3)*
　　x Feast-day sermons
　　xx Church year sermons
　　　Fasts and feasts
　　　Occasional sermons
　　　Sermons
— Jewish authors
　　See Festival-day sermons, Jewish
Festival-day sermons, Jewish
　　sa Rosh ha-Shanah sermons
　　　Sukkoth sermons
　　x Festival-day sermons—Jewish authors
　　　Jewish festival-day sermons
　　xx Fasts and feasts—Judaism
　　　Sermons, Jewish
Festival of Hanukkah
　　See Hanukkah (Feast of Lights)
Festivals *(Indirect)* *(Educational,*
　　　LB3560-3575; Manners and customs,
　　　GT3930-4995)
　　sa Anniversaries
　　　Art festivals
　　　Boy-bishop
　　　Dance festivals
　　　Drama festivals
　　　Family festivals
　　　Fasts and feasts
　　　Folk festivals
　　　Harvest festivals
　　　Holidays
　　　Moving-picture festivals
　　　Music festivals
　　　Pageants
　　　Processions
　　　Tournaments
　　　subdivision Festivals, etc. *under names*
　　　　of cities, e.g. Antwerp—Festivals,
　　　　etc.; *and names of particular*
　　　　festivals, e.g. Fools, Feast of
　　xx Anniversaries
　　　Days
　　　Fasts and feasts
　　　Manners and customs
　　　Pageants
　　　Processions
— Jews
　　　See Fasts and feasts—Judaism
— Juvenile literature
— Management *(GT3935)*
— Pictorial works
— Terminology
Festivals in literature
Festivals of Male Voice Praise
　　xx Music festivals
Festschriften *(Direct)*
　　x Anniversary volumes
　　　Commemorative volumes
　　　Homage volumes
　　　Jubilee volumes
　　　Wedding publications

666

Fetal erythroblastosis
  See Erythroblastosis fetalis
Fetal growth
  See Fetus—Growth
Fetal heart
  xx Heart
Fetal membranes
  sa Amnion
      Chorioallantois
      Chorion
  x Membranes, Fetal
Fetal rickets
  See Rickets, Fetal
Feterita
  See Durra
Fetiales *(JX2025)*
  xx Ambassadors
Fetichism
  See Fetishism
Feticide
  See Abortion
Fetishism *(Ethnology, GN472)*
  sa Animism
      Idols and images
      Nature worship
      Voodooism
  x Fetichism
  xx Animism
      Religion
      Religion, Primitive
      Religions
      Superstition
      Worship
Fetterman Fight, 1866
  x Hundred in the Hands, Battle of the,
      1866
      Philip Kearny, Fort—Massacre, 1866
  xx Cheyenne Indians—Wars
      Dakota Indians—Wars
      Indians of North America—Wars—
      1866-1895
  — Juvenile literature
Fetus *(Physiology, RG600)*
  sa Carcinoembryonic antigens
      Docimasia pulmonum
      Ductus arteriosus
      Maternal-fetal exchange
      Obstetrics
      Urachus
      Wolffian body
      headings beginning with the word Fetal
  x Foetus
      Unborn child
  xx Embryology
      Reproduction
  — Abnormities and deformities
      sa Deformities—Intrauterine diagnosis
  —— Diagnosis
          See Deformities—Intrauterine
              diagnosis
  — Diseases *(RG626-9)*
      sa Blood—Transfusion, Intrauterine
          Cytomegalic inclusion disease
          Dysostosis
          Erythroblastosis fetalis
          Fetus, Effect of radiation on the
          Rickets, Fetal
  —— Diagnosis
      sa Amniocentesis
          Deformities—Intrauterine
              diagnosis
  — Growth
      x Fetal growth
  — Physiology
  — Respiration and cry *(RG600)*
Fetus, Death of the *(RG631)*
  sa Abortion
      Lithopedion

Still-birth
Fetus, Effect of drugs on the
  xx Drugs—Physiological effect
      Pharmacology
Fetus, Effect of radiation on the
  xx Fetus—Diseases
      Radiation—Physiological effect
Fetus (Theology)
  xx Birth (Philosophy)
      Theology, Doctrinal
Feudal castles
  See Castles
Feudal courts *(Direct)*
  sa Manorial courts
  xx Courts
      Feudal law
      Manorial courts
Feudal law *(Direct)*
  sa Allodium
      Banality (Law)
      Feudal courts
      Homage (Feudal law)
      Incorporation (Feudal law)
      Landfriede
  x Droit féodal
      Feudalism—Law
      Law, Feudal
  xx Land tenure—Law
  — Terms and phrases
Feudal tenure
  See Feudalism
      Land tenure
Feudalism *(Indirect)* *(D131; Feudal state,*
      JC109-116)
  sa Chivalry
      Clans and clan system
      Duchies
      Estates (Social orders)
      Homage (Feudal law)
      Immunity (Feudalism)
      Jus primae noctis
      Middle Ages
      Ministerials
      Peasantry
      Scutage
  x Feudal tenure
      Fiefs
  xx Chivalry
      Civilization, Medieval
      Estates (Social orders)
      Land
      Land tenure
      Middle Ages—History
  — Historiography
      xx Middle Ages—Historiography
  — Juvenile literature
  — Law
      See Feudal law
  — Mathematical models
  — Terminology

GEOGRAPHIC SUBDIVISIONS

  — Japan
      sa Daimyo
      x Shogunate
Feuds
  See Vendetta
Feuilletons
  x Serialized fiction
  xx Fiction
      Journalism
      Newspapers
Feuilletons, German, [Russian, etc.]
Fever *(RC106)*
  sa Antipyretics
      Body temperature
      Exanthemata
      Pyrogens

names of fevers, e.g. Malarial fever,
      Scarlatina, Typhoid fever, Typhus
      fever, Yellow fever
  x Hyperthermia
      Pyrexia
  xx Body temperature
      Exanthemata
      Thermometers and thermometry,
      Medical
  Example under Medicine—Practice; Thera-
      peutics
  — Eclectic treatment *(RV211)*
  — Homeopathic treatment *(RX211)*
  — Juvenile literature
Fever, Artificial
  See Fever therapy
Fever, Enteric
  See Typhoid fever
Fever, Eruptive
  See Exanthemata
Fever, Hemoglobinuric
  See Blackwater fever
Fever, Puerperal
  See Puerperal septicemia
Fever, Therapeutic
  See Fever therapy
Fever, Traumatic
  See Traumatic fever
Fever therapy *(RM868)*
  sa Malariotherapy
  x Artificial fever
      Fever, Artificial
      Fever, Therapeutic
  xx Diathermy
      Therapeutics, Physiological
Fever-tick
  See Cattle-tick
Feynman diagrams
  sa Feynman integrals
  xx Matrices
      Problem of many bodies
      Quantum theory
Feynman integrals
  x Integrals, Feynman
  xx Feynman diagrams
      Integrals, Multiple
Fiars prices *(Agricultural prices, HB233.A3)*
  xx Farm produce—Marketing
      Grain trade
      Prices
Fiat automobile *(TL215.F)*
Fiat machine-gun *(UF620.F)*
  xx Machine-guns
Fiat money
  See Currency question
      Legal tender
      Paper money
Fiber bundles (Mathematics)
  x Bundles, Fiber (Mathematics)
  xx Fiber spaces (Mathematics)
      Groups, Continuous
Fiber glass
  See Glass fibers
Fiber glass reinforced plastics
  See Glass reinforced plastics
Fiber optics
  x Optics, Fiber
Fiber plants *(Indirect)* *(SB241-261)*
  sa *specific fiber plants, e.g.* Cotton, Flax,
      Hemp
  xx Botany, Economic
Fiber-reactive dyes
  See Reactive dyes
Fiber reclamation
  x Fibers—Reclamation
      Reclamation of fibers
Fiber reinforced composites
  See Fibrous composites

Fiber spaces (Mathematics)
   sa Fiber bundles (Mathematics)
      Vector bundles
   x Fibre spaces (Mathematics)
   xx Algebraic topology
Fiberboard
   sa Hardboard
      Particle board
   x Building board
      Insulating board
   xx Paperboard
      Wall board
      Wood-using industries
      Wood waste
   — Permeability
   — Standards   *(Direct)*
Fiberboard industry   *(Direct) (TS875)*
   — Waste disposal
Fiberglass
   See Glass fibers
Fiberglass boats
   xx Boat-building
      Boats and boating
      Glass reinforced plastics
   — Testing
Fibers   *(Fiber plants: culture, SB241-261;*
        industry, HD9155-6; Textile fibers,
        TS1540-1549)
   sa Ambary hemp
      Bast
      Coir
      Cotton
      Fibrous composites
      Flax
      Hemp
      Jute
      Linen
      Mitsumata
      Paper
      Paper mulberry
      Ramie
      Retting
      Silk
      Sisal hemp
      Spanish broom
      Textile fibers
      Vulcanized fiber
      Wool
      headings beginning with the word Fiber
   xx Cordage
      Cotton
      Hemp
   — Reclamation
      See Fiber reclamation
Fibers, Carbon
   See Carbon fibers
Fibers, Ceramic
   See Ceramic fibers
Fibers, Glass
   See Glass fibers
Fibers, Graphite
   See Graphite fibers
Fibers, Inorganic
   See Inorganic fibers
Fibers, Polyester
   See Polyester fibers
Fibers, Quartz
   See Quartz fibers
Fibonacci numbers
   x Fibonacci sequence
      Sequence, Fibonacci
   xx Numbers, Theory of
Fibonacci sequence
   See Fibonacci numbers
Fibre spaces (Mathematics)
   See Fiber spaces (Mathematics)
Fibrin   *(QP91)*
   sa Blood coagulation factor XIII

Fibrinolysis
Fibrin stabilizing factor
   See Blood coagulation factor XIII
Fibrinogen   *(QP91)*
   xx Blood
      Hemostatics
   Example under Proteins
Fibrinolysin
   sa Antifibrinolytic agents
   xx Fibrinolytic agents
Fibrinolysis
   sa Fibrinolytic agents
   xx Blood—Coagulation
      Enzymes
      Fibrin
Fibrinolysis inhibitors
   See Antifibrinolytic agents
Fibrinolytic agents
   sa Ceruloplasmin
      Fibrinolysin
      Plasmin
   x Antithrombotic agents
      Fibrinolytic enzymes
      Thrombolytic agents
   xx Enzymes
      Fibrinolysis
Fibrinolytic enzymes
   See Fibrinolytic agents
Fibroblasts
   x Desmocytes
      Fibrocytes
   xx Cells
      Connective tissues
Fibrocytes
   See Fibroblasts
Fibrolite
   See Sillimanite
Fibromas
   xx Tumors
Fibroplasia, Retrolental
   See Retrolental fibroplasia
Fibrosis, Cystic
   See Cystic fibrosis
Fibrosis, Pulmonary
   See Pulmonary fibrosis
Fibrous ceramics
   See Ceramic fibers
Fibrous composites
   sa Reinforced plastics
   x Composites, Fibrous
      Fiber reinforced composites
      Filament reinforced composites
      Reinforced fibrous composites
   xx Composite materials
      Fibers
   — Fracture
      xx Fracture of solids
   — Testing
Fibrous dysplasia of bone   *(RC931.F5)*
   xx Bones—Diseases
Fibrous glass industry
   See Glass fiber industry
Fibrous graphite
   See Graphite fibers
Fibula
   xx Leg
   — Abnormities and deformities   *(QM691)*
Fibula (Archaeology)   *(CC400; Art,*
      NK7306-8)
   sa Brooches
      Clasps
   xx Archaeology
      Brooches
      Clasps
      Jewelry
Fichtelite
Fiction   *(PN3311-3503)*
   sa Adventure stories

      Allegories
      Baseball stories
      Children's stories
      Christian fiction
      College stories
      Crime stories
      Detective and mystery stories
      Dime novels
      Epistolary fiction
      Erotic stories
      Fables
      Fairy tales
      Fantastic fiction
      Feuilletons
      Fishing stories
      Folk-lore
      Ghost stories
      Historical fiction
      Horror tales
      Hunting stories
      Legal novels
      Legends
      Love stories
      Musical fiction
      Nature stories
      Novelists
      Picaresque literature
      Plots (Drama, novel, etc.)
      Radio stories
      Romances
      Romanticism
      Science fiction
      Sea stories
      Short stories
      Sports stories
      Tales
      Western stories
      American fiction, English fiction,
        French fiction, Negro fiction, *and*
        similar headings; also subdivision
        Fiction *under historical events,*
        periods, and characters, etc., e.g.
        Stalingrad, Battle of, 1942-1943—
        Fiction; United States—History—
        1783-1865—Fiction; Napoléon I,
        Emperor of the French, 1769-1821—
        Fiction; *also subdivision* Stories
        under particular subjects, e.g.
        Christian life—Stories; Physicians—
        Stories
   x Novels
      Stories
   xx Literature
   — 18th century
   — 19th century
   — 20th century
   — — Book reviews

      GENERAL SUBDIVISIONS

   — Authorship
      xx Authorship

      GENERAL SUBDIVISIONS

   — Collections   *(Fiction in English, PZ1)*
   — Dictionaries   *(PN41-44)*
   — History and criticism   *(PN3329-3503)*
      sa Psychological fiction
   — Moral and religious aspects   *(PN3347;*
      PN3351)
      xx Religion in literature
      Example under Christian ethics
   — Plots
      See Plots (Drama, novel, etc.)
   — Stories, plots, etc.
   — Technique   *(PN3355-3383)*
      sa Children's stories—Technique
      Detective and mystery stories—
        Technique

Plots (Drama, novel, etc.)
  Psychological fiction
  Western stories—Technique
  xx Authorship
    Prose literature—Technique
— — Juvenile literature
Fiction, Autobiographic *(PN3448.A8;*
    English, PR830.A8; German,
    PT747.A8)
  x Autobiographic fiction
  xx Autobiography
    Biography (as a literary form)
Fiction, Historical
  See Historical fiction
Fiction, Juvenile
  See subdivision Juvenile fiction *under*
    historical events and characters, etc.
Fiction in libraries *(Z711.5)*
  sa Children's literature
  x Libraries—Fiction
  xx Books and reading
    Children's literature
    Libraries and readers
Fictions, Theory of *(Bentham, B1574.B;*
    Logic, BC199.F5; Philosophy and
    religion, BL51; Vaihinger, B3354.V)
  xx Knowledge, Theory of
    Reality
    Truth
Fictions (Law)
  sa Presumptions (Law)
  x Legal fictions
  xx Presumptions (Law)
Fictitious animals
  See Animals, Mythical
Fictitious names
  See Anonyms and pseudonyms
Fictitious societies
  See Imaginary societies
Fictitious titles of books
  See Imaginary books and libraries
Fidā'iyun
  See Fedayeen
Fiddle
  See Violin
Fiddle tunes
  sa Bluegrass music
  xx Country music
    Violin music
Fiddleheads *(Indirect)* *(Botany, QK524.P7;*
    Culture, SB351.F)
  x Ostrich fern
Fiddler-crabs *(QL444.D3)*
  xx Crabs
— Behavior
Fideicommissum *(Direct)* *(HD1236-9)*
  sa Entail
  xx Entail
    Inheritance and succession
    Trusts and trustees
Fideicommissum (Roman-Dutch law)
Fideicommissum (Roman law)
Fidejussio
  See Suretyship and guaranty (Roman law)
Fidelity bonds
  See Insurance, Surety and fidelity
Fidelity insurance
  See Insurance, Surety and fidelity
Fiducia
  sa Constitutum possessorium
    Trusts and trustees
  xx Mortgages (Roman law)
    Pledges (Roman law)
    Roman law
    Sales (Roman law)
    Trusts and trustees
Fiefs
  See Feudalism

Land tenure
Field artillery
  See Artillery, Field and mountain
Field athletics
  See Track-athletics
Field biology
  See Biology—Field work
Field borders
  See Windbreaks, shelterbelts, etc.
Field cameras
  See View cameras
Field-coupled surface waves
  x Surface-coupled electrohydrodynamic
    systems
    Surface-coupled magnetohydrodynamic
    systems
  xx Electrodynamics
    Magnetohydrodynamics
    Surface waves
Field crops *(Indirect)* *(SB183-317)*
  sa Companion crops
    Cover crops
    Double cropping
    Field experiments
    Forage plants
    Grain
    Harvesting time
    Horticulture
    Irrigation farming
    Planting time
    specific crops, e.g. Cotton, Hay, Wheat
  x Crops
    Farm crops
  xx Agriculture
    Farm produce
    Plants
— Accounting
— Costs
— Disease and pest resistance
— Diseases and pests
    sa names of diseases and pests, e.g.
      European chafer
— Drying
— Fertilizers and manures *(S667.F)*
— Judging
— Mathematical models
— Storage
— Tropics
    sa Tropical crops
— Varieties
— Water requirements
Field dependence (Psychology)
  x Field independence (Psychology)
  xx Cognition
    Perception
Field-effect transistors
  x Unipolar transistors
  xx Transistors
Field emission
  sa Field ion microscope
  x Emission, Field
  xx Electron work function
    Electrons—Emission
Field experiments
  sa subdivision Field experiments *under*
    names of crops, e.g. Maize—Field
    experiments
  x Field plot technique
    Field tests
  xx Agricultural research
    Agriculture—Experimentation
    Field crops
Field extensions (Mathematics)
  x Extension fields (Mathematics)
  xx Fields, Algebraic
Field fortification
  See Fortification, Field

Field geology
  See Geology—Field work
Field-glasses *(QC373.F5; Military, UF845)*
  x Binoculars
Field handball
  See Fieldball
Field hockey *(GV1017.H7)*
  xx Hockey
— Juvenile literature
Field hospitals
  See Hospitals, Military
    Medicine, Military
    Red Cross
    War—Relief of sick and wounded
Field houses *(GV405)*
  sa Gymnasiums
  xx Gymnasiums
Field independence (Psychology)
  See Field dependence (Psychology)
Field ion emission microscope
  See Field ion microscope
Field ion microscope
  x Field ion emission microscope
    Ion microscope
  xx Field emission
    Microscope and microscopy
Field marshals
  See Marshals
Field mice *(Agricultural pests, SB994.F5;*
    Zoology, QL737.R6)
  sa California vole
    Sagebrush vole
  x Voles
  xx Mice
— Control
    xx Rodent control
— Diseases
Field of Cloth of Gold, 1520
  x Cloth of Gold, Field of, 1520
Field of view from aeroplanes
  See Aeroplanes—Field of view
Field of view from helicopters
  See Helicopters—Field of view
Field of vision, Measurement of
  See Perimetry
Field orders
  See Orders, Preparation of (Military
    science)
Field plot technique
  See Field experiments
Field plotters *(GA150.5)*
  xx Electronic analog computers
    Geography—Methodology
Field rations
  See Operational rations (Military supplies)
    Survival and emergency rations
Field reeves *(Direct)*
  xx Police, Rural
Field service (Military science) *(U170-175)*
  sa subdivision Field service *under armies,*
    e.g. United States. Army—Field
    service
  xx Military art and science
    Tactics
Field sports
  See Hunting
    Sports
Field telegraph
  See Military telegraph
Field tests
  See Field experiments
Field theories, Unified
  See Unified field theories
Field theory, Quantized
  See Quantum field theory
Field theory (Physics)
  sa Continuum mechanics
    Electric fields

Field theory (Physics) *(Continued)*
    Electromagnetic fields
    Electromagnetic theory
    Gravitation
    Magnetic fields
    Quantum field theory
    Unified field theories
  x Classical field theory
    Continuum physics
  xx Continuum mechanics
    Electromagnetic theory
    Physics
Field theory (Social psychology)
  xx Social psychology
Field trials *(SF425)*
  xx Dog-shows
Field trips by air
  See Aeronautics in education
Field work (Anthropology)
  See Anthropology—Field work
Field work (Biology)
  See Biology—Field work
Field work (Educational method) *(LB2394)*
  sa Aeronautics in education
    Education, Cooperative
    Industrial tours
    Project method in teaching
    School excursions
  xx Education, Cooperative
    Project method in teaching
    School excursions
Field work (Folk-lore)
  See Folk-lore—Field work
Field work (Geography)
  See Geography—Field work
Field work (Geology)
  See Geology—Field work
Field work (Physical geography)
  See Physical geography—Field work
Field work (Rehabilitation counseling)
  See Rehabilitation counseling—Field work
Field work (Social sciences)
  See Social sciences—Field work
Field work (Social service)
  See Social service—Field work
Field work (Social work)
  See Social service—Field work
Fieldball
  x Field handball
    Handball, Field
  — Rules
Fielding (Baseball) *(GV870)*
  x Infield (Baseball)
    Outfield (Baseball)
  xx Baseball
  — Juvenile literature
Fields, Algebraic *(QA247)*
  sa Algebra, Differential
    Algebraic number theory
    Field extensions (Mathematics)
    Ideals (Algebra)
    Modular fields
    Numbers, Theory of
    Quaternions
    Rings (Algebra)
    Valuation theory
  x Algebraic fields
    Algebraic numbers
  xx Algebra, Abstract
    Numbers, Theory of
    Rings (Algebra)
Fields, Electromagnetic
  See Electromagnetic fields
Fife *(History, ML935)*
  xx Flute
Fife and drum music *(M1270)*
  x Drum and fife music
  xx Fife music

    Percussion music
Fife music *(M60-62)*
  sa Fife and drum music
Fife music (Fifes (2)) *(M288-9)*
Fifteen puzzle *(GV1511.F4)*
Fifteenth century
  xx Europe—History—476-1492
    Middle Ages—History
    Renaissance
  — Biography
    See Biography—15th century
  — Forecasts
  — Juvenile literature
Fifth column
  See Subversive activities
    World War, 1939-1945—
    Collaborationists
Fifth grade (Education)
  xx Education, Elementary
Fifth Monarchy Men *(DA420-429)*
Fifth of May (Mexican holiday)
  See Cinco de Mayo (Mexican holiday)
Fifty-two stages (Mahayana Buddhism)
  See Bodhisattva stages (Mahayana Buddhism)
Fig *(Indirect) (SB365)*
  sa Cookery (Figs)
  x Caprifig
  — Diseases and pests *(SB608.F35)*
  — Tariff
    See Tariff on figs
  — Varieties
Fig (in religion, folk-lore, etc.)
  sa Barren fig tree (Parable)
  x Folk-lore of figs
  xx Religion, Primitive
Fig-eater
  See Green June beetle
Fig-insect *(Fig culture, SB365)*
  x Caprifig
Fig-moth *(SB608.F35)*
  x Almond moth
Fig tree, Barren
  See Barren fig tree (Parable)
Fig tree in art
  xx Art
    Trees in art
Fig tree in literature
  xx Trees in literature
Figeater
  See Green June beetle
Fighter-bomber sabres
  See Sabre (Jet fighter planes)
Fighter plane sounds
  xx Aeroplane sounds
    Fighter planes
    Sounds
Fighter planes *(TL685.3)*
  sa 97 Sen (Fighter planes)
    BAC Lightning (Fighter plane)
    BAC TSR 2 (Turbojet fighter planes)
    Bearcat (Fighter planes)
    Black widow (Fighter planes)
    Boeing P-26 (Fighter plane)
    Camel (Fighter planes)
    Corsair (Fighter planes)
    Curtiss Hawk (Fighter planes)
    F-111 (Fighter planes)
    Fighter plane sounds
    Focke-Wulf 190 (Fighter planes)
    Gladiator (Fighter planes)
    Hayabusa (Fighter planes)
    Hayate (Fighter planes)
    Heinkel 100 (Fighter planes)
    Heinkel 112 (Fighter planes)
    Heinkel 162 (Jet fighter planes)
    Hellcat (Fighter planes)
    Hien (Fighter planes)

    Hunter (Turbojet fighter planes)
    Hurricane (Fighter planes)
    Lightning (Fighter planes)
    Messerschmitt 109 (Fighter planes)
    Messerschmitt 110 (Fighter planes)
    Messerschmitt 163 (Fighter planes)
    Messerschmitt 262 (Fighter planes)
    Meteor (Fighter planes)
    MIG (Fighter planes)
    Mirage (Fighter planes)
    Mustang (Fighter planes)
    P-40 (Fighter planes)
    Pfeil (Fighter planes)
    Phantom (Fighter planes)
    Sabre (Jet fighter planes)
    Scimitar (Fighter planes)
    Skyraider (Fighter planes)
    Skyray fighter plane
    Spad (Fighter planes)
    Spitfire (Fighter planes)
    Starfighter (Fighter plane)
    Thunderbolt (Fighter planes)
    Thunderchief (Fighter planes)
    Thunderstreak (Fighter planes)
    Vampire (Turbojet fighter planes)
    Zero (Fighter planes)
  x Pursuit planes
  xx Aeroplanes, Military
  Example under Aeroplanes
  — Flight testing
  — Juvenile literature
  — Pictorial works *(TL685.3)*
  — Piloting
    Example under Aeroplanes—Piloting;
    and under reference from Aeronautics—Piloting; Air pilotage; Piloting (Aeronautics)
  — Tail surfaces
  — Turbojet engines
  — Wings
Fighting
  See Animal fighting
    Battles
    Boxing
    Bull-fights
    Cock-fighting
    Combat
    Dog-fighting
    Dueling
    Fencing
    Gladiators
    Military art and science
    Naval art and science
    Night fighting (Military science)
    Street fighting (Military science)
    Swordplay
    Tournaments
    War
Fighting, Hand-to-hand
  See Hand-to-hand fighting
Fighting (Psychology) *(Child study, BF723.F5)*
  sa Aggressiveness (Psychology)
  x Combativeness
    Pugnacity
  xx Aggressiveness (Psychology)
    Hostility (Psychology)
    Psychology
    Violence
Fighting bull *(SF199.F5)*
  sa Bull-fights
  xx Bull-fights
    Bulls
Fighting on stage
  See Stage fighting
Figural aftereffects *(BF241)*
  x Aftereffects, Figural
  xx Imagery (Psychology)

Perception
Psychology, Physiological
Vision
Figuration
  See Figurative art
Figurative art *(Direct)*
  sa Human figure in art
  x Figuration
  xx Realism in art
Figure drawing
  sa Children in art
    Face
    Head
    Human figure in art
  xx Drawing
    Human figure in art
    Nude in art
  Example under Drawing—Instruction
  — Juvenile literature
Figure of the earth
  See Earth—Figure
Figure painting *(ND1290)*
  sa Genre painting
    Human figure in art
    Portrait painting
  xx Human figure in art
    Nude in art
    Painting
    Portrait painting
Figure skating
  See Skating
Figured bass
  See Thorough bass
Figureheads of ships *(VM308)*
  x Ships—Figureheads
  xx Decoration and ornament
    Ships
Figures of speech *(PN227-8)*
    Here are entered general works and
    works on figures of speech in the Eng-
    lish language. Works treating of figures
    of speech in other languages are en-
    tered under the name of the language,
    with subdivision Figures of speech.
  sa particular figures of speech, e.g.
    Metaphor, Simile
  x English language—Figures of speech
    Speech, Figures of
    Tropes
  xx Rhetoric
    Symbolism
Figurines
  See Bronzes
    Dolls
    Dummy board figures
    Ivories
    Jade
    Ming ch'i
    Terra-cottas
    Ushabti
Fijian language *(PL6235)*
  sa Melanesian languages
  x Viti language
  xx Melanesian languages
Fijian periodicals *(Direct)*
Fijian poetry *(Texts, PL6235.Z77;*
    Translations, PL6235.Z95)
Fijians *(DU600)*
Filament reinforced composites
  See Fibrous composites
Filaments, Solar
  See Sun—Filaments
Filaments for electric lamps
  See Electric lamps, Incandescent—
    Filaments
Filaria and filariasis *(RC142.5)*
  sa Onchocerciasis

Filbert *(Indirect)* *(Botany, QK495.B56;*
    Culture, SB401.F5)
  x Hazel
    Hazelnut
  — Diseases and pests
  — Tariff
    See Tariff on filberts
Files and filing (Documents) *(HF5736-5746)*
  sa Alphabeting
    Card system in business
    Data tapes
    Indexing
    Vertical files (Libraries)
    subdivision Records and
      correspondence *under specific*
      subjects, e.g. Railroads—Records
      correspondence; United States.
      Army—Records and correspondence
  x Data files
    Filing systems
    Indexes, Card
  xx Alphabeting
    Card system in business
    Documentation
    Indexing
    Office furniture
    Office practice
  — Engineering drawings
    xx Engineering drawings
  — Library records
    See Library records
Files and rasps *(TJ1285-7)*
  x Rasps
  xx Hardware
  Example under Tools
  — Standards
Fili (Irish poets) *(PB1321)*
  xx Irish poetry
    Poets
Filial love
  See Filial piety
Filial piety *(BJ1639)*
  x Filial love
  xx Conduct of life
    Ethics
    Parent and child
    Piety
Filiation (Law)
  See Paternity
Filibuster War, Nicaraguan
  See Nicaragua—History—Filibuster War,
    1855-1860
Filibusters *(G539)*
  sa Cuba—History—Insurrection,
    1849-1851
    Nicaragua—History—Filibuster War,
    1855-1860
    Soldiers of fortune
  x Freebooters
  xx Buccaneers
    Pirates
    Soldiers of fortune
    War, Maritime (International law)
Filibusters (Political science) *(JF519)*
  xx Parliamentary practice
    Political science
Filibusters (West Indian buccaneers)
  See Buccaneers
Filicide *(Direct)*
  xx Homicide
    Murder
Filicide (in religion, folk-lore, etc.)
  x Folk-lore of filicide
  xx Religion, Primitive
Filicineae
  See Ferns
Filigrains
  See Water-marks

Filigree
  xx Art metal-work
Filigree lettering *(NK3625.F)*
  xx Lettering
Filing systems
  See Files and filing (Documents)
Filipinos in Mexico, ⌈the United States, etc.⌉
    (Mexico, F1392.F; United States,
    E184.F; United States immigration,
    JV6891.F5-59)
Fill (Earthwork)
  See Fills (Earthwork)
Fill and scour (Geomorphology)
  See Scour and fill (Geomorphology)
Fillers (in paper, paint, etc.) *(TN948.F45)*
  xx Paint
    Paper
    Textile chemicals
Fillets, Fish
  See Fish fillets
Fillets (Engineering)
  xx Engineering
Filling stations
  See Automobiles—Service stations
Fillings (Dentistry)
  sa Dental amalgams
    Inlays (Dentistry)
  x Dental fillings
  xx Dentistry, Operative
Fills, Sanitary
  See Sanitary landfills
Fills (Earthwork)
  sa Embankments
    Hydraulic filling
    Sanitary landfills
  x Earth fills
    Fill (Earthwork)
    Land fills
    Landfills
  xx Earthwork
    Soil mechanics
Film, Television
  See Television film
Film acting
  See Moving-picture acting
Film actors
  See Moving-picture actors and actresses
Film adaptations *(PN1997.85)*
  sa subdivision Film adaptations *under*
    names of literatures and authors
  x Adaptations, Film
    Books, Filmed
    Filmed books
    Films from books
    Moving-picture adaptations
  xx Moving-picture plays
    Moving-pictures and literature
    Moving-pictures—Plots, themes, etc.
    Plots (Drama, novel, etc.)
Film audiences
  See Moving-picture audiences
Film authorship
  See Moving-picture authorship
Film boiling *(QC320.22.F5)*
  x Boiling, Film
    Leidenfrost effect
  xx Ebullition
    Evaporation
    Heat—Transmission
Film catalogs
  See Moving-pictures—Catalogs
    subdivision Film catalogs *under specific*
      subjects, e.g. Geology—Film
      catalogs; Mental hygiene—Film
      catalogs
Film coefficients (Physics)
  xx Boundary layer
    Diffusion

Film coefficients (Physics) *(Continued)*
      Heat—Transmission
      Surface energy
      Surface tension
Film collections
    See Moving-picture film collections
Film coupons, UNESCO
    See UNESCO film coupons
Film dosimetry
    See Photographic dosimetry
Film editing (Cinematography)
    See Moving-pictures—Editing
Film festivals
    See Moving-picture festivals
Film libraries
    See Moving-picture film collections
Film loops
    See Moving-pictures, Loop
Film make-up
    x Moving-picture make-up
    xx Make-up, Theatrical
Film music
    See Moving-picture music
Film posters
    x Moving-picture posters
    xx Playbills
        Posters
Film posters, Czech, [etc.]
    x Czech [etc.] film posters
Film slides
    See Filmstrips
Film stars
    See Moving-picture actors and actresses
Film strip projectors
    See Projectors
Film strips
    See Filmstrips
Filmed books
    See Film adaptations
Films
    See Photography—Films
Films, Cinematographic
    See Moving-picture film
Films, Magnetic
    See Magnetic films
Films, Metallic
    See Metallic films
Films, Monomolecular
    See Monomolecular films
Films, Powdered
    See Powder film
Films, Thin
    See Thin films
Films from books
    See Film adaptations
Films on art
    See Art in moving-pictures
Filmstrip collections *(Z692.F5)*
    x Filmstrip libraries
        Libraries, Filmstrip
Filmstrip libraries
    See Filmstrip collections
Filmstrips
    sa Newspapers on filmstrips
        Slides (Photography)
    subdivision Audio-visual instruction
        under names of languages, e.g.
        English language—Audio-visual
        instruction
    x Film slides
        Film strips
        Slidefilms
    xx Audio-visual materials
        Microphotography
        Slides (Photography)
    — Cataloging
        See Cataloging of filmstrips
    — Catalogs

    — Reviews
Filmstrips in religious education *(BV1535.3)*
    xx Religious education—Audio-visual aids
Filter cloth *(TS1781)*
    xx Filters and filtration
    — Acoustic properties
Filter-presses *(TJ1470-1475)*
    xx Filters and filtration
Filter tips
    See Cigarette filters
Filtered laminar airflow systems
    See Laminar flow clean rooms
Filtering, Kalman
    See Kalman filtering
Filters, Acoustic
    See Acoustic filters
Filters, Digital (Mathematics)
    See Digital filters (Mathematics)
Filters, Light
    See Light filters
Filters, Photographic
    See Photography—Light filters
Filters, Radio
    See Radio filters
Filters and filtration *(Chemical technology,*
    TP156.F5; Chemistry, QD63.F5;
    Water-supply, TD441-9)
    sa Air filters
        Automobiles—Motors—Oil filters
        Chemistry—Manipulation
        Cigarette filters
        Dialysis
        Diatomaceous earth
        Diesel motor—Oil filters
        Filter cloth
        Filter-presses
        Fuel filters
        Oil filters
        Separators (Machines)
        Sewage—Purification—Filtration
        Tractors—Motors—Oil filters
        Trickling filters
        Ultrafiltration
        Vacuum filters
        Water—Purification—Filtration
        Wine and wine making—Filtration
    xx Contamination (Technology)
        Fuller's earth
        Sanitary engineering
        Separators (Machines)
    — Corrosion
    — Patents
    — Testing
Filtration plants
    See Water—Purification—Filtration
Fin whale
    See Finback whale
Final cause
    See Causation
        Teleology
Final utility
    See Marginal utility
Finance *(Direct)*
    sa Amortization
        Bankruptcy
        Banks and banking
        Bonds
        Budget in business
        Business losses
        Business mathematics
        Capital
        Capitalists and financiers
        Church finance
        Commerce
        Controllership
        Credit
        Currency question
        Deflation (Finance)

        Finance, Personal
        Flow of funds
        Foreign exchange
        Income
        Industrial management and inflation
        Inflation (Finance)
        Insurance
        Interest and usury
        International finance
        Investments
        Liquidity (Economics)
        Loans
        Money
        Museum finance
        Open market operations
        Prices
        Profit
        Saving and investment
        Securities
        Self-financing
        Sinking-funds
        Speculation
        Stock-exchange
        Syndicates (Finance)
        War finance
        Wealth
        subdivision Finance *under special*
        subjects, e.g. Colonies—Finance;
        Corporations—Finance; Railroads—
        Finance; Stock companies—Finance
    x Funds
    xx Currency question
        Economics
        Money
    Note under Colonies—Finance
    — Book reviews
    — Law
    — Mathematical models
    — Mathematics
        See Business mathematics
    — Research
        See Financial research
    — Simulation methods
    — Statistics
        x Financial statistics
    — Subject headings
        See Subject headings—Finance
    — Terminology
    — Underdeveloped areas
        See Underdeveloped areas—Finance
    — Vocational guidance
        x Finance as a profession
Finance, Buddhist temple
    See Buddhist temple finance
Finance, Church
    See Church finance
Finance, International
    See International finance
Finance, Local
    See Local finance
Finance, Military
    See War, Cost of
Finance, Municipal
    See Municipal finance
Finance, Personal *(HG179)*
    sa Budgets, Personal
        Children's allowances
        Clergy—Finance, Personal
        Consumer credit
        Estate planning
        Financial security
        Home economics—Accounting
        Insurance
        Investments
        Saving and thrift
    x Personal finance
    xx Family life education
        Finance

— Juvenile literature
Finance, Primitive
  See Economics, Primitive
Finance, Public *(Direct)*
  sa Bonds
    Budget
    Civil list
    Claims
    Corporations, Government—Finance
    Currency question
    Customs administration
    Debts, Public
    Deficit financing
    Expenditures, Public
    Fiscal policy
    Forced loans
    Government business enterprises—
      Finance
    Government lending
    Government monopolies
    Government spending policy
    Grants-in-aid
    Intergovernmental fiscal relations
    Internal revenue
    Investment of public funds
    Legal tender
    Loans
    Local finance
    Metropolitan finance
    Money
    Paper money
    Public depositaries
    Public institutions—Finance
    Repudiation
    Revenue
    Sinking-funds
    State bankruptcy
    Tariff
    Taxation
    War, Cost of
    War finance
    subdivision Appropriations and
      expenditures *under names of*
      departments, institutions, etc.,e.g.
      France. Armée—Appropriations
      and expenditures; United States.
      Dept. of Agriculture—
      Appropriations and expenditures;
      and subdivision Finance, commerce,
      confiscations, etc. *under names of*
      wars, e.g. Spanish Succession, War
      of, 1701-1714—Finance, commerce,
      confiscations, etc.
  x Public finance
  xx Currency question
    Economics
    Money
  Notes under Colonies—Finance; Local fi-
    nance; Municipal finance; War finance
— Accounting *(HJ9701-9995)*
  sa Debts, Public—Accounting
    Government business enterprises—
      Accounting
    Legislative auditing
    Special funds
    Tax accounting
  x Government accounting
    Public accounting
— Electronic data processing
  See Electronic data processing—
    Finance, Public
— Examinations, questions, etc.
— Law
— Mathematical models
— Underdeveloped areas
  See Underdeveloped areas—Finance,
    Public

GEOGRAPHIC SUBDIVISIONS

— Canada
— — Provinces
— France
  sa Intendants

GEOGRAPHIC SUBDIVISIONS

— — To 1789
— — 1789-1871
— — 1871-1918
— — 1918-
— Great Britain
— — To 1688
— — 1688-1815
— — 1815-1918
— — 1918-1945
— — 1945-
— — Accounting
  Example under Accounting

GEOGRAPHIC SUBDIVISIONS

— Islamic countries *(HJ233)*
  x Islamic public finance
    Muslim public finance
— ₍local subdivision₎
— — Law
  Notes under Local finance—Law and
    legislation; Municipal finance—
    Law and legislation
— United States
  x Specie payments
— — To 1789
— — 1789-1800
— — 1801-1861
— — 1861-1875
— — 1875-1900
— — 1901-1933
— — 1933-

GENERAL SUBDIVISIONS

— — States
  sa Budget—United States—States
    Taxation, State
— Washington metropolitan area
  Note under Metropolitan finance
Finance, War
  See War finance
Finance as a profession
  See Finance—Vocational guidance
Finance charges *(Direct)*
  sa Interest and usury
  xx Consumer credit
    Credit
    Loans, Personal
Finance companies, Commercial
  See Commercial finance companies
    Instalment plan
Financial aid administration, Student
  See Student financial aid administration
Financial federations
  See Federations, Financial (Social service)
Financial institutions *(Direct)*
  sa Banks and banking
    Building and loan associations
    Commercial finance companies
    Government financial institutions
    Insurance companies
    Investment trusts
    Pension trusts
  x Financial intermediaries
— Government ownership *(Direct)*
— Investments
  xx Investments
— Taxation *(Direct)*
Financial institutions, International
  sa Banks and banking, International
  x International financial institutions

  xx International finance
Financial intermediaries
  See Financial institutions
Financial journalism
  See Journalism, Commercial
Financial libraries *(Z675.F5)*
  x Libraries, Financial
Financial news
  See Newspapers—Sections, columns, etc.—
    Finance
Financial research *(Direct) (HG152)*
  x Finance—Research
  xx Research
Financial security
  x Security, Financial
  xx Finance, Personal
Financial statements *(Direct) (Balance
    sheet, HF5681.B2)*
  sa Accounts receivable
    Disclosure in accounting
    Ratio analysis
    subdivision Accounting *under special
      subjects, e.g.* Insurance, Life—
      Accounting; Universities and
      colleges—Accounting
  x Balance sheets
    Financial statements, Consolidated
    Income statements
    Operating statements
    Profit and loss statements
  xx Accounting
    Auditing
    Bookkeeping
    Business
    Corporation reports
  Example under Business records
— Examinations, questions, etc.
— Problems, exercises, etc.
— Programmed instruction
— Terminology
Financial statements, Consolidated
  See Financial statements
    Holding companies—Accounting
Financial statistics
  See Finance—Statistics
Financiers
  See Capitalists and financiers
Finback whale
  x Fin whale
    Finner
    Razorback
  xx Whales
— Legends and stories
Finches *(QL696.P2)*
  sa Chaffinches
    Goldfinch (in religion, folk-lore, etc.)
    Goldfinches
    Grass finches
    Greenfinch
    Grosbeaks
    Ortolans
    Snow buntings
    Sparrows
    Towhees
  xx Passeriformes
— Behavior
Finding lists
  See Library catalogs
Finding lost property
  See Lost articles (Law)
Fine arts
  See Art
    Arts
Fine editions
  See Bibliography—Fine editions
Fine-rolls *(DA25)*
Fines (Land titles)
  See Fines and recoveries

Fines (Penalties) (Direct)
    sa Penalties, Contractual
        Tax penalties
    x Penalties (Criminal law)
    xx Costs (Law)
        Criminal law
        Punishment
Fines and recoveries (Direct)
    x Feet of fines
        Fines (Land titles)
        Pedes finium
        Recoveries (Law)
    xx Real property
Finger alphabet
    See Deaf—Means of communication
Finger games
    See Finger play
Finger joint
    — Surgery
Finger marks
    See Fingerprints
Finger millet
    See Ragi
Finger painting
    x Painting, Finger
    xx Children as artists
        Painting
Finger play (GV1218.F5)
    x Finger games
    xx Play
Finger prints
    See Fingerprints
Finger rings
    See Rings
Finger-sucking
    x Thumb-sucking
    xx Infants—Care and hygiene
Fingernail biting
    See Nail-biting
Fingerprints (Anthropology, GN192;
      Criminology, HV6074)
    sa Artificial satellites in fingerprint
        transmission
        Bertillon system
        Dermatoglyphics
        Fortune-telling by fingerprints
    x Dactylography
        Dactyloscopy
        Finger marks
        Finger prints
        Skin—Papillary ridges
    xx Anthropometry
        Crime and criminals—Identification
        Dermatoglyphics
        Identification
    — Juvenile literature
Fingers (QM548)
    sa Hand
        Nails (Anatomy)
        Thumb
    xx Hand
    — Abnormities and deformities (Surgery,
        RD776; Teratology, QM691)
      sa Dupuytren's contracture
      xx Occupational diseases
    — Diseases
    — Wounds and injuries
Fingos
    x Aba-Mbos
        Abambos
        Amafengos
        Amafingos
        Fecanes
        Fingus
        Mfengos
    xx Bantus
        Ethnology—Natal

Fingus
    See Fingos
Finials (TH2495)
    sa Roof crestings
    xx Architectural metal-work
        Building
Finishes and finishing (Finishes, TP934-944;
      Finishing, TT300-345)
    sa Concrete—Finishing
        Cotton finishing
        Lacquer and lacquering
        Metals—Finishing
        Paint
        Paint removers
        Painting, Industrial
        Paper finishing
        Stains and staining
        Textile finishing
        Varnish and varnishing
        Wood finishing
    x Finishing
        Finishing materials
    xx Coating processes
        Coatings
        Manufacturing processes
        Materials
    — Equipment and supplies
Finishing
    See Finishes and finishing
Finishing, Furniture
    See Furniture finishing
Finishing materials
    See Finishes and finishing
Finishing processes, Print
    See Print finishing processes
Finite
    See Infinite
Finite arithmetic
    See Modular arithmetic
Finite automata
    See Sequential machine theory
Finite differences
    See Difference equations
Finite differences, Method of
    See Nets (Mathematics)
Finite element method
    xx Numerical analysis
    — Computer programs
Finite fields (Algebra)
    See Modular fields
Finite groups
    sa Mathieu groups
        Modules (Algebra)
    xx Groups, Theory of
        Modules (Algebra)
Finite number systems
    See Modules (Algebra)
Finland
    — History (DK445-465)
    — — Russian Conquest, 1808-1809
        xx Russo-Swedish War, 1808-1809
    — — Revolution, 1917-1918
    — — — Casualties (Statistics, etc.)
    — — — Personal narratives
    — — — Pictorial works
    — — — Prisoners and prisons
    — — 1939- (DK459.45)
Finner
    See Finback whale
Finnish-American newspapers
    xx Finnish newspapers
Finnish ballads and songs (Collections,
      PH319; History, PH315)
    sa Folk-songs, Finnish
        Songs, Finnish
Finnish baths
    See Sauna

Finnish drama (Direct) (Collections,
      PH347; History, PH311)
Finnish epic poetry
    See Epic poetry, Finnish
Finnish fiction (Direct)
Finnish imprints (Direct)
Finnish incantations
    See Incantations, Finnish
Finnish language (PH101-293)
    xx Finnish languages
Finnish language in Sweden, [etc.]
Finnish languages (PH101-1109)
    sa Estonian language
        Finnish language
        Finno-Ugrian languages
        Karelian language
        Livonian language
        Lydi language
        Olonetsian language
        Vepsish language
        Votish language
    x Balto-Finnish languages
        Finno-Baltic languages
    xx Finno-Ugrian languages
Finnish literature (PH300-498)
Finnish literature (American)
    See American literature—Finnish authors
Finnish literature (Swedish)
    Duplicate entry is made under Swedish
      literature—Finnish authors.
Finnish mythology
    See Mythology, Finno-Ugrian
Finnish newspapers
    sa Finnish-American newspapers
    — Prices (Direct)
Finnish orations (Direct)
Finnish periodicals (History, etc.,
      PN5355.F5)
Finnish poetry (Collections, PH345-6;
      History, PH310)
    sa Epic poetry, Finnish
Finnish poetry (Swedish)
    Duplicate entry is made under Swedish
      poetry—Finnish authors.
Finnish prose literature (Direct)
Finnish spitz (SF429.F4)
    x Spitz, Finnish
Finnish wit and humor (Direct)
    Here are entered collections from several
      authors and individual authors who
      have not written in other literary
      forms.
Finnish wit and humor, Pictorial (Direct)
Finno-Baltic languages
    See Finnish languages
Finno-Hungarian languages
    See Finno-Ugrian languages
Finno-Russian War, 1939-1940
    See Russo-Finnish War, 1939-1940
Finno-Ugrian languages (PH)
    sa Cheremissian language
        Estonian language
        Finnish languages
        Hungarian language
        Ingrian language
        Karelian language
        Lappish language
        Livonian language
        Lydi language
        Mordvinian language
        Ob-Ugrian languages
        Olonetsian language
        Ostiak language
        Permian languages
        Syryenian language
        Ural-Altaic languages
        Vepsish language
        Vogul language

Votiak language
Votish language
x Finno-Hungarian languages
Ugro-Finnish languages
Uralian languages
xx Altaic languages
Finnish languages
Ob-Ugrian languages
Permian languages
Samoyedic languages
Ural-Altaic languages
Finno-Ugrian philology *(PH)*
Finno-Ugrian poetry
Finno-Ugrian studies *(Direct)*
Finno-Ugrians
sa Cheremisses
Estonians
Finns
Hungarians
Karelians
Lapps
Livonians
Mordvinians
Ostiaks
Permians
Syryenians
Veps
Voguls
Votes (People)
Votiaks
x Ugrians
Ugro-Finns
Finns
xx Finno-Ugrians
Finns in Norway, ⌈**the United States, etc.**⌉
Fins *(QL639)*
xx Fishes—Anatomy
Finsen rays
See Phototherapy
Finsen therapy
See Phototherapy
Finsler space
See Spaces, Generalized
Fiords
See Fjords
Fioriture
See Embellishment (Vocal music)
Fioti language
See Congo language
Fipa (African people)
xx Ethnology—Tanzania
Ethnology—Zambia
Fir *(QK495.A14; Sylviculture, SD397.F)*
sa Balsam fir
Bornmueller fir
Douglas fir
Noble fir
Spanish fir
x Firs
— Diseases and pests
sa Douglas-fir tussock moth
Fire *(Chemistry, TP265; Ethnology,*
GN416-417; Folk-lore, GR495)
sa Combustion
Fires
Flame
Fuel
Heat
Heating
Pyromania
Smoke
xx Chemistry
Combustion
Heat
— Juvenile literature
Fire, Greek
See Greek fire

Fire (in religion, folk-lore, etc.)
(Comparative religion, BL453;
Folk-lore, GR495; Folk-lore of the
Indians, E98.F6; Zoroastrianism,
BL1590.F5)
sa Candles and lights
Fire-worshipers
Heat (in religion, folk-lore, etc.)
Homa (Rite)
x Folk-lore of fire
xx Fire-worshipers
Heat (in religion, folk-lore, etc.)
Mythology
Religion, Primitive
Fire-alarms *(Direct)* *(TK7271)*
sa Electric alarms
xx Electric alarms
Electric apparatus and appliances
— Standards
Fire ant, Imported
See Imported fire ant
Fire balls
See Meteors
Fire bean
See Scarlet runner bean
Fire-blight
x Pear-blight
Fire-boats
See Fireboats
Fire bombs
See Incendiary bombs
Fire-boxes
See Locomotives—Fire-boxes
Fire-brick *(TP832.F5)*
xx Bricks
Fire-clay *(Mineral resources, TN941-3;*
Technology, TP838; Testing,
TA455.F5)
xx Clay
Fire companies
See Fire-departments
Fire control (Aerial gunnery)
xx Aerial gunnery
— Equipment
x Airborne fire control systems
xx Aeroplanes, Military—Armament
Fire control (Gunnery) *(UF848)*
sa Position-finders
Range-finding
Target-practice
x Gun fire control
xx Gunnery
Tracking radar
— Equipment
— Optical equipment *(UF849)*
sa Range-finding
Telescopic sights
x Fire control optics
xx Artillery
Optical instruments
Ordnance
Fire control (Naval gunnery) *(VF520)*
sa Range-finding
xx Naval gunnery
Ordnance, Naval
Remote control
— Equipment
— Radar equipment *(VF530)*
x Fire control radar
Radar, Fire control
xx Range-finding
Tracking radar
Fire control optics
See Fire control (Gunnery)—Optical
equipment
Fire control radar
See Fire control (Naval gunnery)—Radar
equipment

Fire damages, Liability for
See Liability for fire damages
Fire-damp *(TN305)*
sa Mine accidents
Mine explosions
Mine fires
Mine ventilation
x Marsh-gas
xx Gases, Asphyxiating and poisonous
Mine accidents
Mine explosions
Mine gases
Fire-departments *(Indirect)* *(TH9500-9599)*
sa Firemen's manuals
Police-fire integration
official reports of fire-departments
under names of cities and towns
x Fire companies
Example under Municipal services
— Communication systems
sa Radio in fire prevention
xx Telecommunication
— Equipment and supplies *(TH9361-9383)*
— — Appraisal
See Fire-departments—Equipment
and supplies—Valuation
— — Standards
— — Valuation
x Fire-departments—Equipment and
supplies—Appraisal
— Examinations, questions, etc.
— Juvenile literature
— Law and legislation *(Direct)*
sa Fire prevention—Laws and
regulations
xx Fire prevention—Laws and
regulations
— Management
— Safety measures
Fire dogs
See Dalmatian dogs
Fire-eating *(GV1559)*
xx Conjuring
Fire ecology *(Indirect)*
sa Prescribed burning
xx Ecology
Forest fires
Forest management
Grassland fires
Prescribed burning
— Juvenile literature
Fire-engines *(TH9371-6; Chemical engines,*
TH9338)
sa Hose-couplings
xx Engines
Fire extinction
— Appraisal
See Fire-engines—Valuation
— Juvenile literature
— Valuation
x Fire-engines—Appraisal
Fire-escapes *(Direct)* *(TH2274)*
sa Life-saving at fires
Life-saving nets
xx Building laws
Fire etching
See Pyrography
Fire extinction *(TH9111-9599)*
sa Fire-engines
Fire extinguishers
Fire sprinklers
Fire streams
Fireboats
Firemen's manuals
Forest fires—Prevention and control
Grassland fires—Prevention and control
Hose-couplings
Insurance engineering

Fire extinction *(TH9111-9599)*
(Continued)
       Mine fires—Prevention and control
   x Fire fighting
   xx Fire prevention
      Fires
      Hydraulics
      Insurance engineering
— Chemical systems *(TH9338)*
   sa Fire extinguishing agents
   xx Fire extinguishing agents
— Competitions
— Explosion systems *(TH9339)*
— Juvenile literature
— Research *(Direct)*
— Safety measures
— Vocational guidance
   See Firemen—Vocational guidance
— Water-supply *(TH9311-9334)*
   Example under Water-supply
— — Problems, exercises, etc.
Fire extinguishers *(TH9362)*
   sa Fire extinguishing agents
   x Extinguishers, Fire
   xx Fire extinction
Fire extinguishing agents *(TP266)*
   sa Fire extinction—Chemical systems
   xx Chemicals
      Fire extinction—Chemical systems
      Fire extinguishers
— Patents
Fire fighters
   See Firemen
Fire fighting
   See Fire extinction
Fire in art *(N8217.F5)*
   xx Art
Fire in literature
Fire insurance
   See Insurance, Fire
Fire investigation *(TH9180)*
   sa Arson investigation
   xx Fires
      Investigations
Fire liability law
   See Liability for fire damages
Fire losses
   See Fires
      Insurance, Fire
Fire-making *(Ethnology, GN416-417)*
Fire-marks *(British insurance, HG9799)*
   x Fire-plates
      Insurance, Fire—Office marks
   xx Insurance, Fire
Fire-plates
   See Fire-marks
Fire prevention *(Direct)* *(TH9111-9599)*
   sa Building, Fireproof
      Electric apparatus and appliances—
         Fires and fire prevention
      Fire extinction
      Fireproofing
      Forest fires—Prevention and control
      Grassland fires—Prevention and control
      Insurance engineering
      Lightning-arresters
      Lightning-conductors
      Lightning protection
      Mine fires—Prevention and control
      Radio in fire prevention
      subdivision Fires and fire prevention
         under names of cities, e.g. London—
         Fires and fire prevention; *and under*
         various classes of institutions and
         buildings, e.g. Factories—Fires and
         fire prevention; Theaters—Fires and
         fire prevention
   x Prevention of fires
   xx Fires

      Insurance engineering
— Inspection *(TH9176)*
— Juvenile literature *(TH9148)*
— Laws and regulations
   sa Fire-departments—Law and
      legislation
      Fireworks—Laws and regulations
      Inflammable liquids—Law and
         legislation
      Inflammable materials—Law and
         legislation
      Inflammable textiles—Law and
         legislation
   xx Fire-departments—Law and
      legislation
      Safety regulations
   Note under Safety regulations
— — Forms
— Outlines, syllabi, etc.
— Programmed instruction
— Research *(Direct)* *(TH9120)*
   sa Fire-testing
   x Fire research
   xx Research, Industrial
— Study and teaching
   x Fire prevention education
— Vocational guidance
   See Firemen—Vocational guidance
Fire prevention education
   See Fire prevention—Study and teaching
Fire proofing
   See Fireproofing
Fire pumps
   See Pumping machinery
Fire research
   See Fire prevention—Research
Fire resistant plastics *(TH1074)*
   x Flame retardant plastics
   xx Fireproofing
      Plastics
— Patents
Fire resistant polymers *(TA455.P58)*
   x Fire retardant polymers
      Flame retardant polymers
   xx Fireproofing
      Polymers and polymerization
— Patents
Fire retardant polymers
   See Fire resistant polymers
Fire sprinklers *(TH9336)*
   x Automatic sprinklers
      Sprinkling systems
   xx Fire extinction
      Sprinklers
Fire streams *(TH9323)*
   xx Fire extinction
      Nozzles
Fire-testing *(TH1091-1098)*
   xx Building, Fireproof
      Building materials—Testing
      Fire prevention—Research
      Fireproofing
      Testing
Fire-worshipers *(BL453; Zoroastrianism,*
   BL1590.F5)
   sa Fire (in religion, folk-lore, etc.)
      Parsees
      Zoroastrianism
   xx Fire (in religion, folk-lore, etc.)
      Parsees
      Religion, Primitive
      Religions
      Worship
Firearms *(Manufacture, TS535-7; Military*
   science, U; Naval science, V)
   Covers works on weapons from which a
   missile, as a bullet, ball, or shell, is
   hurled by the action of explosives.

   sa Air guns
      Allen and Wheelock firearms
      Browning firearms
      Colt firearms
      Espingoles
      Flame throwers
      Gunnery
      Gunpowder
      Gunstocks
      Hunting guns
      Machine-guns
      Mountain guns
      Muzzle-loading firearms
      Ordnance
      Pistols
      Revolvers
      Rifles
      Shooting
      Shooting, Military
      Shot-guns
      Silencers (Firearms)
      Target practice
      subdivsion Firearms *under armies,*
         navies, etc., e.g. United States.
         Army—Firearms; United States.
         Navy—Firearms
   x Gun
      Guns
      Small arms
      Weapons
   xx Arms and armor
      Gunnery
      Shooting
      Shooting, Military
— Cold weather operation
— Collectors and collecting
— Identification *(HV8077)*
   sa Forensic ballistics
   x Identification of firearms
   Example under Identification
— Juvenile literature
— Laws and regulations *(Direct)*
   sa Explosives—Law and legislation
      Munitions—Law and legislation
   x Ammunition—Law and legislation
      Firearms control
      Gun control
   xx Munitions—Law and legislation
      Safety regulations
— Locks *(TS535)*
   x Percussion-lock
— Maintenance and repair *(TS535)*
   xx Gunsmithing
— Patents *(TS535)*
— Private collections *(Direct)*
— Sights *(TS535; Artillery, UF854;*
   Military rifles, UD390)
   sa Telescopic sights
   x Sights for firearms
   xx Ordnance
      Telescopic sights
— Taxation *(Direct)*
   x Pistols—Taxation
      Revolvers—Taxation
— Testing
Firearms, American, ₍British, etc.₎ *(Direct)*
   x American ₍British, etc.₎ firearms
Firearms control
   See Firearms—Laws and regulations
Firearms industry and trade *(Direct)*
   (HD9743)
   Here are entered works on the small-arms
   industry. Works on heavy firearms are
   entered under the heading Ordnance.
   sa Gunsmithing
   xx Armaments
      Munitions
— Licenses *(Direct)*

— Taxation
Firebacks *(Direct)*
  xx Ironwork
    Plaques, plaquettes
Fireboards
  See Dummy board figures
Fireboats *(TH9391)*
  x Fire-boats
  xx Fire extinction
    Ships
    Work boats
  — Juvenile literature
Firebrat
Fireflies *(QL596.M2)*
  x Glow-worms
  xx Beetles
    Bioluminescence
  — Juvenile literature
Fireless cookers *(TX831)*
  x Cookers, Fireless
    Cookery, Fireless
    Hay-boxes
  xx Cookery
    Stoves
Firemen
  sa Negro firemen
    Trade-unions—Firemen
  x Fire fighters
  — Caricatures and cartoons
  — Juvenile literature
  — Language (New words, slang, etc.)
  — Legal status, laws, etc. *(Direct)*
  — — Cases
  — Physical training
    Example under Physical education and
      training
  — Pictorial works
  — Salaries, pensions, etc. *(Direct)*
  — Vocational guidance
    x Fire extinction—Vocational guidance
    Fire prevention—Vocational
      guidance
Firemen, Locomotive
  See Locomotive firemen
Firemen's manuals *(TH9151)*
  xx Fire-departments
    Fire extinction
Fireplaces *(Direct)* *(Architecture,*
    NA3050-3055; Heating,
    TH7421-7434)
  sa Chimneys
    Mantels
  x Chimneypieces
    Grates
  xx Architecture—Details
    Chimneys
    Heating
Fireproof building
  See Building, Fireproof
Fireproof paint
  See Paint, Fireproof
Fireproofing *(Building, TH1061-1093;*
    Fabrics, TP267)
  sa Fire resistant plastics
    Fire resistant polymers
    Fire-testing
    Fireproofing of wood
    Paint, Fireproof
  x Fire proofing
    Flameproofing
  xx Building, Fireproof
    Fire prevention
    Insurance, Fire
Fireproofing of fabrics
  x Fabrics, Fireproofing of
  — Patents
Fireproofing of wood
  x Wood—Fireproofing

  xx Fireproofing
    Wood—Preservation
Fires *(Indirect)* *(TH9448-9)*
  sa Fire extinction
    Fire investigation
    Fire prevention
    Forest fires
    Grassland fires
    Incendiary bombs
    Insurance, Fire—Statistics
    Liability for fire damages
    Life-saving at fires
    subdivision Fires and fire prevention
      under names of cities, e.g. London—
      Fires and fire prevention; *and under*
      various classes of institutions and
      buildings, e.g. Psychiatric hospitals—
      Fires and fire prevention;
      Warehouses—Fires and fire
      prevention. *Particular conflagrations*
      are entered under name of place, e.g.
      London—Fire, 1666
  x Conflagrations
    Fire losses
  xx Accidents
    Disasters
    Fire
  — Juvenile literature
  — Pictorial works
Fires in literature
Fires in mines
  See Mine fires
Fires in ships
  See Ships—Fires and fire prevention
Firesetting, Pathological
  See Pyromania
Firewood
  See Wood as fuel
Fireworks *(TP300-301)*
  sa Flares
    Military fireworks
  x Pyrotechnics
  — Accidents and injuries
    x Fireworks—Injuries
  — Early works to 1800
  — Injuries
    See Fireworks—Accidents and injuries
  — Juvenile literature *(TP270.5)*
  — Laws and regulations *(Direct)* *(TP300)*
    xx Accident law
    Fire prevention—Laws and
      regulations
Firing ranges
  See Bombing and gunnery ranges
    Rifle-ranges
Firm names
  See Business names
Firmeza (Dance)
Firms
  See Business enterprises
Firs
  See Fir
First aid for animals *(SF911)*
  xx Veterinary surgery
First aid in illness and injury *(RC86-88)*
  sa Accidents
    Ambulance service
    Ambulances
    Artificial respiration
    Asphyxia
    Bandages and bandaging
    Burns and scalds
    Drowning, Restoration from
    Emergency medical services
    Loss of consciousness
    Medical emergencies
    Outdoor life—Safety measures
    Resuscitation

    Transport of sick and wounded
    subdivision Ambulance service *under*
      names of cities, e.g. London—
      Ambulance service
  x Ambulance drill
    Emergencies
    Emergencies, Medical
    Injuries
    Wounded, First aid to
  xx Accidents
    Assistance in emergencies
    Drowning, Restoration from
    Home accidents
    Hospitals, Military
    Medical emergencies
    Medicine, Military
    Medicine, Naval
    Nurses and nursing
    Rescue work
    Sick
    Surgery, Military
    Wounds—Treatment
  — Juvenile literature
  — Programmed instruction
  — Study and teaching *(Direct)*
First-born children
  See Children, First-born
First century, A.D.
  xx History, Ancient
First Century Christian Fellowship
  See Oxford Group
First communion *(BX2237)*
  sa Lord's Supper—Admission age
  x Communion, First
    Lord's Supper—First communion
  xx Lord's Supper
    Lord's Supper—Admission age
  — Instruction and study
    xx Catechetics
    Example under references from Courses
      of study; Curricula (Courses of
      study); Study, Courses of
  — Stories
    xx Exempla
First communion sermons
  xx Sermons
First-day covers
  See Covers (Philately)
First editions
  See Bibliography—First editions
    subdivision Bibliography—First editions
      under Literature *and under names of*
      literatures, e.g. English literature—
      Bibliography—First editions
First fruits
  See Annates
    Tithes
First generation children
  See Children of immigrants
First grade (Education)
  xx Education, Primary
First impression (Psychology) *(BF323.F5)*
First-mortgage bonds
  See Mortgage bonds
First of June, 1794, Battle of *(DA87.5 1794)*
First of May
  See May Day (Labor holiday)
First-order logic *(BC128)*
  xx Logic, Modern
    Logic, Symbolic and mathematical
First philosophy
  xx Metaphysics
First year teachers *(Direct)*
  x Beginning teachers
    Teachers, First year
  xx Teachers
  — Attitudes
    xx Attitude (Psychology)

First year teachers *(Direct) (Continued)*
— Correspondence, reminiscences, etc.
Fiscal evasion
See Tax evasion
Fiscal policy *(Direct)*
  sa Monetary policy
  xx Economic policy
    Finance, Public
    Monetary policy
— Mathematical models
— Underdeveloped areas
    See Underdeveloped areas—Fiscal
      policy
Fiscal relations, Intergovernmental
  See Intergovernmental fiscal relations
Fiscal relations, International
  See Intergovernmental fiscal relations
Fiscal year
  x Year, Fiscal
  xx Accounting
    Bookkeeping
Fischer-Tropsch process
  See Coal liquefaction
    Synthine process
Fiscus (Roman law)
Fish
  See Fishes
Fish, Canned
  sa Salmon, Canned
    Sardines, Canned
    Tuna, Canned
  x Canned fish
  xx Fishery products, Canned
    Fishery products—Preservation
    Food, Canned
— Standards *(Direct)*
Fish, Dried
  x Dried fish
  xx Fishery products, Dried
    Fishery products—Preservation
Fish, Frozen
  x Frozen fish
  xx Fishery products—Preservation
    Food, Frozen
— Marketing
— Packaging
Fish, Irradiated
  x Irradiated fish
  xx Fishery products—Preservation
    Food, Irradiated
Fish, Preserved
  See Fishery products—Preservation
Fish, Salted *(Indirect) (SH336.S3)*
  x Salt fish
    Salt preservation of fish
  xx Fishery products—Preservation
    Salting of food
Fish, Smoked
  sa Eels, Smoked
  x Food, Smoked
    Smoked fish
  xx Fishery products—Preservation
— Hygienic aspects
Fish (in religion, folk-lore, etc.) *(BV168.F4)*
  sa Catfishes (in religion, folk-lore, etc.)
    Dolphin (in religion, folk-lore, etc.)
    Fishing (in religion, folk-lore, etc.)
  x Folk-lore of fishes
    Ichthys
  xx Christian art and symbolism
    Jesus Christ—Art
    Religion, Primitive
Fish and game licenses *(Indirect)*
  x Fishing licenses
    Hunting licenses
  xx Licenses
Fish as carriers of disease
  xx Communicable diseases

    Diseases—Transmission
Fish as feed
Fish as food *(Food sources, TX385; Food*
    values, TX556.5)
  sa Cookery (Fish)
    Fish protein concentrate
    Sea food
  xx Fishes
    Food
    Sea food
— Analysis *(TX556.5)*
Fish as laboratory animals
Fish attracting by light
  See Light fishing
Fish by-products
  See Fishery products
Fish control *(Indirect)*
  sa Caribe—Control
  x Coarse fish control
    Fishes—Control
    Rough fish control
  xx Fish-culture
    Fishery management
Fish-culture *(Indirect) (SH)*
  sa Animal introduction
    Aquariums
    Fish control
    Fish ponds
    Fish stocking
    Fishes—Feeding and feeds
    Mariculture
    Tropical fish breeding
  x Fish farming
    Fish hatcheries
    Pisciculture
  xx Animal culture
    Aquaculture
    Aquariums
    Fishes
    Mariculture
— Costs
— Economic aspects *(Direct)*
— Equipment and supplies
— Pests
    See Fishes—Diseases and pests
— Terminology
Fish detection *(SH344.2)*
  sa Echo sounding in fishing
    Sonar in fishing
  x Detection of fish
  xx Fisheries
    Fisheries—Equipment and supplies
Fish distribution
  See Fishes—Geographical distribution
Fish eggs
  See Fishes—Eggs
Fish farming
  See Fish-culture
Fish fillets
  x Fillets, Fish
  xx Fish trade
    Fishery products
Fish flour
  See Fish protein concentrate
Fish genetics
  xx Animal genetics
Fish hatcheries
  See Fish-culture
Fish-hawks
  See Ospreys
Fish impressions
  See Fish prints
Fish inspection *(Direct) (Practice, SH335)*
  x Fisheries—Inspection
    Fishes—Inspection
    Inspection of fish
  xx Fishery law and legislation
    Food adulteration and inspection

Fish law
  See Fishery law and legislation
Fish liver oil
  See Fish-oil
Fish management
  See Fishery management
Fish marking
  See Fish tagging
Fish-meal *(Economics, HD9450-9469;*
    Feeding stuffs, SF99; Preparation,
    SH336.F55)
  xx Fishery products
    Fishery products, Dried
— Analysis
Fish-meal as feed
Fish-meal as food
  xx Food
Fish movement (Christianity)
  xx Church work
    Laity
Fish names
  See Fishes—Nomenclature (Popular)
Fish nets
  See Fishing nets
Fish-of-paradise *(Aquariums, QL78)*
  x Paradise-fish
Fish-oil *(SH335; TP676)*
  sa Whale-oil
  x Fish liver oil
  xx Fishery products
    Marine animal oils
Fish-oil as feed
Fish planting
  See Fish stocking
Fish ponds *(Indirect) (SH159)*
  x Fishponds
    Ponds, Fish
  xx Fish-culture
Fish populations
  x Fishes—Population
    Populations, Fish
  xx Animal populations
    Fisheries
    Fishes—Geographical distribution
— Computer programs
— Mathematical models
— Statistical methods
Fish prints *(NE1340)*
  x Fish impressions
    Fish rubbings
    Gyotaku
  xx Fishes in art
    Prints
— Technique
Fish protein concentrate
  x Fish flour
    FPC
  xx Fish as food
    Fishery products
Fish rubbings
  See Fish prints
Fish sanitation
  See Fishery products—Sanitation
Fish-scrap fertilizer *(S659)*
  xx Fertilizers and manures
    Fishery products
    Organic fertilizers
Fish sounds
  xx Animal sounds
    Sounds
Fish stocking *(Indirect)*
  x Fish planting
    Stocking of fish
    Stocking of streams, etc.
  xx Fish-culture
Fish tagging *(Indirect)*
  x Fish marking
    Fishes—Marking

Fishes—Tagging
  xx Animal marking
    Fisheries—Research
    Fishes—Migration
Fish trade *(Direct)* *(HD9450-9469; SH;*
    Tariff, HF2651.F5)
  sa Fish fillets
    Fishery products
    Shellfish trade
    Wages—Fish trade
  xx Fisheries
    Fisheries—Economic aspects
  — Law and legislation *(Direct)*
    xx Fishery law and legislation
  — Tables and ready-reckoners
    (HF5716.F35)
Fish-traps *(SH344; Primitive, GN423)*
Fish waste
  See Fisheries—By-products
Fish wheels
  See Fishwheels
Fisher *(QL737.C25)*
  xx Martens
  — Juvenile literature
Fisher, Fort
  — Expeditions, 1864-1865 *(E477.63)*
    x Fort Fisher expeditions
Fisher exact test
  x Exact test, Fisher
    Test, Fisher exact
  xx Statistical hypothesis testing
Fisheries *(Indirect)* *(SH)*
  sa Artificial reefs
    Bonito fisheries
    Carp fisheries
    Cod-fisheries
    Coral fisheries
    Crab fisheries
    Eel fisheries
    Electric fishing
    Estuarine fisheries
    Fish detection
    Fish populations
    Fish trade
    Fishery management
    Fishery processing industries
    Fishes
    Fishways
    Gillnetting
    Haddock fisheries
    Hake fisheries
    Halibut fisheries
    Herring-fisheries
    Lift net fishing
    Light fishing
    Lobster fisheries
    Mackerel fisheries
    Marlin fisheries
    Menhaden fisheries
    Mullet fisheries
    Plastics in fisheries
    Pump fishing
    Salmon-fisheries
    Sardine fisheries
    Seining
    Shad fisheries
    Shellfish fisheries
    Smelt fisheries
    Strikes and lockouts—Fisheries
    Trawls and trawling
    Trolling (Fishing)
    Trout fisheries
    Tuna fisheries
  x Commercial fishing
    Fishery methods
    Sea-fisheries
  xx Aquatic resources
    Fishes

    Marine resources
    Natural resources
  Note under Salt-water fishing
  — Accounting *(HF5686.F)*
  — By-products *(TP996.F5)*
    x Fish waste
  — Collective bargaining
    See Collective bargaining—Fisheries
  — Collective labor agreements
    See Collective labor agreements—
      Fisheries
  — Computer programs
  — Economic aspects *(Indirect)*
    sa Fish trade
      Fishery policy
  — Equipment and supplies
    sa Electric fishing
      Fish detection
      Fishhooks
      Fishing boats
      Fishing—Implements and appliances
      Fishing nets
      Fishwheels
      Trawls and trawling
    x Fishery gear
      Fishing gear, Commercial
  — — Prices *(Direct)*
  — Finance
  — Hygienic aspects
  — Information services
  — Inspection
    See Fish inspection
  — Labor productivity
  — Law
    See Fishery law and legislation
  — Licenses
  — Navigation
    See Fisheries navigation
  — Notation
  — Pictorial works
  — Production standards
  — Research *(Indirect)*
    sa Exploratory fishing
      Fish tagging
      Fishery products research
    x Sport fishery research
  — Safety measures
  — Statistical methods
  — Taxation *(Direct)*
  — Vocational guidance
    See Fisheries as a profession
Fisheries, Cooperative *(Indirect)*
  sa Fishes—Cooperative marketing
  x Cooperative fisheries
    Fishery cooperatives
  xx Cooperation
  — Finance
  — Law and legislation *(Direct)*
    xx Fishery law and legislation
Fisheries as a profession
  x Fisheries—Vocational guidance
  xx Fishermen
Fisheries navigation *(Indirect)* *(SH344.1)*
  x Fisheries—Navigation
  xx Fishing boats
    Navigation
Fisherman's knots
  See Fishing knots
Fishermen *(Direct)* *(Labor, HD8039.F65)*
  sa Collective bargaining—Fisheries
    Collective labor agreements—Fisheries
    Fisheries as a profession
    Trade-unions—Fishermen
    Wages—Fishermen
    Whalemen
  — Correspondence, reminiscences, etc.
  — Diseases and hygiene
  — Juvenile literature

  — Language (New words, slang, etc.)
  — Legal status, laws, etc. *(Direct)*
    xx Fishery law and legislation
  — Nutrition
  — Pensions *(Direct)*
  — Songs and music *(M1977.F5;*
    M1978.F5)
Fishermen in art
  xx Art
Fishery cooperatives
  See Fisheries, Cooperative
Fishery gear
  See Fisheries—Equipment and supplies
Fishery harbors
  See Fishing ports
Fishery law and legislation *(Direct)*
    (SH323-7; Fish and game laws,
    SK355-579)
  sa Diving, Submarine—Law and legislation
    Fish inspection
    Fish trade—Law and legislation
    Fisheries, Cooperative—Law and
      legislation
    Fishermen—Legal status, laws, etc.
    Fishery products—Law and legislation
    Oyster-culture—Law and legislation
    Salmon-fisheries—Law and legislation
    Sealing—Law and legislation
    Shrimp fisheries—Law and legislation
    Turtle fishing—Law and legislation
    Whaling—Laws and regulations
  x Fish law
    Fisheries—Law
    Fishing—Law
    Fishing regulations
    Law, Fishery
  xx Fishery policy
    Fishing
    International law
    Territorial waters
    Water—Laws and legislation
    Wildlife conservation—Law and
      legislation
Fishery management *(Indirect)*
  sa Fish control
  x Fish management
  xx Fisheries
    Wildlife management
  — Mathematical models *(SH328)*
Fishery methods
  See Fisheries
Fishery policy *(Indirect)*
  sa Fishery law and legislation
  xx Fisheries—Economic aspects
    Industry and state
Fishery processing industries *(Direct)*
  xx Fisheries
    Fishery products
  — Automation
  — Equipment and supplies
  — Waste disposal
Fishery products *(Indirect)* *(Fisheries,*
    SH335-7; Fishery products,
    HD9450-9469)
  sa Fish fillets
    Fish-meal
    Fish-oil
    Fish protein concentrate
    Fish-scrap fertilizer
    Fishery processing industries
    Klipfish
    Seafood processing
  x Fish by-products
  xx Aquatic resources
    Fish trade
    Marine resources
    Seafood processing
  — Costs

Fishery products *(Indirect)* *(Fisheries, SH335-7; Fishery products, HD9450-9469)* *(Continued)*
— Grading
— Law and legislation *(Direct)*
   xx Fishery law and legislation
— Microbiology
— Packing
— Preservation *(TX612.F5; Fisheries, SH335-7)*
   sa Fish, Canned
      Fish, Dried
      Fish, Frozen
      Fish, Irradiated
      Fish, Salted
      Fish, Smoked
      Fishery products, Canned
      Fishery products, Dried
      Fishery products, Frozen
      Shrimps, Frozen
   x Fish, Preserved
   xx Cold storage
      Food—Preservation
   Example under Canning and preserving; Food supply
— Prices *(Direct)*
— Quality control
— Research
   See Fishery products research
— Sanitation *(QR118)*
   x Fish sanitation
— Standards
— Storage
   x Sea food—Storage
— Transportation

Fishery products, Canned
   sa Crabs, Canned
      Fish, Canned
      Lobsters, Canned
      Oysters, Canned
   x Canned fishery products
      Sea food, Canned
   xx Fishery products—Preservation
      Food, Canned

Fishery products, Dried *(Indirect)*
   sa Fish, Dried
      Fish-meal
   x Dried fishery products
      Seafood, Dried
   xx Fishery products—Preservation

Fishery products, Frozen *(Indirect)*
   x Frozen fishery products
      Sea food, Frozen
   xx Fishery products—Preservation
      Food, Frozen

Fishery products research *(Direct)*
   x Fishery products—Research
   xx Fisheries—Research
      Research
      Research, Industrial

Fishery resources *(Indirect)* *(SH327.5)*
   sa Exploratory fishing
   xx Aquatic resources
      Marine resources

Fishes *(Indirect)* *(QL614-639; Folk-lore, GR745)*
   sa Aquarium fishes
      Aquariums
      Exploratory fishing
      Fish as food
      Fish-culture
      Fisheries
      Fishing
      Ichthyology
      Marine fauna
      Marine fishes
      Poisonous fishes
      Tropical fish

      names of classes, orders, etc. of fishes, e.g. Carp, Ganoidei, Perch, Teleostei
   x Fish
      Pisces
   xx Aquatic animals
      Fisheries
      Ichthyology
      Marine fauna
      Vertebrates
— Age
   x Fishes, Age of
— Anatomy *(QL639)*
   sa Air-bladder (in fishes)
      Branchial arch
      Branchiostegals
      Chloride cells
      Electric organs in fishes
      Fins
      Gills
      Interrenal gland
      Scales (Fishes)
      Weberian apparatus
      subdivision Fishes *under* Digestive organs, Nervous system, Sense-organs
— Bacteriology
   See Fishes—Microbiology
— Behavior
   sa subdivision Behavior *under names of particular fishes, e.g.* Sticklebacks —Behavior
— — Juvenile literature
— Catalogs and collections *(QL618)*
— Classification *(QL618)*
   sa Fishes—Identification
— Collection and preservation *(Fishery exhibitions, SH338-343; Zoology, QL63)*
   xx Taxidermy
      Zoological specimens—Collection and preservation
— Color
   See Color of fishes
— Composition
   xx Fishes—Physiology
— Control
   See Fish control
— Cooperative marketing *(Indirect)*
   x Cooperative marketing of fish
   xx Fisheries, Cooperative
— Cytology
— Development *(QL639)*
   sa Embryology—Fishes
      Larvae—Fishes
— Digestive organs
   See Digestive organs—Fishes
— Diseases and pests *(SH171-9)*
   sa Bacterial gill disease
      Channel catfish virus disease
   x Fish-culture—Pests
— Distribution
   See Fishes—Geographical distribution
— Ecology
— Eggs
   x Fish eggs
   Example under Eggs
— — Juvenile literature
— Embryology
   See Embryology—Fishes
— Evolution *(QL618.2)*
   xx Vertebrates—Evolution
— Fecundity
— Feeding and feeds *(SH156)*
   sa Fishes—Food
   xx Fish-culture
      Fishes—Food
— Field guides
   See Fishes—Identification

— Food *(QL639)*
   sa Fishes—Feeding and feeds
   xx Fishes—Feeding and feeds
— Genetics
— Geographical distribution *(QL619-637)*
   sa Fish populations
   x Fish distribution
      Fishes—Distribution
      Fishes—Zoogeography
   xx Zoogeography
— Growth
— Identification
   sa Fishes—Nomenclature (Popular)
   x Fishes—Field guides
      Fishes—Keys
   xx Fishes—Classification
— Inspection
   See Fish inspection
— Juvenile literature *(QL617)*
— Keys
   See Fishes—Identification
— Larvae
   See Larvae—Fishes
— Legends and stories *(QL795.F7)*
   sa Fishing stories
— Marking
   See Fish tagging
— Microbiology
   x Fishes—Bacteriology
— Migration *(QL639)*
   sa Fish tagging
      Smolting
   x Migration of fishes
— Nervous system
   See Nervous system—Fishes
— Nomenclature *(QL618)*
   xx Zoology—Nomenclature
— Nomenclature (Popular) *(QL618)*
   x Fish names
   xx Fishes—Identification
      Zoology—Nomenclature (Popular)
— Physiology
   sa Fishes—Composition
      Fishes—Reproduction
      Smolting
— Pictorial works *(QL616)*
— Population
   See Fish populations
— Prices *(Direct)*
— Psychology
— Reproduction
   sa Spawning
   xx Fishes—Physiology
      Reproduction
— Research
   See Ichthyological research
— Scales
   See Scales (Fishes)
— Sense-organs
   See Sense-organs—Fishes
— Spawning
   See Spawning
— Tagging
   See Fish tagging
— Terminology
   xx Zoology—Nomenclature
— Transportation
— Tropics
   sa Tropical fish
   Note under Tropical fish
— Zoogeography
   See Fishes—Geographical distribution

Fishes, Age of
   See Fishes—Age

Fishes, Anadromous
   sa Smolting
      Steelhead (Fish)
   x Anadromous fishes

Fishes, Apodal
See Eels
Fishes, Deep-sea
  x Deep-sea fishes
  xx Marine fishes
Fishes, Draught of (Miracle)
  See Miraculous draught of fishes (Miracle)
Fishes, Effect of water pollution on *(Indirect)*
  xx Water—Pollution
  — Juvenile literature
Fishes, Electric
  See Electric organs in fishes
Fishes, Fossil *(QE851-2)*
  sa Acanthodii
  — Juvenile literature
Fishes, Fresh-water *(Indirect)*
  sa names of classes, orders, etc. of
    fresh-water fishes
  x Fresh-water fishes
  xx Fresh-water fauna
Fishes in art
  sa Catfishes in art
    Fish prints
  xx Art
    Fishing in art
Fishhooks
  xx Fisheries—Equipment and supplies
Fishing *(Indirect)* *(SH401-691)*
  sa Aeronautics in fishing
    Arctic char fishing
    Artificial reefs
    Ayu fishing
    Bait
    Bass fishing
    Big game fishing
    Black bass fishing
    Bream fishing
    Brook trout fishing
    Brown trout fishing
    Carp fishing
    Casting (Fishing)
    Channel bass fishing
    Eel fishing
    Electric fishing
    Fishery law and legislation
    Flatfish fishing
    Flies, Artificial
    Fly fishing
    Golden trout fishing
    Grayling fishing
    Hunting and fishing clubs
    Ice fishing
    Largemouth bass fishing
    Marlin fishing
    Pickerel fishing
    Pike fishing
    Rainbow trout fishing
    Roach fishing
    Salmon-fishing
    Salt-water fishing
    Sea bass fishing
    Sea trout fishing
    Shark fishing
    Sheatfish fishing
    Silver salmon fishing
    Smallmouth bass fishing
    Spear fishing
    Spin-fishing
    Steelhead fishing
    Striped bass fishing
    Tarpon fishing
    Tournament fishing
    Trolling (Fishing)
    Trout fishing
    Turtle fishing
    Walleye fishing
  x Angling
    Recreational fishing

    Sport fishing
  xx Aquatic sports
    Fishes
  Example under Sports
  — Anecdotes, facetiae, satire, etc.
    sa Fishing stories
    xx Fishing stories
  — Caricatures and cartoons
  — Early works to 1800
  — Economic aspects *(Direct)*
  — Implements and appliances *(SH451-5)*
    sa Fishing rods
      Fishing tackle
    xx Fisheries—Equipment and supplies
  — Juvenile literature
  — Law
      See Fishery law and legislation
  — Literary collections
  — Pictorial works
    sa Fishing in art
  — Safety measures
  — Terminology
Fishing, Electric
  See Electric fishing
Fishing, Primitive *(Indirect)* *(GN423)*
  sa Harpoons
    Indians of North America—Fishing
  xx Archaeology
    Industries, Primitive
Fishing (in religion, folk-lore, etc.) *(GN423)*
  x Folk-lore of fishing
  xx Fish (in religion, folk-lore, etc.)
    Religion, Primitive
Fishing boats *(Indirect)*
  sa Bugeyes (Boats)
    Dories (Boats)
    Fisheries navigation
    Sharpies (Sailboats)
    Skipjacks
    Trabacolos
  xx Boats and boating
    Fisheries—Equipment and supplies
    Ships
    Work boats
  — Automation
  — Electronic equipment
  — Equipment and supplies
  — Flags, insignia, etc.
  — Hydraulic equipment
  — Maintenance and repair
  — Pictorial works
  — Safety measures
      xx Merchant marine—Safety measures
Fishing contests
  See Tournament fishing
Fishing Creek, Battle of, 1862
  See Mill Springs, Battle of, 1862
Fishing-flies
  See Flies, Artificial
Fishing gear, Commercial
  See Fisheries—Equipment and supplies
Fishing in art
  sa Fishes in art
  xx Fishing—Pictorial works
    Sports in art
Fishing in literature
  sa Fishing in the Bible
Fishing in the Bible
  xx Fishing in literature
    Sea in the Bible
Fishing knots *(Indirect)* *(SH452.9.K6)*
  x Fisherman's knots
  xx Fishing tackle
    Knots and splices
Fishing licenses
  See Fish and game licenses
Fishing lodges *(Direct)*
  xx Architecture, Domestic

    Club-houses
    Dwellings
Fishing lures
  sa Flies, Artificial
  xx Bait
    Flies, Artificial
Fishing nets
  sa Glass fishing floats
  x Fish nets
    Fishnets
  xx Fisheries—Equipment and supplies
    Nets
  — Pictorial works *(SH344.8.N4)*
Fishing ports *(Indirect)* *(TC373)*
  x Fishery harbors
  xx Harbors
Fishing regulations
  See Fishery law and legislation
Fishing rods *(Indirect)* *(SH452)*
  x Rods, Fishing
  xx Fishing—Implements and appliances
    Fishing tackle
Fishing stories
  sa Fishing—Anecdotes, facetiae, satire,
    etc.
  xx Fiction
    Fishes—Legends and stories
    Fishing—Anecdotes, facetiae, satire,
    etc.
    Sports stories
Fishing tackle *(SH447-453)*
  sa Fishing knots
    Fishing rods
  xx Fishing—Implements and appliances
Fishing villages *(Indirect)*
  xx Villages
Fishnets
  See Fishing nets
Fishplates
  See Railroads—Rails—Fastenings
Fishponds
  See Fish ponds
Fishways *(Indirect)* *(SH153)*
  xx Dams
    Fisheries
    Flood dams and reservoirs
  — Costs
  — Specifications
Fishwheels *(Indirect)*
  x Fish wheels
    Salmon wheels
  xx Fisheries—Equipment and supplies
Fissiculata *(QE783.B6)*
  xx Blastoidea
Fission, Nuclear
  See Nuclear fission
Fission (Biology)
  xx Reproduction, Asexual
Fission dating method
  See Radioactive dating
Fission products
  sa Radioactive fallout
    Reactor fuel reprocessing
  xx Nuclear fission
    Radioactive substances
  — Computer programs
  — Decay
      Example under Half-life (Nuclear phy-
        sics); *and under references from*
        Decay, Radioactive; Radioactive
        decay
  — Spectra
Fissionable materials
  See Radioactive substances
Fistula *(RD643)*
Fistula, Anal *(RD643)*
Fistula, Arteriovenous
  sa Arteriovenous anastomosis

Fistula, Arteriovenous *(Continued)*
   x Aneurysms, Arteriovenous
      Arteriovenous aneurysms
      Arteriovenous fistula
   Example under Arteries—Diseases
Fistula, Biliary
   x Biliary fistula
   xx Biliary tract—Diseases
Fistula, Branchial cleft
   x Branchial cleft fistula
   xx Aorta—Diseases
Fistula, Gastric
   x Gastric fistula
Fistula, Intestinal
   x Intestinal fistula
Fistula, Labyrinthine
   x Labyrinthine fistula
   xx Labyrinth (Ear)
Fistula, Lacrimal *(RD643)*
   x Lacrimal fistula
   xx Lacrimal organs—Diseases
Fistula, Recto-urethral
   x Recto-urethral fistula
   xx Rectum—Diseases
      Urethra—Diseases
Fistula, Tracheal
   See Fistula, Tracheoesophageal
Fistula, Tracheoesophageal
   x Fistula, Tracheal
   xx Deformities
      Trachea—Diseases
Fistula, Urinary
   x Urinary fistula
Fistula, Uterine
   xx Uterus—Diseases
Fistula, Vesico-vaginal
   x Vesicovaginal fistula
   xx Bladder—Diseases
Fits, Press
   See Press fits
Fits (Engineering)
   See Tolerance (Engineering)
Fitting, Curve
   See Curve fitting
Fitting, Shrink
   See Shrink fitting
Fitting (Engineering)
   See Machine-shop practice
Fitting out of boats
   See Boats and boating—Equipment and
      supplies
Fitzhugh's Woods, Battle of, 1864 *(E476.35)*
Fiu language
   xx Melanesian languages
Five (The number)
   xx Symbolism of numbers
Five (The number) in art
   xx Art
Five-and-ten-cent stores
   See Variety stores
Five Civilized Tribes *(E78.I5; E78.O45)*
   sa Cherokee Indians
      Chickasaw Indians
      Choctaw Indians
      Creek Indians
      Seminole Indians
   x Indians of North America—Five
      Civilized Tribes
   xx Cherokee Indians
      Chickasaw Indians
      Choctaw Indians
      Creek Indians
      Indians of North America—Indian
         Territory
      Indians of North America—Oklahoma
      Seminole Indians
   — Government relations
   — Land tenure

— Land transfers
— Legal status, laws, etc.
— Tribal citizenship
Five Commandments (Buddhism)
   See Five Precepts (Buddhism)
Five Forks, Va., Battle of, 1865 *(E477.67)*
   sa White Oak Road, Va., Battle of, 1865
Five hundred (Game) *(GV1295.F5)*
Five Nations
   See Iroquois Indians
Five pillars of Islam
   See Pillars of Islam
Five Precepts (Buddhism) *(BQ5485-5525)*
   x Five Commandments (Buddhism)
      Precepts, Five (Buddhism)
   xx Buddha and Buddhism—Discipline
      Buddhist laymen—Discipline
      Buddhist precepts
Five Sacred Wounds
   sa Sacred Heart, Devotion to
      Wound in the Side
   x Five Wounds
      Wounds, Five Sacred
   xx Jesus Christ—Crucifixion
Five-suit bridge *(GV1282.9.F5)*
   xx Bridge whist
      Contract bridge
Five thousand, Feeding of the (Miracle)
   See Feeding of the five thousand (Miracle)
Five Wounds
   See Five Sacred Wounds
Five-Year Plan (Russia)
   See Russia—Economic policy
Fives (Game) *(GV1003)*
Fix-point estimation
   x Point estimation
   xx Estimation theory
Fixation (Histology)
   x Tissue fixation
      Tissues—Fixation
   xx Cytology—Technique
      Histology—Technique
      Tissues—Preservation
Fixed costs
   See Overhead costs
Fixed ideas
   See Eccentrics and eccentricities
      Monomania
      Obsessive-compulsive neuroses
Fixed point theorems (Topology)
      (QA614.5.F5)
   x Points, Fixed (Topology)
   xx Topology
Fixed storage
   See Read-only storage
Fixtures (Law) *(Direct)*
   sa Appurtenances
      Personal property
      Real property
   xx Appurtenances
      Landlord and tenant
      Real property
      Things (Law)
Fixtures (Mechanical devices)
   See Jigs and fixtures
Fjord horse
Fjords *(Indirect)* *(GB454.F5)*
   x Fiords
   xx Coasts
Fjort (African tribe)
   See Bakongo (African tribe)
Flabella *(NK4870)*
   xx Christian art and symbolism
      Fans
Flabellula
FLAC computer
   See Seac computer

Flag Day *(JK1761; LB3531)*
   xx Days
      Holidays
Flag-waving (Exercise) *(GV488)*
   xx Drill (not military)
Flagella (Microbiology)
   xx Bacteria—Motility
      Cilia and ciliary motion
      Spermatozoa—Motility
Flagellants and flagellation *(HV8613-8621)*
   sa Disciplinati
      Fareinistes
   x Flagellation
      Flogging
      Whipping
   xx Asceticism
      Corporal punishment
Flagellata *(QL368.F5)*
   sa Dinoflagellata
      Ebriida
      Silicoflagellata
   xx Infusoria
      Protozoa
Flagellation
   See Corporal punishment
      Flagellants and flagellation
Flageolet *(ML935-6)*
   sa Galoubet
      Penny whistle
      Recorder (Musical instrument)
   xx Flute
      Recorder (Musical instrument)
Flageolet and piano music *(M240-242)*
   x Piano and flageolet music
Flageolet and piano music, Juvenile *(M1405)*
Flageolet and violin music *(M290)*
   x Violin and flageolet music
Flageolet and violin music, Arranged *(M290)*
Flageolet music *(M60-62)*
   xx Flute music
      Recorder music
Flageolet music, Arranged *(M63-64)*
Flageolet music (Flageolets (2)) *(M288-9)*
Flageolet music (Flageolets (2)), Arranged
      (M288-9)
Flagrans crimen *(Direct)*
   x Flagrant délit
   xx Criminal law
      Criminal procedure
      Evidence, Criminal
Flagrant délit
   See Flagrans crimen
Flags *(Direct)* *(Emblems of state, JC345-7;*
      Heraldry, CR101-115; Merchant
      marine signaling, VK385; Military
      science, U360-365, UC590-595;
      Naval science, V300-305)
   sa Church pennants
      Emblems, National
      Guidons
      Signals and signaling
      Standards, Military
      Tankas (Tibetan scrolls)
      United Nations—Emblem and flag
      Yacht flags
      subdivision Flags, insignia, etc. *under*
        subjects, e.g. Steamboat lines—Flags,
        insignia, etc.
   x Banners
      Colors (Flags)
      Ensigns
   xx Emblems, National
      Heraldry
      Signals and signaling
      Standards, Military
   — Juvenile literature
   — Pictorial works
   — Public opinion

— Germany
    x Nuremberg laws

— Great Britain
    x Union Jack

— United States
    sa United States. Army—Flags
        United States. Navy—Flags
    x United States—Flags

— — Catalogs
— — Juvenile literature
Flags of truce
    x Bearers of a flag of truce
        Truce, Flags of
    xx Armistices
        War (International law)
Flake board
    See Particle board
Flake-glass laminates
    x Glass-flake laminates
    xx Glass reinforced plastics
        Laminated plastics
Flame *(Chemistry, QD516; Sound, QC241)*
    xx Combustion
        Fire
Flame hardening *(TN752.F)*
    xx Metals—Heat treatment
        Surface hardening
Flame monitoring systems *(TH6882)*
    xx Gas-burners
Flame photometry
    xx Photometry
        Spectrum analysis
Flame retardant plastics
    See Fire resistant plastics
Flame retardant polymers
    See Fire resistant polymers
Flame scarfing
    See Scarfing (Metals)
Flame spectroscopy
    sa Arc spectra
    xx Spectrum analysis
Flame spraying
    x Spraying, Flame
    xx Protective coatings
Flame throwers *(UG447)*
    xx Firearms
Flamenco *(GV1796.F)*
    x Cante hondo
Flamenco music
    x Cante flamenco
        Cante hondo
Flameproofing
    See Fireproofing
Flamingos *(QL696.P45)*
    x Odontoglossae
— Behavior
— Juvenile literature
Flammable materials
    See Inflammable materials
Flammable textiles
    See Inflammable textiles
Flancs-de-Chien Indians
    See Thlingchadinne Indians
Flandreau Indians
    See Santee Indians
Flanges *(TA492.F5)*
    sa Pipe flanges
— Design and construction
— Standards

Flannel boards
    See Flannelgraphs
Flannelgraphs
    x Flannel boards
    xx Teaching—Aids and devices
Flannellet *(TS1580; Fire protection, TH9446.F6)*
Flaps (Aeroplanes) *(TL673.F6)*
    sa Jet flaps (Aeroplanes)
        Spoilers (Aeroplanes)
    x Aeroplanes—Flaps
        High-lift devices
    xx Aerofoils
        Aeroplanes—Control surfaces
        Ailerons
        Lift (Aerodynamics)
        Spoilers (Aeroplanes)
Flares
    xx Fireworks
        Lighting
        Signals and signaling
Flares, Proton
    See Proton flares
Flares, Solar
    See Solar flares
Flash cards
    See Word recognition
Flash distillation process (Saline water conversion)
    See Saline water conversion—Flash distillation process
Flash-light photography
    See Photography, Flash-light
Flasks
    See Bottles
Flat-coated retriever *(SF429.F)*
    xx Retrievers
Flat-footed flies
    xx Flies
Flat-headed snake
Flat pea *(SB205.F)*
    xx Forage plants
        Peas
Flat racing
    See Horse-racing
Flat roofs *(TH2409)*
    x Roofs, Flat
— Thermal properties
Flatboats
    xx Boats and boating
        River life
— Juvenile literature
Flatfish fishing *(SH691.F5)*
    xx Fishing
Flatfishes *(QL638.P7)*
    sa Halibut
    x Flounders
        Soles
        Turbots
Flatfoot *(RD785)*
    x Pes planus
    xx Foot—Abnormities and deformities
Flathead Indians
    See Salish Indians
Flathead sole *(QL638.P7)*
    x Sole, Flathead
Flatheaded adders
    See Hognose snakes
Flatirons
    See Irons (Pressing)
Flatness measurement
    xx Mensuration
        Surfaces (Technology)
Flats
    See Apartment houses
Flats, Tidal
    See Tidal flats

Flattery, Servile
    See Toadyism
Flatulence
    xx Gastrointestinal gas
        Stomach—Diseases
— Anecdotes, facetiae, satire, etc.
Flatware
    See Tableware
Flatware, Silver
    See Silverware
Flatware, Stainless steel
    See Tableware, Stainless steel
Flatworms
    See Platyhelminthes
Flavins
    sa Flavoproteins
        Quercetin
    xx Coenzymes
        Pigments
Flavonoids
    sa Bioflavonoids
— Analysis
— Spectra
Flavoproteins
    sa Riboflavin
    xx Dehydrogenases
        Flavins
Flavor
    sa Milk—Flavor and odor
    xx Food—Analysis
Flavoring essences *(TP450-453)*
    sa Essences and essential oils
        Sweeteners
        Vanilla
    xx Cookery
        Essences and essential oils
        Food
— Patents
— Specifications *(Direct)*
Flax *(Indirect) (Botany, QK495.L74; Culture, SB253; Technology, TS1700-1731; Trade, HD9155, HE7677.F55, HF5716.F4)*
    sa Flax straw
        Linen
    x Baltic hemp
    xx Fibers
        Linen
        Oilseed plants
        Yarn
    Example under Fiber plants; Textile fibers
— Disease and pest resistance
— Diseases and pests
        sa *specific diseases and pests, e.g.* Flax rust; Flaxwilt
— Drying
— Fertilizers and manures
— Harvesting
— Microbiology
— Varieties
Flax as feed
    xx Flax straw
Flax industry *(Direct)*
    sa Wages—Flax and hemp trade
    xx Textile industry and fabrics
— Equipment and supplies
— Job descriptions
Flax rust
    Example under Flax—Diseases and pests
Flax spinning *(TS1727)*
    xx Spinning
Flax straw
    sa Flax as feed
    xx Flax
        Straw
Flaxseed *(Culture, SB299.F6; Trade, HD9155, HF5716.F5)*
    x Linseed

Flaxseed (Culture, SB299.F6; Trade,
      HD9155, HF5716.F5)
      (Continued)
— Grading
— Varieties
Flaxwilt
   Example under Flax—Diseases and pests
Flea-beetles (QL596.C5; SB608; Pests,
      SB945)
      sa Alder flea-beetle
         Purslane flea-beetle
         Tobacco flea-beetle
      xx Beetles
Fleas (Indirect) (QL503.A7)
      sa Beach-flea
         Oriental rat flea
      xx Diptera
— Control (Indirect) (RA641.F5)
      x Fleas—Extermination
— Extermination
         See Fleas—Control
— Juvenile literature
Fleas as carriers of disease (RA641.F5)
      xx Communicable diseases
         Insects as carriers of disease
Fleas in literature
Fleece
   See Wool
Fleeing (in religion, folk-lore, etc.)
      sa Fleeing in the Bible
      x Folk-lore of fleeing
      xx Religion, Primitive
Fleeing from scene of accident
   See Hit-and-run drivers
Fleeing in the Bible
      x Bible—Fleeing
      xx Fleeing (in religion, folk-lore, etc.)
Fleet ballistic missile weapons systems
      (V990-995)
      sa Atomic submarines
         Polaris (Missile)
      xx Atomic submarines
         Ballistic missiles
         United States. Navy—Weapons
            systems
         Weapons systems
— Production control
Fleet train
   See Naval auxiliary vessels
Fleets, Motor vehicle
   See Motor vehicle fleets
Fleetwood, Battle of, 1863
   See Brandy Station, Battle of, 1863
Flemings (DH491; England, DA122.F6)
**Flemings in France, ⌈Great Britain, South
      Africa, etc.⌉**
Flemish altarpieces
   See Altarpieces, Flemish
Flemish ballads and songs (Collections,
      PT6330-40; History, PT6140)
      sa Ballads, Flemish
         Folk-songs, Flemish
         Songs, Flemish
Flemish drama (Direct)
— 19th century
— 20th century
Flemish drawings
   See Drawings, Flemish
Flemish furniture
   See Furniture, Flemish
Flemish landscape painting
   See Landscape painting, Flemish
Flemish language (PF1001-1199)
      sa Dutch language
      xx Dutch language
         Germanic languages
         Low German language
   Example under Germanic philology
Flemish letters

Flemish literature (Collections,
      PT6215-6397; History, etc.,
      PT6000-6199)
      For literature in the Flemish language
      from 1830 on. The older literature is
      entered under the heading Dutch liter-
      ature.
      sa Belgian literature
      x Belgian literature (Flemish)
      xx Dutch literature
   Example under Germanic philology
   Note under Flemish poetry
Flemish movement (DH491)
Flemish newspapers (History, etc.,
      PN5261-9)
      xx Belgian newspapers
Flemish periodicals (History, etc.,
      PN5261-5270)
      xx Belgian periodicals
Flemish philology
Flemish poetry (Collections, PT6330-6340;
      History, etc., PT6140)
      Cf. note under Flemish literature.
— 20th century
Flemish prose literature
— 19th century
— 20th century
Flemish tapestry
   See Tapestry, Flemish
Flemish wit and humor (PN6222.B4)
Flemish wit and humor, Pictorial
Flesh (Theology)
      xx Man (Theology)
         Theology, Doctrinal
— Biblical teaching
Fleur-de-lis (CR41.F6)
      xx Devices
   Example under Heraldry
Fleurons
   See Type ornaments
Fleurus, Battle of, 1690 (D280.F6)
Fleurus, Battle of, 1794 (DC222.F6)
Flexible gunnery
   See Aerial gunnery
Flexible shafting (TJ1057)
      xx Shafting
— Standards (Direct)
Flexible surfaces, Equilibrium of
   See Equilibrium of flexible surfaces
Flexography (Z252.5.F6)
      x Aniline printing
      xx Printing, Practical
Flexometer (Textile testing, TS1449)
Flexure (Astronomical adjustments, QB154;
      Beams, TG265)
      Here are entered works on the bending
      behavior of materials. Works dealing
      with bending as a forming process are
      entered under Bending.
      sa Elasticity
         Girders
         Strains and stresses
         Strength of materials
   Note under Bending
Flick Trial, Nuremberg, 1947-1949
   See War crime trials—Nuremberg—Flick
      case, 1947-1949
Flicker fusion
      x Critical flicker frequency
         Fusion (Vision)
      xx Vision
Flicorno
   See Fluegelhorn
Fliers, Advertising
   See Advertising fliers
Flies (QL531-8)
      sa Blowflies
         Botflies

         Crane-flies
         Face fly
         Flat-footed flies
         Frit-flies
         Fruit-flies
         Green-bottle flies
         Hessian flies
         Horn fly
         Horseflies
         Housefly
         Lacewing flies
         Louse flies
         Moth-flies
         Robber flies
         Sawflies
         Thickheaded flies
         Tsetse-flies
         Warble-flies
         Winter crane-flies
      x Fly
         Water-flies
      xx Diptera
   Example under Household pests
— Control
         See Fly control
— Extermination
         See Fly control
— Juvenile literature
— Resistance to insecticides
      Example under Resistance to insecticides
Flies, Artificial (SH451-5)
      sa Fishing lures
         Fly-casting
         Fly tying
      x Artificial flies
         Fishing-flies
      xx Fishing
         Fishing lures
— Pictorial works
Flies as carriers of disease (RA641.F6)
      xx Communicable diseases
         Insects as carriers of disease
Flight (Bird flight, QL698; Mechanics of
      flight, TL570-578)
      sa Aeronautics
         Flying-machines
         Stability of aeroplanes
         Wings
      x Birds—Flight
         Flying
      xx Aeronautics
         Animal locomotion
         Animal mechanics
         Birds
         Locomotion
         Wings
— Juvenile literature
— Legends
— Medical aspects
      See Aviation medicine
— Physiological aspects (RC1075)
      x Aviation physiology
         Physiological aspects of flight
      xx Aviation medicine
         Aviation toxicology
— — Age factors
— Pictorial works
— Psychological aspects
      See Aeronautics—Psychology
Flight, Unpowered
   See Gliding and soaring

Flight control *(TL589.4)*
> Here are entered works on systems that govern aircraft and space vehicle attitude, stability, and direction of motion. Works on systems for supervising the navigation of aircraft and space vehicles from one location to another are entered under Guidance systems (Flight)

- *sa* Aeroplanes—Control systems
  Artificial satellites—Control systems
  Automatic pilot (Aeroplanes)
  Automatic pilot (Helicopters)
  Guided missiles—Control systems
  Helicopters—Control systems
  Rockets (Aeronautics)—Control systems
  Space vehicles—Control systems
- *x* Control systems (Flight)
- *xx* Automatic control
  Guidance systems (Flight)
- *Note under* Guidance systems (Flight)

Flight crews *(Direct)*
- *sa* Air lines—Hostesses
  Air pilots
  Flight engineers
  Flight navigators
  Flight radio operators
- *x* Aeroplanes—Crews
  Air crews
  Aircraft crews
  Aircrews
  Flying personnel
- *xx* Air lines—Employees
- — Diseases and hygiene
  See Aviation medicine
- — Juvenile literature
- — Legal status, laws, etc. *(Direct)*
- — Licenses *(Direct)*
- — Pensions *(Direct)*

Flight decks, Aircraft carrier
  See Aircraft carriers—Flight decks
Flight easements
  See Avigation easements

Flight engineering
- *xx* Aeronautical instruments
  Aeroplanes—Maintenance and repair
  Aeroplanes—Motors

Flight engineers *(Direct)*
- *xx* Air lines—Employees
  Flight crews
- — Licenses *(Direct)*

Flight in art
- *sa* Aeronautics in art
- *xx* Art

Flight instruction
  See Flight training
Flight into Egypt
  See Jesus Christ—Flight into Egypt

Flight navigators *(Direct)*
- *x* Air navigators
- *xx* Aeroplanes—Piloting
  Air lines—Employees
  Flight crews
  Navigation (Aeronautics)
- — Legal status, laws, etc. *(Direct)*

Flight radio operators *(Direct)*
- *x* Aeroplanes—Radio operators
- *xx* Flight crews
  Radio in aeronautics
  Radio operators
- — Licenses *(Direct)*

Flight recorders *(TL589.2.F5)*
- *x* Aeroplanes—Flight recorders
  Recorders, Flight
- *xx* Aeronautical instruments

Flight simulators
- *sa* Helicopter flight trainer

Link trainers
- *x* OFT (Flight simulator)
- *xx* Aeronautics, Military—Study and teaching
  Aeroplanes—Piloting
  Flight training
  Synthetic training devices
  Training planes

Flight testing of aeroplanes
  See Aeroplanes—Flight testing
  Aeroplanes, Military—Flight testing
Flight testing of helicopters
  See Helicopters—Flight testing
Flight to Jupiter
  See Space flight to Jupiter
Flight to Mars
  See Space flight to Mars
Flight to Mercury
  See Space flight to Mercury
Flight to the moon
  See Space flight to the moon
Flight tracking
  See Artificial satellites—Tracking
  Balloons—Tracking
  Guided missiles—Tracking
  Space vehicles—Tracking

Flight training *(TL710-713)*
- *sa* Aeroplanes—Piloting
  Flight simulators
  Link trainers
  Space flight training
  Training planes
- *x* Flight instruction
  Flying classes
- *xx* Aeronautics—Study and teaching
  Aeroplanes—Piloting
- — Curricula

Flightless cormorant *(QL696.P4745)*
Flights, Transatlantic
  See Transatlantic flights
Flights, Transpacific
  See Transpacific flights

Flights around the world *(G445)*
- *x* World flights
- *xx* Aeronautics—Flights
  Geography, Aerial
  Voyages around the world

Flint *(Economics, HD9585.F4; Mineral industries, TN948.F5; Mineralogy, QE391.F5)*
Flint implements
  See Stone implements
Flitch of Dunmow
  See Dunmow flitch
Float (Banking)
  See Bank float

Floating batteries *(V890)*
- *sa* Gunboats
- *xx* Artillery
  Batteries
  Coast defenses
  Fortification
  Gunboats
  Naval art and science

Floating bodies *(QA907; QC147)*
- *xx* Hydrostatics
- — Juvenile literature

Floating charges
Floating cranes *(TJ1363)*
- *xx* Cranes, derricks, etc.
  Work boats

Floating ice stations
  See Drifting ice stations
Floating instrument platforms
  See Oceanographic buoys
Floating-point arithmetic *(QA76.6)*
- *x* Arithmetic, Floating-point

- *xx* Electronic digital computers—Programming
Floating theaters
  See Showboats
Floats (Hydraulic engineering)
  See Pontoons
Floats (Parades)
- *xx* Processions
  Vehicles

Flocculation *(QC183)*
- *sa* Coagulation
  Sewage—Purification—Flocculation
  Sonic coagulation
- *xx* Chemistry, Physical and theoretical
  Matter—Properties
  Sedimentation and deposition
- — Patents

Flocculi
  See Sun—Flocculi
Flock
- *xx* Factory and trade waste
  Rags
  Upholstery

Flodden, Battle of, 1513 *(DA784.6)*
Flogging
  See Corporal punishment
  Flagellants and flagellation
Flood, Biblical
  See Deluge
Flood (Hinduism)
  See Deluge (Hinduism)
Flood control *(Indirect)*
- *sa* Flood damage prevention
  Flood dams and reservoirs
  Flood forecasting
  Forest influences
  Levee districts
  Rivers—Regulation
  Stream channelization
- *x* Flood prevention
  Flood protection
  Prevention of floods
- *xx* Floods
  Forest influences
  Hurricane protection
  Hydraulic engineering
  Water resources development
- — Finance
- — Law and legislation *(Direct)*
  - *x* Flood dams and reservoirs—Law and legislation

Flood damage prevention *(Indirect)*
- *x* Flood proofing
  Flood protection
- *xx* Cities and towns—Planning
  Flood control
  Floods
- — Information services *(Direct)*

Flood dams and reservoirs *(Indirect)* *(TC530; Dams, TC540-555; Hydraulics, TC167)*
- *sa* Dikes (Engineering)
  Fishways
  Levee districts
  Sea-walls
  Sluice gates
- *xx* Dams
  Flood control
  Hydraulic structures
  Levees
  Reservoirs
- — Law and legislation
  See Flood control—Law and legislation

Flood forecasting
- *x* Floods—Forecasting
- *xx* Flood control
  Flood routing

Flood forecasting *(Continued)*
    Floods
    Hydrological forecasting
    Stream measurements
Flood insurance
  See Insurance, Flood
Flood plains
  See Floodplains
Flood prevention
  See Flood control
Flood proofing
  See Flood damage prevention
Flood protection
  See Flood control
    Flood damage prevention
Flood routing *(GB1203)*
  sa Flood forecasting
  x Routing, Flood
  xx Floods
    Stream measurements
Floodgates
  See Sluice gates
Floodlighting *(TK4399.F55)*
  xx Electric lighting
    Lighting
Floodplains *(Indirect)* *(GB562)*
    The floodplain of an individual river is
      entered under the name of the valley,
      e.g. Rhine Valley.
  x Flood plains
    River flood plains
  xx Plains
    Valleys
Floods *(Indirect)* *(Engineering, TC404-535;*
    Floods and forests, SD425; Physical
    geography, GB1201-1397; Relief
    work, HV610)
  sa Flood control
    Flood damage prevention
    Flood routing
    Forest influences
    Reclamation of land
    Rivers
    Storm surges
    subdivision Floods *under names of*
      rivers, cities, etc., e.g. Mississippi
      River—Floods
  x Inundations
  xx Flood forecasting
    Meteorology
    Natural disasters
    Rain and rainfall
    Rivers
    Water
  — Forecasting
    See Flood forecasting
  — Mathematical models
  — Statistical methods
Floor area, Industrial
  See Floor space, Industrial
Floor coverings *(Direct)* *(HD9937)*
  sa Carpets
    Linoleum
    Rugs
  xx Flooring
    Interior decoration
  — Maintenance and repair
  — Patents
  — Trade and manufacture *(Direct)*
Floor materials
  See Flooring
Floor polishers
  See Floor polishing machines
Floor polishing machines
  x Floor polishers
  xx Floors—Maintenance and repair
    Household appliances, Electric
  — Maintenance and repair

Floor space, Industrial
  x Floor area, Industrial
  xx Business
    Factories—Design and construction
    Industry
Flooring *(TH2521)*
  sa Floor coverings
  x Floor materials
  xx Building materials
    Floors
  — Costs
    See Flooring—Estimates and costs
  — Estimates and costs
    x Flooring—Costs
  — Safety measures
  — Testing
Flooring, Asphalt
  x Asphalt flooring
Flooring, Concrete
  x Concrete flooring
  xx Concrete construction
Flooring, Plastic
  x Plastic flooring
  xx Plastics
Flooring, Tile
  x Tile flooring
  xx Tiles
Flooring, Wooden
  sa Parquet floors
  x Wood flooring
Floors *(Architecture, NA2970; Building,*
    TH2521)
  sa Bridges—Floors
    Flooring
    Pavements, Mosaic
  xx Architecture—Details
    Building
    Carpentry
  — Corrosion
  — Maintenance and repair
    sa Floor polishing machines
  — Tables, calculations, etc.
  — Thermal properties
Floors, Concrete *(TH2521)*
  xx Concrete construction
  — Tables, calculations, etc.
Floors, Terrazzo
  See Terrazzo
Floors, Wooden
  x Wood floors
  xx Building, Wooden
Floors (Bridges)
  See Bridges—Floors
Flophouses
  See Lodging-houses
Flora
  See Alpine flora
    Bog flora
    Botany
    Cave flora
    Coastal flora
    Desert flora
    Fresh-water flora
    Island flora
    Marine flora
    Marsh flora
    Pond flora
    Wetland flora
Flora, Antarctic
  See Botany—Antarctic regions
Flora, Arctic
  See Botany—Arctic regions
Floral decoration
  See Flower arrangement
Floral design
  See Design, Decorative—Plant forms
Floral games *(Direct)*
  x Games, Floral

    Jeux floraux
  xx Literature—Competitions
    Poetry—Competitions
Florence
  — Flood, 1966
  — — Art
  — History
  — — To 1421
    sa Colle di Val d'Elsa, Italy, Battle
      of, 1269
  — — — Historiography
  — — 1421-1737
    sa Florence—Siege, 1529-1530
  — — — Pictorial works
  — — 1737-
  — Siege, 1529-1530 *(DG738.13)*
  xx Florence—History—1421-1737
Florence in art
Florentine football
  x Calcio fiorentino, Gioco del
    Gioco del calcio fiorentino
  xx Football
    Rugby football
Flores, Battle of, 1591 *(DA87.5 1591)*
Floriculture *(Indirect)* *(SB403-450)*
    Here are entered works on the commer-
      cial growing of flowers and ornamental
      plants. Works on home flower growing
      are entered under Flower gardening.
  sa Annuals (Plants)
    Biennials (Plants)
    Bulbs
    Cold-frames
    Corms
    Cut flowers
    Florists
    Flowers
    Flowers—Marketing
    Greenhouses
    House plants
    Orchid culture
    Perennials
    Plant-breeding
    Plant propagation
    Plants, Ornamental
    Rose culture
    Wild flower gardening
    Window-gardening
    particular types of plants and flowers,
      e.g. Aquatic plants,
      Chrysanthemums, Climbing plants,
      Dahlias, Peonies
  xx Agriculture
    Botany
    Flowers
    Gardening
    Horticulture
    Ornamental horticulture
    Plants
    Plants, Cultivated
  Note under Flower gardening
  — Economic aspects *(Indirect)*
  — Equipment and supplies
  — Exhibitions
    See Flower shows
  — Juvenile literature
  — Standards *(Direct)*
Florida
  — History *(F306-320)*
  — — To 1565
  — — To 1821
  — — Huguenot colony, 1562-1565.
  — — Spanish colony, 1565-1763
  — — English colony, 1763-1784
  — — Revolution, 1775-1783
  — — Spanish colony, 1784-1821
  — — War of 1812
  — — Seminole Wars, 1817-1858

See Seminole War, 1st, 1817-1818
        Seminole War, 2d, 1835-1842
        Seminole War, 3d, 1855-1858
— — Cession to the United States, 1819
— — 1821-1865
— — Civil War, 1861-1865   *(E558)*
— — — Centennial celebrations, etc.
— — 1865-
— — War of 1898
— Hurricane, 1926
— Hurricane, 1928
— Hurricane, 1935
— Hurricane, 1960
— Tornado, 1966
Florida automatic computer
   See Seac computer
Florida fern caterpillar   *(SB945.F6)*
   Example under Caterpillars
Florida language   *(PL6240)*
   x Anudha language
      Gela language
      Nggela language
   xx Melanesian languages
Florida pompano   *(Culture, SH167.P7;*
      Zoology, QL638.C25)
   x Pompano, Florida
Florida velvet bean   *(SB205.B3)*
   xx Beans
Florida War, 1835-1842
   See Seminole War, 2d, 1835-1842
Florin
Florists   *(Indirect)*   *(SB443)*
   xx Floriculture
      Flowers—Marketing
  — Accounting
  — Credit guides   *(HF5585.F6)*
  — Directories   *(SB404)*
  — Juvenile literature
  — Periodicals
     See Flowers—Marketing—Periodicals
Flotation   *(TN523)*
   xx Ore-dressing
      Separation (Technology)
  — Automation
  — Equipment and supplies
  — Problems, exercises, etc.
Flounders
   See Flatfishes
Flour   *(Adulteration, TX595.F6; Food supply,*
      TX393; Food values, TX558.W5;
      Manufacture, TS2120-2159)
   sa Banana flour
      Barley
      Dough
      Graham flour
      Grain
      Grain—Milling
      Maize
      Oats
      Soy-bean flour
      Wheat
   x Breadstuffs
   xx Bread
      Cereal products
      Grain—Milling
      Wheat
  — Analysis and chemistry
   xx Chemistry, Technical
     Example under Chemistry, Analytic
  — Early works to 1800
  — Microbiology
  — Packaging   *(TS2149)*
  — Prices   *(Direct)*
  — Radiation effects
     See Flour, Effect of radiation on
  — Standards
  — Storage
  — Testing

— Transportation
Flour, Effect of radiation on
   x Flour—Radiation effects
   xx Radiation
Flour and feed trade   *(Direct)*   *(HD9056;*
      Tariff, HF2651.F6; Trusts,
      HD2769.M58)
   sa Feed mills
      Feeds—Marketing
   x Feed industry and trade
      Feed trade
      Milling trade
   Example under Food industry and trade
  — By-products
  — Costs
  — Management
  — Prices   *(Direct)*
  — Seasonal variations
  — Tables and ready-reckoners   *(Exchange*
      tables, HG3875.F6)
  — Taxation   *(Direct)*
Flour as feed
Flour-mills   *(Direct)*   *(TS2120-2159)*
   x Grist-mills
   xx Food processing plants
      Grain—Milling
      Milling machinery
      Mills and mill-work
  — Automation
  — Electric equipment
  — Employees   *(Direct)*
     sa Trade-unions—Flour-mill employees
       Wages—Flour-mill employees
  — Equipment and supplies
  — — Appraisal
      See Flour-mills—Equipment and
        supplies—Valuation
  — — Maintenance and repair
  — — Reliability
  — — Valuation   *(TS2149)*
     x Flour-mills—Equipment and
       supplies—Appraisal
  — Fires and fire prevention
  — Heating and ventilation
  — Industrial capacity
  — Laboratory manuals   *(TS2149)*
  — Law and legislation   *(Direct)*
  — Management   *(TS2149)*
  — — Problems, exercises, etc.   *(TS2149)*
  — Production standards
  — Tables, calculations, etc.
  — Taxation   *(Direct)*
Flow, Groundwater
   See Groundwater flow
Flow, Multiphase
   See Multiphase flow
Flow, One-dimensional
   See One-dimensional flow
Flow, Two-phase
   See Two-phase flow
Flow blue china
   See Blue and white transfer ware
Flow charts
   x Flow diagrams
      Flowcharts
   xx Graphic methods
      System analysis
  — Programmed instruction
Flow diagrams
   See Flow charts
Flow graphs
   See Flowgraphs
Flow measurement
   See Flow meters
Flow meters   *(TC177)*
   sa Acoustic velocity meters
      Gas-meters
      Parshall flumes

      Pitot tubes
      Steam-meters
   x Flow measurement
      Flowmeters
      Fluid meters
      Meters, Flow
   xx Hydraulic engineering—Instruments
      Hydraulic measurements
      Stream measurements
      Water-meters
   Note under Hydraulic measurements
  — Patents
  — Standards   *(Direct)*   *(TC177)*
  — Testing
Flow of bulk solids
   See Bulk solids flow
Flow of funds   *(Direct)*
   sa National income
   xx Finance
  — Accounting
     x Social accounting
Flow of gas
   See Gas flow
Flow of water
   See Hydraulics
Flow turning (Metalwork)
   See Metal-spinning
Flow visualization in wind tunnels
   See Wind tunnels—Flow visualization
Flowcharts
   See Flow charts
Flower arrangement   *(SB445-9)*
   sa Bridal bouquets
      Corsages
      Dried flower arrangement
      Driftwood arrangement
      House plants in interior decoration
      Leis
      Wreaths
   x Floral decoration
      Flowers—Arrangement
   xx Cut flowers
      Decoration and ornament
      Flowers
      Table setting and decoration
  — Equipment and supplies
  — Exhibitions
     See Flower arrangement shows
  — Juvenile literature
Flower arrangement, Chinese, ⌐Japanese, etc.⌐
   x Chinese ⌐Japanese, etc.⌐ flower
      arrangement
  — History
  — — Pictorial works
Flower arrangement, Japanese
   x Ikebana
Flower arrangement in art
   xx Art
Flower arrangement in churches
      (SB449.5.C4)
   x Church flower arrangement
   xx Church decoration and ornament
Flower arrangement shows   *(Indirect)*
      (SB449.15)
   x Flower arrangement—Exhibitions
   xx Flower shows
Flower cookery
   See Cookery (Flowers)
Flower drawing
   See Flower painting and illustration
Flower gardening   *(Indirect)*   *(SB403-413)*
      Here are entered works on home flower
      growing. Works on the commercial
      growing of flowers and ornamental
      plants are entered under Floriculture.
   sa Wild flower gardening
   xx Flowers
      Gardening

Flower gardening *(Indirect)* *(SB403-413)*
(Continued)
   Note under Floriculture
   — Juvenile literature
Flower judging
   See Flower shows—Judging
Flower language *(QK84)*
   sa Flowers in literature
      Symbolism of flowers
   x Flowers, Language of
      Language of flowers
   xx Flowers in literature
      Plant lore
      Symbolism of flowers
Flower painting and illustration
   sa Flowers in art
   x Flower drawing
      Flowers, Painting of
   xx Flowers in art
      Painting
   Example under Drawing—Instruction
Flower prints
   See Flowers in art
Flower shows *(SB441)*
   sa Flower arrangement shows
   x Floriculture—Exhibitions
   xx Exhibitions
      Horticultural exhibitions
   — Judging
      x Flower judging
         Flowers—Judging
Flowering bean
   See Scarlet runner bean
Flowering bulbs
   See Bulbs
Flowering cherries *(Botany, QK495.R78; Culture, SB437.5.C5)*
   sa Japanese flowering cherry
   x Cherries, Flowering
   xx Flowering trees
Flowering cornel
   See Flowering dogwood
Flowering dogwood
   x American dogwood
      Flowering cornel
   xx Dogwood
      Flowering trees
Flowering of plants
   See Plants, Flowering of
Flowering plants
   See Angiosperms
      Flowers
Flowering plum in art
   x Plum blossoms in art
   xx Art
Flowering shrubs *(Indirect)*
   xx Ornamental shrubs
   — Pictorial works
Flowering trees *(Indirect)*
   sa Flowering cherries
      Flowering dogwood
   x Trees, Flowering
   xx Ornamental trees
   — Pictorial works
Flowerpeckers
   xx Passeriformes
Flowerpots
   xx Containers
      Plants, Potted
      Pottery
Flowers *(Indirect)* *(Botany, QK; Culture, SB403-450; Manners and customs, GT5160)*
   sa Annuals (Plants)
      Biennials (Plants)
      Cleistogamy
      Color of flowers
      Cookery (Flowers)
      Cut flowers

      Everlasting flowers
      Fertilization of plants
      Floriculture
      Flower arrangement
      Flower gardening
      National flowers
      Nectaries
      Plants, Flowering of
      Provincial flowers
      State flowers
      Wild flowers
      Window-gardening
      names of flowers, e.g. Carnations, Roses, Violets
   x Flowering plants
   xx Botany
      Floriculture
      Inflorescence
      Plants
      Plants, Cultivated
   — Anatomy *(QK653-9; QK692-8)*
      sa Flowers—Morphology
      xx Botany—Anatomy
         Flowers—Morphology
   — Arrangement
      See Flower arrangement
   — Collection and preservation
      sa Flowers—Drying
      xx Plants—Collection and preservation
   — — Juvenile literature
   — Diseases and pests
   — Drying
      sa Dried flower arrangement
      xx Flowers—Collection and preservation
   — Fertilizers and manures
   — Gift-books
   — Identification
      x Identification of flowers
   — Judging
      See Flower shows—Judging
   — Juvenile literature
   — Literary collections
   — Marketing
      sa Florists
      xx Floriculture
   — — Periodicals
      x Florists—Periodicals
   — Morphology *(QK653-9)*
      sa Calyx (Botany)
         Flowers—Anatomy
      xx Botany—Morphology
         Flowers—Anatomy
   — — Atlases
   — Odor
      x Fragrance of flowers
      xx Odors
   — Pictorial works *(QK98)*
   — Quotations, maxims, etc.
   — Tariff
      See Tariff on cut flowers
   — Transportation
Flowers, Artificial
   See Artificial flowers
Flowers, Everlasting
   See Everlasting flowers
Flowers, Forcing of
   See Forcing (Plants)
Flowers, Language of
   See Flower language
Flowers, National
   See National flowers
Flowers, Painting of
   See Flower painting and illustration
Flowers, Protection of
   See Plants, Protection of
Flowers, Provincial
   See Provincial flowers

Flowers, State
   See State flowers
Flowers, Symbolism of
   See Symbolism of flowers
Flowers, Wax
   See Wax flowers
Flowers, Wild
   See Wild flowers
Flowers (in religion, folk-lore, etc.)
   x Folk-lore of flowers
   xx Religion, Primitive
Flowers in art
   sa Design, Decorative—Plant forms
      Flower painting and illustration
      names of specific flowers in art, e.g. Carnations in art
   x Flower prints
   xx Flower painting and illustration
      Plants in art
Flowers in literature
   sa Flower language
      Plant lore
      Roses in literature
      Roses (in religion, folk-lore, etc.)
   x Flowers in poetry
   xx Flower language
      Plant lore
      Plants in literature
Flowers in poetry
   See Flowers in literature
Flowgraphs
   x Flow graphs
      Signal flowgraphs
   xx Graphic methods
      System analysis
   — Programmed instruction
Flowmeter, Laser
   See Laser Doppler velocimeter
Flowmeters
   See Flow meters
Flowoff
   See Runoff
Fluctuations, Cross section (Nuclear physics)
   See Cross section fluctuations (Nuclear physics)
Flue dust
   See Fly ash
Flue gases *(TD885)*
   xx Combustion gases
      Factory and trade waste
   — Purification
Fluegelhorn *(ML975-7)*
   sa Alto horn
   x Flicorno
Fluegelhorn music *(M110.F53)*
   sa Wind quartets (Baritone, fluegelhorn, horn, trumpet)
Flues *(TH2281)*
   sa Chimneys
      Gas appliances—Vents
   x Smoke-pipes
   xx Chimneys
      Ventilation
Fluid amplifiers
   x Amplifiers, Fluid
   xx Fluid dynamics
      Fluidic devices
Fluid bed processes
   See Fluidization
Fluid copying processes *(Z48)*
   x Liquid copying processes
      Spirit duplicating
   xx Copying processes
Fluid couplings
   See Hydraulic couplings
Fluid dynamic measurements
   sa Laser Doppler velocimeter
   x Fluid dynamics—Measurement

Measurements, Fluid dynamic
  xx Physical measurements
Fluid dynamics
  sa Acoustic streaming
    Aerodynamics
    Blades
    Body fluid flow
    Boundary layer
    Boundary layer control
    Bulk solids flow
    Cascades (Fluid dynamics)
    Diffusers
    Eddies
    Electrohydrodynamics
    Fluid amplifiers
    Fluid-film bearings
    Fluidization
    Gas dynamics
    Hydrodynamics
    Ion flow dynamics
    Laminar flow
    Magnetohydrodynamics
    Mass transfer
    Mixing
    Molecular acoustics
    Multiphase flow
    Navier-Stokes equations
    One-dimensional flow
    Plumes (Fluid dynamics)
    Rayleigh waves
    Relativistic fluid dynamics
    Shock waves
    Smoke plumes
    Surface waves
    Viscous flow
    Vortex-motion
    Wakes (Fluid dynamics)
    subdivisions Fluid dynamics *and* Fluid
      models *under subjects, e.g.*
      Turbomachines—Fluid dynamics;
      Geophysics—Fluid models
  xx Fluid mechanics
    Fluids
  — Electromechanical analogies
  — Mathematical models
  — Measurement
    See Fluid dynamic measurements
Fluid dynamics (Space environment)
  sa Rarefied gas dynamics
  x Space flight—Fluid dynamics
    Space fluid dynamics
    Space vehicles—Fluid dynamics
  xx Space environment
Fluid energy mills
  See Jet mills
Fluid fertilizers
  See Liquid fertilizers and manures
Fluid-film bearings
  sa Gas-lubricated bearings
  x Bearings, Fluid-film
    Hydrostatic bearings
  xx Bearings (Machinery)
    Fluid dynamics
    Lubrication and lubricants
Fluid fuel reactors *(TK9203.F5)*
  xx Nuclear reactors
Fluid mechanics
  sa Contact angle
    Diaphragms (Mechanical devices)
    Fluid dynamics
    Fluid power technology
    Fluids
    Hodograph equations
    Hydraulic engineering
    Hydraulics
    Hydrodynamics
    Hydrometer
    Hydrostatics

Splashes
  x Hydromechanics
  xx Continuum mechanics
    Fluids
  — Early works to 1800
  — Experiments
  — Laboratory manuals
  — Problems, exercises, etc.
  — Tables, calculations, etc.
  — Terminology
Fluid meters
  See Flow meters
Fluid power technology
  sa Fluidic devices
    Hydraulic control
    Hydraulic machinery
    Pneumatic control
    Pneumatic machinery
    subdivision Hydraulic drive *under*
      subjects, *e.g.* Diesel locomotives—
      Hydraulic drive
  xx Fluid mechanics
Fluid rotor gyroscopes *(TJ209)*
  x Hydrodynamic gyroscopes
  xx Gyroscope
Fluid therapy *(RM170)*
  sa Hypertonic solutions—Therapeutic use
  x Fluids—Therapeutic use
  xx Body fluids
  — Programmed instruction
Fluidic devices
  sa Fluid amplifiers
  xx Fluid power technology
  — Marketing
  — Patents *(TJ853)*
Fluidization *(TP156.F65)*
  sa Fluidized-bed furnaces
    Fluidized reactors
  x Fluid bed processes
    Fluidized systems
  xx Bulk solids flow
    Catalysis
    Chemical engineering
    Cracking process
    Fluid dynamics
    Particles
    Separation (Technology)
  — Patents
Fluidized-bed furnaces *(TH7140)*
  x Furnaces, Fluidized-bed
  xx Fluidization
    Furnaces
Fluidized reactors
  x Reactors, Fluidized
  xx Fluidization
    Nuclear reactors
Fluidized systems
  See Fluidization
Fluids *(Analytical mechanics, QA901-930;*
    Physics, QC141-168)
  sa Drops
    Fluid dynamics
    Fluid mechanics
    Gases
    Hydraulic engineering
    Hydraulic fluids
    Hydrostatics
    Jets
    Liquids
    Osmosis
    Permeability
    Rotating masses of fluid
    Solvents
  xx Fluid mechanics
    Hydraulics
    Hydrostatics
    Mechanics
    Permeability

Physics
  — Charts, diagrams, etc.
  — Therapeutic use
    See Fluid therapy
  — Thermal properties
  — — Tables, calculations, etc.
Fluids, Drilling
  See Drilling muds
Fluids and humors, Animal
  See Body fluids
Flukes, Liver
  See Liver flukes
Flumes *(Hydraulics, TC175; Irrigation,*
    TC933; Water-power, TJ847)
  sa Irrigation canals and flumes
    Parshall flumes
  xx Channels (Hydraulic engineering)
    Water-power
Fluoborates
Fluorescein *(Chemistry, QD441)*
  sa Sulphonfluorescein
  x Resorcinolphthalein
  xx Dyes and dyeing
    Phthaleins
Fluorescence *(QC477)*
  sa Fluorescent lighting
    Fluorimeter
    Fluorimetry
    Immunofluorescence
    Mössbauer effect
    Optical brighteners
  xx Luminescence
    Radioactivity
Fluorescence analysis
  See Fluorimetry
Fluorescence microscopy
  sa Fluorescent antibody technique
  xx Immunofluorescence
    Microscope and microscopy
Fluorescence spectrometry
  See Fluorescence spectroscopy
Fluorescence spectroscopy *(QH324.F4)*
  x Fluorescence spectrometry
    Spectrometry, Fluorescence
    Spectroscopy, Fluorescence
  xx Spectrum analysis
Fluorescent antibody technique
  xx Antigens and antibodies
    Fluorescence microscopy
    Immunofluorescence
Fluorescent antigen technique
  xx Immunofluorescence
Fluorescent bleaches
  See Optical brighteners
Fluorescent brighteners
  See Optical brighteners
Fluorescent lamp industry *(Direct)*
Fluorescent lamps *(TK4386)*
  x Electric lamps, Fluorescent
  xx Fluorescent lighting
  — Prices *(Direct)*
  — Standards
Fluorescent lighting *(TK4386)*
  sa Fluorescent lamps
  x Electric lighting, Fluorescent
  xx Electric discharge lighting
    Fluorescence
  — Hygienic aspects
    xx Hygiene
      Vision
Fluorescent whitening agents
  See Optical brighteners
Fluoridation of water
  See Water—Fluoridation
Fluorides *(QD181.F1)*
  sa Rare earth fluorides
    Water—Fluoridation
  — Analysis

Fluorides *(QD181.F1)* *(Continued)*
— Physiological effect
  sa Plants, Effect of fluorides on
Fluorimeter
  x Fluorometer
  xx Fluorescence
Fluorimetric analysis
  See Fluorimetry
Fluorimetry
  x Fluorescence analysis
   Fluorimetric analysis
   Fluorometric analysis
   Fluorometry
   Luminescence analysis
  xx Chemistry, Analytic
   Fluorescence
— Safety measures
Fluorine *(QD181.F1)*
  sa Liquid fluorine
  xx Halogens
— Analysis
— Isotopes
— — Decay
— — Spectra
— Physiological effect
  sa Mottled enamel
    Water—Fluoridation
— Spectra
— — Tables, etc.
— Toxicology
  x Fluorine compounds—Toxicology
Fluorine compounds
  sa Organofluorine compounds
— Spectra
— Toxicology
   See Fluorine—Toxicology
Fluorine mica
  x Fluormica
   Fluoromica
  xx Mica
Fluorine organic compounds
  See Organofluorine compounds
Fluorite
  See Fluorspar
Fluormica
  See Fluorine mica
Fluorocarbons
  xx Organofluorine compounds
— Patents
Fluorometer
  See Fluorimeter
Fluorometric analysis
  See Fluorimetry
Fluorometry
  See Fluorimetry
Fluoromica
  See Fluorine mica
Fluoroscopic diagnosis
  See Diagnosis, Fluoroscopic
Fluorosis, Endemic dental
  See Mottled enamel
Fluorspar *(Indirect)* *(Mineral resources,*
    TN948.F6; Mineralogy, QE391.F6)
  x Fluorite
Fluosilicates *(Insecticides, SB951)*
Fluothane
  See Halothane
Flute *(History, ML935-7)*
  sa Czakan
   Fife
   Flageolet
   Galoubet
   Hsiao
   Nāy
   Piccolo
   Recorder (Musical instrument)
   Ryūteki
   Shakuhachi

   Ti tzŭ
   Tibia (Musical instrument)
  x Boehm flute
  Example under Wind instruments
— Construction *(ML936)*
— Fingering charts *(MT348)*
— History *(ML935-6)*
— Juvenile literature *(ML3930.A2)*
— Orchestra studies *(MT346)*
  xx Flute—Studies and exercises
— Studies and exercises *(MT345)*
  sa Flute—Orchestra studies
Flute and bassoon music
  See Bassoon and flute music
Flute and clarinet music
  See Clarinet and flute music
Flute and double-bass music *(M290-291)*
  x Double-bass and flute music
Flute and English-horn music
  See English horn and flute music
Flute and guitar music *(M296-7)*
  sa Potpourris (Flute and guitar)
   Sonatas (Flute and guitar)
   Suites (Flute and guitar)
   Variations (Flute and guitar)
  x Guitar and flute music
Flute and guitar music, Arranged *(M296-7)*
Flute and harp music *(M296-7)*
  sa Concertos (Flute and harp)
   Concertos (Flute and harp with string
    orchestra)
   Flute and harp with orchestra
   Flute and harp with string orchestra
   Rondos (Flute and harp)
   Sonatas (Flute and harp)
   Suites (Flute and harp)
   Variations (Flute and harp)
  x Harp and flute music
Flute and harp music, Arranged *(M296-7)*
Flute and harp with orchestra *(M1040-1041)*
  sa Concertos (Flute and harp)
  xx Concertos (Flute and harp)
   Flute and harp music
   Orchestral music
Flute and harp with string orchestra
   (M1105-6)
  sa Concertos (Flute and harp with string
    orchestra)
  x Harp and flute with string orchestra
  xx Concertos (Flute and harp with string
    orchestra)
   Flute and harp music
   String-orchestra music
Flute and harpsichord music *(M240-242)*
  sa Concertos (Flute and harpsichord with
    string orchestra)
   Flute and harpsichord with string
    orchestra
   Minuets (Flute and harpsichord)
   Sarabands (Flute and harpsichord)
   Sonatas (Flute and harpsichord)
   Suites (Flute and harpsichord)
   Variations (Flute and harpsichord)
  x Harpsichord and flute music
Flute and harpsichord with string orchestra
   (M1105-6)
  sa Concertos (Flute and harpsichord with
    string orchestra)
  xx Concertos (Flute and harpsichord with
    string orchestra)
   Flute and harpsichord music
   String-orchestra music
— Scores *(M1105)*
Flute and horn music *(M288-9)*
  sa Concertos (Flute and horn with string
    orchestra)
   Flute and horn with string orchestra
  x Horn and flute music

Flute and horn with string orchestra
   (M1105-6)
  sa Concertos (Flute and horn with string
    orchestra)
   Variations (Flute and horn with string
    orchestra)
  xx Concertos (Flute and horn with string
    orchestra)
   Flute and horn music
   String-orchestra music
Flute and koto music *(M296-7)*
  x Koto and flute music
Flute and oboe music *(M288-9)*
  sa Concertos (Flute and oboe)
   Concertos (Flute and oboe with
    chamber orchestra)
   Concertos (Flute and oboe with string
    orchestra)
   Flute and oboe with chamber orchestra
   Flute and oboe with orchestra
   Flute and oboe with string orchestra
   Suites (Flute and oboe)
  x Oboe and flute music
Flute and oboe with chamber orchestra
   (M1040-1041)
  sa Concertos (Flute and oboe with
    chamber orchestra)
  xx Chamber-orchestra music
   Concertos (Flute and oboe with
    chamber orchestra)
   Flute and oboe music
Flute and oboe with orchestra *(M1040-1041)*
  sa Concertos (Flute and oboe)
  xx Concertos (Flute and oboe)
   Flute and oboe music
Flute and oboe with string orchestra
   (M1105-6)
  sa Concertos (Flute and oboe with string
    orchestra)
  xx Concertos (Flute and oboe with string
    orchestra)
   Flute and oboe music
   String-orchestra music
— Scores *(M1105)*
Flute and oboe with string orchestra,
  Arranged *(M1105-6)*
Flute and organ music *(MT182-4)*
  sa Sonatas (Flute and organ)
   Variations (Flute and organ)
  x Organ and flute music
Flute and percussion music *(M298)*
  sa Concertos (Flute and percussion with
    string orchestra)
   Flute and percussion with string
    orchestra
   Suites (Flute and percussion)
  x Percussion and flute music
Flute and percussion with string orchestra
   (M1105-6)
  sa Concertos (Flute and percussion with
    string orchestra)
  xx Concertos (Flute and percussion with
    string orchestra)
   Flute and percussion music
   String-orchestra music
Flute and piano music *(M240-242)*
  sa Canons, fugues, etc. (Flute and piano)
   Concertos (Flute and piano with string
    orchestra)
   Flute and piano with string orchestra
   Marches (Flute and piano)
   Passacaglias (Flute and piano)
   Polkas (Flute and piano)
   Recorder and harpsichord music
   Rondos (Flute and piano)
   Saltarellos (Flute and piano)
   Sarabands (Flute and piano)
   Sicilianas (Flute and piano)

Sonatas (Flute and piano)
Suites (Flute and piano)
Variations (Flute and piano)
Waltzes (Flute and piano)
x Piano and flute music
Flute and piano music, Arranged *(M243-4)*
sa Ballets arranged for flute and piano
Concertos (Flute and string orchestra),
Arranged—Solo with piano
Concertos (Flute)—Solo with piano
Concertos (Flute with chamber
orchestra)—Solo with piano
Concertos (Flute with string orchestra),
Arranged—To 1800—Solo with
piano
Concertos (Flute with string orchestra)
—Solo with piano
Concertos (Flute with string orchestra)
—To 1800—Solo with piano
Flute with chamber orchestra—Solo
with piano
Flute with orchestra—Solo with piano
Flute with orchestra—To 1800—Solo
with piano
Flute with string orchestra—Solo with
piano
Rondos (Flute with orchestra),
Arranged—To 1800—Solo with
piano
Suites (Flute with string orchestra),
Arranged—Solo with piano
Suites (Flute with string orchestra)—
Solo with piano
Variations (Flute with orchestra)—Solo
with piano
Flute and piano music, Juvenile *(M1405)*
Flute and piano with string orchestra
(M1105-6)
sa Concertos (Flute and piano with string
orchestra)
xx Concertos (Flute and piano with string
orchestra)
Flute and piano music
String-orchestra music
— Scores *(M1105)*
Flute and recorder music *(M288-9)*
sa Concertos (Flute and recorder with
string orchestra)
Flute and recorder with string orchestra
x Recorder and flute music
Flute and recorder with string orchestra
(M1105-6)
sa Concertos (Flute and recorder with
string orchestra)
xx Concertos (Flute and recorder with
string orchestra)
Flute and recorder music
String-orchestra music
Flute and tabla music *(M298)*
x Tabla and flute music
Flute and trombone music *(M288-9)*
sa Concertos (Flute and trombone with
chamber orchestra)
Flute and trombone with chamber
orchestra
x Trombone and flute music
Flute and trombone with chamber orchestra
(M1040-1041)
sa Concertos (Flute and trombone with
chamber orchestra)
Suites (Flute and trombone with
chamber orchestra)
xx Chamber-orchestra music
Concertos (Flute and trombone with
chamber orchestra)
Flute and trombone music

Flute and trumpet music *(M288-9)*
sa Concertos (Flute and trumpet with
string orchestra)
Flute and trumpet with string orchestra
x Trumpet and flute music
Flute and trumpet with string orchestra
(M1105-6)
sa Concertos (Flute and trumpet with
string orchestra)
xx Concertos (Flute and trumpet with
string orchestra)
Flute and trumpet music
String-orchestra music
Flute and viola d'amore music *(M290-291)*
sa Concertos (Flute and viola d'amore
with string orchestra)
Flute and viola d'amore with string
orchestra
x Viola d'amore and flute music
Flute and viola d'amore with string orchestra
(M1105-6)
sa Concertos (Flute and viola d'amore
with string orchestra)
xx Concertos (Flute and viola d'amore
with string orchestra)
Flute and viola d'amore music
String-orchestra music
Flute and viola music *(M290-291)*
sa Sonatas (Flute and viola)
x Viola and flute music
Flute and violin music *(M290-291)*
sa Concertos (Flute and violin)
Concertos (Flute and violin with string
orchestra)
Flute and violin with orchestra
Flute and violin with string orchestra
Suites (Flute and violin)
x Violin and flute music
Flute and violin with orchestra
(M1040-1041)
sa Concertos (Flute and violin)
xx Concertos (Flute and violin)
Flute and violin music
Orchestral music
— Solos with piano *(M1041)*
xx Trios (Piano, flute, violin), Arranged
Flute and violin with string orchestra
(M1105-6)
sa Concertos (Flute and violin with string
orchestra)
Suites (Flute and violin with string
orchestra)
xx Concertos (Flute and violin with string
orchestra)
Flute and violin music
String-orchestra music
Flute and violoncello music *(M290-291)*
sa Canons, fugues, etc. (Flute and
violoncello)
Concertos (Flute and violoncello with
string orchestra)
Flute and violoncello with string
orchestra
Sonatas (Flute and violoncello)
x Violoncello and flute music
Flute and violoncello with string orchestra
(M1105-6)
sa Concertos (Flute and violoncello with
string orchestra)
xx Concertos (Flute and violoncello with
string orchestra)
Flute and violoncello music
String-orchestra music
— Scores *(M1105)*
Flute, horn, harp with string orchestra
(M1105-6)
sa Concertos (Flute, horn, harp with string
orchestra)

xx Concertos (Flute, horn, harp with string
orchestra)
String-orchestra music
Trios (Flute, horn, harp)
Flute, kettledrums, violin with string orchestra
(M1140-1141)
sa Concertos (Flute, kettledrums, violin
with string orchestra)
xx Concertos (Flute, kettledrums, violin
with string orchestra)
String-orchestra music
Trios (Flute, kettledrums, violin)
Flute music *(M60-62)*
sa Concertos (Flute)
Concertos (Flute with band)
Concertos (Flute with chamber
orchestra)
Concertos (Flute with string orchestra)
Concertos (Flute with wind ensemble)
English horn and flute music
Flageolet music
Flute with band
Flute with chamber orchestra
Flute with instr. ensemble
Flute with orchestra
Flute with string orchestra
Flute with wind ensemble
Marches (Flute)
Passacaglias (Flute)
Piano, flute, zither with percussion
ensemble
Potpourris (Flute)
Recorded accompaniments (Flute)
Recorder music
Rondos (Flute)
Sonatas (Flute)
Suites (Flute)
Variations (Flute)
Quartets, ⌐Trios, etc.⌐, Wind quartets,
⌐trios, etc.⌐ *followed by specifications
which include the flute*
— Interpretation (Phrasing, dynamics, etc.)
(MT140; MT145)
Flute music, Arranged *(M63-64)*
sa Operas arranged for flute
Flute music (Flutes (2)) *(M288-9)*
sa Canons, fugues, etc. (Flutes (2))
Concertos (Flutes (2))
Concertos (Flutes (2) with chamber
orchestra)
Concertos (Flutes (2) with string
orchestra)
Flutes (2) with chamber orchestra
Flutes (2) with orchestra
Flutes (2) with string orchestra
Marches (Flutes (2))
Sonatas (Flutes (2))
Suites (Flutes (2))
Variations (Flutes (2))
x Duets
Note under Chamber music
Flute music (Flutes (2)), Arranged *(M288-9)*
sa Overtures arranged for flutes (2)
Flute music (Flutes (3))
See Wind trios (Flutes (3))
Flute music (Flutes (4))
See Wind quartets (Flutes (4))
Flute music (Flutes (5))
See Wind quintets (Flutes (5))
**Flute, oboe d'amore, viola d'amore with string
orchestra** *(M1105-6)*
sa Concertos (Flute, oboe d'amore, viola
d'amore with string orchestra)
xx Concertos (Flute, oboe d'amore, viola
d'amore with string orchestra)
String-orchestra music
Trios (Flute, oboe d'amore, viola
d'amore)

Flute, oboe, trumpet with string orchestra
    (M1105-6)
    sa Concertos (Flute, oboe, trumpet with
       string orchestra)
    xx Concertos (Flute, oboe, trumpet with
       string orchestra)
       String-orchestra music
       Wind trios (Flute, oboe, trumpet)
Flute, oboe, violin, violoncello with orchestra
    (M1040-1041)
    sa Concertos (Flute, oboe, violin,
       violoncello)
    xx Concertos (Flute, oboe, violin,
       violoncello)
       Orchestral music
       Quartets (Flute, oboe, violin,
       violoncello)
Flute-players *(Direct) (ML937)*
    x Flutists
       Music—Biography
    xx Musicians
    — Biography
Flute-players, Mechanical
    See Automata
Flute, saxophone, harp with string orchestra
    (M1105-6)
    sa Concertos (Flute, saxophone, harp with
       string orchestra)
    xx Concertos (Flute, saxophone, harp with
       string orchestra)
       String-orchestra music
       Trios (Flute, saxophone, harp)
Flute, viola, violoncello with string orchestra
    (M1105-6)
    sa Concertos (Flute, viola, violoncello with
       string orchestra)
    xx Concertos (Flute, viola, violoncello with
       string orchestra)
       String-orchestra music
       Trios (Flute, viola, violoncello)
Flute with band *(M1205-6)*
    sa Concertos (Flute with band)
       Suites (Flute with band)
    xx Band music
       Concertos (Flute with band)
       Flute music
Flute with band, Arranged *(M1257)*
    — Scores and parts *(M1257)*
Flute with chamber orchestra *(M1020-1021)*
    sa Concertos (Flute with chamber
       orchestra)
       Variations (Flute with chamber
       orchestra)
    xx Chamber-orchestra music
       Concertos (Flute with chamber
       orchestra)
       Flute music
    — Solo with piano *(M1021)*
       xx Flute and piano music, Arranged
Flute with chamber orchestra, Arranged
    (M1020-1021)
Flute with instrumental ensemble
    sa Concertos (Flute with instrumental
       ensemble)
    xx Concertos (Flute with instrumental
       ensemble)
       Flute music
       Instrumental ensembles
Flute with orchestra *(M1020-1021)*
    sa Concertos (Flute)
       Polonaises (Flute with orchestra)
       Recorder with orchestra
       Rondos (Flute with orchestra)
       Suites (Flute with orchestra)
       Variations (Flute with orchestra)
    xx Concertos (Flute)
       Flute music
       Orchestral music

— To 1800
— — Solo with piano *(M1021)*
       xx Flute and piano music, Arranged
— Solo with piano *(M1021)*
    xx Flute and piano music, Arranged
Flute with orchestra, Arranged
    (M1020-1021)
    — Scores *(M1020)*
Flute with string orchestra *(M1105-6)*
    sa Canons, fugues, etc. (Flute with string
       orchestra)
       Concertos (Flute with string orchestra)
       Rondos (Flute with string orchestra)
       Suites (Flute with string orchestra)
       Variations (Flute with string orchestra)
    xx Concertos (Flute with string orchestra)
       Flute music
       String-orchestra music
    — Solo with piano *(M1106)*
       xx Flute and piano music, Arranged
Flute with string orchestra, Arranged
    (M1105-6)
Flute with wind ensemble *(M955-7)*
    sa Concertos (Flute with wind ensemble)
    xx Concertos (Flute with wind ensemble)
       Flute music
       Wind ensembles
Flutes (2), glockenspiel with string orchestra
    (M1105-6)
    sa Concertos (Flutes (2), glockenspiel with
       string orchestra)
    x Two flutes and glockenspiel with string
       orchestra
    xx Concertos (Flutes (2), glockenspiel with
       string orchestra)
       String-orchestra music
       Trios (Flutes (2), glockenspiel)
Flutes (2), marimba with string orchestra
    (M1105-6)
    sa Concertos (Flutes (2), marimba with
       string orchestra)
    x Two flutes, marimba with string
       orchestra
    xx Concertos (Flutes (2), marimba with
       string orchestra)
       String-orchestra music
       Trios (Flutes (2), marimba)
    — Scores *(M1105)*
Flutes (2) with chamber orchestra
    (M1020-1021)
    sa Concertos (Flutes (2) with chamber
       orchestra)
    x Two flutes with chamber orchestra
    xx Chamber-orchestra music
       Concertos (Flutes (2) with chamber
       orchestra)
       Flute music (Flutes (2))
Flutes (2) with orchestra *(M1020-1021)*
    sa Concertos (Flutes (2))
    x Two flutes with orchestra
    xx Concertos (Flutes (2))
       Flute music (Flutes (2))
       Orchestral music
Flutes (2) with string orchestra *(M1105-6)*
    sa Canons, fugues, etc. (Flutes (2) with
       string orchestra)
       Concertos (Flutes (2) with string
       orchestra)
       Suites (Flutes (2) with string orchestra)
    x Two flutes with string orchestra
    xx Concertos (Flutes (2) with string
       orchestra)
       Flute music (Flutes (2))
       String-orchestra music
Flutes (3) and harp with orchestra
    (M1040-1041)
    sa Concertos (Flutes (3) and harp)
    xx Concertos (Flutes (3) and harp)

Flutes (3) with band *(M1205-6)*
    sa Concertos (Flutes (3) with band)
    x Three flutes with band
    xx Band music
       Concertos (Flutes (3) with band)
       Wind trios (Flutes (3))
    — Scores and parts *(M1205)*
Flutes (3) with string orchestra *(M1105-6)*
    sa Concertos (Flutes (3) with string
       orchestra)
       Suites (Flutes (3) with string orchestra)
    x Three flutes with string orchestra
    xx Concertos (Flutes (3) with string
       orchestra)
       String-orchestra music
       Wind trios (Flutes (3))
Flutes (4) with band *(M1205-6)*
    sa Concertos (Flutes (4) with band)
    x Four flutes with band
    xx Band music
       Concertos (Flutes (4) with band)
       Wind quartets (Flutes (4))
Flutes (4) with band, Arranged *(M1257)*
    — Scores and parts *(M1257)*
Flutes (4) with orchestra *(M1020-1021)*
Flutists
    See Flute-players
Flutter (Aerodynamics) *(TL574.F6)*
    sa Oscillating wings (Aerodynamics)
    xx Aerodynamics
       Oscillations
       Vibration (Aeronautics)
Fluvial sediment transport
    See Sediment transport
Flux, Neutron
    See Neutron flux
Flux (Metallurgy)
    sa Slag
    xx Slag
    — Analysis *(TN707)*
    — Patents
Fluxgate magnetometer *(QC819)*
    x Saturable core magnetometer
    xx Magnetometer
Fluxions
    See Calculus
Fluxmeter
    xx Electric apparatus and appliances
       Electric measurements
       Galvanometer
Fly
    See Flies
Fly ash
    sa Ashes (Fertilizer)
    x Ash, Pulverized fuel
       Flue dust
       Fuel ash, Pulverized
       Pulverized fuel ash
    xx Coal, Pulverized
       Dust
       Furnaces
       Waste products
Fly-casting *(SH456)*
    xx Casting (Fishing)
       Flies, Artificial
       Fly fishing
Fly control *(Indirect) (RA641.F6;*
    SF593.F6)
    x Flies—Control
       Flies—Extermination
    xx Insect control
    — Biological control *(Indirect)*
       (RA641.F6; SF593.F6)
       xx Insect control—Biological control
Fly disease
    See Trypanosomiasis
Fly dressing
    See Fly tying

Fly fishing
  sa Fly-casting
      Saltwater fly fishing
  xx Fishing
Fly tying
  x Fly dressing
  xx Flies, Artificial
  — Equipment and supplies
Fly-wheels *(TJ541)*
  xx Wheels
Flycatchers *(Birds, QL696.P2)*
  sa specific flycatchers, e.g. Willie wagtail
  xx Passeriformes
Flyers, Advertising
  See Advertising fliers
Flying
  See Flight
Flying, Fear of
  See Fear of flying
Flying, Private
  See Private flying
Flying boats
  See Seaplanes
Flying bombs
  See Guided missiles
Flying classes
  See Aeronautics in education
      Flight training
Flying disks
  See Flying saucers
Flying-fish *(QL638.E9)*
  x Exocoetus
  — Juvenile literature
Flying Fortress (Bombers)
  See B-17 bomber
Flying foxes *(Noxious animals, SB994.F6;*
      Zoology, QL737.C5)
  x Fox-bats
      Fruit-eating bats
  xx Bats
Flying-machines *(TL670-724)*
  sa Aeronautics
      Aeroplanes
      Autogiros
      Gliders (Aeronautics)
      Helicopters
      Ornithopters
      Propellers, Aerial
      Rockets (Aeronautics)
      Strongmobile (Flying automobile)
  xx Aeronautics
      Aeroplanes
      Flight
  — Models
  — Poetry
      See Aeronautics—Poetry
Flying personnel
  See Flight crews
Flying phalangers *(QL737.M3)*
  x Phalangers, Flying
  xx Marsupialia
Flying qualities of aircraft
  See Aeroplanes—Handling characteristics
Flying qualities of helicopters
  See Helicopters—Handling characteristics
Flying qualities of vertically rising aeroplanes
  See Vertically rising aeroplanes—Handling
      characteristics
Flying saucers
  x Flying disks
      Saucers, Flying
      UFO's
      Unidentified flying objects
  xx Aeronautics
  — Caricatures and cartoons
  — Juvenile literature
  — Personal narratives

Flying saucers (in religion, folk-lore, etc.)
  x Folk-lore of flying saucers
  xx Folk-lore of the sky
      Religion, Primitive
Flying spot scanners
  x Scanners, Flying spot
  xx Cathode ray tubes
      Optical data processing
      Scanning systems
Flying squirrels
  — Behavior
  — Juvenile literature
Flying wing (Aeroplanes)
  See Aeroplanes, Tailless
Flyleaf
  See Endpapers
Flysch *(Indirect)*
  xx Geology, Stratigraphic—Cretaceous
      Geology, Stratigraphic—Tertiary
      Sandstone
  — Pictorial works
FM broadcasting
  x FM radio broadcasting
      Frequency modulation broadcasting
      Frequency modulation radio
        broadcasting
  xx Radio broadcasting
      Radio frequency modulation
FM radio
  See Radio frequency modulation
FM radio broadcasting
  See FM broadcasting
FM stereophonic receivers
  See Stereophonic receivers
FN automatic rifles
  See Frabique nationale automatic rifles
Fō dialect
  See Fon dialect
Foà-Kurlov cells
  xx Blood—Corpuscles and platelets
      Lymphocytes
Foam
  sa Antifoaming agents
      Foamed materials
      Plastic foams
  xx Colloids
Foam fractionation (Sewage purification)
  See Sewage—Purification—Foam
      fractionation
Foam fractionation (Water purification)
  See Water—Purification—Foam
      fractionation
Foam glass
  See Cellular glass
Foam inhibitors
  See Antifoaming agents
Foam regulators
  See Antifoaming agents
Foam rubber
  x Rubber foam
      Rubber, Foamed
  xx Foamed materials
      Rubber
Foamed materials
  sa Cellular glass
      Foam rubber
      Plastic foams
      Urethane foam
  xx Foam
      Materials
      Porous materials
Fobs
  See Watch fobs
Foca camera *(TR263.F)*
Focal infection
  x Infection, Focal
  xx Communicable diseases
      Infection

Focal infection, Dental *(RK305; RK351)*
  x Dental focal infection
  xx Teeth—Diseases
Focke-Wulf 190 (Fighter planes)
  x FW-190 (Fighter planes)
  xx Fighter planes
Fodder
  See Feeds
Fodder beet
  See Mangel-wurzel
Foetus
  See Fetus
Fog *(Indirect)* *(Hygiene of atmosphere,*
      RA575; Meteorology, QC929.F7)
  sa Automobile driving in bad weather
      Ice fog
      Smog
  xx Meteorology
      Water
Fog-bells *(VK383)*
  xx Aids to navigation
      Navigation
Fog control *(Indirect)* *(QC929.F7; Airports,*
      TL557.F6)
  x Fog dispersal
      Fog modification
      Fog seeding
  xx Weather control
Fog dispersal
  See Fog control
Fog modification
  See Fog control
Fog seeding
  See Fog control
Fog-signals *(Indirect)* *(VK383)*
  xx Aids to navigation
      Navigation
      Signals and signaling
Fogbow *(QC976.R2)*
  x False white rainbow
      Mistbow
      White rainbow
  xx Meteorological optics
      Rainbow
Foggara
  See Falashas
      Qanat
Fogous
  See Cave-dwellings
Föhn *(QC939.F6)*
  sa Santa Ana winds
  xx Santa Ana winds
      Winds
Fokker airplanes
Fokker-Planck equation
  sa Stochastic differential equations
  x Equation, Fokker-Planck
      Planck-Fokker equation
  xx Differential equations, Partial
      Stochastic differential equations
Folate antagonists
  See Folic acid antagonists
Folded plate structures *(TA660.P63)*
  x Hipped plate structures
      Plate structures, Folded
      Structures, Folded plate
  xx Building
      Plates (Engineering)
      Structural engineering
Folding-machines *(Z261)*
  xx Printing machinery and supplies
  Example under Machinery
Folding of napkins
  See Napkin folding
Folds (Geology) *(QE606)*
  sa Diapirs
      Nappes (Geology)
  xx Geology, Structural

Foliage
   See Leaves
Foliage, Artificial
   See Artificial leaves
Foliage plants *(Indirect)* *(SB431)*
   sa Ferns
       names of individual plants, e.g.
          Begonias
   x Leaf plants
   xx House plants
       Plants, Ornamental
  — Marketing
Foliar diagnosis
   x Leaf analysis
       Leaves—Analysis
   xx Plants—Chemical analysis
       Plants—Nutrition
Foliar feeding *(S662.5)*
   x Foliar fertilization
       Leaf feeding
       Leaves, Feeding of
       Spray application of liquid fertilizers
   xx Liquid fertilizers and manures
Foliar fertilization
   See Foliar feeding
Foliated structures
   See Foliations (Mathematics)
Foliations (Mathematics) *(QA614.5.F6)*
   x Foliated structures
   xx Differential topology
Folic acid antagonists
   x Folate antagonists
   xx Antimetabolites
Folic acid deficiency *(RC627.F6)*
   xx Vitamin B deficiency
Folie à deux *(RC528.F6)*
   xx Psychoses
Folk art *(Direct)* *(N9201-9211;*
    NK801-1094)
      Here are entered (1) material concerning
      the theory, history, social and aes-
      thetic aspects, etc. of all those artistic
      activities and manifestations in the
      fields of decorative art, music, danc-
      ing, theater, etc., which are usually not
      included in the study and literature of
      the fine arts; (2) the more limited, but
      more numerous works dealing with
      popular, decorative, pictorial art, peas-
      ant art, "imagerie populaire" (illustra-
      tion of chap-books, almanacs, broad-
      sides, etc.) Works on the artistic fea-
      tures of the products of handicrafts,
      home industries, etc. (intended for
      sale) are entered under Art industries
      and trade with the addtional heading
      Folk art when applicable.
   sa Art industries and trade
       Art, Primitive
       Arts and crafts movement
       Bodhidharma dolls
       Children as artists
       Santos (Art)
       Tole painting
   x Art, Folk
       Art, Popular
       Peasant art
   xx Art
       Art and society
       Art industries and trade
       Art, Primitive
       Arts and crafts movement
       Children as artists
  — Collectors and collecting *(Direct)*
  — Juvenile literature
Folk classification
   See Classification, Primitive

Folk costume
   See Costume
Folk dance music *(M1627)*
      Here are entered collections of miscel-
      laneous folk dance music. Music for
      individual dances is entered under
      dance form, *e.g.* Square dance music.
      If the collection also contains dance in-
      struction, two headings are used, *e.g.*
      1. Folk dancing. 2. Folk dance music.
      If the collection is for a medium other
      than piano, additional heading is used
      for the medium, *e.g.* 1. Folk dance mu-
      sic. 2. Orchestral music, Arranged.
   x National dances
   xx Dance music
       Folk music
       Music
  Note under Folk dancing
Folk dance music, American, ₍French,
   German, etc.₎ *(M1629-1853)*
      Subdivided by locality.
Folk dance music, Polish
   sa Krakowiaks
Folk dancing *(Indirect)* *(GV1580-1799)*
      Here are entered collections of miscel-
      laneous folk dances which include in-
      structions for the dances.
      If the collection also contains the dance
      music, two headings are used, *e.g.* 1.
      Folk dancing. 2. Folk dance music.
   sa Folk music
       Play-party
       Square dancing
   x National dances
   xx Dancing
       Dancing (in religion, folk-lore, etc.)
       Folk music
       National music
  Note under Folk dance music
  — Pictorial works
Folk dancing, Argentine, ₍French, German,
   etc.₎
      Subdivided by locality.
   sa names of individual folk dances
  — Juvenile literature
Folk-drama *(History, PN1008.D7)*
   sa Carnival plays
       Pastoral drama
       Puppets and puppet-plays
   x Folk-plays
   xx Drama
       Folk literature
       Pastoral drama
Folk-drama, American *(Indirect)*
Folk-drama, English
   sa Mumming plays
Folk-drama, German, ₍Italian, etc.₎ *(Direct)*
   x German ₍Italian, etc.₎ folk-drama
Folk festivals *(Direct)*
   xx Festivals
       Folk-lore
Folk high schools *(Direct)*
   x People's high schools
   xx Adult education
       Education, Secondary
  — Curricula
Folk literature *(Indirect)* *(PN905-1008)*
   sa Chap-books
       Fairy tales
       Folk-drama
       Folk-songs
       Legends
       Literature and folk-lore
       Nursery rhymes
       Proverbs
       Riddles
       Tales

   x Folk-tales
       Literature, Primitive
       Oral literature
       Primitive literature
   xx Literature
  — Jews
   xx Folk-lore—Jews
       Hebrew literature
       Jewish literature
  — Themes, motives *(PN57.A1)*
      For typical plots, motives, etc.
   sa Beard (in religion, folk-lore, etc.)
       Literature, Comparative—Themes,
         motives
       Pharaoh's army (in religion,
         folk-lore, etc.)
       Youngest son (in religion, folk-lore,
         etc.)
   xx Folk-lore—Classification
       Literature, Comparative—Themes,
         motives
Folk literature, Arabic
  — Libya
      x Libyan literature
Folk literature, German, ₍Greek, etc.₎
   (Direct)
   x German ₍Greek, etc.₎ folk literature
  — Themes, motives
Folk-lore *(Indirect)* *(GR)*
   sa Alphabet rhymes
       Amulets
       Animal lore
       Animals, Legends and stories of
       Animism
       Chap-books
       Charms
       Counting-out rhymes
       Devil
       Divining-rod
       Dragons
       Dryads
       Dwarfs
       Elixir of life
       Evil eye
       Fables
       Fairies
       Fairy tales
       Folk festivals
       Folk music
       Folk-songs
       Folklorists
       Geographical myths
       Ghosts
       Ghouls and ogres
       Giants
       Grail
       Halloween
       Incantations
       Legends
       Leopard men
       Mandrake
       Marriage customs and rites
       Myth
       Mythology
       Nursery rhymes
       Oral tradition
       Plant lore
       Proverbs
       Rainbow serpent
       Riddles
       Sacred groves
       Sagas
       Sirens (Mythology)
       Street literature
       Superstition
       Swan-maidens
       Tales
       Valentines

Vampires
Weather-lore
Werwolves
Witchcraft
subdivision Religious life and customs
*under names of countries, states,
cities, etc., e.g.* Germany—Religious
life and customs
x Folk-tales
Folklore
Traditions
xx Animal lore
Ethnology
Fables
Fairy tales
Fiction
Folk-songs
Legends
Mythology
Superstition
— Bio-bibliography *(Z5981-5)*
— Book reviews
— Classification *(GR40; Z5981-5)*
  sa Folk literature—Themes, motives
  x Folk-lore—Themes, motives
  Note under Fairy tales—Classification
— Dictionaries *(GR35; Mythology, BL303)*
— Field work
  x Field work (Folk-lore)
  xx Folk-lore—Theory, methods, etc.
— Indexes
— Jews *(GR98)*
  sa Folk literature—Jews
    Jews in folk-lore
  x Bible—Folk-lore
    Folk-lore, Jewish
    Folk-lore of Jews
    Jewish folk-lore
    Jews—Folk-lore
    Midrash—Folk-lore
    Talmud—Folk-lore
  xx Jews in folk-lore
—— Research *(Direct)*
    xx Jewish studies
— Juvenile literature
— Methodology
  See Folk-lore—Theory, methods, etc.
— Museums
  See Ethnological museums and
     collections
— Study and teaching *(Direct)*
  sa Folk-lore and education
— Themes, motives
  See Folk-lore—Classification
— Theory, methods, etc. *(GR40)*
  sa Folk-lore—Field work
  x Folk-lore—Methodology
Folk-lore, Aryan, ₍Celtic, Gaelic, etc.₎
  x Aryan ₍Celtic, Gaelic, etc.₎ folk-lore
— Juvenile literature
— Slavic ₍etc.₎ influences
Folk-lore, Bohemian
  See Folk-lore, Czech
Folk-lore, Cheremissian
  xx Cheremisses
Folk-lore, Czech
  x Czech folk-lore
    Folk-lore, Bohemian
Folk-lore, Eskimo
  x Eskimos—Folk-lore
Folk-lore, Germanic
  sa Trolls
  x Folk-lore, Teutonic
    Germanic folk-lore
  xx Germanic tribes—Religion
Folk-lore, Gipsy *(DX157)*
  x Gipsy folk-lore

Folk-lore, Glebo
  See Folk-lore, Grebo
Folk-lore, Grebo
  x Folk-lore, Glebo
    Glebo folk-lore
    Grebo folk-lore
Folk-lore, Indian *(E98.F6)*
  Here are entered works on the folk-lore of
  the American Indians. Works relating
  to a particular tribe have duplicate entry under name of tribe. Collections of
  Indian tales, legends, or myths are entered under Indians of North America
  —Legends; Indians of South America
  —Legends; etc.
  sa Incantations, Indian
    Indians of South America—Plant lore
    Totems
  x Indian folk-lore
    Indians—Folk-lore
    Indians of Mexico ₍North America,
     South America, etc.₎—Folk-lore
    Indians of North America—Mythology
  xx Indians—Legends
    Indians of Mexico ₍North America,
     South America, etc.₎—Legends
Folk-lore, Japanese
  sa Seven gods of fortune
  x Japanese folk-lore
Folk-lore, Jewish
  See Folk-lore—Jews
Folk-lore, Kalmuck
Folk-lore, Medical
  See Folk medicine
Folk-lore, Negro *(Africa, GR350; United
    States, GR103)*
  x Negro folk-lore
    Negroes—Folk-lore
Folk-lore, Teutonic
  See Folk-lore, Germanic
Folk-lore and children *(GR43.C4)*
  sa Folk-lore of children
  x Children and folk-lore
    Folk-lore and youth
    Youth and folk-lore
  xx Folk-lore of children
Folk-lore and education *(LB1044.9.F6)*
  x Education and folk-lore
  xx Folk-lore—Study and teaching
Folk-lore and literature
  See Literature and folk-lore
Folk-lore and youth
  See Folk-lore and children
Folk-lore libraries *(Z675.F)*
  x Libraries, Folk-lore
Folk-lore of adzes
  See Adzes (in religion, folk-lore, etc.)
Folk-lore of agriculture *(GR895)*
  x Agriculture, Folk-lore of
    Folk-lore of harvesting
  xx Harvesting
Folk-lore of animals
  See Animal lore
Folk-lore of antlers
  See Antlers (in religion, folk-lore, etc.)
Folk-lore of ants
  See Ants (in religion, folk-lore, etc.)
Folk-lore of apes
  See Apes (in religion, folk-lore, etc.)
Folk-lore of aromatic plants
  See Aromatic plants (in religion, folk-lore,
    etc.)
Folk-lore of ascension
  See Ascension (in religion, folk-lore, etc.)
Folk-lore of beads
  See Beads (in religion, folk-lore, etc.)
Folk-lore of beards
  See Beard (in religion, folk-lore, etc.)

Folk-lore of bears
  See Bears (in religion, folk-lore, etc.)
Folk-lore of bees *(GR750)*
  x Bees, Folk-lore of
Folk-lore of birds *(GR735)*
  sa Birds in literature
    Eggs (in religion, folk-lore, etc.)
    *names of birds followed by the
     specification* (in religion, folk-lore,
     etc.), *e.g.* Woodpeckers (in religion,
     folk-lore, etc.)
  x Birds, Folk-lore of
    Birds (in religion, folk-lore, etc.)
  xx Birds in literature
Folk-lore of birth
  See Birth (in religion, folk-lore, etc.)
Folk-lore of blood
  See Blood (in religion, folk-lore, etc.)
Folk-lore of bones
  See Bones (in religion, folk-lore, etc.)
Folk-lore of bread
  See Bread (in religion, folk-lore, etc.)
Folk-lore of breath and breathing
  See Breath and breathing (in religion,
    folk-lore, etc.)
Folk-lore of brothers and sisters
  See Brothers and sisters (in religion,
    folk-lore, etc.)
Folk-lore of buffaloes
  See Buffaloes (in religion, folk-lore, etc.)
Folk-lore of bulls
  See Bull (in religion, folk-lore, etc.)
Folk-lore of buttocks
  See Buttocks (in religion, folk-lore, etc.)
Folk-lore of candles
  See Candles (in religion, folk-lore, etc.)
Folk-lore of catfishes
  See Catfishes (in religion, folk-lore, etc.)
Folk-lore of cats
  See Cats (in religion, folk-lore, etc.)
Folk-lore of caves
  See Caves (in religion, folk-lore, etc.)
Folk-lore of chickens
  See Chickens (in religion, folk-lore, etc.)
Folk-lore of children *(GR475-487)*
  sa Folk-lore and children
  x Children, Folk-lore of
  xx Folk-lore and children
Folk-lore of circles
  See Circle (in religion, folk-lore, etc.)
Folk-lore of clowns
  See Clowns (in religion, folk-lore, etc.)
Folk-lore of countries
  See Geographical myths
Folk-lore of cows
  See Cows (in religion, folk-lore, etc.)
Folk-lore of cranes
  See Cranes (in religion, folk-lore, etc.)
Folk-lore of crocodiles
  See Crocodiles (in religion, folk-lore, etc.)
Folk-lore of crying
  See Crying (in religion, folk-lore, etc.)
Folk-lore of cuckoos
  See Cuckoos (in religion, folk-lore, etc.)
Folk-lore of curtains
  See Curtains (in religion, folk-lore, etc.)
Folk-lore of dancing
  See Dancing (in religion, folk-lore, etc.)
Folk-lore of darkness
  See Light and darkness (in religion,
    folk-lore, etc.)
Folk-lore of dawn
  See Dawn (in religion, folk-lore, etc.)
Folk-lore of days
  See Days
Folk-lore of deer
  See Deer (in religion, folk-lore, etc.)

Folk-lore of deserts
    See Deserts (in religion, folk-lore, etc.)
Folk-lore of dogs
    See Dogs (in religion, folk-lore, etc.)
Folk-lore of dolls
    See Dolls (in religion, folk-lore, etc.)
Folk-lore of dolphins
    See Dolphin (in religion, folk-lore, etc.)
Folk-lore of donkeys
    See Donkeys (in religion, folk-lore, etc.)
Folk-lore of doves
    See Dove (in religion, folk-lore, etc.)
Folk-lore of dragonflies
    See Dragonflies (in religion, folk-lore, etc.)
Folk-lore of drinking
    See Drinks and drinking (in religion,
        folk-lore, etc.)
Folk-lore of dwellings
    See Dwellings (in religion, folk-lore, etc.)
Folk-lore of eagles
    See Eagle (in religion, folk-lore, etc.)
Folk-lore of effigies
    See Effigies (in religion, folk-lore, etc.)
Folk-lore of eggs
    See Eggs (in religion, folk-lore, etc.)
Folk-lore of excretion
    See Excretion (in religion, folk-lore, etc.)
Folk-lore of fans
    See Fans (in religion, folk-lore, etc.)
Folk-lore of feces
    See Feces (in religion, folk-lore, etc.)
Folk-lore of feet
    See Foot (in religion, folk-lore, etc.)
Folk-lore of felt
    See Felt (in religion, folk-lore, etc.)
Folk-lore of figs
    See Fig (in religion, folk-lore, etc.)
Folk-lore of filicide
    See Filicide (in religion, folk-lore, etc.)
Folk-lore of fire
    See Fire (in religion, folk-lore, etc.)
Folk-lore of fishes
    See Fish (in religion, folk-lore, etc.)
Folk-lore of fishing
    See Fishing (in religion, folk-lore, etc.)
Folk-lore of fleeing
    See Fleeing (in religion, folk-lore, etc.)
Folk-lore of flowers
    See Flowers (in religion, folk-lore, etc.)
Folk-lore of flying saucers
    See Flying saucers (in religion, folk-lore,
        etc.)
Folk-lore of food
    See Food (in religion, folk-lore, etc.)
Folk-lore of foxes
    See Foxes (in religion, folk-lore, etc.)
Folk-lore of gardens
    See Gardens (in religion, folk-lore, etc.)
Folk-lore of gems
    See Gems (in religion, folk-lore, etc.)
Folk-lore of goldfinches
    See Goldfinch (in religion, folk-lore, etc.)
Folk-lore of hair
    See Hair (in religion, folk-lore, etc.)
Folk-lore of hands
    See Hand (in religion, folk-lore, etc.)
Folk-lore of hares
    See Hares (in religion, folk-lore, etc.)
Folk-lore of harvesting
    See Folk-lore of agriculture
Folk-lore of head-gear
    See Head-gear (in religion, folk-lore, etc.)
Folk-lore of healing
    See Healing (in religion, folk-lore, etc.)
Folk-lore of heat
    See Heat (in religion, folk-lore, etc.)
Folk-lore of herbs
    See Herbs (in religion, folk-lore, etc.)

Folk-lore of homosexuality
    See Homosexuality (in religion, folk-lore,
        etc.)
Folk-lore of hoopoes
    See Hoopoes (in religion, folk-lore, etc.)
Folk-lore of horns
    See Horns (in religion, folk-lore, etc.)
Folk-lore of horses
    See Horses (in religion, folk-lore, etc.)
Folk-lore of hunting
    See Hunting (in religion, folk-lore, etc.)
Folk-lore of incubation
    See Incubation (in religion, folk-lore, etc.)
Folk-lore of industry
    x Industrial folk-lore
Folk-lore of initiations
    See Initiations (in religion, folk-lore, etc.)
Folk-lore of insects *(GR750)*
    sa names of insects followed by the
        specification (in religion, folk-lore,
        etc.), *e.g.* Dragonflies (in religion,
        folk-lore, etc.)
Folk-lore of Jews
    See Folk-lore—Jews
        Jews in folk-lore
Folk-lore of kings and rulers
    See Kings and rulers (in religion, folk-lore,
        etc.)
Folk-lore of kissing
    See Kissing (in religion, folk-lore, etc.)
Folk-lore of ladybirds
    See Ladybirds (in religion, folk-lore, etc.)
Folk-lore of lakes
    See Lakes (in religion, folk-lore, etc.)
Folk-lore of lambs
    See Lambs (in religion, folk-lore, etc.)
Folk-lore of laughter
    See Laughter (in religion, folk-lore, etc.)
Folk-lore of lead
    See Lead (in religion, folk-lore, etc.)
Folk-lore of leadership
    See Leadership (in religion, folk-lore, etc.)
Folk-lore of lemons
    See Lemon (in religion, folk-lore, etc.)
Folk-lore of light
    See Light and darkness (in religion,
        folk-lore, etc.)
Folk-lore of lions
    See Lions (in religion, folk-lore, etc.)
Folk-lore of lizards
    See Lizards (in religion, folk-lore, etc.)
Folk-lore of llamas
    See Llamas (in religion, folk-lore, etc.)
Folk-lore of lumbering
    See Lumbering (in religion, folk-lore, etc.)
Folk-lore of markets
    See Markets (in religion, folk-lore, etc.)
Folk-lore of meadows
    See Meadows (in religion, folk-lore, etc.)
Folk-lore of mental illness
    See Mental illness (in religion, folk-lore,
        etc.)
Folk-lore of metal-work
    See Metals (in religion, folk-lore, etc.)
Folk-lore of metallurgy
    See Metals (in religion, folk-lore, etc.)
Folk-lore of metals
    See Metals (in religion, folk-lore, etc.)
Folk-lore of metamorphosis
    See Metamorphosis (in religion, folk-lore,
        etc.)
Folk-lore of mice
    See Mice (in religion, folk-lore, etc.)
Folk-lore of milk
    See Milk (in religion, folk-lore, etc.)
Folk-lore of minerals
    See Minerals (in religion, folk-lore, etc.)

Folk-lore of mines *(Indirect) (GR900)*
    x Lost mines
        Mines and mineral resources—Folk-lore
        Mines, Folk-lore of
Folk-lore of mining
    See Metals (in religion, folk-lore, etc.)
Folk-lore of money
    See Money (in religion, folk-lore, etc.)
Folk-lore of mountains
    See Mountains (in religion, folk-lore, etc.)
Folk-lore of mules
    See Mules (in religion, folk-lore, etc.)
Folk-lore of mushrooms
    See Mushrooms (in religion, folk-lore, etc.)
Folk-lore of nature
    See Nature (in religion, folk-lore, etc.)
Folk-lore of navels
    See Navel (in religion, folk-lore, etc.)
Folk-lore of nets
    See Nets (in religion, folk-lore, etc.)
Folk-lore of night
    See Night (in religion, folk-lore, etc.)
Folk-lore of numbers
    See Counting-out rhymes
Folk-lore of oil
    See Oil (in religion, folk-lore, etc.)
Folk-lore of palms
    See Palms (in religion, folk-lore, etc.)
Folk-lore of paper
    See Paper (in religion, folk-lore, etc.)
Folk-lore of paths
    See Path (in religion, folk-lore, etc.)
Folk-lore of pelicans
    See Pelicans (in religion, folk-lore, etc.)
Folk-lore of pharmacy
    See Pharmacy (in religion, folk-lore, etc.)
Folk-lore of plants
    See Folk-lore of trees
        Plant lore
Folk-lore of polarity
    See Polarity (in religion, folk-lore, etc.)
Folk-lore of pottery
    See Pottery (in religion, folk-lore, etc.)
Folk-lore of poultry
    See Poultry (in religion, folk-lore, etc.)
Folk-lore of rabbits
    See Hares (in religion, folk-lore, etc.)
Folk-lore of railroads *(GR920.R3)*
    x Railroads—Folk-lore
Folk-lore of rain-making
    See Rain-making (in religion, folk-lore, etc.)
Folk-lore of rams
    See Rams (in religion, folk-lore, etc.)
Folk-lore of rape
    See Rape (in religion, folk-lore, etc.)
Folk-lore of ravens
    See Ravens (in religion, folk-lore, etc.)
Folk-lore of regeneration
    See Regeneration (in religion, folk-lore,
        etc.)
Folk-lore of reptiles
    See Serpents (in religion, folk-lore, etc.)
Folk-lore of rice
    See Rice (in religion, folk-lore, etc.)
Folk-lore of rings
    See Rings (in religion, folk-lore, etc.)
Folk-lore of rivers
    See Rivers (in religion, folk-lore, etc.)
Folk-lore of rods
    See Staff (in religion, folk-lore, etc.)
Folk-lore of ropes
    See Rope (in religion, folk-lore, etc.)
Folk-lore of roses
    See Roses (in religion, folk-lore, etc.)
Folk-lore of scorpions
    See Scorpions (in religion, folk-lore, etc.)
Folk-lore of serpents
    See Serpents (in religion, folk-lore, etc.)

Folk-lore of sesame
   See Sesame (in religion, folk-lore, etc.)
Folk-lore of shades and shadows
   See Shades and shadows (in religion,
     folk-lore, etc.)
Folk-lore of ships
   See Ships (in religion, folk-lore, etc.)
Folk-lore of silkworms
   See Silkworms (in religion, folk-lore, etc.)
Folk-lore of skulls
   See Skull (in religion, folk-lore, etc.)
Folk-lore of sleep
   See Sleep (in religion, folk-lore, etc.)
Folk-lore of slings
   See Slings (in religion, folk-lore, etc.)
Folk-lore of snails
   See Snails (in religion, folk-lore, etc.)
Folk-lore of solar eclipses
   See Eclipses, Solar (in religion, folk-lore,
     etc.)
Folk-lore of spiders
   See Spiders (in religion, folk-lore, etc.)
Folk-lore of springs
   See Springs (in religion, folk-lore, etc.)
Folk-lore of staffs
   See Staff (in religion, folk-lore, etc.)
Folk-lore of stars
   See Stars (in religion, folk-lore, etc.)
Folk-lore of stones *(GR800)*
   xx Precious stones
     Stone
Folk-lore of storms
   See Storms (in religion, folk-lore, etc.)
Folk-lore of swallows
   See Swallows (in religion, folk-lore, etc.)
Folk-lore of swine
   See Swine (in religion, folk-lore, etc.)
Folk-lore of swords
   See Swords (in religion, folk-lore, etc.)
Folk-lore of teeth
   See Teeth (in religion, folk-lore, etc.)
Folk-lore of the alphabet
   See Alphabet (in religion, folk-lore, etc.)
Folk-lore of the balance
   See Balance (in religion, folk-lore, etc.)
Folk-lore of the body
   See Body, Human (in religion, folk-lore,
     etc.)
Folk-lore of the color black
   See Black (in religion, folk-lore, etc.)
Folk-lore of the dead
   See Dead (in religion, folk-lore, etc.)
Folk-lore of the deaf
   See Deaf in folk-lore
Folk-lore of the Devanagari alphabet
   See Devanagari alphabet (in religion,
     folk-lore, etc.)
Folk-lore of the drum
   See Drum (in religion, folk-lore, etc.)
Folk-lore of the earth
   See Earth (in religion, folk-lore, etc.)
Folk-lore of the Equator
   See Shellbacks
Folk-lore of the eye
   See Eye (in religion, folk-lore, etc.)
Folk-lore of the foot
   See Foot (in religion, folk-lore, etc.)
Folk-lore of the hand
   See Hand (in religion, folk-lore, etc.)
Folk-lore of the head
   See Head (in religion, folk-lore, etc.)
Folk-lore of the heart
   See Heart (in religion, folk-lore, etc.)
Folk-lore of the hippopotamus
   See Hippopotamus (in religion, folk-lore,
     etc.)
Folk-lore of the moon
   See Moon (in religion, folk-lore, etc.)

Folk-lore of the oak
   See Oak (in religion, folk-lore, etc.)
Folk-lore of the octopus
   See Octopus (in religion, folk-lore, etc.)
Folk-lore of the right of asylum
   See Asylum, Right of (in religion, folk-lore,
     etc.)
Folk-lore of the sea *(GR910)*
   sa Shellbacks
     St. Elmo's fire
   x Ocean (in religion, folk-lore, etc.)
     Sea, Folk-lore of the
   xx Sea stories
     Water (in religion, folk-lore, etc.)
Folk-lore of the sky *(GR620)*
   sa Flying saucers (in religion, folk-lore,
     etc.)
     Moon (in religion, folk-lore, etc.)
     Sky-gods
     Stars (in religion, folk-lore, etc.)
     Sun (in religion, folk-lore, etc.)
   x Sky, Folk-lore of the
     Sky (in religion, folk-lore, etc.)
Folk-lore of the sun
   See Sun (in religion, folk-lore, etc.)
Folk-lore of the swan
   See Swan (in religion, folk-lore, etc.)
Folk-lore of the Tiber River
   See Tiber River (in religion, folk-lore, etc.)
Folk-lore of the tongue
   See Tongue (in religion, folk-lore, etc.)
Folk-lore of the viscera
   See Viscera (in religion, folk-lore, etc.)
Folk-lore of the youngest son
   See Youngest son (in religion, folk-lore,
     etc.)
Folk-lore of thunderstorms
   See Thunderstorms (in religion, folk-lore,
     etc.)
Folk-lore of toads
   See Toads (in religion, folk-lore, etc.)
Folk-lore of transplantation
   See Transplantation (in religion, folk-lore,
     etc.)
Folk-lore of trees *(GR785)*
   sa Christmas trees
     Hawthorn (in religion, folk-lore, etc.)
     Liberty trees
     Oak (in religion, folk-lore, etc.)
     Tree worship
   x Folk-lore of plants
     Trees, Folk-lore of
   xx Druids and Druidism
     Forests and forestry
     Plant lore
     Trees
  — Juvenile literature
Folk-lore of triangles
   See Triangle (in religion, folk-lore, etc.)
Folk-lore of turtles
   See Turtles (in religion, folk-lore, etc.)
Folk-lore of twins
   See Twins (in religion, folk-lore, etc.)
Folk-lore of urine
   See Urine (in religion, folk-lore, etc.)
Folk-lore of vampires
   See Vampires
Folk-lore of volcanoes
   See Volcanoes (in religion, folk-lore, etc.)
Folk-lore of walls
   See Walls (in religion, folk-lore, etc.)
Folk-lore of wands
   See Staff (in religion, folk-lore, etc.)
Folk-lore of war
   See War (in religion, folk-lore, etc.)
Folk-lore of water
   See Water (in religion, folk-lore, etc.)

Folk-lore of wheels
   See Wheels (in religion, folk-lore, etc.)
Folk-lore of wild boars
   See Wild boar (in religion, folk-lore, etc.)
Folk-lore of winds
   See Winds (in religion, folk-lore, etc.)
Folk-lore of wine
   See Wine (in religion, folk-lore, etc.)
Folk-lore of wolves
   See Wolves (in religion, folk-lore, etc.)
Folk-lore of woman *(GR470)*
   x Mothers (in religion, folk-lore, etc.)
     Woman—Folk-lore
     Women in folk-lore
Folk-lore of woodpeckers
   See Woodpeckers (in religion, folk-lore,
     etc.)
Folk-lore of wreaths
   See Wreaths (in religion, folk-lore, etc.)
Folk-lore of writing
   See Writing (in religion, folk-lore, etc.)
Folk-lorists
   See Folklorists
Folk medicine *(Indirect)*
   x Folk-lore, Medical
     Medical folk-lore
   xx Medical anthropology
     Medicine, Magic, mystic, and spagiric
     Medicine, Popular
     Medicine, Primitive
Folk music *(Indirect)*
   sa Country music
     Folk dance music
     Folk dancing
     Folk-songs
   xx Folk dancing
     Folk-lore
     Music
     National music
  — Caricatures and cartoons
  — Phonotape catalogs *(ML157)*
  — ⌐country subdivision¬
      Here are entered collections of folk
      music of various national and ethnic
      origins which consist of instrumen-
      tal music only or of songs and in-
      strumental music. References are
      made to and from Folk music with
      national qualification, *e.g.* Folk mu-
      sic—Mexico *see also* Folk music,
      Mexican; Folk music, Mexican *see*
      also Folk music—Mexico. Addi-
      tional specific references are made
      when needed.
  — Mexico
     Note under Folk music—⌐country sub-
      division¬
Folk music, English, ⌐French, German, etc.¬
   Subdivided by locality.
   x English ⌐French, German, etc.¬ folk
     music
Folk music, Gipsy
   x Gipsy folk music
     Gipsy music
     Music, Gipsy
Folk music, Mexican
   Note under Folk music—⌐country subdivision¬
Folk music, Thai
   sa Pīphāt music
Folk-plays
   See Folk-drama
Folk poetry
   See Folk-songs
Folk-psychology
   See Ethnopsychology

Folk-songs *(Indirect) (Folk poetry,*
PN1341-5; Music, M1627; Music
literature, ML3545)
 sa Ballads
　　Carols
　　Dumy
　　Folk-lore
　　Lays
　　National songs
　　Work-songs
　 x Folk poetry
 xx Ballads
　　Folk literature
　　Folk-lore
　　Folk music
　　Music
　　National music
　　National songs
　　Songs
　　Vocal music
— Accompaniment *(MT68)*
　 xx Musical accompaniment
— Criticism, Textual

GEOGRAPHIC SUBDIVISIONS

— ⌜country subdivision⌝
　　Here are entered collections of folk-
　　songs of various national and ethnic
　　origins which are sung in a particu-
　　lar country. References are made to
　　and from Folk-songs with national
　　qualification, *e.g.* Folk-songs—Ar-
　　gentine Republic *see also* Folk-
　　songs, Argentine; Folk-songs, Ar-
　　gentine *see also* Folk-songs—Ar-
　　gentine Republic. Additional spe-
　　cific references as shown under the
　　following headings are made when
　　needed.

GEOGRAPHIC SUBDIVISIONS

— Albemarle region, N.C.
　　See Folk-songs, American—North
　　Carolina

GEOGRAPHIC SUBDIVISIONS

— Argentine Republic
　　Note under Folk-songs—⌜country sub-
　　division⌝

GEOGRAPHIC SUBDIVISIONS

— Arizona
　 sa Folk-songs, American—Arizona
　　Folk-songs, Spanish—Arizona

GEOGRAPHIC SUBDIVISIONS

— Azores
　　See Folk-songs, Portuguese—Azores

GEOGRAPHIC SUBDIVISIONS

— Brazil
　 xx Folk-songs, Portuguese

GEOGRAPHIC SUBDIVISIONS

— Brittany
　 sa Folk-songs, Breton
　　Folk-songs, French—Ille-et-Vilaine,
　　France (Dept.)

GEOGRAPHIC SUBDIVISIONS

— Bukowina
　　See Folk-songs, German—Bukowina
　　Folk-songs, Romanian—Bukowina

GEOGRAPHIC SUBDIVISIONS

— Canada
　 sa Folk-songs, French-Canadian

GEOGRAPHIC SUBDIVISIONS

— Carinthia
　　See Folk-songs, Austrian—Carinthia

GEOGRAPHIC SUBDIVISIONS

— Czechoslovak Republic
　 sa Folk-songs, German—Czechoslovak
　　Republic

GEOGRAPHIC SUBDIVISIONS

— Estonia
　 sa Folk-songs, Swedish—Estonia

GEOGRAPHIC SUBDIVISIONS

— Faroe Islands
　　See Folk-songs, Faroese

GEOGRAPHIC SUBDIVISIONS

— Finland
　 sa Folk-songs, Swedish—Finland

GEOGRAPHIC SUBDIVISIONS

— Galicia
　 sa Folk-songs, German—Galicia

GEOGRAPHIC SUBDIVISIONS

— Haiti
　 sa Folk-songs, Creole—Haiti

GEOGRAPHIC SUBDIVISIONS

— Iceland
　　See Folk-songs, Icelandic

GEOGRAPHIC SUBDIVISIONS

— Louisiana
　 sa Folk-songs, Creole—Louisiana
　　Folk-songs, French—Louisiana

GEOGRAPHIC SUBDIVISIONS

— Luxemburg
　 sa Folk-songs, French—Luxemburg
　　Folk-songs, German—Luxemburg

GEOGRAPHIC SUBDIVISIONS

— Middle West
　 sa Folk-songs, American—Middle West

GEOGRAPHIC SUBDIVISIONS

— Mississippi Valley
　　See Folk-songs, American—
　　Mississippi Valley

GEOGRAPHIC SUBDIVISIONS

— New Hampshire
　 sa Folk-songs, French—New
　　Hampshire

GEOGRAPHIC SUBDIVISIONS

— New Mexico
　 sa Folk-songs, Spanish—New Mexico

GEOGRAPHIC SUBDIVISIONS

— Ozark Mountains
　　See Folk-songs, American—Ozark
　　Mountains

GEOGRAPHIC SUBDIVISIONS

— Peru
　 sa Mulizas

GEOGRAPHIC SUBDIVISIONS

— Russia
　 sa Folk-songs, German—Russia

GEOGRAPHIC SUBDIVISIONS

— Southwest, New

　 sa Folk-songs, American—Southwest,
　　New
　　Folk-songs, Spanish—Southwest,
　　New

GEOGRAPHIC SUBDIVISIONS

— Southwest, Old
　 sa Folk-songs, American—Southwest,
　　Old

GEOGRAPHIC SUBDIVISIONS

— Styria
　　See Folk-songs, Austrian—Styria

GEOGRAPHIC SUBDIVISIONS

— Texas
　 sa Folk-songs, Spanish—Texas

GEOGRAPHIC SUBDIVISIONS

— The West
　 sa Folk-songs, American—The West

GEOGRAPHIC SUBDIVISIONS

— Transylvania
　 sa Folk-songs, German—Transylvania

GEOGRAPHIC SUBDIVISIONS

— Trinidad
　 x Calypso songs

GEOGRAPHIC SUBDIVISIONS

— Tyrol
　 sa Folk-songs, Austrian—Tyrol

GEOGRAPHIC SUBDIVISIONS

— United States
　 sa Folk-songs, American
　　Folk-songs, French—Louisiana,
　　⌜New Hampshire, United States,
　　etc.⌝
　　Folk-songs, Spanish—Arizona,
　　⌜Southwest, New; etc.⌝
　　Play-party
　 xx Folk-songs, American
Folk-songs, Acadian
　 xx Folk-songs, French-Canadian
Folk-songs, African
　 sa Folk-songs, Angolan
　　Folk-songs, Bambute
　　Folk-songs, Bantu
　　Folk-songs, Ghanaian
　　Folk-songs, Lunda
　　Folk-songs, Thonga
　 x Folk-songs, Negro (African)
　 xx Negro songs
　 Note under Negro songs
Folk-songs, Albanian
　 x Folk-songs, Gheg
Folk-songs, American
　 sa Folk-songs—United States
　 xx Folk-songs—United States
— Arizona
　 xx Folk-songs—Arizona
— Middle West
　 xx Folk-songs—Middle West
— Mississippi Valley
　 x Folk-songs—Mississippi Valley
— North Carolina
　 x Folk-songs—Albemarle region, N.C.
— Ozark Mountains
　 x Folk-songs—Ozark Mountains
— Southwest, New
　 xx Folk-songs—Southwest, New
— Southwest, Old
　 xx Folk-songs—Southwest, Old
— The West
　 xx Folk-songs—The West

Folk-songs, American, [English, French, etc.]
Subdivided by locality. The references indicated here are general in application. Exceptions to this pattern and examples of additional references required in specific cases are shown under the headings below.
Cf. note under Folk-songs (Instrumental settings)
sa Ballads, American, [English, French, etc.]
Folk-songs—United States, [England, France, etc.]
National songs, American, [English, French, etc.]
x American [English, French, etc.] folk-songs
xx American [English, French, etc.] ballads and songs
Ballads, American, [English, French, etc.]
Folk-songs—United States, [England, France, etc.]
National songs, American, [English, French, etc.]
Songs, American, [English, French, etc.]
— Subjects
See Folk-songs, American, [English, French, etc.]—Themes, motives
— Themes, motives
x Folk-songs, American, [English, French, etc.]—Subjects
Folk-songs, Angolan *(M1838.A5)*
xx Folk-songs, African
Folk-songs, Argentine
xx Folk-songs, Spanish American
Note under Folk-songs—[country subdivision]
Folk-songs, Austrian
x Austrian ballads and songs
xx Folk-songs, German
— Carinthia
x Folk-songs—Carinthia
— Styria
x Folk-songs—Styria
— Tyrol
xx Folk-songs—Tyrol
Folk-songs, Bambute *(M1838.C67)*
xx Folk-songs, African
Folk-songs, Bantu
xx Folk-songs, African
Folk-songs, Belgian
sa Folk-songs, Flemish
Folk-songs, Walloon
Folk-songs, Bohemian
See Folk-songs, Czech
Folk-songs, Brazilian
sa Congadas
Folk-songs, Breton
xx Folk-songs—Brittany
Folk-songs, French
Folk-songs, French—Brittany
Folk-songs, British
sa Folk-songs, English
Folk-songs, Scottish
Folk-songs, Welsh
Folk-songs, Bulgarian
xx Folk-songs, Slavic
Folk-songs, Burgundian
x Folk-songs, French—Burgundy
xx Folk-songs, French
Folk-songs, Byelorussian
See Folk-songs, White Russian
Folk-songs, Canadian
sa Folk-songs, French-Canadian
Folk-songs, Catalan
sa Goigs
— Majorca

See Folk-songs, Majorcan
Folk-songs, Creole
— Haiti, [Louisiana, etc.]
xx Folk-songs—Haiti, [Louisiana, etc.]
Folk-songs, Croatian
xx Folk-songs, Slavic
Folk-songs, Yugoslav
Folk-songs, Cuban
xx Folk-songs, Spanish American
Folk-songs, Czech
x Folk-songs, Bohemian
xx Folk-songs, Slavic
Folk-songs, Danish
xx Folk-songs, Scandinavian
Folk-songs, Dutch
sa Folk-songs, Flemish
Folk-songs, Friesian
Folk-songs, English
xx Folk-songs, British
Folk-songs, Eskimo
xx Eskimo—Music
Folk-songs, Faroese
x Folk-songs—Faroe Islands
xx Folk-songs, Scandinavian
Folk-songs, Finno-Ugrian
sa Folk-songs, Ostiak
Folk-songs, Vogul
Folk-songs, Flemish
xx Folk-songs, Belgian
Folk-songs, Dutch
Folk-songs, French
sa Folk-songs, Breton, [Burgundian, French-Canadian, Gascon]
— Brittany
sa Folk-songs, Breton
— Burgundy
See Folk-songs, Burgundian
— Canada
See Folk-songs, French-Canadian
— Gascony
See Folk-songs, Gascon
— Ille-et-Vilaine, France (Dept.)
xx Folk-songs—Brittany
— Louisiana
xx Folk-songs—Louisiana
Folk-songs—United States
— Luxemburg
xx Folk-songs—Luxemburg
— New Hampshire
xx Folk-songs—New Hampshire
Folk-songs—United States
— Provence
sa Folk-songs, Provençal
— Switzerland
See Folk-songs, Swiss (French)
— United States
xx Folk-songs—United States
Folk-songs, French-Canadian
sa Folk-songs, Acadian
x Folk-songs, French—Canada
xx Folk-songs—Canada
Folk-songs, Canadian
Folk-songs, French
Folk-songs, Friesian
xx Folk-songs, Dutch
Folk-songs, Gascon
x Folk-songs, French—Gascony
xx Folk-songs, French
Folk-songs, German *(Direct)*
sa Folk-songs, Austrian
Folk-songs, Jewish (German)
Folk-songs, Low German
x Austrian ballads and songs
— Bukowina
x Folk-songs—Bukowina
— Czechoslovak Republic
xx Folk-songs—Czechoslovak Republic
— Erzgebirge

xx Folk-songs, German—Saxony
— Galicia
xx Folk-songs—Galicia
— Luxemburg
xx Folk-songs—Luxemburg
— Russia
xx Folk-songs—Russia
— Saxony
sa Folk-songs, German—Erzgebirge
— Switzerland
See Folk-songs, Swiss (German)
— Transylvania
xx Folk-songs—Transylvania
Folk-songs, Ghanaian
xx Folk-songs, African
Folk-songs, Gheg
See Folk-songs, Albanian
Folk-songs, Hebrew
See Folk-songs, Jewish (Hebrew)
Folk-songs, Hungarian
x Austrian ballads and songs
Folk-songs, Icelandic
x Folk-songs—Iceland
xx Folk-songs, Scandinavian
Folk-songs, Italian
— Sardinia
See Folk-songs, Sardinian
— Sicily
See Folk-songs, Sicilian
Folk-songs, Japanese
sa Kouta
x Saibara
Folk-songs, Jewish
x Jewish folk-songs
xx Songs, Jewish
Folk-songs, Jewish (German)
xx Folk-songs, German
Folk-songs, Jewish (Hebrew)
x Folk-songs, Hebrew
Hebrew folk-songs
Folk-songs, Jewish (Ladino)
x Folk-songs, Judeo-Spanish
Folk-songs, Ladino
Folk-songs, Sephardic
Judeo-Spanish folk-songs
Ladino folk-songs
Sephardic folk-songs
xx Folk-songs, Spanish
Note under Songs, Sephardic
Folk-songs, Jewish (Yiddish)
x Folk-songs, Yiddish
Yiddish folk-songs
Folk-songs, Judeo-Spanish
See Folk-songs, Jewish (Ladino)
Folk-songs, Kurukh
See Folk-songs, Oraon
Folk-songs, Ladino
See Folk-songs, Jewish (Ladino)
Folk-songs, Low German
xx Folk-songs, German
Folk-songs, Lunda *(M1831.L85; M1832.L85)*
xx Folk-songs, African
Folk-songs, Majorcan
x Folk-songs, Catalan—Majorca
Folk-songs, Spanish—Majorca
Folk-songs, Mexican
sa Corridos
xx Folk-songs, Spanish American
Folk-songs, Moravian
xx Folk-songs, Slavic
Folk-songs, Negro
See Negro songs
Folk-songs, Negro (African)
See Folk-songs, African
Folk-songs, Negro (American)
See Negro songs
Folk-songs, Norwegian
xx Folk-songs, Scandinavian

Folk-songs, Oraon
    x Folk-songs, Kurukh
Folk-songs, Ostiak
    xx Folk-songs, Finno-Ugrian
Folk-songs, Polish
    sa Dumy, Polish
    xx Folk-songs, Slavic
Folk-songs, Portuguese
    sa Fados
        Folk-songs—Brazil
  — Azores
    x Folk-songs—Azores
Folk-songs, Provençal
    xx Folk-songs, Provence
Folk-songs, Romanian
  — Bukowina
    x Folk-songs—Bukowina
Folk-songs, Russian   *(Direct)*
    sa Byliny
        Chastushki
        Folk-songs, White Russian
    xx Folk-songs, Slavic
Folk-songs, Sardinian
    x Folk-songs, Italian—Sardinia
Folk-songs, Scandinavian
    sa Folk-songs, Danish, ⌜Faroese, Icelandic,
        Norwegian, Swedish⌟
Folk-songs, Scottish
    xx Folk-songs, British
Folk-songs, Sephardic
    See Folk-songs, Jewish (Ladino)
Folk-songs, Serbian   *(Direct)*
    xx Folk-songs, Slavic
        Folk-songs, Yugoslav
Folk-songs, Siberian   *(M1766.S4; M1767.S4)*
    xx Folk-songs, Slavic
Folk-songs, Sicilian
    x Folk-songs, Italian—Sicily
    xx Sicilian ballads and songs
Folk-songs, Slavic
    sa Folk-songs, Bulgarian
        Folk-songs, Croatian
        Folk-songs, Czech
        Folk-songs, Moravian
        Folk-songs, Polish
        Folk-songs, Russian
        Folk-songs, Serbian
        Folk-songs, Siberian
        Folk-songs, Slovak
        Folk-songs, Slovenian
        Folk-songs, Ukrainian
        Folk-songs, Wendic
        Folk-songs, Yugoslav
Folk-songs, Slovak
    xx Folk-songs, Slavic
Folk-songs, Slovenian
    xx Folk-songs, Slavic
        Folk-songs, Yugoslav
Folk-songs, Spanish
    sa Coplas
        Folk-songs, Jewish (Ladino)
        Folk-songs, Spanish American
  — Arizona
    xx Folk-songs—Arizona
        Folk-songs—United States
  — Majorca
    See Folk-songs, Majorcan
  — New Mexico
    xx Folk-songs—New Mexico
        Folk-songs—United States
  — Southwest, New
    sa Alabados
    xx Folk-songs—Southwest, New
        Folk-songs—United States
  — Texas
    xx Folk-songs—Texas
        Folk-songs—United States

Folk-songs, Spanish American
    sa Folk-songs, Argentine, ⌜Cuban,
        Mexican, etc.⌟
    xx Folk-songs, Spanish
Folk-songs, Swedish
    xx Folk-songs, Scandinavian
  — Estonia
    xx Folk-songs—Estonia
  — Finland
    xx Folk-songs—Finland
Folk-songs, Swiss (French)
    x Folk-songs, French—Switzerland
        Swiss folk-songs
Folk-songs, Swiss (German)
    sa Yodels
    x Folk-songs, German—Switzerland
        Swiss folk-songs
Folk-songs, Thonga
    xx Folk-songs, African
Folk-songs, Ukrainian
    sa Dumy, Ukrainian
    xx Folk-songs, Slavic
Folk-songs, Vogul
    xx Folk-songs, Finno-Ugrian
Folk-songs, Walloon
    xx Folk-songs, Belgian
Folk-songs, Welsh
    xx Folk-songs, British
Folk-songs, Wendic
    xx Folk-songs, Slavic
Folk-songs, White Russian
    sa Chastushki
    x Folk-songs, Byelorussian
    xx Folk-songs, Russian
Folk-songs, Yiddish
    See Folk-songs, Jewish (Yiddish)
Folk-songs, Yugoslav
    sa Folk-songs, Croatian
        Folk-songs, Serbian
        Folk-songs, Slovenian
    xx Folk-songs, Slavic
Folk-songs (Instrumental settings)
    The specification (Instrumental settings)
        is used also after Folk-songs with na-
        tional qualification.
Folk-tales
    See Folk literature
        Folk-lore
        Legends
        Tales
Folklore
    See Folk-lore
Folklorists   *(GR50)*
    x Folk-lorists
    xx Folk-lore
Folklorists, Women
Folkways
    See Manners and customs
Follicle-stimulating hormone
    xx Gonadotropin
Follicles, Hair
    See Hair follicles
Follies (Architecture)   *(Direct)*
    x Folly (Architecture)
    xx Architecture
        Pavilions
Follis (Coin)
    xx Coins, Roman
Follow-up in teacher training   *(Direct)*
    x Teachers colleges—Follow-up service
    xx Personnel service in higher education
        Teachers college graduates
        Teachers, Training of
Folly
  — Biblical teaching
Folly (Architecture)
    See Follies (Architecture)

Folly in art
    xx Art
Folsom points   *(E98.I4)*
    xx Indians of North America—Implements
        Paleo-Indians
        Projectile points
        Stone implements
Foma (Bantu people)
    xx Ethnology—Zaire
Fomes lignosus
Fon dialect   *(PL8164.Z9)*
    x Djedji dialect
        Fō dialect
        Jeji dialect
    xx Ewe language
Fondue
    xx Chafing-dish receipts
        Cookery (Cheese)
Fontanel
    See Skull
Fontanelle
    See Skull
Fontenoy, Battle of, 1745   *(D293.7.F6)*
    xx Austrian Succession, War of, 1740-1748
Fonts   *(Direct)*   *(NA5070)*
    sa Baptisteries
    x Baptismal fonts
    xx Baptism
        Baptisteries
        Christian antiquities
        Christian art and symbolism
        Church decoration and ornament
        Church furniture
Food   *(Biology, QH521; Chemical technology,*
        TP370-465; Diet, RM214-261;
        Home economics, TX341-641;
        Manners and customs, GT2860;
        Public health, RA601-2; Trade,
        HD9000-9490)
    sa Acorns as food
        Algae as food
        Animal food
        Animals, Food habits of
        Beverages
        Cassava as food
        Cereals as food
        Coloring matter in food
        Condiments
        Cookery
        Diet
        Dietaries
        Eggs as food
        Farm produce
        Fish as food
        Fish-meal as food
        Flavoring essences
        Food mixes
        Fruit
        Gastronomy
        Grain
        Hay as food
        Honey as food
        Insects as food
        Legumes as food
        Macaroni products
        Markets
        Meat
        Milk as food
        Nutrition
        Nuts
        Operational rations (Military supplies)
        Pollen as food
        Poultry as food
        Sea food
        Soy-bean as food
        Straw as food
        Survival and emergency rations
        Vegetables

Food, Freeze-dried   *(Continued)*
  xx Food, Dried
     Freeze-drying
  — Patents
Food, Fried
  x Fried food
  xx Frying
  — Patents
Food, Frozen   *(TP493.5)*
  sa Apple, Frozen
     Baked products, Frozen
     Cold-storage lockers
     Cookery (Frozen foods)
     Desserts, Frozen
     Eggs, Frozen
     Fish, Frozen
     Fishery products, Frozen
     Frozen foods industry
     Fruit, Frozen
     Home freezers
     Meat, Frozen
     Milk, Frozen
     Poultry, Frozen
     Shrimps, Frozen
     Vegetables, Frozen
  x Dehydrofrozen food
     Food, Dehydrofrozen
     Food—Freezing
     Freezing of food
     Frozen food
  xx Food—Preservation
  — Transportation
Food, Irradiated
  sa Fish, Irradiated
  x Irradiated foods
  xx Radiation preservation of food
Food, Precooked
  x Precooked food
Food, Pure
  See Food adulteration and inspection
     Food law and legislation
Food, Raw   *(TX392)*
  sa Vegetarianism
  x Raw food
     Uncooked food
     Unfired food
  xx Diet
     Vegetables
     Vegetarianism
Food, Smoked
  See Cookery (Smoked foods)
     Fish, Smoked
     Meat, Smoked
Food, Wild   *(Indirect)*
  sa Cookery (Wild foods)
     Game and game-birds
     Wildlife as food
  x Wild foods
  xx Game and game-birds
     Plants, Edible
Food (in religion, folk-lore, etc.)
  sa Bread (in religion, folk-lore, etc.)
  x Folk-lore of food
  xx Religion, Primitive
Food additives   *(TX553.A3)*
  sa Edible coatings
     Sweeteners
  x Additive compounds
     Additives, Food
     Chemical additives in food
  xx Food—Analysis
     Food industry and trade
     Food—Preservation
  — Analysis
  — Juvenile literature
  — Law and legislation   *(Direct)*
     xx Food law and legislation
  — Standards   *(Direct)*

— Toxicology
Food adulteration and inspection   *(Indirect)*
     (Economics, HD9000.9; Technical
     works, TX501-595)
  sa Fish inspection
     Food contamination
     Food spoilage
     Fruit inspection
     Meat inspection
     Milk commissions, Medical
     Milk supply
     Oleomargarine
     Poultry inspection
     Vegetable inspection
  x Analysis of food
     Food inspection
     Food—Inspection
     Food, Pure
     Inspection of food
     Pure food
  xx Adulterations
     Consumer protection
     Hygiene, Public
     Sanitary chemistry
  Example under Consumer education
  — Juvenile literature
Food aid programs
  See Food relief
Food allergy   *(RC596)*
  xx Allergy
Food animals
  See Animal food
Food brokers
  xx Grocery trade
     Produce trade
  — Accounting
Food calories
  See Food—Caloric content
Food chains (Ecology)
  xx Animals, Food habits of
     Biological productivity
     Ecology
Food chemistry
  See Food—Analysis
     Food—Composition
Food color
  See Color of food
Food conservation   *(TX357)*
     Here are entered works on the preserva-
     tion and economical use of food, espe-
     cially in war time. Economic works on
     food conditions and supply are entered
     under Food supply; European War,
     1914-1918—Food question; etc.
  sa Canning and preserving
     Food contamination
  x Conservation of food
     Food—Conservation
     Wheat substitutes
  xx Food supply
Food consumption   *(Indirect)*
  xx Food supply
  — Mathematical models
  — Public opinion
  — Underdeveloped areas
     See Underdeveloped areas—Food
        consumption
Food containers
  sa Tin cans
     subdivisions Containers *and* Packaging
        under specific foods, e.g. Milk—
        Containers; Apple—Packaging
  x Food—Containers
  xx Containers
     Food—Packaging
  — Defects
Food contamination
  sa Feed additive residues

     Milk contamination
     Radioactive contamination of food
  x Contaminated food
     Food—Contamination
     Foods, Contaminated
  xx Contamination (Technology)
     Decontamination (from gases,
        chemicals, etc.)
     Food adulteration and inspection
     Food conservation
  — Juvenile literature
Food control
  See Food supply
Food decoration
  See Cookery (Garnishes)
Food for invalids
  See Cookery for the sick
Food for school children
  See School children—Food
Food habits   *(Indirect)*   *(GT2850-2955;*
     TX357)
  sa Children—Nutrition—Psychological
        aspects
     Diet
     Food preferences
     Nutrition
  x Man—Food habits
  xx Diet
     Nutrition
  Note under Human behavior
Food habits of animals
  See Animals, Food habits of
Food handling   *(TX537)*
  sa subdivision Sanitation *under subjects,*
     e.g. Food service—Sanitation;
     Restaurants, lunch rooms, etc.—
     Sanitation
  x Food sanitation
     Handling of food
  xx Sanitation, Household
  — Programmed instruction
  — Research grants   *(Direct)*
     xx Food research
Food in literature
Food in the Bible
  x Bible—Food
Food industry and trade   *(Direct)*
     Here are entered works on the processing
     of food in general and on the market-
     ing of processed food products. Works
     on the processing of specific kinds of
     food products are entered under the
     heading for the specific product.
     Works on the marketing of unprocessed
     agricultural and other commodities
     from the point of view of the com-
     modity dealer are entered under the
     heading Produce trade.
     Works on the marketing of farm produce
     from the point of view of the farmer
     are entered under the heading Farm
     produce—Marketing.
  sa Delicatessen
     Farm produce
     Food additives
     Food prices
     Food supply
     Produce trade
     Snack foods
     Wages—Food industry and trade
     individual processed foods and
        processing industries, e.g. Cheese;
        Coffee processing; Canning and
        preserving—Industry and trade;
        Flour and feed trade
  x Food processing
     Food trade
  xx Agricultural processing

Agriculture
Farm produce
Food supply
Notes under Agricultural processing; Farm
produce—Marketing; Produce trade
— Accounting
— Advertising
See Advertising—Food
— Automation
— By-products
— Collective labor agreements
See Collective labor agreements—
Food industry
— Credit guides
— Defense measures
xx Factories—Protection
War damage, Industrial
— Dust control
— Electric equipment
— Employees
sa Collective labor agreements—Food
industry
x Food processing workers
— Equipment and supplies
— — Appraisal
See Food industry and trade—
Equipment and supplies—
Valuation
— — Catalogs
— — Corrosion
— — Costs *(TP373)*
— — Design and construction
— — Maintenance and repair
— — — Patents
— — Valuation
x Food industry and trade—
Equipment and supplies—
Appraisal
— Finance
— Fires and fire prevention
— Hygienic aspects *(RC965.F)*
— Information services
— Job descriptions
— Juvenile literature
— Labor productivity
— Law and legislation
See Food law and legislation
— Licenses *(Direct)*
— Management
— — Problems, exercises, etc.
— Mathematical models
— Patents
— Production control
Example under Production control
— Production standards
— Quality control
sa Fruit inspection
Vegetable inspection
— Safety measures
— Sanitation *(TP370)*
x Food-plant sanitation
xx Factory sanitation
— Seasonal variations
— Standards *(Direct)*
— Tables and ready-reckoners
— Taxation *(Direct)*
— Technological innovations
— Underdeveloped areas
See Underdeveloped areas—Food
industry and trade
— Vocational guidance
— Waste disposal
Food inspection
See Food adulteration and inspection
Food irradiation
See Radiation preservation of food

Food law and legislation *(Direct)*
(HD9000.7-9)
sa Advertising—Food—Law and
legislation
Canning and preserving—Law and
legislation
Food additives—Law and legislation
Grocery trade—Law and legislation
Meat industry and trade—Law and
legislation
Produce trade—Law and legislation
Products liability—Food
subdivision Law and legislation *under
individual foods, e.g.* Potatoes—Law
and legislation
x Food industry and trade—Law and
legislation
Food—Law and legislation
Food, Pure
Law, Food
Pure food
xx Commercial law
Consumer protection—Law and
legislation
Produce trade—Law and legislation
Example under Public health laws
Food mixes
x Mixes (Cookery)
Prepared food
xx Food
Mixers (Cookery)
Food of animals
See Animals, Food habits of
Food packets, Survival
See Survival and emergency rations
Food pages
See Newspapers—Sections, columns, etc.—
Food
Food-plant sanitation
See Food industry and trade—Sanitation
Food plants
See Plants, Edible
Food poisoning *(Indirect) (RC143)*
sa Animal food—Toxicology
Botulism
Ptomaine poisoning
xx Food—Microbiology
Poisons
Ptomaine poisoning
Putrefaction
Food policy
See Nutrition policy
Food preferences
sa Taste
xx Food habits
Nutrition
Taste
Food preservation
See Food—Preservation
Food preservatives *(TX607-8)*
xx Canning and preserving
Food—Preservation
— Analysis
— Physiological effect *(QP981.P8)*
Food prices *(Direct)*
x Food—Prices
xx Agricultural prices
Cost and standard of living
Food industry and trade
Produce trade
Food processing
See Food industry and trade
Food processing plants *(Indirect) (TP373)*
sa Bakers and bakeries
Canneries
Cheese factories
Creameries
Dairy plants

Flour-mills
Macaroni factories
Milk plants
Packing-houses
Poultry plants
Sugar factories
xx Factories
— Design and construction *(TH4526)*
Food processing workers
See Food industry and trade—Employees
Food relief *(Direct) (HV696.F6)*
sa Diet-kitchens
Emergency food supply
Emergency mass feeding
World War, 1939-1945—Civilian relief
x Food aid programs
Food stamp plan
xx Charities
Disaster relief
Emergency food supply
Public welfare
Surplus agricultural commodities
Unemployed
— Law and legislation *(Direct)*
Food relief, American *(Direct)*
Food research *(TX341)*
sa Food handling—Research grants
x Food—Research
Food sanitation
See Food handling
subdivision Sanitation *under subjects,
e.g.* Food service—Sanitation;
Restaurants, lunch rooms, etc.—
Sanitation
Food service
Here are entered general works on the
quantity preparation and service of
food to those eating away from home.
Works dealing solely with culinary
problems of quantity feeding are en-
tered under Cookery for institutions,
etc.
sa Caterers and catering
Cookery for institutions, etc.
Emergency mass feeding
Industrial feeding
Restaurants, lunch rooms, etc.
subdivision Food service *under
appropriate subjects, e.g.* Air lines—
Food service; Hospitals—Food
service
x Mass feeding
xx Home economics
Note under Cookery for institutions, etc.
— Collective labor agreements
See Collective labor agreements—
Food service
— Cost control *(TX911.3.C65)*
— Employees
See Food service employees
— Equipment and supplies
— — Catalogs
— Examinations, questions, etc.
— Research
See Food service research
— Safety measures
— Sanitation
Example under Food handling; *and under
reference from* Food sanitation
— Study and teaching
— — Audio-visual aids
— Vocational guidance
Food service employees
sa Collective labor agreements—Food
service
School food service directors
Waitresses
x Food service—Employees

Food service employees *(Continued)*
    Food service workers
Food service research *(Direct)*
    x Food service—Research
    xx Research
Food service workers
    See Food service employees
Food spoilage
    xx Food adulteration and inspection
        Food—Microbiology
        Food—Preservation
Food stamp plan
    See Food relief
Food storage pests *(Indirect)* *(SB937)*
    x Storage pests of food
        Stored food pests
    xx Farm produce—Storage—Diseases and
        injuries
        Food—Storage
        Pests
    — Control *(Indirect)*
        xx Pest control
    — Identification
Food substitutes *(TX357; European War,*
        1914-1918: Germany, HC286.2)
    sa Meat substitutes
    x Milk substitutes
        Substitutes for food
    xx Food, Artificial
        Substitute products
    — Patents
Food supply *(Indirect)* *(Economics,*
        HD9000-9019)
    sa Agriculture—Statistics
        Emergency food supply
        European War, 1914-1918—Food
            question
        Famines
        Food conservation
        Food consumption
        Food industry and trade
        Food—Preservation
        Meat industry and trade
        Sino-Japanese Conflict, 1937-1945—
            Food question
        World War, 1939-1945—Food question
        subdivision Preservation *under various*
            food products, e.g. Fishery products
            —Preservation
    x Food control
    xx Food industry and trade
        Produce trade
        Rationing, Consumer
    Note under Food conservation
    — Juvenile literature
    — Mathematical models
    — Pictorial works
    — Public opinion
Food texture
    x Food—Texture
        Texture of food
Food trade
    See Farm produce—Marketing
        Food industry and trade
        Produce trade
Food warmers *(NK4695.F6)*
    x Veilleuses (Pottery)
    xx Porcelain
        Pottery
Foods, Contaminated
    See Food contamination
Fools, Feast of *(GT4995.F6)*
    x Feast of Fools
    Example under Festivals
Fools and jesters *(GT3670)*
    sa Badḥanim
        Clowns
        Hanswurst

        Motley
        Pierrot
    x Court fools
        Jesters
    xx Courts and courtiers
        Favorites, Royal
Fools and jesters in art
    xx Art
Fools and jesters in literature
Foot *(QL950.7; QM549)*
    sa Tendon of Achilles
    x Feet
        Paw
    — Abnormities and deformities *(QM691;*
        Surgical treatment, RD781-9)
        sa Clubfoot
            Flatfoot
            Orthopedic shoes
    — Ankylosis
    — Artificial deformities *(GN477.6)*
    — Care and hygiene
        sa Chiropody
            Safety shoes
        xx Chiropody
    — Diseases *(RC951)*
        sa Drop foot
            Foot—Radiography
            Mycetoma
    — Juvenile literature
    — Radiography
        xx Foot—Diseases
    — Surgery *(RD551-3)*
        sa Amputations of foot
            Chiropody
            Excision of ankle
Foot, Washing of
    See Foot washing (Rite)
Foot (in religion, folk-lore, etc.)
    x Folk-lore of feet
        Folk-lore of the foot
    xx Religion, Primitive
Foot-and-mouth disease *(Indirect)* *(SF793)*
    x Aftosa fever
        Aphthous fever
    xx Cattle—Diseases
    Example under Veterinary medicine
Foot-and-mouth disease virus
    xx Viruses
Foot-ball
    See Football
Foot-binding
    See Footbinding
Foot bridges
    See Footbridges
Foot racing
    See Running
Foot rot in sheep *(SF968)*
Foot soldiers
    See Infantry
Foot trails
    See Trails
Foot washing (Rite) *(BV873.F7)*
    x Feet washing
        Feet, Washing of
        Foot, Washing of
        Washing of feet
    xx Cultus
        Lustrations
        Rites and ceremonies
        Sacraments
        Water (in religion, folk-lore, etc.)
Foot wear
    See Boots and shoes
Football *(GV939-959)*
    Here are entered general works and
        works on American football.
    sa All-Star Football Game
        Australian football

        Backfield play (Football)
        Blocking (Football)
        Canadian football
        Eight-man football
        End play (Football)
        Florentine football
        Football scouting
        Footballs
        Kicking (Football)
        Line play (Football)
        Passing (Football)
        Quarterback (Football)
        Rugby football
        Six-man football
        Soccer
        Super Bowl Game (Football)
        Tackling (Football)
        Touch football
        subdivision Football *under names of*
            schools, colleges, etc.
    x Foot-ball
    xx College sports
    Example under School sports; Sports
    — Accidents and injuries
        x Football accidents
            Football—Injuries
        Example under Accidents; Sports—Acci-
            dents and injuries
    — Anecdotes, facetiae, satire, etc.
    — Attendance
        See Football attendance
    — Caricatures and cartoons
    — Defense *(GV951.1)*
        x Defensive football
    — Economic aspects *(Direct)*
    — History
    —— Juvenile literature
    — Injuries
        See Football—Accidents and injuries
    — Juvenile literature
    — Newsreels
        Additional subdivision by year is used
            when applicable.
        Example under Newsreels
    — Offense *(GV951.8)*
        x Offensive football
    — Pictorial works
    — Rules *(GV955)*
        Example under Sports—Rules
    — Societies, etc.
        See Football clubs
    — Songs and music *(M1977.S718;*
        M1978.S718)
        xx Sports—Songs and music
    — Training *(GV951.85)*
        x Football training
            Training, Football
        Example under Physical education and
            training
Football accidents
    See Football—Accidents and injuries
Football attendance
    x Attendance, Football
        Football—Attendance
Football clubs
    sa names of individual clubs, e.g. New
        York. Football club (National
        League)
    x Football clubs, Professional
        Football—Societies, etc.
        Professional football clubs
Football clubs, Professional
    See Football clubs
Football coaches
    xx Coaches (Athletics)
    — Correspondence, reminiscences, etc.
Football coaching
    xx Coaching (Athletics)

— Audio-visual aids
— Juvenile literature
Football scouting *(GV959)*
   x Scouting, Football
   xx Football
Football stories
   xx Sports stories
Football training
   See Football—Training
Footballs
   xx Balls (Sporting goods)
      Football
Footbinding
   x Foot-binding
Footbridges *(Indirect) (TG428)*
   x Foot bridges
   xx Bridges
      Pedestrians
Footings, Concrete
   See Concrete footings
Footpaths
   See Trails
Footprints, Fossil *(QE845)*
   x Fossil footprints
      Fossil tracks
      Ichnology
      Tracks, Fossil
      Trackways, Fossil
   xx Paleontology
      Sedimentary structures
Foot's resolution, 1829 *(E381)*
Footwear
   See Boots and shoes
Footwear, Protective
   See Safety shoes
Forage *(Animal culture, SF95-99; Military science, UC660-665)*
   sa subdivision Forage *under armies, e.g.* France. Armée—Forage
   xx Armies—Commissariat
      Feeds
Forage harvesting machinery *(Indirect) (S695)*
   x Choppers
      Forage plant harvesters
   xx Forage plants—Harvesting
      Harvesting machinery
Forage plant breeding
   sa Grass breeding
   x Forage plants—Breeding
   xx Plant-breeding
Forage plant harvesters
   See Forage harvesting machinery
Forage plants *(Indirect) (SB193-207)*
   sa Alfalfa
      Beans
      Berseem
      Brome-grass
      Browse
      Bur clover
      Cactus
      Clover
      Cow-peas
      Ensilage
      Flat pea
      Grasses
      Hay
      Heather
      Kafir corn
      Kikuyu grass
      Kudzu
      Legumes
      Lespedeza
      Lotus
      Lupine
      Maize
      Mangel-wurzel
      Millet

Pangolagrass
      Pastures
      Peas
      Prickly-pear
      Rape (Plant)
      Sainfoin
      Serradella
      Sorghum
      Soy-bean
      Stock-ranges
      Sudan grass
      Sweet clover
      Timothy-grass
      Velvet-bean
      Vetch
   xx Agriculture
      Feeds
      Field crops
      Grasses
      Grazing
      Pastures
      Plants
— Analysis
— Breeding
   See Forage plant breeding
— Composition
— Costs
— Diseases and pests
— Drying *(SB198)*
   x Green crop drying
   Example under Drying
— Economic aspects *(Direct)*
— Fertilizers and manures
— Harvesting
   sa Forage harvesting machinery
— Moisture
— Research
— Seed
— Varieties
Foraker act, 1900 (Puerto Rico)
Foraminifera *(Indirect) (QL368.F6)*
   sa Microspheres
   x Thalamophora
   xx Protozoa
— Geographical distribution
— Pictorial works
Foraminifera, Fossil *(Indirect) (QE772)*
   sa Nummulites
   xx Protozoa, Fossil
— Identification *(QE772)*
Forbes Expedition against Fort Duquesne, 1758 *(E199)*
Forbidden-combination check
   See Error-correcting codes (Information theory)
Forbush decreases *(QC485)*
   x Forbush effect
   xx Cosmic rays
      Solar flares
Forbush effect
   See Forbush decreases
Force, Centrifugal
   See Centrifugal force
Force, Centripetal
   See Centripetal force
Force, Electromotive
   See Electromotive force
Force, Vital
   See Vital force
Force (Law)
   See Violence (Law)
Force and energy *(QC73)*
   sa Dynamics
      Energy budget (Geophysics)
      Energy transfer
      Heat, Mechanical equivalent of
      High pressure research
      Mass (Physics)

      Mechanical efficiency
      Mechanics
      Motion
      Pressure
      Quantum theory
      Virtual work
      Vital force
   x Conservation of energy
      Correlation of forces
      Energy
   xx Dynamics
      Mechanics
      Motion
      Physics
      Power (Mechanics)
      Quantum theory
   Note under Energy conservation
— Juvenile literature
— Study and teaching (Higher) *(Direct)*
Force fits
   See Press fits
Force majeure
   See Vis major (Civil law)
Force pumps
   See Pumping machinery
Forced heirs
   See Legitime
      Widow's share
Forced labor *(Direct)*
   sa Contract labor
      Convict labor
      Peonage
      Serfdom
      Service, Compulsory non-military
      Slave labor
      World War, 1939-1945—Conscript labor
   x Compulsory labor
      Conscript labor
      Labor, Compulsory
      Labor, Forced
   xx Crimes against humanity
      Labor and laboring classes
      Native labor
— Personal narratives
Forced labor (International law)
   xx International law
Forced landings (over water)
   See Aeroplanes—Ditching
Forced loans *(Direct) (HJ8047)*
   x Compulsory loans
      Loans, Compulsory
      Loans, Forced
   xx Debts, Public
      Finance, Public
      Loans
Forceps *(RD73.F7)*
   Example under Surgical instruments and apparatus
Forceps, Obstetric *(RG739)*
   xx Labor, Complicated
      Obstetrics—Apparatus and instruments
Forces and couples *(QA823; QA831)*
   x Couples (Mechanics)
   xx Mechanics
      Statics
Forcible entry and detainer *(Direct)*
   x Usurpation (Law)
   xx Actions and defenses
      Eviction
      Landlord and tenant
      Offenses against property
      Possession (Law)
      Possessory actions
      Real property
      Remedies (Law)
      Trespass

Forcing (Plants) *(SB127)*
    sa Cloche gardening
        Greenhouse management
        Hotbeds
        Seeds—Stratification
        Vernalization
    x Flowers, Forcing of
       Fruit, Forcing of
       Vegetables, Forcing of
    xx Gardening
        Greenhouse management
        Greenhouses
        Horticulture
        Plants
Ford automobile *(TL215.F7)*
    sa Anglia automobile
        Capri automobile
        Cobra automobile
        Consul automobile
        Cortina automobile
        Escort automobile
        Fairlane automobile
        Lotus Ford automobile
        Maverick automobile
        Mustang automobile
        Pinto automobile
        Popular automobile
        Prefect automobile
        Taunus automobile
        Torino automobile
        Zephyr automobile
        Zodiac automobile
    Example under Automobiles
Ford Motor Company Strike, Windsor, Ont., 1943
Fore-edge painting *(ND2370)*
    x Decoration, Fore-edge
       Painting, Fore-edge
    xx Art, Decorative
        Book ornamentation
        Decoration and ornament
        Water-color painting
Fore language
    xx Papuan languages
Forebrain
    See Telencephalon
Forecasting *(CB158)*
    x Prediction
    — Juvenile literature
Forecasting, Business
    See Business forecasting
Forecasting, Cyclone
    See Cyclone forecasting
Forecasting, Economic
    See Economic forecasting
Forecasting, Election
    See Election forecasting
Forecasting, Employment
    See Employment forecasting
Forecasting, Forest fire
    See Forest fire forecasting
Forecasting, Hydrological
    See Hydrological forecasting
Forecasting, Income
    See Income forecasting
Forecasting, Ionospheric
    See Ionospheric forecasting
Forecasting, Population
    See Population forecasting
Forecasting, Sales
    See Sales forecasting
Forecasting, Stock price
    See Stock price forecasting
Forecasting, Technological
    See Technological forecasting
Forecasting, Traffic
    See Traffic estimation

Forecasting, Weather
    See Weather forecasting
Forecasts, Long-range weather
    See Long-range weather forecasts
Forecasts (Meteorology), Probability
    See Probability forecasts (Meteorology)
Foreclosure *(Direct)*
    sa Tax-sales
    x Foreclosure sales
       Mechanics' lien foreclosure
       Mortgage foreclosure
       Statutory foreclosure
       Strict foreclosure
    xx Executions (Law)
        Judicial sales
        Mechanics' liens
        Mortgages
Foreclosure sales
    See Foreclosure
Foreign accent
    See English language—Pronunciation by
        foreigners
Foreign affairs
    See International relations
        subdivisions Foreign relations *and*
           Foreign relations administration
        under names of countries
Foreign agents in the United States
    See Foreign propagandists in the United
        States
Foreign agricultural laborers
    See Agricultural laborers, Foreign
Foreign aid program
    See Economic assistance
        Military assistance
        Technical assistance
Foreign aid to agriculture
    See Agricultural assistance
Foreign aid to education
    See Educational assistance
Foreign area studies
    See Area studies
Foreign assistance
    See Economic assistance
        Military assistance
        Technical assistance
Foreign associations, institutions, etc.
    See Associations, institutions, etc., Foreign
Foreign automobiles
    See Automobiles, Foreign
Foreign banks and banking
    See Banks and banking, Foreign
Foreign bodies (Surgery)
    sa subdivision Foreign bodies *under names*
        of organs, e.g. Eye—Foreign bodies
    xx Accidents
        Surgery
        Surgery, Operative
Foreign business enterprises
    See Business enterprises, Foreign
Foreign cars
    See Automobiles, Foreign
Foreign coins
    See Coins, Foreign
Foreign commerce
    See Commerce
Foreign corporations
    See Corporations, Foreign
Foreign correspondents *(Direct)*
    sa Foreign news
    x Correspondents, Foreign
    xx Foreign news
        Journalism
        Journalists
        Liberty of the press
        Newspapers
        Press
        Reporters and reporting

    — Correspondence, reminiscences, etc.
    — Legal status, laws, etc. *(Direct)*
        xx Press law
Foreign correspondents, American, ⌈British, French, etc.⌉ *(Direct)*
Foreign economic policy
    See International economic relations
Foreign economic relations
    See International economic relations
Foreign educational aid
    See Educational assistance
Foreign enlistment *(Direct)*
    sa Mercenary troops
    x Enlistment
    xx Mercenary troops
        Military offenses
Foreign exchange *(HG3811-4000)*
    sa Balance of payments
        Capital flight tax
        Currency convertibility
        Euro-bond market
        Euro-dollar market
        Foreign exchange administration
        Foreign-exchange brokers
        Foreign exchange problem
        Forward exchange
        International clearing
        Sterling area
        Valuta clause
    x Cambistry
       Capital exports
       Capital imports
       Exchange, Foreign
       International exchange
    xx Banks and banking
        Bills of exchange
        Commerce
        Commercial law
        Finance
        Foreign trade promotion
        International finance
        Money
        Stock-exchange
    Note under Exchange
    — Accounting
        x Foreign exchange accounting
        xx Accounting
    — Conflict of laws
        See Conflict of laws—Foreign
           exchange
    — Law *(Direct)*
        sa Emigrant remittances
        x Exchange control
        xx Commercial policy
           Foreign trade regulation
           International travel regulations
           Money—Law
    — — Criminal provisions
    — Mathematical models
    — Tables, etc.
        See Money—Tables, etc.
    — Terminology
Foreign exchange accounting
    See Foreign exchange—Accounting
Foreign exchange administration *(Direct)*
    xx Foreign exchange
Foreign-exchange brokers *(Direct)*
    xx Brokers
        Foreign exchange
Foreign exchange futures
    See Forward exchange
Foreign exchange problem *(Direct)*
    sa French franc area
        Sterling area
    xx Currency question
        Foreign exchange
        International liquidity
    — Underdeveloped areas

See Underdeveloped areas—Foreign
      exchange problem
Foreign freight forwarders
    See Ocean freight forwarders
Foreign income, Taxation of
    See Income tax—Foreign income
Foreign institutions, associations, etc.
    See Associations, institutions, etc., Foreign
Foreign insurance companies
    See Insurance companies, Foreign
Foreign investments
    See Investments, Foreign
Foreign judgments
    See Judgments, Foreign
Foreign labor
    See Alien labor
Foreign language laboratories
    See Language laboratories
Foreign language testing
    See subdivision Examinations, questions,
        etc. under names of languages or
        groups of languages, e.g. English
        language—Examinations, questions,
        etc.; Languages, Modern—
        Examinations, questions, etc.

Foreign law, Pleading and proof of *(Direct)*
  xx Conflict of laws
     Evidence (Law)
     Judicial notice
     Pleading

Foreign licensing agreements
  sa Exclusive licenses
     Patent licenses
     Trade-mark licenses
  x Joint-venture agreements
     Know-how assistance agreements
     Technical assistance agreements
  xx Commerce
     Exclusive licenses
     International business enterprises
     International economic relations
     Investments, Foreign
     Patent licenses
  — Taxation *(Direct)*
Foreign loans
    See Loans, Foreign
Foreign medical graduates
    See Physicians, Foreign
Foreign merchants
    See Merchants, Foreign
Foreign missions
    See Missions, Foreign
Foreign news
  sa Foreign correspondents
  x International news
     News, Foreign
     World news
  xx Foreign correspondents
     International relations
     Journalism
     News agencies
     Newspapers
     Press
  — Censorship
    xx Freedom of information
Foreign offices
  sa names of individual foreign offices, e.g.
     United States. Dept. of State
  xx Diplomatic and consular service
     International law
     International relations
Foreign opinion of the Catholic Church in the
     United States
    See Catholic Church in the United States—
      Foreign opinion
Foreign opinion of the United States
    See United States—Foreign opinion

Foreign physicians
    See Physicians, Foreign
Foreign policy
    See International relations
     subdivision Foreign relations under
      names of countries
Foreign policy and trade-unions
    See Trade-unions and foreign policy
Foreign population
    See Emigration and immigration
     Libraries and foreign population
     subdivisions Emigration and
      immigration under countries, and
      Foreign population under countries,
      cities, etc.
Foreign propagandists in the United States
    (JX1896)
    Here are entered works on foreign agents
     active as propagandists as defined in
     the Foreign agents registration act
     of 1938, as amended. Works on foreign
     business agents are entered under the
     heading Commercial agents.
  x Agents of foreign principals in the
     United States
     Foreign agents in the United States
  xx Diplomatic and consular service
     Propaganda
Foreign property
    See Alien property
Foreign radio stations *(Direct)*
  x Alien radio stations
     Radio stations, Foreign
Foreign relations
    See International relations
     subdivision Foreign relations under
      names of countries, e.g. France—
      Foreign relations
Foreign relations administration
    See subdivision Foreign relations
     administration under names of
     countries, e.g. United States—
     Foreign relations administration
Foreign relations law (United States)
    See United States—Foreign relations—Law
     and legislation
Foreign service
    See Diplomatic and consular service
Foreign students
    See Students, Foreign
Foreign study
  sa Students, Foreign
  xx Education
     Students, Foreign
Foreign teaching positions
    See American teachers in foreign countries
     —Employment
     Teachers in foreign countries—
      Employment
     similar headings
Foreign trade
    See Commerce, and pertinent subjects
     referred to under that heading
Foreign trade control
    See Foreign trade regulation
Foreign trade policy
    See Commercial policy
Foreign trade promotion *(Direct)*
  sa Export controls
     Export credit
     Export premiums
     Fairs
     Foreign exchange
     Foreign trade regulation
     Insurance, Export credit
     Subsidies
     Trade missions
  x Export promotion

     Export trade promotion
  xx Commercial policy
     Export sales
     Foreign trade regulation
     Industry and state
     Subsidies
  — Underdeveloped areas
    See Underdeveloped areas—Foreign
     trade promotion
Foreign trade regulation *(Direct)*
  sa Commercial treaties
     Customs administration
     Export controls
     Foreign exchange—Law
     Foreign trade promotion
     Import quotas
     International clearing
     Tariff—Law
  x Export and import controls
     Foreign trade control
     Import and export controls
     Import restrictions
     International trade control
     International trade regulation
     Prohibited exports and imports
  xx Commercial law
     Commercial policy
     Foreign trade promotion
  — Criminal provisions
Foreign trade zones
    See Free ports and zones
Foreign-trained physicians
    See Physicians, Foreign
Foreign visitors
    See Visitors, Foreign
Foreign workers
    See Alien labor
Foreigners
    See Aliens
     Naturalization
     Visitors, Foreign
     subdivision Foreign population under
      names of countries and cities, e.g.
      Chicago—Foreign population
Foreigners, Church work with
    See Church work with foreigners
Foreigners, Visiting
    See Visitors, Foreign
Foremen *(Direct) (Business management,*
    HF5549; Technology, T56, TS155)
  sa Foremen's unions
     Grievance procedures
  x Supervisors, Industrial
  xx Executives
     Factory management
     Personnel management
     Supervision of employees
     Supervisors
  — Legal status, laws, etc. *(Direct)*
  — Salaries, pensions, etc.
Foremen's unions *(Direct) (HD6490.F6)*
  xx Foremen
     Industrial relations
     Trade-unions
Forenames
    See Names, Personal
Forensic audiology
  x Audiology, Forensic
     Medicolegal audiology
  xx Medical jurisprudence
Forensic ballistics *(HV8077)*
  x Ballistics, Forensic
  xx Criminal investigation
     Evidence, Criminal
     Evidence, Expert
     Evidence (Law)
     Firearms—Identification

Forensic cardiology
   x Cardiology, Forensic
      Medicolegal cardiology
   xx Medical jurisprudence
Forensic chemistry
   See Chemistry, Forensic
Forensic dentistry
   See Dental jurisprudence
Forensic dermatology
   x Dermatology, Forensic
      Dermatology—Jurisprudence
      Medicolegal dermatology
   xx Medical jurisprudence
Forensic gynecology
   sa Forensic obstetrics
   x Gynecology, Forensic
      Gynecology—Jurisprudence
      Medicolegal gynecology
   xx Medical jurisprudence
Forensic hematology
   x Blood—Jurisprudence
      Hematology, Forensic
      Medicolegal hematology
   xx Medical jurisprudence
Forensic hypnotism
   Here are entered works on hypnosis as an
   investigative technique. Works on the
   legal aspects of hypnotism are entered
   under the heading Hypnotism—Jurisprudence.
   xx Hypnotism
   Note under Hypnotism—Jurisprudence
Forensic medicine
   See Medical jurisprudence
Forensic neurology *(RA1147)*
   sa Forensic psychiatry
   x Forensic neuropathology
      Medicolegal neurology
      Neurology, Forensic
      Neurology—Jurisprudence
   xx Medical jurisprudence
Forensic neuropathology
   See Forensic neurology
Forensic obstetrics
   x Medicolegal obstetrics
      Obstetrics, Forensic
      Obstetrics—Jurisprudence
   xx Forensic gynecology
      Medical jurisprudence
Forensic ophthalmology
   x Medicolegal ophthalmology
      Ophthalmology, Forensic
      Ophthalmology—Jurisprudence
   xx Medical jurisprudence
Forensic orations
   sa Forensic oratory
   x Arguments, Legal
      Legal arguments
   xx Forensic oratory
      Law—Addresses, essays, lectures
      Oral pleading
      Orations
      Trial practice
Forensic orations, Imaginary
   x Imaginary forensic orations
Forensic orations in the Bible
Forensic oratory
   sa Forensic orations
      Summation (Law)
   xx Forensic orations
      Oral pleading
      Oratory
Forensic osteology
   x Medicolegal osteology
      Osteology, Forensic
   xx Bones
      Medical jurisprudence

Forensic pathology *(Indirect)* *(RA1058)*
   sa Coroners
      Medical examiners (Law)
   x Pathology, Forensic
   xx Coroners
      Medical examiners (Law)
      Medical jurisprudence
Forensic photography
   See Photography, Legal
Forensic psychiatry *(RA1151)*
   Here are entered works on psychiatry as
   applied in courts of law. Works on the
   legal status of persons of unsound
   mind are entered under the heading
   Insanity—Jurisprudence.
   sa Insane, Criminal and dangerous
      Litigious paranoia
      Traumatic neuroses
   x Psychiatry, Forensic
   xx Criminal psychology
      Forensic neurology
      Insane, Criminal and dangerous
      Insanity—Jurisprudence
      Medical jurisprudence
      Psychology, Forensic
   Note under Insanity—Jurisprudence
Forensic psychology
   See Psychology, Forensic
Forensic radiography *(RA1058.5)*
   x Medicolegal radiography
      Radiography, Forensic
      Radiography—Jurisprudence
   xx Medical jurisprudence
Foreordination
   See Predestination
Forest birds
   x Woodland birds
   xx Forest fauna
Forest clearcutting
   See Clear-cutting
Forest conservation *(Indirect)* *(SD411-428)*
   sa Forest influences
      Forest protection
      Forest reserves
      Reforestation
   x Conservation of forests
      Forest preservation
      Preservation of forests
   xx Conservation of natural resources
      Forest management
Forest credit *(Indirect)*
   x Credit, Forest
   xx Agricultural credit
      Banks and banking
      Credit
Forest ecology *(Indirect)*
   sa Jungle ecology
      Rain forests
      Taiga ecology
      Trees—Growth
      Woody plants
   x Forest flora
      Forests and forestry—Ecology
   xx Botany—Ecology
      Ecology
      Geographical distribution of animals
         and plants
      Woody plants
   — Experiments
   — Juvenile literature
   — Pictorial works
Forest economics
   See Forests and forestry—Economic aspects
Forest entomology
   See Forest insects
Forest fauna *(Indirect)* *(QL112)*
   sa Forest birds
      Forest insects

      Jungle fauna
   x Fauna
   xx Zoology
   — Behavior
   — Juvenile literature
   — Pictorial works
Forest fertilization
   See Forest soils—Fertilization
Forest fire control
   See Forest fires—Prevention and control
Forest fire detection *(SD421)*
   x Forest fires—Detection
   xx Forest fires—Prevention and control
Forest fire fighting
   See Forest fires—Prevention and control
Forest fire forecasting
   x Forecasting, Forest fire
   xx Forest fires—Prevention and control
   — Computer programs
Forest fire insurance
   See Insurance, Forest
Forest fire research *(Indirect)*
   x Forest fires—Research
   xx Research
Forest fires *(Indirect)* *(SD421)*
   sa Fire ecology
      Insurance, Forest
      Prescribed burning
   xx Fires
      Natural disasters
   — Control
      See Forest fires—Prevention and
         control
   — Detection
      See Forest fire detection
   — Economic aspects *(Direct)*
   — Extinction
      See Forest fires—Prevention and
         control
   — Juvenile literature
   — Law and legislation *(Direct)*
      x Forest fires—Prevention and control
         —Law and legislation
      xx Forestry law and legislation
   — Prevention and control *(SD421)*
      sa Aeronautics in forest fire control
         Forest fire detection
         Forest fire forecasting
      x Forest fire control
         Forest fire fighting
         Forest fires—Control
         Forest fires—Extinction
         Lumbering—Fires and fire
           prevention
      xx Fire extinction
         Fire prevention
         Forest protection
   — — Law and legislation
      See Forest fires—Law and
         legislation
   — — Safety measures
   — Research
      See Forest fire research
Forest flora
   See Forest ecology
      Forests and forestry
Forest genetics
   sa Poplar—Genetics
      Tree breeding
      Tree seeds
   x Forests and forestry—Genetic research
      Trees—Genetics
   xx Plant genetics
      Tree breeding
Forest industries
   See Wood-using industries
Forest influences *(SD425)*
   sa Botany—Ecology

Flood control
Forests and forestry
Rain and rainfall
Vegetation and climate
Zoology—Ecology
x Forests and climate
Forests and floods
Forests and rainfall
Forests and water-supply
xx Botany—Ecology
Climatology
Flood control
Floods
Forest conservation
Rain and rainfall
Water-supply
Forest insects *(Indirect)* *(SB761)*
sa Bark-beetles
Wood borers
names of insects, e.g. Pine-moth
x Forest entomology
xx Forest fauna
Forest protection
Insects
Insects, Injurious and beneficial
Trees—Diseases and pests
— Biological control *(Indirect)*
xx Forest insects—Control
— Control *(Indirect)*
sa Forest insects—Biological control
— Identification
— Parasites
See Parasites—Forest insects
Forest insurance
See Insurance, Forest
Forest inventories
See Forest surveys
Forest law
See Forestry law and legislation
Forest litter
xx Forest soils
Humus
Leaf-mold
Forest machinery *(Indirect)*
xx Forestry engineering
— Hydraulic equipment
— Maintenance and repair
— Safety measures
See Forests and forestry—Safety
measures
— Testing
Forest management *(Indirect)*
sa Clear-cutting
Fire ecology
Forest conservation
Forest protection
Forest rangers
Forest thinning
Tree farms
Watershed management
xx Forest policy
Management
Watershed management
— Computer programs
sa TEVAP (Computer program)
— Cost control
— Mathematical models
Forest mapping *(Indirect)* *(SD387.M3)*
x Forests and forestry—Mapping
xx Cartography
Forest surveys
Forests and forestry—Maps
Vegetation mapping
Forest mensuration
See Forests and forestry—Mensuration
Forest nurseries *(Indirect)* *(SD401)*
sa Tree seeds
xx Gardening

Nurseries (Horticulture)
Tree seeds
Forest planting
See Afforestation
Forests and forestry
Forest policy *(SD561-668)*
sa Forest management
Forestry law and legislation
subdivision Forest policy *under names
of countries*
x Forestry and state
Government and forestry
State and forestry
xx Forests and forestry—Economic aspects
Industry and state
Forest preservation
See Forest conservation
Forest products *(Indirect)* *(Economics,
HD9750-9769; Forestry, SD)*
sa Gums and resins
Lumber
Lumber trade
Rubber
Timber
Wood
Wood poles
Wood-pulp
Wood-using industries
xx Botany, Economic
Commercial products
Raw materials
— Economic aspects *(Direct)*
— Juvenile literature
— Marketing
— Prices *(Direct)*
— Quarantine *(Direct)*
xx Plant quarantine
— Standards *(Direct)*
— Taxation *(Direct)*
sa Forests and forestry—Taxation
xx Forests and forestry—Taxation
— Testing
Forest products research *(Direct)*
xx Forestry research
Research
Research, Industrial
Forest protection *(Indirect)*
sa Forest fires—Prevention and control
Forest insects
Plants, Protection of
Trees—Diseases and pests
Trees—Wounds and injuries
x Protection of forests
xx Forest conservation
Forest management
— Law and legislation
See Forestry law and legislation
Forest rangers
sa Park rangers
x Rangers, Forest
xx Forest management
National parks and reserves
Park rangers
Forest regeneration
See Forest reproduction
Forest reproduction *(Indirect)*
Here are entered works on the reproduc-
tion of forests by natural processes.
Works on artificial reproduction are
entered under Reforestation.
x Forest regeneration
Regeneration (Forestry)
xx Reforestation
Forest reserves *(Indirect)* *(SD426-8)*
sa Forests and forestry
National parks and reserves
Wilderness areas
x Forests, National

National forests
xx Forest conservation
National parks and reserves
Natural monuments
Public lands
Wildlife conservation
— Recreational use
xx Outdoor recreation
Forest roads *(Direct)*
x Roads, Forest
xx Roads
— Design and construction
xx Road construction
Forest soils
sa Forest litter
xx Humus
Soils
— Fertilization *(SD408)*
x Fertilizers and manures in forestry
Forest fertilization
xx Fertilizers and manures
Forest surveying
See Forest surveys
Forest surveys *(Indirect)*
sa Forest mapping
x Forest inventories
Forest surveying
Forests and forestry—Surveying
xx Surveys
Vegetation surveys
— Statistical methods
Forest tent-caterpillar
xx Tent-caterpillars
Forest thinning *(SD396.5)*
x Forests and forestry—Thinning
Thinning of forests
xx Forest management
— Computer programs
Forest valuation
See Forests and forestry—Valuation
Forestalling
See Monopolies
Forestation
See Afforestation
Forests and forestry
Reforestation
Foresters *(Direct)* *(SD127)*
sa Forestry as a profession
Police, Rural
xx Forestry as a profession
Police, Rural
— Correspondence, reminiscences, etc.
— Diseases and hygiene
— Salaries, pensions, etc.
Forestier-Certonciny syndrome
See Polymyalgia rheumatica
Forestry and state
See Forest policy
Forestry as a profession
sa Foresters
Lumbering—Vocational guidance
xx Agriculture as a profession
Foresters
— Juvenile literature
Forestry education
See Forestry schools and education
Forestry engineering *(SD388)*
sa Forest machinery
Lumbering
x Forests and forestry—Engineering
xx Agricultural engineering
Engineering
— Handbooks, manuals, etc.
Forestry law and legislation *(Direct)*
(SD561-668)
sa Forest fires—Law and legislation
Plants, Protection of—Law and
legislation

Forestry law and legislation *(Direct)*
    (SD561-668) *(Continued)*
    x Forest law
      Forest protection—Law and legislation
      Forests and forestry—Law
      Government and forestry
      Law, Forestry
      Timber laws and legislation
    xx Forest policy
      Natural resources—Law and legislation
      Plants, Protection of—Law and
        legislation
      Wildlife conservation—Law and
        legislation
    Example under Legislation
  — Colonies
    See Forestry law and legislation,
      Colonial
  — Criminal provisions

GEOGRAPHIC SUBDIVISIONS

  — ₍country₎
  — — Colonies
    Note under Forestry law and legisla-
      tion, Colonial
Forestry law and legislation, Colonial
    Here are entered general and compara-
    tive works only. Works on forestry law
    and legislation of the colonies of an
    individual country are entered under
    the heading Forestry law and legisla-
    tion with subdivision ₍country₎—Colo-
    nies. Works dealing with a specific
    colony are entered under the same
    heading, subdivided by the name of the
    colony.
    x Colonial forestry law
      Colonies—Forestry law and legislation
      Forestry law and legislation—Colonies
Forestry law and legislation (Roman law)
Forestry research *(Indirect)*
    sa Forest products research
      Wood research
    xx Agricultural research
      Research
Forestry schools and education *(Indirect)*
    (SD251-356)
    x Forestry education
      Forests and forestry—Study and
        teaching
    xx Agricultural education
      Agriculture—Study and teaching
      Schools
      Technical education
      Vocational education
Forestry societies *(Indirect)* *(SD1)*
    sa Forests and forestry—Societies, etc. ₍for
      publications of forestry and other
      societies in relation to forestry₎
Forests, National
  See Forest reserves
Forests, Petrified
  See Petrified forests
Forests, Submerged *(GB481-8)*
    x Submerged forests
    xx Forests and forestry
      Geology
      Paleontology
Forests and climate
  See Forest influences
Forests and floods
  See Forest influences
Forests and forestry *(Indirect)* *(SD; Income*
    from state forests, HJ3805; Taxation,
    HJ4167)
    sa Aeronautics in forestry
      Afforestation
      Arboriculture

Brush
Chapparal
Community forests
Cut-over lands
Explosives in forestry
Folk-lore of trees
Forests, Submerged
Hardwoods
Insurance, Forest
Landscape gardening
Lumber
Lumber trade
Lumbering
Mangrove swamps
Moving-pictures in forestry
Natural history—Outdoor books
Plastics in forestry
Pruning
Radioactive tracers in forestry
Rain forests
Reforestation
Slash (Logging)
Taigas
Timber
Timber-line
Tree breeding
Tree farms
Tree felling
Tree planting
Trees
Trees—Growth
Waste lands
Wood
Wood-lots
headings beginning with the words
  Forest *and* Forestry
    x Forest flora
      Forest planting
      Forestation
      Sylviculture
    xx Afforestation
      Agriculture
      Arboriculture
      Forest influences
      Forest reserves
      Natural resources
      Reforestation
      Timber
      Trees
      Water-supply
      Wood
  — Accidents *(Indirect)*
    sa Forests and forestry—Safety
      measures
  — Accounting
  — Anecdotes, facetiae, satire, etc.
  — Computer programs
  — Congresses *(SD118)*
  — Ecology
    See Forest ecology
  — Economic aspects *(Indirect)* *(SD)*
    sa Forest policy
    x Forest economics
      Forests and forestry—Finance
    xx Agriculture—Economic aspects
  — — Mathematical models
  — Engineering
    See Forestry engineering
  — Experimental areas *(SD359)*
  — Finance
    See Forests and forestry—Economic
      aspects
  — Genetic research
    See Forest genetics
  — Government ownership *(Direct)*
    x Government ownership of forests
  — Juvenile literature
  — Labor productivity

  — Law
    See Forestry law and legislation
  — Mapping
    See Forest mapping
  — Maps
    sa Forest mapping
  — Mensuration *(SD551-7)*
    sa Dendrometer
      Forests and forestry—Tables and
        ready-reckoners
      Lumber trade—Tables and
        ready-reckoners
    x Forest mensuration
      Log scaling
      Timber cruising
      Timber—Mensuration
  — — Computer programs
  — — Mathematical models
  — Multiple use
    x Multiple use of forest lands
  — Pictorial works
  — Quotations, maxims, etc.
  — Safety measures *(SD411)*
    x Forest machinery—Safety measures
    xx Forests and forestry—Accidents
  — Societies, etc.
    xx Forestry societies
  — Statistical methods
  — Study and teaching
    See Forestry schools and education
  — Surveying
    See Forest surveys
  — Tables and ready-reckoners
    xx Agriculture—Tables and
      ready-reckoners
      Forests and forestry—Mensuration
  — Taxation *(Direct)*
    sa Forest products—Taxation
    x Timber—Taxation
    xx Forest products—Taxation
      Real property tax
  — Thinning
    See Forest thinning
  — Tools and implements
    xx Tools
  — Valuation *(SD551-7)*
    x Forest valuation
      Timber cruising
  — — Costs
Forests and rainfall
  See Forest influences
Forests and water-supply
  See Forest influences
Forests in art
    xx Art
Forests in literature
    sa Trees in literature
    xx Nature in literature
      Trees in literature
Forfeiture *(Direct)*
    sa Attainder
      Escheat
      Lapse (Law)
    xx Attainder
Forge shops *(Direct)* *(TS225)*
    x Forges
    xx Forging
  — Automation
  — Costs
  — Design and construction *(TS225)*
  — Equipment and supplies
    sa Forging machinery
  — Production control
  — Production standards
Forge shops in art
Forged aluminum
  See Aluminum forgings

Forged steel flanges, Tariff on
   See Tariff on forged steel flanges
Forgery *(Direct)* *(HV6675-6685;*
      Autographs, Z41; Checks,
      HG1696-8)
   sa Blanks in legal documents
      Checks—Criminal provisions
      Counterfeits and counterfeiting
      False certification
      Literary forgeries and mystifications
      Reproduction of money, documents,
         etc.—Law and legislation
      Signatures (Writing)
      Trials (Forgery)
      subdivision Forgeries *under specific*
         subjects, e.g. Postage-stamps—
         Forgeries
   xx Criminal law
      Fraud
      Offenses against property
      Swindlers and swindling
Forgery (Canon law)
Forgery (Roman law)
Forgery of antiquities *(CC140)*
   sa Forgery of works of art
      Piltdown forgery
   x Antiquities, Forgery of
      Archaeological forgeries
   xx Antiquities
      Forgery of works of art
Forgery of hall-marks
   x Hall-mark forgeries
      Hall-marks—Forgeries
   xx Hall-marks
Forgery of inscriptions *(CN99)*
   x Inscriptions—Forgeries
Forgery of manuscripts *(Autographs, Z41;*
      Church history, BX875; Literature,
      PN171.F6-7)
   sa Manuscripts—Certification
   x Manuscripts—Forgeries
      Manuscripts, Forgery of
Forgery of works of art *(N8790)*
   sa Forgery of antiquities
      Literary forgeries and mystifications
      Precious stones, Artificial
   x Art forgeries
      Art—Forgeries
      Art objects, Forgery of
   xx Art
      Forgery of antiquities
      Reproduction of art objects
Forges
   See Forge shops
Forget-me-nots *(Culture, SB413)*
Forgetfulness
   See Memory
Forging *(Manufacture, TS225; Shop work,*
      TT215-240)
   sa Aluminum forgings
      Blacksmithing
      Brass forgings
      Dies (Metal-working)
      Drawing (Metal-work)
      Explosive forming
      Extrusion (Metals)
      Eye-bars
      Forge shops
      Forging machinery
      High energy forming
      Ironwork
      Metal stamping
      Punching machinery
      Rolling (Metal-work)
      Steel forgings
      Welding
   x Drop-forging
   xx Blacksmithing

   Ironwork
      Metal stamping
      Metal-work
   — Handbooks, manuals, etc.
   — Hygienic aspects
   — Problems, exercises, etc.   *(TS225)*
   — Quality control
   — Safety measures
Forging machinery
   xx Forge shops—Equipment and supplies
      Forging
      Metal-working machinery
   — Appraisal
      See Forging machinery—Valuation
   — Automatic control
   — Construction
      See Forging machinery—Design and
         construction
   — Design and construction
      x Forging machinery—Construction
   — Drawing
      See Forging machinery—Drawings
   — Drawings
      x Forging machinery—Drawing
      xx Mechanical drawing
   — Electric driving
   — Electric equipment
   — Hydraulic drive
   — Maintenance and repair
   — Valuation   *(TS225)*
      x Forging machinery—Appraisal
Forgiveness *(BJ1476)*
   sa Pardon
   xx Conduct of life
      Humanity
      Pardon
   — Sermons
Forgiveness of sin *(BT795)*
   sa Absolution
      Confession
      Penance
      Repentance
   x Sin, Forgiveness of
   xx Absolution
      Penance
      Repentance
      Sin
      Theology, Doctrinal
   — History of doctrines
Forgiveness of sin (Islam) *(Koran, BP134.F6)*
   xx Islamic theology
      Sin (Islam)
Fork lift trucks
   xx Conveying machinery
      Hoisting machinery
      Industrial electric trucks
      Industrial power trucks
      Lifting-jacks
      Motor-trucks
   — Maintenance and repair
Forks *(Direct)* *(Household utensils,*
      TX298-9; Silver, NK7230-7240)
   xx Silverware
Form, Literary
   See Literary form
Form, Musical
   See Musical form
Form (Aesthetics) *(BH301.F6)*
   x Aesthetic form
   xx Aesthetics
Form (Logic) *(BC199.F6)*
   x Logical form
   xx Logic
Form (Philosophy)
   sa Structuralism
   xx Idealism
      Matter
      Metaphysics

      Structuralism
Form and matter
   See Hylomorphism
Form criticism (Bible)
   See Bible—Criticism, Form
Form discrimination
   See Form perception
Form factor (Nuclear physics) *(QC794)*
   sa Bootstrap theory (Nuclear physics)
   xx Approximation theory
      Bootstrap theory (Nuclear physics)
      Scattering (Physics)
Form in biology
   See Morphology
Form letters
   xx Commercial correspondence
      Letter-writing
Form of contract *(Direct)*
   sa Statute of frauds
   x Contract, Form of
   xx Contracts
      Formalities (Law)
      Statute of frauds
   Note under Formalities (Law)
Form of juristic acts
   See Formalities (Law)
      Locus regit actum
Form perception
   sa Color and form recognition test
   x Form discrimination
      Shape discrimination
   xx Visual discrimination
Form psychology
   See Gestalt psychology
Form requirements (Law)
   See Formalities (Law)
Forma pauperis
   See In forma pauperis
Formal culture
   See Formal discipline
Formal discipline
   sa Habit
      Memory
      Transfer of training
   x Culture, Formal
      Discipline, Formal
      Formal culture
   xx Education
      Educational psychology
      Habit
      Teaching
      Transfer of training
Formal gardens
   See Gardens
Formal languages *(QA267.3)*
   sa AUTOMATH (Formal language)
   xx Language and languages
      Machine theory
Formaldehyde *(Chemical technology,*
      TP248.F6; Chemistry, QD305.A6;
      Disinfectants, RA766. F6)
   x Formalin
   xx Disinfection and disinfectants
   — Dipole moments
      Example under Dipole moments
   — Spectra
   — Toxicology   *(RA1242.F6)*
Formalin
   See Formaldehyde
Formalism (Russian literature)
   xx Russian literature—20th century—
      History and criticism

Formalities (Law) *(Direct)*

    Here are entered works on legal form requirements *(e.g.* writing, notarization, performance before witnesses) in general. Works on form requirements for specific types of juristic acts are entered under a phrase illustrated by the heading Form of contract. For general collections of legal forms *see* the heading Forms (Law), for collections of forms on individual legal subjects, the subdivision Forms under the respective subjects, *e.g.* Civil procedure—Forms.

    sa Form of contract
    x Form of juristic acts
      Form requirements (Law)
  — Conflict of laws
    See Conflict of laws—Formalities

Formants (Speech)
    x Speech formants
    xx Sound
      Speech
      Voice
      Vowels

Format of books
    See Books—Format

Formation of corporations
    See Incorporation

Formation waters (Oil fields)
    See Oil field brines

Former clergy
    See Ex-clergy

Former jeopardy
    See Double jeopardy

Formic acid *(Chemistry, QD305.A2; Therapeutics, RM666.F6)*

Formicidae
    See Ants

Forming of aluminum
    See Aluminum forming

Formosa serow
    See Japanese serow

Formosan . . .
    See Taiwan . . .

Formosans
    See Taiwanese

Forms, Automorphic
    See Automorphic forms

Forms, Bilinear
    x Bilinear forms

Forms, Binary
    sa Forms, Quadratic
    x Binary forms

Forms, Differential
    See Differential forms

Forms, Normal (Mathematics)
    See Normal forms (Mathematics)

Forms, Quadratic
    sa Diophantine analysis
    x Quadratic forms
    xx Diophantine analysis
      Forms, Binary
      Numbers, Theory of

Forms, Quadrilinear *(QA201)*
    x Quadrilinear forms

Forms, Quaternary
    x Quaternary forms

Forms, Ternary
    x Ternary forms

Forms, Trilinear
    x Trilinear forms

Forms (Business)
    See Business—Forms, blanks, etc.

Forms (Canon law) *(BX1939.F6)*

Forms (Concrete construction)
    See Concrete construction—Formwork

Forms (Frankish law)

Forms (Germanic law)

Forms (Hindu law)

Forms (Jewish law)

Forms (Law) *(Direct)* *(Commercial law: United States, HF1243)*

    Here are entered works on and collections of legal forms in general. Forms relation to special topics or branches of law are entered under the specific heading with subdivision Forms, *e.g.* Corporation law—United States—Forms.

    sa Contracts—Forms
      Conveyancing
      Formularies (Diplomatics)
      Interrogatories
      Legal composition
      Legal correspondence
      Letters patent
    x Legal forms
      Precedents (Law)
    xx Acknowledgments
      Actions and defenses
      Business law
      Commercial law
      Conveyancing
      Legal composition
      Pleading
    Note under Formalities (Law)

Forms (Mathematics) *(QA201; QA243-4)*
    sa Automorphic forms
      Partitions (Mathematics)
    x Quantics
    xx Algebra
      Mathematics

Forms (Precast concrete)
    See Precast concrete—Formwork

Forms, blanks, etc.
    See subdivison Forms, blanks, etc. *under* subjects, *e.g.* Business—Forms, blanks, etc.; Postal service—United States—Forms, blanks, etc.; United States. Air Force—Forms, blanks, etc.

Forms of address *(CR3499-4420)*
    x Address, Forms of
      Address, Titles of
      Titles of address
    xx Etiquette
      Letter-writing
      Salutations
      Titles of honor and nobility

Formula translation (Computer program language)
    See FORTRAN (Computer program language)

Formularies, Medical
    See Medicine—Formulae, receipts, prescriptions

Formularies (Diplomatics) *(CD80)*
    sa Letters patent
    xx Diplomatics
      Forms (Law)

Formulas (Mathematics)
    See Mathematics—Formulae

Formulas for artists
    See Artists' materials—Formulae, tables, etc.

Fornio Indians
    See Fulnio Indians

Fornovo, Battle of, 1495 *(DG541)*
    xx Italy—History—Expedition of Charles VIII, 1494 -1496

Forsterite
    x Boltonite
      White olivine
    xx Chrysolite
      Refractory materials

    Silicates

Fort Ancient culture

Fort Dearborn Massacre, 1812
    See Chicago—Massacre, 1812

Fort Fisher expeditions
    See Fisher, Fort—Expeditions, 1864-1865

Fort Frontenac, Ont.
  — Capture, 1758 *(E199)*

Fort Griswold, Massacre of, 1781
    See Groton Heights, Battle of, 1781

Fort Laramie, Treaty of, 1851
    x Treaty of Fort Laramie, 1851

Fort McHenry, Md., Bombardment of
    See Baltimore, Battle of, 1814

Fort Pillow, Battle of, 1864 *(E476.17)*

Fort Pulaski, Ga.
  — Siege, 1862

Fort Sanders, Battle of, 1863

Fort Stevens, D.C., Battle of, 1864 *(E476.66)*

Fort Ticonderoga, N.Y.
  — Juvenile literature

Fortification *(Indirect)* *(UG400-409)*
    sa Attack and defense (Military science)
      City walls
      Coast defenses
      Earthwork
      Floating batteries
      Intrenchments
      Martello towers
      Military architecture
      Military engineering
      Mines, Military
      Sapping
    subdivision Fortifications, military installations, etc. *under* cities, *e.g.* New York (City)—Fortifications, military installations, etc. *and* Defenses *under countries, e.g.* Great Britain—Defenses
    x Forts
    xx Earthwork
      Military architecture
      Military art and science
      Military engineering
    Notes under Earthwork; Fortification, Primitive
  — Early works to 1800 *(UG400)*
  — United States
    x United States—Fortifications
  — — Juvenile literature

Fortification, Field *(UG403)*
    sa Tanks (Military science)
    x Field fortification
    xx Intrenchments
      Military engineering

Fortification, Primitive *(Direct)* *(GN789)*
    x Hill-forts
    xx Archaeology
      Earthworks (Archaeology)

Fortifications, Attack and defense of
    See Attack and defense (Military science)

Fortín Boquerón, Battle of, 1932
    See Boquerón, Battle of, 1932

Fortín Toledo, Battle of, 1933
    See Toledo, Battle of, 1933

Fortitude *(BV4647.F6)*
    xx Courage
      Morale

FORTRAN (Computer program language)
    sa AUTOSATE
      FAP (Computer program language)
      GASP (Computer program language)
      ROCKET (Computer program)
      SIMSCRIPT (Computer program language)
    x Formula translation (Computer program language)

— Problems, exercises, etc.
— Programmed instruction
Fortran assembly program (Computer program
    language)
    See FAP (Computer program language)
Fortress warfare
    See Attack and defense (Military science)
Fortresses (Bombers)
    See Boeing bombers
Forts
    See Fortification
Fortune
    sa Chance
        Fate and fatalism
        Probabilities
        Success
Fortune, Seven gods of
    See Seven gods of fortune
Fortune, Soldiers of
    See Soldiers of fortune
Fortune-telling *(BF1850-1891)*
    sa Astrology
        Choice by lot
        Clairvoyance
        Crystal-gazing
        Divination
        Dreams
        Palmistry
    xx Amusements
        Catoptromancy
        Clairvoyance
        Divination
        Occult sciences
        Prophecies
        Second sight
        Superstition
Fortune-telling by birthdays
    xx Birthdays
        Divination
Fortune-telling by cards
    x Cartomancy
    xx Card tricks
        Cards
        Divination
Fortune-telling by dice *(BF1891.D5)*
    xx Dice
        Divination
Fortune-telling by fingerprints *(BF1891.F5)*
    xx Divination
        Fingerprints
Fortune-telling by names
    xx Divination
        Names, Personal
Fortune-telling by numbers
    x Arithmomancy
        Numbers, Fortune-telling by
    xx Symbolism of numbers
Fortune-telling by seals
    x Fortune-telling by signets
    xx Seals (Numismatics)
Fortune-telling by signets
    See Fortune-telling by seals
Fortune-telling by tea leaves *(BF1881)*
    xx Divination
Fortunes
    See Income
        Wealth
Forty (The number)
    xx Symbolism of numbers
Forty-five (Game) *(GV1295.F7)*
Forty hours' adoration
    See Forty hours' devotion
Forty hours' devotion *(BX2169)*
    xx Forty hours' adoration
        Forty hours' prayer
Forty hours' prayer
    See Forty hours' devotion

Forty-seven Rōnin
    sa Japan—History—Akō Vendetta, 1702
    x Akō gishi
        Chūshingura Incident, 1703
    xx Japan—History—Tokugawa period,
        1600-1868
Forum, Open
    See Forums (Discussion and debate)
Forums (Discussion and debate)
        (LC6501-6560; Debating,
        PN4177-4191)
    sa Catholic academies
        Evangelical academies
        Group reading
        Radio addresses, debates, etc.
        Seminars
    x Conferences
        Forum, Open
        Group discussion
        Open forum
        Public forums
        Workshops (Group discussion)
    xx Debates and debating
        Discussion
        Meetings
        Radio addresses, debates, etc.
Forward exchange *(HG3853.F6)*
    x Foreign exchange futures
        Futures exchange
    xx Foreign exchange
Forwarders, Freight
    See Freight forwarders
Forwarding agents
    See Freight forwarders
Forwarding merchants
    See Freight forwarders
Fossa axillaris
    See Axilla
Fossil beetles, Fossil birds, Fossil butterflies,
    etc.
    See Beetles, Fossil
        Birds, Fossil
        Butterflies, Fossil
        similar headings
Fossil botany
    See Paleobotany
Fossil dust
    See Diatomaceous earth
Fossil eggs
    See Eggs, Fossil
Fossil excrement
    See Coprolites
Fossil feces
    See Coprolites
Fossil footprints
    See Footprints, Fossil
Fossil man *(Indirect)*
    sa Cro-Magnon man
        Neanderthal race
        Piltdown forgery
        names of fossil hominids by genera and
          species, e.g. Zinjanthropus,
          Pithecanthropus erectus
    x Early man
        Human paleontology
        Man, Fossil
    xx Human evolution
        Man, Prehistoric
        Somatology
    — Catalogs and collections
    — Craniology
Fossil plants
    See Paleobotany
Fossil pollen
    See Pollen, Fossil
Fossil soils
    See Paleopedology

Fossil spores (Botany)
    See Spores (Botany), Fossil
Fossil teeth
    See Teeth, Fossil
Fossil tracks
    See Footprints, Fossil
Fossil wood
    See Trees, Fossil
Fossils
    See Paleontology
Fossils, Living
    See Living fossils
Foster care, Home
    See Foster home care
Foster care, Institutional
    See Children—Institutional care
Foster day care
    sa Day nurseries
        Foster home care
        Visiting housekeepers
    x Child care centers
        Child minders
        Day care
    xx Child welfare
        Children—Institutional care
        Day nurseries
        Family
        Foster home care
        Home
        Visiting housekeepers
    — Licenses *(Direct)*
Foster family care
    See Foster home care
Foster home care *(Direct)* *(HV875)*
    sa Adoption
        Children, Adopted
        Children—Institutional care
        Foster day care
    x Child placing
        Foster care, Home
        Foster family care
    xx Adoption
        Child welfare
        Children—Institutional care
        Family
        Foster day care
        Home
    — Costs
    — Research *(Direct)*
Foucault's pendulum *(QB633)*
    sa Earth—Rotation
    xx Earth—Rotation
        Pendulum
Foul brood, American
    x American foul brood
    xx Bees—Diseases
Foul brood, European
    x European foul brood
    xx Bees—Diseases
Foulahs
    See Fulahs
Fouling of ship bottoms
    sa Marine fouling organisms
    x Ship-bottom fouling
        Ships—Fouling
    xx Marine biology
Fouling organisms
    See Marine fouling organisms
Found art
    See Found objects (Art)
Found objects (Art)
    sa Assemblage (Art)
        Collage
    x Found art
        Objects, Found (Art)
    xx Art, Modern—20th century

Foundation garment industry *(Direct)*
    (HD9969.F65-653)
    sa Corset industry
    xx Underwear industry
Foundation garments *(TT677)*
    sa Corset
    x Corsetry
      Foundations (Clothing)
      Garments, Foundation
    xx Underwear
Foundation stones, Laying of
    See Corner stones, Laying of
Foundations *(Building construction, TH5201;*
    Building design, TH2101;
    Engineering, TA775-787; Hydraulic
    engineering, TC197)
    sa Anchorage (Structural engineering)
      Basements
      Bridges—Foundations and piers
      Caissons
      Coffer-dams
      Compressed air
      Concrete
      Concrete dams—Foundations
      Concrete footings
      Cribwork
      Dams—Foundations
      Earthwork
      Hydraulic structures—Foundations
      Kilns, Rotary—Foundations
      Machinery—Foundations
      Marine engines—Foundations
      Masonry
      Piling (Civil engineering)
      Roads—Foundations
      Rock bolts
      Rolling-mill machinery—Foundations
      Shoring and underpinning
      Soil consolidation
      Soil mechanics
      Steam-boilers, Marine—Foundations
      Steam-turbines—Foundations
      Walls
    xx Architecture—Details
      Building
      Caissons
      Civil engineering
      Earthwork
      Masonry
      Soil consolidation
      Soil mechanics
      Structural engineering
      Underground construction
      Walls
    — Cold weather conditions
    — Contracts and specifications *(TA775)*
    — Problems, exercises, etc.
    — Tables, calculations, etc.
    — Testing
Foundations (Clothing)
    See Foundation garments
Foundations (Endowments)
    See Charitable uses, trusts, and foundations
      Endowments
Foundations of arithmetic
    See Arithmetic—Foundations
Foundations of geometry
    See Geometry—Foundations
Foundations of mathematical analysis
    See Mathematical analysis—Foundations
Foundations of projective geometry
    See Geometry, Projective—Foundations
Founding *(TS229-240)*
    Here are entered general works on melt-
      ing and casting metals.
    sa Aluminum founding
      Bell-founders
      Brass founding

Bronze
Bronze founding
Centrifugal casting
Continuous casting
Copper founding
Cupola-furnaces
Die-casting
Foundry chemistry
Foundry research
Iron-founding
Magnesium founding
Metal castings
Metal-work
Molding (Founding)
Pattern-making
Pattern-making machinery
Precision casting
Risers (Founding)
Steel founding
Type and type-founding
  subdivision Founding *under groups of*
    metals, e.g. Nonferrous metals—
    Founding
  x Casting
    Foundry practice
  xx Brass founding
    Bronze
    Cast-iron
    Iron-founding
    Metal-work
    Pattern-making
  — Accounting *(HF5686.F65)*
  — Hygienic aspects
    Example under reference from Health of
      workers
  — Laboratory manuals
  — Patents
  — Safety measures *(TS233)*
  — Standards *(Direct)*
  — Tables, calculations, etc. *(TS235)*
  — Testing
  — Vocational guidance
    x Founding as a profession
Founding as a profession
  See Founding—Vocational guidance
Foundlings *(Direct)* *(HV835-847)*
  sa Adoption
    Orphans and orphan-asylums
  xx Abandoned children
    Child welfare
    Orphans and orphan-asylums
Foundries *(Direct)* *(TS229-238)*
  sa Coremakers
    Die-casting industry
    Iron molders
    Steel foundries
  — Automation *(TS233)*
  — Dust control
    Example under Dust control
  — Equipment and supplies
    x Foundry supplies
  — — Appraisal
    See Foundries—Equipment and
      supplies—Valuation
  — — Drawing
    See Foundries—Equipment and
      supplies—Drawings
  — — Drawings
    x Foundries—Equipment and
      supplies—Drawing
    xx Mechanical drawing
  — — Standards
  — — Valuation *(TS237)*
    x Foundries—Equipment and
      supplies—Appraisal
  — Fume control
  — Heating and ventilation
  — Management *(TS238)*

  — Production control
  — Production standards
  — Quality control
    Example under Quality control
  — Safety measures *(TS236)*
  — Tables, calculations, etc.
Foundry chemistry *(QD133)*
  x Chemistry, Foundry
  xx Chemistry
    Founding
Foundry ladles
  x Ladles, Foundry
  xx Metallurgical plants—Equipment and
    supplies
  — Standards *(Direct)*
Foundry practice
  See Founding
Foundry research
  xx Founding
    Research, Industrial
Foundry sand
  See Sand, Foundry
Foundry supplies
  See Foundries—Equipment and supplies
Foundry workers
  See Foundrymen
Foundrymen *(Direct)*
  sa Trade-unions—Foundrymen
    Wages—Foundrymen
  x Foundry workers
  xx Metal-workers
  — Collective bargaining
    See Collective bargaining—
      Foundrymen
Fountain pens *(Manufacture, TS1266)*
  xx Pens
Fountains *(Direct)* *(NA9400-9425)*
  sa Drinking fountains
    subdivision Fountains *under names of*
    cities, etc., e.g. Paris—Fountains
  xx Architecture
    Hydraulic structures
Four (The number)
  xx Symbolism of numbers
  — Juvenile literature
Four clarinets with string orchestra
  See Clarinets (4) with string orchestra
Four-color problem
  xx Color in cartography
    Graph theory
Four cornets with band
  See Cornets (4) with band
Four-day week *(Direct)*
  xx Hours of labor
Four flutes with band
  See Flutes (4) with band
Four harpsichords with orchestra
  See Harpsichords (4) with orchestra
Four harpsichords with string orchestra
  See Harpsichords (4) with string orchestra
Four horns with band
  See Horns (4) with band
Four horns with orchestra
  See Horns (4) with orchestra
Four Noble Truths
  sa Eightfold Path
  x Noble Truths, Four
    Truths, Four Noble
  xx Buddhist doctrines
Four picture test
  xx Clinical psychology
    Personality tests
    Picture interpretation tests
    Projective techniques
    Thematic apperception test
Four Satipaṭṭhānāni (Buddhism)
  See Satipaṭṭhāna (Buddhism)

Four saxophones with chamber orchestra
   See Saxophones (4) with chamber orchestra
Four saxophones with string orchestra
   See Saxophones (4) with string orchestra
Four Smṛty-upasthānāni (Buddhism)
   See Satipaṭṭhāna (Buddhism)
Four trumpets with string orchestra
   See Trumpets (4) with string orchestra
Four violins with string orchestra
   See Violins (4) with string orchestra
Fourier analysis   (QA403.5)
   sa Fourier series
      Fourier transformations
      Functions, Orthogonal
      Orthogonal polynomials
      Series, Orthogonal
   x Analysis, Fourier
   xx Mathematical analysis
Fourier integrals
   See Fourier series
Fourier series   (QA404)
   sa Almost periodic functions
      Harmonic analysis
      Harmonic functions
      Integrals, Dirichlet
   x Fourier integrals
      Series, Fourier
      Series, Trigonometric
      Trigonometric series
   xx Calculus
      Fourier analysis
      Harmonic analysis
      Harmonic functions
   — Computer programs
   — Programmed instruction
Fourier transform interferometry
   See Fourier transform spectroscopy
Fourier transform spectroscopy   (QC451)
   x Fourier transform interferometry
      Interference spectrometry
      Multiplex spectrometry
      Spectroscopy, Fourier transform
   xx Fourier transformations
      Interferometer
      Spectrum analysis
Fourier transformations
   sa Digital filters (Mathematics)
      Fourier transform spectroscopy
   x Transformations, Fourier
      Transforms, Fourier
   xx Fourier analysis
      Groups, Theory of
      Harmonic analysis
      Transformations (Mathematics)
   — Computer programs
   — Tables, etc.
Fourteen holy helpers
   x Auxiliary saints
      Helpers, Fourteen holy
      Holy helpers, Fourteen
   xx Saints
Fourteenth century
   xx Europe—History—476-1492
      Middle Ages—History
Fourth dimension   (QA699)
      Here are entered only philosophical and
      imaginative works. Mathematical
      works are entered under the heading
      Hyperspace.
   sa Space and time
   x Space of more than three dimensions
   xx Mathematics
   Note under Hyperspace
Fourth disease
   See Rubella
Fourth grade (Education)
   xx Education, Primary

Fourth of July
   x Independence Day (United States)
      July Fourth
   — Juvenile literature
   — Songs and music   (M1629.3.F6)
      Example under Holidays—Songs and
      music
Fourth of July celebrations   (E286;
      Recitations, PN4305.H7)
   xx Holidays
   — Juvenile literature
Fourth of July orations   (E286)
   xx Orations
Fouta cattle
   See N'Dama cattle
Foval
   See Pearl art glass
Fowl paralysis
   See Avian lymphomatosis
Fowl pest
   See Fowl plague
      Newcastle disease
Fowl plague   (SF995.6.F59)
   x Fowl pest
   xx Poultry—Diseases
      Virus diseases
Fowl plague virus
   xx Myxoviruses
Fowl pox
   See Chicken-pox in poultry
Fowl typhoid   (SF995)
   xx Poultry—Diseases
      Salmonellosis in poultry
Fowling   (Indirect)   (SK311-333)
   sa Decoys (Hunting)
      Duck shooting
      Falconry
      Goose shooting
      Grouse shooting
      Pheasant shooting
      Pigeon shooting
      Shooting preserves
      Upland game bird shooting
      Waterfowl shooting
      Woodcock shooting
   x Bird hunting
      Wildfowling
   xx Falconry
      Game and game-birds
      Hunting
      Shooting
   — Early works to 1800
   — Pictorial works
Fowls
   See Poultry
Fox
   See Foxes
Fox bats
   See Flying foxes
Fox-hunting   (Indirect)   (SK284-7)
   sa Hunters (Horses)
      Melbourne Hunt
      Quorn Hunt
   Example under Hunting
   — Pictorial works
   — Terminology
Fox-hunting in literature
Fox Indians   (E99.F7)
   sa Sauk Indians
   x Meskwaki Indians
      Muskwaki Indians
      Musquakie Indians
      Outagami Indians
   xx Algonquian Indians
      Indians of North America
      Sauk Indians
   — Art

Fox language   (PM1195)
   xx Algonquian languages
Fox squirrel
   xx Squirrels
   — Food
Fox-terriers   (SF429.F5)
   xx Terriers
Fox trot   (GV1796.F6)
Fox trots
      Here are entered collections of fox-trot
      music for various mediums. Individual
      fox trots and collections of fox trots for
      a specific medium are entered under
      the heading followed by specification
      of medium.
Fox trots (Band)   (M1248; M1264)
   xx Band music
   — Scores
Fox trots (Dance orchestra)
   xx Dance-orchestra music
Fox trots (Violin and piano)   (M217-218;
      M221-3)
   xx Violin and piano music
Foxes   (Stories and anecdotes, QL795.F8;
      Zoology, QL737.C2)
   sa Arctic fox
      Fennecs
      Gray fox
      Kit fox
      Red fox
      Silver fox
   x Fox
   — Behavior
      Example under Mammals—Behavior
   — Feeding and feeds
   — Juvenile literature
Foxes (in religion, folk-lore, etc.)
   x Folk-lore of foxes
   xx Religion, Primitive
Foxes in art
   xx Art
Foxglove aphid
Foxholes
   See Intrenchments
Foxhounds   (SF429.F6)
   sa American foxhounds
   Example under Hounds
Foxtail   (Agriculture, SB201.F; Botany,
      QK495.G74; Diseases and pests,
      SB608.F7)
Foyers
   See Entrance halls
FPC
   See Fish protein concentrate
Fractional distillation
   See Distillation, Fractional
Fractional horsepower electric motors
   See Electric motors, Fractional horsepower
Fractionation of cells
   See Cell fractionation
Fractions   (QA117; Methods of teaching,
      QA137)
   sa Series, Farey
   xx Arithmetic
      Mathematics
      Numbers, Rational
   — Juvenile literature
   — Programmed instruction
   — Tables, etc.   (QA117)
Fractions, Continued   (QA295)
   sa Padé approximant
      Processes, Infinite
   x Continued fractions
   xx Processes, Infinite
Fractions, Decimal   (Theory of numbers,
      QA242)
   x Decimal fractions
   — Problems, exercises, etc.

Fractions, Decimal *(Theory of numbers, QA242) (Continued)*
— Programmed instruction
Fracture fixation
   sa Internal fixation in fractures
   xx Fractures
Fracture of metals
   See Metals—Fracture
Fracture of polymeric materials
   See Polymers and polymerization—Fracture
Fracture of solids
   sa Brittleness
     Ceramics—Fracture
     Creep of materials
     Fibrous composites—Fracture
     Glass—Fracture
     Materials—Fatigue
     Metals—Fracture
     Polymers and polymerization—Fracture
     R-curves
     Yield-line analysis
   x Failure of solids
     Solids—Fracture
   xx Brittleness
     Deformations (Mechanics)
     Materials—Fatigue
     Strength of materials
Fractures *(RD101)*
   sa Bones
     Callus
     Fracture fixation
     Internal fixation in fractures
     Pseudarthrosis
     Surgery
     X-rays
     subdivision Fracture *under particular bones, e.g.* Humerus—Fracture; *also subdivision* Fractures *under particular regions of the body, e.g.* Extremities, Lower—Fractures
   xx Bones
     Surgery
   — Juvenile literature
Fractures, Spontaneous *(RD101)*
   xx Bones—Diseases
     Osteopsathyrosis
Frafra language
   See Nankanse language
Fragmentary books
   See Unfinished books
Fragrance of flowers
   See Flowers—Odor
"Fram" Expedition, 1st, 1893-1896 *(G700 1893)*
"Fram" Expedition, 2d, 1898-1902 *(G670 1898)*
Framboesia
   See Yaws
Frame houses, Wooden
   See Wooden-frame houses
Frame-stories *(PN3383.F7)*
   xx Prologues and epilogues
     Short story
     Tales
Framed structures
   See Structural frames
Frames (Structures)
   See Structural frames
Frameworks (Structures)
   See Structural frames
Framing (Building) *(TH2301)*
   sa Half-timbered houses
     House framing
     Roofs
   xx Building
     Half-timbered houses
     Structural frames

Framing of pictures
   See Picture frames and framing
France
   — Bio-bibliography
     Example under Bio-bibliography
   — Colonies
     Example under Colonies
   —— Administration
      Example under Colonies—Administration
   — Commerce
     Example under Commercial statistics
   — Commercial policy
     Example under Commercial policy
   — Court and courtiers
     xx Courts and courtiers
     Example under Favorites, Royal
   — Description and travel
     Example under Geography; Travel
   —— Guide-books
      Example under references from Guide-books; Routes of travel
   —— Maps
      See France—Maps
   — Dictionaries and encyclopedias
     Note under Encyclopedias and dictionaries; *and under reference from* Dictionaries
   — Diplomatic and consular service
     Example under Diplomatic and consular service
   — Economic conditions
     Example under reference from National resources
     Note under Natural resources
   — Foreign relations
     Example under International relations; *and under reference from* Foreign relations
   —— United States
      Note under United States—Foreign relations—Canada, [France, Japan, etc.]
   — Gazetteers
     Example under Geography—Dictionaries
   — Historical geography
     Note under Geography, Historical
   — History *(DC)*
   — History
   —— To 987
     sa Carlovingians
      Merovingians
      Paris—Siege, 886
      Poitiers, Battle of, 732
      Verdun, Treaty of, 843
     xx Carlovingians
      Merovingians
   —— Capetians, 987-1328
     sa Latin Empire, 1204-1261
   —— Medieval period, 987-1515
   —— 13th century
   —— House of Valois, 1328-1589
   —— 16th century
   —— Wars of the Huguenots, 1562-1598
     sa Edict of Nantes
      La Roche-l'Abeille, Battle of, 1569
      St. Germain, Peace of, 1570
     x Huguenot Wars
     xx Edict of Nantes
      Holy League, 1576-1593
      Huguenots in France
   —— Bourbons, 1589-1789
   —— 17th century
     sa Franco-Spanish War, 1635-1659
      Rocroi, Battle of, 1643
   —— 18th century

   —— Regency, 1715-1723
   —— 1789-
   —— Revolution, 1789
     sa Tennis Court Oath, June 20, 1789
   ——— Juvenile literature
   —— Revolution, 1789-1793
   —— Revolution, 1789-1799 *(DC139-195)*
     x French Revolution
      Napoleonic Wars
      Reign of Terror
      Revolution, French
      Terror, Reign of
     xx Émigrés
      Revolutions
   ——— Aerial operations
   ——— Almanacs
   ——— Anecdotes
   ——— Art
   ——— Biography
   ——— Causes and character
     x France—History—Revolution, 1789-1799—Philosophy
   ——— Censorship
   ——— Claims
   ——— Clubs
     sa Girondists
      Jacobins
      Montagnards
   ——— Dictionaries
   ——— Drama
     Example under Drama
   ——— Economic aspects
   ——— Fiction
   ——— Finance, confiscations, etc.
     xx Confiscations
   ——— Foreign public opinion
     Example under Public opinion
   ——— Humor, caricatures, etc.
   ——— Iconography
   ——— Influence
   ——— Influence on literature
   ——— Jews
   ——— Language (New words, slang, etc.)
   ——— Music
   ——— Outlines, syllabi, etc.
   ——— Periodicals
   ——— Personal narratives
   ——— Philosophy
   ——— Philosphy
     See France—History—Revolution, 1789-1799—Causes and character
   ——— Pictorial works
   ——— Poetry
   ——— Portraits
   ——— Propaganda
     xx Propaganda, French
   ——— Quotations, maxims, etc.
   ——— Religious history
     sa Nonjurors, French Catholic
   ———— Historiography
   ——— Sources
   —— 1789-1815
     sa French Expedition to Ireland, 1796-1797
      French Expedition to Wales, 1797
     x Napoleonic Wars
   —— 1789-1900
   ——— Pictorial works
   —— Revolution, 1791
     sa Pillnitz, Declaration of, 1791
   —— Revolution, 1792
     sa Jemmapes, Battle of, 1792
      Valmy, Battle of, 1792
   —— Revolution, 1793
     sa Lyons—Siege, 1793
      Mainz—Siege, 1793
      Torfou, Battle of, 1793

Valenciennes, France—Siege, 1793
— — Revolution, 1794
— — — Pictorial works
— — Revolution, 1795-1799
    sa Vendean War, 1793-1800
    x Directory, French, 1795-1799
      French Directory, 1795-1799
— — Consulate and Empire, 1799-1815
    sa Continental system of Napoleon
    x Napoleonic Wars
— — — 19th century
— — — Invasion of 1814
— — Restoration, 1814-1830
    xx Restorations, Political
— — July Revolution, 1830
    x July Revolution, 1830
— — Insurrection in Lyons, 1834
    x Lyons—Insurrection, 1834
— — February Revolution, 1848
    x Revolution of 1848 in France
— — — Historiography
— — Second Republic, 1848-1852
— — — Art
— — — 1848-1870
— — Coup d'état, 1851
    x Coup d'état of 1851
— — Second Empire, 1852-1870
— — — Caricatures and cartoons
— — Crimean War, 1853-1856
    See Crimean War, 1853-1856
— — Italian Campaign, 1859
    See Italy—History—War of 1859
— — Franco-German War, 1870-1871
    See Franco-German War, 1870-1871
— — Third Republic, 1870-1940
— — Commune, 1871
    See Paris—History—Commune, 1871
— — Occupation and evacuation, 1871-1873
    xx Franco-German War, 1870-1871
— — War with Tunisia, 1881
    See Tunisia—History—French occupation, 1881-1956
— — 20th century
— — — Juvenile literature
— — German occupation, 1914-1918
    Example under Military occupation
— — 1914-1940
— — German occupation, 1940-1945 *(DC397)*
    sa World War, 1939-1945—Deportations from France
— — 1945-
— — — Pictorial works
— — 1958-
— — Revolution

GENERAL SUBDIVISIONS

— — Chronology
    Example under Chronology, Historical

GENERAL SUBDIVISIONS

— — Sources
    Example under reference from Memoirs
— Intellectual life
    Example under Intellectual life
— Kings and rulers
    Example under Queens
— — Religion
— Manufactures
    Example under Manufactures
— Maps
    x France—Description and travel—Maps

— Nobility
    Example under Nobility; Orders of knighthood and chivalry
— Occupations
    Example under Occupations
— Politics and government
    sa Intendants
— Population
    Example under Demography
— Public works
    Example under Civil engineering
— Relations (general) with the United States
    Note under United States—Relations (general) with Canada, [France, Japan, etc.]
— Religion
    Example under Religion
— Statistics, Vital
    xx Vital statistics
— Surveys
    Example under Geodesy
France. Armée
    x Army
    xx Armies
      Military history
      Standing army
— Appropriations and expenditures
    x Army appropriation bills
    Example under Finance, Public
— Commissariat
    Example under Armies—Commissariat
— Examinations
    Example under Examinations
— Forage
    Example under Forage
— Medals, badges, decorations, etc.
    sa Croix de guerre (France)
      Médaille militaire (France)
— Military life
    x Army life
    Example under Soldiers; *and under references from* Army life; Military life
— Organization
    Example under reference from Army organization
— Recruiting, enlistment, etc.
— — European War, 1914-1918
    Example under reference from European War, 1914-1918—Recruiting, enlistment, etc.
— Ski troops
    Example under Ski troops
— Supplies and stores
    Example under Armies—Commissariat; *and under references from* Armies—Supplies; Army supplies
France. Armée. Artillerie
    xx Artillery
France. Armée. Cavalerie
    xx Cavalry
France. Armée. État-major
    Example under Armies—Staffs; *and under references from* General staffs; Military staffs; Staffs, Military
France. Armée. Infanterie
    xx Infantry
France. Conseil d'État
    Example under Administrative courts
France. Marine
    x Naval administration
      Naval policy
      Navy
France. Ministère de la Marine
— Appropriations and expenditures
France in literature *(PN56.F)*
    xx Local color in literature
Franchise
    See Elections

Suffrage
Franchises, Municipal
    See Municipal franchises
Franchises, Retail
    See Franchises (Retail trade)
Franchises, Taxation of
    See Corporations—Taxation
Franchises (Retail trade) *(Direct)*
    x Franchises, Retail
      Retail franchises
    xx Agency (Law)
      Retail trade
      Small business
— Information services
Franciscan Recollets
    See Recollets (Franciscan)
Franciscans *(BX3601-3605; Women, BX4361-4)*
    sa Capuchins
      Fraticelli
      Recollets (Franciscan)
    x Friars, Gray
      Friars Minor
      Gray Friars
      Grey Friars
      Minorites
      St. Francis, Order of
    xx Friars
      Monasticism and religious order
— Bio-bibliography *(Z7840.F8)*
— Manuscripts
— Missions *(BV2280)*
    sa Missions of Piritu
— Spiritual life *(BX3603)*
Franciscans. Second Order
    See Poor Clares
Franciscans in America, [Belgium, France, etc.]
Franciscans in France
    x Cordeliers (Monastic order)
Franciscans in literature
Francium
    xx Alkali metals
      Radioactive substances
Franco-Chinese War, 1884-1885
    See Chinese-French War, 1884-1885
Franco-English War . . .
    See Anglo-French War . . .
Franco-German War, 1870-1871 *(DC281-326)*
    sa Alsace-Lorraine question
      Amiens, Battle of, 1870
      Beaune-la-Rolande, Battle of, 1870
      Belfort, Battle of, 1871
      Belfort, France—Siege, 1870-1871
      Champigny-sur-Marne, France, Battle of, 1870
      Châteaudun, France—Siege, 1870
      Coulmiers, Battle of, 1870
      Dijon—Siege, 1870-1871
      Épinal, Battle of, 1870
      France—History—Occupation and evacuation, 1871-1873
      Frankfurt am Main, Peace of, 1871
      Gravelotte, Battle of, 1870
      Landrecies, France—Siege, 1871
      Le Mans, Battle of, 1871
      Loigny-Poupry, Battle of, 1870
      Longwy, France—Siege, 1871
      Metz—Siege, 1870
      Mézières, France—Siege, 1870-1871
      Montmédy, France—Siege, 1870
      Neuf-Brisach, Alsace—Siege, 1870
      Noisseville, Battle of, 1870
      Orléans, Battle of, 1870
      Paris—Siege, 1870-1871
      Péronne, France—Siege, 1870
      Rambervillers, Battle of, 1870

Franco-German War, 1870-1871
   (DC281-326)   (Continued)
      Sedan Campaign, 1870
      Sélestat, Alsace—Siege, 1870
      Spicheren, Battle of, 1870
      Strassburg—Siege, 1870
      Thiais, France, Battle of, 1870
      Verdun, France—Siege, 1870
      Vionville, Battle of, 1870
      Weissenburg, Battle of, 1870
      Wörth, Battle of, 1870
   x France—History—Franco-German War,
      1870-1871
      Franco-Prussian War, 1870-1871
      Germany—History—Franco-German
         War, 1870-1871
   Example under reference from Wars
   — Aerial operations
   — Armistice   *(DC300)*
   — Causes
   — Claims
   — Drama
   — Fiction
      sa Franco-German War, 1870-1871—
         Juvenile fiction
   — Finance
   — Foreign public opinion
   — Hospitals, charities, etc.
   — Humor, caricatures, etc.
   — Influence on literature
   — Juvenile fiction
      xx Franco-German War, 1870-1871—
         Fiction
   — Juvenile literature
   — Literature and the war
   — Medical and sanitary affairs
   — Personal narratives
   — Pictorial works
   — Poetry
   — Postal service
   — Prisoners and prisons
   — Regimental histories
   — Reparations
   — Sources
Franco-Provençal dialects   *(PC3081-3148)*
   sa Provençal language
   x Dialects
Franco-Prussian War, 1870-1871
   See Franco-German War, 1870-1871
Franco-Russian Alliance   *(D397)*
   x Russo-French Alliance
Franco-Soviet pact, 1935
   x Pacte franco-soviétique, 1935
Franco-Spanish War, 1635-1659   *(DC124.45)*
   sa Pyrenees, Peace of the, 1659
   x French-Spanish War, 1635-1659
      Spanish-French War, 1635-1659
   xx France—History—17th century
      Thirty Years' War, 1618-1648
Franco-Spanish War, 1667-1668
   See Devolution, War of, 1667-1668
Franco-Syrian treaty, 1936
   x Damascus, Treaty of, 1936
Francolins
   sa Erckel francolin
   xx Partridges
Franconia, House of
   See Franconian House
Franconian emperors
   See Germany—History—Franconian House,
      1024-1125
      Holy Roman Empire—History—
         Franconian House, 1024-1125
Franconian House
   sa Germany—History—Franconian House,
      1024-1125
      Holy Roman Empire—History—
         Franconian House, 1024-1125

   x Franconia, House of
      Salian House
   xx Germany—History—Franconian House,
      1024-1125
      Holy Roman Empire—History—
         Franconian House, 1024-1125
Franconian law
   See Law, Frankish
Francs-tireurs
   See Guerrillas
Frangula   *(Experimental pharmacology,*
      QP981.F; Therapeutics, RM666.F)
   sa Buckthorn
   xx Buckthorn
Frank (Fighter planes)
   See Hayate (Fighter planes)
Frankenstein films   *(PN1995.9.F8)*
   xx Moving-pictures
Frankenthal porcelain   *(NK4399.F8)*
   x Porcelain, Frankenthal
Frankfurt am Main, Peace of, 1871   *(DC300)*
   xx Franco-German War, 1870-1871
Frankfurt vocabulary tests
   xx Mental tests
      Vocabulary tests
Frankfurter Gruppe
   See Quadriga (Group of artists)
Franking privilege   *(Direct)   (HE6148;*
      United States, HE6448)
   x Postal service—United States—
      Franking privilege
      Postal service—United States—Penalty
         mail
   xx Postal service
      Postal service—Rates
      Postal service—United States
      Postal service—United States—Rates
   — United States
      x Penalty mail
Frankish law
   See Law, Frankish
Franklin, Tenn., Battle of, 1864   *(E477.52)*
Franklin automobile   *(TL215.F)*
Franklin D. Roosevelt Library, Hyde Park,
N.Y.
   Example under Presidents—United States—
      Archives
Franklin's gull   *(QL696.C46)*
Franks   *(DC64-81; Belgium, DH576;*
      Germany, DD127-134; Italy,
      DG515; Netherlands, DH151)
   xx Germanic tribes
   Example under Teutonic race
   — History
   — — To 768
   — — 768-814
   — — 814-843
   — — 843-987
   — Nobility
      x Nobility, Frankish
Fraternal benefit societies
   See Friendly societies
Fraternal insurance
   See Insurance, Fraternal
Fraternal organizations
   See Friendly societies; Greek letter
      societies; *and similar headings*
Fraternities
   See Greek letter societies
      Initiations (into trades, societies, etc.)
      Secret societies
      Students' societies
Fraternity libraries   *(Direct)   (Z675.F7)*
   x Chapter-house libraries
      Club-house libraries
      Greek letter societies—Libraries
      Libraries, Fraternity
      Libraries, Sorority

      Sorority libraries
   xx Libraries, University and college
Fraternity songs   *(M1960)*
   sa subdivision Songs and music *under*
      names of fraternities, e.g. Phi Kappa
      Psi—Songs and music
   x Sorority songs
   xx Greek letter societies
      Students' songs, American
Fraticelli   *(BX3602)*
   xx Franciscans
Fratricide   *(Direct)*
   xx Homicide
      Murder
Fraud   *(Direct)   (HV6691-9)*
   sa Bad faith (Law)
      Blanks in legal documents
      Cardsharping
      Checks—Criminal provisions
      Diploma mills
      Dolus (Civil law)
      False certification
      False personation
      Forgery
      Fraud investigation
      Fraudulent conveyances
      Impostors and imposture
      Insurance crimes
      Mistake (Law)
      Reformation of instruments
      Restitutio in integrum
      Statute of frauds
      Swindlers and swindling
      Trials (Fraud)
      Whiskey frauds
   x Deceit
      Misrepresentation (Law)
   xx Commercial crimes
      Criminal law
      Deception
      Dolus (Civil law)
      Impostors and imposture
      Mistake (Law)
      Offenses against property
      Simulation (Civil law)
      Swindlers and swindling
      Torts
      Undue influence
      White collar crimes
Fraud (Germanic law)
Fraud (Islamic law)   *(Direct)*
Fraud (Jewish law)
Fraud (Roman-Dutch law)
Fraud (Roman law)
Fraud investigation
   xx Criminal investigation
      Fraud
Fraud orders
   See Postal service—United States—Laws
      and regulations
Frauds, Literary
   See Literary forgeries and mystifications
Frauds, Statute of
   See Statute of frauds
Fraudulent conveyances   *(Direct)*
   sa Assignments for benefit of creditors
      Bulk sales
      Creditors' bills
      Debtor and creditor
      Simulation (Civil law)
   x Actio pauliana
      Bankruptcy, Fraudulent
   xx Assignments for benefit of creditors
      Bankruptcy
      Contracts, Gratuitous
      Creditors' bills
      Debtor and creditor
      Fraud

Simulation (Civil law)
Torts
Fraudulent conveyances (Hindu law)
sa Benami transactions
xx Benami transactions
Fraudulent conveyances (Roman-Dutch law)
Fraudulent conveyances (Roman law)
Fraunhofer lines
xx Absorption spectra
Spectrum, Solar
Fray
See Affray
Frazer Nash automobile
x Frazernash automobile
Frazernash automobile
See Frazer Nash automobile
Freaks
See Deformities
Monsters
Fredericksburg, Battle of, 1862 *(E474.85)*
Fredholm operators
x Operators, Fredholm
xx Linear operators
Fredholm's equation
See Integral equations
Fredonian Insurrection, 1826-1827 *(Texas, F389)*
Free agency
See Free will and determinism
Free banking *(United States, HG2471-8)*
xx Banks and banking
Free choice of employment *(Direct)* *(HD4903)*
x Employment, Free choice of
Freedom of employment
Freedom of occupation
Liberty of employment
Liberty of occupation
Occupation, Free choice of
xx Civil rights
Labor and laboring classes
Labor laws and legislation
Labor supply
Occupations
Personality (Law)
Professions
Free Church of Scotland *(BX9084)*
Free churches
See Dissenters, Religious
Free cities
See Internationalized territories
Free coinage
See Currency question
Silver question
Free diving
See Skin diving
Free earth oscillations *(QE539)*
x Earth oscillations
Free oscillations of the earth
xx Oscillations
Seismology
Free electron theory of metals
sa Effective mass (Physics)
Electric conductivity
Electrons—Emission
Fermi surfaces
x Metals, Free electron theory of
xx Electron gas
Electrons
Energy-band theory of solids
Metals
Free energy relationship, Linear
See Linear free energy relationship
Free enterprise
See Laissez-faire
Free fall, Physiological effect of
See Weightlessness

Free groups
xx Groups, Theory of
Free harbors
See Free ports and zones
Free-law movement
xx Law—Interpretation and construction
Law—Philosophy
Natural law
Free love *(HQ961-7; Socialism and free love, HX546)*
sa Concubinage
Cuckolds
xx Concubinage
Marriage
Sexual ethics
Free material
x Give-aways
"Free on board"
See F.O.B. clause
Free oscillations of the earth
See Free earth oscillations
Free piston engines *(TJ779)*
xx Engines
Gas and oil engines
Gas-turbines
Free ports and zones *(Indirect)* *(HF1418)*
sa Bonded warehouses and goods
Duty-free transit
Harbors—Port charges
x Foreign trade zones
Free harbors
Free zones
xx Bonded warehouses and goods
Commercial policy
Free trade and protection
Harbors
Maritime law
Merchant marine
Shipping
Tariff
Free-radical polymerization
See Addition polymerization
Free schools *(Direct)*
sa Open plan schools
x Alternative schools
xx Education—Experimental methods
Open plan schools
Free seed distribution
See Seed distribution
Free-Soil Party *(JK2336)*
Subdivided by locality, *e.g.* Free-Soil Party. Massachusetts.
Free-Soil Party. Massachusetts
Note under Free-Soil Party
Free speech
See Liberty of speech
Free Spirit, Brethren of the
See Brethren of the Free Spirit
Free thought *(BL2700-2790)*
sa Agnosticism
Bible—Evidences, authority, etc.
Rationalism
Religious liberty
Skepticism
x Thought, Free
xx Christianity—Controversial literature
Deism
God
Irreligion
Liberty of conscience
Rationalism
Theology
— Hymns
Free trade and protection *(HF1701-2701)*
sa Balance of trade
Export controls
Favored nation clause
Free ports and zones

Import quotas
Laissez-faire
Mercantile system
Reciprocity
Second best, Theory of
Shipping bounties and subsidies
Supply and demand
Tariff
Tolls
subdivisions Commercial policy *and* Economic policy *under names of countries*
x Fair trade (Tariff)
Protection
xx Commercial policy
Economic policy
Economics
Mercantile system
Tariff
— Free trade *(HF1701-2580)*
For free trade arguments. Works on the tariff question in a particular country may take this or the succeeding heading in addition to the heading Tariff, *e.g.* 1. Tariff—United States. 2. Free trade and protection—Free trade.
— Protection *(HF1701-2580)*
For arguments in favor of protection.
Free trade areas
See Customs unions
Free verse *(PN1059.F)*
sa Imagist poetry
x Vers libre
xx English language—Versification
Imagist poetry
Poetry
Free will and determinism *(Ethics, BJ1460-1468; Psychology, BF620-628)*
sa Ajivikas
Decision-making (Ethics)
Freedom (Theology)
God—Omniscience
God—Will
Human acts
Inhibition
Libertines (French philosophers)
Life and death, Power over
Necessity (Philosophy)
Pelagianism
Responsibility
Semi-Pelagianism
x Determinism and indeterminism
Free agency
Freedom of the will
Indeterminism
Liberty of the will
xx Conscience
Ethics
Fate and fatalism
Human acts
Law—Philosophy
Necessity (Philosophy)
Philosophy
Predestination
Responsibility
Sin
Theology, Doctrinal
Will
Free will and determinism (Islam) *(BP166.3)*
sa Fate and fatalism (Islam)
God (Islam)—Will
Predestination (Islam)
xx Fate and fatalism (Islam)
Islamic ethics
Islamic theology
Free will and determinism in literature

719

Free zones
  See Free ports and zones
Freeboard, Tables of
  See Load-line
      Ships—Measurement
Freebooters
  See Buccaneers
      Filibusters
      Pirates
Freedmen *(HT731; United States, E185.2)*
  sa Negroes
      Slavery
    x Refugees, Colored
   xx Negroes
      Reconstruction
      Slavery in the United States
      Slavery in the United States—
        Emancipation
Freedmen (Roman law)
Freedmen in Mississippi, ₍North Carolina,
  etc.₎
Freedom
  See Freedom (Jewish theology)
      Liberty
      Slavery
Freedom (Islam) *(BP190.5.F7)*
    x Liberty (Islam)
Freedom (Jewish theology)
    x Freedom
  Example under Jewish theology
Freedom (Theology)
    x Liberty (Theology)
   xx Free will and determinism
      Law and gospel
      Theology, Doctrinal
  — Biblical teaching *(New Testament,*
      BS2545.F7)
  — History of doctrines
  — Juvenile literature
  — Sermons
Freedom of assembly
  See Assembly, Right of
Freedom of association *(Direct) (JC607,*
  JK-JQ)
  sa Assembly, Right of
      Trade-unions
    x Association, Freedom of
      Association, Right of
      Liberty of association
      Right of association
   xx Assembly, Right of
      Associations, institutions, etc.
      Civil rights
      Liberty
      Personality (Law)
Freedom of association (Canon law)
Freedom of contract
  See Liberty of contract
Freedom of debate (Legislative bodies)
  See Legislative bodies—Freedom of debate
Freedom of decision (Ethics)
  See Decision-making (Ethics)
Freedom of employment
  See Free choice of employment
Freedom of information *(Direct)*
  sa Executive privilege (Government
      information)
      Foreign news—Censorship
      Government and the press
      Government information
      Liberty of speech
      Liberty of the press
      Libraries—Censorship
      Moving-pictures—Censorship
      Radio broadcasting
      Radio—Censorship
      Restricted collections in archives

Telecommunication—Law and
  legislation
    x Information, Freedom of
      Intellectual freedom
      Liberty of information
   xx Civil rights
      Liberty of speech
      Liberty of the press
      Telecommunication—Law and
        legislation
Freedom of information (International law)
   xx International law
Freedom of movement *(Direct)*
    x Movement, Freedom of
   xx Civil rights
      Domicile
      Emigration and immigration law
      Industrial laws and legislation
      Labor laws and legislation
      Liberty
      Personality (Law)
Freedom of movement (International law)
   xx International law
Freedom of occupation
  See Free choice of employment
Freedom of religion
  See Religious liberty
Freedom of speech
  See Liberty of speech
Freedom of speech in the church
  See Liberty of speech in the church
Freedom of teaching
  See Teaching, Freedom of
Freedom of testation *(Direct)*
  sa Dower
      Legitime
    x Liberty of testation
      Testation, Freedom of
   xx Inheritance and succession
      Right of property
      Wills
Freedom of the air
  See Airspace (International law)
Freedom of the press
  See Liberty of the press
Freedom of the seas *(European War, D580;*
  International law, JX4423-5;
  Maritime war: International law,
  JX5203-5268)
      Here are entered works dealing with poli-
      tical aspects and theories, also popular
      controversial literature. Works of tech-
      nical or predominantly legal character
      are entered under Maritime law. His-
      torical works and discussions of both
      political and legal aspects are entered
      under both headings.
  sa Jurisdiction over ships at sea
    x Closed sea (Mare clausum)
      Open sea (Mare liberum)
      Sea, Freedom of the
      Seas, Freedom of the
   xx International law
      Maritime law
      Sea-power
      War, Maritime (International law)
Freedom of the will
  See Free will and determinism
Freedom of worship
  See Religious liberty
Freedom Train *(JK4)*
Freehold
  See Land tenure
      Real property
Freeman's Farm, Battle of, 1777
  See Saratoga Campaign, 1777
Freemasonry
  See Freemasons

Freemasons *(HS351-929; United States,*
  HS505-539; Other countries,
  HS551-680)
  sa Antimasonic Party
      Masonic libraries
      Women and freemasonry
      subdivision Freemasonry *under names*
        of persons
    x Freemasonry
      Masons (Secret order)
  Example under Secret societies
  — Addresses, essays, lectures *(HS397)*
  — Art
      sa Freemasons—Medals
  — Biography *(HS399-400)*
  — Cataloging
      See Cataloging of Masonic
        publications
  — Charities *(HS471)*
  — Costumes, supplies, etc. *(HS463-5)*
      Example under Insignia
  — Dictionaries *(HS375)*
  — Directories *(HS381; United States,*
      HS383-7; Other countries,
      HS390)
  — Fiction *(HS435)*
  — Handbooks, manuals, etc.
  — Heraldry
  — History *(HS403-418)*
  — Laws, decisions, etc. *(HS440-447)*
  — Lodge management *(HS396)*
  — Medals *(HS433)*
      xx Freemasons—Art
  — Miscellanea
  — Monitors
      See Freemasons—Rituals
  — Museums and collections
  — Periodicals *(HS351-9)*
  — Poetry *(HS431)*
  — Rituals *(HS455-9)*
      sa Secret societies—Rituals, Cipher
        x Freemasons—Monitors
  — Songs and music *(HS453-4;*
      M1900-1901)
  — Subject headings
      See Subject headings—Freemasons
  — Symbolism *(HS425)*
  — Yearbooks *(HS365)*
Freemasons. Boston
  Note under Freemasons
Freemasons. Constitutions *(HS440-447)*
Freemasons. Knights Templars
  (HS741-760)
  sa Templars
    x Freemasons. Templars
      Knights Templars (Masonic)
   xx Templars
Freemasons. Templars
  See Freemasons. Knights Templars
Freemasons. United States. Scottish Rite.
  National Supreme Council (Negro)
  Note under Freemasons, Negro
Freemasons
    x Masonic orders
Freemasons, Adonhiramite *(HS417.A3)*
    x Adonhiramite masonry
Freemasons, Negro *(HS875-891)*
      Only general works are entered here.
      Works relating to individual colored
      lodges, as well as the literature of col-
      ored freemasonry in any given locality,
      are entered under Freemasons. ₍local
      subdivision₎, *e.g.* Freemasons.
      United States. Scottish Rite. Na-
      tional Supreme Council (Negro)
   xx Negroes
Freemasons and Catholic Church *(HS495)*
  sa Anti-clericalism

x Catholic Church and freemasonry
   xx Secret societies and Catholic Church
Freemasons and Jews
   x Jews and Freemasons
Freemasons and the Orthodox Eastern Church
    (HS495)
   x Orthodox Eastern Church and
    Freemasons
Freemen *(Direct)*
   xx Citizenship
    Municipal government
Freemen (American colonies)
Freemen (Greek law)
Freemen (Roman law)
Freeway airspace utilization
   See Express highways—Airspace utilization
Freeway driving
   See Automobile driving on highways
Freeways
   See Express highways
Freeze-dried food
   See Food, Freeze-dried
Freeze-drying
   sa Food, Freeze-dried
   x Lyophilization
   xx Cryobiology
    Drying apparatus
    Refrigeration and refrigerating
     machinery
  — Patents
Freeze-etching *(QH231)*
   xx Microscope and microscopy—
    Technique
Freezing
   See Cryobiology
    Frost
    Ice
    Plants, Effect of cold on
    Refrigeration and refrigerating
     machinery
    Soil freezing
    Temperature—Physiological effect
    Water-pipes—Freezing
Freezing and opening of rivers, lakes, etc.
   See Ice on rivers, lakes, etc.
Freezing of food
   See Food, Frozen
Freezing of human bodies
   See Cryonics
Freezing of semen
   See Semen, Frozen
Freezing points *(QD545)*
   sa Anti-freeze solutions
Freezing points of solutions
   See Cryoscopy
    Molecular weights
Freezing process (Civil engineering)
   See Soil freezing
Freezing process (Saline water conversion)
   See Saline water conversion—Freezing
    process
Freezing process (Water purification)
   See Water—Purification—Freezing process
Fregatidae
   See Frigate-birds
Freiburg i. B., Battle of, 1644 *(D267.F85)*
   xx Thirty Years' War, 1618-1648
Freight-absorption system
   See Delivered pricing
Freight and freightage *(Direct) (Railroads,*
    HE2301-2500; Shipping, HE593-7)
   sa Aeronautics, Commercial—Freight
    Bills of lading
    Breakage, shrinkage, etc. (Commerce)
    Charter-parties
    Containerization
    Demurrage
    Electric railroads—Freight

Freight forwarders
   Lighterage
   Motor-truck terminals
   Railroads—Freight
   Seatrains
   Stowage
   Tare
   Tonnage
   Transportation, Automotive—Freight
   x Affreightment
    Freight handling
    Freight rates
    Transportation—Freight
   xx Carriers
    Commerce
    Contracts, Maritime
    Maritime law
    Materials handling
    Railroads
    Railroads—Freight
    Tonnage
    Transportation
  Note under Shipping
  — Accounting
  — Claims *(HE1795)*
    x Claims, Freight
  — Classification
    sa subdivision Freight classification
     under means of transportation,
     e.g. Railroads—Freight
     classification
    x Freight classification
    xx Commercial products—Classification
  — Juvenile literature
  — Mathematical models
  — Security measures
  — Tables and ready-reckoners *(TF664)*
    Example under Ready-reckoners
  — Taxation *(Direct)*
    xx Transportation—Taxation
  — Terminology
  — Vocational guidance
Freight-car service
   See Demurrage (Car service)
    Railroads—Freight
    Railroads—Freight-cars
Freight-cars
   See Railroads—Freight-cars
Freight-cars on truck trailers
   x Truck trailers, Freight cars on
   xx Piggyback transportation
    Railroads—Freight
    Transportation, Automotive
Freight classification
   See Freight and freightage—Classification
    subdivision Freight classification *under*
     means of transportation, e.g.
     Railroads—Freight classification
Freight forwarders *(Direct)*
   sa Carriers
    Ocean freight forwarders
   x Forwarders, Freight
    Forwarding agents
    Forwarding merchants
   xx Bailments
    Carriers
    Commercial law
    Freight and freightage
    Hire
    Shipping
  — Taxation *(Direct)*
  — Underdeveloped areas
    See Underdeveloped areas—Freight
     forwarders
Freight handling
   See Freight and freightage
    Railroads—Freight

Freight planes
   See Transport planes
Freight rates
   See Freight and freightage
    subdivision Rates *under means of*
     transportation, e.g. Railroads—Rates
Freight ships
   See Freighters
Freight vessels
   See Freighters
Freighters *(Direct)*
   sa Atomic freighters
    Container ships
    Ore carriers
    Refrigerator ships
    Seatrains
    Tank-vessels
    Tramp steamers
   x Cargo vessels
    Freight ships
    Freight vessels
   xx Merchant marine
    Merchant ships
    Ships
    Steamboats
  — Juvenile literature
  — Passenger traffic
    x Passenger traffic
  — Registers *(Direct)*
  — Safety regulations *(Direct)*
Fréjus, France
  — Flood, 1959
French-American literature *(Direct)*
   xx French literature
French-American newspapers *(United States,*
    PN4885.F7-75)
   xx French newspapers
French-American periodicals *(United States,*
    PN4885.F7-75)
   xx French periodicals
French anatomists
   See Anatomists, French
French and Indian War
   See United States—History—French and
    Indian War, 1755-1763
French architecture
   See Architecture, French
French arts
   See Arts, French
French authors
   See Authors, French
French ballads and songs *(PQ445;*
    Collections, PQ1189)
   sa Ballads, French
    Folk-songs, French
    National songs, French
    Political ballads and songs, French
    Songs, French
    War-songs, French
   x Chansons
  Note under Ballads
French bookbindings
   See Bookbinding—France
French bulldogs *(S429.F8)*
   xx Bulldogs
French cameo glass
   See Cameo glass, French
French-Canadian ballads and songs
    (Collections, PQ3914; History,
    PQ3910)
   sa Ballads, French-Canadian
    Folk-songs, French-Canadian
    Songs, French-Canadian
French-Canadian dialect *(Direct)*
    (PC3601-3649)
   xx French language

French-Canadian drama *(Direct)*
    (Collections, PQ3916; History,
    PQ3911)
French-Canadian fiction *(Collections,*
    PQ3916.F; History, PQ3912)
French-Canadian literature *(Direct)*
    (Collections, PQ3913-3916; History,
    PQ3900-3912)
    x French literature—Canada
    xx American literature (French)
        Canadian literature
        French literature
    — 20th century
French-Canadian periodicals *(Direct)*
French-Canadian poetry *(Collections,*
    PQ3914; History, PQ3910)
    xx American poetry (French)
        Canadian poetry
        French poetry
French-Canadian wit and humor *(Direct)*
    (Collections, PN6178.C3; History,
    PQ3912)
French-Canadians *(F1027)*
    sa Acadians
        Canada—English-French relations
        Canada—History—Rebellion,
          1837-1838
    xx Canadians
    — Biography *(F1005; F1027)*
    — Genealogy *(CS80-89)*
    — Intellectual life
        Example under Intellectual life; Intellec-
         tuals
French-Canadians in Chicago, ⌐Louisiana, New
        England, etc.¬
French Catholic nonjurors
    See Nonjurors, French Catholic
French children's literature
    See Children's literature, French
French children's poetry
    See Children's poetry, French
French clay tobacco-pipes
    See Clay tobacco-pipes, French
French clover
    See Alfalfa
French coins
    See Coins, French
French collages
    See Collages, French
French college verse
    See College verse, French
French color prints
    See Color prints, French
French comic books, strips, etc.
    See Comic books, strips, etc.—French
French courtesans
    See Courtesans, French
French decoration and ornament
    See Decoration and ornament, French
French demonology
    See Demonology, French
French diaries *(Collections, PQ1284)*
    xx Diaries
French didactic poetry
    See Didactic poetry, French
French Directory, 1795-1799
    See France—History—Revolution,
        1795-1799
French drama *(Direct) (Collections,*
    PQ1211-1241; History, PQ500-591)
    sa Jesuit drama, French
        Moralities, French
        Mysteries and miracle-plays, French
    xx Drama
    Note under Theater
    — To 1500 *(Collections, PQ1341-1385;*
        History, PQ511-515)

    Note under Mysteries and miracle-plays,
        English, ⌐French, German, etc.¬
    — 16th century *(Collections, PQ1219;*
        History, PQ521-3)
    — 17th century *(Collections, PQ1220;*
        History, PQ526-8)
    — 18th century *(Collections, PQ1221;*
        History, PQ536-8)
    — 19th century *(Collections, PQ1222;*
        History, PQ541-553)
    — 20th century *(Collections, PQ1223;*
        History, PQ556-8)
    — Belgian authors *(Collections, PQ3846;*
        History, PQ3830)
    — Biography
        See Dramatists, French
French drama (Comedy) *(Collections,*
    PQ1229-1231; History, PQ566-8)
    xx Comedy
French drama (Tragedy) *(Collections,*
    PQ1227; History, PQ561-3)
    xx Tragedy
French drawing
    See Drawing, French
French economic assistance
    See Economic assistance, French
French elegiac poetry
    See Elegiac poetry, French
French endive
    See Belgian endive
French-English War . . .
    See Anglo-French War . . .
French engravers
    See Engravers, French
French epic poetry
    See Epic poetry, French
French epigrams
    See Epigrams, French
French erotic poetry
    See Erotic poetry, French
French essays *(Collections, PQ1290-1291;*
    History, PQ731)
    Here are entered collections of essays by
        several authors.
    xx Essays
French etchers
    See Etchers, French
French etchings
    See Etchings, French
French Expedition to Ireland, 1796-1797
    x Bantry Bay Expedition, 1796-1797
        Brest Expedition, 1796-1797
    xx France—History—1789-1815
        Great Britain—History—Invasions
        Ireland—History—1760-1820
French Expedition to Wales, 1797
    xx France—History—1789-1815
        Great Britain—History—Invasions
        Wales—History
French farces *(Collections, PQ1237.F2;*
    History, PQ584)
    xx Farces
French fiction *(Direct) (Collections,*
    PQ1261-1279; History, PQ631-671)
    sa Love stories, French
        Short stories, French
    xx Fiction
    — To 1500 *(Collections, PQ1391; History,*
        PQ221)
    — 16th century *(Collections, PQ1266;*
        History, PQ643)
    — 17th century *(Collections, PQ1267;*
        History, PQ645)
    — 18th century *(Collections, PQ1268;*
        History, PQ648)
    — 19th century *(Collections, PQ1269;*
        History, PQ651-661)

    — 20th century *(Collections, PQ1271;*
        History, PQ671)
    — Belgian authors *(Collections, PQ3848;*
        History, PQ3842)
        Duplicate entry is made under Belgian
          fiction (French)
        Note under Belgian fiction (French)
    — Cameroon authors
        x Cameroon fiction (French)
          East Cameroon fiction (French)
    — North African authors
        x North African fiction (French)
French folk music
    See Folk music, French
French folk-songs
    See Folk-songs, French
French franc area
    x Zone franc
    xx Currency question
        Foreign exchange problem
        Monetary unions
French glass painting and staining
    See Glass painting and staining, French
French graphic arts
    See Graphic arts, French
French Guiana
    — History
    — — To 1814
    — — 1814-1947
    — — 1947-
French horn
    See Horn (Musical instrument)
French imprints *(Direct)*
    x Imprints (Publications)
    — Book reviews
    — Bookselling
    — Publishing
French in Africa, ⌐Greece, Italy, etc.¬
    — Juvenile literature
    — Legal status, laws, etc.
French in foreign countries
    sa Alien labor, French
    — Legal status, laws, etc.
French in Russia
    xx Émigrés
French in the United States
    xx Émigrés
French Jesuit drama
    See Jesuit drama, French
French language *(PC2001-3761)*
    sa French-Canadian dialect
    x Langue d'oïl
    Example under Romance languages
    — To 1500 *(PC2801-2896)*
        x French language—Old French
          Old French language
    — Early modern, 1500-1700
        (PC2201-2693; PC2901-8)
    — Abbreviations
        See Abbreviations, French
    — Business French *(PC2120.C6;*
        Correspondence, HF5728.F8)
    — Etymology
    — Names
    — — *Note under* Names—Etymology
    — Films for English speakers
    — Grammar
    — — Terminology *(PC2107)*
    — Lexicology
        Note under Lexicology
    — Phonetics
        Example under Phonetics; *and under ref-*
         erence from Phonology
        Note under Phonetic spelling
    — Primers
        See Primers, French
    — Readers (Science)
        Note under Readers

— Rhetoric
    Example under Rhetoric
    Note under Exposition (Rhetoric)
— Scientific French
    See French language—Technical
      French
— Semantics
    Example under reference from
      Etymology
— Slang
    x Trench language (European War)
— Technical French
    x French language—Scientific French
      Scientific French
      Technical French
    xx Technical writing
      Technology—Language
— Terms and phrases
    sa Gallicisms
— Vocabulary
    sa Gallicisms
    Note under Vocabulary
French language in Canada, ₍Haiti, etc.₎
French language in foreign countries
French letters   *(Collections, PQ1285-8;*
    History, PQ711)
  sa Anglo-Norman letters
  xx Letters
French literature   *(Direct) (Collections,*
    PQ1101-1297; History, PQ1-841)
  sa Belgian literature
    Corsican literature
    Encyclopedists
    French-American literature
    French-Canadian literature
    French literature in foreign countries
    Provençal literature
    Swiss literature
  Example under Authors; Literature
— To 1500   *(Collections, PQ1300-1391;*
    History, PQ151-221)
  x Old French literature
— 16th century   *(Collections, PQ1121-5;*
    History, PQ230-239)
  sa Pléiade
— 17th century   *(Collections, PQ1126-1130;*
    History, PQ241-251)
  sa Précieuses
— 18th century   *(Collections, PQ1131-5;*
    History, PQ261-276)
— 19th century   *(Collections, PQ1136-9;*
    History, PQ281-299)
— 20th century   *(Collections, PQ1141;*
    History, PQ301-7)
— African authors
  sa French literature—Negro authors
  x African literature (French)
  xx French literature—Negro authors
— Algerian authors
  x Algerian literature (French)
— American authors   *(Collections,*
    PQ3933-6; History,
    PQ3920-3922)
    Duplicate entry is made under Ameri-
      can literature (French)
  xx United States—Literatures
  Note under American literature (French)
— Anecdotes, facetiae, satire, etc.
— Belgian authors   *(Collections,*
    PQ3840-3853; History,
    PQ3810-3838)
  x Belgian literature (French)
— Bibliography   *(Z2161-2189)*
  sa Catalogs, Publishers'—France
— — Early   *(Z2162; Z2172)*
— — First editions   *(Z2174.F5)*
  x Authors, French—First editions
— Bio-bibliography   *(Z2170)*

— Biography
  See Authors, French—Biography
— Cameroon authors
  x Cameroon literature (French)
    East Cameroon literature (French)
— Haitian authors   *(PQ3948-9)*
    Duplicate entry is made under Haitian
      literature (French)
  Note under Haitian literature (French)
— Jewish authors
  x Jewish literature (French)
— Lebanese authors
  x Lebanese literature (French)
— Libyan authors
  x Libyan literature
— Luxemburg authors
    Here are entered collections of works
      by authors from the Grand Duchy
      of Luxemburg and/or from the Bel-
      gian province of Luxemburg.
  x Luxemburg literature (French)
— Malagasy authors   *(Direct)*
  x Malagasy literature (French)
— Mauritian authors
  x Mauritian literature (French)
— Negro authors
  sa French literature—African authors
  x Negro literature (French)
  xx French literature—African authors
— North African authors
  x North African literature (French)
— North Vietnamese authors
  x North Vietnamese literature (French)
— Protestant authors
— Swiss authors   *(Direct)*
  x Swiss literature (French)
— Translations into English
  Note under Translations
— West Indian authors
  x West Indian literature (French)

GEOGRAPHIC SUBDIVISIONS

— Canada
  See French-Canadian literature
French literature in foreign countries
  (PQ3809)
  xx French literature
French lithographers
  See Lithographers, French
French lithographs
  See Lithographs, French
French logicians
  See Logicians, French
French love poetry
  See Love poetry, French
French love stories
  See Love stories, French
French maxims
  See Maxims, French
French medals
  See Medals, French
French military music
  See Military music, French
French national characteristics
  See National characteristics, French
French newspapers   *(Direct) (History,*
    PN5171-5189)
  sa French-American newspapers
  xx Newspapers
— Indexes   *(AI7)*
— Sections, columns, etc.
  xx Newspapers—Sections, columns, etc.
French newspapers (Belgian)
  See Belgian newspapers
French newspapers (Swiss)
  See Swiss newspapers
French opera
  See Opera, French

French opinion of the United States
  See United States—Foreign opinion, French
French orations   *(Collections, PQ1281-3;*
    History, PQ701)
    Here are entered collections of orations
      by several authors.
  xx Orations
French orators
  See Orators, French
French paintings
  See Paintings, French
French paleography
  See Paleography, French
French paperweights
  See Paperweights, French
French parodies
  See Parodies, French
French part-songs
  See Part-songs, French
French pastoral poetry
  See Pastoral poetry, French
French patriotic poetry
  See Patriotic poetry, French
French periodicals   *(Direct) (History,*
    PN5171-5190)
  sa Children's periodicals, French
    French-American periodicals
  xx Periodicals
  Example under Romance periodicals
— Indexes   *(AI7)*
French periodicals (Belgian)
  See Belgian periodicals
French periodicals (Swiss)
  See Swiss periodicals
French periodicals in foreign countries
French pewter
  See Pewter, French
French philology   *(PC2001-2069)*
  Note under Philology, Modern
French physicists
  See Physicists, French
French pilgrims and pilgrimages
  See Pilgrims and pilgrimages, French
French poetry   *(Direct) (Collections,*
    PQ1161-1201; History, PQ400-491)
  sa Chansons de geste
    Children's poetry, French
    College verse, French
    Didactic poetry, French
    Elegiac poetry, French
    Epic poetry, French
    Epigrams, French
    Erotic poetry, French
    French-Canadian poetry
    Lays
    Parodies, French
    Pastoral poetry, French
    Patriotic poetry, French
    Political poetry, French
    Prose poems, French
    Romances
    Sonnets, French
    Troubadours
    Trouvères
  xx Poetry
  Note under Lyric poetry
— To 1500   *(Collections, PQ1300-1391;*
    History, PQ151-216)
  sa Rondeaus
  x Old French poetry
  xx Trouvères
— 16th century   *(Collections, PQ1173;*
    History, PQ416-418)
  sa Pléiade
— 17th century   *(Collections, PQ1175;*
    History, PQ421-3)
— 18th century   *(Collections, PQ1177;*
    History, PQ426-8)

French poetry (Direct) (Collections,
        PQ1161-1201; History, PQ400-491)
        (Continued)
    — 19th century (Collections, PQ1181-3;
        History, PQ431-9)
    — 20th century (Collections, PQ1184;
        History, PQ441-3)
    — Algerian authors
        x Algerian poetry (French)
    — Alsatian authors
        x Alsatian poetry (French)
    — American authors (Collections, PQ3934;
        History, PQ3930)
        Duplicate entry is made under Ameri-
            can poetry (French)
        Note under American poetry (French)
    — Belgian authors (Direct) (Collections,
        PQ3843; History, PQ3826-9)
        sa Prix Max Rose de poésie
        x Belgian poetry (French)
    — Cameroon authors
        x Cameroon poetry (French)
        East Cameroon poetry (French)
    — Congo authors
        x Congo poetry (French)
    — East Cameroon authors
        x East Cameroon poetry (French)
    — Haitian authors (PQ3940-3949)
        Duplicate entry is made under Haitian
            poetry (French)
        Note under Haitian poetry (French)
    — Malagasy authors
        x Malagasy poetry (French)
    — Negro authors
        x Negro poetry (French)
    — Réunion authors
        x Réunion poetry (French)
    — Swiss authors (Direct)
        x Swiss poetry (French)
French political satire
    See Political satire, French
French portrait painting
    See Portrait painting, French
French portraits
    See Portraits, French
French posters
    See Posters, French
French prints
    See Prints, French
French propaganda
    See Propaganda, French
French property in Alsace, [Egypt, etc.]
French property in foreign countries
French prose literature (Collections,
        PQ1243-1297; History, PQ601-771)
    sa Prose poems, French
    — To 1500 (Collections, PQ1391; History,
        PQ221, PQ607)
French prose poems
    See Prose poems, French
French Protestants
    See Huguenots
        Protestants in France
French Revolution
    See France—History—Revolution,
        1789-1799
French reweaving
    See Reweaving
French rings
    See Rings, French
French salons
    See Salons
French satire
    See Satire, French
French shorthand
    See Shorthand, French
French signing games
    See Singing games, French

French silk
    See Silk, French
French songs
    See Songs, French
French sonnets
    See Sonnets, French
French-Spanish War, 1635-1659
    See Franco-Spanish War, 1635-1659
French-Spanish War, 1667-1668
    See Devolution, War of, 1667-1668
French spinach
    See Orach
French spoliation claims (E336;
        JX238.F72-5)
    xx Claims
French students in Great Britain, [etc.]
French subject headings
    See Subject headings, French
French tales
    See Tales, French
French wall-paper
    See Wall-paper, French
French war-songs
    See War-songs, French
French water-colors
    See Water-colors, French
French wit and humor (Direct) (Collections,
        PN6183-5, PQ1295; History,
        PQ751)
        Here are entered collections from several
            authors and individual authors who
            have not written in other literary
            forms.
French wit and humor, Pictorial
        (NC1490-1499)
    sa Caricatures and cartoons—France
        Comic books, strips, etc.—French
French wood-carving
    See Wood-carving, French
French wood-engravers
    See Wood-engravers, French
Frenchtown, Battle of, 1813
    See Raisin River, Battle of, 1813
Frenulum labii
    See Labial frenulum
Frequencies of oscillating systems
    sa Doppler effect
        Frequency response (Dynamics)
        Frequency stability
        Radio frequency
    x Frequencies of vibrating systems
        Frequency analysis (Dynamics)
        Frequency of oscillation
        Frequency of vibration
        Vibration frequencies
    xx Oscillations
        Vibration
    — Tables, etc.
Frequencies of vibrating systems
    See Frequencies of oscillating systems
Frequency analysis (Dynamics)
    See Frequencies of oscillating systems
Frequency changers (TK2799)
    sa Frequency dividers
        Frequency multipliers
        Frequency synthesizers
    x Frequency converters
    xx Electric current converters
        Electric motors
    — Reliability
Frequency converters
    See Frequency changers
Frequency counts of words
    See Language and languages—Word
        frequency
        subdivision Word frequency under
            individual languages, e.g. English
            language—Word frequency

Frequency curves (HA31)
    xx Correlation (Statistics)
        Curves
        Distribution (Probability theory)
        Probabilities
        Statistics
Frequency detectors
    See Frequency discriminators
Frequency discriminators (TK6565.D4)
    x Discriminators, Frequency
        Frequency detectors
    xx Radio detectors
        Radio frequency modulation
Frequency distribution
    See Distribution (Probability theory)
Frequency dividers
    xx Frequency changers
Frequency meters
    x Meters, Frequency
    xx Electric meters
    — Testing
Frequency modulation, Pulse
    See Pulse frequency modulation
Frequency modulation, Radio
    See Radio frequency modulation
Frequency modulation broadcasting
    See FM broadcasting
Frequency modulation radio broadcasting
    See FM broadcasting
Frequency modulation radios
    See Radio frequency modulation—Receivers
        and reception
Frequency modulation receivers
    See Radio frequency modulation—Receivers
        and reception
Frequency multipliers (TK2799)
    x Static frequency changers
    xx Frequency changers
Frequency of oscillation
    See Frequencies of oscillating systems
Frequency of vibration
    See Frequencies of oscillating systems
Frequency response (Dynamics)
    xx Frequencies of oscillating systems
        Oscillations
        Vibration
Frequency stability
    xx Frequencies of oscillating systems
        Radio frequency
        Stability
Frequency standards
    sa Atomic clocks
        Atomic frequency standards
        Oscillators, Crystal
        Time—Systems and standards
    x Standard frequencies
    xx Standards, Engineering
        Time—Systems and standards
Frequency synthesizers
    x Synthesizers, Frequency
    xx Frequency changers
        Oscillators, Crystal
        Signal generators
Frequency word lists
    See Language and languages—Word
        frequency
        subdivision Word frequency under
            individual languages, e.g. English
            language—Word frequency
Freschwiller, Battle of, 1870
    See Wörth, Battle of, 1870
Fresco painting
    See Mural painting and decoration
Fresh-air charity (Direct) (HV931-941)
    sa Camping
    xx Charities
        Child welfare
        Children—Institutional care

Public welfare
  Social settlements
  Woman—Charities
Fresh water
  sa Drinking water
    Saline water conversion
  xx Water
Fresh-water barriers
  See Saline water barriers
Fresh-water biology *(Indirect)* *(QH96-99)*
  sa Aquariums
    Aquatic pests
    Fresh-water ecology
    Fresh-water fauna
    Fresh-water flora
    Freshwater microbiology
    Limnology
    Water—Bacteriology
    Zooplankton
  x Hydrobiology
  xx Aquatic biology
    Biology
    Fresh-water fauna
    Fresh-water flora
    Limnology
  — Juvenile literature
  — Research
Fresh-water drum
  x Bubbler (Fish)
    Drum, Fresh-water
    Gaspergou
    Perch, White
    Sheepshead (Fish)
    White perch
Fresh-water ecology *(Indirect)*
  sa Freshwater productivity
    Marsh ecology
    Pond ecology
    Stream ecology
    Thermal pollution of rivers, lakes, etc.
  xx Aquatic ecology
    Ecology
    Fresh-water biology
  — Juvenile literature
Fresh-water fauna *(Indirect)* *(Natural history, QH96-99; Zoology, QL141-9)*
  sa Aquariums
    Fishes, Fresh-water
    Fresh-water biology
    Freshwater invertebrates
    Insects, Aquatic
    Mussels, Fresh-water
    Plankton
    Unionidae
    Zooplankton
  x Fauna
  xx Aquatic animals
    Fresh-water biology
    Zoology
  — Identification
  — Juvenile literature
Fresh-water fishes
  See Fishes, Fresh-water
Fresh-water flora *(Indirect)* *(Botany, QK105; Ecology, QK916; Natural history, QH96-99)*
  sa Aquarium plants
    Aquatic plants
    Bog flora
    Fresh-water biology
    Freshwater algae
    Marsh flora
    Phytoplankton
    Plankton
    Pond flora
    Primary productivity (Biology)
    Wetland flora

  x Flora
    Hydrophytes
  xx Botany
    Fresh-water biology
    Wetland flora
  — Identification
Fresh-water mussels
  See Mussels, Fresh-water
    Unionidae
Fresh-water turtles
  sa Box turtle
    Diamondback terrapin
    Ornate box turtle
    Painted turtle
  x Marsh turtles
  xx Turtles
Freshman class (High school)
  See Ninth grade (Education)
Freshmen, College
  See College freshmen
Freshwaster invertebrates *(Indirect)*
  xx Fresh-water fauna
    Invertebrates
Freshwater algae *(Indirect)*
  xx Algae
    Fresh-water flora
    Freshwater phytoplankton
  — Identification
Freshwater invertebrates
  xx Aquatic invertebrates
  — Behavior
  — Identification
Freshwater microbiology *(QR105.5)*
  xx Aquatic microbiology
    Fresh-water biology
    Microbiology
    Water—Microbiology
Freshwater phytoplankton *(Indirect)* *(QK935)*
  sa Freshwater algae
  xx Freshwater plankton
    Phytoplankton
Freshwater plankton *(Indirect)* *(QH96.8.P5)*
  sa Freshwater phytoplankton
    Freshwater zooplankton
  xx Plankton
  — Collection and preservation
Freshwater production rate
  See Freshwater productivity
Freshwater productivity *(Indirect)*
  x Freshwater production rate
  xx Biological productivity
    Fresh-water ecology
Freshwater zooplankton *(Indirect)* *(QL143)*
  xx Freshwater plankton
    Zooplankton
  — Collection and preservation
Fresnel integrals
  See Integrals, Fresnel
Fretting corrosion *(TA407)*
  x False brinelling
    Friction oxidation
    Rubbing corrosion
    Wear oxidation
  xx Corrosion and anti-corrosives
    Friction
    Mechanical wear
    Oxidation
Fretwork *(NK9930)*
  x Scrollwork
    Sorrento work
  xx Art industries and trade
    Decoration and ornament
    Wood-carving
    Woodwork
Frevo (Dance) *(GV1796.F7)*

Friars, Black
  See Dominicans
Friars, Gray
  See Franciscans
Friars *(BX2820)*
  sa Augustinians
    Carmelites
    Dominicans
    Franciscans
    Monasticism and religious orders
  x Mendicant orders
  xx Monasticism and religious orders
  — Controversial literature
Friars in the Philippine Islands
  See Catholic Church in the Philippine
    Islands
    Church lands—Philippine Islands
Friars Minor
  See Franciscans
Friars preachers
  See Dominicans
Friction *(QC197)*
  sa Aerodynamic heating
    Bearings (Machinery)
    Fretting corrosion
    Friction materials
    Frictional resistance (Hydrodynamics)
    Internal friction
    Lubrication and lubricants
    Mechanical wear
    Rolling contact
    Seizing (Metals)
    Skin friction (Aerodynamics)
    Surfaces (Technology)
    Tribology
  xx Bearings (Machinery)
    Machinery
    Mechanics
    Physics
    Tribology
  — Juvenile literature
  — Tables, calculations, etc.
Friction clutches
  See Clutches (Machinery)
Friction gearing *(TJ202)*
  xx Gearing
Friction layer (Meteorology)
  See Planetary boundary layer
Friction materials *(Metallography, TN693.F7)*
  sa Brakes
  xx Brakes
    Friction
    Materials
Friction oxidation
  See Fretting corrosion
Friction welding
  xx Pressure welding
Frictional resistance (Hydrodynamics)
  x Skin friction (Hydrodynamics)
  xx Friction
    Hydrodynamics
    Ship resistance
    Ships—Hydrodynamics
    Surfaces (Technology)
Friday menus
  See Lenten menus
Fried food
  See Food, Fried
Friedel-Crafts reaction *(QD501; Aromatic anhydrides, QD341.A2)*
  xx Chemical reactions
Friedreich's disease
  x Ataxia, Hereditary
    Hereditary ataxia
    Heredo-ataxia
  — Personal narratives

Friend churches
    See Churches, Friend
Friend converts
    See Converts, Friend
Friend meeting-houses
    See Churches, Friend
Friendliness
    See Friendship
Friendly societies *(Indirect)* *(HS1501-1510;*
    Fraternal insurance, HG9201-9245)
    sa Insurance, Assessment
        Insurance, Fraternal
    x Benefit societies
        Fraternal benefit societies
        Fraternal organizations
        Mutual benefit associations
        Societies, Benefit
    xx Charities
        Insurance, Assessment
        Insurance, Social
        Labor and laboring classes
        Societies
        Trade-unions
        Welfare work in industry
  — Accounting *(HF5686.F)*
  — Finance
Friendly visiting *(HV43)*
    sa Elberfeld system
        Social case work
    xx Social case work
        Social service
        Social settlements
Friends, Society of *(BX7601-7795)*
    Subdivided by locality, *e.g.* Friends, So-
    ciety of. Philadelphia.
    sa Churches, Friend
        Friends
        Inner Light
        Seekers (Sect)
        World War, 1939-1945—Friends,
          Society of
        World War, 1939-1945—War work—
          Friends, Society of
    x Quakers
  — Bio-bibliography *(Z7845.F8)*
  — Biography *(BX7790-7795)*
  — Converts
    See Converts, Friend
  — Discipline *(BX7740-7746)*
  — Doctrinal and controversial works
    (BX7730-7732)
  — Education *(LC570-571)*
  — Functionaries
  — History *(BX7630-7728)*
  — — Pictorial works
  — Juvenile literature
  — Language
    xx Language and languages
  — Membership
  — Missions *(BV2535)*
  — Name
    xx Sects—Names
  — Political activity
Friends, Society of. Philadelphia
  Note under Friends, Society of
Friends, Society of (Hicksite) *(BX7751-2)*
    x Hicksites
Friends
    Here are entered works on members of
    the Society of Friends, not as con-
    stituting an ecclesiastical body, but as
    a distinct element or group in the
    population.
    x Quakers
    xx Friends, Society of

Friends, Society of, and world politics
    (BX7748.I65)
    x World politics and the Society of
        Friends
    xx Christianity and international affairs
Friends as scientists
    Here are entered works on the attain-
    ments of Friends as scientists.
    xx Scientists
Friends in literature
    x Quakers in literature
Friends in Pennsylvania, ⌐the United States,
    etc.⌐
Friends of God ("Gottesfreunde")
    (BV5070.F73)
    sa Brothers of the Common Life
Friends of the library *(Direct)* *(Z681.5)*
    xx Library associations
        Public relations—Libraries
Friendship *(BJ1533.F8)*
    sa Fellowship
        Love
        Sympathy
    x Affection
        Friendliness
    xx Conduct of life
        Ethics
        Love
  — Caricatures and cartoons
  — Juvenile literature
  — Quotations, maxims, etc.
Friendship in art
    xx Art
Friendship in literature
Friendship letters
    See International correspondence
Fries Rebellion, 1798-1799 *(E326)*
Friesian cattle
    See Holstein-Friesian cattle
Friesian drama
Friesian essays
Friesian fiction *(Direct)*
Friesian horse *(SF293.F9)*
Friesian language *(PF1401-1497)*
    x Frisian language
    xx Germanic languages
        Low German language
    Example under Germanic philology
  — To 1500
Friesian law
    See Law, Friesian
Friesian letters *(Direct)*
Friesian literature *(PF1501-1558)*
    x Frisian literature
    Example under Germanic philology
  — 20th century
Friesian movement
    A movement which originated in the be-
    ginning of the nineteenth century
    among the Friesians, for the preserva-
    tion and strengthening of Friesian cul-
    ture, language and literature.
Friesian philology *(PF1401-1414)*
    xx Germanic philology
Friesian poetry *(Collections, PF1513)*
Friesians *(DJ401.F5-59)*
Friezes *(NA2965; Decoration, NK2120)*
    sa Metopes
    xx Architecture—Details
        Decoration and ornament
Frigate-birds *(QL696.S6)*
    sa Steganopodes
    x Fregatidae
        Man-of-war birds
    xx Pelecaniformes
Frigates
  — Models
    xx Ship models

Frigidity (Psychology)
    xx Sex (Psychology)
        Sexual disorders
Frigorimeter
    xx Bioclimatology
        Meteorological instruments
        Temperature—Physiological effect
Fringe benefits
    See Non-wage payments
Fringe method, Moiré
    See Moiré method
Fringes (Jewish cultus) *(BM657.F7)*
    x Tsitsit
        Zizith
    xx Bible—Antiquities
        Cultus, Jewish
        Jews—Antiquities
        Jews—Rites and ceremonies
Frisian language
    See Friesian language
Frisian literature
    See Friesian literature
Frit-flies *(SB608.G6)*
    xx Flies
  — Control *(Indirect)*
Friulians *(DG457.F7)*
    x Furlans
    xx Ethnology—Italy
Froebel system of education
    See Kindergarten
Froeschwiller, Battle of, 1870
    See Wörth, Battle of, 1870
Frog-culture *(SH185)*
    sa Frog legs trade
    x Frog-raising
Frog legs trade *(Direct)* *(HD9469.F7-712)*
    xx Frog-culture
Frog-raising
    See Frog-culture
Frogmen
    See Underwater demolition teams
Frogs *(Indirect)* *(Zoology, QL668.E2)*
    sa Bullfrog
        Cookery (Frogs)
        Edible frog
        Green frog
        Wood frog
    x Rana
        Tadpoles
    Notes under Digestive organs—Amphibians,
      ⌐Birds, Fishes, etc.⌐; Generative organs
      —Amphibians, ⌐Birds, Fishes, etc.⌐;
      Sense-organs—Amphibians, ⌐Fishes,
      Insects, Mollusks, etc.⌐
  — Anatomy
  — Food
  — Juvenile literature
  — Legends and stories
  — Physiology
  — Psychology
Frogs, Effect of water pollution on
    xx Water—Pollution
  — Juvenile literature
Frogs as laboratory animals
Frogs as pets
    xx Amphibians as pets
  — Juvenile literature
Fronde *(DC124.4)*
    sa Bordeaux—History—Uprising,
        1652-1653
        Mazarinades
Front-end alignment (Automobile wheels)
    See Automobiles—Wheels—Alignment
Front Morges
    x Morges, Front
Front-screen projection *(TR859)*
    x Alekon-Gerard process
        Jenkins process

Scotchlite process
  xx Cinematography
    Lantern projection
Front-wheel drive (Automobiles)
  See Automobiles—Front-wheel drive
Frontal leukotomy
  See Frontal lobotomy
Frontal lobes
  xx Brain
Frontal lobotomy
  x Frontal leukotomy
    Leucotomy
    Leukotomy
    Lobotomy, Frontal
    Lobotomy, Prefrontal
    Prefrontal lobotomy
  xx Brain—Surgery
Frontal sinus *(Comparative anatomy, QL947;*
    Human anatomy, QM505)
  x Sinus, Frontal
  xx Nose
    Nose, Accessory sinuses of
  — Diseases *(RF421-5)*
  — Surgery *(RF421)*
Frontier and pioneer life *(Indirect) (United*
    States, F596)
  sa Cowboys
    Indians of North America—Captivities
    Indians of South America—Captivities
    Land claim associations
    Overland journeys to the Pacific
    Pioneers
    Ranch life
    Wild men
  x Border life
    Homesteading
    Pioneer life
  xx Adventure and adventurers
    Pioneers
  — Juvenile literature
  — Literary collections
Frontier formalities
  See International travel regulations
Frontier hypothesis
  See Frontier thesis
Frontier patrols
  See Border patrols
Frontier thesis *(E179.5)*
  x Frontier hypothesis
    Turner hypothesis
    Turner thesis
    Turner's frontier hypothesis
  xx United States—Historiography
    United States—History—Philosophy
Frontier workers *(Direct)*
  x Border traffic
    Border workers
    Boundary traffic
  xx Alien labor
    Aliens
    Emigration and immigration
Frontiers
  See Boundaries
    subdivisions Boundaries *and* Frontier
    troubles *under names of countries,*
    states, etc.
Frontispiece *(Z242)*
Frontons
  See Pediments
Fronts (Meteorology)
  sa Air masses
  xx Air masses
    Meteorology
    Weather
Frost *(Direct) (QC929.H6)*
  sa Cryopedology
    Frost protection
    Frost resistant concrete

Frozen ground
  Glaze (Meteorology)
  Ice
  Ice crystals
  Plants, Effect of cold on
  Refrigeration and refrigerating
    machinery
  Thawing
  subdivision Frost damage *under*
    subjects, e.g. Pavements—Frost
    damage; Roads—Frost damage
  x Freezing
  xx Glaze (Meteorology)
    Meteorology
    Temperature—Physiological effect
    Water
  — Measurement
  — Terminology
Frost flakes
  See Ice fog
Frost fog
  See Ice fog
Frost heaving
  xx Frozen ground
  — Measurement
Frost mist
  See Ice crystals
Frost protection
  xx Frost
    Horticulture
    Plants, Effect of cold on
    Plants, Effect of temperature on
Frost resistance of plants
  See Plants—Frost resistance
Frost resistant concrete
  sa Concrete, Effect of temperature on
  x Concrete—Freezing and thawing
    Concrete, Frost resistant
  xx Concrete
    Concrete, Effect of temperature on
    Frost
Frost snow
  See Ice crystals
Frostbite
  sa Chilblains
Frostings, Cake
  See Icings, Cake
Frottage
  See Rubbings
Frozen apple
  See Apple, Frozen
Frozen assets
  See Liquidity (Economics)
Frozen baked products
  See Baked products, Frozen
Frozen blood
  x Blood—Freezing
    Blood, Frozen
  xx Blood—Collection and preservation
Frozen concentrated apple juice
  See Apple juice, Frozen concentrated
Frozen concentrated orange juice
  See Orange juice, Frozen concentrated
Frozen fish
  See Fish, Frozen
Frozen fishery products
  See Fishery products, Frozen
Frozen fog
  See Ice fog
Frozen food
  See Food, Frozen
Frozen food cookery
  See Cookery (Frozen foods)
Frozen-food lockers
  See Cold-storage lockers
Frozen foods industry *(Direct)*
  xx Food, Frozen
  — Waste disposal

Frozen fruit
  See Fruit, Frozen
Frozen fruit juices
  See Fruit juices, Frozen
Frozen ground *(Indirect)*
  sa Frost heaving
    Ice-wedge polygons
    Patterned ground
    Sanitary engineering, Low temperature
    Soil freezing
    Thermokarst
  x Frozen soil
    Permafrost
    Soils, Frozen
  xx Cold regions
    Cryopedology
    Frost
    Soils
    Soils, Effect of temperature on
  — Maps
  — Research
    See Frozen ground research
  — Terminology
  — Testing
  — Thermal properties
Frozen ground research *(Direct)*
  x Frozen ground—Research
  xx Engineering research
    Research
Frozen milk
  See Milk, Frozen
Frozen peas
  See Peas, Frozen
Frozen potatoes
  See Potatoes, Frozen
Frozen semen
  See Semen, Frozen
Frozen shrimps
  See Shrimps, Frozen
Frozen soil
  See Frozen ground
Frozen sperm
  See Semen, Frozen
Frozen stars
  See Black holes (Astronomy)
Frozen vegetables
  See Vegetables, Frozen
Fructofuranosidase
  See Invertase
Fructosans *(QD321)*
  xx Fructose
Fructose *(QD321)*
  sa Fructosans
    Sugar—Inversion
  xx Glycosides
Fructose metabolism *(QP701)*
  xx Metabolism
Fructus
  See Fruits (Civil law)
Fruit *(Indirect) (Culture, SB354-399; Trade,*
    HD9240-9259)
  sa Berries
    Citrus fruits
    Cookery (Fruit)
    Fruit-culture
    Fruit juices
    Fruit trade
    Fruit wines
    Parthenocarpy
    Stone fruit
    Tropical fruit
    particular fruits, e.g. Apple, Orange
  x Fruits
    Pomology
  xx Agriculture
    Botany
    Food
  — Analysis

Fruit *(Indirect)* *(Culture, SB354-399; Trade, HD9240-9259)* *(Continued)*
— Anatomy *(QK660; QK699)*
    sa Fruit—Morphology
       Seeds—Anatomy
    xx Botany—Anatomy
       Fruit—Morphology
       Seeds—Anatomy
— Breeding
    See Fruit breeding
— Canning
    See Fruit—Preservation
— Color
    See Color of fruit
— Cooling
— Cooperative marketing
    xx Fruit—Marketing
— Diseases and pests *(Indirect)*
    (SB608.F8)
    sa Fruit-flies
       Fruit—Storage—Diseases and
         injuries
       Insects, Injurious and beneficial
       Plant diseases
       Scale-insects
       subdivision Diseases and pests *under*
         particular fruits, e.g. Grapes—
         Diseases and pests; *and names of*
         diseases and pests, e.g. Pear
         thrips, Codling-moth
    x Fruit pests
       Fruit—Pests
       Fruit trees—Diseases and pests
    xx Trees—Diseases and pests
    Example under Agricultural pests; Bac-
       teriology, Agricultural; Insects, In-
       jurious and beneficial
— — Atlases
— Drying
    sa Fruit, Dried
    x Drying of Fruit
       Evaporation of fruit
       Fruit—Evaporation
    xx Food—Preservation
       Fruit, Dried
— Early works to 1800
— Evaporation
    See Fruit—Drying
— Fertilizers and manures
    sa Fruit trees—Fertilizers and manures
— Field experiments
— Genetics
— Grading
    sa Fruit grading machinery
— Handling
    See Fruit handling
— Harvesting
— Identification
— Inspection
    See Fruit inspection
— Irrigation
— Judging
— Juvenile literature
— Law and legislation *(Direct)*
    sa Fruit inspection
    x Fruit—Marketing—Law and
       legislation
       Fruit trade—Law and legislation
— Machinery
— Marketing *(SB360)*
    Here are entered works on the market-
    ing of fruit from the point of view of
    the farmer. Works on the marketing
    of fruit from the point of view of the
    commodity dealer are entered un-
    der the heading Fruit trade.
    sa Fruit—Cooperative marketing
       Fruit trade

       subdivision Marketing *under names*
         of fruits, e.g. Apple—Marketing;
         Citrus fruits—Marketing
    x Marketing of fruit
    xx Fruit trade
    Example under Marketing
    Note under Fruit trade
— — Costs
— — Law and legislation
    See Fruit—Law and legislation
— Microbiology
— Moisture
— Morphology *(QK660)*
    sa Fruit—Anatomy
    xx Botany—Morphology
       Fruit—Anatomy
— Packaging
— — Law and legislation *(Direct)*
— — Standards
— Packing
— Patents
— Pests
    See Fruit—Diseases and pests
— Physiology
— Pictorial works *(SB361)*
— Poetry
— Precooling
    xx Fruit—Preservation
       Fruit processing
    Example under Precooling
— Preservation
    sa Fruit—Precooling
       Fruit—Waxing
    x Fruit—Canning
       Preservation of fruit
    xx Fruit processing
    Example under Canning and preserving
— Prices *(Direct)*
    x Fruit trade—Prices
— Processing
    See Fruit processing
— Pruning
    x Fruit trees—Pruning
— Quotations, maxims, etc.
— Radiation effects
    See Fruit, Effect of radiation on
— Research
— Ripening *(SB354-399)*
    x Ripening of fruit
— Seed
— Standards *(Direct)*
— Storage *(SB360)*
    sa subdivision Storage *under names of*
       fruits, e.g. Apple—Storage; Citrus
       fruits—Storage
— — Costs
— — Diseases and injuries *(Indirect)*
    (SB608.F8)
    xx Fruit—Diseases and pests
— Tariff
    See Tariff on fruit
— Taxation *(Direct)*
— Therapeutic use
— Thinning
    See Fruit thinning
— Transportation
    sa subdivision Transportation *under*
       names of fruits, e.g. Apple—
       Transportation; Citrus fruits—
       Transportation
    xx Farm produce—Transportation
— — Diseases and injuries *(Indirect)*
— Varieties
    sa subdivision Varieties *under names of*
       fruits, e.g. Peach—Varieties
    xx Botany—Variation
— Water requirements
— Waxing

    xx Fruit—Preservation
       Fruit processing
       Waxes
— Weed control *(Indirect)*
Fruit, Artificial
    See Artificial fruit
Fruit, Canned
    sa Grapefruit juice, Canned
       Orange juice, Canned
    x Canned fruit
    xx Food, Canned
       Fruit processing
— Grading
— Prices *(Direct)*
Fruit, Dehydrated
    See Fruit, Dried
Fruit, Dried
    sa Fruit—Drying
       Grapefruit juice, Dried
    x Dehydrated fruit
       Dried fruit
       Fruit, Dehydrated
    xx Food, Dried
       Fruit—Drying
       Fruit processing
— Standards *(Direct)*
Fruit, Effect of ozone on
    See Plants, Effect of ozone on
Fruit, Effect of radiation on *(TX612.F7)*
    x Fruit—Radiation effects
    xx Radiation
Fruit, Forcing of
    See Forcing (Plants)
Fruit, Fossil *(QE995)*
    xx Paleobotany
Fruit, Frozen *(TP493.5)*
    sa Fruit juices, Frozen
       specific frozen fruits, e.g. Cranberries,
       Frozen
    x Frozen fruit
    xx Food, Frozen
       Fruit processing
— Prices *(Direct)*
Fruit, Tropical
    See Tropical fruit
Fruit breeding *(SB354)*
    x Fruit—Breeding
    xx Plant-breeding
Fruit-culture *(Indirect)* *(SB354-399)*
    sa Arboriculture
       Berries
       Dwarf fruit trees
       Fruit thinning
       Fruit trees
       Fungi in agriculture
       Grafting
       Horticulturists
       Nurseries (Horticulture)
       Olive industry and trade
       Plant propagation
       Pruning
       Stocks (Horticulture)
       Stone fruit
       Viticulture
       names of fruits
    x Orchards
       Pomology
    xx Agriculture
       Arboriculture
       Fruit
       Gardening
       Horticulture
— Accounting
— Costs
— Early works to 1800
— Finance
— Juvenile literature
— Research *(Direct)*

xx Agricultural research
Fruit-eating bats
  See Flying foxes
Fruit-flies *(Fruit pests, SB945.F8; Zoology,*
     QL537.M6)
  sa Mediterranean fruit-fly
    Melon-flies
    Mexican fruit-fly
  xx Flies
    Fruit—Diseases and pests
  — Behavior
  — Biological control *(Indirect)*
     (SB945.F8)
    xx Fruit-flies—Control
  — Control *(Indirect)* *(SB945.F8)*
    sa Fruit-flies—Biological control
Fruit grading machinery
  xx Agricultural machinery
    Fruit—Grading
Fruit handling *(Indirect)*
  sa Apple handling
  x Fruit—Handling
Fruit in art
  x Fruit prints
  xx Art
Fruit in literature
Fruit inspection *(Indirect)*
  x Fruit—Inspection
    Inspection of fruit
  xx Food adulteration and inspection
    Food industry and trade—Quality
      control
    Fruit—Law and legislation
Fruit jars, Glass
  See Glass fruit jars
Fruit juices *(TP562)*
  sa Apple juice
    Grape juice
    Grapefruit juice, Canned
    Grapefruit juice, Dried
    Lemon juice
    Must
    Orange juice
    Orange juice, Canned
  xx Fruit
    Fruit processing
    Fruit wines
  — Pasteurization
    x Pasteurization of fruit juices
  — Patents
Fruit juices, Canned
  — Prices *(Direct)*
Fruit juices, Concentrated
  sa Apple juice, Frozen concentrated
    Orange juice, Frozen concentrated
Fruit juices, Frozen
  sa Apple juice, Frozen concentrated
    Orange juice, Frozen concentrated
  x Frozen fruit juices
  xx Fruit, Frozen
  — Prices *(Direct)*
  — Transportation
Fruit lecanium *(SB945.F)*
Fruit painting and illustration
  xx Painting
Fruit pests
  See Fruit—Diseases and pests
Fruit prints
  See Fruit in art
Fruit processing *(Indirect)* *(TP374.F)*
  sa Fruit, Canned
    Fruit, Dried
    Fruit, Frozen
    Fruit juices
    Fruit—Precooling
    Fruit—Preservation
    Fruit—Waxing
    Fruit wines

  x Fruit—Processing
  xx Agricultural processing
  — Patents
  — Waste disposal
Fruit thinning
  x Fruit—Thinning
  xx Fruit-culture
Fruit trade *(Direct)* *(HD9240-9259; Tariff,*
    HF2651.F8; Telegraph codes,
    HE7677.F9; Trusts, HD2769.F7)
  Here are entered works on the marketing
    of fruit from the point of view of the
    commodity dealer. Works on the mar-
    keting of fruit from the point of view of
    the farmer are entered under the head-
    ing Fruit—Marketing.
  sa Citrus fruit industry
    Coconut industry
    Fruit—Marketing
    Olive industry and trade
  xx Fruit
    Fruit—Marketing
    Produce trade
  Note under Fruit—Marketing
  — Law and legislation
    See Fruit—Law and legislation
  — Prices
    See Fruit—Prices
  — Tables and ready-reckoners
    (HF5716.F9)
Fruit-tree leaf roller
Fruit tree red spider
  See European red mite
Fruit trees *(Indirect)*
  sa Dwarf fruit trees
    particular fruit trees, e.g. Apple, Cherry
  xx Fruit-culture
    Trees
  — Diseases and pests
    See Fruit—Diseases and pests
  — Fertilizers and manures
    xx Fruit—Fertilizers and manures
  — Pruning
    See Fruit—Pruning
Fruit trees, Training of
  See Espaliers
Fruit wines *(TP561)*
  sa Cider
    Fruit juices
    Perry
    Wine and wine making
  xx Fruit
    Fruit processing
    Wine and wine making
Fruits
  See Fruit
Fruits (Civil law) *(Direct)*
  x Fructus
  xx Possession (Law)
    Real property
    Usufruct
Frustration *(BF575.F7)*
  sa Control (Psychology)
    Rosenzweig picture-frustration test
  x Futility
  xx Attitude (Psychology)
    Emotions
    Personality, Disorders of
  — Testing
Frustration (Child psychology)
  xx Child study
Frustration in literature
  xx Emotions in literature
Frustration of contracts
  See Impossibility of performance
Fryers, Deep fat *(TX657.F7)*
  x Deep fat fryers
  xx Frying

Frying
  sa Food, Fried
    Fryers, Deep fat
  xx Cookery
Fry's art glass
  See Pearl art glass
FT-1 (Fighter planes)
  See Black widow (Fighter planes)
Fu *(PL2519.F8)*
  xx Chinese poetry
    Chinese prose literature
Fuchsia
  — Varieties
Fuchsite *(QE391.F)*
Fuegians *(F2986)*
  sa Alacaluf Indians
    Ona Indians
    Yahgan Indians
  xx Indians of South America
Fuel *(Indirect)* *(Technology, TP315-360)*
  sa Anthracite coal
    Asphalt as fuel
    Bark as fuel
    Benzene as fuel
    Briquets (Fuel)
    Charcoal
    Coal
    Coke
    Combustion deposits in engines
    Gas as fuel
    Heating
    Hecter fuel
    Lignite
    Liquid fuels
    Mennonite grass-burner
    Metal-base fuel
    Motor fuels
    Mud fuel
    Peat
    Petroleum as fuel
    Refuse as fuel
    Sewage-sludge fuel
    Smoke
    Waste products as fuel
    Wood as fuel
    subdivision Fuel *under armies, navies,*
      etc., e.g. United States. Navy—
      Fuel; *and subdivison* Fuel
      consumption *under subjects, e.g.*
      Locomotives—Fuel consumption;
      Steam-boilers—Fuel consumption
  xx Boilers
    Briquets (Fuel)
    Combustion
    Engines
    Fire
    Heating
    Home economics
    Power resources
    Smoke prevention
  — Abstracts
  — Analysis *(TP321)*
  — Costs
  — Patents
  — Prices
  — Research
    See Fuel research
  — Storage
  — Tables, calculations, etc.
  — Testing *(TP321-2)*
    sa Heat of combustion
  — Transportation
Fuel, Colloidal *(TP360)*
  x Colloidal fuel
  xx Coal, Pulverized
    Liquid fuels
    Petroleum
    Petroleum as fuel

Fuel, Liquid
   See Liquid fuels
Fuel ash, Pulverized
   See Fly ash
Fuel-briquet plants
   x Briquet plants
   xx Coal preparation plants
   — Dust control
   — Electric equipment
   — Equipment and supplies
   — Safety measures
Fuel burnup (Nuclear engineering) *(TK9360)*
   x Burnup, Fuel (Nuclear engineering)
   xx Nuclear fuels
Fuel cells *(TK2920)*
   x Electrochemical devices
   xx Direct energy conversion
   Electric batteries
   Electric power production from
      chemical action
   Electrochemistry
   — Juvenile literature
   — Patents
Fuel elements
   See Nuclear fuel elements
Fuel filters
   xx Filters and filtration
Fuel injection pumps
   See Fuel pumps
Fuel oil
   See Petroleum as fuel
Fuel oil burners
   See Oil burners
Fuel pumps
   sa Arc-jet rocket engines—Fuel systems
   Automobiles—Fuel systems
   Diesel motor—Fuel systems
   Gas and oil engines—Fuel systems
   Motor vehicles—Fuel systems
   Rocket engines—Fuel systems
   x Fuel injection pumps
   xx Aeroplanes—Motors
   Automobiles—Motors
   Gas and oil engines
   Gas and oil engines—Fuel systems
   Pumping machinery
   — Maintenance and repair
Fuel research *(Indirect)*
   sa Coal research
   Gas research
   x Fuel—Research
   xx Research
   Research, Industrial
Fuel systems
   See subdivision Fuel systems *under subjects,
      e.g.* Automobiles—Fuel systems
Fuel tanks of aeroplanes
   See Aeroplanes—Fuel tanks
Fuel tanks of rockets
   See Rockets (Aeronautics)—Fuel tanks
Fuel trade *(Direct) (HD9540-9559, etc.;
      TP315)*
   sa Coal trade
   Coke
   Degree days
   Wood
Fuenterrabia, Spain
   — Siege, 1638
Fugalia
   See Regifugium
Fugitive slave law of 1793
   xx Slavery in the United States—Fugitive
      slaves
   Slavery in the United States—Law
Fugitive slave law of 1850
   sa Christiana, Pa.—Riot, 1851
   xx Compromise of 1850

Slavery in the United States—Fugitive
   slaves
Slavery in the United States—Law
Fugitive slaves in the United States
   See Slavery in the United States—Fugitive
      slaves
Fugitives from justice *(Direct)*
   sa Escape (Law)
   Escapes
   Executions in effigy
   xx Arrest
   Contumacy
   Crime and criminals
   Criminal procedure
Fugue *(ML448; MT59)*
   Here are entered works on the fugue as a
      musical form. Scores are entered under
      the heading Canons, fugues, etc.
   sa Canon (Music)
   x Ricercare
   xx Canon (Music)
   Counterpoint
   Musical form
Fugues
   See Canons, fugues, etc.
Fuji (Sect) *(BL1442.S58F8)*
   x Nichiren-shō (Sect)
   xx Nichiren (Sect)
Fuji in art
Fujica camera
   Example under Electric eye cameras
Fuju-fuse (Sect)
   x Fujufuse (Sect)
   xx Buddhist sects
   Nichiren (Sect)
Fujufuse (Sect)
   See Fuju-fuse (Sect)
Fuke (Sect)
   x Fukeshū
   Komushū
   P'u hua tsung
   xx Buddhist sects
   Zen Buddhism
Fukeshū
   See Fuke (Sect)
Fukui, Japan (Fukui Prefecture)
   — Earthquake, 1948
Ful language
   See Fulah language
Fulah Empire *(DT515.9.F8)*
   x Sokoto Empire
   xx Fulahs
   — Juvenile literature
Fulah language *(PL8181-4)*
   x Adamawa dialect
   Ful language
   Fulbe language
   Fulde language
   Fulfulde language
   Peul language
   Poul language
   Example under African languages
Fulah law
   See Law, Fulah
Fulah literature *(Direct)*
Fulah poetry
Fulahs *(GN652.F9)*
   sa Bororo (African people)
   Fulah Empire
   Jaawambe (African people)
   Toucouleurs
   x Felata
   Fellans
   Foulahs
   Fulani
   Fulbe
   Fulfulde
   Peulhs

   xx Ethnology—Sudan (Region)
   Toucouleurs
   — Juvenile literature
Fulani
   See Fulahs
Fulbe
   See Fulahs
Fulbe language
   See Fulah language
Fulde language
   See Fulah language
Fulfillment (Ethics)
   See Self-realization
Fulfulde
   See Fulahs
Fulfulde language
   See Fulah language
Full crew rules
   See Railroads—Full crew rules
Full dentures
   See Complete dentures
Full employment policies
   sa Deficit financing
   Employment agencies
   Employment stabilization
   Government spending policy
   Labor supply
   Public works
   Unemployed
   Work relief
   subdivision Full employment policies
      under names of countries, etc.
   xx Economic policy
   Economic security
   Employment stabilization
   Industry and state
   Manpower policy
   Unemployed
   — Mathematical models
   — Underdeveloped areas
      See Underdeveloped areas—Full
         employment policies
Full-pressure suits (Space environment)
   See Extravehicular space suits
Fuller's earth *(Indirect) (TN948.F9)*
   sa Filters and filtration
   x Attapulgite
   Attapulgus clay
   xx Silicates
Fulling (Textiles)
   See Textile finishing
Fulls (Beaches)
   See Beach ridges
Fulmars
   xx Petrels
Fulminant hyperthermia
   See Malignant hyperthermia
Fulnio Indians
   x Carijó Indians
   Carnijó Indians
   Fornio Indians
   Iate Indians
   xx Indians of South America
   Tapuya Indians
Fulnio language
   xx Indians of South America—Languages
Fulvous tree duck
   x Tree duck, Fulvous
   xx Ducks
Fumaric acid *(QD305.A2)*
Fume control
   sa Smoke prevention
   subdivision Fume control *under specific
      industries and plants, e.g.* Solvents
      industry—Fume control
   x Control of fumes
   xx Aerosols
   Air—Pollution

Contamination (Technology)
Gases, Asphyxiating and poisonous
Smoke

Fumigation *(Plant culture, SB955)*
  sa Disinfection and disinfectants
    Miticides
    Soil fumigation
  xx Communicable diseases
    Disinfection and disinfectants
    Insecticides
    Trees—Diseases and pests
  — Safety measures
  — Standards *(Direct)*
Funafuti language
  See Ellice language
Function, Möbius
  See Möbius function
Function, Secondary
  See Secondary function (Psychology)
Function algebras
  x Algebras, Function
  xx Analytic functions
    Banach algebras
Function generators (Electronic analog computers) *(TK7895.F8)*
  sa Space card (Analog computers)
  xx Electronic analog computers
    Potentiometer
Function spaces
  sa Lp spaces
    Sobolev spaces
  x Spaces, Function
  xx Functional analysis
Function tests, Pulmonary
  See Pulmonary function tests
Function tests (Medicine) *(RC71.8)*
  sa Gastrointestinal function tests
    Heart function tests
    Kidney function tests
    Liver function tests
    Pituitary-adrenal function tests
    Pulmonary function tests
    Thyroid gland function tests
  xx Diagnosis
    Physiology, Pathological
Functional analysis *(QA320)*
  sa Approximation theory
    Digital filters (Mathematics)
    Distributions, Theory of (Functional analysis)
    Function spaces
    Functional equations
    Functor theory
    Hardy spaces
    Hilbert algebras
    Integral equations
    Invariant subspaces
    Lp spaces
    Multipliers (Mathematical analysis)
    Normed linear spaces
    Operator theory
    Perturbation (Mathematics)
    Spectral theory (Mathematics)
    Topological algebras
    Vector spaces
  x Functional calculus
    Functionals
  xx Calculus of variations
    Functional equations
    Integral equations
  — Problems, exercises, etc.
Functional analysis (Social sciences)
  x Functionalism (Social sciences)
    Structural-functional analysis (Social sciences)
  xx Social sciences
    Social systems

Functional burden (Linguistics)
  See Functional load (Linguistics)
Functional calculus
  See Functional analysis
Functional differential equations
  x Differential equations, Functional
  xx Differential equations
    Functional equations
Functional equations *(QA431)*
  sa Differential-difference equations
    Functional analysis
    Functional differential equations
    Integral equations
    Invariant imbedding
    Programming (Mathematics)
  x Equations, Functional
  xx Functional analysis
Functional load (Linguistics)
  x Functional burden (Linguistics)
  xx Phonemics
Functional representation *(JF1057-9)*
  sa Corporate state
    Pressure groups
  x Occupational representation
    Representation, Functional
    Vocational representation
  xx Corporate state
    Gild socialism
    Representative government and representation
  Note under Corporate state
Functionalism (Architecture) *(Direct)*
  x Functionalism in architecture
  xx Architecture, Modern—20th century
Functionalism (Psychology)
  xx Psychology
Functionalism (Social sciences)
  See Functional analysis (Social sciences)
Functionalism in architecture
  See Functionalism (Architecture)
Functionals
  See Functional analysis
Functions *(QA331-351)*
  sa Additive functions
    Approximation theory
    Asymptotic expansions
    Calculus
    Cluster set theory
    Convergence
    Convolutions (Mathematics)
    Distributions, Theory of (Functional analysis)
    Numerical differentiation
    Riemann surfaces
    Wave function
  x Analysis (Mathematics)
  xx Calculus
    Differential equations
    Mathematical analysis
    Mathematics
    Numbers, Complex
    Set theory
  — Computer programs
  — Problems, exercises, etc.
  — Programmed instruction
Functions, Abelian *(QA345)*
  sa Geometry, Algebraic
  x Abelian functions
    Integrals, Abelian
  xx Geometry, Algebraic
Functions, Airy
  See Airy functions
Functions, Algebraic *(QA341)*
  x Algebraic functions
Functions, Almost periodic
  See Almost periodic functions
Functions, Analytic
  See Analytic functions

Functions, Arithmetic
  See Arithmetic functions
Functions, Automorphic *(QA351)*
  sa Eisenstein series
  x Automorphic functions
Functions, Bernoulli's
  See Bernoullian numbers
Functions, Besselian
  See Bessel functions
Functions, Beta
  x Beta functions
  — Tables, etc.
Functions, Characteristic
  sa Distribution (Probability theory)
  x Characteristic functions
  xx Probabilities
Functions, Chebyshev's
  See Chebyshev polynomials
Functions, Circular
  See Trigonometrical functions
Functions, Concentration
  See Concentration functions
Functions, Continuous
  sa Chebyshev systems
  x Continuous functions
Functions, Convex
  See Convex functions
Functions, Coulomb
  See Coulomb functions
Functions, Discontinuous *(QA351)*
  x Discontinuous functions
Functions, Elliptic *(QA343)*
  sa Functions, Modular
    Functions of complex variables
    Integrals, Hyperelliptic
  x Elliptic functions
    Integrals, Elliptic
  xx Functions of complex variables
    Integrals, Hyperelliptic
Functions, Entire *(QA351)*
  sa Value distribution theory
  x Entire functions
    Functions, Integral
    Integral functions
  xx Functions of complex variables
Functions, Error
  See Error functions
Functions, Exponential *(QA342)*
  x Exponential functions
    Functions, Hyperbolic
    Hyperbolic functions
  xx Exponents (Algebra)
    Logarithms
Functions, Gamma *(QA351)*
  x Gamma functions
  Example under Functions, Transcendental
  — Problems, exercises, etc.
Functions, Generalized
  See Distributions, Theory of (Functional analysis)
Functions, Green's
  See Green's functions
Functions, Harmonic
  See Harmonic functions
Functions, Holomorphic
  See Analytic functions
Functions, Hyperbolic
  See Functions, Exponential
Functions, Hyperelliptic
  See Integrals, Hyperelliptic
Functions, Hypergeometric *(QA351)*
  sa Weber functions
  x Hypergeometric functions
  Example under Functions, Transcendental
Functions, Implicit
  x Implicit functions
Functions, Integral
  See Functions, Entire

Functions, Inverse
    x Inverse functions
Functions, Kernel
    See Kernel functions
Functions, L-
    See L-functions
Functions, Lagrangian
    See Lagrangian functions
Functions, Lamé's
    See Lamé's functions
Functions, Legendre's
    See Legendre's functions
Functions, Liapunov
    See Liapunov functions
Functions, Lommel
    See Lommel functions
Functions, Mathieu
    See Mathieu functions
Functions, Meromorphic *(QA331)*
    sa Value distribution theory
    x Meromorphic functions
Functions, Modular *(QA343)*
    sa Functions (Polyhedral)
    x Modular functions
    xx Functions, Elliptic
        Groups, Theory of
        Numbers, Theory of
Functions, Monogenic
    See Analytic functions
Functions, Numerical
    See Numerical functions
Functions, Orthogonal *(QA404.5)*
    sa Orthogonal polynomials
        Series, Orthogonal
        Walsh functions
    x Orthogonal functions
    xx Fourier analysis
        Series, Orthogonal
    Example under Functions, Special
Functions, Parabolic cylinder
    See Weber functions
Functions, Periodic
    See Periodic functions
Functions, Polyhedral
    sa Groups, Theory of
    x Polyhedral functions
    xx Functions, Modular
Functions, Potential
    See Differential equations, Partial
        Harmonic analysis
        Potential, Theory of
        Spherical harmonics
Functions, Production (Economic theory)
    See Production functions (Economic
        theory)
Functions, Recursive
    See Recursive functions
Functions, Regular
    See Analytic functions
Functions, Schlicht
    See Univalent functions
Functions, Set
    See Set functions
Functions, Simple
    See Univalent functions
Functions, Special *(QA351)*
    sa names of specific functions, e.g.
        Functions, Orthogonal;
        Trigonometrical functions
    x Special functions
    xx Mathematical analysis
    — Problems, exercises, etc.
Functions, Spheroidal
    sa Mathieu functions
    x Spheroidal functions
    xx Ellipsoid
        Harmonic functions

Functions, Star-like
    See Star-like functions
Functions, Symmetric
    See Symmetric functions
Functions, Theta *(QA345)*
    x Theta functions
Functions, Toroidal
    See Toroidal harmonics
Functions, Transcendental *(QA351)*
    sa Dilogarithms
        names of specific transcendental
        functions, e.g. Bessel functions;
        Functions, Gamma; Functions,
        Hypergeometric
    x Transcendental functions
Functions, Transfer
    See Transfer functions
Functions, Trigonometrical
    See Trigonometrical functions
Functions, Univalent
    See Univalent functions
Functions, Walsh
    See Walsh functions
Functions, Weber
    See Weber functions
Functions, Zeta *(QA351)*
    x Zeta functions
Functions of complex variables *(QA331)*
    sa Analytic functions
        Arithmetic functions
        Banach spaces
        Bloch constant
        Boundary value problems
        Conformal invariants
        Discontinuous groups
        Functions, Elliptic
        Functions, Entire
        Functions of real variables
        Functions of several complex variables
        Global analysis (Mathematics)
        Hardy spaces
        Kernel functions
        Laurent series
        Quasiconformal mappings
        Series, Lie
        Star-like functions
        Univalent functions
    xx Functions, Elliptic
        Functions of real variables
    — Problems, exercises, etc.
Functions of real variables *(QA331.5)*
    sa Concentration functions
        Convex functions
        Functions of complex variables
        Functions of several real variables
        Set functions
    xx Functions of complex variables
    — Problems, exercises, etc.
Functions of several complex variables
    sa Analytic continuation
        Analytic mappings
        Analytic spaces
        Automorphic forms
        Eisenstein series
        Holomorphic mappings
        Stein spaces
        Teichmüller spaces
    x Several complex variables, Functions of
    xx Functions of complex variables
Functions of several real variables
    x Several real variables, Functions of
    xx Functions of real variables
Functor theory
    sa Categories (Mathematics)
    x Functorial representation
    xx Algebra, Homological
        Categories (Mathematics)
        Functional analysis

        Transformations (Mathematics)
Functorial representation
    See Functor theory
Fund raising *(HG174; Charity organization,*
        HV40-41)
    sa Benefit performances
        Church fund raising
        Educational fund raising
        Federations, Financial (Social service)
        Raffles
        Social service—Finance
        Thrift shops and rummage sales
    x Money raising
    xx Social service—Finance
    — Law and legislation *(Direct)*
Fundamental education *(Direct)*
    xx Community development
        Education
        Underdeveloped areas—Education
Fundamental theology
    See Apologetics
Fundamentalism *(BT82.2)*
    Here are entered works on a twentieth
        century theological movement origi-
        nating in opposition to modernism and
        stressing primary orthodox Christian
        beliefs on Scripture, the creeds, God,
        the person of Jesus Christ, etc. All con-
        troversial literature involving funda-
        mentalism and modernism is entered
        under Modernist-fundamentalist con-
        troversy.
    sa Evangelicalism
        Modernism
        Modernist-fundamentalist controversy
        Neo-orthodoxy
    xx Evangelicalism
        Modernism
        Modernist-fundamentalist controversy
        Neo-orthodoxy
    Note under Modernist-fundamentalist contro-
        versy
Funds
    See Finance
Funds, Special
    See Special funds
Fundus oculi
    x Eyegrounds
        Ocular fundus
    xx Eye
        Ophthalmoscope and ophthalmoscopy
    — Atlases
Funeral directors
    See Undertakers and undertaking
Funeral etiquette
    See Mourning etiquette
Funeral hymns
    sa Dirges
    xx Funeral music
        Hymns
Funeral music
    sa Death in music
        Funeral hymns
        Requiems
    xx Church music
        Music
        Sacred vocal music
Funeral orations *(Greek, PA3264, PA3482)*
    sa Funeral sermons
Funeral rites and ceremonies *(Indirect)*
        (Ethnology, GN486; Manners and
        customs, GT3150-3390)
    sa Ancestor worship
        Cremation
        Dead
        Dokhmas
        Funeral service

Indians of North America—Mortuary
customs
Indians of South America—Mortuary
customs
Lanterns of the dead
Memorial service
Military funerals
Mourning customs
Mourning etiquette
Orientation (Religion)
Scaffold burial
Urns
  x Burial customs
Graves
Mortuary customs
Obsequies
  xx Archaeology
Burial
Cremation
Dead
Manners and customs
Mourning customs
Rites and ceremonies
— Early church, ca. 30-600
    See Funeral rites and ceremonies,
    Early Christian

        GENERAL SUBDIVISIONS

— Art *(N8180)*
— Hittites
    See Funeral rites and ceremonies,
    Hittite
— Jews
    See Funeral rites and ceremonies,
    Jewish
— Terminology
Funeral rites and ceremonies, Basque
  x Basque funeral rites and ceremonies
Funeral rites and ceremonies, Buddhist
    (Direct) (BL1477.8.F8)
  sa Funeral rites and ceremonies, Zen
  x Buddhist funeral rites and ceremonies
  xx Buddha and Buddhism—Rituals
— Public opinion
Funeral rites and ceremonies, Early Christian
    (Direct)
  x Early Christian funeral rites and
    ceremonies
    Funeral rites and ceremonies—Early
    church, ca. 30-600
  xx Church history—Primitive and early
    church, ca. 30-600
Funeral rites and ceremonies, Hittite
    (Direct)
  x Funeral rites and ceremonies—Hittites
    Hittite funeral rites and ceremonies
  xx Hittites—Rites and ceremonies
Funeral rites and ceremonies, Islamic
    (Direct) (BP184.9.F8)
  x Funeral rites and ceremonies, Muslim
    Islamic funeral rites and ceremonies
    Muslim funeral rites and ceremonies
  xx Islamic religious practice
Funeral rites and ceremonies, Jewish
    (Direct) (BM712)
  sa Mourning customs, Jewish
  x Funeral rites and ceremonies—Jews
    Jewish funeral rites and ceremonies
    Jews—Funeral rites and ceremonies
  xx Jews—Rites and ceremonies
Funeral rites and ceremonies, Lappish
  x Lappish funeral rites and ceremonies
Funeral rites and ceremonies, Maori *(Direct)*
  x Maori funeral rites and ceremonies
  xx Maoris—Rites and ceremonies
Funeral rites and ceremonies, Muslim
    See Funeral rites and ceremonies, Islamic

Funeral rites and ceremonies, Shinto *(Direct)*
    (BL2224.25.F8)
  x Shinto funeral rites and ceremonies
  xx Shinto—Rituals
Funeral rites and ceremonies, Slavic *(Direct)*
  x Slavic funeral rites and ceremonies
Funeral rites and ceremonies, Zen *(Direct)*
    (BQ9271.F8)
  x Zen Buddhism—Funeral rites and
    ceremonies
    Zen funeral rites and ceremonies
  xx Funeral rites and ceremonies, Buddhist
Funeral rites and ceremonies in literature
Funeral sermons *(Collections, BV4275)*
  sa Obituaries
  xx Funeral orations
    Sermons
— History and criticism
    Example under Preaching—History
— Outlines
Funeral sermons, Jewish
  xx Sermons, Jewish
Funeral service *(BV199.F8)*
  sa Memorial service
  x Burial service
  xx Church work with the bereaved
    Funeral rites and ceremonies
    Liturgies
    Memorial service
  Note under Memorial service
Fungal cultures
    See Mycology—Cultures and culture media
Fungal genetics *(QK602)*
  x Fungi—Genetics
  xx Genetics
Fungal lung diseases
    See Lungs—Fungi
Fungal toxins
    See Mycotoxins
Fungi *(Indirect) (QK600-635)*
  sa Ascomycetes
    Bacteriology
    Basidiomycetes
    Coenobic plants
    Dermatophytes
    Discomycetes
    Gasteromycetes
    Hypocreales
    Mildew
    Molds (Botany)
    Mushrooms
    Mycology
    Mycotrophy
    Myxomycetes
    Parasites—Fungi
    Pyrenomycetes
    Soil fungi
    Truffles
    Wood-decaying fungi
    Wood-staining fungi
  xx Cryptogams
    Micro-organisms
    Molds (Botany)
    Mushrooms
    Mycology
    Parasitic plants
  Example under Botany
— Analysis
    Example under Plants—Chemical anal-
    ysis
— Anatomy *(QK601)*
    sa Plasmodium (Myxomycetes)
— Catalogs and collections
    See Mycology—Catalogs and
    collections
— Classification
— Collection and preservation
    xx Plants—Collection and preservation

— Cultures and culture media
    See Mycology—Cultures and culture
    media
— Ecology
— Economic aspects
    sa Fungi in agriculture
    Fungi—Industrial applications
    Fungi, Pathogenic
    Fungi, Phytopathogenic
    Fungi—Therapeutic use
    Medical mycology
    Mushrooms, Edible
    xx Botany, Economic
— Genetics
    See Fungal genetics
— Host plants
    See Fungi, Phytopathogenic—Host
    plants
— Identification
— Industrial applications
    sa Yeast
    xx Biochemical engineering
    Fungi—Economic aspects
    Fungi—Physiology
— Physiology *(QK601)*
    sa Fungi—Industrial applications
— Pictorial works
    sa Mushrooms—Pictorial works
— Therapeutic use
    xx Fungi—Economic aspects
Fungi, Edible
    See Mushrooms, Edible
    Truffles
Fungi, Fossil *(QE958)*
  xx Paleobotany
Fungi, Marine
    See Marine fungi
Fungi, Pathogenic *(QR145)*
  sa Adiaspiromycosis
    Fungi, Phytopathogenic
    Medical mycology
    Mushrooms, Poisonous
    Mycotoxins
    Pithomyces chartarum
    Veterinary mycology
  x Fungi, Poisonous
    Pathogenic fungi
  xx Fungi—Economic aspects
    Medical mycology
    Micro-organisms, Pathogenic
    Mycosis
    Parasites
    Veterinary mycology
Fungi, Phytopathogenic *(Indirect)*
  sa Rusts (Fungi)
    Silver leaf disease
  x Fungous diseases of plants
    Phytopathogenic fungi
    Plant fungi
  xx Fungi—Economic aspects
    Fungi in agriculture
    Fungi, Pathogenic
    Micro-organisms, Phytopathogenic
    Plant diseases
    Plant parasites
— Host plants
    x Fungi—Host plants
Fungi, Poisonous
    See Fungi, Pathogenic
Fungi, Predatory
  x Predatory fungi
  xx Fungi in agriculture
Fungi, Thermophilic
    See Thermophilic fungi
Fungi, Wood-decaying
    See Wood-decaying fungi
Fungi, Wood-staining
    See Wood-staining fungi

Fungi as feed
Fungi in agriculture *(Fungus diseases, SB733)*
   sa Anthracnose
      Farm produce—Storage—Diseases and
         injuries
      Farm produce—Transportation—
         Diseases and injuries
      Fungi, Phytopathogenic
      Fungi, Predatory
      Fungicides
      Plant diseases
      Wood-staining fungi
   xx Agricultural microbiology
      Agricultural pests
      Fruit-culture
      Fungi—Economic aspects
      Gardening
      Plant diseases
Fungibles *(Direct)*
   x Res fungibiles
   xx Civil law
Fungicides *(SB951)*
   sa Bordeaux mixture
      Mycostatin
      Seeds—Disinfection
      Systemic fungicides
   x Germicides
   xx Agricultural chemicals
      Fungi in agriculture
      Pesticides
      Seeds—Disinfection
      Trees—Diseases and pests
      Wood preservatives
   — Law and legislation
      See Pesticides—Law and legislation
   — Physiological effect
   — Testing
   — Toxicology
Fungous diseases
   See Medical mycology
Fungous diseases in animals
   See Veterinary mycology
Fungous diseases of plants
   See Fungi, Phytopathogenic
Fungous ear diseases
   See Ear—Fungi
Fungous eye diseases
   See Eye—Fungi
Fungous lung diseases
   See Lungs—Fungi
Fungs *(DT132)*
   xx Ethnology—Sudan
Fungus ants
   x Fungus-growing ants
      Gardening ants
   xx Ants
Fungus-growing ants
   See Fungus ants
Funicular railroads
   See Railroads, Cable
Funnel-beaker culture *(Indirect)*
      (GN776.2-5.F8)
   x TRB culture
   xx Neolithic period
Funnels (Naval architecture)
   See Stacks (Naval architecture)
Funnies
   See Comic books, strips, etc.
Fur *(Anatomy, QL942; Technology,*
      TS1060-1067)
   sa Artificial fur
      Fur garments
      Hatter's fur
      Hides and skins
      Molting
      Rabbit fur
   xx Body covering (Anatomy)
      Hides and skins

— Dressing and dyeing *(TS1061)*
   x Dyes and dyeing—Fur
      Fur dressing
      Fur dyeing
— Grading
— Laboratory manuals *(TS1061)*
— Prices *(Direct)*
— Standards *(Direct)*
— Storage
   x Fur storage
   xx Fur trade
— Taxation *(Direct)*
   xx Luxuries—Taxation
Fur, Artificial
   See Artificial fur
Fur-bearing animals *(Indirect)* *(Animal*
      culture, SF403-5; Trapping, SK283)
   sa Fur farming
      Fur trade
      names of fur-bearing animals, e.g.
         Arctic fox, Beavers, Seals (Animals)
   xx Mammals
      Trapping
      Zoology
      Zoology, Economic
   — Diseases
   — Feeding and feeds *(SF403)*
Fur coats
   See Fur garments
Fur dressing
   See Fur—Dressing and dyeing
Fur dyeing
   See Fur—Dressing and dyeing
Fur farming *(Indirect)* *(SF402-5)*
   sa Mink farming
   xx Animal culture
      Animal industry
      Fur-bearing animals
Fur garments *(TT525)*
   x Clothing, Fur
      Fur coats
      Furriery
      Furs (Clothing)
   xx Clothing and dress
      Fur
      Fur trade
   — Standards
Fur garments in art *(N8217.F8)*
   xx Art
Fur language
Fur money *(Direct)*
   xx Money, Primitive
Fur seal, Northern
   See Northern fur seal
Fur-seal arbitration
   See Bering Sea controversy
Fur seals, Southern
   See Southern fur seals
Fur storage
   See Fur—Storage
Fur trade *(Direct)* *(HD9944)*
   sa Bering Sea controversy
      Fur garments
      Fur—Storage
      Fur works
      names of fur-bearing animals
   x Furriers
   xx Fur-bearing animals
      Trapping
   — Accounting
   — Costs
   — Examinations
   — Juvenile literature
   — Law and legislation *(Direct)*
   — Licenses *(Direct)*
Fur workers *(Direct)*
   sa Wages—Fur workers
   x Furriers

   xx Fur trade
Furan resins *(TP1180.F8)*
   xx Gums and resins, Synthetic
Furiants
      Here are entered collections of furiant
      music for various mediums. Individual
      furiants and collections of furiants for
      a specific medium are entered under
      the heading followed by specification
      of medium.
Furiants (Piano)
   xx Piano music
Furies *(BL820.F8)*
   xx Mythology
      Mythology, Classical
Furlans
   See Friulians
Furnace atmospheres
   See Metallurgical furnaces—Protective
      atmospheres
Furnaces
   sa Electric furnaces
      Fluidized-bed furnaces
      Fly ash
      Glass furnaces
      Image furnaces
      Kilns
      Metallurgical furnaces
      Roller hearth furnaces
      Solar furnaces
      Tube-still heaters
   x Grates
      Steam-boilers—Furnaces
   xx Heating
      Kilns
      Smoke prevention
      Steam-boilers
   — Automatic control
   — Automation
   — Catalogs *(TH7623-4)*
   — Design and construction
   — Fuel consumption
   — Fuel systems *(TJ324.5)*
   — Grates *(Steam-boilers, TJ322-4)*
   — Maintenance and repair
   — Patents
   — Prices *(Direct)*
   — Safety measures
   — Tables, calculations, etc.
Furnaces, Fluidized-bed
   See Fluidized-bed furnaces
Furniture *(Direct)* *(Art, NK2200-2740;*
      Manners and customs, GT450;
      Technology, TS880-887)
   sa Bars (Furniture)
      Bedroom furniture
      Built-in furniture
      Chairs
      Chests
      Children's furniture
      Church furniture
      Cupboards
      Desks
      Dining room furniture
      Dormitories—Furniture, equipment, etc.
      Garden ornaments and furniture
      High schools—Furniture, equipment,
         etc.
      Hospitals—Furniture, equipment, etc.
      Implements, utensils, etc.
      Interior decoration
      Junior high schools—Furniture,
         equipment, etc.
      Library fittings and supplies
      Living room furniture
      Metal furniture
      Miniature furniture
      Mirrors

Office furniture
Plastic furniture
Polishes
Printers' furniture
Public buildings—Furniture, equipment, etc.
Schools—Furniture, equipment, etc.
Stands (Furniture)
Store fixtures
Tables
Unit furniture
Upholstery
Veneers and veneering
Wood-carving
Workbenches
  xx Art, Decorative
Arts and crafts movement
Decoration and ornament
Home economics
House furnishings
Interior decoration
Upholstery
— Building
  See Furniture making
— Catalogs *(NK2265; TS887)*
— Collectors and collecting *(NK2240)*
  Example under reference from Antiques
— Design
  See Furniture design
— Drawing
  See Furniture—Drawings
— Drawings
  x Furniture—Drawing
  xx Furniture design
Mechanical drawing
— Expertising
— Finishing
  See Furniture finishing
— Juvenile literature
— Materials *(TS885)*
— Models
  See Doll furniture
Miniature furniture
— Packing
— Prices
— Private collections *(NK2220)*
— Refinishing
  See Furniture finishing
— Repairing *(TT199)*
  sa Furniture finishing
  xx Furniture finishing
Furniture making
— Specifications
— Standards *(Direct)*
— Testing
Furniture, Amana *(Direct)*
  x Amana furniture
Furniture, Baroque *(Direct)* *(NK2365)*
  x Baroque furniture
  xx Decoration and ornament, Baroque
Furniture, Built-in
  See Built-in furniture
Furniture, Children's
  See Children's furniture
Furniture, Dutch, ⌜English, Flemish, etc.⌝ *(Direct)*
  x Dutch ⌜English, Flemish, etc.⌝ furniture
— Juvenile literature
Furniture, Georgian *(Direct)*
  x Georgian furniture
Furniture, Regency *(Direct)*
  x Regency furniture
Furniture, Renaissance *(Direct)*
  x Renaissance furniture
Furniture, Rococo *(Direct)*
  x Rococo furniture
  xx Decoration and ornament, Rococo

Furniture, Shaker *(Direct)*
  x Shaker furniture
  xx Art industries and trade, Shaker
Furniture building
  See Furniture making
Furniture design *(TT196)*
  sa Chair design
Furniture—Drawings
  x Furniture—Design
  xx Design
Furniture finishing *(Wood industries, TS885; Woodworking crafts, TT199.4)*
  sa Furniture painting
Furniture—Repairing
  x Finishing, Furniture
Furniture—Finishing
Furniture refinishing
Furniture—Refinishing
Refinishing, Furniture
  xx Furniture making
Furniture—Repairing
Wood finishing
Furniture industry and trade *(Direct)* *(HD9773; TS840-887)*
  sa Furniture workers
  Example under Wood-using industries; Woodworking industries
— Accounting *(HF5686.F8)*
— Automation
— Capital productivity
  xx Capital productivity
— Collective labor agreements
  See Collective labor agreements— Furniture industry
— Equipment and supplies
— Finance
— Information services *(Direct)*
— Labor productivity
— Management
— Production standards
— Quality control
— Vocational guidance
Furniture making *(Wood industries, TS880-887; Woodworking crafts, TT194-9)*
  sa Cabinet-work
Furniture finishing
Furniture—Repairing
Upholstery
  x Furniture building
Furniture—Building
  xx Cabinet-work
Joinery
Woodwork
— Amateurs' manuals *(TT195)*
— Juvenile literature
Furniture painting
  xx Furniture finishing
Painting, Industrial
Furniture refinishing
  See Furniture finishing
Furniture workers *(Direct)*
  sa Cabinet-workers
Chair-makers
Trade-unions—Furniture workers
Wages—Furniture workers
  xx Cabinet-workers
Furniture industry and trade
Woodworkers
Furriers
  See Fur trade
Fur workers
Furriery
  See Fur garments
Furs (Clothing)
  See Fur garments
Fürstenberg porcelain *(NK4399.F87)*
  x Porcelain, Fürstenberg

  xx Porcelain, German
Furtum usus
  See Unauthorized use
Furuncle
  x Boil
Furunculosis
  Example under Salmon—Diseases and pests; Trout—Diseases and pests
Furuseto pottery
  See Seto pottery
Fury (Jet fighter planes)
  See Sabre (Jet fighter planes)
Fusain
Fusain (Art)
  See Charcoal-drawing
Fusarium nivale
  See Snow mold
Fusarium wilt of tomatoes
  See Tomato wilt
Fused quartz fibers
  See Quartz fibers
Fused salts
  - *x* Molten salts
Salts, Fused
  xx Salts
— Tables, etc.
Fused silica fibers
  See Quartz fibers
Fusel-oil *(Alcohol, TP593)*
Fuselage (Aeroplanes)
  See Aeroplanes—Fuselage
Fuses, Electric
  See Electric fuses
Fuses (Ordnance)
  x Fuzes (Ordnance)
  xx Electric fuses
Projectiles
Fusible plugs
  xx Steam-boilers
Fusiform rust of pines
  See Pine fusiform rust
Fusion *(QC303)*
Fusion, Latent heat of *(QC303)*
  x Latent heat of fusion
  xx Heat
Fusion, Nuclear
  See Nuclear fusion
Fusion (Vision)
  See Flicker fusion
Fusion of corporations
  See Consolidation and merger of corporations
Fusion piercing drilling *(TN279)*
  xx Boring
Rock-drills
Fusion reactions, Controlled
  See Controlled fusion
Fusion reactors *(TK9204)*
  x Controlled fusion reactors
Controlled thermonuclear reactors
Thermonuclear reactors, Controlled
  xx Atomic power
Controlled fusion
Nuclear reactors
Füssen, Treaty of, 1745 *(DD407.F8)*
  xx Austrian Succession, War of, 1740-1748
Futa cattle
  See N'Dama cattle
Futa Toro
  See Toucouleurs
Futankobe
  See Toucouleurs
Futility
  See Frustration
Futuh
  See Islamic Empire
Futuna language *(PL6435)*
  sa Polynesian languages

Futuna language *(PL6435)* *(Continued)*
    xx Polynesian languages
Future contingents (Logic)
    x Contingentia futura (Logic)
    Contingents, Future (Logic)
    xx Logic
    Many-valued logic
Future estates
    See Future interests
Future interests *(Direct)*
    sa Executory interests
    Expectancies (Law)
    Perpetuities
    Remainders (Estates)
    Reversion
    x Future estates
    xx Estates (Law)
    Expectancies (Law)
    Property
Future life *(Comparative religion, BL535-547; Theology, BT899-904)*
    sa Children—Death and future state
    Eternity
    Future punishment
    Immortality
    Intermediate state
    Rebirth in Western Paradise (Buddhism)
    Resurrection
    Soul
    Spiritualism
    Translation to heaven
    x Eternal life
    Hades
    Life after death
    Life, Future
    Retribution
    xx Death
    Elysium
    Eschatology
    Eternity
    Future punishment
    Heaven
    Immortality
    Intermediate state
    Purgatory
    Resurrection
    Soul
    Note under Eternity
    — Biblical teaching
    — Early works to 1800
    — History of doctrines
    — Meditations
    — Quotations, maxims, etc.
Future life (Assyro-Babylonian religion)
Future life (Buddhism)
    xx Eschatology, Buddhist
Future life (Celtic religion)
Future life (Egyptian religion)
Future life (Finno-Ugrian religion)
Future life (Greco-Roman religion)
Future life (Hinduism) *(BL1215.F8)*
    xx Eschatology, Hindu
Future life (Islam) *(BP166.8)*
    xx Eschatology, Islamic
    — Koranic teaching *(BP134.F8)*
Future life (Norse religion)
Future life (Sumerian religion)
Future life (Zoroastrianism)
Future probation
    See Probation after death
Future punishment *(BT834-8)*
    sa Annihilationism
    Future life
    Hell
    Probation after death
    Purgatory
    Restorationism

Universalism
    x Endless punishment
    Eternal punishment
    Everlasting punishment
    Retribution
    xx Annihilationism
    Death
    Eschatology
    Future life
    Hell
    Punishment
    Purgatory
    Universalism
    — Controversial literature
    — Early works to 1800
    — History of doctrines
Future punishment (Islam) *(BP166.88)*
    xx Eschatology, Islamic
Future time perspective
    See Time perspective
Futures
    See Commodity exchanges
    Hedging (Finance)
    Short selling
    Speculation
Futures exchange
    See Forward exchange
Futurism *(Literature, PN56.F8)*
    sa Constructivism (Russian literature)
Futurism (Art) *(Direct)* *(ND1265)*
    sa Action in art
    Kinetic sculpture
    Letter-pictures
    Post-impressionism (Art)
    xx Action in art
    Aesthetics
    Art
    Art, Modern—20th century
    Modernism (Art)
    Painting
    Post-impressionism (Art)
Futuwwa (Islamic order)
    xx Orders of knighthood and chivalry, Islamic
Futwas
    See Fatwās
Fuyuge
    See Mafulus
Fuyuge language *(PL6621.F8)*
Fuzes (Ordnance)
    See Fuses (Ordnance)
FW-190 (Fighter planes)
    See Focke-Wulf 190 (Fighter planes)
Fyen in literature
Fylfot
    See Swastika
Fyoti language
    See Congo language
G.I. loans
    See Veterans—Loans
G-structures *(QA649)*
    x Structures, G
    xx Geometry, Differential
Gã (African people) *(DT511)*
    xx Ethnology—Ghana
    — Religion
Gã language *(PL8191)*
    x Accra language
    Acra language
    Akra language
    Incran language
    xx Kwa languages
Gab (Artificial language) *(PM8360.G2)*
    xx Languages, Artificial
Gabbro *(Indirect)* *(QE461)*
Gabel
    See Salt—Taxation
    Salt—Taxation—France

Gables *(NA2920)*
    xx Architecture—Details
Gabrieleño Indians *(E99.G15)*
    x Kizh Indians
    Tobikhar Indians
    xx Indians of North America
    Shoshonean Indians
Gabrieleño language *(PM1201)*
    sa Shoshonean languages
    x Tobikhar language
    xx Shoshonean languages
Gabrielsonite *(Indirect)*
Gadabas *(D432.G)*
    xx Ethnology—India
Gadang language
    See Kattang language
Gadarene demoniac (Miracle)
    See Healing of the Gerasene demoniac (Miracle)
Gaddang (Philippine people)
    xx Ethnology—Philippine Islands
Gade (African tribe)
    xx Ethnology—Nigeria
Gadflies
    See Horseflies
Gadgets
    See Implements, utensils, etc.
Gadhang language
    See Kattang language
Gadi Lohars
    See Lohars
Gadiformes
    sa Codfish
    xx Osteichthyes
Gadolinite *(QE391.G)*
Gadolinium
    — Isotopes
    — — Spectra
Gadolinium earths *(QD181.G4)*
Gadsden Purchase *(F786)*
Gadsden treaty, 1853 *(F786)*
Gadsup language
    xx Papuan languages
Gaduliya Lohars
    See Lohars
Gaekwad dynasty
Gaelic ballads and songs *(PB1607; PB1633; PB1648)*
Gaelic folk-lore
    See Folk-lore, Gaelic
Gaelic imprints *(Direct)*
Gaelic language *(PB1501-1599)*
    sa Celtic languages
    Irish language
    Manx language
    x Erse
    xx Celtic languages
    Goidelic languages
    Irish language
Gaelic language (Irish)
    See Irish language
Gaelic literature *(PB1605-1709)*
    sa Celtic literature
    Irish literature
    xx Celtic literature
    Irish literature
    Note under Scottish literature
Gaelic philology
Gaelic poetry *(PB1605-7; PB1631-4; PB1648)*
    Note under Scottish poetry
Gaels
    See Celts
Gaeta, Italy
    — Siege, 1860-1861 *(DG554.5.G2)*
    xx Italy—History—1849-1870
Gafat language *(PJ9285)*
Gaff-topsails (Fishes) *(QL638.A75)*
    xx Catfishes

Gag (Fish)
  xx Sea-bass
Gag (Surgical instrument)
  x Mouth gag
  xx Mouth—Surgery
Gag rule
  See Legislative bodies—Freedom of debate
    subdivision Freedom of debate under
    names of specific legislative bodies,
    e.g. United States. Congress—
    Freedom of debate
Gagaku
  sa Bagaku
Gagauz
  See Gagauzi
Gagauzi
  x Gagauz
  xx Ethnology—Balkan Peninsula
    Oghuz
    Turks
Gagauzi language (PL316)
  xx Turko-Tataric languages
Gage blocks (TJ1166)
  xx Gages
    Measuring instruments
Gages (TJ1166)
  sa Depth gage
    Dial indicator
    Drain-gages
    Electric gages
    Gage blocks
    Indexing (Machine-shop practice)
    Level indicators
    Miter-gages
    Pneumatic gages
    Pressure-gages
    Radioactive gages
    Rain gauges
    Screw-thread gages
    Strain gages
    Surface gages
    Thickness measurement
    Vacuum-gages
  x Gauges
  xx Measuring instruments
    Thickness measurement
    Weights and measures
  — Design and construction
  — Standards (Direct)
Gages (Railroads)
  See Railroads—Gages
Gaging (TP609)
  sa Liquors—Gaging and testing
    Wine and wine making—Gaging and
      testing
  x Gauging
  xx Liquors—Gaging and testing
    Mensuration
  — Tables and ready-reckoners
      (HF5716.L4)
Gagliarde
  See Galliards
Gahuku language
  xx Papuan languages
Gaidamaks
  See Haidamaks
Gaigle (Game) (GV1299.G2)
Gaillardes
  See Galliards
Gainesville, Ga.
  — Tornado, 1936
Gairfowl
  See Great auk
Gaita (ML980)
  x Spanish bagpipe
  xx Bagpipe
Gajo language
  See Gayo language

Gala language
  See Bangala language
Galactic evolution
  See Galaxies—Evolution
Galactic orbits of stars
  See Stars—Orbits
Galactin
  x Lactogenic hormone
    Luteotropic hormone
  xx Pituitary hormones
Galactorrhea
  See Lactation disorders
Galactose (QD321)
  sa Galactose metabolism
  xx Glycosides
Galactose metabolism
  sa Galactosemia
  xx Galactose
    Metabolism
Galactosemia
  xx Galactose metabolism
    Metabolism, Disorders of
Galant automobile
  See Colt Galant automobile
Galapagos albatross (QL696.P63)
Galapagos tortoise (QL666.C584)
Galatians
  sa Celts
    Gauls
  xx Celts
    Gauls
Galatians in art
Galawa language
  See Alawa language
Galaxies
  sa Magellanic Clouds
    Milky Way
    Radio sources (Astronomy)
  x Extragalactic nebulae
    Nebulae, Extragalactic
  xx Nebulae
    Stars
  — Catalogs
  — Evolution
    x Evolution, Galactic
      Galactic evolution
    xx Astronomy
  — Motion in the line of sight (QB857)
    x Galaxies—Radial velocity
  — Problems exercises, etc.
  — Radial velocity
    See Galaxies—Motion in the line of
      sight
Galaxy (Milky Way)
  See Milky Way
Galela language
  See Galelarese language
Galelarese language (PL5323)
  sa Malayan languages
  x Galela language
  xx Malayan languages
Gales
  See Storms
    Winds
Galga
  See Ingush
Galgadung language
  See Kalkatungu language
Galibi Indians (F2460)
  xx Carib Indians
    Indians of South America
Galibi language (PM5976)
  xx Cariban languages
    Indians of South America—Languages
Galicia in literature
Galician dialect
  See Gallegan dialect

Galicians (Spanish)
  See Gallegans
Galilee in literature
Galin-Paris-Chevé method (Music) (MT20)
  xx Music—Instruction and study
    Musical notation
    Sight-reading (Music)
    Sight-singing
    Singing—Methods
Gall
  See Bile
Gall-bladder (Comparative anatomy, QL867;
    Human anatomy, QM351;
    Physiology, QP197)
  sa Bile
  xx Liver
  — Calculi
    See Calculi, Biliary
  — Diseases (RC849-853)
    sa Cholecystitis
      Gall-bladder—Radiography
  — Radiography (RC849)
    xx Gall-bladder—Diseases
  — Surgery
  — — Complications and sequelae
Gall-ducts
  See Bile-ducts
Gall-flies (QL568.C9)
  sa Galls (Botany)
    Violet gall-fly
  x Cynipidae
    Gall wasps
  xx Galls (Botany)
    Hymenoptera
    Wasps
  — Juvenile literature
Gall-gnats (QL537.C4)
  sa Rye gall-gnat
    Saddle gall midge
  x Gall midges
  xx Galls (Botany)
  — Juvenile literature
Gall midges
  See Gall-gnats
Gall sickness
  See Anaplasmosis
Gall-stones
  See Calculi, Biliary
Gall wasps
  See Gall-flies
Galla language (PJ2471-9)
  sa Boran dialect
  x Ilmorna language
  xx Cushitic languages
Gallanty-shows
  See Shadow pantomimes and plays
Gallas (DT390.G2)
  sa Boran (African people)
  x Oromons
Gallegan ballads and songs (Collections,
    PQ9464-5; History, PQ9460)
Gallegan dialect (PC5411-5414)
  x Galician dialect
  Example under reference from Dialects
Gallegan fiction (Direct)
Gallegan literature (Collections, PQ9463-8;
    History, PQ9450-9462)
  x Spanish literature—Galicia
Gallegan philology
Gallegan poetry (PQ9460; PQ9464)
Gallegan wit and humor (Direct)
Gallegans (DP302.G11-12; Cuba, F1789.G3)
  x Galicians (Spanish)
    Gallegos
Gallegos
  See Gallegans
Gallein (QD441)
  xx Coal-tar colors

Galleries (Architecture) *(Direct)*
Galleries (Art)
    See Art—Galleries and museums
Galleys *(VM15-17)*
    xx Prisons
        Ships
    — Juvenile literature
Galleys (Ship kitchens)
    x Ship kitchens
        Ships' kitchens
    xx Kitchens
Galliambic *(PA188.G; PA416.G; PA2337.G)*
    Example under Versification
Galliards
        Here are entered collections of galliard music for various mediums. Individual galliards and collections of galliards for a specific medium are entered under the heading followed by specification of medium.
    x Gagliarde
        Gaillardes
Galliards (Guitar) *(M125-9)*
    xx Guitar music
Gallic acid *(Chemistry, QD341.A2; Therapeutics, RM666.G)*
Gallic language
    See Gaulish language
Gallicanism
    sa Conciliar theory
        Josephinism
        Pragmatic sanction of Charles VII, 1438
    xx Church and state in France
        Councils and synods
        Papacy
Gallicisms *(PB307)*
    sa subdivision Gallicisms *under names of languages, e.g.* English language—Gallicisms
    xx French language—Terms and phrases
        French language—Vocabulary
Galliformes *(Indirect) (QL696.G2)*
    sa Hoactzin
        Pheasants
        Turkeys
    x Gallinae
    — Anatomy
Gallinae
    See Galliformes
Gallipoli Campaign, 1915
    See European War, 1914-1918—Campaigns—Turkey and the Near East—Gallipoli
Gallium *(QD181.G2)*
    — Analysis
    — Electrometallurgy *(TN799.G3)*
    — Isotopes
        x Gallium isotopes
    — — Spectra
    — Metallurgy *(TN799.G3)*
    — Spectra
Gallium alloys
    sa Gallium-tin alloys
Gallium compounds
Gallium isotopes
    See Gallium—Isotopes
Gallium organic compounds
    See Organogallium compounds
Gallium-tin alloys
    x Tin-gallium alloys
    xx Gallium alloys
        Tin alloys
Gallo-Italian dialects *(PC1851-1874)*
    x Dialects
Gallo-Roman architecture
    See Architecture, Gallo-Roman

Gallo-Roman jewelry
    See Jewelry, Gallo-Roman
Gallo-Roman sculpture
    See Sculpture, Gallo-Roman
Gallo-roman terra-cottas
    See Terra-cottas, Gallo-roman
Gallóglaigh
    See Galloglasses
Galloglasses *(Ireland, DA933-7)*
    x Gallóglaigh
        Gallowglasses
    xx Mercenary troops
Gallongs
    x Galongs
    xx Abors
        Ethnology—India—North East Frontier Agency
Galloway cattle *(SF193.G2, SF199.G)*
    sa Belted Galloway
Gallowglasses
    See Galloglasses
Gallows *(Direct)*
    xx Hanging
        Law—Antiquities
Galls (Botany) *(SB767)*
    sa Gall-flies
        Gall-gnats
        Insects, Injurious and beneficial
    x Cecidology
        Insect galls
    xx Gall-flies
        Insects, Injurious and beneficial
        Tumors, Plant
    — Juvenile literature
Galois theory *(Equations, QA211, QA214; Groups, QA171)*
    sa Modular fields
    xx Equations, Theory of
        Groups, Theory of
        Numbers, Theory of
Galongs
    See Gallongs
Galops
        Here are entered collections of galop music for various mediums. Individual galops and collections of galops for a specific medium are entered under the heading followed by specification of medium.
Galops (Band) *(M1248; M1264)*
    xx Band music
Galops (Chamber orchestra) *(M1048; M1060)*
    xx Chamber-orchestra music
Galops (Chorus with piano)
    xx Choruses, Secular, with piano
Galops (Orchestra) *(M1048; M1060)*
    xx Orchestral music
Galops (Piano) *(M31; M32.8)*
    xx Piano music
Galops (Piano, 4 hands)
    xx Piano music (4 hands)
Galops (Piano, 8 hands) *(M213)*
Galoubet *(ML935-7)*
    x Txistu
    xx Flageolet
        Flute
        Recorder (Musical instrument)
Galoubet and tambourin music *(M298)*
    x Tambourin and galoubet music
Galoubet music (Galoubets (2)) *(M288-9)*
Galuth
    See Jews—Diaspora
Galvanic batteries
    See Electric batteries
Galvanic corrosion
    See Electrolytic corrosion

Galvanic skin response
    x Electrodermal response
        Psychogalvanic reflex
        Skin conductance response
        Skin potential response
        Skin response, Galvanic
    xx Electrophysiology
        Reflexes
        Skin
Galvanism
    See Electricity
Galvanized iron
    See Iron, Galvanized
Galvanized steel
    See Steel, Galvanized
Galvanizing *(TS660)*
    sa Iron, Galvanized
        Metals—Pickling
        Steel, Galvanized
        Tin plate
        Zinc coating
        Zinc plating
    xx Plating
        Zinc coating
    — Safety measures
Galvanomagnetic effects
    sa Hall effect
        Magnetoresistance
    xx Electric currents
        Magnetic fields
        Thermomagnetism
        Transport theory
Galvanometer *(QC544.G2)*
    sa Electric measurements
        Fluxmeter
    xx Electric apparatus and appliances
        Electric measurements
Galvanoplastic process
    See Electrotyping
Galvanoplasty
    See Electrometallurgy
        Electroplating
        Electrotyping
Galvanosurgery
    See Electrosurgery
Galvanotropism
    x Electropism
    xx Plants, Effect of electricity on
Galveston
    — Storm, 1900 *(F394.G2)*
        Example under Disasters; Storms
    — — Juvenile literature
Galveston, Battle of, Jan. 1, 1863
Gamant language
    See Kemant language
Gambai dialect *(PL8197)*
    x Kabba Laka dialect
        Ngambai dialect
        Sara Gambai dialect
    xx Sara languages
Gambel quail
    See Gambel's quail
Gambel's quail
    x Gambel quail
    xx Quails
    — Legends and stories
Gambía Indians
    See Moguex Indians
Gambiano Indians
    See Moguex Indians
Gambling *(Direct) (HV6708-6722; Card-playing, Ethics of, GV1245)*
    sa Blackjack (Game)
        Book-making (Betting)
        Boule (Game)
        Cards
        Cardsharping
        Dice

Faro
Horse race betting
Lotteries
Pari-mutuel betting
Probabilities
Raffles
Roulette
Slot machines
Speculation
Trente-et-quarante
Wagers
  x Betting
Games of chance
Gaming
  xx Contracts, Aleatory
Crimes without victims
Criminal law
Ethics
Organized crime
Wagers
— Accounting
— Personal narratives
— Taxation *(Direct)*
  sa Horse-racing—Taxation
Gambling problem (Mathematics)
  See Games of chance (Mathematics)
Gambling systems *(GV1302)*
  x Betting systems
Systems, Gambling
  xx Chance
Probabilities
Statistics
Gambo hemp
  See Ambary hemp
Game and game-birds *(Indirect)* *(Hunting,*
    SK; Ornithology, QL696.G2)
  sa Animal introduction
Band-tailed pigeon
Big game animals
Cookery (Game)
Decoys (Hunting)
Dogs—Training
Falconry
Food, Wild
Fowling
Game bird culture
Game-laws
Game protection
Hunting
Shooting
Shooting preserves
Shore birds
Tinamiformes
Trapping
Water-birds
Waterfowl
Wildlife as food
  particular animals and birds, e.g. Deer,
    Grouse, Rabbits, Woodcock
  x Wild-fowl
  xx Animal introduction
Birds
Ducks
Food, Wild
Grouse
Hunting
Trapping
Zoology
— Age determination
— Diseases
  xx Birds—Diseases
— Feeding and feeds
  xx Animals, Food habits of
Game protection
— Juvenile literature
Game and game-birds, Dressing of
  x Dressing of game
  xx Hunting

Slaughtering and slaughter-houses
Game bird culture *(Indirect)* *(SF508)*
  sa Partridge culture
Pheasant culture
Quail culture
Shooting preserves
Upland game bird culture
Waterfowl culture
  xx Animal culture
Game and game-birds
Game bird management *(Indirect)*
  sa Upland game bird management
  xx Wildlife management
Game birds, Upland
  See Upland game birds
Game calling (Hunting)
  xx Animal sounds
Calls (for animals)
Hunting
Game keepers
  See Gamekeepers
Game-laws *(Direct)* *(SK355-579)*
  sa Birds, Protection of—Law and
    legislation
Poaching
  x Game protection—Law and legislation
Hunting law
Hunting—Law and legislation
  xx Game and game-birds
Game protection
Wildlife conservation—Law and
  legislation
— United States
— — States
Game management
  See Wildlife management
Game meat
  See Wildlife as food
Game-preserves *(Indirect)* *(SK357)*
  sa Shooting preserves
  xx Hunting
Game protection *(Indirect)* *(SK351-579)*
  sa Birds, Protection of
Game and game-birds—Feeding and
  feeds
Game-laws
Gamekeepers
  x Protection of game
  xx Birds, Protection of
Game and game-birds
Hunting
Wildlife conservation
— Juvenile literature
— Law and legislation
    See Game-laws
— Outlines, syllabi, etc.
— Personal narratives
Game reeves
  See Game wardens
Game rooms
  See Recreation rooms
Game theory *(QA269)*
  sa Decision-making
Differential games
Games of chance (Mathematics)
Games of strategy (Mathematics)
Statistical decision
  x Games, Theory of
Theory of games
  xx Mathematical models
Mathematics
— Terminology
Game wardens *(Indirect)*
  x Game reeves
  xx Police, Rural
Gamekeepers
  x Game keepers
  xx Game protection

— Correspondence, reminiscences, etc.
Gamelan *(ML1251)*
  sa Khjai Mendung (Gamelan)
  x Gamelang
  xx Orchestra
Percussion instruments
Gamelan music
Gamelang
  See Gamelan
Games *(Indirect)* *(GV1200-1511;*
    Ethnology, GN454-6; Folk-lore,
    GR480-485; Kindergarten, LB1177;
    Psychology, Educational, LB1137;
    Psychology of play, BF717; School
    management, LB3031)
  sa Amusements
Ball games
Bible games and puzzles
Board games
Cards
Children's parties
Dancing—Children's dances
Educational games
Family recreation
Games for travelers
Geographical recreations
Group games
Indoor games
Kindergarten
Olympic games
Pencil games
Pinball machines
Play
Play-party
Puzzles
Reading games
Schools—Exercises and recreations
Secular games
Singing games
Sports
Targets (Sports)
  specific games, e.g. Backgammon,
    Baseball, Billiards, Chess, Dominoes,
    Tennis, Whist
  x Children—Recreation
Pastimes
Recreations
  xx Amusements
Children's paraphernalia
Entertaining
Physical education and training
Play
Sports
— Terminology

GENERAL SUBDIVISIONS

— Anecdotes, facetiae, satire, etc.
— Early works to 1800 *(GV1227)*
— Juvenile literature
Games, Chinese, ₍Mexican, Oriental, etc.₎
Games, Differential
  See Differential games .
Games, Floral
  See Floral games
Games, Greek and Roman
  sa Secular games
  x Games, Roman
Roman games
Games, Olympic
  See Olympic games
Games, Primitive *(GN454-7)*
  sa Indians of Central America—Games
Indians of Mexico—Games
Indians of North America—Games
Indians of South America—Games
Games, Psychic
  See Psychic games

Games, Rhythmic
   See Games with music
Games, Roman
   See Games, Greek and Roman
Games, Secular
   See Secular games
Games, Theory of
   See Game theory
Games for travelers *(GV1206)*
   x Travelers, Games for
   xx Automobiles—Touring
     Games
     Travel
Games for two *(GV1202.T)*
Games in art
   xx Art
Games in literature
   See Play in literature
Games in religious education *(BV1536.3)*
   xx Bible games and puzzles
     Religious education
Games of chance
   See Gambling
Games of chance (Mathematics) *(QA273)*
   sa Monte Carlo method
   x Gambling problem (Mathematics)
   xx Chance
     Game theory
     Probabilities
Games of strategy (Mathematics) *(QA270)*
   sa Management games
   x Games with rational pay-off
     (Mathematics)
     Rational games (Mathematics)
     Strategy, Games of (Mathematics)
   xx Game theory
     Groups, Theory of
     Mathematical optimization
     Matrices
     Topology
Games with music *(M1993)*
   sa Musical card games
     Singing games
   x Action songs
     Games, Rhythmic
     Rhythmic games
   xx Children's songs
     Play-party
     Singing games
Games with rational pay-off (Mathematics)
   See Games of strategy (Mathematics)
Gametes
   sa Ovum
     Spermatozoa
   xx Embryology
     Reproduction
Gametogenesis
   sa Oogenesis
     Spermatogenesis
   xx Embryology
Gaming
   See Gambling
GAMMA (Electronic computer system)
   x Graphically Aided Mathematical
     Machine
   xx On-line data processing
Gamma decay
   x Decay, Gamma
   xx Gamma rays
     Radioisotopes—Decay
Gamma functions
   See Functions, Gamma
Gamma globulin
   sa Hypergammaglobulinemia
     Immunoglobulins
   xx Antigens and antibodies
     Globulin

Gamma globulin deficiency
   See Agammaglobulinemia
Gamma globulin metabolism
   xx Metabolism
Gamma ray spectrometer *(QC787.S6)*
   xx Spectrometer
   — Calibration
Gamma ray spectrometry
   x Spectrometry, Gamma ray
   xx Angular correlations (Nuclear physics)
     Gamma rays
     Nuclear spectroscopy
     Radiochemistry
     Spectrometer
     Spectrum analysis
   — Charts, diagrams, etc.
   — Computer programs
Gamma rays *(QC490)*
   sa Gamma decay
     Gamma ray spectrometry
   xx Electromagnetic waves
     Ionizing radiation
     Radiation
     X-rays
   — Charts, diagrams, etc.
   — Industrial applications
     sa Radiography, Industrial
   — Measurement
     xx Electromagnetic measurements
   — — Tables, etc.
   — Physiological effect
   — Polarization
     Example under Polarization (Nuclear
       physics)
   — Safety measures
   — Scattering
   — Therapeutic use
     xx Radiotherapy
Gamopetalae *(QK495.G)*
Gaṇagaura
   See Gangaur
Ganda
   See Baganda
Ganda fiction *(Direct)*
Ganda language *(PL8201)*
   x Lu-ganda
     Luganda language
   xx Bantu languages
Gang language
   See Acoli language
Ganga dynasty
   See Gangas
Gangas
   x Ganga dynasty
   xx India—History—1000-1526
     India—History—324 B.C.-1000 A.D.
Gangaur *(BL1213.G3)*
   x Gaṇagaura
   xx Moon (in religion, folk-lore, etc.)
Gangleron
   x Ganglerone
   xx Ganglionic blocking agents
Ganglerone
   See Gangleron
Ganglia, Autonomic
   sa Myenteric plexus
     Solar plexus
   x Autonomic ganglia
   xx Nervous system, Parasympathetic
     Nervous system, Sympathetic
   — Diseases
Ganglia, Basal
   See Basal ganglia
Ganglia, Spinal
   See Spinal ganglia
Ganglion, Gasserian
   See Gasserian ganglion

Ganglion semilunare
   See Gasserian ganglion
Ganglionic blocking agents
   sa Gangleron
     Parasympatholytic agents
     Sympatholytic agents
   xx Autonomic drugs
Ganglionic stimulating agents
   sa Parasympathomimetic agents
     Sympathomimetic agents
   xx Autonomic drugs
Gangrene *(Military surgery, RD153;*
     Pathology, RD628)
   sa Necrosis
   x Mortification (Pathology)
   xx Necrosis
Gangrene, Presenile
   See Thromboangitis obliterans
Gangs *(Direct)* *(HV6437-9; By country,*
     HV6774 -7220)
   sa Hoodlums
   x Crime syndicates
     Gangsters
   xx Boys—Societies and clubs
     Crime and criminals
     Girls—Societies and clubs
     Hoodlums
     Juvenile delinquency
     Social psychology
   — Biography
   — Public opinion
Gangster films
   xx Feature films
     Moving-pictures
   — History and criticism
   — Pictorial works
Gangsters
   See Gangs
     Hoodlums
Ganguela language *(PL8202)*
   x Ngangela language
   xx Bantu languages
Ganja
   See Bhang (Drug)
Gannets
   xx Pelecaniformes
     Steganopodes
   — Behavior
Gannets, Fossil
Ganoidei
   Example under Fishes
Gantrees
   See Gantries
Gantries *(TA660.F7)*
   x Gantrees
   xx Structural frames
Gantry cranes *(TJ1365)*
   xx Cranes, derricks, etc.
Gantt charts
   xx Graphic methods
     Scheduling (Management)
Ganzheit (Philosophy)
   See Whole and parts (Philosophy)
Ganzheit (Psychology)
   See Whole and parts (Psychology)
Gaols
   See Prisons
Gaonic literature
   See Geonic literature
Gap, Energy
   See Energy gap (Physics)
Garage doors
   xx Doors
     Garages
   — Radio control
     x Radio-controlled garage-door
       operators
     xx Mechanically-operated doors

Garages *(NA8348)*
> *sa* Automobile parking
>> Automobiles—Service stations
>> Garage doors
>> Parking garages
> — Design and construction *(TH4960)*
> — Equipment and supplies
> — Fires and fire prevention
> — Law and legislation *(Direct)*
> — Lighting
> — Safety measures

Garand rifle
> *xx* Rifles

Garaŝu Indians
> *See* Pauserna Indians

Garavance
> *See* Chick-pea

Garawi
> *See* Sudan grass

Garbage
> *See* Refuse and refuse disposal

Garbage as feed
> *x* Refuse as feed
> *xx* Refuse and refuse disposal

Garbage as fuel
> *See* Refuse as fuel

Garcinia mangostana
> *See* Mangosteen

Garden apartments *(Direct)*
> *xx* Apartment houses

Garden architecture
> *See* Architecture, Domestic
>> Landscape gardening

Garden borders
> *x* Borders (Gardening)
> *xx* Landscape architecture
>> Plants, Ornamental

Garden cities *(Indirect)* *(HD7526-7630; HT161-5)*
> *sa* Cities and towns—Planning
>> Housing
>> Labor and laboring classes—Dwellings
> *xx* Cities and towns
>> Cities and towns—Planning
>> Greenbelts
>> Housing
>> Labor and laboring classes—Dwellings
>> Welfare work in industry
>> Working-men's gardens
> *Note under* Cities and towns

Garden clubs
> *See* Gardening—Societies, etc.

Garden dormouse
> *x* Dormouse, Garden
> *xx* Dormice

Garden farming
> *See* Truck farming

Garden fertilizers *(S633)*
> *sa* Compost
> *x* Gardening—Fertilizers and manures
> *xx* Fertilizers and manures

Garden fixtures
> *See* Garden ornaments and furniture

Garden lighting *(SB476)*
> *x* Lighting, Garden
> *xx* Electric lighting
>> Garden ornaments and furniture
>> Landscape architecture
>> Lighting, Architectural and decorative

Garden orach
> *See* Orach

Garden ornaments and furniture *(SB473.5)*
> *sa* Garden lighting
>> Stone lanterns
>> Sun-dials
> *x* Garden fixtures
> *xx* Decoration and ornament
>> Furniture

Gardens
> Landscape architecture
> — Pictorial works

Garden paths
> *See* Garden walks

Garden pests *(Indirect)*
> *sa* Insects, Injurious and beneficial
>> Plant diseases
> *xx* Agricultural pests
>> Gardening
>> Insects, Injurious and beneficial
>> Plant diseases
> — Juvenile literature

Garden plants
> *See* Plants, Ornamental

Garden ponds
> *See* Water gardens

Garden pools
> *See* Water gardens

Garden rhubarb
> *See* Rhubarb

Garden shrubs
> *See* Ornamental shrubs

Garden State Parkway
> *Example under* Express Highways; *and under reference from* Parkways

Garden supplies
> *See* Gardening—Equipment and supplies

Garden therapy
> *See* Gardening—Therapeutic use

Garden tools
> *sa* Toolshed
> *xx* Agricultural implements
>> Gardening—Equipment and supplies

Garden trees
> *See* Ornamental trees

Garden vines
> *See* Ornamental climbing plants

Garden walks
> *x* Garden paths
>> Paths, Garden
>> Walks, Garden
> *xx* Gardens
>> Landscape architecture
>> Trails

Garden webworm

Gardeners
> *sa* Wages—Gardeners

Gardenia
> *x* Cape jasmine

Gardening *(Indirect)* *(SB451-466)*
> Here are entered works on the practical operations in the cultivation of fruits, vegetables, flowers and ornamental plants.
> *sa* Acclimatization (Plants)
>> Aquatic plants
>> Artificial light gardening
>> Balcony gardening
>> Bulbs
>> Children's gardens
>> Climbing plants
>> Cloche gardening
>> Cold-frames
>> Color in gardening
>> Container gardening
>> Corms
>> Electrohorticulture
>> Floriculture
>> Flower gardening
>> Forcing (Plants)
>> Forest nurseries
>> Fruit-culture
>> Fungi in agriculture
>> Garden pests
>> Gardens
>> Grafting
>> Greenhouse plants

>> Greenhouses
>> Grounds maintenance
>> Herb gardening
>> Horticulture
>> Horticulturists
>> Insects, Injurious and beneficial
>> Landscape gardening
>> Mulching
>> Nurseries (Horticulture)
>> Organic gardening
>> Patio gardening
>> Plant propagation
>> Plants, Ornamental
>> Plants, Potted
>> Pruning
>> Roof gardening
>> Seaside gardening
>> Topiary work
>> Truck farming
>> Vegetable gardening
>> Weeds
>> Window-gardening
>> Winter gardening
> *x* Bedding (Horticulture)
>> Planting
> *xx* Agriculture
>> Horticulture
>> Plants
>> Plants, Cultivated
> — Anecdotes, facetiae, satire, etc.
> — Caricatures and cartoons
> — Early works to 1800 *(SB92; SB97; SB99)*
> — Equipment and supplies *(SB133)*
>> *sa* Garden tools
>>> Spraying equipment
>> *x* Garden supplies
>> *xx* Agricultural implements
>>> Agricultural machinery
>>> Farm equipment
>>> Horticultural machinery
>>> Tools
> — Examinations, questions, etc.
> — Exhibitions
> — — Judging
> — Fertilizers and manures
>> *See* Garden fertilizers
> — Juvenile literature *(SB55; SB455-7)*
>> *sa* Children's gardens
>> *xx* Children's gardens
>> *Note under* Children's gardens
> — Pictorial works
> — Societies, etc.
>> *x* Garden clubs
>>> Horticulture—Societies, etc.
>> *xx* Horticultural societies
> — Therapeutic use
>> *x* Garden therapy
>>> Horticultural therapy
>> *xx* Occupational therapy

Gardening ants
> *See* Fungus ants

Gardening as a profession
> *See* Horticulture as a profession

Gardening in the shade
> *x* Gardens, Shade
>> Shade gardens
>> Shady gardens

Gardens *(Indirect)* *(SB451-466)*
> *sa* Botanical gardens
>> Children's gardens
>> Church gardens
>> Garden ornaments and furniture
>> Garden walks
>> Rock gardens
>> School gardens
>> Water gardens
>> Working-men's gardens

Gardens (Indirect) (SB451-466)
(Continued)
    x Formal gardens
    xx Gardening
    — Pictorial works (SB465-6)
    — Poetry (PN6110.G2)
    — Quotations, maxims, etc.
Gardens, Glass
    See Glass gardens
Gardens, Japanese, ⌜etc.⌝
    x Japanese ⌜etc.⌝ gardens
Gardens, Miniature (SB419)
    sa Bonkei
       Glass gardens
       Miniature plants
    x Dish gardening
       Miniature gardens
       Tray gardens
    xx House plants
       Miniature objects
       Miniature plants
Gardens, Shade
    See Gardening in the shade
Gardens (in religion, folk-lore, etc.)
    x Folk-lore of gardens
    xx Religion, Primitive
Gardens in art
    xx Art
Gardner machine-gun (Naval, VF410.G2-24)
    xx Machine-guns
Garefowl
    See Great auk
Garfishes
    See Garpikes
Garfowl
    See Great auk
Garhwali dialect
    xx Pahari languages
Garhwali poetry (Direct)
Garia (New Guinea tribe)
    xx Ethnology—New Guinea
Garif Indians
    See Black Carib Indians
Garigliano Valley, Battle of, 1944
    xx World War, 1939-1945—Campaigns—
       Italy
Garlands
    See Wreaths
Garlands of Rāgas (Paintings)
    See Rāgamālā painting
Garlic (Indirect)
    sa Cookery (Garlic)
    — Therapeutic use (RM666.G)
Garment cutting (TT500-678)
    sa Children's clothing—Pattern design
       Dressmaking—Pattern design
       Shirts, Men's—Pattern design
       Tailoring—Pattern design
    xx Clothing and dress
       Cutting
       Dressmaking—Pattern design
       Tailoring
       Underwear
Garment factories
    See Clothing factories
Garment workers
    See Clothing workers
Garments, Foundation
    See Foundation garments
Garments, Leather
    See Leather garments
Garnet (Indirect) (TN997.G3)
    sa Yttrium iron garnet
    Example under Silicate minerals
Garnishes in cookery
    See Cookery (Garnishes)
Garnishment
    See Attachment and garnishment

Garo language (PL4001.G2)
    sa Bodo languages
    x Garrow language
    xx Bodo languages
       Tibeto-Burman languages
Garos (DS485.A84-88; Ethnology,
       GN635.I4)
    sa Missions to Garos
Garpikes (QL638.5)
    x Garfishes
       Garpipes
       Gars
Garpipes
    See Garpikes
Garrets
    See Attics
Garrisons (Indirect) (U370-375)
Garrote (HV8696)
    xx Capital punishment
Garrow language
    See Garo language
Gars
    See Garpikes
Garter snakes (QL666.O6)
    sa Eastern ribbonsnake
       Western ribbonsnake
Gartok Expedition, 1904-1905 (DS785)
Gas (TP700; TP751-764)
    sa Acetylene
       Coal-tar products
       Distillation, Destructive
       Gas manufacture and works
       Gases
       Mineral oils
       Petroleum
       Scrubber (Chemical technology)
       Water-gas
    x Coal-gas
       Illuminating gas
       Producer gas
    xx Coal-tar products
       Distillation, Destructive
       Gases, Asphyxiating and poisonous
    — Analysis
       See Gases—Analysis
    — Electric ignition (TK7291)
       x Electric ignition of gas
       xx Electric apparatus and appliances
    — Heating and cooking (Gas-stoves,
       TH7453-7)
       xx Gas appliances
       Gas as fuel
    — Juvenile literature
    — Law and legislation (Direct)
       x Gas industry—Law and legislation
       Example under Power resources—Law
       and legislation
    — Odorizing (TP754)
       x Odorizing of gas
       xx Gas industry—Safety measures
       Odors
    — Pipe lines
       x Gas pipe lines
    — Research
       See Gas research
    — Storage
    — Testing (TP754)
    — Toxicology (RA1247.G2)
       sa Plants, Effect of gases on
    — War use
       See Gases, Asphyxiating and
       poisonous—War use
Gas, Bose-Einstein
    See Bose-Einstein gas
Gas, Bottled
    See Liquefied petroleum gas
Gas, Gastrointestinal
    See Gastrointestinal gas

Gas, Lattice
    See Lattice gas
Gas, Natural (Indirect) (Fuel, TP350; Gas
       lands, HD242.5; Mineral industries,
       TN880)
    sa Boring
       Condensate oil wells
       Gas industry
       Liquefied natural gas
       Liquefied petroleum gas
       Oil fields
    x Natural gas
    xx Gas industry
       Geology, Economic
       Wells
    — Analysis
    — Cleaning (TN880.5)
    — Companies
       See Gas companies
    — Costs
    — Dehydration
       See Gas, Natural—Drying
    — Drying
       x Gas, Natural—Dehydration
       xx Gases—Drying
    — Geology (Indirect)
       xx Petroleum—Geology
    — Hydrates
       xx Hydrates
    — Laboratory manuals
    — Law and legislation (Direct)
       sa Oil and gas leases
       x Oil and gas law
    —— Terms and phrases
    — Pipe line failures
       x Gas, Natural—Pipe lines—Failures
       Pipe line failures (Natural gas)
       xx Disasters
    — Pipe lines
       xx Gas, Natural—Transportation
    —— Automatic control
    —— Cathodic protection
    —— Communication systems
       xx Telecommunication
    —— Compressor stations
       xx Compressors
       Pumping stations
    ——— Appraisal
       See Gas, Natural—Pipe lines—
       Compressor stations—
       Valuation
    ——— Dust control
    ——— Electromechanical analogies
    ——— Valuation (TN880.5)
       x Gas, Natural—Pipe lines—
       Compressor stations—
       Appraisal
    —— Corrosion
    —— Design and construction (TN880.5)
    ——— Safety measures
    —— Failures
       See Gas, Natural—Pipe line failures
    —— Law and legislation (Direct)
    —— Maintenance and repair
    —— Mathematical models
    —— Quality control
    —— Safety measures
    —— Safety regulations (Direct)
    —— Taxation (Direct)
       xx Gas, Natural—Taxation
    —— Welding
    — Rates
    — Research
    — Storage
       sa Gas, Natural—Underground storage
    — Tables, calculations, etc.
    — Tables, etc.
    — Taxation (Direct)

sa Gas, Natural—Pipe lines—Taxation
— Thermal properties
— Transportation *(HD9580; TN880)*
  sa Gas, Natural—Pipe lines
— Underground storage *(Indirect)*
  x Underground storage of natural gas
  xx Gas, Natural—Storage
— — Mathematical models
— — Models
— — — Testing
— Well drilling
  See Gas well drilling
Gas, Poisonous
  See Gases, Asphyxiating and poisonous
Gas and oil engines *(TJ751-805)*
  sa Aeroplanes—Motors
    Air-ships—Motors
    Automobiles—Motors
      (Compressed-gas)
    Diesel motor
    Free piston engines
    Fuel pumps
    Gasoline locomotives
    Indicators for gas and oil engines
    Jet propulsion
    Junks—Motors
    Motor-boat engines
    Motor-boats—Gasoline engines
    Power (Mechanics)—Statistics
    Wankel engine
  x Gas engines
    Gasoline engines
    Gasoline motors
    Internal combustion engines
    Oil engines
    Petroleum engines
    Producer gas
  xx Engines
    Gas-producers
    Heat-engines
    Motors
— Appraisal
  See Gas and oil engines—Valuation
— Automatic control
— — Problems, exercises, etc. *(TJ789)*
— Bearings
— — Computer programs
— Carburetors
  See Carburetors
— Cold weather operation
— Combustion
  Example under Combustion
— Cooling *(TJ789)*
  sa Aeroplanes—Motors—Cooling
    Automobiles—Motors—Cooling
    Marine engines—Cooling
  Example under Cooling
— Corrosion
— Cylinders
— Defects
— Design
— Drawing
  See Gas and oil engines—Drawings
— Drawings
  x Gas and oil engines—Drawing
  xx Mechanical drawing
— Fuel systems
  sa Fuel pumps
  xx Fuel pumps
— Ignition *(TJ787)*
  sa Magneto
    Spark-plugs
  x Ignition devices
— Juvenile literature
— Lubrication
— Maintenance and repair
— Models
— Mufflers *(TJ789)*

  x Exhaust mufflers
    Mufflers (Gas and oil engines)
— Oil filters
— Patents *(TJ758)*
— Reliability
— Superchargers
  See Superchargers
— Terminology
— Testing
— — Equipment
  See Gas and oil engines—Testing
    equipment
— Testing equipment
  x Gas and oil engines—Testing—
    Equipment
— — Tariff
  See Tariff on gas and oil engine
    testing equipment
— Trade and manufacture *(Direct)*
— Valuation *(TJ759)*
  x Gas and oil engines—Appraisal
— Valve-gears
— Valves
  sa Aeroplanes—Motors—Valves
    Automobiles—Motors—Valves
  xx Valves
Gas and oil leases
  See Oil and gas leases
Gas apparatus and appliances
  See Gas appliances
    Gas manufacture and works—
      Apparatus
Gas appliance vent systems
  See Gas appliances—Vents
Gas appliances *(TP758)*
  sa Gas-burners
    Gas-fixtures
    Gas flow
    Gas—Heating and cooking
    Gas manufacture and works—
      Apparatus
    Gas-meters
    Gas ovens
    Gas toasters
    Stoves, Gas
  x Gas apparatus and appliances
    Gas equipment and appliances
  xx Gas industry
    Gas manufacture and works—
      Apparatus
— Flues
  See Gas appliances—Vents
— Maintenance and repair
— Vents *(TH6835)*
  x Gas appliance vent systems
    Gas appliances—Flues
    Gas vents
    Vents (Gas appliances)
  xx Flues
Gas as fuel *(TP345-350)*
  sa Acetylene as fuel
    Automobiles—Gas-producers
    Automobiles—Motors
      (Compressed-gas)
    Gas—Heating and cooking
    Liquefied petroleum gas
    Oil gas
    Tractors—Gas-producers
  xx Fuel
— Mathematical models
— Rates
  See Gas companies—Rates
— Safety measures
Gas bearings
  See Gas-lubricated bearings
Gas bladder
  See Air-bladder (in fishes)

Gas-burners *(TH7950)*
  sa Argand burner
    Bunsen burner
    Flame monitoring systems
  xx Gas appliances
Gas bursts
  sa Rock bursts
  x Bursts, Gas
    Outbursts, Gas
  xx Mine accidents
    Mine gases
    Rock bursts
Gas chromatography
  x Gas-liquid chromatography
    Vapor-phase chromatography
  xx Chromatographic analysis
— Apparatus and supplies
— Automation
— Industrial applications
  xx Chemistry, Technical
— Programmed instruction
— Tables, etc.
Gas cleaning
  See Gases—Cleaning
Gas companies *(Direct) (Advertising,*
    HF6161.G2; Finance, HG4029.G2;
    Securities, HG4841.G2)
  sa Gas manufacture and works
  x Gas, Natural—Companies
  xx Gas manufacture and works
    Public utilities
  Note under Gas industry
— Accounting *(HF5686.G3)*
— Government ownership *(Direct)*
— Job descriptions
— Rates
  x Gas as fuel—Rates
    Gas rates
Gas-condensate wells
  See Condensate oil wells
Gas condensers *(TP764)*
Gas cooled reactors
  x Reactors, Gas cooled
  xx Atomic power-plants
    Nuclear reactors
Gas cylinders
  x Compressed gas containers
  xx Containers
    Cylinders
    Pressure vessels
Gas-detectors *(HD7264)*
  xx Gas leakage
    Leak detectors
Gas distribution *(TP757)*
  sa Gas-governors
    Gas leakage
    Gas-pipes
    Gases, Compressed
  xx Gas-governors
    Gas-pipes
— Automation
— Cold weather conditions
— Electromechanical analogies
— Laboratory manuals
— Mathematical models
— Reliability
— Safety measures
— Safety regulations *(Direct)*
— Tables, calculations, etc. *(TP753)*
Gas dynamics
  sa Aerodynamics
    Gas flow
    Jets—Fluid dynamics
    Rarefied gas dynamics
    Relaxation (Gas dynamics)
    Thermomolecular pressure
  x Gasdynamics
  xx Fluid dynamics

Gas dynamics *(Continued)*
    Thermodynamics
   — Problems, exercises, etc.
   — Tables, etc.
Gas engineering
   xx Engineering
Gas engines
   See Gas and oil engines
Gas engines, Automotive
   See Automobiles—Motors
      (Compressed-gas)
Gas equipment and appliances
   See Gas appliances
      Gas manufacture and works—
        Apparatus
Gas-fitting *(TH7920-7930)*
   sa Gas-fixtures
      Pipe-fitting
      Plumbing
   xx Pipe-fitting
      Plumbing
   — Law and legislation   *(Direct)*
   — Vocational guidance
Gas-fixtures *(TH7960-7967)*
   sa Incandescent gas-lighting—Fixtures
   xx Gas appliances
      Gas-fitting
Gas flow
   sa Air flow
      Gas-lubricated bearings
      Gas-meters
      Schlieren photography
   x Flow of gas
      Gases, Flow of
   xx Aerodynamics
      Air flow
      Gas appliances
      Gas dynamics
   — Tables, etc.
Gas gangrene *(RC144.G3)*
   xx Clostridium diseases
Gas-governors *(TH7945)*
   sa Gas distribution
   x Gas-regulators
   xx Gas distribution
      Gas-meters
      Governors (Machinery)
Gas holders
   See Gasholders
Gas in war
   See Gases, Asphyxiating and poisonous—
      War use
Gas industry *(Direct)* *(TP751-764)*
   Here are entered general works on industries based on natural or manufactured
   gas. Works on municipal or other
   agencies which distribute to consumers are entered under the heading Gas
   companies. Technical treatises on the
   manufacture of gas are entered under
   the heading Gas manufacture and
   works.
   sa Coke industry
      Gas appliances
      Gas, Natural
      other headings beginning with the word
      Gas
   xx Coke industry
      Gas manufacture and works
      Gas, Natural
   — Abbreviations
   — Automation
   — Defense measures
      xx Factories—Protection
        War damage, Industrial
      Example under references from Defense
        measures; Industrial plant protec-
        tion

   — Employees   *(Direct)*
      sa Trade-unions—Gas industry
        employees
        Wages—Gas industry employees
   — Equipment and supplies
   — — Appraisal
      See Gas industry—Equipment and
        supplies—Valuation
   — — Valuation
      x Gas industry—Equipment and
        supplies—Appraisal
   — Fires and fire prevention
   — Labor productivity
   — Law and legislation
      See Gas—Law and legislation
   — Mathematical models
   — Safety measures   *(TP751.1)*
      sa Gas—Odorizing
   — Taxation   *(Direct)*
   — Vocational guidance
   — Water-supply
Gas lasers *(TA1695)*
   sa Helium-neon lasers
   xx Lasers
   — Amateurs' manuals
   — Laboratory manuals
   — Tables
Gas leakage
   sa Gas-detectors
   x Leakage, Gas
   xx Gas distribution
Gas leases
   See Oil and gas leases
Gas lenses *(QC165.3)*
   xx Gases
      Lenses
Gas-lift (Petroleum)
   See Oil wells—Gas lift
Gas-lighting *(TH7910-7970)*
   sa Acetylene
      Gas manufacture and works
      Incandescent gas-lighting
      Lighting
   xx Lighting
   — Rates
Gas-liquid chromatography
   See Gas chromatography
Gas-lubricated bearings *(TJ1073.5)*
   x Bearings, Gas-lubricated
      Gas bearings
   xx Fluid-film bearings
      Gas flow
Gas-machines *(TP764)*
   sa Gas manufacture and works—
      Apparatus
      Gas-producers
   xx Gas manufacture and works
Gas manufacture and works *(Direct)*
      (TP700-764; Public ownership,
      HD4486-4495)
   sa Coal gasification
      Coal gasification, Underground
      Gas companies
      Gas industry
      Gas-machines
      Gas power-plants
      Gas-producers
      Water-gas
   x Producer gas
   xx Gas
      Gas companies
      Gas-lighting
      Gas-producers
   Example under Chemistry, Technical
   Note under Gas industry
   — Accounting
   — Apparatus
      sa Gas appliances

      Gas-retorts
      Scrubber (Chemical technology)
   x Gas apparatus and appliances
      Gas equipment and appliances
   xx Gas appliances
      Gas-machines
   — By-products   *(TP755)*
      Example under By-products; Waste pro-
        ducts
   — Finance   *(HG4029.G2; Business*
      management, TP751.3)
   — Fires and fire prevention
   — Pilot plants
   — Tables, calculations, etc.
Gas masks   *(Labor hygiene, HD7275; Military*
      science, UG447; Mining, TN297)
   xx Air defenses
      Gases, Asphyxiating and poisonous—
        War use
      Respirators
   — Physiological effect
   — Standards   *(Direct)*
Gas-meters *(TH7940)*
   sa Gas-governors
   x Meters, Gas
   xx Flow meters
      Gas appliances
      Gas flow
Gas myelography
   See Pneumomyelography
Gas ovens
   x Ovens, Gas
   xx Gas appliances
      Stoves, Gas
Gas pipe lines
   See Gas—Pipe lines
Gas-pipes *(TP757)*
   sa Electrolytic corrosion
      Gas distribution
      Pipe flanges
   xx Gas distribution
      Pipe
   — Cleaning   *(TP751.1)*
      x Gas-pipes—Purging
        Purging of gas-pipes
   — Corrosion
      xx Electrolytic corrosion
   — Purging
      See Gas-pipes—Cleaning
   — Standards   *(Direct)*
   — Tables, calculations, etc.
   — Welding
Gas power-plants *(TJ768)*
   x Power-plants, Gas
   xx Gas manufacture and works
Gas-producers *(TP762)*
   sa Acetylene generators
      Automobiles—Gas-producers
      Coal gasification
      Gas and oil engines
      Gas manufacture and works
      Tractors—Gas-producers
   x Producer gas
   xx Gas-machines
      Gas manufacture and works
   — Maintenance and repair
Gas purification
   See Gases—Purification
Gas purifier
   See Scrubber (Chemical technology)
Gas ranges
   See Stoves, Gas
Gas rates
   See Gas companies—Rates
Gas-regulators
   See Gas-governors
Gas research *(Direct)*
   x Gas—Research

xx Chemistry, Technical—Research
   Fuel research
   Research, Industrial
Gas-retorts *(TP764)*
   xx Gas manufacture and works—
      Apparatus
Gas stations
   See Automobiles—Service stations
Gas stoves
   See Stoves, Gas
Gas toasters
   x Toasters, Gas
   xx Gas appliances
      Kitchen utensils
Gas tubes
   sa Diodes
      Ignitrons
      Thyratrons
   xx Electron tubes
   — Noise
Gas tubing *(TP757)*
Gas-turbine automobiles
   See Automobiles, Gas-turbine
Gas-turbine cars
   See Automobiles, Gas-turbine
Gas-turbine disks *(TJ778)*
   x Gas-turbine wheels
      Gas-turbines—Disks
   xx Disks, Rotating
      Gas-turbines
Gas-turbine locomotives
   x Locomotives, Gas-turbine
   xx Gas-turbines
      Locomotives
   — Electric driving
Gas-turbine materials
   See Gas-turbines—Materials
Gas-turbine motor-cars
   xx Railroad motor-cars
   — Testing
Gas-turbine wheels
   See Gas-turbine disks
Gas-turbines *(TJ778)*
   sa Aeroplanes—Turbine-propeller engines
      Aeroplanes—Turbojet engines
      Aircraft gas-turbines
      Automotive gas turbines
      Free piston engines
      Gas-turbine disks
      Gas-turbine locomotives
      Marine gas-turbines
   xx Ducted fans
      Turbines
   — Automatic control *(TJ778)*
   — Blades
   — Combustion
   — Cooling
   — Corrosion
   — Design and construction
   — Disks
      See Gas-turbine disks
   — Drawing
      See Gas-turbines—Drawings
   — Drawings
      x Gas-turbines—Drawing
      xx Mechanical drawing
   — Dynamics *(TJ778)*
   — Erecting work *(TJ778)*
      xx Installation of industrial equipment
   — Incrustations
   — Lubrication
   — Maintenance and repair
   — Materials *(TJ778)*
      sa Metals at high temperatures
      x Gas-turbine materials
      xx Metals at high temperatures
   — Patents
   — Tables, calculations, etc.

   — Testing
   — Vibration *(TJ778)*
   — Welding
Gas-turbines, Aircraft
   See Aircraft gas-turbines
Gas vents
   See Gas appliances—Vents
Gas warfare
   See Gases, Asphyxiating and poisonous—
      War use
Gas welding
   See Oxyacetylene welding and cutting
Gas well drilling
   x Drilling, Gas well
      Gas, Natural—Well drilling
      Well drilling, Gas
   xx Boring
      Gas wells
   — Automation *(TN880.2)*
   — Costs
   — Safety measures
Gas wells *(TN880-883)*
   sa Gas well drilling
      Oil wells
   x Natural gas wells
   xx Oil wells
   — Maintenance and repair
   — Tables, calculations, etc. *(TN880.2)*
   — Testing
Gascon ballads and songs *(PC3428)*
   sa Folk-songs, Gascon
Gascon dialect *(PC3421-8)*
   sa Béarnais dialect
   xx Provençal language
   Example under reference from Dialects
Gascon literature *(PC3428)*
Gascon poetry *(PC3428)*
Gasdynamics
   See Gas dynamics
Gaseous discharge
   See Plasma (Ionized gases)
Gaseous environment (Space environment)
   See Artificial atmospheres (Space
      environment)
Gaseous plasma
   See Plasma (Ionized gases)
Gases *(Chemical technology, TP242-4;*
      Expansion, QC286; Manipulation,
      QD531; Mechanics, QC161-8;
      Specific heats, QC297; Vibrations in
      tubes, etc., QC241)
   sa Artificial atmospheres (Space
      environment)
      Automobile exhaust gas
      Balloon gases
      Bubbles
      Combustion gases
      Diesel motor exhaust gas
      Gas lenses
      Manostat
      Osmosis
      Plants, Gases in
      Pneumatics
      Protective atmospheres
      Virial coefficients
      specific gases, e.g. Acetylene, Argon,
         Helium, Hydrogen, Nitrogen,
         Oxygen
   xx Diffusion
      Fluids
      Gas
      Hydrostatics
      Matter—Properties
      Mechanics
      Physics
      Pneumatics
      Vapors
   — Absorption and adsorption *(QC182)*

      sa Accommodation coefficient
         Getters
      x Absorption of gases
         Adsorption of gases
         Sorption of gases
      xx Absorption
         Plate towers
   — — Mathematical models
   — Analysis *(QD121; Illuminating gas,*
         TP754)
      sa Eudiometer
      x Gas—Analysis
      Example under Chemistry, Analytic
   — Cleaning
      sa Scrubber (Chemical technology)
      x Gas cleaning
      xx Dust—Removal
   — Dehydration
      See Gases—Drying
   — Diffusion
      See Diffusion
   — Drying
      sa Gas, Natural—Drying
      x Gases—Dehydration
   — Expansion
      See Expansion of gases
   — Ionization
      See Ionization of gases
   — Juvenile literature
   — Liquefaction *(QD535)*
      sa Hydrogen
         Liquefied gases
         Liquefied natural gas
         Liquefied petroleum gas
         Liquid air
         Liquid fluorine
         Liquid helium
         Liquid hydrogen
         Liquid nitrogen
         Liquid oxygen
         Low temperature research
      x Liquefaction of gases
      xx Chemistry
         Chemistry, Physical and theoretical
         Heat
         Low temperature engineering
         Low temperature research
         Thermochemistry
   — — Equipment and supplies
   — Occlusion *(QC182)*
      x Occlusion of gases
   — Physiological effect *(Air pollution,*
         RA576; Toxicology, RA1245-7)
      sa Asphyxia
         Gases, Asphyxiating and poisonous
         Plants, Effect of gases on
   — Purification
      sa Air—Purification
      x Gas purification
   — — Adsorption
   — — Patents
   — Separation
      x Air—Separation
      xx Separation (Technology)
   — Spectra *(QC454)*
   — Tables, calculations, etc.
   — Therapeutic use *(RM666.G2)*
      sa Pneumoperitoneum, Artificial
      x Pneumatology (Medicine)
   — — Programmed instruction
   — Thermal properties
   — — Charts, diagrams, etc.
   — — Tables, etc.
   — Viscosity
      See Viscosity

Gases, Asphyxiating and poisonous *(Public health, RA577; Toxicology, RA1245-7)*
  sa Aerosol sniffing
  Asphyxia
  Carbon dioxide
  Carbon monoxide
  Fire-damp
  Fume control
  Gas
  Glue-sniffing
  Hydrogen sulphide
  Mine gases
  Mustard gas
  Tear gas
  x Asphyxiating gases
  Gases, Irrespirable, offensive, and poisonous
  Poison gas
  Poisonous gases
  xx Asphyxia
  Gases—Physiological effect
  Hazardous substances
  Medical jurisprudence
— Laws and legislation *(Direct)* *(RA1245)*
  sa Air conditioning—Safety regulations
  Refrigeration and refrigerating machinery—Safety regulations
  xx Nuisances
— Testing
— Toxicology *(RA1245)*
  x Inhalation toxicology
— War use *(UG447)*
  sa Chemical warfare
  Decontamination (from gases, chemicals, etc.)
  Gas masks
  Tear gas munitions
  x European War, 1914-1918—Gas warfare
  Gas in war
  Gas—War use
  Gas warfare
  Poison gas
  xx Air defenses
  Chemical warfare
  Military art and science
  War (International law)
Gases, Compressed *(TP761.C65)*
  sa Automobiles—Motors (Compressed-gas)
  Liquefied petroleum gas
  x Compressed gas
  xx Gas distribution
— Law and legislation *(Direct)*
— Safety measures
Gases, Electric discharges through
  See Electric discharges through gases
Gases, Expansion of
  See Expansion of gases
Gases, Flow of
  See Gas flow
Gases, Ionization of
  See Ionization of gases
Gases, Ionized
  sa Air, Ionized
  Ion flow dynamics
  Magneto-ionic theory
  Plasma (Ionized gases)
  Rockets (Aeronautics)—Ionization phenomena
  x Ionized gases
  xx Electromagnetism
  Gases, Kinetic theory of
  Ionization of gases
  Particles

Gases, Irrespirable, offensive, and poisonous
  See Gases, Asphyxiating and poisonous
Gases, Kinetic theory of *(QC175)*
  sa Gases, Ionized
  Joule-Thomson effect
  x Kinetic theory of gases
  xx Mathematical physics
  Matter, Kinetic theory of
  Molecular dynamics
  Molecular theory
  Statistical physics
— Programmed instruction
Gases, Liquefied
  See Liquefied gases
Gases, Noble
  See Gases, Rare
Gases, Photoionization of
  See Photoionization of gases
Gases, Poisonous
  See Gases, Asphyxiating and poisonous
Gases, Rare
  sa Argon
  Helium
  Krypton
  Neon
  Radon
  Rare gas compounds
  Xenon
  x Elements, Inert
  Gases, Noble
  Inert elements
  Noble gases
  Rare gases
  xx Nonmetals
— Optical properties
— Physiological effect
Gases at high temperatures
  sa High temperature plasmas
  xx High temperatures
Gases in manure
  See Manure gases
Gases in metals
  sa Aluminum alloys—Hydrogen content
  Degassing of metals
  Deoxidizing of metals
  Iron—Hydrogen content
  Metals—Hydrogen content
  Nonferrous metals—Hydrogen content
  Steel—Hydrogen content
  Steel—Nitrogen content
  Steel—Oxygen content
  Titanium—Hydrogen content
  x Metals, Gases in
  xx Metals—Analysis
Gases in mines
  See Mine gases
Gases in plants
  See Plants, Gases in
Gases in rocks *(QE511)*
  x Rocks, Gases in
  xx Geophysics
  Petrology
Gases in the blood
  See Blood, Gases in
Gasholders
  x Gas holders
  xx Tanks
— Design and construction
— Welding
Gasification of coal
  See Coal gasification
Gasification of coal, Underground
  See Coal gasification, Underground
Gaskets
  xx Machinery
  Packing (Mechanical engineering)
  Sealing (Technology)
  Washers (for bolts and screws)

Gasoline *(TP692.2)*
  sa Aeroplanes—Fuel systems—Vapor lock
  Automobiles—Fuel consumption
  Automobiles—Fuel systems—Vapor lock
  Inflammable liquids
  xx Catalytic reforming
  Cracking process
  Liquid fuels
  Example under Inflammable liquids; Petroleum products
— Anti-knock and anti-knock mixtures *(TP692.2)*
  sa Aeroplanes—Fuel
  x Anti-knock compounds
  High-octane gasoline
  Octane number
  xx Aeroplanes—Fuel
  Motor fuels—Anti-knock and anti-knock mixtures
— Labeling *(Direct)*
— Law and legislation *(Direct)*
— Pipe lines
  x Gasoline pipe lines
  xx Gasoline—Transportation
  Example under Pipe lines
— Prices *(Direct)*
  Example under Price maintenance
— Research
  See Gasoline research
— Storage
  x Gasoline storage
— Taxation *(Direct)* *(HD9579.G3-5)*
  Here are entered works on the taxation of gasoline in general. Works on the taxation of gasoline as a motor fuel are entered under the heading Motor fuels—Taxation.
  sa Motor fuels—Taxation
  x Gasoline tax
  xx Motor fuels—Taxation
— Transportation *(TP692.2)*
  sa Gasoline—Pipe lines
Gasoline automobiles
  See Automobiles
Gasoline consumption of automobiles
  See Automobiles—Fuel consumption
Gasoline engines
  See Gas and oil engines
Gasoline inspection
  See Oil inspection
Gasoline locomotives *(Mining, TN338)*
  xx Gas and oil engines
  Locomotives
  Mine haulage
Gasoline motors
  See Gas and oil engines
Gasoline pipe lines
  See Gasoline—Pipe lines
Gasoline research
  x Gasoline—Research
  xx Research
Gasoline stations
  See Automobiles—Service stations
Gasoline storage
  See Gasoline—Storage
Gasoline stoves
  See Stoves, Gasoline
Gasoline tax
  See Gasoline—Taxation
GASP (Computer program language)
  x General activity simulation program
  xx Digital computer simulation
  FORTRAN (Computer program language)
Gaspergou
  See Fresh-water drum

Gasserian ganglion
  x Ganglion, Gasserian
      Ganglion semilunare
  xx Trigeminal nerve
Gasteromycetes *(QK629.G2)*
  sa Puffballs
  xx Basidiomycetes
      Fungi
Gasteropoda *(Indirect)* *(QL430.4-5)*
      Here are entered systematic studies.
        Popular works on the shelled species of
        gasteropods are entered under Snails.
  sa Abalones
      Amphineura
      Archaeogastropoda
      Heteropoda
      Opisthobranchiata
      Pectinibranchiata
      Prosobranchiata
      Pulmonata
      Snails
      Tentaculitida
      Thecosomata
  x Gastropoda
  xx Mollusks
  Note under Snails
  — Anatomy
    x Snails—Anatomy
  — Behavior
  — Food
    x Snails—Food
  — Identification
  — Laboratory manuals
  — Parasites
    See Parasites—Gasteropoda
  — Physiology
Gasteropoda, Fossil *(QE808-9)*
  sa Murchisoniata
  x Snails, Fossil
  xx Mollusks, Fossil
Gasteropoda (in religion, folk-lore, etc.)
  See Snails (in religion, folk-lore, etc.)
Gasteropoda as carriers of disease
  x Snails as carriers of disease
  xx Animals as carriers of disease
      Communicable diseases
      Parasites—Gasteropoda
Gastrectomy
  See Stomach—Surgery
Gastric biopsy
  See Stomach—Biopsy
Gastric fistula
  See Fistula, Gastric
Gastric intubation
  See Stomach—Intubation
Gastric juice *(QP193)*
  sa Pepsin
      Rennet
  xx Body fluids
      Digestion
      Stomach—Secretions
  Example under Physiology
  — Analysis
Gastric mucosa
  x Mucosa, Gastric
  xx Mucous membrane
      Stomach
Gastric resection
  See Stomach—Surgery
Gastrin *(QP801.H7)*
  xx Gastrointestinal hormones
Gastritis
  See Stomach—Inflammation
Gastroenteritis *(RC840.G3)*
Gastroenteritis of swine, Transmissible
  See Transmissible gastroenteritis of swine
Gastroenterological endocrinology
  See Gastrointestinal hormones

Gastroenterology
  sa Intestines
      Pediatric gastroenterology
      Radioisotopes in gastroenterology
      Stomach
      Veterinary gastroenterology
  x Gastrointestinal tract
  xx Internal medicine
  — Examinations, questions, etc.
Gastroesophageal junction
  See Esophagogastric junction
Gastroesophageal reflux
  Example under Digestive organs—Diseases;
      Esophagus—Diseases
Gastrointestinal agents *(RM355)*
  sa Anthelmintics
      Cholagogues
      Emetics
      Purgatives
  x Drugs, Gastrointestinal
  xx Digestive organs—Diseases
      Pharmacology
Gastrointestinal angiography
  See Digestive organs—Blood-vessels—
      Radiography
Gastrointestinal function tests
  xx Function tests (Medicine)
Gastrointestinal gas
  sa Flatulence
  x Gas, Gastrointestinal
      Intestines, Gases in
  xx Alimentary canal
Gastrointestinal hemorrhage
  x Alimentary canal—Hemorrhage
  xx Hemorrhage
Gastrointestinal hormones
  sa Gastrin
      Secretin
  x Endocrinological gastroenterology
      Gastroenterological endocrinology
  xx Hormones
Gastrointestinal motility
  x Intestines—Motility
      Motility, Gastrointestinal
      Stomach—Motility
  xx Digestion
Gastrointestinal tract
  See Alimentary canal
      Gastroenterology
Gastronomy *(TX631-641)*
  sa Cookery
      Dinners and dining
      Food
      Gluttony
      Menus
      Picnicking
      Topical songs (Gastronomy)
  x Eating
  xx Cookery
      Diet
      Dinners and dining
      Food
  — Early works to 1800 *(TX631-641)*
  — Poetry
Gastrophotography
  xx Gastroscope and gastroscopy
      Photography, Medical
Gastropoda
  See Gasteropoda
Gastroscope and gastroscopy *(RC804.G3)*
  sa Gastrophotography
  xx Stomach—Exploration
Gastrostomy
  See Stomach—Surgery
Gastrotaenia
  xx Aporidea
Gastrotomy
  See Stomach—Surgery

Gastrotricha *(QL391.G2)*
  sa Chaetonotoidea
Gastrulation
  xx Embryology
GAT (Computer program)
  x General analysis technique (Computer
      program)
      Georgetown automatic translation
  xx Electronic digital computers—
      Programming
      Russian language—Machine translating
  Example under Computer programs
Gatang language
  See Kattang language
Gate money (Prisons)
  See Prison release gratuities
Gate receipts, Taxation of
  See Amusements—Taxation
Gates *(Agriculture, S723; Architecture,*
      NA8385-8392; Military architecture,
      NA493-5)
  sa Lich-gates
  xx Fences
Gates, Hydraulic
  See Hydraulic gates
Gatherings, Religious
  See Religious gatherings
Gathmann torpedo gun *(UF630)*
Gatling guns *(UF620.G3; Naval,*
      VF410.G3-34)
  xx Machine-guns
      Mitrailleuses
Gato (Dance) *(GV1796.G)*
Gattermann reaction
  xx Chemical reactions
Gaucho (The word)
Gauchos *(General, F2217; Argentine*
      Republic, F2926; Brazil, F2621;
      Paraguay, F2682.9; Uruguay,
      F2722.9)
  sa Cowboys
  x Herdsmen
  xx Cowboys
  — Costume
  — Language (New words, slang, etc.)
  — Pictorial works
Gauchos in art
Gauchos in literature
Gaudian languages
  See Indo-Aryan languages, Modern
Gaugamela, Battle of, 331 B.C. *(DF234.5)*
  x Arbela, Battle of, 331 B.C.
  xx Macedonia—History—To 168 B.C.
Gauges
  See Gages
Gauging
  See Gaging
Gaul
  — Description, geography
    Example under Geography; Geography,
      Ancient
    Note under Geography, Historical
  — History *(DC21; DC62)*
  — — To 58 B.C.
  — — 58 B.C.-511 A.D.
    sa Alesia, Battle of, 52 B.C.
      Gergovie, Battle of 52 B.C.
      Haute Alsace, Battle of, 58 B.C.
Gaulish calendar
  See Calendar, Celtic
Gaulish language *(PB3001-3029)*
  x Gallic language
  xx Celtic languages
Gauls *(DC62-63)*
  sa Arverni
      Celts
      Galatians
  xx Celts

Gauls (DC62-63) (Continued)
    Galatians
— Religion
Gauls in literature
Gaur
    See Buffaloes
Gauss error function
    See Error functions
Gauss' quadrature formulas
    See Gaussian quadrature formulas
Gaussian mechanical quadrature formulas
    See Gaussian quadrature formulas
Gaussian noise
    See Random noise theory
Gaussian processes
    xx Distribution (Probability theory)
        Stochastic processes
Gaussian quadrature formulas (QA299.4.G3)
    x Gauss' quadrature formulas
        Gaussian mechanical quadrature
            formulas
    xx Numerical integration
Gavdo (Island), Battle of, 1941
    See Matapan, Battle of, 1941
Gavelkind
Gaviiformes
    See Loons
Gavottes
        Here are entered collections of gavotte
        music for various mediums. Individual
        gavottes and collections of gavottes for
        a specific medium are entered under
        the heading followed by specification
        of medium.
Gavottes (Accordion ensemble) (M1362)
    xx Accordion ensembles
Gavottes (Band) (M1248; M1264)
    xx Band music
Gavottes (Bassoon, clarinet, oboe) (M355-9)
    xx Wind trios (Bassoon, clarinet, oboe)
Gavottes (Clarinet, flutes (2)) (M355-9)
    xx Wind trios (Clarinet, flutes (2))
Gavottes (Clarinets (4)) (M455-9)
    xx Wind quartets (Clarinets (4))
Gavottes (Guitar) (M125-9)
    xx Guitar music
Gavottes (Harpsichord, recorders (2))
        (M315-319)
    xx Trios (Piano, recorders (2))
Gavottes (Orchestra) (M1048; M1060)
    xx Orchestral music
— Scores
Gavottes (Organ) (M6-7; M11-13)
    xx Organ music
Gavottes (Piano) (M31; M32.8)
    xx Piano music
Gavottes (Piano, recorders (2)) (M315-319)
    xx Trios (Piano, recorders (2))
Gavottes (Pianos (2)) (M214-215)
    xx Piano music (Pianos (2))
Gavottes (String orchestra) (M1145; M1160)
    xx String-orchestra music
— Scores and parts
Gavottes (Violin and piano) (M217-218;
        M221-3)
    xx Violin and piano music
Gavottes (Violins (3)) (M349-353)
    xx String trios (Violins (3))
Gavottes (Wind ensemble) (M955-7)
    xx Wind ensembles
Gawigl language
    xx Papuan languages
Gay Head Indians (F74.G25)
    xx Algonquian Indians
        Indians of North America
        Wampanoag Indians
Gay lib
    See Gay liberation movement

Gay liberation movement (Direct)
        (HQ76.5-8)
    x Gay lib
        Homophile movement
        Homosexual liberation movement
    xx Homosexuality
Gayal
    x Mithan
    xx Cattle
Gayo language
    x Gajo language
    xx Malayan languages
Gayos (Indonesian people)
    xx Ethnology—Indonesia
Gaza, Battles of, 1917 (D568.7)
    xx European War, 1914-1918—Campaigns
        —Turkey and the Near East—
        Palestine
Gazelles (QL737.U5)
— Behavior
— Legends and stories
Gazels
    x Ghazels
    xx Poetry
Gazels, Arabic, [Urdu, etc.] (Direct)
    x Arabic [Urdu, etc.] gazels
    xx Arabic [Urdu, etc.] poetry
Gazetteers
    See Geography—Dictionaries
        Toponymy
        subdivision Gazetteers under names of
            countries, states, etc.
Gazettes (Direct)
    x Government gazettes
        Official gazettes
    xx Government publications
Gazettes on microfilm
    xx Microfilms
Gaziantep, Turkey
— Siege, 1920-1921
Gbande (African people)
    See Gbandi (African people)
Gbandi (African people)
    x Gbande (African people)
    xx Ethnology—Liberia
Gbandi language (PL8204)
    sa Sango language
    x Bandi language
        Ngbandi language
    xx Mande languages
Gbanya (African tribe)
    See Gonja (African tribe)
Gbari (African tribe)
    See Gwari (African tribe)
Gbari language
    See Gwari language
Gbasa language
    See Bassa language (Liberia)
Gbaya (African people)
    x Bwaka (African people)
        Gbeya (African people)
    xx Ethnology—Africa, West
Gbaya language (PL8205)
    x Gbea language
        Gbeya language
        Ngbaka Gbaya language
Gbea language
    See Gbaya language
Gbeya (African people)
    See Gbaya (African people)
Gbeya language
    See Gbaya language
Gboare (African people)
    See Bachama (African people)
GCA
    See Ground controlled approach
Gciriku language
    See Diriku language

Gdebo language
    See Grebo language
GE 600 series (Computers)
    xx Electronic digital computers
— Programming
Gẽ dialect
    See Mina dialect
Gean
    See Sweet cherry
Gear-cutting machines (TJ187)
    sa Gear-shaping machines
        Gear-shaving machines
        Gearing—Manufacture
    xx Gearing
— Maintenance and repair
    x Gear-cutting machines—Repairing
— Repairing
    See Gear-cutting machines—
        Maintenance and repair
— Standards (Direct)
— Tables, calculations, etc.
Gear pumps (TJ917)
    x Pumps, Gear
    xx Rotary pumps
Gear rolling (TJ184)
    x Roll forming of gears
    xx Gearing—Manufacture
        Rolling (Metal-work)
Gear-shaping machines (TJ187)
    xx Gear-cutting machines
        Shapers
— Standards
Gear-shaving machines
    xx Gear-cutting machines
        Gearing—Manufacture
Gearing (TJ184-204)
    sa Automobiles, Military—Transmission
            devices
        Automobiles—Steering-gear
        Automobiles—Transmission devices
        Boring machinery—Transmission
            devices
        Clutches (Machinery)
        Coal-mining machinery—Transmission
            devices
        Construction equipment—Transmission
            devices
        Couplings
        Diesel locomotives—Transmission
            devices
        Electric locomotives—Transmission
            devices
        Friction gearing
        Gear-cutting machines
        Indexing (Machine-shop practice)
        Locomotives—Transmission devices
        Machine-tools—Transmission devices
        Mechanical movements
        Mining machinery—Transmission
            devices
        Motor-trucks—Transmission devices
        Motor vehicles—Transmission devices
        Odontograph
        Oil well pumps—Transmission devices
        Ships—Transmission devices
        Sprockets
        Tracklaying vehicles—Transmission
            devices
        Tractors—Transmission devices
    x Cog-wheels
    xx Machinery
        Mechanical movements
        Power transmission
        Rolling contact
        Wheels
— Design and construction
— Drawing
    See Gearing—Drawings

748

— Drawings
   x Gearing—Drawing
   xx Mechanical drawing
— Dynamics *(TJ184)*
— Lubrication
— Manufacture
   sa Gear rolling
      Gear-shaving machines
   xx Gear-cutting machines
— — Automation
— Measurement
— Noise
— Notation
— Production standards
— Standards
— Tables, calculations, etc. *(TJ185)*
— Testing *(TJ184)*
— Vibration
Gearing, Bevel *(TJ193-6)*
   x Bevel-gearing
— Standards
Gearing, Helical
   See Gearing, Spiral
Gearing, Involute
   See Gearing, Spur
Gearing, Novikov
   x Novikov gearing
— Design and construction *(TJ202)*
Gearing, Planetary
   sa Harmonic drives
   x Epicyclic gearing
      Planetary gearing
— Design and construction
Gearing, Spiral *(TJ192)*
   sa Spiral milling
   x Gearing, Helical
      Spiral gearing
— Design and construction
— Standards *(Direct)*
Gearing, Spur *(TJ189)*
   x Gearing, Involute
      Spur gearing
— Design and construction
— Standards *(Direct)*
Gearing, Worm *(TJ200)*
   x Worm-gear
— Design and construction
Geckos *(QL666.L2)*
   xx Lizards
Geckos as pets *(SF459.G35)*
   Example under Wild animals as pets
GED tests
   See General educational development tests
Gedaged language
   x Graged language
   xx Melanesian languages
Geddes' comet *(QB723.G)*
Gedebo language
   See Grebo language
Gediz, Turkey
— Earthquake, 1970 *(QE537.2)*
Geese *(QL696.A5; Breeding, SF505; Hunting, SK333.G)*
   sa Bar-headed goose
      Barnacle goose
      Blue goose
      Brent-goose
      Canada goose
      Greylag goose
      Ross's goose
      Snow goose
      White-fronted goose
   x Goose
   xx Poultry
      Waterfowl
— Juvenile literature
Geese, Fossil

Geese in art
   xx Art
Geez language
   See Ethiopic language
Gegenschein
   See Counterglow
Gegs
   See Ghegs
Gehenna
   See Hell (Judaism)
Geiger counters
   See Geiger-Müller counters
Geiger-Müller counters *(QC476)*
   x Counting tubes
      Geiger counters
   xx Ionization chambers
      Nuclear counters
      Radiation
      Radioactivity
      Radioactivity—Instruments
      Radioactivity—Measurement
      Transducers
      Vacuum-tubes
Geikielite
   See Ilmenite
Geishas
   xx Entertainers
Gekū Shintō
   See Ise Shintō
Gel permeation chromatography
   x Chromatography, Gel permeation
   xx Chromatographic analysis
— Laboratory manuals
Gela, Battle of, 1943 *(D763.S5)*
   xx World War, 1939-1945—Campaigns—Italy
Gela language
   See Florida language
Gelada baboon *(QL737.P93)*
   xx Baboons
Gelatin
   sa Cookery (Gelatin)
      Photographic gelatin
— Physiological effect *(QP935.G5)*
Gelatinization
   See Gelation
Gelation
   x Gelatinization
      Gelling
   xx Coagulation
      Colloids
Gelderland in literature
Gelling
   See Gelation
Gels
   See Colloids
Gelsemium *(Therapeutics, RM666.G3)*
Gem carving
   xx Carving (Art industries)
      Gems
      Glyptics
      Sculpture
Gem cutting *(TS752.5)*
   sa Diamond cutting
   x Cutting of gems
      Lapidary art
   xx Cutting
      Gems
      Precious stones
Gematria *(BM525; BS1187; BS2390)*
   sa Cabala
   xx Cabala
      Hermeneutics
      Occult sciences
      Symbolism of numbers
Gembloux, Battle of, 1940 *(D756.5.G)*
   xx World War, 1939-1945—Campaigns—Belgium

Gemini project
   See Project Gemini
Gemmation (Botany)
   See Plants—Reproduction
Gemmation (Zoology)
   See Reproduction, Asexual
Gempei Wars, 1180-1185
   See Japan—History—Gempei Wars, 1180-1185
Gems *(Direct)* *(Art industries, NK7650-7690; Glyptics, NK5505-5735; Manners and customs, GT2250-2280; Manufacture, TS750-757)*
   Here are entered books on engraved stones and jewels, interesting from the point of view of antiquities or art. Works of mineralogical interest are entered under Precious stones.
   sa Cameos
      Chalchihuitl
      Crown jewels
      Gem carving
      Gem cutting
      Glyptics
      Ilmenite
      Intaglios
      Jewelry
      Lapidaries (Medieval literature)
      Portraits on gems
      Precious stones
      Scarabs
   x Jewels
   xx Archaeology
      Art
      Cameos
      Classical antiquities
      Decoration and ornament
      Diamonds
      Engraving
      Glyptics
      Intaglios
      Jewelry
      Mineralogy
      Precious stones
— Collectors and collecting *(NK5530)*
— Juvenile literature
— Private collections *(NK5515)*
— Reproductions, facsimiles, etc.
Gems, American, ₍**Italian, etc.**₎ *(Direct)*
   x American ₍Italian, etc.₎ gems
Gems, Ancient
Gems, Artificial
   See Precious stones, Artificial
Gems, Etruscan *(Direct)*
   x Etruscan gems
GEMS (Computer program language)
   See SIMSCRIPT (Computer program language)
Gems (in religion, folk-lore, etc.) *(GR805)*
   sa Birth-stones
      Lapidaries (Medieval literature)
   x Folk-lore of gems
   xx Religion, Primitive
Gems in literature *(PN6110.G3)*
Gems of art (Game) *(GV1299.G3)*
Gemsbok
   x Cape oryx
      Gemsbuck
   xx Oryx
Gemsbuck
   See Gemsbok
Gen Movement
   xx Youth—Religious life
Genatropin
   See Atropine
Gendarmes
   See Police

Gendarmes (Continued)
    Police, Rural
Gende (Papuan people)
    x Yonu (Papuan people)
    xx Ethnology—New Guinea
       Papuans
Gender
    See Grammar, Comparative and general—
       Gender
       subdivision Gender *under names of*
         languages and groups of languages
Gene, Lethal
    See Lethal mutation
Gene mapping
    See Chromosome mapping
Genealogical correspondence *(CS15)*
    x Correspondence
    xx Letter-writing
Genealogists *(CS8)*
Genealogy *(CS)*
    sa Biography
       Heraldry
       Peerage
       Precedence
       Probate records
       Registers of births, etc.
       Royal descent, Families of
       names of families, e.g. Lincoln family;
         and subdivision Genealogy *under*
         names of places, e.g. United States—
         Genealogy; Plymouth Co., Mass.—
         Genealogy; St. Louis—Genealogy;
         also headings beginning with the
         word Genealogical
    x Ancestry
       Descent
       Pedigrees
    xx Auxiliary sciences of history
       Biography
       Heraldry
       History
       Precedence
    — Forms, blanks, etc. *(CS24)*
    — Juvenile literature
    — Law and legislation *(Direct)*
       sa Copyright
         Names, Personal—Law
         Recording and registration
    — Societies, etc.
       x Family associations
Genealogy in literature
General activity simulation program
    See GASP (Computer program language)
General analysis technique (Computer
       program)
    See GAT (Computer program)
General aptitude test battery
    xx Ability—Testing
       Mental tests
General average
    See Average (Maritime law)
General aviation
    See Private flying
General certificate of education examination
    (Great Britain)
General chapters *(Direct)*
    x Chapters, General
    xx Monasticism and religious orders—
       Government
General confession (Prayer)
    xx Prayers
General Dynamics B-58
    See B-58 bomber
General educational development tests
    sa High school equivalency examination
    x GED tests
    xx Mental tests
       United States. Army—Examinations

General equilibrium (Economics)
    See Equilibrium (Economics)
General Game Playing Program
    See GGPP (Computer program)
General Information Processing System
    See GIPSY (Information retrieval system)
General Integrated Programming System
    See GIPS (Electronic computer system)
General judgment
    See Judgment Day
General Motors Corporation Sit-Down Strike,
    1936-1937
General pact for the renunciation of war, Paris,
    Aug. 27, 1928
    See Renunciation of war treaty, Paris, Aug.
       27, 1928
General practice (Medicine)
    See Physicians (General practice)
General practitioners
    See Physicians (General practice)
General problem solver (Computer program)
    See GPS (Computer program)
General property tax
    See Property tax
General Purpose Simulation System
    See GPSS (Computer program language)
General relativity (Physics) *(QC6)*
    x Relativistic theory of gravitation
       Relativity theory, General
    xx Gravitation
       Physics
       Relativity (Physics)
General semantics *(B820)*
    sa Pragmatics
    x Non-Aristotelian philosophy
       Semantics, General
    xx Education
       Semantics (Philosophy)
    — Juvenile literature
General staffs
    See Armies—Staffs
       under names of countries, the
         designation of the general staff, e.g.
         France. Armée. État-major;
         United States. War Dept. General
         Staff
General stores *(Direct)*
    x Country stores
    xx Retail trade
General strike *(HD5307; Direct action,*
    HD6477)
    Here are entered works dealing with the
    subject of the general strike. For works
    dealing with an individual general
    strike involving an entire country the
    name of the country and the date of
    the strike are included in the heading,
    e.g. General Strike, Great Britain,
    1926; General Strike, Sweden, 1909.
    Works on a strike limited to a single
    city are entered under the name of the
    city with subdivision General Strike,
    date, *e.g.* San Francisco—General
    Strike, 1934.
    sa Strikes and lockouts
       Strikes and lockouts, Sympathetic
    xx Direct action
       Passive resistance
       Political strikes
       Strikes and lockouts
       Strikes and lockouts, Sympathetic
General Strike, Belgium, 1960-1961
General Strike, France, 1968
General Strike, Great Britain, 1926
    (HD5366)
    Note under General strike
General Strike, Hongkong, 1925
General Strike, Russia, 1903

General Strike, Spain, 1917
General Strike, Sweden, 1909
    Note under General strike
General Strike, Sweden, 1971
General vicars
    See Vicars-general
General warrants
    See Warrants (Law)
General Zionism *(DS150.G4-6)*
    x Zionism, General
    xx Zionism
Generalized Data Base Planning System
    See GPLAN (Electronic computer system)
Generalized functions
    See Distributions, Theory of (Functional
       analysis)
Generalized spaces
    See Spaces, Generalized
Generals *(Indirect) (European War, D507;*
    Military biography, U51-54)
    Works dealing with the lives, etc. of gen-
    erals of a particular nationality are en-
    tered here and also under the name of
    the country in question with subhead-
    ing Army—Biography.
    sa Marshals
       Military biography
       Strategi, Greek
    xx Military biography
       Soldiers
    — Anecdotes, facetiae, satire, etc.
    — Correspondence, reminiscences, etc.
    — Health and hygiene
    — Juvenile literature
    — Quotations
Generation
    See Reproduction
Generation, Spontaneous
    See Spontaneous generation
Generation gap
    See Conflict of generations
Generation of geometric forms
    sa Body of revolution
       Revolutions (Descriptive geometry)
    x Geometric forms, Generation of
    xx Geometrical drawing
       Geometry, Descriptive
Generations, Alternating *(QH489)*
    x Alternating generations
       Heterogenesis
Generative grammar
    sa subdivision Grammar, Generative *under*
       names of languages, e.g. English
       language—Grammar, Generative
    x Grammar, Generative
       Grammar, Transformational
       Transformational grammar
    xx Grammar, Comparative and general
       Languages—Psychology
    — Terminology
Generative organs *(Comparative anatomy,*
    QL876-881; Human anatomy,
    QM416-421; Physiology,
    QP251-281)
    sa Change of sex
       Cloaca (Zoology)
       Genito-urinary organs
       Gonads
       Orgasm
       Reproduction
    x Reproductive organs
       Sex organs
       Sexual organs
    xx Genito-urinary organs
       Reproduction
       Sex
    — Abnormities and deformities *(QM691;*
       Female, RG211-215)

sa Laurence-Moon-Biedl syndrome

xx Sexual disorders

— Amphibians, ₍Birds, Insects, etc.₎

Works on the generative organs of a particular class, order, family, genus, or species are entered under Generative organs, subdivided by the larger zoological groups only. When the monograph treats of one of the smaller divisions, additional entry is made under the specific group, e.g. 1. Generative organs—Amphibians. 2. Frogs.

x Amphibians ₍Birds, Insects, etc.₎—Generative organs

— Bacteriology (QR171)

— Cancer

sa Disgerminoma

— Diseases

— — Diagnosis

— Programmed instruction

— Surgery

sa Sterilization (Birth control)

— Transplantation (QP90; QP251)

Generative organs, Effect of radiation on

xx Radiation—Physiological effect

Radioactivity—Physiological effect

Generative organs, Female (Comparative anatomy, QL881; Human anatomy, QM421; Physiology, QP261-281)

sa Gynecology

Obstetrics

Woman—Diseases

names of individual organs

— Abnormities and deformities

— Blood-vessels

— Cancer

— — Diagnosis

— — Programmed instruction

— Diseases

sa Generative organs, Female—Radiography

Menstruation disorders

— — Atlases

— — Diagnosis

sa Vaginal smears

— Examination

sa Vaginal smears

— Innervation

— Juvenile literature

— Radiography

x Generative organs, Female—X-ray examination

xx Generative organs, Female—Diseases

— Surgery

— Tumors

— — Programmed instruction

— X-ray examination

See Generative organs, Female—Radiography

Generative organs, Male (Comparative anatomy, QL878; Human anatomy, QM416; Physiology, QP255-7)

sa names of individual organs

— Diseases

— Surgery

— Tuberculosis

Generator, Van de Graaff

See Van de Graaff generator

Generators, Electric

See Dynamos

Generators, Hall

See Hall generators

Generators, Magnetohydrodynamic

See Magnetohydrodynamic generators

Generators, Random number

See Random number generators

Generators, Vortex

See Vortex generators

Generosity (BJ1533.G4)

Genes

See Heredity

Genes, Complementary

See Complementation (Genetics)

Genetic algebras

x Algebras, Genetic

xx Algebra, Abstract

Biomathematics

Genetic code

sa Genetic transcription

Genetic translation

xx Molecular biology

Molecular genetics

Genetic counseling

xx Counseling

Human genetics

Genetic engineering

x Designed genetic change

Engineering, Genetic

Genetic surgery

— Social aspects (Direct)

Genetic literature

Genetic load

xx Mutation (Biology)

Population genetics

Genetic polymorphisms

x Polymorphism, Genetic

Genetic psychology (BF701-724.8)

Here are entered works on the evolutionary psychology of man in terms of origin and development, whether in the individual or in the species. Works on the psychological development of the individual from infancy to old age are entered under Developmental psychology.

sa Adulthood

Age (Psychology)

Child study

Critical periods (Biology)

Culture conflict

Emotional maturity

Growth

Intelligence levels

Maturation (Psychology)

x Aging—Psychological aspects

Evolutionary psychology

Psychology, Genetic

xx Evolution

Growth

Human genetics

Psychology

Note under Developmental psychology

Genetic recombination

sa Bacterial transformation

Crossing over (Genetics)

Genetic transformation

x Recombination, Genetic

xx Chromosomes

Genetic regulation (QH450)

Here are entered works on the control of the type and rate of cellular processes by regulation of the activity of specific genes controlling individual biochemical reactions. Works on the various mechanisms of cellular control such as structural control, biochemical control, cell differentiation, etc., are entered under Cellular control mechanisms.

sa Genetic translation

xx Biosynthesis

Cellular control mechanisms

Molecular genetics

Note under Cellular control mechanisms

Genetic research (Direct)

x Genetics—Research

xx Research

Genetic surgery

See Genetic engineering

Genetic transcription (QH450.2)

x Transcription (Genetics)

xx Genetic code

Ribonucleic acid synthesis

Genetic transduction

See Transduction

Genetic transformation

sa Bacterial transformation

Transfection

x Transformation (Genetics)

xx Genetic recombination

Microbial genetics

Nucleic acids

Transfection

Genetic translation (QH450.5)

x Translation (Genetics)

xx Genetic code

Genetic regulation

Protein biosynthesis

Geneticists (Direct)

xx Biologists

Microbiologists

Genetics

sa Adaptation (Biology)

Allelomorphism

Animal genetics

Behavior genetics

Breeding

Cell populations

Chromosomes

Complementation (Genetics)

Crossing over (Genetics)

Cytogenetics

Developmental genetics

Ecological genetics

Endocrine genetics

Evolution

Fungal genetics

Heredity

Heredity of disease

Human genetics

Immunogenetics

Karyotypes

Linkage (Genetics)

Microbial genetics

Molecular genetics

Mosaicism

Mutation (Biology)

Natural selection

Nature and nurture

Origin of species

Pharmacogenetics

Plant genetics

Population genetics

Radiogenetics

Somatic hybrids

Translocation (Genetics)

Variation (Biology)

subdivision Genetic aspects under subjects, e.g. Color-sense—Genetic aspects; and headings beginning with the word Genetic

xx Adaptation (Biology)

Biology

Breeding

Chromosomes

Embryology

Eugenics

Evolution

Heredity

Hybridization

Life (Biology)

Mendel's law

Genetics *(Continued)*
    Mutation (Biology)
    Reproduction
    Variation (Biology)
— Abbreviations
— Experiments
— Juvenile literature
— Laboratory manuals
— Mathematical models
    xx Biomathematics
— — Programmed instruction
— Methodology
— Philosophy
— Popular works
— Problems, exercises, etc.
— Programmed instruction
— Research
    See Genetic research
— Statistical methods
— Tables, etc.
Genetics and environment
    See Nature and nurture
Geneva
— Siege, 1602
    x Escalade of Geneva, 1602
— — Poetry
Geneva award
    See Alabama claims
Geneva mechanisms *(TJ181.7)*
    xx Mechanical movements
Geneva protocol, 1924
    xx Arbitration, International
Geniculate bodies
    x Bodies, Geniculate
    Corpus geniculatum
    xx Hearing
    Thalamus
Genii
    See Jinn
Genito-urinary organs
    sa Cloaca (Zoology)
    Generative organs
    x Urogenital organs
    xx Generative organs
    Urinary organs
    Urology
— Abnormities and deformities
    (Comparative anatomy,
    QL871-881, QL991; Human
    anatomy, QM401-421, QM691)
— Bacteriology
    See Genito-urinary organs—
    Microbiology
— Blood-vessels
— Diseases *(RC870-923; Children,*
    RJ466-476; Female, RG)
    sa Endoscope and endoscopy
    Gonorrhea
    Gynecology
    Hydrocele
    Oxaluria
    Spermatorrhea
    Urinary organs—Diseases
    Urine—Analysis and pathology
    Varicocele
    Veterinary urology
    Woman—Diseases
    xx Urology
— — Diagnosis *(RC874)*
    sa Genito-urinary organs—
    Radiography
— — Eclectic treatment *(RV281-6)*
— — Homeopathic treatment *(RX351-6)*
— Foreign bodies
— Microbiology
    x Genito-urinary organs—Bacteriology
— Programmed instruction
— Radiography

    xx Genito-urinary organs—Diseases—
    Diagnosis
— Surgery *(RD571-590)*
    sa Gynecology, Operative
    Surgery, Orificial
    Urethra—Surgery
    x Urological surgery
— Tuberculosis *(RC312.5.G4-5)*
— Tumors *(RC280.G4-5)*
— Wounds and injuries
Genitourinary diseases in animals
    See Veterinary urology
Genius *(BF412-426; Genius and alcoholism,*
    HV5141; Genius and degeneration,
    BF426; Genius and heredity, BF418;
    Genius and insanity, BF423)
    sa Creation (Literary, artistic, etc.)
    Creative ability
    Gifted children
    Originality
    x Genius and insanity
    Greatness
    Insanity and genius
    xx Insanity
    Psychology
Genius and insanity
    See Genius
    Insanity
Genizah
    xx Manuscripts
    Synagogues
Genoa
— General Strike, 1900
— History
— — To 1339
— — 1339-1528
— — 1528-1789
— — 1789-1815
— — 1815-
— Siege, 1800 *(DC224.G4)*
Genocide
    sa Holocaust, Jewish (1939-1945)
    Trials (Genocide)
    xx Crimes against humanity
    International offenses
    Race problems
    Terrorism
Genre (Art)
    sa Farm life in art
    xx Art
Genre painting *(Direct) (ND1450;*
    Water-color, ND2350)
    sa Conversation piece (Portrait painting)
    Narrative painting
    Ukiyoe
    xx Figure painting
    Painting
Genre painting, Dutch, [German, etc.]
    x Dutch [German, etc.] genre painting
Genre paintings *(Direct)*
    xx Paintings
Genre paintings, American, [Dutch, etc.]
    (Direct)
    x American [Dutch, etc.] genre paintings
Gentianales
    See Contortae
Gentians *(Flower culture, SB413.G3)*
Gentiles in the New Testament
    x Bible. N.T.—Gentiles
Gentiles in the Old Testament *(BS1199.N6)*
    x Bible. O.T.—Gentiles
    xx Aliens (Jewish law)
Gentoo language
    See Telugu language

Gentry
    See subdivision Gentry *under names of*
    countries, regions, etc., e.g. Great
    Britain—Gentry; Bedfordshire, Eng.
    —Gentry
Geo-codes
    See Geographical location codes
Geo-electric prospecting
    See Electric prospecting
Geobotanical prospecting
    See Biogeochemical prospecting
Geobotany
    See Phytogeography
Geochemical prospecting *(TN270)*
    sa Biogeochemical prospecting
    xx Geochemistry
    Prospecting
— Statistical methods
Geochemistry *(QE515)*
    sa Biogeochemical cycles
    Biogeochemistry
    Cementation (Petrology)
    Chemical denudation
    Chemical oceanography
    Geochemical prospecting
    Geothermal resources
    Mineralogical chemistry
    Mineralogy, Determinative
    Organic geochemistry
    Rocks—Analysis
    Sediments (Geology)—Analysis
    x Chemical composition of the earth
    Chemical geology
    Earth—Chemical composition
    Geological chemistry
    Geology, Chemical
    xx Chemistry
    Earth sciences
    Petrology
    Physical geography
    Rocks
— Computer programs
— Handbooks, manuals, etc.
— Tables, etc.
Geochronology
    See Geological time
Geochrony
    See Geological time
Geodes *(QE495)*
    xx Concretions
    Geology
    Paleontology
    Rocks
    Sedimentary structures
Geodesic domes
    xx Domes
Geodesy *(Indirect) (QB281-341)*
    sa Aeronautics in geodesy
    Arc measures
    Area measurement
    Astronautics in geodesy
    Astronomy, Spherical and practical
    Azimuth
    Base measuring
    Earth—Figure
    Electronics in surveying
    Geographical positions
    Geography, Mathematical
    Gravimeter (Geophysical instrument)
    Gravity
    Isostasy
    Latitude
    Least squares
    Longitude
    Marine geodesy
    Moon—Figure
    Prismatic astrolabe
    Radar in geodesy

Sea level
Surveying
Triangulation
subdivision Surveys *under names of*
countries, cities, etc., e.g. France—
Surveys; Massachusetts—Surveys
x Degrees of latitude and longitude
Geodetics
xx Arc measures
Astronomy
Earth
Earth—Figure
Geography, Mathematical
Mensuration
Surveying
— Automation
— Computer programs   *(QB297)*
— Early works to 1800
— Mathematics
— Observations
x Geodetic observations
Observations, Geodetic
— Problems, exercises, etc.   *(QB321)*
— Research
See Geodetic research
— Statistical methods
— Tables, etc.   *(QB321)*
Geodesy, Lunar
See Selenodesy
Geodesy as a profession   *(Indirect)*
(QB281.5)
Geodetic observations
See Geodesy—Observations
Geodetic research   *(Direct)*
sa Geodetic satellites
x Geodesy—Research
xx Research
Geodetic satellites   *(TL798.G4)*
xx Artificial satellites
Astronautics in geodesy
Geodetic research
Geodetics
See Geodesy
Geodimeter
xx Distances—Measurement
Kerr cell shutters
Geodynamics   *(QE500-505)*
sa Cryopedology
Earthquakes
Metamorphism (Geology)
Rayleigh waves
Rock mechanics
Sea-floor spreading
x Tectonophysics
xx Geophysics
— Juvenile literature
— Statistical methods
Geognosy
See Geology
Geographers   *(Direct)   (G67-69)*
sa Geography as a profession
Government geographers
xx Earth scientists
Geography
Geographic Incremental Plotting System
See GIPSY (Computer program)
Geographic models
See Geography, Economic—Mathematical
models
Geographical area codes
See Geographical location codes
Geographical atlases
See Atlases
Geographical boundaries
See Boundaries
Geographical dictionaries
See Geography—Dictionaries

Geographical distribution of animals
See Zoogeography
Geographical distribution of animals and
plants   *(QH84)*
sa Forest ecology
Intertidal zonation
Life zones
Paleobiogeography
Phytogeography
Zoogeography
x Biogeography
Geographical distribution of plants and
animals
Plants and animals, Geographical
distribution of
xx Ecology
Natural history
— Juvenile literature
Geographical distribution of fossil animals and
plants
See Paleobiogeography
Geographical distribution of man
See Anthropo-geography
Ethnology
Man—Migrations
Geographical distribution of plants
See Phytogeography
Geographical distribution of plants and animals
See Geographical distribution of animals
and plants
Geographical location codes
sa Grids (Cartography)
x Geo-codes
Geographical area codes
Geographical models
See Geography—Mathematical models
Geographical museums
xx Museums
Geographical myths   *(G100; Folk-lore,*
GR650-690)
sa Lost continents
x Cities, Imaginary
Folk-lore of countries
Imaginary cities
Imaginary islands
Islands, Imaginary
xx Folk-lore
Geography—History
Mythology
Nature (in religion, folk-lore, etc.)
Voyages, Imaginary
Geographical names
See Names, Geographical
Geographical pathology
See Medical geography
Geographical photography
See Photography in geography
Geographical positions   *(Indirect)*
(G109-110; Determination of,
QB201-237)
sa Astronautics in navigation
Geography, Mathematical
Grids (Cartography)
Horizons, Artificial
Latitude
Longitude
Raydist
xx Geodesy
Geography, Mathematical
Grids (Cartography)
Latitude
Longitude
Geographical recreations   *(GV1485)*
x Geography—Games
Recreations, Geographical
xx Games
Geography—Study and teaching

Geographical research
sa Artificial satellites in geographical
research
Astronautics in geographical research
x Geography—Research
xx Geography
Research
Geographical societies   *(G2-56)*
sa Geography—Societies, etc. *[for*
publications of geographical and
other societies in relation to
geography]
xx Societies
Geography   *(G-GF; Ethnology, GN476.4)*
sa Anthropo-geography
Astronomical geography
Atlases
Boundaries
Classical geography
Classification—Books—Geography
Discoveries (in geography)
Ecclesiastical geography
Ethnology
Geographers
Geographical research
Local geography
Man—Influence of environment
Maps
Medical geography
Military geography
Physical geography
Rural geography
Surveying
Voyages and travels
subdivision Description and travel
under names of countries, e.g.
France—Description and travel; *and*
subdivision Description, geography
under names of countries of
antiquity, e.g. Gaul—Description,
geography; Greece—Description,
geography
xx Cosmography
Earth
Earth sciences
World history
— To 400 A.D.
See Geography, Ancient
— 400-1400
See Geography, Medieval
— 15th-16th centuries   *(G113)*
sa Discoveries (in geography)
x Geography—Early works
xx Discoveries (in geography)
— 17th-18th centuries   *(G114; G120-121)*
sa Discoveries (in geography)
x Geography—Early works
xx Discoveries (in geography)
— Atlases
See Atlases
— Bio-bibliography   *(Z6001-6028)*
— Computer programs
— Dictionaries   *(G101-8)*
sa subdivision Gazetteers *under names*
of countries, etc., e.g. France—
Gazetteers
x Gazetteers
Geographical dictionaries
Geography—Gazetteers
—— History
See Toponymy
— Early works
See Classical geography
Geography—15th-16th centuries
Geography—17th-18th centuries
Geography, Ancient
Geography, Medieval
— Examinations, questions, etc.   *(G131)*

Geography *(G-GF; Ethnology, GN476.4)*
(Continued)
— Field work *(G74.5)*
   x Field work (Geography)
— Games
   See Geographical recreations
— Gazetteers
   See Geography—Dictionaries
— History *(G80-99)*
   Only works dealing with the history of
     the science of geography are en-
     tered under this heading.
   sa Discoveries (in geography)
     Geographical myths
     Geography, Ancient
     Geography, Medieval
     Maps, Early
   xx Discoveries (in geography)
— Information services
— Juvenile literature *(G133)*
— Laboratory manuals *(G129)*
— Mathematical models
   x Geographical models
   xx Geography, Mathematical
— Methodology
   sa Field plotters
     Photography in geography
— Models
   See Relief models
— Nomenclature
   See Geography—Terminology
— Philosophy *(G70)*
— Pictorial works *(G136-9)*
   sa Views
   x Geography—Views
     Voyages and travels—Views
   xx Views
— Problems, exercises, etc.
— Programmed instruction
— Punched card systems
   See Punched card systems—Names,
     Geographical
— Radio scripts
   Example under Radio scripts
— Readers
   See Readers—Geography
— Research
   See Geographical research
— Societies, etc.
   xx Geographical societies
   Example under Societies
— Statistical methods
— Statistics
   See Geography—Tables, etc.
— Study and teaching *(Direct) (G72-76)*
   sa Area studies
     Geographical recreations
     Geography rooms and equipment
   xx Area studies
— — Audio-visual aids
   Example under Audio-visual educa-
     tion; Visual aids
— Study and teaching (Elementary)
— Study and teaching (Higher)
— Study and teaching (Primary)
— Study and teaching (Secondary)
— Tables, etc. *(G109-110)*
   sa Distances—Tables, etc.
     Geography, Mathematical—Tables,
     etc.
   x Geography—Statistics
— Teacher training
— Terminology *(G104-8)*
   sa Names, Geographical
   x Geography—Nomenclature
     Topographical terms
   xx Names, Geographical
— Text-books *(G125-7)*
   Example under Text-books

— — Before 1800 *(G125)*
— — 1800-1870 *(G125)*
— — 1870-1945 *(G126-7)*
— — 1945-
— Views
   See Geography—Pictorial works
     Views
Geography, Aerial *(G142)*
   Here are entered works on the effect of
     aviation on geography, as well as
     works on geographical factors in
     aeronautics.
   sa Aeronautics, Commercial
     Airways
     Flights around the world
   subdivisions Description and travel—
     Aerial *under countries, regions, etc.,*
     or Description—Aerial *under cities*
   x Aerial geography
     Air-age geography
     Aviation and geography
     Geography and aviation
Geography, Agricultural
See Agricultural geography
Geography, Ancient *(G82-88)*
   Here are entered works on the geography
     of the ancient world in general. Works
     confined to the geography of Greece
     and Rome are entered under Classical
     geography.
   sa Cities and towns, Ancient
     Vedas—Geography
   subdivision Description, geography
     under names of countries of
     antiquity, e.g. Gaul, Greece *(as*
     distinct from Greece, Modern),
     Rome
   x Ancient geography
     Geography—Early works
     Geography—To 400 A.D.
   xx Classical geography
     Geography, Historical
     Geography—History
     History, Ancient
— Dictionaries *(D54; DE25; G101-3)*
— Maps *(G1033; GA205-213)*
   sa Peutinger table
   x Atlases, Historical
     Historical atlases
     History—Atlases
     Maps, Historical
     War maps
   xx Maps, Early
Geography, Astronomical
See Astronomical geography
Geography, Biblical
See Bible—Geography
Geography, Classical
See Classical geography
Geography, Commercial *(HF1021-9)*
   Here are entered text-books of commer-
     cial geography and treatises on the
     natural resources, commerce, and in-
     dustries of several countries or of the
     world, from the standpoint of com-
     merce.
   sa Geography, Economic
     Trade routes
   x Commercial geography
     World economics
   xx Commerce
     Commercial products
     Geography, Economic
Note under Geography, Economic
— Maps
Geography, Ecclesiastical
See Ecclesiastical geography

Geography, Economic *(HC; HD)*
   Here are entered works which discuss in
     a general way the natural resources,
     commerce, and industries of several
     countries or of the world. Similar
     works concerning one country are en-
     tered under name of country with sub-
     division Economic conditions. *Cf.*
     note under Geography, Commercial.
   sa Agricultural geography
     Geography, Commercial
   x Economic geography
     World economics
   xx Agricultural geography
     Agriculture—Economic aspects
     Commerce
     Commercial products
     Geography, Commercial
     Space in economics
— Juvenile literature
— Maps
   sa subdivision Economic conditions—
     Maps *under names of countries,*
     etc.
   x Natural resources—Maps
— Mathematical models
   x Geographic models
— Methodology
Geography, Historical *(G141; D-F)*
   Here are entered general works which
     show the extent of territory held by
     different states and nations at different
     periods in the world's history.
   Works limited to a particular country or
     region are entered under the name of
     that country or region, with subdivi-
     sion Historical geography, *e.g.* France
     —Historical geography; East (Far
     East)—Historical geography. Under
     names of countries of antiquity, *e.g.*
     Gaul, Greece (as distinct from Greece,
     Modern), Rome, the subdivision De-
     scription, geography is substituted.
   The term Historical geography is some-
     times used in the sense of Anthropo-
     geography. Works of this character are
     entered under Anthropo-geography,
     and Man—Influence of environment.
   sa Classical geography
     Ecclesiastical geography
     Geography, Ancient
     Geography, Medieval
   x Historical geography
   xx Ecclesiastical geography
     History
— Maps
   x Atlases, Historical
     Historical atlases
     History—Atlases
     Maps, Historical
     War maps
Geography, Islamic
See Koran—Geography
Geography, Linguistic
See Linguistic geography
Geography, Local
See Local geography
Geography, Mathematical *(GA)*
   sa Area measurement
     Astronomical geography
     Cartography
     Cartometry
     Cosmography
     Geodesy
     Geographical positions
     Geography—Mathematical models
     Latitude
     Longitude

Map-projection
Nautical astronomy
Surveying
Surveys
x Mathematical geography
xx Astronomical geography
Geodesy
Geographical positions
Mathematics
— Tables, etc. *(GA4)*
xx Geography—Tables, etc.
Geography, Medical
See Medical geography
Geography, Medieval *(G89-95)*
Here are entered geographical works
written during the Middle Ages, as
well as works dealing with the geogra-
phy of that period.
x Geography—400-1400
Geography—Early works
xx Geography, Historical
Geography—History
Middle Ages
— Dictionaries
— Maps
x Atlases, Historical
Historical atlases
History—Atlases
Maps, Historical
Middle Ages—History—Maps
War maps
Geography, Military
See Military geography
Geography, Physical
See Physical geography
Geography, Political
sa Boundaries
Cities and towns
Geopolitics
Territory, National
x Political geography
xx Anthropo-geography
International relations
World politics
Geography, Rural
See Rural geography
Geography, Social
See Anthropo-geography
Geography, Soil
See Soil geography
Geography, Talmudic
See Talmud—Geography
Geography, Urban
See Cities and towns
Geography, Vedic
See Vedas—Geography
Geography and aviation
See Geography, Aerial
Geography and religion
See Religion and geography
Geography as a profession
sa Interns (Geography)
xx Geographers
Geography rooms and equipment
(LB3325.G4)
xx Geography—Study and teaching
Schools—Furniture, equipment, etc.
Geok-Tepe
— Siege, 1880-1881 *(DK856)*
x Denghil Tepe, Siege of, 1880-1881
xx Turkomans
Geologic erosion
See Erosion
Geologic mapping
See Geological mapping
Geological chemistry
See Geochemistry

Geological cycles
See Geology—Periodicity
Geological exhibitions
See Geology—Exhibitions
Geological literature searching
See Information storage and retrieval
systems—Geology
Geological mapping *(QE36)*
sa Geology—Maps
x Geologic mapping
xx Cartography
Geology—Maps
Geological maps
See Geology—ᵣlocal subdivisionᵧ—Maps
Geology—Maps
Geological modeling *(QE43)*
x Modeling, Geological
xx Models and modelmaking
Geological museums *(QE51)*
xx Museums
Geological periodicity
See Geology—Periodicity
Geological physics
See Geophysics
Geological research *(Direct)*
sa Engineering geology—Research
Mohole project
Photography in geology
Sedimentation and deposition—
Research
Upper mantle project
x Geology—Research
xx Research
— Accounting *(HF5686.G35)*
— Juvenile literature
Geological societies *(Indirect)* *(QE1)*
sa Geology—Societies, etc. ᵣfor
publications of geological and other
societies in relation to geologyᵧ
xx Societies
Example under Scientific societies
Geological specimens
— Collection and preservation *(QE50)*
— — Juvenile literature
Geological statistics
See Geology—Statistical methods
Geological surveys *(QE61-350)*
sa Geology—ᵣlocal subdivisionᵧ—Surveys,
e.g. Geology—United States—
Surveys
xx Surveys
Geological time *(QE508)*
sa Earth—Age
Paleoclimatology
Radioactive dating
x Age of rocks
Dating of rocks
Geochronology
Geochrony
Rocks—Age
Time, Geological
xx Chronology
Earth—Age
Geologists *(Direct)* *(QE21-22)*
xx Earth scientists
Naturalists
Scientists
— Correspondence, reminiscences, etc.
Geology *(Indirect)* *(QE)*
sa Aerial photography in geology
Aeronautics in geology
Alluvium
Astronautics in geology
Bitumen—Geology
Boulders
Classification—Books—Geology
Coal—Geology
Continents

Coral reefs and islands
Creation
Crystallography
Deluge
Drift
Earth
Earthquakes
Erosion
Forests, Submerged
Geodes
Geophysics
Geysers
Glaciers
Glaciology
Gondwana (Geology)
Historical geology
Hydrogeology
Military geology
Mineralogy
Moraines
Mountains
Nuclear geophysics
Oceanography
Ore-deposits
Paleoclimatology
Paleogeography
Paleolimnology
Paleontology
Pediments (Geology)
Petroleum—Geology
Petrology
Physical geography
Physical geology
Radioisotopes in geology
Rock glaciers
Rocks
Sand
Sedimentation and deposition
Sediments (Geology)
Slopes (Physical geography)
Speleology
Submarine geology
Submarine topography
Volcanism
Volcanoes
Weathering
x Geognosy
Geoscience
Physiography
xx Creation
Crystallography
Earth
Earth sciences
Geophysics
Natural history
Petrology
Rocks
Science
— Addresses, essays, lectures
Example under Lectures and lecturing;
Speeches, addresses, etc.
— Authorship
— Bibliography
sa Information storage and retrieval
systems—Geology
— Catalogs and collections *(QE51-55)*
— Charts, diagrams, etc.
— Computer programs
— Early works to 1800 *(QE25)*
— Exhibitions
x Geological exhibitions
— Field work *(QE45)*
x Field geology
Field work (Geology)
— — Juvenile literature
— — Safety regulations *(Direct)*
— Film catalogs *(QE40)*
xx Visual education

Geology (Indirect) (QE)
— Film catalogs (QE40) (Continued)
    Example under Moving-pictures—Catalogs; and under references from Catalogs, Film; Film catalogs
— Graphic methods
— Guide-books
    x Guide-books
— History (QE11-13)
    xx Catastrophes (Geology)
— Indexes
— Information services
— International cooperation
— Juvenile literature (QE29)
— Laboratory manuals (QE41)
— Maps (QE33)
    sa Geological mapping
        Geology—⌐local subdivision⌐—Maps
        Magnetism, Terrestrial—Maps
    x Geological maps
        Maps, Geological
    xx Geological mapping
        Magnetism, Terrestrial—Maps
— Mathematical models
— Mathematics (QE33)
    x Mathematical geology
— Nomenclature (QE7)
    sa Geology—Terminology
    xx Geology—Terminology
        Science—Nomenclature
    Example under reference from Nomenclature
— Periodicity
    x Geological cycles
        Geological periodicity
        Varve
    xx Cycles
— Philosophy (QE6)
— Pictorial works
— Research
    See Geological research
— Societies, etc.
    xx Geological societies
— Statistical methods
    x Geological statistics
— Study and teaching (Elementary) (Direct)
— Study and teaching (Higher) (Direct)
— — Finance
— Study and teaching (Secondary) (Direct)
— Terminology
    sa Geology—Nomenclature
    xx Geology—Nomenclature

    GEOGRAPHIC SUBDIVISIONS

— ⌐local subdivision⌐
— — Maps
    x Geological maps
        Maps, Geological
    xx Geology—Maps

    GEOGRAPHIC SUBDIVISIONS

— Moon
    See Lunar geology

    GEOGRAPHIC SUBDIVISIONS

— United States
— — Surveys
    Example under Geological surveys
Geology, Biblical
    See Bible and geology
Geology, Chemical
    See Geochemistry
        Mineralogical chemistry
        Mineralogy, Determinative
        Rocks—Analysis
Geology, Dynamic
    See Geophysics

Geology, Economic (Indirect) (TN260)
    sa Bitumen—Geology
        Building stones
        Coal
        Coal—Geology
        Engineering geology
        Gas, Natural
        Mineral oils
        Mines and mineral resources
        Mining geology
        Ores
        Petroleum
        Petroleum—Geology
        Quarries and quarrying
        Soils
        Stone
        other geological products, e.g. Asbestos, Graphite, Gypsum, Limestone, Peat
    x Economic geology
    xx Physical geology
— Statistical methods (TN260)
Geology, Historical
    See Historical geology
Geology, Lunar
    See Lunar geology
Geology, Military
    See Military geology
Geology, Photography in
    See Photography in geology
Geology, Stratigraphic (QE651-699)
    sa Borings
        Facies (Geology)
        Historical geology
        Lithofacies
        Lunar stratigraphy
        Oil well logging
        Paleontology
        Paleontology, Stratigraphic
        Stratigraphic correlation
    x Age of rocks
        Rocks—Age
        Stratigraphic geology
    xx Historical geology
— Algonkian (QE655)
    sa Geology, Stratigraphic—Huronian
    x Algonkian period
— Archaean (QE653)
    sa Geology, Stratigraphic—Laurentian
        Schists
    x Archaean period
        Archaeozoic period
        Archean period
        Archeozoic period
        Geology, Stratigraphic—Archaeozoic
    xx Geology, Stratigraphic—Pre-Cambrian
— Archaeozoic
    See Geology, Stratigraphic—Archaean
— Caenozoic
    See Geology, Stratigraphic—Cenozoic
— Caledonian
    See Geology, Stratigraphic—Paleozoic
— Cambrian (QE656)
    x Cambrian period
        Geology, Stratigraphic—Primordial
    xx Geology, Stratigraphic—Paleozoic
— Carboniferous (QE671-3)
    sa Geology, Stratigraphic—Mississippian
        Geology, Stratigraphic—Pennsylvanian
    x Carboniferous period
    xx Geology, Stratigraphic—Paleozoic
— Cenozoic (QE690-699)
    sa Geology, Stratigraphic—Quaternary
        Geology, Stratigraphic—Tertiary
        Molasse
    x Caenozoic period

Cenozoic period
    Geology, Stratigraphic—Caenozoic
— Cretaceous (QE685-8)
    sa Flysch
    x Cretaceous period
        Laramie formation
        Montana formation
    xx Geology, Stratigraphic—Mesozoic
— Devonian (QE665)
    x Devonian period
        Old red sandstone (Geology)
        Oriskany formation
    xx Geology, Stratigraphic—Paleozoic
— Diluvial
    See Geology, Stratigraphic—Recent
— Eocene (QE692)
    x Eocene period
    xx Geology, Stratigraphic—Tertiary
— Gothlandian
    See Geology, Stratigraphic—Silurian
— Holocene
    See Geology, Stratigraphic—Recent
— Huronian
    x Huronian epoch
    xx Geology, Stratigraphic—Algonkian
        Geology, Stratigraphic—Pre-Cambrian
— Jurassic (QE681-3)
    x Geology, Stratigraphic—Liassic
        Jurassic period
        Lias
    xx Geology, Stratigraphic—Mesozoic
        Oolite
— Laurentian (QE653)
    xx Geology, Stratigraphic—Archaean
— Liassic
    See Geology, Stratigraphic—Jurassic
— Lower Carboniferous
    See Geology, Stratigraphic—Mississippian
— Lower Silurian
    See Geology, Stratigraphic—Ordovician
— Mesozoic (QE675-688)
    sa Geology, Stratigraphic—Cretaceous
        Geology, Stratigraphic—Jurassic
        Geology, Stratigraphic—Triassic
    x Mesozoic period
— Miocene (QE694)
    x Miocene period
    xx Geology, Stratigraphic—Neocene
        Geology, Stratigraphic—Tertiary
— Mississippian (QE672)
    x Geology, Stratigraphic—Lower Carboniferous
        Geology, Stratigraphic—Subcarboniferous
        Mississippian epoch
    xx Geology, Stratigraphic—Carboniferous
— Neocene (QE694-5)
    sa Geology, Stratigraphic—Miocene
        Geology, Stratigraphic—Pliocene
    x Neocene epoch
    xx Geology, Stratigraphic—Tertiary
— Oligocene (QE693)
    x Oligocene period
    xx Geology, Stratigraphic—Tertiary
— Ordovician (QE662)
    x Geology, Stratigraphic—Lower Silurian
        Geology, Stratigraphic—Silurian, Lower
        Lower Silurian period
        Ordovician formation
        Silurian period, Lower
    xx Geology, Stratigraphic—Paleozoic
— Paleocene

Geometry, Affine
  x Affine geometry
  xx Geometry, Modern
Geometry, Algebraic *(QA564)*
  sa Abelian varieties
    Algebraic spaces
    Algebraic varieties
    Cremona transformations
    Curves, Algebraic
    Embeddings (Mathematics)
    Functions, Abelian
    Geometry, Analytic
    Global analysis (Mathematics)
    Group schemes (Mathematics)
    Linear algebraic groups
    Picard schemes
    Rational equivalence (Algebraic
      geometry)
    Singularities (Mathematics)
    Surfaces
    Surfaces, Algebraic
    Topology
    Transformations (Mathematics)
  x Algebraic geometry
  xx Cremona transformations
    Curves, Algebraic
    Functions, Abelian
    Surfaces
    Topology
    Transformations (Mathematics)
Geometry, Analytic *(QA551-581)*
  sa Algebra—Graphic methods
    Conic sections
    Coordinates
    Curves
    Surfaces
  x Analytical geometry
  xx Algebra—Graphic methods
    Conic sections
    Geometry, Algebraic
  — Examinations, questions, etc.
  — Plane *(QA552)*
    xx Geometry, Plane
  —— Programmed instruction
  — Problems, exercises, etc.
  — Solid *(QA553)*
    xx Geometry, Solid
Geometry, Combinatorial
See Combinatorial geometry
Geometry, Descriptive *(QA501-521)*
  sa Axonometric projection
    Cone
    Engineering graphics
    Generation of geometric forms
    Isometric projection
    Perspective
    Projection
    Shades and shadows
    Stereotomy
  x Descriptive geometry
  xx Geometrical drawing
    Projection
  — Programmed instruction
  — Study and teaching
  —— Audio-visual aids
Geometry, Differential *(QA641-9)*
  sa Almost complex manifolds
    Calculus of tensors
    Congruences (Geometry)
    Connections (Mathematics)
    Convex bodies
    Convex domains
    Convex surfaces
    Coordinates
    Curves
    Differential forms
    Differential topology
    G-structures

    Geometry, Integral
    Geometry, Riemannian
    Holonomy groups
    Hyperspace
    Manifolds (Mathematics)
    Riemannian manifolds
    Spaces, Generalized
    Submanifolds
    Surfaces
    Surfaces, Ruled
    Symmetric spaces
    Transformations (Mathematics)
  x Differential geometry
  — Problems, exercises, etc.
  — Projective *(QA660)*
    x Geometry, Projective differential
    Projective differential geometry
Geometry, Enumerative *(QA607)*
  sa Curves
    Surfaces
Geometry, Hyperbolic *(QA685)*
  x Hyperbolic geometry
    Lobachevski geometry
    Lobatschevski geometry
  xx Geometry, Non-Euclidean
Geometry, Infinitesimal *(QA615-639)*
  sa Calculus
    Calculus of tensors
  x Infinitesimal geometry
  xx Calculus
Geometry, Integral *(QA649)*
  x Integral geometry
  xx Geometry, Differential
Geometry, Kinematic
See Kinematic geometry
Geometry, Line
See Line geometry
Geometry, Modern *(QA473-5)*
  sa Geometry, Affine
    Geometry, Projective
    Inversions (Geometry)
  x Modern geometry
  xx Sphere
  — Plane *(QA474)*
  — Solid *(QA475)*
Geometry, Non-Euclidean *(QA685)*
  sa Geometry—Foundations
    Geometry, Hyperbolic
    Geometry, Riemannian
    Hyperspace
    Parallels (Geometry)
    Screws, Theory of
    Spaces, Generalized
  x Non-Euclidean geometry
  xx Geometry—Foundations
    Parallels (Geometry)
  — Problems, exercises, etc.
Geometry, Plane *(QA451-485)*
  sa Area measurement
    Balbis
    Circle
    Conic sections
    Euclid's Elements
    Geometry, Analytic—Plane
    Golden section
    Triangle
  x Plane geometry
Geometry, Projective *(QA471; QA554)*
  sa Reciprocal polars
  x Projective geometry
  xx Geometry, Modern
  — Foundations
    x Foundations of projective geometry
    xx Axioms
      Mathematics—Philosophy
  — Problems, exercises, etc.
Geometry, Projective differential
See Geometry, Differential—Projective

Geometry, Riemannian
  sa Surfaces of constant curvature
  x Riemann geometry
    Riemannian geometry
  xx Geometry, Differential
    Geometry, Non-Euclidean
    Spaces, Generalized
Geometry, Solid *(QA457; QA491)*
  sa Cone
    Crystallography
    Cube
    Cylinder (Mathematics)
    Geometry, Analytic—Solid
    Polyhedra
    Sphere
    Surfaces
    Tetrahedra
    Volume (Cubic content)
  x Solid geometry
  — Models
Geometry concept *(LB1139)*
  x Conception of geometry
  xx Child study
Geometry of numbers
  x Numbers, Geometry of
  xx Numbers, Theory of
Geometry of paths
See Spaces, Generalized
Geomorphic geology
See Geomorphology
Geomorphological mapping *(Indirect)*
  (GB406)
  xx Cartography
    Geomorphology—Maps
Geomorphological research *(Indirect)*
  (GB409)
  x Geomorphology—Research
  xx Research
Geomorphology *(Indirect)*
  sa Aerial photography in geomorphology
    Astronautics in geomorphology
    Climatic geomorphology
    Earth pyramids
    Erosion
    Landforms
    Volcanism
  x Geomorphic geology
    Physiography
  xx Erosion
    Geology, Structural
    Physical geography
  — Guide-books *(GB406)*
  — Juvenile literature
  — Maps
    sa Geomorphological mapping
  — Mathematical models
  — Mathematics
  — Methodology *(GB406)*
  — Research
    See Geomorphological research
  — Statistical methods
  — Terminology
Geonic literature
  sa Geonim
    Rabbinical literature
    Responsa—To 1040
  x Gaonic literature
  xx Geonim
    Hebrew literature
    Jewish literature
    Talmud
Geonic responsa
See Responsa—To 1040
Geonim
  sa Geonic literature
  xx Geonic literature
    Rabbis
    Talmud

Geophagy
　See Pica (Pathology)
Geophone *(Mine-rescue work, TN297)*
　xx Mine safety—Equipment and supplies
Geophysical instruments
　sa Magnetic instruments
　　Meteorological instruments
　　Riometer
　　Tiltmeter
　x Instruments, Geophysical
　xx Meteorological instruments
　　Physical instruments
　　Scientific apparatus and instruments
Geophysical methods in soil-surveys
　See Soil-surveys—Geophysical methods
Geophysical observatories *(QC808)*
　sa Magnetism, Terrestrial—Observatories
　　Meteorological stations
　　Orbiting geophysical observatories
　　Seismology—Observatories
　　individual observatories
　x Geophysics—Observatories
　　Observatories, Geophysical
　　Stations, Geophysical
　xx Geophysics—Observations
　　Observatories
Geophysical prospecting
　See Prospecting—Geophysical methods
Geophysical research *(Direct)*
　sa Drifting ice stations
　　Radioactive tracers in geophysics
　　Seismological research
　x Geophysics—Research
　xx Research
　Note under Rocket research
Geophysical well logging
　x Logging, Geophysical well
　　Well logging, Geophysical
　xx Prospecting—Geophysical methods
— Problems, exercises, etc.
Geophysics *(Indirect)* *(QC806; QE500-501)*
　sa Astronautics in geophysics
　　Atmospheric electricity
　　Auroras
　　Continents
　　Counterglow
　　Earth currents
　　Earth movements
　　Earth resistance
　　Earth tides
　　Electronics in geophysics
　　Energy budget (Geophysics)
　　Gases in rocks
　　Geodynamics
　　Geology
　　Gravimeter (Geophysical instrument)
　　Information theory in geophysics
　　Magnetism, Terrestrial
　　Magnetohydrodynamics
　　Marine geophysics
　　Mass budget (Geophysics)
　　Meteorology
　　Nuclear geophysics
　　Oceanography
　　Paleogeophysics
　　Plate tectonics
　　Prospecting—Geophysical methods
　　Radiative transfer
　　Rock pressure
　　Seismology
　　Solifluction
　　Van Allen radiation belts
　x Geological physics
　　Geology, Dynamic
　　Physics, Terrestrial
　　Terrestrial physics
　xx Earth
　　Earth sciences

Geology
　Physical geography
　Physics
　Space sciences
— Charts, diagrams, etc.
— Computer programs
— Fluid models *(QC809.F5)*
　x Rotating dishpan
　Example under Fluid dynamics
— International cooperation
　sa International Geophysical Year,
　　　1957-1958
　　International Years of the Quiet Sun,
　　　1964-1965
— Juvenile literature
— Mathematics *(QC809.M37)*
— Observations
　sa Geophysical observatories
　x Observations, Geophysical
— Observatories
　See Geophysical observatories
— Research
　See Geophysical research
— Statistical methods
— Study and teaching (Higher) *(Direct)*
— Tables, etc.
Geophysics, Electronics in
　See Electronics in geophysics
Geopolitics *(Direct)* *(JC319-323)*
　sa Anthropo-geography
　　Boundaries
　　Demography
　　Territory, National
　　World politics
　xx Anthropo-geography
　　Boundaries
　　Demography
　　Geography, Political
　　International relations
　　Political science
　　Territory, National
　　World politics
Georg-Büchner-Preis
　x Büchner-Preis
George, Lake, Battle of, 1755 *(E199)*
　xx Crown Point Expedition, 1755
George Cross *(CR4880)*
　Example under Heroes
George junior republics
　See Junior republics
Georgetown automatic translation
　See GAT (Computer program)
Georgia
— History *(F281-295)*
— — Colonial period, ca. 1600-1775
— — — Juvenile literature
— — Revolution, 1775-1783 *(E263.G3)*
— — 1775-1865
— — War of 1812 *(E359.5.G4)*
— — Creek War, 1836
　　　See Creek War, 1836
— — Civil War, 1861-1865 *(E503; E559)*
— — — Centennial celebrations, etc.
— — 1865-
Georgia (Transcaucasia)
— History
— — To 1801
— — 1801-1917
— — 1917-
Georgia (Transcaucasia) in art
Georgia pine
　See Longleaf pine
Georgian architecture
　See Architecture, Georgian
Georgian art
　See Art, Georgian
Georgian ballads and songs *(Direct)*

Georgian decoration and ornament
　(Transcaucasia)
　See Decoration and ornament, Georgian
　　(Transcaucasia)
Georgian embroidery
　See Embroidery, Georgian
Georgian fiction *(Direct)*
Georgian furniture
　See Furniture, Georgian
Georgian glassware
　See Glassware, Georgian
Georgian illumination of books and
　manuscripts
　See Illumination of books and manuscripts,
　　Georgian
Georgian language *(PK9101-9151)*
　sa Adzhar dialect
　xx Caucasian languages
　　Kartvelian languages
— Dialects
　sa Gurian dialect
Georgian literature *(PK9160-9178)*
　x Grusian literature
Georgian philology
　x Philology, Georgian
　xx Caucasian philology
Georgian poetry *(PK9162; PK9166)*
　sa Revolutionary poetry, Georgian
Georgian silver articles
　See Silver articles, Georgian
Georgian style (Decoration and ornament)
　See Decoration and ornament—Georgian
　　style
Georgian wood-carving
　See Wood-carving, Georgian
Georgians *(DK511.G36)*
　sa Laz
　x Grusinians
　　Ibernians
　　Karthveli
— Religion
Georgians in Moscow
Geoscience
　See Earth sciences
　　Geology
Geoscience electronics
　See Electronics in earth sciences
Geostrophic wind
　xx Winds
　　Winds aloft
Geotechnique
　See Rock mechanics
　　Soil mechanics
Geotechnique, Marine
　See Marine geotechnique
Geotectonics
　See Geology, Structural
Geothermal engineering
　xx Chemical engineering
　　Electric engineering
　　Heat engineering
Geothermal resources *(Direct)*
　sa Geysers
　　Springs
　x Thermal waters
　xx Earth temperature
　　Geochemistry
　　Natural resources
— Maps
Geotropism *(Biology, QH511; Botany,*
　　QK776)
　　Here are entered works on geotropic
　　movements in both animals and plants.
　sa Plants, Effect of weightlessness on
　x Plants, Effect of gravity on
　xx Growth (Plants)
　　Irritability
　　Plants, Effect of weightlessness on

Geotropism *(Biology, QH511; Botany,*
  QK776) (Continued)
    Plants—Irritability and movements
    Tropisms
Gephyra
  See Gephyrea
Gephyrea *(QL391.G5)*
  sa Echiuroidea
  x Gephyra
  xx Annelida
Gepidae *(DD78.G5)*
  xx Germanic tribes
    Goths
Geraniales
  xx Dicotyledons
Geraniums *(SB413.G35)*
  sa Upland geranium
  — Diseases and pests
  — Varieties
Gerasene demoniac (Miracle)
  See Healing of the Gerasene demoniac
    (Miracle)
Gerbera *(Botany, QK495.C; Floriculture,*
  SB413.G)
  x African daisy
    Barberton daisy
    Transvaal daisy
  xx Daisies
  — Diseases and pests
    sa Cyclamen mite
Gerbils *(QL737.R6)*
Gerbils as pets *(SF459.G4)*
  — Juvenile literature
Gere (African people)
  x Dan (African people)
    Guere (African people)
    Ngere (African people)
  xx Ethnology—Ivory Coast
    Ethnology—Liberia
Gere language
  See Dan language
Gergovie, Battle of, 52 B.C. *(DC62)*
  xx Gaul—History—58 B.C.-511 A.D.
Geriatric anesthesia *(RD145)*
  xx Anesthesia
    Geriatrics
Geriatric nursing *(RC954)*
  xx Aged—Care and hygiene
    Nurses and nursing
    Nursing homes
Geriatric ophthalmology *(RE48.2.A5)*
  xx Ophthalmology
Geriatric pharmacology
  See Geriatrics—Formulae, receipts,
    prescriptions
Geriatric psychiatry
  x Aged—Psychiatric care
    Psychiatry, Geriatric
    Psychogeriatrics
  xx Psychiatry
Geriatrics *(RC952-954)*
  sa Aged—Care and hygiene
    Geriatric anesthesia
  x Old age—Diseases
  xx Age factors in disease
    Aged—Care and hygiene
    Old age
  — Formulae, receipts, prescriptions
    (RC953.7)
    x Geriatric pharmacology
  — Vocational guidance
    See Geriatrics as a profession
Geriatrics as a profession
  x Geriatrics—Vocational guidance
  xx Medicine as a profession
Germ cells *(QL964)*
  sa Oogenesis
    Ovum

Spermatogenesis
Spermatozoa
  x Reproductive cells
    Sex cells
  xx Cells
    Embryology
    Heredity
    Oogenesis
    Spermatogenesis
Germ-free life
  See Germfree life
Germ letters
  See Bijas
Germ theory
  See Life—Origin
    Spontaneous generation
Germ theory of disease *(RB214)*
  sa Air—Microbiology
    Bacteria, Pathogenic
    Bacteriology
    Diseases—Causes and theories of
      causation
  x Disease germs
    Germs
    Microbes
  xx Bacteriology
    Communicable diseases
    Diseases—Causes and theories of
      causation
Germ warfare
  See Biological warfare
German (Dance) *(GV1757)*
  x Cotillion
  Example under Square dancing
German almanacs
  See Almanacs, German
German altarpieces
  See Altarpieces, German
German-American literature *(Direct)*
  (Collections, PT3913-3916; History,
  PT3900-3912)
  sa Literature, Comparative—German and
    American
  xx American literature
    German literature
    United States—Literatures
  — Catholic authors
German-American newspapers *(History, etc.,*
  PN4885.G29-34)
  xx American newspapers
    German newspapers
    German newspapers in foreign
      countries
  Note under Newspapers
German-American periodicals
  xx German periodicals
  Note under Periodicals
German-American poetry *(Collections,*
  PT3914; History, PT3910)
  xx American poetry
    German poetry
German-American wit and humor
  (PN6231.G4)
  xx American wit and humor
    German wit and humor
German anacreontic poetry
  See Anacreontic poetry, German
German art objects
  See Art objects, German
German-Austrian Monetary Union of 1857
  See Austrian-German Monetary Union of
    1857
German automobiles
  See Automobiles, German
German ballads and songs *(Direct)*
  (Collections, PT1185, PT1199-1232;
  History, PT507)
  sa Ballads, German

Folk-songs, German
National songs, German
Political ballads and songs, German
Songs, German
War-songs, German
  x Austrian ballads and songs
— Austrian authors
    Duplicate entry is made under Aus-
      trian poetry (German)
  x Austrian ballads and songs (German)
  xx Austrian poetry (German)
— Swiss authors *(Collections, PT3874;*
    History, PT3870)
    Duplicate entry is made under Swiss
      poetry (German)
  x Swiss ballads and songs (German)
  xx Swiss poetry (German)
German Baptist Brethren
  See Church of the Brethren
German Baptists
  See Baptists, German
German-Bohemian literature
  See German literature—Bohemia
German bookbindings
  See Bookbinding—Germany
German-British naval agreement, 1935
  See Anglo-German naval agreement, 1935
German Catholicism *(BX4740)*
    Here are entered works on an antipapal,
      nationalistic movement among Cath-
      olics in Germany started by J. Ronge
      and J. Czerski in 1844. The movement
      was subsequently merged into the
      "free religious" movement.
  x Deutschkatholizismus
  xx Catholic Church in Germany
German church historians
  See Church historians, German
German court epic
  See Court epic, German
German daggers
  See Daggers, German
German Day celebrations
  xx Germans in foreign countries
German decoration and ornament
  See Decoration and ornament, German
German detective stories
  See Dectective and mystery stories,
    German
German drama *(Direct) (Collections,*
  PT1251-1299; History, PT605-709)
  sa Carnival plays
    Mysteries and miracle-plays, German
    Singspiel
  xx Drama
— To 1500 *(Collections, PT1435-1477;*
    History, PT621)
    Note under Mysteries and miracle-plays,
      English, ₍French, German, etc.₎
— Early modern, 1500-1700 *(Collections,*
    PT1263-4; History, PT631-3,
    PT636-8)
— 18th century *(Collections, PT1265;*
    History, PT636-643)
— 19th century *(Collections, PT1266;*
    History, PT651-663)
— 20th century *(Collections, PT1268;*
    History, PT666-8)
— Austrian authors *(Collections,*
    PT3826.D8; History, PT3821)
    x Austrian drama (German)
— Biography
    See Dramatists, German
— Microcard catalogs
— Stories, plots, etc. *(PT626)*
German drama (Comedy) *(Collections,*
  PT1275-7; History, PT676)
  sa Carnival plays

German drama (Tragedy) *(Collections, PT1271-3; History, PT671)*

German drama in foreign countries

German drawing
  See Drawing, German

German emblem books
  See Emblem books, German

German erotic poetry
  See Erotic poetry, German

German essays *(Direct) (Collections, PT1354; History, PT831)*
  Here are entered collections of essays by several authors.

German Expedition to China, 1900-1901 *(DS771.5)*

German farces *(Collections, PT1283.F2; History, PT696)*
  xx Farces

German fiction *(Collections, PT1321-1340; History, PT741-772)*
  sa Detective and mystery stories, German
    Dime novels, German
    Ghost stories, German
    Historical fiction, German
    Horror tales, German
    Love stories, German
    Short stories, German
  — Middle High German, 1050-1500 *(PT230)*
  — Early modern, 1500-1700 *(Collections, PT1313-1314; History, PT753-6)*
  — 18th century *(Collections, PT1315; History, PT759)*
  — 19th century *(Collections, PT1332; History, PT763-771)*
  — 20th century *(Collections, PT1334; History, PT772)*
  — Austrian authors *(Collections, PT3826; History, PT3822)*
    x Austrian fiction (German)
  — Swiss authors
    x Swiss fiction (German)

German folk-drama
  See Folk-drama, German

German folk literature
  See Folk literature, German

German folk music
  See Folk music, German

German genre painting
  See Genre painting, German

German ghost stories
  See Ghost stories, German

German Grand Prix Race
  x Grand Prix, German
  xx Automobile racing
    Grand Prix racing

German Hebrew
  See Yiddish language

German horror tales
  See Horror tales, German

German house names
  See House names, German

German hunting songs
  See Hunting songs, German

German illumination of books and manuscripts
  See Illumination of books and manuscripts, German

German imprints *(Direct)*
  — Publishing

German interludes
  See Interludes, German

German language *(PF3001-5999)*
  sa Low German language
  xx Germanic languages
  — Old High German, 750-1050 *(PF3801-3991)*
    x Old High German language

— Middle High German, 1050-1500 *(PF4043-4350)*
    x Middle High German language
  — — Lexicography
  — Early modern, 1500-1700 *(PF4501-4596)*
  — Business German *(PF3120.C7; Correspondence, HF5728.G3)*
  — Orthography and spelling
    Notes under Phonetic spelling; Spelling reform
  — Pronunciation
    Example under Phonetics
  — Readers (Medicine)
    Note under Readers

German language in foreign countries

German language in Switzerland, ₍etc.₎

German letters *(Collections, PT1348-1352; History, PT811)*

German librarians
  See Librarians, German

German literature *(Direct) (Collections, PT1100-1485; History, PT1-951)*
  sa Austrian literature
    German-American literature
    German literature in foreign countries
    Low German literature
    Swiss literature
  Example under Philology
  — Old High German, 750-1050 *(Collections, PF3985-3991; History, PT183)*
    x German poetry—Old High German, 750-1500
      Old High German literature
  — Middle High German, 1050-1500 *(Collections, PT1375-1479; History, PT175-230)*
    x Middle High German literature
  — Early modern, 1500-1700 *(Collections, PT1121-6; History, PT238-281)*
  — 18th century *(Collections, PT1131)*
  — — History and criticism *(PT285-321)*
    sa Sturm und Drang movement
  — 19th century *(Collections, PT1136)*
  — — History and criticism *(PT341-395)*
    sa Biedermeier
      Young Germany
    xx Young Germany
  — 20th century *(Collections, PT1141; History, PT401-3)*
  — Austrian authors *(Collections, PT3823-9; History, PT3810-3822)*
    x Austrian literature (German)
  — Bibliography *(Z2221-2249)*
    sa Catalogs, Publishers'—Germany
  — — Early *(Z2222; Z2232)*
  — — First editions *(Z2234.F5)*
  — Bio-bibliography *(Z2230-2234)*
  — Catholic authors *(PT89; PT1109.C3)*
    Example under Catholic literature
  — Film adaptations
  — Jewish authors
    x Jewish literature (German)
  — Swiss authors *(Collections, PT3873-6; History, PT3860-3872)*
    x Swiss literature (German)
  — Bavaria
    x Bavarian literature
  — Bohemia
    x German-Bohemian literature
    Note under Bohemian literature
  — Germany, Northern
    xx Low German literature
  — Swabia
    x Swabian literature
  — Switzerland
    xx Swiss literature

German literature in foreign countries *(PT3808-9)*
  xx German literature

German lithographs
  See Lithographs, German

German love stories
  See Love stories, German

German mathematics
  See Mathematics, German

German measles
  See Rubella

German mercenaries *(DD102.7)*
  sa Hanoverian mercenaries
    Hessian mercenaries
    United States—History—Revolution, 1775-1783—German mercenaries
  x Landsknechte
  xx Mercenary troops

German mosaics
  See Mosaics, German

German moving-picture cartoons
  See Moving-picture cartoons, German

German music
  See Music, German

German musicians
  See Musicians, German

German mystery stories
  See Detective and mystery stories, German

German newspapers *(Direct) (History, PN5201-5219)*
  sa Austrian newspapers
    German-American newspapers
    Swiss newspapers
  — Directories *(Z6956.G3)*
  — Prices *(Direct)*
  — Taxation
    xx Newspapers—Taxation

GEOGRAPHIC SUBDIVISIONS

  — Poland
    Duplicate entry is made under Polish newspapers (German)

German newspapers in foreign countries
  sa German-American newspapers

German occupation of Denmark, 1940-1945
  See Denmark—History—German occupation, 1940-1945

German occupation of Netherlands, 1940-1945
  See Netherlands—History—German occupation, 1940-1945

German occupation of Norway, 1940-1945
  See Norway—History—German occupation, 1940-1945

German orations *(Collections, PT1344-5; History, PT801)*
  Here are entered collections of orations by several authors.

German parodies
  See Parodies, German

German part-songs
  See Part-songs, German

German pastoral poetry
  See Pastoral poetry, German

German penmanship
  See Penmanship, German

German periodicals *(Direct) (History, PN5201-5220)*
  sa Austrian periodicals
    Children's periodicals, German
    German-American periodicals
    Swiss periodicals
    Women's periodicals, German
  — Directories *(Z6956.G3)*

German periodicals in foreign countries

German pewter
  See Pewter, German

German philology *(PF3001-3095)*
  xx Germanic philology

German philology *(PF3001-3095)*
   (Continued)
   — Middle High German, 1050-1500
      GENERAL SUBDIVISIONS
   — Political aspects
German physicians' literary writings
   See Physicians' literary writings, German
German poetry *(Direct) (Collections,*
      PT1151-1241; History, PT500-597)
German poetry
   sa Anacreontic poetry, German
      Erotic poetry, German
      German-American poetry
      Parodies, German
      Pastoral poetry, German
      Religious poetry, German
   Note under Lyric poetry
   — Old High German, 750-1050
         See German literature—Old High
            German, 750-1050
   — Middle High German, 1050-1500
         (Collections, PT1391-1429;
         History, PT175-227)
      sa Court epic, German
   — Early modern, 1500-1700 *(Collections,*
      PT1163-5; History, PT525-531)
   — 18th century *(Collections, PT1167-9;*
      History, PT533-5)
   — 19th century *(Collections, PT1171-3;*
      History, PT541-7)
   — 20th century *(Collections, PT1174-5;*
      History, PT551-3)
   — Austrian authors *(Collections, PT3824;*
      History, PT3820)
         Duplicate entry is made under Aus-
            trian poetry (German)
         Note under Austrian poetry (German)
   — Czech authors *(PT3836)*
         x Czech poetry (German)
   — Polish authors
         x Polish poetry (German)
   — Swiss authors *(Collections, PT3874;*
      History, PT3870)
         Duplicate entry is made under Swiss
            poetry (German)
      sa Political poetry, Swiss
         Note under Swiss poetry (German)
German police dogs
   See German shepherd dogs
German-Polish pact, 1934
   See Polish-German pact, 1934
German political posters
   See Political posters, German
German portrait sculpture
   See Portrait sculpture, German
German Presbyterians
   See Presbyterians, German
German propaganda
   See Propaganda, German
German property in foreign countries
German property in Italy, ⌐Sweden,
      Switzerland, etc.⌐
   xx Alien property—Italy, ⌐Sweden,
      Switzerland, etc.⌐
German prose literature *(Direct)*
      (Collections, PT1301-1360; History,
      PT711-871)
German proverbs
   See Proverbs, German
German question (1949-   )
   See German reunification questions (1949-
)
German rearmament
   See Germany—Defenses
German reference books
   See Reference books, German
German Reformed Church (U.S.)
   See Reformed Church in the United States

German refugees
   See Refugees, German
German religious poetry
   See Religious poetry, German
German resistance movement
   See Anti-Nazi movement
German reunification question (1949-   )
      (DD257.25)
   sa Berlin question (1945-   )
      Rapacki plan
   x German question (1949-   )
      German unification question (1949-
)
      Reunification of Germany, Proposed
         (1949-   )
      Unification of Germany, Proposed
         (1949-   )
   xx Germany—History—Allied occupation,
      1945-
      World War, 1939-1945—Peace
   — Historiography
   — Pictorial works
German Russians
   See Russian Germans
German schools
   See Schools, German ⌐for works on German
      schools in foreign countries⌐
      Schools—Germany ⌐for works on
         schools in Germany⌐
German self-portraits
   See Self-portraits, German
German shepherd dogs *(SF429.S6)*
   x Alsatian wolf dogs
      German police dogs
   Example under reference from Shepherd dogs
   — Juvenile literature
   — Legends and stories
German short-haired pointers
   xx Pointers (Dogs)
German shorthand
   See Shorthand, German
German silver
   See Nickel silver
German-Soviet pact
   See Russo-German treaty, 1939
German students in Italy, ⌐the United States,
      etc.⌐
German studies *(Direct) (DD61)*
German subject headings
   See Subject headings, German
German unification question (1949-   )
   See German reunification question (1949-
)
German wirehaired pointers *(SF429.G43)*
   xx Pointers (Dogs)
German wit and humor *(Direct)*
      (Collections, PN6193-5; History,
      PT851)
      Here are entered collections from several
         authors and individual authors who
         have not written in other literary
         forms.
   sa Bavarian wit and humor
      German-American wit and humor
      Low German wit and humor
      Schnaderhüpfel
      Swabian wit and humor
German wit and humor, Pictorial
      (NC1500-1509)
German wood-carving
   See Wood-carving, German
German wood-engravings
   See Wood-engravings, German
Germanic antiquities *(DD51-55)*
   sa subdivision Antiquities, Germanic
      under names of countries, cities, etc.
   x Antiquities, Germanic
      Germanic tribes—Antiquities

   xx Antiquities
Germanic architecture
   See Architecture, Germanic
Germanic art industries and trade
   See Art industries and trade, Germanic
Germanic calendar
   See Calendar, Germanic
Germanic civilization
   See Civilization, Germanic
Germanic demonology
   See Demonology, Germanic
Germanic epic poetry
   See Epic poetry, Germanic
Germanic languages *(PD-PF)*
   sa Anglo-Saxon language
      Danish language
      Dutch language
      English language
      Flemish language
      Friesian language
      German language
      Germanic philology
      Gothic language
      Icelandic and Old Norse languages
      Low German language
      Norwegian language
      Scandinavian languages
      Swedish language
   x Teutonic languages
   — History
      sa Proto-Germanic language
Germanic law
   See Law, Germanic
Germanic legends
   See Legends, Germanic
Germanic literature *(PN821-840)*
      Here are entered chiefly treatises on the
         early literature of the Germanic tribes,
         Goths, Anglo-Saxons, Scandinavians,
         etc.
      sa names of the various literatures which
         form the Germanic group, e.g. Dutch
         literature, English literature, Swedish
         literature
Germanic mythology
   See Mythology, Germanic
Germanic philology *(PD1-71)*
   sa Dutch philology
      English philology
      Friesian philology
      German philology
      Scandinavian philology
      names of various languages and
         literatures which form the Germanic
         group, i.e. Danish, Dutch, English,
         Flemish, Friesian, Gothic, Icelandic
         and Old Norse, Low German,
         Norwegian, Swedish
   xx Germanic languages
      Philology, Modern
   Note under Philology, Modern
Germanic poetry *(PN834)*
   sa Epic poetry, Germanic
Germanic tribes *(Ethnography, GN585.G4;*
      Political institutions, JC29, JC41)
   sa Alemanni
      Bastarnae
      Batavians
      Bavarians
      Cimbri
      Caninefates
      Franks
      Gepidae
      Goths
      Jutes
      Lygii
      Marcomanni
      Missions—Germanic tribes

Quadi
Saxons
Sithones
Suevi
Swabians
Ubii
Vandals
xx Aryans
   Goths
   Migrations of nations
   Teutonic race
— Agriculture
   See Agriculture—Germanic tribes
— Antiquities
   See Germanic antiquities
— Civilization
   See Civilization, Germanic
— History, Military
— Juvenile literature
— Names
— Religion (BL830-875)
   sa Folk-lore, Germanic
      Irminsul
      Mythology, Germanic
      Mythology, Norse
      Salvation (Germanic religion)
   Example under Religion
— Rites and ceremonies
— Weaving
   See Weaving—Germanic tribes
Germanic tribes in the Balkan Peninsula (DR27.G4)
   sa Barbarian invasions of Rome
Germanium (QD181.G5)
Example under Semiconductors
— Analysis
— Electric properties
— Isotopes
   x Germanium isotopes
      Isotopic germanium
— Quenching
   x Quenching of germanium
   xx Cooling
      Metals—Heat treatment
— Spectra
Germanium alloys
   sa Silver-germanium alloys
Germanium crystals
— Electric properties
— Magnetic properties
— Radiation effects
   See Germanium crystals, Effect of radiation on
Germanium crystals, Effect of radiation on
   x Germanium crystals—Radiation effects
   xx Radiation
Germanium detectors
   See Germanium diodes
Germanium diodes (TK7872.V3; Radio, TK6565.V3)
   x Germanium detectors
   xx Crystals
      Diodes
      Electron tubes
      Tunnel diodes
Germanium isotopes
   See Germanium—Isotopes
Germanium organic compounds
   See Organogermanium compounds
Germanium-silver alloys
   See Silver-germanium alloys
Germanization
   xx Assimilation (Sociology)
      Civics
Germans (National characteristics, DD76)
   sa Hessians
      Russian Germans
      Thuringians

Germans in Bohemia
   x Sudeten Germans
Germans in Brazil, [Hungary, Milwaukee, etc.]
— Anecdotes, facetiae, satire, etc.
— Biography
— Education
— Legal status, laws, etc. (Direct)
— Registers
— Religion
Germans in foreign countries
   sa German Day celebrations
Example under Minorities
— Citizenship
— Legal status, laws, etc.
Germans in literature
Germans in Pennsylvania
   See Pennsylvania Germans
Germans in Poland
   xx Drang nach Osten
Example under Minorities
— Legal status, laws, etc.
Germans in Russia
   sa Russian Germans
   xx Drang nach Osten
Note under Russian Germans
Germans in the Czechoslovak Republic
   x Sudeten Germans
Example under Population transfers
— Personal narratives
Germans in the United States
Note under Catholics in Boston, [Canada, Chile, etc.]
— Juvenile literature
Germans in Transylvania
   x Saxons in Transylvania
      Transylvanian Saxons
Germantown, Battle of, 1777 (E241.G3)
Germany
— Antiquities, Roman
   x Romans in Germany
— Constitutional history
   sa Mediatized states
— Defenses
   x German rearmament
      Germany—Rearmament
   Example under reference from Rearmament
— Denazification
   See Denazification
— History (DD)
— — To 843
   sa Marcomannic War, 167-180
      Solicinium, Battle of, 368
— — To 1517
— — 843-918
— — 843-1273
   sa Verdun, Treaty of, 843
— — Saxon House, 919-1024 (DD136-140.7)
   sa Holy Roman Empire—History—Saxon House, 919-1024
   x Ottonian emperors
      Ottonian House
      Saxon emperors
      Saxon House
      Saxony, House of
   xx Holy Roman Empire—History—Saxon House, 919-1024
— — Franconian House, 1024-1125
   sa Franconian House
      Holy Roman Empire—History—Franconian House, 1024-1125
   x Franconian emperors
      Salian emperors
   xx Franconian House
      Holy Roman Empire—History—Franconian House, 1024-1125

— — Hohenstaufen, 1138-1254
— — Interregnum, 1254-1273
— — 1273-1517
   sa Mühldorf, Battle of, 1322
— — 1517-1648
— — 1517-1871
— — 17th century
— — 1618-1648
   sa Thirty Years' War, 1618-1648
   xx Thirty Years' War, 1618-1648
— — 1648-1740
— — 18th century
— — 1740-1806
— — 1789-1900
   x Germany—History—19th century
— — 19th century
   See Germany—History—1789-1900
— — 1806-1815
— — 1815-1866
   sa Schleswig-Holstein question
   xx Young Germany
— — Revolution, 1848-1849
   sa Berlin—History—Revolution, 1848-1849
      Eichsfeld, Ger.—History—Revolution, 1848-1849
   x Revolution of 1848 in Germany
— — — Pamphlets
— — — Refugees
— — 1848-1870
— — 1866-1871
   sa Austro-Prussian War, 1866
— — Franco-German War, 1870-1871
   See Franco-German War, 1870-1871
— — 1871-
— — — Pictorial works
— — 1871-1918
   sa Dual Alliance, 1879
— — — Pictorial works
— — 20th century
— — — Book reviews
— — Revolution, 1918 (DD248)
— — — Posters
— — Allied occupation, 1918-1930 (D650.M5)
   sa Rhine Valley—History—Separatist movement, 1918-1924
   xx Rhine Valley—History
— — 1918-1933
   sa Anschluss movement, 1918-1938
— — — Historiography
— — Kapp Putsch, 1920
   x Kapp Putsch
— — March Uprising, 1921
   x March Action, 1921 (Germany)
      March Uprising, 1921 (Germany)
— — Beer Hall Putsch, 1923
   x Beer Hall Putsch, 1923
      Hitler's Putsch, 1923
      Munich—History—Beer Hall Putsch, 1923
— — 1933-1945
   sa Anschluss movement, 1918-1938
      Anti-Nazi movement
      Munich. Universität—Riot, Feb. 18, 1943
— — — Historiography
— — — Pictorial works
— — — Poetry
— — Great Blood Purge, 1934 (DD247.R56)
   x Blood Purge, 1934
      Great Blood Purge, 1934
      Night of the Long Knives, 1934
      Röhm's Putsch, 1934
— — Allied occupation, 1945-
   sa Denazification

Germany
— History *(DD)*
— — Allied occupation, 1945-
(Continued)
German reunification question
(1949-   )
— — — Caricatures and cartoons
— — — Pictorial works
— Maps
Example under Atlases
— Nobility
Example under Aristocracy
— Politics and government
— — 1945-
sa Denazification
— Rearmament
See Germany—Defenses
— Religious life and customs
Example under Fasts and feasts; Folklore; Religion and sociology
— — Middle Ages, 843-1517
— — Modern period, 1517-
Germany. Heer
Example under Armaments
— Airborne troops
Example under Airborne troops
— Parachute troops
Example under Parachute troops
— Transport of sick and wounded
Example under Transportation, Military
— Transportation
Example under Transportation, Military
Germany. Heer. Feldartillerie
xx Artillery, Field and mountain
Germany. Kriegsmarine
— Juvenile literature
— Medical examinations
Example under reference from Soldiers—Medical examinations
Germany. Reichsarbeitsdienst
Example under Labor service
Germany. Reichsfinanzhof
Example under Tax courts
Germany. Reichstag
— Dissolution
Example under Legislative bodies—Dissolution
Germany, Eastern *(DD731-740)*
Here are entered works concerned with the area of historic Germany approximately east of the Elbe River.
— History
— — 1933-1945
Germany in literature
Germfree life
x Germ-free life
Gnotobiology
Gnotobiotics
xx Biological research
Microbiology
— Technique
Germicidal lamps
xx Air—Purification
Electric lamps
Germicides
See Disinfection and disinfectants
Fungicides
Germinal layers *(QL971)*
sa Parablast
xx Embryology
Germination *(QK740)*
sa Potatoes—Sprouting
Seeds—Stratification
Seeds—Viability
Vernalization
x Seeds—Germination
xx Botany—Embryology
Plant physiology
Seeds—Viability

Germs
See Bacteria
Bacteriology
Germ theory of disease
Micro-organisms
Gerontocracy *(GN492.1)*
xx Aged
Tribes and tribal system
Gerontologists *(Direct)*
xx Social scientists
Gerontology
See Aged
Old age
Gerrymander *(JK1347-8)*
xx Administrative and political divisions
Election districts
Legislative bodies
Representative government and representation
GERT (Network analysis)
x Graphical evaluation and review technique
xx Network analysis (Planning)
Ges languages
See Tapuyan languages
Gesell incomplete man test
x Incomplete man test
xx Child study
Mental tests
Gesso *(NK5080)*
xx Decoration and ornament
Plaster of Paris
Gesta Romanorum *(PA8320-8325)*
xx Fables
Gestagens
See Progestational hormones
Gestalt completion test
See Street gestalt completion test
Gestalt psychology *(BF203)*
sa Bender gestalt test
Street gestalt completion test
Whole and parts (Psychology)
x Configuration (Psychology)
Form psychology
Psychology, Structural
Structural psychology
xx Consciousness
Ejection (Psychology)
Knowledge, Theory of
Perception
Psychology
Senses and sensation
Gestalt test
See Bender gestalt test
Gestalt therapy *(RC489.G4)*
xx Psychotherapy
Gestation
See Pregnancy
Gestogens
See Progestational hormones
Gesture *(Public speaking, PN4165)*
sa Pantomime
Shanghai gesture
Sign language
x Mudra
xx Acting
Elocution
Hand
Movement (Acting)
Nonverbal communication
Oratory
Sign language
— Anecdotes, facetiae, satire, etc.
Gesture in art
xx Art
Gesture in literature
Gesture language
See Deaf—Means of communication

Indians of North America—Sign language
Sign language
Gestures (Buddhism)
See Mudrās (Buddhism)
Gesu
See Gisu (Bantu tribe)
Getas
See Sabots
Getter-ion pumps
See Ion pumps
Getters
sa Ion pumps
xx Gases—Absorption and adsorption
Metals
Vacuum-tubes
Gettysburg, Battle of, 1863 *(E475.53)*
xx Gettysburg Campaign, 1863
Example under War
— Centennial celebrations, etc.
— Juvenile literature
Gettysburg Campaign, 1863 *(E475.51-53)*
sa Gettysburg, Battle of, 1863
x Lee's 2d Northern Invasion
Maryland Campaign, 1863
Pennsylvania Invasion, 1863
Gettysburg Reunion, 1913 *(E475.57)*
Gettysburg Reunion, 1938 *(E475.58)*
x Blue and Gray Reunion, 1938
Getwezi
See Yatvyags
Geysers *(Indirect)* *(QE528)*
sa Springs
x Hot springs
Thermal waters
xx Geology
Geothermal resources
Physical geography
Springs
Water
Water, Underground
GGPP (Computer program)
x General Game Playing Program
Ghadīr al-Khumm
See 'Īd al-Ghadīr
Ghalchah languages *(PK6991.G5)*
sa Iranian languages
Pamir languages
Yazghulami language
Ghana Empire *(DT532.15)*
Ghanaian literature
Ghanaian literature (English)
See English literature—Ghanaian authors
Ghanaian newspapers *(Direct)*
Ghanaian periodicals *(Direct)*
Ghanaian poetry (English)
See English poetry—Ghanaian authors
Ghanaian students in the United States, [etc.]
xx Ghanaians in the United States, [etc.]
Ghanaians in the United States, [etc.]
sa Ghana students in the United States, [etc.]
xx Ghanaian students in the United States, [etc.]
Ghassul culture *(GN775.5.G5)*
xx Man, Prehistoric
Neolithic period
Ghazels
See Gazels
Ghaznawids
See Ghaznevids
Ghaznevids *(DS288.7)*
x Ghaznawids
Ghec-chi language
See Kekchi language
Ghee
xx Butter
Butterfat

— Grading and standardization
— Marketing
Gheel system
   See Mentally ill—Home care
Gheghids
   See Ghegs
Ghegs
   x Gegs
      Gheghids
   xx Albanians
Ghent, Treaty of, 1814 *(E358)*
Ghettos
   See Jews—Segregation
      Negroes—Housing
      Negroes—Segregation
      names of minority groups in particular
        places, e.g. Jews in Morocco;
        Negroes—Philadelphia
Ghibellines
   See Guelfs and Ghibellines
Ghiliaks
   See Gilyaks
Ghoorkas
   See Gurkhas
Ghorids
   See Ghurids
Ghost crabs
   xx Crabs
Ghost dance *(E98.D2)*
   xx Indians of North America—Dances
      Nativistic movements
   — Juvenile literature
Ghost plays
   xx Drama
Ghost stories *(Fiction in English, PZ1-3;*
      History and criticism, PN3435;
      Occult sciences, BF1445-1486)
   sa Horror tales
   x Ghosts—Fiction
   xx Detective and mystery stories
      Fantastic fiction
      Fiction
      Horror tales
Ghost stories, German, ₍etc.₎ *(Direct)*
   x German ₍etc.₎ ghost stories
   xx German ₍etc.₎ fiction
Ghost towns
   See Cities and towns, Ruined, extinct, etc.
Ghosts *(Direct)* *(BF1445-1486; Folk-lore,*
      GR580)
   sa Apparitions
      Demonology
      Hallucinations and illusions
      Hiding-places (Secret chambers, etc.)
      Materialization
      Mediums
      Poltergeists
      Psychical research
      Spiritualism
      Superstition
   x Haunted houses
      Phantoms
      Specters
   xx Apparitions
      Folk-lore
      Hallucinations and illusions
      Psychical research
      Spirits
      Spiritualism
      Superstition
   — Anecdotes, facetiae, satire, etc.
   — Fiction
      See Ghost stories
   — Juvenile literature
   — Poetry *(PN6110.G5)*
Ghosts in art

Ghosts in literature *(PN56.S8)*
   sa Shakespeare, William, 1564-1616—
      Characters—Ghosts
Ghoulie *(GV1282.9.G5)*
   x Train-bridge
   xx Contract bridge
Ghouls and ogres *(GR525; GR560)*
   sa Tengu
   x Ogres
   xx Folk-lore
      Vampires
   — Anecdotes, facetiae, satire, etc.
Ghoya (Bantu tribe)
   x Kubung (Bantu tribe)
      Leghoya (Bantu tribe)
   xx Bantus
      Ethnology—Africa, South
Ghurids *(DS358)*
   x Ghorids
Ghurkas
   See Gurkhas
Ghuzz
   See Oghuz
Gi-Tonga language
   See Tonga language (Inhambane)
Giannuzzi's semilunar bodies
   See Salivary glands
Giant cabbage *(QK495.C9)*
Giant cell tumors
   xx Tumors
Giant chromosomes *(QH605)*
   x Polytene chromosomes
   xx Chromosomes
Giant nuthatch
   xx Nuthatches
Giant panda
   xx Pandas
   — Juvenile literature
   — Legends and stories
Giant pied-billed grebe
   xx Grebes
Giant reed
Giant squids *(QL430.3.O)*
   xx Squids
Giants *(Folk-lore, GR560; Somatology,*
      GN69)
   xx Deformities
      Folk-lore
      Monsters
Giant's cauldrons
   See Potholes
Giants in the Bible *(BS1199.G5)*
   — Juvenile literature
Giardiasis *(Direct)*
   x Lambliasis
      Liambliasis
   xx Medical protozoology
Giarung language
   See Gyarung language
Gibbons *(QL737.P9)*
   xx Apes
   — Juvenile literature
Gibeonites
   xx Ethnology—Palestine
Gibert's disease
   See Pityriasis rosea
Gibraltar
   — Siege, 1779-1783 *(DA87.5 1779)*
Gidabal dialect
   x Gidjabal dialect
      Kitabul dialect
   xx Bandjalang language
Gidayū
   See Jōruri
Gidjabal dialect
   See Gidabal dialect
GIER (Computer)
   xx Electronic digital computers

— Programming
Giessen test *(BF698.8.G5)*
   xx Personality tests
Gift-books (Annuals, etc.) *(AY10-19)*
   sa subdivision Gift-books *under subjects,*
      e.g. Marriage—Gift-books
   x Annuals
      Christmas books
      Keepsakes (Books)
   xx Anthologies
      Souvenirs (Keepsakes)
Gift of tongues
   See Glossolalia
Gift shops
   xx Retail trade
Gift tax
   See Gifts—Taxation
Gift wrapping *(TT870)*
   x Wrapping of gifts
   xx Gifts
      Package goods industry
      Packaging
      Paper work
Gifted children *(LC3991-4000)*
   sa Children as actors
      Children as artists
      Children as authors
      Children as musicians
      Educational acceleration
      Talented students
   x Bright children
      Precocity
      Superior children
      Talented children
   xx Exceptional children
      Genius
      Talented students
   Note under Talented students
   — Education *(Direct)*
      sa High schools—Honors courses
   — — Reading, ₍etc.₎
   — — Research *(Direct)*
      xx Educational research
Gifts *(Direct)* *(Manners and customs,*
      GT3050)
   sa Diplomatic gifts
      Gift wrapping
      Gifts to minors
      Indians of North America—Gifts
      Modus (Civil law)
   x Donations
      Presents
   xx Contracts, Gratuitous
      Manners and customs
   — Juvenile literature
   — Psychology
   — Taxation *(Direct)*
      sa Real property and taxation
      x Gift tax
      xx Inheritance and transfer tax
   — — Deductions
      Example under Tax deductions
   — — Treaties
      See Taxation, Double—Treaties
Gifts, Spiritual *(BT767.3)*
   sa Baptism in the Holy Spirit
      Fear of God
      Glossolalia
   x Charismata
      Gifts of grace
      Gifts of the Holy Spirit
      Grace, Gifts of
      Spiritual gifts
   xx Holy Spirit
      Theology, Doctrinal
      Theology, Practical
   — History of doctrines *(BT767.3)*
Gifts (Canon law)

Gifts (Greek law)
Gifts (Kindergarten)
  See Kindergarten—Methods and manuals
Gifts (Roman-Dutch law)
Gifts (Roman law)
Gifts causa mortis *(Direct)*
    x Donatio mortis causa
      Gifts mortis causa
Gifts causa mortis (Greek law)
Gifts causa mortis (Jewish law)
Gifts causa mortis (Roman law)
Gifts mortis causa
  See Gifts causa mortis
Gifts of grace
  See Gifts, Spiritual
Gifts of money to minors
  See Gifts to minors
Gifts of securities to minors
  See Gifts to minors
Gifts of the Holy Spirit
  See Gifts, Spiritual
Gifts to minors *(Direct)*
    x Gifts of money to minors
      Gifts of securities to minors
   xx Children—Law
      Gifts
      Securities
Giftwares *(Direct)*
Gigging (Textiles)
  See Napping (Textiles)
Gigues
  See Jigs
Gihi language
  See Kissi language
Gii language
  See Kissi language
Gikuyu language
  See Kikuyu language
Gila monster
  — Juvenile literature
Gilbertese language *(PL6245)*
    x Arorai language
   xx Micronesian languages
Gilbertines *(BX3670)*
   xx Monasticism and religious orders
Gild socialism *(HD6479)*
   sa Corporate state
      Functional representation
      Syndicalism
    x Guild socialism
      National gilds
   xx Corporate state
      Socialism
      Syndicalism
   Note under Corporate state
Gilding *(Mechanical trades, TT380; Metal
      manufactures, TS715)*
   sa Bookbinding—Gilding
      Electroplating
      Gold-Plating
      Metals—Coloring
   xx Goldsmithing
      Metals—Coloring
      Painting, Industrial
      Plating
      Stains and staining
Gilds *(Indirect)* *(History, HD6451-6473;
      Modern, HD2341-6)*
   sa Compagnonnages
      Employers' associations
      Journeymen's societies
      Trade and professional associations
      Trade-unions
      particular gilds, e.g. Dunfermline, Scot.
         Weavers' Incorporation; *and
         subdivision* Gilds *under names of
         cities, e.g.* Edinburgh—Gilds
    x Guilds

Labor organizations
      Merchant companies
      Working-men's associations
   xx Brotherhoods
      Confraternities
      Employers' associations
      Labor and laboring classes
      Societies
      Trade and professional associations
      Trade-unions
  — History
  — — Juvenile literature
Gilds, Altar
  See Altar gilds
Gilds, Neighborhood
  See Social settlements
Giliak language
  See Gilyak language
Gill arch
  See Branchial arch
Gill disease, Bacterial
  See Bacterial gill disease
Gill netting
  See Gillnetting
Gill-over-the-ground
  See Ground ivy
Gillingham, Eng.
  — Fire, 1929
Gillnetting *(SH344.6.G5)*
    x Gill netting
   xx Fisheries
Gills *(Anatomy, QL846)*
   sa Branchial arch
      Branchiostegals
      Chloride cells
   xx Branchial arch
      Fishes—Anatomy
      Respiratory organs
Gilsonite *(QE391.G)*
    x Uintaite
   xx Hydrocarbons
Gilts
  See Sows
Gilyak language *(PM67)*
    x Giliak language
      Guiliak language
      Nivkh language
   xx Hyperborean languages
Gilyaks *(Sakhalin Island, GN635.S2)*
    x Ghiliaks
      Nivkhi
   xx Ethnology—Siberia
Gimbala language
  See Congo language
Gimbunda language
  See Mbunda language (Zambia)
Gimini (African people)
  See Djimini (African people)
Gin *(TP607.G4)*
Gin (Cotton machinery)
  See Cotton gins and ginning
Gin rummy
  See Rummy (Game)
Ginger *(Indirect)*
  — Marketing
Gingerbread
  See Cake
Gingivitis
  See Gums—Diseases
Gingko
  See Ginkgo
Ginkgo *(QK495.G48)*
    x Gingko
      Ginkyo
      Maidenhair tree
   xx Gymnosperms
   Example under Living fossils
Ginkgo, Fossil

Ginkyo
  See Ginkgo
Ginseng *(SB295.G5)*
Ginukh dialect *(PK9201.G5)*
   xx Caucasian languages
Gio language
  See Dan language
Gioco del calcio fiorentino
  See Florentine football
Giong
  See Moso (Tribe)
GIPS (Electronic computer system)
    x General Integrated Programming
      System
Gipsies *(Direct)* *(DX101-301; Ethnography,
      GN685-6)*
   sa Missions to Gipsies
      Nawar
      Tinkers
      World War, 1939-1945—Gipsies
    x Gypsies
      Vagabonds
   xx Society, Primitive
      Tribes and tribal system
      Wayfaring life
  — Education *(Direct)*
  — Juvenile literature
  — Language *(DX161)*
   sa Nuri language
    x Gypsy language
      Lovari dialect
      Romany language
  — Literary collections
  — Religious life

   GEOGRAPHIC SUBDIVISIONS

  — Scotland
   xx Clans and clan system
Gipsy . . .
    x Romany . . .
GIPSY (Computer program)
    x Geographic Incremental Plotting
      System
GIPSY (Information retrieval system)
    x General Information Processing System
   xx Information storage and retrieval
      systems
Gipsy caravans
  See Wagons, Gipsy
Gipsy folk-lore
  See Folk-lore, Gipsy
Gipsy folk music
  See Folk music, Gipsy
Gipsy hygiene
  See Hygiene, Gipsy
Gipsy magic
  See Magic, Gipsy
Gipsy medicine
  See Medicine, Gipsy
Gipsy-moth *(SB945.G9)*
    x Gypsy-moth
   xx Moths
   Example under Insects, Injurious and benefi-
      cial; Trees—Diseases and pests
  — Biological control *(Indirect)*
      (SB945.G9)
   xx Gipsy-moth—Control
  — Control *(Indirect)* *(SB945.G9)*
   sa Gipsy-moth—Biological control
Gipsy music
  See Folk music, Gipsy
Gipsy poetry *(DX161)*
   xx Poetry
Gipsy wagons
  See Wagons, Gipsy
Giraffes *(QL737.U5)*
   sa Okapi
   xx Ruminantia

— Juvenile literature
Giraffes, Fossil *(QE882.U3)*
Girders *(TG350-360; Riveting, TA891)*
  sa Box beams
    Bridges
    Building, Iron and steel
    Concrete beams
    Graphic statics
    Grillages (Structural engineering)
    Influence lines
    Plate girders
    Roofs
    Steel, Structural
    Wooden beams
  x Beams
  xx Bars (Engineering)
    Bridges
    Building
    Engineering
    Flexure
    Graphic statics
    Structural frames
  Example under Structural design; Structural
    engineering
— Standards
— Tables, calculations, etc.
— Testing
  Example under Strength of materials
— Vibration
  Example under Structural dynamics
— Welding
Girders, Composite
  See Composite construction
Girders, Continuous *(TG355)*
  sa Bridges, Continuous
    Influence lines
  x Continuous girders
  xx Graphic statics
    Strains and stresses
— Tables, calculations, etc.
Girders, Plate
  See Plate girders
Girdle, Shoulder
  See Shoulder girdle
Girdles of chastity
  See Chastity belts
Giriama (Bantu tribe)
  See Giryama (Bantu tribe)
Giriama language
  See Giryama language
Giribuma (Bantu people)
  See Baboma (Bantu people)
Girl Scouts *(HS3353.G5)*
  xx Girls—Societies and clubs
— Caricatures and cartoons
— Public relations
  x Public relations—Girl Scouts
Girls *(Aids and homes for, HV879-887; Care
    of, HQ777; Ethics, BJ1651-8;
    Manners and customs, GT2540)*
  sa Adolescent girls
    Children
    Church work with children
    Daughters
    Delinquent girls
    Education of women
    Fathers and daughters
    Mothers and daughters
    Sex instruction for girls
    Woman
    Young women
    Youth
  subdivision Juvenile participants *under
    names of wars, e.g.* United States—
    History—Civil War, 1861-1865—
    Juvenile participants; World War,
    1939-1945—Juvenile participants
  xx Children

Parent and child
    Woman
    Young women
    Youth
— Anecdotes, facetiae, satire, etc.
— Biography *(CT3205)*
  sa Children—Biography
    Children in the Bible
  xx Children—Biography
— — Juvenile literature
— Books and reading
  See Books and reading for girls
— Conduct of life *(BJ1631-8)*
— Education
  See Coeducation
    Education of women
— Employment
  See Children—Employment
    Woman—Employment
    Youth—Employment
— Health and hygiene
  xx Hygiene
— Portraits
  xx Children in art
    Children—Portraits
— Prayer-books and devotions
  x Girls—Prayer-books and devotions—
    English
    Prayers for girls
— — English
    See Girls—Prayer-books and
      devotions
— — French, ⌜German, Italian, etc.⌝
— Religious life
— Sexual behavior
— Societies and clubs *(Direct)*
    (HS3341-3365)
  sa 4-H clubs
    Camp Fire Girls
    Gangs
    Girl Scouts
    Science clubs
    Working-women's clubs
    Young farmers' clubs
  x Girls' clubs
  xx Children's clubs
    Clubs
    Social settlements
    Societies
    Woman—Societies and clubs
— Stories
Girls, Delinquent
  See Delinquent girls
Girls as criminals
  See Delinquent girls
Girls' basketball
  See Basketball for women
Girls' clubs
  See Girls—Societies and clubs
Girls in the Bible
  See Children in the Bible
Girls' softball
  See Softball for women
Girls' volleyball
  See Volleyball for women
Giro d'Italia (Bicycle race)
Girón, Playa Invasion, 1961
  See Cuba—History—Invasion, 1961
Girondists *(DC179; Constitutional history,
    JN2474.G5)*
  xx France—History—Revolution,
    1789-1799—Clubs
Giryama (Bantu tribe)
  x Agiryama (Bantu tribe)
    Giriama (Bantu tribe)
  xx Bantus
    Ethnology—Kenya

Giryama language
  x Giriama language
    Kigiryama language
  xx Bantu languages
    Nika language
Gisi language
  See Kissi language
Gisiga language
  x Guissiga language
  xx Chadic languages
Gisira language
  See Shira language
Gisu (Bantu tribe)
  x Bagesu
    Bagishu
    Gesu
  xx Bantus
    Ethnology—Uganda
    Kavirondo (African people)
Gisu language *(PL8207.G55)*
  sa Bukusu language
  x Lugisu language
    Lumasaaba language
    Masaba language
  xx Bantu languages
Gitksan Indians
  See Kitksan Indians
Gitonga language
  See Tonga language (Inhambane)
Giur language
  See Dyur language
Givaro Indians
  See Jivaro Indians
Give-aways
  See Free material
Giving, Buddhist
  See Buddhist giving
Giving, Christian
  See Christian giving
Gizi language
  See Kissi language
Gizima language
  See Kissi language
Gizzard *(QL862)*
  xx Birds—Anatomy
    Stomach
Gizzard shad
  xx Shad
Gjæslingan
— Storm, 1906
Glacial cosmogony
  See Cosmogony, Glacial
Glacial drift
  See Drift
Glacial epoch *(Indirect)* *(QE697-8)*
  sa Cosmogony, Glacial
    Drift
    Drumlins
    Geology, Stratigraphic—Pleistocene
    Loess
  x Ice age
  xx Cosmogony, Glacial
    Earth
    Geology, Stratigraphic—Pleistocene
    Geology, Stratigraphic—Quaternary
    Man, Prehistoric
— Juvenile literature
— Popular works
Glacial erosion *(Indirect)* *(QE575-6)*
  x Ice erosion
  xx Erosion
Glacial landforms *(Indirect)* *(GB581-588)*
  x Glaciated terrain
  xx Landforms
Glaciated terrain
  See Glacial landforms
Glacier bear
  xx Bears

Glacier bear *(Continued)*
    Black bear
Glaciers *(Indirect)* *(QE575-6)*
    sa Boulders
        Erosion
        Glaciology
        Moraines
        Rock glaciers
    xx Boulders
        Drift
        Erosion
        Geology
        Glaciology
        Ice
        Moraines
        Physical geography
        Water
    — Juvenile literature
    — Measurement
    — Pictorial works
    — Popular works
    — Terminology
Glaciology
    sa Aerial photography in glaciology
        Glaciers
    xx Geology
        Glaciers
        Physical geography
    — Forms, blanks, etc.
Gladiator (Fighter planes)
    x Gloster Gladiator
    xx Fighter planes
Gladiatorial War, 73-71 B.C.
    See Rome—History—Servile Wars, 135-71
        B.C.
Gladiators *(DG95; GV35)*
    x Fighting
Gladiators, War of the, 73-71 B.C.
    See Rome—History—Servile Wars, 135-71
        B.C.
Gladiators in art
Gladiolus *(SB413.G5)*
Gladness
    See Cheerfulness
        Contentment
        Happiness
Glagolitic alphabet *(PG91)*
    xx Alphabet
        Slavic languages—Alphabet
Glagolitic literature *(Alphabet, PG91)*
    xx Literature
Gland of Bartholin
    See Bartholin's gland
Gland of Luschka
    See Coccygeal gland
Glanders *(SF796; Human, RC146)*
    sa Epizootic lymphangitis
        Melioidosis
    x Farcy (Glanders)
    xx Epizootic lymphangitis
        Horses—Diseases
Glands *(Comparative anatomy, QL865-8;*
        Human anatomy, QM325-371;
        Physiology, QP190-246)
    sa Secretion
        particular glands, e.g. Carotid gland,
        Cowper's glands, Hemolymph
        glands, Kidneys, Liver
    xx Secretion
    — Diseases *(RC633; RC648-659)*
        sa Cystic fibrosis
    — Juvenile literature
    — Transplantation
        x Glands, Ductless—Transplantation
Glands, Cutaneous
    See Cutaneous glands

Glands, Ductless *(Comparative anatomy,*
        QL868; Human anatomy, QM371;
        Physiology, QP187)
    sa Hormones
        Hormones, Sex
        particular ductless glands, e.g. Thymus
        gland, Thyroid gland
    x Ductless glands
        Endocrine glands
    xx Endocrinology
        Hormones
    — Cancer
    — Diseases
        sa Diabetes
            Glands, Ductless—Radiography
            Turner's syndrome
        x Endocrine diseases
    — — Diagnosis
        x Endocrine diagnosis
    — — Genetic aspects
    — Innervation
    — Programmed instruction
    — Radiography
        xx Glands, Ductless—Diseases
    — Transplantation
        See Glands—Transplantation
Glands, Lacrimal
    See Lacrimal organs
Glands, Mammary
    See Mammary glands
Glands, Odoriferous *(QL943; Insects,*
        QL494-6)
    xx Animal defenses
        Odors
Glands, Salivary
    See Salivary glands
Glands, Sebaceous
    See Sebaceous glands
Glands (Botany) *(QK650; QK703)*
Glands of Brunner
    See Brunner's glands
Glandula uropygalis
    See Uropygial gland
Glandular fever
    See Mononucleosis
Glare, Headlight
    See Headlight glare
Glas automobile *(TL215.G5)*
Glass *(Decorative art, NK5100-5430;*
        Materials of engineering and
        construction, TA450; Optical
        instruments, QC375)
    sa Glass-metal sealing
        Glassware
        Jena glass
        Pyroceramics
    xx Amorphous substances
        Ceramics
        Optical instruments
        Windows
    — Analysis
    — Bonding *(TP858)*
        sa Glass-metal sealing
        xx Sealing (Technology)
    — Corrosion
    — Defects
        Example under reference from Defects
    — Electric properties
    — Fracture
        xx Fracture of solids
    — Grinding
        See Glass grinding and polishing
    — Juvenile literature
    — Melting
        See Glass melting
    — Patents
    — Polishing
        See Glass grinding and polishing

    — Radiation effects
        See Glass, Effect of radiation on
    — Research
        See Glass research
    — Standards
        Example under Materials—Standards
    — Testing
    — Trade-marks
Glass, Cameo
    See Cameo glass
Glass, Carnival
    See Carnival glass
Glass, Cellular
    See Cellular glass
Glass, Colored
    sa Glass painting and staining
    x Colored glass
    xx Glass, Ornamental
        Glass painting and staining
Glass, Custard
    See Custard glass
Glass, Cut
    See Cut glass
Glass, Depression
    See Depression glass
Glass, Effect of radiation on
    x Glass—Radiation effects
    xx Radiation
Glass, Engraved
    See Engraved glass
Glass, Foam
    See Cellular glass
Glass, Millefiori *(NK5430)*
    x Millefiori glass
Glass, Opal
    See Opal glass
Glass, Optical *(QC375)*
    sa Glass grinding and polishing
    x Optical glass
    xx Lenses
        Optical instruments
Glass, Ornamental *(TP863-4)*
        Here are entered works on cut, embossed,
        sand-blast, and other ornamental glass
        used in building.
    sa Engraved glass
        Glass, Colored
        Glass construction
        Glass embossing
        Glass engraving
        Glass etching
        Glass painting and staining
        Sand-blast
    xx Cut glass
        Design, Decorative
Glass, Pearl art
    See Pearl art glass
Glass, Photosensitive
    x Photosensitive glass
Glass, Plate
    See Plate-glass
Glass, Pressed
    See Pressed glass
Glass, Safety *(TP862)*
    x Laminated glass
        Non-shatterable glass
        Safety glass
        Shatter-proof glass
    xx Laminated materials
Glass, Soluble
    See Soluble glass
Glass, Spun
    See Glass fibers
Glass, Stained
    See Glass painting and staining
Glass architecture
    See Glass contrruction

Glass as structural material
  See Glass construction
Glass beads
  xx Beads
     Granular materials
Glass blowing and working *(TP859)*
  sa Bottles
  xx Chemical apparatus
     Chemistry—Laboratory manuals
     Chemistry—Manipulation
     Glass craft
     Glass manufacture
  — Equipment and supplies
Glass bottom boats
  xx Boats and boating
Glass candy containers *(NK5440.C3)*
  x Candy containers, Glass
  xx Containers
Glass cloth
  x Cloth, Glass
  — Standards *(Direct)*
Glass construction *(Architecture, NA4140)*
  x Glass architecture
     Glass as structural material
     Glass in architecture
  xx Architecture
     Building
     Glass, Ornamental
Glass containers
  sa Bottles
     Glass fruit jars
  xx Containers
     Glassware
Glass-crabs *(QL444.D3)*
  xx Crabs
Glass craft *(TT298)*
  sa Glass blowing and working
     Glass embossing
     Glass engraving
     Glass etching
     Glass grinding and polishing
     Glass painting and staining
  xx Handicraft
  — Juvenile literature
Glass doors, Sliding
  x Sliding-glass doors
  xx Doors
Glass electrodes
  See Electrodes, Glass
Glass embossing *(TP863)*
  x Embossing of glass
  xx Glass craft
     Glass, Ornamental
Glass engraving
  sa Engraved glass
  xx Engraving
     Glass craft
     Glass, Ornamental
Glass etching
  xx Etching
     Glass craft
     Glass, Ornamental
Glass factories
  xx Factories
  — Heating and ventilation
Glass fiber industry *(Direct)*
  sa Glass reinforced plastics
  x Fibrous glass industry
  xx Glass manufacture
     Glass trade
  — Automation *(TS1549.G5)*
Glass fiber sculpture *(Direct) (NB1270.G5)*
  xx Glass reinforced plastics
     Plastic sculpture
     Sculpture
Glass fibers
  sa Glass reinforced plastics
     Quartz fibers

  x Fiber glass
     Fiberglass
     Fibers, Glass
     Glass, Spun
     Spun glass
  — Dyeing
     See Dyes and dyeing—Glass fibers
  — Patents
  — Standards *(Direct)*
Glass fishing floats *(Direct)*
  x Glass floats
  xx Fishing nets
     Glassware
  — Collectors and collecting *(Direct)*
Glass-flake laminates
  See Flake-glass laminates
Glass floats
  See Glass fishing floats
Glass fruit jars *(Direct) (NK5440.F7)*
  x Fruit jars, Glass
  xx Glass containers
Glass furnaces
  x Glass melting furnaces
     Glass tank furnaces
  xx Furnaces
     Glass manufacture
     Glass melting
  — Automatic control
Glass gardens *(SB417)*
  sa Miniature plants
     Wardian cases
  x Bottle gardens
     Gardens, Glass
     Plant terrariums
  xx Container gardening
     Gardens, Miniature
     Terrariums
     Wardian cases
Glass grinding and polishing
  x Glass—Grinding
     Glass polishing
     Glass—Polishing
  xx Glass craft
     Glass manufacture
     Glass, Optical
     Grinding and polishing
  — Safety measures
Glass harmonica *(ML1055)*
  x Glasses, Musical
     Harmonica, Glass
     Musical glasses
  — Instruction and study *(MT670)*
Glass-harmonica and lute music *(M298)*
  x Lute and glass-harmonica music
Glass-harmonica and piano music *(M284.G6;*
     M285.G6)
  x Piano and glass-harmonica music
Glass-harmonica music *(M165)*
  sa Canons, fugues, etc. (Glass harmonica)
     Quartets, [Trios, etc.] *followed by*
        specifications which include the glass
        harmonica
Glass in architecture
  See Glass construction
Glass in literature
Glass industry
  See Glass manufacture
     Glass trade
Glass-joining to metals
  See Glass-metal sealing
Glass lampshades
  See Lampshades, Glass
Glass manufacture *(Direct) (TP845-869)*
  sa Annealing of glass
     Glass blowing and working
     Glass fiber industry
     Glass furnaces
     Glass grinding and polishing

     Glass melting
     Glass-workers
     Mirrors
     Optical instruments
     Precious stones, Artificial
     Pressed glass
     Sand, Glass
  x Glass industry
  xx Ceramic industries
  — Accounting
  — Chemistry
  — Collective labor agreements
     See Collective labor agreements—
        Glass manufacture
  — Early works to 1800 *(TP856)*
  — Equipment and supplies
  —— Appraisal
     See Glass manufacture—Equipment
        and supplies—Valuation
  —— Valuation
     x Glass manufacture—Equipment
        and supplies—Appraisal
  — Production standards
  — Quality control
  — Safety measures
  — Safety regulations *(Direct)*
  — Tables, calculations, etc. *(TP857.5)*
  — Vocational guidance
Glass melting
  sa Glass furnaces
  x Glass—Melting
  xx Glass manufacture
Glass melting furnaces
  See Glass furnaces
Glass-metal sealing *(TS718)*
  x Glass-joining to metals
     Glass-to-metal sealing
     Metal-bonding to glass
     Metal-glass sealing
     Metal-to-glass sealing
  xx Glass
     Glass—Bonding
     Metal bonding
     Metals
     Sealing (Technology)
     Welding
Glass painters *(Direct)*
  x Glasspainters
  xx Glass painting and staining
     Painters
Glass painting and staining *(Direct)*
     (NK5300-5410)
  sa Glass, Colored
     Glass painters
     Lumiprints
  x Glass, Stained
     Painted glass
     Stained glass
     Windows, Stained glass
  xx Art
     Arts and crafts movement
     Church decoration and ornament
     Color in the ceramic industries
     Decoration and ornament
     Glass, Colored
     Glass craft
     Glass, Ornamental
     Painting
  Example under Art industries and trade
  — Early works to 1800
  — Technique
Glass painting and staining, Austrian, [French,
  etc.] *(Direct)*
  x Austrian [French, etc.] glass painting
     and staining
Glass painting and staining, Baroque *(Direct)*
  x Baroque glass painting and staining

Glass painting and staining, Gothic (Direct)
  x Gothic glass painting and staining
Glass painting and staining, Medieval
    (Direct)
Glass painting and staining, Renaissance
    (Direct)
  x Renaissance glass painting and staining
Glass painting and staining, Romanesque
    (Direct)
  x Romanesque glass painting and staining
Glass pipe
  See Pipe, Glass
Glass plastics
  See Glass reinforced plastics
Glass polishing
  See Glass grinding and polishing
Glass reinforced plastics
  sa Fiberglass boats
      Flake-glass laminates
      Glass fiber sculpture
  x Fiber glass reinforced plastics
      Glass plastics
  xx Glass fiber industry
      Glass fibers
      Plastics
      Reinforced plastics
— Defects
— Quality control
— Standards (Direct)
— Testing
— Thermal properties (TA455.P55)
Glass research
  x Glass—Research
  xx Research, Industrial
Glass sand
  See Sand, Glass
Glass tank furnaces
  See Glass furnaces
Glass-to-metal sealing
  See Glass-metal sealing
Glass trade (Direct) (HD9623; Tariff,
    HF2651.G5)
  sa Glass fiber industry
      Strikes and lockouts—Glass trade
  x Glass industry
— Accounting
— Prices (Direct)
— Tables and ready-reckoners
    (HF5716.G4)
Glass weights (CJ3413)
  xx Weights and measures, Arabic
Glass-workers (Direct) (HD8039.G5)
  sa Collective labor agreements—Glass
        manufacture
      Trade-unions—Glass-workers
      Wages—Glass-workers
  xx Glass manufacture
— Diseases and hygiene
Glassboro Conference, 1967
Glasses, Musical
  See Glass harmonica
Glasshouse crops
  See Greenhouse plants
Glasshouse plants
  See Greenhouse plants
Glassites
  See Sandemanianism
Glasspainters
  See Glass painters
Glassware (Direct) (Art, NK5101-5430;
    Technology, TP865-8)
  sa Bottles
      Cameo glass
      Crackle
      Cup plates
      Custard glass
      Cut glass
      Depression glass

Engraved glass
Glass containers
Glass fishing floats
Lamp-chimneys, globes, etc.
Lampshades, Glass
Opal glass
Paperweights
Portraits on glassware
Pressed glass
Salt shakers
Saltcellars
Stemware
Sulphides (Art)
  xx Glass
      House furnishings
      Table setting and decoration
      Vases
Example under Art objects
— Collectors and collecting
    (NK5101-5199)
    sa Glassware as an investment
— Packing
— Patents
— Prices
    sa Glassware as an investment
— Private collections (NK5101-5196)
— Repairing (NK5104; TT151)
— Standards (Direct)
— Tables, calculations, etc.
— Trade-marks
Glassware, American, [Canadian, etc.]
    (Direct)
  x American [Canadian, etc.] glassware
Glassware, Ancient (NK5107)
Glassware, Baroque (Direct)
  x Baroque glassware
Glassware, Byzantine (Direct)
  x Byzantine glassware
Glassware, Early Christian (Direct)
  x Early Christian glassware
Glassware, Georgian
  x Georgian glassware
Glassware, Greco-Roman (Direct)
  x Greco-Roman glassware
Glassware, Medieval (Direct)
Glassware, Oriental (NK5172)
Glassware, Renaissance (Direct)
  x Renaissance glassware
Glassware, Victorian (Direct)
  x Victorian glassware
Glassware as an investment
  xx Glassware—Collectors and collecting
      Glassware—Prices
      Investments
Glassware in literature
Glaucoma (RE871)
  sa Cyclodialysis
  xx Eye—Diseases and defects
— Diagnosis
    sa Tonometry
— Surgery
    Example under Surgery; Surgery, Opera-
      tive
Glaucoma in children
  x Congenital glaucoma
      Pediatric glaucoma
Glauconite (QE391.G5)
Glaucous-winged gull
  xx Gulls
Glavda language (PL8207.G6)
Glaze (Meteorology) (Indirect)
    (QC929.G4)
  sa Frost
  xx Condensation
      Frost
      Ice
— Measurement

Glazed brick (TP832.G6)
  xx Bricks
Glazes (TP812; TP823)
  sa Engobes
      Luster-ware
  xx Ceramics
      Color in the ceramic industries
      Glazing (Ceramics)
      Pottery
Glazing (TH8251-8275)
  sa Sealed double glazing
— Accounting
— Estimates and costs (Direct)
— Safety measures
— Vocational guidance
Glazing (Ceramics)
  sa Glazes
  xx Ceramics
      Pottery
Gleaning (Direct) (HD1549)
  xx Agriculture
      Charity laws and legislation
      Harvesting
Glebes
  See Church lands
Glebo (African tribe)
  See Grebo (African tribe)
Glebo folk-lore
  See Folk-lore, Grebo
Glebo language
  See Grebo language
Glees, catches, rounds, etc.
  sa Canons, fugues, etc. (Vocal)
  x Catches
      Rounds
  xx Canons, fugues, etc. (Vocal)
      Part-song
      Song-books
      Vocal music
Glencoe Massacre, 1692 (DA804.7)
Glial cells
  See Neuroglia
Glide path systems (TL696.L33)
  x Glide slope
      Landing path
  xx Aeroplanes—Landing
      Instrument landing systems
      Radio in aeronautics
Glide slope
  See Glide path systems
Glider recognition
  See Gliders (Aeronautics)—Recognition
Glider troops
  See Airborne troops
Gliders (Aeronautics) (TL760-769)
  sa Gliding and soaring
  x Sailplanes (Aeronautics)
  xx Aeroplanes
      Flying-machines
      Gliding and soaring
      Sailing
— Juvenile literature
— Models
    sa Paper airplanes
— — Juvenile literature
— — Radio control
— Piloting (TL765)
— Poetry
    See Aeronautics—Poetry
— Recognition
    x Aircraft identification
      Aircraft recognition
      Glider recognition
      Recognition of gliders
— Standards
    xx Aeroplanes—Standards

Gliding and soaring *(Indirect)* *(TL760; Sport, GV764-6)*
  sa Gliders (Aeronautics)
  x Flight, Unpowered
    Motorless flight
    Soaring (Aeronautics)
    Soaring flight
  xx Aeronautical sports
    Aeronautics
    Gliders (Aeronautics)
  — Personal narratives
Global analysis (Mathematics) *(QA614)*
  sa Jet bundles (Mathematics)
  x Analysis, Global (Mathematics)
  xx Differential topology
    Functions of complex variables
    Geometry, Algebraic
Global learning
  See Global method of teaching
Global method of teaching *(LB1029.G55)*
  sa Reading (Elementary)—Whole-word method
  x Global learning
    Globalism (Education)
  xx Education, Elementary
    Teaching
Global satellite communications systems
  See Artificial satellites in telecommunication
Global temperature changes *(QC903)*
  x Temperature changes, Global
    World temperature changes
  xx Atmospheric temperature
Globalism (Education)
  See Global method of teaching
Globe Mutiny, 1824 *(DU710)*
  Example under Mutiny
Globes *(Direct)* *(G3170)*
  sa Orbs
    World maps
    subdivision Globes *under names of moons and planets (other than Earth) and under certain subjects, e.g.* Mars (Planet)—Globes; Submarine topography—Globes
  x Globes, Terrestrial
    Terrestrial globes
  xx Orbs
    World maps
  — Early works to 1800
  — Handbooks, manuals, etc. *(GA12)*
  — Juvenile literature
  — Trade and manufacture
Globes, Celestial
  sa Astronomy—Charts, diagrams, etc.
  x Celestial globes
  xx Astronomical models
    Astronomy—Charts, diagrams, etc.
  — Early works to 1800
  — Handbooks, manuals, etc.
Globes, Lunar
  See Lunar globes
Globes, Terrestrial
  See Globes
Globidiosis
  See Besnoitiosis
Globular proteins
Globulin
  sa Alpha globulin
    Gamma globulin
    Transferrin
Globus pallidus
  x Pallidum
  xx Basal ganglia
    Brain
Glockenspiel *(History, ML1040)*
  x Bell-lyra
    Orchestral bells

Glockenspiel music *(M147)*
  sa Concertos (Glockenspiel with string orchestra)
    Glockenspiel with string orchestra
    Quartets (Piano, flute, harp, glockenspiel)
    Quintets (Pianos (4), glockenspiel)
    Quintets (Trombone, glockenspiel, percussion)
    Sextets (Glockenspiel, marimba, percussion)
    Trios (Piano, clarinet, glockenspiel)
Glockenspiel with string orchestra *(M1105-6)*
  sa Concertos (Glockenspiel with string orchestra)
  xx Concertos (Glockenspiel with string orchestra)
    Glockenspiel music
    String-orchestra music
Glomerular filtration rate
  xx Kidney function tests
Glomerulonephritis
  xx Immune complex diseases
    Kidneys—Diseases
  — Immunological aspects
Glomfjord Raid, 1942
  xx World War, 1939-1945—Norway
Glonoin
  See Nitroglycerin
Gloominess
  See Sadness
Gloria in excelsis
  Example under Hymns
Glorification (Theology)
  See Glory of God
Glory
  — Biblical teaching
Glory, Divine
  See Glory of God
Glory in literature
Glory of God *(BT180.G6)*
  sa Theophanies
  x Divine glory
    Glorification (Theology)
    Glory, Divine
    God—Glory
    God, Glory of
  xx God
  — Biblical teaching
Glory of God (Judaism)
Glossaries
  See subdivision Glossaries, vocabularies, etc. *under names of languages*
Glossators
  xx Canon law—History
    Roman law—History
Glossematics
  sa subdivision Glossematics *under names of languages and groups of languages*
  x Glossemes
  xx Linguistic analysis (Linguistics)
    Mathematical linguistics
Glossemes
  See Glossematics
Glossolalia *(BL54)*
  sa Baptism in the Holy Spirit
    Pentecostal churches
    Pentecostalism
  x Gift of tongues
    Speaking with tongues
    Tongues, Gift of
  xx Baptism in the Holy Spirit
    Gifts, Spiritual
  — Psychology
    xx Psychology, Religious

Glossopharyngeal nerve *(QL939; QM471; QP366)*
  xx Pharynx
    Tongue
Glossopharyngeal respiration
  xx Respiration
Gloster Gladiator
  See Gladiator (Fighter planes)
Gloster Meteor
  See Meteor (Fighter planes)
Glottis *(Comparative anatomy, QL853; Human anatomy, QM255)*
  sa Vocal cords
  xx Larynx
  — Spasm
    See Laryngismus stridulus
Glove boxes (Safety devices)
  xx Manipulators (Radioactive substances)
    Radioisotopes—Safety measures
Glove industry *(Direct)*
  sa Trade-unions—Glove industry
    Wages—Glove industry
Gloves *(Direct)* *(Costume, GT2170; Manufacture, TS2160; Trade, HD9947)*
  x Mittens
Gloves, Baseball
  See Baseball gloves
Gloves (Surgery) *(RD73.G5)*
  xx Surgical instruments and apparatus
Glow-lamps
  See Electric lamps
Glow-worms
  See Fireflies
Gloxinias
Glucagon
  xx Pancreas—Secretions
Glucic acid
  See Reductones
Glucides
  sa Glucosides
  xx Glucosides
Glucinium
  See Beryllium
Gluck-Piccinni controversy *(ML1727.35)*
  sa Guerre des Bouffons
  xx Guerre des Bouffons
    Opera, French
    Opera, Italian
Glucocorticoids
  xx Adrenocortical hormones
  — Therapeutic use
    xx Hormone therapy
Glucolysis
  See Glycolysis
Glucose *(Chemical technology, TP414; Chemistry, QD321)*
  sa Blood sugar
    Dextran
    Sugar—Inversion
  xx Sugar
Glucose industry *(Direct)* *(TP414)*
  sa Corn-starch
Glucose metabolism *(QP701)*
  xx Metabolism
Glucose synthesis
  xx Biosynthesis
Glucose tolerance tests
  xx Blood sugar
    Diabetes—Diagnosis
Glucosidase synthesis
  xx Protein biosynthesis
Glucosides *(Chemistry, QD325; Pharmacology, QP925)*
  sa Anthocyanin
    Glucides
    Glycosides
    Oligosaccharides

Glucosides (Chemistry, QD325;
    Pharmacology, QP925)
    (Continued)
        Saponins
    xx Glucides
        Glycosides
    Example under Chemistry, Organic
    — Therapeutic use (RM666.G5)
Glucosuria
    See Glycosuria
Glucuronic acid synthesis
    xx Biosynthesis
Glucuronidase
Glue (TP967-8)
    sa Adhesives
        Bone products
        Gluing
    xx Adhesives
        Bone products
Glue-sniffing (HV5822.G5)
    xx Drug abuse
        Gases, Asphyxiating and poisonous
Glued joints
    See Adhesive joints
Gluing
    xx Cabinet-work
        Glue
        Joinery
        Woodwork
Glutamine metabolism
    xx Metabolism
Gluteal region
    See Buttocks
Gluten (Chemistry, QD431; Milling, TS2149)
Gluten-free diet
    xx Celiac disease
        Diet in disease
Gluttons (Animals)
    See Wolverines
Gluttony
    xx Deadly sins
        Gastronomy
Glyceride metabolism
    xx Glycerides
        Lipid metabolism
Glycerides (QD305.A4)
    sa Glyceride metabolism
        Monoglycerides
Glycerin (Chemical technology, TP973;
    Disinfectants, RA766.G6;
    Therapeutics, RM666.G; Trade,
    HD9660.G57-6)
    — Physiological effect (QP915.G5)
Glyceryl trinitrate
    See Nitroglycerin
Glycin
    See Glycine
Glycine
    x Aminoacetic acid
        Glycin
        Glycocoll
    xx Acetic acid
        Amino acids
Glycine (Plant)
    x Ground-nuts
Glycine max
    See Soy-bean
Glycine metabolism
    xx Amino acid metabolism
Glycocoll
    See Glycine
Glycogen (QP701)
    sa Glycogenosis
        Liver—Glycogenic function
        Polysaccharides
    xx Polysaccharides
Glycogen disease
    See Glycogenosis

Glycogen metabolism
    xx Metabolism
Glycogen synthesis
    xx Biosynthesis
Glycogenosis (RJ456.G)
    x Glycogen disease
        Hepatonephromegalia glycogenica
        Thesaurimosis glycogenica
        Von Giercke's disease
    xx Children—Diseases
        Glycogen
        Liver—Diseases
        Liver—Glycogenic function
        Metabolism, Disorders of
Glycols (QD305.A4)
    x Ethylene alcohol
        Ethylene glycol
Glycolysis (QP701)
    x Glucolysis
    xx Blood—Analysis and chemistry
        Blood—Examination
        Pathology
        Sugar in the body
    — Mathematical models
Glycoprotein synthesis
    xx Biosynthesis
Glycoproteins
Glycoside metabolism
    xx Glycosides
        Metabolism
Glycosides
    sa Cardiac glycosides
        Fructose
        Galactose
        Glucosides
        Glycoside metabolism
        Xyloside
    xx Glucosides
    — Therapeutic use
Glycosuria (RC909)
    x Glucosuria
    xx Diabetes
        Sugar in the body
        Urine—Analysis and pathology
Glycozone (RM671.G)
    xx Antiseptics
Glyoxalase
Glyphography (NE2570)
    sa Electrotyping
    xx Electrotyping
        Pictures—Printing
        Plate-printing
Glyptics (NK5500-6050)
    sa Cameos
        Gem carving
        Gems
        Intaglios
        Medals
        Netsukes
        Plaques, plaquettes
        Seals (Numismatics)
    x Glyptography
    xx Art
        Carving (Art industries)
        Engraving
        Gems
        Sculpture
Glyptography
    See Glyptics
Gnadenhutten, Ohio
    — Massacre, 1782 (Moravian Indians,
        E99.M9)
        xx Indians of North America—Wars—
            1775-1783
Gñāni yoga
    See Yoga, Jñāna

Gnatcatchers (QL696.P2)
    sa names of specific gnatcatchers, e.g.
        Blue-gray gnatcatcher
Gnathostomulida
Gneiss (Indirect) (QE461; QE475)
    — Pictorial works (QE475.G55)
Gnetales (QK495.G565)
Gnome project
    See Project Gnome
Gnomes
    See Fairies
Gnomes (Maxims)
    See Aphorisms and apothegms
        Maxims
        Proverbs
Gnomic poetry (PN1059.G)
    sa Priamel
    xx Poetry
        Priamel
Gnomic poetry, Greek (PA3125; PA3453;
    PA3623)
Gnomic poetry, Hebrew (BS1455)
Gnomic poetry, Latin (PA6059.G6;
    PA6135.G6; PA6164)
Gnomic poetry, Welsh (PB2281)
Gnomonics
    See Sun-dials
Gnostic ethics
    x Ethics, Gnostic
Gnosticism (B638; Theology, BT1390)
    sa Mandaeans
    xx Heresies and heretics—Early church,
        ca. 30-600
        Ophites
        Philosophy
        Philosophy, Ancient
        Religions
        Theology, Doctrinal—History—Early
            church, ca. 30-600
        Theosophy
Gnotobiology
    See Germfree life
Gnotobiotics
    See Germfree life
Gnu, White-tailed
    See White-tailed gnu
Gnus
    sa White-tailed gnu
    x Wildebeests
    xx Antelopes
Go (Game) (GV1469.G7)
    x Go-moku
        Gobang (Game)
        Igo (Game)
        Wei chi (Game)
        Wei-ki (Game)
    — Collections of games
    — Examinations, questions, etc.
    — Pictorial works
    — Tournaments
Go-cart racing
    See Karting
Go-Kart racing
    See Karting
Go-Karts (Midget cars)
    See Karts (Midget cars)
Go-moku
    See Go (Game)
Goafing (Mining)
    See Mine filling
Goagiro language
    See Goajiro language
Goajiro Indians (F2270.2.G6)
    x Guajiro Indians
    xx Indians of South America
Goajiro language (PM5981)
    x Goagiro language
    xx Arawakan languages

Indians of South America—Languages

Goal (Psychology)
   xx Motivation (Psychology)

Goals (Sports)
   See Targets (Sports)

Goanese *(DS498)*
   x Goans

Goanese in Uganda, [etc.]

Goans
   See Goanese

Goat breeding
   x Goats—Breeding
   xx Stock and stock-breeding

Goat lice
   xx Lice

Goat lymph *(RM800.L9)*

Goat milk
   See Goat's milk

Goats *(Indirect) (QL737.U5; Animal*
         industries, SF381-5)
   sa Angora goat
      Bouquetin
      Granada goat
      Rocky Mountain goat
   xx Domestic animals
      Ruminantia
      Stock and stock-breeding
   — Behavior
   — Breeding
      See Goat breeding
   — Diseases *(SF968-970)*
      sa Udder—Bacteriology
         Udder—Diseases
      names of specific diseases, e.g.
         Scrapie
   — Feeding and feeds
   — Herd-books
      x Herd-books
   — Juvenile literature

Goats, Fossil

Goat's milk
   x Goat milk
   xx Milk

Gobang (Game)
   See Go (Game)

Gobbing (Mining)
   See Mine filling

Gobbledygook
   See English language—Government jargon

Gobelin tapestry *(NK3049.G7)*
   xx Tapestry

Gober
   See Gobir

Gobir
   x Gober
      Gobirawa
   xx Hausas

Gobirawa
   See Gobir

Goblet cells
   See Exfoliative cytology

Goblets
   See Drinking vessels
      Stemware

Goblins
   See Fairies

Gocart racing
   See Karting

God *(BT98-180; Judaism, BM610)*
   sa Agnosticism
      Anthropomorphism
      Appropriation (Theology)
      Atheism
      Beatific vision
      Causation
      Christianity
      Commandments, Ten—God
      Creation

Deism
Fear of God
Free thought
Glory of God
Holy Spirit
Holy, The
Image of God
Jesus Christ
Judgment of God
Metaphysics
Monarchianism
Monotheism
Myth
Mythology
Natural theology
Nihilianism
Occasionalism
Ontology
Pantheism
Polytheism
Praise of God
Providence and government of God
Rationalism
Religion
Son of God
Teleology
Theism
Theocracy
Theodicy
Theology
Trinities
Trinity
Trust in God
   xx Christianity
      Creation
      Deism
      Metaphysics
      Philosophy
      Religion
      Theism
      Theology, Doctrinal
      Trinity
   — Anger
      See God—Wrath
   — Art *(N8040)*
      sa Gods in art
         Holy Spirit—Art
         Jesus Christ—Art
         Trinity—Art
   — Attributes *(Comparative religion, BL205;*
         Doctrinal theology, BT130-153)
      sa God—Incomparability
         Providence and government of God
         Suffering of God
      x Attributes of God
   — Beauty *(BT153.B4)*
   — Biblical teaching *(BT99)*
   — Caricatures and cartoons
   — Comparative studies
   — Face
      x Face of God
   — — Biblical teaching
   — Fatherhood *(BT153.F3)*
      sa Adoption (Theology)
         Children of God
      xx Children of God
         Fatherhood (Theology)
         Kingdom of God
   — Fear
      See Fear of God
   — Glory
      See Glory of God
   — Goodness *(BT137)*
   — History of doctrines *(BT98)*
   — — 20th century
   — Image
      See Image of God
   — Immanence

      See Immanence of God
   — Immutability *(BT153.I47)*
   — Impassibility
      See Suffering of God
   — Incomparability *(BT153.I6)*
      x Incomparability of God
      xx God—Attributes
      Monotheism
   — Jealousy *(BT153.J4)*
      x God, Jealousy of
      Jealousy of God
   — Judgment
      See Judgment of God
   — Justice
      See God—Righteousness
   — Juvenile literature *(BT107)*
   — Knowableness *(BT98-108)*
      sa Desire for God
      x God—Knowledge
         God, Knowledge of
         God (Theory of knowledge)
         Knowableness of God
         Knowledge of God
      xx Knowledge, Theory of (Religion)
   — — Biblical teaching
   — — History of doctrines
   — Knowledge
      See God—Knowableness
      God—Omniscience
   — Love *(BT140)*
      Here are entered works on God's love
         toward man. Works on the love and
         worship which man accords to God
         are entered under the heading God
         —Worship and love.
      xx Love (Theology)
      Note under God—Worship and love
   — Mercy *(BT153.M4)*
      xx Mercy
   — Motherhood *(BT153.M6)*
   — Name *(BT180.N2)*
      sa Basmalah
         Commandments, Ten—Name of
          God
         God (Judaism)—Name
         Holy Name, Devotion to
         Memra (The word)
      xx Bible—Names
   — — Biblical teaching
   — Omnipotence *(BT133)*
   — Omnipresence *(BT132)*
      sa Presence of God
      x Shekinah
      xx Presence of God
      Note under Presence of God
   — Omniscience *(BT131)*
      x God—Knowledge
         God, Knowledge of
         Knowledge of God
         Omniscience of God
      xx Free will and determinism
      Predestination
   — Pain
      See Suffering of God
   — Passibility
      See Suffering of God
   — Permissive will
      See Theodicy
   — Poetry
   — Praise
      See Praise of God
   — Presence
      See Presence of God
   — Promises *(BT180.P7)*
   — Proof
   — — History of doctrines
   — Proof, Axiological
      See God—Proof, Moral

God (BT98-180; Judaism, BM610)
(Continued)
— Proof, Deontological
    See God—Proof, Moral
— Proof, Empirical (BT98-101)
    x Empirical argument
    xx Experience
       Experience (Religion)
— Proof, Moral
    x Axiological proof of God
       Deontological proof of God
       God—Proof, Axiological
       God—Proof, Deontological
       Moral proof of God
    xx Ethics
— — History of doctrines (BT98)
— Proof, Ontological (BT98-101)
    x Ontological argument
    xx Ontology
— Proof, Teleological (BT98-101)
    x Teleological argument
    xx Teleology
— Providence and government
    See Providence and government of
       God
— Quotations, maxims, etc.
— Righteousness (BT145)
    x God—Justice
       Righteousness of God
— — Biblical teaching
— — History of doctrines
— Sovereignty
    See Providence and government of
       God
— Suffering
    See Suffering of God
— Throne
    See Throne of God
— Transcendence
    See Transcendence of God
— Will
    x Will of God
    xx Free will and determinism
— — History of doctrines
— Will, Permissive
    See Theodicy
— Wisdom (BT150)
    xx Wisdom
— Worship and love (BV4817)
       Here are entered works on the worship
       and love which man accords to
       God. Works on the love which God
       has toward man are entered under
       the heading God—Love.
    sa Bhakti
       Fear of God
       Praise of God
    xx Love (Theology)
       Worship
    Note under God—Love
— Wrath
    sa Judgment of God
    x Anger of God
       God—Anger
       Wrath of God
    xx Sin
— — Biblical teaching
God, Children of
    See Children of God
God, Desire for
    See Desire for God
God, Fear of
    See Fear of God
God, Glory of
    See Glory of God
God, Image of
    See Image of God
God, Immanence of
    See Immanence of God

God, Jealousy of
    See God—Jealousy
God, Kingdom of
    See Kingdom of God
God, Knowledge of
    See God—Knowableness
       God—Omniscience
God, Pain of
    See Suffering of God
God, People of
    See People of God
God, Providence and government of
    See Providence and government of God
God, Suffering of
    See Suffering of God
God (African religion)
God (Brahmanism)
    See God (Hinduism)
God (Chinese religion) (BL1800-1810)
God (Egyptian religion)
    sa Gods, Egyptian
God (Greek religion) (B398.G6; BL795.G6)
God (Hinduism) (BL1200-1225)
    sa Brahman
    x God (Brahmanism)
    xx Hinduism
God (Islam) (BP166.2)
    sa Trust in God (Islam)
    x Allah
    xx Islamic theology
— Attributes
— Knowableness
— Koranic teaching
— Mercy
    xx Mercy
— Name
— Proof
— Will
    xx Free will and determinism (Islam)
— Worship and love
    xx Worship (Islam)
God (Jainism) (BL1356)
    x Paramadevatā
    xx Jainism
— Omniscience
God (Judaism) (BM610)
    sa Fear of God (Judaism)
       Holy Spirit (Judaism)
       Providence and government of God
          (Judaism)
— Attributes
— Juvenile literature
— Knowableness
— Name
    xx God—Name
God (Sikhism) (BL2018.22)
    xx Sikhism
God (Theory of knowledge)
    See God—Knowableness
God (Theosophy) (BP573.G6)
    xx Theosophy
God and man, Mystical union of
    See Mystical union
God in literature
    sa Gods in literature
    xx Gods in literature
       Religion in literature
God is dead theology
    See Death of God theology
Goddesses
    sa Mother-goddesses
    xx Gods
Goddesses, Hindu (BL1216)
Goddesses, Mother
    See Mother-goddesses
Goddesses in art
    See Gods in art

Goddesses in literature
    See Gods in literature
Gödel numbers
    x Numbers, Gödel
    xx Logic, Symbolic and mathematical
       Numbers, Theory of
Gödel's theorem
    x Decidability theory
       Undecidable theories
    xx Arithmetic—Foundations
       Logic, Symbolic and mathematical
       Numbers, Theory of
Godfathers
    See Sponsors
Godmothers
    See Sponsors
Gods (BL473)
    sa Goddesses
       Healing gods
       Kings and rulers (in religion, folk-lore,
          etc.)
       Mother-goddesses
       Mountain-gods
       Myth
       Mythology
       Religions
       Rice-gods
       Sacred marriage (Mythology)
       Sea gods
       Sky-gods
       Titans (Mythology)
       Water-gods
       names of deities, e.g. Athena, Baal
          (Deity)
    x Deities
    xx Mythology
       Mythology, Classical
       Religions
— Costume
    See Idols and images—Costume and
       adornment
— Dictionaries
    See Mythology—Dictionaries
— Language (P141)
Gods, Assyro-Babylonian
    x Assyro-Babylonian gods
    xx Assyro-Babylonian religion
Gods, Buddhist
    sa Angels (Buddhism)
       Bodhisattvas
       Buddhas
    x Buddhist gods
    xx Buddha and Buddhism
Gods, Carthaginian
    See Gods, Punic
Gods, Egyptian (BL2450.G6)
    x Egyptian gods
    xx God (Egyptian religion)
Gods, Greek
    x Greek gods
Gods, Healing
    See Healing gods
Gods, Hindu (Direct)
    sa Gods, Vedic
    x Hindu gods
    xx Hinduism
Gods, Hittite
    x Hittite gods
    xx Hittites—Religion
Gods, Lamaist
    x Lamaist gods
    xx Lamaism
Gods, Phenician
    x Phenician gods
Gods, Punic
    x Carthaginian gods
       Gods, Carthaginian
       Punic gods

Gods, Roman
  x Roman gods
Gods, Semitic
  x Semitic gods
  xx Semites—Religion
Gods, Seven lucky
  See Seven gods of fortune
Gods, Shinto *(BL2226)*
  xx Shinto
Gods, Ugaritic
  x Ugaritic gods
Gods, Vedic *(BL1216-1225)*
  x Vedic gods
  xx Gods, Hindu
     Vedas—Criticism, interpretation, etc.
Gods (in numismatics)
  xx Art and mythology
     Gods in art
     Numismatics
Gods in art
  sa Gods (in numismatics)
     Idols and images
  x Goddesses in art
  xx Art and religion
     God—Art
     Idols and images
Gods in literature
  sa God in literature
  x Goddesses in literature
  xx God in literature
     Religion in literature
Gods of fortune, Seven
  See Seven gods of fortune
God's truce
  See Truce of God
Godwit, Black-tailed
  See Black-tailed godwit
Godwits
  sa Black-tailed godwit
Goethe prize
  x Goethepreis
Goethepreis
  See Goethe prize
Goffering-machines *(TJ1530)*
  xx Machinery
     Textile machinery
  — Patents
Goggles
  See Sun glasses
Goggles, Safety
  See Safety goggles
Gogo language *(PL8208)*
  x Chigogo language
  xx Bantu languages
Gogodala language
  x Gogodara language
  xx Papuan languages
Gogodara language
  See Gogodala language
Gogstad ship
  See Viking ships
Goidelic languages
  sa Gaelic language
     Irish language
     Manx language
  xx Celtic languages
Goigs *(ML3086)*
  xx Folk-songs, Catalan
     Hymns, Spanish
Going away to school
  See Residence and education
Goiter *(Direct)* *(RC656)*
  sa Cretinism
     Substernal goiter
  x Bronchocele
  xx Cretinism
     Graves' disease
     Thyroid gland—Diseases

— Dietary aspects
  See Goiter—Nutritional aspects
— Nutritional aspects
  x Diet and goiter
     Goiter—Dietary aspects
     Nutrition and goiter
Goiter, Exophthalmic
  See Graves' disease
Goiter, Substernal
  See Substernal goiter
Gokenin
  xx Samurai
Gokstad ship
  See Viking ships
Gola languages *(PL8211)*
  x Gora language
     Gura language
Gold *(Chemistry, QD181.A9; Finance,*
     HG289-297, HG551; Mineral
     resources, TN410-429)
  sa Alchemy
     Coinage
     Currency question
     Gold buying
     Gold clause
     Gold mines and mining
     Gold standard
     Goldsmithing
     Jewelry
     Monetary gold confiscations
     Money
     Quantity theory of money
     Silver question
     Spun gold
  x Specie
  xx Coinage
     Currency question
     Money
     Precious metals
     Silver question
  Example under Metals
— Analysis
— Assaying *(TN580.G6)*
     Example under Assaying
— Electrometallurgy *(TN768)*
— Isotopes
     x Gold isotopes
— — Decay
— — Spectra
— Law and legislation *(Direct)*
— Metallurgy *(TN760-769)*
     sa Chlorination
        Cyanide process
        Gold—Milling
     x Gold metallurgy
     Example under Metallurgy
— Milling *(TN762)*
     xx Gold—Metallurgy
— Minting *(HG321)*
— Protective coatings
     See Gold coatings
— Spectra
— Standards of fineness *(HD9747)*
     sa Hall-marks
     xx Coinage
        Hall-marks
— Therapeutic use *(RM666.G7)*
— Transportation
Gold, Cloth of
  See Cloth of gold
Gold alloys *(TS729; Dentistry, RK653)*
  sa Gold-cadmium alloys
     Gold-chromium alloys
     Gold-cobalt alloys
     Gold-copper alloys
     Gold-platinum alloys
     Silver-gold alloys

Gold and ivory sculpture
  See Sculpture, Chryselephantine
Gold articles *(Direct)*
  x Goldwork
  xx Goldsmithing
Gold articles, Chinese, ⌐Norwegian, etc.⌐
     (Direct)
  x Chinese ⌐Norwegian, etc.⌐ gold articles
Gold articles, Prehistoric *(Direct)*
     (GN799.G6)
  x Prehistoric gold articles
  xx Antiquities
Gold articles, Renaissance *(Direct)*
  x Renaissance gold articles
Gold buying
  xx Gold
Gold-cadmium alloys
  x Cadmium-gold alloys
  xx Cadmium alloys
     Gold alloys
Gold-chromium alloys
  x Chromium-gold alloys
  xx Chromium alloys
     Gold alloys
Gold clause *(Direct)*
  sa Valuta clause
  xx Bonds
     Contracts
     Currency question
     Debtor and creditor
     Escalator clause
     Gold
     Industrial management and inflation
     Payment
Gold coatings
  x Gold—Protective coatings
  xx Protective coatings
— Optical properties
Gold-cobalt alloys
  x Cobalt-gold alloys
  xx Cobalt alloys
     Gold alloys
Gold coins
  xx Coins
Gold compounds *(QD412.A9)*
Gold-copper alloys
  x Copper-gold alloys
  xx Copper alloys
     Gold alloys
Gold-cure
  See Alcoholism—Treatment
Gold dredging *(TN422)*
  x Dredging (Gold mining)
  xx Gold mines and mining
— Safety regulations *(Direct)*
Gold exchange standard
  See Gold standard
Gold-eye *(QL638.H5)*
Gold in art
  xx Art
Gold isotopes
  See Gold—Isotopes
Gold-leaf *(TS260)*
Gold metallurgy
  See Gold—Metallurgy
Gold miners *(Direct)*
  xx Gold mines and mining
     Miners
— Diseases and hygiene
— Personal narratives
     See Gold mines and mining—Personal
        narratives
Gold mines and mining *(Indirect)*
     (Economics, HD9536; Mineral
     industries, TN410-429)
  sa Gold dredging
     Gold miners
     Hydraulic mining

775

Gold mines and mining *(Indirect)*
    (Economics, HD9536; Mineral
    industries, TN410-429)
      (Continued)
      Prospecting
      Strikes and lockouts—Gold mining
  xx Gold
      Hydraulic mining
  Example under Mines and mineral resources
  — Accidents
  — Finance
  — Juvenile literature
  — Personal narratives
    x Gold miners—Personal narratives
  — Pictorial works
  — Terminology
Gold ores *(Indirect)*
Gold organic compounds
  See Organogold compounds
Gold plate
  See Plate
Gold-plating *(TS670)*
  xx Gilding
    Plating
Gold-platinum alloys
  x Platinum-gold alloys
  xx Gold alloys
    Platinum alloys
Gold-silver alloys
  See Silver-gold alloys
Gold standard *(HG297)*
  sa Bimetallism
    Currency convertibility
  x Gold exchange standard
  xx Bimetallism
    Currency question
    Gold
    International liquidity
    Money
Gold thread
  sa Spun gold
  xx Spun gold
    Thread
Gold tribe
  See Golds
Gold-weights
  See Goldweights
Goldau, Switzerland
  — Landslide, 1806
Golden age (Mythology)
  xx Mythology, Classical
Golden age (Mythology) in literature
  xx Utopias in literature
Golden bull, 1356 *(JN3270.G8)*
  x Bull, Golden
  xx Electors (Kurfürsten)
Golden eagle
  sa Himalayan golden eagle
  xx Eagles
  — Juvenile literature
  — Legends and stories
Golden Fleece
  See Argonauts
Golden-fronted woodpecker
  xx Woodpeckers
Golden hamster
  See Hamsters
Golden Horde *(DS22.7)*
  x Kipchak (Khanate)
    Kiptchak (Khanate)
  xx Mongols—History
Golden-mantled ground squirrel *(QL737.R68)*
  xx Ground-squirrels
Golden mean
  See Moderation
Golden retrievers
  xx Retrievers
Golden robin
  See Orioles

Golden rose (Papal award)
  xx Decorations of honor, Papal
Golden Rose of Montreux
  x Goldene Rose von Montreux
    Rose d'Or de Montreux
  xx Television broadcasting—Awards
Golden rule *(Comparative religion, BL85;*
    Moral theology, BV4715)
  x Rule, Golden
  xx Christian ethics
Golden section *(QA466)*
  x Extreme and mean ratio
  xx Geometry, Plane
    Ratio and proportion
Golden trout *(QL638.S2)*
  xx Trout
Golden trout fishing
  xx Fishing
    Trout fishing
Goldene Rose von Montreux
  See Golden Rose of Montreux
Goldenrod *(Solidago, QK495.S)*
  sa Sweet goldenrod
  xx Rubber plants
Goldfield Strike, 1907 *(HD5325.M8 1907.G)*
Goldfinch (in religion, folk-lore, etc.)
  x Folk-lore of goldfinches
  xx Christian art and symbolism
    Finches
Goldfinches
  xx Finches
Goldfinches in art
  xx Birds in art
Goldfish *(Fish-culture, SH167.G6; Zoology,*
    QL638.C25, QL638.C94)
  xx Aquarium fishes
  — Diseases and pests
  — Juvenile literature
Goldi
  See Golds
Goldian dialect *(PL461.G)*
  x Nanai dialect
  xx Tungusic languages
Goldman's wood rat
  xx Wood rats
Golds
  x Gold tribe
    Goldi
  xx Ethnology—Manchuria
    Ethnology—Siberia
    Tunguses
Goldsboro, N.C., Battle of, 1862 *(E474.52)*
Goldscheider's disease
  See Epidermolysis bullosa
Goldsmithing *(Indirect)* *(Art industries,*
    NK7100-7695; Manufactures,
    TS720-761)
  sa Engraving (Metal-work)
    Gilding
    Gold articles
    Hall-marks
    Indians—Goldsmithing
    Indians of Mexico—Goldsmithing
    Indians of South America—
      Goldsmithing
    Jewelry making
    Metals—Coloring
    Plate
    Vinaigrettes
  xx Art metal-work
    Arts and crafts movement
    Gold
    Hall-marks
    Jewelry making
    Metal-work
  Example under Toreutic
  — Tables, calculations, etc.

Goldsmithing, British, ⌜**Italian, etc.**⌝ *(Direct)*
  x British ⌜Italian, etc.⌝ goldsmithing
Goldsmithing, Medieval *(Direct)*
Goldsmiths *(Direct)*
  xx Art metal-workers
Goldsmiths, British, ⌜**Italian, etc.**⌝ *(Direct)*
Goldstein rays
  See Canal rays
Goldweights *(Direct)*
  x Gold-weights
  xx Art metal-work
    Brasses
    Weights and measures
Goldweights, Ashanti, ⌜**etc.**⌝
  x Ashanti ⌜etc.⌝ goldweights
Goldwork
  See Gold articles
Golem
  xx Legends, Jewish
    Mysticism—Judaism
  — Drama
  — Fiction
Goletta, Tunis
  — Siege, 1573 *(DT262)*
Golf *(Direct)* *(GV961-987)*
  sa Caddying
    Golf for women
    Grip (Golf)
    Putting (Golf)
    Swing (Golf)
  Example under Sports
  — Anecdotes, facetiae, satire, etc. *(GV967)*
  — Audio-visual aids
  — Caricatures and cartoons
  — Juvenile literature
  — Pictorial works
  — Psychological aspects
  — Rules *(GV971)*
  — Tournaments
      Individual tournaments by name, or
      place, and date, *e.g.* Canadian Open
      Golf Championship Tournament,
      Winnipeg, 1952.
Golf, Miniature *(GV987)*
  sa Bilgo (Game)
  x Miniature golf
Golf balls
  xx Balls (Sporting goods)
Golf-croquet *(GV1017.G)*
Golf for women *(GV966)*
  xx Golf
    Sports for women
  — Caricatures and cartoons
Golf-links *(Direct)* *(GV975)*
  — Construction and care *(GV975)*
    x Greenkeeping
    xx Grasses
      Grounds maintenance
      Lawns
Golgi apparatus
  x Golgi bodies
    Golgi elements
    Golgi material
  xx Cell organelles
    Protoplasm
Golgi bodies
  See Golgi apparatus
Golgi elements
  See Golgi apparatus
Golgi material
  See Golgi apparatus
Goliad, Tex.
  — Massacre, 1836 *(F390)*
Goliards *(Latin verse, PA8065.S8)*
  x Vagantes
    Vagi scholares
Golin dialect
  xx Dom dialects

Marigl dialect
Gólo language *(PL8211)*
  xx Banda languages
Goma (Rite)
  See Homa (Rite)
Gomberg-Bachmann reaction
  xx Chemical reactions
Gonadal dysgenesis
  See Turner's syndrome
Gonadotrophin
  See Gonadotropin
Gonadotropin
  sa Chorionic gonadotropins
    Follicle-stimulating hormone
    Hebin
  x Gonadotrophin
  xx Endocrinology
    Pituitary hormones
  — Therapeutic use *(RM291.2.G6)*
    xx Hormone therapy
Gonads
  sa Ovaries
    Testicle
  x Sex glands
  xx Generative organs
Gond language
  See Gondi language
Gondi language *(PL4631-4)*
  sa Dravidian languages
  x Gond language
  xx Dravidian languages
Gondi poetry *(Texts, PL4634)*
Gondolas
  xx Canal-boats
Gondra, Battle of, 1933
  x Batalla de Gondra, 1933
  xx Chaco War, 1932-1935
Gonds *(DS432.G6)*
  sa Kolams
    Muria
Gondwana (Geology)
  sa Continental drift
  x Gondwanaland
  xx Continental drift
    Geology
    Physical geography
Gondwanaland
  See Gondwana (Geology)
Gong
  See Tamtam
Gongorism *(PQ6066)*
  x Culteranismo
    Cultism
  xx Baroque literature
    Spanish literature—History and
      criticism
Gonin-gumi
  See Goningumi
Goningumi
  sa Tonarigumi
  x Gonin-gumi
  xx Tonarigumi
Goniometry *(QC103)*
  xx Angle
Gonioscopy *(RE79.G)*
  xx Eye—Examination
Gonja (African tribe) *(DT510.42)*
  x Gbanya (African tribe)
    Gonya (African tribe)
  xx Ethnology—Ghana
Gonja language *(PL8215)*
  xx Kwa languages
Gonorrhea *(Indirect) (RC202)*
  sa Conjunctivitis, Infantile
  xx Genito-urinary organs—Diseases
    Venereal diseases
Gonya (African tribe)
  See Gonja (African tribe)

Good and evil *(BJ1400-1408)*
  sa Evil in literature
    Good in literature
    Guilt
    Providence and government of God
    Sin
    Theodicy
  x Evil
  xx Ethics
    Fall of man
    Philosophy
    Polarity (in religion, folk-lore, etc.)
    Suffering
    Temptation
    Theodicy
    Theology, Doctrinal
  — Biblical teaching
Good and evil (Islam) *(BJ1400-1405)*
  xx Islamic ethics
    Islamic theology
Good and evil in art
  sa Good in literature
Good as a theme in literature
  See Good in literature
Good behavior, Security for
  See Surety of the peace
Good behavior (Law) *(Direct)*
  x Behavior, Good (Law)
  xx Certificates of good conduct
    Surety of the peace
Good faith (Canon law)
Good faith (Jewish law)
Good faith (Law) *(Direct)*
  sa Bad faith (Law)
    Ignorance (Law)
    Mistake (Law)
  x Bona fides (Law)
  xx Bad faith (Law)
    Ignorance (Law)
    Mistake (Law)
Good faith (Roman law)
Good Friday *(BV95)*
  xx Church year
    Fasts and feasts
    Holy Week
    Lent
Good Friday music *(Part-songs, M2078.G5,*
    M2088.G5, M2098.G5; Catholic
    liturgical music, M2149.4.G7)
  xx Holy-Week music
Good Friday sermons *(BV95)*
  sa Jesus Christ—Seven last words—
    Sermons
  xx Jesus Christ—Passion—Sermons
    Lenten sermons
    Sermons
Good in literature
  x Good as a theme in literature
  xx Good and evil
    Good and evil in art
Good offices
  See Mediation, International
Good Samaritan (Parable) *(BT378.G6)*
  Example under Jesus Christ—Parables
Good Samaritan laws
  See Assistance in emergencies
Good Samaritan shilling
  x Samaritan shilling
  xx Shilling
Good-will (in business, etc.) *(Direct)*
    (HF5353)
  xx Business
    Industrial property
    Intangible property
  — Taxation *(Direct)*
Good works (Theology)
  sa Antinomianism
    Corporal works of mercy

    Justification
    Merit (Christianity)
    Reward (Theology)
  xx Justification
    Merit (Christianity)
    Reward (Theology)
    Sanctification
    Theology, Doctrinal
  — Early works to 1800
Goodenough draw-a-man test
  See Draw-a-man test
Goods, Confusion of
  See Confusion of goods
Goods, Ecclesiastical
  See Church supplies
Goods in transit, Tariff on
  See Duty-free transit
Goor languages
  See Gur languages
Goorkhas
  See Gurkhas
Goose
  See Geese
Goose (Game) *(GV1469.G)*
Goose hunting
  See Goose shooting
Goose shooting
  x Goose hunting
  xx Fowling
    Waterfowl shooting
Gooseberries *(SB386.G6)*
  — Diseases and pests
Goosefish
  See Angler-fishes
Gophers
  See Ground-squirrels
    Pocket gophers
Gora language
  See Gola language
Gordon Relief Expedition, 1884-1885
  xx Egypt—History—British occupation,
    1882-1936
Gordon Riots, 1780 *(DA510)*
  x No-Popery Riots, 1780
  xx Catholic emancipation
Gordon setters *(SF429.G67)*
  xx Setters (Dogs)
Gorgonacea *(Indirect) (QL377.C6)*
  x Gorgonaria
    Gorgoniaceae
  xx Alcyonaria
Gorgonaria
  See Gorgonacea
Gorgoniaceae
  See Gorgonacea
Gorgons *(BL820.G7)*
  xx Monsters
    Mythology
    Mythology, Classical
Gorillas *(QL737.P9)*
  xx Apes
  — Behavior
    Example under Primates—Behavior
  — Juvenile literature
  — Psychology
Gorillas as pets
Goriunov machine-gun
  x Goryunov machine-gun
  xx Machine-guns
Gorizia, Battle of, 1916 *(D569.G7)*
  xx European War, 1914-1918—Campaigns
    —Italo-Austrian
    Isonzo, Battles of the, 1915-1917
Gorkhali language
  See Nepali language
Gorkhas
  See Gurkhas
Gorlice-Tarnow, Battle of, 1915 *(D557.G6)*

Gormogons *(HS247.G6)*
Gorodki (Game) *(GV903)*
Gorona
  See Korana (African people)
Gorontalo language *(PL5327)*
  sa Malayan languages
  x Gunongtello language
    Gurantala language
    Holontalo language
  xx Malayan languages
Goryōkaku, Battle of, 1868-1869
  See Hakodate, Battle of, 1868-1869
Goryunov machine-gun
  See Goriūnov machine-gun
Goshawk
  xx Birds of prey
    Hawks
  — Juvenile literature
Goshute Indians
  See Gosiute Indians
Gosiute Indians *(E99.G67)*
  x Goshute Indians
  xx Indians of North America
    Numic Indians
    Shoshonean Indians
Gospel, Social
  See Social gospel
Gospel and law
  See Law and gospel
Gospel music
  See Country music
    Hymns, English
    Negro spirituals
    Revivals—Hymns
Gospels enthroned
  See Enthronement of the Gospels
Gossip *(BJ1535.G6)*
  sa Slander
    Talebearing
  xx Slander
Gossypein
  See Gossypol
Gossypol *(Cottonseed feeds, SF99; Cottonseed oil, TP681; Pigment, QD441)*
  x Gossypein
Gothenburg, Sweden, in literature
Gothenburg system *(HV5092-5)*
  xx Liquor laws
    Liquor problem
    Temperance
  Note under Alcoholism
Gothic altarpieces
  See Altarpieces, Gothic
Gothic altars
  See Altars, Gothic
Gothic architecture
  See Architecture, Gothic
Gothic art
  See Art, Gothic
Gothic art industries and trade
  See Art industries and trade, Gothic
Gothic arts
  See Arts, Gothic
Gothic decoration and ornament
  See Decoration and ornament, Gothic
Gothic drawings
  See Drawings, Gothic
Gothic glass painting and staining
  See Glass painting and staining, Gothic
Gothic illumination of books and manuscripts
  See Illumination of books and manuscripts, Gothic
Gothic language *(PD1101-1211)*
  xx Germanic languages
  Example under Germanic philology
Gothic law
  See Law, Gothic

Gothic literature *(Direct)*
  xx Literature
Gothic mural painting and decoration
  See Mural painting and decoration, Gothic
Gothic painting
  See Painting, Gothic
Gothic paintings
  See Paintings, Gothic
Gothic panel painting
  See Panel painting, Gothic
Gothic philology
Gothic revival (Architecture) *(Direct)*
  sa Architecture, Victorian
  xx Architecture, Gothic
    Architecture, Victorian
    Gothic revival (Art)
Gothic revival (Art) *(Direct)*
  Here are entered works on the revival of
    Gothic principles in art during the late
    18th and early 19th centuries.
  sa Gothic revival (Architecture)
  xx Art, Modern
    Arts, Modern
    Romanticism in art
Gothic-roman type controversy *(Z250.5.G6)*
  x Roman-gothic type controversy
  xx Type and type-founding
Gothic sculpture
  See Sculpture, Gothic
Gothic tapestry
  See Tapestry, Gothic
Gothic type
  See Type and type-founding—Gothic type
Gothic wood-carving
  See Wood-carving, Gothic
Gothic writing
  See Writing, Gothic
Goths *(Migrations, D137-8)*
  sa Gepidae
    Germanic tribes
    Visigoths
  x East Goths
    Ostgoths
    Ostrogoths
  xx Germanic tribes
  Example under Teutonic race
Goths in Italy *(DG506-9)*
  sa Barbarian invasions of Rome
  xx Barbarian invasions of Rome
Goths in literature
Goths in the Crimea
Gotland in literature
Gotra (Buddhism) *(BQ4285)*
  xx Buddhist doctrines
Gottorf, Treaty of, May 27, 1768 *(Hamburg, DD901.H27)*
  x Treaty of Gottorf, May 27, 1768
Gotwezi
  See Yatvyags
Gouache painting
  xx Painting
    Water-color painting
Gougerot-Sjogren's syndrome
  See Sjogren's syndrome
Gouges (Woodworking)
  See Chisels
Gouin (African people)
  x Guen (African people)
    Guin (African people)
    Gwin (African people)
    Mbouin (African people)
  xx Ethnology—Upper Volta
    Senufo (African people)
Goura (Musical instrument)
  xx Musical instruments, African
    Musical instruments, Primitive
Gourague language
  See Gurage language

Gourami *(Fish-culture, SH167.G64)*
Gourds *(SB413.G6)*
Gourmantché language
  See Gurma language
Gouro (African people)
  See Guro (African people)
Gouro language
  See Kweni langauge
Gourounsi (African people)
  See Gurunsi (African people)
Gourounsi dialects
  See Gurunsi dialects
Gout *(RC291)*
  sa Arthritis deformans
  x Podagra
  — Dietary aspects
    See Gout—Nutritional aspects
  — Nutritional aspects
    x Diet and gout
      Gout—Dietary aspects
      Nutrition and gout
Governesses *(LC41)*
  xx Children—Management
    Domestic education
Governesses in literature
Government
  See Political science
Government, Comparative
  See Comparative government
Government, Primitive *(GN490)*
  xx Society, Primitive
Government, Resistance to *(JC328)*
  sa Allegiance
    Anomy
    Civil war
    Coups d'état
    Insurgency
    Revolutions
  x Civil disobedience
    Civil obedience
    Higher law
    Non-resistance to government
    Resistance to government
  xx Church and state
    Direct action
    Evil, Non-resistance to
    Insurgency
    Political crimes and offenses
    Political ethics
    Political science
    Revolutions
  — Moral and religious aspects
Government, Resistance to, in literature
Government (Grammar)
  x Grammar, Comparative and general—Government
    Regimen (Grammar)
Government accounting
  See Finance, Public—Accounting
Government advertising *(Direct)*
  x Advertising—Government
    Advertising, Government
  xx Government publicity
Government advisory boards
  See Executive advisory bodies
Government aeroplanes
  See Aeroplanes, Military
    Government aircraft
Government agencies
  See Administrative agencies
Government aircraft *(Direct) (TL723)*
  sa Aeroplanes, Military
  x Aeroplanes, Government
    Aircraft, Government
    Government aeroplanes
    Government-owned aircraft
Government and business
  See Industry and state

Government and forestry
  See Forest policy
    Forestry law and legislation
Government and the press *(Direct)*
  sa Official secrets
  x Press and government
  xx Executive privilege (Government
      information)
    Freedom of information
    Government information
    Government publicity
    Journalism
    Press
    Press law
    Press releases
    Reporters and reporting
Government attorneys *(Direct)*
  sa Attorneys-general
    City attorneys
    County attorneys
    Government litigation
    Judge advocates
    Police legal advisors
    Public prosecutors
  x Attorneys, Government
    Government lawyers
    Lawyers, Government
  xx Lawyers
    Public prosecutors
  — Correspondence, reminiscences, etc.
Government banking
  See Postal savings-banks
Government buildings
  See Public buildings
Government business enterprises *(Direct)*
  sa Corporations, Government
    Government monopolies
    Government ownership
    Government trading
    Municipal ownership
  x Business enterprises, Government
  xx Corporations, Government
    Government competition
    Industry and state
    Public utilities
    Public works
  — Accounting
    xx Finance, Public—Accounting
  — Auditing and inspection
      Here are entered works on the auditing
        of the books of government busi-
        ness enterprises, as well as the in-
        spection and examination of their
        policies, administrative practices,
        and management. For socialist
        countries use Auditing and inspec-
        tion under name of country with
        subdivision Industries, *e.g.* Russia
        —Industries—Auditing and inspec-
        tion.
    x Corporations, Government—
        Auditing and inspection
    xx Industrial management
  — Collective bargaining
    See Collective bargaining—
        Government business
        enterprises
  — Collective labor agreements
    See Collective labor agreements—
        Government business
        enterprises
  — Employees
    xx Civil service
  — Finance
    xx Finance, Public
  — Law and legislation *(Direct)*
    xx Industrial laws and legislation
  — Taxation *(Direct)*

— Underdeveloped areas
    See Underdeveloped areas—
        Government business
        enterprises
Government by commission
  See Municipal government by commission
Government cars
  See Automobiles, Government
Government centralization
  See Decentralization in government
Government competition *(Direct)*
  sa Government business enterprises
  x Competition, Government
  xx Competition
    Corporations, Government
    Government ownership
    Industry and state
Government consultants *(Direct)*
  sa Scientists in government
    Without-compensation personnel
  x Consultants, Government
  — Underdeveloped areas
    See Underdeveloped areas—
        Government consultants
Government contracts
  See Public contracts
Government corporations
  See Corporations, Government
Government correspondence
  sa subdivision Records and
      correspondence *under subjects or
      names of government agencies*
  x Correspondence
  xx Letter-writing
    Public records
Government decentralization
  See Decentralization in government
Government departments
  See Administrative agencies
    subdivision Executive departments
      under names of countries, cities, etc.
Government depositories
  See Public depositaries
Government-developed inventions and patents
  See Patents and government-developed
      inventions
Government documents
  See Government publications
Government employees
  See Civil service
    subdivision Officials and employees
      *under names of countries, cities, etc.,
      e.g.* United States—Officials and
      employees; *and subdivision*
      Government employees *under
      specific subjects, e.g.* Collective
      bargaining—Government employees;
      Collective labor agreements—
      Government employees
Government employees' health insurance
  See Insurance, Government employees'
      health
Government employees' life insurance
  See Insurance, Government employees' life
Government employees' political activities
  See Civil service—Political activity
    United States—Officials and employees
      —Political activity
Government executives *(Direct)*
  xx Executives
    Public officers
  — Correspondence, reminiscences, etc.
Government expenditures
  See Expenditures, Public
Government financial institutions *(Direct)*
  x Public financial institutions
  xx Financial institutions
  — Accounting

Government gazettes
  See Gazettes
Government geographers *(Direct)*
  xx Geographers
Government housing
  See Public housing
Government immunity
  See Government liability
Government information *(Direct)*
  sa Executive privilege (Government
      information)
    Federal government—Information
        services
    Government and the press
    Official secrets
    Security classification (Government
        documents)
  x Government secrecy
    Information, Government
  xx Freedom of information
  — Copyright
    See Copyright—Official information
Government information services
  See Government publicity
Government institutions
  See Public institutions
Government insurance
  See Insurance, Government
Government interns (Legislation)
  See Interns (Legislation)
Government investigations
  See Governmental investigations
Government jargon
  See *subdivision* Government jargon *under
      names of languages, e.g.* English
      language—Government jargon
Government jobs
  See Civil service positions
Government lawyers
  See Government attorneys
Government lending *(Direct)*
  sa Agricultural credit
    Insurance, Government
    Veterans—Loans
  x Government loans
    Loans, Government
  xx Economic assistance, Domestic
    Economic policy
    Finance, Public
    Industry and state
    Loans
Government liability *(Direct)* *(JF1621;
    JK-JQ)*
  sa Act of state
    Compensation for judicial error
    De facto doctrine
    Denial of justice
    Insurance, Government risks
    Liability for school accidents
    Tort liability of municipal corporations
    Tort liability of school districts
    Tort liability of the police
  x Government immunity
    Government responsibility
    Liability of the state
    Sovereign immunity
    State liability
    State responsibility
    Tort liability of the government
    Tort liability of the state
  xx Act of state
    Administrative law
    Administrative responsibility
    Constitutional law
    Eminent domain
    Liability (Law)
    Misconduct in office
    Public law

779

Government liability (Direct) (JF1621;
    JK-JQ) (Continued)
    Torts
    Note under Administrative responsibility
    — Great Britain
        x Crown proceedings
Government liability (International law)
    sa Claims
        Exhaustion of local remedies
            (International law)
        Immunities of foreign states
        State succession
        Tort liability of international agencies
    x International claims
    xx Claims
        International law
        Sovereignty
        State succession
    — Cases
        sa Corfu Channel case
Government librarians (Direct)
    xx Librarians
        Libraries, Governmental,
            administrative, etc.
Government libraries
    See Libraries, Governmental,
        administrative, etc.
Government life insurance
    See Insurance, Government life
Government litigation (Direct)
    x Litigation, Government
    xx Attorneys-general
        Government attorneys
        Procedure (Law)
Government loans
    See Government lending
Government missions
    sa Diplomatic and consular service
        Economic assistance
        Military missions
        Technical assistance
        Trade missions
    x Missions, Government
    xx International relations
        Public administration
Government missions, American, [etc.]
    (Direct)
Government monopolies (Direct)
    (HD3853-6)
    sa names of products, e.g. Salt, Tobacco
    x Monopolies, Government
        State monopolies
    xx Finance, Public
        Government business enterprises
        Government ownership
        Monopolies
        Revenue
        Taxation
    — Employees
Government office practice
    See Office practice in government
Government officials
    See Public officers
Government-owned aircraft
    See Aeroplanes, Military
        Government aircraft
Government-owned automobiles
    See Automobiles, Government
Government-owned corporations
    See Corporations, Government
Government-owned patents
    See Patents, Government-owned
Government ownership (Direct)
    (HD3840-4420)
    sa Corporations, Government
        Government competition
        Government monopolies
        Government trading

Land, Nationalization of
        Municipal ownership
        Railroads and state
        Socialist property
    subdivision Government ownership
        under names of industries, e.g. Coal
        mines and mining—Government
        ownership
    x Nationalization
        Public ownership
        Socialization of industry
        State ownership
    xx Collectivism
        Economic policy
        Economics
        Government business enterprises
        Industry and state
        Political science
        Socialism
Government ownership of coal mines
    See Coal mines and mining—Government
        ownership
Government ownership of electric utilities
    See Electric utilities—Government
        ownership
Government ownership of forests
    See Forests and forestry—Government
        ownership
Government ownership of insurance companies
    See Insurance—Government ownership
Government ownership of mines
    See Mines and mineral resources—
        Government ownership
Government ownership of railroads
    See Railroads and state
Government ownership of retail trade
    See Retail trade—Government ownership
Government ownership of the meat industry
    See Meat industry and trade—Government
        ownership
Government ownership of the petroleum
    industry
    See Petroleum industry and trade—
        Government ownership
Government ownership of the potash industry
    See Potash industry and trade—
        Government ownership
Government ownership of the printing industry
    See Printing industry—Government
        ownership
Government ownership of tobacco manufacture
    and trade
    See Tobacco manufacture and trade—
        Government ownership
Government ownership of wireless telegraph
    See Telegraph, Wireless—Government
        ownership
Government patents
    See Patents, Government-owned
Government positions
    See Civil service positions
Government price control
    See Price regulation
Government price regulation
    See Price regulation
Government procurement
    See Government purchasing
Government property
    sa Socialist property
        Surplus government property
        subdivision Government property under
            names of countries and cities, e.g.
            United States—Government
            property; Portland, Or.—
            Government property
    x Public property
    xx Property
        Public administration

Socialist property
Government property, Surplus
    See Surplus government property
Government property and taxation
    See Taxation and government property
Government publications
    sa Exchanges, Literary and scientific
        Gazettes
        Government publicity
        Maps
        Municipal documents
        Printing, Public
        Security classification (Government
            documents)
        subdivision Government publications
            under names of countries, states,
            counties, cities, etc., e.g. United
            States—Government publications
    x Documents
        Government documents
        Official publications
        Public documents
    xx Government publicity
        Printing, Public
    — Cataloging
        See Cataloging of government
            publications
Government publicity (Direct)
    Here are entered works on the dissemina-
        tion of information by government
        agencies on their activities.
    sa Government advertising
        Government and the press
        Government publications
        Public relations—Municipal government
        Radio broadcasting
    x Government information services
        Information services, Government
        Public relations—Public administration
        Publicity, Government
    xx Government publications
        Propaganda
        Public administration
Government purchasing (Direct)
    sa Brokers in public contracts, etc.
        Public contracts
        Purchasing agents
        subdivision Procurement under
            government agencies, etc., e.g.
            United States. Navy—Procurement;
            United States. Small Business
            Administration—Procurement
    x Government procurement
        Procurement, Government
        Public procurement
        Public purchasing
        Purchasing, Government
    xx Public contracts
        Purchasing
        Sales
    Note under Purchasing
    — Information services
    — Terminology
Government purchasing of real property
    (Direct)
    sa Eminent domain
    x Real property, Government purchasing
        of
    xx Public contracts
        Vendors and purchasers
Government questionnaires
    x Federal questionnaires
        Questionnaires, Government
    xx Industry and state
        Public administration
        Questionnaires
        Statistics

780

Government records
    See Public records
Government regulation of commerce
    See Commercial policy
        Industrial laws and legislation
        Industry and state
        Interstate commerce
        Trade regulation
        methods of regulation, e.g. Bounties,
            Tariff
Government regulation of railroads
    See Interstate commerce
        Railroad law
        Railroads and state
Government responsibility
    See Government liability
Government risks insurance
    See Insurance, Government risks
Government scientists
    See Scientists in government
Government secrecy
    See Executive privilege (Government
        information)
        Government information
        Official secrets
        Security classification (Government
            documents)
Government spending policy *(Direct)*
    sa Expenditures, Public
        Public works
        subdivision Appropriations and
            expenditures *under names of
            countries* [for descriptive and
            statistical works on government
            spending]
    x Public spending policy
    xx Economic policy
        Expenditures, Public
        Finance, Public
        Full employment policies
Government support of science, literature, and
        art
    See State encouragement of science,
        literature, and art
Government surveys
    See Surveys
Government trading *(Direct)*
    x State trading
    xx Commerce
        Commercial policy
        Government business enterprises
        Government ownership
Government vessels
    sa Hospital-ships
        Lighthouse tenders
        Warships
        subdivision Government vessels *under
            names of countries, e.g.* United
            States—Government vessels
    x State ships
        State vessels
    xx Exterritoriality
        Immunities of foreign states
        Maritime law
        Ships
Governmental investigations *(Direct)*
    Here are entered works on investigations
        initiated by the legislative, executive,
        or judicial branches of the government
        and usually conducted by ad hoc or
        permanent bodies for the purpose of
        investigating some particular problem
        of public interest.
    sa Criminal investigation
        Executive privilege (Government
            information)
        Legislative hearings
        Police

names of specific investigative bodies
    x Commissions of inquiry
        Executive investigations
        Government investigations
        Investigations, Governmental
        Judicial investigations
        Legislative investigations
    xx Investigations
        Justice, Administration of
        Legislation
        Legislative bodies—Committees
        Public administration
— United States
    x Congressional investigations
Governments, Legitimacy of
    See Legitimacy of governments
Governments in exile
    sa *subdivision* Governments in exile *under
        names of wars, e.g.* World War,
        1939-1945—Governments in exile
    x Refugee governments
    xx Exiles
        International law
        International relations
        Refugees, Political
        Sovereignty
        State, The
Governor Shirley's War
    See United States—History—King George's
        War, 1744-1748
Governors
        Works on governors of the United States
        are entered under the heading Gover-
        nors—United States. Works on gover-
        nors in other countries are entered un-
        der the name of the country with sub-
        division Governors, *e.g.* Russia—Gov-
        ernors.
        Works on governors of any state or prov-
        ince, including collective biography,
        are entered under the name of the state
        or province with subdivision Gover-
        nors, *e.g.* Louisiana—Governors.
— United States
    xx State governments
        Note under Governors
— — Powers and duties *(JK2447-2458)*
        sa *subdivision* Governors—Powers
            and duties *under names of
            individual states, e.g.* Louisiana
            —Governors—Powers and
            duties
— — Staff
Governors (Machinery) *(TJ1055)*
        This heading covers governing mech-
        anisms used in general machinery.
    sa Electronic control
        Gas-governors
    x Centrifugal regulators
        Regulators
    xx Automatic control
Governors (Steam-engine) *(TJ550-551)*
        This heading covers governing mech-
        anisms applied particularly to steam-
        engines.
    Example under Steam-engines
Gowns, College
    See Academic costume
Gowns, Wedding
    See Wedding costume
Gowrie Conspiracy, 1600 *(DA789)*
Gozan literature
    See Japanese literature—Zen authors
Goze
    xx Minstrels
        Street music and musicians

GPLAN (Electronic computer system)
    x Generalized Data Base Planning
        System
GPS (Computer program)
    x General problem solver (Computer
        program)
    xx Artificial intelligence
        Problem solving
GPSS (Computer program language)
    x General Purpose Simulation System
    xx Digital computer simulation
Graafian follicle *(QL965; QM611)*
    sa Corpus luteum
    xx Embryology
        Ovaries
Graal
    See Grail
Grabens (Geology) *(Indirect)*
    x Fault troughs
    xx Geology, Structural
        Rifts (Geology)
Grace, Gifts of
    See Gifts, Spiritual
Grace (Aesthetics)
Grace (Theology) *(BT760-761)*
    sa Covenants (Theology)
        Law and gospel
        Semi-Pelagianism
        Supernatural (Theology)
        Virtue, Infused
    xx Convenants (Theology)
        Conversion
        Theology, Doctrinal
— Early works to 1800
— History of doctrines
— — Early church, ca. 30-600
— — Middle Ages, 600-1500
Grace at meals *(BV283.G7)*
    x Blessings, Table
        Prayers, Table
        Table blessings
        Table prayers
    xx Prayers
Graces, Expectative
    See Benefices, Ecclesiastical
Graces, The *(Literature, PN57.G6;
        Mythology, BL820.G8)*
Grackles
Grade crossings
    See Railroads—Crossings
Grade labeling
    See Labels
Grade repetition
    x Non-promotion (School)
        Repetition, Grade
    xx Promotion (School)
        Slow learning children
        Underachievers
Grade school . . .
    See Elementary school . . .
Grade separation (Highway engineering)
    See Roads—Interchanges and intersections
Graded schools
    See Ability grouping in education
        Grading and marking (Students)
Gradehede, Battle of, 1157 *(DL170.8)*
Graders (Earthmoving machinery)
    x Grading machinery
        Motor graders
        Road graders
    xx Earthmoving machinery
        Motor vehicles
        Road machinery
        Scrapers (Earthmoving machinery)
— Lubrication
— Maintenance and repair
— Safety measures

Grading

Here are entered works on the division of commercial products into categories of uniform quality to facilitate marketing.

   sa Labels
   Specifications
   Standardization
   Testing
   subdivisions Grading *and* Grading and standardization *under specific commodities, e.g.* Cotton—Grading; Farm produce—Grading; Milk—Grading and standardization
   x Commercial products—Grading
   xx Specifications
   Standardization
   Testing
   — Terminology

Grading and marking (Students)
   (LB3051-3063)
   sa Ability grouping in education
   Mental tests
   Pass-fail grading system
   Promotion (School)
   School credits
   School credits—Outside work
   School reports
   Students, Rating of
   x Graded schools
   Marking (Students)
   Students—Grading and marking
   xx Educational tests and measurements
   Personnel records in education
   School reports
   Students, Rating of
   Note under Students, Rating of
   — Electronic data processing
      See Electronic data processing—Grading and marking (Students)

Grading machinery
   See Graders (Earthmoving machinery)
Graduale romanum
   See Catholic Church. Liturgy and ritual. Gradual
Graduals (Music) (M2079.L416; M2099.L416; M2149)
   xx Catholic Church. Liturgy and ritual. Gradual
   Propers (Music)
Graduate education of women
   See Universities and colleges—Graduate work of women
Graduate examinations
   See Universities and colleges—Graduate work—Examinations
Graduate medical education (Direct) (R840)
   Here are entered works on training at the residency or fellowship level, designed for training medical specialists. Works on advanced medical training, such as refresher courses, designed to keep practicing physicians abreast of developments in the field, are entered under Postgraduate medical education.
   xx Medical education
   Medicine—Specialties and specialists
   Note under Postgraduate medical education
Graduate nursing education (Direct)
   xx Nurses and nursing—Study and teaching
Graduate student mobility
   x Migration of graduate students
   Mobility
   xx Student mobility
Graduate students (Direct)
   sa Graduate teaching assistants
   Women graduate students

subdivision Graduate students *under names of universities, e.g.* Columbia University—Graduate students
   x Students, Graduate
   xx College students
   Universities and colleges—Graduate work
— Science (Direct)
Graduate study in art
   See Art—Graduate work
Graduate study in education
   See Education—Graduate work
Graduate study in special education
   See Teachers of exceptional children, Training of—Graduate work
Graduate teaching assistants (Direct)
   x College teacher aides
   College teacher assistants
   xx College teachers
   Graduate students
Graduate work
   See Universities and colleges—Graduate work
Graduate work in art
   See Art—Graduate work
Graduate work in education
   See Education—Graduate work
Graduate work in special education
   See Teachers of exceptional children, Training of—Graduate work
Graduate work of women
   See Universities and colleges—Graduate work of women
Graduated taxation
   See Taxation, Progressive
Graduates, Junior high school
   See Junior high school graduates
Graduation sermons
   See Baccalaureate addresses
Graeco-Roman law
   See Law, Byzantine
Graffiti (Direct) (GT3912)
   xx Drawings
   Inscriptions
Graffito decoration (Direct)
   x Decoration, Graffito
   Sgraffito decoration
   xx Art, Decorative
   Arts and crafts movement
   Decoration and ornament
   Mural painting and decoration
   Plastering
Graflex camera
   sa Graphic camera
Graft (Game) (GV1299.G7)
Graft (in politics)
   See Corruption (in politics)
Graft copolymers
   x Graft polymers
   xx Polymers and polymerization
Graft polymers
   See Graft copolymers
Grafting (SB125; Implements, S691-3)
   sa Budding
   Plant propagation
   Stocks (Horticulture)
   xx Botany
   Fruit-culture
   Gardening
   Horticulture
   Plant-breeding
   Plant propagation
   Trees
Grafting of bone
   See Bone-grafting
Grafting of skin
   See Skin-grafting

Graged language
   See Gedaged language
Graham flour (Food values, TX558.W5; Milling, TS2149)
   xx Flour
Grahamite (TN885)
Grahamites (TX392)
   xx Vegetarianism
Grahovac, Battle of, 1858
   xx Turco-Montenegrin War, 1858
Grail (Literature, PN57.G7)
   x Graal
   Gral
   Gréal
   Holy Grail
   xx Chalices
   Folk-lore
— Art
— Legends
GRAIL (Electronic computer system)
   x Graphical Input Language
   xx Computer graphics
   Electronic digital computers—Programming
   On-line data processing
Grail movement (Bernhardt) (BP605.B4)
Grail movement (Catholic)
   xx Catholic Church—Societies, etc.
   Woman—Societies and clubs
Grain (Indirect) (Culture, SB189-191)
   sa Cereal products
   Cereals as food
   Lodging of grain
   names of cereal plants, e.g. Maize, Rye, Wheat
   x Breadstuffs
   Cereals
   Corn
   xx Agriculture
   Botany, Economic
   Field crops
   Flour
   Food
   Example under Bulk solids
— Analysis and chemistry
   sa Grain—Moisture
   xx Chemistry, Technical
— Breeding
   See Grain breeding
— Cleaning
— Cooperative marketing
   xx Grain trade
— Costs
— Diseases and pests (Indirect) (SB608.G6)
   sa Cereal rusts
   Grain—Storage—Diseases and injuries
   subdivision Diseases and pests *under names of cereal plants, e.g.* Millet—Diseases and pests; Wheat—Diseases and pests; *also names of pests, e.g.* Chinch-bugs, Mediterranean flour-moth, Rye gall-gnat
   x Grain pests
   Example under Bacteriology, Agricultural; Insects, Injurious and beneficial
— Drying
   sa subdivision Drying *under names of grains, e.g.* Maize—Drying
   x Drying apparatus—Grain
   Grain drying
   Note under Agricultural processing
— Fertilizers and manures
— Field experiments
— Grading

sa *subdivision* Grading *under names of cereal plants*
— Handling
　See Grain handling
— Harvesting
— — Costs
— History
— — Juvenile literature
— Irrigation
— Juvenile literature
— Microbiology
— Milling
　sa Flour
　　Flour-mills
　　Meal
　　Milling machinery
　x Grain milling
　　Milling of grain
　xx Flour
　　Meal
— — Safety measures
— Moisture
　xx Grain—Analysis and chemistry
— Pictorial works
— Prices *(Direct)*
— Research
　See Grain research
— Ripening
　x Ripening of grain
　xx Plant physiology
— Seeds
　See Grain seed
— Storage
　sa Grain aeration
　　subdivision Storage *under names of grains, e.g.* Wheat—Storage
　xx Farm produce—Storage
— — Diseases and injuries *(Indirect)*
　sa Granary weevil
　　Khapra beetle
　　Sawtoothed grain beetle
　xx Farm produce—Storage—Diseases and injuries
　　Grain—Diseases and pests
— — Laboratory manuals
— Tables and ready-reckoners
　See Grain trade—Tables and ready-reckoners
— Transportation *(Railroads, HE2321.G7)*
　sa Grain handling
— Varieties
— Weight and measurement
— Weights and measures *(HF5716.G7; QC89)*
　xx Weights and measures
Grain aeration *(Indirect) (SB190)*
　x Aeration of grain
　　Granaries—Aeration
　xx Grain—Storage
Grain-aphis
　See Grain-louse
Grain as feed
　xx Feeds
Grain beetle, Sawtoothed
　See Sawtoothed grain beetle
Grain bins
　See Granaries
Grain boundaries (Metallography) *(TN690)*
　xx Metallography
Grain breeding *(SB189)*
　sa Barley breeding
　　Maize breeding
　　Millet breeding
　　Oat breeding
　　Rice breeding
　　Rye breeding
　　Sorghum breeding
　　Wheat breeding

x Grain—Breeding
xx Plant-breeding
Grain drying
　See Grain—Drying
Grain elevators *(Direct) (TH4461)*
　sa Granaries
　x Elevators, Grain
　xx Grain handling
— Automation
— Design and construction
— Electric equipment
— Equipment and supplies
— — Appraisal
　　See Grain elevators—Equipment and supplies—Valuation
— — Valuation
　　x Grain elevators—Equipment and supplies—Appraisal
— Fires and fire prevention *(TH9445.G)*
— Management *(SB190)*
— — Problems, exercises, etc. *(SB190)*
— Production standards
— Safety measures
— Ventilation
Grain elevators, Cooperative
　xx Agriculture, Cooperative
Grain handling
　sa Grain elevators
　x Grain—Handling
　xx Bulk solids handling
　　Conveying machinery
　　Grain—Transportation
— Safety measures
Grain-handling machinery
— Maintenance and repair
Grain itch
　See Straw itch
Grain-louse *(SB945.G7; Zoology, QL523.A6)*
　x Grain-aphis
　　Green bug
　　Spring grain-aphis
　　Wheat aphid
　Example under Plant-lice
— Biological control *(Indirect)*
　xx Grain-louse—Control
— Control *(Indirect)*
　sa Grain-louse—Biological control
Grain milling
　See Grain—Milling
Grain pests
　See Grain—Diseases and pests
Grain products
　See Cereal products
Grain research
　sa Rice research
　　Wheat research
　x Grain—Research
　xx Agricultural research
　　Research
　　Research, Industrial
Grain rusts
　See Cereal rusts
Grain seed
　x Grain—Seeds
　xx Seeds
Grain sorghum
　See Sorghum
Grain trade *(Direct) (HD9030-9049; Tariff, HF2651.G8)*
　sa Fiars prices
　　Grain—Cooperative marketing
　　Wheat trade
　x Corn trade
　xx Produce trade
— Accounting *(HF5686.G5)*
— Costs
— Defense measures *(UA929.95.G7)*
— Employees

— Information services
— Law and legislation *(Direct)*
— Mathematical models
— Tables and ready-reckoners *(HF5716.G7; Foreign exchange, HG3875.G7)*
　x Grain—Tables and ready-reckoners
— Taxation *(Direct)*
Grain tribute (China)
Graineries
　See Granaries
Graining *(TT330)*
　sa Painting, Industrial
　　Simulated wood
　xx Painting, Industrial
　　Simulated wood
　　Stains and staining
　　Wood finishing
Grains of paradise
　x Guinea grains
　　Melegueta pepper
　xx Seeds
Gral
　See Grail
Gram (Legume)
　See Chick-pea
Gram stain
　See Gram's stain
Grama grass, Blue
　See Blue grama grass
Gramemes
　See Tagmemes
Grammar
　See Grammar, Comparative and general
　　Language and languages—Grammars
　subdivision Grammar *under names of languages, e.g.* English language—Grammar
Grammar, Comparative and general *(P151-295)*
　Here are entered: 1. Works comparing and classifying the grammars of unrelated languages. Comparative grammar of groups of cognate languages is entered under the names of those groups, with subdivision Grammar, Comparative, *e.g.* Semitic languages—Grammar, Comparative. 2. Works in which the principles of grammar in general are discussed, *i.e.* general, philosophical, or universal grammar.
　sa Conditionals (Logic)
　　Generative grammar
　　Language and languages
　　Linguistic analysis (Linguistics)
　　Parenthesis (Rhetoric)
　　Parts of speech
　　Philology, Comparative
　　Stratificational grammar
　　Tagmemes
　　subdivision Grammar, Comparative *under names of languages*
　x Comparative grammar
　　Comparative linguistics
　　Dialects
　　Grammar
　　Grammar, Philosophical
　　Grammar, Universal
　　Language and languages—Grammar, Comparative
　　Philosophical grammar
　xx Linguistics
　　Philology
　　Philology, Comparative
— Accents and accentuation
　See Accents and accentuation
— Adjective *(P273)*
　x Adjective

Grammar, Comparative and general
(P151-295) (Continued)
— Affixes
x Affixes
— Analogy
See Analogy (Linguistics)
— Apposition
x Apposition (Grammar)
— Article (P277)
x Article
— Aspect
sa subdivision Aspect under names of
languages and groups of
languages, e.g. Russian language—
Aspect
x Aspect (Linguistics)
xx Grammar, Comparative and general
—Verb
— Attribute
x Attribute (Grammar)
— Case (P253)
x Case
— Clauses
x Clauses
xx Grammar, Comparative and general
—Sentences
Grammar, Comparative and general
—Syntax
— Comparison
See Comparison (Grammar)
— Consonants
See Grammar, Comparative and
general—Phonology
— Denominative
x Denominative
— Exercises
— Gender (P271)
x Gender
— Government
See Government (Grammar)
— Honorific
x Honorific
— Infinitive
x Infinitive
— Inflection (P251-9)
x Inflection
Language and languages—Inflection
— Interrogative
sa subdivision Interrogative under
names of languages, e.g. Romance
languages—Interrogative
x Interrogative (Grammar)
— Intonation
See Intonation (Phonetics)
— Mathematical models (P151)
xx Mathematical linguistics
— Negatives
x Negatives (Grammar)
— Noun
x Noun
— Number
x Dual (Grammar)
Number (Grammar)
Plural (Grammar)
— Numerals (P275)
— Particles
x Particles (Grammar)
— Person
x Person (Grammar)
xx Grammar, Comparative and general
—Pronoun
Grammar, Comparative and general
—Verb
— Phonology (P215-240)
sa Phonemics
x Grammar, Comparative and general
—Consonants

Grammar, Comparative and general
—Vowels
Phonology
xx Consonants
Vowels
— — Statistical methods
— Prepositions (P285)
x Prepositions
— Pronoun (P279)
sa Grammar, Comparative and general
—Person
— Reduplication (P245)
x Reduplication (in language)
— Semantics
See Semantics, Comparative
— Sentences
sa Grammar, Comparative and general
—Clauses
x Language and languages—Sentences
— Substitution
x Substitution (Linguistics)
— Syllable (P236)
x Language and languages—Syllable
Syllable
— Syntax (P291-5)
sa Causative (Linguistics)
Grammar, Comparative and general
—Clauses
Phraseology
x Language and languages—Syntax
Syntax
— Tense
x Tense (Grammar)
— Terminology (P152)
— Typology
See Typology (Linguistics)
— Verb (P259; P281)
sa Grammar, Comparative and general
—Aspect
Grammar, Comparative and general
—Person
x Verb
— Voice (P281)
x Voice (Grammar)
— Vowels
See Grammar, Comparative and
general—Phonology
— Word formation (P245)
sa Amalgams (Linguistics)
Morphemics
Portmanteau words
x Morphology (Linguistics)
Word formation
— Word order
sa Languages, Modern—Word order
x Language and languages—Word
order
Word order
Grammar, Generative
See Generative grammar
Grammar, Philosophical
See Grammar, Comparative and general
Grammar, Polyglot
See Language and languages—Grammars
Grammar, Transformational
See Generative grammar
Grammar, Universal
See Grammar, Comparative and general
Grammar schools
See Public schools
Gramme dynamos (TK2441)
xx Dynamos
Grammos-Vitsi, Battle of, 1949
x Vitsi-Grammos, Battle of, 1949
xx Greece, Modern—History—1944-1949
Gramophone
See Phonograph

Gram's stain
x Gram stain
xx Stains and staining (Microscopy)
Granada (City)
— Siege, 1491-1492 (DP164)
Granada (Kingdom)
— History (DP115-118)
— — Spanish Conquest, 1476-1492
(DP121-3)
Granada (City) in literature
Granada (Kingdom) in literature
Granada goat
xx Goats
Granaries (NA8240)
x Grain bins
Graineries
xx Grain elevators
— Aeration
See Grain aeration
— Design and construction
— Heating and ventilation
— Law and legislation (Direct)
Granary weevil
xx Beetles
Grain—Storage—Diseases and injuries
Grand Alliance, War of the, 1689-1697
(D279-280)
Grand jury (Direct)
sa Indictments
Informations
xx Criminal procedure
Indictments
Informations
Jury
Grand Prix, German
See German Grand Prix Race
Grand Prix racing (GV1029)
sa British Grand Prix Race
German Grand Prix Race
Monaco Grand Prix Race
Sebring Grand Prix Race
Watkins Glen Grand Prix Race
xx Automobile racing
— Biography
Grand Remonstrance, 1641 (DA397)
Grand River Ute Indians
See Yampa Indians
Grandfathers
See Grandparents
Grandmothers
xx Grandparents
— Quotations, maxims, etc.
Grandparents
sa Grandmothers
x Grandfathers
xx Family
Fathers
Mothers
— Anecdotes, facetiae, satire, etc.
(PN6231.G8)
— Caricatures and cartoons
— Juvenile literature
Grange
See Patrons of Husbandry
Grangerism
See Illustrated books—Extra-illustrated
Granite (Indirect) (Building stones, TN970;
Petrology, QE462.G7)
Example under Building stones; Petrology;
Rocks; Stone
— Analysis
— Inclusions (QE462.G7)
x Enclaves in granite
Inclusions in granite
— Pictorial works (QE462.G7)
Granite cutters
See Stone-cutters

Granite industry and trade *(Direct)*
  x Granite quarrying
  xx Stone industry and trade
  — Dust control
  — Tables and ready-reckoners
Granite quarrying
  See Granite industry and trade
Granite sculpture *(Direct)*
  xx Sculpture
Granite sculpture, Romanesque *(Direct)*
  x Romanesque granite sculpture
Granodiorite *(QE461)*
  xx Rocks, Igneous
Grants
  See Subsidies
Grants, Land
  See Land grants
Grants-in-aid *(Direct)*
      Here are entered works on grants of
        money made by a central to a local
        government.
  sa Economic assistance, Domestic
      Federal aid to education
      Federal aid to hospitals
      Federal aid to law enforcement
        agencies
      Federal aid to libraries
      Federal aid to outdoor recreation
      Federal aid to the arts
      Federal aid to transportation
      Local finance
      Research grants
      State aid to education
      subdivision Finance *under particular*
        subjects, e.g. Roads—Finance
  x Federal grants
  xx Economic assistance, Domestic
      Federal government
      Finance, Public
      Intergovernmental fiscal relations
      Local finance
Grants-in-aid, Colonial
  x Colonies—Grants-in-aid
  xx Colonies—Finance
Grants-in-aid, International
  See Economic assistance
      International relief
Grant's line (Game) *(GV1469.G3)*
Granular lids
  See Conjunctivitis, Granular
Granular materials
  sa Compacting
      Glass beads
  xx Bulk solids
      Materials
  — Drying
  — Mathematical models
  — Permeability
  — Plastic properties *(TA418.78)*
  — Testing
Granulation tissue
  sa Cicatrices
  xx Wound healing
Granulite *(Indirect)*
  x Leptite
  xx Rocks, Metamorphic
Granulocytes
  xx Leucocytes
  — Mathematical models
Granulocytopenia
  sa Agranulocytosis
  x Granulopenia
Granuloma benignum
  See Sarcoidosis
Granuloma inguinale
  See Granuloma venereum
Granuloma venereum *(RC203.G)*
  x Donovanosis

Granuloma inguinale
  xx Venereal diseases
Granulopenia
  See Granulocytopenia
Grape
  See Grapes
Grape berry moth
Grape culture
  See Viticulture
Grape cure
  See Grapes—Therapeutic use
Grape juice
  xx Fruit juices
  — Analysis
Grape leaf-folder *(SB945.G58)*
Grape leaf-hopper *(SB945.G6)*
  xx Grapes—Diseases and pests
Grape-leaf skeletonizer *(SB945.G)*
Grape pests
  See Grapes—Diseases and pests
Grape products *(Direct)*
  sa Raisins
      Wine and wine making
Grape-scale *(SB945.G)*
  xx Grapes—Diseases and pests
Grape-vine aphis *(SB945.G)*
Grape-vine root-worm *(SB608.G7)*
Grapefruit *(SB370.G7)*
  sa Cookery (Grapefruit)
  x Pomelo
  xx Citrus fruits
  — Marketing
  — Storage
Grapefruit juice, Canned
  xx Fruit, Canned
      Fruit juices
Grapefruit juice, Dried
  xx Fruit, Dried
      Fruit juices
Grapes *(Indirect) (Botany, QK495.V84;*
      Culture, SB387-399; Trade,
      HD9259.G68-7)
  sa Currant grapes
      Muscadine grape
      Viticulture
      headings beginning with the word
        Grape
  x Grape
      Vineyards
  xx Viticulture
      Wine and wine making
  — Disease and pest resistance
  — Diseases and pests *(Indirect)*
      (SB608.G7)
      sa names of diseases and pests, e.g.
        Black rot, Grape leaf-hopper,
        Grape-scale, Phylloxera
      x Grape pests
        Raisins—Diseases and pests
      xx Black rot
      Example under Fruit—Diseases and
        pests; Plant diseases
  — Fertilizers and manures
  — Harvesting
  — Irrigation
  — Marketing
  — Packaging
  — Pruning
      x Grapes—Training
        Grapevine pruning and training
      Example under Pruning
  — Storage
  — Therapeutic use
      x Grape cure
      xx Diet in disease
  — Training
      See Grapes—Pruning
  — Transportation

  — Varieties
  — Water requirements
Grapes in art
  xx Art
Grapevine pruning and training
  See Grapes—Pruning
Graph theory *(QA166)*
  sa Bond graphs
      Four-color problem
      Hypergraphs
      Matroids
      Network analysis (Planning)
  x Theory of graphs
  xx Combinatorial analysis
      Topology
  — Juvenile literature
Graphic algebra
  See Algebra—Graphic methods
Graphic arts *(Direct)*
  sa Drawing
      Engraving
      Painting
      Picture-books
      Printing
      Prints
      Television graphics
  x Art, Graphic
      Arts, Graphic
  xx Art
  — Competitions
  — Marketing
  — Technique
Graphic arts, English, ₍French, Lithuanian,
      etc.₎ *(Direct)*
  x English ₍French, Lithuanian, etc.₎
      graphic arts
Graphic camera
  xx Graflex camera
Graphic data processing
  See Computer graphics
Graphic differentiation
  See Numerical differentiation
Graphic methods *(QA90; Discussion of*
      observations, QA277)
  sa Decision logic tables
      Flow charts
      Flowgraphs
      Gantt charts
      Graphic statics
      Line of balance (Management)
      Mathematics—Charts, diagrams, etc.
      Nomography (Mathematics)
      Organization charts
      Regge trajectories
      subdivision Graphic methods *under*
        subjects, e.g. Physics—Graphic
        methods
  x Graphs
  xx Drawing
      Errors, Theory of
      Geometrical drawing
      Least squares
      Mathematics
      Mechanical drawing
  — Computer programs
  — Juvenile literature
  — Programmed instruction
Graphic Programming System
  See PAGE-1 (Electronic computer system)
Graphic statics *(TG270; Machinery, TJ235)*
  sa Bridges
      Building, Iron and steel
      Girders
      Girders, Continuous
      Influence lines
      Mechanical drawing
      Nomography (Mathematics)
      Roofs

Graphic statics *(TG270; Machinery, TJ235)*
(Continued)
        Strains and stresses
        Strength of materials
   xx Bridge construction
        Girders
        Graphic methods
        Mechanical drawing
        Statics
        Strains and stresses
        Strength of materials
        Structures, Theory of
— Problems, exercises, etc.
Graphical evaluation and review technique
  See GERT (Network analysis)
Graphical Input Language
  See GRAIL (Electronic computer system)
Graphical Remote Access Support System
  See GRASS (Electronic computer system)
Graphically Aided Mathematical Machine
  See GAMMA (Electronic computer
     system)
Graphics, Computer
  See Computer graphics
Graphics, Engineering
  See Engineering graphics
Graphics, Television
  See Television graphics
Graphite *(Indirect)   (TN845; Artificial,*
    TP261.G7)
  sa Graphitization
   x Black-lead
     Plumbago
  xx Carbon
  Example under Geology, Economic
— Radiation effects
    See Graphite, Effect of radiation on
— Testing
Graphite, Effect of radiation on
   x Graphite, Irradiated
     Graphite—Radiation effects
     Radiation—Effect on graphite
  xx Radiation
Graphite, Irradiated
  See Graphite, Effect of radiation on
Graphite fibers
   x Fibers, Graphite
     Fibrous graphite
  xx Carbon fibers
     Inorganic fibers
     Refractory materials
Graphitization *(Cast-iron, TN710; Chemical*
    engineering, TP261.G7; Naturally
    occurring carbon, TN845)
  xx Graphite
Graphology *(BF889-905)*
  sa Drawing, Psychology of
    subdivision Autographs *under names of*
     prominent authors and groups of
     individuals, e.g. Lincoln, Abraham,
     Pres. U.S., 1809-1865—Autographs;
     Composers—Autographs
   x Handwriting
  xx Drawing, Psychology of
     Penmanship
     Writing
Graphophone
  See Phonograph
Graphotyping *(NE2280)*
   x Chalk engraving
  xx Engraving
     Printing, Practical
Graphs
  See Graphic methods
Grappa *(TP599)*
  xx Brandy
Graptolites *(QE779)*
  sa Graptoloidea

Graptoloidea *(QE840.5)*
  xx Graptolites
Grasias
  sa Bhils
   x Dungri-Grasias
  xx Bhils
     Ethnology—India
GRASS (Electronic computer system)
   x Graphical Remote Access Support
     System
  xx Computer graphics
     On-line data processing
Grass breeding
   x Grasses—Breeding
  xx Forage plant breeding
Grass-burner
  See Mennonite grass-burner
Grass finches
   x Weaver finches
  xx Finches
     Weaver-birds
Grass fires
  See Grassland fires
Grass huts *(Direct)*
   x Huts, Grass
  xx Architecture, Domestic
     Dwellings
Grass parakeet
  See Budgerigars
Grass pickerel *(QL638.E7)*
  xx Pickerel
Grass research
  See Grasses—Research
Grass seed
  sa Bromegrass seed
   x Grasses—Seed
  xx Seeds
— Cleaning
— Drying
Grass silage
   x Grasses—Silage
— Analysis
Grass staggers
  See Grass tetany
Grass tetany *(SF967.G7)*
   x Grass staggers
     Staggers, Grass
     Tetany, Grass
  xx Deficiency diseases in domestic animals
     Magnesium metabolism
     Ruminantia—Diseases
Grass waterways
  See Grassed waterways
Grass writing
  See Chinese language—Writing, Cursive
Grassed channels
  See Grassed waterways
Grassed waterways
   x Grass waterways
     Grassed channels
     Vegetated channels
     Vegetated waterways
     Waterways, Grassed
     Waterways, Vegetated
  xx Ditches
     Drainage
     Grasses
     Soil conservation
Grasses *(Indirect)   (Botany, QK495.G74;*
    Culture, SB197-201)
  sa Forage plants
     Golf-links—Construction and care
     Grassed waterways
     Grasslands
     Grazing
     Hay
     Meadows
     Pastures

     Soil-binding
     Turf management
     particular grasses, e.g. Brome-grass,
      Esparto, Quitch-grass; *and headings*
      beginning with the word Grass
   x Agrostology
     Herbage
  xx Agriculture
     Botany, Economic
     Forage plants
     Hay
     Lawns
     Meadows
     Pastures
— Analysis
— Breeding
    See Grass breeding
— Diseases and pests *(Indirect)*
    (SB608.G8)
    sa Asiatic beetle
      Maize rough dwarf virus disease
      Rhodes grass scale
      Snow mold
      Stripe rust
— Drying
    See Hay—Drying
— Fertilizers and manures
    x Meadows—Fertilization
— Harvesting
— Identification
— Juvenile literature
— Pictorial works
— Research *(Direct)*
    x Grass research
— Seed
    See Grass seed
— Silage
    See Grass silage
— Tariff
    See Tariff on grass seed
— Varieties
Grasses, Fossil
  xx Paleobotany
Grasshopper control
  See Locust control
Grasshoppers
  See Locusts
Grassland ecology *(Indirect)   (QH541.5.P7)*
  xx Ecology
Grassland farming
  See Meadows
     Pastures
     Stock-ranges
Grassland fauna *(Indirect)   (QL115)*
  xx Zoology
Grassland fires *(Indirect)*
  sa Fire ecology
     Prescribed burning
   x Grass fires
  xx Fires
— Prevention and control
    xx Fire extinction
     Fire prevention
Grasslands *(Indirect)   (QH541.5.P7;*
    QK938.P7)
  Here are entered works on the natural
  regions of the world in which the characteristic plants are grasses and forbs.
  Works on the management and farming of natural or cultivated grassland
  areas are entered under Meadows,
  Pastures, and Stock-ranges.

  sa Llanos
     Pampas
     Prairies
     Savannas
     Steppes
  xx Grasses

Grassmann's theory of extension
    See Ausdehnungslehre
Grassworm
    See Fall army-worms
Gratefulness
    See Gratitude
Graters, Nutmeg
    See Nutmeg graters
Grates
    See Fireplaces
        Furnaces
Gratings, Diffraction
    See Diffraction gratings
Gratitude   *(Ethics, BJ1533.G8; Theology, BV4647.G8)*
    sa Ingratitude
    x Gratefulness
       Thankfulness
    xx Conduct of life
       Ethics
       Ingratitude
   — Biblical teaching
   — Juvenile literature   *(BV4647.G8)*
   — Quotations, maxims, etc.
Gratitude (Islam)
Gratitude (Jewish theology)
Gratuitous contracts
    See Contracts, Gratuitous
Grauvieh
    See Grey Tirolean cattle
Grauwacke
    See Graywacke
Gravel   *(Indirect)*   *(TN939)*
    xx Aggregates (Building materials)
    Example under Bulk solids
   — Testing
Gravel (Pathology)
    See Calculi, Urinary
Gravel industry
    See Sand and gravel industry
Gravel plants
    See Sand and gravel plants
Gravel roads
    See Roads, Gravel
Gravelines, France
   — Siege, 1644   *(DC127.6)*
Gravelines, Battle of, 1558
Gravelly Run, Va., Battle of, 1865   *(E477.67)*
Gravelotte, Battle of, 1870   *(DC303.4)*
    x Rezonville, Battle of, Aug. 18, 1870
       St. Privat, Battle of, 1870
    xx Franco-German War, 1870-1871
Graves
    See Burial
       Cemeteries
       Epitaphs
       Funeral rites and ceremonies
       Mounds
       Sepulchral monuments
       Tombs
Graves, Military
    See Soldiers' bodies, Disposition of
Graves' disease   *(RC656)*
    sa Exophthalmos
       Goiter
    x Basedow's disease
       Exophthalmic goiter
       Goiter, Exophthalmic
    xx Myxedema
       Thyroid gland—Diseases
Gravestones
    See Sepulchral monuments
Gravette points
    xx Man, Prehistoric
Graveyards
    See Cemeteries

Gravimeter (Geophysical instrument)   *(QB331)*
    x Gravity balance
       Gravity meter
    xx Geodesy
       Geophysics
       Gravity
       Gravity—Measurement
Gravimetric analysis
    See Chemistry, Analytic—Quantitative
Graving-docks
    See Dry-docks
Gravitation   *(Constant of, QB341; Theories of, QC178)*
    Here are entered theoretical works on the phenomenon of gravitation, *i.e.* the attraction between masses anywhere in the universe and determinations of the constant of gravitation. Works relating to measurement of the intensity and direction of the earth's force of attraction are entered under the heading Gravity.
    sa Centrifugal force
       Earth—Density
       Ether (of space)
       General relativity (Physics)
       Mass (Physics)
       Matter
       Potential, Theory of
       Relativity (Physics)
       Weightlessness
    xx Centrifugal force
       Field theory (Physics)
       Matter—Properties
       Physics
       Relativity (Physics)
    Notes under Gravity; Weightlessness
Gravitational collapse
    sa Black holes (Astronomy)
    x Collapse, Gravitational
    xx Stars
Gravitational convection
    See Density currents
Gravitational mass
    See Mass (Physics)
Gravity   *(Indirect)*   *(QB331-9)*
    Here are entered works relating to measurement of the intensity and direction of the earth's force of attraction. Theoretical works on the phenomenon of gravitation and determinations of the constant of gravitation are entered under the heading Gravitation.
    sa Earth—Figure
       Gravimeter (Geophysical instrument)
       Gravity anomalies
       Gravity waves
       Pendulum
    xx Geodesy
       Pendulum
       Specific gravity
       Weights and measures
    Notes under Gravitation; Weightlessness
   — Juvenile literature
   — Measurement
      sa Gravimeter (Geophysical instrument)
   — — Graphic methods
   — Physiological effect   *(QH657; QP82)*
      sa Weightlessness
      Note under Weightlessness
   — Tables, etc.   *(QB331)*
Gravity, Center of
    See Center of mass
Gravity, Local disturbance of
    See Gravity anomalies
Gravity, Specific
    See Specific gravity

Gravity anomalies   *(Indirect)*   *(QB331)*
    x Anomalies, Gravity
       Bouguer anomalies
       Gravity, Local disturbance of
       Isostatic anomalies
    xx Gravity
       Plumb-line deflections
       Prospecting—Geophysical methods
Gravity balance
    See Gravimeter (Geophysical instrument)
Gravity-free state, Physiological effect of
    See Weightlessness
Gravity gradient booms
    x Booms, Gravity gradient
    xx Artificial satellites—Attitude control systems
       Space vehicles—Attitude control systems
Gravity meter
    See Gravimeter (Geophysical instrument)
Gravity prospecting   *(TN269)*
    xx Prospecting—Geophysical methods
Gravity railroads
    See Railroads, Gravity
Gravity switching yards
    See Railroads—Hump yards
Gravity waves   *(Mathematics, QA927)*
    x Waves, Gravity
    xx Gravity
       Hydrodynamics
       Waves
Gravure printing
    See Intaglio printing
Grawi language
    See Šhauri language
Gray
    x Grey
Gray-cheeked thrush, Bicknell's
    See Bicknell's thrush
Gray fox
    xx Foxes
Gray Friars
    See Franciscans
Gray market
    See Black market
Gray mold of strawberries
    See Strawberry gray mold
Gray mullets   *(QL638.M; Fish-culture, SH351.G)*
    sa Black mullets
       Mullet fisheries
       White mullets
    x Mullets, Gray
Gray pine
    See Jack-pine
Gray snapper   *(QL638.L9)*
Gray squirrel
    xx Squirrels
   — Control   *(Indirect)*   *(SB994.S)*
      xx Rodent control
Gray whale
    See Pacific gray whale
Grayfish
    sa Cookery (Grayfish)
Grayling, Michigan
    See Arctic grayling
Grayling, Montana
    See Arctic grayling
Grayling   *(QL638.S2; Culture, SH167.G8)*
Grayling, Arctic
    See Arctic grayling
Grayling fishing   *(SH691.G)*
    xx Fishing
Graywacke   *(Indirect)*
    x Grauwacke
       Greywacke
    xx Sandstone

Grazing *(Indirect) (Forests, SD427.G8;*
      Public lands, HD241)
    sa Forage plants
        Grazing districts
        Pastures
        Stock-ranges
    xx Cattle
        Grasses
        Pastures
        Range management
        Stock-ranges
Grazing districts *(Direct)*
    xx Grazing
        Pastures
        Public lands
        Special districts
        Stock-ranges
Grazing rights
    See Pasture, Right of
Gréal
    See Grail
Grease
    See Lubrication and lubricants
        Oils and fats
Great auk *(QL696.A3)*
    x Gairfowl
        Garefowl
        Garfowl
Great Awakening *(BR520)*
    Here are entered works dealing with the
      revival of religion that occurred in the
      American colonies in the 18th cen-
      tury.
    sa Evangelical Revival
    x Awakening, Great
    xx Evangelical Revival
Great barracuda *(QL638.S77)*
    xx Barracudas
Great Basin tent caterpillar
Great Bear
    See Ursa Major
Great Blood Purge, 1934
    See Germany—History—Great Blood
        Purge, 1934
Great blue heron
    xx Herons
  — Juvenile literature
Great blue shark
    See Blue shark
Great books program
    See Group reading
Great Bridge, Va., Battle of, 1775 *(E241.G)*
Great Britain
    sa Commonwealth of Nations
    Note under Commonwealth of Nations
  — Antiquities, Roman
      x Romans in Great Britain
  — Biography
  — Civil defense
    Example under Civil defense
  — Coast defenses
    Example under Coast defenses
  — Colonies
    sa Commonwealth of Nations
        Imperial federation
    xx Commonwealth of Nations
    Note under Commonwealth of Nations
  —— Commerce
    Example under Colonies
  —— Economic conditions
    Example under Colonies—Economic
      conditions
  — Commercial treaties
    Example under Commercial treaties
  — Constitutional history
    Example under Constitutional history
  — Defenses

Example under Fortification; *and under*
    references from Defenses, Na-
    tional; National defenses
— Economic conditions
    Example under Poverty
—— 1918-1945
    Note under Economic conditions—
      1918-1945
—— 1945-
— Economic policy
— Foreign economic relations
    Example under International economic
      relations
— Foreign relations
—— Treaties
    Example under Treaties

GEOGRAPHIC SUBDIVISIONS

—— Germany
    Example under International relations
— Gentry
    x Squires
    Example under reference from Gentry
— History *(DA)*
    x England—History
—— To 55 B.C.
—— To 449
—— To 1066
——— Juvenile literature
—— To 1485
——— Juvenile literature
—— Roman period, 55 B.C.-449 A.D.
    Example under reference from Ro-
      mans in Germany, ₍Great Brit-
      ain, etc.₎
——— Juvenile literature
—— Anglo-Saxon period, 449-1066
——— Juvenile literature
—— Norman period, 1066-1154
——— Juvenile literature
—— Medieval period, 1066-1485
——— Juvenile literature
—— 1066-1687
—— Angevin period, 1154-1216
——— Juvenile literature
—— Plantagenets, 1154-1399
—— 13th century
—— 14th century
——— Juvenile literature
—— Peasants' Revolt, 1381
    See Tyler's Insurrection, 1381
—— House of Lancaster, 1399-1461
—— Lancaster and York, 1399-1485
    x Great Britain—History—15th
      century
——— Juvenile literature
—— 15th century
    See Great Britain-History—
      Lancaster and York,
      1399-1485
—— Wars of the Roses, 1455-1485
    x Roses, Wars of the, 1455-1485
      Wars of the Roses, 1455-1485
——— Juvenile literature
—— House of York, 1461-1485
—— Modern period, 1485-
—— Tudors, 1485-1603
    x Great Britain—History—16th
      century
——— Juvenile literature
—— 16th century
    See Great Britain—History—
      Tudors, 1485-1603
—— Rebellion of 1569
—— 17th century
    See Great Britain—History—
      Stuarts, 1603-1714
—— Early Stuarts, 1603-1649

——— Juvenile literature
—— Stuarts, 1603-1714
    x Great Britain—History—17th
      century
——— Juvenile literature
—— Civil War, 1642-1649
    sa Bristol, Eng.—Sieges, 1643, 1645
      Hull, Eng.—Siege, 1642
      Leicester, Eng.—Siege, 1645
      Roundway Down, Battle of, 1643
    x Civil War—Great Britain
——— Causes
——— Juvenile literature
——— Pamphlets
    Example under Pamphlets
—— Puritan Revolution, 1642-1660
——— Juvenile literature
—— Commonwealth and Protectorate,
      1649-1660
    x Commonwealth of England
——— Juvenile literature
—— Restoration, 1660-1688
    sa Dutch War, 1672-1678
    x Restoration, 1660-1688
—— 1660-1714
—— Revolution of 1688
—— 1689-1714
—— 18th century
——— Juvenile literature
—— 1714-1837
—— 1760-1789
—— 1789-1820
—— 1800-1837
    sa Copenhagen, Battle of, 1801
—— 19th century
——— Juvenile literature
—— Crimean War, 1853-1856
    See Crimean War, 1853-1856
—— 20th century
——— Juvenile literature
—— Roman period, 55 B.C.-449 A.D.

GENERAL SUBDIVISIONS

—— Invasions
    sa French Expedition to Ireland,
      1796-1797
      French Expedition to Wales, 1797
    x Invasions of Great Britain

GENERAL SUBDIVISIONS

——— Juvenile literature
—— Philosophy
    Example under History—Philosophy
— History, Naval
    Example under Naval battles; Naval his-
      tory; Sea-power
—— Juvenile literature
— Kings and rulers
    sa Anglo-Saxons—Kings and rulers
—— Autographs
—— Juvenile literature
—— Succession
    Example under reference from Succes-
      sion to the crown
— National Health Service
    x National Health Service, Gt. Brit.
—— Salaries, pensions, etc.
— Peerage
    Example under Peerage
— Princes and princesses
    Example under Princes; Princesses
—— Juvenile literature
— Proclamations
    Example under Proclamations
— Queens
    Example under Kings and rulers; Queens;
      and under references from Royalty;
      Rulers; Sovereigns

Greece
— History *(DF1-951; Classical antiquity, DE)*
— — Chremonidean War, 267-262 B.C. *(DF236.5)* *(Continued)*
  x Chremonidean War
  xx Macedonia—History—To 168 B.C.
Greece, Medieval
— History *(DF501-649)*
Greece, Modern
— History *(DF701-951)*
— — 1453-1821
— — 1821-
— — War of Independence, 1821-1829
  sa Mesolóngion, Greece—Siege, 1825-1826
— — — American participation
  xx Greece, Modern—History— War of Independence, 1821-1829—Foreign participation
— — — Anniversaries, etc.
— — — Bulgarian participation
  xx Greece, Modern—History— War of Independence, 1821-1829—Foreign participation
— — — Foreign participation
  sa Greece, Modern—History— War of Independence, 1821-1829—American participation
  Greece, Modern—History— War of Independence, 1821-1829—Bulgarian participation
— — — Foreign public opinion
— — — Pictorial works
— — — Portraits
— — Revolution, 1862
— — War with Turkey, 1897
  See Greco-Turkish War, 1897
— — 1917-1944
  sa Greco-Turkish War, 1921-1922
— — Occupation, 1941-1944
— — 1944-1949
  sa Grammos-Vitsi, Battle of, 1949
— — 1950-
Greece in art
 xx Art
Greece in literature
Greed
 See Avarice
Greek aesthetics
 See Aesthetics, Greek
Greek-American wit and humor
 xx Greek wit and humor, Modern
Greek architecture
 See Architecture, Greek
Greek art metal-work
 See Art metal-work, Greek
Greek astronomy
 See Astronomy, Greek
Greek ballads and songs *(Ancient, PA3445; Modern, PA5255, PA5285)*
 sa Folk-songs, Greek
Greek boundary stones
 See Boundary stones, Greek
Greek bronzes
 See Bronzes, Greek
Greek chronology
 See Chronology, Greek
Greek Church
 See Orthodox Eastern Church
  Orthodox Eastern Church, Greek
Greek civilization
 See Civilization, Greek

Hellenism
Greek costume
 See Costume—Greece
Greek cultus
 See Cultus, Greek
Greek drama *(Collections, PA3461-8; History, PA3131-3239)*
 xx Classical drama
— Chorus
  See Drama—Chorus (Greek drama)
— Incidental music
  xx Music, Greek and Roman
  Music, Incidental
  Opera—History and criticism
— Presentation, Ancient
  See Theater—Greece
— Presentation, Modern *(PA3238)*
Greek drama, Modern *(Direct)*
Greek drama (Comedy) *(Collections, PA3465-6; History, PA3161-3199)*
 xx Comedy
Greek drama (Satyr play) *(PA3160; PA3464)*
 x Satyric drama, Greek
 xx Dionysia
Greek drama (Tragedy) *(Collections, PA3461-3; History, PA3131-3159)*
 xx Tragedy
Greek education
 See Education, Greek
Greek essays, Modern *(Direct)*
Greek fasts and feasts
 See Fasts and feasts—Greek religion
Greek fiction *(Collections, PA3487.E7; History, PA3267)*
 xx Classical fiction
Greek fiction, Modern
Greek fire *(Ancient, TP268-9; Modern, TP300)*
 x Fire, Greek
  Grecian fire
 xx Combustion
  Explosives, Military
Greek folk literature
 See Folk literature, Greek
Greek gods
 See Gods, Greek
Greek historians *(Historiography, DF211-212)*
 x Historians, Greek
Greek hymns
 See Hymns, Greek
  Hymns, Greek (Classical)
Greek imprints *(Direct)*
Greek inscriptions
 See Inscriptions, Greek
Greek ivories
 See Ivories, Greek
Greek language *(PA201-1179)*
 sa Classical philology
  Greek philology
  Hellenism
  Inscriptions, Greek
  Manuscripts, Greek
 xx Classical languages
  Classical philology
  Greek philology
— Alphabet
  sa Inscriptions, Linear B
  Example under Alphabet
  Note under Writing
— Dialects
  Example under reference from Dialects
— Metrics and rhythmics
  Example under Rhythm; Versification; *and under reference from* Meter
— Reduplication

  Example under reference from Reduplication (in language)
— Study and teaching
  Note under Classical education
Greek language, Biblical *(PA695-895)*
 Comprises the language of the Septuagint and the New Testament.
 sa Greek language, Hellenistic (300 B.C.-600 A.D.)
 x Bible—Philology
  Biblical Greek
  New Testament Greek
 xx Bible—Language, style
  Languages—Religious aspects
 Note under Greek language, Hellenistic (300 B.C.-600 A.D.)
Greek language, Byzantine
 See Greek language, Medieval and late
Greek language, Hellenistic (300 B.C.-600 A.D.) *(PA600-691)*
 Works on the language of the Septuagint and the New Testament are entered under Greek language, Biblical.
 x Greek language (Koinē)
  Hellenistic Greek
 xx Greek language, Biblical
Greek language, Medieval and late *(PA1001-1179)*
 Covers the period, *ca.* 600-1821.
 x Greek language, Byzantine
Greek language, Modern *(PA1001-1179)*
 x Romaic language
Greek language, Modern, in the United States, ₍etc.₎
Greek language (Koinē)
 See Greek language, Hellenistic (300 B.C.-600 A.D.)
Greek law
 See Law, Greek
Greek legends
 See Legends, Greek
Greek letter societies *(LJ)*
 sa Fraternity songs
  Hazing
  Initiations (into trades, societies, etc.)
  names of individual societies, e.g. Delta Kappa Epsilon
 x College fraternities
  Fraternal organizations
  Fraternities
  Sororities, Greek letter
 xx Hazing
  Initiations (into trades, societies, etc.)
  Secret societies
  Societies
  Students' societies
  Universities and colleges
— Libraries
  See Fraternity libraries
— Management
Greek letters *(Collections, PA3487.E4; History, PA3042; Teubner collections, PA3403.E6; Translations, PA3601-3671)*
 sa Byzantine letters
 xx Byzantine letters
  Classical letters
Greek letters, Modern
Greek literature *(PA3050-4500)*
 sa Byzantine literature
  Classical literature
  Classical philology
  Greek philology
  Hellenism
 xx Balkan Peninsula—Literatures
  Byzantine literature
  Classical literature
  Classical philology

Greek philology
Example under Literature; Philology
— Criticism, Textual
   Example under Criticism, Textual
— Jewish authors   *(PA3421.G8)*
      Duplicate entry is made under Jewish
         literature (Hellenistic)
   Note under Jewish literature (Hellenistic)
— Study and teaching
   Note under Classical education
— Themes, motives
      For typical plots, motives, etc.
Greek literature, Hellenistic
Greek literature, Modern   *(PA5201-5298;*
      PA5650-5665)
   x Neo-Greek literature
      Romaic literature
Greek manuscripts
   See Manuscripts, Greek
Greek marble sculpture
   See Marble sculpture, Greek
Greek masks
   See Masks, Greek
Greek mathematics
   See Mathematics, Greek
Greek mercenaries   *(DF89)*
   xx Mercenary troops
Greek mirrors
   See Mirrors, Greek
Greek music
   See Music, Greek and Roman
Greek newspapers   *(History, PN5231-9)*
Greek oracles
   See Oracles, Greek
Greek orations   *(Collections, PA3479-3482;*
      History, PA3263-4)
   xx Classical orations
      Oratory, Ancient
Greek orations, Modern
Greek orators
   See Orators, Greek
Greek papyri
   See Manuscripts, Greek (Papyri)
Greek periodicals   *(History, PN5231-5240)*
Greek philology   *(PA1-99)*
   sa Classical philology
      Greek language
      Greek literature
      Inscriptions, Greek
      Manuscripts, Greek
   xx Classical philology
      Greek language
      Greek literature
Greek philology, Medieval and late   *(Direct)*
Greek philology, Modern
Greek philosophy
   See Philosophy, Ancient
Greek poetry   *(Collections, PA3431-3459;*
      History, PA3092-3129)
   sa Byzantine poetry
      Dithyramb
Greek poetry, Modern   *(Collections,*
      PA5280-5289; History,
      PA5250-5255)
Greek pottery
   See Pottery, Greek
Greek prose literature   *(Collections,*
      PA3473-3515; History,
      PA3255-3281)
Greek prose literature, Modern   *(Collections,*
      PA5295; History, PA5265)
Greek revival (Architecture)   *(Direct)*
   xx Architecture, Greek
      Neoclassicism (Architecture)
Greek rhetoric
   See Rhetoric, Ancient
Greek strategi
   See Strategi, Greek

Greek students in the United States, [etc.]
Greek tapestry
   See Tapestry, Greek
Greek temples
   See Temples, Greek
Greek tribes   *(DF251)*
Greek type
   See Type and type-founding—Greek type
Greek vases
   See Vases, Greek
Greek wit and humor   *(Collections,*
      PA3469.W5; History, PA3249)
   xx Classical wit and humor
Greek wit and humor, Modern
   sa Greek-American wit and humor
Greeks   *(DF)*
   xx Aryans
      Mediterranean race
Greeks in Albania, [Bulgaria, Italy, etc.]
— Juvenile literature
Greeks in Asia Minor
   Example under Population transfers
Greeks in foreign countries
Green
Green alder
   See European green alder
Green algae
   See Chlorophyceae
Green belts
   See Greenbelts
Green-bottle flies   *(QL537.M7)*
   xx Flies
Green bug
   See Grain-louse
Green cancer
   See Chloroma
Green crop drying
   See Forage plants—Drying
Green frog
   x Spring frog
   xx Frogs
Green gram
   See Mung bean
Green June beetle
   x Fig-eater
      Figeater
      June beetle, Green
   xx Beetles
Green linnet
   See Greenfinch
Green mallee   *(Botany, QK495.E86; Culture,*
      SD397.G)
   x Mallee, Green
   xx Eucalyptus
Green manuring   *(S661)*
   sa Serradella
   xx Cover crops
      Fertilizers and manures
      Nitrogen—Fixation
      Organic fertilizers
      Soil inoculation
Green peach aphid   *(SB945)*
Green plovers
   See Lapwings
Green soldier-bug   *(SB945.G)*
Green Spring Plantation, Va., Battle of, 1781
Green-striped maple worm
   See Maple worm
Green turtle
   xx Sea turtles
— Juvenile literature
— Legends and stories
Greenback Party
   See National Greenback party
"Greenbackers"
   See National Greenback Party
Greenbacks   *(HG604-5)*
   sa National Greenback Party

   xx Inflation (Finance)—United States
      Legal tender
      National Greenback Party
      Paper money—United States
Greenbelts   *(Direct)*
   sa Garden cities
   x Green belts
   xx Open spaces
Greenfinch
   x Green linnet
   xx Finches
Greenhead
   See Striped bass
Greenhouse crops
   See Greenhouse plants
Greenhouse culture
   See Greenhouse management
Greenhouse gardening
   See Greenhouse management
Greenhouse management   *(Indirect) (SB415)*
      Here are entered works on the culture of
         plants grown in greenhouses and on
         the management of the greenhouses
         themselves.
   sa Artificial light gardening
      Forcing (Plants)
      Greenhouse plants
   x Greenhouse culture
      Greenhouse gardening
      Greenhouses—Management
   xx Forcing (Plants)
      Greenhouse plants
      Greenhouses
      Horticulture
— Costs
Greenhouse plants   *(SB415)*
   sa Greenhouse management
   x Glasshouse crops
      Glasshouse plants
      Greenhouse crops
   xx Gardening
      Greenhouse management
      Horticulture
      Plants, Ornamental
— Diseases and pests   *(SB936)*
— Fertilizers and manures   *(S667.G74)*
— Pictorial works
Greenhouse thrips   *(SB945.T)*
Greenhouse white fly
Greenhouses   *(SB415-416)*
   sa Cold-frames
      Forcing (Plants)
      Greenhouse management
      Growth cabinets and rooms
      Phytotron
      Wardian cases
   x Conservatories
      Hot-houses
   xx Floriculture
      Gardening
      Horticulture
— Catalogs
— Costs
— Heating and ventilation   *(SB416)*
— — Costs
— Management
      See Greenhouse management
— Shading
   x Shading of greenhouses
Greenkeeping
   See Golf-links—Construction and care
Greenland collared lemming
   See Collared lemming
Greenland halibut   *(QL638.P7)*
   x Halibut, Greenland
Greenlandic language
   See Eskimo language

Greens, Edible
  sa *names of edible greens, e.g.* Dandelions,
      Spinach, Water-cress
  x Pot-herbs
    Potherbs
  xx Plants, Edible
    Vegetable gardening
    Vegetables
Green's functions
  x Functions, Green's
  xx Differential equations
    Potential, Theory of
Green's operators
  See Potential, Theory of
Green's theorem
  See Potential, Theory of
Greensand *(Fertilizers, S643; Geology,*
      QE471, QE685)
  xx Sandstone
Greensickness
  See Chlorosis
Greenville, Treaty of, 1795 *(E83.794)*
Greeting cards *(Art, NC1860; Etiquette,*
      BJ2095.G7)
  sa New Year cards
  x Cards, Greeting
  xx Christmas cards
  — Authorship
  — Collectors and collecting *(NC1860)*
  — Juvenile literature
Greetings
  See Salutations
Gregarines
  x Gregarinida
  xx Sporozoa
Gregarinida
  See Gregarines
Gregorian calendar
  See Calendar, Gregorian
Gregorian chant
  See Chants (Plain, Gregorian, etc.)
Gremlin automobile
Grenada, Battle of, 1779 *(E271)*
  xx United States—History—Revolution,
      1775-1783—Naval operations
    West Indies—History—1775-1783
Grenades *(UF765)*
  x Hand-grenades
    Rampart-grenades
    Rifle grenades
  xx Bombs
    Projectiles
  Note under Bombs
Gresham's law *(HG225)*
  xx Money
Grey
  See Gray
Grey Friars
  See Franciscans
Grey kangaroo *(QL737.M3; QL795.K3)*
  x Great grey kangaroo
  xx Kangaroos
Grey-lag goose
  See Greylag goose
Grey seal
  xx Seals (Animals)
  — Juvenile literature
  — Legends and stories
Grey shrew, Pale
  See Pale grey shrew
Grey Tirolean cattle *(SF199.G74)*
  x Grauvieh
    Oberinntal cattle
Greyhounds *(SF429.G8)*
  sa Whippets
  xx Dog racing
  Example under Hounds

Greylag goose *(QL696.A5)*
  x Grey-lag goose
  xx Geese
Greywacke
  See Graywacke
Grid lines
  See Grids (Cartography)
Grid reference systems
  See Grids (Cartography)
Grid systems
  See Grids (Cartography)
Griddle cakes
  See Pancakes, waffles, etc.
Grids, Cattle
  See Cattle guards
Grids (Cartography)
  sa Geographical positions
  x Grid lines
    Grid reference systems
    Grid systems
    Map grids
    Military grid system
  xx Cartography
    Coordinates
    Geographical location codes
    Geographical positions
    Maps
Grids (Cartography) in art
Grids (Electronics)
  See Electron tubes—Grids
    Vacuum-tubes—Grids
Gridwork (Structural engineering)
  See Grillages (Structural engineering)
Grief
  sa Church work with the bereaved
    Consolation
    Crying
  x Sorrow
  xx Bereavement
    Emotions
  — Biblical teaching
Grief in art
  xx Art
Grief in literature
Grierson's Cavalry Raid, 1863 *(E475.23)*
Grievance procedures *(Direct)*
  x Labor grievances
  xx Arbitration, Industrial
    Business agents (Trade-union)
    Foremen
    Industrial relations
    Labor contract
    Mediation and conciliation, Industrial
    Personnel management
    Shop stewards
Grievance procedures (Military law)
  See Complaints (Military law)
Griffins
  x Gryphons
  xx Animals, Mythical
Griffon, Brussels
  See Brussels griffon
Grignard reaction
  See Grignard reagents
Grignard reagents *(QD77)*
  sa Organomagnesium compounds
  x Grignard reaction
  xx Chemical tests and reagents
    Organomagnesium compounds
Gṛihyasūtras *(PK3057; PK3157; PK3257;*
      PK3357; PK3457)
  xx Vedas
Grillages (Structural engineering)
      (TA660.G7)
  x Gridwork (Structural engineering)
  xx Girders
    Structural frames
  — Tables, calculations, etc.

  — Testing
Grilles *(NA3030)*
  xx Architecture—Details
    Doors
    Ironwork
    Windows
  — Patterns
    x Patterns for grilles
Grinders, Meat
  See Meat grinders
Grinding (Size reduction)
  See Size reduction of materials
Grinding and polishing *(TJ1280-1298)*
  sa Burnishing
    Centerless grinding
    Concrete—Finishing
    Electrolytic grinding
    Electrolytic polishing
    Emery-wheels
    Glass grinding and polishing
    Grinding machines
    Grinding wheels
    Honing
    Liquid honing
    Metallographic specimens
    Metals—Finishing
    Polishing wheels
    Sand-blast
    Sharpening of tools
    Stone polishing machinery
    Tumbling (Metal finishing)
    Vibratory finishing (Metal work)
  x Buffing
    Lapping
    Polishing
  — Automation
  — Computer programs *(TJ1280)*
  — Dust control
  — Hygienic aspects
  — Production standards
  — Quality control
  — Safety measures
  — Standards
Grinding machines
  sa Grinding wheels
    Meat grinders
  xx Grinding and polishing
  — Drawing
      See Grinding machines—Drawings
  — Drawings
    x Grinding machines—Drawing
    xx Mechanical drawing
  — Electric equipment
  — Maintenance and repair
  — Mathematical models
  — Safety appliances
Grinding wheels
  sa Diamond wheels
  x Abrasive wheels
    Grindstones
  xx Abrasives
    Grinding and polishing
    Grinding machines
  — Standards *(Direct)*
Grindstones
  See Grinding wheels
Grinnel Expedition, 1st, 1850-1851 *(G665*
      1850)
  Example under reference from Artic expedi-
      tions; Expeditions, Arctic
Grinnel Expedition, 2d, 1853-1855 *(G665*
      1853)
Grip (Golf) *(GV979.G7)*
  xx Golf
Grippe
  See Influenza
Grips (Machines, tools, etc.)
  See Handles

Griquas (DT764.G)
  x Bastaards
  xx Hottentots
     Miscegenation
Grisbåda question (DL658.8)
  x Grisebaa question
Grisebaa question
  See Grisbåda question
Grisons in literature
Grist-mills
  See Flour-mills
Gristle
  See Cartilage
Grit
  See Shot (Pellets)
Gritti's amputation
  See Amputations of leg
Grizzly bear
  xx Bears
  — Juvenile literature
  — Legends and stories
Groceries (Economics, HD9320-9330; Home
     economics, TX341-357)
  — Specifications
Grocers (Economics, HD9320-9330; Home
     economics, TX341-357)
Grocery trade (Direct) (Advertising,
     HF6161.G8; Business, HF6201.G73;
     Cost tables, etc., HF5716.G8;
     Economics, HD9320-9330; Window
     displays, HF5849.G8)
  sa Food brokers
     Self-service stores
     Supermarkets
     Wages—Grocery trade
  Notes under Markets; Show-windows
  — Accounting (HF5686.G8)
  — Costs
  — Equipment and supplies
  — Juvenile literature
  — Law and legislation (Direct)
     xx Food law and legislation
        Trade regulation
  — Mathematical models
Groenendael sheepdog
  See Belgian sheep dog
Groin (QM543; Muscles, QM161)
  xx Abdomen
  — Surgery
  — Tumors
Groins (Shore protection)
  x Groynes (Shore protection)
  xx Hydraulic structures
     Shore protection
Grolier Club, New York
  Example under Clubs
Grommets (Metal-work)
  See Eyelets (Metal-work)
Grooming, Personal
  See Beauty, Personal
     Grooming for men
Grooming for men
  sa Men's clothing
  x Grooming, Personal
     Male grooming
  xx Hygiene
  — Juvenile literature
Grooming for women
  See Beauty, Personal
Grooming of cattle
  See Cattle—Grooming
Grooming of dogs
  See Dog grooming
Grooming of horses
  See Horses—Grooming
Grooming of sheep
  See Sheep—Grooming

Gros Ventres of Montana
  See Atsina Indians
Gros Ventres of the Missouri
  See Hidatsa Indians
Gros Ventres of the Prairie
  See Atsina Indians
Grosbeaks (QL696.P2)
  sa names of grosbeaks, e.g. Cardinal-birds
  xx Finches
     Passeriformes
Groschenromane
  See Dime novels, German
Gross national product (Direct)
  sa Income
     National income
  x National product, Gross
     Social accounting
  xx Economics
     Income
     National income
     Statistics
     Wealth
Grossbeeren, Battle of, 1813
  xx Napoléon I, Emperor of the French,
     1769-1821—Campaigns of
     1813-1814
Grosventre language
  See Atsina language
     Hidatsa language
Grosventres of the Missouri
  See Hidatsa Indians
Grosventres of the Prairie
  See Atsina Indians
Grotesque (Aesthetics, BH301.G74;
     Architecture, NA8460)
  xx Arabesques
     Burlesque (Literature)
     Caricature
     Comedy
     Satire
  — Juvenile literature
Grotesque in architecture (Direct)
Grotesque in art
  xx Art
Grotesque in literature
  sa Ugliness in literature
Groton Heights, Battle of, 1781 (E241.G8)
  sa New London, Conn.—History—
     Burning by the British, 1781
  x Fort Griswold, Massacre of, 1781
Grotrian diagrams
  x Diagrams, Grotrian
  xx Spectrum analysis
Grotto architecture
  See Cave architecture
Grottoes
  See Caves
Ground, Patterned
  See Patterned ground
Ground anchors
  See Guy anchors
Ground bass (ML448)
  x Basso ostinato
     Ostinato
  xx Composition (Music)
     Variation (Music)
Ground controlled approach (TL696.L33)
  x Blind landing
     GCA
     Talk-down system
  xx Aeroplanes—Landing
     Instrument landing systems
     Landing aids (Aeronautics)
     Radar in aeronautics
  Note under Instrument landing systems
Ground cover plants (SB432)
  x Cover plants
  xx Lawns

     Plants, Ornamental
Ground-cushion phenomenon (TA352;
     Aeronautics, TL574.G7)
  sa Ground-effect machines
  x Air-bearing lift
     Ground effect (Aerodynamics)
     Ground pressure (Aerodynamics)
  xx Aerodynamics
     Air jets
     Compressibility
     Lift (Aerodynamics)
     Pneumatics
Ground effect (Aerodynamics)
  See Ground-cushion phenomenon
Ground-effect machine mail
  See Hovermail
Ground-effect machines
  sa Helicopters
     Lift fans
     Vertically rising aeroplanes
  x Air-bearing vehicles
     Air-cushion vehicles
     Ground pressure vehicles, Minimum
     Ground proximity machines
     Hovercraft
  xx Ground-cushion phenomenon
     Lift fans
     Motor vehicles
  — Dynamics (TL574.G7)
  — Juvenile literature
  — Vibration
Ground-hogs
  See Marmots
Ground ivy
  x Gill-over-the-ground
Ground leases
  See Building leases
Ground-nut oil
  See Peanut oil
Ground-nuts
  See Glycine (Plant)
     Peanuts
Ground pressure (Aerodynamics)
  See Ground-cushion phenomenon
Ground pressure vehicles, Minimum
  See Ground-effect machines
Ground proximity machines
  See Ground-cushion phenomenon
Ground radioactive waste disposal
  See Radioactive waste disposal in the
     ground
Ground-rent
  See Rent
     Rent (Economic theory)
Ground simulators (Wind tunnels)
  See Wind tunnels—Ground simulators
Ground-squirrels (QL737.R6)
  sa California ground squirrel
     Golden-mantled ground squirrel
     Richardson ground squirrel
     Thirteen-lined ground squirrel
     White-tailed antelope squirrel
  x Gophers
     Squirrels, Ground
     Susliks
  xx Rodentia
  — Behavior
Ground-squirrels as carriers of disease
     (RA641.G7)
  xx Communicable diseases
     Rodents as carriers of disease
Ground stations (Satellite telecommunication)
  See Earth stations (Satellite
     telecommunication)
Ground substance (Anatomy)
  x Cement substance (Anatomy)
     Interstitial substance
  xx Connective tissues

Ground support (Aeronautics, Military)
    See United States. Navy—Aviation—
        Ground support
Ground support equipment (Ordnance
    rocketry)
    See Ground support systems (Ordnance
        rocketry)
Ground support operations (Ordnance
    rocketry)
    See Ground support systems (Ordnance
        rocketry)
Ground support systems (Astronautics)
    sa Earth stations (Satellite
        telecommunication)
        Launch complexes (Astronautics)
        Space vehicles—Tracking
        Space vehicles—Transportation
    xx Astrionics
        Astronautics
        Electricity in astronautics
Ground support systems (Ordnance rocketry)
    x Ground support equipment (Ordnance
        rocketry)
        Ground support operations (Ordnance
        rocketry)
    xx Rockets (Ordnance)
Ground temperature
    See Earth temperature
Ground tits
    See Wren tits
Ground-to-air missiles
    See Surface-to-air missiles
Ground water
    See Water, Underground
Ground water level
    See Water table
Ground-water recharge
    See Water, Underground—Artificial
        recharge
Ground water surface
    See Water table
Ground water table
    See Water table
Ground wood pulping process
    See Mechanical pulping process
Grounding (Electricity)
    See Electric currents—Grounding
Grounds maintenance
    Here are entered works on the mainte-
    nance of public, industrial, and institu-
    tional grounds and large estates.
    sa Golf-links—Construction and care
        Roadside improvement
        Turf management
    xx Gardening
        Landscape gardening
        Ornamental horticulture
Groundwater barriers
    See Saline water barriers
Groundwater flow *(Indirect) (TC176)*
    sa Seepage
    x Base flow
        Flow, Groundwater
    xx Water, Underground
    — Electromechanical analogies
    — Mathematical models
    — Measurement
Groundwood pulping process
    See Mechanical pulping process
Group counseling
    sa Group guidance in education
        Group psychotherapy
        Self-help groups
    xx Counseling
Group creditors insurance
    See Insurance, Group creditors
Group dental practice *(Direct)*
    x Dental group practice

Group practice in dentistry
    xx Dental clinics
        Dental economics
        Dentistry—Practice
Group discussion
    See Discussion
        Forums (Discussion and debate)
Group dynamics
    See Social groups
Group games
    x Group sports
        Sports for groups
        Team games
    xx Games
Group guidance in education
    xx Group counseling
        Personnel service in education
Group hospitalization
    See Insurance, Hospitalization
Group insurance
    See Insurance, Group
Group legal services
    See Prepaid legal services
Group medical practice *(Direct)*
    sa Clinic managers
        Clinics
        Medical corporations
    x Group practice in medicine
        Medical group practice
    xx Clinics
        Medical cooperation
        Medical economics
        Medicine—Practice
Group method in teaching
    See Group work in education
Group ministry *(BV675)*
    x Co-ministry
        Ministry, Group
        Multiple staff ministry
        Team ministry
    xx Church management
        Pastoral theology
Group practice in dentistry
    See Group dental practice
Group practice in medicine
    See Group medical practice
Group prayer
    See Prayer groups
Group psychoanalysis
    xx Group psychotherapy
        Psychoanalysis
Group psychotherapy *(RC488)*
    sa Family psychotherapy
        Group psychoanalysis
        Moving-pictures in psychotherapy
        Prayer groups
        Psychodrama
    x Collective psychotherapy
    xx Group counseling
        Psychiatry
        Psychotherapy
Group reading *(LC6601-6660)*
    sa Book clubs
        Books and reading
    x Book-study groups
        Great books program
        Reading circles
        Reading groups
    xx Book clubs
        Books and reading
        Forums (Discussion and debate)
Group relations training
    x Encounter groups
        Sensitivity training
        T-groups
    xx Interpersonal relations
        Small groups
        Social interaction

    Social perception
    — Personal narratives
    — Pictorial works *(HM134)*
Group representation (Mathematics)
    See Representations of groups
Group rings
    xx Groups, Theory of
        Rings (Algebra)
Group schemes (Mathematics)
    x Schemes, Group (Mathematics)
    xx Geometry, Algebraic
        Groups, Theory of
Group sports
    See Group games
Group teaching
    See Group work in education
Group work, Church
    See Church group work
Group work, Social
    See Social group work
Group work in architecture
    x Team work in architecture
    xx Architectural practice
        Architecture
Group work in art
    x Team work in art
    xx Art
Group work in education
    x Group method in teaching
        Group teaching
    xx Education
        Teaching
Groupement d'intérêt economique
Groupers
    sa Cookery (Groupers)
Groupies *(Direct)*
    xx Youth
Grouping, Homogeneous
    See Ability grouping in education
Grouping by ability
    See Ability grouping in education
Groupoids
    xx Groups, Theory of
Groups, Age
    See Age groups
Groups, Continuous *(QA385)*
    sa Differential forms
        Differential invariants
        Ergodic theory
        Fiber bundles (Mathematics)
        Topological groups
        Transformations, Infinitesimal
    x Continuous groups
    xx Differential equations
        Lie algebras
Groups, Dimensionless
    See Dimensionless numbers
Groups, Holonomy
    See Holonomy groups
Groups, Infinite
    See Infinite groups
Groups, Kleinian
    See Kleinian groups
Groups, Lie
    See Lie groups
Groups, Mathieu
    See Mathieu groups
Groups, Representation theory of
    See Representations of groups
Groups, Self-help
    See Self-help groups
Groups, Small
    See Small groups
Groups, Social
    See Social groups
Groups, Symmetry
    See Symmetry groups

Groups, Theory of *(QA171)*
    sa Abelian groups
        Algebra, Boolean
        Automorphisms
        Categories (Mathematics)
        Crystallography, Mathematical
        Discontinuous groups
        Eightfold way (Nuclear physics)
        Finite groups
        Fourier transformations
        Free groups
        Functions, Modular
        Galois theory
        Games of strategy (Mathematics)
        Group rings
        Group schemes (Mathematics)
        Groupoids
        Heaps (Mathematics)
        Infinite groups
        Isomorphisms (Mathematics)
        Lattice theory
        Linear algebraic groups
        Lorentz transformations
        Matrix groups
        Modular groups
        Permutation groups
        Quasigroups
        Representations of groups
        Semigroups
        Transformation groups
        Transformations (Mathematics)
    x Substitutions
        Theory of groups
    xx Algebra
        Algebra, Abstract
        Equations, Theory of
        Functions, Polyhedral
        Mathematics
        Numbers, Theory of
  — Problems, exercises, etc.
  — Tables, etc.
Groups, Topological
  See Topological groups
Groups of points *(QA603)*
    sa Convex domains
    xx Set theory
Groups of transformations
  See Transformation groups
Grouse *(Hunting, SK325.G; Zoology,*
       QL696.G2)
    sa Black grouse
        Capercaillie
        Dusky grouse
        Game and game-birds
        Ptarmigans
        Rock ptarmigan
        Ruffed grouse
        Sage grouse
        Sharp-tailed grouse
        Willow ptarmigan
    Example under Game and game-birds
Grouse, Ruffed
  See Ruffed grouse
Grouse hunting
  See Grouse shooting
Grouse shooting
    x Grouse hunting
    xx Fowling
Grout (Mortar) *(TA434)*
    x Cement grout
    xx Grouting
        Mortar
Grouting
    sa Grout (Mortar)
    x Pressure grouting
    xx Concrete construction
        Masonry
        Mortar

Groves, Sacred
  See Sacred groves
Groveton, Battle of, 1862
  See Bull Run, 2d Battle, 1862
Growth *(Biology, QH511; Physiology, QP84)*
    sa Adulthood
        Allometry
        Chemotaxis
        Developmental biology
        Developmental genetics
        Genetic psychology
        Heterosis
        Maturation (Psychology)
        Regeneration (Biology)
        Stature
        subdivision Growth *under subjects, e.g.*
           Bone—Growth; Children—Growth;
           Cities and towns—Growth
    x Development
    xx Developmental biology
        Genetic psychology
        Morphology (Animals)
        Physiology
  — Juvenile literature
Growth (Bacteria)
  See Bacterial growth
Growth (Plants) *(QK731-769)*
    sa Algae—Growth
        Bacterial growth
        Diosmosis
        Geotropism
        Growth cabinets and rooms
        Growth inhibiting substances
        Growth promoting substances
        Heterosis
        Hormones (Plants)
        Hydrotropism
        Meristem
        Phototropism
        Plant regulators
        Regeneration (Botany)
        Rejuvenescence (Botany)
        Tree-rings
        Trees—Growth
        Vernalization
    x Plant growth
        Plants—Growth
    xx Botany
        Diosmosis
        Meristem
        Plant physiology
        Plants
        Rejuvenescence (Botany)
  — Juvenile literature
  — Mathematical models
Growth cabinets and rooms
    x Growth chambers
    xx Botanical research
        Greenhouses
        Growth (Plants)
        Phytotron
Growth chambers
  See Growth cabinets and rooms
Growth disorders
    sa Dwarfism
    xx Metabolism, Disorders of
Growth hormone
  See Somatotropin
Growth inhibiting substances
    sa Hormones (Plants)
    xx Agricultural chemicals
        Growth (Plants)
Growth promoting substances *(QK731)*
    sa Hormones (Plants)
        Indoleacetic acid
        Nerve growth factor
    x Growth substances
    xx Agricultural chemicals

Growth (Plants)
Growth regulating substances
  See Growth regulators
Growth regulators
    sa Plant regulators
    x Growth regulating substances
Growth substances
  See Growth promoting substances
Groynes (Shore protection)
  See Groins (Shore protection)
Gruber-Widal reaction
  See Typhoid fever—Diagnosis—
        Agglutination reaction
Gruinse
  See Gurunsi (African people)
Grumman Albatross
  See Albatross (Amphibian planes)
Grumman Avenger (Bombers)
    xx Bombers
Grumman F6F Hellcat
  See Hellcat (Fighter planes)
Grundlast
  See Reallast
Grundtvigianism *(BR986)*
    x Grundtvigians
    xx Lutheran Church in Denmark
Grundtvigians
  See Grundtvigianism
Grunshi
  See Gurunsi (African people)
Grunwald, Battle of, 1410
  See Tannenberg, Battle of, 1410
Grusi
  See Gurunsi (African people)
Grusi dialects
  See Gurunsi dialects
Grusian literature
  See Georgian literature
Grusinians
  See Georgians
Grussi
  See Gurunsi (African people)
Grussi dialects
  See Gurunsi dialects
Gruyère, Switzerland (District) in literature
Gryphons
  See Griffins
GTO automobile *(TL215.G)*
    xx Pontiac automobile
Guachichile Indians *(F1219)*
    xx Indians of Mexico
Guadalajara, Battle of, 1937 *(DP269.2.G)*
    xx Spain—History—Civil War, 1936-1939
        —Campaigns and battles
Guadalupe fur seal *(QL737.P63)*
    x Juan Fernandez fur seal
        Philippi fur seal
    xx Eared seals
Guadalupe Hidalgo, Treaty of, 1848 *(E408)*
    x Treaty of Guadalupe Hidalgo, 1848
Guaharibo Indians
    x Aharaibu Indians
        Vajaribo Indians
    xx Indians of South America
        Yanoama Indians
Guahibo Indians *(F2319.2.G8)*
    x Guaibo Indians
    xx Indians of South America
Guahibo language *(PM6013)*
    x Guaigua language
        Wa-jibi language
    xx Arawakan languages
        Indians of South America—Languages
Guaiac
  See Guaiacum
Guaiacum
    x Guaiac

Guaibo Indians
   See Guahibo Indians
Guaica Indians
   See Waica Indians
Guaicuruan languages
   See Guaycuruan languages
Guaigua language
   See Guahibo language
Guajajara Indians   *(Brazil, F2520.1.G)*
   xx Indians of South America
       Tenetehara Indians
Guajajara language
   sa Tenetehara dialect
   xx Indians of South America—Languages
       Tenetehara dialect
Guajiro Indians
   See Goajiro Indians
Guana Indians   *(F2230.2.G)*
   xx Indians of South America
Guana language   *(PM6051)*
   xx Indians of South America—Languages
Guanaco
   See Huanaco
Guanajuatite
Guanajuato, Mexico (City)
   — Earthquake, 1784
Guanche language   *(PJ2371)*
   x Canarian language
       Teneriffan language
   xx Berber languages
       Hamitic languages
Guanches   *(Canary Islands, DP302.C36-51;*
       Ethnology, GN661.C2)
   xx Berbers
Guano   *(S649; Trade, HD9484.G9)*
   xx Fertilizers and manures
       Organic fertilizers
   Example under Fertilizer industry
Guar
   xx Legumes
   — Diseases and pests
Guar gum industry   *(Direct)*
Guarana
Guarani Indians   *(F2230.2.G72)*
   sa Caingua Indians
       Chiripá Indians
       Guayaqui Indians
       Pauserna Indians
       Seven Reductions, War of the,
           1754-1756
   xx Indians of Central America
       Indians of South America
   — Legends
Guarani language   *(PM7171-9)*
   sa Guarayo language
       Mbya language
       Siriono language
   xx Guarayo language
       Indians of South America—Languages
Guarani literature   *(Direct)*
Guaranteed annual income   *(Direct)*
   sa Negative income tax
       Wages—Annual wage
   x Annual income guarantee
       Guaranteed income
   xx Economic security
       Income
   — Moral and religious aspects
Guaranteed annual wage
   See Wages—Annual wage
Guaranteed income
   See Guaranteed annual income
Guaranteed wages
   See Wages—Annual wage
Guaranty
   See Suretyship and guaranty
       Warranty

Guaranty, Treaties of   *(JX4171.G8)*
   x Treaties of guaranty
   xx International relations
       Neutrality
       Sovereignty
       Treaties
Guaranty insurance
   See Insurance, Surety and fidelity
Guaranty of bank deposits
   See Banks and banking—Government
       guaranty of deposits
Guarao
   See Warrau Indians
Guarapo
   xx Sugar-cane
Guararapes, Battle of, 1648
   xx Brazil—History—Dutch Conquest,
       1624-1654
Guararapes, Battle of, 1649
   xx Brazil—History—Dutch Conquest,
       1624-1654
Guaraúna language   *(PM6091)*
   sa Cariban languages
   xx Cariban languages
       Indians of South America—Languages
Guarauno Indians
   See Warrau Indians
Guarayo Indians
   xx Indians of South America
Guarayo language   *(PM6096)*
   sa Guarani languages
   xx Guarani language
       Indians of South America—Languages
Guarayú-tá Indians
   See Pauserna Indians
Guard dogs
   See Watchdogs
Guard duty   *(U190-195)*
   sa subdivision Guard duty *under armies,*
       e.g. United States.   Army—Guard
       duty
   x Advance guards
       Outposts
       Patrols
       Picket duty
       Sentinels
   xx Military art and science
Guard fences (Roads)
   See Roads—Guard fences
Guardian and ward   *(Direct)*
   sa Adoption
       Capacity and disability
       Conservatorships
       Executors and administrators
       Interdiction (Civil law)
       Ordinaries
       Parent and child (Law)
       Prodigals (Law)
   x Tutelage
       Wards
   xx Capacity and disability
       Children—Law
       Conservatorships
       Domestic relations
       Interdiction (Civil law)
       Trusts and trustees
   — Domicile
       See Domicile in domestic relations
Guardian and ward (Byzantine law)
   Example under Law, Byzantine
Guardian and ward (Canon law)
Guardian and ward (Islamic law)
   sa Interdiction (Islamic law)
   xx Interdiction (Islamic law)
   Example under Islamic law
Guardian and ward (Jewish law)
Guardian and ward (Roman law)

Guardian angels
   xx Angels
Guardrails (Roads)
   See Roads—Guard fences
Guards, Cattle
   See Cattle guards
Guards, Papal
   See Papal guards
Guarinite
   x Hiordahlite
   xx Silicates
Guarpe Indians   *(F2823.G)*
   x Huarpe Indians
   xx Indians of South America
Guarpe language
   See Allentiac language
Guastec Indians
   See Huastec Indians
Guastec language
   See Huastec language
Guatemala
   — History   *(F1461-1477)*
   — — To 1821
   — — 1821-1945
   — — 1945-
Guatemala-British Honduras dispute
   See British Honduras question
Guatemalan drama   *(Direct)   (Collections,*
       PQ7497; History, PQ7493)
Guatemalan fiction
Guatemalan literature   *(PQ7490-7499)*
   xx Spanish American literature
Guatemalan periodicals   *(PN4989.G)*
Guatemalan poetry   *(Collections, PQ7496;*
       History, PQ7492)
Guato Indians   *(F2520.1.G)*
   x Vuato Indians
   xx Indians of South America
Guava
Guayaki Indians
   See Guayaqui Indians
Guayana Indians   *(F2230.2.G75)*
   xx Indians of South America
Guayaqui Indians   *(F2679)*
   x Aché Indians
       Guayaki Indians
   xx Guarani Indians
       Indians of South America
   Example under Anthropology
Guayaquil Meeting, 1822   *(F2235.36)*
Guaycuru Indians   *(F2230.2.G78)*
   sa Abipone Indians
       Cadioéo Indians
       Mbaya Indians
       Mocobi Indians
       Pilaga Indians
       Tereno Indians
       Toba Indians
   xx Indians of South America
   — Religion and mythology
Guaycuruan languages   *(PM6116)*
   sa Abipone language
       Mbaya language
       Pilaga language
       Toba language (Indian)
   x Guaicuruan languages
   xx Abipone language
       Indians of South America—Languages
       Mbaya language
       Toba language (Indian)
Guaycururú language
   See Mbaya language
Guaymi Indians   *(F1434)*
   xx Chibcha Indians
       Indians of Central America
Guaymi language   *(PM3806)*
   xx Indians of Central America—Languages

Guayule
  xx Rubber
    Rubber plants
  — Diseases and pests *(SB608.G)*
  — Harvesting

Guelfs and Ghibellines *(DG522-3; Germany, DD147)*
  sa Colle di Val d'Elsa, Italy, Battle of, 1269
  x Ghibellines
    Guelphs

Guelphs
  See Guelfs and Ghibellines

Guen (African people)
  See Gouin (African people)

Güenoa language *(PM6126)*
  xx Chana language
    Charrua language
    Indians of South America—Languages

Guere (African people)
  See Gere (African people)

Guerillas
  See Guerrillas

Guérin-Stern syndrome
  See Arthrogryposis

Guernsey cattle *(SF199.G8; Herd-books, SF193.G9)*
  xx Dairy cattle

Guerra de Castas, 1847-1855
  See Yucatan—History—Caste War, 1847-1855

Guerra del Pacifico, 1879-1884
  See War of the Pacific, 1879-1884

Guerre des Bouffons *(ML1727.33)*
  sa Gluck-Piccinni controversy
  x Bouffons, Guerre des
  xx Gluck-Piccinni controversy
    Opera, French
    Opera, Italian

Guerrilla warfare *(U240)*
  x Unconventional warfare
  xx Insurgency
    Military art and science
    Strategy
    Tactics
    War
  Note under Guerrillas

Guerrillas *(Direct)* *(D25.5)*
  Here are entered general and historical works. Works on the military aspects of guerrilla warfare are entered under the heading Guerrilla warfare. International legal aspects of guerrilla warfare are entered under the heading Guerrillas (International law) Municipal criminal law is entered under the heading Guerrillas—Law and legislation.
  sa European War, 1914-1918—Underground movements
    Korean War, 1950-1953—Guerrillas
    United States—History—Civil War, 1861-1865—Guerrillas
    World War, 1939-1945—Underground movements
  x Bushwhackers
    Francs-tireurs
    Guerillas
    Partisans
  — Juvenile literature
  — Law and legislation *(Direct)*
    xx Military offenses
    Note under Guerrillas
  — Personal narratives

Guerrillas (International law) *(JX5123)*
  xx Combatants and noncombatants (International law)
    War crimes
    War (International law)

  Note under Guerrillas

Guerzé language
  See Kpelle language

Guest (Game) *(GV1295.G9)*

Guests
  See Entertaining
    Etiquette
    Hospitality

Guetar Indians
  x Huetar Indians
  xx Indians of Central America

Gueux *(DH187-193)*
  x Beggars, The
  — Songs and music *(PT5484)*
    xx Dutch poetry—1500-1800
      Netherlands—History—Wars of Independence, 1556-1648
      Patriotic poetry, Dutch
      Songs, Dutch

Gugada dialect *(PL7101.G76)*
  x Kukota dialect
  xx Australian languages

Guhu-Samane language

Guichola language
  See Huichol language

Guidance, Student
  See Personnel service in education
    Vocational guidance

Guidance, Vocational
  See Vocational guidance

Guidance in education
  See Personnel service in education

Guidance systems (Flight) *(TL589.4)*
  Here are entered works on systems for supervising the navigation of aircraft and space vehicles from one location to another. Works on systems which govern aircraft and space vehicle attitude, stability, and direction of motion are entered under Flight control.
  sa Flight control
    Proportional navigation
    subdivision Guidance systems *under types of aircraft, e.g.* Guided missiles—Guidance systems
  xx Aeronautical instruments
    Automatic control
    Navigation (Aeronautics)
    Remote control
  Note under Flight control

Guide-books
  See Geology—Guide-books
    Voyages and travels—Guide-books
    subdivision Description—Guide-books *or* Description and travel—Guide-books *under countries, regions, cities, etc., e.g.* France—Description and travel—Guide-books; Levant—Description and travel—Guide-books; Boston—Description—Guide-books

Guide dogs
  x Dog guides
    Seeing Eye dogs
  xx Blind—Travel
    Working dogs
  — Juvenile literature

Guide-posts
  See Signs and sign-boards

Guided missile bases
  x Missile bases
  xx Guided missiles
    Military bases
  — Equipment and supplies

Guided missile frigates
  See Guided missile ships

Guided missile industries *(Direct)*
  sa Strikes and lockouts—Guided missile industries
  x Guided missile production
    Guided missiles industry
    Missile industry
  xx Aerospace industries
  — Accidents

Guided missile production
  See Guided missile industries

Guided missile ships
  x Guided missile frigates
  xx Guided missiles
    Warships

Guided missile sounds
  x Guided missiles—Sounds
  xx Sounds
    Space flight sounds

Guided missiles
  sa Antimissile missiles
    Ballistic missiles
    Guided missile bases
    Guided missile ships
    Surface-to-air missiles
    names of specific missiles, e.g. Bomarc (Missile); Nike rocket; V-1 bomb; V-2 rocket
  x Aeroplanes, Pilotless
    Bombs, Flying
    Flying bombs
    Missiles, Guided
    Pilotless aircraft
  xx Bombs
    Projectiles, Aerial
    Rocketry
    Rockets (Aeronautics)
    Rockets (Ordnance)
    United States. Air Force—Weapons systems
    United States. Navy—Weapons systems
  Note under Ballistic missiles
  — Control systems
    sa Guided missiles—Radio control
    x Missile control systems
    xx Flight control
  — Design and construction
  — Electric equipment
  — Electronic equipment
    xx Electronic control
  — Guidance systems
    x Missile guidance systems
    Example under Guidance systems (Flight)
  — Juvenile literature
  — Maintenance and repair
  — Materials
  — Packaging
  — Pictorial works
  — Pneumatic equipment
  — Radar equipment
    Example under reference from Airborne radar
  — Radio control
    xx Guided missiles—Control systems
  — Reliability
  — Safety measures
  — Sounds
    See Guided missile sounds
  — Testing
  — Tracking
    sa Range instrumentation ships
    x Flight tracking
      Missile tracking
      Tracking
    xx Tracking radar
  — Wings
    xx Wings

Guided missiles industry
    See Guided missile industries
Guides for hunters, fishermen, etc.
    Here are entered works on persons en-
    gaged in the business of guiding hunt-
    ers, fishermen, and other sportsmen.
Guidons *(UC590-595)*
    xx Flags
        Standards, Military
Guild socialism
    See Gild socialism
Guilds
    See Gilds
Guile in literature
    See Deception in literature
Guilford Court House, Battle of, 1781
    (E241.G9)
Guiliak language
    See Gilyak language
Guillain-Barré syndrome
    See Polyradiculitis
Guillemots
    See Murres
Guillotine *(HV8555)*
    xx Capital punishment
        Executions and executioners
Guilt *(BJ1471.5)*
    sa Atonement
        Shame
        Sin
    xx Christian ethics
        Conscience
        Ethics
        Good and evil
        Shame
        Sin
        Subconsciousness
    — Juvenile literature
Guilt (Adat law)
Guilt (Canon law)
Guilt (Jewish law)
Guilt (Law) *(Direct)*
    sa Criminal intent
        Dolus (Civil law)
        Ignorance (Law)
        Negligence
        Pleas (Criminal procedure)
    xx Criminal law
        Criminal liability
Guilt (Roman law)
Guilty, Pleas of
    See Pleas of guilty
Guilty pleas
    See Pleas of guilty
Guin (African people)
    See Gouin (African people)
Guinea (Coin) *(Finance, HG935;*
    Numismatics, CJ2484)
    xx Sovereign (Coin)
    Example under Coins
Guinea Current *(GC296.G8)*
    xx Ocean currents
Guinea-fowl *(SF506)*
    xx Birds, Ornamental
        Poultry
Guinea grains
    See Grains of paradise
Guinea grass *(Botany, QK495.G74; Culture,*
    SB201.G)
Guinea-pig breeding
    sa Guinea-pig breeds
    x Guinea-pigs—Breeding
Guinea-pig breeds
    x Guinea-pigs—Breeds
    xx Guinea-pig breeding
Guinea-pigs *(SF459.G9)*
    — Breeding
        See Guinea-pig breeding

    — Breeds
        See Guinea-pig breeds
    — Juvenile literature
Guinea-pigs as laboratory animals
Guinea-pigs as pets *(SF459.G9)*
    — Juvenile literature
Guineas (Mixed bloods, United States)
    (E184.G8)
    xx Indians of North America—Mixed
        bloods
        Negroes
Guissiga language
    See Gisiga language
Guitar *(ML1015-1018)*
    sa Balalaika
        Bandurria
        Cithern
        Dobro
        English guitar
        Harp-lute guitar
        Hawaiian guitar
        Lyre-guitar
        Ukulele
        Vihuela
    x Spanish guitar
    xx Vihuela
    Example under Stringed instruments
    — Group instruction
        See Guitar—Methods—Group
            instruction
    — Instruction and study *(MT580)*
        sa Guitar music—Teaching pieces
    — Methods *(MT582)*
    —— Group instruction *(MT582)*
        x Guitar—Group instruction
    —— Self-instruction *(MT588)*
        x Guitar—Self-instruction
    — Self-instruction
        See Guitar—Methods—
            Self-instruction
    — Tuning *(History, ML3809; Instruction,*
        MT165)
Guitar, Harp-lute
    See Harp-lute guitar
Guitar, Hawaiian
    See Hawaiian guitar
Guitar and accordion music
    See Accordion and guitar music
Guitar and clarinet music
    See Clarinet and guitar music
Guitar and concertina music
    See Concertina and guitar music
Guitar and double-bass music
    See Double-bass and guitar music
Guitar and drum music *(M298)*
    x Drum and guitar music
Guitar and dulcimer music
    See Dulcimer and guitar music
Guitar and flute music
    See Flute and guitar music
Guitar and harpsichord music *(M276-7)*
    x Harpsichord and guitar music
Guitar and harpsichord music, Arranged
    (M276-7)
Guitar and horn music
    See Horn and guitar music
Guitar and mandolin music
    See Mandolin and guitar music
Guitar and oboe music
    See Oboe and guitar music
Guitar and percussion music *(M298)*
    x Percussion and guitar music
Guitar and percussion music, Arranged
    (M298)
Guitar and piano music *(M276-7)*
    sa Boleros (Guitar and piano)
        Marches (Guitar and piano)
        Polonaises (Guitar and piano)

        Potpourris (Guitar and piano)
        Quadrilles (Guitar and piano)
        Rondos (Guitar and piano)
        Sonatas (Guitar and piano)
        Suites (Guitar and piano)
        Variations (Guitar and piano)
        Waltzes (Guitar and piano)
    x Piano and guitar music
Guitar and piano music, Arranged *(M276-7)*
    sa Concertos (Guitar), Arranged—Solo
        with piano
        Concertos (Guitar)—Solo with piano
        Concertos (Guitar with chamber
        orchestra)—Solo with piano
        Overtures arranged for guitar and piano
        Suites (Guitar with chamber orchestra)
        —Solo with piano
        Suites (Guitar with orchestra)—Solo
        with piano
Guitar and recorder music
    See Recorder and guitar music
Guitar and saxophone music
    See Saxophone and guitar music
Guitar and viola music
    See Viola and guitar music
Guitar and violin music
    See Violin and guitar music
Guitar and violoncello music
    See Violoncello and guitar music
Guitar band
    See Plectral ensembles
Guitar music *(M125-7)*
    sa Canons, fugues, etc. (Guitar)
        Concertos (Guitar)
        Concertos (Guitar with chamber
        orchestra)
        Concertos (Guitar with string
        orchestra)
        Galliards (Guitar)
        Gavottes (Guitar)
        Guitar with chamber orchestra
        Guitar with orchestra
        Guitar with string orchestra
        Hawaiian-guitar music
        Ländler (Guitar)
        Minuets (Guitar)
        Monologues with music (Guitar)
        Overtures (Guitar)
        Passacaglias (Guitar)
        Pavans (Guitar)
        Potpourris (Guitar)
        Recorded accompaniments (Guitar)
        Rondos (Guitar)
        Sarabands (Guitar)
        Sonatas (Guitar)
        Suites (Guitar)
        Tablature (Musical notation)
        Variations (Guitar)
        Waltzes (Guitar)
        Quartets, [Trios, etc.] *followed by*
        specifications which include the
        guitar
    — Teaching pieces *(MT585)*
        xx Guitar—Instruction and study
Guitar music, Arranged *(M128-9)*
Guitar music, Juvenile *(M1385.G7)*
Guitar music (Guitars (2)) *(M292-3)*
    sa Concertos (Guitars (2))
        Concertos (Guitars (2) with chamber
        orchestra)
        Guitars (2) with chamber orchestra
        Guitars (2) with orchestra
        Passacaglias (Guitars (2))
        Rondos (Guitars (2))
        Sonatas (Guitars (2))
        Suites (Guitars (2))
        Variations (Guitars (2))
        Waltzes (Guitars (2))

Guitar music (Guitars (2)), Arranged
    (M292-3)
    sa Overtures arranged for 2 guitars
Guitar music (Guitars (3))
    See Trios (Guitars (3))
Guitar music (Guitars (4))
    See Quartets (Guitars (4))
Guitar music (Guitars (5))
    See Quintets (Guitars (5))
Guitar with chamber orchestra *(M1037.4.G8)*
    sa Concertos (Guitar with chamber
       orchestra)
       Suites (Guitar with chamber orchestra)
    xx Chamber-orchestra music
       Concertos (Guitar with chamber
       orchestra)
       Guitar music
Guitar with orchestra *(M1037.4.G8)*
    sa Concertos (Guitar)
       Suites (Guitar with orchestra)
       Variations (Guitar with orchestra)
    xx Concertos (Guitar)
       Guitar music
       Orchestral music
Guitar with orchestra, Arranged
    (M1037.4.G8)
Guitar with string orchestra *(M1105-6)*
    sa Concertos (Guitar with string
       orchestra)
    xx Concertos (Guitar with string
       orchestra)
       Guitar music
       String-orchestra music
Guitar with string orchestra, Arranged
    (M1105-6)
Guitarists *(Biography: collective, ML399;*
    individual, ML419)
  — Biography
Guitars (2) with chamber orchestra
    (M1037.4.G8)
    sa Concertos (Guitars (2) with chamber
       orchestra)
    x Two guitars with chamber orchestra
    xx Chamber-orchestra music
       Concertos (Guitars (2) with chamber
       orchestra)
       Guitar music (Guitars (2))
Guitars (2) with orchestra *(M1037.4.G8)*
    sa Concertos (Guitars (2))
    xx Concertos (Guitars (2))
       Guitar music (Guitars (2))
Guitars (4) with orchestra *(M1037.4.G8)*
    sa Concertos (Guitars (4))
    xx Concertos (Guitars (4))
       Orchestral music
       Quartets (Guitars (4))
Gujarati ballads and songs
Gujarati essays *(Direct)*
Gujarati language *(PK1841-7)*
    xx Indo-Aryan languages, Modern
Gujarati literature *(PK1850-1888)*
Gujarati newspapers
Gujarati periodicals
Gujarati poetry *(Collections, PK1856)*
Gujarati wit and humor
Gujri language
    See Urdu language
Gula language (Lake Iro, Chad)
    See Kùláál language
Gulf pipefish *(QL638.S9)*
    xx Pipefishes
Gulf States
  — History *(F296)*
  — — To 1803
  — Hurricane, 1969
       sa Nelson Co., Va.—Hurricane, 1969
  — Hurricane, 1970

Gulf Stream *(GC296.G9)*
    xx Ocean currents
Gulf Stream of Japan
    See Kuroshio
Gulfs
    See Bays
Gullah dialect *(PM7875.G8)*
Gulls *(QL696.L3)*
    sa Black-headed gulls
       Black-tailed gull
       California gull
       Glaucous-winged gull
       Herring-gull
       Laughing gull
       Lesser black-backed gull
       Ring-billed gull
    xx Charadriiformes
       Sea birds
       Tubinares
    Example under Water-birds
  — Behavior
Gum arabic *(TP978)*
    x Acacia (Gum)
    xx Adhesives
Gum-bichromate process
    See Photography—Printing processes—Gum
       bichromate
Gum-copal
    See Copal
Gum elastic
    See Rubber
Gum plastics
    x Rubber-modified plastics
    xx Plastics
Gum-wood *(QK495.N98)*
Gumbáingar language *(PL7101.G8)*
    x Kumbainggeri language
    xx Australian languages
Gumbo
    See Okra
Gumbrin
    See Bentonite
Gummosis *(SB741.G8)*
Gums *(QM306)*
    sa Periodontium
    xx Mouth
  — Diseases *(RK401-410)*
       sa Oral manifestations of general
         diseases
         Periodontal disease
       x Gingivitis
       xx Mouth—Diseases
Gums and resins *(Chemical technology,*
    TP977-8; Chemistry, QD419;
    Culture, SB289-291)
    sa Ion exchange resins
       Naval stores
       Oleoresins
       Resinography
       Rosin-oil
       Turpentining
       specific gums and resins, e.g. Copal,
         Kauri gum, Kino
    x Resins
       Rosin
    xx Chemistry, Technical
       Exudation (Botany)
       Forest products
       Plastics
       Protective coatings
  — Analysis
  — Microscopic structure
       See Resinography
  — Permeability
  — Physiological effect *(QP931)*
  — Spectra
  — Tables and ready-reckoners *(HF5716.G)*
  — Therapeutic use *(RM666.G)*

Gums and resins, Artificial
    See Gums and resins, Synthetic
Gums and resins, Synthetic *(Direct)*
    (General, TP977-8; Plastics, TP1180)
    sa Acetal resins
       Acrylic resins
       Alkyd resins
       Epoxy resins
       Furan resins
       Indene resins
       Lucite
       Phenolic resins
       Polyesters
       Resin concrete
       Thermoplastics
       Thermosetting plastics
    x Artificial resins
       Gums and resins, Artificial
       Resins, Synthetic
       Synthetic resins
    xx Chemistry, Technical
       Plastics
       Protective coatings
       Synthetic products
  — Patents
Gun
    See Firearms
       Ordnance
       Rifles
       Shot-guns
Gun, Mountain
    See Mountain guns
Gun-carriages *(UF640-642)*
    xx Ordnance
Gun-carriages, Disappearing *(UF650)*
Gun control
    See Firearms—Laws and regulations
Gun dogs
    See Hunting dogs
Gun fire control
    See Fire control (Gunnery)
Gun-flints *(U888)*
Gun stocks
    See Gunstocks
Gun turrets
    See Aeroplanes, Military—Turrets
       Warships—Turrets
Gunantuna (Melanesian people)
    (Anthropology, GN671.B5; Bismarck
    Archipelago, DU550)
    xx Melanesians
Gunboats
    sa Floating batteries
    xx Floating batteries
       Warships
Guncotton *(TP276)*
    sa Gunpowder
       Nitrocellulose
       Pyroxylin
    xx Explosives
       Gunpowder
       Nitrocellulose
Guncrete
    See Gunite
Gundjun dialect *(PL7101.G86)*
    x Koonjan dialects
       Kunjen dialects
       Ngundjan dialects
    xx Australian languages
Güneş theory (Turkish language)
    See Turkish language—
       History—Güneş theory
Guniam Indians
    See Itenez Indians
Gunite *(TA446)*
    sa Cement gun
    x Guncrete
       Shotcreting

Gunite *(TA446)* *(Continued)*
    Sprayed concrete
    xx Cement gun
    Concrete
    Mortar
Gunja
    See Bhang (Drug)
Gunn effect
    xx Oscillators, Microwave
    Semiconductors
Gunn oscillators
    See Oscillators, Microwave
Gunners, Naval
    See United States. Navy—Gunners
Gunner's mates
    See United States. Navy—Gunners
Gunnery *(UF800; Manuals, drill books, etc.,*
        UF150-302; Naval, VF144-7,
        VF150-302)
    Here are entered general works, and also
        handbooks, manuals, and regulations
        of a general character.
    sa Aerial gunnery
    Ammunition
    Antitank guns
    Artillery
    Ballistics
    Bombing and gunnery ranges
    Explosives
    Fire control (Gunnery)
    Firearms
    Gunpowder
    Naval gunnery
    Ordnance
    Position-finders
    Projectiles
    Range-finding
    Rifle practice
    Shooting, Military
    Target-practice
    Telescopic sights
    xx Artillery drill and tactics
    Ballistics
    Firearms
    Military art and science
    Ordnance
    Projectiles
    Shooting
    Shooting, Military
    Target-practice
    — Tables, calculations, etc.
Gunnery ranges
    See Bombing and gunnery ranges
Gunning
    See Hunting
    Shooting
Gunongtello language
    See Gorontalo language
Gunpowder *(Chemical technology, TP272;*
        Industry, HD9663)
    sa Ammunition
    Compensating-powder
    Guncotton
    Saltpeter
    xx Ammunition
    Explosives
    Firearms
    Guncotton
    Gunnery
    Powders
    Propellants
    Shooting, Military
    — Early works to 1800
    — History
    — — Juvenile literature
    — Juvenile literature
Gunpowder, Smokeless *(TP273)*
    x Powder, Smokeless

Smokeless powder
Gunpowder Plot, 1605 *(DA392)*
Guns
    See Firearms
    Ordnance
    Rifles
    Shot-guns
Guns, Hunting
    See Hunting guns
Guns, Mountain
    See Mountain guns
Gunshot wounds *(RD156)*
    sa subdivision Wounds and injuries *under*
        names of organs and regions of the
        body, e.g. Intestines—Wounds and
        injuries; Knee—Wounds and injuries
    xx Surgery, Military
    Wounds
Gunsmithing *(TS535)*
    sa Firearms—Maintenance and repair
    xx Firearms industry and trade
Gunsmiths *(Direct)*
Gunsmiths, American, [etc.] *(Direct)*
    x American [etc.] gunsmiths
Gunstocks
    x Gun stocks
    Stocks, Gun
    xx Firearms
Gunter's line
    See Slide-rule
Gunwinggu (Australian tribe)
    x Winggu (Australian tribe)
    xx Australian aborigines
Gunwinggu language *(PL7101.G83)*
    xx Australian languages
Gupapuyngu language
    xx Australian languages
Guppies *(Culture, SH167.G)*
Gupta dynasty
    xx India—History—324 B.C.-1000 A.D.
Gur languages *(PL8222)*
    sa Bobo dialects
    Dogon language
    Dompago dialect
    Gurma language
    Gurunsi dialects
    Lele dialect
    Lobi dialects
    Mampruli language
    Moba language
    Mossi languages
    Nankanse language
    Senufo language
    x Goor languages
Gura language
    See Gola language
Gurage language *(PJ9288)*
    x Gourage language
    xx Ethiopian languages
Gurages *(DT380)*
    xx Ethnology—Ethiopia
Gurantala language
    See Gorontalo language
Gurenne language
    See Nankanse language
Gurian dialect *(PK9132)*
    x Guric dialect
    Gurish dialect
    xx Georgian language—Dialects
Guric dialect
    See Gurian dialect
Gurindji (Australian people)
    xx Australian aborigines
    — Government relations
Gurish dialect
    See Gurian dialect
Gurjara-Pratihara dynasty *(DS451.8)*
    x Prathiharas

Pratiharas
    xx India—History—324 B.C.-1000 A.D.
Gurjari language
    See Urdu language
Gurkhali language
    See Nepali language
Gurkhas *(DS485.N4)*
    x Ghoorkas
    Ghurkas
    Goorkhas
    Gorkhas
    xx Ethnology—Nepal
Gurkhas as soldiers
    xx Soldiers
Gurma language
    sa Moba language
    x Gourmantché language
    xx Gur languages
Gurmukhi writing
    See Writing, Old Panjabi
Guro (African people)
    x Gouro (African people)
    Kweni (African people)
    Lo (African people)
    xx Ethnology—Ivory Coast
Guro language
    See Kweni language
Gurumbu (New Guinea tribe)
    See Gururumba (New Guinea tribe)
Gurumsi
    See Gurunsi (African people)
Gurumsi dialects
    See Gurunsi dialects
Gurune language
    See Nankanse language
Gurung language *(PL3801.G8)*
    xx Tibeto-Burman languages
Gurunga
    See Gurunsi (African people)
Gurungs
    xx Ethnology—Nepal
Gurunsi (African people)
    sa Builsa (African tribe)
    x Gourounsi (African people)
    Gruinse
    Grunshi
    Grusi
    Grussi
    Gurumsi
    Gurunga
    xx Ethnology—Upper Volta
Gurunsi dialects
    sa Kasena dialect
    Tamprusi dialect
    x Gourounsi dialects
    Grusi dialects
    Grussi dialects
    Gurumsi dialects
    xx Gur languages
Gururumba (New Guinea tribe)
    x Gurumbu (New Guinea tribe)
    xx Ethnology—New Guinea
Gurus *(Direct)*
    sa Sikh gurus
    xx Hinduism
Gurus, Sikh
    See Sikh gurus
Gusains *(BL1245.G8)*
    xx Hindu sects
Gushers *(TN871)*
    x Oil gushers
    xx Oil wells
Gusii (Bantu tribe)
    x Kisii (Bantu tribe)
    xx Bantus
    Ethnology—Kenya
Gusii language
    x Ekegusii language

Guzii language
   Kisii language
   xx Bantu languages
Gusli *(Russian, ML1015.G8)*
   sa Kanklės
   Kantele (Musical instrument)
   xx Dulcimer
Gust loads
   xx Aerodynamic load
   Atmospheric turbulence
   Wind-pressure
  — Measurement
     xx Aerodynamic measurements
Gut industries
  See Animal gut industries
Gutenberg-Preis der Stadt Leipzig
   xx Book design
Gutta-percha *(Culture, SB291.I5;*
   Manufacture, TS1930; Trade,
   HD9161)
   sa Rubber
   xx Rubber
Gutters *(TH2493)*
   xx Building
   Roof drainage
   Roofs
Guttiferales *(QK495.A12)*
   xx Dicotyledons
Guy anchors
   x Anchors, Deadman
   Anchors, Ground
   Anchors, Guy
   Deadman anchors
   Ground anchors
   xx Anchorage (Structural engineering)
   Civil engineering
Guyana
  — History *(F2361-2391)*
  —— To 1803
     sa English West Indian Expedition,
      1795-1796
  —— 1803-1966
  —— 1966-
Guyanese drama (English)
  See English drama—Guyanese authors
Guyanese literature (English)
  See English literature—Guyanese authors
Guzii language
  See Gusii language
Guzy
  See Oghuz
Gwali language
  See Gwari language
Gwamba language
  See Thonga language
Gwari (African tribe)
   x Gbari (African tribe)
   xx Ethnology—Nigeria
Gwari language
   x Gbari language
   Gwali language
   xx Kwa languages
Gweabo language
  See Jabo language
GWF airplanes *(TL686.G)*
Gwin (African people)
  See Gouin (African people)
Gyarung language *(PL3651.G9)*
   x Giarung language
   xx Tibetan language—Dialects
Gyitkshan Indians
  See Kitksan Indians
Gymnasiums *(GV403-5)*
   sa Field houses
   xx Field houses
   Physical education facilities
  Example under School facilities
  — Apparatus and equipment *(GV407-410)*

   sa Pangymnastikon
Gymnastics *(GV461-475)*
   sa Acrobats and acrobatism
   Balance beam
   Callisthenics
   Chest weights
   Dumb-bells
   Gymnastics for women
   Horizontal bar
   Indian clubs
   Parallel bars
   Physical education and training
   Pyramids (Gymnastics)
   Rings (Gymnastics)
   Schools—Exercises and recreations
   Swedish gymnastics
   Vaulting-horse
   xx Acrobats and acrobatism
   Athletics
   Callisthenics
   Exercise
   Hygiene
   Physical education and training
   Sports
  — Caricatures and cartoons
  — Judging
     xx Sports officiating
  — Rules
  — Terminology
Gymnastics, Medical *(RA781; RM719-721)*
   sa Mechanotherapy
   Swedish gymnastics
   x Exercise therapy
   Kinesiotherapy
   Medical gymnastics
   Movement cure
   Therapeutic exercise
   xx Mechanotherapy
   Swedish gymnastics
Gymnastics for children *(GV464.5)*
   xx Physical education for children
Gymnastics for women *(Direct) (GV464)*
   xx Gymnastics
   Physical education for women
Gymnastics in literature
Gymnobranchiata
  See Nudibranchiata
Gymnolaemata, Fossil
   sa Cryptostomata
   xx Polyzoa, Fossil
Gymnosomata *(QL430.4)*
Gymnosperms *(QK495.G9; Anatomy,*
   QK683.G9; Morphology,
   QK643.G99)
   sa Coniferae
   Ginkgo
   xx Phanerogams
  — Identification
Gymnosperms, Fossil
   sa Cordaitales
   xx Paleobotany
Gynandromorphism
   sa Virilism
   xx Hermaphroditism
   Sex (Biology)
Gynecocracy
  See Matriarchy
Gynecologic endocrinology
  See Endocrine gynecology
Gynecologic nursing
   xx Gynecology
   Nurses and nursing
Gynecologic practice
  See Gynecology—Practice
Gynecological pathology
  See Pathology, Gynecological
Gynecologists *(Direct)*
  — Correspondence, reminiscences, etc.

Gynecology *(Indirect) (RG)*
   sa Endocrine gynecology
   Gynecologic nursing
   Pathology, Gynecological
   Pediatric gynecology
   Veterinary gynecology
   Woman—Diseases
   xx Generative organs, Female
   Genito-urinary organs—Diseases
   Medicine—Practice
   Woman—Diseases
  — Anecdotes, facetiae, satire, etc.
  — Atlases
  — Cases, clinical reports, statistics *(RG106)*
  — Early works to 1800
  — Examinations, questions, etc.
  — Hospitals
     See Hospitals, Gynecologic and
      obstetric
  — Jurisprudence
     See Forensic gynecology
  — Nomenclature
  — Practice
     x Gynecologic practice
     xx Medicine—Practice
  — Psychosomatic aspects
     xx Medicine, Psychosomatic
Gynecology, Forensic
  See Forensic gynecology
Gynecology, Operative *(RG104)*
   sa Clitoridectomy
   x Operative gynecology
   xx Genito-urinary organs—Surgery
  — Complications and sequelae
Gynecology, Osteopathic *(RZ386)*
   xx Osteopathy
Gynecology, Pediatric
  See Pediatric gynecology
Gynogenesis
   xx Parthenogenesis
   Reproduction
Gyotaku
  See Fish prints
Gypsies
  See Gipsies
Gypsum *(Indirect) (TN946)*
   sa Plaster of Paris
   xx Evaporites
   Fertilizers and manures
   Plaster of Paris
  Example under Geology, Economic
  — Drying
  — Standards
Gypsy language
  See Gipsies—Language
Gypsy-moth
  See Gipsy-moth
Gyr falcon
  See Gyrfalcon
Gyrators
   sa Ferrites (Magnetic materials)
   Hall effect
   Wave guides
   xx Electric networks
   Microwave circuits
  — Noise
Gyrfalcon
   x Gyr falcon
   xx Falcons
Gyro compass *(QA862.G9; TL589.C6;*
   VK577)
   sa Automatic pilot (Aeroplanes)
   x Compass, Gyroscopic
   Gyrocompass
   Gyrostatic compass
   xx Aeronautical instruments
   Automatic pilot (Aeroplanes)
   Automatic pilot (Ships)

Gyro compass (*QA862.G9; TL589.C6;*
    VK577) (*Continued*)
  Gyroscope
    Example under Gyroscopic instruments
Gyro horizon
  See Artificial horizons (Aeronautical
    instruments)
Gyro pilot
  See Automatic pilot (Aeroplanes)
    Automatic pilot (Ships)
Gyro stabilizers
  See Gyrostabilizers
Gyro vertical (Instruments)
  See Artificial horizons (Aeronautical
    instruments)
Gyrocompass
  See Gyro compass
Gyrocotylidea (*QL391.P7*)
  xx Cestoda
Gyrodynamics
  See Rotational motion
    Rotational motion (Rigid dynamics)
Gyropilot
  See Automatic pilot (Aeroplanes)
    Automatic pilot (Ships)
Gyroplanes
  See Autogiros
Gyroscope (*QA862.G9*)
  sa Artificial horizons (Aeronautical
    instruments)
    Automatic pilot (Aeroplanes)
    Cryogenic gyroscopes
    Fluid rotor gyroscopes
    Gyro compass
    Gyroscopic instruments
    Gyrostabilizers
    Optical gyroscopes
    Rate gyroscopes
    Stability of aeroplanes
    Stability of helicopters
    Stability of ships
  x Gyrostat
  xx Aeronautical instruments
    Dynamics, Rigid
    Rotational motion (Rigid dynamics)
    Stability of aeroplanes
    Stability of helicopters
    Stability of ships
    Top
Gyroscopic instruments
  sa Astronautical instruments
    names of specific instruments and uses,
      e.g. Automatic pilot (Aeroplanes);
      Gyro compass; Horizons, Artificial;
      Inertial navigation
  xx Aeronautical instruments
    Gyroscope
    Nautical instruments
    Physical instruments
  — Juvenile literature
  — Programmed instruction
Gyrostabilizers
  x Gyro stabilizers
  xx Gyroscope
    Stability
Gyrostat
  See Gyroscope
Gyrostatic compass
  See Gyro compass
Gyrus suprasylvius
  See Suprasylvian gyrus
H-2 locus
  x H-2 system
  xx Immunogenetics
H-2 system
  See H-2 locus
H-guide
  See Dielectric wave guides

H.P. 80 (Jet planes)
  See Victor (Jet planes)
H.P. 115 (Jet planes)
  See Handley Page 115 (Jet planes)
H-spaces
  x Hopf spaces
    Spaces, Hopf
  xx Topological groups
H-T-P test
  See House-tree-person technique
Haagse School
  xx Painting, Modern—19th century
Haar integral
  See Integrals, Haar
Haar measure
  See Integrals, Haar
Haarlem
  — Siege, 1572-1573 (*DH206.H*)
    xx Netherlands—History—Wars of
      Independence, 1556-1648
Haar's measure
  See Integrals, Haar
Haavara
Habad
  x Chabad
    Lubavitch-Chabad
  xx Hasidism
Habans
  See Anabaptists
Habe (African people)
  See Dogons (African people)
Habe language
  See Dogon language
Habeas corpus (*Direct*)
  sa Amparo (Writ)
  xx Civil rights
    Constitutional law
    Criminal procedure
    Detention of persons
    Extraordinary remedies
    Martial law
    Writs
Habeas corpus (International law)
  xx International law
Haberdashery
  See Men's furnishing goods
Habiri
  See Habiru
Habiru
  x Chabiroe
    Habiri
    Khabiri
  xx Ethnology—Mesopotamia
    Jews—Origin
Habit (*BF335-7*)
  sa Formal discipline
    Inhibition
    Instinct
    Nail-biting
  xx Conduct of life
    Ethics
    Formal discipline
    Inhibition
    Instinct
    Psychology
Habit, Clerical
  See Clergy—Costume
Habit, Ecclesiastical
  See Clergy—Costume
Habit, Monastic
  See Monasticism and religious orders,
    Buddhist—Habit
    Monasticism and religious orders—
      Habit
Habit, Riding
  See Riding habit

Habitable atmospheres (Space environment)
  See Artificial atmospheres (Space
    environment)
Habitat improvement, Wildlife
  See Wildlife habitat improvement
Habitat selection
  x Selection of habitat
  xx Animals, Habitations of
    Zoology—Ecology
Habits of animals
  See Animals, Habits and behavior of
Habitual criminals
  See Recidivists
Habituation (Neuropsychology) (*QP374*)
  sa Conditioned response
    Extinction (Psychology)
  xx Conditioned response
    Extinction (Psychology)
Hachi-hachi
  See Hachi-ju-hachi (Game)
Hachi-ju-hachi (Game) (*GV1299.H3*)
  x Eighty-eight (Game)
    Hachi-hachi
    Hana
    Hana-karuta
Hachidaishū
  xx Waka
Hack saws
  See Hacksaws
Hack writers
Hackamore
  xx Harness
    Horse-training
Hackberry (*Celtis, QK495.C*)
Hackensack Indians (*E99.H15*)
  xx Delaware Indians
    Indians of North America
Hackney horse (*SF293.H2*)
Hacks (Carriages)
  See Cab and omnibus service
    Carriages and carts
Hacksaws (*TJ1233*)
  x Hack saws
  xx Metal-cutting
    Saws
  — Standards
Haddock (*QL638.G2; Fisheries, SH351.H18*)
  sa Cookery (Haddock)
  — Diseases and pests
Haddock fisheries (*Indirect*) (*SH351.H18*)
  xx Fisheries
Hades
  See Future life
    Hell
Hadhrami inscriptions
  See Inscriptions, Hadrami
Hadia language (*PL8223*)
Hadith (*BP135*)
    Here are entered works on the oral tradi-
    tions concerning the deeds and sayings
    of Muḥammad, the prophet, solely.
    Works on the oral traditions concern-
    ing the deeds and sayings of Imams
    and Muḥammad, the prophet, are en-
    tered under Hadith (Shiites) Works on
    the traditions of individual Imams are
    entered under the name of the Imam
    with subdivision Hadith.
  sa Iran in the Hadith
    Jews in the Hadith
    Sunna
    Women in the Hadith
  x Tradition (Islam)
  xx Islamic law—Sources
    Islamic literature
    Sunna
  Note under Hadith (Shiites)

— Abrogator and abrogated Hadith
   (BP136.78)
— Authorities (BP136.46-48)
   x Hadith—Transmitters
      Transmitters of Hadith
— Commentaries
   See Hadith—Criticism, interpretation,
      etc.
— Criticism, interpretation, etc. (BP135)
   x Hadith—Commentaries
— Forgeries (BP136.74)
— Language, style
— Prophecies
— Terminology
— Transmitters
   See Hadith—Authorities
Hadith (Shiites) (BP193.25-28)
      Here are entered works on the oral tradi-
      tions concerning the deeds and sayings
      of Imams and Muḥammad, the
      prophet. Works on the oral traditions
      concerning the deeds and sayings of
      Muḥammad, the prophet, solely, are
      entered under Hadith. Works on the
      traditions of individual Imams are en-
      tered under the name of the Imam with
      subdivision Hadith.
   x Imams—Hadith
      Imams—Traditions
      Tradition (Shiites)
   xx Imams
   Note under Hadith
— Authorities (BP193.28)
   x Hadith (Shiites)—Transmitters
— Transmitters
   See Hadith (Shiites)—Authorities
Hadith stories
Hadjerai (African tribe)
   xx Ethnology—Chad
Hadrami inscriptions
   See Inscriptions, Hadrami
Hadran
   xx Sermons, Jewish
      Talmud
Hadron spectroscopy (QC490)
   x Spectroscopy, Hadron
   xx Nuclear spectroscopy
      Spectrum analysis
Hadrons (QC721)
   sa Baryons
      Mesons
   x Strongly interacting particles
— Decay
— Scattering (QC721)
Hadzapi (African people)
   See Tindiga (African people)
Haedong (Sect)
   See Wŏnhyo (Sect)
Haeltzuk language
   See Heiltsuk language
Haemophilus diseases
   See Hemophilus diseases
Haemosporidia
   xx Sporozoa
Haemostasis
   See Hemostasis
Hafirs
   See Reservoirs, Underground
Hafiz (Direct)
   xx Islam—Functionaries
      Koran—Memorizing
      Koran—Recitation
Hafling horse
   x Hafling mountain pony
Hafling mountain pony
   See Hafling horse
Hafnium (QD181.H5)
— Analysis

— Isotopes
— — Decay
— Metallography
Hafnium compounds
Hafnium ores (Indirect)
Hafnium organic compounds
   See Organohafnium compounds
Hafsides (DT199)
   x Hafsite dynasty
   xx Africa, North—History—1517-1882
Hafsite dynasty
   See Hafsides
Hagfish (QL638.1)
   sa Atlantic hagfish
      Pacific hagfish
   x Myxiniformes
      Slime eel
   xx Agnatha
Hagi Rebellion, 1876
   xx Japan—History—Meiji period,
      1868-1912
Hagiography (BX4662)
      Here are entered works on the lives of the
      saints, and how to write them. The
      lives themselves are entered under the
      heading Saints.
   sa Synaxarion
   x Hagiology
   xx Bollandists
      Christian biography
      Saints
Hagiology
   See Hagiography
Hague. Permanent Court of Arbitration
   (JX1925.8)
   xx Arbitration, International
**Hague.   Permanent Court of International
   Justice** (JX1971.5)
Example under International courts
Hague, Treaty of, 1717 (D283.5)
   x Treaty of the Hague, 1717
Hague porcelain (NK4399.H3)
   x Porcelain, Hague
Hai prose
   See Haibun
Haibun
   x Hai prose
Haida Indians (E99.H2)
   x Skittagetan Indians
   xx Indians of North America
— Juvenile literature
Haida language (PM1271-4)
   x Skittagetan languages
Haidamaks (DK508.7)
   x Gaidamaks
      Haydamaks
   xx Brigands and robbers
      Peasant uprisings
Haiduks
   x Hajduks
      Heyducks
Haiduti
   x Khaiduti
Haiga (ND2462)
   x Haikai painting
      Haiku painting
   xx Painting, Japanese
— Technique
Haikai
   sa Haiku
   xx Haiku
      Japanese literature
      Japanese poetry
      Renga
Haikai painting
   See Haiga
Haiku
   sa Haikai

Renga
Senryu
   x Haiku, Japanese
      Hokku
   xx Haikai
      Japanese poetry
— Explication
Haiku, American, ₍English, etc.₎
   xx American ₍English, etc.₎ poetry
Haiku, Japanese
   See Haiku
Haiku painting
   See Haiga
Hail (Indirect) (QC929.H1)
   sa Ice crystals
      Plants, Effect of hail on
   xx Meteorology
      Precipitation (Meteorology)
      Storms
      Water
Hail control (Indirect)
   xx Weather control
Hail insurance
   See Insurance, Hail
Hailam dialect
   See Chinese language—Dialects—Hainan
Hailtsa language
   See Heiltsuk language
Hailtsuk language
   See Heiltsuk language
Hair (Anatomy, Comparative, QL942;
      Anatomy, Human, QM488;
      Anthropology, GN193)
   sa Beard
      Bristles
      Eyelashes
      Molting
      Mustache
      Scalp
      Wigs
   xx Beauty, Personal
      Body covering (Anatomy)
      Color of man
      Head
      Scalp
— Abnormities (QL942; QM488)
   sa Hypertrichosis
   xx Hypertrichosis
— Anecdotes, facetiae, satire, etc.
      (PN6231.H3)
— Care and hygiene (RL91)
   sa Hair preparations
— Diseases (RL91)
   sa Baldness
      Plica polonica
— Dyeing and bleaching (TT973)
   sa Hair dyes
   x Dyes and dyeing—Hair
   xx Hair preparations
      Hairdressing
— Juvenile literature
— Permanent waving
   See Permanent waving
— Transplantation
Hair, Removal of (By electricity, RL115)
   x Depilation
   xx Electrolysis in surgery
Hair (Botany)
   See Trichomes
Hair (in religion, folk-lore, etc.)
   x Folk-lore of hair
   xx Religion, Primitive
Hair-balls (Veterinary medicine, SF851)
Hair-dressing
   See Hairdressing
Hair dyes (TT969)
   x Dyes and dyeing—Hair
      Tints, Hair

Hair dyes (TT969) (Continued)
  xx Hair—Dyeing and bleaching
      Hair preparations
  — Patents
Hair follicles
  x Follicles, Hair
  xx Epithelium
Hair in art
  xx Art
Hair in literature
Hair preparations (TT969)
  sa Hair—Dyeing and bleaching
      Hair dyes
  xx Cosmetics
      Hair—Care and hygiene
      Hairdressing
      Toilet preparations
  — Patents
Hair-work (TT975-6)
Haircutting
  xx Barbers
      Hairdressing
  — Moral and religious aspects (Sikhism,
      BL2018.5.H3)
Hairdressers
  See Beauty operators
Hairdressing (Indirect)
  sa Costume
      Hair—Dyeing and bleaching
      Hair preparations
      Haircutting
      Permanent waving
  x Coiffure
      Hair-dressing
      Headdress
  xx Beauty culture
      Toilet
  — Anecdotes, facetiae, satire, etc.
  — Collective labor agreements
      See Collective labor agreements—
          Hairdressing
  — Hygienic aspects
      xx Hygiene
  — Juvenile literature
  — Terminology
  — Vocational guidance
Hairdressing of Negroes
  x Negro hairdressing
      Negroes—Hairdressing
Hairpin lace (TT805)
  xx Crocheting
      Lace and lace making
Hairy-root disease (SB741.H3)
Haisla Indians (E99.H23)
  x Kitamat Indians
      Kitimat Indians
      Kitlope Indians
  xx Indians of North America
      Kwakiutl Indians
      Wakashan Indians
Haiti
  — History (F1901-1939)
  — — To 1791
  — — Revolution, 1791-1804
      sa Vertières, Battle of, 1803
  — — — Juvenile literature
  — — 1804-
  — — 1804-1844
  — — Revolution, 1843 (F1938.3)
      x Haitian Revolution, 1843
  — — 1844-1915 (F1926)
      sa Las Carreras, Battle of, 1849
  — — American occupation, 1915-1934
      (F1927)
  — — 1934-   (F1928)
Haitian literature (French) (PQ3940-3949)
  Duplicate entry is made under French lit-
      erature—Haitian authors.

Note under French literature—Haitian authors
Haitian orations
Haitian poetry (French) (Collections,
      PQ3946; History, PQ3942)
  Duplicate entry is made under French
      poetry—Haitian authors.
  Note under French poetry—Haitian authors
Haitian Revolution, 1843
  See Haiti—History—Revolution, 1843
Hajduks
  See Haiduks
Hajj
  See Pilgrims and pilgrimages, Muslim—
      Mecca
Ḥajjat al-wadāʿ (BP77.68)
  x Ḥijjat al-wadāʿ
Haka dialect
  See Lai language
Hakas (Tribe) (DS432.H)
  sa Missions to Hakas
  xx Chin tribes
Hake (Zoology, QL638.M)
  sa Pacific hake
Hake fisheries (SH351.H185)
  xx Fisheries
Ḥakili languages
  See Šhauri language
Hakka dialect
  See Chinese language—Dialects—Hakka
Hakke Shintō
  See Shirakawa Shintō
Hakodate, Japan
  — Fire, 1934
Hakodate, Battle of, 1868-1869
  x Goryōkaku, Battle of, 1868-1869
  xx Japan—History—Civil War, 1868
Halacha
  See Jewish law
      Talmud
      Tradition (Judaism)
Halakha
  See Jewish law
      Talmud
      Tradition (Judaism)
Halavah
  See Halvah
Halaya dialect (PL5699)
  xx Bisaya language
      Philippine languages
Halecostomi
  See Pholidophoriformes
Half-breed Indians
  See Indians—Mixed bloods
Half-cent (CJ1836)
  xx Cent
Half-columns (Direct)
  xx Architecture
      Columns
Half-dime (CJ1835)
Half-dollar (United States, CJ1835)
Half-life (Nuclear physics) (QC795)
  sa subdivision Half-life under names of
      radioactive substances, e.g. Lutetium
      —Isotopes—Half-life; also
      subdivision Decay under names of
      radioactive substances, e.g. Fission
      products—Decays;Radium—Decay
  x Radioactive half-life
      Radioisotopes—Half-life
  xx Radioactivity
      Radioisotopes
  — Tables, etc.
Half-timber work
  See Half-timbered houses
Half-timbered houses (NA7175)
  sa Framing (Building)
      House framing
  x Buildings, Half-timbered

Half-timber work
      Houses, Half-timbered
  xx Architecture, Domestic
      Building, Wooden
      Framing (Building)
      House framing
Half-tone process
  See Photoengraving—Halftone process
Half-track vehicles
  See Tracklaying vehicles
Half-way covenant
  See Covenants (Church polity)
Halfbeaks (QL638.H5)
Halftone process
  See Photoengraving—Halftone process
Halfway houses (Direct)
  xx Correctional institutions
      Health facilities
      Mental health services
      Rehabilitation centers
Halhaiin Gol, Battle of, 1939
  x Nomonhan Incident, 1939
  xx Russo-Japanese Border Conflicts,
      1932-1941
Halia language
  xx Melanesian languages
Halibut
  sa Atlantic halibut
      California halibut
      Pacific halibut
  xx Flatfishes
  — Diseases and pests
Halibut, Greenland
  See Greenland halibut
Halibut fisheries (Indirect) (SH351.H2)
  xx Atlantic halibut
      California halibut
      Fisheries
      Pacific halibut
Halides (QD165)
  sa Allyl halides
      Metal halides
      Molybdenum halides
      Transition metal halides
      Zinc halides
Halifax, N.S.
  — Explosion, 1917
  — — Juvenile literature
  — Riots, 1945
Halite
  See Salt
Ḥalitsah (BM720.H3)
  x Chaliza
  xx Levirate
      Marriage (Jewish law)
Hall effect (QC611)
  sa Hall generators
  xx Electric currents
      Electricity
      Galvanomagnetic effects
      Gyrators
Hall generators
  x Generators, Hall
  xx Hall effect
Hall-mark forgeries
  See Forgery of hall-marks
Hall-marks (NK7210)
  sa Clocks and watches
      Forgery of hall-marks
      Gold—Standards of fineness
      Goldsmithing
      Jewelry
      Pewter
      Plate
      Silver—Standards of fineness
      Silversmithing
  x Marks on plate
  xx Gold—Standards of fineness

Goldsmithing
Jewelry
Plate
Silver—Standards of fineness
Silversmithing
— Forgeries
    See Forgery of hall-marks
— Law and legislation (Direct)
Hallah
    xx Priests, Jewish
       Tithes (Jewish law)
       Tithes—Jews
Halley's comet (QB723.H2)
    Note under Comets
Halling (Dance) (GV1796.H2)
Hallow-Eve
    See Halloween
Halloween (GT4965)
    sa Jack-o-lanterns
     x All Hallows' Eve
       Hallow-Eve
    xx Folk-lore
       Manners and customs
    Example under Days
— Juvenile literature
Halloysite (Indirect)
Halls (Direct)
    sa Auditoriums
       Entrance halls
       Music-halls
       Theaters
Halls of residence
    See Dormitories
Hall's rifle
    xx Rifles
Hallstatt period (GN779-780)
    sa Mounds—Rhine Valley
    xx Iron age
       Man, Prehistoric
Hallucinations and illusions (BF1048-1063;
       Psychiatry and psychopathology,
       RC534; Psychology, BF491-3)
    sa Apparitions
       Conjuring
       Deathbed hallucinations
       Ghosts
       Impulse
       Insanity
       Maggid (Cabala)
       Magic
       Mirages
       Optical illusions
       Perception, Disorders of
       Personality, Disorders of
     x Delusions
       Illusions
    xx Apparitions
       Autism
       Ghosts
       Insanity
       Paranoia
       Perception, Disorders of
       Personality, Disorders of
       Psychical research
       Psychology, Pathological
       Subconsciousness
       Visions
Hallucinogenic drugs
    sa Ayahuasca
       Cannabis
     x Consciousness-expanding drugs
       Mind-distorting drugs
       Psychedelic drugs
       Psychotomimetic drugs
    xx Drug abuse
       Psychopharmacology

Hallucinogenic drugs and religious experience
       (BL65.D7)
     x Experience (Religion) and
       hallucinogenic drugs
    xx Medicine and religion
Hallux valgus
    See Toes—Abnormities and deformities
Halmaheran languages (PL7511.H3)
    xx Malay-Polynesian languages
Halo (Art)
    See Nimbus (Art)
Halo-blight (SB608.O2)
Halochromism (QD441)
Halogenation (QD281.H3)
Halogens (QD165)
    sa Astatine
       Bromine
       Carnallite
       Chlorine
       Fluorine
       Iodine
    xx Nonmetals
— Physiological effect
Halophytes
    xx Botany—Ecology
       Coastal flora
       Marshes, Tide
       Plant communities
Halos (Meteorology) (QC976.H1)
    xx Meteorological optics
Halothane (RD86.H3)
     x Fluothane
    xx Anesthetics
       Ethanes
Halukkah
    xx Jews in Palestine—Charities
Halvah
     x Halavah
    xx Confectionery
Ham (Food supply, TX373; Food values,
       TX556.H; Meat industry, TS1962)
    sa Cookery (Ham)
    xx Meat
       Pork
Hamadryas baboon
    xx Baboons
Hamartite
    See Bastnaesite
Hamburger
    See Cookery (Beef)
Hamburgs (Poultry) (SF489.H2)
Hamdanids (DS76)
    xx Muslims
Hameln
— Siege, 1633 (D267.H2)
    xx Thirty Years' War, 1618-1648
Hamesucken
    See Hamsocn
Hamfare
    See Hamsocn
Hamilton-Burr Duel
    See Burr-Hamilton Duel
Hamilton-Cayley theorem
    See Cayley-Hamilton theorem
Hamiltonian operator
     x Operator, Hamiltonian
    xx Differential operators
       Quantum theory
Hamites (Anthropology, GN545; Races,
       HT1581-9)
    sa Barundi
       Berbers
       Borani
       Cushites
       Masai
       Somalis
    xx Berbers
       Mediterranean race

Nilo-Hamitic tribes
Hamitic languages (PJ2301-2551)
    sa Agau language
       Berber languages
       Bilin language
       Cushitic languages
       Guanche language
       Hausa language
       Kunama language
       Nilo-Hamitic languages
       Nubian language
       Quara language
       Rif language
       Sidama language
       Siwa language
       Tamashek language
       Tamazight language
       Zenaga language
     x Languages, Hamitic
    xx Hamito-Semitic languages
Hamito-Semitic languages (PJ991-5)
    sa Hamitic languages
       Semitic languages
     x Semito-Hamitic languages
    xx Afroasiatic languages
Hammer throwing
    xx Weight throwing
Hammer toe
    See Hammertoe
Hammered stringed instruments
    See Stringed instruments
Hammers (TJ1201.H3; Power tool, TJ1305)
    xx Carpentry—Tools
       Metal-work
— Testing
Hammertoe
     x Hammer toe
    xx Toes—Abnormities and deformities
Hammett equation
     x Hammett rule
    xx Linear free energy relationship
Hammett rule
    See Hammett equation
Hammocks (Ethnology, GN415.H;
       Manufacture, TS1781)
Hammond electric organ
    See Hammond organ
Hammond organ (ML597)
     x Hammond electric organ
    xx Electronic organ
       Organ
Hammond organ music
    See Electronic organ music (Hammond
       registration)
Hammudidas
    See Hammudites
Hammudids
    See Hammudites
Hammūdīes
    See Hammudites
Hammudites
     x Hammudidas
       Hammudids
       Hammūdīes
    xx Arabs
       Berbers
       Caliphs
       Middle Ages—History
Hammudites in Spain, [etc.]
Hampshire sheep
    Example under Sheep breeds
Hampshire swine (SF393.H3)
Hampson liquefier (QD535)
Hampton, Va. National Cemetery
    Example under Cemeteries
Hampton Roads, Battle of, 1862 (E473.2)
— Juvenile literature

Hamsocn
"The right of security and privacy in a man's home."—Black, Law dictionary, 4th ed., 1951.
    sa Unlawful entry
    x Hamesucken
       Hamfare
       Hausfrieden
    xx Criminal law
       Privacy, Right of
       Unlawful entry
Hamsters
    x Golden hamster
       Syrian hamster
Hamsters as laboratory animals
    xx Laboratory animals
Hamsters as pets *(SF459.H3)*
Hamyaritic inscriptions
    See Inscriptions, Sabaean
Han dynasty
    See China—History—Han dynasty, 202 B.C.-220 A.D.
Hana
    See Hachi-ju-hachi (Game)
Hana-karuta
    See Hachi-ju-hachi (Game)
Hanafis
    xx Islamic law
       Islamic sects
       Sunnites
Hanbalites
    xx Islamic law
       Islamic sects
       Sunnites
Hand *(Anatomy, QM548; Art, NC774; Piano, MT221; Psychology, BF908-940)*
    sa Fingers
       Gesture
       Left- and right-handedness
       Palmistry
       Thumb
    x Paw
    xx Beauty, Personal
       Fingers
  — Abnormities and deformities *(QM691; Surgery, RD776)*
    sa Syndaktylia
  — Anatomy
  — Care and hygiene
  — Diseases *(RC951)*
    sa Hand—Radiography
  — Fracture
  — Juvenile literature
  — Photography
    See Photography of hands
  — Pictorial works
  — — Juvenile literature
  — Radiography
    xx Hand—Diseases
  — — Atlases
  — Surgery
  — — Juvenile literature
  — Wounds and injuries
Hand (in religion, folk-lore, etc.)
    x Folk-lore of hands
       Folk-lore of the hand
    xx Religion, Primitive
Hand-bags
    See Handbags
Hand bell ringing
    See Handbell ringing
Hand cars
    See Handcars
Hand-grenades
    See Grenades
Hand in art *(N8217.H3)*
    xx Art

Hand irons
    See Irons (Pressing)
Hand-organ
    See Barrel-organ
Hand planes
    See Planes (Hand tools)
Hand press
    See Handpress
Hand-printed Book Project *(Direct)*
    x HPB Project
       Project HPB
    xx Bibliography—Early printed books
       Bibliography, Universal
       Libraries—Automation
Hand-railing *(TH5675-7)*
    x Railing
    xx Carpentry
       Stair building
Hand shadows
    See Shadow-pictures
Hand spinning *(Direct) (TT847)*
    xx Arts and crafts movement
       Handicraft
       Spinning
Hand stamps
    sa Rubber stamps
    x Stamps, Hand
    xx Rubber stamps
Hand stamps (Philately)
    sa Maritime postal hand stamps
    xx Postage-stamps—Collectors and collecting
Hand test *(BF205.H3)*
    xx Personality tests
       Projective techniques
Hand-to-hand fighting *(GV1111-1141)*
    sa Self-defense
    x Fighting, Hand-to-hand
       Man-to-man combat
       Personal combat
    xx Combat
       Self-defense
Hand-to-hand fighting, Oriental
    sa Aikido
       Jiu-jitsu
       Judo
       Karate
       Kempo
       Kendo
    x Oriental hand-to-hand fighting
  — Biography
Hand washing
    xx Hygiene
Hand weaving *(Direct)*
    sa Palm frond weaving
       Reweaving
    x Weaving, Hand
    xx Arts and crafts movement
       Handicraft
       Weaving
  — Juvenile literature
  — Patterns
Handbags
    x Hand-bags
       Pocket-books
       Purses
    xx Clothing and dress
       Leather industry and trade
    Example under Leather goods
Handball *(GV1017.H2)*
    sa Paddleball
Handball, Field
    See Fieldball
Handbell and organ music *(M183-4)*
    x Organ and handbell music
Handbell and organ music, Arranged *(M185-6)*

Handbell music *(M147)*
    xx Handbell ringing
Handbell ringing *(MT710)*
    sa Handbell music
    x Bell ringing
       Hand bell ringing
    xx Bells
       Carillons
Handbells *(Direct)*
    xx Bells
Handbills, Advertising
    See Advertising fliers
Handbooks, vade-mecums, etc. *(AG103-191)*
    Here are entered works of general miscellaneous information: receipts, tables, etc.
    sa Receipts
       Technical manuals
       Text-books
       subdivision Handbooks, manuals, etc. *under subjects*
    x Pocket companions
       Vade-mecums, etc.
    xx Commonplace-books
       Encyclopedias and dictionaries
       Receipts
Handcars
    x Hand cars
       Railroads—Handcars
    xx Railroads—Cars
Handcarts
    x Pushcarts
    xx Carriages and carts
Hande-hui language
    See Ostiak language
Handedness
    See Left- and right-handedness
Handicapped *(Direct)*
    sa Camps for the handicapped
       Church work with the handicapped
       Delinquents
       Disability evaluation
       Invalids
       Mentally handicapped
       Physically handicapped
       Sick
       Socially handicapped
       Veterans, Disabled
       Wages—Handicapped
    x Defective and delinquent classes
       Defectives
       Disabled
    xx Invalids
  — Education *(Direct)*
  — Employment *(Direct)*
    sa Sheltered workshops
       Vocational rehabilitation
    xx Vocational rehabilitation
  — — Mathematical models
  — Housing *(Direct)*
    xx Housing
  — Law and legislation *(Direct)*
  — Means of communication
  — Personal narratives
  — Printing and writing systems
  — Psychology
    x Psychological aspects of disability
  — Recreation
    x Invalids—Recreation
  — Rehabilitation
    See Rehabilitation
       Vocational rehabilitation
  — Religious life
  — Research *(Direct)*
  — — Research grants *(Direct)*
Handicapped and architecture
    See Architecture and the handicapped

Handicapped and libraries
  See Libraries and the handicapped
Handicapped artists
  See Artists, Physically handicapped
Handicapped automobile drivers
  See Automobile drivers, Physically
    handicapped
Handicapped children (Direct)
  sa Aphasic children
    Brain-damaged children
    Mentally handicapped children
    Perceptually handicapped children
    Physical education for handicapped
      children
    Physically handicapped children
    Socially handicapped children
  x Abnormal children
    Children, Abnormal and backward
  xx Child study
    Exceptional children
— Care and treatment (Direct)
— Dental care (Direct)
— Education (Direct) (LC4001-4100)
    sa Teachers of handicapped children
— — Art, ₍etc.₎
— — Audio-visual aids (LC4023)
— — Music
— — Programmed instruction
— — Research (Direct)
    xx Educational research
— — Terminology
— Education (Preschool) (Direct)
      (LC4019.2)
— Family relationships
— Law and legislation (Direct)
    xx Children—Law
— Personal narratives
— Pictorial works
— Recreation
— Rehabilitation (Direct)
— Research (Direct)
— Testing
    sa Illinois test of psycholinguistic
      abilities
Handicapped children, Teachers of
  See Teachers of handicapped children
Handicapped motor bus drivers
  See Motor bus drivers, Physically
    handicapped
Handicapped motor-truck drivers
  See Motor-truck drivers, Physically
    handicapped
Handicapping
  See Horse race betting
Handicraft (Indirect) (TT; Artistic crafts,
    NK)
  sa Artisans
    Arts and crafts movement
    Balsa wood craft
    Bast work
    Bible crafts
    Bread dough craft
    Burlap craft
    Camps—Decoration
    Card weaving
    Collage
    Cork craft
    Cornhusk craft
    Creative activities and seat work
    Decorative balls
    Egg carton craft
    Egg decoration
    Eggshell craft
    Felt work
    Glass craft
    Hand spinning
    Hand weaving
    Hobbies

Indians of North America—Industries
    Industrial arts
    Jewelry making
    Leather work
    Manual training
    Models and modelmaking
    Occupational therapy
    Occupations
    Peanut craft
    Pine needle crafts
    Pipe cleaner craft
    Plastics craft
    Plywood craft
    Pottery craft
    Puppet making
    Raffia work
    Rock craft
    Rush-work
    Salesmen and salesmanship—Handicraft
    Shellcraft
    Sloyd
    Sprang
    Straw work
    String craft
    Toy making
    Wire craft
  x Crafts (Handicrafts)
  xx Arts and crafts movement
    Manual training
    Occupational therapy
    Occupations
    Sloyd
— Anecdotes, facetiae, satire, etc.
— Equipment and supplies
— — Juvenile literature
— Exhibitions
— Film catalogs
— Juvenile literature
— Pictorial works
— Research
— Study and teaching (Direct)
Handkerchiefs (Manufacture, TS1725; Trade,
    HD9930)
  xx Clothing and dress
    Costume
Handles
  x Grips (Machines, tools, etc.)
  xx Implements, utensils, etc.
    Machinery
    Tools
— Standards (Direct)
Handley Page 80 (Jet planes)
  See Victor (Jet planes)
Handley Page 115 (Jet planes)
  x H.P. 115 (Jet planes)
  xx Handley Page airplanes
    Jet planes
    Supersonic planes
Handley Page airplanes
  sa Handley Page 115 (Jet planes)
    Victor (Jet planes)
Handling, Remote (Radioactive substances)
  See Remote handling (Radioactive
    substances)
Handling of bulk solids
  See Bulk solids handling
Handling of cotton
  See Cotton handling
Handling of food
  See Food handling
Handling of materials
  See Materials handling
Handling of snakes (Holiness churches)
  See Snake cults (Holiness churches)
Handloading of ammunition (TS538.3)
  x Reloading of ammunition
  xx Ammunition
    Cartridges

Handloom industry (Direct)
  xx Textile industry and fabrics
Handpress (Z249)
  x Hand press
  xx Printing, Practical
    Printing-press
Hands, Imposition of
  See Imposition of hands
Hands, Laying on of
  See Imposition of hands
Handwriting
  See Autographs
    Graphology
    Paleography
    Penmanship
    Writing
Handyman's manuals
  See Repairing—Amateurs' manuals
Hangars (TL730)
  xx Airports—Buildings
Hanging (HV8579-8581)
  sa Gallows
  xx Capital punishment
    Executions and executioners
  Example under Punishment
Hanging in effigy
  See Executions in effigy
Hanging plants (SB432.5)
  sa Ornamental climbing plants
  x Plants, Hanging
    Trailing plants
  xx Container gardening
    House plants
    Ornamental climbing plants
    Plants, Ornamental
Hanging roofs
  See Roofs, Suspension
Hangnest
  See Orioles
Hangö, Battle of, 1714 (DL743.H)
  xx Northern War, 1700-1721
Hangö, Battle of, 1941
  xx World War, 1939-1945—Campaigns—
    Eastern
Hangover cures
  xx Alcohol—Physiological effect
    Drugs—Physiological effect
    Liquors
Hanha (Bantu tribe)
  See Hanya (Bantu tribe)
Haniwa (NB159.J)
Hanka, Battle of, 1936
  See Khanka, Battle of, 1936
Hankel functions (QA408)
  x Bessel functions (Third kind)
  xx Bessel functions
Hanover, Pa., Battle of, 1863 (E475.51)
Hanover, Treaty of, 1725 (D287.7)
  x Treaty of Hanover, 1725
Hanover horse
  See Hanoverian horse
Hanoverian horse (SF293.H35)
  x Hanover horse
Hanoverian mercenaries (DA500; DA503)
  xx German mercenaries
    Mercenary troops
Hans Christian Andersen Medal
Hansa towns
      Here are entered works dealing collec-
        tively with the towns which were at
        any time members of the Hanseatic
        League. Works relating to the league
        as such are entered under the heading
        Hanseatic League.
  Note under Hanseatic League
Hanseatic League (DD801.H17-25;
    Commerce, HF455-463)
  Cf. note under Hansa towns.

Hanseatic League *(DD801.H17-25;*
      Commerce, HF455-463)
        (Continued)
    xx Commerce
Hansen's disease
    See Leprosy
Hanswurst
    xx Fools and jesters
Hanukkah (Feast of Lights) *(BM695.H3)*
    sa Hanukkah lamp
    x Chanukah
      Dedication, Feast of
      Feast of Dedication
      Feast of Lights
      Feast of the Maccabees
      Festival of Hanukkah
      Lights, Feast of
      Maccabees, Feast of the
    xx Light and darkness (in religion,
        folk-lore, etc.)
  — Juvenile literature
  — Sermons
Hanukkah lamp *(BM657.H3)*
    xx Art, Jewish
      Candles and lights
      Cultus, Jewish
      Hanukkah (Feast of Lights)
      Jews—Antiquities
      Jews—Rites and ceremonies
      Menorah
      Symbolism
Hanunóo
    xx Ethnology—Philippine Islands
Hanunóo language
    xx Mangyan language
      Philippine languages
Hanya (Bantu tribe)
    x Hanha (Bantu tribe)
      Muhanha (Bantu tribe)
    xx Bantus
      Ethnology—Angola
Haploidy
    xx Chromosome numbers
Haplomycosis
    See Adiaspiromycosis
Happening (Art) *(Direct)*
    sa Street theater
    xx Art, Modern—20th century
      Pantomime
Happiness *(BJ1480-1486)*
    sa Cheerfulness
      Contentment
      Joy
      Pleasure
    x Gladness
    xx Cheerfulness
      Contentment
      Ethics
      Hedonism
      Joy
      Pleasure
  — Quotations, maxims, etc.
Happy Land (Buddhism)
    See Western Paradise (Buddhism)
Haptal
    See Ephthalites
Haptens
    xx Antigens and antibodies
Haptics
    See Touch
Hara-kiri
    See Seppuku
Harae (Shinto)
    See Harai (Shinto)
Harai (Shinto)
    x Harae (Shinto)
    xx Shinto-Rituals
Harakiri
    See Seppuku

Harappa culture
    See Indus civilization
Harari language *(PJ9293)*
    x Adari language
      Ararge language
      Harrarjie language
    xx Ethiopian languages
Hararis *(Tanganyika, DT443)*
Harauti language *(PK1921-4)*
    xx Rajasthani language
Harauti philology *(PK1921)*
    xx Hindi philology
Haraya dialect *(PL5701)*
    xx Bisaya language
      Philippine languages
Harbor defenses
    See Coast defenses
Harbor masters *(Direct)*
    xx Harbors
Harbor police *(Direct)*
    xx Harbors—Regulations
      Police
Harbor seal *(QL737.P64)*
    xx Seals (Animals)
Harbor sounds
    See Waterfront sounds
Harbors *(Indirect)* *(Engineering,*
    TC203-324; International law,
    JX4138; Transportation, HE551-560)
    sa Breakwaters
      Docks
      Dredging
      Fenders for docks, piers, etc.
      Fishing ports
      Free ports and zones
      Harbor masters
      Harbors of refuge
      Jetties
      Marinas
      Piers
      Pilots and pilotage
      Port districts
      Sand-bars
      Shore protection
      Wharves
      subdivision Harbor *under names of*
        cities, e.g. New York (City)—Harbor
    x Ports
    xx Channels (Hydraulic engineering)
      Civil engineering
      Commerce
      Communication and traffic
      Docks
      Engineering
      Hydraulic structures
      Hydrography
      Merchant marine
      Navigation
      Shore protection
      Terminals (Transportation)
      Transportation
  — Classification
  — Communication systems
    xx Telecommunication
  — Computer programs
  — Design and construction
  — — Cold weather conditions
  — Finance
    sa subdivision Harbor—Finance *under*
      names of cities
  — Hydrodynamics
    xx Hydrodynamics
  — Juvenile literature
  — Maintenance and repair *(TC205)*
  — — Costs *(TC209)*
  — Management
  — Port charges *(HE951-3)*

    sa subdivision Harbor—Port charges
      under names of cities
    x Port charges
    xx Fees, Administrative
      Free ports and zones
      Maritime law
      Shipping
      Tariff
      Tolls
  — Regulations *(HE951-3)*
    sa Harbor police
      subdivision Harbor—Regulations
      under names of cities
    x Port regulations
    xx Maritime law
      Pilots and pilotage
      Shipping
  — Safety measures
  — Safety regulations *(Direct)*
  — Sanitation
  — Terminology
  — Underdeveloped areas
    See Underdeveloped areas—Harbors
  — Views

GEOGRAPHIC SUBDIVISIONS

  — United States
    x United States—Harbors
Harbors in art
    xx Art
Harbors of refuge *(Indirect)* *(VK369-369.8)*
    Here are entered works on harbors prov-
      ided on stormy coasts for the shelter of
      vessels or small craft in distress or
      seeking safety from storms.
    x Ports of refuge
      Refuge harbors
    xx Anchorage
      Harbors
Hard-core unemployed *(Direct)*
    x Socially handicapped—Employment
    xx Labor supply
      Unemployed
Hard-facing *(TS227)*
    x Hard-surfacing
      Metals—Hard-facing
    xx Metals—Finishing
      Surface hardening
      Welding
  — Automation
Hard-of-hearing children
    See Children, Deaf
Hard-surfacing
    See Hard-facing
Hard woods
    See Hardwoods
Hardanger, Norway, in literature
Hardanger fiddle *(ML760)*
    x Hardangerfele
      Hardingfele
    xx Violin
Hardanger-fiddle music *(M59)*
Hardanger needlework *(TT787)*
    x Norwegian drawn-work
    xx Drawn-work
      Embroidery
      Needlework
Hardangerfele
    See Hardanger fiddle
Hardboard
    sa Particle board
    xx Fiberboard
Hardening, Strain
    See Strain hardening
Hardening, Surface
    See Surface hardening
Hardiness of plants
    See Plants—Hardiness

Hardingfele
  See Hardanger fiddle
Hardness *(Engineering tests, TA407)*
  sa Brinell test
    Microhardness
    Precipitation hardening
Hardness of heart
  x Obduracy
  xx Obstinacy
Hardware *(Direct)* *(Manufacture,*
    TS400-455; Trade, HD9745)
  sa Bolts and nuts
    Building fittings
    Cutlery
    Door fittings
    Files and rasps
    Knives
    Locks and keys
    Nails and spikes
    Saws
    Screws
    Strikes and lockouts—Hardware
      industry
    Tools
    Washers (for bolts and screws)
  xx Iron industry and trade
    Metal trade
  — Accounting *(HF5686.H3)*
  — Catalogs *(TS405)*
  — Credit guides *(HF5585.H3)*
  — Marketing
  — Specifications *(Direct)*
  — Standards *(Direct)*
  — Tables, etc. *(HF5716.H3)*
  — Trade-marks
Hardware industry workers *(Direct)*
Hardware stores *(Direct)*
  xx Retail trade
  — Accounting
  — Credit guides
  — Management
Hardwoods
  sa names of hardwoods, e.g. Walnut
  x Hard woods
  xx Forests and forestry
    Lumber
    Wood
  — Diseases and pests *(Indirect)*
    xx Trees—Diseases and pests
  — Labeling
    sa Mahogany—Labeling
    Example under Labels
Hardy herbaceous perennials
  See Perennials
Hardy spaces
  x Spaces, Hardy
  xx Functional analysis
    Functions of complex variables
Hare (Helicopters)
  See Mi-1 (Helicopters)
Hare and hounds *(Games, GV1063)*
  x Paper-chasing
Hare breeding *(SF454.2)*
  x Hares—Breeding
  xx Stock and stock-breeding
Hare Indians
  See Kawchottine Indians
Harelip *(RD524)*
  x Cleft lip
  xx Lips—Abnormities and deformities
    Surgery, Plastic
Harem *(Barbary States, DT192; Egypt,*
    DT70; Turkey, DR432, HQ1707;
    Women in the Orient, HQ1170)
  xx Polygamy
    Woman—History and condition of
      women

Hares *(Indirect)* *(QL737.R6; Breeding,*
    SF451-5; Hunting, SK341.H3)
  sa Belgian hare
    Coursing
    European hare
    Jack-rabbits
    Rabbits
  xx Jack-rabbits
    Rabbits
  — Breeding
    See Hare breeding
  — Diseases
  — Juvenile literature
Hares, Fossil *(QE882.R6)*
Hares (in religion, folk-lore, etc.) *(Folk-lore,*
    GR730.H; Religion, BL325.H)
  x Folk-lore of hares
    Folk-lore of rabbits
    Rabbits (in religion, folk-lore, etc.)
  xx Religion, Primitive
Hare's Hill, Va., Battle of, 1865
  See Stedman, Fort, Battle of, 1865
Hariani dialect
  See Bangaru dialect
Haridasas *(BL1245.V3)*
  xx Saints, Hindu
    Vaishnavism
    Vedanta
Harijans
  See Untouchables
Harlem, New York (City)
  — Riot, 1935
  — Riot, 1943
  — Riot, 1964
Harlem Heights, Battle of, 1776 *(E241.H2)*
  Example under Battles; *and under reference*
    from Wars
Harlequin *(PN1988.H3)*
  sa Pierrot
  xx Pantomime
    Puppets and puppet-plays
  — Art
Harley-Davidson motorcycle
Harmar's Expedition, 1790 *(E83.79)*
  xx Indians of North America—Wars—
    1790-1794
Harmonic analysis *(QA401-411)*
  sa Bessel functions
    Fourier series
    Fourier transformations
    Harmonic functions
    L1 algebras
    Lamé's functions
    Measure algebras
    Multipliers (Mathematical analysis)
    Spherical harmonics
    Time-series analysis
    Toroidal harmonics
  x Analysis (Mathematics)
    Functions, Potential
    Potential functions
  xx Banach algebras
    Bessel functions
    Calculus
    Fourier series
    Harmonic functions
    Mathematical analysis
    Mathematics
    Time-series analysis
Harmonic analysis (Music) *(MT50)*
  x Music—Harmonic analysis
  xx Harmony
    Music—Theory
Harmonic drives *(TJ202)*
  sa Splines
  x Harmonic speed changers
  xx Gearing, Planetary
    Power transmission

    Splines
Harmonic functions *(QA405)*
  sa Bessel functions
    Fourier series
    Functions, Spheroidal
    Harmonic analysis
    Lamé's functions
    Spherical harmonics
    Toroidal harmonics
  x Functions, Harmonic
    Laplace's equations
    Poisson's equations
    Subharmonic functions
  xx Bessel functions
    Differential equations, Partial
    Fourier series
    Harmonic analysis
    Lamé's functions
    Spherical harmonics
    Toroidal harmonics
  — Problems, exercises, etc.
Harmonic motion
  xx Motion
Harmonic speed changers
  See Harmonic drives
Harmonica, Glass
  See Glass harmonica
Harmonica, Mouth
  See Mouth-organ
Harmonicon, Chemical
  See Pyrophone
Harmonists
  x Rappists
  xx Collective settlements
    Communism
Harmonium
  See Reed-organ
Harmonium, Bichromatic
  See Bichromatic harmonium
Harmonized chant
  See Chants (Anglican)
Harmonometer (Mechanical musical
    instrument)
Harmony *(Acoustics, ML3815; Aesthetics,*
    ML3852; History, ML444;
    Instruction, MT50; Psychology,
    ML3836)
  sa Cadence (Music)
    Chromatic alteration (Music)
    Harmonic analysis (Music)
    Melody
    Modulation (Music)
    Musical intervals and scales
    Organ-point
    Solmization
    Suspension (Music)
    Symmetrical inversion (Music)
    Thorough bass
    Tonality
    Twelve-tone system
  xx Composition (Music)
    Music
    Music—Instruction and study
    Music—Theory
    Thorough bass
    Tonality
  — Mechanical aids *(MT50)*
    x Chromophone
  — Programmed instruction *(MT50)*
Harmony, Keyboard *(MT224)*
  x Keyboard harmony
  xx Improvisation (Music)
    Piano—Instruction and study
Harmony (Aesthetics) *(BH301.H3)*
  xx Aesthetics
    Music
    Music—Philosophy and aesthetics

Harmony (Aesthetics) as a theme in literature
  See Harmony (Aesthetics) in literature
Harmony (Aesthetics) in literature
  x Harmony (Aesthetics) as a theme in
      literature
Harmony (Cosmology)
  See Harmony of the spheres
Harmony of the spheres *(BD645)*
  x Cosmic harmony
      Harmony (Cosmology)
      Music of the spheres
  xx Cosmology
Harness *(Farm implements, S720-721;
      Manners and customs, GT5888)*
  sa Bridle
      Check-rein
      Curb-bit
      Hackamore
      Horse brasses
      Yokes
  xx Horses
      Saddlery
  — Repairing *(TS1032)*
Harness making and trade *(Direct)*
      *(Manufacture, TS1030-1035; Trade,
      HD9780)*
  sa Trade-unions—Harness making and
      trade
  xx Leather industry and trade
      Saddlery
Harness racehorses *(Indirect) (SF343)*
  sa *names of individual racehorses*
  x Pacers and trotters
      Trotters and pacers
  xx Harness racing
      Race horses
  — Training *(SF341)*
      xx Racehorse training
Harness racing *(Indirect)*
  sa Harness racehorses
  x Sulky racing
      Trotting-races
  xx Horse-racing
Harp *(History and construction, ML1005-6)*
  sa Aeolian harp
      Harp-lute guitar
      Kantele (Musical instrument)
      Kokle
  x Irish harp
  Example under Stringed instruments
  — Instruction and study *(MT540-548)*
      sa Harp music—Teaching pieces
  — Orchestra studies *(MT546)*
      xx Harp—Studies and exercises
  — Studies and exercises
      sa Harp—Orchestra studies
Harp and clarinet music
  See Clarinet and harp music
Harp and clarinet with string orchestra
  See Clarinet and harp with string orchestra
Harp and English horn music
  See English horn and harp music
Harp and flute music
  See Flute and harp music
Harp and flute with string orchestra
  See Flute and harp with string orchestra
Harp and harpsichord music *(M282.H37;
      M283.H37)*
  x Harpsichord and harp music
Harp and lute music *(M292-3)*
  sa Concertos (Harp and lute)
      Harp and lute with orchestra
  x Lute and harp music
Harp and lute with orchestra *(M1040-1041)*
  sa Concertos (Harp and lute)
  xx Concertos (Harp and lute)
      Harp and lute music

Harp and oboe music
  See Oboe and harp music
Harp and organ music *(M182-4)*
  sa Harp and organ with string orchestra
  x Organ and harp music
Harp and organ with string orchestra
      (M1105-6)
  sa Concertos (Harp and organ with string
      orchestra)
  xx Concertos (Harp and organ with string
      orchestra)
      Harp and organ music
      String-orchestra music
Harp and percussion music *(M298)*
  sa Concertos (Harp and percussion with
      string orchestra)
      Harp and percussion with string
      orchestra
  x Percussion and harp music
Harp and percussion with string orchestra
      (M1105-6)
  sa Concertos (Harp and percussion with
      string orchestra)
  xx Concertos (Harp and percussion with
      string orchestra)
      Harp and percussion music
      String-orchestra music
  — Scores *(M1105)*
Harp and piano music *(M272-3)*
  sa Concertos (Harp and piano)
      Harp and piano with orchestra
      Sonatas (Harp and piano)
      Variations (Harp and piano)
  x Piano and harp music
Harp and piano music, Arranged *(M272-3)*
  sa Concertos (Harp)—Solo with piano
      Concertos (Harp with string orchestra),
      Arranged—Solo with piano
      Harp with orchestra—Solo with piano
      Harp with string orchestra—Solo with
      piano
Harp and piano with orchestra
      (M1040-1041)
  sa Concertos (Harp and piano)
  xx Concertos (Harp and piano)
      Harp and piano music
Harp and viola music *(M294-5)*
  sa Concertos (Harp and viola with string
      orchestra)
      Harp and viola with string orchestra
  x Viola and harp music
Harp and viola with string orchestra
      (M1105-6)
  sa Concertos (Harp and viola with string
      orchestra)
  xx Concertos (Harp and viola with string
      orchestra)
      Harp and viola music
      String-orchestra music
  — Solos with piano *(M1106)*
      xx Trios (Piano, harp, viola), Arranged
Harp and violin music
  See Violin and harp music
Harp and violoncello music
  See Violoncello and harp music
Harp, harpsichord, piano with string orchestra
      (M1105-6)
  sa Concertos (Harp, harpsichord, piano
      with string orchestra)
  xx Concertos (Harp, harpsichord, piano
      with string orchestra)
      String-orchestra music
      Trios (Harp, harpsichord, piano)
Harp-lute guitar *(ML1015-1018)*
  x Guitar, Harp-lute
  xx Guitar
      Harp
      Lute

Harp-lute guitar and piano music *(M282-3)*
  x Piano and harp-lute guitar music
Harp-lute guitar music *(M142.H2)*
  sa Suites (Harp-lute guitar)
Harp music *(M115-117)*
  sa Chaconnes (Harp)
      Concertos (Harp)
      Concertos (Harp with chamber
      orchestra)
      Concertos (Harp with instr. ensemble)
      Concertos (Harp with string orchestra)
      Harp with chamber orchestra
      Harp with instr. ensemble
      Harp with orchestra
      Harp with string orchestra
      Marches (Harp)
      Potpourris (Harp)
      Sonatas (Harp)
      Suites (Harp)
      Variations (Harp)
      Waltzes (Harp)
      Quartets, ₍Trios, etc.₎ *followed by
      specifications which include the harp*
  — Bibliography *(ML128.H3)*
  — — Graded lists *(ML132.H3)*
      x Harp music—Graded lists
  — Graded lists
      See Harp music—Bibliography—
          Graded lists
  — Teaching pieces *(MT545)*
      xx Harp—Instruction and study
Harp music, Arranged *(M118-119)*
Harp music (Harps (2)) *(M292-3)*
  sa Concertos (Harps (2))
      Concertos (Harps (2) with string
      orchestra
      Harps (2) with orchestra
      Harps (2) with string orchestra
      Sonatas (Harps (2))
      Suites (Harps (2))
Harp music (Harps (2)), Arranged *(M292-3)*
Harp music (Harps (4))
  See Quartets (Harps (4))
Harp seal
  xx Seals (Animals)
Harp, violin, violoncello with orchestra
      (M1040-1041)
  sa Concertos (Harp, violin, violoncello)
  xx Concertos (Harp, violin, violoncello)
      Orchestral music
      Trios (Harp, violin, violoncello)
  — Scores *(M1040)*
Harp with chamber orchestra *(M1036-7)*
  sa Concertos (Harp with chamber
      orchestra)
      Suites (Harp with chamber orchestra)
      Variations (Harp with chamber
      orchestra)
  xx Chamber-orchestra music
      Concertos (Harp with chamber
      orchestra)
      Harp music
Harp with chamber orchestra, Arranged
      (M1036-7)
  — Scores *(M1036)*
Harp with instr. ensemble
  sa Concertos (Harp with instr. ensemble)
  xx Concertos (Harp with instr. ensemble)
      Harp music
      Instrumental ensembles
Harp with orchestra *(M1036-7)*
  sa Concertos (Harp)
      Suites (Harp with orchestra)
      Variations (Harp with orchestra)
  xx Concertos (Harp)
      Harp music
      Orchestral music
  — Solo with piano *(M1037)*

xx Harp and piano music, Arranged

Harp with string orchestra *(M1105-6)*
  sa Concertos (Harp with string orchestra)
    Ländler (Harp with string orchestra)
  xx Concertos (Harp with string orchestra)
    Harp music
    String-orchestra music
  — Solo with piano *(M1106)*
    xx Harp and piano music, Arranged

Harp with string orchestra, Arranged
  (M1105-6)
  — Scores

Harpers Ferry, W.Va.
  — John Brown Raid, 1859 *(E451)*
    x John Brown Raid, 1859
  — — Juvenile literature
  — — Sources

Harpists *(Biography: collective, ML399; individual, ML419)*

Harpoons *(SH387; Primitive, GN447.H29)*
  xx Fishing, Primitive
    Indians of North America—Implements

Harps (2) with orchestra *(M1036-7)*
  sa Concertos (Harps (2))
  xx Concertos (Harps (2))
    Harp music (Harps (2))
    Orchestral music

Harps (2) with string orchestra *(M1105-6)*
  sa Concertos (Harps (2) with string orchestra)
    Suites (Harps (2) with string orchestra)
  xx Concertos (Harps (2) with string orchestra)
    Harp music (Harps (2))
    String-orchestra music

Harpsichord *(History and construction, ML650-697)*
  sa Claviorganum
    Keyboards
    Piano
  x Cembalo
    Clavecin
    Clavicembalo
    Spinet
    Virginal
  xx Piano
  Example under Musical instruments

Harpsichord, Electronic
  See Electronic harpsichord
Harpsichord and bassoon music
  See Bassoon and harpsichord music
Harpsichord and celesta music
  See Celesta and harpsichord music
Harpsichord and English horn music
  See English horn and harpsichord music
Harpsichord and flute music
  See Flute and harpsichord music
Harpsichord and guitar music
  See Guitar and harpsichord music
Harpsichord and harp music
  See Harp and harpsichord music
Harpsichord and lute music
  See Lute and harpsichord music
Harpsichord and mandolin music
  See Mandolin and harpsichord music
Harpsichord and mouth-organ music
  See Mouth-organ and harpsichord music
Harpsichord and oboe d'amore music
  See Oboe d'amore and harpsichord music
Harpsichord and oboe music
  See Oboe and harpsichord music

Harpsichord and organ music *(M182-4)*
  x Organ and harpsichord music

Harpsichord and organ music, Arranged
  (M185-6)

Harpsichord and piano music *(M214)*
  sa Concertos (Harpsichord and piano)

Concertos (Harpsichord and piano with dance orchestra)
  Harpsichord and piano with dance orchestra
  Harpsichord and piano with orchestra
  Harpsichord and piano with wind ensembles
  x Piano and harpsichord music

Harpsichord and piano with dance orchestra
  (M1353)
  sa Concertos (Harpsichord and piano with dance orchestra)
  xx Concertos (Harpsichord and piano with dance orchestra)
    Dance-orchestra music
    Harpsichord and piano music

Harpsichord and piano with orchestra
  (M1010-1011)
  sa Concertos (Harpsichord and piano)
  xx Concertos (Harpsichord and piano)
    Harpsichord and piano music
    Orchestral music

Harpsichord and piano with wind ensemble
  (M915-917)
  xx Harpsichord and piano music
    Wind ensembles

Harpsichord and recorder music
  See Recorder and harpsichord music
Harpsichord and trumpet music
  See Trumpet and harpsichord music
Harpsichord and viola da gamba music
  See Viola da gamba and harpsichord music
Harpsichord and viola d'amore music
  See Viola d'amore and harpsichord music
Harpsichord and viola music
  See Viola and harpsichord music
Harpsichord and viola pomposa music
  See Viola pomposa and harpsichord music
Harpsichord and violin music
  See Violin and harpsichord music
Harpsichord and violoncello music
  See Violoncello and harpsichord music

Harpsichord, flute, harp with string orchestra
  (M1105-6)
  sa Concertos (Harpsichord, flute, harp with string orchestra)
    Suites (Harpsichord, flute, harp with string orchestra)
  xx Concertos (Harpsichord, flute, harp with string orchestra)
    String-orchestra music
    Trios (Harpsichord, flute, harp)

Harpsichord, flute, oboe with string orchestra
  (M1105-6)
  sa Concertos (Harpsichord, flute, oboe with string orchestra)
  xx Concertos (Harpsichord, flute, oboe with string orchestra)
    String-orchestra music
    Trios (Harpsichord, flute, oboe)
  — Scores *(M1105-6)*

Harpsichord, flute, violin with string orchestra
  (M1105-6)
  sa Concertos (Harpsichord, flute, violin with string orchestra)
  xx Concertos (Harpsichord, flute, violin with string orchestra)
    String-orchestra music
    Trios (Harpsichord, flute, violin)

Harpsichord, flutes (2) with string orchestra
  (M1105-6)
  sa Concertos (Harpsichord, flutes (2) with string orchestra)
  x Two flutes, harpsichord with string orchestra
  xx Concertos (Harpsichord, flutes (2) with string orchestra)
    String-orchestra music

Trios (Harpsichord, flutes (2))

Harpsichord makers *(ML651)*
  xx Musical instruments—Makers
  — Biography

Harpsichord music *(M20-39)*
  sa Bourrées (Harpsichord)
    Canons, fugues, etc. (Harpsichord)
    Canons, fugues, etc. (Harpsichords (2))
    Chaconnes (Harpsichord)
    Chorale preludes (Harpsichord)
    Claviorganum music
    Concertos (Harpsichord)
    Concertos (Harpsichord with chamber orchestra)
    Concertos (Harpsichord with instrumental ensemble)
    Concertos (Harpsichord with string orchestra)
    Country-dances (Harpsichord)
    Harpsichord with chamber orchestra
    Harpsichord with instr. ensemble
    Harpsichord with orchestra
    Harpsichord with percussion ensemble
    Harpsichord with string ensemble
    Harpsichord with string orchestra
    Minuets (Harpsichord)
    Polonaises (Harpsichord)
    Rondos (Harpsichord)
    Sonatas (Harpsichord)
    Suites (Harpsichord)
    Thorough bass—Realizations
    Variations (Harpsichord)
    Quartets, ⌈Trios, etc.⌉ *followed by specifications which include the harpsichord*
  x Virginal music
  xx Piano music
  — To 1800
    sa In nomine (Music)

GENERAL SUBDIVISIONS

  — History and criticism *(ML700-742)*
  — Instructive editions *(MT245-7)*
    xx Piano music—Instructive editions

Harpsichord music, Arranged
  sa Chaconnes (Harpsichord), Arranged
  xx Overtures arranged for harpsichord
Harpsichord music, Arranged (Jazz)
  See Harpsichord music (Jazz)

Harpsichord music (4 hands) *(M200-204; M207-212)*

Harpsichord music (Harpsichords (2)) *(M214)*
  sa Concertos (Harpsichords (2))
    Concertos (Harpsichords (2) with string orchestra)
    Harpsichords (2) with orchestra
    Harpsichords (2) with string orchestra
    Sonatas (Harpsichords (2))
    Suites (Harpsichords (2))

Harpsichord music (Harpsichords (2)), Arranged *(M215)*

Harpsichord music (Harpsichords (3)) *(M216)*
  sa Concertos (Harpsichords (3) with string orchestra
    Harpsichord trios (Harpsichords (3))
    Harpsichords (3) with string orchestra

Harpsichord music (Harpsichords (4)) *(M216)*
  sa Concertos (Harpsichords (4))
    Concertos (Harpsichords (4) with string orchestra
    Harpsichords (4) with orchestra
    Harpsichords (4) with string orchestra
    Variations (Harpsichords (4))
  x Harpsichord quartets (Harpsichords (4))

Harpsichord music (Jazz) *(M20-32)*
  x Harpsichord music, Arranged (Jazz)
Harpsichord, piano, violin with orchestra
    (M1040-1041)
  sa Concertos (Harpsichord, piano, violin)
  xx Concertos (Harpsichord, piano, violin)
Harpsichord quartets (Harpsichords (4))
  See Harpsichord music (Harpsichords (4))
Harpsichord realizations of thorough bass
  See Thorough bass—Realizations
Harpsichord trios (Harpsichords (3))
  See Harpsichord music (Harpsichords (3))
Harpsichord with chamber orchestra
    (M1010-1011)
  sa Concertos (Harpsichord with chamber
    orchestra)
  xx Chamber-orchestra music
    Concertos (Harpsichord with chamber
    orchestra)
    Harpsichord music
Harpsichord with instr. ensemble
  sa Concertos (Harpsichord with
    instrumental ensemble)
  xx Concertos (Harpsichord with
    instrumental ensemble)
    Harpsichord music
    Instrumental ensembles
Harpsichord with orchestra *(M1010-1011)*
  sa Concertos (Harpsichord)
    Sarabands (Harpsichord with orchestra)
  xx Concertos (Harpsichord)
    Harpsichord music
    Orchestral music
Harpsichord with percussion ensemble
  xx Harpsichord music
    Percussion ensembles
Harpsichord with string ensemble
    (M910-912)
  xx Harpsichord music
    String ensembles
Harpsichord with string orchestra *(M1105-6)*
  sa Concertos (Harpsichord with string
    orchestra)
  xx Concertos (Harpsichord with string
    orchestra)
    Harpsichord music
    String-orchestra music
  — Scores *(M1105)*
Harpsichords (2) with orchestra
    (M1010-1011)
  sa Concertos (Harpsichords (2))
  x Two harpsichords with orchestra
  xx Concertos (Harpsichords (2))
    Harpsichord music (Harpsichords (2))
    Orchestral music
Harpsichords (2) with string orchestra
    (M1105-6)
  sa Concertos (Harpsichords (2) with string
    orchestra)
  x Two harpsichords with string orchestra
  xx Concertos (Harpsichords (2) with string
    orchestra)
    Harpsichord music (Harpsichords (2))
    String-orchestra music
Harpsichords (3) with string orchestra
    (M1105-6)
  sa Concertos (Harpsichords (3) with string
    orchestra)
  x Three harpsichords with string
    orchestra
  xx Concertos (Harpsichords (3) with string
    orchestra)
    Harpsichord music (Harpsichords (3))
    String-orchestra music
Harpsichords (4) with orchestra
    (M1010-1011)
  sa Concertos (Harpsichords (4))
  x Four harpsichords with orchestra

  xx Concertos (Harpsichords (4))
    Harpsichord music (Harpsichords (4))
    Orchestral music
Harpsichords (4) with string orchestra
    (M1105-6)
  sa Concertos (Harpsichords (4) with string
    orchestra)
  x Four harpsichords with string orchestra
  xx Concertos (Harpsichords (4) with string
    orchestra)
    Harpsichord music (Harpsichords (4))
    String-orchestra music
Harranians *(BL1635)*
  x Sabians
Harrarjie language
  See Harari language
Harriers *(QL696.A2)*
  xx Birds of prey
Harrisburg, Pa.
  — Flood, 1972
    xx Pennsylvania—Hurricane, 1972
  — — Pictorial works
Harrisburg Insurrection, 1838
  See Buckshot War, 1838
Harrisburg Seven (Trial) *(KF224.H27)*
Harrison, Fort, Battle of, 1812 *(E356.H3)*
  xx Indians of North America—Wars—
    1812-1815
Harrison, Fort, Capture of, 1864 *(E477.21)*
Harrower psychodiagnostic inkblot test
    (BF698.8.H35)
  x Inkblot test, Harrower psychodiagnostic
  xx Personality tests
Harrows *(Mechanical engineering and*
    machinery, TJ1482)
  xx Agricultural machinery
Hartree approximation
  See Hartree-Fock approximation
Hartree-Fock approximation *(QC176.8.E4)*
  x Hartree approximation
    Hartree-Fock-Slater approximation
  xx Approximation theory
    Atoms
    Energy-band theory of solids
    Problem of many bodies
  — Tables, etc.
Hartree-Fock-Slater approximation
  See Hartree-Fock approximation
Harvard (Training planes)
  See T-6 (Training planes)
Harvard University. Arnold Arboretum
Example under Arboretums
Harvard University
  — Administration
    Example under Universities and colleges
    —Administration
  — Alumni
  — Anniversaries, etc.
    Example under Anniversaries
  — Athletics
    Example under College sports
  — Basketball
    Example under Basketball
  — Biography
  — Buildings
  — Curricula
  — Degrees
    Example under Degrees, Academic
  — Description
  — — Aerial
  — — Guide-books
  — — Views
  — Dissertations
    Example under Dissertations, Academic
  — Employees
  — — Political activity
  — Endowments
  — Entrance requirements

    Example under references from College
    entrance requirements; Entrance
    requirements
  — Examinations
    Note under Examinations
  — — Mathematics
    Note under Examinations
  — Faculty
  — Finance
  — Football
  — Freshmen
  — Funds and scholarships
    Example under Scholarships; Student
    loan funds
  — Graduate students
  — Graduate work
    Example under Universities and colleges
    —Graduate work
  — Heraldry
  — History
  — — Revolution, 1775-1783
  — — Civil War, 1861-1865
  — Orchestras and bands
  — Poetry
  — Portraits
  — Prizes
  — Public relations
    x Public relations—Harvard University
    Example under Public relations—Schools
  — Registers
  — Religion
    Example under Universities and colleges
    —Religion
  — Riot, April 9, 1969
  — Sanitary affairs
  — Songs and music
    Example under Music in universities and
    colleges; Songs
  — Statistics
    Note under Educational statistics
  — Students
    Example under Students
  — Track-athletics
Harvard University in literature
Harvest festivals *(Direct)* *(GT4380-4499)*
  sa Sukkoth
    Thanksgiving Day
  xx Festivals
Harvesters
  See Harvesting machinery
Harvesting *(Indirect)* *(Agriculture, SB129;*
    Manners and customs,
    GT4380-4499)
  sa Folk-lore of agriculture
    Gleaning
    subdivision Harvesting *under names of*
    specific crops, e.g. Maize—
    Harvesting
  xx Manners and customs
  — Labor productivity
Harvesting machinery *(Indirect)* *(S695-7;*
    Industry, HD9486)
  To cover harvesting machines in general
    and machines for cutting grain in par-
    ticular.
  sa Combines (Agricultural machinery)
    Corn picking machinery
    Cotton-picking machinery
    Forage harvesting machinery
    Haying equipment
    Mowing-machines
    Potato harvesting machinery
    Scythes
    Sickles
    Sugar-cane harvesting machinery
  x Harvesters
    Reapers
  xx Agricultural machinery

Mowing-machines
— Maintenance and repair
— Standards
Harvesting time *(Indirect)*
  xx Field crops
Harz cattle
Hasang Incident, 1938
  See Changkufeng Incident, 1938
Hasheesh
  See Hashish
Hashemites
  See Hashimites
Hashimites
  x Banū Hāshīm
    Hashemites
  xx Arabs
Hashish *(Intoxications, RC568.C2; Materia medica, RS165.H3)*
  x Dagga
    Hasheesh
    Hemp, Indian
  xx Cannabis
    Narcotics
Ḥashwiya
  xx Islamic sects
Hasidic parables
  See Parables, Hasidic
Hasidism *(Direct)* *(BM198)*
  sa Bratslav Hasidim
    Habad
    Parables, Hasidic
    Satmar Hasidim
    Zaddikim
  x Chasidism
  xx Jewish sects
  Note under Judaism
— Apologetic works
— Controversial literature
— Philosophy
  xx Philosophy, Jewish
— Pictorial works
Hasinai Indians
  xx Caddo Indians
    Indians of North America
Haskalah *(Direct)*
  xx Enlightenment
    Judaism
    Liberalism (Religion)
    Reform Judaism
Haskamah
  See Approbations (Hebrew literature)
Hasmonaeans
  See Maccabees
Hasselblad camera
Hasskama
  See Approbations (Hebrew literature)
Hasta (Unit of measure)
  See Cubit
Hastings, Battle of, 1066 *(DA196)*
— Juvenile literature
Hastings embroidery
  xx Embroidery, English
Hat trade *(Direct)* *(HD9948)*
  sa Trade-unions—Hat trade
    Wages—Hat trade
Hatboxes
  sa Bandboxes
  xx Bandboxes
    Boxes
    Hats
Hatch covers
  xx Ships—Equipment and supplies
Hatch davits
  See Davits
Hatchability of eggs
  See Eggs—Hatchability
Hatchettin *(QE391.H)*

Hatching of eggs
  See Eggs—Incubation
Hatchments
  sa Achievements (Heraldry)
  xx Achievements (Heraldry)
    Heraldry
Hate *(BF575.H)*
  xx Emotions
Hath (Unit of measure)
  See Cubit
Haṭha yoga
  See Yoga, Haṭha
Hatigorria language
  See Ao language
Hats *(Manners and customs, GT2110; Manufacture, TS2180-2193)*
  sa Hatboxes
    Hatter's fur
    Millinery
    Safety hats
    Straw industries
  xx Clothing and dress
    Head-gear
    Millinery
  Example under Men's clothing
— Juvenile literature
Hatsang Incident, 1938
  See Changkufeng Incident, 1938
Hatteras Indians
  See Lumbee Indians
Hatters *(Direct)*
  sa Trade-unions—Hat trade
Hatter's fur
  x Hatter's plush
  xx Felt
    Fur
    Hats
Hatter's plush
  See Hatter's fur
Hauling tests *(TE450)*
Haunted houses
  See Ghosts
Hausa folk-lore
  See Folk-lore, Hausa
Hausa language *(PL8231-4)*
  sa Angas language
    Uwana language
  xx Angas language
    Chadic languages
    Hamitic languages
Hausa literature *(Direct)* *(PL8433.5-8434)*
Hausas *(DT518.H3; GN653)*
  sa Gobir
    Mawri (African people)
  x Haussas
— Religion *(BL2480.H3)*
  sa Bori (Cult)
Hausdorff measures
  xx Measure theory
Hausfrieden
  See Hamsocn
Hausfriedensbruch
  See Unlawful entry
Haussas
  See Hausas
Haustorium
  xx Parasitic plants
Haute Alsace, Battle of, 58 B.C.
  xx Gaul—History—58 B.C.-511 A.D.
Havana
— Siege, 1762 *(F1781)*
— Stables
  Example under Stables
Havasupai Indians *(E99.H3)*
  x Supai Indians
  xx Indians of North America
— Religion and mythology

Havasupai language *(PM1311)*
  xx Yuman languages
Haviland china
  xx Porcelain
Havoc bomber
  See A-20 bomber
Havsfjord, Battle of, 872 *(DL464)*
Hawaii
— History *(DU620-629)*
— — To 1893 *(DU627)*
— — Revolution of 1893
— Juvenile literature
— Tidal wave, 1946
  Example under Tidal waves
Hawaii in literature
Hawaiian beet web-worm *(SB608.B4)*
Hawaiian guitar *(ML1015)*
  x Guitar, Hawaiian
  xx Guitar
— Instruction and study *(MT590)*
  sa Hawaiian-guitar music—Teaching pieces
Hawaiian-guitar band
  See Plectral ensembles
Hawaiian-guitar music *(M142.H3)*
  sa Plectral ensembles
  xx Guitar music
— Teaching pieces *(MT590.5)*
  xx Hawaiian guitar—Instruction and study
Hawaiian imprints *(Direct)*
Hawaiian language *(PL6441-9)*
  sa Polynesian languages
  xx Polynesian languages
Hawaiian literature *(Direct)*
  xx United States—Literatures
Hawaiian newspapers *(PN5621-9)*
Hawaiian poetry *(PL6448.5)*
Hawaiian rat
  xx Rats
Hawaiians
  x Owyhees
  xx Ethnology—Hawaii
    Polynesians
— Anthropometry
Hawaiians in the Pacific Northwest, [etc.]
Hawk (Missile)
  xx Surface-to-air missiles
Hawken rifle
  xx Rifles
Hawker airplanes *(TL686.H32)*
Hawker Hunter (Turbojet fighter planes)
  See Hunter (Turbojet fighter planes)
Hawkers and hawking
  See Peddlers and peddling
Hawking
  See Falconry
Hawks *(QL696.A2)*
  sa Goshawk
    Red-tailed hawk
  x Sparrow-hawks
  xx Birds of prey
— Behavior
— Juvenile literature
Hawthorn (in religion, folk-lore, etc.) *(BL457. H3)*
  xx Folk-lore of trees
    Religion, Primitive
Hay *(Indirect)* *(SB198)*
  sa Grasses
    Haying equipment
    Pelleted hay
    Stacks (Hay, grain, etc.)
    names of hay crops, e.g. Alfalfa, Clover
  xx Forage plants
    Grasses
  Example under Field crops
— Drying

Hay *(Indirect)* *(SB198)*
— Drying *(Continued)*
    x Grasses—Drying
— Grading
— Handling
— Harvesting
— — Labor productivity
— Storage
— Terminology
Hay as feed
Hay as food
    xx Food
Hay-boxes
    See Fireless cookers
Hay-fever *(RC743)*
    sa Hay-fever plants
    x Autumnal catarrh
    Catarrh, Autumnal
    Rose-cold
— Homeopathic treatment *(RX326.H3)*
Hay-fever plants *(Indirect)* *(QK100)*
    xx Botany, Medical
    Hay-fever
    Poisonous plants
Hay making equipment
    See Haying equipment
Hay-Pauncefote treaty, 1901 *(JX1398.7)*
Hay trade *(Direct)* *(HD9030-9049)*
— Tables and ready-reckoners
    (HF5716.H4)
Haya (African tribe)
    x Bahaya
    xx Bantus
    Ethnology—Tanganyika
Haya language
    See Ziba language
Haya law
    See Law, Haya
Hayabusa (Fighter planes)
    x Nakajima Ki 43 (Fighter planes)
    xx Fighter planes
Hayagrīva
    xx Buddha and Buddhism
    Horses (in religion, folk-lore, etc.)
    Mythology, Chinese
Hayasa language
    See Khayasa language
Hayate (Fighter planes) *(TL685.3)*
    x Frank (Fighter planes)
    Ki 84 (Fighter planes)
    Nakajima Hayate (Fighter planes)
    Nakajima Ki 84 (Fighter planes)
    xx Fighter planes
Haydamaks
    See Haidamaks
Haying equipment
    x Hay making equipment
    xx Farm equipment
    Harvesting machinery
    Hay
Haymarket Square Riot, 1886
    See Chicago—Haymarket Square Riot, 1886
Haynes automobile
Hayu dialect *(PL3801.V2)*
    sa Tibeto-Burman languages
    Vayu dialect
Ḥazakah
    xx Jewish law
    Possession (Jewish law)
    Presumptions (Jewish law)
Hazan Incident, 1938
    See Changkufeng Incident, 1938
Ḥazanim
    See Cantors, Jewish
Hazara language *(PK6996.H3)*
    x Khazara language
    Khezare language
    xx Iranian languages

Persian language
Hazāras
    xx Ethnology—Afghanistan
    Mongols
Hazardous geographic enviornments *(Direct)*
    (GF85)
    sa Disasters
    x Environments, Hazardous geographic
    xx Disasters
    Human ecology
Hazardous goods
    See Hazardous substances
Hazardous materials
    See Hazardous substances
Hazardous substances *(T55.H3)*
    sa Chemicals—Safety measures
    Explosives—Safety measures
    Gases, Asphyxiating and poisonous
    Inflammable materials
    Poisons
    Radioactivity—Safety measures
    x Dangerous goods
    Dangerous materials
    Hazardous goods
    Hazardous materials
    Toxic and inflammable goods
    xx Industrial safety
    Materials
— Labeling *(Direct)*
— Packaging
— — Law and legislation *(Direct)*
— Standards *(Direct)*
— Transportation
— — Law and legislation *(Direct)*
Hazel
    See Filbert
Hazel mouse
    x Mouse, Hazel
    Muscardine
    Red dormouse
    xx Dormice
Hazelnut
    See Filbert
Hazili dialect
    xx Kunimaipa language
Hazing *(Direct)* *(Annapolis, V415.E9;*
    Student life, LB3604-3615; West
    Point, U410.E9)
    sa Greek letter societies
    Initiations (into trades, societies, etc.)
    Secret societies
    xx Greek letter societies
    Initiations (into trades, societies, etc.)
Ḥazzanim
    See Cantors, Jewish
He-Ne lasers
    See Helium-neon lasers
Head *(Anatomy, Artistic, NC770-773;*
    Anatomy, Human, QM535)
    sa Brain
    Ear
    Eye
    Face
    Hair
    Jaws
    Mouth
    Nose
    Phrenology
    Skull
    xx Brain
    Figure drawing
    Skull
— Abnormities and deformities *(QL991;*
    QM691; Surgical treatment,
    RD763)
    sa Microcephaly
    Example under Abnormalities (Animals);
    Deformities

— Cancer
— Diseases *(RC936)*
    sa Facial pain
    Head—Radiography
    Headache
— — Homeopathic treatment *(RX637)*
— Radiography
    xx Head—Diseases
— Surgery *(RD521-9; Orthopedic, RD763)*
    sa Brain—Surgery
    Skull—Surgery
    Trephining
— Tumors *(RC280.H; RD661-3)*
    sa Cephalaematoma
— Wounds and injuries *(RD131)*
— — Complications and sequelae
— — Mathematical models
— — Research *(Direct)*
Head (in religion, folk-lore, etc.) *(Folk-lore,*
    GR489; Religion, BL325.H25)
    x Folk-lore of the head
    xx Religion, Primitive
Head banging
    xx Child study
    Psychology, Pathological
Head capsule *(QL494)*
    xx Insects—Anatomy
Head-gear *(Indirect)* *(Anthropology,*
    GN419.1; Manners and customs,
    GT2110)
    sa Berets
    Costume
    Hats
    Millinery
    Miters
    x Headdress
    xx Costume
    Millinery
— Terminology
Head-gear (in religion, folk-lore, etc.)
    (BL619.H4)
    x Folk-lore of head-gear
    xx Religion, Primitive
Head-hunters
    xx Ethnology
Head in art *(N8217.H5)*
    xx Art
Head tax
    See Poll-tax
Head waves
    x Conical waves
    Lateral waves
    Refracted waves
    Refraction arrivals
    xx Elastic waves
    Seismic waves
Headache *(RB128; Migraine, RC392)*
    sa Migraine
    xx Head—Diseases
— Homeopathic treatment *(RX301.H5)*
— Psychosomatic aspects
Headdress
    See Hairdressing
    Head-gear
Headings, Subject
    See Subject headings
Headlight glare
    x Automobile headlight glare
    Glare, Headlight
    xx Automobile driving at night
    Automobiles—Lighting
    Reflection (Optics)
Headlights
    See Automobiles—Lighting
    Locomotives—Headlights
Headline writing
    See Newspapers—Headlines

Heads of departments (High schools)
  See Departmental chairmen (High schools)
Heads of state *(D-F; JF251)*
  sa Offenses against heads of state
  x State, Heads of
  xx Dictators
    Executive power
    Kings and rulers
    Presidents
    Statesmen
  — Biography
  — Health and hygiene
  — Interviews
Healey automobile
  See Austin-Healey automobile
Healing, Mental
  See Mental healing
Healing (in religion, folk-lore, etc.)
  sa Faith-cure
    Healing gods
    Healing in the Bible
  x Folk-lore of healing
  xx Medicine and religion
    Religion, Primitive
Healing gods *(BL325.H4)*
  x Gods, Healing
  xx Faith-cure
    Gods
    Healing (in religion, folk-lore, etc.)
    Medicine, Magic, mystic, and spagiric
    Mental healing
    Mythology
Healing in the Bible *(BS680.H4)*
  xx Bible—Medicine, hygiene, etc.
    Healing (in religion, folk-lore, etc.)
Healing of Peter's mother-in-law (Miracle)
  x Peter's mother-in-law, Healing of
    (Miracle)
Healing of the Gerasene demoniac (Miracle)
  x Gadarene demoniac (Miracle)
    Gerasene demoniac (Miracle)
Healing of the man born blind (Miracle)
  x Man blind from his birth (Miracle)
    Man born blind (Miracle)
  Example under Jesus Christ—Miracles; Mira-
    cles
  — Juvenile literature
Healing of the nobleman's son (Miracle)
  xx Nobleman's son (Miracle)
  Example under Jesus Christ—Miracles; Mira-
    cles
Healing of the ten lepers (Miracle)
  x Cleansing of the ten lepers (Miracle)
    Ten lepers, Cleansing of (Miracle)
    Ten lepers, Healing of (Miracle)
  xx Leprosy in the Bible
Healing of wounds
  See Wound healing
Health
  See Hygiene
Health, Bills of
  See Bills of health
Health administration
  See Health services administration
Health agencies, Voluntary
  See Voluntary health agencies
Health and housing
  See Housing and health
Health and welfare federations
  See Community welfare councils
Health attitudes
  xx Attitude (Psychology)
    Hygiene
Health boards *(Indirect) (RA5; Reports,
    RA11-388)*
  x Boards of health
    Public health boards
  xx Hygiene, Public

Public health laws
— Accounting
Health care
  See Medical care
Health care administration
  See Health services administration
Health care costs
  See Medical care, Cost of
Health care institutions
  See Health facilities
Health communication
  See Communication in medicine
Health education *(Direct)*
  sa Cancer education
    Dental health education
    School hygiene
    Schools of public health
    Television in health education
    Venereal disease education
  x Hygiene—Study and teaching
  xx Children—Care and hygiene
    Communication in medicine
    Physical education and training
— Audio-visual aids
— Curricula
— Information services
— Juvenile literature
— Law and legislation *(Direct)*
  xx Educational law and legislation
— Programmed instruction
— Research
— Teacher training
Health education (Elementary) *(Direct)*
Health education (Secondary) *(Direct)*
Health education of women *(Direct)*
  xx Education of women
Health examinations
  See Periodic health examinations
Health facilities *(Direct)*
  sa Ambulances
    Clinics
    Halfway houses
    Hospitals
    Medical centers
    Medical laboratories
    Mental retardation facilities
    Nursing homes
    Poison control centers
    Rehabilitation centers
    Rest homes
    Vaccination centers
  x Health care institutions
    Medical facilities
  xx Hygiene, Public
    Medical care
— Administration
  xx Health services administration
— Classification
— Cost of construction
— Design and construction
— Disinfection
  xx Disinfection and disinfectants
— Law and legislation *(Direct)*
— Planning
— Public opinion
— Waste disposal
Health insurance
  See Insurance, Health
Health manpower
  See Medical personnel
    Public health personnel
Health misconceptions
  See Medical delusions
Health of children
  See Children—Care and hygiene
Health of infants
  See Infants—Care and hygiene

Health of women
  See Woman—Health and hygiene
Health of workers
  See Industrial hygiene
    subdivision Hygienic aspects *under
      names of particular industries, e.g.
      Founding—Hygienic aspects;
      Smelting—Hygienic aspects*
Health-officers *(Direct) (RA5; RA440.8)*
  x Public health officers
  xx Hygiene, Public
    Medicine—Biography
    Public health laws
    Public health personnel
Health personnel
  See Medical personnel
    Public health personnel
Health policy
  See Medical policy
Health professions
  See Medical personnel
Health programs
  See subdivision Health programs *under
    subjects, e.g.* Executives—Health
    programs
Health resorts, watering-places, etc.
    (Indirect) (RA791-954)
  sa Labor rest homes
    Mineral waters
    Sanatoriums
    Seaside resorts
    Summer resorts
    Visitors' taxes
    Winter resorts
  x Spas
    Watering-places
  xx Climatology, Medical
    Hydrotherapy
    Medicine
    Resorts
    Sanatoriums
    Seaside resorts
    Sick
    Summer resorts
    Travel
    Winter resorts
— Atlases
— Economic aspects *(Direct)*
— Law and legislation *(Direct)*
— Pictorial works
Health resorts, watering-places, etc., Ancient
    (RA795)
Health sciences administration
  See Health services administration
Health sciences libraries
  See Medical libraries
Health sciences personnel
  See Medical personnel
    Public health personnel
Health services
  See Medical care
Health services administration *(Indirect)*
  sa Community mental health services—
      Administration
    Health facilities—Administration
    Hospitals—Administration
    Medical centers—Administration
    Nursing homes—Administration
    Public health administration
  x Health administration
    Health care administration
    Health sciences administration
    Medical care—Administration
  xx Public health administration
Health services personnel
  See Medical personnel
    Public health personnel

815

Health surveys

Here are entered works on the techniques employed, and reports, etc. of individual surveys; the latter are entered also under the heading Hygiene, Public, subdivided by the name of the city or other district concerned.

   sa Mental health surveys
   x Public health surveys
  — Statistical methods
   xx Medical statistics

Health thoughts
  See Mental healing

Healths, Drinking of
  See Drinking customs
     Toasts

Heaps (Mathematics)
  xx Groups, Theory of

Hearing *(Anthropology, GN275; Physiology, QP461-9; Psychology, BF251)*
  sa Audiology
    Audiometry
    Auditory adaptation
    Auditory pathways
    Auditory perception
    Bone conduction
    Deafness
    Ear
    Echolocation (Physiology)
    Geniculate bodies
    Labyrinth (Ear)
    Speech perception
    Tympanal organ
  x Acoustics
    Ear—Physiology
    Physiological acoustics
  xx Audiotory pathways
    Bioacoustics
    Deafness
    Ear
    Music—Physiological aspects
    Senses and sensation
    Sound
  — Experiments
  — Testing
    See Audiometry

Hearing aids *(Indirect) (RF300-310)*
  xx Deafness
  — Prices *(Direct)*
  — Testing

Hearing defects
  See Hearing disorders

Hearing disorders
  sa Acoustic trauma
    Deafness
    Ototoxic agents
  x Auditory disorders
    Defective hearing
    Disorders of hearing
    Hearing defects
  xx Ear—Diseases
    Perception, Disorders of
  — Cases, clinical reports, statistics

Hearing disorders in children *(Indirect) (RF122.5.C4)*
  sa Children, Deaf
  xx Communicative disorders in children

Hearing examiners
  See Examiners (Administrative procedure)

Hearing-impaired children
  See Children, Deaf

Hearsay evidence
  See Evidence, Hearsay

Heart *(Comparative anatomy, QL838; Human anatomy, QM181; Physiology, QP101-111)*
  sa Blood—Circulation
    Cardiography

Fetal heart
    Pulse
  xx Blood—Circulation
    Cardiovascular system
    Chest
Example under Anatomy, Human; Physiology; Viscera
Note under Embryology, Human
  — Abnormities and deformities
    sa Atrial septal defects
      Ebstein's anomaly
      Tetralogy of Fallot
      Ventricular septal defects
    x Congenital heart disease
  —— Personal narratives
  —— Radiography
    xx Heart—Radiography
  ——— Programmed instruction
  — Aging
  — Anatomy
  — Atlases
  — Biblical teaching
  — Biopsy *(RC683.5.B5)*
    xx Heart—Examination
  — Blood-vessels
    sa Coronary arteries
    x Cardiac blood-vessels
  —— Atlases
  — Calcification
    x Cardiac calcification
  — Caricatures and cartoons
  — Conduction system
    See Heart conduction system
  — Dilatation
    See Heart—Hypertrophy and dilatation
  — Diseases *(RC666-687)*
    sa Angina pectoris
      Arrhythmia
      Cardiacs
      Cardiology
      Chest—Diseases
      Congestive heart failure
      Cor pulmonale
      Coronary heart disease
      Endocarditis
      Heart block
      Heart failure
      Heart, Fatty
      Heart—Muscle—Diseases
      Heart—Parasites
      Heart—Radiography
      Heart—Valves—Diseases
      Pericarditis
      Rheumatic heart disease
    x Cardiac diseases
    xx Cardiology
  —— Diagnosis *(RC683)*
    sa Angiocardiography
      Auscultation
      Ballistocardiography
      Blood—Circulation, Disorders of
      Cardiac catheterization
      Cardiography
      Electrocardiography
      Electrokymography
      Percussion
      Pulse
      Sphygmograph
  —— Dietary aspects
    See Heart—Diseases—Nutritional aspects
  —— Homeopathic treatment *(RX311-316)*
  —— Jurisprudence *(Direct)*
  —— Mortality
  —— Nutritional aspects
    x Diet and heart disease
      Heart—Diseases—Dietary aspects

Nutrition and heart disease
  —— Personal narratives
  —— Pictorial works
    See Heart—Pictorial works
  —— Prevention
    Example under Medicine, Preventive
  —— Psychosomatic aspects
  —— Public opinion
  —— Research
    See Cardiology—Research
    sa Coronary heart disease—Research
  — Displacement
    x Cardioptosis
  — Enlargement
    See Heart—Hypertrophy and dilatation
  — Examination
    sa Heart—Biopsy
  — Foreign bodies
  — Hydatids
  — Hypertrophy and dilatation *(RC685.H9)*
    x Heart—Dilatation
      Heart—Enlargement
  — Infarction *(RC685.I6)*
    Example under Infarction
  —— Complications and sequelae
  —— Diagnosis
  — Innervation
    x Cardiac nerves
    Example under Nervous system
  — Juvenile literature
  — Massage
    See Cardiac massage
  — Mathematical models
  — Measurement *(Human anatomy, QM181)*
    sa Orthodiagraphy
  — Muscle
    sa Heart conduction system
    x Cardiac muscle
      Heart muscle
      Myocardium
    xx Muscle
  —— Diseases
    x Myocardial diseases
    xx Heart—Diseases
  — Necrosis
    x Cardiac necrosis
  — Palpitation *(RC685.P2)*
    sa Arrhythmia
    x Palpitation of the heart
    xx Arrhythmia
  — Parasites
    x Parasites—Heart
    xx Heart—Diseases
      Medical parasitology
  — Pictorial works
    x Heart—Diseases—Pictorial works
  — Radiography
    sa Heart—Abnormities and deformities —Radiography
    xx Heart—Diseases
  — Rupture *(RC685.R9)*
  — Sounds *(QP111)*
    sa Phonocardiography
    x Auscultation of the heart
    xx Sounds
  — Surgery
    sa Cardiac catheterization
  —— Cases, clinical reports, statistics
  —— Personal narratives
  — Terminology
    See Cardiology—Terminology
  — Transplantation
  —— Personal narratives
  — Tumors
  — Valves
    sa Heart valve prosthesis

Mitral valve
Tricuspid valve
— — Diseases *(RC685.V2)*
   sa Aortic valve stenosis
      Pulmonary stenosis
      Tricuspid valve insufficiency
    x Aortic regurgitation
      Heart valve diseases
      Valvular diseases
   xx Heart—Diseases

Heart, Artificial
  See Perfusion pump (Heart)

Heart, Fatty *(RC685.F; SF811)*
  sa Degeneration, Fatty
   x Fatty heart
  xx Degeneration, Fatty
     Heart—Diseases

Heart (in religion, folk-lore, etc.)
   x Folk-lore of the heart
  xx Religion, Primitive

Heart beat
  sa Arrhythmia
     Pacemaker, Artificial (Heart)
     Pulse
   x Heart rate
  xx Heart conduction system
     Hemodynamics
     Pulse

Heart block
  sa Adams-Stokes syndrome
     Bundle-branch block
   x Cardiac block
  xx Arrhythmia
     Heart—Diseases

Heart catheterization
  See Cardiac catheterization

Heart cherry
  See Sweet cherry

Heart conduction system
  sa Heart beat
     Sinoatrial node
   x Cardiac conduction system
     Conducting system of the heart
     Conduction system of the heart
     Conductive system of the heart
     Connecting system of the heart
     Heart—Conduction system
  xx Heart—Muscle

Heart failure *(RC682)*
  sa Cardiac resuscitation
     Congestive heart failure
   x Cardiac arrest
     Cardiac insufficiency
  xx Heart—Diseases
     Surgery, Operative

Heart function tests *(RC683.5.H)*
  sa Indicator dilution
   x Cardiac function tests
  xx Function tests (Medicine)

Heart massage
  See Cardiac massage

Heart muscle
  See Heart—Muscle

Heart of Jesus, Devotion to
  See Sacred Heart, Devotion to

Heart of Mary, Devotion to
  See Sacred Heart of Mary, Devotion to

Heart patients
  See Cardiacs

Heart rate
  See Heart beat

Heart valve diseases
  See Heart—Valves—Diseases

Heart valve prosthesis
   x Prosthetic heart valves
  xx Heart—Valves
     Prosthesis

Hearth-money *(Direct) (English tax,*
  HJ2612)
   x Chimney-money
     Taxation of hearths
  xx Taxation

Hearts (Game) *(GV1295.H4)*

Heartwater *(SF809.H4)*
  xx Cattle—Diseases
     Rickettsial diseases

Heartworm disease in dogs
  See Canine heartworm disease

Heat *(QC251-338)*
  sa Aerodynamic heating
     Animal heat
     Atmospheric temperature
     Calorimeters and calorimetry
     Cold
     Combustion
     Entropy
     Expansion (Heat)
     Expansion of gases
     Expansion of liquids
     Expansion of solids
     Fire
     Fusion, Latent heat of
     Gases—Liquefaction
     Heat engineering
     High temperatures
     Liquid air
     Metals at high temperatures
     Pyrometers and pyrometry
     Solidification
     Steam
     Surfaces, Isothermic
     Temperature
     Temperature control
     Thawing
     Thermochemistry
     Thermodynamics
     Thermoelectricity
     Thermography (Copying process)
     Thermomagnetism
     Thermometers and thermometry
     Waste heat
   x Equilibrium, Thermal
     Thermal equilibrium
  xx Cold
     Combustion
     Electromagnetic waves
     Fire
     Physics
     Temperature
     Thermochemistry
     Thermodynamics
 — Absorption
    See Heat—Radiation and absorption
 — Conduction *(QC321-3)*
   sa Thermal diffusivity
    x Conduction of heat
 — — Charts, diagrams, etc.
 — — Computer programs
 — — Electromechanical analogies
 — — Measurement
 — Convection *(QC327)*
   sa Convection (Meteorology)
    x Convection of heat
 — Experiments
 — — Juvenile literature
 — Juvenile literature
 — Laboratory manuals *(QC263)*
   xx Calorimeters and calorimetry
 — Notation
 — Physiological effect *(Cells, QH653;*
    Physiology, QP82)
   sa Heatstroke
     Plants, Effect of heat on
     Temperature—Physiological effect

   x High temperatures—Physiological
     effect
     Hyperthermia
  xx Temperature—Physiological effect
 — Problems, exercises, etc.
 — Programmed instruction
 — Radiation and absorption *(QC331-8)*
   sa Cooling
     Radiative transfer
    x Absorption (Heat)
     Heat absorption
     Heat—Absorption
     Radiative heat transfer
   xx Absorption spectra
     Radiation
     Radiative transfer
     Spectrum, Infra-red
 — — Tables
 — Storage devices
    See Heat storage devices
 — Tables
 — Terminology
 — Therapeutic use
    See Thermotherapy
 — Transmission *(QC320-338)*
   sa Ablation (Aerothermodynamics)
     Aeroplanes—Electric equipment—
      Cooling
     Aeroplanes—Electronic equipment—
      Cooling
     Ceilings—Thermal properties
     Exterior walls—Thermal properties
     Film boiling
     Film coefficients (Physics)
     Heat exchangers
     Heat pipes
     Heat-transfer media
     Rayleigh number
    x Heat transfer
     Thermal transfer
     Transmission of heat
   xx Energy transfer
 — — Computer programs
 — — Electromechanical analogies
 — — Instruments *(QC323)*
    x Instruments, Heat transfer
 — — Laboratory manuals
 — — Mathematical models
 — — Measurement
 — — Problems, exercises, etc.
 — — Research *(Direct)*
 — — Tables, calculations, etc.

Heat, Mechanical equivalent of *(QC312)*
   x Mechanical equivalent of heat
  xx Force and energy
     Thermodynamics

Heat, Specific
  See Specific heat

Heat (in religion, folk-lore, etc.)
  sa Fire (in religion, folk-lore, etc.)
   x Folk-lore of heat
  xx Fire (in religion, folk-lore, etc.)
     Religion, Primitive

Heat absorption
  See Heat—Radiation and absorption

Heat accumulators
  See Heat regenerators

Heat as a disinfectant *(RA766.H4)*
  xx Disinfection and disinfectants

Heat barrier
  See Aerodynamic heating
     High temperatures

Heat budget (Geophysics) *(Indirect)*
  sa Atmospheric temperature
     Atmospheric thermodynamics
     Ocean temperature
     Soil temperature
   x Budget, Heat (Geophysics)

Heat budget (Geophysics) *(Indirect)*
(Continued)
     Thermal budget (Geophysics)
    xx Atmospheric temperature
     Earth temperature
     Energy budget (Geophysics)
     Ocean temperature
 — Charts, diagrams, etc.
Heat content
  See Enthalpy
Heat developable paper
  See Thermographic paper
Heat engineering
  sa Combustion engineering
   Geothermal engineering
   Heat-engines
   Heating
  xx Heat
   Mechanical engineering
   Thermodynamics
 — Instruments
   x Instruments, Heat engineering
 — — Appraisal
    See Heat engineering—Instruments
     —Valuation
 — — Valuation *(TJ260)*
   x Heat engineering—Instruments—
    Appraisal
 — Laboratory manuals
 — Mathematical models
 — Safety regulations *(Direct)*
   xx Engineering law
 — Standards
   xx Standards, Engineering
 — Tables, calculations, etc.
 — Terminology
Heat engineering laboratories
  See Thermodynamics laboratories
Heat-engines *(Mechanical engineering,*
     TJ255-265)
  sa Gas and oil engines
   Heat pumps
   Steam-engines
   Stirling engines
   Thermodynamics
  xx Engines
   Heat engineering
   Thermodynamics
 — Problems, exercises, etc.
Heat exchangers *(TP363)*
  sa Air heaters
  xx Chemical engineering—Apparatus and
    supplies
   Heat—Transmission
   Refrigeration and refrigerating
    machinery
 — Automatic control
 — Design and construction
 — Mathematical models
 — Specifications
 — Standards
 — Testing
 — Vibration
 — Welding
Heat function
  See Enthalpy
Heat in animals
  See Estrus
Heat island, Urban
  See Urban heat island
Heat of adsorption
  xx Adsorption
Heat of combustion
  x Combustion, Heat of
  xx Fuel—Testing
   Thermochemistry
Heat of dilution
  See Heat of solution

Heat of hydration
  xx Hydration
   Thermochemistry
Heat of immersion
  See Heat of wetting
Heat of mixing
  xx Mixing
Heat of solution *(QC310)*
  x Heat of dilution
   Solution, Heat of
  xx Calorimeters and calorimetry
   Solubility
   Solution (Chemistry)
   Thermochemistry
Heat of wetting *(QC310)*
  x Energy of immersion
   Heat of immersion
   Immersion, Heat of
  xx Wetting
Heat pipes
   Here are entered works on heat transfer
   cylinders that absorb heat at one end
   by vaporization of a liquid and release
   heat by condensation of the liquid at
   the other end. Works on pipes which
   are components of heating installa-
   tions in structures are entered under
   Heating-pipes.
  xx Heat-transfer media
   Heat—Transmission
   Pipe
  Note under Heating-pipes
Heat pollution of rivers, lakes, etc.
  See Thermal pollution of rivers, lakes, etc.
Heat production in plants
  See Plants, Heat production in
Heat pumps *(TJ266)*
  xx Heat-engines
   Pumping machinery
   Thermodynamics
Heat regenerators
  x Heat accumulators
  xx Heat storage devices
   Stoves
   Waste heat
 — Design and construction
Heat resistant alloys *(TN700)*
  sa Chromium-cobalt-nickel-molybdenum
    alloys
   Nimonic alloys
   Steel, Heat resistant
  x Alloys, Heat resistant
   High temperature metals
   Metals, Heat resistant
   Refractory metals
  xx Alloys
   Heat resistant materials
   Metals at high temperatures
   Powder metallurgy
 — Analysis
 — Testing
 — Welding
Heat resistant concrete
  sa Concrete, Effect of temperature on
  x Concrete, Heat resistant
  xx Concrete
   Concrete, Effect of temperature on
   Heat resistant materials
Heat resistant materials *(TA418.26)*
  sa Ceramic metals
   Heat resistant alloys
   Heat resistant concrete
   Heat resistant plastics
   Refractory materials
  x High temperature materials
  xx Materials
   Materials at high temperatures
 — Corrosion *(TA418.26)*

 — Testing
Heat resistant plastics
  xx Heat resistant materials
   Plastics
Heat resistant steel
  See Steel, Heat resistant
Heat sensitive copying processes
  See Thermography (Copying process)
Heat storage devices
  sa Heat regenerators
  x Heat—Storage devices
   Storage devices, Heat
   Thermal storage devices
  xx Heating
Heat stroke
  See Heatstroke
Heat transfer
  See Heat—Transmission
Heat transfer coefficient
  See Nusselt number
Heat transfer images
  See Thermography (Copying process)
Heat-transfer media
  sa Heat pipes
   Refrigerants
  x Heat-transmission media
   Thermal-transfer media
  xx Heat—Transmission
Heat-transmission media
  See Heat-transfer media
Heat treatment of aluminum alloys
  See Aluminum alloys—Heat treatment
Heat treatment of metals
  See Metals—Heat treatment
Heat treatment of steel
  See Steel—Heat treatment
Heated water discharges into rivers, lakes, etc.
  See Thermal pollution of rivers, lakes, etc.
Heaters, Air
  See Air heaters
Heaters, Tube-still
  See Tube-still heaters
Heath (Botany)
  See Heather
Heath ecology *(Indirect)* *(QH541.5.M6)*
  x Heathland ecology
  xx Ecology
   Moors and heaths
Heathcock
  See Black grouse
Heathenism
  See Paganism
Heather *(QK495.E68)*
  x Heath (Botany)
  xx Forage plants
Heathland ecology
  See Heath ecology
Heaths
  See Moors and heaths
Heating *(TH7010-7641; Manners and*
     customs, GT420)
  sa Air curtains
   Boilers
   Braziers
   Chimneys
   Degree days
   Electric heating
   Fans (Machinery)
   Fireplaces
   Fuel
   Furnaces
   Heat storage devices
   Hot-air heating
   Hot-water heating
   Infra-red rays—Industrial applications
   Insulation (Heat)
   Oil burners
   Radiant heating

Radiators
Soil heating
Solar heating
Steam-heating
Stoves
Ventilation
Waste heat
subdivision Heating and ventilation
under specific subjects, e.g. Factories
—Heating and ventilation; Railroads
—Cars—Heating and ventilation
xx Boilers
Environmental engineering (Buildings)
Fire
Fuel
Heat engineering
Home economics
Sanitation, Household
Stoves
Ventilation
— Caricatures and cartoons
— Climatic factors   *(TH7015)*
xx Engineering meteorology
— Control   *(TH7466.5)*
sa Hot-water heating—Regulators
Induction heating—Regulators
Steam-heating—Regulators
x Heating—Regulators
xx Heating—Equipment and supplies
Thermostat
— Costs
— Equipment and supplies
sa Heating—Control
Strikes and lockouts—Plumbing and
heating industry
— Estimates   *(Direct)   (TH7335-7)*
— Examinations, questions, etc.
— Juvenile literature
— Laboratory manuals
— Law and legislation   *(Direct)*
x Dwellings—Heating and ventilation
—Law and legislation
xx Building laws
— Panel system
See Radiant heating
— Patents
— Regulators
See Heating—Control
— Specifications   *(TH7325)*
— Tables, calculations, etc.   *(TH7225)*
— Vocational guidance
Heating, Aerodynamic
See Aerodynamic heating
Heating, Dielectric
See Dielectric heating
Heating, Infra-red
See Infra-red heating
Heating, Microwave
See Microwave heating
Heating and ventilation industry   *(Direct)*
sa Air conditioning industry
xx Ventilation
Heating from central stations   *(Direct)*
(TH7641)
x Central heating plants
Central station heating
District heating
xx Heating plants
— Automation
— Tables, calculations, etc.   *(TH7641)*

Heating-pipes   *(TH7478)*
Here are entered works on pipes which
are components of heating installa-
tions in structures. Works on heat
transfer cylinders that absorb heat at
one end by vaporization of a liquid and
release heat by condensation of the liq-
uid at the other end are entered under
Heat pipes.
xx Pipe
Plumbing
Note under Heat pipes
— Corrosion
— Tables, calculations, etc.
Heating plants   *(TH7461; TJ395)*
sa Heating from central stations
— Automation
— Equipment and supplies
— Safety regulations   *(Direct)*
Heating research
xx Building research
Engineering research
Heats of vaporization
See Vaporization, Heats of
Heatstroke
x Heat stroke
xx Heat—Physiological effect
Heaven   *(BT844-9; Art, N8150)*
sa Angels
Beatific vision
Empyrean
Future life
Heavenly recognition
Intermediate state
Paradise
xx Death
Elysium
Eschatology
Intermediate state
— Art
— Biblical teaching
— History of doctrines
— Poetry
Heaven (Islam)
See Paradise (Islam)
Heavenly recognition   *(BT847)*
x Recognition, Heavenly
xx Eschatology
Heaven
Heaviside layer
See Ionosphere
Heavy electrons
See Mesons
Heavy hydrogen
See Hydrogen—Isotopes
Heavy metals
xx Metals
Heavy minerals   *(Indirect)*
x Minerals, Heavy
xx Mineralogy
Rocks, Sedimentary
Heavy water
See Deuterium oxide
Heavy water piles
See Heavy water reactors
Heavy water reactors   *(TK9203.H4)*
x Heavy water piles
xx Deuterium oxide
Nuclear reactors
Solid fuel reactors
— Exponential measurements
x Reactor lattices
xx Neutrons
Nuclear engineering
Nuclear fuels
Example under reference from Exponen-
tial measurements

Hebin   *(QP187)*
xx Gonadotropin
Pituitary hormones
Hebrew art
See Art, Jewish
Hebrew artists
See Artists, Jewish
Hebrew astronomy
See Astronomy, Jewish
Hebrew calendar
See Calendar, Jewish
Hebrew chronology
See Chronology, Jewish
Hebrew drama
xx Bible plays
Jewish drama
Hebrew essays
Here are entered collections of essays by
several authors.
Hebrew fiction   *(Direct)*
Hebrew folk-songs
See Folk-songs, Jewish (Hebrew)
Hebrew hymns
See Hymns, Hebrew
Hebrew illumination of books and manuscripts
See Illumination of books and manuscripts,
Jewish
Hebrew imprints   *(Direct)*
Hebrew language   *(PJ4501-5089)*
sa Karaitic dialects
Ladino language
Yiddish language
x Bible—Philology
Jewish language
xx Bible—Language, style
Jews—Languages
Languages—Religious aspects
Example under Semitic languages
— Abbreviations
See Abbreviations, Hebrew
— Alphabet (in religion, folk-lore, etc.)
xx Alphabet (in religion, folk-lore, etc.)
Cabala
— Root   *(PJ4603)*
Example under reference from Roots,
Linguistic
— Vocalization
Example under Vowels
Hebrew language, Mishnaic
See Hebrew language, Talmudic
Hebrew language, Post-Biblical
(PJ5001-5041)
x Hebrew language, Rabbinic
Hebrew language, Rabbinic
See Hebrew language, Post-Biblical
Hebrew language, Talmudic   *(PJ5001-5041)*
x Hebrew language, Mishnaic
Hebrew law
See Jewish law
Hebrew letters
Hebrew libraries
See Jewish libraries
Hebrew literature   *(PJ5001-5060)*
sa Apocalyptic literature
Approbations (Hebrew literature)
Bible
Cabala
Children's stories, Hebrew
Folk literature—Jews
Geonic literature
Jewish literature
Rabbinical literature
Religious literature, Jewish
Talmud
x Jews—Literature
xx Jewish literature
Example under Semitic literature
— Bio-bibliography   *(Z7070)*

Hebrew literature, Medieval (Collections,
    PJ5037; History, PJ5016)
Hebrew literature, Modern (Direct)
    (Collections, PJ5038; History,
    PJ5017-5021)
Hebrew newspapers (PN5650)
    xx Jewish newspapers
    Note under Newspapers
Hebrew paleography
    See Paleography, Hebrew
Hebrew parodies
    See Parodies, Hebrew
Hebrew periodicals (PN5650)
Hebrew philology (PJ4501-4541)
Hebrew poetry (Direct) (Collections,
    PJ5039-5042; History, PJ5022-5)
    sa Azharot
       Parodies, Hebrew
       Piyutim
       Psalmody
       Religious poetry, Hebrew
    x Bible—Poetry
    xx Jewish poetry
Hebrew poetry, Modern (Direct)
Hebrew quotations
    See Quotations, Hebrew
Hebrew songs
    See Songs, Jewish (Hebrew)
       Songs, Zionist
Hebrew theater
    See Theater—Jews
Hebrew wit and humor
    sa Israeli wit and humor
       Jewish wit and humor
    xx Jewish wit and humor
Hebrews
    See Jews
Hebron, Palestine
    — Riot, 1929
Heckelphone (ML990.H4)
    xx Oboe
Heckelphone music (M110.H4)
    sa Wind quartets (English horn,
       heckelphone, oboe, oboe d'amore)
Hecter fuel (TL704.7)
    xx Fuel
       Liquid fuels
Hectograph (Z48)
    xx Copying processes
Heder
    x Cheder
    xx Jews—Education
       Schools, Jewish
Hedgehogs (QL737.I5)
    sa European hedgehog
    — Juvenile literature
    — Legends and stories
Hedgerows
    See Windbreaks, shelterbelts, etc.
Hedges (SB437)
    sa Evergreens
       Fences
       Landscape gardening
       Shrubs
    xx Fences
       Landscape architecture
       Shrubs
       Trees
Hedging (Finance)
    x Futures
    xx Commodity exchanges
       Put and call transactions
       Speculation
       Stock-exchange
Hedonal (Physiology, QP981.H5;
    Therapeutics, RM666.H)

Hedonism (Ethics, BJ1491; Greek
    philosophy, B279)
    sa Altruism
       Egoism
       Happiness
       Lokāyata
       Pleasure
       Self-interest
       Utilitarianism
    x Eudemonism
    xx Asceticism
       Ethics
       Philosophy
       Pleasure
       Utilitarianism
Heel bone
    x Calcaneus
    — Fracture
Heel flies
    See Warble-flies
Hegra
    — Siege, 1940 (D763.N62)
       xx World War, 1939-1945—Campaigns
       —Norway
Hegue language
    See Eudeve language
Heh Miao dialect
    See Hei Miao dialect
Hehe law
    See Law, Wahehe
Hei Miao dialect
    x Heh Miao dialect
       Phö dialect
    xx Miao language
Heidelberg in literature
Heidenhain pouch
    x Heidenhain's pouch
    xx Physiology, Experimental
       Stomach
Heidenhain syndrome
    See Jakob-Creutzfeldt disease
Heidenhain's pouch
    See Heidenhain pouch
Heifers
    xx Cows
    — Feeding and feeds
Heights
    See Altitudes
Heilbronn, Union of, 1633 (D267.H3)
    xx Thirty Years' War, 1618-1648
Heiligerlee, Battle of, 1568
    xx Netherlands—History—Wars of
       Independence, 1556-1648
Heiltsuk language (PM1321)
    sa Wakashan languages
    x Haeltzuk language
       Hailtsa language
       Hailtsuk language
Heinkel 100 (Fighter planes) (TL686.H35)
    x Heinkel 113 (Fighter planes)
    xx Fighter planes
Heinkel 111 (Bomber) (TL685.3)
    xx Bombers
Heinkel 112 (Fighter planes) (TL686.H35)
    xx Fighter planes
Heinkel 113 (Fighter planes)
    See Heinkel 100 (Fighter planes)
Heinkel 162 (Jet fighter planes)
    xx Fighter planes
       Jet planes
Heinkel 177 (Bombers)
    xx Bombers
Heinkel aeroplanes
Heinz bodies
    xx Erythrocytes
Heirlooms (Direct)
    xx Entail
       Inheritance and succession

       Property
       Restraints on alienation
Heirs
    See Inheritance and succession
Heirs, Unworthiness of
    See Unworthiness of heirs
Heisenberg uncertainty principle (QC174.1)
    sa Causality (Physics)
    x Indeterminancy principle
       Uncertainty principle
    xx Quantum theory
Heke's Rebellion, 1844-1846
    See Hone Heke's Rebellion, 1844-1846
Hel Peninsula, Poland, Battle of, 1939
    xx World War, 1939-1945—Campaigns—
       Poland
HeLa cells
    xx Cancer cells
       Uterus—Cancer
Heldensage (PN684; PT204-212)
    sa Byliny
       Chansons de geste
       Legends, Germanic
    x Heroic saga
    xx Heroes
       Legends
Helena, Ark., Battle of, 1863 (E474.9)
Helenium
    See Sneezeweed
Helgoland, Battle of, 1914 (D582.H)
    xx European War, 1914-1918—Naval
       operations
Helicon bass
    See Tuba
Helicopter auto-pilot
    See Automatic pilot (Helicopters)
Helicopter flight simulator
    See Helicopter flight trainer
Helicopter flight trainer
    x Helicopter flight simulator
       Helicopter simulator
    xx Flight simulators
       Helicopters—Piloting
Helicopter recognition
    See Helicopters—Recognition
Helicopter rotors
    See Rotors (Helicopters)
Helicopter simulator
    See Helicopter flight trainer
Helicopter transportation (Direct)
    xx Aeronautics, Commercial
Helicopters (TL716)
    sa Automatic pilot (Helicopters)
       Convertiplanes
       Heliports
       Jet helicopters
       Metropolitan helicopter services
       Mi-1 (Helicopters)
       Rotors (Helicopters)
       Sikorsky helicopter
    xx Aeronautics
       Flying-machines
       Ground-effect machines
    — Aerodynamics
    — Airworthiness
       sa Airworthiness certificates
       x Airworthiness requirements
    — Cargo
       xx Cargo handling
       Example under reference from Cargo
    — Cold weather operation
       x Cold weather operation (Helicopters)
       xx Polar regions—Aerial exploration
    — Control systems
       xx Flight control
    — Design and construction
    — Electric equipment
    — Field of view

x Field of view from helicopters
Helicopters—Range of vision
Range of vision from helicopters
Visual span (Helicopters)
— Flight testing
x Flight testing of helicopters
xx Helicopters—Testing
— Flying qualities
See Helicopters—Handling
characteristics
— Handling characteristics *(TL716)*
x Flying qualities of helicopters
Helicopters—Flying qualities
xx Stability of helicopters
— Juvenile literature
— Landing
— Law and legislation *(Direct)*
xx Aeronautics—Laws and regulations
— Maintenance and repair
— Models
— — Testing
— Motors
— Patents
— Piloting *(TL716.5)*
sa Helicopter flight trainer
Example under Aeroplanes—Piloting;
and under references from
Aeronautics—Piloting; Air pilot-
age; Piloting (Aeronautics)
— Poetry
See Aeronautics—Poetry
— Range of vision
See Helicopters—Field of view
— Recognition
x Aircraft identification
Aircraft recognition
Helicopter recognition
Recognition of helicopters
— Rotors
See Rotors (Helicopters)
— Stability
See Stability of helicopters
— Testing
sa Helicopters—Flight testing
Helicopters, Used
See Used aircraft
Heliochromy
See Color photography
Heliodon *(QC912)*
xx Architecture and climate
Astronomical instruments
Heliograph *(UG582.H4)*
sa Photoheliograph
Spectroheliograph
x Heliotrope (Engineering instrument)
Heliogravure
See Photogravure
Heliometer *(QB97)*
sa Parallax
Planets—Diameters
Sun—Diameters
xx Astronomical instruments
Heliomicrometer *(QB97)*
xx Astronomical instruments
Heliostat *(Optical, QC373.H5; Sun
observations, QB97)*
xx Astronomical instruments
Heliotherapy
See Sun-baths
Heliotrope (Engineering instrument)
See Heliograph
Heliotropism
See Phototropism
Heliotype *(TR937)*
xx Collotype
Photography
Photomechanical processes

Heliozoa *(QL368.H5)*
xx Protozoa
Heliports *(Indirect)* *(TL725.5)*
xx Aeronautics, Commercial
Airports
Helicopters
— Fires and fire prevention
— Planning
Helium *(Aeronautics, TL666; Chemical
technology, TP245.H4; Chemistry,
QD181.H4)*
sa Liquid helium
Solid helium
xx Gases, Rare
Radioactivity
Example under Gases
— Electric properties
— Isotopes
x Helium isotopes
Isotopic helium
— — Decay
— Physiological effect
— Spectra
— Tables, etc.
— Therapeutic use
— Thermal properties
Helium, Solid
See Solid helium
Helium at low temperatures
sa Liquid helium
Solid helium
xx Low temperatures
Helium ions
xx Ions
— Spectra
Helium isotopes
See Helium—Isotopes
Helium-neon lasers *(TA1695)*
x He-Ne lasers
Lasers, Helium-neon
Neon-helium lasers
xx Gas lasers
Hell *(Classical mythology, BL735;
Comparative religion, BL545;
Theology, BT834-8)*
sa Future punishment
Intermediate state
x Endless punishment
Eternal punishment
Everlasting punishment
Hades
Retribution
Sheol
xx Death
Eschatology
Future punishment
Intermediate state
— Art *(N8150)*
— Biblical teaching
— Comparative studies *(BL545; Classical
mythology, BL735)*
— Controversial literature *(BT837)*
— Poetry
— Sermons
Hell (Buddhism)
xx Buddha and Buddhism
— Art
xx Art, Buddhist
Hell (Islam) *(BP166.88)*
xx Eschatology, Islamic
Hell (Judaism) *(BM496.9.H4)*
x Gehenna
xx Eschatology, Jewish
Hell in literature
Hellcat (Fighter planes)
x Grumman F6F Hellcat
xx Fighter planes

Hellenism *(Christianity, BR128.G8; History,
DF77; Judaism, BM176, BM536.G7;
Literature, PN56.H4)*
sa Neoplatonism
*headings beginning with the word
Hellenistic*
x Greek civilization
xx Byzantine studies
Civilization, Greek
Classical philology
Classicism
Greek language
Greek literature
Humanism
Hellenistic art
See Art, Hellenistic
Hellenistic Greek
See Greek language, Hellenistic (300
B.C.-600 A.D.)
Hellenistic portraits
See Portraits, Hellenistic
Hellenistic pottery
See Pottery, Hellenistic
Hellenistic sculpture
See Sculpture, Hellenistic
Hellenists
See Classicists
Helmeted hornbill
xx Hornbills
Helmets *(Direct)* *(Art, N6600-6699;
Military science, U825)*
sa Safety hats
— Testing
Helmholtz double layer
See Electric double layer
Helminthiasis
xx Medical parasitology
Helminthology *(Indirect)* *(QL386-394)*
sa Medical helminthology
Veterinary helminthology
xx Worms
Worms, Intestinal and parasitic
Zoology
Helminths
See Worms, Intestinal and parasitic
HELP (Computer program)
x Hybrid Executive Linkage Program
xx Hybrid computers—Programming
Help-wanted advertising
xx Advertising
Advertising, Classified
Helpers, Fourteen holy
See Fourteen holy helpers
Helpers of Muḥammad, the prophet
See Ansar
Helping behavior
xx Altruism
Interpersonal relations
Helsingborg, Battle of, 1710 *(DL743.H3)*
Hemacytometer *(RB145)*
Hemagglutination
See Blood—Agglutination
Hemagglutinin *(Blood, QP91; Immunity,
QR185)*
sa Phytohemagglutinins
xx Agglutination
Agglutinins
Blood—Agglutination
Immunity
Hematemesis
xx Stomach—Diseases
Stomach—Ulcers
Hematin
See Heme
Hematite *(Indirect)*
x Raddle
xx Iron ores
Hematite crystals

Hematocele
Hematochyluria *(RC918.H4)*
Hematocrit
   xx Blood—Examination
      Erythrocytes
Hematoencephalic barrier
   See Blood-brain barrier
Hematogenic shock
   See Hemorrhagic shock
Hematologic diseases
   See Blood—Diseases
Hematology
   sa Blood
      Immunohematology
      Pediatric hematology
      Radioisotopes in hematology
   xx Internal medicine
   — Atlases
   — Standards *(Direct)*
   — Technique
   — Terminology
Hematology, Forensic
   See Forensic hematology
Hematology, Veterinary
   See Veterinary hematology
Hematoma
   sa Subdural hematoma
   x Blood tumor
   xx Hemorrhage
      Tumors
Hematophilia
   See Hemophilia
Hematopoiesis
   sa Hematopoietic agents
      Hematopoietic system
      Hemoglobin synthesis
   x Blood formation
      Hemopoiesis
   xx Blood
Hematopoietic agents *(RM335)*
   xx Hematopoiesis
      Pharmacology
Hematopoietic system
   sa Marrow
      Reticulo-endothelial system
      Spleen
   x Hemopoietic system
   xx Hematopoiesis
   — Cancer
Hematopoietic system, Effect of radiation on the
   xx Radiation—Physiological effect
Hematoporphyrin *(QP671)*
   x Photodyn
   xx Blood—Pigments
Hematuria *(RC918.H4; SF961)*
Hemba (Bantu people)
   See Bahemba (Bantu people)
Heme
   sa Hemoproteins
      Porphyrin and porphyrin compounds
   x Hematin
   xx Hemoglobin
Hemenway Southwestern Archaeological Expedition, 1886-1894
Hemianopsia *(RE94)*
   xx Blindness
Hemicellulose *(QK865)*
   xx Cellulose
Hemichordata *(QL612)*
   sa Enteropneusta
      Pterobranchia
   xx Animal colonies
Hemiplegia
   xx Paralysis
Hemiptera *(Indirect)* *(QL521-4)*
   sa Heteroptera
      Homoptera

      Plant-lice
      Scale-insects
      Water-scorpions
   x Rhynchota
      Siphonata
   xx Insects
   — Juvenile literature
Hemlock
   See Mountain hemlock
      Western hemlock
Hemlock (Materia medica)
   See Conium
Hemlock looper *(QL561.G6; SB945.H)*
   x Hemlock spanworm
   — Control *(Indirect)*
Hemlock sawfly
Hemlock spanworm
   See Hemlock looper
Hemmingstedt, Battle of, 1500
      xx Denmark—History—1448-1660
         Denmark—History—1448-1660
Hemochromatosis
   sa Addison's disease
      Blood—Diseases
      Hemosiderosis
      Liver—Diseases
   xx Addison's disease
      Blood—Diseases
      Diabetes
      Hemosiderin
      Liver—Diseases
Hemocyanin
   xx Blood—Pigments
Hemocytometer
   xx Blood—Examination
Hemodialysis
   sa Artificial kidney
      Peritoneal dialysis
   x Blood—Dialysis
   xx Dialysis
      Therapeutics
   — Psychological aspects
      xx Sick—Psychology
Hemodynamics
   sa Blood flow
      Blood pressure
      Blood viscosity
      Blood volume
      Cardiac output
      Heart beat
      Regional blood flow
   xx Blood—Circulation
      Cardiac output
Hemoerythrin
   xx Blood—Pigments
Hemoglobin *(QP91)*
   sa Anoxemia
      Bile pigments
      Heme
      Oxyhemoglobin
   x Hemoglobulin
   xx Blood—Pigments
      Blood proteins
      Hemoproteins
   — Physiological effect *(QP951)*
Hemoglobin, Abnormal
   See Hemoglobinopathy
Hemoglobin synthesis
   xx Biosynthesis
      Hematopoiesis
Hemoglobinometry
   xx Blood—Analysis and chemistry
Hemoglobinopathy *(RC641.7.H35)*
   x Hemoglobin, Abnormal
   xx Anemia
   — Genetic aspects
Hemoglobinuric fever
   See Blackwater fever

Hemoglobulin
   See Hemoglobin
Hemogram
   See Blood cell count
Hemolymph
   xx Blood
      Lymphatics
Hemolymph glands *(QL841)*
   xx Glands
Hemolysis and hemolysins *(QR185)*
   sa Hemolytic anemia
      Lysolecithin
   xx Blood
      Immunity
      Serum
Hemolytic anemia
   sa Favism
      Sickle cell anemia
   xx Anemia
      Hemolysis and hemolysins
Hemophilia *(RC642)*
   x Hematophilia
      Hemorrhagic diathesis
   xx Blood—Coagulation, Disorders of
   — Complications and sequelae
Hemophilus diseases
   sa Chancroid
      Hemophilus meningitis
   x Haemophilus diseases
   xx Bacterial diseases
Hemophilus meningitis
   xx Hemophilus diseases
      Meningitis
Hemopoiesis
   See Hematopoiesis
Hemopoietic system
   See Hematopoietic system
Hemoproteins
   sa Cytochrome c
      Hemoglobin
      Myoglobin
   xx Heme
Hemoptysis
   See Hemorrhage
Hemorrhage *(RB144; RD33.3)*
   sa Arteries—Wounds and injuries
      Bloodletting
      Gastrointestinal hemorrhage
      Hematoma
      Hemorrhagic diseases
      Hemostasis
      Hemostatics
      Infarction
      Nosebleed
      Oral hemorrhage
      subdivision Hemorrhage *under names of organs and regions of the body, e.g.* Brain—Hemorrhage
   x Bleeding
      Hemoptysis
   xx Anemia
      Arteries—Wounds and injuries
      Blood
      Surgery, Operative
      Wounds
Hemorrhage, Cerebral
   See Apoplexy
Hemorrhage, Uterine *(Labor, RG711; Pregnancy, RG573; Puerperal state, RG821)*
   sa Menorrhagia
   x Uterus—Hemorrhage
   xx Labor, Complicated
      Uterus—Diseases
Hemorrhagic bronchitis
   See Bronchopulmonary spirochaetosis
Hemorrhagic diathesis
   See Hemophilia

Hemorrhagic disease of newborn *(RJ271)*
   x Morbus haemolyticus neonatorum
Hemorrhagic diseases *(RC633)*
   sa Blood—Coagulation, Disorders of
   x Diseases, Hemorrhagic
      Hemorrhagic disorders
   xx Hemorrhage
Hemorrhagic disorders
   See Hemorrhagic diseases
Hemorrhagic encephalitis
   x Encephalitis, Hemorrhagic
      Strümpell-Leichtenstern encephalitis
Hemorrhagic fever
   sa Dengue
   xx Virus diseases
Hemorrhagic septicemia of cattle *(SF967.H)*
   x Corn-stalk disease
      Shipping fever of cattle
      Stock-yards fever
      Stock-yards pneumonia
   xx Buffaloes—Diseases
      Cattle—Diseases
      Septicemia
Hemorrhagic septicemia of swine
   See Swine plague
Hemorrhagic shock
   x Hematogenic shock
   xx Shock
Hemorrhoids *(RC865)*
   x Piles (Disease)
   xx Rectum—Diseases
      Varix
   — Homeopathic treatment *(RX343)*
Hemosiderin *(QP551)*
   sa Hemochromatosis
   xx Blood—Pigments
Hemosiderosis
   xx Hemochromatosis
      Iron metabolism
      Metabolism, Disorders of
Hemospasia *(RZ999)*
   sa Cupping
      Hyperemia, Artificial
   x Hemospasis
   xx Cupping
      Therapeutics, Cutaneous and external
Hemospasis
   See Hemospasia
Hemostasis
   sa Blood—Coagulation
      Hemostatics
   x Haemostasis
   xx Hemorrhage
Hemostatics *(RD33.3)*
   sa Fibrinogen
      Kino
   x Styptics
   xx Hemorrhage
      Hemostasis
Hemp *(Indirect)* *(Culture, SB255;*
     Technology, TS1733; Trade,
     HD9155)
   Here are entered works on the description, culture, and use of Cannabis
   sativa as a fiber plant. Works on Cannabis sativa as a drug plant are entered
   under Cannabis.
   sa Ambary hemp
      Cordage
      Fibers
      Jute
      Manila hemp
      Ramie
      Rope
      Roselle
      Sisal hemp
      Twine
   xx Fibers

      Linen
      Ramie
      Rope
   Example under Fiber plants; Textile fibers
   Note under Cannabis
   — Control *(Indirect)* *(SB615.H)*
      xx Weed control
Hemp, Indian
   See Hashish
Hemp industry *(Direct)*
   sa Wages—Flax and hemp trade
Hemp industry workers *(Direct)*
Hendecasyllable
   x Endecasyllable
Henequen *(Indirect)* *(Botany, QK495.A484;*
     Culture, SB261.H4)
   sa Twine
   x Mexican sisal
Henkersmahl
   See Last meal before execution
Henna
   x Alhenna
      Egyptian henna
   xx Dyes and dyeing
Henry, Fort, Battle of, 1862 *(E472.96)*
Hens
   See Poultry
Henslow's sparrow *(QL696.P2)*
   xx Sparrows
Heortology
   See Church calendar
      Church year
      Fasts and feasts
      Saints—Calendar
Hepatectomy
   xx Liver—Surgery
Hepatic artery
   — Surgery
Hepatic cirrhosis
   See Liver—Cirrhosis
Hepatic coma *(RC848)*
   x Coma, Hepatic
      Porto-hepatic encephalopathy
   xx Liver—Diseases
Hepatic function tests
   See Liver function tests
Hepatic puncture
   See Liver—Puncture
Hepaticae
   See Liverworts
Hepatitis, Infectious
   x Acute catarrhal jaundice
      Epidemic hepatitis
      Infectious hepatitis
      Infectious jaundice
      Virus hepatitis
   xx Liver—Diseases
Hepatitis, Toxic
   See Toxic hepatitis
Hepatitis associated antigen
   x Australia antigen
      Serum hepatitis antigen
   xx Antigens and antibodies
Hepatolenticular degeneration *(RC394.H4)*
   x Degeneration, Hepatolenticular
      Lenticular degeneration
      Progressive lenticular degeneration
      Wilson's disease
   xx Brain—Diseases
      Liver—Diseases
Hepatoma
   xx Liver—Tumors
Hepatonephromegalia glycogenica
   See Glycogenosis
Hepatoptosis
   See Liver—Displacement
Hephthalite language
   See Ephthalite language

Hephthalites
   See Ephthalites
Heptagon
   x Seven-sided polygon
   xx Polygons
Heptamycin
   xx Antibiotics
Hera (African tribe)
Heraclean tablets *(CN397.H4)*
   x Tablets, Heraclean
   xx Inscriptions, Greeks
   — Language
Heraldic book-plates
   See Book-plates, Heraldic
Heraldic visitations
   See Visitations, Heraldic
Heraldry *(Indirect)* *(National, CR;*
     National: theory, JC345)
   sa Achievements (Heraldry)
      Badges
      Battle-cries
      Canting arms (Heraldry)
      Chivalry
      Color in heraldry
      Crests
      Decorations of honor
      Devices
      Emblems
      Emblems, National
      Escutcheons
      Flags
      Genealogy
      Hatchments
      Insignia
      Knights and knighthood
      Military religious orders
      Mottoes
      Nobility
      Orders of knighthood and chivalry
      Precedence
      Seals (Numismatics)
      Titles of honor and nobility
      Visitations, Heraldic
      subdivision Heraldry *under subjects,*
        e.g. Book industries and trade—
        Heraldry; Popes—Heraldry; *also*
        particular heraldic devices, e.g.
        Collar (in heraldry), Coq gaulois
        (Heraldic device), Eagle (in
        heraldry), Elephant (in heraldry),
        Fleur-de-lis
   x Arms, Coats of
      Blazonry
      Coats of arms
      Pedigrees
   xx Archaeology
      Auxiliary sciences of history
      Biography
      Chivalry
      Crests
      Decorations of honor
      Devices
      Emblems, National
      Genealogy
      History
      Knights and knighthood
      Nobility
      Peerage
      Precedence
      Signs and symbols
      Symbolism
      Titles of honor and nobility
   — Law and legislation *(Direct)*
   — Poetry

     GEOGRAPHIC SUBDIVISIONS

   — United States
      x United States—Heraldry

Heraldry, Ecclesiastical
See Heraldry, Sacred
Heraldry, Ornamental *(CR29-69)*
x Ornamental heraldry
xx Decoration and ornament
Design, Decorative
Heraldry, Sacred *(Indirect) (CR1101-1131)*
sa Popes—Heraldry
x Heraldry, Ecclesiastical
xx Christian antiquities
Christian art and symbolism
Heraldry, School
See School heraldry
Heraldry in literature
Heralds *(CR183-5; Manners and customs, GT5020)*
xx Courts and courtiers
Herb gardening *(SB351.H5)*
xx Gardening
Herbs
Herbage
See Grasses
Herbals
See Botany, Medical
Botany—Pre-Linnean works
Herbs
Materia medica, Vegetable
Medicine, Medieval
Herbaria *(Indirect) (QK75-77)*
Works on herbaria, collectively, are entered here. Publications, descriptions, etc. of individual herbaria are entered under name of herbarium.
sa Botanical museums
Botany—Type specimens
Plants—Collection and preservation
xx Botanical museums
Botany
Plants—Collection and preservation
Herbicides
Here are entered descriptive works on herbicides and their use in weed control. Works on the physiological effect of herbicides on plants are entered under Plants, Effect of herbicides on.
x Weed killers
Weedicides
xx Agricultural chemicals
Pesticides
Weed control
Note under Plants, Effect of herbicides on
— Biodegradation
— Costs
— Economic aspects *(Direct)*
— Environmental aspects *(Direct)*
— Law and legislation
See Pesticides—Law and legislation
— Patents
— Testing
— Toxicology
sa Plants, Effect of herbicides on
xx Spraying and dusting residues in agriculture
Herbivora
sa names of herbivorous animals
— Diseases
Herbs
sa Botany—Pre-Linnean works
Cookery (Herbs)
Dill
Herb gardening
Lavender (Plant)
Tea substitutes
x Herbals
xx Botany, Medical
Botany—Pre-Linnean works
Materia medica, Vegetable
Medicine, Medieval

— Diseases and pests
— Therapeutic use
See Botany, Medical
Materia medica, Vegetable
Medicine, Medieval
Herbs (in religion, folk-lore, etc.)
x Folk-lore of herbs
xx Religion, Primitive
Hercules (Constellation)
See Stars—Clusters
Hercules (Turboprop transports)
x Lockheed Hercules
Turboprop transports
xx Aeroplanes, Military
Jet transports
— Juvenile literature
Hercules in literature
Herd-books
See Cattle—Herd-books
Goats—Herd-books
Swine—Herd-books
Herding behavior in animals
x Congregation in animals
Herding instinct
xx Animals, Habits and behavior of
Instinct
Herding instinct
See Herding behavior in animals
Herdsmen
See Cowboys
Gauchos
Shepherds
Hereditary ataxia
See Friedreich's disease
Hereditary chorea
x Huntington's chorea
xx Chorea
Hereditary diseases
See Heredity of disease
Hereditary metabolic disorders
See Metabolism, Inborn errors of
Hereditary succession
See Inheritance and succession
Heredity *(Biology, QH431; Eugenics, HQ753; Heredity and alcoholism, HV5133; Heredity and child culture, RJ91; Heredity and crime, HV6121-5; Heredity and genius, BF418; Psychology, BF341-6; Sociology, HM121)*
sa Atavism
Biometry
Blood groups
Chromosomes
Consanguinity
Crossing over (Genetics)
Cytoplasmic inheritance
Eugenics
Evolution
Genetics
Germ cells
Heredity of disease
Hybridization
Inheritance of acquired characters
Linkage (Genetics)
Man—Constitution
Mendel's law
Natural selection
Nature and nurture
Population genetics
Prenatal influences
Variation (Biology)
x Ancestry
Descent
Genes
Inheritance (Biology)
Pangenesis
xx Atavism

Biology
Breeding
Children
Diseases—Causes and theories of causation
Eugenics
Evolution
Genetics
Man
Mendel's law
Natural selection
Sociology
— Juvenile literature
— Pictorial works
Heredity, Human *(HQ753; QH431)*
sa Deaf—Marriage
Degeneration
Delinquents
Education and heredity
Human genetics
Mentally handicapped—Marriage
x Heredity in man
xx Delinquents
Eugenics
Family
Heredity of disease
Man—Constitution
Prenatal influences
— Juvenile literature
Heredity and environment
See Nature and nurture
Heredity in man
See Heredity, Human
Heredity of acquired characters
See Inheritance of acquired characters
Heredity of disease *(RB155)*
sa Heredity, Human
Man—Constitution
Medical genetics
Medical record linkage
Metabolism, Inborn errors of
Syphilis, Congenital, hereditary, and infantile
Tuberculosis, Congenital, hereditary, and infantile
Tuberous sclerosis
subdivision Genetic aspects under names of diseases, e.g. Cancer—Genetic aspects
x Diseases, Hereditary
Hereditary diseases
xx Genetics
Heredity
Medical genetics
Heredo-ataxia
See Friedreich's disease
Heredo-retinopathia congenitalis
See Norrie's disease
Hereford cattle *(SF199.H4; Herd-books, SF193.H5)*
xx Beef cattle
Example under Cattle breeds; Cows
Note under Cattle—Herd-books
Herem
See Excommunication (Jewish law)
Herero language *(PL8241)*
x Otjiherero language
Hereros *(DT709; GN657.H)*
x Damaras
Herreros
Ovaherero
Heresies and heretics *(BT1313-1490)*
For general descriptive and historical works. Works on heresy in the abstract are entered under the heading Heresy.
sa In Coena Domini bulls
xx Theology, Doctrinal
— Early church, ca. 30-600 *(BT1313-1470)*

                        sa Adamites
                            Circumcellions
                            Eunomianism
                            Gnosticism
                            Manichaeism
                            Messalians
                            Monarchianism
                            Quartodecimans
                        xx Church history—Primitive and early
                            church, ca. 30-600
                            Theology, Doctrinal—History—Early
                            church, ca. 30-600
    — Middle Ages, 600-1500
            sa Brethren of the Free Spirit
                Sects, Medieval
    — Modern period, 1500-
            sa Sects
Heresies and heretics, Buddhist *(Direct)*
    sa Kakushi Nembutsu
    x Buddhist heresies and heretics
    xx Buddhist doctrines
        Buddhist sects
Heresies and heretics, Islamic *(Direct)*
    (BP167.5)
    x Heresies and heretics, Muslim
        Islamic heresies and heretics
        Muslim heresies and heretics
    xx Islamic sects
        Islamic theology
Heresies and heretics, Jewish
    x Jewish heresies and heretics
    xx Jewish sects
Heresies and heretics, Muslim
    See Heresies and heretics, Islamic
Heresy *(BT1313-1490)*
    sa Apostasy
        Liberty of speech in the church
        Schism
        Trials (Heresy)
    xx Apostasy
        Offenses against religion
        Theology, Doctrinal
    Note under Heresies and heretics
Heresy (Canon law) *(BX1939.H4)*
Hermaphroditism *(RC883)*
    sa Bisexuality
        Gynandromorphism
    x Intersexuality
    xx Sex (Biology)
        Sexual disorders
Hermeneutics *(Classics, PA49; Methodology,*
    BD240-241)
    sa Gematria
        Preunderstanding (Theology)
    x Interpretation
    xx Criticism
Hermeneutics, Biblical
    See Bible—Hermeneutics
Hermeneutics, Talmudic
    See Talmud—Hermeneutics
Hermetic art and philosophy
    See Alchemy
        Astrology
        Magic
        Occult sciences
Hermetic medicines
    See Alchemy
Hermetically sealed double glazing
    See Sealed double glazing
Hermione Mutiny, 1797 *(DA87.7)*
Hermit-crabs *(QL444.D3)*
    xx Crabs
    — Juvenile literature
Hermit-thrush
    See Thrushes
Hermitages *(Direct)*
    sa Hermits
    x Cells of hermits

                Hermits' cells
    xx Hermits
        Monasteries
Hermite polynomials
    x Polynomials, Hermite
    xx Differential equations—Numerical
        solutions
        Orthogonal polynomials
Hermits *(Indirect) (Biography,*
    CT9990-9991; Monasticism,
    BX2845-7)
    sa Augustinians
        Buddhist hermits
        Camaldolites
        Carthusians
        Eremitic life
        Hermitages
        Pillar saints
        Recluses
    x Anchorites
        Eremites
    xx Christian biography
        Eccentrics and eccentricities
        Hermitages
        Monastic and religious life
        Recluses
        Saints
Hermits' cells
    See Hermitages
Hermits in art
    xx Art
Hermits in literature
Hermodactyl *(Drugs, RS165.H5)*
Hernhutters
    See Moravians
Hernia *(RD621-6)*
    sa Femoral hernia
        Hiatal hernia
        Inguinal hernia
        Trusses (Surgery)
        Ventral hernia
        subdivision Hernia *under names of*
            organs, e.g. Lungs—Hernia
    x Bubonocele
        Herniotomy
        Kelotomy
        Rupture
    xx Intestines—Surgery
        Trusses (Surgery)
    — Hospitals *(RD621; RD705)*
Herniotomy
    See Hernia
Hero and Leander
    Example under Literature, Comparative—
        Themes, motives
Hero-worship
    See Heroes
Herodiones *(QL696.A7)*
    sa Herons
        Storks
    x Ardeidae
Heroes
    sa Apotheosis
        Bogatyrs
        Boys as soldiers
        Courage
        Explorers
        Heldensage
        Martyrs
        Mythology
        Saints

                subdivision Juvenile participants *under*
                    names of wars, e.g. United States—
                    History—Civil War, 1861-1865—
                    Juvenile participants; World War,
                    1939-1945—Juvenile participants;
                    also particular civilian and military
                    awards, e.g. George Cross, Medal of
                    Honor
    x Hero-worship
        Heroism
    xx Adventure and adventurers
        Apotheosis
        Courage
        History
        Mythology
        Mythology, Classical
    — Anecdotes, facetiae, satire, etc.
    — Caricatures and cartoons
    — Juvenile literature
Heroes (in numismatics)
    xx Heroes in art
Heroes in art
    sa Heroes (in numismatics)
    xx Art
Heroes in literature *(PN6071.H4)*
    sa Shakespeare, William, 1564-1616—
        Characters—Heroes
Heroes in motion pictures
    xx Moving-pictures
Heroic couplet
    See Heroic verse, English
Heroic poetry
    See Epic poetry
Heroic saga
    See Heldensage
Heroic verse, English *(PE1515)*
    x Heroic couplet
    xx English language—Versification
Heroic virtue
        Here are entered works dealing with the
        exercise of virtue in a pre-eminent de-
        gree, a prerequisite for beatification
        and canonization.
    x Virtue, Heroic
    xx Beatification
        Canonization
        Martyrdom
        Saints
Heroid *(PN1415; German, PT581.H5)*
    xx Imaginary letters
Heroids *(German poetry, PT581.H5; Poetry,*
    PN1415)
Heroin *(HV5822.H4)*
    xx Morphine
        Narcotics
    — Prices *(Direct)*
Heroines
    See Woman—Biography
        Women in literature
        Women in the Bible
Heroism
    See Courage
        Heroes
Herons *(QL696.A7)*
    sa Cattle egret
        European bittern
        Great blue heron
    x Ardeidae
        Egrets
    xx Herodiones
Herpes *(RL281)*
Herpes simplex *(RC147.H6)*
    xx Herpesvirus diseases
Herpes simplex virus
    x Herpes virus hominis
    xx Herpesviruses
Herpes tonsurans maculosus
    See Pityriasis rosea

Herpes virus hominis
  See Herpes simplex virus
Herpes zoster *(RC147.H6)*
  sa Varicella-zoster virus
  x Shingles (Disease)
  xx Herpesvirus diseases
Herpes zoster virus
  See Varicella-zoster virus
Herpesvirus diseases
  sa Chicken-pox
      Herpes simplex
      Herpes zoster
      Pseudorabies
  xx Virus diseases
Herpesviruses
  sa Herpes simplex virus
      Pseudorabies virus
      Varicella-zoster virus
  xx Viruses
Herpetology
  sa Amphibians
      Reptiles
  xx Vertebrates
      Zoology
  — Terminology
Herreros
  See Hereros
Herring *(QL638.C64; Fish-culture, SH167.H5)*
  sa Cookery (Herring)
Herring, Blueback
  See Blueback herring
Herring-fisheries *(Indirect)* *(SH351.H5)*
  xx Fisheries
Herring-gull *(QL696.L3)*
  xx Gulls
  — Juvenile literature
  — Legends and stories
Herrnhuter
  See Bohemian Brethren
      Moravians
Hertzian waves
  See Electric waves
      Microwaves
      Radio waves
Hesperidin
  Example under Bioflavonoids
Hesse
  — History *(DD801.H5-69)*
  — — To 1247
  — — 1247-1567
  — — Landgraviate, 1567-1806
  — — Grand duchy, 1806-1918
  — — 1918-
Hessian flies *(SB945.H3)*
  xx Diptera
      Flies
Hessian mercenaries
  sa United States—History—Revolution, 1775-1783—German mercenaries
  xx German mercenaries
      Mercenary troops
Hessians
  xx Germans
Hessians in the American Revolution
  See United States—History—Revolution, 1775-1783—German mercenaries
Hesychasm *(BT1392)*
  xx Meditation
      Mysticism—Orthodox Eastern Church
      Navel (in religion, folk-lore, etc.)
      Theology, Doctrinal—History
Heteroauxin
  See Indoleacetic acid
Heterocera
  See Moths
Heterocyclic compounds *(QD400-409)*
  x Cycloids, Mixed (Chemistry)

Mixed cycloids (Chemistry)
  xx Cyclic compounds
  Example under Chemistry, Organic — Spectra
Heterogeneous catalysis *(QD505)*
  xx Catalysis
Heterogenesis
  See Generations, Alternating
      Life—Origin
      Spontaneous generation
Heterometry
  xx Chemistry, Analytic—Quantitative
Heteromodal effects
  See Intersensory effects
Heterophoria *(RE776)*
  xx Eye—Diseases and defects
Heteropoda *(Mollusks, QL430.4)*
  xx Gasteropoda
Heteroptera *(Indirect)* *(QL523.H6)*
  sa Chinch-bugs
      Lace-bugs
  xx Hemiptera
Heteroptera, Fossil
  xx Insects, Fossil
Heterosis *(Animal breeding, SF105; Biology, QH421; Breeding, S494; Plant breeding, SB123)*
  xx Breeding
      Fertility
      Growth
      Growth (Plants)
      Hybridization
Heterostylism *(QK926)*
  xx Fertilization of plants
      Plants—Reproduction
      Plants, Sex in
Heterotrophic bacteria
  See Bacteria, Heterotrophic
Heterotropia
  See Strabismus
Heterozygosis *(Biology, QH21-5; Plant breeding, SB123)*
Hetmans *(Direct)*
  xx Cossacks
Hetol *(RM666.H)*
Heulandite *(QE391.H55)*
Heve language
  See Eudeve language
Hevea *(SB291.H)*
  sa Rubber
  x Pará rubber
  xx Rubber
  — Diseases and pests
  — Weed control *(Indirect)* *(SB608.H5)*
Hex signs *(Indirect)*
  sa Barn symbols
  xx Design, Decorative
      Signs and symbols
      Talismans
      Witchcraft in art
Hexactinellida *(QL373.H6)*
Hexadecimal system
  See Sexadecimal system
Hexameter *(P311; English, PE1531.H6; Greek, PA416.H6; Latin, PA2337.H6)*
  Example under Versification
Hexapoda
  See Insects
Heyducks
  See Haiduks
HFB airplanes *(TL686.H)*
Hi-fi systems
  See High-fidelity sound systems
Hiaqui Indians
  See Yaqui Indians
Hiatal hernia
  x Esophageal hernia

  xx Diaphragm—Hernia
      Hernia
Hiba arborvitae *(Botany, QK494.5.C975; Forestry, SD397.H57)*
  x Hiba falsearborvitae
Hiba falsearborvitae
  See Hiba arborvitae
Ḥibat Tsiyon
  See Ḥibbat Zion
Ḥibbat Zion
  x Ḥibat Tsiyon
  xx Zionism
Hibernation *(QL755)*
  sa Animals, Habits and behavior of
      Artificial hibernation
  xx Animals, Habits and behavior of
      Dormancy (Biology)
      Sleep
      Zoology
  — Juvenile literature
Hibiscus
  sa Ambary hemp
Hibiya Kōtō Gakkō
  — Strike, 1969
Hichiriki *(ML990.H5)*
  xx Musical instruments, Japanese
      Oboe
Hickey Plot, 1776 *(E277)*
  xx American loyalists
Hickory *(Forestry, SD397.H6)*
Hicksites
  See Friends, Society of (Hicksite)
Hidage *(Taxation: Great Britain, HJ4337)*
  xx Land value taxation—Great Britain
Hidatsa Indians *(E99.H6)*
  sa Crow Indians
  x Gros Ventres of the Missouri
      Grosventres of the Missouri
      Minitaree Indians
      Minnetaree Indians
  xx Indians of North America
      Siouan Indians
  — Legends *(E99.H6)*
Hidatsa language *(PM1331)*
  x Grosventre language
  xx Siouan languages
Hidden unemployment
  See Disguised unemployment
Hide powder *(TS985)*
  sa Tannins
  xx Collagen
      Hides and skins
      Tanning
      Tannins
Hides and skins *(Direct)* *(Manufactures, TS967; Trade, HD9778)*
  sa Fur
      Hide powder
      Leather
      Tanning
  x Pelts
      Skins
  xx Fur
      Leather
      Tanning
  Example under Animal products
  — Defects
      sa Leather—Defects
      xx Leather—Defects
  — Disinfection *(RA761)*
  — Dressing and dyeing
      x Dyes and dyeing—Hides and skins
  — Standards
  — Tariff
      See Tariff on hides
  — Taxation *(Direct)*

Hides and skins, Effect of radiation on
  (TS967)
  xx Radiation
Hides and skins in the Bible
  x Bible—Hides and skins
Hides and skins industry *(Direct)*
  (HD9778)
Hiding-places (Secret chambers, etc.) *(17th*
    century, England, DA380)
  x Priest's holes
    Secret chambers
    Subterranean passages
  xx Caves
    Ghosts
    Historic houses, etc.
    Labyrinths
    Persecution
Hien (Fighter planes)
  x Kawasaki Ki 100 (Fighter planes)
    Kawasaki Ki 61 (Fighter planes)
  xx Fighter planes
Hieratic inscriptions
  See Egyptian language—Inscriptions
Hieratic writing
  See Egyptian language—Papyri, Hieratic
    Egyptian language—Writing, Hieratic
Hieroglyphic Bibles *(BS560)*
  x Bible—Hieroglyphic Bibles
  xx Bible—Picture Bibles
    Children's literature
    Picture-books for children
Hieroglyphic inscriptions
  See Inscriptions, Hieroglyphic
Hieroglyphic type
  See Type and type-founding—Hieroglyphic
    type
Hieroglyphics *(Egyptian, PJ1091-7)*
  sa Alphabet
    Picture-writing
    Writing—History
  x Ideography
  xx Inscriptions
    Paleography
    Picture-writing
    Writing
Hieroglyphics, Aztec
  See Aztecs—Writing
Hieroglyphics, Egyptian
  See Egyptian language—Writing,
    Hieroglyphic
Hieroglyphics, Maya
  See Mayas—Writing
Hieroglyphics, Mexican
  See Indians of Mexico—Writing
Hieronymites *(BX3680.H5)*
Hieronymites in Spain *(BX3680.H5)*
Higaonan (Philippine people)
  See Bukidnon (Philippine people)
High (Meteorology)
  See Anticyclones
High altitude rocket research
  See Atmosphere, Upper—Rocket
    observations
High-altitude suits
  See Pressure suits
High apartment buildings
  See High-rise apartment buildings
High blood pressure
  See Hypertension
High buildings
  See Tall buildings
High Command Trial, Nuremberg, 1948-1949
  See War crime trials—Nuremberg—High
    Command case, 1948-1949
High energy forming *(TS256)*
  sa Bulging (Metalwork)
    Explosive forming
    Hydrostatic extrusion

    Magnetic forming
  x High energy rate metal forming
    High velocity forming
    Metals—High energy forming
  xx Forging
    Sheet-metal work
High energy fuels
  See Boron as fuel
High energy physics
  See Particles (Nuclear physics)
High energy radiotherapy
  See Radiotherapy, High energy
High energy rate metal forming
  See High energy forming
High-fidelity audio equipment
  See High-fidelity sound systems
High-fidelity sound systems *(TK7882.H5)*
  sa Phonograph—High-fidelity systems
    Radio—High-fidelity systems
    Stereophonic sound systems
  x Hi-fi systems
    High-fidelity audio equipment
  xx Electronics
    Sound—Recording and reproducing
  — Amateurs' manuals
  — Juvenile literature
  — Repairing
  — Testing
High five (Game)
  See Pedro (Game)
High-frequency induction heating
  See Induction heating
High-frequency radio
  See Radio, Short wave
High Gothic art
  See Art, Gothic—High Gothic
High Holidays
  See High Holy Days
High Holy Day sermons
  xx Sermons, Jewish
High Holy Days *(BM693.H5)*
  sa Rosh ha-Shanah
    Shabbat shubah
    Synagogue music—High Holy Day
      services
    Yom Kippur
  x High Holidays
  xx Tishri
High interest-low vocabulary books
  (Z1039.S5)
  sa Retarded readers, Books for
    Slow learning children, Books for
    Socially handicapped children, Books
      for
  x Low vocabulary-high interest books
  xx Children's literature
High jumping
  See Jumping
High license
  See License system
    Liquor laws
    Liquor problem
High-lift devices
  See Flaps (Aeroplanes)
High-octane gasoline
  See Gasoline—Anti-knock and anti-knock
    mixtures
High plains grasshopper
  x Long-winged grasshopper of the plains
  xx Locusts
High potency (Drugs)
  See Homeopathy—Attenuations, dilutions,
    and potencies
High pressure (Engineering)
  See High pressure (Technology)
High pressure (Science) *(QC281)*
  sa Compressibility
    High pressure research

    High pressure (Technology)
    Pressure vessels
  xx Pressure
  — Measurement
    See High pressure measurements
  — Physiological effect
High pressure (Technology) *(TP156.P75)*
  sa Bulging (Metalwork)
    Hydrostatic extrusion
    Materials at high pressures
    Plastics at high pressures
  x High pressure (Engineering)
  xx Chemistry, Technical
    High pressure (Science)
  — Safety measures
High pressure measurements *(QC281)*
  x High pressure (Science)—Measurement
    Measurements, High pressure
High pressure research
  xx Force and energy
    High pressure (Science)
    Pressure
    Research
High-pressure steam
  See Steam, High-pressure
High-pressure system (Meteorology)
  See Anticyclones
High Renaissance art
  See Art, Renaissance—High Renaissance
High-rise apartment buildings *(Direct)*
  x High apartment buildings
    Multistory housing
  xx Apartment houses
    Tall buildings
  — Fires and fire prevention
  — Heating and ventilation
  — Public opinion
High-rise buildings
  See Skyscrapers
    Tall buildings
High school administration
  See High schools—Administration
High school attendance
  See School attendance—High school
High school characteristics index
  x HSCI
High school dropouts *(Direct)*
  x Secondary school dropouts
  xx Dropouts
    Personnel service in secondary
      education
    School attendance
High school education
  See Education, Secondary
High school environment
  x Environment, High school
  xx School environment
High school equivalency certificates
  (LB1627.7)
  xx School credits—Outside work
High school equivalency examination
  x English school certificate examination
    Equivalency examination, High school
  xx Examinations—Questions
    General educational development tests
    School credits—Outside work
High school facilities *(Direct)*
  sa High schools—Buildings
    High schools—Furniture, equipment,
      etc.
  xx School facilities
  — Planning *(Direct)*
    xx Educational planning

High school graduates *(Direct)*
    Here are entered works on high school graduates as a socio-economic group. Works on high school graduates in relation to their alma maters are entered under High schools—Alumni.
    xx High schools—Alumni
  — Employment *(Direct)*
    sa High school students—Employment
High school libraries
  See School libraries (High school)
High school personality questionnaire
    xx Adolescence
      Personality tests
High school placement test
    x Placement test, High school
    xx Educational tests and measurements
High school principals *(Direct)*
    sa Junior high school principals
    x Principals, High school
      Principals, Secondary school
      Principals, Senior high school
      Secondary school principals
      Senior high school principals
    xx School superintendents and principals
  — In-service training
  — Legal status, laws, etc. *(Direct)*
    xx Educational law and legislation
  — Pensions
    See High school principals—Salaries, pensions, etc.
  — Salaries, pensions, etc.
    x High school principals—Pensions
  — Selection and appointment
High school seniors *(Direct)*
    x Seniors, High school
    xx High school students
High school students *(Direct)*
    sa High school seniors
    xx Students
  — Attitudes
    xx Attitude (Psychology)
  — Conduct of life
    xx Student ethics
  — Correspondence, reminiscences, etc.
  — Employment *(Direct)*
    xx Children—Employment
      High school graduates—Employment
  — Health and hygiene *(Direct)*
    xx School hygiene
  — Political activity
    xx Politics, Practical
  — Recreation
  — Social and economic status
    See High school students' socio-economic status
High school students' socio-economic status *(Direct) (LC208.4)*
    x High school students—Social and economic status
    xx Students' socio-economic status
High school teachers *(Direct)*
    x Secondary school teachers
      Senior high school teachers
      Teachers, High school
      Teachers, Secondary school
      Teachers, Senior high school
    xx Teachers
  — Appointment
    See High school teachers—Selection and appointment
  — Attitudes
    xx Attitude (Psychology)
  — Certification *(Direct)*
    xx High school teachers—Legal status, laws, etc.
  — Correspondence, reminiscences, etc.
  — In-service training *(Direct)*

    xx High school teachers, Training of
  — Leaves of absence
  — Legal status, laws, etc. *(Direct)*
    sa High school teachers—Certification
    xx Educational law and legislation
  — Pensions
    See High school teachers—Salaries, pensions, etc.
  — Political activity
    xx Politics, Practical
  — Salaries, pensions, etc.
    x High school teachers—Pensions
  — Selection and appointment
    x High school teachers—Appointment
  — Supply and demand *(Direct)*
  — Tenure *(Direct)*
    xx Employees, Dismissal of
      Employees, Resignation of
  — Work load
High school teachers, Rating of
High school teachers, Training of *(Direct)*
    sa High school teachers—In-service training
  — Audio-visual aids
High school teaching *(Direct)*
    x Secondary school teaching
    xx Teaching
  — Vocational guidance
    See High school teaching as a profession
High school teaching as a profession *(Direct)*
    x High school teaching—Vocational guidance
    xx Teaching as a profession
High school yearbooks
  See School yearbooks
High schools *(Indirect) (LB1603-1694)*
    Subdivided by country or state. Works on high schools of a particular city are entered under name of city, with subdivision Public schools.
    sa Catholic high schools
      Comprehensive high schools
      Education, Secondary
    x Secondary schools
    xx Education
      Education, Secondary
      Public schools
      Schools
  — Accounting
    See Schools—Accounting
  — Accreditation
    Example under Accreditation (Education)
  — Administration *(LB2822)*
    sa Departmental chairmen (High schools)
    x High school administration
    xx School management and organization
  — Alumni
    sa High school graduates
    Note under High school graduates
  — Buildings *(Direct)*
    xx High school facilities
      School buildings
  — Curricula
    sa High schools—Honors courses
    Example under Education—Curricula; *and under references from* Courses of study; Curricula (Courses of study); Study, Courses of
  — Entrance requirements *(LB1627)*
    Example under reference from Entrance requirements
  — Equipment and supplies
    See High schools—Furniture, equipment, etc.
  — Furniture, equipment, etc.

    x High schools—Equipment and supplies
    xx Furniture
      High school facilities
  — Graduate work
    See High schools—Postgraduate work
  — Honors courses
    x Honors courses in high schools
      Honors work in high schools
    xx Gifted children—Education
      High schools—Curricula
  — — Programmed instruction
  — Postgraduate work *(LB1695)*
    x High schools—Graduate work
      Post-graduate work in high schools
      Postgraduate work in high schools
    xx Education, Secondary
  — Schedules
    See Schedules, School
High schools, Junior
  See Junior high schools
High schools, Rural
  See Rural schools
High seas, Jurisdiction over
  See Contiguous zones (Maritime law)
    Maritime law
    War, Maritime (International law)
High society
  See Upper classes
High-speed aerodynamics
  See Aerodynamics, Supersonic
High-speed aeronautics *(TL551.5)*
    sa Aerodynamics, Supersonic
      Aerodynamics, Transonic
      Aeroplanes—Jet propulsion
      Aerothermodynamics
      Hypersonic planes
      Rocket planes
      Rockets (Aeronautics)
      Short take-off and landing aircraft—Jet propulsion
      Supersonic planes
      Transonic planes
      Vertically rising aeroplanes—Jet propulsion
    x Aeronautics, High-speed
      High-speed flight
      Supersonic aeronautics
    xx Aeronautics
High-speed cinematography
  See Cinematography, High-speed
High-speed data processing
  See Real-time data processing
High-speed flight
  See High-speed aeronautics
High speed ground transportation *(Indirect)*
    Here are entered general works on inter-city ground transportation systems differing from the conventional ground modes of transportation of the 1960's both in design and in that they operate at speeds upwards of 300 miles per hour.
    xx Transportation
  — Communication systems
    xx Telecommunication
High-speed photography
  See Photography, High-speed
High-speed radiography
  See Radiography, High-speed
High temperature materials
  See Heat resistant materials
High temperature metallurgy
  See Metals at high temperatures
High temperature metals
  See Heat resistant alloys
High temperature plasmas
    sa Plasma confinement

x Hot plasmas
   Plasmas, High temperature
xx Gases at high temperatures
   Plasma (Ionized gases)
High temperatures *(QC276)*
sa Gases at high temperatures
   Materials at high temperatures
   Metals at high temperatures
   Solar furnaces
x Elevated temperatures
   Heat barrier
   Ultrahigh temperatures
xx Heat
— Measurement
      See Pyrometers and pyrometry
— Physiological effect
      See Heat—Physiological effect
High-tension power distribution
   See Electric power distribution—High
      tension
High treason
   See Treason
High vacuum technique
   See Vacuum
High velocity forming
   See High energy forming
High voltages
xx Electric engineering
   Electricity
— Laboratory manuals
Higher criticism
   See subdivision Criticism, interpretation,
      etc. *under* Bible *and under parts and
      books of the Bible, e.g.* Bible. N.T.
      —Criticism, interpretation, etc.;
      Bible. O.T. Hexateuch—Criticism,
      interpretation, etc.; Bible. N.T.
      Matthew—Criticism, interpretation,
      etc.
Higher education
   See Education, Higher
Higher education and state *(Direct)*
      (LC171-182)
sa Federal aid to higher education
   Universities and colleges—Privileges
      and immunities
x State and higher education
xx Education and state
   Education, Higher
Higher education of women *(Direct)*
sa Professional education of women
   Universities and colleges—Graduate
      work of women
xx Education, Higher
   Professional education of women
Higher law
   See Divine right of kings
      Government, Resistance to
Higher plane curves
   See Curves, Plane
Highland clans
   See Clans and clan system
Highland costume
   See Tartans
Highland fling (Dance) *(GV1796.H)*
Highland pony *(SF315.2.H5)*
xx Ponies
Highlands of Scotland in literature
Highmore's antrum
   See Maxillary sinus
Highrise buildings
   See Tall buildings
Highway accessories
   See Roads—Accessories
Highway accidents
   See Traffic accidents
Highway beautification
   See Roadside improvement

Highway bypasses *(Direct)*
sa Highway relocation
x Bypasses, Highway
xx Express highways
   Highway relocation
   Roads
   Traffic engineering
Highway communications
sa Electronic traffic controls
   Express highways—Communication
      systems
   Traffic signs and signals
x Communications, Highway
   Road communications
xx Roads
Highway construction
   See Road construction
Highway construction workers
   See Road construction workers
Highway departments *(Direct)*
x Road departments
xx Highway engineering
   Highway law
   Roads
— Accounting
— Employees
   sa Highway engineers
Highway design
   See Roads—Design
Highway drainage
   See Road drainage
Highway drawings
   See Roads—Drawings
Highway driving
   See Automobile driving on highways
Highway engineering *(Direct) (TE)*
sa Highway departments
   Highway planning
   Highway relocation
   Highway research
   Road construction
   Roads
   Roadside improvement
   Traffic engineering
x Road engineering
xx Civil engineering
   Highway planning
   Roads
— Management
Highway engineering, Photography in
   See Photography in highway engineering
Highway engineers *(Direct)*
xx Civil engineers
   Engineers
   Highway departments—Employees
— Biography
Highway finance
   See Roads—Finance
Highway guard fences
   See Roads—Guard fences
Highway law *(Direct) (TE315-424)*
      Here are entered works on the law gov-
      erning the laying out, construction,
      and repair of highways and streets as
      well as their use. Works on laws and
      regulations concerning the control of
      traffic on highways and streets are en-
      tered under the heading Traffic regula-
      tions.
sa Automobiles—Laws and regulations
   Bridges—Law and legislation
   Building lines
   Corvée
   Cycling
   Dedication to public use
   Express highways—Law and legislation
   Ferries—Law and legislation
   Highway departments

   Private roads
   Road construction—Safety regulations
   Roads—Right of way
   Servitudes
   Traffic regulations
   Trails—Law and legislation
x Highways
   Law, Highway
   Road law
   Roads—Legislation
   Traffic safety—Law and legislation
xx Servitudes
   Streets
   Transportation—Laws and regulations
— Digests
Highway law (Roman law)
Highway lighting
   See Roads—Lighting
Highway location
   See Roads—Location
Highway patrols
   See Traffic police
Highway planning *(Direct) (TE153)*
sa Highway engineering
x Road planning
xx Highway engineering
   Planning
— Citizen participation
   x Citizen participation in highway
      planning
   xx Social action
Highway post offices
xx Postal service—Transportation,
      Automotive
   Postal service—United States
Highway relocation
sa Highway bypasses
x Relocation of highways
xx Express highways
   Highway bypasses
   Highway engineering
   Roads
   Traffic engineering
Highway research *(Indirect)*
sa Road materials—Testing
   Roads, Experimental
x Road research
   Roads—Research
xx Highway engineering
   Research, Industrial
   Road materials
   Roads
Highway safety
   See Traffic safety
Highway taxes
   See Motor fuels—Taxation
      Transportation, Automotive—Taxation
Highway traffic noise
   See Traffic noise
Highway transport workers *(Direct)*
sa Collective labor agreements—Trucking
      industry
   Motor bus drivers
   Motor bus lines—Employees
   Motor-truck drivers
   Wages—Highway transport workers
x Automotive transport workers
   Motor vehicle drivers
   Motor vehicle operators
   Road transport workers
   Transportation, Automotive—
      Employees
xx Transport workers
   Transportation, Automotive
— Collective bargaining
      See Collective bargaining—Highway
         transport workers
— Juvenile literature

Highway transport workers *(Direct)*
 (Continued)
— Language (New words, slang, etc.)
— Songs and music *(M1977.T87; M1978.T87)*
Highway transportation
 See Transportation, Automotive
Highway user taxes
 See Transportation, Automotive—Taxation
Highwaymen
 See Brigands and robbers
Highways
 See Highway law
 Roads
Hihatl language
 See Chamalal language
Hijacking of aircraft *(Direct)*
 Subdivided by national registry of aircraft.
 x Air lines—Hijacking
 Air piracy
 Seizure of aircraft in transit
 Sky hijacking
 Skyjacking
 xx Crimes aboard aircraft
Ḥijjat al-wadā'
 See Ḥajjat al-wadā'
Hiking *(Indirect)* *(G504)*
 sa Backpacking
 Hitchhiking
 Mountaineering
 Orientation
 Trails
 Vierdaagse (Hike)
 Walking
 x Tramping
 xx Outdoor life
 Walking
— Caricatures and cartoons
— Equipment and supplies
— Juvenile literature
— Songs and music *(M1977.H5; M1978.H5)*
Hilbert algebras
 x Algebras, Hilbert
 xx Functional analysis
 Von Neumann algebras
Hilbert space *(QA691)*
 sa Invariant subspaces
 Spectral theory (Mathematics)
 Von Neumann algebras
 xx Banach spaces
 Hyperspace
Hiligaina dialect *(PL5711)*
 sa Bisaya language
 xx Bisaya language
 Philippine languages
Hill agriculture
 See Hill farming
Hill culture
 See Hillside planting
Hill Damaras *(DT709)*
 x Damaras
Hill farming *(Indirect)* *(S575)*
 sa Hillside planting
 x Alpine agriculture
 Alpine farming
 Hill agriculture
 Mountain agriculture
 Mountain farming
 xx Agriculture
 Mountains
Hill figures *(CC710)*
 x Chalk figures
 Hillside figures
 Turf figures
 xx Archaeology
Hill-forts
 See Fortification, Primitive

Hill reaction
 xx Photosynthesis
Hillbilly music
 See Country music
Hillbilly musicians
 xx Country music
 Musicians
Hillculture
 See Hillside planting
Hillelites
 See Beth Hillel and Beth Shammai
Hillman automobile *(TL215.H5)*
 sa Imp automobile
 Minx automobile
 xx Rootes automobiles
Hillotype *(TR510)*
 xx Color photography
Hillside figures
 See Hill figures
Hillside planting *(Indirect)* *(S627.H5)*
 sa Streambank planting
 x Hill culture
 Hillculture
 Planting
 xx Hill farming
 Soil conservation
Hilsch tubes
 See Vortex tubes
Hiltersried, Battle of, 1433
 xx Bavaria—History—1180-1777
 Hussites
Hima
 See Bahima (African people)
Himalaya Mountains in literature
Himalayan cat *(SF449.H)*
Himalayan golden eagle *(QL696.A2)*
 x Berkut eagle
 Middle Asian golden eagle
 xx Eagles
 Golden eagle
Himalayan languages
 See Tibeto-Burman languages
Himeji Peasant Uprising, 1748
Himyaritic inscriptions
 See Inscriptions, Sabaean
Hinayana Buddhism
 sa Mahāsāṅghikas
 Sarvāstivādins
 x Lesser vehicle (Buddhism)
 Little vehicle (Buddhism)
 Pali Buddhism
 Southern Buddhism
 Southern vehicle (Buddhism)
 Theravada Buddhism
 xx Buddha and Buddhism
 Buddhist sects
— Essence, genius, nature
— Relations
— — Zen Buddhism, [etc.]
Hinckley, Minn.
— Fire, 1894
Hindered rotation theory
 See Molecular rotation
Hindi ballads and songs
Hindi essays
Hindi fiction *(Direct)*
— 20th century
Hindi imprints *(Direct)*
Hindi language *(PK1991-7)*
 Used for Hindustani in the Devanagari character.
 sa Awadhi dialect
 Bangaru dialect
 Bihari language
 Braj language
 Bundeli dialect
 Khari Boli language
 Urdu language

 xx Hindustani language
 Urdu language
— Dialects
— — Deccan *(PK1970)*
 x Dakhini Hindi dialect
 Dakkhini Hindi dialect
 Southern Hindi dialect
 xx Urdu language
— Readers for new literates
 Example under Readers for new literates
Hindi language, Eastern
 See Hindustani language
Hindi language, Western
 See Hindustani language
Hindi letters *(Direct)* *(PK2078.L4)*
Hindi literature *(Direct)*
— To 1500
— 1500-1800
— 19th century
— 20th century
 sa Chayavada
— 1947-

 GENERAL SUBDIVISIONS

— Appreciation *(Direct)*
— Muslim authors
Hindi periodicals *(History, etc., PN5371-5380)*
Hindi philology
 sa Harauti philology
— Research *(Direct)*
Hindi poetry
— To 1500
— 1500-1800
— 19th century
— 20th century
 sa Chayavada
— 1947-
Hindi prose literature *(Direct)*
Hindi wit and humor
Hindoos
 See Hindus
Hindu altars
 See Altars, Hindu
Hindu antiquities *(Direct)*
 When subdivided by place, make a second subject entry under the place, with subdivision Antiquities, Hindu.
 x Antiquities, Hindu
 xx Antiquities
Hindu architecture
 See Architecture, Hindu
Hindu art
 See Art, Hindu
Hindu art objects
 See Art objects, Hindu
Hindu asceticism
 See Asceticism—Hinduism
Hindu astrology
 See Astrology, Hindu
Hindu chant
 See Chants (Hindu)
Hindu children *(Direct)*
 x Children, Hindu
 xx Children
— Religious life *(BL1228.3.C5)*
 x Children—Religious life (Hinduism)
 xx Religious life (Hinduism)
Hindu civilization
 See Civilization, Hindu
Hindu converts to Buddhism
 See Buddhist converts from Hinduism
Hindu converts to Christianity
 See Converts from Hinduism
Hindu cosmology
 See Cosmology, Hindu
Hindu cultus
 See Cultus, Hindu

Hindu decoration and ornament
   See Decoration and ornament, Hindu
Hindu devotional calendars
   x Devotional calendars, Hindu
     Devotional calendars—Hinduism
Hindu devotional literature
   sa Hinduism—Prayer-books and devotions
   x Devotional literature, Hindu
   xx Hindu literature
Hindu devotional literature, Hindi, ⌜Kannada, etc.⌝
Hindu drama *(Direct)*
   xx Drama
     Religious drama
Hindu drawings
   See Drawings, Hindu
Hindu epistemology
   See Knowledge, Theory of (Hinduism)
Hindu eschatology
   See Eschatology, Hindu
Hindu ethics *(BJ121-3)*
   sa Ahiṃsā
     subdivision Conduct of life *under special groups of Hindus, e.g.* Youth, Hindu—Conduct of life
   x Ethics, Hindu
Hindu fasts and feasts
   See Fasts and feasts—Hinduism
Hindu gods
   See Gods, Hindu
Hindu hygiene
   See Hygiene, Hindu
Hindu hymns *(BL1226.3)*
   sa Sivaism—Hymns
     subdivision Hymns *under names of individual Hindu sects, e.g.* Vaishnavism—Hymns
   x Hinduism—Hymns
     Hymns, Hindu
   xx Chants (Hindu)
Hindu hymns, Bengali, ⌜Marathi, etc.⌝
Hindu law
   sa Benami transactions
     Burmese Buddhist law
     Dharma
     Support (Domestic relations law, Hindu)
     specific legal headings with Hindu law *added in parentheses, e.g.* Adoption (Hindu law)
   x Law, Hindu
   xx Law, Oriental
   — Codification
Hindu literature *(BL1145-7)*
   sa Hindu devotional literature
     Hinduism—Sacred books
     Vaishnava literature
   xx Religious literature
Hindu literature, Gujarati, ⌜Hindi, Marathi, etc.⌝
Hindu logic *(BC25-6)*
   x Logic, Hindu
   xx Philosophy, Hindu
Hindu magic
   See Magic, Hindu
Hindu marriage customs and rites
   See Marriage customs and rites, Hindu
Hindu medicine
   See Medicine, Hindu
Hindu meditations
   x Meditations, Hindu
   xx Meditation (Hinduism)
Hindu mendicants
   See Sadhus
Hindu monasticism and religious orders
   See Monasticism and religious orders, Hindu

Hindu music
   See Music, Indic
Hindu mysticism
   See Mysticism—Hinduism
Hindu parables
   See Parables, Hindu
Hindu prayers *(BL1226.8)*
   sa Prayer (Hinduism)
   x Prayers, Hindu
   xx Hinduism—Prayer-books and devotions
     Prayer (Hinduism)
Hindu psychology
   See Hinduism—Psychology
Hindu religious education
   See Religious education, Hindu
Hindu saints
   See Saints, Hindu
Hindu sculpture
   See Sculpture, Hindu
Hindu sects *(Direct)* *(BL1245.A1)*
   sa Alakhiyas
     Bauls
     Bhagavatas
     Dādūpanthīs
     Dharmaṭhākura
     Gusains
     Kālāmukhas
     Kānphaṭas
     Kāpālikas
     Kaulas
     Lingayats
     Mādhvas
     Mahanubhava
     Nagesh sect
     Nātha sect
     Nimbarka (Sect)
     Niranjanis
     Palatu sect
     Pāñcarātra (Sect)
     Radhasoami Satsang
     Sadhs
     Sahajiyā
     Shaktism
     Śiva Nārāyanīs
     Sivaism
     Vaikhanasas
     Vaishnavism
     Vallabhachars
   x Hinduism—Sects
     Sects, Hindu
   xx Brahmanism
     Hinduism
Hindu sermons *(BL1226.5)*
   x Sermons, Hindu
Hindu sermons, Gujarati, ⌜Marathi, etc.⌝
   x Sermons, Gujarati ⌜Marathi, etc.⌝—Hindu authors
Hindu shrines *(Direct)*
   x Shrines, Hindu
Hindu sociology
   See Sociology, Hindu
Hindu symbolism *(BL1215.S9)*
   sa Bijas
     Yantras
   xx Symbolism
Hindu temples
   See Temples, Hindu
Hindu theological anthropology
   See Man (Hinduism)
Hindu wall hangings
   See Wall hangings, Hindu
Hindu women
   See Women, Hindu
Hindu worship
   See Worship (Hinduism)
Hindu youth
   See Youth, Hindu

Hinduism *(Direct)* *(BL1100-1270; India, BL2000-2030; Philosophy, B130-133)*
   sa Advaita
     Ancestor worship (Hinduism)
     Arya-samaj
     Atonement (Hinduism)
     Baptism (Hinduism)
     Bhakti
     Brahma-samaj
     Brahmanism
     Buddha and Buddhism
     Caste—India
     Civilization, Hindu
     Deluge (Hinduism)
     Dev-samaj
     Dharma
     Dvaita (Vedanta)
     Fasts and feasts—Hinduism
     God (Hinduism)
     Gods, Hindu
     Gurus
     Hindu sects
     Jains
     Karma
     Knowledge, Theory of (Hinduism)
     Man (Hinduism)
     Maya (Hinduism)
     Meditation (Hinduism)
     Mysticism—Hinduism
     Nyaya
     Parables, Hindu
     Prayer (Hinduism)
     Purity, Ritual (Hinduism)
     Religious life (Hinduism)
     Revelation (Hinduism)
     Saints, Hindu
     Salvation (Hinduism)
     Sankhya
     Sannyasi
     Soul (Hinduism)
     Spiritual life (Hinduism)
     Śraddhā
     Tantrism
     Temples, Hindu
     Vaiśeṣika
     Vedanta
     Vedas
     Women in Hinduism
     Worship (Hinduism)
     Yoga
   xx Brahmanism
     Religions
   — 20th century *(BL1205)*
   — Asceticism
     See Asceticism—Hinduism
   — Catechisms and creeds
   — Charities
   — Controversial literature *(BL1211)*
   — Essence, genius, nature *(BL1205)*
   — Hymns
     See Hindu hymns
   — Juvenile literature
   — Missions
     Here are entered works on the spread of Hinduism. Works on the spread of Christianity among Hindus are entered under Missions to Hindus.
   — Prayer-books and devotions
     sa Hindu prayers
     xx Hindu devotional literature
   — — English, ⌜French, German, etc.⌝
   — Psychology *(BL1215.P8)*
     x Hindu psychology
     Psychology, Hindu
     xx Psychology
     Psychology, Religious
   — Relations *(BL1230)*

Hinduism *(Direct)* *(BL1100-1270; India, BL2000-2030; Philosophy, B130-133)*
   — Relations *(BL1230)* *(Continued)*
   — — Buddhism, ₍Christianity, Islam, etc.₎
   — Rituals
       sa Bratas
         Chants (Hindu)
         Homa (Rite)
         Marriage customs and rites, Hindu
         Marriage service (Hinduism)
         Mṛtyuñjaya homa
         Rājasūya
         Sacred thread ceremony
         Sandhyā (Hindu rite)
         Sivaratri
         Srāddha (Hindu rite)
         subdivision Rituals *under names of individual Hindu sects, e.g.* Vaishnavism—Rituals
       xx Ritual
   — Sacred books
       xx Hindu literature
   — — Stories
   — Sects
       See Hindu sects
Hinduism and science
   x Science and Hinduism
   xx Religion and science
Hinduism and socialism
   See Socialism and Hinduism
Hinduism and state
   x State and Hinduism
   xx Religion and state
Hinduism and superstition *(BL1235.S9)*
   x Superstition and Hinduism
Hindus *(Civilization, DS421-3; Ethnology, GN635.I4)*
   sa Brahmans
      East Indians
      Missions to Hindus
      Youth, Hindu
   x Hindoos
   xx Aryans
      East Indians
Hindus in Africa, ₍Canada, the United States, etc.₎
   — Juvenile literature
Hindustani drama *(Collections, PK2071; History, PK2041)*
Hindustani language *(PK1931-7)*
      Here are entered works written or published prior to the partition of India in 1947, dealing with the spoken form of Hindi and Urdu as used in large parts of northern India.
   sa Hindi language
      Urdu language
   x Hindi language, Eastern
      Hindi language, Western
   xx Indo-Aryan languages, Modern
Hindustani literature *(PK2030-2158)*
Hindustani music
   See Music, Hindustani
Hindustani periodicals *(History, etc., PN5371-5380)*
Hindustani poetry *(Collections, PK2057-9; History, PK2040)*
Hinge moments (Aerodynamics)
   xx Aerodynamics
      Aeroplanes—Control surfaces
Hinges *(TS400)*
   sa Concrete construction—Hinges
Hino automobile *(TL215.H)*
   x Aichi Hino automobile
Hinomoto (Sect) *(BL2222.H5)*
   xx Shinto sects

Hiordahlite
   See Guarinite
Hip (Rose)
   See Rose hips
Hip arch
   See Pelvic girdle
Hip joint *(QM131)*
   sa Bursae of hip
   — Diseases *(RD772)*
      sa Hip joint—Radiography
         Legg-Calvé-Perthes disease
      x Coxalgia
      Example under Orthopedia
   — Dislocation *(RD101)*
      Example under Dislocations
   — Radiography
      xx Hip joint—Diseases
   — Surgery
      x Excision of hip
Hipped plate structures
   See Folded plate structures
Hippies *(Direct)*
   xx Bohemianism
   — Juvenile literature
   — Personal narratives
   — Pictorial works
   — Religious life
   — — Juvenile literature
Hippocampus (Brain)
   x Ammon's horn
      Cornu ammonis
   xx Cerebral cortex
Hippodrome *(Indirect)*
   sa Circus
   x Theater—Animals
   xx Circus
Hippology
   See Horses
Hippophagy
   See Horse meat
Hippopotamus *(QL737.U5)*
   — Juvenile literature
Hippopotamus (in religion, folk-lore, etc.) *(BL443; BL2450.H5)*
   x Folk-lore of the hippopotamus
   xx Religion, Primitive
Hippuric acid *(QP211)*
   xx Urine
Hire *(Direct)*
   sa Carriers
      Contracts for work and labor
      Freight forwarders
      Independent contractors
      Labor contract
      Leases
      Mandate (Contract)
      Master and servant
      Servants
   xx Bailments
      Carriers
      Independent contractors
      Leases
      Mandate (Contract)
      Master and servant
      Rent
      Wages
Hire (Ancient law)
Hire (Canon law) *(BX1939.H)*
Hire (Jewish law)
Hire (Roman-Dutch law)
Hire (Roman law)
Hire-purchase
   See Sales, Conditional
Hire-purchase plan
   See Instalment plan
Hiring halls
   xx Employment agencies
      Trade-unions

Hirschsprung's disease
   See Megacolon
Hirsutism
   See Hypertrichosis
Hirudinea
   See Leeches
Hirundinidae
   See Swallows
Hishkaryana language
   See Hixkaryana language
Hisingerite
   xx Silicates
HISKAM (Electronic computer system)
Hispanic American . . .
   See Spanish American . . .
Hispanic civilization
   See Civilization, Hispanic
Hispanic studies *(Direct)*
Hispanidad
   See Pan-Hispanism
Hispano-American War, 1898
   See United States—History—War of 1898
Hispanoamericanism
   See Pan-Hispanism
Hispanos
   See Mexican Americans
Hispid cotton rat
   xx Cotton rats
Hiss (Radio meteorology) *(QC973)*
   sa Whistlers (Radio meteorology)
   x Auroral hiss
      Very-low-frequency hiss
   xx Dawn chorus (Radio meteorology)
      Electric interference
      Ionosphere
      Radio meteorology
      Radio noise
      Whistlers (Radio meteorology)
   — Tables, etc.
Hissing
   See Theater—Applause, demonstrations, etc.
Hissing adders
   See Hognose snakes
Histamine
   sa Antihistamines
   xx Amines
   — Analysis
Histamine metabolism
   xx Metabolism
Histiocytosis-X
   See Reticuloendotheliosis
Histochemistry *(QH611)*
   sa Biological chemistry
      Cytochemistry
      Molecular biology
      Physiological chemistry
   xx Biological chemistry
      Cytochemistry
      Histology
      Physiological chemistry
   — Laboratory manuals
   — Technique
Histocompatibility
   sa Immunological tolerance
      Transplantation immunology
   x Tissue compatibility
   xx Immunological tolerance
      Transplantation immunology
Histocompatibility testing
   x Histocompatibility typing
      Tissue typing (Transplantation)
   xx Immunological tolerance
      Tissues—Analysis
Histocompatibility typing
   See Histocompatibility testing

Histology *(QM550-575)*

Here are entered general works on the microscopic anatomy of animal tissues. Studies of particular tissues or organs are entered under the name of the tissue or organ, *e.g.* Bone, Cartilage, Connective tissues, Epithelium, Muscle, Nerves, Kidneys, Pancreas.
Works on plant histology are entered under the heading Botany—Anatomy.

sa Cells
Histochemistry
Historadiography
Microscope and microscopy
Radioactive tracers in histology
Tissues
x Anatomy, Microscopic
Microscopic anatomy
xx Anatomy
Cells
Medicine
Microscope and microscopy
Tissues
— Abstracts
— Atlases
— Examinations, questions, etc. *(QM553)*
— Laboratory manuals *(QM555)*
— Technique
sa Fixation (Histology)
Karyometry
Microtomy

Histology, Pathological *(RB24-35)*
x Pathological histology
xx Pathology
— Atlases
— Technique
Histology, Vegetable
See Botany—Anatomy
Histology, Veterinary
See Veterinary histology

Histoplasmosis
xx Reticulo-endothelial system—Diseases

Historadiography
xx Histology
Radiography
Historia (Liturgy)
See Rimed offices

Historians *(Direct) (D13-15)*
sa Archaeologists
Church historians
Literary historians
Medievalists
xx Historiography
History
Example under Authors; *and under reference from* Writers
— Correspondence, reminiscences, etc.
— Juvenile literature
Historians, Catholic
See Catholic historians
Historians, Church
See Church historians
Historians, Greek
See Greek historians
Historians, Jewish
x Jewish historians
xx Scholars, Jewish
Historians, Latin
See Latin historians
Historians, Negro
x Negro historians
xx Negro authors
Historians, Roman
See Latin historians
Historic bays (International law)
See Territorial waters

Historic houses, etc. *(Architecture, NA7123, NA7205, etc.)*
sa Birthplaces
Hiding-places (Secret chambers, etc.)
Historical markers
Literary landmarks
Musical landmarks
subdivision Historic houses, etc. *under names of countries, cities, etc., e.g.* Baltimore—Historic houses, etc.
x Buildings, Historic
Houses, Historic
xx Historic sites
— Fires and fire prevention *(TH9445.H5)*
Historic sites *(Direct)*
sa Historic houses, etc.
Historic trees
Historical markers
Memorials
Monuments
x Historical sites
xx Archaeology
History
Historic trees *(Indirect)*
sa Bodhi Tree
Liberty trees
x Trees, Historic
xx Historic sites
Trees
Historic waters (International law)
See Territorial waters
Historical art
See History in art
Historical atlases
See Classical geography—Maps
Geography, Ancient—Maps
Geography, Historical—Maps
Geography, Medieval—Maps
subdivision Historical geography—Maps *under names of countries*
Historical charts
See Chronology, Historical—Charts
Historical chronology
See Chronology, Historical
Historical criticism
See Historiography
Historical dictionaries
See History—Dictionaries
Historical drama *(History and criticism, PN1870-1879)*
Used for works dealing with historical or national drama as a distinct type or genre, and for collections of such dramas, including the earlier form, the so-called "chronicle histories."
sa English drama—Early modern and Elizabethan, 1500-1600
x Chronicle history (Drama)
Chronicle play
Drama, Historical
xx Drama
Historiography
Pageants
Historical drama, English
xx English drama
Historical drama, French, ₍German, Italian, etc.₎
Historical fiction *(PN3441)*
Here are entered works about historical fiction. For historical novels, etc. use subdivision History—Fiction (or History—₍period subdivision₎—Fiction) under names of countries, cities, etc. and subdivision Fiction under names of historical events and characters.
x Fiction, Historical
xx Fiction
History

Historical fiction, American, ₍English, German, Spanish, etc.₎
xx American ₍English, German, Spanish, etc.₎ fiction
— Pictorial works
Historical films
xx Feature films
Moving-pictures
Historical geography
See Geography, Historical
Historical geology
sa Geology, Stratigraphic
Paleontology, Stratigraphic
x Geology, Historical
xx Geology
Geology, Stratigraphic
Paleontology, Stratigraphic
— Juvenile literature
Historical libraries *(Direct) (Z675.H5)*
x History libraries
Libraries, Historical
xx Archives
Historical markers *(Direct)*
sa Inscriptions
x Markers, Historical
xx Historic houses, etc.
Historic sites
Inscriptions
Monuments
Signs and sign-boards
Historical materialism
xx Dialectical materialism
History—Philosophy
Historical models
See History—Mathematical models
Historical monuments
See Monuments
Historical museums *(Direct)*
xx Museums
Historical record preservation
See Archives
Historical research
sa Historiography
History—Sources—Publishing
x History—Research
Research, Historical
xx Historiography
Research
— Electronic data processing
See Electronic data processing—Historical research
Historical sites
See Historic sites
Historical societies *(Indirect) (D1)*
sa History—Societies, etc. ₍for publications of historical and other societies in relation to history₎
xx Societies
Example under Learned institutions and societies
Historical sociology *(HM104)*
sa Culture
Society, Primitive
x Sociology, Historical
xx Anthropology
History
Social evolution
Sociology
— Juvenile literature
Historical sources, Publishing of
See History—Sources—Publishing
Historiography *(D13-15)*
sa Diplomatics
Historians
Historical drama
Historical research
History—Methodology
History—Sources—Publishing

Historiography *(D13-15)* *(Continued)*
  Local history
  Moving-pictures in historiography
  Psychoanalysis in historiography
  subdivision Historiography *under
    subjects, e.g.* Art—Historiography;
    Catholic Church—Historiography;
    United States—Historiography;
    United States—History—Civil War,
    1861-1865—Historiography
  x Historical criticism
    History—Criticism
    History—Historiography
  xx Authorship
    Historical research
  — Early works to 1800
  — History
History *(D; History and international law,
    JX1253; History and literature,
    PN50; History and philosophy, B61;
    History and political science, JA78;
    History and sociology, HM36)*
  sa Anthropo-geography
    Archaeology
    Battles
    Biography
    Boundaries
    Chronology
    Church history
    Civilization
    Conspiracies
    Constitutional history
    Coups d'état
    Diplomacy
    Diplomatics
    Discoveries (in geography)
    Ethnology
    Genealogy
    Geography, Historical
    Heraldry
    Heroes
    Historians
    Historic sites
    Historical fiction
    Historical sociology
    Kings and rulers
    Man—Migrations
    Massacres
    Medals
    Migrations of nations
    Military history
    Naval history
    Numismatics
    Political science
    Protohistory
    Race problems
    Restorations, Political
    Revolutions
    Riots
    Seals (Numismatics)
    Sieges
    Social history
    Treaties
    World history
    subdivision History *under specific
      subjects and under names of
      countries, states, cities, etc.*
  x Annals
  xx Auxiliary sciences of history
  — Atlases
    See Classical geography—Maps
      Geography, Ancient—Maps
      Geography, Historical—Maps
      Geography, Medieval—Maps
      subdivision Historical geography
        —Maps *under names of
        countries*
  — Bio-bibliography *(Z6201-9)*

— Biography
    See Biography
— Book reviews
— Chronology
    See Chronology, Historical
— Criticism
    See Historiography
— Dictionaries *(D9)*
    x Historical dictionaries
— Early works to 1800
    See World history—Early works to
      1800
— Errors, inventions, etc. *(D10)*
    sa subdivision History—Errors,
      inventions, etc. *under names of
      countries*
    xx Errors, Popular
      Literary forgeries and mystifications
— Examinations, questions, etc. *(D21)*
    x World history—Examinations,
      questions, etc.
— Historiography
    See Historiography
— Mathematical models
    x Historical models
— Methodology *(D16)*
    sa History—Periodization
      History—Statistical methods
      Oral history
    xx Historiography
— — Juvenile literature
— Outlines, syllabi, etc.
    x World history—Outlines, syllabi, etc.
— Periodicals
    x History, Modern—Periodicals
    Note under Current events
— — Indexes
— Periodization
    x Periodization in history
    xx History—Methodology
      History—Philosophy
— Philosophy *(D16.7-9)*
    sa Buddha and Buddhism—History—
      Philosophy
      Church history—Philosophy
      Civilization
      Demythologization
      Historical materialism
      History—Periodization
      History (Theology)
      subdivision History—Philosophy
        under names of countries, e.g.
        Great Britain—History—
        Philosophy
    x History, Modern—Philosophy
      History, Philosophy of
      Philosophy of history
— Pictorial works
    See World history—Pictorial works
— Poetry *(PN6110.H3)*
    sa Poetry of places
      Political ballads and songs
      Political poetry
    xx Poetry of places
      Political poetry
— Psychological aspects
— Research
    See Historical research
— Satire
    See History, Comic, satirical, etc.
— Societies, etc.
    xx Historical societies
— — Abbreviations
— Sources *(D5)*
    Used only for documents, records, and
      similar materials upon which narra-
      tive history is based.
    sa Archives

Charters
    Diplomatics
    subdivision History—Sources *under
      specific subjects and under names
      of countries, states, cities, etc.,
      e.g.* Catholic Church—History—
      Sources; United States—History—
      Sources
— — Electronic data processing
    See Electronic data processing—
      Historical research
— — Publishing *(Z286)*
    x Historical sources, Publishing of
      Publishing of historical sources
    xx Historical research
      Historiography
      Publishers and publishing
— Statistical methods
    xx History—Methodology
— Study and teaching *(Direct)*
    x World history—Study and teaching
— — Audio-visual aids
— Study and teaching (Elementary)
    (Direct)
— Study and teaching (Secondary) *(Direct)*
— Terminology
— Theology
    See History (Theology)
— Yearbooks
    For non-serial yearbooks add—[date]
    sa News recordings
    x History, Modern—Yearbooks
    xx Chronology, Historical
    Note under Current events
History, Ancient *(D51-90)*
  sa Archaeology
    Bible
    Chronology
    Civilization, Ancient
    Classical dictionaries
    First century, A.D.
    Geography, Ancient
    Inscriptions
    Numismatics
    names of ancient races and peoples, e.g.
      Aryans, Hittites, Mediterranean race;
      and names of countries of antiquity
  x Ancient history
  xx World history
— Biography
    See Biography—To 500
— Chronology *(D54.5)*
    xx Chronology, Historical
— Historiography
— Juvenile literature *(D59)*
— Methodology
History, Biblical
  See Bible—History of Biblical events
History, Church
  See Church history
History, Comic, satirical, etc.
  sa subdivision History, Comic, satirical,
    etc. *under names of countries, states,
    cities, etc.*
  x History—Satire
History, Constitutional
  See Constitutional history
History, Ecclesiastical
  See Church history
History, Economic
  See Economic history
History, Juvenile
  See World history—Juvenile literature
    subdivision History—Juvenile literature
      *under names of countries, regions,
      states, cities, etc.*
History, Local
  See Local history

History, Local (Cataloging)
   See Cataloging of local history
History, Medieval
   See Middle Ages—History
History, Military
   See Military history
History, Modern *(D204-725)*
   sa Civilization, Modern
        Reformation
        Renaissance
   x Modern history
   xx Civilization, Modern
        World history
  — 16th century *(D220-234)*
     sa Sixteenth century
  — 17th century *(D242-280)*
     sa Seventeenth century
  — — Juvenile literature
  — 18th century *(D284-309)*
     sa Eighteenth century
  — — Juvenile literature
  — 19th century *(D351-400)*
     sa Nineteenth century
  — — Caricatures and cartoons
  — 20th century *(D410-725)*
     sa European War, 1914-1918
         Twentieth century
         World War, 1939-1945
  — — Anecdotes, facetiae, satire, etc.
  — 1945-
  — — Caricatures and cartoons

        GENERAL SUBDIVISIONS

  — Chronology
     See Chronology, Historical

        GENERAL SUBDIVISIONS

  — Juvenile literature
  — Periodicals
     See History—Periodicals

        GENERAL SUBDIVISIONS

  — Philosophy
     See History—Philosophy

        GENERAL SUBDIVISIONS

  — Pictorial works
  — Study and teaching
     sa Current events

        GENERAL SUBDIVISIONS

  — Yearbooks
     See History—Yearbooks
History, Natural
   See Natural history
History, Naval
   See Naval history
History, Philosophy of
   See History—Philosophy
History, Universal
   See World history
History (Buddhism) *(BQ4570.H5)*
   sa Buddha and Buddhism—History—
        Philosophy
        Saddharma
        Saddharmavipralopa
   xx Buddhist doctrines
History (Islamic theology)
   xx History (Theology)
       Islamic theology
History (Theology) *(BR115.H5)*
   sa History (Islamic theology)
       Time (Theology)
   x History—Theology
   xx Church and the world
       History—Philosophy
  — Biblical teaching
  — Comparative studies *(BL65.H5)*

— History of doctrines
— — 20th century
History and art
   See Art and history
History and literature
   See Literature and history
History and poetry
   See Literature and history
History and science
   See Science and civilization
History and sex
   See Sex and history
History and social sciences
   See Social sciences and history
History in art
   sa Art and history
   x Historical art
   xx Art
       Art and history
History in literature
History libraries
   See Historical libraries
History teachers *(Direct)*
   xx Teachers
Histrionics
   See Acting
       Theater
Hit-and-run drivers *(Direct)*
   x Fleeing from scene of accident
       Leaving the scene of an automobile
         accident
   xx Automobile drivers
       Traffic accidents
       Traffic violations
Hitch-hiking
   See Hitchhiking
Hitches
   See Slings and hitches
Hitchhiking *(Direct)*
   x Hitch-hiking
   xx Hiking
  — Anecdotes, facetiae, satire, etc.
Hitchiti language *(PM1341)*
   sa Creek language
   x Etcheetee language
       Etchita language
       Ichiti language
   xx Creek language
Hitler's Putsch, 1923
   See Germany—History—Beer Hall Putsch,
       1923
Ḥiṭṭīn, Battle of, 1187 *(D184.8)*
   xx Jerusalem—History—Latin kingdom,
       1099-1244
Hittite funeral rites and ceremonies
   See Funeral rites and ceremonies, Hittite
Hittite gods
   See Gods, Hittite
Hittite language *(P945)*
   sa Luwian language
       Palaic language
   Example under Extinct languages
Hittite law
   See Law, Hittite
Hittite literature *(P945)*
Hittites *(DS66)*
   sa Cypriote syllabary
       Kaskans
   x Chatti
       Kheta
       Khita
   Example under History, Ancient
  — Religion *(BL2370.H5)*
     sa Gods, Hittite
  — Rites and ceremonies
     sa Funeral rites and ceremonies, Hittite
     x Rites and ceremonies—Hittites

Hixkaryana language *(PM6163)*
   x Hishkaryana language
   xx Cariban languages
       Indians of South America—Languages
Hka-kaw
   See Kaw people
Hlengwe language
   See Chopi language
Hmar (Hill tribe) *(DS432.H5)*
   x Mhar (Hill tribe)
       Old Kukis
   xx Ethnology—India
Ho (Munda tribe)
   See Hos
Hoactzin *(QL696.G2)*
   xx Galliformes
Hoarding of money
   sa Misers
   x Money, Hoarding of
   xx Currency question
       Money
Hoards
   See Coin hoards
Hoaxes
   See Imposters and imposture
Hobbies *(GV1201)*
   sa Beachcombing
       Music as recreation
   x Avocations
       Recreations
   xx Amusements
       Collectors and collecting
       Handicraft
       Leisure
       Play
       Recreation
  — Anecdotes, facetiae, satire, etc.
  — Juvenile literature
Hobby-horses
   xx Horses (in religion, folk-lore, etc.)
       Toys
Hobby rooms
   See Recreation rooms
Hobkirk's Hill, Battle of, 1781 *(E241.H)*
Hobo songs *(M1977.H6; M1978.H6)*
   x Tramps—Songs and music
Hoboes
   See Tramps
Hobson-jobson
   x Anglo-Indian dialect
   xx Languages, Mixed
Hochheimer wine
   See Hock (Wine)
Hochkirch, Battle of, 1758 *(DD412.6.H7)*
   xx Seven Years' War, 1756-1763
Höchstädt, Battle of, 1704
   See Blenheim, Battle of, 1704
Hock (Wine) *(TP559.G3)*
   x Hochheimer wine
   xx Wine and wine making
Hock disease
   See Perosis
Hockey *(Direct)* *(GV847)*
   sa Field hockey
       Hockey clubs
       Lawn hockey
       Polo (on skates)
       Ring hockey
       Roller-polo
       Roller-skate hockey
       Stanley Cup (Hockey)
   x Ice hockey
   xx Winter sports
  — Biography
  — — Juvenile literature
  — Juvenile literature
  — Pictorial works

Hockey clubs *(GV848)*
  xx Hockey
Hockey coaching *(GV848.25)*
  xx Coaching (Athletics)
Hodaka motorcycle *(TL448.H)*
Hodgkin's disease *(RC644)*
  sa Lymphogranuloma venereum
  x Lymphadenoma
    Lymphogranuloma
    Lymphogranulomatosis
    Lymphosarcoma
    Pseudoleucemia
  xx Lymphatics—Diseases
    Lymphoma
  — Personal narratives
Hodograph *(QA841)*
  xx Kinematics
Hodograph equations
  x Equations, Hodograph
  xx Differential equations, Partial
    Fluid mechanics
Hofburg Spear
  See Holy Lance
Hoffmann kiln *(TH842.H7)*
  xx Kilns
Hog cholera *(SF973)*
  x Swine fever
  xx Veterinary medicine
  Example under Swine—Diseases
  — Preventive inoculation
Hog houses
  See Swine houses and equipment
Hog Latin
  See Pig Latin
Hog lice
  xx Lice
Hog-nosed snakes
  See Hognose snakes
Hogbacks
  See Cuestas
Hōgen Civil War, 1156
  See Hōgen Insurrection, 1156
Hogen Insurrection, 1156
  x Hōgen Civil War, 1156
  xx Japan—History—Heian period,
    794-1185
Hognose snakes
  sa Eastern hognose snake
    Western hognose snake
  x Blow vipers
    Blowing adders
    Flatheaded adders
    Hissing adders
    Hog-nosed snakes
    Puffing adders
Hogs
  See Swine
Hogue, La, Battle of, 1692 *(D280.H6)*
  — Songs and music
Hohenfriedberg, Battle of, 1745 *(DD407.H7)*
  xx Silesian War, 2d, 1744-1745
Hohokam culture
Hoisting machinery *(TJ1350-1383)*
  sa Capstan
    Cargo handling—Equipment
    Chains
    Conveying machinery
    Cranes, derricks, etc.
    Elevators
    Fork lift trucks
    Marine railways
    Mine hoisting
    Mining machinery
    Stacking machines
    Vacuum lifters
    Winches
    Windlasses
    Wire-rope transportation

  x Lifts
  xx Construction equipment
    Conveying machinery
    Mining machinery
  — Appraisal
    See Hoisting machinery—Valuation
  — Automation
  — Brakes
  — — Patents
  — Design and construction
  — Drawing
    See Hoisting machinery—Drawings
  — Drawings
    x Hoisting machinery—Drawing
    xx Mechanical drawing
  — Dynamics
  — Electric driving
  — Electric equipment
  — Foundations
  — Hydraulic equipment
  — Rigging *(TJ1367)*
    xx Masts and rigging
      Slings and hitches
  — — Patents
  — Safety measures
  — Safety regulations *(Direct)*
  — Standards
  — Tables, calculations, etc.
  — Valuation
    x Hoisting machinery—Appraisal
Hokkerup, Battle of, 1940
  xx World War, 1939-1945—Campaigns—
    Denmark
Hokku
  See Haiku
Holando-Argentino cattle
  x Argentine Friesian cattle
    Dutch Argentine cattle
Hold harmless agreements
  See Indemnity against liability
Holden automobile
Holding companies *(Direct) (Corporations,*
    HD2709-2930; Corporations: United
    States, HD2771-2798; Finance,
    HG4001-4280)
  sa Bank holding companies
    Insurance holding companies
    Public utility holding companies
    Subsidiary corporations
    Trusts, Industrial
  x Companies, Holding
  xx Corporations
    Subsidiary corporations
    Trusts, Industrial
  — Accounting
    x Financial statements, Consolidated
Holiday decorations
  sa Christmas decorations
  x Decorations, Holiday
  xx Decoration and ornament
Holidays *(Indirect) (For shop workers,*
    HV3167; Manners and customs,
    GT3930-4995; National: United
    States, JK1761; Recitations,
    PN4305.H7)
  sa Anniversaries
    Arbor Day
    Bird Day
    Christmas
    Columbus Day
    Dingaan's Day
    Empire Day
    Fasts and feasts
    Flag Day
    Fourth of July celebrations
    John Marshall Day
    John the Baptist's Day
    Labor Day

    Library Day
    May Day
    May Day (Labor holiday)
    Memorial Day
    New Year
    Pan American Day
    Patriot's Day
    Peace Day
    Schools—Exercises and recreations
    St. George's Day
    Sunday legislation
    Thanksgiving Day
    Vacations
    Weekly rest-day
    World Health Day
  x Legal holidays
    National holidays
  xx Anniversaries
    Days
    Fasts and feasts
    Festivals
    Hours of labor
    Manners and customs
    Memorials
    Vacations
  — Jews
    See Fasts and feasts—Judaism
  — Juvenile literature
  — Law and legislation *(Direct)*
    sa Sunday legislation
    xx Sunday legislation
  — Songs and music
    sa Christmas music
      Easter music
      subdivision Songs and music *under*
        special days, e.g. Fourth of July—
        Songs and music; Mother's Day—
        Songs and music

    GEOGRAPHIC SUBDIVISIONS

  — United States
    sa Election Day
      Lincoln Day
      Veterans Day
      Washington's Birthday

    GEOGRAPHIC SUBDIVISIONS

  — — Juvenile literature
Holidays, Jewish
  See Fasts and feasts—Judaism
Holidays with pay
  See Vacations, Employee
Holiness *(BT767)*
  sa Church—Holiness
    Consecration
    Holy, The
    Pentecostal churches
    Pentecostalism
    Perfection
    Sanctification
  xx Sanctification
    Theology, Doctrinal
  — Sermons
Holiness churches *(Direct)*
    Here are entered works dealing with the
      various modern church bodies stress-
      ing the doctrine of holiness.
  sa Church of God
    Snake cults (Holiness churches)
  xx Church of God
    Pentecostal churches
Holism *(B818)*
  xx Evolution
    Whole and parts (Philosophy)
Holland
  See Netherlands
Holland Tunnel
  — Fire, 1949

Hollow bricks
- *sa* Tile construction
- *xx* Bricks
  - Tiles
- *Note under* Tile construction

Hollow charges (Explosives)
- *See* Shaped charges

Hollow ground saws
- *See* Planer saws

Hollow tile construction
- *See* Tile construction

Hollow tiles
> Here are entered works on tiles as building material. Works on the construction of buildings and other engineering structures with tiles are entered under the heading Tile construction.
- *x* Tiles, Hollow
- *xx* Tiles
- *Note under* Tile construction
- — Testing

Hollow ware, Silver
- *See* Silverware

Holly *(QK495.I3)*
- — Varieties

Hollywood, Calif., in literature

Holmes' comet *(QB723.H7)*

Holmium
- — Isotopes
  - *x* Holmium isotopes
    - Isotopic holmium
- — — Decay

Holmium isotopes
- *See* Holmium—Isotopes

Holocain *(RE997.H7)*
- *xx* Local anesthesia

Holocaust, Jewish (1939-1945) *(Direct)*
  (D810.J4; DS135.E83)
- *x* Destruction of the Jews (1939-1945)
    - Extermination, Jewish (1939-1945)
    - Jewish holocaust (1939-1945)
- *xx* Genocide
    - Jews—Persecutions
    - World War, 1939-1945—Atrocities
    - World War, 1939-1945—Jews
- — Historiography
- — Pictorial works
- — Registers of dead

Holocaust, Jewish (1939-1945), in literature
- *xx* Jews in literature

Holocaust (Jewish theology)

Holocephali
- *See* Chimaeriformes

Holographic radar
- *See* Coherent radar

Holographic testaments
- *See* Holographic wills

Holographic wills *(Direct)*
- *x* Holographic testaments
    - Testaments, Holographic
- *xx* Wills

Holography *(QC449)*
- *sa* Acoustic holography
    - Coherent radar
- *x* Laser photography
    - Lensless photography
    - Photography, Lensless
    - Wavefront reconstruction imaging
- *xx* Diffraction
    - Interference (Light)
- — Patents

Holoholo language
- *x* Horohoro language
- *xx* Bantu languages

Holomorphic functions
- *See* Analytic functions

Holomorphic mappings
- *x* Mappings, Holomorphic

- *xx* Functions of several complex variables

Holonomy groups *(QA649)*
- *x* Groups, Holonomy
- *xx* Geometry, Differential

Holontalo language
- *See* Gorontalo language

Holophote *(TC379)*
- *xx* Lighthouses—Lighting

Holothurians *(Indirect)* *(QL384.H7)*
- *sa* Trepang
- *x* Holothurioidea
    - Sea-cucumbers
- *xx* Echinodermata

Holothurians, Fossil *(QE783.H7)*
- *x* Holothurioidea, Fossil
- *xx* Echinodermata, Fossil

Holothurioidea
- *See* Holothurians

Holothurioidea, Fossil
- *See* Holothurians, Fossil

Holstein-Friesian cattle *(SF199.H75;*
  Herd-books, SF193.H7)
- *x* Friesian cattle
- *xx* Dairy cattle

Holstein horse *(SF293.H7)*

Holsteiners in Siena

Holtzman inkblot technique *(BF698.8.H55)*
- *xx* Projective techniques

Holy, The
- *x* Numinous, The
    - Sacred, The
- *xx* God
    - Holiness
    - Mysticism
    - Religion
    - Theism

Holy Alliance *(D383; JX1349)*
- *x* Alliance, Holy
- *Example under* International relations

Holy ark
- *See* Ark of the law

Holy cards *(Direct)* *(Catholic Church,*
  BX2310.H6)
- *x* Cards, Holy
    - Devotional pictures
    - Holy pictures
    - Pictures, Holy
    - Sunday-school cards
- *xx* Christian art and symbolism

Holy Childhood, Devotion to
> Here are entered works dealing with the devotion tendered to the childhood of Jesus, variously referred to as Devotion to the Holy Childhood, Holy Infancy, Child Jesus, Childhood of Jesus, Infancy of Jesus, etc.
- *x* Child Jesus, Devotion to
    - Childhood, Holy
    - Childhood of Jesus, Devotion to
    - Infancy of Jesus, Devotion to
- *xx* Jesus Christ—Childhood

Holy Coat *(BT587.C6-7)*
- *x* Coat, Holy
    - Jesus Christ—Holy Coat
- *xx* Jesus Christ—Relics of the Passion

Holy Cross *(BT465)*
- *x* Cross
    - Jesus Christ—Cross
- *xx* Jesus Christ—Crucifixion
    - Jesus Christ—Relics of the Passion

Holy days
- *See* Fasts and feasts

Holy Family
- *See* Jesus Christ—Family

Holy Ghost
- *See* Holy Spirit

Holy Grail
- *See* Grail

Holy Grail, Spear of the
- *See* Holy Lance

Holy helpers, Fourteen
- *See* Fourteen holy helpers

Holy Hour *(BX2159.H7)*
- *xx* Jesus Christ—Passion

Holy Innocents, Feast of the *(BV50.H6)*
- *sa* Boy-bishop
- *x* Childermas
    - Feast of the Holy Innocents
    - Innocents' Day
    - Innocents, Feast of the Holy
- *xx* Church year
    - Fasts and feasts

Holy Innocents, Massacre of the *(BS2545.H)*
- *x* Innocents, Massacre of the Holy
    - Massacre of the Innocents
- *xx* Jesus Christ—Nativity
    - Magi

Holy Lance
- *x* Destiny, Spear of
    - Hofburg Spear
    - Holy Grail, Spear of the
    - Lance, Holy
    - Longinus, Spear of
    - Passion, Spear of the
    - Spear of Destiny
    - Spear of the Passion
- *xx* Jesus Christ—Relics of the Passion

Holy League (Venice, Spain, and the Pope)
  1570-1571
- *See* Cyprian War, 1570-1571

Holy League, 1576-1593 *(DC120)*
- *sa* France—History—Wars of the
    - Huguenots, 1562-1598
- *xx* Huguenots in France

Holy League against France, 1511-1513
  (DG541)
- *sa* Anglo-French War, 1512-1513

Holy League against the Turks, 1684
  (DR536)

Holy Name, Devotion to *(BX2159.H75)*
- *x* Devotion to the Holy Name
- *xx* God—Name
    - Jesus Christ—Name

Holy Office
- *See* Inquisition

Holy oils
- *sa* Unction
- *x* Oil, Holy
- *xx* Sacramentals
    - Unction

Holy orders
- *See* Clergy—Office

Holy Orthodox Eastern Catholic and Apostolic
  Church
- *See* Orthodox Eastern Church

Holy pictures
- *See* Holy cards

Holy places
- *See* Shrines

Holy Roman Empire
- *sa* Imperial cities (Holy Roman Empire)
- *xx* Church and state in Europe
    - Middle Ages—History
- — Constitutional history
    - *sa* Mediatized states
- — History *(DD125-198.7)*
- — — To 1517
- — — 843-1273
- — — Saxon House, 919-1024
    - *sa* Germany—History—Saxon
        - House, 919-1024
    - *x* Ottonian emperors
        - Ottonian House
        - Saxon emperors
        - Saxon House
        - Saxony, House of

Holy Roman Empire
— History *(DD125-198.7)*
— — Saxon House, 919-1024
   (Continued)
         xx Germany—History—Saxon
               House, 919-1024
— — Salian House, 1024-1125
— — Franconian House, 1024-1125
      sa Franconian House
            Germany—History—Franconian
               House, 1024-1125
      x Franconian emperors
            Salian emperors
      xx Franconian House
            Germany—History—Franconian
               House, 1024-1125
— — Hohenstaufen, 1138-1254
— — Interregnum, 1254-1273
— — 1273-1517
— — House of Luxemburg, 1308-1437
— — 1517-1648
— — 1648-1804
— Kings and rulers
      sa Electors (Kurfürsten)
— — Election
Holy Roman Empire in literature
Holy Saturday music *(Catholic liturgical
            music, M2149.4.H8)*
      xx Holy-Week music
Holy Scriptures
   See Bible
Holy See
   See Papacy
         Popes
Holy Sepulcher *(DS109.4)*
      x Jesus Christ—Tomb
         Sepulcher, Holy
Holy Sepulcher in art
Holy Shroud *(BT587.S4)*
      x Jesus Christ—Holy Shroud
         Shroud, Holy
      xx Jesus Christ—Relics of the Passion
Holy Spirit *(BT120-123)*
      sa Baptism in the Holy Spirit
         Church—Foundation
         Gifts, Spiritual
         Pentecost
         Pentecostalism
         Spirit
         Trinity
      x Holy Ghost
         Paraclete
         Spirit, Holy
      xx God
         Spirit
         Theology, Doctrinal
         Trinity
— Art *(N8055)*
      sa Dove (in religion, folk-lore, etc.)
         Holy Spirit—Symbolism
      xx God—Art
— Early works to 1800
— History of doctrines
— Name
      Example under Names
— Prayer-books and devotions
— Procession
      x Procession (in the Trinity)
         Procession of the Holy Spirit
— Symbolism
      sa Temple of God
      xx Christian art and symbolism
         Holy Spirit—Art
Holy Spirit (Judaism)
      xx God (Judaism)
Holy Thurdsday
   See Maundy Thursday
Holy war (Islam)
   See Jihad

Holy water *(Catholic Church, BX2307;
         Practical theology, BV885)*
      sa Baptismal water
      x Blessed water
         Water, Blessed
         Water, Holy
      xx Sacramentals
         Water (in religion, folk-lore, etc.)
Holy Week *(Ceremonial, BV90; Events,
         BT414)*
      sa Easter
         Good Friday
         Maundy Thursday
         Palm Sunday
      xx Church year
         Jesus Christ—Passion
         Lent
— Prayer-books and devotions
— — English, [French, German, etc.]
Holy-Week music
      sa Good Friday music
         Holy Saturday music
         Tenebrae service music
      xx Sacred vocal music
Holy-Week sermons *(BV90)*
      xx Jesus Christ—Passion—Sermons
         Sermons
Holy Week services
      xx Worship programs
Holy wells *(GR690)*
      sa Springs (in religion, folk-lore, etc.)
      x Wells, Holy
      xx Miracles
         Pilgrims and pilgrimages
         Springs (in religion, folk-lore, etc.)
         Water (in religion, folk-lore, etc.)
Holy Year *(BX961.H6)*
      Here are entered works on the holy or
      jubilee years proclaimed by the popes.
      For special holy years (regular or ex-
      traordinary) add date, *e.g.* Holy Year,
      1925.
      sa Marian Year
         Year of Faith
      x Anno santo
         Jubilee Year
         Year, Holy
         Year, Jubilee
      xx Asylum, Right of
         Indulgences
         Pilgrims and pilgrimages
Hom-idyomo (Artificial language) *(PM8370)*
      xx Languages, Artificial
Homa (Rite) *(BL1226.2)*
      x Goma (Rite)
      xx Fire (in religion, folk-lore, etc.)
         Hinduism—Rituals
         Tantric Buddhism—Rituals
Homage (Feudal law)
      xx Feudal law
         Feudalism
Homage volumes
   See Festschriften
Homatropin *(RE997.H8)*
      xx Atropine
         Mydriatics
Hombo language
   See Ombo language
Home *(HQ503-743; Manners and customs,
         GT2420)*
      sa Broken homes
         Family
         Family life surveys
         Foster day care
         Foster home care
         Home economics
         Home in literature
         Marriage

      xx Family
         Marriage
— Quotations, maxims, etc.
— Sounds
      See Household sounds
Home accidents *(Direct) (TX150)*
      sa First aid in illness and injury
      x Accidents, Home
      xx Accidents
         Domestic engineering
— Prevention *(TX150)*
      x Household safety
      xx Safety education
Home air conditioning
   See Dwellings—Air conditioning
Home and school *(LC225)*
      sa Parent-student counselor relationships
         Parent-teacher relationships
         Parents' and teachers' associations
      x School and home
      xx Education
         Parent-teacher relationships
         Parents' and teachers' associations
— Juvenile literature
Home appliances
   See Household appliances
Home buying
   See House buying
Home care programs, Hospital-based
   See Hospitals—Home care programs
Home construction
   See House construction
Home decoration
   See Interior decoration
Home delivery of books
   See Direct delivery of books
Home demonstration work *(Direct)*
      xx Agricultural extension work
         Home economics extension work
Home economics *(Indirect) (TX)*
      sa Cleaning machinery and appliances
         Clothing and dress—Care
         Consumer education
         Cookery
         Cost and standard of living
         Dairying
         Dishwashing
         Entertaining
         Food
         Food service
         Fuel
         Furniture
         Heating
         House cleaning
         House furnishings
         Household appliances
         Household appliances, Electric
         Household linens
         Household pests
         Interior decoration
         Laundry
         Marketing (Home economics)
         Mobile home living
         Needlework
         Receipts
         Servants
         Sewing
         Storage in the home
         Television in home economics
         Ventilation
         Visiting housekeepers
      x Domestic economy
         Domestic science
         Household management
         Household science
         Housekeeping
      xx Consumer education
         Family life education

Home
— Accounting (TX326)
   x Budgets, Family
      Budgets, Household
      Family budgets
      Household budgets
      Household expenses
   xx Cost and standard of living
      Finance, Personal
      Statistics
— Anecdotes, facetiae, satire, etc.
— Bibliography
   sa Information storage and retrieval
      systems—Home economics
— Biography
— Caricatures and cartoons
— Competitions
— Early works to 1800 (TX144)
— Equipment and supplies (TX298-9)
   sa Bedding
      House furnishings
   x Home economics, Rural—Equipment
      and supplies
— Examinations
— Exhibitions
— International cooperation
   x International cooperation in home
      economics
— Juvenile literature
— Research
    See Home economics research
— Study and teaching (Direct)
   sa Home economics extension work
      Home economics students
— — Audio-visual aids
— Study and teaching (Higher) (Direct)
— Teacher training (Direct)
— Terminology
Home economics, Rural
   x Rural home economics
   xx Country life
      Farm life
— Equipment and supplies
    See Home economics—Equipment
      and supplies
Home economics as a profession (TX165)
   sa Dieticians—Vocational guidance
Home economics centers
   x Homemaking centers
      Homemaking departments
   xx School buildings
— Safety measures
Home economics extension work (Direct)
   sa Home demonstration work
      Nutrition extension work
   xx Home economics—Study and teaching
Home economics literature searching
    See Information storage and retrieval
      systems—Home economics
Home economics research
   x Home economics—Research
   xx Research
      Research, Industrial
Home economics students (Direct)
   xx Home economics—Study and teaching
      Students
— Personality
    See Home economics students—
      Psychology
— Psychology
   x Home economics students—
      Personality
Home economics teachers
   xx Teachers
Home education
    See Correspondence schools and courses
      Domestic education
      Self-culture

Home freezers
   sa Cold-storage lockers
   xx Cold-storage lockers
      Food, Frozen
      Refrigeration and refrigerating
         machinery
Home furnishings
    See House furnishings
Home furnishings industry and trade
    See House furnishings industry and trade
Home games
    See Indoor games
Home geography
    See Local geography
Home in literature
   xx Home
Home labor (Direct) (HD2331-6)
   sa Cottage industries
      Sweating system
   x Industries, Home
   xx Artisans
      Cottage industries
      Industry—History
      Labor and laboring classes
      Manufactures
      Sweating system
      Woman—Employment
   Note under Cottage industries
— Law and legislation (Direct)
   xx Labor laws and legislation
Home libraries
    See Libraries, Private
Home loan banks
    See Federal home loan banks
Home missions
    See Missions, Home
Home nursing (RT61)
   sa Care of the sick
      Hospitals—Home care programs
      Tuberculous—Home nursing
   xx Care of the sick
      Nurses and nursing
Home ownership (HD7287)
   sa Farm ownership
      House buying
   xx House buying
      Housing
      Real estate business
Home purchase
    See House buying
Home range
   xx Animal populations
Home repairing
    See Repairing—Amateurs' manuals
Home room guidance (Direct) (LB1620.7)
   x Homeroom guidance
   xx Personnel service in secondary
      education
Home room guidance (Elementary) (Direct)
    (LB1027.7)
   xx Personnel service in elementary
      education
Home rule (District of Columbia)
   xx Municipal home rule
Home rule (Ireland) (DA947-962)
   sa Curragh Mutiny, 1914
      Fenians
      Irish question
   xx Irish question
Home rule (Scotland) (DA765)
Home rule (Wales)
Home rule for cities
    See Municipal home rule
Home sites
    See Homesites
Home sounds
    See Household sounds

Home storage
    See Storage in the home
Home study courses
    See Correspondence schools and courses
      Self-culture
      Singing—Methods—Self-instruction
      subdivision Self-instruction *under*
         names of languages; and subdivision
         Methods—Self-instruction *under*
         names of musical instruments
Home visiting (Church work)
    See Visitations (Church work)
Home visiting (Religious education)
    See Visitations (Religious education)
Home workshops
    See Workshops
Homeland (Theology)
   x Fatherland (Theology)
      Native land (Theology)
   xx Theology, Doctrinal
— Biblical teaching (BS680.H58)
Homeland in literature
Homemaker service
    See Visiting housekeepers
Homemaking centers
    See Home economics centers
Homemaking departments
    See Home economics centers
Homeomorphisms (QA613.7, QA614)
   xx Manifolds (Mathematics)
      Topological spaces
      Transformation groups
Homeopathic hospitals
    See Homeopathy—Hospitals and
      dispensaries
Homeopathic physicians
    See Physicians, Homeopathic
Homeopathic research (Direct)
   x Homeopathy—Research
   xx Medical research
      Research
Homeopathy (RX)
   sa Electrohomeopathy
      Medicine, Biochemic
      Obstetrics, Homeopathic
      Pharmacopoeias, Homeopathic
      Pharmacy, Homeopathic
      Surgery, Homeopathic
      Sycosis (Homeopathy)
      Veterinary medicine, Homeopathic
      subdivision Homeopathic treatment
         under names of diseases and groups
         of diseases, e.g. Diphtheria—
         Homeopathic treatment; Children—
         Diseases—Homeopathic treatment;
         Nervous system—Diseases—
         Homeopathic treatment
   x Homoeopathy
   xx Medicine
      Medicine—Practice
— Attenuations, dilutions, and potencies
    (RX81)
   x High potency (Drugs)
— Biography (RX61-66)
   xx Physicians
      Physicians, Homeopathic
— Hospitals and dispensaries (RX6)
   x Dispensaries, Homeopathic
      Homeopathic hospitals
      Hospitals, Homeopathic
   xx Hospitals
— Law and legislation (Direct)
   xx Medical laws and legislation
— Materia medica and therapeutics
    (RX601-675)
   x Homeopathy—Therapeutics
   xx Materia medica
      Therapeutics

Homeopathy *(RX)* *(Continued)*
— Popular works *(RX76)*
— Practice *(RX71-75)*
— Research
    See Homeopathic research
— Study and teaching *(Direct)*
— Therapeutics
    See Homeopathy—Materia medica
       and therapeutics
Homeostasis
  sa Water-electrolyte balance (Physiology)
  xx Biological control systems
     Biological physics
     Body fluids
     Physiological chemistry
     Physiology
— Programmed instruction
Homeowners insurance
  See Insurance, Homeowners
Homeric civilization
  See Civilization, Homeric
Homeroom guidance
  See Home room guidance
Homes, Broken
  See Broken homes
Homes, Mobile
  See Mobile homes
Homes (Institutions)
  See Almshouses
     Asylums
     Blind—Institutional care
     Charities
     Children—Institutional care
     Deaf—Institutional care
     Institutional care
     Old age homes
     Orphans and orphan-asylums
     Soldiers' homes
     Woman—Institutional care
     subdivisions Benevolent and moral
       institutions and societies *and*
       Charities *under names of cities, e.g.*
       Albany—Charities
Homes for the aged
  See Old age homes
Homesickness
  See Nostalgia
Homesites
  x Architecture, Domestic—Location
     Home sites
     Location of homes
Homestead law *(Direct)* *(Homestead and*
    exemption, HD1337; Land law,
    HD197-205)
  x Homesteading
     Law, Homestead
     Scrip
  xx Exemption (Law)
     Land tenure—Law
     Restraints on alienation
— United States
    sa Pre-emption rights (United States)
    x Land scrip (United States)
      Scrip, Land (United States)
    xx Public lands
Homestead Strike, 1892 *(HD5325.15*
    1892.H)
Homesteading
  See Frontier and pioneer life
     Homestead law
Homework *(LB1048)*
  xx Study, Method of
Homicide *(Direct)* *(HV6499-6535)*
  sa Assassination
     Crime passionnel
     Death by wrongful act
     Euthanasia
     Filicide

Fratricide
     Homicide investigation
     Infanticide
     Murder
     Parricide
     Poisoning
     Suicide
     Trials (Homicide)
     Uxoricide
  x Manslaughter
  xx Criminal law
     Murder
     Offenses against the person
     Violent deaths
Homicide (Greek law)
Homicide (Islamic law) *(Direct)*
Homicide (Jewish law)
Homicide (Roman law)
Homicide in literature
Homicide investigation
  xx Criminal investigation
     Homicide
Homiculture
  See Eugenics
Homiletical illustrations *(BV4224-4230)*
  sa Allegories
     Christian life—Pictures, illustrations,
       etc.
     Christian life—Stories
     Exempla
     Fables
     Legends
     Parables
     Short stories
     Tales
  x Catechetical illustrations
     Illustrations, Homiletical
     Sermons—Illustrations
  xx Anecdotes
     Exempla
     Preaching
     Religion—Quotations, maxims, etc.
     Tales
  Note under Story sermons
Homiletical illustrations, Buddhist
  xx Preaching, Buddhist
Homiletical illustrations, Islamic
  sa Exempla, Islamic
  x Homiletical illustrations, Muslim
     Islamic homiletical illustrations
     Muslim homiletical illustrations
  xx Preaching, Islamic
Homiletical illustrations, Jewish
  xx Preaching, Jewish
Homiletical illustrations, Muslim
  See Homiletical illustrations, Islamic
Homiletical stories
  See Story sermons
Homiletics
  See Preaching
Homilies
  See Sermons
Homing pigeons *(Animal culture, SF469;*
    Military art and science, UH90)
  sa European War, 1914-1918—Pigeons
     Pigeon post
     Pigeon racing
     World War, 1939-1945—Pigeons
  x Carrier pigeons
     Racing pigeons
  xx Pigeons
— Breeding
    xx Pigeon breeding
    Example under Breeding
Hommel
  See Noordsche balk
Homoeopathy
  See Homeopathy

Homogeneous grouping
  See Ability grouping in education
Homogenized milk
  See Milk, Homogenized
Homografts
  sa Bone-grafting
     Post-mortem homografts
     Skin-grafting
  x Allogeneic homografts
     Allografts
  xx Transplantation of organs, tissues, etc.
Homological algebra
  See Algebra, Homological
Homology (Biology) *(QH367.5)*
  xx Anatomy, Comparative
     Biology—Classification
     Evolution
     Morphology
     Phylogeny
Homology theory *(QA611)*
  sa Algebra, Homological
     K-theory
     Sheaves, Theory of
  x Cohomology theory
     Contrahomology theory
  xx Abelian groups
     Algebraic topology
     Sheaves, Theory of
Homonymous authors
  x Authors, Homonymous
  xx Anonyms and pseudonyms
Homonyms
  sa subdivision Homonyms *under names of*
     languages
  x Homophones
  xx Synonyms
Homophile Movement
  See Gay Liberation Movement
Homophones
  See Homonyms
Homoptera *(Indirect)* *(QL523.H7)*
  sa Auchenorrhyncha
     Cicada
     Leaf-hoppers
     Plant-lice
     Scale-insects
  xx Hemiptera
— Classification
— Juvenile literature
Homosexual liberation movement
  See Gay liberation movement
Homosexuality *(Direct)* *(Medical*
    jurisprudence, RA1141;
    Neuropsychiatry, RC558; Social
    pathology, HQ76)
    Works on the criminal manifestation of
      homosexuality are entered under the
      heading Sodomy.
  sa Bisexuality
     Church work with homosexuals
     Gay liberation movement
     Lesbianism
     Sodomy
  xx Sex
— Anecdotes, facetiae, satire, etc.
— Personal narratives
Homosexuality (in religion, folk-lore, etc.)
  x Folk-lore of homosexuality
  xx Religion, Primitive
Homosexuality and art
  x Art and homosexuality
Homosexuality and employment *(Direct)*
  x Employment and homosexuality
Homosexuality and Islam
  x Islam and homosexuality
  xx Sex and religion
Homosexuality and literature
  x Literature and homosexuality

Homosexuality in animals (QL761)
    xx Sexual behavior in animals
Homosexuality in literature
    xx Sex in literature
Homosexuality in motion pictures
    xx Moving-pictures
Homosexuality in the Bible
    x Bible—Homosexuality
Homotopy theory (QA611)
    sa Loop spaces
    x Deformations, Continuous
    xx Topology
        Transformations (Mathematics)
Honda motorcycle (TL448.H6)
Hondschoote, Battle of, 1793 (DC220.5)
Honduran fiction (Direct)
Honduran literature (PQ7500-7509)
    xx Spanish American literature
Honduran newspapers
Honduran periodicals
Honduran poetry (Direct) (PQ7506)
Honduras
    — History
    — — To 1838 (F1507)
        sa Trinidad, Battle of, 1827
    — — 1838-1933 (F1507.5)
    — — Revolution, 1919
    — — 1933-   (F1508)
        sa Salvador-Honduras Conflict, 1969
Honduras-Salvador Conflict
    See Salvador-Honduras Conflict, 1969
Hone Heke's Rebellion, 1844-1846
    x Heke's Rebellion, 1844-1846
Honesty (Child psychology, BF723.H7;
        Ethics, BJ1533.H7)
    sa Business ethics
        Cheating (Education)
        Truthfulness and falsehood
        Wealth, Ethics of
    x Dishonesty
    xx Business ethics
        Conduct of life
        Ethics
        Truthfulness and falsehood
Honey (Indirect) (SF539; Foods,
        TX560.H7)
    sa Bee culture
        Bees
        Cookery (Honey)
        Honeydew
        Mead
    xx Bee culture
        Bees
        Natural sweeteners
    — Analysis
    — Law and legislation (Direct)
    — Taxation (Direct)
    — Therapeutic use
Honey-ants (QL568.F7)
    xx Ants
        Hymenoptera
Honey as food
    xx Food
Honey-bearing plants
    See Honey plants
Honey buzzards
    xx Buzzards
Honey cookery
    See Cookery (Honey)
Honey-creepers (QL696.P2)
Honey-eaters (Birds, QL696.P2)
Honey-guides
Honey Hill, S.C., Battle of, 1864 (E477.44)
Honey locust (SB397)
    x Thorn tree
Honey plants (Indirect) (SF535)
    x Honey-bearing plants
        Nectar plants

    xx Bee culture
        Botany, Economic
Honeybees
    See Bees
Honeycombs
    sa Beeswax
    xx Bees
Honeydew (SF539)
    xx Honey
Honeymoon (Direct)
    xx Marriage
Honeysuckle
    — Diseases and pests
Honeysuckle clover
    See White clover
Hong Kyŏng-nae Incident, 1811-1812
    xx Korea—History—1637-1864
Hongkong
    — Riots, 1967
    — Siege, 1941
        xx World War, 1939-1945—Hongkong
Honing
    sa Liquid honing
    xx Grinding and polishing
Honmiti
    — Doctrines
        xx Shinto theology
Honor (Ethics, BJ1533.H8)
    sa Business ethics
        Courts of honor
        Dignity
        Dueling
    xx Business ethics
        Chivalry
        Conduct of life
        Ethics
        Knights and knighthood
Honor, Courts of
    See Courts of honor
Honor, Decorations of
    See Decorations of honor
Honor in literature
Honor system
    See Self-government (in education)
Honorary citizenship (Direct)
    xx Citizenship
Honorary degrees
    See Degrees, Academic
Honorary titles
    See Titles of honor and nobility
Honorific
    See Grammar, Comparative and general—
        Honorific
        subdivision Honorific under names of
            languages and groups of languages
Honors courses in colleges
    See Universities and colleges—Honors
        courses
Honors courses in high schools
    See High schools—Honors courses
Honors work in colleges
    See Universities and colleges—Honors
        courses
Honors work in high schools
    See High schools—Honors courses
Hooded crow
    xx Crows
Hooded skunk
    xx Skunks
Hooden horse (GT4985)
Hoodlums
    sa Gangs
    x Gangsters
        Hooligans
    xx Crime and criminals
        Gangs
        Juvenile delinquency
    — Public opinion

Hoods
    See Academic costume
Hoofs (QL942)
    x Hooves
    xx Horses
        Horses—Anatomy
    — Diseases (SF901)
    — Juvenile literature
Hook order
    See Social hierarchy in animals
Hooked rugs
    See Rugs, Hooked
Hooke's coupling (TJ183)
Hooking
    sa Rugs, Hooked
    xx Fancy work
Hooks (TS440-445; Strength of materials,
        TA492.H6)
Hooks and eyes (Manufacture, TS2301.H;
        Trade, HD9969.H5-53)
    xx Fastenings
Hookworm disease (RC199.95)
    x Ankylostomiasis
        Uncinariasis
    xx Anemia
        Medical parasitology
    Example under Tropics—Diseases and hygiene
Hookworms (RC199.95)
    x Ankylostomia
        Uncinaria
    xx Nematoda
        Worms, Intestinal and parasitic
Hooligans
    See Hoodlums
Hoop exercises (GV490)
    x Hoops
    xx Calisthenics
Hoopah Indians
    See Hupa Indians
Hoopoes (QL696.C7)
    xx Coraciiformes
Hoopoes (in religion, folk-lore, etc.)
    x Folk-lore of hoopoes
    xx Religion, Primitive
Hoops
    See Hoop exercises
Hoops, Baling
    See Baling hoops
Hoosier (Nickname) (F257)
    Example under Nicknames
Hootzools
    See Huculs
Hooves
    See Hoofs
Hop-aphis (SB608.H8)
    xx Hops—Diseases and pests
Hop flea-beetle (SB608.H8)
    xx Hops—Diseases and pests
Hop industry and trade
    See Hops
Hop pickers (Direct)
    x Hop picking
    xx Hops
Hop picking
    See Hop pickers
Hope (Moral theology, BV4638; Philosophy,
        BD216)
    sa Despair
    xx Despair
        Faith
        Theological virtues
    — Biblical teaching
    — History of doctrines
    — Meditations
    — Sermons
Hope in literature
Hopedale Community
    Example under Collective settlements

Hopewell culture
   xx Indians of North America—Antiquities
      Mound-builders
   — Juvenile literature
Hopf algebras
   x Algebras, Hopf
   xx Algebraic topology
Hopf spaces
   See H-spaces
Hopi Indians *(E99.H7)*
   sa Pueblo Indians
   x Moki Indians
      Moqui Indians
      Tusayan Indians
   xx Indians of North America
      Pueblo Indians
      Shoshonean Indians
   Example under Ethnology
   — Antiquities
   — Art
      Example under Indians of North America
         —Art
   — Juvenile literature
   — Land tenure
   — Legends
   — Names
   — Religion and mythology
   — Social life and customs
   — — Pictorial works
Hopi language *(PM1351)*
   sa Shoshonean languages
   x Moki language
   xx Shoshonean languages
"Hopped-up" motors
   See Automobiles, Racing—Motors
Hops *(Indirect)* *(Brewing, TP585; Culture,
      SB295.H8)*
   sa Hop pickers
   x Hop industry and trade
   — Diseases and pests *(Indirect)*
      (SB608.H8)
      sa Hop-aphis
         Hop flea-beetle
   — Harvesting
Hopscotch *(GV1218.H)*
Horae (Books of hours)
   See Hours, Books of
Horde
   See Nomads
Hordeolum *(RE155.H6)*
   x Sty
      Stye
   xx Eyelids—Diseases
      Sebaceous glands—Diseases
   — Psychosomatic aspects
Horgen culture *(GN775.5.H6)*
   xx Neolithic period
Horizon, Dip of *(VK572)*
   x Dip of the horizon
Horizon sensors, Infra-red
   See Infra-red horizon sensors
Horizons, Artificial *(VK584.H)*
   x Artificial horizons
   xx Geographical positions
      Nautical instruments
   Example under Gyroscopic instruments
Horizontal bar *(GV527)*
   x Bar, Horizontal
   xx Gymnastics
Horizontal property
   See Condominium (Housing)
      Condominium (Office buildings)
Hormée, 1652-1653
   See Bordeaux—History—Uprising,
      1652-1653
Hormonal peptides
   See Peptide hormones

Hormonal steroids
   See Steroid hormones
Hormone antagonists
   x Antihormones
   xx Antigens and antibodies
Hormone receptors
   x Receptors, Hormone
   xx Endocrinology
Hormone research
   x Hormones—Research
   xx Research
Hormone therapy *(RM283-298)*
   sa Adrenocortical hormones—Therapeutic
      use
      Estrogen—Therapeutic use
      Glucocorticoids—Therapeutic use
      Gonadotropin—Therapeutic use
      Steroid hormones—Therapeutic use
   x Endocrine therapy
      Hormones—Therapeutic use
   xx Therapeutics
Hormones *(QP801.H7)*
   sa Cortin
      Ecdysone
      Endocrinology
      Gastrointestinal hormones
      Glands, Ductless
      Hormones, Sex
      Insect hormones
      Metabolic regulation
      Peptide hormones
      Pheromones
      Pituitary hormone releasing factors
      Pituitary hormones
      Steroid hormones
      Sympathin
      Thyroid hormones
      Thyroxine
      Toxohormone
   xx Endocrinology
      Glands, Ductless
      Metabolic regulation
      Secretion
   — Analysis
   — Juvenile literature
   — Research
      See Hormone research
   — Therapeutic use
      See Hormone therapy
Hormones, Sex
   sa Progestational hormones
      names of hormones, e.g. Androgens,
         Progesterone, Testosterone
   x Female sex hormone
      Male sex hormone
      Sex hormones
   xx Androstane
      Endocrinology
      Glands, Ductless
      Hormones
      Steroid hormones
Hormones (Plants) *(QK731)*
   sa Plant regulators
   x Phytohormones
      Plant hormones
   xx Agricultural chemicals
      Botanical chemistry
      Growth inhibiting substances
      Growth (Plants)
      Growth promoting substances
      Plants
   — Research
      See Plant hormone research
Horn (Musical instrument) *(ML955-8)*
   sa Alpenhorn
      Alto horn
      Lur
      Shophar

      Tuba
   x French horn
   xx Tuba
   Example under Wind instruments
   — Juvenile literature
   — Orchestra studies *(MT426)*
      xx Horn (Musical instrument)—Studies
         and exercises
   — Studies and exercises *(MT425)*
      sa Horn (Musical instrument)—
         Orchestra studies
Horn and bassoon music
   See Bassoon and horn music
Horn and clarinet music
   See Clarinet and horn music
Horn and flute music
   See Flute and horn music
Horn and guitar music *(M296-7)*
   x Guitar and horn music
Horn and guitar music, Arranged *(M296-7)*
Horn and oboe music *(M288-9)*
   x Oboe and horn music
Horn and organ music *(M182-4)*
   x Organ and horn music
Horn and percussion music *(M298)*
   x Percussion and horn music
Horn and piano music *(M255-7)*
   sa Rondos (Horn and piano)
      Sonatas (Horn and piano)
      Suites (Horn and piano)
      Variations (Horn and piano)
   x Piano and horn music
Horn and piano music, Arranged *(M258-9)*
   sa Concertos (Horn)—Solo with piano
      Concertos (Horn with string orchestra)
         —Solo with piano
      Concertos (Horn with string orchestra)
         —To 1800—Solo with piano
      Horn with orchestra—Solo with piano
      Variations (Horn with orchestra)—Solo
         with piano
Horn and violin music *(M290-291)*
   x Violin and horn music
Horn and violoncello music *(M290-291)*
   x Violoncello and horn music
Horn carving *(NK6020)*
   xx Carving (Art industries)
Horn fly *(Agriculture, SF810.H6; Zoology,
      QL537.M7)*
   xx Flies
   — Control *(Indirect)*
Horn music *(M80-84)*
   sa Concertos (Horn)
      Concertos (Horn with band)
      Concertos (Horn with chamber
         orchestra)
      Concertos (Horn with string orchestra)
      Horn with band
      Horn with chamber orchestra
      Horn with instrumental ensemble
      Horn with orchestra
      Horn with string orchestra
      Hunting music
      Recorded accompaniments (French
         horn)
      Sonatas (Horn)
      Quartets, [Trios, etc.], Wind quartets,
      [trios, etc.] *followed by specifications
      which include the horn*
Horn music (Horns (2)) *(M288-9)*
   sa Concertos (Horns (2))
      Concertos (Horns (2) with string
         orchestra)
      Horns (2) with orchestra
      Horns (2) with string orchestra
      Sonatas (Horns (2))
Horn music (Horns (3))
   See Wind trios (Horns (3))

Horn music (Horns (4))
  See Wind quartets (Horns (4))
Horn music (Horns (5))
  See Wind quintets (Horns (5))
Horn players *(ML399; ML419)*
Horn shark
  x Horned shark
    Hornshark
  xx Sharks
**Horn, trombones (2), trumpets (2) with string
    orchestra** *(M1105-6)*
  sa Concertos (Horn, trombones (2),
    trumpets (2) with string orchestra)
  xx Concertos (Horn, trombones (2),
    trumpets (2) with string orchestra)
    String-orchestra music
    Wind quintets (Horn, trombones (2),
    trumpets (2))
Horn with band *(M1205)*
  sa Concertos (Horn with band)
  xx Band music
    Concertos (Horn with band)
    Horn music
Horn with band, Arranged *(M1257)*
  — Scores *(M1257)*
Horn with chamber orchestra *(M1028-9)*
  sa Concertos (Horn with chamber
    orchestra)
  xx Concertos (Horn with chamber
    orchestra)
    Horn music
Horn with instrumental ensemble
  xx Horn music
    Instrumental ensembles
Horn with orchestra *(M1028-9)*
  sa Concertos (Horn)
    Rondos (Horn with orchestra)
    Variations (Horn with orchestra)
  xx Concertos (Horn)
    Horn music
    Orchestral music
  — Solo with piano *(M1029)*
    xx Horn and piano music, Arranged
Horn with orchestra, Arranged *(M1028-9)*
Horn with string orchestra *(M1105-6)*
  sa Concertos (Horn with string orchestra)
  xx Concertos (Horn with string orchestra)
    Horn music
    String-orchestra music
Horn with string orchestra, Arranged
    (M1105-6)
  — Scores *(M1105)*
Hornbeam, European
  See European hornbeam
Hornbills *(QL674; QL696.C7)*
  sa Helmeted hornbill
  xx Coraciiformes
Hornblende *(Indirect)* *(QE391.H)*
  xx Amphiboles
  Example under Mineralogy
Hornbooks *(Z1033.H8)*
  xx Primers
Horned frogs
  See Horned toads
Horned larks
  See Larks
Horned lizards
  See Horned toads
Horned owl
  xx Owls
  — Behavior
  — Juvenile literature
Horned pout
  See Black bullhead
    Brown bullhead
Horned shark
  See Horn shark

Horned toads *(QL666.L2)*
  x Horned frogs
    Horned lizards
    Lizards, Horned
  xx Toads
  — Juvenile literature
Hornet automobile
Hornets
  See Paper wasps
Hornpipe (Dance)
Hornpipes
    Here are entered collections of hornpipe
    music for various mediums. Individual
    hornpipes and collections of hornpipes
    for a specific medium are entered un-
    der the heading followed by specifica-
    tion of medium.
Hornpipes (Orchestra) *(M1048; M1060)*
  xx Orchestral music
Hornpipes (Piano)
  xx Piano music
Hornpipes (Violin and piano) *(M211-213;
    M217-218)*
  xx Violin and piano music
Horns *(QL942)*
  sa Antlers
  Example under Animal weapons
  — Juvenile literature
Horns, Cutaneous *(RL427)*
  sa Molting
  x Cornua cutanea
    Cutaneous horns
  xx Keratosis
Horns, Removal of
  See Dehorning
Horns (2) and oboes (2) with string orchestra
    (M1140-1141)
  sa Concertos (Horns (2) and oboes (2)
    with string orchestra)
  x Two horns and oboes (2) with string
    orchestra
  xx Concertos (Horns (2) and oboes (2)
    with string orchestra)
Horns (2) with orchestra *(M1028-9)*
  sa Concertos (Horns (2))
  x Two horns with orchestra
  xx Concertos (Horns (2))
    Horn music (Horns (2))
    Orchestral music
Horns (2) with string orchestra *(M1105-6)*
  sa Concertos (Horns (2) with string
    orchestra)
  x Two horns with string orchestra
  xx Concertos (Horns (2) with string
    orchestra)
    Horn music (Horns (2))
    String-orchestra music
Horns (3) with band *(M1205-6)*
  sa Concertos (Horns (3) with band)
  x Three horns with band
  xx Concertos (Horns (3) with band)
Horns (3) with orchestra *(M1028-9)*
  sa Concertos (Horns (3))
  x Three horns with orchestra
  xx Concertos (Horns (3))
    Orchestral music
    Wind trios (Horns (3))
Horns (4) with band *(M1205-6)*
  sa Concertos (Horns (4) with band)
  x Four horns with band
  xx Concertos (Horns (4) with band)
Horns (4) with orchestra *(M1028-9)*
  sa Concertos (Horns (4))
  x Four horns with orchestra
  xx Concertos (Horns (4))
    Orchestral music
    Wind quartets (Horns (4))
  — Scores *(M1028)*

Horns (in religion, folk-lore, etc.)
  x Folk-lore of horns
  xx Religion, Primitive
Hornshark
  See Horn shark
Hornstone
  See Chert
Horodlo, Treaty of, 1413
  xx Lithuania—History
    Poland—History—Jagellons, 1386-1572
Horohoro language
  See Holoholo language
Horology *(TS540-549)*
  sa Chronometer
    Clocks and watches
    Days
    Sun-dials
    Time
  x Hours (Time)
  xx Time
    Time measurements
Horoscopes *(BF1728.A2)*
  xx Astrology
Horoscopy
  See Astrology
Horror
  sa Fear
  xx Emotions
    Fear
Horror films
  xx Feature films
    Moving-pictures
  Note under Moving-pictures—Plots, themes,
    etc.
  — History and criticism
  — Juvenile literature
Horror tales
  sa Ghost stories
  x Terror tales
  xx Detective and mystery stories
    Fiction
    Ghost stories
Horror tales, American, ₍German, etc.₎
    (Direct)
  x American ₍German, etc.₎ horror tales
  xx American ₍German, etc.₎ fiction
Hors d'oeuvres
  See Cookery (Appetizers)
Horse
  See Horses
Horse, Vaulting
  See Vaulting-horse
Horse bean
  See Broad bean
Horse brasses *(GT5888)*
  xx Brasses
    Harness
    Metal-work
Horse-breaking
  See Horse-training
Horse breeders' societies *(SF277)*
  xx Livestock associations
Horse breeding *(Indirect)* *(SF290-294)*
  sa Horse breeds
    Horses—Stud-books
    Pony breeding
    Stallions
  x Horses—Breeding
    Stud-farms
  xx Stock and stock-breeding
Horse breeds *(Indirect)*
  sa names of specific breeds, e.g. Arabian
    horse, Clydesdale horse, Tennessee
    walking horse
  x Breeds of horses
    Horses—Breeds
  xx Horse breeding
    Horses

Horse breeds *(Indirect)* *(Continued)*
Example under Livestock breeds
— Juvenile literature
Horse buying
x Horse purchasing
xx Purchasing
Horse-chestnut *(QK495.A)*
Horse drawn railroads
See Horse railroads
Horse flies
See Horseflies
Horse meat *(Foods, TX556.H8)*
x Hippophagy
xx Meat
Horse purchasing
See Horse buying
Horse race betting *(Indirect)* *(SF331)*
sa Book-making (Betting)
Pari-mutuel betting
x Handicapping
xx Gambling
Horse-racing
Wagers
Horse racetracks
See Racetracks (Horse-racing)
Horse-racing *(Direct)* *(SF321-359;*
Gambling, HV6718)
sa Harness racing
Horse race betting
Horses—Paces, gaits, etc.
Jockeys
Race horses
Racetracks (Horse-racing)
Steeplechasing
x Flat racing
xx Racing
Example under Sports
— Anecdotes, facetiae, satire, etc.
— Caricatures and cartoons
— Employees
sa Jockeys
— Juvenile literature
— Law and legislation *(Direct)*
— Moral and religious aspects
— Pictorial works
— Taxation *(Direct)*
xx Gambling—Taxation
— Terminology
Horse-racing societies *(Indirect)* *(SF335)*
Horse-radish *(SB307.H)*
x Horseradish
— Diseases and pests
sa Horse-radish flea-beetle
Horse-radish web-worm
Horse-radish flea-beetle
xx Horse-radish—Diseases and pests
Horse-radish web-worm *(SB608.H82)*
xx Horse-radish—Diseases and pests
Horse railroads *(Direct)* *(TF16; Street*
railways, TF830)
x Horse drawn railroads
Railroads, Horse
Tramways
xx Railroads
Railroads, Local and light
Horse sense
See Common sense
Horse Shoe, Battle of the, 1814 *(E83.813)*
x Horse Shoe Bend, Battle of, 1814
Horseshoe Bend, Battle of, 1814
Tohopeka, Battle of, 1814
xx Creek War, 1813-1814
Horse Shoe Bend, Battle of, 1814
See Horse Shoe, Battle of the, 1814
Horse show jumping
See Show jumping
Horse-shows *(Indirect)* *(SF295-7)*
sa Horses—Judging

Horses—Showing
Jockeys
Rodeos
Show jumping
Show riding
Three-day event (Horsemanship)
x Horses—Exhibitions
xx Livestock exhibitions
— Juvenile literature
— Pictorial works
Horse stealing *(HV6646-6665)*
xx Larceny
Thieves
Horse tick fever
See Equine piroplasmosis
Horse trails
See Trails
Horse-training *(Animal culture, SF287;*
Trained animals, GV1831.H8)
sa Cavalletti
Dressage
Hackamore
Racehorse training
x Horse-breaking
Horses—Training
xx Animals, Training of
— Early works to 1800
— Personal narratives
Horseback riding clubs
See Riding clubs
Horseflies *(QL537.T2)*
sa Deerflies
x Gadflies
Horse flies
xx Flies
— Control *(Indirect)* *(SF593.F6)*
— Identification
Horsehair *(Manufactures, TS1747.H6)*
Horsemanship *(SF309; Cavalry, UE470-475)*
sa Coaching
Dressage
Driving
Horsemen
Horses—Paces, gaits, etc.
Jumping (Horsemanship)
Riding clubs
Riding habit
Rodeos
Show riding
Three-day event (Horsemanship)
Trail riding
Vaulting (Horsemanship)
x Equestrianism
Equitation
Riding
xx Locomotion
— Caricatures and cartoons
— Juvenile literature
— Pictorial works
— Terminology
— Vocational guidance
Horsemanship in art
xx Art
Horsemanship in literature
Horsemen *(Indirect)* *(SF280)*
sa Cowboys
Jockeys
x Horsewomen
xx Horsemanship
Horses
— Biography
— Correspondence, reminiscences, etc.
— Juvenile literature
Horsemen in art
xx Art
Horses in art
Horsemint *(QK495.M)*

Horsepower (Mechanics) *(Machinery, TJ173;*
Steam-engines, TJ475-8)
xx Engines
Mechanical engineering
Steam engineering
Steam-engines
Horseradish
See Horse-radish
Horses *(Indirect)* *(QL737.U6; Cruelty to*
horses, HV4749-4755; Folk-lore,
GR715; Horse raising, SF277-359;
Industry, HD9434; Manners and
customs, GT5885; Military service,
UC600-695, UE460-475, UF370)
sa Draft horses
Harness
Hoofs
Horse breeds
Horsemen
Hunters (Horses)
Mares
Mules
Mustang
Polo ponies
Ponies
Race horses
Remount service
Show jumpers (Horses)
Stallions
headings beginning with the word
Horse
x Farriery
Hippology
Horse
xx Domestic animals
Driving
Stock and stock-breeding
Example under Ungulata
— Age *(SF869)*
— Age determination
Example under Age determination
(Zoology)
— Anatomy *(SF765)*
sa Hoofs
Example under Veterinary anatomy
— — Atlases
— Behavior
— Breeding
See Horse breeding
— Breeds
See Horse breeds
— Diseases *(SF951-9)*
sa Abortion in animals
African horse sickness
Dourine
Epizootic lymphangitis
Equine encephalomyelitis
Equine infectious anemia
Equine influenza
Equine piroplasmosis
Glanders
Lameness in horses
Laminitis
Trypanosomiasis
Tuberculosis in horses
Veterinary medicine
Veterinary surgery
Example under Veterinary medicine
— Early works to 1800
— Exhibitions
See Horse-shows
— Feeding and feeds
Example under Feeding; Feeds
— Grooming
x Grooming of horses
— Judging *(SF297)*
xx Horse-shows
— Juvenile literature

— Lameness
   See Lameness in horses
— Law *(Direct)*
— Legends and stories *(PZ10.3;*
   QL795.H7)
— Paces, gaits, etc. *(SF289)*
   sa Dressage
   xx Animal locomotion
      Horse-racing
      Horsemanship
— Photography
   See Photography of horses
— Physiology
— Pictorial works *(SF303)*
— Pictures, illustrations, etc. *(Animal*
   culture, SF303, SF337; Art,
   N7660)
   sa Horses in art
   xx Horses in art
   Note under Horses in art
— Poetry
— Psychology
   Example under Animal intelligence; Psy-
   chology, Comparative
— — Juvenile literature
— Showing *(SF295)*
   sa Show jumping
      Show riding
   xx Horse-shows
— Stud-books *(SF293)*
   sa Ponies—Stud-books
      Race horses—Names
   x Stud-books
   xx Horse breeding
— Taxation *(Direct)*
— Terminology
— Training
   See Horse-training
— Transportation *(Military service,*
   UC680-695)
Horses, Fossil *(QE882.U6)*
Horses (in heraldry)
Horses (in religion, folk-lore, etc.)
   (Folk-lore, GR715; Religion,
   BL443.H)
   sa Hayagrīva
      Hobby-horses
   x Folk-lore of horses
   xx Religion, Primitive
Horses in art *(N7660)*
   Here are entered treatises on the horse as
   represented in art. Works made up
   wholly or largely of representations of
   the horse are entered under the head-
   ing Horses—Pictures, illustrations,
   etc.
   sa Horsemen in art
      Horses—Pictures, illustrations, etc.
   xx Animals in art
      Art
      Horses—Pictures, illustrations, etc.
— Juvenile literature
Horses in literature
   xx Animals in literature
Horses in moving-pictures
   xx Moving-pictures
Horseshoe Bend, Battle of, 1814
   See Horse Shoe, Battle of the, 1814
Horseshoe pitching
   See Quoits
Horseshoeing *(SF907; Military service,*
   UC640-645)
   x Farriery
   xx Blacksmithing
Horseshoers
   sa Trade-unions—Horseshoers
   xx Blacksmiths

Horsewomen
   See Horsemen
Horticultural exhibitions *(SB59.5)*
   sa Flower shows
   xx Agricultural exhibitions
Horticultural machinery *(Indirect)* *(S678.7)*
   sa Gardening—Equipment and supplies
   xx Agricultural machinery
Horticultural research *(Indirect)*
   sa Banana research
      Insect cages
   x Horticulture—Research
   xx Agricultural research
Horticultural societies *(Indirect)* *(SB1-13)*
   sa Gardening—Societies, etc. *ṛfor*
      publications of horticultural and
      other societies in relation to
      horticultureȷ
   x Horticulture—Societies, etc.
   xx Societies
Horticultural therapy
   See Gardening—Therapeutic use
Horticulture *(Indirect)*
   Here are entered works on the scientific
   and economic aspects of the cultivation of fruits, vegetables, flowers and
   ornamental plants.
   sa Acclimatization (Plants)
      Agricultural pests
      Arboriculture
      Bulb industry
      Bulbs
      Cloche gardening
      Cold-frames
      Electro-horticulture
      Floriculture
      Forcing (Plants)
      Frost protection
      Fruit-culture
      Gardening
      Grafting
      Greenhouse management
      Greenhouse plants
      Greenhouses
      Horticulturists
      Hydroponics
      Insects, Injurious and beneficial
      Landscape gardening
      Mulching
      Mushroom culture
      Nurseries (Horticulture)
      Organic farming
      Ornamental horticulture
      Plant propagation
      Plants, Potted
      Pruning
      Puddling (Horticulture)
      Seed industry and trade
      Truck farming
      Vegetable gardening
   xx Agriculture
      Field crops
      Gardening
      Plants
— Biography
   See Horticulturists
— Economic aspects *(Direct)*
— Labor productivity
— Laboratory manuals
— Research
   See Horticultural research
— Safety measures
— Societies, etc.
   See Gardening—Societies, etc.
      Horticultural societies
— Taxation *(Direct)*
— Terminology
— Vocational guidance

   See Horticulture as a profession
Horticulture as a profession *(SB51)*
   x Gardening as a profession
      Horticulture—Vocational guidance
   xx Agriculture as a profession
      Horticulturists
Horticulturists *(Direct)* *(SB61-63)*
   sa Horticulture as a profession
   x Horticulture—Biography
   xx Agriculturists
      Botanists
      Fruit-culture
      Gardening
      Horticulture
— Biography
Hos *(DS432.H6)*
   x Ho (Munda tribe)
      Larka Kols
   xx Ethnology—India—Bihar (State)
      Mundas
Hose *(TS2301.H7; Fire hose, TH9380)*
   sa Sprinklers
   xx Rubber industry and trade
— Testing *(TH9380; TS2301.H7)*
Hose-couplings *(TH9380; TS2301.H7)*
   xx Fire-engines
      Fire extinction
      Hydrants
Hosiery *(Manufacture, TT679-695)*
   x Stockings
   xx Clothing and dress
   Example under Costume; Display of merchan-
      dise; Dry-goods; Manufactures; Tex-
      tile industry and fabrics
— Dyeing
   See Dyes and dyeing—Hosiery
— Specifications *(Direct)*
Hosiery, Cotton *(TT681)*
   x Cotton hosiery
Hosiery, Nylon *(TT681)*
   x Nylon hosiery
Hosiery, Silk *(TT681)*
   x Silk hosiery
Hosiery dyeing
   See Dyes and dyeing—Hosiery
Hosiery industry *(Direct)* *(Industry,*
   HD9969.H6-8; Manufacture,
   TT679-695)
   xx Clothing trade
      Textile industry and fabrics
   Example under Display of merchandise
— Accounting
— Automation
— Collective labor agreements
   See Collective labor agreements—
      Hosiery industry
— Costs
— Job descriptions
— Labor productivity
— Management
— Prices *(Direct)*
— Production standards
Hosiery workers *(Direct)*
   sa Trade-unions—Hosiery workers
      Wages—Hosiery workers
   xx Textile workers
Hospital accreditation
   See Hospitals—Accreditation
Hospital administration
   See Hospitals—Administration
Hospital administration as a profession
   x Hospitals—Administration—Vocational
      guidance
Hospital administrators *(Direct)* *(RA972.5)*
   xx Hospitals—Administration
      Hospitals—Staff
Hospital and community
   x Community and hospital

Hospital and community *(Continued)*
  xx Community life
Hospital attendants
  See Hospitals—Staff
Hospital beds
  xx Beds and bedsteads
      Hospitals—Furniture, equipment, etc.
Hospital care *(Direct)*
  sa Aged—Hospital care
      Children—Hospital care
      Coronary care units
      Hospitals—Home care programs
      Intensive care units
      Monitoring (Hospital care)
  xx Insurance, Hospitalization
      Medical care
  — Costs
      x Hospitals—Rates
  — Length of stay
      See Hospital utilization—Length of
          stay
Hospital central service department
  See Hospitals—Central service department
Hospital chaplains
  See Chaplains, Hospital
Hospital dental service *(Direct)*
  x Dental service in hospitals
      Hospitals—Dental service
  xx Sick—Dental care
Hospital dietary department
  See Hospitals—Food service
Hospital emergency service
  See Hospitals—Emergency service
Hospital endowments
  See Endowments
Hospital evacuation
  x Evacuation of hospitals
      Hospitals—Evacuation
  xx Hospitals—Administration
Hospital housekeeping *(RA975.5.H6)*
  xx Hospitals—Administration
Hospital infections
  See Cross infection
Hospital interns
  See Interns (Medicine)
Hospital laundries
  See Laundries, Hospital
Hospital libraries *(Direct) (Z675.H7)*
  sa Bibliotherapy
  x Libraries, Hospital
  xx Hospitals
      Institution libraries
      Medical libraries
  — Administration
  — Standards *(Direct)*
Hospital personnel administration
  See Hospitals—Personnel management
Hospital pharmacies *(RA975.5.P5)*
  xx Drugstores
      Hospitals
      Pharmacy
  — Law and legislation *(Direct)*
Hospital records
  sa Medical records
  x Hospitals—Records
  xx Medical records
Hospital research
  See Hospitals—Research
Hospital schools
  x Preventorium schools
  xx Children—Hospitals
      Hospitals
      Schools
Hospital service (War)
  See Hospital-ships
      Hospitals, Military
      Hospitals, Naval and marine
      Red Cross

War—Relief of sick and wounded
Hospital-ships *(Naval medicine, VG450)*
  sa subdivision Hospital-ships *under navies,*
      e.g. United States. Navy—
          Hospital-ships
  x Hospital service (War)
  xx Government vessels
      Hospitals
      Hospitals, Naval and marine
      Medicine, Naval
      Ships
      Surgery, Naval
Hospital social work
  See Medical social work
Hospital training-schools
  See Nursing schools
Hospital use
  See Hospital utilization
Hospital utilization *(Direct)*
  x Hospital use
  — Length of stay
      x Hospital care—Length of stay
          Hospitals—Length of stay
          Length of stay in hospitals
Hospitalers *(BX2825)*
  x Hospitallers
  xx Hospitals
      Military religious orders
      Monasticism and religious orders
      Nurses and nursing
  — Religious life
Hospitality *(BJ2021-8)*
  x Guests
  xx Entertaining
      Etiquette
  — Anecdotes, facetiae, satire, etc.
Hospitality (Islam)
  x Islamic hospitality
      Muslim hospitality
  xx Islamic etiquette
Hospitality (Judaism)
  xx Jews—Rites and ceremonies
Hospitalization insurance
  See Insurance, Hospitalization
Hospitallers
  See Hospitalers
Hospitals *(Indirect) (RA960-996)*
  sa Alcoholics—Hospitals and asylums
      Almshouses
      Care of the sick
      Catholic hospitals
      Children—Hospitals
      Clinics
      Dispensaries
      Epileptics—Hospitals
      Extended care facilities
      Homeopathy—Hospitals and
          dispensaries
      Hospital libraries
      Hospital pharmacies
      Hospital schools
      Hospital-ships
      Hospitalers
      Incurables—Hospitals and asylums
      Medical centers
      Medicine, Clinical
      Military religious orders
      Nervous system—Diseases—Hospitals
      Nose—Diseases—Hospitals
      Nurses and nursing
      Nursing homes
      Operating rooms
      Orthopedia—Hospitals and institutions
      Prison hospitals
      Psychiatric hospitals
      Throat—Diseases—Hospitals
      Volunteer workers in hospitals

subdivision Hospitals *under names of*
  cities, e.g. New York (City)—
      Hospitals, *and under names of*
      various diseases, e.g. Diphtheria—
      Hospitals; Smallpox—Hospitals;
      Tuberculosis—Hospitals and
      sanatoriums
  x Benevolent institutions
      Infirmaries
  xx Care of the sick
      Charities
      Charities, Medical
      Dispensaries
      Health facilities
      Hygiene, Public
      Institutional care
      Medical centers
      Medicine
      Nurses and nursing
      Public institutions
      Public welfare
      Sick
  — Accounting *(HF5686.H7)*
      Example under Institution management
  — Accreditation *(RA971)*
      x Accreditation of hospitals
          Accrediting of hospitals
          Hospital accreditation
      xx Hospitals—Inspection
  — Administration
      sa Hospital administrators
          Hospital evacuation
          Hospital housekeeping
          Medical appointments and schedules
      x Hospital administration
          Hospitals—Management and
              regulation
      xx Health services administration
  — — Mathematical models
  — — Study and teaching
  — — Tables, etc.
  — — Vocational guidance
          See Hospital administration as a
              profession
  — Air conditioning *(RA969)*
  — — Costs
  — Anecdotes, facetiae, satire, etc.
  — Attendants
      See Hospitals—Staff
  — Cardiovascular services
      sa Coronary care units
      x Cardiovascular services in hospitals
  — Caricatures and cartoons
  — Central service department
      sa Hospitals—Furniture, equipment, etc.
      x Central service department
          (Hospitals)
          Hospital central service department
      xx Hospitals—Furniture, equipment, etc.
  — — Automation
  — Cleaning
  — Collective bargaining
      See Collective bargaining—Hospitals
  — Collective labor agreements
      See Collective labor agreements—
          Hospitals
  — Construction *(RA967)*
      sa Coronary care units
          Intensive care units
      x Hospitals—Design and construction
      xx Architecture
          Architecture—Designs and plans
  — Cost of operation
      x Hospitals—Operating costs
  — Dental service
      See Hospital dental service
  — Design and construction
      See Hospitals—Construction

— Disinfection
    xx Disinfection and disinfectants
— Electric equipment
— Emergency service *(RA975.5.E5)*
    sa Ambulances
        subdivision Hospitals—Emergency
          service *under names of cities*
    x Emergency rooms
      Emergency services in hospitals
      Hospital emergency service
    xx Emergency medical services
      Medical emergencies
— Employees
    See Hospitals—Staff
— Evacuation
    See Hospital evacuation
— Federal aid
    See Federal aid to hospitals
— Finance
    sa Federal aid to hospitals
— Fires and fire prevention *(TH9445.H7)*
— Food service *(RA975.5.D5)*
    x Dietary departments of hospitals,
        etc.
      Hospital dietary department
    xx Hospitals—Furniture, equipment, etc.
    Example under Food service
— Furniture, equipment, etc. *(RA968)*
    sa Hospital beds
      Hospitals—Central service
        department
      Hospitals—Food service
    xx Furniture
      Hospitals—Central service
        department
— — Costs
— — Tables, etc.
— Heating and ventilation *(RA969)*
— Home care programs
    x Home care programs, Hospital-based
    xx Chronically ill—Care and treatment
      Home nursing
      Hospital care
      Hospitals—Outpatient services
— Hygiene *(RA969)*
    sa Cross infection
      Laundries, Hospital
— Inspection *(RA971)*
    sa Hospitals—Accreditation
— Job descriptions
— Juvenile literature *(RA965)*
— Labor productivity
— Landscape architecture *(RA967.7)*
    xx Landscape architecture
— Laundry service
    See Laundries, Hospital
— Laws and legislation *(RA974)*
    sa Federal aid to hospitals
      Hospitals (Canon law)
      Hospitals—Staff—Legal status, laws,
        etc.
      Tort liability of hospitals
— Length of stay
    See Hospital utilization—Length of
      stay
— Lighting
— Location *(RA967.7)*
— Management and regulation
    See Hospitals—Administration
— Nephrological services
    sa Artificial kidney
    x Nephrological services in hospitals
    xx Kidneys—Diseases
— Noise control *(RA969.7)*
— Nurses
    See Hospitals—Staff
      Nurses and nursing
— Operating costs

    See Hospitals—Cost of operation
— Outpatient services *(RA974)*
    sa Hospitals—Home care programs
      Medical emergencies
    x Ambulatory care
      Outpatient services in hospitals
— Personnel management
    x Hospital personnel administration
    xx Hospitals—Staff
    Example under Personnel management
— Poetry
— Radiological services
    sa Diagnosis, Radioscopic
      Radiotherapy
    x Radiological services in hospitals
    xx Radiology
— Rates
    See Hospital care—Costs
— Records
    See Hospital records
— Research
    x Hospital research
— Safety measures
— Sociological aspects
    xx Sociology
— Specifications *(RA967.5)*
— Staff *(RA972)*
    sa Collective bargaining—Hospitals
      Hospital administrators
      Hospitals—Personnel management
      Interns (Medicine)
      Strikes and lockouts—Hospitals
      Trade-unions—Hospitals
    x Hospital attendants
      Hospitals—Attendants
      Hospitals—Employees
      Hospitals—Nurses
      Resident physicians
    xx Medical personnel
— — Housing *(Direct)*
— — In-service training *(Direct)*
    xx Employees, Training of
      Medical education
— — Juvenile literature
— — Legal status, laws, etc. *(Direct)*
    xx Hospitals—Laws and legislation
— — Medical care
— — Salaries, pensions, etc.
    xx Wages—Medical personnel
— Taxation *(Direct)*
— Tort liability
    See Tort liability of hospitals
— Vocational guidance
— Waste disposal
Hospitals, Convalescent *(RA973)*
    sa Convalescence
      Rest homes
    xx Convalescence
      Rest homes
      Sanatoriums
Hospitals, Disaster
    See Disaster hospitals
Hospitals, Field
    See Hospitals, Military
      Medicine, Military
      War—Relief of sick and wounded
Hospitals, Gynecologic and obstetric
    (RG12-16)
    sa Maternity homes
    x Gynecology—Hospitals
      Hospitals, Maternity
      Lying-in hospitals
      Maternity hospitals
      Mother and child—Hospital care
      Obstetrics—Hospitals
      Woman—Hospitals
    xx Maternal health services
— Administration

Hospitals, Homeopathic
    See Homeopathy—Hospitals and
      dispensaries
Hospitals, Indian
    See Indians of North America—Hospitals
Hospitals, Insane
    See Psychiatric hospitals
Hospitals, Maternity
    See Hospitals, Gynecologic and obstetric
Hospitals, Medieval *(RA964)*
Hospitals, Military *(Indirect)* *(UH460-485)*
    sa First aid in illness and injury
      subdivisions Hospitals, charities, etc.
      and Medical and sanitary affairs
      under names of wars and campaigns,
      e.g. United States—History—Civil
      War, 1861-1865—Hospitals,
      charities, etc.; South African War,
      1899-1902—Medical and sanitary
      affairs
    x Field hospitals
      Hospital service (War)
      Hospitals, Field
      Military hospitals
      Veterans' hospitals
    xx Medicine, Military
      Military art and science
      Surgery, Military
      Veterans—Medical care
      War—Relief of sick and wounded
— Construction
    See Hospitals, Military—Design and
      construction
— Design and construction
    x Hospitals, Military—Construction
— Outpatient services

— United States
    x United States. Army—Hospitals
Hospitals, Mobile
    x Mobile hospitals
      Portable hospitals
Hospitals, Naval and marine *(Indirect)*
    (Marine, RA975, RA980-993; Naval,
    VG410-450)
    sa Hospital-ships
    x Hospital service (War)
      Marine hospitals
      Naval hospitals
    xx Medicine, Naval
      Naval art and science
      Surgery, Naval
      Veterans—Medical care
      War—Relief of sick and wounded
Hospitals, Ophthalmic and aural *(RE3; Ear,*
    nose and throat, RF6)
    x Aural hospitals
      Eye—Hospitals
      Ophthalmic and aural hospitals
    xx Ear—Diseases
      Eye—Diseases and defects
Hospitals, Rural *(Indirect)* *(RA975)*
    x Rural hospitals
Hospitals, Veterinary
    See Veterinary hospitals
Hospitals (Canon law)
    xx Hospitals—Laws and legislation
Host-parasite relationships
    sa Host-virus relationships
    x Parasite-host relationships
    xx Parasitism
Host plants
    sa Weed control—Biological control
      subdivision Host plants *under names of*
      parasites or groups of parasites, e.g.
      Leaf-hoppers—Host plants
    xx Agricultural pests

Host plants *(Continued)*
    Insect-plant relationships
    Insects, Injurious and beneficial
    Plant diseases
    Weeds
Host-virus relationships
    sa Virus-vector relationships
    x Virus-host relationships
    xx Host-parasite relationships
        Virus diseases
        Viruses
Hostage Trial, Nuremberg, 1947-1949
    See War crime trials—Nuremberg—Hostage
        case, 1947-1949
Hostages *(Law of war, JX5143)*
    xx War (International law)
Hostilities
    See War
        War, Declaration of
        War (International law)
        War, Maritime (International law)
Hostility (Psychology)
    sa Fighting (Psychology)
    xx Aggressiveness (Psychology)
        Psychology
Hot-air baths
    See Baths, Hot-air
Hot-air engines
    See Air-engines
        Caloric engines
Hot-air heating *(TH7601-7635)*
    x Warm-air heating
    xx Heating
    — Ducts
        See Air ducts
Hot-air treatment
    See Thermotherapy
Hot-atom chemistry
    xx Chemistry
        Nuclear chemistry
Hot-beds
    See Hotbeds
Hot cakes
    See Pancakes, waffles, etc.
Hot dog rolls
    xx Baked products
        Bread
Hot laboratories (Radioactive substances)
    (Radiochemical laboratories,
    QD604.8)
    x Laboratories, Hot (Radioactive
        substances)
    xx Atomic energy research—Laboratories
        Radiochemical laboratories
    — Equipment and supplies
    — Safety measures
"Hot motors"
    See Automobiles, Racing—Motors
Hot pepper
    See Chili
Hot plasmas
    See High temperature plasmas
Hot pursuit (International law)
    xx Search, Right of
Hot shot
    xx Munitions
Hot spring ecology *(Indirect)*
    x Hot springs
    xx Ecology
Hot springs
    See Geysers
        Hot spring ecology
        Springs
Hot stage microscope
    xx Microscope and microscopy
Hot water
    This heading is used only with subdivi-
        sions.

— Therapeutic use *(RM253)*
    sa Salisbury treatment
    xx Hydrotherapy
Hot-water bags, Tariff on
    See Tariff on hot-water bags
Hot water discharges into rivers, lakes, etc.
    See Thermal pollution of rivers, lakes, etc.
Hot-water heaters
    See Water heaters
Hot-water heating *(TH7511-7549)*
    xx Heating
    — Regulators *(TH7541)*
        xx Heating—Control
    — Tables, calculations, etc.
Hot-water heating (Jewish law)
Hot water rockets
    xx Rockets (Aeronautics)
Hot-water supply *(TH6551-6568)*
    sa Kitchen-boiler explosions
        Solar water heaters
        Water heaters
    xx Plumbing
Hot-wire anemometer
    xx Anemometer
Hotbeds
    sa Soil heating
    x Hot-beds
    xx Forcing (Plants)
        Plants, Effect of heat on
Hotchkiss machine-gun *(UF620.H8)*
    sa Benet-Mercié machine-gun
    xx Machine-guns
Hotchkiss revolving cannon *(UF620.H8)*
    xx Machine-guns
Hotel administration
    See Hotel management
Hotel bellmen *(TX926)*
    x Bellboys, Hotel
        Bellhops, Hotel
        Bellmen, Hotel
        Motel bellmen
    xx Hotels, taverns, etc.—Employees
Hotel detectives
    See House detectives
Hotel doormen *(TX926)*
    x Doormen, Hotel
        Motel doormen
    xx Hotels, taverns, etc.—Employees
Hotel housekeeping *(TX912)*
    sa Hotel laundry service
    xx Hotel management
Hotel laundry service *(TX911.5)*
    xx Hotel housekeeping
        Laundry
        Linen supply service
Hotel maids *(TX928)*
    x Chambermaids, Hotel
        Maids, Hotel
        Motel maids
    xx Hotels, taverns, etc.—Employees
Hotel management
    sa Coffee-house management
        Hotel housekeeping
        Motel management
        Stewards
    x Hotel administration
        Hotels, taverns, etc.—Management
    — Study and teaching
        sa Hotel management schools
    — Vocational guidance
Hotel management schools *(Direct)*
    xx Hotel management—Study and
        teaching
Hotels, taverns, etc. *(Indirect)*
    (Architecture, NA7800-7850;
    Manners and customs,
    GT3770-3899)
    sa Coffee-houses

        House detectives
        Lodging-houses
        Motels
        Music-halls (Variety-theaters, cabarets,
            etc.)
        Restaurants, lunch rooms, etc.
        Tourist camps, hostels, etc.
        subdivision Hotels, taverns, etc. *under*
            names of cities, e.g. San Francisco—
            Hotels, taverns, etc.
    x Ale-houses
        Boarding-houses
        Cafés
        Dramshops
        Inns
        Public houses
        Rooming houses
        Saloons
        Taverns
    xx Liquor problem
        Liquor traffic
        Restaurants, lunch rooms, etc.
        Temperance
    — Accounting *(HF5686.H75)*
    — Anecdotes, facetiae, satire, etc.
    — Collective labor agreements
        See Collective labor agreements—
            Hotels, taverns, etc.
    — Employees *(Direct) (TX911; TX930)*
        sa Hotel bellmen
            Hotel doormen
            Hotel maids
            Hotels, taverns, etc.—Personnel
                management
            Porters
            Restaurants, lunch rooms, etc.—
                Employees
            Trade-unions—Hotels, taverns, etc.
            Wages—Hotels, taverns, etc.
            Waiters
            Waitresses
        x Motels—Employees
    — — Accidents
    — — Supplementary employment
    — Finance
    — Fires and fire prevention *(TH9445.H)*
    — Furniture, equipment, etc. *(TX912)*
        sa Bars (Furniture)
    — Law
        sa subdivision Hotels, taverns, etc.—
            Law *under names of cities*
        x Innkeeper and guest
            Restaurants, lunch rooms, etc.—Law
        xx Bailments
    — Management
        See Hotel management
    — Parking facilities
        xx Automobile parking
    — Personnel management *(TX911.3.P4)*
        xx Hotels, taverns, etc.—Employees
    — Rates
    — Safety measures
    — Sanitation
    — Social aspects
    — Terminology
    — Valuation *(Direct)*
    — Vocational guidance
Hotels, taverns, etc., in literature
Hothouses
    See Greenhouses
Hotin, Battle of, 1621
    xx Turkey—History—1453-1683
Hotin, Battle of, 1673
    xx Poland—History—Elective monarchy,
        1572-1763
HOTRAN (Computer program)

Hotspur (Destroyer)
　Example under World War, 1939-1945—Naval operations
Hottentot language *(PL8251-4)*
　sa Korana language
　xx Bushman languages
Hottentots *(Ethnography, GN660.H6; South Africa, DT764.H6)*
　sa Bondelswarts (African tribe)
　　Bushmen
　　Griquas
　　Korana (African people)
　　Missions to Hottentots
　　Tannekwe (African tribe)
　— Name
　— Religion *(BL2480.H6)*
Houbara *(QL696.L7)*
　x Hubara
　xx Bustards
Houdans (Poultry) *(SF489.H7)*
Hound Dog (Missile)
Hounds *(SF429.H6)*
　sa Coursing
　　particular breeds of hounds, e.g.
　　　Basset-hounds, Deer-hounds, Foxhounds, Greyhounds, Irish wolf-hounds, Russian wolf-hounds
Hour-glasses *(QB214)*
　xx Time measurements
Hour of birth
　See Birth, Hour of
Houroûfîs
　See Hurufis
Hours, Books of *(Art, ND3363; Catholic Church, BX2080)*
　sa Primers (Prayer-books)
　x Books of hours
　　Horae (Books of hours)
　xx Catholic Church. Liturgy and ritual. Hours
　　Catholic Church—Prayer-books and devotions
　　Christian art and symbolism
　　Decoration and ornament
　　Illumination of books and manuscripts
　　Illustrated books
　　Liturgies
　　Prayer-books
　　Prayers
Hours (Time)
　See Chronology
　　Days
　　Horology
　　Sun-dials
　　Time
Hours of labor *(Direct) (HD5106-5250)*
　sa Children—Employment
　　Collective farms—Income distribution
　　Daylight saving
　　Eight-hour movement
　　Four-day week
　　Holidays
　　Night work
　　Overtime
　　Rest periods
　　Shift systems
　　Sunday legislation
　　Sunday opening of libraries
　　Vacations, Employee
　　Weekly rest-day
　　Woman—Employment
　x Children—Hours of labor
　　Labor, Hours of
　　Woman—Hours of labor
　　Working-day
　xx Children—Employment
　　Labor and laboring classes
　　Labor laws and legislation

　　Weekly rest-day
　　Woman—Employment
　— Mathematical models
　— Public opinion
Housatonic Indians
　See Stockbridge Indians
Housatunnuk Indians
　See Stockbridge Indians
House-boats *(Boating, GV836; Naval architecture, VM335)*
　sa Shantyboats and shantyboaters
　x Houseboats
　xx Boats and boating
　　River boats
　　River life
　— Law and legislation *(Direct)*
House built upon a rock (Parable)
　x House built upon sand (Parable)
House built upon sand (Parable)
　See House built upon a rock (Parable)
House buying
　sa Home ownership
　　House selling
　x Home buying
　　Home purchase
　　House purchasing
　xx Home ownership
　　House selling
　　Real estate business
　— Caricatures and cartoons
House cleaning *(Vacuum cleaners, etc., TH7692-8)*
　sa Bathrooms—Cleaning
　xx Cleaning
　　Home economics
　　Sanitation, Household
House construction *(TH4805-4835)*
　sa Drainage, House
　　Dwellings—Maintenance and repair
　　Dwellings—Remodeling
　　House framing
　　House painting
　　special kinds of house construction, e.g.
　　　Concrete houses, Prefabricated houses
　x Building, House
　　Construction, House
　　Home construction
　　Residential construction
　xx Architecture, Domestic
　　Building
　　Dwellings
　— Amateurs' manuals *(TH4815)*
　— Anecdotes, facetiae, satire, etc.
　— Contracts and specifications *(Direct)*
　　xx Building—Contracts and specifications
　— Costs
　　See House construction—Estimates and costs
　— Estimates and costs *(Direct)*
　　x House construction—Costs
　— Juvenile literature
House decoration
　See Interior decoration
House detectives *(Direct)*
　x Hotel detectives
　xx Detectives
　　Hotels, taverns, etc.
　　Police, Private
　— Correspondence, reminiscences, etc.
House drainage
　See Drainage, House
　　Plumbing
　　Sanitation
　　Sewerage
House-dust mite

House fittings
　See Building fittings
House flags
　See Steamboat lines—Flags, insignia, etc.
House fly
　See Housefly
House framing *(TH2301-2398)*
　sa Half-timbered houses
　　Wooden-frame houses
　xx Carpentry
　　Framing (Building)
　　Half-timbered houses
　　House construction
House furnishings *(Direct)*
　sa Candlesticks
　　Carpets
　　Chamber pots
　　Clocks and watches
　　Cushions
　　Furniture
　　Glassware
　　Household appliances
　　Interior decoration
　　Kitchen utensils
　　Lamps
　　Pottery
　　Rugs
　　Silver
　　Trivets
　x Home furnishings
　　Household goods
　xx Home economics
　　Home economics—Equipment and supplies
　　Interior decoration
　— Storage
　— Testing *(TX315)*
　— Trade-marks
House furnishings industry and trade *(Direct)*
　x Home furnishings industry and trade
　　Housefurnishings industry and trade
　xx Interior decoration
House inscriptions
　See Architectural inscriptions
　　House marks
House marks
　sa Barn symbols
　　Kolam
　x House inscriptions
　　Inscriptions, House
　　Marks, House
　xx Devices
　　Industrial design coordination
　　Signs and sign-boards
　　Symbolism
　　Tokens
House-martin *(QL396.P2)*
　x Martins
　xx Swallows
House mothers
　See Housemothers
House moving
　See Moving of buildings, bridges, etc.
House names
　xx Names
House names, German, [etc.]
　x German [etc.] house names
House of Yahweh
　See Temple of God

House organs *(Direct)* *(HF6121.H6)*
> Here are entered works treating of the history, purpose, etc. of periodical publications published by individual business concerns to disseminate information promoting their interests and success. Works on periodical publications issued by employees and devoted to their interests are entered under the heading Employees' magazines, handbooks, etc.

    xx Advertising—Periodicals
        Business—Periodicals
        Journalism, Technical
    Note under Employees' magazines, handbooks, etc.
House organs, Interior
    See Employees' magazines, handbooks, etc.
House painting *(TT320-324)*
    sa Painting, Industrial
        Texture painting
    xx House construction
        Painting, Industrial
    Note under Do-it-yourself work
    — Amateurs' manuals *(TT320)*
    — Contracts and specifications *(TT320)*
    — Defects
    — Equipment and supplies
    — — Drawing
        See House painting—Equipment and supplies—Drawings
    — — Drawings
        x House painting—Equipment and supplies—Drawing
        xx Mechanical drawing
    — Estimates *(TT320)*
    — Tropical conditions
        x Tropical house painting
        Example under Tropics; *and under reference from* Tropical conditions
    — Vocational guidance
House plans
    See Architecture, Domestic—Designs and plans
House plants *(SB419)*
    sa Artificial light gardening
        Foliage plants
        Gardens, Miniature
        Hanging plants
        Plants, Potted
        Wardian cases
        Window-gardening
    xx Botany
        Container gardening
        Floriculture
        Plants
        Window-gardening
    — Diseases and pests *(Indirect)* *(SB608.H84)*
    — Juvenile literature
    — Pictorial works
House plants in interior decoration
    xx Flower arrangement
        Interior decoration
House purchasing
    See House buying
House sanitation
    See Sanitation, Household
House selling
    sa House buying
    xx House buying
        Real estate business
House sparrow
    See English sparrow
House spirits
    See Household shrines
House style
    See Industrial design coordination

House-to-house fighting
    See Street fighting (Military science)
House trading
    See Trade-in housing
House-tree-person technique *(BF698.8.H6)*
    x H-T-P test
    xx Projective techniques
Houseboats
    See House-boats
Housefly *(QL537.M7; RA641.F6)*
    x House fly
    xx Flies
    — Behavior
    — Control
        See Housefly control
    — Extermination
        See Housefly control
Housefly control *(Indirect)* *(RA641.F6)*
    x Housefly—Control
        Housefly—Extermination
Housefurnishings industry and trade
    See House furnishings industry and trade
Household appliances
    sa Irons (Pressing)
        Salesmen and salesmanship—Household appliances
    x Domestic appliances
        Home appliances
        Household equipment
        Household goods
    xx Home economics
        House furnishings
    — Collectors and collecting *(Direct)*
    — Juvenile literature
    — Maintenance and repair
    — — Problems, exercises, etc.
    — Terminology
Household appliances, Electric *(Direct)* *(Economics, HD9697; Technology, TK7018-7301)*
    sa Electric blankets
        Electric irons
        Electric water heaters
        Floor polishing machines
        Vacuum cleaners
    x Domestic electric apparatus
        Electric apparatus and appliances, Domestic
        Electric household appliances
    xx Electric apparatus and appliances
        Home economics
    Example under Electric industries
    — Accounting
    — Amateurs' manuals
        See Electric apparatus and appliances—Amateurs' manuals
    — Maintenance and repair *(TK7018; Amateurs' manuals, TK9901)*
    — — Vocational guidance
    — Marketing
    — Noise
    — Prices *(Direct)*
    — Safety measures
    — Standards
    — Testing *(TK7018)*
Household budgets
    See Home economics—Accounting
Household equipment
    See Household appliances
Household expenses
    See Cost and standard of living
        Home economics—Accounting
Household gods
    See Household shrines
Household goods
    See House furnishings
        Household appliances
        Kitchen utensils

Household goods carriers
    See Storage and moving trade
Household linens
    sa Bedding
        Drapery
        Table-cloths
    x Household textiles
        Linens, Household
    xx Home economics
        Textile industry and fabrics
    — Storage
Household management
    See Home economics
Household moving
    See Moving, Household
Household pests *(Indirect)* *(TX325)*
    sa specific pests, e.g. Cockroaches, Flies
    x Vermin
    xx Home economics
        Insects, Injurious and beneficial
        Pests
Household repairs
    See Repairing—Amateurs' manuals
Household safety
    See Home accidents—Prevention
Household sanitation
    See Sanitation, Household
Household science
    See Home economics
Household shrines
    sa Lares
    x House spirits
        Household gods
    xx Religion, Primitive
        Shrines
Household sounds
    x Dwellings—Sounds
        Home sounds
        Home—Sounds
    xx Sounds
Household supplies
    x Domestic supplies
        Supplies, Household
Household textiles
    See Household linens
Household utensils
    See Implements, utensils, etc.
        Kitchen utensils
Household workers
    See Servants
Housekeepers, Visiting
    See Visiting housekeepers
Housekeeping
    See Home economics
Housekeeping, Industrial
    See Industrial housekeeping
Housekeeping service (Social work)
    See Visiting housekeepers
Housemaids
    See Servants
Housemothers
    sa Residence counselors
    x House mothers
        Matrons of dormitories
    xx Children—Institutional care
        Dormitories—Staff
Houses
    See Architecture, Domestic
        Dwellings
Houses, Adobe
    See Adobe houses
Houses, Apartment
    See Apartment houses
Houses, Brick
    See Brick houses
Houses, Concrete
    See Concrete houses

Houses, Demountable
　See Prefabricated houses
Houses, Half-timbered
　See Half-timbered houses
Houses, Historic
　See Historic houses, etc.
Houses, Portable
　See Buildings, Portable
Houses, Prefabricated
　See Prefabricated houses
Houses, Single story
　See Single story houses
Houses, Sod
　See Sod houses
Houses, Stone
　See Stone houses
Housing　*(Direct)*　*(HD7286-7390)*
　　Here are entered works on the social and
　　economic aspects of the housing prob-
　　lem. Treatises on the architecture,
　　construction, equipment, etc. of dwell-
　　ings for the working classes are en-
　　tered under Labor and laboring classes
　　—Dwellings.
　sa Aged—Dwellings
　　Discrimination in housing
　　Emergency housing
　　Garden cities
　　Handicapped—Housing
　　Home ownership
　　Housing authorities
　　Housing management
　　Housing, Rural
　　Housing surveys
　　Industrial housing
　　Labor and laboring classes—Dwellings
　　Lodging-houses
　　Mobile homes
　　Negroes—Housing
　　Public housing
　　Real estate management
　　Relocation (Housing)
　　Rent strikes
　　Rent—Taxation
　　Residential mobility
　　Self-help housing
　　Slums
　　Tenement-houses
　　Youth—Dwellings
　x Low income housing
　　Slum clearance
　xx Cities and towns—Planning
　　Garden cities
　　Labor and laboring classes—Dwellings
　　Municipal engineering
　　Social problems
　Note under Housing surveys; Labor and labor-
　　ing classes—Dwellings
　— Accounting
　　See Housing management—
　　　Accounting
　— Cases
　　x Housing—Law and legislation—
　　　Cases
　— Finance
　　sa Buildings—Repair and reconstruction
　　　—Finance
　　　Deeds of trust
　　　Mortgages
　　　Settlement costs
　　x Housing finance
　　xx Mortgages
　— Information services　*(Direct)*
　— Juvenile literature
　— Law and legislation
　　xx City planning and redevelopment
　　　law
　——— Cases

　　See Housing—Cases
　— Management
　　See Housing management
　— Mathematical models
　— Personal narratives
　— Public opinion
　— Research
　　See Housing research
　— Subject headings
　　See Subject headings—Housing
　— Underdeveloped areas
　　See Underdeveloped areas—Housing
Housing, Animal
　See Animal housing
Housing, Cooperative　*(Direct)*　*(HD7287.7)*
　sa Apartment houses, Cooperative
　x Cooperative housing
　　Mutual housing
　xx Cooperation
　— Auditing and inspection
　— Finance
Housing, Discrimination in
　See Discrimination in housing
Housing, Naval
　See United States.　Navy—Barracks and
　　quarters
Housing, Negro
　See Negroes—Housing
Housing, Rural　*(Direct)*
　sa Cottages
　　Country homes
　　Farm buildings
　x Agricultural laborers—Housing
　　Rural housing
　xx Housing
　— Finance
　　x Housing finance
　　xx Mortgages
　— Law and legislation
　— Pictorial works
Housing, Student
　See Student housing
Housing and health　*(RA770)*
　x Health and housing
　xx Hygiene, Public
Housing authorities　*(Direct)*
　xx Housing
　　Public housing
　— Officials and employees
　—— Salaries, allowances, etc.
Housing finance
　See Housing—Finance
　　Housing, Rural—Finance
　　Public housing—Finance
Housing for government employees
　See subdivision Officials and employees—
　　Housing *under names of countries,*
　　cities, etc.
Housing for physically handicapped
　xx Architecture and the physically
　　handicapped
　　Physically handicapped
Housing for the aged
　See Aged—Dwellings
Housing management　*(TX960)*
　x Housing—Management
　xx Apartment houses
　　Housing
　　Management
　　Real estate management
　— Accounting
　　x Housing—Accounting
　— Examinations, questions, etc.
　— Forms, blanks, etc.
　— Law and legislation　*(Direct)*
Housing projects, Government
　See Public housing

Housing research　*(Direct)*
　x Housing—Research
　xx Research
Housing surveys
　　Here are entered works on the methods
　　and techniques of housing surveys. In-
　　dividual surveys are entered under the
　　heading Housing, subdivided by the
　　name of the area surveyed.
　xx Housing
Houssatonnoc Indians
　See Stockbridge Indians
Houthulst, Battle of, 1918
　xx European War, 1914-1918—Campaigns
　　—Belgium
Hova dialect
　See Merina dialect
Hovas
　x Merina (African people)
Hoven
　See Bloat in animals
Hovercraft
　See Ground-effect machines
Hovermail　*(HE6239.H6)*
　x Ground-effect machine mail
　xx Postal service
Howard Plan
　xx Education
　　Education of women
　　Education, Secondary
Howitzers　*(UF470-475; UF560-565; Naval,*
　　VF390-395)
　xx Ordnance
Howler monkeys
　x Howling monkeys
　xx Monkeys
　— Juvenile literature
Howling monkeys
　See Howler monkeys
Howlite　*(QE391.H)*
Hoysala dynasty, ca. 1006-ca. 1346
　xx India—History—1000-1526
HPB Project
　See Hand-printed Book Project
HSCI
　See High school characteristics index
Hsi-hsia language
　See Tangut language
Hsiang chi (Game)
　See Chinese chess
Hsiao　*(ML980)*
　xx Flute
Hsiung-nu
　See Jou-jan (Tatar tribe)
HU-16 (Amphibian planes)
　See Albatross (Amphibian planes)
Hu ch'in　*(ML531)*
　xx Violin
Hu ch'in music　*(M175.H8)*
　xx Violin music
Hua-yen (Sect)
　See Kegon (Sect)
Huabi Indians
　See Huave Indians
Huabi language
　See Huave language
Huacas　*(Panaman antiquities, F1565;*
　　Peruvian antiquities, F3429)
Hualapai Indians
　x Hualapi Indians
　　Walapai Indians
　　Walapi Indians
　xx Indians of North America
　　Yuman Indians
Hualapi Indians
　See Hualapai Indians
Huamachuco, Battle of, 1883
　xx War of the Pacific, 1879-1884

Huambisa language
   x Ssimaku language
   xx Indians of South America—Languages
      Jivaran languages
Huanaco *(Animal culture, SF401.H; Zoology,*
      QL737.U5)
   x Guanaco
Huanca Indians *(F3430.1.H)*
   x Wanka Indians
   xx Indians of South America
Huancavilca Indians
   xx Indians of South America
   — Art
Huarás, Peru
   — Earthquake, 1941
Huarpe Indians
   See Guarpe Indians
Huastec Indians *(F1221.H)*
   x Guastec Indians
      Huaxtec Indians
   xx Indians of Mexico
      Mayas
   — Art
Huastec language *(PM3831)*
   x Guastec language
      Huaxtec language
   xx Maya language
Huave Indians *(F1221.H)*
   x Huabi Indians
   xx Indians of Mexico
Huave language *(PM3836)*
   x Huabi language
   xx Indians of Mexico—Languages
Huaxtec Indians
   See Huastec Indians
Huaxtec language
   See Huastec language
Hubara
   See Houbara
Hubbardston, Battle of, 1777
   See Hubbardton, Battle of, 1777
Hubbardton, Battle of, 1777 *(E241.H8)*
   x Hubbardston, Battle of, 1777
   xx Burgoyne's Invasion, 1777
Hucha de Oro prize
   See Premio Hucha de Oro
Huckaback *(TS1580)*
Huckleberries *(SB386.H)*
Hucksters
   See Peddlers and peddling
Hucul horse
   x Hutzul horse
      Huzul horse
Huculs *(DB350.7)*
   x Hootzools
      Huzuls
   xx Ethnology—Carpathian Mountains
      Ukrainians
al-Hudaybiyah, Treaty of, 628 *(DS232)*
Hudhayl tribe
   x Banū Hudhayl
   xx Arabs
Hudson automobile *(TL215.H)*
Hudson-Fulton Celebration, 1909 *(F127.H8)*
   xx Steamboats
Hudson River School
Huella (Dance) *(GV1796.H75)*
Huetar Indians
   See Guetar Indians
Huguenot wars
   See France—History—Wars of the
      Huguenots, 1562-1598
Huguenots *(BX9450-9459)*
   x French Protestants
   Example under Christianity; Reformation; Ref-
      ugees, Religious
   — Songs and music

Huguenots in France *(BX9450-9459; History,*
      DC111-130)
   sa Edict of Nantes
      France—History—Wars of the
         Huguenots, 1562-1598
      Holy League, 1576-1593
      St. Bartholomew's Day, Massacre of,
         1572
      St. Germain, Peace of, 1570
   xx Camisards
      St. Bartholomew's Day, Massacre of,
         1572
Huguenots in Germany, [the Netherlands,
   Switzerland, etc.]
Huia
   xx Starlings
Huichol Indians *(E99.H78; Mexico,*
      F1221.H)
   sa Cora Indians
   xx Cora Indians
      Indians of Mexico
      Indians of North America
      Piman Indians
   — Art
   — Government relations
   — Religion and mythology
Huichol language *(PM3841)*
   x Guichola language
   xx Indians of Mexico—Languages
Huiliche Indians
   See Huilliche Indians
Huilliche Indians
   x Huiliche Indians
      Hullicos
   xx Araucanian Indians
      Indians of South America
Huisache girdler *(Insect pests, SB945.H)*
Huitoto language
   See Witoto language
Hula (Dance) *(GV1726.H)*
Hula language *(PL6621.H8)*
   xx Papuan languages
Huli (Papuan people)
   xx Ethnology—New Guinea
      Papuans
Hull, Eng.
   — Siege, 1642
      xx Great Britain—History—Civil War,
         1642-1649
Hull pottery
Hullicos
   See Huilliche Indians
Hulls (Naval architecture) *(VM)*
   sa Planing hulls
   xx Naval architecture
      Ship-building
      Shipfitting
   — Maintenance and repair
   — Welding
Hulmecas
   See Olmecs
Huma
   See Bahima (African people)
Huma Indians
   See Yuma Indians
Human acts *(BV4618)*
   sa Free will and determinism
      Sin
      Virtue
   x Acts, Human
   xx Christian ethics
      Free will and determinism
Human anatomy
   See Anatomy, Human

Human behavior
   Here are entered general works on the
   observable patterns of human actions
   and reactions. Works on the general
   science of and explanation of behavior are entered under Psychology.
   Material on particular types of behavior are entered under the specific subject, *e.g.* Drinking and traffic accidents; Food habits; Leadership.
   sa Displacement (Psychology)
      Electronic behavior control
      Psychobiology
   x Behavior (Psychology)
   xx Human biology
      Psychology
      Social sciences
   — Anecdotes, facetiae, satire, etc.
   — Mathematical models *(BF39)*
      x Behavioral models
      xx Psychology—Methodology
      Example under Mathematical models
Human biology
   sa Anatomy, Human
      Embryology, Human
      Human behavior
      Human ecology
      Human genetics
      Human mechanics
      Medicine
      Physiology
      Psychology
      Somatology
   xx Biology
      Man
   — Laboratory manuals
   — Social aspects *(Direct)*
Human body
   See Body, Human
Human capital *(Direct) (Economic theory,*
      HB501.5)
   sa Labor supply
   x Man—Economic value
   xx Capital
      Labor economics
      Labor supply
Human cell culture
   xx Cell culture
Human centrifuge
   xx Acceleration (Physiology)
      Centrifuges
Human chromosome abnormalities
   xx Chromosome abnormalities
      Medical genetics
Human chromosomes
   xx Chromosomes
      Human genetics
   — Nomenclature
Human cold storage
   See Cryonics
Human curiosities
   See Deformities
Human dissection *(QM34)*
   sa Anatomy, Human—Laboratory manuals
   x Anatomy, Practical
      Practical anatomy
   xx Anatomy, Human—Laboratory manuals
      Dissection
Human ecology *(Indirect)*
   sa Anthropo-geography
      Closed ecological systems
      Community life
      Conservation of natural resources
      Environmental policy
      Hazardous geographic environments
      Man—Influence of environment
      Man—Influence on nature
      Population

Social psychology
Sociology
x Ecology, Human
Ecology, Social
Environment
Environment, Human
Human environment
Social ecology
Survival (Human ecology)
xx Anthropo-geography
Conservation of natural resources
Ecology
Environmental policy
Human biology
Social sciences
Sociology
— Moral and religious aspects *(GF80)*
— Public opinion
— Study and teaching *(Direct)*
  sa Nature study
  x Environmental education
  Environmental studies
Human embryology
See Embryology, Human
Human engineering
Here are entered works on engineering
design with reference to man's
anatomical, physiological, and psycho-
logical capabilities and limitations.
Works in which human engineering is
used in the sense of man's relation to
his job are entered under the heading
Psychology, Applied and other appro-
priate headings.
  sa Aeroplanes—Piloting—Mathematical
  models
  Human information processing
  Life support systems (Space
  environment)
  Man-machine systems
  Space cabin simulators
  Space vehicles—Piloting—Mathematical
  models
  x Biotechnology
  Ergonomics
  Human factors in engineering design
  xx Bioengineering
  Design, Industrial
  Environmental engineering
  Industrial engineering
  Machinery—Design
  Psychology, Applied
  Psychology, Physiological
— Programmed instruction
Human environment
See Human ecology
Human evolution *(QH368)*
  sa Fossil man
  xx Evolution
  Man—Origin
— Juvenile literature
Human experimentation in medicine
  (R853.H8)
  x Experimentation on man, Medical
  Medical experiments on humans
  xx Medical ethics
  Medical research
  Medicine, Experimental
Human experimentation in psychology
  x Experimentation on man, Psychological
  Psychological experimentation on
  humans
  xx Psychological research
  Psychology, Experimental
  Psychology—Experiments
Human factors in engineering design
See Human engineering

Human fertility
See Fertility, Human
Human figure in art *(N7570-7649; Design,*
  NK1550; Drawing, NC760-775;
  Painting, ND1290-1337; Sculpture,
  NB1930)
  sa Action in art
  Anatomy, Artistic
  Breast in art
  Figure drawing
  Figure painting
  Men in art
  Nude in art
  Women in art
  xx Anatomy, Artistic
  Art
  Composition (Art)
  Drawing
  Figurative art
  Figure drawing
  Figure painting
  Nude in art
Human figure in literature *(PN56.H)*
Human genetics
  sa Dermatoglyphics—Genetic aspects
  Genetic counseling
  Genetic psychology
  Human chromosomes
  Human population genetics
  Medical genetics
  xx Genetics
  Heredity, Human
  Human biology
— Information services
— Methodology
— Moral and religious aspects
— Social aspects *(Direct)*
Human geography
See Anthropo-geography
Human information processing
  x Information processing, Human
  xx Bionics
  Human engineering
  Information theory in psychology
  Perception
Human information processing (Child
  psychology) *(BF723.I)*
  x Information processing in children
  xx Cognition (Child psychology)
Human interaction
See Social interaction
Human leopards
See Leopard men
Human locomotion
  sa Action in art
  Locomotion, Disordered
  Man—Attitude and movement
  Running
  Swimming
  Walking
  xx Human mechanics
  Locomotion
Human magnetism
See Animal magnetism
Human mechanics
  sa Human locomotion
  Sitting position
  x Human movements
  Kinesiology
  Movements of man
  xx Animal mechanics
  Biomechanics
  Human biology
Human movements
See Human mechanics
Human operators (Systems engineering)
See Man-machine systems

Human paleontology
See Fossil man
Human parasitology
See Medical parasitology
Human physiology *(QP34-38)*
  xx Physiology
— Problems, exercises, etc.
Human population genetics *(Indirect)*
  xx Human genetics
  Population genetics
Human relations
See Interpersonal relations
Human reproduction *(Indirect)* *(QP251)*
  sa Embryology, Human
  xx Reproduction
Human resource development
See Education
  Manpower policy
Human rights
See Civil rights
Human sacrifice
See Sacrifice, Human
Human science
See Anthroposophy
Human skeleton *(QM101)*
  xx Skeleton
— Juvenile literature
— Radiography
Human subsystems (Systems engineering)
See Man-machine systems
Human torpedoes
See Kaiten (Torpedoes)
  Midget submarines
Humane education *(Direct)* *(HV4712)*
  x Animals, Treatment of—Study and
  teaching
  Education, Humane
  xx Education
  Moral education
Humane societies
See Animals, Treatment of—Societies, etc.
  Charitable societies
  Child welfare
  Vivisection—Societies, etc.
  subdivision Benevolent and moral
  institutions and societies *under*
  names of cities
Humane treatment of animals
See Animals, Treatment of
Humanism *(B778; Modern, B821)*
  sa Ciceronianism
  Civilization
  Classical education
  Classical philology
  Culture
  Devotio moderna
  Hellenism
  Humanistic ethics
  Humanities
  Learning and scholarship
  Philosophical anthropology
  Renaissance
  xx Civilization
  Classical education
  Classical philology
  Culture
  Education, Humanistic
  Learning and scholarship
  Literature
  Philosophical anthropology
  Philosophy
  Renaissance
— 20th century *(B821)*
  sa Lokāyata
  x Humanitarianism (Religion)
  xx Philosophy, Modern

Humanism, Religious

Here are entered works dealing with a movement, originating in American Unitarianism, which stressed the idea that man can satisfy all his religious needs from within himself and discarded in its advanced thought all theistic concepts.

    sa Christianity and religious humanism
    x Religious humanism
    xx Man (Theology)
        Philosophy, Modern
        Religions
        Unitarianism
Humanism and the Catholic Church
    See Catholic Church and humanism
Humanism in art
    sa Ut pictura poesis (Aesthetics)
    xx Art
Humanism in literature
Humanist ethics
    See Humanistic ethics
Humanistic education
    See Education, Humanistic
Humanistic ethics *(BJ1360)*
    x Ethics, Humanistic
        Humanist ethics
    xx Ethics
        Humanism
Humanistic psychology
    xx Personality
        Psychology
Humanistic writing
    See Writing, Humanistic
Humanists *(Direct) (PA83-85)*
Humanitarian conventions
    See War victims—Law and legislation
Humanitarianism (Religion)
    See Arianism
        Humanism—20th century
        Jesus Christ—Divinity
        Positivism
        Socinianism
        Trinity
        Unitarianism
Humanities

The studies or branches of learning, collectively, which deal with man and his affairs as contrasted with (1) nature (natural science) and (2) theology and religion. Corresponds, in general, with "Geisteswissenschaften," humanistic studies, polite learning, etc., including art and letters, classical studies, the social sciences, history and philosophy. The heading is to be used only for works treating of so many of these branches that it is not practicable to make subject entries for each of them.

    sa Classical education
        Education, Humanistic
        Science and the humanities
    xx Classical education
        Humanism
    — Methodology
Humanities and religion
    See Religion and the humanities
Humanities and science
    See Science and the humanities
Humanity *(Virtues, BJ1533.H)*
    sa Benevolence
        Charity
        Forgiveness
        Kindness
        Sympathy
    xx Charity
        Conduct of life
        Ethics

Kindness
Humanity, Religion of
    See Positivism
Humber automobile
    xx Rootes automobiles
Humblebees
    See Bumblebees
Humboldt Bay Indians
    See Wiyot Indians
Humbug
    See Impostors and imposture
        Swindlers and swindling
Humectants
    x Moisture controlling agents
    xx Moisture
    — Patents
Humerus *(Comparative anatomy, QL821;*
        Human anatomy, QM117)
    xx Arm
        Bones
    Example under Skeleton
    — Dislocation
        See Shoulder joint—Dislocation
    — Fracture *(RD557)*
        Example under Fractures
Humic acid *(QD341.A2)*
Humidity *(Indirect) (QC915-917)*
    sa Air conditioning—Climatic factors
        Cooling towers—Climatic factors
        Evaporation (Meteorology)
        Moisture
        Plants, Effect of humidity on
    x Air, Moisture of
        Atmospheric humidity
    xx Meteorology
        Moisture
        Weather
    — Physiological effect
        sa Plants, Effect of humidity on
Humiliati *(BX3680.H8)*
    sa Waldenses
    x Barettini
    xx Waldenses
Humility *(BV4647.H8)*
    sa Meekness
    xx Meekness
Humility (Judaism)
Humility in literature
Humin *(S598)*
Hummel
    See Noordsche balk
Humming-birds *(QL696.T6)*
    xx Apodiformes
        Birds
    — Juvenile literature
    — Pictorial works
Humor
    See Wit and humor
Humor and Islam
    See Islam and humor
Humor and religion
    See Religion and humor
Humor in advertising
    x Advertising, Humor in
    xx Advertising
        Wit and humor
Humor in education
    x Education, Humor in
    xx Education—Philosophy
        Wit and humor
Humorists *(PN6147)*
    sa Satirists
    xx Wit and humor
    Example under Authors
    — Juvenile literature
Humorists, American, [English, French, etc.]
Humorous illustrations
    See Caricatures and cartoons

Wit and humor, Pictorial
Humorous monologues
    See Humorous recitations
Humorous poetry
    sa Doggerel
        Limericks
        Nonsense-verses
    x Humorous verse
        Light verse
    xx Poetry
        Wit and humor
Humorous poetry, English, [etc.] *(Direct)*
    x English [etc.] humorous poetry
    xx English [etc.] poetry
        English [etc.] wit and humor
Humorous recitations
    x Humorous monologues
        Recitations, Humorous
    xx Recitations
        Wit and humor
Humorous songs
    sa Bawdy songs
        Nonsense songs
    x Comic songs
        Songs, Humorous
    xx Songs
Humorous verse
    See Humorous poetry
Hump yards
    See Railroads—Hump yards
Humpback salmon
    See Pink salmon
Humpback whale *(QL737.C424)*
    xx Whales
Humus *(S598)*
    sa Compost
        Forest litter
        Forest soils
        Wood waste as mulch, soil conditioner, etc.
    x Mold, Vegetable
        Mould, Vegetable
        Muck
        Organic matter in soil
        Soil organic matter
        Soils—Organic matter
        Vegetable mold
    xx Compost
        Fertilizers and manures
        Organic fertilizers
        Soils
        Soils—Composition
Hundred Days, 1815
    See Napoléon I, Emperor of the French, 1769-1821—Elba and the Hundred Days, 1814-1815
Hundred in the Hands, Battle of the, 1866
    See Fetterman Fight, 1866
Hundred Years' War, 1339-1453 *(DC96-105)*
    sa Agincourt, Battle of, 1415
        Brétigny, Treaty of, 1360
        Calais—Siege, 1346
        Crécy, Battle of, 1346
        Poitiers, Battle of, 1356
        Roosebeke, Battle of, 1382
        Troyes, Treaty of, 1420
    — Sources
Hungarian-Austrian Compromise, 1867
    See Austro-Hungarian Compromise, 1867
Hungarian ballads and songs *(PH3125)*
    sa Folk-songs, Hungarian
        Songs, Hungarian
Hungarian-Croatian Compromise, 1868
    See Croato-Hungarian Compromise, 1868
Hungarian drama *(Collections, PH3165-3171;*
        History, PH3084-3096)
    — 20th century
Hungarian fiction *(Direct)*

Hungarian imprints *(Direct)*
Hungarian language *(PH2001-2800)*
    x Magyar language
    xx Finno-Ugrian languages
Hungarian language in foreign countries
Hungarian literature *(Collections,*
        PH3132-3188; History,
        PH3001-3123)
    x Magyar literature
  — To 1800 *(Collections, PH3141; History,*
        PH3036)
  — 20th century
    sa Népi írók mozgalom
Hungarian literature in foreign countries
Hungarian mythology
  See Mythology, Finno-Ugrian
Hungarian newspapers *(History, PN5168.H8)*
Hungarian orations *(Direct) (Collections,*
        PH3180)
Hungarian periodicals *(History, PN5168.H8)*
Hungarian poetry *(Collections,*
        PH3151-3164; History,
        PH3062-3082)
  — 20th century
Hungarian Presbyterians
  See Presbyterians, Hungarian
Hungarian property in Great Britain, ⌐the
    Czechoslovak Republic, etc.¬
Hungarian students in Italy, ⌐the United
    States, etc.¬
  — Sources
Hungarian tiles
  See Tiles, Hungarian
Hungarians
  sa Magyars
    Palocs
    Szeklers
  xx Finno-Ugrians
    Magyars
Hungarians in Cleveland, ⌐Romania, etc.¬
  — Education
  — Juvenile literature
Hungarians in foreign countries
  — Juvenile literature
Hungarians in the United States
  sa United States—History—Civil War,
        1861-1865—Hungarian participation
Hungary
  — History *(DB901-975)*
  — — To 894
  — — 894-1000
  — — 1000-1683
  — — — Juvenile literature
  — — 1526-1683
      sa Kanisza, Battle of, 1601
        Szöny, Hungary, Peace of, 1642
  — — 1683-1848
  — — Uprising of 1848-1849
      x Revolution of 1848 in Hungary
      xx Austria—History—Revolution,
        1848-1849
  — — — Juvenile literature
  — — — Pictorial works
  — — — Polish participation
  — — 1849-1867
  — — 1867-1918
  — — 20th century
  — — Revolution, 1918-1919
  — — 1918-1945
  — — — Juvenile literature
  — — 1945-
  — — — Pictorial works
  — — Revolution, 1956
Hunger *(QP141)*
  sa Appetite
  xx Appetite
Hunger in art *(N8217.H8)*
  xx Art

Hunger in literature
Hunkpapa Indians *(E99.H795)*
  xx Dakota Indians
    Indians of North America
    Teton Indians
Huno Indians
  See Puquina Indians
Huns *(D141-3)*
  sa Ephthalites
  xx Barbarian invasions of Rome
Hunsdiecker degradation
  See Hunsdiecker reaction
Hunsdiecker reaction
  x Hunsdiecker degradation
  xx Chemical reactions
Hunt roman
  See Type and type-founding—Hunt roman
Hunter (Turbojet fighter planes)
  x Hawker Hunter (Turbojet fighter
      planes)
  xx Fighter planes
    Jet planes
Hunters (Horses)
  xx Fox-hunting
    Horses
  — Pictorial works
Hunting *(Indirect) (Hunting sports, SK;*
     Manners and customs,
     GT5810-5899)
  sa Aeronautics in hunting
    Beagling
    Big game hunting
    Bird dogs
    Camping
    Coursing
    Decoys (Hunting)
    Falconry
    Fowling
    Game and game-birds
    Game and game-birds, Dressing of
    Game calling (Hunting)
    Game-preserves
    Game protection
    Hunting and fishing clubs
    Hunting dogs
    Hunting with bow and arrow
    Market hunting (Game hunting)
    Poaching
    Tracking and trailing
    Trapping
    headings beginning with names of
      animals and birds hunted, e.g. Deer
      hunting, Duck shooting,
      Fox-hunting, Moose hunting, Otter
      hunting
  x Chase, The
    Field sports
    Gunning
  xx Game and game-birds
    Trapping
  Example under Sports
  Note under Shooting
  — Accidents and injuries
    sa Hunting—Safety measures
    x Hunting accidents
      Hunting—Injuries
  — Anecdotes, facetiae, satire, etc.
    sa Hunting stories
  — Caricatures and cartoons
  — Collections
    See Hunting—Museums and
      collections
  — Early works to 1800
  — Forms, blanks, etc.
  — Implements and appliances *(SK273-5)*
    sa Hunting guns
  — — Collections

    See Hunting—Museums and
      collections
  — Injuries
    See Hunting—Accidents and injuries
  — Juvenile literature
  — Law and legislation
    See Game-laws
  — Moral and religious aspects
    xx Animals, Treatment of
      Ethics
  — Museums and collections
    x Hunting—Collections
      Hunting—Implements and appliances
      —Collections
    xx Museums
  — Pictorial works *(SK271)*
  — Quotations, maxims, etc.
  — Safety measures
    x Hunting safety
    xx Hunting—Accidents and injuries
Hunting, Primitive *(Indirect) (GN422)*
  sa Indians of Central America—Hunting
    Indians of North America—Hunting
    Indians of South America—Hunting
  xx Industries, Primitive
  — Juvenile literature
Hunting (in numismatics) *(CJ161.H)*
Hunting (in religion, folk-lore, etc.) *(GN422)*
  sa Dog Mass
  x Folk-lore of hunting
  xx Religion, Primitive
Hunting accidents
  See Hunting—Accidents and injuries
Hunting and fishing clubs *(Indirect)*
      (Fishing clubs, SH403; Hunting
      clubs, SK3)
  xx Fishing
    Hunting
Hunting customs *(GT5810-5850)*
  xx Manners and customs
Hunting dogs *(SF428.5)*
  sa Bird dogs
    particular breeds of hunting dogs
  x Gun dogs
    Sporting dogs
  xx Dogs
    Hunting
    Working dogs
Hunting game for sale
  See Market hunting (Game hunting)
Hunting guns *(Indirect) (SK274)*
  sa Hunting rifles
    Shot-guns
  x Guns, Hunting
    Sporting guns
  xx Firearms
    Hunting—Implements and appliances
Hunting in art *(N8250)*
  xx Art
Hunting in literature *(PN56.H)*
Hunting law
  See Game-laws
Hunting-leopards
  See Cheetahs
Hunting licenses
  See Fish and game licenses
Hunting lodges
  xx Architecture, Domestic
    Club-houses
Hunting museums *(Indirect)*
  xx Museums
Hunting music
  sa Bugle-calls
    Hunting songs
    Trumpet-calls
  xx Horn music
    Instrumental music
    Music

Hunting music *(Continued)*
    Trumpet-calls
    — History and criticism *(ML3780)*
Hunting rifles *(Indirect)* *(SK274)*
    x Sporting rifles
    xx Hunting guns
        Rifles
Hunting safety
    See Hunting—Safety measures
Hunting songs *(M1977.H8; English poetry,*
        PR1195.H9; History, etc., ML3780)
    xx Hunting music
        Songs
Hunting songs, German, [etc.]
    x German [etc.] hunting songs
Hunting stories
    xx Fiction
        Hunting—Anecdotes, facetiae, satire,
            etc.
        Sports stories
Hunting trophies
    x Trophies, Hunting
    xx Taxidermy
    — Exhibitions
Hunting with bow and arrow *(Indirect)*
    (SK36)
    x Bow hunting
    xx Bow and arrow
        Hunting
Huntington's chorea
    See Hereditary chorea
Hunzukuts
    See Burusho
Hupa Indians *(E99.H8)*
    x Hoopah Indians
    xx Athapascan Indians
        Indians of North America
Hupa language *(PM1361-4)*
    xx Athapascan languages
        Indians of North America—Languages
Hur Rebellion, 1942-1947
    See Sind—History—Hur Rebellion,
        1942-1947
Hurdle-racing *(GV1067)*
    xx Obstacle racing
        Racing
        Running
        Track-athletics
Hurdle racing (Horse racing)
    See Steeplechasing
Hurdy-gurdies (2) with instr. ensemble
    sa Concertos (Hurdy-gurdies (2) with
        instr. ensemble)
    x Two hurdy-gurdies with instr. ensemble
    xx Concertos (Hurdy-gurdies (2) with
        instr. ensemble)
        Hurdy-gurdy music (Hurdy-gurdies (2))
        Instrumental ensembles
Hurdy-gurdies (2) with orchestra
    (M1039.4.H87)
    sa Concertos (Hurdy-gurdies (2))
    x Two hurdy-gurdies with orchestra
    xx Concertos (Hurdy-gurdies (2))
        Hurdy-gurdy music (Hurdy-gurdies (2))
Hurdy-gurdy *(ML760)*
    Not to be confused with the barrel and
    piano organs used chiefly by street
    musicians.
    xx Viol
Hurdy-gurdy music *(M59)*
    sa Concertos (Hurdy-gurdy with chamber
        orchestra)
        Hurdy-gurdy with chamber orchestra
        Nonets (Hurdy-gurdies (2), clarinets
            (2), horns (2), violas (2), violoncello)
        Trios (Harpsichord, bagpipe,
            hurdy-gurdy)

Hurdy-gurdy music (Hurdy-gurdies (2))
    (M286-7)
    sa Concertos (Hurdy-gurdies (2))
        Concertos (Hurdy-gurdies (2) with
            instr. ensemble)
        Hurdy-gurdies (2) with instr. ensemble
        Hurdy-gurdies (2) with orchestra
        Suites (Hurdy-gurdies (2))
Hurdy-gurdy with chamber orchestra
    (M1039.4.H87)
    sa Concertos (Hurdy-gurdy with chamber
        orchestra)
    xx Chamber-orchestra music
        Concertos (Hurdy-gurdy with chamber
            orchestra)
        Hurdy-gurdy music
Huri (Papuan people)
    xx Ethnology—Papua-New Guinea (Ter.)
Hurling (Game) *(GV1017.H8)*
Huron, S.D.
    — Tornado, 1884
Huron Indians *(E99.H9)*
    x Wyandot Indians
    xx Indians of North America
        Iroquoian Indians
    — Antiquities
    — Legends
    — Missions
    — Religion and mythology
    — Wars
        sa Blue Licks, Battle of the, 1782
            Crawford's Indian Campaign, 1782
Huron language *(PM1366)*
    sa Iroquoian languages
    xx Iroquoian languages
Huronian epoch
    See Geology, Stratigraphic—Huronian
Hurri
    See Hurrians
Hurrian language
    See Mitannian language
Hurrians *(DS59.H)*
    sa Subarians
    x Hurri
        Kharri
        Khurrians
    xx Mitannians
        Subarians
Hurribomber
    See Hurricane (Fighter planes)
Hurricane (Fighter planes)
    x Hurribomber
    xx Fighter planes
Hurricane control
    See Hurricane protection
Hurricane protection *(Direct)*
    sa Afforestation
        Agricultural credit
        Building laws
        Disaster relief
        Flood control
        Hydraulic engineering
        Insurance, Disaster
        Public works
        Shore protection
        Zoning
    x Hurricane control
        Hurricane rehabilitation, Long-range
    xx Disaster relief
        Hurricanes
        Public works
        Regional planning
Hurricane rehabilitation, Long-range
    See Hurricane protection
Hurricane waves
    See Storm surges

Hurricanes *(QC941-959)*
    Here are entered mainly works on storms
    in the neighborhood of the West In-
    dies. *Cf.* note under Storms.
    sa Cyclones
        Hurricane protection
        Storm surges
        Storms
        Typhoons
        subdivision Hurricane *under names of*
            countries, cities, etc.
    xx Meteorology
        Meteorology, Maritime
        Storms
        Typhoons
        Winds
    Note under Cyclones
    — Kinetic energy
        x Kinetic energy of hurricanes
        xx Dynamic meteorology
    — Mathematical models
Hürtgen, Battle of, 1944
    xx World War, 1939-1945—Campaigns—
        Germany
Hurufis
    x Houroûfis
    xx Islamic sects
        Shiites
Husband and wife *(Direct)*
    sa Antenuptial contracts
        Community property
        Curtesy
        Desertion and non-support
        Divorce
        Dower
        Dowry
        Marriage law
        Married women
        Separate property
        Separation (Law)
        Support (Domestic relations)
        Tenancy by the entirety
    x Matrimonial regime
    xx Desertion and non-support
        Domestic relations
        Marriage law
        Married women
    Notes under Husbands; Married women;
        Wives
    — Conflict of laws
        See Conflict of laws—Husband and
            wife
    — Taxation *(Direct)*
        sa Community property—Taxation
            Income tax—Joint returns
Husband and wife (Ancient law)
Husband and wife (Canon law)
Husband and wife (Hindu law)
Husband and wife (Islamic law)
Husband and wife (Jewish law)
Husband and wife (Lübeck law)
Husband and wife (Magdeburg law)
    Example under Magdeburg law
Husband and wife (Roman law)
Husband and wife (Saxon law)
Husbandmen, Wicked (Parable)
    See Wicked husbandmen (Parable)
Husbandry
    See Agriculture
Husbandry, Patrons of
    See Patrons of Husbandry
Husbands
    Here are entered works on husbands in
    general. Works on legal relations be-
    tween husband and wife are entered
    under the heading Husband and wife.
    xx Marriage
    — Anecdotes, facetiae, satire, etc.

— Prayer-books and devotions *(BV283.H8)*
　　x Husbands—Prayer-books and
　　　　devotions—English
— — English
　　　　See Husbands—Prayer-books and
　　　　　　devotions
Huskies, Siberian
　　See Siberian huskies
Husky, Siberian
　　See Siberian huskies
Husqvarna motorcycle *(TL448.H)*
　　xx Motorcycles
Hussite Bibles
　　See Bible—Versions, Hussite
Hussites *(BX4913-4918)*
　　sa Adamites
　　　　Hiltersried, Battle of, 1433
　　　　Lipan, Battle of, 1434
　　　　Lord's Supper—Communion in both
　　　　　　elements
　　　　Moravians
　　　　Utraquists
　　Example under Reformation
Hustler (Bombers)
　　See B-58 bomber
Huts, Grass
　　See Grass huts
Hutu
　　See Bahutu
Hutzul horse
　　See Hucul horse
Huzul horse
　　See Hucul horse
Huzuls
　　See Huculs
Huzvaresh
　　See Pahlavi language
Hwang-ho in art
Hwaŏm (Sect)
　　See Kegon (Sect)
Hwarangdo *(CR6095)*
　　xx Chivalry
　　　　Ethics, Korean
　　　　National characteristics, Korean
Hyacinths *(SB413.H9)*
Hyaenas
　　See Hyenas
Hyaline membrane disease *(RJ274)*
　　xx Lungs—Diseases
　　　　Respiratory distress syndrome
Hyangga
　　x Saenaennorae
　　　Sanoega
　　　Sinoega
　　xx Korean poetry
Hybrid computers
　　sa Digital-to-analog converters
　　　　Electronic analog computers
　　　　Electronic digital computers
　　x Computers, Hybrid
　　xx Computers
— Programming
　　　sa HELP (Computer program)
　　　xx Programming (Electronic computers)
Hybrid corn *(Indirect)*
　　xx Maize breeding
　　　　Maize—Varieties
　　Note under Maize breeding
Hybrid Executive Linkage Program
　　See HELP (Computer program)
Hybrid fuel rockets
　　See Hybrid propellant rockets
Hybrid integrated circuits *(TK7874)*
　　x Integrated circuits, Hybrid
　　xx Integrated circuits
Hybrid propellant rockets *(TL783.45)*
　　x Hybrid fuel rockets
　　　　Rocket motors, Hybrid propellant

　　xx Rockets (Aeronautics)
Hybrid sorghum
　　xx Sorghum breeding
　　　　Sorghum—Varieties
Hybridism
　　See Hybridization
Hybridity of races
　　See Miscegenation
Hybridization *(QH421-5)*
　　sa Genetics
　　　　Heterosis
　　　　Leopons
　　　　Mendel's law
　　　　Nucleic acid hybridization
　　　　Telegony
　　x Hybridism
　　xx Biology
　　　　Breeding
　　　　Heredity
　　　　Mendel's law
　　　　Origin of species
　　　　Telegony
Hybridization, Vegetable *(QH423)*
　　x Plants—Hybridization
　　　　Vegetable hybridization
　　xx Botany
　　　　Plant-breeding
Hydatid disease
　　See Echinococcosis
Hydatids *(RC242)*
　　　　Here are entered general works only.
　　　　　　Works on hydatids in particular organs
　　　　　　are entered under name of organ, with
　　　　　　subdivision Hydatids, *e.g.* Kidneys—
　　　　　　Hydatids; Liver—Hydatids.
　　x Bladder-worm
　　xx Medical parasitology
　　　　Worms, Intestinal and parasitic
Hyden Coal Mine Disaster, Hyden, Ky., 1970
Hydralazine
　　xx Cardiovascular agents
　　　　Hypertension
Hydrangea
Hydrants *(Fire prevention, TH9365)*
　　sa Hose-couplings
Hydrate process (Saline water conversion)
　　See Saline water conversion—Hydrate
　　　　process
Hydrates *(QD181.H1)*
　　sa Gas, Natural—Hydrates
　　xx Complex compounds
Hydration *(QD63.H)*
　　sa Heat of hydration
　　　　Water of hydration
Hydraulic accumulators
　　x Accumulators, Hydraulic
　　xx Hydraulic machinery
Hydraulic brakes
　　xx Brakes
　　　　Hydraulic machinery
Hydraulic cement
　　See Cement
Hydraulic circuits
　　x Circuits, Hydraulic
　　xx Hydraulic machinery
— Computer programs
Hydraulic conductivity of soils
　　See Soil permeability
Hydraulic control
　　xx Automatic control
　　　　Fluid power technology
　　　　Hydraulic machinery
Hydraulic conveying *(TJ898)*
　　x Hydraulic transport
　　xx Conveying machinery
　　　　Materials handling
— Automation

Hydraulic couplings
　　x Fluid couplings
　　xx Couplings
　　　　Oil hydraulic machinery
Hydraulic drive
　　See subdivision Hydraulic drive *under
　　　　subjects, e.g.* Diesel locomotives—
　　　　Hydraulic drive; Machine-tools—
　　　　Hydraulic drive
Hydraulic elevators
　　See Elevators
Hydraulic engineering *(Indirect) (TC)*
　　sa Blasting, Submarine
　　　　Boring
　　　　Channels (Hydraulic engineering)
　　　　Drainage
　　　　Dredging
　　　　Flood control
　　　　Hydraulic filling
　　　　Hydraulic laboratories
　　　　Hydraulic machinery
　　　　Hydraulic mining
　　　　Hydraulic structures
　　　　Hydraulics
　　　　Hydrodynamics
　　　　Hydrostatics
　　　　Irrigation engineering
　　　　Plastics in hydraulic engineering
　　　　Pontoons
　　　　Pumping machinery
　　　　Reclamation of land
　　　　Retaining walls
　　　　Rivers
　　　　Shore protection
　　　　Stream measurements
　　　　Tidal power
　　　　Underwater construction
　　　　Underwater drilling
　　　　Water-jet
　　　　Water-supply engineering
　　　　Wells
　　　　names of rivers, etc., e.g. Mississippi
　　　　　　River; Rhone River—Power
　　　　　　utilization; Niagara Falls—Power
　　　　　　utilization
　　x Engineering, Hydraulic
　　xx Civil engineering
　　　　Engineering
　　　　Fluid mechanics
　　　　Fluids
　　　　Hurricane protection
　　　　Hydraulics
　　　　Rivers
　　　　Shore protection
　　　　Water
　　　　Water-power
— Early works to 1800 *(TC144)*
— Electromechanical analogies
— Equipment and supplies
　　　x Hydraulic equipment
— — Testing
— Examinations, questions, etc.
— Instruments *(TC177)*
　　　sa Aeroplanes—Hydraulic equipment
　　　　　Flow meters
　　　　　Hydraulic measurements
　　　　　Liquid level indicators
　　　　　Radioisotopes in hydraulic
　　　　　　engineering
　　　xx Hydraulic measurements
— Laboratory manuals
— Law and legislation *(Direct)*
— Pictorial works
— Problems, exercises, etc.
— Research *(Direct)*
　　　x Hydraulic research
　　　xx Engineering research
— Safety measures

Hydraulic engineering *(Indirect) (TC)*
(Continued)
— Standards *(Direct)*
— Tables, calculations, etc. *(TC151)*
Hydraulic engineering laboratories
See Hydraulic laboratories
Hydraulic equipment
See Hydraulic engineering—Equipment and
supplies
Hydraulic fill dams
See Earth dams
Hydraulic filling
xx Earthwork
Fills (Earthwork)
Hydraulic engineering
Hydraulic fluids *(TJ844)*
sa Petroleum products
xx Fluids
Hydraulic machinery
Petroleum products
Hydraulic fracturing
See Oil wells—Hydraulic fracturing
Hydraulic gates
sa Sluice gates
x Gates, Hydraulic
Water gates
xx Hydraulic structures
Hydraulic jacks *(TJ1435)*
x Jacks, Hydraulic
xx Lifting-jacks
— Testing
Hydraulic jump *(TC175)*
xx Hydraulics
Hydraulic laboratories *(Direct) (TC158)*
x Hydraulic engineering laboratories
xx Engineering laboratories
Hydraulic engineering
— Equipment and supplies
Hydraulic machinery *(TJ840-890)*
sa Archimedean screw
Centrifugal pumps
Hydraulic accumulators
Hydraulic brakes
Hydraulic circuits
Hydraulic control
Hydraulic fluids
Hydraulic motors
Hydraulic servomechanisms
Hydraulic turbines
Jet pumps
Oil hydraulic machinery
Pumping machinery
Turbines
Water mills
Water-wheels
subdivision Hydraulic equipment *under
subjects, e.g.* Aeroplanes—Hydraulic
equipment; Tractors—Hydraulic
equipment
xx Fluid power technology
Hydraulic engineering
Machinery
Water-power
— Electric driving
— Juvenile literature
— Problems, exercises, etc.
— Reliability
Hydraulic measurements
Here are entered works on scientific and
technical measurement of properties
and behavior of liquids, including
equipment used in measurement.
Works on particular measuring instru-
ments are entered under names of in-
struments, *e.g.* Flow meters, Hydrom-
eter, Water-meters.
sa Flow meters
Hydraulic engineering—Instruments
Hydrometer

Stream measurements
Water-meters
x Hydrometry
xx Hydraulic engineering—Instruments
Hydraulics
— Electromechanical analogies
— Problems, exercises, etc.
Hydraulic mining *(Gold, TN421)*
sa Dredges
Gold mines and mining
Manganese mines and mining,
Submarine
x Placer-mining
xx Gold mines and mining
Hydraulic engineering
Manganese mines and mining,
Submarine
Mining engineering
Hydraulic models *(TC163)*
sa Dams—Models
Hydrologic models
Metallurgical furnaces—Models
x Models, Hydraulic
xx Engineering models
Hydraulic structures
Hydraulic turbines—Models
Hydraulics
Hydrologic models
Models and modelmaking
Hydraulic motors *(TJ855-7)*
sa Oil hydraulic machinery
Turbines
Water-wheels
xx Hydraulic machinery
Motors
Turbines
— Design and construction
Hydraulic organ *(ML553)*
sa Barrel organ, Hydraulic
x Hydraulus
Water organ
xx Organ
Hydraulic power plants
See Water-power
Water-power electric plants
Hydraulic presses *(TJ1460)*
x Presses, Hydraulic
xx Power presses
— Automatic control *(TJ1460)*
— Numerical control
xx Automatic control
— Safety measures *(TJ1460)*
Hydraulic propulsion
See Jet boat engines
Hydraulic rams *(TJ905)*
x Rams, Hydraulic
xx Pumping machinery
Hydraulic research
See Hydraulic engineering—Research
Hydraulic servomechanisms *(TJ857)*
x Servomechanisms, Hydraulic
xx Hydraulic machinery
Oil hydraulic machinery
Servomechanisms
Hydraulic structures
sa Aqueducts
Artesian wells
Breakwaters
Bridges—Foundations and piers
Caissons
Canals
Coffer-dams
Cribwork
Culverts
Dams
Desilting basins
Dikes (Engineering)
Docks

Draft tubes
Earthquakes and hydraulic structures
Embankments
Flood dams and reservoirs
Fountains
Groins (Shore protection)
Harbors
Hydraulic gates
Hydraulic models
Intakes (Hydraulic engineering)
Irrigation canals and flumes
Jetties
Levees
Lighthouses
Locks (Hydraulic engineering)
Piers
Pipe lines
Pumping stations
Reservoirs
Reservoirs, Underground
Rock traps (Hydraulic engineering)
Sea-walls
Sewerage
Spillways
Tunnels
Water tunnels
Weirs
Wharves
xx Hydraulic engineering
Structural engineering
— Cold weather conditions
— Construction
See Hydraulic structures—Design and
construction
— Design and construction
x Hydraulic structures—Construction
— Electric equipment
— Foundations
xx Foundations
— Ice prevention *(TC180)*
xx Ice prevention
— — Patents *(TC180)*
— Inspection
— Maintenance and repair
— — Costs *(TC180)*
— Patents
— Protection
— — Patents
— Testing
— Vibration
Hydraulic torque converters
sa Automobiles—Transmission devices,
Automatic
Tractors—Transmission devices,
Automatic
x Torque converters, Hydraulic
xx Oil hydraulic machinery
Torque
Hydraulic transmission
See Oil hydraulic machinery
Hydraulic transport
See Hydraulic conveying
Hydraulic turbines *(TJ870-875)*
sa Draft tubes
x Water turbines
xx Hydraulic machinery
Turbines
— Automatic control
— Bearings
— Design and construction
— Dynamics *(TJ873)*
— Erecting work
— Maintenance and repair
— Models
xx Hydraulic models
— Reliability
— Testing
— Vibration

Hydraulics *(TC160-179)*
  sa Atomization
    Channels (Hydraulic engineering)
    Fire extinction
    Fluids
    Hydraulic engineering
    Hydraulic jump
    Hydraulic measurements
    Hydraulic models
    Hydrodynamics
    Hydrostatics
    Jets
    Nozzles
    Seepage
    Surge tanks
    Venturi tubes
    Water—Air entrainment
    Water—Distribution
    Water hammer
  x Flow of water
    Water—Flow
  xx Fluid mechanics
    Hydraulic engineering
    Jets
    Liquids
    Mechanics
    Physics
    Water—Distribution
  Note under Hydrodynamics
  — Abbreviations
  — Graphic methods
  — Laboratory manuals
  — Mathematics
  — Notation
  — Problems, exercises, etc.
  — Tables, calculations, etc. *(TC179)*
  — Terminology
Hydraulus
  See Hydraulic organ
Hydrazine *(QD181.N15)*
  xx Disinfection and disinfectants
Hydrazines *(QD305.A8; QD341.A8)*
  — Physiological effect
Hydrazoic acid
  See Hydronitric acid
Hydriae *(NK4650.H9)*
  xx Vases, Greek
    Vases, Roman
Hydriodic acid *(QD181.I1)*
  x Iodide of hydrogen
Hydro-aeroplanes
  See Seaplanes
Hydro-electric plants
  See Water-power electric plants
Hydrobiology
  See Aquatic biology
    Fresh-water biology
    Marine biology
Hydroboration
  xx Reduction, Chemical
Hydrobotany
  See Aquatic plants
Hydrobromic acid *(QD181.B7)*
Hydrocal
  xx Cement
Hydrocarbon research *(Indirect)*
  x Hydrocarbons—Research
  xx Research
Hydrocarbons *(QD305.H5-8; QD341.H9)*
  sa Alkylation
    Bitumen
    Caustobioliths
    Cracking process
    Gilsonite
    Methyl groups
    Mineral oils
    Paraffins
    Petroleum products

    Petroleum, Synthetic
    Synthine process
  xx Bitumen
  — Analysis
  — Nomenclature
    Example under Chemistry—Nomenclature
  — Purification
  — Research
    See Hydrocarbon research
  — Spectra *(QC463.H9)*
  — Storage
  — Tables, etc.
Hydrocele *(RC898)*
  xx Genito-urinary organs—Diseases
Hydrocephalus *(RC391)*
  x Water on the brain
  xx Brain—Diseases
  — Personal narratives
Hydrochloric acid *(Chemical technology, TP217.H8; Chemistry, QD181.C5)*
  x Muriatic acid
  — Molecular rotation
Hydrocortisone
  x Compound F
    Cortisol
    Hydrocortone
  xx Adrenocortical hormones
    Cortisone
Hydrocortone
  See Hydrocortisone
Hydrocyanic acid *(Chemistry, QD181.C15; Disinfectants, RA766.H8)*
  x Prussic acid
  xx Disinfection and disinfectants
  — Physiological effect *(QP913.C15)*
  — Therapeutic use *(RM666.H8)*
  — Toxicology *(RA1242.H9)*
Hydrocyanic acid gas
Hydrocyclones
  See Separators (Machines)
Hydrodynamic gyroscopes
  See Fluid rotor gyroscopes
Hydrodynamic impact on seaplanes
  See Seaplanes—Hydrodynamics
Hydrodynamic short range weather forecasting
  x Dynamic short range weather forecasting
    Weather forecasting, Hydrodynamic short range
  xx Hydrodynamic weather forecasting
Hydrodynamic weather forecasting
  sa Hydrodynamic short range weather forecasting
    Numerical weather forecasting
  x Dynamic weather forecasting
    Weather forecasting, Dynamic
  xx Dynamic meteorology
    Hydrodynamics
    Meteorology—Mathematical models
    Weather forecasting
Hydrodynamics *(QA911-929)*
  Here are entered works on the theory of the motion of fluids. Works dealing with the technical application of the science are entered under Hydraulics.
  sa Blades
    Boundary layer (Meteorology)
    Buoyant ascent (Hydrodynamics)
    Cavitation
    Channels (Hydraulic engineering)
    Electrohydrodynamics
    Frictional resistance (Hydrodynamics)
    Gravity waves
    Harbors—Hydrodynamics
    Hydrodynamic weather forecasting
    Hydroelasticity
    Hydrofoil boats—Hydrodynamics

    Hydrostatics
    Jets
    Magnetohydrodynamics
    Mixing
    Pipe—Hydrodynamics
    Rotating masses of fluid
    Sailboats—Hydrodynamics
    Seaplanes—Hydrodynamics
    Ship resistance
    Ships—Hydrodynamics
    Siphons
    Sloshing (Hydrodynamics)
    Tank-vessels—Hydrodynamics
    Turbulence
    Underwater explosions
    Viscosity
    Vortex-motion
    Water hammer
    Water waves
    Waves
  xx Dynamics
    Fluid dynamics
    Fluid mechanics
    Hydraulic engineering
    Hydraulics
    Liquids
    Mathematical physics
    Mechanics
    Mechanics, Analytic
  — Computer programs
  — Electromechanical analogies
  — Simulation methods
Hydroelasticity
  sa Planing hulls
    Ships—Hydrodynamic impact
    Sloshing (Hydrodynamics)
    Vibration (Marine engineering)
  xx Elastic waves
    Elasticity
    Hydrodynamics
Hydrofluoric acid *(QD181.F1)*
  — Patents
Hydrofoil boats *(VM362)*
  x Hydrofoils (Vessels)
  xx Boats and boating
  — Hydraulic equipment
  — Hydrodynamics
    xx Hydrodynamics
  — Juvenile literature
  — Law and legislation *(Direct)*
  — Maintenance and repair
Hydrofoils
  See Planing hulls
Hydrofoils (Vessels)
  See Hydrofoil boats
Hydrogen *(Chemical technology, TP245.H9; Chemistry, QD181.H1)*
  sa Interstellar hydrogen
    Iron—Hydrogen content
    Liquid hydrogen
    Metals—Hydrogen content
    Nonferrous metals—Hydrogen content
    Steel—Hydrogen content
    Titanium—Hydrogen content
    Water—Electrolysis
    Zirconium alloys—Hydrogen content
  xx Gases—Liquefaction
    Nonmetals
  Example under Gases
  — Analysis
    sa Hydrogen-ion concentration—Measurement
  — Dipole moments
  — Isotopes
    sa Deuterium
    x Heavy hydrogen
      Hydrogen isotopes
    xx Tracers (Chemistry)

Hydrogen *(Chemical technology, TP245.H9;*
  Chemistry, QD181.H1)
    (Continued)
— Purification
— Spectra
— Tables, etc.
— Thermal properties
Hydrogen bomb
  sa Atomic bomb
      Radioactive fallout
  x Thermonuclear weapons
  xx Atomic bomb
      Atomic warfare
      Atomic weapons
      Bombs
      Nuclear fusion
— Testing
Hydrogen bonding
  xx Chemistry, Physical and theoretical
      Molecular association
Hydrogen in aluminum alloys
  See Aluminum alloys—Hydrogen content
Hydrogen in iron
  See Iron—Hydrogen content
Hydrogen in metals
  See Metals—Hydrogen content
Hydrogen in steel
  See Steel—Hydrogen content
Hydrogen in titanium
  See Titanium—Hydrogen content
Hydrogen-ion concentration *(QD561)*
  sa Buffer solutions
      Ionization
      Soil acidity
      Water—Electrolysis
  xx Ionization
      Water—Electrolysis
— Measurement
    xx Hydrogen—Analysis
Hydrogen isotopes
  See Hydrogen—Isotopes
Hydrogen nucleus
  See Protons
Hydrogen peroxide *(Chemistry, QD181.H1;*
      Disinfectants, RA766.H9;
      Therapeutics, RM648.H)
  sa Hydrogen peroxide rockets
  xx Disinfection and disinfectants
Hydrogen peroxide as a propellant
  See Hydrogen peroxide rockets
Hydrogen peroxide rockets
  x Hydrogen peroxide as a propellant
      Rockets, Hydrogen peroxide
  xx Hydrogen peroxide
      Liquid propellant rockets
      Rockets (Aeronautics)
Hydrogen sulphide *(QD181.S1)*
  x Sulphureted hydrogen
  xx Gases, Asphyxiating and poisonous
      Mine gases
— Analysis
— Spectra
— Toxicology
Hydrogenase
Hydrogenation *(QD281.H8)*
  sa Coal liquefaction
      Hydrogenolysis
      Petroleum, Synthetic
Hydrogenolysis
  xx Hydrogenation
      Hydrolysis
Hydrogeological surveys
  xx Hydrogeology
      Surveys

Hydrogeology
    Here are entered general works on the
    study of ground water in relation to its
    geologic environment. Works on the
    hydrogeology of special geographic
    areas are entered under Water, Under-
    ground.
  sa Aerial photography in hydrogeology
      Aquifers
      Artesian basins
      Hydrogeological surveys
      Radioactive tracers in hydrogeology
  xx Geology
      Hydrology
      Water, Underground
— Equipment and supplies
— Maps
— Mathematical models
— Statistical methods
Hydrographic charts
  See Nautical charts
Hydrographic surveying *(VK591-7)*
  sa Drags (Hydrography)
      Hydrography
      Hydrography—Observers' manuals
      Marine geodesy
      Navigation
      Oceanographic research ships
      Surveyors, Marine
  x Marine surveying
      Maritime surveying
      Nautical surveying
      Surveying, Marine
  xx Hydrography
      Navigation
      Surveying
Hydrography *(Indirect) (GB651-2597;*
      Marine, VK)
    Here are entered works on the results of
    the investigation of coast waters, riv-
    ers, and lakes, primarily with reference
    to navigation.
    Other works in the title of which the word
    "hydrography" occurs in the sense of
    water resources for other purposes
    than navigation are entered under Wa-
    ter-power, Water-supply, Water, Un-
    derground.
  sa Coastwise navigation
      Drags (Hydrography)
      Harbors
      Hydrographic surveying
      Hydrology
      Hydronymy
      Inland navigation
      Lakes
      Navigation
      Ocean currents
      Rivers
      Sounding and soundings
      Stream measurements
      Submarine topography
      Tides
  xx Hydrographic surveying
      Hydrology
      Oceanography
      Physical geography
      Rivers
  Notes under Water, Underground; Water-
      power; Water-supply
— Graphic methods
    xx Hydrography—Tables, etc.
— Observers' manuals *(VK593.5)*
    xx Hydrographic surveying
— Tables, etc.
    sa Hydrography—Graphic methods
— Terminology

Hydroida
  x Hydroidea
  xx Hydrozoa
Hydroida, Fossil *(QE779)*
Hydroidea
  See Hydroida
      Hydromedusae
      Hydrozoa
Hydrologic cycle *(GB688-690)*
  x Cycle, Hydrologic
      Water cycle
  xx Cycles
      Energy budget (Geophysics)
      Mass budget (Geophysics)
Hydrologic models *(GB665)*
  sa Hydraulic models
  x Hydrology—Models
  xx Hydraulic models
      Models and modelmaking
Hydrological forecasting *(GB678)*
  sa Flood forecasting
  x Forecasting, Hydrological
Hydrological instruments
  x Instruments, Hydrological
— Appraisal
    See Hydrological instruments—
        Valuation
— Maintenance and repair
— Testing
— Valuation
    x Hydrological instruments—Appraisal
Hydrological research
  See Hydrology—Research
Hydrological stations *(Indirect)*
  x Stations, Hydrological
  xx Hydrology—Research
Hydrology *(Indirect)*
    Here are entered works treating of water
    in all its aspects. Works on under-
    ground waters are entered under the
    heading Water, Underground. The
    heading Oceanography is used for
    works on ocean waters.
  sa Aerial photography in hydrology
      Astronautics in hydrology
      Classification—Books—Hydrology
      Hydrogeology
      Hydrography
      Hydrometeorology
      International Hydrological Decade,
        1965-1974
      Military hydrology
      Oceanography
      Radar in hydrology
      Radioactive substances in rivers, lakes,
        etc.
      Radioisotopes in hydrology
      Water
    headings beginning with the words
        Hydrological *and* Water
  xx Earth sciences
      Hydrography
— Computer programs
— Early works to 1800
— Electromechanical analogies *(GB665)*
— Juvenile literature
— Laboratory manuals
— Mathematical models
— Models
    See Hydrologic models
— Research *(Direct)*
    sa Hydrological stations
        Watersheds—Research
    x Hydrological research
— Statistical methods
— Tables, calculations, etc.
— Terminology
— Text-books

Hydrolysis *(QD501; Organic chemistry, QD281.H)*
  sa Hydrogenolysis
    Lysosomes
    Protein hydrolysates
    Sugar—Inversion
  xx Solvolysis
  — Problems, exercises, etc. *(TP156.H82)*
Hydromagnetic waves
  See Magnetohydrodynamics
Hydromechanics
  See Fluid mechanics
Hydromedusae *(QL377.H9)*
  sa Discophora (Coelenterata)
    Hydrozoa
    Siphonophora
  x Hydroidea
  xx Coelenterata
    Hydrozoa
    Medusae
Hydromel *(GT2920)*
  sa Mead
  xx Mead
Hydrometallurgy *(TN688)*
  xx Metallurgy
Hydrometeorological cycles
  See Hydrometeorology—Periodicity
Hydrometeorological periodicity
  See Hydrometeorology—Periodicity
Hydrometeorology *(Indirect)*
  sa Aeronautics in hydrometeorology
    Depth-area-duration
      (Hydrometeorology)
    Moisture index
  xx Hydrology
    Meteorology
  — Mathematical models
  — Periodicity
    x Hydrometeorological cycles
      Hydrometeorological periodicity
    xx Cycles
Hydrometer *(QC111)*
  x Areometer
  xx Fluid mechanics
    Hydraulic measurements
    Hydrostatics
    Specific gravity
  Note under Hydraulic measurements
Hydrometry
  See Hydraulic measurements
Hydronephrosis *(RC918.H8)*
  xx Kidneys—Diseases
    Urine—Retention
Hydronitric acid *(QD181.N1)*
  x Hydrazoic acid
Hydronium ions
  See Oxonium ions
Hydronymy
  xx Hydrography
    Names, Geographical
    Toponymy
    Water
Hydropathy
  See Hydrotherapy
Hydroperitoneum
  See Ascites
Hydrophobia
  See Rabies
Hydrophone
  xx Electroacoustic transducers
    Sound—Apparatus
    Underwater acoustics—Instruments
Hydrophytes
  See Algae
    Fresh-water flora
    Marine flora

Hydroplanes *(VM341-9)*
  Here are entered works dealing with boats that skim over the surface of the water but do not rise in the air. Works on planes designed to rise from and alight on water are entered under the heading Seaplanes.
  sa Planing hulls
    Seaplanes
  xx Motor-boats
  Note under Seaplanes
Hydroponics
  x Agriculture, Soilless
    Chemiculture
    Plants—Soilless culture
    Soilless agriculture
    Water farming
  xx Horticulture
    Plants, Effect of chemicals on
    Plants—Nutrition
Hydrostatic bearings
  See Fluid-film bearings
Hydrostatic extrusion *(TS255)*
  xx Extrusion (Metals)
    High energy forming
    High pressure (Technology)
Hydrostatic pressure
  x Underwater pressure
  xx Pressure
  — Physiological effect *(QP82.2.P7)*
Hydrostatics *(Analytic, QA905-7; Experimental, QC147)*
  sa Compressibility
    Floating bodies
    Fluids
    Gases
    Hydrometer
    Rayleigh number
    Rotating masses of fluid
    Saline water conversion—Piezodialysis
      process
    Soil percolation
    Specific gravity
    headings beginning with the word
      Hydrostatic
  xx Capillarity
    Fluid mechanics
    Fluids
    Hydraulic engineering
    Hydraulics
    Hydrodynamics
    Liquids
    Mechanics
    Mechanics, Analytic
    Physics
    Statics
Hydrotherapy *(RM801-822)*
  sa Baths
    Baths, Moor and mud
    Baths, Partial
    Health resorts, watering-places, etc.
    Hot water—Therapeutic use
    Mineral waters
    Spondylotherapy
  x Hydropathy
    Kneipp cure
    Water-cure
    Water—Therapeutic use
  xx Baths
    Medicine—Practice
    Physical therapy
    Therapeutics, Physiological
    Water
  — Early works to 1800 *(RM810)*
Hydrothermal deposits *(Indirect)*
  x Deposits, Hydrothermal
  xx Mineralogy
    Ore-deposits

  — Mathematical models
Hydrothermal electric power systems *(TK1005)*
  x Combined hydroelectric and steam power systems
    Electric power-plants—Combined hydroelectric and steam
    Power systems, Hydrothermal electric
    Water-power electric plants—Combination with steam plants
  xx Electric power production
    Interconnected electric utility systems
Hydrothorax *(RM276)*
  xx Pleura—Diseases
Hydrotropism
  xx Growth (Plants)
    Plant-water relationships
    Plants—Irritability and movements
    Tropisms
Hydroxylamine *(QD181.N15; QD305.A8)*
  — Spectra
Hydroxylation *(Chemical engineering, TP156.H85; Organic chemistry, QD281.H85)*
  xx Chemical reactions
Hydroxytryptamine
  See Serotonin
Hydrozoa *(QL377.H9)*
  sa Anthomedusae
    Hydroida
    Hydromedusae
    Siphonophora
  x Hydroidea
  xx Coelenterata
    Hydromedusae
Hydrozone *(RM671)*
  xx Antiseptics
Hydruria *(SF871; SF995)*
Hyenas *(QL737.C2)*
  sa Spotted hyena
  x Hyaenas
Hygiene *(Domestic, RA771; Ethical aspects, BJ1695; Personal, RA773-790)*
  sa Air
    Athletes—Hygiene
    Baths
    Beauty, Personal
    Boys—Health and hygiene
    Breast—Care and hygiene
    Breathing exercises
    Callisthenics
    Charm
    Children—Care and hygiene
    Climatology, Medical
    Diet
    Disinfection and disinfectants
    Exercise
    Fluorescent lighting—Hygienic aspects
    Food
    Girls—Health and hygiene
    Grooming for men
    Gymnastics
    Hairdressing—Hygienic aspects
    Hand washing
    Health attitudes
    Infants—Care and hygiene
    Infants (Newborn)—Care and hygiene
    Local officials and employees—Health and hygiene
    Men—Health and hygiene
    Mental hygiene
    Military hygiene
    Mouth—Care and hygiene
    Narcotics
    Naval hygiene
    Periodic health examinations
    Physical education and training
    Physiology

Hygiene *(Domestic, RA771; Ethical aspects, BJ1695; Personal, RA773-790)*
(Continued)

    Political prisoners—Health and hygiene
    Prisoners of war—Health and hygiene
    Relaxation
    Rest
    Sanitation
    School hygiene
    Shaving
    Sleep
    Solar radiation—Physiological effect
    State governments—Officials and
       employees—Health and hygiene
    Stimulants
    Temperance
    Travel—Hygienic aspects
    Tropics—Diseases and hygiene
    Ventilation
    Veterinary hygiene
    Water—Pollution
    Water, Underground—Hygienic aspects
    Woman—Health and hygiene
    Youth—Health and hygiene
  x Cleanliness
    Health
    Hygiene, Social
    Personal hygiene
    Social hygiene
  xx Climatology, Medical
    Longevity
    Medicine
    Medicine, Preventive
    Sanitation
    Woman—Health and hygiene
  Note under Physical fitness
— Audio-visual aids
— — Catalogs
— Authorship
   See Medical writing
— Early works to 1800 *(RA775)*
— Film catalogs
   Example under Moving-pictures—Catalogs
— Juvenile literature *(QP36-38)*
— Posters
— Quotations, maxims, etc.
— Study and teaching
   See Health education
— Terminology *(RA423)*
Hygiene, Dental
  See Teeth—Care and hygiene
Hygiene, Gipsy
  x Gipsy hygiene
Hygiene, Hindu *(RA529; RA776)*
  x Hindu hygiene
Hygiene, Industrial
  See Industrial hygiene
Hygiene, Islamic
  sa Koran—Medicine, hygiene, etc.
  x Hygiene, Muslim
    Islamic hygiene
    Muslim hygiene
Hygiene, Jewish *(RA561)*
  sa Bible—Medicine, hygiene, etc.
  x Jewish hygiene
    Jews—Hygiene
Hygiene, Maya *(F1435.M4)*
  x Maya hygiene
    Mayas—Hygiene
Hygiene, Mental
  See Mental hygiene
Hygiene, Military
  See Military hygiene
Hygiene, Muslim
  See Hygiene, Islamic
Hygiene, Naval
  See Naval hygiene

Hygiene, Public *(Direct) (RA; Comprehensive treatises, RA425; General documents, RA11-388)*

  sa Burial
    Cemeteries
    Charities, Medical
    Cities and towns—Planning—Hygienic
      aspects
    Communicable diseases
    Community health services
    Community health services for children
    Community mental health services
    Cremation
    Dental public health
    Diseases—Reporting
    Disinfection and disinfectants
    Drinking cups—Hygienic aspects
    Dust—Removal
    Environmental health
    Epidemics
    Food adulteration and inspection
    Health boards
    Health facilities
    Health-officers
    Hospitals
    Housing and health
    Industrial hygiene
    Meat inspection
    Medical care
    Medicine, Preventive
    Mental health planning
    Milk supply
    Occupational diseases
    Pollution
    Public comfort stations
    Public health advisory groups
    Public health laboratories
    Public health nursing
    Quarantine
    Railroads—Sanitation
    Recreation areas—Hygienic aspects
    Refuse and refuse disposal
    Regional medical programs
    Sanitary districts
    Sanitary engineering
    Sanitation
    School hygiene
    Sewage disposal
    Ships—Sanitation
    Slaughtering and slaughter-houses
    Social medicine
    Soils—Bacteriology
    Swimming pools
    Theaters—Sanitation
    Vaccination
    Veterinary hygiene
    Water-supply
  subdivision Sewerage *under names of*
    cities, e.g. Vienna—Sewerage
  x Hygiene, Social
    Public health
    Public hygiene
    Sanitary affairs
    Social hygiene
  xx Medicine, Preventive
    Medicine, State
    Quarantine
    Sanitation
    Social problems
  Note under Health surveys
— Abstracts
— Accounting
— Administration
   See Public health administration
— Authorship
   See Medical writing
— Congresses *(RA422)*
— Evaluation

— Examinations, questions, etc.
— Exhibitions *(RA438)*
— Finance
  xx Medical economics
— Information services *(Direct)*
— International cooperation
  sa World Health Day
  x International cooperation in public
    health
  xx International agencies
    Medical assistance
    Public health laws, International
  Example under International cooperation
— Law and legislation
   See Public health laws
— Mathematical models
— Methodology
— Problems, exercises, etc.
— Research
   See Public health research
— Research grants
   See Public health research—Research
    grants
— Statistical methods
— Statistical services
— Study and teaching *(Direct)*
— Underdeveloped areas
   See Underdeveloped areas—Public
    health
— Vocational guidance
   See Public health as a profession

GEOGRAPHIC SUBDIVISIONS

— United States
  x United States—Sanitary affairs
Hygiene, Rural *(Direct) (RA427; RA771)*
  sa Medicine, Rural
  x Public health, Rural
    Rural hygiene
    Rural public health
  xx Medicine, Rural
— Maps
Hygiene, Sexual *(HQ31-58; Men, RC881; Women, RG121)*
  sa Birth control
    Conception—Prevention
    Promiscuity
    Prostitution
    Sex instruction
    Sexual ethics
    Venereal diseases
  x Hygiene, Social
    Sexual hygiene
    Social hygiene
  xx Conception—Prevention
    Prostitution
    Sex instruction
    Sexual ethics
    Venereal diseases
Hygiene, Social
  See Hygiene
    Hygiene, Public
    Hygiene, Sexual
    Prostitution
    Venereal diseases
    related subjects referred to under these
    headings
Hygiene, Tropical
  See Tropics—Diseases and hygiene
Hygiene, Veterinary
  See Veterinary hygiene
Hygiene in literature
Hygrometry *(QC915-917)*
  x Psychrometers
  xx Meteorological instruments
    Meteorology
— Charts, diagrams, etc.
— Tables, etc. *(QC917)*

Hyksos *(DT86)*
    x Shepherd kings
    xx Egypt—History—To 332 B.C.
Hylemorphism
    See Hylomorphism
Hylomorphism *(BD648)*
    x Form and matter
    Hylemorphism
    Matter and form
    xx Matter
    Metaphysics
    Peripatetics
    Substance (Philosophy)
Hylozoism
    Here are entered works dealing with the theory that all matter has life and that life as such is a property of matter.
    sa Animism
    Panpsychism
    xx Animism
    Panpsychism
    Philosophy
Hymen (Gynecology) *(Anatomy, QM421; Obstetrics, RG519)*
Hymenomycetes *(QK629.H9)*
    sa Polyporales
    xx Basidiomycetes
Hymenoptera *(Indirect)* *(QL563-9)*
    sa Ants
    Bees
    Chalcid wasps
    Gall-flies
    Honey-ants
    Mason-bees
    Sawflies
    Stingless bees
    Symphyta
    Wasps
    xx Insects
    — Catalogs and collections
    — Juvenile literature
Hymenoptera, Fossil *(QE832.H9)*
    xx Insects, Fossil
Hymn festivals *(BV341)*
    xx Hymns
    Music festivals
    Worship programs
Hymn playing
    See Hymns—Accompaniment
Hymn tunes
    Here, with appropriate subdivisions, are entered works about hymn tunes. Collections of hymn tunes (without accompanying text) are entered under the heading Tune-books.
    sa Chorale
    Old Hundredth (Tune)
    Tune-books
    xx Hymns
    Tune-books
    Note under Tune-books
Hymn writers *(BV325)*
    x Hymnists
    xx Hymns—History and criticism
    Poets
Hymnists
    See Hymn writers
Hymnology
    See Hymns

Hymns *(BV301-525; Hymns with music, M2115-2145)*
    Here are entered general collections of hymns as well as hymns of a particular Christian denomination, with qualification, when appropriate, by language, *e.g.* Hymns, English. Duplicate entry is made for the latter under the name of the denomination with subdivision Hymns, *e.g.* Baptists—Hymns.
    sa Advent hymns
    Bible—Use in hymns
    Canticles
    Carols
    Christian poetry
    Christmas—Poetry
    Easter hymns
    Funeral hymns
    Hymn festivals
    Hymn tunes
    Lenten hymns
    Psalmody
    Religious poetry
    Revivals—Hymns
    Seamen—Hymns
    Soldiers—Hymns
    Sunday-schools—Hymns
    Tune-books
    names of hymns, e.g. Gloria in excelsis
    x Christian hymns
    Hymnology
    xx Canticles
    Christian poetry
    Church music
    Devotional exercises
    Liturgies
    Poetry
    Psalmody
    Religious poetry
    Sacred songs
    Sacred vocal music
    Theology, Practical
    — Accompaniment *(MT240)*
        sa Chants (Plain, Gregorian, etc.)—Accompaniment
        x Hymn playing
        xx Chants (Plain, Gregorian, etc.)—Accompaniment
        Musical accompaniment
    — Concordances
        See Hymns—Indexes
    — Devotional use
        xx Devotional exercises
    — Dictionaries *(ML102)*
    — Discography *(ML156.4.R4)*
    — History and criticism *(BV310-340; Music, ML3086, ML3186)*
        sa Hymn writers
    — Indexes
        x Hymns—Concordances
    — Metrics and rhythmics *(BV335)*
        x Hymns—Versification
        xx Versification
    — Orchestrations
    — Versification
        See Hymns—Metrics and rhythmics
Hymns, Afrikaans, [**Danish, English, etc.**]
    x Afrikaans [Danish, English, etc.] hymns
Hymns, American
    See Hymns, English
Hymns, Arikara, [**Choctaw, Cree, etc.**]
    x Arikara [Choctaw, Cree, etc.] hymns
    Indians of North America—Hymns
Hymns, Bohemian
    See Hymns, Czech
Hymns, Buddhist
    See Buddhist hymns

Hymns, Byzantine
    See Hymns, Greek
Hymns, Czech
    x Bohemian hymns
    Czech hymns
    Hymns, Bohemian
Hymns, Danish
    sa Hymns, Norwegian
    xx Hymns, Norwegian
Hymns, Early Christian *(BV320)*
    x Early Christian hymns
    xx Christian literature, Early
Hymns, English
    sa Sikh hymns, English
    x American hymns
    Gospel music
    Hymns, American
    Note under Hymns
    — Juvenile literature
Hymns, German
    sa Chorale
    Chorale prelude
    Chorales
    Hymns, Low German
    x German hymns
Hymns, Greek
    Here are entered Christian hymns in the Greek language, whether ancient, Byzantine or modern. Pre-Christian classical hymns are entered under the heading Hymns, Greek (Classical)
    x Greek hymns
    Hymns, Byzantine
    xx Byzantine poetry
Hymns, Greek (Classical)
    x Greek hymns
    xx Music, Greek and Roman
    Note under Hymns, Greek
Hymns, Hebrew
    sa Hymns, Yiddish
    Jews—Hymns
    Piyutim
    x Hebrew hymns
    Hymns, Jewish
    Jewish hymns
    xx Hymns, Yiddish
    Jews—Hymns
Hymns, Hindu
    See Hindu hymns
Hymns, Islamic
    See Islamic hymns
Hymns, Jaina
    See Jaina hymns
Hymns, Jewish
    See Hymns, Hebrew
    Hymns, Yiddish
    Jews—Hymns
Hymns, Kafir
    See Hymns, Xosa
Hymns, Low German
    x Low German hymns
    xx Hymns, German
Hymns, Muslim
    See Islamic hymns
Hymns, Norwegian
    sa Hymns, Danish
    x Norwegian hymns
    xx Hymns, Danish
Hymns, Ramadan
    See Ramadan hymns
Hymns, Revival
    See Revivals—Hymns
Hymns, Sikh
    See Sikh hymns
Hymns, Sivaite
    See Sivaism—Hymns
Hymns, Spanish
    sa Alabados

Hymns, Spanish *(Continued)*
    Goigs
    x Spanish hymns
Hymns, Xosa
    x Hymns, Kafir
Hymns, Yiddish
    sa Hymns, Hebrew
        Jews—Hymns
    x Hymns, Jewish
        Jewish hymns
        Yiddish hymns
    xx Hymns, Hebrew
        Jews—Hymns
Hymns (Instrumental settings)
Hymns to Apollo
    xx Music, Greek and Roman
Hyoid bone
    sa Branchiostegals
    x Lingual bone
    xx Bones
Hyperadrenocorticism
    sa Hyperaldosteronism
    x Adrenocortical hyperplasia
        Hypercorticism
    xx Adrenal cortex—Diseases
Hyperaldosteronism
    x Aldosteronism
        Conn's disease
    xx Hyperadrenocorticism
Hyperbaric oxygenation
    x Oxygenation, Hyperbaric
    xx Compressed air—Therapeutic use
        Oxygen therapy
Hyperbola *(Analytical geometry, QA559; Plane geometry, QA485)*
    xx Conic sections
Hyperbole
Hyperbolic differential equations
    See Differential equations, Hyperbolic
Hyperbolic functions
    See Functions, Exponential
Hyperbolic geometry
    See Geometry, Hyperbolic
Hyperbolic navigation *(VK560)*
    sa Decca navigation
        Loran
        Loran charts
        Raydist
        Shoran
    xx Electronics in aeronautics
        Electronics in navigation
        Navigation
Hyperboloid *(QA561)*
    xx Quadrics
        Surfaces
Hyperborean languages *(PM1-95)*
    sa Aglemiut dialect
        Ainu language
        Aleut language
        Chukchi language
        Eskimo language
        Gilyak language
        Kamchadal language
        Koryak language
        Yuit language
        Yukaghir language
    x Paleoasiatic languages
        Paleosiberian languages
        Uralian languages
Hyperboreans
    See Arctic races
Hyperbrachycephaly *(GN71)*
    xx Brachycephaly
        Craniology
Hypercalcemia
    xx Calcium metabolism disorders
        Metabolism, Disorders of

Hypercapnia
    xx Blood—Analysis and chemistry
        Carbon dioxide—Physiological effect
Hypercholesteremia
    x Cholesteremia
    xx Cholesterol metabolism
        Metabolism, Disorders of
Hypercinesia
    See Hyperkinesia
Hypercircle method
    x Method of the hypercircle
    xx Approximation theory
        Boundary value problems
        Elasticity
        Hyperspace
        Mathematical physics
Hyperconjugation *(QD471)*
    x No-bond resonance
    xx Mesomerism
Hypercorticism
    See Hyperadrenocorticism
Hyperdulia
    See Mary, Virgin—Cultus
Hyperelliptic functions
    See Integrals, Hyperelliptic
Hyperelliptic integrals
    See Integrals, Hyperelliptic
Hyperemia *(RB145)*
Hyperemia, Artificial *(RM184)*
    xx Hemospasia
Hyperemia, Cerebral
    See Brain—Congestion
Hyperergic encephalomyelitis
    See Allergic encephalomyelitis
Hyperfine interactions *(QC762)*
    sa Hyperfine structure
        Isotone shift
        Isotope shift
    x Interactions, Hyperfine
    xx Electron paramagnetic resonance
        Hyperfine structure
        Magnetic fields
        Nuclear magnetism
        Nuclear spectroscopy
Hyperfine structure *(QC173)*
    sa Hyperfine interactions
    x Structure, Hyperfine
    xx Atomic spectra
        Hyperfine interactions
        Level-crossing spectroscopy
        Nuclear moments
Hyperfragments
    xx Nuclear physics
Hyperfunctions *(QA324)*
    xx Analytic functions
        Distributions, Theory of (Functional analysis)
Hypergammaglobulinemia *(RC647.H9)*
    xx Blood—Diseases
        Gamma globulin
Hypergeometric functions
    See Functions, Hypergeometric
Hyperglycemia
    sa Obese-hyperglycemic syndrome
    x Hyperglycosemia
    xx Blood—Analysis and chemistry
        Blood sugar
Hyperglycemic-obese syndrome
    See Obese-hyperglycemic syndrome
Hyperglycosemia
    See Hyperglycemia
Hypergraphs
    xx Graph theory
Hyperinsulinism
    See Insulin shock
Hyperkeratosis
    See X disease in cattle

Hyperkinesia
    x Hypercinesia
        Hyperkinesis
    xx Psychomotor disorders
Hyperkinesis
    See Hyperkinesia
Hyperlipemia
    x Hyperlipidemia
    xx Blood—Diseases
        Lipid metabolism disorders
Hyperlipidemia
    See Hyperlipemia
Hyperlipoproteinemia *(Indirect)* *(RC632.H88)*
    xx Blood—Diseases
        Lipid metabolism disorders
        Lipoproteins
        Protein metabolism disorders
Hypernatremia
    xx Metabolism, Disorders of
        Sodium in the body
Hyperons
    x Y-particles
    xx Baryons
Hyperopia
    x Farsightedness
    xx Eye—Diseases and defects
Hyperostosis frontalis interna
    x Calvarial hyperostosis
        Cranial hyperostosis
        Metabolic craniopathy
        Morel's syndrome
        Morgagni's syndrome
        Stewart-Morel syndrome
    xx Skull—Abnormities and deformities
Hyperparathyroidism
    sa Osteitis fibrosa
    xx Parathyroid glands—Diseases
Hypersensitivity, Delayed
    See Cellular immunity
Hypersensitivity (Immunology)
    See Allergy
Hypersonic aerodynamics
    See Aerodynamics, Hypersonic
Hypersonic aircraft
    See Hypersonic planes
Hypersonic planes
    x Aeroplanes, Hypersonic
        Hypersonic aircraft
        Planes, Hypersonic
    xx Aerodynamics, Hypersonic
        High-speed aeronautics
Hypersonic speeds
    See Aerodynamics, Hypersonic
Hypersonic wind tunnels
    sa Hypervelocity guns
    xx Aerodynamics, Hypersonic
        Wind tunnels
Hypersonics
    See Aerodynamics, Hypersonic
Hyperspace *(QA691)*
    Only mathematical works are entered here. Philosophical and imaginative works are entered under the heading Fourth dimension.
    sa Hilbert space
        Hypercircle method
        Polytopes
        Space and time
        Spaces, Generalized
    x Algebraic configurations in hyperspace
        Space of more than three dimensions
    xx Geometry
        Geometry, Differential
        Geometry—Foundations
        Geometry, Non-Euclidean
        Mathematics
        Space and time

Note under Fourth dimension
Hypersplenism *(RC645)*
  xx Spleen—Diseases
Hypersusceptibility
  See Anaphylaxis
Hypertension
  sa Hydralazine
    Hypotensive agents
    Nephrosclerosis
    Portal hypertension
    Pulmonary hypertension
    Renal hypertension
  x Blood pressure, High
    High blood pressure
    Vascular hypertension
  xx Blood—Circulation, Disorders of
  — Diagnosis
  — Psychosomatic aspects
Hypertension in pregnancy *(RG580.H9)*
  xx Pregnancy, Complications of
Hyperthermia
  See Fever
    Heat—Physiological effect
Hyperthyroidism
  x Thyrotoxicosis
  xx Thyroid gland—Diseases
Hypertonic solutions
  xx Solution (Chemistry)
  — Therapeutic use
    xx Fluid therapy
      Intravenous therapy
Hypertrichosis *(RL431)*
  sa Hair—Abnormities
  x Hirsutism
  xx Hair—Abnormities
  — Psychosomatic aspects
Hypertrophy *(RB140)*
  sa Acromegaly
    Kidneys—Hypertrophy
    Muscles, Hypertrophy of
    Prostatic hypertrophy
    Tongue, Hypertrophy of
Hypervelocity guns
  xx Ballistic ranges
    Hypersonic wind tunnels
    Shock tubes
Hyperventilation
  xx Respiration
Hypervitaminosis
  xx Vitamins
Hyphen
  xx Punctuation
Hyphomycosis
  sa Hyphomycetes
  xx Hyphomycetes
    Medical mycology
    Veterinary mycology
Hypnopaedia
  See Sleep-learning
Hypnosis
  See Hypnotism
Hypnotic susceptibility
  xx Hypnotism
Hypnotics *(RM325)*
  sa Barbiturates
    Narcotics
  xx Insomnia
  — Toxicology
Hypnotism *(BF1111-1156; Hypnotism and crime, HV6110; Psychiatry, RC490-499)*
  sa Animal magnetism
    Crystal-gazing
    Forensic hypnotism
    Hypnotic susceptibility
    Hypnotism and crime
    Magnetic healing
    Mental suggestion

    Mesmerism
    Mind and body
    Personality, Disorders of
    Psychoanalysis
    Rigidity (Psychology)
    Stanford hypnotic susceptibility scale
    Subconsciousness
    Therapeutics, Suggestive
  x Autosuggestion
    Braidism
    Hypnosis
  xx Animal magnetism
    Clairvoyance
    Medicine
    Mental suggestion
    Mesmerism
    Mind and body
    Mind-reading
    Personality, Disorders of
    Psychical research
    Psychoanalysis
    Psychology, Physiological
    Second sight
    Somnambulism
    Subconsciousness
    Thought-transference
    Trance
  — Jurisprudence *(Direct)*
    Here are entered works on the legal aspects of hypnotism. Works on hypnosis as an investigative technique are entered under the heading Forensic hypnotism.
    sa Hypnotism and crime
    x Hypnotism and law
      Law and hypnotism
    xx Hypnotism and crime
      Psychology, Forensic
    Note under Forensic hypnotism
  — Moral and religious aspects *(Catholic Church, BX1759.5.H8)*
  — Sounds
    xx Sounds
  — Therapeutic use
    xx Therapeutics, Suggestive
  — — Cases, clinical reports, statistics
Hypnotism and crime
  sa Hypnotism—Jurisprudence
  x Crime and hypnotism
  xx Crime and criminals
    Criminal psychology
    Hypnotism
    Hypnotism—Jurisprudence
Hypnotism and law
  See Hypnotism—Jurisprudence
Hypnotism in dentistry
  xx Anesthesia in dentistry
    Dentistry
Hypnotism in obstetrics
  xx Anesthesia in obstetrics
    Obstetrics
Hypnotism in surgery *(RD85.H9)*
  xx Anesthesia
    Surgery
Hypoacoustic children
  See Children, Deaf
Hypochlorinators
  xx Water—Purification
Hypocholesteremic agents
  See Anticholesteremic agents
Hypochondria *(RC552.H8)*
  x Hypochondriasis
  xx Insanity
    Psychology, Pathological
  — Anecdotes, facetiae, satire, etc.
Hypochondria in literature
  xx Anxiety in literature
    Fear in literature

Hypochondriasis
  See Hypochondria
Hypochromic anemia *(RC641.7.H9)*
  sa Iron deficiency anemia
  x Anemia, Microcytic hypochromic
    Microcytic hypochromic anemia
  xx Anemia
Hypocreales *(QK623.P9)*
  xx Fungi
Hypocrisy *(Ethics, BJ1535.H8; Theology, BV4627.H8)*
  xx Conduct of life
    Ethics
Hypocupraemia
  See Hypocupremia
Hypocupremia
  x Copper deficiency disease
    Hypocupraemia
    Hypocuprosis
  xx Copper in the body
    Deficiency diseases in domestic animals
Hypocuprosis
  See Hypocupremia
Hypocycloids
  See Epicycloids and hypocycloids
Hypodermic injections
  See Injections, Hypodermic
Hypodermic needles
  sa Hypodermic syringes
  Example under Medical instruments and apparatus
Hypodermic syringes
  xx Hypodermic needles
Hypogaeic acid *(QD305.A2; Botanical chemistry, QK866.P3)*
Hypogammaglobulinemia
  See Agammaglobulinemia
Hypogastric plexus
  — Surgery
Hypoglycemia *(Disease, RC857)*
  sa Cookery for hypoglycemics
    Insulin shock
  x Hypoglycemosis
  xx Blood sugar
    Insulin
    Pancreas—Diseases
Hypoglycemosis
  See Hypoglycemia
Hypogonadism
  sa Klinefelter's syndrome
  xx Sexual disorders
Hypoleucemia
  See Leucopenia
Hypoleucia
  See Leucopenia
Hypoleucocytosis
  See Leucopenia
Hypophosphatasia
  xx Phosphorus metabolism disorders
Hypophosphites *(Therapeutics, RM666.H9)*
  xx Materia medica
Hypophysectomy
  x Pituitary body—Excision
Hypophysis cerebri
  See Pituitary body
Hypospadias
  xx Penis
    Urethra
Hypostatic union *(BT205)*
  sa Jesus Christ—Natures
  x Union, Hypostatic
  xx Jesus Christ—Natures
    Jesus Christ—Person and offices
  — History of doctrines
Hyposulphites *(QD181.S1)*
Hypotension
  x Blood pressure, Low
    Low blood pressure

Hypotension *(Continued)*
  xx Blood—Circulation, Disorders of
Hypotensive agents
  sa Kinins
    Vasodilators
  x Antihypertensive agents
  xx Cardiovascular agents
    Hypertension
Hypothalamic hypophysiotropic hormones
  See Pituitary hormone releasing factors
Hypothalamo-hypophyseal system
  xx Hypothalamus
    Neuroendocrinology
    Pituitary body
Hypothalamus *(QM455)*
  sa Hypothalamo-hypophyseal system
    Supraoptic nucleus
  xx Brain
Hypothecation
  See Bottomry and respondentia
    Chattel mortgages
    Liens
    Mortgages
    Pledges (Law)
Hypothermia
  sa Artificial hibernation
  x Hypothermy
  xx Body temperature
    Cryobiology
Hypothermy
  See Hypothermia
Hypothesis *(Logic, BC183)*
  sa Statistical hypothesis testing
  x Assumption
    Supposition
  xx Logic
    Reasoning
    Science—Methodology
Hypothesis testing (Statistics)
  See Statistical hypothesis testing
Hypothyrea
  See Hypothyroidism
Hypothyreosis
  See Hypothyroidism
Hypothyroidism
  sa Myxedema
  x Hypothyrea
    Hypothyreosis
  xx Thyroid gland—Diseases
  — Mathematical models
Hypovitaminosis
  See Avitaminosis
Hypoxemia
  See Anoxemia
Hypoxia
  See Anoxemia
Hypsometric colors
  See Color in cartography
Hypsometry
  See Altitudes—Measurement
Hypsometry, Barometric
  See Barometric hypsometry
Hypurina language
  See Ipurina language
Hyracoidea *(QL737.U7)*
Hysterectomy
  sa Uterus—Surgery
  x Uterus—Excision
  xx Uterus—Surgery
  — Complications and sequelae
  — Moral and religious aspects
    (BX1759.5.H9)
Hysteresigraph *(QC755.675.H9)*
  xx Hysteresis
    Magnetic instruments
Hysteresis *(QC761)*
  sa Hysteresigraph
    Hysteresis loop

  xx Elasticity
    Magnetic induction
Hysteresis loop
  xx Dielectrics
    Hysteresis
    Magnetic induction
    Magnetic materials
    Magnetism
Hysteria *(RC532)*
  sa Aerophagy
    Astasia and astasia-abasia
    Demoniac possession
    Demonomania
    Ecstasy
    Paralysis, Hysterical
    Trance
    Witchcraft
  x Insanity, Hysterical
  xx Ecstasy
    Insanity
    Psychology, Pathological
  Example under Neuroses
Hysteria, Epidemic *(RC532)*
  sa Chorea, Epidemic
  x Epidemic hysteria
    Epidemics, Mental
    Mental epidemics
  xx Chorea, Epidemic
Hysteria (Social psychology)
  x Mass hysteria
    National hysteria
  xx Fear
    Social psychology
I ching and science
  x Science and I ching
I.D. cards
  See Identification cards
I.G. Farben Trial, Nuremberg, 1947-1948
  x War crime trials—Nuremberg—I.G.
    Farben case, 1947-1948
    War crime trials—Nuremberg
    (Subsequent proceedings, case no. 6)
  xx War crime trials—Nuremberg,
    1946-1949
    World War, 1939-1945—Atrocities
I-hsien, China (Shantung Province)
  — Siege, 1632-1633
I.T.A.
  See Initial teaching alphabet
Iai language *(PL6253.Z91)*
  xx Melanesian languages
Iaido
  x Iainuki
  xx Kendo
Iainuki
  See Iaido
Iamalele language
Iambic tetrameter
Iapygian language
  See Messapian language
Iare language
  xx Papuan languages
Iate Indians
  See Fulnio Indians
Iatmul language
  xx Papuan languages
Iatmuls
Iatrogenic diseases *(RC90)*
  sa Drugs—Side effects
  x Diseases, Iatrogenic
  xx Medicine, Psychosomatic
    Therapeutics—Complications and
    sequelae
Iatromathematical school
  See Iatrophysical school
Iatrophysical school *(R148)*
  x Iatromathematical school
  xx Astrology

    Medicine
Ibadites *(Direct)*
  xx Islamic sects
IBAL (Computer program language)
  x Illiac III Basic Assembler Language
  xx Assembler language (Computer
    program language)
    Illiac computer—Programming
Ibanag language *(PL5721)*
  xx Philippine languages
Ibans (Bornean people)
  x Sea Dyaks (Bornean people)
  xx Dyaks
    Etnology—Borneo
Ibatan language
  See Batan language
Ibembe language
  See Bembe language (Lake Tanganyika)
Iberian architecture
  See Architecture, Iberian
Iberian bronzes
  See Bronzes, Iberian
Iberian language *(P1081)*
Iberian pottery
  See Pottery, Iberian
Iberians *(DP53.I2)*
  sa Basques
    Celtiberi
    Ilergetes
Ibernians
  See Georgians
Ibero-Insular race
  See Mediterranean race
Ibex
  See Bouquetin
Ibibios *(Nigeria, DT515)*
  sa Anang (African tribe)
    Ubium (African people)
Ibis *(QL696.A7)*
IBM 360 (Computer)
  xx Electronic digital computers
  — Programming
    sa AEMOVE (Computer program)
    MERMAC (Electronic computer
    system)
    POKER 360 (Electronic computer
    system)
  — — Problems, exercises, etc.
IBM 370 (Computer)
  xx Electronic digital computers
  — Programming
IBM 650 (Computer)
  xx Electronic digital computers
  — Programming
IBM 1130 (Computer)
  xx Electronic digital computers
  — Programming
IBM 1401 (Computer)
  xx Electronic digital computers
  — Programming *(QA76.8.I; Business,*
    HF5548)
  — — Programmed instruction
IBM 1440 (Computer)
  xx Electronic digital computers
IBM 1620 (Computer)
  xx Electronic digital computers
  — Programming
IBM 1800 (Computer)
  xx Electronic digital computers
  — Programming
IBM 3965 (Computer)
  xx Electronic digital computers
  — Programming
IBM 7030 (Computer)
  x IBM Stretch computer
    Project Stretch
    Stretch computer
  xx Electronic digital computers

IBM 7040 (Computer)
   xx Electronic digital computers
   — Programming
IBM 7044 (Computer)
   xx Electronic digital computers
IBM 7090 (Computer)
   xx Electronic digital computers
   — Programming
IBM 7094 (Computer)
   xx Electronic digital computers
   — Programming
IBM aperture card systems
   See Microfilm aperture card systems
IBM Stretch computer
   See IBM 7030 (Computer)
IBM System/3 (Computer)
   xx Electronic digital computers
   — Programming
Ibo art
   See Art, Ibo
Ibo language *(PL8261)*
   sa Izi language
   x Igbo language
   xx Kwa languages
Ibo law
   See Law, Ibo
Ibo poetry *(Direct)*
Ibo tribe *(DT515)*
   sa Missions to Ibos
   — Juvenile literature
   — Religion
Icarex camera
ICBM
   See Intercontinental ballistic missiles
Ice *(Indirect) (GB2401-2597)*
   sa Building, Ice and snow
     Dry ice
     Glaciers
     Glaze (Meteorology)
     Ice caves
     Ice coring rigs
     Ice crystals
     Ice on rivers, lakes, etc.
     Icebergs
     Pingos
     Saline water conversion—Freezing
       process
     Sea ice
     Transportation, Military—Cold weather
       conditions
   x Freezing
   xx Frost
     Physical geography
     Water
   — Bacteriology *(QR107)*
     sa Water—Bacteriology
     xx Water—Bacteriology
   — Classification
   — Control
     See Ice prevention
   — Electric properties
     Example under reference from Electric
       properties of materials
   — Hygienic aspects *(RA599)*
   — Juvenile literature
   — Manufacture *(TP490-495)*
     sa Refrigeration and refrigerating
       machinery
     x Ice-machinery
       Ice making
     xx Ice industry
       Refrigeration and refrigerating
       machinery
   — — Patents
   — Measurement
   — Pictorial works
   — Prevention
     See Ice prevention

— Testing

GEOGRAPHIC SUBDIVISIONS

— Antarctic regions
   x Ice, Polar
     Polar ice

GEOGRAPHIC SUBDIVISIONS

— Arctic regions
   x Ice, Polar
     Polar ice

GEOGRAPHIC SUBDIVISIONS

— Greenland
   x Ice, Polar
     Polar ice

GEOGRAPHIC SUBDIVISIONS

— Newfoundland
   Example under Icebergs
Ice, Polar
   See Ice—Antarctic regions
     Ice—Arctic regions
     Ice—Greenland
     similar headings
Ice accidents
   xx Accidents
     Rescue work
Ice age
   See Glacial epoch
Ice and snow building
   See Building, Ice and snow
Ice-boats *(GV843)*
   xx Boats and boating
     Sailing
     Winter sports
Ice breaking operations *(VK1299.5-6)*
   sa United States. Navy—Ice breaking
   x Icebreaking operations
   xx Aids to navigation
     Ice-breaking vessels
Ice-breaking vessels *(VM451)*
   sa Atomic icebreakers
     Ice breaking operations
   x Steamboats, Ice-breaking
   xx Ice on rivers, lakes, etc.
     Ships
   — Juvenile literature
Ice bridges
   See Ice crossings
Ice carnivals
   See Winter sports
Ice carving *(NK6030)*
   xx Sculpture
Ice caves *(GB602)*
   xx Ice
Ice climbing
   See Snow and ice climbing
Ice control
   See Ice prevention
Ice control (Roads)
   See Roads—Snow and ice control
Ice control on bridges
   See Bridges—Snow and ice control
Ice coring rigs
   xx Boring machinery
     Ice
Ice-cream freezers
   xx Refrigeration and refrigerating
     machinery
Ice cream, ices, etc. *(TX795)*
   sa Confectionery
     Ice cream industry
     Milkshakes
   x Ices
   xx Confectionery
     Desserts, Frozen
   — Law and legislation *(Direct)*

   xx Dairy laws
Ice cream industry *(Direct)*
   xx Ice cream, ices, etc.
   — Accounting
   — Employees *(Direct)*
   — Equipment and supplies
Ice crossings
   x Ice bridges
   xx Bridges
     Ice on rivers, lakes, etc.
     Roads, Ice
Ice crystals
   sa Ice fog
     Snow crystals
   x Frost mist
     Frost snow
     Ice needles
     Ice prisms
     Poudrin
   xx Frost
     Hail
     Ice
   — Spectra
Ice drift
   See Sea ice drift
Ice erosion
   See Glacial erosion
Ice excavation
   sa Ice tunneling
   xx Civil engineering—Cold weather
     conditions
     Excavation
     Ice tunneling
Ice field drift
   See Sea ice drift
Ice fishing *(SH459)*
   xx Fishing
     Winter sports
Ice fog *(QC929.F7)*
   x Air hoar
     Frost flakes
     Frost fog
     Frozen fog
     Rime fog
   xx Fog
     Ice crystals
Ice hockey
   See Hockey
Ice-houses *(Commercial, NA6360; Private,*
     NA8350)
Ice industry *(Direct) (Cutting, storage,*
     TP498; Trade, HD9481)
   sa Dry ice
     Ice—Manufacture
     Wages—Ice industry
   — Accounting *(HF5686.14)*
Ice islands
   sa Arlis II (Drifting ice station)
     Drifting ice stations
   x Islands, Ice
   xx Drifting ice stations
     Icebergs
     Sea ice
Ice-machinery
   See Ice—Manufacture
     Refrigeration and refrigerating
       machinery
Ice making
   See Ice—Manufacture
Ice navigation *(VK545)*
   sa Sea ice
   xx Navigation
     Seamanship
Ice needles
   See Ice crystals
Ice on aeroplanes
   See Aeroplanes—Ice prevention

Ice on electric lines
   See Electric lines—Ice prevention
Ice on rivers, lakes, etc. *(Indirect) (Lakes,
    GB1601-1797; Rivers,
    GB1201-1397)*
   sa Ice-breaking vessels
     Ice crossings
     Lakes—Temperature
     Rivers—Temperature
   x Freezing and opening of rivers, lakes,
     etc.
     Lakes, Freezing and opening of
     Rivers, Freezing and opening of
   xx Ice
     Lakes—Temperature
     Meteorology
     Rivers—Temperature
Ice on ships
   See Ships—Ice prevention
Ice palaces *(NA6890)*
Ice prevention *(TA197)*
   sa Aeroplanes—Ice prevention
     Electric lines—Ice prevention
     Hydraulic structures—Ice prevention
     Roads—Snow and ice control
     Ships—Ice prevention
     Telegraph lines—Ice prevention
     Telephone lines—Ice prevention
   x Ice control
     Ice—Control
     Ice—Prevention
   xx Engineering meteorology
   — Patents
Ice prisms
   See Ice crystals
Ice rinks
   See Skating rinks
Ice roads
   See Roads, Ice
Ice seamanship
   See Seamanship—Cold weather conditions
Ice skating
   See Skating
Ice sports
   See Winter sports
Ice stations, Drifting
   See Drifting ice stations
Ice tunneling
   sa Ice excavation
   xx Civil engineering—Cold weather
     conditions
     Ice excavation
     Tunneling
Ice-wedge polygons
   x Contraction-crack polygons
   xx Frozen ground
     Patterned ground
Icebergs *(GB2401-2597; Navigation,
    VK1299)*
   sa Ice islands
     Ice—[local subdivision], *e.g.* Ice—
      Newfoundland
     International ice patrol
     Sea ice
   xx Ice
     Physical geography
     Sea ice
   — Juvenile literature
Icebreakers, Atomic
   See Atomic icebreakers
Icebreaking operations
   See Ice breaking operations
Iceland pony *(SF315.2.I3)*
   xx Ponies
Iceland spar *(QE391.I)*
   xx Polarization (Light)
     Refraction, Double

Icelanders
   xx Scandinavians
Icelanders in Canada, [Wisconsin, etc.]
   — Biography
Icelandic-American literature *(PT7526-7545)*
Icelandic and Old Norse languages
    (PD2201-2392)
   sa Faroese dialect
     Norn dialect
     Norwegian language
     Scandinavian philology
   x Icelandic language
     Norse languages
     Old Icelandic language
     Old Norse language
   xx Germanic languages
     Scandinavian languages
   Example under Germanic philology
Icelandic and Old Norse letters
   x Old Norse letters
Icelandic and Old Norse literature
    *(Collections, PT7220-7262; History,
    PT7101-7211)*
   sa Eddas
     Faroese dialect—Texts
     Norwegian literature
     Sagas
     Scalds and scaldic poetry
     Scandinavian literature
     Scandinavian philology
   x Icelandic literature
     Norse literature
     Old Icelandic literature
     Old Norse literature
   xx Norwegian literature
     Sagas
     Scalds and scaldic poetry
     Scandinavian literature
   Example under Germanic philology
Icelandic and Old Norse philology
   xx Scandinavian philology
Icelandic and Old Norse poetry *(Collections,
    PT7230-7252; History,
    PT7170-7174)*
   sa Eddas
     Lausavísur
     Rímur
     Scalds and scaldic poetry
   x Old Norse poetry
   xx Icelandic poetry
Icelandic and Old Norse prose literature
    (Direct)
Icelandic drama *(Collections, PT7470-7477;
    History, PT7411)*
Icelandic fiction *(Collections, PT7485-7;
    History, PT7413)*
Icelandic language
   See Icelandic and Old Norse languages
     Icelandic language, Modern
Icelandic language, Modern *(PD2401-2447)*
   x Icelandic language
Icelandic literature
   See Icelandic and Old Norse literature
     Icelandic literature, Modern
Icelandic literature, Modern *(Collections,
    PT7451-7495; History,
    PT7351-7438)*
   x Icelandic literature
Icelandic manuscripts
   See Manuscripts, Icelandic and Old Norse
Icelandic newspapers *(PN5355.I3)*
Icelandic periodicals *(PN5355.I3)*
Icelandic poetry
   sa Icelandic and Old Norse poetry
   xx Scandinavian poetry
   — Early modern, 1500-1700 *(Collections,
    PT7465-7; History, PT7410)*

Icelandic poetry, Modern *(Collections,
    PT7465-7; History, PT7410)*
Icelandic prose, Modern *(Collections,
    PT7480-7495; History,
    PT7412-7419)*
Ices
   See Ice cream, ices, etc.
ICES (Electronic computer system)
    (TA345.5.I2)
   sa STRUDL (Electronic computer system)
   x Integrated Civil Engineering System
     (Electronic computer system)
   xx Electronic data processing—Civil
     engineering
     Electronic digital computers—
      Programming
     On-line data processing
Ichigenkin *(ML1015-1018)*
   xx Koto
     Musical instruments, Japanese
Ichigenkin music *(M142.I3)*
Ichiti language
   See Hitchiti language
Ichnology
   See Footprints, Fossil
Ichthyol *(Physiological effect, QP915.I2;
    Therapeutics, RM666.I2)*
Ichthyological research
   x Fishes—Research
     Ichthyology—Research
   xx Research
Ichthyologists *(Indirect)*
   xx Zoologists
Ichthyology
   sa Fishes
   xx Fishes
     Zoology
   — Research
     See Ichthyological research
Ichthyomorpha
   See Urodela
Ichthyosauria *(QE862.I2)*
   xx Reptiles, Fossil
Ichthyosis follicularis
   See Keratosis
Ichthys
   See Fish (in religion, folk-lore, etc.)
Icila (African dance)
Icing of aeroplanes
   See Aeroplanes—Ice prevention
Icing of electric lines
   See Electric lines—Ice prevention
Icing of ships
   See Ships—Ice prevention
Icings, Cake
   sa Cake decorating
   x Cake icing
     Frostings, Cake
   xx Cake decorating
Icon painting *(Direct)*
   x Painting, Icon
   xx Icons
     Miniature painting
     Painting
   — Byzantine [etc.] influences
Iconoclasm *(8th century, BR238)*
   x Iconoclasm—History
   xx Idols and images—Worship
   — History
     See Iconoclasm
   — Sources
Iconography
   See Art
     Christian art and symbolism
     Idols and images
     Portraits

special subjects, e.g. Musicians—
Portraits; Saints—Art; *and*
subdivisions Iconography, Portraits,
and Portraits, caricatures, etc. *under*
names of persons
Iconostases *(Direct)* *(NA5082)*
  xx Screens (Church decoration)
Icons *(Direct)* *(Russian art, N7956)*
  sa Icon painting
  x Eikons
  Ikons
  xx Christian art and symbolism
  Jesus Christ—Art
  Mary, Virgin—Art
  Saints—Art
— Private collections *(Direct)*
Icons, Byzantine
  x Byzantine icons
Icons, Russian, ⌐**Serbian, etc.**⌐
  x Russian ⌐Serbian, etc.⌐ icons
Icosahedra *(QA491)*
  xx Polyhedra
Icterus (Ornithology)
  See Orioles
Icterus (Pathology)
  See Jaundice
Id (Psychology)
  xx Psychoanalysis
  Psychology
'Īd al-Aḍḥā *(BP183.66)*
  xx Islamic sermons
'Īd al-Fiṭr *(BP186.45)*
  x Bairam
  'Īd al-Ṣadaqah
  al-'Īd al-Ṣaghīr
'Īd al-Fiṭr sermons *(BP183.645)*
  xx Islamic sermons
'Īd al-Ghadīr *(Direct)* *(BP186.9)*
  x Ghadīr al-Khumm
  xx Shiites
'Īd al-Ṣadaqah
  See 'Īd al-Fiṭr
al-'Īd al-Ṣaghīr
  See 'Īd al-Fiṭr
Idafat
  See subdivision Noun *under names of*
  languages and groups of languages
Iddingsite *(QE391.I)*
Idea (Philosophy) *(Plato, B398.I3)*
  sa One (The One in philosophy)
  x Ideas (Philosophy)
  Ideas, Theory of
  Theory of ideas
  xx Knowledge, Theory of
  Philosophy
Ideal states
  See Utopias
Idealism *(B823; By country, B851-4695;*
  United States, B941)
  sa Dualism
  Form (Philosophy)
  Immanence (Philosophy)
  Materialism
  Neo-Kantianism
  Pragmatism
  Realism
  Transcendentalism
  Vijñaptimātratā
  Yogācāra (Buddhism)
  xx Animism
  Dualism
  Materialism
  Monism
  Personalism
  Philosophy
  Positivism
  Realism
  Transcendentalism

Idealism, American, ⌐**English, French, etc.**⌐
Idealism in art *(N61-79)*
  sa Naturalism in art
  Realism in art
  Romanticism in art
  xx Aesthetics
  Art
  Naturalism in art
  Realism in art
  Romanticism in art
Idealism in literature *(PN56.I4)*
  sa Naturalism in literature
  Realism in literature
  Romanticism
  xx Aesthetics
  Naturalism in literature
  Realism in literature
  Romanticism
Ideals (Algebra) *(QA247)*
  x Algebraic ideals
  xx Fields, Algebraic
  Rings (Algebra)
Ideals (Philosophy) *(B105.I3)*
  xx Philosophy
Ideals (Psychology)
  sa Example
  Influence (Psychology)
  xx Concepts
  Example
  Exempla
Ideas, Association of
  See Association of ideas
Ideas, Reproduction of
  See Reproduction (Psychology)
Ideas, Theory of
  See Idea (Philosophy)
Ideas (Philosophy)
  See Idea (Philosophy)
Identification *(Direct)* *(Anthropology,*
  GN192; Medical jurisprudence,
  RA1055; Penology, HV8073)
  sa Fingerprints
  Medical jurisprudence
  Palmprints
  subdivision Identification *under*
  subjects, e.g. Amphibians—
  Identification; Firearms—
  Identification; Legal documents—
  Identification
  xx Medical jurisprudence
Identification, Friend or foe (Electronic
  equipment)
  See Aeroplanes—IFF equipment
Identification (Greek law)
Identification (Psychology)
  sa Reference groups
  xx Defense mechanisms (Psychology)
  Internalization
  Psychology
Identification (Religion) *(BV4509.5)*
  x Identity (Religion)
  Self-realization (Religion)
  xx Love (Theology)
  Man (Theology)
Identification cards
  x I.D. cards
Identification marks on freight-cars
  See Railroads—Freight-cars—Markings
Identification marks on military vehicles
  See Vehicles, Military—Markings
Identification of automobiles
  See Automobiles—Identification
Identification of birds
  See Birds—Identification
Identification of cactus
  See Cactus—Identification
Identification of cattle
  See Cattle—Marking

Identification of criminals
  See Crime and criminals—Identification
Identification of documents
  See Legal documents—Identification
Identification of firearms
  See Firearms—Identification
Identification of flowers
  See Flowers—Identification
Identification of handwriting
  See Writing—Identification
Identification of rocks
  See Rocks—Identification
Identification of seeds
  See Seeds—Identification
Identification of shrubs
  See Shrubs—Identification
Identification of the dead
  See Dead—Identification
Identification of trees
  See Trees—Identification
Identification of typewriting
  See Typewriting—Identification
Identification of weeds
  See Weeds—Identification
Identification of wood
  See Wood—Identification
Identification of woody plants
  See Woody plants—Identification
Identification papers for employees
  See Labor passports
Identity *(Logic, BC199.I4; Theory of*
  knowledge, BD236)
  xx Comparison (Psychology)
  Individuality
  Knowledge, Theory of
  Logic
  Ontology
  Resemblance (Philosophy)
Identity, Loss of
  See Depersonalization
Identity (Psychology)
  sa Ego (Psychology)
  xx Ego (Psychology)
  Personality
  Self
— Juvenile literature
Identity (Religion)
  See Identification (Religion)
Ideography
  See Chinese language—Writing
  Hieroglyphics
  Pasigraphy
  Picture-writing
Ideology
  xx Knowledge, Theory of
  Perception
  Philosophy
  Psychology
  Senses and sensation
  Thought and thinking
Idiocy *(Indirect)* *(RC571; Charities,*
  HV3004-8; Children, HV891-901)
  sa Amaurotic family idiocy
  Cretinism
  Epilepsy
  Insanity
  x Idiots
  xx Delinquents
  Insanity
  Mentally handicapped
  Psychology, Pathological
Idioms
  See subdivisions Idioms, corrections, errors
  and Provincialisms *under names of*
  languages
Idiopathic femoral necrosis *(Direct)*
  (RC931.I3)
  x Aseptic femoral necrosis

Idiopathic femoral necrosis *(Direct)*
  (RC931.I3) *(Continued)*
    Avascular femoral necrosis
    Ischaemic femoral necrosis
  xx Femur—Diseases
Idiopathic hemorrhagic sarcoma
  See Kaposi's sarcoma
Idiot asylums
  See Mentally handicapped—Institutional
    care
Idiots
  See Idiocy
Ido *(PM8391-4)*
  xx Languages, Artificial
Ido (African language)
  See Ijo language
Idocrase
  See Vesuvianite
Idolatry
  See Idols and images—Worship
Idols and images *(Art, NB960-1113)*
  sa Commandments, Ten—Images
    Dolls (in religion, folk-lore, etc.)
    Gods in art
    Ming ch'i
    Ushabti
  x Iconography
    Images and idols
    Religious art
    Statuettes
  xx Animism
    Art and religion
    Art, Primitive
    Fetishism
    Gods in art
    Magic
    Religion, Primitive
    Sculpture, Primitive
    Symbolism
  — Costume and adornment
    x Gods—Costume
  — Worship *(BL485)*
    sa Commandments, Ten—Other gods
      Iconoclasm
    x Idolatry
    xx Worship
Idoma language *(PL8263)*
  x Oturkpo dialect
IDS (Computer program language)
  x Integral Data Store
  xx COBOL (Computer program language)
Iduna language
Idyllic poetry
  See Pastoral poetry
Idzebu language
  See Yebu language
Idzo language
  See Ijo language
Iemanjá (Cultus) *(BL2590.B7)*
  x Yemanjá (Cultus)
  xx Religion, Primitive
Ifa *(BF1779.I4)*
  xx Divination
    Geomancy
IFF systems
  See Aeroplanes—IFF equipment
Iffland-Ring
  See Ifflandring
Ifflandring
  x Iffland-Ring
  xx Theater—Awards
Ifugaos *(DS666.I15)*
Igala (African tribe)
  See Igara (African tribe)
Igalikite
Igara (African tribe)
  x Igala (African tribe)
  xx Ethnology—Nigeria

— Religion
Igbo art
  See Art, Ibo
Igbo language
  See Ibo language
Igelites *(TP986.I)*
  xx Vinyl polymers
Igloolikmiut
  See Iglulirmiut (Eskimo tribe)
Igloos
  x Iglus
  xx Building, Ice and snow
    Dwellings
    Eskimos
Igluligmiut
  See Iglulirmiut (Eskimo tribe)
Iglulingmiut
  See Iglulirmiut (Eskimo tribe)
Iglulirmiut (Eskimo tribe)
  x Igloolikmiut
    Igluligmiut
    Iglulingmiut
Iglus
  See Igloos
IgM
  See Immunoglobulin M
Igneous rocks
  See Rocks, Igneous
Igneous rocks, Alkaline
  See Alkalic igneous rocks
Ignimbrite *(Indirect)* *(QE462.I35)*
  x Welded tuff
  xx Volcanic ash, tuff, etc.
Ignition devices
  See Automobiles—Ignition
    Gas and oil engines—Ignition
    Magneto
    Spark-plugs
Ignitrons
  xx Gas tubes
    Mercury-arc rectifiers
Ignorance (Canon law)
Ignorance (Law) *(Direct)*
  sa Good faith (Law)
    Mistake (Law)
  xx Criminal liability
    Good faith (Law)
    Guilt (Law)
    Mistake (Law)
Igo (Game)
  See Go (Game)
Igorot *(DS666.I2)*
  sa Bontoks (Philippine people)
    Isneg
  x Igorrotes
Igorot language *(PL5731-4)*
  sa Kankanay dialect
  x Benguetano language
    Igorrote language
  xx Philippine languages
Igorrote language
  See Igorot language
Igorrotes
  See Igorot
Iguana, Marine
  See Marine iguana
Ihansalen
  See Ahansala
Iijima Seishi Strike, 1958
IITRAN (Computer program language)
  x Illinois Institute of Technology
    translator (Computer program
    language)
Ijaw (African people)
  See Ijo (African people)
Ijaw language
  See Ijo language

Ijca Indians *(F2270.2.I5)*
  xx Chibcha Indians
    Indians of South America
Ijo (African people)
  x Ijaw (African people)
  xx Ethnology—Nigeria
Ijo language *(PL8276)*
  sa Kolokuma dialect
    Nembe language
  x Bonny language
    Djo language
    Dzo language
    Ejo language
    Ido (African language)
    Idzo language
    Ijaw language
    Ijoh language
    Iyo language
    New Calabar language
    Ojo language
    Oru language
    Udzo language
Ijoh language
  See Ijo language
Ijtihād (Islamic law)
  See Islamic law—Interpretation and
    construction
Ik (African people) *(DT429)*
  x Teuso (African people)
  xx Ethnology—Kenya
    Ethnology—Sudan
    Ethnology—Uganda
Ikat
Ikebana
  See Flower arrangement, Japanese
Ikeya-Seki comet *(QB727)*
Ikhshidids
  x Ikshidids
  xx Egypt—History—640-1250
Iki-kukwe language
  See Mwamba language
Ikinyi-Kiusa language
  See Ngonde language
Ikkō uprisings *(BL1442.S5)*
  — Juvenile literature
Iklig *(ML3730)*
  xx Musical instruments, Primitive
Ikoflex camera *(TR263)*
  xx Zeiss cameras
Ikons
  See Icons
Ikonta camera *(TR263.I3)*
  xx Zeiss cameras
Ikota
  See Kota (African tribe)
Ikounka
  xx Berbers
    Ethnology—Morocco
Ikshidids
  See Ikhshidids
Ikuno Uprising, 1863 *(DS881.3)*
  xx Japan—History—Restoration,
    1853-1870
Ila (Bantu tribe)
  x Ba-ila
    Mashukulumbwe
    Shukulumbwe
  xx Bantus
    Ethnology—Zambia
Ila language *(PL8281)*
Ilali language
  See Teke language
Ilamba language
  See Nilamba language
Ilaoquatsh Indians
  See Clayoquot Indians
Ileal conduit surgery
  xx Urinary organs—Surgery

Ileitis
 See Ileum—Diseases
Ileitis, Regional
 See Regional ileitis
Ileostomy
 xx Ileum—Surgery
 — Complications and sequelae
Ilergetes
 xx Iberians
Ileum
 xx Intestine, Small
 — Diseases
  sa Regional ileitis
  x Ileitis
 — Surgery
  sa Ileostomy
Ileus
 See Intestines—Obstructions
Iliac artery
 xx Arteries
 — Ligature
  xx Arteries—Ligature
Ilimaussite (Indirect) (QE391.I4)
Iliofemoral joint
 xx Femur
  Ilium
Iliopsoas muscle
Ilium
 sa Iliofemoral joint
  Sacroiliac joint
 xx Pelvis
 — Fracture
Iliushin 62 (Jet transports)
 xx Jet transports
Illegal contracts (Direct)
 sa Immoral contracts
 x Contracts, Illegal
 xx Contracts
  Immoral contracts
  Nullity
Illegal contracts (Jewish law)
Illegal libraries (Direct)
 x Libraries, Illegal
 xx Libraries and state
  Library legislation
  Prohibited books
  Subversive activities
Illegal literature
 See Underground literature
Illegal strikes
 See Wildcat strikes
Illegality (Direct)
 sa Justification (Law)
 x Unlawfulness
 xx Criminal law
  Law
Illegitimacy (Direct) (HQ998-9; Statistics,
  HB903.I6)
 sa Acknowledgment of children
  Legitimation of children
  Paternity
  Unmarried fathers
  Unmarried mothers
 x Bastardy
  Legitimacy (Law)
 xx Children—Law
  Parent and child (Law)
  Paternity
  Sex and law
 — Personal narratives
Illegitimacy (Canon law)
Illegitimacy (Germanic law)
Illegitimacy (Islamic law) (Direct)
Illegitimacy (Jewish law)
 See Mamzer
Illegitimacy and crime (Direct)
 x Crime and illegitimacy
 xx Crime and criminals

Illegitimacy in literature
Illiac computer (QA76.8.I5; Engineering,
  TK7889.I5)
 x Illinois automatic computer
  MISTIC (Computer)
 xx Electronic digital computers
 — Programming (QA76.8.I5)
  sa IBAL (Computer program language)
Illiac III Basic Assembler Language
 See IBAL (Computer program language)
Illicit coining
 See Counterfeits and counterfeiting
Illicit distilling
 See Distilling, Illicit
Illinium
 See Promethium
Illinois
 — History (F536-550)
 — — To 1778
 — — 1778-1865
 — — War of 1812
 — — Black Hawk War, 1832
   See Black Hawk War, 1832
 — — Civil War, 1861-1865 (E505)
 — — 1865-
Illinois automatic computer
 See Illiac computer
Illinois Indians (E99.I2)
 xx Algonquian Indians
  Indians of North America
 — Land transfers (F542)
 — Missions (E99.I2)
  Example under Indians of North America
   —Missions
Illinois Institute of Technology translator
  (Computer program language)
 See IITRAN (Computer program language)
Illinois language (PM1371)
 sa Algonquian languages
 xx Algonquian languages
Illinois test of psycholinguistic abilities
 x ITPA
 xx Children—Language
  Handicapped children—Testing
  Language and languages—Ability
   testing
Illite (Indirect)
 xx Clay
  Mica
  Mineralogy
  Silicates
Illiteracy (Indirect) (LC149-160)
 sa Education and crime
  Elementary education of adults
  Libraries and new literates
  Mental tests for illiterates
  New literates, Writing for
  Right to Read program
 x Literacy
 xx Education
  Education and crime
 — Juvenile literature
Illlumination
 See Lighting
ILLOD-(NOR-B) (Computer program)
 xx Switching theory
Illuminati (HS142)
 sa Alumbrados
  Enlightenment
 xx Mysticism
Illuminating gas
 See Gas
Illumination (Buddhism)
 See Enlightenment (Buddhism)
Illumination of books and manuscripts
  (Direct) (ND2890-3416)
 sa Alphabets
  Hours, Books of

 Initials
 Miniature painting
 Missals
 Paleography
 x Manuscripts, Illuminated
  Miniatures (Illumination of books and
   manuscripts)
  Ornamental alphabets
 xx Alphabets
  Art
  Art, Medieval
  Arts and crafts movement
  Books
  Christian art and symbolism
  Decoration and ornament
  Design, Decorative
  Illustration of books
  Initials
  Manuscripts
  Missals
  Painting
  Paleography
 — Catalogs (ND2895-9)
 — Collectors and collecting (Direct)
 — Exhibitions (ND2893)
  sa Bibliographical exhibitions
  xx Bibliographical exhibitions
 — Specimens, reproductions, etc.
  (ND3345-3399)
  xx Illustrated books
**Illumination of books and manuscripts,
  Ancient**
**Illumination of books and manuscripts,
  Byzantine** (Direct)
 x Byzantine illumination of books and
  manuscripts
**Illumination of books and manuscripts,
  Carlovingian** (Direct)
 x Carlovingian illumination of books and
  manuscripts
**Illumination of books and manuscripts,
  Cistercian** (Direct)
 x Cistercian illumination of books and
  manuscripts
**Illumination of books and manuscripts,
  English, ⌐German, Spanish, etc.¬**
  (Direct)
 x English ⌐German, Spanish, etc.¬
  illumination of books and
  manuscripts
**Illumination of books and manuscripts,
  Georgian** (Direct)
 x Georgian illumination of books and
  manuscripts
Illumination of books and manuscripts, Gothic
  (Direct)
 x Gothic illumination of books and
  manuscripts
Illumination of books and manuscripts, Hebrew
 See Illumination of books and manuscripts,
  Jewish
**Illumination of books and manuscripts,
  Islamic** (ND2955)
 x Illumination of books and manuscripts,
  Muslim
  Islamic illumination of books and
  manuscripts
  Muslim illumination of books and
  manuscripts
Illumination of books and manuscripts, Jewish
  (Direct)
 x Hebrew illumination of books and
  manuscripts
  Illumination of books and manuscripts,
  Hebrew
  Jewish illumination of books and
  manuscripts

Illumination of books and manuscripts,
   Medieval *(Direct)*
Illumination of books and manuscripts, Mogul
   (Direct)
   x Mogul illumination of books and
      manuscripts
Illumination of books and manuscripts, Muslim
   See Illumination of books and manuscripts,
      Islamic
Illumination of books and manuscripts,
   Norman *(Direct)*
   x Norman illumination of books and
      manuscripts
Illumination of books and manuscripts,
   Oriental
   x Oriental illumination of books and
      manuscripts
Illumination of books and manuscripts,
   Ottonian *(Direct)*
   x Ottonian illumination of books and
      manuscripts
Illumination of books and manuscripts,
   Renaissance
   x Renaissance illumination of books and
      manuscripts
Illumination of books and manuscripts,
   Romanesque *(Direct)*
   x Romanesque illumination of books and
      manuscripts
— Byzantine [etc.] influences
Illusions
   See Hallucinations and illusions
Illusions, Optical
   See Optical illusions
Illustrated books *(Z1023)*
   sa Emblem books
      Hours, Books of
      Illumination of books and manuscripts
         —Specimens, reproductions, etc.
      Toy and movable books
   x Books, Illustrated
   xx Engravings
      Illustration of books
— 15th and 16th centuries
— 17th century
— 18th century
— 19th century
— 20th century

      GENERAL SUBDIVISIONS

— Extra-illustrated
   x Extra-illustrated books
      Grangerism
   xx Bibliography—Rare books
      Privately printed books

      GENERAL SUBDIVISIONS

— Facsimiles
Illustrated books, Children's
   sa Caldecott medal books
      Picture-books for children
      Toy and movable books
   x Children's books
      Children's illustrated books
      Illustrated children's books
   xx Children's literature
      Children's paraphernalia
      Picture-books for children
Illustrated children's books
   See Illustrated books, Children's
Illustrated periodicals
   sa Newspapers—Illustrations
   x Magazine illustration
      Periodicals, Illustrated
      Periodicals—Illustrations
   xx Journalism, Pictorial
      Newspapers—Illustrations
      Photography, Journalistic

Illustration, Biological
   See Biological illustration
Illustration, Botanical
   See Botanical illustration
Illustration, Medical
   See Medical illustration
Illustration, Scientific
   See Scientific illustration
Illustration, Technical
   See Technical illustration
Illustration, Zoological
   See Zoological illustration
Illustration of books *(Direct) (NC960-996;*
   By country, NC975-995)
   sa Archaeological illustration
      Caricature
      Drawing
      Engraving
      Illumination of books and manuscripts
      Illustrated books
      Photomechanical processes
      Scientific illustration
      Technical illustration
      subdivision Illustrations *under specific*
         subjects, individual authors and
         literatures, e.g. Beatitudes—
         Illustrations; Shakespeare, William,
         1564-1616—Illustrations; Lithuanian
         literature—Illustrations
   x Book illustration
      Books, Illustrated
   xx Art
      Art, Decorative
      Books
      Decoration and ornament
      Drawing
— Exhibitions *(NC15)*
   sa Bibliographical exhibitions
      Book industries and trade—
         Exhibitions
   xx Bibliographical exhibitions
      Book industries and trade—
         Exhibitions
— Subjects
   See Illustration of books—Themes,
      motives
— Themes, motives
   x Illustration of books—Subjects
Illustrations, Homiletical
   See Homiletical illustrations
Illustrations, Humorous
   See Caricatures and cartoons
      Wit and humor, Pictorial
Illustrators *(Direct) (NC)*
   sa Pen drawing
   xx Artists
— Interviews
Illyrian antiquities
   x Antiquities, Illyrian
      Illyrians—Antiquities
   xx Antiquities
Illyrian language (Slavic)
   See Serbo-Croatian language
Illyrian languages *(PA2393)*
   sa Messapian language
Illyrian movement
   See Illyrism
Illyrian wars *(DG246)*
   xx Rome—History—Republic, 265-30 B.C.
Illyrians *(D90.I3)*
— Antiquities
   See Illyrian antiquities
Illyrism *(DB370.5)*
   x Illyrian movement
   xx Languages—Political aspects
      Panslavism
Ilmenite *(Indirect)*
   x Geikielite

      Menacantite
      Menaccanite
      Menachanite
      Titanic iron ore
   xx Gems
      Iron ores
      Titanium ores
Ilmorna language
   See Galla language
Ilocano language
   See Iloko language
Ilocanos
   See Ilokanos
Iloco language
   See Iloko language
Ilokanos *(DS666.I6)*
   x Ilocanos
Iloko fiction *(Direct)*
Iloko language *(PL5751-4)*
   sa Nabaloi dialect
   x Ilocano language
      Iloco language
   xx Philippine languages
Iloko literature *(PL5751)*
Ilomba *(SD397.14)*
   x Akomu
      Boxboard (Tree)
      Cardboard (Tree)
Ilongot (Philippine tribe) *(DS666.I4)*
ILS
   See Instrument landing systems
Ilumbu language
   See Lumbu language (Gabon)
Image, Body
   See Body image
Image (Theology)
   sa Image of God
   xx Christian art and symbolism
      Communication (Theology)
Image converters *(TK7872.I6)*
   x Electron image converter tubes
      Image tubes
   xx Electron optics
      Electron tubes
      Image intensifiers
      Photoelectronic devices
Image furnaces
   x Arc image furnaces
      Optical furnaces
   xx Furnaces
Image iconoscope *(TR882)*
   x Television pick-up tubes
   xx Cathode ray tubes
      Electron optics
      Image intensifiers
      Television camera tubes
      Television cameras
Image intensifiers
   sa Electron microscope
      Electronography
      Image converters
      Image iconoscope
      Television camera tubes
      Television picture tubes
   xx Electroluminescence
      Electron optics
      Electron tubes
      Electronography
      Information display systems
      Phosphorescence
      Photoelectronic devices
Image of God
   x God—Image
      God, Image of
   xx God
      Image (Theology)
      Man (Theology)
— Early works to 1900

— History of doctrines
Image quality in radiography
   See Radiography—Image quality
Image tubes
   See Image converters
Imagery, Eidetic
   See Eidetic imagery
Imagery (Psychology) *(BF367)*
   sa After-images
      Eidetic imagery
      Figural aftereffects
   x Images, Mental
      Mental images
   xx Imagination
Images, Mental
   See Imagery (Psychology)
Images and idols
   See Idols and images
Imaginal buds
   See Imaginal disks
Imaginal cells
   See Imaginal disks
Imaginal disks *(QL494.5)*
   x Cells, Imaginal
      Disks, Imaginal
      Imaginal buds
      Imaginal cells
   xx Insects—Metamorphosis
      Larvae—Insects
Imaginary animals
   See Animal lore
      Animals, Mythical
Imaginary battles
   See Imaginary wars and battles
Imaginary book-plates
   See Book-plates, Imaginary
Imaginary books and libraries *(Z1024)*
   sa Imprints (in books), Fictitious
      Literary forgeries and mystifications
   x Books, Imaginary
      Fictitious titles of books
      Imaginary libraries
      Libraries, Imaginary
   xx Anonyms and pseudonyms
      Bibliography
      Imprints (in books), Fictitious
      Literary forgeries and mystifications
Imaginary cities
   See Geographical myths
Imaginary conversations
   xx Conversation
      Dialogues
Imaginary forensic orations
   See Forensic orations, Imaginary
Imaginary imprints
   See Imprints (in books), Fictitious
Imaginary islands
   See Geographical myths
Imaginary letters
   sa Heroid
Imaginary libraries
   See Imaginary books and libraries
Imaginary quantities
   See Numbers, Complex
Imaginary revolutions
   x Revolutions, Imaginary
   xx Imaginary wars and battles
      Revolutions
Imaginary societies
   x Fictitious societies
      Societies, Imaginary
   xx Societies
Imaginary travels
   See Voyages, Imaginary
Imaginary voyages
   See Voyages, Imaginary

Imaginary wars and battles *(U313; Military situation in special countries, UA; Naval, V253; Peace literature, JX1964; World politics, D445)*
   sa Imaginary revolutions
      Prophecies
   x Imaginary battles
      Wars and battles, Imaginary
   xx Battles
      Military art and science
      Naval art and science
      War
Imagination *(BF408; Artistic, N61-79)*
   sa Creation (Literary, artistic, etc.)
      Creative ability
      Fantasy
      Imagery (Psychology)
      Originality
      Originality (in literature)
      Reproduction (Psychology)
   xx Educational psychology
      Intellect
      Psychology
      Reproduction (Psychology)
   — Juvenile literature
Imagism
   See Imagist poetry
Imagist poetry
   sa Free verse
   x Imagism
   xx Free verse
      Poetry
Imamate *(BP166.94)*
   sa Imams
   xx Islam
Imamites
   See Shiites
Imams
   sa Hadith (Shiites)
   xx Imamate
   — Hadith
      See Hadith (Shiites)
   — Traditions
      See Hadith (Shiites)
Imams as teachers
   xx Teachers
Imari porcelain *(NK4399.I4)*
   x Porcelain, Imari
   xx Arita porcelain
Imbecility
   See Mentally handicapped
Imbeddings, Topological
   See Topological imbeddings
Imbeddings (Mathematics)
   See Embeddings (Mathematics)
Imerina dialect
   See Merina dialect
Imidoesters *(QD305.I6)*
Imitation *(BF357)*
   sa Example
      Influence (Psychology)
   xx Influence (Psychology)
      Psychology
Imitation (in art)
   xx Art
      Pictures—Copying
Imitation (in literature) *(PN166)*
   sa Originality (in literature)
      Plagiarism
   xx Authorship
      Literature
      Originality (in literature)
      Parody
      Plagiarism
      Quotation
Imitation (in music) *(ML430)*
   x Music, Imitation in
   xx Composition (Music)

Imitation of Jesus Christ
   See Jesus Christ—Example
Imitation wood
   See Simulated wood
Imjin-gang, Battle of, 1951
   xx Korean War, 1950-1953
Immaculate Conception *(BT620)*
   sa Mary, Virgin
      Virgin birth
   xx Virgin birth
   — Art
      See Mary, Virgin—Art
   — Early works to 1800
   — History of doctrines
   — Sermons
      x Immaculate Conception, Feast of the
         —Sermons
Immaculate Conception, Feast of the *(BV50.I6)*
   x Feast of the Immaculate Conception
   xx Church year
      Fasts and feasts
   Example under Mary, Virgin—Feasts
   — Sermons
      See Immaculate Conception—Sermons
Immaculate Heart of Mary
   See Sacred Heart of Mary, Devotion to
Immanence (Philosophy)
   xx Consciousness
      Experience
      Idealism
      Knowledge, Theory of
      Metaphysics
      Transcendentalism
Immanence of God *(BT124)*
   sa Jesus Christ—Mystical body
      Mystical union
      Mysticism
      Transcendence of God
   x Divine immanence
      God—Immanence
      God, Immanence of
   xx Mysticism
      Pantheism
      Transcendentalism
Immediate memory
   See Short-term memory
Immemorial usage
   See Prescription (Law)
      Time immemorial (Law)
Immersion, Baptismal
   See Baptism
Immersion, Heat of
   See Heat of wetting
Immersion (Judaism)
   See Purity, Ritual (Judaism)
Immersion technique (Education)
   See Concentrated study
Immigrant in literature
   See Immigrants in literature
Immigrant labor
   See Alien labor
Immigrant remittances
   See Emigrant remittances
Immigrants
   See Emigration and immigration
      Immigrants in literature
      subdivision Emigration and immigration
         *under names of countries; and
         subdivision* Foreign population *under
         names of countries, cities, etc.*
Immigrants' children
   See Children of immigrants
Immigrants in literature
   x Immigrant in literature
      Immigrants
   xx Emigration and immigration

Immigrants' narratives
See United States—Emigration and
immigration—Personal narratives
Immigrants' reminiscences
See United States—Emigration and
immigration—Personal narratives
Immigration
See Emigration and immigration
Immigration law
See Emigration and immigration law
Immobilization of animals
See Animal immobilization
Immoral conditions (Law)   *(Direct)*
x Conditions, Immoral (Law)
xx Conditions (Law)
Immoral consideration
See Immoral contracts
Immoral contracts   *(Direct)*
sa Illegal contracts
Undue influence
Usury laws
x Contracts contra bonos mores
Contracts, Immoral
Immoral consideration
xx Contracts
Illegal contracts
Lesion (Law)
Undue influence
Immoral literature
See Literature, Immoral
Immortality   *(Comparative religion, BL530;*
Egyptian religion, BL2450.I5;
Theology, BT919-925)
sa Annihilationism
Future life
Tree of life
x Life after death
xx Eschatology
Future life
Soul
— Biblical teaching
— Comparative studies
— Controversial literature
— Early works to 1800
— History of doctrines
Example under Theology, Doctrinal—
History
— Sermons
Immortality, Conditional
See Annihilationism
Immortality (Buddhism)   *(BL1475.I5)*
xx Eschatology, Buddhist
Immortality (Judaism)   *(BM645.I5)*
xx Eschatology, Jewish
Immortality (Philosophy)   *(BD419-423)*
xx Philosophy
Immortelle
See Everlasting flowers
Immune complex diseases
sa Glomerulonephritis
Serum sickness
xx Immunopathology
Immune complexes
sa Complements (Immunity)
x Antibody-antigen complexes
Antigen-antibody complexes
xx Allergy
Cellular immunity
Complements (Immunity)
Immune serum globulin
See Immunoglobulins
Immune serums   *(RM279)*
x Antisera
xx Biological products
Immunology
Immunities and privileges
See Privileges and immunities

Immunities of foreign sovereigns
See Immunities of foreign states
Immunities of foreign states
sa Diplomatic privileges and immunities
Exterritoriality
Government vessels
x Immunities of foreign sovereigns
Jurisdictional immunities of foreign
states
Sovereign immunity (International law)
State immunities (International law)
xx Government liability (International law)
Jurisdiction (International law)
Privileges and immunities
Sovereignty
Immunity   *(QR181-5)*
sa Agglutination
Allergy
Anaphylaxis
Antigens and antibodies
B cells
Cellular immunity
Communicable diseases
Complements (Immunity)
Conglutination
Hemagglutinin
Hemolysis and hemolysins
Immunization
Immunochemistry
Inoculation
Serum
Serumtherapy
T cells
Toxins and antitoxins
Vaccination
subdivision Preventive inoculation
under names of certain diseases, e.g.
Plague—Preventive inoculation;
Typhoid fever—Preventive
inoculation
xx Bacteriology
Communicable diseases
Immunology
Inoculation
Medicine, Preventive
Pathology
Serumtherapy
Toxins and antitoxins
Vaccination
Immunity, Ecclesiastical
See Privileges and immunities, Ecclesiastical
Immunity, Parliamentary
See Legislative bodies—Privileges and
immunities
Immunity, Political
See Legislative bodies—Privileges and
immunities
Immunity (Canon law)
See Privileges and immunities, Ecclesiastical
Immunity (Exemption)
See Privileges and immunities
Immunity (Feudalism)   *(JC116.I3)*
xx Feudalism
Immunity (Plants)
See Plants—Disease and pest resistance
Immunity from self-incrimination
See Self-incrimination
Immunization   *(Indirect)*
Here are entered works on any process,
active or passive, that leads to in-
creased immunity. Works on active
immunization with a vaccine are en-
tered under Vaccination
xx Immunity
Note under Vaccination
Immunization centers
See Vaccination centers

Immunoassay
sa Radioimmunoassay
xx Antigens and antibodies—Analysis
Immunology
Immunochemistry
xx Biological chemistry
Chemistry
Immunity
— Laboratory manuals   *(QR183)*
— Technique
Immunocompetent cells
x Immunologically competent cells
xx Cells
Immunology
Immunodiffusion
xx Immunology
Immunoelectrophoresis
xx Electrophoresis
Immunohematology
Serum diagnosis
Immunofluorescence
sa Fluorescence microscopy
Fluorescent antibody technique
Fluorescent antigen technique
xx Antigens and antibodies
Fluorescence
Immunology—Technique
— Standards   *(Direct)*
Immunogenetics
sa Carcinoembryonic antigens
H-2 locus
Rheumatoid factor
xx Genetics
Immunology
Serology
Immunoglobulin A
xx Immunoglobulins
Immunoglobulin E
xx Immunoglobulins
Immunoglobulin G
xx Immunoglobulins
Immunoglobulin M   *(QR186.8.M2)*
x IgM
xx Immunoglobulins
Immunoglobulins
sa Antigens and antibodies
Immunoglobulin A
Immunoglobulin E
Immunoglobulin G
Immunoglobulin M
Macroglobulins
x Immune serum globulin
xx Antigens and antibodies
Gamma globulin
Plasma proteins
Immunohematology
sa Compatibility testing (Hematology)
Immunoelectrophoresis
xx Hematology
Immunology
— Examinations, questions, etc.
Immunological adjuvants
See Adjuvants, Immunological
Immunological deficiency syndromes
xx Immunopathology
Immunological diseases
See Immunopathology
Immunological disorders in children
See Pediatric immunopathology
Immunological phylogeny
See Immunotaxonomy
Immunological research   *(Indirect)*
x Immunology—Research
Research, Immunological
xx Research
Immunological taxonomy
See Immunotaxonomy

Immunological tolerance
- *sa* Antilymphocytic serum
  - Histocompatibility
  - Histocompatibility testing
  - Transplantation immunology
- *x* Tolerance, Immunological
- *xx* Histocompatibility
  - Immunology
  - Transplantation immunology
  - Transplantation of organs, tissues, etc.

Immunologically competent cells
- *See* Immunocompetent cells

Immunology
- *sa* Antigens and antibodies
  - Cellular immunity
  - Cellular recognition
  - Immune serums
  - Immunity
  - Immunoassay
  - Immunocompetent cells
  - Immunodiffusion
  - Immunogenetics
  - Immunohematology
  - Immunological tolerance
  - Immunopathology
  - Immunosuppressive agents
  - Immunotaxonomy
  - Phagocytosis
  - Phytohemagglutinins
  - Radiation immunology
  - Serology
  - Transplantation immunology
  - Veterinary immunology
  - *subdivision* Immunological aspects
    - *under diseases, e.g.* Cancer—
    - Immunological aspects
- *xx* Serology
- — Atlases
- — Examinations, questions, etc.
- — Laboratory manuals
- — Popular works
- — Programmed instruction
- — Research
  - *See* Immunological research
- — Standards
- — Technique
  - *sa* Immunofluorescence
    - Radioactive tracers in immunology

Immunopathology
- *sa* Agammaglobulinemia
  - Allergy
  - Autoimmune diseases
  - Immune complex diseases
  - Immunological deficiency syndromes
  - Mast cell disease
  - Pediatric immunopathology
- *x* Immunological diseases
- *xx* Immunology
  - Pathology
- — Atlases
- — Research *(Direct)*

Immunophylogeny
- *See* Immunotaxonomy

Immunosuppressive agents
- *xx* Chemotherapy
  - Immunology

Immunosympathectomy
- *xx* Sympathectomy

Immunotaxonomy *(QR185.153)*
- *x* Immunological phylogeny
  - Immunological taxonomy
  - Immunophylogeny
  - Taxonomy, Immunological
- *xx* Biology—Classification
  - Immunology
  - Phylogeny

Immunotherapy
- *sa* Serumtherapy

- *xx* Therapeutics

Imp automobile *(TL215.14)*
- *xx* Hillman automobile

Impact *(QA935; QC131)*
- *sa* Blast effect
  - Elasticity
  - Shock (Mechanics)
  - Splashes
  - Structural dynamics
- *xx* Blast effect
  - Materials—Dynamic testing
  - Shock (Mechanics)
- — Measurement
- — Physiological effect
  - *sa* Crash injuries
    - Falls (Accidents)

Impact, Ion
- *See* Ion bombardment

Impact limiter
- *See* Cushioning materials

Impact phenomena (Nuclear physics)
- *See* Collisions (Nuclear physics)

Impact tubes
- *See* Pitot tubes

Impassibility of God
- *See* Suffering of God

Impeachments *(Direct)* *(Executive, JF295;*
Procedure, JF475; States,
JK2700-9599; United States: Civil
service, JK751-2; Impeachable
offenses, JK446; Judiciary, JK1595;
Powers and procedure of Congress,
JK1079, JK1268; President,
JK593-5)
- *sa* Privileges and immunities
  - Recall
  - Trials (Impeachment)
- *xx* Administrative responsibility
  - Criminal justice, Administration of
  - Legislative bodies as courts
  - Political crimes and offenses
  - Privileges and immunities
  - Public administration

Impedance, Acoustic
- *See* Acoustic impedance

Impedance, Mechanical
- *See* Mechanical impedance

Impedance (Electricity)
- *sa* Electric resistance
  - Reactance (Electricity)
- *xx* Electric currents, Alternating
  - Electric resistance
  - Electricity
  - Reactance (Electricity)

Impedance plethysmography
- *x* Electric impedance plethysmography
- *xx* Electrophysiology
  - Plethysmography

Impediments (Canon law)
- *See* Impediments to marriage (Canon law)
  - Irregularities (Canon law)

Impediments to marriage *(Direct)*
- *sa* Abduction
  - Adoption
  - Adultery
  - Affinity (Law)
  - Age (Law)
  - Banns
  - Bigamy
  - Consanguinity
  - Marriage—Dispensations
  - Marriage with deceased wife's sister
- *x* Marriage—Impediments
- *xx* Marriage law

Impediments to marriage (Canon law)
- *sa* Marriage, Mixed
- *x* Impediments (Canon law)
- *xx* Marriage (Canon law)

Impediments to marriage (Canon law, Oriental)
- *xx* Canon law, Oriental

Impediments to marriage (Jewish law)

Impellers *(TJ267.16)*
- *x* Turbomachines—Impellers
  - Turbomachines—Rotors
- *xx* Turbomachines

Impennes
- *See* Penguins

Imperatives (Logic)
- *See* Commands (Logic)

Imperator (Roman title) *(DG83.5.16)*

Imperial cities (Holy Roman Empire)
- *x* Imperial towns
- *xx* Holy Roman Empire

Imperial federation *(JN276; History, DA18)*
- *sa* Commonwealth of Nations
- *x* Federation, Imperial
- *xx* Commonwealth of Nations
  - Federal government
  - Great Britain—Colonies
  - Imperialism
  - Persons (International law)

Imperial Poetry Contest (Japan)
- *See* Utakaihajime

Imperial preference

Imperial towns
- *See* Imperial cities (Holy Roman Empire)

Imperial Trans-Antarctic Expedition,
1914-1917 *(G850 1914)*

Imperialism *(Constitutional history: Great*
Britain, JN276; United States, E713,
JK304; Political theory, JC359)
- *sa* Caesarism
  - Chauvinism and jingoism
  - Drang nach Osten
  - Imperial federation
  - Militarism
  - *subdivision* Foreign relations *under*
    - *names of countries*
- *x* Colonialism
  - Expansion (United States politics)
- *xx* Caesarism
  - Chauvinism and jingoism
  - Militarism
  - Political science
- — Juvenile literature

Imperium (Roman law)
- *xx* Jurisdiction (Roman law)

Impermanence (Buddhism) *(BQ4261)*
- *x* Anicca (Buddhism)
  - Anitya (Buddhism)
- *xx* Buddhist doctrines

Impersonal judgment
- *See* Judgment (Logic)

Impersonating an officer *(Direct)*
- *xx* False personation

Impersonation
- *sa* False personation
  - Impersonators, Female
  - Impersonators, Male
  - Transvestism

Impersonation (Law)
- *See* False personation

Impersonation in literature

Impersonators, Female
- Here are entered works on men impersonating women. Works on women
  impersonating men are entered under
  the heading Impersonators, Male.
- Works on impersonation of the opposite
  sex as a manifestation of sexual perver-
  sion are entered under the heading
  Transvestism.
- *x* Female impersonators
- *xx* Acting
  - Actresses

Impersonators, Female *(Continued)*
>> Costume
>> Impersonation
Impersonators, Male
>> *Cf.* note under Impersonators, Female.
>> *x* Male impersonators
>> *xx* Acting
>> Actors
>> Costume
>> Impersonation
>> *Note under* Impersonators, Female
Impetigo *(RL283)*
>> *xx* Pyoderma
Imphal, Battle of, 1944
>> *xx* World War, 1939-1945—Campaigns—
>>> Burma
Imphee
>> *See* Sorgo
Implant dentures
>> *x* Dental implantation
>> Oral implantology
>> *xx* Prosthodontics
Implantation, Ion
>> *See* Ion implantation
Implantation of ovum
>> *See* Ovum implantation
Implanted cardiovascular instruments
>> *See* Cardiovascular instruments, Implanted
Implements, utensils, etc. *(Direct)*
>>> *(Primitive, GN446-7)*
>> *sa* Agricultural implements
>> Agricultural machinery
>> Bone implements
>> Handles
>> Kitchen utensils
>> Stone implements
>> Tools
>> *subdivision* Implements *under* Indians,
>>> Mound-builders, *and similar*
>>> *headings; and names of particular*
>>> *implements, utensils, etc., e.g.*
>>> Knives, Mortars, Scythes
>> *x* Gadgets
>> Household utensils
>> Utensils
>> Vessels (Utensils)
>> *xx* Furniture
>> Tools
>> — Collectors and collecting
>> — Juvenile literature
>> — Terminology
Impletol
>> *x* Procaine hydrochloride
>> *xx* Local anesthesia
>> Novocaine
Implicit functions
>> *See* Functions, Implicit
Implied powers (Constitutional law) *(Direct)*
>> *sa* Executive power
>> Judicial power
>> Legislative power
>> War and emergency powers
>> *xx* Constitutional law—Interpretation and
>>> construction
>> Executive power
>> Judicial power
>> Legislative power
Import and export controls
>> *See* Foreign trade regulation
Import controls
>> *See* Import quotas
>> Tariff
Import licenses
>> *See* Import quotas
Import quotas *(Direct)* *(HF1401-1650)*
>> *x* Import controls
>> Import licenses
>> Import restrictions

Quotas, Import
>> *xx* Commercial policy
>> Foreign trade regulation
>> Free trade and protection
Import restrictions
>> *See* Foreign trade regulation
>> Import quotas
Imported fire ant *(SB945.I4)*
>> *x* Fire ant, Imported
>> *xx* Ants
>> — Control *(Indirect)*
>>> *xx* Ant control
Imports
>> *See* Commerce
>> Tariff
Importunate widow (Parable)
>> *See* Unjust judge (Parable)
Imposition (Typography)
>> *See* Printing, Practical—Imposition, etc.
Imposition of hands *(Christian sacraments,*
>>> *BV873.L3; Jewish sacrifices, BM715)*
>> *x* Hands, Imposition of
>> Hands, Laying on of
>> Laying on of hands
>> *xx* Ordination
>> Rites and ceremonies
Impossibility of performance *(Direct)*
>> *sa* Accident (Casus fortuitus)
>> Rebus sic stantibus clause
>> Vis major (Civil law)
>> *x* Frustration of contracts
>> Supervening impossibility
>> *xx* Contracts
>> Discharge of contracts
>> Performance (Law)
>> Rebus sic stantibus clause
Impostors and imposture *(Direct)*
>>> *(CT9980-9981; Criminal,*
>>> *HV6751-6761)*
>> *sa* Fraud
>> Quacks and quackery
>> Swindlers and swindling
>> *x* Charlatans
>> Delusions
>> Hoaxes
>> Humbug
>> Pretenders
>> *xx* Crime and criminals
>> Fraud
>> Swindlers and swindling
Impotence *(RC889)*
>> *xx* Sexual disorders
Impotence (Canon law)
Impotence (Jewish law)
Impoundment of appropriated funds, Executive
>> *See* Executive impoundment of
>>> appropriated funds
Imprecation
>> *See* Blessing and cursing
Impregnation, Artificial
>> *See* Artificial insemination
Impresarios *(ML429)*
>> *sa* Concert agents
>> Theatrical agencies
>> *xx* Concert agents
>> Opera
Impression materials, Dental
>> *See* Dental impression materials
Impressionism *(Aesthetics, BH301.I6)*
>> *xx* Style, Literary
Impressionism (Art) *(Direct)* *(ND1265)*
>> *sa* Abstract impressionism
>> Neo-impressionism (Art)
>> Post-impressionism (Art)
>> *xx* Aesthetics
>> Art, Modern—19th century
>> Modernism (Art)
>> Painting

Post-impressionism (Art)
>> — Juvenile literature
Impressionism (Music) *(ML197)*
>> *x* Music, Impressionism in
>> *xx* Music
>> Music—History and criticism—20th
>>> century
>> Music—Philosophy and aesthetics
>> Style, Musical
Impressions in paste
>> *See* Prints in paste
Impressment *(War of 1812, E357.2-3)*
>> *sa* Shanghaiing
>> *x* Press-gangs
>> *xx* Naval history
>> Seamen
>> Ships—Manning
Imprinting (Psychology)
>> *xx* Birds—Behavior
>> Child study
>> Critical periods (Biology)
>> Education—Experimental methods
Imprints, Imaginary
>> *See* Imprints (in books), Fictitious
Imprints (in books) *(Z242.I3)*
>> *sa* Colophons
>> *x* Printers' imprints
>> Publishers' imprints
>> *xx* Book industries and trades
>> Books
>> Cataloging
>> Colophons
>> Printing—History
>> Title-page
Imprints (in books), Fictitious
>> *sa* Imaginary books and libraries
>> Literary forgeries and mystifications
>> *x* Imaginary imprints
>> Imprints, Imaginary
>> *xx* Anonyms and pseudonyms
>> Imaginary books and libraries
>> Literary forgeries and mystifications
Imprints (Publications)
>> *See* English imprints; French imprints; *and*
>>> *similar headings; and subdivision*
>>> Imprints *under names of countries,*
>>> *states, cities, etc., e.g.* United States
>>> —Imprints; Philadelphia—Imprints
Imprisonment *(Direct)*
>> *sa* Arrest
>> Debt, Imprisonment for
>> False imprisonment
>> Juvenile detention homes
>> Penal colonies
>> Preventive detention
>> Prisons
>> Reformatories
>> Workhouses
>> *xx* Corrections
>> Criminal justice, Administration of
>> Detention of persons
>> Prisons
>> Punishment
Imprisonment, False
>> *See* False imprisonment
Imprisonment for debt
>> *See* Debt, Imprisonment for
Impromptu speaking
>> *See* Extemporaneous speaking
Impromptu theater
>> *See* Improvisation (Acting)
Improper integrals
>> *See* Integrals, Improper
Impropriation
>> *See* Secularization
Improvements (Real property)
>> *See* Betterments

Improvisation (Acting) *(PN2071.I5)*
    sa Commedia dell'arte
     x Impromptu theater
       Theater, Impromptu
    xx Acting
       Commedia dell'arte

Improvisation (Music) *(MT68)*
    sa Chance composition
       Harmony, Keyboard
     x Extemporization (Music)
    xx Music
       Music—Performance

Impulse *(Instinct, BF695)*
    sa Inhibition
    xx Emotions
       Hallucinations and illusions
       Inhibition
       Instinct
       Psychology
       Will

Impurities (Technology)
    See Contamination (Technology)

In
    See Jen

In Coena Domini bulls
     x Bulls, In Coena Domini
       Coena Domini bulls
    xx Bulls, Papal
       Heresies and heretics
       Maundy Thursday

In convertendo (Music)
    See Psalms (Music)—126th Psalm

In exitu Israel (Music)
    See Psalms (Music)—114th Psalm

In-flight feeding (Space flight)
    See Menus for space flight

In forma pauperis *(Direct)*
    sa Appeals in forma pauperis
       Legal aid
       Public defenders
     x Forma pauperis
       Pauperis, In forma
       Poor persons procedure
    xx Costs (Law)
       Legal aid

In fraudem legis
    See Evasion (Law)

In-line data processing
    See On-line data processing

In nomine (Music)
    xx Harpsichord music—To 1800
       Masses—To 1800
       Viol music—To 1800

In-plant data collection systems, Automatic
    See Automatic data collection systems

In pleno parliamento (The phrase)
    xx Latin language—Terms and phrases

In rem actions
    See Actions in rem

In-service training
    See Employees, Training of
       subdivision In-service training *under*
         subjects, e.g. Librarians—In-service
         training; Teachers—In-service
         training

In te, Domine, speravi, non confundar in
    aeternum, in justitia tua libera me,
    Inclina (Music)
    See Psalms (Music)—31st Psalm

INAC (Computer)
    xx Electronic digital computers

Inarticulata, Fossil

Inaudible sound
    See Ultrasonics

Inauguration Day *(JK536-550)*
    sa Presidents—United States—
       Inauguration

       subdivision Inauguration *under names*
         of presidents
    xx Presidents—United States—
       Inauguration

Inboard-outboard engines
     x Inboard-outdrives
       Outboard drives
       Stern drives
       Transom drives
    xx Motor-boat engines
    — Maintenance and repair

Inboard-outdrives
    See Inboard-outboard engines

Inborn errors of metabolism
    See Metabolism, Inborn errors of

Inbreeding *(Animal breeding, SF105;*
    Inbreeding and degeneration,
    HV4981; Principles of breeding,
    S494)
    sa Breeding
       Consanguinity
       Miscegenation
    xx Breeding
       Consanguinity

Inca language
    See Kechua language

Inca law
    See Law, Inca

Inca music
    See Incas—Music

Incan language
    See Callahuaya language
       Kechua language

Incandescent electric lighting
    See Electric lighting, Incandescent

Incandescent gas-lighting *(TH7953-5)*
     x Incandescent mantles
    xx Gas-lighting
       Lighting
    — Fixtures *(TH7953-5)*
       xx Gas-fixtures

Incandescent lamps
    See Electric lamps, Incandescent

Incandescent lamps, Iodine
    See Iodine incandescent lamps

Incandescent lighting
    See Electric lighting, Incandescent

Incandescent mantles
    See Incandescent gas-lighting

Incantations *(Demonology, BF1558;*
    Folk-lore, GR540; Religious
    invocations, BL)
    sa Blessing and cursing
       Mantras
     x Spells
    xx Folk-lore
       Magic
       Occult sciences
       Superstition

Incantations, Aramaic, [Finnish, Latin, etc.]
     x Aramaic [Finnish, Latin, etc.]
       incantations

Incantations, Buddhist
    See Buddhist incantations

Incantations, Indian
     x Indian incantations
       Indians—Incantations
       Indians of North America—
         Incantations
    xx Folk-lore, Indian

Incapacity, Estimation of
    See Disability evaluation

Incapacity (Law)
    See Capacity and disability

Incardination (Canon law) *(BX1939.I44)*
    sa Excardination (Canon law)
    xx Benefices, Ecclesiastical (Canon law)
       Clergy (Canon law)

       Excardination (Canon law)
       Ordination (Canon law)

Incarnation *(BL510; Christology, BT220)*
    sa Theophanies
     x Jesus Christ—Incarnation
       Kenosis (Theology)
    xx Avatars
       Jesus Christ
       Theology, Doctrinal
       Theophanies
    — Early works to 1800
    — History of doctrines

Incas *(F3429; F3442)*
    sa Kechua Indians
       Peru—History—Insurrection of
         Tupac-Amaru, 1780-1781
       Peru—History—To 1548
       Yanaconas
    xx Indians of South America
    — Art *(F3429.3.A7)*
    — Comparative studies
    — Drama
    — Fiction
    — Juvenile literature
    — Languages
       sa Kechua language
    — Law
       See Law, Inca
    — Legends *(F3429.3.L)*
    — Music *(ML3575)*
      x Inca music
       Music, Inca
    — Religion and mythology *(F3429.3.R38)*

Incendiarism
    See Arson
       Pyromania

Incendiary bombs
     x Bombs, Incendiary
       Fire bombs
    xx Bombs
       Explosives, Military
       Fires
    Note under Bombs

Incense *(Christian worship, BV197.16)*
    xx Essences and essential oils
       Odors

Incense burners and containers *(Direct)*
    (NK6078)
     x Burners, Incense
       Incense containers
    xx Containers

Incense-burning parties, Japanese
    See Japanese incense ceremony

Incense cedar
     x California white cedar
       White cedar
    xx Cedar
    — Diseases and pests

Incense ceremonies, Japanese
    See Japanese incense ceremony

Incense containers
    See Incense burners and containers

Incense-smelling parties, Japanese
    See Japanese incense ceremony

Incentive (Psychology)
    sa Reinforcement (Psychology)
       Rewards and punishments in education
    xx Motivation (Psychology)

Incentives in education
    See Rewards and punishments in education

Incentives in industry *(Direct)*
    sa Bonus system
       Employee competitive behavior
       Employee ownership
       Performance awards
       Profit-sharing
       Rewards (Prizes, etc.)
       Wages

Incentives in industry (*Direct*)
(*Continued*)
   x Employee incentives
     Labor incentives
   xx Employee competitive behavior
     Employee morale
     Personnel management
  — Mathematical models
Incest (*Anthropology, GN480.3; Sociology,*
     HQ71)
   xx Consanguinity
     Crimes without victims
     Sex crimes
Incest in literature (*PN56.155*)
   xx Sex in literature
Incidental music
  See Music, Incidental
Incidental questions (Conflict of laws)
  See Preliminary questions (Conflict of laws)
Incineration (*Direct*)
  sa Cremation
     Incinerators
   xx Refuse and refuse disposal
  — Accounting
Incinerators
   x Destructors, Refuse
     Refuse destructors
     Refuse incinerators
   xx Incineration
     Smoke prevention
  — Corrosion
  — Mathematical models
Incipits
   xx Colophons
     Incunabula
     Manuscripts
     Titles of books
Incitement to war
  See Crimes against peace
Inclina Domine (Music)
  See Psalms (Music)—86th Psalm
Inclined passenger lifts
  See Elevators, Private residence
Inclined planes
  sa Wedges
   x Ramps
   xx Machinery
     Power transmission
  — Juvenile literature
Inclinometer (*Aeronautical instruments,*
     TL89)
   xx Aeronautical instruments
     Oil wells—Equipment and supplies
Inclosures (*Great Britain, HD594.6*)
  sa Waste lands
   x Enclosures
   xx Land tenure—Law
     Real property
Inclusion disease, Cytomegalic
  See Cytomegalic inclusion disease
Inclusions in granite
  See Granite—Inclusions
Inclusions in iron
  See Iron—Inclusions
Inclusions in steel
  See Steel—Inclusions
Income (*Direct*) (*Theory, HB601; National*
     income, HC)
  sa Capital
     Consumption (Economics)
     Discretionary income
     Distribution (Economic theory)
     Farm income
     Gross national product
     Guaranteed annual income
     Multiplier (Economics)
     National income
     Negative income tax
     Profit

     Purchasing power
     Retirement income
     Wages
   x Distribution of income
     Fortunes
     Income distribution
   xx Economics
     Finance
     Gross national product
     Profit
     Property
     Purchasing power
     Wealth
  — Accounting
    See Income accounting
  — Juvenile literature
  — Mathematical models
  — Programmed instruction
  — Public opinion
  — Statistical methods
  — Underdeveloped areas
    See Underdeveloped areas—Income
Income accounting
  sa National income—Accounting
   x Income—Accounting
   xx Accounting
Income distribution
  See income
Income forecasting
   x Forecasting, Income
   xx Economic forecasting
Income statements
  See Financial statements
Income tax (*Direct*) (*HJ4621-4831; United*
     States, HJ4651-5)
  sa Capital gains tax
     Copyright—Royalties—Taxation
     Damages—Taxation
     Deferred compensation—Taxation
     Dividends—Taxation
     Excess profits tax
     Interstate commerce—Taxation
     Non-wage payments—Taxation
     Old age pensions—Taxation
     Profit-sharing—Taxation
     Real property and taxation
     Rent—Taxation
     Tithes
     Undistributed profits tax
     Unjust enrichment tax
     Usufruct—Taxation
     Wages—Taxation
     Withholding tax
   x Direct taxation
     Personal income tax
     Taxation of income
   xx Internal revenue
     Taxation
     Taxation, Progressive
     Tithes
     Wages—Taxation
     Wealth
Example under Agriculture—Taxation
Note under Income tax, Municipal
  — Accounting
    Example under Tax accounting
  — Auditing
    See Tax auditing
  — Cases
  — — Digests
     See Income tax—Digests
  — Consolidated returns
     See Corporations—Taxation—
       Consolidated returns
  — Deductions
     Example under Tax deductions
  — — Charitable contributions

   x Charitable contributions as tax
     deductions
     Charities—Taxation
  — — Educational expenses
     See Income tax—Deductions—
       Expenses
  — — Expenses
    sa Expense accounts and taxation
     x Expenses as tax deductions
     Income tax—Deductions—
       Educational expenses
     Income tax—Deductions—
       Medical expenses
     Income tax—Deductions—Repairs
    xx Expense accounts
  — — Interest
     x Interest as tax deductions
  — — Losses
     x Business losses as tax deductions
     Carry-back of business losses
     Carry-over of business losses
     Losses as tax deductions
  — — Medical expenses
     See Income tax—Deductions—
       Expenses
  — — Political contributions
     x Political contributions as tax
       deductions
  — — Repairs
     See Income tax—Deductions—
       Expenses
  — — Taxes
     x Taxes as tax deductions
  — Digests
     x Income tax—Cases—Digests
  — Examinations, questions, etc.
     x Income tax—Law—Examinations,
       questions, etc.
  — Foreign income
    sa Corporations, Foreign—Taxation
     Investments, Foreign—Taxation
     Taxation, Double
     x Foreign income, Taxation of
     Taxation of foreign income
  — Joint returns (*Direct*)
     x Joint returns (Income tax)
    xx Husband and wife—Taxation
     Tax returns
  — Law
    sa Rewards (Prizes, etc.)—Taxation
     Scholarships—Taxation
     Single people—Taxation
  — — Examinations, questions, etc.
     See Income tax—Examinations,
       questions, etc.
  — Mathematical models
  — Public opinion
  — Rates and tables
  — Retirement contributions
     x Retirement contributions as tax
       deductions
  — Treaties
     See Taxation, Double—Treaties
  — Withholding
     See Withholding tax
Income tax, Municipal (*Direct*)
     Divided by country or state. Works on
     the income tax of a particular city are
     entered under the heading Income tax,
     divided by the name of the city.
   x City income tax
     Municipal income tax
   xx Local taxation
Incommunicants
  See Louisets
Incomparability of God
  See God—Incomparability

Incompatibility of offices *(Direct)*
  sa Conflict of interests (Public office)
  xx Conflict of interests (Public office)
    Constitutional law
    Separation of powers
Incompatibility of offices (Canon law)
Incompatibles (Pharmacy) *(RM143)*
  sa Medicines, Antagonism of
  xx Chemistry, Medical and pharmaceutical
    Medicines, Antagonism of
    Pharmacy
    Prescription writing
Incomplete books
  See Unfinished books
Incomplete man test
  See Gesell incomplete man test
Incomplete sentence test
  See Sentence completion test
Incomplete works of art
  See Unfinished works of art
Inconel
  xx Chromium-iron-nickel alloys
Inconfidencia mineira, 1789
  See Minas Gerais, Brazil—History—
    Revolution, 1789
Inconnu (Fish) *(QL638.S2)*
Incontinence, Urinary stress
  See Urinary stress incontinence
Incorporated bar
  See Integrated bar
Incorporated farms
  See Farm corporations
Incorporation *(Direct)*
  sa Articles of incorporation
    Certificates of incorporation
    Charters
    De facto corporations
    Municipal incorporation
    Promoters
  x Federal incorporation
    Formation of corporations
  xx Corporation law
  — Popular works
Incorporation, Certificates of
  See Certificates of incorporation
Incorporation, Municipal
  See Municipal incorporation
Incorporation (Feudal law)
  xx Feudal law
Incorporeal property
  See Intangible property
Incorrigibles (Juvenile delinquency)
  xx Delinquents
    Juvenile delinquency
Incran language
  See Gã language
Increment, Unearned
  See Unearned increment
Incremental System Programming Language
    (Electronic computer system)
  See ISPL (Electronic computer system)
Incrustation removal
  See Descaling
Incrustations (Saline water conversion plants)
  See Saline water conversion plants—
    Incrustations
Incrustations (Steam-boilers)
  See Steam-boilers—Incrustations
Incrusted cameos
  See Sulphides (Art)
Incubation (in religion, folk-lore, etc.)
    (BL325.I5)
  x Folk-lore of incubation
  xx Faith-cure
    Medicine, Magic, mystic, and spagiric
    Religion, Primitive
    Revelation

Incubation of eggs
  See Eggs—Incubation
Incubators *(SF495-7)*
  sa Poultry houses and equipment
  x Brooders
  xx Eggs—Incubation
    Poultry houses and equipment
  — Catalogs *(SF497)*
Incubators (Pediatrics)
Incumbrances (Law)
  See Encumbrances (Law)
Incunabula *(Z240-241)*
  sa Bibliography—Rare books
    Block-books
    Colophons
    Incipits
    Printers' marks
    Printing—History
    Registers (in early printed books)
  x Bibliography—Early printed books—
      15th century
    Early printed books
  xx Bibliography
    Bibliography—Rare books
    Books—History—1400-1600
    Printing
    Printing—History
  — Bibliography *(Z240-241)*
  —— Catalogs *(Z240)*
  —— Union lists
  — Cataloging
    See Cataloging of incunabula
  — Facsimiles *(Z241)*
    xx Block-books—Facsimiles
      Printing—Specimens
    Example under Facsimiles
  — Music *(ML112)*
    x Music—Incunabula
Incurable diseases
  x Diseases, Incurable
  — Psychological aspects
Incurables
  — Hospitals and asylums *(HV3000-3003)*
    xx Asylums
      Charities, Medical
      Hospitals
      Sick
Indecent assault *(Direct)*
  x Indecent liberties
  xx Assault and battery
    Sex crimes
Indecent exposure *(Direct)*
  x Exposure of person
  xx Exhibitionism
    Sex crimes
  Note under Exhibitionism
Indecent liberties
  See Indecent assault
Indeclinable words
  See subdivision Indeclinable words *under
    individual languages or groups of
    languages, e.g.* Aryan languages—
    Indeclinable words
Indefinite sentence
  See Indeterminate sentence
Indemnification claims (1933-   )
  See Restitution and indemnification claims
    (1933-   )
Indemnity *(JX5326)*
  sa Alien property—Valuation
    Reparations
    Requisitions, Military
  xx Compensation (Law)
    Damages
    International law
Indemnity against liability *(Direct)*
  sa Insurance, Liability
  x Hold harmless agreements

  xx Conditions (Law)
    Insurance, Liability
    Liability (Law)
Indemnity insurance
  See Insurance, Liability
Indene resins *(TP1180.I5)*
  xx Gums and resins, Synthetic
Indentured servants *(HD4871-5; United
    States, HD4875.U5)*
  x Servants, Indentured
  xx Contract labor
    Redemptioners
    Slave labor
Indentures
  See Deeds
    Trust indentures
Independence
  See Autonomy
Independence (Mathematics)
  xx Logic, Symbolic and mathematical
Independence Day (Costa Rica)
Independence Day (India)
Independence Day (Israel)
Independence Day (Philippine Islands)
  x Philippine Independence Day
Independence Day (United States)
  See Fourth of July
Independency (Church polity)
  See Congregationalism
Independent administrative agencies
  See Independent regulatory commissions
Independent agencies
  See Independent regulatory commissions
Independent churches *(Direct)*
  sa Community churches
    Non-institutional churches
  x Churches, Nondenominational
    Churches, Undenominational
    Nondenominational churches
    Undenominational churches
  xx Community churches
    Sects
Independent contractors *(Direct)*
  sa Agency (Law)
    Contracts for work and labor
    Employers' liability
    Hire
    Labor contract
    Liability (Law)
    Master and servant
  x Contractors, Independent
    Vicarious liability
  xx Agency (Law)
    Contracts for work and labor
    Employers' liability
    Hire
    Labor contract
    Liability (Law)
    Master and servant
Independent contractors (Roman law)
Independent Labour Party (Gt. Brit.)
    (HD8395)
Independent ocean freight forwarders
  See Ocean freight forwarders
Independent Order of Odd-fellows
  See Odd-fellows, Independent Order of
Independent Party
  See National Greenback Party
Independent regulatory commissions *(Direct)*
  sa Public service commissions
  x Commissions, Independent regulatory
    Commissions of the federal government
    Independent administrative agencies
    Independent agencies
    Quasi-judicial agencies
    Regulatory commissions
  xx Administrative agencies
    Administrative law

Independent school trustees
  See Private school trustees
Independent schools
  See Private schools
Independent study (LB1049)
  x Study, Independent
  xx Study, Method of
    Tutors and tutoring
    Universities and colleges—Honors
      courses
Independent telephone companies
  See Telephone—United States
Independent treasury (United States,
      HG2535-9)
  x Subtreasury bill, 1840
    Subtreasury system
    Treasury, Independent
  — Caricatures and cartoons
  — Speeches in Congress (HG2539)
Independent unions (Direct)
  sa Company unions
  x Local independent unions
  xx Trade-unions
Indeterminancy principle
  See Heisenberg uncertainty principle
Indeterminate analysis
  See Diophantine analysis
Indeterminate sentence (Direct) (HV8715)
  sa Probation
  x Indefinite sentence
    Sentence, Indeterminate
  xx Criminal law
    Criminal procedure
    Judgments
    Judgments, Criminal
    Juvenile courts
    Prison sentences
    Probation
    Punishment
    Sentences (Criminal procedure)
Indeterminism
  See Free will and determinism
Index expurgatorius
  See Index librorum prohibitorum
Index librorum prohibitorum (Z1020)
  sa Censorship
  x Index expurgatorius
  xx Catholic Church—Bibliography
    Catholic Church—Discipline
    Catholic literature
    Censorship
    Condemned books
    Expurgated books
    Liberty of the press
    Prohibited books (Canon law)
Index maps
  sa subdivision Index maps under names of
      countries, regions, cities, etc.
  xx Maps
Index numbers (Economics) (HB225)
    Here are entered general works on the
    construction and use of index num-
    bers. Specific types or the index num-
    bers themselves are entered under
    their subjects.
  sa Price indexes
  x Numbers, Index
  xx Economics
    Prices
Index of refraction
  See Refractive index
Indexes (AI)
  sa Abstracting and indexing services
    Citation indexes
    Periodicals—Indexes
    Permutation indexes
    Reverse indexes
    Subject headings

  subdivision Indexes under specific
    subjects, e.g. Engineering—Indexes
  x Indices
  xx Bibliography
    Concordances
  — Evaluation
  — Prices
Indexes, Card
  See Card system in business
    Catalogs, Card
    Files and filing (Documents)
Indexing (Z695.9; Business filing and
    indexing, HF5735-5746)
  sa Automatic indexing
    Chain indexing
    Coordinate indexing
    Cross references (Cataloging)
    Files and filing (Documents)
    Municipal government—Records and
      correspondence—Indexing
    Punched card systems
    Subject cataloging
    Thesauri
  subdivision Abstracting and indexing
    under specific subjects, e.g.
    Chemistry—Abstracting and
    indexing
  xx Abstracting
    Bibliography
    Cataloging
    Documentation
    Files and filing (Documents)
    Thesauri
  — Programmed instruction
  — Standards
Indexing, Automatic
  See Automatic indexing
Indexing (Machine-shop practice) (TJ1167)
  xx Gages
    Gearing
    Machine-shop practice
    Machine-tools
Indexing and abstracting services
  See Abstracting and indexing services
Indexing vocabularies
  See Subject headings
    Thesauri
India
  — Climate
    Example under Tropics—Climate
  — Famines
    Example under Famines
  — History (DS401-498)
  — — To 324 B.C.
    sa Cheras
  — — — Juvenile literature
  — — 324 B.C.-1000 A.D.
    sa Chalukyas
      Chandela dynasty
      Cholas
      Gangas
      Gupta dynasty
      Gurjara-Protihara dynasty
      Indo-Scythians
      Kalabhras
      Kalinga, Battle of, 260 B.C.
      Maitrakas
      Pala dynasty
      Pallavas
      Pandyas
      Paramaras
      Rashtrakutas
      Satakani dynasty
      Vakataka dynasty
      Vellals
      Yadava dynasty
  — — — Juvenile literature
  — — 1000-1526

    sa Gangas
      Hoysala dynasty, ca. 1006-ca.
        1346
      Kakatiya dynasty
      Khilji dynasty
      Pala dynasty
      Pandyas
      Paramaras
      Sharqi dynasty
      Yadava dynasty
  — — 1000-1765
  — — 1500-1765
    sa Ahmadnagar (Kingdom)
      Marathas
      Mogul Empire
      Panipat, Battle of, 1526
      Panipat, Battle of, 1556
  — — 18th century
    sa Panipat, Battle of, 1761
      Plassey, Battle of, 1757
  — — British occupation, 1765-1947
    sa Chota Nagpur, India—History—
        Insurrection, 1831-1832
      Maratha War, 1775-1782
      Maratha War, 1803
      Maratha War, 1816-1818
      Nepalese War, 1814-1816
  — — — Juvenile literature
  — — Rohilla War, 1774
    See Rohilla War, 1774
  — — Mysore War, 1790-1792 (DS474.1)
    x Mysore War, 1790-1792
  — — Mysore War, 1799 (DS475.3)
    x Mysore War, 1799
  — — 19th century
    sa Wahhabi movement (India)
  — — Mutiny, 1809
  — — Burmese Wars, 1824-1852
    See Burmese War, 1824-1826
      Burmese War, 1852
  — — Afghan Wars, 1838-1919
    See Afghan Wars
  — — Sikh Wars, 1845-1849
    See Sikh War, 1845-1846
      Sikh War, 1848-1849
  — — Sepoy Rebellion, 1857-1858
    sa Arrah—Siege, 1857
      Delhi—Siege, 1857
      Kanpur—Siege, 1857
      Lucknow—Siege, 1857
    x Indian Mutiny, 1857-1858
      Sepoy Rebellion
  — — — Atrocities (DS478)
  — — — Personal narratives
  — — Sikkim Expedition, 1861
    See Sikkim Expedition, 1861
  — — Sikkim Expedition, 1888
    See Sikkim Expedition, 1888
  — — Chitral Campaign, 1895
  — — Tirah Campaign, 1897-1898
    x Tirah Campaign, 1897-1898
  — — 20th century
  — — — Anecdotes, facetiae, satire, etc.
  — — — Pictorial works
  — — Waziristan Campaign, 1919-1920
    x Waziristan Campaign, 1919-1920
  — — 1947-
    sa India-Pakistan Conflict, 1965
      India-Pakistan Conflict, 1971
      Refugees, East Indian
      Refugees, Pakistan
      Sino-Indian Border Dispute, 1957-
  — Kings and rulers
    x Maharajahs
  — Scheduled tribes
    sa Asurs
      Koras
      Untouchables

x Scheduled tribes (India)
xx Tribes and tribal system
Untouchables
India in literature
India ink *(TP948.I6)*
xx Ink
Water-color painting
India-Pakistan Conflict, 1965
x Indian-Pakistan Conflict, 1965
Indo-Pakistan Conflict, 1965
Pakistan-Indian Conflict, 1965
xx India—History—1947-
— Biography
— Caricatures
See India-Pakistan Conflict, 1965—
Humor, caricatures, etc.
— Humor, caricatures, etc.
x India-Pakistan Conflict, 1965—
Caricatures
— Pictorial works
— Public opinion *(Indirect)*
India-Pakistan Conflict, 1971-
sa Bangladesh—History—Revolution, 1971
x Indo-Pakistan Conflict, 1971-
Pakistan-Indian Conflict, 1971-
xx India—History—1947-
— Biography
— Diplomatic history
— Personal narratives
— Pictorial works
India rubber
See Rubber
India rubber industry
See Rubber industry and trade
Indian . . .
x Amerindian . . .
Indian appropriations
See Indians of North America—
Appropriations
Indian baskets
See Basketwork
subdivision Basket making *under*
Indians of North America; Indians
of South America; *and similar*
headings
Indian belts
See Wampum belts
Indian blankets
See Indians of North America [South
America, etc.]—Textile industry and
fabrics
Indians—Textile industry and fabrics
Indian buffalo
See Water buffalo
Indian captivities
See Indians of Central America—Captivities
Indians of North America—Captivities
Indians of South America—Captivities
Indian-Chinese Border Dispute, 1957-
See Sino-Indian Border Dispute, 1957-
Indian civilization
See Indians—Culture
Indian clubs *(Exercises, GV491-3)*
sa Callisthenics
xx Callisthenics
Gymnastics
Example under Physical education and training
Indian corn
See Maize
Indian-corn paper
See Paper, Maize
Indian drama *(Direct)*
xx Drama
Indian elephant
xx Elephants
— Behavior
— Juvenile literature
— Legends and stories

— Pictorial works
— — Juvenile literature
Indian ethics
See Indians of North America—Ethics
Indian folk-lore
See Folk-lore, Indian
Indian hospitals
See Indians of North America—Hospitals
Indian incantations
See Incantations, Indian
Indian languages
See Indians—Languages
Indians of Mexico [North America,
etc.]—Languages
Indian literature *(Direct)*
Here are entered collections in the lan-
guages of the American Indians. Col-
lections in a single language are en-
tered under their own heading, *e.g.*
Aztec literature.
x Indian literature (American Indian)
Indians—Literature
xx Literature
Note under Indian poetry
— United States
xx United States—Literatures
Indian literature (American Indian)
See Indian literature
Indian literature (Canadian)
See Canadian literature—Indian authors
Indian literature (East Indian)
See Indic literature
Indian literature (English)
See American literature—Indian authors
Indian meal
See Corn meal
Indian millet
See Durra
Indian music (American Indian)
See Indians—Music
Indian Mutiny, 1857-1858
See India—History—Sepoy Rebellion,
1857-1858
Indian mythology (American Indian)
See Indians—Religion and mythology
Indian-Negro relations
See Negro-Indian relations
Indian numeration
See Numeration, Indian
Indian occupation of Alcatraz Island, Calif.,
1969-1971
See Alcatraz Island, Calif.—History—Indian
occupation, 1969-1971
Indian orations
See Indians of North America—Oratory
Indian paint fungus
xx Wood-decaying fungi
Indian-Pakistan Conflict, 1965
See India-Pakistan Conflict, 1965
Indian poetry
Cf. note under Indian literature.
sa Cherokee poetry
Chippewa poetry
Dakota poetry
similar headings
xx Poetry
Indian ponies *(Animal culture, SF315;*
Indians of North America, E98.H55)
sa Appaloosa horse
x Indians of North America—Ponies
xx Indians of North America—Domestic
animals
Indians of North America—
Transportation
Mustang
Ponies
— Juvenile literature

Indian reservations
See Indians of North America—
Reservations
names of reservations, e.g. Shoshoni
Indian Reservation, Wyo.
Indian rice
See Wild rice
Indian rupee
See Rupee, Indian
Indian scholarships
See Indians of North America—
Scholarships, fellowships, etc.
Indian studies
See Indians—Study and teaching
Indian trade factories
See Indians of North America—Trading
posts
Indian trails *(Direct) (E98.T7)*
sa Portages
x Indians of North America—Trails
Trails, Indian
xx Portages
Roads
Trails
Indian warfare *(E98.W2; U240)*
Here are entered treatises on the Indian
method of fighting and instructions for
campaigns against the Indians. Works
on Indian wars are entered under Indi-
ans of Mexico [North America, South
America, etc.]—Wars and under
names of specific Indian wars.
sa Indians of North America as soldiers
Scalping
x Indians of North America—Military
capacity and organization
Warfare, Indian
xx Indians of North America—Wars
— Juvenile literature
Indiana
— History *(F521-535)*
— — To 1787
— — Revolution, 1775-1783
— — War of 1812
— — War with Mexico, 1845-1848
(E409.5.I7)
— — Civil War, 1861-1865 *(E506)*
— Tornado, 1965
Indianapolis
— Explosion, 1963
— Social conditions
Note under Social surveys
Indianists *(E57)*
xx Indians—Historiography
Indians *(E51-99)*
Here are entered works on the aboriginal
peoples of the Western Hemisphere,
including Eskimos.
For convenience, the Western Hemi-
sphere has been divided into five basic
geographical regions: North America,
Mexico, Central America, West Indies
and South America. Works pertaining
to Indian groups located within the
confines of one of these regions are
entered under Indians of the pertinent
region, *e.g.* Indians of North America,
Indians of Mexico.
Names of Indian linguistic families are
distinguished as such (and from the
names of single languages or tribes) by
the termination *an* or *ian*.
sa Paleo-Indians
x American aborigines
American Indians
Amerinds
Indians—Ethnology
Stone age—America

Indians *(E51-99) (Continued)*
   xx Man, Prehistoric—America
   Example under Ethnology; *and under reference from* Aborigines
   Note under Indians of North America
— Agriculture *(E59.A)*
— Antiquities *(E58; E59.A63; E61)*
   sa Indians—Pottery
      Man, Prehistoric—America
      Paleo-Indians
   xx America—Antiquities
      Archaeology
— — Juvenile literature
— Architecture *(E59.A67)*
   xx Architecture
— — Juvenile literature
— Arms and armor
   xx Arms and armor, Primitive
— Art *(E59.A7)*
   sa Indians—Metal-work
      Indians—Sculpture
   x Art, Indian
   xx Art, Primitive
— — Exhibitions
— Basket making
   xx Basket making
      Indians—Industries
— Biography
— Boats *(E59.C2)*
   xx Boats and boating
      Navigation, Primitive
— Calendar
— Cartography *(E59.C25)*
   xx Cartography, Primitive
— City planning
   xx Cities and towns—Planning
— Civilization
   See Indians—Culture
— Color *(E59.C)*
   xx Color of man
— Costume and adornment *(E98.C8)*
— Culture *(E59.C95)*
   x Civilization, American
      Civilization, Indian
      Civilization, Pre-Columbian
      Indian civilization
      Indians—Civilization
      Pre-Columbian civilization
— — Chinese influences
— — Hindu influences
— Diseases
— Dwellings *(E59.D9)*
   xx Dwellings
— Early works to 1800
— Economic conditions *(E59.E)*
— Education *(E57.E4)*
   Example under Education, Primitive
— Ethnology
   See Indians of North America;
      Indians of South America; *and*
      similar headings
— Folk-lore
   See Folk-lore, Indian
— Food *(E59.F)*
   Example under Food
— Games *(E59.G3)*
— Goldsmithing
   xx Goldsmithing
      Indians—Metal-work
— Government relations *(E59.G)*
   sa Indians, Treatment of
   xx Indians, Treatment of
— Historiography
   sa Indianists
— History *(E58)*
— — Juvenile literature
— Illustrations

   See Indians—Pictures, illustrations, etc.
— Implements *(E59.I4)*
   xx Industries, Primitive
— Incantations
   See Incantations, Indian
— Industries
   sa Indians—Basket making
      Indians—Metal-work
— Land tenure
   x Indians—Land titles
      Indians—Real property
   xx Land tenure
— Land titles
   See Indians—Land tenure
— Languages *(PM1-7356)*
   x Indian languages
— — Texts *(PM102)*
— Legal status, laws, etc.
   Here are entered works containing, or treating of legislation enacted by Western colonial powers or national governments, governing the status of, and relations to Indian tribes and individuals in general. Laws governing the Indians of individual regions or individual tribes are entered under pertinent headings followed by the subdivision Legal status, laws, etc., *e.g.* Indians of North America—Oklahoma—Legal status, laws, etc.; Cherokee Indians—Legal status, laws, etc. Works on the native law of Indian tribes are entered under a heading appropriate for the respective legal system, *e.g.* Law, Cheyenne.
   sa subdivision Legal status, laws, etc.
      under names of groups of Indians and names of individual Indian tribes, e.g. Indians of North America—Legal status, laws, etc.; Cherokee Indians—Legal status, laws, etc.
— Legends *(E59.F6)*
   sa Folk-lore, Indian
   x Legends, Indian
— Libraries
   See Libraries and Indians
— Literature
   See Indian literature
— Marriage customs and rites
   x Marriage customs and rites, Indian
   xx Indians—Social life and customs
— Mathematics
   See Mathematics, Indian
— Medicine
   sa Medicine-man
   xx Medicine, Primitive
— Metal-work
   sa Indians
      Indians—Goldsmithing
      Silversmithing
   xx Art metal-work
      Indians—Art
      Indians—Industries
      Metal-work
— Missions *(E59.M65)*
   x Missions, Indian
— Mixed bloods
   x Half-breed Indians
      Mixed bloods (American Indians)
   xx Miscegenation
— Money *(E59.M7)*
— Mortuary customs *(E59.M8)*
   x Mortuary customs
— Music *(E59.M9; ML3547)*
   x Indian music (American Indian)

      Music, Indian (American Indian)
      Music—Indians
      Musical instruments—Indians
   xx Music, Primitive
— Mythology
   See Indians—Religion and mythology
— Names *(E59.N)*
   Notes under Names, Anglo-Saxon, ₍Arabic, Celtic, etc.₎; Names, Geographical—Anglo-Saxon, ₍Celtic, Latin, etc.₎
— Numeration
   See Numeration, Indian
— Origin *(E61)*
   sa Indians—Transpacific influences
      Nephites
   x Indians of Mexico ₍North America, South America, etc.₎—Origin
— Physical characteristics *(E59.P53)*
— Picture-writing
   See Picture-writing, Indian
— Pictures, illustrations, etc.
   x Indians—Illustrations
      Indians in art
— Poetry *(E59.P7)*
   Here are entered collections of poetry about Indians. Collections of poetry written by Indians in Indian languages are entered under Indian poetry. Collections of poetry written by Indians are entered under American poetry—Indian authors; Mexican poetry—Indian authors; etc.
— Pottery *(E59.P8)*
   sa Plumbate ware
   xx Indians—Antiquities
      Pottery
      Pottery, Primitive
— Psychology
— Real property
   See Indians—Land tenure
— Relations with Negroes
   See Negro-Indian relations
— Religion and mythology *(E59.R38)*
   x Indian mythology (American Indian)
      Indians—Mythology
      Mythology, Indian (American Indian)
   xx Mythology
      Religion, Primitive
   Example under Religion
— Rites and ceremonies
   x Rites and ceremonies—Indians
— Sculpture
   x Indians—Stone-sculpture
   xx Indians—Art
      Sculpture
      Sculpture, Primitive
— Silversmithing
   xx Indians—Metal-work
      Silversmithing
— Social life and customs *(E59.S)*
   sa Indians—Marriage customs and rites
   x Customs, Social
      Social customs
   xx Manners and customs
      Society, Primitive
— Statistics *(E59.S7)*
— Stone-sculpture
   See Indians—Sculpture
— Study and teaching *(Direct)*
   x Indian studies
— — Audio-visual aids
— Textile industry and fabrics *(E59.T35)*
   x Indian blankets
   xx Weaving
— Transpacific influences

x Transpacific influences on Indians
xx America—Discovery and exploration
　　　—Pre-Columbian
　　Indians—Origin
　　Man—Migrations
— Transportation
— Treaties
　xx Treaties
— Writing *(E59.W9)*
　sa Picture-writing, Indian
　xx Alphabet
　　Picture-writing, Indian
　　Writing
Indians, East
　See East Indians
Indians, Treatment of
　sa Indians—Government relations
　　Indians of North America—
　　　Government relations
　xx Indians—Government relations
— Juvenile literature

GEOGRAPHIC SUBDIVISIONS

— Canada
　x Indians of North America—
　　Treatment
　　Indians of North America,
　　Treatment of
　xx Indians of North America—
　　Government relations

GEOGRAPHIC SUBDIVISIONS

— Latin America
　sa Encomiendas (Latin America)

GEOGRAPHIC SUBDIVISIONS

— Mexico
　sa Indians of Mexico—Government
　　relations
　　Indians of Mexico—Taxation
　xx Indians of Mexico—Government
　　relations

GEOGRAPHIC SUBDIVISIONS

— United States
　sa Indians of North America—
　　Government relations
　x Indians of North America—
　　Treatment
　　Indians of North America,
　　Treatment of
　xx Indians of North America—
　　Government relations
Indians and libraries
　See Libraries and Indians
Indians in art
　See subdivision Pictures, illustrations, etc.
　　under Indians; Indians of Central
　　America; Indians of North America;
　　and similar headings
Indians in literature *(PN56.I; American
　　literature, PS173.I6)*
　xx Indians of North America—Poetry
Indians in motion pictures
　xx Moving pictures
Indians of Canada
　See Indians of North America—Canada
Indians of Central America *(F1434-5)*
　Subdivided by countries or regions, *e.g.*
　　Indians of Central America—
　　Guatemala; Indians of Central
　　America—Mosquitia.
　sa Black Carib Indians
　　Boruca Indians
　　Bribri Indians
　　Cakchikel Indians
　　Carib Indians
　　Choco Indians

Chorti Indians
Cuna Indians
Guarani Indians
Guaymi Indians
Guetar Indians
Ixil Indians
Jacalteca Indians
Kekchi Indians
Lacandon Indians
Mam Indians
Mangue Indians
Mayas
Mosquito Indians
Nicarao Indians
Otomi Indians
Paya Indians
Pipil Indians
Pokomam Indians
Pokonchi Indians
Quichés
Sumu Indians
Talamanca Indians
Terraba Indians
Tzeltal Indians
Xicaque Indians
Xinca Indians
x Indians of Central America—Ethnology
— Agriculture
　xx Agriculture, Primitive
— Amusements
　See Indians of Central America—
　　Games
　　Indians of Central America—
　　Social life and customs
— Anthropometry *(F1434.A55; F1434.2.A)*
— Antiquities *(F1434)*
　sa Indians of Central America—Pottery
— Architecture *(F1434.2.A)*
　sa Indians of Central America—
　　Dwellings
— Art *(F1434.2.A)*
　sa Indians of Central America—
　　Goldsmithing
　　Indians of Central America—
　　Metal-work
　　Indians of Central America—
　　Sculpture
　　Indians of Central America—
　　Wood-carving
　　Mayas—Art
　x Art, Indian
— Astronomy
　x Astronomy, Central American
　　Indian
　　Astronomy, Maya
　xx Astronomy
— Boats
　xx Boats and boating
　　Canoes and canoeing
　　Indians of Central America—
　　Transportation
　　Navigation, Primitive
— Captivities
　x Indian captivities
— Children
　xx Children
— Commerce
　sa Indians of Central America—Trading
　　posts
　xx Commerce
— Costume and adornment *(F1434.2.C)*
— Culture
　sa Indians of Central America—Social
　　life and customs
— Customs
　See Indians of Central America—
　　Social life and customs
— Dances

　sa Moros y Cristianos (Dance)
　xx Dancing (in religion, folk-lore, etc.)
　　Indians of Central America—
　　Religion and mythology
　　Indians of Central America—Social
　　life and customs
— Dwellings
　xx Dwellings
　　Indians of Central America—
　　Architecture
— Economic conditions
— Ethnology
　See Ethnology—Central America
　　Indians of Central America
— Games
　x Indians of Central America—
　　Amusements
　　Indians of Central America—
　　Recreations
　　Indians of Central America—Sports
　xx Games, Primitive
　　Indians of Central America—Social
　　life and customs
— Goldsmithing
　xx Indians of Central America—Art
— Health and hygiene *(Direct)*
　xx Medical anthropology
— Hunting
　xx Hunting, Primitive
— Illustrations
　See Indians of Central America—
　　Pictures, illustrations, etc.
— Industries
　sa Indians of Central America—
　　Metal-work
　　Indians of Central America—Paper
　　making and trade
— Labor service
　xx Labor service
— Languages *(PM3001-4566)*
　sa Boruca language
　　Bribri dialect
　　Cakchikel language
　　Chorti language
　　Doraskean languages
　　Guaymi language
　　Ixil language
　　Jacalteca language
　　Kekchi language
　　Lenca language
　　Maya language
　　Mayan languages
　　Mosquito language
　　Otomi language
　　Pipil language
　　Pokomam language
　　Pokonchi language
　　Quiché language
　　Quichean languages
　　Talamanca language
　　Terraba language
　　Tlascalteca language
　　Xinca language
— Legal status, laws, etc.
— Legends *(F1434.2.F6; Mayas,
　　F1435.3.F6)*
— Magic
　x Magic, Indian
　xx Indians of Central America—
　　Religion and mythology
— Marriage customs and rites
　xx Indians of Central America—Social
　　life and customs
　　Marriage customs and rites
— Masks
　xx Masks
— Metal-work *(F1434.2.M4)*
　xx Art metal-work

Indians of Central America (F1434-5)
— Metal-work (F1434.2.M4)
(Continued)
    Indians of Central America—Art
    Indians of Central America—
       Industries
    Metal-work
— Missions (F1434.2.M6)
— Mixed bloods
   sa Black Carib Indians
— Mortuary customs
— Music (ML3572)
— Names
   x Names, Geographical—Indian
   Names, Indian
    Notes under Names, Anglo-Saxon,
      [Arabic, Celtic, etc.]; Names, Geo-
      graphical—Anglo-Saxon, [Celtic,
      Latin, etc.]
— Paper making and trade
   xx Indians of Central America—
      Industries
— Pictures, illustrations, etc.
   x Indians in art
   Indians of Central America—
      Illustrations
— Pottery (F1434.2.P6)
   sa Plumbate ware
   xx Indians of Central America—
      Antiquities
— Recreations
    See Indians of Central America—
      Games
— Religion and mythology (F1434.2.R3)
   sa Indians of Central America—Dances
   Indians of Central America—Magic
— Rites and ceremonies
   x Rites and ceremonies—Indians
— Sculpture
   x Indians of Central America—
      Stone-sculpture
   xx Indians of Central America—Art
   Sculpture
   Sculpture, Primitive
— Social life and customs
   sa Indians of Central America—Dances
   Indians of Central America—Games
   Indians of Central America—
      Marriage customs and rites
   x Indians of Central America—
      Amusements
   Indians of Central America—
      Customs
   xx Indians of Central America—Culture
— Sports
    See Indians of Central America—
      Games
— Stone-sculpture
    See Indians of Central America—
      Sculpture
— Textile industry and fabrics
   x Indians of Central America—
      Weaving
   xx Textile industry and fabrics
— Trading posts
   x Trading posts (Central American
      Indian)
   xx Indians of Central America—
      Commerce
— Transportation
   sa Indians of Central America—Boats
— Weaving
    See Indians of Central America—
      Textile industry and fabrics
— Women
   xx Woman—History and condition of
      women
— Wood-carving
   xx Indians of Central America—Art

— Wood-carving
— Writing
   sa Mayas—Writing
Indians of Mexico (F1219-1220)
   Subdivided by states, e.g. Indians of Mex-
      ico—Yucatan.
   sa Acaxee Indians
   Akwa'ala Indians
   Azteco-Tanoan Indians
   Aztecs
   Basket-Maker Indians
   Cahita Indians
   Cazcan Indians
   Chiapanec Indians
   Chichimeca-Jonaz Indians
   Chichimecs
   Chinantec Indians
   Chontal Indians
   Cocopa Indians
   Cora Indians
   Guachichile Indians
   Huastec Indians
   Huave Indians
   Huichol Indians
   Kickapoo Indians
   Lacandon Indians
   Mam Indians
   Matlatzinca Indians
   Mayas
   Mayo Indians
   Mazahua Indians
   Mazatec Indians
   Mixe Indians
   Mixtec Indians
   Nahuas
   Olmecs
   Opata Indians
   Otomi Indians
   Pame Indians
   Papago Indians
   Pipil Indians
   Popoloca Indians
   Popoluca Indians (Vera Cruz)
   Seri Indians
   Tarahumare Indians
   Tarasco Indians
   Teco Indians
   Tepanecas
   Tepehua Indians
   Tepehuane Indians
   Tezcucan Indians
   Tlahuica Indians
   Tlascalan Indians
   Toltecs
   Totonacos
   Trique Indians
   Tzeltal Indians
   Tzotzil Indians
   Uto-Aztecan Indians
   Yaqui Indians
   Zacateca Indians
   Zapotec Indians
   Zoque Indians
   x Indians of Mexico—Ethnology
   Note under Indians
— Agriculture (F1219.3.A)
— Amusements
    See Indians of Mexico—Games
— Anthropometry (F1219.3.A)
— Antiquities (F1219)
   sa Indians of Mexico—Implements
   Indians of Mexico—Pottery
   Indians of Mexico—Pyramids
   Indians of Mexico—Seals
      (Numismatics)
— Architecture (F1219.3.A6)
   x Architecture, Aztec
   Aztec architecture

— Arms and armor (F1219.3.A)
   sa Throwing-sticks
— Art (F1219.3.A7)
   sa Indians of Mexico—Bone carving
   Indians of Mexico—Metal-work
   Indians of Mexico—Sculpture
   Indians of Mexico—Wood-carving
   Tarasco Indians—Art
   subdivision Art under names of
      tribes
   x Art, Indian
— Astronomy
   x Astronomy, Maya
   Astronomy, Mexican Indian
   xx Astronomy
— Biography
— Bone carving
   xx Bone carving
   Indians of Mexico—Art
— Children
   xx Children
— Commerce
— Costume and adornment (F1219.3.C)
— Craniology (F1219.3.C8)
— Culture (F1219-1220)
— Dances (F1219.3.D2)
   sa Moros y Cristianos (Dance)
— Dentistry
   xx Dentistry
   Indians of Mexico—Medicine
— Diseases
   xx Indians of Mexico—Health and
      hygiene
— Education (Direct)
   x Indians of Mexico—Schools
— Ethnology
    See Ethnology—Mexico
    Indians of Mexico
— Fishing
— Folk-lore
    See Folk-lore, Indian
— Games
   x Indians of Mexico—Amusements
   Indians of Mexico—Recreations
   Indians of Mexico—Sports
   xx Games, Primitive
   Indians of Mexico—Social life and
      customs
— Goldsmithing
   xx Goldsmithing
   Indians of Mexico—Metal-work
— Government relations
   sa Indians of Mexico—Taxation
   Indians, Treatment of—Mexico
   xx Indians, Treatment of—Mexico
— Health and hygiene (Direct)
   sa Indians of Mexico—Diseases
— History (F1219)
— Illustrations
    See Indians of Mexico—Pictures,
      illustrations, etc.
— Implements
   sa Metates
   x Indians of Mexico—Stone
      implements
   xx Indians of Mexico—Antiquities
— Industries
   sa Indians of Mexico—Metal-work
   Indians of Mexico—Paper making
      and trade
— Kinship
   xx Indians of Mexico—Social life and
      customs
   Kinship
— Labor service
   xx Labor service
— Land tenure

Swinomish Indians
Tabeguache Indians
Taensa Indians
Tahltan Indians
Takelma Indians
Takulli Indians
Tanai Indians
Tanoan Indians
Taos Indians
Tawakoni Indians
Tepehuane Indians
Têtes de Boule Indians
Teton Indians
Tewa Indians
Thlingchadinne Indians
Tigua Indians
Timiskaming Indians
Timucua Indians
Tinne Indians
Tlakluit Indians
Tlingit Indians
Tolowa Indians
Tonikan Indians
Tonkawa Indians
Tsattine Indians
Tsilkotin Indians
Tsimshian Indians
Tubatulabal Indians
Tukkuthkutchin Indians
Tukuarika Indians
Tulalip Indians
Tunica Indians
Tunxis Indians
Tuscarora Indians
Tutelo Indians
Tututni Indians
Twana Indians
Ugalakmiut Indians
Uinta Indians
Umatilla Indians
Umpqua Indians
United States—Civilization—Indian
    influences
Ute Indians
Uto-Aztecan Indians
Vuntakutchin Indians
Wachuset Indians
Waco Indians
Wahpekute Indians
Wahpeton Indians
Wailaki Indians
Wakashan Indians
Walla Walla Indians
Walpapi Indians
Wamesit Indians
Wampanoag Indians
Wanapum Indians
Wappinger Indians
Wappo Indians
Warm Spring Apache Indians
Wasco Indians
Washo Indians
Wawenock Indians
Wea Indians
Welsh Indians
Wenrohronon Indians
Wichita Indians
Wiminuche Indians
Winnebago Indians
Wintun Indians
Wiyot Indians
Woodland Indians
Wyam Indians
Yahuskin Indians
Yakima Indians
Yakonan Indians
Yamassee Indians
Yampa Indians

Yana Indians
Yankton Indians
Yanktonai Indians
Yavapai Indians
Yokayo Indians
Yokuts Indians
Yuchi Indians
Yukian Indians
Yuma Indians
Yuman Indians
Yurok Indians
Zuñi Indians
  x American aborigines
    American Indians
    Indians—Ethnology
    Indians of North America—Ethnology
    Indians of North America—United
      States
    Indians of the United States
    North American Indians
  Note under Indians
— Aesthetics (E98)
    xx Aesthetics
— Agriculture (E98.A3)
    sa Indians of North America—
      Domestic animals
      Indians of North America—
      Irrigation
    xx Agriculture, Primitive
— — Juvenile literature
— Amusements
    See Indians of North America—
      Games
      Indians of North America—Social
      life and customs
— Anecdotes, facetiae, satire, etc.
— Animals, Domestic
    See Indians of North America—
      Domestic animals
— Anthropometry (E98.A55)
    sa Indians of North America—
      Craniology
    xx Anthropometry
      Indians of North America—
      Craniology
      Indians of North America—Physical
      characteristics
— Antiquities (E98.A6)
      Antiquities of a particular tribe are en-
      tered under name of tribe; antiqui-
      ties of a locality, under name of lo-
      cality.
    sa Arrow-heads
      Hopewell culture
      Indians of North America—
      Implements
      Indians of North America—Pottery
      Kitchen-middens
      Mississippian culture
      Mound-builders
      Mounds
    xx Indians of North America—
      Industries
      United States—Antiquities
— — Collectors and collecting (Direct)
— — Conservation and restoration
— — Juvenile literature
— — Private collections (Direct)
— Appropriations (E91-93)
    x Appropriations, Indian
      Indian appropriations
    xx Indians of North America—
      Government relations
— Architecture (E98.A65)
    sa Indians of North America—
      Dwellings
      Kivas

    xx Indians of North America—
      Dwellings
— Arms and armor (E98.A65)
    sa Bow and arrow
      Slings
      Throwing-sticks
      Tomahawks
    xx Arms and armor, Primitive
— Art (E98.A7)
    sa Indians of North America—
      Embroidery
      Indians of North America—
      Metal-work
      Indians of North America—
      Sculpture
      Indians of North America—
      Wood-carving
      Mound-builders—Art
      Sandpaintings
      subdivision Art under names of
      Indian tribes, e.g. Hopi Indians—
      Art
    x Art, Indian
    xx Art, Primitive
— — Juvenile literature
— Astronomy
— Basket making (E98.B3)
    x Indian baskets
    xx Basket making
      Indians of North America—
      Industries
— Beadwork
    See Beadwork
      Indians of North America—
      Costume and adornment
      Indians of North America—
      Textile industry and fabrics
      Wampum belts
— Bibliography (Z1209-1210)
    sa Indians of North America—Wars—
      Bibliography
— Biography (E89-90)
    Example under Biography
— — Juvenile literature
— Blankets
    See Indians of North America—
      Textile industry and fabrics
— Boats (E98.C2)
    sa Eskimos—Boats
    x Birch-bark canoes
    xx Boats and boating
      Canoes and canoeing
      Indians of North America—
      Transportation
      Navigation, Primitive
— Burial
    See Indians of North America—
      Mortuary customs
— Calendar (E98.C14)
— Captivities (E85-87)
    x Indian captivities
    xx Frontier and pioneer life
— — Juvenile literature
— Census (E98.C3)
    xx Census
— Children (E98.C5)
    xx Children
— — Juvenile literature
— Citizenship (E91-93)
      Here are entered works on United
      States citizenship of American Indi-
      ans. Works on tribal citizenship are
      entered under names of particular
      Indian tribes with subdivision
      Tribal citizenship, e.g. Chickasaw
      Indians—Tribal citizenship.

Indians of North America *(E77-99)*
— Citizenship *(E91-93) (Continued)*
    sa subdivision Tribal citizenship *under*
      names of particular Indian tribes,
      e.g. Chickasaw Indians—Tribal
      citizenship
    xx Citizenship
— Civil rights
    xx Civil rights
— Civilization
    See Indians of North America,
      Civilization of *[for material on*
      efforts to civilize the race]
    Indians of North America—
      Culture *[for literature dealing*
      with the cultural condition of
      the Indian at a given time or
      period]
— Claims *(E98.C6)*
    xx Indians of North America—Legal
      status, laws, etc.
— Claims (against the Indians) *(E98.C62)*
    x United States—Claims against
      Indians of North America
— Commerce *(E98.C7)*
    sa Indians of North America—Trading
      posts
    xx Commerce
— Copper implements
    See Indians of North America—
      Implements
— Costume and adornment *(E98.C8)*
    sa Moccasins
      Wampum
      Wampum belts
    x Indians of North America—
      Beadwork
      Indians of North America—
      Footwear
    xx Costume
      Wampum
— Councils *(E98.C)*
— Courts *(E93)*
    xx Courts
      Indians of North America—Legal
      status, laws, etc.
— Craniology *(E98.C85)*
    sa Indians of North America—
      Anthropometry
    xx Craniology
      Indians of North America—
      Anthropometry
      Indians of North America—Physical
      characteristics
— Crime *(E98.C87)*
    sa Indians of North America—Juvenile
      delinquency
    xx Crime and criminals
      Indians of North America—Social
      conditions
— Culture *(E98.C9)*
    Here is entered literature dealing with
      the cultural condition *(e.g.* arts, in-
      dustries, religion and mythology,
      etc.) of the Indian at a given time or
      period. Works treating of the efforts
      to civilize the race are entered un-
      der the heading Indians of North
      America, Civilization of.
    sa Plaquemine culture
    x Indians of North America—
      Civilization
    Note under Indians of North America,
      Civilization of
— Customs
    See Indians of North America—Social
      life and customs
— Dances *(E98.D2)*

    sa Butterfly dance
      Calumet dance
      Corn maidens' dance
      Eagle dance
      Ghost dance
      O-kee-pa (Religious ceremony)
      Snake-dance
      Sun-dance
      Sunflower dance
      Urine dance
      Wolf ritual
    xx Dancing (in religion, folk-lore, etc.)
      Indians of North America—Religion
      and mythology
      Indians of North America—Social
      life and customs
— — Juvenile literature
— Diseases *(E98.D6)*
    sa Indians of North America—
      Hospitals
— Domestic animals
    sa Indian ponies
    x Indians of North America—Animals,
      Domestic
    xx Domestic animals
      Indians of North America—
      Agriculture
— Drama
    Example under Drama
— Dwellings *(E98.D9)*
    sa Indians of North America—
      Architecture
      Pueblos
    x Teepees
      Tepees
      Tipis
      Wigwams
    xx Dwellings
      Indians of North America—
      Architecture
— — Juvenile literature
— Economic conditions *(E98.E2)*
    sa Indians of North America—
      Employment
      Indians of North America—Public
      welfare
— Education *(Canada, LC2629; United*
    States, E97)
    sa Indians of North America—
      Scholarships, fellowships, etc.
    particular schools, e.g. Carlisle, Pa.
      United States Indian School
    x Indians of North America—Schools
— — Law and legislation
— Embroidery *(E98.E5)*
    x Embroidery, Indian
    xx Indians of North America—Art
      Indians of North America—Textile
      industry and fabrics
— Employment *(E59.E3)*
    xx Indians of North America—
      Economic conditions
— Ethics
    x Ethics, Indian
      Indian ethics
— Ethnology
    See Ethnology—North America
      Indians of North America
— Factory system
    See Indians of North America—
      Trading posts
— Fiction
    sa subdivision Fiction *under names of*
      Indian tribes, e.g. Iroquois Indians
      —Fiction
— Financial affairs *(E98.F3)*
    sa subdivision Financial affairs *under*
      names of tribes

    xx Indians of North America—Property
— Fishing *(E98.F)*
    xx Fishing, Primitive
— — Juvenile literature
— Five Civilized Tribes
    See Five Civilized Tribes
— Flint implements
    See Indians of North America—
      Implements
— Folk-lore
    See Folk-lore, Indian
— Food *(E98.F7)*
    Notes under Ethnobotany; Ethnozoology
— — Juvenile literature
— Footwear
    See Indians of North America—
      Costume and adornment
      Moccasins
— Games *(E98.G2)*
    x Indians of North America—
      Amusements
      Indians of North America—
      Recreations
      Indians of North America—Sports
    xx Games, Primitive
      Indians of North America—Social
      life and customs
— Gifts
    sa Potlatch
    xx Gifts
      Indians of North America—
      Government relations
      Indians of North America—Social
      life and customs
— Government relations *(E91; United*
    States, E93)
    Here are entered works on the Indian
      policy and relations with the Indi-
      ans of the United States Govern-
      ment.
    Works on government relations with
      Indians of a particular state have a
      secondary subject entry under Indi-
      ans of North America subdivided
      by name of the state, *e.g.* Indians of
      North America—California.
    sa Indians of North America—Canada
      —Government relations
      Indians of North America—Gifts
      Indians, Treatment of—United States
      subdivision Government relations
      under names of tribes, e.g. Dakota
      Indians—Government relations;
      and names of agencies, e.g. Red
      Cloud Indian Agency
    xx Indians of North America—Land
      transfers
      Indians of North America—Treaties
      Indians, Treatment of—United States
      Native races
— — To 1789
— — 1789-1869
— — 1869-1934
— — 1934-
    sa Alcatraz Island, Calif.—History—
      Indian occupation, 1969-1971

GENERAL SUBDIVISIONS

— — Juvenile literature
— Handicraft
    See Indians of North America—
      Industries
— Health and hygiene *(Direct) (RA801)*
    sa Indians of North America—
      Hospitals
    xx Medical anthropology
— History *(E77)*
    sa Indians of North America—Wars

—— Colonial period, ca. 1600-1775 *(E77)*
—— Civil War, 1861-1865 *(E540.I3)*
— Hospitals *(RA981.A35)*
    x Hospitals, Indian
      Indian hospitals
    xx Indians of North America—Diseases
      Indians of North America—Health
        and hygiene
— Hunting *(E98.H)*
    sa Buffalo jump
    xx Hunting, Primitive
      Indians of North America—
        Industries
      Indians of North America—Social
        life and customs
—— Juvenile literature
— Hymns
    See Hymns, Arikara, [Choctaw, Cree,
      etc.]
— Illustrations
    See Indians of North America—
      Pictures, illustrations, etc.
— Implements *(E98.I4)*
    sa Folsom points
      Harpoons
      Scottsbluff points
      Throwing-sticks
      Tomahawks
    x Indians of North America—Copper
      [Flint, Metallic, Stone]
      implements
    xx Indians of North America—
      Antiquities
      Indians of North America—Quarries
      Stone implements
— Incantations
    See Incantations, Indian
— Industries *(E98.I5)*
    sa Indians of North America—
      Antiquities
    subdivisions Basket making, Hunting,
      Metal-work, Pottery, Quarries,
      Textile industry and fabrics,
      Trading posts, Trapping *under*
      Indians of North America
    x Indians of North America—
      Handicraft
      Indians of North America—
      Manufactures
    xx Handicraft
      Industries, Primitive
— Irrigation
    xx Indians of North America—
      Agriculture
      Irrigation
— Juvenile delinquency *(E98.C87)*
    xx Indians of North America—Crime
      Juvenile delinquency
— Juvenile literature *(E77; Readers,*
    PE1127.I5)
— Kinship
    xx Indians of North America—Social
      life and customs
      Kinship
— Land tenure *(E98.L3)*
    sa subdivision Land tenure *under*
      names of tribes, e.g. Ute Indians
      —Land tenure
    x Indians of North America—Land
      titles
      Indians of North America—Real
      property
    xx Indians of North America—Legal
      status, laws, etc.
      Indians of North America—Property
      Land tenure
— Land titles

    See Indians of North America—Land
      tenure
— Land transfers *(E91-93)*
    sa subdivisions Government relations,
      Property, Treaties *under* Indians
      of North America; *and*
      subdivision Land transfers *under*
      names of Indian tribes, e.g.
      Dakota Indians—Land transfers
    xx Indians of North America—Legal
      status, laws, etc.
      Indians of North America—Treaties
—— Juvenile literature
— Languages *(PM1-7356)*
    sa names of languages, e.g. Algonquian
      languages, Chippewa language,
      Hupa language
    x Indian languages
— Leather work
    sa Parfleches
    xx Leather work
— Legal status, laws, etc.
    sa Indians of North America—Probate
      law and practice
    subdivisions Claims, Courts, Land
      tenure, Land transfers, Pensions,
      Property, Suffrage, Treaties, Wills
      under Indians of North America;
      and subdivision Legal status, laws,
      etc. *under names of tribes, e.g.*
      Cherokee Indians—Legal status,
      laws, etc.
    Example under Indians—Legal status,
      laws, etc.
—— Digests
— Legends *(E98.F6)*
    sa Folk-lore, Indian
      subdivision Legends *under names of*
      Indian tribes, e.g. Iroquois Indians
      —Legends
    x Indians of North America—
      Mythology
      Legends, Indian
    Note under Folk-lore, Indian
—— Juvenile literature
— Liquor problem *(E98.L7)*
    xx Liquor problem
— Magic *(E98.M2)*
    x Magic, Indian
    xx Indians of North America—Religion
      and mythology
— Manufactures
    See Indians of North America—
      Industries
— Masks *(E98.M3)*
    xx Masks
— Medals *(E98.M35)*
— Medical care *(Direct)*
— Medicine *(E98.M4)*
    sa Medicine-man
    xx Medicine, Primitive
—— Juvenile literature
— Metal-work
    sa Indians of North America—
      Silversmithing
    xx Art metal-work
      Indians of North America—Art
      Indians of North America—
      Industries
      Metal-work
— Metallic implements
    See Indians of North America—
      Implements
— Military capacity and organization
    See Indian warfare
      Indians of North America as
      soldiers
— Mines and mining

— Missions *(E98.M6)*
    sa Jesuits—Missions
      subdivision Missions *under names of*
      Indian tribes, e.g. Illinois Indians
      —Missions
    x Missions, Indian
    xx Missions
—— Juvenile literature
— Mixed bloods *(E99.M693)*
    sa Guineas (Mixed bloods, United
      States)
      Jackson Whites
      Wesorts
    x Mixed bloods (American Indians)
    xx Miscegenation
— Money *(E98.M7)*
    sa Wampum
    xx Money
      Shell money
      Wampum
— Mortuary customs *(E98.M8)*
    x Indians of North America—Burial
      Mortuary customs
    xx Burial
      Funeral rites and ceremonies
— Museums *(E56)*
    xx Archaeological museums and
      collections
      Ethnological museums and
      collections
    Example under Museums
— Music *(E98.M9; ML3557)*
    This heading covers general works on
      the music of the North American
      Indians and also works dealing with
      the music of a particular tribe. The
      latter are entered also under name
      of tribe.
    x Music, Indian (North America)
    xx Music, Primitive
— Mythology
    See Folk-lore, Indian
      Indians of North America—
      Legends
      Indians of North America—
      Religion and mythology
— Names *(E98.N2)*
    sa subdivision Names *under particular*
      tribes, e.g. Delaware Indians—
      Names
    x Names, Geographical—Indian
      Names, Indian
    Notes under Names, Anglo-Saxon,
      [Arabic, Celtic, etc.]; Names,
      Geographical—Anglo-Saxon,
      [Celtic, Latin, etc.]
— Oratory *(E98.O7)*
    x Indian orations
    xx Orations
      Oratory
— Origin
    See Indians—Origin
— Pensions *(E98.P3)*
    xx Indians of North America—Legal
      status, laws, etc.
      Indians of North America—Public
      welfare
— Periodicals *(E77)*
— Philosophy *(E98.P5)*
— Physical characteristics *(E98.P53)*
    sa Indians of North America—
      Anthropometry
      Indians of North America—
      Craniology
    x Indians of North America—
      Somatology
— Pictorial works *(E77.5)*

Indians of North America *(E77-99)*
— Pictorial works *(E77.5)*
   (Continued)
    sa subdivision Pictorial works *under*
      names of tribes
— — Juvenile literature
— Picture-writing
   See Picture-writing, Indian
— Pictures, illustrations, etc. *(E77)*
   x Indians in art
    Indians of North America—
      Illustrations
   Example under Pictures
— Poetry *(E98.P74)*
   sa Indians in literature
    subdivision Poetry *under names of*
      Indian tribes, e.g. Dakota Indians
      —Poetry
— Ponies
   See Indian ponies
— Portraits *(E89)*
   This heading covers general collections of portraits of Indians and also
   works containing portraits of Indians of a particular tribe or of the
   tribes of a specific locality. The latter are entered also under the name
   of the tribe or under the local subdivision, *e.g.* a work which deals
   with portraits of Indians of Oregon
   will appear under: 1. Indians of
   North America—Portraits. 2. Indians of North America—Oregon.
— Pottery *(E98.P8)*
   xx Indians of North America—
    Antiquities
    Indians of North America—
      Industries
    Pottery
— — Juvenile literature
— Probate law and practice
   xx Indians of North America—Legal
    status, laws, etc.
— — Digests
— Property *(E98.P9)*
   sa Indians of North America—Financial
    affairs
    Indians of North America—Land
      tenure
   xx Indians of North America—Land
    transfers
    Indians of North America—Legal
      status, laws, etc.
— Psychology *(E98.P95)*
— Public welfare
   sa Indians of North America—Pensions
   xx Indians of North America—
    Economic conditions
    Public welfare
— Quarries *(E98.I5)*
   sa Indians of North America—
    Implements
   xx Indians of North America—
    Industries
    Quarries and quarrying
— Race identity
   x Racial identity of Indians of North
    America
   xx Ethnopsychology
    Race awareness
— Real property
   See Indians of North America—Land
    tenure
— Recreations
   See Indians of North America—
    Games
— Religion and mythology *(E98.R3)*
   sa Corn maidens' dance
    Indians of North America—Dances

Indians of North America—Magic
   Katcinas
   Peyotism
   Totems
   subdivision Religion and mythology
    under names of tribes
   x Indians of North America—
    Mythology
    Mythology, Indian (American
      Indian)
   xx Mythology
    Religion, Primitive
   Example under Religion
— Reservations *(E78; E91-93; E99)*
   sa names of reservations, e.g. Shoshoni
    Indian Reservation, Wyo.
   x Indian reservations
    Reservations, Indian
— Rites and ceremonies
   sa Butterfly dance
    Peyotism
    names of special ceremonies, e.g.
      O-kee-pa (Religious ceremony);
      and subdivision Rites and
      ceremonies *under names of tribes*
   x Rites and ceremonies—Indians
— Sanatoriums
— Scholarships, fellowships, etc. *(Direct)*
   x Indian scholarships
   xx Indians of North America—
    Education
— Schools
   See Indians of North America—
    Education
   particular schools, e.g. Carlisle,
    Pa. United States Indian
    School
— Sculpture
   x Indians of North America—
    Stone-sculpture
   xx Indians of North America—Art
    Sculpture
    Sculpture, Primitive
— Secret societies *(E98.S75)*
   xx Secret societies
— Sign language *(E98.S5)*
   x Gesture language
   xx Sign language
— — Juvenile literature
— Silversmithing
   xx Indians of North America—
    Metal-work
    Silversmithing
— Social conditions
   sa Indians of North America—Crime
    Indians of North America—Urban
      residence
— Social life and customs
   sa Indians of North America—Gifts
    Indians of North America—Kinship
    Potlatch
    subdivisions Dances, Games,
      Hunting *under* Indians of North
      America; *and subdivision* Social
      life and customs *under names of*
      Indian tribes, e.g. Omaha Indians
      —Social life and customs
   x Indians of North America—
    Amusements
    Indians of North America—Customs
— — Juvenile literature
— Societies, etc. *(E77)*
— Somatology
   See Indians of North America—
    Physical characteristics
— Sports
   See Indians of North America—
    Games

— Statistics
   sa subdivision Statistics *under names of*
    Indian tribes
— Stone implements
   See Indians of North America—
    Implements
— Stone-sculpture
   See Indians of North America—
    Sculpture
— Suffrage *(E91-93)*
   xx Elections
    Indians of North America—Legal
      status, laws, etc.
    Suffrage
— Taxation
   sa subdivision Taxation *under names of*
    individual Indian tribes, e.g.
    Cherokee Indians—Taxation
— Textile industry and fabrics *(E98.T35)*
   sa Indians of North America—
    Embroidery
   x Indian blankets
    Indians of North America—
      Beadwork, ₍Blankets, Weaving₎
   xx Blankets
    Indians of North America—
      Industries
    Textile industry and fabrics
    Weaving
— Trading posts *(E98.C7)*
   x Indian trade factories
    Indians of North America—Factory
      system
    Trading posts (North American
      Indian)
   xx Indians of North America—
    Commerce
    Indians of North America—
      Industries
— — Juvenile literature
— Trails
   See Indian trails
— Transportation
   sa Indian ponies
    Indians of North America—Boats
— Trapping *(E98.T75)*
   xx Indians of North America—
    Industries
    Trapping
— Treaties *(E95)*
   sa Indians of North America—
    Government relations
    Indians of North America—Land
      transfers
    names of specific treaties, e.g. Penn's
      treaty with the Indians, 1682; *and*
      subdivision Treaties *under names*
      of Indian tribes, e.g. Iroquois
      Indians—Treaties
   xx Indians of North America—Land
    transfers
    Indians of North America—Legal
      status, laws, etc.
    Treaties
— Treatment
   See Indians, Treatment of—United
    States, ₍Canada, etc.₎
— Tribal government
   sa subdivision Tribal government *under*
    names of Indian tribes, e.g.
    Iroquois Indians—Tribal
    government
   Example under Tribal government
— Urban residence
   sa subdivision Urban residence *under*
    names of tribes
   xx City and town life

Indians of North America—Social
conditions
Urbanization
— Wars (E81-83)
sa Indian warfare
Indians of North America as seamen
Indians of North America as soldiers
subdivision Wars under names of
Indian tribes, e.g. Dakota Indians
—Wars
xx Indians of North America—History
Notes under Indian warfare; United
States—History
—— 1600-1750 (E82)
sa Ackia, Battle of, 1736
Chickasaw Indians—Wars,
1739-1740
Eastern Indians, Wars with,
1722-1726
Esopus Indians—Wars, 1655-1660
Esopus Indians—Wars, 1663-1664
King Philip's War, 1675-1676
Natchez Indians—Wars, 1716
Pequot War, 1636-1638
Tuscarora Indians—Wars,
1711-1713
United States—History—King
George's War, 1744-1748
United States—History—King
William's War, 1689-1697
United States—History—Queen
Anne's War, 1702-1713
Wappinger Indians—Wars,
1655-1660
—— 1750-1815 (E81)
sa Cherokee Indians—Wars,
1759-1761
Dunmore's Expedition, 1774
Pontiac's Conspiracy, 1763-1765
Tippecanoe, Battle of, 1811
United States—History—French
and Indian War, 1755-1763
—— 1775-1783 (E83.775)
sa Blue Licks, Battle of the, 1782
Crawford's Indian Campaign,
1782
Gnadenhutten, Ohio—Massacre,
1782
Shawnee Indians—Wars,
1775-1783
Sullivan's Indian Campaign, 1779
Yuma Indians—Wars, 1781-1782
—— 1790-1794 (E83.79)
sa Big Bottom, Ohio—Massacre,
1791
Harmar's Expedition, 1790
St. Clair's Campaign, 1791
Wayne's Campaign, 1794
xx Delaware Indians
—— 1812-1815 (E83.812)
sa Creek War, 1813-1814
Harrison, Fort, Battle of, 1812
—— 1815-1875 (E81)
sa Black Hawk War, 1832
Creek War, 1836
Mill Creek Indians—Wars,
1857-1865
Pacific coast Indians, Wars with,
1847-1865
Paiute Indians—Wars, 1860
Rogue River Indian War,
1855-1856
Seminole War, 1st, 1817-1818
Seminole War, 2d, 1835-1842
Seminole War, 3d, 1855-1858
Spirit Lake, Iowa—Massacre,
1857
Temecula—Massacre, 1847

—— 1862-1865 (E83.863)
sa Birch Coulee, Battle of, 1862
Dakota Indians—Wars, 1862-1865
Platte Bridge, Battle of, 1865
Sand Creek, Battle of, 1864
Shoshoni Indians—Wars,
1863-1865
—— 1866-1895 (E83.866)
sa Apache Indians—Wars,
1883-1886
Bannock Indians—Wars, 1878
Butte, Battle of the, 1877
Cheyenne Indians—Wars, 1876
Dakota Indians—Wars, 1876
Dakota Indians—Wars, 1890-1891
Fetterman Fight, 1866
Modoc Indians—Wars, 1873
Nez Percé Indians—Wars, 1877
Red River War, 1874-1875
Tukuarika Indians—Wars, 1879
Ute Indians—Wars, 1879
——— Juvenile literature
—— 1868-1869 (E83.866)
sa Beecher Island, Battle of, 1868
x Washita Campaign, 1868-1869
—— Bibliography
xx Indians of North America—
Bibliography
—— Juvenile literature
—— Pictorial works
— Weaving
See Indians of North America—
Textile industry and fabrics
— Wills (E98.W5)
xx Indians of North America—Legal
status, laws, etc.
— Women (E98.W8)
xx Woman—History and condition of
women
— Wood-carving (E98.W85)
xx Indians of North America—Art
Wood-carving
— Writing (E98.W9)
sa Picture-writing, Indian
subdivision Writing under names of
Indian tribes
xx Picture-writing, Indian
Writing
— Alaska
xx Arctic races
— California
x Mission Indians of California
— Canada
x Indians of Canada
—— Government relations
xx Indians of North America—
Government relations
— Indian Territory
sa Five Civilized Tribes
— Oklahoma
sa Five Civilized Tribes
—— Legal status, laws, etc.
Note under Indians—Legal status,
laws, etc.
— United States
See Indians of North America
Indians of North America, Civilization of
(E97)
Here is entered literature dealing with ef-
forts to civilize the Indians. Works on
the cultural condition of the race at a
given time or period are entered under
the heading Indians of North America
—Culture.
x Indians of North America—Civilization
Note under Indians of North America—Cul-
ture

Indians of North America, Treatment of
See Indians, Treatment of—United States,
[Canada, etc.]
Indians of North America as seamen
sa United States. Navy—Indians
World War, 1939-1945—Indians
xx Indians of North America—Wars
Indians of North America as soldiers
(E98.M5)
sa European War, 1914-1918—Indians
United States. Army—Indian troops
World War, 1939-1945—Indians
x Indians of North America—Military
capacity and organization
xx Indian warfare
Indians of North America—Wars
Soldiers
Indians of South America (F2229-2230)
Subdivided by countries or regions, e.g.
Indians of South America—Chile; In-
dians of South America—Amazon
Valley.
sa Abipone Indians
Accawai Indians
Achagua Indians
Akwē-Shavante Indians
Alacaluf Indians
Amahuaca Indians
Andaqui Indians
Anserma Indians
Apalai Indians
Apalakiri Indians
Apiacá Indians
Apinagé Indians
Arara Indians
Araucanian Indians
Arawak Indians
Arawakan Indians
Arecuna Indians
Arhuaco Indians
Ashluslay Indians
Atacameño Indians
Aymara Indians
Bakairi Indians
Barasana Indians
Boro Indians
Bororo Indians
Botocudo Indians
Cadioéo Indians
Caingua Indians
Calchaqui Indians
Callahuaya Indians
Campa Indians
Cañari Indians
Canella Indians
Cara Indians
Caraja Indians
Carib Indians
Cashibo Indians
Catio Indians
Catoquina Indians
Cayapa Indians
Cayapo Indians
Chacobo Indians
Chamacoco Indians
Chamí Indians
Chanca Indians
Chané Indians
Charrua Indians
Chibcha Indians
Chimu Indians
Chiquito Indians
Chiriguano Indians
Chiripá Indians
Choco Indians
Chono Indians
Choroti Indians
Chupacho Indians

Indians of South America *(F2229-2230)*
(Continued)

Cobaría Indians
Cocama Indians
Colla Indians
Colorado Indians (Ecuador)
Comechingone Indians
Craho Indians
Crao Indians
Crichaná Indians
Cubeo Indians
Cumana Indians
Cupisnique Indians
Desana Indians
Diaguita Indians
Fuegians
Fulnio Indians
Galibi Indians
Goajiro Indians
Guaharibo Indians
Guahibo Indians
Guajajara Indians
Guana Indians
Guarani Indians
Guarayo Indians
Guarpe Indians
Guato Indians
Guayana Indians
Guayaqui Indians
Guaycuru Indians
Huanca Indians
Huancavilca Indians
Huilliche Indians
Ijca Indians
Incas
Ipurucotó Indians
Iscaycinca Indians
Itenez Indians
Jivaro Indians
Juruna Indians
Kagaba Indians
Kaingangue Indians
Kamaiurá Indians
Kariri Indians
Kechua Indians
Kreen-Akrore Indians
Kuikuru Indians
Lengua Indians
Lule Indians
Machiganga Indians
Macusi Indians
Manacica Indians
Manta Indians
Masacali Indians
Mataco Indians
Maue Indians
Mayna Indians
Mbaya Indians
Mbya Indians
Mochica Indians
Mocobi Indians
Moguex Indians
Moro Indians
Morochucan Indians
Motilon Indians
Moxo Indians
Mundurucu Indians
Muzo Indians
Ona Indians
Otavalo Indians
Otuquis Indians
Oyampi Indians
Oyana Indians
Oyaricoulet Indians
Paez Indians
Palenque Indians
Pampean Indians
Pancararu Indians
Pasto Indians

Patamona Indians
Pauishana Indians
Pauserna Indians
Payagua Indians
Pehuenche Indians
Pilaga Indians
Piro Indians (Peru)
Pocra Indians
Puelche Indians
Puquina Indians
Puruha Indians
Querandi Indians
Quijo Indians
Quillacinga Indians
Quimbaya Indians
Ranqueles Indians
Sanavirona Indians
Shapra Indians
Sharanahua Indians
Shokleng Indians
Sipibo Indians
Siriono Indians
Tairona Indians
Tamanac Indians
Tapajó Indians
Tapirapé Indians
Tapuya Indians
Tenetahara Indians
Teque Indians
Tereno Indians
Timbira Indians
Toba Indians
Tonocote Indians
Trio Indians
Tucano Indians
Tucuna Indians
Tunebo Indians
Tupari Indians
Tupi Indians
Tupinamba Indians
Txicaos Indians
Tzoneca Indians
Uaboi Indians
Umotina Indians
Urubu Indians
Vilela Indians
Waica Indians
Waiwai Indians
Wapisiana Indians
Warrau Indians
Witoto Indians
Xikrin Indians
Yabarana Indians
Yagua Indians
Yahgan Indians
Yakalamarure Indians
Yanaconas
Yanoama Indians
Yaruro Indians
Yecuana Indians
Yuko Indians
Yunca Indians
Yurucari Indians
Zamucoan Indians
   x American aborigines
      American Indians
      Indians—Ethnology
      Indians of South America—Ethnology
   xx Indians of the West Indies
— Agriculture *(F2230.1.A3)*
   xx Agriculture, Primitive
— Amusements
    See Indians of South America—
       Games
       Indians of South America—Social
        life and customs
— Anthropometry *(F2230.1.A)*
— Antiquities *(F2229)*

   sa Indians of South America—
      Implements
      Indians of South America—Pottery
   xx Indians of South America—
      Industries
— Architecture *(F2230.1.A)*
— Arms and armor
   sa Throwing-sticks
   xx Arms and armor, Primitive
— Art *(F2230.1.A7)*
   sa Indians of South America—
      Metal-work
      Indians of South America—Sculpture
— Astronomy
   x Astronomy, South American Indian
   xx Astronomy
° — Basket making *(F2230.1.B)*
   x Indian baskets
   xx Basket making
      Indians of South America—
      Industries
— Blankets
    See Indians of South America—
       Textile industry and fabrics
— Boats *(F2230.1.B6)*
   xx Boats and boating
      Canoes and canoeing
      Indians of South America—
      Transportation
      Navigation, Primitive
° — Burial
    See Indians of South America—
       Mortuary customs
— Calendar *(F2230.1.C2)*
— Captivities
   x Indian captivities
   xx Frontier and pioneer life
— Census
   xx Census
— Children *(F2230.1.C5)*
— — Juvenile literature
— Colonization
— Costume and adornment *(F2230.1.C8)*
— — Pictorial works
— Craniology *(F2230.1.C85)*
— Culture
   sa Indians of South America—Social
      life and customs
— Customs
    See Indians of South America—Social
       life and customs
— Diseases
— Economic conditions
— Education *(LC2658-2679)*
— Ethnology
    See Ethnology—South America
      Indians of South America
— Folk-lore
    See Folk-lore, Indian
— Food *(F2230.1.F)*
— Games *(F2230.1.G2)*
   x Indians of South America—
      Amusements
      Indians of South America—
      Recreations
      Indians of South America—Sports
   xx Games, Primitive
      Indians of South America—Social
      life and customs
— Goldsmithing
   xx Goldsmithing
      Indians of South America—
      Metal-work
— Health and hygiene *(Direct)*
   xx Medical anthropology
— History
— Hunting
   xx Hunting, Primitive

Indians of South America—
  Industries
Indians of South America—Social
  life and customs
— Illustrations
    See Indians of South America—
      Pictures, illustrations, etc.
— Implements (F2230.1.I4)
    x Indians of South America—Stone
      implements
    xx Indians of South America—
      Antiquities
      Stone implements
— Industries
    sa Indians of South America—
      Antiquities
      Indians of South America—Hunting
    subdivisions Basket making,
      Metal-work, Pottery, Textile
      industry and fabrics under Indians
      of South America
    xx Industries, Primitive
— Juvenile literature
— Kinship (F2230.1.K5)
    xx Indians of South America—Social
      life and customs
      Kinship
— Land tenure
    sa subdivision Land tenure under
      names of tribes, e.g. Aymara
      Indians—Land tenure
    x Indians of South America—Land
      titles
      Indians of South America—Real
      property
    xx Indians of South America—Property
— Land titles
    See Indians of South America—Land
      tenure
— Languages (PM5001-7356)
    Subdivided by countries or regions,
      e.g. Indians of South America—
      Languages—Brazil; Indians of
      South   America—Languages—
      Orinoco Valley.
    sa Abipone language
      Accawai language
      Achagua language
      Aguaruna dialect
      Alacaluf language
      Allentiac language
      Amahuaca language
      Araona language
      Arasa language
      Araucanian language
      Arawak language
      Arawakan languages
      Arecuna language
      Aymara language
      Bakairi language
      Bauré language
      Bora language
      Bororo language
      Cacán language
      Callahuaya language
      Campa language
      Campa languages
      Cañarian language
      Canella language
      Canichana language
      Capanahua language
      Carib language
      Cariban languages
      Catio language
      Cavineño language
      Cayapo language
      Chacobo language
      Chayahuita language

Chechehet language
Chibcha language
Chibchan languages
Chimu language
Chiquito language
Choco language
Chuntaquiro language
Cocama language
Culina language
Cumana language
Ese Ejja language
Fulnio language
Galibi language
Goajiro language
Guahibo language
Guajajara language
Guana language
Guarani language
Guaraúna language
Guarayo language
Guaycuruan languages
Güenoa language
Hixkaryana language
Huambisa language
Ipurina language
Iranxe language
Itonama language
Kagaba language
Kaingangue language
Kamarakoto language
Kariri language
Kechua language
Lorenzan language
Machiganga language
Macú language
Macusi language
Masacali language
Mataco language
Matsigenka language
Mbaya language
Mbya language
Movima language
Muinane language
Mundurucu language
Murui language
Nomatsiguenga language
Ona language
Otomaco language
Oyana language
Parentintim language
Pasto language
Pemón dialects
Pilaga language
Puquina language
Saliva language
Siriono language
Tacanan languages
Taparita language
Tapuyan languages
Taurepan language
Tereno language
Toba language (Indian)
Tucano language
Tucuna language
Tupi language
Tzoneca language
Uaiuai language
Urubu language
Vejoz language
Witoto language
Yaruro language
Yunca language
Yurucarean language
Zamucoan languages
— Legal status, laws, etc.
— Legends (F2230.1.F6)
    sa Folk-lore, Indian

    subdivision Legends under names of
      Indian tribes, e.g. Tupi Indians—
      Legends
    Note under Folk-lore, Indian
— Magic (F2230.1.M3)
    xx Indians of South America—Religion
      and mythology
— Marriage customs and rites
    x Marriage customs and rites, Indian
    xx Indians of South America—Social
      life and customs
— Masks
    xx Masks
— Medicine (F2230.1.M4)
— Metal-work
    sa Indians of South America—
      Goldsmithing
      Indians of South America—
      Silversmithing
    xx Art metal-work
      Indians of South America—Art
      Indians of South America—
      Industries
      Metal-work
— Missions (F2230-3799)
    sa Missions of Pititu
    subdivision Missions under names of
      Indian tribes, e.g. Moro Indians—
      Missions
    x Missions, Indian
— Mixed bloods (F2230.1.M)
    x Mixed bloods (American Indians)
— Mortuary customs (F2230.1.M)
    x Indians of South America—Burial
      Mortuary customs
    xx Burial
      Funeral rites and ceremonies
— Music (F2230.1.M9; ML3575)
    This heading covers general works on
      the music of the South American
      Indians and also works dealing with
      the music of a particular tribe. The
      latter are entered also under name
      of tribe.
    xx Music, Primitive
— Names (F2230.1.N)
— Origin
    See Indians—Origin
— Philosophy
    xx Philosophy, Primitive
— Pictorial works
— Picture-writing
    See Picture-writing, Indian
— Pictures, illustrations, etc.
    x Indians of South America—
      Illustrations
— Plant lore
    xx Folk-lore, Indian
      Plant lore
— Pottery (F2230.1.P8)
    xx Indians of South America—
      Antiquities
      Indians of South America—
      Industries
— Property
    sa Indians of South America—Land
      tenure
— Psychology
— Real property
    See Indians of South America—Land
      tenure
— Recreations
    See Indians of South America—
      Games
— Religion and mythology (F2230.1.R3)
    sa Indians of South America—Magic
    subdivision Religion and mythology
      under names of tribes

Indians of South America *(F2229-2230)*
— Religion and mythology *(F2230.1.R3)*
(Continued)
    xx Mythology
— Rites and ceremonies
    sa subdivision Rites and ceremonies
      under names of tribes
— Sculpture
    x Indians of South America—
      Stone-sculpture
    xx Indians of South America—Art
      Sculpture
      Sculpture, Primitive
— Silversmithing
    xx Indians of South America—
      Metal-work
      Silversmithing
— Social life and customs *(F2230.1.S7)*
    sa Indians of South America—Games
      Indians of South America—Hunting
      Indians of South America—Kinship
      Indians of South America—Marriage
      customs and rites
    x Indians of South America—
      Amusements
      Indians of South America—Customs
    xx Indians of South America—Culture
— Sports
    See Indians of South America—
      Games
— Statistics
    sa subdivision Statistics *under names of*
      Indian tribes
— Stone implements
    See Indians of South America—
      Implements
— Stone-sculpture
    See Indians of South America—
      Sculpture
— Textile industry and fabrics
    (F2230.1.T3)
    x Indian blankets
      Indians of South America—Blankets
      Indians of South America—Weaving
    xx Indians of South America—
      Industries
      Textile industry and fabrics
      Weaving
— Transportation
    sa Indians of South America—Boats
— Wars
    Note under Indian warfare
— Weaving
    See Indians of South America—
      Textile industry and fabrics
— Weights and measures
    xx Weights and measures
— Women
    xx Woman—History and condition of
      women
— Writing *(F2301.W)*
    sa Picture-writing, Indian
    xx Writing
Indians of the United States
See Indians of North America
Indians of the West Indies *(F1619)*
    Subdivided by names of islands, *e.g.* Indi-
    ans of the West Indies—Cuba.
    sa Arawak Indians
      Black Carib Indians
      Carib Indians
      Ciboney Indians
      Indians of South America
      Lucayan Indians
      Quisqueyano Indians
      Taino Indians
— Agriculture
— Anthropometry *(F1619)*
— Antiquities

    sa Elbow-stones
— Commerce
    xx Commerce
— Implements
— Languages *(PM5071-9)*
    sa Taino language
— Legal status, laws, etc.
— Pottery
— Religion and mythology *(F1619)*
— Wars
    sa St. Vincent—History—Carib War,
      1795-1796
Indic aesthetics
  See Aesthetics, Indic
Indic demonology
  See Demonology, Indic
Indic drama *(Modern collections, PK5437-8;*
    Modern history, PK5421)
Indic fiction
Indic fiction (English)
  See English fiction—Indic authors
Indic languages
    Here are entered works on the languages
    of India in general, and works not con-
    fined to the Indo-Aryan languages, or
    to any other special group or language.
    sa Dravidian languages
      Indo-Aryan languages
      Indo-Aryan languages, Modern
      Indochinese languages
      Iranian languages
      Mon-Khmer languages
      Munda languages
      Pisacha languages
      Tibeto-Burman languages
— Alphabet
    sa Devanagari alphabet
Indic literature *(Direct)*
    Here are entered works dealing with the
    literature of India in general, works on
    Indo-Aryan literature, and other
    works not confined to the literature of
    a single language.
    x East Indian literature
      Indian literature (East Indian)
      Indo-Aryan literature
    xx Iranian literature
Indic manuscripts
  See Manuscripts, Indic
Indic miniature painting
  See Miniature painting, Indic
Indic miniature paintings
  See Miniature paintings, Indic
Indic orations (English)
  See English orations—Indic authors
Indic philology
Indic philosophy
  See Philosophy, Indic
Indic poetry *(Direct)*
Indic prose literature *(Direct)*
Indic studies *(PK11)*
Indic wit and humor
    sa Assamese wit and humor
      Bengali wit and humor
      Kannada wit and humor
      Marathi wit and humor
      Panjabi wit and humor
      Telugu wit and humor
Indican *(Physiological chemistry, QP801.I4;*
    Secretions, QP211; Veterinary
    medicine, SF771)
    xx Physiological chemistry
      Urine—Analysis and pathology
Indicating instruments
  See Recording instruments
Indicator dilution
    x Indicator dilution technics
    xx Heart function tests

Indicator dilution technics
  See Indicator dilution
Indicator plants
  See Plant indicators
Indicators (Biology)
    sa Plant indicators
      Water quality bioassay
    x Biological indicators
    xx Ecology
Indicators and test-papers *(Analytic*
    chemistry, QD77)
    sa Chemical tests and reagents
      Methylene blue
      Resazurin
    x Test-papers, Chemical
    xx Chemical tests and reagents
      Chemistry, Analytic
      Chemistry—Laboratory manuals
      Volumetric analysis
Indicators for gas and oil engines *(TJ759)*
    xx Gas and oil engines
Indicators for steam-engines *(TJ478)*
    x Steam-engine indicators
    xx Steam-engines
Indices
  See Indexes
Indictments *(Direct)*
    sa Grand jury
      Informations
      Joinder of offenses
    x Accusation
    xx Criminal procedure
      Grand jury
      Informations
      Prosecution
Indifference, Religious
  See Indifferentism (Religion)
Indifferentism (Ethics) *(BJ1535.I)*
    xx Ethics
Indifferentism (Ethics) in literature
Indifferentism (Religion) *(BT33)*
    sa Communicatio in sacris
      Liberalism (Religion)
      Religious tolerance
      Unionism (Religion)
    x Indifference, Religious
      Religious indifference
    xx Dogma
      Irreligion
      Liberalism (Religion)
      Rationalism
      Religious liberty
      Religious tolerance
      Theology, Doctrinal
Indigenous church administration
    Here are entered works dealing with the
    transfer of church administration in
    the mission field from missionaries to
    native Christians.
    sa Native clergy
    x Church administration, Indigenous
      Missions—Devolution
      Missions, Foreign—Devolution
      Native church administration
    xx Church polity
      Church work
Indigenous clergy
  See Native clergy
Indigenous labor
  See Native labor
Indigestion
  See Dyspepsia
Indignation
  See Anger
Indignitas
  See Unworthiness of heirs (Roman law)

Indigo *(Agriculture, SB287.I4; Economics, HD9019.I; Technology, TP923-4)*
   xx Dyes and dyeing
Indirect costs
   See Overhead costs
Indirect discourse
   See subdivision Indirect discourse *under names of languages and groups of languages, e.g.* English language—Indirect discourse
Indirect discourse in literature
   x Discourse, Indirect, in literature
Indirect taxation
   See Internal revenue
       Tariff
       Taxation
Indium *(Chemistry, QD181.I5)*
   — Analysis
   — Isotopes
   — Metallurgy
   — Spectra
Indium alloys
   sa Indium-thallium alloys
Indium compounds *(QD181.I5)*
Indium deposits
   See Indium ores
Indium ores *(Indirect)*
   x Indium deposits
Indium-thallium alloys
   x Thallium-indium alloys
   xx Indium alloys
       Thallium alloys
Individual instruction
   See Individualized instruction
Individual judgment (Theology)
   See Particular judgment (Theology)
Individual sports
   See Sports for individuals
Individualism *(Philosophy, B824; Political theory, JC571; Sociology, HM136)*
   sa Collectivism
       Communism
       Laissez-faire
       Personalism
       Persons
       Self-interest
       Socialism
       Solidarity
   xx Collectivism
       Economics
       Equality
       Personalism
       Persons
       Political science
       Self-interest
       Socialism
       Sociology
Individuality *(BF697)*
   sa Conformity
       Identity
       Personality
       Secrecy (Psychology)
       Self
   x Individuation (Psychology)
   xx Conformity
       Consciousness
       Personality
       Psychology
       Self
Individualized instruction
   sa Open plan schools
   x Individual instruction
   xx Open plan schools
       Slow learning children
       Tutors and tutoring
   — Evaluation
Individualized reading instruction
   x Reading instruction, Individualized

   xx Reading
Individuals (Philosophy)
   See Individuation
Individuation
   sa Self (Philosophy)
   x Individuals (Philosophy)
       Particulars (Philosophy)
   xx Philosophy
       Scholasticism
       Universals (Philosophy)
       Whole and parts (Philosophy)
Individuation (Psychology)
   See Individuality
Indo-Aryan languages *(PK101-2899)*
   sa Aryan languages
       Indo-Iranian languages
       Iranian languages
       Pali language
       Pisacha languages
       Prakrit languages
       Sanskrit language
       Saurashtra language
       Vedic language
   xx Aryan languages
       Indic languages
       Indo-Iranian languages
       Iranian languages
       Old Persian language
   — Writing
       sa Brahmi alphabet
           Kharosthi alphabet
Indo-Aryan languages, Middle
   x Middle Indo-Aryan languages
Indo-Aryan languages, Modern *(PK1501-2845)*
   sa Assamese language
       Bengali language
       Bhili language
       Bihari language
       Changari language
       Dingal language
       Dumaki language
       Gujarati language
       Hindustani language
       Kashmiri language
       Khari Boli language
       Konkani language
       Lahndi language
       Marathi language
       Nepali language
       Oriya language
       Panjabi language
       Pisacha languages
       Sindhi language
       Sinhalese language
   x Gaudian languages
   xx Indic languages
Indo-Aryan literature
   See Indic literature
Indo-Aryan manuscripts
   See Manuscripts, Indic
Indo-Aryan philology *(PK101-119)*
   sa Aryan philology
       Indo-Iranian philology
       Iranian philology
       Pali philology
       Sanskrit philology
   x Philology, Indic
       Philology, Indo-Aryan
   xx Aryan philology
       Indo-Iranian philology
       Iranian philology
       Pali philology
Indo-European languages
   See Aryan languages
Indo-European philology
   See Aryan philology

Indo-Europeans
   See Aryans
Indo-Germanic languages
   See Aryan languages
Indo-Germanic peoples
   See Aryans
Indo-Iranian languages *(PK1-9201)*
   sa Aryan languages
       Indo-Aryan languages
       Iranian languages
       Mundzhan language
       Pisacha languages
       Wakhi language
   xx Aryan languages
       Indo-Aryan languages
Indo-Iranian philology *(PK1-17)*
   sa Aryan philology
       Indo-Aryan philology
       Iranian philology
   x Philology, Indo-Iranian
   xx Aryan philology
       Indo-Aryan philology
       Iranian philology
   Note under Oriental philology
Indo-Pakistan Conflict, 1965
   See India-Pakistan Conflict, 1965
Indo-Pakistan Conflict, 1971-
   See India-Pakistan Conflict, 1971-
Indo-Russian Treaty, 1971
   See Indo-Soviet Treaty of Peace, Friendship, and Cooperation, 1971
Indo-Scythians
   sa Saka
       Yüeh-chih
   xx India—History—324 B.C.-1000 A.D.
       Scythians
Indo-Soviet Treaty of Peace, Friendship, and Cooperation, 1971
   x Indo-Russian Treaty, 1971
       Russo-Indian Treaty, 1971
       Soviet-Indian Treaty, 1971
Indochina, French
   — History
   — — 1945-
       sa Refugees, Vietnamese
   — — Indochinese War, 1946-1954 *(Direct)* *(DS553.1)*
       x Indochina War, 1946-1954
       Indochinese War, 1946-1954
       xx Vietnam—History—1945-
   — — — Campaigns *(Direct)* *(DS553.3)*
       sa Dien Bien Phu, Vietnam, Battle of, 1954
   — — — Peace *(DS553.6)*
   — — — Personal narratives *(DS553.5)*
   — — — Prisoners and prisons
Indochina, French, in literature
Indochina War, 1946-1954
   See Indochina, French—History—Indochinese War, 1946-1954
Indochinese languages *(PL3521-9)*
   sa Ahom language
       Austroasiatic languages
       Chinese language
       Dungan language
       Min-chia language
       Mon-Khmer languages
       Moso language
       Tai languages
       Tibeto-Burman languages
   x Sino-Tibetan languages
       Tibeto-Chinese languages
   xx Austroasiatic languages
       Indic languages
       Mon-Khmer languages
       Tai languages
       Tibeto-Burman languages
Indochinese philology

Indolacetic acid
   See Indoleacetic acid
Indole acetic acid
   See Indoleacetic acid
Indoleacetic acid
   x Heteroauxin
     Indolacetic acid
     Indole acetic acid
   xx Acetic acid
     Growth promoting substances
Indonesia
   — History
   — — To 1478   *(DS641)*
   — — 1478-1798   *(DS642)*
   — — 1798-1942   *(DS643)*
   — — British occupation, 1811-1816
   — — 20th century
   — — Japanese occupation, 1942-1945
        (DS643.5)
   — — 1945-
   — — Revolution, 1945-1949
   — — — Personal narratives
   — — 1950-1966
   — — 1966-   *(DS644.4)*
Indonesia in literature
Indonesian language   *(PL5071-9)*
   sa Malay language
   x Bahasa Indonesia
   xx Malay language
     Malayan languages
Indonesian languages
   See Malay-Polynesian languages
     Malayan languages
Indonesian newspapers   *(Direct)*
Indonesian periodicals   *(Direct)*
Indonesian prose literature   *(Direct)*
Indonesian students in Europe, [etc.]
   xx Indonesians in Europe, [etc.]
Indonesians in Europe, [etc.]
   sa Indonesian students in Europe, [etc.]
Indoor baseball   *(GV881)*
   sa Softball
   xx Baseball
     Softball
Indoor games   *(GV1221-9)*
   sa Amusements
     Psychic games
   x Home games
     Rainy day games
   xx Amusements
     Games
Indoor photography
   See Photography, Indoor
Indoor soccer   *(GV943.9.I6)*
   x Salon soccer
   xx Soccer
Indore process
   See Compost
Indorsement advertising
   See Testimonials in advertising
Indorsements   *(Direct)*
   sa Accommodation indorsements
   x Endorsements
   xx Negotiable instruments
Indorsements, Accommodation
   See Accommodation indorsements
Indubitability
   See Certainty
Induced labor (Obstetrics)
   See Labor, Induced (Obstetrics)
Induced mutations in breeding
   See Mutation breeding
Induced radioactivity   *(QC795)*
   x Artificial radioactivity
   xx Nuclear reactions
     Radioactivity

Inductance   *(QC638)*
   Here are entered works relating to the
     constants of coils (mutual and self-
     inductance), their calculation or meas-
     urement.
   sa Mutual inductance
     Reactance (Electricity)
     Self-inductance
   xx Electric measurements
     Electrodynamics
     Electromagnetism
     Induction (Electricity)
Induction (Electricity)   *(Electromagnetic,*
     QC631-8; Electrostatic, QC581)
   Here are entered works relating to cur-
     rents or static charges of electricity in-
     duced in conductors by the presence of
     other currents or charges in the neigh-
     borhood.
   sa Condensers (Electricity)
     Electric charge and distribution
     Inductance
   xx Electric discharges through gases
     Electricity
     Electrostatics
Induction (Logic)
   sa Induction (Mathematics)
   x Inductive logic
     Logic, Inductive
   xx Inference (Logic)
     Logic
     Reasoning
   Note under Logic
Induction (Magnetism)
   See Magnetic induction
Induction (Mathematics)
   x Mathematical induction
   xx Induction (Logic)
     Mathematics
   — Problems, exercises, etc.
Induction accelerator
   See Betatron
Induction coils   *(QC645)*
   sa Condensers (Electricity)
     Mutual inductance
     Resistance-coils
     Self-inductance
   xx Electric apparatus and appliances
Induction hardening   *(TN672; TN752.I5)*
   xx Induction heating
     Metals—Heat treatment
     Surface hardening
Induction heating   *(TK4601)*
   sa Induction hardening
   x High-frequency induction heating
   xx Electric heating
   — Regulators
     xx Heating—Control
   — Safety measures
Induction motors
   See Electric motors, Induction
Induction of labor (Obstetrics)
   See Labor, Induced (Obstetrics)
Induction pumps
   See Electromagnetic pumps
Inductive logic
   See Induction (Logic)
Indulgences   *(Direct)*   *(BX2279-2283)*
   sa Absolution
     Catholic Church—Discipline
     Crusade bulls
     Holy Year
     Marian Year
     Purgatory
     Scapulars
   x Jubilee indulgences
   xx Absolution
     Catholic Church—Discipline

     Church discipline
     Pilgrims and pilgrimages
     Purgatory
Indulgences (Canon law)   *(BX1939.I45)*
Indus civilization   *(DS425)*
   x Harappa culture
     Indus Valley civilization
     Indus Valley culture
Indus Valley civilization
   See Indus civilization
Indus Valley culture
   See Indus civilization
Industrial accidents   *(Direct)*
   sa Disability evaluation
     Dust explosion
     Electricity, Injuries from
     Employers' liability
     Mine accidents
     Occupations, Dangerous
     Workmen's compensation
     subdivisions Accidents, Safety
     appliances, *and* Safety measures
     under particular industries or
     occupations, e.g. Railroads—
     Accidents; Mining engineering—
     Safety measures
   x Accidents, Industrial
     Accidents, Occupational
     Industrial injuries
     Labor and laboring classes—Accidents
     Occupational accidents
   xx Accidents
     Disability evaluation
     Employers' liability
     Factory inspection
     Factory laws and legislation
     Industrial hygiene
     Industrial safety
     Insurance, Accident
     Insurance, Employers' liability
     Occupations, Dangerous
     Personal injuries
   — Prevention
     See Industrial safety
   — Study and teaching
     See Safety education, Industrial
Industrial administration
   See Industrial management
Industrial advertising
   See Advertising, Industrial
Industrial alcohol
   See Alcohol, Denatured
Industrial allocations
   See Priorities, Industrial
Industrial arbitration
   See Arbitration, Industrial
Industrial archaeology   *(Indirect)*   *(T37)*
   Here are entered works on the organized
     study of the physical remains of indus-
     tries of the 18th and 19th centuries,
     including industrial buildings, machin-
     ery, tools, etc.
   x Antiquities, Industrial
   xx Archaeology
     Industrial buildings—History
     Industrial equipment—History
     Technology—History
Industrial architecture
   See Architecture, Industrial
Industrial art libraries   *(Z675.T3)*
   sa Industrial arts—Bibliography
     Technical libraries
   xx Industrial arts—Bibliography
     Technical libraries
Industrial arts   *(T-TX)*
   sa Agriculture
     Art industries and trade
     Artisans

Arts and crafts movement
Classification—Books—Technology
Do-it-yourself work
Engineering
Industries, Primitive
Inventions
Machinery
Machinery in industry
Manual training
Manufactures
Manufacturing processes
Mechanical engineering
Mills and mill-work
Occupations, Dangerous
Patents
Research, Industrial
Technical education
Technology
   names of specific industries, arts,
     trades, etc., e.g. Bookbinding,
     Printing, Ship-building; *and*
     subdivisions Industries,
     Manufactures, Occupations *under*
     names of countries and cities, e.g.
     Birmingham, Eng.—Industries;
     Lowell, Mass.—Manufactures;
     United States—Occupations
  x Arts, Useful
    Discoveries (in science)
    Industries
    Mechanic arts
    Trades
    Useful arts
  xx Handicraft
    Manufactures
    Technical education
    Technology
— Bibliography *(Z7911-7916)*
  sa Industrial art libraries
  xx Industrial art libraries
    Technology—Bibliography
— Biography *(T39-40)*
  sa Inventors
  xx Inventors
— Competitions *(T65.3)*
— Congresses *(T6)*
— Early works to 1800
— Exhibitions
  See Exhibitions
— Film catalogs
  See Technology—Film catalogs
— History *(T15-35)*
  sa Industries, Primitive
    Inventions
    Lost arts
  xx Lost arts
    Technology—History
— International cooperation
— Juvenile literature
— Museums
  See Industrial museums
— Pictorial works
— Programmed instruction
— Research
— Study and teaching
  sa Area vocational-technical centers
    Television in vocational education
  Example under Accreditation (Education); Universities and colleges—Accreditation
— — Audio-visual aids
— Teacher training
— Terminology *(T9-10)*
  xx Technology—Terminology
Industrial arts shops
  See School shops
Industrial arts teachers *(Direct)*
  xx Teachers

— Salaries, pensions, etc.
— Supply and demand *(Direct)*
Industrial banking
  See Industrial loan associations
    Loans, Personal
Industrial buildings *(Direct)*
    (NA6400-6581)
  sa Employees' buildings and facilities
    Factories
    Mercantile buildings
    Nuclear reactors—Containment
    Office buildings
  x Buildings, Industrial
  xx Architecture, Industrial
    Plant engineering
— Details
— — Drawings *(TH4516)*
  xx Structural drawing
— Heating and ventilation
  x Industrial buildings—Ventilation
— History
  sa Industrial archaeology
— Hygienic aspects
— Landscape architecture
  xx Landscape architecture
— Lighting
— Maintenance and repair
— — Costs
— Ventilation
  See Industrial buildings—Heating and ventilation
Industrial buying
  See Industrial procurement
Industrial cafeterias
  See Industrial feeding
Industrial canteens
  See Industrial feeding
Industrial capacity *(Direct)*
  sa subdivision Industrial capacity *under specific industries, e.g.* Machinery—Trade and manufacture—Industrial capacity
  x Capacity, Industrial
    Manufacturing capacity
  xx Industry
    Manufactures
— Mathematical models
Industrial ceramics
  See Ceramics
Industrial chaplains
  See Chaplains, Industrial
Industrial chemistry
  See Chemical engineering
    Chemistry, Technical
Industrial cinematography
  See Cinematography, Industrial
Industrial clothing
  See Work clothes
Industrial combinations
  See Trusts, Industrial
Industrial communication
  See Communication in management
Industrial concentration
  sa Competition
    Conglomerate corporations
    Consolidation and merger of corporations
    Industrial organization
  x Concentration, Industrial
    Economic concentration
  xx Big business
    Competition
    Consolidation and merger of corporations
    Industrial organization
    Industries, Size of
    Oligopolies
    Trusts, Industrial

Industrial conciliation
  See Mediation and conciliation, Industrial
Industrial contamination
  See Contamination (Technology)
Industrial costs
  See Costs, Industrial
Industrial councils
  See Works councils
Industrial counseling
  See Employee counseling
Industrial courts
  See Labor courts
Industrial dentistry
  xx Dentistry
    Medicine, Industrial
Industrial dermatitis
  See Occupational dermatitis
Industrial design
  See Design, Industrial
Industrial design coordination *(T324)*
  sa Advertising cards
    Design protection
    House marks
    Letterheads
    Railroads—Freight-cars—Markings
    Service marks
    Trade-marks
  x Coordination of industrial designs
    Corporate design coordination
    Corporate image and design
    Corporate style
    Design coordination, Industrial
    Designs (Industrial publicity)
    House style
    Visual designs (Industrial publicity)
  xx Design, Industrial
    Emblems
    Industrial property
    Industrial publicity
Industrial design departments
  See Design, Industrial—Management
Industrial designers *(Direct)*
  sa Design, Industrial—Vocational guidance
  x Designers, Industrial
  xx Design, Industrial
Industrial development bonds *(Direct)*
  xx Bonds
    Industrial promotion
    Municipal bonds
Industrial development centers
  See Industrial productivity centers
Industrial discipline
  See Labor discipline
Industrial diseases
  See Occupational diseases
Industrial disputes
  See Labor disputes
Industrial districts *(Direct)*
  Here are entered works on self-contained industrial areas within which utilities, transportation, and other general services are offered to a group of individual companies.
  x Industrial estates
    Industrial parks
    Research parks, Industrial
  xx Industrial sites
    Real estate business
— Buildings
— Finance
— Law and legislation *(Direct)*
  xx Real property
Industrial drawing
  See Mechanical drawing
Industrial economics
  See Industrial organization (Economic theory)

Industrial education
　　See Manual training
　　　Technical education
Industrial efficiency
　　See Efficiency, Industrial
Industrial electric tractors
　　See Industrial electric trucks
Industrial electric trucks
　　sa Fork lift trucks
　　x Electric industrial trucks
　　　Electric tractors, Industrial
　　　Electric trucks, Industrial
　　　Industrial electric tractors
　　xx Conveying machinery
　　　Electric motors
　　　Electric vehicles
　　　Industrial power trucks
　　　Materials handling
　　　Motor-trucks
　— Automation
　— Batteries
　— — Standards (Direct)
Industrial electrochemistry
　　See Electrochemistry, Industrial
Industrial electronics (TK7881)
　　sa Electronic control
　　　Electronic instruments
　　　Industrial television
　　x Electronics in industry
　　　Factories—Electronic equipment
　　xx Electronic apparatus and appliances
　　　Electronics
　　　Factories—Electric equipment
　— Problems, exercises, etc.
Industrial engineering (Indirect)
　　　Here are entered works on the application
　　　of engineering principles and tech-
　　　niques to the design, installation and
　　　improvement of integrated systems
　　　employing men, materials, and equip-
　　　ment for a high level of productivity at
　　　an optimum cost. Works dealing with
　　　the planning and control of the me-
　　　chanical means of shape, condition,
　　　and relationship of materials toward
　　　changing the greater effectiveness and
　　　value are entered under Production
　　　engineering.
　　sa Automation
　　　Costs, Industrial
　　　Engineering economy
　　　Human engineering
　　　Industrial project management
　　　Industrial relations
　　　Industrial statistics
　　　Methods engineering
　　　Operations research
　　　Plant layout
　　　Production control
　　　Production engineering
　　　Psychology, Industrial
　　　Quality control
　　　Standardization
　　　Systems engineering
　　　Wages and labor productivity
　　　Work measurement
　　x Engineering, Industrial
　　　Management engineering
　　xx Efficiency, Industrial
　　　Engineering
　　　Factory management
　　　Industrial management
　　　Simplification in industry
　　Note under Production engineering
　— Abbreviations
　— Mathematics
　　xx Engineering mathematics
　— Notation

　　x Industrial engineering symbols
　— Problems, exercises, etc.
　— Statistical methods (T57.35)
　　xx Industrial statistics
　— Vocational guidance
　　　See Industrial engineering as a
　　　　profession
Industrial engineering as a profession
　　x Industrial engineering—Vocational
　　　guidance
Industrial engineering symbols
　　See Industrial engineering—Notation
Industrial engineers (Direct)
　　xx Engineers
Industrial engineers, Japanese, [etc.]
　　x Japanese [etc.] industrial engineers
Industrial equipment (Direct)
　　sa Factories—Equipment and supplies
　　　Industrial equipment leases
　　　Installation of industrial equipment
　　　Office equipment and supplies
　　　Pollution control equipment
　　　Replacement of industrial equipment
　　　subdivision Equipment and supplies
　　　　under names of industries, e.g.
　　　　Petroleum industry and trade—
　　　　Equipment and supplies
　　x Capital equipment
　　　Equipment, Capital
　　　Equipment, Industrial
　　xx Industry
　— Corrosion (TS191)
　— Estimates and costs (Direct)
　— History
　　sa Industrial archaeology
　— Maintenance and repair
　　xx Plant maintenance
　— — Mathematical models
　— Prices
　— Valuation
　　x Industrial equipment valuation
Industrial equipment, Replacement of
　　See Replacement of industrial equipment
Industrial equipment leases (Direct)
　　sa Computer leases
　　x Equipment leasing
　　　Leases, Industrial equipment
　　xx Industrial equipment
　　　Lease and rental services
Industrial equipment valuation
　　See Industrial equipment—Valuation
Industrial espionage
　　See Business intelligence
Industrial estates
　　See Industrial districts
Industrial exhibitions
　　See Exhibitions
Industrial feeding (Direct)
　　x Canteens (Industrial)
　　　Employee food service
　　　Factory canteens
　　　Industrial cafeterias
　　　Industrial canteens
　　　Industrial lunchrooms
　　　Industry—Food service
　　xx Food service
　　　Restaurants, lunch rooms, etc.
　　Note under Canteens (War-time, emergency,
　　　etc.)
　— Management
Industrial films
　　See Moving-pictures in industry
Industrial folk-lore
　　See Folk-lore of industry
Industrial gaming
　　See Management games
Industrial health
　　See Occupational diseases

Industrial health engineering
　　See Industrial hygiene
Industrial housekeeping
　　x Factory housekeeping
　　　Housekeeping, Industrial
　　xx Buildings—Cleaning
　　　Factory sanitation
　　　Plant maintenance
Industrial housing (Direct) (HD7289.5)
　　　Here are entered works on housing prov-
　　　ided by an industry to its employees.
　　　Works on communities in which all or
　　　the major portion of the property and
　　　businesses are owned by one industry
　　　are entered under Company towns.
　　x Employee housing
　　xx Housing
　　　Labor and laboring classes—Dwellings
　　Note under Company towns
Industrial hygiene (Direct) (HD7260-7780)
　　sa Factories—Safety measures
　　　Factory sanitation
　　　Industrial accidents
　　　Mine sanitation
　　　Occupational diseases
　　　subdivision Diseases and hygiene under
　　　classes of workers, e.g. Potters—
　　　Diseases and hygiene; and
　　　subdivision Hygienic aspects under
　　　names of industries, processes, or
　　　occupations, e.g. Wool trade and
　　　industry—Hygienic aspects; Welding
　　　—Hygienic aspects
　　x Health of workers
　　　Hygiene, Industrial
　　　Industrial health engineering
　　　Occupational health and safety
　　　Occupations—Hygienic aspects
　　xx Environmental health
　　　Hygiene, Public
　　　Industrial management
　　Note under Medicine, Industrial
　— Classification
　— Examinations, questions, etc.
　— Forms, blanks, etc.
　　x Medicine, Industrial—Forms, blanks,
　　　etc.
　— Instruments
　— Laboratory manuals
　— Law and legislation (Direct)
　　sa Factory laws and legislation
　　　Medicine, Industrial—Law and
　　　legislation
　　　Painting, Industrial—Law and
　　　legislation
　　　Ventilation—Laws and regulations
　　x Factory sanitation—Law and
　　　legislation
　　xx Factory laws and legislation
　　　Labor laws and legislation
　　Example under Public health laws
　— Posters
　— Research (Direct)
Industrial injuries
　　See Industrial accidents
Industrial installation
　　See Installation of industrial equipment
Industrial insurance
　　See Insurance, Industrial
Industrial laws and legislation (Direct)
　　(HD3621-7)
　　　Here are entered works of a comprehen-
　　　sive character which deal with laws
　　　and legislation regulating industry.
　　　Works on the theory of state regula-
　　　tion of industry are entered under In-
　　　dustry and state; Laissez-faire.
　　sa Competition, Unfair

Factory laws and legislation
Freedom of movement
Government business enterprises—Law
and legislation
Labor laws and legislation
Occupations, Dangerous
Patent laws and legislation
Standardization—Law and legislation
Trade-marks
Trade regulation
x Government regulation of commerce
Law, Industrial
xx Economic policy
Industry and state
— Digests
— Underdeveloped areas
See Underdeveloped areas—Industrial
laws and legislation
Industrial lighting
See Factories—Lighting
Industrial loan associations
x Banks and banking, Industrial
Industrial banking
xx Banks and banking
Credit
Instalment plan
Loans, Personal
Industrial location
See Industries, Location of
Industrial lunchrooms
See Industrial feeding
Industrial maintenance
See Plant maintenance
Industrial management *(Direct)*
Here are entered works on the application
of the principles of management to in-
dustrial enterprises, including, in addi-
tion to the production aspects, office
management, marketing, financial
controls, etc.
Works limited to technical control of
manufacturing processes are entered
under the heading Factory manage-
ment.
sa Assembly-line methods
Big business
Business
Business consultants
Business intelligence
Classification—Books—Industrial
management
Communication in management
Controllership
Delegation of authority
Efficiency, Industrial
Employment stabilization
Executives
Executives, Training of
Factory management
Government business enterprises—
Auditing and inspection
Industrial engineering
Industrial hygiene
Industrial management and inflation
Industrial organization
Industrial procurement
Industrial productivity
Industrial relations
Industrial sociology
Industries, Location of
Industries, Size of
Labor productivity
Management audit
Management committees
Management games
Management rights
Managerial economics
Marketing

Marketing management
Materials management
New business enterprises
Office management
Personnel management
Physical distribution of goods—
Management
Production control
Production management
Production standards
Ratio analysis
Sales management
Service industries—Management
Shift systems
Shipment of goods
Simplification in industry
Small business—Management
Technological innovations
Welfare work in industry
Works councils
x Industrial administration
Management, Industrial
Rationalization of industry
Scientific management
xx Business
Industrial organization
Industry
Management
Organization
Technology
— Anecdotes, facetiae, satire, etc.
— Audio-visual aids
— — Catalogs
— Examinations, questions, etc.
— Graphic methods *(T60.G7)*
— Handbooks, manuals, etc.
— Information services
— International cooperation
— Mathematical models
sa DYNAMO (Computer program
language)
xx Business mathematics
— Methodology
— Problems, exercises, etc.
— Programmed instruction
— Quotations, maxims, etc.
— Research
— Statistical methods
— Study and teaching *(Direct)*
— Terminology
— Vocational guidance
See Industrial management as a
profession

GEOGRAPHIC SUBDIVISIONS

— Russia
sa Socialist competition
Stakhanov movement
Industrial management and inflation
sa Currency convertibility
Gold clause
Payment
Revalorization of debts
Valuta clause
x Inflation and industrial management
Inflation (Finance) and industrial
management
xx Currency question
Finance
Industrial management
Inflation (Finance)
Payment
Industrial management as a profession
x Industrial management—Vocational
guidance
Industrial management games
See Management games

Industrial materials
See Materials
Industrial mediation
See Mediation and conciliation, Industrial
Industrial medicine
See Medicine, Industrial
Industrial melanism
xx Melanism
Industrial mental health
See Industrial psychiatry
Industrial meteorology
See Industry and weather
Industrial microbiology *(QR53)*
sa Microbial mutation breeding
Microbiological synthesis
Sanitary microbiology
subdivision Microbiology *under
subjects, e.g.* Petroleum—
Microbiology; Textile fibers—
Microbiology
x Microbiology, Industrial
xx Microbiology
— Safety measures
Industrial microscopy
sa Metallography
subdivision Microscopy *under special
industries and industrial products*
x Microscopy, Industrial
xx Microscope and microscopy
Industrial missions
See Missions—Industrial work
Industrial mobilization *(Indirect) (UA18)*
sa Military supplies
Munitions
subdivision Military aspects *under
names of industries, e.g.* Chemical
industries—Military aspects; Clock
and watch making—Military aspects
x Defenses
Industries
Mobilization, Industrial
xx Armaments
Economic policy
Military art and science
War—Economic aspects
Industrial morale
See Employee morale
Industrial museums *(Indirect) (T179-183)*
x Art industries and trade—Museums
Industrial arts—Museums
Technological museums
Technology—Museums
xx Museums
Industrial noise *(Direct) (TA365)*
sa *subdivision* Noise *under industrial
subjects, e.g.* Steel-works—Noise
x Factories—Noise
Factory noise
xx Noise
Industrial nuisances
See Nuisances
Industrial nursing *(RC966)*
sa Public health nursing
xx Medicine, Industrial
Nurses and nursing
Public health nursing
Industrial ophthalmology
x Ophthalmology, Industrial
xx Medicine, Industrial
Industrial organization *(Direct)*
sa Industrial concentration
Industrial management
Works councils
x Industry—Organization
Organization, Industrial
xx Industrial concentration
Industrial management
Industry

Industrial organization *(Direct)*
  (Continued)
    Organization
Industrial organization (Economic theory)
  x Industrial economics
  xx Industry
    Microeconomics
Industrial painters
  See Painters, Industrial
Industrial painting
  See Painting, Industrial
Industrial parks
  See Industrial districts
Industrial photochemistry
  See Photochemistry—Industrial applications
Industrial photography
  See Photography, Industrial
Industrial plant protection
  See Factories—Protection
    subdivision Defense measures *under*
      industries and plants, e.g. Gas
      industry—Defense measures;
      Petroleum industry and trade—
      Defense measures
Industrial plants
  See Factories
Industrial poisons
  See Industrial toxicology
Industrial police
  See Police, Private
Industrial power trucks *(Manufacture,*
    TL296; Material handling, TS155)
  sa Fork lift trucks
    Industrial electric trucks
    Straddle trucks
  x Industrial tractors
    Industrial trucks
    Motor-trucks, Industrial
    Power trucks, Industrial
  xx Materials handling
    Motor-trucks
  — Hydraulic drive
  — Parts
  — Safety measures
  — Safety regulations *(Direct)*
Industrial priorities
  See Priorities, Industrial
Industrial process control
  See Process control
Industrial processing
  See Manufacturing processes
Industrial procurement *(Direct)*
  sa Make-or-buy decisions
    Priorities, Industrial
    Purchasing agents
    Purchasing departments
    Small orders
  x Buying, Industrial
    Industrial buying
    Industrial purchasing
    Procurement, Industrial
    Purchasing, Industrial
  xx Industrial management
    Purchasing
  Note under Purchasing
  — Accounting
  — Auditing and inspection
  — Automation
  — Management
  — Mathematical models
Industrial production
  See Industry
    Overproduction
    Supply and demand
Industrial productivity
  sa Automation
    Capital productivity
    Labor productivity
    Machinery in industry

    Productivity accounting
    Technological innovations
  x Productivity, Industrial
  xx Efficiency, Industrial
    Industrial management
    Industry
    Production (Economic theory)
Industrial productivity centers *(Direct)*
  x Industrial development centers
    Productivity centers
  xx Economic development
    Research, Industrial
    Technical assistance
Industrial project management
  sa Network analysis (Planning)
  x Project management
    Project management, Industrial
  xx Factory management
    Industrial engineering
    Management
Industrial promotion *(Direct)*
  sa Industrial development bonds
  xx Boards of trade
    Industry
    Small business
  — Information services *(Direct)*
  — Underdeveloped areas
    See Underdeveloped areas—Industrial
      promotion
Industrial property *(Direct)*
  Here are entered works dealing collectively with several categories of intangible property rights connected with
  industry, commerce, and agriculture,
  as, ownership of patents, trade-marks,
  business names, etc.
  sa Business names
    Competition, Unfair
    Design protection
    Good-will (in business, etc.)
    Industrial design coordination
    Marks of origin
    Models (Patents)
    Patent laws and legislation
    Service marks
    Trade-marks
  x Proprietary rights
  xx Intangible property
  — Cases
  — Criminal provisions
    sa Copyright infringement
  — Forms
  — Taxation *(Direct)*
Industrial property (International law)
  xx International law
Industrial psychiatry
  x Industrial mental health
    Psychiatry, Industrial
  xx Medicine, Industrial
    Psychiatry
    Psychology, Industrial
Industrial psychology
  See Psychology, Industrial
Industrial publicity
  sa Advertising
    Industrial design coordination
    Public relations
  x Publicity, Industrial
  xx Industry
    Public relations
    Publicity
Industrial purchasing
  See Industrial procurement
Industrial radiochemistry
  See Radiochemistry—Industrial applications
Industrial radiography
  See Radiography, Industrial

Industrial railroads
  See Railroads, Industrial
Industrial rationing
  See Priorities, Industrial
Industrial recreation *(HD7395.R4)*
  sa Vacations, Employee
  x Employee recreation
    Recreation, Industrial
  xx Recreation
    Welfare work in industry
Industrial relations *(Direct) (HD6961)*
  Here are entered works dealing with employer-employee relations in general.
  Works on special aspects of this relationship are entered under specific
  headings, *e.g.* Arbitration, Industrial;
  Collective bargaining; Employees' representation in management; etc. The
  heading Labor laws and legislation is
  used for material on the legal aspects.
  Works on the technique of personnel
  management and relations from the
  employers' point of view are entered
  under the heading Personnel management while those descriptive of the social and economic conditions of labor
  are entered under Labor and laboring
  classes.
  sa Arbitration, Industrial
    Business agents (Trade-union)
    Collective bargaining
    Company towns
    Company unions
    Employee counseling
    Employee-management relations in
      government
    Employees' magazines, handbooks, etc.
    Employees, Reporting to
    Employees' representation in
      management
    Featherbedding (Industrial relations)
    Foremen's unions
    Grievance procedures
    Industrial sociology
    Labor contract
    Labor disputes
    Labor laws and legislation
    Management rights
    Mediation and conciliation, Industrial
    Personnel directors
    Personnel management
    Shop stewards
    Strikes and lockouts
    Trade-unions
    Unfair labor practices
    Works councils
  x Capital and labor
    Employee-employer relations
    Employer-employee relations
    Labor and capital
    Labor-management relations
    Labor relations
  xx Industrial engineering
    Industrial management
    Industry
    Labor and laboring classes
    Labor economics
  Note under Supervision of employees
  — Audio-visual aids
    Example under Visual aids
  — Caricatures and cartoons
  — Programmed instruction
  — Public opinion
  — Research *(Direct)*
    x Industrial relations research
    xx Research, Industrial
  — Simulation methods
Industrial relations as a profession

Industrial relations councils
    See Works councils
Industrial relations research
    See Industrial relations—Research
Industrial research
    See Research, Industrial
Industrial revolution
    See Industry—History
        subdivisions Economic conditions *and*
          Industries *under names of countries*
Industrial safety *(Direct)* *(T55)*
    sa Clothing, Protective
        Dam safety
        Hazardous substances
        Industrial accidents
        Industrial safety committees
        Mine safety
        Safety appliances
        Safety education, Industrial
        Safety engineers
        Safety signs
        subdivisions Safety appliances *and*
          Safety measures *under subjects, e.g.*
          Cotton machinery—Safety
          appliances; Factories—Safety
          measures
    x Industrial accidents—Prevention
        Occupational health and safety
        Safety engineering
        Safety, Industrial
        Safety measures
        Safety of workers
    xx Accidents—Prevention
        Plant engineering
  — Classification
  — Film catalogs
  — Laboratory manuals
  — Law and legislation *(Direct)*
    sa Factory laws and legislation
        Mine safety—Law and legislation
        Safety regulations
        Ventilation—Laws and regulations
        subdivision Safety regulations *under*
         particular subjects, e.g. Machinery
         —Safety regulations
    xx Accident law
        Employers' liability
        Factory laws and legislation
        Safety regulations
        Note under Safety regulations
  — Pictorial works
  — Posters
  — Standards
  — Study and teaching
        See Safety education, Industrial
Industrial safety committees
    xx Industrial safety
Industrial safety education
    See Safety education, Industrial
Industrial safety engineers
    See Safety engineers
Industrial salvage
    See Salvage (Waste, etc.)
Industrial scale removal
    See Descaling
Industrial schools
    See Manual training
        Reformatories
        Trade schools
Industrial security measures
    See Industry—Security measures
Industrial security program (United States)
    xx Labor and laboring classes—United
        States—1914-
        Loyalty security program, 1947-
Industrial sites *(Direct)*
    sa Industrial districts
    x Factory sites

    xx Factories—Location
        Industries, Location of
        Plant engineering
        Real property
Industrial sociology *(HD6971-4)*
    Here are entered works on social rela-
    tions within industry, as distinguished
    from labor-management relations.
    Works about the impact of industry on
    culture and societal changes, and
    works about the social responsibilities
    of businessmen are entered under In-
    dustry—Social aspects.
    sa Industry—Social aspects
    x Sociology, Industrial
    xx Industrial management
        Industrial relations
        Industry—Social aspects
        Personnel management
        Psychology, Industrial
        Sociology
        Work
    Note under Industry—Social aspects
  — Research *(Direct)*
    xx Sociological research
Industrial statistics *(HC; Special industries,*
      HD9000-9999; Theory, HA40.16)
    sa Industrial engineering—Statistical
        methods
        subdivision Industries *under names of*
         countries, cities, etc.
    x Industry—Statistical methods
       Industry—Statistics
    xx Industrial engineering
        Statistics
  — Problems, exercises, etc.
Industrial storage racks
    See Storage racks
Industrial stores
    See Company stores
Industrial supply houses
    x Industry—Equipment and supplies
Industrial surveys *(HC28)*
    Here are entered works on the techniques
    employed. Reports, etc. of individual
    surveys are entered under the city or
    district concerned, with subdivision
    Industries.
    x Industry—Surveys
Industrial technicians
    See Technicians in industry
Industrial television
    x Television in industry
       Television, Industrial
       Television—Industrial applications
    xx Closed-circuit television
        Industrial electronics
        Microwave communication systems
Industrial tours
    x Factory tours
       Plant tours
    xx Business education
        Employees, Training of
        Field work (Educational method)
        School excursions
        Technical education
Industrial toxicology *(RC963.5)*
    x Industrial poisons
       Poisons, Industrial
    xx Occupational diseases
        Toxicology
Industrial tractors
    See Industrial power trucks
Industrial traffic management
    See Shipment of goods
Industrial trucks
    See Industrial power trucks

Industrial trusts
    See Trusts, Industrial
Industrial unions
    See Trade-unions
Industrial vacuum
    See Vacuum technology
Industrial wastes
    See Factory and trade waste
       Waste products
Industrial water-supply
    See Water-supply, Industrial
Industrial welfare work
    See Welfare work in industry
Industrialization
    Works on the industrialization of in-
    dividual countries or regions are en-
    tered under the name of the area fol-
    lowed by the subdivision Industries.
    sa Technical assistance
        Underdeveloped areas
        United Nations—Economic assistance
        United Nations—Technical assistance
    xx Economic development
        Economic policy
        Industry
        Technical assistance
  — Mathematical models
Industrialized building *(Direct) (TH1000)*
    sa Buildings, Prefabricated
        Modular construction
        Precast concrete construction
    x Industrialized construction
       System building
       Systems building
    xx Building
        Construction industry—Management
Industrialized construction
    See Industrialized building
Industries
    See Industrial arts
       Industrial mobilization
       Industry
       names of specific industries, e.g.
        Aerospace industries; Construction
        industry; *and subdivision* Industries
        under names of countries, cities, etc.
Industries, Chemical
    See Chemical industries
Industries, Electric
    See Electric industries
Industries, Home
    See Home labor
Industries, Location of *(Direct) (HD58)*
    sa Business relocation
        Factories—Location
        Industrial sites
        Store location
    x Industrial location
       Location in business
       Location of industries
       Plant location
    xx Cities and towns—Planning
        Community development
        Factories—Location
        Industrial management
        Space in economics
  — Mathematical models
Industries, Primitive *(GN429-434)*
    sa Agriculture, Primitive
        Arms and armor, Primitive
        Australian aborigines—Industries
        Bone implements
        Bow and arrow
        Fishing, Primitive
        Hunting, Primitive
        Indians—Implements
        Indians of North America—Industries
        Indians of South America—Industries

Industries, Primitive *(GN429-434)*
(Continued)
    Man, Prehistoric
    Matting
    Nets
    Pottery, Prehistoric
    Pottery, Primitive
    Stone implements
    Weaving
  x Primitive technology
    Technology, Primitive
  xx Archaeology
    Ethnology
    Industrial arts
    Industrial arts—History
    Society, Primitive
Industries, Seasonal
  See Seasonal industries
Industries, Service
  See Service industries
Industries, Size of
  sa Big business
    Economies of scale
    Industrial concentration
    Small business
  x Size of industries
  xx Big business
    Industrial management
    Industry
    Small business
Industry *(HC; HD)*
  sa Big business
    Business losses
    Business mortality
    Businessmen
    Color in industry
    Costs, Industrial
    Cottage industries
    Efficiency, Industrial
    Employees' representation in
      management
    Entrepreneur
    Floor space, Industrial
    Industrial capacity
    Industrial equipment
    Industrial management
    Industrial organization
    Industrial organization (Economic
      theory)
    Industrial productivity
    Industrial promotion
    Industrial publicity
    Industrial relations
    Industrialization
    Industries, Size of
    Interindustry economics
    Machinery in industry
    Moving-pictures in industry
    New business enterprises
    Production (Economic theory)
    Research, Industrial
    Seasonal industries
    Seasonal variations (Economics)
    Substitution (Economics)
    Technology
    Turnover (Business)
    Underdeveloped areas—Industries
    Water-supply, Industrial
    subdivision Industries *under names of*
      countries, regions, cities, etc.
  x Industrial production
    Industries
  xx Economics
    Overproduction
    Technology
  — Auditing and inspection
  — Classification

  sa subdivision Industries—Classification
    under names of countries, e.g.
    United States—Industries—
    Classification
  — Costs
    See Costs, Industrial
  — Defense measures *(Direct)*
    xx Civil defense
  — Equipment and supplies
    See Industrial supply houses
  — Food service
    See Industrial feeding
  — History *(HD2321)*
    sa Commerce—History
      Factory system
      Home labor
      Machinery in industry
    x Industrial revolution
    xx Economic history
  — — Juvenile literature
  — Information services
    sa subdivision Industries—Information
      services *under names of countries,*
      cities, etc., e.g. Europe—
      Industries—Information services
  — Juvenile literature
  — Organization
    See Industrial organization
  — Security measures *(Direct) (HV8290;*
    Protection of classified
    information, UB249)
    x Industrial security measures
      Security measures, Industrial
      Security measures (Military
      information)
    xx Factories—Protection
    Example under reference from Security
      measures
  — Social aspects *(Direct)*
    Here are entered works about the im-
    pact of industry on culture and soci-
    etal changes, and works about the
    social responsibilities of business-
    men. Works on social relations
    within industry, as distinguished
    from labor-management relations,
    are entered under Industrial soci-
    ology
    sa Industrial sociology
    x Business and social problems
      Business—Social aspects
    xx Industrial sociology
      Social change
    Note under Industrial sociology
  — — Public opinion
  — Statistical methods
    See Industrial statistics
  — Statistics
    See Industrial statistics
      subdivision Industries *under*
      names of countries, cities, etc.,
      e.g United States—Industries
  — Subject headings
    See Subject headings—Industry
  — Surveys
    See Industrial surveys
      subdivision Industries *under name*
      of city or district concerned
  — Terminology
Industry (Psychology)
  See Work
Industry and art
  See Art and industry
Industry and climate
  See Industry and weather
Industry and colleges
  See Industry and education

Industry and education *(Direct)*
  sa Education, Cooperative
  x Education and industry
    Industry and colleges
  xx Universities and colleges
Industry and music
  See Music in industry
Industry and state *(Indirect)*
  (HD3611-3790)
  sa Agriculture and state
    Bounties
    Commercial policy
    Concessions
    Corporate state
    Economic policy
    Fishery policy
    Foreign trade promotion
    Forest policy
    Full employment policies
    Government business enterprises
    Government competition
    Government lending
    Government ownership
    Government questionnaires
    Industrial laws and legislation
    Insurance—State supervision
    Labor laws and legislation
    Labor policy
    Laissez-faire
    Mercantile system
    Price regulation
    Priorities, Industrial
    Public interest
    Public service commissions
    Railroads and state
    Right to labor
    Subsidies
    Trade regulation
    Transportation and state
    specific industries or commercial
      products
  x Business and government
    Government and business
    Government regulation of commerce
    Law, Industrial
    State and industry
  xx Economic policy
    Laissez-faire
    Socialism
    Technology and state
  Note under Industrial laws and legislation
Industry and the church
  See Church and industry
Industry and war
  See War—Economic aspects
Industry and weather
  sa Degree days
    Engineering meteorology
    Unemployment, Seasonal
  x Industrial meteorology
    Industry and climate
    Weather and industry
  xx Engineering meteorology
    Man—Influence of climate
    Weather
Industry in art *(N8218)*
  xx Art and industry
Industry in literature *(PN56.I)*
  xx Economics in literature
Indwelling of God
  See Mystical union
Inebriates
  See Alcoholics
Inebriety
  See Alcoholism
    Drunkenness (Criminal law)
Inefficiency, Intellectual *(BF435-7)*
  sa Fatigue, Mental

Mental tests
Mentally handicapped children
Pedantry
 x Intellectual inefficiency
Stupidity
 xx Ability
Delinquents
Education
Fatigue, Mental
Intellect
Mental deficiency
Mentally handicapped
Psychology
Inelastic cross sections *(QC173)*
 sa Cross sections (Nuclear physics)
Elastic cross sections
 x Cross sections, Inelastic
 xx Collisions (Nuclear physics)
Elastic cross sections
Inequalities (Mathematics) *(QA295)*
 xx Processes, Infinite
— Programmed instruction
Inequality
 See Equality
Inert elements
 See Gases, Rare
Inertia, Moments of
 See Moments of inertia
Inertia, Products of
 See Moments of inertia
Inertia (Mechanics)
 sa Mass (Physics)
Momentum (Mechanics)
 xx Acceleration (Mechanics)
Mass (Physics)
Mechanics
— Measurement
Inertial guidance
 See Inertial navigation systems
Inertial guidance sensors
 See Inertial navigation systems
Inertial mass
 See Mass (Physics)
Inertial navigation
 x Navigation, Inertial
 xx Dead reckoning (Navigation)
Nautical instruments
Navigation
 Example under Gyroscopic instruments
Inertial navigation (Aeronautics) *(TL588.5)*
 x Navigation, Inertial (Aeronautics)
 xx Aeronautical instruments
Dead reckoning (Navigation)
Navigation (Aeronautics)
Inertial navigation (Astronautics)
 sa Stellar inertial navigation systems
 x Navigation, Inertial (Astronautics)
 xx Astrodynamics
Navigation (Astronautics)
Space vehicles—Guidance systems
Inertial navigation systems
 x Inertial guidance
Inertial guidance sensors
 xx Nautical instruments
Infallibility (Philosophy) *(BD234)*
 sa Popes—Infallibility
 xx Knowledge, Theory of
Philosophy
Infallibility of the church
 See Catholic Church—Infallibility
Church—Infallibility
Infallibility of the Pope
 See Popes—Infallibility
Infamy (Canon law)
Infamy (Law)
 sa Civil death
Political rights, Loss of
 xx Civil death

Civil law
Criminal law
Political rights, Loss of
Punishment
Infamy (Roman law)
Infancy of animals
 See Animals, Infancy of
Infancy of Jesus, Devotion to
 See Holy Childhood, Devotion to
Infant and maternal health services
 See Maternal health services
Infant baptism *(BV813)*
 sa Children—Conversion to Christianity
Predestination
 x Pedobaptism
 xx Baptism
Infant salvation
— Early church, ca. 30-600
 xx Church history—Primitive and early
church, ca. 30-600
Infant communion *(BV828)*
 x Children's communion
Communion, Infant
Lord's Supper—Infant communion
 xx Lord's Supper
Infant education
 See Education, Preschool
Infant formulas
 xx Infants—Nutrition
— Standards
Infant mortality
 See Children—Mortality
Infants—Mortality
Infants (Newborn)—Mortality
Infant salvation *(BT758)*
 sa Children—Conversion to Christianity
Children—Death and future state
Infant baptism
Limbo
Predestination
 xx Children—Death and future state
Limbo
Salvation
Infant sudden death
 See Sudden death in infants
Infant welfare
 See Maternal and infant welfare
Infanticide *(Direct)* *(HV6537-6541)*
 sa Abortion
 xx Criminal law
Homicide
Murder
Offenses against the person
Infanticide (Roman law)
Infanticide in literature
Infantile conjunctivitis
 See Conjunctivitis, Infantile
Infantile paralysis
 See Poliomyelitis
Infantile scurvy
 See Scurvy, Infantile
Infantilism *(RJ135)*
 sa Childishness
 x Progeria
 xx Childishness
Infantry *(UD)*
 sa France. Armée. Infanterie
United States. Army. Infantry
 similar headings
 subdivision Militia *under states of the
United States, e.g.* Massachusetts—
Militia
 x Foot soldiers
— Equipment *(UD370-375)*

Infantry drill and tactics *(UD157-302)*
Here are entered general works only.
Works on the army of any particular
country are entered under the name of
the country, with subheading Army.
Infantry—Drill and tactics.
 sa Night fighting (Military science)
Skirmishing
Target-practice
 xx Drill and minor tactics
Military art and science
Tactics
Infantry landing craft
 See Landing craft
Infants *(Psychology, BF723.16; Social groups,
HQ769-785)*
 sa Children
Children, First-born
Crawling and creeping
 x Babies
 xx Children
— Anecdotes, facetiae, satire, etc.
— Bathing
 xx Infants—Care and hygiene
— Care and hygiene *(RJ61; RJ101)*
 sa Baby sitters
Finger-sucking
Infants—Bathing
Nurseries
Prenatal care
 x Health of infants
 xx Children—Care and hygiene
Hygiene
Nurses and nursing
— — Anecdotes, facetiae, satire, etc.
— Charities, protection, etc.
 See Maternal and infant welfare
— Clothing *(TT635-645)*
 sa Layettes
 xx Children's clothing
— — Tariff
 See Tariff on infants' clothing
— Crying
 See Crying
— Discipline
 See Discipline of infants
— Diseases *(RJ)*
 sa Craniotabes
Dehydration in infants
Spasms
 x Diseases of children
 xx Children—Diseases
Medicine—Practice
— — Diagnosis *(RJ50)*
 xx Diagnosis
— — Homeopathic treatment *(RX501-531)*
— Growth *(RJ131)*
— — Testing
— Insurance
 See Insurance, Child
— Juvenile literature
— Law
 See Children—Law
— Mortality *(Public health, RJ59, RJ598;
Vital statistics, HB1323.I4)*
 sa Dehydration in infants
Infants (Newborn)—Mortality
Insurance, Child
Mothers—Mortality
Still-birth
Sudden death in infants
 x Infant mortality
Mortuary statistics
 xx Children—Mortality
Mortality
— Nutrition *(RJ216)*
 sa Bottle feeding
Breast feeding

903

Infants *(Psychology, BF723.I6; Social groups, HQ769-785)*
— Nutrition *(RJ216)* *(Continued)*
    Infant formulas
    Infants—Weaning
    Lactated food
    Milk
    Milk depots
    Wet-nurses
  x Baby foods
    Infants, Food for
    Nutrition of children
  xx Children—Nutrition
    Milk, Human
— Quotations, maxims, etc.
— Weaning *(RJ216)*
  x Weaning of infants
  xx Infants—Nutrition
— Weight *(GN63)*
  x Weight in infancy
  xx Body weight
Infants, Food for
  See Infants—Nutrition
Infants (Newborn)
  sa Infants (Premature)
— Care and hygiene
  xx Hygiene
— Diseases
  sa names of special diseases, e.g.
    Asphyxia neonatorum;
    Erythroblastosis fetalis
— — Diagnosis
— Mortality
  x Infant mortality
    Neonatal death
  xx Infants—Mortality
— Physiology
— Surgery
  x Neonatal surgery
    Surgery, Neonatal
  xx Children—Surgery
Infants (Premature) *(RJ250)*
  x Birth, Premature
    Premature infants
  xx Infants (Newborn)
    Labor (Obstetrics)
Infants (Still-born)
  See Still-birth
Infants and drugs
  See Drugs and infants
Infarction *(RB144)*
  sa subdivision Infarction *under names of organs of the body, e.g.* Heart—Infarction
  xx Embolism
    Hemorrhage
    Thrombosis
Infection
  sa Airborne infection
    Communicable diseases
    Cross infection
    Focal infection
    Metastasis
  xx Diseases—Causes and theories of causation
    Medical microbiology
Infection, Airborne
  See Airborne infection
Infection, Focal
  See Focal infection
Infectious abortion
  See Brucellosis in cattle
Infectious anemia
  sa Equine infectious anemia
  x Anemia, Infectious
    Swamp fever
  xx Anemia

Infectious arthritis
  x Arthritis, Infectious
  xx Collagen diseases
Infectious avian encephalomyelitis
  See Avian encephalomyelitis
Infectious bovine rhinotracheitis *(SF967.I48)*
  x Bovine rhinotracheitis, Infectious
    Red nose
    Rhinotracheitis, Infectious bovine
  xx Mucosal diseases of cattle
Infectious bronchitis in poultry
  x Chick bronchitis, Infectious
    Poultry bronchitis, Infectious
  xx Bronchitis
    Poultry—Diseases
Infectious diseases
  See Communicable diseases
Infectious enteritis in pigs
  See Necrotic enteritis
Infectious enterotoxemia
  See Enterotoxemia
Infectious equine encephalomyelitis
  See Equine encephalomyelitis
Infectious hepatitis
  See Hepatitis, Infectious
Infectious jaundice
  See Hepatitis, Infectious
Infectious necrotic hepatitis
  See Braxy
Infectious polyneuritis
  See Polyradiculitis
Inference (Logic) *(BC199.I47)*
  sa Induction (Logic)
    Prediction (Logic)
    Probabilities
    Syllogism
  xx Logic
Inferior colliculus
  xx Mesencephalon
Inferiority complex
  sa Attention-seeking
  xx Neuroses
    Personality, Disorders of
Infertility
  See Sterility
Infibulation *(GN481)*
  xx Circumcision
    Vagina
Infield (Baseball)
  See Fielding (Baseball)
Infiltrometer
  xx Soil absorption
Infinitary languages
  x Languages, Infinitary
  xx Logic, Symbolic and mathematical
Infinite *(Mathematics, QA9; Metaphysics, BD411)*
  sa Eternity
    Ontology
    Space and time
  x Finite
    Infinity
— Juvenile literature
Infinite groups *(QA171)*
  x Groups, Infinite
  xx Groups, Theory of
Infinite processes
  See Processes, Infinite
Infinite products
  See Products, Infinite
Infinite series
  See Series, Infinite
Infinitesimal calculus
  See Calculus
Infinitesimal geometry
  See Geometry, Infinitesimal
Infinitesimal transformations
  See Transformations, Infinitesimal

Infinitive
  See Grammar, Comparative and general—Infinitive
  subdivision Infinitive *under names of languages and groups of languages*
Infinity
  See Infinite
Infirmaries
  See Hospitals
Inflammable liquids *(Dangerous industries, HD3623-4)*
  sa Oil inspection
    names of inflammable liquids, e.g. Gasoline, Petroleum
  x Combustible liquids
    Liquids, Inflammable
  xx Gasoline
    Inflammable materials
    Oil inspection
    Petroleum
— Law and legislation *(Direct)*
  xx Fire prevention—Laws and regulations
— Safety measures
— Transportation
Inflammable materials *(TA407)*
  sa Inflammable liquids
  x Flammable materials
  xx Hazardous substances
— Law and legislation *(Direct)*
  xx Fire prevention—Laws and regulations
Inflammable textiles
  x Cloth
    Flammable textiles
    Textile fabrics
    Textiles
  xx Textile industry and fabrics
— Law and legislation *(Direct)*
  xx Fire prevention—Laws and regulations
Inflammation *(Pathology, RB131; Treatment, RC104)*
  sa Antiphlogistics
    Myositis
    Suppuration
    subdivision Inflammation *under names of organs of the body, e.g.* Eye—Inflammation
Inflatable boats *(VM360)*
  xx Boats and boating
Inflatable space structures
  See Expandable space structures
Inflatable structures
  See Air-supported structures
Inflation (Finance) *(Direct)*
  sa Currency question
    Escalator clause
    Industrial management and inflation
    Inflation (Finance) and accounting
    Insurance and inflation
    Paper money
    Price regulation
    Wage-price policy
  xx Circular velocity of money
    Currency question
    Economic policy
    Finance
    Money
— Mathematical models
  sa Phillips curve
— Underdeveloped areas
  See Underdeveloped areas—Inflation

GEOGRAPHIC SUBDIVISIONS

— France
  sa Assignats

— United States
   sa Greenbacks
Inflation (Finance) and accounting
   x Accounting and inflation (Finance)
   xx Accounting
      Inflation (Finance)
Inflation (Finance) and industrial management
   See Industrial management and inflation
Inflation (Finance) and insurance
   See Insurance and inflation
Inflation and industrial management
   See Industrial management and inflation
Inflation and insurance
   See Insurance and inflation
Inflection
   See Grammar, Comparative and general—
      Inflection
      Languages, Modern—Inflection
      subdivision Inflection *under names of*
      languages and groups of languages
Inflexibility (Psychology)
   See Rigidity (Psychology)
Inflorescence *(QK652; QK691)*
   sa Flowers
      Involucre
   xx Botany—Anatomy
Influence, Undue
   See Undue influence
Influence (Psychology)
   sa Conformity
      Example
      Imitation
      Persuasion (Psychology)
      Social facilitation
   xx Conformity
      Ethics
      Example
      Exempla
      Ideals (Psychology)
      Imitation
      Persuasion (Psychology)
Influence lines *(TG270)*
   xx Bridges
      Girders
      Girders, Continuous
      Graphic statics
      Strains and stresses
      Structural frames
      Trusses
Influence machines
   See Electric machines
Influenza *(Direct) (RC150)*
   sa Asian flu
      Equine influenza
   x Grippe
   xx Cold (Disease)
      Virus diseases
— Bacteriology *(QR201.I6)*
— Complications and sequelae
— Homeopathic treatment *(RX326.I)*
— Prevention
   sa Influenza vaccines
— Research
   See Influenza research
Influenza research *(RC150)*
   x Influenza—Research
   xx Medical research
      Research
Influenza vaccines *(Indirect) (QR189.5.I)*
   sa Equine influenza vaccines
   x Influenza virus vaccines
   xx Influenza—Prevention
      Influenza viruses
Influenza virus vaccines
   See Influenza vaccines

Influenza viruses *(QR201.I6)*
   sa Influenza vaccines
   xx Myxoviruses
Informants, Linguistic
   See Linguistic informants
Information, Freedom of
   See Freedom of information
Information, Government
   See Government information
Information centers
   See Information services
Information display systems
   sa Aeronautical instruments—Display
      systems
      Airports—Traffic control—Display
      systems
      Astronautical instruments—Display
      systems
      Automatic checkout equipment—
      Display systems
      Cathode ray tubes
      Image intensifiers
      Radar indicators
   x Data display systems
      Display systems, Information
      Dynamic display systems
   xx Computer input-output equipment
      Computers—Optical equipment
      Optical data processing
      Photoelectronic devices
      Recording instruments
— Marketing
— Psychological aspects
   xx Reading, Psychology of
      Recognition (Psychology)
      Visual discrimination
Information libraries *(Z675.G7)*
   x Overseas information libraries
      Overseas libraries
   xx Intellectual cooperation
      Libraries, Governmental,
      administrative, etc.
Information libraries, American, ₍British, etc.₎
Information measurement
   sa Uncertainty (Information theory)
   x Information measures (Information
      theory)
      Informational measure
      Measure of information
      Shannon-Wiener information measure
      Signals (Information theory)
   xx Information theory
Information measures (Information theory)
   See Information measurement
Information networks *(Direct)*
   sa Library information networks
   x Automated information networks
      Networks, Information
   xx Data transmission systems
      Exchanges, Literary and scientific
      Information services
      Information storage and retrieval
      systems
      Intellectual cooperation
Information networks, Library
   See Library information networks
Information processing, Human
   See Human information processing
Information processing in children
   See Human information processing (Child
      psychology)
Information processing language (Computer
      program language)
   See IPL (Computer program language)
Information processing systems
   See Information storage and retrieval
      systems

Information retrieval systems
   See Information storage and retrieval
      systems
Information science
   sa Documentation
      Electronic data processing
      Information services
      Information storage and retrieval
      systems
      Library science
   xx Communication
— Abbreviations
— Research *(Direct)*
— Study and teaching *(Direct)*
— — Audio-visual aids
— Terminology
Information services *(Direct) (AG500-551)*
   sa Archives
      Bibliographical services
      Data libraries
      Documentation
      Exchange of bibliographic information
      Information networks
      Information storage and retrieval
      systems
      Libraries
      Machine-readable bibliographic data
      Reference services (Libraries)
      Research
      Selective dissemination of information
      Statistical services
      subdivision Information services *under*
      special subjects or organizations, e.g.
      Child welfare—Information services;
      United Nations—Information
      services
   x Information centers
   xx Documentation
      Information science
      Libraries
      Reference services (Libraries)
      Research
— Cost control
— Economic aspects *(Direct)*
— International cooperation
— Job descriptions
Information services, Government
   See Government publicity
Information services employees *(Direct)*
   sa Wages—Information services employees
Information storage and retrieval systems
      Subdivided by subject, *e.g.* Information
      storage and retrieval systems—Elec-
      tronics; Information storage and re-
      trieval systems—Metallurgy.
   sa Automatic indexing
      Ballots Project
      BASIS-E (Information retrieval system)
      Computers
      Data libraries
      Data tapes
      DRL (Computer program language)
      Electronic data processing
      GIPSY (Information retrieval system)
      Information networks
      KONKAT (Information retrieval
      system)
      Libraries—Automation
      LIBRIS (Information retrieval system)
      Machine-readable bibliographic data
      Magnacard data processing system
      Management information systems
      Microfilm aperture card systems
      MINSK-ARDIS (Information retrieval
      system)
      Permutation indexes
      Project Spires
      Punched card systems

Information storage and retrieval systems
(Continued)

  Selective dissemination of information
  SESAM (Information retrieval system)
  SMART (Information retrieval system)
  SYNTOL (Information storage and
   retrieval system)
 x Automatic data storage
  Automatic information retrieval
  Automation in documentation
  Data processing
  Data storage and retrieval systems
  Information processing systems
  Information retrieval systems
  Machine data storage and retrieval
  Mechanized information storage and
   retrieval systems
 xx Abstracting and indexing services
  Bibliography
  Classification
  Computers
  Data libraries
  Documentation
  Information science
  Information services
  Language data processing
  Libraries—Automation
  Library science
— Aeronautics
 x Aeronautical literature searching
 xx Aeronautical libraries
— Agriculture
 sa Punched card systems—Agriculture
 x Agricultural literature searching
 xx Agricultural libraries
  Agriculture—Documentation
— Biology
 sa Punched card systems—Biology
 x Biological literature searching
 xx Biology—Bibliography
— Chemistry   *(Z699.5.C5)*
 sa Punched card systems—Chemistry
 x Chemical literature searching
 xx Chemical libraries
— Cities and towns
— — Planning
  xx Cities and towns—Planning—
   Bibliography
— Code numbers
 x Code numbers (Information storage
  and retrieval)
— Code words
 sa subdivision Code words *under*
  topical subdivisions, e.g.
  Information storage and retrieval
  systems—Engineering—Code
  words
 x Code words (Information storage
  and retrieval)
— Costs
— Electronics   *(Z699.5.E5)*
 x Electronics literature searching
 xx Electronics—Information services
  Electronics libraries
  Engineering libraries
 Note under Information storage and retrieval systems
— Engineering
 sa Project SHARP
 x Engineering literature searching
 xx Engineering libraries
— — Code words
  Example under Information storage
   and retrieval systems—Code
   words
— Evaluation
— Geology
 x Geological literature searching
 xx Geology—Bibliography

— Home economics
 x Home economics literature searching
 xx Home economics—Bibliography
— Law   *(Direct)*
 sa Statutes—Word frequency
 x Legal literature searching
 xx Law—Bibliography
  Law libraries
— Materials
 x Materials literature searching
 xx Engineering libraries
— Mathematical models
 xx Mathematical models—Bibliography
— Medicine
 sa MEDLARS
 x Medical literature searching
 xx Medical libraries
  Medicine—Bibliography
— Metallurgy   *(Z699.5.M4)*
 x Metallurgical literature searching
 xx Engineering libraries
 Note under Information storage and retrieval systems
— Meteorology
 x Meteorological literature searching
 xx Meteorological libraries
  Meteorology—Bibliography
— Naval art and science
 sa Project SHARP
 x Naval literature searching
 xx Libraries, Naval
— Nursing
 x Nursing literature searching
 xx Nursing libraries
— Patent documentation   *(Z699.5.P3)*
 xx Patent searching
— Programmed instruction
— Science   *(Z699.5.S3)*
 x Scientific literature searching
 xx Scientific libraries
— Slavic literature   *(Z699.5.S6)*
 x Slavic literature searching
 xx Slavic literature—Bibliography
— Technology   *(Z699.5.T4)*
 x Technical literature searching
 xx Technical libraries
  Technology—Bibliography
— Terminology
— Water-supply   *(Z699.5.W3)*
 x Water-supply literature searching

Information theory
 sa Automatic control
  Coding theory
  Data transmission systems
  Error-correcting codes (Information
   theory)
  Information measurement
  Language and languages
  Machine translating
  Mathematical linguistics
  Modulation theory
  Punched card systems
  Rate distortion theory
  Semantics
  Signal theory (Telecommunication)
  Speech processing systems
  Statistical communication theory
  Switching theory
  Telecommunication
 x Communication theory
 xx Communication
  Cybernetics
— Nomenclature
— Problems, exercises, etc.   *(Q360)*
Information theory in aesthetics
 sa Information theory in music
 xx Aesthetics
  Cybernetics

  Perception
  Psychology
Information theory in biology
 xx Biology
  Biomathematics
Information theory in economics
 xx Econometrics
Information theory in geophysics   *(QC806)*
 xx Geophysics
Information theory in music
 xx Information theory in aesthetics
  Music
Information theory in optics   *(QC370)*
 xx Optics
Information theory in physics   *(QC28)*
 xx Physics
Information theory in psychology
 sa Human information processing
 xx Cybernetics
  Perception
  Psychology
  Psychology, Physiological
Information theory in sociology
 xx Sociology
Information theory in translating
 xx Translating and interpreting
Informational measure
 See Information measurement
Informations   *(Direct)*
 sa Grand jury
  Indictments
  Joinder of offenses
  Quo warranto
 x Accusation
 xx Criminal procedure
  Grand jury
  Indictments
  Prosecution
  Public prosecutors
  Quo warranto
Informers   *(Direct)*
 x Police informers
 xx Complaints (Criminal procedure)
  Crime prevention
  Criminal investigation
  Prosecution
Infra-red albedo
 x Albedo, Infra-red
 xx Infra-red rays
  Terrestrial radiation
— Diurnal variation
 x Diurnal infra-red albedo variations
  Diurnal variation (Infra-red albedo)
Infra-red apparatus and appliances
 sa Infra-red drying apparatus
  Infra-red horizon sensors
 xx Infra-red technology
Infra-red astronomy
 x Astronomy, Infra-red
 xx Astronomy
  Infra-red rays
Infra-red broiling
 See Broiling
Infra-red drying apparatus   *(TP363)*
 xx Drying apparatus
  Infra-red apparatus and appliances
Infra-red heating   *(Chemical engineering,*
  TP363; Electric engineering,
  TK4635)
 x Heating, Infra-red
 xx Electric heating
  Infra-red technology
Infra-red horizon scanners
 See Infra-red horizon sensors
Infra-red horizon sensors
 x Horizon sensors, Infra-red
  Infra-red horizon scanners
 xx Infra-red apparatus and appliances

Remote sensing systems
Infra-red photography
   See Photography, Infra-red
Infra-red rays
   sa Atmospheric radiation
      Infra-red albedo
      Infra-red astronomy
      Infra-red technology
      Terrestrial radiation
   x Rays, Infra-red
   xx Electromagnetic waves
      Spectrum, Infra-red
   — Industrial applications
      xx Electric heating
         Heating
         Infra-red technology
   — Military applications
      xx Infra-red technology
   — Therapeutic use
Infra-red rays in medicine *(RM857)*
   xx Radiology, Medical
Infra-red spectrometry
   xx Spectrometer
      Spectrum, Infra-red
   — Laboratory manuals
   — Programmed instruction *(QC457)*
   — Tables, etc.
Infra-red spectrum
   See Spectrum, Infra-red
Infra-red technology
   sa Infra-red apparatus and appliances
      Infra-red heating
      Infra-red rays—Industrial applications
      Infra-red rays—Military applications
      Photography, Infra-red
   xx Infra-red rays
Infrasonic waves *(QC243.5)*
   x Waves, Infrasonic
   xx Sound-waves
Infringement of copyright
   See Copyright infringement
Infused virtue
   See Virtue, Infused
Infusion therapy
   See Intravenous therapy
Infusoria *(QL368-9; Early works, QL365)*
   sa Ciliata
      Flagellata
   xx Animalcules
      Protozoa
Infusorial earth
   See Diatomaceous earth
Ingalik Indians *(E99.I5)*
   x Inkalik Indians
      Ten'a Indians
   xx Athapascan Indians
      Indians of North America
      Tinne Indians
Ingalik language *(PM1373)*
   x Inkalik language
      Ten'a language
   xx Athapascan languages
      Tinne languages
Ingavi, Battle of, 1841 *(F3324)*
   xx Bolivia—History—1825-1879
      Peru—History—1829-1919
Ingelheim dooms
   See Ingelheim law
Ingelheim law
   x Ingelheim dooms
   xx Law—Germany (Middle Ages)
Ingermans
   See Ingrians
Ingers
   See Ingrians
Ingestion
   xx Absorption (Physiology)
      Phagocytosis

Ingot molds
Ingots, Aluminum
   See Aluminum ingots
Ingots, Brass
   See Brass ingots
Ingots, Bronze
   See Bronze ingots
Ingots, Nonferrous
   See Nonferrous ingots
Ingots, Steel
   See Steel ingots
Ingram's Rebellion (Virginia)
   See Bacon's Rebellion, 1676
Ingratitude
   sa Gratitude
   x Thanklessness
      Ungratefulness
      Unthankfulness
   xx Conduct of life
      Ethics
      Gratitude
Ingrian language
   x Izhorskii
   xx Finno-Ugrian languages
Ingrians
   x Ingermans
      Ingers
      Izhortsy
   xx Ethnology—Russia
Ingrowing nails
   See Nails, Ingrowing
Inguinal hernia
   xx Hernia
Ingush *(DK34.I)*
   x Galga
   xx Ethnology—Caucasus
Ingush language *(PK9201.I6)*
   xx Caucasian languages
Ingush literature *(Direct)*
   xx Daghestan literature
Ingush poetry *(Direct)*
Inhalation anesthesia *(Indirect)* *(RD85.I48)*
   x Anesthesia, Inhalation
   xx Anesthesia
Inhalation therapy
   sa Aerosol therapy
      Aerotherapy
      Oxygen therapy
   x Respiratory therapy
   xx Aerotherapy
      Therapeutics
   — Complications and sequelae
   — Examinations, questions, etc.
Inhalation toxicology
   See Gases, Asphyxiating and poisonous—
      Toxicology
Inheritance (Biology)
   See Heredity
Inheritance (Theology)
   xx Salvation
      Theology, Doctrinal
   — Biblical teaching
Inheritance and succession *(Direct)*
      (Economics, HB715)
   sa Benefit of inventory
      Charitable bequests
      Claims against decedents' estates
      Co-heirs
      Contracts to make wills
      Curtesy
      Decedents' estates
      Decedents' family maintenance
      Disinheritance
      Distribution of decedents' estates
      Dower
      Droit d'aubaine
      Election (Wills)
      Entail

      Escheat
      Estate settlement costs
      Estates (Law)
      Estates, Unclaimed
      Executors and administrators
      Fideicommissum
      Freedom of testation
      Heirlooms
      Inheritance and transfer tax
      Inquisitiones post mortem
      Kings and rulers—Succession
      Land tenure
      Legacies
      Legitime
      Mejora
      Primogeniture
      Probate law and practice
      Renunciation of inheritance
      Restraints on alienation
      Reversion
      Separation of patrimony
      Substitution of heirs
      Testamentary trusts
      Trusts and trustees
      Unborn children (Law)
      Unworthiness of heirs
      Widow's allowance
      Widow's share
      Wills
      Worthier title
   x Bequests
      Descent and distribution
      Descents
      Heirs
      Hereditary succession
      Intestacy
      Intestate succession
      Law of succession
      Succession, Intestate
   xx Probate law and practice
      Real property
      Universal succession
   — Mathematical models
   — Sources
Inheritance and succession (Adat law)
      (Direct)
Inheritance and succession (Angoni law)
   Example under Law, Angoni
Inheritance and succession (Canon law)
      (BX1939.I)
Inheritance and succession (Canon law, Eastern)
Inheritance and succession (Frankish law)
Inheritance and succession (Germanic law)
Inheritance and succession (Greek law)
Inheritance and succession (Hindu law)
Inheritance and succession (Islamic law)
      (Direct)
Inheritance and succession (Jewish law)
      (Direct)
   sa Primogeniture (Jewish law)
Inheritance and succession (Lübeck law)
Inheritance and succession (Magdeburg law)
   Example under Magdeburg law
Inheritance and succession (Oriental law)
Inheritance and succession (Primitive law)
      (Direct)
Inheritance and succession (Roman law)
Inheritance and succession (Saxon law)
   Example under Law, Saxon
Inheritance and transfer tax *(Direct)*
      (HJ5801-5819)
   sa Decedents' estates—Taxation
      Gifts—Taxation
      Real property and taxation
      Settlements (Law)—Taxation
   x Death-duties
      Estate tax

Inheritance and transfer tax *(Direct)*
    (HJ5801-5819) *(Continued)*
      Inheritance tax
      Legacies, Taxation of
      Succession taxes
      Taxable transfers
      Taxation of legacies
      Transfer tax
    xx Estate planning
      Inheritance and succession
      Internal revenue
      Probate law and practice
      Taxation
      Taxation, Progressive
  — Deductions
  — Examinations, questions, etc.
  — Popular works
  — Treaties
    See Taxation, Double—Treaties
Inheritance of acquired characters
    x Acquired characters, Heredity of
      Acquired characters, Inheritance of
      Heredity of acquired characters
    xx Heredity
Inheritance tax
  See Inheritance and transfer tax
Inhibition *(Psychology, BF335-7)*
    sa Habit
      Impulse
    xx Free will and determinism
      Habit
      Impulse
      Neurology
      Psychology
      Will
Inhibition (Writ)
  See Prohibition (Writ)
Inhibitors, Chemical
  See Chemical inhibitors
Inhibitors, Enzyme
  See Enzyme inhibitors
Inhuman treatment (Divorce)
  See Legal cruelty
Initial teaching alphabet *(LB1181)*
    x Alphabet, Initial teaching
      I.T.A.
    xx English language—Alphabet
      Reading (Elementary)
Initial value problems *(QA378)*
    sa Boundary value problems
    x Problems, Initial value
    xx Boundary value problems
      Differential equations
  — Numerical solutions
    xx Numerical analysis
Initialisms
  See Acronyms
Initials *(NK3600-3640; Illumination,*
    ND3335)
    sa Alphabets
      Artists' marks
      Illumination of books and manuscripts
      Lettering
      Monograms
      Printing—Specimens
      Type and type-founding
    xx Alphabets
      Illumination of books and manuscripts
      Lettering
      Monograms
      Printers' ornaments
      Type and type-founding
      Type ornaments
Initiations (in religion, folk-lore, etc.)
    (BL615)
    sa Baptism
      Circumcision
      Installation (Rabbis)

      Komo (Secret order)
      Profession (in religious orders,
        congregations, etc.)
      Puberty rites
      Sacred thread ceremony
    x Folk-lore of initiations
    xx Education, Primitive
      Installation (Clergy)
      Occult sciences
      Religion, Primitive
      Rites and ceremonies
Initiations (into trades, societies, etc.)
    (Labor, HD4889)
    sa Greek letter societies
      Hazing
      Secret societies
    x Fraternities
      Trades, Initiations into
      Youth dedication
    xx Greek letter societies
      Hazing
      Rites and ceremonies
      Secret societies
Initiative, Right of *(Direct)*
    xx Administrative law
      Executive power
      Legislation
      Political science
      Public law
Initiative and referendum
  See Referendum
Injection-gneiss
  See Migmatite
Injection molding of plastics *(TP1150)*
    xx Plastics—Molding
Injections *(Therapeutics, RM163-176)*
    sa Ampuls
      Parenteral therapy
  — Caricatures and cartoons
Injections, Anatomical *(Biology, QH324;*
    Comparative anatomy, QL812;
    Human anatomy, QM39)
    sa Anatomical specimens
Injections, Bronchial
    x Bronchia, Injections into
    xx Lungs—Diseases
Injections, Hypodermic *(RM169)*
    x Hypodermic injections
      Injections, Subcutaneous
    xx Therapeutics
  — Programmed instruction
Injections, Intra-arterial
    sa Arterial catheterization
    x Intra-arterial injections
Injections, Intra-articular
    x Intra-articular injections
    xx Therapeutics
Injections, Intradermal
    x Intradermal injections
Injections, Intramuscular
    x Intramuscular injections
Injections, Intraperitoneal *(RM180)*
    x Intraperitoneal injections
    xx Peritoneum
Injections, Intravenous *(RM170)*
    sa Intravenous anesthesia
Injections, Saline *(RM178)*
    x Saline injections
Injections, Spinal
    x Intraspinal injections
      Spinal injections
Injections, Subcutaneous
  See Injections, Hypodermic
Injectors *(Steam-boilers, TJ387)*
    x Steam-injectors
    xx Boilers
      Jet pumps
      Pumping machinery

      Steam-boilers
Injunctions *(Direct)* *(Labor law, HD7819;*
    Theory, JF721; United States
    judiciary, JK1542)
    sa Interdict (Civil law)
      Labor injunctions
    x Anti-injunction law
    xx Actions and defenses
      Civil procedure
      Constitutional law
      Equitable remedies
      Extraordinary remedies
      Interdict (Civil law)
      Provisional remedies
Injunctions, Labor
  See Labor injunctions
Injuries
  See Accidents
    First aid in illness and injury
    Traumatism
    Wounds
    subdivision Wounds and injuries *under*
      names of organs and regions of the
      body, e.g. Brain—Wounds and
      injuries; Chest—Wounds and injuries
Injuries, Crash
  See Crash injuries
Injuries, Whiplash
  See Whiplash injuries
Injuries (Law)
  See Accident law
    Damages
    Employers' liability
    Medical jurisprudence
    Personal injuries
    Torts
Injuries from electricity
  See Electricity, Injuries from
Injuries from sports
  See Sports—Accidents and injuries
Injurious and beneficial animals
  See Zoology, Economic
Injurious insects
  See Insects, Injurious and beneficial
Injurious occupations
  See Occupations, Dangerous
Ink *(Paleography, Z112; Technology,*
    TP946-950)
    sa India ink
      Inkstands
      Printing-ink
    xx Writing—Materials and instruments
Ink bottles *(Direct)*
    xx Bottles
Ink brushwork
  See Brush drawing
Ink drawing
  See Pen drawing
Ink drying
  See Printing-ink—Drying
Ink slabs
  See Ink-stones
Ink sticks
  See Inksticks
Ink-stones *(TP948.I6)*
    x Ink slabs
Inkalik Indians
  See Ingalik Indians
Inkalik language
  See Ingalik language
Inkblot test, Harrower psychodiagnostic
  See Harrower psychodiagnostic inkblot test
Inkblot test, Rorschach
  See Rorschach test
Inkermann, Battle of, 1854 *(DK215.5)*
    xx Crimean War, 1853-1856
Inkstands *(Direct)*
    xx Ink

— Collectors and collecting *(Direct)*

Inksticks
   x Ink sticks
   xx Art objects, Oriental

Inkwells *(NK6035)*
— Collectors and collecting *(Direct)*
— Prices

Inland marine insurance
   See Insurance, Inland marine

Inland navigation *(Indirect) (Engineering, TC601-791; Transportation, HE617-720)*
   sa Bridges—Navigation clearances
      Canals
      Inland water transportation
      Intracoastal waterways
      Lakes
      Rivers
      Towing
      Work boats
      subdivision Navigation *under names of canals, rivers, etc.*
   x Interior navigation
      Navigation, Inland
   xx Commerce
      Communication and traffic
      Hydrography
      Inland water transportation
      Intracoastal waterways
      Navigation
      Shipping
      Transportation
      Water resources development
   Note under Waterways
— Collective labor agreements
   See Collective labor agreements—
      Inland water transportation
— Employees
   See Inland water transportation—
      Employees
— Examinations, questions, etc.
— Laws and regulations *(HE586-7)*
   sa Bridges—Law and legislation
      Ferries—Law and legislation
      International rivers
      Motor-boats—Safety regulations
      subdivision Navigation—Laws and regulations *under names of waterways, e.g.* Danube River—Navigation—Laws and regulations; Panama Canal—Navigation—Laws and regulations
   x Inland rules of the road
      Navigation—Law and legislation
      Navigation laws
      Rule of the road, Inland
      Rules of the road, Inland
— Problems, exercises, etc.
— Safety measures

     GEOGRAPHIC SUBDIVISIONS

— United States
Inland revenue
   See Internal revenue
Inland rules of the road
   See Inland navigation—Laws and regulations
Inland shipping
   See Inland water transportation
Inland transportation insurance
   See Insurance, Inland marine

Inland water transportation *(Direct)*
   Works on shipping on individual lakes, rivers, etc. are entered under the heading Shipping subdivided by the name of the river, etc., *e.g.* Shipping—Danube River.
   sa Inland navigation

Wages—Inland water transportation
   x Inland shipping
      Shipping, Inland water
      Water transportation, Inland
   xx Commerce
      Inland navigation
      Shipping
      Transportation
   Note under Shipping
— Accounting
— Collective labor agreements
   See Collective labor agreements—
      Inland water transportation
— Communication systems *(VM479)*
   xx Telecommunication
— Cost of operation
— Employees
   sa Collective labor agreements—Inland water transportation
   x Inland navigation—Employees
      Inland water transportation workers
   xx Boatmen
      Merchant marine—Officers
      Merchant seamen
      Transport workers
— Finance
— Fires and fire prevention
— Juvenile literature
— Labor productivity
— Law and legislation *(Direct)*
— Mathematical models
— Passenger traffic
— Production standards
— Rates
— Taxation *(Direct)*
— Time-tables
   x Time-tables (Transportation)
— Transit charges
   xx Tolls
Inland water transportation workers
   See Inland water transportation—
      Employees
Inland waterway vessels *(Direct)*
   sa Canal-boats
      Lake steamers
      River boats
   xx Ships
      Work boats
— Appraisal
   See Inland waterway vessels—
      Valuation
— Cargo
   sa Cargo handling
   xx Stowage
— Designs and plans
— Equipment and supplies
— Fires and fire prevention *(VK1258)*
— Handling
— Inspection *(Indirect)*
— Measurement
— Pictorial works
— Registration and transfer *(Direct)*
   x Registration of inland waterway vessels
   xx Recording and registration
      Ship registers
— Valuation
   x Inland waterway vessels—Appraisal
Inlaying in wood
   See Marquetry
Inlays (Dentistry)
   xx Dentistry, Operative
      Fillings (Dentistry)
      Prosthodontics
Inmates of institutions *(Direct)*
   x Institutions, Inmates of
      Public institutions—Inmates
— Sexual behavior

Inmeas dialect
   See Isinai dialect
Inner Light *(BX7748.I6)*
   x Light, Inner
   xx Assurance (Theology)
      Authority (Religion)
      Experience (Religion)
      Friends, Society of
      Revelation
Inner missions *(Germany, BV2950)*
   x Missions, Inner
Innkeeper and guest
   See Hotels, taverns, etc.—Law
Innocence (Theology)
   xx Baptism
      Simplicity
Innocents, Feast of the Holy
   See Holy Innocents, Feast of the
Innocents, Massacre of the Holy
   See Holy Innocents, Massacre of the
Innocents' Day
   See Holy Innocents, Feast of the
Innovations, Agricultural
   See Agricultural innovations
Innovations, Diffusion of
   See Diffusion of innovations
Innovations, Educational
   See Educational innovations
Innovations, Medical
   See Medical innovations
Innovations, Technological
   See Technological innovations
Inns
   See Hotels, taverns, etc.
Innuit
   See Eskimos
Inoculation
   sa Immunity
      Medicine, Preventive
      Serumtherapy
      Smallpox, Inoculation of
      Vaccination
      subdivision Preventive inoculation *under names of certain diseases, e.g.* Anthrax, Plague, Rabies, Typhoid fever
   x Preventive inoculation
   xx Communicable diseases
      Immunity
      Medicine, Preventive
      Serumtherapy
      Vaccination
Inoculation of legumes
   See Legume inoculation
Inoculation of plants
   See Plant inoculation
Inoculation of soils
   See Soil inoculation
İnönü, Battle of, 1921
   xx Greco-Turkish War, 1921-1922
      Turkey—History—Revolution, 1918-1923
Inoperculates
   See Discomycetes
Inorganic chemistry
   See Chemistry, Inorganic
Inorganic fibers
   sa Asbestos fibers
      Carbon fibers
      Ceramic fibers
      Graphite fibers
   x Fibers, Inorganic
   xx Textile fibers
Inorganic polymers *(QD196)*
   xx Polymers and polymerization
Inosite *(QD321)*
Input equipment (Computers)
   See Computer input-output equipment

Input-output analysis
   See Interindustry economics
      Linear programming
      Production functions (Economic
        theory)
      Recursive programming
Input-output equipment (Computers)
   See Computer input-output equipment
Inquests, Coroners'
   See Coroners
Inquiry, Courts of
   See Courts-martial and courts of inquiry
Inquiry (Theory of knowledge) *(BD183)*
   xx Knowledge, Theory of
Inquisition. Spain
   x Spanish Inquisition
   Note under Inquisition
Inquisition *(BX1700-1745)*
      Subdivided by locality, *e.g.* Inquisition.
        Spain.
   sa Auto-da-fe sermons
      Martyrs
      Persecution
      Torture
   x Holy Office
   xx Catholic Church
      Church discipline
      Church history
      Church history—Middle Ages,
        600-1500
      Persecution
      Torture
Inquisition, Islamic
   See Miḥna
Inquisition, Motazilite
   See Miḥna
Inquisitiones post mortem *(English counties,*
      DA670; English genealogical
      records, CS434-6; English records,
      DA25)
   x Post-mortem inquisitions
   xx Inheritance and succession
      Registers of births, etc.
Inquisitiveness
   See Curiosity
Inro *(Direct) (NK6080)*
   sa Netsukes
Insane
      This heading is used only with legal sub-
        divisions. Other material is entered un-
        der Mentally ill.
   — Care and treatment
      See Mentally ill—Care and treatment
   — Colonization
   — Commitment and detention
   — Legal status, laws, etc.
      See Insanity—Jurisprudence
        Mental health laws
Insane, Criminal and dangerous *(Direct)*
      (Insanity and crime, HV6133;
      Prisons, HV8741-2)
   sa Criminal liability
      Forensic psychiatry
      Insanity—Jurisprudence
      Insanity, Moral
   x Crime and insanity
      Criminal insane
      Insanity and crime
   xx Crime and criminals
      Forensic psychiatry
      Insanity—Jurisprudence
      Insanity, Moral
Insane, Killing of the
   x Killing of the insane
   xx Euthanasia
Insane hospitals
   See Psychiatric hospitals

Insanity *(Indirect) (Insanity and crime,*
      HV6133; Insanity and degeneration,
      HV4977; Insanity and genius,
      BF423)
      Here are entered works on the legal as-
        pects of mental disorders. Popular
        works and works on regional or social
        aspects of mental disorders are entered
        under Mental illness. Systematic de-
        scriptions of mental disorders are en-
        tered under Psychology, Pathological.
        Works on clinical aspects of mental
        disorders, including therapy, are en-
        tered under Psychiatry.
   sa Dementia
      Depression, Mental
      Eccentrics and eccentricities
      Epilepsy
      Genius
      Hallucinations and illusions
      Hypochondria
      Hysteria
      Idiocy
      Manic-depressive psychoses
      Melancholia
      Monomania
      Negativism
      Neuroses
      Nymphomania
      Personality, Disorders of
      Psychiatry
      Psychology, Pathological
      Psychoses
      Schizophrenia
      Stupor
      Suicide
   x Genius and insanity
      Insanity and genius
      Lunacy
      Madness
      Mania
   xx Brain—Diseases
      Degeneration
      Delinquents
      Eccentrics and eccentricities
      Hallucinations and illusions
      Idiocy
      Manic-depressive psychoses
      Mental illness
      Personality, Disorders of
      Psychiatry
      Psychology, Pathological
      Psychoses
   Example under Nervous system—Diseases
   Notes under Mental illness; Psychoses
   — Bibliography
      See Mental illness—Bibliography
   — Diagnosis and semiology
      See Mental illness—Diagnosis
   — Jurisprudence *(Direct) (RA1151)*
      Here are entered works on the legal
        status of persons of unsound mind.
        Works on the law affecting the wel-
        fare of the insane are entered under
        the heading Mental health laws.
        Works on psychiatry as applied in
        courts of law are entered under the
        heading Forensic psychiatry
      sa Capacity and disability
        Criminal liability
        Forensic psychiatry
        Insane, Criminal and dangerous
        Insanity, Moral
        Interdiction (Civil law)
        Liability (Law)
        Litigious paranoia
      x Insane—Legal status, laws, etc.
        Law and mental illness

      Mental illness and law
      Mentally ill—Legal status, laws, etc.
   xx Insane, Criminal and dangerous
      Insanity, Moral
      Status (Law)
   Example under Medical jurisprudence
   Notes under Forensic psychiatry; Mental
      health laws
   — Jurisprudence (Canon Law)
   — Jurisprudence (Jewish law)
   — Jurisprudence (Roman law)
   — Negroes
      See Negroes—Insanity
Insanity, Delusional
   See Paranoia
Insanity, Hysterical
   See Hysteria
Insanity, Moral
   sa Insane, Criminal and dangerous
      Insanity—Jurisprudence
   x Moral insanity
   xx Crime and criminals
      Degeneration
      Insane, Criminal and dangerous
      Insanity—Jurisprudence
      Psychology, Pathological
Insanity, Periodic and transitory
   sa Personality, Disorders of
   x Insanity, Transitory
Insanity, Religious
   x Religious insanity
   xx Psychology, Religious
Insanity, Transitory
   See Insanity, Periodic and transitory
Insanity and art
   See Art and mental illness
Insanity and crime
   See Insane, Criminal and dangerous
Insanity and genius
   See Genius
      Insanity
Insanity in literature
   See Mental illness in literature
Inscriptions *(Direct) (CN)*
   sa Architectural inscriptions
      Brasses
      Brick stamps
      Chronograms
      Cuneiform writing
      Epitaphs
      Graffiti
      Hieroglyphics
      Historical markers
      Monograms
      Petroglyphs
      Picture-writing
      Runes
      Seals (Numismatics)
      Signatures (Writing)
      Tablets (Paleography)
   x Epigraphy
   xx Archaeology
      Auxiliary sciences of history
      Historical markers
      History, Ancient
      Paleography
   — Forgeries
      See Forgery of inscriptions
      GEOGRAPHIC SUBDIVISIONS
   — Crete
      x Inscriptions, Minoan
        Minoan writing
      xx Inscriptions, Linear B
      GEOGRAPHIC SUBDIVISIONS
   — Mycenae
      x Inscriptions, Mycenaean

Insect culture
  See Insect rearing
Insect forms in art and archaeology
  sa Scarabs
  xx Archaeology
Insect galls
  See Galls (Botany)
Insect genetics
  xx Animal genetics
Insect hormones
  sa Insect control
  xx Hormones
    Insect control
Insect metamorphosis
  See Insects—Metamorphosis
Insect-plant relationships
  sa Fertilization of plants by insects
    Host plants
    Insects—Food
    Plant parasites
  x Plant-insect relationships
  xx Insects
    Insects, Injurious and beneficial
    Plant parasites
Insect pollenizers
  See Fertilization of plants by insects
Insect populations
  x Populations, Insect
  xx Arthropod populations
    Insect societies
    Insects—Geographical distribution
    Invertebrate populations
Insect radiosterilization *(SB973)*
  x Radiosterilization of insects
  xx Insect sterilization
    Radiobiology
Insect rearing *(Indirect)*
  x Entomology—Cultures and culture
    media
    Insect culture
    Insects—Cultures and culture media
    Insects—Rearing
    Mass rearing of insects
    Rearing of insects
Insect repellents
  See Insect baits and repellents
Insect societies
  sa Ants
    Bees
    Insect populations
    Termites
    Wasps
  x Insects, Social
    Social insects
  xx Animal societies
    Animals, Habits and behavior of
    Insects
    Insects—Behavior
  — Juvenile literature
Insect song
  See Insect sounds
Insect sounds
  sa Sound production by insects
  x Insect calls
    Insect song
  xx Animal sounds
    Insects
    Nature sounds
    Sound production by insects
Insect sterilization
  sa Insect chemosterilization
    Insect radiosterilization
  x Sterile-male technique (Insect control)
    Sterilization of insects
  xx Agricultural chemistry
    Insect control—Biological control
    Insects, Effect of radiation on
  — Mathematical models

Insect traps *(SB959)*
  sa Insect cages
  x Light traps
Insect venom
  sa Bee venom
  xx Venom
  — Physiological effect *(QP941)*
Insecticidal plants
  See Plants, Insecticidal
Insecticide research
  See Insecticides—Research
Insecticide resistance
  See Resistance to insecticides
Insecticides *(SB951)*
  sa Fumigation
    Insect baits and repellents
    Insects, Injurious and beneficial
    Miticides
    Mothproofing
    Plants, Effect of insecticides on
    Plants, Insecticidal
    Resistance to insecticides
    Systemic insecticides
    names of insecticides, e.g. Pyrethrum,
      Sheep-dip
  xx Agricultural chemicals
    Insects, Injurious and beneficial
    Pesticides
    Trees—Diseases and pests
    Wood preservatives
  — Biodegradation
    x Insecticides—Biodeterioration
    Example under Biodegradation
  — Biodeterioration
    See Insecticides—Biodegradation
  — Economic aspects *(Direct)*
  — Equipment and supplies
  — Law and legislation
    See Pesticides—Law and legislation
  — Patents
  — Physiological effect
  — Research
    x Insecticide research
    xx Agricultural research
  — Terminology
  — Testing
  — Toxicology
    x Wildlife, Effect of insecticides on
    Example under Toxicology
Insecticides, Systemic
  See Systemic insecticides
Insectivora *(Indirect) (QL737.I5)*
  sa *names of insectivorous animals, e.g.*
    Moles (Animals)
  xx Mammals
Insectivora, Fossil *(QE882.I5)*
  sa Deltatheridia
Insectivorous plants *(Direct) (QK917)*
  x Carnivorous plants
  xx Botany
    Botany—Ecology
    Plants
    Plants—Irritability and movements
  — Juvenile literature
Insects *(Indirect) (QL461-599; Folk-lore,*
    GR750)
  sa Anoplura
    Beetles
    Dermaptera
    Diptera
    Electric organs in insects
    Entomology
    Fertilization of plants by insects
    Forest insects
    Hemiptera
    Hymenoptera
    Insect baits and repellents
    Insect-plant relationships

    Insect societies
    Insect sounds
    Lac-insects
    Lepidoptera
    Mecoptera
    Neuroptera
    Odonata
    Orthoptera
    Scale-insects
    Ants, Butterflies, Moths, Wasps, *and*
      similar headings
  x Hexapoda
  xx Arthropoda
    Entomology
    Invertebrates
    Soil fauna
  Example under Zoology
  — Anatomy *(QL494)*
    sa Head capsule
      Wings
      subdivision Insects *under* Digestive
        organs, Nervous system,
        Sense-organs
  — Behavior
    sa Insect societies
      Parasitic insects
      Pheromones
      subdivision Behavior *under particular*
        insects, e.g. Ants—Behavior
    x Insect behavior
  —— Juvenile literature
  — Biological control
    See Insect control—Biological control
  — Cages
    See Insect cages
  — Catalogs and collections *(QL468)*
  — Classification *(QL468)*
  — Collected works
    See Entomology—Collected works
  — Collection and preservation *(QL465)*
    sa Zoological specimens—Collection
      and preservation
    x Preservation (Natural history)
      Specimens, Preservation of
    xx Museums
      Natural history—Technique
      Zoological specimens—Collection
        and preservation
  —— Juvenile literature
  — Color
    See Color of insects
  — Congresses
    See Entomology—Congresses
  — Control
    See Insect control
  — Cultures and culture media
    See Insect rearing
  — Development *(QL494.5)*
    sa Cocoons
      Ecdysis
      Insects—Metamorphosis
      Larvae—Insects
      Molting
      Pupae
  — Diseases
    sa Parasites—Insects
  — Eggs
  — Embryology
    See Embryology—Insects
  — Evolution
  — Extermination
    See Insect control
  — Food
    xx Insect-plant relationships
  — Generative organs
    See Generative organs—Insects
  — Geographical distribution *(QL469-491)*
    sa Insect populations

xx Zoogeography
— Identification
— Juvenile literature *(QL467)*
— Laboratory manuals
    See Entomology—Laboratory manuals
— Larvae
    See Larvae—Insects
— Metamorphosis *(QL494.5)*
    sa Diapause
        Imaginal disks
        Larvae
    x Insect metamorphosis
    xx Insects—Development
        Metamorphosis
— — Juvenile literature
— Microbiology
— Migration *(QL496)*
    x Migration of insects
— — Juvenile literature
— Nomenclature *(QL353-4)*
    xx Zoology—Nomenclature
— Nomenclature (Popular) *(QL355)*
    xx Zoology—Nomenclature (Popular)
— Physiology *(QL495)*
    sa Dormancy in insects
        Insects, Effect of radiation on
        Pheromones
— Pictorial works *(QL466)*
— Rearing
    See Insect rearing
— Research
    See Entomological research
— Resistance to insecticides
    See Resistance to insecticides
— Sense-organs
    See Sense-organs—Insects
— Society publications
    See Entomology—Societies, etc.
Insects, Aquatic *(QL496)*
    x Aquatic insects
    xx Aquatic animals
        Aquatic invertebrates
        Fresh-water fauna
— Juvenile literature
Insects, Color of
    See Color of insects
Insects, Destructive and useful
    See Insects, Injurious and beneficial
Insects, Effect of radiation on
    sa Insect sterilization
    x Radiation—Effect on insects
    xx Insects—Physiology
        Radiation—Physiological effect
Insects, Fossil *(QE831-2)*
    sa Beetles, Fossil
        Butterflies, Fossil
        Heteroptera, Fossil
        Hymenoptera, Fossil
        Orthoptera, Fossil
        Thrips, Fossil
Insects, Injurious and beneficial *(Indirect)*
    (SB821-945)
    sa Agricultural pests
        Farm produce—Storage—Diseases and
            injuries
        Farm produce—Transportation—
            Diseases and injuries
        Fertilization of plants by insects
        Forest insects
        Galls (Botany)
        Garden pests
        Host plants
        Household pests
        Insect control
        Insect-plant relationships
        Insecticides
        Insects as carriers of disease
        Insects as carriers of plant diseases

Insects as food
    Plant inspection
    Plants—Disease and pest resistance
    Veterinary entomology
    Weed control—Biological control
    names of insects, e.g. Argentine ant,
        Boll-weevil, Book-worms,
        Gipsy-moth; *and subdivision*
        Diseases and pests *under names of*
        crops, plants, trees, etc., e.g. Fruit—
        Diseases and pests; Grain—Diseases
        and pests; Roses—Diseases and
        pests; Pine—Diseases and pests;
        Trees—Diseases and pests
    x Economic entomology
        Entomology, Economic
        Injurious insects
        Insects, Destructive and useful
    xx Agricultural pests
        Agriculture
        Fruit—Diseases and pests
        Galls (Botany)
        Garden pests
        Gardening
        Horticulture
        Insecticides
        Parasites
        Pests
        Trees—Diseases and pests
        Vegetables—Diseases and pests
        Zoology, Economic
— Biological control
    See Insect control—Biological control
— Control
    See Insect control
— Extermination
    See Insect control
— Identification
— Law and legislation *(Direct)*
Insects, Parasitic
    See Parasitic insects
Insects, Social
    See Insect societies
Insects, Sound production by
    See Sound production by insects
Insects and plant diseases
    See Insects as carriers of plant diseases
Insects as carriers of disease *(RA639-641)*
    sa Cockroaches as carriers of disease
        Fleas as carriers of disease
        Flies as carriers of disease
        Insects as carriers of plant diseases
        Lice as carriers of disease
        Mites as carriers of disease
        Mosquitoes
        Ticks as carriers of disease
        Tsetse-flies
        Veterinary entomology
    x Medical entomology
    xx Animals as carriers of disease
        Communicable diseases
        Diseases—Transmission
        Insects, Injurious and beneficial
Insects as carriers of plant diseases *(SB931)*
    sa Virus diseases of plants
    x Insects and plant diseases
    xx Insects as carriers of disease
        Insects, Injurious and beneficial
        Plant diseases
        Virus diseases of plants
Insects as food
    xx Food
        Insects, Injurious and beneficial
Insects as pets *(SF459.I5)*
— Juvenile literature
Insects in art
Insecurity (Psychology)
    See Security (Psychology)

Inselbergs *(Indirect)*
    xx Mountains
Insemination, Artificial
    See Artificial insemination
Insensibility
    See Loss of consciousness
Inserts, Concrete
    See Concrete inserts
Insider trading in securities *(Direct)*
    xx Directors of corporations
        Securities
Insight (Buddhism)
    See Vipaśyanā (Buddhism)
Insignia *(Direct)* *(Jeweled, NK7400-7419;*
    Military, UC530-535; Naval, VC345;
    Royalty, CR4480; Secret societies,
    HS159-160)
    sa Armed Forces—Insignia
        Armies—Insignia
        Badges
        Baseball insignia
        Buttons
        Campaign insignia
        Decorations of honor
        Devices
        Emblems, National
        Maces, Ceremonial
        Military religious orders—Insignia
        Orders of knighthood and chivalry—
            Insignia
        Patriotic societies—Insignia
        Regalia (Insignia)
        Sashes (Costume)
        Schools—Insignia
        Universities and colleges—Insignia
    subdivisions Insignia *and* Medals,
        badges, decorations, etc. *under*
        armies and navies, e.g. United States.
        Army—Insignia; United States.
        Army—Medals, badges, decorations,
        etc.; *and subdivision* Costumes,
        supplies, etc. *under names of secret*
        societies, e.g. Freemasons—
        Costumes, supplies, etc.
    x Badges of honor
        Jewels
    xx Decorations of honor
        Devices
        Emblems
        Emblems, National
        Heraldry
        Societies
    Note under Regalia (Insignia)
Insignia, Municipal
    See Municipal insignia
Insignia, Royal
    See Regalia (Insignia)
Insolation
    See Solar radiation
Insolvency
    See Bankruptcy
Insomnia *(RC548)*
    sa Hypnotics
        Narcotics
        Sleep
    x Sleeplessness
        Wakefulness
    xx Sleep
        Sleep deprivation
        Sleep disorders
Inspection, Engineering
    See Engineering inspection
Inspection by sampling
    See Sampling
Inspection for disarmament
    See Disarmament—Inspection
Inspection of buildings
    See Building inspection

Inspection of disarmament
    See Disarmament—Inspection
Inspection of factories
    See Factory inspection
Inspection of fish
    See Fish inspection
Inspection of food
    See Food adulteration and inspection
Inspection of fruit
    See Fruit inspection
Inspection of meat
    See Meat inspection
Inspection of oil
    See Oil inspection
Inspection of poultry
    See Poultry inspection
Inspection of schools
    See School management and organization
Inspection of steam-boilers
    See Steam-boiler inspection
Inspection of stock
    See Stock inspection
Inspection of vegetables
    See Vegetable inspection
Inspiration   *(Psychology, BF410; Theology,*
    BT125)
    sa Bible—Inspiration
        Breath and breathing (in religion,
            folk-lore, etc.)
        Creation (Literary, artistic, etc.)
        Creative ability
        Enthusiasm
        Mormons and Mormonism—Sacred
            books—Inspiration
        Revelation
    xx Bible—Inspiration
        Creation (Literary, artistic, etc.)
        Supernatural
        Theology, Doctrinal
Inspirationists   *(HX656.A4)*
Installation (Clergy)   *(BV4290)*
        Here are entered works dealing with the
        installation of a clergyman as the pas-
        tor of a church. Works dealing with the
        ordination of a clergyman *(i.e.* his first
        entrance into the clerical office) are
        entered under the heading Ordination.
        Whenever ordination and installation
        are simultaneous, preference is given
        to the heading Ordination.
    sa Catholic Church—Clergy—Installation
        Initiations (in religion, folk-lore, etc.)
        Installation (Rabbis)
        Installation sermons
    x Clergy—Installation
    xx Installation sermons
    — Anniversary sermons   *(BV4290)*
Installation (Rabbis)
    x Rabbis—Installation
    xx Initiations (in religion, folk-lore, etc.)
        Installation (Clergy)
    — Anniversary sermons
Installation of carpets
    See Carpet laying
Installation of industrial equipment
        (TS191.3)
    sa Gas-turbines—Erecting work
        Machinery—Erecting work
        Metal-working machinery—Erecting
            work
        Steam-turbines—Erecting work
    x Industrial installation
        Installing of industrial equipment
    xx Industrial equipment
        Plant engineering
    — Estimates and costs   *(Direct)*
    — Prices   *(Direct)*   *(TS191.3)*
    — Production standards

— Safety measures
Installation sermons   *(BV4290)*
    sa Installation (Clergy)
    xx Installation (Clergy)
        Sermons
Installation service (Church officers)
        (BV199.15)
    xx Church officers
        Liturgies
        Worship programs
Installing of industrial equipment
    See Installation of industrial equipment
Instalment contracts   *(Direct)*
        Here are entered works dealing with con-
        tracts where, by the terms of the con-
        tract, a partial delivery is contem-
        plated, or where a thing is delivered
        periodically or continuously. Works
        on the law of sale of consumer goods
        purchased on the instalment plan are
        entered under Sales, Conditional.
    x Instalment sales
    xx Contracts
        Sales
Instalment credit companies
    See Commercial finance companies
        Instalment plan
Instalment land contracts   *(Direct)*
    x Land contracts
    xx Sales, Conditional
        Vendors and purchasers
Instalment plan   *(Direct)*   *(HF5568)*
    sa Commercial finance companies
        Industrial loan associations
        Insurance, Group creditors
        Layaway plan
        Sales, Conditional
    x Accounts receivable finance companies
        Commercial credit companies
        Credit companies
        Finance companies, Commercial
        Hire-purchase plan
        Instalment credit companies
        Sales-finance companies
    xx Business
        Consumer credit
        Credit
        Layaway plan
        Purchasing
        Sales, Conditional
    Example under Consumer education
    Note under Consumer credit
    — Public opinion
Instalment sales
    See Instalment contracts
Instant coffee
    See Soluble coffee
Instant sweet potatoes
    See Sweet potato flakes
Instant tea
    See Soluble tea
Instantaneous photography
    See Photography, Instantaneous
Instinct   *(Psychology, BF685; Zoology,*
        QL781)
    sa Animal intelligence
        Habit
        Herding behavior in animals
        Impulse
        Orientation
        Psychology, Comparative
        Self-preservation
        Sublimation
    x Animal instinct
        Intelligence of animals
    xx Animal intelligence
        Animals, Habits and behavior of
        Habit

Psychology
Psychology, Comparative
— Juvenile literature
Institutes, Farmers'
    See Farmers' institutes
Institutes, Teachers'
    See Teachers' institutes
Institution building
    xx Social change
        Social institutions
        Social policy
Institution libraries   *(Direct)*   *(Z675.16)*
    sa Blind, Libraries for the
        Hospital libraries
        Prison libraries
        Reformatory libraries
    x Libraries, Institution
Institution management   *(Charities, HV40;*
        Home economics, TX147)
    sa Church management
        Office management
        subdivision Accounting *under types of*
            institutions, e.g. Hospitals—
            Accounting
    x Management, Institution
    xx Management
        Office management
Institutional care   *(Direct)*
    sa Almshouses
        Hospitals
        Nursing homes
        Old age homes
        Orphans and orphan-asylums
        Psychiatric hospitals
        subdivisions Care and treatment,
            Institutional care *and* Hospitals and
            asylums *under classes of persons*
    x Benevolent institutions
        Charitable institutions
        Homes (Institutions)
    xx Charities
        Public institutions
        Public welfare
Institutional church
    See Church work
Institutional economics   *(HB99.5)*
    xx Economics
Institutional investments   *(Direct)*
    sa Endowments—Program-related
        investments
    xx Investments
    — Social aspects   *(Direct)*
Institutional market   *(Direct)*
    xx Marketing
Institutional missions   *(Direct)*
        (BV2000-3705)
    x Missions, Institutional
    xx Church work
        City missions
        Evangelistic work
        Missions, Home
Institutional research (Education)
    See Education, Higher—Research
Institutionalism (Religion)
    xx Church polity
        Church work
Institutions, Catholic
    See Catholic institutions
Institutions, Charitable and philanthropic
    See Charities
Institutions, Ecclesiastical
    See Religious and ecclesiastical institutions
Institutions, Inmates of
    See Inmates of institutions
Institutions, International
    See International agencies
        International cooperation

special *international congresses,*
  societies, etc.
Institutions, Open-air
  See Open-air institutions
Institutions, Public
  See Public institutions
Institutions, Religious
  See Religious and ecclesiastical institutions
Institutions, Social
  See Social institutions
Institutions, State
  See Public institutions
Institutions, associations, etc.
  See Associations, institutions, etc.
Institutions, associations, etc., Foreign
  See Associations, institutions, etc., Foreign
Instruction
  See Education
    Teaching
    subdivision Instruction and study *under*
      Music *and under names of musical*
      instruments
Instruction, Camps of
  See Military training camps
Instructional change
  See Curriculum change
Instructional materials
  See Teaching—Aids and devices
Instructional materials centers
  sa Audio-visual library service
    Instructional materials personnel
    Selection of nonbook materials
  x Audio-visual materials centers
    Media centers (Education)
    Schools
  xx Audio-visual library service
    Libraries, University and college
    School libraries
  — Administration
  — Design and construction
  — Standards *(Direct)*
Instructional materials personnel *(Direct)*
  sa Audio-visual education
  x Audio-visual materials personnel
    Audio-visual specialists
    Educational media personnel
    Media service personnel in education
  xx Audio-visual education
    Instructional materials centers
    School management and organization
Instructional supervision
  See School supervision
Instructional systems analysis
  See Educational surveys
Instructional technology
  See Educational technology
Instructions to juries *(Direct)*
  sa Special issues
    Verdicts
  x Prayers and instructions
  xx Civil procedure
    Criminal procedure
    Jury
    Trial practice
Instructive games
  See Educational games
Instructive toys
  See Educational toys
Instructors
  See College teachers
Instrument approach systems
  See Instrument landing systems
Instrument flight
  See Instrument flying
Instrument flying *(TL711.B6)*
  sa Instrument landing systems
    Link trainers
    Omnirange system

Runway localizing beacons
    Tacan
  x Blind flying
    Instrument flight
  xx Aeronautical instruments
    Aeroplanes—Piloting
  — Charts, diagrams, etc.
  — Examinations, questions, etc.
Instrument industry *(Direct)*
  sa Optical industry
    Scientific apparatus and instruments
    Wages—Instrument industry
    names of categories of instruments, e.g.
      Chemical apparatus; Optical
      instruments
  xx Engineering instruments
    Scientific apparatus and instruments
  — Accounting
  — Automation
  — Employees *(Direct)*
    x Instrument manufacture—Employees
Instrument landing systems *(TL696.L33)*
    Here are entered general works on sys-
    tems of landing aeroplanes by instru-
    ments when visibility is low or practi-
    cally nonexistent, and also works on
    the specific system known as ILS (in-
    strument landing system) Works on
    other individual systems are entered
    under specific headings, *e.g.* Ground
    controlled approach.
  sa Distance measuring equipment (Aircraft
    to ground station)
    Glide path systems
    Ground controlled approach
    Runway localizing beacons
    Surveillance radar
  x Blind landing
    ILS
    Instrument approach systems
  xx Aeroplanes—Landing
    Electronics in aeronautics
    Instrument flying
    Landing aids (Aeronautics)
  Example under Aids to air navigation
  — Charts, diagrams, etc.
    xx Aeronautical charts
  — Maintenance and repair
Instrument-making
  See Instrument manufacture
Instrument manufacture *(Direct) (TS500)*
  x Instrument-making
    Physical instruments—Trade and
    manufacture
  xx Engineering instruments
    Measuring instruments
    Scientific apparatus and instruments
  — Automation
  — Employees
    See Instrument industry—Employees
  — Problems, exercises, etc.
  — Production standards
  — Quality control
  — Technological innovations
  — Vocational guidance
Instrument platforms, Floating
  See Oceanographic buoys
Instrument transformers, Electric
  See Electric instrument transformers
Instrumental analysis *(QD73)*
  xx Chemistry, Analytic
    Chemistry, Physical and theoretical
    Physical instruments
    Physical measurements
  — Laboratory manuals
Instrumental behavior
  See Operant behavior

Instrumental conditioning
  See Operant conditioning
Instrumental ensembles *(M900-949;*
      M960-985)
    Here are entered compositions for ten or
    more solo instruments belonging to
    various families of instruments.
    When used in conjunction with a specific
    solo instrument(s) or solo voice(s), the
    designation instrumental ensemble
    may stand for any number and combi-
    nation of various solo instruments.
    Compositions for ten or more solo bowed
    stringed instruments or for ten or more
    solo wind instruments are entered re-
    spectively under String ensembles and
    Wind ensembles.
    Compositions for ten or more plectral in-
    struments are entered under Plectral
    ensembles unless the instruments in-
    volved are guitars, harps or a combina-
    tion of those two instruments, in which
    case the compositions are entered un-
    der Instrumental ensembles.
    Compositions for ten or more percussion
    instruments are entered under Percus-
    sion music.
  sa Bassoon with instr. ensemble
    Canons, fugues, etc. (Instrumental
      ensemble)
    Chorale preludes (Instrumental
      ensemble)
    Clarinet with instr. ensemble
    Concertos (Clarinet with instr.
      ensemble)
    Concertos (Harp with instr. ensemble)
    Concertos (Harpsichord with
      instrumental ensemble)
    Concertos (Hurdy-gurdies (2) with
      instr. ensemble)
    Concertos (Oboe with instr. ensemble)
    Concertos (Piano with instrumental
      ensemble)
    Concertos (Trumpet with instr.
      ensemble)
    Concertos (Violin and violoncello with
      instr. ensemble)
    Concertos (Violin with instr. ensemble)
    Concertos (Violoncello with instr.
      ensemble)
    Flute with instr. ensemble
    Harp with instr. ensemble
    Harpsichord with instr. ensemble
    Horn with instrumental ensemble
    Hurdy-gurdies (2) with instr. ensemble
    Jigs (Instrumental ensemble)
    Monologues with music (Instrumental
      ensemble)
    Oboe with instr. ensemble
    Organ with instr. ensemble
    Overtures (Instrumental ensemble)
    Percussion and piano with instrumental
      ensemble
    Piano with instr. ensemble
    Pianos (2) with instr. ensemble
    Polkas (Instrumental ensemble)
    Polonaises (Instrumental ensemble)
    Reels (Instrumental ensemble)
    Suites (Instrumental ensemble)
    Suites (Pianos (2) with instrumental
      ensemble)
    Symphonies (Instrumental ensemble)
    Trumpet with instr. ensemble
    Variations (Instrumental ensemble)
    Viola with instr. ensemble
    Violin and viola with instr. ensemble
    Violin and violoncello with instr.
      ensemble

Instrumental ensembles *(M900-949; M960-985) (Continued)*
  Violin with instr. ensemble
  Violoncello with instr. ensemble
 x Ensembles (Music)
 Note under Chamber music
Instrumental ensembles, Arranged
Instrumental ensembles, Juvenile *(M1413-1417)*
Instrumental masses
 See Organ masses
Instrumental music *(Indirect) (M5-1459)*
 sa Accordion ensembles
  Band music
  Chamber music
  Chamber-orchestra music
  Dance music
  Dance-orchestra music
  Hunting music
  Jazz nonets
  Jazz quartets
  Jazz quintets
  Jazz septets
  Jazz sextets
  Jazz trios
  Military music
  Mouth-organ ensembles
  Orchestral music
  Percussion music
  Plectral ensembles
  Salon-orchestra music
  String-orchestra music
  Piano music, Violoncello and harpsichord music, *and similar headings*
 x Music, Instrumental
 xx Music
 — To 1800
 — — Discography *(ML156.4.I5)*
 — Bibliography
 — — Graded lists *(ML132.I5)*
   x Instrumental music—Graded lists
 — Graded lists
  See Instrumental music—Bibliography —Graded lists
 — History and criticism *(ML460-547)*
  sa Bands (Music)
   Musical instruments
   Orchestra
   various forms of instrumental music, e.g. Sonata, Symphony
  xx Musical instruments
 — Instruction and study *(MT170)*
  sa subdivision Instruction and study *under names of musical instruments, e.g.* Piano— Instruction and study
  x Musical instruments—Instruction and study
  xx Music—Instruction and study
 — Studies and exercises *(MT170)*
 — Studies and exercises (Jazz) *(MT170)*
 — Thematic catalogs *(ML128.I65)*
Instrumentation and orchestration *(History, ML455; Instruction, MT70)*
 sa Arrangement (Music)
  Musical instruments
 x Orchestration
 xx Arrangement (Music)
  Chamber orchestra
  Composition (Music)
  Music
  Music—Instruction and study
  Music—Theory
  Musical instruments
  Orchestra

Instrumentation and orchestration (Band) *(ML455; MT73)*
 xx Bands (Music)
  Military music—History and criticism
  Wind instruments
Instrumentation and orchestration (Dance orchestra) *(MT86)*
 xx Dance music—History and criticism
  Dance orchestra
  Jazz music
Instrumentmen, Naval
 See United States. Navy—Instrumentmen
Instruments, Acoustic impedance
 See Acoustic impedance—Instruments
Instruments, Aeronautical
 See Aeronautical instruments
Instruments, Agricultural
 See Agricultural instruments
Instruments, Astronautical
 See Astronautical instruments
Instruments, Astronomical
 See Astronomical instruments
Instruments, Atomic absorption spectroscopy
 See Atomic absorption spectroscopy— Instruments
Instruments, Ballistic
 See Ballistic instruments
Instruments, Dental
 See Dental instruments and apparatus
Instruments, Drawing
 See Drawing instruments
Instruments, Earth science
 See Earth science instruments
Instruments, Electric
 See Electric apparatus and appliances
Instruments, Electronic
 See Electronic instruments
Instruments, Engineering
 See Engineering instruments
Instruments, Engineering geology
 See Engineering geology—Instruments
Instruments, Geophysical
 See Geophysical instruments
Instruments, Heat engineering
 See Heat engineering—Instruments
Instruments, Heat transfer
 See Heat—Transmission—Instruments
Instruments, Hydrological
 See Hydrological instruments
Instruments, Internal friction
 See Internal friction—Instruments
Instruments, Magnetic
 See Magnetic instruments
Instruments, Marine
 See Nautical instruments
Instruments, Mathematical
 See Mathematical instruments
Instruments, Measuring
 See Measuring instruments
Instruments, Medical
 See Medical instruments and apparatus
Instruments, Meteorological
 See Meteorological instruments
Instruments, Military topography
 See Military topography—Instruments
Instruments, Moisture measuring
 See Moisture—Measurement—Instruments
Instruments, Musical
 See Musical instruments
Instruments, Nautical
 See Nautical instruments
Instruments, Negotiable
 See Negotiable instruments
Instruments, Oceanographic
 See Oceanographic instruments
Instruments, Ophthalmological
 See Eye, Instruments and apparatus for

Instruments, Optical
 See Optical instruments
Instruments, Percussion
 See Percussion instruments
Instruments, Physical
 See Physical instruments
Instruments, Printing
 See Printing, Practical—Instruments
Instruments, Radiochemical
 See Radiochemistry—Instruments
Instruments, Scientific
 See Scientific apparatus and instruments
Instruments, Surgical
 See Surgical instruments and apparatus
Instruments, Surveying
 See Surveying—Instruments
Instruments, Underwater acoustics
 See Underwater acoustics—Instruments
Instruments, Veterinary
 See Veterinary instruments and apparatus
Instruments of war
 See Munitions
Insubordination *(Direct) (Military, UB789; Naval, VB880)*
 sa Mutiny
 xx Military offenses
  Naval offenses
Insubordination (Canon law)
Insular fauna
 See Island fauna
Insular flora
 See Island flora
Insulating board
 See Fiberboard
Insulating materials
 sa Cellular glass
  Electric insulators and insulation
  Insulating oils
 xx Building materials
Insulating oils *(TK3441.O5)*
 x Oils, Insulating
  Transformer oil
 xx Electric insulators and insulation
  Insulating materials
  Mineral oils
  Oils and fats
 — Testing
Insulating paper
 x Paper, Insulating
 xx Electric insulators and insulation
  Paper
Insulating varnish *(TK3441.V3)*
 x Varnish, Insulating
 xx Electric insulators and insulation
Insulation (Electric)
 See Electric insulators and insulation
Insulation (Heat) *(TH1715)*
 sa Aircraft cabins—Insulation
  Clothing, Cold weather
  Cold storage—Insulation
  Exterior walls—Thermal properties
  Mineral wool
  Railroads—Cars—Insulation
  Refrigerator-cars
  Ships—Insulation
  Steam-pipe coverings
 x Thermal insulation
 xx Exterior walls—Thermal properties
  Heating
 — Laboratory manuals
 — Standards
Insulation (Sound)
 See Soundproofing
Insulin *(QP951)*
 sa Hypoglycemia
  Insulin shock
 xx Antidiabetics
 — Physiological effect

— Standards
Insulin hypoglycemia
    See Insulin shock
Insulin shock
    sa Insulin shock therapy
    x Hyperinsulinism
        Insulin hypoglycemia
    xx Diabetes
        Hypoglycemia
        Insulin
        Shock
Insulin shock therapy
    xx Insulin shock
        Shock therapy
Insuloma
    See Islands of Langerhans—Tumors
Insurance (Direct) (HG8011-9970)
    sa Collective farms—Insurance
        Insurance and inflation
        Insurance companies
        Insurance departments
        Insurance policies
        Insurance surveys
        Reinsurance
        Revalorization of insurance
        Saving and thrift
        Self-insurance
    x Assurance (Insurance)
        Insurance, Mutual
        Mutual insurance
        Underwriting
    xx Estate planning
        Finance
        Finance, Personal
— Abbreviations
— Accounting (HG8077)
    x Insurance companies—Accounting
— Adjustment of claims
    x Adjustment of claims
        Claims, Adjustment of
— Agents (HG8091-8102)
    sa Insurance, Accident ₍Fire, Life, etc.₎
        —Agents
        Insurance as a profession
    x Insurance agents
        Insurance—Salesmanship
    xx Insurance as a profession
        Insurance companies—Employees
    Example under Commercial agents
— — Directories
        See Insurance—Directories
— — Psychology
— Anecdotes, facetiae, satire, etc.
        (PN6231.I6)
— Biography
— Caricatures and cartoons
    x Insurance—Cartoons
— Cartoons
        See Insurance—Caricatures and
            cartoons
— Dictionaries (HG8025)
— Directories (HG8021)
    x Insurance—Agents—Directories
        Insurance companies—Directories
— Examinations, questions, etc.
— Finance (HG8076-8)
    sa Insurance companies—Investments
        Insurance—Reserves
— Government ownership (Direct)
    x Government ownership of insurance
        companies
    xx Insurance, Government
— History (HG8027-8039)
— Management
        See Insurance companies—
            Management
— Mathematics (HG8781-2)
    sa Actuaries

Insurance—Rates and tables
        Insurance—Statistical methods
    x Actuarial science
    xx Business mathematics
— Periodicals (HG8011-8015)
— Plans (HG8051)
— Policies
        See Insurance policies
— Premiums
        See Insurance—Rates and tables
— Rates and tables (HG8065-7)
        Includes works on the theory and com-
            putation of premiums, as well as
            lists of rates in force.
    sa subdivision Rates and tables under
        particular branches of insurance
    x Actuarial statistics
        Insurance—Premiums
        Insurance statistics
    xx Insurance—Mathematics
— Reserves
    x Insurance reserves
        Premium reserves
        Reserves (Insurance)
    xx Corporation reserves
        Insurance—Finance
        Insurance law
        Reserves (Accounting)
— Risk
        See Risk (Insurance)
— Salesmanship
        See Insurance—Agents
— Self-insurance
        See Self-insurance
— Societies, etc. (By country, HG8522,
        etc.; International, HG8016)
— State supervision (HG8111-8117)
    sa Insurance law
    x Insurance and state
        State and insurance
    xx Consumer protection
        Industry and state
        Insurance law
— Statistical methods
    x Actuarial statistics
        Insurance statistics
    xx Insurance—Mathematics
— Statistics (HG8045)
    x Actuarial statistics
        Insurance statistics
— Taxation (HG8119-8123)
    x Insurance companies—Taxation
— Vocational guidance
        See Insurance as a profession
— War risks (HG8055)
    x Insurance, War
        Risks (Insurance)
        War insurance
        War risks (Insurance)
— Yearbooks (HG8019)
Insurance, Accident (Direct)
        (HG9301-9343; Industrial,
        HD7101-2)
    Cf. note under Insurance, Employers' lia-
        bility.
    sa Disability evaluation
        Industrial accidents
        Insurance, Athletic accident
        Insurance, Employers' liability
        Insurance, Liability
        Insurance, Life—Disability benefits
        Insurance, Travelers'
        Workmen's compensation
    x Accident insurance
        Labor and laboring classes—Insurance
    xx Disability evaluation
        Insurance, Casualty
        Insurance, Liability

— Adjustment of claims (HG9323.A3)
    x Adjustment of claims
        Claims, Adjustment of
— Agents
    xx Insurance—Agents
— Medical examinations (HG8886-8891)
    x Examinations, Medical
        Insurance, Employers' liability—
            Medical examinations
        Medical examinations
— Rates and tables (HG9323.R3)
— Statistics (HG9310)
— War risks
Insurance, Aeronautical
    See Insurance, Aviation
Insurance, Agricultural (Direct)
        (HG9966-9)
    sa Farm risks
        Insurance, Forest
        Insurance, Windstorm
    x Agricultural insurance
    xx Insurance, Casualty
— Crops (Direct) (HG9968.C6-8)
    x Crop insurance
        Insurance, Crop
    Example under Insurance, Government
— Hail
        See Insurance, Hail
— Lightning
        See Insurance, Lightning
— Livestock (Direct) (HG9968.L5-8)
    x Cattle insurance
        Insurance, Livestock
        Livestock insurance
— Public opinion
— Research
— Windstorm
        See Insurance, Windstorm
Insurance, Aircraft mortgage (Direct)
    x Aircraft mortgage guaranty
    xx Aircraft mortgages
        Insurance, Credit
        Insurance, Mortgage guaranty
Insurance, Art (HG9970.A)
    x Art insurance
Insurance, Assessment (Direct) (HG8826;
        HG9201-9245)
    sa Friendly societies
    x Assessment insurance
    xx Friendly societies
        Insurance, Life
— Rates and tables (HG9221.R3)
Insurance, Athletic accident
    x Athletic accident insurance
    xx Athletics
        Insurance, Accident
Insurance, Atomic hazards (Direct)
    x Atomic insurance
    xx Atomic energy—Economic aspects
        Insurance, Liability
Insurance, Automobile (Direct)
        (HG9970.A4-68)
    sa Insurance, No-fault automobile
        Insurance, Uninsured motorist
        Unsatisfied judgment funds (Traffic
            accidents)
    x Automobile insurance
        Automobiles—Insurance
    xx Insurance, Casualty
        Insurance, Liability
— Anecdotes, facetiae, satire, etc.
— Digests
— Mathematics
— Policies
— Public opinion
— Risks
Insurance, Aviation (HG9970.A7)
    sa Insurance, Life—Aviation risks

Insurance, Aviation *(HG9970.A7)*
(Continued)
Salvage (Aeroplanes)
x Aeronautics—Insurance
Aeroplanes—Insurance
Air-ships—Insurance
Aviation insurance
Insurance, Aeronautical
Insurance, Transportation
xx Insurance, Travelers'
— War risks
Insurance, Bank deposit
See Insurance, Deposit
Insurance, Bicycle
x Bicycle insurance
xx Insurance, Casualty
Insurance, Liability
Insurance, Boiler *(HG9963.B5-8)*
x Boiler insurance
xx Insurance, Casualty
Steam-boilers
Insurance, Burglary *(Direct)* *(HG9970.B8)*
Here are entered works on insurance against robbery and theft, as well as burglary in the legal sense. (This conforms to insurance usage)
x Burglary insurance
Insurance, Robbery
Insurance, Theft
Robbery insurance
Theft insurance
xx Burglary protection
Insurance, Casualty
Insurance, Burial *(Direct)* *(HG9466-9479)*
x Burial clubs
Burial insurance
Clubs, Burial
xx Insurance, Industrial
Insurance, Business *(Direct)*
x Business insurance
Company insurance
Corporate insurance
Insurance, Corporate
Insurance, Business interruption *(Direct)* *(HG9970.B85)*
sa Insurance, Strike
x Business interruption insurance
Insurance, Profits
Insurance, Use and occupancy
Profits insurance
Use and occupancy insurance
xx Insurance, Casualty
Insurance, Business life *(Direct)*
(Economics, HG8937; Law, K)
sa Stock purchase agreements (Close corporations)
x Business insurance
Business life insurance
Insurance, Partnership
Partnership insurance
xx Insurance, Life
— Forms
Insurance, Casualty *(Direct)* *(HG9956-9970)*
sa Insurance, Accident
Insurance, Agricultural
Insurance, Automobile
Insurance, Bicycle
Insurance, Boiler
Insurance, Burglary
Insurance, Business interruption
Insurance, Computer
Insurance, Disaster
Insurance, Earthquake
Insurance, Employers' liability
Insurance, Explosion
Insurance, Flood
Insurance, Government risks
Insurance, Hail

Insurance, Liability
Insurance, Lightning
Insurance, Machinery
Insurance, Plate-glass
Insurance, Property
Insurance, Strike
Insurance, Surety and fidelity
Insurance, Title
Insurance, Windstorm
x Casualty insurance
xx Insurance, Property
Note under Insurance, Group
— Adjustment of claims *(HG9956)*
— Agents
— Inspectors
Insurance, Child *(HG9271-7)*
x Child insurance
Infants—Insurance
Insurance, Infant
xx Children—Mortality
Infants—Mortality
Insurance, Life
Insurance, Computer *(Direct)*
x Computer insurance
Computer software insurance
xx Insurance, Casualty
Insurance, Property
Insurance, Consumer credit
See Insurance, Credit
Insurance, Contractors'
See Contractors—Insurance requirements
Insurance, Corporate
See Insurance, Business
Insurance, Credit *(Direct)* *(HG9970.C6-89)*
sa Insurance, Aircraft mortgage
Insurance, Export credit
Insurance, Investment guaranty
Insurance, Mortgage guaranty
Insurance, Ship mortgage
x Credit insurance
Insurance, Consumer credit
Insurance, Loan
Loan insurance
xx Credit
Insurance, Creditors group
See Insurance, Group creditors
Insurance, Crop
See Insurance, Agricultural—Crops
Insurance, Dental *(Direct)*
x Dental care, Prepaid
Dental insurance
xx Dental care
Insurance, Health
Insurance, Deposit *(HG1662)*
Here are entered works on private insurance of bank deposits. Works on government insurance of bank deposits are entered under Banks and banking—Government guaranty of deposits.
sa Banks and banking—Government guaranty of deposits
x Bank deposit insurance
Deposit insurance
Insurance, Bank deposit
Insurance, Savings
Savings insurance
xx Bank deposits
Insurance, Property
Insurance, Depreciation
See Insurance, Replacement cost
Insurance, Disability *(Direct)*
x Disability insurance
Insurance, Invalidity
Invalidity insurance
Old age, survivors and disability insurance
xx Insurance, Social

Insurance, Disaster *(Direct)*
sa Insurance, Earthquake
Insurance, Explosion
Insurance, Fire
Insurance, Flood
Insurance, Hail
Insurance, Lightning
Insurance, Windstorm
x Disaster insurance
xx Disaster relief
Hurricane protection
Insurance, Casualty
Insurance, Dowry
See Insurance, Marriage endowment
Insurance, Drug
See Insurance, Pharmaceutical services
Insurance, Earthquake *(Direct)* *(HG9970.E3)*
x Earthquake insurance
xx Insurance, Casualty
Insurance, Disaster
Insurance, Employers' liability *(Direct)* *(HG9964.E4-7)*
Here are entered works on the insurance of an employer's liability for compensation to his employees in case of accident.
sa Disability evaluation
Industrial accidents
x Employers' liability insurance
xx Employers' liability
Insurance, Accident
Insurance, Casualty
Insurance, Liability
Workmen's compensation
Note under Insurance, Accident
— Adjustment of claims
— Medical examinations
See Insurance, Accident—Medical examinations
— Rates and tables
— Statistics
Insurance, Endowment
See Insurance, Life—Endowment policies
Insurance, Explosion
x Explosion insurance
xx Explosions
Insurance, Casualty
Insurance, Disaster
Insurance, Fire
Insurance, Export
See Insurance, Inland marine
Insurance, Export credit *(Direct)*
x Export credit guarantees
Export credit insurance
xx Export credit
Foreign trade promotion
Insurance, Credit
Insurance, Fidelity
See Insurance, Surety and fidelity
Insurance, Fire *(Direct)* *(HG9651-9899)*
sa Fire-marks
Fireproofing
Insurance engineering
Insurance, Explosion
Insurance, Lightning
x Fire insurance
Fire losses
xx Building, Fireproof
Insurance, Disaster
Insurance, Lightning
Insurance, Property
— Accounting *(HG9678-9)*
— Adjustment of claims *(HG9721-7)*
x Adjustment of claims
Claims, Adjustment of
— Agents *(HG9706-9)*

918

Manuals of individual companies are entered under the company alone.

xx Insurance—Agents
— Classification of risks (HG9687)
   x Classification of risks
— Dictionaries (HG9665)
— Finance (HG9674-9)
— History (HG9660)
— Inspectors (HG9711-9717)
— Maps and surveys (HG9771)
   x Insurance, Fire—Surveys
   xx Surveys
— Office marks
   See Fire-marks
— Periodicals (HG9651)
— Plans (HG9665; HG9882)
— Policies (HG9695-9)
   Example under Insurance policies
— Premiums
   See Insurance, Fire—Rates and tables
— Programmed instruction
— Rates and tables (HG9685-9691)
   Includes works on the theory and computation of premiums, as well as lists of rates in force.
   Rates of a particular district are entered here and also under Insurance, Fire—[local subdivision]
   x Insurance, Fire—Premiums
— Risks (HG9731.A-Z)
   sa Electric engineering—Insurance requirements
   x Risks (Insurance)
— Self-insurance
   Example under Self-insurance
— Societies, etc. (By country, HG9753; International, HG9653)
— State supervision (HG9739)
   x Insurance and state
— Statistics (HG9663)
   xx Fires
— Surveys
   See Insurance, Fire—Maps and surveys
— Taxation (Direct) (HG9735)
— War risks (HG9731.W3)
— Yearbooks (HG9655)
Insurance, Flood (Direct) (HG9970.F55-554)
   x Flood insurance
   xx Insurance, Casualty
   Insurance, Disaster
   Insurance, Property
Insurance, Forest (HG9970.F)
   x Forest fire insurance
   Forest insurance
   Insurance, Timber
   Timber insurance
   xx Forest fires
   Forests and forestry
   Insurance, Agricultural
Insurance, Fraternal (Direct)
   x Fraternal insurance
   xx Friendly societies
Insurance, Government (Direct)
   sa Insurance—Government ownership
   Insurance, Social
   other types of insurance underwritten by government authorities, e.g. Banks and banking—Government guaranty of deposits; Insurance, Agricultural—Crops; Insurance, War risk
   x Government insurance
   xx Government lending
   Note under Insurance, Government risks

Insurance, Government employees' health (Direct)
   x Government employees' health insurance
   xx Insurance, Health
Insurance, Government employees' life (Direct)
   x Government employees' life insurance
   xx Insurance, Government life
   Insurance, Life
Insurance, Government life (Direct)
   sa Insurance, Government employees' life
   x Government life insurance
   Veterans' insurance
   xx Insurance, Life
Insurance, Government risks (Direct) (HG8059.G6)
   Here are entered works on insurance protection against risks involving government agencies, especially losses and claims connected with government-owned property or resulting from wrongful actions of government officials and employees. Works on insurance underwritten by government authorities are entered under Insurance, Government.
   x Government risks insurance
   xx Government liability
   Insurance, Casualty
Insurance, Group (Direct) (HG8059.G7; Life, HG8830)
   Here are entered works on group insurance in general and on group life insurance. Works on group insurance in other specific fields are entered under Insurance, Casualty; Insurance, Hospitalization; etc.
   sa Insurance, Group creditors
   x Group insurance
   xx Insurance, Life
Insurance, Group creditors
   x Creditors group insurance
   Group creditors insurance
   Insurance, Creditors group
   xx Consumer credit
   Instalment plan
   Insurance, Group
   Insurance, Life
Insurance, Guaranty
   See Insurance, Surety and fidelity
Insurance, Hail (Direct) (HG9968.H2-5)
   x Hail insurance
   Insurance, Agricultural—Hail
   Storm insurance
   xx Insurance, Casualty
   Insurance, Disaster
Insurance, Health (Direct) (HG9383-9399; Industrial, HD7101-2)
   sa Insurance, Dental
   Insurance, Government employees' health
   Insurance, Hospitalization
   Insurance, Life—Disability benefits
   Insurance, Mental health
   Insurance, Pharmaceutical services
   Medical care
   Medicine, Preventive—Law and legislation
   Workmen's compensation
   x Health insurance
   Insurance, Sickness
   Labor and laboring classes—Insurance
   Medical care, Prepaid
   Medical service, Prepaid
   Prepaid medical care
   Sickness insurance
   Socialized medicine

   xx Insurance, Social
   Medical care
   Medicine, Preventive—Law and legislation
— Adjustment of claims
— Conflict of laws
   See Conflict of laws—Insurance, Health
— Criminal provisions
   xx Insurance crimes
— Employees
— Mathematics
— Medical examinations (HG8886-8891)
   x Examinations, Medical
   Medical examinations
— Public opinion
— Rates and tables (HG9389.R3)
Insurance, Homeowners (Direct) (HG9970.H6-64)
   x Homeowners insurance
   xx Insurance, Multiple-line
Insurance, Hospitalization (Direct)
   sa Hospital care
   x Group hospitalization
   Hospitalization insurance
   Socialized medicine
   xx Insurance, Health
   Note under Insurance, Group
Insurance, Indemnity
   See Insurance, Liability
Insurance, Industrial (Direct) (Finance, HG9251-9262; Labor, HD7090-7250)
   Here are entered works on life insurance whose premiums are collected in small weekly or monthly instalments. Works on industrial insurance in the sense of social insurance are entered under Insurance, Social.
   sa Insurance, Burial
   x Industrial insurance
   xx Insurance, Life
— Adjustment of claims (HG9257.A3)
— Agents (HG9255)
— Finance
— Policies
— Rates and tables (HG9257.R3)
Insurance, Infant
   See Insurance, Child
Insurance, Inland marine (Direct) (HG9903)
   x Export insurance
   Inland marine insurance
   Inland transportation insurance
   Insurance, Export
   Insurance, Transportation
   Transportation insurance
   xx Insurance, Marine
   Insurance, Property
Insurance, Invalidity
   See Insurance, Disability
Insurance, Investment guaranty (Direct) (HG4538)
   x Investment guaranty insurance
   xx Insurance, Credit
   Insurance, Property
   Investments, Foreign
Insurance, Legal costs
   See Insurance, Litigation
Insurance, Legal services
   See Prepaid legal services
Insurance, Liability (Direct) (Employers' liability, HG9964.E)
   sa Indemnity against liability
   Insurance, Accident
   Insurance, Atomic hazards
   Insurance, Automobile
   Insurance, Bicycle

Insurance, Liability (Direct) (Employers'
  liability, HG9964.E)
  (Continued)
    Insurance, Employers' liability
    Insurance, Malpractice
    Insurance, Products liability
  x Indemnity insurance
    Insurance, Indemnity
    Liability insurance
  xx Indemnity against liability
    Insurance, Accident
    Insurance, Casualty
    Liability (Law)
— Adjustment of claims
— Policies
— Rates and tables
Insurance, Life (Direct) (HG8751-9200)
  sa Annuities
    Death—Proof and certification
    Insurance, Assessment
    Insurance, Business life
    Insurance, Child
    Insurance, Government employees' life
    Insurance, Government life
    Insurance, Group
    Insurance Group creditors
    Insurance, Industrial
    Insurance, Mortgage life
    Insurance, Savings-bank life
    Life insurance stocks
    Life insurance trusts
    Mortality, Law of
    Survivors' benefits
  x Actuarial science
    Insurance, Postal life
    Life insurance
    Postal life insurance
— Accounting (HG8848)
    Example under Financial statements
— Adjustment of claims
— Agents (Direct) (HG8876-8883)
    xx Insurance—Agents
— — Correspondence, reminiscences, etc.
— Aviation risks
    x Risks (Insurance)
    xx Insurance, Aviation
— Congresses (HG8755)
— Directories (HG8758)
    x Insurance companies—Directories
— Disability benefits (HG8811.D6)
    xx Insurance, Accident
    Insurance, Health
— Endowment policies (HG8818)
    sa Insurance, Marriage endowment
    x Endowment insurance
    Insurance, Endowment
    xx Insurance, Life—Policies
— Examinations, questions, etc.
— Finance (HG8844-8850)
— History (HG8761)
— Juvenile literature
— Licenses
— Mathematics (HG8781-8793)
    sa Insurance, Life—Rates and tables
    Probabilities
    x Actuarial science
    xx Mortality
    Vital statistics
— — Problems, exercises, etc.
— Medical examinations (HG8886-8891)
    x Examinations, Medical
    Medical examinations
— Periodicals (HG8751)
— Plans (HG8816-8830)
— Policies (HG8861-6)
    sa Insurance, Life—Endowment policies
    Insurance, Life—Tontine policies
— Premiums
    See Insurance, Life—Rates and tables

— Public opinion
— Rates and tables (HG8851-3)
    Includes works on the theory and com-
    putation of premiums, as well as
    general tables of rates in force.
    Rates and tables of particular com-
    panies are entered under the com-
    pany alone.
    x Insurance, Life—Premiums
    Present-value tables
    xx Insurance, Life—Mathematics
— Records and correspondence
— Sales letters
    Example under Sales letters
— Societies, etc. (By country, HG8941,
    etc.; International, HG8754)
— State supervision (HG8916-8919)
    x Insurance and state
— Statistics (HG8766)
— Taxation (HG8910-8914)
    x Insurance companies—Taxation
— Tontine policies (HG8817)
    x Tontine policies
    xx Insurance, Life—Policies
— War risks (HG8811.W2)
    Here are entered works on the war risk
    in private life insurance policies.
    Works on life insurance written by
    the government for members of the
    Armed Forces are entered under
    the heading Insurance, War risk.
    sa Insurance, War risk
    x Insurance, War
    Risks (Insurance)
    War insurance
    War risks (Insurance)
    xx Insurance, War risk
    Veterans
— Yearbooks (HG8756)
Insurance, Lightning (Direct)
  sa Insurance, Fire
  x Insurance, Agricultural—Lightning
    Lightning insurance
    Storm insurance
  xx Insurance, Casualty
    Insurance, Disaster
    Insurance, Fire
Insurance, Litigation (Direct) (HG9970.L6)
  x Insurance, Legal costs
    Litigation insurance
  xx Costs (Law)
Insurance, Livestock
  See Insurance, Agricultural—Livestock
Insurance, Loan
  See Insurance, Credit
Insurance, Machinery (HG9963.M)
  x Machinery insurance
  xx Insurance, Casualty
    Insurance, Property
Insurance, Malpractice (Direct)
  x Malpractice insurance
  xx Insurance, Liability
Insurance, Manufacturers' liability
  See Insurance, Products liability
Insurance, Marine (Direct) (HE961-971)
  sa Average (Maritime law)
    Bottomry and respondentia
    Insurance, Inland marine
    Salvage
  x Abandonment (Marine insurance)
    Insurance, Transportation
    Marine insurance
    Transportation insurance
  xx Commerce
    Contracts, Maritime
    Insurance, Property
    Maritime law
    Merchant marine

    Shipping
— Accounting (HE967)
— Adjustment of claims (HE965-7)
— History (HE964)
— Policies (HE967)
— Rates
— War risks (HE966)
    x Insurance, War
    Risks (Insurance)
    War insurance
    War risks (Insurance)
Insurance, Marriage endowment (HG9281-7)
  x Dowry insurance
    Insurance, Dowry
    Marriage endowment insurance
  xx Insurance, Life—Endowment policies
Insurance, Maternity (Direct) (HG9291-5)
  x Maternity insurance
    Motherhood insurance
  xx Insurance, Social
    Maternal and infant welfare
Insurance, Mental health (Direct)
  x Insurance, Psychiatric
    Mental health insurance
    Mental illness insurance
    Psychiatric insurance
  xx Insurance, Health
Insurance, Military
  See Insurance, War risk
Insurance, Mortgage guaranty (Direct)
  (HG9970.M6)
  sa Insurance, Aircraft mortgage
    Insurance, Ship mortgage
  x Mortgage guaranty insurance
  xx Insurance, Credit
    Insurance, Property
    Insurance, Title
    Mortgages
Insurance, Mortgage life
  xx Insurance, Life
    Mortgages
Insurance, Moving-picture (Direct)
  x Moving-picture insurance
    Moving-pictures—Insurance
Insurance, Multiple-line (Direct)
  sa Insurance, Homeowners
    Insurance, School
  x Insurance companies—Multiple-line
    underwriting
    Multiple-line insurance
Insurance, Mutual
  See Insurance
Insurance, No-fault automobile (Direct)
  x No-fault automobile insurance
  xx Insurance, Automobile
Insurance, Partnership
  See Insurance, Business life
Insurance, Pharmaceutical services (Direct)
  x Drug benefit plans
    Drug insurance
    Insurance, Drug
    Insurance, Prescription
    Pharmaceutical services insurance
    Prepaid prescription drug plans
    Prescription insurance
  xx Insurance, Health
Insurance, Physicians'
  See Physicians—Insurance requirements
Insurance, Plate-glass (HG9963.P6)
  x Plate-glass insurance
  xx Insurance, Casualty
Insurance, Postal life
  See Insurance, Life
Insurance, Prescription
  See Insurance, Pharmaceutical services
Insurance, Products liability
  x Insurance, Manufacturers' liability
    Manufacturers' liability insurance

920

Products liability insurance
   xx Insurance, Liability
      Products liability
Insurance, Profits
   See Insurance, Business interruption
Insurance, Property *(Direct)*
   sa Insurance, Casualty
      Insurance, Computer
      Insurance, Deposit
      Insurance, Fire
      Insurance, Flood
      Insurance, Inland marine
      Insurance, Investment guaranty
      Insurance, Machinery
      Insurance, Marine
      Insurance, Mortgage guaranty
      Insurance, Windstorm
   x Property insurance
   xx Insurance, Casualty
   — Agents
   — Policies
   — Rates and tables
Insurance, Psychiatric
   See Insurance, Mental health
Insurance, Replacement cost *(Direct)*
   sa Insurance and inflation
      Revalorization of insurance
   x Actual cash value insurance
      Insurance, Depreciation
      Replacement cost insurance
Insurance, Robbery
   See Insurance, Burglary
Insurance, Savings
   See Insurance, Deposit
Insurance, Savings-bank life *(Direct)*
   x Savings-bank insurance
      Savings-bank life insurance
   xx Insurance, Life
      Savings-banks
Insurance, School *(Direct)*
   x School insurance
   xx Insurance, Multiple-line
      School plant management
Insurance, Self
   See Self-insurance
Insurance, Ship mortgage *(Direct)*
      (VM299.5-7)
   x Ship mortgage insurance
   xx Insurance, Credit
      Insurance, Mortgage guaranty
Insurance, Sickness
   See Insurance, Health
Insurance, Social *(Direct)* *(HD7090-7250)*
   sa Friendly societies
      Insurance, Disability
      Insurance, Health
      Insurance, Maternity
      Insurance, Unemployment
      Old age pensions
      Social insurance courts
      Social security taxes
      Survivors' benefits
      Workmen's compensation
   x Insurance, State and compulsory
      Insurance, Working-men's
      Medical assistance programs
      Old age, survivors and disability
         insurance
      Social insurance
      Social security
      State and insurance
   xx Economic security
      Insurance, Government
      Non-wage payments
      Pensions
      Social legislation
   Note under Insurance, Industrial
   — Accounting

— Auditing and inspection
— Biography
— Cases
— — Digests
     See Insurance, Social—Digests
— Conflict of laws
     See Conflict of laws—Insurance,
        Social
— Criminal provisions
— Digests
   x Insurance, Social—Cases—Digests
— Employees
— Finance
— Public opinion
— Research
— Statistical services
— Study and teaching *(Direct)*
Insurance, Social (International law)
   xx International law
Insurance, State and compulsory
   See Insurance, Social
Insurance, Strike *(Direct)* *(HG9964.S6)*
   sa Insurance, Unemployment
   x Strike insurance
   xx Insurance, Business interruption
      Insurance, Casualty
      Insurance, Unemployment
      Strikes and lockouts
Insurance, Surety and fidelity *(Direct)*
      (Economics, HG9970.S4-8; Law, K)
   sa *subdivision* Officials and employees—
      Bonding *under names of countries,*
      cities, etc.
   x Bonding of employees
      Bonds, Fidelity
      Bonds, Surety
      Fidelity bonds
      Fidelity insurance
      Guaranty insurance
      Insurance, Fidelity
      Insurance, Guaranty
      Surety and fidelity insurance
      Surety bonds
      Surety companies
   xx Insurance, Casualty
      Judicial bonds
      Suretyship and guaranty
   — Self-insurance
Insurance, Survivors
   See Survivors' benefits
Insurance, Theft
   See Insurance, Burglary
Insurance, Timber
   See Insurance, Forest
Insurance, Title *(Direct)* *(HG9970.T4-68)*
   sa Insurance, Mortgage guaranty
      Title companies
   x Title guaranty
      Title insurance
   xx Insurance, Casualty
      Land titles
      Real property
Insurance, Tornado
   See Insurance, Windstorm
Insurance, Transportation
   See Insurance, Aviation
      Insurance, Inland marine
      Insurance, Marine
      Insurance, Travelers'
Insurance, Travelers' *(Direct)*
   sa Insurance, Aviation
   x Insurance, Transportation
   xx Insurance, Accident
Insurance, Unemployment *(Direct)*
      (HD7095-6)
   sa Insurance, Strike
      Supplemental unemployment benefits
      Unemployment, Seasonal

   x Labor and laboring classes—Insurance
      Unemployment compensation
      Unemployment insurance
   xx Insurance, Social
      Insurance, Strike
      Unemployed
   — Case studies
     Example under reference from Case stud-
       ies
   — Examinations, questions, etc.
   — Finance
   — Public opinion
Insurance, Uninsured motorist *(Direct)*
   x Uninsured motorist insurance
   xx Insurance, Automobile
Insurance, Use and occupancy
   See Insurance, Business interruption
Insurance, War
   See Insurance, Life—War risks
      Insurance, Marine—War risks
      Insurance, War risk
      Insurance—War risks
Insurance, War damage
   See War damage compensation
Insurance, War risk *(Direct)* *(UB370-375)*
      Here are entered works on life and disa-
      bility insurance written by the govern-
      ment for members of the Armed
      Forces. Works on government insur-
      ance of property against damage from
      enemy action are entered under the
      heading War damage compensation.
      Works on war risk in private insurance
      policies are entered under Insurance
      and under the names of certain types
      of insurance, with subdivision War
      risks.
   sa Insurance, Life—War risks
   x Insurance, Military
      Insurance, War
      Risks (Insurance)
      War insurance
      War risk insurance
   xx Insurance, Life—War risks
      Pensions, Military
   Example under Insurance, Government
   Note under Insurance, Life—War risks
Insurance, Windstorm *(Direct)*
   x Insurance, Agricultural—Windstorm
      Insurance, Tornado
      Storm insurance
      Tornado insurance
      Windstorm insurance
   xx Insurance, Agricultural
      Insurance, Casualty
      Insurance, Disaster
      Insurance, Property
Insurance, Working-men's
   See Insurance, Social
Insurance agents
   See Insurance—Agents
Insurance and inflation
   x Inflation and insurance
      Inflation (Finance) and insurance
   xx Inflation (Finance)
      Insurance
      Insurance, Replacement cost
Insurance and state
   See Insurance, Fire—State supervision
      Insurance, Life—State supervision
      Insurance—State supervision
Insurance as a profession
   sa Insurance—Agents
   x Insurance—Vocational guidance
   xx Insurance—Agents
   — Juvenile literature
Insurance companies *(Direct)*
   sa Insurance holding companies

Insurance companies *(Direct)*
(Continued)
    Insurance stocks
    Lloyds associations
    x Companies, Insurance
    xx Financial institutions
    Insurance
— Accounting
    See Insurance—Accounting
— Collective labor agreements
    See Collective labor agreements—
        Insurance companies
— Costs
— Directories
    See Insurance—Directories; Insurance,
        Life—Directories; *and similar*
        headings
— Employees *(Direct)*
    sa Collective labor agreements—
        Insurance companies
    Insurance—Agents
    Trade-unions—Insurance companies
    Wages—Insurance companies
— Equipment and supplies
— Investments
    x Insurance company investments
    xx Insurance—Finance
    Investments
— Licenses *(Direct)*
— Management
    x Insurance—Management
— Multiple-line underwriting
    See Insurance, Multiple-line
— Taxation
    See Insurance—Taxation; Insurance,
        Life—Taxation; *and similar*
        headings
Insurance companies, American, [British, etc.]
    (Direct)
    x American [British, etc.] insurance
        companies
Insurance companies, Foreign *(Direct)*
    x Foreign insurance companies
    xx Corporations, Foreign
Insurance company investments
    See Insurance companies—Investments
Insurance contracts
    See Insurance policies
Insurance crimes *(Direct)*
    sa Insurance, Health—Criminal provisions
    x Crimes, Insurance
    xx Criminal law
    Fraud
    Insurance law
Insurance departments *(Direct)*
    x Corporate insurance departments
    Corporations—Insurance departments
    xx Insurance
Insurance engineering *(TH9201-9237)*
    sa Building, Fireproof
    Fire extinction
    Fire prevention
    xx Building, Fireproof
    Fire extinction
    Fire prevention
    Insurance, Fire
    Safety appliances
Insurance holding companies *(Direct)*
    xx Holding companies
    Insurance companies
Insurance law *(Direct) (HG8115, etc.;*
    Burial, HG9471; Fire, HG9734;
    Health, HG9393; Life, HG8906-9)
    sa Insurance crimes
    Insurance policies
    Insurance—Reserves
    Insurance—State supervision
    Revalorization of insurance
    Warranty

    x Law, Insurance
    xx Commercial law
    Contracts, Aleatory
    Insurance—State supervision
— Conflict of laws
    See Conflict of laws—Insurance
— Examinations, questions, etc.
— Programmed instruction
Insurance law, International
    Here are entered works dealing with in-
    surance laws adopted or proposed by
    international convention or treaty.
    sa Conflict of laws—Insurance
    x International insurance law
    xx Conflict of laws—Insurance
    International law
Insurance libraries *(Z675.17)*
    x Libraries, Insurance
Insurance policies *(Direct)*
    sa subdivision Policies *under various kinds*
        of insurance, e.g. Insurance, Fire—
        Policies
    x Contracts, Insurance
    Insurance contracts
    Insurance—Policies
    Policies of insurance
    Policy of insurance
    xx Contracts
    Insurance
    Insurance law
Insurance reserves
    See Insurance—Reserves
Insurance statistics
    See Insurance—Rates and tables
    Insurance—Statistical methods
    Insurance—Statistics
Insurance stocks *(Direct)*
    sa Life insurance stocks
    xx Insurance companies
    Stocks
Insurance surveys
    xx Insurance
Insurance trusts
    See Life insurance trusts
Insured mail *(Direct)*
    x Postal service—Insurance
Insurgency *(Direct) (JC328.5)*
    sa Government, Resistance to
    Guerrilla warfare
    Internal security
    Peasant uprisings
    Subversive activities
    Terrorism
    x Counterinsurgency
    Rebellions
    xx Civil war
    Government, Resistance to
    Internal security
    Political crimes and offenses
    Revolutions
— Mathematical models
Insurrections
    See Revolutions
    Slavery in the United States—
        Insurrections, etc.
    particular insurrections, e.g. Whiskey
        Insurrection, 1794
Intaglio printing
    x Gravure printing
    xx Printing
    Prints—Technique
Intaglios *(Direct) (NK5730)*
    sa Gems
    Seals (Numismatics)
    xx Gems
    Glyptics
Intakes (Hydraulic engineering)
    xx Hydraulic structures

INTAL (Artificial language)
    See International auxiliari linguo (Artificial
        language)
Intangible assets
    See Intangible property
Intangible property *(Direct)*
    sa Business names
    Choses in action
    Copyright
    Good-will (in business, etc.)
    Industrial property
    Licenses
    Patents
    Trade-marks
    x Incorporeal property
    Intangible assets
    Intangibles
    xx Property
— Accounting
— Taxation *(Direct)*
    sa Taxation of bonds, securities, etc.
    x Taxation of intangible property
    xx Property tax
Intangible property (Canon law)
Intangibles
    See Intangible property
Intarsia
    See Marquetry
Integer programming
    xx Programming (Mathematics)
INTEGRAL (Network analysis)
    xx Network analysis (Planning)
Integral calculus
    See Calculus, Integral
Integral Data Store
    See IDS (Computer program language)
Integral equations *(QA431)*
    sa Calculus, Operational
    Functional analysis
    Integral transforms
    Stochastic integral equations
    Volterra equations
    x Equations, Integral
    Fredholm's equation
    xx Functional analysis
    Functional equations
— Numerical solutions
    xx Numerical calculations
Integral equations, Nonlinear
    x Nonlinear integral equations
    xx Nonlinear theories
Integral error function
    See Error functions
Integral functions
    See Functions, Entire
Integral geometry
    See Geometry, Integral
Integral operators
    x Operators, Integral
    xx Integrals
    Operator theory
Integral transforms
    sa Mellin transform
    x Transforms, Integral
    xx Integral equations
    Transformations (Mathematics)
Integralismo
    See Fascism—Brazil
Integrals *(QA308-311)*
    sa Bernstein polynomials
    Convolutions (Mathematics)
    Dilogarithms
    Integral operators
    Integrals, Fresnel
    Overlap integral
    Resonance integral
    xx Calculus, Integral
    Mathematics—Tables, etc.

— Problems, exercises, etc.
— Programmed instruction
Integrals, Abelian
    See Functions, Abelian
Integrals, Definite *(QA311)*
    sa Error functions
      Numerical integration
Integrals, Dirichlet
    x Dirichlet integrals
    xx Fourier series
Integrals, Double
    See Integrals, Multiple
Integrals, Elliptic
    See Functions, Elliptic
Integrals, Feynman
    See Feynman integrals
Integrals, Fresnel
    x Fresnel integrals
    xx Integrals
Integrals, Generalized *(QA312)*
    sa Integrals, Haar
      Measure theory
      Wiener integrals
    xx Calculus, Integral
Integrals, Haar
    x Haar integral
      Haar measure
      Haar's measure
    xx Integrals, Generalized
      Invariants
      Measure theory
Integrals, Hyperelliptic
    sa Functions, Elliptic
    x Functions, Hyperelliptic
      Hyperelliptic functions
      Hyperelliptic integrals
    xx Functions, Elliptic
Integrals, Improper
    x Improper integrals
Integrals, Multiple *(QA311)*
    sa Feynman integrals
    x Double integrals
      Integrals, Double
      Multiple integrals
      Triple integrals
    xx Probabilities
Integrals, Stochastic
    x Stochastic integrals
    xx Stochastic processes
Integrals, Wiener
    See Wiener integrals
Integrated bar *(Direct)*
    Here are entered works on state or local
    bar associations, membership in which
    is compulsory as a condition to prac-
    tice law in the area.
    x Bar integration
      Incorporated bar
      State bar
      Unified bar
    xx Bar associations
      Lawyers
      Practice of law
    — Digests
Integrated churches
    See Church and race problems
Integrated circuits
    sa Hybrid integrated circuits
      Linear integrated circuits
    x Circuits, Integrated
    xx Electronic circuits
      Microelectronics
    — Radiation effects
        See Integrated circuits, Effect of
          radiation on
    — Reliability
    — Tables
    — Testing

Integrated circuits, Effect of radiation on
    x Integrated circuits—Radiation effects
    xx Radiation
Integrated circuits, Hybrid
    See Hybrid integrated circuits
Integrated Civil Engineering System
      (Electronic computer system)
    See ICES (Electronic computer system)
Integrated curriculum
    See Interdisciplinary approach in education
Integrated data processing
    See Electronic data processing
Integration, Faculty
    See Faculty integration
Integration, Numerical
    See Numerical integration
Integration, Racial
    See Race problems
Integration, Social
    See Social integration
Integration (Theory of knowledge)
    xx Knowledge, Theory of
Integration in education
    See Articulation (Education)
      School integration
Integration in higher education
    See Segregation in higher education
Integrators *(QA75)*
    sa Planimeter
    xx Analog computers
Integrity
    See Self-respect
Intellect *(Psychology, BF)*
    sa Age and intelligence
      Creation (Literary, artistic, etc.)
      Imagination
      Inefficiency, Intellectual
      Knowledge, Theory of
      Logic
      Maze tests
      Memory
      Mental tests
      Perception
      Reason
      Reasoning (Psychology)
      Self-organizing systems
      Senses and sensation
      Thought and thinking
      Wisdom
    x Intelligence
      Mind
    xx Knowledge, Theory of
      Psychology
      Reasoning (Psychology)
      Thought and thinking
    — Dietary aspects
        See Intellect—Nutritional aspects
    — Nutritional aspects *(QP398)*
      x Diet and intellect
        Intellect—Dietary aspects
        Nutrition and intellect
      xx Psychology, Physiological
Intellect and age
    See Age and intelligence
Intellect and personality
    See Personality and intelligence
Intellectronics
    See Artificial intelligence
      Bionics
Intellectual cooperation *(AS4; League of*
    Nations, JX1975; Political theory,
    JC362)
    sa Authorship—Collaboration
      Cataloging, Cooperative
      Congresses and conventions
      Cultural relations
      Educational exchanges
      Endowment of research

      Exchange of persons programs
      Exchanges, Literary and scientific
      Information libraries
      Information networks
      International correspondence
      International education
      International Education Year, 1970
      International Geophysical Year,
        1957-1958
      International Years of the Quiet Sun,
        1964-1965
      Internationalism
      Library cooperation
      University cooperation
      subdivision Relations (general) *under*
        names of countries, e.g. United
        States—Relations (general) with
        Latin America
    x Cooperation, Intellectual
      Cultural exchange programs
    xx International cooperation
      International education
      Library cooperation
Intellectual freedom
    See Censorship
      Freedom of information
      Liberty of speech
      Teaching, Freedom of
Intellectual inefficiency
    See Inefficiency, Intellectual
Intellectual life
    sa Learning and scholarship
      Popular culture
      subdivision Intellectual life *under*
        particular classes of people and
        under names of countries, cities, etc.,
        e.g. French-Canadians—Intellectual
        life; Jews—Intellectual life; France—
        Intellectual life; London—Intellectual
        life
    xx Culture
    Note under Popular culture
Intellectual property
    See Copyright
      Inventions
      Patents
Intellectuals *(Direct)* *(HM213)*
    sa Professions
      subdivision Intellectual life *under*
        particular classes of people and
        under names of countries, cities, etc.,
        e.g. French-Canadians—Intellectual
        life; Jews—Intellectual life; United
        States—Intellectual life
    xx Professions
    — Biography
    — Books and reading
    — Interviews
Intellectuals and communism
    See Communism and intellectuals
Intellectuals in literature
    xx Characters and characteristics in
      literature
Intelligence
    See Intellect
Intelligence, Artificial
    See Artificial intelligence
Intelligence, Business
    See Business intelligence
Intelligence and age
    See Age and intelligence
Intelligence levels *(Direct)*
    xx Educational psychology
      Genetic psychology
    — Blind
      sa Stanford-Ohwaki-Kohs tactile block
        design intelligence test for the
        blind

Intelligence levels (Direct)
— Blind (Continued)
    x Blind—Intelligence
— Chinese
    x Chinese intelligence
— Deaf
    x Deaf—Intelligence
— Javanese
    x Javanese intelligence
— Jews
    x Jewish intelligence
       Jews—Intelligence
— Negroes
    x Negro intelligence
       Negroes—Intelligence
— Shilluks
    x Shilluk intelligence
— Testing
    See Mental tests
Intelligence of animals
    See Animal intelligence
       Instinct
       Psychology, Comparative
Intelligence service (Direct)
    sa Espionage
       Military intelligence
       Secret service
    x Counterintelligence
    xx Public administration
       Research
       Secret service
Intelligent machines
    See Artificial intelligence
       Conscious automata
       Logic machines
Intelligibility of speech
    See Speech, Intelligibility of
Intemperance
    See Alcoholism
       Liquor problem
       Temperance
Intendants (Intendants de province,
       JS4843.I6)
    xx Finance, Public—France
       France—Politics and government
       Justice, Administration of—France
       Local government—France
Intension (Philosophy)
    See Semantics (Philosophy)
Intensity, Earthquake
    See Earthquake intensity
Intensive care units
    sa Coronary care units
    xx Hospital care
       Hospitals—Construction
Intensive programs in education
    See Concentrated study
       Educational acceleration
Intent, Criminal
    See Criminal intent
Intention, Declaration of
    See Declaration of intention
Intention (Islam)
    xx Islamic theology
       Man (Islam)
Intention (Logic) (BC199.I5)
    xx Logic
       Reasoning
Intention (Theology)
    x Purity of intention
       Right intention
    xx Spiritual life
Intentionalism
    x Act psychology
    xx Psychology
Inter-American conferences
    sa particular conferences and congresses
    x International American conferences

       Pan American conferences
    xx Pan-Americanism
Inter-American conventions
    See Pan-American treaties and conventions
Inter-American cooperation
    See Pan-Americanism
Inter-American relations
    See Pan-Americanism
Inter-American societies
    See Pan American societies
Inter-American treaties
    See Pan-American treaties and conventions
Inter-college cooperation
    See University cooperation
Inter-library loans (Direct) (Z713)
    sa Exchanges, Literary and scientific
       Libraries—Circulation, loans
    x Book lending
       Books, Lending of
       Loans, Inter-library
    xx Exchanges, Literary and scientific
       Libraries—Circulation, loans
       Library cooperation
— Law and legislation (Direct)
    xx Library legislation
— Terminology
Inter vivos trusts
    See Living trusts
Interaction, Social
    See Social interaction
Interaction (Philosophy) (B824.1)
    xx Philosophy
Interaction analysis in education
    sa Communication in education
       Microteaching
    x Analysis, Interaction (Education)
       Interaction process analysis in
       education
       Teacher-pupil interaction
    xx Observation (Educational method)
       Social interaction
       Teacher-student relationships
       Verbal behavior
Interaction of atmosphere and ocean
    See Ocean-atmosphere interaction
Interaction process analysis in education
    See Interaction analysis in education
Interactions, Electromagnetic
    See Electromagnetic interactions
Interactions, Hyperfine
    See Hyperfine interactions
Interanimal memory transfer
    See Memory transfer
Intercept method
    See Saint Hilaire method
Interception of communications, Unauthorized
    See Eavesdropping
Intercession (Islam) (BP166.825)
    xx Eschatology, Islamic
Intercessor (Theology)
    See Mediator (Theology)
Interchange of bibliographic information
    See Exchange of bibliographic information
Interchange of librarians
    See Librarians, Interchange of
Interchange of patents and technical
       information
    See Exchanges of patents and technical
       information
Interchange of persons
    See Exchange of persons programs
Interchange of population
    See Population transfers
Interchange of students
    See Students, Interchange of
Interchange of teachers
    See Teachers, Interchange of

Interchange of visitors
    See Exchange of persons programs
Interchangeable mechanisms (TJ233;
       TJ1180)
    x Mechanisms, Interchangeable
    xx Machine parts
       Machinery
       Unit construction
Interchanges (Highway engineering)
    See Roads—Interchanges and intersections
Interchurch cooperation
    See Interdenominational cooperation
Intercoastal shipping (Direct) (HE751)
    sa Coastwise shipping
    xx Coastwise shipping
       Shipping
Intercommunication systems
    sa Closed-circuit television
       Loud-speakers
       Microwave communication systems
       Police communication systems
       Public address systems
       subdivision Communication systems
       under subjects, e.g. Railroads—
       Communication systems
    x Intercoms
       Interoffice communication systems
    xx Electro-acoustics
       Electronic apparatus and appliances
       Public address systems
       Sound—Recording and reproducing
       Telecommunication
Intercommunion (BX9.5.I5)
    sa Close and open communion
       Communicatio in sacris
       Simultaneum
       Unionism (Religion)
    xx Christian union
       Church membership
       Church—Unity
       Close and open communion
       Ecumenical movement
       Interdenominational cooperation
       Lord's Supper
       Sects
       Unionism (Religion)
Intercoms
    See Intercommunication systems
Interconnected electric utility systems
    sa Hydrothermal electric power systems
    x Electric power pooling
       Electric utility systems, Interconnected
       System interconnection, Electric power
    xx Electric power distribution
       Electric power-plants
       Electric power systems
       Electric utilities
— Automation
    x Automatic load dispatching (Electric
       power)
    xx Automatic control
       Electric power distribution
       Electric power-plants—Load
       Machine accounting
— Mathematical models
Interconnection (Plumbing)
    See Cross-connections (Plumbing)
Intercontinental ballistic missile bases
       (Indirect)
    sa Air bases
       Bombing and gunnery ranges
    xx Air bases
       Astronautics, Military
       Intercontinental ballistic missiles
       Weapons systems
Intercontinental ballistic missiles
    sa Intercontinental ballistic missile bases

924

names of specific intercontinental
  ballistic missiles, e.g. Atlas (Missile);
  Minuteman (Missile)
  x ICBM
  xx Atomic weapons
    Ballistic missiles
Intercontinental bombers
  See Supersonic bombers
Intercorrelation of traits
  See Trait intercorrelations
Intercostal muscles
  xx Muscles
Intercropping
  See Companion crops
Intercultural communication
  sa Technical assistance—Anthropological
    aspects
  x Communication, Intercultural
  xx Communication
    Culture
    East and West
    Technical assistance—Anthropological
      aspects
  — Juvenile literature
Intercultural education *(CB199)*
  sa Education, Bilingual
    Race awareness
  x Education, Intercultural
  xx Acculturation
    Assimilation (Sociology)
    Comparative education
    Race problems
Intercultural relations
  See Cultural relations
Interdenominational cooperation *(BV625)*
  sa Churches—Interdenominational use
    Community churches
    Federated churches
    Intercommunion
    Local church councils
    Missions—Interdenominational
      cooperation
  x Cooperation, Interchurch
    Cooperation, Interdenominational
    Interchurch cooperation
  xx Christian union
    Church and social problems
    Church work
    Sects
Interdict (Canon law) *(BX1939.I5)*
  sa Excommunication
  xx Catholic Church—Discipline
    Censures, Ecclesiastical
    Excommunication
    Punishment (Canon law)
Interdict (Civil law) *(Direct)*
  sa Injunctions
    Possessory actions
  xx Catholic Church—Discipline
    Censures, Ecclesiastical
    Excommunication
    Punishment (Canon law)
Interdict (Roman-Dutch law)
Interdict (Roman law)
Interdiction (Civil law) *(Direct)*
  sa Capacity and disability
    Guardian and ward
    Prodigals (Law)
  xx Capacity and disability
    Guardian and ward
    Insanity—Jurisprudence
    Persons (Law)
    Prodigals (Law)
Interdiction (Islamic law)
  sa Guardian and ward (Islamic law)
  xx Guardian and ward (Islamic law)
Interdisciplinarity in education
  See Interdisciplinary approach in education

Interdisciplinary approach in education
  x Integrated curriculum
    Interdisciplinarity in education
    Interdisciplinary studies
  xx Curriculum planning
    Universities and colleges—Curricula
Interdisciplinary studies
  See Interdisciplinary approach in education
Interdivisional transfer pricing
  See Transfer pricing
Interest (Law)
  sa Damages
  xx Civil law
Interest (Psychology) *(BF321)*
  sa Attention
    Attention-seeking
    Curiosity
    Interest inventories
    Personality-interest test
  xx Attention
    Educational psychology
    Psychology
Interest and usury *(Direct) (Banking*
    practice, HG1621-3; Theory of
    interest, HB531-9)
  sa Discount
    Prime rate
    Usury laws
  x Loan sharking
    Usury
  xx Banks and banking
    Capital
    Distribution (Economic theory)
    Economics
    Finance
    Finance charges
    Loans
    Usury laws
  — Mathematical models
  — Problems, exercises, etc.
  — Tables, etc. *(HG1626-1638)*
    sa Annuities—Tables
      Banks and banking—Tables, etc.
      Investments—Tables, etc.
    x Amortization tables
      Amortization—Tables, etc.
      Mortgages—Tables, etc.
      Tables, Interest
    xx Annuities—Tables
Interest and usury (Islamic law) *(Direct)*
Interest and usury (Jewish law)
Interest and usury (Roman-Dutch law)
Interest and usury (Roman law)
Interest as tax deductions
  See Income tax—Deductions—Interest
Interest centers approach to teaching
  See Open plan schools
Interest groups
  See Pressure groups
Interest inventories *(LB1027.5)*
  x Interest measures
  xx Interest (Psychology)
    Personnel service in education
Interest measures
  See Interest inventories
Interfaces, Chemistry of
  See Surface chemistry
Interfacings (Clothing)
  xx Clothing and dress
    Sewing
Interference (Aerodynamics)
  xx Aerodynamics
Interference (Electricity)
  See Electric interference
Interference (Light) *(QC411)*
  sa Electric waves
    Holography
    Iridescence

  x Newton's rings
  xx Light
    Optics
    Wave-motion, Theory of
Interference (Sound) *(QC233)*
  sa Acoustic holography
Interference microscope *(QH212.I5)*
  xx Microscope and microscopy
Interference spectrometry
  See Fourier transform spectroscopy
Interferometer *(QC411)*
  sa Fourier transform spectroscopy
    Polarization interferometer
Interferons
  xx Antibiosis
    Virus inhibitors
    Viruses
  — Standards *(Direct)*
Interglossa (Artificial language) *(PM8398)*
  xx Languages, Artificial
Intergovernmental fiscal relations *(Direct)*
  sa Grants-in-aid
    Intergovernmental tax relations
  x Federal revenue sharing
    Federal-state fiscal relations
    Fiscal relations, Intergovernmental
    Fiscal relations, International
    International fiscal relations
    Revenue sharing
    State-local fiscal relations
  xx Federal government
    Finance, Public
    International cooperation
    International relations
    Local finance—Law and legislation
Intergovernmental tax relations *(Direct)*
  sa Taxation and government property
    Taxation, Double
  x Federal revenue sharing
    Federal-state tax relations
    Revenue sharing
    State-local tax relations
    Tax relations, Intergovernmental
    Tax sharing
  xx Federal government
    Intergovernmental fiscal relations
    Taxation
Interim certificates *(Direct)*
  sa Stock certificates
  xx Commercial documents
    Securities
    Stock certificates
Interindustry economics
  sa Diversification in industry
    PASSION (Computer program)
  x Input-output analysis
  xx Economics, Mathematical
    Industry
    Linear programming
  — Computer programs
Interior ballistics
  See Ballistics, Interior
Interior decoration *(Direct) (Art,*
    NK1700-3505; Home economics,
    TX311-317)
  sa Antiques in interior decoration
    Chandeliers
    Church decoration and ornament
    Color in architecture
    Color in interior decoration
    Coverlets
    Drapery
    Floor coverings
    Furniture
    House furnishings
    House furnishings industry and trade
    House plants in interior decoration
    Interior decorators

Interior decoration *(Direct) (Art, NK1700-3505; Home economics, TX311-317) (Continued)*
  Library decoration
  Lighting, Architectural and decorative
  Mural painting and decoration
  Paper-hanging
  Plastics in interior decoration
  Room layout (Dwellings)
  School decoration
  Screens
  Staircases
  Stove-plates
  Tapestry
  Textile fabrics in interior decoration
  Texture painting
  Upholstery
  Wall-paper
  x Arts, Decorative
    Decoration, Interior
    Decorative arts
    Home decoration
    House decoration
  xx Art
    Decoration and ornament
    Environmental engineering (Buildings)
    Furniture
    Home economics
    House furnishings
    Upholstery
  Notes under Do-it-yourself work; Interior decoration—Amateurs' manuals
  — Amateurs' manuals
      Here are entered works on the practical, technical aspects of interior decoration. Works on the planning and art work are entered under the heading Interior decoration.
  — Caricatures and cartoons
  — Juvenile literature
  — Practice
  — Psychological aspects
Interior decoration as a profession *(NK2116)*
Interior decoration in art
  xx Art
Interior decorators *(Direct)*
  x Interior designers
  xx Interior decoration
Interior designers
  See Interior decorators
Interior navigation
  See Inland navigation
Interior valleys
  See Polje (Geomorphology)
Interlingua (International Auxiliary Language Association)
  Cf. note under Interlingua (Latin without inflections)
  xx Languages, Artificial
  Note under Interlingua (Latin without inflections)
Interlingua (Latin without inflections)
      Here are entered works on the artificial language evolved by Giuseppe Peano through a simplification of classical Latin. Works dealing with the artificial language promoted by the International Auxiliary Language Association are entered under Interlingua (International Auxiliary Language Association).
  xx Languages, Artificial
    Latin language—Glossaries, vocabularies, etc.
  Note under Interlingua (International Auxiliary Language Association)

Interlocking signals
  See Railroads—Signaling—Interlocking systems
Interlocutory decisions *(Direct)*
  x Interlocutory decrees
    Interlocutory judgments
    Interlocutory orders
  xx Judgments
Interlocutory decrees
  See Interlocutory decisions
Interlocutory judgments
  See Interlocutory decisions
Interlocutory orders
  See Interlocutory decisions
Interludes *(Drama, PN1934)*
  xx Drama
Interludes, English, ⌐German, etc.⌐
  x English ⌐German, etc.⌐ interludes
Interludes, Spanish
  sa Entremés
Intermarriage
  See Consanguinity
    Interracial marriage
    Marriage, Mixed
Intermarriage (Racial)
  See Interracial marriage
Intermaxillary bones *(Comparative anatomy, QL821; Human anatomy, QM105)*
Intermediaries in public contracts, etc.
  See Brokers in public contracts, etc.
Intermediate frequency amplifiers
  xx Tuned amplifiers
Intermediate-range ballistic missiles
  sa names of specific intermediate-range ballistic missiles, e.g. Jupiter missile
  x IRBM
  xx Ballistic missiles
Intermediate school districts
  See School districts
Intermediate schools
  See Junior high schools
    Middle schools
Intermediate service units (Education) *(LB2813)*
  x Regional service agencies (Education)
  xx County school systems
Intermediate state *(BT830)*
  sa Death
    Eschatology
    Future life
    Heaven
    Hell
    Probation after death
    Purgatory
    Soul
  xx Death
    Eschatology
    Future life
    Heaven
    Hell
    Probation after death
    Purgatory
    Soul
  — Biblical teaching
Intermediate state (Islam) *(BP166.82)*
  xx Eschatology, Islamic
Intermedin
Interment
  See Burial
Intermetallic compounds
  xx Metals
  — Magnetic properties
  — Thermal properties
Intermittent fever
  See Malarial fever
Intermodal transportation
  See Containerization

Intermunicipal law
  See Conflict of laws
Internal combustion engines
  See Alcohol motors
    Gas and oil engines
Internal conversion (Nuclear physics)
  sa Auger effect
    Beta rays
    Electrons—Emission
    X-rays
  xx Electromagnetic theory
    Electrons
    Nuclear physics
    Quantum theory
  — Tables, etc.
      x Internal conversion coefficients
Internal conversion coefficients
  See Internal conversion (Nuclear physics)—Tables, etc.
Internal fixation in fractures
  x Intramedullary nailing
    Medullary nailing
    Metal implants
  xx Fracture fixation
    Fractures
Internal friction *(QC191)*
  x Anelasticity
  xx Damping (Mechanics)
    Elastic solids
    Elastic waves
    Friction
    Vibration
  — Instruments *(QC191)*
      x Instruments, Internal friction
Internal friction (Liquids)
  See Viscosity
Internal improvement movement
  See Public works
Internal medicine
  sa Cardiology
    Endocrinology
    Gastroenterology
    Hematology
    Nephrology
  x Medicine, Internal
  xx Medicine—Practice
  — Cases, clinical reports, statistics
  — Examinations, questions, etc. *(RC58)*
  — Programmed instruction
Internal migration
  See Migration, Internal
Internal reflection spectroscopy
  x Spectroscopy, Internal reflection
  xx Absorption spectra
    Reflection (Optics)
Internal revenue *(Indirect) (HJ5001-5231)*
  sa Bonded warehouses and goods
    Distillery warehouses
    Income tax
    Inheritance and transfer tax
    Licenses
    Octroi
    Revenue-stamps
    Stamp-duties
    Tolls
    names of services or articles taxed, e.g. Amusements—Taxation; Liquor traffic—Taxation; Oleomargarine—Taxation
  x Excise
    Fee system (Taxation)
    Indirect taxation
    Inland revenue
    Revenue, Internal
  xx Finance, Public
    Taxation
  — United States
      x United States—Internal revenue

United States—Revenue

Internal revenue law *(Direct)* *(United States, HJ3251)*
  x Excise
  Law, Internal revenue
  Revenue law
Internal revenue stamps
  See Revenue-stamps
Internal rotation (Molecular)
  See Molecular rotation
Internal security *(Direct)*
  sa Insurgency
  Loyalty oaths
  Subversive activities
  x Security, Internal
  xx Insurgency
  Subversive activities
  — Cases

GEOGRAPHIC SUBDIVISIONS

  — United States
  sa Loyalty-security program, 1947-
Internal transfer pricing
  See Transfer pricing
Internal waves
  x Boundary waves (Oceanography)
  Waves, Internal
  xx Ocean waves
Internalization
  sa Identification (Psychology)
  xx Psychoanalysis
International administration
  See International agencies
  International organization
International administrative courts
  x Administrative courts, International
  Administrative international courts
  xx Administrative courts
  International courts
International affairs and Christianity
  See Christianity and international affairs
International affairs and religion
  See Religion and international affairs
International agencies
  Here are entered works on public international organizations and agencies of international government. Particular organizations are entered under their respective names.
  sa Hygiene, Public—International cooperation
  International officials and employees
  International organization
  Medicine—International cooperation
  United Nations—Economic assistance
  United Nations—Technical assistance
  x Associations, International
  Institutions, International
  International administration
  International associations
  International institutions
  International organizations
  International unions
  Organizations, International
  Specialized agencies of the United Nations
  United Nations—Specialized agencies
  xx International cooperation
  International organization
  — Abbreviations
  — Acronyms
  — Finance
  — Information services *(Direct)*
  — Membership
  — Privileges and immunities

  sa subdivision Privileges and immunities *under names of individual international organizations, e.g.* International Labor Office—Privileges and immunities
  x International officials and employees—Privileges and immunities
  xx Diplomatic privileges and immunities
  Privileges and immunities
  — Rules and practice
  — Tort liability
  See Tort liability of international agencies
  — Voting
  xx Voting
International agencies in America, ⌈**Europe, etc.**⌉
International agreements
  See International obligations
  Treaties
International agricultural cooperation
  sa Agricultural assistance
  International farm youth exchange project
  x Agricultural cooperation, International
  International cooperation in agriculture
  xx Agriculture
  Technical assistance
International air traffic rules
  See Air traffic rules, International
International airport charges
  See International airports—Landing fees
International airports *(Direct)* *(TL726.15)*
  sa names of individual international airports, e.g. John F. Kennedy International Airport
  x Airports of entry
  xx Airports
  Ports of entry
  — Landing fees
  x International airport charges
  International airports—Port charges
  Port charges
  xx Airports—Landing fees
  — Port charges
  See International airports—Landing fees
International alphabet
  See Phonetic alphabet
  Transliteration
International American conferences
  See Inter-American conferences
International and municipal law *(Direct)* *(JK-JQ; JX1248)*
  Here are entered works dealing with the relation of international law to the internal or national law of a state or states. Works on the law of municipal corporations are entered under the heading Municipal corporations.
  sa Contracts (International law)
  Treaties—Accession
  Treaties—Ratification
  Treaties—Reservations
  x Municipal and international law
  xx Constitutional law
  International law
International Antarctic Expedition, 1901-1903 *(Scientific results, Q115)*
International arbitration
  See Arbitration, International
International arbitration and award
  See Arbitration and award, International
International associations
  See International agencies
  International cooperation—Societies, etc.

particular international agencies, congresses, societies, etc.
International auxiliari linguo (Artificial language)
  x INTAL (Artificial language)
  xx Languages, Artificial
International baccalaureate
  x Baccalaureate, International
  xx Examinations—Questions
  International education
  Universities and colleges—Entrance requirements
International banking
  See Banks and banking, International
International bibliography
  See Bibliography, International
International bimetallism
  See Bimetallism
International boundaries
  See Boundaries
International broadcasting
  sa individual broadcasting activities, e.g. Radio Free Europe; Voice of America (Radio program)
  x Broadcasting, International
  xx Radio broadcasting
International business enterprises
  sa Corporations, Foreign
  Foreign licensing agreements
  Investments, Foreign
  x Business enterprises, International
  Multinational corporations
  xx Business enterprises
  Commerce
  Corporations
  International economic relations
  — Accounting
  — Finance
  — Research *(Direct)*
  — Simulation methods
  — Taxation *(Direct)*
International civil service
  See International officials and employees
International claims
  See Claims
  Government liability (International law)
International clearing *(Direct)*
  x Clearing agreements
  Clearing, International
  xx Balance of payments
  Foreign exchange
  Foreign trade regulation
  International finance
  — Conflict of laws
  See Conflict of laws—International clearing
International coinage
  See Coinage, International
International commissions of inquiry
  See Commissions of inquiry, International
International competition
  See Competition, International
International conciliation
  See Mediation, International
International Confederation of Free Trade Unions
  Example under International labor activities
International conferences, congresses and conventions
  See Congresses and conventions
International cookery
  See Cookery, International
International cooperation *(JC362; International bureaus, etc., JX1995)*
  Here are entered general works on international cooperative activities with or without the participation of governments.

International economic relations
International financial institutions
    See Financial institutions, International
International fiscal relations
    See Intergovernmental fiscal relations
International forwarding agents
    See Ocean freight forwarders
International Geophysical Year, 1957-1958
      (Direct) *(QC801.3)*
    sa Project Vanguard
    xx Geophysics—International cooperation
       Intellectual cooperation
    — Juvenile literature
International grants-in-aid
    See Economic assistance
       International relief
International Hydrological Decade, 1965-1974
      (Direct)
    xx Hydrology
       International cooperation
International ice patrol
    xx Icebergs
International institutions
    See International agencies
       International cooperation
       particular international congresses,
         societies, etc.
International insurance law
    See Insurance law, International
International inventory of musical sources
    xx Music—Bibliography
International jurisdiction
    See Jurisdiction (International law)
International labor activities
    sa names of individual labor organizations,
      e.g. International Confederation of
      Free Trade Unions; World
      Federation of Trade Unions
    xx Labor and laboring classes
       Trade-unions
International Labor Day
    See May Day (Labor holiday)
International labor laws and legislation
    See Labor laws and legislation, International
International Labor Office
    — Privileges and immunities
      Example under Diplomatic privileges and
      immunities; International agencies
      —Privileges and immunities
International language
    See Diplomacy—Language
       Language, Universal
International law
    sa Act of state
      Aggression (International law)
      Air traffic rules, International
      Airspace (International law)
      Alien property
      Aliens
      Allegiance
      Angary, Right of
      Annexation (International law)
      Arbitration, International
      Asylum, Right of
      Atomic ships (International law)
      Atomic weapons (International law)
      Autonomy
      Bills of exchange (International law)
      Boundaries
      Chicanery (International law)
      Children (International law)
      Citizenship (International law)
      Civil procedure (International law)
      Civil rights (International law)
      Civil war
      Claims
      Colonies (International law)
      Comity of nations

Concordats
Condominium (International law)
Conquest, Right of
Consular law
Consuls
Criminal liability (International law)
Criminal procedure (International law)
Denial of justice
Design protection (International law)
Diplomatic and consular service
Diplomatic documents
Diplomatic protection
Diplomatic protests
Diplomats
Dismemberment of nations
Drago doctrine
Effectiveness and validity of law
Embargo
Eminent domain (International law)
Equality of states
Equity (International law)
Executions (International law)
Executive agreements
Exhaustion of local remedies
    (International law)
Exhibitions (International law)
Expatriation
Exterritoriality
Extradition
Fishery law and legislation
Forced labor (International law)
Foreign offices
Freedom of information (International
    law)
Freedom of movement (International
    law)
Freedom of the seas
Government liability (International law)
Governments in exile
Great powers
Habeas corpus (International law)
Indemnity
Industrial property (International law)
Insurance law, International
Insurance, Social (International law)
International and municipal law
International cooperation
International courts
International obligations
International offenses
International organization
Intervention (International law)
Investments, Foreign (International
    law)
Judicial assistance
Jurisdiction (International law)
Jurisdiction over ships at sea
Labor laws and legislation, International
Lis pendens (International law)
Maritime law
Medical laws and legislation,
    International
Military law
Natural law
Naturalization
Naval law
Necessity (International law)
Neutrality
Notification (International relations)
Nuisances (International law)
Occupancy (International law)
Ocean bottom (Maritime law)
Papacy (International law)
Passports
Persons (International law)
Pirates
Political crimes and offenses
Postliminy

Prescription (International law)
Presumptions (International law)
Promissory notes (International law)
Property (International law)
Protectorates
Public health laws, International
Radioactive substances—Transportation
    (International law)
Radioactive waste disposal
    (International law)
Recognition (International law)
Refugees, Political
Refugees, Political—Legal status, laws,
    etc.
Religious liberty (International law)
Repatriation
Salvage
Salvage (Aeroplanes)
Sanctions (International law)
Self-defense (International law)
Servitudes (International law)
Ships—Nationality
Slave-trade
Slavery (International law)
Sovereignty
Space law
State bankruptcy
State succession
Tax evasion (International law)
Territorial waters
Territory, National
Third parties (International law)
Time (International law)
Trade-marks (International law)
Transit by land (International law)
Transportation, Automotive—Laws and
    regulations, International
Transportation—Laws and regulations,
    International
Treaties
Ultimatums
Uti possidetis (International law)
War (International law)
War, Maritime (International law)
Warships—Visits to foreign ports
Water-rights (International law)
subdivisions Law and legislation *and*
    Laws and regulations *under topics of*
    international concern; and
    subdivision International status
    under names of countries, regions,
    etc., e.g. Antarctic regions—
    International status
  x Law, International
    Law of nations
    Nations, Law of
  xx International organization
    International relations
    Natural law
    Public law
    Space law
— Book reviews
— Cases *(JX63-91)*
— Classification
  x Classification—International law
— Codification *(JX1261-1283)*
— History *(Direct)*
— Interpretation and construction
— Philosophy
  x Philosophy of international law
  xx Jurisprudence
    Natural law
— Research *(Direct)*
— Sources *(JX63-91)*
  sa Treaties
— Study and teaching *(Direct)*
— Terminology *(JX1226)*

International law, Private
    See Conflict of laws
International law (Islamic law)
    x Islamic international law
International lawn tennis championship
    See Davis cup
International librarianship
    See Comparative librarianship
International liquidity
    sa Balance of payments
        Foreign exchange problem
        Gold standard
        Special drawing rights
    xx Balance of payments
        International finance
        Liquidity (Economics)
International loans
    See Loans, Foreign
International marriages
    See Marriages, International
International mediation
    See Mediation, International
International medical laws and legislation
    See Medical laws and legislation,
        International
International money
    See Coinage, International
International museums *(AM)*
    xx International cooperation
        Museums
International news
    See Foreign news
International obligations *(JX4171.O3)*
    sa Treaties
    x International agreements
    xx International law
        Treaties
    Note under Contracts (International law)
International offenses
        Here are entered works on the criminal
        law aspects of violations of interna-
        tional law. Works on exterritorial
        crimes and on the conflict of jurisdic-
        tions in the administration of criminal
        law are entered under the heading
        Criminal jurisdiction.
    sa Aggression (International law)
        Assaulting a foreign official
        Crimes against humanity
        Crimes against peace
        Criminal liability (International law)
        Criminal procedure (International law)
        Genocide
        Sovereignty, Violation of
        Terrorism
        War crimes
    x Criminal law, International
        International criminal law
    xx Criminal law
        International law
International officials and employees
    (JX1995)
    sa subdivision Officials and employees
        *under names of international
        agencies, e.g.* International
        Telecommunication Union—Officials
        and employees
    x Civil service, International
        International civil service
        Officials and employees, International
    xx International agencies
        International organization
        Public officers
    — Privileges and immunities
        See International agencies—Privileges
            and immunities

subdivision Privileges and
    immunities *under names of
    individual international
    agencies*
International organization
        Here are entered works on theories and
        efforts leading toward world-wide or
        regional political organization of na-
        tions.
    sa Church and international organization
        Concert of Europe
        International agencies
        International cooperation
        International law
        International officials and employees
        International police
        International trusteeships
        Latin American federation
        Mandates
        Reconstruction (1914-1939)
        Reconstruction (1939-1951)
        Regionalism (International
            organization)
        Security, International
        World politics
        names of specific organizations, e.g.
            League of Nations, Pan American
            Union
    x Federation, International
        International administration
        International federation
        Organization, International
        World federation
        World government
        World organization
    xx Congresses and conventions
        International agencies
        International cooperation
        International law
        International relations
        Peace
        Political science
        Security, International
        World politics
    Note under Internationalism
    — Study and teaching *(Direct)*
International organization and the church
    See Church and international organization
International organizations
    See International agencies
International payments, Balance of
    See Balance of payments
International Polar Expedition, 1882-1883
    (G670)
International police *(JX1981.P7)*
    sa United Nations—Armed Forces
    x Peacekeeping forces
        Police, International
    xx International cooperation
        International organization
        International relations
        Sanctions (International law)
        Security, International
        United Nations—Armed Forces
International politics
    See World politics
International press law
    See Press law, International
International private law
    See Conflict of laws
International propaganda
    See Propaganda, International
International public health laws
    See Public health laws, International
International railroad law
    See Railroad law, International

International relations
        Here are entered works dealing with the
        theory of international intercourse.
        Historical accounts are entered under
        the headings World politics; Europe—
        Politics; etc. Works dealing with for-
        eign relations from the point of view of
        an individual state are entered under
        the name of the state with subdivision
        Foreign relations.
    sa Alliances
        Ambassadors
        Arbitration, International
        Balance of power
        Boundaries
        Catholic Church—Relations
            (diplomatic)
        Comity of nations
        Commissions of inquiry, International
        Competition, International
        Concordats
        Congresses and conventions
        Consuls
        Cultural relations
        Diplomacy
        Diplomatic and consular service
        Diplomatic documents
        Diplomatic negotiations in international
            disputes
        Diplomatic protection
        Diplomats
        Disarmament
        Executive agreements
        Foreign news
        Foreign offices
        Geography, Political
        Geopolitics
        Government missions
        Governments in exile
        Great powers
        Guaranty, Treaties of
        Intergovernmental fiscal relations
        International cooperation
        International courts
        International economic relations
        International law
        International organization
        International police
        Jihad
        Mediation, International
        Military missions
        Monroe doctrine
        Munitions
        National security
        Nationalism
        Neutrality, Armed
        Notification (International relations)
        Orders in council
        Pacific settlement of international
            disputes
        Pan-Pacific relations
        Peace
        Peaceful change (International
            relations)
        Plebiscite
        Propaganda, International
        Reconstruction (1914-1939)
        Reconstruction (1939-1951)
        Refugees, Political
        Religion and international affairs
        Security, International
        Treaties
        Ultimatums
        Warships—Visits to foreign ports
        World politics

names of international alliances, congresses, treaties, etc., e.g. Holy Alliance; Vienna. Congress, 1814-1815; Berlin, Treaty of, 1878; and subdivisions Foreign relations and Foreign relations administration under names of countries, e.g. France—Foreign relations; Great Britian—Foreign relations— Germany; United States—Foreign relations administration
   x Foreign affairs
     Foreign policy
     Foreign relations
   xx National security
   Note under World politics
  — Book reviews
  — Mathematical models
  — Methodology
  — Moral and religious aspects
  — Psychological aspects
    xx Political psychology
  — Public opinion
  — Research (Direct)
  — Simulation methods
  — Vocational guidance

International relief (Direct)
  sa Disaster relief
    Duty-free importation of relief supplies
    Refugees, Political
    War relief
    subdivisions Civilian relief or Hospitals, charities, etc. under names of wars, e.g. European War, 1914-1918— Hospitals, charities, etc.; World War, 1939-1945—Civilian relief
   x Grants-in-aid, International
    International grants-in-aid
    Relief (Aid)
    Relief, International
   xx Charities
    Economic assistance
    Public welfare
International rivers (JX4150)
   x Rivers, Right of navigation of
   xx Inland navigation—Laws and regulations
    Rivers
    Water—Laws and legislation
International sales
  See Export sales
International sanitary regulations
  See Public health laws, International
International security
  See Security, International
International Settlements, Bank for
  See Bank for International Settlements
International Six Days Trial (GV1060)
   xx Motorcycle racing
International space cooperation
  See Astronautics—International cooperation
International teaching positions
  See American teachers in foreign countries —Employment
    Teachers in foreign countries— Employment
    similar headings
International Telecommunication Union
  — Officials and employees
    Example under International officials and employees
International territories
  See Internationalized territories
International trade
  See Commerce
International trade control
  See Foreign trade regulation

International trade regulation
  See Foreign trade regulation
International transit
  See Transit, International
International travel regulations
  sa Admission of nonimmigrants
    Aliens
    Customs administration and tourists
    Emigration and immigration law
    Foreign exchange—Law
    Passports
    Public health laws, International
   x Frontier formalities
    Travel regulations, International
   xx Aliens
    Customs administration
    Travel
International treaty for the limitation and reduction of naval armament, London, 1930
  See London naval treaty, 1930
International tribunals
  See International courts
International trusteeships (Direct)
  sa Mandates
    State succession
   x Nonselfgoverning territories
    Trust territories
    Trusteeships, International
    United Nations—International trusteeships
   xx International organization
    Internationalized territories
    Mandates
    Protectorates
    State succession
    World War, 1939-1945—Territorial questions
International unification of civil law
  See Civil law—International unification
International unification of law
  See Law—International unification; and subdivision International unification under particular branches of the law, e.g. Civil law—International unification
International unification of private law
  See Civil law—International unification
International unions
  See International agencies
International upper mantle project
  See Upper mantle project
International visitors
  See Visitors, Foreign
International voluntary work camps
  See Work camps
International words
  See Language and languages—Foreign words and phrases
International Years of the Quiet Sun, 1964-1965 (QC801.4)
   x IQSY
   xx Geophysics—International cooperation
    Intellectual cooperation
    Solar activity
Internationalism (JC361)
   Here are entered works on internationalism as an attitude, in contrast to extreme nationalism; also works on cosmopolitanism as opposed to provincialism.
   Works on measures advocated by internationalists are entered under International cooperation; International organization; etc.
  sa International education
    Nationalism
   x Cosmopolitanism

   xx Intellectual cooperation
    International cooperation
    International education
    Nationalism
Internationalism in literature
Internationalized territories (JX4068.16)
  sa International trusteeships
    Mandates
   x Free cities
    International territories
    Territories, International
   xx Sovereignty
Internment camps
  See Concentration camps
Internment of warships
  See Warships, Internment of
Interns (LC1051-1064)
   x Internship
   xx Professional education
Interns (Business) (Direct)
   x Business interns
   xx Apprentices
    Employees, Training of
  — Law and legislation (Direct)
Interns (Civil service) (Direct)
   x Civil service interns
   xx Apprentices
    Civil service—Study and teaching
    Employees, Training of
Interns (Clinical psychology)
   xx Clinical psychology
Interns (Criminal justice administration) (Direct)
   x Criminal justice interns
   xx Criminal justice, Administration of— Study and teaching
Interns (Education) (Direct)
  sa Student teaching
   x Teaching internship
   xx Student teachers
    Teachers, Training of
Interns (Geography)
   x Student trainee program (Geography)
   xx Geography as a profession
Interns (Legislation) (Direct)
   x Government interns (Legislation)
    Legislative interns
   xx Legislation
    Legislative bodies—Officials and employees
Interns (Library science)
  sa Librarians—In-service training
   x Library interns
   xx Librarians—In-service training
    Library education
Interns (Medicine) (RA972)
   x Hospital interns
    Medical interns
   xx Hospitals—Staff
Interns (Meteorology)
   x Student trainee program (Meteorology)
   xx Meteorology as a profession
    Meteorology—Study and teaching
Interns (Psychiatry)
   xx Psychiatric hospitals
    Psychiatrists
    Psychiatry—Study and teaching
Internship
  See Interns
Interoceanic canals
  See Canals, Interoceanic
Interoceanic ship-railroads
  See Ship-railroads
Interoception
   xx Perception
    Reflexes
Interoffice communication systems
  See Intercommunication systems

Interpellation *(Direct)*
    x Questions (Parliamentary practice)
    xx Ministerial responsibility
        Parliamentary practice
Interpersonal attraction
    x Attraction, Interpersonal
    xx Interpersonal relations
Interpersonal perception
    See Social perception
Interpersonal relations *(HM132)*
    sa Atomic bomb shelters—Psychological
        aspects
        Communication—Psychological aspects
        Competition (Psychology)
        Conflict of generations
        Dependency (Psychology)
        Group relations training
        Helping behavior
        Interpersonal attraction
        Intimacy (Psychology)
        Machiavellianism (Psychology)
        Personal space
        Social exchange
        Social perception
        Teacher-student relationships
    x Human relations
    xx Conduct of life
        Family life education
        Psychology
        Psychology, Applied
        Social distance
        Social psychology
    — Juvenile literature
    — Quotations, maxims, etc.
Interplanetary communication
    See Interstellar communication
Interplanetary magnetic field
    x Magnetic field, Interplanetary
    xx Magnetic fields (Cosmic physics)
Interplanetary propulsion
    See Space vehicles—Propulsion systems
Interplanetary voyages *(TL789-790)*
    sa Outer space—Exploration
        Rockets (Aeronautics)
        Space flight
        Space flight in literature
        Space flight to Jupiter
        Space flight to Mars
        Space flight to Mercury
    x Interstellar voyages
        Moon, Voyages to
        Space travel
        Voyages, Interplanetary
        Voyages to the moon
    xx Aeronautics
        Astronautics
        Rockets (Aeronautics)
        Space flight
        Voyages, Imaginary
    Note under Space flight
    — Juvenile literature
Interpleader
    See Actions and defenses
Interpolation *(QA281)*
    sa Approximation theory
        Numerical integration
        Spline theory
    xx Algebra
        Approximation theory
        Mathematics
        Numerical analysis
    — Tables, etc. *(QA281)*
Interpretation
    See Hermeneutics
Interpretation, Biblical
    See Bible—Criticism, interpretation, etc.

Interpretation, Literary
    See subdivision Explication *under specific*
        literatures, e.g. English literature—
        Explication; English poetry—
        Explication
Interpretation, Musical
    See Music—Interpretation (Phrasing,
        dynamics, etc.)
Interpretation, Photographic
    See Photographic interpretation
Interpretation and construction (Law)
    See Law—Interpretation and construction
Interpretative reading
    See Oral interpretation
Interpretative speech
    See Oral interpretation
Interpreters
    See Translators
Interpreting and translating
    See Translating and interpreting
Interpretive dancing
    See Modern dancing
Interracial adoption *(Direct)*
    x Mixed race adoption
        Trans-racial adoption
    xx Adoption
        Race problems
Interracial marriage *(Direct) (HQ1031)*
    x Intermarriage
        Intermarriage (Racial)
        Marriage, Interracial
    xx Culture conflict
        Marriage, Mixed
        Miscegenation
Interreligious relations
    See Religions—Relations
Interrenal body
    See Interrenal gland
Interrenal gland
    x Interrenal body
    xx Fishes—Anatomy
        Kidneys
Interrogation
    See Questioning
Interrogative (Grammar)
    See Grammar, Comparative and general—
        Interrogative
        subdivision Interrogative *under names*
        of languages and groups of languages
Interrogator-transpondor systems
    See Aeroplanes—IFF equipment
        Distance measuring equipment (Aircraft
        to ground station)
Interrogatories *(Direct)*
    xx Discovery (Law)
        Forms (Law)
        Pre-trial procedure
        Questionnaires
        Witnesses
Interrogatories (Criminal procedure)
    See Preliminary examinations (Criminal
        procedure)
Interruption (Psychology) *(BF378.I65)*
    x Zeigarnik effect
    xx Memory
        Motivation (Psychology)
Interscholastic athletics
    See School sports
Intersections (Highway engineering)
    See Roads—Interchanges and intersections
Intersensory effects
    sa Synesthesia
    x Heteromodal effects
    xx Perception
Intersexuality
    See Hermaphroditism
Interstate agreements *(Direct) (JK2441)*
    x Agreements, Interstate

        Compacts, Interstate
        Cooperation, Interstate
        Interstate compacts
        Interstate cooperation
    xx Interstate relations
        State governments
        Uniform state laws
Interstate commerce *(Commission reports,*
    HE2708; Discussion, HE2757; Law
    and cases, HE2710-2712; Rates,
    HE1843, HE1853)
    Here are entered works on interstate
    commerce in general and in the United
    States.
    Works dealing with interstate commerce
    in other countries organized on a fed-
    eral basis are entered under Interstate
    commerce—[local subdivision] *e.g.* In-
    terstate commerce—Australia.
    sa Bills of lading
        Carriers
        Employers' liability—United States
        Railroad law—United States
        Railroads and state—United States
        Restraint of trade
        Trade regulation
        Use tax
    x Commerce clause (United States.
        Constitution)
        Government regulation of commerce
        Government regulation of railroads
    xx Carriers
        Commerce
        Railroads and state
        Railroads—Rates
        Restraint of trade
        Transportation—Laws and regulations
        Trusts, Industrial
    — Taxation *(Direct)*
        xx Income tax

        GEOGRAPHIC SUBDIVISIONS

    — Australia
        Note under Interstate commerce
Interstate compacts
    See Interstate agreements
Interstate controversies *(Direct)*
    x Controversies, Interstate
        Interstate disputes
    xx Constitutional law
        Federal government
        Interstate relations
        State governments
Interstate cooperation
    See Interstate agreements
Interstate disputes
    See Interstate controversies
Interstate relations *(Direct)*
    sa Interstate agreements
        Interstate controversies
    xx Federal government
        State governments
Interstellar communication
    sa Astronautics—Communication systems
        Radio astronomy
    x Interplanetary communication
        Outer space communication
        Space communication
        Space telecommunication
    xx Life on other planets
        Radio astronomy
        Telecommunication
    — Tables, etc.
Interstellar extinction
    See Interstellar reddening
Interstellar hydrogen
    xx Hydrogen
        Interstellar matter

Radio astronomy
— Atlases (QB790)
Interstellar matter (QB500)
    sa Cosmic dust
       Interstellar hydrogen
       Interstellar reddening
       Nebulae
       Planetary nebulae
    xx Astrophysics
       Cosmogony
       Ether (of space)
       Interstellar reddening
       Light—Scattering
       Matter
       Space environment
— Optical properties
— Tables, etc.
Interstellar reddening
    sa Interstellar matter
    x Extinction, Interstellar
      Interstellar extinction
      Reddening, Interstellar
    xx Absorption of light
      Interstellar matter
Interstellar voyages
    See Interplanetary voyages
Interstitial fauna
    xx Marine fauna
      Seashore biology
Interstitial substance
    See Ground substance (Anatomy)
Intertemporal law
    See Retroactive laws
Intertidal zonation (Indirect)
    x Eulittoral zonation
      Littoral zonation, Intertidal
      Tidal zonation
      Zonation, Intertidal
    xx Geographical distribution of animals
       and plants
      Seashore ecology
Intertype
    xx Printing machinery and supplies
      Type-setting machines
Interurban railroads
    See Street-railroads
Intervals (Music)
    See Musical intervals and scales
Intervention (Civil procedure) (Direct)
    sa Joinder of parties
    x Third parties (Civil procedure)
    xx Civil procedure
      Joinder of parties
      Parties to actions
      Third parties (Law)
Intervention (Federal government) (Direct)
    x Federal intervention
    xx Federal government
      Intervention (International law)
Intervention (International law) (JX4481)
    sa Drago doctrine
      Intervention (Federal government)
      Jurisdiction (International law)
      Monroe doctrine
      Neutrality
    x Military intervention
    xx Diplomatic protection
      International law
      Neutrality
      War (International law)
Intervention (Psychology)
    See Operant behavior
Interventricular heart block
    See Bundle-branch block
Intervertebral disk
    xx Vertebrae
— Diseases
    sa Intervertebral disk displacement

— Hernia
— Radiography
— Surgery
Intervertebral disk displacement (RD771.16)
    x Slipped disk
    xx Intervertebral disk—Diseases
— Personal narratives
Interviewing (Charities, HV43; Evidence,
    BF761-8)
    sa Counseling
      Employment interviewing
      Interviewing in psychiatry
      Interviews
      Medical history taking
      Questioning
      Social case work
    x Social psychotechnics
    xx Applications for positions
      Counseling
      Evidence
      Personnel management
      Psychology, Applied
      Social case work
      Social psychology
— Examinations, questions, etc.
— Programmed instruction
Interviewing (Journalism) (PN4784.16)
    xx Journalism
      Reporters and reporting
Interviewing in corrections
    xx Corrections
— Programmed instruction
Interviewing in ethnology
    xx Ethnology—Methodology
Interviewing in law enforcement
    sa Police questioning
    xx Law enforcement
      Police questioning
— Programmed instruction
Interviewing in marketing research
    xx Marketing research
Interviewing in psychiatry
    xx Interviewing
      Psychotherapist and patient
      Psychotherapy
Interviews
    sa subdivision Interviews under classes of
      persons, e.g. Authors—Interviews
    xx Interviewing
Interviews, Parent-teacher
    See Parent-teacher conferences
Intestacy
    See Inheritance and succession
Intestate succession
    See Inheritance and succession
Intestinal absorption
    xx Absorption (Physiology)
      Digestion
Intestinal and parasitic worms
    See Worms, Intestinal and parasitic
Intestinal fistula
    See Fistula, Intestinal
Intestinal infections
    See Intestines—Bacteriology
Intestinal irrigation
    See Enema
Intestinal obstructions
    See Intestines—Obstructions
Intestinal worms
    See Worms, Intestinal and parasitic
Intestine, Large
    sa Cecum
      Colon (Anatomy)
      Rectum
    x Bowel, Large
      Large bowel
      Large intestine
    xx Intestines

— Cancer
— Radiography
— Surgery
Intestine, Small
    sa Duodenum
      Ileum
      Jejunum
    x Small intestine
    xx Intestines
— Diseases
— Innervation
— Radiography
— Surgery
— — Complications and sequelae
— Ulcers (RC862.U5)
Intestines (Comparative anatomy, QL863;
    Human anatomy, QM345;
    Physiology, QP156)
    sa Appendix (Anatomy)
      Defecation
      Intestine, Large
      Intestine, Small
      Mesentery
      Myenteric plexus
      Omentum
      Peritoneum
      Viscera
    xx Abdomen
      Gastroenterology
    Example under Digestive organs; Viscera
— Bacteriology (QR171)
    sa Escherichia coli infections
    x Enteric infections
      Intestinal infections
    xx Intestines—Micro-organisms
    Example under Bacteria, Pathogenic
— Biopsy
— Blood-vessels
— — Diseases
— Cancer
— Diseases (RC860-862)
    sa Appendicitis
      Bilious diseases and biliousness
      Constipation
      Diarrhea
      Digestive organs—Diseases
      Dysentery
      Enteritis
      Enteroptosis
      Intestines—Radiography
      Intestines—Tuberculosis
      Malabsorption syndromes
      Melaena
      Regional enteritis
— — Diagnosis (RC803-5)
— — Psychosomatic aspects
    Example under Medicine, Psy-
      chosomatic
— Indigitation
    See Intestines—Intussusception
— Infarction
— Innervation
— Intubation
— Intussusception
    sa Intussusception in children
    x Intestines—Indigitation
      Intestines—Invagination
      Intussusception, Intestinal
— Invagination
    See Intestines—Intussusception
— Micro-organisms (QR155-171)
    sa Intestines—Bacteriology
    xx Micro-organisms
— Motility
    See Gastrointestinal motility
— Obstructions
    x Ileus
      Intestinal obstructions

Intestines *(Comparative anatomy, QL863;*
Human anatomy, QM345;
Physiology, QP156)
— Obstructions *(Continued)*
Obstructions, Intestinal
xx Intestines—Surgery
— Radiography
xx Intestines—Diseases
— Surgery *(RD540-544)*
sa Appendicitis
Hernia
Intestines—Obstructions
Intestines—Wounds and injuries
xx Abdomen—Surgery
— Tuberculosis *(RC312.5.T7)*
xx Intestines—Diseases
— Wounds and injuries
xx Intestines—Surgery
Example under Gunshot wounds
Intestines, Gases in
See Gastrointestinal gas
Intimacy (Psychology)
xx Emotions
Interpersonal relations
Intocostrin
See Curare
Intolerance
See Fanaticism
Liberty of conscience
Religious liberty
Toleration
Intonarium
See Tonarius
Intonation (Phonetics) *(P222)*
sa Oral interpretation
subdivision Intonation *under names of*
languages and groups of languages
x Grammar, Comparative and general—
Intonation
Language and languages—Intonation
Linguistics—Intonation
Tone (Phonetics)
xx Oral interpretation
Phonetics
Intoxicants
See Alcohol
Alcoholic beverages
Liquors
Stimulants
Intoxication
See Alcoholism
Drunkenness (Criminal law)
Liquor problem
Narcotic habit
Temperance
Intoxication, Ammonia
See Ammonia intoxication
Intra-airport transportation *(TL725.3.I6)*
xx Airports
Transportation
Intra-arterial injections
See Injections, Intra-arterial
Intra-articular injections
See Injections, Intra-articular
Intracoastal navigation
See Intracoastal waterways
Intracoastal waterways *(Indirect) (United*
States, TC623.4-624)
Here are entered works on inland water-
ways, natural, artificial, or both closely
following a coastline, improved or con-
structed for the purpose of connecting
points on the same coast. Works on the
economic aspects are entered under
the heading Coastwise shipping.
sa Canals
Inland navigation
x Intracoastal navigation

Waterways, Intracoastal
xx Canals
Coastwise navigation
Inland navigation
Waterways
Note under Waterways
Intracostal muscles
xx Respiratory muscles
Intracranial aneurysms *(RC693)*
xx Aneurysms
Brain—Blood-vessels
Intracranial pressure
x Pressure, Intracranial
xx Brain—Diseases
Intracranial stimulation
See Brain stimulation
Intracranial tumors
xx Brain—Tumors
Intradermal injections
See Injections, Intradermal
Intramedullary nailing
See Internal fixation in fractures
Intramercurial planets
See Planets, Intramercurial
Intramural sports *(GV710)*
x Sports, Intramural
xx College sports
School sports
Intramuscular injections
See Injections, Intramuscular
Intraocular pressure
x Pressure, Intraocular
xx Eye
Intraperitoneal injections
See Injections, Intraperitoneal
Intraspinal injections
See Injections, Spinal
Intratracheal anesthesia *(RD85.I)*
x Anesthesia, Endotracheal
Anesthesia, Intratracheal
Endotracheal anesthesia
Intrauterine blood transfusion
See Blood—Transfusion, Intrauterine
Intrauterine contraceptives *(RG137.3)*
xx Contraceptives
Intravenous anesthesia *(RD85.I)*
x Anesthesia, Intravenous
xx Injections, Intravenous
Intravenous catheterization *(RC683.5.I5)*
x Catheterization, Intravenous
Venous catheterization
xx Blood pressure—Measurement
Intravenous therapy
Intravenous therapy
sa Hypertonic solutions—Therapeutic use
Intravenous catheterization
x Infusion therapy
xx Parenteral therapy
Therapeutics
Intrenching tools *(UG380)*
xx Tools
Intrenchments *(Field fortification, UG403;*
Trenches and trench warfare,
UG446)
sa Attack and defense (Military science)
Fortification, Field
Mines, Military
Sapping
x Entrenchments
Foxholes
Trench warfare
xx Camps (Military)
Fortification
Military art and science
Military engineering
Military field engineering
Obstacles (Military science)

Intrinsic factor (Physiology)
xx Cyanocobalamine
Introduction of speakers
xx After-dinner speeches
Lectures and lecturing
Oratory
Public speaking
Speeches, addresses, etc.
Introits
xx Propers (Liturgy)
Introits (Music)
xx Propers (Music)
Psalms (Music)
Introspection
x Self-observation
xx Observation (Psychology)
Psychology
Introspection (Theory of knowledge)
See Self-knowledge, Theory of
Introversion *(BF175)*
sa Autism
Extraversion
Maudsley personality inventory
xx Extraversion
Personality
Psychiatry
Psychology, Physiological
Intrusion, Saltwater
See Saltwater encroachment
Intrusion alarm systems
See Electronic alarm systems
Intrusions (Geology) *(Indirect)*
sa Batholiths
Dikes (Geology)
Laccoliths
Necks (Geology)
Sills (Geology)
Stocks (Geology)
x Intrusive bodies
Pluton
xx Geology, Structural
Rocks, Igneous
Intrusive bodies
See Intrusions (Geology)
Intubation
See subdivision Intubation *under subjects,*
e.g. Larynx—Intubation; Trachea—
Intubation
Intuition *(BD181)*
x Intuitionalism
xx Consciousness
Knowledge, Theory of
Philosophy
Rationalism
Intuition (Psychology) *(BF311)*
sa Perception
xx Consciousness
Perception
Psychology
Senses and sensation
Intuition of duration
See Time perception
Intuitionalism
See Intuition
Intuitionistic mathematics
xx Constructive mathematics
Mathematics
Intumescences (Botany) *(Plant pathology,*
SB732)
Intussusception, Intestinal
See Intestines—Intussusception
Intussusception in children
xx Intestines—Intussusception
Inuit
See Eskimos
Inulase *(Plant physiology, QK896)*
Inulin *(QD321)*

Inundations
  See Floods
Invalid cookery
  See Cookery for the sick
Invalidity insurance
  See Insurance, Disability
Invalids
  sa Convalescence
    Handicapped
    Self-help devices for the disabled
  xx Convalescence
    Handicapped
    Nurses and nursing
    Sick
  — Occupations
    sa Occupational therapy
    xx Occupational therapy
      Occupations
  — Recreation
    See Aged—Recreation
      Handicapped—Recreation
      Sick—Recreation
Invariance principles (Physics)
  See Symmetry (Physics)
Invariant imbedding *(QA431)*
  xx Functional equations
    Invariants
    Mathematical physics
    Radiation
Invariant subspaces
  x Subspaces, Invariant
  xx Functional analysis
    Hilbert space
Invariants *(QA201; Theory of numbers,*
    QA244)
  sa Integrals, Haar
    Invariant imbedding
Invariants, Conformal
  See Conformal invariants
Invariants, Differential
  See Differential invariants
Invasion of privacy
  See Privacy, Right of
Invasions of China
  See China—History—Invasions
Invasions of Great Britain
  See Great Britain—History—Invasions
Invasions of Rome, Barbarian
  See Barbarian invasions of Rome
Invective *(English literature, PR1111.I65)*
  sa Satire
  x Abuse
    Vituperation
  xx Satire
  — Anecdotes, facetiae, satire, etc.
Invention (Rhetoric)
  See Originality (in literature)
Inventions *(Direct) (History, T15-35;*
    Patents, T201-339)
  sa Creation (Literary, artistic, etc.)
    Exchanges of patents and technical
      information
    Inventors
    Musical inventions and patents
    Patents
    Patents and government-developed
      inventions
    Research, Industrial
    Technological innovations
    Technology transfer
  x Discoveries (in science)
    European War, 1914-1918—Inventions
    Intellectual property
  xx Civilization
    Industrial arts
    Industrial arts—History
    Machinery
    Patents

Research, Industrial
  Technology
  Note under Technological innovations
  — Caricatures and cartoons
  — Juvenile literature
  — Philosophy
  — Problems, exercises, etc.
Inventions, Employees' *(Direct)*
  sa Patents and government-developed
    inventions
  x Employees' inventions
    Inventions of employees
    Shop rights (Patent law)
  xx Master and servant
    Patent laws and legislation
Inventions of employees
  See Inventions, Employees'
Inventories *(Direct) (HF5681.S8)*
  sa Commercial finance companies
    Inventory control
    Inventory shortages
    subdivision Inventories *under subjects,*
      e.g. Materials—Inventories; Meat
      industry and trade—Inventories
  x Stock in trade
    Stock-taking
  xx Accounting
    Bookkeeping
    Inventory control
  Example under Business records
  — Accounting
  — Programmed instruction
  — Taxation *(Direct)*
  — Valuation *(Direct)*
Inventories, Retail
  x Retail inventories
  xx Product management
    Retail trade
Inventories in libraries
  See Libraries—Inventories
Inventories of archives
  See Archives—Inventories, calendars, etc.
Inventories of decedents' estates *(Direct)*
  xx Decedents' estates
    Liquidation
    Registers of births, etc.
Inventors *(Direct) (T39-40)*
  sa Engineers
    Industrial arts—Biography
    Women as inventors
  xx Engineers
    Industrial arts—Biography
    Inventions
  — Anecdotes, facetiae, satire, etc.
  — Juvenile literature
Inventors, Negro
  See Negro inventors
Inventory control
  sa Economic lot size
    Inventories
    Materials management
    Stores or stock-room keeping
    Warehouses
    subdivision Inventory control *under*
      industries, processes, etc., e.g.
      Booksellers and bookselling—
      Inventory control
  x Control, Inventory
    Inventory management
    Stock control
  xx Inventories
    Physical distribution of goods
    Production control
  — Mathematical models
Inventory management
  See Inventory control
Inventory shortages *(Direct)*
  sa Shoplifting

  x Shortages, Inventory
  xx Inventories
    Retail trade
    Retail trade—Security measures
    Shoplifting
Invergordon Mutiny, 1931 *(DA89)*
Inverse functions
  See Functions, Inverse
Inverse matrices
  See Matrix inversion
Inverse of a matrix
  See Matrix inversion
Inverse problems (Differential equations)
  xx Differential equations
Inversion, Matrix
  See Matrix inversion
Inversion, Symmetrical
  See Symmetrical inversion (Music)
Inversion geometry
  See Inversions (Geometry)
Inversion of atmospheric temperature
  See Temperature inversions
Inversion of sugar
  See Sugar—Inversion
Inversions (Geometry) *(QA473)*
  sa Involutes (Mathematics)
  x Inversion geometry
  xx Circle
    Geometry, Modern
    Sphere
    Transformations (Mathematics)
Invertase *(Organic chemistry, QD321;*
    Physiological chemistry, QP601)
  sa Sugar—Inversion
  x Fructofuranosidase
Invertebrate populations *(Indirect)*
  sa Insect populations
    Plankton populations
    Starfish populations
  — Statistical methods
Invertebrates *(Indirect) (QL362-599)*
  sa Animal colonies
    Aquatic invertebrates
    Arachnida
    Arthropoda
    Brachiopoda
    Coelenterata
    Crustacea
    Cryptozoa
    Ctenophora
    Echinodermata
    Freshwater invertebrates
    Insects
    Marine invertebrates
    Mesozoa
    Mollusks
    Myriapoda
    Polyzoa
    Protozoa
    Pseudocoelomata
    Sponges
    Worms
  Example under Zoology
  — Anatomy *(QL363)*
    sa Cement glands
  — — Atlases
  — Behavior
    sa subdivision Behavior *under names of*
      particular invertebrates, e.g.
      Sea-urchins—Behavior
  — — Juvenile literature
  — Catalogs and collections
  — Collection and preservation
  — Cultures and culture media
    xx Laboratory animals
      Small animal culture
  — Diseases
  — Identification *(QL362.5)*

Invertebrates *(Indirect)* *(QL362-599)*
(Continued)
— Juvenile literature
— Laboratory manuals
— Larvae
    See Larvae—Invertebrates
— Physiology *(QL364)*
— Psychology
Invertebrates, Fossil *(QE770-832)*
    sa names of individual fossil phyla, classes,
       orders, etc., e.g. Coelenterata, Fossil
— Identification
— Type specimens *(QE770)*
    x Type specimens (Invertebrates,
       Fossil)
    xx Paleontology—Catalogs and
       collections
    Type specimens (Natural history)
Inverters, Electric
    See Electric inverters
Investigations
    Here are entered works on the technique
      of investigations in general. Works
      dealing with investigations in a specific
      field are entered under specific subject
      headings, *e.g.* Criminal investigation.
    sa Criminal investigation
    Fire investigation
    Governmental investigations
Investigations, Governmental
    See Governmental investigations
Investiture *(Church history, BX1198)*
    sa Bishops
    Church and state
    Concordat of Worms, 1122
    Consecration of bishops
    Simony
    xx Bishops
    Catholic Church—Government
    Church and state
    Church polity
    Consecration of bishops
Investment advisers *(Direct)*
    x Investment counselors
    xx Investments
— Legal status, laws, etc. *(Direct)*
Investment and saving
    See Saving and investment
Investment banking *(Direct)*
    sa Development banks
    Over-the-counter markets
    Syndicates (Finance)
    x Banks and banking, Investment
    Investment banks
    xx Banks and banking
    Investments
    Securities
— Accounting
Investment banks
    See Investment banking
Investment casting
    See Precision casting
Investment clubs *(HG4530)*
    sa Investment trusts
    xx Investment trusts
Investment companies
    See Investment trusts
    Small business investment companies
Investment counselors
    See Investment advisers
Investment guaranty insurance
    See Insurance, Investment guaranty
Investment in real estate
    See Real estate investment
Investment of public funds *(Direct)*
    x Public funds, Investment of
    xx Finance, Public
    Investments
    Legal investments

— Law and legislation *(Direct)*
— Mathematical models
Investment tax credit *(Direct)*
    xx Capital investments
    Depreciation allowances
    Tax credits
Investment trusts *(Direct)* *(HG4530)*
    sa Face-amount certificate companies
    Investment clubs
    Real estate investment trusts
    x Investment companies
    Mutual funds
    Profit-sharing trusts
    Unit trusts
    xx Financial institutions
    Investment clubs
    Investments
    Securities
    Trust companies
— Accounting *(HF5686.I58)*
— Juvenile literature
— Taxation *(Direct)*
Investments *(Direct)* *(HG4501-5990)*
    sa Annuities
    Art objects as an investment
    Bank investments
    Bonds
    Brokers
    Building and loan associations
    Capital investments
    Financial institutions—Investments
    Glassware as an investment
    Institutional investments
    Insurance companies—Investments
    Investment advisers
    Investment banking
    Investment of public funds
    Investment trusts
    Jewelry as an investment
    Legal investments
    Loans
    Mortgages
    Pension trusts—Investments
    Pewter as an investment
    Porcelain as an investment
    Pottery as an investment
    Prints as an investment
    Prospectus writing
    Real estate investment
    Saving and thrift
    Securities
    Speculation
    Stock-exchange
    Stocks
    University investments
    Venture capital
    x Portfolio
    xx Capital
    Estate planning
    Finance
    Finance, Personal
    Loans
    Saving and investment
    Saving and thrift
    Speculation
    Note under Investments, American, ₍French,
      etc.₎
— Accounting *(HF5686.I6)*
— Caricatures and cartoons
— Electronic data processing
    See Electronic data processing—
      Investments
— Law and legislation *(Direct)*
— Mathematical models
— Mathematics
    x Mathematics of investment
    xx Business mathematics
    Example under Mathematics

— Psychological aspects
— Tables, etc. *(HG4537)*
    x Bonds—Tables, etc.
    xx Interest and usury—Tables, etc.
— Taxation *(Direct)*
    sa Capital gains tax
    Investments, American, ₍French,
      etc.₎—Taxation
Investments, American, ₍French, etc.₎
    (Direct)
    Here are entered works dealing with for-
      eign investments originating in in-
      dividual countries and made in the
      country, if any, indicated by the sub-
      division. Works on investments origi-
      nating in several countries are entered
      under Investments, Foreign. Works on
      domestic investments are entered un-
      der Investments.
— Taxation *(Direct)*
    xx Investments—Taxation
Investments, Bank
    See Bank investments
Investments, Foreign *(Direct)* *(HG4538)*
    sa Corporations, Foreign
    Debts, External
    Foreign licensing agreements
    Insurance, Investment guaranty
    Loans, Foreign
    Technical assistance
    x Capital exports
    Capital imports
    Foreign investments
    xx Business enterprises, Foreign
    Commerce
    International business enterprises
    International economic relations
    International finance
    Securities
    Technical assistance
    Note under Investments, American, ₍French,
      etc.₎
— Law and legislation *(Direct)*
— — Underdeveloped areas
    See Underdeveloped areas—
      Investments, Foreign—Law
      and legislation
— Taxation *(Direct)*
    x Taxation of foreign investments
    xx Income tax—Foreign income
— Underdeveloped areas
    See Underdeveloped areas—
      Investments, Foreign
Investments, Foreign (International law)
    sa Calvo doctrine and clause
    Drago doctrine
    xx International law
Investments (Canon law)
    xx Catholic Church—Finance
Investors
    See Capitalists and financiers
Invisible reweaving
    See Reweaving
Invisible world
    See Spirits
Invisible writing
    See Writing, Invisible
Invocation of martyrs
    See Martyrs—Cultus
Invocation of saints
    See Saints—Cultus
Invoices *(Direct)*
    sa Consular invoices
    x Billing
    Bills (Invoices)
    xx Bookkeeping
    Commercial documents
    Commercial law

Sales
Shipment of goods
Invoices, Consular
See Consular invoices
Involucre
xx Botany—Morphology
Inflorescence
Involutes (Mathematics) *(QA557)*
xx Curves
Inversions (Geometry)
Example under Locus (Mathematics)
Ioánnina, Greece
— Siege, 1912-1913 *(DR46.8)*
xx Balkan Peninsula—History—War of
1912-1913
Iodates *(QD181.I1)*
Iodide incandescent lamps
See Iodine incandescent lamps
Iodide of hydrogen
See Hydriodic acid
Iodides *(QD191.I1)*
Iodimetry
See Iodometry
Iodine *(Chemical technology, TP245.I6;*
Chemistry, QD181.I1)
sa Iodine compounds
Sandell-Kolthoff reaction
xx Halogens
Example under Counter-irritants
— Analysis
— — Automation
— Isotopes
x Radioactive iodine
Radioiodine
— — Decay
— — Half-life
— Physiological effect *(QP913.I1)*
— Spectra
— Therapeutic use *(RM666.I6)*
sa Iodine compounds—Therapeutic use
Iodine compounds
sa Organoiodine compounds
xx Iodine
— Therapeutic use
xx Iodine—Therapeutic use
Iodine in soils
See Soils—Iodine content
Iodine in the blood
See Iodine in the body
Iodine in the body
x Iodine in the blood
Iodine incandescent lamps
x Incandescent lamps, Iodine
Iodide incandescent lamps
xx Electric lamps, Incandescent
Lamps
Iodine metabolism
xx Metabolism
Iodine organic compounds
See Organoiodine compounds
Iodochloroxyquinoline
See Vioform
Iodocrase
See Vesuvianite
Iodoform
— Physiological effect *(QP15.I6)*
Iodometry
x Iodimetry
xx Chemistry, Analytic
Iodopsin
xx Retina
Iolite
See Cordierite
Iomud horse
See Yomud horse
Ion acoustic waves
x Ion plasma waves
Ion waves

Ionic waves
xx Electrons
Ions
Plasma waves
Ion bombardment
sa Ion implantation
Sputtering (Physics)
x Bombardment, Ion
Impact, Ion
Ion impact
Ionic bombardment
xx Collisions (Nuclear physics)
Ions
Sputtering (Physics)
Ion columns
See Meteor trails
Ion exchange *(Chemical engineering,*
TP156.I6; Chemistry, QD561)
sa Charge transfer
Ion-permeable membranes
Saline water conversion—Ion exchange
process
Sephadex
Sewage—Purification—Ion exchange
process
Water—Purification—Ion exchange
process
x Base-exchange
Exchange adsorption
xx Adsorption
Ionization
Ion exchange membranes
See Ion-permeable membranes
Ion exchange resins
xx Gums and resins
— Patents
— Radiation effects
See Ion exchange resins, Effect of
radiation on
Ion exchange resins, Effect of radiation on
x Ion exchange resins, Irradiated
Ion exchange resins—Radiation effects
Radiation—Effect on ion exchange
resins
xx Radiation
Ion exchange resins, Effect of temperature on
Ion exchange resins, Irradiated
See Ion exchange resins, Effect of radiation
on
Ion flow dynamics *(QC717)*
sa Magnetohydrodynamics
Plasma (Ionized gases)
x Ionic flows
xx Electrodynamics
Electron optics
Fluid dynamics
Gases, Ionized
Magnetohydrodynamics
Ion impact
See Ion bombardment
Ion implantation
x Implantation, Ion
Solids—Ion implantation
xx Ion bombardment
Solids, Effect of radiation on
Ion microscope
See Field ion microscope
Ion-permeable membranes
sa Electrodialysis
x Ion exchange membranes
Permeable membranes (Electrodialysis)
Permselective membranes
xx Electrodialysis
Ion exchange
Membranes (Technology)
— Testing
Ion plasma waves
See Ion acoustic waves

Ion power
See Ion rockets
Ion propulsion
See Ion rockets
Ion pumps
x Getter-ion pumps
Penning pumps
Pumps, Ion
Sputter-ion pumps
xx Getters
Pumping machinery
Vacuum-pumps
Ion rockets *(TL783.63)*
x Electrostatic propulsion systems
Ion power
Ion propulsion
Ionic propulsion
xx Direct energy conversion
Electric rocket engines
Ions
Rockets (Aeronautics)—Ionization
phenomena
— Propellant feed systems
x Propellant feed systems of ion
rockets
Ion waves
See Ion acoustic waves
Ionians
xx Ethnology—Greece
Ionic bombardment
See Ion bombardment
Ionic columns
See Columns, Ionic
Ionic crystals
sa Polarons
Example under Crystals
— Spectra
Ionic equilibrium
x Equilibrium, Ionic
xx Ionization
Ionic flows
See Ion flow dynamics
Ionic mobility
x Mobility of ions
xx Ions—Migration and velocity
Ionic polymerization
See Addition polymerization
Ionic propulsion
See Ion rockets
Ionic solutions
sa Buffer solutions
x Solutions, Ionic
xx Ions
Solution (Chemistry)
Ionic waves
See Ion acoustic waves
Ionization *(QC702)*
sa Auger effect
Collisions (Nuclear physics)
Cosmic ray showers
Hydrogen-ion concentration
Ion exchange
Ionic equilibrium
Ionization chambers
Photoionization
Rockets (Aeronautics)—Ionization
phenomena
Scintillation counters
Scintillators
Sporadic E (Ionosphere)
Stopping power (Nuclear physics)
xx Collisions (Nuclear physics)
Hydrogen-ion concentration
Ionization chambers
sa Bubble chamber
Cloud chamber
Geiger-Müller counters
Nuclear counters

Ionization chambers *(Continued)*
    Spark chamber
    x Counting tubes
    xx Electronic measurements
        Ionization
        Nuclear counters
        Radiation
        Radioactivity
        Radioactivity—Instruments
        Radioactivity—Measurement
Ionization constants *(QD561)*
    x Constants, Ionization
    — Measurement *(QD561)*
    —— Laboratory manuals *(QD561)*
Ionization in rocketry
    See Rockets (Aeronautics)—Ionization
        phenomena
Ionization of gases *(QC702-721;*
        Atmosphere, QC918)
    sa Active nitrogen
        Air, Ionized
        Gases, Ionized
        Meteor trails
        Photoionization of gases
    x Gases—Ionization
        Gases, Ionization of
    xx Atmospheric electricity
        Atmospheric nucleation
        Electric discharges through gases
        Radioactivity
    — Tables, etc.
Ionized air
    See Air, Ionized
Ionized gases
    See Gases, Ionized
Ionizing radiation *(Biology, QH652;*
        Medicine, RA1231.R2; Physics,
        QC474-492, QC795.95-795.55;
        Physiology, QP356.5)
    sa Alpha rays
        Beta rays
        Cosmic rays
        Gamma rays
        Ultra-violet rays
        X-rays
    x Radiation, Ionizing
    xx Radiation
        Radioactivity
    — Measurement
Ionones *(QD305.A6)*
Ionosphere
    sa D region
        Dawn chorus (Radio meteorology)
        F region
        Hiss (Radio meteorology)
        Ionospheric electron density
        Ionospheric forecasting
        Sporadic E (Ionosphere)
        Thermosphere
        Whistlers (Radio meteorology)
    x Heaviside layer
        Kennelly-Heaviside layer
    xx Air, Ionized
        Atmosphere
        Thermosphere
    — Electromechanical analogies
    — Observations
Ionospheric drift
    sa Equatorial electrojet
        Geomagnetic micropulsations
        Van Allen radiation belts
    x Drift, Ionospheric
    xx Magnetism, Terrestrial
        Radio meteorology
    — Charts, diagrams, etc.
    — Tables, etc.
Ionospheric electron density
    x Electron density, Ionospheric

    xx Electrons
        Ionosphere
    — Charts, diagrams, etc.
    — Measurement *(QC879)*
Ionospheric forecasting *(QC879)*
    sa Ionospheric radio wave propagation
    x Forecasting, Ionospheric
    xx Ionosphere
        Ionospheric radio wave propagation
        Weather forecasting
Ionospheric radio wave absorption
    x Radio wave absorption in the
        ionosphere
    xx Radio meteorology
        Radio waves
    — Charts, diagrams, etc.
    — Observations
Ionospheric radio wave propagation
    sa Ionospheric forecasting
        Magneto-ionic theory
        Sporadic E (Ionosphere)
    x Radio wave propagation in the
        ionosphere
    xx Ionospheric forecasting
        Magneto-ionic theory
        Radio meteorology
        Radio wave propagation
        Radio waves
        Sporadic E (Ionosphere)
    — Charts, diagrams, etc.
    — Mathematical models
    — Observations *(QC802-3)*
    — Tables, etc.
Ionospheric research
    sa Ariel (Artificial satellite)
        Atmosphere, Upper—Radiosonde
        observations
    xx Atmosphere, Upper—Rocket
        observations
        Research
    — International cooperation
        x International cooperation in
            ionospheric research
Ionospheric sounds
Ions *(Electrochemistry, QD561; Physics,*
        QC702-721)
    sa Ammonium ions
        Bromide ions
        Carbonium ions
        Charge exchange
        Cloud chamber
        Complex ions
        Copper ions
        Deuterium ions
        Electric discharges through gases
        Electrolysis
        Electrons
        Helium ions
        Ion acoustic waves
        Ion bombardment
        Ion rockets
        Ionic solutions
        Metal ions
        Oxonium ions
        Particle accelerators
        Plasma (Ionized gases)
        Rare earth ions
        Silver ions
        Space charge
        Thermionic emission
        Ylides
    xx Electrolysis
        Electrons
        Matter—Properties
        Physics
        Solution (Chemistry)
    — Migration and velocity *(QD561)*
        sa Activity coefficients

        Ionic mobility
    x Migration of ions
    xx Chemistry, Physical and theoretical
    — Scattering
    — Spectra
    —— Tables, etc.
Iowa
    — Description and travel
    —— Poetry
        Note under Poetry of places
    — History *(F616-630)*
    —— War with Mexico, 1845-1848
    —— Civil War, 1861-1865 *(E507)*
Iowa Indians *(E99.I6)*
    xx Indians of North America
        Siouan Indians
Iowa language *(PM1376)*
    sa Siouan languages
    xx Siouan languages
Iowa picture interpretation test
    x Picture interpretation test, Iowa
    xx Mental tests
        Picture interpretation tests
Iowa tests of educational development
    xx Educational tests and measurements
Ipecac
    See Ipecacuanha
Ipecacuanha *(Therapeutics, RM666.I7)*
    x Ipecac
    xx Emetics
Ipitinere Indians
    See Amahuaca Indians
IPL (Computer program language)
    x Information processing language
        (Computer program language)
    xx List processing (Electronic computers)
        Mathematical linguistics
Ipurina language
    x Hypurina language
        Jupurina language
        Kangütü language
        Kankiti language
    xx Arawakan languages
        Indians of South America—Languages
Ipurocotó Indians *(Brazil, F2520.1.I)*
    x Purigotos
    xx Carib Indians
        Indians of South America
IQSY
    See International Years of the Quiet Sun,
        1964-1965
Irakov (African tribe)
    See Wambulu (African tribe)
Iramba language
    See Nilamba language
Iran
    — History *(DS270-318)*
    —— To 640 A.D.
        sa al-Qādisīyah, Battle of, 637
    —— Medieval and modern, 640-
        sa Ṭāhirids
    —— 640-1500
        sa Buwayhids
            Muzaffarids
            Timurids
    —— 16th-18th centuries
    —— 19th century
    —— War with Great Britain, 1856-1857
        (DS307.5)
    —— 1905-1911
    —— 1909-
    —— 1945-
Iran in literature
Iran in the Hadith
    xx Hadith
Iranche language
    See Iranxe language

Iranian languages *(PK6001-6996)*
  sa Aryan languages
     Avesta language
     Baluchi language
     Ephthalite language
     Hazara language
     Indo-Aryan languages
     Kabuli-Persian language
     Khorezmi language
     Kurdish language
     Median language
     Old Persian language
     Ossetic language
     Pahlavi language
     Pamir languages
     Parthian language
     Persian language
     Pushto language
     Tajik language
     Talysh language
     Tat language
     Yaghnobi language
     Yüeh-chih language
  x Eranian languages
  xx Aryan languages
     Baluchi language
     Ghalchah languages
     Indic languages
     Indo-Aryan languages
     Indo-Iranian languages
     Pahlavi language
     Pamir languages
     Persian language

Iranian literature *(PK6001-6996)*
  sa Indic literature
  x Eranian literature
  xx Pahlavi literature
  Example under Oriental literature

Iranian philology *(PK6001-6996)*
  sa Aryan philology
     Indo-Aryan philology
     Indo-Iranian philology
  x Eranian philology
  xx Aryan philology
     Indo-Aryan philology
     Indo-Iranian philology

Iranian studies *(Direct) (DS271.8)*

Iranians
  x Persians
  xx Ethnology—Iran

Iranians in the United States

Iranxe language
  x Iranche language
  xx Indians of South America—Languages

Iraq
  — History
    — — Revolt of 1920
    — — Revolution, 1958
      — — — Anniversaries, etc.
      — — — Pictorial works
    — — Revolutions, 1963

Iraq in literature

Iraqi newspapers *(Direct)*

Iraqw (African tribe)
  See Wambulu (African tribe)

Iraqw language
  xx Cushitic languages

Iraya language
  See Mangyan language

IRBM
  See Intermediate-range ballistic missiles

Ireland
  — Famines
    Example under Famines
  — History *(DA900-995)*
    — — To 1172
    — — To 1603
      — — — Juvenile literature

    — — English Conquest, 1166-1186
    — — 1172-
    — — 1172-1603
    — — 16th century
    — — 1558-1603
    — — 1595-1612
    — — 17th century
    — — 1603-1625
    — — 1625-1649
    — — Rebellion of 1641
    — — 1649-1660
    — — 1649-1775
    — — 1660-1688
    — — 1660-1690
    — — 1688-1689
    — — War of 1689-1691
    — — 1691-
    — — 18th century
    — — 1760-1820
       sa French Expedition to Ireland, 1796-1797
    — — French invasion, 1798
    — — Rebellion of 1798
       x Wexford Rebellion, 1798
    — — The Union, 1800
    — — 1800-1837
    — — 19th century
    — — Emmet's Rebellion, 1803
    — — 1837-1901
       sa Fenians
    — — Rising of 1848
    — — 20th century
    — — 1910-1921
      — — — Juvenile literature
    — — Sinn Fein Rebellion, 1916
       x Easter Rebellion, 1916
        Sinn Fein Rebellion, 1916
      — — — Atrocities
      — — — Juvenile literature
    — — 1922-
    — — Civil War, 1922-1923
  — Unification
    See Irish unification question

Ireland in art
Ireland in literature
Irenge (African people)
  See Murle (African people)

Irenics
  See Christian union

Iridectomy
  xx Eye—Surgery
     Iris (Eye)

Iridescence
  xx Interference (Light)
     Structural colors

Iridium *(Chemistry, QD181.I7)*
  xx Platinum group
  — Analysis
  — Isotopes
    x Iridium isotopes
    — — Decay
    — — Spectra
  — Spectra

Iridium isotopes
  See Iridium—Isotopes

Iridocyclitis
  xx Eye—Diseases and defects
     Iritis

Iris (Eye) *(Comparative anatomy, QL949; Human anatomy, QM511)*
  sa Iridectomy
     Iritis
  xx Eye
  — Examination

Iris (Plant) *(SB413.I8)*
  — Diseases and pests *(SB608.I7)*
  — Varieties *(SB413.I8)*

Irish *(General biography, CT790-808; Historical biography, DA915-916; History, DA900-990)*
  sa Scotch-Irish
  — Caricatures and cartoons

Irish-American newspapers *(PN4885.I)*
  xx Irish newspapers

Irish-American wit and humor *(PN6158-6161)*
  Here are entered collections from several authors and individual authors who have not written in other literary forms.
  xx American wit and humor
     Irish wit and humor

Irish ballads and songs *(Direct) (History of Irish literature, PB1331-3; Irish collections, PB1345-1353)*
  sa Ballads, Irish
     Folk-songs, Irish
     Political ballads and songs, Irish
     Songs, Irish

Irish ballads and songs (English) *(Collections, PR8860; History, PR8780)*
  Duplicate entry is made under English poetry—Irish authors.

Irish bulls
  See Bulls, Colloquial
     Irish wit and humor

Irish Confederation, 1642-1648 *(DA943)*
  x Kilkenny Confederation

Irish crochet lace *(TT805)*
  xx Lace and lace making

Irish diaries (English)
  See English diaries—Irish authors

Irish drama

Irish drama (English) *(Collections, PR8864-8870; History, PR8783-8795)*
  Duplicate entry is made under English drama—Irish authors.
  Note under English drama—Irish authors

Irish fiction (English) *(Collections, PR8875-6; History, PR8797-8807)*
  Duplicate entry is made under English fiction—Irish authors.
  Note under English fiction—Irish authors

Irish harp
  See Harp

Irish in Boston, [Rhode Island, the United States, etc.]
  — Juvenile literature
  — Registers

Irish in foreign countries

Irish in literature *(PN56.I; English literature, PR151.I)*
  Example under Literature, Comparative—Themes, motives

Irish in the American Revolution
  See United States—History—Revolution, 1775-1783—Irish participation

Irish Land League *(Economic history, HD625; History of Ireland, DA951)*
  x Land League, Irish

Irish land question
  See Land tenure—Ireland

Irish language *(PB1201-1299)*
  sa Celtic languages
     Gaelic language
     Shelta
  x Erse
     Gaelic language (Irish)
  xx Celtic languages
     Gaelic language
     Goidelic languages
  — To 1100 *(PB1218)*
    x Irish language—Old Irish

Irish language *(PB1201-1299)*
  (Continued)
  — Middle Irish, 1100-1550 *(PB1218)*
  — Old Irish
      See Irish language—To 1100
  — Revival
      Example under Languages—Revival
Irish literature *(PB1306-1449)*
      Comprises literature in the Irish language
      and literature written by Irish authors
      in English or other languages.
    sa Celtic literature
      Gaelic literature
    x British literature
    xx Celtic literature
      Gaelic literature
  — To 1100 *(Collections, PB1347-1351;*
      History, PB1321)
  — American authors *(PS153.I7)*
      Duplicate entry is made under Ameri-
      can literature (Irish)
      Note under American literature (Irish)
Irish literature, Epic
    See Epic literature, Irish
Irish literature (English) *(Direct)*
      (PR8700-8899)
      Duplicate entry is made under English
      literature—Irish authors.
    Note under English literature—Irish authors
Irish newspapers *(History, PN5141-9)*
      Here are entered works on newspapers
      published in Ireland, and on newspa-
      pers in the Irish language, or devoted
      to Irish interests, published outside of
      Ireland.
    sa Irish-American newspapers
    x British newspapers
    Note under Irish periodicals
Irish newspapers (English) *(History,*
      PN5141-9)
      Duplicate entry is made under English
      newspapers—Irish.
    Note under English newspapers—Irish
Irish orations (English)
    See English orations—Irish authors
Irish periodicals *(History, PN5141-5150)*
    Cf. note under Irish newspapers.
    x British periodicals
Irish periodicals (English) *(History,*
      PN5141-5150)
      Duplicate entry is made under English
      periodicals—Irish.
    Note under English periodicals—Irish
Irish philology
Irish poetry *(Direct)* *(History, PB1331-3)*
      Comprises poetry in the Irish language
      and poetry written by Irish authors in
      English or other languages.
    sa Fili (Irish poets)
      Triads (Literature)
    x British poetry
Irish poetry (English) *(Collections,*
      PR8849-8863; History,
      PR8761-8781)
      Duplicate entry is made under English
      poetry—Irish authors.
    Note under English poetry—Irish authors
Irish question *(DA947-965)*
    sa Fenians
      Home rule (Ireland)
      Land tenure—Ireland
      Phoenix Park Assassination, 1882
    xx Fenians
      Home rule (Ireland)
Irish setters *(SF429.I7)*
    xx Setters (Dogs)
Irish terriers *(SF429.I8)*
    xx Terriers

Irish type
    See Type and type-founding—Irish type
Irish unification question
    x Ireland—Unification
Irish university question
    See Education—Ireland
      Universities and colleges—Ireland
Irish water spaniel *(SF429.I83)*
    xx Spaniels
Irish wit and humor *(PN6178.I6)*
      Here are entered collections from several
      authors and individual authors who
      have not written in other literary
      forms.
    sa Bulls, Colloquial
      Irish-American wit and humor
    x Bulls, Irish
      Irish bulls
Irish wit and humor, Pictorial
      (NC1470-1479)
Irish wolf-hounds *(SF429.I85)*
    Example under Hounds
Irish wolf-hounds in literature
Iritis *(RE352)*
    sa Iridocyclitis
    xx Eye—Diseases and defects
      Iris (Eye)
Irminsul
    xx Germanic tribes—Religion
      Tree worship
Iroha karuta *(GV1299.I7)*
Iron *(Chemistry, QD181.F4; Manufactures,*
      TS300-445; Metallography,
      TN693.I7; Properties, testing, etc.,
      TA464-479)
    sa Building, Iron and steel
      Cast-iron
      Iron—Hydrogen content
      Iron ores
      Ironwork
      Soils—Iron content
      Steel
      Wrought-iron
    Example under Transition metals
  — Analysis *(QD133)*
    sa Cast-iron—Analysis
      Iron ores—Analysis
      Steel—Analysis
    xx Steel—Analysis
  — Brittleness
  — Corrosion
    x Rust
  — Electrometallurgy *(TN706)*
  — Fatigue
  — Heat treatment
    sa Iron—Quenching
  — Hydrogen content *(TN707)*
    x Hydrogen in iron
      Iron, Hydrogen in
    xx Gases in metals
      Hydrogen
      Iron
  — Inclusions
    x Inclusions in iron
  — Isotopes
    x Iron isotopes
      Isotopic iron
  — Juvenile literature
  — Magnetic properties
  — Metallography *(TN693.I7)*
    Example under Metallography
  — Metallurgy *(TN703-757)*
    sa Puddling
      Sintering
  — — Juvenile literature *(TN705)*
  — — Mathematical models
  — Physiological effect *(QP913.F4;*
      Therapeutics, RM666.I8)

    sa Plants, Effect of iron on
      Note under Pharmacology
  — Quenching *(TN752.Q4)*
    xx Cooling
      Iron—Heat treatment
  — Radiation effects
      See Iron, Effect of radiation on
  — Radiography
      Example under Radiography; Radiogra-
      phy, Industrial
  — Specifications *(TA466)*
  — Spectra
      Example under Spectrum analysis
  — Standards *(Direct)*
  — Tables, calculations, etc. *(TA685;*
      TS307-9)
  — Testing *(TA464-479)*
  — Therapeutic use *(RM666.I8)*
  — Transportation
Iron, Effect of radiation on
    x Iron—Radiation effects
    xx Radiation
Iron, Galvanized *(TS660)*
    x Galvanized iron
    xx Galvanizing
      Metal coating
      Sheet-iron
Iron, Hydrogen in
    See Iron—Hydrogen content
Iron, Phosphoric salts of *(RM666.I8)*
    x Pyrophosphate of iron
Iron, Structural *(Engineering, TA684-5;*
      Manufacture, TS350)
    sa Bridges, Iron and steel
      Building, Iron and steel
      Columns, Iron and steel
      Plates, Iron and steel
      Ships, Iron and steel
      Steel, Structural
    x Structural iron
    xx Bridges, Iron and steel
      Building, Iron and steel
      Building materials
      Steel, Structural
  — Tables, calculations, etc. *(TA685)*
Iron, Wrought
    See Wrought-iron
Iron age *(Indirect)* *(GN779-780)*
    sa Archaeology
      Bronze age
      Hallstatt period
      La Tène period
    x Prehistory
    xx Archaeology
      Bronze age
Iron alloys *(TN756-7)*
    sa Meehanite metal
      specific iron alloys, e.g. Iron-cobalt
      alloys, Iron-nickel alloys
  — Analysis
  — Corrosion
  — Electrometallurgy
  — Metallography *(TN693.I7)*
  — Metallurgy
Iron-aluminum alloys *(TA479.A4)*
    x Aluminum-iron alloys
  — Corrosion
Iron and steel bridges
    See Bridges, Iron and steel
Iron and steel building
    See Building, Iron and steel
Iron and steel columns
    See Columns, Iron and steel
Iron and steel plates
    See Plates, Iron and steel
Iron and steel ships
    See Ships, Iron and steel

Iron and steel workers *(Direct)*
    sa Collective bargaining—Iron industry
       Collective bargaining—Steel industry
       Collective labor agreements—Iron
          industry
       Collective labor agreements—Steel
          industry
       Strikes and lockouts—Steel industry
       Trade-unions—Iron and steel workers
       Wages—Iron and steel workers
    x Iron workers
       Steel workers
    xx Iron industry and trade
       Metal-workers
       Steel industry and trade
    — Diseases and hygiene
      xx Iron industry and trade—Hygienic
         aspects
       Steel industry and trade—Hygienic
         aspects
    — Juvenile literature
    — Medical care
    — Medical examinations
      x Physical examination of iron and
         steel workers
      xx Medicine, Industrial
    — Pensions
Iron bacteria *(QR84)*
    xx Bacteria
Iron catalysts
    xx Catalysts
Iron-chromium alloys
    See Chromium-iron alloys
Iron-clad vessels
    See Armored vessels
Iron-cobalt alloys
    sa Vanadium permendur
    x Cobalt-iron alloys
    xx Cobalt alloys
    Example under Iron alloys
Iron compounds
    — Radiation effects
      See Iron compounds, Effect of
         radiation on
Iron compounds, Effect of radiation on
    x Iron compounds—Radiation effects
    xx Radiation
Iron-copper alloys
    x Copper-iron alloys
    xx Copper alloys
Iron Cross *(CR5351)*
Iron Crown of Italy
    See Order of the Crown of Italy
Iron Crown of Lombardy *(CR5511)*
    xx Crowns
Iron crystals
Iron curtain lands
    See Communist countries
Iron deficiency anemia
    xx Anemia
       Hypochromic anemia
    — Diagnosis
Iron dynasty, China
    See China—History—Liao dynasty,
       907-1125
    See Khitan Mongols
Iron electrodes
    See Electrodes, Iron
Iron electroplating
    See Iron plating
Iron-founding *(TS229-240)*
    sa Cast-iron
       Cupola-furnaces
       Founding
       Pattern-making
       Stove industry and trade
    x Casting
    xx Cast-iron

    Founding
    Iron industry and trade
    — Costs
Iron group *(QD172.F4)*
    Example under Metals
Iron in soils
    See Soils—Iron content
Iron in the body *(QP535.F4)*
    sa Iron metabolism
       Transferrin
    xx Physiological chemistry
       Transferrin
    Example under Minerals in the body
Iron industry and trade *(Direct)*
         (HD9510-9529)
    sa Cast-iron
       Enameled ware
       Hardware
       Iron and steel workers
       Iron-founding
       Ironwork
       Rolling-mills
       Steel industry and trade
       Wrought-iron
    x Ferrous metal industries
       Steel industry and trade
    xx Metal trade
    — Accidents
    — Automation
    — By-products
    — Collective bargaining
      See Collective bargaining—Iron
         industry
    — Collective labor agreements
      See Collective labor agreements—Iron
         industry
    — Costs
    — Fume control
    — Government ownership *(Direct)*
    — Hygienic aspects
      sa Iron and steel workers—Diseases
         and hygiene
    — Labor productivity
    — Management
    — Mathematical models
    — Prices
      Example under Prices
    — Problems, exercises, etc.
    — Safety measures
    — Tables and ready-reckoners *(HF5716.18)*
    — Taxation *(Direct)*
    — Vocational guidance
Iron isotopes
    See Iron—Isotopes
Iron lung
    x Drinker respirator
    xx Artificial respiration
       Poliomyelitis
Iron-manganese alloys
    sa Ferromanganese
    x Manganese-iron alloys
    xx Manganese alloys
Iron metabolism
    sa Hemosiderosis
    xx Iron in the body
       Metabolism
Iron mines and mining *(Indirect) (Mining,*
         TN400-409)
    — Costs
    — Labor productivity
    — Production standards
    — Safety measures *(TN295)*
Iron molders *(Direct) (Founders' wages,*
         HD4966.F8; Trade-union periodicals,
         HD6350.I7)
    sa Coremakers
       Trade-unions—Iron molders
    xx Coremakers

    Foundries
Iron-molybdenum alloys
    x Molybdenum-iron alloys
       Molybdenum-steel alloys
    xx Molybdenum alloys
Iron-nickel alloys *(Metallurgy, TN757.N;*
         Testing, TA479.N)
    sa Iron-nickel-phosphorus alloys
    xx Nickel alloys
    Example under Iron alloys
Iron-nickel-cobalt alloys
    sa Kovar
    x Fernico
    xx Cobalt alloys
       Nickel alloys
Iron-nickel-copper alloys
Iron-nickel-phosphorus alloys
    xx Iron-nickel alloys
       Nickel alloys
       Phosphorus compounds
Iron-nickel-silicon alloys
Iron ores *(Indirect) (TN400-409)*
    sa Hematite
       Ilmenite
       Maghemite
       Magnetite
       Pyrites
       Pyrrhotite
       Taconite
    xx Iron
    — Analysis *(QD133)*
      xx Iron—Analysis
      Example under Metallurgical analysis
    — Standards *(Direct)*
    — Taxation *(Direct)*
    — Transportation
Iron organic compounds
    See Organoiron compounds
Iron oxides *(QD181.F4)*
    — Magnetic properties
Iron-palladium alloys
    x Palladium-iron alloys
    xx Palladium alloys
    — Magnetic properties
Iron pipe
    See Pipe, Iron
Iron plating
    x Iron electroplating
    xx Electroplating
Iron quartermaster
    See Automatic pilot (Ships)
Iron roofing
    See Roofing, Iron and steel
Iron salts *(QD181.F4)*
Iron-silicon alloys *(TA479.S5)*
    sa Ferrosilicon
       Silicon steel
    x Silicon-iron alloys
    xx Silicon alloys
    — Magnetic properties
    — Testing *(TA479.S5)*
Iron sulphate
    See Ferrous sulphate
Iron sulphur proteins *(QP552.I7)*
    x Sulphur iron proteins
    xx Organoiron compounds
       Organosulphur compounds
       Proteins
Iron-tin alloys
    x Tin-iron alloys
    xx Tin alloys
Iron-titanium alloys
    See Titanium-iron alloys
Iron-tungsten alloys
    sa Ferrotungsten
    x Tungsten-iron alloys
    xx Tungsten alloys

Iron workers
See Iron and steel workers
Iron-works *(Direct)* *(TS300-360)*
— Equipment and supplies
— Pictorial works
— Pilot plants
Ironclads
See Armored vessels
Ironing
See Laundry
Irons, Electric
See Electric irons
Irons (Pressing)
sa Electric irons
x Box irons
Flatirons
Hand irons
Pressing irons
Sadirons
xx Household appliances
Pressing of garments
— Collectors and collecting *(Direct)*
Ironstone
See Tiger's eye
Ironwork *(Direct)* *(Engineering*
construction, TA890-891; Mechanic
trades, TT215-240; Ornamental
ironwork, NK8200-8299)
sa Architectural ironwork
Blacksmithing
Firebacks
Forging
Grilles
Welding
xx Art metal-work
Arts and crafts movement
Blacksmithing
Decoration and ornament
Forging
Iron
Iron industry and trade
Metal-work
Wrought-iron
Example under Toreutic
— Private collections
Irony *(Aesthetics, BH301.I7; Drama,*
PN1680)
x Sarcasm
xx Cynicism
Rhetoric
Satire
Tragic, The
Irony in art
Irony in literature
Iroquoian Indians *(E99.I69)*
sa Caughnawaga Indians
Cayuga Indians
Cherokee Indians
Conestoga Indians
Huron Indians
Iroquois Indians
Mohawk Indians
Neutral Nation Indians
Oka Indians
Oneida Indians
Onondaga Indians
Seneca Indians
St. Regis Indians
Tuscarora Indians
xx Indians of North America
Iroquoian languages *(PM1381-4)*
sa Cherokee language
Huron language
Iroquois language
Mohawk language
Oneida language
Onondaga language
Seneca language

xx Cherokee language
Huron language
Iroquois language
Mohawk language
Oneida language
Onondaga language
Seneca language
Iroquois Indians *(E99.I7)*
sa Caughnawaga Indians
Cayuga Indians
Mohawk Indians
Oka Indians
Oneida Indians
Onondaga Indians
Seneca Indians
Tuscarora Indians
x Agoneaseah Indians
Five Nations
Massawomeke Indians
Mengwe Indians
Six Nations
xx Indians of North America
Iroquoian Indians
Mingo Indians
— Art
— Fiction
Example under Indians of North America
—Fiction
— Government relations
— Juvenile literature
— Land transfers
— Law and legislation
— Legends
Example under Indians of North America
—Legends
— Missions
— Religion and mythology
— Social life and customs
— — Juvenile literature
— Treaties
Example under Indians of North America
—Treaties; Treaties
— Tribal government
Example under Indians of North America
—Tribal government
— Wars
sa Sullivan's Indian Campaign, 1779
Iroquois language *(PM1381-4)*
sa Iroquoian languages
xx Iroquoian languages
Iroquois law
See Law, Iroquois
Iroquois poetry
Irradiated blood
See Blood irradiation
Irradiated fish
See Fish, Irradiated
Irradiated foods
See Food, Irradiated
Irradiation
sa Radioactivation analysis
xx Radiation
Irrational numbers
See Numbers, Irrational
Irrationalism (Philosophy) *(B824.2)*
xx Belief and doubt
Philosophy
Rationalism
Irregularities (Canon law)
x Impediments (Canon law)
xx Clergy (Canon law)
Ordination (Canon law)
Irreligion
Here are entered works dealing with a
condition of complete absence of reli-
gion.
sa Agnosticism
Atheism

Free thought
Indifferentism (Religion)
Non church-affiliated people
Rationalism
Secularism
xx Belief and doubt
Religion
Irreligion and society
See Irreligion and sociology
Irreligion and sociology
x Irreligion and society
Society and irreligion
Sociology and irreligion
xx Religion and sociology
Irreversible processes
x Processes, Irreversible
xx Dynamics
Equilibrium
Molecular dynamics
Statistical mechanics
Thermodynamics
Irrigation *(Indirect)* *(Agriculture, S613-615;*
Economic history, HD1711-1741;
Irrigation engineering, TC801-937)
sa Alkali lands
Arid regions
Dams
Dry farming
Indians of North America—Irrigation
Irrigation farming
Irrigation water
Plants—Water requirements
Reservoirs
Saline irrigation
Sewage irrigation
Sprinkler irrigation
Trickle irrigation
Water-storage
Windmills
subdivision Irrigation *under names of*
crops, e.g. Cotton—Irrigation
xx Agriculture
Engineering
Reclamation of land
Reservoirs
Soils
Waste lands
Water in agriculture
Water resources development
Water-storage
Water-supply
— Automation
— Finance
— Juvenile literature
— Management *(TC812)*
— Mathematical models
— Rates
— Research
See Irrigation research
— Tables, calculations, etc.
Irrigation, Overhead
See Sprinkler irrigation
Irrigation, Sewage
See Sewage irrigation
Irrigation (Medicine)
sa Enema
xx Asepsis and antisepsis
Therapeutics
Irrigation agriculture
See Irrigation farming
Irrigation canals and flumes *(TC930-933)*
sa Desilting basins
xx Canals
Flumes
Hydraulic structures
— Linings
x Linings of irrigation canals
— Maintenance and repair

— Tables
Irrigation districts *(Direct)*
   xx Special districts
Irrigation engineering *(TC801-937)*
   sa Plastics in irrigation
      Qanat
   x Engineering, Irrigation
   xx Agricultural engineering
      Hydraulic engineering
   — Tables, calculations, etc.
Irrigation farming *(Indirect) (SB112)*
   x Irrigation agriculture
      Paddy field culture
   xx Agriculture
      Arid regions agriculture
      Field crops
      Irrigation
   — Economic aspects *(Direct)*
   — — Mathematical models
   — Juvenile literature
Irrigation laws *(Direct) (United States, HD1727-9; Other countries, HD1741)*
   x Law, Irrigation
   xx Reclamation of land—Law and legislation
      Water—Laws and legislation
      Water-rights
   — Colonies
      See Irrigation laws, Colonial

GEOGRAPHIC SUBDIVISIONS

   — [country]
   — — Colonies
      Note under Irrigation laws, Colonial
Irrigation laws, Colonial
   Here are entered general and comparative works only. Works on irrigation laws of the colonies of an individual country are entered under the heading Irrigation laws with subdivision [country]—Colonies. Works dealing with a specific colony are entered under the same heading, subdivided by the name of the colony.
   x Colonial irrigation laws
      Colonies—Irrigation laws
      Irrigation laws—Colonies
Irrigation research *(Indirect)*
   x Irrigation—Research
   xx Agricultural research
      Research, Industrial
      Water conservation—Research
Irrigation water
   xx Irrigation
      Water
      Water-supply
Irritability *(Cells, QH647)*
   sa Excitation (Physiology)
      Geotropism
      Phototropism
      Plants—Irritability and movements
   x Animals, Irritability of
      Animals, Movements of
      Compensatory motion
      Motion, Compensatory
      Movements of animals
   xx Animals, Habits and behavior of
      Biology
      Cells
Irritation
   sa Counter-irritants
Isala (African people)
   See Sisala (African people)
Isamurang language
   See Batan language
Isano oil
   x Boleko oil

Isano seed oil
Isano seed oil
   See Isano oil
Isatis tinctoria
   See Woad
Isazai
   xx Ethnology—India
Iscaycinca Indians *(F3430.1.I)*
   xx Indians of South America
Ischaemic femoral necrosis
   See Idiopathic femoral necrosis
Ischemia
   xx Blood—Circulation, Disorders of
Ischemia, Cerebral
   See Cerebral ischemia
Ischias
   See Sciatica
Ise, Japan, in literature
Ise Bay
   — Typhoon, 1959
Ise Shintō *(BL2221.9.I8)*
   x Gekū Shintō
      Outer Shrine Shinto
      Watarai Shintō
   xx Shinto
Iseksawan
   See Seksawa (Berber tribe)
Ishigakibaru, Battle of, 1600 *(DS894.965)*
   x Bungo Ishigakibaru, Battle of, 1600
Ishikawa, Japan (Prefecture), in literature
Ishkashmi dialect *(PK6996.I7)*
   sa Zebaki dialect
   xx Pamir languages
      Zebaki dialect
Ishmaelites
   Not to be confused with the Mohammedan sect, Ismailites.
Isi-Lololo
   See Fanakalo
Isi-Piki
   See Fanakalo
Isi-Xosa language
   See Xosa language
Isinai dialect *(PL5801)*
   x Inmeas dialect
   xx Philippine languages
Ising model *(QC174.85.I8)*
   x Lenz-Ising model
   xx Ferromagnetism
      Phase transformations (Statistical physics)
Isinglass *(TS2301.I8)*
Iskra (Training planes)
   xx Training planes
Isla de Pinos, Battle of, 1596 *(F1799.I8)*
   x Pines, Isle of, Battle of, 1596
Islam *(Direct) (BP1-223)*
   Here are entered works on the religion of which Muḥammad is the prophet. Works on the community of believers in this religion are entered under Muslims. Works on the cultural system or civilization erected on the foundations of this religion are entered under Civilization, Islamic. Works on the group of countries in which the majority of the people are Muslims or in which Islam is the established religion are entered under Islamic countries.
   sa Caliphate
      Dervishes
      Imamate
      Jerusalem in Islam
      Koran
      Mahdism
      Miḥna
      Muslims
      Palestine in Islam

      Prophets, Pre-Islamic
   special headings with Islam *added in parentheses, e.g.* Angels (Islam); *and subdivision* Islam *under special topics, e.g.* Marriage—Islam; *also headings beginning with the words* Islamic *and* Muslim
   x Islamism
      Mohammedanism
      Muhammadanism
      Muslimism
      Mussulmanism
   xx Religions
   — 1800-
   — 20th century *(BP163)*
   — Apologetic works *(BP170)*
      x Apologetics, Islamic
      Apologetics, Muslim
      Islamic apologetics
      Muslim apologetics
   — Appreciation *(BP163)*
   — Biography *(BP70-80)*
      sa Architects, Muslim
      Educators, Muslim
      Muslim converts
      Saints, Muslim
      Scientists, Muslim
      Theologians, Muslim
      x Islamic biography
      Muslim biography
      xx Muslims
   — Catechisms and creeds *(BP45)*
   — — Arabic, [English, etc.]
   — Charities
      sa Zakat
      x Alms and almsgiving (Islam)
   — Clergy
      See Islam—Functionaries
   — Controversial literature *(BP169)*
   — Early works to 1800 *(BP160)*
   — Education *(Direct) (LC901-915)*
      sa Religious education, Islamic
      Students, Muslim
      Women, Muslim—Education
      x Education, Islamic
      Education, Muslim
      Islamic education
      Muslim education
      Muslims—Education
   — Essence, genius, nature
   — Evangelistic work
      See Daʻwah (Islam)
   — Five pillars
      See Pillars of Islam
   — Functionaries *(BP185)*
      sa Hafiz
      Ulama
      x Islam—Clergy
      Islamic religious functionaries
      Muslim religious functionaries
      xx Pastoral theology (Islam)
   — Government *(BP185)*
      sa Mosques—Organization and administration
   — Historiography *(BP49)*
      xx Islamic research
   — Hymns
      See Islamic hymns
   — Influence
   — Juvenile literature
   — Manuscripts
   — Marriage
      See Marriage—Islam
   — Missions *(Direct) (BP170.3)*
      Here are entered works on the spread of Islam. Works on the spread of Christianity among Muslims are entered under Missions to Muslims.

Islam *(Direct) (BP1-223)*
— Missions *(Direct) (BP170.3)*
    (Continued)
        sa Da'wah (Islam)
        x Islamic missions
            Missions, Islamic
            Missions, Muslim
            Muslim missions
— Origin *(BP55)*
— Pictures, illustrations, etc.
— Pillars
        See Pillars of Islam
— Prayer-books and devotions *(BP183.3)*
        Subdivided by language.
        sa Islamic prayers
            Koran—Prayers
        xx Islamic devotional literature
            Prayer (Islam)
— Psychology
        sa Faith (Islam)—Psychology
        x Islamic psychology
            Muslim psychology
            Psychology, Islamic
            Psychology, Muslim
        xx Psychology, Religious
— Quotations, maxims, etc.
— Relations *(BP171)*
        sa Religious tolerance (Islam)
— — Bahaism, ₍Buddhism, etc.₎
— — Christianity *(BP172)*
        sa Islam—Relations—Coptic Church
            Islamic literature—Christian
                interpretations
            Jesus Christ—Islamic
                interpretations
            Mary, Virgin—Islamic
                interpretations
            Missions to Muslims
— — Coptic Church *(BP172.5.C6)*
        xx Islam—Relations—Christianity
— Research
        See Islamic research
— Rites and ceremonies
        See Islamic religious practice
— Sects
        See Islamic sects
— Study and teaching *(Direct)*
        x Islamic studies
— Terminology
— Unity *(BP170.82)*
— Universality *(BP170.8)*
Islam and art *(BP190.5.A7)*
        sa Islam and the performing arts
        x Art and Islam
        xx Art and religion
            Art, Islamic
Islam and astronautics *(BP190.5.A8)*
        x Astronautics and Islam
        xx Cosmology, Islamic
            Islam and science
            Religion and astronautics
Islam and birth control
        See Birth control—Religious aspects—Islam
Islam and communism
        See Communism and Islam
Islam and economics *(BP173.75)*
        x Economics and Islam
        xx Sociology, Islamic
Islam and homosexuality
        See Homosexuality and Islam
Islam and humor *(BP190.5.H8)*
        x Humor and Islam
        xx Religion and humor
Islam and labor *(HD6338.4)*
        x Labor and Islam
        xx Religion and labor
Islam and literature
        x Literature and Islam
        xx Religion and literature

Islam and medicine
        See Medicine and Islam
Islam and music *(BP190.5.M8)*
        x Music and Islam
        xx Religion and music
Islam and philosophy
        sa Koran and philosophy
        x Philosophy and Islam
        xx Philosophy and religion
            Philosophy, Islamic
Islam and poetry
        x Poetry and Islam
        xx Religion and poetry
Islam and politics *(Direct) (BP173.7)*
        x Politics and Islam
        xx Islam and state
Islam and race problems
        x Race problems and Islam
        xx Islam and social problems
Islam and science *(BP190.5.S)*
        sa Islam and astronautics
            Koran and science
            Medicine and Islam
        x Science and Islam
        xx Religion and science
Islam and slavery
        See Slavery and Islam
Islam and social problems *(Direct)*
        (HN40.I)
        sa Islam and race problems
        x Religion and social problems
            Social problems and Islam
        xx Sociology, Islamic
Islam and socialism
        See Socialism and Islam
Islam and state *(Direct) (BP173.6)*
        sa Islam and politics
            Jihad
        x State and Islam
        xx Nationalism and religion
            Religion and state
— Koranic teaching
        xx Koran—Political science
Islam and the performing arts *(BP190.5.P4)*
        x Performing arts and Islam
        xx Islam and art
Islam and world politics *(BP173.5)*
        x World politics and Islam
Islam in literature
Islamic . . .
        x Mohammedan . . .
            Moslem . . .
Islamic angelology
        See Angels (Islam)
Islamic antiquities *(Direct)*
        sa Inscriptions, Islamic
        x Antiquities, Islamic
            Antiquities, Muslim
            Muslim antiquities
        xx Antiquities
Islamic apologetics
        See Islam—Apologetic works
Islamic architects
        See Architects, Muslim
Islamic architecture
        See Architecture, Islamic
Islamic arms and armor
        See Arms and armor, Islamic
Islamic art
        See Art, Islamic
Islamic art industries and trade
        See Art industries and trade, Islamic
Islamic art metal-work
        See Art metal-work, Islamic
Islamic art objects
        See Art objects, Islamic
Islamic arts
        See Arts, Islamic

Islamic authors
        See Muslim authors
Islamic biography
        See Islam—Biography
Islamic bookbinding
        See Bookbinding, Islamic
Islamic calendar
        See Calendar, Islamic
Islamic children
        See Muslim children
Islamic chronology
        See Chronology, Islamic
Islamic cities and towns
        See Cities and towns, Islamic
Islamic civilization
        See Civilization, Islamic
Islamic coins
        See Coins, Islamic
Islamic converts
        See Muslim converts
Islamic converts to Christianity
        See Converts from Islam
Islamic cosmology
        See Cosmology, Islamic
Islamic costume
        See Costume, Islamic
Islamic countries *(DS36-40)*
        sa Arab countries
        x Muslim countries
        Note under Islam
— History, Naval
Islamic courts
        See Courts, Islamic
Islamic cultus
        See Cultus, Islamic
Islamic decoration and ornament
        See Decoration and ornament, Islamic
Islamic demonology
        See Demonology, Islamic
Islamic devotional calendars
        x Devotional calendars—Islam
            Devotional calendars, Islamic
            Devotional calendars, Muslim
            Muslim devotional calendars
Islamic devotional literature *(BP188.2)*
        sa Exempla, Islamic
            Islam—Prayer-books and devotions
            Islamic meditations
        x Devotional literature, Islamic
            Devotional literature, Muslim
            Muslim devotional literature
Islamic education
        See Islam—Education
Islamic educators
        See Educators, Muslim
Islamic Empire
        Here are entered works dealing with the
            Near East alone, or the Near East,
            North Africa and Islamic Spain as a
            whole, during the period 622-1517,
            i.e., from the rise and expansion of Is-
            lam to the creation of the Ottoman
            Empire.
        sa Abbasids
            Almohades
            Mamelukes
            Omayyads
            Saracens
            Songhai
        x Arab Empire
            Empire, Islamic
            Futuḥ
            Muslim Empire
            Near East—History—622-1517
— Biography
— History
— — 622-661 *(DS38.1)*
— — 661-750 *(DS38.5)*

—— 750-1258 (DS38.6)
—— 1258-1517 (DS38.7)
— Juvenile literature
Islamic enamel and enameling
    See Enamel and enameling, Islamic
Islamic epistemology
    See Knowledge, Theory of (Islam)
Islamic eschatology
    See Eschatology, Islamic
Islamic ethics (BJ1291)
    sa Blasphemy (Islam)
        Free will and determinism (Islam)
        Good and evil (Islam)
        Islamic etiquette
        Koran—Ethics
        Pillars of Islam
        Sin (Islam)
        subdivision Conduct of life under
            special groups of Muslims, e.g.
            Women, Muslim—Conduct of life
    x Ethics, Islamic
        Ethics, Muslim
        Muslim ethics
    xx Philosophy, Islamic
        Religion and ethics
— Early works to 1800 (BJ1291)
— Quotations, maxims, etc. (BJ1291)
Islamic etiquette (BJ2020)
    sa Hospitality (Islam)
        Mosque etiquette
    x Etiquette, Islamic
        Etiquette, Muslim
        Muslim etiquette
    xx Islamic ethics
Islamic exempla
    See Exempla, Islamic
Islamic fasts and feasts
    See Fasts and feasts—Islam
Islamic funeral rites and ceremonies
    See Funeral rites and ceremonies, Islamic
Islamic heresies and heretics
    See Heresies and heretics, Islamic
Islamic holy war
    See Jihad
Islamic homiletical illustrations
    See Homiletical illustrations, Islamic
Islamic homiletics
    See Preaching, Islamic
Islamic hospitality
    See Hospitality (Islam)
Islamic hygiene
    See Hygiene, Islamic
Islamic hymns (BP183.5)
    sa Ramadan hymns
    x Hymns, Islamic
        Hymns, Muslim
        Islam—Hymns
        Muslim hymns
Islamic illumination of books and manuscripts
    See Illumination of books and manuscripts,
        Islamic
Islamic inscriptions
    See Inscriptions, Islamic
Islamic international law
    See International law (Islamic law)
Islamic ivories
    See Ivories, Islamic
Islamic law (Direct)
    sa Hanafis
        Hanbalites
        Malikis
        Rif law
        Shafiites
        Sunnites
        Taqlīd

special legal headings and subdivisions
    with Islamic law added in
    parentheses, e.g. Aliens (Islamic
    law); Guardian and ward (Islamic
    law); Wills (Islamic law); Woman—
    Legal status, laws, etc. (Islamic law)
    x Civil law (Islamic law)
        Koran—Law
        Law, Arab
        Law in the Koran
        Law, Islamic
        Sharia (Islamic law)
    xx Law, Oriental
        Law, Semitic
— Examinations, questions, etc.
— Interpretation and construction
    x Analogy (Islamic law)
        Ijtihād (Islamic law)
        Qiyās (Islamic law)
— Sources
    sa Fatwās
        Hadith
        Koran
Islamic learning and scholarship (Indirect)
    sa Muslims as scientists
        Muslims—Intellectual life
        Scholars, Muslim
    x Learning and scholarship—Muslims
        Muslim learning and scholarship
        Muslims—Learning and scholarship
    xx Muslims—Intellectual life
Islamic legends
    See Legends, Islamic
Islamic libraries
    x Libraries, Islamic
        Libraries, Muslim
        Muslim libraries
Islamic literature (BP87-89)
    sa Hadith
        Ismaili literature
        Koran
        Muslim authors
        Shiite literature
        Sunna
    x Muslim literature
    xx Religious literature
— Christian interpretations (BP172)
        Here are entered works about Chris-
        tian interpretations of Islamic liter-
        ature. Studies by Christian authors
        on Islamic literature are entered un-
        der Islamic literature—History and
        criticism.
    xx Christianity and other religions—
        Islam
        Islam—Relations—Christianity
— History and criticism
        Note under Islamic literature—Christian
        interpretations
Islamic logicians
    See Logicians, Muslim
Islamic magic
    See Magic, Islamic
Islamic majolica
    See Majolica, Islamic
Islamic marriage customs and rites
    See Marriage customs and rites, Islamic
Islamic martyrs
    See Muslim martyrs
Islamic meditations
    x Meditations, Islamic
        Meditations, Muslim
        Muslim meditations
    xx Islamic devotional literature
Islamic metal-work
    See Metal-work, Islamic
Islamic miniature painting
    See Miniature painting, Islamic

Islamic missions
    See Islam—Missions
Islamic monasticism and religious orders
    See Monasticism and religious orders,
        Islamic
Islamic mosaics
    See Mosaics, Islamic
Islamic mural painting and decoration
    See Mural painting and decoration, Islamic
Islamic mysticism
    See Mysticism—Islam
Islamic New Year (BP186.2)
    x Muslim New Year
        New Year, Islamic
        New Year, Muslim
Islamic numismatics
    See Numismatics, Islamic
Islamic orders of knighthood and chivalry
    See Orders of knighthood and chivalry,
        Islamic
Islamic painting
    See Painting, Islamic
Islamic paintings
    See Paintings, Islamic
Islamic pastoral theology
    See Pastoral theology (Islam)
Islamic philosophers
    See Philosophers, Muslim
Islamic philosophy
    See Philosophy, Islamic
Islamic pilgrims and pilgrimages
    See Pilgrims and pilgrimages, Muslim
Islamic pottery
    See Pottery, Islamic
Islamic prayers (BP183.3)
    sa Prayer (Islam)
    x Muslim prayers
        Prayers, Islamic
        Prayers, Muslim
    xx Islam—Prayer-books and devotions
        Prayer (Islam)
Islamic prayers, Arabic, [Bengali, etc.]
    x Arabic [Bengali, etc.] Islamic prayers
Islamic preaching
    See Preaching, Islamic
Islamic press
    See Press, Islamic
Islamic psychology
    See Islam—Psychology
Islamic public finance
    See Finance, Public—Islamic countries
Islamic religious education
    See Religious education, Islamic
Islamic religious functionaries
    See Islam—Functionaries
Islamic religious practice (BP174)
    sa Cultus, Islamic
        Fasts and feasts—Islam
        Funeral rites and ceremonies, Islamic
        Mysticism—Islam
        Pastoral theology (Islam)
        Pillars of Islam
        Purity, Ritual (Islam)
        Religious life (Islam)
        Sharia (Islamic religious practice)
        Worship (Islam)
    x Islam—Rites and ceremonies
        Muslim religious practice
        Theology, Practical (Islam)
    xx Rites and ceremonies
— Shiites
        See Shiite religious practice
Islamic research (Direct) (Civilization,
    D199.3; Religion, BP42-3)
    sa Islam—Historiography
    x Islam—Research
        Muslim research
        Research, Islamic

Islamic research   *(Direct)   (Civilization,*
D199.3; Religion, BP42-3)
(Continued)
Research, Muslim
Islamic rugs
See Rugs, Islamic
Islamic saints
See Saints, Muslim
Islamic scholars
See Scholars, Muslim
Islamic scientists
See Scientists, Muslim
Islamic sculpture
See Sculpture, Islamic
Islamic sects   *(Direct)   (BP191-223)*
sa Ahl-i Ḥadīth
Ahmadiyya
Assassins (Ismailites)
Badawiyah
Batinites
Bektashi
Dīn-i Ilāhī
Hanafis
Hanbalites
Ḥashwīya
Heresies and heretics, Islamic
Hurufis
Ibadites
Ismailites
al-Jahmīyah
Karramites
Kharijites
Khojahs
Malikis
Motazilites
al-Muʻaṭṭilah
Murīdīyah
Nosairians
Sālimīyah
Shabak
Shafiites
Shiites
Sunnites
Wahhabis
Zaidites
x Islam—Sects
Muslim sects
Sects, Islamic
Sects, Muslim
Islamic sermons   *(BP183.6)*
sa ʻĪd al-Aḍḥā sermons
ʻĪd al-Fiṭr sermons
Laylat al-Miʻrāj sermons
Ramadan sermons
Wedding sermons, Islamic
x Muslim sermons
Sermons, Islamic
Sermons, Muslim
xx Preaching, Islamic
Islamic sermons, Arabic, ₍Indonesian, Turkish,
etc.₎   *(BP183.6)*
x Sermons, Arabic, ₍Indonesian, Turkish,
etc.₎—Islamic authors
Sermons, Arabic, ₍Indonesian, Turkish,
etc.₎—Muslim authors
Islamic shrines   *(Direct)   (BP187)*
sa Pilgrims and pilgrimages, Muslim
x Muslim shrines
Shrines, Islamic
Shrines, Muslim
xx Pilgrims and pilgrimages, Muslim
Islamic sociology
See Sociology, Islamic
Islamic students
See Students, Muslim
Islamic studies
See Islam—Study and teaching
Islamic tales
See Tales, Islamic

Islamic taxation
See Taxation—Islamic countries
Islamic textile industry and fabrics
See Textile industry and fabrics, Islamic
Islamic theologians
See Theologians, Muslim
Islamic theological anthropology
See Man (Islam)
Islamic theology   *(BP166)*
sa Authority (Islam)
Basmalah
Eschatology, Islamic
Faith (Islam)
Fate and fatalism (Islam)
Forgiveness of sin (Islam)
Free will and determinism (Islam)
God (Islam)
Good and evil (Islam)
Heresies and heretics, Islamic
History (Islamic theology)
Intention (Islam)
Koran—Theology
Man (Islam)
Merit (Islam)
Miracles (Islam)
Mysticism—Islam
Predestination (Islam)
Revelation (Islam)
Salvation (Islam)
Spirits (Islam)
Taqlīd
x Kalam
Muslim theology
Theology, Islamic
Theology, Muslim
xx Theology, Doctrinal
— Early works to 1800
Islamic wedding sermons
See Wedding sermons, Islamic
Islamic women
See Women, Muslim
Islamic women saints
See Saints, Muslim women
Islamic wood-carving
See Wood-carving, Islamic
Islamic youth
See Youth, Muslim
Islamism
See Islam
Island arcs   *(Indirect)   (QE511.2)*
x Volcanic arcs
xx Geology, Structural
Islands
Plate tectonics
Island ecology
xx Ecology
— Juvenile literature
Island fauna
x Fauna
Insular fauna
xx Evolution
Islands
Zoogeography
Zoology—Ecology
Zoology—Variation
— Pictorial works
Island flora
x Flora
Insular flora
xx Botany—Ecology
Botany—Variation
Evolution
Islands
Phytogeography
Islands   *(Direct)   (GB471-8; Folk-lore,
GR675; Lost islands, G555)*
sa Barrier islands
Coral reefs and islands

Island arcs
Island fauna
Island flora
— Juvenile literature

GEOGRAPHIC SUBDIVISIONS

— United States
sa United States—Insular possessions
Islands, Artificial
See Artificial islands
Islands, Ice
See Ice islands
Islands, Imaginary
See Geographical myths
Islands in literature
Islands of Langerhans
x Langerhans, Islands of
xx Pancreas
— Tumors
x Insuloma
Isles de Pierres Indians
See Sinkiuse-Columbia Indians
Islet cell tumor, Ulcerogenic
See Zollinger-Ellison syndrome
Isleta Indians   *(E99.I8)*
xx Indians of North America
Pueblo Indians
Tanoan Indians
Isleta language   *(PM1387)*
xx Tanoan languages
Ismail, Russia
— Siege, 1790   *(DR555.7)*
Ismaili
See Ismailites
Ismaili literature   *(PJ891.I55)*
xx Arabic literature
Islamic literature
Persian literature
Ismailians
See Ismailites
Ismailites   *(BP195.I8)*
sa Assassins (Ismailites)
Batinites
Fatimites
Nosairians
x Ismaili
Ismailians
xx Assassins (Ismailites)
Islamic sects
Shiites
Note under Ishmaelites
Isneg   *(DS666.I7)*
x Apayao
Apoyao
xx Igorot
Isneg language   *(PL5805)*
x Apayao language
xx Philippine languages
Isoagglutination
See Blood—Agglutination
Isoantigens
xx Antigens and antibodies
Isobaric spin
x Isospin
Isotopic spin
Spin, Isobaric
xx Nuclear physics
Quantum theory
Isobars
See Atmospheric pressure
Isobars, Nuclear
See Nuclear isobars
Isocephaly (Craniology)
See Brachycephaly
Isochromatic photography
See Photography, Orthochromatic
Isoenzymes
x Isozymes

xx Enzymes

Isogonic lines

    See Magnetism, Terrestrial

Isohemagglutination

    See Blood—Agglutination

Isohypse

    See Contours (Cartography)

Isolated organ perfusion (Physiology)

    See Isolation perfusion (Physiology)

Isolating mechanisms

    x Isolation, Biotic

    xx Evolution

        Reproduction

        Species

Isolation, Biotic

    See Isolating mechanisms

Isolation, Perceptual

    See Sensory deprivation

Isolation, Social

    See Social isolation

Isolation (Hospital care)

    See Communicable diseases—Hospitals

Isolation (Philosophy) *(B824.3)*

    xx Alienation (Philosophy)

        Philosophy

Isolation hospitals

    See Communicable diseases—Hospitals

Isolation perfusion (Physiology)

    x Isolated organ perfusion (Physiology)

        Organs (Anatomy)—Perfusion

        Perfusion, Isolation (Physiology)

        Regional perfusion

    xx Biology—Technique

        Perfusion (Physiology)

        Preservation of organs, tissues, etc.

    — Laboratory manuals

Isolators, Ferrite

    See Ferrite isolators

Isomerase

    xx Phosphorus metabolism

Isomerism *(QD471)*

    sa Isomerization

        Mesomerism

        Stereochemistry

        Tautomerism

    xx Chemistry, Physical and theoretical

        Molecular rotation

        Stereochemistry

Isomerism (Nuclear physics)

    See Nuclear isomers

Isomerization

    xx Isomerism

        Petroleum—Refining

        Rearrangements (Chemistry)

Isomers, Nuclear

    See Nuclear isomers

Isomers (Nuclear physics)

    See Nuclear isomers

Isometric drawing

    See Isometric projection

Isometric exercise

    x Isometrics (Exercise)

        Resistance exercise

    xx Exercise

Isometric projection *(Mathematics, QA505; Mechanical drawing, T365)*

    x Isometric drawing

        Projection, Isometric

    xx Axonometric projection

        Geometry, Descriptive

        Mechanical drawing

        Projection

Isometrics (Exercise)

    See Isometric exercise

Isometrics (Mathematics)

    xx Transformations (Mathematics)

Isomorphisms (Mathematics) *(Category theory, QA169; Group theory, QA171)*

    xx Categories (Mathematics)

        Groups, Theory of

        Set theory

Isonipecaine

    x Demerol

        Dolantin

        Eudolat

    xx Narcotics

Isonzo, Battles of the, 1915-1917 *(D569.I7)*

    sa Gorizia, Battle of, 1916

    xx European War, 1914-1918—Campaigns —Italo-Austrian

Isoperimetrical problems

    See Calculus of variations

Isopoda *(Indirect)* *(QL444.I8)*

    xx Arthrostraca

        Crustacea

        Malacostraca

    — Identification

Isoptera

    See Termites

Isospin

    See Isobaric spin

Isostasy *(QB283; Geology, QE511; Gravity, QB331)*

    xx Earth—Figure

        Geodesy

Isostatic anomalies

    See Gravity anomalies

Isothermal transformation diagrams *(TN690)*

    x S curves (Metallurgy)

        Time-temperature-transformation curves (Metallurgy)

        TTT curves (Metallurgy)

    xx Phase diagrams

        Physical metallurgy

Isothermic curves

    See Curves, Isothermic

Isothermic surfaces

    See Surfaces, Isothermic

Isotherms

    See Atmospheric temperature

Isotone shift *(QC794)*

    sa Isotope shift

    x Shift, Isotone

    xx Hyperfine interactions

        Isotope shift

        Nuclear spectroscopy

Isotope dilution analysis *(QD608)*

    x Isotopic dilution analysis

    xx Radiochemical analysis

        Radioisotopes

Isotope enrichment

    See Isotope separation

Isotope separation *(QD466; Engineering, TK9350)*

    sa Calutron

        Nuclear fuels

    x Isotope enrichment

        Separation of isotopes

    xx Isotopes

        Radiochemistry

        Separation (Technology)

Isotope shift *(QC794)*

    sa Isotone shift

    xx Atomic spectra

        Hyperfine interactions

        Isotone shift

Isotopes *(QD466)*

    sa Calutron

        Isotope separation

        Isotopic power generators

        Nuclear isobars

        Packing fractions

        Radioactive tracers

        Radioisotopes

        Tracers (Chemistry)

    subdivision Isotopes *under names of elements or groups of elements, e.g.* Carbon—Isotopes; Uranium— Isotopes

    xx Nuclides

        Radioactive substances

    — Catalogs *(TP202)*

    — Industrial applications

    — Mass

        Example under Atomic mass

    — Physiological effect

    — Tables, etc.

    — Therapeutic use

Isotopic actinium

    See Actinium—Isotopes

Isotopic antimony

    See Antimony—Isotopes

Isotopic beryllium

    See Beryllium—Isotopes

Isotopic boron

    See Boron—Isotopes

Isotopic bromine

    See Bromine—Isotopes

Isotopic cadmium

    See Cadmium—Isotopes

Isotopic carbon

    See Carbon—Isotopes

Isotopic cerium

    See Cerium—Isotopes

Isotopic cesium

    See Cesium—Isotopes

Isotopic dilution analysis

    See Isotope dilution analysis

Isotopic europium

    See Europium—Isotopes

Isotopic germanium

    See Germanium—Isotopes

Isotopic helium

    See Helium—Isotopes

Isotopic holmium

    See Holmium—Isotopes

Isotopic indicators

    See Radioactive tracers

Isotopic iron

    See Iron—Isotopes

Isotopic lanthanum

    See Lanthanum—Isotopes

Isotopic lutetium

    See Lutetium—Isotopes

Isotopic manganese

    See Manganese—Isotopes

Isotopic mercury

    See Mercury—Isotopes

Isotopic platinum

    See Platinum—Isotopes

Isotopic polonium

    See Polonium—Isotopes

Isotopic power generators

    sa subdivision Isotopic power generators *under subjects, e.g.* Automatic meteorological stations—Isotopic power generators; Space vehicles— Isotopic power generators

    x Radioisotopic power generators

    xx Atomic power-plants

        Isotopes

        Radioisotopes—Decay

Isotopic praseodymium

    See Praseodymium—Isotopes

Isotopic protactinium

    See Protactinium—Isotopes

Isotopic radon

    See Radon—Isotopes

Isotopic rubidium

    See Rubidium—Isotopes

Isotopic silicon
  See Silicon—Isotopes
Isotopic spin
  See Isobaric spin
Isotopic sulphur
  See Sulphur—Isotopes
Isotopic tellurium
  See Tellurium—Isotopes
Isotopic thallium
  See Thallium—Isotopes
Isotopic thorium
  See Thorium—Isotopes
Isotopic thulium
  See Thulium—Isotopes
Isotopic uranium
  See Uranium—Isotopes
Isotopic vanadium
  See Vanadium—Isotopes
Isotopic xenon
  See Xenon—Isotopes
Isotta automobile
Isotype (Picture language) *(PM8999)*
Isozymes
  See Isoenzymes
ISPL (Electronic computer system)
  x Incremental System Programming
    Language (Electronic computer
    system)
Israel
  — History
  — — 1948-1949
  — — Suez Campaign, 1956
      See Sinai Campaign, 1956
  — Name
    xx Bible—Names
      Jews—Name
Israel, Election of
  See Jews—Election, Doctrine of
Israel, Ten lost tribes
  See Lost tribes of Israel
Israel, Twelve tribes of
  See Twelve tribes of Israel
Israel and the Diaspora
  sa Jews in the United States—Attitudes
    toward Israel
  x Diaspora
  xx Jews—Diaspora
    Jews in Africa, ⌐Germany, Poland, etc.⌐
    Zionism
Israel-Arab Border Conflicts, 1949-
    (Direct)
  sa Fedayeen
  x Arab-Israel Border Conflicts, 1949-
    Israeli-Arab Border Conflicts, 1949-
  xx Jewish-Arab relations
    Jewish-Arab relations—1949-1967
    Sinai Campaign, 1956
  — Pictorial works
Israel-Arab War, 1948-1949 *(Direct)*
    (DS126.9-99)
  sa Jerusalem—Siege, 1948
  x Arab-Israel War, 1948-1949
    Jewish-Arab War, 1948-1949
  — Aerial operations
  — Armistices
  — Campaigns and battles
  — Charities
      See Israel-Arab War, 1948-1949—
        Civilian relief
  — Civilian relief
    x Israel-Arab War, 1948-1949—
        Charities
      Israel-Arab War, 1948-1949—Social
        work
  — Destruction and pillage
    x Israel-Arab War, 1948-1949—Pillage
  — Diplomatic history
  — Humor, caricatures, etc.

  xx Israel-Arab War, 1948-1949—
      Pictorial works
  — Influence and results
  — Juvenile literature
  — Naval operations
  — Personal narratives
  — Pictorial works
    sa Israel-Arab War, 1948-1949—
        Humor, caricatures, etc.
  — Pillage
      See Israel-Arab War, 1948-1949—
        Destruction and pillage
  — Propaganda
  — Registers of dead
  — Social work
      See Israel-Arab War, 1948-1949—
        Civilian relief
Israel-Arab War, 1956
  See Egypt—History—Intervention, 1956
    Sinai Campaign, 1956
Israel-Arab War, 1967-   *(Direct)*
  x Arab-Israel War, 1967-
    Six Day War, 1967
  xx Jewish-Arab relations—1949-1967
  — Aerial operations
    x Israel-Arab War, 1967-   —Battles,
        sieges, etc.
      Israel-Arab War, 1967-   —
        Military operations
  — Battles, sieges, etc.
      See Israel-Arab War, 1967-   —
        Aerial operations
  — Biography
  — — Juvenile literature
  — Caricatures
      See Israel-Arab War, 1967-   —
        Humor, caricatures, etc.
  — Causes
  — Diplomatic history
  — Humor, caricatures, etc.
    x Israel-Arab War, 1967-
        Caricatures
  — Influence and results
  — Juvenile literature
  — Maps
  — Military operations
      See Israel-Arab War, 1967-   —
        Aerial operations
  — Naval operations
  — Occupied territories
    sa Israel-Arab War, 1967-   —
        Territorial questions
  — — Pictorial works
  — Pictorial works
  — Poetry
  — Public opinion   *(Direct)*
  — Registers, lists, etc.
  — Registers of dead
  — Religious aspects
  — Sources
  — Territorial questions   *(Direct)*
    xx Israel-Arab War, 1967-   —
        Occupied territories
Israel in art
Israel in literature
Israel prize
  x Peras Yisrael
Israeli-Arab Border Conflicts, 1949-
  See Israel-Arab Border Conflicts, 1949-
Israeli literature   *(Direct)*
Israeli newspapers
  Note under Newspapers
Israeli poetry   *(Direct)*   *(PN849.I8)*
Israeli pound
  See Pound, Israeli
Israeli wit and humor   *(Direct)*   *(PN6222.I8)*
  xx Hebrew wit and humor
    Jewish wit and humor

Israelis
  xx Jews
Israelis in the United States, ⌐etc.⌐
Israelites
  See Jews
Israelites (Bohemia)
  See Abrahamites (Bohemia)
ISS 714 (Computer)
  xx Electronic digital computers
Issus, Battle of, 333 B.C.
Istanbul
  x Constantinople
  — Riot, 1955
  — — Pictorial works
  — Siege, 1203-1204   *(D164)*
    sa Crusades—Fourth, 1202-1204
    xx Crusades—Fourth, 1202-1204
      Latin Empire, 1204-1261
  — Siege, 1422
  — Siege, 1453   *(DF645-9)*
Istanbul in literature
Italian-American newspapers   *(History,
    PN1885.I)*
  xx American newspapers
    Italian newspapers
Italian-American periodicals   *(History,
    PN1885.I)*
  xx American periodicals
    Italian periodicals
Italian architecture
  See Architecture, Italian
Italian art
  See Art, Italian
Italian art objects
  See Art objects, Italian
Italian ballads and songs   *(Collections,
    PQ4217-4219; History,
    PQ4119-4123)*
  sa Folk-songs, Italian
    National songs, Italian
    Political ballads and songs, Italian
    Sicilian ballads and songs
    Songs, Italian
    War-songs, Italian
Italian bronzes
  See Bronzes, Italian
Italian children's literature
  See Children's literature, Italian
Italian children's poetry
  See Children's poetry, Italian
Italian copper articles
  See Copper articles, Italian
Italian cypress
Italian didactic poetry
  See Didactic poetry, Italian
Italian drama   *(Direct)*   *(Collections,
    PQ4227-4245; History,
    PQ4133-4160)*
  — To 1700   *(PQ4137-9)*
  — 18th century   *(PQ4141)*
  — 19th century   *(PQ4143)*
  — 20th century   *(PQ4145)*
Italian drama (Comedy)   *(PQ4149)*
  sa Commedia dell' arte
  xx Comedy
Italian drama (Tragedy)   *(PQ4147)*
  xx Tragedy
Italian drawing
  See Drawing, Italian
Italian elegiac poetry
  See Elegiac poetry, Italian
Italian essays   *(Collections, PQ4260; History,
    PQ4183.E8)*
  Here are entered collections of essays by
  several authors.
Italian farces   *(Collections, PQ4236-8;
    History, PQ4155-9)*

Italian fiction *(Direct)* *(Collections,*
PQ4251-7; History, PQ4169-4181)
    sa Short stories, Italian
  — To 1400 *(PQ4171)*
  — 15th century *(PQ4171-2)*
  — 16th century *(PQ4172)*
  — 17th century *(PQ4172)*
  — 18th century *(PQ4173)*
  — 19th century *(PQ4173)*
  — 20th century *(PQ4174)*
Italian folk-drama
    See Folk-drama, Italian
Italian gems
    See Gems, Italian
Italian goldsmithing
    See Goldsmithing, Italian
Italian imprints *(Direct)*
  — Book reviews
  — Union lists
Italian language *(PC1001-1977)*
    sa Sardinian language
    Example under Romance languages
  — To 1300 *(PC1715)*
  — Dialects
  —— Judeo-Italian
      xx Jews—Languages
  — Euphemism
  — Primers
      See Primers, Italian
  — Pronunciation
      Example under references from
        Phonology; Pronunciation
  — Scientific Italian
      See Italian language—Technical
        Italian
  — Technical Italian
      x Italian language—Scientific Italian
      Scientific Italian
      Technical Italian
      xx Technical writing
      Technology—Language
Italian language in Costa Rica, [Switzerland,
etc.]
Italian letters *(Collections, PQ4259; History,*
PQ4183.L4)
Italian literature *(Direct)* *(Collections,*
PQ4201-4263; History,
PQ4001-4199)
    sa Patriotic literature, Italian
    Revolutionary literature, Italian
    Sardinian literature
    Example under Romance literature
  — To 1400
  — 15th century *(PQ4075)*
  — 16th century *(PQ4079-4080)*
  — 17th century *(PQ4081-2)*
  — 18th century *(PQ4083-4)*
  — 19th century *(PQ4085-6)*
  — 20th century *(PQ4087)*
  — Bibliography *(Z2341-2369)*
    sa Catalogs, Publishers'—Italy
  —— Early *(Z2342; Z2352)*
  — Bio-bibliography *(Z2350-2354)*
  — Catholic authors
  — Competitions
    sa Premio letterario "Libera Stampa"
    Premio letterario "Mario Pettenon"
    Premio letterario Massarosa
    Premio Strega
  — History and criticism
    sa Marinism
  — Jewish authors
    Duplicate entry is made under Jewish
      literature (Italian)

GEOGRAPHIC SUBDIVISIONS

  — Calabria
    x Calabrian literature

GEOGRAPHIC SUBDIVISIONS

  — Corsica
    sa Corsican literature

GEOGRAPHIC SUBDIVISIONS

  — Liguria
    x Ligurian literature

GEOGRAPHIC SUBDIVISIONS

  — Sicily
    x Sicilian literature
    Sicilian poetry

GEOGRAPHIC SUBDIVISIONS

  — Switzerland
    xx Swiss literature
Italian majolica
    See Majolica, Italian
Italian mosaics
    See Mosaics, Italian
Italian mural painting and decoration
    See Mural painting and decoration, Italian
Italian museum directors
    See Museum directors, Italian
Italian newspapers *(Direct)* *(History,*
PN5241-9)
    sa Italian-American newspapers
Italian opera
    See Opera, Italian
Italian opinion of the United States
    See United States—Foreign opinion, Italian
Italian panel painting
    See Panel painting, Italian
Italian paste
    See Macaroni products
Italian patriotic literature
    See Patriotic literature, Italian
Italian periodicals *(Direct)* *(History,*
PN5241-5250)
    sa Italian-American periodicals
    Example under Romance periodicals
Italian philology *(PC1001-1977)*
Italian poetry *(Direct)* *(Collections,*
PQ4207-4225; History,
PQ4091-4131)
    sa Children's poetry, Italian
    Didactic poetry, Italian
    Elegiac poetry, Italian
    xx Poetry
  — To 1400 *(PQ4094-9)*
    x Dolce stil nuovo
    Sicilian poetry
    Stile nuovo (Italian poetry)
  — 15th century *(PQ4101)*
    sa Strambotto
  — 16th century *(PQ4103)*
  — 17th century *(PQ4105)*
  — 18th century *(PQ4107)*
  — 19th century *(PQ4109)*
  —— Caricatures and cartoons
  — 20th century *(PQ4113)*
Italian portrait sculpture
    See Portrait sculpture, Italian
Italian propaganda
    See Propaganda, Italian
Italian property in Cyrenaica, [the United
States, Tripolitania, etc.]
Italian prose literature *(Direct)*
(Collections, PQ4247-4263; History,
PQ4161-4185)
  — Early to 1700
  — 18th century
  — 19th century
  — 20th century
Italian question, 1849-1870
    See Italy—History—1849-1870

Italian quilting
    See Trapunto
Italian revolutionary literature
    See Revolutionary literature, Italian
Italian romances
    See Romances, Italian
Italian schools
    See Schools, Italian *[for works on Italian*
      schools in foreign countries]
    Schools—Italy *[for works on schools in*
      Italy]
Italian students in the United States, [etc.]
Italian wit and humor *(PN6203-5)*
    Here are entered collections from several
    authors and individual authors who
    have not written in other literary
    forms.
Italian wit and humor, Pictorial
Italian wood-engravings
    See Wood-engravings, Italian
Italians
  — Caricatures and cartoons
Italians in Africa, [Boston, Portugal, etc.]
  — Juvenile literature
  — Religious life
Italians in foreign countries
  — Legal status, laws, etc. *(Direct)*
Italians in the United States
    sa Missions to Italians in the United
      States
    Example under Emigration and immigration
Italic inscriptions
    See Inscriptions, Italic
Italic languages and dialects *(PA2420-2550)*
    sa Etruscan language
    Faliscan language
    Latin language
    Venetic language
    x Dialects
    xx Latin language
Italic type
    See Type and type-founding—Italic type
Italic writing
    See Writing, Italic
Italics
    sa Type and type-founding—Italic type
    xx Type and type-founding—Italic type
Italo-Ethiopian War, 1895-1896 *(DT387.3)*
    sa Adowa, Battle of, 1896
    x Abyssino-Italian War, 1895-1896
    Ethiopian-Italian War, 1895-1896
    Italy—History—War with Ethiopia,
      1895-1896
  — Public opinion *(Direct)*
Italo-Ethiopian War, 1935-1936 *(DT387.8)*
    x Ethiopian-Italian War, 1935-1936
    Italy—History—War with Ethiopia,
      1935-1936
  — Aerial operations
  — Causes
  — Diplomatic history
  — Drama
  — Hospitals, charities, etc.
  — Naval operations
  — Personal narratives
Italo-Turkish War, 1911-1912
    See Turco-Italian War, 1911-1912
Italy
  — Commercial policy
    Example under Commercial policy
  — Diplomatic and consular service
  —— United States
    Note under Diplomatic and consular
      service
  — History *(DG)*
  —— To 476
    sa Aurunci
    Samnites

Iẓhorskiĭ language
  See Ingrian language
Izhortsy
  See Ingrians
Izi language
  x Izzi language
  xx Ibo language
      Kwa languages
İzmir (City)
  — Fire, 1922
      xx Greco-Turkish War, 1921-1922
  — Riot, 1955
Izumo Taisha (Sect)
  x Taishakyo
  xx Shinto sects
Izzi language
  See Izi language
Jaawambe (African people)
  xx Ethnology—Africa, French-speaking
      West
      Fulahs
Jabêm language
  See Jabim language
Jabim language *(PL6251)*
  sa Melanesian languages
  x Jabêm language
      Yabin language
  xx Melanesian languages
Jabo (African people) *(DT630.5.J3)*
Jabo language *(PL8287)*
  x Gweabo language
Jaborandi *(Pharmacy, RS165.J2;*
      Therapeutics, RM666.J15)
Jaca (African people)
  See Bayaka (African people)
Jacalteca Indians *(Guatemala, F1465.2.J3;*
      Mexico, F1221.J3)
  xx Indians of Central America
      Mayas
Jacalteca language *(PM3889)*
  xx Indians of Central America—Languages
      Maya language
Jacaranda wax scale
  x Wax scale, Jacaranda
Jack Cade's Rebellion
  See Cade's Rebellion, 1450
Jack-in-the-box
  xx Toys
Jack-Jack (African people)
  See Alagya (African people)
Jack-o-lanterns
  xx Halloween
      Pumpkin
Jack-pine *(SD397.P575)*
  x Gray pine
  — Diseases and pests
      sa Jack-pine budworm
Jack-pine budworm
  xx Jack-pine—Diseases and pests
Jack-pine warbler
  See Kirtland's warbler
Jack-rabbits *(QL737. R6)*
  sa Black-tailed jack-rabbit
      Hares
  xx Hares
      Rabbits
  — Juvenile literature
Jackals *(QL737.C2)*
Jackass penguin *(QL696.S5)*
  x Blackfooted penguin
      Cape penguin
  xx Penguins
  — Legends and stories
Jackdaw
  — Legends and stories
  — Psychology *(QL785.5.B6)*
Jackets
  See Coats

Jackets, Record
  See Phonorecord jackets
Jacks
  See Lifting-jacks
Jacks, Hydraulic
  See Hydraulic jacks
Jacks (Game)
Jackson-Dickinson Duel
  x Dickinson-Jackson Duel
Jackson Whites *(E184.J)*
  xx Indians of North America—Mixed
      bloods
      Mulattoes
Jackstraws (Game) *(GV1511.J3)*
Jacobean architecture
  See Architecture, Jacobean
Jacobean decoration and ornament
  See Decoration and ornament, Jacobean
Jacobi polynomials
  x Polynomials, Jacobi
  xx Orthogonal polynomials
Jacobi varieties *(QA333)*
  x Varieties, Jacobi
  xx Riemann surfaces
Jacobins (Dominicans)
  See Dominicans
      Dominicans in France
Jacobins *(DC178)*
  x Breton Club
  xx France—History—Revolution,
      1789-1799—Clubs
  Example under Clubs
Jacobite ballads and songs
  See Jacobites—Poetry
Jacobite Expedition, 1707 *(DA814.2)*
Jacobite Rebellion, 1715 *(DA814.3)*
  x Scotland—History—Jacobite Rebellion,
      1715
Jacobite Rebellion, 1719 *(DA814.4)*
Jacobite Rebellion, 1745-1746 *(DA814.5)*
  x Scotland—History—Jacobite Rebellion,
      1745-1746
  — Juvenile literature
Jacobites *(DA813-814)*
  sa Lancashire Plot, 1689-1694
      Nonjurors
  — Poetry *(English poetry, PR1195.H5;*
      Scottish poetry, PR8661.J3)
      x Jacobite ballads and songs
Jacobsen reaction
  x Jacobsen rearrangement
  xx Chemical reactions
Jacobsen rearrangement
  See Jacobsen reaction
Jacobson's organ *(QL947)*
Jacquard knitting machines *(TT685)*
  xx Knitting-machines
  — Automatic control
Jacquard weaving *(TS1500)*
  xx Looms
      Weaving
Jacquemarts
  See Jaquemarts
Jacquerie, 1358 *(DC99.3)*
  sa Peasantry—France
  Example under Peasant uprisings
Jactitation of title *(Direct)*
  xx Land titles
      Possessory actions
Jade *(Indirect)* *(Art industries, NK5750;*
      Mineralogy, QE391.J2)
  x Figurines
      Nephrite
      Statuettes
  — Collectors and collecting *(Direct)*
Jade art objects *(Direct)*
  x Art objects, Jade
      Jades

  — Collectors and collecting *(Direct)*
Jades
  See Jade art objects
Jaffa in literature
Jaffa Riot, 1921 *(DS126)*
Jagane language
  See Yahgan language
Jagataic language *(PL55.J3)*
  x Chagatai language
      Old Uzbek language
      Tschagataj language
      Uzbek language (Old)
      Yagatai language
  xx Turko-Tataric languages
Jagataic literature *(Direct)*
Jagellon dynasty
  sa Poland—History—Jagellons, 1386-1572
  x Yagello dynasty
  xx Poland—History—Jagellons, 1386-1572
Jagga language
  See Chaga language
Jaggas
  See Wachaga
Jaguar automobile *(TL215.J)*
  Example under Sports cars
Jaguars *(QL737.C2)*
Jaguars, Fossil
Jah Hut (Malaysian people)
  xx Ethnology—Malaysia
      Sakai
  — Religion
Jahad
  See Jihad
al-Jahmīyah *(BP195.J3-32)*
  x Djahmiyya
  xx Islamic sects
Jahn-Teller effect
  x Teller-Jahn effect
  xx Coupled mode theory
      Crystal field theory
      Energy levels (Quantum mechanics)
Jahre prize
  x Anders Jahre prize
Jai alai
  See Pelota (Game)
Jail-fever
  See Typhus fever
Jails
  See Prisons
Jaina architecture
  See Architecture, Jaina
Jaina art
  See Art, Jaina
Jaina devotional literature *(Direct)*
  sa Jaina prayers
  x Devotional literature, Jaina
  xx Jaina literature
Jaina ethics *(BJ1290)*
  sa Ahiṃsā
  x Ethics, Jaina
Jaina hymns *(BL1377.3)*
  x Hymns, Jaina
      Jainism—Hymns
Jaina legends
  See Legends, Jaina
Jaina literature *(Direct)* *(BL1315-1317)*
  sa Jaina devotional literature
Jaina logic *(B162.5; Ancient, BC25-26)*
  x Logic, Jaina
  xx Jainism
      Nyaya
      Philosophy, Jaina
Jaina meditations
  x Meditations, Jaina
Jaina monasticism and religious orders
  See Monasticism and religious orders, Jaina
Jaina mysticism
  See Mysticism—Jainism

Jaina philosophy
   See Philosophy, Jaina
Jaina prayers
   x Prayers, Jaina
   xx Jaina devotional literature
Jaina religious practice *(BL1376)*
   sa Religious life (Jainism)
   x Theology, Practical (Jainism)
   xx Jainism
Jaina sculpture
   See Sculpture, Jaina
Jaina sects
   sa Terehpanth (Jaina sect)
   x Sects, Jaina
   xx Jainism
Jaina shrines *(Direct)*
   x Shrines, Jaina
Jaina temples
   See Temples, Jaina
Jaina women
   See Women, Jaina
Jainas
   See Jains
Jainism *(Direct)* *(BL1300-1365)*
   sa Ajivikas
     Architecture, Jaina
     God (Jainism)
     Jaina logic
     Jaina religious practice
     Jaina sects
     Monasticism and religious orders, Jaina
     Mysticism—Jainism
     Prayer (Jainism)
     Soul (Jainism)
     Women in Jainism
   — Hymns
     See Jaina hymns
   — Influence
   — Relations
   — — Buddhism, [etc.]
   — Rituals
   — Sacred books
Jainism in literature
Jains *(BL1300-1365)*
   sa Saraks
   x Jainas
   xx Brahmanism
     Buddha and Buddhism
     Hinduism
     Religions
Jaipurī dialect *(PK2215-2218)*
   xx Rajasthani language
Jakob-Creutzfeldt disease
   x Heidenhain syndrome
     Spastic pseudosclerosis
     Subacute spongiform encephalopathy
   xx Central nervous system—Diseases
Jakri (African people)
   See Jekri (African people)
Jakun (Malayan people)
   xx Ethnology—Malaysia
Jakut language
   See Yakut language
Jalap *(Pharmacy, RS165.J; Therapeutics, RM666.J)*
   x Convolvulin
     Jalapin
Jalapin
   See Jalap
Jalčen
   See Solons (Tungusic tribe)
Jaloof language
   See Wolof language
Jam *(TX612.J3)*
   xx Cookery (Fruit)
   — Standards *(Direct)*
Jamaa Movement
Jamaica

— History *(F1861-1895)*
— — Maroon War, 1795-1796
   xx Maroons
— — Slave Insurrection, 1831
— — Insurrection, 1865
— Hurricane, 1944
Jamaica pepper
   See Allspice
Jamaican literature (English)
   See English literature—Jamaican authors
Jambos
   See Anuaks
James Bond films
   xx Moving-pictures
Jameson's Raid, 1895-1896 *(DT929)*
   xx South African War, 1899-1902
     Transvaal—History—1880-1910
Jamestown weed
   See Datura
Jamming (Radio)
   See Radio—Interference
Jamunda Indians
   See Uaboi Indians
Jangstēn language
   See Thādo language
Janissaries
   See Janizaries
Janitors *(Direct)* *(TX339)*
   sa Charwomen and cleaners
     Sacristans
     School custodians
     Sextons
   x Building superintendents
     Custodian-engineers
     Custodians
     Superintendents of buildings and
       grounds
   xx Building-service employees
     Charwomen and cleaners
   — Collective labor agreements
     See Collective labor agreements—
       Janitors
Janizaries *(Turkish army, UA816; Turkish history, DR448)*
   x Janissaries
Jankau, Battle of, 1645 *(D267.J)*
   xx Thirty Years' War, 1618-1648
Jansenists *(BX4720-4735)*
   sa Convulsionaries
     Fareinistes
     Old Catholic Church
   — Catechisms and creeds
Jansonists *(BX7990.J3)*
   xx Collective settlements
     Communism
Japan
— Civilization
— — Occidental influences
     Note under Civilization
— Emperors
   sa Jinshin Revolt, 672
     Kokutai
   x Japan—Kings and rulers
     Japanese emperors
   xx Emperors
— — Cultus
     See Emperor worship, Japanese
— — Protection
— — Public opinion
— — Tombs
— — Visits *(Direct)*
   xx Royal visitors
     Visits of state
— Empresses
   x Empresses, Japanese
     Japan—Kings and rulers
     Japanese empresses
— Foreign relations

— — United States
     Note under United States—Foreign
       relations—Canada, [France, Ja-
       pan, etc.]
— History *(DS801-897)*
     Example under reference from Shogunate
— — To 645
     sa Na no Kuni
— — — Anecdotes, facetiae, satire, etc.
— — — Historiography
— — — Pictorial works
— — To 1333
— — To 1868
     sa Korea—History—Japanese
       invasions, 1592-1598
       United States Naval Expedition to
       Japan, 1852-1854
— — — Pictorial works
— — Taika period, 645-649
     x Taika reforms
— — 645-794
     sa Jinshin Revolt, 672
— — — Historiography
— — Heian period, 794-1185
     sa Hōgen Insurrection, 1156
— — — Historiography
— — Tengyō Revolt, 938-940
     x Masakado's Revolt, 938-940
       Taira Masakado Revolt, 938-940
       Tengyō Revolt, 938-940
       Tenkei Revolt, 938-940
— — Earlier Nine Years' War, 1051-1062
     (DS854)
— — Gempei Wars, 1180-1185
     x Gempei Wars, 1180-1185
— — — Anecdotes
— — Kamakura period, 1185-1333
     sa Japan—History—Attempted
       Mongol invasions, 1274-1281
     x Kamakura shogunate
— — 1185-1868
— — — Anecdotes, facetiae, satire, etc.
— — Attempted Mongol invasions,
     1274-1281
     xx Japan—History—Kamakura
       period, 1185-1333
— — — Pictorial works
— — 1333-1600
     sa Ashikaga Shogunate
       Ōnin War, 1467-1477
— — — Anecdotes, facetiae, satire, etc.
— — — Juvenile literature
— — Period of northern and southern courts
     (Yoshino period), 1336-1392
     (DS864.5)
— — Period of civil wars, 1480-1603
     (DS868)
     sa Kawanakajima War, 1553-1564
— — — Anecdotes, facetiae, satire, etc.
— — Azuchi-Momoyama period, 1568-1603
     sa Shizugatake, Battle of, 1583
— — Tokugawa period, 1600-1868
     sa Forty-seven Rōnin
       Osaka—Siege, 1614-1615
       Sekigahara, Battle of, 1600
       Shimabara Uprising, 1637-1638
— — — Anecdotes, facetiae, satire, etc.
— — — Historiography
— — Akō Vendetta, 1702
     xx Forty-seven Rōnin
— — 1787-1868
— — Restoration, 1853-1870
     sa Ee ja nai ka Uprising, 1867
       Ikuno Uprising, 1863
       Mito, Japan (Fief)—History
       Wadaryō, Battle of, 1864
     x Meiji Restoration
— — — Anecdotes, facetiae, satire, etc.

— — — Historiography
— — — Juvenile literature
— — Civil War, 1868
    sa Hakodate, Battle of, 1868-1869
    x Boshin War, 1868
— — — Personal narratives
— — — Pictorial works
— — Meiji period, 1868-1912
    sa Hagi Rebellion, 1876
      Kabasan Uprising, 1884
      Saga Rebellion, 1874
      Satsuma Rebellion, 1877
      Shimpūren Rebellion, 1876
— — — Anecdotes, facetiae, satire, etc.
— — — Centennial celebrations, etc.
— — — Juvenile literature
— — — Pictorial works
— — War with China, 1894-1895
    See Chinese-Japanese War,
      1894-1895
— — 20th century
    sa Korea—History—Chōsen,
      1910-1945
— — — Caricatures and cartoons
— — War with Russia, 1904-1905
    See Russo-Japanese War,
      1904-1905
— — Taishō period, 1912-1926
    x Taishō period, 1912-1926
— — — Pictorial works
— — 1912-1945
    sa Sino-Japanese Conflict, 1937-1945
    xx Sino-Japanese Conflict, 1937-1945
— — Shōwa period, 1926-
    x Shōwa period, 1926-
— — March Incident, 1931
    x March Incident, 1931 (Japan)
— — February 26 Incident, 1936
    x February 26 Incident, 1936
      Japan—History—Nī-nīroku jiken,
      1936
      Nī-nīroku jiken, 1936
— — — Personal narratives
— — Nī-nīroku jiken, 1936
    See Japan—History—February 26
      Incident, 1936
— — 1945-
— — — Anecdotes, facetiae, satire, etc.
— — — Juvenile literature
— — — Pictorial works
— — Allied occupation, 1945-1952
— — 1952-
— Kings and rulers
    See Japan—Emperors
      Japan—Empresses
— Relations (general) with the United States
    Note under United States—Relations
      (general) with Canada, ₍France, Ja-
      pan, etc.₎
Japan clover
  See Lespedeza
Japan Current
  See Kuroshio
Japan Expedition of the American Squadron,
    1852-1854
  See United States Naval Expedition to
    Japan, 1852-1854
Japan gold-size *(TP937.7)*
  xx Carriage and wagon painting
    Varnish and varnishing
Japan in art
Japan in literature
Japanese *(DS830)*
— Origin
Japanese architecture
  See Architecture, Japanese
Japanese associations, institutions, etc.
  See Associations, institutions, etc., Japanese

Japanese ballads and songs
  sa Enkyoku
    Katōbushi
    Kouta
    Shigin
    Sōka
Japanese beetle *(QL596.S3; Insect pests,*
    SB945.J3)
  x Popillia japonica
  xx Beetles
— Control
  See Japanese beetle control
Japanese beetle control *(Indirect)*
    (SB945.J3)
  x Japanese beetle—Control
— Biological control *(Indirect)* *(SB945.J3)*
Japanese block-books
  See Block-books, Japanese
Japanese bronzes
  See Bronzes, Japanese
Japanese Buddhist stories
  See Buddhist stories, Japanese
Japanese cherry
  See Japanese flowering cherry
Japanese chess
  See Shogi
Japanese-Chinese Conflict, 1937-1945
  See Sino-Japanese Conflict, 1937-1945
Japanese-Chinese War, 1894-1895
  See Chinese-Japanese War, 1894-1895
Japanese chins (Dogs)
  See Japanese spaniels
Japanese cloisonné
  See Cloisonné, Japanese
Japanese courtesans
  See Courtesans, Japanese
Japanese cultus
  See Cultus, Japanese
Japanese deer
  See Sika deer
Japanese diaries *(Collections, PL771)*
Japanese drama *(Collections in European*
    languages, PL887-8; History in
    European languages, PL871;
    Japanese, PL734-5, PL771-7)
  sa Jōruri
    Kabuki plays
    Kōwaka plays
    Kyōgen plays
    Nō plays
Japanese emperor worship
  See Emperor worship, Japanese
Japanese emperors
  See Japan—Emperors
Japanese empresses
  See Japan—Empresses
Japanese encephalitis
  x Encephalitis Type B
  xx Encephalitis, Epidemic
Japanese encephalitis vaccine *(QR189.5.E5)*
Japanese epigrams
  See Epigrams, Japanese
Japanese fan painting
  See Fan painting, Japanese
Japanese fan paintings
  See Fan paintings, Japanese
Japanese fencing
  See Kendo
Japanese fiction *(Collections in European*
    languages, PL890; History in
    European languages, PL873;
    Japanese, PL736-740, PL781-2)
— Heian period, 794-1185
— Edo period, 1600-1868
— 19th century
— 1868-
Japanese flower arrangement
  See Flower arrangement, Japanese

Japanese flowering cherry *(SB435)*
  x Cherry, Japanese
    Japanese cherry
  xx Flowering cherries
Japanese folk-lore
  See Folk-lore, Japanese
Japanese gardens
  See Gardens, Japanese
Japanese imprints *(Direct)*
— Publishing
Japanese in California, ₍**Taiwan, the United**
    States, etc.₎
— Biography
— Economic conditions
— Education
— Juvenile literature
— Legal status, laws, etc.
— Personal narratives
— Pictorial works
— Portraits
— Religious life
Japanese in foreign countries
— Biography
— Employment
— Legal status, laws, etc.
— Salaries, pensions, etc.
Japanese in San Francisco
  xx Aliens
  Example under Emigration and immigration
Japanese in the United States
  sa Missions to Japanese in the United
    States
  x Nisei
  xx Deportation
— Race identity
  xx Race awareness
Japanese incense ceremony *(GT3032)*
  x Incense-burning parties, Japanese
    Incense ceremonies, Japanese
    Incense-smelling parties, Japanese
Japanese industrial engineers
  See Industrial engineers, Japanese
Japanese lacquer and lacquering
  See Lacquer and lacquering, Japanese
Japanese language *(PL501-700)*
  sa Ryukyu language
— Ability testing *(LB1577.J3)*
— Epithets *(PL659)*
  x Makurakotoba
— Punctuation
  sa Kunten
— Study and teaching *(Direct)*
Japanese larch
  xx Larch
Japanese letters *(Direct)*
Japanese literature *(Direct)* *(PL701-898)*
  sa Haikai
    Kibyoshi-bon
— To 794 *(Collections, PL755.1; History,*
    PL726.1)
— To 1600
— To 1868
— Heian period, 794-1185
— — Pictorial works
— 1185-1600
— Edo period, 1600-1868
— 1868-
— Meiji period, 1868-1912
— 20th century
  sa Shirakaba School
— Taishō period, 1912-1926

    GENERAL SUBDIVISIONS

— Cataloging
  See Cataloging of Japanese literature

    GENERAL SUBDIVISIONS

— Korean authors

Japanese literature *(Direct) (PL701-898)*
  (Continued)
  — Zen authors
      x Gozan literature
      xx Zen literature
Japanese literature (Chinese)
  See Chinese literature—Japanese authors
Japanese literature (English) *(PR9900.J)*
      Duplicate entry is made under English
        literature—Japanese authors (or Eng-
        lish poetry—Japanese authors)
      Notes under English literature—Japanese au-
        thors; English poetry—Japanese au-
        thors
Japanese macaque *(QL737.P93)*
      xx Macaques
          Monkeys
Japanese medlar
  See Loquat
Japanese messianism
  See Messianism, Japanese
Japanese morning glory
      x White-edge morning glory
      xx Morning-glories
Japanese newspapers *(PN5401-9)*
  — Circulation
  — Illustrations
Japanese newspapers in foreign countries
Japanese paper folding
  See Origami
Japanese periodicals *(PN5401-5410)*
  — Anecdotes, facetiae, satire, etc.
Japanese philology *(PL501-699)*
Japanese poetry *(Direct) (Collections in
        European languages, PL884-6;
        History in European languages,
        PL867-870; Japanese, PL717-720,
        PL756-770)*
      sa Epigrams, Japanese
          Haikai
          Haiku
          Renku
          Ryukyu poetry
          Senryu
          Shigin
          Waka
Japanese poetry (Chinese)
  See Chinese poetry—Japanese authors
Japanese political posters
  See Political posters, Japanese
Japanese polo
  See Polo, Japanese
Japanese pottery
  See Pottery, Japanese
Japanese printmakers
  See Printmakers, Japanese
Japanese prints
  See Prints, Japanese
Japanese property in foreign countries
Japanese property in Korea, ₍Manchuria, etc.₎
      xx Alien property—Korea, ₍Manchuria,
          etc.₎
Japanese quail
      xx Quails
  — Anatomy
      Example under Birds—Anatomy
Japanese quail as laboratory animals
      (SF407.J3)
Japanese reference books
  See Reference books, Japanese
Japanese river fever
  See Tsutsugamushi disease
Japanese rock gardens
  See Rock gardens, Japanese
Japanese-Russian Border Conflicts, 1932-1941
  See Russo-Japanese Border Conflicts,
        1932-1941
Japanese-Russian War, 1904-1905
  See Russo-Japanese War, 1904-1905

Japanese satire
  See Satire, Japanese
Japanese screen painting
  See Screen painting, Japanese
Japanese screen paintings
  See Screen paintings, Japanese
Japanese scrolls
  See Scrolls, Japanese
Japanese serow *(QL737.U53)*
      x Formosa serow
Japanese spaniels
      x Chins, Japanese (Dogs)
          Japanese chins (Dogs)
      xx Spaniels
Japanese students in foreign countries
Japanese students in the United States, ₍etc.₎
Japanese studies *(Direct)*
      sa Japanologists
      xx Area studies
Japanese sword guards
  See Sword guards, Japanese
Japanese tea ceremony *(GT2910)*
      sa Chashitsu (Japanese tearooms)
      x Cha-no-yu
          Tea ceremony, Japanese
      xx Drinking customs
          Tea
  — History
  — — Anecdotes, facetiae, satire, etc.
  — Pictorial works
  — Utensils *(GT2915)*
      sa Raku pottery
      xx Pottery, Japanese
Japanese wit and humor *(Direct)*
      Here are entered collections from several
        authors and individual authors who
        have not written in other literary
        forms.
      sa Kyōka
          Rakugo
Japanese wit and humor, Pictorial
Japanese women's writings
  See Women's writings, Japanese
Japanese wrestling
  See Sumo
Japanning *(TP942)*
      sa Metals—Finishing
          Tole painting
          Varnish and varnishing
      xx Lacquer and lacquering
          Varnish and varnishing
Japanologists
      xx Japanese studies
          Scholars
Japp-Klingemann reaction
      xx Chemical reactions
Jaqai
      xx Ethnology—New Guinea
Jaqaru language
  See Cauqui dialect
Jaquemarts
      x Jacquemarts
      xx Bells
          Church architecture
          Tower-clocks
Jarabe (Dance) *(GV1796.J)*
      x Jarave (Dance)
Jarai
      x Djarai
      xx Ethnology—Vietnam
Jarai language *(PL4498.J3)*
      xx Malayan languages
          Mon-Khmer languages
Jarave (Dance)
  See Jarabe (Dance)
Jarchas
  See Muwashshah

Jarecoune Indians
  See Arecuna Indians
Jargons
  See Languages, Mixed
Jaricuna Indians
  See Arecuna Indians
Jarosławice, Battle of, 1914
      xx European War, 1914-1918—Campaigns
          —Eastern
Jarot language
  See Jarut language
Jars, Apothecary
  See Apothecary jars
Jarut language
      x Jarot language
      xx Mongolian languages
Jaryas
  See Muwashshah
Jasper *(QE391.J)*
Jasperoid *(Indirect) (QE475.J3)*
      x Limestone quartzite
          Silicified limestone
      xx Limestone
          Quartz
Jass (Game) *(GV1295.J3)*
      sa Penuchle (Game)
Jassen
  See Jazyge
Jassidae
  See Leaf-hoppers
Jassy, Battle of, 1944
      x Kishinev, Battle of, 1944
      xx World War, 1939-1945—Campaigns—
          Romania
Jat caste
  See Jats
Jatavs *(DS432.J25)*
      xx Caste—India
          Untouchables
Jaṭkī language
  See Lahndi language
JATO
  See Aeroplanes—Assisted take-off
Jats
      x Jat caste
      xx Caste—India
          Ethnology—India
Jatu dialect
  See Bangaru dialect
Jatvingi
  See Yatvyags
Jaunde language
  See Ewondo language
Jaundice *(RC851; Infants, RJ276)*
      sa Kernicterus
      x Icterus (Pathology)
      xx Bilious diseases and biliousness
Jaundice, Spirochaetal
  See Weil's disease
Java gum disease
  See Leaf scald of sugar-cane
Java Sea, Battle of the, 1942 *(D774.J)*
      xx World War, 1939-1945—Naval
          operations
Javanese
Javanese ballads and songs *(Direct)*
Javanese drama *(Collections, PL5177;
        History, PL5173)*
      sa Ludruk plays
          Wayang plays
Javanese in Sumatra, ₍Surinam, etc.₎
Javanese intelligence
  See Intelligence levels—Javanese
Javanese language *(PL5161-9)*
      sa Balinese language
          Malayan languages
          Sassak language
      xx Malayan languages

954

— Old Javanese
  See Kawi language
Javanese literature *(PL5170-5189)*
Javanese newspapers *(PN5449.J3)*
Javelin automobile
Javelin throwing *(GV1093)*
  xx Track-athletics
Javelinas
  See Peccaries
Jaw bone, Musical *(ML1040)*
  x Musical jaw bone
Jaw joint
  See Temporomandibular joint
Jawa motorcycle
Jawboning
  See Wage-price policy
Jawi alphabet *(PL5052)*
  x Malay alphabet
  xx Alphabet
    Arabic alphabet
    Malayan languages—Alphabet
Jaws *(Comparative anatomy, QL821; Human anatomy, QM105; Physiology, QP311)*
  sa Mandible
    Mandibular condyle
    Mastication
    Maxilla
    Micrognathia
    Prognathism
    Temporomandibular joint
  xx Craniology
    Head
    Mouth
    Skull
— Abnormities and deformities *(RD763)*
— Biopsy
— Cancer
— Diseases *(RC936)*
  sa Jaws—Radiography
— Fracture *(RD526)*
— Necrosis *(Phosphorus poisoning, RA1231.P5)*
  x Phossy jaw
  xx Phosphorus—Toxicology
  Example under Necrosis
— Radiography
  xx Jaws—Diseases
— Surgery *(RD526)*
— Tumors *(RC280.J; RD661)*
  sa Odontogenic cysts
    Odontogenic tumors
— Wounds and injuries
Jayhawk *(GR830)*
Jays *(QL696.P2)*
  sa Blue jay
    Steller's jay
  x Cyanocitta
— Behavior
Jay's treaty, 1794 *(E314)*
Jaywick, Operation
  See Operation Jaywick
Jazyge
  x Jassen
  xx Alani
    Ethnology—Hungary
Jazz dance
  xx Dancing
Jazz emsembles
  sa Suites (String quartet with jazz emsemble)
Jazz ensemble with chamber orchestra *(M1040-1041)*
  sa Concertos (Jazz ensemble with chamber orchestra)
    Monologues with music (Jazz ensemble with chamber orchestra)
  xx Chamber-orchestra music

Concertos (Jazz ensemble with chamber orchestra)
Jazz ensembles
— Scores *(M1040)*
Jazz ensemble with orchestra *(M1040-1041)*
  sa Concertos (Jazz ensemble)
  xx Concertos (Jazz ensemble)
    Jazz ensembles
Jazz ensembles *(M900-949; M960-985)*
    Here are entered single jazz compositions for ten or more solo instruments, also collections of jazz compositions for any number or combination of solo instruments.
  sa Choruses, Sacred (Mixed voices) with jazz ensemble
    Clarinet with jazz ensemble
    Concertos (Clarinet with jazz ensemble)
    Concertos (Jazz ensemble)
    Concertos (Jazz ensemble with chamber orchestra)
    Concertos (Percussion with jazz ensemble)
    Dance-orchestra music
    Jazz ensemble with chamber orchestra
    Jazz ensemble with orchestra
    Monologues with music (Jazz ensemble)
    Percussion with jazz ensemble
    Piano with jazz ensemble
    Suites (Jazz ensemble)
  x Ensembles (Music)
  xx Dance-orchestra music
Jazz music *(Indirect)* *(ML3561)*
  sa Blues (Songs, etc.)
    Instrumentation and orchestration (Dance orchestra)
    Ragtime music
    Jazz quintets, Jazz septets, *and similar headings; and various headings for instrumental music followed by the qualifying adjective* (Jazz), *e.g.* Piano music (Jazz); *also subdivisions* Methods (Jazz) *and* Studies and exercises (Jazz) *under names of instruments or groups of instruments, e.g.* Saxophone—Studies and exercises (Jazz); Wind instruments—Methods (Jazz)
  x Be bop music
    Bebop music
    Soul music
    Swing music
  xx Dance music—History and criticism
    Music
    Music—History and criticism—20th century
— Interpretation (Phrasing, dynamics, etc.) *(MT75)*
— Juvenile literature *(ML3930)*
— Pictorial works
— Terminology *(ML108)*
Jazz musicians
  xx Musicians
— Biography
— Correspondence, reminiscences, etc.
  See Musicians—Correspondence, reminiscences, etc.
— Juvenile literature
— Portraits
  See Musicians—Portraits
Jazz nonets
  xx Instrumental music
Jazz octet with orchestra *(M1040-1041)*
  sa Concertos (Jazz octet)
    Jazz octets
  xx Concertos (Jazz octet)
    Jazz octets

Orchestral music
Jazz octets
  sa Concertos (Jazz octet)
    Jazz octet with orchestra
  xx Concertos (Jazz octet)
    Jazz octet with orchestra
Jazz quartet with orchestra *(M1040-1041)*
  sa Concertos (Jazz quartet)
  xx Concertos (Jazz quartet)
    Jazz quartets
    Orchestral music
Jazz quartets
  sa Concertos (Jazz quartet)
    Jazz quartet with orchestra
  xx Instrumental music
    Quartets (Piano, percussion, vibraphone, double bass)
Jazz quintet with orchestra *(M1040-1041)*
  sa Concertos (Jazz quintet)
  xx Concertos (Jazz quintet)
    Jazz quintets
Jazz quintets
  sa Concertos (Jazz quintet)
    Jazz quintet with orchestra
  xx Instrumental music
    Jazz music
Jazz septets
  xx Instrumental music
    Jazz music
Jazz sextets
  xx Instrumental music
Jazz trio with orchestra *(M1040-1041)*
  sa Concertos (Jazz trio)
  xx Concertos (Jazz trio)
    Jazz trios
    Orchestral music
Jazz trios
  sa Concertos (Jazz trio)
    Jazz trio with orchestra
    Suites (Jazz trio)
  xx Instrumental music
Jealousy *(Psychology, BF575.J4)*
  sa Envy
  xx Emotions
    Envy
— Poetry
Jealousy (Child psychology)
  xx Child study
— Juvenile literature
Jealousy of God
  See God—Jealousy
Jeans (Clothing)
  x Blue jeans
    Levis
  xx Clothing and dress
    Denim
    Overalls
    Trousers
    Work clothes
Jebel Mūsa, Syria, Defense of, 1915 *(D568.6)*
  xx European War, 1914-1918—Campaigns—Turkey and the Near East
Jeep automobile
  x Jeep vehicle
    Willys jeep
  xx Automobiles, Military
    Motor-trucks
    Tractors
Jeep vehicle
  See Jeep automobile
Jeffrey pine
Jehad
  See Jihad
Jehovah, Day of
  See Day of Jehovah
Jehovah, Servant of
  See Servant of Jehovah

Jeji dialect
  See Fon dialect
Jejunostomy
  sa Esophagojejunostomy
  xx Jejunum—Surgery
Jejunum
  xx Intestine, Small
  — Surgery
    sa Jejunostomy
Jekri (African people)
  x Itsekiri (African people)
    Jakri (African people)
  xx Ethnology—Nigeria
  — Juvenile literature
Jelly *(TX612.J4)*
  xx Cookery
    Cookery (Fruit)
Jellyfish
  See Medusae
Jemez Indians *(E99.J4)*
  xx Indians of North America
    Pueblo Indians
    Tanoan Indians
Jemmapes, Battle of, 1792 *(DC222.J3)*
  xx France—History—Revolution, 1792
Jen *(B127.J4)*
  x In
    Jin
  xx Philosophy, Confucian
Jena, Battle of, 1806 *(DC230.J4)*
Jena glass *(QC375)*
  xx Glass
Jena in art
Jena plan *(LB1029.J)*
  xx Education—Experimental methods
    Vocational education
Jenkins' Ear, War of
  See Anglo-Spanish War, 1739-1748
Jenkins process
  See Front-screen projection
Jenny (Training planes)
  See JN-4D (Training planes)
Jeopardy, Double
  See Double jeopardy
Jequirity *(Pharmacy, RS165.J; Therapeutics,
    RH666.J)*
Jerboas *(QL737.R6)*
  xx Mice
Jerky
  See Beef, Dried
Jersey cattle *(SF199.J5; Herd-books,
    SF193.J5)*
  xx Dairy cattle
Jersey pine
  See Scrub-pine
Jerusalem
  — History
  — — Latin kingdom, 1099-1244
        (D175-195)
      sa Ḥiṭṭīn, Battle of, 1187
      x Latin kingdom of Jerusalem
      xx Crusades
        Latin Orient
  — Siege, 70 A.D. *(DS122.8)*
      sa Jews—History—Rebellion, 66-73
  — Siege, 586 B.C.
  — Siege, 701 B.C.
      xx Jews—History—953-586 B.C.
  — Siege, 1948
      xx Israel-Arab War, 1948-1949
        Palestine—History—1929-1948
Jerusalem. Temple
  sa Tabernacle
  Example under Architecture, Jewish; Archi-
    tecture, Oriental
  — Symbolism
      See Temple of God

Jerusalem artichoke *(SB211.J)*
  x Topinambur
  xx Artichokes
Jerusalem in Islam
  xx Islam
    Palestine in Islam
Jerusalem in literature
  sa Jerusalem in the Bible
    Jerusalem in the Midrash
Jerusalem in the Bible
  xx Bible—Theology
    Jerusalem in literature
    Religion and geography
Jerusalem in the Midrash *(BM518.J4)*
  xx Jerusalem in literature
    Midrash
Jesness inventory
  xx Criminal behavior, Prediction of
    Personality tests
Jest-books
  See Chap-books
    Wit and humor
Jesters
  See Fools and jesters
Jests
  See Wit and humor
Jesuats *(BX3760.J)*
Jesuit architecture
  See Architecture, Jesuit
Jesuit art
  See Art, Jesuit
Jesuit drama
  xx Drama
Jesuit drama, French, ₍etc.₎ *(Direct)*
  x French ₍etc.₎ Jesuit drama
  xx French ₍etc.₎ drama
Jesuit War, 1754-1756 (South America)
  See Seven Reductions, War of the,
    1754-1756
Jesuits *(BX3701-3755; Women, BX4371-4)*
  sa Bollandists
  x Jesus, Society of
    Society of Jesus
  xx Counter-Reformation
    Monasticism and religious orders
  — Bio-bibliography *(Z7840.J5)*
  — Biography *(BX3755)*
  — Controversial literature
  — Dictionaries
  — Education *(LC493)*
      Example under Education
  — History *(BX3706-3749)*
  — Missions *(BV2290)*
      sa Catholic Church—Missions
      xx Indians of North America—Missions
      Example under Missions; Monasticism
        and religious orders—Missions
  — Portraits
  — Spiritual life *(BX3703)*
      Example under Monastic and religious
        life
Jesuits' bark
  See Cinchona
Jesuits in Brazil
  — Occupations
      Example under Monasticism and reli-
        gious orders—Occupations
Jesuits in England, ₍France, Maryland, etc.₎
  — Heraldry
Jesuits in literature
Jesuits in Paraguay *(BX3714.P2; F2684)*
  sa Seven Reductions, War of the,
    1754-1756
  xx Seven Reductions, War of the,
    1754-1756
Jesus, Society of
  See Jesuits

Jesus Christ *(BT198-590)*
  sa Antichrist
    Atonement
    Christianity
    Crosses
    Incarnation
    Logos
    Lord's Supper
    Mercersburg theology
    Messiah
    Millennium
    Redemption
    Salvation
    Second Advent
    Trinity
  x Christ
    Christology
  xx Christianity
    God
    Theology, Doctrinal
    Trinity
  — Addresses, essays, lectures
  — Anthroposophical interpretations
  — Apparitions and miracles (Modern)
      (BT580)
      xx Apparitions
  — Appearances *(BT490)*
      Here are entered works dealing with
        the appearances of Jesus Christ
        after His resurrection.
      sa Theophanies
      xx Jesus Christ—Forty days
        Jesus Christ—Resurrection
        Theophanies
  — Appreciation
  — Art *(N8050-8054)*
      sa Bible—Picture Bibles
        Bible—Pictures, illustrations, etc.
        Christian art and symbolism
        Fish (in religion, folk-lore, etc.)
        Icons
        Jesus Christ—Iconography
        Lord's Supper—Art
        Magi—Art
        Mary, Virgin—Art
      x Jesus Christ in art
        Jesus Christ—Nativity—Art
        Jesus Christ—Passion—Art
        Jesus Christ—Pictures, illustrations,
          etc.
      xx God—Art
        Mary, Virgin—Art
      Example under Bible—Pictures, illustra-
        tions, etc.; Christian art and sym-
        bolism
  — Ascension *(BT500)*
      sa Ascension Day
      x Ascension of Christ
  — — History of doctrines *(BT500)*
  — Atonement
      See Atonement
  — Attitude towards Jewish dietary laws
      xx Jews—Dietary laws
  — Attitude towards the Old Testament
      xx Jesus Christ—Knowledge and
        learning
  — Attitude towards women *(BT590.W6)*
      xx Woman (Theology)—Biblical
        teaching
  — Baptism *(BT350)*
  — Beatitudes
      See Beatitudes
  — Betrayal *(BT435)*
      x Betrayal of Christ
      xx Jesus Christ—Biography—Passion
        Week
        Jesus Christ—Passion
  — Biography *(BT298-500)*

sa Mysteries of the Rosary
x Jesus Christ—Life
—— Apocryphal and legendary literature
(BT520)
xx Christian literature, Early
——— Juvenile literature
—— Devotional literature (BT306.28-5)
—— Drama
See Jesus Christ—Drama
—— Early life (BT310-330)
sa Jesus Christ—Childhood
Jesus Christ—Flight into Egypt
——— Juvenile literature
See Jesus Christ—Childhood—
Juvenile literature
—— Early works to 1800 (BT300)
—— History and criticism (BT303)
—— Juvenile literature (BT302)
—— Meditations
—— Passion Week (BT414)
sa Jesus Christ—Betrayal
Jesus Christ—Passion
xx Jesus Christ—Passion
——— Juvenile literature
—— Public life (BT340-500)
—— Sources
sa Jesus Christ—Historicity
xx Jesus Christ—Historicity
—— Sources, Biblical (BT298-9)
Here are entered works purporting
to give a life of Jesus Christ in the
words of the four Gospels, har-
monized into a continuous nar-
rative.
—— Sources, Jewish (BT305)
xx Christianity and other religions—
Judaism
— Birth
See Jesus Christ—Nativity
— Blessing of children
— Brethren (BT313)
sa Jesus Christ—Family
Mary, Virgin—Virginity
x Brethren of Jesus
Brothers of Jesus
Jesus Christ—Brothers
xx Apostles
Jesus Christ—Family
Mary, Virgin—Virginity
— Brothers
See Jesus Christ—Brethren
— Buddhist interpretations
x Jesus Christ in Buddhism
Jesus Christ—Interpretations,
Buddhist
xx Christianity and other religions—
Buddhism
— Burial (BT460)
x Jesus Christ—Descent from the cross
— Cartoons, satire, etc.
— Character (BT304)
x Jesus Christ—Personality
—— Juvenile literature
— Childhood (BT320-325)
sa Holy Childhood, Devotion to
xx Jesus Christ—Biography—Early life
—— Juvenile literature
x Jesus Christ—Biography—Early
life—Juvenile literature
Jesus Christ—Juvenile literature
— Chronology (BT303)
— Cleansing of the Temple
— Commandments
See Summary of the Law (Theology)
— Conflicts (BT303)
Here are entered works dealing with
the controversies which Jesus
Christ had with His opponents.

— Cross
See Holy Cross
Jesus Christ—Crucifixion
— Crucifixion (BT450-455)
sa Five Sacred Wounds
Holy Cross
x Crucifixion of Christ
Jesus Christ—Cross
—— Art
—— Role of Jews
See Jesus Christ—Passion—Role of
Jews
— Cultus (Direct)
sa Precious Blood, Devotion to
Sacred Heart, Devotion to
— Descent from the cross
See Jesus Christ—Burial
— Descent into hell (BT470)
— Devotional literature
— Divinity (BT214-215)
sa Arianism
Socinianism
Trinity
Unitarianism
x Divinity of Christ
Humanitarianism (Religion)
xx Arianism
Jesus Christ—Natures
Socinianism
Unitarianism
— Drama (BT555)
sa Christmas plays
Easter—Drama
Passion-plays
x Jesus Christ—Biography—Drama
Jesus Christ—Nativity—Drama
Jesus Christ—Passion—Drama
xx Religion in literature
— Education (BT330)
— Entry into Jerusalem (BT415)
sa Palm Sunday
xx Palm Sunday
— Ethics (BS2417.E8)
sa Summary of the Law (Theology)
xx Christian ethics
— Evangelistic methods (BT590.E8)
xx Evangelistic work
— Exaltation (BT200-201)
— Example (BT304.2)
Here are entered works dealing with
Jesus Christ as an example or pat-
tern to be followed.
x Imitation of Jesus Christ
—— Biblical teaching
— Family (BT313)
sa Jesus Christ—Brethren
x Family, Holy
Holy Family
xx Jesus Christ—Brethren
— Fiction (BT560)
xx Religion in literature
— Flight into Egypt (BP315)
x Flight into Egypt
xx Jesus Christ—Biography—Early life
— Forty days (BT485)
Here are entered works descriptive of
the forty days between the resurrec-
tion and the ascension.
sa Jesus Christ—Appearances
— Forty days in the wilderness
See Jesus Christ—Temptation
— Foundation of the church
See Church—Foundation
— Friends and associates (BS2430-2520)
— Genealogy (BT314)
xx Bible—Genealogy
— Hindu interpretations
x Jesus Christ in Hinduism

Jesus Christ—Interpretations, Hindu
xx Christianity and other religions—
Hinduism
— Historicity (BT303)
sa Jesus Christ—Biography—Sources
xx Jesus Christ—Biography—Sources
— History of doctrines (BT198)
sa Antiochian school
Example under Theology, Doctrinal—
History
—— Early church, ca. 30-600
x Jesus Christ—Interpretations,
New Testament
Jesus Christ—New Testament
interpretations
—— Middle Ages, 600-1500
—— 16th century
—— 17th century
—— 18th century
—— 19th century
— Holy Coat
See Holy Coat
— Holy Shroud
See Holy Shroud
— Humanity (BT218)
sa Precious Blood, Devotion to
xx Jesus Christ—Natures
— Humiliation (BT220)
— Humor
x Jesus Christ—Wit and humor
xx Religion and humor
— Iconography (BT590.I)
xx Jesus Christ—Art
— Incarnation
See Incarnation
— Influence (BT303)
— Intellectual life (BT590.I6)
— Intercession (BT255)
xx Mediator (Theology)
— Interpretations, Buddhist
See Jesus Christ—Buddhist
interpretations
— Interpretations, Hindu
See Jesus Christ—Hindu
interpretations
— Interpretations, Islamic
See Jesus Christ—Islamic
interpretations
— Interpretations, Jewish
See Jesus Christ—Jewish
interpretations
— Interpretations, Negro
See Jesus Christ—Negro
interpretations
— Interpretations, New Testament
See Jesus Christ—History of doctrines
—Early church, ca. 30-600
— Islamic interpretations (BP172)
sa Jesus Christ—Koranic teaching
x Jesus Christ in Islam
Jesus Christ—Interpretations, Islamic
Jesus Christ—Muslim interpretations
xx Christianity and other religions—
Islam
Islam—Relations—Christianity
—— Juvenile literature
— Jewish interpretations (BM620)
sa Jesus Christ—Passion—Role of Jews
x Jesus Christ—Interpretations, Jewish
xx Judaism
— Journeys (BT590.J7)
— Juvenile literature
See Jesus Christ—Childhood—
Juvenile literature
— Kingdom (BT94)

Jesus Christ *(BT198-590)*
— Kingdom *(BT94) (Continued)*
    Here are entered works dealing with the kingdom of Jesus Christ as represented by His followers. Works treating of Jesus as king are entered under Jesus Christ—Royal office. Works treating of the kingdom of Jesus as being a part of the kingdom of God, or being the same as the Kingdom of God, are entered under Kingdom of God.
    sa Jesus Christ—Mystical body
    xx Jesus Christ—Mystical body
        Jesus Christ—Royal office
        Kingdom of God
— Kingship
    See Jesus Christ—Royal Office
— Knowableness *(BT205)*
    x Jesus Christ, Knowledge of
        Knowableness of Jesus Christ
        Knowledge of Jesus Christ
    xx Knowledge, Theory of (Religion)
— Knowledge and learning *(BT590.K6)*
    sa Jesus Christ—Attitude towards the Old Testament
— Koranic teaching *(BP134.J37)*
    xx Jesus Christ—Islamic interpretations
— Language *(BT590.L3)*
    Here are entered works dealing with the problem of the language used by Jesus Christ, specifically whether He spoke Hebrew, Aramaic, or Greek.
— Last Supper
    See Last Supper
— Last words
    See Jesus Christ—Seven last words
— Life
    See Jesus Christ—Biography
— Logos doctrine
    See Logos
— Lord's prayer
    See Lord's prayer
— Lord's Supper
    See Lord's Supper
— Meditations
— Messiahship *(BT230-240)*
    sa Messiah
    Note under Messiah
— Miracles *(BT364-5)*
    sa names of miracles, e.g. Healing of the man born blind (Miracle); Healing of the nobleman's son (Miracle)
    x Bible—Miracles
    xx Miracles
— Miscellanea *(BT295; Occult, BT308)*
— Mormon interpretations
    xx Mormons and Mormonism
— Music
    See Jesus Christ in music
— Muslim interpretations
    See Jesus Christ—Islamic interpretations
— Mystical body
    sa Church—Foundation
        Communion of saints
        Jesus Christ—Kingdom
        Mystical union
        Priesthood, Universal
    x Mystical body of Christ
    xx Church
        Immanence of God
        Jesus Christ—Kingdom
        Jesus Christ—Primacy
    Note under Mystical union
— — History of doctrines

— Name *(BT590.N2)*
    sa Holy Name, Devotion to
        Servant of Jehovah
        Son of God
        Son of Man
    x Jesus Christ—Titles
        Jesus prayer
    xx Bible—Names
    Example under Names, Personal
— — Juvenile literature
— — Meditations
— — Sermons
— — — Outlines
— Nativity *(BT315)*
    sa Christmas
        Epiphany
        Holy Innocents, Massacre of the
        Star of Bethlehem
        Virgin birth
    x Jesus Christ—Birth
        Nativity of Christ
    xx Christmas
— — Art
    See Jesus Christ—Art
— — Drama
    See Jesus Christ—Drama
— — Sermons
    See Christmas sermons
— Natures
    sa Hypostatic union
        Jesus Christ—Divinity
        Jesus Christ—Humanity
    xx Hypostatic union
— Negro interpretations
    x Jesus Christ—Interpretations, Negro
    xx Negroes—Religion
— New Testament interpretations
    See Jesus Christ—History of doctrines —Early church, ca. 30-600
— New Thought interpretations *(BT304.92)*
    xx New Thought
— Oriental interpretations *(BT304.94)*
— Parables *(BT373-8)*
    sa names of parables, e.g. Good Samaritan (Parable)
    x Parables, Biblical
        Parables, Christian
    xx Bible—Parables
        Parables
— — Meditations
— — Pictures, illustrations, etc. *(N8180)*
    x Jesus Christ—Pictures, illustrations, etc.
— Passion *(BT430-465)*
    sa Holy Hour
        Holy Week
        Jesus Christ—Betrayal
        Jesus Christ—Biography—Passion Week
        Jesus Christ—Relics of the Passion
        Lent
        Paschal mystery
        Precious Blood, Devotion to
        Stations of the Cross
    xx Jesus Christ—Biography—Passion Week
        Suffering of God
— — Art
    See Jesus Christ—Art
— — Drama
    See Jesus Christ—Drama
— — Juvenile literature
— — Manuscripts
— — Meditations
— — Music
    See Passion-music
— — Role of Jews

    x Jesus Christ—Crucifixion—Role of Jews
    xx Jesus Christ—Jewish interpretations
— — Sermons
    Here are entered sermons dealing exclusively with the passion of Jesus Christ.
    sa Good Friday sermons
        Holy-Week sermons
        Lenten sermons
    Note under Lenten sermons
— Person and offices *(BT200-201; BT304)*
    sa Hypostatic union
        Nihilianism
        Subordinationism
— — Early works to 1800
— — Juvenile literature
— — Sermons
— Study *(BT203)*
— Personality
    See Jesus Christ—Character
— Pictures, illustrations, etc.
    See Jesus Christ—Art
    See Jesus Christ—Parables—Pictures, illustrations, etc.
— Poetry *(BT550)*
    xx Religion in literature
        Religion in poetry
— Popular works
— Prayers *(BV229-234)*
    sa Lord's prayer
    xx Bible—Prayers
— Pre-existence *(BT200-201)*
    xx Logos
— Preaching *(BT590.P7)*
— Preaching at Nazareth
    x Jesus Christ—Rejection at Nazareth
— Precious Blood
    See Precious Blood, Relics of the
— Presentation
    sa Candlemas
    xx Candlemas
— — Sermons
— Priesthood *(BT260)*
    xx Atonement
        Priesthood
— Primacy
    sa Jesus Christ—Mystical body
        Jesus Christ—Royal office
        Logos
    x Primacy of Jesus Christ
    xx Creation
— Procession *(BT114)*
    Here are entered works on the eternal procession of God the Son from God the Father.
    x Procession (in the Trinity)
        Trinity—Procession
— Prophecies *(BT370)*
    Here are entered works dealing with prophecies made by Jesus Christ. Works dealing with prophecies concerning Jesus Christ are entered under the heading Messiah—Prophecies.
    xx Bible—Prophecies
    Example under Prophecies
— Prophetic office *(BT252)*
— Psychiatry *(BT590.P8)*
— Psychology *(BT590.P9)*
— Rationalistic interpretations *(BT304.95)*
    xx Christianity—Controversial literature
— Rejection at Nazareth
    See Jesus Christ—Preaching at Nazareth
— Relics of the Passion *(BT465)*
    sa Holy Coat

Holy Cross
Holy Lance
Holy Shroud
Precious Blood, Relics of the
  xx Jesus Christ—Passion
     Relics and reliquaries
— Resurrection (BT480-490)
  sa Easter
     Paschal mystery
  x Resurrection of Christ
  xx Easter
     Resurrection
— — Biblical teaching
— — Juvenile literature
— — Meditations (BT481)
— — Sermons
— Rosicrucian interpretations (BF1623.R7)
  xx Rosicrucians
— Royal office (BT270)
  sa Jesus Christ—Kingdom
  x Jesus Christ—Kingship
  xx Jesus Christ—Primacy
  Note under Jesus Christ—Kingdom
— — History of doctrines
— Sacred Heart, Devotion to
  See Sacred Heart, Devotion to
— Sayings
  See Jesus Christ—Words
— Second Advent
  See Second Advent
— Sending of the twelve (BT360)
  x Mission of the twelve apostles
     Sending of the twelve apostles
  xx Apostles
— Sermon on the mount
  See Sermon on the mount
— Seven last words (BT455-6)
  x Jesus Christ—Last words
     Seven last words
  xx Jesus Christ—Words
— — Drama
— — Sermons
     xx Good Friday sermons
— Significance
— Similitudes (BT590.S5)
— Sinlessness
— Spiritualistic interpretations (BT304.96)
  sa Bible and spiritualism
— Summary of the Law
  See Summary of the Law (Theology)
— Teaching methods (BT590.T5)
  xx Religious education
— Teachings (BS2415-2417)
  x Teachings of Jesus
— Temptation (BT355)
  x Jesus Christ—Forty days in the
     wilderness
— — History of doctrines
— Theosophical interpretations (BT304.97)
  xx Bible and theosophy
     Theosophy
— Titles
  See Jesus Christ—Name
— Tomb
  See Holy Sepulcher
— Transfiguration (BT410)
  x Transfiguration of Christ
— Trial (BT440-445)
— — Apocryphal and legendary literature
  xx Christian literature, Early
— Typology
  See Typology (Theology)
— Wit and humor
  See Jesus Christ—Humor
— Words (BT306)
  sa Jesus Christ—Seven last words
  x Jesus Christ—Sayings
— — Meditations

Jesus Christ in fiction, drama, poetry, etc.
  x Jesus Christ in literature
Jesus Christ in literature
  See Jesus Christ in fiction, drama, poetry,
     etc.
Jesus Christ, Knowledge of
  See Jesus Christ—Knowableness
Jesus Christ in art
  See Jesus Christ—Art
Jesus Christ in Buddhism
  See Jesus Christ—Buddhist interpretations
Jesus Christ in Hinduism
  See Jesus Christ—Hindu interpretations
Jesus Christ in Islam
  See Jesus Christ—Islamic interpretations
Jesus Christ in moving-pictures
  xx Moving-pictures
Jesus Christ in music
  x Jesus Christ—Music
  xx Music
Jesus Christ the King, Feast of (BV64.J4)
  x Christ the King, Feast of
     Feast of Jesus Christ the King
  xx Church year
     Fasts and feasts
Jesus Freaks
  See Jesus People
Jesus Movement
  See Jesus People
Jesus People (Direct) (BV3793)
  sa Children of God (Movement)
  x Jesus Freaks
     Jesus Movement
     Street Christians
  xx Pentecostalism
     Revivals
     Youth—Religious life
— Pictorial works
Jesus prayer
  See Jesus Christ—Name
Jet (Art objects, NK5755)
Jet aeroplanes
  See Jet planes
Jet-assisted take-off (Aircraft)
  See Aeroplanes—Assisted take-off
Jet boat engines
  x Cone propulsion (Boats)
     Hydraulic propulsion
     Marine jet engines
     Marine jet propellers
     Marine jet propulsion
     Water-jet engines
  xx Jet propulsion
     Jet pumps
     Motor-boat engines
Jet boats (VM348.5)
  x Boats, Jet-propelled
     Jet-propelled boats
  xx Motor-boats
Jet bundles (Mathematics) (QA614)
  xx Global analysis (Mathematics)
     Manifolds (Mathematics)
     Vector bundles
Jet engine noise
  See Jet planes—Noise
Jet engine sounds
  See Jet plane sounds
Jet flaps (Aeroplanes)
  xx Air jets
     Flaps (Aeroplanes)
Jet flow
  See Jets—Fluid dynamics
Jet fuel
  See Jet planes—Fuel
Jet helicopters
  xx Helicopters
— Identification marks

Jet mills
  x Fluid energy mills
  xx Milling machinery
Jet nacelles (Aeroplane)
  See Aeroplanes—Nacelles
Jet nozzles
  xx Nozzles
Jet plane noise
  See Jet planes—Noise
Jet plane sounds
  x Jet engine sounds
     Jet planes, Military—Sounds
  xx Aeroplane sounds
     Noise
     Sounds
Jet planes
  sa Avro 707 (Jet planes)
     BAC Lightning (Fighter plane)
     BAC TSR 2 (Turbojet fighter planes)
     Delfin (Training planes)
     Fairey Delta (Jet planes)
     Handley Page 115 (Jet planes)
     Heinkel 162 (Jet fighter planes)
     Hunter (Turbojet fighter planes)
     Jet transports
     Messerschmitt 262 (Fighter planes)
     Meteor (Fighter planes)
     Provost (Training planes)
     T2J (Training planes)
     Vampire (Turbojet fighter planes)
     Victor (Jet planes)
  x Aeroplanes, Jet propelled
     Jet aeroplanes
     Jet propelled aeroplanes
— Design and construction
— Flight testing
— Fuel
  sa Boron as fuel
  x Jet fuel
     Jet propellants
  xx Aeroplanes—Fuel
     Motor fuels
— Juvenile literature
— Motors
  See Aeroplanes—Jet propulsion
     Aeroplanes—Ramjet engines
     Aeroplanes—Turbojet engines
— Noise
  x Aircraft noise
     Jet engine noise
     Jet plane noise
  xx Aerodynamic noise
— Piloting
— Radar equipment
  xx Radar in aeronautics
— Thrust reversers (TL709.5.T5)
  x Thrust reversers (Jet plane)
  xx Aeroplanes—Landing
Jet planes, Military
  sa B-58 bomber
  x Military jets
  xx Aeroplanes, Military
— Maintenance and repair
— Pictorial works (TL685.3)
— Sounds
  See Jet plane sounds
Jet propellants
  See Jet planes—Fuel
Jet propelled aeroplanes
  See Aeroplanes—Jet propulsion
     Jet planes
Jet-propelled boats
  See Jet boats
Jet propelled short take-off and landing aircraft
  See Short take-off and landing aircraft—Jet
     propulsion

Jet propelled vertically rising aeroplanes
  See Vertically rising aeroplanes—Jet
    propulsion
Jet propulsion
  sa Aeroplanes—Jet propulsion
    Jet boat engines
    Rockets (Aeronautics)
    Rockets (Ordnance)
    Short take-off and landing aircraft—Jet
      propulsion
    Vertically rising aeroplanes—Jet
      propulsion
  xx Gas and oil engines
    Rockets (Aeronautics)
  — Juvenile literature
Jet pumps *(TJ901)*
  sa Ejector pumps
    Injectors
    Jet boat engines
    Short take-off and landing aircraft—Jet
      propulsion—Ejectors
    Vertically rising aeroplanes—Jet
      propulsion—Ejectors
  x Momentum pumps
  xx Hydraulic machinery
    Pumping machinery
Jet stream *(QC935)*
  sa Clear air turbulence
  xx Atmosphere, Upper
    Atmospheric circulation
    Meteorology
    Winds
    Winds aloft
Jet transports *(TL685.7)*
  sa Boeing 707 (Jet transports)
    Boeing 720 (Jet transport)
    Boeing 727 (Jet transports)
    Boeing 747 (Jet transports)
    C-5A (Jet transports)
    Caravelle (Jet transports)
    Comet (Jet transports)
    Electra (Turboprop transports)
    Hercules (Turboprop transports)
    Iliushin 62 (Jet transports)
    McDonnell Douglas DC-10 (Jet
      transport)
    Supersonic transport planes
    Tupolev 134 (Jet transport)
  x Jetliners
    Turbine-powered transports
    Turbojet transports
    Turboliners
  xx Jet planes
    Supersonic transport planes
    Transport planes
  — Design and construction
  — Identification marks
  — Juvenile literature
  — Landing
  — Piloting
Jetliners
  See Jet transports
Jetons
  See Jettons
Jets *(Hydraulic engineering, TC173)*
  sa Air jets
    Atomization
    Density currents
    Hydraulics
    Plasma jets
    Spinnerets (Textile machinery)
  xx Atomization
    Capillarity
    Fluids
    Hydraulics
    Hydrodynamics
    Liquids
  — Fluid dynamics *(QA911)*

  sa Coanda effect
  x Jet flow
  xx Gas dynamics
Jets, Plasma
  See Plasma jets
Jettatura
  See Evil eye
Jetties *(TC535)*
  sa Breakwaters
    Sand-bars
    Shore protection
    subdivision Jetties *under names of*
      rivers, e.g. Mississippi River—Jetties
  xx Breakwaters
    Dikes (Engineering)
    Harbors
    Hydraulic structures
    Reclamation of land
    Sea-walls
    Shore protection
  — Terminology
Jettison
  sa Average (Maritime law)
    Salvage
    Ships—Cargo
    Wreck
  xx Average (Maritime law)
    Contracts, Maritime
    Salvage
    Ships—Cargo
    Wreck
Jettons *(CJ5450)*
  sa Tokens
  x Jetons
  xx Numismatics
    Tokens
Jeu de paume, Serment du
  See Tennis Court Oath, June 20, 1789
Jeux floraux
  See Floral games
Jeux-partis *(Old French verse, PQ1323.J4)*
  x Partimen
  xx Provençal poetry
    Troubadours
Jeverland cattle *(Herd-books, SF193.J6)*
  xx Dairy cattle
Jeweled bindings
  See Bookbinding—Jeweled bindings
Jewelers *(Direct) (Art, NK7100-7695;*
    Manufactures, TS720-770; Trade,
    HD9747)
  sa Clock and watch makers
    Trade-unions—Jewelers
  xx Art metal-workers
Jewelers' supplies *(TS760)*
Jewelry *(Direct) (Art industries,*
    NK7100-7695; Manners and
    customs, GT2250-2280;
    Manufacture, TS720-770; Taxation,
    HJ5783)
  sa Bracelets
    Brooches
    Cameos
    Crown jewels
    Ear-rings
    Fibula (Archaeology)
    Gems
    Hall-marks
    Necklaces
    Nose ornaments
    Paste jewelry
    Pendants (Jewelry)
    Pins and needles
    Rings
  x Jewels
  xx Art
    Art industries and trade
    Art metal-work

    Arts and crafts movement
    Costume
    Decoration and ornament
    Gems
    Gold
    Hall-marks
    Silver
  Example under Art objects
  — Catalogs *(NK7399; TS759)*
  — Collectors and collecting
    sa Jewelry as an investment
  — Prices *(Direct)*
    sa Jewelry as an investment
  — Private collections *(NK7303)*
  — Repairing *(TS740)*
    xx Jewelry making
    Example under Repairing
  — Taxation *(Direct)*
    xx Luxuries—Taxation
  — Trade-marks
Jewelry, Ancient *(NK7307)*
  — Juvenile literature
Jewelry, Byzantine, ⌈Chinese, Egyptian,
    Gallo-Roman, etc.⌉ *(Direct)*
  x Byzantine ⌈Chinese, Egyptian,
    Gallo-Roman, etc.⌉ jewelry
Jewelry, Japanese
  sa Magatama
Jewelry, Medieval *(Direct)*
Jewelry, Prehistoric *(Direct)*
  x Prehistoric jewelry
Jewelry, Victorian *(Direct)*
  x Victorian jewelry
Jewelry as an investment
  xx Investments
    Jewelry—Collectors and collecting
    Jewelry—Prices
Jewelry making *(TS740-761)*
  sa Enamel and enameling
    Engraving (Metal-work)
    Goldsmithing
    Jewelry—Repairing
    Silversmithing
  xx Goldsmithing
    Handicraft
    Silversmithing
  — Amateurs' manuals *(TT212)*
  — Juvenile literature
Jewelry trade *(Direct) (HD9747)*
  Example under Display of merchandise
  — Accounting *(HF5686.J6)*
  — Credit guides *(HF5585.J4)*
  — Hygienic aspects
  — Tables and ready-reckoners
  — Vocational guidance
  — — Juvenile literature
Jewels
  See Crown jewels
    Gems
    Insignia
    Jewelry
    Precious stones
Jewish almanacs
  See Almanacs, Jewish
Jewish apologetics
  See Judaism—Apologetic works
Jewish-Arab relations
  sa Arabs in Palestine
    Israel-Arab Border Conflicts, 1949-
    Propaganda, Zionist
  x Arab-Jewish relations
    Palestine problem, 1917-
  xx Arabs in Palestine
  — 1949-1967
    sa Israel-Arab Border Conflicts, 1949-
      Israel-Arab War, 1967-
      Sinai Campaign, 1956

— Caricatures and cartoons
— Moral and religious aspects
Jewish-Arab War, 1948-1949
　　See Israel-Arab War, 1948-1949
Jewish architecture
　　See Architecture, Jewish
Jewish art and symbolism
　　sa Liturgical objects—Judaism
　　　Magen David
　　　Menorah
　　　Symbolism in the Bible
　　　Synagogue art
　　　Temple of God
　　x Jewish symbolism and art
　　xx Art, Jewish
　　　Christian art and symbolism
　　　Symbolism
　　　Symbolism in art
Jewish artists
　　See Artists, Jewish
Jewish asceticism
　　See Asceticism—Judaism
Jewish astronomy
　　See Astronomy, Jewish
Jewish bankers
　　See Banks and banking—Jews
Jewish Bibles
　　See Bible. O.T.—Versions, Jewish
Jewish Biblical criticism
　　See Bible. O.T.—Criticism, interpretation,
　　　etc., Jewish
Jewish calendar
　　See Calendar, Jewish
Jewish cantors
　　See Cantors, Jewish
Jewish capitalists and financiers
　　See Capitalists and financiers—Jews
Jewish chant
　　See Chants (Jewish)
Jewish charities
　　See Jews—Charities
Jewish children
　　sa Religious camps, Jewish
　　x Children, Jewish
　　　Jews—Children
　　xx Children
　— Prayer-books and devotions　*(BM666)*
　　　x Children—Prayer-books and
　　　　devotions, Jewish
　　　　Jewish children—Prayer-books and
　　　　devotions—English
　——— English
　　　　See Jewish children—Prayer-books
　　　　　and devotions
　——— French, ⌈German, Italian, etc.⌉
Jewish children's sermons
　　See Children's sermons, Jewish
Jewish Christian Science
　　See Jewish Science
Jewish Christians　*(BR158)*
　　Here are entered works dealing with
　　　Christians of Jewish antecedence.
　　sa Converts from Judaism
　　　Maranos
　　x Christians, Jewish
　— Early church, ca. 30-600　*(BR195.J8)*
　　　sa Ebionism
　　　xx Church history—Primitive and early
　　　　church, ca. 30-600
　　　　Ebionism
　　　　Elkesaites
Jewish chronology
　　See Chronology, Jewish
Jewish civilization
　　See Jews—Civilization

Jewish community centers
　　See Community centers, Jewish
Jewish converts
　　See Proselytes and proselyting, Jewish
Jewish converts to Christianity
　　See Converts from Judaism
Jewish cosmology
　　See Cosmology, Jewish
Jewish costume
　　See Costume, Jewish
Jewish councils and synods
　　x Councils and synods, Jewish
　　　Jewish synods
　　　Synods, Jewish
　　xx Jews—Politics and government
Jewish courts
　　See Courts, Jewish
Jewish creeds
　　See Creeds, Jewish
Jewish criminals
　　x Jews as criminals
　　　Jews—Crime
　　xx Crime and criminals
Jewish cultus
　　See Cultus, Jewish
Jewish Day of Atonement
　　See Yom Kippur
Jewish deeds
　　See Deeds, Jewish
Jewish devotional calendars
　　x Devotional calendars, Jewish
　　　Devotional calendars—Judaism
Jewish devotional literature
　　sa Jews—Prayer-books and devotions
　　x Devotional literature, Jewish
Jewish drama
　　sa Hebrew drama
　　　Yiddish drama
Jewish engravings
　　See Engravings, Jewish
Jewish ethics
　　See Ethics, Jewish
Jewish etiquette
　　sa Synagogue etiquette
　　　Table etiquette, Jewish
　　x Etiquette, Jewish
　　xx Ethics, Jewish
Jewish families
　　xx Family
Jewish fasts and feasts
　　See Fasts and feasts—Judaism
Jewish festival-day sermons
　　See Festival-day sermons, Jewish
Jewish fiction
Jewish fiction (American)
　　See American fiction—Jewish authors
Jewish folk-lore
　　See Folk-lore—Jews
　　　Jews in folk-lore
Jewish folk-songs
　　See Folk-songs, Jewish
Jewish funeral rites and ceremonies
　　See Funeral rites and ceremonies, Jewish
Jewish heresies and heretics
　　See Heresies and heretics, Jewish
Jewish historians
　　See Historians, Jewish
Jewish holidays
　　See Fasts and feasts—Judaism
Jewish holocaust (1939-1945)
　　See Holocaust, Jewish (1939-1945)
Jewish homiletics
　　See Preaching, Jewish
Jewish hygiene
　　See Hygiene, Jewish
Jewish hymns
　　See Hymns, Hebrew
　　　Hymns, Yiddish

　　Jews—Hymns
Jewish illumination of books and manuscripts
　　See Illumination of books and manuscripts,
　　　Jewish
Jewish intelligence
　　See Intelligence levels—Jews
Jewish language
　　See Hebrew language
　　　Yiddish language
Jewish law
　　sa Commandments (Judaism)
　　　Commandments, Six hundred and
　　　　thirteen
　　　Commandments, Ten
　　　Courts, Jewish
　　　Equality before the law—Biblical
　　　　teaching
　　　Ḥazakah
　　　Jews—Dietary laws
　　　Mamzer
　　　Responsa
　　　Revelation on Sinai
　　　Sabbath legislation
　　　Sabbatical year (Judaism)
　　　Semikhah
　　　*special legal headings with Jewish law
　　　　added in parentheses, e.g.* Aliens
　　　　(Jewish law), Contracts (Jewish law),
　　　　Larceny (Jewish law), Torts (Jewish
　　　　law)
　　x Bible—Law
　　　Biblical law
　　　Civil law (Jewish law)
　　　Halacha
　　　Halakha
　　　Hebrew law
　　　Jews—Law
　　　Law, Hebrew
　　　Law in the Bible
　　　Law, Jewish
　　　Law—Jews
　　　Law, Mosaic
　　　Mosaic law
　　xx Law, Oriental
　　　Law, Semitic
　　Note under Bible and law
　— Interpretation and construction
　　　sa Eruv
　— Juvenile literature
　— Language
　　　xx Law—Language
　— Literary history
　　　Example under Jurisprudence—History;
　　　　Legal literature—History and criti-
　　　　cism
　— Philosophy
　— Popular works

　— Palestine
　　　Here are entered works dealing with
　　　　that part of Jewish law operative
　　　　only in Palestine.

　—— Cases
　　　Note under Responsa
Jewish law and technology
　　See Technology and Jewish law
Jewish lawyers
　　See Lawyers, Jewish
Jewish learning and scholarship　*(Direct)*
　　(DS113)
　　sa Jews as scientists
　　　Jews—Intellectual life
　　　Kallah
　　　Talmudic academies
　　x Jews—Learning and scholarship

Jewish learning and scholarship *(Direct)*
   (DS113) (Continued)
   Learning and scholarship—Jews
   xx Jews—Intellectual life
   — Juvenile literature
Jewish legends
  See Legends, Jewish
Jewish Legion *(D568.7)*
   xx European War, 1914-1918—Campaigns
    —Turkey and the Near East—
    Palestine
   European War, 1914-1918—Jews
Jewish letters
Jewish libraries *(Z675.J4)*
  x Hebrew libraries
   Libraries, Hebrew
   Libraries, Jewish
Jewish literature *(Direct)*
  sa Apocalyptic literature
   Bible
   Cabala
   Folk literature—Jews
   Geonic literature
   Hebrew literature
   Midrash
   Proverbs, Jewish
   Rabbinical literature
   Religious literature, Jewish
   Talmud
   Yiddish literature
  x Jews—Literature
   Judaica
  xx Hebrew literature
Jewish literature (American)
  See American literature—Jewish authors
Jewish literature (Arabic)
   Duplicate entry is made under Arabic lit-
   erature—Jewish authors.
  Note under Arabic literature—Jewish authors
Jewish literature (Dutch)
  See Dutch literature—Jewish authors
Jewish literature (English)
   Duplicate entry is made under English
   literature—Jewish authors.
  Note under English literature—Jewish authors
Jewish literature (Ethiopic)
Jewish literature (French)
  See French literature—Jewish authors
Jewish literature (German)
  See German literature—Jewish authors
Jewish literature (Hellenistic) *(Collections,*
  PA3421.G8)
   Duplicate entry is made under Greek lit-
   erature—Jewish authors.
  Note under Greek literature—Jewish authors
Jewish literature (Italian)
   Duplicate entry is made under Italian lit-
   erature—Jewish authors.
  Note under Italian literature—Jewish authors
Jewish literature (Portuguese) *(PQ9025.J4)*
   Duplicate entry is made under Por-
   tuguese literature—Jewish authors.
  Note under Portuguese literature—Jewish au-
   thors
Jewish literature (Spanish) *(PQ6056)*
   Duplicate entry is made under Spanish
   literature—Jewish authors.
  Note under Spanish literature—Jewish authors
Jewish liturgical music
  See Synagogue music
Jewish magic
  See Magic, Jewish
Jewish marriage customs and rites
  See Marriage customs and rites, Jewish
Jewish medals
  See Medals, Jewish
Jewish medicine
  See Medicine, Jewish

Jewish merchants
  See Merchants, Jewish
Jewish migrations
  See Jews—Migrations
Jewish music
  See Music, Jewish
   Music—Jews
Jewish musicians
  See Musicians, Jewish
Jewish-Negro relations
  See Negro-Jewish relations
Jewish New Year
  See Rosh ha-Shanah
Jewish newspapers *(Direct)*
  sa Hebrew newspapers
   Yiddish newspapers
  x Jews—Newspapers
Jewish parables
  See Parables, Jewish
Jewish Pentecost
  See Shavu'oth (Feast of Weeks)
Jewish periodicals *(Direct)*
  xx Jews—Periodicals
Jewish philosophy
  See Philosophy, Jewish
Jewish poetry *(Direct)*
  sa Badḥanim
   Hebrew poetry
Jewish poetry (Arabic)
  See Arabic poetry—Jewish authors
Jewish poetry (Spanish)
  See Spanish poetry—Jewish authors
Jewish prayers
  sa Prayer (Judaism)
  x Prayers, Jewish
  xx Jews. Liturgy and ritual
   Prayer (Judaism)
Jewish prayers for rain
  See Prayers for rain, Jewish
Jewish preaching
  See Preaching, Jewish
Jewish property in Austria, ₍Italy, the
  Czechoslovak Republic, etc.₎
Jewish proselytes and proselyting
  See Proselytes and proselyting, Jewish
Jewish proverbs
  See Proverbs, Jewish
Jewish question *(DS141-151)*
  sa Antisemitism
   Jews—Economic conditions
   Jews—Employment
   Jews—Legal status, laws, etc.
   Marriage, Mixed
   Refugees, Jewish
   Zionism
  xx Zionism
  Note under Jews—Political and social condi-
   tions
Jewish question (1948-)
Jewish quotations
  See Quotations, Jewish
Jewish rabbis
  See Rabbis
Jewish refugees
  See Refugees, Jewish
Jewish religious education of preschool
  children
  See Religious education of preschool
   children, Jewish
Jewish religious functionaries
  See Judaism—Functionaries
Jewish-Roman War, 66-73
  See Jews—History—Rebellion, 66-73
Jewish-Roman Wars, 168 B.C.-135 A.D.
  See Jews—History—168 B.C.-135 A.D.
Jewish scholarships
  See Jews—Scholarships, fellowships, etc.

Jewish schools
  See Schools, Jewish
Jewish Science *(BM729.J4)*
   Here are entered works dealing with a
   movement that, negatively, seeks to
   counteract Christian Science with a
   Jewish counterpart and, positively, re-
   veals to the Jew the sources of health,
   serenity, and peace of mind within his
   own faith.
  x Christian Science, Jewish
   Jewish Christian Science
   Science, Jewish
  xx Christian Science
   Faith-cure
   Mental healing
  Note under Judaism
Jewish scientists
  See Scientists, Jewish
Jewish sculpture
  See Sculpture, Jewish
Jewish sects *(BM175)*
  sa Conservative Judaism
   Essenes
   Hasidism
   Heresies and heretics, Jewish
   Karaites
   Orthodox Judaism
   Pharisees
   Qumran community
   Reconstructionist Judaism
   Reform Judaism
   Sabbathaians
   Sadducees
   Zadokites
   Zealots (Jewish party)
  x Jews—Sects
   Sects, Jewish
Jewish sermons for children
  See Children's sermons, Jewish
Jewish shrines
  x Shrines, Jewish
Jewish sociology
  See Sociology, Jewish
Jewish students
  See Students, Jewish
Jewish studies *(Direct)*
  sa Folk-lore—Jews—Research
Jewish symbolism and art
  See Jewish art and symbolism
Jewish synods
  See Jewish councils and synods
Jewish table etiquette
  See Table etiquette, Jewish
Jewish teachers
  x Teachers, Jewish
Jewish theological seminaries
  See Rabbinical seminaries
Jewish theology *(BM600)*
   Here are entered systematic works on the
   doctrines and dogmas of the Jewish
   religion. Works dealing with Jewish
   faith and practice are entered under
   the heading Judaism.
  sa Bible. O.T.—Criticism, interpretation,
   etc., Jewish
   Creeds, Jewish
   Judaism
   Revelation on Sinai
   Samaritan theology
   Talmud—Theology
  special headings with Jewish theology
   added in parentheses, e.g. Freedom
   (Jewish theology)
  x Theology, Jewish
  Note under Judaism
Jewish war-songs
  See War-songs, Jewish

Jewish way of life *(BM723)*
    sa Family—Religious life (Judaism)
        Students, Jewish—Religious life
        Women, Jewish—Religious life
    x Life, Jewish way of
        Religious life (Judaism)
        Way of life, Jewish
    xx Ethics, Jewish
        Jews—Rites and ceremonies
        Jews—Social life and customs
        Sociology, Jewish
— Stories *(BM723)*
Jewish wit and humor *(PN6231.J5)*
    sa Hebrew wit and humor
        Israeli wit and humor
        Purim parodies
        Schlemiel in literature
    xx Hebrew wit and humor
Jewish wit and humor, Pictorial
Jewish women
    See Women, Jewish
Jewish youth
    See Youth, Jewish
Jews *(DS101-151; Anthropology, GN547)*
    sa Anglo-Israelism
        Ashkenazim
        Benjamin (Tribe of Israel)
        Falashas
        Israelis
        Kemants
        Missions to Jews
        Naphtali (Tribe of Israel)
        Patriarchs (Bible)
        Prophets
        Sephardim
        Youth, Jewish
        headings beginning with the word
        Jewish
    x Hebrews
        Israelites
        Judaica
    xx Christianity
        Judaism
    Example under Semites
— Anecdotes, facetiae, satire, etc.
    sa Rabbis—Anecdotes, facetiae, satire,
        etc.
    Example under Ethnic wit and humor
— Anthropometry
    x Anthropometry—Jews
— Antiquities *(DS111)*
    sa Ark of the Covenant
        Bible—Antiquities
        Brazen serpent
        Breastplate of the High Priest
        Dancing (in religion, folk-lore, etc.)
        Ephod
        Fringes (Jewish cultus)
        Hanukkah lamp
        Menorah
        Numismatics—Jews
        Phylacteries
        Priests, Jewish—Vestments
        Tabernacle
    xx Bible—Antiquities
— Apologetic works
    See Judaism—Apologetic works
— Bio-bibliography *(Hebrew and Yiddish,*
    Z7070)
— Biography *(Collective, DS115)*
    sa Artists ₍Musicians, Scientists, etc.₎,
        Jewish
        Jews in Brooklyn, ₍Germany, etc.₎—
        Biography
        Pseudo-Messiahs
        Rabbis
        Women, Jewish
    x Judaism—Biography

    xx Rabbis
— Cabala
    See Cabala
— Charities *(HV3191-2)*
    sa Jews in Africa, ₍Germany, Poland,
        etc.₎—Charities
        Orphans and orphan-asylums—Jews
    x Jewish charities
— Children
    See Jewish children
— Chosen people
    See Jews—Election, Doctrine of
— Civil rights
    See Jews—Legal status, laws, etc.
— Civilization *(DS112-113)*
    sa Civilization, Medieval—Jewish
        influences
    x Civilization, Jewish
        Jewish civilization
    xx Civilization, Semitic
— — Arab influences
    xx Civilization, Arab
— Clothing and dress
    See Costume, Jewish
— Colonization *(Direct)*
    xx Agricultural colonies
— Commerce *(Ancient, HF369)*
— Conversion to Christianity *(BV4922)*
    Here are entered works dealing
    theoretically with the conversion of
    Jews to Christianity.
    xx Conversion
— Converts to Christianity
    See Converts from Judaism
— Courts
    See Courts, Jewish
    See Rabbinical courts
— Craniology *(GN130.J4)*
    x Craniology—Jews
— Crime
    See Jewish criminals
— Customs
    See Jews—Social life and customs
— Dancing
    See Dancing—Jews
— Diaspora
    Here are entered works dealing with
    the dispersion of the Jewish people
    beyond the confines of Palestine,
    together with a description of life,
    attitude and outlook in their new
    surroundings.
    sa Israel and the Diaspora
        Jews—Migrations
        Proselytes and proselyting, Jewish
    x Diaspora of the Jews
        Dispersion of the Jews
        Galuth
        Jews—Dispersion
        Jews in foreign countries
    xx Jews—Migrations
        Jews—Political and social conditions
        Jews—Restoration
        Man—Migrations
        Minorities
— Dictionaries and encyclopedias
    (DS102.8)
    sa Judaism—Dictionaries
    xx Judaism—Dictionaries
    Note under Encyclopedias and dictionar-
    ies; *and under reference from* Dic-
    tionaries
— — Juvenile literature
— Dietary laws *(BM710)*
    sa Jesus Christ—Attitude towards
        Jewish dietary laws
        Kosher restaurants
        Meat inspection (Jewish law)

        Passover (Jewish law)
        Slaughtering and slaughter-houses—
        Jews
        Wine and wine making (Judaism)
    x Dietary laws, Jewish
        Kasher food
        Kashruth, Laws of
        Kosher food
    xx Cookery, Jewish
        Diet
        Jewish law
— Directories
— Dispersion
    See Jews—Diaspora
— Divorce
    See Divorce (Jewish law)
— Doctrine of election
    See Jews—Election, Doctrine of
— Economic conditions
    xx Jewish question
        Jews—Political and social conditions
— Education *(Ancient, LA47; Modern,*
    LC701-775)
    sa Heder
        Jews in Africa, ₍Germany, Poland,
        etc.₎—Education
        Jews—Scholarships, fellowships, etc.
        Religious education, Jewish
        Schools, Jewish
        Students, Jewish
        Talmud Torahs
    x Judaism—Education
— Election, Doctrine of *(BM613)*
    x Chosen people (Jews)
        Election of Israel
        Israel, Election of
        Jews—Chosen people
        Jews—Doctrine of election
        Jews—Mission
    xx Election (Theology)
        Judaism—Relations
        Nationalism and religion
        People of God
— Emigration and immigration
    See Jews—Migrations
— Employment
    x Jews—Occupations
    xx Jewish question
— Ethics
    See Ethics, Jewish
— Exodus
    See Exodus, The
— Fasts and feasts
    See Fasts and feasts—Judaism
— Festivals
    See Fasts and feasts—Judaism
— Folk-lore
    See Folk-lore—Jews
— Funeral rites and ceremonies
    See Funeral rites and ceremonies,
        Jewish
— Genealogy *(CS3010)*
— History *(DS101-135)*
— — To 1200 B.C.
    sa Exodus, The
        Pharoah's army (in religion,
        folk-lore, etc.)
— — To 953 B.C.
— — To 586 B.C.
    sa Treaties in the Bible
        Twelve tribes of Israel
— — To 70 A.D.
    xx Judaism—History—To 70 A.D.
        Palestine—History—To 70 A.D.
— — — Juvenile literature
— — 1200 B.C.-953 B.C.
— — 953-586 B.C. *(DS121)*
    sa Jerusalem—Siege, 701 B.C.

Jews (DS101-151; Anthropology, GN547)
— History (DS101-135) (Continued)
— — Babylonian captivity, 598-515 B.C.
    x Babylonian captivity, Jewish
      Babylonian exile, Jewish
    xx Jews in Babylonia
— — 586 B.C.-70 A.D.
    sa Maccabees
— — 168 B.C.-135 A.D. (DS122)
    x Jewish-Roman Wars, 168
      B.C.-135 A.D.
      Roman-Jewish Wars, 168
      B.C.-135 A.D.
— — — Miscellanea
— — Rebellion, 66-73
    x Jewish-Roman War, 66-73
      Roman-Jewish War, 66-73
    xx Jerusalem—Siege, 70 A.D.
— — — Juvenile literature
— — 70-
— — 70-1789 (DS124)
— — 1789-1945
— — 1945-

      GENERAL SUBDIVISIONS

— — Chronology
    sa Chronology, Jewish
    xx Chronology, Jewish

      GENERAL SUBDIVISIONS

— — Juvenile literature
    x Jews—History, Juvenile

      GENERAL SUBDIVISIONS

— — Pictorial works
— — Study and teaching (Direct)
— History, Juvenile
    See Jews—History—Juvenile literature
— Hygiene
    See Hygiene, Jewish
— Hymns (BM679)
    sa Hymns, Hebrew
      Hymns, Yiddish
      Piyutim
    x Hymns, Jewish
      Jewish hymns
    xx Hymns, Hebrew
      Hymns, Yiddish
      Music—Jews
      Synagogue music
— Intellectual life
    sa Jewish learning and scholarship
    xx Jewish learning and scholarship
    Example under Intellectual life; Intellec-
      tuals
— Intelligence
    See Intelligence levels—Jews
— Kings and rulers
    sa Kings and rulers—Biblical teaching
— Labor and laboring classes
    See Labor and laboring classes—Jews
— Languages
    sa Arabic language—Dialects—
      Judeo-Arabic
      Hebrew language
      Italian language—Dialects—
      Judeo-Italian
      Judeo-Persian language
      Karaitic dialects
      Yiddish language
— Law
    See Jewish law
    See Jews—Legal status, laws, etc.
— Learning and scholarship
    See Jewish learning and scholarship
— Legal status, laws, etc. (Direct)
    sa Restitution and indemnification
      claims (1933-   )

headings beginning Jews in . . . e.g.
    Jews in Barcelona, [Bulgaria, etc.]
  x Jews—Civil rights
    Jews—Law
    Law—Jews
    Refugees, Jewish—Legal status, laws,
      etc.
  xx Civil rights
    Jewish question
    Jews—Persecutions
  Notes under Jews—Segregation; Race
    discrimination
— — Germany
    x Nuremberg laws
— Legends
    See Legends, Jewish
— Literature
    See Hebrew literature
    See Jewish literature
— Lost tribes
    See Lost tribes of Israel
— Marriage
    See Marriage—Jews
— Medicine
    See Medicine, Jewish
    See Physicians, Jewish
— Mental illness
    See Mental illness—Jews
— Migrations
    sa Jews—Diaspora
      Refugees, Jewish
    x Jewish migrations
      Jews—Emigration and immigration
      Migrations, Jewish
    xx Jews—Diaspora
      Migrations of nations
      Refugees, Jewish
— Mission
    See Jews—Election, Doctrine of
— Missions
    See Proselytes and proselyting, Jewish
— Music
    See Music—Jews
— Name (BM7292.N)
    sa Israel—Name
    xx Bible—Names
    Example under Names
— Nationalism
    See Nationalism—Jews
— Newspapers
    See Jewish newspapers
— Nobility
— Numismatics
    See Numismatics—Jews
— Occupations
    See Jews—Employment
— Origin (GN547)
    sa Habiru
— Periodicals (AP91-93; Historical, DS101,
    DS133; United States, E184.J5)
    sa Jewish periodicals
— Persecutions
    sa Blood accusation
      Holocaust, Jewish (1939-1945)
      Jews—Legal status, laws, etc.
      Refugees, Jewish
      Siedlce, Poland—Massacre, 1906
      World War, 1939-1945—Jews—
      Rescue
    xx Antisemitism
      Persecution
      Political atrocities
— Philosophy
    See Philosophy, Jewish
— Political and social conditions
    (DS111-135; Early economic
    conditions, HC35; Early social
    conditions, HN10.H4)

Here are entered works relating to
questions affecting the social and
political life of the Jews themselves
in contradistinction to the heading
Jewish question which is used for
works on the relation of Jews to
non-Jews in general and in continental Europe in particular.
    sa Jews—Diaspora
      Jews—Economic conditions
      Jews in Africa, [Germany, Poland,
      etc.]—Political and social
      conditions
      Jews—Segregation
      Zionism
    x Jews—Social conditions
    xx Zionism
— — To 70 A.D. (DS112)
    Note under Sociology, Biblical
— — 1948-
— Politics and government (Ancient, JC67)
    sa Jewish councils and synods
      Zealots (Jewish party)
— Prayer-books and devotions (Devotional
    works, BM724; Prayer and service
    books, BM665-9)
    sa Women, Jewish—Prayer-books and
      devotions
    x Judaism—Devotional exercises
    xx Jewish devotional literature
— — English, [French, German, etc.]
— Priests
    See Priests, Jewish
— Psychology
— Public opinion
    Here are entered works dealing with
    public opinion about Jews. Works
    on public opinion of Jews are en-
    tered under Public opinion—Jews.
    x Judaism—Public opinion
— Radicalism
    See Radicalism—Jews
— Recreation
— Relations with Negroes
    See Negro-Jewish relations
— Religion
    See Judaism
— Religious education
    See Religious education, Jewish
— Rescue, 1939-1945
    See World War, 1939-1945—Jews—
      Rescue
— Restoration (BS649.J5)
    Here are entered works dealing with
    the belief—whether held by Jews or
    by Christians—that, in fulfillment
    of Biblical prophecy, the Jews
    would some day return to Palestine,
    and thereby also meet a require-
    ment for the realization of eschato-
    logical expectations.
    sa Jews—Diaspora
      Messianic era (Judaism)
      Zionism
    xx Zionism
— Rites and ceremonies (Direct)
    (BM700-720)
    sa Bar mitzvah
      Cohanim
      Confirmation (Jewish rite)
      Fringes (Jewish cultus)
      Funeral rites and ceremonies, Jewish
      Hanukkah lamp
      Hospitality (Judaism)
      Jewish way of life
      Jews in Africa, [Germany, Poland,
      etc.]—Rites and ceremonies
      Marriage customs and rites, Jewish

Menorah
Mikveh
Redemption of the first-born
Reform Judaism—Ceremonies and
practices
Slaughtering and slaughter-houses—
Jews
x Judaism—Ceremonies and practices
Judaism—Rituals
Minhagim
Rites and ceremonies—Jews
—— Juvenile literature
— Ritual
See Jews. Liturgy and ritual
See Jews—Social life and customs
— Scholarships, fellowships, etc. (Direct)
x Jewish scholarships
xx Jews—Education
— Sects
See Jewish sects
— Segregation
Works on the history and policy of seg-
regation within a particular country
or geographical area are entered un-
der the heading Jews in [locality],
e.g. Jews in Poland. Legal material
is entered under the heading Jews—
Legal status, laws, etc.
x Ghettos
xx Antisemitism
Discrimination in housing
Jews—Political and social conditions
— Sex customs
See Sex customs—Jews
— Social conditions
See Jews—Political and social
conditions
— Social life and customs (DS112-113)
sa Community centers, Jewish
Excommunication (Jewish law)
Jewish way of life
Sex customs—Jews
x Customs, Social
Jews—Customs
Jews—Ritual
Social customs
xx Manners and customs
—— Juvenile literature
— Societies, etc. (DS101; HS2226-2230;
United States, E184.J5)
sa Young Men's Hebrew Association
x Jews in the United States—Societies,
etc.
— Statistics, Vital
— Ten lost tribes
See Lost tribes of Israel
— Territorialism
sa Zionism
x Territorialism (Jewish movement)
xx Zionism
— Tithes
See Tithes—Jews
— Women
See Women, Jewish
— Yearbooks (DS101; England, DS135.E5;
United States, E184.J5)
— Zionism
See Zionism
Jews. Liturgy and ritual (BM660-675)
sa Amen (Liturgy)
Chants (Jewish)
Cultus, Jewish
Jewish prayers
Marriage service (Judaism)
Piyutim
Religious poetry, Hebrew
Synagogue music
Worship (Judaism)

x Jews—Ritual
Judaism—Liturgy and ritual
xx Cultus, Jewish
Music—Jews
Synagogue music
— Juvenile literature
Jews. Liturgy and ritual. Day of
Atonement prayers
sa Synagogue music—Day of Atonement
services
Jews. Liturgy and ritual. Festival prayers
sa Synagogue music—Festival services
Three Festivals
Jews. Liturgy and ritual. High Holy Day
prayers
sa Synagogue music—High Holy Day
services
Jews. Liturgy and ritual. Memorial services
sa Synagogue music—Memorial services
Jews. Liturgy and ritual. New-Year prayers
sa Synagogue music—New-Year services
Jews. Liturgy and ritual. Passover prayers
sa Synagogue music—Passover services
Jews. Liturgy and ritual. Sabbath prayers
sa Synagogue music—Sabbath services
Jews. Liturgy and ritual. Seli hot
sa Synagogue music—Seli hot services
Jews Liturgy and ritual. Seliḥot
sa Synagogue music—Seliḥot services
Jews. Liturgy and ritual. Synagogue
dedication services
See Synagogue dedication services
Jews, Kurdish, [Yemenite, etc.]
x Kurdish [Yemenite, etc.] Jews
Jews, Negro
See Negro Jews
Jews, Russian
x Russian Jews
xx Jews in the United States
Jews, Sephardic
See Sephardim
Jews and alcohol
See Alcohol and Jews
Jews and Freemasons
See Freemasons and Jews
Jews as criminals
See Jewish criminals
Jews as educators
See Educators, Jewish
Jews as engineers
See Engineers, Jewish
Jews as farmers
Jews as lawyers
See Lawyers, Jewish
Jews as scientists (Q128)
Works on the attainments of Jews as
scientists are entered here. Works
mainly biographical are entered under
the heading Scientists, Jewish.
xx Jewish learning and scholarship
Jews as seamen
x Seamen, Jewish
xx Seamen
Jews as soldiers
sa Cantonists
subdivision Jews under names of wars,
e.g. World War, 1939-1945—Jews
xx Soldiers
Jews as statesmen
See Statesmen, Jewish
Jews in Africa, [Germany, Poland, etc.]
sa Israel and the Diaspora
— Anecdotes, facetiae, satire, etc.
— Caricatures and cartoons
— Charities
xx Jews—Charities
— Education (LC741-750)
xx Jews—Education

— Juvenile literature
— Legal status, laws, etc.
— Persecutions
—— Public opinion
— Pictorial works
— Pictures, illustrations, etc.
— Political activity
xx Politics, Practical
— Political and social conditions
xx Jews—Political and social conditions
— Registers
— Rites and ceremonies
xx Jews—Rites and ceremonies
Jews in art (N7415)
Jews in Babylonia
sa Jews—History—Babylonian captivity,
598-515 B.C.
Jews in Barcelona
Example under Jews—Legal status, laws, etc.
Jews in Brooklyn
— Biography
xx Jews—Biography
Jews in Bulgaria
Example under Jews—Legal status, laws, etc.
Jews in England
See Jews in Great Britain
Jews in folk-lore
sa Folk-lore—Jews
Wandering Jew
x Folk-lore of Jews
Jewish folk-lore
xx Folk-lore—Jews
Jews in foreign countries
See Jews—Diaspora
Jews in Germany
— Biography
xx Jews—Biography
National socialism
— History
—— To 1096
—— 1096-1800
—— 1800-1933
—— 1933-1945
—— 1945-
— Pictorial works
Jews in Great Britain
x Jews in England
Jews in literature (English literature,
PR151.J5; German literature,
PT149.J4)
sa Holocaust, Jewish (1939-1945), in
literature
Jews in the Koran
Judaism in literature
Schlemiel in literature
xx Characters and characteristics in
literature
Literature
Jews in Morocco
x Mellahs
Example under reference from Ghettos
Jews in Palestine
— Charities
sa Halukkah
Jews in Poland
sa Siedlce, Poland—Massacre, 1906
Note under Jews—Segregation
Jews in public life (Direct)
sa Statesmen, Jewish
Jews in Russia
sa Cantonists
Jews in the Hadith
xx Hadith
Jews in the Koran (BP134.J4)
xx Jews in literature
Jews in the New Testament

Jews in the United States *(E184.J5;*
        Immigration, JV6895.J6)
    sa Jews, Russian
        United States—History—Civil War,
            1861-1865—Jews
        United States—History—Revolution,
            1775-1783—Jewish participation
    — Attitudes toward Israel
        xx Israel and the Diaspora
    — Societies, etc.
        See Jews—Societies, etc.
Jezides
    See Yezidis
Język maszynowe rozmowy
    See MARO (Computer program language)
Ji (Sect) *(BL1442.J5)*
    x Jishū
    xx Buddhist sects
Jicaque Indians
    See Xicaque Indians
Jicarilla Apache Indians
    See Jicarilla Indians
Jicarilla Indians *(E99.J)*
    x Jicarilla Apache Indians
    xx Apache Indians
        Athapascan Indians
        Indians of North America
    — Economic conditions
Jicarilla language *(PM1389)*
    xx Athapascan languages
Jie (African tribe)
    xx Ethnology—Uganda
        Nilo-Hamitic tribes
Jig (Dance) *(GV1796.J5)*
        Here are entered works on the jig. Music
        for the dance is entered under the
        heading Jigs followed by specification
        of medium.
Jig saws
    x Scroll saws
    xx Saws
Jigger
    See Chigoe
Jiggermen
    See Potters
Jiggers (Mites)
    See Chiggers (Mites)
Jigging
    See Ore-dressing
Jigs
        Here are entered collections of jig music
        for various mediums. Individual jigs
        and collections of jigs for a specific
        medium are entered under the heading
        followed by specification of medium.
    x Gigues
Jigs (Instrumental ensemble)
    xx Instrumental ensembles
Jigs (Mechanical devices)
    See Jigs and fixtures
Jigs (Orchestra) *(M1048)*
    xx Orchestral music
    — Scores *(M1048)*
Jigs (Piano) *(M32)*
    xx Piano music
Jigs (String orchestra) *(M1145; M1160)*
    xx String-orchestra music
Jigs (Violin and piano) *(M217-218; M221-3)*
    xx Violin and piano music
Jigs (Violin with string orchestra)
        (M1105-6)
    xx Violin with string orchestra
Jigs and fixtures *(TJ1185)*
    sa Collets
    x Fixtures (Mechanical devices)
        Jigs (Mechanical devices)
    xx Machine-tools
    — Design and construction

— — Computer programs *(TJ1187)*
— Drawing
        See Jigs and fixtures—Drawings
— Drawings
        x Jigs and fixtures—Drawing
        xx Mechanical drawing
— Standards *(Direct)*
Jigsaw puzzles
    xx Puzzles
Jihad *(BP182)*
    x Holy war (Islam)
        Islamic holy war
        Jahad
        Jehad
        Muslim holy war
    xx International relations
        Islam and state
        Pillars of Islam
        War
        War and religion
Jihi
    See Compassion (Buddhism)
Jimini (African people)
    See Djimini (African people)
Jin
    See Jen
Jindjibandji language
    x Jindjiparndi language
    xx Australian languages
Jindjiparndi language
    See Jindjibandji language
Jinghpaw language
    See Kachin language
Jingoism
    See Chauvinism and jingoism
Jinn *(GR582)*
    x Genii
        Jinni
        Jinns
    xx Demonology
        Spirits (Islam)
    — Koranic teaching
Jinni
    See Jinn
Jinns
    See Jinn
Jinrikimen
    See Rickshaw men
Jinshin Revolt, 672
    xx Japan—Emperors
        Japan—History—645-794
Jishū
    See Ji (Sect)
Jita language
    x Kijita language
    xx Bantu languages
Jitney buses
    See Motor buses
Jitterbug dancing *(GV1796.J)*
    x Swing dancing
    xx Dancing
Jiu-jitsu *(GV475)*
        Here are entered works on the various
        Japanese schools on the art of self-
        defense prior to their unification by
        Chigorō Kanō in 1882.
    sa Judo
        Kempo
    x Jujitsu
    xx Athletics
        Hand-to-hand fighting, Oriental
        Physical education and training
        Self-defense
        Wrestling
    — Juvenile literature
Jivaran languages *(PM6273)*
    sa Aguaruna dialect
        Huambisa language

    xx Aguaruna dialect
Jivaro Indians *(F3722.1.J5)*
    x Givaro Indians
        Shuara Indians
        Xivaro Indians
    xx Indians of South America
    — Legends
    — Religion and mythology
JN-4D (Training planes)
    x Jenny (Training planes)
    xx Aeroplanes, Military
        Training planes
Jñāna (Buddhism)
    See Wisdom (Buddhism)
Jñāna yoga
    See Yoga, Jñāna
Jo-jotte (Game) *(GV1295.J6)*
Job analysis *(HF5549.5.J6)*
        Here are entered works on the process of
        making a detailed study of a job to de-
        termine the duties, facilities required,
        conditions of work, and the qualifica-
        tions needed for its performance.
        Works on the appraisal of the relative
        value of individual jobs in an organiza-
        tion for wage determination, promo-
        tions, etc., are entered under Job
        evaluation.
    sa Job descriptions
        Job evaluation
        Medical personnel—Classification
    x Analysis, Job
    xx Job evaluation
        Occupations
    Note under Job evaluation
Job descriptions *(Industrial management,*
        T58; Occupational descriptions
        Collective)
    sa subdivision Job descriptions *under*
        names of occupations, trades and
        institutions, e.g. Clothing trade—Job
        descriptions; United States. Navy—
        Job descriptions
    x Assignment specifications
    xx Job analysis
        Occupations
Job design
    See Work design
Job discrimination
    See Discrimination in employment
Job evaluation *(HF5549.5.J62)*
        Here are entered works on the appraisal
        of the relative value of individual jobs
        in an organization for wage determina-
        tion, promotions, etc. Works on the
        process of making a detailed study of a
        job to determine the duties, facilities
        required, conditions of work, and the
        qualifications needed for its perform-
        ance are entered under Job analysis.
    sa Job analysis
    x Evaluation, Job
        Job rating
        Rating, Job
    xx Job analysis
        Occupations
        Personnel management
    Note under Job analysis
Job openings
    See Job vacancies
Job performance standards
    See Performance standards
Job rating
    See Job evaluation
Job résumés
    See Résumés (Employment)
Job satisfaction
    sa Schaffer job satisfaction test

Teaching satisfaction
  xx Attitude (Psychology)
    Employee morale
    Labor and laboring classes
    Personnel management
    Satisfaction
    Work
Job training
  See Occupational training
Job vacancies *(Direct)*
  x Employment opportunities
    Job openings
  xx Employment agencies
    Employment (Economic theory)
    Labor supply
    Unemployed
  — Information services
Jobs
  See Occupations
    Professions
JOBSHOP (Computer program)
Jockeys
  xx Horse-racing
    Horse-racing—Employees
    Horse-shows
    Horsemen
  — Biography
  — Correspondence, reminiscences, etc.
Joconde (Game)
  x Mona Lisa (Game)
Jodel
  See Yodel and yodeling
Jodo-shin-shu
  See Shin (Sect)
Jogging *(GV494)*
  xx Running
Johannesburg
  — Riots, 1941
John Brown Raid, 1859
  See Harpers Ferry, W.Va.—John Brown
    Raid, 1859
John-dory
  See Dory (Fish)
John F. Kennedy International Airport
  Example under International airports
John Marshall Day *(E302.6.M4)*
  x Marshall Day
  xx Holidays
John Newbery medal books
  See Newbery medal books
John Peter Zenger award
  xx Journalism—Awards
John the Baptist's Day *(BV70.J)*
  x St. John the Baptist's Day
    St. John's Day
  xx Holidays
Johne's disease *(SF810.J6)*
  x Paratuberculosis of cattle
    Paratuberculous enteritis
    Pseudotubercular enteritis
  xx Cattle—Diseases
    Pseudotuberculosis
JOHNNIAC computer
  xx Electronic digital computers
Johnniac open shop system (Electronic
  computer system)
  See JOSS (Electronic computer system)
Johnson County Cattle War, 1892
  See Johnson County War, 1892
Johnson County Invasion, 1892
  See Johnson County War, 1892
Johnson County War, 1892
  x Johnson County Cattle War, 1892
    Johnson County Invasion, 1892
    Powder River Invasion, 1892
    Rustler War, 1892
Johnson grass *(Indirect)* *(SB201.J5)*

Johnson light machine-gun
  xx Machine-guns
Johnson semiautomatic rifle
  xx Rifles
Johnsonville Campaign, 1864
Johnstown, Pa.
  — Flood, 1889
  — — Juvenile literature
Joinder in issue
  See Joinder of issue
Joinder of actions *(Direct)*
  sa Separate actions
  xx Actions and defenses
    Separate actions
Joinder of issue *(Direct)*
  x Joinder in issue
    Joining of issue
    Litis contestatio
    Litiscontestation
    Similiter (Pleading)
  xx Civil procedure
    Pleading
Joinder of issue (Canon law)
Joinder of issue (Roman law)
Joinder of offenses *(Direct)*
  sa Compound offenses
  xx Compound offenses
    Criminal procedure
    Indictments
    Informations
Joinder of parties *(Direct)*
  sa Intervention (Civil procedure)
  x Third parties (Civil procedure)
    Third party practice
  xx Intervention (Civil procedure)
    Parties to actions
Joiners
  sa Cabinet-workers
  xx Carpenters
    Woodworkers
Joinery *(TH5662-3)*
  sa Cabinet-work
    Carpentry
    Clamps (Joinery)
    Furniture making
    Gluing
    Woodwork
  xx Carpentry
    Woodwork
  — Examinations, questions, etc.
Joining of issue
  See Joinder of issue
Joint adventures *(Direct)*
  x Adventures, Joint
    Joint undertakings
    Joint ventures
    Ventures, Joint
  xx Commercial law
    Partnership
  — Taxation *(Direct)*
"Joint and several"
  See Correality and solidarity
Joint and several contracts
  See Contracts, Joint and several
Joint authors
  See Authorship—Collaboration
Joint family *(Direct)*
  x Joint household
    Undivided family
  xx Domestic relations
    Family
Joint français Strike, 1970
Joint heirs
  See Co-heirs
Joint household
  See Joint family
Joint occupancy of buildings
  x Mixed use of buildings

    Multiple use of buildings
    Multipurpose buildings
    Occupancy of buildings, Joint
  xx Buildings
Joint operations (Military science)
  See Amphibious warfare
    Landing operations
    Unified operations (Military science)
Joint production committees
  See Works councils
Joint returns (Income tax)
  See Income tax—Joint returns
Joint-stock companies
  See Stock companies
Joint tenancy *(Direct)*
  sa Apartment houses, Cooperative
    Condominium (Housing)
    Condominium (Office buildings)
    Copyright (Joint tenancy)
    Partition
    Patents (Joint tenancy)
    Tenancy by the entirety
  x Co-ownership
    Cotenancy
  xx Land tenure—Law
    Property
    Real property
Joint tenancy (Roman law)
Joint testaments
  See Joint wills
Joint tortfeasors *(Direct)*
  x Joint torts
  xx Correality and solidarity
    Torts
Joint torts
  See Joint tortfeasors
Joint undertakings
  See Joint adventures
Joint-venture agreements
  See Foreign licensing agreements
Joint ventures
  See Joint adventures
Joint wills *(Direct)*
  x Joint testaments
  xx Wills
Joint wiping *(Plumbing, TH6295)*
  xx Plumbing
Jointer (Woodworking machine)
  xx Planing-machines
Jointless rails (Railroads)
  See Railroads—Continuous rails
Joints *(Comparative anatomy, QL825;*
    Human anatomy, QM131)
  sa Bursae mucosae
    Cartilage
    Ligaments
    Pseudarthrosis
    Synovia
    names of anatomical joints, e.g. Elbow,
      Knee, Wrist
  x Articulations
  xx Bones
    Skeleton
  — Atlases
  — Diseases *(RD686)*
    sa Arthritis
      Arthritis deformans
      Arthrogryposis
      Charcot joints
      Joints—Radiography
    x Arthropathy
    xx Arthritis deformans
  — Dislocation
    See Dislocations
  — Examination
    sa Arthroscopy
  — Paracentesis
    See Arthrocentesis

Joints *(Comparative anatomy, QL825;*
     Human anatomy, QM131)
       (Continued)
  — Puncture
    See Arthrocentesis
  — Radiography
    xx Joints—Diseases
  — Surgery *(RD551; RD684; RD686)*
    sa Arthrodesis
      Arthroplasty
      Excision (Surgery)
      Synovectomy
  — Tuberculosis *(RC312.5.J)*
  — Tumors
Joints, Riveted
  See Riveted joints
Joints (Engineering)
  sa Adhesive joints
    Bolted joints
    Bolts and nuts
    Bridges, Concrete—Joints
    Bridges—Floors—Joints
    Concrete construction—Joints
    Electric cables—Joints
    Expansion joints
    Fastenings
    Pipe joints
    Precast concrete construction—Joints
    Press fits
    Riveted joints
    Sewer-pipe—Joints
    Shrink fitting
    Splines
    Timber joints
    Universal joints (Mechanics)
    Welded joints
  xx Engineering
  — Drawing
    See Joints (Engineering)—Drawings
  — Drawings
    x Joints (Engineering)—Drawing
    xx Mechanical drawing
  — Patents
  — Programmed instruction
  — Standards
  — Testing
Joints (Geology) *(QE605)*
  xx Geology, Structural
Jok language
  See Chokwe language
Jokes
  See Wit and humor
Joloano language
  See Sulu language
Jolof language
  See Wolof language
Jōmon culture *(GN776.3.J6)*
  sa Pottery, Jōmon
  x Jōmonshiki culture
  xx Neolithic period
  — Juvenile literature
Jōmon pottery
  See Pottery, Jōmon
Jōmonshiki culture
  See Jōmon culture
Jonah, Sign of
  See Sign of Jonah
Jonaz-Chichimeca Indians
  See Chichimeca-Jonaz Indians
Jongleurs
  See Jugglers and juggling
    Minstrels
    Troubadours
    Trouvères
Joost-van-den-Vondel-Preis
Jordan
  — History
  —— Intervention, 1958

Jordan algebras
  x Algebras, Jordan
  xx Algebra, Abstract
    Algebras, Linear
Jordan curves
  See Curves, Jordan
Jordans
  See Chamber pots
Joropo (Dance) *(GV1796.J7)*
  xx Tango (Dance)
Jōruri
  x Gidayū
  xx Japanese drama
    Monologue
    Monologues with music (Shamisen)
Joseph E. Drexel Preis
  xx Journalism—Awards
Josephinism *(BR815)*
  x Josephism
  xx Catholic Church in Austria
    Church and state in Austria
    Gallicanism
Josephism
  See Josephinism
JOSS (Electronic computer system)
  x Johnniac open shop system (Electronic
    computer system)
  xx On-line data processing
Jössehärad polska (Dance)
Jota *(Dancing, GV1796.J; Musical history,*
    ML3447)
Jotas
    Here are entered collections of jota music
    for various mediums. Individual jotas
    and collections of jotas for a specific
    medium are entered under the heading
    followed by specification of medium.
Jotas (Orchestra) *(M1049)*
  xx Orchestral music
Jou-jan (Tatar tribe) *(DS25)*
  x Hsiung-nu
  xx Tatars
Jou-tchen language
  See Ju-chên language
Joule-Thomson effect *(QC286)*
  x Joule-Thomson expansion
    Thomson-Joule effect
  xx Gases, Kinetic theory of
Joule-Thomson expansion
  See Joule-Thomson effect
Journalism *(Direct) (PN4700-5650)*
    Also subdivided by topic, *e.g.* Journalism
    —Automobile industry and trade;
    Journalism—Automobiles.
  sa Amateur journalism
    Broadsides
    Canards (Journalism)
    College and school journalism
    Copy-reading
    Copyright—Newspaper articles
    Crime and the press
    Editing
    Editorials
    Feuilletons
    Foreign correspondents
    Foreign news
    Government and the press
    Interviewing (Journalism)
    Journalistic ethics
    Liberty of the press
    Moving-picture journalism
    Musical criticism
    News-letters
    Newspaper court reporting
    Newspaper layout and typography
    Newspaper publishing
    Newspaper reading
    Newspapers

    Periodicals
    Periodicals, Publishing of
    Press
    Press and propaganda
    Press conferences
    Press councils
    Radio journalism
    Reporters and reporting
    Science news
    Sports journalism
    Television broadcasting of news
  x Literature as a profession
    Writing (Authorship)
  xx Publicity
Note under Editing
  — Agriculture
    See Journalism, Agricultural
  — Anecdotes, facetiae, satire, etc.
    (PN4838)
  — Authorship
    xx Authorship
  — Automobile industry and trade
    Note under Journalism
  — Automobiles
    Note under Journalism
  — Awards
    sa John Peter Zenger award
      Joseph E. Drexel Preis
    xx Rewards (Prizes, etc.)
  — Biography
    See Journalists
  — Commerce
    See Journalism, Commercial
  — Competitions *(PN4798)*
  — Education
    See Journalism, Educational
  — Exhibitions and museums
  — Film catalogs
  — Juvenile literature
  — Labor
    See Journalism, Labor
  — Medicine
    See Journalism, Medical
  — Merchant marine
    See Journalism, Maritime
  — Negroes
    See Negro press
  — Outdoor life
    See Journalism, Outdoor
  — Philosophy *(PN4731)*
  — Political aspects *(PN4751)*
    sa Press and politics
    xx Press and politics
  — Religion
    See Journalism, Religious
  — Research
  — Social aspects *(PN4749)*
    x Press—Social aspects
  — Societies, etc.
    x Newspapers—Societies, etc.
      Press associations
      Press clubs
      Press—Societies, etc.
  — Sports
    See Sports journalism
  — Study and teaching *(Direct)*
  —— Audio-visual aids
  — Terminology
Journalism, Aeronautical
  x Aeronautical journalism
  xx Journalism, Technical
Journalism, Agricultural *(Direct)*
    (PN4784.A3)
  x Agricultural journalism
    Dairy journalism
    Journalism—Agriculture
    Journalism, Dairy

Note under Newspapers—Sections, columns, etc.

Journalism, Commercial *(Direct)*
  (PN4784.C7)
  x Commercial journalism
    Financial journalism
    Journalism—Commerce
    Trade journalism
Journalism, Communist *(Direct)*
  x Communist journalism
Journalism, Dairy
  See Journalism, Agricultural
Journalism, Educational
  x Educational journalism
    Journalism—Education
Journalism, Ethnic
  See Ethnic press
Journalism, Industrial
  See Journalism, Technical
Journalism, Labor *(Direct)*
  sa Press, Labor
  x Journalism—Labor
    Journalism, Trade-union
    Labor journalism
    Trade-union journalism
Journalism, Legal *(Direct)*
  sa Newspaper court reporting
  x Legal journalism
Journalism, Maritime *(Direct)*
  x Journalism—Merchant marine
    Maritime journalism
Journalism, Medical *(PN4784.M4)*
  x Journalism—Medicine
    Medical journalism
Journalism, Military *(Direct)*
  x Armed Forces—Journalism
    Armed Forces newspapers
    Army newspapers
    Military journalism
  xx War correspondents
Journalism, Negro
  See Negro press
Journalism, Outdoor *(PN4784.O9)*
  x Journalism—Outdoor life
    Outdoor journalism
Journalism, Pictorial
  sa Illustrated periodicals
    Photography, Journalistic
  x Photojournalism
    Pictorial journalism
Journalism, Prison *(Direct)*
  sa Prison periodicals
  x Prison journalism
Journalism, Religious *(Direct)*
  (PN4888.R4)
  sa Press, Baptist
    Press, Catholic
    Press, Lutheran
  x Catholic journalism
    Journalism—Religion
    Religious journalism
  xx Advertising—Churches
    Mass media in religion
    Press, Catholic
    Religion and the press
    Religious literature—Authorship
    Religious newspapers and periodicals
Journalism, Scientific *(PN4888.S)*
  x Scientific journalism
Journalism, Socialist *(Direct)*
  x Socialist journalism
Journalism, Technical *(PN4784.T3)*
  sa Employees' magazines, handbooks, etc.
    House organs
    Journalism, Aeronautical
  x Journalism, Industrial
    Technical journalism

Journalism, Trade-union
  See Journalism, Labor
Journalism and education
  x Education and journalism
Journalism and literature *(Direct)*
  x Literature and journalism
Journalism and moving-pictures
  sa Moving-picture journalism
  x Moving-pictures and journalism
Journalism as a profession *(PN4797)*
  — Juvenile literature
Journalistic ethics *(Direct)* *(PN4756)*
  sa Confidential communications—Press
    Sensationalism in newspapers
  x Ethics, Journalistic
  xx Ethics
    Journalism
    Journalists
    Newspapers
    Professional ethics
Journalistic libraries
  See Newspaper office libraries
Journalistic photography
  See Photography, Journalistic
Journalists *(Direct)* *(PN4820-4823;*
    PN4841-5650; Great Britain,
    PN5122-3; United States, PN4871-4)
  sa Foreign correspondents
    Journalistic ethics
    Negro journalists
    News photographers
    Strikes and lockouts—Journalists
    Wages—Journalists
    War correspondents
    Women journalists
    subdivision Journalists *under names of*
      wars, e.g. United States—History—
      Civil War, 1861-1865—Journalists
  x Commentators
    Editors (Journalism)
    Journalism—Biography
    Literature as a profession
    Radio journalists
  Example under reference from Writers
  — Biography
  — Collective bargaining
      See Collective bargaining—Journalists
  — Collective labor agreements
      See Collective labor agreements—
        Journalists
  — Correspondence, reminiscences, etc.
      (PN4820-4823; PN4841-5650)
    sa subdivision Personal narratives *under*
      names of wars, e.g. World War,
      1939-1945—Personal narratives
  — Legal status, laws, etc. *(Direct)*
    xx Press law
  — Prayer-books and devotions
  — Taxation *(Direct)*
Journalists, Slavic
  x Slavic journalists
Journals (Machinery)
  See Bearings (Machinery)
Journeymen *(Direct)*
  xx Artisans
Journeymen's fraternities
  See Journeymen's societies
Journeymen's gilds
  See Journeymen's societies
Journeymen's societies *(Indirect)*
  sa Compagnonnages
  x Journeymen's fraternities
    Journeymen's gilds
    Yeomanry gilds
  xx Gilds
    Trade and professional associations
Journeys
  See Voyages and travels

Voyages around the world
  subdivision Description and travel
    under names of countries, regions,
    etc.
Jovian atmosphere
  See Jupiter (Planet)—Atmosphere
Jowar
  See Durra
Joy
  sa Happiness
  xx Emotions
    Happiness
  — Biblical teaching
  — Quotations, maxims, etc.
Joy in literature
Ju 87 (Bombers)
  See Stuka (Bombers)
Ju-chên (Tribe)
  x Juchen (Tribe)
    Jŭrčed (Tribe)
    Jurchen (Tribe)
    Jurchid (Tribe)
  xx Ethnology—Manchuria
    Tunguses
Ju-chên language
  x Džurdžin language
    Jou-tchen language
    Jučen language
    Jurchi language
    Nütschi language
  xx Tungusic languages
Juan Fernandez fur seal
  See Guadalupe fur seal
Juanambú River, Battle of the, 1814
  xx Colombia—History—War of
    Independence, 1810-1822
Juaneño Indians *(E99.J)*
  x Acagchemin Indians
  xx Indians of North America
    Shoshonean Indians
  — Religion and mythology
Juar
  See Durra
Jubbulpore, India (City)
  — Riots, 1961
Jubilate Deo omnis terra, Servite Domino
    (Music)
  See Psalms (Music)—100th Psalm
Jubilate Deo omnis terra, psalmum dicite
    (Music)
  See Psalms (Music)—66th Psalm
Jubilee (Judaism)
  x Year of Jubilee (Judaism)
  xx Agricultural laws and legislation
    (Jewish law)
    Sabbatical year (Judaism)
Jubilee indulgences
  See Indulgences
Jubilee singers *(ML400)*
Jubilee volumes
  See Festschriften
Jubilee Year
  See Holy Year
Jučen language
  See Ju-chên language
Juchen (Tribe)
  See Ju-chên (Tribe)
Juchitán, Battle of, 1866
  xx Mexico—History—European
    intervention, 1861-1867
Judaica
  See Jewish literature
    Jews

Judaism *(Direct)*

Here are entered works on Jewish faith and practice in which the main stream of orthodox Judaism is treated and no cleavage is stressed. Systematic works on the doctrines and dogmas of Judaism are entered under the heading Jewish theology.

Polemic works limited to any one of the sects, schisms, or cleavages within Judaism are entered under the name of such a movement, *e.g.* Hasidism, Jewish Science, Reform Judaism.

sa Cabala
Chief Rabbinate
Circumcision
Commandments, Six hundred and thirteen
Commandments, Ten
Communism and Judaism
Confession—Judaism
Cultus, Jewish
Fasts and feasts—Judaism
Haskalah
Jesus Christ—Jewish interpretations
Jews
Messiah
Mysticism—Judaism
Mythology, Jewish
Parables, Jewish
Parchment—Religious use
Printing, Hebrew—Religious aspects
Proselytes and proselyting, Jewish
Religious literature, Jewish
Religious Zionism
Sabbath
Sabbath legislation
Synagogues
Synedrion
Urim and Thummim
Zionism and Judaism
special headings with Judaism *added in parentheses, e.g.* Repentance (Judaism); *also headings beginning with the word* Jewish

x Jews—Religion
xx Cultus, Jewish
Jewish theology
Religions
Semites—Religion
Note under Jewish theology

— 20th century *(BM565)*
— Apologetic works *(BM648)*

Here are entered works defending the Jewish religion and Judaism in general.

x Apologetics, Jewish
Jewish apologetics
Jews—Apologetic works
— Asceticism
See Asceticism—Judaism
— Biography
See Jews—Biography
— Caricatures and cartoons
— Ceremonies and practices
See Jews—Rites and ceremonies
— Clergy
See Judaism—Functionaries
— Controversial literature *(BM585; Christian apologetics, BT1120; Mohammedan apologetics, BT173.J8)*

Here are entered works against the Jewish religion.

xx Apologetics
— Devotional exercises
See Jews—Prayer-books and devotions
— Dictionaries

sa Jews—Dictionaries and encyclopedias
xx Jews—Dictionaries and encyclopedias
— Early works to 1900
See Judaism—Works to 1900
— Education
See Jews—Education
— Functionaries *(BM652)*
sa Cantors, Jewish
Marbits Torah
Rabbis
Scribes, Jewish
x Jewish religious functionaries
Judaism—Clergy
— History
—— To 140 B.C.
See Judaism—History—To 70 A.D.
—— To 70 A.D. *(BM165)*

Here are entered works dealing with Judaism on a developmental or evolutionary basis from its beginnings to the downfall of the Jewish state in 70 A.D.

sa Jews—History—To 70 A.D.
x Judaism—History—To 140 B.C.
xx Palestine—History—To 70 A.D.
—— Pre-Talmudic period, 586 B.C.-10 A.D.
See Judaism—History—Post-exilic period, 586 B.C.-210 A.D.
—— Post-exilic period, 586 B.C.-210 A.D. *(BM176)*

Here are entered works dealing with the history of Judaism from the exile to the downfall of the Jewish state and the earliest redaction of Jewish law in the Mishnah.

x Bible—History of inter-testamental events
Judaism—History—Greco-Roman period, 332 B.C.-210 A.D.
Judaism—History—Inter-testamental period, 140 B.C.-30 A.D.
Judaism—History—Pre-Talmudic period, 586 B.C.-10 A.D.
xx Palestine—History—To 70 A.D.
—— Greco-Roman period, 332 B.C.-210 A.D.
See Judaism—History—Post-exilic period, 586 B.C.-210 A.D.
—— Inter-testamental period, 140 B.C.-30 A.D.
See Judaism—History—Post-exilic period, 586 B.C.-210 A.D.
—— Tannaitic period, 10-220
See Tannaim
—— Talmudic period, 10-425 *(BM177)*

Here are entered works dealing with the history of Judaism during the redaction of the Jewish law, approximately the first five centuries of the Christian era.

sa Talmud—Theology
xx Tannaim
Note under Judaism—History of doctrines

—— Medieval and early modern period, 425-1789

Here are entered works dealing with the history of Judaism from the completion of the Talmud in the fifth century of the Christian era to the time of the emancipation of the Jews in the eighteenth century.

—— Modern period, 1500- *(BM190)*

Here are entered works dealing with the history of Judaism from the time of the emancipation of the Jews in the eighteenth century of the Christian era down to present times.

— History of doctrines

Here are entered works dealing with two or more individual tenets of Jewish faith. Works dealing with a single tenet are entered under the specific heading, *e.g.* Atonement (Judaism). Works limited to a particular period of history are entered under the specific heading, *e.g.* Judaism—History—Talmudic period, 10-425.

— Influence
— Juvenile literature
— Liturgical objects
See Liturgical objects—Judaism
— Liturgy and ritual
See Jews. Liturgy and ritual
— Pictures, illustrations, etc.
— Public opinion
See Jews—Public opinion
— Quotations, maxims, etc.
xx Quotations, Jewish
— Reconstructionist movement
See Reconstructionist Judaism
— Reform movement
See Reform Judaism
— Relations
sa Jews—Election, Doctrine of
—— Buddhism, [Christianity, Islam, etc.]
— Rituals
See Jews—Rites and ceremonies
— Study and teaching
sa Rabbinical seminaries
— Terminology
— Works to 1900

Here are entered general works on Judaism written before 1900. For specific aspects *see* the specific subdivision.

x Judaism—Early works to 1900
Judaism, Conservative
See Conservative Judaism
Judaism, Orthodox
See Orthodox Judaism
Judaism, Reconstructionist
See Reconstructionist Judaism
Judaism, Reform
See Reform Judaism
Judaism and art *(BM538.A7)*
sa Art, Jewish
x Art and Judaism
xx Art and religion
Art, Jewish
Judaism and communism
See Communism and Judaism
Judaism and evolution
See Evolution and Judaism
Judaism and labor
sa Labor laws and legislation (Jewish law)
x Labor and Judaism
xx Church and labor
Labor and laboring classes—Jews
Judaism and parapsychology
x Parapsychology and Judaism
xx Psychical research
Judaism and philosophy
x Philosophy and Judaism
xx Philosophy and religion
Philosophy, Jewish
Judaism and psychology
x Psychology and Judaism

Judaism and science *(BM538.S3)*
  sa Evolution and Judaism
  x Science and Judaism
  xx Religion and science
Judaism and social problems *(HN40.J5)*
  x Religion and social problems
    Social problems and Judaism
  xx Church and social problems
    Social problems
    Sociology, Jewish
Judaism and socialism
  See Socialism and Judaism
Judaism and state *(BM538.S7)*
  sa Zionism
  x State and Judaism
  xx Nationalism and religion
    Religion and state
Judaism and Zionism
  See Zionism and Judaism
Judaism in literature
  xx Jews in literature
    Religion in literature
Judean sibyl
  See Babylonian sibyl
Judenburg Mutiny, 1918
Judeo-German language
  See Yiddish language
Judeo-Persian language
  x Persian language—Dialects—
    Judeo-Persian
  xx Jews—Languages
Judeo-Persian literature *(Direct)*
Judeo-Persian poetry *(Direct)*
Judeo-Spanish folk-songs
  See Folk-songs, Jewish (Ladino)
Judeo-Spanish language
  See Ladino language
Judesmo
  See Ladino language
Judge advocates *(Direct)*
  xx Government attorneys
  — Salaries, pensions, etc. *(Direct)*
Judge-made law *(Direct)*
  x Judicial law
    Judicial legislation
    Law, Judge-made
  xx Common law
    Judicial power
    Judicial process
    Lacunae in law
    Law—Interpretation and construction
    Legislation
    Legislative power
Judges *(Direct)* *(JF700-721; JK1507-1599;*
    etc.)
  sa Courts
    Disqualification of judges
    Judgments
    Judicial corruption
    Judicial discretion
    Judicial ethics
    Judicial process
    Justice, Administration of
    Justices of the peace
    Law officers (Courts-martial)
    Lay judges
    Police magistrates
    Women as judges
  x Chief justices
    Magistrates
  xx Courts
    Courts—Officials and employees
    Judicial power
    Justice, Administration of
    Law—Biography
    Lawyers
  Example under Law—Biography
  — Appointment, qualifications, tenure, etc.

  x Judicial tenure
    Selection of judges
  — Correspondence, reminiscences, etc.
  — Costume *(GT6230-6280)*
    x Legal dress
  — Directories
    x Law—Directories
  — Discipline
    xx Judicial ethics
  — Portraits
  — Retirement
    Example under Retirement
  — Salaries, pensions, etc.
    x Judicial compensation
  — Travel regulations
    Example under reference from Travel
      regulations
Judges (Canon law)
Judges (Germanic law)
Judges (Islamic law)
  sa Cadis
Judging (Sports)
  See Sports officiating
Judgment
  sa Attitude change
    Common sense
    Conservation (Psychology)
    Similarity judgment
    Size judgment
    Weight judgment
  xx Knowledge, Theory of
    Language and languages
    Psychology
    Thought and thinking
    Wisdom
  — Ability testing
Judgment, Last
  See Judgment Day
Judgment, Practical
  See Practical judgment
Judgment (Ethics)
  x Moral judgment
  xx Ethics
Judgment (Logic) *(BC181)*
  sa Fallacies (Logic)
    Negation (Logic)
    Prediction (Logic)
    Reasoning
  x Impersonal judgment
  xx Logic
    Reasoning
Judgment Day *(BT880-881)*
  sa Particular judgment (Theology)
    Second Advent
  x Day of Judgment
    Doomsday
    General judgment
    Judgment, Last
    Last Judgment
  xx End of the world
    Eschatology
    Judgment of God
    Second Advent
  — Art *(N8120)*
    Example under Bible—Pictures, illustra-
      tions, etc.
  — Biblical teaching
    sa Day of Jehovah
  — Comparative studies
  — Early works to 1800
  — Sermons
Judgment Day (Egyptian religion)
Judgment Day (Islam) *(BP166.85)*
  xx End of the world (Islam)
    Eschatology, Islamic
Judgment Day in literature
Judgment notes *(Direct)*
  xx Promissory notes

Judgment of God
  sa Judgment Day
  x God—Judgment
  xx God
    God—Wrath
  — Biblical teaching
Judgment of the soul (Theology)
  See Particular judgment (Theology)
Judgments *(Direct)*
  sa Alternative convictions
    Arrest of judgment
    Confession of judgment
    Conflict of judicial decisions
    Dismissal and nonsuit
    Executions (Law)
    Indeterminate sentence
    Interlocutory decisions
    Judgments by default
    Judicial opinions
    Jurisdiction
    Res judicata
    Scire facias
    Stare decisis
    Supplementary proceedings
  xx Civil procedure
    Courts
    Criminal procedure
    Estoppel
    Judges
    Judicial process
    Jurisdiction
    Stare decisis
  — Forms
Judgments, Criminal *(Direct)*
  sa Acquittals
    Indeterminate sentence
    Sentences (Criminal procedure)
  x Criminal judgments
    Judgments of conviction
  xx Criminal courts
    Criminal procedure
Judgments, Declaratory *(Direct)*
  x Declaratory judgments
  xx Declaratory acts
Judgments, Foreign *(Direct)* *(JX6607)*
    Here are entered works dealing with the
      legal status in one country or state of
      the judicial decisions of other coun-
      tries or states in general.
    Works relating to the enforcement by one
      state or country of the judicial acts of
      another are entered under the heading
      Judicial assistance.
  sa Judicial assistance
  x Foreign judgments
  xx Civil procedure (International law)
    Conflict of laws
    Judicial assistance
Judgments (Canon law) *(BX1939.J8)*
Judgments (Roman law)
Judgments by default *(Direct)*
  x Default judgments
  xx Contumacy
    Default (Law)
    Judgments
Judgments by default (Roman law)
Judgments by peers
  See Jury
Judgments of conviction
  See Judgments, Criminal
Judica me, Deus (Music)
  See Psalms (Music)—43d Psalm
Judicial assistance *(Direct)*
    Here are entered works relating to the
      enforcement by one state or country of
      judicial acts of another state or coun-
      try.

Judicial assistance *(Direct)* *(Continued)*
>> To be distinguished from the French "assistance judiciare" for which "legal aid" is the English equivalent.
>> Works dealing with the treatment of nationals of one country in the civil courts of another are entered under the heading Civil procedure (International law)
>> *sa* Extradition
>> Judgments, Foreign
>> Legalization
>> Letters rogatory
>> *xx* Civil procedure
>> Civil procedure (International law)
>> Criminal procedure
>> International law
>> Judgments, Foreign
>> *Note under* Judgments, Foreign

Judicial assistance (Canon law)
Judicial behavior
>> *See* Judicial process

Judicial bonds *(Direct)*
>> *sa* Insurance, Surety and fidelity
>> Security for costs
>> *x* Court bonds
>> *xx* Security (Law)
>> Suretyship and guaranty
Judicial compensation
>> *See* Judges—Salaries, pensions, etc.

Judicial corruption *(Direct)*
>> *x* Corruption, Judicial
>> *xx* Bribery
>> Judges
>> Judicial ethics
>> Misconduct in office

Judicial councils *(Direct)*
>> *xx* Courts
>> Justice, Administration of
Judicial decision-making
>> *See* Judicial process
Judicial decisions, Conflict of
>> *See* Conflict of judicial decisions
Judicial decisions, Recall of
>> *See* Recall of judicial decisions

Judicial discretion *(Direct)*
>> *sa* Administrative discretion
>> Law—Interpretation and construction
>> *x* Discretion, Judicial
>> Discretion (Law)
>> Discretion of court
>> *xx* Administrative discretion
>> Judges
>> Law—Interpretation and construction

Judicial discretion (Canon law)
Judicial discretion (Roman law)
Judicial districts *(Direct)*
>> *sa* Courts
>> *xx* Administrative and political divisions
>> Justice, Administration of

Judicial error *(Direct)*
>> *sa* Compensation for judicial error
>> *x* Criminal justice, Errors of
>> Errors of criminal justice
>> Justice, Miscarriage of
>> Miscarriage of justice
>> *xx* Criminal justice, Administration of
>> Justice, Administration of
>> Trials

Judicial error (Canon law)
Judicial error (Roman law)
Judicial error in literature
Judicial ethics *(Direct)*
>> *sa* Judges—Discipline
>> Judicial corruption
>> *x* Ethics, Judicial
>> *xx* Judges
>> Law and ethics

Legal ethics
>> Professional ethics
Judicial functions of legislative bodies
>> *See* Legislative bodies as courts
Judicial investigations
>> *See* Governmental investigations
Judicial law
>> *See* Judge-made law
Judicial legislation
>> *See* Judge-made law

Judicial notice *(Direct)*
>> *sa* Foreign law, Pleading and proof of
>> *x* Notice, Judicial
>> Notoriety
>> *xx* Evidence (Law)
Judicial officers
>> *See* Courts—Officials and employees

Judicial opinions *(Direct)*
>> *sa* Advisory opinions
>> Dissenting opinions
>> *x* Opinions, Judicial
>> *xx* Judgments
>> Law reports, digests, etc.

Judicial opinions (Islamic law) *(Direct)*
Judicial power *(Direct)* *(JF265; JF700-723; JK-JQ)*
>> *sa* Courts
>> Delegation of powers
>> Implied powers (Constitutional law)
>> Judge-made law
>> Judges
>> Judicial review
>> Legislative bodies as courts
>> Separation of powers
>> *x* Judiciary
>> Power, Judicial
>> *xx* Constitutional law
>> Courts
>> Implied powers (Constitutional law)

Judicial power (Canon law)
Judicial power (Islamic law) *(Direct)*
Judicial power and political questions
>> *See* Political questions and judicial power

Judicial process *(Direct)*
>> *sa* Evidence (Law)
>> Judge-made law
>> Judgments
>> Law—Interpretation and construction
>> Stare decisis
>> *x* Decision-making, Judicial
>> Judicial behavior
>> Judicial decision-making
>> *xx* Judges
>> Law—Interpretation and construction
>> Law—Psychology
>> Procedure (Law)

Judicial process (Islamic law) *(Direct)*
Judicial process (Primitive law) *(Direct)*
Judicial review *(Direct)* *(JF711; United States, JK1541)*
>> *sa* Amparo (Writ)
>> Legislative power
>> Political questions and judicial power
>> Separation of powers
>> *x* Review, Judicial
>> *xx* Constitutional law
>> Courts
>> Delegation of powers
>> Executive power
>> Judicial power
>> Legislation
>> Legislative power
>> Rule of law
>> Separation of powers

Judicial review of administrative acts *(Direct)*
>> *sa* Abuse of administrative power

Actions and defenses (Administrative law)
>> Administrative remedies
>> Equitable remedies
>> Exhaustion of administrative remedies
>> Extraordinary remedies
>> *xx* Administrative acts
>> Administrative courts
>> Administrative law
>> Administrative procedure
>> Appellate procedure
>> Rule of law

Judicial sales *(Direct)*
>> *sa* Foreclosure
>> Tax-sales
>> *x* Sales, Judicial
>> *xx* Executions (Law)
>> Sales
>> Tax-sales
>> — Cases

Judicial sales (Roman law)
Judicial separation
>> *See* Separation (Law)

Judicial statistics *(Direct)*
>> *sa* Criminal statistics
>> *x* Courts—Statistics
>> Justice, Administration of—Statistics
>> Law—Statistics
>> Legal statistics
>> *xx* Statistics
Judicial tenure
>> *See* Judges—Appointment, qualifications, tenure, etc.
Judiciary
>> *See* Courts
>> Judicial power
Judiciary, State
>> *See* Courts—United States—States

Judo *(GV475)*
>> Here are entered works on the art of self-defense as unified by Chigorō Kanō in 1882.
>> *sa* Karate
>> *xx* Hand-to-hand fighting, Oriental
>> Jiu-jitsu
>> Self-defense
>> — Accidents and injuries
>> *x* Judo—Injuries
>> — Caricatures and cartoons
>> — History
>> — — Pictorial works
>> — Injuries
>> *See* Judo—Accidents and injuries
Jugambe dialect
>> *See* Jugumbir dialect
Jugendstil
>> *See* Art nouveau

Jugglers and juggling *(GV1541-1561)*
>> *sa* Conjuring
>> Magic
>> *x* Jongleurs
>> Legerdemain
>> Sleight of hand
>> *xx* Conjuring
>> Tricks
Jugoslav . . .
>> *See* Yugoslav . . .
Jugoslavs
>> *See* Yugoslavs
Jugs
>> *See* Pitchers
Jugs, Toby
>> *See* Toby jugs

Jugtown pottery *(NK4340.J7)*
Jugular vein
Jugumbir dialect
>> *x* Jugambe dialect
>> Yugumbir dialect

Yukambe dialect
  xx Bandjalang language
Jugurthine War, 111-105 B.C. *(DG255)*
Juhani (Arab tribe)
  See Juhaynah (Arab tribe)
Juhaynah (Arab tribe)
  x Juhani (Arab tribe)
  xx Arabs
Jujitsu
  See Jiu-jitsu
Jujube (Plant) *(SB379.J8)*
Jukado
  xx Self-defense
Jukaghir language
  See Yukaghir language
Juke boxes
  See Jukeboxes
Jukeboxes
  x Coin operated machines
    Juke boxes
  xx Musical instruments (Mechanical)
    Phonograph
Jukon language
  See Jukun language
Juku language
  See Jukun language
Jukun language *(PL8301)*
  x Jukon language
    Juku language
    Kurorofa language
  xx Benue-Congo languages
Julian calendar
  See Calendar, Julian
Jullundur Mutiny, 1920
July
  Example under Months
July Fourth
  See Fourth of July
July Handicap (Horse race) *(SF357.J8)*
  x Rothmans July Handicap (Horse race)
July Revolution, 1830
  See France—History—July Revolution, 1830
Jumano Indians *(E99.J9)*
  xx Indians of North America
    Pueblo Indians
Jump rope
  See Rope skipping
Jumping *(GV529)*
  sa Barrel jumping
    Ski jumping
  x High jumping
  xx Athletics
    College sports
    Sports
Jumping (Horsemanship)
  sa Cavalletti
    Show jumping
  xx Horsemanship
  — Juvenile literature
  — Pictorial works
Jumping bail
  See Bail
Jumping jacks
  xx Toys
Jumping plant-lice *(QL523.P8)*
  Example under Plant-lice
Junction transistors *(TK7872.T73)*
  sa Tunnel diodes
  x Transistors, Junction
  xx Electric current rectifiers
    Transistors
    Triodes
    Tunnel diodes
  — Noise
June beetle, Green
  See Green June beetle

June devotions
  See Sacred Heart, Devotion to
June grass
  See Kentucky bluegrass
Juneau, Alaska, in art
Jungle ecology *(Indirect)* *(QH541.5.J8)*
  xx Ecology
    Forest ecology
    Rain forests
  — Juvenile literature
Jungle fauna
  x Fauna
  xx Forest fauna
    Zoology—Tropics
  — Juvenile literature
Jungle fowl
  sa Burmese red jungle fowl
  x Junglefowl
  xx Pheasants
Jungle warfare *(U167.5.J)*
  xx Military art and science
    Strategy
    Tactics
    War
Jungle zoos
  See Open-air zoos
Junglefowl
  See Jungle fowl
Junin, Battle of, 1824 *(F3446)*
Junior class (High school)
  See Eleventh grade (Education)
Junior college libraries *(Direct)* *(Z675.J8)*
  sa Municipal university and college libraries
  x Libraries, Junior college
  xx Libraries, University and college
    Municipal university and college libraries
Junior college students *(Direct)*
  xx Students
Junior college trustees
  x Junior colleges—Trustees
    Trustees, Junior college
  xx College trustees
    Junior colleges—Administration
Junior colleges *(Indirect)* *(LB2328)*
  sa Municipal junior colleges
  xx Education, Higher
    Universities and colleges
  — Accounting
  — Administration
    sa Junior college trustees
  — Curricula
  — Faculty
    x Faculty (Education)
    xx College teachers
  — Finance
    x Tuition
  — Statistics
    Note under Educational statistics
  — Trustees
    See Junior college trustees
Junior high school facilities *(Direct)*
  sa Junior high schools—Furniture, equipment, etc.
  xx School facilities
  — Planning *(Direct)*
    xx Educational planning
Junior high school graduates *(Direct)*
  x Graduates, Junior high school
  — Employment *(Direct)*
Junior high school principals *(Direct)*
  x Principals, Junior high school
  xx High school principals
    School superintendents and principals
  — Legal status, laws, etc. *(Direct)*
    xx Educational law and legislation

Junior high school students *(Direct)*
  x Junior high schools—Students
  xx Students
  — Books and reading
  — Social and economic status
    See Junior high school students' socio-economic status
Junior high school students' socio-economic status *(Direct)* *(LC208.4)*
  x Junior high school students—Social and economic status
  xx Students' socio-economic status
Junior high school teachers *(Direct)*
  xx Teachers
Junior high school teachers, Training of *(Direct)*
Junior high schools *(Indirect)* *(LB1623)*
  sa Middle schools
  x High schools, Junior
    Intermediate schools
  xx Education, Secondary
  — Accreditation
  — Administration
    xx School management and organization
  — Curricula
  — Equipment and supplies
    See Junior high schools—Furniture, equipment, etc.
  — Furniture, equipment, etc.
    x Junior high schools—Equipment and supplies
    xx Furniture
    Junior high school facilities
  — Students
    See Junior high school students
Junior police
  See School safety patrols
Junior republics *(HV876)*
  sa School city, state, etc.
  x George Junior Republics
  xx Children—Institutional care
    Self-government (in education)
Juniorate *(BX903)*
  xx Monasticism and religious orders—Education
Juniper *(QK495.J9)*
  — Identification
Junk
  See Waste products
Junk mail
  See Advertising, Direct-mail
Junk trade *(Direct)*
  sa Secondhand trade
  x Waste trade
  xx Secondhand trade
  — Sounds
    xx Sounds
Junkers airplanes
Junkers Ju 87 (Bombers)
  See Stuka (Bombers)
Junks *(VM101)*
  x Chinese junks
  xx Ships
  — Motors
    xx Gas and oil engines
    Marine engines
Jupiter (Planet) *(Descriptive astronomy, QB661; Theoretical astronomy, QB384)*
  sa Space flight to Jupiter
  — Atmosphere *(QB661)*
    x Jovian atmosphere
  — Juvenile literature *(QB661)*
  — Mass *(QB661)*
  — Observations *(QB661)*
  — Orbit
  — Satellites
    See Satellites—Jupiter

Jupiter (Planet)   (Descriptive astronomy,
        QB661; Theoretical astronomy,
        QB384)   (Continued)
— Tables   (QB384)
Jupiter missile
    x Jupiter rocket
    Example under Intermediate-range ballistic
        missiles
Jupiter rocket
    See Jupiter missile
Jupurina language
    See Ipurina language
Jur language
    See Dyur language
Jura horse
    xx Draft horses
Jurak language
    See Nenets language
Jurakuyaki
    See Raku pottery
Jurassic period
    See Geology, Stratigraphic—Jurassic
        Paleobotany—Jurassic
        Paleontology—Jurassic
Jürčed (Tribe)
    See Ju-chên (Tribe)
Jurchen (Tribe)
    See Ju-chên (Tribe)
Jurchi language
    See Ju-chên language
Jurchid (Tribe)
    See Ju-chên (Tribe)
Juridical psychology
    See Law—Psychology
        Psychology, Forensic
Jurisdiction   (Direct)   (JX4173-4195)
    sa Appeal as from an abuse
        Conflict of judicial decisions
        Conflict of laws
        Courts
        Criminal jurisdiction
        Denial of justice
        Judgments
        Political questions and judicial power
        Privileges and immunities
        Prohibition (Writ)
        Venue
    xx Competent authority
        Conflict of judicial decisions
        Courts
        Judgments
        Law
        Venue
— Conflict of laws
        See Conflict of laws—Jurisdiction

        GEOGRAPHIC SUBDIVISIONS

— Rome
        See Jurisdiction (Roman law)

        GEOGRAPHIC SUBDIVISIONS

— United States
        sa Removal of causes
Jurisdiction, Consular
    See Consular jurisdiction
Jurisdiction, Domestic
    See Jurisdiction (International law)
Jurisdiction, Exterritorial
    See Exterritoriality
Jurisdiction, International
    See Jurisdiction (International law)
Jurisdiction, Non-contentious
    See Non-contentious jurisdiction
Jurisdiction, Territorial
    sa Leased territories
        Territorial waters
    x Territorial jurisdiction
    xx Territory, National

Jurisdiction, Voluntary
    See Non-contentious jurisdiction
Jurisdiction (Canon law)   (BX1939.J85)
    sa Appeal as from an abuse
        Bishops (Canon law)
        Delegation of powers (Canon law)
        Privilegium fori
    xx Bishops (Canon law)
Jurisdiction (Germanic law)
Jurisdiction (International law)
    sa Arbitration, International
        Conflct of laws—Jurisdiction
        Immunities of foreign states
        International courts
    x Domestic jurisdiction
        International jurisdiction
        Jurisdiction, Domestic
        Jurisdiction, International
    xx Arbitration, International
        Conflict of laws—Jurisdiction
        International courts
        International law
        Intervention (International law)
        Sovereignty
— Cases
        sa Sabbatino case
Jurisdiction (Roman law)
    sa Imperium (Roman law)
    x Jurisdiction—Rome
Jurisdiction over aircraft   (Direct)
    xx Aeronautics—Laws and regulations
        Aeroplanes—Nationality
        Airspace (International law)
Jurisdiction over ships at sea
    sa Blockade
        Contraband of war
        Search, Right of
        Seizure of vessels and cargoes
    xx Freedom of the seas
        International law
        Maritime law
        Ships—Nationality
        War, Maritime (International law)
Jurisdictional disputes (Trade-unions)
    See Trade-unions—Jurisdictional disputes
Jurisdictional immunities of foreign states
    See Immunities of foreign states
Jurisprudence
    sa Effectiveness and validity of law
        International law—Philosophy
        Law
        Law and politics
        Law—Methodology
        Law—Philosophy
        Legal certainty
        Public law
        Sociological jurisprudence
    xx Law
        Law—Philosophy
        Natural law
        Political science
— History   (Direct)
        sa subdivision Literary history under
            particular legal systems, branches
            of law, and legal subjects, e.g.
            Jewish law—Literary history
        x Law—Literary history
— Research
Jurisprudence, Comparative
    See Comparative law
Jurisprudence, Dental
    See Dental jurisprudence
Jurisprudence, Doctor of
    See Doctor of laws degree
Jurisprudence, Ethnological
    See Ethnological jurisprudence
Jurisprudence, Medical
    See Medical jurisprudence

Jurisprudence, Veterinary
    See Veterinary jurisprudence
Juristic acts   (Direct)
    sa Administrative acts
        Capacity and disability
        Contracts
        Declaration of intention
        Declaratory acts
        Rescission (Law)
        Simulation (Civil law)
    x Acts, Juristic
        Juristic transactions
        Transactions, Juristic
    xx Contracts
— Interpretation and construction
        Example under Law—Interpretation and
            construction
Juristic acts (Canon law)
Juristic acts (Roman law)
Juristic persons   (Direct)
    sa Charitable uses, trusts, and foundations
        Corporation law
        Corporations, Government
        Corporations, Nonprofit
        Criminal liability of juristic persons
        Municipal corporations
        Unincorporated societies
    x Artificial persons
        Conventional persons
        Legal persons
        Persons, Artificial
        Persons, Conventional
        Persons, Juristic
        Persons, Legal
    xx Persons (Law)
— Criminal liability
        See Criminal liability of juristic
            persons
— Nationality
        See Corporations—Nationality
Juristic persons, Foreign
    See Corporations, Foreign
Juristic persons (Canon law)
Juristic persons (Hindu law)
Juristic persons (International law)
    See Persons (International law)
Juristic persons (Roman law)
    sa Universitates (Civil law)
Juristic psychology
    See Law—Psychology
        Psychology, Forensic
Juristic transactions
    See Juristic acts
Jurists
    See Lawyers
Juruks
    See Yuruks
Juruna Indians   (F2520.1.J)
    x Yuruna Indians
    xx Indians of South America
Jury   (Direct)   (JF723; England, JN923;
        United States, JK1736)
    sa Grand jury
        Instructions to juries
        Jury commissioners
        Law and fact
        Nisi prius
        Summation (Law)
        Verdicts
    x Judgments by peers
        Trial by jury
        Trial by peers
    xx Civil procedure
        Courts
        Criminal courts
        Criminal procedure
        Law and fact
        Lay judges

NOTICE TO PURCHASERS

<u>Library of Congress Subject Headings</u>, 8th edition, 1975

Adolescence
CANCEL:
  --Stories
Adultery
CANCEL:
  --Stories
Automobiles
  --Service stations (<u>Direct</u>) (<u>TL153</u>)
ADD:
          x Automobile filling stations
            Automobile service stations
            Filling stations
            Gas stations
            Gasoline stations
            Service stations, Automobile
            Stations, Service (Automobiles)
         xx Automobile industry and trade
            Automobiles--Apparatus and
                supplies
            Garages
            Petroleum industry and trade
  ----Equipment and supplies
  ----Heating and ventilation
  ----Juvenile literature
  ----Law and legislation (<u>Direct</u>)
          xx Petroleum law and legislation
Beatitudes
CANCEL:
  --Stories (<u>BT382</u>)
SUBSTITUTE: FOR:
Bible   Bible
  --Zoology   --Zoology
      See Bible--Natural history   See Bible--Natural history
Bible. Manuscripts   x Bible--Codices
    x Bible--Codices   Bible--Manuscripts
      Bible--Manuscripts   --Catalogs
  --Catalogs   x Bible--Catalogs
      x Bible--Catalogs   --Facsimiles
  --Facsimiles
Bible. Manuscripts, Coptic, ⌐Greek,
        Latin, etc.⌐
Birds
  --Food
ADD:
      <u>Example</u> <u>under</u> Food

SUBSTITUTE:
Choruses, Sacred (Mixed voices 4 pts.)
    with orchestra
  --To 1800
  ----Vocal scores with piano (M2023)
     xx Choruses, Sacred (Mixed
       voices, 4 pts.) with piano
SUBSTITUTE:
Choruses, Sacred (Mixed voices, 6 pts.)
    with orchestra
  --Vocal scores with pianos (2)
     (M2023)
     xx Choruses, Sacred (Mixed
       voices, 6 pts.) with
       pianos (2)
SUBSTITUTE:
Choruses, Secular (Mixed voices,
    8 pts.) with chamber orchestra
  --Vocal scores with piano (M1533)
     xx Choruses, Secular (Mixed
       voices, 8 pts.) with piano
  --Vocal scores with pianos (2)
     (M1533)
     xx Choruses, Secular (Mixed
       voices, 8 pts.) with piano
Christian giving
CANCEL:
  --Stories
Church history
  --Primitive and early church,
      ca. 30-600
ADD:
     sa Canon law--Early church,
       ca. 30-600
Concertos (Horns (2))
  --Solos with piano
ADD:
     xx Trios (Piano, horns (2)),
       Arranged
SUBSTITUTE:
Concertos (Violoncellos (2))
    (M1016-1017)
  sa Violoncellos (2) with chamber
     orchestra
     Violoncellos (2) with orchestra
  xx Violoncello music (Violoncellos
     (2))
     Violoncellos (2) with orchestra
SUBSTITUTE:
Continuo
  See Continuo used as part of the
    specification of medium in
    headings, e.g. Trio-sonatas
  (Violins (2), continuo)

FOR:
Choruses, Sacred (Mixed voices, 4 pts.)
    with orchestra
  --To 1800
  ----Scores (M2020)
     xx Choruses, Sacred (Mixed
       voices, 4 pts.) with piano
FOR:
Choruses, Sacred (Mixed voices, 6 pts.)
    with orchestra
  --Vocal scores with 2 pianos (M2023)
     xx Choruses, Sacred (Mixed voices,
       6 pts.) with 2 pianos

FOR:
Choruses, Secular (Mixed voices, 8 pts.)
    with chamber orchestra
  --Vocal scores with piano (M1533)
     xx Choruses, Secular (Mixed voices,
       8 pts.) with piano
     xx Choruses, Secular (Mixed voices,
       8 pts.) with piano

FOR:
Concertos (Violoncellos (2)) (M1016-1017)
  sa Violoncellos (2) with chamber
     orchestra
     Violoncellos (2) with orchestra
     Violoncellos (2) with orchestra

FOR:
Continuo
  See Continuo used as part of the
    specification of medium in
    headings, e.g.

English poetry
  --Translations from foreign
          literature
ADD:
      Example under Translations
CANCEL:
      Note under Translations
Exempla
CANCEL:
   sa First communion--Stories
Express service
  --United States
ADD:
      x United States--Express service
First communion
CANCEL:
  --Stories
CANCEL:
      xx Exempla
France
  --History
CANCEL:
  ----Revolution
French literature
  --Translations into English
ADD:
      Example under Translations
CANCEL:
      Note under Translations
Girls
CANCEL:
  --Stories
Great Britain
  --History
  ----Restoration, 1660-1688
ADD:
      xx Restorations, Political
Hinduism
  --Sacred books
CANCEL:
  ----Stories
Inland navigation
  --United States
ADD:
      x United States--Inland navigation
Jewish way of life
CANCEL:
  --Stories (BM723)
Ländler (Violins (2), violoncello
ADD:
   xx String trios (Violins (2),
        violoncello)

Lord's Supper
CANCEL:
  --Stories
Mermaids
CANCEL:
  --Stories
Minorities
CANCEL:
  --Stories
Napoléon I, Emperor of the French,
      1769-1821
ADD:
  --Addresses, sermons, etc. (DC203)
SUBSTITUTE:
  --Art patronage
      Example under Art patronage;
          Art patrons
  --Books and reading (Z989)
      Example under Book collectors;
          Books and reading
SUBSTITUTE:
  --Coronation
      Example under Coronations
  --Death and burial (DC212)
      x Napoléon I, Emperor of the
          French, 1769-1821--Funeral
  --Juvenile literature
CANCEL:
      x Napoléon I, Emperor of the
          French, 1769-1821--Relics
ADD:
  --Literary art (DC215.5)
ADD:
  --Medals (CJ6155.N3-5)
ADD:
  --Museums, relics, etc. (DC2039)
      x Napoléon I, Emperor of the
          French, 1769-1821--Relics
SUBSTITUTE:
  --Quotations
  --Relationship with women (DC204)
      x Napoléon I, Emperor of the
          French, 1769-1821--Women
Nativism
ADD:
    xx Anti-Catholicism--United States
New Hampshire
  --History
ADD:
  ----Revolution, 1775-1783 (E263.N4)
ADD:
  ----Civil War, 1861-1865 (E520)

Napoléon I, Emperor of the French,
      1769-1821
FOR:
  --Art patronage
      Example under Art partonage; Art
          patrons
      Example under Book collectors;
          Books and reading
FOR:
  --Coronation
      Example under Coronations
      x Napoléon I, Emperor of the French,
          1769-1821--Funeral
FOR:
  --Quotations
      x Napoléon I, Emperor of the French,
          1769-1821--Women

New York (State)
  --History
ADD:
  ----Revolution, 1775-1783 (<u>E263.N</u>6)
ADD:
  ------Juvenile literature
  ----War of 1812
CANCEL:
  ------Centennial celebrations, etc.
ADD:
  ----Civil War, 1861-1865 (<u>E523</u>)
ADD:
  ------Centennial celebrations, etc.
SUBSTITUTE:
Pakhto language
  <u>See</u> Pushto language
Pakistan
  --History
  ----Civil War, 1971
        <u>See</u> Bangladesh--History--
            Revolution, 1971

Penance
CANCEL:
  --Stories
Periodicity
  <u>See</u> Cycles
CANCEL:
  --Juvenile literature
Piano music (Pianos (2)), Arranged
ADD:
  <u>sa</u> Piano with band--2-piano scores
ADD:
      Piano with orchestra--2-piano
        scores
ADD:
      Piano with orchestra, Arranged--
        2-piano scores
ADD:
      Piano with string orchestra--
        2-piano scores
Piano music (Pianos (3))
ADD:
  <u>sa</u> Pianos (3) with string orchestra
Play-party
ADD:
  <u>xx</u> Folk-songs--United States
Postage stamps
CANCEL:
  --United Nations
CANCEL:
      <u>See</u> United Nations--Postal
            service

FOR:
Pakhto language
  <u>See</u> Pushto language
  --History
  ----Civil War, 1971
        <u>See</u> Bangladesh--History--
            Revolution, 1971

Postal service
  --United States
ADD:
    sa Parcels-post--United States
ADD:
        Postal savings-banks--
          United States
  ----Rates
ADD:
      sa Parcels-post--United
            States
Purāṇas
CANCEL:
  --Stories
Quintets (Celesta, flutes (2), harps (2))
ADD:
    xx Celesta music
Quintets (Pianos (2), percussion, double
        bass)
ADD:
    xx Piano music (Pianos (2))
Rabbis
CANCEL:
  --Stories
Race problems
  --Economic aspects
CANCEL:
      (Direct)
SUBSTITUTE: FOR:
Radar (Direct) (TK6575)   Radar (Direct) (TK65.75)
SUBSTITUTE: FOR:
Radioactive substances in rivers, lakes,   Radioactive substances in rivers, lakes,
        etc. (Direct) (TD427.R3)   etc. (Direct) (TD247.R3)
Rocks
CANCEL:
  --Classification and nomenclature
        (QE425)
Rome
  --History
ADD:
  ----Empire, 30 B.C.-284 A.D.
ADD:
  ----Empire, 30 B.C.-476 A.D.
Russia
  --History
ADD:
  ----Kandiyevka Uprising, 1861
ADD:
        x Kandeevka Uprising, 1861
ADD:
        Kandiyevka Uprising, 1861
  ----February Revolution, 1917
CANCEL:
  ------Historiography

Russia--History (Continued)
ADD:
  ----1917-
ADD:
  ------Historiography
SUBSTITUTE:
Seventh-Day Adventists
   xx Adventists
      Sabbatarians
  --Converts
      See Converts, Seventh-Day
            Adventist
  --Education
Songs with instr. ensemble
  --To 1800
ADD:
      Example under reference from
            Songs--16th-17th centuries
Spanish fiction
  --Translations into Italian
ADD:
      Example under Translations
CANCEL:
      Note under Translations
Survivors' benefits
ADD:
   x Widows' pensions
Transportation, Military
ADD:
   sa subdivisions Transport of sick
      and wounded, Transport
      service and Transportation
      under armies, e.g. Germany.
      Heer--Transport of sick and
      wounded; United States. Army
      --Transport service; Germany.
      Heer--Transportation
SUBSTITUTE:
United States
  --History
  ----Civil War, 1861-1865
  ------Registers of dead
         xx United States--History--
            Civil War, 1861-1865--
            Casualties (Statistics,
            etc.)
  --Officials and employees
  ----Leave regulations
ADD:
      sa Sick leave--United States
United States. Navy
  --Barracks and quarters
ADD:
   xx Navy-yards and naval stations
      --United States

FOR:
Seventh-Day Adventists
   xx Adventists
      Sabbatarians
   See Converts, Seventh-Day Adventists

FOR:
United States
  --History
  ----Civil War, 1861-1865
  ------Registers of dead
         sa United States--History--
            Civil War, 1861-1865--
            Casualties (Statistics,
            etc.)

Upanishads
CANCEL:
  --Stories (<u>BL1120</u>)
Variations (Cornet, trombones (3),
       trumpets (3), tuba)
ADD:
   <u>xx</u> Wind octets (Cornet, trombones
       (3), trumpets (3), tuba)
Vietnamese Conflict, 1961-
  --War work
  ----Seventh-Day Adventists
CANCEL:
       <u>x</u> Vietnamese Conflict, 1961-
          --War work--Churches
Violin with instr. ensemble
ADD:
   <u>sa</u> Concertos (Violin with instr.
       ensemble)
ADD:
   <u>xx</u> Concertos (Violin with instr.
       ensemble)
ADD:
     Instrumental ensembles
ADD:
     Violin music
War and emergency powers
  --United States
ADD:
    <u>xx</u> Presidents--United States
ADD:
Washington (State)
ADD:
  --History (<u>F886-900</u>)
ADD:
  ----To 1889
ADD:
  ----1889-
Young women
CANCEL:
  --Stories
ADD:
Zabirmawa (African people)
ADD:
  <u>See</u> Zarma (African people)